VOLUME 6   Cathedrals to Civil War

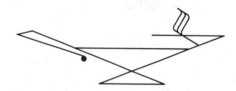

THE ENCYCLOPEDIA
AMERICANA
INTERNATIONAL EDITION

COMPLETE IN THIRTY VOLUMES   FIRST PUBLISHED IN 1829

AMERICANA CORPORATION   International Headquarters: Danbury, Connecticut 06816

Library of Congress Cataloging in Publication Data
Main entry under title:

The Encyclopedia Americana.

Includes bibliographical references and index.
1. Encyclopedias and dictionaries.
AE5.E333   1980   031   79–55176
ISBN 0–7172–0111–2

BERNARD G. SILBERSTEIN, FROM RAPHO GUILLUMETTE

THE MAJESTIC GOTHIC CATHEDRAL of Salisbury, England, as seen through morning mists rising from the Avon.

CATHEDRALS AND CHURCHES

CATHEDRALS AND CHURCHES, kə-thē′drəlz, chûrch′əz, are buildings for Christian worship. A cathedral is the home church of a bishop and the administrative center of a diocese. By virtue of the bishop's importance, most cathedrals are large, but size in itself does not make a church a cathedral. In Athens the Little Metropolitan Church (12th century) was the city's cathedral until the 19th century, though it is smaller than most private houses.

Like other forms of architecture, churches throughout history have been shaped by their purpose—specifically by the forms of worship they are meant to house. While churches do provide for individual and private devotion, their chief purpose is to accommodate congregational worship. Thus the expected size of the congregation becomes important. Likewise, the particular type of ritual dictates the arrangement of the spaces within the church, and as the ritual changes, so do the spatial requirements. Thus, for example, the Catholic Mass calls for a different form of building than is required for Presbyterian services. The effect of the liturgy on church architecture is easily demonstrable in both historic and modern churches.

A less tangible but nevertheless significant factor in church design is the philosophy of the several branches of Christianity. The vast height of Gothic cathedrals and their colorful half-light create a setting perfectly expressive of the mystical devotion and exaltation of medieval Christianity. These cathedrals would hardly be appropriate for churches devoted to the austerities of John Calvin's Reformation philosophy.

Early Christian Churches. During its first few centuries, Christianity grew slowly, surviving periodic persecutions. When, in 313 A. D., Constantine granted toleration to the Christian religion, the time to build the first churches had arrived.

Basilican Plan. The early Christian basilica was well suited to the needs of the church. A basilica is a hall-like structure designed around a longitudinal axis. In its most typical form, as in the old Church of St. Peter's in Rome (now destroyed), the main building was preceded by an enclosed court, or *atrium,* open to the sky, with the baptismal font in its center. Until a person had been accepted into the church through the sacrament of baptism, he was not allowed to enter the church proper. A *narthex,* or vestibule, linked the atrium and the church. The main part of the building consisted of a *nave,* or central aisle, flanked by two side aisles, or in the largest basilicas, four side aisles. The long nave and aisles provided space for the congregation and directed attention to the more sa-

1

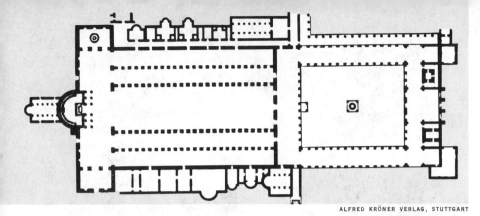

EARLY BASILICAS, as shown in the floor plan of the old Church of St. Peter's, Rome, were divided between a main building and an enclosed court, or atrium (*right*), with the baptismal font.

cred zones beyond them. The nave terminated in a triumphal arch at a *bema,* a space situated at right angles to the nave. If the bema projected beyond the side walls of the church, it was called a *transept.* Beyond the bema was a semicircular *apse,* the church sanctuary, corresponding to the nave in width. The altar was set at the entrance to the apse, or sometimes in the transept in front of it. A bench for the higher clergy encircled the apse, with the bishop's throne in the center on the axis of the church. The lower clergy were accommodated in the bema.

Thus the basilica provided clear divisions for the Christian hierarchy—the catechumens in the atrium, laity in the nave, lower clergy including deacons and choristers in the bema, and higher clergy and bishop in the apse. The form proved so satisfactory to the needs of the church that it persisted in Rome almost unchanged for centuries.

No question has been more hotly debated by scholars of church architecture than the origin of the basilica. Some scholars trace it to pagan basilicas such as the Basilica Ulpia in Trajan's Forum and the Basilica Julia in the Forum Romanum, both in Rome. These buildings also were hall-like and were divided into a nave and side aisles. In the Basilica Ulpia, apses terminated the ends of the nave. But the pagan basilica served secular needs; it was commonly entered from the side, not from one end; and while the plans of some pagan basilicas do correspond in part to the Christian basilica, others, like the Basilica of Maxentius (also called the Basilica of Constantine) in the Roman Forum are quite different.

Other scholars argue that the source of the early Christian basilica was the Roman house. Smaller Roman houses had an atrium with walks on either side of a central pool that might correspond to the aisles of a church. Toward the end of the atrium were alcoves that might suggest transepts, and the *tablinum,* where the Romans venerated their household gods, occupied a position similar to the apse in the Christian basilica. Certainly, as we learn from the Acts of the Apostles, Christians first gathered for worship in the home of one of the congregation. We know, too, that the space in the church preferred by the laity was at first the aisles rather than the nave. This custom might be traced to the Roman house in which the atrium was open to the sky in the center, whereas the walks at the sides were protected from sun and rain. However, no single source seems to account for all the elements of the Christian basilica.

Early Christian basilicas were oriented (arranged in relation to the points of the compass) from the beginning. This custom did not orig-

inate with Christianity. The pyramids at Giza in Egypt and the Mesopotamian temple towers were also oriented. The axis of the Parthenon in Athens was so placed that the rays of the rising sun would enter the east door to light the gold and ivory statue within. It seems to have been the custom for early Christian priests to face east when celebrating the Lord's Supper (Communion), a custom probably borrowed from earlier religions. The priest normally faced the congregation from behind the "Lord's Table," or altar. The laity therefore looked west, and in the early churches the sanctuary was at the west end of the building. This was the case in the old St. Peter's in Rome, and is true of the present church.

Then, perhaps during the 6th century, the custom changed, and it became standard for both the priest and the congregation to face east. The priest stood in front of the altar with his back toward the congregation during much of the Mass. The altar thereafter was located at the east end of the church and the door at the west. This practice became so regular that "east end" became synonymous with "sanctuary" and "west end" with "entrance" in speaking of church architecture. The history of church orientation is neatly summed up in San Lorenzo, f.l.m., in Rome. (These letters stand for the Italian *fuori le mura,* "outside the walls." The earliest churches were built over the graves of the saints to whom they were dedicated, and the cemeteries were outside the old walls of Rome.) The original Church of San Lorenzo (5th century) had its apse to the west. Several centuries later, after the custom had changed, a new church was built with its apse to the east, back to back with the old apse. Eventually both apses were removed, the eastern door closed, and the old church became the eastern sanctuary of the enlarged building.

Structurally, the interiors of early Christian basilicas were simple. Colonnades divided the nave from the side aisles. Sometimes the colonnade held lintels, or beams, as in Santa Maria Maggiore in Rome; sometimes it supported a light arcade with arches springing directly from the capitals of the columns rather than from intervening blocks of entablature. This departure from earlier Roman precedent exists in San Paolo, f.l.m., restored on its original lines after a fire in the early 19th century. Over the colonnade or arcade, light walls rose above the aisle roofs to create a clerestory pierced with windows to light the nave. The clerestory in turn held a simple timber roof. Probably the roof beams and trusses were originally left visible, but later they were generally concealed by paneled ceilings. The only vault was the half dome over the apse.

Most of the great imperial Roman buildings had been vaulted and were therefore more massive and monumental in construction. But after the constant revolution and economic chaos of the 3d century, the Christians of the 4th century could not afford the costly vaulted style. Nor could they always afford new columns and other architectural members for their basilicas. They therefore took them from pagan temples, or perhaps from other, older buildings, that had outlived their usefulness. Often no uniform set of columns was available, so they appropriated whatever columns, capitals, and architraves they could find. Some columns in San Lorenzo, f.l.m., are stout, others slender; their heights vary and are pieced out by thinner or thicker bases. Some blocks of the architraves are richly carved, but the patterns on adjacent blocks contrast, indicating that they came from different sources. This hodgepodge of styles gives a certain naïve charm to these early basilicas.

The floors of the early basilicas were laid in marble slabs, which possibly had faced the concrete of earlier Roman buildings. In the floor, and sometimes in the furniture, disks of colored marble helped to create a luxurious appearance. Such disks were easily obtained by cutting slices from the shaft of a column. The polychromy of the interior was then completed by mosaics on the walls above the nave arcade, on the triumphal arch, and particularly in the half dome of the apse. These mosaics, made of small bits of colored glass, presented patterns, Christian symbols, saintly figures, or scenes from the Scriptures.

A noted series of Scriptural themes is preserved in Santa Maria Maggiore, Rome. Particularly fine apse mosaics are in Santa Pudenziana, Santi Cosmo e Damiano, and Sant'Agnese, f.l.m., all in Rome. The apse mosaic in Sant'Agnese, dating from the 7th century, shows the strong Byzantine influence that extended to Rome itself after the collapse of the Roman Empire in the west in the 5th century. The figures are unrealistic, though they are less formalized, less conventional, less hieratic than they later became in Byzantine mosaics. See BYZANTINE ART AND ARCHITECTURE.

The highly colorful interiors of early Christian basilicas were not matched by the exteriors. The outside of the buildings were quite plain. Tiled roofs covered the volumes of nave, aisles, bema, and apse. Greek and Roman temples, which were essentially monuments serving as shrines for the cult image, had beautifully planned and decorated exteriors. The Christian basilica, however, had to meet the needs of congregational use, and its builders lavished their attention on the interior, largely ignoring the exterior.

No basilica in Rome has been preserved in its entirety, but there are many surviving naves, or at least nave arcades and apses. Perhaps the most complete impression of what the basilicas were like may be obtained from San Paolo, f.l.m. The present church of San Clemente, although it was built in the 12th century, has, however, the only early Christian atrium left in Rome. Since it has no bema, the space for the clergy has encroached on the nave, and is there defined by low parapet walls in slabs of varicolored marbles. Below the present church there was excavated an earlier basilica that contains a number of rare fresco paintings. Below it is the

COLONNETTES ON PIERS lead to ribbed vaulting above the nave of St. Étienne (Abbaye-aux-Hommes) at Caen.

original Roman pavement with the remains of the house said to have belonged to St. Clement and the ruins of a Mithraic temple across the street. Some early basilicas had cloisters attached to them, although these were generally later additions. Examples are San Lorenzo, f.l.m., St. John Lateran, and San Paolo, f.l.m. The small columns in the last two churches are varied in form—some cylindrical and undecorated, some fluted, some spiral, and many with patterns inset with bits of red, blue, or gold glass or stone.

The basilica was the major church form of the early Christian period. The type spread to the Byzantine world where it is seen in the churches of Sant'Apollinare in Classe and Sant'Apollinare Nuovo, both in Ravenna, Italy. The greater wealth of Byzantium, however, permitted Emperor Justinian and his architects to develop the more monumental vaulted domed basilica. The basilica form is also found in some early churches in Syria and the Near East. There, however, the dearth of timber tended to encourage vaulting in place of wooden roofs.

Central Plan. In addition to basilicas, the early Christians constructed a few churches on the central plan, designed around a vertical, instead of a longitudinal, axis. Central-plan churches may be circular, octagonal, or in the form of a Greek cross with four equal arms. However, they do not lend themselves well to congregational worship. The vertical axis creates a focal point in the center of the building. Unless the altar, the religious center of the church, is placed there, it will lose its prominence. In the service of the Mass it is generally preferable to have the congregation in front of the altar, rather than on either side of or behind it. In buildings of the central type, three quarters of the interior

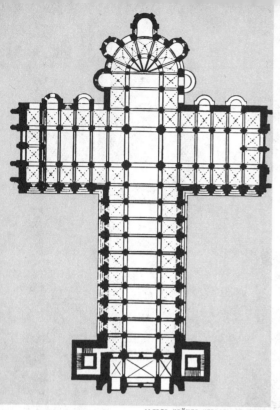

SANTIAGO DE COMPOSTELA (floor plan, *left*; clock tower, *right*), is a Romanesque pilgrimage cathedral.

space is useless for this primary Christian service. This difficulty probably accounts for the comparative rarity of the central type in churches of the Western world.

However, for buildings intended primarily as commemorative monuments, or for individual and private devotion, the central plan is quite appropriate. When used as a baptistery, the form is not only valid but desirable, since the congregation will then group itself around the font in the center. The churches of Santo Stefano Rotondo and Santa Costanza in Rome are both circular in plan, the former with a timber roof, the latter domed. Santa Costanza was intended primarily as a commemorative building, as was the Greek-cross church of St. Simeon Stylites at Kalat Seman, Syria. Four equal arms radiate from an octagon that has at its center the column on top of which St. Simeon is said to have lived.

Dark Ages. The final collapse of the Roman Empire in the West (476 A. D.) ushered in five centuries commonly called the Dark Ages. During this time the peoples who had overthrown the empire were very slowly developing their own cultures. Little remains of the architecture of this time; the few buildings that have been preserved are small. It is probable that most of them, including perhaps some of larger dimensions, were constructed in timber and were replaced by more permanent structures in later centuries.

The still-extant plan of the 9th century monastery of St. Gall, in Switzerland, shows a large and complex basilican church with apses at both ends, surrounded by the living quarters, guest houses, stables, and shops of a self-supporting community. Charlemagne's chapel at Aachen, Germany (built 796–804) is the most monumental extant church of the period. Its similar-

ity to the Byzantine Church of San Vitale at Ravenna indicates the dominance of Byzantine civilization at this time, even in the domain of the most powerful ruler of the Western world. A few churches from the Dark Ages still exist in Spain, generally basilican in plan and with traces of Islamic influence. Santa Maria de Naranco near San Miguel is a good example. England also is comparatively rich in remains from this time. Parts of the little church at Jarrow are associated with the Venerable Bede (about 673–735). Towers, like the one at the parish church of Earl's Barton, Northamptonshire, with its decorative ribbons of stone, are the most striking features of these buildings. Some, like the church at Bradford-on-Avon, are remarkably tall in comparison to their area but have doors wide enough only for one person to enter at a time.

Romanesque. The economic revival of the 11th century ushered in the next great age of church building. Feudalism fostered a group of diverse styles, with each region developing its own particular forms. The Tuscan Romanesque is distinct from Lombard Romanesque; the domed churches of Aquitaine with their traces of the Byzantine are different from the Provençal churches with their faint memories of Roman architecture. But for all its diversity of style, the Romanesque has some unifying elements. The major churches are large and generally have stone walls pierced by small windows. Round arched arcades, tier upon tier, support either wooden roofs or ponderous stone vaulting. Each part of the church is conceived as a unit, connected to other areas but distinct and complete in itself.

Tuscany. The cathedral group at Pisa was begun in 1063. The structure continues the tradition of the basilica with its nave and aisles, arcades, and timber roof. However, the transepts have been extended and a choir added beyond them, thus changing the plan into a Latin-cross form. The atrium was abandoned, but the baptistery was built as a separate building in front, and on the axis, of the church. This places the font in the same position relative to the church and the altar that it had occupied since early Christian times. The Corinthian columns of the interior of the cathedral perpetuate Roman precedent, but the colorful mosaics characteristic of the basilica have been replaced by alternating bands of light and dark marble. Arcades on small columns rise one above another on the facade of the church, and in the form of engaged arcades create a rhythm along the sides. The white exterior walls are also banded with stripes of green marble. Clearly, the exterior of the church had begun to challenge the interior in importance.

Sicily. Quite different from the Cathedral at Pisa is Monreale Cathedral (built 1174–1189) in Sicily. Successive occupations left their marks on Sicilian architecture. The mosaics and columns of the interior of Monreale are almost completely Byzantine, but the external arcading is composed of pointed Saracenic arches interlaced in the fashion of Normandy and topped by the Lombard arched corbel table. Sicilian Romanesque churches generally stress decoration more than structure.

Lombardy. The opposite is true in Lombardy. Sant'Ambrogio in Milan (11th century) has a domical ribbed vault supported on membered piers with colonnettes corresponding to each rib of the vault above. This type of structure provided the germ from which Gothic vaults later developed. It also raised problems of buttressing that caused the elimination of the clerestory; consequently, Lombard churches are very dark. A common decorative element was the arched corbel table, a fringe of small arches resting on corbels or brackets that sometimes appear under the eaves of a roof or mark the several stories of a tower.

Germany. In Germany during the Romanesque period a combination of forms appeared, some drawn from German architecture of the Dark Ages, some from Byzantine precedent, and many from contemporary Lombard work. An instance of Byzantine influence is seen in the triple apses (two of them terminating the transepts) in St. Mary in the Capitol in Cologne (11th century).

By far the most dramatic German churches are the great cathedrals of the Rhineland—Worms, Speyer, and Mainz—built mainly in the 11th and 12th centuries. The plan of such large cathedrals was sometimes complicated by two transepts and by the addition of a western apse to the usual one at the east end of the nave. Towers or lanterns rise where the transepts meet the nave, and additional pairs of towers may flank the apses or terminate the transepts. The picturesque silhouette created by this duplication of members probably derived from the complex plans of such monastic churches of the Dark Ages as St. Gall in Switzerland.

A familiarity with Lombard architecture is evident from the use of arched corbel tables in German churches. Since the Holy Roman Empire was essentially German and claimed north Italy as one of its major territories, this connection with Italian architecture is understandable. The system of ribbed vaults, alternate membered piers, and pilaster strip buttresses frequently

ROBERT DOISNEAU, FROM RAPHO GUILLUMETTE

CHARTRES CATHEDRAL, with its massive stained-glass windows, including the 13th-century rose window.

found in German Romanesque churches is unmistakably Lombard. The Germans, however, sometimes omitted one or more members, thus weakening the remorseless logic of the Lombard scheme as exemplified in Sant'Ambrogio. Unlike Lombard churches of the time, German churches relied on thick walls for buttressing as well as support, and thus were able to preserve a clerestory to light the nave.

Normandy. Normandy also fell under Lombard influence in the Romanesque period. The great prestige of northern Italy at this time was due in part to its great universities, such as the one at Pavia. Some of the most important prelates of Normandy, and subsequently of England, were born and trained in Lombardy, and they helped to carry the Lombard style northward. Hence the abbeys at Caen have a modified form of Lombard structure. La Trinité, or the Abbaye-aux-Dames (1062), and St. Étienne, or the Abbaye-aux-Hommes (1064), were founded by William the Conqueror and Matilda, his queen, in gratitude for being given permission by the church to marry despite their blood relationship. The Abbaye-aux-Hommes has the ribbed vaults (added later), the membered piers with a colonnette for each rib, the alternate system, and the pilaster buttresses of Lombardy. The Normans, however, added another rib crossing the nave of the church over each slightly smaller intermediate pier, converting the Lombard 4-part system, with four triangles of vaulting in each compartment, into a 6-part system. They also raised the vaults above the aisle roofs to allow for a clerestory. These vaults were supported and buttressed by walls so thick that narrow passages could be left within them.

The builders of the Abbaye-aux-Dames, apparently pleased with this rhythmic alternation of pier and vault, used a system of vaulting (added later) that is structurally 4-part, but has a purely decorative intermediate rib added to simulate the visual effect of St. Étienne. The facades of both churches are flanked by twin towers marking the ends of the aisles, and the central door in turn expresses the nave. Moreover, the 3-level door and window arrangement of the facade of St. Étienne expresses the vertical divisions of the interior—nave arcade, triforium gallery, and clerestory. The motive of the twin-towered facade stems ultimately from such early Christian churches as Tourmanin in Syria, and foreshadows the later Gothic facade. For decoration, the Normans relied on moldings carved with geometric patterns and on interlacing arcades, but even these appear only sparingly.

England. When the Normans conquered England in 1066 they replaced the more modest Saxon architecture with monumental churches whose imposing character no doubt impressed the subject people with the superiority of Norman culture. None of the great English cathedrals preserves its Norman construction throughout but Norman naves or transepts are common. The nave of St. Albans and the transepts at Winchester Cathedral show the style at its most austere. The nave arcades, triforium gallery, and clerestory are ponderous, their severity hardly mitigated even by moldings. On the other hand, the Norman style in England is somewhat richer than in France, with massive walls supported by multiple concentric arches each broader than the one below, and often molded with bands of geometric patterns. The piers may be composed of groups of engaged columns, as in the nave of Ely Cathedral, with rather less rigid adherence to structure than in the Abbaye-aux-Hommes.

Most English churches were unvaulted, but the finest of the Norman buildings, Durham Cathedral, is an exception. The vaults of its nave (1133) are basically 4-part, but every other transverse rib is omitted, creating a rhythm that is echoed in the alternation of the piers below. Carved moldings and interlacing arcades on the aisle walls add richness. Durham is remarkable for the bluntly pointed arches of its nave vaults, which begin to anticipate the Gothic style. So, also, the half arches in the gallery level behind each main pier foretell the Gothic flying buttress. The same device was used simultaneously in La Trinité in Caen, France.

Generally, the English Norman style is less adventurous in structure than its continental counterpart, but no church in Normandy rivals the majesty of Durham. For the expression of pure power, few buildings anywhere can equal Durham Cathedral.

Monastic and Pilgrimage Churches. The Romanesque was the monastic age. The most influential orders were the Cluniac, begun in the 10th century; the Cistercian and Carthusian, founded

in the 11th century; and the Benedictine, which was already five centuries old. The Cluniac order, which had a great abbey church at Cluny that has been almost completely destroyed, fostered pilgrimages to the shrine of St. James (Cathedral of Santiago) at Santiago de Compostela in northwestern Spain. Well-defined pilgrimage routes to this popular shrine led across France and converged on the Pyrenees. Along these routes was built a series of great churches such as St. Sernin in Toulouse (11th century). In the Santiago cathedral (begun 1075) the massive nave arcades support a barrel vault, abutted on either side by half barrel vaults that eliminate the possibility of lighting the nave by clerestory windows. Neither mosaics nor colored marbles relieve this somber but powerful interior.

Santiago, like Pisa, has a Latin-cross plan with nave, aisles, transepts, choir, and apse. The aisles, however, not only flank the nave, but continue around the sides and ends of the transepts, along the choir, and curve around the semicircle of the apse to form an ambulatory—a continuous path around the church. These aisles were designed not merely to provide additional space for the laity, but also to serve as a path for the processions that by this time had become an important part of the service. At an appropriate moment, the officiating priest and his acolytes would leave the high altar in the apse; the remaining clergy, including the choir, would then fall in behind him, to be followed in turn by the laity. The procession, perhaps singing Gregorian chants, would then file completely around the church, stopping from time to time at the subsidiary altars before returning to the chancel to continue the service.

The plan of Santiago was further elaborated by no less than five small chapels, which originally radiated out from the ambulatory. In addition, there are two chapels protruding from the east side of each transept. In contrast to the early Christian basilica, which had a single altar, Santiago had not less than 10 altars. These smaller chapels could not accommodate a full congregation except as a pause in the processions. But they did serve for individual devotions, and they made it possible for several Masses to be said simultaneously—a real necessity since many of the higher clergy connected with Santiago were expected to celebrate Mass frequently.

In the pilgrimage churches each altar would normally enshrine a relic of the saint to whom the chapel was dedicated. Pilgrims at Santiago were conducted through the church by some member of the church staff, who instructed them in the stories and powers of each saint. At these altars, the pilgrims offered veneration and perhaps gave alms. Although not restricted to monastic churches, elaborate processions, multiple altars, and relics were usually most in evidence there.

The relics were enormously valuable assets to the church, particularly if some of them were believed to have miracle-working properties. Whoever felt that he had been helped by visiting a shrine might bequeath to the church a part or all of his estate. Most of the wealth offered at the shrines was devoted to enlarging and beautifying the church. Canterbury Cathedral offers a dramatic illustration of the wealth of pilgrimage churches. Soon after the remains of St. Thomas à Becket had been enshrined in its

GEORGES MARTIN, FROM RAPHO GUILLUMETTE

ST. PETER'S GREAT DOME, designed by Michelangelo, is partly obscured by the east facade of the basilica.

choir, Canterbury became the most important pilgrimage site in England. (Chaucer's *Canterbury Tales* are told by pilgrims en route to the shrine.) When, early in the 16th century, Henry VIII suppressed the English monasteries, including Canterbury, he fell heir to their remaining wealth. The gold and precious stones taken from the shrine itself filled two chests, each said to be so heavy that four men were needed to carry it. In addition, 26 wagons were required to carry off the slightly less valuable property.

Obviously, assets of such value required the protection of a fireproof building. It may be partly for this reason that wooden roofs were replaced by more costly stone vaults which, in turn, required more massive walls and piers to hold them. But fire was not the only hazard. Relics were a constant temptation to thieves and even to rival churchmen. The Abbot of Peterborough pried up one of the paving stones on which Becket's blood had been spilled, and took it back with him to his own monastery. He hoped that Peterborough might win some share of Becket's popularity. To protect the wealth of Canterbury the monks loosed a pack of watchdogs in the cathedral at night. See also ROMANESQUE ARCHITECTURE.

Gothic. The Gothic period extended from the late 12th century through the 14th century in Italy, and included the 15th century in Spain and northern Europe. During this period the feudal system weakened as the power of the monarchies increased. This, coupled with a gradual improvement in the road system, led to more unified architectural styles within the several countries. Despite some local variations of style, there were no longer major differences between the provinces. The Romanesque had produced distinct and contrasting architectural features in Provence, Aquitaine, Burgundy, and Normandy, but the French Gothic developed as a unified style.

During the Gothic era towns grew in importance, partly as a result of their alliance with royal power against the feudal barons. The burghers eagerly defended the civic rights and liberties that had been granted to the cities by the king. As one approaches Chartres or Amiens, Beauvais or Reims, the cathedral can be seen high above the roofs of the town, like a rock emerging from the sea. Its prominence symbolizes the dominant role played by the church in the community.

Even though the cost of these churches was met primarily by the bishop, the townsfolk bore their share in its building. The merchant or trade guilds might undertake the responsibility for a chapel dedicated to the patron saint of their guild, or for some part of the stained-glass windows or the sculpture. At Chartres, the townsfolk unhitched the oxen from the carts that were loaded with stone for the cathedral, and themselves dragged the burden to the building site, so that they might claim a personal part in its construction.

Cities rivaled one another in the size and height of their cathedrals. The builders of Notre Dame in Paris raised the vaults about 125 feet (38 meters) above the pavement; Amiens, begun somewhat later, reached a height of 137 feet (41 meters), while still later Beauvais topped both of them with vaults 157 feet (48 meters) high. In Italy, both Siena and Florence claimed the special protection of the Virgin. Siena built its sumptuous cathedral in her honor first, only to have the Florentines undertake a much larger project. Thereupon the Sienese made plans to convert their new building into the transept of a new, immensely larger church. They completed little more than the foundations before the wave of cathedral building ebbed, but the civic rivalry is quite clear.

That the communities of the Gothic period shared in building the great cathedrals does not mean that these churches had no architects as such. On the contrary, though the architect might have been called a master mason or a clerk of the works, his name was recorded in most cases. He was a well-known and respected craftsman.

The achievement of the Gothic era was in lightening the massiveness of the Romanesque, increasing and dramatizing the height of the building, and refining the heavy Romanesque piers and walls with small windows to convert the building into a cage of glass and stone. The plan of Chartres, a Gothic cathedral, has the same elements as the Romanesque cathedral at Santiago, but the piers are smaller and more widely spaced. Isolated buttresses replace the continuous wall. Windows fill the walls between the buttresses in the aisles, and on the clerestory level the space between the piers. The nave vaults are so high that flying buttresses are necessary to transmit the outward thrust of the nave vaults over the aisle roofs to the lofty tower buttresses beyond the aisles.

These changes create an entirely different spatial effect from that of the Romanesque. The earlier style had defined each part—nave, aisles, ambulatory, or chapels—as a volume distinct and complete in itself. In the Gothic, these volumes flow into one another. The translucence of the vast window area creates a minimal separation of interior and exterior space in the Gothic church. The projecting tower buttresses, flying buttresses, spires, and pinnacles make the building seem to merge with the surrounding space. Greek temples were finite and complete, as definite and measurable as the Olympian deities to whom they were dedicated. The Gothic cathedral, on the other hand, is indefinite in outline, immeasurable as the infinity of the Christian concept of God, who is at the same moment within His temple and present throughout the cosmos. The Greek temple was proportioned to man, but in the vast height of Chartres the individual man loses significance. The unearthly beauty of the multicolored light pouring through the stained-glass windows creates an atmosphere of mystical Christianity. No nobler expression of this spirit exists than French cathedrals of the early 13th century, such as Chartres.

French Gothic. The Gothic style developed in France during the late 12th century as an outgrowth of the Romanesque styles of Normandy and particularly of the Île de France, the royal demesne. Early Gothic churches retained the 6-part vaults, the triforium galleries over the aisles, and something of the heaviness of its predecessor. For example, Notre Dame in Paris has 6-part vaults, a triforium gallery, and a noble facade that looks like a translation into Gothic shapes of the facade of St. Étienne in Caen. But in the 13th century cathedral at Reims, the vaults have become 4-part, with the galleries replaced by the narrow passage of a blind triforium, and the facade more plastic and decorative than that of Notre Dame.

English Gothic. From France the new style spread in all directions. Each country created its own version of Gothic architecture. English Gothic developed almost as early as French, but the English cathedral is quite different in conception. During the Early English period (1150–1250), although the Gothic pointed arch was adopted, the heavy walls of the Romanesque tend to linger on. These were abandoned in the so-called Decorated period (1250–1350) when the small lancet windows of the Early English style were replaced with broad, richly traceried openings, which in turn gave way in the Perpendicular period (1350–1500) to windows latticed with vertical mullions and horizontal transoms.

Although the English used the basic French structure of membered piers, buttresses, and ribbed vaults, they did not attempt the daring height of the French cathedrals. The vaults of Westminster Abbey rise about 100 feet (30 meters), but this is the most French of the English churches, rebuilt by the Francophile king, Henry III, between 1245 and 1260. Usually the vaults of the English cathedrals are about 80 feet (24 meters) high, half the height of those of Beauvais. Because this lower vaulting made the buttress problem less acute, flying buttresses are comparatively rare in English Gothic churches.

In most respects, Canterbury Cathedral is characteristic of the English Gothic style. In addition to a central transept, it has a second transept farther east, producing an archiepiscopal cross plan. The additional transept provides space for more altars. Twin towers flank the facade, as at Notre Dame, but the tower over the central transept—"Bell Harry," as it is called at Canterbury—overtops them. In the French cathedral, the exterior focus is at the west end; in England it is at the center. The French cathedral rises from the middle of the town with houses and shops close around it. But the English cathedral is set off within its own lawns and trees, visible from all angles, and this fact makes the emphasis on the central tower seem logical.

The reason for this characteristic difference between the French and the English Gothic styles is that most of the English cathedrals were monasteries (minsters), and so were set within the monastic grounds. For the same reason there is usually a cloister, and often other monastic buildings, attached to the English church. Generally there is a chapter house for meetings, and, in the church proper, choir screens to separate the part of the building intended primarily for the monks from those areas in which the laity normally worshiped. These screens, which often break the vista down the length of the English minsters, emphasize the multiple functions of the building. All this tends to give to the English churches a less dramatic, perhaps less public character than the French cathedrals. Canterbury seems almost private, even intimate, in comparison to the grandeur of Chartres or of Notre Dame.

In one respect, Canterbury minster is not typically English. It preserves the rounded apse, perhaps because that part was designed by a French architect, William of Sens, in the 12th century. During the Norman period, English churches regularly had apses. In the Gothic period, a square east end replaced the apse and its radiating chapels, as can be seen in Lincoln minster. Why the English made this change is not known. Conceivably, the English monks felt the necessity of proper orientation not merely of

PHILIP GENDREAU

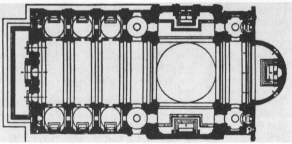

IL GESÙ, the Baroque mother church of the Jesuit order in Rome, was designed with side chapels rather than aisles and with a wide nave and short transepts. The design concentrated the congregation in full view and good hearing of the priest at a time when sermons were becoming increasingly important in the Catholic service.

ARCHIVES PHOTOGRAPHIQUES, PARIS

the church as a whole, but of each chapel. Radial chapels cannot be correctly oriented, but chapels on the eastern sides of the transepts, or at the ends of aisles in a square east end, are correct in this matter. There is, however, no proof of this hypothesis.

In English Gothic churches the central chapel of the east end is commonly dedicated to the Virgin, and is known as the Lady Chapel. As the Middle Ages progressed, devotion to the Virgin grew steadily until she was almost as much beloved by the people as Christ himself. Services in her honor grew more and more elaborate and were sung by the full choir. In Gloucester Cathedral the Lady Chapel was enlarged so much that it forms a nearly independent church.

Other Gothic Styles. Germany at first accepted the Gothic style reluctantly, retaining much of the Romanesque spirit with the occasional addition of Gothic details. In some instances, however, as in Cologne Cathedral, they almost copied French models, in this case Amiens Cathedral. The *Hallenkirchen,* or hall churches, are more original. In them, the aisles rise nearly as high as the nave.

Spain also produced both imitative and free versions of Gothic. Thus, León Cathedral was inspired by Chartres, though it can hardly be called a close copy of its model. Seville Cathe-

dral, on the other hand, has such original features as nearly flat roofs (made possible by the climate of southern Spain) and somewhat Moorish details, a reminder of the centuries of Moorish occupation of this part of Spain.

The Gothic spirit in architecture was foreign to Italy. The Cistercians introduced a rather austere version of that style in the early 13th century, seen in churches such as San Galgano, near Siena. More typical is the Cathedral of Florence, vast and gaunt in its interior, and with vaults secured by iron tie rods instead of external buttressing as in French structures. The nearly flat roofs, also, contrast with the steep pitched roofs of the north. Chartres had been built of native gray limestone; Florence's polychromed exterior is sheathed in white marble with bands and panels of green or red marble.

The immense Cathedral of Milan, despite its glistening white marble and flat roofs, is perhaps the closest Italian approximation of the northern Gothic style. This 5-aisled church has a wealth of buttresses crowned by a forest of pinnacles that tend to stress verticality in contrast to the predominantly horizontal lines of Florence Cathedral. The interlacing lines of the tracery show the influence of the 15th century Flamboyant style of French Gothic, though modified by the German masons who built Milan. Before the

ST. PAUL'S, in London, designed by Christopher Wren, unifies many divergent architectural influences.

cathedral was finished, the Renaissance had been born in Florence, but this new style touched only a few details on the facade of Milan. See also GOTHIC ARCHITECTURE.

Renaissance and Post-Renaissance. In the Romanesque and Gothic periods, the building of churches had been the dominant concern of architecture. The revival of Roman architecture, a basic factor in the complex movement known as the Renaissance in Italy, was certainly not hostile to Catholicism, yet comparatively few churches were built.

Filippo Brunelleschi, the foremost Florentine architect of the early 15th century, rejected the Gothic style as barbaric. In his design for San Lorenzo in Florence (begun 1419), he reverted instead to the early Christian basilica, a form that he would have considered Roman and that, in fact, had been born in the late years of the Roman Empire. In this church, light columns and arcades support thin clerestory walls that hold, instead of Gothic vaults, a wooden roof and its flat ceilings. Roman round arches replace pointed arches; Corinthian capitals are surmounted by blocks of the classic entablature. If these details seem a bit naïve, they represent the efforts of an earnest student to understand the forms of the past. In one significant point, Brunelleschi abandoned his precedent. Marble floors and wall mosaics had made the basilicas colorful. But Brunelleschi, associating polychromy with medieval buildings, made his interior monochromatic with gray stone set off against white plaster.

Further study brought a more complete understanding of principles behind the forms of Roman architecture. Leon Battista Alberti's · design of Sant'Andrea in Mantua (1470) adopted a barrel-vaulted nave, whose clearly defined space extends into barrel-vaulted chapels at either side.

St. Peter's, Rome. When, early in the 16th century, Pope Julius II determined to replace the venerable early Christian basilica of St. Peter's in Rome, he gave the commission to Donato Bramante. Bramante boasted that he would put the Pantheon on top of the Basilica of Constantine; in other words, that he intended to raise a huge dome above barrel- and groin-vaulted forms drawn from the Roman basilica. This would have produced a church of the central type— four equal arms of a Greek cross radiating from the defined space under the main dome, the whole complex fitting in a square plan. Bramante lived to see the foundations laid and the walls begin to rise.

After his death a series of architects was appointed, some of whom suggested converting his Greek-cross plan into a Latin cross. But little was done until Michelangelo was put in charge in 1547. He returned to Bramante's scheme but made the voids more open and the supports more massive to hold the great dome that he envisioned. This was to be raised above the body of the church on a cylinder or drum of masonry to make the full curve of the dome visible externally. Michelangelo, a sculptor, thought in terms of form, not structure. The necessary buttressing for the dome of St. Peter's is provided by chains embedded in the masonry. The dome was completed (1588–1592) after Michelangelo's death by Giacomo della Porta, who modified it in some details but without altering the essentials.

The Protestant Reformation had forced a rebuttal from the Roman Catholic Church. The Council of Trent, sitting when Michelangelo was made architect of St. Peter's, formulated the church's position in the Catholic Counter-Reformation. It emphasized the unity of the church and its complete power and authority in religious matters. The unity and power of the dome of St. Peter's is the perfect architectural expression of this position.

Much of the effect that Michelangelo had in mind for his dome was lost when the present nave was added to St. Peter's (built 1606–1626) by Carlo Maderna. The decision to abandon Bramante's and Michelangelo's central type church in favor of the basilican Latin cross form was made, not by any architect but by the Papacy itself. For the reasons discussed above, the central type lends itself less successfully to congregational worship than does the basilican form. Moreover, St. Peter's, as it then existed, did not cover all the ground occupied by the nave of the former basilica. The inclusion of this ground, hallowed by centuries of use, may have been a reason behind the decision to add the present nave.

Maderna could only prolong the eastern arm of Michelangelo's design by adding three more large bays to it; the dimensions and the architectural organization were already fixed. His design for the facade also preserves Michelangelo's intentions, except that Maderna gave up the free-standing colonnade envisioned by his predecessor to avoid bringing the facade any farther forward than necessary. As it is, the projection of the facade tends to screen the dome and even the drum from view as one approaches the church. Consequently, the dome is far less effective from the front than from the Vatican gardens behind St. Peter's.

The last major addition to the great complex was the regularization of its approaches. Gian Lorenzo Bernini designed first a trapezoidal piazza and then the elliptical colonnades (1656–1663) that seem to gather in the faithful at the front of the church. On festive occasions, the pope appears at a balcony on the facade of St. Peter's to bless the thousands of Catholics gathered in the huge colonnaded piazza. See also RENAISSANCE ARCHITECTURE.

Jesuit Influence. Another innovation of the Counter-Reformation was the establishment in 1540 of the Society of Jesus, commonly called the Jesuit order, by St. Ignatius of Loyola. Its military organization made it a powerful weapon in the church's struggle to stem the spread of heresy. Il Gesù in Rome (begun 1568), the mother church of the order, is typical of many late 16th century churches in Rome and elsewhere. Its designer, Giacomo Barozzi da Vignola, recognized that the traditional church with its nave and side aisles would not wholly meet contemporary needs.

While most of the rituals of Catholicism remained unchanged, processions had declined in importance, and the sermon had gained prominence. In fact, the Jesuits sometimes had preachers in two pulpits presenting the sermon as a dialogue between them. Preaching, of course, was well known in the Middle Ages. The dramatic sermons of Peter the Hermit at Clermont-Ferrand, France, had done much to launch the first crusade in 1095, and the Dominican order, founded in 1215, was composed of preaching friars. Nevertheless, the spatial complexity of the Gothic cathedral was hardly an ideal setting for the spoken word. The congregation must be able to see and hear the speaker clearly if it is to follow his argument or discourse.

To achieve the more unified and concentrated space required for these purposes, Vignola contracted the transepts until they hardly project beyond the walls of the church. He broadened the nave and replaced the side aisles by lateral chapels. The chapels were primarily for private devotion, but the congregation was concentrated in the wide nave and shallow transepts with full vision of the pulpit.

Protestantism and Anglicanism. The sermon played an even more dominant role after the various branches of Protestantism began to emerge in the early 16th century. When, in 1517, Martin Luther posted his theses on the doors of Wittenberg Cathedral, he unwittingly started the Protestant Reformation. One effect of the Reformation was a partial return to the simpler forms of worship that were ascribed to early Christianity. The elaborate rituals that had grown up in the Catholic Church were suppressed, as were the sumptuous vestments of the clergy. With the Protestant emphasis on the individual's direct responsibility to God rather than through the church as intermediary, processions and formalism gave way to plainness. Veneration of relics and of everything associated with them was so strongly disapproved that the more ardent Puritans of the 16th century destroyed untold numbers of images of saints in sculpture and stained glass.

When Henry VIII rejected the authority of the pope over the Church in England, he insisted that this did not alter the fundamental Catholic faith of Anglicanism or its descent from the

J. ALLAN CASH, FROM RAPHO GUILLUMETTE

ST. PATRICK'S in New York City, a major example of the 19th-century Gothic Revival in the United States.

apostolic succession. But in fact, under his successor Edward VI, the English Church drifted far toward Protestantism. There was a brief reversion to Catholicism under Mary Tudor before the middle course of Anglicanism was established under Elizabeth I.

Where the new faiths—Lutheran, Calvinist, Anglican—became dominant, services were usually held in already existing churches. Features of the older buildings that were adapted to Catholic ritual were simply ignored. England, for example, had an abundance of parish churches that without change could be used for Anglican services. When Protestant faiths began to build their own meetinghouses, the plainness of worship called for corresponding severity in architecture. A simple boxlike auditorium was needed, with a pulpit in a dominant position, and perhaps galleries to the sides and rear for additional seating, as in some of the Huguenot meetinghouses in France. This added space became necessary as the emphasis on preaching required pews to seat the congregation. Medieval churches had had no seats except choir stalls for the clergy. The congregation either stood or kneeled during the Mass. The benches or box pews introduced during the Reformation required more room per person in the interior of the church. The plainness and generally utilitarian character of Protestant churches of the 16th century gave them little architectural interest.

Churches of Christopher Wren. When the great fire of 1666 wiped out most of the city of London, it destroyed half a hundred churches. The rebuilding of these churches fell to the lot of Sir Christopher Wren, the royal architect. The destroyed medieval churches had occupied irregular plots of ground and, surrounded by other

THOMPSON, FROM ART REFERENCE BUREAU

COVENTRY CATHEDRAL, completed in 1962, replaced a Gothic cathedral destroyed by bombing in World War II.

buildings, had only a small access to the street. Wren showed remarkable ingenuity in contriving a variety of orderly plans for the old irregular sites.

Generally, he omitted the separate sanctuary, placing the altar instead at one end of the main volume. Consequently, the altar, and sacramental worship, lost some of their prominence. The pulpit, on the other hand, gained in importance. The interiors of such churches as St. Mary-le-Bow, Cheapside, and St. Bride's, Fleet Street, are light in color with some decorative gilding. Their clear glass windows made it possible for the congregation to follow the service in prayer books, whereas the medieval churches, because of their stained-glass windows, had been too dark for reading even if books had been available. Because little more than the entrance of these churches was visible from the street, Wren designed a great variety of towers and steeples to rise above the surrounding buildings. The tower of St. Mary-le-Bow is square in plan through the belfry level, with circular colonnaded stories above becoming progressively smaller and crowned by a pyramid.

Wren designed St. Paul's Cathedral (built 1668–1710) to replace the medieval church. He would have preferred a central-plan building, but English conservatism forced a longitudinal plan. The length, and the presence of a western transept, come from English sources. The dome, with a continuous colonnade in the drum, is more structural than Michelangelo's dome for St. Peter's and no less effective as a visual focus of the whole building. The western towers and steeples, also seen in Wren's parish churches,

indicate an Italian baroque influence, while the paired colonnade of the porch derives from the east front of the Louvre in Paris. And yet Wren's genius welded these diverse sources into an original and unified design. St. Paul's is the only major cathedral of the Western world to be completed within the lifetime of the designing architect.

Wren's successors of the 18th century continued to design well-lighted parish churches with prominent towers and steeples. St. Martin's-in-the-Fields, in Trafalgar Square, London (built 1721–1726), by James Gibbs, adds a colonnaded portico in front of the church. It was Gibbs' influence that transmitted a modified Wren manner to the English colonies.

Early Churches in the United States. The earliest extant church in the United States is St. Luke's in Smithfield, Va. (1632). As one would expect for this time, this Anglican church continues the late Gothic tradition in brick. The Old Ship Meeting House in Hingham, Mass. (1681), is a Puritan building, an unpretentious structure, square in plan, with a pyramidal hipped roof topped with a small belfry. Galleries surround three sides of the boxlike interior whose exposed roof timbers are curved like the beams of a wooden ship. Box pews fill the floor and galleries to seat the congregation during the long sermons. There is no altar in the traditional sense. However, a pulpit occupies the center of one wall. It is raised well above the floor, so that the minister could dominate his congregation on the floor and in the galleries.

With the advent of the Georgian style in the 18th century, both Protestant and Anglican churches followed the Gibbsian style. That there is no important architectural difference suggests how similar to Protestantism Anglican worship had become. St. Paul's Chapel in New York City (built 1764–1766), designed by Thomas Mc-Bean, has a colonnaded portico at one end and a tower and steeple at the other. St. Paul's is Anglican, but equally fine steeples may be seen on the First Baptist Church in Providence, R. I., and on the Puritan Old South Meeting House in Boston.

19th Century. The 19th century was an age of eclecticism. Churches, like other buildings, were designed after the manner of past architectural styles. Thus the Madeleine in Paris (built 1807–1842), by Barthélemy Vignon, was shaped like a Roman temple with free-standing colonnades around it and a pediment terminating the gable roof over the entrance. No one would guess from this Roman exterior that the interior is composed of three domes. The Madeleine is exceptional in the completeness of its Roman temple form. More commonly, 19th century designs preserve only details of past styles—a pedimented portico, a motif like a triumphal arch, or an arcade.

Gothic Revival. The most important religious development of the 19th century in its effect on architecture was the revival in the Anglican Church known as the Oxford movement. After its separation from the Roman Catholic Church under Henry VIII, Anglicanism had moved far away from its Catholic background. By the 18th century, itself hardly a religious age, the established church had become an almost empty form. Ministers carried out their duties in a perfunctory manner, and laymen attended church more from habit and social duty than from religious conviction. The consecrated interiors of churches

THE STARKLY MODERN Roman Catholic Cathedral of Tokyo, designed by the noted Japanese architect Kenzo Tange and completed in 1965, retains and dramatizes the traditional cruciform plan of early cathedrals.

were so little revered that part of St. Paul's Cathedral became a semipublic thoroughfare known as Paul's Walk. Sacramental worship was all but abandoned. A bishop could refer to the sacrament of baptism as a venerable custom in which he could see no harm. Clearly something needed to be done if Anglicanism was to be considered a religion at all.

The Oxford movement began with Bishop John Keble's sermon on "National Apostasy," preached at the Assizes of Oxford in 1833. Keble called for a return to the purity and fervor of medieval faith. The ensuing religious revival brought about a renewed emphasis on the sacraments and, consequently, a partial return to older ritual. To be sure, processions did not play the role that they had in the medieval church, and the veneration of relics was not revived, but the trend toward a return to religious forms as they had existed before the Reformation was unmistakable. The new spirit led some people to the Roman Catholic Church, as in the cases of John Henry Cardinal Newman and Augustus Welby Northmore Pugin, the foremost Gothic Revival architect.

The religious revival had the effect of reviving also the architectural forms that had been created as a setting for earlier, more formal worship. Pugin, indeed, identified Gothic architecture as Christian architecture. The Cambridge Camden Society was formed in 1839 to advise prospective church builders on the proper liturgical disposition of the church and its furnishings. Its periodical, the *Ecclesiologist*, dispensed advice on matters pertaining to the sanctity of the chancel and the necessity of separating it from the space for the laity; the proper placement of the altar, the lectern, and the pulpit; and proper orientation, although this last point was not always followed.

Pugin's work, such as St. George's in Southwark, is liturgically correct. The deep chancel is distinct from the nave and screened from it, as in English medieval churches. Galleries were generally abandoned, and in Pugin's designs the forms of Gothic architecture—its piers, vaulted or timber roofs, tracery, buttresses, and pinnacles—are followed with much understanding. But Pugin could not resurrect the medieval craftsmanship that had given such freshness to the old designs. However scholarly his work, it does not quite recapture the vitality of medieval churches.

The new movement was felt also in the Protestant Episcopal Church in the United States. There, its principal exponent in architecture was Richard Upjohn, whose design for Trinity Church in New York City (built 1839–1846), may be the first relatively pure Gothic design in the country. Its frank expression of nave, aisles, chancel, and tower come from English parish churches of the Perpendicular style, and yet it is not a copy of any specific building. The deep chancel, the absence of galleries, and the general adaptation to the spirit of the new liturgy are complete.

Because of the pivotal position of Trinity parish in the Episcopal Church, its example was widely followed throughout the United States. For poorer parishes, Upjohn devised a simple design to be executed in wood. The windows have pointed arches and the tower has a plain spire, but the significance of this design lies in its careful provision for the new liturgy. Money

13

GREEK REVIVAL pillars were used in the early 19th century Congregational Church of Litchfield, Conn.

might be saved by the use of cheaper materials and simpler construction, and by abandoning decoration, but never at the expense of a deep chancel.

Probably the largest Gothic Revival church in America is St. Patrick's Cathedral in New York City (built 1850–1879), by James Renwick. Here, instead of the Gothic style of English parish churches, is the full continental cathedral form with apse, transepts, and twin western towers. Like Trinity Church, the vaulted form of the ceiling is not constructed of stone and has no outward lateral thrust. Hence there was no need for flying buttresses, and Renwick quite properly omitted them.

When Henry Hobson Richardson designed Trinity Church in Boston (begun 1872), he turned to the Romanesque style for inspiration, in the belief that the ruggedness of the earlier style was suited to a young and vigorous country. Elements derived from the Spanish Romanesque Cathedral of Salamanca and from the French Romanesque styles of Auvergne and Provence are identifiable, but these eclectic traces are subordinate to a powerful organization of masses and volumes. Because the church was built for the great Episcopal preacher Phillips Brooks, the architect gave it a kind of Greek-cross plan with a short, wide nave, broad, shallow transepts, and almost no aisles. Brooks in his pulpit was visible and could be heard from every seat in the church.

20th Century. Eclecticism continued to dominate church architecture from 1890 to 1930. The firm of Cram, Goodhue, and Ferguson was especially associated with the Gothic style, regardless of the sect to be served. They designed All Saints Church (Episcopal) in Boston, the First Baptist Church in Pittsburgh, the Cathedral of Bryn Athyn (Swedenborgian) near Philadel-

phia, and the chapel of the United States Military Academy (nonsectarian) at West Point, N. Y.

The source of most of these designs is the later phases of Gothic architecture, either English or French. Ralph Adams Cram seemed to resume the architectural thought of his Gothic forebears after a lapse of four centuries. These modern Gothic designs are distinct from churches of the Gothic Revival in that they have a certain facility of handling and a freedom and freshness that recapture much of the spirit as well as the forms of the past and adapt them to modern purposes. Why this should be so is not clear. Cram's knowledge of Gothic was profound, but so was Pugin's.

There are two factors that may have given Cram his advantage. By the late 19th century, faster travel made it possible for architects frequently to visit the buildings of the past and refresh their memories of them. Also, Cram and his contemporaries were able to study architectural masterpieces of the past through photographs, which are better able to capture their true flavor than the line engravings on which architects of the Gothic Revival had to rely. Between 1880 and 1900 photographs had replaced engravings in architectural books and journals.

Cram's individual designs, such as the nave of the Cathedral of St. John the Divine in New York City, were sometimes scholarly restudies—in this case of Bourges Cathedral. Without losing the spirit of the past, Bertram Goodhue in St. Thomas' Church, New York City, felt free to modify details. Riverside Church, also in New York City, was designed by the firm of Allen and Collens as a setting for the sermons of Harry Emerson Fosdick. Although the church has some echoes of Laon Cathedral in France, the broad auditorium is hardly Gothic in its handling of space, or in the steel construction concealed within the Gothic buttresses of stone.

Perhaps because the Episcopal and Protestant churches had chosen the Gothic style, the firm of Maginnis and Walsh preferred some phase of the Romanesque for their Catholic churches, such as St. Catherine's in Somerville, Mass. Nor was the Georgian style neglected; the Village Chapel in Pinehurst, N. C., and the First Baptist Church in Plainfield, N. J., both by Hobart Upjohn, are as perfect in proportion and as exquisite in detail as any churches of the 18th century.

Even when these designs—Gothic, Georgian, or Romanesque—most closely approximate historical precedent, they are still adapted to 20th century needs. In St. Thomas' Church in New York City, the aisles have dwindled in size from their Gothic precedent because processions no longer have a large role in most Episcopal services. The auditorium of Riverside Church has no model in the Gothic. But the most important difference between 20th century churches and those of all earlier periods is the provision made in almost all 20th century churches for Sunday school, lay meetings, and other semisocial activities. Until the 20th century, churches had provided for several types of worship, but nothing more. Sunday school and church social activities are given as much space in the First Baptist Church in Plainfield, N. J., as the church proper occupies. In Riverside Church the lofty tower houses offices, lecture rooms, and

FRANK LLOYD WRIGHT'S First Unitarian Church in Madison, Wis., an example of contemporary church architecture.

other facilities, and even a gymnasium and a garage have their places in the complex. Clearly modern churches must be designed to provide for more than a few services on Sundays.

Not all churches of the 20th century are based on historic styles. Frank Lloyd Wright's Unity Church in Oak Park, Ill. (1903–1905), shows none of the nostalgia for the past that may be felt in St. John the Divine. Its modern material, concrete, as well as its rectilinear forms and skylit interior are far from Gothic mysticism, but reflect instead the rationalism of the Unitarian faith. Le Corbusier's Chapel of Notre Dame du Haut at Ronchamps, France, forms a shrine enclosed by the free-flowing forms of walls and roof.

Finally, mention should be made of a liturgical development affecting architecture in the Anglican Church. Instead of services being performed entirely by the clergy for the laity, some parishes have made an effort to give individual laymen a larger role and a more direct responsibility in the services. This has fostered a trend toward bringing the altar out of the chancel and placing it where the congregation may surround it. The priest celebrating the Eucharistic service may face part of his congregation across the altar, thus reversing the change in ritual that took place in the 5th century.

Advocates of these changes maintain that they are returning to practices of the very early church. If these changes should be widely accepted, they could lead to the abandonment of the basilican form, with its longitudinal axis, in favor of churches in some variety of the central type.

See also ECCLESIASTICAL ART.

EVERARD M. UPJOHN, *Columbia University*

Bibliography

Biéler, André, *Architecture in Worship* (Edinburgh 1965).
Bumpus, Thomas F., *The Cathedrals and Churches of Italy* (New York 1926).
Christ-Janer, Albert W., and Foley, M. M., *Modern Church Architecture* (New York 1962).
Clarke, Basil F. L., *Church Builders of the Nineteenth Century* (New York 1938).
Conant, Kenneth J., *Carolingian and Romanesque Architecture, 800–1200* (Baltimore 1959).
Dorsey, Stephen P., *Early English Churches in America, 1607–1807* (New York 1952).
Frankl, Paul, *Gothic Architecture* (Baltimore 1962).
Gardner, Arthur, *An Introduction to French Church Architecture* (New York 1938).
Hamlin, Talbot F., ed., *Forms and Functions of Twentieth Century Architecture*, 4 vols. (New York 1952).
Hempel, Eberhard, *Baroque Art and Architecture in Central Europe* (Baltimore 1965).
Hitchcock, Henry Russell, *Architecture Nineteenth and Twentieth Centuries* (Baltimore 1958).
Krautheimer, Richard, *Early Christian and Byzantine Architecture* (Baltimore 1965).
Short, Ernest H., *History of Religious Architecture*, 3d ed. rev. (New York 1951).
Short, Ernest H., ed., *Post-War Church Building* (London 1947).
Summerson, John, *Architecture in Britain, 1530–1830* (Baltimore 1954).
Webb, Geoffrey, *Architecture in Britain: The Middle Ages* (Baltimore 1956).
Wittkower, Rudolf, *Art and Architecture in Italy, 1600–1750* (Baltimore 1958).

For Specialized Study

Addleshaw, George William O., and Etchells, Frederick, *The Architectural Setting of Anglican Worship* (London 1948).
Briggs, Martin S., *Puritan Architecture and Its Future* (London 1946).
Bruggink, Donald J., and Droppers, C. H., *Christ and Architecture; Building Presbyterian/Reformed Churches* (Grand Rapids, Mich., 1965).
Clapham, Alfred W., *English Romanesque Architecture* (New York 1965).
Davies, John G., *The Architectural Setting of Baptism* (London 1962).
Dolbey, George W., *The Architectural Expression of Methodism* (London 1964).
Faulkner, Charles D., *Christian Science Church Edifices* (Chicago 1946).
Fiddes, Victor H., *The Architectural Requirements of Protestant Worship* (Toronto 1961).
Hammond, Peter, *Liturgy and Architecture* (New York 1961).
Kretzmann, Paul E., *Christian Art in the Place and in the Form of Lutheran Worship* (St. Louis 1921).
Kubler, George, and Soria, Martin, *Art and Architecture in Spain and Portugal and Their American Dominions, 1500–1800* (Baltimore 1959).
Lowrie, Walter, *Art in the Early Church* (New York 1947).
Perkins, E. Benson, and Hearn, Albert, *The Methodist Church Builds Again* (London 1946).
Reed, Henry Hope, *In the Shadow of St. Barbara and St. Thomas; Catholic Church Architecture in America* (New York 1956).
Sinnott, Edmund Ware, *Meeting House and Church in Early New England* (New York 1963).
Swift, Emerson H., *Roman Sources of Christian Art* (New York 1951).
White, James F., *The Cambridge Movement: The Ecclesiologists and the Gothic Revival* (New York 1962).

CATHER, kath'ər, **Willa** (1873–1947), American novelist and short-story writer, who celebrated the pioneer traditions of the Nebraska prairies and the deserts of the Southwest. Miss Cather once told an interviewer that "the years from 8 to 15 are the formative period in a writer's life, when he unconsciously gathers basic material." These were roughly the years she spent in Webster county, Nebraska, the land she later left for the city but which she could never truly escape, and for which, consciously or not, she became a spokesman. All her fiction (and this is true even of those short stories and novels not set in the West) was built around pioneer traits and themes: courage and struggle, sensitivity to the land, child-parent ties and adolescent restlessness, the debilitating aridity of small-town life on the prairies, the quest for ancestors, and the sense of the legendary and historical past. She became a champion of these elements of an older society against the modern, industrial, materialistic world.

Life. Willa Cather was born in Back Creek Valley, near Winchester, Va., on Dec. 7, 1873. When she was a child, her father moved his family to a ranch near Red Cloud, Nebr., and after a year of homesteading settled in the little frontier village itself. Miss Cather grew up among the immigrant farmers of the region and was educated at home, in schools in Red Cloud and Lincoln, and at the University of Nebraska, where she supported herself by writing drama criticism for the *Nebraska State Journal.*

Fond of music and intellectual pursuits (she was a Latin scholar), Miss Cather left Nebraska at 22 for Pittsburgh, Pa., where her first job was editorial work on *The Home Monthly.* To find more time for writing poetry and stories, she left journalism to teach Latin and English in Pittsburgh high schools. A collection of stories, *The Troll Garden* (1905), which included the famous *Paul's Case,* so impressed the great publisher and editor S. S. McClure that he offered Miss Cather an editorial position on *McClure's Magazine.* She then moved to New York, where she became the brilliant managing editor of that reform-minded magazine.

On a visit to Boston, Miss Cather met the New England author Sarah Orne Jewett, who urged her to give up journalism entirely. "It is impossible for you to work so hard," Miss Jewett wrote, "and yet to have your gifts mature as they should." Willa Cather took heed and in 1912 gave up a comfortable income in journalism for the riskier but more rewarding career of novelist. The same year she paid a prolonged visit to her brother Douglass in Arizona, and on the way back east spent two months in Red Cloud refreshing childhood memories. For the next 15 years, she and Edith Lewis, her future biographer, shared a Greenwich Village apartment. During these years Miss Cather wrote eight novels; she finished two more novels, a book of short stories, and a volume of miscellaneous essays before she died in New York City on April 24, 1947.

Writings. Willa Cather wrote a graceful, measured prose that gives immense dignity to her fiction. Always she searched for the essential forms of experience and for her own distinctively austere, restrained literary methods of embodying them.

"O Pioneers!". Willa Cather's first successful novel was *O Pioneers!* (1913), the first of three books dealing with the Nebraska frontier—"the kind of country I love," as she wrote much later, with its "old neighbors, once very dear." Alexandra Bergson, the Swedish farmgirl heroine, could doubtless be traced to a prototype in the river country south of Red Cloud and the high plains region called "The Divide." The early death of Alexandra's parents leaves her the head of the family and the narrative centers on her struggle to hold the land and to keep her younger brothers Oscar and Lou on the farm.

"My Ántonia." The story of *My Ántonia* (q.v., 1918), also set in Nebraska, is filtered through the eyes of the narrator, Jim Burden, a pioneer from Virginia, whose prosperous family helps the unfortunate immigrant Shimerda family from Bohemia; but the novel unquestionably revolves around the fortunes of Ántonia Shimerda. In spite of difficulties encountered as a hired girl and desertion by a lover, she retains her steady, honest, joyous character and returns with her illegitimate child to her brother's farm, aware that the earth has a hold she cannot shake off. Eventually, Ántonia marries Cuzak, a good-natured, hard-working fellow immigrant, and raises a large family.

"A Lost Lady." One of the finest short novels in American literature, *A Lost Lady* (1933) is the story of the charming, cultivated Marian Forrester of Sweet Water, Nebr., as seen by the rather naïve Niel Herbert, a youthful admirer. After the death of her husband, a railroad pioneer, Mrs. Forrester slowly degenerates. Niel watches in disillusionment as she gives in to the blandishments of the town's shrewd and unscrupulous upstart, Ivy Peters, before she disappears. She is heard of again only when rumors circulate about her death in Argentina.

"Death Comes for the Archbishop" and "Shadows on the Rock." Miss Cather climaxed her career with *Death Comes for the Archbishop* (q.v., 1927), a novel based on the lives of two historical French clerics, which re-creates the difficult early years of the Roman Catholic Church in the Southwest. Into *Death Comes for the Archbishop,* Willa Cather poured all her talent for interpreting and illuminating the pioneer vision. Her heroes, the intellectual Bishop Latour and his friend the practical Father Vaillant, struggle successfully against Indian indifference to religion, Spanish corruption, and the harshness of the land to establish their faith.

Roman Catholicism also plays an important part in *Shadows on the Rock* (1931), set in 18th century Quebec. The novel tells of the love of Cécile Auclair, daughter of an apothecary, and Pierre Charron, a *coureur de bois.* Nuns, a missionary, and two rival bishops—the old Bishop Laval and his young successor Monseigneur de Saint-Vallier—are background characters.

RICHARD M. LUDWIG
Princeton University

Bibliography

Bennett, Mildred R., *The World of Willa Cather* (Lincoln, Nebr., 1961).
Bloom, Edward A., and Bloom, Lillian D., *Willa Cather's Gift of Sympathy* (Carbondale, Ill., 1962).
Brown, Edward Killoran, and Edel, Leon, *Willa Cather: A Critical Biography* (New York 1953).
Daiches, David, *Willa Cather: A Critical Introduction* (New York 1962).
Lewis, Edith, *Willa Cather Living* (New York 1953).
Randall, John H., *The Landscape and the Looking Glass: Willa Cather's Search for Value* (Boston 1960).
Sergeant, Elizabeth Shepley, *Willa Cather: A Memoir* (Lincoln, Nebr., 1963).
Van Ghent, Dorothy, *Willa Cather* (Minneapolis 1964).

CATHERINE I (1684–1727) was empress of Russia from 1725 to 1727. The daughter of a Lithuanian peasant, she was born Marfa Skavronskaya in Jacobstadt (now Jekābpils, Latvia) on April 5, 1684. As a servant in the home of a Lutheran pastor, she received a rudimentary education. Her first husband was a Swedish dragoon. When the district where she lived was surrendered to the Russians by the Swedes, she was taken as a prisoner of war by the Russian marshal Boris P. Sheremetev. She was taken from Sheremetev by Prince Aleksandr D. Menshikov, at whose house she was seen by Emperor Peter (I) the Great in 1705. She immediately became Peter's mistress and inseparable companion. She bore him 11 children, most of whom died in infancy. Of those who survived, Anna, born in 1708, became duchess of Holstein and mother of Emperor Peter III, and Elizabeth, born in 1709, was the future Empress Elizabeth I.

Catherine (in Russian, Yekaterina) was the great feminine influence in the life of Peter the Great, and she alone could calm his nervous rages. Peter married her in 1712 and officially acknowledged their children as his own. Catherine was crowned empress-consort in a magnificent ceremony in May 1724 and was proclaimed reigning empress on Jan. 28, 1725, immediately after Peter's death. Catherine's claim to the throne was supported by regiments of the palace guards. They brushed aside the demands of other claimants who, in the views of many, had stronger rights to the throne than Peter's widow.

No lasting institutional changes were introduced under Catherine. The Supreme Privy Council, which was established in 1726 and actually ruled Russia in the name of the inexperienced Empress, did not legally restrict the autocracy and was suppressed by Catherine's successors. Foreign affairs were largely directed by Baron Andrei I. Ostermann, who made a close alliance with Austria the keystone of his policies.

Catherine died in St. Petersburg on May 6, 1727. The brief reign of this robust, gay, and shrewd woman must be regarded as a postscript to that of Peter the Great.

PETER CZAP, JR., *Amherst College*

CATHERINE II (1729–1796), empress of Russia from 1762 to 1796, was known as *Catherine the Great.* She was born Princess Sophia Augusta Frederika of Anhalt-Zerbst in Stettin (now Szczecin, Poland) on April 21, 1729. In 1744 she was betrothed to Grand Duke Peter, nephew and heir of Empress Elizabeth of Russia. In June 1744 she embraced the Orthodox faith, being rechristened Yekaterina (Catherine) Alekseyevna, and on Aug. 10, 1745, she was married to the Grand Duke. During 17 unhappy years of married life with Peter, Catherine endured public humiliations and threats of divorce, which she survived only because she enjoyed good relations with Empress Elizabeth. The marriage resulted in the birth of one child in 1754, the future Emperor Paul I, toward whom Catherine displayed near loathing. However, she was capable of maternal affection, as can be seen in her relations with her grandson, the future Emperor Alexander I. As grand duchess, Catherine cultivated good relations at the court and nurtured her desire for power.

At the death of Elizabeth on Dec. 25, 1761, the Grand Duke ascended the throne as Peter III. Peter showed open contempt for Russia and its people. His decision to send Russian troops

BETTMANN ARCHIVE

Catherine II (Catherine the Great) of Russia

against Denmark to benefit the duchy of Holstein, of which he was duke, precipitated a plot to remove him from the throne. Catherine, though no more Russian than her husband, displayed her sympathy for the Russian national feelings of Peter's subjects. A minor German princess with no blood tie to the ruling dynasty, Catherine had an extremely weak claim to the throne, but her closest supporters, officers of the palace guard, brushed aside all obstacles, including a plan to install Catherine as regent for her son Paul. She was acclaimed reigning empress on June 28, 1762. The deposed Peter was subsequently murdered, possibly with Catherine's tacit consent.

Reigning Empress. Catherine's German origin and the unusual circumstances of her accession made it necessary for many of her early measures to be directed toward consolidating her power. She became a defender of the Orthodox faith and the nation, and took various steps to win the political support of the nobility. Unlike her immediate predecessors, Catherine took a personal interest in state affairs and was a diligent monarch. Her early pronouncements on statecraft and reform met the highest standards of the Enlightenment. Many of these sentiments, however, proved little more than rhetorical flourishes when the time came to implement progressive programs or abolish the worst social abuses in the realm. At the same time that she declared herself to be a disciple of Voltaire and Diderot, she handed over tens of thousands of state peasants into personal bondage by distributing them as gifts to her favorites and members of the nobility.

Catherine conducted an animated correspondence with the leading thinkers and statesmen of her time and, in addition to her famous *Memoirs,* wrote plays, fables, satires, and political and historical tracts. However, she imposed the first formal censorship in Russia. Her persecution of the writers Aleksandr Radishchev and Nikolai Novikov reveals her true attitude toward freedom of expression. Catherine was an avid collector of art works, and those in the Hermitage became the foundation of a Russian national collection of world art.

She was sensuous and was never restrained by conventional moral standards. As empress she had a succession of 10 lovers, all of whom held positions in the government. At least three of them, Grigori Orlov, Grigori Potemkin, and Platon Zubov, exercised great political influence.

Internal Affairs. Catherine conceived of a grandiose reform of the Russian government based on her celebrated Nakaz (Instruction) of 1767, a document that owed its chief ideas to the writings of Montesquieu and Cesare Beccaria. A legislative commission met from 1767 to 1768 to act on Catherine's proposals but was dismissed by the Empress before it had a chance to draft a single reform. Local and central administration demanded reform, nevertheless. In 1775 new agencies of provincial administration were created by decree, and in 1785 the Charter of the Towns endeavored to organize the urban population for greater self-government. Both reforms increased the number of officials and administrative cost but did little to raise government standards.

The Charter of the Nobility of April 1785 had a more substantial effect on the social and political structure of the empire. Increased exactions by the nobles had led to mass flights of serfs and to frequent, scattered peasant uprisings, culminating in the revolt of 1773–1774, led by Yemelyan Pugachev. This revolt demonstrated the urgent need for reforms, but its failure ended any hope of improvement. By the new charter the nobility were organized into self-governing corporations to deal with local affairs, and the power of noblemen over serfs living on their estates, great as it was, was further broadened.

Foreign Affairs. The foreign policy of Catherine was chiefly concerned with Poland, Turkey, and Sweden, and, at the end of her reign, with limiting the influence of the French Revolution. A Russo-Prussian alliance concluded in April 1764 was aimed at maintaining a weak and divided Poland. Catherine intervened more seriously in Polish affairs in 1768 and provoked the alarm of Turkey, Austria, and Sweden. Austria was accommodated by being made a party to a partition of Poland in 1772, which cost Poland one third of its territory. Polish attempts at reform and at reducing Russian influence in the country resulted in a Russian invasion and a second partition in 1793, followed by a final partition in 1797, which erased Poland from the map of Europe. Two wars with Turkey, 1768–1774 and 1787–1792, ended with Russian annexation of the Crimea, portions of the Caucasus, and of territories between the Dniester and Bug rivers, and freedom of passage for Russian merchant vessels through the Bosporus and the Dardanelles. Catherine's grand design to restore the Byzantine Empire and create a kingdom of Dacia in the Balkans remained unfulfilled, but her territorial gains mark her foreign policy as perhaps her greatest achievement. Catherine died of apoplexy in St. Petersburg on Nov. 6, 1796.

PETER CZAP, JR., *Amherst College*

Bibliography

Anthony, Katherine, *Catherine the Great* (New York 1925).
Grey, Ian, *Catherine the Great* (Philadelphia 1962).
Maroger, Dominique, ed., *The Memoirs of Catherine the Great* (London 1955).
Oldenbourg, Zoé, *Catherine the Great* (New York 1965).
Thompson, Gladys, *Catherine the Great and the Expansion of Russia* (New York 1950).

CATHERINE DE MÉDICIS, də mā′də-sēs (1519–1589), queen of France, who was the dominant personality during France's religious wars and the mother of three kings of France and of two queens (Spain, Navarre). Catherine was born in Florence, Italy, on April 13, 1519, the daughter of Lorenzo de' Medici, Duke of Urbino, and the niece of Pope Leo X. She was married in 1533 to the Duke d'Orléans, who in 1547 became king of France as Henry II. Catherine was at first unable to conceive a child, and there were rumors that she would be repudiated. After 1544, however, she bore 10 children, of whom seven lived, and her position became more secure. But domestic happiness was denied her because of Henry's infatuation with his mistress, Diane de Poitiers. Catherine, who deeply admired her husband, bore his infidelities with dignity. During her 26 years of marriage she played no part in affairs of state, but her husband's tragic death in 1559 changed this dramatically.

The Reigns of Francis II and Charles IX. For the next three decades Catherine was either regent or chief adviser to her incapable sons (Francis II, reigned 1559–1560; Charles IX, reigned 1560–1574; and Henry III, reigned 1574–1589). Strong-willed, tireless, and intelligent, she pursued one goal: the preservation of the monarchy's power in the mounting chaos of civil war. She was unprincipled and had no loyalties except to her dynasty: to serve it was to serve France. Her religious convictions were nominally Catholic but basically indifferent. She was a woman of the Renaissance in her patronage of the arts. Her building projects included the Tuileries.

Catherine's policies were directed at persuading Catholics and Huguenots (French Calvinists) to coexist in peace. But having only a weak monarchy with which to confront the religious fanaticism of both parties, she was unable to pursue a consistent policy. During the reign of Charles IX she vacillated between toleration and persecution of Calvinism. She sought to promote reconciliation until 1567, then tried to crush the Huguenots by force. When this failed, she granted them liberties by the generous Peace of St.-Germain (1570). But this was followed by the massacre of the Huguenots on St. Bartholomew's Day, Aug. 24, 1572, for which Catherine bore prime responsibility. Henceforth she was distrusted by Catholics and Protestants alike.

The Reign of Henry III. Henry III was not dominated by his mother, but he failed to rule in his own right. Catherine had constantly to steel his nerve and to oversee the vital negotiations with Catholics and Calvinists that were the monarchy's main means of survival. Her dealings with Henry of Navarre, the leader of the Huguenots and the husband of her daughter Marguerite de Valois, helped to restrain the crown's Huguenot foes. By her negotiations with the Catholic League she sought heroically, if unsuccessfully, to protect her son from the domination of his most zealous Catholic subjects. She also restrained her youngest son, the Duke d'Anjou, whose ambitions for a crown in the Low Countries had threatened to drag France into war with Spain,

Catherine died at Blois on Jan. 5, 1589. Her improvisations had not prevented religious war, but they had preserved the monarchy.

EDMUND H. DICKERMAN
University of Connecticut

Further Reading: Héritier, Jean, *Catherine de Medici,* tr. by Charlotte Haldane (New York 1963).

CATHERINE DE'RICCI, dä rēt'chē, **Saint** (1522–1590), Italian mystic and nun. Of noble family, Alessandra was born in Florence on April 23, 1522. On becoming a Dominican nun in 1535, she took the name Catherine. She spent her entire religious life in the convent at Prato, near Florence, serving as prioress from 1552 until her death there on Feb. 2, 1590. A stigmatic who experienced ecstasies and other mystical graces, she exerted widespread influence through personal contacts and extensive correspondence. Her spirituality was much influenced by that of Savonarola. She was canonized in 1746. Her feast is February 13.

JOHN F. BRODERICK, S. J.
Weston College, Mass.

CATHERINE OF ALEXANDRIA, al-ig-zan'drē-ə, **Saint,** Christian martyr, who has been a favorite subject of canvases and icons through the ages. All the details of her life, and perhaps her very existence, belong to the realm of legend.

The two earliest extant sources of her life were composed centuries after the events they purport to record and have no historical value. According to them Catherine belonged to a noble or royal Christian family of Alexandria, Egypt, or perhaps Cyprus. Immediately after baptism she enjoyed a vision of her mystical espousal with Christ. During a persecution, she was seized in Alexandria. At her trial the 18-year-old, highly educated virgin managed to confound 50 philosophers in a religious debate. Thereupon she converted them and the empress and 200 guards as well. She was starved and tortured on a spiked wheel for causing the conversions, but miraculously she remained unharmed. Emperor Maximian, or his son Maxentius, then had her beheaded (Nov. 24 or 25, 305).

By the 8th century veneration for Catherine had penetrated to Rome, and by the 11th century she had become one of the most popular saints. Her feast, November 25, was dropped from the universal liturgical calendar in 1969 because of doubts about her existence.

JOHN F. BRODERICK, S. J.
Weston College, Mass.

CATHERINE OF ARAGON, ar'ə-gon (1485–1536), was the first queen of King Henry VIII of England. She was the daughter of Ferdinand and Isabella, king and queen of Spain. Her parents and Henry VII of England negotiated a marriage that brought her to England in 1501 to be the bride of Henry's older son Arthur, Prince of Wales. The marriage took place in November. However, Arthur died in April 1502 without the marriage having been consummated.

Negotiations began at once for a marriage between Catherine and Henry, the King's second son. For this proposed marriage to a deceased brother's widow a papal dispensation was granted. Formal betrothal followed. During the remaining years of Henry VII's reign Catherine remained in England, virtually a prisoner, while King Henry negotiated with her father over a dowry and other matters of dynastic politics.

On the death of Henry VII in 1509, Henry VIII quickly married Catherine. They lived together happily for some years, and she assumed certain responsibilities in government during Henry's absence on campaigns in France.

From January 1510 to November 1518, Catherine bore Henry six children, two of them boys, but all were stillborn or died in infancy except Mary, who later became queen of England. In the 1520's Catherine's physical condition made it clear that she would bear no more children. Meanwhile Henry had entered into various extramarital unions with other women.

About 1526, Henry began a love affair with Anne Boleyn and made plans for marrying her. His plans depended on gaining from Pope Clement VII a judgment that his marriage to Catherine had been invalid from the beginning. The request for such an invalidation was not unusual among European royal families, but the Pope did not wish to provoke Emperor Charles V, Catherine's nephew. So the Pope began proceedings to consider Henry's request for annulment but managed the hearings in such a way that years passed without conclusive action.

Henry persisted in his search for a papal decision in his favor. He attempted to put pressure on the Pope by legislative action in parliament that deprived the Pope of judicial authority in England and also of financial privileges. Henry's wish to marry Anne Boleyn increased and led to action by Thomas Cranmer, newly created Archbishop of Canterbury, who in 1533 decided that he could convene a court that would decide the matter. His court declared the marriage to Catherine invalid and validated a previous secret marriage between Henry and Anne Boleyn (q.v.). Catherine died on Jan. 7, 1536, shortly before the execution of Anne.

FREDERICK G. MARCHAM
*Goldwin Smith Professor of English History
Cornell University*

CATHERINE OF BOLOGNA, bō-lō'nyä, **Saint** (1413–1463), Italian spiritualist, who experienced visions, revelations, and other mystic graces. She was born in Bologna, Italy, on Sept. 8, 1413. A member of the noble Virgi family, she received a good humanistic education at the court of the Estes in Ferrara, where in 1432 she joined the newly built monastery of the Poor Clares. She was the mistress of novices there for many years and served as abbess in Bologna for all but three years from 1456 until her death on March 9, 1463.

Catherine wrote Latin and Italian verse and prose and composed devotional works and hymns. Her most famous work is *Le sette arme* (*Seven Spiritual Weapons*). Her paintings and miniatures are in several Italian museums. Her feast day is March 9.

JOHN F. BRODERICK, S. J.
Weston College, Mass.

CATHERINE OF BRAGANZA, brə-gan'zə (1638–1705), was the Portuguese wife of King Charles II of England. She was born at Villa Viçosa, Alentejo, Portugal, on Nov. 25, 1638. The treaty of June 23, 1661, which settled her marriage to Charles, was a link in the centuries-long chain of Anglo-Portuguese alliances. In spite of her plain appearance and scanty education, Catherine seemed an ideal bride: her dowry included the ports of Tangier and Bombay, as well as mahogany, sugar, and gold worth about £330,000. In return, England had to furnish soldiers for Portugal's struggle for independence from Spain and to agree to protect Portugal's trading colonies in the Far East from the Dutch.

Although Charles was far from being a model husband, he steadfastly defended his queen against the members of Parliament who accused her of seeking to poison the king. Catherine survived her husband and, though she retired from the court, remained in England through the early years of William and Mary's rule. In 1692, however, she returned to Portugal, where she actively promoted the Anglo-Portuguese treaty of 1703. Then, in the year before her death, Catherine governed the kingdom as regent for her ailing brother Pedro II. She died in Lisbon on Dec. 31, 1705.

JOHN FERGUSON
Columbia University

CATHERINE OF GENOA, jen'ō-ə, **Saint** (1447–1510), Italian mystic noted for her service to the poor and sick. She was born to the powerful Fieschi family in Genoa. In 1473, during an unhappy political marriage to Giuliano Adorno, a nobleman noted for his immorality, she experienced a sudden overwhelming illumination that endowed her with a permanent spiritual outlook. She then began a life of extraordinary asceticism and mysticism. Soon after, her husband went bankrupt and repudiated his former ways, becoming a Franciscan monk. Thereafter the couple devoted themselves to the poor and to the sick in the Pammatone hospital in Genoa, where Catherine was administrative head from 1490 to 1496. The *Treatise on Purgatory* and *Dialogue* attributed to her are spiritual classics. She died in Genoa on Sept. 15, 1510, and was canonized in 1737. Her feast day is celebrated on September 15.

CATHERINE OF SIENA, syâ'nä, **Saint** (c. 1347–1380), Italian mystic and Doctor of the Church. She was born in Siena, Italy. A twin and the 23d of 25 children of Giacomo and Lapa Benincasa, she reportedly experienced the first of her many visions at the age of 7. Rebelling against the constant urgings of her family, who wished her to marry, Catherine finally displayed her determination to dedicate her life to Christ by cutting off her hair and taking a private vow of virginity. After joining the secular Third Order of St. Dominic about 1365, she secluded herself for three years in her room, devoting her time to frequently ecstatic prayer, fasting, and other mortifications. Toward the end of this period, she experienced a vision of her mystical marriage with Christ, who ordered her to engage in active works of charity.

Thereafter a contemplative in action, Catherine revealed remarkable qualities of leadership and initiative. A large group of disciples, including secular and religious priests, as well as lay people, gathered around her. Much of her time was spent giving religious instructions, aiding the poor, and nursing the sick. While tending the plague-stricken in 1374, she contracted the pestilence herself. She gained the reputation of a miracle worker and attracted many lay and ecclesiastical leaders, who sought her counsel and advice.

Catherine thus became embroiled in the political-ecclesiastical issues of her day. The object of many attacks because of her intense convictions, she successfully defended her orthodoxy before the general chapter of the Dominicans at Florence in 1374. To promote a crusade against the Turks she strove for years to unify Western Christians. During a visit to Pisa for this purpose in 1375, she received the stigmata. She visited the papal court at Avignon in a vain and probably unofficial attempt to mediate peace between Florence and the Papal States, but her exhortations may well have been a cause of Pope Gregory XI's resolve to return to Rome. Once there, he sought her efforts to end hostilities, but these were again unsuccessful.

Her almost exclusively spiritual outlook limited her political vision and effectiveness. She supported Pope Urban VI, but her efforts could not prevent the start and spread of the Western Schism which grew out of Urban's election. Her plans for reforming the Roman Curia were not put into effect. The poor reputations long suffered by the Avignon popes were in part caused by her ill-founded denunciations. She died in Rome on April 29, 1380. Her writings include the *Dialogues,* a spiritual classic containing her doctrines, and some 381 letters. Catherine, canonized in 1461, is, along with St. Francis of Assisi, Italy's principal patron saint. Her feast is celebrated on April 30.

JOHN F. BRODERICK, S. J.
Weston College, Mass.

CATHERINE OF SWEDEN, Saint (1331 or 1332–1381). The daughter of St. Bridget of Sweden (q.v.), she was born in Ulfasa. In 1343 she married a nobleman and lived with him in continence until his death in 1351. For more than 20 years thereafter she was her mother's closest companion, sharing her ascetic life in Rome and accompanying her on pilgrimages in Italy and to the Holy Land. After returning to Sweden with Bridget's corpse in 1374, she became the first abbess at Vadstena, the Brigittine convent. Between 1375 and 1380 she promoted the cause of her mother's canonization in Rome, and secured papal approval of the Brigittine rule. She died in Vadstena on March 24, 1381. Although she was never formally canonized, she is commemorated as a saint by the Brigittines, who celebrate her feast on March 24.

JOHN F. BRODERICK, S. J.
Weston College, Mass.

CATHERINE OF VALOIS, và-lwà' (1401–1437), was the wife of Henry V of England, mother of Henry VI, and grandmother of Henry VII, founder of the House of Tudor. Born in Paris on Oct. 27, 1401, Catherine was the youngest daughter of the mad French king Charles VI and Isabella of Bavaria. Although the English had tried earlier to arrange a marriage treaty uniting Henry V and Catherine, they did not succeed until May 1420. By this marriage Henry V became the "adopted" heir to the French throne, while Catherine's brother—the future Charles VII—was disinherited.

The new queen was crowned at Westminster in February 1421 and before the year was out gave birth to a son at Windsor. But Henry V died at Vincennes in August 1422. Passed over as regent for her infant son in favor of his uncles, Catherine retired to the countryside.

In 1428, Parliament passed an act forbidding anyone to marry Catherine without the consent of king and council, though by this time she may have already married the Welshman Owen Tudor. By Owen, Catherine had four children, the eldest of whom was the father of Henry VII. She died at Bermondsey Abbey on Jan. 3, 1437.

JOHN FERGUSON
Columbia University

CATHERINE TEKAKWITHA, kath′ər-ən tek-ə-kwith′ə (1656–1680), Mohawk Indian Catholic, who was the first North American Indian to be a candidate for sainthood. She was born Tekakwitha in Ossernenon (now Auriesville); N. Y. Her mother, a Catholic Algonquin, was captured by the Mohawks and married to one of their pagan sachems. The smallpox epidemic of 1660 left Tekakwitha an orphan with impaired eyesight and pockmarks. Reared by her uncle, she first came into contact with Christian missionaries in 1667, when three Jesuit priests stayed at her uncle's home. She lived thereafter in a Christian manner and, against Indian custom, refused to marry.

Tekakwitha did not receive formal instruction in Catholicism until some years later. In 1676 she was baptized by her instructor, Jacques de Lamberville, a Jesuit priest, and given the name Catherine. Indian opposition to her conversion forced her to move to Caughnawaga, a Christian Indian village near Montreal, Canada, where she lived in great austerity and piety. In 1679 she took a perpetual vow of chastity, an unusual step even among Christianized Indians. She died in Caughnawaga on April 17, 1680. In 1932 the beatification cause of the "Lily of the Mohawk," as Catherine came to be called, was introduced in Rome.

JOHN F. BRODERICK, S. J., *Weston College*

CATHERINE THE GREAT. See CATHERINE II.

CATHERWOOD, Frederick (1799–1854), British-American architect, artist, and engineer, whose drawings first brought the ruins of the ancient

CATHERWOOD'S drawing of a Mayan stela in Copán.

PEABODY MUSEUM, HARVARD UNIVERSITY

Maya of Central America and Mexico to the world's attention. He was born in London on Feb. 27, 1799. He was apprenticed to an architect when he was 16 and later studied at the Royal Academy, where he became influenced by the works of Piranesi. From 1821 to 1835 he traveled in Greece, Egypt, and Syria as an artist attached to archaeological field parties.

Catherwood went to the United States in 1836 and accompanied the explorer John Lloyd Stephens to Central America in 1839–1840 and to Yucatan in 1841–1842. The results of these explorations were published in *Incidents of Travel in Central America* (1841) and *Incidents of Travel in Yucatan* (1843), with drawings by Catherwood. In 1844, Catherwood published by himself his famous album of engravings, *The Views of Ancient Monuments of Central America, Chiapas, and Yucatan*. His drawings combine a delightful romanticism with great fidelity to detail. Modern archaeological work has attested to their accuracy.

Catherwood spent his last 10 years in commercial engineering ventures. He was drowned at sea on Sept. 27, 1854, while crossing the Atlantic.

GORDON R. WILLEY
Author, "Introduction to American Archaeology"

Further Reading: Von Hagen, Victor Wolfgang, *Frederick Catherwood, Arch[t]* (New York 1950).

CATHETER, kath′ə-tər, is a thin tubular instrument usually used for drawing off fluid from a body cavity or an organ, such as the bladder. Sometimes a catheter is used for injecting a liquid or gas into the body. For example, a radio-opaque dye may be injected through a catheter into the tiny blood vessels of the heart so that they may be easily seen on X-ray photographs.

CATHODE, kath′ōd, a solid material, usually a metal or metallic compound, that emits electrons in a controlled environment, usually a vacuum or a gas, when energy is supplied to it.

A *thermionic cathode* is supplied energy in the form of heat, such as the heat produced by passing an electric current through a wire. When heated to a high temperature, the cathode emits electrons; this process is called thermionic emission. Thermionic cathodes supply the free electrons used in the vacuum tubes of radio receivers. Thermionic cathodes also are the source of electron beams used in cathode-ray tubes.

A *photocathode* is supplied energy in the form of light. When light strikes the cathode, it emits electrons; this process is called photoelectric emission. Photocathodes are used in electron multiplier tubes, in some types of television camera tubes, and in infrared detectors.

GLENN M. GLASFORD, *Syracuse University*

CATHODE-RAY TUBE, an electron-tube device that presents a visual display on a luminescent surface. The most familiar form of the cathode-ray tube is the television picture tube, which presents the picture on the home television screen.

Engineers and technicians use visual data presented by cathode-ray oscilloscopes to aid them in designing, testing, and repairing electronic equipment. The military services use cathode-ray tubes to aid in navigation and to detect enemy vessels and aircraft; the radar scope and the visual indicator used in sonar are

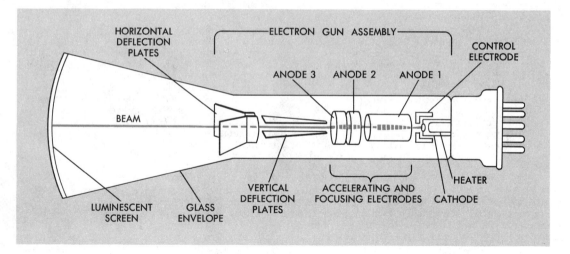

HORIZONTAL DEFLECTION PLATES — ELECTRON GUN ASSEMBLY — CONTROL ELECTRODE — ANODE 3 — ANODE 2 — ANODE 1 — BEAM — LUMINESCENT SCREEN — GLASS ENVELOPE — VERTICAL DEFLECTION PLATES — ACCELERATING AND FOCUSING ELECTRODES — CATHODE — HEATER

cathode-ray tube screens. (See also RADAR—1. *Principles.*) The cathode-ray tube also is used with computer systems to provide a visual display of computer output data; sometimes, a cathode-ray tube is used with a light pen and a computer so that diagrams can be used as a medium of communication between the computer and its user. The diagrams on the face of the tube provide communication in graphic form and thus supplement the conventional use of printed data.

How a Cathode-Ray Tube Works. The cathode-ray tube provides a visual display in the following way: (1) its thermionic cathode produces a stream of electrons; (2) an electric field accelerates the stream of electrons to a desired velocity, or energy level; (3) an electron lens focuses the stream of electrons into an electron beam that has a very small cross section; (4) an electric or magnetic field is used to deflect the focused beam through a prescribed angle; (5) the deflected beam hits a small area of a transparent glass surface coated on the inside with a phosphorescent material that emits light when an electron beam strikes it with sufficient energy; and (6) if the electron beam is swept rapidly and repeatedly across the cathode-ray tube screen, a line of varying intensity is produced rather than a sequence of discrete spots. A complete image of the television type is formed by producing a number of lines on the screen.

Types. There are two basic types of cathode-ray tubes. One, the *electrostatic* cathode-ray tube, is often used in cathode-ray oscilloscopes; the other type, the *electromagnetic* cathode-ray tube, is often used in home TV sets.

Electrostatic Cathode-Ray Tube. In an electrostatic cathode-ray tube, electric fields are used for focusing and for deflecting the electron beam. The section of the tube that is responsible for producing, accelerating, focusing, and deflecting the electron beam is called an *electron gun* (see illustration).

With a typical electrostatic electron gun, the electrons emitted from the cathode pass through a small circular aperture in the grid, or control electrode. Variations of the voltage applied to this grid control the beam current, which is the number of electrons passing through the grid aperture per unit time. Approximately zero voltage with respect to the cathode voltage

results in maximum beam current, while a highly negative voltage reduces it to zero. The beam, which is unfocused at this stage, enters the region of anode 1 and is accelerated to a velocity directly proportional to the voltage applied to this anode. The center section of the beam passes through a second aperture into the region of anode 2 and is decelerated to a lower velocity because of the lower potential in this region. The beam then enters the region of anode 3, which is approximately at the potential of anode 1; in this region, its velocity is again increased. The electric field in the regions between anodes 1 and 3, because of the variation of applied potentials, provides the focusing action. The beam may have been diverging before it entered the region of anode 2, but it is made to converge before leaving the region of anode 3, allowing most of the beam current to pass through a small limiting aperture that defines the final limit of the size of the beam cross section.

When a potential difference is applied between the first pair of deflection plates, electrons in the beam are deflected toward whichever plate is the more positive, the deflection being directly proportional to the applied potential and inversely proportional to the velocity of the electrons. This first pair of plates, called *vertical deflection plates*, deflect the beam upward or downward. Another potential difference is applied between the second pair of plates, which are oriented at right angles to the first pair. This potential difference causes the beam to be deflected toward whichever plate is the more positive. This pair of deflection plates, called *horizontal deflection plates*, deflect the beam to the left or to the right of the axis of the tube. Thus, by applying a combination of time-varying voltages to the two sets of deflection plates, the beam can be made to follow any path to the screen.

Electromagnetic Cathode-Ray Tube. An electromagnetic cathode-ray tube is one in which beam deflection is produced by a magnetic rather than an electric field. The beam may be focused by electrostatic or electromagnetic means.

A magnetically focused tube has a focus coil, which is a coil of wire oriented radially to the axis of the tube. The turns of the coil are enclosed in a magnetically shielded case that encircles the neck of the tube. There is a small air gap between the case and the tube; the magnetic flux leakage across this gap produces a short longitudinal magnetic field within the neck of the tube. This field has a focusing action analogous to that of the electrostatic system.

Horizontal deflection of the beam is provided by currents in segments of a coil oriented parallel to the axis of the tube. These coil segments produce a magnetic field directed to the left or to the right of the axis of the tube, depending on the direction of the applied current. Vertical deflection of the beam is provided by currents in other coil segments oriented at right angles to the first group. These coil segments produce a magnetic field directed upward or downward, depending on the direction of the applied current. Deflection of the beam depends on the coil current and other factors.

A typical electromagnetic cathode-ray tube has a rectangular viewing area that is used efficiently when the beam is swept horizontally across the screen at a rate many times that of its vertical rate, as is done in television. In general it is possible to get, efficiently, much wider deflection angles with magnetic deflection that with electrostatic deflection. Hence, it is possible to use a much shorter electromagnetic cathode-ray tube to obtain a given amount of beam deflection. For this reason, the television picture tube is usually of this type.

GLENN M. GLASFORD, *Syracuse University*

CATHODE RAYS, kath′ōd, are negatively charged particles emitted from a cathode. These particles, now called electrons, were identified by the English physicist Joseph J. Thomson in 1897. The term "cathode ray" was used to denote these particles before Thomson identified them as electrons.

Cathode rays are used in devices such as cathode-ray tubes, television image pickup tubes, electron microscopes, and particle accelerators. Cathode rays also are used in many types of recording, copying, or display devices.

In normal usage, the cathode rays are focused into a narrow beam by elements of an electron gun, using electric or magnetic fields or both, and accelerated to a high velocity by means of an electric field directed along the axis of travel of the beam. Once focused, the beam may be deflected by means of other electric or magnetic fields, which force it to follow a prescribed path. The term "electron beam" is used in preference to the term "cathode rays" when reference is made to moving electrons.

GLENN M. GLASFORD, *Syracuse University*

CATHOLIC ACTION MOVEMENT, as defined by Pope Pius XI, "the participation of the laity in the apostolate of the Church's hierarchy." He gave the movement a charter, a spirit, and an apocalyptic urgency. In 1957, Pius XII asserted that all national and international groups "belong to Catholic Action" in a way "to preserve their autonomy" while at the same time forming "a federated unit." In the United States, the National Councils of Catholic Men and Women and the Confraternities of Christian Doctrine are the largest federated lay groups.

Pope John XXIII (reigned 1958–1963) applied the term "lay apostolate" to Catholic lay activity, both organized and unorganized, and by the use of this formula helped to end quibbles over terms and jurisdiction. On Nov. 18, 1965, the Second Vatican Council voted for the promulgation of the Decree of the Apostolate of the Laity, which outlines a developing theology of the laity, and offers guidelines to lay leadership. In order to expand cooperation among lay groups and foster greater understanding between the clergy and the laity, the Roman Catholic Church has established the Council of the Laity.

HARRY J. SIEVERS, S. J.
Loyola Seminary, Shrub Oak, N. Y.

CATHOLIC CHURCH is a term that is part of the formal title of the Roman Catholic Church (see CATHOLIC CHURCH, ROMAN). It is also applied to the Eastern Orthodox Church and is used by some Protestant churches in the Apostles' Creed. The term "Catholic" means "universal." The early Christian writings, beginning with the New Testament, assume that the Gospel is to be proclaimed throughout the world and that Christians will be found everywhere.

The first use of the word "Catholic" in the surviving early Christian literature is in the letter to the Smyrnaeans by St. Ignatius of Antioch (about 107 A. D.): "Wherever the bishop appears, there let the congregation be gathered, just as where Jesus Christ is, there is the Catholic Church. Without the bishop, it is not lawful either to baptize or to hold the lovefeast (*agapē*)". Emphasis upon episcopal authority, concern for the validity of the sacraments, and the presupposed indwelling presence of Christ in the church are already evident in this brief statement of the bishop of Antioch on his way to martyrdom in Rome. Here, as in later usage, the "Catholic" church is understood to mean the whole or "universal" church as distinct from the local congregation. Catholic belief or teaching is the faith held "everywhere, always, and by all." It is the teaching of Holy Scripture as set forth by the universal church. The authoritative theological meaning of the term "Catholic" was most natural and came into general use at an early date. As heresies arose, it was used to distinguish the "true" church.

Thus another definition of "Catholic" arose, as meaning opposed to limited, sectarian, heretical, or schismatic views or groups. This usage prevailed for almost 10 centuries, up to the final separation between East and West, after which the Eastern Churches distinguished themselves by using the title "Orthodox." This left the title "Catholic" to be maintained (and claimed) by Rome and the West. In modern Protestant usage, "Catholic" is sometimes included in the doctrinal definitions of the Reformed Churches, and its use in the Apostles' Creed is still maintained—some groups preferring to translate it by "Universal." In the Book of Common Prayer the third article of the creed reads: "I believe in the Holy Catholic Church, the Communion of Saints."

The Roman Catholic Church has steadfastly maintained the ancient title, often without contest by other churches. But the modern revival of ecumenical theology has emphasized the importance of the title, as among Anglicans, Old Catholics, and even Eastern Orthodox. Thus the term "Greek Catholic Church" is popularly used. The Ecumenical Movement of the 20th century aroused fresh interest in the ancient title among Christians generally.

FREDERICK C. GRANT
Union Theological Seminary

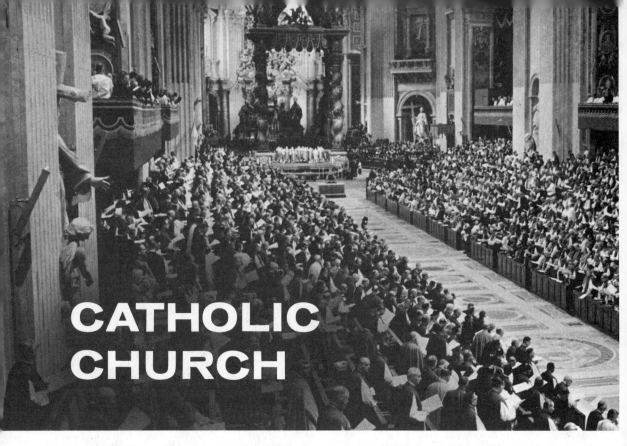

CATHOLIC CHURCH

ECUMENICAL COUNCIL VATICAN II opens with papal Mass in St. Peter's, Rome, on Sept. 14, 1965.

CONTENTS

CATHOLIC CHURCH, Roman. Catholicism means a way of life, a personal commitment to God through Christ with all the social and individual responsibilities that flow from this commitment. The doctrine or teaching of the Catholic church maps the Christian way of life, directs personal commitment, and reinforces Christian responsibilities. Thus the church has always stressed doctrine. It is appropriate, then, to begin a discussion of Catholicism with its doctrine.

1. Doctrine

The New Testament is full of Christ's commands "to preach the gospel," "to teach," or, more precisely, "to make disciples of all nations" (Matthew 28:19–20), "to witness" (Acts 1:8). In his first letter to the Corinthians (9:16), St. Paul insists on the fulfillment of these commands: "Woe to me if I do not preach the gospel." He further cautions the early Christians to accept and act upon only those teachings which emanate from Christ himself.

Because Catholicism has understood itself to be a religion of revelation, it has emphasized belief in God's revelation, especially as finally communicated by Christ. Indeed, Christ himself *is* God's ultimate revelation to man; and Christ's church is viewed as the mediator of God's revelation. This view does not, however, create a dichotomy between the church's role and Christ's unique mediation, because Christ is "the one mediator." (This point is made explicit in Vatican Council II, Constitution on the Church, section 9.)

TEACHING AUTHORITY

"In order to keep the gospel forever whole and alive within the church, the apostles left bishops as their successors, handing over their own teaching authority to them" (Vatican Council II, Constitution on Divine Revelation, section 7). It is only because the apostles received their commission from Christ that the bishops, as their successors, possess the mission to teach all nations and to preach the gospel to every creature (Vatican Council II, Constitution on the Church, section 24). Thus when all the bishops of the world meet as a "college" in union with the pope, Peter's successor and the bishop of Rome, they constitute the church's most solemn teaching instrumentality—an ecumenical council (see COUNCIL). Although many councils have been held throughout the church's history, the teachings of these councils have been considered normative and final only when confirmed by the pope. An ecumenical council is as extraordinary and rare a means of communicating divine revelation, however, as is a papal pronouncement on matters of faith or morals. But before a pope exercises his unique teaching authority he always consults the bishops, and indeed the laity, since his role is within the college of bishops, not

KEYSTONE PRESS AGENCY, INC.

through the framework of Hebraic, Hellenic, medieval, and modern modes of thought, enabling each successive ecumenical council, as well as all the church's other teaching instrumentalities, to enrich its understanding of basic dogmas without producing new revelation. Catholics believe that the Holy Spirit guides and safeguards the teaching church in this process, so that it is infallible in its teaching on faith and morals. Infallibility does not, of course, involve sinlessness nor does it save the church from the need for constant reform. Still less does it imply a complete understanding of the mysteries contained in revelation. These ultimately must remain beyond full human grasp.

SCOPE AND PURPOSE

Catholic doctrine deals principally with God's saving action in human history; it is thus concerned with man, to whom God revealed himself. Not only is man God's noble creature, but historically he is an innately frustrated noble creature. As originally created, man was perfectly integrated, in harmony with God, himself, and the universe. By an act of sin (which most theologians believe was basically that of pride), man destroyed this integrity: he lost his special harmony with God, with self, with creation. Human nature henceforth, in terms of God's original design, became deficient. This is what is meant by original sin. It is called sin since it flowed from sin and leads to other sin. Although original sin is inherited and not personally committed, it is sin in a profound sense since it is the state of total alienation from God. Because man's whole being is a dynamism toward God, alienation is the frustration of that dynamism. This means that man needs to be saved, to be reformed, so that his energy can reach its intended goal. See also ORIGINAL SIN.

In spite of original sin, man is still man. His human powers are not destroyed, nor is he totally depraved. His mind can still think and his will can still produce some natural virtue. Harmony with nature or union with God is nevertheless beyond his human grasp. To attain his final goal, the full sharing of the divine life and total fulfillment in God, man needs divine help. This assistance is available in grace—God's helpful presence—but man must respond to this help freely and humanly. Thus the good works man performs through God-given grace and faith enlarge his capacity for ultimate happiness with God. In confronting this option man is able freely and definitively to accept or reject God's help. Utter refusal of grace is called damnation or hell.

And yet God wills the salvation of all (I Timothy 2:4). This salvation is not something spiritual for the soul alone. It is for the human person, both body and soul. Accordingly "resurrection of the body" has always been essential to the Christian creed. While the manner of this resurrection remains mysterious, it is held that after the last judgment of all men "will come the time of the restoration of all things." "The human race as well as the entire world, which is intimately related to man and achieves its purpose through him, will be perfectly reestablished in Christ." (Vatican Council II, Constitution on the Church, section 48, paraphrasing Ephesians 1:10).

Catholic doctrine is, therefore, preeminently a doctrine of salvation. In the solemn words of

outside it; and, since both the pope and the college of bishops are protected by the same Holy Spirit, contradiction between them cannot occur.

Generally the church employs more ordinary means to communicate revelation: local councils, pastoral letters or decrees, preaching and catechetical instruction. The church frequently draws upon the Bible, the Word of God, given to the church for the fulfillment of its teaching ministry. Together with the Bible, though not necessarily separate from it, is sacred tradition. Basically, sacred tradition originated with the apostles, but it "develops in the church with the help of the Holy Spirit" (Constitution on Divine Revelation, section 8) and assumes many forms. The past declarations of the college of bishops and of its center, the pope, are part of tradition. So too are the teachings common to the ancient churchmen known as the "Fathers of the Church." Even the consensus of theologians constitutes part of tradition, as does that of the whole body of the faithful. These various forms of tradition do not, however, have equal weight. For this reason, theologians have continued to expend much effort in attempting to determine the precise weight of any given teaching. A distinction is made, for example, between those teachings which are considered "solemn," such as that on the Trinity, and those beliefs which are commonly held, such as the idea of guardian angels.

Although Catholics believe that divine revelation was complete at the death of the last apostle, they also believe that our understanding of revelation constantly deepens and grows. As human culture has developed, new insights into the meaning of revelation have also developed. In this way doctrinal development has advanced

Vatican Council II, God "did not abandon men after they had fallen in Adam, but ceaselessly offered them helps to salvation, in anticipation of Christ the Redeemer" (Constitution on the Church, section 2).

SIGNS OF SALVATION

The church teaches because it thinks with Christ and makes explicit the revelation of Christ. The church actively communicates the life of Christ and does this in symbolic signs, or sacraments. These are not merely dramatic presentations of abstract truths, but conveyers of living reality.

The sacraments are seven: *Baptism,* the symbol of death and resurrection to new life (through stylized immersion in water), makes one a member of the church. The *Eucharist,* the sacred meal, or Holy Communion, symbolizing and truly making present Christ as our food, reenacts bloodlessly His sacrifice. The Eucharistic Sacrifice, or the Mass, is the central act of Catholic worship. Through it the People of God, gathered in community, join themselves to Christ the High Priest, in his own act of total self-giving to the Father. *Confirmation,* the outward sign of which is anointing with strengthening oil, prepares one for a life of Christian responsibility and maturity. *Matrimony,* the symbol of the love of Christ and His church, binds together a man and a woman in human marriage. *Holy Orders,* the symbol of official dedication, empowers certain members of the mystical body to perform Christ's priestly action for all. *Penance,* the symbol of the forgiving judgment of the church in the name of Christ, renews the life of grace in the souls of the faithful. *Anointing of the Sick,* or *Extreme Unction,* the symbol of healing anointing, helps the Christian in serious illness or old age before he faces the ordeal of death. See also Section 3. *Liturgy;* and separate article SACRAMENTS.

SOME FUNDAMENTAL DOCTRINES

From a theological viewpoint some doctrines are more fundamental than others since the others are derived from them. First of all, and implicit in all doctrine, is the teaching that a transcendental God exists (which is not to deny His immanence), who made personal contact with man in history. In the early written record of this contact, the Old Testament, His name was given: Yahweh, the living God. Though human reason is able to reach knowledge of his existence, human experience suggests that this is a precarious enterprise and that, in the practical order, man needs divine revelation. The Catholic Church, in claiming to be the "one true Church of Christ," claims to be the Christ-founded interpreter of divine revelation. At the same time the church recognizes that other Christian churches share much of God's truth. Vatican Council II affirmed that "Catholics must joyfully acknowledge and esteem the truly Christian endowments from our common heritage which are to be found among our separated brethren" (Vatican Council II, Decree on Ecumenism, section 4).

The First Principle. In its interpretation of divine revelation, the church views God as the first principle and ground of being. All things come from Him by way of creation. Still, the notion of creation does not deny the theory of evolution, on which revelation sheds no direct light one way or the other. The Biblical account of the origin of the world is seen as a religious message rather than a scientific statement. Phrased in the imagery and literary forms of the time and situation of the writers, the Bible unfolds for us not the scientific history of the cosmos, but the religious meaning of the world's birth, in whatever form it took place.

God is not only the creator of the world, He is also its loving preserver and intelligent planner. At the end of time, human history will prove to have been directed by Providence, and the love and wisdom of God will be manifest.

The Trinity. The one God is triple by reason of three inner personal principles. These three persons are called the Father, Son (or Word), and Holy Spirit. This Trinity does not multiply God, who is one, but does put in the divine oneness three distinct intelligent principles of action. Even with faith the human mind can do little more than accept this truth as a mystery. See also TRINITY.

The Incarnation. Salvation came to man by putting a richer humanity within his reach, and it came in an astounding but truly fitting way: one of the persons of the divine Trinity entered into salvation history as a man. This is known as the Incarnation. This truth is not some mythological expression of the fact that in all men there lies some "divine spark," which, by effort, can be fanned into flame. For the Catholic the Incarnation quite literally means that God became man so that one man, Jesus of Nazareth, was quite literally God. But not only was Jesus truly God; He was just as truly man. Nothing human was missing from Him except sin. Since He was God, He could not be alienated from God. Hence in Him there could be no sin, either original or personal.

The motive of Jesus, the God-man, in His earthly life was redemptive. That is to say, He wished to save man from his innate futility and frustration. He did this by presenting Himself to the Divinity as the proxy of all men and bore the penalty of all on His shoulders. He offered Himself in a sacrificial ordeal in order to enter into His divine heritage, and did this as man. He willingly accepted death on the cross. But death was only a passing from imperfect human life into a risen life in divine glory.

The meaning of Jesus' work is man's reorientation to God. Man can share in God because Christ shares in God. Man need only share in the humanity of the Christ (which title, literally, means God's "anointed"), which is the common humanity of all men. Man cannot achieve this by his own effort, but God can make him a sharer. The Holy Spirit does this in a supreme gesture of love. To those who see Jesus as the Son of God and accept Him as Lord and Saviour, the Spirit communicates the humanity of Christ. This is a radical change for man, a rebirth, a new being, a new creation. God initiates it; and man, through faith and conversion, cooperates with God's initiative. See also GRACE OF GOD.

Visible Body of Christ. Because of Christ's redemption, there is a new humanity, a new People of God present in the world. Those who accept this gift of redemption form a visible body in the world. This body—the Body of Christ, the Mystical Body—is a visible community produced and upheld by the Holy Spirit. It is the church. For the Catholic, to share in the life of Christ, which is man's salvation, is to be in the church.

Within the church there are two bodies: the body of bishops assisted by priests who share, though not fully, in the bishops' priestly prerogatives; and the body of the faithful, each of whom shares somehow in the priesthood of Christ. These latter, the laity, do not perform certain functions of the bishops and other clergy, but they "make up the body of Christ under one Head" and are "called to sanctity and have an equal privilege of faith" (Constitution on the Church).

The church recognizes also its links with those who are baptized but not in full unity with it. Similarly the church acknowledges a special relationship with those others, outside the Christian tradition, who "sincerely seek God and, moved by grace, strive by their deeds to do His will as it is known to them" (Constitution on the Church, section 16). They are saved by their link, realized or not, with Christ.

Hierarchy. Catholic doctrine holds that the church is hierarchically structured. Its hierarchy makes it an institutional, organized, and visible community. The hierarchy, or ruling group, is the college, or collectivity, of bishops. In positing this, Catholics do not differ greatly from the Orthodox Eastern churches or from Anglo-Catholics. Catholics may insist more than some others, however, that this element is not merely a historical accident, but depends on the will of Christ. The college of bishops perpetuates itself by conferring sacramental Orders on chosen Christians. The apostles were the first bishops, ordained by Christ, and it is only from them that other bishops receive their ordination. This is known as the apostolic succession, a basic teaching of Catholicism.

Primacy of Peter. All bishops are equally bishops. Together they form the college of bishops, which is not the sum of separate independent bishops but a single spiritual power in the church, which all bishops share equally. This power was given first to Peter (Matthew 16:16–20) and then to the other apostles, who shared in the power of Peter. The power of the pope, then, is an episcopal, or bishop's, power and not a totally different one. The Catholic view of hierarchy differs from other views by its insistence that the college of bishops is united not only inwardly by the action of the Holy Spirit, but outwardly by a visible solidarity with the pope, who by reason of the direct succession of his powers from the first bishop of Rome, St. Peter, is the prime bishop. This is the doctrine of papal primacy. By it the bishop of Rome is acknowledged as the first among the bishops, not only in rank and dignity, but in pastoral authority as well. See also PAPACY.

Infallibility. A word must be said about infallibility, both that of the pope and that of the college of bishops. Definition of doctrine is made rarely, usually only when there is danger of widespread misunderstanding of revelation. Not all pronouncements of the college of bishops or of the pope are solemn definitions of revelation. Normally they are ordinary communications of revelation which, if necessary, can be reformed. Indeed, most episcopal and papal messages are directive norms rather than formal statements of doctrine. Because these messages are dignified by the teaching authority of the bishops, they demand acceptance. Even though acceptance of these messages may not be as absolute as that accorded solemn definitions, Catholics respond out of fidelity to Christ who acts through his representatives, the bishops.

Doctrine of Solidarity. The redemption brought by Christ involves the union of those who accept Christ with the visible body which He established for all. This brings with it the concept of solidarity, the union of those in the visible church on earth and those who have passed on from earthly life. The "faithful departed" are considered to be still in Christ-unity and therefore in unity with the church. This doctrine is today called the "communion of saints," although the phrase has had different meanings at various times.

Saints. The doctrine of solidarity in Christ implies a mutual influence of all those in Christ. Those who have left the earthly Christ-society and have attained full unity with the risen Lord retain links with members still on earth. This union is, in fact, "strengthened through the exchange of spiritual goods." Furthermore, these departed members, having reached ultimate union, "are present to the Lord, and through Him and with Him and in Him they do not cease to intercede with the Father for us" (Constitution on the Church, section 49). Thus it is a family spirit that prompts Catholics to pray to their brothers who are with the Lord. When the Catholic prays to these brothers, the saints, he does not pray as he prays to God. Rather he simply asks that they pray to God for him. The saint is not some minor divinity but a holy member of Christ's body joined to all the other members. In and through the one Saviour the saint intercedes for those in union with him. Just as a person on earth may ask another to pray for him, the Catholic expands this common custom when he asks the saints to do the same. See also INTERCESSION; SAINT.

Mary. Of all the saints saved by the Redeemer, Mary, His mother, is the most revered. Both Catholic and Orthodox traditions are at one in their devotion to Mary: God chose her to be the first point of contact between historical man and his salvation, which is Christ Jesus. It is in recognition of the peculiar unity between son and mother that she is so esteemed. Because she is the mother of Christ, who is God, Mary was conceived free of original sin (a doctrine called the Immaculate Conception); and after her life on earth she was taken up, body and soul, into heaven (a doctrine known as the Assumption). Traditionally she is thought of as mother of all Christians, who are incorporated into Christ through His human nature, and thus she is accorded the title "Mother of the Church."

Catholic and Orthodox expressions of devotion to Mary can bewilder and even shock other Christians. The rhetoric sometimes used can be exalted, highly poetic, even flamboyant. Accordingly Vatican Council II cautions all Catholics "to carefully and equally avoid the falsity of exaggeration on the one hand, and the excess of narrowmindedness on the other" (Constitution on the Church, section 67). At the same time the Council reminds the faithful that "true devotion consists neither in fruitless and passing emotion, nor in a certain vain credulity, but it proceeds from true faith."

Purgatory. The solidarity of the redeemed with Christ and with each other can again be seen in the Catholic teaching concerning purgatory. In her teaching the church first considers the two dimensions of sin: (1) the upset of God's designed order and (2) the alienation of the sinner from God. In God's act of pardon the second effect, alienation, disappears. But the disturbance of order remains. This disturbance consists in a person's acceptance of his own pleasure as the norm of conduct without regard for God's true norms.

Since sin produced this imbalance, balance can be achieved again only when man freely sacrifices his own pleasure to compensate for his overindulgence of it.

Those who die in God's union (the state of grace) want to restore the balance upset by sin. Preparing for the state of full union with God, they are in a temporary state of purgation, or of righting the disorder they have caused. They wish to compensate for their lack of effort before death. This state, called purgatory, is not a hell but a vestibule of heaven. The church prays for the souls in purgatory, asking God to accept the merits of Christ to make up for the shortcomings of those who are in Christ.

CHURCH AND STATE

Catholics form a community or society. This society has been structured partly by God, partly by man. The human part can be changed, but the part established by God cannot be. Catholics at the same time are members of a secular community or society, which also claims the allegiance of its members. In this respect Catholics are in the same situation as other religious citizens. Any religious person gives his allegiance first to God. If this allegiance were to conflict with his allegiance to the civic community, the second allegiance would be suspended. This situation has occurred on occasion throughout human history. Victims of religious persecution have always been regarded as noble and heroic souls, not traitors, though they were convicted by human laws.

The basic question is not how the believing community is related to the civic commonwealth, but rather what the relationship of transcendent faith is to the secular order. Catholic doctrine firmly recognizes the need of secular human society for the common good. Catholics consider this the law of nature. Hence Catholics, like everyone else, have an obligation to obey the secular authority. Both fellowship in Christ and fellowship in secular society are necessary. But the transcendent dimension of human destiny is unconditionally imperative, while its earthly counterpart is not.

Yet the religious claims on the believer cannot make him incapable of fulfilling his civic obligations, since both are ultimately from one God. "In their own spheres, the political community and the church are mutually independent and self-governing. Yet by a different title each serves the social and personal vocation of the human beings" (Vatican Council II, Constitution on the Church in the Modern World, section 75). Since the believer and citizen are a single person, there cannot be a total separation of the believer from the citizen. Thus, there are meanings of the phrase "separation of Church and State" that are too doctrinaire and totalistic to be acceptable.

The solution to possible problems of conflict between allegiances is along the lines of concord of the two communities. Each must act in harmony, respect, and collaboration with the other. This concord will vary historically according to the structures of different commonwealths, and must be worked out according to concrete situations. Neither church nor state is to be thought of as a subservient instrument of the other. The principle of rendering "to Caesar the things that are Caesar's, and to God the things that are God's" (Matthew 22:21) recognizes the autonomy of the two communities. Vatican Council II's Constitution on the Church in the Modern World states explicitly that "the church does not lodge its hope in privileges conferred by civil authorities; indeed it stands ready to renounce the exercise of certain legitimately acquired rights if it becomes clear that their use raises doubts about the sincerity of its witness or new conditions of life demand some other arrangement." In turn, it demands the right to "preach the faith with true freedom, to teach its social doctrine, and to discharge its duty among men without hindrance." Further, it "consolidates peace among men, to God's greater glory; for it is the Church's task to uncover, cherish and ennoble all that is true, good and beautiful in the human community."

MORALITY

Christian morality is in general a reformulation of the Ten Commandments of the Old Testament, as St. Paul stated in his letter to the Galatians (5:13–26) and his first letter to the Corinthians (5:9–13). Catholics believe that Christ fulfilled the Old Law and that life in Christ is their norm of action. In their love for Christ and their union with Him they aim to be Christlike, and this is their deepest law.

What differentiates Catholic morality from that of others is principally its formal source. Christ is "the Way, the Truth, and the Life" (John 14:6). Philosophers justify a code of ethics by argument and reason. The Catholic, too, may be a philosopher, and when he is he will follow the philosopher's method. As a Catholic, however, he accepts Christ in faith as the norm and reason for his conduct. Non-Catholic Christians generally hold the same position. However, the Catholic views his membership in the Body of Christ, which is the church, as his link to Christ. Hence moral guidance will be given authentically and definitively by the teaching church, to which God has given the authority to interpret the natural law derived from man's God-given nature.

Accordingly, there exists in Catholic morality the obligation to hear the church. "He who hears you hears me, and he who rejects you rejects me, and he who rejects me rejects him who sent me" (Luke 10:16). The moral directives made by the church are, for the Catholic, not mere counsels but strict obligations, showing the will of God. This does not minimize the importance of conscience, which Vatican II calls "the most secret core and sanctuary of a human being" (Constitution on the Church, section 16); this is so because "authentic freedom is an exceptional sign of the divine image in man" and "man's dignity demands that he act according to a knowing and free choice" (Constitution on the Church).

Here on earth man, even while a member of the church, is in a state of pilgrimage toward the fullness of restoration and revelation of the sons of God (Romans 8:19–22). In his process of fulfillment in Christ he is confronted with many large and small choices. Whether the choices are in the personal or in the social realm he will follow his conscience as enlightened by Christ's teaching in the concrete specifics of such choices. This does not emancipate him from personal or social responsibility but indeed makes his commitment to both more demanding and man-sized. The role of the teaching church is not to diminish conscience but to help the Christian develop his conscience maturely so that he truly acts out of love and truth and not out of whim and egotism.

ST. PAUL, in a portrayal by the 13th century Florentine artist Cimabue (*left*).

ST. PETER, with keys of heaven and cross-staff, in 7th century icon (*right*).

Thus faith, living through hope, charity, justice, and the other virtues, becomes something richer, more meaningful, and more absorbing than the initial intellectual assent. Morality, on the other hand, involves something higher and yet more intimate than a series of mere commands and prohibitions.

GUSTAVE WEIGEL, S. J.
Formerly Professor of Ecclesiology,
Woodstock College
C. J. McNASPY, S. J.
Associate Editor, "America" and "Catholic Mind"

Bibliography

Abbott, Walter M., ed., *The Documents of Vatican II* (New York 1966).
Adam, Karl, *The Spirit of Catholicism* (New York 1935).
Congar, Yves, *The Mystery of the Church* (London 1965).
Corbishley, Thomas, *Roman Catholicism* (New York 1950).
Gelpi, Donald, *Life and Light* (New York 1965).
Hasseveldt, Roger, *The Church, a Divine Mystery,* tr. by William Storey (Chicago 1954).

2. History

The worldwide diffusion of modern Christianity is in sharp contrast to its humble origins. Its founder, Jesus of Nazareth, was born in Palestine around 8–4 B. C. His life and teaching were recorded by his earliest followers in the New Testament. During his public ministry, Jesus preached, worked a number of miracles, and manifested himself as the Messiah, or Christ— the anointed of God. His preaching eventually brought him into conflict with the Palestinian authorities, who crucified him about 30 A. D. because they expected that his death would end his influence. The opposite occurred. His disciples began to proclaim that "God has raised Jesus from the dead" (Acts 2:32) and has sent him "to turn away every one of you from his sins" (Acts 3:26).

EARLY CHURCH

The preaching of this Gospel, or good news, was soon accepted by many in Jerusalem and elsewhere. At Antioch in the mid-1st century, "the disciples were for the first time called Christians" (Acts 11:26). At first Christians constituted a sect within Judaism: they followed Jewish practices, such as praying in the temple, but celebrated their own unique service, the Eucharist, as well. Christianity and Judaism soon diverged because of their doctrinal incompatibility. A church meeting at Jerusalem (about 49 A. D.) decided that a Christian need not submit to circumcision and other Jewish practices (Acts 15: 1–35). This decision, based on doctrinal considerations, effectively opened Christianity to the non-Jewish world.

Persecution and Growth. During the 1st century, missionaries such as St. Paul were able to win converts and organize churches in Asia Minor, Greece, Italy, and North Africa. This intensive missionary activity was aided by the Roman Empire's transportation system and by the use of Greek, the language of the New Testament, as the common commercial language. Although early Christian writers speak of an atmosphere of religious expectancy that made many receptive to the Gospel, conversions were neither instantaneously nor effortlessly made.

Paganism was the official state religion. Christianity was suspect, and Christians were subjected to persecution for a variety of reasons: they were accused of disloyalty to the state because of their refusal to participate in the official pagan rites; Christian rites were grossly misrepresented as acts of fanaticism and immorality; Christians were even blamed for natural disasters, such as famine and epidemic. Nero (reigned 54–68), for example, blamed the Christians for burning Rome, and executed many including Saints Peter and Paul. The Emperor Trajan (reigned 98–117), on the other hand, ordered that Christians were not to be sought out but must be tried if denounced. Thus a Christian was at the mercy of his enemies. At the trials of Christians, magistrates attempted to persuade them, by promises or by threats, to renounce their faith. Although many preferred torture, exile, or death to apostasy, some faltered. Generally, persecutions were sporadic and local, but empire-wide persecutions were ordered by the emperors Decius (reigned 249–251) and Diocletian (reigned 284–305).

Doctrinal Development. The church's doctrinal development is discernible in the corpus of early Christian literature. This literature includes letters from one bishop or church to another, such as those of Ignatius of Antioch (q.v.), which discussed particular problems. A second type of literature, the catechetical, was designed to instruct prospective or recent converts in the principal Christian doctrines. In the 2d century, Christian literary effort assumed an apologetic purpose. The apologists, such as Justin Martyr (q.v.), attempted to convince their contemporaries of the civic loyalty of Christians and to explain Christian belief and practice. These writings may not have convinced the pagans or Jews, but they furnish important information about the early church. Theological writing developed in reaction to Gnosticism, a syncretistic religious movement that was potentially a greater threat to Christianity than the persecutions. Writers such as Irenaeus of Lyon pointed out the radical incompatibility between Gnosticism, which promised salvation through ritual knowledge (gnosis), and Christianity, which preached salvation through the revelation given by Christ. An indirect but important benefit of these polemical writings was the emergence of genuine theological reflection. See GNOSTICISM.

The 3d century development of Christian theology was occasioned by the necessity of presenting Biblical revelation in a form intelligible to intellectuals and by the correlative desire to achieve a systematic presentation of revelation. Basically this was part of a continuing process of transculturation; the Christian principles expressed in the Hebraic mentality of the New Testament were gradually developed by Greek thought, in accordance with Hellenistic philosophical categories. This endeavor emanated from catechetical schools, the most famous of which were at Antioch in Syria and Alexandria in Egypt, but the theological orientation of the two differed. Antioch, employing a literal interpretation of Scripture, emphasized Christ's human nature; Alexandria, relying on an allegorical interpretation of Scripture, stressed the divinity of Christ. These different approaches, intensified by rivalry between the sees, clashed in the Christological controversies that emerged in the 4th century.

Organizational Development. Early Christian literature indicates the development of church organization in the early centuries. The local church considered itself the assembly of those called by God to the faith and thus a focalization of the universal church. The authority of the church, according to a letter attributed to Clement of Rome (about 95), descended from God through Christ and the apostles to the leaders of the church, who thus exercised divine authority. Local authority was vested in a bishop and a college of presbyters, assisted by deacons (I Timothy 3:1–13, 5:17–22); the role of the bishop, according to Ignatius of Antioch, was monarchical. Subsequent writings, such as the *Pastor of Hermas* (or *Shepherd* of Hermas; about 140), indicate a well-established hierarchical structure of bishops, priests, and deacons. By the 3d century other offices, such as lector and acolyte, had been introduced.

When St. Peter left Jerusalem, he lived for a time in Antioch before journeying to Rome where he held the position of primate. Catholics believe that the primacy of Peter is continued in his successors through the office of bishop of Rome. The significance and exercise of the Roman primacy underwent a long process of development. An early indication of the authority of the Roman church is Clement of Rome's letter to the church at Corinth attempting to settle a dispute among its members. Similarly, Ignatius of Antioch gave special recognition to the Roman church as "presiding in love, maintaining the law of Christ"; and in answer to the Gnostic leaders' claims to special revelation, Irenaeus (about 180) pointed out that the true doctrine was the possession of the apostolic churches, especially that church "founded by the two most glorious apostles, Peter and Paul," with which "every church must agree." Such recognition is remarkable, since the popes of this period were not so outstanding as the writers who acknowledged their office; furthermore, the fact that such acknowledgment was even given by those who differed from Roman decisions on particular questions is unique.

Controversy and Councils. Under Constantine (reigned 306–337), Christianity became privileged. He credited the Christian God with his victory over Maxentius at the Milvian Bridge (312) and hoped that, in return for religious toleration, the Christians would aid him in unifying the empire. Constantine felt responsible for preserving unity within the church. When Arius, a priest of Alexandria, created a controversy by teaching that Christ was not properly the Son of God, but only the highest of creatures and unequal to the Father, Constantine summoned all bishops to a council that met at Nicaea in 325. After considerable debate, a creed was accepted that professed belief in Jesus Christ as "begotten, not made, of one substance (*homoousios*) with the Father." Constantine expected the Nicene creed to settle the Arian controversy, but acrimonious debate about the *homoousios* continued for decades. Eventually, because of the efforts of Saints Basil, Gregory of Nyasa, and Gregory of Nazianzus, the Nicene creed received universal recognition at the Council of Constantinople in 381. The Council of Nicaea also acknowledged the special status of the patriarchal sees of Rome, Antioch, and Alexandria. But because of the civic importance of Constantine's newly erected capital of Constantinople, the bishops of the "New Rome" claimed an honorific primacy second only to that of the see of Rome; this claim set the stage for future rivalry between sees in the East, and ultimately between Constantinople and Rome.

From the time of Constantine, Christianity gained ground, while paganism waned, despite the efforts of Emperor Julian (reigned 361–363) to restore it. Under Theodosius (reigned 379–395) paganism was outlawed, and Christianity became the official state religion. At Theodosius' death, the empire was divided between his two sons into two parts—East and West. In the East, because of the close alliance between church and state begun under Constantine, the emperors frequently intervened in ecclesiastical disputes, and the Eastern church came increasingly under imperial control; in the West, because of the breakdown of imperial authority, the church's autonomy and prestige were intensified.

While the basic issue in the Christological controversies of the 5th and 6th centuries was the validity of varying philosophical presentations concerning Christ, a number of other tensions became manifest. These arose over the intervention of the emperor in church affairs, the rivalry among the Eastern patriarchal sees, and, at the same time, the acknowledgment of the Roman primacy implied by the Eastern appeals to Rome in doctrinal and disciplinary disputes.

The Council of Ephesus in 431 taught that Mary must be honored under the title "mother of God" (*Theotokos*), against the teaching of Nestorius that Mary was merely "mother of Christ" (*Christotokos*). Against the teaching of Eutyches that Christ's human nature was absorbed by His divinity, the Council of Chalcedon in 451 accepted the *Tome* of Pope Leo I and declared that Christ is "truly God and truly man." Chalcedon s decision failed to satisfy those who held the monophysite position of Eutyches; their opposition, however, was more anti-imperial than heretical. Justinian's attempt at the Second Council of Constantinople in 553 to impose a doctrinal statement broad enough to satisfy everyone was only partially successful.

The Church as a Temporal Power. From the 4th century on, the church in the West developed in a different direction than the church in the East. The migration, or "invasion," of the barbarian tribes that crossed the Rhine completely disrupted the Western Empire. In the resulting state of disorder, the 5th century church emerged as the only effective organization, in both spiritual and temporal matters. Pope Leo I (reigned 440–461), for example, exercised the primacy for the East as well as the West in his decisions and defended Rome from barbarian depredations.

The barbarians were either pagans or Arian Christians hostile to Catholicism. At the end of the 5th century, a Frankish tribe under Clovis was converted from paganism to Catholicism. Gradually the Franks became dominant in northern Europe, and their Catholic faith spread.

The Church as a Spiritual Force. While the Western church was concerned with the ordering of man's life in the temporal world, its theologians discussed man's salvation. Against Pelagius, who claimed that man is naturally able to live without sin, St. Augustine (354–430) taught that man's justification depends on grace, a free gift of God. Augustine was undoubtedly the greatest theological writer of the early Western church; his *Confessions* and the *City of God* still influence theological thought.

Although monasticism existed in Judaism and other religions, Christian monasticism originated in 3d century Egypt. It was founded to enable men to live the Gospel counsels perfectly, and many felt that this was possible only by withdrawing from worldly concerns. Two basic types of monasticism developed: the solitary life, advocated by St. Anthony of Egypt, in which each hermit lives alone; and the communal life, organized and directed by St. Pachomius, in which monks live and work as a group following a rule. Monasticism spread from Egypt eastward and northward to Palestine, Syria, and Asia Minor, where the monastic directives of St. Basil (q.v.) were followed.

In the West, a Latin translation of St. Athanasius' *Life of St. Anthony* inspired many to lead a monastic life. Communities were established in 4th century Italy and Gaul, and as Christianity spread, monasticism became rooted throughout the West. The greatest figure of Western monasticism was St. Benedict (about 480–547); after living as hermits at Subiaco, Italy, he and his followers built a monastery on Monte Cassino. The Rule of St. Benedict gradually predominated in the West. In the history of western Europe from the 6th to the 12th century, the monasteries were practically the only stable institutions. They preserved and propagated the influence of both civilization and Christianity.

The first six centuries of Christian history closed with Pope Gregory the Great (reigned 590–604), whose pontificate recapitulated the currents at work during the preceding centuries and exemplified the ideals that influenced succeeding centuries in the church. After serving as civil prefect of Rome, Gregory disposed of his family inheritance and became a monk; he always remained a monk at heart, even after his appointment as papal legate to Constantinople and his election as pope. During his pontificate he defended the primatial rights of the Roman see, worked for civil peace in a period of turmoil, sent St. Augustine of Canterbury with missionaries to England, and administered the patrimonial possessions of the papacy. Through his writings, such as the *Pastoral Care* and the *Dialogues,* Gregory's influence continued throughout the Middle Ages.

JOHN C. FORD, C. S. C.
Holy Cross College, Washington, D. C.

MEDIEVAL CHURCH

The medieval church is the church of the West in the period between late antiquity (about 600) and the beginning of the Reformation (1517). It is impossible, however, to limit the medieval church with chronological accuracy; its history neither began nor ended abruptly. In Italy, for example, the medieval element in church life was greatly transformed by the Renaissance, while in Germany it was the Reformation that was most influential in displacing it. Since the medieval church varied in character with the passage of time and with the national culture of the different peoples who composed it, to generalize about it is difficult. The church in medieval Ireland, for example, was very different in spirit and structure from the church in England. Yet common to both, and to the other national churches, was an adherence to Latin Christianity; the medieval church was Latin, not only in its cultural origins but also in its law, its theology, and its religious expression—both biblical and liturgical. Its formation was inspired by the cultural supremacy of Rome. The medieval church was a religious community in transition. Its spirituality was derived from ancient Christianity, but it was rapidly becoming a centralized institution with the office of the Roman pontiff as its core. But the pope presided over more than the church, he presided over Christendom—the Christian nations of the West.

The most pressing problem of the church from the 5th to the 8th century was the conversion of the pagan and the Semi-Arian people of northern Europe. This it accomplished by missionary enterprises of the first quality—St. Patrick in Ireland and St. Augustine of Canterbury in England. St. Boniface Christianized the East Franks in the 8th century, while Saints Cyril and Methodius were apostles to the Slavic peoples in the 9th century. This vast apostolic work, substantially completed by the mid-10th century, was basic to the realization of Christendom as a unified society: universally Catholic, coextensive with modern Europe, and Latin in cultural roots. The conversion of these barbarian peoples provided a common bond between them and the Latin peoples to the south. It also led to their unification under the papacy and to the creation of the church of the Middle Ages.

The Concept of Christendom. The religious unity realized in the early Middle Ages was cemented by a political unity. On Christmas Day, 800, Pope Leo III crowned the Frankish king Charlemagne in the basilica of St. Peter at Rome. This conferring of the imperial dignity by the papacy secured the unity in the religious and political orders that was the presupposition of medieval Christendom. The coronation signified not only that the emperor of the Romans, as Charlemagne and his successors were styled, would have an obligation to protect the church in the temporal order and to promote its spiritual welfare, but also that the pope had the right to confer the imperial crown. At the same time, it signified a new orientation for the church. Up to that time the papacy had looked to the east and to the Byzantine emperor for protection. After Charlemagne's coronation the popes looked to the north for support.

Political Structure. The modern conception of church and state as two distinct entities did not exist in the Middle Ages. Christendom was a structure unified religiously, culturally, and politically and rested on pope and emperor. The pope was believed to be superior by the will of Christ. As all bishops stood under the pope, so all princes theoretically stood under the emperor. Both powers were supreme; neither was absolute, for both stood before the law of God and the voice of conscience. Relations between the two powers were constantly in a state of flux; their interests conflicted, and their spheres of influence overlapped. As the Middle Ages grew older, tension mounted until it exceeded the strength of the structure of society.

Social Structure. Church and society were neither differentiated nor separated from one another in the Middle Ages. The two blended. The philosophy of the medieval church was concerned with the hereafter, but its actions were directed toward the temporal; the church did not retreat from the world, nor was the world withdrawn from the church. The two coalesced at so many points that the separation became blurred. Abuses that marked church life in the Middle Ages—overinvolvement in secular concerns and undue preoccupation with the affairs of princes and nations—were, to a large extent, due to the obscurity of the demarcation.

Medieval society was monolithic in religion; religious pluralism was not admitted. In the early medieval period, church and crown were generally tolerant of diversity of religious persuasion. Heresy was not approved, but neither was it persecuted. By the late 12th century, however, Christendom had become a more closed, sensitive society. It became suspicious of religious thought (for example, Jewish and Albigensian) that was at variance with the common faith of Christendom. Aberrations were thus regarded as a threat to church, realm, and society itself. Hence the Inquisition was established by Emperor Frederick II and Pope Gregory IX to prosecute and persecute religious dissenters.

Ecclesiastical Structure. In its earliest stages the medieval church was relatively unorganized; the primacy of the see of Rome was generally admitted by the faithful, but the bonds between it and the local or national churches were loose. By reason of its apostolic origins, the church of Rome enjoyed a preeminent position as the final court of appeal in matters of faith and morals. In the mid-11th century a dramatic change overtook the church and its structure: the motivating force was the reaction of Pope Gregory VII (reigned 1073–1085) to the absorption of the bishops into the constitutional structure of the empire. Secularization had gone as far as it could go without extinguishing that "liberty of the Church" that "the justice of God" demanded. In the reform that Pope Gregory directed against the right of Emperor Henry IV to invest bishops the papal program ultimately succeeded in bringing the hierarchy of Germany—and ultimately of all Christendom—under the authority of the pope. This was the beginning of ecclesiastical centralization: at this time the words "Curia Romana" (Roman court) came into general use with regard to the ruling bodies in the church, and the title "Vicar of Christ" was commonly attributed to the pope. At this time, too, the college of cardinals, electors of the pope since 1059, emerged as a power in church administration. Subsequently the church's government tended to become more centralized, bureaucratic, and oligarchic. Under the growing influence of Roman law, canon law became more and more universal in scope and extent.

Power Structure. By the opening years of the 13th century the Holy See virtually presided over the whole Western world. Innocent III (reigned 1198–1216) demonstrated the international significance of the medieval papacy when he settled the feudal dispute between King Philip Augustus of France and King John of England. Further, he condemned the Magna Carta as an illicit intrusion on his overlordship in England. Maintaining that it was his right to give the imperial crown to whomsoever he would, because the empire pertained to the papacy by reason of its translation from the Greeks to the Romans to the Germans, and by reason of papal coronation and anointing, he constituted himself supreme judge in the so-called Throne Controversy between Otto IV and Philip of Swabia. Yet at the end of that century, Boniface VIII (reigned 1294–1303), despite the pretensions to universal jurisdiction that he expressed in his famous bull *Unam sanctam* (1302), witnessed the nadir of the papacy. His long struggles with Philip IV of France ended at Anagni, Italy, where Philip's men actually attacked the person of the Pope, and Boniface died a month later.

Educational Structure. The whole tenor of ecclesiastical education in the Middle Ages was Latin. Knowledge of Greek had become rare early in the Middle Ages; by the mid-9th century Duns Scotus (see ERIGENA, JOHANNES SCOTUS) was the only Greek scholar in the West. Contact with the rich tradition of Byzantium was cut off. Certain classical authors, such as Virgil, were known, but interest centered on the four Latin Fathers: Jerome, Ambrose, Augustine, and Gregory. These authors were fundamental to both ascetical doctrine and Biblical exegesis. The study of Holy Scripture was "the queen of the sciences," not only because all learning was to be derived from its sacred pages, but basically because all learning was ordered to its comprehension and interpretation.

The earliest medieval schools of sacred doctrine were monastic. Here Biblical exegesis was cultivated in the tradition of Origen and Gregory the Great, an approach to Scripture that depreciated the literal (historical) sense of the sacred page, caused the religious mind to withdraw from history, and led to a development of a comprehension of the Bible that was largely arbitrary. These attitudes colored the religious mind of the medieval church with the conviction that the spiritual, the invisible, the inaccessible transcended the material, the visible, the tangible. Biblical exegesis also affected liturgy. Every liturgical action, word, and object was found to have a transferred meaning, apart from its own history and objectivity, in the allegorical order.

The monastic schools, such as Reichenau, Corbie, and Fulda, developed a Biblical theology that was meaningful in its own historical context. It was based on a study of the Bible that aimed at goodness. The questions that it posed were traditional and received traditional answers from the Church Fathers. Little room was left for expanding the scope of theology, and by the 11th century monastic education was exhausted. New schools arose in cities such as Lyon, Paris, and Laon in close proximity to the cathedrals and their administration. Their concern was more humanistic and secular than Biblical and religious; but their success and achievements were noteworthy. By the end of the 12th century a new theological method had developed: the dialectics of Aristotle were applied to the content of Christian revelation, and theological vistas were opened. A methodological technique, aimed at systematizing all Christian doctrine according to logical categories, was perfected. The power of this system of thought, called scholasticism, was great enough to create a distinct phase in the history of the medieval church: within its intellectual frame the university as an institution emerged, and an illustrious line of doctors—Albert the Great (Albertus Magnus), Thomas Aquinas, Duns Scotus—developed. Their thinking was to shape the church for the next five centuries. See SCHOLASTICISM.

Abuses and Achievements of Christendom. The church of the Middle Ages was a creative force. Under its auspices and with its support the University of Paris developed as the most renowned theological center in the world, and St. Dominic was able to found the Order of Preachers as an instrument for educating the faithful in the Gospel. The constitution of his organization was remarkable for the stress that it placed on liberal education, especially in theology, and for the freedom that its members enjoyed in electing their own superiors. At the same time St. Francis of Assisi founded, with papal approval, an order of "little brothers" to imitate the poverty and humility of Christ. The true Gospel simplicity which animated his foundation inspired the Christian world with new vitality at a time when its energies were almost depleted. The inspirational power of the medieval church is most vividly revealed in her art (painting, sculpture, book illumination) and architecture (Romanesque and Gothic).

Although the central Christian teaching of the medieval church was dogmatically pure, it was transmitted to and comprehended by the faithful in a distorted manner. The church suffered acutely from poor education among its lower clergy and the simple laity. Since both Bible and liturgy were in Latin, a language that was not understood by the majority, the tendency was to bypass the Gospel in favor of more picturesque, imaginative, and appealing religious forms. Thus devotion to saints, and all that it involved—relics, pilgrimages, devotions—grew by leaps and bounds; and devotion to Mary took a position of ascendancy that, in retrospect, seems exaggerated and disproportionate. The drift of medieval religion was toward exteriority. Good works were rewarded with indulgences that remitted punishment in the afterlife.

In a certain sense the medieval church was victimized by legalism and moralism; it was overconscious of sin and death. But on the other hand it was able to supply the faithful with an inspiring vision of life and of faith; it gave man an objective substance on which to form his conscience and to live his life. It also gave him a vigorous concept of the sacred and the mystical. Medieval religion had its defects; but it was able to civilize man and to elicit from him true human goodness. It made man transcend himself in greatness of life. There were abuses in this ancient church; but the corporal and the spiritual works of mercy were not forsaken. Its genius lay in preserving the past; it was not, however, alert to the future and its needs. This is probably why it decayed.

ROBERT E. MCNALLY, S. J.
Fordham University

RENAISSANCE AND REFORMATION

As the French monarchy more and more dominated the papacy the church's moral and temporal authority declined. Pope Clement V (reigned 1305–1314) decided to forsake Rome and reside in France. Thus, the bishop of Rome was enthroned in Lyon and in 1309 moved to Avignon. This city and its environs, including the Comtat de Venaissin, were purchased from Joanna I of Naples in 1348; and the popes, all Frenchmen, remained there until 1378. Their absence from Rome is known as the Babylonian Exile of the church. Deprived of revenues from the papal states, the popes of Avignon perfected a system of taxation and collation of benefices that made the papacy the greatest western fiscal power. The maintenance of a brilliant court, the increase of curial personnel, and efforts to finance military undertakings in support of territorial claims did much to lessen papal prestige. The papacy also was confronted with nascent nationalism in the political sphere, nominalism in the philosophical sphere, and the conciliar movement, which threatened to destroy the total authority of the pope.

Nationalism. The suppression of the Knights Templars was an early example of national interests overriding the church's universalism. In 1307, Philip the Fair of France, with ecclesiastical approval, arrested the grand master of the order, Jacques de Molay, and over 2,000 knights. At the Council of Vienne (1311–1312) Pope Clement V in the bull *Vox in excelso* suppressed the Templars. Its properties were confiscated and its leaders executed.

The final struggle between pope and emperor also occurred during this period. Pope John XXII (reigned 1316–1334), a former chancellor of King Charles II of Naples, favored the French-supported candidate, Duke Frederick of Austria, over Louis of Bavaria in a contested imperial election. John excommunicated Louis in March 1324, after his coronation as emperor, but the conflict preoccupied the papacy until Louis' death in 1347. The quarrel was complicated by the question of apostolic poverty as practiced by the mendicant orders. A large number of Franciscans sided with Louis against the Pope, including William of Occam, a leading nominalist. The Parisian professors Marsilius of Padua and John of Jandun also supported the Emperor, and a vigorous literary feud ensued over the church-state relationship. Marsilius violently attacked the medieval theory of church and state in *Defensor pacis*, advocating laicism and democratic principles in the church. For

Marsilius ecclesiastical authority resided in the Christian community; the highest court of the church, the general council, could be summoned by civil authorities, and the laity were to have a right to be seated and heard at the council.

The struggle between the pope and the emperor had its counterpart in England. During the Hundred Years' War the English became increasingly suspicious of the French controlled papacy and lessened papal authority through legislation. Parliament declared all papal appointments to English benefices invalid and established severe penalties for appealing to ecclesiastical courts outside of England. John Wycliffe, a professor of theology at Oxford, declared that the church was not composed of a hierarchy and the faithful, but was an invisible communion of the predestined. Many of his doctrines were spread by a group called the Lollards. In 1401, by an act of Parliament, the Inquisition was introduced in England.

St. Bridget of Sweden, St. Catherine of Siena, and Petrarch finally convinced Pope Gregory XI (reigned 1370–1378) to return to Rome (January 1377). Since that time the popes have resided in the .Vatican, not as formerly in the Lateran Palace. Gregory's successor, Urban VI, plunged the church into an even greater crisis in 1378. Urban, the last pope not a cardinal at the time of his election, was the former archbishop of Bari. Several months after his election 13 French cardinals, claiming the election invalid due to duress, returned to Avignon. In August 1378 they elected a new pope, Clement VII (reigned 1378–1394), a cousin of the French King. Thus began the Great Western Schism, which divided the Catholic world into two hostile camps; central and northern Italy, Hungary, England, northern Germany, and Scandinavia adhered to the Roman popes. Two series of popes, one in Avignon and the other in Rome, continued to excommunicate each other and their followers for almost 40 years (1378–1417).

Conciliarism. Early efforts to heal the schism failed. Later, in March 1409, 13 cardinals of both obediences, together with some 200 bishops and 200 abbots, convened in Pisa and elected a new pope, Alexander V. Since the rivals, Gregory XII and Benedict XIII, refused to resign, three popes claimed rightful rule to Christendom. In 1414, pressured by Emperor Sigismund, John XXIII, Alexander V's successor, summoned the ecumenical Council of Constance (1414–1418). Three tasks confronted the last great assembly of the Christian West: the termination of the schism; the condemnation of the errors of Wycliffe and Jan Hus; and the reform of the church. Dominated by partisans of the conciliar theory, who maintained that a general council wielded supreme authority in the church, the council deposed all three contenders and elected Cardinal Odo Colonna as Martin V (reigned 1417–1431). The Czech reformer Jan Hus and his colleague John of Prague, although not guilty of the charges against them, were condemned and burned, and a civil war raged in Bohemia until 1436 as a result. The teachings of Wycliffe were also condemned, but little or nothing was done to abolish ecclesiastical abuses.

The council declared the superiority of a council over the pope in the decree *Haec sancta* and urged the frequent holding of councils, but Martin and his successors repudiated this. The contest between the pope and the conciliarists culminated at the Council of Basel (1431–1437). The first 25 sessions of this Council together with the Council of Ferrara-Florence (1438–1442) form what is considered the 17th General Council. Its main achievement was a temporary reunion between the Latin and the Greek churches.

Nominalism. During the 14th and 15 centuries the scholastic theology of the high Middle Ages was radically altered with the rise of the system known as nominalism. It opposed extreme formalism and stressed the absolute omnipotence of God: advocating the notion that God could in no way be man's debtor, it paved the way for the rejection of the medieval merit and penitential system. Indicative of a trend toward individualism and subjectivism in theology were the writings of the 14th century Rhenish mystics Meister Eckhart, Johannes Tauler, and Heinrich Suso. A proliferation of sects appeared: the Friends of God, the Brethren of the Free Spirit, and the Beghards and Beguines. In Germany and the Low Countries the Brethren of the Common Life fostered a more personal approach to the divine. This laicized theology found its finest expression in the *Imitation of Christ*, written in 1420 by Thomas à Kempis. The great humanist, biblicist, and critic of church abuses, Erasmus of Rotterdam, was influenced by these trends. His Greek edition of the New Testament (1516) and his translations of the Fathers paved the way for the Reformation.

Innovations. A number of new devotional practices appeared during the late Middle Ages. The Angelus, the custom of reciting certain prayers at the ringing of a bell, became widespread after 1456 when Pope Callistus III ordered church bells rung at noon to remind the faithful of the Turkish peril. The Way of the Cross (Stations) took on a more definite form, and devotion to Mary increased. The feasts of the Visitation and the Immaculate Conception were instituted, and the rosary was popularized. It was the granting of indulgences, the temporal remission of punishment due to sin, however, that gained the greatest popularity. Papal grants of indulgence for the dead first appeared in the mid-15th century. The Jubilee indulgence, a grant of special graces for those visiting the city of Rome, was held every 25 years.

The invention of movable type made possible an increase in the number of printed Bibles. During the incunabular period of printing (1450–1500) almost 100 editions of the Vulgate appeared. Some 14 editions of the Bible had been printed in German before 1518. In church architecture a new style, borrowed from ancient Greek and Roman models, succeeded the earlier Gothic. The Renaissance style aimed at spaciousness and emphasized decorations, leafwork, and friezes.

While the Renaissance, with its glorification of nature, was in many ways inimical to the church, nonetheless under Pope Nicholas V (reigned 1447–1453), Rome rather than Florence became the center for the revival of classical learning. Nicholas founded the Vatican Library, Pius II (reigned 1458–1464) was a leading humanist, and Giovanni de' Medici, son of Lorenzo the Magnificent of Florence, became Pope Leo X (reigned 1513–1521). Under Julius II (reigned 1503–1513), Bramante began the construction of St. Peter's Basilica, and Michelangelo painted the Sistine Chapel.

Spain, which by the early 16th century had become the greatest nation in Europe, was thought to have owed much of its power to an insistence on "racial purity" and religious orthodoxy. The Inquisition was revived under Isabella and Ferdinand and began to function in Seville in 1480. In 1483 the Pope appointed the Dominican Tomás de Torquemada grand inquisitor. The chief victims of the Spanish Inquisition were Jews and Muslims; the former were expelled in 1492, the latter in 1502. The last death sentence was passed in Seville in 1781.

The Dominican preacher Savonarola typified the identification of political with religious reform on the eve of the Reformation. He was hanged for heresy in Florence and his body burned. (Since 1955 the Dominicans have sought his canonization.)

Protestant Reform. While Spain and the areas under its control retained the medieval faith, the 16th century witnessed Catholicism's loss of most of northern Europe. The Reformation arose from many causes: the far-reaching deterioration of religious and moral strength, a lack of precision in central questions of belief and of a sense of pastoral responsibility among the clergy, and lost opportunities for reform. The fact that it happened was due to a great extent to the personality and work of the German-born Augustinian Martin Luther (1483–1546). He was ordained in 1507 and received his doctorate in theology in 1512. During the next two years, while lecturing on the Psalms and the Pauline Epistles at the University of Wittenberg, he developed his doctrine that Scripture is the sole source of revelation and that man is justified by faith rather than the performance of good works. The sale of indulgences for the construction of St. Peter's Basilica occasioned the first public enunciation of his new theology. The 95 theses, distributed in 1517, led to his condemnation by Rome in 1520. During the same year he published his most violent attacks on the Roman Church, rejecting the primacy of the pope, the sacramental system, and the sacrificial nature of the Mass.

In 1529 at the second Diet of Speyer the protest of many of the Imperial Cities and territories in the empire against the continuation of Catholic practices gave birth to the expression "Protestantism." The Lutheran form of Protestantism spread to Sweden in 1527, to Finland and Denmark in 1536, and to Norway in 1545. Important Reformers outside of Germany were Ulrich Zwingli in Switzerland and Martin Bucer in Alsace. Both accepted the principles of justification by faith alone and the Bible as the sole source of revelation. Both identified the reform with improved social and moral conditions. The French-born theologian John Calvin led the second generation of Reformers. Directing the movement from Geneva he gave to Protestantism a more systematic theology and closer-knit organization, adapting it to the social virtues of the emerging commercial classes. Calvin's *Institutes of the Christian Religion* (1536) stressed faith in God's special guidance in the affairs of man. Whereas Luther taught an absolute trust in a redeeming Saviour, Calvin taught assent to the will of God. By the end of the century Calvinism had taken root in France, Scotland, the Netherlands, Poland, and Hungary.

The Reformation in England was largely an act of state. Henry VIII originally opposed the doctrines of Luther. His *Defense of the Seven Sacraments* won for him from Pope Leo X the title Defender of the Faith. It was the claim that his marriage to Catherine of Aragon was invalid because of her previous marriage to his brother Arthur that led to a break with Rome. In 1531 the convocation of the clergy, not without protest, voted to recognize the king as head of the church "as far as the law of Christ allows." On May 23, 1533, the Archbishop of Canterbury declared Henry's marriage to Catherine null, thus validating his marriage with Anne Boleyn. The Act of Supremacy of November 3, 1534, transferred all legal rights and duties of the pope to the crown. Since Bishop John Fisher of Rochester and Sir Thomas More refused to swear to the Act of Supremacy, they were beheaded in 1535. With Parliament's consent a statute of April 4, 1536, suppressed 291 lesser monasteries. Between 1537 and 1540 the larger monasteries were dissolved. It was not until the reign of Edward VI that elements of continental Protestantism were introduced. An English Communion Rite composed by Cranmer was prescribed in 1548. The Book of Common Prayer appeared in 1549. Both changed not only the language but the doctrinal content of the liturgy.

Catholic efforts to stem the reform were hindered by papal involvement in political struggles and by a failure to fathom the depth of the new theory of salvation. The gradual exclusion of Erasmian reform ideas and the establishment of the Inquisition eliminated moderating influences and prepared the way for the Council of Trent and the militancy of the newly founded Jesuits.

JOHN P. DOLAN, *University of South Carolina*

MODERN PERIOD

By the 17th century, Europe's religious map had taken its present shape. The Catholic Counter-Reformation kept Austria, southern Germany, Poland, most of Hungary and the non-Orthodox Slavic lands loyal to Rome. Between the Reformation and the Thirty Years' War, effective Roman reaction was begun by Pope Paul III, who created a reform commission (1536), approved the Society of Jesus (1540), and convoked the Council of Trent (1545–1563), which passed decrees on Scripture, original sin, the sacraments, seminary training, preaching, indulgences, and reform of clerical life.

Pope Paul IV (reigned 1555–1559) curbed abuses in religious orders, finance, ecclesiastical behavior, and political interference. Pius IV (reigned 1559–1565) continued the reform, which was exemplified in the actions of his nephew St. Charles Borromeo (q.v.). St. Pius V (reigned 1566–1572) vigorously implemented Trent's decrees, standardized the catechism and liturgical books, encouraged the growth of colleges and seminaries, and worked politically against Protestantism: he excommunicated Elizabeth I of England and organized a successful crusade against the Turks.

Gregory XIII (reigned 1572–1585) sent Jesuits to England and sponsored a futile invasion of Ireland (1580). The Gregorian calendar (1582) is named for him. Sixtus V (reigned 1585–1590) subsidized the Spanish Armada (1588), thus widening the breach between England and Rome. Gregory XV (reigned 1621–1623) founded the central mission office, the Congregation for the Propagation of the Faith, in an age of missionary expansion. New and reformed religious orders arose: contemplative Carmelites under St. Teresa of Ávila and St. John of the Cross, and Capuchin Franciscans; Oratorians like St. Philip Neri and Caesar Baronius further contributed to church reform.

Secular rulers both helped and hindered Catholic reformation. Emperor Charles V delayed the opening of Trent and, in the Peace of Augsburg (1555), acknowledged the right of a prince to determine the religion of his people. France, torn by religious civil war (1562–1598), was the scene of the bloody massacre of Protestants (Huguenots) on St. Bartholomew's Day, 1572. Although toleration was granted to the Huguenots by the Edict of Nantes, it was revoked in 1685. Philip II of Spain was generally a papal ally, but his alliance with Rome compromised Catholics in countries hostile to Spain.

A spiritual revival within Catholicism was popularized by the writer St. Francis de Sales (q.v.). St. Vincent de Paul (q.v.) founded organizations for charitable and educational work. But there were spiritual excesses. Jansenism taught that human nature was corrupt and man powerless to avoid sin without special grace. A second development, quietism, blended mystical religious and libertarian practices. Because of these religious disputes, religion was held up to ridicule just as the Enlightenment burst upon Europe. Men looked to science and modern philosophy for answers formerly sought in religion. Politically, the emphasis shifted from the impotent empire to nation-states.

Seventeenth and Eighteenth Centuries. England's break with Rome, begun by Henry VIII, was consummated by Elizabeth I. Catholics were persecuted, as Protestants had been under Mary I. James I continued Elizabeth's policies; the 1605 Gunpowder Plot led to penal legislation against "Papists." Guy Fawkes Day (November 5), the anniversary of the foiling of the plot, became a national holiday. English Catholicism was torn by dissension and English Catholics were compromised by identification of their religion with Spain; their support of Charles was to lead to further difficulties under the Protectorate and Commonwealth. Charles II was more lenient, but the 1673 Test Act excluded Catholics from public office, and the 1678 "Popish Plot" cast suspicion on Catholic loyalty. James II, a Catholic, issued declarations of toleration in 1687 and 1688, but these were declared illegal exercises of royal power, and James was deposed (1688). Under William and Mary the 1689 Toleration Act benefited Protestant dissenters, but laws against Catholics increased until the first Catholic Relief Act was passed in 1778. Catholic Emancipation did not exist fully until as late as 1829.

The 17th and 18th centuries on the Continent saw the church at odds with the national monarchies. "Gallicanism," the assertion of the autonomy of the French church, and similar movements toward church nationalism in other countries, plagued Rome. The Enlightenment, which emphasized reason and anthropocentricism, dominated European thought. Deism became popular, and the Continental Masonic lodges emerged as centers for the new ideas. The first papal condemnation of Freemasonry dates from 1738. The Jesuits, a casualty of the Enlightenment and nationalism, were banned by governments in France, Portugal, Spain, and Italy under

Clement XIII (reigned 1758–1769). Clement XIV (reigned 1769–1774), pressured by the Bourbon courts, suppressed them in 1773. Thus the papacy's position was weakened in Europe, and missionary work in areas as far spread as China and the Americas was virtually halted.

When Pius VI (reigned 1775–1799), who had survived the French Revolution, died Napoleon's prisoner, the church was shaken to its foundations. Pius VII (reigned 1800–1823) was also Napoleon's captive from 1809 to 1814; Napoleon incorporated the Papal States into the French Empire, and in 1801 signed a concordat, which was to govern relations between France and the church until 1905. The 1815 Congress of Vienna restored the Papal States, and a series of conservative popes cooperated with the restoration settlement. The romantic movement exalted the power and person of the pope and encouraged Roman centralization. The Jesuits, restored in 1814, were another strong conservative force.

Nineteenth Century. The 19th century industrial and scientific revolution gave birth to the liberal and socialist movements. Catholicism was at odds with both. Except in the United States, Ireland, and Poland, the church's hold on the middle and working classes weakened. Theology was at a low ebb; apart from Louvain and the Roman schools, no Catholic university existed in the world until toward the end of the century. German scholars were looked on with suspicion; efforts like that of the French priest Félicité de Lamennais to accommodate the church to democratic ideas were rebuffed. Advances in Biblical criticism and the evolutionary theory of Charles Darwin challenged traditional ideas.

The popes supported established powers against nationalist uprisings. Their possession of the Papal States alienated them from the Italian national movement and made them politically dependent on Austria and France. Thus began the "Roman Question," which bedeviled relations with Italy until the 1929 Lateran Treaty set up the state of Vatican City. Pius IX (reigned 1846–1878) began as a paternalist but was ousted from Rome by the 1848 revolution and returned only with French help. Most of the Papal States were taken by Italy after the 1859 war with Austria; Rome itself fell in 1870. Popes from then until 1929 considered themselves "prisoners of the Vatican."

Pius IX reacted to the spirit of the times with the 1854 definition of the Immaculate Conception, designed to honor the Virgin Mary, but also to proclaim papal authority and provide a theological basis for condemnation of contemporary exaltation of human nature. The first Vatican Council (1869–1870), which stated Catholic opposition to rationalism and defined papal primacy and infallibility as dogmas of faith, was similarly motivated. At Pius' death the church in Germany was in conflict with Prince Bismarck, and the ensuing Kulturkampf lasted over a decade.

Leo XIII (reigned 1878–1903) restored peace with Germany but failed to obtain Catholic support for the French Third Republic. His encyclical letters on politics evidenced appreciation of the changing complexion of political and economic life. The 19th century was also a period of extensive missionary activity, which was greatly facilitated by the efforts of the major nations to establish colonies in all parts of the

POPE PAUL VI making an eloquent plea for world peace in an address before the United Nations Assembly in New York City on Oct. 4, 1965.

world. The Catholic Church in the United States began to be noticed. Its membership had grown from 25,000 in 1785 to 12,041,000 in 1900. The church prospered in America, where it emerged as a church of the workingman when the working classes of Europe had largely deserted the church. European liberals looked with envy on its constitutional freedom.

Twentieth Century. St. Pius X (reigned 1903–1914) contended with the Modernist crisis, an outgrowth of the rapidly paced scholarly developments in Biblical criticism and the newly emphasized subjective elements in religious faith. In France the church was disestablished, the 1801 concordat was denounced (1905), and religious orders were expelled. Catholic piety flourished with renewed devotion to the Eucharist, and liturgical reforms were begun. Under Benedict XV (reigned 1914–1922) the code of canon law was published in 1917. His efforts to mediate among the powers in World War I failed, however, and he was not represented at the Versailles peace conference.

Pius XI (reigned 1922–1939) sent a postwar relief mission to the Soviet Union but failed to establish relations with the Soviets and remained to the end an implacable enemy of Bolshevism. The 1929 Lateran Treaty with Italy ended the Roman Question by making the pope sovereign of Vatican City. Relations with Italian dictator Benito Mussolini were often strained, however, and the Pope condemned government interference with the church in Italy, as well as in Germany where Adolf Hitler had come to power in 1933. Both countries dissolved Catholic political parties. In Spain the church was sympathetic to the 1936 revolt of Francisco Franco, though Basques and other Catholics supported the republicans. Pius XI maintained a cautious reserve throughout the war but strongly criticized destruction of church property and the murder of priests and nuns. His encyclical *Casti connubii* (1930) enunciated doctrines on marriage, and *Quadragesimo anno* (1931) further explained the church's social teaching.

Pius XII (reigned 1939–1958) was a diplomat who tried to prevent, and then to mediate, World War II, but he has been criticized for not taking more direct action. His reign was notable for the far-ranging statements he made on a variety of topics of contemporary concern and advances made in the study of the nature of the church, exegesis, and liturgy. In the postwar years Catholic political parties revived in Europe, and Christian Democracy became a strong force in Germany, Italy, and France.

James Hennesey, S. J.
Fordham University

ERA OF ECUMENISM

Pope John XXIII. At the time of his election (Oct. 28, 1958) jovial Pope John XXIII, aged 77, was thought to be a "transitional" pope, but he soon advanced the church's social teaching in a great encyclical, *Mater et magistra;* revitalized the work for peace with a still greater encyclical *Pacem in Terris* (the first ever addressed to "all men of good will"); and only 90 days after his election he announced plans for the greatest religious event of the century, the 21st Ecumenical Council, known as Vatican II (1962–1965).

Appalled that two thirds of humanity knew little or nothing of Christianity, that communism controlled one third of the earth, and that Christians (less than a third of humanity) were so divided, Pope John set out to revitalize the church. He chided the "prophets of doom" and began a program of *aggiornamento* (updating). He invited Eastern Orthodox and Protestant churches to send observer-delegates to the council (where they were given positions of honor) and initiated dialogue with atheists. He authorized use of modern languages in the administration of the sacraments, asked North America's bishops to give one tenth of their priests for work in Latin America, and established a commission for revision of the Code of Canon Law. He founded the Secretariat for Promoting Christian Unity and named biblical scholar Augustin Cardinal Bea its president. Six weeks before he died Pope John had the Secretariat's first version of the Vatican II's Decree on Ecumenism sent to all the council fathers for study. In its final form, the decree, promulgated by Pope Paul VI (Nov. 21, 1964), marked the church's full and formal entry into the ecumenical movement. When Pope John died on June 3, 1963, he was one of the most beloved popes in history.

Pope Paul VI. On his election (June 21, 1963) Pope Paul VI promised to continue John's work. Although he reserved to himself the questions of birth control, mixed marriage, and clerical celibacy, Pope Paul continued the council, promulgated its 16 documents, and followed up with decrees of implementation. He advanced the church's social teaching in the encyclical *Populorum progressio*, personally addressed the United Nations General Assembly (Oct. 4, 1965), and tirelessly worked for peace. As a pilgrim visiting the Holy Land (Jan. 2–4, 1964), the first pope to do so since St. Peter, he sent 220 peace messages to heads of state and others; he attended the 38th International Eucharistic Congress in Bombay (Dec. 3–5, 1964) and the 50th Anniversary celebration of the shrine in Fatima, Portugal (May 13, 1967).

Pope Paul had to deal with Catholics reluctant to abandon old positions as well as the "emerging layman," "new breed" youth, and others impatient with the pace of church reform. Clearly committed to Vatican II, *aggiornamento*, and ecumenism, Pope Paul strove to win all in the church to these programs. At the close of Vatican II he announced the introduction of the cause of beatification for both Pope John XXIII and Pope Pius XII. After seven years of study, he reformed the Roman Curia and established its new form in the constitution Government of the Universal Church (*Regimini ecclesiae universae;* Aug. 15, 1967); abolished the Index of Forbidden Books; and established the Secretariat for Non-Christians and the Secretariat for Non-Believers (for dialogue with Marxists and other atheists). He reaffirmed the church's traditional view on clerical celibacy in the encyclical *Sacerdotalis caelibatus* (June 24, 1967). The first pope in more than 500 years to meet with the Ecumenical Patriarch (Athenagoras in Jerusalem, 1964), on Dec. 7, 1965, the Pope in Rome and the Patriarch in Istanbul issued a common declaration removing the mutual sentences of excommunication made in 1054.

Second Vatican Council. Vatican II marked the end of the Counter-Reformation (that is, the end of polemical focus in theology) and the full approbation of positive movements that had built up in the church (liturgical, Biblical and kerygmatic, ecumenical, social, and apostolic). Unlike earlier councils, Vatican II was not called to condemn anybody or anything. It met to put the core of the Christian message in focus, to find forms appropriate for the church's life, to set the face of the church to the future.

The first session (Oct. 11-Dec. 8, 1962) produced the Message to Humanity (Oct. 20), Biblical in flavor and strong in stress on service. The second session (Sept. 29-Dec. 4, 1963) produced the Constitution on the Sacred Liturgy (see Section 3. *Liturgy,* below) and the Decree on the Media of Social Communication. The third session (Sept. 14–Nov. 21, 1964) produced the pivotal document of Vatican II, the Dogmatic Constitution on the Church, as well as the Decree on Ecumenism, and the Decree on Eastern Catholic Churches. Pope Paul VI followed up the council's doctrine on episcopal collegiality by announcing norms for the Synod of Bishops, which he established at the request of the council fathers, and which began its first meeting in Rome on Sept. 29, 1967. The synod was composed of 197 prelates of which 135 were elected representatives of national episcopal conferences.

The final session of Vatican II (Sept. 14–Dec. 8, 1965) saw the completion of 11 documents: Decree on the Bishops' Pastoral Office (implemented by Pope Paul in a document of July 11, 1966, increasing the powers of bishops, and again August 6 when, to update the episcopacy, he asked bishops to resign at 75); Decree on Priestly Formation (seminary reform); Decree on the Renewal and Adaptation of the Religious Life (soon followed by meetings of orders and congregations to make detailed application); Declaration on Non-Christian Religions (with a section on Jews stating that the Bible does not teach that they are "repudiated or cursed by God"); Declaration on Education; Dogmatic Constitution on Divine Revelation (including approval of common Christian Bible translation work, thus opening the way to worldwide collaboration with the United Bible Societies); Decree on the Apostolate of the Laity; Pastoral Constitution on the Church in the Modern World; Decree on the Ministry and Life of Priests; Decree on Missionary Activity; and the Declaration on Religious Freedom (the chief architect of which was the late American theologian, John Courtney Murray, S. J.). The documents of Vatican II are a charter of hope for Christianity and the world. See also VATICAN COUNCIL, SECOND.

WALTER ABBOTT, S. J.
Editor of "Documents of Vatican II"

Bibliography

Daniélou, J. and Marrou, H., *The Christian Centuries: The First Six Hundred Years* (New York 1964).
Dolan, John P., *History of the Reformation* (New York 1965).
Dvornik, Francis, *The Ecumenical Councils* (New York 1961).
Hales, Edward E. Y., *Revolution and Papacy 1769–1846* (New York 1960).
Hughes, Philip, *A History of the Church,* 3 vols. (London 1947).
Huizinga, Johan, *The Waning of the Middle Ages* (London 1924).
Jalland, Trevor, *Church and Papacy* (New York 1944).
Lotz, Johannes Baptist, *How the Reformation Came* (New York 1965).
Mollat, Guillaume, *The Popes at Avignon 1305–1378* (London 1963).
Rynne, Xavier, *Vatican II* (New York 1967).
Schillebeeckx, Edward, *The Real Achievement of Vatican II* (New York 1967).

3. Liturgy

The Constitution on the Sacred Liturgy, promulgated by the Second Vatican Council on December 4, 1963, states that "in the liturgy the whole public worship is performed by the mystical body of Christ, that is, by the head and members. From this it follows that every liturgical celebration—because it is an action of Christ the priest and of his body, which is the Church—is a sacred action surpassing all others; no other action of the Church can equal its efficacy by the same title and to the same degree." Thus liturgy goes far beyond cult or ritual in the narrow sense. It is infinitely more complex: "Rightly, then, the liturgy is considered as an exercise of the priestly office of Jesus Christ." The liturgy actualizes this priesthood by means of sacred signs and symbols, but the liturgy is more than ritual, it is an *admirabile commercium,* a wonderful exchange, the expression of man's response to God's gracious saving act.

THEOLOGY OF THE LITURGY

Many Catholics formerly identified the liturgy with mere ceremony, or viewed it as a code of laws governing the external performance of sacred services. Still others identified it with vestments, or Gregorian chant, or church music. But all these views were superficial and failed to touch upon the substance, the reality of what the liturgy is.

Nature of the Liturgy. The liturgy springs from what the church itself is, and since it is impossible to define the church adequately, it is equally impossible to define the liturgy. Like man himself the church resists or transcends definition. The church is simultaneously structured community and communion, event and activity; it not only is, it does. Among its activities is the celebration of the liturgy, and this activity, as the Constitution on the Liturgy emphasizes, is the summation and synthesis of all the other activities of the church. It is the expression of the church's whole life, and that life is directed toward making Christ present in the world. From the very beginning, the church has recognized that the liturgy is the principal means of accomplishing this. The liturgy gives glory to God and brings peace, that is, salvation, to men. Neither one of these activities is isolated from the other: the church believes that the very act of saving men gives glory to God; the act of glorifying God brings salvation to men.

Thus liturgy is an act of worship, but it is distinguished from worship in the broad sense. Worship is the response that man makes to God for all that God is and has done. Man gives recognition to God in the form of praise, thanksgiving, petition, sacrifice: these may be expressed publicly or privately, alone or in community, inwardly felt or outwardly expressed. Regardless of the manner in which these prayers are offered, they are equally acts of worship. Liturgy, on the other hand, is public worship, not by any one man or group of men, but by the community that is the church. Since the liturgy is the embodiment of the church's attitude toward God—that specialized form of worship that involves the entire community—it is always outwardly expressed. A liturgy that is purely internal is, therefore, a contradiction. Similarly, a liturgy that is only external is an empty formality. Liturgy is an action, the action of Christ in the church, an action that employs signs and symbols but that is not imprisoned by them, an action that does what it signifies but does far more than the signs—the words and the actions—can adequately convey. It is an action that involves the whole man, his mind, heart, and will, body and emotions.

Just as liturgy is not simply worship, it is inadequate to define it as rite, although these terms are often used interchangeably. "Roman Liturgy" and "Roman Rite," for example, are used to express the same thing. Strictly speaking, however, the Roman Rite is only one of the many ways of celebrating the liturgy. Since the liturgy basically celebrates the mystery of salvation, or the redemptive activity, in symbolic form, the form may vary from one rite to another, but the celebration is always the same. Thus there are many rites, but only one liturgy, one act of the church. The death of the Lord is proclaimed one way in Alexandria, another in Rome, and still another way in Antioch: the words and the gestures are quite distinct, but the drama is unchanging.

In all the rites the mystery of salvation is enacted principally through the Eucharist, or Mass,

ST. GILES shown in a 15th century painting in the act of celebrating Mass before the altar of St. Denis.

then through the other sacraments, and finally through the Divine Office, which is the public prayer of the church. Although this article is primarily concerned with the Roman Rite—that form of the liturgy which had its beginnings at Rome but spread throughout the world to become the most prevalent of all the Christian rites—the theology outlined concerning the liturgy is equally applicable to all the rites.

The Sacraments. The Sacrament of the Eucharist, which is the Mass, is the principal sacrament. The other six sacraments are closely related to the Eucharist: Baptism and Confirmation equip a person to celebrate the Eucharist by making him a member of the church; Penance reconciles the Catholic to the church after he has fallen into sin; Matrimony is the sign of the union between Christ and His church; the Anointing of the Sick is the sacrament that restores the sick man to health so that he may again participate in the Eucharist with his brethren in the church; Holy Orders makes a man capable of performing the ministry of the Eucharist for his fellow Christians.

Like the Eucharist these sacraments are acts of public worship, and together with the Eucharist form the most important part of the liturgy. St. Augustine calls the sacraments the "visible word," because they are made up of words and actions: the words give meaning to the actions and, in a very real way, are actions in themselves.

The sacraments are effective signs of God's action in Christ and man's response to that action, also in Christ. Unlike the commentators of the recent past, modern theologians stress the personal aspect of the sacraments. They view the sacraments, not as the action of God alone but as the joint action of Christ in His church, of the priest who celebrates them, and of the faithful Christian, the concelebrant, who takes part in them. Contemporary theologians point out that men do not just *receive* the sacraments, they *participate* in them.

The Principal Sacrament. The Eucharist, or Mass, is the sacred rite that reenacts the Last Supper. Thus the Mass is a sacramental offering of sacrifice to God. The Constitution on the Liturgy beautifully expresses the meaning of the Mass: "At the Last Supper, on the night when he was betrayed, our Saviour instituted the Eucharistic sacrifice of his body and blood. He did this in order to perpetuate the sacrifice of the cross throughout the centuries until he should come again, and so to entrust to his beloved spouse, the Church, a memorial of his death and resurrection: a sacrament of love, a sign of unity, a bond of charity, a paschal banquet in which Christ is received, the mind is filled with grace, and a pledge of future glory is given us."

Divine Office. The Divine Office, or daily prayer of the church, is next in importance after the Eucharist and the other sacraments. It is not, however, a separate or isolated activity. The Office actually complements the sacraments and continues the work of the redemption because it shares in the prayer of Christ. The Constitution on the Liturgy describes the prayer of Christ as: "Christ Jesus, high priest of the new and eternal covenant, taking human nature, introduced into this earthly exile that hymn which is sung throughout all ages in the halls of heaven." This hymn of praise and thanksgiving goes on for all eternity. Christ is its first and greatest celebrant. But He does not sing alone—He associates all creation with Him in singing it, especially the rational, human part of creation. This hymn takes many forms: it resounds in the Mass and the sacraments, but it finds more direct and ordered expression in the Divine Office. This is done by means of psalms, hymns, and canticles.

Originally the Office was the prayer of the layman. The clergy did not even attend it. It was divided into two parts, morning and evening prayer, or Lauds and Vespers. In the course of centuries, however, the Office, like the Mass, became a clerical specialty. Unlike the Mass it remains so even today. In theory it is "the prayer of the church," but in practice it is not. A complete and radical reform of the Office has been called for by many in order that it keep pace with the reform of the Mass and the sacraments.

Liturgical Year. The celebration of the Mass and the Office is set in a framework that is known as the liturgical year, or the year of the church. This year does not correspond to the current calendar year, but rather turns about the feast of Easter, or, as it was called in ancient times, Pascha, the paschal feast. The preparation for Easter and the celebration and the prolongation of the feast take up the greater part of the year. The purpose of the liturgical year is to commemorate and celebrate the mystery of the redemption. Even the feasts of Christmas and Epiphany are regarded more as celebrations of the redemptive event than as commemorations of the temporal birth of Christ. The feasts of the Blessed Virgin and the saints, which round out the year, are in the main much later additions to the original nucleus. They too derive all their meaning from the redeeming work of Christ.

Sunday, the day of the Lord, is the pivot on which the liturgical year turns, precisely because Sunday is the day on which the Lord rose from the dead and sent the Holy Spirit upon the church. In a most complete way it is the day of the resurrection, recalling not only the event itself but all its consequences.

Through the liturgical year the redemptive events, or mysteries, as they are called, are made present in such a way that the faithful may make contact with them and be filled with the graces these mysteries contain. The sacred mysteries of the life, death, and resurrection of Christ reach the faithful through the symbolic commemoration of these events. By means of the readings, prayers, and chants of the Mass and Office the inward reality of these mysteries is made clear, and the faithful are stimulated to live by these mysteries, to reproduce them in their lives.

All the liturgy revolves around the Paschal Mystery, the mystery of the death-resurrection of Christ. Pope Pius XII's encyclical *Mediator Dei* (On the Sacred Liturgy, Nov. 20, 1947) points out that "the liturgical year is Christ himself." The liturgical year is a natural device that assures the remembrance of the great events of salvation. But these events cannot be separated from Christ, who accomplished them.

THE HISTORY OF THE LITURGY

The Institution of the Eucharist. The Eucharist, or Mass, is always the reenactment of the Last Supper, or the Lord's Supper. Whether or not the Last Supper was a Passover celebration is a question that engages scholars, but one that will probably never be resolved satisfactorily. It is clear, however, that the supper occurred during the time of year, and in the same week, that the Jews celebrated Passover, and it is probable that the meal was held in the atmosphere of the paschal feast. In Christ's time, just as today, the Jews commemorated the deliverance of their ancestors from Egypt at the Passover feast. By participating in this annual memorial of the Exodus the Jew could share in the experience of deliverance that his fathers had enjoyed; at the same time, he could look forward to a fuller deliverance, a more perfect Exodus to come. This spirit undoubtedly permeated the thinking of the disciples at the Last Supper and, indeed, was carried over into the Eucharistic feast celebrated by the early Christians.

The events that occurred at the Last Supper are recorded in the New Testament in the writings of Matthew, Mark, Luke, and Paul. None of these accounts tell exactly what Jesus said or did because the evangelists were preoccupied with the meaning the Eucharist had to the Christian community rather than detailed history. In fact, since the Eucharist was celebrated each week long before the evangelists wrote their accounts of the Last Supper, many scholars believe that these accounts were transcriptions of the Eucharistic celebration of the period. Although the accounts are not in complete harmony, all four agree that during the meal Christ took a piece of bread into his hands, pronounced the customary thanksgiving and blessing over it, broke it, and then, as he gave it to his disciples, said: "Take and eat, this is my body." After

MASS is celebrated at the U. S. Air Force Academy at an altar prescribed by new church rules for joint clergy and lay participation in the ritual.

the meal had been eaten, Christ took the "cup of blessing," pronounced a longer blessing over that, and as he passed it around to his disciples, said: "Take and drink, this is the cup of my blood," or "This is the new covenant in my blood."

Through this series of actions and words Christ acted out a prophecy or parable in the Hebraic style. He symbolically dramatized his coming sacrifice and, at the same time, gave it meaning by interpreting it through his words. Although Christ's actions were those of any ordinary head of a house at such a gathering, his words imparted deeper meaning to his acts, and his disciples' response—their taking and eating, their taking and drinking—completed the meaning of both his words and his actions.

The Eucharist as a Memorial. The word "memorial" had much more meaning to the Jews of Christ's time than it does to men of the 20th century. Today the word "memorial" has a purely subjective connotation: it implies someone or something no longer present that is recalled to mind through an effort of will. To the ancient Jew, on the contrary, the liturgical memorial was an objective representation that made the past event present in some way. The New Testament clearly indicates that Christians of the apostolic age believed that they encountered the Risen Christ in the Eucharistic feast.

Neither Matthew nor Mark mentions Christ's command "do this in commemoration of me," but both Luke and Paul do. This discrepancy has led some scholars to deny that Jesus ever said these words. It is highly significant, however, that they appear in St. Paul's first letter to the Corinthians (11:25), which is the oldest account. In this Epistle, Paul reports that Christ said: "Do this . . . as a remembrance of me," and adds "As often as you eat this bread and drink the cup, you proclaim the death of the Lord until he comes." Paul goes on to say that he received this account "from the Lord." This statement shows that the early Christians believed that Christ had commanded His disciples to repeat His supper. Whether or not Christ actually pronounced these exact words, then, is purely an academic question. The disciples of Jesus Christ acted as though He had said them.

How exactly they obeyed His command is uncertain. It is known that the Eucharist was connected with the ordinary family meal for some time. On the first day of the week the early Christians gathered in the home of one of their members, usually a house with a room of sufficient size to accommodate such a gathering. Sunday was a day of great significance to the early Christians; not only had the Holy Spirit been sent to the Apostles on this day (that is, Pentecost), but more importantly it was the day of the Lord's Resurrection. Thus the early Christians prayed in the synagogue on the Sabbath, the last day of the week, and on the first day of the week they commemorated the Risen Lord's sacrifice at a fraternal meal at which the bishop officiated.

St. Paul's words, "In the same way, after the supper, he took the cup . . .," indicate that at first the blessing of the bread was separated from the blessing of the cup by the actual meal. Before long, however, the two consecrations were joined together, and the prayer or blessing over the cup became the blessing for both. The actual meal, or agape, either preceded or followed the Eucharist. At one time it was believed that the first part of the Eucharistic service that is now called the Liturgy of the Word, was derived directly from the synagogue service. Modern scholars, however, are more cautious about this assertion, and suggest that, at most, the synagogue service only influenced the form of the Liturgy of the Word.

The Eucharist as a Formal Liturgical Service. By the end of the 1st century the fraternal meal, or agape, became totally separated from the Eucharistic service. The increase in the number of Christians with the resulting problems and abuses contributed to this development of the Eucharist as a formal liturgical service. Another factor was the inability of the non-Jewish, or Gentile, converts to relate the Eucharist to an ordinary meal. Unlike the Jews, their traditions did not include a family meal of religious significance.

In spite of this, the Eucharist continued to be regarded as a meal—a very special, stylized meal at which the Lord is the host, inviting men to sit down with him at table. The altar on which Christ's sacrifice on the cross is reenacted is not an altar in the pagan sense: it is the table of the Lord on which is offered, not a bloody victim, but something that is primarily life-giving food. Like other food, the bread and wine of the Eucharist are blessed and eaten. The Eucharist is a sacrifice in the form of a meal. Eating the food is an essential part of the total sacrificial action; without the taking and eating, the memorial does not exist. Communion is not an optional append-age to the sacrifice; it is an integral part of it. The meal is the sacrifice; the sacrifice is the meal.

The oldest fairly complete description of the Mass as a formal liturgical service is that of the 2d century apologist St. Justin. Although Justin lived in Rome, the service he recorded is not simply a local liturgy, because this phenomenon had not yet evolved, but the form of the Eucha-rist used throughout the Roman Empire, both East and West. The ordinary Sunday Eucharist consisted of two parts: the Liturgy of the Word, as it is now called, and the Eucharistic Liturgy.

The Liturgy of the Word began with readings from both the Old and New Testament. Justin fails to mention the number of passages read, as well as whether psalmody was used. Most scholars agree, however, that there were three scriptural readings, the first two of which were ended by Psalms. Indeed, the use of Psalms prob-ably predates Justin's time. The "President of the Brethren" then delivered a homily based on the readings. A prayer in common, which corre-sponded to the modern "Prayer of the Faithful," completed the first part of the service.

The Eucharistic Liturgy commenced with the kiss of peace. Since the kiss, which was actually an embrace, could be exchanged only by baptized Christians, the catechumens, or those not yet formally received into the church, had already left. Thus the kiss of peace symbolized the fellowship in Christ of the Christians who were about to reenact his sacrifice. The bread and wine needed for the Eucharistic meal had been brought by the people and deposited with the deacons at the door of the house-church. The bread used then, and for many centuries follow-ing, was leavened bread baked in the form of small loaves by the women of the congregation. At this point in the service, the bread and wine were carried to the altar table where the bishop would reenact the words and actions of Christ at the Last Supper. When the offering was over, the president of the brethren said the Eucharistic Prayer, a prayer of praise, blessing, and thanks-giving, which was completely extempore. This prayer continued to be composed according to the president's ability until the 4th century, when the traditional prayers were recorded and then be-came fixed. The Eucharistic Prayer ended with a doxology, and the people responded with "Amen."

Communion followed immediately after the Prayer was completed. Although Justin does not describe the manner in which communion was re-ceived, later writers indicate that the people re-ceived the consecrated bread in their hands and communicated themselves; they then sipped the consecrated wine from the chalice held by one of the deacons.

The Development of Regional Rites. In St. Justin's time each church was allowed to arrange the de-tails of the Mass in any manner it preferred, as long as the main elements were present: the Liturgy of the Word and the Liturgy of the Eu-charist. But the universal, fluid rite gradually gave place to standardized regional rites. This evolution occurred mainly because of the rapid growth of the church. Until the 4th century the bishop was the only chief celebrant of the Eucharist. The presbyters had been his concele-

brants. As Christianity spread, the bishops found it necessary to establish more churches. This multiplication of parishes required the bishops to delegate priests as the celebrants of the Eucha-rist on the local level. Unlike the bishop, how-ever, the local priests did not compose the prayers of the Eucharistic service; rather they copied the prayers used in the cathedral church and recited these at their own services. The books into which the prayers were collected were called *sacramentaries,* the forerunners of the later missal and the modern sacramentary.

The changed conditions brought about by the Peace of the Church under Emperor Constantine also had far-reaching effects upon the liturgy. The church buildings became larger, finer, and more elaborately decorated. The services natu-rally tended to keep pace with the architecture, and as the 4th century drew to a close the austere primitive service yielded to a more highly de-veloped liturgy.

The great centers of Christian influence at Rome, Antioch, and Alexandria, as well as in southern France, developed certain elaborate liturgical practices that all the churches in the surrounding regions imitated. By the end of the 4th century there were four major rites, or litur-gical families. All the liturgies of Christendom, whether Catholic, Orthodox, or Protestant, stem from these four parent rites: Antiochene, Alex-andrian, Roman, or Gallican.

The Mass of the Roman Rite. The Roman Rite, the most widespread of all, began as the local liturgy of the church of Rome. Originally austere, with little external ritual, it slowly absorbed something of the ceremonial color and pageantry of the imperial court. Although it still remained less complex than the other rites, as the church-houses were everywhere replaced by splendid basilicas, the services became longer and more involved. And whereas formerly there were no proper vestments as such, or special tableware, church vessels and vestments began to assume a distinctive ecclesiastical character.

Other changes of far-reaching consequence occurred in the last part of the patristic period. Ceremonial developed, that is, entrance proces-sions, offertory processions, communion proces-sions, and special chants to accompany the pro-cessions. The *schola,* or special choir required to sing this complex music, soon began to sing the responses that once belonged exclusively to the people. A little later the loaves of leavened bread were replaced by small unleavened wafers, which effectively destroyed the symbolism of the shared loaf. Instead of placing the consecrated bread in the communicant's hand so that he could communicate himself, the celebrant now placed the small wafer on the person's tongue.

The position of the altar was also changed. It was pushed back until it was placed against the rear wall of the sanctuary. The celebrant no longer faced the people, but stood in front of the altar with his back toward them. There are sev-eral explanations for this change: the Roman Rite borrowed the custom of facing east, and there-fore away from the people, from the Gallican Rites, which, in turn, had borrowed it from the East. Another explanation is that the custom of placing large shrines behind the altar made it impossible for the priest to stand there. What-ever the reason, this custom removed the people still further from the altar and the sanctuary, heightened the air of mystery that surrounded the altar, and, inevitably, made the liturgy more remote and inaccessible. The distance between altar and nave represented the progressively widening gap between clergy and laity.

Although the Mass of the Roman Rite had originally been confined to the city of Rome and its environs, it began to spread to the rest of Europe in the 6th and 7th centuries. St. Augustine of Canterbury brought the Roman Rite to the Anglo-Saxon missions of southern England in 596. A century later it infiltrated the churches of France. Early in the 9th century, by a decree of Charlemagne, the Roman Rite as modified by Alcuin was adopted in all the churches of the realm. Despite the fact that the Roman Rite had replaced the Gallican Rite almost universally, customs of the Gallican rites were transferred to the Roman liturgy. Many of its ceremonials and prayers are still used in the Roman Rite. The procession on Palm Sunday and the use of incense, for example, are of Gallican origin. The Roman service books that were sent beyond the Alps returned greatly transformed. The Gallicanized books rapidly became the norm and standard of worship in Rome itself, and by the end of the Middle Ages prevailed throughout western Europe.

The Decline of the Liturgy. What had once been the corporate communal worship of the whole people of God had, by 1517, become an elaborate, formal ritual performed by specialists. The people no longer took a direct part in the rites; they assisted at them. While the clergy performed the official liturgy, the people filled in the time with the rosary and other private and individual devotions. These things, good in themselves, were inadequate substitutes for the liturgy itself. Furthermore, the practice of communion, which is the heart and soul of liturgical participation, had so declined that the Fourth Lateran Council in 1215 made it compulsory for the faithful to communicate at least once a year. Communion was the only real participation left to the average layman: he could not understand the service because it was recited in Latin; even if books had existed containing translations of the Latin, few laymen were able to read, supposing that they could afford to buy them; and the peoples' participation in the chants had long ago ceased.

By the end of the Middle Ages the liturgy, as such, had ceased to be an effective force in the lives of the people. Although the Council of Trent was convoked in 1545 to effect reform in the church, it did not actually reform the liturgy. It suppressed some abuses and provided an *editio typica*, or standard for the liturgical books, but far more was needed. Because of the lack of knowledge of the liturgy at that time, it could hardly be restored. The Roman Rite was frozen into a rigid mold: all the essential elements remained, but there was no savor, no warmth, and no vitality evident.

Liturgical Reform and Renewal. Interest in the nature of the liturgy was rekindled in the 17th and 18th centuries. By the 19th century, liturgical studies, along with a renewed appreciation of the Scriptures, were sparked by the fresh inquiry into the nature of the church itself. Thus the liturgy was again viewed as the act of the priestly church. Once this line of reasoning was established, it moved toward a natural conclusion: if the liturgy is the act of the church, then it is the act of the whole church, the people as well as the clergy, because the church is precisely "God's holy people." If it is the act of the people, the people should participate directly in the liturgy.

The decades before the 1960's were, therefore, marked by extensive study of the whole idea of the liturgy, its general structure, and its component elements. Books, periodicals, and articles appeared, and conferences and lectures were given, in all the modern European languages, as well as in Latin, examining the liturgy from every possible point of view—historical, pastoral, doctrinal, spiritual. From a study of what the liturgy was, the scholars progressed to a study of what the liturgy should be. Without this vast literary effort the restoration of the liturgy would never have been seriously considered, let alone actually begun.

By his decree on frequent and daily communion in 1905, as well as by his encouragement of the people's participation in the Mass, Pius X gave a great impetus to the liturgical renewal. But the credit for launching the modern liturgical movement belongs to a Belgian Benedictine, Dom Lambert Beauduin (1873–1960). The object of this liturgical movement was to make the faithful more conscious of the liturgy and especially of the Mass. The first step in this educational program was to make the vernacular missal available to the laity in small, inexpensive editions equipped with a detailed commentary on the liturgy. These missals, which were left in the churches, were probably the most effective means of making the faithful aware of the liturgy, and awakening in them a love for it.

As time progressed the faithful clearly realized that this was not enough; even with missal in hand the layman was still not participating actively. The desire for greater participation found expression in the dialogue, or recited, Mass, which gained acceptance in some parts of Europe. By 1958 it was not only accepted but was highly recommended by the Instruction on Sacred Music and the Liturgy. The main obstacle, however, still remained—the Latin language. More and more the leaders of the reform movement realized that the Mass could not become the genuine prayer of the people until at least the people's parts were in their own language. This was not to be realized until Vatican II promulgated the Constitution on the Liturgy.

The Constitution on the Liturgy is the culmination of decades of scholarly inquiry. Its purpose is to renew the liturgy. The liturgy, however, cannot be renewed if those who celebrate it are not themselves renewed. The real purpose of the Constitution, then, is to renew the church through a renewal of the liturgy. Thus the entire concern of the Constitution is pastoral: it is concerned with the life of the church and the spiritual growth of its members.

The Constitution goes to the root of the problem by providing for complete reform of the rites themselves. The guiding principle of liturgical celebration is no longer conformity to liturgical books, but intelligibility to the people: "in the revision of the liturgy the rites should be distinguished by a noble simplicity; they should be short, clear, and unencumbered by useless repetitions. They should be within the people's powers of comprehension and normally should not require much explanation."

The chief importance of the Constitution on the Liturgy is that it establishes the principle that the liturgy is the activity of the whole church, not just of a part of the church. It stresses the communal nature of the liturgy. Never again will the people be silent spectators of someone else's activity. Instead they will be active participants in an activity that belongs to them.

WILLIAM J. O'SHEA, S. S.
Catholic University of America

Further Reading: Crichton, John D., *The Church's Worship* (New York 1964); Dalmais, Irenée H., *Introduction to the Liturgy,* tr. by Roger Capel (Baltimore 1961); Jungmann, Josef A., *The Mass of the Roman Rite* (New York 1961); Miller, John H., *Fundamentals of the Liturgy* (Notre Dame, Ind., 1966).

4. Organization

The Roman Catholic Church is organized upon a unity of belief and of worship, and under a common hierarchical government of bishops in union with the pope, the bishop of Rome. At the same time, it reflects a wide diversity of differences preserved in the many structural facets of the various communities which make up the Catholic communion. These different communities, or particular churches, acknowledge the supreme authority of the pope, but in matters of worship, ecclesiastical discipline, and administrative direction they are largely self-determining. In general organization, then, the Catholic Church preserves an essential unity of faith, but simultaneously fosters a variety of cultural and historical expressions of the Christian life.

The institutional structures of the apostolic church laid the foundation for the development of the modern organization. By sharing and exercising Christ's authority after His death, the Apostles built up the church in definite hierarchical forms that reflected the order of contemporary Jewish communities. The Apostles themselves, and their successors, occupied a special presidential position in the early church. St. Peter exercised leadership among the Apostles in the name of the Lord. Local communities, beginning at Antioch and spreading through the known world, were distinctive in character, but were joined together in the body of Christ (Colossians 1:13–18). Various functions within these communities, such as preaching, teaching, and presiding at the Eucharist, were eventually stabilized into permanent ministries.

From the 2d to the 4th century, internal growth and the need for adaptation to social circumstances wrought organizational changes. Local communities were centralized into dioceses under the rule of a single bishop; ecclesiastical offices were established to absorb diverse ministries; and stable forms of consultation and cooperation among bishops were made possible by regional and provincial synods. These advances, coupled with the emergence of major centers of Christian influence in the capitals and apostolic sees, shaped the development of the church. After Constantine issued the Edict of Milan, in 313, and after the codifications of law by the emperors Theodosius II (promulgated 438) and Justinian (promulgated 533–534), the patterns of Roman civil government were discernible in the ranks of ecclesiastical institutions.

From earliest times the decisions of local and universal councils, the writings of the Church Fathers and popes, and selections from Roman civil law were honored as a body of customary law. To regulate and protect the church in the Middle Ages, compilations of these norms, or

"canons," were made and enforced, and they became the substance of ecclesiastical law. The Code of Canon Law promulgated in 1917 remains substantially in force. Since the Second Vatican Council (1962–1965), however, extensive revision has been undertaken. The Code contains detailed norms for church government.

THE CHURCH AND THE CHURCHES

Within the universal church, many particular ecclesiastical communities, or churches, both territorial and personal in extension, are autonomous and equal at law.

The Particular Churches. In the 3d and 4th centuries the ancient patriarchates of Alexandria, Antioch, and Rome became major centers of influence in the church. In the following century Constantinople gained predominance in the East; from the Council of Chalcedon (451), the church was organized around a pentarchy of five patriarchates (Jerusalem was added honorarily).

The particular churches which have derived from these patriarchal sees are characterized by certain distinctive elements. They are communities of the faithful that have preserved their ecclesiastical unity and tradition. Their hierarchy of bishops is autonomous, yet directly in communion with Rome. Their established discipline derives from the particular law and custom by which the church's administration and personal traits are chiefly regulated. They preserve a spiritual patrimony that is embodied in their varied national characteristics, forms of devotion, and spirituality. They use a particular and distinctive form of liturgy, language, type of popular piety, and calendar of feasts. In the late 1960's over 20 particular churches were formally acknowledged in the Catholic communion. These churches are frequently referred to as "rites."

From the patriarchal see of *Alexandria* the Coptic and Ethiopian churches are derived; they follow the Alexandrian rite. Deriving from the ancient patriarchate of *Antioch* are the Malankar, Maronite, and Syrian churches of the Antiochene rite. The Chaldean rite, which also derives from Antioch by a later tradition, comprises the Chaldean and Malabar churches. From the ancient see of *Constantinople* are derived the churches of the Byzantine rite: Albanian, Belorussian, Bulgarian, Chinese, Estonian, Finnish, Japanese, Georgian, Greek, Italo-Albanian, Melkite, Rumanian, Russian, Ruthenian, Slovak Byzantine, Ukrainian, and Yugoslavian. The Latin church, largest and most numerous of the churches, exists for the most part in those countries Christianized from *Rome.*

Structure of the Particular Church. The organizational structure of the church evolved in order that its priests and bishops could fulfill their primary goal—the ministry to the people. This pastoral concern manifests itself in the way in which authority is delegated. Clerical jurisdiction is determined by the groupings of people served, rather than by territorial extension.

Parish. A parish is a stable, local community of Catholics entrusted to the spiritual care of a parish priest, or pastor. The bishop may appoint assistant priests (curates) or an administrator to assist the parish priest. The role of the laity is expressed in parochial councils and parish organizations. The modern structure of the parish, which dates from the decisions of the Council of Trent (1545–1563), is primarily territorial in extension. In essence, however, the parish is the basic sacramental community in the church and may follow the personal lines of natural communities. A territorial parish, for example, includes all Catholics in a given area; a national parish may include all Catholics of the same nationality within a country, and embraces many territorial parishes. For purposes of cooperation and supervision, parishes are grouped to form a *deanery* (in the Eastern rites, *protopresbyterate*).

Diocese. A diocese (Eastern rite, *eparchy*) is a well-defined territorial division of the church; it is composed of a large number of parishes and is under the jurisdiction of a bishop. Although the term "diocese," as derived from Roman civil government, was current in the 4th century, it did not become exclusively applied to ecclesiastical territories until the 13th century.

The central governing office of a diocese is the *chancery* or *curia*. A number of chancery officials assist the bishop in governing the diocese. The *vicar general* (Eastern rites, *syncellus*) shares the jurisdiction of the bishop of the diocese, takes charge when he is absent, and exercises general administrative care. The *officialis* (Eastern rites, *vicar judicial*) supervises the tribunal of justice, or court, and processes cases for the adjudication of the synodal judges. The *chancellor* acts as an ecclesiastical notary; he indexes, arranges, and preserves material for the archives. In the United States many of the powers of the bishop are delegated to the chancellor.

Other diocesan officers include the parish priest *consultors*, whose advice must be obtained by the bishop in certain major matters; the *synodal examiners*, who administer the canonical examinations of the clergy; the *promotor of justice*, who is charged with the prosecution of criminal cases and those harming the public order; and the *defender of the bond*, who pleads for the validity of marriage and holy orders in cases of nullity. The Eastern rites have a special office for temporal administration called the *econome*. Most dioceses provide other offices to coordinate the works of charity or social service, education, hospitals, and so forth.

The Second Vatican Council decided that each diocese should form a pastoral council, composed of representatives of the laity, the clergy, and religious, in order to advise the bishop in all areas of diocesan apostolic work. The diocesan priests are represented in a senate of the priests.

In mission territories, areas that are similar to a diocese but not of sufficient population or stability to be so designated, are constituted *vicariates*. They are administered by a bishop and a prefect apostolic, both of whom are responsible to the pope.

An *abbey nullius* (in the Eastern rites, *exarchy*) is an autonomous community surrounding a monastery and ruled by an abbot who is independent of the local bishop.

Archdiocese or Province. An archdiocese, which is almost always a metropolitan see, is a diocese whose bishop is directly responsible to the pope. Although it serves as a supervisory unit for all the dioceses, called suffragan dioceses, that fall within its boundaries, thus constituting an ecclesiastical province, it has no direct jurisdiction over these dioceses. The archbishop summons councils of all the suffragan bishops within his province; and in cases of abuse or the neglect of canonical visitation, he may intervene. When a suffragan bishopric becomes vacant, the archbishop sees that the consultors (or cathedral

ROMA-WAAG, FROM PIX

NEWLY ELEVATED CARDINALS concelebrate Mass with Pope Paul VI in St. Peter's Basilica in Vatican City.

chapter) elect an administrator within the time allotted by canon law. In judicial matters, the metropolitan tribunal is a court of appeals.

Religious Communities. Groups of men and women who live a community life, who are bound by the vows of poverty, chastity, and obedience, and who are engaged either in contemplation or in apostolic service are organized outside the parochial structures. They are ruled by their own elected superiors, some subject to the bishops, others only to the pope.

Patriarchates. Each of the particular churches is ultimately ruled either by its own patriarch, with jurisdiction over all the bishops, clergy, and the people of the rite, or by a major archbishop with less extensive power. The pope is the patriarch of the West, or of the Latin rite. The lesser patriarchs within the Latin rite—Lisbon, Venice, the Americas—bear honorary titles. The Latin patriarchates of the East have all been suppressed, except that of Jerusalem, which is honorary. The Melkites, Copts, Chaldeans, Syrians, Armenians, and Maronites have Catholic patriarchs; the other Oriental rites have major archbishops. The patriarch governs the particular church or rite through the offices of the *patriarchal curia*.

THE POPE AND THE BISHOPS

The pope has supreme, full, and universal jurisdiction over the entire church and the faithful, by divine right, as the successor of St. Peter. He has and exercises this primacy as the head of the college of bishops, who succeed to the role of the apostolic college. With him, they constitute the supreme government of the church.

The Organs of Episcopal Collegiality. Authority over the universal church in teaching, sanctifying, and ruling is extraordinarily and singularly exercised in ecumenical councils. It is ordinarily exercised by the bishops in their solicitude for the whole church or by the pope singularly.

The Synod of Bishops. By the decree of Pope Paul VI, *Apostolica sollicitudo* (Sept. 16, 1965), a synod of bishops for the universal church was set up in response to the wishes of Vatican Council II. The synod, a central ecclesiastical institution, is made up of elected representatives from the episcopate. It is a permanent structure, but meets only when convoked by the pope. Its ordinary work is handled through the office of a general secretary.

The National and Regional Conferences of Bishops. Episcopal conferences are councils of the bishops of particular nations or territories. Their statutes, which have been approved by the Holy See, make their decisions (passed by a two-thirds majority vote) legally binding for those within their jurisdiction. Offices such as the United States Catholic Conference constitute the executive organs of episcopal conferences.

The College of Cardinals. The cardinals constitute the senate of the pope. Though the title "cardinal" is largely honorary, by virtue of their ecclesiastical office cardinals become the pope's principal consultants and, as members of the college of cardinals, exercise the privilege of electing a new pope whenever the office becomes vacant. All the cardinals are bishops. In modern times the number of cardinals remained at 70, as decided by Pope Sixtus V (reigned 1585–1590), until Pope John XXIII (reigned 1958–1963) raised it to 85. Since then the number has been decided by the reigning pope.

The Roman Curia. The Roman Curia is a complex of congregations, offices, tribunals, and secretariates through which the pope directs the central government of the church. Although the Curia has an ancient history, its present organization was determined by Pope Paul VI, in the apostolic constitution *Regimini ecclesiae universae*, Aug. 15, 1967, as amended May 8, 1969.

The heads and members of curial departments are drawn from the clergy and laity throughout the world. These men, who have had outstanding pastoral or technical experience, are assigned for five-year terms of office. With the exceptions of the cardinal vicar general of Rome, the chamberlain, and the major penitentiary, all department heads must resign on the death of the pope. They may be either reassigned by the new pope or replaced within three months of his election. Each congregation is headed by a cardinal prefect, a secretary, and an undersecretary, all papal appointees. Seven bishops, from various countries, are assigned as members of each congregation. They are apprised of the ongoing work of the congregation, and must attend its annual plenary session. Lesser officials and consultors aid in expediting ordinary affairs.

As part of the Roman Curia, but governed by their own special constitutions, are the Council of the Laity and the Papal Commission for Promoting Justice and Peace.

THE SACRED CONGREGATIONS

The Sacred Congregation for the Teaching of the Faith safeguards and promotes the teaching of faith and morals in the whole Catholic world.

The Sacred Congregation for the Oriental Churches examines any and all questions that pertain to persons, discipline, or the liturgies of the Oriental churches. The Oriental patriarchs and the cardinal president of the Secretariat for Promoting Christian Unity are ex officio members.

The Sacred Congregation for Bishops provides for the election of bishops and for the general affairs of dioceses. The establishment of new dioceses and the convocation of particular councils fall within its purview.

The Sacred Congregation for the Sacraments and for Divine Worship (replacing two separate congregations in 1975) oversees all matters that pertain to the administration of the sacraments, and all matters connected wih the liturgy.

The Sacred Congregation for the Causes of Saints deals with beatification and canonization of saints.

The Sacred Congregation for the Clergy is competent in all concerns of the diocesan clergy.

The Sacred Congregation for Religious and Secular Institutes is entrusted with the affairs of all groups of religious, both men and women, who are members of an officially recognized institute.

The Sacred Congregation for Catholic Education oversees seminaries, universities, Catholic schools, and all institutions of catechetical or religious instruction.

The Sacred Congregation for the Evangelization of the Nations or Propaganda Fide aids in promoting and maintaining missions throughout the world. It coordinates the work of the major mission societies, such as The Mission Aid Society.

THE SECRETARIATS

The Papal Secretariat and the Papal Council for the Church's Public Affairs is the central coordinating commission of the Curia and the direct agent of the pope in the care of the universal church. Papal nuncios and delegates, accredited to civil governments and national churches, are supervised by this secretariat.

The Secretariat for Promoting Christian Unity specifically directs projects to establish Christian unity.

The Secretariat for Non-Christians is concerned with fostering understanding and mutual respect in the church's relations with non-Christians.

The Secretariat for Non-Believers is engaged in the study of atheism in order to explore more deeply its rationale and, insofar as possible, to establish dialogue with non-believers.

THE SACRED TRIBUNALS

The Supreme Tribunal of the Apostolic Signatura supervises the courts of the church and is itself a court of final appeal.

The Sacred Roman Rota principally handles actions seeking annullment of marriages, though it also adjudicates some criminal cases and litigation over property.

The Sacred Apostolic Penitentiary is competent over cases of conscience that may not be handled in the public forum.

THE SACRED OFFICES

The Apostolic Chancery expedites and preserves ecclesiastical documents.

The Prefecture of the Holy See's Economic Affairs coordinates the administration of the properties of the Holy See.

The Apostolic Chamber and **The Administration of the Patrimony of St. Peter** fulfill tasks of special administration.

The Prefecture of the Apostolic Palace handles papal audiences and general affairs of Vatican City.

The Central Statistics Office gathers and transmits data to assist the pope and the bishops.

WILLIAM BASSETT
Catholic University of America

Bibliography

Abbo, John, and Hannan, J., *The Sacred Canons* (St. Louis 1957).

Abbott, Walter M., ed., *The Documents of Vatican II* (New York 1974).

Bassett, William, *The Determination of Rite* (Rome 1966).

Heston, Edward, *The Holy See at Work* (Milwaukee 1950).

Rahner, Hugo, *The Parish*, tr. by R. Kress (Westminster, Md., 1958).

Rahner, Karl, and Ratzinger, J., *The Episcopate and the Primacy*, tr. by K. Barker (New York 1962).

Stanley, David M., *The Apostolic Church in the New Testament* (Westminster, Md., 1965).

5. Activities

The core activity of the Roman Catholic Church is missionary in nature. Catholics have always been conscious of the command of Christ to "Go therefore and make disciples of all nations" (Matthew 28:19). This missionary concern has probably never been better vocalized than by St. Paul: "Woe to me if I do not preach the gospel" (I Corinthians 9:16). Christ equally stressed the need "to teach." Thus, once the "good news" has been carried to the people of the earth, the church labors to reinforce faith through education. This section, then, deals with both the initial phase of the church's evangelical mission—preaching the gospel—and its secondary phase—educating its members to greater knowledge and awareness of God.

MISSIONS

The Second Vatican Council's Decree on the Missionary Activity of the Church asserts: "It is God's plan that the whole body of men which makes up the human race should be joined in one Body of Christ, should be built up together in one Temple of the Holy Spirit. . . . the missionary activity of the church must be declared absolutely necessary. In no other way but through it is the plan of God sedulously accepted and obediently carried into operation for the glory of God."

Carrying out this plan, the decree states, is the obligation of every member of the church: ". . . the whole Church is missionary." The reasons for the church's strong emphasis on a continuous state of mission are theologically and Biblically founded. They are theological because the church views itself as "the universal sacrament of salvation" (Vatican II's Dogmatic Constitution on the Church, section 1). A sacrament, by definition, is a visible sign. The term "sacrament" is thus applied since the church is a sign and instrument of the grace which unites all men supernaturally to God and to one another. The church proclaims its intention to accomplish the salvation of all men in accordance with the directions of its founder, Jesus Christ: "Go into the whole world and preach the gospel to every creature" (Mark 16:15).

The Decree on Missionary Activities defines mission as "the term usually given to those undertakings by which the heralds of the Gospels are sent out by the church and go forth into the world to carry out the task of preaching the Gospels and planting the church among peoples or groups who do not yet believe in Christ." In order to plant the church among the more than 2 billion people of the world who do not yet believe in Christ, the church looks to its history and the great missionaries of the past for inspiration; it searches the directives of its popes and bishops for guidelines; and it constantly attempts to better prepare its more than 100,000 professional missionaries for their task.

History of Missionary Endeavors. From its first days a catholicity, or universality, of concern for mankind has been a mark of the church. St. Paul carried Christianity to the Gentiles; Spain lays claim to Christianity through the Apostle James the Greater; the tradition of the Malabar Christians of India is that their forebears received the faith from the Apostle Thomas.

Early Efforts. The centuries following the Apostolic Age were equally rich in missionary activity. Facilitated by the *Pax Romana* (the peace of the Roman Empire, which extended roughly from the 1st through the 2d century A. D.), the Roman Empire's excellent roads, the widespread use of Latin and Greek, and the fact that the Mediterranean world was the largest cultural center of mankind, Christianity constantly expanded. By the time of Emperor Diocletian's great persecution in 303, Christianity had penetrated not only three continents, but all

social classes. Diocletian began his purge with his court and discovered his own wife and daughter to be Christian. At this time almost the entire northern coast of Africa was Christian; Asia Minor was better than half Christianized; episcopal sees flourished on both sides of the Persian Gulf; in France, Lyon, Tours, Arles, and Toulouse were strong Christian centers; and churches flourished among the Germans and Celts. The details of Spanish evangelization are not known, but Spain was represented by 19 bishops at the Council of Elvira, which was held about 300.

The next era of missionary history has been called the period of the apostles to the nations. Although there were small scattered Christian communities before these men arrived, it was they who successfully established Christianity in various regions: St. Martin of Tours (316–397) in France, St. Patrick (about 450) in Ireland, and St. Columban (died 615), who also toiled in Ireland, but who made missionary journeys to Gaul, Switzerland, Germany, and northern Italy as well. St. Augustine of Canterbury, a Roman, went to England in 596 and became the first archbishop of Canterbury; the Anglo-Saxon St. Boniface (died 754) became the Apostle of Germany; St. Ansgar (Anscar), who died in 865, converted Scandinavia; and the Macedonian brothers, Saints Cyril (827–869) and Methodius (825?–885), became the Apostles of the Slavs. This period came to a close when John of Montecorvino (1247–1330) went to Peking as the first archbishop of China.

Missionary work from this time on underwent a subtle change. The growth of nationalism, coupled with the age of discovery, catapulted the European nations into a contest for individual prestige. The papacy, already weakened, was about to be further debilitated by the Reformation. Missionary work in this context became the responsibility not of individuals, but of religious orders: Dominicans, Franciscans, Mercedarians, and the recently founded Jesuits. The last group took a fourth vow of special obedience to the Holy See, and succeeding popes used the Jesuits as shock troops to counter the Reformation in Europe and to advance the frontiers of Christianity in Asia, in the Americas, and in Africa.

American Missions. Columbus' discovery of the New World opened vast new mission fields. Missionaries marched with conquistadores. In 1493, Pope Alexander VI granted the Spanish sovereigns proprietary rights in the Americas. At the same time he reminded Ferdinand and Isabella of their Christian duty to convert the native inhabitants and to pay the church's expenses. But church and state soon came into conflict. The crown had ordered that the Indians be left free, and the missionaries were charged with civilizing and Christianizing them. But the Indians were parceled out to the colonists for work in mines and fields. They were virtual slaves. Bartolomé de Las Casas (1474–1566), a Dominican missionary, appealed to the royal court at Madrid, and he was appointed "Protector of the Indians."

To avoid further exploitation of the Indians, the missionaries founded "reductions." These were self-sufficient colonies where the Indians were Christianized, learned to farm and practice trades, and lived apart from the Spanish colonists. The missionaries' protectiveness had one

JESUIT MISSIONARY shares work of India's untouchables in constructing a dispensary for the villagers.

bad effect: because royal decrees kept the Indians free, Africans were imported for work on the plantations, occasioning a new slavery in the Americas.

Missions in the Orient. A number of attempts were made to establish the church in China. Cathay was not penetrated, however, until the Portuguese were allowed to found a trading post on a Kwantung island called Macao (which was soon to become the center of China's foreign commerce). The Jesuits made Cathay their mission center for the Far East. The Jesuit who made the breakthrough was Matteo Ricci (1552–1610). He had prepared himself by an intensive study of the Chinese language and culture, but it took 20 years of persistent effort before Ricci was able to get to Peking. There his gifts of a clock and a spinet won the favor of Emperor Wan Li. Ricci and his companions were allowed to remain in the capital, and Chinese intellectuals flocked to talk with the "Sage of the West." His prestige was such that it enabled other Jesuits to set up bases in other parts of the country. By 1650 there were a quarter of a million Chinese converts.

In India the Jesuit Roberto de Nobili adopted the dress and manner of life of the Brahmans and outdid them in austerity; he made thousands of converts among the upper classes. Father Alexander de Rhodes (1591–1660) mastered the Annamese language of Indochina. Among his early converts were 200 Buddhist monks. Within a century of the discovery of the Philippines, 2 million inhabitants had become Catholics. In Manila the Jesuit College of San José was founded in 1601 and the Dominican College of Santo Tomás in 1611.

Missions in the United States. Missioners penetrated the American southwest from Mexico. In 1542 the Franciscan Juan de Padilla was killed

by Indians on a Kansas prairie. Several Spanish attempts to colonize Florida failed until St. Augustine was founded in 1565. From this center missionaries spread out to convert the hostile Indians. By 1625 there were 43 churches in the vicinity of Santa Fe, New Mexico. In 1570, 34 years before the arrival of the English, Spanish missionaries attempted to found a colony near what was to be Jamestown, Va. A school for Indian boys was started. Disaster struck the following year when Indians put to death the Jesuits there.

France was late in entering the competition for colonies in the New World. In 1608, Samuel de Champlain founded Quebec, but Canada was never colonized in the strict sense because France was exclusively interested in the fur trade, not in settlement. In 1611 two Jesuits began work among the Micmac Indians of Nova Scotia, and from then on the Jesuits were to be associated in a special way with the Indian apostolate in Canada and in the northern part of the United States. Many missionaries were put to death: 39 in New Mexico; 16 in Florida; 13 in Texas; 11 in Mississippi; 9 in Virginia; 6 in California; 5 in Georgia; 3 in New York; 2 each in Illinois, Michigan, and Wisconsin; 1 each in Alabama, Louisiana, Maine, and Nebraska. Eight of these have been canonized

Father Junípero Serra (1713–1784) pioneered in California. The missions he founded along El Camino Real were the keys to this state's development—San Diego, Carmel, San Gabriel, Santa Clara, San Luis Obispo, Ventura, San Juan Capistrano, and San Francisco. A great defender of the Indians, he once traveled 2,400 miles (3,800 kilometers) to Mexico City to get redress from the viceroy when a Spanish commandant practiced cruelty on some Indians. He taught the Indians how to sow and harvest; he turned battlefields into rich farmlands. His successors founded 12 more missions, including Los Angeles.

Another great figure in the Indian missions was Father Pierre De Smet (1801–1873). He worked among the Crow, Cheyenne, Arapahoe, Sioux, and others. He was the foremost American authority on Indians, and his letters, diaries, and maps have been of great value to historians. He undertook a number of peace missions for the government. In 1868, without escort, he penetrated the Sioux stronghold on the Powder River to end the warfare between the United States and the Sioux under Sitting Bull. He once estimated that he had traveled 260,929 miles (around 420,000 kilometers) by foot, horseback, and canoe in serving the Indians.

Modern Mission Efforts. In the 19th century mission activity advanced considerably. Many new European mission-sending societies were founded, and the Jesuits were restored in 1814 after having been suppressed. With the growth of mission personnel, areas once neglected were penetrated. Central and East Africa were evangelized, and work was begun in such diverse places as Siam, Ceylon, Formosa, the Pacific Islands, Mongolia, Korea, Japan, and Borneo.

At the turn of the 20th century the church in the United States was still a missionary church, but in 1908, Pope Pius X issued a decree ending its status as a mission country. Three years later Father James Anthony Walsh of Boston and Father Thomas Frederick Price, who was a missionary in North Carolina, submitted a plan to the American hierarchy for the foundation of an American mission-sending society. The archbishops of the United States in April 1911 voted the establishment of the Catholic Foreign Mission Society of America. On June 29, 1911, Pope Pius X gave formal approval to the new organization, and the founders were authorized to open a seminary and recruit students. Property was obtained in Westchester county, New York, and named Maryknoll—a title which became the popular name for the society. In 1918 the first mission band of four left for China. As the society grew, additional fields were added, and today Maryknollers are working in Korea, Japan, Hong Kong, Taiwan, the Philippines, Hawaii, Tanzania, Kenya, Mexico, Guatemala, El Salvador, Venezuela, Colombia, Peru, Bolivia, and Chile.

Following World War II many European societies established branches in the United States in order to obtain personnel and funds to carry on their work. New emphasis was placed on restoring the church in Latin America, where a grave shortage of priests existed. This period also saw the rapid expansion of the lay mission movement, which Pius XII called "the sleeping giant." John XXIII issued a call for lay volunteers for Latin America, thus PAVLA (Papal Volunteers for Latin America) was formed. In the postwar period a decline of missionary activity occurred in Communist-controlled countries (China, Mongolia, North Korea, and North Vietnam). In some of the new African countries severe handicaps afflicted mission work. In the Democratic Republic of Congo (the former Belgian Congo), for example, 106 priests, 24 brothers, and 37 sisters were murdered. The Muslims in the Sudan began a persecution of Christians; Buddhists in Ceylon and Burma halted mission work by expelling foreign clergy. But for 19 centuries Christian apostles have been building on ruins, and the work goes on.

Papal Policy. The *Letters and Instructions* of Pope Gregory the Great (about 540–604) are the earliest extant papal directives concerning missions, and they also present a philosophy of operation that is still applied. He wisely advised St. Augustine of Canterbury to accommodate to pagan customs and practices in order to evangelize Britain. Gregory instructed Augustine to make free use of the Gallican liturgy; to leave pagan temples standing, but to destroy pagan idols; and to adapt pagan rites, if innocent, for Christian feasts, because "if they are not deprived of such external joys, they will understand more easily the inner joy of faith" (Bede, *Historia ecclesiastica*, 1:30).

During the age of discoveries this principle of cultural relevancy was almost totally ignored. Three Jesuits, St. Francis Xavier in Japan, Matteo Ricci in China, and Roberto de Nobili in India, successfully revived accommodation in their missionary endeavors but aroused much opposition in Europe. In the early 18th century the Holy See forbade the use of all but a Western expression of Catholicism in missionary regions, and it was not until recent times that the church returned to Gregory the Great's philosophy. In 1919, Pope Benedict XV issued the important missionary encyclical, *Maximum illud* (*The Greatest Endeavor*), which insisted on the use of accommodation or adaptation and, further, on the establishment of a native clergy and hierarchy in missionary regions. No country, he reasoned, had ever been converted except by its own clergy. Pope Pius XI expanded this policy. His encyclical *Rerum ecclesiae* (1926) reexamined every aspect of the mission apostolate. John XXIII's missionary encyclical *Princeps pastorum* (*On the Catholic Missions*, 1959) is the most recent of the 30 papal encyclicals of modern times that together constitute the church's mission policy. This thinking was synthesized in the Vatican II Decree on Missionary Activities.

Organization. Missionary activities have always been directly supervised by the Roman pontiff. In the Middle Ages the missions were heavily funded by a system of royal patronage (*Patronato Real*) which reached a zenith of both effectiveness and abuse during the age of discoveries. Portugal and Spain contributed greatly to missionary activities in the new lands but soon usurped the church's administrative rights. Their excessive unilateral actions, as well as the disorganized and uncoordinated activities of missionary orders, caused Pope Gregory XV to institute the Sacred Congregation for the Propagation of the Faith (*Propaganda Fide*) in 1622.

At first Propaganda's jurisdiction was all-inclusive in the missionary field, but it was modified by Pius X in 1908. In August 1967 its official title was changed to the Congregation for the Evangelization of Missions or for the Propagation of the Faith. This Congregation designates and supervises missionary territory throughout the world, appoints directors to missionary regions, supervises certain missionary orders of religious, and has limited judicial functions. In addition, it has exclusive jurisdiction over all the mission seminaries in the world.

Raising and distributing funds for missions is the function of the Papal Society for the Propagation of the Faith. Founded in 1823, the society is represented by national offices throughout the world and is directed by a superior general council appointed by the pope. The society furnishes aid to the home missions in the United States (inner-city missions, Indian missions, and others), Asia, Latin America, Europe, Africa, and the Middle East.

Missionary Training. The study of missiology—the systematized and scientific investigation into the apostolic aspect of the church—has led, in recent years, to a specialized training program for missionaries. Although the Urban College for the training of foreign missionaries was founded in Rome in 1627, in earlier times men like St. Francis Xavier relied upon their zeal alone. Today's missionary is prepared before entering the field. He is tutored in the language and ethnology of the country to which he is assigned and receives a broad education in anthropology, economics, medicine, sociology, and psychology. Faculties of missiology have been established in seminaries throughout the world to study this important field.

ALBERT J. NEVINS, M. M.
Maryknoll, New York

Bibliography

Campbell, Robert E., ed., *The Church in Mission* (New York 1965).
Grassi, Joseph A., *A World to Win: The Missionary Methods of Paul the Apostle* (New York 1965).
Hillman, Eugene, *The Church as Mission* (New York 1965).
Houtart, François, and Pin, E., *The Church and the Latin American Revolution* (New York 1965).
Luzbetak, Louis, *The Church and Cultures: An Applied Anthropology for the Religious Worker* (Techny, Ill., 1963).

EDUCATION

Philosophy of Catholic Education. The special and distinctive objective of Catholic education has always been to prepare men for eternal life, but preparation for life in this world has been stressed consistently. While the emphasis on "this-worldly" as against "other-worldly" preparation has varied from place to place and from time to time, the two elements have been involved in Catholic education.

Among noteworthy 20th century documents setting forth a Catholic philosophy of education are the 1929 encyclical of Pope Pius XI, *Divini illius Magistri* (*On the Christian Education of Youth*), and the Declaration on Christian Education adopted by the Second Vatican Council and promulgated by Pope Paul VI on Oct. 28, 1965. These and other documents agree in pointing to three major agents in education: the family (regarded as the primary agent), the state, and the church. The role of the state is seen as protecting the rights of parents and others in education, carrying out its own educational activities in line with parental wishes, and operating educational institutions required by the common good. The church's right to educate is seen as arising from its existence as a human society and from the mandate to teach given it by Christ.

In this view the Catholic school is the special expression of the church's teaching mission. The Declaration on Christian Education states: "No less than other schools does the Catholic school pursue cultural goals and the natural development of youth." It adds, however: "But it has several distinctive purposes . . . to create for the school community a special atmosphere animated by the gospel spirit of freedom and charity, to help the adolescent in such a way that the development of his own personality will be matched by the growth of that new creation which he became by baptism. It strives to relate all human culture eventually to the news of salvation so that the light of faith will illuminate the knowledge which students gradually gain of the world, of life, and of mankind."

History of Catholic Education. The way in which the church's educational mission has been carried out has varied substantially over the centuries. The first Christians were part of a pagan society that was culturally Hellenic and politically Roman. Well-to-do Christians studied in pagan schools and sought religious education from other sources, mainly the family and the church. The writings of the early Church Fathers assume that religious education ideally was begun in the home and later was expanded under the guidance of the bishop.

The earliest Christian instructional writings were of a catechetical nature, designed to teach Christians about their religion or to prepare the catechumens, the candidates for baptism, for admission to the church. Eventually, Christian catechetical schools developed, the most distinguished of which was in Alexandria. It was directed successively by Clement of Alexandria (died about 215) and Origen (died about 254). Since Christians were determined to use what was best in pagan culture, while at the same time ordering it to Christianity, which to them represented the higher synthesis, it is not surprising that Greek philosophy and science were studied at the catechetical schools in preparation for the study of theology.

Early Middle Ages. The barbarian invasions of the Roman Empire at the onset of the early Middle Ages caused learning to become almost entirely the preserve of the ecclesiastical structure. The monasteries were particularly involved in education: the rule of St. Benedict of Nursia (q.v.), for example, required a minimum of two hours reading each day by the monks. The monasteries also established schools for the training of monastic aspirants. Among the best-known monastic schools of this period were those at Tours in France, Fulda in Germany, Jarrow in northern England, Monte Cassino in Italy, Iona in Scotland, and Clonmacnoise in Ireland. In addition to schools, most monasteries had scriptoria where books were copied by hand and frequently were elaborately illustrated (see BOOK OF KELLS).

Other church schools that existed in this period included cathedral schools for the education of the clergy, maintained by bishops, and some parish schools. Secular subjects, the so-called seven liberal arts, were studied in both monastic and cathedral schools before "divine learning" was undertaken. The latter included the Scriptures, liturgical works, the writings of the Fathers of the Church and other Christian scholars, the decrees of popes, bishops, and church councils, and the works of spiritual writers. Although the education provided in these schools was intended primarily for the preparation of ecclesiastics, some laymen, usually noblemen, were educated there. Alcuin, master of the Cathedral School of York and later of Charlemagne's Palace School, and Remigius of Auxerre were outstanding educational leaders of this period.

Later Middle Ages. Christian humanism and Christian education reached new heights in the 11th, 12th, and 13th centuries under the impetus of the rise of towns and commerce, the growing need for literacy, and the medieval belief in the divine origin and ultimate unity of all knowledge. Though the monastic schools continued to be important institutions, they lost their preeminence to urban-centered cathedral and professional schools, and to the new universities.

The medieval universities developed out of cathedral and professional schools as organizations of students or teachers or both who incorporated themselves for the study of law, medicine, and theology, and the teaching of the liberal arts. The leading universities founded by the year 1300 were those of Paris and Montpellier, Bologna and Salerno, Salamanca, Lisbon-Coimbra, Oxford, and Cambridge. By 1500 more than 75 universities had been founded.

Most of the professors and students of the universities were ecclesiastics. The medieval universities were truly international institutions—their members were linked by a common religious faith, a common language (Latin), and a common interest in the pursuit of knowledge. A university graduate was entitled to teach anywhere. From the universities emerged the system of philosophic thought known as Scholasticism, which is best represented in the works of Thomas Aquinas, Abelard, Anselm, Albertus Magnus, Bonaventure, Duns Scotus, and many others.

Renaissance. The impact of the Renaissance on education was manifested in a rejection of the spiritual emphasis of the Middle Ages, for which was substituted a humanistically oriented emphasis on the Greek and Roman classics. Special importance was given to literary studies intended to develop proficiency in speaking and writing

Latin. Subjects such as history, mathematics, astronomy, music, and philosophy were part of the curriculum, but their position was subordinate to the study of classical literature.

Both the Protestant Reformation and the Catholic Reform were related to the Renaissance, either incorporating its ideals or reacting against them, and this was as applicable to education as to other fields. The most important educational force in the Catholic Reform was the Society of Jesus. The Jesuit educational program blended the classical literary education of the Renaissance with the spiritual concern of the Middle Ages. The *ratio studiorum*, or plan of studies, on which the program in all Jesuit schools was based, made classical and humanistic studies the groundwork preceding the student's entrance into the university for advanced training in philosophy, theology, law, or medicine.

The 16th through the 19th Century. Educational leadership in this period no longer lay with Catholic thinkers, but some did contribute significant theoretical or practical innovations. The Brothers of the Christian Schools (Christian Brothers), founded by St. Jean Baptiste de La Salle in 1684, innovated free education for the sons of artisans and the poor. De La Salle established one of the first training schools for lay teachers. Other religious communities that carried on large educational programs included the French Oratorians, the Vincentians, and the Sulpicians (whose specialty was, and has remained, seminary education). New religious teaching communities of women included the Sisters of Notre Dame, the School Sisters of Notre Dame, the Visitandines, the Sisters of Charity of St. Vincent de Paul, the Sisters of St. Joseph, and the Sisters of Mercy of St. Charles Borromeo. The French bishop François Fénelon, in *A Treatise on the Education of Girls* (1687), not only dealt with a long-neglected subject but put forward ideas well in advance of his and later times. John Henry Cardinal Newman in England and Félix Dupanloup in France were notable educational theorists of the 19th century whose writings helped to revolutionize education.

Catholic Education in the United States. The Franciscan missionaries who accompanied the Spanish settlers to Florida set up the first school in what is now the United States, at St. Augustine in 1606. Catholic education did not prosper in the colonial period, however, particularly in the British colonies, where Catholics were the objects of repressive legislation. Maryland's Act to Prevent the Growth of Popery (1704), for example, made any Catholic who kept a school or instructed children liable to deportation. Nevertheless, efforts were made to establish schools. Jesuits founded schools in Maryland in 1640 and 1673, and a Catholic school was established in New York in 1634. But these efforts were seldom long-lived.

After the Revolutionary War, Catholics were encouraged by a new spirit of toleration and increased their educational undertakings. The growth of the Catholic population (30,000 at the time of the Revolution, 195,000 by 1820, and 1,606,000 by 1850) made this essential. Though the location of the first parochial school in the United States is debated, it is generally agreed that the major impetus and model for the tuition-free parish school came from Elizabeth Seton and her Sisters of Charity, who started their school at St. Joseph's parish in Emmitsburg, Md., in 1810.

Adding to the pressure for Catholic schools was the Protestant orientation of the 19th century public schools. Catholic leaders were alarmed by the loss of the faith among the new Catholic immigrants and their children, and perhaps another motive, though one less consciously recognized, was to soften the cultural shock caused by the transition from Europe and to facilitate the assimilation process.

Growth and Expansion. The creation of a Catholic school system in the United States derived its principal impetus from the four councils of the American Catholic hierarchy held at Baltimore in 1829, 1852, 1866, and 1884. The last, the Third Plenary Council of Baltimore, set the objective that "every Catholic child in the land shall have within its reach the means of education"; it directed each Catholic parish to establish a parochial school, and it required Catholic parents to send their children to such schools "unless it is evident that a sufficient training in religion is given either in their own homes, or in other Catholic schools."

By 1900 about 45% of the 8,000 Catholic parishes in the country had parochial schools, and parochial secondary schools numbered 53. Central or diocesan high schools, the first of which was established in Philadelphia in 1890, grew more slowly. Private high schools and academies conducted by religious communities had existed earlier than either the parish or diocesan secondary institutions, but their growth was retarded by shortages of funds and students. After 1840 many Catholic colleges for men conducted by religious communities came into existence. Catholic colleges for women did not appear until the closing years of the 19th century, but their expansion has since been extremely rapid.

By 1920, parochial elementary schools numbered 6,551, with 41,581 teachers and 1,759,673 students. Catholic parochial, diocesan, central, and private high schools numbered 1,552 and enrolled 129,848 students. Impressive as this growth was, it pales beside the expansion of the next 40 years, particularly during the period after World War II, when the number of students in Catholic schools rose from 2,396,000 (1940) to 5,253,791 (1960), an increase of 219%. (In the same period public school enrollment increased 142%.)

Higher Education. In the late 1960's over 300 Catholic colleges and universities were in operation in the United States and enrolled more than 400,000 students. Significant trends in Catholic higher education included the development of boards of trustees, which often had a majority of lay members and were independent of the religious communities that had founded the institutions; the increased sharing of facilities and faculties by two or more schools; and outright mergers of schools, designed to halt an unhealthy proliferation of Catholic colleges and to strengthen already existing institutions. Laymen, who for some years had been in the majority on Catholic college and university faculties, were being appointed to top administrative positions, including the presidency, at these schools.

Catholic seminaries in the United States numbered about 600, with an enrollment of about 40,000, by the late 1960's. There was a pronounced trend among the seminaries—as among the colleges and universities—toward interinstitutional cooperation and mergers, including the transfer of seminaries to the campuses of large Catholic and non-Catholic universities. Laymen assumed more prominent roles as faculty members at these institutions.

Educational Associations. A number of institutions and organizations have been active in fostering the professional growth of Catholic education in the United States. The largest, the National Catholic Educational Association, was founded in 1904, with headquarters in Washington, D. C. The NCEA provides professional services and acts as a medium for the exchange of ideas and information among its members. Also active, particularly as a national-level spokesman for the hierarchy in educational matters, has been the Education Department of the United States Catholic Conference. Several religious orders, such as the Jesuits, maintain educational associations to provide information and services geared to the interests of their schools. Since the mid-1950's the National Sister Formation movement and its organizational embodiment, the Sister Formation Conference, have done notable work in upgrading the professional training of nuns. The Confraternity of Christian Doctrine, which is responsible for the religious education of all Catholics not in Catholic schools, has endeavored to provide this instruction, but its work has frequently been hampered by lack of financial resources and trained personnel.

Problems of Catholic Education. The rapid expansion of Catholic schools created difficult problems. Emphasis was too often put on expansion of services rather than on the quality of the education provided. But studies conducted in the 1960's at the National Opinion Research Center and at the University of Notre Dame with Carnegie Corporation support, indicate that Catholic school students were at least not inferior to public school students in academic achievement.

The administrative decentralization inherent in a parochial system of education has also created difficulties for Catholic schools, since it has placed educational decisions in the hands of pastors, who are usually not trained educators. This has been partly corrected by the development of strong diocesan offices of education. A trend toward policy-making school boards, often with laymen in the majority, on both the diocesan and the parish level, showed a marked increase in the 1960's. Providing salaries that attract and hold qualified lay persons, who are increasingly needed in Catholic schools, is a major unmet challenge to the hard-pressed financial resources of the system. An even more basic problem of Catholic education is represented by the large number of Catholic children and young people who are not in Catholic schools and whose religious education is in many cases slighted. This situation has led some to suggest that the Catholic schools are using up a disproportionate amount of time, energy, and resources, and that funds and personnel should be reallocated in order to provide for the religious education of all rather than just those in Catholic schools.

Growing feeling in the Catholic community that the government has a responsibility to support the education of all children, not just those in public schools, has led to renewed emphasis on efforts to obtain financial assistance, either for the schools or their students, from public sources. The issue has been made even more acute for Catholics by the infusion of large sums of federal money into education, and the prospect of more to come.

The enactment of the Elementary and Secondary Education Act of 1965, which provided some benefits for disadvantaged parochial school pupils, represented a compromise, but it seemed certain that the issue would arise again as the federal government increased its role in the support of education. Decisions by the U. S. Supreme Court that in some cases upheld the provision of services and support to church-related education but in others confirmed lower court rulings that denied such benefits have complicated the situation.

Catholic Education in Other Countries. Although the U. S. Catholic school system is the largest in the world, extensive Catholic educational programs exist in many countries. Wherever it has been permitted to do so, the church has operated schools, supplementing these with catechetical and religious formation programs. Education has been a major component of missionary efforts, and substantial Catholic school systems have grown up in a number of places in Africa and Asia as well as in Europe and the Americas.

The Catholic educational effort differs in many particulars from one country to another. A number of European countries have integrated the Catholic schools into the overall national educational system and give full or almost full financial support to them. In England, for instance, if a Catholic school chooses integration into the government education system, it receives government support in return. Similar arrangements operate in the Netherlands and West Germany.

Catholic education has experienced hardships in a number of Communist and totalitarian countries. In some places Catholic schools have been closed down entirely; elsewhere they are forced to fight for their survival against severe pressures and tight restrictions. Seminary education has been a special target for harassment in some European Communist countries.

RUSSELL SHAW
National Catholic Educational Association

Bibliography

Burns, James, C. S. C., and Kohlbrenner, Bernard, *A History of Catholic Education in the United States* (New York 1937).
Fichter, Joseph N., S. J., *Parochial School: A Sociological Study* (Notre Dame, Ind., 1958).
Greeley, Andrew M., and Rossi, Peter H., *The Education of Catholic Americans* (Chicago 1966).
Lee, James Michael, ed., *Catholic Education in the Western World* (Notre Dame, Ind., 1967).
McCluskey, Neil G., S. J., ed., *Catholic Education in America: A Documentary History* (New York 1964).
Millar, L. H. *Christian Education in the First Four Centuries* (London 1946).
Rashdall, Hastings, *The Universities of Europe in the Middle Ages*, ed. by F. M. Powicke and A. B. Emden (New York and London 1936).

6. The Church in the United States

The Roman Catholic Church is the largest single religious denomination in the United States. Its listed membership in 1966 was 46,-246,175, or 23.7% of the total population. Its hierarchy, headed in rank by seven cardinals, is second in number only to that of Italy.

MODERN STRUCTURE

Ecclesiastical authority on the national level is exercised through the National Conference of Catholic Bishops (NCCB). Organized in November 1966 along lines suggested by the Second Vatican Council (1962–1965), it is headed by a president, elected for a 5-year term, a vice president, and a 38-member administrative committee.

Its authority is binding on all bishops in certain matters. In one much-noted instance, the NCCB relieved U.S. Catholics of the obligation to abstain from meat on Fridays.

In civil-religious matters the NCCB acts through its secretariat, the United States Catholic Conference (USCC), formerly the National Catholic Welfare Conference (NCWC; 1922–1966). A civil corporate entity, the USCC has a treasurer and seven major departments: education, legal, immigration, social action, lay organizations, youth, and press. Its numerous subdivisions supervise the whole range of national Catholic activities. The Catholic Relief Service–USCC distributes food, clothing, and medicine to the needy overseas without regard to creed; its 1966 program had a value of $181,-714,276.00. Charities within the U.S. (child welfare, family counseling, health, services for unmarried mothers, neighborhood center programs, and care of the aged) are conducted on the diocesan level.

Two national lay organizations have their headquarters at the USCC: the National Council of Catholic Men (membership of 9 million) and the National Council of Catholic Women (membership of 10 million). These and other lay groups have played an increasingly significant role in the work of the U.S. church since Vatican II promulgated the Decree on the Apostolate of the Laity in 1965. The council's directives in other areas have been implemented as well: the renewal of the church's corporate worship; ecumenical dialogues and interreligious cooperation; socioreligious programs in depressed urban and rural areas; racial justice; renewal of religious communities; reorganization of seminaries; scriptural catechetics; establishment of diocesan priests' senates; and the involvement of lay people in the church's administration.

Apart from its parish structure, the principal achievement of U.S. Catholicism has been its school system, which is the largest private educational system in the world. The Confraternity of Christian Doctrine (CCD) in each diocese and parish conducts classes in religion for about 5 million of the approximately 8 million Catholic children attending public schools. The 1 million Catholic students in secular colleges and universities are served by the Newman Apostolate.

U.S. Catholics have exerted moral influence affirmatively in the areas of social justice, family life, and decency in literature and films; negatively, in opposition to communism, artificial birth control, abortion, euthanasia, and divorce and remarriage. U.S. Catholics generally and officially favor religious liberty and separation of church and state; at the same time they seek federal aid to parochial schools as a constitutional right. Politically, most Catholics have been Democrats, reflecting their working-class origins. With their increasingly middle-class, suburban status that pattern, however, may change. Of the 12 Catholics elected to Congress in 1966 for their first terms, for example, 10 were Republicans.

EARLY MISSIONARY HISTORY

Spanish Missions. Roman Catholicism first entered the United States in Florida, when Pedro Menéndez de Avilés founded the settlement of San Agustín (St. Augustine) and its Mission Nombre de Dios on Sept. 8, 1565. The secular priests with him began the permanent history of

RENI PHOTOS

IMMACULATE CONCEPTION SHRINE, in Washington, D. C., national center for Roman Catholics in America.

the service of Catholic priests in what is now the United States. During the next 120 years Spanish Franciscans founded a chain of 35 missions, which stretched northward along the Georgia coastal islands and westward across the Florida peninsula. By 1655, 26,000 Christian Indians could be counted. These missions were destroyed by the English under Col. James Moore of Carolina in 1702–1704, and were never revived successfully during Spanish occupation.

West of Florida, the missionary incursions into what is now the United States emanated from New Spain (Mexico): in 1598 the Franciscans began evangelizing New Mexico. By 1630 they had established two dozen missions, extending as far west as Arizona, at which 90 friars served some 50,000 Indians. The Texas missions were formally opened at the same time that the French were entering the lower Mississippi, where they established the Catholic settlement of New Orleans. From the founding of San Antonio and the Alamo mission in 1718 until the missions were secularized in the 1790's, some 160 friars worked in the Texas missions. The Arizona and Baja (Lower) California missionary efforts bore the stamp of a remarkable Tyrolean Jesuit priest Eusebio Francisco Kino (Kühn), who arrived in Primería Alta in 1687. By 1765 the Jesuits had 13 missions in Baja California, and after Charles III expelled them from New Spain in 1767, Franciscans took their place. When Spain occupied Alta California in 1769, the friars also moved north. By 1823 they had founded 21 missions along a 600-mile (965-km) stretch of coast between San Diego and San Francisco Solano; the first 9 were founded by their great leader Junípero Serra before his death in 1784. Thus, over a span of two and a half centuries and across a distance of 3,000 miles (4,800 km) the

Catholic religion was firmly implanted early in the history of the United States.

French Missions. As most of the southern arc of American states originally drew its Catholicism from Spain and Mexico, the northeast corner of the future republic received its first Catholic influence from Canada. For 105 years prior to the founding of New Orleans in 1718, French Jesuits, Franciscan Récollets, Capuchins, and diocesan priests had traversed the heart of the continent and preached to such Indian tribes as the Hurons and the Iroquois.

British Colonial Missions. In contrast to their position elsewhere on the continent prior to the Revolution, Catholics formed a small and frequently despised minority in the British colonies. Even in Maryland, founded by the Catholic Calverts in 1634, Protestants outnumbered the Catholic colonists ten to one by the beginning of the 18th century. John Adams said in 1765 that a Roman Catholic in British America was "as rare as a comet or an earthquake." As late as 1785 a survey by the Marquis de Barbé-Marbois revealed only 32,500 Catholics in the infant United States —less than 1% of the total population. Between 1634 and 1773, when the Society of Jesus was suppressed, 186 Jesuit missionaries of English and American origin served this minority. Despite their small numbers, Catholics were everywhere regarded with suspicion and, on occasion, open hostility. Proscriptions against them were incorporated into the colonial charters, and penal laws imported from England were enacted against them. Significantly, when Catholics enjoyed brief periods of political power in Maryland (1649) and in New York (1683), they enacted edicts of religious freedom. Catholics unanimously supported the American cause during the Revolution. Several achieved national distinction, including Charles Carroll, a signer of the Declaration of Independence, and Daniel Carroll and Thomas FitzSimons, who participated in the Constitutional Convention of 1787.

EARLY NATIONAL CHURCH

In 1784 the Holy See named John Carroll (q.v.) of Maryland superior of the American missions. In December 1790 he was installed as bishop of Baltimore, the first Catholic bishop in the United States. Under his charge were 25 priests, most of them members of the suppressed Jesuit order. With the new century the ranks of the clergy were swelled by immigrant priests from France, Ireland, Spain, the Low Countries, and the German states. Among the numerous French clergy were Sulpician fathers. In October 1791 they founded and staffed St. Mary's Seminary, Baltimore, thus providing a continuing source of native clergy. In 1808 Baltimore was raised to the rank of a metropolitan see and Boston, New York, Philadelphia, and Bardstown (later Louisville) were created as suffragan sees.

PROBLEMS OF GROWTH

By 1820 the Catholic population had grown to 195,000. Immigration, mostly from Ireland and Germany, caused this expansion; and by 1860, Roman Catholicism was the largest single Christian denomination in the U.S. This extraordinary growth occasioned many acute problems.

Lay Trusteeism. Following the Protestant example, in many early parishes, lay trustees administered parochial property. Inspired by rebellious priests or ethnic antagonisms, trustees often attempted to extend their control to ecclesiastical matters, including the appointment and dismissal of pastors. Since the church's canon law vests this power solely in bishops, serious conflicts resulted. Interdict, excommunication, or schism occurred in Philadelphia, St. Augustine, New Orleans, Charleston, Norfolk, and Buffalo before the bishops gained the upper hand. Trusteeism finally waned in the 1860's.

Nativism. As Catholic immigrants poured in by the thousands, native Americans, worried by the threat posed to their economic security, began opposing them on what seemed their most vulnerable ground—religion. "Popery" was openly and widely attacked as a peril to the republic, and violence resulted. A Massachusetts convent was burned (1834) and riots in Philadelphia took 13 lives (1835). The anti-Catholic movement took on a political character in the 1850's with the founding of the American, or Know-Nothing, party. After several successes at the polls, however, the Know-Nothing cause faded as the nation turned its attention to the slavery crisis. Organized anti-Catholicism on a large scale did not appear again until the 1880's, when the American Protective Association (APA) was founded, and again with the post-World War I Ku Klux Klan. The election of John F. Kennedy to the presidency in 1960 suggests that anti-Catholic nativism is no longer a significant force.

Education. Between 1820 and 1860, nonsectarian, common, free schools gradually replaced church-affiliated schools as the main agency of public education. The common schools were Protestant-oriented, and many used textbooks that were anti-Catholic, reflecting the nativism of the times. The response of the Catholic bishops was to found parochial schools, where Catholic values prevailed. Despite its cost, a parochial school system was vigorously supported by the bishops at the three plenary councils of Baltimore (1852, 1866, 1884) and equally supported by the majority of Catholics. In 1870, Bishop Augustin Verot secured an arrangement with the city of Savannah, Ga., which agreed to support the Catholic schools by public funds, and religious instruction was permitted to be given in the buildings after school hours; this "Savannah Plan" remained in force until 1916. Other shortlived accommodations with local school systems were secured, but it was not until the federal Elementary and Secondary Education Act (Public Law 89-10) of 1965 was passed that parochial school children began receiving widespread public financial support on a limited basis.

CIVIL WAR TO 1900

Generally, Catholics took no stand on the institution of slavery prior to the Civil War. Both Northern and Southern bishops argued that involuntary servitude was not necessarily evil, and the laity took no part in abolitionism, whose leaders, in some instances, were anti-Catholic as well as antislavery. With the outbreak of war, Catholics chose sides according to their sections, and thousands fought in the conflict. The church's organizational unity was maintained throughout the war, and at its close 45 bishops met in plenary council at Baltimore (1866). They adopted plans for the religious care and instruction of the freed Southern Negroes, but for a variety of reasons these plans failed. Only in Florida and Georgia were any successes of note scored during the Reconstruction period.

Between 1870 and 1900, Irish and German immigration continued to predominate, but after 1880 the number of arrivals from eastern and southern Europe rose markedly. Although the Germans tended to settle in rural areas, most Catholic immigrants remained in the industrial centers of the East and Middle West, imparting to U. S. Catholicism its still predominantly urban pattern. Hundreds of so-called national parishes were opened. Here immigrants were served by their own priests in their own languages. This development kept large numbers of immigrants in the church but impeded their Americanization. Friction between the national groups, particularly Catholics of Irish and German birth, marked the last two decades of the century.

Daunted by a lingering nativism among the Protestant majority, most Catholics of this period exhibited what has been styled a "siege" or "ghetto" mentality, and few figured prominently in the nation's public life. Only in municipal politics and the trade-union movement were Catholics in positions of influence before 1900. The church was strongly identified with the working class and assured its continued influence among the workers in 1887, when the bishops, led by James Cardinal Gibbons, archbishop of Baltimore, exempted the Knights of Labor (the first major U. S. labor organization) from the church's general condemnation of secret, oath-bound societies. Some historians have attributed the nonradical character of the U. S. labor movement since that date, as well as the absence of a labor party as such, to the moderating influence of the Catholic Church in this area.

The U. S. church was represented by 49 bishops at the First Vatican Council in Rome (1869–1870), at which the force of their interventions was mainly pastoral and showed more concern with practice than theory. At home U. S. Catholics failed to make a contribution, in proportion to their numbers, to the nation's intellectual and cultural life during the 19th century. This failure can be attributed to the church's preoccupation with the flood of immigrants, and the time-consuming need to provide churches, schools, and charitable institutions for the mounting Catholic population. This so-called brick and mortar era persisted until the 1940's. Catholic historians in the 1950's cited it as the chief reason for Catholics' failure to forge a distinct intellectual tradition. Nevertheless, the church's preoccupations did not lead to a neglect of higher education: 32 Catholic colleges and universities, still in operation, were opened between 1791 and the Civil War. In 1889 a group of progressive bishops, headed by Cardinal Gibbons, succeeded in founding the Catholic University of America, at Washington, D. C. Gibbons, the first U. S. cardinal (1886), perhaps best represented the Catholic mind to most Americans during the near half century (1877–1921) that he occupied the see of Baltimore. He was forward-looking and desirous of accommodating Catholicism to the national spirit. Gibbons stoutly defended the orthodoxy of the U. S. church when conservatives in Paris and Rome accused it, in 1897–1899, of promoting a liberalized Christianity, styled Americanism.

20TH CENTURY

On June 29, 1908, the maturing U. S. church was removed from the jurisdiction of the Roman Congregation for the Propagation of the Faith and placed under the authority of the Roman Curia. This meant that the Holy See no longer viewed the United States as a missionary area. A break with the past that was more keenly felt by Catholic leaders came with the passage by Congress (1924) of the National Origins Act. This act radically limited the immigration quota of countries that had supplied the bulk of Catholic immigrants. When the act went into effect in 1929, the U. S. church was enabled to concentrate on programs of internal development. The principal Catholic national organization of this time, the National Catholic Welfare Conference, was founded in 1919 and reorganized in 1922. Successful both as an episcopal conference and as a secretariat, the NCWC was studied and imitated by other national hierarchies.

A longtime Catholic apathy to the struggle of Negroes for racial justice was broken in 1947–1948 when Cardinals Joseph E. Ritter of St. Louis and Patrick A. O'Boyle of Washington, D. C., desegregated their archdiocesan schools. The civil rights pace quickened in the 1960's, though Catholics generally followed rather than led movements for improvement in race relations.

The spiritual and intellectual maturity of the mid-century U. S. church was evidenced by the increase of male vocations to the contemplative life (e. g., Trappists); the spread of the liturgical reform movement; the academic prestige of universities such as Notre Dame, Georgetown, and Fordham; and the quality of research and writing in such journals and reviews as *Theological Studies, Catholic Historical Review, Worship, America,* and *Commonweal.*

The U. S. church reached ecclesiastical adulthood at the Second Vatican Council (1962–1965); its 250 prelates formed the second-largest hierarchy in attendance at the council, and the many and trenchant interventions they made on pastoral matters reflected their experience of living in a pluralistic society. Their vigorous support of the Declaration on Religious Freedom (Dec. 8, 1965), drafted in great part by the late American Jesuit, John Courtney Murray, helped make the U. S. Catholic experience the norm for worldwide church-state relations.

Vatican II profoundly influenced the shaping of the U. S. church after 1962. Once characterized by critics as authoritarian, exclusive and monolithic, the church exhibited, after the council, a remarkable vitality and variety, which resulted from several factors. Among these, in addition to many structural changes within the church, were a modification of ancient disciplines, a more demanding and articulate laity, a pervading spirit of openness and self-criticism, a renewed and vigorous sacramental life, advances in Biblical theology, a surge in the respectability of the Catholic intellectual, and a flourishing liturgical art. These changes did not occur without accompanying problems, and even shocks, but by and large the direction taken by the post conciliar church received the support of most U. S. Catholics.

MICHAEL V. GANNON, *University of Florida Author of "Cross in the Sand: The Early Catholic Church in Florida, 1513–1870."*

Further Reading: Ellis, John T., *American Catholicism* (Chicago 1956); id., *A Guide to American Catholic History* (Milwaukee 1959); Shaughnessy, Gerald, S. M., *Has the Immigrant Kept the Faith?* (New York 1925).

CATHOLIC EMANCIPATION ACT, passed in 1829, a major step toward the elimination of political discrimination against Catholics in Britain and Ireland. After its passage the only government offices denied Catholics were those of lord chancellor of England, lord lieutenant of Ireland, and the crown. Catholics had previously expected political emancipation after the Act of Union in 1800, which created the United Kingdom of Great Britain and Ireland. On this occasion the opposition of George III proved decisive. Subsequent attempts also failed in the face of obstruction from the crown, influential political figures, and the Church of England.

In 1823, however, prospects for reform improved when Daniel O'Connell, a vigorous Irish Catholic lawyer with great popular appeal, founded the Catholic Association. In spite of government attempts to outlaw it, the organization quickly produced effective grass roots support of Catholic candidates for Parliament.

In 1828, O'Connell easily won an election contest against the Protestant incumbent in county Clare. Although O'Connell's Catholicism prevented him from being seated in the House of Commons, the Clare election forced the Duke of Wellington, who was prime minister, to recognize the strong Irish sentiment for emancipation. Wellington and most of his supporters were personally opposed to permitting Catholics to sit in Parliament, but the danger of revolt among the Irish Catholics was so great that a change of policy was considered necessary. A bill introduced by Sir Robert Peel became law in April 1829. Although Irish small landowners were disenfranchised and the franchise qualifications raised to £10 in an effort to minimize the number of Catholics elected to Parliament, the act was a victory for O'Connell and the Catholic Association.

JOHN W. OSBORNE, *Rutgers University*

CATHOLIC LIBRARY ASSOCIATION, an organization of librarians and bookmen interested in the promotion and encouragement of Catholic literature and librarianship through mutual cooperation, publication, education, and the dissemination of information. Its over 4,000 members in the United States and 26 other countries represent all types of library service. There are more than 40 regional and local chapters of the association in the United States and Canada.

The association is organized into a number of specialized sections, arranged according to a particular area of interest. They include units on cataloging and classification; children's libraries; high school, college, and university libraries; hospital, seminary, and parish libraries; and library education.

In 1959 the CLA established the Regina Medal to honor individuals who have made a significant contribution to children's literature. The medal is presented at a special luncheon during the annual convention. The association also awards a scholarship each year for study leading toward an advanced degree in library science. In addition, the organization publishes or sponsors a number of booklists, manuals, classification schedules, and subject heading lists, besides setting standards for the selection of books for Catholic libraries of all categories. The major publications of the CLA are the *Catholic Library World* (the official journal), the *Catholic Periodical Index*, the *Guide to Catholic Literature*, and the annual *CLA Handbook and Membership Directory*.

The Catholic Library Association was founded in 1921 as a section of the National Catholic Education Association. It continued to work within the parent group until 1931, when it was reestablished as an independent organization. Since then it has broadened its field of activity to cover every aspect of Catholic library service. The association is governed by a 10-member executive board chosen by general vote among the membership. The advisory council is made up of the officers of the association and board members; past presidents, editors, and representatives to other library organizations; directors of Catholic library educational programs; and chairmen of sections, of committees, and of regional units. The official headquarters of the organization and the office of the executive director are located at Haverford, Pa. National conventions have been held annually since 1921.

JAMES J. KORTENDICK, S. S.
Catholic University of America

CATHOLIC UNIVERSITY OF AMERICA, the national pontifical university of the United States. It is the only university belonging to the hierarchy of the United States, which governs it under authority of the Holy See through a board of trustees composed of all the residential archbishops of the country and some priests and laymen. As a result of a decree of the Third Plenary Council of Baltimore (1884) and by virtue of a charter from Pope Leo XIII, it opened in 1889. At first only advanced ecclesiastical sciences were offered, but the secular disciplines were soon added in accordance with the original intention. The university has schools of sacred theology, philosophy, canon law, civil law, arts and sciences (19 departments), education, social service, engineering and architecture (8 departments), music, and nursing, as well as the undergraduate college of arts and sciences.

The university administers a program of affiliation embracing over 700 seminaries, colleges, and secondary schools. It has a press for learned publications, a division of adult education, and several specialized institutes. Its library contains more than 700,000 volumes. The university is a charter member of the Association of American Universities. The college has a chapter of Phi Beta Kappa and other national scholastic honor societies.

The university, which is located on 140 acres in the northeast section of Washington, D. C., is flanked by the National Shrine of the Immaculate Conception and surrounded by 87 residences of religious orders. Five sixths of the faculty (450 full-time and 150 part-time members) and three fourths of the student body are lay people, who represent every state in the Union and about 70 foreign countries.

ROBERT TRISCO
Catholic University of America

CATILINE, kat′ə-lĭn (c. 108–62 B.C.), was a Roman politician, who was notorious because of the abortive conspiracy he organized in 63 B.C. Catiline (Lucius Sergius Catilina) was born to a patrician family that had been long obscure. In his early years he seems to have been in the circle of Marius and, in fact, he married a relative of that great general. But when civil war broke out and Sulla appeared a likely victor, Catiline abandoned his former friends and became a supporter of Sulla. In the proscriptions and murders that followed Sulla's victory in 82, Catiline played a conspicuous role. Among his victims was his own brother-in-law.

Catiline's new prominence speeded his career. The quaestorship came in 70, the praetorship in 68, and the governorship of the province of Africa in 67. The consulship, however, continued to elude him. A late application prevented Catiline's candidacy in 66; in 64 and 63 he was defeated at the polls. If he possessed any conspiratorial leanings, they were certainly not yet apparent to his contemporaries.

The Catilinarian Conspiracy. Defeat in 63, however, drove Catiline to more desperate measures. He set about acquiring a wider and more volatile following. His demagogic speeches promised abolition of debts and hinted at a redistribution of property. It was not only the destitute who listened, but even indebted members of the nobility. The effects of Sulla's dictatorship lay behind the Catilinarian conspiracy. Sulla had dispossessed many Romans, who were now in a desperate situation and were prepared to follow Catiline. Others who had benefited from Sulla's victory 20 years before had squandered their holdings and mortgaged their property to the hilt. Many ex-soldiers and desperadoes, placed on farms by Sulla, had failed as farmers. They were now looking for adventure and release. Catiline's support grew. A plot was hatched to seize control of the state in 63. Despite later suspicions, it appears certain that neither Caesar nor Crassus supported any attempt to abolish debts or to overthrow the government.

In 63, Cicero was consul and was therefore responsible for executive authority. Fortunately, his agents were well placed and kept him informed of all Catiline's plans. In October, Cicero revealed details of the conspiracy, which included the presence of armed men in Etruria under Gnaeus Manlius. The Senate, sufficiently alarmed, passed its "ultimate decree" empowering the consul to save the state by whatever means necessary. Catiline joined Manlius openly in Etruria in November. Other conspirators remained in Rome, prepared to create havoc through murder and arson. In December, however, Cicero received conclusive proof of the conspiracy and arrested the ringleaders in the city. The Senate was swayed by Cato's powerful speech, and the conspirators were promptly executed. Mobilization followed against Catiline, Manlius, and their levies in Etruria. In January 62, government forces crushed the remaining insurgents, and Catiline was killed in the fighting.

Evaluation. Catiline is traditionally pictured as a monstrous villain interested only in murder, devastation, and social revolution. But this picture comes from the heavily biased speeches of Cicero. Sallust's monograph on Catiline is equally hostile, but it too depends largely on Cicero's speeches. Whatever Catiline's own motives, his movement exposed real social ills. He was certainly ruthless and unscrupulous. But he was also a man of great physical strength, imposing personality, powerful eloquence, immensely appealing charm, and the courage of his convictions. His face breathed fire and determination, Sallust reports, even after death.

ERICH S. GRUEN
University of California at Berkeley

CATINAT, kȧ-tē-nȧ', **Nicolas de** (1637–1712), French general, who was a marshal of France. He was born in Paris on Sept. 1, 1637, the son of a lawyer. After studying law, he entered the army and won the attention of Louis XIV by his valor at the storming of Lille in 1667, which gained him a promotion. Sent as a lieutenant general against the Duke of Savoy, Catinat won the battles of Staffarda (1690) and Marsaglia (1693), occupied Savoy and a part of Piedmont, and was made a marshal in 1693. His humanity and mildness often led him to spare the vanquished in these regions, contrary to the commands of the Marquis de Louvois, the minister of war.

In 1701, Catinat was put in command of the French army in Italy against Prince Eugène of Savoy, but here he was less successful. Short of money and provisions and hampered by orders from court, he was defeated at Carpi on July 6 and at the Battle of Chiari on September 1. Catinat's representations at court were not believed, and he fell into disgrace. He died at St.-Gratien on Feb. 25, 1712.

CATLIN, kat'lən, **George** (1796–1872), American painter and traveler, whose paintings, engravings, and writings present an eyewitness record of Indian life in North and South America. He was born in Wilkes-Barre, Pa., on July 26, 1796. He had little formal education. After serving an apprenticeship in a lawyer's office, he set up his own practice in Luzerne, Pa., in 1820. Although he had no training in art, Catlin began to make a reputation as an amateur painter and portraitist. In 1823 he gave up his legal practice, moved to Philadelphia, and set himself up as a professional portrait painter.

The turning point in Catlin's career came in 1829, when he saw a delegation of Indians from the West. He was so impressed by the group that he determined to devote himself to painting Indians and their way of life in their own territories. In the 1830's he spent considerable time among the Indian tribes of the Plains and the Northwest. Most of the nearly 600 paintings that he finished during this period are in the Smithsonian Institution in Washington, D. C.

In 1839, accompanied by several Indians, Catlin made a tour of the eastern United States, France, and England, exhibiting a selection of his paintings. During the 1850's he made two more extended trips, painting the Indians of the California coast and of Central and South America. Most of these paintings are in the American Museum of Natural History in New York City.

Catlin published a number of volumes about his travels, illustrating them with engravings from his sketches and paintings. His early travels are described in *Letters and Notes on the Manners, Customs, and Condition of the North American Indians* (1841). His later publications include *My Life Among the Indians* (1867) and *Last Rambles Among the Indians of the Rocky Mountains and the Andes* (1867). Catlin died in Jersey City, N. J., on Dec. 23, 1872.

FREDERICK A. SWEET
The Art Institute of Chicago

Further Reading: De Voto, Bernard A., *Across the Wide Missouri* (Boston 1947); McCracken, Harold, *George Catlin and the Old Frontier* (New York 1959); Plate, Robert, *Palette and Tomahawk: The Story of George Catlin* (New York 1962); Ross, Marvin, ed., *Episodes from Life Among the Indians and Last Rambles* (Norman, Okla., 1959).

Catnip

(Nepeta cataria)

ROCHE

CATNIP is a sturdy, perennial garden herb of the mint family (Labiatae), native to Europe and Asia. Catnip (*Nepeta cataria*) grows to 3 feet (1 meter) high and bears gray, aromatic leaves and dense clusters (spikes) of tiny white or purplish flowers. The plant, whose odor is attractive to cats, contains a volatile oil (principally nepetalactone), nepetalic acid and related compounds, and tannin. The dried leaves and stems are marketed to cat owners.

DONALD WYMAN
The Arnold Arboretum, Harvard University

CATO, kā'tō, **Marcus Porcius** (234–149 B. C.), Roman statesman, also known as *Cato the Elder* or *Cato the Censor,* who made important military, political, and literary contributions to Rome. Born in Tusculum of a plebeian family, he went to Rome and sought public office at the request of his patrician neighbor and future patron, L. Valerius Flaccus, who had been greatly impressed by Cato's many abilities and moral character.

Cato was elected quaestor for 204 and went to Sicily. Subsequently, he was elected plebeian aedile (199) and then praetor (198). He held the consulship in 195. In 184, Cato was elected censor, sharing the office with Valerius Flaccus.

Cato fought in the Second Punic War (218–201), and he later volunteered for service in the First Syrian War (192–189). He was instrumental in defeating the forces of Antiochus III at Thermopylae in 191, when the Roman force turned the pass and defeated the enemy.

Cato's Traditionalism. Cato was an intensely nationalistic, proud Roman who distrusted things Greek and hated the luxury-loving attitude that was taking over Roman life. In 195 he opposed the repeal of the wartime law (*Lex Oppia*), which rationed possession of silver plate and jewelry, and as censor he taxed heavily the dress and ornaments of women of fashion, as well as vehicles and slaves. He humiliated enemies by removing them from the Senate on moral grounds. Cato also attacked the Scipionic circle and its adherents, who were most responsible for the Hellenization of Roman character. He attacked his former commander in the Syrian War, M. Acilius Glabrio, friend of the Scipios, for misappropriation of funds, costing Glabrio the censorship he sought (189). Cato then brought a similar charge against Lucius Scipio, brother of Scipio Africanus. The latter countered by defiantly tearing up the account books and asserting his and his brother's proper behavior

(187). Cato pressed on during his censorship: Lucius was only saved from a prison term by a tribune's veto; and Africanus, accused of treasonable dealings with Antiochus, freed himself of the charge, but in doing so lost influence, then retired in disgust from the city, and died within the year (184).

Cato was the most successful, influential spokesman for the archconservative and nationalistic element in Rome, but in his fight against foreign ideas and influences, he waged a losing battle. Romans were greatly impressed by the highly sophisticated Eastern peoples, especially the Greeks, and the upper classes increasingly grafted onto Roman culture the manners and customs as well as the learning of these peoples.

Works. In his literary pursuits Cato was equally hostile to Hellenism and what he considered the moral degradation of his day. He is regarded as the father of Latin prose because, contrary to earlier practice, he wrote in Latin instead of Greek and made it fashionable. His *Origines,* in 7 books, was designed to cover the history of all Latin cities, including Rome, beginning with the time of the kings. Cato's work exalts the aristocracy, shows an obvious antidemocratic bias, and emphasizes the virtues of traditional Roman character. He was determined to show that Rome's heritage was as illustrious as that of the Greeks and that the Romans did more with their heritage. Of Cato's speeches, fragments of about 80 of the original 150 have survived. For the edification of his eldest son, Cato wrote an encyclopedia, which included essays on agriculture, medicine, rhetoric, military science, and law. Cato's only extant work is *De agricultura* (*Concerning Agriculture*), which, written in his archaic and simple style, indicates many old Roman customs and superstitions and insists upon the value of hard work and the ancient virtues.

Cato and Carthage. Cato is perhaps best remembered for his opposition to the Carthaginians. After the defeat of Hannibal in 202 he carefully watched the developments in Carthage and was quick to support its African foes. Sent as a member of a senatorial commission to Carthage in 153, he was alarmed at the recovery of the city, which, although militarily no longer a rival of Rome, was rapidly becoming a threat economically. Hereafter, Cato, when speaking upon any subject whatsoever, ended his speech by saying, "In my opinion Carthage ought to be destroyed." Ironically, he supported Scipio Aemilianus' command in the third Punic War (149–146), though Aemilianus belonged by adoption to the Scipio family that Cato had prosecuted. Cato did not live to see the city razed.

RICHARD E. MITCHELL, *University of Illinois*

CATO, kā'to, **Marcus Porcius** (95–46 B. C.), Roman statesman, also known as *Cato the Younger* or *Cato Uticensis,* who was the great-grandson and conscious imitator of Cato the Elder. In an era when public morality was rapidly disintegrating, Cato stood out for his uncompromising rigor and his conspicuous Stoic virtue.

In 63, while only in his 30's, Cato delivered a powerful speech in the Senate, advocating the execution of the Catilinarian conspirators. The speech was so convincing that it swayed the Senate against Julius Caesar's argument for their imprisonment. Antagonism between Caesar and Cato continued throughout their careers, as Cato's eloquence and vigor made him the leading conservative spokesman against the intrigues of Caesar and the ambitions of Pompey.

Cato's unbending obstructionism, however, damaged his own cause. In 60 his opposition drove Pompey, Caesar, and Crassus together in their powerful triumvirate. His refusal to allow the revision of a public contract with the tax collectors caused the monied interests to split with the Senate and further divided the republic.

Cato sought in vain to block Caesar's bill for land distribution in 59. The tribune Clodius managed to remove him temporarily in 58 by appointing him governor of Cyprus. Cato was aware that this was designed to eliminate opposition to Clodius' popular program, but his strong sense of public obligation dictated that he carry out this task, which he performed in exemplary fashion.

Much of Cato's energy in the 50's was consumed in fruitless resistance to Caesar, Pompey, and their followers. He became praetor in 54, but his unwillingness to engage in bribery or demagoguery brought him defeat in the consular elections for 51.

When civil war erupted in 49, Cato chose the side of Pompey, not out of any love for the man but because he saw Pompey as the last hope for the republic against Caesarian autocracy. During the war he served in Sicily until expelled by the Caesarians. He joined Pompey in Greece and, after Pompey's defeat in 48, went to Africa to help organize the resistance. With typical lack of judgment he selected Metellus Scipio—a man of illustrious family but no military ability—as general. As a result, the Caesarian forces gained a crushing victory at Thapsus in 46. Cato, who was holding the town of Utica (from which he received the surname *Uticensis*), could not endure the prospect of a Caesarian dictatorship. He chose instead to commit suicide.

Cato proved to be much more formidable in death than in life. Admirers honored his memory, wrote books on his life, and transformed him into a martyr for republicanism. His posthumous reputation helped inspire his nephew and son-in-law, Brutus, to become one of the assassins of Caesar in 44.

ERICH S. GRUEN
University of California at Berkeley

Marcus Porcius Cato, the Younger.

ALINARI, FOR ART REFERENCE BUREAU

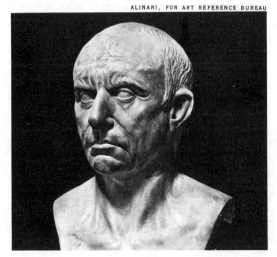

CATO, kā'tō, a blank verse tragedy in five acts by Joseph Addison, first performed in London in 1713. The play is set in the governor's palace at Utica, and is based on the last days of the Roman statesman Marcus Porcius Cato (q.v.), his struggle against the would-be dictator Julius Caesar, and his determination to die rather than outlive his country's freedom. *Cato* was an extraordinary success—primarily because contemporary audiences thought they recognized references to current political rivalries. The Whigs saw in Cato a representation of the Duke of Marlborough; to the Tories, Marlborough was Julius Caesar. The Whigs cheered whenever an actor mentioned the word "liberty"; the Tories, resenting the innuendo, cheered louder.

CATONSVILLE, kā'tənz-vil, in central Maryland, is an unincorporated residential suburb of Baltimore, in Baltimore county. It adjoins Baltimore on the southwest. The growth of the Baltimore metropolitan area has brought small industries to the perimeter of Catonsville. Chemical, electrical, steel, and cotton duck products are manufactured. Educational institutions in Catonsville include Catonsville College, St. Charles College, and a branch of the University of Maryland. Patapsco Valley State Park provides recreational facilities for the community.

The area was settled by Quakers in the 1720's, and the village was known as Johnnycake until about 1800, when it was renamed for Richard Caton, a son-in-law of Charles Carroll, one of Maryland's signers of the Declaration of Independence. Government is by an elected county executive and a council. Population: 54,812.

FLORENCE C. WILMER
Catonsville Community College

CATOSTOMIDAE, kat-ə-stom'ə-dē, the *suckers,* a family of fishes in the order Eventognathi, to which many of the freshwater fishes of the world belong. The family has about 100 species in North America, one species in Siberia, and at least one in China.

The body of a sucker varies from thick and heavy to long and slender. The scales are smooth-edged, the head scaleless, and the jaws toothless. The mouth is so constructed that it can form a tubelike sucker through which food, consisting of plants and small animals, is drawn from the bottom of lakes and streams, the chosen habitat of suckers. The largest members of the family are the various buffalo fish, which may reach 3 feet (1 meter) in length.

Suckers are taken commercially in gill and trap nets and afford some sport fishing. During spawning migrations into the shallow waters of lakes and streams, many are speared. The flesh, though bony, is sweet. A considerable fishery of suckers centers along the Great Lakes and adjacent streams.

C. W. COATES, *New York Aquarium*

CATRON, kā-trən, **John** (1786?–1865), American jurist, who sided with the majority of the Supreme Court in the Dred Scott case (1857). This decision denied the right of Negroes to citizenship and held unconstitutional the 1820 Missouri Compromise prohibiting slavery north of the line 36° 30'. Catron had written to President-elect James Buchanan, asking Buchanan to use his influence to persuade Justice Robert

C. Grier (who favored delay) to participate in a decision on the merits of the case, so that the issue could be conclusively settled.

Born in Wythe county, Va., of poor parents, Catron lived in Virginia and Kentucky before settling in Tennessee in 1812. After serving under Andrew Jackson in the War of 1812, he was admitted to the Tennessee bar in 1815 and became a successful Nashville lawyer specializing in disputed land titles. Appointed to the state's highest court in 1824, he wrote a strong opinion in 1829 upholding the disbarment of a lawyer for killing a man in a duel. In 1831 he became the state's first chief justice, serving until his court was abolished in 1834 by constitutional change. Resuming law practice and politics, he supported Jackson's struggle against the Bank of the United States and led the Tennessee campaign for Martin Van Buren's election to the presidency.

On March 4, 1837, just before Van Buren's inauguration, Jackson appointed Catron to the Supreme Court. Catron did not emulate his associate, John A. Campbell, in resigning from the court on the outbreak of the Civil War, and so had to leave Tennessee. He did not return there until shortly before his death, in Nashville, on May 30, 1865.

LEO PFEFFER, *Long Island University*

CAT'S-EYE, any of several semitransparent gemstones that, when cut in a rounded shape, show a line of reflected light that resembles the narrowed pupil of a cat's eye. This *chatoyancy*—from a French word that means "to shine like the eyes of a cat"—is produced by fibrous inclusions of other minerals in the stone or by the fibrous structure of the gemstone itself. Greenish chrysoberyl with tiny, needlelike inclusions produces a valuable cat's-eye. Such stones are found in Ceylon and Brazil. Common cat's-eye is fibrous quartz, or chalcedony, which sometimes contains inclusions of asbestos; it is of little value. (*Tigereye* is a yellow chalcedony from South Africa.) Cat's-eye has also been cut from other minerals.

A CAT'S-EYE stone of chrysoberyl, with the stone cut in cabochon shape to show the line of light that causes the stone to resemble an actual cat's eye.

RUSS KINNE, FROM PHOTO RESEARCHERS

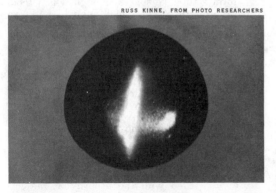

CATSKILL, kats'kil, is a village in eastern New York, the seat of Greene county. It is situated on the west side of the Hudson River, 30 miles (48 km) south of Albany. The village is a summer resort and a gateway to Catskill Mountain resorts. Its factories produce women's wear and machinery, and the village is a shipping center for apples and grapes, grown in the vicinity. St. Anthony's Seraphic Seminary, a Franciscan institution, is situated there.

Catskill was settled about 1680 by Derrick Teunis van Vechten, whose homestead, built in 1690, still stands. The village is governed by a board of trustees. Population: 5,317.

CATSKILL MOUNTAINS, kats'kil, a group of low mountains in southeastern New York, west of the Hudson River, mainly in Greene and Ulster counties. The Catskills, a section of the Appalachian Plateaus, are characterized by bulky masses between the summits, few valleys, and deep gorges, called "cloves," with many waterfalls. The region is drained northward to the Mohawk River by Schoharie Creek, eastward to the Hudson by Esopus, Catskill, and other creeks, and southwestward to the Delaware River by headstreams of that river, which flow from the Catskills. Ashokan reservoir, on Esopus Creek, and Schoharie reservoir are part of the New York City water supply system. Although the highest of the richly forested peaks rise only a little over 4,000 feet (1,220 meters), the sloping summits, clearly visible from the shores of the Hudson, present striking scenery. The highest peak is Slide Mountain, 4,204 feet (1,282 meters).

In preglacial times the Catskill region was a level plateau, standing above a sea that covered much of the surrounding area. The present contours of the mountains were determined by weathering, stream erosion, and outward-moving valley glaciers associated with the continental ice sheets of 20,000 to 50,000 years ago. The sandstones and other rocks of the Catskills, well exposed by cliffs and gorges, present geologists with significant records of the rock system of Devonian times.

The Catskills are primarily a resort area and vacationland, both summer and winter. They offer an abundance of recreational facilities, including several state camping areas, a state ski center at Belleayre Mountain, miles of trout streams, a network of hiking trails, golf courses, and resort hotels. The Catskill Forest Preserve covers approximately 700,000 acres (283,500 hectares) of which about 40% is owned by the state of New York.

Industries in the region produce business machines, electrical machinery, clothing, processed foods, and stone, clay, and glass products. New superhighways linking the area to the New York City market are helping to bring other small industries. The major agricultural activities are dairying, fruit growing, and poultry raising.

History. In addition to its other attractions, the Catskill area is rich in history. It is dotted with historic sites such as the Senate House (1676) in Kingston, where the first session of the New York State Senate was held in 1777; the Bronck House Museum (1663), home of Jonas Bronck, for whom the Bronx, one of the five boroughs of New York City, was named; and Hasbrouck Memorial House (1712) in New Paltz, one of several Huguenot houses preserved in that city. Other places of interest are Roxbury, the birthplace of the nature writer John Burroughs and of the financier Jay Gould, and Palenville, the legendary home of Rip Van Winkle, hero of Washington Irving's short story of the

J. A. AND R.H. GLENN

THE CATSKILL MOUNTAINS often display rounded summits. The deep ravines between them are called "cloves."

same name. James Fenimore Cooper and William Cullen Bryant, as well as Irving and Burroughs, wrote extensively about the Catskills. The Hudson River school of painters, including Thomas Cole, Asher Durand, and Frederick Church, painted many Catskill scenes and held an important position in American art of the 19th century. Since 1900, Woodstock has been well known as a colony of artists, writers, and musicians.

The Catskills were discovered in 1609 by Henry Hudson as he voyaged up the Hudson River in the *Half Moon*. Almost within a decade the Dutch made the first settlements in the area, which they continued to hold until the English took control in the 1660's.

EDGAR TOMPKINS
Albany Public Library

CATT, kat, **Carrie Lane Chapman** (1859–1947), American reformer, who helped secure the enfranchisement of women. Born in Ripon, Wis., on Jan. 9, 1859, she grew up on the Wisconsin and Iowa frontiers. After graduating from Iowa State College in 1880, she became a school administrator in Mason City, Iowa. In 1885, she married Leo Chapman, the editor of a local newspaper. He died the following year and in 1890 she married George Catt, a civil engineer, with whom she moved to New York City.

After joining the Iowa woman suffrage organization in 1887, Mrs. Catt rose rapidly in the national movement. In 1900 she succeeded Susan B. Anthony as president of the National American Woman Suffrage Association. She resigned in 1904 because of her husband's illness, but after his death in 1905 she led the movement in New York State, and in 1915 she reassumed the national presidency. A gifted administrator and a persuasive speaker, she devised the famed "Winning Plan"—emphasizing work on state and national levels and through both political parties—which resulted in ratification of the 19th Amendment in 1920, which extended the suffrage to women. She later was a founder of the League of Women Voters and was active also in the world peace movement. She died in New Rochelle, N. Y., on March 9, 1947.

PAUL S. BOYER
University of Massachusetts

CATTAIL, a hardy perennial reed with dense velvety brown spikes. Cattails are widely distributed in marshy places throughout the world. There are 15 species, all classified in the genus *Typha* of the cattail family Typhaceae.

The common cattail, *T. latifolia*, grows to 8 feet (2.5 meters) in height. It has long, slender leaves and a dark brown flower spike 6 to 12 inches (15 to 30 cm) long and 1 inch (2.5 cm) wide. The flower spike is made up of hundreds of closely packed petalless flowers that appear in July and August. A short, narrow length of male flowers is borne on the upper end of the spike, and the female flowers that comprise the "cat's tail" are borne below. After the pollen is shed, only the withered stalk that bore the male flowers remains above the spike of female flowers, which produces small hairy fruits.

Cattail (*Typha latifolia*)

J. J. SMITH

THE CATTALO is a hybrid developed by crossing North American bison (buffalo) with domestic cattle.

CATTALO, kat'əl-ō, are hybrid animals produced by crossing cattle with bison ("buffalo"). The purpose of these crosses is to obtain livestock that can withstand the cold winters of northern ranges better than cattle. Cattalo have been bred in both the United States and Canada since about 1900, but Canadian scientists have conducted the most extensive research. The work was greatly hindered in early years by the high percentage of sterile cattalo bulls. In subsequent years, however, the percentage of fertile bulls has been increased.

Cattalo are of various colors, and about half of the animals in the Canadian research herd are without horns. They tend to grow rapidly from birth to weaning, but in the feedlot, where they are fattened for market, they gain less rapidly on the average than beef cattle. Some individual cattalo, however, actually outgain beef cattle in the feedlot. By breeding these outstanding individuals, Canadian researchers hope to establish a herd of high performance.

NED D. BAYLEY
U. S. Department of Agriculture

CATTANEO, kät-tä'nä-ō, **Danese di Michele** (1509?–1573), Italian sculptor, who was noted for his portrait busts. He was born in Colonnata, near Carrara, and studied in Rome under Jacopo Sansovino, whose style deeply influenced Cattaneo's earlier works. After the sack of Rome by the forces of Charles V in 1527, he fled to Florence, where he executed a marble bust of Alessandro de' Medici. After returning to Rome about 1530, he accompanied Sansovino to Venice; there he produced sculptures for the Libreria di San Marco, a statue of St. Jerome (c. 1530) in San Salvatore, and a statue of Apollo for the fountain in the Zecca. In Padua, in 1547, he executed a bust of Pietro Cardinal Bembo for the prelate's tomb in Sant'Antonio.

Cattaneo's two most important works are the memorial altar (1565) for Giano Fregoso in Sant'-Anastasia, Verona, and the allegorical figures and reliefs in marble for the funeral monument (1572) of Leonardo Loredan in Santi Giovanni e Paolo, Venice. Both works were sculptured with the aid of his pupil Gerolamo Campagna. Cattaneo was also a poet; his *Dell'amor di Marfisa* (1562), an epic, was praised by Tasso. He died in Padua in 1573.

CATTELL, kə-tel', **James McKeen** (1860–1944), American psychologist, who was an early worker in the field of intelligence testing. He was born in Easton, Pa., on May 24, 1860. He received his B. A. from Lafayette College and did graduate work at Göttingen and Leipzig under the famed European psychologist Wilhelm Wundt. After two years at Johns Hopkins he returned to Leipzig in 1883 to be Wundt's assistant, a post he held for five years. He taught psychology at Columbia University for almost three decades, beginning in 1891. In 1924 he founded the Psychological Corporation and served as its leader until his death.

Cattell was a pioneer in American psychology. He served as the first president of the American Psychological Association in 1895. He was the first psychologist to use the term "mental test" and developed one of the first intelligence tests. Cattell was a firm believer in the application of psychological techniques to practical problems. Under his guidance the Psychological Corporation became a leader in the development of new tests for use in education and industry. He died in Lancaster, Pa., on Jan. 20, 1944.

MICHAEL G. ROTHENBERG
Columbia University

CATTELL, kə-tel', **Raymond Bernard** (1905–　　），Anglo-American psychologist, who is noted primarily for his work in the development of psychological tests. He was born in Staffordshire, England, in 1905. He took a degree in chemistry and a Ph. D. and a D. Sc. in psychology at the University of London. After moving to the United States he taught psychology at Columbia University and Harvard. In 1945 he became research professor of psychology and director of the Laboratory of Personality Assessment at the University of Illinois.

Committed to the idea that human motivation and personality can be studied on a quantitative, experimental, and mathematical basis, Cattell devoted most of his efforts to the development of tests to measure individual differences in what he calls the "primary source traits of personality." He designed the "Sixteen Personality Factor Questionnaire," an instrument noted for the use of analytic mathematical methods in its construction. Cattell's books include *The Description and Measurement of Personality* (1946), *Personality and Motivation Structure and Measurement* (1957), and *The Scientific Analysis of Personality* (1965).

MICHAEL G. ROTHENBERG
Columbia University

CATTERMOLE, kat'ər-mōl, **George** (1800–1868), English watercolorist, painter, and book illustrator. He was born in Dickleborough, near Diss, Norfolk, on Aug. 8, 1800. As a youth he contributed architectural drawings to John Britton's *Cathedral Antiquities of England*. He exhibited at the Royal Academy from 1819 to 1827 and at the Society of Painters in Water Colours from 1822 to 1850, when he began painting in oil. He was given a gold medal for his oil paintings at the Paris Exhibition of 1855.

Cattermole brilliantly illustrated Sir Walter Scott's *Waverly Novels* and *Cattermole's Historical Annual—the Great Civil War of Charles I and the Parliament* (2 vols., 1841–1845), with text by his brother Richard Cattermole. He died in London on July 24, 1868.

Cattle, on their way to summer pasture, ford the Milk River in southern Alberta.

CATTLE

CATTLE. Cattle are the most important of all live-stock animals. They supply approximately 50% of the world's meat and 95% of the world's milk, and their hides are used to produce 80% of the leather used for shoes and other products. All domestic cattle are members of the genus *Bos* in the cattle family (Bovidae). See also BOVIDAE.

CONTENTS

1. Domestication and History

In addition to the genus *Bos,* the cattle family includes the bison *(Bison),* the yak *(Poephagus),* the gaur group *(Bibos),* the Indian buffalo *(Bubalus),* the anoa *(Anoa)* of the Sunda archipelago, and the African buffalo *(Syncerus).* However, these so-called genera are so closely related to the genus *Bos* that the members can interbreed and produce fertile offspring. Such interbreeding may have been important in the development of the many domesticated breeds of cattle that we know today.

The domestication of cattle probably began before 4000 B.C., but nothing is known of its initial phases. Most authorities believe that cattle probably originated in Central Asia and spread from there into Europe, China, and Africa. Local varieties developed in all these areas. Because of constant interbreeding among the varieties and also with the widely distributed wild cattle, the exact center of domestication is not known.

In their first close relationship to man, cattle were probably crop-robbers during the period when man advanced from food gathering to food production. Wild cattle doubtless liked the cultivated crops and interfered with man's efforts to raise them by eating the readily available plants. The growing of crops, however, tied man to the land, and he soon learned that by building pens and stables he could tame cattle and use them for a variety of purposes. Their meat and milk were food; their hides made tough shields; their dung was not only a valuable fuel in areas where wood was scarce but also was used for building purposes. The cattle could be fed the straw and coarse leaves left over after the crops were harvested.

Cattle also became beasts of burden at an early stage of their domestication. They were put to work in the fields, hauling sleds and wheeled transport. They were also used to tread out the grain on threshing floors in ancient Egypt. The Egyptians fattened cattle by forcible feeding, a practice which they also used on hyenas and antelopes.

The hunting of wild cattle was a favorite sport in Egypt and other lands, and bull sports became popular tests of bravery. In ancient Crete bull "leaping" was a popular spectator sport. In this dangerous activity the contestant seized a charging wild bull by its horns and allowed the bull to throw him up into the air in such a manner that the athlete could somersault over the bull's back.

Both bulls and cows also played important roles in ancient religious ceremonies. In some regions the cattle were sacrificed, while in other areas they were considered sacred. A cult in which the bull was a prominent religious symbol flourished in Minoan Crete.

Introduction to the Americas. Cattle were first brought to the Americas by the Norsemen who landed in "Vinland" around 1000 A.D., but this settlement was abandoned after several years. Many importations followed. Christopher Columbus brought cattle to America on his second voyage in 1493; cattle of Spanish descent were brought from the West Indies to Veracruz, Mexico, in 1525; Portuguese traders brought cattle and hogs to Newfoundland and Nova Scotia in 1553; and a sizable shipment of British cattle reached Jamestown, Virginia, in 1611. Subsequent importation and breeding led to the establishment of herds of British breeds in all of Britain's North American colonies.

The practice of cattle raising had crossed the Alleghenies into Ohio and Kentucky by 1800 and was well established in Illinois and Missouri by 1860. In the early 19th century there was an active importation of cattle from Mexico into the United States, and by 1870 there were cattle producers throughout the country. The Great Plains became well known as cow country soon after 1880. The "longhorn" cattle imported by Spanish settlers went northwest from the South, and the British breeds spread westward from the East.

The cattle of Spanish origin brought into South America spread throughout the continent and gradually evolved into several local breeds. Later, British breeds were also brought into South America and became concentrated in the plain and plateau areas where there was an abundance of grass. Recently, large numbers of both beef and dairy cattle from Europe, Britain, and the United States, along with some zebu cattle, have also been imported into South America.

Further Reading: Sanders, Alvin H., *The Cattle of the World* (Washington 1926); Zeuner, Friedrich E., *A History of Domesticated Animals* (New York 1963).

2. Breeds of Cattle

There are two obvious breed groups of cattle in the world: the humped cattle, or zebu (*Bos indicus*), group which are found in tropical regions, and the breeds which descended from an extinct wild type, the aurochs (*Bos primigenius*), and are now found throughout the temperate regions of the world.

TROPICAL BREEDS

The zebu with its long face, steep horns, and hump appears to have developed in the tropics during the earliest times of domestication. Zebu breeds are now distributed throughout tropical Africa and Asia. The hump, which consists of muscle tissue, is a genetically fixed characteristic of these cattle, and it is already well developed in the calf at birth. Its function is unknown.

Principal breeds in the zebu tropical group include the Red Sinhi, Sahiwal, Dhonne, Kankrej (Guzerat), Gir, Krishna Valley, and Nellore of India and Pakistan; the Ankole, Ngonda, Boran, Africander, and Jiddu of Africa; the Damascus and Iraqui of the Middle East; the Khurasani, Kuronem, and Tajik of the USSR; the Chinese Yellow of China; and the Indo-Brazil of South America. All of these breeds have distinguishing characteristics. The nature and diversity of these characteristics are suggested in the following examples.

BEEFMASTER BULL. The beefmaster is an American beef breed developed from Brahman, Hereford, and Shorthorn cattle.

BEEFMASTER BREEDERS UNIVERSAL

AMERICAN-INTERNATIONAL CHAROLAIS ASSOCIATION

CHARBRAY BULL. The Charbray, an American beef breed still in its formative stage, is being developed for ruggedness and heavy musculature.

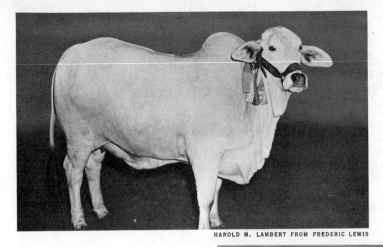

BRAHMAN COW. Brahman cattle, developed in the United States from four types of Indian cattle, are more resistant to heat and humidity than most other breeds.

HAROLD M. LAMBERT FROM FREDERIC LEWIS

BRAHMAN BULL. Brahman cattle were used for developing other breeds, including the Beefmaster and Brangus breeds.

HAROLD M. LAMBERT FROM FREDERIC LEWIS

Boran. Found in southern Ethiopia and adjoining parts of Somalia and Kenya, Boran cattle have been selected for their beef qualities, particularly on ranches in northern Kenya. Mature cows weigh from 760 to 920 pounds (345–420 kg) and bulls from 1,180 to 1,440 pounds (535–650 kg). They are usually white or gray, but occasionally are red or spotted. The cows produce moderate amounts of milk.

Sahiwal. The Sahiwal is a zebu milking breed of India and Pakistan. Cattle of this breed are usually reddish brown with white markings. They are low set and well muscled. Cows weigh about 900 pounds (410 kg) and bulls about 1,200 pounds (545 kg). Milk production is usually about 5,000 pounds (2,275 kg) a year, but some cows have produced more than 10,000 pounds (4,540 kg) in a single year. The butterfat content is from 4.3 to 6%. The Sahiwal has been introduced into many tropical countries, including the Philippines, and it has been crossed with the Jersey breed to produce the Jamaica Hope breed of Jamaica.

Kankrej. The Kankrej is another zebu breed found in India and Pakistan. Known as the Guzerat breed in the United States, it was used in the development of the Brahman breed. Kankrej cattle are gray and have lyre-shaped horns. They are approximately the same size as Sahiwal cattle, but they do not produce as much milk.

Krishna Valley. The Krishna Valley breed is one of several short-horned zebu breeds of India and Pakistan. Cattle of this breed are deep and blocky and vary in color from white to gray. Cows weigh about 700 pounds (320 kg) and bulls about 1200 pounds (545 kg). Krishna Valley cattle have been developed primarily for draft purposes; their milk production is only about one half as much as the Sahiwal.

Dhonne. A striking breed of zebu cattle, Dhonne cattle have Dalmatian-like spots. Native to the northern portion of West Pakistan, they are similar in size and milk production to the Krishna Valley breed. They too are most prized as draft animals.

Ankole. The Ankole breed of cattle, found in Uganda and adjacent areas of East Africa, is known for its extremely long horns. These horns extend from the head at right angles to the body and then curve upward. The distance between the tips of the horns is sometimes as much as 52 inches (1.3 meters).

BREEDS OF TEMPERATE CLIMATES

Bos primigenius is considered to be the wild cattle from which most of the domesticated breeds in the temperate climates of the world have evolved. These now extinct cattle were commonly known as "aurochs." Their external appearance is well known. The bulls were large, up to 6½ feet (2 meters) at the shoulder, and they often had very long horns. The bull was black with a light stripe along the back and light curly hair between the horns, while the cows were mostly brownish red, occasionally diffused with black. As early as 2500 B.C. there were already several well-characterized breeds which descended from the aurochs. One of these, the *Bos longifrons*, is considered by some as the source of present Alpine, Jersey, and Shorthorn cattle.

GALLOWAY BULL. The Galloway breed is one of the oldest beef breeds developed in Britain. It is a sturdy breed, but it is not raised widely by ranchmen in the United States.

BRAHMAN-HEREFORD STEER. Brahman Hereford steers, found in the southern United States, combine the superior beef qualities of Herefords with the hardiness of Brahman cattle.

SHORTHORN STEER. The Shorthorn, the heaviest breed of beef cattle, is raised in many parts of the world.

ABERDEEN-ANGUS STEER. The Aberdeen-Angus breed, noted for the distribution of fat in its high quality beef, is found throughout the world.

CHAROLAISE STEER. The Charolaise breed, one of the most important breeds of cattle in France, has been imported into the United States and used to develop the Charbray breed of beef cattle.

BRANGUS STEER. The Brangus breed, five-eighths Angus and three-eighths Brahman, was developed in the United States to combine the meat qualities of the Angus with the hardiness of the Brahman.

SANTA GERTRUDIS BULL. The Santa Gertrudis breed, developed from crosses of Shorthorn and Brahman cattle, was the first recognized American breed.

HEREFORD STEER. Hereford cattle, known for their white faces and superior quality meat, are very popular in the United States and are also raised in many other regions of the world.

SIMMENTAL COW. An important dual-purpose breed, the Simmental breed is used for draft as well as for milk and meat in parts of Central Europe and Russia.

FOOD AND AGRICULTURE ORGANIZATION OF THE UNITED NATIONS

MILKING SHORTHORN COW. The Milking Shorthorn breed, related to the Shorthorn beef breed, is used for both milk and beef production.

STROHMEYER & CARPENTER

Today there are more than 250 recognized cattle breeds in the world. The most important of these are grouped into three major classes according to their use: beef, dual purpose, and dairy.

Beef Breeds. Many of the most important and best-known breeds of beef cattle found in the temperate regions of the world are derived from breeds that originated in Britain. These breeds have spread throughout much of the temperate world and have gradually developed into many local breeds. In the 20th century, several new beef breeds were also developed in the United States.

Aberdeen-Angus. Cattle of the Aberdeen-Angus breed are distinguished from most other breeds by their black color, smooth haircoats, and polled, or hornless, heads. They have short legs, short compact bodies, well-developed backs and loins, and wide, deep rear quarters. They produce carcasses of high quality and are well known for the marbling, or dispersion, of fat in their meat.

Aberdeen-Angus cattle are well liked by cattlemen because they mature early and bring top prices. The cows produce adequate milk to support a calf. Because of their black skin pigment, they show a marked resistance to eye troubles that plague many beef cattle. Mature cows may weigh as much as 1,600 pounds (725 kg) and bulls as much as 2,000 pounds (900 kg).

Originating in the northeastern part of Scotland, Aberdeen-Angus cattle descended from two polled strains known as Angus doddies and Buchan humlies. Crossing and recrossing of these strains with selection for beef production eventually led to the Aberdeen-Angus breed. They were first imported into the United States in 1873. They were crossed with Texas Longhorns and the resulting offspring made such a favorable impression that further importations were made. The breed developed most rapidly in the Corn Belt states, but recently it has been growing in popularity in the Eastern states and in the western range country.

Angus cattle are also numerous in Canada, Argentina, Britain, New Zealand, and Australia. They are also raised in Russia and are used for producing crossbreeds in Japan.

Hereford. Hereford cattle are very commonly referred to as "white-faced" cattle. Their white faces and their red body color have become distinctive trademarks. The superior meat qualities of Hereford cattle over the meat of early Longhorns and of other nondescript cattle coming to the market so impressed cattle buyers that the mere presence of the white face on cattle was taken as an indication of higher value.

Ranchers like the sturdy qualities of Hereford cattle and their adaptability to range conditions. Herefords can withstand the heat and drought of many semiarid regions and can endure the cold of the exposed range in the winter. They can walk long distances to water and will scatter themselves

DEVON COW. The Devon, first bred in England, is now a popular dual-purpose breed in many parts of the world, including South America.

over the areas where grass is available. They have also proved their ability to put on flesh rapidly in the feedlots.

Hereford cattle originated in the area of England known as Herefordshire, where excellent grass and meadow crops favored their development. In the 16th and 17th centuries they were valued primarily as draft animals and were slaughtered for meat only after their useful life was finished. They were extremely large solid red cattle with widespread horns.

In the mid-18th century a group of breeders began to develop the meat producing qualities of these cattle. They reduced the extreme size of the breed and improved their symmetry, thickness, and smoothness. Cows now weigh about 1,500 pounds (680 kg) and bulls about 1,900 pounds (860 kg). Breeders also fixed the white-face characteristic along with white on the top of the neck, breast, underline, lower legs, and lower part of the tail.

Herefords are raised in large numbers in Britain, North and South America, Australia, and New Zealand. They are also raised to some extent in the USSR.

Henry Clay is credited with being one of the first importers of Herefords into the United States in 1817. As a result of many later importations and the favorable acceptance of the qualities of Herefords on the western ranges, the breed spread rapidly throughout the country. Later in the 19th century, a few United States breeders developed hornless breeds of Hereford cattle that have become increasingly popular and are known as Polled Herefords.

Shorthorn. The Shorthorn is the heaviest breed of beef cattle: the bulls may reach a weight of 2,200 pounds (1,000 kg), and the cows may weigh as much as 1,700 pounds (770 kg). They are more rectangular in form than most beef cattle. Their haircoat is most often various shades of red, but roan, a mixture of red and white, is also common. They may also be completely white or may be spotted with red and white.

The Shorthorn breed of cattle originated in the English counties of Northumberland, Durham, York, and Lincoln, but their first real development occurred in the valley of the Tees River, and they became known as Teeswater cattle. Teeswater cattle were large and had wide backs and deep, wide forequarters. They produced liberal amounts of milk and fattened quickly when fed liberally. They were introduced into northern Scotland in the 19th century and were intensively developed by breeders in that area. They were gradually introduced into many other countries and are raised extensively in North and South America, New Zealand, and Australia. They are also found in certain areas of France and the USSR.

The first importation of Shorthorns from England into the United States was made in 1783, but the more influential importations were made between 1817 and 1850. Most of these cattle were imported into Kentucky and Ohio. The cattle were fattened on grass and corn and then driven overland to Philadelphia and Baltimore markets. About 1850 the popularity of certain bloodlines of Shorthorns increased, and modest fortunes were made and lost in the boom of prices and their subsequent collapse as the popularity disappeared.

Scotch Shorthorns were first imported into the United States in 1857. These cattle became more popular than other bloodlines, and Scotch Shorthorns soon became widely distributed throughout the Central states. They were also used to some extent on the western ranges.

Shorthorn cattle are considered to have mild dispositions that make them easy to handle. They are well known for their milking ability as compared to other beef breeds. They are particularly adapted to farming areas where there is an abundance of feed. Shorthorns cross well with other breeds for the production of commercial cattle, and some ranchers on the western ranges of the United States have used Shorthorn bulls to improve the size and weight of the calf crop. Shorthorn bulls have also been used in the hot and humid areas of the United States for improving the productivity of native stock and of the Brahman cattle. Their main concentration in the United States is, however, in the corn belt states.

Galloway. One of the oldest breeds of beef cattle developed in Britain, the Galloway comes from the province of Galloway in Scotland. The breed was introduced into Canada in 1853 and was later brought into the United States.

Black in color and hornless, Galloways resemble Aberdeen-Angus cattle in general appearance except that the coat of the Galloway is usually very curly. The breed was developed for its ability to produce under rigorous range conditions. They have heavy hides for withstanding cold climates, and the calves survive adverse weather at calving time better than those of most other breeds. Their popularity with ranchmen has been limited, however.

Scotch Highland. The Scotch Highland breed was developed in the mountains of western Scotland, where many of the peaks exceed 4,000 feet (1220 meters) in elevation. The cattle have widespread horns and long shaggy coats of brown hair.

Colors of black, red, and brindle are also not uncommon. Scotch Highland cattle are noted in their native land for their ability to withstand cold temperatures without housing and to survive on scant feed supplies; the cows are good mothers. There have been several importations into the United States, but this breed has been popular among only a few enthusiastic breeders.

Sussex. Developed in the counties of Sussex and Kent in southern England, Sussex cattle were originally used for draft purposes. As beef cattle they are noted for their rapid growth. They are horned and dark red in color. Outside of England they have been raised most frequently in South Africa, South West Africa, and in Rhodesia. Only a few have been introduced into the United States.

Charolais. The Charolais is one of the most important breeds of French cattle. Charolais cattle have a reputation for extremely rapid growth and for yielding large amounts of lean beef. They are among the largest of beef cattle. Their color is a light cream or white. Charolais cattle have been introduced into the United States and they are increasing in popularity.

Brahman. Brahman cattle were developed in the United States as a result of interbreeding four strains of cattle from India: the Guzerat, the Nellore, the Gir, and the Krishna Valley. Indian cattle were first introduced into South Carolina in 1849. Later introductions were made in Georgia, Louisiana, and Texas.

These cattle were introduced for the specific purpose of crossing them with other breeds that were not well adapted to the subtropical conditions of the Gulf Coast region. Brahmans can withstand hot and humid weather, are resistant to insects, and are free from eye trouble. For a time they were raised primarily in the Gulf Coast region; since 1942, however, they have spread to 46 of the 50 states. As recently as 1946 a group of cattle of Indian descent was brought into Texas from Brazil. No special effort has been made to keep the various strains separate, and they have blended into a single breed, the Brahman. They are now used with success in some of the high western altitudes, including such areas of California, Nevada, and Montana.

Brahman cattle are easy to distinguish from all other breeds. Like other zebu cattle they have a distinct hump over the shoulders and an excess of loose skin under the throat, on the dewlap, and in the region of the navel and sheath. The ears are long and drooping. The prevailing color is gray, but red, red spotted with white, gray spotted with white, and even black, brown, or white are not uncommon.

Santa Gertrudis. The best-known beef breed developed in the United States is the Santa Gertrudis. Its name is derived from the Santa Gertrudis division of the King Ranch in Texas, where the breed was developed. The foundation cattle for the breed were Shorthorn-Brahman crossbreds. After nearly 30 years of selection, inbreeding, and line-breeding, the Santa Gertrudis became the first distinctly American breed to be generally recognized.

Santa Gertrudis cattle are large. Mature cows frequently attain 1,600 pounds (725 kg), and mature bulls often weigh 2,000 pounds (900 kg). They are a deep cherry red in color. Developed purposely for adaptation to subtropical climates and semiarid ranching conditions, they make large gains on grass and can scavenge a living in areas of scant forage. They have been exported to several South and Central American countries and to Africa.

Beefmasters. Beefmasters were developed on the Lasater ranches of Texas and Colorado. The foundation cattle were crosses of Brahman, Hereford, and Shorthorn. In selecting breeding stock, the Lasaters emphasized weight, conformation, thriftiness, milk production, disposition, and fertility. They paid no attention to color, but the majority of Beefmasters are dun, brown, reddish brown, or red with some white.

Brangus. Another beef breed developed in the United States is the Brangus. Brangus are three-eighths Brahman and five-eighths Angus. They are black and hornless. They were developed to obtain the hardiness of the Brahman for southern conditions and for the meat qualities of the Angus.

Charbray. The Charbray breed is still in the formative stage. The foundation cattle were produced by crossing Charolaise cattle with Brahman cattle. The resultant Charbray cattle are horned, but the characteristic Brahman hump is almost nonexistent. They are creamy white in color. Cows weigh from 1,700 to 2,200 pounds (770–1,000 kg) and bulls from 2,500 to 3,200 pounds (1125–1450 kg). The breed is being developed for ruggedness and heavy musculature.

Dual-Purpose Cattle. Many of the cattle breeds found in Russia, Europe, and South America serve two purposes: the production of good quality beef and the production of comparatively large amounts of milk.

Simmental. The Simmental breed is probably the most important of the dual-purpose breeds. In fact, it is a triple-purpose breed since it is used for draft as well as for beef and milk. Simmental cattle originated in Switzerland and are very numerous throughout Central Europe and the USSR. They are the predominant breed of cattle in Austria, Czechoslovakia, the highlands of Germany, Switzerland, and Yugoslavia. They have also been imported into Brazil as well as into North America. They are usually maintained on high mountain pastures during the summer and kept in villages in the winter.

Simmental cattle vary in color from light orange or a straw color to spotted red and solid red. The head is usually white with colored markings on the forehead. Cows weigh about 1,600 pounds (725 kg) and bulls from 2,100 to 2,500 pounds (950–1,135 kg). The average milk production of the cows is about 8,900 pounds (4,050 kg), and the butterfat content is 4%. The males are known for their good beef qualities and for their fast rate of growth.

Red Poll. Red Poll cows are capable of producing comparatively large amounts of milk, and the calves grow into desirable beef animals. The breed originated from the crossing and merging of the native stocks of Norfolk and Suffolk counties in England. They were first imported into the United States in 1873. Approximately 300 head were imported by 1900, and a few have been imported as recently as 1950.

Red Polls are red in color and hornless, as the name implies. They are medium-sized and intermediate in disposition between the quieter beef cattle and the more active dairy cattle. Very acceptable milk and butterfat production has been attained by individual Red Poll cows, but they do not equal the best cows of the dairy breeds in production. They have proved adaptable to farming conditions where farmers desire to use cattle for both milk and beef. Red Polls are most numerous in the Midwest, but they are also found in the East and in the irrigated areas of the West and in

HOLSTEIN-FRIESIAN COW. Holsteins are the most popular type of dairy cattle in the United States generally.

the South. In addition to their homeland and the United States, Red Polls are also found in Canada, Argentina, Brazil, Australia, New Zealand, Sweden, and Norway.

Devon. The Devon breed derives its name from the county in England where it was developed. The first importations to North America were made by an agent of the Plymouth Colony in 1623. Later importations were made about 1800 into New England and Maryland. At the present time the greatest number of Devons in the United States are in the South, particularly in the Gulf states. Devons are also found in South America and in Australia.

Devons are smaller than some other British breeds. They are red in color and usually horned. They appear to thrive in humid regions. Devon cows are considered to be good milk producers, and some owners claim that this breed can produce young, tender beef from grass and that it does not need feeding in the feedlot.

Milking Shorthorn. The Milking Shorthorn is a variety of the Shorthorn breed that developed from the Shorthorns that remained in England as contrasted to the beef Shorthorns that developed in Scotland. Because many of the Shorthorns imported into the United States were from England and of the dual-purpose, or milking, type, the foundation for Milking Shorthorns in the United States was established at the same time as the foundation for beef Shorthorns. Their color is the same as that found in beef Shorthorns.

Dairy Breeds. Several breeds of cattle are raised principally for their dairy products, although some may also provide good beef and veal.

Holstein-Friesian. These cattle originated in the northern part of the Netherlands. The breed is commonly called Holstein in North America and Friesian in other parts of the world.

Cattle of the Holstein-Friesian breed are found throughout the temperate regions of the world. Large numbers are found in Canada, Europe, Britain, the USSR, New Zealand, Australia, and Japan. They are also the most productive cattle of Israel, where dairying is highly developed. With proper care and management, Holsteins also produce well in the dry arid climates of northern Africa and in the higher altitudes of the tropics, particularly in Central and South America. India and Pakistan are also studying management methods that would allow the expansion of the Holstein breed in those countries.

The earliest Dutch settlers brought Holsteins to America, but the main importations were made in the latter half of the 19th century. No Holsteins have been imported into the United States from Europe since 1905.

The most numerous breed of dairy cattle in the United States, Holsteins are easily recognized by their black and white markings and their large

JERSEY CATTLE originated on Jersey, an island in the English Channel off the coast of France. They are now widely raised in many tropical countries as well as in many temperate regions. *(Above)* A Jersey cow. *(Below)* A Jersey bull.

AYRSHIRE COW. The Ayrshire originally bred in Scotland, is now a popular dairy breed in North America, Britain, Australia, New Zealand, and in parts of Europe and South America.

STROHMEYER & CARPENTER

GUERNSEY COW. The Guernsey, noted for its yellowish milk, is a highly popular dairy breed in the United States. It originated on Guernsey, an island that is located in the English Channel.

STROHMEYER & CARPENTER

size. Mature cows often weigh 1,500 pounds (680 kg) and sometimes as much as 2,000 pounds (900 kg). Bulls usually weigh from 2,000 to 2,400 pounds (900 to 1,100 kg). There are a few naturally polled (hornless) Holsteins, but most of them have horns that are removed by the dairymen when the calves are still very young.

Holsteins are famous for their production of large quantities of milk. The average production of fully grown cows is about 14,000 pounds (6,350 kg) of milk a year, or 6,800 quarts (6,430 liters), with an average butterfat content of 3.7%. The butterfat and protein percentage of their milk is usually lower than that of the other dairy breeds. Nevertheless, because of the large amount of milk that they produce, their average butterfat production is 520 pounds (235 kg) a year.

Although Holsteins have been developed in the United States almost entirely for dairy production, they also provide a large amount of meat. The calves are often slaughtered for veal, and the cows, after they are no longer productive as dairy animals, have a high salvage value for beef. In recent years, the popularity of Holstein steers in beef cattle feedlots has been steadily increasing. For many years, they have provided the main source of beef in the Netherlands, West Germany, and Britain.

Jersey. Jersey cattle originated on the island of Jersey, which is in the English Channel just off the coast of France. They were probably introduced to Jersey from France sometime prior to 1100 A.D. In the mid-20th century, they are raised widely in the temperate zones, particularly in Britain, Europe, Asia, New Zealand, and Aus-

tralia. They have also been introduced in rather large numbers into tropical countries, including India and Central and South American countries.

The first Jerseys were introduced into America after they had been used for milk on sailing vessels coming to this country. As with the Holsteins, however, the importations which formed the major foundation of the breed in the United States were made during the latter part of the 19th century. Unlike the Holsteins, however, some importations have been made continuously since that time. Jersey cattle spread rapidly throughout the dairy areas of the country.

Jersey cattle are famous for the richness of their milk. The butterfat content of Jersey milk averages 5.2%. In recent years, considerable emphasis has also been placed on increasing the pounds of milk they produce. Their current average milk production is 8,600 pounds (3,900 kg) or 4,200 quarts (4,000 liters) a year.

Mature Jersey cows weigh about 1,000 pounds (454 kg); the bulls weigh 1,500 pounds (680 kg). Their color varies from a light gray to dark brown or fawn. They often have extensive black markings, and they may occasionally be marked with patches of white. They mature rapidly and may be put into the milking herd at younger ages than most other dairy cattle.

Guernsey. Guernsey cattle originated on the island of Guernsey, which lies about 22 miles (35 km) north of Jersey and about 30 miles (48 km) from France. A colony of monks is reported to have introduced the cattle from Brittany and Normandy in northern France to the island. Although Guernsey cattle were brought to the United

States on sailing vessels in earlier years, the first importations of note occurred in 1830 and 1831 when two heifers and one bull were brought in. Descendants of the bull and of one of the heifers are in Guernsey herds today. Other importations which formed the foundation of the breed in the United States were made up to 1914. A few animals have been introduced since that time, but very few have been imported since 1930. Numerous Guernseys are found in Britain, and some are also found in South America and Australia.

The Guernsey ranks between the Holstein and Jersey in size, milk production, and in richness of milk. Cows average about 1,100 pounds (500 kg) in weight. Bulls average 1,700 pounds (770 kg). The average annual milk production is about 9,400 pounds (4,270 kg), or 4,600 quarts (4,350 liters). The percentage of butterfat is 4.8.

Guernsey milk is well known for its yellow color. This color is associated with the occurrence of yellow pigment in the skin of these cattle. Their haircoats are, however, fawn-colored and white.

Ayrshire. Ayrshires originated in the county of Ayr, Scotland. They were first recognized as a dairy breed in 1814, but prior to that date they were often referred to as "Cunningham" or "Dunlop" cattle. They were improved by crossing with other breeds, one of which was the Teeswater, the forerunner of the Shorthorn.

Prior to 1840 only about 17 head of Ayrshires were imported into the United States. During the next 20-year period, about 200 more were imported. The early Ayrshire breeders were located in New England, but the breed eventually became established throughout the country.

Ayrshires are also numerous in Britain, Sweden, Finland, Norway, Canada, New Zealand, Australia, and several South American countries.

Mature Ayrshire cows produce an average of 10,800 pounds (4,900 kg), or 5,200 quarts (4,900 liters), of milk a year. The butterfat content of the milk is 4.1%.

Ayrshires are red, mahogany, or brown with numerous well-defined areas of white. They are medium in size. The cows average about 1,150 pounds (525 kg) in weight and the bulls 1,800 pounds (820 kg). They are well known for their stylish upright horns, and early breeders paid a great deal of attention to shaping and forming the horns for show purposes. More recently, however, the presence of horns has been considered a disadvantage on dairy farms because of the danger of the cows injuring one another. Therefore, as with the other dairy breeds, most of the horns are now removed at an early age. Since the late 1940's, breeding for naturally hornless Ayrshire cattle has been promoted.

Brown Swiss. Switzerland is the native home of the Brown Swiss breed of dairy cattle. Most of the early improvements of this breed took place in the canton of Schwyz in the 19th century. The earlier origins of the breed are not known, but there is reason to believe that the Pinzgau breed from Germany was used in its development. The Brown Swiss breed spread to most of the countries of Central Europe and the USSR. It is also raised in higher altitudes of South America, India, and Pakistan.

The first Brown Swiss cattle were brought to the United States in 1869. However, importations were stopped in 1906 because of outbreaks of foot-and-mouth disease in continental Europe. From only 155 head known to have been imported, the breed has grown and spread rapidly throughout the country.

Brown Swiss produce a yearly average of 12,-000 pounds (5,500 kg), or 5,800 quarts (5,500 liters), of milk. The butterfat content of their milk is about 4.1%. They are similar to the Holsteins in their usefulness for veal and beef production. In their early years in Switzerland and also in the United States they were often used for draft purposes on the farm. In America, however, they have

BROWN SWISS COW. A breed from Switzerland.

STROHMEYER & CARPENTER

U. S. DEPARTMENT OF AGRICULTURE

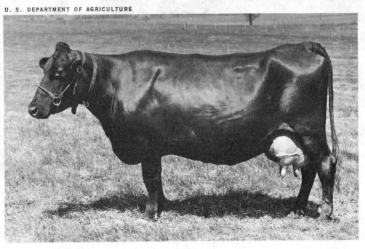

RED DANISH COW. Red Danish cattle are widely raised in Denmark, but they are rapidly diminishing in the United States.

been developed entirely for dairy purposes for more than fifty years.

Brown Swiss are large and rugged. Cows will average about 1,400 pounds (635 kg) in weight and bulls about 1,900 pounds (860 kg). Their color varies from light brown with a silvery cast to extremely dark brown. They usually have distinctly lighter color on parts of their heads and in a stripe down their backs.

Red Danish. Red Danish cattle have been intensively improved for dairy purposes in Denmark. A few are also found in northern Europe and in the USSR. They were first imported into the United States in 1935.

Imported bulls were mated with other breeds in the United States, and the offspring were also bred to Red Danish bulls. This "back crossing" procedure was continued until nearly all the herds became almost entirely Red Danish. Most of the cattle have been raised in Michigan, although there are a few herds in Indiana, Alaska, and several other states.

The yearly average production of Red Danish cows in the United States is 11,500 pounds (5,225 kg) of milk, or 5,600 quarts (5,300 liters). The butterfat content of the milk is 4.0%. As the name indicates, Red Danish cattle are red. The cows weigh about 1,300 pounds (590 kg) and the bulls about 1,800 pounds (820 kg). They have been used extensively in dairy cattle crossbreeding research. However, because of the presence of foot-and-mouth disease in Denmark, only four bulls have been imported since 1935. This limited source of breeding stock discouraged United States breeders, and the numbers of these cattle are rapidly diminishing.

Swedish Red and White. The Swedish Red and White breed has been developed since 1920 from crosses of the Swedish Red Spotted breed and the Ayrshire. Very numerous in Sweden, this breed has been selected for milk production, and it compares in production to the Ayrshires of the United States. It also has very good beef qualities.

Kholmogor. Kholmogor cattle are considered one of the best dairy breeds of the USSR. Their improvement started before the 18th century, and they have been raised throughout the country. They have also been exported to Poland, Finland, and the Baltic countries.

Cattle of the Kholmogor breed are usually black and white spotted, solid black, or red with white spots. They are the largest of all Russian breeds. Cows weigh 1,100 to 1,200 pounds (500–550 kg) and bulls from 1,600 to 2,000 pounds (725–900 kg). Their milk production is comparable to that of the Holsteins found in Russia.

Further Reading: Briggs, Hilton M., *Modern Breeds of Livestock* (New York 1958); Mason, I. I., *A World Dictionary of Breeds, Types, and Varieties of Livestock* (Farnham Royal, England, 1957); U. S. Department of Agriculture, *Beef Cattle Breeds for Beef and for Beef and Milk* (Washington 1958); U. S. Department of Agriculture, *Dairy Cattle Breeds* (Washington 1962).

3. Cattle Industry

Cattle numbers are increasing in nearly every country in the world. The world population of cattle, including buffalo, is about one billion head. The population of cattle in a country, of course, does not always indicate the amount of commercial production of beef and milk. In many countries cattle are used very little for milk and meat but are used primarily for draft, and in some African countries cattle are symbols of wealth. In India, cattle are used for milk and as draft animals but are not used extensively for beef.

COMMERCIAL IMPORTANCE

The production of cattle throughout the world has increased steadily since World War II. This increase, a result of rising standards of living with an accompanying demand for meat, has been particularly rapid in the USSR and in South America. Only minor increases occurred in North America and Oceania. It is evident that countries with deficient supplies of beef have undertaken programs to improve their self-sufficiency, and surplus producing countries are increasing their production to meet the growing home demand and to gain a larger share of the expanding world market.

World milk production has also increased since World War II, but not so rapidly as beef production. The chief milk producing regions are Europe, North America, and Oceania. The major producers in Europe are France, West Germany, Britain,

ANGUS CATTLE are exhibited in a ring at a cattle show in Lexington, Kentucky.

AMERICAN ANGUS ASSOCIATION

HERD OF CATTLE driven along a snow-covered road to a ranch near Seligman, Arizona.

Italy, the Netherlands, Denmark, and the USSR. Production in Oceania is about equally divided between Australia and New Zealand.

Although some countries have had problems of milk surplus from time to time, the total world production in the mid-1960's has not been enough to provide each person in the world with a pint of milk a day. Milk production in western Europe, North America, and Oceania accounts for 55% of the world output, but these regions have only about 20% of the world's population. The less developed countries, such as those in Latin America, Africa, and Asia, have more than 60% of the world's population, but they only produce 20% of the world's milk.

Japan is an example of a country which has put great emphasis on increasing its milk production. The numbers of dairy cattle in that country have increased rapidly. To feed them, Japanese farmers buy large quantities of imported grains.

NUMBERS OF CATTLE BY CONTINENTS AND BY LEADING COUNTRIES

Africa	**112,500,000**
Ethiopia...................... 21,996,000	
Asia	**376,200,000**
India........................207,119,000	
China (mainland)............... 63,000,000	
Pakistan..................... 29,762,000	
USSR (European and Asian)	**66,400,000**
Europe	**107,800,000**
France....................... 17,978,000	
North America	**135,700,000**
United States................. 93,899,000	
Mexico....................... 17,254,000	
Oceania	**22,800,000**
South America	**156,100,000**
Brazil....................... 68,879,000	
Argentina................... 43,385,000	
World total	**977,500,000**

Source: U.S. Department of Agriculture, *Agricultural Statistics 1966.* The numbers given are the averages for the period 1955-1960. They include domesticated buffalo as well as cattle.

In 44 major producing countries, cattle produced 60 billion pounds (27.2 billion kg) of beef and veal in a typical year in the mid-1960's. In 18 of the leading dairy countries cows produced nearly 400 billion pounds (182 billion kg), or 194 billion quarts (184.3 billion liters), of milk.

In South America the emphasis is primarily on beef production, and Argentina, in particular, exports large quantities of meat. Australia also exports large amounts of beef, and New Zealand exports both beef and dairy products. In Europe and Britain most of the beef comes from dairy cattle. The USSR had a wide range of cattle types, but most are of the dual purpose or dairy types.

United States Production. In the United States alone in the mid-1960's, more than 55 million head of cattle and calves were sent to slaughter annually. The receipts from the sale of these animals amount to nearly $9 billion. Receipts from the sale of milk amount to more than $5 billion. The income from cattle represents 30% of the gross farm income. To produce this great volume of animals and products, beef and dairy cattle raisers in the United States raise and maintain about 100,000 head of cattle and calves. This number increased steadily in the 1960's. However, the increases have been in beef cattle only; the number of dairy cattle has declined. The cattle consume hay, silage, pasture, and grain in amounts equivalent to the feed value of 240 million tons (218 million metric tons) of corn.

Distribution of Cattle in the United States — Beef Cattle. The United States is the world's largest producer and consumer of beef and milk. Beef cattle numbers increased most rapidly in the feed-producing areas, that is, in the western ranges where pasture is available and in the north central section where large amounts of locally produced grain are available in addition to pasture. When cattle raising first began, these parts of the country were far removed from the main concentrations of

DISTRIBUTION OF BEEF AND DAIRY CATTLE IN THE UNITED STATES

	Beef Cattle[1]	Dairy Cattle[2]
North Atlantic States	732,000	2,457,000
East North Central States	6,988,000	3,746,000
West North Central States	28,439,000	3,101,000
South Atlantic States	5,116,000	1,142,000
South Central States	22,916,000	2,051,000
Western States	16,984,000	1,609,000
Alaska	4,000	2,000
Hawaii	216,000	15,000
TOTAL	81,395,000	14,123,000

[1] U.S. Department of Agriculture, *Livestock and Meat Statistics* (Supplement for 1965 to Statistical Bulletin No. 333, August 1966).

[2] U.S. Department of Agriculture, *Milk Production and Dairy Products* (Annual Statistical Summary, 1966).

people, and, even today, the average pound of meat travels 1,000 miles (1,610 km) from where it is produced to where it is consumed. In the early days cattle were driven in large herds over trails to market or, later, to the railroads. Today they are moved by railroads and trucks to the slaughter plants and then to retail stores. In 1966 there were approximately 81 million head of beef cattle on farms in the United States, and the number was steadily increasing.

Dairy Cattle. In contrast to beef cattle raising, milk production for use as fluid milk or cream tended to cluster near centers of human population. This occurred in the days before modern refrigeration was available, and the quick movement of milk to market was necessary if the milk was to stay sweet. Today, with efficiently cooled milk trucks and railroad cars, milk is often moved halfway across the country.

Milk production for use as butter and cheese, however, did not have to be transported so quickly to the consumer. Therefore, farms producing milk for these purposes were concentrated in the more remote areas of the Northeast and North Central states, where there were good pastures and plenty of grain for feed. Butter plants and cheese factories were developed in these areas to receive the growing production of milk. More recently evaporated milk, condensing, and drying plants have developed in these areas.

Consequently, a dairy belt developed in the United States, and, despite the growth of dairying in the South and West, it still exists from New England through New York, southeastern Pennsylvania, and central Maryland, across northeastern Ohio to Michigan, Wisconsin, southeastern Minnesota, northern Illinois, and eastern Iowa. Southern Wisconsin has the heaviest population of milk cows per square mile.

RAISING AND MARKETING BEEF CATTLE

The raising and marketing of beef cattle are carried out by a large variety of methods. Many small farmers keep only one or two cows and use them for both beef and milk, while, on the other hand, huge ranches, like those found in the western United States, may maintain breeding herds of several thousand head. There are also feedlot operators who specialize in fattening cattle and may handle more than 20,000 head at one time.

In general beef cattle producers tend to specialize in one or two systems of operation. Some operate breeding herds and sell all their calves as feeders, except for the calves that they need as replacements in the herd, while others buy the feeders and grow and fatten them. The particular system that the beef producer chooses depends on the type and size of his farm, the kinds of markets available, and the amount of money available for

investment and expenses. Specific feeding and management practices depend on the age of the cattle and on the purpose for which the particular group of cattle is being kept.

Breeding Herd. The breeding herd consists of cows that are usually either pregnant or nursing a calf. The cows are turned on pasture or range during the summer. The pasture provides a low-cost feed, and, if it is not too crowded with cows, it will provide the herd with excellent nutrition. Salt and minerals are the only substances that usually need to be added to the cow's diet. Pastures in the Corn Belt will often carry one cow per acre (0.4 hectare), but in the western range country, 20 to 40 acres (8 to 16 hectares) are often used for each cow.

The winter season is the most crucial period for managing the breeding herd. In many areas the herd must be provided with shelter in the form of open sheds or barns. The cows can often graze on crop fields during the winter, but they usually must be provided with some hay and silage and, when necessary, a supplemental feeding of grain.

Calf Crop. Beef cattle producers speak of the calves born in any one year as their "calf crop." Most beef calves are born on pasture in the spring. On the range, calves receive no special care unless it is necessary. The mothers nurse their calves and the calves continue on the range until they are weaned. Dehorning, castration, marking, branding, and vaccination are all done at the time of round-up.

On farms, as contrasted to the range, calves are handled in several ways. They may be allowed to graze with the cows, or they may be fed grain in addition to the grass they get from pasture and the milk they get from their mothers. Sometimes the calves are kept in a lot and fed separately from their mothers. In these cases the mothers are brought twice daily to the calves for nursing.

Spring calves are usually weaned in the fall at the end of the pasture season. After weaning, the calves are put on feeds that will keep them growing satisfactorily until the fattening period.

Fall-born calves are generally more difficult to raise than those born in the spring. They have to be fed harvested feeds, and they require more shelter than the spring calves.

Feeder or Fattening Cattle. The calves may be fattened on pasture or may be sold as feeders to cattlemen who specialize in fattening them for slaughter. The peak sales of feeder cattle occur in the fall. The pasture season ends at this time of year, and cattlemen are looking for feeder calves to consume the already harvested crops of hay, silage, and feed grains. They buy the feeders directly from the cattle raiser, at auction markets, or through agents who buy for them. The feeders are sold in classes according to sex, age, weight, and grade. The grades range from fancy to inferior and are based on the expected ability of the feeder to gain weight rapidly and to yield a large amount of high quality beef.

The calves are fed hay, silage, and pasture throughout their first winter. They are pastured the following summer and then fattened by feeding them heavily for 60 to 100 days. With this procedure, the cattle reach the market at 18 to 20 months of age and weigh approximately 1,000 pounds (455 kg). They are then considered finished cattle, and they are ready for sale to meat packers.

Finished Beef Cattle. Finished beef cattle may be sold directly to a slaughterhouse, or they may be sold to meat packers through a public auction, local dealer, or central market. In the early years of beef marketing in the United States, cattle were driven or carried on the railroads for long distances to slaughtering plants near the large cities of the Midwest or the East. Recently, however, there has been a growing trend to locate the slaughtering plants in the cattle-feeding areas and to ship only the carcasses to the large urban markets.

Finished cattle are also sold according to sex, age, weight, and grade. The grades are based on the expected quality and yield of meat. They are ranked in order of merit: prime, choice, good, standard, commercial, and utility. Approximately 40% of the cattle are sold as choice.

RAISING AND MARKETING DAIRY CATTLE

The labor requirements in raising and caring for dairy cattle are approximately 15 times as great as for beef cattle. The increased attention that dairy cattle need starts with the newborn calf and continues during the lifetime of the cow.

The Cow. Most dairy cows are milked twice a day under highly sanitary conditions. With the exception of a few very small farms, nearly all cows are milked with machines. The machines must be carefully operated if the milk is to be withdrawn without injury to the udder (see section 5. *Anatomy and Physiology*: Mammary System). The udder is prepared for milking by washing and massaging. It is then rapidly milked out. As the machines are removed the udder is massaged to be sure that all the milk has been withdrawn.

Milking cows can be housed in several different ways. Some are kept in individual stalls or stanchions, while others are allowed to roam in and out of large well-bedded sheds. Many are milked while in their stalls, but an increasing number are milked in special buildings that are known as milking parlors.

Dairy cows producing nearly 11,000 pounds (5,000 kg) of milk a year will eat as much as six tons (5.5 metric tons) of hay, silage, or pasture and more than a ton (0.9 metric ton) of grain and oilseed meal. Milking cows are usually fed all the forage they can eat, together with enough grain and oilseed meal to meet their nutrient requirements. In addition, the cows receive salt and minerals, particularly calcium and phosphorus.

For the first few days after the cows give birth to their calves, they are fed carefully measured amounts of grain and oilseed meal. Later, these feeds are given to them liberally, because if adequate nutrients are not available during the first several months of lactation, a high-producing cow will take food nutrients from her body and secrete them in her milk. During the second month after the birth of her calf, the cow's daily milk production usually reaches its maximum. After that time the production declines steadily, and the amount of feed given the cow is reduced accordingly.

Most dairy cows are milked until about two months before they are to have their next calves. At that time milking is discontinued and the cows are fed enough forages and grain to prepare them for the next lactation period.

Several days before her calf is to be born the cow is separated from the rest of the herd. She is put in a roomy, well-bedded stall or a well-protected grassy lot. She is observed carefully until the calf is born and is assisted in the birth, if necessary.

The Calf. Most calves will be standing and nursing within one hour after birth. Help is given to those that are too weak to nurse. The calf is taken from its mother when it is 12 to 18 hours old. This is the easiest age at which to separate the two. The calf learns to drink easily at this age, and the mother responds better to milking if separated from her calf.

The calf is fed its mother's milk (colostrum) for at least three days. It is then fed whole milk from the herd until it is 5 days old. After that it can be continued on whole milk or gradually shifted to commercial milk replacers, and it can be offered hay and grain. Careful feeding during the first 20 days of a calf's life is important. After the calf is 20 days old it begins to eat increasing amounts of grain and hay. At 3 months of age it can be weaned entirely from milk or milk replacers and fed the same feeds as are given to the dairy herd. At 9 months of age it usually will continue to grow rapidly if it is given all the high quality hay and silage or pasture that it can eat.

Calves need dry and clean individual pens during the first month of their lives. After that age they can be grouped with other calves of similar age. They are usually dehorned within a few days after birth, and each calf is identified with a permanent ear tag or tattoo. Extra teats on the udder are usually removed between the ages of one and two months.

Record Keeping. One of the important practices in raising and caring for dairy cattle is to keep careful production records. These records are the basis for determining the proper amount of feed for milking cows and for deciding which cows do not produce enough milk to be profitable, and which dairy bulls have the best milk-producing daughters.

Beef from Dairy Cattle. Dairy cattle provide about 30% of the beef and veal marketed in the United States. The veal calves are usually sold at weights between 100 and 200 pounds (45 and 90 kg). Dairy cows, when no longer productive as milk producers, are usually sent directly to slaughter without further feeding or fattening. They usually grade as standard, commercial, or utility. There is also a growing practice of raising dairy steers and fattening them in the feedlot.

PRODUCTS OF THE CATTLE INDUSTRY

The world production of beef and veal, outside of the United States, is approximately 64 billion pounds (30 billion kg) a year. The consumption of milk is 650 billion pounds (300 billion kg); in the major milk producing countries 78% of this is used for fluid milk and butter, 15% for cheese, 3% for canned milk, and 4% for dry whole milk and ice cream.

Meat and milk from cattle provide nearly 25% of the food energy and 40% of the protein available to the United States consumer. These foods also provide large amounts of vitamins and minerals. The annual consumption of these products in the United States is nearly 20 billion pounds (about 9 billion kg) of beef and veal and 125 billion pounds (nearly 57 billion kg) of milk. This amounts to 100 pounds (45 kg) of beef and veal per person, 302 pounds (135 kg) of milk and cream for drinking purposes, over 6 pounds (3 kg) of butter, nearly 10 pounds (4.5 kg) of cheese, 18 pounds (8 kg) of ice cream, 11 pounds (5 kg) of canned milk, and 6 pounds (3 kg) of dry milk powders.

In addition to meat and milk products cattle yield a large number of useful by-products after slaughtering. The blood is made into plywood adhesives, is used for livestock feeds, and provides materials for textile printing and dyeing. The bones are ground into special bone meals that are used for water treatment, for calcium, for phosphates, for copper molds, for livestock feeds, and for fertilizers. Bones and sinews are also used in glues and in neat's-foot oil. The hooves, horns, and dewclaws are made into protective colloids, plaster retarders, and fertilizer. The hair is used for felting, and the ear hair makes "camel's hair" brushes. The fat is used in candy, margarine, and baking industries. The glands are important sources of chemicals for preparing pharmaceuticals. The hides are used for leather and glue. Calf skins yield gelatin. Calf stomachs provide rennet for cheese manufacture.

Dairy products are also used for purposes other than food. The casein in milk is used in coldwater paints, waterproof glues, face creams, buttons, and combs. The lactic acid is put into soft drinks, drugs, and insecticides and is also used in tanning and dyeing leather and in dyeing textiles.

Bibliography

Anderson, Arthur L., *Introductory Animal Husbandry* (New York 1958).
Cole, Harold H., *Introduction to Livestock Production,* 2d ed. (San Francisco 1962).
Morrison, Frank B., *Feeds and Feeding,* 3d ed. (Ithaca, N.Y., 1966).
Snapp, Roscoe R., and Neumann, A. L., *Beef Cattle* (New York 1960).
U.S. Department of Agriculture, *Agricultural Statistics* (Washington, annually).
U.S. Department of Agriculture, *The Farm Beef Herd* (Washington, 1958).
U.S. Department of Agriculture, *Feeding Dairy Cattle* (Washington, 1961).
U.S. Department of Agriculture, *Improving Your Dairy Herd* (Washington, 1967).
U.S. Department of Agriculture, *Livestock and Meat Statistics* (Washington, annually).
U.S. Department of Agriculture, *Raising Dairy Calves and Heifers* (Washington, 1962).
U.S. Department of Agriculture, *World Beef Trends* (Washington, annually).

4. Breeding

The principles of breeding are the same for both beef and dairy cattle. The gestation period of cattle is about 280 days. The objective is for each cow to have one calf a year. This means that she must be mated with a bull in the third month subsequent to calving.

Improvement of Beef Cattle. Most beef producers prefer to have their cows calve on pasture in the spring. Therefore, their breeding season is during the summer months. They usually use one bull for about every 20 to 30 cows.

Improvement of beef cattle through breeding is usually directed toward increasing the number and birth weights of calves and toward producing cattle with rapid growth, improved efficiency in utilizing feed, and greater meat value of their carcasses. In order to accomplish this, the breeder must keep accurate records of births and weights at various ages. With these records he can then sort out his best cattle, save them for breeding stock, and send the rest to market. The keeping of these records of performance is not presently a general practice among beef cattle breeders, but the more progressive breeders either keep their own records or belong to an organization which does it for them.

Improvement in Dairy Cattle. Dairy cows usually produce slightly more milk if they give birth to their calves in the fall. The cooler weather and the regularity of winter feeding is responsible for the additional production. However, because of the year-round demand for milk on most markets, dairymen are breeding their cows to freshen all year around. This is possible because with modern dairy management the calves can be cared for in any season.

Improvement of dairy cattle through breeding is aimed at increasing milk production, obtaining an optimum butterfat content in the milk, and improving the physical traits of a cow that might help production or contribute to length of life. Record keeping and performance measures are equally as important for dairy cattle breeding as for beef cattle.

Systems of Mating. In addition to selecting outstanding breeding stock cattle breeders use several systems of mating: outbreeding, inbreeding, linebreeding, and crossbreeding. Most cattlemen use outbreeding, that is, they mate the best animals but make sure they are unrelated, but some breeders do mate related animals in a system called inbreeding. Inbreeding is difficult to carry out successfully with cattle, and only a few breeders have produced outstanding herds with it. Linebreeding, a form of inbreeding where matings are made between descendants of an outstanding ancestor, is often practiced; however, the extent to which real improvement can be made by linebreeding as compared to outbreeding is a matter of debate among cattle breeders.

Research has shown that crossbreeding, that is, the mating of animals from different breeds, is a successful system of mating for beef cattle. Crossbred steers grow faster and yield as much high quality meat as other steers. Crossbred cows produce more calves and have more milk for their calves than other beef cows. For these reasons crossbreeding is a rapidly growing practice among beef producers. On the other hand, research has not revealed substantial benefits from the crossbreeding of dairy cattle. See also BREEDING.

Artificial Insemination. One of the most rapidly growing practices in cattle breeding is artificial insemination. A few outstanding bulls are kept at a central location, and specially trained technicians, using carefully developed scientific techniques, inseminate the cows in a large number of herds. In this manner, several thousand calves can be sired by one bull in one year instead of the usual 20 to 50 calves produced by natural mating. Through artificial insemination the inheritance of an unusually superior bull can be passed on to many more offspring than was previously possible. Approximately 48% of the dairy cows in the United States are bred by artificial insemination. The practice is also increasing rapidly for beef cattle.

Further Reading: Gregory, Keith E., *Beef Cattle Breeding* (Washington 1964); Rhoad, Albert O., *Breeding Beef Cattle for Unfavorable Environments* (Austin, Texas, 1955); Rice, Victor A., and others, *Breeding and Improvement of Farm Animals* (New York 1957).

5. Anatomy and Physiology

The anatomical structures of beef cattle and dairy cattle are identical. In fact, many years ago, a scientist reconstructed the skeleton of a champion beef steer and that of a champion dairy cow, and it was found to be impossible to tell the difference between the two skeletons without reading the labels.

The difference between beef and dairy cattle is in the degree of fleshiness and in the development of the udder. Beef cattle are bred to be blocky and thick in shape with smooth muscles and flesh covering the angularity of their bones. Dairy cattle are much thinner in their fleshing. Their hip bones, ribs, shoulder bones, and other points of the skeleton are usually prominent.

The most interesting parts of cattle anatomy and physiology are the digestive system and the mammary system.

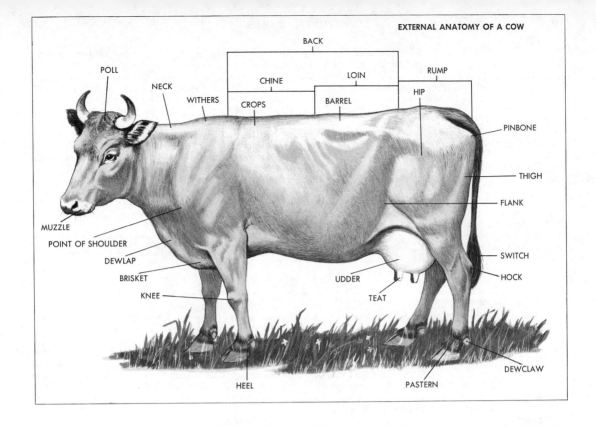

BACK

POLL
NECK
WITHERS
CHINE
CROPS
LOIN
BARREL
RUMP
HIP
PINBONE
THIGH
FLANK
MUZZLE
POINT OF SHOULDER
DEWLAP
BRISKET
KNEE
SWITCH
HOCK
UDDER
TEAT
DEWCLAW
HEEL
PASTERN

Digestive System. Cattle are ruminants along with other animals such as sheep, goats, bison, deer, antelope, giraffes, and camels. As ruminants, cattle chew a cud and have a complex stomach especially adapted for eating large quantities of forages.

Teeth. The location of the teeth in cattle is an interesting aspect of their digestive anatomy. Cattle have teeth for grinding in the rear of their mouths on both the upper and lower jaws. However, they have teeth only on the lower jaw in the front of their mouths. The upper jaws in front are covered with thick pads of cartilage. When cows eat grass, they wrap their tongue tightly around the stems and break the grass off between their lower teeth and the cartilaginous pads. For this reason, cattle do not crop plants as close to the ground as do sheep and other herbivorous animals that have biting teeth on both the upper and lower jaws.

Stomach. Cattle have four stomachs: (1) a rumen, or paunch; (2) a reticulum; (3) an omasum; and (4) an abomasum.

Cattle chew their food only enough to moisten it and form it into masses suitable for swallowing. The swallowed portions go into the paunch and the reticulum. In both of these stomachs the food is mixed and softened and enormous numbers of special kinds of bacteria and protozoa start the process of breaking down the coarse stems and leaves of forage into food the cattle can use.

Later the cattle regurgitate or "cough up" balls of the partially digested food from the paunch and reticulum. These balls are known as *cuds,* and the cattle chew them thoroughly, swallow them, cough them up again, and chew them again. This repeated chewing is called *ruminating.* Cattle spend as much as eight hours a day ruminating their food, or chewing their cuds.

After chewing, the cuds are swallowed and pass into the rumen, where bacteria and protozoa continue to help cattle digest the large quantities of hay and other forages that they eat. The nutrients of forages are enclosed in hard and thick cell walls of cellulose, and digestive fluids cannot easily reach the nutrients. Bacteria and protozoa attack the cellulose walls and break them down, thus permitting the digestive fluids to reach the forage nutrients. The microorganisms also change the cellu-

THE COW'S STOMACH in cross section, showing the four parts: rumen, reticulum, omasum, and abomasum. Food partially digested in the rumen and reticulum is coughed up and rechewed. It is then swallowed and passes through the first two "stomachs" and on into the omasum and abomasum where digestion is completed.

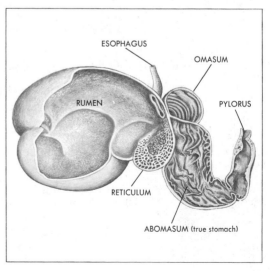

ESOPHAGUS
OMASUM
RUMEN
PYLORUS
RETICULUM
ABOMASUM (true stomach)

lose into simpler compounds that can be used by cattle as food. The action of the microorganisms also generates considerable heat, and this heat is sometimes helpful in keeping cattle warm.

After the action of the bacteria and protozoa is completed, the food products are passed on through the reticulum into the other two stomachs where digestion continues. After digestion is completed, the products are passed into the small intestine.

The stomachs of newly born calves are not fully developed for digesting grain and forage. For this reason, calves must be fed milk or milk substitutes. Their ability to digest coarse feeds gradually increases until at three months of age they are ready to eat the same feeds as the dairy herd.

Mammary System — Udder. The udder of the cow is made up of four mammary glands, each of which is known as a *quarter*. The udder is suspended from the cow's body by a strong central ligament that in some cows must support not only the empty weight of the udder but also more than 50 pounds (22.5 kg) of milk. Skin and connective tissues bind the sides of the udder to the cow's body and restrict its movement when the cow walks.

Nutrients for making milk are brought to the cow's udder by the blood in two large arteries which pass through the front and rear quarters and deposit the chemicals in the mammary cells. The blood leaves the udder in three large veins. Scientists estimate that 100 quarts (95 liters) of blood flow through the udder of a high-producing dairy cow in an hour.

The portions of the mammary glands in which the milk is actually secreted are filled with clusters of grapelike structures called *alveoli*. These alveoli are made up of tiny mammary cells that draw the chemicals from the blood, recombine some of them, and then secrete the result into the ducts in the form of milk.

The secretion of milk goes on continuously until the udder is so full that the pressure of the milk in the udder stops any more secretion. Once the pressure is relieved by withdrawing the milk at milking time, the secretion starts again.

"Let-Down" of Milk. Successful milking of a cow depends on the dairyman's skill in getting the cow to "let down" her milk. To do this, he must understand certain aspects of the cow's behavior and physiology, particularly the effect of nervous stimuli on the udder.

Cows become used to the time when they are to be milked. They recognize the time by certain acts of the farmer, such as rattling the milking pails, washing the udder to get it ready for milking, or starting the engine of the milking machine. Any of these can signal the cow's brain that it is milking time.

The nervous stimuli cause the brain of the cow to send signals to the pituitary gland at the base of the brain. The pituitary gland secretes a hormone called oxytocin that is carried through the blood stream to the udder. In the udder, oxytocin acts on the cells and literally forces the milk out into the main ducts. At this time, if the cow is milked immediately and rapidly, all the milk can be easily withdrawn. Most efficient farmers start milking each cow about one minute after washing the udder since they know it takes about one minute for the nerves, the brain, and the hormones to prepare the udder for milking.

If the farmer fails to prepare the udder properly and fails to milk the cow in accordance with her "let down" of milk, he not only has more difficulty in withdrawing the milk, but he seldom gets as much out of the cow as he would have with correct milking procedures. Also, if the cow is frightened or upset during milking time, another hormone, called epinephrine, is secreted into the blood stream. This hormone counteracts the oxytocin and the "let down" of milk either doesn't occur or is stopped.

Additional hormones secreted by the cow also affect her ability to produce milk. At least one hormone brings about the development of the ducts in the udder, while others affect the growth of the alveoli and the milk-secreting cells. Hormones also are at least partially responsible for the fact that a cow produces the most milk per day during the second month after she calves.

Further Reading: Craplet, Camille C., *The Dairy Cow* (London 1963); McCabe, Terrence W., and Mitchell, Harley W., *Animals That Give People Milk* (Chicago 1957); Smith, Vearl R., *Physiology of Lactation*, 5th ed. (Ames, Iowa, 1959).

6. Diseases

Cattle are subject to a wide variety of infectious and nutritional diseases that can cause serious economic losses. The most important of the diseases that commonly affect cattle are discussed below.

Foot-and-Mouth Disease. This is a highly infectious disease that is one of the most dreaded of all livestock diseases. It is caused by a virus and it affects hogs and sheep as well as cattle. The main symptom of the disease is blisters in the mouth and on the feet. The animals may also become lame. The disease causes a severe loss in meat and milk production and sometimes even death.

The first outbreak of foot-and-mouth disease in the United States occurred in 1870. There have been eight other outbreaks in the United States, the last in 1929. In all but two of the outbreaks, this disease was wiped out within a few months. However, nearly two years of quarantining, destruction of infected and exposed herds, and cleaning and disinfection of premises were necessary to stamp out the infections found in 1914 and 1924.

The disease continues to exist in Africa, Asia, Europe, and South America, and only the utmost vigilance by agents of the U.S. Department of Agriculture keeps it from invading the United States. Cattle, swine, sheep and goats, and the fresh, chilled, or frozen meats of these animals cannot be imported unless they are from countries free from the disease.

In addition to preventing the importation of infected animals, the U.S. Department of Agriculture operates a foot-and-mouth disease research laboratory on an island off the eastern coast. This laboratory is working on new and more effective means of controlling the disease if a new outbreak should occur.

Mastitis. This is the most costly of all cattle diseases. It is particularly serious in dairy herds because it affects the udder and sharply reduces milk production. Mastitis may be caused by several bacteria, including *Streptococcus agalactiae*, *Micrococcus pyogines*, and *Escherichia coli*. Nearly 20% of cows have mastitis at least once a year.

Mastitis exists in two forms, acute and chronic. In both forms of mastitis, the mammary cells are replaced with fibrous tissue, and in advanced cases the udder becomes useless. In acute mastitis the infected quarter of the udder is hot, tense, hard, and tender. Milk secretion stops almost completely. Fever, dullness, and loss of appetite may also occur.

Chronic mastitis is not so easily recognized. Inflammation and infection of the udder usually involve only a small portion of the milk-secreting tissue. The udder may appear normal, but flakes or clots may appear in the milk. The butterfat and protein content of the milk is usually reduced, and the salt content increases.

Calf Scours. The most destructive disease of calves is calf scours. The typical symptom is diarrhea. The most fatal form of the disease appears at birth or within 6 to 72 hours after birth. The calf may be found dead or cold, weak, and dying. Sometimes, however, newborn calves may have mild diarrhea for 10 to 30 days and then recover with little assistance. However, most calves that have scours become unthrifty, grow slowly, and are highly susceptible to pneumonia.

A variety of organisms can cause scours. The disease occurs more frequently in large herds than in very small herds of one or two cows. Calf pens, calving stalls, barnyards, trucks, and other facilities may be contaminated by the infectious agents. Lack of Vitamin A in the cow's diet may reduce the resistance of the calf to scours, and what are known as noninfectious scours may be caused by improper feeding.

Pneumonia. The symptoms of pneumonia include dullness, coughing, rapid breathing, high temperature, and a nasal discharge. A complete or partial loss of appetite may also occur. Death may result in a few hours or days if treatment is not successful. Pneumonia may affect both cows and calves. In mature cattle it is often a secondary infection that invades the animal after another disease has weakened it. The organisms that cause pneumonia can usually be combated with the proper antibiotics; but if treatment is to be most effective it must be started early.

Screwworm. Screwworm flies lay their eggs in the wounds of cattle. The eggs hatch in 12 to 24 hours, and the tiny maggots feed in the living flesh. Infested animals usually die unless they are treated promptly. On the range prompt treatment of infested cattle has been difficult, costly, and often impossible.

The successful war against screwworm is probably one of the more spectacular accomplishments in cattle protection in recent years. To control these ravaging insects, scientists developed a procedure which prevents the females from reproducing. Male flies are reared in large numbers in a laboratory and then sterilized by exposure to gamma rays from radioactive cobalt. The sterile males are released from airplanes over the screwworm infested areas. Wild females, once mated to a sterile male, do not mate again and therefore cannot reproduce.

As a result of a campaign begun in 1957, in which many billions of sterile flies were produced and released, screwworms have been eradicated in the southeastern United States and in most of the Southwest.

Brucellosis. Brucellosis is a cattle disease that may infect humans. It is caused by the bacteria, *Brucella abertus.* The disease is commonly known as *Bang's disease* and as *undulant fever,* and in cattle it may also be known as *infectious abortion* because it causes cows to lose their calves before the normal time for birth. The infection may spread rapidly through a herd and from one herd to another. The birth of weak calves and other abnormal occurrences during birth may result from brucellosis infection. No effective treatment for cattle infected with brucellosis has been found.

Since 1934 there has been a nationwide program for the control and eradication of brucellosis in the United States. Infected animals are slaughtered and many healthy animals, mostly calves, are vaccinated. During the early years of the campaign, the infection rate was above 6% of all cattle tested, but by 1965 annual losses from this disease had been reduced by 75%. See also BRUCELLOSIS.

Milk Fever. A nutritional disease of high-producing dairy cows, milk fever occurs occasionally during calving but most often in the first few days after calving when the cow is coming into full production of milk. The condition is produced by a rapid lowering of calcium, or lime, in the blood. The symptoms are paralysis, inability to rise, and partial or total loss of consciousness. Despite the name of the disease, fever is not a usual symptom.

This ailment used to cause rapid death in as many as 90% of the cows affected. Fortunately, with modern methods of treatment, only a few dairy cattle now die from the disease.

Treatment for milk fever consists of injecting a calcium-glucose solution into the blood system. To counteract a common lack of blood sugar in affected cows, dextrose is often added to the solution. Immediately after treatment the cow brightens up and usually makes a good recovery in 1 or 2 hours. No effective methods of prevention are known.

Ketosis. Another nutritional disease, ketosis most often occurs in the early months of lactation. During this period of peak milk production, it is difficult to feed high-producing cows enough to meet their needs. When a deficiency is prolonged, ketosis may occur. It also occurs occasionally in cows that are not lactating and even in steers.

The more obvious symptoms of ketosis involve the nervous reactions of the animal. The cattle may be excitable, may stagger and sway when they walk, or may be listless. During the early stages of the disease, the cattle also develop a peculiar aroma on their breaths which experienced dairymen learn to detect. The aroma comes from the abnormal amounts of ketone bodies formed in the blood because of a metabolic abnormality. These ketone bodies are volatile and are excreted from the lungs as well as in the urine. Milk production usually drops markedly in cows affected with ketosis. Ketosis can be treated by injections of glucose and feeding of drugs.

Pinkeye. Pinkeye, also known as infectious keratitis, affects the eyelids of cattle. The linings of the lids become red and congested. The eyes are closed, and the animals show evidence of pain, especially in bright sunlight. They usually lose weight because they cannot see to graze. Some animals may become permanently blind.

Pinkeye is most commonly seen in the summer. The infection is usually introduced into uninfected herds by newly purchased animals that are either infected or have been exposed to infection while in transit. It may also be transmitted by flies and gnats.

Anaplasmosis. Anaplasmosis is an infectious disease caused by a protozoa *(Anaplasma morginale)* that infects the red blood cells and causes anemia. The disease is transmitted by bloodsucking insects such as mosquitoes, horseflies, and ticks. It occurs in the northern areas, but it is especially troublesome in warmer climates.

The severity and duration of the disease vary greatly. Symptoms may be so mild as to go unnoticed by the casual observer. In severe cases the animal usually becomes thin, and the pulse and breathing rate increase. As the disease progresses, there is drooling from the mouth, discharge of mucus from the nostrils, and increasing weakness. The disease is most severe in mature cattle, and as many as 50% of the affected animals have died in some outbreaks.

Certain antibiotics can suppress the multiplication of the protozoa and can rid carrier animals of infection, and they are often used to treat the disease. Blood transfusions are also useful in many cases, but, to be effective, 2 to 3 gallons (7.5 to 11 liters) of whole blood must be injected into the sick animal.

Bloat. This is a digestive disorder in which the cattle's paunch and reticulum are swollen by stomach gases. The disease can kill cattle in a few hours. Its occurrence has increased rapidly after 1930, probably as a result of new feeding practices—particularly the increased use of alfalfa and other legumes for feed.

Tuberculosis. Tuberculosis was once widely prevalent in the United States. In 1917 the disease was found in 40% to 80% of the cattle in some of the badly infected areas, and a campaign against the disease was started. By 1940, the incidence had been reduced to less than 0.5% in the United States, in Puerto Rico, and in the Virgin Islands, and by the 1970's it was virtually eliminated in the United States.

The tubercle bacilli causing cattle tuberculosis are not the same as the bacteria causing human tuberculosis. However, humans are slightly susceptible to the cattle disease, and therefore, the control of cattle tuberculosis is beneficial to the human population as well as to the cattle industry.

Tick Fever. Another serious cattle disease in the early days of the United States was tick fever. This costly disease probably entered the country as early as the 17th century by way of the West Indies and Mexico. Trailherds from Texas carried the pestilence and cause of death to cattle into Indian territory, Missouri, Kansas, and Arkansas. Farmers suspected that the tick was the carrier of this disease, and researchers found the protozoan parasite *(Babesia bigemina)* that was the cause of the disease and confirmed that the tick *(Boophilus annulatus)* was the carrier of the parasite. This research not only opened the way to eradicating tick fever but also showed the way for revealing the causes of human diseases such as malaria, yellow fever, typhus, bubonic plague, and Rocky Mountain spotted fever. Today tick fever is no longer a significant disease of cattle in the United States.

Pleuropneumonia. Pleuropneumonia was one of the first serious diseases to affect cattle in the United States. A highly contagious disease, it was introduced into the United States by a cow from a British ship in 1843. Forty years later an extensive campaign to combat the disease began, and 5 years later the disease had been eradicated from the United States at a cost of $1.5 million. However, constant vigilance is necessary to prevent the disease from reentering the country since it does still exist throughout a large part of the world. Many governments have active campaigns to eradicate the very costly disease.

Pleuropneumonia is caused by a virus, *Asterococcus mycoides.* Known in Germany as "lung plague," this disease causes an inflammation of the lungs and the lining of the thoracic cavity. Animals affected with pleuropneumonia often develop high fevers, lose weight, and drop in milk production. Many of them die.

Further Reading: Bailey, Jackson W., *Veterinary Handbook for Cattlemen,* 4th ed. (Springer Pub. 1972); U. S. Department of Agriculture, *Animal Diseases: The Yearbook of Agriculture 1956* (USGPO 1956).

NED D. BAYLEY
U. S. Department of Agriculture

CATTLEYA, kat′lē-ə, any of a large group of tropical American orchids highly valued for their big, showy flowers. Cattleyas grow about 12 inches (305 mm) tall. Their flowers, which are often 7 to 8 inches (180 to 200 mm) across, grow singly or in small clusters and are usually brightly colored. See also ORCHID.

CATTON, kat′ən, **Bruce** (1899–1978), American historian of the Civil War. Charles Bruce Catton was born in Petoskey, Mich., on Oct. 9, 1899. He grew up in northern Michigan hearing the tales of aged veterans of the Virginia campaigns. These he later described vividly in *Mr. Lincoln's Army* (1951), *Glory Road* (1952), and *A Stillness at Appomattox* (1953); these volumes constituted his famous trilogy on the Army of the Potomac, of which the last volume won the Pulitzer Prize.

Catton left Oberlin College to serve in the Navy during World War I. A journalist until World War II, he then became a government information officer. Afterward he wrote for *The Nation,* but his interest in the Civil War quickened.

Although he became editor of *American Heritage* magazine in 1954, Catton subsequently increased his literary production. His works included *U.S. Grant and the American Military Tradition* (1954), *This Hallowed Ground* (1956), *Grant Moves South* (1960), *The Coming Fury* (1961), *The Terrible Swift Sword* (1963), and *Never Call Retreat* (1965). *The American Heritage Picture History of the Civil War* (1960), for which he wrote the narrative, received a special Pulitzer Prize. He also edited many volumes. Admired by specialists and general readers alike, Catton portrayed events in terms of what they meant for individuals whose emotions the reader could share. Thus, he recreated not only the actual past but also the feelings of those who participated. Commenting on American fascination with the Civil War, he said that Americans view it "not as an excuse to wave the flag, but as an experience that may teach us something useful for today." He died in Frankfort, Mich., on Aug. 28, 1978.

BERTRAM WYATT BROWN
Case Western Reserve University

CATULLUS, kə-tul′əs, **Gaius Valerius** (c.84–c. 54 B.C.), Roman poet, whose love lyrics served as models for later European poets. There is little certain knowledge of his life. According to ancient sources, he was born in 87 B.C. and died at the age of 30; one datum or the other must be in error, since there are clear references in his poems to events after 57 B.C. However, since his 116 extant poems—most of them short, a few of them fragmentary—tend to be self-revealing to an extent unusual in world literature, a fairly plausible biography can be constructed mainly on their evidence.

First Poems. A native of Verona, Catullus went to Rome, apparently in his early 20's. During his first years there he shared the more or less Bohemian life of a group known as the "New Poets," who were attempting to introduce into Latin the meters and poetical techniques of the Greek lyric and short epic, especially those characteristic of the Alexandrian age. To this period may belong such poems as the *Hymn to Diana* (No. 34) and the marriage songs, or epithalamia (Nos. 61 and 62). Catullus' success in the adopted forms probably contributed to his being called *doctus,* which means not only "learned" but also "skillful, technically adept."

Love Poems. In the late 60's B. C., Catullus fell passionately in love with an older woman. Called "Lesbia" in his poems, she is almost universally identified as Clodia Pulchra, wife of the consul Metellus Celer and sister of Clodius Pulcher, one of Cicero's bitterest political enemies. Clodia's family was aristocratic, ruthless, and dissolute, and Catullus' relationship with her was probably brief and undoubtedly disastrous. The first poem he wrote to her, "He who sits near you seems the equal of a god" (No. 51), is a translation from Sappho of Lesbos and may have suggested the pseudonym Lesbia. At its most passionate the affair produced such pieces as "Let us live, my Lesbia, and let us love" (No. 5), "How many kisses are enough?" (No. 7), and the songs on his lady's pet sparrow and its death (Nos. 2 and 3).

These poems were followed by a long series of lyrics containing scabrous attacks on the poet's more favored rivals in love and voicing his own doubt and torment. Typical of these are "Miserable Catullus, stop playing the fool" (No. 8); "I hate and love. If you ask me why,/ I have no answer, but I feel it to be so and I am in agony" (No. 85); and the meditative, prayerful "O gods, if it be yours to pity, deliver me from this love, this plague, this ruin, this foul disease" (No. 76). Revulsion fills what is presumably one of Catullus' last comments on his grand passion: "O Caelius, our Lesbia, that Lesbia, she whom Catullus only/ Loved, more than he loved self or any other,/ Now in the gutters and the darkened byways/ Rolls with the random sons of Father Remus" (No. 58). Similarly, disgust is voiced in his message of farewell, in which the poet wishes Clodia good luck with her lovers, "three hundred of whom she clasps in one embrace, loving none sincerely, but draining them all over and over" (No. 11).

Later Poems. About 57 B. C., perhaps to escape from the scene of so much personal suffering, Catullus went to the Roman province of Bithynia in Asia Minor as a member of the governor's staff. His stay in Bithynia, while disappointing financially, was poetically productive. Visiting his brother's grave near the site of Troy, he composed the famous *Ave atque vale* (*Hail and Farewell!*, No. 101). He also became acquainted with the orgiastic cult of the Asiatic Great Mother and composed *Attis* (No. 63), a long poem in hectic rhythm telling how a Greek youth, carried away by divine frenzy, castrates himself in the goddess' honor and disappears forever into the forest.

Catullus must have returned to Rome in time for the trial, early in 56 B. C., of his friend and rival in love, Marcus Caelius Rufus (doubtless the "Caelius" mentioned in No. 58). Caelius, accused by Clodia of trying to poison her, was defended by Cicero. Cicero's defense speech, still extant, apparently resulted in Caelius' acquittal and the total ruin of Clodia's reputation. It may have been on this occasion that Catullus expressed his approval of Cicero in the poem beginning "Most eloquent of Romulus' grandsons" (No. 49).

Probably during the very last years of Catullus' life he wrote a series of epigrammatic poems attacking Julius Caesar and his political henchmen. At some point, however, Catullus apologized and was invited to dinner by Caesar. Also from this period are the rather stilted translation of Callimachus' lost poem, *Berenice's Hair* (No.

66), and the longest of Catullus' extant poems, *The Marriage of Peleus and Thetis.* This *epyllion,* or small-scale epic is chiefly notable for the extensive description of Theseus' desertion of Ariadne, a scene that forms part of the decoration of Peleus and Thetis' marriage bed. Lastly, there are a number of vehement attacks on miscellaneous individuals. These poems contain much obscenity and scatology; their interest lies not in their content but in the skill with which the poet poured unpromising material into a delicate poetic mold.

Style and Influence. Catullus used various metrical forms, and his extant poems are arranged according to meter. His characteristic meter, however, is the hendecasyllabic, or 11-syllable, line. (An example of this meter in English is Tennyson's "Here I come to the test, a tiny poem/ All composed in the meter of Catullus.") He also was fond of the elegiac couplet and had much influence on such later elegists as Ovid and Propertius.

Catullus' reputation in later antiquity was minor but secure. During the Middle Ages, however, even in the period of courtly love poetry, when Ovid was the "master of the art of loving," Catullus was almost completely ignored. His poetry was preserved in only one late medieval copy, except for which his work would probably have been lost forever.

In the 14th and 15th centuries, the revival of learning saw a revival of interest in Catullus. He became a model for love poets writing both in Renaissance Latin and in the vernacular languages. His epithalamia (which had been the forerunners of others written in Latin) were the models for the marriage songs of the English poets Edmund Spenser, Ben Jonson, and Robert Herrick.

Interest in Catullus intensified in the 19th century, when some critics ranked him among the few greatest lyricists of all time because of his emotional vehemence, sincerity, and lack of restraint. It should be noted, however, that his occasional touches of self-mockery, his concern with form and erudition, and his predilection for the less pleasant aspects of life are far removed from 19th century romantic idealism.

RICHMOND Y. HATHORN
Author of "Tragedy, Myth, and Mystery"

Bibliography

Editions of Catullus' works include *Complete Poems,* tr. by Jack Lindsay (London 1948); *Poems,* selected and ed. by Hugh V. Macnaghten and A. B. Ramsay (London 1948); *Poems* (in English translation), ed. by William A. Aiken (New York 1950); *Works,* ed. by Elmer Truesdell Merrill (Cambridge, Mass., 1951); *Carmina,* ed. by Roger A. B. Mynors (New York 1958); *The Lesbia of Catullus,* arranged and tr. by J. H. A. Tremenheere (New York 1962); *The Complete Poetry,* tr. by Frank O. Copley (Ann Arbor, Mich., 1964); *The Poetry of Catullus,* tr. by C. H. Sisson (New York 1967).

Duckett, Eleanor S., *Catullus in English Poetry* (Northampton, Mass., 1925).
Emperor, John B., *The Catullian Influence in English Lyric Poetry* (Columbia, Mo., 1928).
Fordyce, Christian J., *Catullus, a Commentary* (New York 1961).
Frank, Tenney, *Catullus and Horace* (New York 1928).
Harrington, Karl P., *Catullus and His Influence* (Boston 1923).
Havelock, Eric P., *The Lyric Genius of Catullus* (Toronto 1939).
Quinn, Kenneth, *The Catullan Revolution* (London 1959).
Slater, David A., *The Poetry of Catullus* (Manchester, Eng., 1912).
Wheeler, Arthur L., *Catullus and the Traditions of Ancient Poetry* (Berkeley, Calif., 1934).
Wright, Frederick A., *Three Roman Poets* (New York 1938).

CATULUS, kat′yə-ləs, was the name of a prominent plebian family in Rome. Gaius Lutatius Catulus, consul in 242 B.C., commanded the Roman fleet when operations resumed against Carthage in the First Punic War. In the Battle of the Aegates Islands off the west coast of Sicily in 241, he gained an easy victory over the Carthaginian fleet, bringing the war to an end after 23 years of fighting. He went on to conduct peace negotiations. The resulting treaty, which awarded Sicily to Rome, bore his name.

QUINTUS LUTATIUS CATULUS (c. 150–87 B.C.) was a statesman who possessed the highest intellectual and aesthetic gifts. Both the Romans and the Greeks admired his mastery of their languages and the purity of his style. His writings, now almost entirely lost, included speeches, poetry, and memoirs. He earned a widespread reputation as a philosopher and became the center of his own philosophic and literary circle. Together with this broad range of abilities, however, there was some pettiness in his character.

Catulus held the consulship in 102. In the next year he and Marius, Rome's leading general, defeated the Germans at Vercellae in Cisalpine Gaul, saving Rome from invasion. On his return, Catulus claimed the lion's share of the credit for the victory, and as a result his relations with Marius became embittered. Catulus, whose instincts were conservative and aristocratic, then moved closer to Sulla politically. In 87, when Marius controlled Rome, Catulus suffered prosecution. The outcome was foredoomed, and he committed suicide. The anti-Marian tradition in Roman source material derives largely from the memoirs of men like Catulus and Sulla.

QUINTUS LUTATIUS CATULUS, son of Quintus Lutatius, inherited the conservatism of his father. A supporter of Sulla, he was consul in 78 B.C. and crushed the insurrection of Lepidus after Sulla's death in that year. Catulus continued to be a bulwark of the oligarchy and led the opposition to Pompey's military commands in 67 and 66. He became censor in 65, but he was defeated by Caesar in the election for the office of pontifex maximus in 63. He inherited neither the military nor the intellectual talents of his father, but his voice was a sober and steady influence in the Senate until his death about 60 B.C.

ERICH S. GRUEN
University of California at Berkeley

CATV. See COMMUNITY ANTENNA TELEVISION.

CAUCA RIVER, kou′kä, a stream in western Colombia. It rises in the central range of the Andes, near Popayán, and flows 600 miles (965 km) north into the Magdalena River. Its upper course, between the central and western Andes, cuts through a fertile valley known as the Valle del Cauca. North of Cartage the river breaks through the mountains into the Caribbean plain.

The chief crop of the densely populated Valle del Cauca is sugarcane. Other important products are cacao, tobacco, and livestock. Coffee is grown on the slopes of the Andes. The Cauca Valley Corporation, formed in the 1950's and modeled on the Tennessee Valley Authority, has done much to improve agricultural techniques, reclaim land, provide electricity, and stimulate industrial growth in the region. The city of Cali is the industrial center of the Valle del Cauca and the third-largest city in Colombia.

CAUCASIAN LANGUAGES, kô-kā′zhən, a family of languages spoken in the region of the Caucasus Mountains, which form a natural boundary between European Russia and Asia Minor. Although these languages are spoken by small groups of neighboring people, they are, in many instances, mutually unintelligible. Most of the languages of the Caucasian family have remained practically unknown outside their own territory, except Georgian, the most important of the languages, which had its own rich literature as early as the 4th and 5th centuries.

Structurally, the Caucasian language family (also known as *Alarodian* or *Japhetic*) belongs to the agglutinative group of languages. In agglutinative languages, root words are modified by juxtaposition only, that is, the verb or noun is not changed internally (as in inflected languages), but is altered by the incorporation of a prefix, infix (a small word within the main word), or suffix. (English agglutinated words include "*re*form," "mother-*in*-law," and "care*less*.")

The Caucasian family of languages is divided into four groups: (1) the Western, or Abkhaz-Adigeh, group, which consists of Abkhazian (more than 70,000 speakers), Abazinian (more than 20,000 speakers), Adigeh (about 80,000 speakers), and Kabardinian-Circassian (about 225,000 speakers); (2) the Eastern or Chechenian-Ingush group, which consists of Chechenian (about 420,000 speakers, and Ingush (over 100,000 speakers); (3) the Dagestan group, which consists of Awarian (about 260,000 speakers), Dargwa (about 150,000 speakers), Lezginian (about 200,000 speakers), Tabassaran (about 34,000 speakers), and Lakian (about 60,000 speakers); and (4) the Southwestern, or Kartvelian, group, which consists of Georgian (about 2,610,000 speakers) and several Georgian dialects including Kartlian, Mingrelian, Laz, and Svanian.

Until relatively recently, many of these peoples speaking Caucasian languages employed a modified Arabic or Latin alphabet. Today, however, with the exception of the Georgians, who use a special 33-letter alphabet, most of them use the Cyrillic-Russian alphabet with certain modifications, such as the addition of special letters to represent sounds that do not exist in Russian. The present Abkhazian Cyrillic alphabet contains 58 letters; the Abazinian, 73; the Adigeh, 66; the Kabardinian-Circassian, 59; the Chechenian, 49; the Ingush, 46; the Awarian, 51; the Dargwa, 46; the Lezginian, 50; the Tabassaran, 56; and the Lakian, 55.

It has been discovered that various important ancient languages have certain affinities with the Caucasian language family. Among the ancient peoples who apparently spoke languages belonging to the Caucasian family were the Elamites, the inhabitants of the region to the north of the Persian Gulf and to the east of the Lower Tigris, corresponding roughly with the modern Persian province of Khuzistan; the Khatti, predecessors of the Indo-European Hittites of ancient Asia Minor; the Lycians and the Carians, non-Hellenic peoples who lived in western Asia Minor during the middle centuries of the first millennium B.C.; and, perhaps, the Sumerians, the probable inventors of cuneiform writing, the earliest systematic script.

See also CYRILLIC ALPHABET; LANGUAGES OF THE WORLD.

DAVID DIRINGER; *Author of "The Alphabet"*

CAUCASOID, kô′kə-soid, one of the major racial groups of mankind found in Europe, the Americas, North Africa, the Middle East, and India. "Caucasoid" or "Caucasian" is often equated with "white," but this is inaccurate because the group includes many populations of dark complexion. The term was coined by Johann Friedrich Blumenbach in the 18th century because the skull he took as typical for the group was that of the Georgian women from the Caucasus. Blumenbach thought the type may have originated in the Caucasus, but in fact no one knows.

Skin color among Caucasoids varies from pale, reddish-white to dark brown. Head hair varies from silky straight to curly. It is almost never woolly, rarely frizzly, and the individual hairs are seldom as coarse or as sparsely distributed as in Mongoloids. In males, the hair on the face and over the rest of the body is usually well developed. All forms of head shape occur, but the general tendency is to broadheadedness (brachycephaly). The nose tends to be comparatively narrow and projecting. The cheekbones are generally not prominent, and the lips tend to vary from thin to moderately developed. The face tends to be straight (orthognathic), and the forehead is comparatively high.

REPRESENTATIVE CAUCASOID POPULATIONS

Basic Mediterranean: Best seen among the Portuguese, Spaniards, and some English and Welsh; in North Africa among the Hamitic-speaking peoples; in Arabia; and among the Berbers of Morocco.

Atlanto-Mediterranean: Principal element in the population of North Africa; strongly represented in Iraq, Israel, parts of Arabia, and the eastern Balkans, and to some extent in Portugal, Spain, and the British Isles.

Irano-Afghan Mediterranean: The principal element in the populations of Iran, Afghanistan, the Turkoman country, found also in parts of India, Arabia, and North Africa.

Nordic: The characteristic type of Scandinavia, found with varying frequencies in Iceland, Frisian Islands, British Isles, Belgium, the Netherlands, and the north central European plain, which is bounded by Russia on the east, and Poland and Northern Germany on the west.

Alpine: The populations concentrated along a mountainous range extending from France along the Alps, through the Balkans and into the mountains of Asia Minor, and northwest into Russia and Siberia. The type is found sporadically throughout Europe.

Dinaric: Sometimes called *Adriatic* or *Illyrian.* The type is found from eastern Switzerland through the Austrian Tyrol, Yugoslavia, and Albania.

Armenoid: Found in Asia Minor to the east and southeast of the Black Sea.

Hamitic: Essentially Basic Mediterraneans, ranging over the greater part of North and East Africa. They comprise the Northern Hamites; the Libyans, or Mediterranean Berbers of Cyrenaica, Tripolitania, Tunisia, and Algeria; the Atlantic Berbers of Morocco such as the Kabyles; the West Saharan Berbers, or Tuaregs; the Tibu of East Sahara; the Fula or Fulani of Nigeria; and the extinct Guanche of the Canary Islands. The Eastern Hamites comprise the ancient and modern Egyptians, now much mixed with Arabic elements, and the Nubians, Beja, Galla, Somali, Danakil, and most Ethiopians.

East Baltic: A type found in Germany, Poland, the Baltic States, and Finland.

Lapps: A type found in Northern Scandinavia, in the highlands of Sweden, the tundra of northern Finland, the Norwegian coastal provinces of Troms and Finmark, and a great part of the Russian Kola Peninsula.

Indo-Dravidians: Distributed widely throughout India and Ceylon.

Polynesian: Pacific populations living within an area bounded by Hawaii in the North, the Fiji Islands in the Southwest, and to New Zealand and Easter Island in the East.

ASHLEY MONTAGU, *Author of*
"Introduction to Physical Anthropology"

Further Reading: Kroeber, A. L., *Anthropology* (New York 1948); Montagu, Ashley, *Introduction to Physical Anthropology,* 3d ed. (Springfield, Ill., 1960).

CAUCASUS, kô′kə-səs, one of the world's great mountain systems, located in the USSR. It occupies the isthmus between the Black Sea in the west and the Caspian Sea in the east. The Caucasus (Russian *Kavkaz*) is considered by some geographers to be a natural boundary between Europe and Asia. The highest peak is the Elbrus, in the central part of the system, with an elevation of 18,481 feet (5,633 meters). Covering a territory of 170,000 square miles (440,000 sq km) including its piedmont, the Caucasus is a region of great natural diversity.

Divisions and Structure—Greater Caucasus. The main axis of the mountain system, the Greater Caucasus, extends about 700 miles (1,100 km) northwest-southeast from the Taman Peninsula, between the Black Sea and the Sea of Azov, to the Apsheron Peninsula on the Caspian Sea. The northern piedmont is an extensive region of lowlands and plateaus extending from the Greater Caucasus north to the Kuma-Manych river depression. This depression also runs northwest-southeast, parallel to the main mountain axis, between the lower reaches of the Don River and the Caspian Sea. The western part of the northern piedmont consists of the alluvial plains of the Kuban River and lesser streams draining into the Sea of Azov. The central part of the piedmont is occupied by the Stavropol upland, a limestone and sandstone plateau rising to 2,730 feet (832 meters). To the southeast of the plateau, in the Beshtau region, is a cluster of laccoliths (dome-shaped hills) rising to 4,593 feet (1,400 meters). Some of the Soviet Union's best-known mineral springs (Pyatigorsk, Yessentuki, and Kislovodsk) are in these hills. The eastern part of the piedmont consists of a semiarid plain between the Terek and Kuma rivers and, farther south, the parallel Terek and Sundzha hill ranges, rising to 3,038 feet (926 meters). The anticlinal structure of these ranges is associated with the oil deposits of the Grozny area.

The mountain system of the Caucasus resulted from the Alpine mountain-making movement that took place in Europe in the Tertiary period. The northern slopes of the Greater Caucasus, in contrast to the steeper southern slopes, rise gently from the piedmont through a series of sloping plains and foothills to the main mountain ranges. The central ranges present a core of Precambrian and Paleozoic crystalline rocks amid Jurassic schists. The highest peaks are situated in the so-called watershed range and in the parallel lateral range, just to the north. In addition to the Elbrus, at the western end of the cluster of high peaks, are the Ushba (15,403 feet; 4,695 meters), the Dykh-Tau (17,070 feet; 5,203 meters), the Shkhara (16,594 feet; 5,058 meters), and, on the east, the Kazbek (16,558 feet; 5,047 meters).

The crustal upheaval that gave rise to the Caucasus was accompanied by volcanic activity. Both the Elbrus and the Kazbek are thought to be dead volcanoes. Mud volcanoes are still active at the Taman and the Apsheron ends of the Greater Caucasus ranges. Limestone plateaus and foothills often display karst forms.

Lesser Caucasus. South of the central ranges there is a longitudinal depression made up of a series of river valleys that separate the Greater Caucasus from a mountain region sometimes called the Lesser Caucasus. The longitudinal depression begins in the northwest on the Black Sea in the Colchis swamps. The swamps are associated with the Greek legend of the Golden Fleece. Across

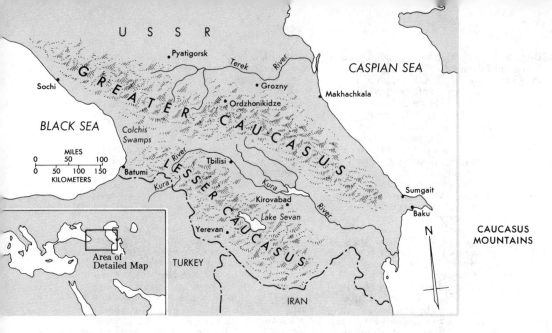

CAUCASUS
MOUNTAINS

the Surami Pass (3,113 feet; 949 meters), the depression continues southeast along the valley of the Kura River, which opens onto the broad Kura-Aras plain on the Caspian Sea.

Unlike the Greater Caucasus, the Lesser Caucasus does not have a well-defined northwest-southeast alignment. It consists of a system of short fold mountains and the Armenian volcanic uplands that link with the neighboring mountainous regions of Turkey and Iran. The highest point within the Soviet part of the Lesser Caucasus is Mt. Aragats, an extinct volcano rising to 13,418 feet (4,090 meters). Mt. Ararat, a similar cone that is 16,916 feet (5,156 meters) high, is nearby, across the Soviet border in Turkey. A prominent physical feature in the Armenian uplands is Lake Sevan, the largest lake of the Soviet Caucasus region.

Climate. Because the Caucasus covers such a large area, there are a wide variety of climates and vegetation in the region. There are dramatic contrasts in precipitation: as much as 100 inches (254 cm) of precipitation a year on the slopes facing the Black Sea in the west as contrasted with only 12 inches (30 cm) in the semiarid lowlands bordering on the Caspian Sea in the east. In addition the Greater Caucasus range functions as a major climatic barrier against polar air masses moving southward across the Russian plain, especially in winter. In the shelter of the mountains, a humid subtropical climate is found in the Colchis lowland on the Black Sea and, to a lesser extent, in the Lenkoran area on the Caspian Sea.

On the northern slopes of the Greater Caucasus, there is a piedmont steppe, followed by a forest steppe and forest zone, followed by alpine meadows and, finally, by the zone of permanent snow and ice. This glacier zone of the Caucasus, coinciding with the area of high peaks between the Elbrus and the Kazbek, contains 1,400 glaciers covering a total area of 772 square miles (2,000 sq km). One of the largest glaciers, the Dykh-Su, descending from the Dykh-Tau and Shkhara peaks, is more than 9 miles (15 km) long.

Animal and Plant Life. The highly diversified fauna and flora of the Caucasus include a number of endemic forms. The forest zone of the northern slopes is inhabited by the Caucasian red deer and the Transylvanian wild boar. The alpine zone is inhabited by the tur, a Caucasian wild goat.

The Caucasian rhododendron, an evergreen shrub that covers large areas on the southern slopes near the Black Sea, is believed to be a relict of ancient Tertiary vegetation.

Mineral and Power Resources. The Caucasus is a region of rich mineral resources. The petroleum deposits of Baku (on the Apsheron Peninsula), Grozny, and Maikop were the principal sources of Soviet oil until they were eclipsed by the development of more extensive fields between the Volga River and the Urals in the 1950's. Gas deposits around Stavropol are among the Soviet Union's main sources of natural gas, supplying Moscow and Leningrad by pipelines. Tyrny-Auz, on the slopes of the Elbrus, is a producer of tungsten and molybdenum.

South of the Greater Caucasus are the rich manganese mines of Chiatura, among the world's largest, and the important copper and molybdenum mines of Armenia. Aluminum-bearing minerals, such as alunite and nephelite syenite, are exploited as a source of aluminum.

Industrial development in the Caucasus has also been furthered by the existence of a hydroelectric power potential in its mountain streams, especially on the wetter and more precipitous southern slopes. The principal power projects are on the Kura River (at Mingechaur), the Rioni and Inguri rivers, and the Razdan River, which flows out of Lake Sevan in Armenia.

Agriculture. The climatic contrasts between the northern slopes of the Caucasus exposed to the Russian winter and the protected southern slopes are reflected in agriculture. The Kuban plain, in the northern piedmont, is one of the Soviet Union's main winter wheat regions. With increasing aridity toward the east, crop growing makes way for livestock raising, mainly sheep. South of the Greater Caucasus, tea and citrus fruits (mainly lemons) are grown in the humid subtropical Colchis area, and cotton is grown on irrigated land of the Kura-Aras plain to the east. Caucasian wines and brandies are considered among the best in the Soviet Union.

Transportation. In addition to being a climatic

barrier, the Greater Caucasus is also a barrier to transportation. The only motor highway crossing the mountains is the Georgian Military Highway, 129 miles (207 km) long, between Ordzhonikidze in the northern piedmont and Tbilisi, in the south. An old invasion route using natural gorges, the road has been open to wheeled traffic since 1799. It crosses the central range in the Krestovy Pereval (Pass of the Cross) at 7,835 feet (2,388 meters).

Two other land routes to the west, the Military Ossetian Highway and the Military Sukhumi Highway, are not usable by motor traffic across the central range. Railroads between European Russia and Transcaucasia skirt the Greater Caucasus; an older line runs around the eastern end of the system along the Caspian Sea; a newer railroad (completed during World War II) extends along the Black Sea coast.

Ethnic and Language Divisions. Throughout history the Caucasus has served as a refuge for persecuted peoples who fled into the mountain valleys to seek protection against invaders. Wave upon wave of settlement has produced a complex ethnic pattern that is reflected in the ethnically oriented political subdivisions of the Soviet Union.

The northern slopes and piedmont of the Caucasus fall within the Russian federated republic, reflecting the predominance of the Russians, who moved into this area starting in the 18th century. The area of Russian settlement encloses several non-Russian minorities on the northern slopes of the Caucasus. Among these minorities are the Circassian peoples of the North Caucasian language group, who number 300,000. Some live in the Adyge Autonomous Oblast. Others make up the Cherkess component of the Karachai-Cherkess Autonomous Oblast and the Kabardian component of the Kabardian-Balkar Autonomous Soviet Socialist Republic. The related Karachai and Balkar peoples speak a Turkic language. The Ossetian people, who are of Iranian language stock, live on both slopes of the Caucasus, in the North Ossetian ASSR of the Russian republic and in the South Ossetian Autonomous Oblast of Georgia. The related Chechen and Ingush peoples, who also speak a North Caucasian language, are joined in the Chechen-Ingush ASSR.

The easternmost of the minority areas on the northern slopes of the Caucasus is Dagestan, a conglomerate of several ethnic groups, notably the Turkic-speaking Kumyks and several North Caucasian language groups (Avars, Darghins, and Lezghians).

The area south of the Greater Caucasus is divided more simply among three constituent republics of the Soviet Union: Georgia, in the west; Turkic-speaking Azerbaidzhan, in the east; and Armenia. In Georgia, ethnic subdivisions have been set apart for the Ossetians in the South Ossetian Autonomous Oblast; for the Abkhaz, a North Caucasian language group related to the Circassians, and for the Adzhars, who are Muslim Georgians. As a result of overlapping ethnic areas, Armenia separates an Azerbaidzhani exclave, the Nakhichevan ASSR, from the rest of Azerbaidzhan. An Armenian exclave, in turn, the Nagorno-Karabakh Autonomous Oblast, is included in the Azerbaidzhan SSR.

See also ARMENIAN SOVIET SOCIALIST REPUBLIC; AZERBAIDZHAN SOVIET SOCIALIST REPUBLIC; GEORGIAN SOVIET SOCIALIST REPUBLIC.

THEODORE SHABAD
Editor of "Soviet Geography"

CAUCHON, kō-shôn′, **Pierre** (c. 1371–1442), French bishop, who conducted the trial of Joan of Arc. He was born near Reims and became rector of the University of Paris in 1403. At the court of Charles VI, Cauchon joined the Burgundian party. He was banished from Paris in 1414 but returned in 1418 with the rebellious Duke of Burgundy, John the Fearless. Named bishop of Beauvais in 1420, Cauchon helped the Duke of Bedford extend English control over most of northern France.

When Joan of Arc was captured in Compiègne in 1430, Cauchon selected and headed the panel of judges that tried her at Rouen. Prejudice and Anglo-Burgundian political interests dictated her conviction on grounds of heresy and witchcraft. Cauchon's direction of the trial earned him posterity's opprobrium.

He was named bishop of Lisieux in 1432 and attended the Council of Basel in 1435. He spent his last years defending England's position in France. He died at Rouen on Dec. 18, 1442.

EDMUND H. DICKERMAN
University of Connecticut

CAUCHY, kō-shē′, **Augustin Louis** (1789–1857), French mathematician and physicist, who was the founder of the theory of functions of a complex variable. Born at Paris on Aug. 21, 1789, Cauchy received his early education from his father, a devout Catholic and a government official before the French Revolution. He then concentrated on science, graduating from the École Polytechnique in 1807, studying at the École des Ponts et Chaussées for three years, and serving as an engineer for another three years. After 1813 he devoted himself to teaching and research in mathematics and science. By 1815 he had already established his reputation by proving a famous conjecture of Fermat on figurate numbers, a proof which had eluded mathematicians for more than a century. In 1816 he unashamedly accepted the chair of geometry left vacant by the politically inspired ouster of Gaspard Monge from the Académie des Sciences.

From 1816 to 1830, Cauchy published numerous papers and books in mathematics. Three of these—*Cours d'analyse* (1821), *Résumé des leçons sur le calcul infinitésimal* (1823), and *Leçons sur le calcul différentiel* (1829)—reformed and established the calculus on a rigorous foundation. The limit concept and the definition of continuous functions introduced by Cauchy may still be found in modern texts on the calculus. In *Sur l'application du calcul de résidus* (1827) he founded the theory of functions of a complex variable. This memoir contains Cauchy's discoveries on integrals with complex number limits and also the well-known "Cauchy integral theorem," which is the core of complex variable analysis.

In 1830, Cauchy followed King Charles X into exile after the July Revolution, and he was called to tutor Charles' son in 1833. He returned to France in 1838, but still believing in the legitimate monarchy, he refused to take the oath of loyalty to the government. Nevertheless, through special dispensation, he was named to the chair of astronomy at the Sorbonne, a post he held until his death at Sceaux on May 23, 1857. During his career Cauchy wrote over 700 memoirs on such topics as the wave theory of light, hydrodynamics, planetary motions, theory of numbers, and differential equations.

CARL B. BOYER, *Brooklyn College*

CAUCUS, kô-kəs, a general term for a policy-making meeting of members of a political party. The term has various shades of meaning, depending on the nature of the business transacted at such a meeting. Undertones of disrepute are associated with the word because of the early American practice of holding clandestine caucuses to select candidates and determine issues without public discussion.

The congressional caucus for nominating U. S. presidential candidates in the first quarter of the 19th century was later discredited and gave way to national party conventions. Nominating caucuses in state legislatures gave way to conventions and later to direct primary elections. Legislative caucuses on the national and state levels in the United States remain useful tools for determining party strategy, but their decisions are not necessarily binding on legislators. In Britain the term "caucus" usually refers to a system of party organization.

The Changing Meaning of Caucus. The earliest documented use of the term caucus in the United States was in a history of the American Revolution published by William Gordon in Boston in 1788. Gordon wrote that "more than fifty years ago, Mr. Samuel Adams' father, and twenty others, one or two from the north end of the town, where all the ship business is carried on, used to meet, make a caucus, and lay their plan for introducing certain persons into places of trust and power." Gordon noted that the terms "caucus and caucusing" were in common usage in Boston before the 1780's, "but my repeated applications to different gentlemen have not furnished me with a satisfactory account of [their] origin." No satisfactory explanation has ever been provided. By various authorities the origin of the word has been traced, inconclusively, to *caulkers*, engaged in ship building; to the medieval Latin *caucus*, after the Greek *kaukos*, a drinking vessel; and to the Algonkian Indian *caucausu*, elder, counselor.

The most famous description of the early Boston caucuses, though not an eyewitness account, was recorded by John Adams in his diary in February 1763. Adams reported that "the Caucas Clubb meets at certain Times in the Garret of Tom Daws, the Adjutant of the Boston Regiment. He has a large House, and he has a moveable Partition in his Garrett, which he takes down and the whole Clubb meets in one Room. There they smoke tobacco till you cannot see from one End of the Garrett to the other. There they drink Phlip [i.e., flip] I suppose, and there they choose a Moderator, who puts Questions to the Vote regularly, and Selectmen, Assessors, Collectors, Wardens, Fire Wards, and Representatives are regularly chosen before they are chosen in the Town."

Whatever the etymology of the word "caucus," the definition that Adams provided is the meaning that came to be accepted in the United States; its connotation of smoke-filled rooms where public decisions were made in advance by an influential group of leaders survived. In 1810 a North Carolina Federalist congressman defined a caucus as "a private night meeting of a party, in which particular measures are discussed and determined on for reasons which do not admit of being disclosed in public."

In the late 1800's the term "caucus" was used in New England and some Western states to mean a primary election, but the use of the word in connection with informal meetings of party leaders continued in the designation "parlor caucuses." Increasingly in American political life "caucus" is used to mean a political conference designed to determine party strategy. Thus, state delegations to national presidential nominating conventions hold caucuses to decide floor strategy and votes; Democratic governors assemble periodically in a caucus; or Republicans in the U. S. House of Representatives meet in the Republican conference.

British Usage. In Britain, "caucus" came into use in the 1870's as a term, largely of reproach, applied to a closely disciplined system of party organization of one's political opponents. Borrowed from the United States, the designation was meant to imply a "political machine" rather than a conference. The term was first applied by Prime Minister Benjamin Disraeli (Earl of Beaconsfield) to the Liberal Association organization initiated by Joseph Chamberlain in Birmingham, from which the plan of organization spread throughout the country. The term passed quickly into general usage in reference to the new Liberal machinery of representative party associations.

THE CAUCUS IN U. S. HISTORY

Although in the United States the terms "conference" and "caucus" are increasingly being used interchangeably, in certain earlier periods caucuses were more sharply defined, had clear and continuing rules of operations, and wielded extensive powers in the nation's political life. This was especially true on the level of national politics with respect to congressional caucuses.

There were two main periods when congressional caucuses were particularly influential elements in the political structure of national politics: the first was from 1800 to 1824, when the congressional nominating caucus controlled the choice of presidential candidates; the second was from 1910 to 1920, when the legislative caucus exercised its most powerful influence on congressional actions.

The Congressional Nominating Caucus. The formation of national political parties in the United States in the 1790's required that procedures be devised for nominating presidential and vice presidential candidates. As early as 1796 the Jeffersonian Republicans reportedly held a caucus of Republican members of Congress to decide on a vice presidential nominee to be run on the ticket with Thomas Jefferson, whom consensus had made their first choice. Although no agreement was reached at this meeting, it initiated a precedent, and in 1800 the Republican congressmen met in a nominating caucus and agreed on a party slate of Jefferson and Aaron Burr. Federalist members of Congress in 1800 also held a caucus and agreed to support John Adams and Charles C. Pinckney.

The congressional nominating caucus was continued by the Jeffersonian Republicans from 1800 to 1824, and all the candidates for president and vice president that the Republicans nominated until 1824 were successful. Thus, the Republican congressional caucus, which selected the nominees of the dominant party, came to exercise a powerful influence in American politics. After the Federalist defeat in 1800 and the resultant decline in Federalist membership in Congress, that party abandoned the congressional nominating caucus.

Initially, both Republicans and Federalists had attempted to keep their nominating caucuses secret. However, in 1804 reports of the Republican caucus proceedings were published in the newspapers, and members of Congress wrote freely about the practice. That year, for the first time, the nominating caucus appointed a committee to promote the election of the party's nominees; this was the earliest version of a national party committee in the United States. By 1808 the congressional caucus had become so decisive that political maneuvering and competition for its nomination was one of the most keenly contested aspects of the presidential campaign.

The powerful role of the congressional nominating caucus provoked vigorous protests against the practice. One observer complained that "an intriguing character has nothing therefore to perform, but to secure the good will of a majority of the members of Congress, and his success is inevitable." Protests against the nominating caucus generally came from those who disapproved of the caucus choice, and many contemporaries defended the practice on the grounds that congressmen were a representative group well qualified to make presidential nominations. Nevertheless, criticism of the system continued.

Decline of the Nominating Caucus.
The caucus system broke down in the presidential election of 1824. Supporters of presidential aspirants who had little chance to win the caucus nomination carried their campaign directly to the people. They aroused widespread popular resentment against the institution that was increasingly denounced as "King Caucus." For the first time, in 1824, the nominee of the Republican congressional caucus, William H. Crawford, was not elected. But because no national system of concentrating support behind a particular candidate had replaced the caucus, no candidate in 1824 received a majority of electoral votes; the election was decided in the House of Representatives, which chose John Quincy Adams.

The breakdown of the nominating caucus marked the end of the first American party system, in which the role of the members of Congress, especially through the caucus, had provided the principal national party machinery. The vacuum created by the collapse of the caucus was not immediately filled. However, in 1832, following the lead of the Anti-Masonic party, the Jacksonian Democrats and the National Republicans held national nominating conventions, and a new institution in American politics was established.

Early State Nominating Caucuses.
During the Federalist-Jeffersonian period, state caucuses paralleled the congressional nominating caucus. In many states party members of state legislatures met in caucuses to nominate candidates for state offices, representatives to Congress, and presidential electors. These caucuses were also frequently open to party leaders from throughout the state. In some instances such party caucuses established statewide systems of party committees or other party machinery. In short, the party caucus was a key device in determining state party nominations and in the creation of formal party machinery. State caucuses, at times, also attempted to influence the nomination of the congressional caucus by announcing support for particular candidates.

On the state level the transition from caucus nomination to a convention system occurred earlier than on the national level. New Jersey initiated a state nominating convention in 1800, and a growing trend from caucus to convention on the state level strengthened the opposition to the national nominating caucus. However, after the introduction of the national convention, parties in some states continued to use the state party caucus to choose delegates to national conventions.

The Congressional Legislative Caucus.
Although the nominating caucus was the most significant and influential use of the caucus device in Congress during the early national period, party members in Congress occasionally held party caucuses to consider legislative issues and nominees for officers chosen by Congress. These were frequently informal gatherings and had no rules of procedure. The development of the committee system from 1816 onward largely superseded the legislative caucus, and the standing committee system became the established method of conducting congressional business.

Woodrow Wilson, writing in 1885, saw no controllable party organization within Congress, where party discipline was slack and indefinite in dealing with legislation: "The only bond of cohesion is the caucus, which occasionally whips a party together for cooperative action against the time for casting its vote upon some critical question." However, the occasional caucus, which Wilson saw as weak in the late 1800's, emerged strong in the early 1900's, and for the period between 1910 and 1920 was the most significant device employed for the consideration of legislative policy in Congress.

The reemergence of "King Caucus" in the 20th century followed the successful revolt in Congress against the power of the Republican speaker of the House, Joseph G. Cannon, in 1910. The caucus had previously been used primarily to nominate party candidates for the speakership and other House offices. But depriving the speaker of much of his power opened the way for the revival of powerful party caucuses.

After capturing the House in the congressional elections of 1910, the Democrats used the secret caucus to establish strong party control over Congress. Under this system the caucus established direct control over legislative action. Every major measure was discussed and differences settled in a party caucus. Rules adopted by the Democratic caucus in 1909 provided that a caucus decision adopted by two thirds of the party membership in the House was binding on all Democrats with the following exceptions: questions involving interpretation of the Constitution, contrary pledges made to a member's constituents before election, or contrary instructions received on nomination.

Modern Functions.
After World War I, the party caucus system gradually disintegrated. Party caucuses in Congress are held primarily on the eve of the meeting of each new Congress for nominating candidates for the elective offices of the House. Nomination by the majority party caucus is tantamount to election. Party caucuses rarely are held to determine the party stand on legislative issues, and they are not binding on members.

The Democratic caucus rarely meets to decide legislative matters, but the Republican conference of the House of Representatives has met regularly since the early 1950's to discuss policy and exchange ideas. The adoption by Republicans of the name conference rather than caucus is indicative of the declining use of the older term. The Republican policy committee is an adjunct of the Republican House conference, having been established by the conference.

STATE LEGISLATIVE CAUCUSES

Legislative caucuses operate with varying degrees of power and effectiveness on the state level in the United States. Because the existence and operation of state caucuses is closely related to two-party politics, they never remain static. An authoritative survey of American state legislatures, made by the American Political Science Association's committee on American legislatures in 1954, showed that majority party caucuses in state legislatures functioned in 25 senates and 24 houses, existed but had little significance in 8 senates and 9 houses, and were nonexistent in 15 senates and 14 houses. Minority party caucuses were found in 25 states, but were reported to be of importance in only 15 states. Majority and minority caucuses are most commonly found in states with competitive 2-party systems. Party caucuses generally do not exist in 1-party states, although there may be factional caucuses within the majority party.

The states that had strong majority party caucuses during the 1960's were Colorado, Connecticut, Delaware, Idaho, Indiana, Massachusetts, Nevada, New Jersey, New York, Pennsylvania, Rhode Island, Washington, and Wyoming. In these 13 states, majority party caucuses met frequently, sometimes daily, and played a major role in the legislative process. In some instances caucuses serve as places where debates on bills are held by the majority party, differences are settled, and the party members decide the fate of legislative proposals. In New Jersey, where the majority caucus in both House and Senate meet daily, the caucus controls the legislative program and makes all crucial legislative decisions. In the states in which a majority party caucus functions but does not attempt to exert any significant control over the legislative program, the caucus usually meets once a year, primarily for organizational purposes.

The evidence that the legislative caucus exerts, or attempts to exert, a strong influence on the legislative process in only 13 states suggests the decline of the legislative caucus on the state level in the United States, as it already has declined on the national level. On the local level, party caucuses may be found in such a variety of circumstances and places as to make generalizations about them impossible.

See also CONVENTION, POLITICAL; DEMOCRATIC PARTY; ELECTIONS.

NOBLE E. CUNNINGHAM, JR.
University of Missouri

Bibliography

Butterfield, Lyman H., ed., *The Adams Papers: Diary and Autobiography of John Adams*, vol. 1, pp. 238–240 (Cambridge, Mass., 1961), on the early Boston caucuses.
Cunningham, Noble E., Jr., *The Jeffersonian Republicans in Power* (Chapel Hill, N. C., 1963).
Dallinger, Frederick W., *Nomination for Elective Office in the United States* (New York 1897).
Galloway, George B., *History of the House of Representatives* (New York 1961).
Zeller, Belle, ed., *American State Legislatures: Report of the Committee on American Legislatures: American Political Science Association* (New York 1954).

CAUDATA, kô-dā′tə, one of three orders of living Amphibia, the other two being the Salientia (such as frogs and toads) and the Gymnophiona (rare, wormlike animals of the tropics). The Caudata (by some authorities called the Urodela) include the tailed Amphibia (salamanders and newts). Various species are found in North America, Europe, and Asia.

Most members of the order have a superficial resemblance to lizards, but unlike lizards they have a moist skin and lack scales. Being amphibians, they cannot live in a dry environment. Some species are found in moist earth under logs and stones, while others live in streams and lakes.

The eggs of Caudata are usually larger than those of frogs and toads. Development takes place in moist earth or water. The larval stages have external gills, but in most species the gills are lost at the time of metamorphosis into the adult stage. A few species, such as the axolotl (*Siredon*) of Mexico and the western United States and the mud puppy (*Necturus*) of the eastern United States, are aquatic and possess gills throughout their adult life. The red spotted newt of eastern America (*Diemictylus*) passes its larval life in water. At the time of metamorphosis it changes into the red eft and spends several years on land, where it undergoes a second change in body structure and coloration, after which it returns to water to spend the rest of its life. The largest member of the order is the giant salamander of Japan, which reaches a length of 5 feet (1.6 meters) or more. Most species, however, are between 4 and 10 inches (10 and 25 cm) long.

Except for some Asiatic and Mexican species, which are used for food, the animals of this order are of little or no economic importance. They are, however, of considerable interest to zoologists because they possess many primitive vertebrate structures and because they provide both adults and embryos for experimental purposes.

JOHN A. MOORE, *Columbia University*

Further Reading: Bishop, Sherman C., *Handbook of Salamanders* (Ithaca, N. Y., 1947); Conant, Roger, *A Field Guide to Reptiles and Amphibians* (Boston 1958); Noble, Gladwyn, K., *Biology of the Amphibia* (New York 1931); Stebbins, Robert C., *Amphibians and Reptiles of Western North America* (New York 1954).

CAUDILLO, kou-the′lyō, the Spanish word for "chief," usually refers to a leader of irregular armed forces or a political boss with a military following loyal to him personally. In Spain, *caudillo* has meant the leader of a political party with military backing—for example, Gen. Francisco Franco; it resembles the term *Il Duce* used for Benito Mussolini in Italy. In Spanish America, and to a lesser extent in Brazil—where *caudilho* is the Portuguese equivalent—the term has acquired a wider range of meanings, but the central concept remains that of a strong political boss whose following is highly personalist and frequently militaristic.

The early years of independence in Spanish America have been called the Age of the Caudillos because the new nations often were dominated by powerful local leaders whose armies made and unmade governments. Many of these early caudillos emerged as leaders in the wars for independence and were loyal to the ideals of the independence movement. The caudillos of the succeeding generation tended to be less idealistic and used power for personal gain or to reward unscrupulous followers.

The economic prosperity of the late 1800's produced a third variety—typified by Antonio Guzmán Blanco of Venezuela, José Balta of Peru, and Porfirio Díaz of Mexico, whose power rested on control of the professional armed forces. These caudillos ruled through a system of thinly disguised force and manipulated elections, although they often carried out reform programs.

Populist politics of the 1900's produced still another type, such as José María Velasco Ibarra of Ecuador and, in some respects, Juan Perón of Argentina, who relied on armed force but derived much of their power from demagogic appeals to dissatisfied elements of the population.

HAROLD E. DAVIS, *American University*

CAUDWELL, kôd'wel, **Christopher** (1907–1937), pen name of Christopher St. John Sprigg, British author. He founded the journal *Aircraft Engineering* and wrote several books on aviation, including *The Airship* (1931) and *Great Flights* (1935). He was also the author of eight popular detective novels, such as *The Perfect Alibi* (1934), centering on the fictional detective Charles Venable. In *Illusion and Reality: A Study of the Sources of Poetry* (1937), Caudwell analyzed, from a Marxist viewpoint, the role of the bourgeois artist in relation to the proletariat, maintaining that since language is a social product, the study of society is important to an understanding of poetry. Among his other works are *Studies in a Dying Culture* (1938) and *Poems* (1939). After the outbreak of the Spanish Civil War he joined the British battalion of the International Brigade in Spain, where he died on March 5, 1937.

CAUGHNAWAGA, kog-nə-wog'ə, is an Indian town in southern Quebec, Canada, on Lake St. Louis in the St. Lawrence River about 10 miles (16 km) south of Montreal. The town was founded by Jesuit missionaries in 1667 as a refuge for Christian Iroquois Indians who might be molested by non-Christian tribes. The Indians engage in farming and make snowshoes and lacrosse sticks. In 1890 the rule by tribal chief was changed to municipal government by mayor and council. Population: (1961) 2,240.

CAULAINCOURT, kō-laN-kōōr', **Armand Augustin Louis de** (1773–1827), French general and diplomat. He was born in Caulaincourt on Dec. 9, 1773, the son of a general. Though he was of noble birth, the Marquis de Caulaincourt surrendered his commission in the army in the French Revolution, and served as a common soldier. Rising rapidly through the ranks, he won the attention of Napoleon Bonaparte, who sent him on a diplomatic mission to Russia in 1801.

From 1807 to 1811, Caulaincourt (who was made a duke in 1808) headed the French embassy in St. Petersburg. Strongly opposing Napoleon's planned invasion of Russia, he asked to be recalled in 1811. Yet during the retreat after the French defeat, Caulaincourt loyally accompanied Napoleon on the dangerous journey back to France. He handled the important negotiations at the Congress of Châtillon, and during the Hundred Days he returned as Napoleon's foreign minister. After the Bourbon restoration in 1815 he was saved from exile by Czar Alexander I. He died in Paris on Feb. 19, 1827.

RICHARD M. BRACE, *Oakland University*

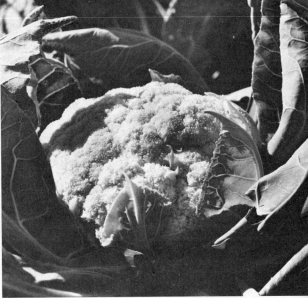

GRANT HEILMAN

Cauliflower

CAULIFLOWER, kô'li-flou-ər, is a low, thick, fleshy-stemmed food plant with a dense white or sometimes purple flowering head. It is popular in both Europe and North America, where it is eaten either raw or boiled. Primitive forms of cauliflower were evidently cultivated in the Middle East in pre-Christian times. Selections adapted to the cooler climate of northern Europe were developed during the Middle Ages. These have yielded the modern varieties.

Cauliflower is grown as a summer annual. For an early crop, seedlings are started under glass and transplanted outdoors after danger of frost has passed. Harvest is generally 60 to 100 days after planting. A late crop can be seeded directly outdoors in June or July for autumn harvest. Cauliflower grows best during mildly cool weather in fertile, well-watered soil. It is cut before the flower buds open. Unlike broccoli, once the head is cut, regeneration from side shoots does not take place.

Cauliflower is more difficult to raise and more troublesome to tend than other members of the cabbage species, such as common cabbage, broccoli, and Brussels sprout. The head becomes stunted or discolored either by near-freezing or by unduly hot weather. Stunted heads that slowly form in hot weather may have a bitter flavor. Varieties have been developed that are reasonably heat-tolerant. If the growing head is left exposed, the top part tends to bronze or turn purple. To avoid the color change, the heads are usually blanched by tying one or more of the large upper leaves over the developing head. Also, to prevent damage to the heads by the cabbage worm, it is sometimes necessary to apply an insecticide that does not contaminate the cauliflower head.

Cauliflower, *Brassica oleracea botrytis* L., is a member of the mustard family (Cruciferae). Snowball, in several forms, is a popular variety. There are also purple-headed cauliflowers that do not require blanching.

ROBERT W. SCHERY
Lawn Institute, Marysville, Ohio

CAULONIA, kou-lô′nyä, is a town in southern Italy, in Reggio di Calabria province, 37 miles (60 km) southwest of Catanzaro. It lies 5 miles (8 km) from the Ionian Sea, on a hill, at an elevation of about 1,000 feet (305 meters). The surrounding agricultural region produces citrus fruits, olives, and grapes. About 9 miles (14 km) northeast of the modern town are the ruins of ancient Caulonia.

Ancient Caulonia was founded in the 7th century B. C. by Greek colonists and became a flourishing town of Magna Graecia, though it was always a dependency of Croton, a powerful colony farther up the coast. Caulonia was destroyed in 389 B. C. by Dionysius I of Syracuse during his conquest of southern Italy, and the inhabitants moved to Syracuse. Caulonia was later rebuilt, but it never regained its former prosperity. Population: (1961) 3,891.

CAUSALITY, kô-zal′ə-tē, in philosophy, involves the effect of one event, process, or entity upon another. It is the necessary connection of events through cause and effect.

The Early Tradition. Philosophical inquiry into causality is a crucial part of the history of Western thought. Plato and Aristotle introduced a distinctively philosophical feature into the early discussion of "why things are as they are" by wondering about the nature of causality itself. This is a different question from "What causes X?" which is usually a scientific inquiry. The philosophical question about causality is "What is, or what is meant by, a cause?"

Aristotle gave cause (q. v.) a far broader definition than it is generally given today. He distinguished between four types of causes: material cause, the matter from which an entity is formed; formal cause, the pattern or essence imposed upon the matter; efficient cause, the force or agent producing the thing; and final cause, the purpose or end for which it was produced.

Medieval philosophers adopted Aristotle's notion of four causes and regarded an effect as flowing from the nature or essence of its cause. Three theses about the nature of causality were held to be indisputable: nothing can come from nothing; nothing can give what it does not have; and a cause must have at least as much perfection (or being) as it gives to its effects.

The metaphysical views of René Descartes (1596–1650) concerning causality closely resembled the medieval view. However, Descartes felt that the physical (nonmental) world was strictly determined in a mechanical fashion—that it was virtually a mechanical system "operated" by the First Cause, God. Sir Isaac Newton (1642–1727) had a similar view, observing that the regular causal connections observed in nature were the working out of requirements issuing from God.

Gottfried Wilhelm von Leibniz (1646–1716) believed that there were an infinite number of created individual substances (monads), which did not interact causally with each other, but acted in accordance with a preestablished harmony, set up by the Prime Monad, God, between all finite things. Benedict de Spinoza (1632–1677) also believed that all things stemmed from one cause, of which everything in the world was a manifestation and expression.

Skeptical Tradition. The tradition within which David Hume was to raise "skeptical" questions about the nature of causality can be viewed as starting with John Locke (1632–1704). Locke equated cause with "active power," the capacity to initiate motion or to think. He observed that it was not possible to get a clear notion of active power from experience of physical objects (ideas of sensation)—in other words, that cause could not be clearly experienced as operating in nature—and that the notion of cause must come from the operations of the understanding (ideas of reflection).

George Berkeley (1685–1753) noted that Locke's thesis entailed the view that men could not know there were causal agents in the physical world, since the only experience they had of causality was of the operations of their own minds thinking and willing. The regularity with which some perceptions succeeded others in men's minds was the pattern set by God in nature, the "divine language" of the Author of Nature speaking to man.

David Hume (1711–1776) claimed that there were no clear perceptions of active power, or cause, either physical or mental. What he found when he analyzed cause and effect situations were successions of perceptions constantly conjoined. Experience led him to expect that these perceptions would always be so joined. But the relationship between the perceptions was not one of logical necessity. In logic one could deduce B from A: if A; then, necessarily, B. But one could not by pure logic deduce from the concept of a cause what any of its effects would be. A newly created Adam, Hume remarked, could not possibly have logically deduced from his first experience of water that if he held his head in it long enough he would drown.

The link between a cause and its effect, Hume continued, must be supplied by experience. At its best, however, experience reveals what happens to be the case in the world, not what necessarily is the case. Experience merely teaches that certain events constantly occur in sequence, and one seems dependent on the other. Necessity cannot be experienced, and there is, therefore, no certainty whatsoever that a supposed effect B must be produced by a supposed cause A—that when the wind blows, the leaves must move. Causality is merely the expectation, derived from past experience, that this will be the case.

Thus primitive man and sophisticated man are basically akin in the naïveté of their causal beliefs. Primitive man, with his limited observational resources, may very well believe that night is the cause of day, since he observes that day regularly follows night. Sophisticated man still thinks in terms of cause and effect; but, capable of a greater range of observation, he considers both day and night effects, and other phenomena, such as the rotation of the earth, as causes. The most sophisticated scientist bases his causal beliefs on even more extended observation, but the principle of causality used in his analyses—that one event necessarily follows or precedes another because, in experience, they have always been conjoined—is the same process of reasoning used by the primitive man.

Immanuel Kant (1724–1804) viewed Hume's analysis as damaging to belief in the universality and necessity of basic scientific truths. He resolved the dilemma between the credibility of scientific laws and the questionable nature of cause by designating cause as a necessary, unavoidable, a priori category of the mind. One of the conditions enabling man to think about or judge objects of experience, Kant contended, is that he categorizes some of them as causes, some as effects. Furthermore, it would be impossible to imagine an empirical counterinstance to the claim that every event has a cause. The causal connections in nature were necessarily imposed on it by human judgment, and men could not think of nature without imposing that structure on it.

The discussion of causality continues today. Emphasis is directed to questions of whether such diverse entities as human nature and microunits of matter are causally describable, and whether scientific investigation should proceed on the assumption that things are definitely determined by their "causes" or that it is merely probable that one thing flows from another.

JOHN P. DREHER, *Lawrence University*

Further Reading: Hume, David, *A Treatise of Human Nature*, ed. by Lewis A. Selby-Bigge (New York 1941); Kant, Immanuel, *Critique of Pure Reason*, tr. by Norman Kemp Smith (New York 1965); Lerner, David, ed., *Cause and Effect* (New York 1965).

CAUSE, in the philosophy of Aristotle, is a special generic term referring to the four principles through which one arrives at knowledge of any entity. In distinguishing between the material, formal, efficient, and final causes of a substance, Aristotle attempted to take into account everything necessary to produce it.

Background. The theories of the pre-Socratic philosophers postulated the elements from which all things were formed: earth, air, fire, and water. This view corresponds somewhat to Aristotle's concept of a material cause; however, it was too limited to account for an ordered cosmos and its intelligibility.

Plato's concept of the causes of things in part resembles Aristotle's formal cause. In his treatment of the problem, however, Plato made the mistake of treating the essences of entities (the Platonic Forms or Ideas) as though they were substances in their own right.

The Four Causes. Aristotle found unacceptable Plato's view that the essence of entities resides in a separate realm of Forms. He attempted to describe the existence of all things in terms of the things themselves, without postulating a special metaphysical realm. According to Aristotelian analysis, all material things (sensible substances) are composed of matter and form. Matter, or the *material cause,* is the "stuff" of which a thing is made—brick is the material cause of a house. It is important to note here that "matter" is a relative term for Aristotle; by it he means the materials of a thing relative to the structure that holds them together. Thus, the elements are the material cause of tissues; tissues are the material cause of organs; and organs are the material cause of the living body.

The form of an entity, either its "shape" or its structural plan, is its *formal cause.* The blueprints, or the actual structure of a house, are the formal causes of the house. The formal and material causes are generally inseparable for Aristotle—each requires the other.

Although each individual entity is a composite of matter and form, these two categories do not sufficiently account for why things are what they are. There must be an agent or force that imposes the form on the matter. That something is Aristotle's *efficient cause,* the *vis a tergo,* or "push from behind." The builder of a house (or the builder in the act of building) is the efficient cause of the house. This cause most closely corresponds to the ordinary meaning of "cause" today.

Just as the "push from behind" pushes the substance to change in a specific direction, that direction is predetermined by the *vis a fronte,* or "pull from the front": the entelechy, or *final cause.* This cause is the end, purpose, or goal at which the process of change aims and terminates. The final cause of a house might be "being comfortable to live in."

Present-Day Implications. The Aristotelian account of causation is not generally used in modern analysis of cause, which is interested in clarifying statements concerning cause in ordinary and scientific discourse. However, the subject of final causes (teleological explanation) is still vigorously discussed, particularly in the life and social sciences. See also CAUSALITY.

JOHN P. DREHER
Lawrence University

Further Reading: Bréhier, Émile, *History of Philosophy: The Hellenic Age* (Chicago 1963); McKeon, Richard, *Introduction to Aristotle* (New York 1947); Ross, William D., *Aristotle,* rev. ed. (New York 1955).

CAUSTIC, kôs'tik, an agent that causes local tissue destruction when it is applied to the skin. Caustics are used to remove certain skin lesions such as warts and some moles. They are sometimes also used to treat fungal infections and some types of open wounds. For example, silver nitrate can "burn off" warts and granulation tissue, while phenol may be used on dog or snake bites. Both silver nitrate and phenol are bactericidal; that is, they kill bacteria. In addition, phenol is an anesthetic.

Many inorganic alkalis and acids are caustics. The most commonly used are caustic soda (sodium hydroxide), caustic potash (potassium hydroxide), sulfuric acid, and nitric acid. There are also many organic caustic agents, among which are phenol, glacial acetic acid, and trichloroacetic acid.

Some caustics are also escharotics; that is, they not only destroy tissue but also cause the subsequent formation of a scab (eschar) which is ultimately replaced by a scar. Nitric acid, for example, produces a yellow scab over the affected area. Alkalis such as caustic soda, however, are not escharotics since they redissolve most of the precipitated material from which the scab might otherwise form.

Caustics should be stored out of the reach of young children, because if swallowed they may damage the upper digestive tract sufficiently to cause fatal hemorrhaging.

CAUSTIC POTASH. See POTASSIUM—*Potassium Hydroxide.*

CAUSTIC SODA. See SODIUM—*Sodium Hydroxide.*

CAUTERETS, kō-tre', is a resort village in France. It is in the department of the Hautes-Pyrénées, near the Spanish border, 20 miles (32 km) southwest of Lourdes. In the summer people come to take the waters of its sulfurous springs for throat and respiratory ailments, rheumatism, and skin diseases. In the winter Cauterets is a resort for winter sports and mountain climbing. The valley in which the village is located is covered with chestnut forests. There are fine views of the surrounding mountains. Cauterets won fame in the 16th century, when Margaret of Navarre, sister of Francis I of France, held her literary court and wrote much of her *Heptaméron* there. Population: (1975) 1,065.

Steve Cauthen at age 18 in 1978 won racing's triple crown—the Kentucky Derby, Preakness, and Belmont.

CAUTHEN, koth'ən, **Steve** (1960–   ), American jockey, who was the first to ride mounts earning $6 million in one year. He was born in Covington, Ky., on May 1, 1960. His father was a blacksmith and his mother a horse trainer. By the time he was two he was riding ponies and by 12 had begun to learn the jockey's trade. He received his jockey's license at 16 and soon after won his first race.

Cauthen rose to prominence in 1977, winning 488 races for purses worth more than $6 million. Three times in 1976–1978 he brought home six winners in a nine-race program. In 1978 he rode Affirmed to triple-crown laurels with victories in the Kentucky Derby, Preakness, and Belmont stakes. In 1979, Cauthen went to England as a contract rider and in races there and in Europe brought his career wins to the 1,000 mark.

CAUVERY RIVER, kô'və-rē, a river of southern India that rises in the Brahmagiri Hills, southwest of Mercara in the state of Mysore. It is also known as the *Kaveri River*. It is about 475 miles (760 km) long and cannot be navigated by large vessels. The river flows southeast to Sivasamudram island near the Mysore-Madras border, where it divides into twin arms that descend to the Carnatic plain in abrupt falls of 320 feet (97 meters) called the Cauvery Falls. Traversing the Carnatic, the river empties into the Bay of Bengal through a wide, fertile delta approximately 4,000 square miles (10,360 sq km) in area. A hydroelectric complex at the falls serves the Kolar gold mines and the cities of Mysore and Bangalore. The river, often called the "Ganges of the south," is considered sacred by the Hindus, especially at Sivasamudram and Seringapatam. The Cauvery has an extensive irrigation system, and one canal, the Grand Ancient, dates from the 2d century.
H. J. STEWARD, *University of Toronto*

CAVAFY, kä-vä'fē, **Constantine P.** (1863–1933), Greek poet, who, little known during his lifetime, has come to be regarded as a major figure in 20th century literature. He was born in Alexandria, Egypt, on April 17, 1863. His family name is also spelled Kavafis or Kabaphes. He wrote in Greek, although he lived most of his life in Alexandria and made only two brief trips to Greece. In Lawrence Durrell's *Alexandria Quartet*, Cavafy is the unnamed but omnipresent poet. He died in Alexandria on April 29, 1933.

Cavafy published little during his lifetime. A volume of 14 poems appeared in 1904 and was reissued with an additional seven poems in 1909. The subject matter of all his poems is Greek, early Alexandrian, and Byzantine. With precisely balanced irony, many of his poems superimpose on the 20th century the events and people of the ancient world, especially of the Homeric age and the Alexandria of the Ptolemys.

Cavafy's work was introduced to English readers in E. M. Forster's *Pharos and Pharillon* (1923). Some of Cavafy's poetry was translated into English by John Mavrogordato in 1952, and *The Complete Poems of Cavafy*, translated by Rae Dalven, with an introduction by W. H. Auden, was published in 1960.
HORACE V. GREGORY, *Coauthor of "History of American Poetry 1900–1940"*

CAVAIGNAC, kä-ve-nyàk', **Louis Eugène** (1802–1857), French republican general, who crushed the June 1848 insurrection. He was born in Paris on Oct. 15, 1802, into a family of republican sentiment. His father, Jean Baptiste Cavaignac, as a member of the National Convention, had voted for the death of Louis XVI. Although handicapped by this background and by his own discreet but unquestioned republicanism, Eugène Cavaignac was successful in making his way as a professional army officer.

Trained as an engineer at the École Polytechnique, he was commissioned a second lieutenant in 1826 and fought his first campaign in Greece two years later. Cavaignac was the first in his regiment to hail Louis Philippe following the Revolution of 1830. His republican convictions reemerged rapidly, causing him minor career difficulties. In 1832 he was sent to Algeria, where, except for 1838–1839, he was stationed until 1848. He distinguished himself as a combat officer during the long campaigns of the Algerian conquest. By 1848, Cavaignac had risen to the rank of brigadier general and had been given command of the province of Oran.

Cavaignac and the Revolution of 1848. The Second Republic, lacking generals of undoubted loyalty to republican ideals, showered him with honors. Promoted to divisional general following the February Revolution in 1848, he was first made governor general of Algeria and then offered the war ministry in the republican provisional government, which he declined. In April 1848, General Cavaignac was elected to the National Assembly by two departments, one of them Paris, where the ardent republicanism of his brother, Godefroy, who had died in 1845, was well remembered. Following an abortive invasion of the National Assembly by a mob on May 15, Cavaignac accepted a new offer of the war ministry. Five weeks later the social tensions in Paris culminated in the working-class uprising of June 23–26, which, in a way, was a repetition of the February Revolution. To deal with the outbreak, the National Assembly gave Cavaignac dictatorial powers on June 24.

Cavaignac's role in putting down the insurrection remains controversial. It is clear that, ignoring political and humane considerations, he concentrated on the technical military problems and on restoring the army's honor, supposedly lost in the surrender of February. He therefore first allowed the insurrection to develop and then crushed it with massed columns backed by artillery. However successful from the military and morale-building viewpoints, Cavaignac's strategy made the June Days the bloodiest revolution in French history prior to the Paris Commune of 1871.

In the months that followed, Cavaignac maintained a state of siege, closing obstreperous newspapers, taming and harassing political clubs, and deporting some 3,500 insurgents without benefit of a public trial. Yet with respect to the legislature, Cavaignac used his emergency powers with discretion, working through the National Assembly and respecting both its liberty and its increasingly conservative predilections. Though the June insurrection unquestionably ended the dynamic and socially explosive phase of the revolution, recent research has stressed not only Cavaignac's sincere republicanism but also his attempts to steer modest reforms through a reluctant legislature. Yet his was scarcely a government to capture the imagination; in the contest for president of the republic in December 1848, Cavaignac garnered only about 1,450,000 votes as against nearly 6 million for his major opponent Louis Napoléon.

Throughout the Second Republic, Cavaignac continued to sit as a moderate republican representative. In semiretirement after Louis Napoléon's coup d'etat of December 1851, he died on his estate at Ourne, on Oct. 28, 1857. His son Jacques Godefroy Cavaignac was to become a prominent figure in the Third Republic.

PETER AMANN
State University of New York at Binghamton

CAVAILLON, kȧ-vȧ-yôn', is a town in southeastern France, in Vaucluse department, 14 miles (22 km) southeast of Avignon. The town is situated near the Durance River in an irrigated district that produces excellent fruits and early vegetables and is especially noted for melons.

The ancient Cabellio, Cavaillon contains the remains of a Roman arch dating from the 1st century A. D. The town was the seat of a bishopric from the 5th to 18th century. The Church of St.-Véran, formerly the cathedral, is a Romanesque structure dating from the 12th century, with later additions. The 18th century synagogue is notable for the wooden decoration in the interior. Population: (1962) 12,062.

CAVALCANTI, kä-väl-kän'tē, **Guido** (1250/1255–1300), Florentine poet and philosopher. He was a friend of Dante, who in the *Divine Comedy* characterized Cavalcanti's lyric verse as "our tongue's glory." Cavalcanti's family belonged to the Guelph faction, but he was married by arrangement to Beatrice, the daughter of Farinata degli Uberti, the leader of the Ghibellines. With the outbreak of fighting between the "Black" Guelph's and the "Whites" in 1300, he was exiled to Sarzana as a leader of the Whites. He contracted malaria there and was allowed to return to Florence, where he died in August 1300.

About 50 of Cavalcanti's poems survive; they include sonnets, ballades, and *canzoni*. His love poems, addressed usually to a lady whom he calls "Primavera" ("Springtime"), are generally poignant and somber. Their style is the *dolce stil novo* praised by Dante, on whom Cavalcanti exercised considerable influence.

CAVALCASELLE, kä-väl-kä-sel'lä, **Giovanni Battista** (1820–1897), Italian art historian, whose method, based on encyclopedic knowledge of painting and conscientious attention to detail, has profoundly influenced modern art criticism. He was born in Legnago on Jan. 22, 1820. As a youth he studied at the Academia in Venice. After serving in Garibaldi's forces in the revolution of 1848, he went to Paris and then to London, where he collaborated with Joseph Archer Crowe on *Notices of the Lives and Works of the Early Flemish Painters* (1857); *A New History of Painting in Italy* (5 vols., 1864–1871), their masterwork; *Titian* (1877); and *Raphael* (1882–1885).

Cavalcaselle returned to Italy in 1859. In 1863 he was named inspector of fine arts for the ministry of education in Rome and held this office until 1895. He died in Rome on Oct. 31, 1897.

CAVALIER, kav-ə-lēr', was a term applied derisively to the king's partisans, the Royalists, in the English Civil War. Originally derived from the Latin *caballarius*, meaning "horseman," it acquired the more specific meaning of a knight or mounted soldier, and at a later date any dashing soldier or person. In the United States the term was applied to Southern gentlemen planters or gentlemen soldiers, especially of the Civil War period. See also CIVIL WAR, ENGLISH.

CAVALIER POETS, kav'ə-lēr', the group of lyric poets among the followers of Charles I and his exiled son, from the first actual warfare with the Commonwealth until the Restoration. The term is also applied more broadly to other poets of the time, such as Robert Herrick and John Donne, who wrote in the same style, but it is properly used only for those loyalists who were preeminently court gentlemen and fighters for the king. Generally the Cavalier poets were a highly sophisticated and urbane group, whose love lyrics and songs were charmingly frank, graceful, and witty.

Characteristics. One of the lesser known but extremely patriotic Cavalier poets was James Graham, 1st Marquess of Montrose, several of whose works reflect his fierce devotion to the royalist cause. In general, however, light gracefulness was a mark of the Cavaliers, as in Montrose's most famous lyric, which begins "My dear and only love." In singleness and loftiness of devotion, in the actual sacrifice of his life for the cause, and in the natural, incidental place of literature in his career, Montrose is perhaps the ideal Cavalier poet.

Richard Lovelace, author of the best-known Cavalier lyric, "Tell me not, sweet, I am unkind," and of *To Althea, from Prison,* illustrates in his life the tragedy that often underlay this graceful verse. He impoverished himself to give his fortune to the king. On returning from the wars abroad, he was imprisoned, and his "Lucasta," Lucy Sacheverell, believing him dead, married someone else. Lovelace died worn out by suffering and poverty.

A similarly typical fate was that of Sir John Suckling, who spent his fortune for the king, became an exile, and died abroad. Although he wrote several plays, his fame is founded on his Cavalier poems. In his life and in his writing he is neither so noble nor so pathetic as Montrose and Lovelace; he is a roisterer at heart, as can clearly be seen even in the exquisite *A Ballad Upon a Wedding*. But he is master of the reckless tone that finally characterized the school, the tone that had been caught so finely by George Wither in his "Shall I, wasting in despair?" Suckling, in such lines as "Out upon it, I have loved three whole days together," turns the bravado note into a pretty compliment; in his best lyric, the song from *Aglaura*, "Why so pale and wan, fond lover?" he carries it to its logical conclusion of recklessness.

In addition to Herrick and Donne, among the many poets who wrote in the Cavalier manner, though not under strict Cavalier conditions, Edmund Waller should be mentioned for his two perfect lyrics *On a Girdle* and *Go, Lovely Rose*. But far more important is Thomas Carew, one of the most gifted minor poets of the time. In Carew's verse the Cavalier compliment is most elaborate and most noble, as in the incomparable *To Celia*, beginning "Ask me no more," and in the epitaphs on Lady Mary Villiers, where he is indeed more the scholar than the Cavalier. "Give me more love or more disdain" and "He that loves a rosy cheek" are other examples of his felicity. Carew had in full measure the rhetorical grace of the true Cavalier, the secret of splendid openings and cadences—an unacademic art that began not in literary imitation but in courtly conversation—the fine compliment paid to beauty that need not be abashed by praise.

Development of Cavalier Poetry. In literary tradition the Cavalier poets took their descent from Sir Thomas Wyatt; Henry Howard, Earl of Surrey; Sir Philip Sidney; Sir Walter Raleigh; and those other "makers" of the Tudor and Elizabethan courts, who naturalized the Provençal lyric and its love system on English soil. This influence had been strong in Chaucer's time, but only with the later group did lyric poetry become well established as an accomplishment among the gentlemen of the English court and take on a genuinely native manner.

The early Elizabethan court poets, even in their narrowest imitations of the French sonneteers, had some of the largeness of the age in their manner and spoke consciously to an audience. At the end of Elizabeth's reign, Renaissance scholarship and culture had spread through the nation, and what remained the peculiar inheritance of the courtly poet was undergoing a refinement. In John Lyly's novel *Euphues* (1580), for example, the story is taken into the drawing room, where the feminine influence is dominant, imposing the exquisiteness that is the end of all courtly love. See COURTLY LOVE.

By a similar transition, the courtly poets, letting go the larger subjects and the public manner, made the quality of their verse the very qualities of graceful society—the personal compliment, the brief sallies that general conversation demands, the quick turns in which grace and wit count, the method of versification that restrains beneath an even manner all feeling that is too personal or too deep. The presence of the ladies is felt, but not the presence of one woman alone; the lover must find ways to woo his lady under the very eyes of her teasing comrades.

This development of the court poetry was occasioned, no doubt, by the natural growth of culture and the perfecting of manners in English society as a whole. Some impression, however, was made upon the court by the change from Elizabeth's manlike rule to the gentle influence of Charles' refined queen. The influence of Henrietta Maria, however, was not altogether admirable. Refining though it was, it took the direction of effeminacy and, in the *précieuse* fashion that it fostered, of insincere pedantry. William Habington in his *Castara* (1634) illustrates the overrefinement of theme to which the graceful court verse at this moment might have been doomed.

However, the personality of Charles, which enlisted the loyalty of the courtiers, his tragic end, and the exile of his family and his followers, gave back to the courtly verse the vitality it was losing and, in addition, some new characteristics that distinguished it as Cavalier poetry. Loyalty to Charles and to his son, unlike loyalty to Elizabeth, was more personal than patriotic and served to revive some of the most ideal aspects of chivalry. Charles became not so much the sovereign of a country as the head of an order of knights, and his exiled son became their leader under all skies. The sufferings that were the cost of the Cavaliers' loyalty, their sense of a lost cause, and their long tradition of proud breeding that would bear all with outward lightness combined to form the pathos and the grace of the best of their poetry.

JOHN ERSKINE, *Author of*
"The Kinds of Poetry and Other Essays"

Further Reading: Skelton, Robin, *Cavalier Poets* (New York 1962).

CAVALIERI, kä-vä-lyâ′rē, **Emilio de′** (1550?–1602), Italian composer. He was born in Rome and became an organist. From 1584 he lived in Florence. Cavalieri's melodic compositions, differing from the contrapuntal style of his time, stressed monody, which he used to reveal the artistic force of the text. He also was one of the first composers to use figured bass accompaniment and *stile recitatavo*.

Cavalieri's masterwork, *La rappresentazione di anima e di corpo* (1600), is regarded by some musicologists as the first oratorio. His other stage works include *Il satiro* (1590), *La disperazione di Fileno* (1590), and *Il giuoco della cieca* (1595). Cavalieri died in Rome on March 11, 1602.

CAVALIERI, kä-vä-lyâ′rē, **Francesco Bonaventura,** (1598–1647), Italian mathematician, physicist, and astronomer. He is noted for having developed the method of indivisibles used in calculating the areas and volumes of geometric figures.

Cavalieri was born in Milan and entered the Order of St. Jerome (Hieronymites) at the age of 15. After studying at the University of Pisa, he occupied the chair of astronomy at the University of Bologna from 1629 until his death there on Dec. 3, 1647.

Cavalieri was one of the most influential mathematicians of his time and was responsible for the introduction of logarithms into Italy. He is credited with deriving the familiar formulas of physics for finding the focal length of a lens from the lens curvature. He is best known, however, for his development of the method of indivisibles, which was a first step in the direction of the integral calculus. This method is based on the assumption that a line is made up of an infinite number of points, a surface is made up of an infinite number of lines, and a volume is made up of an infinite number of surfaces—much as a deck of cards is made up of the individual cards. The value of this method is illustrated by the well-known "theorem of Cavalieri" in solid geometry, which states that if two solids have equal altitudes and if all plane sections parallel to their bases and at equal distance from their bases have equal areas, then the two solids have the same volume.

CARL B. BOYER
Brooklyn College

CAVALLA, kə-val′ə, is a name applied to several marine fishes but most often to members of the genus *Scomberomorus,* such as the king mackerel or kingfish (*Scomberomorus cavalla*), the Spanish mackerel (S. *maculatus*), and the cero (S. *regalis*). These long, tunalike fishes have widely forked, powerful tails and small finlets following their dorsal and anal fins. Their bodies are generally silvery; some species may be spotted. Streamlined, speedy swimmers, they range in large schools throughout the world, mainly in tropical or temperate areas.

The name "cavalla" occasionally is also given to crevalle or jack members of the family Carangidae, especially to *Caranx hippos.* Jacks have a variety of body forms, but they usually have keeled, bony shields preceding their tails, and they live near reefs.

Both the mackerels and the jacks are popular food fishes that reach over 100 pounds (45 kg). They are of sport and commercial importance, especially in the southeastern United States.

EDWIN S. IVERSEN
University of Miami

CAVALLERIA RUSTICANA, kä-väl-lä-rē′ä rōōs-tē-kä′nä, is a one-act opera by Pietro Mascagni, first performed on May 17, 1890, at the Costanzi in Rome. The work was an instant triumph without parallel in operatic history, and in a very short time is was performed in every operatic center, major and minor.

The libretto by Ottaviano Targioni-Tozzetti is based on the play *Cavalleria Rusticana* (1884; *Rustic Chivalry*) by Giovanni Verga. Verga, who fashioned his play from a short story he had written in 1880, was a leading exponent of naturalism in Italian literature. Mascagni's opera introduced naturalism (*verismo*) to the operatic stage and initiated a whole school of opera dealing with the violent passions of humble people.

The action takes place in a Sicilian village on Easter morning. Before the curtain rises, Turridu (tenor) sings a love song in praise of Lola (mezzo-soprano), the wife of Alfio (baritone), a carter. Santuzza (soprano) has been seduced and abandoned by Turridu, but she hopes to win him back. When she learns that Turridu is pursuing Lola, Santuzza reveals her anguish to Turridu's mother, Lucia (contralto). Encountering Turridu on his way to church, Santuzza upbraids him for his faithlessness and begs him to return to her, but he insists on following Lola into the church. Because Santuzza has been excommunicated, she may not enter the church. Santuzza reveals to Alfio that Turridu is pursuing Lola, thereby arousing the husband's violent jealousy. After the playing of the famous *Intermezzo,* during which the stage is empty, Turridu comes out of church and invites the villagers to drink with him. Alfio refuses and challenges Turridu to a duel. Turridu accepts, then bids his mother an emotional farewell and goes to meet Alfio. Soon a voice is heard crying that Alfio has killed Turridu, and Santuzza faints.

Although Mascagni's music lacks subtlety, the melodies are impetuous and intense. Many passages of the score have won wide popularity, especially the *Intermezzo.* The best-known vocal numbers are Turridu's arias *Siciliana, Brindisi,* and *Addio alla mamma,* and Santuzza's aria *Voi lo sapete* and her agitated duets with Turridu and Alfio.

WILLIAM ASHBROOK
Author of "Donizetti"

CAVALLI, kä-väl′lē, **Pietro Francesco** (1602–1676), Italian composer, who wrote the first popular Venetian operas. He also composed sacred choral works and chamber cantatas. Cavalli was born P. F. Caletti-Bruni in Crema, Lombardy, on Feb. 14, 1602. (In 1640 he adopted the name of his noble patron, Federico Cavalli.) He studied with Monteverdi in Venice, where at St. Mark's he became second organist (1640), first organist (1665), and chapel master (1668).

Cavalli composed 42 operas, beginning in 1639. His first success in Italy was *La Didone* (1642); his first throughout Europe was *Egisto* (1646). His most popular opera, *Giasone* (1649), continued to be performed long after his death, in Venice, on Jan. 14, 1676.

Whereas in Monteverdi's early operas the musical forms were determined by the text, Cavalli's works, along with Luigi Rossi's, introduced the *bel canto* aria (short flowing melodies in dance rhythm), using abstract musical procedures that had little relationship to the text. Cavalli's harmonies are less striking than Monteverdi's and his style less sensitive, but his operas have drive and a dramatic use of vocal and instrumental forces.

ADRIENNE FRIED, *Choral Director*
Dalcroze School of Music, New York City

CAVALLINI, kä-väl-lē′nē, **Pietro** (1250?–?1330), Italian painter and mosaicist, who, with Giotto and Cimabue, was one of the major innovators of the naturalism that began to replace Byzantine stylization in the late 13th and early 14th century.

Much of Cavallini's work has been lost through deterioration or destruction. However, Ghiberti in his *Commentaries,* written a century after Cavallini's death, gives a careful account of Cavallini's work, and provides an indication of his stature. Cavallini did most of his major works in Rome, where his patron was Bertholdo Stefaneschi. He is first mentioned in connection with the decoration in 1273 of Santa Maria Maggiore, and in 1291 he signed the apse mosaic in Santa Maria in Trastevere. Cavallini's fresco cycle in San Paolo fuori le Mura (1282–1297) is known only through copies. He also worked in San Giorgio in Velabro, sometime after 1295. In 1308 he was in Naples, and it was perhaps the king of Naples who sent him to Assisi to decorate the Church of San Francesco. Cavallini completed the large *Ascension* on the entrance wall of the upper church, and his influence dominates the frescoes of the upper section of the nave walls.

MARTICA SAWIN
Parsons School of Design, New York City

A CAVALRY CHARGE by Scottish Dragoons at the Battle of Waterloo.

CAVALRY, kav′əl-rē, a term formerly restricted to military forces mounted on horseback, is now often broadened to include mechanized and armored, and sometimes airborne, forces. With the decline of the horse in warfare these have assumed many of the characteristics and missions of the earlier cavalry. The basic characteristics are mobility and shock, which often are decisive in battle. Other than attack, missions include reconnaissance, counterreconnaissance, delaying action, raid, and pursuit.

The term "cavalry," which is derived from the Latin word for horse (*caballus*), came into general use during the 16th century to denote all types of mounted troops. These included dragoons, who rode to battle but usually fought dismounted; light cavalry, or hussars, used primarily for reconnaissance, screening, and liaison missions; and heavy cavalry (sometimes called cuirassiers), used primarily for shock effect. These same distinctions persist in mechanized and armored cavalry. The "armored infantryman," or *Panzergrenadier* (German), for example, is descended from the dragoon, riding to battle in an armored personnel carrier but usually fighting on foot. Of the major armies of the world, only the Russian and the Chinese Communist retain any major quantities of horse cavalry.

Early History. The development of cavalry followed the breeding of horses large and sturdy enough to carry an armed man. By about 772 B. C. lancers and mounted bowmen had begun to appear in the Assyrian army, but the Persians were apparently the first to employ horsemen with bow or javelin as a principal arm. The first use of cavalry in appreciable strength in western Europe seems to have been Leuctra, Greece, in 371 B. C., when Epaminondas used it to secure his flanks. Philip II of Macedon (reigned 359– 336 B. C.) was the first to employ cavalry as an

arm of decision. Fixing the enemy by frontal attack with a powerful infantry phalanx, he would destroy his fore with a cavalry charge against a flank. Inheriting Philip's army and traditions, Alexander the Great (reigned 336–323 B. C.) scored notable successes with cavalry against the Persians and Indians.

Since the fighting in this era devolved mainly on the front rank of compact formations, a few horsemen riding bareback, holding reins and gripping with their knees, might penetrate the first rank or so, only to be pulled from their horses by men in the interior of the phalanx. Since horses were relatively scarce and valuable, only the wealthy nobility could afford them, thus limiting the numbers of cavalry but also early establishing it as an elite arm.

Although Rome was slow to develop efficient cavalry, bitter experience at the hands of Hannibal (particularly at Cannae in 216 B. C.) finally prompted Roman leaders to correct the deficiency. Roman cavalry drove Hannibal's horsemen from the field at Zama, North Africa, in 202 B. C. and helped effect the fall of Carthage.

Saddles, then stirrups, appeared in the first centuries of the Christian era and increased the effectiveness of cavalry. The Goths probably used both in annihilating a Roman army at Adrianople in Asia Minor in 378 A. D.

Cavalry survived for a time, as Roman civilization survived, under the Byzantine Empire. But in the west the rise of the feudal system, wherein warfare was the province of the nobility, produced such a reliance on armor for mount and rider that horsemen ceased to have the mobility expected of cavalry.

Europe was thus virtually defenseless as the Mongols under Genghis Khan in the early 13th century approached with a mounted army whose horsemen roamed far and deep, maneuvering swiftly in widely separated columns and concentrating unexpectedly on the enemy's flank or rear. Only troubles back in Asia spared European civilization from the Golden Horde of mounted Mongols.

The European cavalryman, meanwhile, had become obsessed with his superiority to the point of folly. Lacking maneuverability, he was ripe for defeat by infantry using powerful new weapons, such as the longbow, dramatically unleashed at the Battle of Crécy, France, in 1346, and old weapons such as the pike, which the Swiss phalanx emplaced in the ground at an angle to stop horsemen. These developments sent cavalry into sharp decline.

Middle History. The advent of weapons utilizing gunpowder during the 16th and 17th centuries halted cavalry's decline, both by augmenting cavalry with artillery and by substituting the pistol for the lance. Advancing at a trot in columns several ranks deep, the horsemen would fire by rank at close range, then wheel to the rear to reload.

Gustavus Adolphus of Sweden (reigned 1611–1632) improved on this method by training his cavalry to advance at a gallop, with only the front rank firing, then applying the sword. During this same period, the French introduced a cavalryman who fought dismounted, the dragoon. Frederick the Great of Germany (reigned 1720–1786) further improved the performance of cavalry by ceaseless training and iron discipline.

Napoleon Bonaparte in the early 19th century developed the concept of coordination between a cavalry screen, which covered the advance of his army, and a cavalry reserve. The screen having located the enemy, Napoleon fixed his foe with light cavalry and advance guard, then massed his artillery to blast a hole through which the cavalry reserve poured, slashing the enemy irresistibly and running down escapees. There were notable failures, as at Eylau in 1807, when the cavalry was committed too soon; at Leipzig in 1813, when it was too weak; and at Waterloo in 1815, when rough terrain and an uphill charge muted the effect. But until the campaign in Russia in 1812 eliminated many of Napoleon's veteran troops and horses, French cavalry in close coordination with artillery and infantry was the scourge of Europe.

The agricultural and financial exhaustion of Europe after the Napoleonic Wars, followed by development of artillery and small arms effective at long range, again produced a sharp decline in the effectiveness of cavalry. The Charge of the Light Brigade (1854) at Balaklava in the Crimean War was celebrated more for losses and romance than for achievement.

Americans in the U. S. Civil War and the Indian Wars provided cavalry a final grand employment, yet the use was less in the traditional sense of overwhelming charge than in lesser missions such as reconnaissance, screening, delaying, and raids. Seldom was cavalry effective against the improved weapons of entrenched infantry; thus, in deliberate attack cavalry usually fought dismounted.

Modern History. Cavalry accomplished little either in the Franco-Prussian War (1870–1871) or the Russo-Japanese War (1904–1905), yet European nations at the start of World War I had large bodies of cavalry. It was organized in separate divisions on which the belligerents depended for exploiting a break in the enemy lines,

in the manner of Napoleon, after vastly improved infantry and artillery weapons had blasted a path through the lines.

As it turned out, cavalry was reduced to impotence by the unexpected advantage the new weapons afforded the defense and by the impediments presented by long lines of entrenchments, barbed wire entanglements, and ground churned by bombardment, along with the use of aviation for surveillance. Refusing to fight dismounted, most cavalry was frittered away in small segments. Only in two cases were there decisive cavalry engagements. In Palestine three divisions of British cavalry poured through after infantry and artillery had blasted a gap in the Turkish right, and on the eastern front a single German cavalry division delayed the Russian advance long enough for the Germans to concentrate and win the Battle of Tannenberg.

Of the major combatants in World War I, all but the Germans failed to discern the twilight of cavalry and the ascendancy of tanks. In Britain, France, and the United States, old-time cavalrymen fought to retain cavalry in some form, either augmented by light tanks and armored cars or transported to battle in vans, while relegating the tank to an infantry-support role.

German World War II campaigns against Poland, the Low Countries, and France demonstrated incontestably the end of the horse as a decisive instrument of war, its place assumed by tanks and self-propelled artillery operating in close conjunction with aerial bombardment. Both Russia and the western Allies subsequently used armored divisions much as the Germans had done, and in many cases mechanized cavalry units with light tanks and armored cars. The latter were useful for reconnaissance and for screening the flanks of larger forces.

Of the horse cavalry units operating in Europe at the start of World War II, those of Poland and France were swiftly annihilated. Russian cavalry lost heavily against German armor, but the Russians learned to infiltrate their horsemen through thinly stretched German lines and launch surprise attacks against rear installations. Both the Chinese and Japanese used large bodies of mounted troops, but they seldom were decisive. The United States lost a cavalry regiment of the Philippine Scouts in defense of Bataan. Of two cavalry divisions in the U. S. Army at the start of the war, one was disbanded while the other, the 1st Cavalry Division, left its horses behind to fight in the Pacific as an infantry unit.

In the U. S. Army and most other major armies following World War II, the names, traditions, missions, and internal organization (squadrons and troops) of the old cavalry units passed to armored regiments and divisions and to mechanized reconnaissance units. All have mobility, while armor provides shock and the ability to pursue and destroy. During the war in Vietnam in the 1960's, the United States organized the 1st Cavalry Division (Airmobile), which by means of the helicopter achieved the old cavalry characteristics of quick strikes against enemy flanks and rear. But as the utility and availability of the helicopter increased, regular infantry divisions took on some of the same capabilities, so that true air cavalry, separate and distinct from other arms, was yet to emerge.

CHARLES B. MACDONALD
Deputy Chief Historian
U. S. Department of the Army

CAVAN, kav'ən, 10th Earl of (1865–1946), British field marshal, who commanded the Italian Tenth Army in the final offensive on the Italian front in World War I. He was born Frederic Rudolph Lambart, son of the 9th Earl of Cavan, on Oct. 16, 1865. He graduated from the Royal Military College at Sandhurst and served in the South African War.

In World War I he commanded the 14th Corps and the Guards Division in France before being sent to Italy in 1918 with British reinforcements for the Italian armies. The Tenth Army, made up of Italian and British troops under his command, played a major part in the Battle of Vittorio Veneto (Oct. 24–Nov. 5, 1918) that ended the war in Italy. Cavan was chief of the imperial general staff from 1922 to 1926. He was made a field marshal in 1932. He commanded the troops at the coronation of King George VI in 1937. Cavan died in London on Aug. 28, 1946.

CAVAN, kav'ən, in Ireland, is an inland county stretching along the border with Northern Ireland. It is one of three counties of the province of Ulster that did not become part of Northern Ireland when Ireland was divided in 1920. Cavan is primarily rural. The Erne River flows south through the center of the county, forming many beautiful lakes. The highest point is Cuilcagh (2,188 feet, or 667 meters), a hill in northwest Cavan where the Shannon River rises in what is known as the Shannon Pot. Potatoes and oats are the major crops; cattle and pigs are raised; and bacon is produced in Cavan, the county town. There are gypsum deposits in the county that are mined to make plaster and cement.

Cavan town grew up around a Franciscan friary founded about 1300 by a chieftain of the O'Reillys. Only the friary's belfry tower remains. Several famous members of the O'Reilly family are buried at Cavan. Most of the town was destroyed in 1690 by the English forces of William III. There is a modern Roman Catholic cathedral, built in 1942. Near Bailieborough in the southeastern part of the county is the ancestral home of Gen. Philip H. Sheridan, the noted Union officer in the American Civil War. Population: (1966) 53,815.

THOMAS FITZGERALD
Department of Education, Dublin

CAVATINA, kav-ə-tē'nə, in opera and oratorio, a simple air composed in one section and without repetition of words or phrases. In instrumental music, it is a songlike piece or movement. The word *cavatina* is a diminutive of the Italian *cavata* (literally, "extraction") and means "epigrammatic sentence." Hence, a cavatina is a little musical sentence.

Cavatinas were frequently used in 18th and 19th century operas. Notable examples include *Largo al factotum,* for baritone, and *Una voce poco fa,* for soprano, from Rossini's *Barber of Seville; Come per me serena,* for soprano, from Bellini's *La Sonnambula; Udite, o rustico,* for basso buffo, from Donizetti's *L'elisir d'amore;* and *Salut! demeure chaste et pure,* for tenor, from Gounod's *Faust.*

Be Thou Faithful unto Death, from Mendelssohn's oratorio *St. Paul,* is listed in the orchestral score as a cavatina, but it is more often classified as an aria. The title "cavatina" is also given to the fifth movement of Beethoven's great String Quartet in B-Flat Major, Opus 130.

CAVAZZOLA, kä-vät-tsōl'lä, Paolo (1486–1522), Italian painter of the Veronese school, whose nickname was *Morando.* A native of Verona, he studied with Francesco Bonsignore, from whom he learned how to mold figures and work in precise chiaroscuro, and with Domenico Morone, from whom he derived his rich metallic coloring. He was influenced by Venetian painters and by Raphael. Cavazzola eventually developed his own style, marked by both freedom and severe harmony and by a fullness of form associated with Roman art.

Most of Cavazzola's work was frescoes for churches in Verona, including an *Annunciation* in San Nazaro e Celso and two archangels in Santa Maria in Organo. He also painted scenes from the Passion, the *Baptism of Christ, Madonna and St. John the Baptist,* and portraits of Giulia Trivulzio and of a "Gentleman." According to Vasari, Cavazzola died prematurely as a result of overwork caused by his excessive ambition to attain greatness. He died in Verona on Aug. 13, 1522.

CAVE, Edward (1691–1754), English printer, who published the first modern English magazine. He was born at Newton, Warwickshire, on Feb. 27, 1691. He began his career as an apprentice to a London printer, who sent him to Norwich to put out a weekly paper. By 1725, Cave was writing country news for London papers and London news for country journals. In 1731 he opened a printing shop in London as "R. Newton," and founded the *Gentleman's Magazine,* containing essays and news items that he often signed "Sylvanus Urban, Gent." The magazine featured reports of parliamentary debates that Cave and others, notably Samuel Johnson, wrote from hearsay accounts. This was Johnson's first regular literary employment. The reports caused trouble for Cave, although he disguised them as debates of a mythical parliament of Lilliput, and had to be discontinued. Cave published other works by Johnson, including the *Rambler* and *Irene.* He died in London on Jan. 10, 1754.

CAVE, George (1856–1928), English judge and political leader, who became lord chancellor in 1922. He was born in London on Feb. 23, 1856, and graduated with honors from Oxford in 1878. Two years later he was called to the bar by the Inner Temple, and he became a king's counsel in 1904. He was elected to Parliament in 1906 as a Unionist member for the Kingston division of Surrey, a seat he retained until 1918, when he was created 1st Viscount Cave and entered the House of Lords. As a member of the Commons, he had gained much influence through his lucidity and fairness and had played a prominent role in many crucial issues, including the Parliament bill (1911) and the Home Rule bill (1912).

In 1914 he was appointed attorney general to the Prince of Wales. In 1915 he became privy councillor and solicitor general, and also was knighted. He dealt with the difficult and unfamiliar tasks arising out of World War I, such as the conduct of prize cases and the trial for high treason of Sir Roger Casement in 1916. In that same year he became home secretary in the cabinet of Lloyd George. The greatest honor of his career was his appointment by Bonar Law as lord chancellor, the presiding justice of England's highest court. He served from 1922 until a few days before his death. He died at Burnham-on-Sea, Somerset, on March 29, 1928.

NEW MEXICO DEPARTMENT OF DEVELOPMENT

CARLSBAD CAVERNS, in southeastern New Mexico, are limestone solution caves, among the largest in the world. The huge mineral formations within the caverns include Giant Dome, a 62-foot-high stalagmite (above) that resembles the Leaning Tower of Pisa.

HARVY CAPLIN, FROM CARLSBAD CHAMBER OF COMMERCE

CAVE, a natural opening within the earth, generally extending beyond the zone of light. Caves are found in many types of rock but are most common in limestone, dolomite, and gypsum, which are readily dissolved by ground water. Sandstones having considerable quantities of lime cement between their grains also give rise to caves produced by the dissolving action of ground water. Such caves are called solution caves. Caves in the form of lava tubes, some several miles long, are common in extensive lava fields, particularly in the western part of North America. These caves are formed when successive lava beds from volcanic eruptions cool and solidify, trapping liquid lava that leaves open tubes when it escapes to flow to the surface. A third type of cave is found along seashores or lakeshores where the shoreline is cliffed or steep in slope. Waves attack zones of weakness in the face of the shore, and cut openings in the rocks which eventually develop into large cavelike passages.

Small caverns also develop along fissures, joints, or faults where slight movements of the rock give rise to small openings. Collections of broken rock debris at the foot of steep slopes or cliffs often contain large interconnected voids that are referred to as caves.

Origin of Solution Caves. The origin of solution caves in limestone and related rocks is complex, and scientists are not in full accord as to the exact sequence of events that lead to the formation of such caves. In all solution caves at least three related phases of development are recognized: (1) In the first phase, openings are developed in the rock by solution and are integrated to form cavern passages. (2) The second phase involves the filling of these passages with clay, silt, sand, or gravel, the source of which is the surface soils or rock in the vicinity of the cave. At times these deposits of cave earth accumulate to such an extent that they completely fill the primitive passages of the cave. (3) The

third stage is a reverse of the second and results in the partial removal of the earth fill by streams flowing in the cave. The streams also modify and enlarge the primitive passages. Simultaneously, the reopened passages receive deposits of calcite or other minerals that are carried through the rocks in solution. The deposition of these minerals on or from the walls and ceilings of passages develops beautiful stalactites, stalagmites, columns, flowstone, or other formations that are attractions in many caves opened for public inspection. During this stage the ceilings of many cavern passages are weakened by stresses exerted upon them so that they no longer can support their own weight and collapse, forming large piles of rock known as *breakdown*.

While the three phases of development outlined are recognized by most scientists, there are two schools of thought as to the timing and position of each phase. One school believes that all three stages occur simultaneously at or near the top of the groundwater in the earth. According to this view (known as the one-cycle theory), water descending from the surface of the earth into the ground dissolves the limestone to form cavern openings. At the same time, some of the water containing large amounts of dissolved materials precipitates these materials on reaching the openings, forming stalactites, flowstone, and other cavern formations. Earth fills, also, are brought in from the surface by the descending waters at the same time that the passages are being enlarged by solution. The other school believes that each phase is distinct and separate; this view is known as the two-cycle theory. The first phase occurs well below the top of the groundwater; the second phase at or near the top of the groundwater level; and the third phase in the zone between the top of the groundwater and the surface of the earth.

Age of Caverns. The age of caverns is still an unsolved problem. Many estimates have been based on the rate of growth of stalactites, on fossil remains in the cavern fills, and on the rate of solution within the cavernous limestones. The figures arrived at by these methods have been of little consequence, as they are not directly tied to the origin of the cave and at best are minimum ages. Work in the Appalachians and Ozarks, however, indicates that caverns are closely related to erosion levels of the earth's surface and that they were probably developed simultaneously. On this basis some caverns in central and eastern North America originated as far back as the Cretaceous period of geologic time, with most of the Appalachian caves dating from the end of the Tertiary period.

Description. Caves have many different shapes and patterns of passages. In most caves, passages are formed primarily along joints. Faults and bedding planes are secondary in controlling the direction of passages but often are important in developing the shape of the passages. In plan, most caves are either a series of simple sinuous or subangular passages, or a complex maze of interlacing, relatively straight passages, similar in layout to city blocks. The latter plan is generally found in caves developed at the point where the rocks are gently bowed upward. Passages are usually arranged vertically in levels. In caves in mountainous regions these levels are often separated by more than 100 feet (30 meters) of rock. Each level of passages is relatively horizontal, both in flat-lying or steeply dipping limestones.

In size, the cavern passages range from small openings that require crawling to pass through, up to giant galleries several hundred feet wide and long. Most passages, though relatively small, have enough room to permit walking. Floors are generally formed of smooth or stream-scoured earth fills which in some caves are covered with broken fragments of fallen rock. Pits, some small with gently sloping sides, others 50 feet (15 meters) or more across with vertical sides over 200 feet (60 meters) deep, interrupt the floor in many cavern passages. In some passages, deposits of calcite in the form of smooth sheets or low sinuous dams (rimstone) cover the floor. Most cavern walls are bare rock, at times with a thin covering of wet clay. In a small percentage of cavern passages, beautiful deposits of minerals known as *formations* occur, and in many commercialized caves they are the principal tourist attraction. Those formations hanging from the ceiling are *stalactites;* those deposited upright on the floor are *stalagmites;* while those deposited in sheets or layers on the walls or floors are *flowstone.*

Atmospheric conditions in caves are uniform. At the entrance, temperatures and humidity approximate surface conditions. Beyond a short zone of transition the temperature and humidity show little variation. At most times the temperature within the cave is close to the mean annual surface temperature of the region in which the cave is located. Humidity is close to 100% except in some caves with abundant gypsum or other mineral deposits, where humidity generally is low. In caves with passages connecting two or more surface openings, strong air circulation takes place between entrances, giving rise to what is known as a "blowing" cave. If the circulation alternates in direction at an entrance, successively blowing in and out, the phenomenon is known as a "breathing" cave. Another unique meteorological feature of some small

caves, particularly lava caves, is the large accumulation of ice throughout the year, even though the surface temperature rises very high in summer. Several of these caves are located in desert areas in the southwestern United States and many of them are well known in the mountains of Europe and Asia.

Location. Caves are generally located in areas known as karst lands. *Karst* is the surface expression of the subterranean solution of limestone that develops caverns. Karst landscapes are pitted with sinkholes, vertical shafts, and long blind valleys that lack surface outlets. Karst soils are usually thin, and bare bands of limestone, known as *karren* or *lapiez,* form much of the surface. Most of the streams that drain karst areas flow underground through cavernous passages, often reaching the surface in the form of large springs.

North America. The most famous of the karst and cavern areas in North America are in Kentucky and Tennessee. In these states, and in adjacent areas of Indiana and Illinois, there are over 20,000 square miles (50,000 sq km) of limestone that are "karstified." Sinkholes dot much of the landscape and in places there are as many as 1,000 sinks per square mile. On the plateau surrounding Mammoth Cave in central Kentucky there are sinkholes over 1 mile in diameter with steep slopes over 300 feet (90 meters) deep that have resulted from the collapse and subsequent solution of underground chambers. Passages in these caves are mainly large galleries extending for miles; gypsum is often present. The large caves in this region, like most in the eastern United States, are in limestones assigned in geologic age to the Mississippian system. Within this cavern area are some of North America's most famous caves.

Mammoth Cave, discovered in 1799, and the connecting Flint Ridge System, have over 150 miles (242 km) of known passageways. Mammoth Cave National Park was created in 1936. In the same region with Mammoth Cave are five other large commercial caves, including Crystal Cave, which was owned and developed by Floyd Collins, whose death in a small cave nearby attracted worldwide attention in 1925. In central Tennessee, Higginbotham Cave, which rivals Mammoth in size, is one of the largest noncommercial caves in the United States. Wyandotte Cave in southern Indiana is one of America's oldest known commercial caves, having been discovered in 1798. It was operated for saltpeter until 1850, when it was opened to the public. In eastern Kentucky, near Mt. Vernon, is the Great Saltpeter Cave which, along with Mammoth Cave, was the source of much of the niter used for gunpowder during the War of 1812 and the Mexican War. It was first dug for saltpeter in 1794.

In the Appalachian Mountains there are numerous cave areas. In general, the caves are smaller but more highly decorated than those in the plateaus of Kentucky and Tennessee. The Great Appalachian Valley, extending from New Jersey to Alabama, is floored with limestone of the Ordovician age and contains numerous beautiful caves, the most famous being Luray Caverns in Virginia, which was discovered in 1878. Weyers (Grand) Cave near Waynesboro, Va., is probably the oldest existing commercial cave in America, having been opened to the public in 1804. Madison Cave, close by, is reputed to

HOW CAVES ARE FORMED

1. SOLUTION CAVES

| Solution caves form in limestone and related rocks. By solution, openings are developed in rock and are integrated to form cavern passages. | The cavern passages fill with clay, silt, sand, or gravel that comes from the surface soil or from rock in the vicinity of the cave. | Streams flowing in the cave partially remove the earth fill and further enlarge and modify the passages. Mineral deposits form in the cave. |

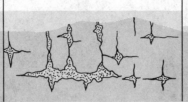

2. LAVA TUBES

| Lava flowing from volcano cools at the surface, trapping liquid lava. | Lava breaks through hardened crust and drains away, leaving empty tube. | Repeated outbreaks may produce a lava tunnel that extends for miles. |

3. SHORELINE CAVES

| Shoreline caves occur in cliffs or steep shores facing seas or lakes. | Waves attack and begin to cut openings in weak areas in the shore face. | In time the waves enlarge the openings and produce long passages. |

have been opened commercially shortly before the 19th century, but for a brief period only.

In southeastern West Virginia is a region of limestones of the Mississippian age that contains immense caverns similar to those found in Kentucky. Within this area is Organ Cave, made famous by Thomas Jefferson's description of fossil bones found in it in 1799. Elsewhere throughout the Appalachian Mountains and plateau are many limestone valleys and ridges with thousands of small, little-known caves in them.

In the central United States, the Ozark region of southern Missouri and northern Arkansas is an important cavern region. Although there are numerous large caves and large springs in this area, other karst features are generally lacking. Other important cavern regions of the Midwest are the Black Hills of South Dakota and the Driftless Area of southwestern Wisconsin. In southeastern New Mexico and western Texas are large areas of limestone, Permian and Cretaceous in age,

that contain large, deep caverns, including the famous Carlsbad Caverns, reputed to be the largest in the world. Limestones continue south through the interior of Mexico and are very cavernous, ending in Yucatán, where there are deep well-like pits, known as *cenotes*, in the karst. These *cenotes* served as sacrifice pits for the ancient Mayas. Another famous West Indian cave and karst area is northwestern Puerto Rico, where the ground is so honeycombed with subterranean passages that it has been described as a "lot of cave held together by a little limestone." Similar conditions exist in western and central Cuba and in central Jamaica, which is well-known for its "Cockpit" country.

Europe and Asia. Northern Italy and Yugoslavia are renowned for their large caverns and sinkholes. The Pyrenees of southern France, near Grenoble, contain the world's deepest known cave, called the Resea de la Pierre Saint-Martin, with a reported depth of 3,842 feet (1,171 meters)

THE BLUE GROTTO of Capri, Italy, is a famous shoreline cavern, named for the brilliant blue light that filters into the grotto from its entrance.

below its entrance. In eastern Belgium and western Germany are caverns that are well known because of the remains of ancient man found in them. In the Urals, the Caucasus, and other parts of the southern USSR are extensive caverns and karst, some of which are important for the presence of radium. Other noted cavern areas are in central England, North Africa, southeast Asia, the islands of the East Indies, and in parts of southern and southeastern Australia.

Commercial Aspects. Most people who visit caves tour those that have been developed for commercial purposes. Commercial caves have graded paths, elevators, and in the case of Postumia Grotto in Italy, an electric tramway to make passage through the cave safe. Electric lights are now extensively used but, formerly, kerosene lanterns or pine torches were the main source of illumination. In the United States there are about 130 caves opened commercially, and throughout the rest of the world there is probably an equal number. Thirteen caves in the United States have been set aside as parts of national parks or monuments, including such famous ones as Carlsbad (New Mexico), Mammoth (Kentucky), and Wind and Jewel (South Dakota).

Aside from their interest as tourist attractions, caves are being commercially exploited only to a limited degree at present. However, prior to the development of modern chemical methods they were an important source of saltpeter, used in the manufacture of gunpowder. In all the American wars up to the Civil War, caves in the Appalachian Mountains and adjacent areas in Tennessee and Kentucky were worked extensively for saltpeter. During the Civil War a large part of the Confederate Army's gunpowder was made from saltpeter dug from caves in Virginia, West Virginia, Tennessee, Alabama, and Georgia. The saltpeter, in the form of calcium nitrate, is contained in the earth fills on the floors of caves. It was removed by leaching with water and mixing with wood ashes to produce potassium nitrate. Natural caves have been considered for use as shelters in warfare but in general have been found unsuitable because of the irregular size of passages and the danger of flooding. Large deposits of sand, clay, and guano (the accumulated excrement of birds or bats) in many caves have proved to be economically valuable.

Speleology. The study of caves is known as speleology, and those who explore caves are called speleologists or spelunkers. In the United States the scientific study of caverns and related features was not systematized until the late 1930's. In France, Germany, Austria, Italy, Yugoslavia, and England, serious study has been devoted to caves since the latter part of the 19th century. In 1895 the Société de Spéléologie was founded in France, and similar societies soon were established in several European countries. In the United States the National Speleological Society, founded in 1939, has brought together most of those interested in caverns of the Western Hemisphere. In addition to the countries listed above, speleological societies exist in Spain, Switzerland, Bulgaria, Czechoslovakia, the USSR, and Belgium.

WILLIAM E. DAVIES
U. S. *Geological Survey*

CAVE LIFE

Several species of animals are found in caves; they are classified in three groups according to their degree of dependence on cave conditions. Those that commonly enter caves but must regularly return to the surface, like bats, are called *trogloxenes*, or "cave visitors." Animals that can complete their life cycles either in caves or in suitable habitats above ground are called *troglophiles*, or "cave guests." Those that live in caves and nowhere else are called *troglobites*, or "cave dwellers." The first two groups are distributed mostly near the entrance; permanent cave dwellers live deeper within the cave.

Environmental Zones. Cave environmental zones may be described in terms either of temperature or of light. The entrance of a cave is a variable-temperature zone, the extent of which depends upon such factors as the size and exposure of the entrance, volume of air and water (if any) entering the cave, and extremes of seasonal temperature. Farther inside the cave, air and water temperature reach nearly complete stability, approximately uniform for the latitude and elevation of the cave; this is the constant-temperature zone. The light zones of a cave are the entrance or twilight zone, and beyond that, the zone of total darkness.

A third factor strongly influencing the distribution of cave fauna is the presence or absence of water, whether as cave streams, water dripping from the roof, or the existence of a water table higher than the floor of the cave. More important, often, is the question of whether surface water can enter the cave, particularly during spring floods. This is critical because growth of green plants is restricted in caves to the twilight zone. Consequently, the bulk of organic matter upon which cave dwellers depend must either be washed into the cave as leaves, logs, and so forth, or it must drop or blow into the entrance. Two important additions to the food supply may occur: animals traveling back and forth, such as bats and cave crickets, may deposit substantial amounts of guano upon which other cave life can feed; and carcasses of animals may be trapped by accident.

Temporary Inhabitants. The most conspicuous of cave animals are bats, which in northern regions hibernate in caves and in southern regions use them in summer for breeding. Individual caves in the southwest United States may harbor as many as 30 million bats, principally free-tailed or guano bats (*Tadarida brasiliensis*). In Carlsbad Caverns National Park, New Mexico, on a summer evening, as many as half a million bats fly from a section of the cave remote from the tourist area and emerge from the huge entrance. After spending the night devouring flying insects within a 50-mile (80-km) radius, they return about dawn. The guano deposits were so great that about 100,000 tons were removed and sold for fertilizer before the national park was established.

A marked movement of temporary cave dwellers to the surface occurs on nights when temperature and humidity outside are favorable. Pack rats, cave crickets, and eyed salamanders forage outside the entrance. Many of the insects found in caves in winter, including moths, fungus gnats, and mosquitoes, leave in spring, but populations of daddy longlegs, certain spiders, pseudoscorpions, millipedes, and snails may occupy portions of the variable-temperature zone the year round.

Permanent Inhabitants. Troglobites include a variety of unusual creatures: eyeless fish, white crayfish, blind salamanders, blind beetles, and white, eyeless flatworms, amphipods, and isopods. Surface-dwelling species of animals most closely related to troglobites show a tendency toward the same physical characteristics: reduced eyes and pigment, thinner skin or exoskeleton, elongated or otherwise modified tactile organs, and reduced but efficient activity and metabolism. They are considered to be "preadapted" to cave conditions as the ancestors of present-day cave dwellers must have been.

Most types of cave fauna are small, scarce, and so locally distributed that even biospeleologists find them with difficulty. Some are caught in baited traps, others by dragging fine-mesh nets through underground pools. Because of their rarity or the lack of present knowledge about them, cave animals should be left undisturbed, and extreme care should be taken to avoid polluting cave environments.

CHARLES E. MOHR
Coauthor of "The Life of the Cave"

Further Reading: Halliday, William R., *Depths of the Earth: Caves and Caverns of the United States* (Evanston, Ill., 1966); Mohr, Charles E., and Poulson, Thomas L., *The Life of the Cave* (New York 1966); Moore, George W., and Nicholas, Brother G., *Speleology* (Boston 1964); National Speleological Society, *Bulletins* (Washington 1940–).

FRENCH GOVERNMENT TOURIST OFFICE

SPELEOLOGISTS descend a vertical shaft in the Gorges du Tarn, France, to begin scientific studies of a cave.

CAVE ART. See PALEOLITHIC ART.

CAVE CRICKET, a relatively large insect usually found in dark places such as caves and basements or in hollow logs. It is also called *camel cricket*. It has a robust brown or gray body, is usually wingless, and has long antennae. Some cave crickets are carnivorous, while others feed on vegetable matter. Cave crickets are classified in the family Stenopelmatidae of the order Orthoptera. They are closely related to sand crickets, Jerusalem crickets, and the wetas of Australia and New Zealand.

ROSS HUTCHINS
State Plant Board of Mississippi

CAVE DWELLERS are people who occupy caves or dwell beneath cliff overhangs. Archaeologists who have studied tools, food debris, and human bones in such sites have ascertained that men have occupied caves since earliest times.

Earliest Examples. In Africa the earliest inhabited caves are Swartkrans and Sterkfontein in the Transvaal province of the Republic of South Africa. These date from the end of the lower Pleistocene time, about one million years ago. Here the bones of the fossil man *Australopithecus* and various stone tools he might have made have been found together with the fossilized bones of other animals. Some of the animal bones have been broken in such a way as to suggest that early man had learned to split them to extract the marrow.

Another cave of similar age is the Vallonnet Cave in France, where both stone tools and fossilized animal bones are present. These caves were probably not occupied continuously but visited from time to time by their inhabitants. The accumulation of bones in them indicates that the caves also may have been used by such animals as bears, leopards, or hyenas when they were not occupied by man.

In the middle Pleistocene time, about 500,-000 years ago, the Choukoutien Cave near Peking was inhabited by the fossil man originally known as "Peking man" and now called *Homo erectus*. Stone tools, the bones of this early man, and animal bones have been found. There is some evidence of cannibalism on the part of *Homo erectus* at Choukoutien. Here also the earliest evidence of the use of fire has been found. It is not known whether fires were actually made at this time, or if embers were simply collected from fires started by natural causes. Whatever its source, fire would have been useful for warmth, perhaps for preparing food, and certainly for driving off wild animals. Since *Homo erectus* lived by hunting for meat and collecting vegetable food, he moved from one area to another at different seasons of the year, sometimes living in caves and at other times in the open.

Later Caves. Many more caves are known from the upper Pleistocene time than from the earlier periods. They are found across southern Europe and in Asia and Africa. During the first part of the upper Pleistocene, 35 to 70 thousand years ago, a population of so-called Neanderthal men was very widespread. Neanderthal fossils are known from caves such as La Ferrassie in France, Krapina in Yugoslavia, Kiik-Koba in the Crimea, Shanidar in Lebanon, Teshik-Tash in Uzbekistan, Ma-Pa in China, Jebel Irhoud in Morocco, and many others. By this time fire was in common use. In some places there is again evidence of cannibalism. For the first time in the prehistoric record, intentional burial was practiced, and ceremonial goods were often included in the graves. At Teshik-Tash, for example, a child's grave was surrounded with the skulls of five or six goats. This attention to burial and the apparent ceremony attached to it have been interpreted as evidence for belief in an afterlife.

Archaeological Discoveries. The caves in Europe, Asia, and North Africa occupied by the Neanderthals usually contain large stone scrapers, probably used on wood and skins, as well as triangular points that were often flaked on one face, and other stone tools. At the same time, south of the Sahara in what is now South Africa, sites such as the Cave of Hearths and Montagu Cave were occupied by people who made stone tools of the kind called Acheulian. Notable among these were hand axes—large almond-shaped tools flaked on both faces—in addition to cleavers and a variety of smaller tools. Some sites, such as Montagu Cave, were visited regularly to make use of a nearby source of stone, known as quartzite. Tools were made in the cave and taken elsewhere to be used.

By the latter part of the upper Pleistocene, from about 10,000 to 35,000 years ago, the number of Neanderthals had decreased, and members of the species *Homo sapiens*, who were physically identical to modern man, had become widely distributed. With the retreat of the glaciers at the end of the Pleistocene epoch, man occupied vast areas of Europe and Asia and had emigrated to the New World via the Bering Strait land bridge. In Europe the stone tool assemblages of this time are referred to as the Upper Paleolithic. Much of the archaeologists' knowledge about these industries comes from caves such as Abri Pataud and Combe Capelle in France and Grimaldi in Italy.

One of the most impressive features of this period is the painting on the cave walls in France, Spain, and Italy. (See PALEOLITHIC ART.) In some of the caves there are also clay models of animals. The art usually depicts the same kinds of animals as those whose bones are found in the debris in the caves. The paintings and sculptures found deep in the inner parts of caves are usually interpreted as having been used in rituals to ensure the hunters' success. On the other hand, the paintings and engravings in well-lighted portions of the caves may have been done for purely aesthetic reasons.

In other parts of Europe, as well as Asia and Africa, caves continued to be used as intermittent shelters for nomadic groups as they moved about their territory following game and searching for nuts, seeds, roots, and other vegetable foods. This kind of activity continued in some areas almost to the present day.

In the New World caves were often used as shelters. Some of these, such as Bat Cave in New Mexico or Danger Cave in Utah, have contributed substantially to our knowledge of the archaeology of North America, since they contain perishable materials like basketry or netting that are not found in more exposed sites.

See also ARCHAEOLOGY; CAVE; CLIFF DWELLERS.

CHARLES M. KELLER
The Robert H. Lowie Museum of Anthropology
University of California at Berkeley

Further Reading: Bataille, Georges, *Lascaux: or, The Birth of Art* (New York 1955); Cornwall, Ian W., *World of Ancient Man* (New York 1964); De Sieveking, A., and De Sieveking, G., *Caves of France and Northern Spain* (Chester Springs, Pa., 1962); Willey, Gordon R., and Phillips, Philip, *Method and Theory in American Archaeology* (Chicago 1957).

CAVEAT EMPTOR, kā'vē-at emp'tər, a Latin phrase meaning "let the buyer beware," is a doctrine pertaining to the law of sales that developed in medieval times. It was believed that the buyer should not rely on the representations of the seller regarding the merchandise sold but, instead, should inspect the goods and make his own decision. Under this doctrine the buyer takes the risk on an item he purchases and cannot complain of a defect. Unless there is either fraud or warranty (guarantee) by the seller, the rule applies to the sale of personal property (that is, not real estate) where the buyer and seller have equal access to information about the item and the buyer is able to make personal inspection.

The doctrine of caveat emptor has been greatly limited in modern times as a result of changes in marketing conditions and the growing complexity of industrial processes. Formerly goods were relatively simple, and the buyer and seller met face to face, each having equal opportunity to inspect and understand the nature of the product. Today, however, owing to scientific and industrial development, many products are so complicated that only experts can evaluate them, and the buyer has to rely on the knowledge and good faith of the seller. Thus there is today, in fact if not in form, a rejuvenation of the Roman legal principle of "caveat venditor" (let the seller beware), which places the responsibility for defects upon the seller.

PETER D. WEINSTEIN
Member of the New York Bar

CAVELL, kav'əl, **Edith** (1865–1915), English nurse, who pioneered in modern nursing in Belgium and was executed by the Germans during World War I for helping fugitive Allied soldiers.

Born near Norwich, England, on Dec. 4, 1865, the eldest daughter of a country parson, she became a governess in Brussels and then returned to England, where she trained as a nurse at the London Hospital and worked in north and east London. Nursing in Belgium at the time lagged far behind that in England, and when Dr. Antoine Depage, surgeon to the king, started a training school for nurses in Brussels in 1907, he invited Miss Cavell to become its matron. By the outbreak of World War I, she had established Belgian nursing on modern lines.

During the Allied retreat from Mons and Charleroi in August 1914, many soldiers, cut off from their units, disguised themselves as civilians, thereby rendering themselves liable to be shot as spies, together with—according to German orders —any civilians who befriended them. They had no money, food was running short, and reprisals were threatened on the civilian population if they did not give them up. Several prominent Belgians formed an organization to help them escape. Fugitives were rounded up, escorted into Brussels, and then guided across the frontier into the neutral Netherlands.

Edith Cavell was asked to hide fugitives in her hospital and willingly consented, helping 200 of them to get away. German suspicion grew, however, and on Aug. 5, 1915, Miss Cavell was arrested along with 34 others. She was kept in solitary confinement for nine weeks, during which she was tricked into a confession. It has been said that she implicated her codefendants, but there is little evidence that she revealed anything not already known to the Germans.

The trial of the accused lasted only two days, but no legal right was denied them. Edith Cavell and four others, two women and two men, were sentenced to death, and many others to long periods of hard labor. They all had offended against the laws promulgated by the Germans under international law to ensure the safety of the German armed forces. Miss Cavell refused to defend herself and agreed that her sentence was just.

The sentences were passed in secret, and the military governor, determined to make an example of someone and possessed by a passionate hatred of England, deliberately expedited the sentences on Miss Cavell and Philippe Baucq, an architect, in order to preclude any appeal for mercy. The news leaked out, however, and the American legation made a desperate appeal to save Miss Cavell; but the governor, acting within his strict legal rights, refused. She and Baucq were shot at dawn on Oct. 12, 1915.

The execution of a woman—moreover of a nurse—aroused emotions around the world, and in the Allied countries she was looked upon as a martyr. Politically unwise though this act was, the Germans were legally if not morally justified in what they did. Edith Cavell, in following the dictates of her conscience, had compromised her immunity as a nurse and had violated the law. Or as the English theologian Hastings Rashdall wrote in another context: "It may be the duty of an individual to do something which nevertheless it may be the right and duty of other individuals to shoot her for doing."

A. E. CLARK-KENNEDY, M. D.
Author of "Edith Cavell"

Edith Cavell

BELGIAN SCHOOL OF NURSING, BRUSSELS

CAVENDISH, kav'ən-dish, **George** (1500?–?1561), English biographer, who is best known for his *Life of Cardinal Wolsey* (1557), one of the most interesting short biographies in English. He served as gentleman usher to Thomas Cardinal Wolsey from about 1527 until the latter's death in 1530. He then retired to his house at Glemsford, Suffolk, where he lived quietly with his wife, a niece of Sir Thomas More, until his death.

Cavendish's biography of Wolsey may have been read in manuscript by Shakespeare, whose view of the cardinal corresponds to Cavendish's. It was first published in crude form in 1641; a more polished edition was issued by the Universal Library in 1885.

CAVENDISH, kav'ən-dish, **Georgiana** (1757–1806), English beauty and wit, whose marriage to William, 5th Duke of Devonshire, enabled her to become the leader of fashion in late 18th century England. Georgiana Cavendish was born on June 9, 1757, the eldest daughter of John, 1st Earl Spencer.

Her marriage to the Duke of Devonshire in June 1774 was regarded in society as the most enviable one in England, and she swiftly capitalized on the advantages it brought her. Her physical charm was enhanced by vivacity, as several portraits by Thomas Gainsborough and Sir Joshua Reynolds attest, and she had the intelligence and style to endear herself to such men of genius as Samuel Johnson, Horace Walpole, and Richard Brinsley Sheridan. She died in London on March 30, 1806.

CAVENDISH, kav'ən-dish, **Henry** (1731–1810), English chemist and physicist, who is best known for his research in gas chemistry and electrical theory, and for the determination of Newton's gravitational constant.

Life. The elder son of Lord Charles Cavendish and Lady Anne Gray, Cavendish was born at Nice on Oct. 10, 1731. He was educated at Hackney School (1742–1748) and Peterhouse College, Cambridge (1749–1753), which he left without taking a degree, perhaps because of reservations about the religious declaration then required of all degree candidates. One of the wealthiest men of his day, he spent most of his life in and around London, maintaining houses in Clapham Common and at Bloomsbury and a library in Soho.

Henry
Cavendish

(From an en-
graving of the
19th century)

GRANGER COLLECTION

After leaving Cambridge, Cavendish became an assistant in his father's laboratory, where he began a series of profound and wide-ranging researches that he pursued relentlessly for more than 50 years. Elected a fellow of the Royal Society of London in 1760, he seems to have been an extremely shy man whose social contacts were limited almost exclusively to the weekly lunches at the society. He never married, and his fear of women bordered on neurosis. (On one occasion, after he happened to meet a housemaid on the stairs of his home, he ordered a separate staircase to be built for his exclusive use.) His introvertedness, combined with a slight speech defect, evidently made him appear both withdrawn and ludicrous. Nonetheless, he was considered by many of his contemporaries to be the greatest scientist of his day, a view amply confirmed by the subsequent development of science. He died a recluse at his home in London, on March 10, 1810.

Contributions to Science. Characteristically, Cavendish was reluctant to publish any results or theories that were not polished to perfection. As a result, the papers published during his lifetime form only a small fraction of his actual output. It was only when the physicist Clerk Maxwell edited Cavendish's manuscripts that the scope of his contributions to science and his extraordinary genius came to be fully appreciated.

One of the first to introduce quantitative techniques into chemistry, he spent several years studying the properties of "inflammable air" (hydrogen) and "fixed air" (carbon dioxide). In his "Three Papers Containing Experiments on Factitious Air" (published in the *Philosophical Transactions* of the Royal Society for 1766), he made the discovery that hydrogen was a separate substance. He then studied the solution of metals in oxidizing acids and analyzed the presence of minerals in natural water supplies. This latter research led him to the discovery of calcium carbonate in hard water. In his paper "Experiments on Air" (*Philosophical Transactions*, 1784), he

described the famous experiment by which he discovered that water could be synthesized from hydrogen and oxygen. By putting a mixture of these two gases into a narrow glass tube and introducing an electric spark (a technique developed by Volta in 1776), he observed the obvious explosion and the formation of water droplets, accompanied by a contraction of the volume of the gaseous mixture. A year later, he did similar experiments, producing nitric acid from a mixture of nitrogen, oxygen, and water vapor, discovering, almost accidentally, that nitrogen was a constituent of nitric acid. From a quantitative analysis of these experiments, he rightly concluded that "common air" (the atmosphere) is four-fifths nitrogen and one-fifth oxygen.

While it is true that Cavendish, as an adherent of the phlogiston theory, did not explain the composition of water in terms familiar to modern chemists and even misunderstood the nature of gases, there is no doubt that he was the first chemist to produce water from hydrogen and oxygen and to understand that the production of water was essentially related to the loss of the combined weights of the gases.

Cavendish's work on electrical theory was also of paramount importance. A proponent of Franklin's one-fluid theory of electricity, Cavendish suggested that every charged body was surrounded by an "electric atmosphere." This was a major step toward the formulation of an electrical field theory. He discovered the idea of electric potential (which he termed "compression") and, along with Priestley, discovered the law that electrostatic attractions and repulsions between particles are functions of the inverse square of the distance between them. He also demonstrated that the charge on an electrified hollow sphere is "lodged intirely on its surface."

Cavendish also made major contributions to thermometry and the theory of heat (working especially on vapor pressures, thermometer calibration, latent heat, freezing mixtures, and heterogeneous equilibria), meteorology, and terrestrial magnetism. He is perhaps known best of all for the torsion balance that bears his name, and with which, in 1798, he determined Newton's gravitational constant and the density of the earth. This is described in his celebrated paper "Experiments to Determine the Density of the Earth" (1798).

L. L. LAUDAN, *University College, London*

Further Reading: Berry, Arthur T., *Henry Cavendish* (London 1960); Cavendish, Henry, *Scientific Papers,* ed. by James Clerk Maxwell and others, 2 vols. (Cambridge, England, 1921); Wilson, George *The Life of the Hon. Henry Cavendish* (London 1851).

CAVENDISH, kav'ən-dish, **Margaret** (1624–1674), English writer, who is best known for her autobiographical record of the manner in which young ladies of means were reared in 17th century England. She was born at St. John's, near Colchester, Essex, the youngest of the eight children of Sir Thomas Lucas. From 1643 to 1645, during the Civil War, she served Queen Henrietta Maria as maid of honor in Paris. While in attendance on the queen she met and married William Cavendish, later Duke of Newcastle. Her writings also include poems, essays, plays, and a memoir of her husband. She died in London on Jan. 7, 1674.

CAVENDISH, Spencer Compton. See DEVONSHIRE, 8TH DUKE OF.

CAVENDISH, kav′ən-dish, **Thomas** (1560?–1592), English buccaneer and the third circumnavigator of the globe. He was born near Harwich, in southeastern England. Having squandered his inheritance at court, Cavendish hoped to recoup his losses by highjacking the treasure ships streaming from America to Spain. In 1585 he joined Sir Richard Grenville's expedition to establish a colony in North America. But Cavendish did not remain with the unlucky men who settled on Roanoke Island. Instead, he returned to England, where he made preparations for a voyage around the world.

On July 21, 1586, his fleet of three ships put out from Plymouth. Generally following Sir Francis Drake's route of 1577–1580, the fleet dropped down to the Cape Verde Islands before heading west. For almost six weeks the ships battled the wild seas of the South Atlantic before they passed into the Pacific. Here the English managed to destroy six Spanish vessels, including one with cargo worth £20,000. Then, on Nov. 4, 1587, they captured the *Great St. Anne* with an enormous treasure. When they had taken what they could, the captors anxiously set out for home. They arrived on Sept. 10, 1588, having taken some seven months less time than either Magellan or Drake.

Although the trip reestablished Cavendish's fortunes, the cost of life at court soon dissipated them. In 1591 he sailed with five vessels for China. But bad luck haunted the voyage from the start, the crew refused to go on, and Cavendish died at sea in June 1592.

JOHN FERGUSON, *Columbia University*

CAVENDISH LABORATORY, kav′ən-dish lab′rə-tôr-ē, the name given to the first building for experimental physics at the University of Cambridge, England, but now used to denote all the buildings used by the physics department at Cambridge. The original laboratory was opened in 1874 with funds provided by the 8th Duke of Devonshire, Spencer Compton Cavendish, whose family name was given to the building. Henry Cavendish, the famous 18th century physicist, was a grandson of the 2d Duke of Devonshire.

The Cavendish chair of experimental physics is held by the head of the physics department at Cambridge and has been occupied successively by James Clerk Maxwell (1871–1879), Lord Rayleigh (1879–1884), J. J. Thomson (1884–1919), Ernest Rutherford (1919–1937), Lawrence Bragg (1938–1953), and Nevill Mott 1954–   ).

Many accomplishments of paramount importance in the history of physics are associated with the Cavendish Laboratory. Among them are the discovery of the electron (J. J. Thomson), the invention of the mass spectrometer (Francis W. Aston), the development of the cloud chamber (C. T. R. Wilson), the first artificial disintegration of the nucleus (J. D. Cockcroft and E. T. S. Walton), and the discovery of the neutron (James Chadwick). The first 15 years after Rutherford's appointment were extraordinarily fruitful and saw the opening up of the structure of the nucleus as a new field of experimental research as well as the eager adoption of the new ideas of quantum mechanics and its development by Cambridge theorists such as P. A. M. Dirac, R. H. Fowler, A. H. Wilson, and N. F. Mott.

In addition to teaching experimental and theo-retical physics, the laboratory now sponsors research in such areas as radio astronomy, particle physics, solid state physics, and crystallography. The early work of Francis Crick and M. F. Perutz on molecular biology was also carried out in the Cavendish Laboratory.

SIR NEVILL MOTT
University of Cambridge

CAVENTOU, kȧ-väN-tōō, **Joseph Bienaimé** (1795–1877), French chemist, who, along with Pierre Pelletier, isolated and synthesized quinine and other pharmacologically important alkaloids. This work was important in the early development of chemotherapy.

In 1820, Caventou and Pelletier studied various types of *Cinchona* bark, a bark known by the Peruvian natives to contain medicinal properties useful in the treatment of fevers, especially malaria. After much experimentation and analysis, they succeeded in isolating an alkaloid they called "quinine." They reported that this was the active ingredient in *Cinchona* responsible for the alleviation of fevers. They also reported many of the physical and chemical properties of quinine, and went on to synthesize the compound and prepare it on a large industrial basis. The manufacture and use of quinine spread rapidly throughout the world, and the drug was widely used to treat malaria until the mid-20th century.

Before their work on *Cinchona*, Caventou and Pelletier studied ipecac roots and isolated emetine, a drug used to treat dysentery. They also isolated two poisonous alkaloids—strychnine and brucine—from the nux vomica plant.

CAVIAR, kav′ē-är, the salted roe, or eggs, of certain large fish, especially members of the sturgeon family. Caviar is served as a gourmet delicacy; the eggs, either whole or pressed, are usually served slightly chilled. Sturgeon eggs are either black or slate gray, depending on the species. Red caviar is made from the roe of salmon, especially chum and silver salmon.

After the eggs are removed from the ovaries, they are strained and salted before being packaged. The amount of salt added depends on the quality of the eggs. The best quality roe is only slightly salted and is called malossol.

About 95% of the black caviar in the United States is imported from Iran, where the sturgeon is caught along the shores of the Caspian Sea. The three main species producing black caviar are the beluga, which has the largest eggs; the osetra, which has medium-sized eggs; and the sevruga, which has the smallest eggs. Of the more than 66 tons (60 metric tons) of caviar imported from Iran each year, most is preserved and pasteurized and sold in jars. The rest is sold fresh. Until 1954 about 90% of all the sturgeon caviar in the United States was imported from Russia. That year, however, trade agreements between Iran and Russia were not renewed, and American importers, instead of continuing to obtain caviar from Russia, provided a new market for Iranian caviar.

Red caviar sold in the United States comes mostly from the Pacific Northwest and British Columbia. About 350,000 pounds (59,000 kg) of this type of caviar are consumed in the United States each year.

ARNOLD H. HANSEN-STURM
Romanoff Caviar Company

CAVIGLIA, kä-vē′lyä, **Enrico** (1862–1945), Italian field marshal, who held major commands in both world wars. He was born in Finalmarina, Liguria, on May 4, 1862. He was educated at the Turin military academy and took part in Italian colonial campaigns. In World War I, Caviglia commanded the 24th Corps, which broke the Austrian lines on the Bansizza plateau (1917), and later led the 8th Army, which played a prominent role in the final Italian victory at Vittorio Veneto (1918).

After the war he led the troops that expelled Gabriele d'Annunzio's army of adventurers from the free state of Fiume (1920). He was promoted field marshal in 1926. In World War II, Caviglia took command of Rome after Italy's capitulation to the Allies (1943) and helped negotiate the city's surrender to the Germans. He died in Finalmarina on March 22, 1945.

CAVITATION, kav-ə-tā′shən, is a violent agitation of a liquid caused by the rapid formation and collapse of vapor bubbles. It occurs when the liquid's pressure fluctuates slightly above and below its vapor pressure, as may happen in the vicinity of a ship's propeller or in the working fluid of hydraulic machinery. Cavitation results when a liquid moves rapidly from a region of lower fluid pressure, where it vaporizes and forms vapor bubbles (cavities), to a region of higher pressure, where the bubbles collapse forcefully.

Cavitation can pit metal parts and dangerously weaken them, and it also can reduce the efficiency of pumps, turbines, ship propellers, and other hydraulic machinery. It is sometimes accompanied by a noticeable noise arising from the formation and collapse of the bubbles. Cavitation noise is a handicap in naval actions because it facilitates the detection of a ship or submarine by the enemy's sonar.

CAVITE, kä-vē′tā, is a city in the Philippines, located on the island of Luzon. It is the capital of the province of Cavite. Its position on a peninsula in Manila Bay, 8 miles (13 km) south of Manila, has made it a trade center.

Originally an old walled Spanish town, Cavite was the scene of Filipino insurrections before its liberation in 1898. The naval base of Sangley Point just north of the city was seized on Jan. 2, 1942, by the Japanese in World War II and was retaken on Feb. 13, 1945, by United States forces after heavy bombardment.

When the Philippines became independent in 1946, the base at Sangley Point was retained by the U. S. Navy as an operational area. Population: (1960) 54,891.

CAVO-RELIEVO, kä′vō rē-lē′vō, in sculpture, is a kind of relief in which no part of the figure rises above the general surface of the surrounding material. It is done by deeply incising the figure's outlines. (See also INTAGLIO.) The bounding line is marked by a wedge-shaped groove. The slope of one side of the wedge is the boundary of the design, and the other slope disappears in the general rounding of the figures.

Cavo-relievo (an alternate spelling is *cavorilievo*) was commonly used in decorating the walls of ancient Egyptian temples. This type of relief is sometimes called *coelanaglyphic* (hollow relief) sculpture, and a fine example is preserved in the Temple of Amon-Ra, Karnak.

CAVOUR, kä-vōōr′, **Count di** (1810–1861), Italian statesman and chief architect of a united Italy. Camillo Benso di Cavour was born on Aug. 10, 1810, in Turin, until 1814 the capital of the Italian departments of the French Empire and later capital of the kingdom of Sardinia. He was named after his godfather, Camillo, Prince Borghese, brother-in-law of Napoleon I. The family, originally from Chieri, near Turin, traced its origins to the 12th century. His father, Michele, held several important government positions. His mother, Adèle de Sellon, belonged to a Genevan Calvinist patrician family renowned for its liberalism and humanitarianism.

Early Life. Cavour entered the military academy in Turin at the age of 10. At 14 he was made a page to Charles Albert, heir to the Sardinian throne. When he was 16, he was commissioned a second lieutenant in the engineers. While serving in various garrisons, Cavour read, among other works, those of Auguste Comte, François Guizot, Benjamin Constant, Adam Smith, Jeremy Bentham, and David Ricardo. In 1830, through Anna Giustiniani, the one love of his life, he met *Carbonari* conspirators in Genoa. In consequence of preventive measures taken by Sardinian authorities in the wake of the July 1830 revolution in France, Cavour was transferred to the forbidding fort of Bard. Charles Albert, now king, allowed him to resign in November 1831.

For the next 16 years Cavour managed his father's estates. Introducing improvements tried out in Britain, Cavour increased the income of his father, his own income, and that of the tenants. With the guidance of a Swiss friend, he ventured into business, founding banks, building railroads and factories, and engaging in export-import trade. He established a society for agricultural improvement; another for the diffusion of education among working-class children; and a whist club in Turin that became a center for the spread of progressive ideas. Cavour also traveled extensively. In Paris, London, and Geneva, he met Alexis de Tocqueville, the historian Simonde de Sismondi, and the economists Pellegrino Rossi and Nassau Senior.

Cavour's visits abroad provided material for early articles on free trade, the British corn laws and poor laws, the Irish question, and railroads. When Sardinian press laws were liberalized in 1847, Cavour founded *Il Risorgimento*, which became the main organ of Sardinian and Italian liberal opinion and to which he was the chief contributor. From then on, politics was his main concern. Early in 1848 he was active in advocating constitutional government. Following demonstrations caused by news of the February revolution in Paris, a constitution was granted by Charles Albert. At the supplementary elections held in June, Cavour was elected to the newly established parliament. In articles and speeches he advocated war against Austria and the formation of a unitary state that would include the whole of northern Italy. After the defeat of the Sardinians by the Austrians at Custoza, near Verona, and the signing of an armistice, he opposed renewal of the war in 1849 and supported the new king, Victor Emmanuel II. In 1850 he joined the cabinet, and in 1852, as head of a liberal coalition formed by his own right-of-center moderates and by Urbano Rattazzi's left-of-center democrats, he became prime minister.

Cavour's Liberalism. Cavour belonged to the world of European liberalism. Like de Tocqueville in France, John Stuart Mill in Britain, and Friedrich Dahlmann in Germany, he believed in liberty, progress, and moderation. Revolutionary in relation to traditional absolutism, Cavour was conservative in relation to leftist authoritarianism. He rejected dogmatism of all kinds. In his writings and speeches, he demonstrated that he preferred the modern scientific method to traditional a priori methods of thought. Baptized a Roman Catholic, he advocated freedom of conscience for all and was close to Protestantism in postulating the primacy of the individual conscience over external authority. "Free church in a free state" was the formula he adopted from the Swiss, Alexandre Vinet. He considered freedom of the mind and freedom of the press the most important liberties. The key to political liberty he found in constitutionalism: parliamentary government, separation of powers, checks and balances, and the separation not only of church and state but also of the state and the economy. Since liberty leads to pluralism and is thus a source of division and a cause of tension, he considered moderation the essential value for the survival of a free society. He preferred evolution to revolution and was convinced that the former requires a constitutional frame.

Unlike other moderates, whose fear of democracy led them into conservatism, Cavour was ready to accept democracy. Next to Britain, the home of liberalism, he admired Switzerland and the United States. An advocate of free enterprise, he was not a dogmatic upholder of laissez-faire. He stood for sound public finance but never made a fetish of balanced budgets. No regionalist or separatist, he felt greater loyalty to Italy than to the Sardinian state.

But unlike Giuseppe Mazzini and Vincenzo Gioberti, Cavour was no integral nationalist. His task, as he saw it, was to unify as much of the Italian nation as possible. Unlike Italian conservatives, he thought a unitary state preferable to a federal one. Unlike most Italian republicans, he was convinced that foreign aid was necessary to expel Austria from Italy.

The Statesman. During the difficult period immediately following the 1848–1849 crisis, internal reforms were Cavour's main concern. A loan from a British bank helped reorganize Sardinian finances and pay war indemnities to Austria. Commercial treaties brought an increased flow of trade. Highways and railroads were built, and ports and canals were improved. These developments, together with the reform of the banking system, the expansion of credit, and the formation of joint-stock companies, promoted economic expansion. Bigger revenues made possible the strengthening of the armed forces. Public education was improved at all levels. Privileges enjoyed by the Catholic Church were abolished. As a result of a law of 1855 dissolving monasteries and redistributing the incomes of the clergy, Cavour was excommunicated, but king and parliament stood by him.

The Crimean War (1853–1856) enabled Cavour to enter the international arena. An alliance with Britain and France led to the sending of a Sardinian expeditionary force of 18,000 men to the Crimea. Losses were heavy, but Cavour had gained the confidence of British and French leaders. At the Paris peace congress of 1856, he brought up Italian problems. In that year, exiles from other Italian states, many of them republicans, organized a National Society with the aim

THE GRANGER COLLECTION

Count di Cavour

of backing Cavour in his endeavors to free all of Italy from the Austrians.

The French Emperor Napoleon III was scheming to replace Austrian with French influence in Italy. Contacts established late in 1857 led to a meeting at Plombières-les-Bains between the emperor and Cavour. They agreed that should Austria attack Sardinia, France would come to the rescue; northern Italy would be annexed to Sardinia; the Pope would become president of an Italian federation; and Savoy and Nice, French-speaking districts held by Sardinia, would be ceded to France. In April 1859, war followed an Austrian ultimatum to Sardinia, largely engineered by Cavour. After the French-Sardinian victory of Solferino, the French emperor, concerned about internal and external problems, signed an armistice giving Sardinia only the Lombard section of Austrian-held territories in Italy. Feeling betrayed by Napoleon III, Cavour resigned, but he was induced to resume the premiership in January 1860.

Following successful revolutions in the smaller states of central Italy, provisional governments had been organized by Cavour's friends in the National Society. An agreement with France in March 1860 made possible the merger of these states with Sardinia. Savoy and Nice were transferred to France. Early in May, Garibaldi led an expedition to overthrow the Bourbon king of the Two Sicilies in southern Italy. Cavour maneuvered in order, on the one hand, to facilitate the success of the expedition with British support; on the other, to prevent the consolidation of Garibaldi's dictatorship in the liberated areas. Sardinian troops occupied parts of the Papal States and the Two Sicilies. On March 17, 1861, the proclamation of the kingdom of Italy crowned Cavour's efforts. Exhausted, he died a few weeks later, on June 6, 1861. A friendly friar gave him absolution and a nation mourned him.

M. SALVADORI, *Smith College*

Bibliography

Delzell, C. F., *The Unification of Italy, 1859–1861* (New York 1965).
Mack Smith, Denis, *Cavour and Garibaldi, 1860* (Cambridge, England, 1954).
Salvadori, M., *Cavour and the Unification of Italy* (Princeton 1961).
Thayer, W. R., *Life and Times of Cavour* (Boston 1911).
Whyte, A. J., *The Early Life and Letters of Cavour, 1810–1848* (London 1925).
Whyte, A. J., *Political Life and Letters of Cavour, 1848–1861* (London 1930).

N. LIGHTFOOT, FROM PHOTO RESEARCHERS

THE PATAGONIAN CAVY, or mara, is also called the Patagonian hare. It is the largest of the cavies.

CAVY, kā′vē, the common name for rodents of the family Caviidae. Cavies are native to South America from Colombia to Patagonia. They are heavy-bodied, short-tailed or tailless animals and feed on vegetable matter.

Forest cavies range from Colombia to northern Argentina and Uruguay. They are short-legged animals measuring from 9 to 14 inches (23–35.5 cm) in length and from 1 to 1½ pounds (450–700 grams) in weight. Wild forms are brownish to grayish in color. Forest cavies live in groups of 5 to 10 at the edge of forests or in grassy fields near water. Domesticated by Peruvian Indians before the time of the Incas, they are now common as pets and laboratory animals (see also GUINEA PIG).

Savannah cavies differ from forest cavies mostly in tooth pattern. They nest in rock caves and termite mounds. *Rock cavies,* or mocos, are found in rocky, semiarid areas of Brazil, where they are hunted for meat. Their coat is grayish, with white mottling.

Patagonian cavies, or maras, resemble hares and are the largest of the cavies. They range from 28 to 31 inches (72–80 cm) in length and from 20 to 35 pounds (9–16 kg) in weight. Maras live in groups of 3 to 40 in arid areas.

The family Caviidae contains 16 species, which are grouped into 5 genera: *Cavia* (forest cavies), *Galea* (savannah cavies), *Kerodon* (rock cavies), and *Dolichotis* and *Pediolagus* (Patagonian cavies).

FERNANDO DIAS DE AVILA-PIRES
Universidade do Brasil

CAWDOR, kô′dər, is a village in Nairnshire, Scotland, about 70 miles (113 km) northwest of Aberdeen. It is the site of Cawdor Castle, seat of the earls of Cawdor.

The moated castle, on the bank of the Cawdor Burn, a tributary of the Nairn River, is the traditional site of the murder of King Duncan I of Scotland by Macbeth, earl of Cawdor, in 1040. The tradition is without basis in fact. The castle's central tower and its battlements and drawbridge date from 1454; they are the only remaining original portions. The surrounding buildings were built in the 16th century.

The legend of Duncan's murder here is retold in Shakespeare's tragedy *Macbeth.* In the play, the Thane of Cawdor, a feudal lord who does not appear on stage, is condemned to death by Duncan, and his lands and title are bestowed on Macbeth as the witches had prophesied.

CAWEIN, kā-wīn′, **Madison Julius** (1865–1914), American poet. He was born in Louisville, Ky., on March 23, 1865. His verse, depicting mostly scenes and people of his native Kentucky, is often musical and pleasing and displays a good command of meter, but it tends toward overornamentation and excessive use of adjectives. He published his *Complete Poetical Works,* in five volumes, in 1907, and *Selected Poems,* with a foreword by William Dean Howells, in 1911. A posthumous volume, *The Cup of Comus,* appeared in 1915. Cawein died in Louisville on Dec. 8, 1914.

CAWNPORE. See KANPUR.

CAWOOD, kā′wŏod, is an unincorporated village in southeastern Kentucky, in Harlan county, 110 miles (177 km) southeast of Lexington and 4 miles (6 km) north of the Virginia border. It is situated in the densely forested Cumberland Mountains. The region is one of the principal producing areas of the extensive eastern Kentucky coalfield. Lumbering and the mining of bituminous coal are Cawood's principal industrial activities.

CAXAMARCA. See CAJAMARCA.

CAXIAS DO SUL, kə-shē′əs thōō sōōl, is a city in southern Brazil. Founded about 1870 and called *Caxias* until 1944, it is one of the centers of Italian immigrant settlement in the state of Rio Grande do Sul. A road and railroad connect it with Pôrto Alegre, 60 miles (95 km) south.

Local farm products form the basis of the city's principal industries—winemaking, cattle and hog slaughtering, and lard manufacture. Agates are found nearby. Population: (1960) 60,607.

CAXTON, William (1422?–1491), English printer, who was the first to print books in the English language. He also made a major contribution to English literature as a translator and editor, and to a large extent he shaped the literary tastes and reading habits of his own times and of succeeding generations.

Life. Born in Kent, in the wide wooded area known as the Weald, Caxton came of good yeoman stock and received a sound education. He went to London in 1438 as an apprentice to Robert Large, a prominent mercer who became lord mayor. Large died in 1441, and Caxton went into business on his own in Bruges. He rose to the position of governor of all the English merchants in the Low Countries, wielding extensive power and sometimes acting in a diplomatic capacity for the English king.

At the age of 50, Caxton relinquished his post as governor and entered the service, in Bruges, of Margaret, Duchess of Burgundy and sister of Edward IV of England. It was probably during a visit to Cologne in 1471–1472 that Caxton first saw a printing press at work. Returning to Bruges about 1474, he joined Colard Mansion in printing *The Recuyell of the Histories of Troy* (in Caxton's own translation from the French), the first book printed in the English tongue.

Ɛ haue deupſed aboue the thynges that appertyne
Ꝟ Ꝟnto the formes of the cheſſe men and of their offi
ces. that is to Ꝟete as Ꝟel of noble men as of the compn
peple / Than hit appertyneth that Ꝟe ſholð deupſe ſhortlp
hoꝶ they pſſue and goon out of the places Ꝟhere they be
ſette . Ꝛnd firſt Ꝟe ought to ſpeke of the forme and of
the faꞇon of the cheꝗuer after that hit repreſenteth and

COURTESY OF THE NEW YORK PUBLIC LIBRARY

CAXTON'S printing, from 2d edition (c.
1483) of *Game and Playe of the Chesse*.

Caxton went back to London in 1475 or
1476 and rented premises in the precincts of
Westminster Abbey, known as the Almonry.
There he labored as a printer for the next 15
years. Caxton died in London in 1491, just after
completing a translation of St. Jerome's *Lives
of the Fathers*.

Work. Caxton's work in printing is characterized by complete integrity and by an unflagging
industry—an especially remarkable trait in that,
by the standards of his time, he was an old man
when he began his new career. About 100
books, totaling 18,000 leaves, have been traced
to his press, and about one third of these were
his own translations. His choice of books to
publish was determined largely by his own
fondness for romance and chivalry. While he
did not ignore demand, he was sufficiently
wealthy not to be subservient to it.

Caxton, a scrupulous editor and corrector,
was a writer of idiomatic and robust style. His
prologue to *The Dictes and Sayings of the
Philosophers* (1477), probably the first book
printed in England, is an example of the quiet
humor that characterizes Caxton's writing. Among
his other publications were Chaucer's *Canterbury Tales* (two editions), *The Golden Legend*
(1483), and *The Noble Histories of King Arthur
and of Certain of His Knights* (1485).

GRANT UDEN
Author of "The Knight and the Merchant"

Further Reading: Blades, William, *The Life and
Typography of William Caxton*, 2 vols. (New York
1960); British Museum, *Printing and the Mind of Man*
(London 1963); Bühler, Curt F., *The 15th Century Book*
(Philadelphia 1960); id., *William Caxton and His Critics*
(Syracuse, N. Y., 1960).

CAYCE, kā'sē, is a city in central South Carolina,
in Lexington county. It is about 1 mile (2 km)
southwest of Columbia, from which it is 'separated by the Congaree River. The city is an
industrial center manufacturing cement blocks,
crushed granite, processed silica, fabricated steel,
iron and brass foundry products, chemicals,
plastics, lumber, caskets, dolls, packed meats,
salad dressing, jellies, and candy. The Cayce
house, built in 1765, was a stronghold for both
sides in the Revolution. Cayce has a council-
manager government. Population: 9,967.

CAYENNE, kī-en', is the capital, largest city, and
chief port of French Guiana, an overseas department of France on the north central coast of
South America. The city is situated on the island of Cayenne, formed by the estuary of the
Comté River and small branches including the
Cayenne River. The climate is hot and humid,
with a fairly constant year-round temperature of
80° F (27° C) and an annual rainfall of more
than 100 inches (254 cm). Most of the people
of French Guiana live on the island of Cayenne
and other smaller centers of population in the
coastal lowlands, the remainder of the country
(90% of the land mass) being a heavily forested
highland. The capital city itself holds about
half the total population.

Cayenne's industries include sawmills, rum
distilleries, and small plants that process foods
and other local products. The chief exports are
gold, lumber, rum, and rosewood essence. The
coastal district has a good system of roads that
extend from Cayenne northwestward to St.
Laurent-du-Maroni, a small city on French
Guiana's border with Surinam (Netherlands
Guiana) and southeastward to the Brazilian
border. The airport at Rochambeau, near Cayenne, has international service. Points of interest
in Cayenne include botanical gardens, a museum,
and the Pasteur Institute, which was founded in
1940 to conduct research on tropical diseases
and now is concerned also with food and nutrition. Public educational facilities include a secondary school and a boys' vocational school.

The date of Cayenne's founding is uncertain,
although records of French settlement of the
area go back to the early decades of the 17th
century. Devil's Island, one of the Îles du
Salut, off the coast northwest of Cayenne, was
the best known of the penal settlements in
French Guiana to which French convicts were
deported from the mid-1800's until all finally
were closed in the 1940's. Population: (1962)
18,010.

GREGORY RABASSA, *Columbia University*

CAYEY, kä-yā', is a town in southeastern Puerto
Rico, 25 miles (40 km) south of San Juan.
Situated in the Sierra de Cayey, it has a cool
climate and is a summer resort. Coffee, sugarcane, and tobacco are grown in the area. The
tobacco is considered the finest produced in
Puerto Rico. The manufacture of cigars is the
town's chief industry. Population: 19,738.

CAYLEY, kā'lē, **Arthur** (1821–1895), English
mathematician, who worked on the theory of
algebraic invariants, the theory of matrices, and
the development of higher dimensional geometry.
Born at Richmond, Surrey, on Aug. 16, 1821,
Cayley spent his first eight years chiefly in St.
Petersburg (now Leningrad), Russia, where his
father was a merchant. In 1829 he returned
with his parents to live near London, where he
attended private school and King's College, London University. At 17 he entered Trinity College, Cambridge, where he graduated senior
wrangler in mathematics and became a fellow
of the college in 1842. This appointment was
not renewed; and since no new position was
offered to him in mathematics and he preferred
not to take holy orders, Cayley studied law at
Lincoln's Inn and was called to the bar in 1849.
He practiced law for the next 14 years, but he
much preferred mathematics research and pub-

lished more than 200 mathematical papers during this period.

Following changes in the statutes of the university, Cayley became in 1863 the first Sadlerian professor of pure mathematics at Cambridge, a post he held until his death there on Jan. 26, 1895. At Cambridge he continued his research, often in collaboration with James Joseph Sylvester, on algebraic invariants, elliptic and Abelian functions, geometry, and the theory of matrices. The fundamental "Hamilton-Cayley" theorem in the theory of matrices, which he established, appropriately recalls his name. Although he published only one book—*Elementary Treatise on Elliptic Functions* (1876)—his record of over 900 published papers is almost unmatched in the history of mathematics.

CARL B. BOYER, *Brooklyn College*

CAYLEY, kā′lē, **Sir George** (1773–1857), British scientist and inventor, who founded the science of aerodynamics and formulated the concept of the modern airplane. He was born at Scarborough, England, on Dec. 27, 1773. By 1799 he had designed the first flying machine of modern configuration—with fixed wings, control surfaces on the tail, and an auxiliary means of propulsion. In 1809–1810, in *Nicholson's Journal,* Cayley published the theoretical basis of aerodynamics from which all subsequent aerodynamics derives. He also built a number of model and full-scale gliders, and in one of the latter he sent his coachman as a passenger on the first true gliding flight in history (1853).

Cayley's work in aeronautics extended over calculations for lift and thrust; 3-axis automatic stability; control in pitch and yaw; streamlining; the construction of monoplanes, biplanes, and triplanes; the construction and propulsion of streamlined airships, for which he was the first to advocate compartmentation into multiple gas cells; and the production of winged artillery missiles, which he both made and tested.

Spurred on by the suggestion of a young acquaintance, Cayley in 1843 made the first complete design for a convertiplane: first the machines' four helicopter blade systems would raise it vertically, and then, when the two airscrews took over for propulsion, the blade systems would be flattened into sustaining wings.

Cayley's influence in history was exerted by means of his publications, and through those who studied his work, especially W. S. Henson, who designed the prophetic aerial steam carriage in 1842–1843, and John Stringfellow, who built his model triplane in 1868, which led directly to the modern biplane.

Cayley was also a distinguished inventor and worker in other fields: he invented the caloric (hot-air) engine (1807), which was used extensively in industry during the 19th century, and the caterpillar tractor (1825), which he patented and which led to the tracked vehicles and tanks of today. His researches extended to acoustics, electricity, optics, railroad safety devices, and land drainage (on which he was a leading authority). In 1838 he founded the Polytechnic Institute for adult education in London, which still flourishes. Cayley also represented Scarborough for a short time as a member of Parliament. He died at Brompton, England, on Dec. 15, 1857.

C. H. GIBBS-SMITH
Author of "The Aeroplane: An Historical Survey"

CAYMAN ISLANDS, kā′mən, a British colony in the Caribbean Sea. The group consists of three small islands—Grand Cayman, Little Cayman, and Cayman Brac—with a total area of 100 square miles (259 sq km). Grand Cayman, the largest and most populous, lies about 180 miles (290 km) northwest of Jamaica and 70 miles (110 km) southwest of Little Cayman, which is separated from Cayman Brac by a channel 7 miles (11 km) wide.

Most Caymanians are of mixed African and European descent. Many are seamen employed by overseas shipping companies. Turtles, turtle products, and rope are the islands' main exports, and two thirds of the trade is with the United States. Georgetown, the capital and chief port, is on Grand Cayman.

Grand Cayman and Little Cayman are low-lying, but Cayman Brac has a massive central limestone bluff rising to 140 feet (43 meters). The coasts are largely rockbound, protected by coral reefs, though Grand Cayman has a 6-mile (10-km) beach.

The islands were discovered by Columbus in 1503 and were first known as Las Tortugas (The Turtles). Ceded to Britain by Spain in 1670, they were settled from Jamaica in the 1700's. They are governed by an administrator and executive council and by a partially elected legislative assembly. Population: (1960) 7,622.

RICHARD E. WEBB
British Information Services, New York

CAYUGA INDIANS, kē-ōō′gə, a tribe of Iroquoian-speaking Indians who, at the time of their first European contacts, lived near Lake Cayuga in what is now New York state. During the American Revolution many Cayuga Indians moved to Canada, where their descendants live today. Others scattered to Ohio, Wisconsin, and Indian Territory (now Oklahoma). By the mid-1960's only about 300 Cayuga still lived in New York; the majority, around 1,000, lived in Ontario. In 1670 most of the tribe lived in three villages: Goiogouen, Tiohero, and Onnontare, all on the east side of Lake Cayuga.

The Cayuga were a member of the confederation of the Five (later Six) Nations of the Iroquois, the famous "League of the Iroquois." Their economy, religion, and social organization closely resembled those of the other member tribes. By 1550 they, like the others, were living in villages of up to 1,000 inhabitants, fortified with log palisades and defensive trenches.

The leadership of the league was composed of 50 representatives, called sachems, drawn from the villages and clans of the member tribes. Representation was not equal; the Cayuga had 10 delegates while the other tribes had as many as 14 or as few as 8. Decisions had to be unanimous, however, so majority rule was of little importance. The league was referred to as the "long house," after the long, bark-covered frame structure common to all of the member tribes.

The league maintained peaceful relations among its members, and enforced its terms of peace, by warfare and adoption of captives among outside tribes. The Cayuga played an important role in these activities until, weakened by a series of disastrous battles with the Susquehannah and their allies in 1667 and 1673, they and the Oneida and Onondaga (all members of the league) signed a declaration of neutrality with the French and British in 1688. After this time the political independence of the league declined rapidly, setting the stage for the later dispersal of the tribes. See also IROQUOIS INDIANS.

RICHARD A. GOULD
American Museum of Natural History

CAYUGA LAKE, kȧ-ōō′gȧ, is one of the Finger Lakes in west central New York. It is the longest —about 40 miles (64 km)—of the group, and the second-largest—about 66 square miles (171 sq km)—with steep banks cut by inflowing streams. It averages 2 miles (3 km) wide. The Seneca River, at its northern end, connects it with Seneca Lake to the west. This section of the river is canalized as part of the state barge system. The city of Ithaca, the home of Cornell University, lies at the southern end of the lake.

Surrounding Cayuga Lake is a farming and fruit-growing region with many resorts and recreational areas. Cayuga Lake State Park is near the village of Seneca Falls, at the north end of the lake. Taughannock Falls, Buttermilk Falls, and Robert H. Treman state parks are situated near Ithaca.

CAYUGAN SERIES, kē-ōō′gȧn, the series of rocks deposited in the Cayugan epoch of the late Silurian, about 400 million years ago. Named for Lake Cayuga in New York, it succeeds the Lockportian stage of the Niagaran series and underlies the Devonian Helderbergian series. Mineral salts of Cayugan age were formed by the evaporation of marine waters that flowed into subsiding basins in southern Michigan, Pennsylvania, and West Virginia. Halide (NaCl) is a major source of rock salt, and associated Cayugan salts produce brines for chemical industries.

Cayugan rocks in the northern Appalachian Mountains are principally limestones. Geologists in recent years have moved down the upper limit of the series, because the supposedly Cayugan limestone at Manlius, N. Y., was found to be of the same age as the Devonian Gedinnian series of Europe. Recognition of equivalent beds has been difficult, and some rocks thought to be Lockportian may be Cayugan carbonates. The series is equivalent to most of the Ludlovian series of western Europe. See also SILURIAN PERIOD.

MARSHALL KAY
Columbia University

CAZAMIAN, kȧ-zȧ-myäN′, **Louis** (1877–1965), French scholar. He was born at St.-Denis, Réunion, on April 2, 1877. In 1900 he took a degree in English at the École Normale Supérieure in Paris, and he received his doctorate of letters there in 1903. After lecturing at several French universities, he was appointed professor of modern English literature and civilization at the Sorbonne in 1909. He also lectured at several American universities.

Among his works translated into English are *Modern England* (1911); *Carlyle* (1914); *History of English Literature* (with Émile Legouis, 1927; rev. ed., 1956), which became a standard college text in the United States; *The Development of English Humor* (2 vols., 1930 and 1952); and *A History of French Literature* (1955). Cazamian died at St.-Haon-le-Châtel, Loire department, France, on Sept. 5, 1965.

CAZEMBE, kä-zem′be, was the most powerful pre-colonial kingdom in the central African savanna. The name, also spelled *Kazembe*, was taken from the title of the tribe's rulers. Early in the 18th century the king of the Lunda sent a military expedition eastward to the Luapulu Valley, south of Lake Mweru. Soon afterward he gave the title *cazembe* to one of his subordinates there.

Later cazembes acted independently of the Lunda kings, although they remained on good terms and periodically sent gifts. In a series of military campaigns, they established control over a large area, including the entire Central African copper belt. The cazembes exacted tribute from the conquered peoples. Ivory trade with the Arabs and Portuguese and valuable copper mines enriched the kingdom.

The first Portuguese expedition to visit the Cazembe capital arrived in 1798. The kingdom declined in the later 19th century as a result of succession disputes and the intrusion of Arab slave traders from the east coast. By about 1900 the defunct Cazembe kingdom had been divided between the Congo Free State of Belgium's Leopold II (now the Democratic Republic of Congo) and the British South Africa Company's Northern Rhodesia (now Zambia).

LEONARD M. THOMPSON
University of California at Los Angeles

CB RADIO, or Citizens Band radio, is a form of voice radio communication used primarily by ordinary persons to talk informally with others, as while driving an automobile. CB radio includes 40 channels, or frequencies, on which to send or receive voice messages. Channel 9 is reserved for emergency use, channel 19 is widely used by truck drivers and motorists, and the other 38 channels are for general use. A CB radio transmitter and receiver are inexpensive and simple to operate. The unit, or rig, typically is installed in a car, truck, boat, or home and is connected with a power source, such as the car battery. A license to operate may·be obtained from the Federal Communications Commission.

CB radio has undergone a phenomenal growth. The first CB license was granted in 1947. In the next 25 years, only 850,000 CB licenses were issued. However, in one month in 1976 there were more than 540,000 CB license applications in the United States. By mid-1970's, more than 15 million CB radios were in use. See also RADIO— *Special Applications of Radio*.

CEANOTHUS, sē-ə-nō′thəs, is a large genus of shrubs and small trees of the buckthorn family (Rhamnaceae). Most species have alternate leaves about 1 inch (25 mm) long and tiny flowers borne in dense clusters (panicles or racemes). Most species are deciduous, but a few are evergreen.

Two species are native to eastern North America: the New Jersey tea (*Ceanothus americanus*) and the inland ceanothus (*C. ovatus*). The New Jersey tea grows about 3 feet (1 meter) tall and has white flowers. It is so named because its leaves were used as a substitute for tea leaves during the Revolutionary War. The inland ceanothus is similar to the New Jersey tea.

The larger members of the genus are the blueflowered species native to California and Oregon. A popular one is the blueblossom (*C. thyrsiflorus*), which grows 30 feet (9 meters) tall and has flower clusters 3 inches (75 mm) long. Another blueflowered species is *C. delilianus,* which grows 6 feet (1.8 meters) tall and has evergreen leaves that may be 3 inches (75 mm) long. Several hybrids of this species, such as the Leon Simon, are well known as ornamentals.

DONALD WYMAN
The Arnold Arboretum, Harvard University

CEARÁ, sā-ə-rà′, is a state in northeastern Brazil, on the Atlantic Ocean, only 1,700 miles (2,635 km) from Africa. Ceará is one of seven states that make up Brazil's northeast region. These states all have a humid tropical climate on the coast, but the interior (the *sertão*) is semiarid and plagued by severe intermittent droughts. There is a deficiency of transportation and communication facilities and of industry. The droughts (one in 1877, which was followed by a plague, cost 57,000 lives) and the lack of jobs have caused extensive migration to the Amazon region, to the southeast, and to Brasília. In spite of this movement, the state has increased rapidly in population, as has its capital and chief port, Fortaleza (1960 population, 354,942). Other important cities are Juàzeiro do Norte, Sobral, and Crato. The sandy and mediocre coastal soils produce cotton, sugar, coffee, and rice, while the upland *sertão* grazes cattle and goats and grows caroa fiber and carnauba wax. Population: (1960) 3,337,856.

LAURENCE R. BIRNS
The New School for Social Research, New York

CEAUSESCU, chou-shes′kōō, **Nicolae** (1918–   ), Rumanian Communist leader. Born in Scornicesti in the region of Oltenia on Jan. 26, 1918, he participated widely in Communist party activities in his youth. Following the Communist victory in Rumania after World War II, he first served in posts connected with the army. In 1948 he was elected a full member of the Communist party's central committee, and in 1954 he entered the central committee secretariat and the politburo, becoming a full member of the politburo in 1955. In 1965, after the death of Gheorghe Gheorghiu-Dej, Ceausescu was elected to replace him as secretary general of the central committee. In 1967 he became head of state as well.

Ceausescu proved to be an active and able administrator. Continuing the policies of his predecessor, he emphasized industrial development and resistance to Soviet domination.

BARBARA JELAVICH and CHARLES JELAVICH
Indiana University

CEBU, sā-bōō′, one of the Visayan Islands, is located in the center of the Philippines It is separated laterally from Negros by Tañon Strait and from Bohol by Bohol Strait. The Visayan and Camotes seas converge on its northern shores. Its length, northeast to southwest, measures 139 miles (224 km), but its width is only 20 miles (32 km). The island's total area is 1,702 square miles (4,408 sq km). There is an off-center spine of mountains, traversed by six passes, the best passes running from Sibonga, just south of Cebu city on the eastern coast, across the island to Dumanjug. The province of Cebu includes Cebu island, Bantayan, Mactan, and the Camotes group.

Cebu has one of the Philippines' two principal copper mines, the largest open-pit operation in eastern Asia; and in 1955, a copper-processing plant was built at Toledo. Low-grade coal is also mined. There is a cement and fertilizer plant at Naga and a petroleum installation on Mactan off Cebu city. But Cebu's major manufacturing activity is the processing of sugar and its by-products.

There is little level land in Cebu, and the soil erodes rapidly; therefore, the land must be cultivated intensively to support its population—over 700 persons per square mile (270 per sq km)—densest of the larger provinces. Because corn is more adaptable than rice to such conditions, 89% of the food crop area and 76% of the total land cultivated is in corn. Until 1959, Cebu led the Philippines in corn yield. Cebu also grows tobacco and coconuts and is a base for commercial fishing in the Visayan Sea.

Cebu island is the source of Cebuano, an important vernacular language of the Philippines.

It was on Mactan, in 1521, that Magellan was slain when he tried to exact tribute from the chieftain Lapulapu. Later, Magellan's cross was discovered and enshrined in Cebu city. In 1565, Miguel López de Legazpi, on orders to convert the Filipinos, established the first permanent Spanish settlement among them on Cebu, where he remained until he moved to Manila in 1570. This settlement on Cebu ultimately became Cebu city. Population: (1960) 1,332,847.

LEONARD CASPER
Boston College

CEBU, sā-bōō′, capital of Cebu province in the central Philippines, is located on the eastern coast of Cebu Island. Its site attracted Miguel López de Legazpi, who in 1565 made it the first permanent Spanish settlement in the Philippines. As a commercial port, Cebu rivals Manila, and in culture it is nearly as cosmopolitan. It has two radio stations, for broadcasts in English and Cebuano, three daily newspapers, a normal school, and three universities. Imposing residences surround Osmeña Park and the capitol, along the Guadalupe River. Lahug Airfield lies between the railroad and the hills. In the harbor area stand the remains of 16th century Fort San Pedro. Cebu has an oil storage depot as well as rubber goods, corn products, and beverage factories.

In reprisal for guerrilla resistance, Cebu city was nearly razed by the Japanese in 1942. It was also severely damaged by postwar typhoons. Gradually, the buildings were rebuilt in concrete. Population: (1960) 251,146.

LEONARD CASPER
Boston College

CECCHETTI, chā-kāt′tē, **Enrico** (1850–1928), Italian ballet dancer and teacher. His students included Pavlova, Markova, Nijinsky, and other immortals of classical ballet.

He was born in Rome on June 21, 1850, into a family of dancers. After studying with Giovanni Lepri, he made his debut at La Scala in Milan in *Gods of Valhalla* in 1870 and toured Europe as a premier dancer for a number of years. He became second ballet master at the Russian Imperial Theater in 1890 and instructor at the Imperial School in 1892. Later he opened private schools in St. Petersburg and in London. In 1925 he was appointed ballet master at La Scala, where he last appeared publicly in 1926.

Among the roles that Cecchetti created were those of Blue Bird and Carabosse in *Sleeping Beauty.* Although his talents for choreography were limited, his techniques and teaching methods were of lasting influence. He died in Milan on Nov. 13, 1928.

CECCO D'ASCOLI, chāk′kō däs′kō-lē (1257?–1327), Italian poet and astrologer. His real name was Francesco degli Stabili. Cecco was born in Ascoli about 1257. He lectured on astrology at Bologna and other Italian universities and compiled commentaries on the astronomical and astrological works of Johannes de Sacrobosco and Alcabizio. Since astrology was regarded by the church as inimical to the doctrines of grace and free will, Cecco was declared a heretic and was forced to leave Bologna.

In 1324, Cecco moved to Florence, where he became astrologer to Duke Charles of Calabria. There he wrote the four books of *L'acerba,* an allegorical poem of encyclopedic compass and superstitious view, which is noted chiefly because it defends astrology against Dante's theological attacks on it in the *Divine Comedy.* The work also deals with meteorology, physiognomy, minerals, and moral problems. It was declared heretical, and Cecco was burned at the stake in Florence on Sept. 16, 1327.

CECIL, ses′əl, is the name of one of the most durable and distinguished families in England. In the last 400 years it has contributed three preeminent statesmen to Britain's government and several political leaders of distinct although less importance.

The Cecils rose to local prominence in Northamptonshire in the years immediately preceding the accession of Henry VII, the first Tudor king of England. Dedicated Protestants from the time of the Reformation, they profited from the Tudor dynasty and the spoils afforded by confiscation of monastic lands.

Richard Cyssel (Cecil) went to court during the reign of Henry VII. His son, Sir William Cecil (1520–1598), 1st Baron Burghley, became the chief minister of Elizabeth I and founded the family fortunes.

Burghley had two sons, half brothers. The elder son, Thomas (1542–1623), was an able army commander. He succeeded his father as 2d Baron Burghley and was created 1st Earl of Exeter.

Robert Cecil (1565?–1612), Burghley's younger son, was associated with his father in Elizabeth's government. He became increasingly powerful after Burghley's death in 1598, and after acting in behalf of the Stuart succession at the end of Elizabeth's reign, he became the chief minister of James I. Thus father and son occupied the same position of predominant influence in successive reigns. Robert Cecil was created 1st Earl of Salisbury in 1605.

The contemporary Cecils in the British peerage are descended in two lines from the two sons of Burghley. However, the family's political abilities are particularly marked in the Salisbury rather than in the Exeter line. In the 19th century an important new strain came into the Salisbury line when James Brownlow William Cecil (1791–1868), 2d Marquess of Salisbury, married the daughter and heiress of Bamber Gascoyne, the son of Sir William Crisp Gascoyne, who was a business magnate and lord mayor of London.

Robert Arthur Talbot Gascoyne-Cecil (1830–1903), the oldest son of the marriage, succeeded his father as 3d Marquess of Salisbury and was three times prime minister of Britain between 1885 and 1902. He was the last member of the House of Lords to form a government.

The 3d Marquess of Salisbury had five sons, three of whom achieved unusual prominence in British public life. James Edward Hubert Gascoyne-Cecil (1861–1947), 4th Marquess of Salisbury, served in the House of Commons from 1885 to 1903 and in the House of Lords thereafter. Robert Cecil (1864–1958), the third son, won the Nobel Peace Prize in 1937 and was created Viscount Cecil of Chelwood. Hugh Richard Heathcote Cecil (1869–1956), the fifth son, was a Conservative leader of the House of Commons from 1894 to 1906 and from 1910 to 1937. He was created 1st Baron Quickswood in 1941.

The 4th Marquess of Salisbury had two sons, both of whom distinguished themselves. Robert Arthur James Gascoyne-Cecil, 5th Marquess of Salisbury, was Conservative leader in the House of Lords for more than 20 years. His younger brother, Lord David Cecil, was Goldsmiths' professor of English literature at Oxford University and a distinguished author.

See also BURGHLEY, *1st Baron;* CECIL, LORD DAVID; CECIL, LORD ROBERT; SALISBURY, 1ST EARL OF; SALISBURY, 3D MARQUESS OF; SALISBURY, 5TH MARQUESS OF.

LESLIE G. PINE
Former Editor of "Burke's Peerage"

CECIL, ses′əl, **Lord David** (1902–   ), English biographer and literary critic, whose interests center largely on the British writers of the 19th and 20th centuries. He was born Edward Christian David Gascoyne Cecil in London on April 9, 1902, the younger son of the 4th Marquess of Salisbury. Educated at Eton and Christ Church, Oxford, he was elected a fellow of New College in 1939 and became Goldsmith's professor of English literature in 1948.

Writings. Cecil's criticism is not formal or technical but rather has the virtues of an older kind of appreciative sympathetic essay. His studies of English authors include *The Stricken Deer: The Life of Cowper* (1929), *Sir Walter Scott* (1933), *Jane Austen* (1935), *Hardy, the Novelist* (1943), and *Max* (1964), the life of Sir Max Beerbohm. Cecil also wrote a comprehensive, 2-part biography of the 19th century British statesman Lord Melbourne, *The Young Melbourne* (1939) and *Melbourne* (1954; also entitled *Lord M.*). He edited *The Oxford Book of Christian Verse* (1940) and coedited, with Allen Tate, *Modern Verse in English 1900–1950* (1958).

ALFRED SCHWARZ, *Wayne State University*

CECIL, ses'əl, **Lord Robert** (1864–1958), British political leader, who won the Nobel Peace Prize in 1937 for his consistent advocacy of support for the League of Nations.

Early Career. Cecil was the son of the 3d Marquess of Salisbury, prime minister of Britain. He was born Edgar Algernon Robert Cecil on Sept. 14, 1864, and was a practicing lawyer and private secretary to his father before entering Parliament in 1906. His political career was strongly independent from the outset; he joined the extreme opposition to Irish home rule, believed in free trade in spite of his party's conversion to protection, and supported the privileges of the House of Lords against the agitation to check its powers.

During World War I, Cecil was undersecretary and then assistant secretary for foreign affairs. In 1916, in a memorandum to the British cabinet, he urged the need for an international body in which disputes between nations might be publicly discussed and pressure brought to bear on an aggressor. He felt that war might have been avoided in 1914 if efforts to call an international conference to consider the crisis had succeeded, and he sought to prevent a repetition of that catastrophe.

League of Nations. As a result of his memorandum a parliamentary committee produced the first British plans for a League of Nations; and Cecil and General Jan Smuts of South Africa were the British representatives concerned with League questions at the Paris Peace Conference in 1919. Privately, Cecil thought that the American draft proposals presented at the conference by President Wilson were verbose, but because of Wilson's eminence he accepted them as the only possible basis for the League of Nations Covenant, which ultimately was part of the Versailles settlement.

In 1923, Cecil was created Viscount Cecil of Chelwood. Between the wars he was a Conservative cabinet minister (lord privy seal in 1923–1924 and chancellor of the Duchy of Lancaster in 1924–1927), periodically a British representative to the League, and an active member of various League committees. The signatories of the Versailles Treaty were committed to disarmament, and Cecil wished to see this promise honored as a guarantee of peace; he resigned from the cabinet in 1927 because he felt Britain was not working wholeheartedly enough toward this end. During the 1929 election he urged that candidates, irrespective of party, be supported or opposed according to their attitude to the League.

Later Years. Cecil was out of office in the 1930's when the League's failure to prevent Japanese, Italian, and German aggression undermined its authority, but he urged collective action against any power that resorted to war. In 1935 he helped organize the "peace ballot," a survey of British public opinion that revealed wide support for his point of view. But the British government preferred to negotiate unilaterally with the Axis aggressors. For his steadfast support of collective security he was awarded the 1937 Nobel Peace Prize.

Cecil took little part in public life after 1939. In 1941 he published *The Great Experiment,* an autobiography combining personal recollections with a history of the League. He died in London on Nov. 24, 1958.

JOHN BROWN, *University of Edinburgh*

CECILIA, Saint, sə-sēl'yə, Roman Christian martyr. Her life and cult have presented hagiographers with more thorny problems than those of any other early Roman saint. The celebration of a feast in her honor in Rome by the 4th century guarantees her historical existence, but little is known with any certainty about the details of her life. The earliest extant sources are late and completely unreliable, consisting largely of a recasting of stories in Victor of Vita's *Historia persecutionis Africanae provinciae* (about 486), an account of the martyrdom of African Christians by the Vandals. Modern estimates place Cecilia's death between 177 and 362. She may have been a Christian member of the illustrious Caecilii family. As a benefactress of the church, she may have been buried at some early date alongside the popes and martyrs in the crypt of Callistus; later Cecilia came to be venerated herself as a virgin and martyr.

The most popular version comes from the legend-filled and chronically vague *Passio,* or account of her martyrdom. According to this source, Cecilia, born into a noble Roman family, was a Christian from infancy. She was married to Valerianus, a pagan noble, whom she converted to Christianity. Valerianus and his brother Tiburtius were then martyred. After an attempt to suffocate Cecilia in her bath failed, she was ordered decapitated. She lived, however, for three days after being struck with the ax and was then buried, presumably in the Catacomb of Callistus.

Devotion to Cecilia spread widely after Pope Paschal I transferred her remains from the cemetery of Praetextatus to the Church of St. Cecilia in the Trastevere section of Rome in 821. At this time the skull was placed apart in a reliquary; yet when the sarcophagus was opened in 1599 the body was said to repose intact. Because a sentence in the *passio* was changed in the liturgy for Cecilia's feast (which has been celebrated on November 22 since the 6th century), Cecilia has become the patron saint of musicians. She is often depicted playing a small organ, viola, harp, or other musical instrument.

JOHN F. BRODERICK, S. J.
Weston College, Mass.

CECROPIA MOTH, si-krō'pē-ə, one of the largest North American moths, commonly occurring east of the Rocky Mountains. Cecropia moths sometimes attain a wingspread of over 6 inches (15 cm). Their wings are mostly dark reddish-brown, and the outer halves of both wings are alternately banded by dusky shades of white, red, black, and gray. There is a single whitish crescent-shaped mark near the center of both the fore and hind wings and a small eyespot near the tip of each fore wing. The antennae of the male have longer branches than those of the female, and thus appear more bushy.

The cecropia larva feeds on a wide variety of broad-leaved trees and shrubs such as apple, elm, maple, and wild cherry. When mature, the larva constructs a large, brownish, somewhat spindleshaped cocoon that is attached along one side to a branch. It passes the winter as a pupa inside the tough, papery cocoon. The adult moth emerges in the spring, but it has no mouthparts and survives only a few days—just long enough for mating and laying eggs.

The cecropia, *Hyalophora cecropia,* belongs to the silkworm moth family (Saturniidae).

DON R. DAVIS, *Smithsonian Institution*

CECROPS, sē'krops, in Greek legend, was the first king of Attica and the founder of Athens. According to some authorities he was believed to have been an *autochthon* (one who sprang from the soil); to others, he was half man and half snake; and to still others, he was a hero of the Pelasgians, an ancient Greek people.

As the first king of Attica, Cecrops is said to have founded a confederacy of 12 Greek cities, to whose inhabitants he introduced religion and morals, social life and marriage, and the art of writing. He ended the practice of offering bloody sacrifices to the gods and introduced the custom of burying the dead. As the founder of Athens, Cecrops is said to have built its citadel, the Acropolis, which in ancient times was named *Cecropia* in his honor and was the site of his grave and shrine.

Cecrops was married to Agraulos, daughter of Actaeus, and had a son, Erysichton, and three daughters, Agraulos, Herse, and Pandrosos.

During Cecrops' reign, Poseidon (Roman, Neptune) and Athena (Roman, Minerva) vied for the possession of Athens. The winner was to be the one who produced a gift of the greater benefit to mankind. Cecrops chose Athena because she planted an olive tree, whereas Poseidon brought forth a horse.

CECUM, sē'kəm, the large pouch at the junction of the ileum (the last segment of the small intestine) and the ascending colon (the first segment of the large intestine). The human cecum is usually 2½ inches (6.3 cm) long and nearly 3 inches (7.5 cm) across. In some other animals, especially rabbits, the secum is comparatively large and plays an impotrant role in digestion.

At the point where the ileum empties into the cecum there is a circular band of muscle tissue. This band, the ileocecal sphincter, opens at the approach of food material from the small intestine and then closes to prevent the mass from backing up into the small intestine. Protruding from the cecum, a little below the ileocecal sphincter, is the vermiform appendix, a hollow, fingerlike structure ranging in length from about 2 to 8 inches (5 to 20 cm). In man, the appendix is believed to be a rudimentary structure with no known function, but in some other animals it is well developed and aids in digestion.

JEFFREY WENIG
ENDO Laboratories

CEDAR, sē'dər, is the common name applied to a number of trees of several different genera and families, including the true cedars (*Cedrus*), the red cedars (*Juniperus*), the West Indian cedar (*Cedrela*), the white cedars (*Chamaecyparis* and *Thuja*), the California incense cedar (*Libocedrus*), and the Japanese cedar (*Cryptomeria*). However, it is considered scientifically incorrect to refer to any genus other than *Cedrus* as simply "cedar." All others require additional qualifying terms, such as "red," "incense," or "Japanese."

True cedars (*Cedrus*) are members of the pine family (*Pinaceae*). They are stately trees, 120 to 150 feet (35 to 45 meters) tall, with bunches of short, needlelike leaves and erect cones. They occur naturally from the Mediterranean region to the western Himalayas of Asia. The true cedars are among the best of evergreens for ornamental use; they also are utilized as general construction lumber. The Atlas cedar (*C. atlantica*), native to northern Africa, is pyri-

PHILIP GENDREAU

CEDAR OF LEBANON (*Cedrus libani*) is a true cedar.

midal in shape, becoming almost as wide as it is tall. The deodar cedar (*C. deodara*), with its drooping branch tips, is more tender and graceful. It is native to the Himalayas. The Cedar of Lebanon (*C. libani*) is native to Asia Minor and is the tree Solomon used in building his temple.

Red cedars are actually junipers of the cypress family (*Cupressaceae*). They are dense evergreen trees, narrow to pyramidal in shape. They have small, scalelike leaves and small, berrylike fruits. The common red cedar (*Juniperis virginiana*), found throughout the eastern United States, grows to 100 feet (30 meters) high. The western red cedar (*J. scopulorum*), of the Rocky

NORTHERN WHITE CEDAR (*Thuja occidentalis*) is not a true cedar, but is a member of the arborvitae group.

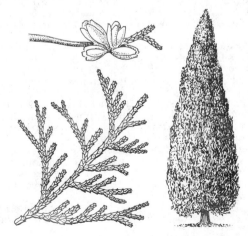

Mountains area, grows to about 40 feet (12 meters) high. The wood of the red cedar is soft, durable, and weather resistant; it is used in cedar chests, pencils, and cigar boxes.

The *West Indian cedar* (*Cedrela odorata*), native to the West Indies but widely distributed through the tropical Americas, is a member of the mahogany family (Meliaceae). It grows to 100 feet (30 meters) high and has large, divided leaves. It bears clusters of yellowish flowers and dry, capsular fruits. The wood of this tree is reddish brown, fragrant, durable, and insect repellent. It is the principal cedar wood of commerce and the wood most often used in cigar boxes.

The *white cedar* (*Chamaecyparis thyoides*), a member of the cypress family, is an evergreen tree found in swampy areas from Maine to Florida. It grows to about 75 feet (23 meters) high and has a loose, open pattern of growth. The white cedar has small, scalelike leaves and rounded, berrylike fruits. ·Its wood is sometimes used for shingles.

Occasionally the name "white cedar" is applied to the arborvitae (*Thuja*) of the cypress family. The arborvitae have flat sprays of scalelike leaves and bear very small cones. The common arborvitae (*T. occidentalis*) grows to 60 feet (18 meters) high and is widely distributed in the eastern United States. The giant arborvitae (*T. plicata*) of western North America may grow to 180 feet (55 meters) in height. The wood of these trees is durable, but it splits easily. It is therefore generally restricted to use as shingles.

The *California incense cedar* (*Libocedrus decurrens*), of the cypress family, is an evergreen tree of Oregon and northern California. It grows to 135 feet (40 meters) high, has flat, scalelike leaves, and is branched down to the ground. The leaves give off an aromatic fragrance when crushed. Its wood has been used for cedar chests and pencils.

The *Japanese cedar* (*Cryptomeria japonica*), native to Japan, is a member of the bald cypress family (Taxodiaceae). It is a showy, pyramidal, evergreen tree, up to 125 feet (38 meters) high. It is used for lumber and as an ornamental.

DONALD WYMAN
The Arnold Arboretum, Harvard University

CEDAR APPLES, sē'dər, are galls, or swellings, produced by the apple rust fungus (*Gymnosporangium juniperi-virginianae*) on twigs of the red cedar (*Juniperus*) and several other junipers. First appearing in early June, cedar apples develop rapidly, and by September they are large, brown, leathery to corklike, generally rounded structures, 1 to 2 inches (2 to 5 cm) in diameter, dotted with tiny pits. With the coming of warm spring rains, stringy, orange-colored horns, 1 to 1½ inches (2.5 cm) long, rise from the pits to form a flowerlike mass known as cedar flowers. The horns contain thick-walled spores (teliospores) that germinate and produce thin-walled basidiospores, which are released to infect apple trees (and a few other related fruit trees). The basidiospores, also called sporidia, germinate and penetrate the apple tree's tissues to produce lesions (rust spots) that ruin the leaves and fruits. The fungus then produces fertilization spores (pycniospores, or spermatia). After fertilization, the fungus pushes through the plant's tissues to release aeciospores, which reinfect cedar trees and begin a new cycle.

E. S. HARRAR
School of Forestry, Duke University

CEDAR CITY, sē'dər, is a tourist center and the chief commercial city of southwestern Utah. It is in Iron county, 230 miles (370 km) southwest of Salt Lake City. The city is the gateway to many of Utah's national parks and monuments. Cedar Breaks National Monument, Bryce Canyon National Park, and Dixie National Forest are to the east, and Zion National Park is about 30 miles (48 km) to the south.

Cedar City is in a large livestock and agricultural area. There are several iron mines to the west. Local industries include coal and iron mining, lumbering, and brick making, and the city has creameries and bottling, canning, and meat-packing plants. The College of Southern Utah, a coeducational 4-year liberal arts institution, is in Cedar City.

Mormons founded the community in 1851 and discovered iron ore. It was here that iron was first refined west of the Mississippi River. Government is by mayor and council. Population: 8,946.

CEDAR CREEK, Battle of, sē'dər krēk, in the American Civil War, fought on Oct. 19, 1864, about 15 miles (24 km) southwest of Winchester, Va. Union Gen. Philip H. Sheridan had driven a Confederate army led by Gen. Jubal A. Early south up the Shenandoah Valley. Sheridan then withdrew northward, destroying crops and other property. He left his troops encamped along Cedar Creek, commanded by Gen. Horatio G. Wright, while he visited Washington, D. C., for a conference.

Early moved his troops rapidly northward and surprised the Union army in an attack at dawn, dispersing part of it in confusion. Sheridan reached Winchester on his return trip and learned of the reversal. He rode to the battlefield and rallied the troops, who counterattacked and routed the Confederates. The victory ended the Confederates' control .of the Shenandoah Valley, which they had held for three years. Thomas Buchanan Read's poem *Sheridan's Ride* celebrates the general's role.

CEDAR FALLS, sē'dər, a city in northeastern Iowa, is in Black Hawk county, on the Cedar River, 6 miles (9.6 km) west .of Waterloo. The city is situated in an agricultural region, but has some industry. Its chief manufactured products are rotary pumps, farm equipment, golf-course equipment, humidifiers, air-conditioning and heating grilles and registers, tools and dies, stanchions, gates, feeders, wagons, hullers, and truckloading equipment.

Cedar Falls is the site of the State College of Iowa and is the home of the Cedar Falls Bible Conference.

First settled in 1844, Cedar Falls was incorporated as a city in 1865. It is governed by a mayor and council. Population: 29,597.

CEDAR GROVE, sē'dər, an unincorporated township in northeastern New Jersey, is in Essex county, in the vicinity of the Watchung Mountains, 9 miles (15 km) northwest of Newark. It is primarily a residential community. Manufactured products include instruments and small parts, brushes, machine tools, fabrics, and plastics. Cedar Grove is the site of Essex County Overbrook Hospital, an institution for the mentally ill. The township has a council-manager form of government. Population: 15,582.

CEDAR KEY, sē′dər, is a small island off the northwestern Florida coast, 90 miles (145 km) northwest of Tampa. A highway bridge connects it with the mainland. Cedar Key, a city (population, 714) on the island, was a major port of Florida's west coast in the mid-19th century, Cedar Key State Historical Memorial here has a museum featuring exhibits of the activities of the early seaport.

CEDAR LAKE, sē′dər, is in western Manitoba, Canada, west of Lake Winnipeg, near the border of Saskatchewan. It is 40 miles (64 km) long and 32 miles (51 km) broad at its widest point. Its area is 285 square miles (738 sq km). The Saskatchewan River enters the lake on the west side and leaves it on the east to pour over the Grand Rapids into Lake Winnipeg. The lake is named for a dense stand of cedar on its shores. The surrounding country is forested with balsam, spruce, birch, poplar, tamarack and pine.

CEDAR LAKE, sē′dər, a town in northwestern Indiana, is in Lake county, 19 miles (30 km) south of Gary, at the south end of Cedar Lake. The town is a summer resort and a trade center in an agricultural region where oats, corn, and wheat are raised. It is the seat of a Franciscan monastery and retreat. Cedar Lake was incorporated in 1965. Population: 7,589.

CEDAR RAPIDS, sē′dər rap′ədz, the second-largest city in Iowa, is on the Cedar River, 102 miles (164 km) northeast of Des Moines. It is the seat of Linn county. Cedar Rapids is a trade and distribution center and the principal industrial city of eastern Iowa. Situated in a large agricultural area, it has many food-processing establishments. It also produces highway construction machinery, earth-moving equipment, milk-processing machinery, radio transmitters and receivers, electronic equipment, paper products, packed meats, cereals, corn products, poultry and livestock feeds, and pharmaceuticals. The city is a major producer of popcorn and has what is considered to be the world's largest cereal mill. Cedar Rapids is one of the leading U. S. export cities; its products find markets in over 100 countries.

The city is the home of two 4-year colleges. Coe College, founded in 1851, is coeducational, and Mount Mercy College is a Roman Catholic institution for women. City and county public buildings are situated on Municipal Island, a narrow strip of land in the main channel of the river. Cedar Rapids has a symphony orchestra, community theater, and art center. The Masonic Library of Iowa there maintains a large collection of books on Freemasonry. Grant Wood, the painter, lived and taught in Cedar Rapids, and many of his canvases are owned by residents of the city.

Nearby points of interest include the Amana Colonies, a group of villages 18 miles (29 km) southwest, founded in the 1850's by members of a German religious sect; and the Herbert Hoover Birthplace and Library in West Branch, 28 miles (45 km) southeast.

The place was first settled in 1838. Cedar Rapids was incorporated as a town in 1849 and as a city in 1856. Its has the commission form of government. Population: 110,642.

JAMES C. MARVIN
Cedar Rapids Public Library

KARL H. MASLOWSKI, FROM PHOTO RESEARCHERS

Cedar waxwing

CEDAR WAXWING, sē′dər waks′wing, a small, tree-dwelling bird found in North America from Alaska and Newfoundland southward to northern Oklahoma. In the winter it migrates southward, sometimes as far as northern South America. It is also called *cedarbird.*

The cedar waxwing has handsome, sleek, fawn-gray and cinnamon-brown plumage with a feathered crest, velvety black eye patches, and a yellow-tipped tail. Its secondary flight feathers have a red, waxy appearance, from which the bird derives its name. During migration, cedar waxwings form large compact flocks. These flocks can strip an ornamental berry bush in a very short time. The food of cedar waxwings consists primarily of berries, fruits, and blossoms, but they also eat insects.

During the breeding season the cedar waxwing builds a cap-shaped nest of twigs and dry grass 4 to 5 feet (1.2 to 1.5 meters) above the ground in trees. Three to five pale bluish gray eggs are laid. The female incubates the eggs, but both sexes care for the young.

The cedar waxwing, *Bombycilla cedrorum,* belongs to the family Bombycillidae in the order Passeriformes. This order also includes other perching birds such as pipits, sparrows, and shrikes.

KENNETH E. STAGER
Los Angeles County Museum of Natural History

CEDARBURG, sē′dər-bûrg, is a city in southeastern Wisconsin, in Ozaukee county. It is situated 17 miles (27 km) north of Milwaukee, near the shore of Lake Michigan. Cedarburg is a residential and trading center. It was first settled in 1842 and was incorporated as a city in 1921. Government is by a mayor and a city council. Population: 7,697.

CEDARHURST, sē′dər-hûrst, is a village in southeastern New York, near the south shore of Long Island. A residential suburb of New York City, it is situated in Nassau county, near the boundary of the borough of Queens, New York City, 17 miles (27 km) southeast of the borough of Manhattan. The village was settled in 1680 and incorporated in 1910. Government is by mayor and council. Population: 6,941.

CEDARTOWN, sē′dər-toun, an industrial city in Georgia, the seat of Polk county, is situated 61 miles (96 km) northwest of Atlanta. Its manufactured products include tire-cord fabric, cotton yarn, woolen cloth, shirts, cheese, vitamins, chemicals, paper products, furniture, disc plows and harrows, butane gas cylinders, and prefabricated homes. Cedar, pine, poplar, and oak timber is plentiful in the region. High-grade iron ore deposits are mined nearby, and limestone is present in large quantities.

Cedartown is built on the site of a Cherokee Indian meeting ground. It was incorporated in 1854 and has a council-manager form of government. Population: 9,253.

CEFALÙ, chà-fä-lōō′, is a town and commune in Italy, on the north coast of the island of Sicily, 46 miles (74 km) east of Palermo. Cefalù is best known for its great cathedral, built by Roger II, Norman king of Sicily in the 12th century. Begun in 1131, the cathedral presents the appearance of a northern Norman church. Its vast interior, 295 feet (90 meters) long, shows examples of Sicilian and Arab workmanship.

The apse of the cathedral is its greatest glory. There the art of the mosaic makers in the Byzantine tradition reached a height unsurpassed in any of the other great centers of art in Sicily. The dominant figure of the mosaic in the apse is an immense, severe head of Christ. Below the head of Christ, the Virgin and four archangels appear. The two bottom rows of mosaics represent the apostles. The mosaics of the apse were completed in 1148. Population: (1961) of the town 10,360; (1966 est.) of the commune, 12,770.

GEORGE KISH
University of Michigan

CEILING, the interior overhead surface of a room. Strictly speaking, a ceiling is the decorative covering that partially or wholly hides the structural elements of a roof or the floor of an upper story. A ceiling is usually a flat surface made of some

BEAMED CEILING of the gallery of Francis I in the Fontainebleau Palace, France, is intricately paneled.

JEAN ROUBIER

light material, such as wooden planks or panels or plaster, which may be carved and painted. Loosely speaking, the term "ceiling" may be extended to mean the underside of a flat roof or of the floor above even when the structural elements are uncovered. For a detailed discussion of roofs, see ROOF.

Ancient and Medieval. The timber roofs of ancient Greek temples were sometimes open and sometimes hidden by coffered ceilings; that is, they were covered by a flat surface made of decorative, deep-set, geometric panels. The same kinds of roof and ceiling continued into the Roman period, with the addition of barrel vaults, groined vaults, and domes. In simpler buildings the roof beams might be covered with planks and plaster, which were sometimes adorned with paintings and reliefs.

Medieval buildings had open timber roofs; vaults; flat ceilings of planks, plaster, or shallow wooden panels; or beamed ceilings in which the structural beams stood out from the covering material.

Renaissance and After. During the Renaissance, ceilings began largely to replace open timber roofs and vaulting; in major buildings they were often extremely sumptuous. The beamed ceilings of Italian palaces were coffered, with large panels, which were generally rectangular but often included a round or oval panel in the center. The panel moldings were ornately carved and gilded, and the surfaces often bore pictures, such as those by Paolo Veronese in the Sala del Collegio of the Ducal Palace in Venice. The somberly rich beamed ceiling of the gallery of Francis I at Fontainebleau has smaller coffers of dark, ungilded wood.

The flat, white, plaster ceilings of Knole Park, Kent, are typical of the Elizabethan and Jacobean style. Their broad, shallow moldings define geometric or floral shapes that have no relation to the hidden roof beams but sometimes intersect to create an effect reminiscent of the patterns of medieval rib vaulting.

In the French rococo style of the early 18th century, the ceiling curved down into the walls instead of joining them at a right angle. In the Hôtel de Soubise, Paris, this transition is effected by painted panels of complex shapes framed in delicate, feminine C-scrolls.

During the late 18th century, European ceilings were influenced by a new interest in classical archaeology, as exemplified by English ceilings in the Adam style (q.v.). Such ceilings as those at Syon House, London, or Mellerstain, Scotland, have an exquisite linear delicacy in their combination of small painted panels with refined white moldings of urns, garlands and festoons of small bell-shaped corn husks, and radiating sunbursts against a tinted background.

During the 19th century, ceilings commonly repeated older styles. With the rise of functionalism (q.v.) in the early 20th century, they were stripped of most decoration. Technological advances, however, have found new functions for the ceiling—it may incorporate an indirect lighting system, acoustical features, or a ventilation system. Synthetic tiles and other new materials broadened design possibilities. Most 20th century ceilings are as simple in design as their function permits, relying on the natural textures and colors of materials to provide visual interest.

EVERARD M. UPJOHN
Columbia University

CELA, sä'lä, **Camilo José** (1916–   ), Spanish writer, noted for the grim realism and biting satire of his novels. He was born in Iria-Flavia on May 11, 1916, of a Spanish father and an English mother. He studied law in Madrid and England. His novels, which describe the seamy side of life in 20th century Spain, include *La familia de Pascual Duarte* (1942; Eng. tr., *Pascual Duarte's Family*, 1947), *La colmena* (1951; Eng. tr. *The Hive*, 1953), and *Mrs. Caldwell habla con su hijo* (1953). He also published several volumes of short stories, poems, and essays.

ČELAKOVSKÝ, che'lä-kôf-skē, **František Ladislav** (1799–1852), Czech poet and literary scholar. He was born at Strakonice, Bohemia, on March 7, 1799. He edited religious and literary journals and lectured on Czech language and literature at the University of Prague. Forced to leave Prague for political reasons, he accepted a professorship at the University of Breslau, in 1842, but the changed political situation after 1848 permitted him to return to the University of Prague. He died in Prague on Aug. 5, 1852.

Čelakovský's numerous works include *Poems* (1822), *Slavic Folk Songs* (1822–1827), *Echoes of Russian National Songs* (1829), *Echoes of Czech National Songs* (1839), and *Popular Philosophy of the Slavic Nations in Their Proverbs* (1851).

CELANDINE, sel'ən-dīn, a weedy biennial or perennial plant, whose acrid yellow sap has been used in medicine as a cathartic and a depressant. When taken in large quantities, the sap is poisonous, and grazing livestock are known to have been killed by eating the plants.

The celandine grows from 1 to 2 feet (30 to 60 cm) tall. Its leaves are composed of many segments 1 to 2 inches (25 to 50 mm) long, and the yellow flowers, which may be 1 inch (25 mm) wide, are borne in loose clusters. Although the celandine is originally native to Europe and western Asia, it has become naturalized in North America and ranges from Quebec to Missouri.

The celandine, *Chelidonium majus*, belongs to the poppy family. A close relative, *Stylophorum diphyllum*, is known as the celandine poppy, and a member of the buttercup family, *Ranunculus ficaria*, is called the lesser celandine.

DONALD WYMAN
The Arnold Arboretum, Harvard University

CELAYA, sä-lä'yä, is a city in Mexico, in the state of Guanajuato, about 125 miles (200 km) by road northwest of Mexico. It was founded in 1570 and was the first important city to be liberated from the Spanish after Mexico's declaration of independence in 1810. Celaya was the birthplace of one of Mexico's great architects, Francisco Eduardo Tresguerras (1765–1833), among whose buildings in the city are the churches of El Carmen and San Francisco. Celaya is noted for its production of sweets, especially a caramel sauce called *cajeta*. Other local industries are textile and flour milling, tanning, and distilling. Population: (1960) 58,851.

CELEBES. See SULAWESI.

CELEBES SEA, sel'ə-bēz, between Indonesia and the Philippines in Southeast Asia. It is 165,000 square miles (427,350 sq km) in area. The sea is bounded on the north by Mindanao island and the Sulu Archipelago of the Philippines, on the south by Sulawesi (formerly Celebes) island of Indonesia, and on the west by Borneo. To the east it passes into the Pacific Ocean.

A deep-basin sea, it has raised beaches, wave-cut terraces, and little sedimentation from rivers. It is also characterized by a rapid surface circulation of warm and salty waters reaching down to a depth of about 5,500 feet (1,540 meters). Below the sill dividing the Celebes basin from neighboring seas is a slow-moving, dense, saline circulation. The many kinds of marine forms in the sea include crabs, shrimps, and mussels.

THOMAS R. WILLIAMS
The Ohio State University

CELEBREZZE, sel-ə-brēz'ē, **Anthony Joseph** (1910–   ), American public official. Born in Anzi, Italy, on Sept. 4, 1910, he grew up in Cleveland, Ohio. After study at John Carroll University he earned a law degree at Ohio Northern University in 1936. As a lawyer in Cleveland, he engaged actively in civic and political affairs, with a period of Navy service during World War II. He was elected as a Democrat to the Ohio senate in 1950 and reelected in 1952. In 1953 he was elected mayor of Cleveland.

Celebrezze was one of the city's most popular and constructive mayors, winning reelection in 1955, 1957, 1959, and 1961 (in the last year capturing more than 73% of the vote). His administration helped develop Cleveland as a world trade center and promoted urban renewal, harbor and transportation improvements, and welfare and recreational services. After serving as president of the American Municipal Association (1958–1959) he was appointed by President Dwight D. Eisenhower to the President's Advisory Committee on Intergovernmental Relations. From 1962 to 1965 he served as secretary of health, education, and welfare, and in 1965 he became a judge on the Sixth United States Court of Appeals.

DAVID LINDSEY
California State College at Los Angeles

Celandine

ROCHE

JANE LATTA

CELERY

The edible stalks (*far left*) and flowering head (*left*).

ARTHUR AMBLER—NATIONAL AUDUBON SOCIETY

CELERY, sel'ə-rē. Celery (*Apium graveolens*) is a member of the carrot family (Umbelliferae) and is related to parsley and parsnip. In the wild state it is a tough, coarse plant containing a bitter, poisonous juice. Wild celery is native to wet, marshy places in Europe, northeastern Africa, and western Asia to the Himalaya. It also has been found growing wild in California and New Zealand, presumably escaped from cultivation.

Cultivated celery (*A. graveolens* var. *dulce*) is a biennial plant with a thick root, compacted stem, and compound (divided) leaves. The leaves are borne on long, succulent leafstalks (petioles) that are the celery of commerce.

In ancient writings celery is mentioned only as a medicinal plant. The earliest record of its cultivation as a food plant was in France in 1623, when it was used primarily as a flavoring herb in broths and soups.

Cultivation. The seed of celery is small and requires a fine seedbed for good germination. About 2 to 3 months are needed for the seedlings to grow large enough for transplanting in the field. Growth of the crop should be uniformly rapid throughout the growing season to ensure good yields and tender, edible leafstalks. This requires deep, fertile soil, irrigation, and a mild growing season. Celery is grown on sandy loam and muck soils in Florida, on muck soils in New York and Michigan, and on alluvial ("water-deposited") soils in California.

The growing leafstalks can be bleached by mounding up soil or other cover around them to block the light and prevent the development of green chlorophyll. This practice, however, is now seldom used. Some varieties tend to lose chlorophyll as they approach maturity, while others remain green. The former, which have been decreasing in importance, are earlier (planted earlier in the year), less vigorous, more easily bleached, and have thinner leafstalks that are inferior in both eating and keeping qualities to the green varieties.

If the celery plant is exposed to low temperatures for a few weeks, it will change from a vegetative growth to a reproductive type of growth. The stem will elongate and produce a branched inflorescence (flower shoot) which results in an inedible plant.

The celery's root system is highly branched but occupies a very limited area of soil. Consequently, if moisture or fertility becomes limited, growth is checked and undesirable fiber accumulates in the leafstalks, making them unpalatable.

Celery is an expensive crop to grow, requiring about 335 man-hours per acre, which exceeds that of any other vegetable. The annual United States crop value exceeds $60 million, with the states of California and Florida leading in production.

JOHN P. McCOLLUM
University of Illinois

CELESTA, sə-les'tə, a keyboard instrument like a small upright piano. It was invented by Auguste Mustel of Paris in the 1880's. The hammers of

CARROLL MUSICAL INSTRUMENT SERVICE CORP.

Celesta

the celesta, or *céleste* (from the Italian word for "heavenly"), strike metal plates over wooden resonating boxes to produce delightful, pure, bell-like tones. Its range is upward from middle C.

A *céleste*, or *voix céleste*, is also an organ stop using the same elements as the keyboard instrument to give a similar effect. Some pianos have a soft pedal called a céleste.

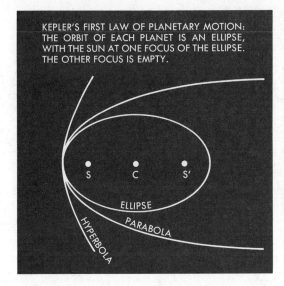

KEPLER'S FIRST LAW OF PLANETARY MOTION: THE ORBIT OF EACH PLANET IS AN ELLIPSE, WITH THE SUN AT ONE FOCUS OF THE ELLIPSE. THE OTHER FOCUS IS EMPTY.

HYPERBOLA
PARABOLA
ELLIPSE
S C S'

KEPLER'S SECOND LAW: EACH PLANET REVOLVES AROUND THE SUN IN A PATH THAT SWEEPS OVER EQUAL AREAS OF THE ORBITAL PLANE IN EQUAL INTERVALS OF TIME.

EQUAL AREAS
SUN

CELESTIAL·MECHANICS grew from the basic concept that a planet travels in an elliptical orbit (greatly exaggerated above). The sun (S) is not at the center (C) of the orbit but at one of its two foci; the other focus (S') is empty. Newton showed that celestial bodies could also have hyperbolic or parabolic orbits.

AS A PLANET MOVES about the sun, its velocity changes. Thus, when the planet is closer to the sun, it travels a greater distance in a certain time interval than it does in an equal interval when it is farther away. However, a line connecting planet and sun would sweep over equal areas of space in the same intervals.

CELESTIAL MECHANICS, sə-les'chəl mə-kan'iks, is the branch of science concerned with the investigation of the movement of bodies in space. It supplies the link between the observed motions of celestial bodies and the physical descriptions of these bodies, such as their mass and sometimes their shape. Founded three centuries ago by the English scientist Isaac Newton, it bears contributions from many of the leading mathematicians and astronomers of the 18th and 19th centuries. With the emergence of astrophysics and the movement from applied to pure mathematics, interest in celestial mechanics declined for a while, but in the present age of artificial satellites and space vehicles it has experienced a vigorous revival. Almost every facet of the subject has been affected by research since the launching of the first satellite in 1957.

Basic Concepts. Nearly all of celestial mechanics is based on Newtonian mechanics—that is, on Newton's *three laws of motion*, first published in his *Principia Mathematica* in 1657. The laws state that: (1) any particle of matter will continue in a state of rest, or of uniform motion in a straight line, unless it is compelled by some external force to change that state; (2) the rate of change of the momentum of a particle is proportional to the force applied to the particle and takes place in the same direction as that force; and (3) the mutual actions of any two bodies are always equal and oppositely directed.

Earlier in the 17th century the German astronomer Johannes Kepler, using the planetary observations made by the Danish astronomer Tycho Brahe, had formulated his three laws of planetary motion. The laws state that: (1) the orbit of each planet is an ellipse, with the sun situated at one focus of the ellipse; (2) each planet revolves about the sun in a path such that a line joining the planet to the sun sweeps over equal areas of the orbital plane in equal intervals of time; and (3) with a as the semimajor axis of

any planetary orbit, and P as the time the planet takes to make one revolution about the sun, the quantity P^2/a^3 is the same for all planetary orbits. (The point in a planet's orbit when it is closest to the sun is called *perihelion*, and the semimajor axis a is the distance between the center of the ellipse and the perihelion.)

Newton proved that as a consequence of Kepler's laws and his own laws of motion, the force acting to keep a planet in its orbit must be directed toward the sun. He proved also that this force obeyed his *law of universal gravitation*, which states that any two particles of matter attract each other with a force that is proportional to the product of their masses and inversely proportional to the square of the distance between them. Newton showed further that if any two bodies move subject only to their mutual attraction, then Kepler's laws are valid in a description of the motion of one body about the other—with the addition that hyperbolic or parabolic orbits are also possible, and that the third law should be modified to state that the quantity $(m_1 + m_2)P^2/a^3$ is always the same. (Here, m_1 and m_2 denote the masses of the two bodies.) An important limitation is that each body should be a rigid sphere. Newton showed that at points outside such a body, the gravitational force is the same as it would be were the total mass of the body concentrated at its own center; the body is indistinguishable from a particle in such calculations.

Problems of Motion. In Newtonian mechanics it is not difficult to write down the basic equations that must be solved in order to describe the motion of a celestial body. Difficulties arise only in the solution of these equations, and are of a mathematical nature.

The problem of determining the motion of two bodies that are attracted to each other, as formulated above, is called the *problem of two bodies*. It has been solved completely, and the solution is known as *Keplerian motion*. However,

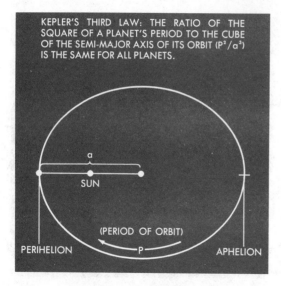

a

SUN

(PERIOD OF ORBIT)

PERIHELION   P   APHELION

THE PERIOD-DISTANCE RELATIONSHIP of planetary
orbits is described by Kepler's third law. If the
period of a planet—the time it takes to complete a revolution—is determined, the semimajor axis of its orbit
can then be calculated relative to that of the earth.
The shape of the ellipse, however, could vary greatly.

this solution has only limited application in practice. For example, the motion of the moon around
the earth can be described in terms of Keplerian
motion, but only rather inaccurately. The principal difficulty is that the attraction of a third
body, the sun, is involved as well. With three
bodies involved, there are deviations (called *perturbations*) from Keplerian motion. The *problem
of three bodies* has proved as yet to be intractable, except in special instances.

Newton demonstrated the power of his mechanics by accounting for some of the principal
perturbations in the motion of the moon, but the
problem of evolving mathematical formulas that
could be used to calculate the position of the
moon accurately enough to satisfy observing astronomers remained one of the foremost challenges to mathematicians. Not until 1887 did the
American mathematician George W. Hill lay the
foundations of a fresh approach to the problem,
enabling satisfactory theories to be constructed.

It was fortunate that the observations that
were available to Kepler were accurate enough
for him to develop his laws of planetary motion
but not accurate enough to show the perturbations that are caused by the attractions of the
other planets. These perturbations can be considerable. One of the most notable triumphs of
celestial mechanics occurred when the observed
perturbations in the motion of the planet Uranus
enabled the English astronomer John Couch
Adams and the French astronomer Jean Lever-
rier, in 1845 and 1846, to predict the existence
and calculate the position of Neptune.

Some special solutions to the problem of
three bodies were found by the French mathematician Joseph Lagrange. For one solution, the
three bodies lie at the apexes of an equilateral
triangle. Later, asteroids known now as the Trojan asteroids were discovered that lay, on the
average, in the plane of Jupiter's orbit but 60°
ahead of or behind the planet, thus forming equi-

lateral triangles with the sun and Jupiter. There
is also a famous simplified version of the problem
of three bodies, called the *restricted problem of
three bodies,* in which two bodies (for example,
the sun and Jupiter) move around each other
while a third (such as an asteroid) moves subject
to their attraction but without affecting their motions. This problem is important astronomically,
since it represents a good approximation to some
actual situations in the solar system. It has also
attracted the attention of many mathematicians,
notably Henri Poincaré (1854–1912) of France,
who may be said to have started the purely
mathematical branch of celestial mechanics.

Problems of Long-Term Prediction of Positions.
An important part of celestial mechanics is the
prediction of positions of heavenly bodies for
publications in the almanacs used by astronomers.
The lengthy formulas that are used in this work
may contain over a thousand terms, yet they are
only approximate. They satisfy conditions adequately over a few hundred years, but they certainly do not apply to the motions of the planets
over thousands, millions, or billions of years. Has
the solar system existed in its present state ever
since the planets were formed? Is it possible for
planets or satellites to escape their positions or
be captured by one another? Questions of this
kind involve difficult concepts, such as stability,
and they cannot be answered satisfactorily at the
present time.

By making some approximations in the basic
equations it is possible to gain evidence that the
planetary orbits have not changed their general
character in the past few million years. This is
known as the method of *secular perturbations.*
In special systems, such as that of the restricted
problem of three bodies, orbits that repeat themselves are studied. These *periodic orbits*—which,
by definition, are known for all time—form an
important part of the mathematical study of celestial mechanics.

Very little is known, on the other hand, of
the properties of orbits that are not periodic.
However, new mathematical methods have been
evolved in the 1960's that make it possible to
make statements about some nonperiodic motions
that also are valid for all time. The Russian
mathematician V. I. Arnold, for example, proved
that if the sun of a model solar system is sufficiently massive compared with its planets, and
if the planetary orbits are sufficiently close to
being circles and are inclined at sufficiently small
angles to one another, then such a configuration
can persist for all time. One difficulty in applying
this result lies in giving a quantitative meaning
to the word "sufficiently." Nevertheless, it must
be considered one of the most important new developments in the subject.

An argument against applying such a result to
the actual solar system is that the basic equations
of motion may not be valid over long periods of
time. Newtonian mechanics itself has proved inadequate in some situations. Furthermore, the
planets and satellites are subject to forces more
complicated than those given by the law of gravitation. In many cases in celestial mechanics,
nongravitational forces also are important; atmospheric drag or radiation pressure, for example,
is important when considering the motion of an
artificial satellite. In the case of planetary motion, the effects of such forces are at present
negligible, but their cumulative effect over billions of years cannot be dismissed.

THE FORCE OF GRAVITY is universal. Two particles of matter attract each other with a force directly proportional to the product of the two masses (M times m), and inversely proportional to the square of the distance (R) between them. (G stands for a universal constant.)

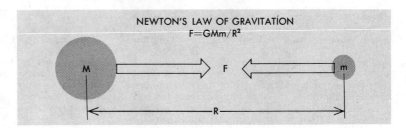

NEWTON'S LAW OF GRAVITATION
$$F = GMm/R^2$$

M F m

R

Relativistic Mechanics. In 1905 it was shown by Albert Einstein that the assumptions of Newtonian mechanics were untenable, although their lack of validity becomes obvious only when speeds comparable to the speed of light are considered. Modifications in the classical results of celestial mechanics are therefore small and can be considered as small perturbations. Nevertheless, they are observable in some cases and will become more important as observing equipment becomes more accurate and especially as electronic equipment is more widely used.

For example, it is predicted by Einstein's theory of general relativity that the elliptic orbit of a planet will rotate slowly in space. This phenomenon is called the *advance of perihelion*. The largest effect, as determined mathematically, is in the orbit of Mercury; the perihelion of its orbit would advance through 43 seconds of a degree in a century (taking, at this rate, nearly 3 million years for a complete rotation). It happens that theories of the motion of Mercury based on Newton's laws do show a disparity, when compared with observations, that could be accounted for by this small modification based on relativistic mechanics. This is considered one of the crucial tests of the theory of relativity. The test is not completely established, however. The American physicist Robert Dicke, in 1966, claimed that the relativistic effect should be smaller and that part of the motion of the perihelion of Mercury results from the fact that the sun is not perfectly spherical.

Celestial Mechanics Today. There are two main reasons for the revival of interest in celestial mechanics. One is the advent of high-speed electronic computers. A computer is able to perform long, complicated, repetitive calculations very quickly and reliably and can carry out logical operations. Apart from purely numerical work, it can also be used to develop and manipulate algebraic formulas. Consequently, many problems that were not seriously considered previously have become solvable, and it has been possible to develop new methods of attack. Modern space programs would be impossible without the speed and accuracy of these computers.

An important field that has been opened is the performance of experiments by means of a computer. For example, in order to get a better idea of the behavior of orbits in the problem of three bodies, it is possible to compute many orbits and pick out regularities that may give clues about general properties of the orbits. For many purposes (as in the calculation of the positions of some of the planets), the numerical solutions found by computers will be used in place of the approximate formulas used in the past. Computers have their limitations, however. In particular, the longer the calculation, the smaller (in general) will be the accuracy of the final result. Therefore, although they have supplemented and

eased analytical celestial mechanics, computers are more likely to stimulate than replace it.

A second reason for the resurgence of celestial mechanics is the advent of the exploration of space by satellites and space vehicles. In the past, the worker in celestial mechanics has had to be content with the orbits of natural bodies. Now he must also deal with problems concerning the design and control of artificial orbits. In the same way that the orbit of Uranus was used to reveal the existence of another planet, it is possible to study the motion of an artificial satellite of the earth to find out details of the structure of the atmosphere and irregularities in the gravitational field and the shape of the earth. Thus, satellite observations are important in geodesy.

Similarly, satellites sent into orbit around the moon have been used to determine with increased accuracy the mass of the moon and details about its gravitational field and its shape. Space vehicles passing close to Venus and Mars have yielded, through the interpretation of their orbits, more precise values for the physical properties of those planets. New problems have been created by the space age, and more accurate solutions are now required. A welcome consequence has been that in addition to being a matter of interest to astronomers and mathematicians, celestial mechanics has become important to engineers. The subject is no longer merely another branch of astronomy. See also ASTRONOMY; GRAVITATION; GRAVITY.

J. M. A. DANBY
North Carolina State University

Further Reading: Danby, John M. A., *Fundamentals of Celestial Mechanics* (New York 1962); Pollard, Harry, *Mathematical Introduction to Celestial Mechanics* (New York 1966); Van de Kamp, Peter, *Elements of Astromechanics* (San Francisco 1964). Van de Kamp's is the best book for beginners. The development of celestial mechanics was only possible after the invention of the calculus, so there are no references of consequence that do not require knowledge of the calculus.

CELESTIAL NAVIGATION. See NAVIGATION–*Celestial Navigation*.

CELESTIAL SPHERE, sə-les'chəl sfēr, the imaginary sphere on which the stars seem to be projected, with the earth at the center of the sphere. In ancient times the sky was often pictured as a sphere that rotated from east to west once every 24 hours. Since all astronomical bodies (excepting the members of the solar system) are so far away from the earth that they appear essentially fixed in the heavens, the concept of the sky as a sphere remains a useful artifice for astronomers and for those engaged in astronautics. The stars, considered as fixed points on the celestial sphere, make an excellent reference system for the determination of time and for navigational and other purposes.

The celestial sphere's apparent rotation is,

of course, produced by the rotation of the earth about its axis. Thus, if the earth's North and South poles are projected out toward the celestial sphere, they become the points about which the sphere seems to rotate.

The Equatorial Coordinate System. Suppose that an observer of the daily rotation of the celestial sphere is stationed at the earth's equator. He will note that all the stars he can see appear to rise and set and that they do so perpendicularly to the horizon. An observer at the North or South Pole will note that all the stars he can see appear to circle the celestial pole, parallel to the equator, and that they never set. For an observer somewhere between the poles and the equator, some stars seem to rise and set obliquely to the horizon, and some stars are circumpolar—that is, they stay above the horizon as they circle the celestial pole. For example, an observer 40° north of the equator sees all the stars that lie within 40° of the pole on the celestial sphere as circumpolar stars.

These facts indicate a convenient technique by which an observer may determine his latitude on the earth's imaginary geographical grid. The entire grid can be projected upon the celestial sphere, thus providing a fixed reference system in the sky. Since the earth rotates, however, it must be understood that the projection is made at a given instant during that rotation. Astronomers have established the time of projection as the moment when the center of the sun's disk is directly above the equator in the spring. This instant is called the *vernal equinox*. It occurs on or about March 22 every year.

The coordinate reference system thus defined is called the *equatorial system*. In this system, celestial latitude is referred to as *declination* and celestial longitude is referred to as *right ascension*. The celestial equator is divided into 24 time zones or *hour circles*. Stars are cataloged according to this system, with the right ascension of each star given in hours, minutes, and seconds, and the declination given in degrees, minutes, and seconds north or south of the celestial equator.

Suppose that a star of known declination and right ascension passes through the zenith·of an observer—that is, directly above his point of observation (called the *substellar point*). Since the star's position is known in terms of the equatorial system, the observer's position at that instant is also known in terms of the earth's geographical grid. With the aid of mathematics, this method of position determination can also make use of stars that do not pass through the zenith of the observer. The method is very useful for navigational purposes, in which case it is known as *celestial navigation*.

Other Coordinate Systems. The sun, moon, and planets are near enough to the earth to move with respect to the apparent motion of the celestial sphere. During the course of a year, the sun's path also moves north and south of the celestial equator, as a result of the tilt of the earth's axis with respect to the plane of its orbit around the sun. The sun's yearly path on the celestial sphere is therefore the plane of the earth's orbit extended to that sphere. This plane is called the *ecliptic*. A useful reference system known as the *ecliptic coordinate system* is based on the ecliptic as a reference plane. Another coordinate system, the *galactic coordinate system*, is based on the plane of our Milky Way galaxy. All of these coordinate systems (including a local horizon that defines positions in terms of altitude and azimuth) can be projected onto the celestial sphere. Therefore coordinates from one system can be transformed to those of another system by means of simple spherical trigonometry.

See also AZIMUTH; NAVIGATION—*Celestial Navigation*.

LAURENCE W. FREDRICK
University of Virginia

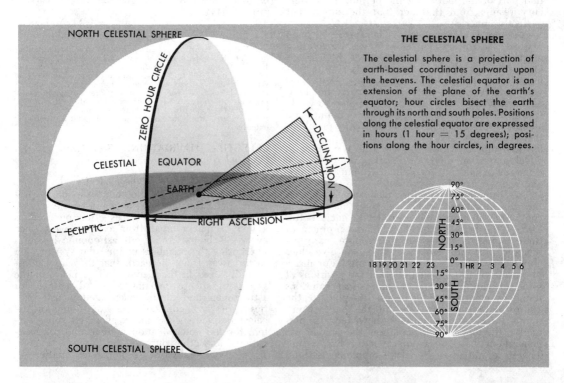

THE CELESTIAL SPHERE

The celestial sphere is a projection of earth-based coordinates outward upon the heavens. The celestial equator is an extension of the plane of the earth's equator; hour circles bisect the earth through its north and south poles. Positions along the celestial equator are expressed in hours (1 hour = 15 degrees); positions along the hour circles, in degrees.

CELESTINA, thä-lä-stē'nä, a novel in dialogue form that ranks as one of Spain's greatest literary masterpieces. The oldest extant published version of the book (Burgos 1499) bears the title *Comedia de Calisto y Melibea,* but there almost certainly was an earlier version. Fernando de Rojas (died 1541?) wrote most of *La Celestina,* but studies of its sources, themes, and syntax support the belief that the first part was written by an unknown author before 1499.

The diabolic bawd Celestina is the central character. Through guile, a perceptive grasp of psychology, and a talent for persuasion, she is able to arrange the tragic love affair between the young aristocrat Calisto and the beautiful Melibea. The lovers die—Calisto by accident, Melibea by suicide.

Influences on *La Celestina* include Roman (especially Terentian) comedy, Petrarch, medieval Spanish literature, notably the *Libro de buen amor* by Juan Ruiz. Markedly medieval are *La Celestina's* moral purpose and the mores and language of Celestina and her companions. A realistic work, *La Celestina* is a forerunner of the picaresque novel.

DONALD W. BLEZNICK
University of Cincinnati

CELESTINE I, sel'əs-tīn, **Saint** (died 432), pope from 422 to 432. A Roman, he served as archdeacon before his consecration as pope on Sept. 10, 422. He recognized Nestorius as bishop of Constantinople in 428, but when he heard that Nestorius refused to believe in Mary as the Mother of God, but believed only that she was the mother of Christ the man, Celestine sent St. Cyril of Alexandria to investigate. Using the papal commission, Cyril presided over the Council of Ephesus (June–July 431) and excommunicated Nestorius for heresy, as well as John of Antioch. The Pope approved the deposition of Nestorius but sent an emissary to bring peace between Cyril and John of Antioch.

Celestine's relations with the church in Africa became strained because of his intervention. He supported Bishop Anthony of Fussala over the protest of St. Augustine. However, he admired Augustine and protected his theology against the Pelagian doctrines, which denied the concept of original sin. He sent a mission to Britain, where the heresy had found support.

These activities are known principally through Celestine's letters. The so-called *Chapters on Grace* are not of his composition, though they represent papal thought of the time. Celestine died on July 27, 432. His feast day is April 6.

FRANCIS X. MURPHY, C. SS. R.
Academia Alfonsiana, Rome

CELESTINE II, sel'əs-tīn (died 1144), was pope in 1143–1144. His reign was marked by the settlement of a quarrel between his predecessor Innocent II and King Louis VII of France. He was born Guido de Castellis and was a pupil of Abelard. He served in the papal curia under several popes and stood loyally by Innocent II against antipope Anacletus II. Guido was a cardinal priest of St. Mark when he was elected pope in 1143 as Celestine II.

Celestine was an old man when he took office, and his reign was brief. He died on March 8, 1144.

JOSEPH S. BRUSHER, S. J.
University of Santa Clara, Calif.

CELESTINE II, sel'əs-tīn, was antipope in 1124. He was elected in a compromise between candidates of the Frangipane and Pierleone families. He was born Theobold Buccapecu and was a cardinal priest before his election. When the Frangipanes pressed their candidate's claim, the cardinals abandoned Celestine. Although he is not officially recognized, it seems hard to call him an antipope.

JOSEPH S. BRUSHER, S. J.
University of Santa Clara, Calif.

CELESTINE III, sel'əs-tīn, was pope from 1191 to 1198. Born Giacinto Bobo in Rome, about 1106, he studied theology in Paris under Abelard and attempted to defend his master at the Council of Sens in 1140. Created a cardinal in 1144, he served in the Roman curia and was sent on legations to Spain in 1154 and 1172.

He undertook numerous missions for the exiled Pope Alexander III, and on March 30, 1191, at the age of 85, was himself elected to the papacy. His advanced age made it difficult for him to control the Roman aristocracy, and as a result the city of Tusculum was destroyed. He crowned Henry VI emperor, but broke relations with him when Henry invaded Sicily and threatened the independence of the papacy. He failed to take action against the Emperor for the murder of the bishop of Liège and the imprisonment of Richard I of England who, as a returning crusader, was under papal protection. To avert possible violence at the conclave after his death, he proposed that the cardinals accept his designation of John of St. Prisca as his successor and offered to resign in his favor in 1197, but the cardinals refused this revolutionary offer. Celestine died on Jan. 8, 1198.

FRANCIS X. MURPHY, C. SS.R.
Academia Alfonsiana, Rome

CELESTINE IV, sel'əs-tīn (died 1241), pope in 1241. Born Goffredo Castiglioni, he was named a cardinal in 1227. When Pope Gregory IX died in 1241, his war with Frederick II had reached the outskirts of Rome. To keep Frederick from influencing the papal election, Matteo Orsini, a Roman senator, kept the cardinal-electors in Rome. They compromised after two months on Goffredo. He died, however, 17 days later.

ANDREW J. CHRISTIANSEN, S. J.
Loyola Seminary, Shrub Oak, N. Y.

CELESTINE V, sel'əs-tīn, **Saint** (1215–1296), pope from July 5 to Dec. 13, 1294. He was born Peter of Morrone, in Isernia, Italy. He joined the Benedictine order in 1235 and was a founder of the Celestines (1264). Most of his life was spent as a hermit and itinerant preacher. In July 1294 he wrote to a cardinal in Perugia denouncing the incapacity of the conclave meeting there to choose a successor to Pope Nicholas IV. Impressed by the letter, the cardinals elected him; he was crowned Celestine V on August 29.

Charles II of Anjou and a host of adventurers took advantage of Celestine's inexperience, administrative incompetence, and unworldliness to exploit the papal resources by means of appointments, pensions, and other privileges. Charles secured the rank of cardinal for a number of his favorites and the appointment of his son Louis to the see of Lyon.

Realizing his inadequacy for the papacy, Celestine issued a bull declaring the pope's right to resign and forthwith did so on Dec. 13, 1294. He was succeeded by Boniface VIII, who revoked most of Celestine's concessions and kept him in papal custody until his death in Anagni on May 19, 1296, lest he be used by Boniface's enemies. Celestine was canonized by Clement V on May 15, 1313, and his feast is observed on May 19.

MICHAEL V. GANNON, *University of Florida*

CELESTITE, sel′ə-stīt, is mineral strontium sulfate. Large deposits of celestite are a useful source of strontium. Celestite occurs in fibrous form or as tabular or prismatic crystals, usually in sedimentary rocks such as sandstone and limestone. Barium often substitutes for strontium in varying proportions.

The transparent to translucent crystals of celestite have a glassy luster and are usually colorless or white but sometimes have a bluish tinge. Fine crystals have been found in Sicily, Czechoslovakia, and Britain. The best occurrences are in the United States.

Composition, $SrSO_4$; hardness, 3–3.5; specific gravity, 3.9; crystal system, orthorhombic.

CELIAC DISEASE, sē′lē-ak, is a chronic disorder of infants and children characterized by an impaired absorption of food materials. The major symptom is diarrhea, and the stool is generally fatty, bulky, and foul-smelliing. Associated with the diarrhea is a loss of nutrients, leading to nutritional deficiencies. The major problem is concerned with the malabsorption of fat.

For many years, the cause of celiac disease was unknown, but it is now recognized that afflicted patients are usually sensitive to certain proteins, called glutens, which are found in wheat, rye, and oats. There is some evidence suggesting that the disease is due to an inherited defect of some kind, but the exact mechanism is still unknown. Celiac disease occurs almost exclusively in white children. It is uncommon in Negroes and has never been found in Orientals. In recent years, a malabsorption disorder of adults has been recognized as a sensitivity to gluten. This disorder, once called non-tropical sprue, is now called adult celiac disease.

Symptoms. The severity of celiac disease may vary enormously, from a mild digestive disturbance to a serious and debilitating wasting disease. The onset usually occurs gradually at the end of the first year of life and becomes full blown in the second year. In addition to the diarrhea, the child often has a poor appetite and does not grow normally. He may also become irritable and moody. As he grows older, retardation in growth and development becomes more evident, and there is a weight loss, usually most marked in the limbs and around the buttocks and groin. Although the face often remains full and plump, the child often looks pale, and there may be a puffiness around the eyes. The abdomen is generally enlarged and distended.

Treatment. Treatment consists of placing the child on a gluten-free diet. If this diet is strictly followed, there may be a complete remission of the symptoms, and by the replacement of lost nutrients all signs of deficiency disappear. Most children improve spontaneously in adolescence and adult life, although there may an occasional later recurrence.

LOUIS J. VORHAUS, M. D.
Cornell University Medical College

CELIBACY, sel′ə-bə-sē, is the state of being unmarried, usually because of religious motives. As a Christian institution, celibacy is the voluntary renunciation of marriage for the purpose of practicing perfect chastity. The Roman Catholic Church requires all religious and clerics in major orders to be celibate, but grants certain privileges to clerics of the Eastern rites. Outside the Christian tradition religious celibacy is practiced by members of the Hindu, Jain, and Buddhist ascetic orders, who consider it a high form of austerity.

Ancient peoples frequently imparted religious significance to celibacy but rarely considered it fitting as a permanent condition of life. The continence or virginity that certain cults demanded of their priests and priestesses (for example, the Roman Vestal Virgins) was a form of corporal purification and related to worship. Although both the Greeks and Romans had a special veneration for their virgin goddesses, they exhibited only contempt for unmarried persons. Old Testament Jews considered marriage a duty and looked upon a large family as a sign of divine favor. However, Jewish monks—the Essenes and members of the Qumran community—practiced celibacy, primarily for religious reasons.

Early Christian View. Through the teaching and example of Christ and St. Paul, celibacy and virginity came to be viewed as virtues. Christ, born of a virgin, dedicated his entire life to the service of God and man. He knew neither marriage nor carnal love; He commended celibacy as a practice, particularly for those seeking the kingdom of heaven (Matthew 19:12); He presented virginity as a state of eschatological beatitude, which he likened to the angelic life (Matthew 22:30; Luke 20:34–36; Mark 12:25). At the same time He made it clear that only those few who were called to a life of celibacy could accept this difficult teaching (Matthew 19:11–12).

Following the precepts of his Master, St. Paul praised and practiced celibacy as the more perfect condition of life which, he believed, better enables men to serve God freely (I Corinthians 7:25–35). Although he desired all Christians to follow his example (I Corinthians 7:7), Paul admitted that those not in the ministry had a right to marry. Thus Paul's advice had special significance for those in the ministry. He clearly indicated his desire that his coworkers in the ministry exert restraint in exercising their right to marry, when he prescribed that a bishop or a priest be blameless and be married only once (I Timothy 3:2).

Despite the fact that clerical celibacy is highly recommended in the New Testament, there is no evidence that it either derives from a divine precept or that the church imposed it as a requirement prior to the 4th century. It is known that as early as the 1st century ascetics were living in continence "in honor of the flesh of Christ." Perfect continence came to be regarded as an essential part of the asceticism that became highly developed during the 2d century and later was to evolve into monasticism.

Medieval Legislation. The law of clerical celibacy took on definite form, both in the East and the West, during the 4th century. Legislation in the East was codified by the Christian emperors Theodosius II and Justinian I. Somewhat less rigorous and more liberal than in the West, it prohibited bishops from marrying, but allowed priests, deacons, and subdeacons, if married before ordination, to retain their wives. No cleric, however, was permitted to remarry after his wife's death. In 692 the Council of Trullo not only confirmed this legislation but adopted an even stricter view: absolute continence was enjoined upon all bishops, and if a bishop-elect was married he had to separate from his wife, who was to enter a monastery. This decree is still in force in most Eastern churches, but some Eastern Catholic rites have adopted a discipline similar to that of the Roman church.

The first known decree on clerical celibacy in the West is that of the Council of Elvira (about 300), which imposed absolute continence on "all bishops, priests, deacons, and all clerics engaged in the ministry." This legislation did not go into effect, however, until the latter part of the 4th century when subsequent councils and papal decrees imposed it absolutely. In the 5th century, Pope Leo the Great extended the obligation of celibacy to subdeacons.

The period following the decline of the Carolingian Empire was characterized by a general moral decay that could not but help affect clerical celibacy. Like many other doctrines, it was attacked as unnecessary. St. Peter Damian (1007–1072) refuted such arguments against celibacy that were typical of those times in his *Liber Gomorrhianus* and *De coelibatu sacerdotum ad Nicolaum II.* Although abuses among 11th and 12th century clergymen abounded, they were met with vigorous protests and remedial measures by popes such as Leo IX and Nicholas II. It was the courageous and energetic action of Pope Gregory VII, however, that restored clerical celibacy to its original state.

The First and Second Lateran Councils (1123; 1139) further strengthened the laws of celibacy by declaring invalid, without exception, all marriages attempted by clerics in sacred orders. The law was confirmed and extended to subdeacons by Pope Alexander II in 1180. Pope Paul VI abolished the order of subdeacon in 1972, and candidates for the priesthood now assume the obligation of celibacy when they become deacons.

The Council of Trent to Vatican II. Despite such strict legislation, clerical celibacy came under attack again at the end of the Middle Ages, and particularly during the Renaissance when a new decline in morality permeated the church. The most serious campaign against celibacy, however, was waged from outside the church by Martin Luther and other leaders of the Protestant Reformation. Luther not only condemned celibacy but declared void the vow of chastity of all priests, both religious and secular. John Calvin admitted the value of celibacy but objected to its imposition as an obligation on the clergy.

To counteract the effects of the Reformation and to suppress widespread abuses in the church, the Council of Trent (1563) reaffirmed the value and suitability of clerical celibacy. This Tridentine legislation was incorporated into the Code of Canon Law when it was revised in 1917, and has since been in force. In his encyclical *Sacra virginitas* (*Consecrated Virginity*, 1954), Pius XII reminded all Catholics of the excellence of celibacy and consecrated virginity. Vatican II also reasserted approval of the institution of celibacy, but it did make provisions for the order of diaconate to be opened to married men of mature age. Even before Vatican II, however, Pius XII— as well as his successors John XXIII and Paul VI

—had departed from traditional church policy when he granted dispensations from the vow of chastity to married Protestant ministers who had been converted to Catholicism and who wished to be ordained priests.

The Encyclical "Sacerdotalis Caelibatus." With the many changes wrought in the Catholic Church by Vatican II, it was inevitable that the institution of clerical celibacy would once more be questioned. Certain quarters of the church expressed the view that priestly celibacy be made optional. After Pope Paul VI had given consideration to the matter, he fulfilled his promise to the Council Fathers and wrote an encyclical on celibacy, *Sacerdotalis caelibatus*, which was issued to the whole church on June 24, 1967. In it Paul VI reaffirmed the church's traditional teaching and rejected modern objections raised against it. The Pope maintained that celibacy, far from being detrimental to the physical and psychological development of the priest's personality, supports him "in his exclusive, definitive, and total choice of the unique and supreme love of Christ." Although, like Vatican II, the Pope conceded that virginity is not demanded by the very nature of the priesthood, he emphasized the contemporary relevance of priestly celibacy.

BERNARDINO M. BONANSEA, O. F. M.
Catholic University of America

CELINA, sə-lī′nə, a city in western Ohio, the seat of Mercer county, is 85 miles (137 km) northwest of Columbus. It is situated on Grand Lake and is a summer resort. Celina has canneries, and it manufactures furniture, bicycles, lawnmowers, and metal products. It is the site of Western Ohio College, founded in 1962. Celina, settled in 1834, is governed by a mayor, council, and city manager. Population: 7,779.

CÉLINE, sā-lēn′, **Louis Ferdinand** (1894–1961), French novelist, whose nihilistic distaste for humanity and his seemingly careless style were precursors of black humor and the literature of the absurd. Céline, whose real name was Louis Ferdinand Destouches, was born at Courbevoie, near Paris, on May 27, 1894. Trained as a physician he practiced medicine in a low-income area of Paris.

Céline's first and by far his best novel, *Voyage au bout de la nuit* (1932), was a triumph. The hero, Dr. Ferdinand Bardamu, Céline's alter ego, relates his odyssey of revolt, despair, and anarchy in a new, controversial language that ranges from slang to scatology. Subsequent books, such as *Mort à crédit* (1936), also mix autobiography and invention in violent, nihilistic chronicles suggestive of the "nausea" of Sartre.

Intensely anti-Semitic, as shown by his virulent pamphlets and picaresque novel *Guignol's Band* (1944), Céline was suspected of sympathizing with the German occupation of France during World War II and fled to Germany and Denmark. Returning to France in 1951, he became a recluse and a doctor for the poor. He published his somewhat fictionalized versions of his wartime adventures in *D'un château l'autre* (1957) and *Nord* (1960). Céline died in Paris on July 3, 1961.

EDWIN JAHIEL, *University of Illinois*

Further Reading: Hindus, Milton, *Crippled Giant* (New York 1950); Ostrovsky, Erika, *Céline and His Vision* (New York 1966).

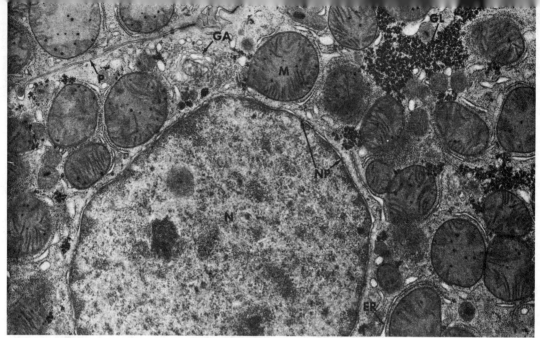

ELECTRON MICROGRAPH of a bat liver cell, showing nucleus (N) and nuclear pores (NP), mitochondria (M), endoplasmic reticulum (ER), Golgi apparatus (GA), glycogen, granules (GL), and plasma membrane (P).

CELL. The living tissue of almost every organism is composed of fundamental living units called cells. A very small organism may consist of only a single cell; such unicellular forms include bacteria, protozoa, some algae, and the gametes (reproductive stages) of higher organisms. (See MICROBIOLOGY.) Larger organisms, on the other hand, are subdivided into cells that are relatively autonomous but cooperate in the functioning of the plant or animal. The fact that both plants and animals are made up of cells is the basis of the *cell theory*. It was first recognized in 1838-39 by the German biologists Matthias J. Schleiden, who had studied plants, and Theodor Schwann, who worked on animals. See also ANIMAL—1. *Animal Characteristics;* PLANTS AND PLANT SCIENCE—2. *Anatomy.*

While a unicellular organism must perform all activities necessary for its nourishment and reproduction, these activities are fulfilled by the entire population of cells in a higher organism; therefore, the component cells may become specialized in their cooperative functions. Within such an organism, a *tissue* is a population of cells with the same specialized function. The cells of muscle tissue, for example, are specialized for movement and those of bone and connective tissue, for structural support. Corresponding to such differences in function, cells of different tissues differ widely in structure.

Cells vary greatly in size. Although some nerve cells have axons that are several feet long, a typical animal cell such as that described in the following section has an overall diameter of perhaps 20 microns (roughly 1/1000 inch). Cells of this size can be seen only with the aid of a microscope.

A typical animal cell is described immediately below, and the distinguishing characteristics of the basically similar plant cell are discussed in the following section. For a description of bacterial cells, which are considerably simpler in structure, see BACTERIA AND BACTERIOLOGY—2. *Bacterial Anatomy.*

ANIMAL CELL STRUCTURE

Although cells vary widely in their structure and function, the conditions for life impose certain basic requirements upon the composition and activities of all cells. Essential components include the *nucleus,* which serves as a control center, the *cytoplasm,* which does the work, and an enveloping *plasma membrane.*

Nucleus. The nucleus is usually a spherical or ovoid body occupying about 1/10 of the cellular volume. It contains the *chromosomes,* which consist principally of *deoxyribonucleic acid* (DNA) and of basic proteins called *histones.* The chromosomes carry the cell's genetic information and play a central role in the regulation of the cell's activities. See also CHROMOSOME; MITOSIS.

Nucleolus. The nucleus usually contains two spherical bodies, the *nucleoli,* which are rich in *ribonucleic acid* (RNA) and deficient in DNA. There is generally one nucleolus for each set of chromosomes; hence, the normal diploid cell contains two sets of chromosomes and two nucleoli. This equality of numbers follows from the fact that the nucleolus is formed in association with a *nucleolar organizer* carried by one chromosome in each set. This organizer is probably the region of the chromosome where ribosomal RNA is synthesized. Ribosomal RNA is one of the principal components of the cell organelles known as ribosomes, described below.

Nuclear Membrane. The nucleus is limited by a *nuclear envelope,* or *membrane,* which consists of two thin *unit membranes* separated by a small gap. This complex envelope is perforated by numerous nuclear pores, which probably provide for exchange of materials between nucleus and cytoplasm. This exchange is probably controlled by a dense material that fills the orifice of each pore.

Unit Membranes. Each of the two unit membranes of the nuclear envelope is a trilaminar (3-layered) structure composed of a protein layer, a lipid layer, and another protein layer. This important basic structure, which occurs in many other parts of the cell, varies in thickness from about 60 to 120A (angstrom units). Unit membranes limit the movement of molecules both within the cell and between the cell and its environment. They also possess means of permitting certain molecules to pass through themselves, either passively through minute pores or actively by a "pumping" mechanism.

Cytoplasm. The cytoplasm surrounds the nucleus and performs most of the active functions of the cell. Although the composition of cytoplasm varies from one cell type to another, certain basic substructures are present in most cells.

Ribosomes. Ribosomes are particles, about 250A in diameter, that synthesize proteins. They are composed of large RNA molecules, which are produced by the nucleolus, and of various proteins. If the proteins synthesized by the ribosomes are to remain in the soluble part of the cytoplasm, or *ground substance*, the ribosomes remain free within this matrix. In a rapidly growing cell, for example, most of the ribosomes are found in the ground substance; the proteins produced here permit the cell to increase its bulk between divisions. If the proteins must be segregated from the ground substance, however, the ribosomes become attached to the outer surface of membrane-enclosed sacs in the cytoplasm.

Endoplasmic Reticulum. These ribosome-studded sacs are the *cisternae* of the rough-surfaced (or granular) endoplasmic reticulum (rough ER). The membranes are similar to the unit membranes of the nuclear envelope. In fact, the outer membrane of the envelope is frequently continuous with the membranes of the rough ER and may itself be covered with ribosomes. Proteins that are synthesized by the ribosomes of the rough ER pass directly into the membrane. Some of them remain here to provide material for membrane growth. But many proteins pass into the cavity of the cisterna where they remain segregated from the other components of the cytoplasm. The segregated proteins are either stored for later use within the cell or secreted from the cell for the benefit of the organism.

The smooth-surfaced (or agranular) endoplasmic reticulum is distinguished from the rough-surfaced component by its lack of ribosomes. It frequently is composed of tortuous tubules, also bounded by unit membranes. Although the functions of the smooth ER are somewhat obscure, it probably provides for the segregation and transport of certain kinds of molecules (sugar, fats, salts, steroids, and proteins) within the cytoplasm.

Golgi Apparatus. The *Golgi apparatus*, or *Golgi complex*, is another cytoplasmic organelle composed of spaces enclosed by unit membranes. The structure was originally identified in 1898 by the Italian biologist Camillo Golgi through its ability to cause a visible precipitate from silver salts. The electron microscope has revealed the Golgi apparatus to be a stack of flat cisternae surrounded by both irregular and spherical vesicles. Several Golgi complexes may be present in a cell, sometimes comprising a larger, continuous network. Among the roles tentatively assigned to the Golgi bodies is the "packaging" of newly synthesized protein from the endoplasmic reticulum and the complexing of such proteins with other kinds of molecules.

Mitochondria. Mitochondria (singular, *mitochondrion*) are discrete cytoplasmic bodies present in all aerobic (oxygen-using) cells. They are generally 1 to 2 microns long and about ½ micron in diameter, and possess two unit membranes, one enclosing the other. One membrane forms the outer wall of the elongate structure, and the other, the internal membrane, which has a much larger surface area, is highly convoluted —either into flattened folds called *cristae* or into small tubules. The enzymes that mediate the formation of the high-energy molecule adenosine triphosphate (ATP) by the process of oxidative phosphorylation are contained within the mitochondrion, probably in well-ordered complexes attached to the surfaces of the inner membranes. The ATP provides available energy for a multitude of cellular processes.

Lysosomes. Another component generally found in animal cells is the lysosome. Hydrolytic enzymes, such as the acid phosphatases, are contained within these membrane-enclosed bodies, where they will not destroy other parts of the cytoplasm. The lysosome may combine with food vacuoles, and the hydrolytic enzymes then break up (digest) various large molecules into small molecular subunits, which can be used by the cell.

TWO CENTRIOLES (CN) *(left)*, perpendicular to one another and surrounded by microtubules (Mt). Microvilli of an intestinal absorptive cell *(right)*, covered by the plasma membrane, increase the surface area of the cell.

DR. BRECK BYERS   DR. KEITH R. PORTER

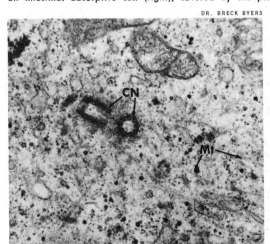

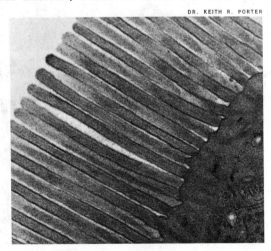

Other Cytoplasmic Inclusions. Other cytoplasmic inclusions are present with considerable variability between different cell types. *Food vacuoles* are membrane-limited sacs containing the products of phagocytosis. Other vacuoles may be involved in water balance. *Glycogen* is a form of polymeric glucose, serving as a stored food supply, especially in animal cells. *Pigment granules* are particularly prominent in epidermal cells, but are also found in older cells of internal organs. *Fats* and other lipids are seen as nearly spherical droplets within the cytoplasm. In fat tissue, a droplet may become so enormous that the rest of the cell contents are limited to a thin covering surrounding the droplet, with the nucleus flattened against one side of the cell membrane. Products of protein synthesis by the rough endoplasmic reticulum are usually enclosed in membrane-limited sacs; *zymogen granules*, for example, are packages of hydrolytic enzymes in the acinar cells of the pancreas.

Structural Elements. Other elements of the cytoplasm provide the structural framework for support and movement within the cell. Muscle tissue, for example, is composed chiefly of numerous *fibers* containing a contractile protein complex of *actin* and *myosin*. More primitive systems for movement may also involve cytoplasmic fibers. Thus, the framework of the mitotic spindle is composed of microtubules, which are extremely long, straight, apparently hollow rodlets about 250A in diameter. Various other cytoplasmic complexes, which are characterized by a dynamic supporting system, also contain microtubules. *Microfibrils* are even smaller than microtubules and seem to lack a hollow center. They may also play a role in cytoplasmic support and mobility.

Centrioles. The cells of animals and of certain lower plants contain a pair of centrioles. Electron microscopy reveals their complex organization: each consists of a cylinder of nine sets of three microtubules parallel to the cylindrical axis. Centrioles are found not only at the poles of the mitotic spindle (where they probably control the activities of this complex of microtu-

bules), but they also are the *basal bodies* for specialized organelles called *cilia* and *flagella*. Both cilai and flagella are long projections from the surface of the cell and like the centrioles they contain microtubules (a ring of nine sets of two, plus two near the center). Cilia and flagella whip violently through the surrounding medium and thus cause the cell to move through the medium, or, if the cell is fixed, cause the medium to move past the cell.

Plasma Membrane. The plasma membrane, or cell membrane, also appears as a unit membrane, but its structure may include an outer covering believed to consist of mucopolysaccharides (sulfur-containing polymers of sugar, sometimes combined with proteins). This membrane must control not only the exchange of materials between the cell and its environment but also the adhesiveness between cells.

The plasma membrane regulates with great specificity the passage of ions into and out of the cell. This is particularly important in nerve cells, where a sudden great change in the concentration of certain ions results in a reversal of the electrical potential difference across the membrane and the propagation of an *action potential,* or *nerve impulse,* which travels down the long cell axon and excites the adjoining cell either by electrical or chemical stimulation.

The rate of exchange of molecules between the cytoplasm and its environment is partly dependent on the surface area of the plasma membrane. Thus, cells that absorb large quantities of material generally have their surface area increased, either by extensive folding of the cell membrane, or as in the cells lining the intestine, by fingerlike projections called *microvilli.*

Larger materials must enter the cell by a drastic change in the shape of the plasma membrane. Particles such as food or bacteria may be ingested by *phagocytosis,* a process in which folds in the membrane engulf the particles; this results in the formation of a food vacuole. Proteins and other macromolecules may enter the cell by a similar process, called *pinocytosis,* in which a small depression in the membrane

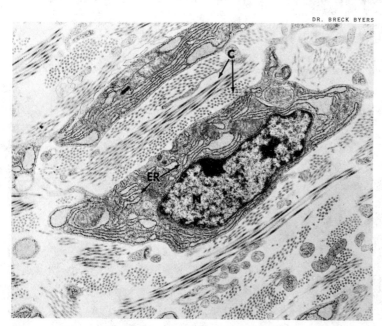

DR. BRECK BYERS

FIBROBLAST CELL of a chick embryo, showing nucleus (N), collagen fibrils (C) in both longitudinal and cross section, and endoplasmic reticulum (ER) containing the protein precursor of the collagen fibrils.

breaks off and enters the cell as a tiny vesicle.

Other specializations of the plasma membrane involve the contacts between adjacent cells. In the usual situation, there is an apparent 200A gap—probably filled by mucopolysaccharide—between the outer limits of the two unit membranes. A *tight junction* is a region where this apparent gap is closed, permitting small molecules to pass relatively freely between the cytoplasms of the two cells. A *desmosome* is an adhesive complex that is reinforced by fibrils diverging into the cytoplasm of the two cells.

PLANT CELL STRUCTURE

Most of the organelles of animal cells are also present in plant cells. One important exception is the centriole, which is absent from the cells of all higher plants except in the reproductive stages of a few plants. Plant cells have two structures—a cell wall and plastids—not found in animal cells, and the vacuoles of most plant cells are much larger than those of animal cells.

Cell Wall. The cell wall of plants is usually considered to consist of an extensible *primary wall,* which is formed during cell division, and a more rigid *secondary wall,* which is formed during cell differentiation. *Cellulose* is an important component of the wall. Many cell walls have perforations containing *plasmodesmata,* which are minute connections between the plasma membranes of adjacent cells.

Plastids. A unique class of organelles in plant cells are the plastids. Some of these ovoid structures store materials such as starch, oil, or protein. The most familiar form of plastid is the chloroplast, which carries on photosynthesis. It has a complex structure of internal membranes, and the entire chloroplast is limited by a double set of membranes like that of the mitochondrion. See also CHLOROPLAST.

Vacuoles. The vacuoles of plant cells are frequently so large that they nearly fill the cell, and the cytoplasm makes up only a thin layer against the cell wall, with thin strands transversing the vacuole. Hydrostatic pressure within the vacuole and within the cell as a whole forces the plasma membrane firmly against the cell wall, thus producing the rigidity of nonwoody plant tissues known as *turgor.*

METABOLISM

The living cell contains an enormous variety of organic molecules in dynamic interaction. The larger molecules may be assigned to certain categories on the basis of the smaller units of which they are formed. *Proteins* are specifically ordered polymers of L-amino carboxylic acids; they are not only structural elements of cells, but they also make up the important class of compounds called *enzymes,* which catalyze biochemical reactions. *Nucleic acids* are linear polymers of *nucleotides* and contain coded information for the synthesis of proteins. Lipids are important both in metabolism and in membrane structure; they include *fats,* which are esters of long-chain carboxylic acids with glycerol, and *steroids,* which are derivatives of a complex ring system.

The enzymes of intermediary metabolism catalyze the conversion of smaller organic molecules from one form to another. The basic materials for these processes are ultimately derived from *carbohydrates* produced by photosynthesis in green plants. Enzymes in the cytoplasmic matrix of the plant cell use these carbohydrates for the

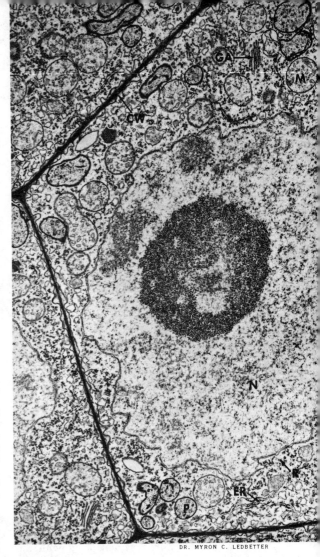

DR. MYRON C. LEDBETTER

PLANT CELL, showing large nucleus (N) with densely staining nucleolus; mitochondria (M), proplastids (P), Golgi apparatus (GA), ribosomes (R), and cell wall (CW).

production of energy and for conversion into other kinds of molecules. Similar conversions occur in the cells of animals, which ingest these plant materials. But animals also frequently depend upon plants for the synthesis of certain other kinds of molecules; the *essential amino acids* required for protein synthesis are particularly important.

Energy Production. Although some useful energy is obtained by the cell from these enzymatic conversions within the cytoplasmic ground substance, the greatest amount of such energy is produced within the mitochondria. Here, ordered complexes of enzymes and cytochromes convert acetate residues (derived from various foods) into carbon dioxide and water. The energy freed by this degradation is used to synthesize ATP, which then provides energy for various cellular processes such as muscle contraction, active transport, and macromolecular synthesis. See also ATP.

Enzyme Synthesis. Without enzymes to increase the rate of the biochemical reactions, the metabolic processes of the cell could not proceed rapidly enough to maintain life. Studies of bacteria and other simple organisms have shown that the synthesis of enzymes (as well as that of the other proteins) is controlled very specifically by the genes. The genes themselves are part of the DNA molecules of chromosomes. See also CHROMOSOME; GENES, NATURE AND ACTION OF; NUCLEIC ACIDS.

The genes of the cell contain information for many more enzymes than are synthesized or used by the cell at any one time; this reserve capability permits the cell to adapt to a variety of environmental conditions; for example, the cell may suddenly need to begin synthesizing a molecule that had formerly been present or to begin degrading one formerly absent. The series of enzymes necessary for one of these tasks comprises a *biochemical pathway*. One mode of controlling such pathways is *allosteric inhibition* of enzyme activity, in which the final product of a pathway binds with a specific site on the enzyme responsible for the first conversion in the pathway, thereby inhibiting the first step and thus all further steps in the pathway. Another mode of control is *enzyme induction;* in this case, the concentration of a specific metabolite in the cell controls the synthesis of the enzymes needed for its metabolism. This control mechanism may be important in the cells of higher organisms, where it may be the basis of differentiation, whereby various kinds of cells are developed with different structures appropriate to their different functions.

REPRODUCTION

The reproduction of cells is chiefly characterized by a striking series of nuclear events called mitosis. In mitosis each chromosome in the cell is duplicated. The cell then divides, with one of the duplicate chromosomes remaining in each daughter cell. In this way two cells with identical chromosomal complements are formed. See also MITOSIS.

Cell organelles other than chromosomes also reproduce in preparation for cellular reproduction, but this generally does not occur with the same precision as the division of the chromosomes. The synthesis of proteins for the growth of membrane systems apparently occurs on ribosomes directly attached to membranes. The synthesis of ribosomes themselves involves the nucleolar synthesis of RNA, but the site of production of ribosomal proteins has not yet been established. The mitochondria have been shown to divide in the living cell. The partitioning of various other cytoplasmic components, such as the endoplasmic reticulum and the Golgi apparatus, is a somewhat random process in most cases. A new pair of centrioles, on the other hand, is formed in intimate association with the old, and the pairs are specifically directed to the two daughter cells by their positions at the poles of the mitotic spindle.

The reproduction of plant cells must also provide for the formation of new chloroplasts. These organelles, as well as other food-storing plastids, are derived from a precursor population of proplastids. Their replication and subsequent differentiation into chloroplasts are partially autonomous from the genes of the nucleus; proplastids and chloroplasts contain their own complements of coded DNA and of protein-synthesizing components. Similarly, there is some evidence that the mitochondria and the centrioles in other cells contain DNA and may function as partially autonomous cellular organelles.

DIFFERENTIATION AND GROWTH

In all but the simplest multicellular organisms there is a division of labor among cells known as differentiation. Groups of cells become specialized to perform particular functions. In most cases studied, all of the cells in the organism retain all of the genes originally present within the nucleus; however, only some of these genes influence the morphology and behavior of any particular kind of cell.

In many developing organisms there are interactions called *inductions* between groups of actively dividing cells resulting in their differentiation from one another. As the organism grows and matures, cells continue to undergo mitosis and become differentiated for specialized roles.

In plants, *meristems* are populations of proliferative cells which give rise to all tissues in the immediate vicinity, for they are unable to migrate within the organism. These new cells are relatively small; the plant increases in size by enlargement of the differentiating cells.

There are also regions of cellular multiplication in animals. Nerve cells are formed only during embryonic development; such differentiated cells must survive for the life of the organism because they cannot be replaced. Cellular renewal, on the other hand, is the rule in epithelial tissues, which serve as coverings or linings for other tissues. The intestinal epithelium, which covers projections (villi) into the cavity of the gut, is renewed by mitosis in the indentations between the villi. The epidermis (outer layer of skin) constantly loses cells from its surface; these cells are replaced by mitotic division in the basal layer. New blood cells are produced in the bone marrow.

The problem of aging at the cellular level is intimately associated with that of growth and differentiation. There is no aging in a culture of rapidly growing bacteria; all of the component cells continue to grow and divide as long as growth requirements are satisfied. Similarly, as long as mitosis continues in a proliferative tissue of a multicellular organism, there is a replacement of cells that are accidentally damaged or that are destined by their mode of differentiation to be lost. Such cells are themselves always young, although aging may occur in the tissue as a whole when the vital organization is disrupted by deposits of extraneous material or by scar tissue. Cells of the nervous system, on the other hand, are nonmitotic, and therefore are not rejuvenated by cell division. Aging at the cellular level is a serious problem in such tissue.

Aging and senescence of the organism as a whole also results from defects in the mechanisms of tissue renewal and repair. When this results in uncontrolled proliferation of cells—called *cancer*—the same mechanisms that normally protect the organism may instead destroy it. If, on the other hand, cellular proliferation fails to keep pace with differentiation, the tissue becomes unable to fulfill its vital functions.

BRECK BYERS and K. R. PORTER
Harvard University

Further Reading: Bourne, Geoffrey H., ed., *Cytology and Cell Physiology* (New York 1964); de Robertis, E. D. P., and others, *Cell Biology* (Philadelphia 1965); Fawcett, Don W., *Cell: Its Organelles and Inclusions* (Philadelphia 1966); Loewy, Ariel G., and Siekevitz, Philip, *Cell Structure and Function* (New York 1963).

CELL, Electric. See BATTERY.

BENVENUTO CELLINI'S works include the gold and enamel Rospigliosi Cup (*upper left*) and saltcellar (*lower left*) made for Francis I of France. His statue of Jove (*right*) is in a niche in the base of his bronze statue, *Perseus.*

CELLINI, chăl-lē'nĕ, **Benvenuto** (1500–1571), Florentine goldsmith and sculptor, who was one of the most noted craftsmen of his time. He is known today primarily for his colorful autobiography, *The Life of Benvenuto Cellini* (posthumously published, 1728).· This remarkable work, in presenting its author as a boastfully adventurous figure who was proudly devoted to his art and quarreled fiercely with both his rivals and his patrons, gives a vivid, tumultuous picture of the Renaissance in 16th century Italy.

Life. Cellini was born in Florence on Nov. 3, 1500, the son of an architect and musician. Desspite his father's wish that he become a flutist, he apprenticed himself to the Florentine goldsmith Antonio di Sandro Marcone. At the age of 16, the hot-tempered Cellini was exiled to Siena for participating in a duel. Shortly thereafter, he went to Bologna, Pisa, and Rome. In 1521 his father called him back to Florence, but he became involved in other quarrels and fled to Rome. There the Medici pope Clement VII, a Florentine, took a liking to him and enabled him to open a workshop. Showered by nobles and prelates with commissions for jewelry, medallions, and other small objects, Cellini soon became the most sought-after goldsmith in Rome.

During the siege and sack of Rome by the troops of the Holy Roman Emperor Charles V in 1527, Cellini took refuge with the pope and cardinals at the Castel Sant' Angelo. In his autobiography he claims that while defending the castle he killed the leader of the attacking troops, Charles, Duke de Bourbon, Constable of France, and wounded the Duke of Orange.

In 1529, after a brief visit to Florence, Cellini returned to Rome, where Pope Clement appointed him "master of stamping" at the papal mint.

However, after murdering the soldier who had killed his brother Cecchino in self-defense (Cecchino's erratic temperament was not unlike Cellini's), and after killing Pompeo, a Milanese goldsmith who was seeking the Pope's favor, Cellini fled to Naples.

When the new pope, Paul III, absolved Cellini of Pompeo's murder, Cellini returned to his former post in Rome; but constant persecution by Paul's illegitimate son, Pier Luigi Farnese, drove him back to Florence, where he designed some coins for Alessandro de' Medici. After trips to Venice and Paris, he returned to Rome in 1535, only to be imprisoned by Farnese in the Castel Sant'Angelo, charged with having stolen jewels belonging to Pope Clement. Cellini made a daring attempt to escape, lowering himself by a chain of sheets from the high walls of the castle, but he was caught and thrown in a dungeon. He was finally released at the request of Ippolito II Cardinal d'Este, for whom he made a seal (1539).

In 1540, at the invitation of King Francis I, Cellini went to France, where Francis granted him yearly pensions and use of the castle of Petit Nesle, which became his home and workshop. He executed several works in gold for the king, including a famous saltcellar (1539–1543; now in the Kunsthistorisches Museum, Vienna) and larger pieces of sculpture for the Palace of Fontainebleau. However, Cellini was constantly harassed by the King's mistress, Madame d'Étampes, and by the King's changeable attitude. After five years, he decided to return to Florence.

Even there Cellini did not find the serenity he was then seeking. Though Duke Cosimo de' Medici gave him protection and numerous commissions, including the noted statue of *Perseus*

(1545–1554; in the Loggia dei Lanzi of the Piazza della Signoria), Cellini became exasperated by bitter quarrels with the rival artists Bandinelli and Ammannati and by the demands of the Duke. In 1557 he was sent to prison on charges of immorality.

In another quixotic change, Cellini took preliminary religious vows in 1558, but he obtained release from them two years later and about 1564 married his housekeeper, Piera de' Parigi, by whom he had two children. At the same time, Catherine de Médicis, the widow of Francis' son, Henry II, invited Cellini to return to France to work on Henry's tomb. It is unclear whether he declined because he was refused permission by Duke Cosimo, as he claimed in his autobiography, or because of his marriage, as some writers speculate. Cellini died in Florence on Feb. 13, 1571, and was buried in the Church of the Annunziata.

Writings. Cellini's renown is closely linked to the great popularity of the *Vita di Benvenuto Cellini* (*The Life of Benvenuto Cellini;* Eng. tr., by J. A. Symonds, 1888), which he wrote between 1558 and 1566, and which records his life up to 1562. The book, dictated extemporaneously, uses the everyday language of Florence—colorful, idiomatic, at times ungrammatical. It clearly and forcefully conveys through both exaggerated storytelling and accurate autobiographical detail the many and various facets of its author's complex personality.

After an introductory section describing a distant ancestor, Fiorino da Cellino, after whom, Cellini claims, Florence was named, the *Vita* recounts Cellini's life and travels. It is filled with vignettes, wild stories, and historical descriptions concerning well-known personages with whom Cellini came in contact—men such as Clement VII, Paul III, Francis I, Cosimo de' Medici, and Michelangelo. It tells of Cellini's visions in the dungeon of Sant'Angelo, of his difficulties in casting the *Perseus*, of Pope Clement's financial worries after the sack of Rome, and of Cosimo romping with his jester. It ends with the mourning at the death of Cosimo's brother in 1562.

The *Vita* was first translated into English in 1771, into German (by Goethe, who greatly admired it) in 1796, and into French in 1822. It forms the basis of the Berlioz opera *Benvenuto Cellini* (1837).

Though Cellini quite possibly intended to be truthful, even his English translator, J. A. Symonds, who argued strongly for his veracity, admitted exaggeration in the *Vita*. What emerges from the work is a larger-than-life hero who towers above all others. He is courageous, fiercely independent, energetic, and single-mindedly devoted to Art (for whom he will meet all challenges), and at the same time, vindictive, superstitious, and enormously boastful. Cellini regards everybody and everything as an obstacle that stands in his path to glory, an obstacle that he, favored by God, will overcome. He is not bound by any law, moral or otherwise, and has been singled out by Providence to do great deeds. This self-portrait, whether accurate or not, affords valuable insights into Cellini's time.

Art. Cellini's artistic energies were primarily devoted to work in gold, outstanding for its intricate design and skillful execution. Only a few of his pieces have survived him, and many have been falsely attributed to him. The most famous of the surviving works is the gold and enamel saltcellar made for Francis I. The piece is unusually large for its kind—over 10 inches (25 cm) high and 13 inches (33 cm) wide, and its style is reminiscent of Michelangelo, whom Cellini revered. The saltcellar is dominated by large nude figures of Neptune and Mother Earth, resting in the precariously balanced poses typical of mannerist art. Neptune guards a salt container in the shape of a beautifully wrought ship surrounded by sea horses and many kinds of fish. Mother Earth presides over a pepper container in the shape of an ornamented Ionic building surrounded by many small land animals. On the pedestal are relief figures symbolizing times of the day (recalling Michelangelo's Medici tombs) and the winds.

Among Cellini's other works in precious metals, no longer extant, were medals, coins, jewels, jewel boxes, seals, candlesticks (including 12 silver ones for Francis I, 1544), and a famous morse (clasp) for Pope Clement (1530–1531). His helmet designs, now in the Uffizi Gallery, Florence, are particularly fanciful.

Under the spell of Michelangelo, Cellini tried to excel in sculpture, an art he took up after he was 40. He seemed uncomfortable, however, in handling large pieces, and he tended to allow the goldsmith's love of detail to take precedence over the emphasis on form and unity required by his new art. In the bronze *Nymph of Fontainebleau* (1543–1544; now in the Louvre, Paris), originally designed for the entrance to Fontainebleau, an awkward contrast exists between the long, manneristic body of the nymph and the detailed, naturalistic groups of hounds, deer, and boars surrounding her. Cellini's superiority in working on a smaller scale is also evident when his famous bronze *Perseus* is compared with the small, charming wax and bronze preliminary models of the work, which possess a litheness and a youthful quality that are lacking in the completed statue.

Cellini's best piece of sculpture is the bronze bust of Bindo Altoviti (1550; now in the Gardner Museum, Boston). He also executed a large bronze portrait bust of Duke Cosimo (1545–1548; Bargello Museum, Florence).

Of Cellini's pieces in marble, probably the best known is a life-sized marble crucifix (1556–1562; now at the church of the Escorial, Spain), composed of a white marble figure on a black marble cross. The work, which was originally intended for Cellini's own tomb, is manneristic, with the head of Christ hanging awkwardly over a long, slender body. Two other marbles, on mythological themes, *Apollo and Hyacinth* (1546) and *Narcissus* (1547–1548), are in the Bargello Museum.

CHARLES SPERONI
University of California at Los Angeles

Bibliography

The standard edition of Cellini's *Vita*, in Italian, was edited with critical comment by Orazio Bacci (Florence 1901); the standard English translation, by John Addington Symonds, first published in 1888, was reedited, with introduction and notes, by John Pope-Hennessy (New York 1949).

Fletcher, Jefferson B., *Literature of the Italian Renaissance* (Port Washington, N. Y., 1964).

Klein, Robert, and Zerner, Henri, *Italian Art, 1500–1600* (New York 1966).

Matt, Leonard von, and Mariana, Valerio, *Renaissance Art in Rome* (New York 1961).

Pope-Hennessy, John, *Italian Renaissance Sculpture* (New York 1958).

Rossi, Filippo, *Italian Jeweled Arts*, tr. by Elizabeth Mann Borgese (New York and London 1957).

CELLO. See VIOLONCELLO.

CELLOPHANE, sel'ə-fān, is a transparent, tough, flexible film prepared from wood pulp and used extensively in food packaging. It is essentially a form of pure cellulose. Cellophane was developed in 1908 by the French chemist Jacques Edwin Brandenberger, who derived the name from the words *cellulose* and *diaphanes,* a Greek word meaning "transparent."

In the production of cellophane, the wood pulp is first treated with sodium hydroxide and then shredded, aged, and reacted with carbon disulfide. This series of reactions results in the formation of a cellulose derivative, sodium cellulose xanthate, which is then dispersed in dilute sodium hydroxide to form a thick, syrupy solution called viscose. After aging, the viscose is extruded through a long thin slot into a bath of sulfuric acid and sodium sulfate. The bath coagulates the viscose into a film; carbon disulfide and hydrogen sulfide are evolved, and the cellulose is regenerated. The film is led through a series of tanks where it is washed, chemically purified, and combined with a softener or plasticizer. The wet, softened film is then dried to a controlled moisture content.

Finally, the cellophane is moisture-proofed by the application of specially designed coating lacquers, some of which are heat sealable. The original coatings developed in the 1920's and 1930's were based on nitrocellulose lacquers, but polyvinylidene chloride (Saran) coatings have now been developed that are more moisture-proof and better looking.

J. W. RINKER
E. I. du Pont de Nemours & Company, Inc.

CELLULASE, sel'yə-lās, is a class of enzymes that attack cellulose, the principal material of land plant cell walls. Cellulase degrades cellulose to short fragments with 6 to 10 or so glucose residues. These are then degraded to glucose by the enzyme cellobiase, which invariably accompanies cellulase but is not able to attack high-molecular-weight cellulose.

Cellulases occur in organisms that use cellulose as a source of carbon in their nutrition. Examples include wood-rotting fungi, certain bacteria, and protozoa that live symbiotically in the rumen of the cow and in the guts of snails, shipworms, and many insects.

Two cellulases with molecular weights of 11,400 and 51,000 have been prepared in pure form from the fungus *Polyporus versicolor*.

JAMES BONNER
California Institute of Technology

CELLULOID, sel'yə-loid, is a durable plastic mixture of cellulose nitrate and camphor. It usually contains 3 parts cellulose nitrate, 1 part camphor, and minor quantities of dye and alcohol. Celluloid was invented in 1856 by Alexander Parkes and was first manufactured successfully in 1868 by the brothers I. S. and J. W. Hyatt. Since it softens at about 85° C, it is readily shaped into articles such as combs, tool handles, and billiard balls. Photographic film base was formerly composed of celluloid but is now made of less flammable plastics. Since 1939, world production of celluloid has decreased in favor of less expensive plastics.

HARRISON H. HOLMES
E. I. du Pont de Nemours & Co.

CELLULOSE, sel'yə-lōs, is the principal structural material in the cell walls of land plants. Cotton fiber is over 90% cellulose; wood, roughly 50%; straw, 30%. Cellulose occurs commonly in useful form in such seed fibers as cotton and kapok; in such stem (bast) fibers as flax, ramie, jute, and hemp; and in wood, bagasse, rice hulls, and various other plant products. Many useful products, such as plastics or fabrics, are derived from cellulose, but the manufacture of paper is the largest single commercial use of cellulose. See also PLASTICS—*Synthetic Plastics;* PAPER.

Structure. An analysis of cellulose shows it to contain 44.4% carbon, 6.2% hydrogen, and 49.4% oxygen. This analysis suggests the empirical formula $C_6H_{10}O_5$. Pure cellulose can be hydrolyzed to form D-glucose, $C_6H_{12}O_6$, with a yield of about 95%. These and other studies indicate that the structural unit of cellulose is anhydroglucose, $C_6H_{10}O_5$, that is, D-glucose minus a water molecule (H_2O). The anhydroglucose unit is repeated many times to build a chainlike molecule. The bond between the anhydroglucose units is through oxygen and is a beta-glucoside linkage from the first carbon atom of one unit to the fourth carbon atom of the next unit. Each anhydroglucose unit has three hydrox, OH, groups, which are involved in producing commercially important cellulose derivatives such as cellulose nitrate, cellulose acetate, and ethyl cellulose.

The structure within the white area of the accompanying illustration of the cellulose molecule is the anhydroglucose unit. The value of h varies from 600 to 1,000 in wood pulp to more than 3,500 in cotton fibers. Commercially regenerated cellulose, which is brought into solution and then resolidified, is believed to be degraded to the extent that it retains 600 to 1,000 anhydroglucose units per chain.

The beta-glucoside linkage of cellulose differs from the alpha-glucoside linkage found in starch only in the three-dimensional arrangements of the groups attached to the carbon atoms involved in the joining of adjacent anhydroglucose units. This beta linkage can be hydrolyzed and broken by the microorganisms existing in the digestive tracts of herbivorous animals. The process of digestion forms D-glucose, which is then available to the animal as a food material. Humans and carnivorous animals lack the enzyme supply necessary for the hydrolysis of the beta linkage. They have instead only the enzymes that are able to hydrolyze the alpha-glucoside linkage of starch and therefore cannot digest cellulose.

Formation. Cellulose is formed in plants by the process of photosynthesis, a complex series of steps which is still imperfectly understood. As a result of photosynthesis, carbon dioxide and water are combined with the help of enzymes to form glucose; the glucose units are then further combined into carbohydrate structures, of which starch and cellulose are examples.

The chemical changes of carbohydrate formation are endothermic ("energy absorbing") in balance, and the energy absorbed from sunlight is stored in plants in the form of chemical energy. It may be released either through the digestion and metabolism of living organisms or, in the form of heat, through the burning of wood, coal, or other plant products.

Microfibrils. X-ray diffraction studies have shown that cellulose fibers contain long, overlapping microfibrils, or chains, that are held to each other by van der Waals' forces and by hydrogen

CELLULOSE is a chainlike molecule composed of many glucose molecules. Because the joining of glucose molecules is accompanied by the loss of an H atom and an OH group (HOH, or water), the linked glucose residues are also known as anhydroglucose.

bonding (see also BOND, in chemistry). Aggregates of these chains form strong, pliable plant fibers. The chains form chance groupings of crystalline regions separated by noncrystalline, or amorphous, regions. In the crystalline areas there is a tight and orderly arrangement of the chains, while in the amorphous zones the chains are much more loosely and haphazardly arranged. A single chain may go through several crystalline and several amorphous regions. Cotton and ramie fibers are believed to be about 70% crystalline, whereas regenerated cellulose may be only about 40% crystalline. Moisture absorption and most forms of chemical attack occur first in the amorphous regions, apparently because the loose and random chains are more accessible to the reagent.

American cotton is about 91% cellulose and 8% water, the balance consisting of wax, pectic matter, and minerals. Dried wood contains about 60% cellulose and hemicellulose (a chemical relative of cellulose) with 25% to 30% of lignin, as well as small percentages of sap, resins, waxes, pentosans, gums, and mineral matter.

Physical and Chemical Properties. Cellulose is insoluble in water and organic solvents such as benzene, alcohol, ether, acetone, and chloroform. About 85% of cellulose from wood pulp is insoluble in 17.5% sodium hydroxide solution. This is arbitrarily designated as *alpha-cellulose* and is the material that is commonly used in preparing regenerated cellulose and various cellulose derivatives.

The treatment of cellulose with dilute sodium hydroxide solution produces a swelling in the fiber with attendant rounding out of the original, somewhat flattened structure and an increase in luster. This is essentially what has occurred in mercerized cotton. The chain structures in the fiber also appear to be loosened so as to facilitate further attack by chemical reagents.

Cellulose is soluble in Schweitzer's reagent, a mixture of copper II hydroxide and concentrated ammonium hydroxide. When the solution is forced through holes in a spinneret into an acid bath, a fiber of degraded cellulose is regenerated. An early silk substitute produced by this method is still used for some knitted and woven fabrics.

Cellulose degradation involves a reduction of the chain length, and usually a weakening of the fiber. It results from heating, severe mechanical manipulation, or chemical attack. If cellulose is heated in dilute acid solution, hydrolysis to D-glucose results.

Regenerated Cellulose. *Viscose rayon* is a commercial form of regenerated cellulose. Wood pulp or cotton linters is soaked in 18% sodium hydroxide solution to swell the fiber and remove the soluble portion. Then the alkali cellulose is shredded, aged, and stirred in a mixer with carbon disulfide. After several hours crumbs of cellulose xanthate are obtained, in which the xan-

$$\text{thate grouping } -O-\overset{\overset{\displaystyle S}{\|}}{C}-S-Na$$

is substituted for one or more of the active hydrogen atoms (in hydroxyl groups) in each anhydroglucose unit. The crumbs are dissolved in a sodium hydroxide solution to produce a thick liquid called viscose. This is aged, filtered, de-aerated, and forced through holes in a spinneret into an acidic spinning bath. Acid action causes the removal of the xanthate grouping and the solidification in fiber form of regenerated cellulose. If the viscose is forced into the spinning bath through a slit rather than a spinneret, a sheet of *cellophane* is formed.

Substituents. The three hydroxyl groups attached to each anhydroglucose unit primarily determine the reactions of cellulose that are important to industry. The hydrogen atom of each hydroxyl group can be replaced by some other structure, such as an ester or ether grouping. If each of the three hydroxyl hydrogens of the unit is replaced, the maximum degree of substitution (3.0) is achieved. The derivatives of cellulose that are commercially valuable are seldom fully substituted.

The introduction of substituents greatly changes the physical and chemical properties of cellulose and increases the number of possible solvents. It makes possible a wide range of plastics, textile fibers, explosives, lacquers, food thickeners, adhesives, and other products. A typical substitution reaction is the formation of ethyl cellulose from cellulose, sodium hydroxide, and ethyl chloride.

Cellulose Derivatives. *Cellulose nitrate* was the first of the commercially important cellulose derivatives, as well as the first synthetically produced plastic. It was introduced in 1865 under the name *celluloid*. To prepare it, cellulose was nitrated in a mixture of nitric and sulfuric acids and the product was combined with camphor as a plasticizer. Today cellulose nitrate, in degrees of substitution ranging from 2.4 to 2.8, is used as lacquer, photographic film, plastics, and explo-

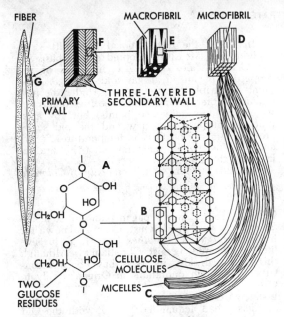

CELLULOSE IN PLANT FIBERS. Glucose subunits combine into cellulose molecules (A). Bundles of the molecules, partly arranged in lattices (B) that form micelles (C), make up microfibrils (D). Microfibrils and microporosities (in black) compose the macrofibril (E) elements of wall layers (F) of a fiber cell wall (G).

sives. Cellulose derivatives with the lower degrees of substitution remain flammable, but they are not explosive.

Cellulose acetate is the most widely used of the cellulose derivatives. It is an ester prepared by treating cellulose with acetic anhydride in acetic acid solution, using a sulfuric acid catalyst. The most useful product has a degree of substitution of about 2.2 and is soluble in acetone and other organic solvents. It is tough, moisture resistant, and low in flammability; it is used for acetate rayon textile fibers, molding plastics, and photographic film.

Cellulose propionate is prepared by treating cellulose fibers with propionic anhydride in propionic acid. The product is more stable than cellulose acetate, can be used with many different plasticizers, and requires much less plasticizer than cellulose acetate. It has high toughness and shock resistance and good moisture resistance. This ester is especially useful for injection molding since it has good flow characteristics over a wide range of temperatures. Cellulose propionate is used for telephone housings, radio cabinets, automobile parts, pens and pencils, toys, television parts, and similar products. It is virtually nonflammable.

Cellulose acetate butyrate is a mixed ester produced by treating cellulose fibers with a mixture of acetic anhydride, butyric anhydride, acetic acid, and butyric acid. The degree of substitution is 0.7 to 0.8 for the acetate radical and 1.2 to 1.5 for the butyrate radical. This mixed cellulose ester is particularly valuable for its toughness, weather resistance, high-luster surface, and transparency. It needs relatively little plasticizer, has low water absorption and good electrical properties, and is easily formed by injection molding, extrusion, or vacuum molding. The flammability is low. It is used for such parts as tool handles, steering wheels, instrument housings, lenses for automobile taillights and turn lights, railroad sig-

nals, and street lamp globes. It is also used in photographic film, protective coating solutions, and lacquers.

Ethyl cellulose is an ether derivative of cellulose made by treating cellulose fibers with sodium hydroxide and ethyl chloride (see illustrative equation given earlier). Ethyl cellulose plastics are tough over a wide temperature range and have good dimensional stability, good surface luster, excellent resistance to water and strong alkalis, and good resistance to oils and grease. They have the lowest density of any commercial cellulose derivatives and have high flexibility. Ethyl cellulose plastics are used for such varied purposes as football helmets, packaging materials, automobile parts, special adhesives, and paper coatings. Ethyl cellulose is also used as a toughening agent for plastics.

Both ethyl cellulose and methyl cellulose with low degrees of substitution are employed as thickening agents in foods, in pharmaceuticals, and in latex dispersions such as water-base paints.

Carboxymethylcellulose contains one or more —OCH_2COOH groups per anhydroglucose unit. These groups may be in the form of the sodium salt —OCH_2COONa; this derivative is produced by treating cellulose fibers with sodium hydroxide and monochloroacetic acid, $ClCH_2COOH$. It is used as a textile and paper sizing agent, as a cleaning aid in synthetic detergents, and as a thickener for printing pastes, cosmetics, latex paints, and food products.

Otto W. Nitz
Stout State University, Menomonie, Wis.

CELLULOSE ACETATE, sel'yə-lōs as'ə-tāt, a thermoplastic resin of cellulose. Fibers made of cellulose acetate are widely used in the production of a strong, silklike material that is easily dyed and wears well. The resin is also used in lacquers, protective coatings, artificial leather, transparent sheeting, and cigarette filters and in the production of plastics and acetate film.

Cellulose acetate occurs as odorless white flakes or as a powder; it softens at temperatures of from 60° to 97° C (140° to 207° F) and melts at about 260° C (500° F). It is soluble in acetone, ethylene dichloride, ethyl acetate, cyclohexanol, and nitropropane.

Cellulose acetate is produced by treating cellulose from wood pulp or cotton with acetic acid and acetic anhydride in the presence of sulfuric acid. The product of this reaction, which is acetylated cellulose, is then partially hydrolyzed. In the final product, each of the glucose subunits of the cellulose contains an average of 2 to 2.5 acetate groups.

Fibers of cellulose acetate are made by forcing an acetone solution of the compound through small openings in a spinneret into a warm-air stream, which causes the solvent to evaporate from the filaments. In the production of cellulose acetate films, the solution is coated on a drum, and when the solvent evaporates, the remaining film is removed. The films are used as a support for photographic film, for magnetic tape for sound recording, for packaging, and for laminating.

For use as a plastic, cellulose acetate is usually combined with plasticizers and dyes or pigments. The plastics are tough and have a high mechanical strength and relatively low flammability. They are widely used in handles for tools and cutlery, in toys, and in containers for radios and other appliances.

CELLULOSE NITRATE, sel′yə-lōs nī′trāt, is a flammable substance produced by the reaction of cellulose with nitric acid. It is also known as *nitrocellulose*. Its high molecular weight and solubility in organic liquids make it useful in molded articles, propellants, explosives, and protective films. In coated upholstery fabrics, photographic film base, and small celluloid articles, cellulose nitrate has for the most part been replaced by less flammable cellulose acetate and other plastics.

In the manufacture of cellulose nitrate, purified cotton linters or softwood cellulose is stirred into a mixture of nitric acid, sulfuric acid, and water. After a few minutes the excess acid is removed in a centrifuge, and the cellulose nitrate is steeped for 24 hours or more in boiling water to remove residual acid. Finally, it is rinsed with alcohol.

The chemical composition of cellulose nitrate is tailored to specific uses, principally by varying the degree of nitration of the starting cellulose. This is done by adjusting the water content of the nitrating acid. The theoretical maximum nitrogen content, 14.1% by weight, is not attained in practice. The nitrogen contents of commercial grades of cellulose nitrate are: 12.6–13.4% for smokeless gun propellants and high-energy rocket propellants; 11.8–12.2% for gelatin dynamite, collodion, household cement, and lacquer finishes for metal and wood; 11.3–11.7% for moisture-resistant coatings on paper and cellophane; and 10.9–11.2% for fast-drying printing inks, celluloid, sealers, and fillers.

HARRISON H. HOLMES
E. I. du Pont de Nemours & Co.

CELSIUS, sel′sē-əs, **Anders** (1701–1744), Swedish astronomer, who devised the Celsius (centigrade) thermometer scale. Celsius was born in Uppsala on Nov. 27, 1701. He was the most distinguished member of a well-known scientific family. In 1730 he was appointed professor of astronomy at Uppsala, holding the post until his death there on April 25, 1744. He published detailed observations of the aurora borealis in 1733 and was the first to associate the phenomenon with the earth's magnetic field. In 1740 he was appointed director of a new observatory, where he pioneered in the measurement of stars' brightness by photometric devices.

In 1742, Celsius described the thermometric scale used universally by scientists today. In it the temperature interval between the freezing and boiling points of water is divided into a hundred degrees. This "centigrade scale" is now usually known as the "Celsius scale" (abbreviated "C"). Celsius originally set the freezing point of water at 100° C and the boiling point at 0° C, but later reversed them.

ISAAC ASIMOV
Boston University Medical School

CELSIUS SCALE, sel′sē-əs, the temperature scale commonly used for scientific measurements and the scale used for all purposes in most countries of the world. The Celsius scale, also called the *centigrade scale*, was long defined on the basis of two fixed points: the freezing point of water, which was assigned a temperature of 0°, and the boiling point of water, which was assigned a temperature of 100°. It is named in honor of Anders Celsius (q.v.), a Swedish astronomer who first advocated such a scale.

In 1954 the International Committee on Weights and Measures adopted a new basis for the Celsius scale, defining it in terms of the properties of an ideal gas and a single fixed point—the triple point of water. Under the new definition the boiling and freezing points of water are only reference points, but for most practical purposes the new and the old scales are the same. The Celsius temperature $T(°C)$ and the Fahrenheit temperature $t(°F)$ are related by the expression $t = \%T + 32$.

MICHAEL McCLINTOCK, *University of Colorado*

Further Reading: Zemansky, Mark W., *Heat and Thermodynamics* (New York 1957).

CELSUS, sel′səs, was a pagan philosopher of the 2d century A. D. A Platonist, Celsus is known for his *True Discourse* (*Alethes Logos*), an incisive literary polemic against Christianity. Although this work was lost, its ideas have been reconstructed through quotations in Origen's reply to Celsus, *Against Celsus* (*Contra Celsum*), in 8 books, written in 246.

Celsus had acquainted himself with the Old Testament, the Gospels, and Christian apologetic writings and apparently had made personal contact with Christians to learn their beliefs. Yet his statements show that he did not fully grasp the differences between Christianity, Gnosticism, Judaism, and heterodox teachings. There are indications of Platonic influences in his concept of God, and Stoic influences are discernible in his cosmology. He considered absurd the Christian teachings on creation, the Incarnation, and the Crucifixion. Further, he regarded Christianity as a ghetto religion whose followers were: "grubs gathering in a filthy corner contending with one another as to which is the greater sinner." A champion of Hellenic ideals, Celsus viewed Christianity as a threat to the state and advised that, for the public welfare, it be eliminated.

HERMIGILD DRESSLER
Catholic University of America

CELSUS, sel′səs, **Aulus Cornelius** (1st century A. D.), Roman encyclopedist, whose writings include not only the most complete Roman medical text of his time but also a history of early medicine. He was the author of a comprehensive work dealing with agriculture, military science, rhetoric, philosophy, jurisprudence, and medicine, but only the section on medicine has survived. This section, *De medicina*, (translated by W. G. Spencer in London in 1935) covers the whole of medicine including surgery, nutrition, pharmacology, hygiene, and mental diseases. It draws largely on earlier Greek medical writers, and it is responsible for what we know today about the medical and surgical practices of the Hellenistic period. The preface is especially noteworthy as the earliest history of ancient medicine. Well-read in philosophy and medical theories, Celsus avoided dogmatic conclusions and steered a middle course between conflicting medical ideas, often accepting the opinions of Hippocrates.

JERRY STANNARD, *University of Kansas*

CELT, selt, a member of a group of peoples who spread over much of Europe and to the British Isles in pre-Roman times. See CELTIC PEOPLES; CELTIC LANGUAGES; CELTIC MYTHOLOGY.

CELTES, Conradus. See CELTIS, CONRADUS.

CELTIBERIA, selt′ə-bir′ē-ə, was an ancient territory in north central Spain, inhabited by the Celtiberi, a hybrid people created by the mixture of Celts who migrated across the Pyrenees and peoples of Iberian stock. The Celtic migrations occurred as early as 1000 B. C. and as late as 600 B. C. The name "Celtiberi," loosely used in antiquity, can be specifically applied to certain tribes: the Arevaci, Belli, Titti, and Lusones.

The Celtiberi lived in the mountainous districts. Frequent family feuds conditioned them to a life of fighting and hardship, and they were ideally suited for service in formal military units as light-armed infantry and cavalry. They were first employed in this capacity by the Carthaginians in the late 3d century B. C. during the Second Punic War.

The Celtiberi first came into contact with the Romans in the Second Punic War, and in the period that followed the two fought many battles. The wars were characterized by Roman atrocities, and the Celtiberi finally yielded to Rome after Numantia, their most important city, fell to Scipio Aemilianus in 133 B. C. During this period the Romans adopted the Celtiberian sword, equally good for cutting and thrusting, which became standard equipment for the legionnaire.

RICHARD E. MITCHELL, *University of Illinois*

CELTIC CHURCH, sel′tik, is a term denoting the early medieval churches of Ireland, Britain (Wales), and Brittany—areas of settlement by Celtic tribes. This church had its roots in Ireland, where Celtic society survived the impact of the Roman conquest. The tribal and rural nature of that society precluded the establishment of urban centers similar to those upon which the diocesan, or episcopal, organization of the church on the European continent was based. The Celtic church was thus organized on monastic, rather than diocesan lines, with powers of jurisdiction in the hands of the abbots. Monastic bishops, subject to the abbots, only had powers of ordination. Celtic monks were noted for their highly disciplined, almost hermitlike lives of learning, piety, and asceticism. They clung tenaciously to tradition, as exemplified by their adherence to a method of dating Easter that had been abandoned elsewhere. There were few Mass texts in their liturgy, which was replete with long litanies of the saints. However, this monastic way of life, founded largely through the efforts of St. Columba and St. Columbanus (q.q.v.), did not completely replace the previously established diocesan organization. Even in Ireland, where the diocesan church had from the first been adapted to the unique character of Celtic society, episcopal churches continued to exist alongside monastic ones.

Although the Celtic church differed from the Roman church on questions of organization, liturgy, and discipline, it was in accord in matters of doctrine, and missionaries from the Celtic church were responsible for converting large areas of Europe to Christianity. In Welsh and Irish monasteries the study of Latin and of the Bible was considerably in advance of the average standard in early medieval Europe. Nevertheless, the "unorthodox" life in Celtic monasteries often brought them into conflict with ecclesiastical authority. Ultimately, Brittany conformed with Rome in the 9th century, Wales in the 11th, and Ireland in the 12th.

LUDWIG BIELER, *University College, Dublin*

CELTIC LANGUAGES, sel′tik. The Celtic languages form the westernmost group of the Indo-European family of languages, all of which seem to have descended from a common origin or are at least characterized by a closely related system of phonetics and morphology as well as by a common vocabulary and the same syntactical structure. The Celtic languages, which have been spoken by different branches of the Celtic peoples (q.v.) from prehistoric times to the present day, belong to the so-called *centum* group of Indo-European languages. The *centum* group (Italic, Germanic, Greek, Venetic, and Illyrian, as well as Tocharian and Hittite) have preserved the Indo-European palatal consonants as occlusives, while in the so-called *satem* group (Albanian, Armenian, Balto-Slavic, and Indo-Iranian), these consonants became sibilants. So we have in Welsh *cant* (hundred) and in Latin *centum,* as opposed to Avestic *satam,* all three forms going back to an Indo-European **kmtóm.* (The asterisk [*] indicates that a word form is conjectured and reconstructed.)

Phonetic Characteristics. The most notable phonetic characteristics that set off the Celtic languages from the other members of the Indo-European family are as follows:

(1) The dropping of the initial and intervocalic *p*: compare Latin *pater* (father) with Old Irish *athir;* Gaulish *are-* (beside) and Irish and Welsh *ar* with Greek περί, παρά; Gaulish *ver-* (over), Irish *for,* and Old Welsh *guor* with Greek ὑπέρ.

(2) Indo-European medial aspirates *bh, dh, gh,* and *ǵh* have fallen together with the simple voiced stops: compare Old Irish *-biur* (I carry) with English *I bear,* Latin *ferō,* and Greek φέρω; Old Irish *-tíag* (I go) with Greek στείχω.

(3) Indo-European labialized velar *gᵘ* has become *b*: compare Old Irish *bó* (cow) and Welsh *buwch* with Greek βοῦς and Sanskrit *gauh;* the change of the Indo-European labialized voiceless guttural *kᵘ* and of *k + ᵘ* to *p* is only found in Gaulish and Brythonic (see later discussion).

(4) Indo-European vocalic *r* and *l* appear before stops and *r, l, m,* and *n,* as *ri* and *li:* compare Gaulish *ritu-* (ford) and Welsh *rhyd* with Latin *portus* (harbor) and German Furt (ford); Gaulish *litanos* (broad), Old Welsh *litan,* and Old Irish *lethan* with Greek πλάτανος (planetree).

(5) Indo-European *ē,* has been changed to *ī:* compare Gaulish *rīx* (king), Old Irish *rí* (king), and Welsh *rhi* (prince) with Latin *rēx* (king).

(6) Indo-European *ō* has been changed to *ā* and in final syllables to -*ū:* compare Gaulish *gnātos* (familiar), Old Irish *gnáth* (known), and Welsh *gnawd* (customary) with Latin (*g)nōtus* and Greek γνωτός; compare Old Irish *cú* (dog) and Welsh *ci* with Sanskrit *śvā,* forms derived from Indo-European *ḱuō(n).*

(7) Indo-European *ei* has become *ē:* compare Gaulish *dēuos* (divine), Old Irish *día,* (god), and Old Welsh *duiu-tit* (god-head) with Latin *divus* (godlike) and Sanskrit *dēva-h.*

Morphology. The Old Celtic morphology must have been very archaic: the neuter gender as well as the dual of the noun was preserved, while the verb shows a similar rich inflection as do Greek and Sanskrit. Celtic and Indo-Iranian are the only Indo-European languages that have preserved the distinction between masculine and feminine gender in the numerals *three* and *four:* *three,* Old Irish (m.) *trí* and (f.) *téoir,* Welsh and Breton (m.) *tri* and (f.) *teir,* Sanskrit (m.)

tráyah and (f.) *tisráh; four,* Old Irish (m.) *cethair* and (f.) *cethéoir,* Welsh (m.) *pedwar* and (f) *pedeir,* Breton (m.) *pevar* and (f.) *peder,* Sanskrit (m.) *čatvarah* and (f.) *čátasrah,* Indo-European (m.) **kʷetuores* and (f.) **kʷetesores.*

The closest analogies, however, are found between Celtic and Italic. It is true that the passive and deponent formations in *-r* are found not only in Celtic and Italic but also in Venetic, Indo-Iranian, Phrygian, Armenian, Hittite, and Tocharic. The genitive singular in *ī* of masculine and neuter *o*-stems is also found in Venetic and Messapic (Illyrian); but the assimilation of an initial Indo-European *p-* to a following *kʷ* is an innovation only found in Italic and Celtic: Indo-European **penkʷe* (five) becomes Latin *quinque* and Old Celtic **quenque,* hence Old Welsh *pimp,* Breton *pemp,* Old Irish *cóic.* The superlative in **-samo-* is only found in Celtic and Italic: Gaulish *Belisama* (the very shining one), Old Welsh *hinham* (oldest, from **senisamos*), Old Irish *nessam* (nearest), Oscan *nessimas* (nearest; nom. pl. fem.) Latin *maximus* (greatest). Both Italic and Celtic had subjunctives in *-ā* and *-s* under similar morphological and phonetic conditions; both have (independently) created a *b-*future: Latin *amābō* (I shall love), Old Irish *léiciub* (I shall leave); and both formed verbal nouns in *-tiō(n)* and used the old verbal adjective in *-to-* to form a passive preterite.

All those morphological agreements point to very old relations between Celtic and Italic. A close neighborhood in prehistoric times would be sufficient to explain them. On the other hand, the vocabularies of both languages, though they show some interesting agreements [Old Irish *dí* (of, from) = Latin *dē;* Old Irish *den* (strong) = Latin *bonus* (good), archaic *duenos*], are not so similar as to justify the assumption of a former genealogical Celto-Italic unity.

The vocabulary of Celtic and Germanic shows far more identical words: Gothic *ailps* (oath) = Old Irish *oeth;* Gothic *rūna* (secret) = Old Irish *rún;* Gothic *freis* (free) = Welsh *rhydd;* Gothic *haipi* (field) and English *heath* = Welsh *coed* (wood); Old English *wudu* (wood) = Gaulish *vidu-* and Old Irish *fid.* Many of these words may be Celtic loans in Germanic, as for certain Gothic *andbahts* (servant), hence German *Amt* from Gaulish *ambactus;* or Gothic *reiki* (empire) from Gaulish **rīgion.* But the morphology of both languages is very different. This difference points to rather late relations between Celts and Germans after their morphology had already been fixed.

The numerous religious terms common to Celtic and Indo-Iranian are rather to be explained as survivals from the Indo-European past, while the many agreements among Celtic and Baltic and Slavonic vocabularies may be the result of the wanderings of the Urnfield people.

CELTIC LANGUAGE GROUPS

The Celtic languages fall into two main groups: Goidelic (called Gaelic today) and British (also called Brythonic). *Ancient Goidelic* is characterized by (1) the preservation of Indo-European *kʷ* and *k + ˣ* as *qu: equos* (horse); (2) the change of Indo-European sonant *m, n* before stops to *em, en: *kenton* (hundred); (3) the preservation of initial *sr-: srutus* (stream). *Ancient Brythonic* is characterized by (1) the change of Indo-European *kʷ* and *k + ˣ* to *p: epos* (horse); (2) the change of Indo-European

sonant *m, n,* before stops to *am, an: kanton* (hundred); (3) the change of initial *sr-* to *fr-: frutus* (stream).

Celtic languages may also be divided into Old, or continental, Celtic, spoken on the European mainland, and insular Celtic, spoken on the British Isles. The cleavage into Brythonic and Goidelic runs through each of these divisions.

Continental Celtic (often called Gaulish) mostly belongs to the Brythonic group, but the language of the Celtiberians and of some other Spanish Celts can be shown to have belonged to the Goidelic group. All we have left of Gaulish, as spoken in Gaul, Spain, northern Italy, and the rest of Europe, are about 60 inscriptions, some in the North Etruscan alphabet of the 2d century B.C. and some in the Greek alphabet or in the Latin alphabet of Roman imperial times, to which have been added over 60 graffitos from La Graufesenque (Aveyron) with lists and accounts of potters. The Goidelic inscriptions of the Celtiberians are mostly in the Iberic alphabet.

Apart from Celtic words recorded by classical writers, there have been preserved a large number of personal and place-names in literature, on coins, and on Greek and Latin inscriptions all over Europe. Celtic place-names are found as far east as the Dniester (*Carro-dūnon,* Wagon-fortress), the Dobruja, and Galatia Asia Minor, and as far north as Westphalia. They are mostly compounds with *-dūnon* (fortified place), *-brigā* (height, fortress), *-magos* (field), or *-ialon* (clearing), or derivatives from personal names with the suffix *-ācon* (Latin *-ācum*). Though there must have been dialectic differences in such a huge territory, almost no trace of such differences appears in the numerous place-names and proper names on inscriptions; St. Jerome tells us that the speech of the Galatians in Asia Minor bore a strong resemblance to the language he had heard spoken in the neighborhood of Trier (386 A.D.).

No written trace of the rich oral Gaulish literature has survived. More than 200 Celtic words have been preserved in the Romance languages, mostly plant names and terms referring to agriculture and peasant life. Celtic speech seems to have died out in Gaul in the course of the 5th century A.D., but probably survived much longer in parts of Switzerland. The Celtic idiom spoken in Brittany today is not a survival of Gaulish but the language spoken by those Brythons who were driven out of southwestern England by the Saxons in the 5th and 6th centuries A.D. and came to Armorica in northern France.

Insular Celtic shows a much greater divergence between Goidelic and Brythonic than does continental Celtic. The chief differences developed only from the 6th century A.D. onward, so that today an Irish speaker could not make himself understood to a Welsh speaker, while in St. Patrick's time mutual communication could not have been difficult.

Goidelic, or Gaelic. The name "Goidelic" comes from the ancient name of the people, the *Goídil,* known to the Romans by the name of *Scotti.* The territorial subdivisions of Gaelic are (1) Irish, or Irish Gaelic (native *Gaedhealg*), in Ireland; (2) Scottish Gaelic (native *Gáidhlig*), sometimes called Erse (= Irish) in the northern and western Highlands of Scotland and the adjacent western islands, where it was introduced by the Irish settlers (called in Latin *Scotti*), from about the 6th century A.D.; (3) Manx (native *Gailck*), the language formerly spoken in the Isle of Man, now extinct. Linguistically these are really nothing more than dialects of one language, Old Irish; we possess no monuments of Scottish Gaelic and Manx in the oldest period. Until the end of the 18th century, though spoken Irish and Scottish Gaelic had diverged to a considerable extent, the same literary language as passed current in Ireland continued to be employed by Scottish writers.

Irish. Of all the Celtic languages, Irish is by far the most important, because of its wealth of archaic features and abundance of linguistic material. The language of some of the Ogam (q.v.; Ogham) inscriptions (5th to 7th century A. D.) is almost as archaic as that of continental Celtic. Altogether there are about 370 inscriptions —short writings on gravestones and boundary stones, almost exclusively containing proper names —most of which have been found in the southern half of Ireland. The 48 found in Britain, chiefly in Wales, are the work of colonists from southern Ireland. The Ogam alphabet consists of from one to five strokes or notches scored on either side of the edge of an upright stone, originally, no doubt, on wooden staves.

The Irish literary tradition begins with Old Irish written in Latin cursive script, from about 600 to 900 A. D. Much Old Irish linguistic material has been preserved, in slightly modernized form, in Middle Irish manuscripts. Middle Irish, distinguished from Old Irish chiefly by the weakening of vowels in unaccented syllables and the reduction of flexional forms, extends to about 1400. The language was not the popular language but rather that of literature; the literate classes had at their command a standard form of Irish, which educated men understood everywhere. As a result of the English conquests, there came about the dissolution of the standard literary language. Since the 16th century a dialect with well defined characteristics has been spoken throughout the southern half of Ireland. Northern Irish is subdivided into two lesser dialects, one of them in Connacht, the other (strongly influenced by Scottish Gaelic) in Ulster. Irish is still spoken in the southwest, west, and northwest of Ireland. In the mid-19th century 4 million out of 7 million persons spoke Irish as their mother tongue, of whom 1 million spoke only Irish. After World War II the number of Irish speakers among a population of approximately 4,300,000 was only 740,000, most of whom were bilingual.

Scottish Gaelic. Scottish Gaelic was differentiated from Irish chiefly on account of the strong Norse influence. The sound shifting of the voiced *b, d, g,* to the voiceless stops *p, t, c,* was accompanied by a change of the historic voiceless stops *p, t, c,* which are, when initial, pronounced with a following strong aspiration, and, when they follow the stressed vowel, become the preaspirated occlusives *chp, cht, chk,* a curious parallel to the prehistoric Germanic sound shifting. Before World War II, out of a population of 4,842,980, the number of Gaelic speakers was about 137,000, 7,000 of whom spoke only Gaelic. There were perhaps 30,000 speakers of Gaelic and another language in Canada.

Manx. Manx stands in a much closer relation to Scottish Gaelic than to Irish. It is written in a kind of phonetic spelling, based on Anglo-Scottish orthography. Its most distinctive feature is a peculiar stress system. Many dissyllabic words with a final long syllable shifted their stress to the second syllable as a result of Anglo-Norman influence; the same happened in Southern Irish. Somewhat later, long terminations of those words that had escaped the accent shift were shortened, probably under the influence of Scottish Gaelic. The Manx vocabulary contains a fairly great number of Norse and English loan words. In 1875 there were still 12,340 people out of a population of 41,048 (exclusive of the capital, Douglas) on the Isle of Man who used Manx as their everyday language; among them were 190 who spoke nothing but Manx. In the second half of the 20th century Manx was extinct.

British, or Brythonic. The term "British" or "Brythonic" comes from *Brittones* (welsh *Brython*), a by-form of Latin *Britanni,* the inhabitants of the Roman province Britannia. It comprises (1) Welsh (native *Cymraeg*), so called from the Celtic people the *Volcae,* whose name was extended by the Germans to all their western neighbors, in this case to the inhabitants of Wales; (2) Cornish (native *Kernewek*), the language of Cornwall, extinct since the end of the 18th century; (3) Breton (native *Brezonek*), the several dialects of Brittany.

Welsh. Welsh is the most important language of the Brythonic group. Old Welsh (from 800 to 1100 A. D.) is known to us almost entirely by means of glosses, isolated words, and proper names, but some Old Welsh texts have been preserved in Middle Welsh dress. Middle Welsh (from 1100 to 1500) is much more simplified than Old or Middle Irish. There remain only faint traces of case forms (mostly in the formation of the plural), and the dual and the neuter gender. The inflexion of the verb does not show as many archaic traces as that of the Irish verb. Spoken Welsh may be divided into North and South Welsh, each of which is further divided into two groups. Before World War II, out of a total population of 2,472,377, there were over 900,000 Welsh speakers.

Cornish. Cornish, which stood in a much closer relation to Breton than to Welsh, can be divided into Old Cornish (from 900 to 1100), known only by glosses and proper names, Middle Cornish (until 1600), and Late Cornish.

Breton. Breton is divided into Old Breton (from the 9th to the 11th century), known likewise only by glosses and proper names, Middle Breton (until the 16th century), and Modern Breton, which is composed of four chief dialects of Léon, Cornouailles, Tréguier, and Vannes. The last named differs greatly from the others, chiefly by preserving the old British stress on the former penult, which is now, after the loss of the final syllables, the final syllable.

Pictish. Pictish, the language of the Picts (Latin *Picti*) in the north of Britain, has left scarcely any traces beyond 16 "Pictish" inscriptions in an unknown language and a few proper names, some of which seem to be non-Celtic and some Goidelic and British. It is not impossible that a Goidelic dialect was spoken in Pictland before the coming of the Scots.

INSULAR CELTIC VARIATIONS

Differences Between Goidelic and Brythonic. The chief differences between insular Goidelic and Brythonic are as follows:

(1) While continental Celtic (Gaulish) seems to have preserved the free Indo-European accent, as in such Gaulish place names as *Némausus* (French *Nîmes*), *Tricasses* (*Troyes*), *Bitúriges*

(*Bourges*), and *Eburóvices* (*Evreux*), the accent rules in insular Celtic have become mechanical. In Irish the stress always fell on the first syllable, causing the loss of vowels in post-tonic syllables, but in Brythonic it fell on the penult before the loss of final syllables. Afterward it was again shifted to the new penult: compare Old Irish *Ériu* (Ireland) from Goidelic *Ēveriū*, genitive *Érenn* from **Ēveriónos*. The same **Ēveriónos* became in Welsh *Iwérddon*.

(2) Initial *s-* was preserved in Irish but became *h-* in Brythonic: compare Gaulish *senos* (old) and Old Irish *sen* with Welsh and Breton *hen*. The treatment of the *s-* groups also varies a great deal in Irish and Brythonic.

(3) In Irish the continental Celtic voiceless stops *t* and *k* became voiceless spirants *th* and *ch* in intervocalic position, while in Brythonic the continental Celtic intervocalic stops *p, t, k,* became voiced stops *b, d, g:* compare Gaulish *catu-* (battle) with Old Irish *cath* and Welsh *cad*.

(4) Continental Celtic *j* and *w* are lost in Irish but preserved in Britannic: compare continental Celtic **jewnkos* (young) with Old Irish *óac* (archaic *óëc*) and Welsh *ieuanc* (young).

(5) The vowels of accented syllables are better preserved in Goidelic than in Britannic: compare Gaulish *dūnon* (fort) with Old Irish *dún* and Welsh *din;* Gaulish *oinos* (one) with Old Irish *oín, oén,* and Welsh and Breton *un*.

(6) Owing to contact with the Romans, there were not only many more Latin words introduced into Britain than into Ireland, but the Brythonic languages became much simplified in their grammatical structure and preserve far less archaic traits than Goidelic.

Differences from Other Indo-European Languages. While the syntax of continental Celtic, or Gaulish, does not seem much different from that of the other Indo-European languages, as far as we are able to judge from the few inscriptions, the general character of insular Celtic seems completely different. (1) Where the autonomy of the single word seems especially characteristic of Indo-European, it is rather the group of closely connected words that forms the principal unit in insular Celtic. This characteristic explains why the same rules that govern the fate of intervocalic consonants or of nasals + consonants are also applied to initial consonants within certain groups of words in accordance with the original endings of preceding words; compare Old Irish *fer cáech* (a blind man), genitive *fir chaích*, with Gaulish **viros caicos*, genitive **virī caicī*, where the initial *c* is treated like intervocalic *c* if the preceding noun ended in a vowel. Thus the original endings still exercise their influence upon the initials of a following word long after the endings themselves have been lost. Without these changes, so-called initial mutations, there would be no such thing as syntax in insular Celtic. They have taken the place of the original word inflection, which has thus been supplanted by so-called group inflection, characteristic of some non-Indo-European languages, such as Basque and most languages of the Caucasus. The same group inflection appears in verbal forms that incorporate not only a pronominal object, a construction also found in some Indo-European languages, but at the same time a pronominal subject as well as relative and local particles; as for example, Old Irish *amal as-i-n-d-beir-som* (as he says it), from earlier **eks-is-en-ide-e(d)-beret-somos*, literally (in-the-way out-he-in which-here-it-brings-he).

(2) The fixed position of the verb at the head of the sentence, which is not obligatory in any other Indo-European language, is likewise found in Berber, Egyptian, and Semitic.

(3) Indo-European languages are characterized by a highly subjective verb, which normally treats events as actions; they also have developed a nominative case as the distinct expression of the subject. In insular Celtic the agent (logical subject) of the action, that the verb expresses often appears in an impersonal, passive construction also found in Egyptian, Berber, Basque, and many Caucasian and Arctic languages. Note the passive construction even of the verb *to be,* as in Old Irish *is di Ult(a)ib dom* (it is of the Ulstermen to me = I am an Ulsterman).

(4) The insular Celtic system of tenses and aspects, particularly the use of the progressive (periphrastic) tenses to denote the aspect (also used in English), is not Indo-European but has parallels in Basque, Egyptian, and Berber.

(5) There is no present participle, its function being discharged by the verbal noun, as in Egyptian and Berber.

(6) The so-called inflected prepositions (Old Irish *dom,* to me, *duit,* to you, *dó,* to him) have their exact parallel in Berber, Egyptian, and Semitic. Prehistory and anthropology show the existence of more than one pre-Celtic element in the British Isles: remainders of the Paleolithic inhabitants of western Europe, many traces of a widespread Arctic Mesolithic culture, Mediterranean invaders from northwest Africa (the bearers of Megalithic culture), and finally, during the Bronze Age, Dinaric brachycephalic immigrants from Spain, hailing ultimately from the Middle East, the so-called bell-beaker folk. See also CELTIC LITERATURE.

The great importance of Celtic linguistical studies lies in the fact that here we have an excellent chance of studying the effects of racial and linguistic blendings. It is at last being realized, according to John Rhys, that "the Celtic world commands one of the chief portals of ingress into the pre-Aryan foreworld, from which it may well be that we modern Europeans have inherited far more than we dream."

JULIUS POKORNY
Author of "Historical Reader of Old Irish"

Bibliography

General Works

Aberdeen, University of, *Scottish Gaelic Studies* (London 1926–   ).
Jackson, Kenneth Hurlstone, *Language and History in Early Britain* (Edinburgh 1953).
Lewis, Henry, and Pedersen, Holgar, *Concise Comparative Celtic Grammar* (Göttingen 1937).

Old and Middle Irish

Condon, T., Greene, D., and Quin, E. C., *Contributions to a Dictionary of the Irish Language* (Dublin 1939–   ).
Hessen, Hans, *Irish Lexicon* (Halle 1933–1940).
Pokorny, Julius, *Historical Reader of Old Irish* (Halle 1923).
Royal Irish Academy, *Dictionary of the Irish Language* (Dublin 1913).
Strachan, John, *Old Irish Paradigms and Selection from the Old Irish Glosses,* 3d ed. (Dublin 1929).
Thurneysen, Rudolf, *Grammar of Old Irish,* tr. by D. A. Binchy and Osborn Bergin, rev. ed. (Dublin 1946–1949).
Thurneysen, Rudolf, *Old Irish Reader* (Dublin 1949).

Modern Irish

de Bhaldraithe, Thomas, *English-Irish Dictionary* (Dublin 1959).
Christian Brothers, *Irish Grammar* (Dublin 1905).
Dinneen, P. S., *Irish-English Dictionary,* rev. ed. (Dublin 1927).

Henry, John Patrick, *Handbook of Modern Irish* (Dublin 1904–1906).

Mackenna, Lambert, *English-Irish Dictionary*, 2d ed. (Dublin 1943).

O'Cuír, Brian, *Irish Dialects and Irish-speaking Districts* (Dublin 1951).

O'Nolan, Gerald, *Grammar of Modern Irish* (Dublin 1934).

O'Rahilly, T. F., *Irish Dialects, Past and Present* (Dublin 1932).

Wagner, Heinrich, *Linguistic Atlas and Survey of Irish Dialects* (Dublin 1958).

Scottish Gaelic

Calder, George, *Gaelic Grammar* (Glasgow 1937).

Dieckhoff, H. C., *Pronouncing Dictionary of Scottish Gaelic* (Edinburgh 1932).

Dwelly, Edward, *Illustrated Gaelic-English Dictionary*, 4th ed. (Stirling, Scotland, 1941).

Macbain, Alexander, *Etymological Dictionary of the Gaelic Language*, 2d ed. (Stirling, Scotland, 1911).

Manx

Goodwin, Edmund, *First Lessons in Manx* (Dublin 1901).

Jackson, Kenneth Hurlstone, *Contributions to the Study of Manx Phonology* (Edinburgh 1955).

Kelly, John, *English and Manx Dictionary* (Douglas, Isle of Man, 1866).

Kneen, J. J., *Grammar of the Manx Language* (London 1931).

Welsh

Anwyl, Edward, *Welsh Accidence and Welsh Syntax* (London 1897–1900).

Anwyl, Edward, and Spurrell, William, *Welsh-English Dictionary*, 10th ed. (Carmarthen, Wales, 1930).

Bowan, John T., and Rhys Jones, T. J., *Teach Yourself Welsh* (New York 1960).

Evans, D. Simon, *Grammar of Middle Welsh* (Dublin 1964).

Geirisdur Prifysgol Cymru, *Dictionary of the Welsh Language* (Cardiff 1950–1952).

Gwynn-Jones, T., *Welsh-English and English-Welsh Dictionary* (Cardiff 1950).

Jenkins, Myrddin, *Welsh Tutor* (Cardiff 1959).

Morris-Jones, John, *Elementary Welsh Grammar* (Oxford 1921).

Smith, A. S. D. (Caradar), *Welsh Made Easy* (Wrexham, Wales, 1925).

Strachan, John, *Introduction to Early Welsh* (Manchester, England, 1909).

Cornish

Jenner, Henry, *Handbook of the Cornish Language* (London 1904).

Morton-Nance, R., *Cornish for All* (St. Ives, England, 1938).

Smith, A. S. D. (Caradar), *Cornish Simplified* (St. Ives, England, 1939).

Breton

Hardie, D. W. F., *Handbook of Modern Breton* (Cardiff 1948).

Hemon, Roparz, *Dictionnaire breton-français* (Brest 1941).

Hemon, Roparz, *Dictionnaire français-breton* (La Baule, France, 1950).

Hemon, Roparz, *Grammaire bretonne* (Brest 1941).

CELTIC LITERATURES, sel'tik, are literatures in the traditional languages of the insular Celts, including Irish Gaelic, Scottish Gaelic, Manx, Welsh, Cornish, and Breton. (Breton is considered an insular Celtic language because the Brythons, who spoke it, originally lived in England before the Anglo-Saxon invasions in the 5th and 6th centuries forced them to flee to France.) We have no remains of continental Celtic literature. However, our knowledge of the art and national character of the continental Celts, as described by ancient Greek and Latin writers, suggests that in many respects continental Celtic literature must have resembled that of the insular Celts.

The chief characteristics of Celtic literature are as follows:

(1) The Celtic peoples stand almost alone in that they used prose for epic narrative and reserved the verse form for lyric poetry. When the French Arthurian epics became known to the Welsh, they were changed from verse to prose; and the prose form of the Teutonic sagas and French romances is the result of Celtic influence.

(2) Although there is relatively little Celtic drama, the prose epics are often interspersed with dialogues in verse.

(3) Celtic poetry is frequently deficient in the architectonic quality, in the sense of structural unity. The poets do not seem to have the ability to produce large, continuous compositions, but devote their attention to harmonious detail. In the longer poems or tales, image is added to image, fancy piled on fancy, but we feel the want of any organic progression of thought and feeling. Celtic poets are masters of detail rather than of the whole, just as Celtic artists were masters in decoration and craftsmanship but with few exceptions, such as Irish illumination, did not produce great representative works of art.

(4) Celtic devotion to detail explains why, in so many beautiful poems, we do not have elaborate or sustained description but rather a succession of impressionistic pictures and images. To the poets the half-said thing is dearest; they avoid the obvious and the commonplace. A thousand years later this "impressionism" would be rediscovered in France; that it happened on old Celtic soil is certainly no mere coincidence. The Celts are distinguished among the Indo-European peoples by high mental excitability accompanied by quickness and mobility of thought. Also their language shows more of a tendency to break thought into small parts than does any other Indo-European language.

(5) Celtic nature poetry stands quite alone in medieval European literature. Nowhere else do we find such a sensitiveness to nature's various moods and such a capacity for bringing human moods into relation with those of nature. Celtic nature poetry is sentimental and highly imaginative, but never rationalistic. Often nature is described with a loving fidelity that has no object but itself.

(6) The irrational plays a far greater part in Celtic literature than in other literatures. Celtic literature is full of tales of magic and the supernatural; the distinction between natural and supernatural has not yet been clearly drawn. Dreams and visions belonged to the stock of the poet's repertoire, and even today some of the folk stories are actual daydreams. The Celtic storyteller had a vastly greater power of imagination and a much more subtle sense of the uncanny than the storyteller in other European countries. The fantastic exaggeration found in early epic tales was sometimes done for the fun of the thing, but by no means for this reason alone. The strong sense for the irrational was also a characteristic of continental Celtic art.

(7) Though the Celts appear in their literature as warlike people, gay and sensuous, fond of bright colors and eager for life, there is, after all, a vestige of truth in the myth of the "Celtic twilight," in which the Celts appeared to the rest of Europe as a result of the forgeries of the Scottish poet James Macpherson (q.v.) in the middle of the 18th century. In the earliest Celtic poems we occasionally find an intense, passionate yearning for that which is not possessed, for dead friends, for vanished youth, for the satisfaction that life can never give. But those elegies form merely a small part of the early Celtic literature. Only in modern times has the tragic fate of the Celts, who have

struggled to maintain their identity as peoples, caused a change in their outlook. Political persecution and social depression could not be without effect upon the literary production.

(8) While poets of other nations usually endeavor to translate the remote into terms of the present, Celtic poets invariably depict the remote as remote, producing in this way the sense of mystery and atmosphere of glamour found in so many Celtic romances.

Irish Gaelic Literature. This division of the Celtic literatures is treated in a separate article under the heading GAELIC LITERATURE.

Scottish Gaelic Literature. The Scots, who came from Ireland to Scotland in the 6th century, long spoke the same Gaelic as their relatives in Ireland. Gradually, in the Scottish Highlands and the western islands a Scottish Gaelic oral language began to diverge from classical Irish Gaelic, and a rich oral literature developed. The ballads, mostly derived from older prose stories, are concerned chiefly with the deeds of the Irish heroes Fionn Mac Cumhail (see FIONN MAC CUMHAIL), who is called Fingal in Scotland, Oisín (Ossian), and Oscar, members of the Fenians, a band of warriors who are often represented as fighting invaders from overseas. Since about the 12th century, Vikings often take the place of older, supernatural foes. No less interesting than the Ossianic ballads (and far more important to the folklorists) are the numerous charms and incantations collected by Alexander Carmichael in his immortal *Carmina Gadelica* (2d ed., 1928–1942).

Until the beginning of the 18th century, however, the literary language of the Scottish Highlands and the western islands continued to be the Gaelic of Ireland. The classical Gaelic poetry is the same in both countries. The subjects treated are about identical, since the literature of Scotland in its earlier stages drew its inspiration and themes from the motherland. The official poets and men of learning attached to the chiefs of Scottish clans went to Ireland for their bardic training. The family bards occupied an honored position in the Scottish social system; they kept alive the pride of race and ministered to it, especially by panegyrics.

We get the first glimpse of a special Scottish Gaelic literary tradition in an old and precious collection of poems known as the *Book of the Dean of Lismore*, written between 1512 and 1529 and collected by Sir James Macgregor, dean of Lismore in Argyll. Though the subject matter of the poems does not differ much from the contemporary Irish literature, the curious phonetic orthography and stylistic peculiarities enable us to form a fair idea of the dialects spoken in Scotland. The most important part of the collection consists of 28 Ossianic ballads. Thus the dean's book gives clear evidence that already at that time Ossianic poetry was recited and known in Gaelic Scotland and that it was very similar to the type known from later tradition. The use of the ballad for epic purpose originally was foreign to the Celtic poetic genius; no doubt its adoption was the result of Viking influence in both Ireland and Scotland.

Toward the close of the 16th century, owing to the decline of the trained professional poets and of the bardic organization, a new school of poets arose. The complicated syllabic meters of classical Gaelic were abandoned, and new meters came into existence. This modern poetry was usually regulated by stress, each line having a fixed number of stressed syllables—in other words, a certain rhythm. The foremost representatives of this new mode were Mary Macleod (called in Gaelic, Mairi Nighean Alasdair Ruaidh) and John Macdonald (Iain Lom).

More than 130 poets are mentioned between 1645 and 1830, many of them men of really great ability. Their language was the current Scottish Gaelic of their day. While the classic poetry was addressed to the aristocracy, the modern poetry was addressed to the people. The greatest original genius was Alexander Macdonald (Alasdair Mac-Mhaighstir Alasdair), who struck an entirely new note in Scottish Gaelic literature. In his descriptive poems he gave an expression to an intimate love of nature, similar to that found in early Irish lyrics. In 1741 he published the first Scottish Gaelic vocabulary, which was the first book printed in Scottish Gaelic. Other poets of great merit were Duncan Bán MacIntyre (Donnachadh Bán) and the great satirist Robert Mackay, called Rob Donn. The most outstanding writer of hymns and sacred poems was Dugald Buchanan. The poets of the new school were born, not made. Their poetry is spontaneous; it has the notes of freedom and sincerity, and great beauty of form; the style is direct and clear. The poets delight in manly vigor and beauty, in prowess in war and the hunt, in singing of festivity and of music. There is no trace of "Celtic mysticism" or of "Celtic gloom," not even in the lyrical outburst that followed the Forty-five (the Jacobite uprising against the English in 1745), when the Gaelic people of Scotland were left dependent on a foreign—and to them distasteful—culture. The dominant note in such poetry is emphatic personal loyalty to their beloved prince. In the dawn of the 19th century every district in the Highlands still had its native poet; today few bards of high reputation are left.

James Macpherson, the well-known forger of Ossianic ballads, does not occupy a place among the classical Gaelic poets, because his Gaelic texts are mere retranslations from the English and are full of offenses against idiom, being written in an unnaturally strained language. Yet he was an Anglo-Celtic poet of real genius and, after all, an heir to the ancient Celtic bards. Though his overflowing sentimentality corresponds rather to the general tendency of the early romantic movement than to the Celtic character, there is a decided Gaelic atmosphere in his work, and his sentimental nature poetry is doubtless an old Celtic heritage. His great mission was to make people aware of the existence of Celtic tradition, and the Ossianic revival led to the diligent collection of Ossianic poetry in the Highlands and the Western Islands. Efforts such as these were of lasting importance in the salvation of this tradition from oblivion.

Unfortunately there is not much Scottish Gaelic prose literature worth mentioning. The whole Gaelic Bible appeared in 1807; the earlier editions of 1767 and 1783 show too much Irish influence. But we have a great amount of valuable Gaelic folk tales published (see *Bibliography*), not to mention various collections of proverbs.

Manx Literature. There is no early literature extant in Manx. Of the many Ossianic poems known among the Manx people, only one fragment (and that possibly of an earlier period) has been preserved. Most of the existing literature of native origin consists of ballads and carols, locally called carvels. Only a small part of these has been published. There is, in addition, a fair amount of folklore, tales, and proverbs.

Literature translated into Manx is almost entirely religious. The earliest book known to have been written in Manx is a translation of the Book of Common Prayer, written between 1625 and 1630 (but published only in 1895). The first printed book is *The Principles and Duties of Christianity* (1699) by Bishop Thomas Wilson. The complete Old Testament appeared in 1772, and the New Testament appeared in 1775.

Among nonreligious translations may be mentioned a paraphrase of portions of Milton's *Paradise Lost* by Thomas Christian (1794) and *Aesop's Fables* by Edmund Faragher (1901).

Welsh Literature. The oral folk culture of Wales goes back to Megalithic times. Early Welsh written poetry is found mainly in four manuscripts commonly called *The Four Ancient Books of Wales,* namely the *Black Book of Carmarthen,* the *Book of Aneirin,* the *Book of Taliesin,* and the *Red Book of Hergest,* all written after the close of the 12th century. Most of the poems in these manuscripts are attributed to four poets: Aneirin, Taliesin, Myrddin (the Merlin of romance), and Llywarch Hen, who are all called *cynfeirdd* (early poets). Metrically their work shows the main characteristics of Welsh syllabic verse. The rhythmic effect is attained chiefly by the use of internal rhyme and consonantal correspondences. The first three poets belong to the "Men of the North," the British tribes who, until the mid-7th century, owned the south of Scotland and the northeast of England. The *Gododin* (*Gododdin*) of Aneirin, a poem on the Battle of Catraeth (probably modern Catterick), about 600 A.D., is not a narrative poem, but rather a succession of lyrical laments on the disastrous effects of the battle. Though largely modernized, the *Gododin* and several historical poems attributed to Taliesin show distinct traces of direct copying from a 9th century original. It has been claimed on internal evidence that the *Gododin* is actually the work of Aneirin (c.600). The Myrddin poems, as well as his name, are late and spurious. Llywarch Hen is not the author of the poems attributed to him, but merely the chief character of a lost saga, produced about 850 in Powys or mid-Wales. The poems are steeped in magic and have a prevailingly elegiac quality.

The next period, that of the *gogynfeirdd* (rather early poets), from about 1150 to 1350, is the time of the bardic court poetry. The bards were court officials with closely defined duties and recognized privileges. Their tendency to preserve the exclusiveness of their caste by multiplying the difficulties of their craft led to an exaggerated formalism and the substitution of verbal ingenuity for passion and imagination. Yet their poetry often succeeded in expressing not systematically but rather by suggestion the whole range of their emotions. Noun is piled on noun and adjective on adjective, so that one must feel their poetry rather than understand it.

The father of modern Welsh poetry is the 14th century Dafydd (Davydd) ap Gwilym, the greatest poet produced by Wales. He broke the tyranny of the bardic schools and freed poetic language from the fetters of conventional archaic diction by writing in the ordinary language of his educated countrymen. He introduced popular fresh themes and established the new metrical form called *cywydd*. His love poems are derived from Provençal poetry through the channels opened by the *clerici vagantes* (wandering scholars), but are far more realistic. The highest summit of his poetic art he attains, however, in his nature poems.

Unfortunately the authority of the bardic schools soon re-established the old formal strictness, though the *cywydd* remained and flourished. After centuries of decline the bardic organization finally collapsed. The Calvinistic Methodism of the 18th century, which produced masterpieces of hymnology, and the literary renascence that was in strong opposition to Methodism, led to an extraordinary outburst of poetry. Here belongs Ceiriog (pen name of John Ceiriog Hughes), one of the chief lyric poets of Wales.

From about 1850 the accentual free meters gained more and more ground. The so-called new poet school was inaugurated by Sir John Morris-Jones with his excellent translations from Heine. W. J. Gruffydd, one of the first to revolt against the prevailing puritanism, wrote poems of singular beauty. T. Gwynn Jones showed that the old tradition could answer to any demand that was made upon it. His translation of Goethe's *Faust* is a masterpiece.

R. Williams Parry and Cynan are among the best contemporary poets. Modern Welsh lyrical poetry occupies an honorable place among the literatures of the great nations of Europe.

A gift for gnomic poetry and a fondness for the epigram have been characteristic of Welsh literature since the 12th century. There are hundreds of examples of the *englyn* (a four-line stanza), many of them comparable to the Greek epigram at its best. Among the countless folk songs must be mentioned the anonymous *penhillion* (stanzas for singing to the harp), often quite heartrending in their perfect simplicity. In these, as in many other poems of the 19th century, we find for the first time a note of melancholy, that "nostalgia of the infinite" resulting from the hopeless social conditions and the influence of Calvinistic theology, which has often been quite wrongly ascribed to the Celts as such.

There was no Welsh drama until the 19th century, when this genre made a promising start. The interludes, or miracle plays, of Twm o'r Nant in the 18th century hardly deserve that name.

Welsh prose begins with the *Laws of Howel* (*Hywel*) *Dda* (10th century). The vast body of Arthurian legend was widely known on the Continent even before Geoffrey of Monmouth wrote in Latin between 1135 and 1139 the *History of the Kings of Britain.* The sources of the Arthurian verse epics of the 12th century French poet Chrétien de Troyes must have been Welsh and Cornish documents as well as spoken narratives. The earliest attempt at turning prose to artistic purposes is found in the *Four Branches of the Mabinogi,* preserved in the *White Book of Rhydderch* written in the late 13th or early 14th century. The first four tales (forming the *Mabinogion* proper) preserve old British mythical traditions, partly influenced by Irish mythology; the others are old British tales referring to Roman times, British Arthurian tales, and translations or adaptations of Norman French originals. The translation of the Welsh Bible (1588) laid the foundation for modern Welsh prose. The 19th century novels of Daniel Owen are not much inferior to the work of Dickens. In the 20th century the short stories of Kate Roberts and the novels of T. Rowland Hughes are real works of genius.

More is printed in Welsh—in books, papers, and magazines—than in all the other Celtic languages together. Methodism has saved the Welsh language but has killed much of the old folk culture of Wales.

Cornish Literature. Though the preserved remains of nonreligious literature in Cornish are very scanty, there must have existed a large number of old Celtic legends in Cornwall during the Middle Ages. Arthur's treacherous nephew Modret bears a purely Cornish name; in the story of Arthur, Cornwall plays a very important part. Similarly the topography of the Tristan saga in the sources of the Anglo-Norman writer Béroul is predominantly Cornish. The form of many Celtic names in the French epics shows that they must have been derived from written Cornish and Welsh sources. There cannot be much doubt that the world owes to Cornwall and Wales the "Matter of Britain." Owing to Norman Conquest, Cornwall (where the French encountered a Celtic population dominated by an English aristocracy) grew to be a trilingual country, so that it is probably to Cornwall and not to Brittany that we owe the transmission of the Celtic legends to the Continent.

Unfortunately the only nonreligious literary remains are a few Cornish conversations, some songs, proverbs, and epigrams, and a folk tale, the story of John of Chy-an-Hur (*The Ram's House*), the plot of which is well known in Ireland and elsewhere. Apart from a long poem on the Passion, the religious literature consists chiefly of mystery plays of learned origin, imitated from English sources. There are also fragments of translations, such as chapters of Scripture, the Lord's Prayer, and the Commandments. During the Reformation neither the Book of Common Prayer nor the Scriptures were translated into Cornish; and when the Methodist movement came, it was too late. Some enthusiasts lately have attempted a kind of revival of Cornish, which has produced some fine lyrics and a mystery play.

Breton Literature. The earliest piece of connected Breton has been preserved in a manuscript of the 14th century. It seems to be a fragment of a love song, similar to the contemporary French chansonette. No other examples of the rich Breton poetry of the Middle Ages have been preserved. The earliest Breton printed work, a Breton-Latin-French dictionary, the *Catholicon* by Jean Lagadeuc, was published in 1499. French seems to have been the language of the aristocracy and the medium of culture; hence the oldest texts are either translated or imitated from French. The early literature is almost exclusively religious, such as *The Hours* (1486) and *The Mirror of Death* (1519).

The bulk of Breton literature before the 19th century consists of mystery and miracle plays. Brittany is the only Celtic land where the theater, though not of native growth and only introduced from France, has met with an immense popular favor. Upwards of 150 Breton mystery plays are known to exist. The oldest, the *Life of St. Nonn*, belongs to the end of the 15th century and is modeled on a Latin version. The mysteries are adaptations mostly from French or Latin and are full of French words. From the 18th century we also find plays dealing with romances of chivalry, such as the *Tragedy of the Four Sons of Aymon* (of which no less than 15,000 copies were sold), *Huon de Bordeaux*, and *Robert the Devil*. Their subject matter is likewise taken from French sources, and their chief interest lies in the fact they are the last creations of the theater of the Middle Ages.

Only the 19th century brought an original Breton literature. The movement was led by Jean François Le Gonidec, the author of the first Breton translation of the Bible (1868), the first scientific Breton grammar, *Grammaire celto-bretonne* (1807), and an excellent dictionary (1821). Ardent patriots endeavored to create a national literature. At about the same time, the attention of the whole world of letters was directed to Brittany, when Hersart de la Villemarqué (1815–1895) published his famous collection *Barzaz Breiz* (The Poetry of Brittany) in 1839. The work gave rise to a protracted and heated discussion, which is almost as famous as that caused by Macpherson's Ossian forgeries. Today we know that Villemarqué transformed the material that he had collected, eliminating anything that he believed to be crude and gross. He transferred modern poems to medieval times, rearranged others, and composed some himself. But at least he had a fluent command of Breton, and his book is not only a great and really beautiful work of art, but also linguistically much superior to that of Macpherson. Just as in Scotland, Villemarqué's poems gave the signal for a serious study of the popular Breton ballads, legends, and folk tales that form the real literature of Brittany. The most famous collections we owe to F. M. Luzel and Anatole Le Braz.

It is usual to divide popular Breton poetry into *gwerziou* and *soniou*. The *gwerziou* (complaints) are short ballads or complaints, village tales in verse of a highly dramatic quality and usually of tragic interest. The *soniou* (songs) consist of love songs, satires, carols, and sailors' songs, and sometimes show traces of French influence. Breton folk tales and legends are extremely valuable from the folkloristic point of view and show some very archaic traits. In 1839 there also appeared *Kanaouennou eur C'hernewad* (*Poems of a Man from Cornouailles*) the first book by Prosper Proux, one of the few original Breton poets of the 19th century. Another great poet of that time was Auguste Brizeux, author of *Telen Arvor* (*The Harp of Brittany*).

An important new literary movement in the 20th century was inaugurated by linguistic specialists including such men as Émile Ernault, François Vallée (Abhervé), and René le Roux (Meven Mordiern). In 1918 there came into being a small circle of intellectual writers, whose work found expression in the pages of the journal *Gwalarn* (Northwest), which appeared from 1925 to 1944 and was continued from 1946 as *Al Liamm* (*Bond*). In 1921 appeared *War an Daoulin* (*À Genoux*), a small volume of poetry by Jean Pierre Calloc'h, written in the Vannes dialect and furnished with a French translation. This poetry is mystic and Catholic and completely free from the platitudes of Calloc'h's contemporaries. Thence a new poetry came into existence, worthy of the best that other countries have produced. Among the younger poets may be mentioned Xavier de Langlais, Maodez Glanndour, and Roparz Hémon. Some of the finest examples of Celtic nature poetry are found among the poems of Roperzh Er Mason, *Chal ha Dichal* (*Flood and Ebb Tide*).

Other new developments in Breton literature were short stories and novels by Jakez Riou, Roparz Hémon, Kenan Kongar, and Youenn Drezen.

A modern theater was created by Tangi Malmanche, Xavier de Langlais, and Roparz Hémon. Some of their work almost equals that of the Anglo-Irish poets such as Yeats and Synge. The patriotic efforts of all those idealists is the more to be admired because they had no help whatever from any official circles. The French government was very hostile to all their efforts and refused to tolerate the Breton language either in public schools or in public institutions, fearing a resurgence of the centuries-old Breton separatist movement.

JULIUS POKORNY
Author of "Historical Reader of Old Irish"

Bibliography
General Works
Jackson, Kenneth Hurlstone, *Celtic Miscellany* (London 1951).
Rhys, Grace, *Celtic Anthology* (London 1927).

Scottish Gaelic
Campbell, John Francis, *Popular Tales of the West Highlands*, 2d ed., 4 vols. (Paisley, Scotland, 1890–1893).
Campbell, John Lorne, *Highland Songs of Forty-five* (Edinburgh 1933).
Christensen, Reidar T., *The Vikings in Irish and Gaelic Tradition* (Oslo 1932).
Mackenzie, John, *The Beauties of Gaelic Poetry*, 2d ed. (Edinburgh 1907).
Mackenzie, John, and Calder, George, *Gaelic Songs by William Ross*, rev. ed. (Edinburgh 1937).
Maclean, Magnus, *Literature of the Highlands*, 2d ed. (London 1925).
McKay, John G., *More West Highland Tales* (Edinburgh 1940).
Watson, James Carmichael, ed., *Gaelic Songs of Mary Macleod* (Glasgow 1934).
Watson, William J., *Scottish Verse from the Book of The Dean of Lismore* (Edinburgh 1937).

Manx
Clague, John, *Manx Reminiscences* (Castletown, Isle of Man, 1911).
Moore, Arthur William, *Manx Ballads and Music* (Douglas, Isle of Man, 1896).
Moore, Arthur William, *Manx Folklore* (Douglas, Isle of Man, 1891).
Moore, Arthur William, *Manx Names* (Douglas, Isle of Man, 1903).

Welsh
Bell, H. C., and Bell, C. C., *Welsh Poems of the Twentieth Century in English Verse* (Wrexham, Wales, 1925).
Bell, Harold Idris, *The Development of Welsh Poetry* (New York and London 1936).
Bell, Harold Idris, *Welsh Literary Renascence of the Twentieth Century* (New York 1953).
Clancy, Joseph P., *Medieval Welsh Lyrics* (New York 1965).
Ellis, Thomas Peter, *Welsh Tribal Law and Custom in the Middle Ages* (New York and London 1926).
Ellis, Thomas Peter, and Ellis, Lloyd, J., *The Mabinogion* (New York and London 1929).
Graves, Robert, *White Goddess*, rev. ed. (New York 1966).
Jackson, Kenneth Hurlstone, *Studies in Early Celtic Nature Poetry* (London and New York 1935).
Jackson, Kenneth Hurlstone, ed., *Early Welsh Gnomic Poems* (Mystic, Conn., 1961).
Parry, Thomas, *History of Welsh Literature* (Oxford 1955).
Parry, Thomas, ed., *Oxford Book of Welsh Verse* (New York and London 1962).
Williams, Gwyn, *Introduction to Welsh Poetry* (New York 1953).

Cornish
Halliday, Frank Ernest, ed. and tr., *Legend of the Rood* (London 1955).
Norris, Edwin, *Ancient Cornish Drama* (Oxford 1859).

Breton
Cadic, François, *Chants de Chouans* (Paris 1949).
Le Braz, Anatole, *La légende de la mort chez les bretons armoricains* (Paris 1902).
Le Braz, Anatole, *Le théâtre celtique* (Paris 1902).
Loth, Joseph, *Chrestomathie bretonne* (Paris 1890).
Luzel, F. M., *Contes populaire de Basse-Bretagne* (Paris 1887).

CELTIC MYTHOLOGY, sel'tik mi-thol'ə-jē.

The mythology of the Celts is perhaps best known in modern times because of its influence on Irish and Welsh folklore and literature. However, the term "Celtic mythology" covers the mythology of peoples who once inhabited much of continental Europe as well as the British Isles (see CELTIC PEOPLES). Celtic mythology is steeped in magic and the supernatural. Neither the Celts nor related barbarians possessed philosophical or ethical concepts of religion. Rather, their concern lay in the proper functioning of magic, exerted through ritual, to procure prosperity in the land, freedom from disease, and victory in war. Thus Celtic paganism may best reflect the nature of what all European peoples must once have held sacred, and there are many links with Italic, German, and even Aryan mythology.

The Structure of Celtic Mythology. Among the Celts, the Otherworld seems to have been conceived as a magical counterpart to the world of men, with a similar social structure and possibilities for overlordship. A significant feature of the Celtic deities was their distinctly local character. Each tribe possessed its one all-powerful god, who was an eponymous ancestor (having the same name as the tribe), protector, and provider. Some deities obtained a more universal recognition, but in general the welfare of any one Celtic tribe was influenced by its particular local god. Many of these gods, often of immense size and appetites, had similar attributes. Thus Dagda, "the good god" in Ireland, may be compared with Esus, "master" in a beneficent sense, in Gaul.

Dagda, as the all-competent father, protector, and benefactor of the tribe, represents the basic type of Celtic male deity. He is pictured with a never-empty cauldron, signifying eternal plenty and fertility. Magical cauldrons symbolizing abundance were attributed to other gods as well.

Each local god possessed all-embracing powers, and there were no gods with powers limited to a single focus, such as war, wisdom, or beauty, as in Greek and Roman mythology. However, there is evidence, particularly in Ireland, of an association of gods similar to the Greek and Roman pantheons. This association was known in Ireland as the Túatha Dé Danann, or "the peoples of the goddess Danu." Dagda, Gobniu, and another Irish god, Lug, belonged to this group. According to legend, the Túatha Dé Danann defeated older established deities, particularly through the prowess of these three gods. Overcome in turn by the Milesians, the forerunners of the present-day Irish, the Túatha Dé Danann retreated to the hills and became associated with the fairy folk so noted in Irish folklore today.

Goddesses, while mates of tribal gods, also had special relationships with tribal kings, particularly in Ireland. At the beginning of a reign, the goddess appeared as a beautiful maiden who accepted the youthful king. But with the decline of the king's physical powers, the goddess awaited his death in the guise of a dreadful hag. The mythological stories around this theme imply the king's ritual death by burning or stabbing. There are indications, also, that goddesses were identified more closely with natural topography or territory than with society. The same goddess might have several names in reference to her particular role. As death-foreboding hag, her names are always horrific compared with those appropriate for other functions. Thus there were

Nemain (panic), Morrígan (queen of demons), and Badb Catha (battle raven). On the other hand, the river goddess names Boann (Boyne) and Sequanna (Seine) imply fruitfulness. Dedications to Matronae, "the mothers," show placid scenes of three seated women surrounded by baskets of fruit, small animals, and infants. The number "three" was regarded as sacred and having magical powers.

Sacred Festivals. The major Celtic festivals, especially in Ireland, commemorated the change in seasons from warm to cold. *Samain,* celebrated on the day that is November 1 in the modern calendar, was the greatest festival in Ireland, marking the end of one year and the beginning of the next. Rituals were undertaken to ensure a prosperous year. Perhaps the most significant period of this festival took place the preceding night, corresponding to Halloween, when it was believed that the world of men was overrun by the forces of magic. At the festival of *Samain* the marriage of Dagda with Morrígan or with Boann was celebrated.

The second major Irish festival was *Beltine,* celebrated on the first of May at the beginning of the warm season. Great fires were kindled at this festival, probably dedicated to the god Belenus, who was associated with the welfare of sheep and cattle. Other seasonal festivals were Imbolc, celebrated on February 1, and Lugnasad, on August 1. Imbolc, perhaps particularly connected with sheep tending, corresponds to the Christian feast of St. Brigid or Brigit. The Celtic Brigit, a daughter of Dagda, was a powerful fertility goddess. Lugnasad, founded by Lug in honor of a goddess, still survives.

Sacrifices were prominent in Celtic ritual, and human and animal sacrifices took place at the sacred festivals. One Irish myth concerns the sacrifice of the son of a sinless couple to make amends to the gods for an unfortunate marriage between a king and a foreign woman. As the boy is about to be sacrificed, a woman appears leading a cow, which is offered up instead.

The practitioners of Celtic ritual and magical lore were most widely known as druids. The druids held a dominant position in Celtic society, for it was they who invoked the magical powers to ensure prosperity and success. Descriptions of hide-clad druids undergoing trances in order to forecast events resemble accounts of shamans in other cultures—for example, the medicine men of the North American Indians. See also DRUID.

After the inclusion of much Celtic territory in the Roman Empire, Celtic deities were often identified with Roman gods. As a result, Roman sculpture was adapted to the portrayal of largely native deities. Moreover, many Latin dedicatory inscriptions incorporating a great number of Celtic names have been found in the British Isles, the Iberian Peninsula, and the Rhineland.

Although the Celts once covered a large area of the European continent, much of the information about their mythology comes only from the British Isles, particularly Ireland and Wales. Nevertheless, it is clear that the elements of Celtic mythology relate to a common Indo-European heritage from which much of Western mythology derives. See also CELTIC LANGUAGES; GAELIC LITERATURE.

T. G. E. POWELL, *University of Liverpool*
Further Reading: Powell, Thomas G. E., *The Celts* (London 1958); Sjoestedt, Marie L., *Gods and Heroes of the Celts,* tr. by Myles Dillon (London 1949); Ross, Anne, *Pagan Celtic Britain* (London 1967).

CELTIC PEOPLES, kel'tik pē'pəlz. The Celts were a group of peoples, bound by a common Indo-European cultural and linguistic heritage, who spread over much of Europe from the 2d millennium B.C. to about the 1st century B.C. They included the Gauls, the Galatians, and the Belgae, as well as the ancestors of the present-day Irish, Scottish, and Welsh. All these peoples spoke related languages, and this linguistic association, as well as other distinctive ethnological characteristics, have helped identify the Celtic peoples (see CELTIC LANGUAGES).

The Celts were recognized by Greek geographers from the late 6th century B.C. as a major barbarian nation living in the area north of Massilia (Marseille). Herodotus wrote of them in the mid-5th century B.C. as one of the most westerly European peoples, inhabiting the Upper Danube region. The name "Celt" is thus known earliest in the Greek form, *Keltoi,* and this term was used up to the time of Julius Caesar. From the 3d century B.C., however, the names *Galatae* (Galatians) and *Galli* (Gauls) were increasingly used by Classical writers.

Areas of Celtic Settlement. Three major cultures, Urnfield, Hallstatt, and La Tène, are associated with Celtic settlements in Europe, and it is through archaeological evidences of these cultures that the extent of Celtic expansion can in part be inferred.

Evidence of Celtic names in the Iberian Peninsula is found in the *Massilot Periplus,* a work of the late 7th or early 6th century B.C., which describes a voyage along the coasts of Spain. The presence of Celtic names in this area is best explained by the spread of the Urnfield culture, denoting a migration from the Upper Rhône region into Catalonia and beyond, beginning about 700 B.C.

The introduction of an iron-using economy in the 8th century B.C. gave rise to the Hallstatt culture, widespread in the Upper Danubian region and extending to the Rhine and into eastern France. By the mid-6th century B.C., the Greek colony of Massilia was maintaining trade contacts with barbarian Celtic rulers in the area of modern Württemberg, Baden, and Burgundy. The wealth found in princely tombs in this region, including native goldwork and imported Greek and Etruscan bronzes, indicates the existence of a stable and prosperous Celtic nation.

During the 5th century B.C., certain shifts in the centers of economic activity, particularly to the iron-producing region of the Middle Rhine, combined with continued Mediterranean influences on native culture to encourage the formation of the La Tène culture, noted for its remarkable decorative art style. It was as the bearers of this culture that the Celts came more fully into historical view. About the beginning of the 4th century B.C., they descended on the rich lands of northern Italy, reaching Rome about 390 B.C. This move into Italy was the most spectacular step in a general expansion of Celtic tribes throughout the 4th and 3d centuries that reached to Bohemia, the Carpathians, and the Ukraine. Celtic inroads through the Balkans followed. Delphi was sacked in 279 B.C., and some of these migrant Galatians moved into Asia Minor, where they were finally subdued, although they retained something of their national characteristics and language until the 4th century A.D.

In Italy the Cisalpine Gauls were finally checked by the Romans at the battle of Telamon in 225 B.C. By 192 B.C., Roman supremacy had been established as far as the Alps. A further move into Celtic territory, the Transalpine province of Provence, was undertaken by the Romans in 124 B.C. Meanwhile, the reduction of the Celtiberian stronghold of Numantia had occurred in 133 B.C. Subsequent Latin inscriptions show many Celtic names in the north and west of the Iberian Peninsula. The Gallic War, undertaken in 58 B.C. by Julius Caesar, saw the end of Celtic independence on the European mainland.

The date and nature of the initial Celtic settlement of the British Isles is disputed. In one view, the Celtic languages may have been lodged in these islands since the early or mid-2d millennium B.C. If this view is correct, there well may be a correlation between Celtic settlements in the British Isles and antecedents of early continental Bronze Age cultures. There is, however, an alternate theory that Celtic-speaking peoples of mixed Urnfield and Hallstatt cultures, coming mainly from the region of the Lower Rhine and the Seine, intermittently settled Britain between the 8th and 5th century B.C. Ireland probably first received Gaulish settlers, of the La Tène Culture, in the 3d century B.C. Others came later as refugees. It is uncertain if any further significant immigration into Britain took place until the arrival of the Belgae, Celtic tribes from northwestern Gaul, about the beginning of the 1st century B.C.

Celtic strongholds in Britain eventually fell to Roman domination. Caesar's two expeditions to that island in 55 and 54 B.C. paved the way for the invasion by Emperor Claudius in 43 A.D. With the eventual stabilization of frontiers along Hadrian's Wall in northern England about 128 A.D., only the poor, warlike tribes north of this line and the inhabitants of Ireland remained to preserve a Celtic way of life.

Celtic Society. Celtic society and economy were remarkably homogeneous, as evidenced from archaeological findings, Classical texts, and the literature of the Celtic peoples themselves. Celtic life was essentially rural, dependent on stock raising and agriculture in varying degrees from region to region. Iron-smelting and crafts were generally conducted on a local basis. Long-distance trade and the development of fine metal workmanship and decorative arts required special circumstances and substantial local patronage. No real towns existed, although in the 1st century B.C., larger groups of people than before were drawn together for purposes of trade and communal safety. These settlements are the subject of wide modern archaeological study.

The social unit among the Celts revolved around kinship, reckoned to various degrees but essentially to the descendants of a common great-grandfather traced through the male line. The tribe, or "people," was made up of freemen ruled by a king and subdivided into a warrior nobility and a farming class. The druids, practitioners of Celtic ritual, were recruited from noble families and ranked above them. Caesar's distinction of *druides* (men of cult and learning), *equites* (warriors), and *plebs* (commoners) in Gaulish society is thus classic. Freemen were normally vassals of wealthier men, and this system continued through the vassalage of weaker kings to stronger. In this way the large confederation of Caesar's opponents in Gaul and the kingdoms of early medieval Ireland were built up.

Celtic Warfare. The warrior class played a sig-

HURAULT—LOUVRE, PARIS

A Celtic helmet of bronze overlaid with gold, of the 4th century B.C.

A statuette of a Celtic god with a boar, carved in limestone in the 1st century B.C., from France.

HURAULT—MUSEE NATIONALE, ST. GERMAIN-EN-LAYE

LIBRARIES, MUSEUMS, AND ARTS COMMITTEE, LIVERPOOL

A Celtic gold coin of the 1st century A.D., from Great Britain.

WÜRTTEMBERG LANDESMUSEUM, STUTTGART

A Gallo-Roman stone relief depicts horses arranged in groups of three.

nificant role in Celtic society, and their methods of warfare are a subject of great interest. From the 4th to the 1st century B. C., the Celts fought mainly on foot with iron swords, spears, and long shields. Light chariots with paired horses were used for display, intimidation, and transportation rather than for actual combat. The same was true of the ridden horse, and although in Caesar's time Gaulish *equites* were numerous, there was no true cavalry in the sense of drilled formations. Warriors fought naked as a matter of ritual. Battles often began with champions issuing personal challenges and boasting of their prowess and lineage. The ideal Celtic warrior is represented as having great stature and muscular strength, blond coloring, golden hair, and ruddy cheeks. Recklessness in battle and excess in feasting and drinking were highly esteemed. Greek sculpture has memorialized the type in the noted statue *The Dying Gaul*.

Celtic Art. Surviving artifacts are evidence of notable artistic achievements by Celtic society. The unique art style of the La Tène Culture drew on trans-Alpine, Mediterranean, and Oriental sources for its abstract geometric designs and stylized bird and animal forms. But the distinctive feature of Celtic art is the use of curvilinear designs of spirals and scrolls. It was particularly in fine metalwork that this art style received its greatest expression. Human representation was largely confined to formalized heads and faces in otherwise abstract designs. After the La Tène culture declined in continental Europe, the Celts developed a new medium for their art in native coinage. This coinage was based on Greek prototypes, but coin design soon gave expression to Celtic elaborations of the head.

The Celtic Heritage. The Celtic heritage that was maintained beyond the northwestern frontiers of the Roman Empire laid the foundations for two national traditions surviving today in Ireland and Wales. In Ireland, Celtic institutions continued with some modifications to the 16th century, and a great body of prose and verse literature both oral and written was cherished. Gaelic, the Irish branch of the Celtic language, with some influence from Church Latin, developed into the modern tongue still spoken, though decreasingly. See GAELIC LITERATURE.

In Britain, a complex situation arose with the withdrawal of Roman arms early in the 5th century. An important factor in the survival of the Celtic heritage in this area was the transference of partly Romanized British-speaking tribes from southern Scotland to what is now Wales. This was a defense against Irish raiding and settlement, but it also provided a stronghold in the west when all the northern territories were lost either to Gaelic-speaking Scots (who were Irish settlers in western Scotland) or to Anglo-Saxons who had pushed north from Northumbria. The surviving British population in the west was called "Welsh," from an Anglo-Saxon word meaning "foreigner." The Welsh, already Christianized, developed their own culture in opposition, and a distinguished literature flourished over many subsequent centuries, continuing along with the Welsh language to modern times.

T. G. E. POWELL, *University of Liverpool*

Further Reading: Piggott, Stuart, *Ancient Europe* (Edinburgh 1966); Powell, T. G. E., *The Celts* (London 1958); Tierney, J. J., *The Celtic Ethnography of Posidonius* (Dublin 1960).

CELTIS, tsel'tis, **Conradus** (1459–1508), German humanist and Latin poet. He was born in Wipfeld, near Schweinfurt, on Feb. 1, 1459, the son of a wine maker. His real name was Konrad Pickel. Celtis ran away from home and studied under Agricola in Heidelberg. He became a wandering scholar and taught in Erfurt, Rostock, and Leipzig.

Celtis' first important work was *Ars versificandi et carminum* (1486). This book created a sensation, causing Celtis to be crowned by Maximilian I in 1487 as the first poet laureate of Germany. He later was professor of rhetoric and poetry at Ingolstadt (1492–1497) and at Vienna (1497–1508). He died in Vienna, Feb. 4, 1508.

Celtis discovered and published the Latin plays and poems of the nun Roswitha (Hroswitha); the *Tabula Peutingeriana*, the famous map of the Roman Empire; and other Latin works. He planned a great historical work on Germany, but only portions were published. His Latin poems were considered masterpieces.

CELTUCE, a variety of lettuce, has a fleshy edible stem that tastes somewhat like celery and lettuce.

BURPEE SEEDS

CELTUCE, sel'təs, is a variety of lettuce cultivated for its fleshy edible stem. The stems, sometimes together with the young leaves, are served fresh as a salad green or cooked as a vegetable. The name "celtuce" was coined from "celery" and "lettuce" because the flavor of celtuce is similar to that of both lettuce and celery. However, celtuce is in no way related to celery. Celtuce, which is known technically as *Lactuca sativa* var. asparagina (or var. angustana), belongs to the composite family (Compositae). Celery is a member of the parsley family (Umbelliferae).

Cultivated lettuces probably originated in Asia Minor from one of the native wild species. Since Roman times many different varieties have been developed, including many leafy forms as well as celtuce. Like other forms of lettuce, celtuce is a fast-growing annual that matures in about 80 days. In hot weather it has a tendency to bolt (form an elongated flowering stalk) and turn bitter.

ROBERT W. SCHERY, *Director, The Lawn Institute*

CEMENT production begins with the blasting of limestone from an open quarry. Limestone is one source of lime, a basic ingredient of cement.

CEMENT, si-ment', may be any bonding agent such as glue, mucilage, certain plastics, putty, solder, asphalt, and hydraulic cement. However, the use of hydraulic cements in the construction and road-building industries has become so important that the unmodified term "cement" now refers almost exclusively to these products.

A hydraulic cement is a bonding agent that reacts with water to form a hard stonelike substance that is resistant to disintegration in water. Most hydraulic cements are specific combinations of silicates and aluminates of lime. Many other combinations of mineral oxides would qualify as hydraulic cements but cannot compete for use in ordinary construction because of their cost. Most hydraulic cement is used in the form of concrete, which consists of cement, water, sand, and gravel or crushed stone. The cement is the bonding agent, and the other rock materials, which are called *aggregates,* act as filler.

Three classes of cements have been developed commercially: natural cements (including hydraulic limes), aluminous cements, and portland cements.

NATURAL CEMENTS

History. In the United States, the need for a water-resistant mortar became imperative with the development of canals as major arteries of transportation. With the beginning of construction of the Erie Canal in 1817, a search for natural cement rock resulted in the discovery of a suitable deposit near Fayetteville, N. Y. Canals were being built in many parts of the country, and other deposits were discovered and processed in widely scattered locations, including Pennsylvania, Maryland, West Virginia, Virginia, Kentucky, Wisconsin, and Illinois. A mill built in 1828 in Rosendale, Ulster county, N. Y., became the center of the industry, and the term "Rosendale cement" came to be synonymous with natural cement.

The first natural cement was made in small, upright, wood-burning kilns that were fired for about a week, after which the clinker was ground between millstones by waterpower. In 1899 nearly 10 million barrels (1.7 million metric tons) of natural cement were produced in the United States, but because of the increased production of portland cement, production of natural cement had dropped by 1918 to less than half a million barrels (85,000 metric tons). Since then

production has again increased and is now more than 3 million barrels (513,000 metric tons) annually.

Manufacture. When carbon dioxide is removed from pure limestone (calcium carbonate) by prolonged heating, a process known as *calcining,* the resulting quicklime (calcium oxide) slakes rapidly in water with the evolution of considerable heat, and the product (calcium hydroxide) forms a putty that does not set under water. Its use as a plaster or mortar is dependent on its interaction with carbon dioxide in the air and the resulting formation of a moderately hard bond of calcium carbonate. The calcined product of such a limestone, which has a high calcium content, is a natural cement called *fat lime.*

When the limestone contains up to 25% of an argillaceous (clay-containing) material, such as shale, the calcined product reacts slowly with water, there is no rapid evolution of heat, and a hard product is formed that does not disintegrate under water. The calcined products with a relatively low 10 to 20% silica and alumina content are usually called *hydraulic limes,* while those with a silica and alumina content of 20 to 35% are referred to simply as natural cements. Magnesia may be present in both kinds in concentrations of 10 to 25%.

ALUMINOUS CEMENT

The commercial development of aluminous or high-alumina cement is associated principally with the work of J. Bied of France, during the first quarter of the 20th century. This research was initiated in the hope of finding a cement that would be resistant to groundwaters rich in sulfates, such as gypsum. A product eventually was obtained that not only possessed the desired properties of sulfate resistance but also hardened more rapidly than the portland cement of that period. The cement was first put on the market in 1918. Aluminous cement is made by heating a mixture of limestone and bauxite until it is molten. The finely ground product, consisting principally of aluminates of lime, has the property of reacting rapidly with water to form a hard mass that is resistant to water and sulfate solutions. Its rapid rate of hardening, faster than ordinary portland cement, makes it particularly suitable for use in repair of roads where traffic diversion must be as brief as possible. Its resistance to the action of salt has led to its use in roads that are exposed to ice and snow. Another important application is in the insulation of furnaces where high temperatures are encountered.

PORTLAND CEMENT

History. About 98% of the cement produced in the United States is portland cement, which is not a brand name but a type of hydraulic cement. The name was given in 1824 by Joseph Aspdin, a bricklayer of Leeds, England, to a hydraulic lime that he patented, because when set with water and sand, it resembled a natural limestone quarried on the Isle of Portland in England.

At about the same time it was discovered that an excellent cement could be made by pulverizing the nodules, called *grappiers,* which occasionally became sintered (that is, formed into a nonporous solid without melting) when hydraulic lime was fired. The resulting cement, produced from the formerly discarded grappiers, was of much higher quality than that obtained from the unsintered material. This fact was firmly established by the English cement manufacturer L. C. Johnson in 1845, and the term "portland cement" has since been applied solely to the cement made from the sintered material. This period marks the real beginning of the portland cement industry.

The first portland cement made in the United States was produced in 1876 by David Saylor at Coplay, Pa. It was made in vertical kilns similar to those used for burning lime. The increasing demand for both quantity and quality led to the introduction of the rotary kiln in 1899. This kiln had been invented in 1885 by Frederick Ransome in England but had not been enthusiastically received there.

The production of portland cement is a major industry in the United States, increasing from 8 million barrels (1.4 million metric tons) in 1900 —when it trailed natural cement slightly in output—to almost 400 million barrels (68.4 million metric tons) annually. (A 376-pound, or 171-kg, barrel is the standard unit of weight for hydraulic cement in the United States, even though no cement, except for export, is now shipped in barrels. The 94-pound, or 42.7-kg, bag now in general use contains one fourth of a barrel.) The leading cement-producing countries are the United States, the USSR, West Germany, Japan, and France.

Manufacture. The raw materials of portland cement consist principally of a lime-containing material such as limestone, marl, chalk, or shells, and an argillaceous material such as clay, shale, ashes, or slag. The concentration of the constituent calcium oxide, silica, alumina, and ferric oxide must be exact within very narrowly defined limits. These restrictions sometimes necessitate the introduction of other types of rock besides those immediately available, such as a high-calcium limestone, sandstone, or iron ore. On other locations, the available material must be treated to remove excessive amounts of silica, iron oxide, carbon, magnesia, alumina, or alkalies.

All raw materials must be ground to a fine powder intimately mixed before burning. In a modern cement plant this is a prodigious task: the rock has to be blasted out of the mountain, fed into a crusher that takes blocks as large as a grand piano, and broken, hammered, and pulverized to the fineness of flour. The clay or shale and other materials then must be thoroughly mixed with the lime rock. Blending of the rock may begin in the quarry and continue as the raw materials flow into each crusher or mill. In the *dry process,* all grinding and blending is done with dry materials, and the final mixing is accomplished chiefly in the grinding mills. In the *wet process,* the final grinding and blending is carried out in a water slurry, and the mixing is accomplished both in the grinding mills and by stirring in large vats. In both processes, rigid control of the composition of the final kiln feed is attained through chemical analysis of the raw materials at various stages and the subsequent blending of mixtures.

The water is partially removed from slurries by various processes: by gravity-settling of the solids in a thickener; by filtration of the water through canvas-covered rotating drums, the interiors of which are under reduced pressure; and by evaporation of the water in various kinds of heat exchangers. Often, however, the slurry is fed directly into the kilns, and the water is removed by evaporation, aided by chains or baffle plates inserted in the back ends of the kilns.

In Europe, the shaft or vertical kiln is still used extensively because it can be operated with greater fuel economy than the rotary kiln. It is claimed that improvements have been made that make the shaft kiln competitive with the rotary kiln with respect to uniformity and quality of clinker produced. A sinter-grate kiln is also used in which the nodulized charge containing coal or coke is burned on a traveling grate. Ignition is produced by a downblast of burning oil and continued by drawing hot air down through the moving charge by means of an exhaust fan.

The rotary kiln has completely replaced the vertical kiln in the United States. The kiln is usually between 300 and 400 feet (92 to 122 meters) in length, although there are some that are more than 600 feet (183 meters) long. The kiln is set at an inclination of about ½ inch per foot (4.3 cm per meter) and rotated at a speed of between 30 and 90 revolutions per hour, causing the load to work its way downward toward the discharge end. There heat is introduced, usually by a blast of ignited powdered coal and air, or less commonly with fuel oil or gas. During the passage of the mixture down the length of the kiln, several reactions take place at various temperature levels.

The liquefaction of some compounds during the burning process causes the charge to agglomerate into nodules of various sizes (usually ¼ to 1 inch in diameter) that are characteristically black, glistening, and hard. This material is known as *portland cement clinker.* The charge drops from the end of the kiln into some form of cooler and is then ground, usually with 4 to 5% gypsum (hydrous calcium sulfate), to a powder so fine that most of it will pass through a sieve that will retain water. More specifically, the fineness is specified by a minimum average surface area of 1,600 to 1,800 sq cm per gram, depending on the type of cement being made. The purpose of the gypsum is to make the mixture of the cement with water and aggregate (as in fresh concrete mix) remain fluid and workable over a period of several hours. Without the addition of gypsum, the mixture might set before it had been properly placed in the forms.

In the modern cement plant the many operations involved in cement production are increasingly defined and controlled by instrumentation

IN HUGE ROTARY KILNS, which may measure more than 12 feet in diameter, cement undergoes the several changes of the final phase of manufacture. The slowly revolving kilns are set at a slight inclination, down which cement moves to the discharge end.

and automation. From the quarry to the mills to the kilns, the process is in the hands of the operator in the control room, surrounded by dials, flow meters, and closed-circuit television consoles.

Chemistry of Cement Production. The heart of the manufacturing process consists of a number of chemical reactions brought about by the high temperatures in the kiln. By these reactions, the compounds emerging from the kiln in the clinker are totally different from those of the raw material. During the 2 to 4 hours of passage through the kiln, the temperature of the charge gradually increases until it reaches about 1425 to 1540°C (2600 to 2800°F).

Evaporation of free water from the raw materials begins immediately on entering the kiln, but combined water in the clay is retained up to a temperature of about 540°C (1000°F). Magnesium carbonate decomposes to magnesium oxide and carbon dioxide at about 600°C (1100°F), calcium carbonate to calcium oxide and carbon dioxide at about 900°C (1650°F). The initial interactions of the component oxides—principally lime, silica, alumina, and ferric oxide—begin at the surface of the grains even before any liquid has formed, but such action is minimal. Liquid begins to appear at temperatures just under 1320°C (2400°F), the amount and composition depending on the temperature and composition of the raw mix. At maximum temperatures, about 20 to 30% of the charge is in the form of a liquid, which consists principally of the alumina and ferric oxide components, together with the alkalies and portions of the lime, silica, and magnesia.

Interaction between the lime and silica becomes rapid at 1375°C (2500°F) with the formation of dicalcium silicate, which is slowly converted in part to tricalcium silicate. If the temperature fails to exceed 1375°C, the dicalcium silicate may invert on cooling to an inactive form which, because of a large increase in volume, results in a "dusting" of the clinker with consequent loss in hydraulic value.

If the clinker is cooled slowly, the alumina and ferric oxide components have time to crystallize, and they emerge in the form of tricalcium aluminate and tetracalcium aluminoferrite. Magnesia appears as the oxide, and alkalies as sulfates. With rapid cooling, the liquid may solidify as "undercooled" liquid or glass. Hence, the rate of cooling determines the relative amounts of crystalline and amorphous phases present.

It is essential that the components of the cement raw mix be accurately proportioned because each compound or phase in the clinker exerts its peculiar influence on the final properties of the cement when used in mortar or concrete.

Composition. The principal compounds in portland cement are: tricalcium silicate ($3CaO \cdot SiO_2$), which is chiefly responsible for initial set and early strength of the cement-water paste; dicalcium silicate ($2CaO \cdot SiO_2$), which hardens slowly but contributes notably to strength at ages over a month; tricalcium aluminate ($3CaO \cdot Al_2O_3$), which liberates a large amount of heat during the first few days of hardening and is rapidly attacked by sulfate solutions; the iron-containing phase (a solid solution that approaches the composition $4CaO \cdot Al_2O_3 \cdot Fe_2O_3$), which is valuable as a flux in manufacture; magnesia (MgO), which, if present in excessive amount, may cause expansion of structures exposed to moisture after a number of years; and calcium oxide or free lime (CaO), which results from incomplete reaction in the kiln and, if present in amounts over 2 or 3%, may cause unsoundness and expansion in the cement paste. In addition to the above clinker compounds, gypsum or calcium sulfate hydrate ($CaSO_4 \cdot 2H_2O$) is interground with the clinker to control the rate of set of the cement-water paste.

Hydration of Cement. The usefulness of portland cement for making concrete depends on a series of reactions between its components and water. The most important of these reactions is the hydration of the calcium silicates to form a colloidal gel of calcium silicate hydrate that solidifies to a hard mass. This material forms a continuous phase that surrounds and encloses each piece of aggregate in concrete, and bonds the whole into a rocklike structure. The behavior of the material will be determined by many factors, including the composition and fineness of the cement; the cement-water ratio of the paste; the grading and nature of the aggregate; the time, temperature, and manner of curing; and the presence of entrained air.

Types of Portland Cement. Five types of portland cement are included in the standard specifications of the American Society for Testing Materials and the Federal Specifications Board. The properties of each depend in great part on the relative proportions of the compounds described in the preceding section. Typical compositions of the five standard types of portland cement are given in the table on page 158.

TYPES OF PORTLAND CEMENT

	Type I	Type II	Type III	Type IV	Type V
$3CaO \cdot SiO_2$	45	44	53	28	38
$2CaO \cdot SiO_2$	27	31	19	49	43
$3CaO \cdot Al_2O_3$	11	5	11	4	4
$4CaO \cdot Al_2O_3 \cdot Fe_2O_3$	8	13	9	12	9
$CaSO_4$	3.1	2.8	4.0	3.2	2.7
MgO	2.9	2.5	2.0	1.8	1.9
Free CaO	0.5	0.4	0.7	0.2	0.5

Type I is for use in general concrete construction where the special properties specified for Types II, III, IV, and V are not required. Type II is for use in general concrete construction exposed to moderate sulfate action or where moderate heat of hydration is required. Type III is for use where high early strength is required. Type IV is for use where low heat of hydration is required. Type V is for use where high sulfate resistance is required.

All types of portland cement may be obtained with or without a specific agent that allows air to be entrained in the paste when the cement is mixed with water and aggregate. The purpose of the entrained air is to improve the durability of the concrete, especially under conditions where cycles of freezing and thawing are encountered.

In addition to the standard types of portland cement, many modified cements have been manufactured. White portland cement is made for special architectural uses and differs from regular portland cement principally in having a low content of ferric oxide. Oil-well cement, made for sealing oil wells, must be slow-setting and able to resist high temperatures and pressures. The substitution of some iron oxide for clay has been found to improve the resistance to sulfate waters, and such cements are manufactured under the names of Ferrari and iron-ore cement.

Most important of the modified portland cements are the slag and pozzolanic cements made by intergrinding from 15 to 85% of granulated blast furnace slag or pozzolanic material with the portland cement clinker or in some cases with slag and lime or slag and anhydrite.

Pozzolana was named for a fine volcanic rock from Mount Vesuvius that the ancient Romans found valuable in improving the quality of mortars. The name is now given to a variety of naturally occurring materials such as volcanic ash, trass, Santorin earth, and pumicite, and it is also applied to artificially prepared materials, such as burned clays or diatomaceous earth, that have the capacity to combine in water with lime to form a calcium silicate.

ROBERT HERMAN BOGUE
Author of "The Chemistry of Portland Cement"

Bibliography

Bogue, Robert H., *The Chemistry of Portland Cement*, 2d ed. (New York 1955).
Cement and Concrete Institute, *Third International Symposium on the Chemistry of Cement* (London 1953).
Davis, A. C., *A Hundred Years of Portland Cement, 1824–1924* (London 1924).
Lea, Frederick M., and Desch, C. H., *The Chemistry of Cement and Concrete*, 2d ed. (London 1956).
Lesley, Robert W., *History of the Portland Cement Industry in the United States* (New York 1924).
Meade, Richard K., *Portland Cement*, 3d ed. (Easton, Pa., 1926).
National Bureau of Standards, Monograph 43, *Proceedings of the Fourth International Symposium on the Chemistry of Cement* (Washington 1962).
Royal Swedish Institute for Engineering Research, *Symposium on the Chemistry of Cements* (Stockholm 1938).

CEMENTATION PROCESS. See STEEL—2. *Steelmaking Processes* (Early Processes).

CEMETERIES, National. See NATIONAL CEMETERIES.

CENCI, chen'chē, **Beatrice** (1577–1599), Italian tragic heroine of history and legend. Born in Rome on Feb. 6, 1577, she was one of 12 children of the powerful and wealthy Roman nobleman Francesco Cenci, notorious for his violence and licentiousness. In the course of one of his frequent quarrels with his family, Francesco imprisoned Beatrice and her stepmother in 1595 in the remote castle of La Petrella between Rome and Naples. Cruelly treated and unsuccessful in attempts to escape, Beatrice found refuge in a love affair with her father's castellan, Olimpio Calvetti. With her lover, two of her brothers, and her stepmother, she plotted her father's murder. On Sept. 9, 1598, the act was committed.

The truth soon leaked out, and the Cenci were arrested. Under torture the conspirators confessed and in a dramatic trial were condemned by a papal court, despite desperate efforts to obtain mercy from Pope Clement VIII. The tragedy reached its climax on Sept. 11, 1599, when Beatrice and her stepmother were beheaded and her brother Giacomo put to death by slow torture.

Beatrice has been idealized many times in works of prose, poetry, and painting, which include her portrait by Guido Reni, Shelley's verse-drama *The Cenci,* and romances by Stendhal, Dumas, and Francesco Domenico Guerazzi.

RANDOLPH STARN
University of California at Berkeley

CENCI, The, chen'chē, a 5-act tragedy by Percy Bysshe Shelley, composed in 1819 and published in 1820. The play, which was not performed publicly until 1922 because of censorship, is generally regarded as the best English verse tragedy of the 19th century.

The Cenci was based on a manuscript purporting to be an accurate historical account of events in Rome during the reign of Pope Clement VIII (1592–1605). It portrays Count Francesco Cenci's sadistic torture of his family, culminating in his rape of his innocent daughter Beatrice, and the plot by Beatrice, her brother, and her stepmother to have him killed. Before resorting to murder, Beatrice and her family appeal in vain to nobles and churchmen, who temporize either out of fear or for their own advantage. But after two hired assassins kill the wicked old man, the Pope orders the conspirators to be tortured and executed as parricides. The play shows the corruption of a strong, virtuous person—Beatrice—by concentric forces of an evil social order epitomized by her father and the Pope. In her final vision of evil, Beatrice imagines that God, who she had once hoped would save her, is nothing but a cosmic magnification of the evil power embodied in her dead father.

The Cenci is written in stark, simple blank verse, embellished with Shakespearean echoes. The action follows the rising and falling 5-act pattern of Elizabethan tragedy, the turning point being Beatrice's decision to take justice into her own hands. By so doing, she falls victim to the same corrupting megalomania that affects her father—seeing herself as God's scourge.

DONALD H. REIMAN
Editor of "Shelley and His Circle"

CENERENTOLA, La, chä-nä-rän'tō-lä, a 2-act opera by Gioacchino Rossini, based on the Cinderella story. It was first performed at Rome on Jan. 25, 1817. Although Jacopo Ferretti's libretto is untimately derived from Charles Perrault's fairy tale, the opera's plot differs widely from the usual version of the story. In *La Cenerentola,* there is no stepmother, fairy godmother (her offices are filled by a philosopher-magician, Alidoro), pumpkin, or, most surprisingly, glass slipper. In the opera, Cenerentola's identity as the beautiful stranger at the ball is established by means of a pair of matching bracelets. The slipper motif was dropped in deference to the Roman censors of 1817, who would not countenance the display of a female ankle on the stage.

Cenerentola and her ugly sisters, Clorinda and Tisbe, live with their foolish father, Don Magnifico. Alidoro, the tutor of Prince Ramiro, tells them his master will marry the loveliest girl at the forthcoming ball. Ramiro and his valet, Dandini, having exchanged clothes, call at Don Magnifico's house. The ugly sisters fawn over Dandini; Cenerentola and Ramiro are taken with each other. At the palace, Cenerentola makes a splendid appearance, thanks to Alidoro, but her relatives fail to recognize her and are much put out by the "stranger's" success. Before she leaves, Cenerentola gives Ramiro one of a pair of bracelets. At home, Cenerentola is tormented by her overbearing family. A storm, conveniently raised by Alidoro, causes Ramiro's coach to halt at Don Magnifico's house. Ramiro sees the matching bracelet on Cenerentola's arm and asks for her hand. She accepts him and also forgives her family for their past behavior.

Rossini's score sparkles with music that makes great demands on vocal technique. There is a fine overture, some hilarious buffo arias, and a dazzling final rondo for Cenerentola.

WILLIAM ASHBROOK
Author of "Donizetti"

CENNINI, chä-nē'nē, **Cennino di Drea** (1370?–?1440), Italian painter and writer on art, who is known chiefly for his treatise on art, *Il libro dell'arte* (about 1400; Eng. tr., *The Craftsman's Handbook,* 1932). He was born near Florence and may have been a student of Agnolo Gaddi, a disciple of Giotto.

Cennini's treatise was the first Italian attempt to explain the techniques of Giotto and his school. It expounds the view that painting is among the highest human endeavors because, in the process of revealing the hidden qualities of objects, painting combines imagination and manual skill. Cennini advises the aspiring artist to study with a master for as long as possible and to develop a steady hand by temperate living. He also gives considerable technical information. None of Cennini's paintings is known to survive.

CENOTAPH, sen'ə-taf, a monument or tablet erected in honor of a person whose body is buried elsewhere or cannot be recovered. Cenotaphs have been erected since ancient times; wealthy Egyptians might have a cenotaph built in the sacred city of Abydos, where his spirit could dwell with the God Osiris while still maintaining a link with his native town. Cenotaphs are often erected in honor of those who have perished in defense of their country. In the United States one of the best known cenotaphs of this kind is the Soldier's and Sailor's Monument in New York City.

CENOZOIC ERA, sē-nə-zō'ik, the last great division of geologic time. It began about 70 million years ago and extends to the present. The name Cenozoic—from Greek *kainos,* "recent," and *zōē,* "life"—was coined in 1840 by the English geologist John Phillips (who spelled it Kainozoic). The era is divided into the Tertiary and Quaternary periods. The Tertiary is further divided into the Paleocene, Eocene, Oligocene, Miocene, and Pliocene epochs, in order of increasing recency. The Quaternary consists of the Pleistocene epoch and

ERA	PERIOD	
CENOZOIC	QUATERNARY	
	TERTIARY	
MESOZOIC	CRETACEOUS	
	JURASSIC	
	TRIASSIC	
PALEOZOIC	PERMIAN	
	CARBON-IFEROUS	PENNSYLVANIAN
		MISSISSIPPIAN
	DEVONIAN	
	SILURIAN	
	ORDOVICIAN	
	CAMBRIAN	
PRE-CAMBRIAN TIME		

recent times (the past 10,000 years). The spans of the epochs in the Tertiary period have been estimated as 10, 20, 15, 13, and 10 million years, respectively; of the Pleistocene, 2 million years. These estimates are based on the ratios of isotopes produced by radioactive decay in the rocks of the successive epochs.

Geology of the Era. The Cenozoic rocks of North America are found in several contrasting regions. The coast of the Gulf of Mexico is underlain by sands and clays that dip seaward, increasing in thickness to a maximum of 6 or 7 miles (about 10 km) in a trough beneath the shore of the western Gulf Coast. Salt domes penetrate the beds, rising from pre-Cenozoic layers in the deep subsurface; oil is derived in Mississippi, Louisiana, and Texas from the flanks of these domes. The Florida peninsula is underlain by Cenozoic limestones that were deposited in shallow seas on a gradually subsiding surface. The Atlantic coast has a layer of seaward-dipping Cenozoic sedimentary rocks, a few thousand feet thick, and extending northeastward to the Grand Banks of Newfoundland.

The distribution and character of Cenozoic rocks along the Pacific coast of North America are much more varied, because there was active deformation and volcanism in that belt throughout the era. In the eastern part of the belt, marine sediments pass into nonmarine rocks and into lavas such as those that form broad plateaus along the Columbia River. In the western interior states, deposits laid by streams and lakes accumulated in basins that were bounded by rising fault blocks to the west. In Utah, Wyoming, and Colorado, freshwater lakes were filled with sediments. Some of the shales there are so rich in organic matter that they are a great potential source of oil. Volcanism also produced local lava flows and fragmental deposits. Stream-laid sediments spread eastward from the Rocky Mountains.

Studies of lavas of the Pliocene and Pleistocene have revealed that reversals of the earth's magnetic field have taken place. Moreover, the reversals recorded in the rocks on the margins of oceanic rifts show that the ocean floors have been spreading, at rates of up to 2 inches (5 cm) a year, over the past several million years.

Fauna and Flora of the Era. Life in the earliest Cenozoic differed from that of late Mesozoic times in various degrees. There were the minor modifications from ancestor to descendant that are invariably present in geologic succession; but the abrupt changes, in which characteristic life forms vanish completely without leaving lineal descendants, are much more definitive. The ammonoid cephalopods are an example. Some of these animals may have survived the Mesozoic (and some Paleocene rocks may mistakenly be called Cretaceous because of the presence of their fossils), but they never attained the abundance in the Cenozoic that they had in earlier times. The dinosaurs—the great reptiles of the Mesozoic—have never been found in Paleocene rocks in North America, and only doubtfully in Europe.

The ordinary life forms of the Cenozoic soon became quite unlike those of the preceding era. In the seas, the differences at first were negative ones, such as the absence of ammonites. Orbitoid foraminifera—disc-shaped one-celled animals like the nummulites that fill the limestone of the pyramids—grew in the warmer seas. (A few had also lived during the Cretaceous, however.) On land, the forests of the Paleocene contained many of the deciduous trees that dominate present forests of similar climates—poplars, oaks, maples, birches, and their associates. The sequoia, a conifer whose present range is very limited, was spread over larger regions in the Paleocene. Grasses and herbaceous plants that still abound grew on the plains.

It was in the vertebrate inhabitants of the forests and plains that the Cenozoic introduced the greatest changes. Mammals had existed during the Mesozoic as little animals, obscure in number and size as compared to the great dinosaurs and other reptiles. With the coming of Cenozoic times, however, most forms of reptiles became extinct; only a few survived, such as turtles, snakes, and crocodiles. In contrast, many different varieties of mammals soon developed. Some of them became immense and grotesque and eventually died out. Thus, amblypods—huge, clumsy, hoofed beasts somewhat resembling the hippopotamus but only distantly related—did not survive the Eocene. Titanotheres—elephantlike creatures with long nasal projections resembling tusks— roamed the plains during the Oligocene; their fossils are preserved in the clays of the South Dakota Badlands.

The mammals ancestral to the modern elephant were small and undistinguished in Miocene times; as the size of their descendants increased, their tusks and trunks grew longer. The descendants of a little, doglike Eocene mammal became larger, acquired a longer head and legs and high-crowned teeth, and developed a one-toed hoof, until at last the modern horse appeared. The record of man's ancestors is not as well established, but they may have been tree-dwellers. The remains of man-ape forms that date from Miocene times have been found in scattered regions, but the first traces of modern man occur in the Pliocene or early Pleistocene—a small fraction of the time since the beginning of the Cenozoic era.

See also GEOLOGY—*Geologic Time Scale;* and articles on Cenozoic periods and epochs.

MARSHALL KAY, *Columbia University*

CENSOR, a Roman magistrate whose responsibilities included taking the census of Roman citizens, assessing their property, inspecting public morals, and regulating public finance. According to the Roman tradition, the first census was taken by King Servius Tullius in the 6th century B. C. The consuls and dictators of the early republic also took censuses. The first actual censors were elected in 443 B. C. Two in number, they were usually ex-consuls, and they could veto each other's acts. Originally, the office was open only to patricians, who, the tradition says, created it to weaken the consulship, which the plebeians were demanding. A plebeian first held the office of censor in 351 B. C., and the *Lex Publilia* of 339 B. C. required that one censor should always be a plebeian.

Responsibilities. The chief function of the censor was to make a list of Roman citizens and to assess their property. The census was the basis of civic life and served as the foundation for voting, taxation, and military conscription. The Romans felt that citizens' responsibility for military duty and possession of voting and other privileges should be in direct relation to their property qualifications; the more one had to lose, the more one ought to be relied upon to defend the state, and correspondingly, the more influence one ought to have in the affairs of state. The censors evaluated the property of each citizen and assigned him to a tribe and a century. They listed the very wealthiest citizens, who were qualified to serve the state as cavalry (*equites*), and reviewed the *equites* in the Forum. If a man's person, horse, or equipment was not suitable for service, he might be removed from the list or fined. Individuals who did not cooperate with the censors or who gave false information could be brought to trial by the censors themselves.

The tenure of office of the censors in the early republic is unknown, but in the later period censors were elected every five years. According to tradition, in 434 B. C. they began the practice of resigning from office at the end of 18 months, but this probably did not really begin until after the censorship of Appius Claudius Caecus, who held office in 312–307 B. C. At the end of their period in office, the censors performed the religious ceremony of purifying the population (the *lustrum,* or cleansing).

Censors gradually assumed control over public morality (*cura morum*) through their revision of the list of citizens; and because they assigned the state contracts, they assumed a general concern for the state's economy. By the *Lex Ovinia* (passed about 312 B. C.) they even extended their control to the Senate. The Ovinian law empowered the censors to revise the list of senators and to remove from it any member who had violated the law or who was guilty of moral laxity.

Decline of the Office. In the late republic (about 80 B. C.) Sulla made election to the office of quaestor the prerequisite for entry into the Senate, thus taking control over the Senate out of the hands of the censors. They never fully recovered their influence. Under the empire few censors were appointed, although at times emperors performed their function. The office lost all significance when Emperor Domitian (reigned 81–96 A. D.) became censor for life.

RICHARD E. MITCHELL, *University of Illinois*

Further Reading: Suolahti, Jaakko, *The Roman Censors: A Study on Social Structure* (Helsinki 1963).

CENSORSHIP, sen'sər-ship, in the narrow and original sense of the term, is a system under which official censors must give permission before communications of a specified type can lawfully be made. Such *preventive* censorship may be applied to books, newspapers, and other writings intended for circulation to the public; to movies and stage plays; to private letters flowing through controllable channels, such as correspondence with prisoners and with soldiers in combat zones; and indeed to any communication of a type that, as a matter of practical administration, can be subjected to official scrutiny before completion.

Preventive censorship is not the only way to restrict communication. Specified types of publication such as obscene material and attacks on racial or religious groups, which are deemed by the lawmakers to be contrary to the public interest, may be made criminal. Or they may be barred from government-controlled facilities such as public libraries and the mails. Books and magazines may be subjected to boycott by private organizations, which circulate lists of disapproved publications and urge nonpatronization of merchants who sell them. Such systematic limitations on the individual's access to information or ideas are also, in current parlance, frequently referred to as censorship; and that usage will be followed here, the narrower term "preventive censorship" being applied as indicated above.

Preventive censorship, by definition, can only be imposed by law. It is adopted when the government believes the public interest requires not only discouragement but also complete suppression of information or ideas thought to be dangerous. Its widespread use began shortly after the advent of the printing press in the 15th century opened the way to mass communication. At the time, government by consent of the governed was unknown, and the security and authority of both church and state could be seriously threatened by mobilization of demands for redress of grievances and by propagation of seditious or heretical doubts about the legitimacy of secular or ecclesiastical power. Preventive censorship of all printing therefore became common, and it has endured to the present day, supplemented by similar control of movies, radio, and television as those media appeared, in countries that do not practice full self-government.

Censorship in the broad sense exists to some extent in all parts of the world. In Western democracies relatively few restraints are imposed, particularly by means of preventive censorship. The same is true in India. In the Soviet Union and other European Communist states, on the other hand, governments exercise strict preventive censorship of the press and apply a variety of controls on the work of poets, novelists, and other nonjournalistic writers. As most of these governments control the news media, official disapproval of any item results in automatic suppression. Where private newspapers are tolerated, they are closely supervised by ministries of information. In China and Cuba the press is frankly regarded as an instrument of government.

Somewhat milder, but nevertheless strict, controls are found elsewhere. In Spain, for example, where preventive censorship has been abolished by law, the press is required to print all information distributed by the government without reporting its origin. All Spanish journalists are trained in state-operated schools, and official

rules for their conduct are enforced by a jury of professional ethics directed by the ministry of information. In Pakistan all incoming wire service reports are routed through the information ministry and are subject to automatic censorship.

In many African nations government monopoly is a result of the general economic stringency that makes private financing of news media impossible. Countries that have inherited British traditions tend to show greater respect for the concept of press freedom, but even they exhibit great official sensitivity to criticism. Their governments do not hesitate to manage the press to the extent that political turbulence or other public exigency appears to demand. Politically centralized states such as Algeria and the United Arab Republic control the press either directly or through the dominant political party. South Africa and Rhodesia have private newspapers but exercise the power to ban those that strongly oppose government policy.

JUDICIAL CONTROL OF CENSORSHIP IN THE UNITED STATES

Censorship in the United States and legal restrictions on it developed against a background of previous British practice.

British Background. The evolution of self-government in England through the gradual strengthening of the House of Commons was accompanied by increasing opposition to preventive censorship. In 1644, John Milton attacked such censorship eloquently in *Areopagitica*, a plea for repeal of the Licensing Act of 1643, which forbade the printing or sale of any book without prior official approval. This act survived Milton's assault, but growing resistance to it interrupted its effectiveness until it finally expired in 1695. That date has been said to mark the definite establishment of freedom of the press in England.

Abolition of preventive censorship of printed matter was clearly a great gain for freedom in England, for the conservatism of the official censor had shown itself to be intrinsic. As Milton pointed out, even if a censor is intelligent and broadminded (and it is hard to get such a man to undertake the unpleasant job) it is safer for him to resolve his doubts by ruling against publication. The very fact that he has power to suppress information makes him vulnerable to the inference that failure to do so implies approval— even though the inference is wholly unfair. On the other hand, a suppressed document will not ordinarily come to the attention of those who would object to its suppression, and if it does, the censor can smother objections.

Expiration of the English Licensing Act did not terminate censorship in the broader sense. As late as 1769, Blackstone wrote in his *Commentaries on the Law of England:* "The liberty of the press is indeed essential to the nature of a free state; but this consists in laying no *previous* restraints upon publication, and not in freedom from censure for criminal matter when published." Even preventive censorship was not completely abolished. No play, for instance, could be put on in public without the prior permission of the Lord Chamberlain. Only in 1966, when the Lord Chamberlain suggested that his censorship duties were no longer appropriate, did a joint committee of the Lords and Commons weigh the problem and unanimously recommend an end to the theater licensing system.

In Britain, despite the existence of parliamentary power to impose censorship, a strong tradition against it has resulted in very broad freedom of expression in point of fact. In the United States a similar tradition, reinforced by constitutional guarantees administered by the courts, enables any individual to question the legal validity of official restraints on expression.

The Supreme Court and Free Expression. The 1st Amendment to the Constitution forbids Congress to abridge "the freedom of speech, or of the press, or the right of the people peaceably to assemble, and to petition the Government for a redress of grievances." The Supreme Court has held that these provisions are made binding on the state and local governments by the due process clause of the 14th Amendment. In a series of decisions beginning in 1927 with *Fiske* v. *Kansas,* the court interpreted the constitutional guarantees so broadly that freedom of expression probably enjoys more solid legal protection in the United States than anywhere else.

The key idea underlying the court's decisions is that freedom of expression is not merely a personal liberty but is an essential part of the mechanism of government by the people. Their right to vote is not enough by itself to give them effective control of official actions and policies. They must also be able to take part in the formation of public opinion by engaging in vigorous and wide-ranging debate on controversial matters. The political processes whereby new officials are elected to replace old ones and changes in the law are made in response to public demand would not function if the incumbent government could enact and enforce laws stifling criticism of itself. And, should that happen, faith in the justice of the laws and the honesty and competence of government personnel would be so greatly impaired that general civil disobedience and even revolution might ensue. Censorship that hinders peaceable opposition to the government in the short run creates the long-run danger of violent opposition. The Supreme Court, therefore, recognizes that restraints on expression impinge on the broad public interest in preserving an open society.

Justices Oliver Wendell Holmes and Louis D. Brandeis were the first members of the court to articulate this conception of the public value of free expression. In *Abrams* v. *United States* (1919), Justice Holmes declared it to be "the theory of our constitution" that "the ultimate good desired is better reached by free trade in ideas." This was the first of a series of great dissenting opinions that progressively expounded the connection between freedom of expression and an open society. Justice Brandeis, in a minority opinion in *Whitney* v. *California* (1927), declared: "Those who won our independence . . . knew that order cannot be secured merely through fear of punishment for its infraction; that it is hazardous to discourage thought, hope and imagination; that repression breeds hate; that hate menaces stable government; that the path of safety lies in the opportunity to discuss freely supposed grievances and proposed remedies; and that the fitting remedy for evil counsels is good ones."

Justice Holmes and Brandeis did not maintain, however, that there can be no legal restraints on expression. Their view was that it should be suppressed only in the rare situations where there is a "clear and present danger" that it will lead to serious public harm too rapidly for its harmful

tendency to be dispelled by the "fitting remedy" of further discussion. (The classic illustration is a false cry of "Fire!" in a crowded theater to create a panic.) This clear and present danger test was later adopted by the whole court and has been applied (with some variation to fit special circumstances) in a wide variety of cases involving words which, though not harmful in themselves—as is a libel that destroys personal reputation—are feared because of their tendency to induce illegal conduct. The court has also embraced the underlying Holmes-Brandeis philosophy that public harm can and usually will result from censorship.

Moreover, the court has assumed a special responsibility for protection of the 1st Amendment freedoms. Embracing this idea, it has limited censorship to cases of strong necessity, and even there the court has held its scope to a minimum.

The Mass Media. In *Near* v. *Minnesota* (1931), the Supreme Court held invalid a state statute that provided for injunction of continued publication of any "malicious, scandalous, and defamatory newspaper, magazine, or other periodical," unless "published with good motives and for justifiable ends." The newspaper that was the object of the legislation had published a series of highly intemperate accusations of corruption in the city administration. The court held that although libelous statements might be punished, suppression of the newspaper was unconstitutional censorship. Newspapers have also been held to be immune from taxation designed to limit their circulation. In *Grosjean* v. *American Press Co.* (1936), a 2% gross receipts tax on publications having a weekly circulation exceeding 20,000 was struck down as an abridgment of press freedom.

The "Pentagon Papers" case, *New York Times* v. *United States* (1971) reaffirmed the Supreme Court's reluctance to approve the use of injunctions to suppress publication of politically controversial material. The government sought to prevent newspapers from publishing a large number of secret documents concerning the early years of the Vietnam War, copies of which had been unlawfully released to the newspapers. Most of the justices (a) agreed with the government's contention that the public interest would be damaged if certain of the documents were published; (b) held open the possibility that criminal penalties might be imposed, not only for the initial release but also for the later publication; and (c) recognized that suppression would be justified in more urgent circumstances, such as keeping secret the sailing dates of military transports in wartime. By a vote of 6 to 3, however, the court held that the First Amendment prevented suppression of the documents in question.

In radio and television the same full freedom from government control is precluded because the number of broadcasting channels is limited. Some governmental regulation is required, and in the United States it takes the form of licensing by the Federal Communications Commission (FCC), established by statute in 1934. Although the FCC statute specifically forbids censorship, the commission does have the duty, in considering renewal of each 3-year operating license, to evaluate a station's overall performance to determine whether better service to the public might be rendered by a competing applicant. Because such evaluation may include a review of program content, anticipation of review doubtless has a restraining influence on broadcasters. On the other hand, the commission follows a conscious policy of promoting public access to different viewpoints through its "fairness doctrine," which calls for presentation of contrasting positions on controversial issues of public importance, and by limiting the merger of stations, or of stations and newspapers, into a single ownership.

The licensing system results in materially greater freedom than the alternative system of government monopoly that has been employed in many other countries. Where all broadcasting facilities are owned by the government, full preventive censorship is automatic, though it may be very liberally applied in practice, as it was by the British Broadcasting Corporation (a government agency that held a monopoly until the Television Act of 1954 provided for the licensing of broadcasters by the Independent Television Authority).

The moving picture is the only mass medium that may be subjected to preventive censorship in the United States. Some years after movies made their appearance, the Supreme Court ruled, in *Mutual Film Corp.* v. *Ohio Industrial Comm.* (1915), that they were predominantly commercial entertainments rather than political expressions and therefore were excluded from 1st Amendment guarantees. State and local censorship agencies were established in many places with power to suppress films or order deletions from them before exhibition. The usual conservatism that characterizes preventive censorship was aggravated in many cases by the makeup of the censorship boards. In Chicago, for instance, the board was for a time composed of widows of policemen.

The Supreme Court subsequently rejected the distinction between "the informing and the entertaining." In 1948 it declared in *Winters* v. *New York*, a case involving crime literature: "What is one man's amusement teaches another's doctrine." Later the same year, by way of dictum in *United States* v. *Paramount Pictures*, it said: "We have no doubt that moving pictures, like newspapers and radio, are included in the press whose freedom is guaranteed by the 1st Amendment." In *Burstyn* v. *Wilson* (1952) it set aside a particular censorship order as unconstitutional, and thereafter it intervened against a number of such orders. Under the impact of these and other rulings, preventive censorship of movies apparently withered. By 1965 preventive censorship legislation was on the books in only four states and 43 cities, and it was not actively enforced in 28 of the cities.

Individual Expression. Constitutional protection is not limited to the mass media. It extends to individuals and groups who, through lack of easy access to newspapers, magazines, radio, and television, must express their viewpoints primarily through pamphlets, handbills, loudspeaker trucks, street-corner speeches, and parades or other public demonstrations. Religious sects (particularly Jehovah's Witnesses) and organizations protesting racial discrimination have often employed these methods. Such activities are typically subject to a wide variety of local regulations, designed primarily to preserve the streets for traffic and the parks for recreation but susceptible to use to prevent the dissemination of unpopular ideas.

The Supreme Court has intervened repeatedly to prevent the use of these regulations for censorship purposes. In a case involving pamphlet distribution by Jehovah's Witnesses within a city, it has held that such distribution cannot be subjected to licensing by an official such as the city manager if licenses are to be issued or denied at the uncontrolled discretion of the official. The same ruling was made on a New York City ordinance for the licensing of public worship meetings in the streets, where a license had been denied to a person who had previously engaged in "scurrilous attacks on Catholics and Jews."

In 1948 the court held invalid a city ordinance prohibiting the use of loudspeakers without permission of the police chief. But the following year a general municipal prohibition against sound trucks was upheld as a noise control measure, the censorship element being absent because there was no licensing provision enabling a city official to pick and choose among applicants for licenses.

Censorship is not involved in ordinary regulations governing use of the streets and other public places. Thus the courts will not interfere with enforcement of a law that regulates the time and place of parades if the law's intent is only to protect the flow of traffic. But such a law is invalid if, by selective prosecution or other discriminatory administration, it is used as an instrument of censorship. The littering of streets is also a matter of legitimate public concern and can be prohibited; but the Supreme Court has held that because of the great importance of allowing free expression, handbill distribution may not be prohibited in order to prevent littering by persons who receive the handbills and throw them away.

Organizational Activity. The constitutional policy against censorship has also been extended in another way. In the United States, one of the major modes of participating in public controversy is through support of private organizations that seek to influence public opinion and governmental action. The proliferation of such organizations is a notable aspect of American life. Some concentrate on a specific field, such as birth control; some deal with problems such as racial discrimination or world peace, which have wider ramifications; and some are broad-spectrum organizations, such as political parties, which cover the whole range of social and economic issues. These organizations provide a medium for opinion expression by the many people who lack the time or the knowledge or the courage to speak or write themselves. By donating money they finance the operations of the organization's spokesmen, who share their values and objectives and who in effect serve as their delegates.

Some of these organizations have been frequent targets of censorship efforts because they provide attractive channels for the expression of unpopular viewpoints on highly charged issues. The customary anonymity of rank and file supporters provides shelter against such reprisals as discharge from employment, eviction from homes, withdrawal of credit, and verbal or physical attack.

Constitutional guarantees against such censorship have come into play on two levels. One level concerns the question of whether the organization as such or its leaders may be punished for words without deeds—that is, for advocacy of unlawful acts such as revolution or sabotage to achieve the organizational objectives. It is well settled that any objectives whatever, no matter how extreme and radical a change of the existing order they involve, may lawfully be advocated so long as illegal methods are not urged. The doctrine was upheld in *Fiske* v. *Kansas* (1927) in respect to advocacy of state socialism, and in *Stromberg* v. *California* (1931) regarding display of a red flag as a symbol of opposition to organized government. When illegal methods are advocated, however, the clear and present danger rule is applied. In *Dennis* v. *United States* (1951), the Supreme Court thus upheld the convictions of 11 persons who reorganized the Communist party of the United States after World War II, on evidence that they had conspired to promote revolution, in violation of the Smith Act (1940). In the context of the Cold War, which created an appreciable possibility that a revolt might be supported by the great military power of the USSR, the clear and present danger test was deemed satisfied even though immediate revolution was not shown to be contemplated. Relaxation of the usual immediacy requirement was held justified by the gravity of the danger, the secrecy of the party's activities, and its rigid discipline over its members. But the convictions of 14 second-string party leaders, based on a finding that they had conspired to advocate revolution "as an abstract doctrine," were set aside in *Yates* v. *United States* (1957). In 1961 the court upheld the Subversive Activities Control Act of 1950, which in effect outlawed the party itself as a foreign-controlled revolutionary organization.

The second level of constitutional protection concerns the question of whether the government may weaken opinion organizations by discouraging people from supporting them. Official attacks have usually taken that indirect form because of the difficulty of satisfying the clear and present danger rule in proceedings against the organizations themselves. Most of the litigation involving censorship problems in this area has arisen from legislative investigations leading to (a) public identification of individuals connected with organizations thought to be subversive and (b) compilation and publication of lists of such organizations. Federal and state legislative committees, particularly the House Committee on Internal Security (formerly the House Committee on Un-American Activities), have engaged in both operations. Since 1948 the attorney general has published lists of subversive organizations. Some states have compelled disclosure of membership in secret oath-bound organizations, such as the Ku Klux Klan. In the deep South many official investigations have aimed at identifying supporters of such civil rights groups as the National Association for the Advancement of Colored People.

The Supreme Court has repeatedly been asked to hold that legislative investigations conducted for the purpose of exposing and thereby discouraging membership are unconstitutional abridgments of freedom of expression. In the field of subversive activities, the court declared in *Watkins* v. *United States* (1957) that investigation for the sole purpose of exposure (and not for the usual purpose of learning the need for proposed legislation) is beyond the constitutional competence of the legislature. But it also held, in *Barenblatt* v. *United States* (1959), that the motivation of Congress and its committees is not a proper subject of judicial inquiry, and it therefore refused to excuse witnesses from answering questions about Communist party membership on the broad ground that the exposure purpose of the investigation rendered it unlawful. Even so, witnesses were accorded substantial protection. Through restrictive interpretation the court reversed all but a few of the contempt convictions arising out of refusal to answer committee questions on 1st Amendment grounds; and it upheld the refusal of witnesses who claimed their privilege against self-incrimination under the 5th Amendment.

Sharper limits have been imposed on local investigations of civil rights organizations. In 1958, in *NAACP* v. *Alabama* and *Bates* v. *Little Rock*, the court denied the right of officials to demand NAACP membership and contributor lists, declaring that there is a "close nexus" between freedom of speech and associational privacy. Even where NAACP lists were demanded as an aid to investigate possible Communist infiltration into that organization, the court (observing that the NAACP is a "wholly legitimate organization") held the demand unlawful in *Gibson* v. *Florida Legislative Investigation Committee* (1963).

Libel. For a long time it was thought that no problems of censorship were presented by laws protecting individuals from words damaging their reputations. Enforcement of criminal libel laws and the award of damages for false and defamatory utterances did not seem to involve the danger of suppressing public discussion of controversial issues.

In the ordinary defamation case this is still true. But in 1964 the Supreme Court found the evils of censorship to exist in the award of damages for innocent but erroneous charges of misconduct by public officials. The New York *Times* had carried a paid advertisement complaining of wrongful repression of Negro protest by the police of Montgomery, Ala., in the bitter racial struggles of 1960. The police chief, on proof that a few out of a long list of factual charges were inaccurate, obtained a $500,000 damage judgment. The Supreme Court set it aside in *New York Times* v. *Sullivan*, holding that contrary to the usual rule in libel cases, a charge of official misconduct is not actionable unless made "with knowledge that it was false or with reckless disregard of whether it was false or not." The decision was compelled by the danger that the press might otherwise be deterred from quick and full coverage of controversial issues and cease to function as a watchdog against misgovernment. In 1967 the same rule was extended in *Associated Press* v. *Walker* to statements about private persons participating in public controversy.

A special problem is raised by group libel statutes, which penalize attacks on racial and religious groups and thus, unlike the usual libel laws, are not limited to defamation of identifiable individuals. In 1952, in *Beauharnais* v. *Illinois*, the Supreme Court upheld a state group libel statute over a vigorous dissent which called it "expansive state censorship." Inasmuch as hostility to minority groups does hamper the just operation of a democratic system based on majority rule, there is a public interest in minimizing race hatred. But the question of whether censorship for that purpose is constitutional cannot be considered settled, in view of the more recent decisions such as the *Sullivan* case, which reflect increasing emphasis on the protection of open controversy in all fields including intergroup relations.

Free Press v. Fair Trial. Perhaps the most extreme application of the constitutional policy against censorship has been made in cases involving claims of interference with judicial proceedings. Particularly in jury cases there is a possibility that adjudication will be influenced by mobilization of public opinion on behalf of one of the parties, or by publication of facts, such as the past arrests or convictions of an accused defendant, that are not admissible in court but may affect the jurors. Even in non-jury cases, judges (particularly elected judges) may be affected by criticism.

Although the Supreme Court sets aside convictions infected by widespread publicity against the defendants, as in *Sheppard* v. *Maxwell* (1966), and recognizes the validity of statutes penalizing courthouse demonstrations, as in *Cox* v. *Louisiana* (1965), it denies the power to punish, as a contempt of court, criticisms of judicial behavior even in pending cases, as in *Wood* v. *Georgia* (1962), unless there is clear and present danger of obstructing justice.

Creative Expression. The forms of censorship heretofore considered have related almost exclusively to direct participation in public affairs through statements of fact and opinion. But works of fiction can also convey powerful messages on social problems. The Greek regime that took power by a military coup in the spring of 1967 recognized the dangerous potentialities of the theater by imposing rigid censorship. Such books as *Uncle Tom's Cabin, Huckleberry Finn, Oliver Twist,* and *1984* have played their part in molding public opinion on slavery, poverty, crime, and authoritarian government. The Holmes-Brandeis philosophy, which relates free expression to preservation of an open society, therefore clearly applies to novels, movies, plays, and art.

Censorship problems have arisen mainly in two areas: books and movies thought to convey an antisocial message; and obscenity.

In the first area the Supreme Court has uncompromisingly held that censorship may not be based on the substantive content of the message. In *Burstyn* v. *Wilson* (1952) it reversed an order suppressing an Italian film entitled *The Miracle,* which portrayed the Nativity in a manner found by the New York State censorship agency to be sacrilegious and offensive to Roman Catholics. A similar ruling was made on the French film *Lady Chatterley's Lover,* which had been censored on the ground that it glorified sexual immorality. In *Kingsley International Pictures Corp.* v. *Board of Regents* (1959) the court held there was no clear and present danger that the film would incite the commission of adultery.

In the second area, obscenity, the clear and present danger test has not been applied. Here, censorship efforts are not based on the danger that depiction of sexual acts will incite illicit behavior. (There is grave doubt that it has that effect; respectable authority declares that it usually tends to have the opposite effect because it provides a substitute sexual outlet.) The objection is that the publication itself is harmful.

So far as verbal—as opposed to pictorial—expression is concerned, the Supreme Court has adopted a very liberal test. A book or other publication may not be suppressed as obscene because it may be harmful to such particular groups in the community as adolescents, or because of particular passages (as opposed to the quality of the book as a whole). Rather, "It must be established that (a) the dominant theme of the material taken as a whole appeals to a prurient interest in sex; (b) the material is patently offensive because it affronts contemporary community standards relating to the description or representation of sexual matters; and (c) the material is utterly without redeeming social value." This test was applied in *Memoirs* v. *Massachusetts* (1966) to prevent suppression of *Memoirs of a Woman of Pleasure* (commonly known as *Fanny Hill*), written in England by John Cleland about 1750 and banned in numerous countries since then. The book contains explicit descriptions of sexual acts, both normal and abnormal, and the court assumed that it failed to pass the first two branches of the test; but "redeeming social value" was found to exist, on the basis of expert testimony that the book had literary merit and had played a part in the development of the English novel.

It is still possible to censor "hard core" obscenity. On the same day that it decided the *Fanny Hill* case the court, in *Mishkin* v. *New York,* upheld convictions for selling pulp magazines that depicted sexuality in various deviant forms and that had been found to be of no literary merit. But the court has gone very far to conform obscenity censorship to the modern view that the state should not intervene to protect consenting adults in sexual matters. And in *Stanley* v. *Georgia* (1969) it was held that a man cannot be punished for keeping a movie film in his own home, for his personal amusement, no matter how obscene it is.

On the other hand, the court has held that even though a book or magazine may not be censorable as obscene by reason of its content, the manner of its sale may be punishable. In *Ginzburg* v. *United States* (1966), a 5-year prison term was imposed for flamboyant and salacious advertising in the marketing of two periodicals and of a book that, though devoted to sexual matters, would not have been deemed obscene had the defendant not engaged in "the sordid business of pandering."

Material that is unsuitable for children but harmless to adults cannot be suppressed entirely (*Butler* v. *Michigan,* 1957) but its distribution to children can be forbidden (*Ginsberg* v. *New York,* 1968).

In the area of pictorial expression, the law is partly unclear. Pictures can bring the observer closer to the sexual act than words, and they have greater capacity to shock. They may also be more susceptible to pandering. Although magazines featuring nudist pictures have been protected against censorship, portrayal of sexual behavior in moving pictures or still photographs may well be vulnerable as constituting a fairly close approach to "peep show" enactment of sexual scenes by living performers. The latter can doubtless be censored as a direct violation of the taboo on public sexual display.

EXTRAJUDICIAL CENSORSHIP

The censorship methods already considered are dependent, in one way or another, on judicial enforcement. For example, a licensing system is backed up by criminal prosecution for unlicensed publication. So courts have been in a position to hold such censorship within the strict limits demanded by the public value of free expression, and, under the Supreme Court's leadership, the limits have become very strict indeed.

The same high standards are not and as a practical matter cannot be enforced where censorship is imposed without the help of courts. Limitation of such censorship depends more on a general tradition of tolerance than on legal safeguards, for the courts can intervene only when someone sues to limit the censors.

Postal and Customs Censorship. When written material flows in volume through a government agency as a matter of routine, censorship can be imposed rather easily. This potentiality was seen by President Washington, who once advocated the free delivery of mail because he feared that imposition of fees would lead to federal control of content; and as Justice Holmes observed in 1922, "Use of the mails is almost as much a part of the right of free speech as the right to use our tongues." Until after the Civil War, postal censorship in the United States was unauthorized by law. In 1835 even Sen. John C. Calhoun of South Carolina opposed a bill to exclude abolitionist propaganda from the mails, declaring that the 1st Amendment would be violated.

In 1865, however, a postal censorship law was enacted. In 1873, largely because of the moralist crusades of Anthony Comstock, the law was broadened and strengthened, particularly for sex literature. Although first-class mail is not subject to inspection, reduced-rate mail such as magazines and newspapers (which have been granted the much lower second-class rates to encourage free circulation of information and opinion, and which in many cases would be financially foreclosed from mass distribution without this indirect subsidy) may be examined by postal employees. If considered obscene, seditious, or otherwise unmailable, the offending publication may be returned to the sender, or, in some cases, destroyed. The federal government also has the power to deny second-class mailing privileges to the publisher, thus affecting future issues as well as past ones, though the Supreme Court has curtailed this practice. Other administrative techniques include informal warning visits to publishers by postal inspectors. (Such visits numbered 9,554 in 1965.) Criminal prosecution is available for all classes of mail but is used only in clear cases, and relatively rarely.

There has been occasional judicial intervention. In *Hannegan* v. *Esquire, Inc.* (1946) the Supreme Court set aside an order denying second-class rates to a magazine containing material said to be vulgar and risqué though not obscene. The contention that the low rates are only for publications that contribute affirmatively to the public welfare was rejected. In *Lamont* v. *Postmaster General* (1966) the court terminated the practice of withholding delivery of foreign propaganda (such as mainland China magazines) unless the addressee responded affirmatively to a postcard from the post office, asking if he wished to receive it. But so long as the system remains in effect, a substantial number of lawful publications (works by Freud, Kinsey, Margaret Mead, and even Aristophanes have at one time or another been excluded) will doubtless continue to encounter difficulty.

The U. S. Customs Bureau, in its inspection of all incoming freight and luggage for tax purposes, also engages in censorship of obscene and seditious material by seizing objectionable items. Since 1930, however, the bureau has been required by statute to establish in court the legality of the seizure if the importer challenges it. The casual tourist does not ordinarily find it worthwhile to engage in such litigation, but the 1930 law has materially benefited commercial importers. A series of decisions upsetting Customs Bureau determinations, highlighted by the 1933 decision of federal district Judge John M. Woolsey, allowing James Joyce's *Ulysses* to be imported, has led to perceptible liberalization of the bureau's standards as compared with those of the Post Office.

Information About the Government. Although the term "censorship" is ordinarily applied only to obstruction of communication between two willing parties, it is also sometimes extended to the withholding of information by the government. No one contends that every public official should work in a fishbowl; the public interest often requires that internal policy discussions, negotiations with foreign governments, and military plans be kept at least temporarily confidential. It is generally agreed, on the other hand, that the government should not conceal its operations for the sole purpose of protecting itself from criticism by the people, whose agent it is. The public's right to know is basic to intelligent opinion and voting, and the government's power over its own officers and employees, enabling it to exercise monopoly control over the release of such information, has sometimes been abused. Because public trials are guaranteed by the Constitution and most legislative proceedings are well publicized, the problem has arisen mainly in the executive branch.

Secrecy of military information is accomplished mainly through the classification process. Documents are classified as "top secret," "secret," "confidential," or "restricted," and are so marked. The classification determines the scope of permissible circulation within the government as well as release to the press. Military censorship in the United States during World War II was accomplished primarily through this system and by censorship of mail and telegrams entering and leaving the country. The press was left legally free to print what it liked, though it ordinarily refrained from publishing items that the government indicated might be harmful. After the war there was increasing complaint against overclassification resulting from the great number of federal employees—estimated at more than a million —empowered to classify, coupled with the customary conservatism of the censor. Congress in 1958 broadened access to public records, and in 1966 a greatly strengthened "right to know" statute sharply reduced the discretionary power of federal officials to withhold information. The statute provides for judicial review and puts the burden of proof on the government. Similar statutes exist in a number of states.

Public Libraries. Libraries must necessarily purchase books on the basis of content, and censorship is said to exist if there is a conscious effort to prevent or restrict the reading of lawful material because of moral, partisan, or doctrinal disapproval. The American Library Association (ALA) has vigorously maintained that librarians have the right and duty to provide full access to all viewpoints on all problems and issues, including such controversial matters as communism and fascism, and to resist outside pressures toward "a coercive concept of Americanism" (ALA *Bill of Rights*, 1948). The ALA has also condemned the practice of labeling materials to indicate that the librarian considers them subversive or otherwise dangerous, its position being that the presence of a book in a library does not imply endorsement of its contents and that the responsibility of evaluation rests on the reader (ALA *Statement on Labeling,* 1951). Its bimonthly *Newsletter on Intellectual Freedom* publicizes departures from those standards and provides significant moral support to local librarians confronted by community criticism. When conformist pressures became acute in the early 1950's under the stimulus of congressional disloyalty investigations conducted by Senator Joseph R. McCarthy and others, President Eisenhower strongly endorsed the ALA position in a widely publicized letter on intellectual freedom.

Censorship by selective acquisition doubtless exists to some extent, but on the whole it has not crippled library service. A number of libraries, however, have followed the compromise practice of keeping controversial books on a "closed shelf" behind the librarian's desk and making them available only on request. In some places they are lent only to certain classes of readers, such as adults or married persons.

Public School Textbooks. Another quantitatively important censorship possibility exists with respect to textbooks. About half of the annual sales of hard-cover books are made to public agencies or are subject to their approval. Half the states have central textbook commissions, and the others rely on local boards. As in the case of libraries, approval is necessarily based on content, and there are frequent pressures to deviate from the sole standard of educational utility, largely because of the fear that juvenile readers may need special protection against undue candor about sex or political ideas considered wrong and dangerous. Much controversy has also centered on race relations, books thought to place undue emphasis on civil rights, and, elsewhere, books that have been criticized as implying Negro inferiority.

Private Censorship. Though censorship is ordinarily associated with official action, a significant part is played by private organizations that endeavor to suppress particular books and other materials, usually on moral grounds. Insofar as they address themselves directly to the potential reader or moviegoer and condemn the material as unworthy of patronage, they do not engage in censorship. Typically, however, they exert their efforts against distribution channels in order to eliminate the power of individual choice; and this is censorship. Often they seek to induce action on the part of public officials who have censorship powers, such as movie censors, postal and customs authorities, and, particularly librarians and textbook agency personnel. They lobby for stronger obscenity legislation and encourage prosecutions under existing law (which have a strong deterrent effect even when there is an acquittal, because it usually costs a bookdealer more to defend a criminal charge than to discontinue the sale of one or a few challenged books or magazines).

Such organizations have also worked independently of government, through boycott of offending merchants. For example, lists of disapproved books and magazines have been distributed to members of the organization and the public, with a request to make no purchases at all from bookstores, drugstores, or other retailers that sell any item on the list. Such action has often been highly effective.

The historic prototype was the *Index of Prohibited Books,* published by the Roman Catholic Church from 1559 until its discontinuance in 1966, which in its latest revision listed more than 4,000 works forbidden to Catholics as heretical or otherwise sinful. For a time the *Index* was used for preventive censorship in some countries, through laws penalizing publication and sale of any listed work, but even after withdrawal of legal sanctions such works were often avoided by dealers.

In the United States, Anthony Comstock's Society for the Suppression of Vice became prominent in the latter part of the 19th century, as did the New England Watch and Ward Society. The best known modern organizations are the National Organization for Decent Literature, established in 1938 by the Catholic bishops of the United States, and the nondenominational Citizens for Decent Literature, organized in 1956, which has concentrated on appeals for official censorship to prevent sale of sex literature to juveniles.

The courts have sometimes curbed private censorship. In 1926, for example, the New England Watch and Ward Society's attempts to force withdrawal of magazines by threats to prosecute dealers were enjoined as an illegal boycott, in *American Mercury, Inc.* v. *Chase.* But in a number of communities, private organizations have succeeded in keeping out of retail stores, libraries, and the schools such serious novels as *The Catcher in the Rye, Brave New World,* and *The Grapes of Wrath,* and issues of such reputable magazines as *McCall's* and *Reader's Digest.*

Self-Censorship. One form of accommodation to official and private censorship has been the establishment of voluntary standards by industrial associations, with central offices to interpret the rules and monitor violations. The best known of these is the agency created by the American film producers, originally known as the Hays Office and redesignated the Motion Picture Production Code Administration, which reviews films before release and accords its "seal of approval" only to those that satisfy its fairly strict rules on sex, violence, and moral teaching. For some years after 1927, when 17 producers agreed to follow the Hays Office rules, local movie houses generally refused to exhibit films that failed to comply with them. In the 1950's and 1960's, however, the effectiveness of such censorship was weakened by the influx of foreign films, the defection of one major film producer (United Artists), and the producers' loss of control of distribution through application of the antitrust laws. Similar self-censorship efforts have been made by television broadcasters and comic book publishers.

LOUIS LUSKY
School of Law, Columbia University

Bibliography

Chafee, Zechariah, Jr., *Free Speech in the United States* (Cambridge, Mass., 1941).
Craig, Alec, *Suppressed Books: A History of the Conception of Literary Obscenity* (Cleveland 1963).
Downs, Robert, ed., *The First Freedom* (Chicago 1960).
Emerson, Thomas I., and others, *Political and Civil Rights in the United States,* 3d ed. (Boston 1967).
Ernst, Morris L., and Schwartz, Alan U., *Censorship* (New York 1964).
Haiman, Franklin S., *Freedom of Speech* (New York 1965).
Hudon, Edward G., *Freedom of Speech and Press in America* (Washington, D. C., 1963).
Swayze, Harold, *Political Control of Literature in the USSR, 1946–1959* (Cambridge, Mass., 1962).
Wiggins, James R., *Freedom or Secrecy,* rev. ed. (New York 1964).

CENSUS, sen'səs, in general terms, a count or tally of population, lands, or other items. The term derives from the Latin *censere* (to assess). Official national censuses are carried out and financed by governments to provide nations with statistical profiles of their people, including their demographic, economic, and social characteristics. Censuses of population, housing, agriculture, business and industry, government, and the like supply the essentials for good national administration and development, and extend the statistical base for studying and solving man's current and future problems.

Official censuses are compulsory, and in almost all countries the data obtained are confidential. The censuses cover specified areas and are taken at a precise time. As a general rule, both the day and a particular time, called the "census moment," are fixed for the census. People may be counted according to their regular or legal residence (a de jure census) or according to the place where they are found at the time of enumeration (a de facto census).

Although some elements in the conduct of various censuses may differ, preparatory operations are usually similar for all. First, legal authority for the census is obtained, and then the funds necessary are provided. Questions are chosen, sampling plans selected, questionnaires designed and tested, and national boundaries and boundaries of subdivisions and enumeration areas are determined. Instructions are written for the guidance of field workers, and the work load is planned so that publication of the results will not be delayed.

After the preparatory operation, the data-collection phase begins. As soon as preliminary counts are available, initial reports are normally issued to meet the needs of the users as quickly as possible. These may be followed by advance reports of selected figures from the final tabulations, or by parts of books which will eventually be combined into complete volumes. A final step, after all reports have been issued, is the review and evaluation of the census operation—a process that may include resurveys and other checks of the adequacy of the enumeration as to coverage and accuracy of information, and of the accuracy of the field transcription, the coding, and the processing. Thus the groundwork is laid for a more effective operation in the next census.

Historical Background. Before the 17th century, partial enumeration of heads of families, households, hearths, male citizens of military age, and taxpayers were undertaken from time to time in many jurisdictions throughout the world. The earliest enumerations were either property surveys taken by magistrates or other civil officials to provide a basis for taxation, or registration surveys to identify individuals for military service or work-force conscription.

Knowledge of these very early censuses has been preserved over the ages in various historical documents and records. The Bible includes accounts of the enumeration of military men among the Israelites at the time of the Exodus (about 1500 B. C.) and during the reign of David (five centuries later). Chinese records dating from 2275 B. C. reveal that the number of taxpaying households was recorded, at intervals, until 1712 A. D., at which time censuses of individuals are thought to have been undertaken. Some authorities believe that some form of census may have existed in China as early as 3000 B. C. Egyptian registrations date from very early times, too, with complete registrations reported during the 14th century B. C. Similar registrations in Persia, and in the valley of the Nile during the reign of Amasis (570–526 B. C.), were reported by Herodotus. Solon is credited with introducing the Egyptian idea of registrations into Athens, where Attic Greeks developed it into a systematic record of the citizenry, some portions of which were preserved in stone. The first census of Athens was taken by Demetrius of Phalerum in 317 B. C.

The most complete enumerations in ancient times were conducted by the Romans. During the reign of Servius Tullius (578–535 B. C.), magistrates known as censors were charged with making registers of people and property for taxation and military purposes. The practice was continued at intervals for over 400 years and was extended, in 5 B. C. by Emperor Augustus, to include the entire Roman Empire. Figures passed down in the writings of Roman historians have contributed significantly to the study of the growth of the Roman population.

The collapse of the Roman Empire brought an end to the first known series of periodic censuses. The feudal system that followed rendered the revival of census taking, even when practicable, less necessary. Charlemagne made an effort to revive such accountings in the 9th century, and in 1086 A. D., William the Conqueror set up a censuslike record of the names of English proprietors, with a description of the value and extent of their lands, in the Domesday Book. Genghis Khan had censuses made of the people and possessions in territories overrun by his armies during the late 12th and early 13th centuries. One of the earliest complete censuses of a city was taken in Nuremberg in 1449.

Provincial and municipal enumerations continued to be taken in various countries and municipalities throughout the 15th and 16th centuries. Surviving records of the ancient Inca civilization in Peru and historical writings of the Spanish conquistadors indicate that the first known censuses in the Western Hemisphere may have been made in Peru. The first post-Columbian census in the Americas was conducted in Peru in 1548 by the Spanish, and the first census in North America, taken in 1576, provided counts for Spain's American possessions.

After colonies were established in North America, the need for statistical information about colonial markets led to census taking in Virginia in 1624–1625 and again in 1634–1635. New York took a census in 1698, and other colonies gradually followed suit.

Development of Modern Methods. The modern concept of the census as a scientifically designed instrument to be used for the purpose of obtaining a statistical base for studying social and economic trends began to develop in the early 1700's, and what has been claimed to be the first census in the modern manner was conducted in 1666 in the colony of New France, in what is now Canada. Thereafter, census taking was continued throughout the French regime until it ended in 1763. In 1851, Canada instituted a regular decennial census, taking its first dominion-wide census in 1871.

In Europe the first modern census was that taken of the population in Iceland in 1703, but because its publication was delayed for many

Nuns, aiding the U. S. Census Bureau in the 1970 count, interview a mother at her window in New York City.

years, the Swedish census of 1750 is regarded as the first regularly taken and periodically published population record. Like other western European censuses, it was made up from the parish registers. Various other partial censuses were taken in Europe during the 18th century, and certain Italian states conducted very accurate enumerations. In 1810 a modern census was undertaken in Prussia. Norway followed in 1815, Austria in 1818, Greece in 1836, Belgium in 1846, Italy in 1861, and Russia in 1897. In Great Britain, the publication in 1798 of Sir John Sinclair's surveys of population, agriculture, trade, and industry, compiled by inquiries to the clergy of the Anglican Church, led to the establishment of a census office in 1800, and in the spring of 1801, Great Britain's first population census was taken. But the first censuses of British agriculture and industry were not taken until 1907. France also took its first census in 1801, and another in 1806, but reliable census-taking methods were not adopted in that country until 1836.

United States Censuses and Surveys. The first census of the United States, taken in 1790, was unique among early modern censuses: it was the first to be conceived as an integral part of the machinery of government. The Constitution provided for a population census to be taken "within three Years after the first Meeting of the Congress of the United States, and within every subsequent Term of ten Years" (Article I, Section 2); and without lapse, such an enumeration has been made every 10 years since 1790. The census was first designed to provide a basis for determining the number of representatives each state would have in Congress.

The content of the census as well as the methods of taking it changed as the nation's needs and interests did. The first inquiry on manufactures was made in 1810. Questions on agriculture, mining, and fisheries were added in 1840. In 1850 the census included immigration and nativity statistics for the first time. These became increasingly important as the basis for

the establishment of immigration quotas.

After 1900, censuses in certain fields that had previously been taken concurrently with the decennial census came to be taken more frequently. The census of manufactures was taken at 5-year intervals from 1900 to 1920 and at 2-year intervals through 1940. After a lapse during World War II, new legislation provided for censuses of manufactures, mineral industries, and other businesses to be taken on a 5-year basis. The transportation census was first taken for 1963. The 1967 census of business has been expanded to include a census of the construction industry. Censuses of government, providing statistics on government organization, public employment, finances, and related matters, were taken every 10 years from 1902 until 1942. Since 1957, they have been taken on a 5-year basis. Censuses of religious bodies were taken at intervals until 1936, but none thereafter.

Current surveys on census subjects were authorized by Congress as the need for intercensal statistics arose. As a result, the United States Bureau of the Census began compiling comprehensive statistics of population, housing, manufactures, business, construction, governments, foreign trade, and the like, at weekly, monthly, quarterly, and annual intervals.

Changes in Census Methods. The first 12 censuses of the United States, 1790–1900, were conducted without a permanent census office although a group of professionals had developed. The field supervisors for the first nine censuses, 1790–1870, were the marshals of the U. S. judicial districts, and the enumerators and counters were the deputy marshals. In the census of 1880, however, the enumeration responsibility was transferred to census supervisors appointed for each census district, the temporary field organization established on the old judicial district lines was discontinued, and a census office was established. In addition, this reorganization led to improved choice of subjects to be investigated and more detailed presentation of the results. This census, therefore, is generally con-

BUREAU OF THE CENSUS, U. S. DEPARTMENT OF COMMERCE

CENSUS BUREAU COMPUTER is used to process statistical data stored on reels of magnetic tape.

sidered to be the first modern census of the United States.

In 1902, Congress enacted the Permanent Census Act, creating the Bureau of the Census. Thereafter, great strides were made in developing efficient census taking and in tabulating and publishing the results. Machine tabulation had been introduced in 1890. In the 1940 census, sampling techniques for collecting some of the census information were used for the first time.

Other notable advances in census-taking techniques were developed after World War II, including the use of electronics in new statistical computing machines. The electronic Universal Automatic Computer (UNIVAC) acquired by the Census Bureau in 1951 was the first electronic computing machine developed for large-scale statistical use. The Fosdic system (Film Optical Sensing Device for Input to Computers), which transfers information from microfilm copies of census questionnaires to magnetic tape that can be used in the electronic computer, was employed extensively in the 1960 censuses. This method eliminates both hand punching of cards and the subsequent transfer of the data from punched cards to tape. A later development was the Computer Document Recorder, which converts computer tape directly into readable microfilm records that can be easily stored and also used to produce readable paper prints.

A number of new procedures were used in the 1970 census to improve the accuracy of the count and the quality of the data. In major metropolitan areas, residential address lists were established in advance of the census. A questionnaire was mailed to each address prior to census day, with the request that the form be filled out and mailed back in the envelope provided. Four households out of five received a "short form" containing 23 questions, while every fifth household received a longer form containing several additional questions. Public cooperation was such that 86% of the forms were mailed back. About 80% of these were properly filled out and needed

no follow-up. However, if no questionnaire was returned or if an unacceptable one was received, an enumerator called at the address to obtain the necessary information.

In nonmetropolitan areas, letter carriers left a short-form questionnaire at each residence where they regularly delivered mail. Householders were instructed to fill out the questionnaire and hold it for an enumerator who would call for it later. At every fifth household the enumerator asked the additional sample questions used on the longer form in the metropolitan area.

Modern Foreign Censuses. After World War II, efforts by international organizations, particularly the United Nations, to coordinate the timing and contents of censuses in various countries resulted in a trend toward increasing uniformity. The scope of the inquiry in population censuses was enlarged to include more questions on occupation, industry, type of job activity, educational level and literacy, language spoken and ethnic characteristics, and marriage and birth rates. Some questions varied significantly, however, according to areas of the world and populations involved. In Europe, questions concerning marriage and number of children were more common than in other areas, but questions about income and ethnic or national background were much less common.

In certain countries with populations of varied ethnic and religious backgrounds, questions were frequently included concerning tribal affiliation, principal language, religion, refugee status, or migration. For example, in the Sierra Leone census of population of 1963, tribal affiliation and literacy in any of four languages were recorded for each respondent. The Indian census of 1961 contained questions on religion, asking for the caste or tribe as well as the main faith of the respondent.

The most apparent differences among countries in the contents and procedures of population censuses were necessitated by special problems that arose in particular areas. In many Asian countries, all the dwellings in defined urban areas and in villages had to be numbered before the census was actually taken to ensure systematic coverage of all dwellings. In India, Pakistan, and certain African countries with large floating populations, the enumeration was started in the early morning hours of the census day in order to count the people at their sleeping sites. In Jordan, which has a significant nomadic population, a similar problem was resolved in 1961 by locating Bedouin tribal encampments through the desert police and enumerating all groups within as short an interval as possible.

In most areas of the world the number of censuses of housing, agriculture, business, and industry increased steadily after World War II.

Uses of Census Statistics. Census statistics have extremely wide and varied uses. Government plans and decisions, national electoral distribution, social welfare programs, and employment, immigration, housing, and other legislation develop from census information about people and the economic and social characteristics of their environment. In wartime, censuses of manufactures and agriculture provide vital information on industrial facilities and critical materials, and the population census provides a basis for determining military manpower potential. This is perhaps the only remaining similarity between ancient enumerations and the modern census. Industries are established on the basis of census data; certification by census records of age, citizenship, and residence help an individual obtain a job, social security benefits, inheritances, or passports; and the public derives innumerable indirect benefits from the improvements, economies, and efficiencies produced by public and private groups because of their use of timely and accurate census statistics.

UNITED STATES BUREAU OF THE CENSUS

The Bureau of the Census was created as a permanent census office in 1902, and it operates under congressional authority. It is the major statistical agency of the federal government and is responsible for providing periodic censuses of population, housing, agriculture, manufactures, mineral industries, business, governments, and transportation, as well as periodic surveys of most of these same fields; population estimates and projections; and statistics on foreign trade, construction, and housing vacancies. The bureau performs statistical services for other government agencies and for private users under certain conditions. It prepares special tables of information already collected and conducts a personal census records service, furnishing certificates of age and place of birth to individuals. The bureau also acts as consultant to foreign governments and trains foreign technicians in census and other statistical methods. The information furnished the bureau is confidential and may not be used for any purpose except to compile statistical totals.

The bureau's headquarters is at Suitland, Md., and there is a Census Operations Office at Jeffersonville, Ind., and a Personal Census Service Branch at Pittsburg, Kans. Twelve field offices are located in major cities throughout the United States. For national population and housing censuses, a temporary field organization is set up. The number of temporary field employees has decreased with the use of the self-enumeration system.

Major Programs. The population census, taken decennially since 1790, is the oldest United States census program. From its initial use as a basis for apportioning congressional representation and direct taxes among the states, it has grown to include much detail on the number and characteristics of the population. This information is shown for metropolitan areas, counties, cities, towns, and special areas such as census tracts and blocks, and is especially valuable in analyzing the population with respect to age, education, employment, income, and family status. The census also provides data on which current estimates and projections of growth are in part based.

A housing census has been taken decennially since 1940. Before that time, some housing information had been obtained as part of the population census. The housing census deals with vacancies, financing, number of rooms, condition of plumbing facilities, lighting, refrigeration, heating equipment, and the like.

Agriculture censuses were taken every 10 years from 1840 to 1920. Now taken every 5 years, they provide extensive data including a count of farms, an inventory of agricultural land and its use, the amount and sale of farm produce, kinds and numbers of livestock and poultry, farm machines and facilities, farm workers, and a record of important cash expenditures.

A census of manufactures was first taken in 1810, and all subsequent decennial censuses except that of 1830 contained questions on manufactures. After 1900, as the industrial capacity of the country increased, manufacturing censuses became more frequent. They are currently taken every five years, giving statistics for over 400 industries, including number of plants or factories, their locations, number of workers, payroll, cost of materials, new plant and equipment expenditures, and amount of value added to a product by the manufacturing process.

Questions on mining first appeared in the 1840 census. Thereafter, a census of mineral industries was taken every 10 years until 1940.

METROPOLITAN MAPPING PROGRAM, based on census data, is one of the operations of the Census Bureau.

Currently taken every 5 years, this census gives statistics on the value of mineral products, the industrial and geographical structure of mining, costs of development and operation, and the labor, materials, and capital required.

The retail, wholesale, and service trades are later additions to the census series. The first business census of these trades was taken in 1929; thereafter it was taken at various intervals before and after World War II. It is now conducted every five years, giving statistics on the number of establishments, sales or receipts, employees, and payrolls.

Information on state and local governments was first obtained in 1850, and data were given at 10-year intervals until the 1950's, when the census was made quinquennial. It includes a count of all local governments, with basic facts about finances and employment from each.

Statistics on construction activity and transportation are relatively new full-time responsibilities of the bureau. Since 1959, reports have been issued on the value of new construction, housing units started and authorized by building permits, and sale of houses. The 1968 census of the construction industry, taken for 1967, is the first such census. With regard to transportation, the bureau is authorized to collect only those statistics not already provided by other government agencies such as the Interstate Commerce Commission and the Department of Transportation. The first transportation census, taken for 1963, covered the physical and geographical distribution of commodities shipped, a national survey of travel by individuals, a truck inventory and use survey, and a bus and truck carrier survey.

Foreign trade data have been compiled since 1941 from statements required of importers and exporters. The findings yield information on foreign trade by commodity and country; statistics on gold and silver trade, on trade with Puerto Rico and with U. S. possessions, and on trade by customs districts; and data on sea and air shipments, as well as vessel shipments by port of loading and unloading.

The bureau publishes important general works including *The Statistical Abstract of the United States*, an annual statistical summary of the social, political, and economic organization of the United States; the *Pocket Data Book, USA*, issued biennially; *Historical Statistics of the United States, Colonial Times to 1957* (prepared with the Social Science Research Council); the *County and City Data Book*, a selection of over 140 statistics for every county and every city of over 25,000—with data for metropolitan areas and states; *County Business Patterns*, an annual report series of employment, payrolls, and employment units by industry for counties and metropolitan areas; and *Business Cycle Developments*, a monthly compilation of useful economic indicators. The Bureau also publishes a quarterly catalog with 12 monthly supplements as a comprehensive guide to published and unpublished statistics.

A. Ross Eckler, *Director*
U. S. Bureau of the Census

Further Reading: United Nations, *Handbook of Population Methods:* vol. 1, *General Aspects of a Population Census* (New York 1958); id., *World Facts and Figures* (New York 1962); U. S. Bureau of the Census, *Historical Statistics of the United States* (Washington 1960); id., *1960 Censuses of Population and Housing; Procedural History* (Washington 1966).

CENT. See Coins — *Coins of the United States.*

CENT NOUVELLES NOUVELLES, sän nōō-vel' nōō-vel', a collection of facetious and racy tales written in the French vernacular of the 15th century. Of unkown authorship, *Les cent nouvelles nouvelles* was probably influenced by fabliaux and the *Decameron.* The stories, which are the direct antecedents of modern short stories, are important historically because they give detailed descriptions of contemporary manners and customs. Among the narrators are obscure and untitled men, who figure side by side with some of the great names in French history. The tales were first told at the table of the dauphin, later Louis XI, in the castle of Genappe (Belgium) during his exile. They appeared in manuscript about 1462 and were first published in Paris by Antoine Vérard in 1486. The arrangement of this collection of tales has been attributed to Antoine de la Sale and Louis XI.

CENTAUR, sen'tôr, in Greek mythology, one of a race of creatures that were half man and half horse, usually depicted as having the head, neck, arms, and chest of a man and the body, legs, and tail of a horse. They lived chiefly around Mt. Pelion in Thessaly and were believed to be the offspring of Ixion and a cloud. The Centaurs, accordingly, were also known as Ixionidae.

According to the most accepted version of the account of their origin, Ixion, king of the Lapithae in Thessaly, fell in love with Hera, wife of Zeus, and arranged a meeting intending to seduce her. However, Zeus fashioned a cloud in the shape of Hera and carried it to the meeting place. Ixion embraced the cloud, and from this union were born the Centaurs. The most famous of the Centaurs was Chiron (q. v.), who was the teacher of Jason, Aesculapius, and Hercules.

At the wedding of Ixion's son Pirithous and Hippodamia, one of the Centaurs became intoxicated and tried to abduct the bride. A battle ensued in which many Centaurs were slain; the others were driven from Thessaly.

CENTAUR. See Centaurus.

CENTAUREA, sen-tôr'ē-ə, any of a large group of annual and perennial plants, many of which are cultivated for their decorative flower heads. Centaureas make up the genus *Centaurea* of the composite family. The most popular species are generally of European or Asian origin.

One of the best-known centaureas is the cornflower (*C. cyanus*), also known as bachelor's button. It is a European annual, from 1 to 2 feet (30 to 60 cm) tall, with small blue, white, or pink flower heads. Another popular species, the sweet sultan (*C. moschata*) is an Oriental annual about 2 feet (60 cm) tall with fragrant purple, white, or yellow flower heads about 2 inches (50 mm) across. A native American species, the basket flower (*C. americana*), grows 6 feet (1.8 meters) tall and bears pink or purplish flower heads, 5 inches (13 cm) wide.

Three perennial species of less horticultural interest are the dusty miller (*C. cinerea*), which has yellow or purple flower heads, and the mountain bluet (*C. montana*) and the knapweed (*C. nigra*), both of these varieties having blue flower heads.

Donald Wyman
The Arnold Arboretum, Harvard University

CENTAURUS, sen-tô′rəs, is a large constellation of the Southern Hemisphere. Its name is derived from the race of centaurs, half man and half horse, which appears in Greek mythology. A small part of Centaurus is visible in northern latitudes during the spring, but the constellation cannot be seen in full except from a position near or below the equator.

Centaurus extends into the Milky Way and contains many interesting celestial objects. The brightest of these are the two 1st-magnitude stars, α and β Centauri. The former, known to navigators as Rigel Kent, is actually a binary or double star. It has the distinction of being, with one exception, our sun's closest stellar neighbor in space; it is only 4.3 light-years away. The exception is an 11th-magnitude star, too faint to be seen with the naked eye, which is a third member of the α Centauri system and which lies slightly closer to the sun. This star is often referred to as Proxima Centauri.

The 4th-magnitude object called ω Centauri is actually a large globular cluster containing thousands of stars. This cluster, at a distance of about 22,000 light-years, is one of the closest of about 120 such globular clusters found in the vicinity of the Milky Way galaxy. It is also one of the very few globular clusters that can be observed with the naked eye. See also CONSTELLATION; STARS.

CENTAURY, sen′tô-rē, the common name for a small group of mostly annual, European plants of the gentian family. In the United States only one species, *Centaurium scilloides*, is raised as an ornamental, grown primarily in rock gardens. It is a tufted plant about 4 inches (10 cm) tall with rounded opposite leaves about ¾ inches (1.9 cm) in diameter. Its bright rose-colored or white flowers are very small and are borne in loose spikes. The plant is propagated by seed and grows best in a sandy loam.

C. umbellatum is a European species that escaped from cultivation in North America and now ranges from Quebec and Michigan southward to Georgia and Indiana. It is a short plant with rose-purple flowers.

DONALD WYMAN
Arnold Arboretum, Harvard University

BROWN BROTHERS

Machinery Hall at Philadelphia's Centennial Exposition.

CENTENNIAL EXPOSITION, the world's fair held in Philadelphia, Pa., from May 10 to Nov. 10, 1876, to celebrate the 100th anniversary of the Declaration of Independence. An association of Philadelphians proposed an international exhibition of arts, manufactures, and agricultural products. Congress authorized it and appointed a commission from the states, and individual and public subscriptions made it possible. In about 200 buildings erected on 236 acres of Fairmount Park, 49 nations and 26 states displayed representative work to almost 10 million visitors, who paid a 50-cent admission charge.

There were no amusements, but the crowds were fascinated by working models, with moving parts, of new machines—among them, the self-binding reaper, typewriter, telephone, air brake, refrigerator car, and duplex telegraph that transmitted two messages simultaneously over one wire. All the machinery in the fair was powered by a single steam engine built by George H. Corliss.

A landmark in industrial history, the exposition showed Europeans the American technique of mass production by means of interchangeable parts. It ushered in the modern age of machine invention and made many people aware of new inventions. It had such concrete effects as giving impetus to American bicycle manufacturing. Less significant economically but still important, it popularized Japanese decoration and recognized women's crafts. The Pennsylvania Museum of Art is the only remaining building.

CENTER, Geographic. See CENTROGRAPHY.

CENTER LINE is a city in Michigan, in Macomb county, 10 miles (16 km) north of Detroit, of which it is a residential suburb. Center Line has metalworking and tool plants and is the site of a U.S. Army arsenal. Settled in 1857, it was incorporated as a village in 1925 and as a city in 1936. It is governed by a mayor and council. Population: 10,379.

The constellation Centaurus

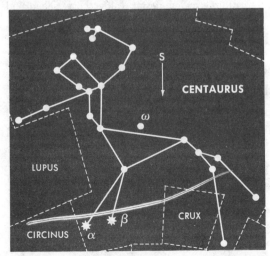

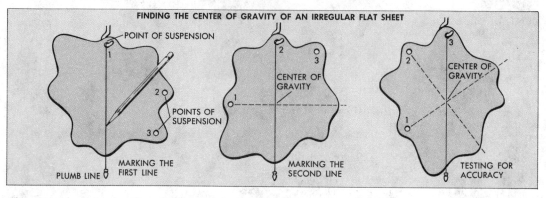

FINDING THE CENTER OF GRAVITY OF AN IRREGULAR FLAT SHEET

The center of gravity of an irregular flat sheet is given by the intersection of plumb lines from two suspension points.

CENTER OF BUOYANCY. See Hydrostatics; Ship.

CENTER OF GRAVITY, the point at which the gravitational attraction of a body may be considered to be concentrated. Since gravitational attraction depends on mass, the mass of the body may also be considered to be concentrated at this point. For this reason, the center of gravity is also known as the center of mass.

The fact that all the mass and weight of a body may be taken to be acting at a single point greatly simplifies many calculations. For example, the motion of a spinning baton thrown into the air appears to be rather complex. Actually, while the baton rotates about its center of gravity, the center of gravity itself moves through a simple arc.

The center of gravity of a body may or may not be a point on or within the body. For bodies of regular geometrical shape and uniform density, it is at their geometrical center. Thus, the center of gravity of an automobile tire or a hollow cube would not be a point on the tire or cube, while the center of gravity of a solid cube would be located at a point of the cube.

When an object is suspended, the center of gravity always lies directly below the point of suspension. This fact can be used to find the center of gravity of an irregularly shaped flat object. If the object is suspended successively from two points and lines are drawn on the object indicating the positions of plumb lines hung from the points of suspension, the two lines will intersect at the center of gravity. A third point of suspension will provide a third line also going through this point as a check.

A standing object is stable when its center of gravity is directly over its base; it is unstable when its center of gravity is over a point outside its base.

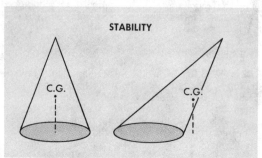

STABILITY

The location of the center of gravity of an object determines whether it will be stable in a given position or not. The more stable an object is, the less likely it is to tip over. As long as the center of gravity is over the base of the object, it will be stable. The lower the center of gravity is, the more one can tip the object and still have the center of gravity remain over the base, causing the object to return to its original position after it has been displaced. Likewise, a larger base makes an object more stable. Thus, the cone on the left in the accompanying drawing will be stable because its center of gravity is directly over its base. If it were squashed down so that the area of its base increased and its center of gravity was lower, its stability would be even greater. The cone on the right, however, is unstable and will tip over because its center of gravity does not lie above its base.

CENTER OF MASS. See Center of Gravity.

CENTER OF POPULATION. See Centrography; United States—10. *Population Growth and Characteristics.*

CENTERBOARD. See Yachts and Yachting—*Principles of Sailing.*

CENTERVILLE, a city in southern Iowa, the seat of Appanoose county, is 73 miles (113 km) southeast of Des Moines, in the Chariton River valley. It is the trade and manufacturing center of an agricultural region raising cattle, hogs, sheep and poultry. The area has valuable deposits of coal, shale, clay, limestone, gypsum.

Centerville's products include camp trailers, farm equipment, electrical appliances, food wrappings, fertilizer, beverages, boxes, and clay concrete, metal, shale, and wood products. Other industries are processing of grain, meat, and milk products; printing, and limestone quarrying. There is a municipal airport.

It is the seat of Centerville Community College, a 2-year coeducational institution, founded in 1930. An annual fall festival, Pancake Day, attracts as many as 50,000 visitors.

Centerville is built around an 8-block city square, laid out in 1846. First called Chaldea and then Senterville, it received its present name in 1847. The city was incorporated in 1855 and is governed by a mayor and council. Population: 6,531.

Dorothy Owen
Drake Public Library

CENTERVILLE, a borough in southwestern Pennsylvania, in Washington county, is on the west bank of the Monongahela River, 28 miles (45 km) south of Pittsburgh. Bituminous coal mining is its chief industry. The first settlers came to the site of Centerville in 1766. It was incorporated in 1895. Government is by mayor and council. Population: 4,175.

CENTIGRADE SCALE. See CELSIUS SCALE.

CENTIMETER, sen'tə-mē-tər, a unit of length in the metric system. It is defined as 1/100 of a meter, the basic unit of the metric system. One centimeter is equal to about 0.3937 inch. See also WEIGHTS AND MEASURES.

CENTIMETER-GRAM-SECOND SYSTEM, a system of units in the metric system in which the centimeter, the gram, and the second are the basic units. See METRIC SYSTEM.

CENTIPEDE, sent'ə-pēd, any of a large class of arthropods found throughout all warm and temperate regions of the world. Commonly known as *hundred-legger,* the centipede is recognized by its long, flattened body with many segments and a pair of walking legs on each typical segment.

Structure. The centipede has a distinct head, which has a pair of sensory antennae, a pair of toothed chewing jaws (mandibles), and two pairs of accessory jaws (maxillas), which handle food and hold it to the mouth. Eyes are usually not present, but when they do occur, they usually are no more than a small clump of simple eyes (ocelli). The eyes of the house centipede and its relatives, which are active in the daytime, are faceted and resemble the compound eyes of insects.

The upper and lower surfaces of the centipede's trunk segments are armored with thickened plates and joined by a flexible membrane. In each typical trunk segment, these membranes are perforated by a pair of openings called spiracles. They supply air to the tubes of the respiratory system.

The first trunk segment has a pair of curved hollow pincers, or poison claws, that have sharp perforated tips. A paralyzing poison is injected through them into captured prey.

Although one genus of centipedes reaches a length of 1 foot (30 cm), most are only 1 to 2 inches (2.5–5 cm) long.

Reproduction. The sexes are separate in centipedes. The sex openings are on a genital segment, the next to the last body segment. Fertilization probably is accomplished by the male depositing a mass of sperm on a small web, and the female taking it up. Some centipedes lay their eggs in the soil, while in other species the female curls her body around the egg mass to protect it and prevent it from drying out.

Natural History. Most centipedes are found underground, under stones or bark or leaf litter, in rocky crevices, and in damp, dark corners of human dwellings during the daytime. They come out at night to feed on small insects, worms, and slugs that frequent small crevices in soil, rocks, or bark. Some centipedes capture toads, snakes, and lizards, and in captivity, these centipedes have been fed mice.

A few species of centipedes are marine, and they live between tidemarks under stones or seaweeds, in rocky crevices, or in empty barnacles or worm tubes. None of the centipedes live in fresh water.

TWEEDIE, FROM PHOTO RESEARCHERS

Centipede

Centipedes cannot tolerate drying because they lack effective devices for closing the respiratory openings. Therefore they minimize the water loss by coming out only at night and by hiding in the daytime.

Economic Importance. All centipedes are carnivorous, but a few also feed on plants and when extremely numerous they may injure plant crops. Most centipedes are incapable of biting through human skin, and they almost always seek to escape rather than to bite. If picked up, some centipedes will bite readily, causing sharp pain that subsides quickly. The bite of a large centipede, however, can cause fiery pain, a fever, and painful swelling that may last for three weeks.

Classification. Centipedes form the class Chilopoda of the phylum Arthropoda. They are closely related to the millipedes, which make up the class Diplopoda.

RALPH BUCHSBAUM and MILDRED BUCHSBAUM
University of Pittsburgh

CENTLIVRE, sent-liv'er, **Susanna** (1667?–1723), English playwright, who invented the character Simon Pure, the source of the expression "simonpure." Perhaps born in Ireland she left home at an early age and appeared for a time as an actress. In 1706 she married Joseph Centlivre, possibly her third husband, who was a cook in the household of Queen Anne.

Mrs. Centlivre wrote 19 plays, the first of which was the tragedy *The Perjur'd Husband* (1700). Her comedies include *The Gamester* (1705); the *Busy Body* (1709), with its character Marplot, a prototype of the well-meaning blunderer; *The Wonder! A Woman Keeps a Secret* (1714); and *A Bold Stroke for a Wife* (1718), in which Simon Pure appears. Alexander Pope, Mrs. Centlivre's literary enemy, referred to her as "the cook's wife in Buckingham Court." She died in London on Dec. 1, 1723.

CENTO, sen'tō, a literary work, most commonly in verse, put together from lines composed by other authors. *Cento* in Latin means "patchwork." Centos were very popular in the decadent period of Latin literature. Rules for their composition were formulated by Ausonius (310?–395), author of the sensational *Cento nuptialis,* composed of lines taken from Virgil. Another 4th century example is the *Cento Vergilianus,* by Proba Falconia, in which Biblical stories are narrated in lines from Virgil.

BANGUI, on the Ubangi River, is the capital of the Central African Empire. Place de la République is at the lower left, with the Fontaine Lumineuse in its center circle.

CENTRAL AFRICAN EMPIRE, formerly the Central African Republic, is an independent country in central Africa. Once that part of French Equatorial Africa known as Ubangi-Shari, the country attained independence as the Central African Republic on Aug. 13, 1960. In December 1976 it was renamed Central African Empire. It has retained extensive economic and commercial links with France, on which it has been dependent for much of its foreign aid. Situated more than 300 miles (480 km) from the sea, it is one of the most remote and underdeveloped countries on the African continent.

The People. The Central African Empire has an estimated population (1971) of 1,637,000. About 90% of the population is rural and is unevenly distributed throughout the country. The only large population concentrations are found along the Ubangi River and near the border with Chad. The capital and major port is Bangui, situated on the Ubangi River.

The population of the country is composed of various ethnic groups that migrated into the interior of Africa to escape the slave trade over a period of two centuries. There is no one dominant tribe in the country. In the southern part of the country, along the northern banks of the Ubangi River, intermixing has produced largely Bantu-speaking cultures. In the east, Nilotic cultural and physiological influences are clearly marked in the population. In the north, the people tend to be taller and more robust.

The principal ethnic groups are the Azande, Yakoma, Sango, and Banziri, who inhabit the banks of the Ubangi River and its tributary, the M'Bomou River; the Banda, inhabiting the upper reaches of the Ouaka, Kotto, and Gribingui rivers; the Mandjia-Baya, principally inhabiting the administrative regions of upper Sangha, Ouham, and Ouham-Pende; and the Sara, found mainly in the north, near the frontiers of Chad.

French is the official language of the country. Sango, which is spoken in all parts of the country, serves as a linguistic bridge between the various ethnic groups. About 70% of the people of the Central African Empire are tribal animists in religion. There are 170,000 Catholics, 110,000 Protestants, and 50,000 Muslims in the country.

The educational system of the Central African Empire is modeled along French lines. About 45% of all school-age children were attending classes in the mid-1960's, most of them enrolled in primary schools. The literacy rate is estimated to be between 5% and 10% of the population.

Although the country has no institutions for higher education, a number of technical and vo-

---

INFORMATION HIGHLIGHTS

Official Name: Central African Empire.
Head of State: Emperor.
Head of Government: Emperor.
Area: 240,534 square miles (622,984 sq km).
Boundaries: *North*, Chad; *east*, the Sudan; *south*, Congo (Brazzaville) and Zaire; and *west*, Cameroon.
Population: 1,637,000 (1971 est.).
Capital: Bangui (1971 population, 187,000).
Major Languages: French (official); Sango.
Major Religions: Tribal; Christianity; Islam.
Monetary Unit: Franc CFA.
Weights and Measures: Metric system.
Flag: Four narrow horizontal stripes (blue, white, green, and yellow), divided by a narrow red vertical stripe at the center. A yellow five-pointed star is in the upper left corner.
National Anthem: *La Renaissance (The Rebirth).*

cational schools provide instruction in public administration, mechanical skills, agronomy, and teaching. The United Nations Educational, Scientific, and Cultural Organization (UNESCO) operates a regional center for the instruction of teacher-training personnel and school counselors in Bangui. A few hundred students from the Central African Empire attend colleges and universities in France, the United States, and other countries.

The Land and Natural Resources. The country is a vast, well-watered plateau, with an average elevation of about 2,000 feet (610 meters). It is drained by two major river systems, with the northerly one draining into the Shari basin and eventually into Lake Chad, and the southerly into the Ubangi River, a confluent of the Congo River. The Ubangi River forms the southern border of the country and is its main artery of traffic.

The country is covered principally by savanna-type vegetation. In the southwestern corner of the country is a dense equatorial rain forest, while semiarid conditions prevail in the northeastern tip.

The climate of the country is hot and humid, although it is often quite cool in the western highlands. Average annual temperatures at Bangui range between a low of 72° F (22° C) and a high of 92° F (33° C). Rainfall is heaviest from June to October. Annual rainfall in the Ubangi River valley is about 70 inches (1,800 mm). In the extreme northeastern portion of the country rainfall averages only about 31 inches (790 mm) a year.

Almost every type of tropical animal is represented in the Central African Empire. Elephants are especially numerous. The country's soils are generally poor, although a diversity of common tropical and subtropical crops are grown.

Until recently the only known minerals in the country were diamonds and gold. Deposits of iron ore, zinc, copper, and tin have now been discovered, and their potential value is under study. Traces of uranium have been found in the southeastern part of the country, and active exploration is in progress.

The Economy. The Central African Empire is a predominantly agricultural country, whose population is engaged mainly in subsistence farming. The chief food crops are manioc, millet, sorghum, and maize. Cotton and coffee, the major commercial crops, account for about 45% of the value of the country's exports. Other cash crops include peanuts and palm kernels.

Since 1961 the economy has been increasingly dominated by diamond mining, with industrial and gem diamonds representing almost half of the total value of exports. Most consumer and producer goods must be imported. Industry is limited and is centered primarily on the processing of beverages, textiles, footwear, plastic goods, bicycles, and soap. There are several lumber mills in operation.

Most of the country's exports are purchased by France, Israel, and the United States. Over half of the country's imports come from France. Other import suppliers include the countries of the European Common Market (notably West Germany and the Netherlands), the United States, Britain, and Senegal.

The Central African Empire has an extensive system of rivers, which are used to carry

CARL FRANK

CEREMONIAL DANCE is performed by young tribal women in the northern part of the Central African Empire.

a large percentage of its trade. There are about 11,000 miles (17,700 km) of roads, of which about 50 miles (80 km) are paved. Airports are located at Bangui, Berbérati, and Bouar, and secondary airports are found throughout the country.

The country has been plagued by a number of economic problems upon the solution of which its future prosperity largely depends. There is an increasingly serious agricultural problem. An estimated 93% of the country's population is normally engaged in some aspect of agriculture. Between 1960 and 1965, however, the production of grain cotton and fibers, long the staple export commodity, declined alarmingly as more than 100,000 persons involved in growing and processing cotton turned to other pursuits. The total number of acres devoted to cotton declined, as did the yield per acre. Late planting, progressive negligence of fields, shifts to more profitable cash crops such as coffee, excessive taxes and levies, and the siren call of the diamond mines were all factors in the downward trend.

The country's relatively sudden diamond boom, though immensely profitable, caused severe dislocations in the economy because it diverted thousands of farmers from subsistence and commercial farming to diamond mining. The government was unable to capitalize on the diamond boom; much of the production was smuggled out, and only a small percentage was mined by companies that the government could effectively control. Finally, neither the source beds nor the main producing areas had been fully surveyed. Therefore no one knew how long the diamond boom would last. With the government increasingly relying on revenue from diamond production, serious problems would arise if the supply were to diminish unpredictably.

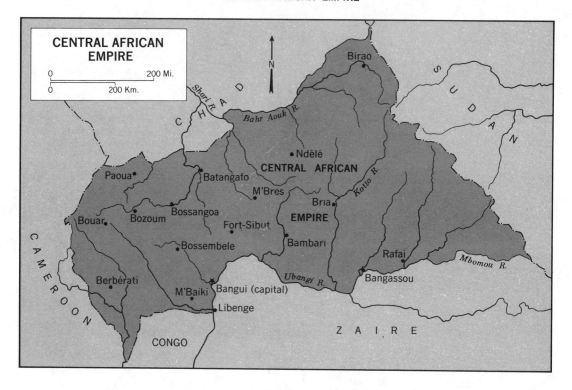

The government faces the problem of modernizing and developing its communications system. The relative geographical isolation of the country means that improved links with its neighbors and the sea are essential to its development. It was once endowed with the best north-south route in equatorial Africa, but the road system seriously degenerated after the country achieved independence in 1960. No new roads were opened, and irregular and poor maintenance caused extensive deterioration of the existing network.

Increased amounts of foreign aid were needed if the new republic's economy was to grow to any extent. Between 1958 and 1966 foreign aid to the Central African Republic amounted to over $60 million, of which France contributed about one third, the European Development Fund about one fourth, and the United States and West Germany the balance. Israel provided youth training in the Central African Republic's "Pioneer Youth" program, and Israelis performed tasks similar to those of the U. S. Peace Corps.

History and Government. Between the 14th and 17th centuries migrants from the Congo region began to arrive along the valley of the Ubangi River. Until the 19th century, the area of the present-day Central African Empire was also lightly populated by small Bantu-speaking groups that had originally moved south from the areas now forming Chad and Sudan. However, it was the slave trade that brought the country most of its population. Various groups fleeing the slave raiders came from the coastal areas, from the north, and from the Nile basin and settled in the interior, which slavers could reach only with great difficulty.

Between 1805 and 1830 the Baya, who came from Chad and Sudan, settled on the plains of the Shari and Logone rivers. They were followed by the Mandjia from the Congo, who populated the area between the Ubangi and Shari rivers. During this same period, the Banda fled from what is now Somaliland, where their numbers had been decimated by the slave trade, and moved upon the Mandjia and west toward the towns of Ouadda and Bambari as well as south along the valleys of the Chinko and M'Bari rivers. Thirty years later, beginning in 1860, massive migrations brought in the Azande, Lissongo, M'Baka, Mondjombo, Pamde, M'Bimo, and Kaja, all fleeing slave parties and seeking refuge in the dense forests. During the latter part of the 19th century, much of the northeast and eastern parts of the country fell under the sway of the Mahdist state, which controlled most of the areas of present Sudan and Chad from 1881 to 1898. At the turn of the century, when European colonial powers had begun to enter the area, two military adventurers, Rabeh and Senoussi, briefly ruled the savanna area of the country.

European Rule. The first French penetration of the area occurred in 1887. Four years later, Albert Dolisie founded Bangui on the northern bank of the Ubangi River. In 1910 the territory, known as Ubangi-Shari, was made a colony within French Equatorial Africa (an administrative federation based in Brazzaville, grouping Chad, Ubangi-Shari, Gabon, and the French Congo). French administration of Ubangi-Shari was marred by the forced labor practices of the concessionary companies and by various exploitative activities carried on without restraint from Paris. It was not until shortly after World War II that forced labor was finally abolished in French Equatorial Africa.

During World War II, Ubangi-Shari, together with the rest of French Equatorial Africa and French-administered Cameroon, rallied to the Free French cause. After the war, a complete change in French colonial policy and the crea-

Col. Eddine Ahmed Bokassa took the title emperor when he created the Central African Empire in December 1976.

tion of representative institutions stimulated the development of several rival political groups in the territory. After 1951 the party that dominated all others was the Mouvement pour l'Évolution Sociale de l'Afrique Noire (MESAN), founded by Barthélemy Boganda, a former priest turned politician.

Boganda became the head of the territory's first responsible government in 1957. He advocated the creation of a "United States of Latin Africa," which would unite the countries of French Equatorial Africa with Angola and the Belgian Congo. Ubangi-Shari voted to become a self-governing republic within the French Community in 1958. Boganda became the first president of the country, which had changed its name to the Central African Republic. Following Boganda's death in an airplane crash in March 1959, the government was taken over by David Dacko, his cousin and close associate.

Independence. President Dacko favored an independent federation of the four territories of French Equatorial Africa, but after Gabon and Congo (Brazzaville) decided against the project, he led his country to independence on Aug. 13, 1960. Between 1960 and 1966 the Dacko government found itself increasingly unable to cope with the new country's worsening economic situation, a gradual disintegration of MESAN (which had become the country's sole political party), and mounting inefficiency and corruption in the government.

During the night of Dec. 31, 1966–Jan. 1, 1967, Col. Jean-Bedel Bokassa, chief of the general staff of the Central African Republic, staged an almost bloodless coup d'etat and removed President Dacko and his government from power. Colonel Bokassa claimed the coup was necessary to forestall a leftist coup by a "people's

army" organized with the aid of Communist China; to prevent disorder; and to restore confidence in the government.

Shortly after the coup, Colonel Bokassa assumed the presidency. The constitution was abrogated, and the National Assembly was dissolved. Bokassa established a revolutionary council composed of civilians and military men and moved to consolidate his regime. He promised that full civilian rule would be restored at an indeterminate time in the future, when free elections might place honest and trustworthy men in office. President Bokassa instituted financial and administrative austerity measures designed to increase governmental efficiency. Among the new measures were those requiring ministers to work several days each month in the fields and those cutting back such bureaucratic perquisites as government-furnished automobiles and free housing.

The Central African Republic became a member of the United Nations in 1960. It also joined a number of African organizations and became an associate member of the European Common Market.

Colonel Bokassa, who changed his name from Jean-Bedel Bokassa to Eddine Ahmed Bokassa upon conversion to Islam, gradually assumed almost total control of the country as army chief of staff and head of 14 of the government's 16 ministries, with power to dissolve the National Assembly at will. On Dec. 4, 1976, it was announced that he had changed the name of the country to Central African Empire, that it would be a parliamentary monarchy, and that President Bokassa had become Emperor Bokassa I.

VICTOR T. LE VINE[*]
Washington University, St. Louis, Mo.

Further Reading: Ballard, John A., "Four Equatorial States," in Gwendolen M. Carter, ed., *National Unity and Regionalism in Eight African States* (Ithaca, N. Y., 1966); Thompson, Virginia, and Adloff, Richard, *The Emerging States of French Equatorial Africa* (Stanford, Calif., 1960); Le Vine, Victor T., "The Central African Republic: Insular Problems of an Inland State," *Africa Report*, vol. 10, no. 10, pp. 17–23 (Washington 1965).

MANIOC, one of the chief products of the Central African Empire, is a nutritious starch obtained by pounding the rootstocks of the cassava, as shown below.

LAKE ATITLÁN lies at the foot of San Pedro, one of Guatemala's inactive volcanoes.

CENTRAL AMERICA, as geographers use the term, is an isthmus that connects North America and South America. Some say it extends from Tehuantepec in Mexico to the border between Panama and Colombia; others, making a greater concession to political boundaries, say it includes the land from Guatemala through Panama. The isthmian residents themselves count as Central Americans only the people of the five republics of Guatemala, El Salvador, Honduras, Nicaragua, and Costa Rica, along with those of the colony called British Honduras, or Belize. The Panamanians, however, have been invited to join both the Organization of Central American States and the Central American Common Market, which consist of these five lands, so that eventually the indigenous and the geographical conceptions of Central America may come to be the same.

The Central American isthmus from Guatemala through Panama meanders somewhat, but runs generally from northwest to southeast. It lies between 7° and 19° N and between 77° and 93° W, but most of the quadrangle so bounded is covered by the Pacific Ocean and the Caribbean Sea. The air distance from the Guatemala border with Mexico to the Panama border with Colombia is about 1,150 miles (1,850 km). The width of the isthmus varies from 50 to 250 miles (80–400 km).

Central America for more than 10 million years has served as a pathway for plants and animals making their way from one American continent to the other; thus it has become a biological transition zone. For over 10,000 years the isthmus served as a land bridge for human beings migrating from North America to South America. Central American Indian groups 500 years ago spoke about 40 languages; over one fourth of the groups were descended from the stock of the ancient Maya, who had developed one of the very highest of the autochthonous civilizations of the Americas. The Spaniards, who conquered most of the Indians in the 16th century, brought the isthmus its first political unity (though Panama was soon separated from the remainder). The Africans who were then brought in as slaves or who later migrated from West Indian islands helped to make the population a three-way mix of peoples, varying considerably in ratios from one region to another.

Independence from Spain brought political disunity and conditions often bordering on anarchy, from which the isthmus is now making recovery. The Panama Canal and roads and railways connecting the two seas will soon be joined by a highway to restore disrupted continent-to-continent transport by land. Nations that have depended upon coffee, banana, and cotton exports are seeking to diversify their economies. The Central American Common Market and the Organization of Central American States both hold promise for new unity. But the future remains clouded by a remarkably high isthmian birthrate (the population increases by more than 3% each year) and by the reluctance of the more privileged classes to concede greater opportunities for the masses in each land.

1. The People

The attitudes displayed by one class toward another in Central American society bear no direct correspondence to either ancestry or physiognomy. Acceptance of one person by another is based upon the cultural traits of customs, behavior, and language rather than on physical appearance or actual racial background. Persons called Indians, it is true, may be assumed to have a high proportion of Indian blood. Those labeled *ladinos*, on the other hand, may also be individuals of Indian parentage who have simply chosen to desist from the Indian style of living and so to have become "Latins," or Europeans.

Races. The mixing of the races in Central America goes on apace, only a few of the ethnic groups holding themselves aloof from the process. The Spaniards who came here, as well as a sprinkling of other Europeans, North Americans, and Asians who followed them, have mingled quite freely, until their mestizo descendants far exceed the Caucasoids. Africans brought in as slaves during the colonial period have melted quite completely into the general stream (so that their presence in relatively large numbers in the past is not even noted in most demographic accounts of the region). *Zambo* (part Indian, part

180

Negro) immigrants or progeny from the colonial epoch, such as the Black Caribs and Miskitos, are still in separate evidence along the Caribbean coasts, the former in Belize, Guatemala, and Honduras, the latter in Nicaragua. Nineteenth and 20th century immigrants from the West Indies, some white but mostly Negro and mulatto, live chiefly along the same coasts and in the Panama Canal Zone, many of them speaking English and practicing Protestantism, but nevertheless involved in the merging process.

Everywhere except the Caribbean coast, the Canal Zone, and the highland central zone of Costa Rica, Indian ancestry predominates. In Costa Rica's so-called Meseta Central (Central Plateau), European physical features are most in evidence, though the Indian factor may be more properly considered submerged than eliminated. In the remaining portions of Panama, Costa Rica, Nicaragua, and Honduras, as well as the greater part of El Salvador, the people are nearly all mestizos, with an unknowable component of African ancestry in the mix. In western El Salvador and Guatemala the Indian race and culture remain very much as they were in pre-Columbian times. Here, in nearly every town, distinctions are made between Indian and *ladino* families, with the former nearly always the more disadvantaged.

Languages and Religions. Guatemalan Indians speak 11 languages of the Mayan stock. Most notable among their groups are the Quiché, the Mam, and the Cakchiquel. Their religion is a blend of Spanish Catholicism and pre-Columbian paganism, expressed in a variety of degrees. Yet even in Guatemala the Spanish language and a purer Spanish Catholicism now prevail, the proportion of *indígenas* (Indians who have not adopted a European way of life) in the population having dropped from 54% in 1950 to 43% in the mid-1960's. Other Central American Indian languages are on the verge of extinction where they are not already lost, except for those of the *zambo* Black Caribs and Miskitos and of some Chibcha-related peoples of Costa Rica and Panama, the most distinctive of whom are the San Blas Cuna east of the Panama Canal.

Spanish is the language of the Europeanized isthmian inhabitant as Spanish Catholicism is in the great majority of cases his religion. Religious toleration is common (only Costa Rica retains a tie between church and state), and Protestantism is found as a small but growing minority in every land.

Economic and Social Conditions. Greater than racial or religious problems in this isthmus are those of the poor who form the masses on very hand. Almost all Central America's rural inhabitants suffer from the great economic disparity between themselves and the very few who own most of the land. Every government has undertaken some kind of land reform program, turning over unused or expropriated farms to poor *campesinos* (peasants) on easy terms. A few states have also experimented with minimum-wage legislation for agricultural work. The wages are too low, however, and the land reform programs too slow to affect the lives of many. The minority of persons who have moved into cities to take up manufacturing, commercial, construction, or service occupations have done better than their rural countrymen, especially with new growth sponsored by the Central American Common Market since 1961. However, in most cases even

they must live on extremely small incomes, their lot only slightly ameliorated by inadequate urban housing projects.

The problems of the poor in four of the isthmian countries are the problems of the uneducated. In the realm of learning, Costa Rica and Panama have moved far ahead, until fewer than one fifth of their people remain unlettered. In the other four republics, the lack of schools and high dropout rates where there are schools have produced illiteracy rates of from one half to nearly three quarters of the adults. Since the 1940's, the governments concerned have taken measures to alleviate this condition, though Guatemala and Nicaragua have lagged behind. Appropriations for education now form one fifth to one fourth of the budget in each isthmian country. But it will be some time before Guatemala's *indígenas*, nine tenths of whom over the age of seven have not attended first grade, catch up with Costa Rica's and Panama's 94%-literate urbanites.

Central America's rapid population growth, further encouraged by improved sanitation and the conquest of diseases, remains a threat to every educational and economic reform program. Yet these lands (excepting possibly El Salvador) were not overcrowded in the 1960's, and there remains the hope that a new willingness to develop their own resources may provide the impetus needed for a much better life for the average isthmian inhabitant.

2. The Land and Natural Resources

The Central American environment is determined by its position in the low northerly latitudes, its tendency as an isthmus to meander, the warm waters on either side, and its plenitude of mountains.

Climate. The relative nearness of all isthmian terrain to warm ocean waters means that in the season when the sun's overhead action is strong (generally from May to October), most regions receive very ample rain. On the Caribbean side, especially where the winding coast receives the full impact of northeasterly trade winds, there is heavy precipitation throughout most of the year. Where the mountains run high, temperatures become cool, but only moderately so; snow is very uncommon. The interior of the isthmus tends to be drier than either coast, and here a few zones are quite arid.

Physical Features. Some of the mountains are very ancient; most of those in Guatemala, northern Nicaragua, and Honduras are believed to have stood long ago with those of the state of Chiapas, Mexico, as the backbone of a large Middle American island. Others in all parts of the isthmus are geologically young. Most notable of them are the dozens of volcanoes, ranging in height from 2,776 to 13,816 feet (846 to 4,210 meters), many still active from time to time. Where the isthmus is broader, the volcanoes are situated on the Pacific side, but they continue into slender Costa Rica and Panama. In Nicaragua there lies a trough of lowland from the Gulf of Fonseca through Lakes Managua and Nicaragua to the lakes' San Juan River drainage on the Caribbean side. Before the digging of the Panama Canal at the point where the isthmus is most narrow, many engineers favored the Nicaraguan low-altitude trough for a canal.

Plant and Animal Life. The North American pine family, having come to Nicaragua but never crossed its trough, illustrates Central

America's position as a biological transition zone. Many plants (even some subarctic species found only on mountain peaks) have apparently battled their way through the isthmus as easily as most of the animals, and are now found on both of its extremities in great profusion.

Mangrove and palm trees are found in abundance along both shores of the isthmus. On the so-called Mosquito Coast (the Caribbean lowland of Nicaragua and northeastern Honduras) there is much grassland studded with pines. Elsewhere, the Caribbean side is covered with tropical rain forest, while the Pacific side generally maintains a much thinner coverage of deciduous woods. In middle altitudes north of the Nicaraguan trough, uncultivated land is usually covered with mixed forests in which oak and pine trees predominate. In the same altitudes in Costa Rica and Panama are found some of the same woods, but without the pine. Only a few zones in Costa Rica and Guatemala reach to alpine meadows above the tree line. A few districts in Guatemala and Honduras are dry enough for a show of cactus.

Migrations of the animals, especially the mammals, are better understood than migrations of the plants and are very complicated. From South America, for example, the isthmian fauna is enriched by opossums, porcupines, and armadillos, which have reached the United States; by agoutis, anteaters, and spider and howler monkeys, which have stopped in Mexico; by tree sloths and capuchin monkeys, which have gone no farther than Honduras; and by marmosets, which extend only through Panama. From North America, foxes and also jaguars, mountain lions, and other cats have reached the southern continent, and coyotes are found today wherever the northern-oriented Indian lived in pre-Columbian times. Central America's tapirs and two species of peccaries, as well as its raccoon-related coatis and kinkajous, came originally from the north, but are now better known to the isthmus and South America. Migration has also brought to the isthmus a great variety of birds, reptiles, and amphibians. In contrast, freshwater fishes are much underrepresented, because their migration was blocked by high land and salt water.

Economic Potential. Gold, silver, lead, zinc, and copper have been among Central America's exports; some nickel, coal, and iron ore have been found; and nearly every one of the states has been engaged in a search for petroleum. But in all likelihood, the chief source of Central America's income will remain its products of forest and field. Mahogany, pine, and cedar exports are important from several zones on the Caribbean; their development calls for wise, conservation-minded planning. Agricultural industry, on the other hand, seems to offer new prospects both that the nations will be able to feed themselves more adequately and that there will be an increase in the quantity and variety of their exports. When warm-weather pests and diseases are controlled, Central America's combination of sun, rain, and fine soils can produce some of the world's best coffee, bananas, and cotton, along with a number of other negotiable items.

3. History

If farming and related activities remain Central America's greatest contribution in the world to come, such an occurrence will be but an extension of the isthmus' past history. The Span-

iards who ruled here looked for gold and silver where they could be found, but grew wealthy chiefly from exports of cacao and indigo. And long before their day, both highland and lowland Maya, as well as many of their neighbors, depended on maize for a living, valued the cacao bean and the chocolate beverage derived from it, and learned how to cultivate chayote, papaya, and avocado.

The Maya. These people were the first to leave an identifiable mark on Central American history. They lived in the northwestern end of the isthmus, excelling other Western Hemisphere groups in writing, mathematics, and astronomy, and leaving witness of their skill in architecture, sculpture, and painting. Their period of highest magnificence, it now seems likely (though the matter of Maya-Christian date correlations has not been finally settled), was from the 3d century A. D. through the 9th. Until more of their writing can be deciphered, single theories regarding their decline seem premature. It is likely that great movements of peoples and a number of other factors were involved. In any event, the peoples of the isthmus continued farming as the Maya had and as many do today.

The Colonial Period. The first European vessel believed to have sailed along isthmian shores was that of Rodrigo de Bastidas, off eastern Panama in 1501. In the following year, Columbus traced most of the Caribbean coast. In 1509, Spanish settlers arrived in Panama; from there, Santo Domingo, and Mexico, they moved into other Central American regions in 1524.

For a time, each province pertained to an *audiencia* (court) situated in the capital from which it had been conquered: Guatemala to Mexico City, Honduras to Santo Domingo, Nicaragua to the *audiencia* of Panama organized in 1538. A short-lived Audiencia de los Confines (1543–1565) included all the isthmus at first, but Panama was removed from its jurisdiction in 1550 and given its own ruling body again in 1567. The Audiencia de Guatemala (1570–1821) included the land from Costa Rica through Chiapas. Here many Spaniards became wealthy through the chiefly agricultural labor of their Indian tributaries and Negro slaves. And here, with the acculturation of the Indians toward European ways and the blending of three races, evolved the way of living of most Central Americans of today.

Panama retained its separate *audiencia* until 1751, after which it was ruled from Bogotá, Colombia, until 1903. Belize, the Mosquito Coast, and the Bay Islands, unoccupied by the Spaniards, came under British control in the 17th and 18th centuries; the latter two were finally relinquished in 1859–1860, but Belize was elevated to the status of a British colony (British Honduras) in 1862. British Hondurans and Panamanians have thus remained outside the mainstream of Central American development, though both have shown interest in new patterns for isthmian integration.

Independence. Central America (aside from these marginal regions and Chiapas, which adhered to Mexico) attempted unity after its 1821 proclamation of independence from Spain, and failed. Neither Manuel José Arce, first president (1825–1828) of the federation of Central American states, nor Francisco Morazán, the second (1830–1839), could contain the dissension and local jealousies and patriotisms. In

CENTRAL AMERICA

AGRICULTURE, INDUSTRY and RESOURCES

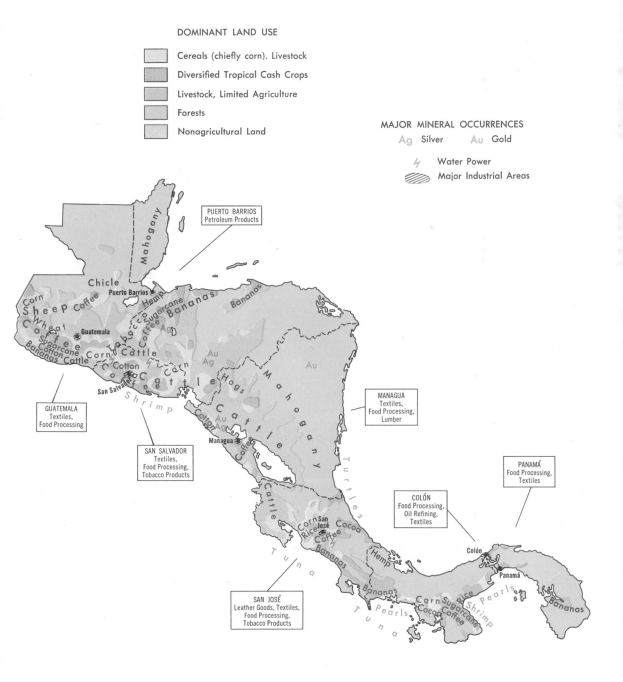

DOMINANT LAND USE

- Cereals (chiefly corn), Livestock
- Diversified Tropical Cash Crops
- Livestock, Limited Agriculture
- Forests
- Nonagricultural Land

MAJOR MINERAL OCCURRENCES

Ag Silver   Au Gold

⚡ Water Power

Major Industrial Areas

PUERTO BARRIOS
Petroleum Products

GUATEMALA
Textiles,
Food Processing

SAN SALVADOR
Textiles,
Food Processing,
Tobacco Products

SAN JOSÉ
Leather Goods, Textiles,
Food Processing,
Tobacco Products

MANAGUA
Textiles,
Food Processing,
Lumber

PANAMÁ
Food Processing,
Textiles

COLÓN
Food Processing,
Oil Refining,
Textiles

© Copyright HAMMOND INCORPORATED, Maplewood, N. J.

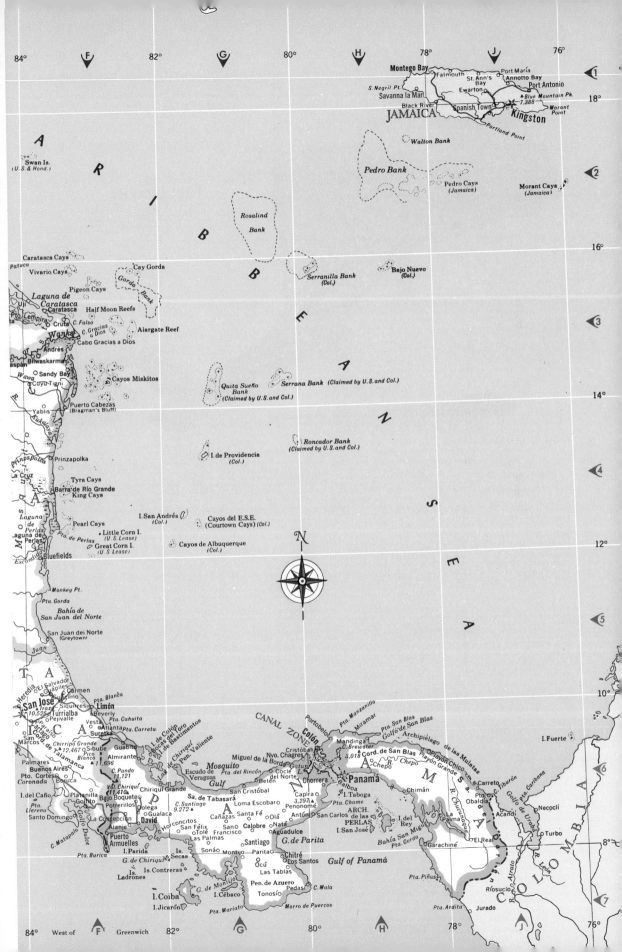

CENTRAL AMERICA

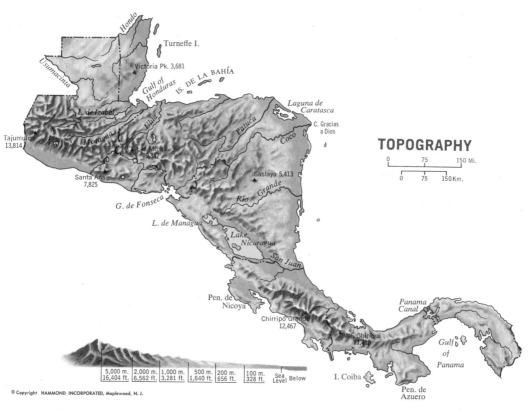

TOPOGRAPHY

| 0 | 75 | 150 Mi. |
| 0 | 75 | 150 Km. |

| 5,000 m. | 2,000 m. | 1,000 m. | 500 m. | 200 m. | 100 m. | Sea | Below |
| 16,404 ft. | 6,562 ft. | 3,281 ft. | 1,640 ft. | 656 ft. | 328 ft. | Level | |

© Copyright HAMMOND INCORPORATED, Maplewood, N. J.

BELIZE
Total Population, 116,000

CITIES and TOWNS

Belize City (cap.), 32,867 ....C 2
Belize City, *45,572 ....C 2
Benque Viejo, 1,607 ....C 2
Cayo, 1,890 ....C 2
Corozal, 3,171 ....C 1
Hill Bank, 78 ....C 2
Monkey River, 417 ....C 2
Orange Walk, 2,157 ....C 1
Punta Gorda, 1,789 ....C 2
San José, 365 ....C 2
San Pedro, 170 ....D 2
Stann Creek, 5,287 ....C 2

OTHER FEATURES

Ambergris (cay), †572 ....D 1
Belize (river) ....C 2
Bokel (cay) ....D 2
Cockscomb (mts.) ....C 2
Corker (cay), †360 ....D 2
Glovers (reef) ....D 2
Half Moon (cay) ....D 2
Hondo (river) ....C 1
Honduras (gulf) ....D 2
Mauger (cay) ....D 2
New (river) ....C 2
Saint Georges (cay), †34 ....D 2
Sarstún (river) ....C 3
Turneffe (isl.), 99 ....D 2

CANAL ZONE
Total Population, 55,600

CITIES and TOWNS

Balboa, 3,139 ....H 6
Cristóbal, 817 ....G 6

COSTA RICA
Total Population, 1,700,000

CITIES and TOWNS

Alajuela, 19,620 ....E 6
Atenas, 963 ....E 6
Atlanta ....F 6
Bagaces, 1,175 ....E 5
Beverly ....F 6
Boruca, †1,049 ....F 6
Buenos Aires, †4,624 ....F 6
Cañas, 2,991 ....E 5

Carmen ....F 5
Cartago, 18,084 ....F 6
Chomes, ‡1,991 ....E 5
Ciudad Quesada, 3,696 ....E 5
El Salvador ....F 5
Esparta, 2,860 ....E 5
Filadelfia, 1,574 ....E 5
Golfito, 6,859 ....F 6
Grecia, 4,862 ....E 5
Guácimo, 5,731 ....F 5
Guápiles, 983 ....F 5
Heredia, 19,249 ....E 5
Las Juntas, 827 ....E 5
Liberia, 6,087 ....E 5
Limón, 19,432 ....F 6
Miramar, 1,122 ....E 5
Nicoya, 3,196 ....E 5
Orotina, 1,749 ....E 5
Palmares, 1,529 ....E 5
Paquera ....F 6
Paraíso, 4,427 ....F 6
Pejivalle ....F 6
Platanilla ....F 6
Playa Bonita ....E 6
Puerto Cortés, 1,757 ....F 6
Puntarenas, 19,582 ....E 6
Quepos, 1,858 ....E 6
San Ignacio, 315 ....E 6
San José (cap.), 177,969 ....F 5
San José, *339,094 ....F 5
San Marcos, 411 ....E 6
San Ramón, 6,444 ....E 5
Santa Cruz, 3,849 ....E 5
Santa Rosa, ‡1,750 ....E 5
Santo Domingo, 3,333 ....F 6
Sibube ....F 6
Siquirres, 2,157 ....F 5
Turrialba, 8,629 ....F 6
Vesta ....F 6

OTHER FEATURES

Blanca (point) ....F 5
Blanco (cape) ....E 6
Blanco (mt.) ....F 6
Burica (point) ....F 6
Cahuita (point) ....F 6
Caño (isl.) ....F 6
Carreta (point) ....F 6
Chirripó Grande (mt.) ....F 6
Coronada (bay) ....F 6
Cuilapa Miravalles (volcano)......E 5
Dulce (gulf) ....F 6
Góngora (mt.) ....E 5
Guionos (point) ....E 6
Irazú (mt.) ....F 6
Judas (point) ....E 6

Llerena (point) ....F 6
Matapalo (cape) ....F 6
Nicoya (gulf) ....E 6
Nicoya (pen.) ....E 6
Papagayo (gulf) ....E 5
Salinas (bay) ....D 5
San Juan (river) ....E, F 5
Santa Elena (cape) ....D 5
Talamanca (range) ....F 6
Velas (cape) ....D 5

EL SALVADOR
Total Population, 3,151,000

CITIES and TOWNS

Acajútla, 3,662 ....B 4
Ahuachapán, 13,261 ....B 4
Atiquizaya, 6,346 ....C 3
Chalatenango, 5,332 ....C 3
Chinameca, 5,778 ....C 4
Cojutepeque, 11,415 ....C 4
Estanzuelas, 2,083 ....C 4
Ilobasco, 4,716 ....C 4
Intipucá, 2,401 ....D 4
Jucuarán, 1,103 ....C 4
La Libertad, 4,943 ....C 4
La Palma, 1,464 ....C 3
La Unión, 11,432 ....D 4
Metapán, 3,435 ....C 3
Nueva San Salvador (Santa
   Tecla), 27,039 ....C 4
Puerto de la Concordia...............C 4
San Francisco Gotera, 3,668......C 4
San Miguel, 40,432 ....D 4
San Salvador (cap.), 317,570......C 4
Santa Ana, 72,839 ....C 4
Santa Rosa de Lima, 4,618........D 4
Santa Tecla, 27,039 ....C 4
San Vicente, 15,433 ....C 4
Sensuntepeque, 5,063 ....C 4
Sonsonate, 23,666 ....C 4
Suchitoto, 4,447 ....C 4
Texistepeque, 1,339 ....C 3
Usulután, 12,467 ....C 4
Zacatecoluca, 12,232 ....C 4

OTHER FEATURES

Fonseca (gulf) ....D 4
Güija (lake) ....C 3
Lempa (river) ....C 4
Remedios (point) ....B 4
Santa Ana (mt.) ....C 4

GUATEMALA
Total Population, 4,864,000

CITIES and TOWNS

Amatitlán, 12,225 ....B 3
Antigua, 13,576 ....B 3
Asunción Mita, 6,341 ....C 3
Cahabón, 939 ....C 3
Chahal, 323 ....C 3
Chajul, 4,187 ....B 3
Champerico, 3,823 ....A 3
Chichicastenango, 2,099 ....B 3
Chimaltenango, 9,077 ....B 3
Chinaja ....B 2
Chiquimula, 14,760 ....C 3
Chisec, 812 ....B 3
Coatepeque, 13,657 ....A 3
Cobán, 9,073 ....B 3
Comalapa, 9,202 ....B 3
Cubulco, 1,676 ....B 3
Cuilapa, 3,657 ....B 3
Cuilco, 728 ....B 3
Dolores, 630 ....C 2
El Cambio ....C 2
El Porvenir ....B 2
El Progreso, 3,458 ....B 3
Escuintla, 24,832 ....B 3
Flores, 1,503 ....C 2
Gualán, 4,425 ....C 3
Guatemala (cap.), 572,937 ....B 3
Huehuetenango, 10,185 ....B 3
Ipala, 3,190 ....C 3
Izabal ....C 3
Iztapa, 751 ....B 4
Jacaltenango, 3,873 ....B 3
Jalapa, 10,035 ....B 3
Jutiapa, 7,747 ....B 3
La Gomera, 1,397 ....B 3
La Libertad, 770 ....B 2
Livingston, 3,026 ....C 3
Los Amates, 1,131 ....C 3
Masagua, 1,100 ....B 3
Matías de Gálvez ....C 3
Mazatenango, 19,506 ....B 3
Momostenango, 3,148 ....B 3
Morales, 1,710 ....C 3
Nejapa ....B 3
Ocós, 576 ....A 3
Panzós, 1,803 ....C 3
Puerto Barrios, 22,242 ....C 3
Quezaltenango, 45,195 ....B 3
Quezaltepeque, 2,578 ....C 3
Rabinal, 4,155 ....B 3
Retalhuleu, 14,366 ....B 3
Río Hondo, 1,300 ....C 3
Sacapulas, 1,407 ....B 3
Salamá, 4,442 ....B 3
San Andrés, 939 ....B 2
San Felipe, 2,916 ....B 3

*City and suburbs.   †Population of sub-district.   ‡Population of district.

BELIZE: Total pop.—1970 off. est.; capital (& with suburbs)—1968 off. est.; other pops—1960 final census. **CANAL ZONE:** Total, cap., 1967 off. est.; other pops—1960 final census. **COSTA RICA:** Total pop.—1968 off. est.; cap. (& with suburbs)—1965 off. est.; other pops— 1963 final census. **EL SALVADOR:** Total pop.—1967 off. est.; capital—1966 off. est.; other pops—1961 final census. **GUATEMALA:** Total pop.—1967 off. est.; other pops—1964 census. **HONDURAS:** 1968 off. est. **NICARAGUA:** Total pop.—1966 off. est.; cap.—1965 off. est.; other pops—1963 final census. **PANAMA:** Total, cap. & Colón—1970 OE; other pops—1960 final census.

San José, 5,771 .... B 4
San Juan de Dios .... B 2
San Luis, 763 .... C 2
San Luis Jilotepeque, 5,795 .... C 3
San Marcos, 5,569 .... B 3
San Martín Jilotepeque, 2,806 .... B 3
San Mateo Ixtatán, 2,892 .... B 3
San Miguel .... C 2
San Pedro Carchá, 3,966 .... B 3
Santa Ana, 239 .... C 2
Santa Ana Mixtán .... B 4
Santa Cruz del Quiché, 6,472 .... B 3
Santa Rosa de Lima, 734 .... B 3
Sipacate .... B 4
Sololá, 3,957 .... B 3
Tacaná, 900 .... A 3
Tejutla, 973 .... B 3
Totonicapán, 7,292 .... B 3
Yaloch .... C 2
Zacapa, 11,173 .... C 3

OTHER FEATURES

Atitlán (lake) .... B 3
Atitlán (volcano) .... B 3
Azul (river) .... C 2
Chixoy (river) .... B 2
Dulce (Izabal) (lake) .... C 3
Güija (lake) .... C 3
Honduras (gulf) .... D 2
Izabal (lake) .... C 3
Minas (mts.) .... C 3
Motagua (river) .... C 3
Pasión (river) .... B 2
Petén-Itzá (lake) .... B 2
San Pedro (river) .... B 2
Sarstún (river) .... C 3
Tacaná (volcano) .... A 3
Tajumulco (volcano) .... B 3
Tres Puntas (cape) .... C 3
Usumacinta (river) .... B 2

HONDURAS

Total Population, 2,412,916

CITIES and TOWNS

Ahuás .... E 3
Amapala, 3,491 .... D 4
Balana .... E 3
Balfate, 602 .... D 3
Belén, 201 .... C 3
Brus Laguna, 1,247 .... E 3
Caratasca .... F 3
Catacamas, 4,751 .... E 3
Cedros, 1,177 .... D 3
Chichicaste .... E 3
Choloma, 6,678 .... C 3
Choluteca, 17,350 .... D 4
Colorado .... D 3
Comayagua, 11,247 .... D 3
Comayagüela .... D 3
Concepción de María, 653 .... D 4
Concordia, 644 .... D 3
Copán, 2,190 .... C 3
Corquín, 2,817 .... C 3
Cruta .... F 3
Danlí, 8,242 .... D 3
Donel .... E 3
El Dulce Nombre, 145 .... E 3
El Paraíso, Copán, 1,787 .... C 3
El Paraíso, El Paraíso, 5,758 .... D 4
El Porvenir, 529 .... D 3
El Progreso, 8,718 .... D 3
El Triunfo, 2,136 .... D 4
Goascorán, 1,184 .... D 4
Gracias, 2,484 .... C 3
Guaimaca, 2,620 .... D 3
Gualpatanta .... E 3
Guanaja, 1,253 .... E 2
Guarita, 599 .... C 3
Guayape, 610 .... D 3
Iriona, 119 .... E 2
Jacaleapa, 992 .... D 3
Jesús de Otoro, 2,775 .... C 3
Jutiapa, 1,711 .... D 3
Juticalpa, 7,912 .... D 3
La Ceiba, 33,934 .... D 3
La Concepción .... E 3
La Esperanza, 2,000 .... C 3
La Guata, 281 .... D 3
La Paz, 5,542 .... D 3
La Protección, 820 .... D 3
Lauterique, 272 .... D 4
Limón, 1,934 .... E 3
Manto, 943 .... D 3
Marcala, 1,968 .... C 3
Melcher .... D 3
Morazán, 3,924 .... D 3
Morocelí, 1,472 .... D 3
Nacaome, 4,376 .... D 4
Namasigüe, 1,024 .... D 4
Naranjito, 3,291 .... C 3
Nueva Armenia, 866 .... D 4
Nueva Ocotepeque, 4,608 .... C 3
Olanchito, 5,008 .... D 3
Omoa, 1,384 .... C 3
Paso Real .... E 3
Patuca .... E 3
Pespire, 1,758 .... D 4
Puerto Castilla .... D 3
Puerto Cortés, 21,600 .... D 2
Roatán, 1,883 .... D 2
Sabanagrande, 1,657 .... D 4
Salado .... D 3
San Esteban, 763 .... D 3
San Francisco, 1,122 .... D 3
San Francisco de la Paz, 1,971 .... D 3
San Juan de Flores, 1,174 .... D 3
San Luis, 2,631 .... C 3
San Marcos, 1,576 .... C 3
San Pedro Sula, 90,538 .... C 3
San Pedro Zacapa, 765 .... D 3
Santa Bárbara, 6,129 .... C 3
Santa Cruz de Yojoa, 1,833 .... D 3
Santa Rita, 3,976 .... D 3
Santa Rosa de Aguán, 1,701 .... E 2
Santa Rosa de Copán, 9,109 .... C 3
Siguatepeque, 9,462 .... D 3
Sinuapa, 822 .... C 3
Sonaguera, 1,344 .... D 3
Sulaco, 1,071 .... D 3
Tegucigalpa (cap.), 205,560 .... D 3
Tegucigalpa, *239,930 .... D 3
Tela, 14,103 .... D 3
Teupasenti, 829 .... D 3
Tocoa, 1,605 .... E 3
Trinidad, 2,817 .... C 3
Trujillo, 4,656 .... E 3
Uji .... F 3
Utila, 967 .... D 2
Villa de San Antonio, 2,287 .... D 3
Yocón, 269 .... D 3
Yorito, 869 .... D 3
Yoro, 4,129 .... D 3
Yuscarán, 1,854 .... D 4

OTHER FEATURES

Aguán (river) .... D 3
Bahía (isls.), 9,702 .... D 2
Bonacca (Guanaja) (isl.), 2,039 .... E 2
Brus (lagoon) .... E 2
Camarón (cape) .... E 2
Caratasca (cays) .... F 2
Caratasca (lagoon) .... F 3
Choluteca (river) .... D 4
Coco (river) .... E 3
Colón (mts.) .... E 3
Esperanza (mts.) .... E 3
Falso (cape) .... F 3
Fonseca (gulf) .... D 4
Gorda (bank) .... F 3
Gorda (cay) .... F 3
Guanaja (isl.), 2,039 .... E 2
Half Moon (reefs) .... F 3
Honduras (cape) .... E 2
Honduras (gulf) .... D 2
Patuca (point) .... E 3
Patuca (river) .... E 3
Paulaya (river) .... E 3
Pigeon (cays) .... F 3
Pija (mts.) .... D 3
Roatán (isl.), 6,552 .... D 2
San Pablo, Sierra de (mts.) .... E 3
Segovia (Coco) (river) .... F 3
Sico (river) .... E 3
Sulaco (river) .... D 3
Swan (isls.), 28 .... F 2
Ulúa (river) .... D 3
Utila (isl.), 1,111 .... D 2
Vivario (cays) .... F 3
Wanks (Coco) (river) .... F 3
Yojoa (lake) .... D 3

NICARAGUA

Total Population, 1,783,000

CITIES and TOWNS

Acoyapa, 1,755 .... E 5
Alamikamba .... E 4
Barra de Río Grande .... F 4
Bilwaskarma .... F 3
Bluefields, 9,292 .... F 4
Boaco, 4,656 .... E 4
Bocay .... E 3
Bonanza, 2,175 .... E 4
Bragman's Bluff (Puerto Cabezas), 5,983 .... F 3
Cabo Gracias a Dios, 511 .... F 3
Camoapa, 2,617 .... E 4
Chichigalpa, 6,657 .... D 4
Chinandega, 22,409 .... D 4
Ciudad Darío, 3,851 .... D 4
Comalapa, 441 .... E 4
Condega, 2,229 .... D 4
Corinto, 9,177 .... D 4
Cuicuina .... E 4
Cuyu Tigni .... F 3
Diriamba, 10,499 .... D 5
El Gallo .... E 4
El Jicaral, 239 .... D 4
El Jícaro, 1,114 .... D 4
El Sauce, 2,944 .... D 4
El Viejo, 7,190 .... D 4
Esquipulas, 1,636 .... E 4
Estelí, 12,742 .... D 4
Granada, 28,507 .... E 5
Greytown (San Juan del Norte), 199 .... F 5
Jalapa, 1,368 .... E 4
Jinotega, 7,693 .... E 4
Jinotepe, 9,113 .... D 5
Juigalpa, 6,146 .... E 4
La Conquista, 364 .... D 5
La Cruz, 155 .... E 4
Laguna de Perlas .... F 4
La Libertad, 1,355 .... E 4
La Paz Central, 4,431 .... D 4
La Paz de Oriente, 828 .... E 5
La Trinidad, 2,340 .... D 4
León, 44,053 .... D 4
Managua (capital), 262,047 .... D 4
Managua, *274,278 .... D 4
Masatepe, 4,831 .... D 5
Masaya, 23,402 .... D 5
Matagalpa, 15,030 .... E 4
Mateare, 1,254 .... D 4
Morrito, 324 .... E 5
Moyogalpa, 1,252 .... E 5
Muleculus .... E 4
Muy Muy, 691 .... E 4
Muy Muy Viejo .... E 4
Nagarote, 5,241 .... D 4
Nandaime, 5,051 .... E 5
Ocotal, 4,339 .... D 4
Ocotal .... E 4
Palsagua .... E 4
Playa Grande .... D 4
Poneloya, 995 .... D 4
Poteca .... E 4
Prinzapolka, 230 .... F 4
Puerto Cabezas, 5,983 .... F 3
Quilalí, 710 .... E 4
Rama (El Rama), 600 .... E 4
Rivas, 7,721 .... E 5
San Carlos, 1,547 .... E 5
Sandy Bay .... F 3
San Francisco .... E 5
San Jorge, 1,657 .... E 5
San Juan del Norte, 199 .... F 5
San Juan del Sur, 2,103 .... D 5
San Miguelito, 885 .... E 5
San Pedro .... E 4
San Rafael del Norte, 1,298 .... E 4
San Rafael del Sur, 2,411 .... D 5
San Ramón, 436 .... E 4
Santa Cruz .... E 4
Santo Domingo, 1,779 .... E 4
Santo Tomás, 1,530 .... E 5
Siuna, 3,743 .... E 4
Somotillo, 1,435 .... D 4
Somoto, 3,967 .... D 4
Telpaneca, 1,019 .... D 4
Terrabona, 690 .... E 4
Teustepe, 764 .... E 4
Tipitapa, 3,600 .... E 4
Tunki .... E 4
Waspán, 973 .... E 3
Yablis .... F 4

OTHER FEATURES

Alargate (reef) .... F 3
Coco (river) .... E 3
Cosegüina (point) .... D 4
Dariense (range) .... E 4
Dipilto (range) .... D 4
Escondido (river) .... F 4
Fonseca (gulf) .... D 4
Gorda (point) .... F 5
Gracias a Dios (cape) .... F 3
Grande (river) .... E 4
Huapí (mts.) .... E 4
Isabelia (range) .... E 4
King (cays) .... F 4
Kukalaya (river) .... F 4
Managua (lake) .... E 4
Miskito (cays) .... F 3
Monkey (point) .... F 5
Nicaragua (lake) .... E 5
Ometepe (isl.), 12,556 .... E 5
Pearl (cays) .... F 4
Perlas (lagoon) .... F 4
Prinzapolca (river) .... F 4
Salinas (bay) .... D 5
San Juan (river) .... E, F 5
San Juan del Norte (bay) .... F 5
Segovia (Coco) (river) .... E 3
Solentiname (isls.) .... E 5
Tuma (river) .... E 4
Tyra (cays) .... F 4
Wanks (Coco) (river) .... F 3
Waspuk (river) .... E 3
Wawa (river) .... F 3
Zapatera (isl.) .... E 5

PANAMA

Total Population, 1,463,500

CITIES and TOWNS

Aguadulce, 6,010 .... G 6
Alanje, 650 .... F 6
Almirante, 3,521 .... F 6
Antón, 2,684 .... G 6
Bajo Boquete, 2,611 .... F 6
Belén, 39 .... G 6
Bocas del Toro, 2,459 .... F 6
Calobre, 524 .... G 6
Cañazas, 1,105 .... G 6
Capira, 1,067 .... G 6
Carreto, 181 .... J 6
Chepo, 1,664 .... H 6
Chimán, 535 .... H 6
Chiriquí Grande, 98 .... F 6
Chitré, 9,120 .... G 7
Chorrera, 13,696 .... H 6
Coclé del Norte, 204 .... G 6
Colón, 66,300 .... H 6
David, 22,924 .... F 6
Dolega, 831 .... F 6
El Real, 1,071 .... J 6
Garachiné, 1,326 .... H 6
Guabito, 734 .... F 6
Gualaca, 1,380 .... F 6
Horconcitos, 1,079 .... F 6
La Concepción, 6,532 .... F 6
La Palma, 1,885 .... H 6
Las Palmas, 753 .... G 6
Las Tablas, 3,504 .... G 7
Loma Escobar (La Pintada), 848 .... G 6
Los Santos, 3,165 .... G 7
Mandinga, 51 .... H 6
Miguel de la Borda, 179 .... G 6
Miramar, 153 .... H 6
Montijo, 753 .... G 6
Natá, 2,319 .... G 6
Nuevo Chagres, 336 .... G 6
Ocú, 1,617 .... G 7
Olá, 149 .... G 6
Panamá (cap.), 405,300 .... H 6
Parita, 1,464 .... G 6
Pedasí, 988 .... G 7
Penonomé, 4,266 .... G 6
Playón Chico, 1,178 .... H 6
Playón Grande, 78 .... H 6
Portobelo, 591 .... H 6
Potrerillos, 1,082 .... F 6
Puerto Armuelles, 10,712 .... F 6
Puerto Obaldía, 402 .... J 6
San Carlos, 415 .... H 6
San Cristóbal, 123 .... G 6
San Félix, 608 .... G 6
San Francisco, 800 .... G 6
Santa Fé, 446 .... G 6
Santiago, 8,746 .... G 6
Soná, 3,176 .... G 6
Tocumen .... H 6
Tolé, 811 .... G 6
Tonosí, 559 .... G 7

OTHER FEATURES

Azuero (pen.) .... G 7
Bastimentos (isl.), 376 .... G 6
Brewster (mt.) .... H 6
Burica (point) .... F 6
Cébaco (isl.), 238 .... G 7
Chepo (river) .... H 6
Chiriquí (gulf) .... F 7
Chiriquí (lagoon) .... G 6
Chiriquí (volcano) .... F 6
Chucunaque (river) .... J 6
Coiba (isl.), 176 .... F 7
Colón (isl.), 3,315 .... G 6
Contreras (isls.) .... F 7
Darién (mts.) .... J 6
Escudo de Veraguas (isl.) .... G 6
Gatun (lake) .... G 6
Gorda (point) .... H 6
Jicarón (isl.) .... F 7
Ladrones (isls.) .... F 7
Manzanillo (point) .... H 6
Montijo (gulf) .... G 7
Mosquito (gulf) .... G 6
Mulatas (arch.) .... J 6
Panamá (gulf) .... H 7
Pando (mt.) .... F 6
Parida (isl.), 79 .... F 6
Parita (gulf) .... G 6
Perlas (arch.), 2,872 .... H 6
Puercos (prom.) .... H 7
Rey (isl.) .... H 6
Rincón (point) .... G 6
San Blas (gulf) .... H 6
San Blas (range) .... H 6
San José (isl.) .... H 6
San Miguel (bay) .... H 6
Santiago (mt.) .... G 6
Secas (isls.) .... G 7
Tabasará (mts.) .... G 6
Taboga (isl.), 928 .... H 6
Tiburón (cape) .... J 6
Valiente (pen.) .... G 6

CENTRAL AMERICA

Great Corn (isl.), 1,896 .... F 4
Guardian (bank) .... D 6
Little Corn (isl.) .... F 4
Mosquito Coast (reg.) .... E 4
Rosalind (bank) .... G 2

1839 the confederation broke up and its five provinces became the independent states of Guatemala, El Salvador, Honduras, Nicaragua, and Costa Rica.

Contention between the states was softened in 1856–1857, when all fought the attempt of the filibuster William Walker (q.v.) to make himself president of Nicaragua. Rivalries continued, however, even when new leaders arose who favored union; it was a battle between two unionist rulers that took the life of Justo Rufino Barrios, president of Guatemala, who attempted to force his own plan in 1885. Serious multilateral moves toward unity came again in 1906–1907, when the Central American Court of Justice was created, but after 10 years the court foundered when its decisions concerning canal rights displeased the governments of Nicaragua and the United States.

In the 19th century, Britain had maintained influence in this region through the importance of British trade. With the independence of Panama in 1903 and the consequent creation of the Canal Zone and construction of the canal, the United States had become sensitive to every isthmian movement. Salvador Mendieta (1879–1958), the principal Central American proponent of union during his lifetime, nevertheless argued that the Central American people, with their provincialisms, dictatorships, and anarchy, were chiefly responsible for their own political and economic weakness. As though to heed his words, these people on their own initiative since 1951 (though with help from the United States, especially since the rise of Cuba's Fidel Castro) have begun again the processes that will tend to make them one.

The Organization of Central American States, founded in 1951 and steadily active since 1955, has established a wide background of cooperation in almost every endeavor, from university instruction to public health to a common currency. The Central American Common Market, in the making since 1961, and the Central American Bank for Economic Integration, giving the Common Market support, are bringing great change to the isthmian economy. They are not simple devices for free trade, but means for a logical development of the isthmus' resources for the benefit of its inhabitants. Panama, though her economy has special characteristics because of the canal, began negotiating possible entry into the Common Market in 1966. If the advances which encouraged that move can gain headway over the growth of population, and if ways can be found to make sure that new wealth reaches all isthmian people, there will quickly develop the first lasting basis for union that Central America has known.

FRANKLIN D. PARKER
The University of North Carolina at Greensboro

Bibliography

Adams, Richard N., *Cultural Surveys of Panama-Nicaragua-Guatemala-El Salvador-Honduras* (Washington, D. C., 1957).

Clark, Sydney, *All the Best in Central America* (New York 1964).

Dozier, Craig L., *Indigenous Tropical Agriculture in Central America* (Washington, D. C., 1958).

Karnes, Thomas L., *The Failure of Union: Central America, 1824–1960* (Chapel Hill, N. C., 1961).

Martz, John D., *Central America: The Crisis and the Challenge* (Chapel Hill, N. C., 1959).

Parker, Franklin D., *The Central American Republics* (New York and London 1964).

Pincus, Joseph, *The Central American Common Market* (Washington, D. C., 1962).

Rodríguez, Mario, *Central America* (New York 1965).

Valle, Rafael Heliodoro, *Historia de las ideas contemporáneas en Centro-América* (Mexico City 1960).

CENTRAL ASIA. See ASIA (Introduction).

CENTRAL CITY, a town in north central Colorado, is situated 26 miles (42 km) northwest of Denver, along the steep slopes of Gregory Gulch in the Front Range of the Rocky Mountains. It is the seat of Gilpin county. Once a booming gold town, Central City is now a cultural and tourist center noted for the drama and opera festivals held here each summer in the restored Opera House, originally completed in 1878. Other attractions are Teller House, which still reflects the taste of an elegant frontier hotel; the Central Gold Mine and Museum; and the "Glory Hole," a mining pit about 1,000 feet (300 meters) wide and 300 feet (90 meters) deep.

Central City became a center of mining activity in 1859, when the discovery of gold touched off a stampede. By the late 1870's the gold rush had leveled off. The small amount of gold now produced here is a by-product of the mining of other minerals in the area, including lead, zinc, and uranium. Restoration of early buildings began in 1932 with the formation of the Central City Opera Association, which sponsors the yearly festivals, featuring noted opera singers. The town was incorporated in 1864 and has a mayor-council form of government. Population: 228.

ALYS FREEZE
Public Library, City and County of Denver

CENTRAL FALLS is a city in northeastern Rhode Island, in Providence county, on the Blackstone River. It adjoins Pawtucket on the east. An industrial center, it manufactures apparel, textiles, machinery, chemicals, glass, jewelry, plastics, and toys. Cogswell Memorial Clock Tower, 70 feet (21 meters) high, in Jenks Park, is a familiar landmark. Central Falls was incorporated with the town of Lincoln in 1871 and became a separate city in 1895. Government is by mayor and council. Population: 18,716.

THE CENTRAL CITY Opera House once welcomed some of the greatest 19th-century singers and actors. Now restored, it houses a yearly opera and drama festival.

MYRON WOOD, FROM PHOTO RESEARCHERS

CENTRAL INTELLIGENCE AGENCY, an organization established to provide for the security of the United States. It was created by the National Security Act of 1947, which also unified the three military departments—Army, Navy (and Marine Corps), and Air Force—under a secretary of defense. To integrate federal policies and procedures relating to defense, the National Security Council was established. The functions of the Central Intelligence Agency (CIA)—necessarily described in vague terms—were to correlate, evaluate, and disseminate intelligence and "to perform, for the benefit of the existing intelligence agencies, such additional services of common concern as the National Security Council determines can be more efficiently accomplished centrally."

Personnel and Funds. In creating the CIA, Congress specified that both the director and deputy director would be appointed by the president, subject to confirmation by the Senate. In 1949, Congress also gave complete discretionary power over CIA personnel and funds to the director of the CIA. Because all of CIA's activities are secret and because the agency follows the policy of neither denying nor confirming reports, there is little official information available to the public about its size, organization, or appropriations.

The size of its building, located in Langley, Va., suggests that the often-quoted estimate of 10,000 persons at headquarters may be approximately correct. How many agents and operatives are employed in various foreign countries of the world is quite uncertain. Estimates of annual expenditures vary widely—from $500 million to $4 billion. CIA funds are hidden in the annual appropriations of other agencies, and limited supervision is exercised through subcommittees of the armed services and appropriations committees of Congress. Periodic efforts to create a congressional watchdog group modeled on the Joint Atomic Energy Committtee have failed.

Historical Background. Since its founding the government of the United States has recognized the importance of gathering information, but before World War II its methods were somewhat disorganized and unprofessional. The war, navy, and state departments gathered information, but their activities were so rudimentary that even as late as the Civil War, Allan Pinkerton, a well-known detective, was hired to gather intelligence for President Lincoln and his generals. On the eve of World War II most information still came from state department representatives and from military and naval attachés in U. S. embassies abroad. More than any other single event, the attack on Pearl Harbor explains the creation of the CIA. The congressional investigation into that disaster disclosed that the information necessary to anticipate the attack was available, but that there was a failure in evaluation, interpretation, and dissemination of the information.

But even before Pearl Harbor, President Franklin D. Roosevelt had appointed Col. (later Maj. Gen.) William J. Donovan coordinator of information and instructed him to collect and analyze all strategic intelligence for the president and other interested agencies. After the outbreak of hostilities General Donovan's office became the Office of Strategic Services (OSS). For the first time, the United States had an organization devoted to intensive strategic intelligence research and special operations behind enemy lines. At the end of the war President Harry S Truman ordered OSS disbanded, but he established the Central Intelligence Group by executive order on Jan. 22, 1946. Under the thoroughgoing reorganization provided by the National Security Act of 1947, the Central Intelligence Group formed the nucleus of the CIA.

In 1967, the CIA was only one of nine agencies that were collectively referred to as "the intelligence community." The others included the National Security Agency and the Federal Bureau of Investigation.

CIA Activities. Under its power to perform "services of common concern" to the intelligence community, CIA has engaged in a variety of activities; some have been hailed as great successes and others have been condemned as failures. Among the actions that have been regarded as successes was the work of CIA's agents in bringing down Iran's Premier Mohammed Mossadegh in 1953 after the latter attempted with Communist aid to overthrow the shah. In 1954 anti-Communist forces in Guatemala, with the aid of supplies from the United States, overthrew the regime of Jacobo Arbenz Guzmán.

Beginning in 1960, a series of revelations damaged the CIA's reputation. Ironically, one of its greatest triumphs led to one of its greatest embarrassments when, on May 1, 1960, a U-2 high-altitude observation plane piloted by Francis Gary Powers was brought down over Soviet territory. In 1961 the CIA's reputation was further tarnished by the failure of the Bay of Pigs invasion of Cuba.

Investigations during the mid-1970's implicated the CIA in many questionable activities, and its cloak of secrecy was partially torn away. Several former CIA employees were convicted in connection with the Watergate affair. In 1975, President Gerald Ford named Vice President Nelson Rockefeller to head an investigation of the organization. The latter's commission found that the CIA had engaged in "plainly unlawful" domestic spying activities.

Congress also investigated the CIA. A Senate committee headed by Sen. Frank Church (D-Idaho) established that the CIA had plotted to assassinate Prime Minister Fidel Castro of Cuba and Premier Patrice Lumumba of the Congo, and that it was implicated in attempts on three other foreign leaders. Although four of the five were assassinated, the committee found no evidence that any died as a result of U. S. plotting. Evidence suggested that Presidents Eisenhower, Kennedy, and Nixon were aware of the plots. The CIA recruited organized crime figures to kill Castro.

Although the CIA was supposedly barred by its charter from engaging in domestic operations, investigations revealed long and widespread abuses of the civil rights of Americans—wiretaps, buggings, break-ins, and mail openings. The CIA maintained records on 1.5 million Americans. The Senate committee called for strict limitations on covert activities by the CIA and tighter oversight of its affairs.

HARRY L. COLES, *Ohio State University*

Bibliography
Blackstock, Paul W., *The Strategy of Subversion: Manipulating the Politics of Other Nations* (Chicago 1964).
Dulles, Allen, *Craft of Intelligence* (New York 1963).
Marchetti, Victor, and Marks, John, *The CIA and the Cult of Intelligence* (New York 1974).
Ransom, Harry Howe, *Central Intelligence and National Security* (Cambridge, Mass., 1958).
Tully, Andrew, *CIA, the Inside Story* (New York 1962).
Wise, David, and Ross, Thomas B., *The Invisible Government* (New York 1964).

CENTRAL PARK, overlooking Central Park Lake, with Fifth Avenue's apartment buildings in the background.

CENTRAL PARK, in New York City, comprises an oblong area in the center of Manhattan, from West 59th Street to West 110th Street and from Fifth Avenue to Central Park West. Surrounded by apartment buildings, it is New York City's most popular park. It is third in size among the city's parks, extending 2½ miles (4 km) from north to south and ½ mile (0.8 km) from east to west. Of its 840 acres (340 hectares), 150 acres (61 hectares) are water.

The park is an outstanding example of landscape architecture. Working with a naturally diversified terrain, man has created flower beds, lawns, heavily wooded areas, three lakes, and two ponds; miles of bicycle and bridle paths, and walking trails, baseball diamonds, football, hockey, and soccer fields; and other recreational facilities.

Features. The Mall, a broad 1,500-foot (457-meter) avenue, is the scene of the free Guggenheim Memorial Concerts presented during the summer and the site of public events throughout the year. The Sheep Meadow, a large open plain off Central Park West, is the center of free musical performances which have drawn tens of thousands of persons. The outdoor Delacorte Shakespeare Theatre presents free performances of Shakespeare's plays. The park's largest lake (21.8 acres, or 8.8 hectares) has been famous for boating since 1860. Just north of the lake is the Ramble, a wilderness area threaded by paths.

The Central Park Zoo, off Fifth Avenue at 64th Street, completed in 1934, now also includes a Children's Zoo, where adults are admitted only if accompanied by a child. The zoo buildings are situated on either side of the Arsenal, built as a state arsenal in 1848, which now houses the city parks department. The Wollman Memorial Skating Rink, an amphitheater for ice-skating, is near the southeast corner of the park, as is a pavilion for chess and checker playing. At the north end of the park is the Harlem Meer, a small lake with a boathouse. Nearby are the sites of blockhouses of the American Revolution and the War of 1812 and of Fort Fisk and Fort Clinton.

The park contains hundreds of monuments and plaques, many by world-famous artists, to the memory of statesmen, writers, and children, and even in honor of animals and birds. Others commemorate historic military events. Hundreds of varieties of plants, shrubs, and trees, many very rare, represent years of care and add color and beauty to the walks, rambles, and promenades.

History. In 1844, William Cullen Bryant, editor of the *Evening Post,* expressed the need for a park in the face of spreading urbanization. Others joined him, and in 1853 the state legislature authorized the purchase of some 624 acres (253 hectares) of land between 59th and 106th Streets. Six years later, permission was given to extend the purchase to 110th Street. The entire cost was about $5 million. In a nationwide competition in 1858, Calvert Vaux and Frederick Law Olmsted won first prize of $2,000 for a plan for the park. Work had begun the year before, with the removal from the area of hundreds of hovels and of hog farms and bone-boiling works, and the draining of sumps, creeks, and open sewers. In the following years millions of trees and shrubs were planted, and roads, bridges, paths, and irrigation systems were built.

The park remains essentially as planned by Vaux and Olmsted, although some changes have taken place. Early in the 20th century, carriage roads were converted and paved for use by automobiles. Tennis courts and baseball diamonds were constructed. In 1925 the Heckscher Playground at the southern end of the park was donated. This was the first of several private gifts, including the Wollman Memorial Skating Rink (1950) and the Delacorte Shakespeare Theatre (1963).

After Robert Moses was appointed parks commissioner in 1934, many changes were made in Central Park. A system of playgrounds for small children was created. The sheep that had grazed in the Sheep Meadow were removed and a restaurant was built in the area. A cafeteria and a terrace with tables were built in the zoo. In June 1965 the park was named a national historic landmark.

LEO HERSHKOWITZ
Queens College, City University of New York

CENTRAL POWERS, a military coalition in World War I of Germany, Austria-Hungary, Bulgaria, and the Ottoman Empire. Their opponents were the Allies, led by France, Britain, Russia, and the United States. See WORLD WAR I.

CENTRAL TREATY ORGANIZATION, a mutual defense alliance between Turkey, Iran, Pakistan, and Britain. It came into existence as the Baghdad Pact in 1955, through a treaty of mutual assistance between Iraq and Turkey, acceded to later in the same year by Iran, Pakistan, and Britain. Iraq's pro-Western government was overthrown in 1958, and the following year that country withdrew from the pact. Its headquarters were moved from Baghdad to Ankara, Turkey, and in 1959 the organization was renamed the Central Treaty Organization (CENTO).

The United States, although not an official member, has been closely associated with CENTO since its inception. It sends observers to many of CENTO's meetings; it helps finance various CENTO activities; and it contributes an equal share to the organization's staff.

Organization. CENTO has a fairly elaborate organizational structure. Its main organs are the council of ministers, which meets at least once a year, and the deputy council of ministers, consisting of the ambassadors accredited to Turkey from Iran, Pakistan, and Britain and a senior Turkish official, which meets every two weeks and serves as an interim governing body. CENTO has a secretariat headed by a secretary-general and a scientific council, which among other activities directs the organization's Institute of Nuclear Sciences at Teheran. There is also an economic committee, which ·has important subcommittees in such fields as health, trade, and communications. CENTO has a military committee but although the matter has been frequently raised at meetings of the council of ministers, it has no military command structure and no combat troops have been assigned to the organization.

Functions. At its origin CENTO seemed to be primarily an anti-Soviet alliance, linking the "Northern Tier" countries of the Middle East with the North Atlantic Treaty Organization (NATO) and the Southeast Asia Treaty Organization (SEATO). For many reasons, however, CENTO has failed to develop as a security arrangement and has given increasing attention to economic development and technical cooperation within the region. The Middle Eastern members have been increasingly dissatisfied with it because it has not helped them to meet their real security needs and has been of limited usefulness even in providing economic assistance. In September 1965, Pakistan invoked the treaty in connection with its war with India, but Iran and Turkey gave Pakistan little more than verbal support, and Britain, like the United States, refrained from taking a ·position in support of either belligerent country.

In the economic field CENTO's main achievements have been in transportation and communications. A spectacular achievement in this respect was the inauguration in June 1965 of a 3,060-mile (7,925-km) microwave telephone line linking Ankara, Teheran, and Karachi, the longest line of its kind in the world.

The dissatisfaction of the Middle Eastern members of CENTO with the organization and perhaps also their desire to operate more independently of Britain and the United States led to the formation in July 1964 of an organization known as Regional Cooperation for Development to accelerate regional cooperation outside the framework of CENTO.

NORMAN D. PALMER
University of Pennsylvania

CENTRALIA, sen-trāl′yə, an industrial city in south central Illinois, is in Marion county, 93 miles (149 km) southeast of Springfield. It is a distribution point for a rich agricultural region and a center of large-scale oil production. There are many oil fields in the surrounding area. The city has railroad shops and it manufactures stoves, furnaces, fiber glass products, paper, potato chips, and candy. It is the seat of Kaskaskia Junior College, a 2-year coeducational institution. A state school for retarded children is in the city.

In 1851 the Illinois Central Railroad sent surveyors to the site. Settlement began two years later. Centralia, named for the railroad, was incorporated in 1859. By the 1960 census, the center of population in the United States was situated at a point 6½ miles (10 km) northwest of the city. Government is by a city manager. Population: 15,217.

LAURA C. LANGSTON, *Centralia Public Library*

CENTRALIA, sen-trāl′yə, a city in southwestern Washington, is in Lewis county, 22 miles (35 km) south of Olympia. It is situated in a lumbering area, which also has dairy, poultry, and berry farms. Centralia manufactures lumber products, gloves, cement products, and abrasives. There is a forestry research laboratory and a 2-year college. A point of interest is the Borst Blockhouse, built in 1855 as a defense against Indians.

Settled in the 1850's as Centerville, Centralia adopted its present name in 1883 and was incorporated in 1889. It is governed by commission. In 1919, the city was the scene of a gunfire attack on an American Legion parade marching past the hall of the Industrial Workers of the World (IWW). Four Legionnaires were killed and one IWW member was lynched. Population: 10,054.

CENTREVILLE, a city in southwestern Illinois, is in St. Clair county, 11 miles (19 km) southeast of East St. Louis. The community is principally residential. Scott Air Force Base is 12 miles (19 km) to the east.

The area around Centreville was settled about 1805. In 1957 the city was incorporated from part of Centreville township. Government is by mayor and council. Population: 11,378.

CENTRIFUGAL FORCE. See CENTRIPETAL AND CENTRIFUGAL FORCE.

CENTRIFUGE, sen′trə-fūj, a machine for subjecting an experimental sample or object to sustained centrifugal force. A wide range of centrifuges have been built for separating gas molecules that differ in mass, for separating solid particles from liquids, and for separating two or more liquids that have different densities. Centrifuges have also been designed for subjecting men, plants, and animals to centrifugal force. Since centrifugal force has the same properties as the earth's gravitational force, the force exerted on a sample or object in a centrifuge is generally compared directly with the pull of gravity. Thus, centrifuges are described as exerting a force of two or three times to over five million times the force of gravity (2 or 3 g to over 5,000,000 g).

How a Centrifuge Works. The simplest centrifuge is merely a bucket attached to a rope that is swung around one's head. Most centrifuges, while employing exactly the same principle, have metal rotors that spin on a shaft driven by either electric motors or air or oil turbines.

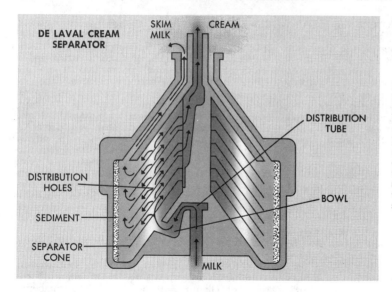

DE LAVAL CREAM SEPARATOR

SKIM MILK · CREAM

DISTRIBUTION TUBE

DISTRIBUTION HOLES

SEDIMENT

SEPARATOR CONE

BOWL

MILK

In the De Laval cream separator, milk is pumped into the bottom of the centrifuge bowl. As the rotor turns, the milk rises through distribution holes in the closely spaced separator cones (shown in cross section). When the milk strikes the separator cones, the cream globules coalesce and move upward toward the cream spout. The skim milk moves downward and outward and then flows upward to the skim milk spout.

According to Newton's first law, a moving object continues in a straight line unless a force is exerted to deflect it. When an object is moved in a circular path, the reaction against the deflecting force (the pull of the rope on the bucket) is the centrifugal force (which also holds the water in the bucket). The centrifugal force exerted on a particle in a centrifuge is given by:

$$F = 0.00001117 \, (\text{rpm})^2 \times R \times M$$

where the force (F) is expressed in grams, the speed (rpm) is in revolutions per minute, the radius (R) (distance between the axis of rotation and the particle) is in centimeters, and the particle mass (M) is given in grams. Note that the force is directly proportional to the radius (which means that at a fixed speed if the radius is doubled or halved, the force is correspondingly doubled or halved) and is proportional to the square of the speed (doubling the speed increases the centrifugal force at a given radius by a factor of four). For high-speed centrifuges the diameter is limited by the strength of the alloys used. As the speed is increased, the diameter must be decreased, and to a close approximation the maximum speed is inversely proportional to the diameter. The fact that centrifugal force is proportional to the square of the speed allows very high gravitational fields to be reached in small diameter rotors.

Industrial Centrifuges. Centrifuges are used industrially to cast metal pipe, to recover crystalline precipitates such as table sugar, to separate small pieces of lean meat from particles of fat, to concentrate slurries, and to dry laundry. The most familiar industrial centrifuge is the cream separator. In the earth's gravitational field droplets containing butterfat, being lighter than skim milk, rise slowly to the top of whole milk. Centrifugal force may be used to achieve this separation much more rapidly and in a continuously flowing stream. A cream separator rotor contains a series of closely spaced cones or separators. As milk flows between these, droplets of cream need only rise a short distance before impacting the separator surface where the particles coalesce and flow toward the axis of the rotor as a mass. Skimmed milk collects along the inner surfaces of the separators and cream collects against the outer surfaces. These separated fluids are led continuously out of the rotor through separate spouts.

Preparative Laboratory Centrifuges. In research and in clinical studies, preparative centrifuges are used to separate particles ranging in size from blood cells and flocculent precipitates to protein molecules or low molecular weight substances on the basis of either sedimentation rate or buoyant density. Both types of separations are made in each of the three types of centrifuge rotors that have been developed. These rotor types are: the *swinging-bucket rotor*, in which the centrifuge tubes are vertically oriented during rest and swing out to a horizontal position during rotation; the *fixed-angle*, or *angle-head, centrifuge*, in which the centrifuge tubes do not change orientation with respect to the axis during rotation; and the *zonal centrifuge rotor*, which does not use centrifuge tubes but is a hollow pressure vessel that is usually filled and emptied while spinning.

Sedimentation Rate. The rate of sedimentation of a particle in a centrifugal field depends on the particle size, the difference in density between the particle and the suspending medium, and the viscosity of the medium. The sedimentation rate is proportional to the square of the radius; therefore, doubling the diameter of a particle increases its sedimentation rate by four.

If only one particle species is present in a suspension, it may be sedimented completely to the bottom of a centrifuge tube and recovered as a pellet. If two or more species are present, these may be partially separated by sedimenting the most rapidly moving species and then removing the overlying fluid and the slower particles suspended in it. The sedimented pellet will, however, contain some of the slower particles. These may be removed by resuspending the pellet and resedimenting the rapidly sedimenting particles several times. Centrifugation of this type is used to separate red cells and leucocytes from blood plasma, to remove unsoluble precipitates from suspension, and to separate subcellular particles.

Zonal Centrifugation. Higher resolution separations may be achieved by a technique termed "zonal centrifugation." In a centrifugal field particles having different sedimentation rates move different distances, often forming discrete zones which are recovered at the end of the experiment. It is evident that a particle whose density exactly matches that of the suspending solutions will neither float nor sink in a centrifugal field. If the suspending solution is a density gradient, then a particle may float or sink through the gradient until it finds the level where the liquid density and the particle density (or buoyant density) are equal. This level is termed the *isopycnic level*. Particles of one density may thus be concentrated into a narrow band, and if particles having different densities are present, these may separate into several bands. This technique, also termed *isopycnic centrifugation*, is widely used to separate subcellular particles, viruses, and DNA molecules.

For large-scale separations in liquid density gradients a new type of centrifuge, termed a *zonal centrifuge*, has been developed at the Oak Ridge National Laboratory in Tennessee. It has hollow rotors divided internally into sector-shaped compartments by vertical septa. Special seals are attached to the rotors to allow fluids to be pumped into and out of the rotors during rotation. While spinning at a relatively low speed, a liquid density gradient that is pumped in is held against the rotor wall by centrifugal force. When the rotor is filled with the gradient, which is usually a sucrose or cesium chloride solution, the sample is introduced to the rotor center. The rotor is then accelerated to high speed to separate particles on the basis of either their sedimentation rate or their isopycnic density. After the separation has been completed, the rotor is decelerated to low speed, and a dense fluid is pumped to the rotor edge. This displaces the gradient, and the separated particle zones which it contains, toward the axis and out through the fluid line seal where it is collected as a series of discrete fractions.

Zonal centrifuges have been used for the high-resolution separation of subcellular particles including nuclei, mitochondria, lysosomes, fragments of endoplasmic reticulum, chloroplasts, glycogen, polysomes, ribosomes, viruses, macroglobulins, RNA, and DNA. Zonal centrifuges are especially useful for the purification of large quantities of virus for vaccine purposes. Continuous flow zonal centrifuges have been developed in which the virus-laden fluid flows through a high-speed rotor containing an imprisoned liquid gradient. As the virus particles sediment out of the stream they band isopycnically in the gradient and are recovered in a highly concentrated and purified form. This method is now in routine use for the purification of influenza vaccines.

High-resolution centrifugal separations have revolutionized cell biochemistry by allowing large quantities of cell substructures to be isolated in sufficient quantity for analysis by conventional methods. A large part of present knowledge on the localization of activities and functions in cells has therefore been gained by using centrifugal separations.

Separative Centrifugation. Swinging-bucket centrifuges are frequently used for separating large particles. At speeds up to approximately 3,000 rpm, buckets containing up to a liter are widely used for blood fractionation and for the sedimentation of coarse precipitates. As the speed is increased, the volume that can be centrifuged in the bucket or cup drops off sharply until only a few milliliters may be centrifuged at 65,000 rpm.

A considerable increase in the volume which can be centrifuged at a given speed is achieved by using solid rotors containing sealed plastic centrifuge tubes held at a fixed angle. By far the largest number of rotors used in the range of 5 to

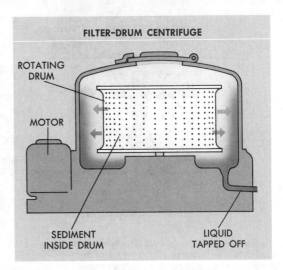

FILTER-DRUM CENTRIFUGE

ROTATING DRUM

MOTOR

SEDIMENT INSIDE DRUM

LIQUID TAPPED OFF

In the filter-drum centrifuge, liquid passes through the perforations, while solid particles remain in the drum.

65,000 rpm are of this type. In a titanium angle rotor, for example, approximately 162 milliliters of a suspension may be centrifuged at 50,000 rpm. The force exerted (226,000 times that of gravity) is sufficient to sediment protein molecules such as gamma globulin in a few hours. The shape of the tube, however, limits sedimentation rate separations to particles that do not aggregate when they collide with the wall of the centrifuge tube.

Analytical Ultracentrifuge. While estimates of particle size and weight can be made in each of the several rotor types described, precise measurements are made by centrifuging the suspension in a cell fitted with transparent quartz or sapphire windows and by recording the rate of sedimentation or the position and shape of an isopycnic band photographically or with a scanning photomultiplier cell. These optical centrifuges are called "analytical ultracentrifuges." The term "ultracentrifuge" refers to any centrifuge operating over 20,000 rpm. The first analytical ultracentrifuge was used by Theodor Svedberg and J. G. Nichols in 1923 and led to the discovery that proteins have characteristic molecular weights.

Three types of measurements may be made in analytical ultracentrifuges: sedimentation rate, sedimentation equilibrium, and buoyant density. Electrically driven analytical ultracentrifuges operating at speeds up to 60,000 rpm are widely available and are routinely used to study, by sedimentation-rate measurements, changes in the proportion of albumin, globulin, and macroglobulins occurring in human plasma in disease.

Accurate determinations of molecular weight may be made at very much lower speed (usually about 6,000 rpm) under conditions where an equilibrium is reached between sedimentation toward the cell periphery and back diffusions in the opposite direction. No sharp boundary is formed; instead, a continuous concentration gradient is seen. From the shape and slope of the curve, and accurate measurement of rotor speed, the molecular weight may be calculated. Molecular weights between 40 and 50,000,000 have been determined in this manner.

Isopycnic centrifugation, in either preformed gradients or gradients formed by sedimentation of

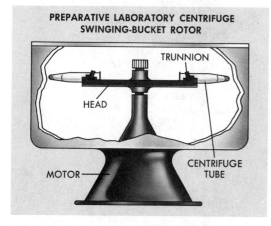

**PREPARATIVE LABORATORY CENTRIFUGE
SWINGING-BUCKET ROTOR**

TRUNNION

HEAD

MOTOR

CENTRIFUGE
TUBE

In the swinging-bucket rotor, the tubes are vertical at rest and swing to a horizontal position during rotation.

gradient solutes during centrifugation, is widely used to determine the buoyant density of nucleic acids, proteins, viruses, and subcellular particles. Solutions of cesium chloride provide sufficiently dense solutions to allow DNA molecules to be sharply banded. Accurate determinations of the ratio of the nucleotides of which the molecule is composed may be obtained from the banding densities. In addition, the width of the band provides an indication of the molecular weight of the DNA molecules.

Analytical ultracentrifuges, and other high speed centrifuges as well, are operated in a high vacuum to prevent heating due to air friction. Heavy armor is provided around the vacuum chamber to stop fragments in case the rotor explodes at high speed.

Physiological Research Centrifuges. During recovery from high-speed dives in aircraft, launching or reentry of space vehicles, or aircraft or automobile accidents the human body may be subject to rapid acceleration or deceleration, frequently with adverse effects. To study this problem centrifuges have been built which will rotate experimental animals and men at low speeds. Acceleration producing a force acting along the long axis of the body from head to seat is called positive ($+G$); that acting from seat to head is called negative ($-G$), and that acting perpendicular to the long axis is called G_z acceleration. A $+G$ acceleration of 5 or 6g lasting more than 3 or 4 seconds will produce "blackout" and later unconsciousness. Acceleration in the opposite direction ($-G$) produces more serious and longer lasting effects on the brain. Higher $+G_z$ acceleration can be withstood in a prone position than in other positions, over 8g being experienced during launch for orbital flight. Large experimental centrifuges for human use allow the effect of rate of acceleration, position, use of anti-g suits, and conditioning on circulation, vision, and performance to be studied in the laboratory.

NORMAN G. ANDERSON
Oak Ridge National Laboratory, Tenn.

Further Reading: Anderson, Norman G., *The Development of Zonal Centrifuges* (Wash. D. C. 1966); Schachman, H. K., *Ultracentrifugation in Biochemistry* (New York 1959); Svedberg, Theodor, and Pederson, K., *Ultracentrifuge* (New York 1940).

CENTRIOLE. See CELL–*Cytoplasm* (Centrioles).

CENTRIPETAL AND CENTRIFUGAL FORCE, sen-trip'ə-təl, sen-trif'yə-gəl. According to Newton's first law of motion, a body in motion will continue to move in a straight line unless it is acted upon by a force. Thus, when a body travels in a circular path, a force is necessary to hold it in that path, such as the force of gravity on the satellite of a star or the force exerted by a man's hand when he whirls a ball at the end of a string. This force, which causes an orbiting body to continually swerve toward the center of its orbit, is called *centripetal* ("center-seeking") force.

According to Newton's third law of motion, when two bodies interact, the forces that they exert on each other are equal but opposite in direction. Thus, corresponding to the centripetal force exerted (through the string) by the man's hand on the whirling ball, there is an opposite, *centrifugal* ("center-fleeing") force exerted by the whirling ball on the man's hand. Centrifugal force and centripetal force are not distinct forces that could conceivably exist separately; instead, they are two aspects of a single phenomenon.

Centrifugal force should not be confused with the apparent force—actually an example of the so-called coriolis force—by which fluids in a "centrifugal" pump are "impelled" radially by a rotor. This apparent force is a convenient postulate, which makes it appear that motion follows the same rules in an accelerated frame of reference (the rotor) as it follows in an unaccelerated one.

CENTROGRAPHY, sen-trog'rə-fē, is the branch of geography that deals with the location of geographic centers of any distribution of people, natural resources, agricultural products, or other variables on the earth. The location of these centers, or average positions, of various distributions is particularly valuable in planning the location of future schools, factory and office buildings, highways, public transportation, and other facilities.

Types of Centers. Although there are many different types of centers, only two are widely used. These are the so-called *center of gravity*, which is used mostly for the analysis of the movement of a population over a period of time, and the *median center*, which is used primarily for planning the location of future facilities.

Center of Gravity. The geographical concept of center of gravity is derived from the concept of the same name used by physicists to denote the balancing point of a material body. The U. S. Bureau of the Census first applied this concept to human populations in the first *Statistical Atlas of the United States* in 1874, and in every subsequent major census bureau publication. The definition of the center of population used by the census bureau is "that point upon which the United States would balance if it were a rigid plane, without weight, with the population distributed thereon with each individual having equal weight." An alternative definition of this center is that point at which the sum of the squared distances from the point to each member of the population is a minimum. If one were working with a set of numbers, instead of populations distributed over an area, the second definition would be the definition of the arithmetic mean—the familiar "average"—and so the center of gravity is also called the *arithmetic mean center*.

There are two main reasons for the usefulness of the center of gravity. First, it is an ex-

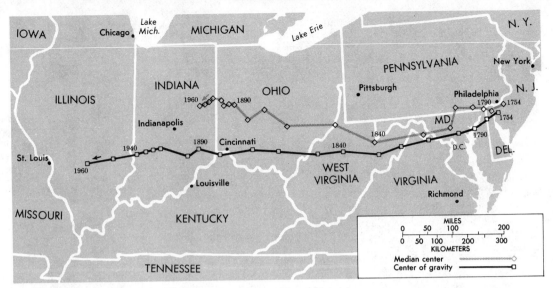

CENTERS OF GRAVITY AND MEDIAN CENTERS of the U. S. population (excluding Alaska and Hawaii) charted for each census between 1754 and 1970 show a movement westward. From 1940 to 1970 the center of gravity moved westward rapidly, while the median center changed very little. The center of gravity is more affected by movements over large distances, and it reflects the fact that a relatively small proportion of the population moved, but that most of those who moved traveled westward for large distances.

tremely sensitive measure and will change, even though the change may be minute, with any movement within the population. This sensitivity makes it a very useful device for studying general trends in the movement of population over long periods of time. In addition, since it is the most often used centrographic measure, there is a vast library of previously computed centers of gravity of populations of all kinds. For example, the center of gravity of population for each state in the United States has been computed for each census since 1880. Since 1920, centers of gravity have been computed for wage earners, foreign-born, native white, Negro, urban, and rural populations. In addition, centers of gravity have been computed for the distribution of farms, farm acreage, and many manufactured and agricultural products.

Second, the center of gravity is also useful because it possesses the statistical properties of the arithmetic mean, which is particularly important when the entire population cannot be studied and sampling techniques must be used.

Median Center. The first applications of the concept of a median center were based on the property of a median to divide a distribution in half. Thus, the median point was defined as the intersection of two perpendicular lines, each of which divides the population in half. However, in 1902, J. F. Hayford recognized that the location of this intersection depends on the direction in which the lines lie, and that the differences in the positions of the various median centers were not small enough to be ignored. Hayford, therefore, redefined the median center as the point at which the sum of the distances from the point to each of the members of the population is a minimum. This is similar to the definition of the center of gravity, except that for the median center the distances are not squared.

If each member of the population were to travel in a straight line from his home to some point, the total amount of travel would be least

if that point were the median point. Thus the median point is sometimes called the *point of minimum aggregate travel* or the *point of minimum average travel*. It is this minimum travel property that makes the median center useful in determining locations for schools, offices, warehouses, and other facilities.

Modal Center and Harmonic Mean Center. Two other types of centers have found increasing use in recent years. These are the modal center and the harmonic mean center. The *modal center* is defined as the location of the unit of area that has the greatest density of population. The practical difficulty in working with this concept is that a center is defined as a point but density must be defined in terms of an area. To avoid this difficulty many centrographers have adopted the *harmonic mean center,* often called the peak of potential of population; although more difficult to define and compute, it is more precise mathematically and is usually located at the same place as the modal center.

History. Historically, the study of centrography began with the work of Hilgard and the U. S. Bureau of the Census in the 1870's. Around the turn of the century, the Russian chemist Dmitri Mendeleyev (or Mendeleev) began investigations of the center of gravity of the population of Russia. The Mendeleyev Centrographical Laboratory was formed in Leningrad in 1925 by several of his countrymen who had become interested in his studies.

The study of centrography as a distinct field reached its peak in the 1920's and 1930's. During this period there was an international race, led by centrographers in the United States, the Soviet Union, and Italy, to see who could compute and analyze the greatest number of centers of all kinds. By the late 1930's, however, the study of centrography fell into disfavor, partially because it could not live up to the absurd claims made for it by some of its proponents, particularly those in the Soviet Union. A re-evaluation of the field was made in the late 1950's when the Israeli geographer Roberto Bachi and the American geographer William Warntz, as well as others, recognized that centrography, while not important as an independent field of study, is one of the most useful tools in an overall system of quantitative geographic analysis.

DAVID S. NEFT, *Author of*
"Statistical Analysis for Areal Distributions"

Bibliography

Bachi, R., "Statistical Analysis of Geographical Series," *Revue de l'Institut International de Statistique*, vol. 36 (The Hague 1957).
Hayford, J.F., "What Is the Center of an Area, or the Center of a Population?" *Journal of the American Statistical Association*, vol. 8 (Washington 1902).
Hilgard, J.E., "The Advance of Population in the United States," *Scribner's Monthly*, vol. 4 (New York 1872).
Scates, D.E., "Locating the Median of the Population in the United States," *Metron*, vol. 11 (Rome 1933).
Sviatlovsky, E.E., and Eells, W.C., "The Centrographical Method and Regional Analysis," *Geographical Review*, vol. 27 (New York 1937).
Warntz, W., and Neft, D.S., "Contributions to a Statistical Methodology for Areal Distributions," *Journal of Regional Science*, vol. 2 (Philadelphia 1960).

CENTROSOME. See CELL.

CENTUM AND SATEM LANGUAGE GROUPS,

ken'tǝm, sä'tǝm, the two divisions of the Indo-European linguistic family. The distinction between divisions is that in the *centum* group, certain original archaic guteral sounds—*k-* (*kh-*), *g-* (*gh-*)—were retained as guttural consonants, while in the *satem* group these consonants changed into sibilants.

Because the word for "hundred" in the various languages is one of the words in which this change occurs, *centum*, the Latin word for hundred, and *satem*, the Iranian, have been chosen to designate the two groups. The *centum* group generally consists of such west Indo-European tongues as Greek, the Romance languages (principally French, Italian, Spanish, and Portuguese), Celtic, and the Germanic languages (including English). The *satem* group consists of such east Indo-European languages of eastern Europe and Asia as Ancient Indian (Sanskrit), Iranian (Avestic), Slavonic, and Baltic.

A few ancient languages, however, do not follow the geographical pattern of these groups. These languages include Agnean and Hittite, both ancient Indo-European languages once spoken in Asia Minor. While both languages are eastern geographically and should belong to the *satem* group, they appear to belong to the *centum* group because in Agnean the word for "hundred" is *känt* and in Hittite there were words like *kuit*, which corresponded to the Latin *quid*.

DAVID DIRINGER, *Author of "The Alphabet"*

CENTURION,

sen-tōōr'ē-ǝn, a professional officer in the Roman army. Every Roman legion (nominally 6,000 men) was divided into 60 centuries, each of which was commanded by a centurion. The centuries of a legion were grouped into 10 cohorts with 6 centuries in each cohort. Each of the 6 centuries in a cohort had a different rank or grade. However, except for the first cohort, the difference in rank was not significant. The best centurions were ordinarily put into the first cohort, and within that cohort the highest rank was that of *primipilus*.

The centurions were normally promoted from the ranks of the common soldiers and were usually responsible for discipline in the army. They were well paid and received a greater share of the spoils than the common soldiers. The post was so lucrative that many centurions were able to enter the equestrian class when they retired. Under the republic centurions did not normally advance to become higher officers, but by the time of Augustus there were military tribunes and prefects who had been promoted from the centurionship.

ARTHER FERRILL, *University of Washington*

CENTURY PLANT. See AGAVE.

CEPHALIC INDEX,

sǝ-fal'ik, one of the many indices used in anthropometry. The skull is measured with spreading calipers, and the ratio of head length to head breadth is expressed by the formula:

$$\text{Cephalic index} = \frac{\text{Maximum head breadth} \times 100}{\text{Maximum head length}}.$$

The cephalic index was develolped in 1840 by the Swedish anthropologist Anders Retzius. He and other anthropologists derived averages for various populations in an attempt at race classification based on head form. However, the cephalic index has proved to be of only limited value for this purpose, as there is much overlap of racial ranges. Also, the two components of length and breadth reflect many structural and functional factors which are inherited through a large number of genes. Consequently, its major use is to indicate possible relationships between small population groups.

PRISCILLA C. WARD
American Museum of Natural History

CEPHALOCHORDATA. See AMPHIOXUS.

CEPHALONIA,

sěf-ǝ-lō'nē-ǝ, is the largest and most mountainous of Greece's Ionian Islands. The Greek form of the name is Kefallinía. Cephalonia has an area of 290 square miles (750 sq km). With several smaller islands, it forms the Greek department of Cephalonia. The island is located in the Ionian Sea, off the western coast of Greece. It has long been known for its wine, olives, and olive oil. The island's most important city is Argostoli.

Following the classical era, when four cities—Same, Pale, Crane, and Pronnoi (Proni)—were the chief centers of civilization on the island, Cephalonia came under Roman and then Byzantine control. The Norman Robert Guiscard took it in 1082. In 1194 it fell to an Italian, Matteo Orsini. His descendants ruled until 1324. In 1357 Cephalonia came under the control of another line of Italian nobles, the Tocco family, who were deposed by the Turks in 1479. Catalan mercenaries seized the island in 1481, Venice took it in 1483, the Turks recaptured it in 1485. Venice retook Cephalonia in 1500 and held it until 1797.

In 1797, France conquered all of the Ionian Islands. The French were driven out in 1799 by a joint Russian-Turkish force. In 1800, Cephalonia joined the other Ionian Islands in the Septinsular Republic. France reasserted control in 1807 only to be driven out in 1809 by Britain. In 1815, Cephalonia became part of the United States of the Ionian Islands, a British protectorate. In 1864, Britain ceded it and all the other Ionian Islands to Greece. Population: (1961) of the department, 46,314; of the island, 39,793.

GEORGE J. MARCOPOULOS, *Tufts University*

ANATOMY OF THE CEPHALOPODS

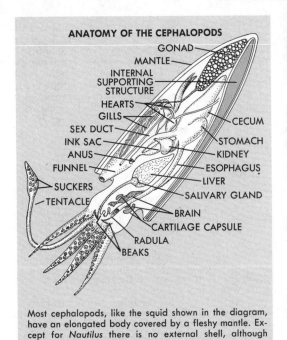

GONAD
MANTLE
INTERNAL SUPPORTING STRUCTURE
HEARTS
GILLS
SEX DUCT
INK SAC
ANUS
FUNNEL
SUCKERS
TENTACLE
CECUM
STOMACH
KIDNEY
ESOPHAGUS
LIVER
SALIVARY GLAND
BRAIN
CARTILAGE CAPSULE
RADULA
BEAKS

Most cephalopods, like the squid shown in the diagram, have an elongated body covered by a fleshy mantle. Except for *Nautilus* there is no external shell, although many species have an internal supporting structure.

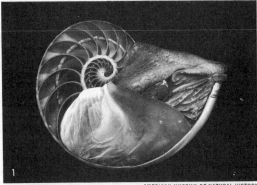

AMERICAN MUSEUM OF NATURAL HISTORY

ANNAN PHOTO FEATURES

ALL CEPHALOPODS have tentacles surrounding the mouth. In the chambered nautilus (1) the tentacles are smooth and very small; in the octopus (2) the tentacles are large and are equipped with one or more rows of suckers.

CEPHALOPOD, sef'ə-lə-pod, any of a small class of marine mollusks that includes the squids, cuttlefishes, and octopuses. Cephalopods are found in all seas throughout the world, living near the surface as well as at great depths. Some species are of great importance. Many, especially the squid *Todarodes pacificus,* are widely eaten in Japan and elsewhere. Squids are also used as bait in many fisheries.

Cephalopods range in size from the tiny squid *Idiosepius pygmaeus,* which is less than 1 inch (25 mm) in length, to the giant squids (*Architeuthis*), which attain a total length of more than 60 feet (18 meters) and are the largest of all living invertebrates.

Cephalopods may vary greatly in color. Their coloration is due to special pigment sacs, called chromatophores, which are made to expand or contract by the nervous system. Under the chromatophores are special reflecting cells, the iridocytes. Each species has several types of chromatophores containing different pigments, and by displaying various combinations of chromatophores, the cephalopod can become almost any color. It is also capable of changing color very rapidly, and by contracting all of the chromatophores, the animal can become almost invisible. In addition to chromatophores and iridocytes, many species have light-producing organs, or photophores, which may be used to light the animal's way through the water, to attract prey, to scare away predators, or to attract mates.

Structure. Most cephalopods have a somewhat elongated body covered by a fleshy tissue called the "mantle." Surrounding the mouth is a circlet of 8, 10, or more fleshy appendages, the arms and tentacles. Except in Nautilus, they are equipped with one or more rows of suckers. In some squids they also have clawlike hooks.

Located near the mouth is a pair of eyes. The cephalopod's eye is more complex than that of any other invertebrate. In all except *Nautilus,* it is very large and in many ways similar to that of a mammal.

The cephalopod's organs of locomotion are the fins and a tubular siphon called the "funnel." Fins are found in all cephalopods except *Nautilus* and some octopuses, but the swimming action of these structures is rather feeble. The main means of locomotion is the expulsion of a jet of water from the funnel, but many octopuses also use their arms and tentacles for crawling.

Unlike other mollusks, most cephalopods lack an external shell. The shell is retained only by *Nautilus,* the thin shell of the paper nautilus (*Argonauta*) functioning primarily as an egg case. In all other cephalopods the shell is internal. In the cuttlefish *Sepia* it is chalky, and in the squid *Loligo* it is thin and chitinous. In *Octopus* it consists of two slender vestigial rods, and in *Spirula* it is coiled and chambered. The tiny squid *Idiosepius* has no internal shell at all.

The cephalopod's digestive tract is rather simple and generally consists of a pair of parrotlike beaks; a toothed rasping organ called the "radula"; two pairs of salivary glands, of which the posterior pair produces a strong neurotoxin; a long esophagus, often with a distinct crop; a stomach; a spiral cecum; a large and small intestine; and an anus, often with flaps.

The respiratory structures are two feathery gills suspended inside the mantle cavity. The circulatory system has three hearts: a systemic heart and two branchial hearts, one located at the base of each gill. The blood contains a blue respiratory pigment called hemocyanin.

The cephalopod's nervous system is more highly developed than that of any other invertebrate. There is a true brain enclosed in a cartilaginous capsule, and studies of octopuses have shown that these animals possess a relatively high degree of intelligence. In many squids the mantle is ennervated by a pair of giant dorsal nerve axons. These contain fibers that are among the largest nerve fibers of any living animal and they are often used in neurological research.

Feeding and Defense. Cephalopods are active predators, feeding on many marine organisms, including worms, shrimp, fish, and even young whales. Octopuses capture prey by jumping on it with their mantle outspread, and some squids seize their victims with their arms and tentacles. Cephalopods kill fish by biting out chunks of flesh with their sharp beaks or by paralyzing them with the neurotoxin. Octopuses sometimes use their radula for boring through the shells of clams or other mollusks. In other cephalopods the radula is used for tearing the victim's flesh into small pieces and then forcing the pieces into the esophagus.

Cephalopods are preyed on by many animals, including whales and large sea birds. An octopus may escape a predator by releasing a cloud of ink, or sepia, from its funnel. The ink also tends to paralyze the predator's sensory organs so that it cannot follow the fleeing octopus. Squids use their ink to form "dummy" images of themselves, puzzling their predators while they shoot off with their pigment sacs contracted.

Reproduction. In the male cephalopod the sperm is contained in complex packets, or spermatophores, which are transferred to the female by means of a specially modified nuptial arm, the hectocotylus. In some, such as *Tremoctopus*, the arm, along with its sperm packets, may be cast off and retained within the female's mantle cavity.

The eggs of a cephalopod contain large quantities of yolk and they may be very tiny or as much as 1 inch (25 mm) in length. In *Octopus* and its allies, the fertilized eggs are attached to the bottom, and in *Argonauta*, they are retained in an egg case. In some species the eggs are simply released into the water.

Unlike other mollusks, cephalopods have no trochophore or veliger stage, although some species do have a larval stage. The larvae of some squids, such as *Chiroteuthis*, have a weird appearance, with a stalked head, eyes, and slender body equipped with several pairs of fins.

Evolution and Classification. The class Cephalopoda is an ancient one, first appearing in the Upper Cambrian period, about 600 million years ago. It reached its greatest diversity and size in the late Paleozoic and Mesozoic periods, from about 270 to 235 million years ago. Of the three great groups of fossil cephalopods, only one group still survives—it is represented by the chambered nautilus (*Nautilus pompilius*) and its allies.

The cephalopods are generally divided into three subclasses: Nautiloidea, Ammonoidea, and Coleoidea. This last subclass is divided into five orders: Belemnoidea, Sepioidea, Teuthoidea, Vampyromorpha, and Octopoda. There are about 150 genera of living cephalopods and they are divided into about 650 species.

GILBERT L. VOSS
Institute of Marine Sciences, Miami, Fla.

CEPHALOTHIN, sef-ə-lō'thin, is a valuable antibiotic used in the treatment of many bacterial infections, especially staphylococcal infections. It is effective against a wider range of microorganisms than most of the penicillins, and some patients who are allergic to the penicillin group of antibiotics have been able to tolerate cephalothin. It is a semisynthetic antibiotic, produced by a chemical modification of a product of the fungus *Cephalosporium.*

ANDRES GOTH, M. D.
University of Texas Southwestern Medical School

CEPHALUS, sef'ə-ləs, in Greek legend, was a young hunter, the son of Deion, King of Phocis, and Diomede. He was happily married to Procris. Eos (Aurora), goddess of the dawn, fell in love with him but could not win his affection. Procris, however, began to doubt her husband's fidelity.

Procris received from Artemis (Diana), goddess of the chase, a dog and a spear, which she gave to Cephalus. When the dog was about to catch the swiftest fox in the country, both animals were changed into stone.

Cephalus, while hunting, would rest in a shady place and call upon Aura, goddess of the breeze, to cool him. Learning of this, Procris again suspected his fidelity. One day, as she spied on him from behind some bushes, Cephalus mistook her for an animal and killed her with his spear.

CEPHEID VARIABLE, sē'fē-əd, one of a class of pulsating stars that undergo very regular changes in brightness. The name derives from the first recognized pulsating star, δ Cephei in the constellation Cepheus.

Cepheid variables are of great interest because their absolute brightness and their pulsations are correlated in a simple fashion: the brighter the star, the longer is its period of pulsation. The American astronomer Henrietta Leavitt first pointed out this relation in 1907. Once this so-called period-luminosity relation is calibrated, it is possible to compute the distance to any Cepheid by measuring its apparent brightness and its period of pulsation. Cepheids are one of astronomy's major distance indicators.

Definite classes or groups of pulsating stars have been identified. The original Cepheids, now referred to as *classical Cepheids,* have periods ranging from 1 day to 50 days. Similar stars that are about 2 magnitudes fainter are called *W Viriginis stars.* Variables having periods of less than 1 day are called *RR Lyrae stars, short-period Cepheids,* or *cluster variables.* See also STARS.

LAURENCE W. FREDRICK
University of Virginia

CEPHEUS, sē'fē-əs, is an autumn constellation of the Northern Hemisphere. In Greek mythology Cepheus was an Ethiopian king, husband of Cassiopeia and father of Andromeda. The constellation is near the north celestial pole, between Ursa Minor and Cassiopeia.

Cepheus is an inconspicuous formation; its brightest star, Alderamin, has a magnitude of only 2.43. However, the constellation is notable because one of its stars, δ Cephei, is the first star that was observed to pulsate, or vary in brightness. The class of stars it typifies, the Cepheid variables, were therefore named for this constellation. See also CONSTELLATION.

CEPHISODOTUS, sef-i-sod′ō-təs, the name of two Greek sculptors of the 4th century B.C. The elder was possibly an older brother (some say the father) of Praxiteles, while the younger was Praxiteles' son.

The elder Cephisodotus devoted his talent to statues of gods. His work represents the transition from Phidias to Praxiteles. Among his notable achievements was his group of Eirene, goddess of peace, holding the infant Plutus, god of wealth. The exquisite marble statue in the Glyptothek in Munich is said to be a copy of this work.

The younger Cephisodotus was known chiefly for his portrait sculpture, particularly of Menander and Lycurgus.

CERACCHI, chä-räk′kē, **Giuseppe** (1751–1802), Italian sculptor, who had a reputation in his time second only to Canova's. He was born in Rome on July 4, 1751. In 1775, after studying with Tommaso Righi, he went to London, where he won praise for his work, including the statues *Strength* and *Temperance* on the facade of Somerset House and portrait busts of Lord Shelburn, Viscount Keppel, Sir Joshua Reynolds, and others.

Ceracchi visited the United States in 1790 and 1792 and became friendly with George Washington and Alexander Hamilton, whose portrait busts he did. Others who sat for him were Benjamin Franklin, and Thomas Jefferson.

On his return to Europe, Ceracchi modeled in Milan several busts of Napoleon, who then invited him to Paris. In Paris, disillusioned with Napoleon, he joined in a conspiracy against Napoleon's life and was guillotined on Jan. 30, 1802.

CERAM, sa′räm, is the second-largest of the Moluccas, islands in eastern Indonesia. It extends about 210 miles (338 km) east and west and about 45 miles (72 km) north and south, and has a total land area of about 7,190 square miles (18,625 sq km). In Indonesia the island's name is frequently spelled *Seram*.

Ceram has a narrow coastal plain and a rugged mountain range covering most of the interior. The tallest peak is Mt. Biniya, which rises over 8,000 feet (2,440 meters). Much of the coastal area is composed of mangrove swamps. Although Ceram has many rivers, not even the larger ones are navigable during the dry season.

Ceram's population, particularly in the interior areas, is of mixed Malay-Papuan stock. Malay is the dominant coastal language; in the interior there are some 35 different Ceramese dialects, stemming from a Papuan base. Most of the coastal peoples practice Islam or Christianity, whereas in the interior animism prevails. Wahai (1961 population, 8,781) is Ceram's capital; Bula (1961 population, 3,116) and Piru (1961 population, 23,-633) are important commercial centers.

From the island's dense tropical forests come ironwood and other forest products. These, along with copra, are the island's chief exports, although a small oil field exists at Bula. Sago is the staple food, supplemented in the interior by hunting and on the coast by fishing. There are no roads, but Bula possesses a small airport.

Ceram came under Dutch influence in the mid-17th century and remained a part of the Netherlands East Indies until it was incorporated into Indonesia at the time of independence in 1945. Population: (1961) 73,453.

ROBERT C. BONE, *Florida State University*

CERAMICS, sə-ram′iks, is a term that was originally applied to products made from natural earths that had been exposed to high temperatures. Today, the field of ceramics covers a widely diversified group of products of specialized industries, including glass, enamels, refractories, cements, limes and plasters, cermets, electronic ceramics, high and low tension electrical insulators, structural clay products, nuclear ceramics, whitewares, as well as certain abrasives.

Nature of Ceramic Materials. Ceramics are inorganic, nonmetallic materials that have been subjected to heat treatment. They are generally hard brittle materials that withstand compression very well but do not hold up well under tension compared to the metals. They are abrasive-resistant, heat resistant (refractory), and can sustain large compressive loads even at high temperatures. Many ceramics are chemically inert even at high temperatures, as is shown by their good oxidation and reduction resistance at these temperatures. The nature of the chemical bond in ceramics is generally ionic in character, and the anions play an important role in the determination of the properties of the material. Typical anions that are important constituents of ceramic materials are carbides, borides, nitrides, and oxides.

KINDS OF CERAMICS

There are a great number of different types of ceramic materials, and these may be grouped according to their methods of production or uses. Some common types of ceramics are whiteware, which includes china and porcelain; structural clay products; glass; and refractory materials, which are capable of withstanding very high temperature.

Pottery is a generic name for all fired clay ware. However, the term may be used more specifically to designate colored, porous articles fired at a relatively low temperature. Earthenware is sometimes distinguished from pottery as being white or buff-colored. Both pottery and earthenware are soft, or nonvitreous, ceramics that are capable of absorbing more than 3% moisture.

China is glazed or unglazed vitreous (hard and nonabsorbent) whiteware that is used for nontechnical purposes. It includes products such as dinnerware and works of art. The china-making process is one in which the ceramic body is first "bisque fired" (or "biscuit fired") to harden, or mature, the material; the object is then glazed and "glost fired" to fix the glaze. The glost firing is done at a substantially lower temperature than the bisque firing.

Porcelain, as defined in the modern United States ceramics industry, is glazed or unglazed vitreous ceramic whiteware that is used for technical purposes. In countries other than the United States, the terms china and porcelain are used

---

The modern ceramics industry produces a wide variety of products serving many different uses, from domestic tableware to missile nose cones. The present article surveys the industry as a whole and describes briefly the major types of ceramics. For additional information the reader is referred to the following separate articles, several of which discuss ceramics as an art form.

Brick	Pipe
Cermet	Porcelain
Composite Materials	Potter's Wheel
Glass	Pottery
Glassmaking	Terra-cotta

almost interchangeably. The true, or hard-fired porcelain, first produced in China, was brought to Europe by Marco Polo. It was called porcelain because of its translucency and similarity to the sea shell Porcellana.

Typical porcelain products are electrical, chemical, mechanical, structural, and thermal ware. In the production of porcelain ware, the ceramic body and the glaze are usually matured together in a single high-temperature firing. Because only a single firing operation is required, porcelain is more economical to produce than china. However, more colors are available for chinaware because of the lower maturing temperature used in the glost firing.

Structural ceramic products include common building brick, facing brick, paving brick, hollow tile, roofing tile, drain tile, conduits, sewer pipe, flower pots, stoneware, and terra-cotta. In order to minimize transportation costs of both raw materials and the finished products, these items are almost always made near the point of use from native clays mined from local deposits.

Almost all structural clay products are made either by the stiff-mud or soft-mud process. These processes differ only in the amount of water used in the clay to develop the plasticity required for extrusion. Large pieces are generally made by the stiff-mud process so that they will not slump after forming. The clays are crushed, disintegrated, extruded through a steel die, and then cut off to the desired length with a wire. They are dried and fired to a temperature of from 980° to 1095°C (1800° to 2000°F), depending on the maturing temperature of the clay.

Salt glazing is a commonly used technique in the manufacture of structural clay products. The salt is introduced toward the end of the firing to give a vitreous coating to the product. This technique is used, for the most part, on structural tile and conduits.

DEVELOPMENTS IN CERAMICS

The impetus for the many current developments in ceramics has arisen from the critical demands of many industries for improved materials. Particularly stringent requirements have come from the aerospace industry, where weight-strength ratios, and thermal shock, dielectric, abrasive, and refractory properties are critical. The applications of ceramic materials in the aerospace industry include the use of alumina ceramics for missile and rocket nose cones. Silicon carbide or molybdenum disilicide are used in rocket nozzles, ceramic coatings are used on metal parts of rockets and satellites, and ceramic materials are used for thermal insulation in the spacecraft.

Ceramic fuel elements are of increasing importance in the generation of nuclear power. Approximately 90% of newly planned nuclear electric power installations will contain enriched uranium dioxide (UO_2), a ceramic material, as the fuel element. Many of the structural elements of the reactors, from the construction materials to the control rods (which are usually boron compounds or rare-earth oxides), are also ceramic materials.

Laser materials are also part of the field of ceramics. The most widely used laser is a specially doped single crystal or ruby. The dopant is chromium, and this ion responds to high intensity xenon light with the emission of a coherent monochromatic pulse of light from the end of the laser crystal. The ends of the laser are parallel and silvered; one end is less silvered than the other. The light is reflected back and forth by the silvered ends until the intensity is great enough to permit the emission of the high intensity beam through the less silvered end of the crystal. Many glass compositions incorporating special dopants are being developed to replace single crystals, or at least to extend the range of frequencies of the laser beam. Lasers are being used for machining, drilling of refractory materials such as diamonds, welding, and in some types of surgery, such as the repair of detached retinas.

Piezoelectric materials develop an electrical charge when they are subjected to a mechanical stress; and conversely, when an electrical charge is imposed, a mechanical strain develops. Some classes of ceramic materials, notably barium titanate and lead zirconate-titanate, exhibit this phenomenon. Such materials are the active elements of phonograph cartridges, sonar, and ultrasonic devices.

Glass ceramics are special glass compositions that are thermally treated before forming operations to devitrify or precipitate a crystalline phase from the material. The crystalline phase that is precipitated out is designed to give that material special properties such as zero thermal expansion for applications involving high thermal-shock applications. Magnetic phases may be precipitated to produce magnetic glasses, or high dielectric phases to produce high-capacitance materials such as barium titanate.

Magnetic ceramics, which are ferrites, were discovered in the Netherlands during World War II and were a well-kept secret until after the war. Ferrites are complex multiple oxides of iron oxide. The magnetic properties of these compounds vary, depending on the metallic oxide that is combined with the iron oxide. Permanent-type ceramic magnets are primarily of the barium ferrite type, although lead ferrites and strontium ferrites are also used. These compounds are also insulators, and they are widely used in small direct-current motors for automobiles. Nickel-zinc ferrites and manganese ferrites, in combination with other compounds, are used in computer memory cores, television yokes, antennae, and in telecommunication systems.

Cermets are a class of materials containing both ceramics and metal. These materials were developed in an attempt to combine the best properties of both types of materials. Metals have high tensile strength and good thermal shock properties, but even the refractory metals have low resistance to oxidation and poor strength at elevated temperatures. By combining the metals with ceramics, which have good strength and oxidation resistance at high temperatures, superior materials can be obtained. A common group of cermets contains alumina (Al_2O_3) and chromium in varying proportions. Cermets are used in jet engines, brake shoe linings, and oxidation-resistant parts.

Nonlinear dielectric ceramics, which are electrical insulating materials, have been very important in the miniaturization of electronic parts and have permitted the development of increasingly sophisticated electrical circuitry. These materials are also used in capacitors. Barium titanate, lead zirconate-titanate, lead niobates, and combinations of titanates are typical nonlinear dielectric ceramics.

Refractory ceramics have been developed for use in the oxygen-processing method of steelmaking. These processes required new or improved refractory materials for containing the steel under severe conditions. "Direct-bonded" and fused cast types of chrome magnesite refractories as well as high-purity magnesia and tar-bonded dolomites have been developed. Such refractories have allowed utilization of existing furnaces, while permitting higher temperatures and more severe oxidation and reduction conditions than were possible with the old refractories. Other special high-temperature refractories have been developed that far exceed the capacities of the more conventional refractories. The new materials include borides, nitrides, and carbides. For example, hafnium carbide melts at 3900°C (7030°F). In addition to their ability to withstand extremely high temperatures, these materials are also very hard and resistant to abrasion.

Dry-film lubricants are an important class of materials that are used at temperatures where conventional lubricants cannot function. Molybdenum disulfide, MoS_2, and graphite suspended in a carrier, such as low-melting glass, are examples of this class of materials. New glasses are being developed that become fluid at high temperatures and are good lubricants.

Composite materials are made up of a combination of two or more types of materials. A common type of composite material has whiskers or fibers embedded in a metal or ceramic matrix. Single crystal fibers of sapphire, which have great strength, are added to metals and ceramics to improve their mechanical properties and their response to high temperatures. Glass fibers are used to reinforce plastics and metals, and they give remarkable strength advantages. For example, glass-reinforced plastics are used to construct the bodies of boats and cars and are used in aircraft shells.

Glass-fiber-reinforced plastics, glass ceramics, and alumina ceramics are being used in nose cones and radomes. The alumina ceramics have good insulating properties for the radar housings, and they are mechanically strong and have good temperature resistance.

Special glasses containing soda, lime, silica, and alumina have been developed which, after forming operations, are dipped into molten salt baths of potassium nitrate. This permits ion substitution at the surface of the glass. On cooling, the surface of the glass is put in high compression with respect to the center of the glass. This phenomenon increases the strength of the glass, and glasses with flexural strengths of 80,000 to 1,000,000 pounds per square inch have been produced. By using this technique on the glaze, very strong dinnerware may be produced.

Ceramic materials are being used in personnel armor to defeat the penetration of bullets. Aluminum oxide compounds are the most widely used for this purpose. Such ceramic materials are also being used as armor in helicopters and other aircraft.

Improvements in the beneficiation of ceramic raw materials are probably no less important than the development of new ceramic materials. For example, kaolins that have been subjected to bleaching and particle size selection are being used instead of the more expensive titanium dioxide in the coating of fine paper; and improved particle selection of flint has made possible the development of higher strength porcelains. There have been improvements in the selection and grinding of nepheline syenite for fluxing glasses and ce-

The handle is made separately and attached to the cup.

ramics. Potting clays have been improved by particle selection and purification.

HISTORY

Pottery-making probably began in the Neolithic period with hand-molded vessels that were baked in the sun or in campfires. Because ceramic materials are chemically inert, they are extremely resistant to deterioration, even after long exposure or burial. Historians have relied heavily on ceramic articles in tracing the development of ancient civilizations, as well as the migrations of peoples. For example, the various historical eras of Mesopotamia, Persia, and Egypt have been characterized by the pottery pieces that have been discovered.

In Neolithic times Egyptian ware was characteristically red in color. It progressed in quality in the predynastic era to highly polished red ware with patterns and figures, and during the protodynastic era, glazed vases were made of copper-bearing compounds giving blue and green colors. During the dynastic period, the pottery became very decorative, particularly during the reign of Amenhotep III.

Chinese ceramic authorities state that their pottery was first made during the reign of Hoang-ti, who ascended the throne in 2698 B.C. True porcelain, however, was probably not perfected until the beginning of the Sung dynasty (960–1279 A.D.) although porcelainlike pottery had been made much earlier. The Chinese also made enamelled ware. The cobalt blue colors used on such ware were learned from the Arabs. However, porcelain was the most common type of ceramic, and it was used for centuries for all classes of wares.

Prehistoric Greek pottery was usually of a single color which depended largely on the firing of the ware. Some of this ware was quite highly polished. Designs first appeared on the pottery in about 2200 B.C. By about 2000 B.C. silvery ware appeared, and other types of lusterware appeared about 1100 B.C. In this period from about 500 B.C. to 320 B.C. Greek ceramic ware commonly showed black figures on red backgrounds or red figures on black backgrounds. Some other pieces were all black with the decorations either incised or stamped in. On other ware a slip of white clay was applied, and on this slip detailed scenes were painted with tempera colors. In Hellenistic times, from about 300 B.C. to 100 B.C., relief work became popular and replaced the painting. During this time red glazed ware was also very common.

Roman pottery was greatly influenced by the pottery of the Greeks. The most common pottery of the Romans was a red ware called *terra sigillata*, which had an alkaline glaze.

The most notable contributions of the later Europeans to ceramics were the development of the European porcelains—the Jasper ware of Josiah Wedgwood, the bone china of England, and the soft paste Medici ware of France and Italy. The development of the hard-paste porcelain at Meissen, Germany by Johann Böttger in 1719 marked the real beginning of the European porcelain and was Europe's most important contribution to the development of ceramics.

The Indians of the Americas produced soft pottery, which archaeologists have uncovered in tombs in the southern and western United States, Mexico, and Central and South America.

When the Europeans first settled in the United States, some low-quality pottery was produced. With the arrival of skilled English and Scottish potters a real pottery industry developed, and New Jersey, particularly Trenton, became one of the leading centers for ceramics in the country. In the early 1900's large ceramics plants were built in western Pennsylvania and eastern Ohio because natural gas and coal were available for fuel.

MALCOLM G. McLAREN, *Rutgers University*

Bibliography

Hove, John E., and Riley, W. C., *Modern Ceramics* (New York 1965).
Kingery, W. David, *Introduction to Ceramics* (New York 1960).
Lee, P. William, *Ceramics* (New York 1961).
Nelson, Glenn C., *Ceramics: A Potter's Handbook* (New York 1966).
Van Schoick, Emily C., ed., *Ceramic Glossary* (Columbus, Ohio 1963).

CERARGYRITE, sə-rär'jə-rīt, is mineral silver chloride and an ore of silver. The cubic crystals are transparent to translucent. They have a pearly gray color or are colorless, but darken rapidly to violet-brown when exposed to light. Large deposits occur in Chile, Peru, Bolivia, and Mexico. Among the U.S. sites where it has been an important ore are Leadville, Colo., the Comstock Lode in Nevada, and San Bernardino county, Calif.

Composition, AgCl.; hardness, 2–3; specific gravity, 5.5; crystal system, isometric.

CERBERUS, sûr'bər-əs, in Greek mythology, was the watchdog of Hades. His job was to keep the living from entering and the dead from leaving. He was supposed to have had three heads, the tail of a snake, and snakes coiled around his neck. Cerberus figures most prominently as the 12th and final labor of Hercules (Herakles), who brings Cerberus back from the lower world (Hades).

CEREAL, sir'ē-əl. The word "cereal" is derived from Cerealia, the name given ancient Roman ceremonies held in the honor of Ceres, the goddess of grain. Cereals are members of the grass family, grown for their edible seeds. They include wheat, oats, rye, barley, corn, millet, and rice. For a discussion of their uses and information on their cultivation, see GRAINS.

CEREBELLUM, a major division of the brain. See BRAIN.

CEREBRAL HEMORRHAGE. See APOPLEXY.

CEREBRAL PALSY, ser'ə-brəl pôl'zē, is a disorder in which muscular control and coordination are impaired due to brain damage. In many patients, speech and hearing are also affected, and the patient may also be mentally retarded. Cerebral palsy is usually first noted in infancy or early childhood.

It is estimated that there are probably more than half a million cases of cerebral palsy in the United States. Each year there are six new cases for every 100,000 people. Of these six, roughly two are feebleminded and four have normal intelligence. Of these four, one is mildly affected, two are moderately affected, and one is severely affected. People who are mildly affected require very little attention and should perform more or less normally in school or at work. A moderately involved patient may require some assistance in his daily activities and may also need physical, occupational, or speech therapy, though he is usually able to attend either public school or a special school for the handicapped. The moderately involved patient may also require more intensive care at regular intervals to prevent him from becoming severely involved. The severely involved patient is either predominantly or totally dependent on outside help and may be either homebound or institutionalized, depending on his mental state and other factors.

Types of Cerebral Palsy. The various forms of cerebral palsy are sometimes classified into four major groups according to the type of disability. Some patients have a combination of two or more of these types, depending on the area and degree of brain involvement.

Well over half of all patients exhibit at least a partial spastic weakness of one or more extremities. In this type, known as *spastic* cerebral palsy, the muscles are under a continuous state of tension, with increased reflex activity. About 40% of all patients have the *athetoid* type, with disorganized spontaneous muscular movements. In these patients the extremities move involuntarily in many different directions.

The *ataxic* form, which occurs in relatively few patients, is manifested as a disturbance in balance while walking or standing. These patients may fall often and frequently cannot move about without assistance. In patients with the *tremor* type, there is a spontaneous vibration, or trembling, of one or more of the extremities.

The various forms of cerebral palsy are also often further divided into four groups on the basis of the particular extremities involved. In *monoplegia*, only one limb is affected. In *hemiplegia*, there is involvement of an arm and a leg on the same side of the body. *Diplegia*, or *paraplegia*, indicates involvement of either both arms or both legs. In *quadriplegia*, all four limbs are affected.

Cause. The brain damage that produces cerebral palsy may result from a variety of causes. Sometimes it occurs before birth as the result of a disease or injury that affects the fetus in the mother's uterus. Difficulties during childbirth may also produce brain damage. In later life, it may result from various infections, vascular diseases, or head injuries.

Each type of cerebral palsy is caused by damage to a different area of the brain. Damage to the motor regions of the cerebral cortex results in the spastic type, while damage to the basal ganglia (special masses of gray matter at the base of the brain produces the athetoid type. The ataxic and tremor types are caused by damage to the cerebellum. Associated difficulties in speech, hearing, or vision are usually due to damage of the brain centers governing these functions. Similarly, mental retardation results when areas of the cerebral cortex concerned with intelligence and other higher functions are affected.

Treatment. Many drugs have been used to help relieve spasticity, but these usually have met with only short-term success. The primary goal in treating cerebral palsy is to maintain or improve the functioning of the patient by the use of such services as phyiscal therapy, occupational therapy, speech therapy, and social and psychological counseling. In addition, the application of braces or other appliances may be helpful, and in some cases surgery is used.

Physical therapy for the cerebral palsy patient includes exercise programs aimed at preventing permanent muscle and joint tightness and attempting to improve muscular strength, control, and coordination. Although such programs may be started while the patient is in a hospital or other institution, a home program of therapy should be continued with help from the patient's family.

Occupational therapy may be of significant value to the mildly affected patient and may help a moderately involved patient to care for himself more effectively. Appropriate social and psychological counseling throughout the patient's life can be important in helping him adjust to his condition. Generally, optimum physical benefits cannot be achieved until the patient has adjusted to his social and psychological problems.

Speech therapy can be of particular value in assisting the patient's family in communicating with him. It is most helpful for patients with either aphasia or dysarthria. Aphasia, caused by damage to the speech center of the brain, is a difficulty in comprehension, expression, or both. Dysarthria is a difficulty in articulation and is caused by abnormal functioning of the muscles of the face and mouth.

Various kinds of appliances, such as braces, splints, and standing tables, may be helpful in preventing deformities, controlling involuntary movements, supporting the patient's weight, and enabling him to walk. A number of surgical procedures can also be of value in helping a patient achieve maximum functioning. Such operations include lengthening the heel cords when there is severe tightness of the calf muscles, releasing thigh muscles that are contracted, and fusing certain joints, such as the ankle or wrist. Also, it might be hepful to cut certain nerves supplying severely spastic and tightened muscles, and muscle transplants may occasionally be helpful. Patients with athetoid cerebral palsy may be helped by cryosurgery, in which the damaged tissue is destroyed by chilling it to a very low temperature.

Prognosis. Although there is no cure for cerebral palsy, the patient should be given maximum opportunity in both his home and educational environment to achieve as high a functional level as possible. Many patients can live relatively normal, productive lives if optimal use of their abilities can be realistically combined with appropriate therapy and satisfactory adjustments to their disabilities.

KENNETH ARCHIBALD, M. D.
Temple University School of Medicine

CEREBROSPINAL MENINGITIS. See MENINGITIS.

CEREBRUM, one of the major divisions of the brain. See BRAIN.

CEREMONY, a formal act or series of acts conducted with more or less elaborate ritual that marks the sacredness or solemnity of an occasion. The word derives from the Latin *caerimonia* (ritual), which may have been first used to describe an official act by which the inhabitants of Caere, an ancient Etruscan city, were granted Roman citizenship. In highly stratified societies, ceremonies often determine the relations between the members of that society.

See also CONVENTION; ETIQUETTE; LITURGY; PROTOCOL; and references listed under the Index entry *Rite and Ritual.*

CERENKOV, Pavel Alekseyevich. See CHERENKOV, PAVEL ALEKSEYEVICH.

CERES, sir'ēz, in Roman mythology, was an earth goddess, the patroness of agriculture, especially of fruit and grain. She was known to the Greeks as *Demeter.*

Ceres was the daughter of Saturn (Greek, Cronus) and Rhea, and a sister of Jupiter (Greek, Zeus), by whom she was the mother of Proserpina (Greek, Persephone).

While Proserpina was gathering flowers in Enna, in Sicily, a region of perpetual spring, she was admired by Pluto (Greek, Hades), who carried her off to his domain in the lower world, or the abode of the dead. In her anger, Ceres caused the earth to become barren, and she set out in search of her daughter. Disguised as an old woman, Ceres came to Eleusis, in Attica, where she was received hospitably by King Celeus, who gave her the care of his ailing infant son, Triptolemus (or Demophoön). She cured the boy but was prevented by his mother, Metaneira, from putting him in a fire to make him immortal. Ceres revealed her identity and took the boy away in her chariot. She taught him the arts of agriculture, which he gave to the world, and on his return home he built a temple to Ceres and instituted the Eleusinian mysteries in her honor.

Pluto, urged by the gods, consented to give up Proserpina, but before he allowed her to return, he tricked her into eating some pomegranate seds. Because of this, Proserpina was required to spend one third of the year in Hades. Nevertheless, Ceres rejoiced at her daughter's return and restored fertility to the earth.

CERES, sir'ēz, in astronomy, is the largest of the minor planets, or asteroids. It is named for the Roman goddess of agriculture. Ceres was the first asteroid to be discovered; it was observed by the Italian astronomer Giuseppe Piazzi in 1801 as he searched for the planet that had been predicted by Bode's law to exist between the orbits of Mars and Jupiter. Its orbit was later calculated by the German mathematician Karl Friedrich Gauss.

Ceres has a diameter of 593 miles (955 km). It travels around the sun in 4.6 years, with its mean distance from the sun being about 257 million miles (414 million km). Ceres' apparent magnitude at mean opposition is about +7. See also ASTEROID; SOLAR SYSTEM.

CEREUS, si′rē-əs, is a small genus of cactuses, mostly native to South America and the West Indies. These cactuses are normally tall and treelike, with brightly colored funnel-shaped flowers that open at night. Their fleshy fruits are usually red and in some species they are edible. Probably the best known species is the hedge cactus (*Cereus peruvianus*), which reaches a height of 50 feet (15 meters) and is widely grown as a feature plant of cactus gardens in tropical regions. It has long spines and white flowers 6 inches (15 cm) long.

Contrary to its name, the night blooming cereus is not a member of this genus. Actually, the name is applied to 3 different species, the most popular of which is *Hylocereus undatus,* a plant native to tropical America. It has a high-climbing stem with 3 wavy ribs and bears white flowers that are often 12 inches (30 cm) long. The red fruits are edible and about 4½ inches (11.5 cm) long.

DONALD WYMAN
Arnold Arboretum, Harvard University

CERF, sûrf, **Bennett Alfred** (1898–1971), American publisher and editor, president of Random House. Cerf was born in New York City and studied at Columbia University. He worked in journalism and publishing until 1925 when, with Donald S. Klopfer, he bought the Modern Library, a series of inexpensive reprints of literary classics, which they made into a successful enterprise. In 1927 they founded Random House, publisher of notable trade titles, including Joyce's *Ulysses* (1934) and of the *Random House Dictionary of the English Language* (1966). Cerf edited many books, chiefly collections such as the book of humor *Try and Stop Me* (1945) and *Encyclopedia of American Humor* (1954).

An enthusiastic raconteur, Cerf also lectured, was a panelist on the television show *What's My Line?*, and wrote a syndicated column, *Cerfboard.* He died in Mount Kisco, N. Y., Aug. 27, 1971.

CERIGNOLA, chä-rē-nyô′lä, is a town and commune in southeastern Italy, in Foggia province in the region of Apulia. The town is situated 23 miles (37 km) southeast of the city of Foggia on some low hills at an elevation of about 400 feet (120 meters). It serves as a marketing center for a region where grapes, olives, almonds, and grains are grown and sheep are raised. The town has an agricultural school and is the seat of a bishop.

On April 28, 1503, the Spanish, in their conquest of the Kingdom of Naples, won a decisive victory over the French near Cerignola. Population: (1961) of the town, 43,345; (1966 est.), of the commune, 48,488.

CERIUM, sir′ē-əm, symbol Ce, is the most abundant of the metallic rare-earth elements. The metal was discovered in 1803 by the German chemist Martin Heinrich Klaproth and by the Swedish chemists Jöns Jakob Berzelius and Wilhelm Hisinger. The name "cerium" was derived from the name of the asteroid Ceres, which was discovered two years earlier.

Properties. Cerium is a soft steel-gray metal, which may ignite if scratched with a file. If undisturbed, the metal is only slowly oxidized by dry air at low temperatures. The atomic number of cerium is 58, and its atomic weight is 140.12. It has 14 known isotopes, ranging from ^{133}Ce to ^{146}Ce. ^{140}Ce constitutes about 88% of the naturally occurring isotopes and ^{142}Ce about 11%.

Each of the rare-earth, or lanthanide, elements has a common valence of $+3$; however, cerium is an exception in that it can also have a valence of $+4$. The higher oxidation state is useful for separating cerium from the other rare earths and also makes it possible for cerium to form very strong oxidizing agents, such as $Ce(ClO_4)_4$.

Cerium melts at 795° C (1463° F) and boils at 3469° C (6240° F). It displays four allotropic forms, depending on the temperature. The pure metal is somewhat harder than magnesium, with a tensile strength of about 15,000 lb/sq in and a hardness of 35 on the Brinell hardness scale.

Preparation. Cerium metal is generally prepared by the reduction of very pure metal fluoride or chloride either by electrolysis or calcium metal reduction. Refinement techniques include zone refining and vacuum distillation processes. The purity of commercial cerium is generally about 99.9%.

Uses. The uses of pure cerium are limited. However, misch metal, which is a mixture of rare-earth metals, is used in flints for cigarette lighters, as an additive to remove oxides from cast iron and steel, and as a gas adsorbent in electronic tubes. The oxides of cerium are used in the ceramics and carbon industries, but most applications involve mixed rare-earth oxides.

Occurrence. Cerium is found in numerous minerals, the most important of which are monazite and bastnaesite. Monazite ore is the principal source for the metal's commercial production.

DOUGLAS V. KELLER, JR.
Syracuse University

CERMET, sûr′met, is a material made from two dissimilar materials, one a ceramic and the other a metal, that has physical properties intermediate between those of its two components. Ceramic materials are very strong at high temperatures; however, they are quite brittle and do not withstand impact well. Metals, on the other hand, are quite ductile and have high impact strength, but they are weak at high temperatures. By combining metal and ceramic, it is possible to obtain a material that maintains its strength at high temperatures and is not as brittle as a ceramic.

Cermets are produced by the techniques of powder metallurgy. The metal and ceramic are combined on a microscale by mixing very fine powders of two components. The mixture of powders is compacted into the desired shape under high pressure and then heated (sintered) to form a solid. Most cermets look like metals, and a microscopic examination is necessary to determine the presence of the ceramic.

Nickel/titanium-carbide cermets have been studied extensively as materials for possible use in jet engines, and titanium carbide may be combined with several metals to produce hard, tough tool bits for machining operations. Chromium-bonded alumina has a high resistance to oxidation at high temperatures as well as high thermal shock resistance; it is used for thermocouple tubing and for temperature-sensing probes in melting metals. Cermets of aluminum and uranium dioxide are used as fuel elements in nuclear reactors.

JAMES R. TINKLEPAUGH
College of Ceramics, Alfred University

CERRO DE PASCO, ser'rô thâ päs'kō, a mining center in Peru, is the capital of Pasco department. It is situated high in the Andes in the central part of the country, 110 miles (177 km) northeast of Lima, to which it is connected by railroad and highway. Cerro de Pasco's elevation, about 14,000 feet (4,267 meters) above sea level, makes it one of the highest cities in the world.

Rich silver ores first discovered at Cerro de Pasco in 1630 led to the founding of the city. The mines yielded well until late in the 1800's. In the early 1900's it gained new importance with the exploitation of other minerals—copper, gold, lead, zinc, and bismuth. The main product, copper, is smelted at La Oroya, a town 20 miles (32 km) to the southeast, and from there is shipped to Lima over a rail line designed by the United States engineer Henry Meiggs (1811–1877). Population: (1972) 47,178.

GREGORY RABASSA, *Columbia University*

CERRO GORDO, Battle of, ser'rô gôr'thō, in the Mexican War, fought on April 17-18, 1847, about 40 miles (64 km) west of Veracruz, Mexico. Gen. Winfield Scott, the American commander, captured Veracruz on March 29 after a 20-day siege and moved his army westward toward Mexico City, 270 miles (434 km) distant. Gen. Antonio López de Santa Anna, the Mexican commander, fortified strong positions on hills near the hamlet of Cerro Gordo, manned by a force of 12,000. On April 18, Scott's troops made a general attack and the Mexicans fled, suffering heavy losses, especially in prisoners. The American losses were light.

CERTIFIED PUBLIC ACCOUNTANT. See ACCOUNTING.

CERTIORARI, sûr-shē-ə-râr'ē, in law, is a writ, or formal legal document, issued by a higher court to request the record of a proceeding in an inferior court or administrative body so that the higher court may determine whether the inferior tribunal acted beyond its powers or in violation of the parties' legal rights. The writ is usually obtained by the unsuccessful party. It is not a matter of right, so its issuance is within the discretion of the higher court. Hence "denial of certiorari" by the U. S. Supreme Court does not of itself determine any legal issue. The other avenue to the Supreme Court is by appeal, in which case the court must review a case properly before it, provided a "substantial federal question" is presented.

LINDA ALDEN MOODY
School of Law, Columbia University

CERUSSITE, sə-rus'īt, is mineral lead carbonate and an important ore of lead. It occurs in the upper zone of lead veins in association with galena and is found in fibrous crystalline aggregates and in massive or earthy form. The transparent to translucent crystals are white or light yellow to gray, but inclusions sometimes make them green, blue, or black. They are brittle and have a diamondlike luster. Cerussite is a widespread mineral, and good occurrences are too numerous to list; some the the notable localities are in Germany, Sardinia, Siberia, and Australia. In the United States cerussite is mined in Arizona, Colorado, and other Western states.

Composition, $PbCO_3$; hardness, 3–3.5; specific gravity, 6.5–6.6; crystal system, orthorhombic.

CERVANTES, ther-vän'täs, **Miguel de** (1547–1616), Spanish writer, who was Spain's greatest literary genius and among the most esteemed figures in world literature. His works, the greatest of which is *Don Quixote* (q.v.), exemplify the fusion of Renaissance humanism and aesthetics with the disillusion, skepticism, and critical attitudes of the baroque period. Cervantes' style is a harmonious balance between the affected rhetoric of the 16th century and the natural spoken language. His role in Spanish literature is similar in several respects to that of Lope de Vega (1562–1635). Both stood at the crossroads between the Renaissance and the baroque; both splendidly synthesized the ideas and habits of their fellow Spaniards; and both were the creators of modern literary genres in Spain: Cervantes in the novel and Lope in the theater. However, there the comparison ends, for Lope had worthy competitors but Cervantes was without peers.

LIFE

Miguel de Cervantes Saavedra was born in Alcalá de Henares, a town near Madrid. He was baptized on Oct. 9, 1547; although the exact day of his birth is not known, it is believed that he was born on September 29, the day of San Miguel (Saint Michael), whose name he bears. Miguel was the fourth of seven children born to Leonor de Cortinas and Rodrigo de Cervantes, a member of the minor nobility, who evidently was unsuccessful in his practice of surgery. In 1551, seeking a livelihood, the father moved his family from town to town in Spain—to Valladolid, Córdoba, Seville, and Madrid.

Cervantes probably studied with the Jesuits in Córdoba or Seville, and perhaps spent two years at the University of Salamanca, the oldest Spanish university. In 1568–1569 he studied in Madrid with Juan López de Hoyos, a humanist, who probably instilled in the young man a desire for knowledge and a love of freedom. In 1569, by publishing three poems in which Cervantes honored the death of Isabel of Valois, the third wife of Philip II, López de Hoyos revealed his affection for his disciple. The same year, Cervantes went to Rome in the service of Guilio Acquaviva, who became a cardinal in 1570. Scholars can only speculate as to Cervantes' reason for going to Italy. It could have been to seek adventure, to make his way in the world, or to escape punishment for a youthful indiscretion.

Military Career. In 1570, Cervantes became a soldier, and on Oct. 7, 1571, fought in the naval battle of Lepanto, in which the forces of Don Juan of Austria, half brother of Philip II of Spain, defeated the Turks. Cervantes fought bravely aboard the galley *Marquesa* and received a wound in the chest and another that permanently maimed his left hand. This injury to his hand earned him the title "Cripple of Lepanto," a nickname of which he was very proud. After his recuperation in Messina, Sicily, he returned to active duty in the campaigns of Corfu and Navarino (1572) and Tunis (1573).

In September 1575 he and his brother Rodrigo set out on the galley *Sol* for Spain, carrying letters written by Don Juan of Austria and the Duke of Sesa, viceroy of Sicily, recommending him for promotion. The *Sol* was captured by Barbary pirates, and for five years Cervantes was a slave of the Moors in Algiers. His brother was ransomed two years after their capture, but Miguel's ransom was set much higher because the

Cervantes (left), the creator of Don Quixote. The artist Daumier's concept of the Don and his faithful squire Sancho Panza is pictured above.

Moors thought he was a more important captive in view of the influential letters of recommendation they found in his possession. Four times he participated in unsuccessful attempts to escape from captivity. Finally, on Sept. 19, 1580, two Trinitarian monks effected his release with the payment of 500 escudos raised by their order and Cervantes' family.

Return to Spain. When Cervantes returned to Madrid, he found his family in dire poverty and his war service forgotten. He held several temporary and ill-paid administrative posts of little consequence. Then he returned energetically to literature, and between 1583 and 1587 wrote his pastoral novel *La Galatea*, a number of plays, and some poetry. During this time he had a love affair with an actor's wife named either Ana Franca de Rojas or Ana de Villafranca, and from this union was born Isabel de Saavedra. On Dec. 12, 1584, he married Catalina de Salazar Palacios of Esquivias, near Toledo. She was a girl almost half his age, and her dowry consisted of a house and some land not far from Madrid. From 1585 to 1587 the couple lived in Esquivias, paying occasional visits to Madrid to tend to matters related to Cervantes' writings. The marriage proved to be a failure, and toward the end of 1587, Cervantes left his wife. During the next 20 years he led a nomadic existence, traveling about Spain in an effort to eke out a livelihood.

In Seville, Cervantes became a purchasing agent for the Spanish Armada, which Philip II was outfitting for his attack on England. Cervantes was not really a suitable choice for this post or others like it. He squabbled with peasants who refused to pay a share of their crops to the government; he was accused of mismanaging funds; he lost money because of bank failures; he was excommunicated by the church for expropriating its wheat; and he was brought to trial several times and imprisoned at least twice (1592 and 1597) because of fiscal irregularities. In 1590 he had sought and been denied a post in the American possessions of Spain. During one of his incarcerations (probably the second one, which was in a Sevillian jail) Cervantes conceived the idea for or began to write *Don Quixote*. His prologue to this work states that it was "engendered in some dismal prison where wretchedness is rooted and every dismal noise resides." The scoundrels and criminals he encountered in prison appeared in his fiction, their behavior and language realistically portrayed.

Last Years. In 1603 or 1604, Cervantes went to live with his two sisters, his illegitimate daughter, and a niece in Valladolid, where Philip III had established his court. The first part of *Don Quixote* was published early in 1605. During the evening of June 27 of the same year, Gaspar de Ezpeleta, a nobleman, was mortally wounded outside Cervantes' house, and Cervantes and several members of his family were arrested and charged with complicity in Ezpeleta's death. Although they were exonerated of this crime, there is evidence to indicate that the morality of the family, especially that of the women, was held in low esteem.

Cervantes moved to Madrid when the court returned there in 1606, and he remained there the rest of his life. In the next 11 years, his major works appeared: in 1613, *Exemplary Tales* (*Novelas ejemplares*); in 1614, *Journey to Parnassus* (*Viaje del Parnaso*), a volume of poems; and in 1615, the second part of *Don Quixote* and *Eight Comedies and Eight Interludes* (*Ocho comedias y ocho entremeses*), a collection of plays. He finished *Persiles and Sigismunda* (*Persiles y Sigismunda*) not long before his death in Madrid on April 23, 1616. Despite his attainment of wide recognition as an outstanding literary figure in the final years of his life, Cervantes continued to be harassed by poverty and was bitterly disillusioned over the conduct of his illegitimate daughter.

WRITINGS

Poetry. Cervantes wrote a substantial amount of poetry using Italianate as well as traditional Spanish meters. He composed poems on contemporary events, love poems, laudatory verses dedicated to contemporary poets, and such patriotic compositions as the poems on the "Invincible Armada." He frequently included pastoral poetry in his novels and plays. In his longest poem, *Journey to Parnassus*, an allegory consisting of almost 3,000 verses in tercets, Cervantes praises the chief poets of his epoch and presents an appreciation of his own works and of the literary genres then in vogue. Despite his heroic efforts to excel in poetry, he was aware of his shortcomings in this genre. He was a good poet but could not rival such contemporaries as Fernando de Herrera, Luis de León, Góngora, Quevedo, and Lope de Vega.

Drama. Cervantes was probably Spain's best dramatist prior to the advent of Lope de Vega. In his prologue to *Eight Comedies and Eight Interludes,* Cervantes states that between 1581 and 1587 he wrote some 20 or 30 plays. Of these only two are extant: *The Algerian Affair* (*El trato de Argel*), a series of scenes lacking in dramatic unity, based on his captivity in Algiers; and *The Siege of Numancia* (*El cerco de Numancia*), an allegorical dramatization in praise of Spanish heroism. *The Siege of Numancia* is based on a historical episode in the 2d century B. C., in which 4,000 Numantians, preferring death to surrender and dishonor, resisted 80,000 Roman soldiers during a long siege that ended with the complete annihilation of the besieged.

In *Eight Comedies and Eight Interludes,* Cervantes demonstrates his acceptance of some of Lope de Vega's dramatic theories, including the use of three acts instead of four, the abandonment of the dramatic unities, and the use of a variety of themes. He accepts Lope's principle of verisimilitude by introducing, for comic relief, the figure of the *gracioso,* a servant who parodies the actions of his master.

Cervantes' fame as a dramatist derives chiefly from his interludes (*entremeses*), short comic pieces often satirical in nature. His models for the interludes were the popular one-act plays of Lope de Rueda (1510?–1565), some of which Cervantes saw performed in his youth. Cervantes surpassed all other writers of interludes. His are notable for their realistic, lively dialogue, true-to-life characters, benevolent humor that never becomes bitter even when it is satirical, and natural, unaffected style. *The Marvelous Puppet Show* (*El retablo de las maravillas*), generally considered the best of his interludes, is a sharp satire exposing the hypocrisy of the inhabitants of a Spanish town, who, in order to demonstrate the purity of their lineage, pretend to see nonexistent action on an empty puppet stage. Other interludes by Cervantes deal with the amorous rivalry between a soldier and a sacristan, in which the latter wins; marital spats and cuckoldry; and a humorous version of the way in which a village elects a mayor.

Novels and Stories. Cervantes' first published work was *La Galatea* (1585), a run-of-the-mill example of the pastoral novels that were so popular in the 16th century. *La Galatea*'s plot is complicated and loosely knit, its action is slow, and its style lacks the liveliness, grace, and vigor of Cervantes later prose writings. However, there is present in *La Galatea* the idealism that was a fundamental constant in his later works.

The *Exemplary Tales* are contemporaneous with *Don Quixote.* Had Cervantes never written his great masterpiece, these short stories, which Cervantes called *novelas,* would have been sufficient to ensure their author's place among the Spanish literary giants. Cervantes borrowed the word *novela* from the Italian *novella* (a short story or tale), the form used in the *Decameron* of Boccaccio and by other Italian masters. However, although he utilized the external structure of the short story successfully cultivated by the Italian *novellieri,* Cervantes owes no substantive debt to their writings; his *Exemplary Tales* are as uniquely his own creation as is *Don Quixote.*

In his prologue to this collection of 12 tales Cervantes rightfully claims the distinction of being the first to write short stories in Castilian. The prologue further informs the reader that he uses the word "exemplary" in the title because each story will teach some profitable lesson. Realism predominates in some tales, idealism in others, and in some stories realism and idealism are inextricably intertwined. The stories demonstrate Cervantes' ability to depict with superb perspicacity the life of his fellow Spaniards. Among the best known of them are: *The Gypsy Maid* (*La gitanilla*), in which the love affair between the beautiful gypsy girl Preciosa and a young gentleman romantically unfolds amid vividly drawn scenes of gypsy life; *Rinconete and Cortadillo* (*Rinconete y Cortadillo*), a delightful story of the adventures of two youths in a section of Seville infested by scoundrels and thieves; *The Dialogue of the Dogs* (*El coloquio de los perros*), a satire narrated by the talking dogs Cipion and Berganza; *Master Glass* (*El licenciado vidriera*), a satirical censure of contemporary life by a madman who believes himself made of glass; *The Jealous Estremenian* (*El celoso extremeño*), the tale of a rich old man who tries to keep his very young bride from committing adultery; and *The Illustrious Kitchen Maid* (*La ilustre fregona*), the story of the love between a noble young man and an aristocratic girl disguised as a scullery maid.

Three days before his death, Cervantes wrote the last lines of his extensive Byzantine novel *The Exploits of Persiles and Sigismunda* (*Los trabajos de Persiles y Sigismunda*), which was published in 1617. In this baroque novel filled with adventures of sheer fantasy, the author pays little heed to the psychology of the characters.

"Don Quixote." The greatest work in Spanish literature is Cervantes' *The Ingenious Gentleman Don Quixote of La Mancha* (*El ingenioso hidalgo Don Quijote de la Mancha*), known simply as *Don Quixote,* the first part of which was published in Madrid in January 1605. Part I is divided into four very unequal sections and consists of 52 chapters. It gained a good measure of immediate popularity, as evidenced by the six subsequent editions that appeared in that year. During Cervantes' lifetime, 16 editions of Part I were published, including translations into English and French, and hundreds of copies were shipped to the New World. In 1614, using the pseudonym Alonso Fernández de Avellaneda, an unknown author (whose identity has still not been uncovered) published an apocryphal continuation of the adventures of *Don Quixote.* The publication of this book undoubtedly urged Cervantes into finishing the second part of his masterpiece, which he published at the end of 1615. Part 2, which was not divided into sections, consists of 4 chapters.

In the prologue to the first part of *Don Quixote,* Cervantes informs the reader that his work is "an invective against books of chivalry." It is quite possible that Cervantes initially planned to parody the novels of chivalry that had enjoyed tremendous popularity in the 16th century but were becoming unfashionable by the beginning of the 17th century. The influence of such romances of chivalry as Montalvo's *Amadis of Gaul* and Francisco de Moraes' *Palmerin of England* is patent in *Don Quixote.*

The novel describes a series of adventures in which Don Quixote, like a knight-errant in a chivalric novel, endeavors to right the injustices of the world about him. On his first expedition, Don Quixote is alone and rather promptly returns home battered and bruised. He then convinces the laborer Sancho Panza to accompany him as his squire, and the two set out on a round of adventures that take up the rest of the first part of the book. Despite failure after failure, the knight and his squire persevere.

Several apparently extraneous episodes slow down the progress of the main story. Included in Part I are imitations of the kinds of short novels then fashionable: the pastoral, as exemplified in the story of Marcela and Crisóstome; the Moorish, in the narration of the captive; the sentimental, in the story of Cardenio and Lucinda; the exemplary, in the story of foolish curiosity; and the picaresque, in the episode of the galley slaves.

In Part 2, Cervantes yielded to readers' criticism and abandoned the technique of intercalaing stories. The second part contains less action and makes greater use of dialogue, and gives the reader deeper insight into the psychology of the two main characters. Don Quixote gradually becomes disillusioned, and on his deathbed regains his sanity and confesses the folly of his past adventures.

Don Quixote is the idealistic reformer, selfless and of sterling morality; Sancho is materialistic and self-seeking, but loyal to his master and capable of sincere and generous acts. As the novel progresses, they affect and complement each other, not unlike a husband and wife who have lived together for many years. The two protagonists represent a composite of all men who embody in varying degrees the quixotic and the materialistic. At the end of the novel the two characters reverse their roles: Don Quixote returns to sanity, and Sancho, in tears, pleads with his master to remain in the service of his lady Dulcinea and continue helping humanity.

Cervantes' unique skill in creating people of flesh and blood extends to the minor characters, whose variety is boundless. This profoundly human work, which spendidly captures the reality of early 17th century Spain, is written in a beautiful, natural, and stately style. Its universal appeal has made it the world's most famous and most often published novel.

DONALD W. BLEZNICK, University of Cincinnati

Bibliography

Arbó, Sebastián Juan, Cervantes, tr. by Ilsa Barea (New York 1955).
Bell, Aubrey, F. G., Cervantes (Norman, Okla., 1947).
Croft-Cooke, Rupert, Through Spain with Don Quixote (New York 1960).
Entwistle, William J., Cervantes (New York 1940).
Fitzmaurice-Kelly, James, Miguel de Cervantes Saavedra: A Memoir (Oxford 1913).
Flores, Angel, and Benardete, Mercedes J., eds., Cervantes Across the Centuries (New York 1948).
Frank, Bruno, A Man Called Cervantes, tr. from the German by H. T. Lowe-Porter (New York 1935).
Ford, Jeremiah D. M., and Lansing, Ruth, Cervantes: A Tentative Bibliography (Cambridge, Mass., 1931).
Grismer, Raymond L., Cervantes: A Bibliography, 2 vols. (New York 1946; Minneapolis 1963).
Lewis, D. B., Wyndham, The Shadow of Cervantes (New York 1962).
Mac Eóin, Gary, Cervantes (Milwaukee 1950).
Madariaga, Salvador de, Don Quixote: An Introductory Essay in Psychology, tr. by the author and Constance H. M. de Madariaga (New Town, Wales, 1935).
Ortega y Gasset, José, Meditations on Quixote, tr. by Evelyn Rugg and Julián Marías (New York 1963).
Predmore, Richard L., The World of Don Quixote (Cambridge, Mass., 1967).
Riley, Edward C., Cervantes' Theory of the Novel (New York 1962).
Schevill, Rudolph, Cervantes (New York 1919).
Van Doren, Mark, Don Quixote's Profession (New York 1958).
Watts, Henry Edward, Life of Miguel de Cervantes (London 1891).

CÉSAIRE, sā-zâr', **Aimé** (1913–   ), Martinican Negro poet writing in French, one of the leading spokesmen of Négritude. He was born in Martinique on June 25, 1913, and was educated in Paris. Césaire introduced the term Négritude in his Cahier d'un retour au pays natal (1939–1956). By Négritude he understood the "simple recognition of the fact of being a Negro and the acceptance of this fact and of its cultural and historical consequences."

The themes of Césaire's poetry are revolt, denunciation of colonialism, and the recovery of the lost dignity of the Negroes. The imagination is visionary, and the rhythms often syncopated. In two lyrical plays, Et les chiens se taisaient (1956) and La tragédie du roi Christophe (1963), Césaire criticizes the apathy of the Caribbean masses and extols the courage of its leaders.

Césaire's active political involvement in Martinique is paralled by his work as a historian. Discours sur le colonialisme (1956) analyzes colonial mentality, and the biography Toussaint Louverture (1962) glorifies the Haitian patriot.

EMILE SNYDER
University of Wisconsin, Madison

CESALPINO, chä-zäl-pē'nō, **Andrea** (1525–1603), Italian botanist, physician, and philosopher, who is best known for his classification of plants and his early studies of blood circulation. In his De plantis (1583), Cesalpino divided plants into woody and herbaceous kinds and classified them according to the number of seeds, the position of the embryo in the seed, and other characteristics. In all, Cesalpino classified plants into 32 groups, some corresponding to modern families.

As a physician, Cesalpino stated that there is a perpetual movement of blood from the veins into the heart and from the heart into the arteries. He also maintained that blood passes through the lungs on its way from the right to the left side of the heart. However, Cesalpino stated his views very cautiously and never formulated a convincing theory of blood circulation, as did William Harvey.

Cesalpino was born in Arezzo, Italy, in 1525. He was professor of botany and director of the botanical garden at Pisa and later physician to Pope Clement VIII. Although he was a careful, critical, and original observer, he stated all his views in an Aristotelian manner and thus severely limited himself. He died in Rome on March 15, 1603.

WILLIAM T. STEARN
British Museum (Natural History)

Further Reading: Pagel, Walter, William Harvey's Biological Ideas, pp. 169–209 (New York 1966).

CESAREAN SECTION, sə-zâr'ē-ən, is the delivery of a baby through an incision in the mother's abdomen. The name is apparently derived from an ancient Roman law, Lex caesarea, requiring dying women to be operated on in the last weeks of pregnancy in an effort to save the child—and not, as commonly believed, from the method of Julius Caesar's birth.

A cesarean section is usually performed because the mother's pelvis is too small to allow the baby's head to pass through it, as would occur during normal delivery. Although a cesarean section may be performed before the mother's labor pains begin, it is more often done after she has had pain for several hours and it has been shown that the baby's head cannot descend. This waiting period is known as a "test of labor." Other reasons for performing a cesarean section include severe hemorrhaging from the uterus, an abnormal positioning of the baby, or high blood pressure or diabetes in the mother.

There is great controversy among doctors about how to deliver subsequent babies after a woman's first child has been delivered by cesarean section. If the reason for the first operation was a too-small pelvis, then all later deliveries of normal-sized babies must be by cesarean. But many doctors give a test of labor after a woman has had a cesarean for reasons other than a too-small pelvis. The chief danger of a test of labor under these conditions is the possibility of a ruptured uterus. Although this danger is slight for the mother, it may be serious for the baby.

In choosing the appropriate time to perform the second cesarean section, it is important to make sure that the baby is developed enough to survive after birth. This may be determined through X rays, but it is considered best to wait for labor pains to begin or for the membranes surrounding the baby to break spontaneously. At that time the physician may decide to have a test of labor or to perform the cesarean. If the delivery promises to be easy, the baby should be permitted to come through the natural passages.

J. P. GREENHILL, M.D.
Michael Reese Hospital, Chicago

CESARI, chä′zä-rē, **Giuseppe** (1568?–1640), Italian painter of the mannerist school, also known as *Cavaliere d'Arpino.* He was born in Arpino or Rome and won riches and renown through the work he did for popes, cardinals, nobles, and French kings. He retained the idealistic, artificial, mannerist style, although with imagination and vigor, against the more lifelike naturalistic style newly developed by his pupil Caravaggio. Cesari's best works are in Rome — frescoes in the Capitol, the Borghese Chapel of Santa Maria Maggiore, and the Olgisti chapel in Santa Prassede; the huge *Ascension* in St. John Lateran; and designs for mosaics in the dome of St. Peter's. Cesari died in Rome on July 3, 1640.

CESENA, chä-zâ′nä, is a city in northern Italy, in the Emilia-Romagna region. It is the market center of a prosperous farming district, some 20 miles (30 km) from the Adriatic. The outstanding single monument of Cesena is the Malatesta Library, one of the oldest and most perfectly preserved private libraries of medieval Europe. The library building, completed in 1452, is in pure Renaissance style. Above Cesena stands the 14th century fortress called La Rocca. Cesena's golden age was from 1379 to 1465. Population: city (1961), 31,153; commune (1966 estimate), 83,852.

GEORGE KISH
University of Michigan

CESIUM, sē′zē-əm, symbol Cs, is a soft, metallic element. It was discovered in 1860 by the German chemists Robert Bunsen and Gustav Kirchhoff. During the spectroscopic analysis of water, they detected the two blue lines of cesium; hence the name of the element, which was derived from *caesius,* the Latin word for "sky blue."

Properties. Cesium is a silver-white, ductile metal that is not much harder than cold butter. It explodes in the presence of water and burns brightly in humid air. It melts at 28.5°C (83.3°F)

and boils at 670°C (1238°F); its specific gravity is 1.90. Cesium is located in column 1A of the periodic table and is the heaviest of the common alkali metals. It has an oxidation number of $+1$. Its atomic number is 55, and its atomic weight is 132.91. There are 22 known isotopes of cesium with masses ranging from ^{123}Cs to ^{144}Cs. All naturally occurring cesium is ^{133}Cs.

Cesium is the most electropositive element. Because of its very low ionization potential, it reacts far more vigorously with oxidizing agents than do the other alkali metals. Like sodium and potassium, cesium forms many soluble salts with the mineral acids. Complex cesium ions are not common.

Occurrence. Cesium occurs in nature in highly concentrated deposits as the ore pollucite, which contains up to 28% of the metal. It is found in Canada, Africa, Sweden, and the USSR. Small amounts of cesium are also found in ores such as carnallite and lepidolite.

Production. Pollucite is usually handpicked from pegmatite deposits and then put through a complex separation process that eventually produces cesium chloride. The cesium chloride, together with a reducing metal such as calcium or lithium, is then heated in a vacuum furnace and the cesium allowed to boil off. Further vacuum distillations result in the production of cesium that is more than 99.9% pure.

Uses. Cesium, in small quantities, is used in some photoelectric radio tubes as the photosensitive material and in special vacuum tubes as a getter material to remove oxygen, water, and other substances. Research has also been conducted on the use of cesium as a fuel for deep-space ion-propulsion rocket engines.

DOUGLAS V. KELLER, JR.
Syracuse University

CÉSPEDES, thās′pā-thās, **Pablo de** (1538–1608), Spanish painter, sculptor, architect, and poet. He was born in Córdoba and attended the University of Alcalá de Henares, where he studied theology and Oriental languages. Later he went to Rome and, under the direction of Federigo Zuccaro, studied the works of Raphael, Michelangelo, and other artists. In 1560, while he was in Rome, the Inquisition of Valladolid instituted proceedings against him, but these were ultimately dropped. He returned to Spain in 1577 and was made a canon of Córdoba Cathedral. One of his most celebrated paintings is a *Last Supper,* in the Córdoba cathedral. He also painted a series of frescoes in the Seville cathedral. Céspedes wrote a number of poems and essays on art, including the poem *The Art of Painting,* which contains a eulogy of Michelangelo. Céspedes died in Córdoba on July 26, 1608.

CESSPOOL, ses′pool, an underground pit for receiving untreated wastes piped from households or commercial establishments. It is used in areas where there are no sewers. The pit is surrounded by naturally porous soil or emplaced porous material that filters the liquid portion of the waste before it joins the groundwater.

To construct a cesspool, a pit is excavated, and perforated sidewalls are built in the pit to support the adjacent soil. A cover is placed over the pit, with an opening for removing the solid wastes that fill it up. The cover, which is buried under backfill, must be sturdy and able to withstand corrosion.

A cesspool can pollute water wells, especially if there is fractured limestone or similar rock at the site. A few feet of sand or gravel adjacent to the cesspool usually will provide enough filtration to remove the danger of polluting the groundwater. The cesspool should be located as far as possible, preferably downhill, from the nearest well, and it should not be ventilated. The pipe to the cesspool should have tight joints to prevent the escape of wastes.

KENNETH W. COSENS, *Ohio State University*

CESTODA, ses-tō′də, a subclass of Cestoidean parasitic flatworms commonly known as *tapeworms*. Adult cestodes consist of a head (scolex), equipped with hooks and suckers for attachment to the host, and a ribbonlike, segmented body (strobila), usually joined by a narrow neck. They live in the intestines of vertebrate animals, and, since cestodes lack both a mouth and a digestive system, they absorb digested material directly through their body walls.

Each body segment (proglottid) develops both male and female organs and may fertilize itself or another segment. The embryos (onchospheres) pass to the outside to be swallowed by an appropriate host. Most cestodes require one or two intermediate hosts for the larva in addition to the final host of the adult. In some two-host types, the embryo in the intermediate host develops into a baglike form (bladder worm, or cysticercus) containing a single head. In some species, the baglike form (called a coenurus, or hydatid in *Echinococcus*) produces additional heads.

CESTRUM, ses′trəm, a large genus of tropical shrubs and small trees often grown for their attractive, usually fragrant, flowers. The species most often cultivated in the United States is *Cestrum nocturnum,* often called the night-blooming jessamine because its flowers open at night. This species, native to the West Indies, is a shrub about 12 feet (3.5 meters) tall with lustrous leaves from 4 to 8 inches (10 to 20 cm) long. Its flowers are greenish white, with a very heavy fragrance.

Another popular species, *C. parqui*, is sometimes called the willow-leaved jessamine. Native to Chile, it is a shrub from 6 to 10 feet (1.8 to 3 meters) tall with yellowish green flowers. Like the night jessamine, it is grown outdoors only in warm climates. In northern regions it is grown in greenhouses.

DONALD WYMAN
The Arnold Arboretum, Harvard University

CETACEA, sē-tā′shē-ə, an order of wholly aquatic mammals found in all seas and in certain tropical and temperate river systems. Though in a broad sense the term "whales" is applied to all members of the order, only the larger cetaceans are popularly called whales. Small cetaceans are referred to as either "dolphins" (especially in classical literature) or "porpoises" (by whalers and many zoologists).

Cetaceans range in size from about 4 feet (1200 mm) in length and 80 pounds (36 kg) in weight for the smaller porpoises to about 100 feet (30 meters) and 135 tons (122 metric tons) for the blue whale, the largest animal that ever lived. Coloration varies from solid black, to yellows, pinks, browns, or grays marked with spots or streaks, to vividly contrasting patterns of black and white.

Modern cetaceans are typified by a streamlined shape, paired pectoral (front) flippers containing limb bones and digits, and horizontal tail flukes without supporting bones. All cetaceans possess a fatty blubber coat that serves both as a food reservoir and as insulation. Breathing occurs through paired or single blowholes ("nostrils") on the top of the head, except in the sperm whale whose blowhole is located at the front of the snout.

The cetaceans are divided into two basic types: the *baleen,* or *whalebone, whales* and the *toothed whales* (which include the porpoises). Baleen whales possess a water-straining device, the baleen, consisting of a comblike row of fringed, horny plates hanging from each side of the roof of the mouth. Toothed whales feed largely on fish or squid and usually have numerous conical teeth lining the jaw margins.

CLASSIFICATION OF THE ORDER CETACEA

Suborder Archaeoceti (ancient whale ancestors—extinct)
Suborder Mysticeti (baleen, or whalebone, whales)
    Family Cetotheriidae (extinct)
    Family Balaenopteridae (finback, blue, humpback, and other rorqual whales)
    Family Balaenidae (right whales)
    Family Eschrichtiidae (gray whales)
Suborder Odontoceti (toothed whales)
    Superfamily Squalodontoidea (extinct toothed whales)
    Family Physeteridae (pygmy sperm and sperm whales)
    Family Hyperodontidae (beaked whales)
    Family Platanistidae (river porpoises)
    Family Stenidae (roughtooth porpoises)
    Family Phocoenidae (harbor and finless porpoises)
    Family Delphinidae (various river and oceanic porpoises; pilot and killer whales)
    Family Monodontidae (beluga and narwhal)

Gestation (pregnancy) ranges from 9 to 16 months. Birth and nursing (on milk) occur at sea, and the young grow rapidly.

Toothed whales commonly live in complex social orders within large schools; baleen whales seldom aggregate except during feeding or breeding. See also WHALE.

KENNETH S. NORRIS
University of California at Los Angeles

CETSHWAYO, ket-chwȧ′yō (1826–1884), was the fourth and last of the Zulu kings. His name is also spelled *Cetewayo.* An intelligent and conciliatory man, he was, like many other African rulers of the period, the victim of forces beyond his control.

White farmers in neighboring territories coveted his land, feared his army, and were shocked at a social system they did not understand. For a time he was able to play the Afrikaner Transvaal Republic off against the British colony of Natal, but in 1877, Britain annexed the Transvaal. Thereafter, the Zulu kingdom was regarded as a menace to South African security.

Although a Natal commission reported in favor of Cetshwayo's claims in his boundary dispute with the Transvaal, the British high commissioner forced the Zulu king into a war by demanding that he disband his army in 1878. British and colonial forces invaded Zululand. The Zulu won a great victory at Isandhlwana before they were overwhelmed in 1879.

Cetshwayo was captured, deposed, and exiled, and his kingdom was divided into 13 petty states, supervised by a British resident. Cetshwayo was allowed to return home, without royal status, in 1883. He died in Eshowe in February 1884.

LEONARD M. THOMPSON
University of California at Los Angeles

CETUS, sē'təs, is an autumn constellation that lies partly in the Northern but mainly in the Southern Hemisphere. In Greek mythology, Cetus (Latin for "whale") was the sea monster from which Perseus rescued Andromeda.

Although it is one of the largest constellations, Cetus contains no 1st-magnitude stars. The most important star in the constellation is Mira (the Wonderful), a variable star that was discovered in 1596 by the German theologian and astronomer

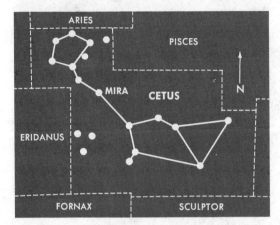

David Fabricius. Mira has a period of about 330 days and may drop in brightness from the 2d to the 10th magnitude, fading below the point of visibility. See also CONSTELLATION; MIRA.

CEUTA, thä'ōo-tä, a fortified city in North Africa, is a territory of Spain. The city occupies an enclave of 7.5 square miles (19 sq km) on the coast of Morocco, at the Mediterranean entrance to the Strait of Gibraltar. Situated only about 16 miles (26 km) south of Gibraltar, Ceuta is the closest African port to Europe.

The city stands on a narrow peninsula that runs east-west and is dominated by Mt. Acho (636 feet or 194 meters). Mt. Acho is probably ancient Abila (Abyla), which according to tradition constituted with Gibraltar the classical Pillars of Hercules. Ceuta's name in Arabic is *Sabta*, which probably derives from the name of the Roman colony on the peninsula, Ad Septem Fratres (Seven Brothers), so called from the seven hills rising there in a group.

Little remains of Ciudad Antigua, the old part

of Ceuta, on the western side of the peninsula. The modern town lies to the east on the slopes of Almina. Shipping is the major industry, followed by fishing and food processing. Ceuta is also important as a military station and a refueling port for ships.

Ceuta's strategic location has made it a prized possession throughout history. It has served both as the springboard for Muslim invasions of Spain and for Iberian inroads into Morocco. The site of Ceuta was first settled by the Phoenicians. Subsequently a Roman colony, the town was captured by the Vandals in the 5th century, passed to the Byzantine Empire in the 6th century, and fell to the Visigoths in 618. Taken by the Arabs in 711, it passed under a succession of Muslim dynasties before it was captured by Portugal in 1415. It passed into the possession of Spain in 1580 and has remained Spanish ever since, except for a brief British occupation from 1810 to 1814. Ceuta is regarded as an integral part of Spain. For administrative purposes, it is included in the province of Cádiz. Population: (1960) 73,182.

M. E. YAPP, *University of London*

CÉVENNES, sā-ven', a mountain range in France, is the principal range between the Alps and the mountains of the Auvergne. Lying mainly west of the Rhône River, it forms the watershed between the river systems of the Rhône and the Loire and Garonne. Its general direction is from northeast to southwest, beginning in the Monts du Vivarais near St.-Étienne, and extending under different local names as far as the Canal du Midi, which divides the Cévennes from the slopes of the Pyrenees.

The entire arc of the range extends into nine departments; the central mass, forming the Cévennes proper, rises in Hérault, Gard, and Lozère. The average height of the mountains is between 3,000 and 4,000 feet (900 and 1,200 meters), but Mont Lozère reaches 5,584 feet (1,702 meters), and Mont Mézenc, the highest peak of the chain, rises to 5,755 feet (1,754 meters).

The Roman name for the region was Cebenna. One of the least accessible parts of France, the Cévennes served as a refuge for Huguenots (French Calvinists) after the revocation of the Edict of Nantes in 1685. From 1702 to 1704 the Camisards waged a guerrilla war there against Louis XIV.

CEYLON. See SRI LANKA.

CEUTA, at the entrance to the Strait of Gibraltar, is an important refueling port.

CÉZANNE worked for seven years, from 1898 to 1905, on *Grandes Baigneuses.* It is often considered the culminating masterpiece of his series of bathers.

PHILADELPHIA MUSEUM OF ART—WILSTACH COLLECTION

CÉZANNE, sā-zản', **Paul** (1839–1906), French painter, whose work is the culmination of a more than 500-year-old tradition in European painting. The classical spirit, romanticism, and naturalism were all absorbed into his style. In his late works he achieved a condensation of form so great that the structural elements of shape and color frequently dominate the natural subject.

Cézanne, however, considered nature the only source of inspiration. But his work also reveals his intense study of the old masters (especially those in the Louvre in Paris) as can be seen in his many sketches from paintings, sculptures, and casts. Yet it would be inaccurate to see Cézanne as a "classicist"; his nature was passionate' and his paintings are the result of an arduous struggle within himself and with his subjects.

Because art after 1910 developed in the direction of nonrepresentational expression, Cézanne is often cited as a forerunner of the abstract tendencies in the modern idiom. This is true only to a degree, because the artist considered himself a *"peintre impressioniste"* and his paintings "constructions after nature." It is rather the strong formal structure and composition in his art that tie him to various trends in 20th century art.

Early Years. Cézanne was born at Aix-en-Provence on Jan. 19, 1839. His father, Louis Auguste Cézanne, and his mother, Élisabeth (Aubert), were of humble origin. Through his industry and business acumen Louis Auguste became, first, the owner of a hat factory and eventually a well-to-do banker. He dominated the family, and his sensitive son lived in constant fear of displeasing him.

Paul spent the formative years from age 13 to 19 at the Collège Bourbon (now Lycée Mignet) in Aix. Through the school, his patriarchal family, and the conservative Catholic town, he absorbed the humanist values of classical and of French culture, and his thought and character were determined by these values. As a result, Cézanne offers the contradictory image of a small-town bourgeois who was also a great and completely independent innovator in art. At school he developed a deep friendship with Émile Zola, which lasted for many years. After the traditional instruction in art at the Collège he attended the École des Beaux-Arts in Aix, where, under Joseph Marc Gibert, he drew from casts and from the model. In 1859, at his father's insistence, Cézanne began the study of law at the University of Aix, but at night he attended the Academy of Art.

Finally, in 1861, Cézanne persuaded his father to let him go to Paris. He attended the Académie Suisse, and in the afternoons went to the Louvre where his real teachers—the great colorists Titian, Veronese, Tintoretto, and Rubens and the classicist Poussin—began to exert their lifelong influence. After 6 months, refused admission to the École Nationale des Beaux-Arts, Cézanne went back to Aix, discouraged, only to return to Paris in 1862, determined to become a painter.

At the Académie Suisse he met Camille Pissarro, 10 years his senior, a man of warm humanity and a skillful, naturalistic painter who took the groping and awkward Cézanne under his tutelage. At the Café Guerbois, Cézanne joined the circle of the admired leader of the young generation, Édouard Manet. Their spirit encouraged Cézanne's direction toward independence, but it was his discovery of Delacroix that helped him form the bridge between the great colorists of the past and the modern epoch.

Middle Years. Between 1864 and 1869 Cézanne lived alternately in Aix and in Paris. In 1869 he met Hortense Fiquet, a girl of the working class, who served as his model and by whom he had a son, Paul, born in 1872. During the Franco-Prussian War of 1870–1871, Cézanne avoided military service by staying at L'Estaque near Aix.

THE ART INSTITUTE OF CHICAGO (PHOTO FROM WILDENSTEIN & CO., INC.)

MADAME CÉZANNE IN A YELLOW ARMCHAIR, completed in 1894, is constructed in planes of color that foreshadow the later development of cubism.

The scenery around this small town on the Bay of Marseille remained one of his favorite subjects for painting. After a brief return to Paris at the end of the war Cézanne went to Pontoise where he worked—often before the same subject—together with Pissarro. It was during this period that Cézanne developed his impressionist style. In Auvers-Sur-Oise, where he stayed for a time at the home of Dr. Paul Gachet, an amateur artist and friend of the impressionists, Cézanne also did some etching.

The first exhibition of the impressionist painters took place in Paris in 1874; Cézanne's broadly painted picture *The House of the Hanged Man* (1873) aroused the special ridicule of the critics. At the third impressionist show (1877) he exhibited 16 paintings. Again the critics singled him out for scathing attacks, which deeply wounded Cézanne and enhanced his natural shyness and misanthropy. His work, however, began to arouse the interest of a few collectors—Dr. Paul Gachet, Count Doria, and especially Victor Choquet, who eventually bought 31 of his paintings. After 1877 he alternated between L'Estaque, Aix, and Paris.

About 1876, in addition to the still lifes, landscapes, and occasional portraits that Cézanne continued to produce, he began the series of studies of bathers that thereafter absorbed him. With this theme he transcended the nature-oriented art of the impressionists, envisaging a new art more like "Poussin entirely redone from nature."

In 1886, Cézanne finally married Hortense Fiquet. The same year his father died and left him a considerable fortune, which, however, made very little change in his life as a thrifty, suspicious recluse. It was also in 1886 that Cézanne ended his friendship with Zola, who had used him as a model for an artist-failure in his novel *L'Ouevre.* This deprived Cézanne of the only close friend he ever had.

Late Years. About 1890 recognition began to come to Cézanne, just when he was developing his last, most dynamic, and at the same time most "abstract" style. He was invited in 1891 to show three paintings with the avant-garde group "Les Vingt" in Brussels, and he also exhibited at the Salon des Indépendents in Paris. The dealer Ambroise Vollard gave Cézanne his first one-man show in 1895 and a second in 1898. He began to receive visits from admiring young artists; one was the poet Joachim Gasquet, who later published his conversations with the painter. He was also visited by and exchanged letters with the young painter-friend of Gauguin and van Gogh, Émile Bernard, who published his reminiscences in the *Mercure de France* in 1904. In the works of the painters of the next generation, especially Gauguin and Bernard, one can discern the structural style of Cézanne as an influence.

In 1895, Cézanne bought a cabin near Aix-en-Provence, in the mountainous region near the Château Noir and the quarry of Bibémus, where he developed in complete loneliness his last and strongest style. He sold the place in 1899 and built himself a studio house on the Chemin des Lauves in Aix, where he could work on his large canvases of the bathers. During these last years he regularly exhibited at the Salon des Indépendants, the Salon d'Automne, and at the Libre Esthétique in Brussels, now a center of modern art. In the fall of 1906 he fell ill when he was caught in a rainstorm while painting, and he died on October 22. In this last period he could rightly say to Gasquet, "Perhaps I was born too early. I was more the painter of your generation than of mine."

Work. One can discern three phases in the art of Cézanne: a youthful romantic period from about 1864 to 1872; an impressionist period from about 1872 to 1882; and a final period, in which his ideas were increasingly condensed and intensified and which ended only with his death.

Romantic Period. During the first period Cézanne's paintings frequently have violent and erotic subjects, with an undulating, somewhat baroque design, painted with a heavily loaded brush or occasionally with the palette knife. Besides the impact of the Venetian colorists, the influence of Delacroix and Daumier is evident. A growing tendency toward a direct interpretation of nature came from the influence of Courbet. Gradually the clumsy but expressive manner becomes more static, and objects are examined from a closer distance and gain in volume. The breakthrough to a more objective view of reality, recreated in simplified, monumental shapes, can be seen in his first completely resolved masterpieces: *The Black Clock* (1869–1871) and *The Railway Out* (1870–1871).

Impressionist Period. The impulse toward impressionism came to Cézanne primarily through the influence of Pissarro, his qualified admiration for Manet, and his contact with the other impressionists, especially Monet and Renoir. In some respects Cézanne followed the general impressionist guidelines, painting out-of-doors with a sunlit prismatic palette and with a division of local color to be recomposed by the viewing eye. His pictures differ from those of the other impressionists by their more severe composition, a predilection for shapes already strongly structured in nature, an increasing use of blue as a ground base for all colors, and a greater loneliness in his painted scenes. The range of his subjects includes still lifes, landscapes, portraits, and figure compositions.

Especially in the still lifes of the late 1870's, the emergence of a new formal discipline can be observed. Shapes and their distances from each other and the color harmonies of objects become the essential qualities of the paintings. His purpose, as he told Maurice Denis, was "to make out of impressionism something solid like the art of the museums." To achieve this, "one must not copy nature but represent it. This is done ·by coloristic equivalents" accomplished "not so much by modelling as by modulating."

Late Work. In the last and longest phase of Cézanne's career as a painter, one observes a steady reduction of imitative naturalism. "Treat nature by the cylinder, the sphere, the cone," he wrote to Bernard in 1904. His statement clarifies his own adjustment between the rich variety of natural forms and the underlying structure that has its origin in the artist's mind—an adjustment that leads toward greater abstraction. His late work also shows a subtle balance between the deep space of nature and the flat picture plane, as well as a heightened contrast between purple and green, red and violet. His brush stroke takes on a controlled slanting direction independent of the painted shapes, enhancing the feeling of a rhythmically woven texture. Portraits, still lifes, and nudes in landscape settings were his major subjects. In the bathers series, for example the *Grandes Baigneuses* (1905), he aimed at a unification of figure composition with landscape painting. A classical idyll is attempted, with the color blue used not naturalistically, but as a harmonizing and vitalizing element throughout. Cézanne's increasing concern with the spiritual, rather than the real, can best be observed in his many late watercolors. They have an almost Oriental economy; only a few evocative essentials are depicted; and space and color relationships are established with much of the white paper ground left untouched.

The "classical" or highly organized quality of many of the still lifes and landscapes are only one aspect of Cézanne's late work. One notices also in some of his portraits, such as *The Boy with the Red Vest* (1888–1890), and in some of the Château Noir and the Quarry Bibémus landscapes, a new impetuosity mingled with a feeling of loneliness and desperation. Here the deepest characteristic of Cézanne's art is revealed: his struggle for *réalisation*—one of his favorite terms —achieved by the transformation of a passionately experienced nature into a suprapersonal, objectified image of reality.

ALFRED NEUMEYER
Author of "Cézanne's Drawings"

Bibliography

Badt, Kurt, *The Art of Cézanne,* tr. by Sheila Ann Ogilvie (Berkeley, Calif., 1965).
Bernard, Émile, *Souvenirs sur Paul Cézanne* (Paris 1912).
Denis, Maurice, *Nouvelles Théories* (Paris 1922).
Denis, Maurice, *Théories* (Paris 1913).
Dorival, Bernard, *Cézanne* (Paris 1948).
Gasquet, Joachim, *Cézanne* (Paris 1921).
Loran, Erle, *Cézanne's Composition* (Berkeley, Cal., 1946).
Neumeyer, Alfred, *Cézanne's Drawings* (New York 1958).
Novotny, Fritz, *Cézanne* (London 1937).
Perruchot, Henri, *La vie de Cézanne* (Paris 1956).
Rewald, John, ed., *Cézanne Letters* (London 1941).
Rewald, John, *Paul Cézanne* (New York 1948).
Schapiro, Meyer, *Paul Cézanne* (New York 1952).
Venturi, Lionello, *Cézanne, son art, son oeuvre,* 2 vols., (Paris 1936).

CHAADAYEV, chä-ä-dä'yef, **Pyotr Yakovlevich** (1794?–1856), Russian philosopher, who was the first to discuss Russia's isolation from the West. He was born in Moscow on May 27, probably in 1794. An aristocrat, he attended the University of Moscow before becoming an army officer. After traveling·in western Europe (1823–1826), he led a secluded life in Moscow, writing in French his eight *Lettres philosophiques.* The first letter was published in the review *Telescope* in 1836; it incurred official wrath, and Chaadayev was declared insane and forbidden to publish more. He died in Moscow on April 14, 1856.

Chaadayev was deeply religious and intensely patriotic. He advances in *Lettres philosophiques* the concept of Russia's divine mission to help Christianity progress toward the unity of men in the kingdom of God on earth. The first letter, influenced by French Catholic writers, scolds his backward Orthodox countrymen for their sinfully egoistic isolation from the West and insists that unity must be through the Church of Rome. The later letters were more favorable to Russia.

CHABANEL, shà-bà-nel', **Saint Noël** (1613–1649), French Jesuit missionary and martyr. He was born in Saugues, Haute-Loire, France, on Feb. 17, 1613, the son of a notary. He joined the Jesuits in 1630, taught college rhetoric, and was ordained a priest. In 1643 he sailed to Canada as a missionary. After a year in Quebec, he labored among the Hurons and Petuns. Despite his inability to master the native dialect and his abhorrence of Indian customs, he took a vow to remain in this post, if his superiors permitted.

On Dec. 8, 1649, while traveling through the wilderness near the southeast corner of Nottawasaga Bay in Ontario, he was separated from his escort when a band of hostile Iroquois approached and caused the group to flee in panic. Later that day a lone Huron apostate tomahawked him and cast his body into the water. With seven other missionaries to the Indians, known collectively as the North American Martyrs, he was canonized in 1930. Their common feast is September 26. A sanctuary erected at Midland, Ontario, in honor of him and four others martyred in Canada is the site of popular pilgrimages.

JOHN F. BRODERICK, S. J.
Weston College, Mass.

CHABAS, shà-bàs', **Paul Émile** (1869–1937), French painter, who was best known for his studies of nude bathers, particularly his *Matinée de Septembre* (*September Morn,* 1912). He was born in Nantes on March 7, 1869. He studied with Adolphe Bouguereau and Tony Robert-Fleury and began to exhibit his work at the salons of the Société des Artistes Français in 1892. Among the best known of his early works are *La marchande de rêves* (1897) and *Joyeux ébats* (1899).

September Morn, which caused a sensation when first shown in New York City in 1913, was bought by a Russian, hidden during the Russian Revolution, rediscovered in Paris in 1935, and finally purchased by the Metropolitan Museum of Art, New York. His other nude studies include *Crépuscule, La baigneuse,* and *Nageuse.* Chabas was elected to the Académie des Beaux-Arts in 1920 and served as president of the Société des Artistes Français. He died in Paris on May 10, 1937.

CHABLIS, shä-blē′, is a pale, greenish gold wine of Burgundy, France, known for its clean, dry, flinty taste. The entire district where Chablis is produced measures only about 10 miles (16 km) long by 6 miles (10 km) wide, so the supply of this wine is very limited. Unfortunately, the name is frequently used to label other dry white wines that do not have the distinctive character of true Chablis.

From the village of Chablis and its dwindling vineyards on slopes thinly covered with chalky soil, some 158,000 gallons (600,000 liters) of the fine Chablis are produced annually. The great growths are named for their vineyards, all planted on one slope visible from the village square: Le Bougras, Les Preuses, Vaudesir, Grenouille, Les Clos, Valmur, and Blanchots. After them come 22 first growths, labeled Chablis followed by the vineyard names. In addition, about 336,000 gallons (1.3 million liters) of more ordinary Chablis and Petit Chablis are produced annually in surrounding villages. See also WINE.

ALEXIS LICHINE, *Author of*
"Encyclopedia of Wines & Spirits"

CHABRIER, shȧ-brē-ā′, **Emmanuel** (1841–1894), French composer. He was born Alexis Emmanuel Chabrier in Ambert, Puy-de-Dôme, Auvergne, on Jan. 18, 1841. He was trained for the law, and from 1862 to 1880 worked in the French ministry of the interior in Paris. Meanwhile, he studied music with private teachers. Though he had been writing music for many years, he had no ambition to become a full-time composer until 1879, when a performance of Wagner's *Tristan und Isolde* convinced him to give up his government post and concentrate on music. His first important composition was *Dix pièces pittoresques* (1880), for piano. His first great success, and still his most frequently heard work, was *España*, a rhapsody that had its premiere performance in 1883.

Chabrier's subsequent major compositions include the opera *Gwendoline* (1886), which was strongly influenced by Wagner, and the charming opéra-comique *Le roi malgré lui* (1887). His best-known piano pieces are *Joyeuse marche* (1888), which he later orchestrated, and *Bourrée fantasque* (1891), of which orchestrations were made by Felix Mottl and Charles Koechlin. George Balanchine used the music of *Bourrée fantasque* for a ballet (1949) of that name. Chabrier died in Paris on Sept. 13, 1894.

DAVID EWEN
Author of "The World of Great Composers"

CHACHALACA, chä-chȧ-lä′kȧ, a noisy fowl that lives mostly in the forests of Central and South America. A chickenlike bird, the chachalaca can be domesticated and may become an important protein-rich food in tropical lands.

One species, the common chachalaca (*Ortalis vetula*), extends into the United States and is found from the lower Rio Grande Valley of Texas through Mexico to northern Nicaragua and Honduras. It has also been introduced into the Sapelo and Blackbeard islands of Georgia. A slender bird, the common chachalaca is usually about 2 feet (60 cm) long. It is brownish-green and has a short black bill, red streaks on its neck, long slender legs, and a long tail that is tipped with white.

Chachalacas are gregarious birds. Their *cha-cha-la-ca* calls are harsh and clamorous, especially in the early morning and evening. The chachala-

RUSS KINNE, FROM PHOTO RESEARCHERS
Chachalaca

ca's nest, made of sticks and leaves, is usually set low in a tree. The female lays two white eggs and incubates the eggs for about 22 days.

Chachalacas make up the genus *Ortalis*. Together with their relatives, the guans, they are in the family Cracidae in the order Galliformes.

CARL WELTY
Beloit College, Wis.

CHACMA. See BABOON.

CHACO, chä′kō, a vast stretch of infertile alluvial lowland plain in the south central part of South America, at an elevation of 200 to 900 feet (60–300 meters). On the east the region is defined by the Paraguay and Paraná rivers, and on the west by the foothills of the Andes. On its northern border it merges with the tropical forests of Bolivia, and its southern boundary is the Río Salado in Argentina. Known also as the *Gran Chaco*, the area is divided into three parts: the Chaco Boreal (100,000 square miles, or 250,000 sq km), most of which has belonged to Paraguay since 1938 (see CHACO WAR), with the western and northern fringes remaining in Bolivian hands; the Chaco Central (50,000 square miles, or 130,000 sq km), situated between the Pilcomayo and Bermejo rivers and ceded to Argentina by Bolivia in 1889; and the Chaco Austral (100,000 square miles, or 250,000 sq km), situated south of the Bermejo, an original part of Argentina.

The Chaco is humid in its tropical parts and semiarid away from its rivers. In the drier areas (turned into swamps during the 3-month rainy period) xerophytic prickly scrub growth called *monte* has an extensive range. In the wetter areas, jaguars and large marsh deer abound. The area supports fewer than 500,000 people, a large percentage of whom are concentrated in the Argentine cities of Resistencia and Formosa. Lumbering, the extraction of tannin from the quebracho tree, cattle grazing, cotton culture, and oil prospecting are the principal economic activities of the region.

LAURENCE R. BIRNS
The New School for Social Research, New York

CHACO CANYON NATIONAL MONUMENT, chä′kō, is in northwestern New Mexico, in the canyon of the Chaco River. It was established in 1907 to preserve ruins of Indian villages representing the height of prehistoric Pueblo civilization, about 1000 A. D., in the present United States. Of the 13 major ruins the most completely excavated is Pueblo Bonito, dating from about 920 A. D. It is semicircular in form, with the central part of its 4-story walls backed close under the rim of the canyon. Its 800 rooms rise in terraces along the walls, facing two central plazas. The total population of the villages within the 33.6-square-mile (87-sq-km) area of the monument is believed to have been about 6,000.

CHACO WAR, chä′kō, an armed conflict in 1932–1935 between Bolivia and Paraguay, fought over territory in the Chaco (q.v.) region. A truce and finally a settlement were arranged through mediation by other American nations. The treaty of 1938 favored Paraguay, the military victor, but both countries experienced economic hardship and political upheavals after the war.

Throughout the 19th century Bolivia and Paraguay had failed to agree on a boundary line separating their territories in the vast, largely uninhabited Chaco area, although there were several unsuccessful efforts to resolve the issue in the 1870's and 1880's. Both nations had historic claims to the disputed territory and economic motives for acquiring it.

Interest in the area increased after World War I because of Paraguayan settlements there, especially by Mennonites, and because of rumors of petroleum deposits. Both countries sent garrisons into the region, and after an armed clash in 1928 both prepared for war. Peace efforts of the League of Nations and American countries, notably Chile, brought a truce. But four years later the bloodiest 20th century war in the Americas began.

Chaco Canyon National Monument—Pueblo Bonito ruins.

The Bolivian Army, trained by German officers, was larger and better equipped, but the Paraguayans had the advantage of better adaptation to the terrain and of fighting nearer home bases. Bolivian troops, accustomed to high altitudes, were more susceptible to endemic diseases of the hot, humid lowlands. Both sides suffered heavy casualties—about 100,000 dead in all.

After the League of Nations failed at arbitration, mediation by Argentina, Brazil, Chile, Peru, Uruguay, and the United States brought about an armistice in 1935. Paraguay and Bolivia agreed to a definitive treaty at Buenos Aires, Argentina, in 1938. By its terms, Paraguay, which held most of the disputed area when hostilities ceased, received about three fourths of the land. Bolivia was granted the rest plus an outlet on the Pilcomayo River, a tributary of the Paraguay. Argentina, which had unofficially supported Paraguay during the negotiations, received most of the credit for effecting a settlement.

The effects of the war were important in the postwar politics of both belligerents, especially as wartime leaders became political leaders. In Bolivia the postwar reaction was expressed in the National Revolutionary Movement (MNR), which ultimately brought about the revolution of 1952. In Paraguay it produced the reform party Febrerista, deriving its name from a coup d'etat led by the war hero Col. Rafael Franco in February 1936.

HAROLD E. DAVIS, *American University*

Further Reading: Zook, David, Jr., *The Conduct of the Chaco War* (New York 1950).

CHACONNE, shä-kôn′, a musical form, probably derived from a Spanish dance. It usually has three slow beats to a measure and a ground bass, and is composed in short sections of four to eight measures. The chaconne is virtually indistinguishable from the passacaglia, which was derived from a Spanish or Italian dance. The keyboard music of the 17th and early 18th century abounds in chaconnes and passacaglias by such composers as Buxtehude, Couperin, and Handel. The most famous examples, both by Bach, are the chaconne in the last movement of the D-Minor Suite for Violin, and the Passacaglia and Fugue in C Minor, usually performed on the organ.

The Chaco War involved the boundary claims shown.

```
BOLIVIA                          BRAZIL
        Otuquis R.
    GRAN
    CHACO                   Paraguay R.
Yacuiba
  • La Esmeralda            Apa R.
                    PARAGUAY
    Pilcomayo
Bermejo      River
                        Asunción •
ARGENTINA
                River
——— Present boundary
                          Uruguay R.
·········· Maximum Paraguayan        MILES
           claim                  0  50 100 150
– – – Maximum Bolivian    Paraná   0  100  200
           claim                   KILOMETERS
```

MARKETING of products, chiefly agricultural, takes place in and around the new market at Fort-Lamy, Chad's capital and largest city.

CHAD, chad, is a republic in Africa. One of the former territories of French Equatorial Africa, it achieved independence on Aug. 11, 1960. Its name is also spelled *Tchad*. The country commands a strategic position in the heart of Africa at the crossroads of the famed eastern trans-Saharan routes. It is an ethnically diversified nation, euphemistically referred to as "Africa's melting pot." Chad, like the other countries of the Sudanic belt (Sudan, Niger, Mali, and Mauritania) is confronted with the problem of harmonizing the cultures of two distinct worlds—the Semitic-Islamic world of the north and the Negro-African world of the south. Indelibly marked by this dual personality, Chad actually belongs neither to the Middle East nor to Subsaharan Africa. The problems of both worlds are compounded in it, as the two cultures sometimes blend but often clash.

The People. Chad's population, estimated at nearly 4 million, is divided into 11 main ethnic groups and numerous subgroups. Regional cultural and ethnic differences form the single most important political cleavage, complicating and slowing national unity. The Shari River is the approximate line of demarcation between the two main cultural and ethnic groups: to the north are the Muslims, Berbero-Negroids, and Arabo-Negroids; to the south are the Subsaharan Negroes, comprising more than 50% of the total population.

Population densities, as well as ethnic and cultural differences and economic specializations, often follow the country's geography. The average population density is 5.4 per square mile (2.1 per sq km), but it is 15.5 per square mile (6 per sq km) in the three southern prefectures and only 3.1 per square mile (1.2 per sq km) in the three northern Saharan ones.

The main Islamic groups of the north include the Arabs, who are chiefly cattle raisers; the Wadaians, near the Sudan border, who are farmers; and the Toubous, who are desert nomads. The principal Negro group is the Sara, which is the largest single group in the country. Inhabiting the Shari and Logone river valleys, they are primarily farmers.

Chad's people are primarily nomadic or rural. Only about 5% live in urban centers, most of which have less than 5,000 inhabitants. Fort-Lamy (renamed N'Djemena in 1973; pop., 1973: 192,962) is the capital and largest city, at the confluence of the Shari and Logone rivers. Other important cities include Fort-Archambault (renamed Sarh in 1972; pop., 1972 est.: 43,700), a tourist and hunting center; and Moundou and Abécher, which are trading centers.

Islam, introduced in the area in the 19th century, is the religion of most of the people of northern Chad. South of the Shari River, traditional African beliefs predominate, with anthropomorphism as a general characteristic. Christianity, primarily Roman Catholicism, has been adopted by about 5% of the country's population.

French is Chad's lingua franca as well as its official tongue. Arabic-based dialects, especially Turku, are spoken throughout the north. Bantu-based Sara dialects are the language of the people of the southern part of the country.

The educational system is patterned after the French. It includes mandatory, though not yet universal, primary schooling, followed by a choice of secondary, commercial, or technical school. The literacy rate is about 5% of the adult population. Children attend school in greater numbers

---

INFORMATION HIGHLIGHTS

Official Name: Republic of Chad.

Head of State: President.

Head of Government: President.

Legislature: National Assembly.

Area: 495,752 square miles (1,284,000 sq km).

Boundaries: *North,* Libya; *east,* Sudan; *south,* Central African Republic; *west,* Nigeria, Cameroon, and Niger.

Population: 3,869,000 (1973 est.).

Capital: Fort-Lamy (renamed N'Djemena in 1973).

Major Languages: French (official), Arabic, and African tribal languages.

Major Religions: Islam, animism, Christianity.

Monetary Unit: Franc CFA.

Weights and Measures: Metric system.

Flag: Blue, yellow, and red vertical stripes.

National Anthem: La Tchadienne.

each year; the percentage of school-age children enrolled in school leaped from 4.4% in the mid-1950's to nearly 35% (225,000) in the mid-1960's.

Primary schools are functioning in every provincial capital and are being established in many of the smaller towns, particularly in the populous, sedentary south. Secondary, normal, commercial, and technical schools are attended by more than 10,000 pupils. Some 6,000 pupils attend the *lycées* of Fort-Lamy, Bengor, Abécher, Fort-Archambault, Moundou, Pala, and Moussoro.

The National University, with 300 students, was opened in 1971. A number of students are sent abroad to study, chiefly in France.

The Land. Chad covers a landlocked area 900 miles (1,450 km) from the nearest seaport. The country forms a vast, generally arid depression, sloping westward toward the nearly triangular Lake Chad. Three distinct climatic zones in Chad affect population, ethnic concentration, and economic specialization.

Nearly the entire northern half of the country is desert. The sandy terrain slopes gently down the Tibesti Mountains, which reach 11,204 feet (3,415 meters) at Mt. Emi Koussi. Human life here is as sparse as vegetation and as nomadic as the shifting dunes. This area is the domain of the camel and its Toubou master. Extreme temperatures prevail in the Saharan zone, with occasional downpours totaling about 8 inches (20 cm) annually.

Below the desert region begins a less arid steppe zone, with infrequent summer rainfall totaling up to about 30 inches (76 cm) a year. A sparse vegetation of acacia, mimosa, and palm trees thrives in this region. The terrain slopes westward from the 5,000-foot (1,500-meter) Wadai plateau to the shores of Lake Chad. The lake, which drains the Chadian basin, is fed by two permanent rivers, the Shari and Logone, as well as by several ephemeral streams. At high water the lake measures 10,000 square miles (25,900 sq km). The lake region is rich in cattle and has a varied fauna.

In the south, which has the highest population density, one finds a typical semitropical savanna. Here the rainfall ranges from 35 to 48 inches (89 to 122 cm) annually, allowing the growth of baobab bushes and thickets of other plants. Temperature and humidity are high. Agriculture, fishing, and animal husbandry constitute the main economic activities. The rich fauna, including elephants, lions, buffalo, and leopards, attracts tourists and hunters.

The Economy. Chad is primarily an agricultural country. The rural economy employs about 80% of the active nongovernmental labor force. Millet and sorghum are the chief subsistence crops. Peanuts, dates, paddy rice, and cassava are also produced. The main cash crop is cotton, which accounts for about 80% of the nation's exports. Peanuts are the only other export crop.

Herding is the predominant economic activity in the Saharan and steppe regions of Chad. The herds include 4 million cattle, 4 million goats and sheep, 500,000 donkeys and horses, and 250,000 camels. Nearly 100,000 tons of fish are caught yearly in the rivers and lakes.

Manufactures include leather, textiles, beer, carbonated drinks, sugar, radios, bicycles, and

CHAD Map Index

Population: 3,869,000
Area: 495,752 square miles (1,284,000 sq km)

CITIES AND TOWNS

Abécher, 21,000...C3	Oum Hadjer, 1,209.C3
Abou Deia, 1,100..B3	Pala, 10,500.....A4
Adré, 3,100......C3	
Am Dam, 1,002....C3	PHYSICAL FEATURES
Am-Timan, 3,200...C3	Aouk, Bahr (riv.)....C3
Ati, 6,600......B3	Azoum, Bahr
Baibokoum, 3,138..B4	(dry riv.).....C3
Biltine, 4,000.....C3	Batha (riv.).......B3
Bokoro, 3,000.....B3	Chad (lake)......B3
Bongor, 11,000...B3	Domar (dry riv.)...B2
Bousso, 3,600....B3	Emi Koussi (mt.)...B2
Doba, 10,000....B4	Ennedi (plat.).....C2
Faya (Largeau),	Fittri (lake)......B3
5,385........B2	Ghazal, Bahr el
Fort-Archambault	(dry riv.).......B2
(Sarh), 44,000...B4	Haouach, Wadi
Fort-Lamy	(dry riv.).......C2
(N'Djemena)	Kanem (reg.),
(cap.), 91,688...B3	261,108......A3
Kélo, 10,000.....B4	Logone (riv.)......B3
Koumra, 10,000....B4	Maro (dry riv.)...B2
Lai, 6,500......B4	Mbéré (riv.)......B4
Largeau, 5,385...B2	Pendé (riv.)......B4
Léré, 3,332......A4	Sahara (des.).....B1
Mao, 4,015......B3	Salamat (riv.)....B4
Massakori, 3,000..B3	Sara, Bahr (riv.)..B4
Melfi, 2,008......B3	Shari (riv.).......B3
Mongo, 5,000....B3	Tibesti (mts.).....B1
Moundou, 29,000..B4	Wadai (reg.),
Moussoro......B3	314,775......C3

Total pop.—1973 off. est.; city pops.—1964, 1963, 1961 off. est.; regions—1961 off. est.

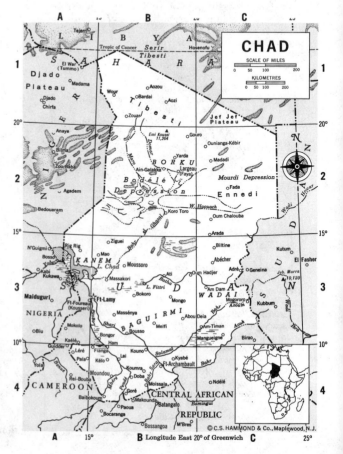
© C.S. HAMMOND & Co., Maplewood, N.J.

VILLAGE WELL near Kélo in southern Chad. The bottleshaped granary at right is for the storage of millet.

MARC & EVELYNE BERNHEIM, FROM RAPHO GUILLUMETTE

shoes, and skins are processed. Chad's balance of trade registers a yearly deficit that is met by aid from France, its major trading partner. France buys most of Chad's cotton at a subsidized price. Imports include consumer goods, motor vehicles, machinery, and petroleum products.

Government. A parliamentary constitution, promulgated in 1959, was replaced by a presidential constitution in 1962. In 1964 the constitution was amended to allow only one party, the Parti Progressiste Tchadien (PPT), confirming a situation that had existed since 1962. Under the constitution, the president was to be assisted by a Council of Ministers. A unicameral National Assembly with 75 members popularly elected for 5-year terms chose the president, who was then confirmed by popular referendum. After the coup of April 1975, a 9-member Supreme Military Council and head of state replaced the constitutional establishment.

History. Chadians like to refer to their country as Africa's Mesopotamia because civilization here also began between two rivers, the Shari and Logone, and because the area is presumed to be the starting point of the Bantu southern migrations. The alluvial shores of the rivers still proudly guard the secrets and achievements of those who inhabited them. Archaeological remains, including pottery dating back to the beginning of the Christian era and ironcraft, suggest that the region was an important trading center as early as the 4th century A. D.

In the 7th century, Sao tribes began to invade the delta region in Chad, where they soon established their hegemony, defending it against encroachments by the Boulalas. In the 11th century the Arabian geographer el-Bikri reported the existence in Chad of a kingdom known as Kanem, which was ruled by the Sef, a Berber Muslim dynasty.

Kanem and Bornu Empires. In 1220 the Kanem empire began to extend its sovereignty over much of present-day Chad. After a century of wars and anarchy, the empire was lost to the Boulalas. In the 14th century, however, the exiled king created a new sultanate at Bornu and attempted to regain control of Kanem. For nearly three centuries the empires of Bornu and Kanem vied for the hegemony of the Chadian basin. Toward the end of this period they also had to contend with the raids of the rising Hausa states in the west. Bornu finally reconquered Kanem in the 16th century and the united empire exercised suzerainty over the vassal kingdoms of Kano and Wadai and was in constant commercial relationship with North Africa and the Nile basin. The main export was slaves.

Until the 19th century the Kanem-Bornu empire resisted the persistent attacks of the Baguirmi kingdom and their allies, the Boulalas. The unified Hausa states succeeded in invading Bornu in 1808. Its fleeing *mai* (king) appealed to a relative, Mohammed al-Amin al-Kanemi, for help. The victorious al-Kanemi subsequently became the actual leader of the kingdom, taking the title of *shehu*, while the *mai*, his authority reduced, became a figurehead. Al-Kanemi established his headquarters at Kukawa, which became the most active slave market of Central Africa, dealing mostly through the north with the Ottoman Empire. The last Sef *mai* was assassinated in 1846, thus bringing to an end a dynasty dating back to the 11th century. A period of disorder and anarchy followed, involving struggles among the various kingdoms of the greater Chadian area. The Sudanese adventurer Rabeh capitalized on this dissension and ultimately seized control of much of the region.

European Rule. The Englishmen Dixon Denham and Hugh Clapperton were the first European explorers to enter the Chadian basin. They did so in 1822. In 1870 and 1871 many Germans, including Heinrich Barth and Gustav Nachtigal, explored or visited the area. The French entered the region in 1893, and within 16 years Chad was under their control. It was made a colony within the federation of French Equatorial Africa in 1920.

During World War II, Chad became a strategic field of operation for the Free French forces of Gen. Charles de Gaulle in their fight against the German forces in the Fezzan. Chad also provided the Free French with some of their best soldiers. The colony was then administered by Félix Éboué, one of the most outstanding French Negro statesmen.

Chad was granted its own territorial assembly after World War II. It was also authorized to send representatives to the French Parliament, one of whom was the Socialist Gabriel Lisette.

Independence. A former trade unionist, François Tombalbaye (he later changed his first name to Ngarta), became Chad's first prime minister (1959) and first president (1960), ultimately combining the two positions into one. Under his leadership, Chad became an independent republic on Aug. 11, 1960. In 1962, Tombalbaye banned all political parties except his ruling Parti Progressiste Tchadien, but bloody regional and ethnic clashes continued, notably between northern Muslims and southern Bantus. The Muslims also waged intermittent warfare against the government, which received military aid from France.

On April 13, 1975, Tombalbaye was killed in a military coup d'etat, and on April 16, Brig. Gen. Félix Malloum was named to head the governing Supreme Military Council. Amid deadly civil strife, Malloum was forced into exile in March 1979. In August, rival groups agreed on a national union government, with Goukouni Oueddei, leader of the Liberation Front, as president.

ALFRED G. GERTEINY*, *University of Bridgeport*

Bibliography

Cornet, Charles, *Au Tchad* (Paris 1911).
Lapie, Pierre, *My Travels Through Chad*, tr. by Leslie Buell (London 1943).
Lebeuf, J. P., *La civilisation du Tchad* (Paris 1950).
Le Rouvreur, Albert, *Sahéliens et Sahariens du Tchad* (Paris 1962).

CHAD, Lake, in central Africa, at the boundaries of Cameroon, Chad, Niger, and Nigeria. It is fed primarily by the Shari and Logone rivers. The lake has no visible outlet, but remains fresh as a result of subterranean drainage. The area of the lake is shrinking, but varies greatly in size: it averages between 4,000 to 10,000 square miles (10,000 to 26,000 sq km), depending on the seasonal rainfall.

Lake Chad lies between the desert in the north and the savanna in the south. Rainfall over the lake averages about 25 inches (640 mm) in the south and 5 inches (130 mm) in the north. The lake is very shallow, especially in the north.

The lake was first seen by Europeans when it was reached by the British explorers Dixon Denham, Hugh Clapperton, and Walter Oudney in 1823.

HUGH C. BROOKS
St. John's University, New York

CHADWICK, Florence (1918–   ), American professional distance swimmer, who was the first woman to swim the English Channel both ways. Her time of 13 hours 20 minutes, from Cape Gris-Nez, France, to Dover, England, on Aug. 8, 1950, established a speed record for women. She conquered the route from England to France, against the tides, three times: 1951, 1953, and 1955. Her time of 13 hours 47 minutes for the 21-mile swim from Catalina Island to the California mainland in 1952 broke the speed record for any swimmer. In 1953 she swam the Strait of Gibraltar, the Dardanelles, and the Bosporus.

Born in San Diego, Calif., on Nov. 9, 1918, the 5-foot 6-inch, 150-pound brunette began swimming at the age of 6. Miss Chadwick was, physiologically, unusually resistant to cold.

HAROLD PETERSON, *"Sports Illustrated"*

CHADWICK, George Whitefield (1854–1931), American composer in the romantic style. He was born in Lowell, Mass., on Nov. 13, 1854, and received his training in Boston and in Germany. In 1876–1877 he headed the music department at Olivet College in Michigan. Later he served as organist of the South Congregational Church in Boston for a number of years.

In 1882 he began to teach harmony and composition at the New England Conservatory of Music. He became director of the conservatory in 1897. Chadwick died in Boston on April 4, 1931.

Chadwick's numerous compositions include the *Rip Van Winkle* overture (1879); the operas *Tabasco* (1894) and *Judith* (1901); the familiar *Symphonic Sketches* (1895–1904); and the symphonic ballad *Tam O'Shanter* (1915). He also wrote choral works, cantatas, chamber music, incidental music, some 100 songs, and an influential textbook, *Harmony:* (1897), which went into many editions.

CHADWICK, Sir James (1891–1974), British physicist, who was awarded the Nobel Prize in physics in 1935 for the discovery of the neutron. In 1946 he received the U. S. Medal for Merit for his contribution to the successful outcome of the U. S. wartime Manhattan Project, on which he had led the British team. He received the Copley Medal in 1950 and the Franklin Medal in 1951, and was knighted in 1945.

Chadwick was born in Manchester on Oct. 20, 1891, and was educated at the universities of Manchester, Berlin, and Cambridge. At Manchester he studied under Ernest Rutherford, and after Rutherford had moved to the Cavendish professorship at Cambridge (1919), Chadwick rejoined him there. Eventually he took over from Rutherford the exacting task of directing most of the experimental research in nuclear physics carried out in the laboratory during its most fruitful period, from 1925 to 1935. Chadwick was professor of physics at the University of Liverpool (1935–1948) and master of Gonville and Caius College, Cambridge (1948–1958). He died in Cambridge, England, on July 24, 1974.

Chadwick's discovery of the neutron in 1932 marked the beginning of the modern era in the experimental study and theoretical understanding of the atomic nucleus. As a young student in Berlin (1914), he had been the first to obtain the energy spectrum of the beta particles from radioactive substances, thus posing the problem that led Wolfgang Pauli to postulate the existence of the neutrino in 1931. In 1920, Chadwick was the first to determine the electric charge on the nucleus by an absolute measurement of alpha particle scattering. His work in collaboration with Rutherford was mainly in the field of artificial nuclear transmutation, using alpha particles as projectiles. Rutherford had been the first to detect such an effect, with nitrogen, in 1919. Later, with his own students, Chadwick continued this work and investigated nuclear transmutations produced by neutrons and gamma rays.

NORMAN FEATHER, *University of Edinburgh*

CHAEREMON, kē-rē′mon, Greek tragic poet of the 4th century B. C. Chaeremon's tragedies are known only from 11 fragments that are still extant. These fragments contain excellent descriptions of flowers and fair women, reflecting Chaeremon's love of beauty. They also show that his poetry was more lyrical than was appropriate for a tragic playwright. This appears to have been the opinion of Aristotle, who, in his *Rhetoric*, described Chaeremon's *Centaur* as not a true tragedy in the traditional sense but rather a rhapsody compounded from all meters and meant to be read rather than acted.

CHAERONEA, ker-ō-nē′ə, was the westernmost city of the ancient district of Boeotia in central Greece. Part of the fortifications of the acropolis, which date from the 4th century B.C., and a small theater are preserved about 4 miles (6 km) north of Levádhia.

The plain of Chaeronea lies between the Petrakhos Ridge and the site of Chaeronea on the west and the Cephissus River on the east. The Macedonians under Philip II defeated a united Greek force here in 338 B.C. The chief opponents of the Macedonians were the Athenians, who held the mountainous left flank, and the Thebans, who were in the plain along the Cephissus. The 300 warriors of the famed Sacred Band of Thebes held their positions and were annihilated by the Macedonian cavalry under the command of Alexander, the son of Philip. A gigantic marble lion, restored in 1902, marks the mass grave of the Sacred Band. The result of the battle was the virtual subjugation of all Greece to Macedonia.

The second great battle at Chaeronea occurred in 86 B.C., when the Romans under Sulla overwhelmed the numerically superior army of Mithridates VI of Pontus. This was the last battle against Rome on behalf of the freedom of the Greek states.

JAMES R. WISEMAN, *University of Texas*

CHAETOGNATHA, kē-tog′nə-thə, is a phylum of marine worms commonly known as *arrowworms.* They are found in all oceans. Large numbers live at the surface, where they form a part of the drifting plankton, but others may be found at depths of more than 3,200 feet (1,000 meters).

Characteristics. At maturity, arrowworms range in size from about 0.24 to 2.4 inches (0.6–6 cm). They have a transparent, tubular body, which is divided into head, trunk, and tail segments. The head has seizing spines, or chaetae, which are used for grasping tiny marine animals, and sometimes even other arrowworms. The mouth is located on the underside of the head. One or two pairs of delicate, lateral fins lie along the trunk and tail segments, and a caudal fin is found at the end of the tail segment.

The arrowworm's body is covered by a cuticle formed by the underlying epidermal cells. A complex set of muscles in the head is used to help catch and swallow prey, and four lengthwise muscles extending along the trunk and tail are used in swimming.

The arrowworm's digestive tract is straight and extends from the mouth to the anus, located at the junction of the trunk and tail segments.

The nervous system consists of a large ganglion, or nerve mass, in the head with branches that pass around the gut and a pair that extends to the large nerve center on the ventral surface.

Reproduction. The reproductive system consists of a pair of ovaries in the trunk segment and testes in the tail segment. Although arrowworms are hermaphroditic (each individual has both male and female sex organs), cross fertilization may take place in some species. Sperm are transferred to the ovaries, and after fertilization the eggs pass down the oviduct and into the sea. Development of the embryo is rapid, and the young are hatched in two days. There is no characteristic larval stage.

E. LOWE PIERCE, *University of Florida*

CHAETOPODA, kē-top′ə-də, is a term often applied to the annelid worms that bear two separate bundles of bristles on each side of every body segment. One group, the oligochaetes, are freshwater and terrestrial forms; an example is the common earthworm. The other group, the polychaetes, are mainly marine; an example is the common sandworm, or clamworm. The term Chaetopoda is sometimes restricted to the polychaetes. See also ANNELIDA; OLIGOCHAETA; POLYCHAETA.

CHAFARINAS ISLANDS, chä-fä-rē′näs, is an island group belonging to Spain, in the Mediterranean Sea off the northeastern coast of Morocco. The three small islands—Congreso, Isabel II, and Rey—are about 30 miles (48 km) southeast of the Spanish enclave of Melilla in Morocco, and are under direct Spanish administration. Congreso is the largest island, and only Isabel II is inhabited.

Called Tres Insulae by the Romans and Zafran by the Arabs, they were a haunt of the Barbary pirates until annexed by Spain in 1848. They are also known as the Zafarin or Zaffarine Islands.

CHAFER, chā′fər, any of several beetles of the Scarabaeidae family that gnaw or chafe the stems and leaves of plants. In the United States the principal chafers are the May beetle (called "June bugs" in some areas) and the rose chafer, both of which may be severe pests. The larva is white and has a C-shaped body. It passes the winter deep in the soil. In the spring, the last-stage larva crawls near to the soil's surface and pupates. In a few days the adult emerges from the pupa.

R. H. ARNETT, JR., *Purdue University*

ANATOMY OF A CHAETOGNATH

TAIL — TRUNK — HEAD

SEMINAL VESICLE — ANUS — OVARY — INTESTINE — SEIZING SPINES — TESTIS — POSTERIOR FIN — VENTRAL GANGLION — CAUDAL FIN — OPENING OF OVIDUCT — ANTERIOR FIN — COLARETTE

Chaffinch

CHAFFINCH, chaf'inch, a species of finch native to Europe and Asia. The chaffinch, including its many subspecies, ranges from the British Isles to western Sibera and from Scandinavia to northern Africa and Asia Minor. It is also found in the Azores and the Canary Islands.

About 6 inches (15 cm) long, the male chaffinch is pinkish brown below, slate-blue on the crown and nape, and rich chestnut on the upper back. Its wings and tail are gray-brown, and it has two white wing bars and white outer tail feathers that are particularly noticeable in flight. The females and the young chaffinches are duller and browner.

The most abundant of the European finches, the chaffinch favors woodlands but also inhabits farmyards, gardens, and parks. It feeds on the seeds of grasses and weeds and on small fruits and insects. It builds its nest of grasses, mosses, and lichens in thick cover close to the ground. The female lays 4 or 5 eggs. Incubation takes 12 days, and both parents care for the young.

The chaffinch, *Fringella coelebs,* is a member of the family Fringillidae in the order Passeriformes.

JOSEPH BELL, *New York Zoological Society*

CHAGA, chä'gə, Bantu-speaking people inhabiting the slopes of Mount Kilimanjaro in northern Tanzania. Their name is also spelled Chagga. They number over 300,000. Culturally, the Chaga are closely related to the Pare, Taveta, Teita, and Nyika peoples.

The Chaga subsist primarily by agriculture and make extensive use of irrigation and animal fertilizer to improve their fields. Among the variety of food crops produced in the Chaga's well-developed farming system are yams, bananas, and maize. But the Chaga are best known for the quantity and quality of their coffee. This cash crop is exported to American and other Western and world markets through a network of marketing and processing cooperatives. The Chaga's managerial skills have enabled them to become one of the best African examples of progressive change in a traditional way of life. Their principal large town, Moshi, is the site of a cooperative-owned commercial college.

ROBERT A. LYSTAD, *Johns Hopkins University*

CHAGALL, shə-gäl', **Marc** (1887–   ), Russian-French painter, whose works are fantasies saturated with the emotions, ideas, and images of Jewish folklore and religion blended with the customs of Russian provincial life. With Matisse, Picasso, Braque, Rouault, and Klee, Chagall is regarded as one of the "old masters" of 20th century painting.

Chagall was never a part of any art movement, and he adhered to no theoretical school of art. His work differs totally in meaning and substance from the work of his contemporaries. At a time when literary and emotional references in painting were regarded with mistrust, Chagall's powerful and original vision, although crowded with these elements, gained the highest respect of the art world.

In Chagall's paintings, angels, lovers, flowers and animals are freed from earthly gravity to take part in an exuberant dance in space, a never-ending free fall under a romantic moon. His world of private dreams and fantasies was described by the critic Roger Fry as "an entirely miraculous one where anything may happen at any moment. The Greeks had one flying horse, the Arabs had one magic carpet, but Chagall has one universe of movement. Man, of course, has always dreamt of flying, but Chagall doesn't bother about balance, stress, motors, or fuel. He creates a whole world of flying creatures and invests them with his own emotional expressions."

Early Life. Marc Chagall was born in the village of Liozno, near Vitebsk, Russia, on July 7, 1887. His parents and relatives were all followers of Baal Shem Tov, founder of the Hasidic sect, a branch of the Jewish religion that interpreted God as a deity of song, dance, and gaiety. Heaven was a setting for a never-ending *simcha,* the celebration that frees man from the dreary earthly prologue to his divine existence. The Hasidic sect, like other revivalist groups, prepared for the next world by living out their philosophy in this one. Thus, on the Sabbath, Chagall's father and relatives, clad in their prayer shawls, seemed to the young boy like a company of luminous saints engaged in the dancing, chanting, and general celebrations that followed prayers. In describing one of these childhood memories that helped to shape his special reality and personal imagery, Chagall later wrote: "The ceiling suddenly opens and a winged creature descends with a great commotion, a swish of fluttering wings. I think an angel. I can't open my eyes ... it is too bright, too luminous." Chagall's vision was also conditioned by the Hasidic belief that God exists everywhere, in everything: "He comes down and dwells among the downtrodden. Thus all, animals and humans, are invested with a heavenly spirit."

After a childhood and adolescence spent entirely in his native village, Chagall left home at the age of 20 to attend the Imperial School of Fine Arts in St. Petersburg (now Leningrad). Miserably poor, he often went without eating and slept on park benches. Finding the academic instruction of the school uninspiring, Chagall began to attend the classes of the theatrical designer León Bakst. There he encountered an attitude of greater freedom and the stimulus of ideas that increased his confidence in his own aesthetic vision. His first mature works, all based on elemental human themes, were of this period, and include *Death* (1908), and *Birth* (1909).

With the aid of an art patron in St. Petersburg, Chagall studied in Paris from 1910 to 1914. His contact with the works of Picasso, Juan Gris, Braque, Delaunay, and Matisse made a lasting impression on him. The writers Blaise Cendrars, André Salmon, and Guillaume Apollinaire became his friends. Paris broadened Chagall's outlook and enlarged his technical skill, but he clung to his own visual reality. From the abstract movement then current in France, he borrowed only what served his own purposes. The techniques of cubism, for example, which could help free his subjects from the hold of physical space, were utilized in such paintings as *I and My Village* (1911), *The Violinist* (1913,) and *Paris Through My Window* (1913).

At the outbreak of World War I in 1914, Chagall returned to Russia. The demands of the revolution and his own artistic interests kept him there until 1922. He was named commissar of fine arts for Vitebsk by the Bolshevik government that came to power in 1917, and he helped to organize an art school and a museum in the city. Eventually differences with the local authorities led him to resign. In Moscow, he painted murals and designed sets and costumes for the Granowsky Yiddish Theater.

Middle Years. In 1922, Chagall left Russia with his wife Bella, whom he married in 1915. After a brief stay in Berlin, where he began his autobiography, *Ma vie*, Chagall and his wife settled in Paris. The work of the next 18 years, produced in great profusion, was a fully mature reflection of Chagall's overpowering, poetical universe. Among the masterpieces that brought him to the forefront of modern art are *Over Vitebsk* (1923), *Double Portrait* (1925), *The Circus* (1931), and *Lovers with Rooster* (1933).

Between 1923 and 1931, Chagall illustrated Gogol's *Dead Souls* (published in 1948), the *Fables of La Fontaine* (published in 1952), and the *Bible* (published in 1956), all commissioned by the art dealer and publisher Ambroise Vollard. Chagall became almost as well known for his graphic work as for his paintings and probably executed more lithographs and etchings than any of his contemporaries, with the possible exception of Picasso.

With the surrender of France to Germany in 1940, Chagall, now a French citizen, left the country. With the help of the Museum of Modern Art in New York City, he went to the United States, where he remained until 1948. During this period he also visited Mexico, where he designed his first ballet, Massine's *Aleko* (1942). He also designed sets and costumes for Ballet Theatre's production of *Firebird* (1945).

During Chagall's stay in the United States he painted some of his best-known works, including *The Juggler* (1943) and *Cockcrow* (1944). In 1946 the Museum of Modern Art arranged a major retrospective exhibit of his work, which was also seen at the Art Institute in Chicago. Chagall's wife Bella died in the United States in 1944.

Postwar Years. In 1948, Chagall returned to France. He lived for a year in the Montmartre section of Paris, and then moved to Vence, on the south coast. With Valentina Brodsky, whom he married in 1952, he settled in the neighboring town of St.-Paul-de-Vence in 1960.

Chagall's painting style remained essentially the same through the whole course of his career. Such works as *Red Roofs* (1953) and *Girl with*

MARC CHAGALL utilized the techniques of cubism to serve his own imaginative vision in *I and My Village.*

Blue Face (1960) are distinguishable as late paintings only by an increased feeling of light and open space, achieved partly by the use of transparent, overlapping forms.

His great international fame brought Chagall many important commissions in several countries. Among the best known are the 12 stained-glass windows for the synagogue of the Hadassah–Hebrew University Medical Center in Jerusalem, installed in 1962. These windows, representing the 12 tribes of Israel, established Chagall as one of the outstanding artists in this medium. He also designed windows for a church in Fulton, N. Y., and for the Roman Catholic cathedral at Metz, France. In 1964, Chagall completed the ceiling decorations for the Paris Opéra. He also executed two large mural paintings for the Metropolitan Opera House at Lincoln Center, New York City, in 1966. The same year he designed sets and costumes for the Metropolitan Opera's new production of Mozart's *Magic Flute*. Chagall's prolific production of graphic work culminated in the *Exodus* portfolio of 1966.

On July 7, 1973, Chagall's 86th birthday, a museum devoted exclusively to his works was opened in Nice, France. It was called the National Museum of the Marc Chagall Biblical Message, and it was the first state-built museum in France to house the production of a single living artist.

JOSEPH K. FOSTER, *Author of*
"Marc Chagall: Posters and Personality"

Further Reading: Foster, Joseph K., *Chagall: Posters and Personality* (New York 1966); Kloomok, Isaac, *Marc Chagall, His Life and Work* (New York 1951); Lassaigne, Jacques, *Chagall* (Paris 1957); Meyer, Franz, *Marc Chagall* (New York 1964); Sweeney, James J., *Marc Chagall* (New York 1946).

CHAGAS' DISEASE, chä'gäs, is a disorder that occurs primarily in South and Central America and is caused by the protozoan parasite *Trypanosoma cruzi.* The disease was named for Carlos Chagas, who discovered the parasite in Brazil in 1909. The parasite is transmitted to people by insects and cannot be passed directly from one person to another. An insect picks up the parasite by biting an infected animal. The parasite then enters the insect's digestive tract and is later passed out with its waste matter. Humans become infected if the contaminated waste matter comes into contact with their mucous membranes or with a break in the skin.

The initial lesion in Chagas' disease most often involves the eye, which becomes swollen, red, and inflamed. Sometimes the first symptom is a small, purplish red sore on the skin. After several weeks the sore crusts over and gradually subsides, leaving a small pigmented scar. After the initial attack the disease often becomes chronic, with intermittent fever, swelling of the body, enlargement of the lymph glands, and skin rashes. Sometimes the heart is involved, causing shortness of breath, chest pain, and palpitations. Sometimes the central nervous system is involved and convulsions develop.

There is no satisfactory treatment for Chagas' disease. In many cases the symptoms eventually subside spontaneously, but sometimes the disease continues to progress until the patient dies, usually due to heart failure.

Louis J. Vorhaus, M.D.
Cornell University Medical College

CHAGOS ARCHIPELAGO, chä'gōs, is a group of British-owned islands in the Indian Ocean, about 250 miles (400 km) south of the Maldive Islands. Formerly a dependency of Mauritius, the islands were transferred in 1965 to a newly created colony called the British Indian Ocean Territory.

The five main coral atolls are Diego Garcia, Peros Banhos, Salomon, Three Brothers, and Six Islands. The last two are uninhabited. Diego Garcia, which is about 100 miles (160 km) to the southeast of the group, is the largest, and its crescent shape encloses a lagoon that forms a harbor. The island was a British air base during World War II and in 1965 became a British-American defense facility. Expansion of the U. S. naval base, with new airport and harbor facilities, was approved by the Senate in July 1975. More than 1,200 residents of Diego Garcia, Île du Coin, and Boddam islands were transferred to Mauritius, which subsequently offered to move these people to its dependency, the Agalega Islands, 600 miles (970 km) to the north. See also British Indian Ocean Territory.

CHAGRES RIVER, chä'grās, in Panama and the Panama Canal Zone. The Panama Canal follows most of its course. The river rises in the Cordillera de San Blas of northeastern Panama and flows to a point 9 miles (14 km) upstream from Gamboa, where it is dammed to form Madden Lake, the supplementary reservoir of the canal. At Gamboa it becomes a part of the canal. This section of the river is dammed at Gatun to form Gatun Lake, from which it flows into the Caribbean.

At Gatun it leaves the canal and flows a short distance to the Caribbean Sea. In its natural state the Chagres was a torrential river subject to flooding. Its waters are now controlled by Madden Dam.

CHAIN, Ernst Boris (1906–   ), German-English biochemist, who shared the 1945 Nobel Prize in medicine with Howard W. Florey and Alexander Fleming "for the discovery of penicillin and its curative value in a number of infectious diseases."

Chain was born in Berlin, Germany, on June 19, 1906. He emigrated to England in 1933 and spent his first years there at the School of Biochemistry at Cambridge under Sir Frederick Gowland Hopkins. In 1935 he went to the Sir William Dunn School of Pathology, at Oxford, at the invitation of Florey. There Chain worked first on the mode of action of snake venom and later on the enzyme hyaluronidase, which promotes diffusion of substances in tissues by breaking down a tissue-cementing substance (hyaluronic acid). Chain also made an important early contribution to the knowledge of the mode of action of lysozyme, an antibacterial enzyme that attacks the cell walls of certain bacteria and brings about their lysis (disintegration).

Florey's interest in lysozyme led Florey and Chain to plan a systematic investigation of antibacterial substances produced by microorganisms. One of the first substances to be chosen for study was penicillin, which had been described first by Fleming in 1928. Florey and Chain and a group of colleagues at Oxford extracted and purified penicillin and demonstrated for the first time its remarkable chemotherapeutic properties. Their work marked the beginning of the modern antibiotic era.

From 1948 to 1961, Chain was director of a research center at the Instituto Superiore di Sanità in Rome, where he studied problems in microbial fermentation and the mode of action of insulin. During this time he became a consultant to the Beecham Research Laboratories Ltd., where the nucleus of the penicillin molecule, 6-aminopenicillanic acid, subsequently was isolated. The preparation of this nucleus led to the production of new penicillins of clinical value. In 1961, Chain became professor of biochemistry at Imperial College, University of London.

E. P. Abraham
Sir William Dunn School of Pathology, Oxford

CHAIN, a cable made of a series of metal links or rings fitted together. Three main types of industrial chain may be distinguished by the shape of link that they employ. Stud links are preferred for chain cable on ships, because the joint in the middle adds weight, prevents entangling, and reduces the chance of deformation. The so-called "short" or "open" links are used for ordinary purposes of hauling and lifting. Pitched or calibrated links, designed to fit accurately into a sprocket wheel or similar device, serve for power transmission.

Chains are manufactured from many different metals and alloys, and are for the most part cut and shaped by machinery and are electrically welded. But large chains of wrought iron, which is often preferred for strength, are made by hand. Each link is then cut to standard length from the bar of metal, flattened or *scarfed* at both ends, and bent into a U-shape. After it has been heated in the furnace and threaded into its place in the chain, the ends are welded together with a hammer. Finally, any unevenness in the weld may be removed by further hammering with concave shaping-tools called *dollies.*

Early History. The origin of the chain is unknown, but its possibility may have been suggested by the entangling of hooks or the use of a double hook for connection. Chains dating from before 2500 B. C. have been found in the royal cemetery at Ur in Mesopotamia; their links consist of rings folded in half and tucked into each other. About a millennium later an Egyptian tomb relief shows chained prisoners, and the gold chain of office which Pharaoh gives to Joseph in Genesis (41:42) represents a well-attested Egyptian practice and illustrates the long history of the modern ornamental chain. In the 8th century B. C. the Assyrians had heavy cast-bronze chains with S-shaped links.

In the Roman Empire bronze chains were used for mooring galleys. Slim chains of various metals, such as those used in the pendant oil lamps found at Pompeii, were part of the equipment of the well-to-do home. Unruly slaves as well as prisoners were held in chains of iron. Only prison chains are named in the New Testament, and supposed links from the chains of the Apostles were treasured as relics in early Christendom.

Outside the Roman Empire, the skill of Celtic smiths is illustrated by a chain dating from about 50 B. C. found in North Wales. Its links had been hammered, apparently with internal dies, into a figure eight, thus anticipating the modern stud link.

Middle Ages and Renaissance. In the Middle Ages, agriculture, the building industry, and transportation all employed iron chains increasingly for purposes which involved a possible breaking strain in rope. Other uses ranged from the closing of harbor entrances by a chain boom to the hanging of cooking vessels over the open hearth. Chains were forged on the blacksmith's anvil, and were sufficiently common to figure in late-medieval English inventories. In a Worcestershire inventory a plow chain was valued at sixpence, the same amount as a secondhand pair of shears. In 1634 one of the earliest English patents was issued to a blacksmith for chain-making, and in colonial America chains also continued to be a regular product of the smithy.

Development of Modern Chains. At the end of the 18th century new methods of making bar iron rendered the material for chains more plentiful, and new uses were developed. In 1801 James Finley built his chain-hung suspension bridge at Uniontown, Pa., and in 1817 Samuel Brown in England patented flat links strong enough for large spans. Brown used these links for the once-famous chain pier at Brighton, and Thomas Telford employed them on the 580-foot (177-meter) Menai Strait Bridge in Wales, where they lasted for more than a century. Although John A. Roebling used steel-wire cable instead of chain for his bridges in the mid-19th century, some bridges, such as the London Tower Bridge (1894) were still being chain hung. Many modern suspension bridges, especially in Europe, have eye-bar chain suspension cables made of high tensile strength steel. Besides inventing flat links, Samuel Brown, who was a retired naval officer, also invented chain cable, an anchor chain which he patented in 1816 after sailing a ship to the West Indies equipped throughout with chain-rigging and cable. The rapid growth of the world's shipping in numbers and tonnage provided an enormous demand for chain.

The demand for chains on ships, together with the need for chain couplings on railroads and for hoisting chains at warehouses and building sites,

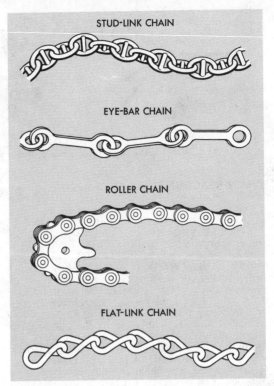

STUD LINK CHAIN is used as heavy-duty cable on ships because it is strong and unlikely to foul. Eye-link chain and flat-link chain were developed in the 19th century for use on suspension bridges. Roller chain is commonly seen in bicycle transmissions.

made chains a key product. The English "Black Country" of South Staffordshire became the principal center of production for large chains, which were made at domestic forges operated by masters who often exploited the labor of women and children under barbarous conditions. By the 1890's the work was beginning to be transferred to factories, where it was under better control, but in 1909 chain making was still one of the four notorious "sweated industries" for which the first Trade Boards were set up as a remedy.

In America, where some factory production had been established at an early date—at the Pittsburgh Rolling Mill, for example, in 1811—Pennsylvania became the main manufacturing center for light chains, especially in the neighborhood of York with its strong German handicraft tradition.

In the 20th century many new types of chain have been developed for power transmission, beginning with the roller chain for the bicycle and extending to most mechanisms in which the distance between the shafts that require connection is of moderate length. Chains used with sprocket wheels are also preferred to belts where no slipping can be tolerated, and are employed in many conveyor systems. For marine purposes electrically welded steel chains and high-tensile molded chains of cast steel have gained ground in recent years.

THOMAS KINGSTON DERRY
Coauthor of "A Short History of Technology"

CHAIN MAIL. See ARMOR.

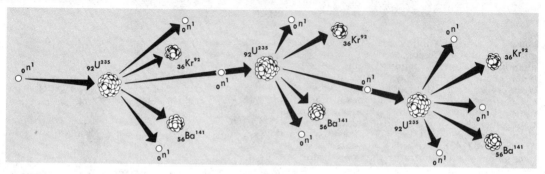

A CHAIN REACTION requires that at least one of the neutrons released in each reaction cause another reaction.

CHAIN REACTION, a process that, once started, is self-perpetuating. Conditions necessary for the process are evident in the case of an ordinary coal fire. The coal is stable until it is heated to its kindling temperature. Combustion then releases energy, which under certain circumstances can heat more coal to the burning point, thus starting a chain reaction. A single piece of coal will usually not sustain a fire because most of the liberated energy is lost to the surroundings. In a pile of coal, however, most of the energy lost from one piece is absorbed by its neighbors. Enough energy is maintained by the pile to keep the temperature above the point necessary for burning, while the surplus energy escaping from the pile can be used for other purposes.

In general, any chain reaction involves some reaction that requires triggering to start and that gives off more energy than it takes to trigger it. The structural configuration or other conditions must then be such that the energy given off and absorbed in the material is released in the right form and in sufficient quantity to trigger more reactions.

Nuclear Chain Reactions. Since 1945 the best-known type of chain reaction has been that produced by the fission of uranium or plutonium. In that year the atomic bomb blasts signaled a new era in production of energy. The energy source in fission is in the atomic nucleus. Strictly speaking, ordinary chemical interactions produce atomic or molecular energy, while fission yields nuclear energy. The large atomic nuclei of several heavy elements are only slightly stable against breakdown into nuclei of much lighter elements. When a nucleus of the uranium isotope with mass 235 absorbs a slow neutron, it breaks almost in half into two lighter nuclei, such as barium and krypton, at the same time releasing several neutrons. Most of the nuclear energy is released in the form of the kinetic energy of the neutrons and of the lighter nuclei which spring apart. The kinetic energy serves to heat the material, but the neutrons provide the trigger needed to cause other nuclei to undergo fission, thus maintaining the chain reaction. Although only about 0.1% of the mass of the uranium is converted to other forms of energy in the process, this is sufficient to fuel a large city power plant while consuming only about an ounce of uranium per hour.

Ordinary uranium contains less than 1% of the isotope 235. The common isotope, with mass 238, can absorb a neutron without undergoing fission. Instead, the nucleus gives off an electron, becoming plutonium 239 by this beta decay. If this nucleus then absorbs a second slow neutron it will also undergo fission. Nuclear bombs or reactors can be fueled with either uranium 235 or plutonium 239. The former is separated from natural uranium by complicated, expensive procedures, and the latter must be manufactured in nuclear reactors, since it does not exist naturally.

The production of a chain reaction with either uranium 235 or plutonium 239 involves the same considerations that we have already described. A small piece of either metal will remain stable in spite of the fact that fission is spontaneously taking place. Each such fission produces on the average about 2.5 neutrons, but these have fairly high energy and so can travel through considerable material without interacting with an atomic nucleus. To sustain a chain reaction, at least one neutron from each fission must cause another fission.

Critical Size. The escaping neutrons can be made effective by reflecting them back into the material, or by making the material large enough so that the neutrons are slowed down and captured. There is a "critical mass"—or more properly, a "critical size"—such that at least one neutron from each fission is captured, starting the chain reaction. To produce nuclear explosions, small pieces of fissionable material, each stable by itself, are shot together to form a piece larger than the critical size. If each fission provides neutrons to trigger more than one other fission, and each such process takes a small fraction of a millionth of a second, then the number of fissioning nuclei increases exponentially, yielding the enormous energy of a bomb blast before the material itself is blown apart.

Nuclear Reactors. For the continuous production of fission energy in nuclear power plants, the average number of neutrons per fission used to maintain the chain reaction must be exactly one. If the number is less than one, the reaction will stop; if it remains more than one, the reaction rate will steadily increase. The arrangement of materials must be such that the system is in dynamic equilibrium, maintaining the chain reaction at a chosen level. Such systems, called nuclear reactors, contain the fissionable material in a solution or in a solid array interspersed with other elements that slow the neutrons. In some reactors the level of the chain reaction is maintained by movable cadmium rods that absorb neutrons. In others the temperature of the fuel mixture determines its density in such a way that too much activity disperses the fissionable material, thus controlling the chain reaction. See also NUCLEAR ENERGY—1. *Nuclear Fission.*

CLIFFORD E. SWARTZ
State University of New York, Stony Brook

CHAIN SNAKE is a name sometimes given to the king snake. See KING SNAKE.

CHAIN STORES are a relatively modern phenomenon, present to some degree in all retail-store merchandise lines and also in the service industries. An important segment of the American economy, chain stores account for approximately 37% of all retail trade in the United States. They have made a substantial contribution to living standards and to styles of living by presenting to consumers a wide variety of goods efficiently and economically.

A chain or chain store organization consists of two or more centrally owned units that handle on the same level of distribution (wholesale or retail) substantially similar lines of merchandise. While avoiding the term "chain," the U. S. Census of Business considers a store a member of a multiunit organization "if it is one of two or more stores in the same general kind of business operated by the same firm." For example, a firm is classified as multiunit if it operates two or more food stores. But a firm operating one drugstore, one hardware store, and one furniture store is not classified as a chain, and all the individual stores in this case are regarded, for official enumeration purposes, as single units.

Kinds of Chains. Common usage appears to relate the term "chain" to retail stores, and tends to neglect the existence of many chains of public utilities, banks, hotels, motion-picture theaters, finance company offices, and of other types. The distinctive attribute of a chain is central ownership. Regular chains are thus distinguished from cooperative or voluntary chains, in which the retailer members preserve individual ownership (for example, some widely known food, drug, and auto-parts stores).

The regular chain has full control over its retail units, assumes full financial responsibility for them, bears all loss when a unit is closed, and retains all profit made by each store. In a voluntary chain, on the other hand, cooperation with the central organization is contractual. The individual store assumes full financial responsibility for its acts. All profit earned by the store is retained by its owner. When a store is forced to close its doors, it is considered commercially and legally a failure, and the total loss is borne by the owner and his creditors.

Some voluntary chains are sponsored by wholesalers, some are operated cooperatively by a group of affiliated retailers, and still others are franchised outlets of regular retail chains. Closely akin to chain operations are various franchise operations (for example, motels and highway restaurants).

Kinds of Business. In some lines of business in the United States, regular chains dominate the trade; in others their position is not greatly different from their average share of the market for total retail trade; and in still others they are of negligible importance. The greatest strength during the late 1960's was in department stores, grocery stores, and women's ready-to-wear clothing stores. On the other hand, the chain store share of total sales in several lines is quite weak. These include hardware stores, gasoline service stations, eating and drinking places, and franchised passenger-car dealers.

Geographical Classes of Chains. Substantially all stores in *local chains* are located in or near the same metropolitan area. In the United States most of these organizations are in the food and drug fields. Also rather common among local chains are department stores, clothing stores, furniture and appliance establishments, gasoline service stations, and liquor stores.

Chains are classified as *sectional* if their stores are located in some one major part of the country, such as New England. Many of these chains are large, and often they are at least as well known within their area of operation as are some still larger organizations.

The interests of *national* chains are much broader than any one section, although they do not necessarily cover the entire country. Illustrative are the Great Atlantic & Pacific Tea Company; Sears, Roebuck & Company; Safeway Stores Company; J. C. Penney Company; Kroger Company; and F. W. Woolworth Company. Some of these companies may also be regarded as *international* because of their extensive operations in other countries.

Urban Concentration. During the early periods of development—prior to the 1920's—chains in the United States tended to concentrate in large urban areas. While some chains are now situated in virtually all United States cities of any significant size, marked concentration in the largest population centers continues to be the rule. This is explained in part by the fact that certain prominent chains, especially in shopping goods lines (for example, home furnishings and wearing apparel), operate only in large cities. Also, in convenience lines (for example, groceries, drugs, and hardware), the number of different chains competing with each other tends to be much larger in large markets than in small markets. The smaller the city, the easier it is for independents to complete with chains, especially in advertising and other forms of promotional activity.

Degree of Vertical Integration. Chains are divided into several classes based upon the degree of vertical integration (control of retailing or wholesaling, or manufacturing, or a combination of these activities).

One group consists of units without wholesale distribution or manufacturing facilities, which therefore confine their activities to retailing. In this group belong many local chains of only a limited number of units.

A second group consists of chains with warehouses or wholesale distribution centers. This arrangement is typical in many lines where the volume of goods sold by the chain makes purchasing directly from the manufacturer economically feasible. Warehousing facilities are needed to serve the individual stores much in the same way that wholesalers provide an assembling, sorting, and dispersion service for independent stores.

The third type consists of chains that have integrated their activities still further by the performance of manufacturing activities. This group overlaps with the second in that its members ordinarily also operate wholesale distribution centers. Complete or partial ownership of subsidiary manufacturing companies is common among national general merchandise chains, as is strong control over the activities of supplying manufacturers by furnishing specifications and taking all or a substantial part of their output. Large chains in the grocery, shoe, and men's apparel classification are also involved to a significant degree in the manufacture of many private brands or store-controlled items. Sears, Roebuck and Company, for example, has substantial ownership interest in many of the companies that are its major suppliers.

GENERAL ORGANIZATIONAL CHARACTERISTICS

In national, sectional, and local chains, major authority and responsibility tend to be centralized in the home office or in branch or regional headquarters organizations, rather than delegated to individuals serving in store units. Individual store managers are chiefly responsible for sales and customer service. They depend on headquarters officials to perform such merchandising activities as planning, negotiations with suppliers, technical assistance in advertising and display, and, in many cases, much of the stock control, accounting, and data-processing work.

Compared with single-unit firms, chains are characterized by elaborate systems of supervision and control. These systems are designed to hold individual operating units accountable for reasonable standards of performance and to keep the home office informed at all times about operating results in each of the individual units. This continuous information process requires detailed reports and the personal supervision of individual units by a district superintendent, who in turn usually reports to a divisional or regional official, or directly to headquarters in local chains.

The elaborate, complex, and somewhat inflexible nature of the control machinery necessary to administer a widely scattered business enterprise consisting of hundreds or thousands of store units has been responsible for an important modern trend among the larger chains. This trend is the substantial decentralization of authority and responsibility into regional or divisional headquarters. For example, Sears, Roebuck & Company and the Great Atlantic & Pacific Tea Company are operated much like a group of regional organizations. They are unified by major policy decisions of the headquarters organization but are separately responsible within a defined geographical area for the major part of the buying, selling, and sales promotion activities.

A similar rather common development, attributable to substantial variations in local competition and to larger average size of stores, is the upgrading of the job of store manager. Once regarded as a mere operating and personnel manager of the store unit, he now frequently has a much wider range of responsibility, more freedom to adapt his store to local conditions, and merchandising responsibility for much larger sales volume than was traditionally the situation among large, centrally managed chains.

Competitive Factors. Because some chains operate in almost every kind of business (while others operate in a limited field) and because they use almost every method of store operation or merchandising technique, no competitive advantages or disadvantages are common to all multiunit organizations. Certain competitive circumstances, however, characterize all large, centrally managed chains.

Advantages. By ordering merchandise for many retail units through a central office that negotiates with suppliers, the large chain is able to buy on more favorable terms than is the single-unit store in the same line of business. Because the manufacturer's marketing costs are relatively low when disposing of large quantities to one customer, chains are able to obtain the lowest prices and to obtain other allowances related to quantity buying. These allowances include advertising funds and compensation for special store displays. Large chains also have the benefit of considerable buying skill, a natural result of functional specialization. Situated at the central or district headquarters are merchandising experts, who spend all of their time maintaining market contacts, collecting and interpreting marketing information, viewing offerings of vendors, determining the suitability of merchandise for sale by the company, and conducting negotiations.

Certain economies result in relatively low operating costs. One of the most significant economies among chains with warehouses is derived from combining or integrating wholesaling and retailing operations. Through the coordination of these activities, stores are supplied from a single chain warehouse that does not have to compete directly with other suppliers, as is the case with wholesalers who sell to independent retailers. No salesmen need call upon the store managers to solicit business, credit problems are eliminated, and deliveries can be effectively scheduled.

Another economy is curtailment of consumer services. As compared with its typical independent competitor, the chain tends to sell to a greater extent on a cash basis. It tends to deliver only bulky or expensive items or to make a charge for delivery when it is provided. It tends to emphasize self-service or self-selection merchandising techniques.

Many chains gain economies by limiting the composition of their stocks. By concentrating offerings on those items for which there is a widespread demand, they attain higher than typical rates of stock turnover. This turnover reduces the risk of merchandise deterioration or style obsolescence, requires less storage space per unit of sales, and lowers capital costs and insurance costs on inventories.

Low merchandise costs stemming from large purchasing power and relatively low operating costs are often associated with a belief that a small percentage of net profit will increase sales to a maximum and yield large total dollar profits. This results in another important competitive characteristic: the ability to feature price appeal.

When chains are in competition with independent neighborhood stores, they have significant advertising advantages. For example, a grocery chain with stores in all parts of a city can utilize major advertising media in a manner not possible for smaller competitors with highly localized markets.

Large chains have highly skilled real estate departments and, because of excellent credit ratings, are able to command the most favorable merchandising sites in established business districts and in new shopping centers.

Limitations. No single disadvantage applies to every large chain store organization, but certain limitations may be highlighted because of their tendency to restrict further development.

Standardization of operating procedures, although essential and usually economical, has limited chains in fields where individualized management attention is of unusual importance. Large national chains are nonexistent in the hardware trade, for example, partly because of the great diversity of items that must be handled and the close supervision and care necessary to maintain balanced stocks. In any trade in which contract work is involved, large chains are at a disadvantage, because each contract presents a particularized pricing problem. The need for outside sales promotion and installation also introduces complications.

The common practices of restricting consumer services and limiting assortments, while reducing expenses of operation, limit the consumer appeal of many chains. Large numbers of consumers insist upon and are willing to pay for the wider range of services and facilities offered by many independent stores.

Within the lines of trade in which chains are of the greatest relative importance, many companies are only weakly differentiated from each other. In spite of excellent opportunities for research and experimentation, innovations have tended to be imitative rather than imaginative. Many chains have copied operating methods and techniques that apparently have worked well for others, thus contributing to a type of monotonous uniformity and a lack of exciting and dynamic merchandising.

ORIGIN AND DEVELOPMENT

The present type of chain store is of comparatively recent origin. The chain idea of distribution, however, has many forerunners and prototypes. As early as 200 B.C., a Chinese businessman owned a chain of a great many units. A poster found in Pompeii, which was destroyed in 79 A.D., advertised for lease a firm consisting of 900 retail shops. The Mitsui system of apothecary shops in Japan dates from 1643, and the company has been one of the wealthiest and most powerful businesses in that country.

In the Americas, the Hudson's Bay Company began to operate a chain of trading posts before 1750. But in the United States the development of the modern chain was not started until the Great Atlantic & Pacific Tea Company was founded in 1858. (The second A & P store was opened a year later.) The second of the existing chains is Park & Tilford, which began business in 1840 but did not open a second store until 1860. The Jones Brothers Tea Company was established in 1872, and the F. W. Woolworth Company proved the validity of the chain principle in the variety business about 1880.

Although a number of chains were established during the latter half of the 19th century, their real growth occurred during the 20th century. Even as late as 1919, the estimated volume of chains was less than 5% of total retail sales, but by 1929 this proportion had increased sixfold to about 30%. The phenomenal development of the chains during the 1920's is explained by economic and social factors. The time was ripe for applying mass methods on a widespread basis in retail distribution, where efficiency had not generally kept pace with industrial mass production techniques. The number of people living in cities was about twice that at the beginning of the century, and a large amount of the city growth came during the 1920's.

Mergers and Acquisitions. The economic power of certain large chains has been considerably enlarged by the acquisition of other organizations in the same or similar lines of trade. For example, in the period 1949–1958, 10 large food chains were particularly active in acquiring other companies. These 10 corporations acquired 107 food chains, which all together, in the year prior to acquisition, operated 1,474 stores, 42 manufacturing establishments, and 64 wholesale distribution warehouses. Merger activity was also obvious in the shoe trade, the automotive accessory field, and the apparel trades. Because most acquisitions involved mergers of one chain with another

chain, they did not substantially affect the total competitive position of multiunit organizations. An exception was the department store field, where some acquired firms were large single-unit stores.

The general tendency was toward greater concentration of ownership among the very largest firms in the trades affected. Some mergers were forestalled early in the negotiations or were dissolved through action of the Federal Trade Commission or the U. S. Department of Justice, the latter using the terms of the Clayton Antitrust Act. The grounds for action under the Clayton Act were that "the effect of such acquisition may be substantially to lessen competition, or tend to create a monopoly."

Legal Limitations. Most of the current legal limitations in large-scale retailing were originally enacted as an aspect of the anti-chain store movement of the late 1920's and the 1930's. The chains' ability to obtain discriminatory advantages in purchasing was limited by the Robinson-Patman Act (1936). The chain's freedom to engage in loss-leader pricing (selling an item below cost to attract customers) was curtailed to some extent by state pricing legislation. The state statutes were known as fair trade laws, and they permitted resale price maintenance in which manufacturers set minimum retail prices.

In addition, many states have taxed chain store organizations in some special manner with the intent, at least in part, of restricting the growth of chains and the multiplication of their store units. At one time such laws were in effect in 29 states, yet in the late 1960's only 11 states had chain store taxes based on graduated license fees.

CHAIN STORES OUTSIDE THE U. S.

Chains in other countries follow largely the same pattern as in the United States. In Canada, chains are defined for census purposes as having four or more centrally owned units. There is more concentration in some lines of trade, especially grocery stores. Corporate chains in this field grew from 29.6% in 1951 to 47% in all stores in 1965. Voluntary chains also grew, increasing from 10% to 38.2% of the stores in the grocery field during the same period. A large decline occurred in the independent grocery store, which fell from 60.4% to 14.8%.

The greatest growth has been in the voluntary chain as Canadian independents and wholesalers have organized to compete with corporate chains. Some corporate chains have diversified and now own wholesale establishments that in turn sponsor voluntary chains.

Outside North America, chain stores are found mainly in Europe and South America. Many food, variety, and department-store chains are owned by resident entrepreneurs. Also, many are either wholly or partially owned by U. S. firms.

WILLIAM R. DAVIDSON
Ohio State University
Coauthor of "Retailing Management"

Bibliography

Beckman, Theodore N., and Davidson, William R., *Marketing* (New York 1967).
Beckman, Theodore N., and Nolen, H. C., *The Chain Store Problem* (New York 1938).
Davidson, William R., and Doody, Alton F., *Retailing Management* (New York 1966).
Lebhar, Godfrey, *Chain Stores in America* (New York 1963).
Lebhar-Friedman Publications, *Chain Store Age* (New York, monthly).

CHAIR, a movable seat with a back, and with or without arms, intended to hold one person. Although it is one of the oldest furniture forms, the chair has only come into common use within the last 300 years. Prior to the 17th century, chairs were so uncommon that they were generally considered symbols of authority and dignity. Most people sat on stools, benches, or on the tops of chests that doubled for storage. Even in the houses of the rich, the few chairs were reserved for the head of the household and distinguished visitors. Today when we speak of the "chairman" or in parliamentary procedure address "the chair," our words reflect the importance that people used to attach to this article of furniture and the person it held.

Ancient Chairs. The earliest known chairs were those used by the ancient Egyptians. The legs of Egyptian chairs were often representations of the legs of animals, terminating in paws or hoofed feet. Egyptian chairs were made of costly materials—ebony, ivory, and gilded woods, sometimes carved and painted in brilliant colors—and were covered with rich textiles or animal skins.

The Greeks developed a remarkably beautiful type of chair known as the *klysmos*, frequently seen in Greek vase paintings. It is an armless chair, the rear leg and back of which, seen in profile, form a continuous line shaped like an S; the front leg is a c-curve. The *klysmos*, perhaps the most beautiful design ever evolved for a chair, was revived early in the 19th century and again in the 20th century.

A type of chair particularly associated with the Romans is the curule, or X-framed chair. Curules, either made of wood and ivory or cast in metal, were used by Roman magistrates.

Medieval Chairs. Curule chairs continued to be used throughout the Middle Ages. Other medieval chairs had tall paneled backs and sides or were set under canopies of figured damask or cut velvet. These features helped to protect against the cold in drafty medieval halls. Loose cushions made the chairs more comfortable.

Seventeenth Century. In the 17th century there were a number of developments in the design of chairs, some of them influenced by trade with the Orient. After the Portuguese returned from India with chairs having caned panels in their backs and seats, caned chairs became very popular throughout Europe and in the American colonies. They allowed air to circulate and were thought to discourage vermin, that might breed in chairs of solid wood.

The chief advance of the century, however, traced by many scholars to the influence of the East, was the reintroduction of sinuous curved shapes. For centuries most European chairs had been designed as patterns of straight lines, the backs, seats, and arms, making very little accommodation to the soft and flexible contours of the human body. Chinese furniture, however, included chairs with curved backs. Pictorial lacquered screens of the 17th century showing European traders loading Chinese treasure on their ships suggest that some of these Chinese chairs may have been introduced to Europe. Whatver their derivation, chairs with curved backs became fashionable during the 17th century. At the same time, straight turned legs gave way to arched "cabriole" legs.

Only at the end of the 17th century did upholstery come into common use. Earlier, in the 16th century, a few chairs had been entirely covered with fabric—even their legs and arms—and decorated with large metal studs.

Eighteenth Century. Upholstery was increasingly used during the 18th century. "Easy chairs" began to be made; they had padded and upholstered backs, seats, and arms (and sometimes upholstered wings to shield the sitter from drafts). Upholstered chairs generally were covered with a hard-finished wool cloth, or with decorative panels of needlework or tapestry. Since silks and velvets were very expensive and relatively perishable, they were used only in the grander houses.

Still, upholstered chairs were much less comfortable than were side and arm chairs made entirely of wood. Household inventories from the 18th century show that side chairs were made in sets of as many as 12, 18, or 24. From 18th century paintings and written accounts we know that these sets of chairs generally were ranged around the perimeter of the room and only brought forward as needed. These side chairs, although they look like modern dining room chairs, were used all over the house—in the parlor or drawing room and in the bedrooms. Special rooms set aside for the sole purpose of eating did not become usual until late in the century, even in large houses.

Nineteenth and Twentieth Centuries. During the 19th century the design of chairs began to reflect rapidly expanding technology. The first patent for coiled springs, made of iron or steel wire twisted into spirals, was granted to Samuel Pratt of London in 1828. They were soon used for upholstered chairs, which became deeper, softer, and larger and were called "overstuffed chairs." Other new materials such as thin laminated woods, which could be bent into intricate shapes, papier-mâché, and prefabricated metal forms were experimented with by 19th century designers. Probably the most successful was Michael Thonet of Vienna, whose "bentwood" chairs continued to be manufactured in huge numbers in the 20th century.

The English designer William Morris, founder of the arts and crafts movement (q.v.), designed the "Morris chair." Its movable back made it a forerunner of modern reclining chairs.

During the 20th century, functionalism (q.v.) and the hope of bringing good design to mass-produced furniture brought increased simplicity to chair design. New materials, notably plastic, made possible new forms. Many of the outstanding chair designs of the 20th century were made by architects, including Alvar Aalto, Marcel Breuer, and Eero Saarinen to harmonize with the architecture of the "international style."

Country or Cottage Chairs. The many revolutions in taste between the 17th and 20th century had little effect except on chairs intended for the rich and fashionable. Throughout these centuries there was a strong continuity in the design of "low-style" chairs. They commonly had straight legs and backs, sometimes turned but rarely carved. Their frames were made of native woods and sometimes painted; their seats were made of solid wood, rush, or cane. These "country" or "cottage" chairs are so conservative in design that it is sometimes hard to date them accurately within fifty or a hundred years. Perhaps the most important design innovation in "low-style" chairs during the 18th century was the Windsor chair, which was so simple that it readily lent itself to mass production. See also FURNITURE.

J. STEWART JOHNSON, *Newark Museum of Art*

CHAIR OF ST. PETER (*Cathedra Petri*), by Bernini, surmounts an altar in St. Peter's Basilica, Rome.

CHAIR OF ST. PETER, an ornate chair or throne, also known as the *Cathedra Petri*, that stands in the center of the apse of the Basilica of St. Peter's in Rome. It is decorated with reliefs symbolizing the divine institution of the pastoral authority of St. Peter and the popes who succeeded him. The original chair is of wood and ivory and dates from the 9th century or even earlier. In 1657–1666 the baroque sculptor Giovanni Lorenzo Bernini (q.v.) created a splendid case entirely enclosing the chair. It is decorated in marble, gilt bronze, and stucco. In its present setting the chair forms part of Bernini's culminating ensemble for the interior of the Basilica of St. Peter's. Supported by enormous bronze figures, it rises aloft against the brilliant sunburst that serves as its foil.

WAYNE DYNES, *Vassar College*
Further Reading: Battaglia, R., *La Cattedra Berniniana de San Pietro* (Rome 1943); Wittkower, Rudolf, *Gianlorenzo Bernini, Sculptor of the Roman Baroque*, 2d ed. (London 1967).

CHAITANYA, chī-tun'yə (1485–1533), was a Hindu saint, mystic, and theistic reformer, who played an important part in the Vishnuism movement in Bengal, India. He founded a cult devoted to the worship of the god Vishnu in his form as Krishna (q.v.). His name is sometimes spelled *Caitanya*. He was also known as *Guaranga*.

Born at Nabadwip into a pious Brahman family, Chaitanya even as a child evidenced a deep interest in the *Bhagavad Gita* (q.v.). As an adult he entered the second ("householder") stage of Hindu life and was twice married, but while visiting the great religious center at Bodh-Gaya, he underwent a transforming experience that called him to a life of total religious commitment.

Chaitanya projected a simple but intense love of Krishna that attracted devotees. His teaching emphasized the supreme importance of devotion (*bhakti*) to Krishna, and the forms of worship practiced by his followers included chanting and eurhythmic movements. Chaitanya's social teaching stressed love, noninjury to living creatures (*ahimsa*), and equal treatment for all persons irrespective of caste. He was deified in his own lifetime as an incarnation (*avatar*) of Krishna.

PETER A. PARDUE,*Columbia University*

CHAKA, chä'ka (1787?–1828), a Zulu warrior, was the founder of the Zulu kingdom in southeastern Africa. The preferred spelling of his name is *Shaka*. In Chaka's youth the small autonomous chiefdoms that had existed among the Nguni for several centuries were being forcefully amalgamated into confederacies. He started his career as a soldier under Dingiswayo, head of the Mthethwa Confederacy.

In 1816, Chaka seized control of the Zulu chiefdom from his half brother and began to transform it—conscripting the young men into regiments, segregating them from civil society, toughening them with an iron discipline, and arming them with short stabbing spears in place of assegais (javelins). He began a career of conquest in 1818, creating a single, centralized, despotic kingdom between the Tugela and Pongola rivers. He devasted the country to the south, while refugee bands carried the devastation as far north as Lake Tanganyika. Chaka was assassinated in 1828 by two half brothers, one of whom, Dingane, succeeded him as king of the Zulu.

LEONARD M. THOMPSON
University of California at Los Angeles

CHALCANTHITE, kal-kan'thīt, is a hydrous copper sulfate mineral. It occurs in massive form and as azure crystals that are transparent to translucent and have a glassy luster. Although rare elsewhere, it is found in sufficient abundance in Chile to be an important ore of copper there.

Composition, $CuSO_4 \cdot 5H_2O$; hardness, 2.5; specific gravity, 2.3; crystal system, triclinic.

CHALCEDON, kal'sə-don, was an ancient Greek city in Bithynia, on the eastern shore of the Bosporus opposite Byzantium (modern Istanbul). The site is now occupied by the city of Kadıköy, Turkey. Chalcedon, also spelled *Calchedon*, was founded about 676 B.C. by Greeks from Megara, antedating Byzantium by 17 years. Its position was much less favorable than Byzantium's commercially because the Bosporus currents made ship landings difficult and also diverted toward Byzantium the tuna, a main source of wealth. Hence Chalcedon was called "city of the blind." It did, however, benefit from passing trade and had sources of copper and semiprecious stones.

Chalcedon belonged to the Athenian League in the 5th century B.C.; under Spartan rule from 405 and Persian from 387, it sided with Persia against Alexander the Great. It was made part of Alexander's empire but regained its freedom in 281. A Roman ally after 197, it was involved in the disaster of 73 B.C., when Mithridates VI of Pontus defeated a Roman army and captured a Roman fleet there. Under the Roman Empire it was a free city within the province of Bithynia.

Chalcedon was captured by Khosrau (Chosroes) II of Persia in 616 and destroyed by the Turks in 1075. Nothing is now visible of the ancient city. See also CHALCEDON, COUNCIL OF.

D. J. BLACKMAN
University of Bristol, England

CHALCEDON, Council of, kal'sə-don, the Fourth Ecumenical Council of the Catholic Church. It was held in the Church of St. Euphemia at Chalcedon, near Constantinople, on Oct. 8–31, 451. Emperor Marcian suggested the council in a letter to Pope Leo I. It met first on Sept. 1, 451, at Nicaea in Bithynia but was moved to Chalcedon to enable the Emperor to supervise its proceedings.

Attended by some 350 Eastern bishops, 3 papal legates and 2 African bishops in exile, the council attempted to end the disputes concerning the two natures in Christ. The disagreements arose from the differing theological approaches of Alexandria, which depended on the doctrine of St. Cyril, and of Antioch, which was considered the root of Nestorianism and was condemned at Ephesus in 431. The council also hoped to stem the ecclesiastical maneuverings represented in the deposition of Flavian, patriarch of Constantinople, by the patriarch of Alexandria, Dioscorus, at what Pope Leo I had stigmatized as the "Robber Synod" (*latrocinium*) of Ephesus in 449.

Pope Leo opposed a council held in the East because the Western bishops could not attend, on account of the barbarian invasions; but he capitulated to the Emperor and sent three legates: Bishops Paschasinus of Lilybeum and Licentius of Ascoli, and the priest Bonifatius, who presided at the council under the guidance of 19 imperial commissioners. In accordance with the Pope's instructions, the first four sessions were devoted to the trial of Dioscorus and the instigators of the Robber Synod. Dioscorus was deposed for contempt of ecclesiastical authority. For doctrine, the two synodical letters of St. Cyril were read along with Pope Leo's famous *Tome to Flavian*. Some Egyptian bishops objected to phrases in the papal explanation, and a new definition was hammered out by a committee under Anatolius of Constantinople. This was proclaimed on October 25.

The sessions of October 26–31 dealt with disciplinary matters, restored the bishops deposed at the Robber Synod, and issued the 28th canon, which declared Constantinople second in patriarchal rank after Rome. Because of canon 28, Leo I refused to confirm the council's acts until March 21, 453, after the monks in Egypt, who looked on the deposition of Dioscorus as a repudiation of the theology of St. Cyril, rebelled against the council.

The theological definition of Chalcedon was an amalgam of the teaching of Cyril, John of Antioch, Flavian of Constantinople, and Theodoret of Cyr with the Western tradition of Tertullian and St. Augustine summed up in Leo's *Tome*. It defined the one Christ as both God and man, consubstantial with the Father, and of one substance with man, one being in two natures, united without confusion or change.

FRANCIS X. MURPHY, C. SS. R.
Academia Alfonsiana, Rome

CHALCEDONY, kal-sed'ə-nē, is a variety of the silicate mineral, quartz. Also called *calcedony*, it is named for the ancient Greek city of Chalcedon. It is semitransparent to translucent, with a waxy luster, and is used for ornament. Chalcedony is cryptocrystalline; the individual crystals are so fine that they cannot be observed even through a microscope. The crystals are arranged in fibers to form parallel bands. Differently colored varieties are known by a number of names. Thus, red chalcedony is *carnelian*, brown is sard, green is *chrysoprase*, and a green variety with small red spots of jasper in it is called *heliotrope* (*bloodstone*). In *agate*, layers of chalcedony alternate with layers of opal or granular quartz.

CHALCID FLY, kal'sid, any of a group of tiny wasps that are parasitic in or on other insects. The larvae of some chalcid flies are so small that they can develop within the eggs of other insects. Others parasitize aphids and the immature stages of moths, butterflies, beetles, fleas, and bugs. Chalcid flies are less than 0.1 inch (0.3 cm) long and often are metallic blue or green in color. Some adults are wingless.

Many chalcid flies have strange habits. Some kinds are parasitic on other parasites of insects, while one kind, the fairy fly, swims underwater and deposits its eggs in the eggs of dragonflies. Another chalcid, the wheat straw-worm, spends its larval stage feeding in the stems of wheat and other grasses where it produces gall-like enlargements. Other chalcids live in ant nests where they attack the ant pupae.

One of the most interesting chalcids is the fig wasp (*Blastophaga psenes*), which is the sole pollinator of the flowers of the Smyrna fig. Since the flowers do not develop into fruit unless they are pollinated, the Smyrna fig industry is entirely dependent on this wasp. See also FIG; FIG WASP.

Chalcids belong to the superfamily Chalcidoidea, a large group containing many families, in the order Hymenoptera.

ROSS HUTCHINS
State Plant Board of Mississippi

CHALCIDICE, kal-sid'i-sē, is a *nomos* (department) and very mountainous peninsula in northeastern Greece. The *nomos* of Chalcidice (Greek, *Khalkidhikí*), which occupies the southern part of the peninsula, has an area of 1,158 square miles (2,998 sq km), and its capital is Políyiros.

Although corn, cereal, grain, tobacco, and olives are grown, the peninsula is most important economically for its beehives and metal mines. Mount Áthos, situated near the tip of Aktí, the easternmost of the three prongs that jut out from the peninsula, is the peninsula's highest mountain, with an elevation of 6,670 feet (2,033 meters). The Mount Áthos district is mentioned in ancient literature but is most celebrated for its numerous monasteries, the first of which was established in 963. See also ÁTHOS, MOUNT.

The original inhabitants of Chalcidice were mainly Thracians, but many Greek settlers arrived in the 7th and 6th centuries B. C., especially from the Euboean cities of Chalcis and Eretria. Olynthus and Potidea, the two most important cities of Chalcidice, were located on Pallene, the western prong. The dispute between Corinth and Athens over the control of Potidea was one of the factors that led to the opening of the Peloponnesian War in 431 B. C. After 348 B. C., Chalcidice was under Macedonian control. Olynthus was a major state in the 5th and early 4th centuries B. C., but it was destroyed by Philip II of Macedonia in 348 B. C. Population: (1961) of the *nomos*, 79,849.

JAMES R. WISEMAN
University of Texas

CHALCIS, kal'sis, is a city on the Greek island of Euboea and the capital of the *nomos* (department) of Euboea. Chalcis (Greek, *Khalkís*) is located on the Euripus channel, which separates it from mainland Greece by only 130 feet (40 meters). It was a trade center in antiquity and remains an important commercial port and tourist center. The city has soap, cement, and brick factories, distilleries, and flour mills.

The area is known to have been inhabited from at least the Early Bronze Age (approximately 3200–1900 B.C.). Although Chalcis was the most famous Euboean city in antiquity, it is still unexcavated. Most authorities agree that the ancient site is occupied by the modern town, but it may have been somewhat to the south where the classical acropolis has been identified.

Chalcis reached the height of its importance in the Archaic period (8th to early 5th century B.C.) and was the chief opponent of nearby Eretria in the Lelantine War (late 8th to early 7th century B.C.). This war was ostensibly fought for possession of the fertile Lelantine Plain but was more likely concerned with maritime supremacy. It eventually involved most of the major states of Greece. Little is known, however, of the conduct of the war, and even the identity of the victor is disputed.

Chalcis founded many colonies in Chalcidice (to which peninsula it gave its name), in the islands of the Sporades, in Sicily, and in Italy. The city was especially famous for its metalwork and pottery. Chalcis may have been the first city to adapt the Phoenician alphabet to the writing of Greek.

Chalcis was defeated in 506 B.C. by Athens, which settled 4,000 colonists in the Lelantine Plain. Chalcis was mainly under the control of Athens or Boeotia until 338 B.C., when the whole of Euboea came under the rule of Philip II of Macedonia. During the Hellenistic period the Macedonians considered the citadel of Chalcis one of the three most strategic garrisons (with Acrocorinth and Demetrias) in Greece. The city fell to the Turks in 1470 and became a part of the Greek kingdom in 1830. Population: (1961) 24,745.

JAMES R. WISEMAN
University of Texas

CHALCOCITE, kal'kǝ-sīt, a copper sulfide mineral, is one of the most important ores of copper. It is usually found in a massive or granular form in zones of sulfide deposits. The crystals of chalcocite are prismatic, opaque, and dark lead-gray, tarnishing to brown-black on exposure; they have a metallic luster. Distinct crystals are rarely observed in the deposits, but some beautiful specimens have been found at Cornwall, England, and Bristol, Conn.

Chalcocite occurs as an ore in Italy, southwest Africa, Mexico, Chile, and Peru. In the United States large deposits have been found and mined in several Western states.

Composition, Cu_2S; hardness, 2.5–3; specific gravity, 5.5–5.8; crystal system, orthorhombic.

CHALCOPYRITE, kal-kǝ-pī'rīt, a copper-iron sulfide mineral, is one of the most important ores of copper. It is commonly found in sulfide veins, often in association with pyrite and galena. The wedge-shaped chalcopyrite crystals are brittle and brass-yellow (often with a bronze or iridescent tarnish), with a metallic luster. Hence, the mineral is sometimes called "fool's gold."

Chalcopyrite has the widest occurrence of any copper mineral. Among the many localities where it is mined are Britain, Sweden, Czechoslovakia, South Africa, Canada, and Chile. In the United States it is mined in Utah, Montana, Arizona, Tennessee, and elsewhere.

Composition, $CuFeS_2$; hardness, 3.5–4; specific gravity, 4.1–4.3; crystal system, tetragonal.

CHALDEA, kal-dē'ǝ, was an ancient land in southern Babylonia, on the Persian Gulf near the delta of the Tigris and Euphrates rivers. In the Bible the name came to be applied to all of Babylonia.

The Chaldeans were a seminomadic people from Arabia who occupied the city of Ur "of the Chaldeans" (Genesis 11:28) and adjacent areas. References to them in the annals of the king of Assyria date back to 884–859 B.C. In 721, despite great opposition, a Chaldean ruler seized the Babylonian throne and held it for 10 years. His efforts to incite the western states against Assyria are related in Isaiah 39. In 597 and 586 B.C., under Nebuchadnezzar II, they subdued Judaea and captured Jerusalem. The Chaldean dynasty held sway until the Persian invasion of 539 B.C.

The name "Chaldean" was applied in the Book of Daniel, and by many writers of antiquity, to Babylonian magi who were learned in astronomy but devoted also to astrology and magic.

CHALET, sha-lā', a wooden house typical of the Swiss Alps and nearby mountainous regions of France, Bavaria, and the Tirol. "Chalet" (meaning "little castle" in French) originally referred to a herdsman's hut but came to mean any mountain villa, cottage, or ski hut.

The chalet is designed for a cold, snowy climate. It is usually a low building with one or more overhanging upper stories supported by brackets. A wide, low-pitched roof projects as much as several feet beyond the walls and may cover stables and barns as well as the house. The walls are of heavy horizontal planks interlocking at the corners and often only roughly finished. Small windows may look out on narrow balconies, which, with the brackets, may be elaborately carved.

CHALEUR BAY, shǎl-ûr', in eastern Canada, is an inlet of the Gulf of St. Lawrence, between the Gaspé Peninsula on the north and New Brunswick on the south. It is about 90 miles (144 km) long and up to about 20 miles (32 km) wide. The bay is famous for mackerel fishing. The Matapédia and Restigouche rivers, which enter from the west, are notable salmon streams. The principal towns on the bay are Campbellton, Dalhousie, and Bathurst in New Brunswick, and New Carlisle in Quebec. The bay was discovered in July 1534 by Jacques Cartier, who gave it its name because of the heat his party endured there.

CHALGRIN, shǎl-graɴ', **Jean François Thérèse** (1739–1811), French architect, who is best known for his plans for the Arch of Triumph in Paris, which was begun under his supervision in 1806 and completed after his death. He was born in Paris and studied there with Giovanni Niccolò (Jean Nicolas) Servandoni. In 1758 he won the Grand Prix de Rome, and in 1770 he was elected to the Academy of Architecture. His studies in Italy awakened in him a passion for the simplicity of classical Greek architecture, which is reflected in most of his work.

In Paris he built the Palace La Vrillière (now de Rothschild), reconstructed the Church of St. Sulpice, and designed the Church of St. Philippe-du-Roule. He also executed major alterations on the Collège de France and remodeled the Luxembourg Palace to serve as headquarters for the Directory. He died in Paris on Jan. 20, 1811.

Feodor Chaliapin in the title role of *Boris Godunov.*

CHALIAPIN, shu-lyä′pyin, **Feodor Ivanovich** (1873–1938), Russian basso, who was one of the great operatic singing actors. On stage his magnificent bearing dominated the scene, and he was gifted with a voice of great lyric beauty and remarkable coloristic palette. He is best remembered for his unsurpassed interpretation of the title role in Moussorgsky's *Boris Godunov,* but his influence on the entire Russian operatic repertory cannot be underestimated.

Feodor Chaliapin, whose name is also spelled Fyodor Shalyapin, was born in Kazan, Russia, on Feb. 13, 1873. After being trained in vocal and acting techniques by Dimitri Usatov, he made his debut in Glinka's *A Life for the Tsar* in Tiflis in 1892. It was not, however, until 1896, when he joined Mamontov's private opera company in Moscow, that he began to develop his brilliant characterizations in such great Russian operas as Moussorgsky's *Khovanshchina* and Borodin's *Prince Igor.*

In 1899, Chaliapin joined the Imperial Opera in Moscow. Two years later he appeared in Boito's *Mefistofele* at La Scala, Milan, where his unconventional style did not please prevailing taste. The same unenthusiastic response greeted his debut at the Metropolitan Opera in New York City in 1907. However, his performances of Russian opera in 1913–1914 in London met with great success.

When Chaliapin left Russia in 1921, the Soviet government made several unsuccessful attempts to persuade him to go back and finally deprived him of his property. He returned to the Metropolitan Opera in 1921, achieving great acclaim for his interpretations of Boris and of King Philip in Verdi's *Don Carlos.* After 1929 he settled in Paris.

Chaliapin appeared in England in 1931 in the title role of Massenet's *Don Quichotte.* In the early 1930's he impersonated Cervantes' hero in a motion picture, for which the music was composed by Jacques Ibert. Chaliapin also made numerous concert appearances throughout Europe. He died in Paris on April 12, 1938.

GEORGE JELLINEK
Author of "Callas, Portrait of a Prima Donna"

Further Reading: Chaliapin, Feodor, *Man and Mask* (London 1932); Pleasants, Henry, *The Great Singers* (New York 1966).

CHALICE, chal′is, in modern ecclesiastical usage, the liturgical vessel containing the consecrated wine of the Eucharistic rite. In the Middle Ages chalices had a somewhat wider range of functions; the ministerial chalice dispensed the wine to the congregation when communion was still taken in both forms (that is, both bread and wine). Vessels of this type were generally of gold or parcel-gilt silver; humble materials were forbidden. Large offertory chalices were placed in churches to receive wine donated by the faithful. In baptismal rites, a special chalice was used for mixing the candidate's symbolic draft of milk and honey. Funerary chalices were available for placement in the tombs of the clergy.

The early Christians borrowed their chalice forms from the vessel shapes in standard use during ancient times. There were two main types. One had a base, stem, and a tall cup; the other also had these features, but the cup was broad and flanked by two handles. A striking example of the first type is the Antioch Chalice, a late 4th or early 5th century piece now exhibited at the Cloisters of the Metropolitan Museum of Art, New York. This chalice has two silver cups—a plain inner one set in an outer cup which is decorated with an openwork pattern of grapevines encircling figures and animals. In later versions of this type the base was enlarged to form a visual and functional counterpart to the cup. This altered version appeared in the 8th century Tassilo Chalice, with figures outlined in black in the niello technique. This chalice is displayed at the Abbey of Kremsmünster, Austria. The second type, which became rare by the 10th century, is best seen in an 8th century Irish work, the Ardagh Chalice, now in the National Museum of Ireland, in Dublin.

In the Gothic period of the 13th to the 15th century, the cup became smaller, while the stem grew higher and the central knop, or decorated knob, more prominent. These changes not only reflected the desire for greater ostentation, but also represented a change in the liturgy, in that communion was normally taken in one form only. The Renaissance saw a further increase in decorative richness, with the stem and knop developing a variety of lobed and sculptural shapes. In this way the original significance of the cup was

CHALICE, of copper alloy, gilded, with silver inlay, of the 9th century.

CHALK CLIFFS on the English Channel coast near Eastbourne. Wave action has eroded the cliffs, leaving a cross section of seven hills known as the Seven Sisters.

obscured. It is not surprising that modern artisans have reacted against this trend by producing chalices of an austere simplicity closely akin to the functionalist work of other modern designers. Early medieval chalices, such as the Merovingian Grimfridus Chalice in the Dumbarton Oaks Collection in Washington, D. C., have served as patterns for these modern pieces.

Before chalices may be used in the Roman Catholic Church, canon law prescribes that they be consecrated by a bishop or abbot.

WAYNE DYNES
Vassar College

CHALK, chôk, is a soft, finely granular, easily pulverized variety of limestone (mineral calcium carbonate). It frequently contains a small admixture of clay minerals; and sometimes (as in the chalks of southern England) of nodules of silica, flint, or chert. The color of chalk ranges from pure white to grayish or buff.

Chalk is a marine deposit that consists primarily of shells of minute organisms such as Foraminifera, and of coccoliths (algal structures). The name of the Cretaceous period, which began about 135 million years ago and from which chalk dates, derives from the Latin word *creta,* meaning "chalk." Cretaceous chalk forms the cliffs of Dover along the English Channel. Chalk in the Cenomanian, Turonian, and Senonian stages of the Cretaceous System of rocks extends from Flamborough Head, Yorkshire, to Dorset. Similar chalk encircles the Paris Basin in France and appears interruptedly northward to Denmark.

The best known chalk formations in North America also belong to the Upper Cretaceous. On the coast of the Gulf of Mexico, a chalk belt extends for hundreds of miles northeast and southwest from Austin, Texas. It is a few hundred feet thick at the surface and continues beneath the surface toward the Gulf. Similar chalk crops out in Alabama and in the northern Mexican states of Chihuahua, Coahuila, and Tamaulipas. Chalk of about the same age is found in Kansas and Nebraska and westward in Colorado and Wyoming.

Chalk is widely used as one of the principal constituents in the making of cement. It forms an important source of agricultural limestone and is burned to produce quicklime (calcium oxide). Chalk is used in smaller quantities, after purification, as "whiting" in cleaning substances (especially for metalware), in rubber materials and putty, and to allay stomach acidity. The common chalk of the schoolroom, however, is a manufactured substance that is not generally made from natural chalk.

See also CALCIUM; CEMENT; LIMESTONE.

MARSHALL KAY
Columbia University

CHALK RIVER, a village in southeastern Ontario, Canada, is the site of an important atomic research station. The village is situated in Renfrew county, on the Chalk River, 95 miles (153 km) northwest of Ottawa. In 1945 a heavy-water reactor was established here; four other reactors were built between 1945 and 1960. The Chalk River Nuclear Laboratories installation, operated by Atomic Energy of Canada Limited, is Canada's major nuclear research plant. Chalk River was incorporated in 1954. Population: 1,094.

CHALLENGER EXPEDITION, the first circumnavigation of the world's oceans made primarily for scientific purposes. H. M. S. *Challenger,* a steam corvette of 2,300 tons, sailed from England under Capt. George S. Nares in December 1872. During her voyage of 3½ years and 69,000 miles, a scientific staff consisting of C. Wyville Thomson and five other civilians, with the assistance of the ship's officers and men, made the first comprehensive collection of oceanographic data from surface to bottom in all the oceans.

After the ship's return under Capt. Frank Thomson in May 1876, the vast collections of animals and plants, of samples from the sea floor, and of specimens of seawater were sorted in Edinburgh under C. Wyville Thomson's supervision. Descriptions and interpretations by scientists from all over the world were published from 1881 to 1895 in 50 large volumes edited by Thomson until his death early in 1882 and thereafter by John Murray, one of the naturalists on the expedition. The cruise of the *Challenger* and the report of its scientific results cost the British government about £200,000.

The Challenger Expedition contributed unequally to the founding of the four major branches of ocean science: marine biology, submarine geology, chemistry of seawater, and physical oceanography. Though it was preceded by American, Scandinavian, and other British investigations, the Challenger Expedition's collections of deep-sea organisms were much more comprehensive than anything obtained earlier, and the 40 zoological volumes of its report still form the basis of marine biology. Similarly, the geological volumes laid the groundwork for modern studies of the configuration of the ocean basins and the distribution and composition of bottom sediments. In sea-water chemistry, the Challenger Expedition confirmed results established a decade earlier. For physical oceanography, though the expedition gathered valuable data and began studies of the relation between pressure and the measurement of temperature, it missed the opportunity to explain the ocean currents.

HAROLD L. BURSTYN
Carnegie-Mellon University

247

CHALLONER, chal'ə-nər, **Richard** (1691–1781), English Catholic, who led the movement to revitalize Catholicism in 18th century England. He was born in Lewes, Sussex, on Sept. 29, 1691, and as a boy adhered to the Presbyterian faith of his father. When he was about 13, he was converted to Catholicism while living with a Catholic family. He was sent to the English College at Douai, France, in 1705 and was ordained in 1716.

He remained at Douai, serving as professor, vice president, and prefect of studies, until 1730, when he returned to England for missionary work. Forced to work in secret under an assumed name to escape indictment under the anti-Catholic penal laws, he was nevertheless successful in bolstering the faith of English Catholics. In 1741 he was appointed bishop of Debra and coadjutor to Dr. Benjamin Petre, vicar-apostolic of the London district. He succeeded Dr. Petre in 1758, and for the next 23 years administered Catholic activities in 10 counties, the Channel Islands, and British North America. Indicted under more rigorously enforced penal laws in 1765, he escaped imprisonment when the indictments were withdrawn on a technicality. During the anti-Catholic Gordon Riots of June 2–8, 1780, he fled to the house of a friend, but died shortly after his return to London, on Jan. 12, 1781.

Challoner's major works, standard for many years, include revisions of the Douay-Rheims Bible and the English catechism, a translation of St. Augustine's *Confessions,* and *Meditations for Every Day in the Year* (1758).

SISTER A. M. SAWKINS
Marygrove College, Detroit

CHALMERS, chä'mərz, **Alexander** (1759–1834), Scottish editor, journalist, and biographer.

He was born on March 29, 1759, in Aberdeen, Scotland, where he received a classical and medical education. He went to London about 1777 and became editor of the *Public Ledger* and the *London Packet.*

He was particularly noted as an editor of reference works, including *The British Essayists* (45 vols., 1803); *The English Poets from Chaucer to Cowper* (1810); and *The General Biographical Dictionary* (32 vols., 1817), the fullest body of biographical information published in England up to that time. His literary work also included the editing of works by Fielding, Johnson, Pope, Gibbon, and Lord Bolingbroke. He published a *Glossary to Shakespeare* (1797) and an annotated edition of Shakespeare's works (1809). He died in London on Dec. 10, 1834.

CHALMERS, chä'mərz, **James** (1841–1901), Scottish Congregational missionary and explorer. He was born at Ardrishaig, Argyllshire, in the Highlands, on Aug. 4, 1841. Accepted by the London Missionary Society at the age of 21, he mastered the Rarotongan language for work in the South Seas. He was ordained in 1865 and went to Rarotonga in the Cook Islands, where for 10 years he worked to develop an indigenous church and fostered teacher training. In 1877 he went to New Guinea, where he served with salutary effect, often as the first white man ever seen by the uncivilized natives. He helped to establish a British protectorate over southeastern New Guinea. He explored the South Sea Islands (1879–1886), gaining valuable information.

His work is best known through his vivid *Work and Adventure in New Guinea* (1885), and *Pioneering in New Guinea* (1887). On April 7, 1901, he was killed and eaten by cannibals at Dopima, off the south coast of Papua.

JAMES H. SMYLIE
Union Theological Seminary, Richmond, Va.

CHALMERS, chä'mərz, **Sir Mackenzie Dalzell** (1847–1927), British public official and judge whose drafts for the Bills of Exchange Act and Sale of Goods Act in the late 19th century also had great influence on commercial legislation in the United States. He was born at Nonington, Kent, England, on Feb. 7, 1847, and educated at King's College, London, and Trinity College, Oxford. He was called to the bar in 1869 and in the same year joined the civil service in India, serving until 1872. Later he returned there as legal member of the viceroy's council in 1896–1898. In 1902 he became first parliamentary counsel and in 1903 permanent undersecretary of state for the home department in Britain. As a judge, he received an unusual promotion from a county court to the High Court in 1920.

In a distinguished career of public service, his most important work was the drafting of parliamentary acts. The Bills of Exchange Act, (1882), set forth a new and more flexible interpretation of the use of negotiable instruments. It became the model for the act proposed by the Commissioners on Uniform Laws in the United States (1896), adopted by all U. S. jurisdictions at that time except Alaska, Puerto Rico, and the Philippines. Also influential were his drafts for the Sale of Goods Act (1893) and the Marine Insurance Act (1906). He died in London on Dec. 22, 1927.

CHALMERS, chä'mərz, **Thomas** (1780–1847), Scottish clergyman and professor, who was a leader in the establishment of the Free Church of Scotland. He was born at Anstruther, Fife, on March 17, 1780, and was licensed to preach in the Church of Scotland in 1799. When he was 30, he underwent a remarkable religious change from moralistic moderatism, which almost bordered on atheism, to evangelicalism, and his ministry was marked by eloquent preaching that made him internationally known. He was also noted for his emphasis on social and economic improvement. Strongly attracted to science, he related the Gospel to scientific and industrial development in popular lectures.

In 1823, Chalmers was appointed to the chair of moral philosophy at the University of St. Andrews and in 1828 to the chair of theology at the University of Edinburgh. Even as a professor he continued to organize new churches and to encourage missions.

Although Chalmers in general advocated the maintenance of established churches through government aid, he always upheld the right of church self-government independent of civil control. Thus, as the state intruded more and more into church affairs, he threw his support to the Free Church of Scotland, becoming its first moderator in 1843. He died near Edinburgh about May 30, 1847.

Chalmers' most important works include *On the Adaptation of External Nature* (1833) and *Institutes of Theology* (1849).

JAMES H. SMYLIE
Union Theological Seminary, Richmond, Va.

CHALMETTE NATIONAL HISTORICAL PARK, shal-met', on the eastern bank of the Mississippi River just below New Orleans, La., commemorates Andrew Jackson's defeat of the British in the Battle of New Orleans on Jan. 8, 1815, in the War of 1812. The park covers 136 acres (55 hectares). One section preserves a part of the battle area and includes the Chalmette Monument, a marble obelisk commemorating the victory. Another section is a military cemetery. The park is named for Ignace de Lino de Chalmette, owner of the land at the time of the battle and a volunteer in the war. It was established in 1907 as Chalmette Monument and Grounds and renamed in 1939.

CHALON-SUR-SAÔNE, shäl-lôn'-sür sōn, a city in east central France, astride the Saône River where it turns south to join the Rhône, in Saône-et-Loire department. It is about midway between Dijon and Mâcon, in the center of the famous Burgundy wine district.

The Saône lowland is a rich agricultural area and produces much wheat, corn, and a great variety of vegetables and fruits. Chalon's industries include the manufacture of electrical and electronic equipment, boilers, engineering products, glass, knitwear, hosiery, apparel, chemicals, plastics, agricultural equipment, and sugar and other processed agricultural products.

Chalon-sur-Saône was an ancient Roman town (Latin, Cabillonum) and was built at a crossroads where the Saône could be easily forded. It has a number of prized architectural monuments, especially the St.-Vincent Cathedral, started in the 13th century. Population: (1962) 40,056.

HOMER PRICE
Hunter College, New York

CHÂLONS-SUR-MARNE, shä-lôn' sür märn, is a city in northeastern France, about 95 miles (153 km) northeast of Paris, on the Marne River. It is the capital of the Marne department, and near the center of the Champagne wine district. Although the excellent wines of this district are its most famous agricultural product, the region is a rich farming area that yields a variety of commodities. In addition to the important wine trade, especially in Champagne, the city manufactures a variety of goods, including beer, electrodes, wallpaper, bronze powder, industrial detergents and other chemicals, precision instruments, sugar, knitwear, and hosiery.

The superb St. Étienne cathedral, dating from the 13th century but much restored under Louis XIV, boasts a magnificent Romanesque tower and several very beautiful 13th century stained-glass windows. Behind the town hall stands another exceptional church, the 13th century Notre-Dame-en-Vaux, with four towers and exceptionally fine stained-glass windows. Population: (1962) 39,658.

HOMER PRICE
Hunter College, New York

CHALUKYA, chä'look-yə, was a ruling dynasty of southern India. It ruled over much of the western Deccan—parts of present Madhya Pradesh, Maharashtra, Mysore, and Andhra Pradesh—from about 535 to 750 A. D. and again from 973 to 1189 A. D. Its early capital was Vatapi (Badami), where Pulakesin I (reigned about 535–566 A. D.) had established himself as an independent ruler. The small kingdom became an empire when Pulakesin II (reigned 610–640 A. D.) conquered the Pallavas

of Kanchi and their feudatories. He defeated the north Indian ruler, Harsha of Kanauj, between 629 and 634 A. D. and barred his southward expansion. Pulakesin II appointed his brother, Kubja Visnuvardhana, governor in the east, where an independent Chalukya kingdom later arose in the Vengi area (eastern Andhra Pradesh). It became a pawn in the various Deccan struggles.

Pulakesin II was one of the great rulers of his time and his fame was widespread. He exchanged embassies with Persia, an event commemorated by a fresco in an Ajanta cave. Also, the Chinese Buddhist pilgrim, Hsüan Tsang, visited the kingdom around 641 A. D. and described him as a mighty and able ruler. However, the struggle which he initiated against the Pallavas continued until the Chalukyas were defeated by the Rastrakutas of the Deccan in the 8th century.

The later Chalukyas, called the Chalukyas of Kalyana, regained their independence under Taila II (reigned 973–997), who overthrew the Rastrakutas. The following years were ones of warfare with the Cholas of Tanjore, who, under Rajaraja I and Rajendra I, devastated large areas of the empire from about 993 to 1021 A. D. The Chalukyas revived their fortunes under Vikramaditya VI (reigned 1076–1126), but the empire soon ended. After 1190 A. D., it split into the kingdom of Dorasamudra ruled by the Hoysalas, the kingdom of Devagiri founded by the Yadavas, and the kingdom of Warangal, which was governed by the Kakatiyas.

Though engaged in constant warfare, the Chalukyas supported the arts, and under their patronage a distinct style of temple building developed which reached its apex under the rule of the Hoysalas.

B. G. GOKHALE
Wake Forest College

Further Reading: Ganguly, Dhirendra C., *The Eastern Chalukyas* (London 1937); Nilakanta Sastri, K. A., *History of Southern India,* 2d ed. (London 1959).

CHALYBES, kal'i-bēz, an ancient people of northern Asia Minor, on the southeastern shore of the Black Sea. To the Greeks they were semilegendary figures. Skillful miners and metal-workers, they were supposed to have discovered iron-working. Aeschylus described them as wild and inhospitable. Strabo placed them in the mountains above Trapezus (modern Trabzon; also Trebizond), and traces of early iron workings have been discovered in the area. But the Greeks had only a vague idea about the Chalybes and where they lived.

D. J. BLACKMAN
Bristol University, England

CHALYBITE. See SIDERITE.

CHAM, chäm, a Malayo-Polynesian people whose kingdom, Champa, existed for over a thousand years in central Vietnam. The art of the Cham, profoundly influenced by Indian culture, is known mainly from their temples. The Cham were absorbed by the Vietnamese as they moved south, and it is estimated that somewhat less than 50,000 Cham remain in Cambodia and Vietnam, with the majority, about 35,000, in southern and central South Vietnam. The Cham today are mostly Muslim and live by agriculture. They were allotted one seat in the 1966 South Vietnam constituent assembly. See also CHAMPA.

ELLEN J. HAMMER
Author of "Vietnam: Yesterday and Today"

CHAMARS, chȧ-märz', one of the largest caste groups of Hindu India. They constitute a "low," or Shudra (Sudra), caste because their traditional occupation, leatherwork, requires contact with dead animals and so is considered polluting. However, they are not untouchables. The caste has a complicated hierarchy of subcastes. It is found in all parts of northern India, where it forms the bulk of the labor force in some areas.

CHAMBA, chum'bə, a district in northern India, was formerly a princely state. Situated in the rugged foothills of the Himalaya, Chamba district forms part of Himachal Pradesh territory and has an area of 3,127 square miles (8,099 sq km). The capital is also called Chamba.

The princely state of Chamba was founded in the 6th century. It was nominally independent, but fell under the influence of the Mughul (Mogul) Empire, and in 1846 of Britain. Chamba has been a district of Himachal Pradesh since 1948. Population: (1962) of the the district, 210,579; of the town, 8,609.

CHAMBAL RIVER, chum'bəl, in west central India, forming part of the Rajasthan-Madhya Pradesh boundary. About 550 miles (885 km) long, it rises in the southern Vindhya Range and flows northeast to form the main tributary of the Jumna River. Its passage across the plateau country of Madhya Bharat Patar is marked by a series of gorges and by the Chambal ravine system below its junction with the Banas River. It has two major water development projects, the Chambal Valley Project near Kota, which was begun in 1952 as part of India's first 5-year plan, and the damming of the gorge at the entrance of the Kanjarda Plateau, which formed a large artificial lake, Gandhi Sagar.

H. J. STEWARD, *University of Toronto*

CHAMBER MUSIC is a kind of ensemble music of an intimate character, designed for performance in a room or chamber as opposed to a concert hall or opera house. The term usually refers to instrumental music, written for from two to eight players, with one player to a part, and traditionally performed without a conductor. When the designation "chamber music" originated during the late 16th and early 17th centuries, this type of music was performed predominantly in the homes of the aristocracy and the well-to-do. This custom persisted through the 19th century, when the public concert became popular, and chamber works began to be presented more frequently in the concert hall, where they are most often heard today. However, private performances of chamber works by amateur groups are still given in the intimate surroundings to which this kind of music is best suited.

The various combinations possible in chamber music ensembles are generically named according both to the number of players participating and to the types of instruments that are used for a given work. A group of three players is known as a *trio;* a group of four, a *quartet;* a group of five, a *quintet,* and so on. (An exception to this rule is the *sonata,* performed by two players, with one violin or other instrument and piano.) Ensembles that consist only of string instruments, which have traditionally been the bulwark of chamber music groups, include the *string trio* (violin, viola, and cello) and the *string quartet* (two violins, viola, and cello). When other instruments appear in a

chamber music ensemble, their presence is indicated in the work's generic title. Thus, a *piano trio* is made up of a violin, cello, and piano; a *woodwind quintet* consists of a flute, oboe, clarinet, bassoon, and French horn.

HISTORY

Baroque and Transitional Period. The history of chamber music begins about 1570. At that time, French vocal pieces, known as *chansons,* were transcribed in Italy for small groups of instruments and were called *canzoni.* Numerous changes in form and style during the 17th century resulted in various versions of the form. Dance forms and rhythms began to be introduced into this early type of chamber music, and the term *sonata* was gradually substituted for "canzone."

The first great master of string chamber music was the Italian composer Arcangelo Corelli, in whose works two versions of the form became standard: *sonata da chiesa* (church sonata), marked by four movements, slow-fast-slow-fast, and *sonata da camera* (chamber sonata), characterized by dancelike movements, including *allemande and gigue.* These baroque sonatas existed in two principal instrumental combinations: the *solo sonata:* one violin or other instrument, with basso continuo, using a bass instrument and harpsichord accompaniment; *sonata a tre* (later *trio sonata*): two violins or other instruments and basso continuo. Between 1681 and 1700, Corelli composed about 60 trio sonatas.

Through the baroque period, ending about 1750, hundreds of composers wrote sonatas, using Corelli's works as models. Among the outstanding chamber works of the time are those of George Frideric Handel, Johann Sebastian Bach, and Antonio Vivaldi. These composers, of course, expressed their individuality in terms of technique, lyric melody, and counterpoint. However, all their works were based on the use of the basso continuo, in which the written-out bass line, performed by a cello or other bass instrument, provided a foundation of indicated harmonies that were realized and elaborated by the harpsichordist.

Several major changes in the technique of chamber music composition took place about 1750. These changes included the virtual abandonment of the basso continuo and a weakening of the early 18th century doctrine that favored adherence to a single mood within a movement. New forms emerged in which there were harmonic and melodic contrasts, as well as changes of mood within a movement. Also, a new texture developed gradually, in which all parts were written out, and new forms emerged in accord with a new doctrine that demanded harmonic and melodic (or mood) contrasts within a single movement. These developments resulted in the modern string quartet, piano trio, and similar combinations in and the final emergence of the classical style.

Classical Period. The string quartet was the major and most popular form of chamber music in the classical period and it has retained its position of importance in modern times. The string quartet was usually written in four movements: the sonata-form movement (exposition, development, recapitulation, and coda), slow movement, minuet or scherzo, and fast final movement. Early in the classical period one instrument dominated the others; later in the period this domination was largely eliminated, and all four instruments shared equally in the unfolding of the texture.

Franz Joseph Haydn was the first major composer of classical chamber music, producing 76 string quartets as well as numerous other chamber works. Many of his later string quartets (1788–1799) are staples in the repertoire. Wolfgang Amadeus Mozart was at first influenced by and then served as a model for his older contemporary, Haydn. Mozart's chamber works include 26 string quartets, as well as several string quintets, and piano trios, over 30 sonatas for piano and violin, and more than a dozen other chamber compositions.

Ludwig van Beethoven further developed the styles, textures, and forms of Haydn and Mozart. He contributed new elements of dramatic contrast, wide-ranging harmonies, and a powerfully expressive content that was purely his own. Beethoven's 17 string quartets, 15 sonatas, septet (for clarinet, horn, bassoon, violin, viola, cello, and double bass), and a dozen miscellaneous works form the backbone of the chamber music repertoire. He also excelled in piano trios, of which he composed 12. In the classical piano trio the third movement was usually omitted and the piano tended to dominate the texture; however, in Beethoven's later trios, the listener may sense a strong polarity between the piano and the strings—a polarity that came to full effect in the chamber music of Johannes Brahms approximately half a century later.

Romantic Period. In the romantic period, extending roughly from 1825 to 1900, the framework if not the content of the classical forms was retained. Most of the major instrumental composers of the time, with the exception of Hector Berlioz, Frédéric Chopin, and Franz Liszt, produced a sizable quantity of chamber music. In each case the stylistic traits that distinguished their orchestral works are also present in their chamber music. Franz Schubert's 15 string quartets, two piano trios, string quintet, and octet for strings and winds are rich in harmonic color. The six string quartets, string octet, and two piano trios of Felix Mendelssohn are marked by classical perfection of form. In half a dozen works Robert Schumann dramatized the conflicts between dreamy romanticism and forthright moods. Profundity mixed with sentiment and classical forms filled with romantic content distinguish the works of Brahms, whose 24 compositions for various combinations of instruments are among the greatest works of the period. Tchaikovsky brought his skill as an orchestrater to three quartets and a piano trio, and several of the 30 chamber works of Antonín Dvořák rival those of Schubert in their melodious expressiveness.

The 20th Century. Chamber music in the 20th century is characterized by a multiplicity of styles. Neoromantic idioms and expressive content mark the works of Sergei Prokofiev, Dimitri Shostakovich, and Walter Piston. The compositions of Darius Milhaud, Roy Harris, and Paul Hindemith are marked by their adherence to modified classical forms. Béla Bartók's six quartets stand alone in their originality, richness of instrumental effects, and expressive power. Contemporary American composers of chamber music who have used the serial, or 12-tone, technique introduced by Arnold Schönberg include Leon Kirchner and Elliott Carter. The emotional impact of contemporary chamber music is undeniable. Its ability to remain in the repertoire, however, has yet to be determined.

HOMER ULRICH, *Author of "Chamber Music"*

CHAMBER OF COMMERCE, a voluntary organization of businessmen devoted to promoting their common interests and reflecting business opinion as it relates to matters of community, state, regional, and national concern. Chambers of commerce are found throughout the world and are strongly entrenched in American life at many levels. They are the direct descendants of the merchant guilds of medieval times. The first association to take the name "chamber of commerce" was organized in Marseille, France, in 1599.

Early History in the United States. The first American chamber of commerce was organized in New York City in 1768 with the purpose of "encouraging commerce, supporting industry, adjusting disputes relative to trade and navigation, and producing such laws and regulations as may be found necessary for the benefit of trade in general." These general objectives still characterize the movement.

A handful of chambers of commerce were organized in seaboard cities prior to 1800, but during the 19th century they multiplied rapidly, sometimes calling themselves "boards of trade." Various efforts to bring them together in a federation through such bodies as the National Board of Trade (organized 1868) proved ineffective because of the variety of geographical and other interests that had to be accommodated.

On the initiative of the Boston Chamber of Commerce and with the approval and active support of President William H. Taft and his secretary of commerce and labor, a national convention was called in 1912 to consider ways in which businessmen and their organizations could form an effective national clearinghouse of business opinion. The result was the organization of a federally chartered Chamber of Commerce of the United States of America in July 1912. Although governmentally approved, it was not—in contrast to many of its European counterparts—governmentally sponsored. This was important in view of the organization's liaison role between government and the business community.

Learning from the mistakes of its predecessors, the national Chamber was organized on a democratic basis from the bottom up. As part of this philosophy, it submitted major policy questions to referendum votes by its membership. The first referendum involved adoption of a resolution supporting adoption of a scientific national budget by the federal government. The Chamber's support of this measure and educational efforts on its behalf contributed significantly to its adoption. Similar Chamber support was extended to the enactment of the Federal Reserve Act, the strengthening of the American merchant marine, and the creation of a Bureau of Domestic and Foreign Commerce within the U. S. Department of Commerce.

Chamber Activities. The national Chamber, representing an underlying membership of some 3 million firms and individuals in affiliated organizations, is recognized as a spokesman for a significant element of the business community. In addition to representing their interests before governmental bodies, it keeps members informed of governmental developments. In general, the national Chamber is dedicated to strengthening and supporting private enterprise, individual initiative, and responsibility. It places corollary emphasis on economy in government and the need to protect the private sector against encroachment by the federal government.

In performing these functions, the national Chamber, with headquarters in Washington, D. C., can call on a staff of some 850 persons. Their activities are organized by departments. The program development departments are manned by specialists in fields as varied as education and community development, national defense, and communication and transportation. The public affairs and organizational services departments provide assistance to local and state chambers, including instruction in how to manage them. The communications departments embrace the various activities through which the national Chamber keeps its membership and the public abreast of matters of current interest. Included in these activities are an audio-visual department, a news department, and the Chamber's major periodical, *Nation's Business*, with a circulation of many hundreds of thousands. The administrative services departments handle building operations, data processing, and general services.

Weekly publications, including *Washington Report* and *Congressional Action*, provide current, authoritative information on developments in the nation's capital. Other reports, studies, and research papers are directed to specific public policy issues, economic trends, labor relations, and general organizational problems. A weekly *Newsletter* keeps local chambers informed of developments at state and lower levels. These activities embrace many areas aside from legislation and include community development, city beautification, and fire safety.

Among the many organizations involved in the chamber of commerce movement, the Junior Chamber of Commerce, popularly known as the "Jaycees," is perhaps best known. Limited to members between 21 and 36 years of age, this organization, founded in 1920, has concerned itself particularly with community betterment programs.

The lesser-known International Chamber of Commerce, organized in 1919 and directed from Paris, has an active United States affiliate. With a worldwide membership, the International Chamber concerns itself with the broad issues of international trade and finance. It has been recognized as an authoritative spokesman on such matters before the United Nations.

ARTHUR M. JOHNSON, *Harvard University*
Author of "Government-Business Relations"

CHAMBERLAIN, Sir Austen (1863–1937), English political leader. A cabinet officer intermittently from 1902 to 1931, he was foreign secretary under Stanley Baldwin (1924-1929). Chamberlain won a Nobel Peace Prize in 1925, but the prized office of prime minister eluded him.

He was born Joseph Austen Chamberlain in Birmingham on Oct. 16, 1863. The elder son of Joseph Chamberlain and the half brother of Neville Chamberlain (qq.v.), he was always conscious of being the family's political heir. Chamberlain was educated at Cambridge and in Berlin and Paris. Elected to Parliament in 1892, he held a number of government posts, including chancellor of the exchequer (1903–1905, 1919–1921), secretary of state for India (1915–1917), and first lord of the admiralty (1931).

As foreign secretary he was one of the main architects of the Locarno Pact of 1925, by which France, Germany, and Belgium accepted their existing frontiers as permanent, and Britain and Italy agreed to guarantee these boundaries. As a result, French fears of Germany were temporarily stilled, and Germany entered the League of Nations. This easing of tension enhanced Chamberlain's prestige, and he was a corecipient of the Nobel Peace Prize that year. However, there was no settlement of Germany's eastern boundaries, and Chamberlain's reputation declined in the 1930's as the international harmony proved illusory.

Chamberlain was close to becoming prime minister in the 1920's. He became the Conservative party leader in 1921, but resigned in 1922, when the Conservatives, against his wishes, withdrew from the coalition government of Lloyd George, and he refused to join Andrew Bonar Law's purely Conservative administration. Thus, he missed the chance to become prime minister when illness forced Law from office in 1923. Chamberlain remained in Parliament until he died in London on March 16, 1937.

JOHN BROWN, *University of Edinburgh*

CHAMBERLAIN, George Earle (1854–1928), American public official. Born on Jan. 1, 1854, near Natchez, Miss., he received B. A. and LL. B. degrees from Washington and Lee University. In 1876 he went to Oregon. He was elected to the state legislature in 1880 and later served as district attorney and attorney general. As governor (1903–1909), he blocked private exploitation of valuable timber on state school lands. Elected as a Democrat to the U. S. Senate in 1908 and 1914, he was chairman of the committee on military affairs during World War I and was influential in pushing through measures for selective service, food control, and war financing. His criticism of the war department lost him President Wilson's support. He died on July 9, 1928, in Washington, D. C.

CHAMBERLAIN, Houston Stewart (1855–1927), Anglo-German author. He was born in Southsea, Hampshire, on Sept. 9, 1855, and went to Germany in 1870 to study German culture. In 1908 he married Eva, a daughter of Richard Wagner, as his second wife. Chamberlain was best known for *The Foundations of the Nineteenth Century* (1911), a scholarly but biased historical study, which, through its espousal of German superiority and anti-semitism, influenced the development of National Socialist thought. His other works include *Richard Wagner* (1897), studies of Kant (1905) and Goethe (1912), and *The Wagnerian Drama* (1915). He died in Bayreuth, Germany, on Jan. 9, 1927.

CHAMBERLAIN, Joseph (1836–1914), British political leader. He was one of Britain's greatest public figures in the late 19th and early 20th centuries.

Chamberlain was born in London on July 8, 1836, of a prosperous Birmingham family. At 16 he became a businessman in Birmingham in partnership with a cousin, and at 38 he retired with a substantial assured income. As mayor of Birmingham from 1873 to 1875, he secured municipal ownership of the gas and water supply and carried out schemes of slum clearance. For most of his subsequent career the city provided him a safe political base and along with its surrounding area returned him or the candidates he endorsed to Parliament.

Chamberlain first became nationally known as a leader of the nonconformist agitation of the National Education League against the 1870 Education Act, which seemed to perpetuate the Anglican Church's hold over English education. The contacts he formed during this campaign led to the foundation in 1877 of the National Liberal Federation, a union of local Liberal party organizations that played an important part in the Liberal party's election victory in 1880.

Initially, William Ewart Gladstone and other official Liberal leaders regarded the federation with suspicion as a new and perhaps sinister influence over the parliamentary party, and as Chamberlain played a major role in its affairs during its early years, the federation contributed to his reputation for radicalism.

Chamberlain meanwhile had entered Parliament in 1876, and from 1880 to 1885 he was president of the Board of Trade in Gladstone's second government. Although his desire for social reform put him to the left of most of his colleagues, he was widely regarded as a future leader of the Liberal party. For the 1885 election he brought forward an "unauthorized program" (so-called because it expressed only his own views), and in language unusually extreme for a cabinet minister he argued the need for new social policies, especially for education and land reform. In 1886, Chamberlain was driven to the right in politics, by his refusal to accept the Irish nationalist demand for a separate parliament in Dublin responsible for internal affairs. As a compromise he proposed to the Home Rule members the creation of Irish county boards responsible to a central board, which would control neither the police nor the administration of justice.

In 1886, despite his differences with the Liberal majority, Chamberlain accepted the presidency of the Local Government Board in Gladstone's brief third ministry. But when the Liberals split over Ireland, Chamberlain and the Marquess of Hartington, who had been opposed on most other issues, led the minority of the party that joined the Conservatives to defeat the home rule bill and thereby destroy the government.

From 1886 to 1892, Chamberlain and the other Liberal Unionists supported the Conservative government, and cooperation with the Conservatives continued during the period of Liberal rule from 1892 to 1895. In 1895 the 3d Marquess of Salisbury, a Conservative, formed a Unionist government in which Chamberlain was colonial secretary and increasingly the most influential minister. Chamberlain had not abandoned his interest in domestic reform, and he was the main influence behind passage of the Workmen's Compensation Act of 1897. He also advocated the need for some form of old-age pensions, although he was unable to devise any practicable scheme.

Chamberlain's colonial policy was striking and controversial. Despite the criticism of Salisbury, he began a forward policy in West Africa that resulted in the creation of the modern boundaries of Nigeria. He also attempted a drastic solution to the conflict in South Africa between Britain and the Boer republic of the Transvaal. He was rightly suspected of complicity in the Jameson raid of 1896, an attempted coup d'etat in the Transvaal that Cecil Rhodes, the premier of Cape Colony, organized, and in 1899 his unwillingness to make concessions and his threats to use force contributed to the outbreak of the Boer war. About the same time his concern over Britain's inability to halt Russia's penetration of China led him to advocate alliances with Germany and the United States, which both countries spurned.

In 1903, Chamberlain resigned from the cabinet to campaign for a policy of tariff protection. He was convinced that new economic bonds instead of free trade were necessary to preserve the unity of the British Empire. He was also worried by the effects of increasing German and American competition on British industry and believed that tariffs would supply the revenue necessary for social reform. His own party was converted by his arguments but not the country, which was alarmed that protection might lead to a rise in the cost of living. The Liberal opposition seized the issue, and in the general election of 1906 it won a sweeping victory over the Unionist party. A few months later, in July 1906, Chamberlain was incapacitated by a stroke. He lived for eight more years in Birmingham with physical disabilities that prevented him from ever appearing in public. He died there on July 2, 1914.

Chamberlain was married three times and had two famous sons—Austen Chamberlain (q.v.) and Neville Chamberlain (q.v.).

JOHN BROWN, *University of Edinburgh*

Further Reading: Fraser, Peter, *Joseph Chamberlain* (Cranbury, N. J., 1967); Garvin, James Louis, and Amery, H. Julian, *The Life of Joseph Chamberlain*, 4 vols. (London 1932–1951); Petrie, Sir Charles, *The Chamberlain Tradition* (New York 1939).

CHAMBERLAIN, Sir Joseph Austen. See CHAMBERLAIN, SIR AUSTEN.

CHAMBERLAIN, Joshua Lawrence (1828–1914), American general, who served four terms as governor of Maine. He was born in Brewer, Me., on Sept. 8, 1828. He graduated from Bowdoin College and from Bangor Theological Seminary. In 1862 he joined the Union Army as lieutenant colonel of the 20th Maine Infantry. Chamberlain took part in many major battles of the Civil War and was wounded three times. He received the Congressional Medal of Honor for leading his regiment in the defense of Little Round Top, a key position in the Battle of Gettysburg. In June 1864 he was promoted brigadier general on the field by General Grant, and in 1865 he was brevetted major general.

Chamberlain was governor of Maine from 1866 to 1870 and president of Bowdoin College from 1871 to 1883. Later he engaged in railroad building in Florida. He died on Feb. 24, 1914.

CHAMBERLAIN, Mellen (1821–1900), American lawyer and historian. He was born in Pembroke, N. H., on June 4, 1821. He graduated from Dartmouth College in 1844 and took his law degree at Harvard in 1848. While serving as chief justice of the municipal court of Boston, he was named in 1878 librarian of the Boston Public Library, where his special knowledge of early American history proved invaluable. He wrote important chapters in Justin Winsor's *Narrative and Critical History of America*, vol. 6 (1888), and was the author of *John Adams, the Statesman of the American Revolution* (1890). He died in Chelsea, Mass., on June 25, 1900.

BLACK STAR

NEVILLE CHAMBERLAIN, after signing the Munich Pact (1938), waves the agreement on his return home.

CHAMBERLAIN, chām′bər-lən, **Neville** (1869–1940), British prime minister, whose policies failed to avert the outbreak of World War II in Europe in 1939. The younger son of Joseph Chamberlain (q.v.), Arthur Neville Chamberlain was born in Birmingham, England, on March 18, 1869. He was educated at Rugby and Mason College, Birmingham. He achieved mixed results in business ventures, turned to politics, and in 1911 was elected to the Birmingham city council. He was lord mayor of Birmingham in 1915 and 1916 and was elected to the Commons in 1918 as a Conservative from Birmingham.

Entering Parliament at age 49, Chamberlain rose rapidly. He was minister of health (1923–1924, 1924–1929, 1931), chancellor of the exchequer (1923–1924, 1931–1937), and prime minister (1937–1940), succeeding Baldwin.

Prime Minister. Chamberlain confronted the threat to peace posed by Germany and Italy. Seeking to appease Adolf Hitler and Benito Mussolini, he first negotiated a treaty with Italy accepting the conquest of Ethiopia on condition that Italy withdraw from the Spanish Civil War. Turning to the Czech question, Chamberlain conferred with Hitler and Mussolini. In the Munich pact (1938), signed also by France, Chamberlain accepted Hitler's territorial claims to predominantly German areas of Czechoslovakia. Though Chamberlain assured Britain that his concession had brought "peace in our time," Hitler soon broke his agreement and occupied the rest of Czechoslovakia.

After Germany invaded Poland on Sept. 1, 1939, Chamberlain honored a pledge to stand by Poland and led Britain into war two days later. Although his policies were discredited, he held on as prime minister until May 1940, when he resigned and was succeeded by Winston Churchill. He died in Heckfield on Nov. 9, 1940.

Character and Political Philosophy. As befitted the son of the most famous Liberal Radical of the late 19th century, Neville Chamberlain was keenly interested in the amelioration of social conditions. But unlike his father, he brought little passion or demagogy to his work. His political character was thus very different from that of most of his opponents in the Labour party, for whom the demonstration of public passion on behalf of the working classes was a political creed. To Labourites, Chamberlain's concern with administrative minutiae, financial probity, and individual responsibility (which he feared the careless extension of state welfare might undermine) appeared as inhuman indifference to the poor. Chamberlain was by temperament a businessman and a civil servant before he was a politician; although he did much to extend welfare services between the wars, his contribution was that of rationalization and was not based on a desire to change quickly and radically the existing qualities of social life.

If to his domestic politics he brought little of the fervor of his Birmingham Radical upbringing, this quality was surprisingly present when he turned to foreign affairs. His "appeasement" has seldom been discussed in this light, and most of his critics have misrepresented his position. The urgent desire to negotiate with Hitler and Mussolini did not, in Chamberlain's case, spring from pacifism. He strongly supported sanctions against Mussolini's invasion of Ethiopia in 1935 and was a vocal supporter of rearmament after 1934. Nor was he ignorant of the menace of the dictators. Few people linked the need for rearmament more strongly with the ambitions of Germany. But the crucial characteristic of Chamberlain's support of rearmament lay in his vision of such rearmament as a support for negotiations that would institute a general peace. Chamberlain believed that a lasting peace would be possible when British rearmament had helped demonstrate to the dictators that the alternatives to negotiation were unthinkable.

Chamberlain's willingness to negotiate with Hitler was thus more than a result of a sense of military weakness and a refusal to regard the German minority in Czechoslovakia as worth fighting over—although these considerations were present. It sprang also from a passionate desire to avert the horror of war and a firm belief in the possibility of a lasting general peace. This policy of "negotiation through strength" was always potentially self-defeating. The more Britain rearmed, the less sincere her desire for peace might appear; the more she spoke of peace, the less credible the deterrence of rearmament might become. When the British declared war on Germany, Chamberlain's policy had failed. The deterrent was to be used, and he above all men was stricken by the catastrophe that he had striven to prevent. This repugnance to war made him appear to many to be unfitted for wartime politics; he resigned after the obvious discontent within his own party was combined with the refusal of the Labour party to join any government led by him.

On reflection, Chamberlain's apparent coldness is not easily distinguished from a strong sense of integrity and public service. If his self-confidence and rigidity of will were placed in policies now generally believed mistaken, they were policies supported by most of his contemporaries and ones that Chamberlain defended more intelligently than most.

A. J. BEATTIE, *London School of Economics*

Further Reading: Feiling, Keith, *Life of Neville Chamberlain* (London 1946); Macleod, Iain, *Neville Chamberlain* (London 1961).

CHAMBERLAIN, chăm'bər-lin, **Owen** (1920–   ), American physicist, who shared the 1959 Nobel Prize for physics with Emilio Segrè for their discovery of the antiproton. Owen Chamberlain was born in San Francisco, Calif., on July 10, 1920, the son of Dr. W. Edward Chamberlain, a prominent radiologist. His father had unusual interest in and understanding of physics; his mother came from a pioneer California family. Owen obtained his bachelor's degree at Dartmouth College in 1941 and from there went to the University of California at Berkeley as a graduate student of physics with a special interest in possible biological applications.

In his graduate studies he came in contact with Professor Emilio Segrè and soon joined him in research. At that time the work for the Manhattan Project, which was to develop the atomic bomb, was rapidly gaining momentum. In 1942 Chamberlain moved with a group of students under the leadership of Segrè to Los Alamos near Santa Fe, N. Mex., the newly established research center of the Manhattan Project. He remained there until the end of the war, investigating spontaneous fission of the heavy elements and nuclear cross sections of interest for the atomic bomb project. He also participated in the test of the first atomic bomb near Alamogordo, N. Mex.

At the end of the war he moved to Chicago to finish his graduate studies under Enrico Fermi. Fermi had collected a brilliant group of young people, several from Los Alamos, eager to work under his guidance. The interruption in formal classwork caused by the war had not prevented them from gaining extensive scientific experience at Los Alamos or in other projects. Thus, they formed an unusually mature group, out of which came several distinguished physicists. Chamberlain obtained his Ph. D. in 1949 from the University of Chicago. His thesis was on neutron diffraction by liquids, using the newly developed neutron piles as a source. This work paralleled the X-ray diffraction in liquids studied by the Debye school in the 1930's.

The University of California at Berkeley offered Chamberlain a teaching appointment, and he returned to Berkeley where he rejoined Segrè and several other of his Los Alamos colleagues and friends, notably Clyde Wiegand, who was finishing his doctoral work at Berkeley.

They undertook a series of experiments on nucleon-nucleon scattering which extended over a long period of time. Nucleons are the particles that make up the nucleus, that is, protons and neutrons. Particularly noteworthy were experiments in which the nucleons were polarized; that is, a large fraction of the particles in the beams used had their spins parallel to each other. The purpose of this work was to try to better understand the forces at play between two protons or a proton and a neutron. Although the problem has not yet been solved, these studies made a major contribution to its progress.

When the Bevatron accelerator of the Lawrence Radiation Laboratory went into operation, the opportunity arose for deciding the old question, opened by Dirac's theory of 1928. This was the question whether the proton has an antiparticle, or charge conjugate particle—that is, a particle of the same mass and spin and described by the same statistics, but having an opposite electric charge. Experiments by Chamberlain, Segrè, Wiegand, and Thomas Ypsilantis gave proof of the existence of such a particle, now called the antiproton. Other antiparticles were found later and it is clear that there is symmetry between our world of particles and a theoretically possible world of antiparticles. Subsequently, Chamberlain worked on the preparation and use of polarized proton targets.

EMILIO SEGRÈ, *University of California*
Nobel Prize Winner in Physics

CHAMBERLAIN, chăm'bər-lin, **Wilt** (1936-   ) American basketball player, who broke many scoring records and is ranked among the greatest players of all time. Standing over 7 feet tall, he was nicknamed "Wilt the Stilt."

Wilton Norman Chamberlain was born in Philadelphia, Pa., on Aug. 21, 1936. In high school his height and scoring ability drew national attention. At the University of Kansas in the first game of his varsity career he scored 52 points. After his junior year at college Chamberlain joined the Harlem Globetrotters for a year before signing in 1958 with the Philadelphia Warriors of the National Basketball Association.

In 1960 he was the first NBA player to be named the league's outstanding rookie and most valuable player in the same year. For seven years he led the NBA in scoring, averaging 39.6 points per game. On March 2, 1962, he scored an unprecedented 100 points in a 169–147 Philadelphia win over the New York Knickerbockers in Hershey, Pa. In 1965 the Warriors (then in San Francisco) traded Wilt to the Philadelphia 76ers. In each of three years with the 76ers he was named the NBA's most valuable player. In 1968 he was traded to the Los Angeles Lakers, with whom he played until joining the San Diego Conquistadors as a coach for the 1973–1974 season.

The first player to amass 30,000 points, he had a career average of over 30 points and led the league in rebounding for 11 seasons.

MICHAEL QUINN, *"Newsday"*

WILT CHAMBERLAIN, one of basketball's top stars.

CHAMBERLAIN, a medieval officer in France and England. From the time of the Merovingian kings of France (481–751 A. D.) the *camerarius*, or keeper of the chamber, had charge of the chamber where the royal treasure and archives were kept. His duties extended over the domestic management of the palace and occasionally to command of the royal army. But the financial aspect of the office was most important because that led to the multiplication of chamberlains who acted solely as treasury officers both within and outside the royal households. More or less honorary chamberlains multiplied also because the title seemed the obvious designation for those who served in dignified offices in the royal household. But there was always a master, or great, chamberlain who was a nobleman and leading dignitary of the court, although in England he ceased to be responsible for the chamber where the treasure was kept.

The dignitaries of the Old English kingdom are not to be identified with those of the Empire, as those of France are. But there was correspondence among all three offices. The titles both of *bower-thegn* and *bed-thegn* (servants in the king's chambers in Anglo-Saxon England) were translated in Latin as *camerarius* or *cubicularius* (chamber servant), and there is no clear distinction between them. A similar confusion existed in France, where the *cubiculaire* or *chambellan*, who attended the king in his chambers, were of inferior rank to the *chambrier*, who was in charge of the royal treasury. *Chambellans* were in principle concerned only with the domestic service of the king, but the *grand chambellan* in the course of time became a court official of the highest rank. The chambrier, on the other hand, ceased to exercise any effective functions by the 13th century.

In England, by the time of Edward the Confessor, one of the household chamberlains had special responsibility for the king's treasury, and that arrangement was continued after the Conquest. Henry I's acquisition of Normandy resulted in the creation of a separate treasury, which was permanently located in England, while the chamber accompanied the king across the English Channel.

One of the results of King John's expulsion from Normandy was that the chamber became localized in England. Under Henry III, besides a hereditary chamberlain with ceremonial functions, chamberlains of a new type were appointed. Nominally they were in charge of the chamber. But they tended to become mere dignitaries who were intimates of the king (Piers Gaveston, the favorite of Edward II, for example), and it became necessary to appoint vice chamberlains to perform the actual duties of the office. Finally, with the evolution of the modern state, the king's chamber ceased to be the great spending department, and the chamberlains no longer had any significant financial functions. The pure sinecures were abolished in the 18th century.

The hereditary Lord Great Chamberlain of England survives, but with only ceremonial functions. His office is to be distinguished from that of the Lord Chamberlain, who is head of the royal household, with a vice chamberlain and large staff. Until that function was abolished in 1968, he licensed stage plays in Britain.

HENRY GERALD RICHARDSON
Author, "The Governance of Mediaeval England"

CHAMBERLAND, shän-ber-län′, **Charles Édouard** (1851–1908), French bacteriologist, best known for his work in devising a type of filter known as the porcelain candle. This filter, made from unglazed porcelain, was designed so that when liquid was forced through it, microscopic organisms would be strained out while ultramicroscopic organisms would be allowed to pass through with the liquid. This was the first device that enabled scientists to separate ultramicroscopic organisms from microscopic ones, and it was heralded as one of the outstanding advances in the study of ultramiscroscopic organisms.

Chamberland was born in Chilly-le-Vignable, France, on March 12, 1851. He was interested in many areas of bacteriology and worked with several famous French bacteriologists. While working with Louis Pasteur and Pierre Roux at the Pasteur Institute in Paris he used weakened bacterial cultures for therapeutic and immunological research. He also helped them demonstrate the presence of rabies virus in the blood of infected persons. Chamberland also worked with Pasteur and Jules Joubert in discovering the bacterium that causes a type of edema. This was the first discovery of an anaerobic disease-producing organism.

In 1904, Chamberland became assistant director of the Pasteur Institute. He died in Paris on May 2, 1908.

DAVID OTTO, *Stephens College*

CHAMBERLIN, chăm′bər-lən, **Thomas Chrowder** (1843–1928), American geologist, who proposed the planetesimal hypothesis of the origin of the solar system. Chamberlin was born in Mattoon, Ill., on Sept. 25, 1843. He was professor of geology at Beloit College, in Wisconsin, and became chief state geologist of Wisconsin in 1876. His work gained him recognition as the outstanding American glacial geologist, and he was made chief of the glacial division of the U. S. Geological Survey in 1882, serving until 1907. In 1887 he became president of the University of Wisconsin, where he reorganized the curriculum, giving more prominence to science. Tiring of administrative work, he resigned in 1892 and served as head of the department of geology at the University of Chicago until 1919. He died in Chicago on Nov. 15, 1928.

Chamberlin's speculations on the causes of glacial periods led him to investigate the origin of the atmosphere and ultimately the evolution of the solar system. In order to explain very ancient glacial periods, he felt it necessary to reject the prevailing nebular theory of a molten origin of the earth and to develop (from 1903 on), with the aid of the astronomer Forest Ray Moulton, the hypothesis that the earth had formed and grown slowly to its present size by the accumulation of infalling small bodies ("planetesimals"). Chamberlin attempted to explain the entire history of the earth in terms of his hypothesis; and he believed that this history had been marked by brief episodes of worldwide earth movements separated by long periods of stability, which provided a natural basis for the correlation of strata.

A bold and imaginative thinker, Chamberlin had a great influence on geologists as first editor of the *Journal of Geology* (1893–1928). He popularized the method of "multiple working hypotheses" as the most fruitful in science.

LEROY E. PAGE, *Wayne State University*

CHAMBERS, Sir Edmund Kerchever (1866–1954), English literary critic, who was one of Britain's greatest Shakespeare scholars. He was born in Berkshire, England, on March 16, 1866, and was educated at Corpus Christi College, Oxford. In 1892 he joined the National Education Department.

Chambers edited *English Pastorals* (1895) and and *The Oxford Book of Sixteenth Century Verse* (1932). His scholarly writings include *The Mediaeval Stage* (1903), *The Elizabethan Stage* (1923), *William Shakespeare* (1930), and *Shakespearean Gleanings* (1944). Chambers was knighted in 1925. He died at Devon, England, on Jan. 21, 1954.

CHAMBERS, Ephraim (1680–1740), English writer and encyclopedist. He was born in Kendal, Westmorland, England. After leaving school he was apprenticed to a maker of globes and mathematical instruments in London. This experience stimulated his interest in science and inspired in him the idea of compiling an encyclopedia. The result was his famous *Cyclopaedia, or an Universal Dictionary of Arts and Sciences*. The first edition was published in 1728 in two volumes. Other editions appeared in 1738, 1739, 1741, and 1746. A French translation was the basis of the 35-volume *Encyclopédie* (1751–1780) compiled by Denis Diderot and Jean Le Rond d'Alembert. Revised and enlarged editions of the English work were prepared by George L. Scott (1753) and, in four volumes, by Abraham Rees (1781–1786), who later used it as a basis for his *Cyclopaedia* (1819). Chambers died at Islington on May 15, 1740.

CHAMBERS, Robert (1802–1871), Scottish publisher and author. He was born in Peebles on July 10, 1802. In 1813 his family moved to Edinburgh, and his interest in that city led to his writing *Traditions of Edinburgh* (2 vols., 1823; new ed., 1868). He joined his brother William (1800–1883) in editing the successful *Chambers's Journal*, and with him founded the publishing firm of W. & R. Chambers in 1832.

Chambers' most significant work, *Vestiges of the Natural History of Creation* (1843–1846), was published anonymously, and its authorship was not disclosed until 1884, long after his death. He also wrote *Book of Days*, (2 vols., 1862–1864), a compendium of anecdotes and curiosities related to the calendar. Chambers died at St. Andrews on March 17, 1871.

CHAMBERS, Whittaker (1901–1961), American editor and author, and a former Communist spy whose testimony in August 1948 during a sensational and controversial congressional investigation led eventually to the conviction of Alger Hiss for perjury. For Chambers the Hiss trial was the climax of a troubled life. He was born in Philadelphia on April 1, 1901, the son of a stormy marriage between a former actress and a newspaper artist. Reared in Lynbrook, N.Y., he had an unhappy childhood. Before joining the Communist party in 1925, Chambers had changed his name (from Jay Vivian to Whittaker), stayed at Williams College less than a week, and had been an erratic student (although one with considerable literary ability) at Columbia University.

After seven years in the Communist party, Chambers went "underground," eventually as part of a Washington espionage ring. He left the party in 1938 and confessed to the State Department but offered no proof. From 1939 to 1948 he worked for *Time* magazine, becoming a senior editor.

In 1948, Chambers described his Communist past to the House Committee on Un-American Activities and named Hiss an accomplice. Hiss, a Harvard law school graduate and former State Department official, was then president of the Carnegie Endowment for International Peace. Hiss denied under oath that he had delivered government documents to Chambers, and sued for libel. When Chambers produced microfilm to support his charge, Hiss was indicted for perjury (the statute of limitations prevented an espionage indictment). The first trial, in 1949, ended in a hung jury but the second, ending in January 1950, resulted in his conviction. The Hiss case contributed to public fear of Communist infiltration in the government and became a major political issue. Representative (later Vice President) Richard M. Nixon of California was instrumental in developing evidence against Hiss and thus enhanced his political career.

After the Hiss trial, Chambers published his autobiography, *Witness* (New York 1952), later became senior editor of the conservative *National Review*, and lived on his Maryland farm. He died in Westminster, Md., on July 9, 1961.

KEITH W. OLSON, *University of Maryland*

CHAMBERS, Sir William (1726–1796), English architect, who practiced a refined classical style for domestic and official buildings and was a pioneer of rococo design in the Oriental manner.

Life. Chambers, the son of an English merchant of Scottish descent, was born in Göteborg, Sweden, and educated at Ripon, in England. He traveled to India and China during seven years with the Swedish East India Company. After studying architecture in Paris and Rome, he settled in London in 1755. He was appointed architectural tutor to the Prince of Wales (later George III), a post that opened the way to a successful practice and to a number of official appointments. Chambers was a founding member of the Royal Academy (1768). He died in London on March 8, 1796.

Works. Chambers' most important building in the classical style is Somerset House (begun 1775), a prototype of government office buildings. His Oriental style is exemplified in designs for ornamental buildings (1757–1762) at Kew Gardens, of which the charming Chinese pagoda still survives. The Royal State Coach, still used at coronations, was designed by him.

Chambers' writings include *Designs of Chinese Buildings* (1757) and *Treatise on Civil Architecture* (1759).

BRUCE ALLSOPP
University of Newcastle upon Tyne, England

CHAMBERS, in law, refer to the private quarters in which judges transact judicial business that does not require or cannot await treatment in court. Such transactions began in 17th century England as a means of reaching judges on vacation, that is, in the period between court terms. Although the word usually refers to private offices in court buildings, a judge's chambers—for the purpose of exercising judicial authority—are wherever he happens to be, within his geographical jurisdiction, when exigencies demand his attention.

DOV GRUNSCHLAG, *Member, New York Bar*

CHAMBERSBURG is a borough in southern Pennsylvania, seat of Franklin county, 50 miles (80 km) southwest of Harrisburg. It is a trading center for a fruit-producing area in the Cumberland valley. Its industries include food processing plants and manufactures of clothing, drop-forging equipment, power transmission machinery, containers, and paper products. Chambersburg is the seat of Wilson College for women.

The site was settled in 1732 by Col. Benjamin Chambers. The original town area was laid out in 1764, and the borough was chartered in 1803. Early Scotch-Irish settlers were followed by Pennsylvania Germans, attracted by the fertile land.

In the Civil War, Confederate Gen. Robert E. Lee and his commanders, conferring in the town square, made the decision to turn his army east, which brought on the Battle of Gettysburg (July 1–3, 1863). During the war the Confederates raided the town three times; it was the only Northern town burned in the war.

Chambersburg is governed by a mayor and council. Population: 17,315.

HELEN MARGARET COOPER, *Wilson College*

CHAMBÉRY, shäN-bā-rē′, is a city in eastern France and, after Grenoble, the largest city in the French Alps. It is the capital of the Savoie department. Chambéry is situated about 55 miles (90 km) east of Lyon, in a depression or valley that unites Lake Bourget (and hence the upper Rhône Valley) with Isère River drainage. It is on the main route leading toward Mont Cenis and the Mont Cenis Tunnel. Chambéry's valley separates the Bauges Massif to the northeast from the Grande Chartreuse Mountains on the southwest. It is a fertile valley; grapes and other fruit grow there in abundance and cattle graze on its slopes.

Chambéry is a major rail center and a manufacturing city. Its varied industries produce cement, steel (structural steel as well as other grades), metal products, glass, chocolate and other confections, men's clothing, shoes, vermouth, spaghetti, and many other items. The city is a tourist center and a starting point for excursions in all directions. The fashionable health resort of Aix-les-Bains is nearby, on the shores of Lake Bourget.

The city was the capital of the duchy of Savoy. Of great interest to tourists are the Savoy Museum of History and Archaeology and the 16th century palace of the dukes of Savoy. The palace chapel is known for its fine stained-glass windows. Population: (1962) 41,011.

HOMER PRICE, *Hunter College, New York*

CHAMBEZI RIVER, cham-bē′zē, in northern Zambia, East Africa. It rises in the highlands south of Lake Tanganyika and flows southeast and then southwest to Lake Bangweulu, a course of about 300 miles (480 km). It emerges from the lake as the Luapula River. Its name is also spelled *Chambeshi.*

CHAMBLEE, cham-blē′, a city in Georgia, in De Kalb county, is 10 miles (16 km) northeast of Atlanta. It is a manufacturing, warehousing, and distribution center. Products include electrical equipment, farm machinery, lumber, abrasives, and medical supplies. Chamblee was incorporated in 1922. Government is by mayor and council. Population: 9,127.

CHAMBLY, shäN-blē′, a city in Quebec, Canada, is on the Chambly Basin (a widening of the Richelieu River), 14 miles (22 km) east of Montreal. It manufactures insoles, corrugated paper, canned foods, pottery, and agricultural chemicals. Chambly is the site of Fort Chambly National Historic Park. The fort, built by the French in 1665 and rebuilt in 1710, has been restored since the founding of the park in 1940. The towns of Chambly and Fort Chambly were joined to form the city of Chambly in 1965. Population: 11,469.

CHAMBORD, shäN-bôr′, **Count de** (1820–1883), Bourbon claimant to the French throne. He was born Henri Charles Ferdinand Marie Dieudonné de Bourbon, in Paris, on Sept. 29, 1820, the only son of the murdered Duke de Berry and the grandson of the Count d'Artois, who became king of France as Charles X; he also held the title Duke de Bordeaux. His youth was sheltered. He was trained by emigré legitimists and developed into a saintly and unworldly person.

Chambord was briefly styled king as Henry V after the revolution of 1830 but followed his grandfather into forced exile in Britain and later Austria. In 1844 he issued a manifesto outlining what was his lifelong position: while claiming to be legitimate king of France, he disavowed violence in "regaining" his throne.

In 1871 the election of a monarchist parliament in the wake of the collapse of the Second Empire gave promise of restoring the monarchy, provided that the Orleanists and Legitimists could unite behind a constitutional king. Elaborate negotiations ultimately broke down over Chambord's insistence on substituting the white flag of the Bourbons for the tricolor, which cloaked the real issue of the royal prerogative. The election of Marshal MacMahon as president of the Third Republic in 1873 sent Chambord back to permanent exile at Frohsdorf, Austria, where he died on Aug. 24, 1883. His inflexibility had ended all serious hope of a monarchist restoration in France.

PETER AMANN
State University of New York at Binghamton

CHAMBORD, shäN-bôr′, is a château in France, the largest and one of the most magnificent in the Loire Valley. The château occupies the site of a castle of the counts of Blois, which was razed by Francis I in 1519 to make way for the present building. It is uncertain why Francis wanted to build a château at Chambord, on low, marshy land only 10 miles (15 km) from Blois. But he was passionately interested in its construction; neither wars nor economic crises interrupted the work.

Chambord is one of the finest examples of French Renaissance architecture. Located in a vast park, the white structure is striking in its unity of style and richness of decoration. Fundamentally, it consists of a central building with four large towers, and a vast wall enclosing a courtyard. The two most admired features are the staircase and the terrace-roof. The staircase, decorated in the Italian style, mounts from the center of the hall of guards in two spirals, which parallel each other but never meet. Inspired by Italian models, the terrace-roof has a lantern light, numerous gables and dormer windows, 800 capitals, 365 chimneys, and many shafts.

Throughout the 16th and 17th centuries Chambord was a favorite residence of the French kings and the scene of colorful and famous events. Louis XV put it at the disposal of Stanislav I Lesczyński, his father-in-law, the dethroned king of Poland. Thenceforth it was held by a number of noble families. It was bought by the French government in 1932.

BRYCE LYON, *Brown University*

CHAMBRE ARDENTE, shäN-brär-dänt', was a name applied to several French courts exercising special jurisdiction. The first *chambre ardente* ("burning chamber") tried nobles accused of political crimes. The court sat in a darkened chamber lighted only by torches; the walls were draped entirely in black. The name *chambre ardente* was also popularly applied to courts established by Henry II (reigned 1547–1559) for the purpose of collaborating with the Roman Inquisition in the prosecution of Protestants. They were so named because they often sentenced people to be burned at the stake.

In 1679–1680 the *chambre ardente* was employed by Louis XIV to prosecute the perpetrators of numerous crimes of poisoning; it sentenced some of the leading aristocrats of the realm to be burned at the stake. The name was still later applied to a commission founded in 1780 to enact ferocious penalties for crimes by slaves in the island of Martinique. Finally, special judicial bodies known as *chambres de justice*, convened from the 16th through the 18th centuries, were sometimes called *chambres ardentes*.

LIONEL ROTHKRUG, *University of Michigan*

CHAMELEON, kə-mēl'yən, any of about 90 species of lizards of the family Chamaeleontidae, found throughout Africa, Spain, Arabia, the Middle and Near East, India, and Ceylon. They are considered by some authorities to be most closely related to the Agamidae, an Old World family of lizards that parallels the New World iguanids. The name "chameleon" is commonly misapplied to iguanid lizards of the genus *Anolis,* the anoles of the southern United States, Mexico, Central America, and northern South America, which are often sold as pets.

Coloration. The coloration of chameleons is generally cryptic and is traced in a variety of yellows, browns, greens, and blues—often in some sort of pattern. Some species even resemble leaves, with a color pattern suggesting the veins of a leaf. The chameleon's ability to change color is proverbial but overrated. Many other lizards change color as well and certain fishes do much better. The color change does not absolutely match the background; it is a behavioral response involving a direct reaction of the skin (modified system) affected by fright, temperature change, and similar stimuli. The actual mechanism involves the movement of pigment granules in the outer layers of the skin, resulting in a decrease or increase of pigment visibility.

Body Structure. The largest species of chameleon occurs in East Africa and Madagascar. It is nearly 2 feet (60 cm) long. An adult pigmy chameleon measures about 2 inches (5 cm) from snout to tail. Chameleons have a large head, short neck, underset body, and downward curving tail.

The spectacular modifications in chameleons are best understood as specializations for life in

FRENCH GOVERNMENT TOURIST OFFICE

CHÂTEAU DE CHAMBORD, a magnificent example of French Renaissance architecture, is set in a vast park.

trees. All 70 or more species of the genus *Chamaeleo* live in trees and bushes, although the much smaller specimens of the genus *Brookesia* (formerly *Rhampholeon*) may be found on the ground and sometimes even hiding under stones. The head, body, and tail show marked compression. The limbs project sideways and backward and are so jointed that all four feet can easily grasp a slender branch located immediately below the body. The grasping feet are formed by two opposable groups of digits. On the forelimbs, the two outer digits are opposed to the three inner ones, while on the hind limbs, the three outer digits are opposed to the two inner ones. This arrangement provides an ideal mechanism for clamping onto cylindrical twigs. The tail of most species is elongate and adapted to grasping a branch to provide additional support for the animal when it is resting or shooting at prey with the tongue.

The body of a chameleon is covered with scales that are generally small and granular. Some species have rows of enlarged shields along both sides of the trunk, and a row of enlarged spines often forms a crest along the middle of the back, or a "beard" along the middle of the lower jaw.

Head. The skull of chameleons is highly specialized. A variety of bony crests and horns on the head contribute to the animal's weird appearance. One to four bony horns project from a beaklike snout (rostrum) only in males, or in males and females of different species. These structures are true horns, since they are never shed and they have a bony core and a keratinous (horny) cover. Other forms have two or more crests on the back of the skull. Soft tissue specializations found in various species include one

CHAMELEONS of all kinds have feet adapted for grasping branches and projectile tongues for capturing prey. (*Left*) Jackson's chameleon; (*right*) brown chameleon.

or two leaflike flaps on the tips of the nose, an inflatable set of throat pouches, and flaps at the back of the head that can be moved by muscles.

Eyes. Vision is a much more important sense than smell for a chameleon. The eyes are highly specialized. Their relatively small openings are located at the tips of conical projections that are formed by fused eyelids. The entire assemblage may be moved independently on the left and right sides, so that the animals may watch objects to the front and to the rear simultaneously. When the two eyes are directed forward, there is a considerable overlap of the visual field that permits true stereoscopic vision and an estimate of distance and direction. These are important factors for an animal that has to project its tongue over some distance to capture prey.

Tongue. The tongue is aimed entirely by visual cues. It is ordinarily folded on the tip of the bone supporting the tongue and is shot off this support by the contraction of a complexly folded bundle of intrinsic extensor muscles. The entire process takes less than a third of a second. The folded retractor muscles, as well as a tendon and the blood vessels and nerves supplying the tip of the tongue, all unfold during projection and are returned when the retractor muscles are activated.

Behavior—Feeding. Chameleons feed on various insects; the larger species also rob hatchlings from bird nests. The remarkable projectile tongue, which may be shot forth at prey over a distance often greater than the length of the animal, compensates for the slow motion of these animals. Some species have been found to possess special attractant glands, whose contents, when smeared on a branch, act as bait for flies and other insects.

Locomotion. Chameleons move with a characteristic slowness that makes them unique among the lizards. Even a "rapidly" moving chameleon hardly takes a dozen steps a minute. It often rocks back and forth on a branch; the reason for this behavior is not clear. The forelegs appear to be placed by visual cues, but the hind legs are positioned in a semi-automatic fashion.

Reproduction. Various specializations of the head often represent secondary sex characteristics or isolating devices. The males use such devices in displaying to each other, and these peculiarities are also involved in sex recognition and in restricting mating to within a given species. The animals not only display themselves, but males will lock their horns and fight to force each other off a branch.

Some species lay eggs that are buried in the ground by a laborious process, since the feet of a chameleon are not adapted to rapid digging. Other species are ovoviviparous: they retain the eggs through their development and give birth to live young. Both the egg complement and the number of young vary widely from species to species—from 4 to about 40. Sperm storage has been reported in some species.

CARL GANS
State University of Buffalo, N. Y.

CHAMFORT, shän-fôr´, **Sébastien Roch Nicolas** (1741–1794), French writer. He was born near Clermont, Auvergne, on April 6, 1741, and received free schooling at the Collège des Grassins. An illegitimate child, he took Chamfort for his pen name. Noted for his wit, Chamfort was patronized by the nobility, introduced at the court of Louis XVI, and elected to the French Academy in 1781. But he was a bohemian and revolutionary at heart.

At the beginning of the French Revolution, Chamfort, a protégé of the Count de Mirabeau, was secretary of the Jacobin Club. However, he eventually came into conflict with Marat and Robespierre. Threatened with imprisonment, he died of self-inflicted wounds on April 13, 1794, in Paris.

Collections of Chamfort's works include *Pensées, maximes et anecdotes* (1803) and *Oeuvres complètes* (5 vols., 1824–1826).

CHAMINADE, shà-mē-nàd´, **Cécile Louise Stéphanie** (1857–1944), French composer and pianist. She was born in Paris on Aug. 8, 1857. A pupil of Benjamin Godard in composition, she began to compose at the age of eight, and her work attracted the interest of Georges Bizet. From the age of 18 she appeared in concerts, frequently playing her own piano compositions. In 1908 she made a successful tour of the United States.

Her best-known compositions include *Callirhoë*, a ballet symphony performed with great success at Marseille in 1888; *Les Amazones* for chorus and orchestra (1888); and such songs as *Madrigal, Chanson slave, Ritournelle, Fleur de matin,* and *Sans amour.* In addition to many works for solo piano, she wrote a concert piece for piano and orchestra and two piano trios. She died in Monte Carlo, Monaco, on April 18, 1944.

CHAMISSO, shä-mis′ō, **Adelbert von** (1781–1838), German writer and botanist, who was the leading lyric poet among the Berlin romanticists. Originally a member of the French aristocracy, he was born Louis Charles Adélaïde de Chamisso on Jan. 30, 1781, at the castle of Boncourt in Champagne. At the outbreak of the French Revolution, his family fled to Berlin, where Adelbert (also spelled Adalbert) spent most of his life. He served in the Prussian Army from 1798 to 1806 and during this period helped found the Nordsternbund, a society of Berlin romantic poets. From 1804 to 1806 he was coeditor of the society's journal, *Musenalmanach,* in which his first poems appeared.

About 1812, Chamisso began to study natural science, and from 1815 to 1818 he was a botanist on Otto von Kotzebue's scientific voyage around the world. Chamisso's diary of this trip was published in 1821. Upon his return to Germany, he was appointed curator of the Berlin Botanical Gardens, a post he held until shortly before his death, in Berlin, on Aug. 21, 1838.

The most famous of Chamisso's works is the prose tale *Peter Schlemihls wundersame Geschichte* (1814); Eng. tr., *The Wonderful History of Peter Schlemihl* (1825), which tells of a man who sold his shadow to the devil, with many unhappy consequences. *Schlemihl* has become a synonym for an unlucky fellow who gets worsted in all his dealings. Chamisso's best-known poetry is the cycle of love lyrics *Frauenliebe und Leben* (1830), which was set to music by Robert Schumann. Chamisso also wrote a number of poems idealizing the common man, most notably the nostalgic ballad *Das Schloss Boncourt* (1827). He was influenced in these writings by the French political poet Pierre Béranger, whose *Chansons* he translated into German in 1838.

SOL LIPTZIN, *Author of* "*A Historical Survey of German Literature*"

Further Reading: Fitzell, Henry J., *The Hermit in German Literature, 1749–1835* (Chapel Hill, N. C., 1961); Liptzin, Sol, *Lyric Pioneers of Modern Germany* (New York 1928).

CHAMOIS, sham′ē, an agile, goatlike animal native to the mountains of middle and southern Europe and southwestern Asia. Because of extensive hunting, its numbers have been greatly reduced in areas such as the Alps. The chamois (*Rupicapra rupicapra*) stands about 31 inches (785 mm) high at the shoulders and ranges up to 110 pounds (50 kg) in weight. Its tail is quite short, being generally less than 1½ inches (40 mm) long. Both sexes bear slender, black horns, rarely more than 8 inches (200 mm) in length, which rise straight from the forehead and curve back at the tips to form a hook. The summer coat, which averages about 1½ inches (40 mm) in length, is reddish brown. The winter coat grows to 8 inches (200 mm) in length and is blackish brown.

During the summer the chamois is found at high mountain elevations, where it feeds on herbs and flowers. In the winter the chamois descends to wooded areas at lower elevations to feed on mosses, lichens, and shoots.

Females and young usually live together in herds of 15 to 30 animals, with the older, solitary males joining the herds during the mating season in the fall. Usually one young is born in the spring after a gestation period (pregnancy) of about 6 months. The young are able to walk shortly after birth. Sexual maturity occurs at

ANNAN PHOTO FEATURES

Chamois

about 3 years of age, and some chamois may live for 20 or more years.

The chamois was the original source of "shammy" leather, but modern commercial chamois is made from the skins of domestic sheep and goats.

The chamois is classified in the goat subfamily (Caprinae) of the cow family (Bovidae) and is often categorized, along with several closely related animals, as a goat-antelope.

CHAMOMILE, kam′ə-mīl, a plant (*Matricaria chamomilla*) of the composite family, from which a medicinal oil of the same name is extracted. Chamomile is an annual that grows to a height of 2 feet (⅔ meter). Its name is derived from a Greek word meaning "earth apple," suggested by the applelike odor of the plant's flowers.

All parts of the plant contain active ingredients, but chamomile oil is obtained from the flower heads. The oil is used as a mild tonic, and in large doses it causes vomiting. Methoxycoumarin, which is a constituent of the oil, is claimed to relieve spasms, but there appears to be no rational pharmacological basis for the medical use of chamomile.

JOHN C. KRANTZ, JR. *United States Pharmacopoeia*

CHAMONIX, shà-mô-nē′, is a valley in southeastern France, in the department of Haute-Savoie, in the Savoy Alps. The valley of Chamonix (or *Chamouni*) is traversed by the Arve River. The eastern wall of the valley is formed by Mont Blanc (15,781 feet, or 4,807 meters) and other massive peaks of the same range. On the west are Mont Brévent and the Aiguilles Rouges.

Glaciers, including the Mer de Glace, one of the largest in the Alps, descend close to the cultivated fields of the valley. The soil is not very fertile, but it is assiduously farmed and yields grain, flax, and potatoes. Cattle are grazed on upland meadows.

Of the numerous towns and villages in the valley, Chamonix-Mont-Blanc is the most important. About 37 miles (59 km) southeast of Geneva, it is a year-round tourist center. The ascent of Mont Blanc is usually made from here. Population: (1962) of the town, 5,412.

CHAMORRO VARGAS, chä-môr′rō vär′gäs, **Emiliano** (1871–1966), Nicaraguan general and public official. He was born in Acoyapa, Nicaragua, on May 11, 1871. An army leader and a member of the Conservative party, he participated in the revolt that deposed José Santos Zelaya in 1909. Chamorro was Nicaraguan envoy to the United States (1913–1916; 1921–1923); in 1914 he signed the Bryan-Chamorro Treaty (ratified 1916), which gave the United States an option to build a canal through Nicaragua. (See also NICARAGUA—*10. History.*) He was president of Nicaragua from 1917 to 1920 and again in 1926, when the United States resumed its earlier occupation of the country.

Chamorro carried out other diplomatic assignments and served as a national senator. From 1933 until his death he was the leader of the Conservatives; he consistently opposed Liberal administrations, notably that of Anastasio Somoza. Chamorro died in Managua on Feb. 26, 1966.

CHAMP DE MARS, shän də mȧrs, in Paris, France, a park on the left bank of the Seine River, between the river and the École Militaire. It was built between 1765 and 1767 as the military school's exercise and parade ground and was made into a park in 1913. It is about 1,100 yards (1,000 meters) long and about 550 yards (500 meters) wide. The Eiffel Tower was built at the river end in 1889.

In 1790, Louis XVI and his family met on the Champ de Mars in the Fête de la Fédération, in which the King swore to defend the constitution. In June 1794 the grounds were the scene of the Festival of the Supreme Being, in which the populace affirmed Robespierre's new state religion. In 1815, Napoleon I proclaimed a liberalized constitution there.

CHAMPA, cham′pə, was an ancient Cham kingdom on the east coast of Vietnam. Founded in 192 A. D., it extended from north of Hué almost 300 miles (482 km) south to Camranh Bay.

The Cham were an Indonesian people deeply influenced by Indian culture. Their kingdom was first mentioned in Chinese annals in the 3d century A. D. under the name of Lin-yi. Lin-yi was composed of four small states, Amaravati (Quangnam), Vijaya (Binhdinh), Kauthara (Nhatrang), and Panduranga (Phanrang), all bent on invading Chinese-held territory in Vietnam, then called Annam by the Chinese.

The first great king, Bhadravarman, emerged around 400 A. D. and was the founder of Mison, the sacred city. The Cham incessantly raided the Chinese territories until 446 A. D., when in retaliation the Chinese destroyed their capital. Champa threw off Chinese dominance in the 6th century and subsequently flourished despite raids by the Chinese, Khmer, and Javanese. After gaining its independence from China in 939 A. D. and for the next few centuries, Vietnam found itself vying with Champa for supremacy. During the 12th century, Champa invaded the Khmer kingdom in Cambodia, sacked its capital, Angkor, and soon fell under Khmer rule.

Champa was invaded by the Mongols in the 13th century, and in 1312 was briefly a vassal state of Vietnam. It regained its independence under King Che Bong Nga (1360–1390), whose fleet pillaged Hanoi in 1371. After the king's death, Champa declined. When the Vietnamese emperor Le Thanh Tong captured the Cham capital of Vijaya near Binh Dinh in 1471, Champa was virtually destroyed. What remained disintegrated into principalities which the Vietnamese absorbed as they advanced south. Today only remnants of the once powerful kingdom survive in impoverished villages in South Vietnam and in Cambodia. See also CHAM.

JOSEPH BUTTINGER
Author of "Vietnam: A Dragon Embattled"
Further Reading: Buttinger, Joseph, *The Smaller Dragon: A Political History of Vietnam* (New York 1958); Hall, Daniel G., *History of South-East Asia* (New York 1955).

CHAMPAGNE, shän-pȧn′yə, is a region of France to the east of Paris. It includes all of the department of Marne as well as parts of Haute-Marne, Aisne, Seine-et-Marne, Yonne, Meuse, Ardennes, and Aube. Its name is derived from the Latin *campania* (plain). The region is generally flat, but low hills relieve the monotony of the landscape and provide a suitable environment for the growing of vines. Along the valley of the meandering Marne River the countryside has an open, rolling beauty. The forest of Clairvaux is well known for the ruins of St. Bernard's Cistercian Abbey of Clairvaux.

Champagne has always occupied an important position in the history of France. Attila and the Huns were defeated by Roman armies on the plains of Champagne in 451. In 496 at Reims, a city in Champagne, St. Remi baptized Clovis I, the founder of the Merovingian line. The early Capetian kings of France established the tradition of going to the cathedral of Reims to be crowned. During the 11th century the powerful counts of Champagne began a series of fairs, at the towns of Provins, Troyes, Bar-sur-Aube, and Lagny-sur-Marne, that made Champagne the center of European trade and finance. These fairs continued to be held through the 12th and 13th centuries.

Early in the 14th century Champagne came under the rule of the French kings, and since the 16th century, whenever France has been invaded from the east, Champagne has been the scene of battles. The region suffered most severely during World War I, when for over four years German and French armies fought along the Marne River.

The cathedral of Notre Dame at Reims is the best known edifice in Champagne. It is a magnificent example of French Gothic architecture, notable for its monumental and symmetrical plan. Heavily damaged by German artillery in World War I, it was fully restored by 1938. The town of Troyes also has a Gothic cathedral of note, interesting for its facade and off-center clock tower. An abbey at Hautvillers is now the property of the venerable bottling firm of Moët and Chandon, which is world-famous as a producer of Champagne wine.

BRYCE LYON, *Brown University*

CHAMPAGNE, sham-pȧn′, is a white wine of the region of France that was formerly the province of Champagne. Almost all the wine of this region is processed to be effervescent, and therefore champagne generally means a sparkling white wine. The grapes are grown on the chalky plain between the cities of Reims and Épernay. The plain is dominated by a humped hill known as the Mountain of Reims. The best vineyards are planted on its slopes, on the Côte de Bouzy and the Côte des Blancs, and on the slopes of the

Marne valley, above Ay. True champagne is the finest wine of its kind, and no bottle is permitted the name on its label unless its content was harvested and blended within this specific district of France.

The vineyards of Champagne are planted with the black Pinot Noir grape, excepting the 15-mile (25-km) stretch of the so-called "white" slopes, which are planted with White Pinot and Chardonnay grapes. The Pinot Noir grape produces the noble red wines of Burgundy, but for champagne the grape yields a less robust, more acid white wine well suited to the blending and sugaring that give champagne its distinctive character. The golden color of the wine results from quickly separating the skins from the grapes after they have been crushed.

Some of the wine from the White Pinot and Chardonnay grapes of the white slopes is made into Blanc de Blancs, a champagne that is paler in color. In this region growers do not process their own wines. Instead, they sell them to local wine-receiving centers in Épernay and Reims, where they are blended and kept in cellars stretching for miles underground.

In the spring the wine is racked, that is, drawn off from the lees, or dregs. It is then ready to be bottled and to undergo the secondary fermentation that will impart its sparkle. A small quantity of cane sugar is added to each bottle, and when this turns to alcohol, carbon dioxide is generated. A pressure of 5 or 6 atmospheres is built up in the bottles, requiring stout bottles and thick corks. The wine lies in cool cellars for about four years, until the time is ripe for *remuage* (moving the sediment) and *dégorgement* (removing the sediment).

The first procedure entails putting the bottles in racks, necks pointing slightly downward, and shaking and tilting the bottles daily until they reach an upside-down position, with the deposit close to the cork. The *dégorgeur* takes the bottle, eases off the cork, and permits the sediment to shoot out, propelled by the pressure in the bottle. The performance of these highly skilled, time-consuming practices is the reason for the comparatively high cost of champagne.

Two alternative methods of inducing sparkle are the quite respectable but second-class bulk champagne process called *Charmat*, giving the wine its secondary fermentation in glass-lined vats instead of in bottles, and the crude practice of carbonization—injecting carbon dioxide, as is done with effervescent soft drinks.

After *dégorgement*, each bottle is refilled and sweetened with a liqueur of wine and sugar to suit various tastes. Percentages of sweetening by volume are indicated by such descriptive terms on the labels at *Brut* (very dry), 0-1½%; *Extra Dry* (really only fairly dry), 1-2%; and *Sec*, 8-10%. See also WINE.

ALEXIS LICHINE, *Author of "Encyclopedia of Wines & Spirits"*

CHAMPAIGN, sham-pān′, is a city in east central Illinois, in Champaign county, 126 miles (203 km) south of Chicago. It is a trade, manufacturing, and education center in a rich agricultural area. The campus of the University of Illinois straddles the line dividing Champaign from the adjoining city of Urbana. The university, a coeducational institution chartered in 1867, plays an important part in the economic and social life of the two communities. Champaign has a wide

PIPER-HEIDSIEGK

CHAMPAGNE CORKS receive wire coverings to withstand pressures from the sparkling wine in the bottles.

variety of industrial establishments producing drop forgings, alloy castings, bleachers (seating for athletic events), cement products, academic apparel, athletic equipment, soybean oil, and other processed foods.

Originally called West Urbana, Champaign was founded about 1855 with the coming of the Illinois Central Railroad. It was incorporated as a city in 1860. The city has the council-manager form of government. Population: 56,532.

KATHRYN J. GESTERFIELD
Champaign Public Library

CHAMPAIGNE, shäN-pån′yə, **Philippe de** (1602–1674), French painter, who is known especially for portraits and religious scenes painted in a powerful, though austere, style that combines elements of naturalism and classicism. His name is sometimes spelled *Champagne*. He was born in Brussels on May 26, 1602. In 1621 he moved to Paris, where he assisted Nicolas Poussin in decorating the Luxembourg Palace. Champaigne was patronized by Marie de Médicis, Louis XIII, and Cardinal Richelieu, for whom he painted a series of frescoes in the dome of the Sorbonne church. The influence of Rubens and van Dyck is seen in the paintings of this period, including *Adoration of the Shepherds* (1630; Wallace Collection, London) and a portrait of Richelieu (1635; National Gallery, London).

After 1647, when he came under the influence of the pious austerity of Jansenism, Champaigne banished all traces of baroque emotionalism from his work and evolved a style of sober restraint and subtle coloring. A masterpiece of this period is *Ex Voto* (1662; Louvre, Paris), a portrait of his daughter, who was a nun. Champaigne died in Paris on Aug. 12, 1674.

CHAMPEAUX, shän-pō′, **William of** (c. 1070–1122), French bishop and early scholastic writer. He was born at Champeaux near Melun, France, about 1070, studied at the Cathedral school in Paris under Anselm of Laon, and by 1095 was himself the master of the school. He was among the most brilliant teachers of the period; Peter Abelard (q.v.) was one of his students. In 1103, Champeaux became archdeacon of Paris, but in 1108 resigned his post to enter the Augustinian monastery of Canons Regular of St. Victor in Paris. He continued to teach publicly, however, and established the famous scholastic tradition of the Victorines. In 1113 he was appointed bishop of Châlons-sur-Marne. Here he established a close friendship with St. Bernard of Clairvaux whom he consecrated as abbot in 1125. He died at Châlons-sur-Marne on Jan. 18 or 25, 1122.

Although William compiled a book of *Sentences* in the tradition of Anselm of Laon, and was one of the pioneers of early scholastic systematic theology, little of his writing survives. His philosophic position has been gleaned mainly from Peter Abelard's work, *Historia Calamitatum*, in which Abelard traces their quarrel over universals. William, who was an ultrarealist, maintained that an identical nature exists in every individual of the species: thus the nature of Plato is that of Socrates. Abelard countered that if Socrates had the same nature as Plato, then Socrates must be Plato and William's view must ultimately lead to monism or pantheism. Abelard's criticisms eventually forced William to modify his position to that of making nature merely similar in every individual. Thus Socrates and Plato would share the same (similar but not identical) nature.

James A. Weisheipl, O. P.
Mediaeval Institute, University of Toronto

CHAMPERTY, cham′pər-tē, in law, is an illegal agreement between a party to a lawsuit and a person who otherwise has no interest in the suit, by which the distinterested person undertakes to bear the costs of the litigation and in return receives a portion of any proceeds recovered. A lawyer's contingent-fee agreement, whereby he derives his fees from a fixed percentage of the proceeds or, in the case of no recovery, collects no fee at all, is not champertous in most states of the United States unless the attorney has also

agreed to maintain the litigation costs. Champerty has been rejected in several states as antiquated and contrary to notions of contractual freedom. See also Barratry.

Linda Alden Rodgers, *Columbia Law School*

CHAMPION, cham′pē-ən, **Gower** (1921–   ), American dancer, choreographer, and theatrical director. He was born in Geneva, Ill., on June 22, 1921, and began dancing at 16 in nightclubs and musical revues with Jeanne Tyler. Later he danced with Marjorie Celeste Belcher, whom he married in 1947. The dance team of Marge and Gower Champion, noted for its vitality, creative choreography, and precision, met with great success in nightclubs, on Broadway and television, and in such films as *Mr. Music* (1950), *Show Boat* (1952), and *Everything I Have Is Yours* (1952). Champion choreographed and directed the Broadway productions *Bye, Bye Birdie* (1960), *Carnival* (1961), and *Hello Dolly!* (for which he won a 1964 Antoinette Perry award). In 1966 he staged *I Do, I Do* on Broadway.

CHAMPLAIN, shän-plaN′, **Samuel de** (1567?–1635), French explorer and colonizer, who is generally considered the true founder of New France and hence of Canada. He was born in Brouage, Saintonge, France. During the Wars of Religion he fought on the Huguenot side under Henry of Navarre. Then, in 1598, he took service under the king of Spain and visited Central America, where he conceived the idea of a Panama canal.

Exploration and Colonization. He was appointed a royal geographer by his old captain, now Henry IV, on his return to France. In this capacity he made his first visit (1603) to the Gulf of St. Lawrence and he sailed up the St. Lawrence River to the Lachine Rapids. The following year he accompanied the Sieur de Monts to Acadia and spent the next three years mapping the Atlantic coast from Nova Scotia to Martha's Vineyard. His interest in colonization as well as exploration was first revealed at Port Royal (now Annapolis Royal, Nova Scotia), where he sought to make the little band of Frenchmen self-sufficient by gardening, fishing, and hunting.

In 1608, after French interest in North America shifted from Acadia to the St. Lawrence Valley, he commanded the expedition that founded Quebec, and he was to devote the rest

SAMUEL DE CHAMPLAIN was the first European to explore Lake Champlain, which he reached in the company of an Indian war party in 1609. This drawing by J. D. Kelly is in the Château de Ramezay in the city of Montreal.

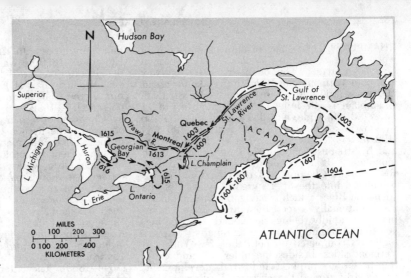

CHAMPLAIN first explored the Gulf of St. Lawrence in 1603. Between 1604 and 1607 he mapped the Atlantic coast of North America from Nova Scotia to Martha's Vineyard. He founded the settlement of Quebec in 1608. His major explorations inland were made between the years 1613 and 1616.

of his life to making that establishment the first permanent French settlement in North America. In 1609, having agreed to help the friendly Montagnais, Algonkin, and Huron Indians against their enemies, he accompanied a war party up the Richelieu River to Lake Champlain, which he was the first white man to explore. With his European arms he helped them to defeat the Iroquois in a skirmish near the site of Fort Ticonderoga on the New York shore. This casual encounter was to confirm the French alliance with the Algonkin and the Huron and to earn for them the lasting enmity of the Iroquois, who for nearly a century thereafter were to threaten the extermination of the French settlements on the St. Lawrence.

Champlain spent the winter of 1609–1610 in France seeking support for the colony from the court and the French merchants. In 1612 he was appointed commandant in New France, and in the following year he made his way up the Ottawa River as far as Allumette Island, in an effort to induce the Algonkin to come once more to trade with the French at the rapids (Montreal). It was on this trip that he lost his astrolabe while portaging. It was discovered in 1867 and is now in the museum of the New-York Historical Society. Champlain found baseless the report of his guide, Nicolas Vignau, a French boy who had spent the winter of 1611–1612 with the Algonkin, that one could go in 17 days from Montreal to the "Northern Sea." Vignau claimed to have seen there the wreckage of an English ship—a "'moccasin-telegraph" echo of Henry Hudson's discovery of the bay that bears his name. Champlain was dissuaded from going farther on this occasion by the Algonkin, who wished to keep their profitable role of middlemen between the French and the Huron.

In 1615, however, Champlain again set out up the Ottawa, and by way of the Mattawa River reached Lake Nipissing, the French River, and Georgian Bay, following the route that was to become the main highway of the French fur trade. In the Huron country south of Georgian Bay he was induced to join his hosts in a war party against the Iroquois, which took him to the Onondaga stronghold near the site of Syracuse, N. Y., by way of Lake Simcoe, the Trent River, Lake Ontario, and the Oneida River. Despite Champlain's efforts to induce his allies to practice European siege warfare, the Huron attack was repulsed. Champlain was wounded and had to spend the winter with the Huron, before returning to Quebec in the spring.

Growth of the Colony. Chhamplain's exploring days were over, but he had acquired a working knowledge of the main Indian trade routes from Acadia to the Great Lakes, as well as great prestige among the Indians. While he devoted himself to maintaining and building up the French establishment at Quebec, he sent young men such as Étienne Brulé and Jean Nicolet into the hinterland to learn the Indian tongues and to induce the Indians to trade with the French. His constant efforts to enlist support from the French court for the struggling colony were rewarded in 1627, when he was named governor of New France under the Company of New France (known as the Company of One Hundred Associates). Cardinal Richelieu organized this new company to make good the deficiencies of earlier companies, which had failed to keep their engagements to promote colonization as well as the fur trade.

But in 1628, Quebec was threatened by David Kirke, an Anglo-French privateer who intercepted the men and provisions sent out from France for Quebec. The following year Champlain was forced to surrender his starved-out post to the English privateers. However, thanks in part to Champlain's efforts, Quebec was restored to France by the Treaty of St.-Germain-en-Laye (1632), and Champlain devoted his few remaining years to rebuilding the establishment, which had been allowed to fall into ruins by the English traders. He founded Trois-Rivières, halfway between Quebec and the future site of Montreal, in 1634. He died on Christmas Day, 1635, in Quebec, where he was buried.

Champlain was an extraordinary combination of explorer, fur trader, colonizer, and profoundly religious man, who induced both the Recollets (Reformed Franciscans) and the Jesuits to commence their notable missionary labors in New France and Huronia. He is regarded by both English and French-speaking Canadians as the founder of their country.

The best edition of Champlain's numerous writings is that of Henry P. Biggar, *The Works of Samuel de Champlain,* 6 vols. (Toronto 1922–1936).

Mason Wade, *University of Western Ontario*

Further Reading: Bishop, Morris, *Champlain: The Life of Fortitude* (New York 1948); Brebner, J. Bartlet, *The Explorers of North America, 1492–1806* (New York 1933; paperback ed., New York 1955).

CHAMPLAIN, Lake, sham-plān', a natural body of water in New York and Vermont, with a part in Quebec, Canada. The boundary between New York and Vermont runs through the lake for about 100 miles (160 km) north to south. In all, Lake Champlain is 107 miles (172 km) long, up to 14 miles (23 km) wide, and 435 square miles (1,126 sq km) in area. Its greatest depth is 399 feet (122 meters). The lake is fed by Lake George and by streams from the Adirondack and Green mountains. It is connected with the Hudson River by the Champlain Barge Canal and drains northward into the St. Lawrence by way of the Richelieu River, which is navigable through locks.

Traditionally a recreation area, Lake Champlain is rapidly being developed for boating, year-round fishing, and winter sports. Express highways completed on both the New York and Vermont sides, besides the older rail and canal transportation, promise industrial development, particularly around the cities of Burlington, Vt., and Plattsburgh, N. Y.

Because Lake Champlain lies in a long valley connecting the middle St. Lawrence and the Hudson valleys at near sea level, its control was an important military objective in early American history. Samuel Champlain, for whom the lake is named, discovered it in 1609 and fought a battle with the Iroquois Indians at Ticonderoga that year. The French and Indian War (1754–1760) brought European armies and navies to fight more sophisticated battles on the lake. In 1758, 5,000 French and Canadian troops routed 15,000 British and provincial soldiers who attacked them at Fort Ticonderoga. The next year the British captured the fort and built a fleet with which they conquered Lake Champlain.

In the American Revolution, a Continental army invaded Canada down Lake Champlain in 1775. Benedict Arnold built an American fleet on the lake and with it won the Battle of Valcour Island (1776), thus holding off a British invasion for a crucial year. In 1777 a British army and fleet took Lake Champlain and held it until the Treaty of Paris (1783) made most of it part of the United States.

During the War of 1812, Lake Champlain was a warpath of nations for the last time. Commodore Thomas Macdonough's total destruction of a British fleet in Plattsburgh Bay (1814) was the decisive battle of the second war with England.

HARRISON K. BIRD
Author of "Navies in the Mountains"

CHAMPOLLION, chän-pô-lyoN', **Jean François** (1790–1832). He was born at Figeac, France, on Dec. 23, 1790. He received his formal education at Grenoble and the Collège de France (Paris), but the bulk of his prodigious knowledge was acquired through individual study and work with tutors, several of whom were famous scholars.

At the age of 18 he was appointed professor of history at Grenoble. Later, returning to Paris, he continued his attempts to decipher the ancient Egyptian scripts and played a major role in deciphering the hieroglyphic text of the Rosetta Stone. In his *Lettre à Monsieur Dacier,* read before the Académie des Inscriptions in September 1822, Champollion actually elucidated all the basic principles of Egyptian hieroglyphic writing

Champollion went to Italy in 1824 to study the Egyptian material at Turin and to acquire a collection for the Louvre in Paris, where he subsequently became the first conservator of Egyptian antiquities. In 1828–1829 he worked in Egypt. In 1830 he was elected to the Académie des Inscriptions et Belles-Lettres, and the next year the first chair of Egyptology was created for him at the Collège de France. He died in Paris on March 4, 1832.

Champollion's many manuscripts were purchased by the French government and deposited in the Bibliothèque Nationale. The foundation for all subsequent Egyptological study was contained in three basic works: the epoch-making *Précis du système hiéroglyphique des anciens égyptiens* (1824), and the posthumous *Grammaire* (1836) and *Dictionnaire* (1841; corrected, completed, and arranged by his brother, Jacques Joseph Champollion-Figeac). His study of the monuments of the Nile Valley resulted in the 4-volume *Monuments de l'Égypte et de la Nubie* (1835–1845) and much later in the *Notices descriptives* (1844–1889). The latter made available the texts from which his grammatical and lexical conclusions had been drawn, enabling scholars to see for themselves the extent to which the young Frenchman had "created" Egyptology.

CAROLINE PECK, *Brown University*

CHAMPS ÉLYSÉES, shän-zā-lē-zā, an avenue in Paris, perhaps the city's finest promenade. The Champs Élysées ("Elysian Fields") extends from the Place de la Concorde to the Arc de Triomphe. At the lower end, the Horses of Marly frame the view down the avenue. The park that extends from here to the Rond-Point des Champs Élysées is flanked by the Grand and Petit Palais and the Théâtre de Marigny. The upper end, toward the arch, is lined with busy cafés, shops, hotels, and movie theaters.

CHAMSON, shän-sôN', **André** (1900–   ), French novelist and essayist. He was born in Nîmes on June 6, 1900, and studied at the École des Chartes in Paris. Chamson's early novels, dealing with the austere life of Protestant peasants in his native Cévennes mountains, include *Roux le bandit* (1925), *Les hommes de la route* (1927), and *Le crime des justes* (1928). He was active in the Resistance in World War II, and his concern with contemporary political and philosophical problems is reflected in such later works as *La galère* (1939), *Les puits des miracles* (1945), *L'homme qui marchait devant moi* (1948), *La neige et la fleur* (1951), and *La petite Odyssée* (1965).

Chamson also worked as a museum curator and in 1959 became director of the Archives de France. He was elected to the French Academy in 1956.

CHAN-CHAN, chän chän, was the capital city of the Chimú civilization of Peru. Situated in the Moche Valley, on the northern coast, about 2 miles (3 km) from modern Trujillo, the city flourished for several centuries during a peak of early Peruvian culture. The ruins cover about 8 square miles (21 sq km).

Chan-Chan was constructed almost entirely of adobe brick, often decorated with painted plaster reliefs. Distinguishable still are the remains of the rectilinear street plan, high walls, temples, pyramids, reservoirs, and an advanced system of irrigation. The city probably housed more than 250,000 people. The culture was based on agriculture. In 1470, Chan-Chan was conquered by the Incas and abandoned.

CHANCE, Britton (1913–   ), American biophysicist and physical biochemist, who pioneered in the study of rapid biologic reactions of certain enzymes and in the measurement of biologic reactions by means of spectrophotometric and fluorometric techniques. He also investigated the control and regulation of metabolism and the mechanism of energy transfer associated with biologic oxidations and photosynthesis.

Contributions to Science. In the early 1940's, Chance studied catalase and peroxidase, two hemoprotein enzymes. His experiments permitted the first direct demonstration of an enzyme-substrate complex as well as the measurement of the most rapid biologic reaction then known. After working on the design of electronic circuits to measure the intensity of light, he extended his use of rapid and sensitive spectrophotometric methods from the study of pure enzymes to the study of hemoproteins bound to mitochondria, which are cell organelles involved in cellular oxidation. He developed a technique for measuring the absorbancy changes of pigments associated with cellular organelles, and, together with his colleagues, defined and characterized the transitions undergone by respiratory pigments during the process by which the energy of food molecules is used in the formation of ATP, the immediate source of energy in living organisms. Through their work, they established the foundations of the present knowledge of energy-transfer reactions in biologic systems.

Applying similar techniques in measuring the fluorescence of pyridine nucleotides from organs such as the heart, brain, and liver, Chance clarified the chemical definition of cellular metabolism during various physiological states. His recognition of the fluctuations of intracellular metabolites and his ability to express his observations in mathematical terminology suitable for digital and analogue computer simulation added a further means of explaining the many facets of multiple enzyme systems.

Chance also applied his techniques to the study of photosynthesis in green plants and to the study of bacteria capable of carrying on photosynthesis. In particular, his examination of temperature-independent photooxidation reactions provided a significant guidepost for future research.

Life. Chance was born in Wilkes-Barre, Pa., on July 24, 1913. He attended Haverford School and the University of Pennsylvania, where he received his Ph. D. in physical chemistry in 1940. He continued his studies at Cambridge University in England, receiving Ph. D. and D. Sc. degrees in biology, and later at the Nobel Institute in Stockholm.

In 1949, Chance became director of the Johnson Research Foundation and chairman of the department of biophysics and physical biochemistry at the University of Pennsylvania School of Medicine.

RONALD W. ESTABROOK
University of Pennsylvania School of Medicine

CHANCE, Frank LeRoy (1877–1924), American baseball star, who was one of the game's most successful playing managers. The "Peerless Leader" managed the Chicago Cubs to four National League pennants (1906–1908 and 1910) and to two World Series championships (1907 and 1908). He was the first baseman in the famous Tinker-to-Evers-to-Chance double-play combination. He was elected to the Baseball Hall of Fame in 1946.

Born in Fresno, Calif., on Sept. 9, 1877, Chance became known as "Husk" for his 200-pound frame. He joined the Cubs in 1898 as a catcher, moved to first base in 1903, and managed from 1905 to 1912. A fiery competitor, he was the leading Cub hitter at .327, .310, .316, and .319 from 1903 to 1906. His career average was .297. His 1906 team won 116 games, still a major league record for a 154-game season, and finished 20 games in front. In the 1908 World Series, Chance batted .421 and stole five bases. It is said that he challenged every new Cub player to a fistfight and that he never lost. In 1913 and 1914, Chance was playing manager for the New York Yankees. He died in Los Angeles on Sept. 15, 1924.

HAROLD PETERSON, *"Sports Illustrated"*

CHANCE, a novel by Joseph Conrad (q.v.), published in 1913. One of Conrad's later works, it was his first popular success. The story, as in many of Conrad's novels, is narrated by the seaman Marlow; it focuses on Flora de Barral, one of the sensitive and troubled protagonists characteristic of Conrad's later novels. She suffers from the shame of her father's imprisonment for fraud and from the hatred of her embittered governess. Flora marries Captain Roderick Anthony of the ship *Ferndale*, and they take two sea voyages together accompanied by Flora's father, who has returned from prison under the alias "Smith" with the intention of alienating Flora from Anthony and securing her love for himself alone. At the climax "Smith" attempts to poison Anthony, but his plot is discovered, and, in despair, he takes the poison himself and dies.

CHANCEL, chan'səl, in architecture, that part of the church reserved for the clergy and choir, usually the eastern end of the building. In traditional churches the chancel includes the sanctuary, or area containing the main altar and seats of the presiding clergy (an area originally called a "chancel") and the area for the singers (an area called a "choir") between the sanctuary and the nave. In some modern churches, where the choirs sit above the back of the nave, the chancel includes only the sanctuary. The chancel is set off from the nave by a barrier, which before the Reformation was usually a carved screen (*cancellus* in Latin) and is today generally a balustrade or railing.

CHANCELLOR, John William (1927–   ), American journalist, television newscaster, and government official. He was born in Chicago, Ill., on July 14, 1927; briefly attended the University of Illinois; and joined the staff of the Chicago *Sun-Times* in 1948. In 1950 he began to report crimes, fires, and racial incidents for a Chicago affiliate of the National Broadcasting Company, and in 1958 he was assigned to the Vienna bureau of NBC News.

Chancellor became NBC's London correspondent in 1959 and its Moscow correspondent in 1960. He was host of NBC-TV's *Today* show in 1961–1962, but returned to Europe as Brussels correspondent in 1963. He then served in Washington, D. C., as White House correspondent in 1964–1965. From 1965 to 1967 Chancellor was director of the Voice of America, after which he returned to NBC News.

CHANCELLOR, chan′sə-lər, **Richard** (died 1556), English mariner, who established the first trade between England and Russia. He was captain of a ship and "pilot-general" in an expedition led by Sir Hugh Willoughby in 1553 to seek a northeast passage to India. When other vessels missed an appointed rendezvous off the coast of Norway, Chancellor sailed into the White Sea and landed near Archangel, Russia.

Chancellor traveled overland to Moscow and was received by Czar Ivan IV. He arranged for the entry of English ships into Russian ports and for trading opportunities for English merchants. When he returned to England in 1554, the Muscovy Company was formed that to carry on the enterprise. Chancellor sailed again to Archangel in 1555 and passed the winter in Moscow. On his return voyage to England, he perished when the vessel on which he was sailing foundered off the coast of Scotland.

CHANCELLOR, chan′sə-lər, any of a number of diverse officers of church, state, or academic administration whose functions derive from the medieval office of that name. The title of chancellor was first applied to scribes in the Roman imperial system and subsequently adopted by the secular and ecclesiastical governments of medieval Europe.

Chancellor (*cancellarius*) was the title given by the Carolingian kings of France to the royal chaplain whose duties were the custody of his lord's seal and the direction of a scriptorium (writing office). In time the office in France and elsewhere became vested in the higher clergy— the archbishop of Mainz being archchancellor of the medieval Empire; the archbishop of Cologne, archchancellor of Italy; and the archbishop of Treves (Trier), archchancellor of Gaul and Arles (Burgundy). The two latter offices were honorific, but the archbishop of Mainz had real functions, even though in practice they were discharged by a vice chancellor.

In the emerging German principalities the chancellor was one of the most important ministers, and in the German Empire of 1871 the *Reichskanzler* (Reichschancellor) became in effect prime minister and has remained so.

In France the Carolingian office was continued by the Capetian kings, and the office of chancellor did not lapse until the French Revolution. It was revived by Napoleon but was finally abolished in 1848.

Chancellor of England. In England the organization of a royal scriptorium charged with preparing royal writs preceded the reign (1042– 1066) of Edward the Confessor. Although little is known of its staffing and processes, the old English administrative system, with its devotion to formal diplomatic instruments, was evidently well organized, and historians frequently refer to an English chancery of that period. However, the term is, strictly speaking, anachronistic, for there is no evidence to suggest that the title of chancellor existed in England as it did in France at that time. Some evidence suggests that it was borne by a royal chaplain during the Confessor's reign, but that his duties were connected with the scriptorium is uncertain. The fact that the title is not found in any Norman document before 1066 but does appear in the early years of the Norman Conqueror's reign in England would seem a further indication that the Confessor used the title, and historians infer that he borrowed it from France—possibly in connection with his adoption of the use of a great seal.

The early English chancellors, like their predecessors who did not bear that title, were royal chaplains, and the office was a steppingstone to a bishopric. Not until the 12th century were the office and a bishopric held simultaneously, and the conjuncture was rare until the 14th century. Three lay chancellors appear in rapid succession in the years 1340–1345, but laymen only exceptionally held the office before 1529, when Sir Thomas More was appointed.

After More's death laymen generally held the office, and from 1625 the chancellor of England has invariably been a layman. As lord chancellor, he presides over the House of Lords. As head of the English judiciary, he must be a lawyer of distinction, and consequently his appointment, though a party one, cannot be purely political. (For the evolution and nature of the chancellor's equitable jurisdiction, see CHANCERY.)

Chancellor of the Exchequer. Originally the chancellor of the exchequer was the clerk in charge of the duplicate royal seal kept in the exchequer. He appears with the present title in the first half of the 13th century, but his office did not assume importance until 1714, when the office of treasurer was permanently in commission, but with the first lord of the treasury and chancellor of the exchequer as the principal commissioners. From 1730, the first lord was identical with the prime minister, and the chancellor of the exchequer became the effective head of the treasury. Because the House of Commons controls finance, he must be a member.

Ecclesiastical and Academic Chancellors. In the 11th century the Curia of the Roman Catholic Church adopted the title of chancellor from the empire and applied it to its own administrative office (see CHANCERY, ROMAN CATHOLIC CHURCH), while in cathedral chapters another chancellor appeared as one of the principal officers. The title of chancellor given to the principal officer of a university is derived from the cathedral chapter's early guardianship of education. Thus the nascent university of Paris came under the authority of the chancellor of the cathedral of Paris and only at a much later date, with royal assistance, obtained its own independent chancellor. The university at Oxford was modeled on that at Paris, but because Oxford was not a cathedral city, the university lay outside the authority of a cathedral chancellor. Nevertheless the chancellor of the university was an officer of the bishop of Lincoln and only gradually escaped episcopal control. The office followed a parallel course at Cambridge.

New universities established in England or under English influence have had their chief officers designated chancellor. But the office, both in ancient and modern universities, has become honorific, and its functions are performed by a vice chancellor.

Of the variety of officials to whom the title of chancellor has been given, the most important remaining one is the diocesan chancellor of the Anglican and Roman Catholic churches. The former combines the medieval duties of vicargeneral and official. The title is post-Reformation, and the office, which is judicial, is usually filled by a layman. The latter may be described broadly as the head of the bishop's secretariat.

HENRY GERALD RICHARDSON, *Coauthor of The Governance of Mediaeval England"*

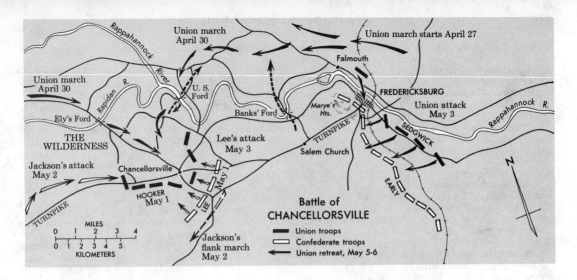

Battle of
CHANCELLORSVILLE

- Union troops
- Confederate troops
- Union retreat, May 5-6

CHANCELLORSVILLE, Battle of, chan′sə-lərz-vil, in the Civil War, fought May 1–4, 1863, in north central Virginia about 50 miles (80 km) southwest of Washington, D. C. It was the last great Confederate victory won by Gen. Robert E. Lee and his indomitable corps commander Lt. Gen. Thomas J. "Stonewall" Jackson. This battle is remarkable for the outstanding skill, courage, and tactical genius displayed by these two great leaders who fought and won against heavier odds than they had ever before encountered. Unfortunately for the South, these two generals were destined never again to go into battle together, for it was on this field that Jackson fell, severely wounded.

Almost five months before, at Fredericksburg, the Confederate Army of Northern Virginia had administered a severe defeat to the Army of the Potomac, then commanded by Maj. Gen. Ambrose E. Burnside. The Union attacks on that date, Dec. 13, 1862, had been repulsed with casualties totaling more than 12,600 men. After this defeat President Abraham Lincoln had been forced to select a new commander.

He chose Maj. Gen. Joseph Hooker, popularly known as "Fighting Joe." The new commander had been confronted immediately with a severe morale problem, but by judicious granting of furloughs and by other measures, he brought the Union Army of the Potomac back to a condition of combat readiness. Furthermore, by the end of April, the strength of that army had been increased until it numbered 134,000 men. This gave the North an unusual preponderance of strength, for General Lee, at this time, did not have the entire Army of Northern Virginia serving with him. Lt. Gen. James Longstreet had been dispatched with two divisions to the Suffolk area in southeastern Virginia. Lee had under his command in the Fredericksburg area a total of only about 60,000 men to confront Hooker's army of over twice that strength.

Hooker's Plan. The plan that General Hooker evolved for bringing Lee's army to battle was excellent. The Army of the Potomac was organized into seven corps of two or three divisions each. With three corps, Hooker would march westward, on a wide turning movement, well beyond Lee's left flank, cross the Rappahannock and the Rapidan, then swing east toward the Confederate positions overlooking Fredericksburg. As the movement progressed, new fords of the Rappahannock and more direct routes would be opened up, so that additional Union corps could cross the river. This massing of troops on General Lee's left flank should force the Confederate army either to accept battle at a great disadvantage or to retreat southward toward Richmond. In addition, two Union corps were to cross below Fredericksburg to launch an attack at a critical moment or join in a pursuit to the southward.

Lee's Reaction. Most generals, outflanked and with an army of only six divisions opposed to a much larger force approaching from the west, and with another threatening from across the river in front, would surely have retreated southward to another defensive position, but not Lee. On April 29, learning of the movement against his left flank, he dispatched one division in that direction, then another division, and finally, on May 1, three more divisions under Gen. "Stonewall" Jackson toward that threatened flank, thus leaving only one Confederate division to try to hold Fredericksburg against two Union corps.

Jackson's action upon arrival on the scene was also fully characteristic of him. Instead of waiting to be attacked in a hastily prepared defensive position, he launched a counterattack. This unexpected and forceful assault so surprised and unnerved General Hooker that he halted his own advancing troops. Some of the Union corps commanders, being closer to the scene of action and thus better able to judge events, protested vigorously, but to no avail. Thus the first day of battle, May 1, which should have brought a large, threatening army down upon Gen. Lee's left flank, had ended in a Southern counterattack, leaving the initiative completely in the hands of the Confederates.

Jackson's Flank Attack. Southern plans for the next day, May 2, were prepared at a night meeting of Lee and Jackson. No one else was present at that conference, so no one knows who first suggested the daring plan that was adopted. It called for a further subdivision of the Confederate army in the face of their enemy. Jackson was to take three of the Confederate divisions on a long march around in front of the Union army using a little-known road, then fall upon Hooker's opposite (western) flank in a surprise assault. It was a bold, risky plan that might not have been undertaken if the action of the preceding day had not clearly indicated that "Fighting Joe" Hooker had become unnerved, overcautious, and apprehensive of the future. The danger inherent in such a plan was that it would leave Lee with only two divisions to hold the line all day against Hooker's army. It called for the working of a gigantic bluff by Lee to keep the Union army from learning what was happening and to prevent them from carrying out an attack on his little force.

When, at 5:15 P. M. on May 2, Jackson's men burst forth from the tangled mass of undergrowth and stubby little trees known as the Wilderness, the attack came as a tremendous shock to the Union soldiers posted on that distant flank. For a time it seemed that nothing could halt the power and speed of the assault. But that night the Confederate cause was dealt a shattering blow. While on reconnaissance between the lines, "Stonewall" Jackson was shot and severely wounded by some of his men firing into the darkness. On May 10, eight days later, he died of pneumonia. The South would never find another leader to take his place.

The Final Actions. On the next day, May 3, the two Confederate wings were able to unite, preparatory to advancing in a concerted attack on the morrow. During part of this day General Hooker was out of action. He had been leaning against a pillar of the Chancellor House when a cannonball struck it, rendering him unconscious. It would have been far better for the Union cause if he had then relinquished command, but he refused.

On this same day, Maj. Gen. John Sedgwick, commanding the Union troops already across the river near Fredericksburg, attacked. Although calls for help from Hooker had left Sedgwick with only one Union corps, his men valiantly stormed Marye's Heights and drove Maj. Gen. Jubal A. Early's lone Confederate division before them toward Chancellorsville, as far as Salem Church. This new threat from the east forced General Lee to suspend his attack on Hooker and turn back to assist Early. On May 4, General Sedgwick was attacked, and, not receiving any aid from Hooker, he was forced to retreat. These two engagements are sometimes separately designated as the Battles of Marye's Heights and Salem Church, but in fact they were part of the larger Battle of Chancellorsville.

General Lee then turned again to attack Hooker but discovered that the main Union army was retiring to safety across the river. In this long, complex battle, Union casualties totaled about 17,000, while the South lost about 13,000 men. It was the last great Confederate victory in Virginia and the prelude to Lee's second invasion of the North.

JOSEPH B. MITCHELL
Author of "Decisive Battles of the Civil War"

Bibliography

Bigelow, John, Jr., *The Campaign of Chancellorsville* (New Haven 1910).
Esposito, Col. Vincent J., ed., *The West Point Atlas of American Wars*, vol. 1 (New York 1959).
Freeman, Douglas S., *R. E. Lee: A Biography* (New York 1934–1935).
Freeman, Douglas S., *Lee's Lieutenants* (New York 1942–1944).
Henderson, Col. Lt. Gen. George F. R., *Stonewall Jackson and the American Civil War* (New York 1932).
Johnson, Robert U., and Buel, Clarence C., eds., *Battles and Leaders of the Civil War*, vol. 3, new ed. (New York 1956).
Stackpole, Lt. Gen. Edward J., *Chancellorsville* (Harrisburg, Pa., 1958).
Steele, Maj. Matthew F., *American Campaigns* (Harrisburg, Pa., 1958).
Williams, Kenneth P., *Lincoln Finds a General*, 3 vols. (New York 1949–1952).

CHANCERY, chan'sə-rē, a system of jurisprudence administered by courts of equity. It had its beginnings in 13th century England. The courts of that day, known as common-law courts, paid such rigid deference to forms, precedents, and procedural niceties that injustice often resulted. A person thus aggrieved would have no remedy except a plea to the grace of the king, who would refer such petitions to his secretary, the "chancellor." In due course, these petitions came to be presented directly to the chancellor by the suitors, and thus gradually, at a time that history cannot fix precisely, the court of chancery became established.

Chancery provided relief only in those cases in which the common-law remedies were inadequate or nonexistent. Thus, if a poor man was sued in a common-law court by a wealthy but dishonest lord of the realm, the poor man might obtain "equitable relief" from chancery if he could demonstrate that his adversary had bribed the jurors. If a contract was breached, a common-law court could grant only money damages, whereas chancery could require "specific performance" by the defaulting party. Such orders, requiring a party to act or refrain from acting, are still peculiarly equitable and are known as "injunctions."

The court of chancery and the common-law courts thus existed side by side in England, each with a distinct jurisdiction and procedure, and each applying rules of law that were distinct, though complementary. Under the Judicature Acts of 1873 and 1876, however, the court of chancery was made a division of the high court of justice, which is itself one of two departments of the supreme court of judicature.

In the United States, development of equity jurisprudence followed quite naturally from the colonies' adoption of the English common law. Though some states adhered to the early English practice and established separate common-law and chancery (equity) courts, the trend today in every state except Delaware and Tennessee has been to merge the two. In the other states and in the federal jurisdiction, despite merger, the term "equity" retains its vitality. The nature of the relief remains the same; its administration has merely been made more effective.

LINDA ALDEN RODGERS
School of Law, Columbia University

CHANCERY, chan'sə-rē. In the Roman Catholic Church the Apostolic Chancery is the office responsible for drafting and sending out pontifical letters. The most important of these documents are called "bulls" (see BULL, PAPAL). The chancery, headed by a cardinal chancellor, is one of the offices included in the Roman Curia. The name "chancery" is also applied to the administrative headquarters of a diocese.

CHANCHIANG, jän'jyäng', is a major seaport in South China, situated on northeast Luichow Peninsula in Kwangtung province. The name is also spelled *Tsamkong*. Facing the Kwangchow Wan and sheltered by Tunghai and Naochow islands, the port of Chanchiang is second only to Canton in the area, and serves a large part of Southwest China.

The completion of the Litang-Chanchiang railway linking the port with the Kweichow-Kwangsi railway resulted in a rapid growth of the trade and manufacturing of Chanchiang in the 1950's and 1960's. A navigation channel, 30 feet (9 meters) wide and 25 miles (40 km) long, links the port with the sea. A 1,280-foot (390-meter) deepwater pier and a 1,122-foot (342-meter) pier for smaller vessels have been constructed, capable of accommodating simultaneously one 25,000-ton (22,500-metric ton) oil tanker, two 10,000-ton (9,000-metric ton) vessels, and three 5,000-ton (4,500-metric ton) vessels and of handling 1,700,000 tons (1,530,000 metric tons) of cargo annually. Chanchiang is one of China's major producers of calcium phosphate, ammonium chloride, and caustic soda.

In October 1899, a French fleet entered the Chanchiang embayment and forced China to lease to France what was subsequently known as the Kwangchow Wan Territory, a 325-square mile (840-sq km) area including Chanchiang and the nearby coastal strip and offshore islands. During World War II, the Japanese occupied the area from 1942 to 1945. French rule came to an end in August 1945 when the termination of the lease was signed in Chungking. Population: (1958) 170,000.

KUEI-SHENG CHANG, *University of Washington*

CHANCROID, shang'kroid, is a venereal infection caused by the bacterium *Hemophilus ducreyi*. Chancroid is generally much less common than syphilis and other venereal diseases, and it is important that it be distinguished from these diseases as well as from nonvenereal infections that occur in the genital area. Through careful examination by a physician and special laboratory tests to identify the disease-producing bacterium, chancroid can be easily diagnosed.

The symptoms of the disease generally develop from a few days to two weeks after a person has had sexual relations with an infected individual. The first sign of chancroid is a small red papule on the genitals or surrounding skin. Within a few days the papule enlarges and develops pus in its center. It soon opens and drains, leaving a painful ulcer surrounded by a swollen red area. Unlike the chancre of syphilis, the ulcer is soft. Often, the infection spreads, and secondary eruptions appear. Unless the case is treated, the lymph nodes in the groin become enlarged and may develop abscesses.

If chancroid is diagnosed early and treatment is started immediately, the disease can be quickly cured. It is generally treated with sulfonamides or broad spectrum antibiotics, such as chlortetracyline (aureomycin), oxytetracyline (terramycin), or chloramphenicol.

LOUIS J. VORHAUS, M. D.
Cornell University Medical College

CHANDA, chän'də, is a historic town of central India, in southern Maharashtra state. It is situated about 85 miles (137 km) southeast of Nagpur and was the old capital of the ancient Gond dynasty that ruled the area from the 12th century until its incorporation into the Mughul (Mogul) empire. The Gonds continued to reign as feudatories until they were ousted by the Marathas in 1751. The city is surrounded by a stone fortification 10 feet (3 meters) thick and has many ancient ruins, royal tombs, and statuary. Chanda is a commercial and rail center and produces textiles and bamboo, gold, and silver work. Population: (1962) 95,690.

Brass chandelier (late 18th century) from the Netherlands.

CHANDELIER, shan-də-lir', any lighting fixture suspended from a ceiling or other high place. The principal use of the chandelier is to provide light, which may be done by candles, oil lamps of either a simple or a complex type, gas, or electricity. But many chandeliers are designed and decorated so that they are ornamental as well as utilitarian.

Early History. The early history of the chandelier, as of all lighting fixtures, is obscure and lost in antiquity. Probably the earliest examples were simply branches hung from the ceiling of a cave to hold a pine knot or other resinous piece of wood in a fork or prong. Iron frames of a simple nature were probably the next step, an improvement that prevented burning the form.

During prehistoric times simple lamps were fashioned from stone and clay. These had an open reservoir to hold an animal oil or vegetable oil and a channel into which a wick could be laid. The wick, made of rush, hemp, or some similar substance, was ignited in the oil. This kind of lamp could be suspended by leather thongs or other materials and thus formed the ancestors of the true chandeliers. The Egyptians fashioned these simple lamps of clay and bronze and often suspended them from frames. Some frames were highly elaborate in ancient Greece and Rome, where bronze was the favorite material.

Middle Ages. During the Middle Ages true chandeliers became more popular adjuncts to everyday life. They were generally made of iron, bronze, or brass, and they incorporated the whole range of Gothic design into their forms. They most often burned a type of candle, but hanging spout lamps were also known. Candle-burning lamps were composed of a shaft with a hook at the top fastened either to a chain or to the ceiling, and arms that radiated from the central shaft. Three or four arms were commonly used,

Simple proportions typical of the neoclassic style are maintained in this late 18th century New England piece of tinned sheet metal (*above*). Contrasting with this severity of style is the elaborate design of the English (or Irish) chandelier of the same period (*right*).

and each arm terminated in a socket or nozzle that actually held the candle in place.

Renaissance. During the Renaissance, chandeliers became more elaborate. The same materials that had been used in the Middle Ages were generally in use except in Italy, where some relatively simple fixtures were made of glass. In addition to containing more candle arms to provide greater light, chandeliers of this period became more ornamental and elaborate. The float lamp, which was known as early as the 7th century, became widely popular. It consisted of a cylindrical vessel, usually of glass, abruptly flared at the top, which could be used as a reservoir. This vessel was partially filled with water on which floated a thin layer of oil. In the oil a wick was floated on a dish of cork, wood, or paper. These float lamps were set into frames and hung by chains. Some of these chandeliers were very elaborate—especially those fashioned for use in churches. Float lamps were also popular at this time in both the Middle East and the Orient.

Baroque. During the baroque period chandeliers became still more ornate. The grotesque and human forms common to all the arts of this period were often incorporated into chandeliers. A standard form of candle chandelier with a heavy ball as an integral part of the shaft was developed. From the ball detachable candle arms were extended. Brass was the most common material for chandeliers of this type, although pewter and sometimes silver were also used. Toward the middle of the 17th century the shaft was expanded by placing another ball or even two balls above the first, so that two or three rows of candle arms could be used.

The 18th Century. The 18th century probably brought the chandelier to its greatest opulence and importance. All materials from previous periods continued to be used, but glass chandeliers became a special luxury item. The great glass industries of England and Ireland produced chandeliers of extraordinary beauty and bril-

liance of design. The earliest of these were derived from Italian, especially Venetian, chandelier designs. They were composed of a heavy central shaft, sometimes with cut glass decoration, from which several arms radiated. The arms were occasionally notched or cut in some manner, but usually without glass drops or pendants. By the 1740's a glass drip pan was commonly placed under the candle socket and often decorated with cut glass pendants.

As the century progressed, chandeliers became increasingly elaborate, and strings of beads as well as cut swags began to ornament the area between the candle arms. The number of candles was increased to 12, 24, or more. This type of chandelier was fixed on the ceiling to a pulley that allowed it to be pulled down for cleaning and refilling with candles. In the summer they were often not used because of the amount of heat they generated. These elaborate glass chandeliers found a waiting market in the Orient and in the English colonies.

Because of English guild regulations, silver chandeliers were hallmarked by the individual silversmiths. For this reason we know the names of some individual designers of silver chandeliers; almost none of the glass chandeliers can be traced to their designers. However, only a few silver chandeliers survive. Some of the elaborate 18th century brass chandeliers were also marked with a maker's name, or were in some way engraved so that it is possible to identify and date them. The same is true of pewter ones.

The 18th century saw the widespread production of furniture design books in England and in France. Many of these books included engravings of chandeliers. While the rococo style dominated around midcentury, highly complex chandeliers were executed in carved and gilded wood and ormolu. In some instances, rococo chandeliers were further ornamented with cut glass or rock crystal drops. In the neoclassic 1760's, elaborate chandeliers continued to be popular; they were often based on antique Greek and Roman models.

Not all the chandeliers produced during the 18th century were in the grand tradition. Country craftsmen, using wood and tinned sheet iron, often fashioned chandeliers with simple beauty that were aesthetically pleasing. These were generally made to hold candles but a few surviving examples held primitive pottery lamps.

The 19th and 20th Centuries. During the 19th century, a great revolution in artifiical lighting took place. At the beginning of the 1800's, traditions of the preceding century held sway, with the production of highly elaborate candle-burning chandeliers in ormolu and glass. The Empire style was dominant in the design of these pieces, which were often virtually covered with emblems and symbols borrowed from antiquity. However, gas, which had been in limited use during the 18th century, began to enjoy a wider vogue. Because of technical improvements and especially the innovations of the Industrial Revolution, it was now possible to supply gas at a cost that made it practical to use in residences.

Historical revivalism, the borowing of elements from varied earlier sources, became the dominant design trend by the mid-19th century. Enormous and fanciful chandeliers for both candles and gas were produced in styles that ranged from Gothic to Renaissance, Louis XV, and Louis XVI. During the second half of the century elements from these different styles were often combined in one piece. This trend, called eclecticism, resulted in the creation of chandeliers so elaborate that they seemed to defy their function of providing light.

The introduction of kerosine in the 1850's brought a further change to chandelier production. Glass kerosine-burning lamps were fitted into a great variety of frames made of brass, copper, or iron. Kerosine provided a far more intense light than either candles or gas. Most of these chandeliers were also designed in the vocabulary of historical revivalism.

Toward the end of the 19th century the *art nouveau* movement began to dominate design in Europe. In addition, the invention of the incandescent light bulb by Thomas Alva Edison brought the greatest innovation to lighting yet known. Chandeliers based on natural forms such as flowers were designed to hold electric bulbs.

In the 20th century the chandelier in its original form, as a suspended object of illumination, lost some of its popularity, and it began to be used more for decoration only. Illumination, direct or diffused, from the ceiling came to be provided instead by spotlights or hidden lights. However, many people continued to favor the warm glow and romantic atmosphere associated with chandeliers.

JOSEPH T. BUTLER, *Author of*
"Candleholders in America, 1650–1900"

CHANDERNAGORE, chun-dər-nə-gôr′, is a town in the state of West Bengal, India, on the Hooghly River, 21 miles (34 km) north of Calcutta. It was established by the French as a trading center in 1673, and was ceded to France by the Mughul (Mogul) emperor Aurangzeb, in 1688. Seized by the British in 1757 and again in 1794, it was each time restored to French rule. France yielded the enclave to India in 1950, and the transfer became final on April 11, 1952. Jute milling is the major industry. Population: (1961) 67,105.

CHANDIGARH'S Secretariat Buildings, like the planned city itself, was designed by architect Le Corbusier.

CHANDIGARH, chun′dē-gär, is the capital of Punjab and Haryana states in northwestern India. The city is located at the foot of the Siwalik Hills, 30 miles (48 km) north of Ambala and 70 miles (113 km) south of Simla, a hill station in the Lesser Himalaya. Chandigarh is situated in an area of considerable natural beauty, and its climate is mild. There are good railroad and air connections to other Punjab and Haryana cities and to New Delhi.

Chandigarh was built after the 1947 partition of Punjab granted the former capital, Lahore, to Pakistan. Work on the site commenced in 1950, and Chandigarh replaced Simla as capital in 1953. In 1966, Punjab was divided into Punjab and Haryana states, and Chandigarh, which is on their common border, became the capital of both states. The city and a 10-mile area surrounding it was constituted a union territory.

The city is the creation of the French architect Le Corbusier and is one of the three planned cities in India (the other two are New Delhi and Gandhinagar, in Gujarat state). The city is laid out in 30 rectangular sections which are integrated by a grid of highways. Twenty-four sections are residential. Chandigarh has boldly styled government buildings and residential quarters that contrast sharply with any found in India. The central monument is an open hand, 50 feet (8 meters) high, which symbolizes the harmony among men. To the northeast of the city is a large artificial lake, and the garden on Pinjora, a replica of Srinigar's Shalimar garden, is nearby. Population: (1961) 99,262.

ROBERT C. KINGSBURY, *Indiana University*

CHANDLER, chan′dlər, **Albert Beniamin** (1898–), American public official, known as "Happy" Chandler. Born in Corydon, Ky., on July 14, 1898, he served in the U. S. Army during World War I. Holding a B.A. from Transylvania College (1921) and an LL.B. from the University of Kentucky (1924), Chandler began law practice at Versailles, Ky., and simultaneously coached football at Centre College. Turning to politics as a Democrat, he rose rapidly from the Kentucky senate (1930–1931) to lieutenant governor (1931–1935) and then to governor (1935–1939). In 1939 he was appointed to the U. S. Senate to fill an unexpired term, and he was then elected to the seat in 1940. Reelected in 1942, he resigned in 1945 to become high commissioner of baseball, and his six years in that office were marked by frequent controversies with the club owners.

After several years of private life he was returned to the governorship (1955–1959). In his terms as governor he introduced direct primary elections, sponsored an extensive public highway building program, improved Kentucky's school system, and initiated a retirement system for state employees and public school teachers. An ebullient and colorful man who loved politics, Chandler was an unsuccessful contender for the Democratic presidential nomination in 1956 and for the Senate and governorship in other years.

DAVID LINDSEY
California State College at Los Angeles

CHANDLER, Raymond (1888–1959), American novelist and screenwriter, famous for his tough, literate crime novels, in which his hero is the private detective Philip Marlowe. Chandler was born in Chicago on July 23, 1888. He grew up in England and attended Dulwich College near London. In 1912 he left England for California, and in 1914 he went to Canada to join the Canadian Gordon Highlanders. After World War I he returned to Los Angeles, where he entered the oil business.

When Chandler lost his job during the Depression, he turned to writing, publishing his first story in the magazine *Black Mask* in 1933. The first of his seven novels, *The Big Sleep*, appeared in 1939. With *Farewell My Lovely* (1940), *The High Window* (1942), and *The Lady in the Lake* (1943), he became internationally famous. Chandler also wrote several screenplays, including *Double Indemnity* (1944). Chandler died in La Jolla, Calif., on March 26, 1959.

DOROTHY GARDINER
Author of "West of the River"

CHANDLER, William Eaton (1835–1917), American lawyer, journalist, and public official. He was born in Concord, N. H., on Dec. 28, 1835, and received a law degree from Harvard in 1854. As a journalist on the Concord *Monitor and Statesman*, he was nicknamed the "stormy petrel" of state politics. A supporter of the Union cause in the Civil War, he was elected speaker of the state's house of representatives in 1863.

Chandler held appointments under presidents Abraham Lincoln and Andrew Johnson in the navy and treasury departments. He was elected a Republican national committeeman in 1867, and subsequently helped direct several presidential campaigns; after the election of 1876, he helped swing disputed electoral votes to Rutherford B. Hayes. Later a supporter of James G. Blaine's presidential aspirations, he was named secretary of the navy (1882) by President Chester A. Arthur in an attempt to conciliate the Blaine faction of the party. As secretary, he began a modern shipbuilding program. He left office in 1885 amid accusations regarding contract favoritism. From 1887 to 1901 he was a U. S. senator from New Hampshire. He died in Concord on Nov. 30, 1917.

RONALD A. WELLS, *Simmons College*

CHANDLER, Zachariah (1813–1879), American senator, who was a leading Radical Republican in the Civil War period. He was born in Bedford, N. H., on Dec. 10, 1813. After a common school and academy education, he went west. He settled in Detroit, where he started a general store and became a rich man. In 1851 he was elected Whig mayor of Detroit, but the next year he was defeated in the race for governor. Chandler was a founder of the Republican party at Jackson, Mich., in 1854, and in January 1857 he was elected to the U. S. Senate.

Chandler became powerful as chairman (1861–1875) of the Committee on Commerce, in which post he controlled the flow of federal money into the growing Midwest. Aided by this position, he consolidated his hold as Republican boss of Michigan. During the Civil War he was an unrelenting foe of the Confederates, of Britain (which built their ships), and of the antiwar Copperheads. During the Grant era when he was a "Stalwart" and chairman of the Republican Congressional Committee, Chandler was as noted for his partisanship as for his fine style of living and his huge bewhiskered figure. In 1875, after Chandler had failed to win reelection to the Senate, Grant appointed him secretary of the interior. But President Hayes, whose election Chandler helped engineer in 1876 as chairman of the Republican National Committee, turned him out. He was reelected senator in 1879. He died in Chicago on Nov. 1, 1879, a highly popular figure.

JOSEPH A. BOROMÉ
The City College, New York

CHANDLER is a city in Arizona, in Maricopa county, 25 miles (40 km) southeast of Phoenix. The city is a winter resort and a trading center in the irrigated farmlands of the Salt River Valley. Cotton, alfalfa, citrus fruits, sugarbeets, and safflower are the principal crops. Chandler's industries include cotton processing, sugar refining, electronics, and the cutting and polishing of diamonds. Gila River Indian Reservation is just west of the city. Williams Air Force Base, established in 1941, is 10 miles (16 km) to the east. Chandler was founded in 1912 and incorporated in 1920. It is governed by a council and manager. Population: 13,763.

CHANDOS, shan'dos, is a title in the English peerage that is borne by members of the Brydges family.

SIR JOHN BRYDGES, 1ST BARON CHANDOS, (1490?–1557), served with Henry VIII in France and was knighted there in 1513. A supporter of Edward VI and Mary, he helped suppress Sir Thomas Wyatt's rebellion. As lieutenant of the Tower of London in 1553–1554, he had custody of Wyatt and Lady Jane Grey. He was created 1st Baron Chandos in 1554. He died at Sudeley Castle, Gloucestershire, on April 12, 1557.

JAMES BRYDGES, 1ST DUKE OF CHANDOS (1673–1744), was born on Jan. 1, 1673, the son of the 8th Baron. As paymaster general of the forces abroad during the War of the Spanish Succession, he amassed a great personal fortune from war taxes. He was made Viscount Wilton and Earl Carnarvon in 1714 and Marquess of Carnarvon and 1st Duke of Chandos in 1719. George Frideric Handel composed the oratorio *Esther* in the Duke's service, and Alexander Pope satirized Cánons, Chandos' magnificent home in Middlesex. Chandos died on Aug. 9, 1744.

CHANDOS, shan'dos, **Sir John** (died 1370), English soldier in the Hundred Years' War. He fought at Cambrai in 1337 and helped defeat the French at Crécy in 1346 and at Poitiers in 1356. At Poitiers his vigilance saved the life of his friend and commander, Edward the Black Prince. Soon afterward he was appointed "regent and lieutenant" of the king of England in France and vice-chamberlain of the royal household. Given the lands of the Viscount of St.-Sauveur in the Cotentin, Chandos became constable of Guienne in 1362. Commanding the English forces at Auray, he won a victory there in 1364 and took as prisoner the French hero Bertrand Du Guesclin. In 1367 he fought once more under the Black Prince at Nájera, Spain, defeating the French and again capturing Du Guesclin. He was named seneschal of Poitou in 1369. Chandos was one of the original Knights of the Garter. He was wounded in battle at Lussac-les-Châteaux near Poitiers and died at Mortemer, France, on Jan. 1, 1370.

CHANDRAGUPTA, chun-drə-gōōp'tə, was the first historical emperor of India and the founder of the Maurya dynasty in the early 4th century B.C. He is often known as *Chandragupta Maurya.* After Alexander the Great retreated from India in 325 B.C., Chandragupta overthrew Dhana Nanda, ruler of Magadha, a large Gangetic empire. He was crowned sometime between 324 and 322 B.C. and became emperor with the aid of Brahman Chanakya (Kautilya), author of the *Arthrasastra,* the celebrated manual on ancient Indian polity.

Around 305 B.C., Chandragupta defeated Alexander's general Seleucus Nicator in the Punjab, and through a pact with him acquired four Greek satrapies in Afghanistan and Baluchistan. His empire included all of northern India and stretched as far north as Kabul in Afghanistan. It was prosperous and highly organized and it was expanded by his son Bindusura and by his grandson Asoka.

B. G. GOKHALE, *Wake Forest University*

CHANDRAGUPTA I, chun-drə-gōōp'tə (reigned c. 320–c. 330 A.D.), was king in India, the first Gupta to assume the title of emperor. Grandson of Srigupta, the earliest known Gupta, he began his rise to power when he married Kumaradevi, a Licchavi princess of what is now Nepal. The beginning of the Gupta dynasty dates from 319–320 A.D., the year of Chandragupta's wedding or accession, or both. His rule extended over parts of Bengal, Bihar, and Uttar Pradesh.

B. G. GOKHALE, *Wake Forest University*

CHANDRAGUPTA II, chun-drə-gōōp'tə, was a ruler of the Gupta empire in northern India, who reigned about 380 to about 413 A.D. He was the son of Samudragupta. He wrested Gujarat (mainland Gujarat) and Saurastra (peninsular Gujarat) from the Sakas, removing the last traces of foreign rule from India and giving the Guptas control of Indian trade with the Roman world. The Chinese Buddhist pilgrim Fa Hsien visited India at this time and commented on the kingdom's prosperity and benign administration. It is believed that the Sanskrit poet Kalidasa stayed at the court and that the legends surrounding the shadowy emperor Vikramaditya refer to Chandragupta II.

B. G. GOKHALE, *Wake Forest University*

CHANDRASEKHAR, chun-drə-shā'kər, **Subrahmanyan** (1910–   ), American astrophysicist and theoretical physicist, who established powerful mathematical methods of wide scope. Born in Lahore (now in Pakistan) on Oct. 19, 1910, Chandrasekhar early showed considerable mathematical powers, which he soon turned to astronomical problems. In 1930 he went to Trinity College, Cambridge, where he was influenced by A. S. Eddington, R. H. Fowler, and E. A. Milne. One of his earliest papers concerned the physical interpretation of the broad bright lines in the spectra of expanding stars. A series of investigations on stellar interiors and stellar models led to his important treatise *An Introduction to the Study of Stellar Structure* (1939).

Chandrasekhar went to the University of Chicago in 1937. He did important research on white dwarf stars, the chemical composition of stars, and the theory of radiation transfer in the atmospheres of stars and planets. His extensive work on the stability of stellar systems resulted in *Principles of Stellar Dynamics* (1943). Later he made mathematical investigations into the difficult problems of convection and turbulence in fluids and the stability of fluid motions in the presence of rotation, magnetic forces, and heat sources.

JOSEPH ASHBROOK
Editor of "Sky and Telescope"

CHANEL, shȧ-nel', **Gabrielle Bonheur** (1883–1971), French fashion designer and perfume manufacturer, famous for the simple, elegant "Chanel look." She was born on Aug. 19, 1883, at Saumur, Maine-et-Loire. In 1914 she went to Paris and with a sister opened a small hat shop.

During the 1920's, "Coco" Chanel became an established dress designer and recognized leader of fashion. She replaced the long-skirted, elaborately decorated dresses of the pre-World War I era with the "Chanel look," distinguished by the casually elegant comfort of simple wool jersey suits with straight collarless jackets and short skirts, the whole set off by ropes of fake pearls and other jewels. The House of Chanel later also made textiles and perfume, including Chanel No. 5. In 1938, Chanel gave up designing, but in 1954 she triumphantly reintroduced the Chanel look. The musical *Coco* (1969) was based on her life. She died in Paris on Jan. 10, 1971.

CHANEY, chā'nē, **Lon** (1883–1930), American motion picture actor. He was born in Colorado Springs, Colo., on April 1, 1883. His parents were deaf-mutes, and from learning to communicate with them by means of gestures and facial expression he developed an exceptional ability in pantomime that was fully exploited on the silent screen. In his most famous roles, as the hunchback Quasimodo in *The Hunchback of Notre Dame* (1923) and in *The Phantom of the Opera* (1925), Chaney played disfigured, twisted men who excited both revulsion and pity. For such roles he created his own elaborate makeup and, when necessary, designed devices to contort his body. Although his reputation rests mainly on his performances as grotesque characters in thrillers, several of them made with the great horror-film director Tod Browning, he was also successful without disguise, as in *The Big City* (1928) and *Laugh Clown Laugh* (1928). Chaney died on Aug. 26, 1930, in Los Angeles, Calif.

CHANG CHIH-TUNG, jäng jûr dŏong (1837–1909), was a Chinese government official and one of the first Chinese to realize the need for modern technological development in China. He was born in Nanpi, Hopeh province, on Sept. 2, 1837, and died on Oct. 4, 1909.

Brilliant and incorruptible, Chang was governor-general of Kwangtung-Kwangsi from 1884 to 1889, and of Hupei-Hunan from 1889 to 1907. He repeatedly urged the government to adopt policies that would protect China's frontiers against Western encroachment, and he helped keep South China free of the Boxer Rebellion in 1900. Although an advocate of Western-style industrial development, he insisted on retention of the Chinese values embodied in Confucianism.

JAMES R. SHIRLEY
Northern Illinois University

CHANG HSÜEH-LIANG, jäng shü-e′ lyäng (1898–), known as the "Young Marshal," is a former Manchurian warlord held in custody by the Chinese Nationalists since 1936. He became ruler of Manchuria in 1928, when his father, Chang Tso-lin (q.v.), was assassinated by the Japanese. He united China by accepting the authority of the Chinese central government, but lost Manchuria to Japan in 1932.

Chang was assigned to fight the Communists in the northwest, but he gradually came to favor a united front against Japan. He arrested Chiang Kai-shek at Sian on Dec. 12, 1936 and held him until the front was agreed upon. Chang was arrested after Chiang Kai-shek's release.

JAMES R. SHIRLEY
Northern Illinois University

CHANG TANG, jäng däng, is a high plain on the central and northwestern plateau of Tibet. It is an undissected plateau stretching about 700 miles (1,125 km) east and west and about 300 miles (480 km) north and south, with an elevation exceeding 17,000 feet (5,200 meters). Its surface is a windswept waste of salt lakes, great swamps, and barren mountains. Very few people live here and vegetation is scant. Because of the high elevation, the climate is very cold; freezing temperatures persist for at least 8 months of the year. The largest lake is Tengri Nor, with an area of 950 square miles (2,460 sq km). The Chang Tang area is probably one of the world's most inhospitable and least known places.

CHENGTSU WU, *Hunter College, New York*

CHANG TSO-LIN, jäng tsō lin (1873–1928), known as the "Old Marshal," was the Chinese warlord who controlled Manchuria from 1911 to 1928. He was born in Haicheng, Fengtien, the present Liaoning province. He was appointed governor of Fengtien in 1916 and became inspector general of all Manchuria in 1918. From 1920 on, he took part in the warlord battles that wracked China. He had gained control of Peking by 1926, but when the Kuomintang revolutionary forces advanced on the capital in 1928, he ordered his men to retreat. Japanese officers who feared that he might turn against Japanese interests in China bombed his railroad car as it neared Shengyang (Mukden) on June 4, 1928, and he died of wounds shortly after. His power was inherited by his son, Chang Hsüeh-liang (q.v.).

JAMES R. SHIRLEY
Northern Illinois University

CHANGAN. See SIAN.

CHANGCHOW, jäng′jō′, is a city in Kiangsu province, China, located between Nanking and Shanghai and connected with them by rail. Situated on the Grand Canal, Changchow is also known as *Wuchin* or *Wutsin*.

Modern industries, first developed in Changchow in the 1930's, were greatly expanded in the 1950's and 1960's. Among them, textiles, silk, food processing, and locomotive manufacturing are the major ones.

Located in the rich agricultural region of the Yangtze delta, Changchow is one of the famed scenic spots of Kiangnan (the lower Yangtze plain). Historical sites such as the Tien-ning Buddhist temple, Hung-mei Ko classical library, and Wen-pi pagoda have drawn tourists for centuries. Population: (1957) 300,000.

CHENGTSU WU, *Hunter College, New York*

CHANGCHUN, chäng′chŏon′, in the center of the Manchurian plain, is the capital of Kirin province in northeastern China. It is connected by railroad with Harbin in the north, with Korea via the border city of Tumen, and with Talien (part of Lüta), the seaport on the southern tip of Liaotung Peninsula. It is one of the major industrial cities of China. The first automobile manufacturing plant built in China is located in the southwestern part of the city. Other industries include machinery, cotton textiles, precision tools, and food processing.

As the cultural center of Kirin province, Changchun is the home of several institutions of higher education, scientific research institutes, and motion picture studios. The city is known for its broad tree-lined streets and its South Lake Park. Population: (1957) 975,000.

CHENGTSU WU, *Hunter College, New York*

CHANGE OF LIFE. See MENOPAUSE.

CHANGE RINGING is the art or science of producing variations in the ringing of a set of swinging bells. A set, known as a *ring,* may contain from 3 to 12 bells. The highest in tone, number one, is called the *treble;* the lowest, the *tenor.* Ringing the bells down the scale from treble to tenor is called ringing in *rounds.* In change ringing, the ringers, one for each bell, produce rhythmic permutations (*changes*) in the striking order. On three bells (*sixes*), it is possible to ring six changes, repeating the first at the end: 1 2 3/ 2 1 3/ 2 3 1/ 3 2 1/ 3 1 2/ 1 3 2/ 1 2 3. On 12 bells (*maximus*) the total number of possible changes is almost 480 million and would take about 38 years to ring.

A sequence of not less than 5,040 changes constitutes a true *peal;* any smaller number is a *touch.* Normally, the ringers limit their ringing to combinations they regard as most musical.

Scientific change ringing developed in England in the 17th century. *Grandsire,* one of the oldest methods, originated about 1640. Other early methods were composed by Fabian Stedman, who wrote a book on change ringing in 1668. The first complete peal of 5,040 changes was accomplished at the church of St. Peter Mancroft, Norwich, on May 2, 1715, in 3 hours and 18 minutes. See also BELL; CHIMES AND CARILLONS.

JAMES R. LAWSON, *Carillonneur*
The Riverside Church, New York City

CHANGELING, The, a tragedy by Thomas Middleton and William Rowley. The best of their collaborative dramas, it was first produced in 1624 and published in 1654.

The Changeling is a powerful psychological study of passion, particularly concerned with the consequences of crime. The heroine, Beatrice Joanna, falls in love with the honorable Alsemero and persuades her servant Deflores to murder her fiancé Alonzo. Deflores, violently impassioned with Beatrice, uses the murder to gain control over her; but the two are ultimately discovered, and Deflores kills Beatrice and himself. The play takes its title from a subplot in which one character poses as a half-wit and which ironically echoes the main plot.

CHANGKIAKOW, jäng'jyä'kō, a city in the northwestern corner of Hopeh province, China, is strategically located near one of the passes through the Great Wall of China. The city is sometimes known as *Changyüan* or *Wanchüan* in Chinese, and as *Kalgan* in the West.

Historically important as a center of trade between the pastoral Mongols and the agricultural Chinese, Changkiakow is today a transportation center connected by railroads with Peking to the east, Inner Mongolia to the west, and the Mongolian People's Republic to the north.

Major commodities traded here include tea, grains, fur, and skins, as well as silk and cotton fabrics. Industries include the manufacture of machinery and mining tools, food processing, and tanning. A special kind of mushroom produced here is well known in China as *kowmo*. Tsuerh Shan, to the west of Changkiakow, is a scenic resort. Population of Changkiakow: (1957) 480,000.

Chengtsu Wu
Hunter College, New York

CHANGPAI SHAN, chäng'bī'shän, is a mountain chain located in Kirin province, China, near the China-Korea border. The highest peak is Paitou Shan (White Head Mountain), which rises to 9,190 feet (2,801 meters) above sea level. This mountain, which was formed by volcanic action, is the site of Tienchih (Heavenly Lake), a famous crater lake. Paitou Shan is called Paektu San in Korean.

The lower ranges of Changpai Shan are considerably eroded. They have gentle slopes covered by dense forests. The lakes and streams in this mountain area have good power potential. Mineral deposits include coal and oil shale.

Chengtsu Wu
Hunter College, New York

CHANGSHA, chäng'shä', in China, is the capital city of Hunan province. Located on the east bank of the lower Siang (Hsiang) River, it is the political, economic, and cultural center of the province and the leading port on the river. The Siang River, which can accommodate fairly large vessels, flows into the Tungting Lake and therefore is connected to the Yangtze River. Changsha is also an important stop on the Peking-Canton railroad. Changsha, meaning "long sand" in Chinese, is named for the elongated sandy isle of Suiluchow in the Siang River.

Since the Tungting Lake Plain is one of the major "rice bowls" in China, Changsha has become one of the leading rice markets. Changsha is also the outlet for most of the native products

of the Siang basin, namely lumber, pigs, tung oil, and tea. Some handicraft products from Changsha are nationally well known, such as *Siang hsiu* (Siang embroidery), buttons, ya-yung-peh (special type of bed spread), pottery and ceramics, and leather products. Modern industries include machinery, food processing, and textiles. Antimony and lead are processed here.

Changsha is also one of the leading historical and cultural centers of China. On the west bank of the river, opposite the city, stands the beautifully landscaped Yolu hill. It is the home of historic Yolu College, in which the great philosopher of the Sung dynasty (960–1279), Chu Hsi, taught. Population: (1957) 703,000.

Chengtsu Wu
Hunter College, New York

CHANGSHU, chäng'shoo', a city in Kiangsu province, China, is located in the Yangtze delta between Shanghai and Nanking. It is one of the historic cities of this rich agricultural region. The climate is generally hot and humid, spring and autumn being the pleasantest seasons of the year. Rice, corn, wheat, tea, and mulberry leaves for silkworms are the major agricultural products of the area, and Changshu is a market for them. The city's traditional industries are for the most part handicrafts. Since Changshu is located approximately 45 miles (72 km) northwest of Shanghai, its modern industry is linked to Shanghai's. Cotton textiles, one such modern industry, has been established for many years in Changshu. Population: (1953) 101,400.

Chengtsu Wu
Hunter College, New York

CHANGTEH, chäng'du', is a city in northern Hunan province, China. It is located on the lower Yüan River, which flows into Tungting Lake. In the past, Changteh was a focal point for transportation and communication between northern China and the southwestern provinces of Kweichow and Yünnan. Today it is important as the commercial outlet for commodities such as lumber, tung oil, and herb medicine from the Yüan River drainage basin. Changteh's industries include textiles, food processing, and tanning. Population: (1953) 94,800.

Chengtsu Wu
Hunter College, New York

CHANGTU, chäng'doo', a city in eastern Tibet, is the capital of the Changtu Area, an autonomous district within the Tibet Autonomous Region of China. Both the city and the area are often called *Chamdo*. A land of towering mountains interrupted by deep river canyons (containing the upper courses of the Yangtze, Mekong, and Salween rivers), the Changtu Area is one of China's most inaccessible regions.

A modern road connecting Lhasa, Tibet's capital, with Szechwan province, was built across this region in the 1950's at great cost. Changtu is situated on this highway at the confluence of the Omuchu and Chiachu rivers, both tributaries of the Lungtzan Kiang (the upper Mekong).

The Changtu Area did not belong traditionally to Tibet, but was one of China's frontier regions. It was organized into the province of Sikang in 1939, and after the abolition of that province, in 1955, was made part of Tibet.

Chengtsu Wu
Hunter College, New York

ST. PETER PORT on the Channel Island of Guernsey, with part of Castle Cornet in the foreground. The castle stands at the entrance to the harbor.

DE WYS

CHANNEL ISLANDS, a group of islands in the English Channel, off the northwest coast of France. They are a possession of the British Crown, but they are not a part of the United Kingdom. Their total area is 75 square miles (194 sq km), and the population in 1971 was 126,363.

In order of size, the islands are Jersey, Guernsey, Alderney, Sark, Herm, Brechou, Jethou, and some islets with no permanent inhabitants. The only towns are St. Helier in Jersey, St. Peter Port in Guernsey, and St. Anne in Alderney.

The Channel Islands (*Îles Anglo-Normandes*) are the only portions of the old Duchy of Normandy still belonging to the Crown, to which they have been attached since the Norman Conquest (1066). They are divided into two autonomous communities, known as the Bailiwick of Jersey, of which the Écréhous and Minquiers, islets, are a part, and the Bailiwick of Guernsey which includes Alderney, Sark, Herm, Brechou, Jethou, Lihou, and Burhou. Each Bailiwick has its own laws, and Jersey, Guernsey, Alderney and Sark have each a constitution.

The People. The families of many of the inhabitants have lived in the islands for centuries, but there has been a constant influx of population, mainly from other parts of the British Isles and from Normandy and Brittany. The income tax, from which Sark is exempt, is much lower than in the United Kingdom, and no estate duties are levied. These and other advantages attract many residents, and the islands have long been a sanctuary for refugees. There is also much emigration, and Channel Islands names are not uncommon in Canada, Australia and New Zealand.

Protestants outnumber Roman Catholics, who, however, form a strong minority. In the country districts of Jersey and Guernsey and throughout Sark, some people speak, in addition to English, old Norman-French dialects, but to a decreasing extent. The use of French is not widespread.

The Land. Noted for their natural beauty, the islands are, for the most part, undulating and of moderate height, reaching a maximum of 454 feet (138 meters) in Jersey. Steep-sided valleys with small streams are numerous, while rugged cliffs and sandy bays are typical of the coast. The climate is mild, the average February temperature in Jersey and Guernsey being 43°F (6°C). In August it is 63°F (17°C) in Jersey and 60°F (16°C) in Guernsey. The average annual rainfall is 33 inches (838 mm) in Jersey and 36 inches (914 mm) in Guernsey. On sunny days, particularly in spring and summer, the landscape is extremely bright and the sea almost as blue as the Mediterranean.

Animal Life. Many species of birds have been recorded. Alderney, where sea-bird life is of exceptional interest, has two gannetries, one on Les Étacs and one on Ortac, rocks off the coast. Fish are not very plentiful, but special mention should be made of the ormer (abalone), a shellfish considered a great delicacy. Crabs are numerous and lobsters fairly so. Green lizards occur in Jersey and Guernsey and frogs in Jersey, Guernsey, Alderney and Sark; but grass snakes, toads, wall lizards, and palmated newts are confined to Jersey. Mammals include red squirrels in Jersey, stoats and hedgehogs in Jersey and Guernsey, moles in Jersey and Alderney, and rabbits in nearly all the islands.

Economic Life. The only cattle, usually tethered, are Jerseys in Jersey and Guernseys in Guernsey, Alderney, and Sark. They differ greatly, are renowned for their milk, and are exported to many parts of the world.

Truck farming is extensive, much seaweed being used as a manure. In Guernsey, greenhouses cover a very wide area. Important exports, mostly to the United Kingdom, include potatoes, tomatoes, cauliflower, fruit, and flowers.

Bank of England paper currency and United Kingdom coinage are legal tender, but the Bailiwick of Jersey has also local £10, £5, and £1 notes, and that of Guernsey, local £5 and £1 notes. The Channel Islands introduced decimal currency on Feb. 15, 1971, the same date as that chosen for the purpose by the United Kingdom. Thus each Bailiwick has its new ½ penny, 1 penny, and 2, 5, 10, and 50 pence coins. Each Bailiwick, too, has its own postal service and stamps of various designs, colors, and denominations. United Kingdom stamps are not valid there.

Tourist traffic is heavy in summer. Fast passenger steamers maintain regular services and a brisk trade is carried on by small freighters of various flags. The busy airports of Jersey and Guernsey are suitable for large aircraft.

Places of Interest. Places of major interest include Mont Orgueil and Elizabeth Castles and the Fishermen's Chapel in Jersey; Castle Cornet, the Little Chapel, and Hauteville House (Victor Hugo's home) in Guernsey; Telegraph Bay in Alderney; and the Seigneurie in Sark.

In Alderney, the streets of the little town of St. Anne are largely stone-paved and there is a fine 19th century church designed by Sir George Gilbert Scott. In Sark, often called the gem of the Channel Islands, the importation of automobiles is prohibited and tourists see the island on foot or in horse-drawn vehicles.

The islands are rich in prehistoric remains. Of a number of megalithic monuments, the most remarkable is the tumulus-covered passage grave of the Hougue Bie in Jersey. At La Cotte, a rock shelter in the same island, the discovery in 1910 of teeth of Neanderthal man is regarded by anthropologists as an event of great importance. At a lower level, proof of previous occupation by Pre-Mousterian man has likewise been found. Herm, a vacation resort, has prehistoric remains and a remarkable shell beach.

Government. The islands are governed by non-party legislative assemblies, which in Jersey, Guernsey, and Alderney are called States and in Sark the Chief Pleas. In these assemblies, the Lieutenant-Governors of Jersey and of Guernsey, appointed by the Crown as the personal representatives of the British Sovereign, have a voice, but no vote.

The Bailiff of Jersey and the Bailiff of Guernsey, also appointed by the Crown, are Presidents of the States and of the Royal Court of their respective islands; Alderney has an elected President and the holder of the highest position in Sark, if a man, is known as the Seigneur, and if a lady, as the Dame.

World War II. The Channel Islands were the only British territory to come under German control during World War II. Before German forces occupied them in July 1940, thousands of people had been evacuated to England. During the Occupation, some 2,000 British subjects were deported to Germany. Large numbers of prisoners and paid workers were brought from the Continent to build extensive fortifications, two vast underground hospitals, and other works. After the Liberation in May 1945, generous financial help was received from the British government. See also ALDERNEY; GUERNSEY; JERSEY; SARK.

H. TEULON PORTER
Member of the Société Jersiaise

Further Reading: Balleine, George, *The Bailiwick of Jersey*, new ed. (London 1962); Hooke, Wilfred, *The Channel Islands* (London 1953); Le Huray, C. Philip, *The Bailiwick of Guernsey* (London 1952); Uttley, John, *A Short History of the Channel Islands* (New York 1967); Wood, Alan and Mary, *Islands in Danger* (New York 1956).

CHANNEL ISLANDS NATIONAL MONUMENT, off the coast of southern California, includes two small islands, Santa Barbara and Anacapa. It was established in 1938 to protect a large sea lion rookery, colonies of nesting seabirds, and other unusual animal and plant life. Most of the monument is open ocean. The islands comprise less than 2 square miles (5 sq km) of the monument's total area, which is about 28 square miles (73 sq km).

CHANNEL-PORT AUX BASQUES, chan'əl pôrt ō bask, is a town on the southwest coast of Newfoundland, Canada, 7 miles (11 km) southeast of Cape Ray. It is the western terminus of the Newfoundland division of the Canadian National Railways and is linked with North Sydney, N. S., by a railway ferry. Channel-Port aux Basques is also an important fishing port. It was incorporated in 1945 from the separate communities of Channel and Port aux Basques. Population: 5,942.

CHANNELVIEW is an unincorporated community in eastern Texas, in Harris county, about 12 miles (19 km) east of Houston, of which it is a suburb. It is near Galveston Bay, just north of the Houston Ship Channel. The manufacture of petrochemicals, plastics, and fabricating materials are the chief industries. San Jacinto State Park, 2 miles (3 km) south, is the site of the decisive battle (April 1836) of the war for Texas independence in which Mexican forces under Santa Anna were defeated. The park's San Jacinto Monument commemorates the battle.

CHANNING, Carol (1923–), American actress, singer, and comedienne, best known as the warmly exuberant star of the musical comedies *Gentlemen Prefer Blondes* (1949) and *Hello Dolly!* (1963). She was born in Seattle, Wash., on Jan. 31, 1923, and began her acting career in summer stock in 1940. After several years in supporting stage roles and satirical nightclub acts, she attained stardom as Lorelei Lee, the coy gold digger in *Gentlemen Prefer Blondes*, which ran for nearly two years on Broadway. She also appeared on stage in *Wonderful Town* (1953), and *Show Girl* (1961); in the films *The First Traveling Saleslady* (1956) and *Thoroughly Modern Millie* (1967); and in various television shows.

Miss Channing's performance as Dolly Gallagher Levi, the brassy ambitious widow in *Hello Dolly!* earned her the 1964 Antoinette Perry best actress award.

CHANNING, Edward (1856–1931), American historian. He was born on June 15, 1856, in Dorchester, Mass., and grew up in the intellectual atmosphere of the Channing clan. His father, William Ellery Channing (1818–1901), was a poet, of uncertain talent. Channing was a product of Harvard, where he studied with Henry Adams and received his doctorate in 1880. He remained at Harvard throughout his life, as instructor and professor. As a friend of Harvard presidents Charles Eliot and Abbott Lowell he helped develop the Harvard graduate school system. Students, however, found him unpleasantly sarcastic and strict in the classroom.

Channing's reputation as a distinguished scholar rests on his 6-volume *History of the United States* (1905–1925), the last volume of which, *The War of Southern Independence,* brought him a Pulitzer Prize. He intended to write an 8-volume account from the Norse voyages to the close of the 19th century, but when he died in Cambridge, Mass., on Jan. 7, 1931, he was still working on the seventh volume. Channing's work, which also included the early monograph *Town and County Governments in the English Colonies* (1884) and *A Student's History of the United States* (1898), was characterized by prodigious research, a striving for objectivity, and a freshness of view.

Some of his judgments, particularly on American pre-Civil War literature, show New England prudery and a lack of humor. But though arid in style, his volumes have withstood the test of time better than many works of his generation. His expert training of graduate students, marked by open-mindedness, was an important contribution to the maturing of American historiography.

BERTRAM WYATT-BROWN
Case Western Reserve University

CHANNING, Edward Tyrrell (1790–1856), American educator. He was born in Newport, R. I., on Dec. 12, 1790, a brother of William Ellery Channing and Walter Channing. He helped found the *North American Review,* one of the most important periodicals of the 19th century, and in 1818 he became the editor. The next year Channing was appointed Boylston professor of rhetoric and oratory at Harvard University, a post he held for 32 years. He died in Cambridge, Mass., on Feb. 8, 1856.

Channing's scholarship and teaching skill made him one of the most influential professors of his time. Among his students were Ralph Waldo Emerson and Henry David Thoreau.

CHANNING, William Ellery (1780–1842), American theologian, who was a leader of the Unitarian movement in New England. Shortly after graduating from Harvard, he became pastor of the Federal Street Congregational Church in Boston in 1803. His sermon *Unitarian Christianity,* delivered in Baltimore in 1819, led to his recognition as one of the founders of Unitarianism. An opponent of slavery, he achieved eminence as a philosopher, theologian, preacher, and philanthropist, and "Channing Unitarianism" was an acknowledged influence on the works of Emerson, Bryant, Longfellow, Lowell, and Holmes.

Philosophy. Channing's philosophy combined both rationalistic and mystical elements in its insistence that reason is itself a form of revelation and that supernatural revelation must be justified to the dictates of human reason. This union of mystical and rational interests is clarified in Channing's contention that God is to be loved, not feared. A lovable God must be a unipersonal God (as opposed to the Trinity) whose nature can be clearly conceived by man, whose qualities are essentially the same as human qualities, and with whom the establishment of personal relations is therefore possible.

Channing held that the most important knowledge is derived from the apprehension of eternal truths and from an awareness of the nature of the soul, rather than from sense experience. He saw humanity's great task as moral improvement, to which government could give little aid. The business of the state is to keep order. The state cannot abolish man's natural rights, which are of divine origin; it can only violate them. Thus slavery is evil, and domination by any individual or group is inconsistent with the natural rights of man. Channing thus adhered to the political philosophy that every free society must constitutionally limit the powers of society in order to protect individual rights.

Unitarianism. Initially Channing hoped that his ideas about the nature of man, although anti-Calvinistic, could still be compatible with the framework of Congregationalism. But the development of factions within the church, intensified after his 1819 sermon, led him to acknowledge the inevitability of creating a new religious group. In 1820 he formed a conference of liberal ministers, out of which grew the American Unitarian Association, established in 1825.

Later Years. Channing's later years were spent less in preaching and more in expounding his views through essays. His philosophy extended beyond purely religious questions. He was an advocate of public education and strongly espoused the development of an American literature, deploring the tendency of American writers to pattern their works after those of English authors. His last audible words, "I have had many messages from the spirit," are a summary of his life. He died in Bennington, Vt., on Oct. 2, 1842.

ROBERT LEET PATTERSON, *Duke University*

CHANNING, William Henry (1810–1884), American clergyman and reformer. Channing was born in Boston, Mass., on May 25, 1810. He was the nephew of William Ellery Channing (1780–1842).

Channing graduated from the Harvard Divinity School and entered the Unitarian ministry in 1833. A temperamental if dedicated person, Channing served a number of churches, lived at Brook Farm for a short time, and in 1847 headed the Religious Union of Associationists. In 1852 he went to Rochester, N. Y., as a Unitarian preacher. After 1854 he spent most of his life in England. During the Civil War, however, he returned to the United States and became a pastor in Washington, D. C., and was involved in the Underground Railroad for fugitive slaves. He was chaplain of the House of Representatives in 1863–1864. Channing died in London on Dec. 23, 1884.

CHANSON, shän-sôn′, in music, is the generic term for all French secular song. The art chanson of the Middle Ages and the Renaissance may be traced as far back as the 11th and 12th centuries, to the Provençal songs of the troubadours. From these beginnings developed the polyphonic song form that emerged in the 15th century and reached its height in the 16th century.

The development of the 15th and 16th century chanson may be divided into five stylistic subperiods. The first, from about 1390 to 1450, was the period of the English and early Burgundian chanson. These chansons were generally composed for solo voice with instrumental accompaniment. The chief composers of the period were John Dunstable, Guillaume Dufay, and Gilles Binchois, whose works have elegance, beauty, and refinement.

The years from about 1450 to 1480 form the period of the early Parisian chansons, many of which originated in Burgundy. Among the outstanding composers of these chansons, which were similar in form and style to those of the previous era, were Phillipe Caron and Johannes Ockeghem. The next period, from 1480 to 1505, took its name *Odhecaton*, from the title of a famous collection of songs published in 1501. Most chansons at this time were written for from three to five voices without accompaniment. The leading composers included Josquin Deprès, Heinrich Isaac, and Jacob Obrecht.

The chansons of about 1505 to 1549 were strongly influenced by two Italian forms, the frottola and the madrigal. Both types were written for from three to five voices and were frequently homophonic in style. This movement away from pure polyphony in chansons was led by such composers as Nicolas Gombert and Jean Mouton. The composition of the new chansons coincided with the rise of the music-printing industry, and they were the first to be widely available.

The period from about 1549 to 1630 was the era of the "humanist" chanson, and the chanson *vers mesurés* (measured verse) was the chief form. In this type of song the rhythm of the music followed the metrical pattern of the poetry to which it was set. Claude Le Jeune and Jacques Mauduit were the chief composers of this type of chanson. These songs marked the end of the development of the formal Renaissance chanson.

FRANKLIN B. ZIMMERMAN
Author of "Henry Purcell: His Life and Times"

CHANSONS DE GESTE, shän-sôn' də zhest', are French epic poems of the Middle Ages. Roughly 80 *chansons de geste* ("songs of deeds") survive. Dating from the 11th to the 15th century, they are mostly by unknown authors. The best known is the *Chanson de Roland*, probably composed in the 11th century. See ROLAND SONG.

Evolution. Early in the 8th century the Old French word "geste" came to designate a historical work. The *Gesta regum Francorum* and *Gesta Dagoberti*, Latin histories of "the deeds of the kings of the Franks" and "the deeds of Dagobert," are reflected in Old French versified histories, such as the *Geste de Charlemagne*. This *geste* is typical of the Old French *épopée*, an epic poem composed in *laisses* (assonant stanzas), concerning parts of the life of an eponymic hero and incorporating historical material and fictional embellishment.

There is considerable evidence that *chansons de geste* existed in the 10th century, but the earliest extant manuscripts date from the late 11th century. In the 12th century the genre was developed and brought to its culmination. In the 13th century the *chansons* began to lose their earlier purity, and those of the next two centuries represent the decadent stage of the art.

Contents. Throughout this entire period little distinction was observed between documented history and fiction, and the *chansons de geste* present a curious mixture of fact and fantasy, of authenticated history and wild fabrication. The *chansons* generally deal with the great deeds of noble heroes; but a medieval poet might adapt the exploits of several heroes of existing *chansons*, rearrange them, and add them to the deeds of his own hero. Thus, more than a dozen historical figures serve as models for the description of Guillaume in *Guillaume d'Orange*, although he himself was a historical personage. Similarly, different poets' depictions of specific characters are often inconsistent: the hero of one *chanson* may be the villain of another. Consequently no *chanson de geste* is entirely accurate historically, though hardly any is entirely fictional; yet they may have been generally regarded as valid history by their medieval audiences.

The themes of the *chanson de geste* gradually changed during its development. As the chief form of literary expression of the French aristocracy throughout the 12th and 13th centuries, the poems emphasized the virtues of the strong military hero and reflected the aspirations and ancestral pride of the leading families in the centuries following the glories of the Carolingian period. The central themes were valor, loyalty, and the dignity of warlike actions and attitudes. But the *chansons* of the 14th and early 15th centuries, although they continued to extol the military virtues, did so with less spontaneity; at the same time the theme of courtly love, which had never before been a major concern, gained prominence. This development reflected the growing importance of the *roman courtois* (courtly romance), which finally displaced the *chanson de geste* as the dominant literary form.

Classification. Most of the extant *chansons de geste* are traditionally grouped into three cycles: the *Geste du Roi;* the *Geste de Garin de Monglane,* which is also called the *Geste de Guillaume d'Orange;* and the *Geste de Doon de Mayence.* This classification is first recorded by Bertran de Bar-sur-Aube, an early 13th century author of two well-known *chansons de geste.* Another 13th century poet, Jean Bodel, is credited with first referring to these French epics as a national genre, the *Matière de France,* distinguishing them from the *Matière de Bretagne* (the Arthurian legends) and the *Matière de Rome* (literature transmitted from Greek and Roman antiquity).

"Geste du Roi." The *Geste du Roi* consists of the epics celebrating Charlemagne and his court and family and their struggles against the Saracens. The *chansons* composing this *geste* are, as a group, the oldest and the best, although the three cycles overlap considerably in both quality and date of composition. The oldest and finest individual *chanson,* the *Chanson de Roland,* belongs to this cycle.

Scholars have divided the *Geste du Roi* into six subdivisions, the first of which deals with Charlemagne's mother, Bertha, and with the life of Charlemagne himself before the appearance of the knight Roland. To this group belong *Bertha Greatfoot* (*Berte aus grans piés*) and *Aspremont,* the latter describing a fictitious campaign against a Saracen king in Calabria. The second group, known as the feudal epic, describes Charlemagne's struggles against rebellious vassals; it includes *Ogier the Dane.* In the third group are the poems describing Charlemagne and his nobles on a legendary trip to the Holy Land. The best known of this group, the *Pèlerinage de Charlemagne,* affords the first example of alexandrine verse in French poetry. The fourth group, including *Aiquin, Fierabras,* and *Otinel,* deals with events before the Spanish war between the Christians and the Saracens; the fifth concerns the war in Spain and includes the *Chanson de Roland.* The sixth subdivision treats events between Roland's death in 778 and that of Charlemagne in 814.

"Geste de Garin de Monglane." Of the two other great cycles, the *Geste de Garin* is generally ranked the more important because it is a continuation of the *Geste du Roi.* The central hero of this cycle is Guillaume d'Orange (Duke William Shortnose); the poems celebrate the Duke's battles against the Saracens or against rebellious vassals of his suzerain, Louis le Débonnaire, Charlemagne's son. Among the famous *chansons* in this cycle are *Girard de Viane, Aliscans, La chanson de Guillaume, Le moniage Guillaume, La prise d'Orange,* and *Le charroi de Nîmes.* See GUILLAUME D'ORANGE.

"Geste de Doon de Mayence." The third great cycle deals with revolts against Charlemagne by members of the family of the archtraitor Ganelon, who fatally betrayed Roland at Roncevaux; therefore it is somtimes called *"la faulse geste."* Most of the central figures of the cycle, including Ogier the Dane, Ganelon, Huon de Bordeaux, and Renaud de Montauban, are grandsons of Doon de Mayence (Mainz). The most important is Renaud, after whom one of the *chansons* is named; other famous *chansons* of this cycle are *Huon de Bordeaux* and *Les quatre fils Aymon.*

Although most of the *chansons* belong primarily to one or another of the three cycles, some of them have many connections with *chansons* in other cycles. For instance, *Le couronnement de Louis,* which clearly belongs to the *Geste du Roi,* is also closely and significantly linked to the *Geste de Garin de Monglane.*

Minor Cycles. Besides the three great cycles there are seven or eight secondary cycles; these are shorter but not necessarily of lesser quality or interest. They include the *Geste des Lorrains,* which consists of five long *chansons* including the famous *Garin de Lorrain;* the *Geste du Nord,* which includes the *Chanson de Raoul de Cambrai,* the most interesting of all the regional *chansons;* and the *Geste bourguignonne,* of which *Girard de Roussillon* is the best-known chanson. Still other *chansons* defy grouping; an example is *Audigier,* a parody of chivalry, which has no relation to any cycle.

The chief flaw of this system of classification is that it tends to conceal and undervalue the historical development of the *chanson de geste.* Each *chanson* was, of course, composed independently. The first of a cycle often celebrated the deeds of a conspicuous hero; later poems would deal with the hero's childhood or youth or with his father, grandfather, or sons. Consequently, the order of composition of the *chansons* seldom corresponds with the chronological order of the events they describe.

Performance. The *chansons de geste* were originally sung or chanted, usually to aristocratic audiences, by jongleurs, troubadours, or trouvères. Some performers accompanied themselves with simple string instruments; others were accompanied by one or more musicians. The simple and unobtrusive melodies, no longer extant, were repeated at intervals of one or two lines throughout the performance. Although they grew out of a noble tradition and were intended for courtly audiences, and although commoners consequently have almost no significance in the stories, the *chansons* were sometimes performed to inspire or entertain troops of soldiers or pilgrims.

Artistic Features. The *chansons,* which range in length from about 1,000 to 20,000 lines, are written in *laisses,* stanzas unified by assonance but lacking uniform length and paragraphic unity. *Laisses* range in length from 7 to more than 70 lines, all sharing assonance of the last stressed syllable. Although the lines of some *chansons* are alexandrine or octosyllabic, the decasyllabic line with a caesura after the fourth or sixth syllable is so predominant that it has been termed the "epic verse."

A salient characteristic of the epics is their deep religious and national feeling. With the exception of the *Roland,* however, the poems reveal only a rudimentary knowledge of literary construction. As a rule, the narrative is rambling and diffuse; the versification is rough; the characters lack shading, being all good or all bad; and moral problems are all but nonexistent.

Yet despite these many defects the *chansons* express an undeniable primitive force and sincerity as well as profound religious sentiment. Above all, they express intense love of the native soil, a noble patriotism that is unexcelled in the poetry of more civilized epochs. They were, undoubtedly, largely influential in fostering the spirit of Christian chivalry that flowered during the Crusades.

Origins. According to Léon Gautier, one of the foremost authorities on the *chansons de geste,* the natural epic requires four conditioning circumstances. The first is a primitive period when science and criticism are virtually nonexistent, history and legend are easily confounded, and credulity is general. The second is a national and religious environment in a country that has achieved a measure of national unity, as was the case in France when the *chanson de geste* was, in effect, the great war cry of Christianity against Islamic invasion, and when religious and patriotic concepts were difficult to distinguish. The third is extraordinary and grievous events. Tragedy is the prime element of the epic. A defeat and a heroic death are the subjects of most of these virile songs, replete with blood and tears and almost devoid of joy. With grief there is room only for saintliness, as that of Charlemagne, Guillaume, and Renaud. The fourth is heroes who are the personification of an entire nation in a historical epoch. Just as Achilles personified the Greek people at a certain stage of its history, so Roland represents the chivalric French of the 10th and 11th centuries.

Although all of these conditions obtained when the *chanson de geste* originated, its precise development is still in doubt, and contradictory hypotheses have been put forth to explain it. One of the earlier theories stressed mystical and romantic origins and underplayed the historical background of the poems. This was countered by the so-called "realistic" interpretation, which held that the chansons developed through a popular oral tradition firmly based on (though exaggerating) historical events. The basic modern theories are those of Joseph Bédier and Ferdinand Lot. Bédier's "individualist" theory maintains that the *chansons* were the works of individual poets, though based on popular tales; and it denies almost completely their historical validity, asserting that they combined and exploited poetic themes belonging not to a particular nation or culture but to all nations and all times. Lot was among the first to desert the individualist theory; he became the proponent of the "traditionalist" theory, which reasserts the importance of an oral tradition and upholds, with qualifications, the historical accuracy of the epics.

ELIE R. VIDAL
California State College at Hayward

Further Reading: Bédier, Joseph, *Les légendes épiques: recherches sur la formation des chansons de geste,* 3d ed., 4 vols. (Paris 1926–1929); Crosland, Jessie, *The Old French Epic* (Oxford 1951); Siciliano, Italo, *Les origines des chansons de geste* (Paris 1951); Zumthor, Paul, *Histoire littéraire de la France médiévale. VIᵉ–XIVᵉ siècles* (Paris 1954).

CHANT, in its broadest sense, is any vocal music, but especially liturgical vocal music, that is meant to be a heightened projection of a prose text. Because of the importance of the text, chant is usually free in rhythm and is unaccompanied. It differs from song in that the melody follows no inner structural principle but is regulated by the meaning of the text.

The liturgical vocal music of almost all Eastern, early Western, and early New World peoples is called chant. There is, for example, Hindu, Buddhist, Muslim, ancient Hebrew, American Indian, and Negro chant. Christian chant is of several varieties corresponding to the different liturgies that developed in the early church. Gregorian chant (q.v.), also called plainsong, is used by the Roman Catholic Church and is the most widespread. Other Western chants include the Ambrosian (used in Milan, see AMBROSIAN MUSIC) and the virtually extinct Mozarabic (Spain) and Gallican (France). Eastern chants include the Syrian, Byzantine (see BYZANTINE MUSIC), Coptic, Ethiopian, Armenian, and Russian.

The term "chant" refers more narrowly to melodies used in Anglican churches for singing psalms and canticles. During the Reformation the Latin texts that accompanied Gregorian chant were translated into English, and for them composers such as Tallis and Byrd wrote melodies derived from the eight monophonic psalm tones of Gregorian chant. Their work generally retained the free, oratorical Gregorian rhythm but used four-part harmony based on the work of Italian composers and had a strict metrical pattern at the cadences, or ends of sections. These Anglican "simple" tone chants followed the Gregorian practice of fitting a complete chant to a psalm verse. Later composers wrote new double, triple, or quadruple chants, not based on Gregorian models, that required two or more verses to be complete. Many of these later chants had metrical rhythms that forced artificial accentuation of the text. In the 19th century the relation of notes to syllables was indicated by "pointing," or marking the text. Recently, composers have tried to return to the rhythmic freedom of the Gregorian examples. All Anglican chants, however, err in that they begin with models intended for Latin texts instead of constructing new chants related to the nature of the English language.

REMBERT G. WEAKLAND, *Abbot Primate, O. S. B.*

CHANT ROYAL, shäṇ rwȧ-yȧl', a French poetic form (also called *chanson royale*) popular from the 14th to the 16th century. Related to the ballade, it is longer and formally more demanding, consisting usually of five 11-line stanzas followed by an envoi of 5 lines. The standard rhyme scheme for each stanza is *a b a b c c d d e d e;* for the envoi, *d d e d e.* Because the same rhyme sounds are used in all stanzas, the traditional chant royal has only 5 rhyme sounds in 60 lines. The lines are generally decasyllabic, mingling masculine and feminine rhymes in various ways. The last line of the first stanza also concludes each other stanza and the envoi; it is called the *refrain.*

The name of the chant royal probably derives directly or indirectly from its supremely demanding form, which especially suits it to lofty subjects. Elaborate, courtly, and grandiose, *chants royaux* are conventionally addressed to a divinity, king, or nobleman, who is invoked by his title at the opening of the envoi.

Chants royaux of the 14th century did not employ a refrain; many such poems were written in honor of the Virgin Mary. The finest *chants royaux* were written by Eustache Deschamps (1340?–?1407) and Clément Marot (1495?–1544). The form was revived briefly in the late 19th century.

ELIE R. VIDAL
California State College at Hayward

CHANTAL, shän-tȧl', **Saint Jane Frances de** (1572–1641), French founder of the Visitation nuns. She was born in Dijon, France, on Jan. 23, 1572, the daughter of a prominent lawyer. She married Christophe de Rabutin, Baron de Chantal, in 1592. After his death in 1601, she spent the next nine years raising her four children. Together with St. Francis of Sales, her spiritual director since 1604, she founded the Visitation nuns at Annecy in 1610, and herself became a nun. Pope Paul V approved the order in 1618. For a few years the archbishop of Lyon restricted the nuns to a contemplative life. After that they visited the sick and poor. Their boarding schools for upper class girls were popular and served to speed the order's rapid growth. St. Jane died in Moulins on Dec. 13, 1641. She was canonized in 1767. Her feast day is August 21.

JOHN F. BRODERICK, S. J.
Weston College, Mass.

CHANTECLER, shän-tə-klâr', is a poetic drama in four acts by the French poet and playwright Edmond Rostand. First produced in Paris in 1910, it is a somewhat contrived dramatization of a barnyard fable spoofing contemporary society. The first English translation was made in 1910 by Gertrude Hall.

Chantecler the cock, the hero of the play, believes that his song directly evokes the day. When he learns that he is wrong, he continues to sing, in order to proclaim, if not to summon, the dawn. The other characters include various barnyard animals satirizing social types of Rostand's day, such as Patou, the idealistic dog; and La Faisane, the hen pheasant, representing woman, the enchantress, who attempts to divert man from his work but is ready to die for him.

CHANTERELLE. See MUSHROOM.

CHANTEY, shan'tē, a traditional sailors' song, particularly the cadenced work songs of English and American sailors. "Forecastle songs," in contrast to chanteys (or shanties), were sung simply for entertainment and are often nautical variants of old English, Irish, and Scots ballads. Most English-language chanteys date from the sailing-vessel days of the 18th and early 19th centuries. In addition to "deep sea chanteys," the United States has traditional chanteys and songs from riverboat and Great Lakes vessels.

Chanteys set the cadence of such tasks as pumping, hoisting anchor, and reefing sails, and were classified according to rhythm as "short drag" chanteys, "halliard" chanteys, and "windlass," or "capstan," chanteys. The verses were commonly sung solo by a "chantey man," with the refrain sung by the crew.

Further Reading: Colcord, Joanna C., *Songs of American Sailormen* (New York 1964); Hugill, Stan, ed., *Shanties from the Seven Seas* (New York 1961).

CHANTILLY, shän-tē-yē', is a small town in France in the Oise department, 25 miles (40 km) north of Paris. Not far from the Nonette River and situated in gently rolling country, Chantilly is a celebrated Parisian resort and a center for film making and for the manufacture of lace. It is the site of the races of the French Jockey Club. But Chantilly is even better known for its château.

The original château at Chantilly was built in the 14th century; much rebuilding and restoration has taken place since then. Its main section, called the Grand Château, was destroyed in the French Revolution and not restored until 1840. The adjoining Petit Château, built around 1560, has survived intact and is a fine example of French Renaissance architecture.

Chantilly began acquiring a reputation for elegance and beauty in the late 15th century, when it came into the possession of the house of Montmorency. In the 17th century it was acquired by the house of Condé, under which it was to know its most brilliant period. The Prince de Condé (1621–1686), called the Great Condé, lavished money and care upon the château and the surrounding park. Leading men of letters, including Racine, Molière, La Fontaine, Boileau, and La Bruyère, were entertained there. Louis XIV accepted an invitation to Chantilly and went with his whole court—a party of 5,000 people— in April 1671. The château, with its library and art collections, was given to the Institut de France in 1886. Population: (1962) 8,106.

BRYCE LYON, *Brown University*

CHANTREY, chan'trē, **Sir Francis Legatt** (1781– 1841), English sculptor. He was born in Jordanthorpe, Derbyshire, on April 7, 1781, the son of a carpenter. After being apprenticed to a carver and gilder, he studied at the Royal Academy in London.

In 1808, Chantrey won a commission to do a statue of George III for the Guildhall, London. His later work included busts of George IV (Windsor and Brighton), William Pitt (London), George Washington (State House, Boston), and, most notably, Sir Walter Scott (Abbotsford). He also did equestrian statues of George IV and the Duke of Wellington (both in London). His most celebrated work is the *Sleeping Children*, a sentimental memorial to the two children of the Rev. W. Robinson, in Lichfield Cathedral.

Chantrey became a member of the Royal Academy in 1818 and was knighted in 1835. He died in London on Nov. 25, 1841, leaving the Chantrey Bequest to the Royal Academy to buy works of art executed in Britain.

CHANTRY, chan'trē, the endowment of a priest to provide for the celebration of masses for the prosperity of the living or the repose of the dead. The post generally involved other duties, especially teaching school, and chantry schools were numerous. The term was also applied to the small chapels added to a large church where the priest held Mass.

Prior to the Reformation, chantries were numerous, almost every family of importance having founded one or more. Among the most interesting was the chantry of William of Wykeham in Winchester Cathedral, and a chapel erected on a bridge at Bradford on Avon. Chantries were finally dissolved in England by Edward VI, and nearly all endowments went to the crown.

CHANUKAH. See HANUKKAH.

CHANUTE, shə-nōōt', **Octave** (1832–1910), American engineer, aviation pioneer, and writer. He was born in Paris, France, on Feb. 18, 1832, and went to the United States in the fall of 1838. Chanute became one of the outstanding civil engineers in the United States, specializing in railroad work; but his fame now rests on his great influence in aeronautics, especially in the dissemination of reliable information about achievements in Europe and America. His classic, *Progress in Flying Machines,* was published in New York in 1894. It was the first proper technical assessment of the aviation pioneers.

In 1896, Chanute designed his famous stable biplane hang-glider, with its excellent rigging; this machine proved to be a turning point in glider design. Chanute became a valued friend and encourager of the Wright brothers, but technically they only owed their rigging system to him. A lecture that he gave in Paris in 1903 proved to be one of the decisive turning points in the revival of European aviation. He showed, by photographs and descriptions, the gliding successes of the Wrights; this spurred the Europeans to rivalry in airplane design and production. Chanute died in Chicago on Nov. 23, 1910.

C. H. GIBBS-SMITH
Author of "Aviation: An Historical Survey"

CHANUTE, shə-nōōt', is a city in southeastern Kansas, in Neosho county, on the Neosho River, about 110 miles (177 km) southwest of Kansas City. The city's basic industries are petroleum and wax refining and cement production. Its smaller industries include the manufacture of pump jacks, trailer parts, and work clothing.

Chanute has a community junior college and the Safari Museum, commemorating the explorers Martin and Osa Johnson. Mrs. Johnson was born in Chanute.

Settled in 1868 and incorporated in 1873, the city is named for Octave Chanute, a railroad consulting engineer, who became a pioneer in aviation. It has a commission-manager government. Population: 10,341.

CHAO PHRAYA, chou prä-yä, Thailand's major river. It derives its existence from four tributaries, the Ping, the Wang, the Yom, and the Nan, which rise in Thailand's northern hills. The length of the Chao Phraya proper, which is also called the *Menam,* meaning "river," is 226 miles (365 km), and it traverses Thailand's largest and most fertile plain as it flows toward the Gulf of Siam, entering it some 25 miles (40 km) below Bangkok. The river basin, subject to flooding in the rainy season, is the country's rice bowl.

Geologists surmise that centuries-long silting has created the Chao Phraya delta out of the upper reaches of the old Gulf of Siam. As silting persists, constant dredging alone renders the Chao Phraya estuary navigable. For ages the river has served as Thailand's cheapest and most convenient means of transport, and the advent of railroads and highways at the turn of the century in no way lessened its importance. Several multipurpose dams have been built, tapping its potential for irrigation, flood control, and hydroelectric power.

PRACHOOM CHOMCHAI
Chulalongkorn University

CHAOS, kā′os, in Greek mythology, was the void that existed before the creation of the universe, out of which the natural world, the gods, and mankind came into being.

In early Greek tradition, the first gods, Uranus (Heaven) and Gaea (Earth), arose from Chaos, and they in turn gave birth to the Titans, sons and daughters who personified the various powers of nature and abstractions of good and evil. In later Greek tradition, Chaos was conceived of as an unformed mass that contained all the seeds of nature.

In figurative usage, the word "chaos" has come to mean utter disorder or confusion.

CHAPAIS, sha-pe′, **Sir Thomas** (1858–1946), Canadian public official and historian. Joseph Amable Thomas Chapais was born at St.-Denis-de-la-Bouteillerie, Quebec, on March 23, 1858. After graduating from Laval University in 1879, he was admitted to the bar. He was appointed to the Quebec Legislative Council in 1892 and served as the council's speaker in 1895. In 1897 he became minister of colonization and mines in the Flynn cabinet.

Chapais was appointed to the Senate of Canada in 1919. He was minister without portfolio in Maurice Duplessis' Union Nationale cabinet from 1936 to 1939.

Chapais, who edited *Le Courier du Canada* from 1884 to 1901, was also a noted historian and a professor at Laval University. His chief historical work was *Cours d'histoire du Canada* (8 vols., 1919–1933). In 1935 he was knighted for his work as a historian. Chapais died at his birthplace, St.-Denis, on July 15, 1946.

CHAPARRAL, shap-ə-ral′, a term used to describe dense thickets of shrubby plants occurring in semiarid areas. Most of the plants range from 10 to 15 feet (3 to 4.5 meters) in height, and some may be evergreen. Chaparral is a common vegetation form in the southwestern United States and usually grows in locations receiving between 10 to 20 inches (250 to 500 mm) of rainfall per year. Common chaparral plants include scrub oak (*Quercus dumosa*), mesquite (*Prosepis glandulosa*), and several species of sage (*Salvia*) and manzanita (*Arctostaphylos*). Certain mammals and birds, such as the California deer mouse (*Peromyscus californicus*) and the wrentit (*Chamaea fasciata*), may be found in close association with chaparral. Because chaparral occurs in dry areas where it is readily subject to wind-swept flames, it is quite often involved in fires that cause serious damage to homes in southern California and other populated areas.

CHAPBOOK, a piece of cheap, popular literature in the form of a pamphlet that was formerly sold by a chapman, or peddler. Chapbooks were the late 15th through 18th century counterparts of today's magazines, comic books, and paperbacks. In contrast to the large, heavy, hardbound books of the time, generally expensive and confined to libraries, chapbooks were small (usually 5½ by 4½ inches), portable booklets consisting of a single signature of 4 to 32 pages, which were cheaply printed and often illustrated with crude woodcuts.

Most chapbooks were unsigned and undated. Neither literary nor subtle, they present a picture of common taste. Their contents ranged from the latest notorious murder or bawdy ballad through nursery rhymes, fairy tales, witchcraft, and school lessons to Bible tales and the lives of saints. When penny magazines and other inexpensive periodicals became available after 1800, chapbooks died out.

CHAPEL, a small place of prayer or worship. The word derives from the medieval Latin *cappella*, "cape," and its present usage stems from the veneration of the cape of St. Martin of Tours, which Martin is supposed to have shared with a beggar and which was later seen worn by Christ in a vision. The place where the cape was kept as a relic came to be known as the Cappella di San Martino (Chapel of St. Martin). The word was gradually applied to other buildings containing relics and then to a variety of religious buildings that were smaller or had fewer privileges than churches.

Various types of chapels developed at different periods. The *royal chapel* was attached to a court and under the direct jurisdiction of a ruler. The *proprietary chapel*, founded by an important person or by a group, was often on an estate and privately supported and controlled. The *chapel of ease* was open for preaching, prayer, administration of the sacraments, and funerals, for the convenience of people too far from the mother church of the parish (as in colonial Virginia), but was subordinate to the mother church. The *dissenter chapel* was designated by the established church for worship by nonconformists, as in England in the 17th and 18th centuries. *Institutional chapels* are attached to seminaries, universities and other schools, and hospitals. They are sometimes under private control and often have very imposing edifices.

In addition, large churches or synagogues may maintain individual chapels with separate relics or altars set aside for special purposes such as weddings, baptisms, and funerals. In Roman Catholic and some Anglican churches such chapels are often dedicated to the Virgin Mary and called *Lady Chapels.*

JAMES H. SMYLIE
Union Theological Seminary, Richmond, Va.

A ROMAN CATHOLIC CHAPEL designed to reflect the liturgical reforms of Vatican II and built in 1967 at Cranwell Preparatory School in Lenox, Mass.

PETER MCLAUGHLIN, ARCHITECT—PHOTO BY ALEXANDRE GEORGES

CHAPEL HILL is a town in north central North Carolina, in Orange county, 24 miles (39 km) northwest of Raleigh. It is situated in a corn- and tobacco-raising area of the Piedmont section of the state. The town is the home of the University of North Carolina, chartered in 1789, which was the first state university in the United States. Chapel Hill has maintained the atmosphere of a college town in spite of the expansion of the university and the community. It is the seat of several research firms but has no large industries. The Carolina Playmakers, founded in 1918, provides a community theater program open to both students and citizens of the town.

Chapel Hill was founded in 1792 and grew up around the university campus. It was incorporated in 1851. The town is governed by a manager and council. Population: 25,537.

ELIZABETH D. GEER
Chapel Hill Public Library

CHAPELAIN, shȧ-plaɴ′, **Jean** (1595–1674), French poet and critic, who was a founding member of the Académie Française. He was born in Paris on Dec. 4, 1595. In the early 1620's he attracted attention by his critical writings, especially a preface (1623) to Giambattista Marino's *Adone.* His *Ode* to Richelieu won him the cardinal's favor, and when Richelieu founded the Académie Française in 1635 he selected Chapelain as a member.

Chapelain became very influential within the Académie, for which he drew up the first regulations. He also wrote the Académie's *Sentiments* (1638) on Corneille's *Le Cid;* the *Sentiments,* which attacked Corneille for ignoring the Aristotelian "unities," was important in establishing the neoclassical cult of regularity. Chapelain drew up plans for the Académie's famous dictionary of the French language, which was first published in 1693, after his death.

Chapelain's most ambitious undertaking was an epic poem, *La Pucelle,* celebrating Joan of Arc. Begun in 1630, the poem was eagerly awaited, but when the first 12 cantos were published in 1656 they met with critical disapproval so virulent that the last 12 were not published until 1882. The epic, notable only for its meticulous adherence to neoclassical rules, vitiated Chapelain's reputation. He died in Paris on Feb. 22, 1674.

KENNETH DOUGLAS, *Author of*
"A Critical Bibliography of Existentialism"

CHAPIN, chā′pin, **Roy Dikeman** (1880–1936), American industrialist, who helped make the automobile industry a major part of the U. S. economy. He was born in Lansing, Mich., on Feb. 23, 1880. After attending the University of Michigan, he joined the Olds Motor Works in 1901. In that year he drove the first motorcar that made the trip from Detroit to New York entirely under its own power.

Chapin advanced rapidly in the automobile industry and became president of the Hudson Motor Company in 1910. He introduced the Essex in 1919, and he offered closed cars at prices competitive with the touring car in 1922. Other companies followed his lead, and the touring car rapidly disappeared from the American scene.

Chapin served as chairman of the highway transportation committee of the Council of National Defense in 1917–1918, and he was the secretary of commerce in 1932–1933. He was president of Hudson Motor Company when he died in Detroit on Feb. 16, 1936.

CHAPLAIN, chap′lən, a person appointed to fulfill a religious ministry for an individual, a group, or a particular institution. The term originally designated the custodian of a chapel, and like "chapel," it derives from the Latin *cappella,* meaning, "cape." It was initially applied to the guardian of the cape of St. Martin of Tours, which was used as a pledge of victory in battle and for the verification of oaths. As various types of chapels developed, the office of chaplain was expanded, and some chaplains exercised great ecclesiastical and political power.

Throughout history chaplains have served royalty, nobility, and others in the church hierarchy, performing religious services or acting as personal advisers. They also came to be used in the armed forces, hospitals, prisons, and educational institutions.

The *military chaplaincy* is an ancient office with wide modern applications. In the United States, military chaplains are commissioned officers of the Department of the Defense and are supervised by the Chief Chaplains Office. Military chaplains must be approved by some denominational body and must attend a chaplains' school. The military chaplain conducts worship, provides religious education, and offers personal counseling. The office of *hospital chaplain* is also an old one, serving the physically or emotionally ill. A hospital chaplain may be a part-time or a full-time staff member and is often under some form of ecclesiastical discipline. He may receive some special schooling. *Prison chaplains* minister to those separated from society by law. *Educational chaplains* are usually ministers, priests, or rabbis assigned to a campus chapel or to a denominational foundation near a campus. These chaplains guide students and instructors in attempting to place learning and maturing in a religious context.

In modern society a new type of chaplain known as the *industrial chaplain* has emerged to meet the spiritual needs of managers and workers in an industrialized, mass society where there is often a loss of personal identification and self-awareness. The "worker priests" of France are examples of this concept of the chaplain's role in present-day life.

JAMES H. SMYLIE
Union Theological Seminary, Richmond, Va.

CHAPLEAU, shȧp-lō′, **Sir Joseph Adolphe** (1840–1898), Canadian public official. He was born in Ste.-Thérèse, Lower Canada (Quebec), on Nov. 9, 1840, and educated at Masson College and the seminary of St. Hyacinthe. In 1861 he became a member of the bar and in 1873 queen's counsel. He represented Terrebonne as a Conservative in the Quebec legislature and served as solicitor general, provincial secretary, and prime minister (1879–1882) of Quebec. He was secretary of state for Canada for 10 years (to 1892) and then lieutenant governor of Quebec until 1898. Chapleau, who was knighted in 1896, died on June 13, 1898, in Montreal.

CHAPLEAU, shȧ-plō′, is an unincorporated township in northeastern Ontario, Canada. It is in Sudbury district, about 100 miles (160 km) north of Sault Ste. Marie.

Chapleau is a divisional point on the transcontinental line of the Canadian Pacific Railway. Lumber, timber, and plywood are its major products, and there is a phosphorus extraction plant in the township. Population: 3,785.

CHAPLIN, Charlie (1889–1977), British film actor, whose "little tramp" character was the most popular comic figure of the 20th century. Charles Spencer Chaplin was born in London on April 16, 1889, into a family of music hall performers. His parents separated when he was a boy, and both he and his half brother Sydney were sent to live in the Lambeth Workhouse.

Early Career. While still a youth, Charles joined a music hall act called Fred Karno's Comedians, and by the time he was 19 had become a starring performer. When the troupe was on tour in the United States in 1913, Mack Sennett saw Chaplin's performance and hired him to work for his Keystone studios in Hollywood. In less than a year Chaplin made 35 one-reel comedies. However, Chaplin disliked the violence and speed of the Sennett slapstick. "Nothing transcends personality," Chaplin once said, and the personality he wanted to develop was that of the "little tramp" —the elegant ragamuffin in a derby hat, baggy pants, oversized shoes, and tightly fitting coat, who sported a toothbrush moustache and carried a bamboo cane—that he had introduced in his second one-reeler, *Kid Auto Races at Venice* (1914).

By the time Chaplin signed a contract with the Essanay company in 1915 at 10 times his Keystone salary, he was already internationally famous for his little tramp's shuffling walk, nervous smile, and formal mannerisms. In the 14 one-reel comedies he made for Essanay, Chaplin combined elements of pathos and comedy for the first time in motion pictures. In 1916, Chaplin was hired by the Mutual company, again with a huge salary increase. The films he made in 1916–1917 for Mutual—*The Floor Walker, One A. M., The Pawnshop, Easy Street,* and *The Immigrant*—are generally acknowledged to be Chaplin's best short films.

Later Career. In 1918, Chaplin built his own studio and signed a $1 million contract with First National Films to produce eight motion pictures. Among the eight were the enormously popular *Shoulder Arms* (1918) and Chaplin's first feature-length film, *The Kid* (1921), which introduced the child star Jackie Coogan. In 1923, Chaplin, Mary Pickford, Douglas Fairbanks, Sr., and D. W. Griffith founded United Artists Corporation, which produced the feature-length "little tramp" pictures: *The Gold Rush* (1925), *The Circus* (1928), *City Lights* (1931), *Modern Times* (1936), and *The Great Dictator* (1940).

After World War II, Chaplin abandoned the "little tramp." He wrote, produced, directed, and acted in *Monsieur Verdoux* (1947), *Limelight* (1952), and *A King in New York* (1957) and wrote and directed *A Countess from Hong Kong* (1967). These films, however, failed to win the acclaim his earlier efforts had received.

Chaplin was identified with liberal causes, and in 1952, while vacationing abroad, he was notified by the U. S. attorney general that his reentry into the United States would be challenged. With his fourth wife, the former Oona O'Neill, and their children, he settled in Switzerland. In 1972, however, he was given a special honorary Academy Award, and he was knighted by Queen Elizabeth II in January 1975. He published *My Autobiography* in 1964. Chaplin died in Corsier-sur-Vevey, Switzerland, on Dec. 25, 1977.

HOWARD SUBER
University of California at Los Angeles
Further Reading: Cotes, Peter, and Niklaus, Thelma, *The Little Fellow* (1951; reprint, Citadel Press 1966); Huff, Theodore, *Charlie Chaplin* (1951; reprint, Arno 1972).

CHARLIE CHAPLIN in *The Gold Rush* (1925), one of the silent films in which he played his "tramp" role.

CHAPMAN, Frank Michler (1864–1945), American ornithologist, active in the education of the public about birds. Chapman was born in Englewood, N. J., on June 12, 1864. He became deeply involved in the awakening of public interest in birds that occurred in the United States in the early part of the 20th century. As founder and editor of *Bird-Lore,* a popular nature magazine, he was also a leader in the Audubon movement to end the widespread destruction of North American birds.

As chairman of the Department of Ornithology at the American Museum of Natural History in New York from 1920 to 1942, Chapman initiated the exhibition of birds in natural groupings and was among the first to make extensive photographic studies of birds. He was also the author of numerous technical books on birds. Chapman died in New York City on Nov. 15, 1945.

DEBORAH HOWARD
Massachusetts Audubon Society

CHAPMAN, George (1559?–1634), English poet and dramatist, famous for translating Homer's *Iliad* (1611) and *Odyssey* (1614). Chapman was an important Elizabethan dramatist in his own right, and is possibly the "rival poet" referred to in Shakespeare's sonnets.

Life. Chapman was born at Hitchin, Hertfordshire. Information about his early life is scanty, but it is probable that he studied at Oxford and later Cambridge, but left both universities without taking a degree. He was briefly imprisoned twice: in 1600 for debt, and in 1605 for his play *Eastward Ho!* (written in collaboration with Ben Jonson and John Marston), which offended King James I for its satire on the Scots. He regained some favor in court and wrote a royal masque in 1614. Chapman received the patronage at various times of Henry, Prince of Wales, and Robert Carr, the Earl of Somerset;

however, much of his life was spent in financial difficulty. Chapman died in London on May 12, 1634.

Translations. The most famous tribute to Chapman's translation of Homer is John Keats' sonnet *On First Looking into Chapman's Homer* (1816). The translations, which include the *Iliad,* the *Odyssey,* and *Hymns* (1624) and minor poems ascribed to Homer, have been criticized as rough and inexact, filled with conceits more Elizabethan than Homeric, but most critics defer to the spirit and vigor of Chapman's work and to his fine poetic impulse. In addition, Chapman translated works of Hesiod, Petrarch, Juvenal, and Musaeus.

Plays. Between 1596 and 1612, Chapman contributed to Elizabethan drama a number of "humours" comedies, in which characters were defined by and ridiculed for the dominant trait responsible for their foolishness. Among his outstanding comedies were *The Blind Beggar of Alexandria, All Fools,* and *The Widow's Tears.* His tragedies, which were mostly melodramas about social decay and the breakdown of Renaissance values, included *Bussy D'Ambois, The Conspiracy and Tragedy of Charles Duke of Byron,* and *The Tragedy of Chabot Admiral of France.*

Poetry. Chapman's poems *The Shadow of Night* (1594) and *Ovid's Banquet of Sense* (1595) foreshadowed the metaphysical school of poetry, with their strong intellectual cast, their logical rather than sensuous imagery, and their exploration of anxiety and paradox. Chapman also completed, though not brilliantly, Christopher Marlowe's unfinished poem *Hero and Leander* (1598). An excellent edition of Chapman's poems was edited by Phyllis Brooks Bartlett in 1941.

RICHARD E. HUGHES
Author of "Literature: Form and Function"

CHAPMAN, John (1774–1845), American pioneer and folk hero, known as "Johnny Appleseed." He was born in Leominster, Mass., on Sept. 26, 1774. Almost from the moment he ventured onto the Pennsylvania frontier in 1797 he was a legendary folk figure. He actually did plant tiny apple orchards on the frontier from the Allegheny River to the Saint Marys River.

JOHN CHAPMAN was known in legend as "Johnny Appleseed." This artist's sketch appeared in *A History of the Pioneer and Modern Times of Ashland County from the Earliest to the Present Date,* by H. S. Knatt, in 1863.

BROWN BROTHERS

JOHNNY APPLESEED.

Procuring apple seeds from the pomace of cider presses, Johnny was able to establish a large number of orchards in the course of his wanderings. But so much legend is mixed with fact that it is difficult to ascertain how many orchards—or what distinct contribution he made to American pomology. He was certainly influential in hastening the spread of apple orchards westward.

Chapman became interested in Swedenborgianism, and until his death he was an active missionary for that religious philosophy. It was, however, his role as a true frontiersman enduring the hardships of the new country and living the life of an altruistic orchardist in a day when men were seeking to claim large blocks of western land that has assured him a warm and affectionate place in American frontier history. Johnny Appleseed died on March 10, 1845, in Allen county in northeastern Indiana.

THOMAS D. CLARK, *University of Kentucky*
Author of "Frontier America"

Further Reading: Botkin, Benjamin A., *A Treasury of American Folklore* (New York 1944); Price, Robert, *Johnny Appleseed, Man and Myth* (Bloomington, Ind., 1954).

CHAPMAN, John Jay (1862–1933), American essayist and poet. He was born in New York City on March 2, 1862. He graduated from Harvard in 1884 and was admitted to the New York bar in 1888. After 10 years of active practice, he gave up law for literature. His essays and speeches reveal him to be a keen observer and an original thinker.

Chapman's works include *Emerson, and Other Essays* (1898); *Causes and Consequences* (1898); *The Maid's Forgiveness* (1908), a play; *A Sausage from Bologna* (1909), a play; *Learning, and Other Essays* (1910); *The Treason and Death of Benedict Arnold* (1910), a play; *William Lloyd Garrison* (1913); *Notes on Religion* (1915); *Greek Genius and Other Essays* (1915); *A Glance Toward Shakespeare* (1922); *Letters and Religion* (1924); *Dante* (1927); and *John Jay Chapman and His Letters,* edited by M. A. DeW. Howe (1937). Chapman died in Poughkeepsie, N. Y., on Nov. 4, 1933.

CHAPMAN'S HOMER. See CHAPMAN, GEORGE.

CHAPPED SKIN is a popular term for skin that is dry and cracked. It is usually associated with redness, itching, scaling, and sensation of burning. Chapped skin occurs most frequently on the back of the hands and is in most cases due to exposure to cold weather. It may also be caused by the use of harsh detergents or other agents that remove the oily coating of the skin, allowing too much water to evaporate from the outer skin layers.

Chapped skin is treated by keeping the affected parts dry and warm and by applying lanolin or lotions or ointments designed to coat the skin.

SIDNEY HOFFMAN, M. D.
St. John's Episcopal Hospital, Brooklyn, N. Y.

CHAPPELL, chap'əl, an English family who were the proprietors of Chappell & Co., a firm of music publishers, concert agents, and piano manufacturers. This firm was established in 1811 in New Bond Street, London, by Samuel Chappell and two business partners. After Chappell's death in 1834, his sons William, Thomas Patey,

CHAPULTEPEC CASTLE, in Mexico City, in an aerial view showing the public park that surrounds it. The castle has been a museum since 1937.

EWING GALLOWAY

and S. Arthur Chappell carried on and greatly expanded the business. The Chappell family played an important part in London's musical life; it was instrumental in the founding of the Philharmonic Society (1813) and in the building of St. James's Concert Hall (1858).

William Chappell (1809–1888), the best-known member of the family, was a music antiquarian who did much to revive an interest in traditional English melodies. His published works include *Collection of National English Airs* (2 vols., 1838–1840) and *Popular Music of the Olden Time* (2 vols., 1855–1859).

CHAPTAL, shȧp-tȧl′, **Jean Antoine Claude** (1756–1832), French chemist, industrialist, and administrator. He was born at Nogaret on June 4, 1756, the son of a pharmacist and the nephew of a renowned physician in Montpellier. He finished his education in 1777 and in 1781 was named to a chair of chemistry at Montpellier. With a legacy from his uncle, he began the manufacture of sulfuric acid, soda, and alum, and was so successful in this enterprise that he was raised to a position of nobility by King Louis XVI.

In 1795 the Revolutionary government called him to Paris to make saltpeter. When Napoleon came to power, Chaptal was asked to draw up a plan of national education. In 1800 he became minister of the interior; in this capacity he expanded the dye industry in France, widened the manufacture of ceramics. In 1811 he ordered the general adoption of the metric system of weights and measures. In this year, also, he was created Count de Chanteloup.

Chaptal contributed to education in chemistry through several textbooks. In his *Éléments de chimie* (1790) he proposed the name "nitrogen," meaning "that which forms niter," for the element then called "azote." *La chimie appliquée aux arts* was published in four volumes in 1806, and a companion book on agriculture appeared in 1825. He published a survey of French industries in 1819.

EDUARD FARBER
Editor of "Great Chemists"

CHAPTER, in ecclesiastical affairs, is an assembly of the members of a religious order or congregation. The term came into use because of the monastic practice of assembling daily to read a chapter of the law. At these meetings the superior proposed any business needing the consent of the brethren. The general chapter of large religious communities, such as the Benedictines, meets biyearly to elect a superior general and to amend the rules of the order. Such general chapters are composed of the superiors of individual houses or provinces.

In Europe, though not in the United States, "chapter" has an added ecclesiastic meaning as a college of clerics, called canons, whose function it is to worship God in a cathedral or church. A cathedral chapter has the added purpose of serving as a bishop's council. In England, deans and chapters originally had the right to choose the bishop, but in the 16th century Henry VIII reserved this right as a prerogative of the crown. See also RELIGIOUS ORDERS AND CONGREGATIONS.

CHAPULTEPEC, chä-pōōl-tä-pek′, is a rocky hill in Mexico City that has given its name to a castle on the site, the surrounding woods and park, and the battle that was fought here. *Chapultepec* means "grasshopper hill" in the Nahautl language. The hill is about 3 miles (5 km) southwest of the city's main plaza and rises nearly 200 feet (60 meters) above it. North and west of the hill, before the Spanish conquest and in colonial times, was a woods (*bosque*) of ancient giant bald cypresses. Several hundred of these trees remain, and to them have been added thousands of other trees and shrubs of many varieties.

In 1783 the Spanish viceroy Matías de Gálvez began building a summer residence on the top of the Cerro (hill) de Chapultepec. His son and successor, Bernardo de Gálvez, continued the work until it was stopped by a royal order in 1786. The *castillo* (castle), as it was called, was then abandoned and subsequently fell into ruins. Restoration was undertaken in 1840, and in 1842 the national military academy was installed in one wing.

The last important battle of the war between the United States and Mexico took place at Chapultepec on Sept. 13, 1847. After bombarding the recently fortified hill on the 12th and the early morning of the 13th, Gen. Winfield Scott directed the final U. S. asault, which was from the west and south, avoiding the craggy declivities on the other sides. At the end of 90 minutes of fighting the castle was surrendered by its commander, Gen. Nicolás Bravo, and Mexico City fell the next day. The Mexican losses were about 1,800 killed, wounded, and captured, while the U. S. losses were about 500.

289

During the French intervention of the 1860's, Emperor Maximilian and Empress Carlota remodeled and enlarged the castle and had the grounds terraced, roadways cut, and hilltop gardens laid out. Sumptuous furnishings were imported, and the imperial couple lived briefly in the palace. In the following decades, Porfirio Díaz enlarged the park and had an artificial lake constructed. He and succeeding presidents used the castle as a residence until 1933. Since 1934 the presidential mansion has been the Casa Crema at Los Pinos, in the southwest corner of the old park. The National Museum of History occupies the castle, to which several additions have been made.

In 1961–1964 the park was enlarged to the north and west, and the national museums of anthropology, natural history, and modern art were transferred here into new quarters of outstanding architectural quality. Today the enlarged Bosque de Chapultepec, with its three lakes, well-kept drives, shady walks, bridle paths, ornamental fountains, zoological and botanical gardens, museums, and historical monuments constitutes one of the world's largest and most beautiful city parks.

DONALD D. BRAND, *The University of Texas*

CHAPULTEPEC, chä-pōōl-tä-pek′, **Act of** a resolution passed at the Inter-American Conference on Problems of War and Peace held in the Chapultepec section of Mexico City from Feb. 21 to March 8, 1945. Concerned with principles of security of the Western Hemisphere, the Act of Chapultepec declared that "every attack of a state against the integrity or inviolability of the territory, or against the sovereignty or political independence of an American state shall . . . be considered an act of aggression against the other states," and called for a meeting of consultation to agree on measures to deal with the act of aggression.

This agreement extended the Declaration of Reciprocal Assistance passed in July 1940, at the Inter-American meeting in Havana, in that the Act of Chapultepec provided for action against attack from within the hemisphere as well as from a non-American state.

While the act was designed as a wartime measure and was prompted in part by a fear of an expansionist policy on the part of neutral Argentina at the expense of neighboring Uruguay, its principle was incorporated into the Inter-American Treaty of Reciprocal Assistance (Rio Pact) concluded in 1947.

JOHN FINAN, *The American University*

Further Reading: Thomas, Ann V., and Thomas, Aaron J., *The Organizaiton of American States,* (Dallas, Texas, 1963); Mecham, John Lloyd, *The United States and Inter-American Security, 1889–1960* (Austin, Texas, 1961).

CHAR, chär, any of several species of the genus *Salvelinus,* including the lake trout, the brook trout, the Arctic char, and the Dolly Varden. They are found in both marine and fresh waters of the north temperate and Arctic zones of North America, Europe, and Asia. Like their close relatives the true trouts (genus *Salmo*), chars are excellent game and food fishes.

The slim, bony, chars are distinguished from the true trouts by their pattern of teeth. Chars have only a few teeth at he front end of the bone (vomer) in the middle of the roof of the mouth, while true trouts have teeth along most of its length. In addition, chars have smaller and more numerous scales than true trouts do.

The brook trout (*Salvelinus fontinalis*) and the lake trout (*S. namaycush*) are native only to North America, while the Dolly Varden (*S. malma*) occurs indigenously from northern California to Alaska and from eastern Russia to Japan. The Arctic char (*S. alpinus*) is found in the polar region; it occurs farther north than any other char or trout, having been taken well above the Arctic Circle. The brook and lake trouts are confined to freshwater, but the Arctic char and the Dolly Varden can either be landlocked in freshwater or else spend the spring and summer in the sea and the fall spawning time time in freshwater.

Chars make up the genus *Salvelinus* of the family Salmonidae in the order Clupeiformes.

JAMES C. TYLER
Academy of Natural Sciences of Philadelphia

CHARACIN, kar′ə-sən, a family of fish that inhabits fresh and brackish waters. The fish are also known as *characids.* Some are found in Central and South America, and one group is found only in Africa. Curiously, one group is found in both South America and Africa, bolstering the theory that these two continents were once joined. Species such as tetras and deadly piranhas are popular with tropical fish hobbyists.

Most characins are small; they range in size from 1 inch to 5 feet (2.5 to 150 cm). Many are brilliantly colored. They usually have strong, highly efficient teeth, although some species are toothless. Most characins have an adipose fin, which distinguishes them from carp and other related fishes. Some have broadly anal and dorsal fins; and several small species have large pectoral fins, which they beat rapidly to fly short distances over the water. All characins have specialized anterior vertebrae, called the Weberian apparatus, that probably function in the perception of sound and pressure.

Some characin are voracious predators, even eating other characin; others are omnivorous, while still others are strict vegetarians. Most strew their eggs among aquatic plants and abandon them. In a few species, however, the males tend the eggs until they hatch.

Characins constitute the family Characidae in the order Cypriniformes. They are related to minnows, carp, and catfish.

EDWIN S. IVERSEN, *University of Miami*

CHARACTER, kar′ik-tər, in literature, a personage in a novel, short story, drama, or poem. The term "character" also denotes the essential qualities and personality traits of a fictional or real individual. The ability to create compelling and believable characters is one of the hallmarks of the literary artist.

A character in a work of fiction may be realized in a number of ways. He may be a "flat," two-dimensional figure or a "round," three-dimensional figure. A flat character, sometimes known as a "type character," is usually lightly sketched, without much detail. A round character is generally a complex personality, a fully realized individual. The chief character or hero of a piece of fiction or drama is usually three-dimensional and is known as the *protagonist.* His adversary, if any, is known as the *antagonist.*

Most novels and plays have flat characters to offset round ones. In some fiction, including mystery and adventure stories, where plot is more important than character development, most characters are flat.

CHARACTER originally denoted a die for stamping coins as well as the device stamped upon them. It comes directly from ancient Greek. In contemporary English the word retains this sense, and it may be used to refer to letters of the alphabet or other signs in written language. However, through the years it acquired, among others, the additional meaning of the unique, differentiating aspects of an individual or group of individuals or of a literary work.

Immanuel Kant first invested the word "character" with an ethical quality, by proposing that it be used solely to designate man's nonmaterial aspect, which he achieves through ethical striving. This particular meaning has evolved to connote an evaluation of personality in terms of some code or standard of moral conduct. This development makes "character" less useful and less current in psychological investigation than it was in the 19th and early 20th centuries.

The popular meaning is now loaded with value judgements and psychologists prefer the term "personality," which has remained more neutrally toned. It is interesting to note that the definition of "personality" is very close to the ancient meaning of "character" as referring to the unique, differentiating aspects of an individual.

MICHAEL G. ROTHENBERG, *Columbia University*

CHARACTER READER, a device that scans printed information and automatically recognizes each character that it encounters. The character reader, which was developed for fast and accurate entry of information into a modern electronic computer, can identify letters, numbers, and special characters at rates up to 2,500 characters per second.

How a Reader Works. A character reader advances the document, finds the area to be read, and identifies the characters on the document. The character recognition patterns are converted to electrical signals, which are transferred to the computer for processing.

Document advance depends entirely on mechanical equipment. The document is moved from a stacker, which holds unread documents, to a read station. The area to be read on the document is located by the character reader by contrast detection, recognition of special symbols on the document, recognition of a standardized document format, and other methods.

At the read station, characters are sensed by either optical or magnetic devices. An *optical character reader* has a powerful light source and a lens system for distinguishing black and white patterns. A *magnetic character reader* senses characters that are printed with a special magnetic ink containing iron oxide particles.

The magnetic or optical sensors at the read station convert printed information into electrical signals. Each signal uniquely represents a character or a character segment. The particular electrical signal is compared with a set of standard signals for identification by matching. After a match is established, an appropriate electrical signal is sent from the character reader to the computer.

Special typefaces have been designed for ease of machine recognition, because the most important means for distinguishing characters is by their shape. In a special typeface, there is as much difference as possible between the shapes of characters. Some character readers recognize several different typefaces, but operation is simpler when only one type face is to be read.

Uses. Magnetic character readers process checks for banks. Individual and bank identifications are printed on checks before they are used. When a used check arrives at the bank of origin, the amount is read by a clerk who uses a machine to print the amount on the check in magnetic ink. Then the character reader reads the check and supplies full posting information to the computer.

Optical character readers are used for many tasks, such as reading credit card charges, public utility bills, and insurance premium bills. Since the reader gets information from a company-prepared form, such as a charge card or computer print-out, it only needs to recognize the typeface used by the company.

IVAN FLORES, *Stevens Institute of Technology*

CHARACTERISTICS, published in 1711 (rev. ed. 1714), is the chief work of the English moral philospher Anthony Ashley Cooper, 3d Earl of Shaftesbury. Fully titled *Characteristics of Men, Manners, Opinions, and Times,* the book is composed of five previously published treatises—on virtue, the paradoxes of state, enthusiasm, the moralist, and common sense—and a sixth treatise answering criticisms of the preceding ones. The style is intended to be conversational, but often seems artificial and pedantically discursive to the modern reader.

Characteristics reflects the influence of Plato and the Stoics. It places Shaftesbury as an important link between the Cambridge Platonists of the 17th century and the moral intuitionists of the 18th century and as the founder of the "moral sense" school of philosophy. The book bases goodness and beauty neither on revelation nor fashion but in the divine and absolute perfection of Nature, whose harmony proves the existence of a benevolent deity. What man sees as flaws would seem so if he could know the whole pattern of the universe. In opposition to the egoistic Hobbes, Shaftesbury sees man as naturally social and emotionally inclined to find such concepts as justice and mercy personally satisfying and hence beautiful. A virtuous life achieves a balance between "natural affections" (the inclination toward public good) and "self-affections" (the inclination toward private good), and so produces happiness. Personal pleasure and public welfare are thus interdependent in the ordered, harmonious balance of the universe; the good and the beautiful are ultimately one.

GEORGIA DUNBAR, *Hofstra University*

CHARACTERIZATION, in literature, is the presentation of the attitudes and behavior of imaginary persons in order to make them credible to the author's audience. Characterization is a unique feature of such fictional forms as the short story, novel, drama, and narrative poetry. Criticism regards good characterization as an important criterion of excellence in fiction.

An author may choose one of three methods to present a character. He may directly describe a character's personality, as do omniscient novelists, such as Henry Fielding in *Tom Jones* (1749); he may have the reader deduce the personality of a character from his actions, as in drama, thus enabling a character such as Shakespeare's Hamlet to remain enigmatic; or he may present the inner workings of a character's mind, showing the character's psychological reactions to the situations in which he becomes involved. Examples of the latter method of characterization are found in such stream-of-consciousness novels as William Faulkner's *The Sound and the Fury* (1929).

A character may be drawn with a few marked personality traits or with a complex collection of them. In Ben Jonson's "comedies of humours," or in the comedies of Molière, each character has a single dominant trait. This approach carried to extreme results in caricature. Usually the major characters in a work of fiction tend to be what E. M. Forster called "round characters," while minor ones tend to exhibit only a few dominant traits.

A character may also be either static, showing little change, or dynamic, that is, significantly affected by the events of the narrative. Most novels and full-length plays concern the development of dynamic characters, while static characters are more often the subjects of one-act plays and short stories.

C. HUGH HOLMAN
Coauthor of "A Handbook to Literature"

CHARADES, shə-rādz′, is a parlor game for two groups of players known as *actors* and *audience*, who take turns at pantomiming and guessing an idea within a set time. The audience first selects a subject (for example, book title, quotation, event) and then informs one of the actors of the choice. The actor, through expressive bodily or facial movements, attempts to convey the idea to his teammates. He may use prearranged signals to indicate that his team's guesses are "hot" (close) or "cold" (way off) or to show the number of words or syllables in the idea. A member of the audience keeps time from the moment the actor indicates that he is ready to begin, and if time is called before the opponents guess correctly, the actor must stop. Actors and audience change sides until everyone has a chance to be the actor. The winning team is the one that uses the least time to guess all the ideas used.

FRANK K. PERKINS, *Boston "Herald"*

CHARAS, the name used in the Far East for a narcotic resin obtained from the hemp plant. See HEMP.

CHARCOAL is an amorphous, porous form of carbon made by the destructive distillation of almost any carbonaceous material. It may be prepared from wood, bone, corn cobs, rice hulls, nutshells, fruit seeds, and vegetable wastes such as bagasse and lignin.

Production. Originally, charcoal was produced by stacking hard or soft wood in piles or long rows that were covered with earth; a small opening was left in the top through which a fire was lighted, and the wood was allowed to smolder for about 10 days. The hole was then closed, the fire smothered, and the charcoal collected.

In commercial plants, the raw materials are carbonized in retorts or kilns, and the by-products of the process, such as methyl alcohol, acetic acid, and wood tar, are collected by condensation and then further distilled and purified.

Uses. Charcoal is used to some extent as a domestic fuel, both for heating and cooking. Because of its low sulfur content, it is used to replace coke in the processing of some types of iron. Wood charcoal is also used for making black gunpowder, for carburizing steel, in the production of calcium carbide, sodium cyanide, and carbon tetrachloride, and for making arc electrodes.

Activated Charcoal. Activated charcoal is produced by heating animal bones or certain types of vegetable charcoal to temperatures of 800 to 900° C (1470–1650° F) in steam or carbon dioxide. This treatment results in the formation of a highly developed internal pore structure with a very large surface area that may be as high as 2,000 square meters per gram (714,000 sq ft per ounce). In the form of an adsorbent powder, activated charcoal is used to decolorize sugar and to purify drinking water, oils, and a variety of substances in the chemical, food, and pharmaceutical industries.

The granular form of activated charcoal is used to adsorb gases in the purification of chemicals and industrial gases. It is used in air conditioning systems to remove odors and irritants. Activated charcoal, in conjunction with chemicals, is used in industrial and military gas masks. In the exhaust systems and coolant gas systems of nuclear reactor installations, activated charcoal adsorbs and holds radioactive contaminants until the isotope decays.

PAUL B. EATON, *Purdue University*

CHARCOT, shàr-kō′, **Jean** (1867–1936), French explorer, who made important discoveries in Antarctica. He was born in Neuilly-sur-Seine on July 15, 1867. He was a physician but turned to exploration and oceanographic studies. Charcot led expeditions in 1903–1905 and 1908–1910 that explored the western side of the Antarctic Peninsula and discovered the island that is named for him. His maps of the region were of great value in enlarging the knowledge of the continent.

On later voyages he studied the submarine life of the north Atlantic Ocean, English Channel, and Mediterranean Sea. He perished when his vessel, the *Pourquoi Pas?* was wrecked off the coast of Iceland on Sept. 16, 1936.

CHARCOT, shàr-kō′, **Jean Martin** (1825–1893), French clinician and teacher who was distinguished for his work in clinical neurology. He described the painful gastric crises and destructive joint lesions (Charcot's joints) in locomotor ataxia, a syphilitic affliction of the nervous system. He clearly differentiated amyotrophic lateral sclerosis (a progressive muscular wasting disease) and distinguished paralysis agitans (Parkinson's disease) from multiple sclerosis. A group of symptoms in multiple sclerosis, consisting of intention tremor, nystagmus (constant involuntary movement of the eyeball), and scanning speech (pronouncing words slowly) is referred to as Charcot's triad. He also pioneered in the clinical studies of hysteria, hypnosis, and other aspects of psychiatry. Freud was one of his students.

Charcot was born in Paris on Nov. 29, 1825. He earned a medical degree at Paris in 1853, and in 1862 became a physician at the renowned neurological Salpêtrière hospital. There he was appointed professor of pathological anatomy in 1872 and in 1882 became the first professor of nervous diseases.

Charcot achieved fame with his dramatic public clinics. Patients were presented on a stage equipped with footlights and spotlights, while Charcot explained their case histories and clinical signs, acting out their various gaits, tics, and postures for his audiences. He illustrated the pathological findings with lantern slides.

The clinical versatility of Charcot was shown in his descriptions of disease states involving systems other than the nervous system. Clinicians today are familiar with Charcot's biliary fever, caused by obstruction of the common bile duct, and with Charcot-Leyden crystals, observed in the sputum of asthmatic patients. In 1867 he published a book on old age, which foreshadowed geriatrics. Charcot also introduced the study of medical history and disease as illustrated in the arts. He died on Aug. 16, 1893.

IRVING SOLOMON, M. D.
Mount Sinai School of Medicine, New York

CHARD, Swiss. See BEET—*Swiss Chard.*

CHARDIN, shàr-daN′, **Jean** (1643–1712), French author and traveler, who was noted for his fascinating account of his travels in Persia and India, published as *Voyage en Perse et aux Indes orientales* (1711). He was born in Paris on Nov. 26, 1643. In 1664 he traveled to the East to buy diamonds, spending several years in Isfahan, Persia, where he was engaged less in trade than in study, and where he made use of his connections at the royal court to gain valuable political information about Persia. Returning to France in 1670, he went to the East again a year later. After another four years in Isfahan, he traveled home, via India, in 1677.

In 1681, Chardin fled France to avoid persecution as a Protestant, and settled in London. In 1683 he was sent to Holland as representative of the English East India Company and as plenipotentiary of King Charles II. Chardin was knighted, as Sir John Chardin, in 1681. He died in London on Dec. 25, 1712.

CHARDIN, shàr-daN′, **Jean Baptiste Siméon** (1699–1779), French painter, who was one of the great 18th century masters of genre and still-life subjects. He was born in Paris, on Nov. 2, 1699, the son of a cabinetmaker. He studied under Pierre Jacques Cazes, a painter of historical scenes, and Noël Nicolas Coypel, who specialized in mythological subjects. Chardin's first work consisted primarily of still lifes and animal paintings in the style of such Flemish artists as Jan Fyt and Frans Snyders. An early painting, *The Rayfish* (1728; Louvre, Paris), was highly praised by the critic Denis Diderot. Chardin was admitted to the Royal Academy of Painting and Sculpture in 1728.

Still-life paintings continued to occupy Chardin throughout his life, but in the 1730's he also began to paint genre subjects in the style of the 17th century masters in the Low Countries, such as Gabriel Metsu and Pieter de Hooch. His own wife and son often served as models for his scenes from the life of the *petite bourgeoisie*, and his genre work has a tender charm that never descends to sentimentality or ancedote.

Chardin rapidly gained popularity among the leading collectors in Europe, and in 1740 he was presented to Louis XV. The King so admired his recently completed *Benediction* and *Industrious Mother* (both in the Louvre) that he added them to his own collection. In 1757, Louis granted Chardin one of the apartments in the Louvre that were reserved for favored artists. Another powerful patron was the Marquis de Marigny, who commissioned Chardin to paint decorations for the Château de Choisy and the Château de Bellevue. Two panels originally

PHOTOGRAPHIE GIRAUDON

JEAN B. CHARDIN'S Le Bénédicité, in the Louvre.

painted for Choisy, the *Attributes of the Arts* and the *Attributes of Music*, are now in the Louvre.

Chardin gained widespread popularity with engraved copies of his work made by Charles Nicolas Cochin and with copies in oil that Chardin later made himself. The pastels that he painted late in life when his sight began to fail are considered among the best of the 18th century. Chardin died in Paris on Dec. 6, 1779.

WILLIAM GERDTS, *University of Maryland*

Further Reading: Rosenberg, Pierre, *Chardin* (Cleveland 1963).

CHARDONNET, shàr-dô-nä′, **Comte de** (1839–1924), French scientist and industrialist who invented a process for making rayon. Louis Marie Hilaire Bernigaud de Chardonnet was born at Besançon on March 1, 1839. After graduating from the École Polytechnique of Besançon in 1861, he went to work in the laboratory of de Ruolz, an inventor, whose niece Chardonnet married in 1865.

While observing Pasteur's studies of silkworms, Chardonnet decided to imitate their spinning process, using a liquid that hardens in air. In 1884 he obtained "a textile material similar to silk" from the solution of a cellulose nitrate in a mixture of alcohol and ether. This artificial silk, called rayon, won the Grand Prix at the Paris Exposition of 1889.

The production of the material was protected by many patents in Chardonnet's name. His early efforts were to perfect the spinning apparatus; the techniques for solvent recovery, denitrification, and waste water treatment came much later. The removal of the nitro groups from the spun fibers reduced both the fire hazards and the difficulties in dyeing. Loss of solvents in storage was reduced by covering the surfaces with floating disks of wood or metal. A description of the entire device for producing rayon was published in January 1924, shortly before Chardonnet's death, in Paris, on March 25, 1924.

EDUARD FARBER, Editor of "Great Chemists"

CHARDZHOU, chär-jō'o͞o, is a city in the Turkmen republic of the USSR, and the capital of Chardzhou oblast. It is a transportation center on the Amu-Darya river, and a junction of two railway lines.

The old section of the city has narrow streets winding between low houses. The modern section contains tree-lined boulevards flanked by large, multistoried buildings. The area surrounding the city is a partially irrigated desert famous for its melons. City factories process silk, cotton, and Astrakhan fur, as well as phosphate from nearby mines. The inhabitants are mostly Turkmen and Russian.

Founded in the 1880's, Chardzhou (at various times known also as Chardzhui and Leninsk-Turkmenski) was once part of the khanate of Bukhara, a Russian protectorate annexed by the USSR in 1924. Population: (1965) 80,000.

                                        ELLSWORTH RAYMOND
                                        New York University

CHARENTE, shà-räNt', is an inland department in the western part of central France. It derives its name from the Charente River, by which it is traversed. Its area is 2,306 square miles (5,973 sq km), and its capital is Angoulême. Its terrain is generally uneven, with hills, sandy plains, and meadows.

The celebrated Cognac brandy is made from a white wine in the districts of Champagne, Cognac, Jarnac, Rouillac, and Aigre. The winegrowers themselves carry on the distillation, each estate having stills and the necessary apparatus. The paper made at Angoulême is said to be the best in France. In addition to brandy and paper, the department produces sacking, cloth, cordage, hats, corks, naval guns, leather, gunpowder, flour, and earthenware. Population: (1962) 327,658.

CHARENTE-MARITIME, shà-räNt' mà-rē-tēm', is a department on the west coast of France. Until 1941 it was called Charente-Inférieure. It is 2,792 square miles (7,231 sq km) in area, and its capital is the port of La Rochelle.

The soil of the department is fertile. The cultivation of vineyards is an important industry; other agricultural products include hemp, flax, saffron, oats, wheat, maize, rye, potatoes, and fruit. The pastures are good and support cattle, horses, and sheep. Along the coast are extensive salt marshes. Industries include the manufacture of salt, brandy, machinery, porcelain and faience wares, and oyster, sardine, mussel, and pilchard fisheries. The department's chief harbors are those of Rochefort and La Rochelle. Population: (1962) 470,897.

CHARENTE RIVER, shà-räNt', in western France. Rising in the department of Haute-Vienne, the Charente flows in a generally westward direction past Angoulême and Cognac and empties into the Bay of Biscay about 10 miles (15 km) south of Rochefort, opposite the Île d'Oléron. Its 225-mile (360-km) course is navigable up to Angoulême, but the river carries little commercial traffic.

The spacious valley of the Charente is one of the most beautiful in France. The river meanders slowly among meadows and hillsides wooded with poplar and chestnut trees. The wines of the region, particularly around Cognac, are of inferior quality, but they are distilled to yield the best brandy in Europe.

CHARES, kâr'ēz, Greek sculptor of the early 3d century B.C. A native of Lindus, Rhodes, he was a pupil of Lysippus and became the recognized head of the school of Rhodes, which in his day was the leading Greek state. Chares was the sculptor of the Colossus of Rhodes (q.v.), one of the Seven Wonders of the World. Representing the Rhodian sun god Helios, it was the largest statue of ancient times, carved between 292 and 280 B.C., but was soon destroyed by an earthquake.

CHARGAFF, chär'gaf, **Erwin** (1905–   ), Austrian-American biochemist, whose work with nucleic acids ushered in the modern era of biochemical genetics. Chargaff found that the parts of a nucleic acid molecule, known as "bases," occur in pairs. This discovery overthrew the prevailing theory that they occur in groups of four and opened the way for the Watson-Crick structural model of deoxyribonucleic acid (DNA).

Work. Prior to his work on nucleic acids, Chargaff had already made important contributions in blood clotting phenomena and in lipid chemistry. For his work with nucleic acids, he devised accurate micro-methods for estimating the amounts of the individual purine and pyrimidine bases in DNA. The purine bases had been found to be adenine (A) and guanine (G), and the pyrimidine bases were known to be thymine (T) and cytosine (C). Chargaff, in 1949, found that the sum of the bases of a DNA molecule equals the sum of the T bases and that the sum of the G bases equals the sum of the C bases. This observation provided the foundation for the theory of base pairing, stating that an A base always pairs with a T base and a G base always pairs with a C base. This theory, together with later observations, led to the proposal in 1953 by J. D. Watson and F. H. C. Crick that DNA consists of a double helix, with the two strands linked together by their paired bases.

Life. Chargaff was born in Vienna, Austria on Aug. 11, 1905. After earning his Ph. D. in 1928 at the University of Vienna he held the Milton Campbell Research Fellowship at Yale University. Between 1930 and 1934 he was at the University of Berlin and the Pasteur Institute in Paris. In 1935 he joined the staff of Columbia University and became a full professor in 1952.

Chargaff's publications include scientific papers and a book, *Essays on Nucleic Acids* (1963). In collaboration with J. N. Davidson, he edited the authoritative work *The Nucleic Acids* (3 vols., 1955–1960).

                                        SAMUEL GRAFF, *Columbia University*

CHARGE, in physics. See ELECTRICITY—2. *Electrostatics.*

CHARGÉ D'AFFAIRES, shär-zhä-də-fâr', a diplomatic representative who is placed in charge of an embassy or legation during the temporary absence of the ambassador or minister plenipotentiary. Distinction is made between this type of representative, known more fully as chargé d'affaires *ad interim*, and a chargé d'affaires *en titre*, who holds permanent appointment. The latter position ranks lower than ambassador, minister plenipotentiary, and resident minister. He is accredited not to the host country's head of state but to its minister of foreign affairs, and he holds his credentials from the minister of foreign affairs of his own country. See also AMBASSADOR.

EGYPTIAN CHARIOT is shown in this detail from an 18th dynasty (1570–1304 B. C.) relief from Tell el Amarna.

CHARGE OF THE LIGHT BRIGADE, a heroic incident in the Battle of Balaklava in the Crimean War. The charge took place on Oct. 25, 1854. During the siege of Sevastopol a Russian force attacked the British wing of the Allied army, whose supply base was the small seaport of Balaklava. The main attack by General Ryzhov's cavalry division was checked by the well-directed uphill charge of Gen. Sir James Y. Scarlett's Heavy Brigade—which was outnumbered four to one by the Russians.

At the beginning of the action some Turkish batteries commanding a valley between two ridges had been overrun by the Russians. Lord Raglan, the British commander in chief, ordered that the guns be retaken, but faulty reconnaissance and muddled orders resulted in the launching of the Light Brigade of Lord Cardigan in a frontal instead of a flanking attack. The doomed squadrons, raked by head-on fire as well as cannon and infantry fire from the flanking ridges, actually rode down the Russian gunners. But the charge was not supported, and less than a third of the light brigade rode back—covered by the intervention of Algerian infantry.

Of the 673 cavalrymen in the attack, only 195 answered the next muster, but many were absent because their horses were casualties. There were actually 113 killed and 134 wounded; 475 horses were killed.

Alfred, Lord Tennyson's ballad *The Charge of the Light Brigade* immortalized the action.

WILLIAM E. D. ALLEN
Coauthor of "Caucasian Battlefields"

CHARI RIVER. See SHARI.

CHARING CROSS, char'ing krôs, in London, England, is the area between the north end of Whitehall and the west end of the Strand, adjoining Trafalgar Square. It is one of London's major traffic centers. Road distances from London often are measured from Charing Cross.

The locality was the site of a hamlet (Cherringe or Charing) where Edward I erected the last of a series of 13 crosses, marking the places where the body of his queen, Eleanor of Castile (who died in Nottinghamshire in 1290), rested on the journey to Westminster Abbey, where she was buried. The cross was torn down in 1647, and the present equestrian statue of Charles I was erected on its site in 1676. The modern "Eleanor Cross," in the courtyard of the Charing Cross railway station, dates from 1863.

CHARIOT, char'ē-ət, most commonly a two-wheeled light vehicle that was drawn by two horses. Chariots were used in war, hunting, travel, and racing.

The earliest known chariot was used in war by the Sumerians in the 2000's B. C. and was a heavy, four-wheeled wagon drawn slowly, usually by four oxen or asses. The wheels were made of solid wood, bound together by crosspieces and banded with leather or copper. These chariots were designed to hold a driver and a chariot-warrior, armed with javelin, axe, and spear. By 1500 B. C. the light horse-drawn chariot had made its appearance as a decisive element in warfare. The Hyksos presumably used it in conquering and controlling Egypt and it was certainly the primary weapon in the successful expulsion of the Hyksos by the Egyptians.

The Egyptian chariot, whether used for war, travel, or state appearances, was essentially of the same construction: two wheels (usually with six spokes, though there are some with four or eight), an axle, a pole springing from the axle, and a body mounted on the axle and pole. A yoke, to which the span was harnessed with a wide breast strap and wooden collar for pulling, was attached to the end of the pole. Chariot bodies were often decorated, sometimes with very elaborate silver and gold patterns. Though Pharaoh was portrayed alone in his chariot, it is probable that when the vehicle was used in war there was always a chariot-warrior, who carried a shield and weapons, with the driver. Chariots seldom attacked directly but swept the flanks and the rear.

Essentially similar chariots were in use in ancient China and all over the ancient Middle East, especially in Syria, Palestine, and Assyria, and they spread through Greece and Rome as far west as Britain and Ireland. The Greeks and Romans, however, soon abandoned them as an instrument of war and limited their use to processions and racing. Roman emperors rode in triumph in chariots drawn by as many as ten horses. The Greek Olympic games in the 7th century B. C. began with chariot races. Rome had professional drivers grouped in factions. They raced up to twenty times a day with four to twelve competing teams of usually four horses. Betting was organized and extensive, and rioting by disgruntled partisans of one faction or the other was not infrequent.

RICHARD A. PARKER
Brown University

CHARISMA, kə-riz′mə, is the quality of personality that sets an individual apart from ordinary men so that he is recognized as having otherworldly or at least uniquely exceptional powers and qualities. Charismatic qualities may be found in the leaders of such varied groups as priests, politicians, revolutionists, artists, and socialites.

A leader is said to have charisma not only because he has a calling to fulfill a mission, but also because there is spontaneous recognition on the part of his followers of his uncommon and unusual characteristics, abilities, and personality. This recognition, which is based on irrational feelings and emotions, seems to flow from a quality resembling divine grace in the leader.

The term "charisma" has a wide range of applications, but it is never used to refer to a leader's cause or the end for which he strives. It has reference only to leadership qualities. For example, despite the dissimilarity in their political aims, Adolf Hitler and Franklin D. Roosevelt can both be classified as leaders who had a strong charisma.

In sociological analysis, the term has been used to characterize a certain type of authority. Max Weber, a German sociologist, suggested that there are three kinds of authorities. Two of these, the traditional and the rational, or legal, types, are more or less stable. The third, the charismatic authority, is transitory, unstable, and often a response to a revolutionary social situation. An example of this type of charismatic authority is Napoleon I of France.

Social crises arising out of rapidly changing beliefs, values, and modes of behavior or out of economic and political instability are particularly apt to produce charismatic leaders. Such leadership, therefore, often carries with it the idea of mass excitement and collective fervor. It always challenges ordinary, established practices and generally results in radical societal changes.

The character of the charismatic authority tends to be undemocratic because the leader demands rather than seeks recognition. The leader does not necessarily represent his followers' opinions or even their interests, although there is usually an elating unity between leader and followers. This relationship is precarious and the charismatic leader is likely to lose his authority if his mission fails.

Since charismatic authority is transitory and personal, problems of political continuity necessarily accompany such a phenomenon. It is difficult, for example, to find and justify a successor to such a leader and to maintain his charismatic fervor while ordinary, routine, and stable relations are being reestablished.

MARLIS KRÜGER and FRIEDA SILVERT
City College, New York

CHARITON, kar′ə-ton, was a Greek writer of romances, who lived not later than the 2d century A. D., probably in Aphrodisias, Caria, in southwestern Asia Minor. His romance *Chaereas and Callirhoë* is the earliest surviving Greek novel. In this story, Chaereas, a citizen of Syracuse, mistakenly believes that he has killed his wife Callirhoë during a violent quarrel. He is filled with anguish and remorse, and upon learning that she is still alive but has been sold into slavery, he sets out to find and rescue her. After many harrowing adventures, Chaereas and Callirhoë are reunited and return to Syracuse.

CHARITY is the last and greatest of the Christian virtues and is so recognized by moralists in many religions and by nonreligious thinkers. The cardinal virtues were named by Plato as prudence, temperance, fortitude (or courage), and justice. These were elaborated by Aristotle and the Stoics and in the Middle Ages were taken over as the foundation of morals. Superimposed upon them were the three Christian virtues: faith, hope, and charity (as listed by Paul in I Corinthians 13:13). The whole chapter by Paul is a paean of divine love, which human beings should imitate, participate in, and emulate. Thus charity is a part—the chief part—of the "imitation of God"—that is, righteousness—which the Stoics had enjoined and the Christians had made central to all ethics. See also CARDINAL VIRTUES.

Love and Almsgiving. The Greek word used by Paul and the earliest Christians was *agapê,* which meant self-giving love; the alternative, *erōs,* though originally not limited to sexual or possessive love, had come to denote what Renaissance poets and artists called "profane" love, in contrast to "divine" or "heavenly" love. Nowhere in the New Testament is "love" used to mean almsgiving. I Corinthians 13 seems to consider a worldly concern for the poor and to contrast it with pure love. Moreover, "charity" fell short of the highest and purest love, with the result that modern English translators of the Bible have substituted "love" for "charity." But in the Middle Ages the Latin word *caritas,* from which charity is derived, was filled with the richest meanings of self-denial and self-sacrifice for the sake of others. It was only in the post-Reformation period that charity became identified with almsgiving. To the Reformers, giving alms was a pretended means of winning merit, and this led to the rejection of "charity" in Biblical texts and hence in general religious usage among Protestants. But the word is too rich in meaning to be abandoned: pure charity is the noblest of virtues.

The Practice of Charity. The Old Testament stresses charity (Deuteronomy 15:7–15; Isaiah 58:6–7). Obedience to God and care for the needy were cardinal demands upon Jewish piety. The love of God and love of one's neighbor, summarized in the Old Testament, are reinforced in the Talmud and other Jewish writings.

In ancient Greece the practice of charity grew out of the emphasis placed on hospitality and the "sacredness" of the wayfarer, whose rights must be maintained. The beggar must not be passed by or driven from one's door. In Rome the wealthy and the state aided the needy.

In other religions the giving of alms was viewed as a solemn duty, as in Buddhism, where to this day many poor persons and ascetics are supported by the dole provided by generous givers. Muslim law enforces the duty of giving to the poor and the dedication of property for pious or charitable purposes. In all religions charity has tended to provide a self-return. The beggar prays for the donor, and the generous giver feeds three: "himself, his hungering neighbor, and me," the divine being who encourages the charity.

In all lands, the care of the needy is becoming more and more a social obligation, and the state or community is undertaking it. But the religious motivation ("charity") is not always found in "social welfare."

FREDERICK C. GRANT
Union Theological Seminary

CHARLEMAGNE, shär′lə-mān (742?–814), was king of the Franks, first emperor and greatest ruler of the Carolingian dynasty, which bears his name. Charlemagne means Charles the Great in French. He is also known as Charles I, both as king of France and as emperor of the Holy Roman Empire.

By the time of his coronation as emperor in 800, Charlemagne's ceaseless military campaigns had brought many tribes under his rule—from the Avars along the Danube to the Bretons on the Atlantic coast, from the Frisians and Saxons who lived along the North Sea to the Bavarians in southern Germany, the Lombards of northern Italy, and the mixed peoples of the Spanish March. Although Charlemagne's realm was held together by his own power and was not, in the modern sense, a territorial state, it was the largest realm the West had known since the 4th century.

Charlemagne's reign was known for the Carolingian Renaissance, a rebirth of the imperial, scholarly, and law-making traditions of the Roman Empire. His vast empire was given legal codes. Scholars were encouraged to explore the great works of the past and to create new works. Tribal forms of government began to give way and the forms of government that characterized the Middle Ages—especially feudalism—began to take shape.

Charlemagne's Inheritance. The exact place and year of Charlemagne's birth is uncertain, but it is likely that he was born in 742 and that the place of his birth was Aachen (Aix-la-Chapelle in French), now in West Germany. His paternal grandfather was Charles Martel. His father was Pepin III (known as Pepin the Short), king of the Franks. His mother's name was Bertha.

The shaping of Charlemagne's political attitudes and political future began when he was a boy. In 750 his father, Pepin III, began negotiating an alliance with Pope Zacharias (reigned 741–752) in which the Pope recognized Pepin as king of the Franks. In 754 the bond with the papacy was further strengthened when Pope Stephen III (reigned 752–757) crowned Pepin and his sons, Charlemagne and Carloman, jointly as kings of the Franks and Patricians of the Romans. Sometime between 754 and 756, probably in 756, Pepin promised the papacy extensive land holdings in central and northern Italy and pledged his support and that of his heirs to defend papal rights in this area if challenged. This promise is known as the Donation of Pepin.

When Pepin died in 768, his titles and land holdings were shared by his two sons. Carloman was given southern and central France (including eastern Aquitaine), Alsace, and the regions around Orléans, Paris, and Reims. Charlemagne received the rest, from the Atlantic coast of Aquitaine to Thuringia. Charlemagne was crowned a second time, at Noyon.

King of the Lombards. In 770, much against the will of Pope Stephen IV, who feared a coalition against the papacy, Charlemagne's mother, Bertha, entered a diplomatic arrangement with the Lombards, who controlled most of Italy. The alliance was sealed in 770 by the marriage of Charlemagne to a daughter of Desiderius, the Lombard king. But the alliance did not endure. Within a year Charlemagne had expelled his wife. When his brother Carloman died in 771, Carloman's widow fled with their children to Lombardy, and Charlemagne seized Carloman's lands. Thereby he became sole king of all the Franks. Having no further need of the Lombard alliance, he divorced Desiderata, his Lombard wife. He was later to have several other wives and concubines.

The terms of the Donation of Pepin now came into play, for it was the papacy's fear of the Lombards that had prompted the arrangements made in the Donation. In 772, Pope Adrian I appealed to Charlemagne for military help, protesting that Desiderius, Charlemagne's father-in-law and king of the Lombards, had usurped control of papal lands. Adrian invoked Charlemagne's oath to defend the Roman Church.

Charlemagne's first move was to offer Desiderius a substantial financial settlement on the condition that he withdraw from the lands claimed by the papacy. When Desiderius refused to comply, Charlemagne renewed the Donation of Pepin and invaded Italy. This was the first of Charlemagne's five military expeditions into Italy, and the most successful. Desiderius was captured and imprisoned in a Frankish monastery. Carloman's widow and children fell into Charlemagne's custody and disappeared. The Lombard duchies of northern Italy submitted to Charlemagne, who assumed the title of king of the Lombards.

Emperor. In 781, Charlemagne used the papacy's special powers to strengthen his position by persuading Pope Adrian I to crown his sons Pepin and Louis kings, respectively, of Italy and Aquitaine. But his support of Adrian's successor, Leo III, who came to the papal throne in 795, won Charlemagne the imperial crown. Leo III had not been able to reconcile the factions that split at his election. The crisis reached a head in 799 when Pope Leo, charged by his enemies with both perjury and adultery, was waylaid during a religious procession in Rome and brutally attacked. Charlemagne's envoys in Rome rescued Leo from his attackers and sent him to Gaul. Charlemagne interviewed him at Paderborn and then dispatched him back to Rome with a commission of inquiry to look into the charges against him. Later Charlemagne went to Rome himself. He would have presided at Leo's trial, but the Pope was allowed to clear himself of the charges against him on canonical grounds, without trial, by taking an oath of purgation before Charlemagne and a synod. After punishing Leo's enemies, Charlemagne was ritually crowned and adored as emperor by the Pope on Christmas Day, 800. At the same time, Leo also crowned Charlemagne's son Charles as king of the Franks.

The final step in Charlemagne's political ascendancy came in 812. As a result of a Frankish naval defeat of the Byzantine forces, and after palace revolutions in Constantinople, the Byzantine emperor, Michael I, acknowledged Charlemagne as emperor. Charlemagne died on Jan. 28, 814, at Aachen.

Empire Builder. Although some of the territory in Charlemagne's empire came to him through inheritance and through diplomatic negotiations and alliances, he won other parts by conquest. He had first invaded Italy in 773–774. His next three invasions (776, 780–781, 786–787) consolidated his conquests there and settled his conflicts with the papacy.

Charlemagne made one expedition into Spain, in 778, fighting both the Arabs and the Christian Basques, who inflicted upon him the famous defeat of Roncevalles. Forced to retreat, he left Spain north of the Ebro River to local governors, encouraging them to make guerrilla war against the Arabs. He organized the Spanish March.

Beginning in 778, Charlemagne strove to supplant Breton tribal authorities with agents of his royal government. He himself led two expeditions to quell the ensuing Breton revolts in 786 and again in 799.

The most dangerous and protracted struggles of Charlemagne's reign occurred in the East. From 773 on, the Saxons launched periodic attacks on Frankish lands, once penetrating as far as Cologne under their leader Wittekind. Their raids inflicted great destruction, and Charlemagne responded with fire and sword. In 785 he brought Wittekind to a settlement, set forth in Charlemagne's capitulary *De partibus Saxoniae*, in which, among other things, he prescribed death for any Saxon who refused to be baptized. Acceptance of the Franks' God signified submission to their king, Charlemagne. However, the settlement provided only a pause in the fighting. Almost every year between 792 and 800 there was a Saxon revolt against the Franks. A final outburst occurred in 804.

Charlemagne was able to win clearer victories along the Saale and Danube rivers over the Bavarians and their allies, the Avars. Duke Tassilo, the ruler of Bavaria, conspired with Arechis of Benevento against Charlemagne. The duke also entered into a pact with the Avars in 781. In 787, Charlemagne invaded Bavaria, seized and imprisoned Tassilo, and divided his duchy among his counts. In 794, at the Synod of Frankfurt, Charlemagne forced Tassilo publicly to abdicate his authority over Bavaria.

Charlemagne launched an elaborate campaign against the Avars by land and river. Forced to retreat in 791, he left command of his army to his son, Pepin of Italy. In 795 the Franks seized the camp of the leader of the Avars, called the Khagan, and with it enormous treasure. The Franks had to put down further Avar revolts in 796 and again in 805. As in Saxony, conversion to Christianity followed conquest. Charlemagne made the city of Salzburg, now in Austria, a missionary center for work among the Avars. In 805 the leader of the Avars was converted and entered Charlemagne's custody.

By means of these conquests and by endless negotiations and alliances Charlemagne created the Frankish empire.

Administration. The rapid extension of Charlemagne's control over many diverse and widely separated peoples required administrative improvisation of a high order. In some lands, like the duchy of Benevento, he subjected the local rulers to his service by oaths of fealty. In other areas, as in Bavaria, he supplanted the local rulers with his own agents. Along his frontiers he erected buffer provinces, called marches, commanded by counts with virtually autonomous powers. These "margraves" (as such counts were called) erected a military cordon, or line of defense, between the Franks and hostile peoples outside the empire.

In Frankish lands, Charlemagne developed the administrative system of his predecessors, making counts and bishops his agents in local government. He introduced the *missi dominici* (teams of inspectors), each consisting of one count and one bishop, who went as his personal envoys through a number of counties, supervising fiscal and legal matters.

Of his many specific changes, Charlemagne's reform of the Frankish monetary system in 790–794 was perhaps the most important. By increasing the weight of the pound and reserving to the crown the exclusive mintage of silver, he began the monometallic system of currency that prevailed in western Europe until the 13th century.

Law. Besides introducing the capitulary as a form of legal promulgation in 779, Charlemagne had written copies prepared of the tribal laws of the Saxons, Thuringians, and Frisians. He also supplemented the Bavarian code and, after 800, revised the codes of the two chief Frankish tribes, the Ripuarians and the Salians. He also encouraged the study of Church law. In the *Codex Carolinus*, he made a collection of 8th century papal letters to Frankish kings, which was invaluable for later studies of canon law.

Religion and Learning. Charlemagne's father had encouraged the purification of liturgical texts. Under Charlemagne himself a critical study of the liturgy led to a scrutiny of Scriptural texts and, ultimately, to the highly accurate Alcuinian Rescension (or edition) of the Scriptures, prepared under the supervision of Alcuin, the Anglo-Saxon scholar. Careful editions were also prepared of ancient and patristic writings.

The papal alliance was, from the beginning, essential to this work. For although the Franks differed with the papacy on political issues, they accepted the authority of the church in matters of faith and religious practice. Charlemagne sought and received from Adrian I books of liturgical order, an authentic copy of the Benedictine rule, and an authoritative collection of canon law texts. The Carolingian concepts of the king as the vicar of God, of his realm as in some sense a reflection of the Heavenly Kingdom, and of royal ceremonies as a sort of divine liturgy made these theological and liturgical studies an integral part of Charlemagne's effort to establish a reign of law and order.

Charlemagne was convinced that right government, that is, government upheld by divine favor, must follow a pattern that careful study could uncover in Christianity's holy books. This conviction led to stringent regulations about education of the clergy. Ordination of illiterates was forbidden. He assembled the so-called Palatine Academy to prepare textual criticism and to teach the clergy of the royal chapel, from among whom bishops were usually chosen.

Alcuin, the Anglo-Saxon scholar, was Charlemagne's closest academic adviser between 782 and 796. The Lombard scholar Paul the Deacon, Peter of Pisa, Agobard of Spain, Leidrad of Bavaria, Theodulf the Visigoth, and the eunuch Elissaeus (the Byzantine tutor in Greek) gathered at Charlemagne's court both as intellectual ornaments representing his far-flung empire and as theological strategists in what Charlemagne, inspired by St. Augustine's *City of God*, considered his war against the Devil for peace and justice.

The normal conduct of government, court ceremonies and architecture, as well as Charlemagne's intervention in great theological disputes (such as the Adoptionist conflict in Spain and the iconoclastic controversy in Byzantium) show the impact of the scholars' work. Indeed, the blending of modes of thought from many lands was ultimately the most lasting achievement of Charlemagne's reign. The scholars' letters, treatises, and canon law collections survived, together with the legislation Charlemagne issued under their counsel. Their teachings disciplined the great theologians and lawyers in the reign of Charlemagne's grandson Charles the Bald. The missionary work among the eastern tribes pressed the frontier of Christendom beyond the Elbe River and gave that region the cultural stamp that still appears in its retention of the Latin rite of the Christian church rather than the Eastern rite.

Weaknesses in the Empire. The intellectual accomplishments of Charlemagne's empire endured, but the empire they were meant to sustain crumbled. In Charlemagne's day, western Europe was just emerging from a period of political and cultural anarchy. His predecessors, in the aftermath of the barbarian invasions, had laid foundations on which Charlemagne built the illusion of a vast and powerful empire. Like most barbarian kingdoms, Charlemagne's realm was actually a personal union. The empire was an agglomeration of kingdoms and provinces, a confederation of tribes, having nothing in common besides personal subjection to Charlemagne.

Charlemagne had gathered the empire; he could divide it as he chose. In 806, he prepared a division of the empire among his three sons. But two of the sons predeceased him, and shortly before his own death Charlemagne crowned as emperor his son Louis the Pious. Consequently, Louis inherited the empire intact, but he partitioned it among his own sons. This act unleashed the tribal divisions, the increasing independence of great nobles, and the latent power of the protofeudal classes that Charlemagne had both held in check and encouraged to his own advantage. The system of local administration, the cordon of marches, and all other administrative supports of Charlemagne's personal union dissolved in a welter of civil wars.

Still, the assertion of independent power by the great nobles marked progress toward a new and higher system of government as well as the decay of a primitive order. The splintering of Charlemagne's empire signified the end of tribal government in which the realm was, in effect, the personal property of the king. It indicated the beginning of the state as a permanent, territorial unit bound up with, but still separate from, individual kings. Thus began the distinction, extremely faint at first, between king and kingdom that lies at the heart of constitutional forms of government.

Achievement. In most of his works, Charlemagne built on precedents. His special talents lay, not in innovation, but in development. Pepin the Short had introduced the Roman mode of chant and the purification of liturgical texts, which under Charlemagne evolved into a broad revival of law, theology, and rhetoric. Charlemagne's involvement in Roman affairs was rooted in negotiations that began under Charles Martel and matured in Pepin's alliance with Pope Stephen III. His role as patron of Christian missions among the pagan tribes between the Weser and Elbe rivers likewise continued policies of Charles Martel and Pepin. It was as though Charlemagne's predecessors had stretched a canvas, made preliminary designs, and left him the greater work of the final design and painting.

By his conquests, Charlemagne takes his place with the Byzantine emperors and the caliphs of Baghdad and Cordova as a great ruler. He entered into diplomatic negotiation with all of them. The silks, balsam, musk, and spices that, according to a chronicle ascribed to Einhard, went with Charlemagne to his tomb at Aachen in 814 gave evidence of the wide contacts of his realm.

Posterity overlooks Charlemagne's slaughter of the Saxons, his probable murder of his brother Carloman's children, his treachery toward Desiderius, his Lombard father-in-law, and his moral laxity, which scandalized even the barbaric age in which he lived. Posterity remembers the victories and the broad movement of government reform and learning that accompanied them, which has been called the Carolingian Renaissance.

K. F. MORRISON, *University of Chicago*

Bibliography

Buckler, Francis William, *Harunu'l-Rashid and Charles the Great* (Cambridge, Mass., 1931).
Bullough, Donald, *The Age of Charlemagne* (London 1965).
Fichtenau, Heinrich, *The Carolingian Empire*, tr. by Peter Munz (New York and London 1957).
Grant, Arthur James, ed. and tr., *Early Lives of Charlemagne* (London 1926).
Sullivan, Richard Eugene, *The Coronation of Charlemagne: What Did It Signify?* (Boston 1959).

CHARLEROI, shàr-lə-rwä′, is a city in south central Belgium, on the Sambre River, in Hainaut province. It is a leading industrial center. Originally the village of Charnoy, it took its present name in 1666 in honor of Charles II, king of Spain.

In the mid-20th century Charleroi's prosperity suffered as the coal mines of the region proved unable to meet the competition of new fields opened near the Netherlands border in the Flemish Campine. The chief problem appeared to be the narrowness, irregularity, and depth of the veins and the obsolescence of the machinery used to work them. Government subsidies, which slowed the closing of marginally producing mines, were being phased out during the 1960's. Unemployment and social unrest resulted, exacerbated by the distrust of the Walloon inhabitants for what they considered to be the increasing influence of Flemings in Belgium as a whole. Despite these difficulties, the Charleroi region has remained an important coal center. The city is also at the heart of a large iron ore mining and steel and machinery manufacturing area. Glassmaking and brewing are undertaken on a large scale.

As an early locus of Belgium's industrial revolution, Charleroi played an influential role in the development of social welfare work, to which its Université du Travail testifies. The city possesses a small airport and excellent rail and water communications. Its location has frequently caused it to be the site of warfare. Fortified by Vauban under Louis XIV during a period of French occupation, Charleroi later passed to the Austrians, from whom it was seized by French Revolutionaries in 1794. During the German invasion in 1914, the city witnessed bitter fighting. Not extensively defended in World War II, it avoided severe destruction at that time. Population: (1965) 25,139.

JONATHAN E. HELMREICH
Allegheny College

CHARLEROI, shär′lə-roi, is an industrial borough in southwestern Pennsylvania, in Washington county. It is on the west bank of the Monongahela River, 22 miles (35 km) south of Pittsburgh. Situated in a coal-mining and dairy-farming region, Charleroi is a center for the production of steel, glass, mining equipment, paper cartons, and beverages.

Named for Charleroi, the mining and industrial center in Belgium, the borough was laid out in 1890. It was incorporated in 1892, and it has a mayor-council form of government. Population: 6,723.

CHARLES

CHARLES: Rulers bearing the name Charles are entered according to realm, as follows:

CHARLES I (1887–1922), emperor of Austria and (as Charles IV) king of Hungary, was born at Persenburg in Lower Austria on Aug. 17, 1887, the son of Archduke Otto and Maria Josepha, Princess of Saxony. His grandfather was the brother of Emperor Francis Joseph. Charles was educated chiefly by foreign tutors. At the age of 18 he joined the army as a lieutenant, and subsequently held various military posts. On Oct. 21, 1911, Charles married Princess Zita of Bourbon-Parma. The eldest of their eight children, Otto, was later to become head of the Habsburg house. With the assassination of Archduke Francis Ferdinand at Sarajevo on June 28, 1914 (which led to the outbreak of World War I), Charles became their apparent. He held various military commands during the war.

On Nov. 21, 1916, at the death of Francis Joseph, Charles succeeded to the thrones of the Dual Monarchy. He was never crowned in Austria or Bohemia, but in response to Magyar demands, he was crowned king of Hungary on Dec. 30, 1916, in an elaborate ceremony. In March 1917, he became involved in an ill-fated attempt to enter into separate peace negotiations with France, through the mediation of his brothers-in-law, the Princes Sixtus and Xavier of Bourbon-Parma. In May, when he summoned the Parliament of Austria, the various national groups that were united under the imperial crown clamored for reform.

On Oct. 16, 1918, Charles issued a proclamation calling for the conversion of the Dual Monarchy into a federated state, but such a reform no longer sufficed to quiet internal revolution. With military defeat, Charles laid down his governmental powers in Austria on Nov. 11, and in Hungary on Nov. 13, 1918, though he never formally abdicated.

Charles went into exile in Switzerland the next year, under British protection. In 1921 he made two unsuccessful attempts to regain the Hungarian throne. Captured during the last attempt, he was exiled to Madeira, where he died of pneumonia on April 1, 1922.

ERNST C. HELMREICH, *Bowdoin College*

Charles the Bold, Duke of Burgundy

CHARLES (1433–1477), Duke of Burgundy, known as *Charles the Bold*. The son of Philip the Good of Burgundy, Charles was born at Dijon on Nov. 10, 1433. He was made a knight of the Golden Fleece and Count of Charolais. Estranged briefly from his father, he turned to Louis XI of France, who appointed him governor of Normandy in 1461. Their cooperation soon broke down, however, when Charles suspected the King of plotting to poison him. From then on Charles and Louis were inveterate foes. When several feudal magnates rebelled against the King in the War of the Common Weal in 1465, Charles allied himself with them and led an attack on Paris. By the Peace of Conflans, Louis reaffirmed Burgundy's claims to some disputed cities on the Somme.

When Philip died in 1467, Charles became Duke of Burgundy. His ambition was to create a strong, centralized state between France and the Holy Roman Empire and ultimately to obtain a crown. This last dream faded when Emperor Frederick III reneged on an earlier promise in 1473. To attain his other goal, Charles centralized the administration of his loose-knit patrimony, reorganized its finances and its army, and created a *parlement* and States-General on the French model.

Charles crushed internal resistance in Liège in 1467 and later in Flanders. He acquired Alsace in 1469 and Gelderland in 1473 and then turned to the conquest of Lorraine. The acquisition of this province would have created the middle state that Charles desired, by joining Burgundy to Artois, Luxemburg, and the Netherlands. But Louis XI thwarted Charles' designs by campaigns and by subsidies to Burgundy's enemies, the Swiss cantons and Lorraine. Only in 1475, when Louis agreed to a 9-year truce, could Charles turn to settling old scores with the Swiss. But his increasingly rash campaigns against them in 1476 met with disastrous defeat. When Charles besieged Nancy, trying to conquer Lorraine, he met his death on Jan. 5, 1477.

The legacy of Charles the Bold was the dissolution of the Burgundian state. His daughter Mary was forced to marry Maximilian of Habsburg to preserve her lands in Flanders, and Burgundy was annexed by Louis XI.

EDMUND H. DICKERMAN
University of Connecticut

CHARLES I (1600–1649), king of England, Scotland, and Ireland, was the only reigning British monarch to die on the scaffold. (His grandmother, Mary, Queen of Scots, was also executed, but she was a prisoner in England.) At his trial, Charles was accused of being a "man of blood" and the enemy of his people.

Early Life. Charles was born on Nov. 19, 1600, at Dunfermline in Scotland, the second son of King James VI of Scotland and his Queen, Anne of Denmark. When Charles' father was called from Scotland to the throne of England as King James I in 1603, Charles was not at first brought to London with him, for he was such a frail child that his life was almost despaired of. He suffered from weak joints throughout his youth and a nervous stutter throughout his life.

On Nov. 6, 1612, on the death of his elder brother, Henry, Charles became the heir apparent to the throne. He was educated by Scottish and English tutors and acquired a taste for art.

Marriage. In line with his policy of peace, King James, from 1617 onward, projected an alliance with Spain through the marriage of Charles to the Infanta Maria, daughter of Philip III. When he was 18, the prince entered into an intimate friendship with his father's favorite, George Villiers, 1st Duke of Buckingham (see VILLIERS), who also supported the idea of a Spanish alliance. In February 1621, Prince Charles and Buckingham visited Madrid, where Charles fell in love with the languorous Spanish princess. Negotiations for the marriage broke down because of excessive Spanish demands, however, and the two Englishmen returned home the following fall, deeply humiliated and breathing fire against the Spanish empire. By the time Charles succeeded to the throne on March 27, 1625, England was at war with Spain, and an alliance with France had been sealed by the new King's proxy marriage to the French King's sister, Henrietta Maria. On June 13, Charles welcomed his bride, whom he had never seen before, at Canterbury.

Parliaments and Their Dissolution. Charles I not only inherited the war against Spain but also soon became involved in an unsuccessful war against France. Because his wars could not be waged without the aid of money voted by the House of Commons, the early Parliaments of Charles' reign were in a strong position to enforce their wishes on the executive and to air new and old grievances. Many members of the Commons were critical of Charles' ecclesiastical policy. They particularly resented the wide-ranging powers of the bishops, and they wanted the church "purified" of Catholic practices.

The leaders of the Commons did not at first criticize the King personally. They blamed the Duke of Buckingham and other "evil advisers" for the war policy and the incompetent manner in which it was carried out. They tried to impose their wishes by refusing the King money. When Charles' third Parliament met, in March 1628, however, they complained about forced loans, illegal levying of customs duties (known as "tunnage and poundage"), and forced billeting of soldiers in households. In particular they protested that the King had no right to imprison his subjects without showing cause why he did so. The Commons set out their various grievances in a constitutional document known as the Petition of Right (q.v.), to which the King was obliged to give his assent in June.

After the assassination of the Duke of Buckingham in the summer of 1628, Charles tried to adjourn the Parliament that met in the following January. Leading members, however, held the speaker of the House of Commons down in his chair while they voted three resolutions condemning the actions of the monarchy as illegal. Charles retaliated by dissolving Parliament, and for the next 11 years he governed without calling another one.

The "Eleven Years' Tyranny." Charles' critics described the period of executive rule as the "eleven years' tyranny." In fact Charles was no more obliged than Queen Elizabeth I had been to call parliaments if he did not wish to; and on the whole, the country was peaceful and prosperous without them at this time.

Some administrative reforms were attempted, and an increase in customs receipts combined with a pacific foreign policy enabled the King to manage without parliamentary grants. Charles raised funds to pay for his navy by "ship money" —a tax which, while it was declared legal by the law courts, aroused widespread resentment among owners of property who had to pay it.

The Civil War. Charles simultaneously antagonized his Scottish Presbyterian subjects by pursuing an ecclesiastical policy designed to make the Scottish and English churches conform with one another. When the Scots openly resisted the ordered changes, Charles began a war against them, in 1639 (see BISHOPS' WARS). His ill-equipped army was defeated, and in April 1640 he was finally obliged to call another Parliament. Prepared to concede almost nothing, he dissolved it in less than a month. His army was again beaten by the Scots that summer, however, and in November, his money all but exhausted, he summoned the so-called Long Parliament.

Taking advantage of the King's difficulties, the leaders of the Long Parliament exacted a reversal of most of his policies. They compelled him to abandon "ship money" and "tunnage and poundage." They made him promise to call Parliaments regularly. They deprived him of important royal prerogatives and forced him to assent to the punishment of his "evil counsellors"— above all to the execution of his chief minister, Thomas Wentworth, Earl of Strafford.

Conflict between the Long Parliament and the King slowly came to a head. On Jan. 4, 1642, the King attempted to arrest five leading members of Parliament on charges of high treason. The attempt failed, but it galvanized the opposition to him. Thereupon Charles retired to the north of England and prepared to make war on Parliament to reestablish his authority. The fighting that followed is known as the First Civil War.

Charles did not lead his armies in any of the fighting. He possessed some very capable generals—notably his nephew, Prince Rupert of the Palatinate—but he confused them with his orders and unjustly blamed them when they suffered defeat. The Royalist cause was ruined in two stunning defeats, at Marston Moor on July 2, 1644, and at Naseby on June 14, 1645.

The First Civil War ended in 1646, when the city of Oxford, Charles' headquarters, surrendered to besieging Parliamentarian forces. Charles escaped in disguise from Oxford and, promising concessions to the Scottish Presbyterians, gave himself up to a Scottish army that had entered England in 1644 to support the Parliamentarians.

Execution of the King. Charles was a prisoner first of Parliament (to whom the Scots delivered

Charles I of England, Scotland, and Ireland

Charles II of England, Scotland, and Ireland

him) and then of the English Army. For two and a half years he vainly negotiated with Parliament to regain his throne, but the Parliamentary leaders regarded him as unlikely to keep his promises. In fact, he made it perfectly clear in correspondence with his wife, who had fled to France, and with other intimates that he would stop at no deception to win back power and safeguard the authority of the church. In December 1647 he signed a secret treaty with a group of Scots that brought about the Second Civil War, in which the Royalists were again defeated. The victorious Parliamentary army then demanded the King's trial and execution.

At his trial in London, Charles refused to recognize the authority of the court or to plead before it. He asserted that he had always stood for the true liberties of his people and was opposed to arbitrary government. Charles was condemned to death as a traitor, and on Jan. 30, 1649, he was beheaded in Whitehall. He met his fate with majestic dignity. "Death is not terrible to me," he said. "I bless my God that I am prepared."

Character. Charles was neither a bloody nor a cruel ruler. He loved his family, and in spite of his nervous disabilities, he always behaved like a king. He was a noble patron of the arts and tried to care for and protect his poorer subjects. But fundamentally he was uncertain of himself, unable to make up his mind, too easily subject to the will of others. He depended heavily on Buckingham and later on his Queen, with whom he belatedly fell in love but he betrayed his wisest servants. His personal weaknesses rather than his policies brought him to his tragic end. See also CIVIL WAR, ENGLISH.

MAURICE ASHLEY
University of Loughborough, England
Author of "Life in Stuart England"

Further Reading: John, Evan, *King Charles I* (New York 1952); Kenyon, John P., *The Stuarts* (London 1958); Roots, Ivan, *Commonwealth and Protectorate: The English Civil War and Its Aftermath* (New York 1966); Wedgwood, Cicily V., *A Coffin for King Charles* (New York 1964).

CHARLES II (1630–1685), king of England, Scotland, and Ireland, regained the English throne his father had lost and defended it for 25 years against threats of revolution. Having no legitimate children himself, he secured the succession of his brother, James, and thus continued the Stuart dynasty.

Early Life. Charles was born in London on May 29, 1630. He was the eldest son of Charles I and Queen Henrietta Maria. The Civil War began when he was 12, and he received scant education thereafter. At 15 he was sent to the west of England in a vain attempt to rally the Royalists there. At the end of the war he fled first to the Scilly Isles, then to the island of Jersey, and finally to exile in France. In July 1648, following the outbreak of the Second Civil War, Charles sailed from Holland to England with a Royalist fleet, but sickness and unpromising circumstances in England forced him to abandon his planned invasion. The Royalist forces capitulated and Charles' father was executed.

In England the monarchy was abolished, but in February 1649, a month after the execution of Charles I, the Scots proclaimed Charles II their king. Charles arrived in Scotland in June 1650, determined that the Scottish Presbyterian leaders would regain his English throne by defeating the Parliamentarians under Oliver Cromwell. He was crowned at Scone on Jan. 1, 1651, but he ruled in Edinburgh only a few months. In August he led a Scottish army into England, was overwhelmingly defeated at the battle of Worcester.

A King in Exile. For nine years Charles wandered about Europe, enjoying himself as best he could and mastering the art of dissimulation. As long as Cromwell lived, all Charles' attempts to overthrow the Protectorate failed. After Cromwell's death in 1658, however, the English Parliamentarians and Cromwell's generals quarreled. Disenchantment rapidly spread through the country, and Charles was almost unanimously welcomed back. He arrived in London on his 30th birthday, May 29, 1660.

Charles as King. Henceforth Charles' aim was

to avoid being "sent on his travels again." Accordingly he played off his ministers and advisers against each other; he accommodated his wishes to his Parliaments', and he sought the protection of Louis XIV of France, the most powerful king in Europe. For seven years Charles' principal ministers were Edward Hyde, 1st Earl of Clarendon, and others who had served his father. But Charles balanced them with younger men who had served him during his exile. He also employed some of those former Cromwellians who had helped restore him to his throne. As a supreme act of conciliation, he allowed his first Parliament, elected on a wave of loyalty, to sit intermittently for 17 years.

The Treaty of Dover. In 1667, Clarendon, with whom Charles had grown bored, became a scapegoat for England's unsuccessful prosecution of a war against the Dutch. Charles selected a number of new ministers at that time, but he became in effect his own chief executive. As such, in May 1670 he concluded a treaty with France through the agency of his sister Henrietta Anne, the wife of the French King's brother. Charles agreed to renew the war against the Dutch in alliance with the French. He also agreed to declare himself, at an appropriate time, a Roman Catholic and to accept French assistance in returning his subjects to the Roman Church.

What Charles' precise motives were is obscure. Some historians consider the promise to become a Roman Catholic to have been merely a ruse to get extra money from Louis XIV. Be that as it may, the plot against the Dutch failed; the English Navy was humiliated again, and opinion in England swung increasingly against France and Catholicism.

Internal Policy. Despite his foreign policy Charles may not himself have been a convinced Catholic. He believed in religious toleration and tried vainly to offset the bigoted "Churchmanship" of the Anglican majority in his Parliaments by issuing two Declarations of Indulgence. But anti-Catholicism was stronger than he was. In 1673, Parliament forced him to agree to the Test Act, whereby only members of the Church of England were allowed to hold office; and three Parliaments in succession demanded that Charles' brother, James, Duke of York, who was known by 1673 to be a Roman Catholic, should be excluded from the throne.

Charles fought a long, astute, and ultimately successful battle of wits against these "Exclusionists." He loosened their hold on the influential city of London by obliging Parliament to meet in Oxford in 1681, and after the two houses of Parliament had quarreled with each other there, he dissolved the body and dispensed with it altogether.

Charles' success was due partly to the excesses of the rebellious Exclusionists, or Whigs. Just as in 1678 a story of an imaginary plot (known as "the Popish Plot") had strengthened the hands of the Exclusionists, so also in 1683 a conspiracy of obscure Whigs allegedly to murder the King and his brother ("the Rye House Plot") revived the monarchy by arousing ancient loyalties. Charles used the plot as a pretext for excuting formidable and innocent opponents, and he governed virtually as a despot thereafter.

Character. Charles was a strong-minded, even ruthless king, as his treatment of both his ministers and his enemies showed. But at the same time he was tactful, affable, and cunning in handling delicate political situations. He was extremely witty, and his cynicism was notorious. "He has a very ill opinion of men and women," wrote Gilbert Burnet, "and so is infinitely distrustful; he thinks the world is governed wholly by interest."

Charles was married in 1662 to a Portuguese princess, Catherine of Braganza, with French approval. They had no children, but Charles, who was tall, dark, and charming, had at least 14 illegitimate children by various mistresses.

Charles had a remarkable constitution and great stamina, but he abused his strength. He died on Feb. 5, 1685, at the age of 54. On his deathbed he was received into the Roman Catholic Church by the same priest (Father Hudlestone) who had helped him escape from England in his youth after the battle of Worcester. He apologized to the courtiers for taking "a unconscionable time" dying.

MAURICE ASHLEY
University of Loughborough, England
Author of "Life in Stuart England"

Bibliography
Airy, Osmund, *Charles II* (London 1904).
Bryant, Arthur, *King Charles II* (London 1931).
Chapman, Hester W., *The Tragedy of Charles II* (Boston 1964).
Kenyon, John P., *The Stuarts* (London 1958).
Ogg, David, *England in the Reign of Charles II*, 2 vols. (New York 1955).

CHARLES I and II, chärlz, in the sequence of French kings generally designate Charlemagne (reigned 768–814) and Charles the Bald (reigned 840–877); Charles the Bald was also Emperor Charles II of the Carolingian empire. Less frequently, Charles I and II of France respectively designate Charles the Bald and Charles the Fat (reigned 884–887); in the sequence of Carolingian emperors Charles the Fat is known as Charles III.

CHARLES III (879–929), king of France, who was called *Charles the Simple*. He was born on Sept. 17, 879, the posthumous son of King Louis II of France and his second wife, Adelaide.

Charles' claim to the throne was long in dispute. It was set aside in 880 in favor of the claims of his half brothers, Louis III and Carloman. In 884, Charles' cousin, Charles the Fat, gained the throne. In 888, Charles was by-passed once more when a faction of West Frankish nobles elected Count Odo of Paris as king.

In 893 a group led by Archbishop Fulk of Reims revolted against Odo's rule, proclaimed Charles king, and had him consecrated. The ensuing conflict ended in a compromise: Charles and Odo were declared joint kings.

At Odo's death in 898, Charles became sole ruler. But he proved unable to cope with the crises of his time. In 911 he was forced to cede part of Neustria as a virtually autonomous duchy (Normandy) to the Norman leader, Rollo. In 923, embroiled in a civil war, he had to cede Lorraine to Henry the Fowler of Germany. He struggled futilely against two usurpers, Robert of Paris (who was proclaimed king in 922) and Raoul of Burgundy (who was proclaimed king in 923).

From 923 until his death at Péronne on Oct. 7, 929, Charles was forced to live as a prisoner of the Count of Vermandois. A legitimist faction recalled Charles' son, Louis IV, from exile in England and established him as king.

K. F. MORRISON, *University of Chicago*

CHARLES IV (1294–1328), king of France, known as *the Fair*. He was the third and youngest son of Philip IV and Joan of Navarre to reign as king of France and Navarre. (He reigned as Charles I in the latter kingdom.) Charles became king in January 1322, succeeding his brother Philip V, who had no sons.

Administrative innovations and aggressive fiscal policies had made his able predecessor unpopular, and Charles began his reign on a more conservative note. He debased the coinage moderately but sought to avoid unpopular taxes. A border incident and the reluctance of Edward II of England to render homage for his French fief of Gascony led to wars with England in 1324–1325 and again in 1326–1327. The French were easily victorious. Efforts to suppress a rebellion in Flanders, however, were less successful.

Charles owed his crown to a principle that had gained acceptance in his predecessor's reign —that no woman could occupy the French throne. After he contracted a fatal illness early in 1328, this rule was extended to bar any male whose claim to the throne was through a woman. When he died at Vincennes on Feb. 1, 1328, his cousin Philippe de Valois assumed the regency. In April, when Charles' posthumous child proved to be a daughter, Philippe succeeded to the French throne (but not to that of Navarre) as Philip VI. Charles IV was thus the last French king in the direct line of the Capetian dynasty, which had ruled since 987.

JOHN HENNEMAN
McMaster University, Hamilton, Ontario

CHARLES V (1338–1380), king of France. Although he was frail and sickly, Charles was the ablest ruler of France between Philip IV and Louis XI. His intelligence and dedication earned him the sobriquet "the Wise." Charles was born at Vincennes on Jan. 21, 1338. He began his apprenticeship as a ruler under trying circumstances. When his father, John II, was captured by the English at Poitiers in 1356, Charles, now the regent for his father, was left to face internal rebellion and an English invasion. By craft and patience he thwarted the efforts of the States-General under Étienne Marcel to vitiate royal power, crushed the Jacquerie (a peasant uprising), and outmaneuvered the wily Charles of Navarre, who sought the French crown for himself. But he could not expel the English and was forced to accept the Peace of Brétigny in 1360, which left England in control of one third of France.

Charles ascended the throne in 1364 and spent the rest of his short life recovering his father's losses to the English king, Edward III, and the Black Prince, Edward's son. They key to national revival lay in strengthening France's inefficient royal government. Charles ignored the right of the States-General to control annual grants and secured for the crown a regular income by collecting hearth and sales taxes. To avoid dependence on nobles of dubious loyalty, Charles chose able jurists as royal advisers and administrators. Provided with a regular income, he was able to reorganize the royal army, hitherto composed of unreliable feudal levies and treacherous mercenaries. The free companies, mercenaries who had been hired to fight the English, had remained to plunder their former employer after the peace of 1360. By the Ordonnance of 1374, Charles enrolled these troops in regular companies under royal captains. When paid regularly they formed a loyal army, even in sustained campaigns.

His internal reforms completed, Charles declared war on England in 1369. By the time of his death in 1380 he had recovered all of his patrimony except Calais and a narrow strip of territory in Guyenne. Charles wisely never took the field himself but in 1370 appointed a minor Breton noble, Bertrand du Guesclin, *connétable* of France. Leading the reorganized army and capitalizing on the overextension of English power, Guesclin gradually expelled the invader. By refusing pitched battles, Guesclin avoided the earlier disasters of Crécy and Poitiers. These tactics were not heroic, but they were effective. Charles died at Vincennes on Sept. 16, 1380.

EDMUND H. DICKERMAN
University of Connecticut

CHARLES VI (1368–1422), king of France, whose reign was one of the most unfortunate in French history. He was born in Paris on Dec. 3, 1368. Ascending the throne in 1380 at the age of 12, he was subjected to the tutelage of his uncles, the dukes of Anjou, Burgundy, and Berry, great feudal magnates, who used the monarchy for selfish ends. Their oppressive taxation provoked resentment and riots (1380–1382), and their foreign ambitions in Flanders, Naples, and Milan further sapped the monarchy's resources.

Charles declared his majority in 1388. He dismissed his uncles from the council and recalled the former servants of Charles V to court. These Marmousets, as they were called, sought to restore order and put an end to princely despotism. Charles himself did not rule, but pursued the pleasures of court. In 1392 he went insane, a condition from which he emerged only sporadically for the rest of his reign.

The King's incapacity allowed his uncles to return to power. France gradually sank into near anarchy. The magnates controlled much of the kingdom, collected taxes, received pensions, appointed their followers as royal officers, and plundered the treasury. Louis, Duke d'Orléans, the King's brother, and Philip the Bold, Duke of Burgundy, soon emerged as leaders of hostile factions. Both sought to exploit the monarchy by dominating the King. When Philip of Burgundy died in 1404, he was succeeded by his son, John the Fearless. The latter arranged Louis' assassination in 1407.

The Count of Armagnac succeeded Louis as leader of the opposition to John the Fearless, and in 1411 civil war broke out between the Burgundian and Armagnac factions. When John was driven from Paris in 1414, he invited the intervention of Henry V of England. The defeat of the Armagnac nobles by the English at Agincourt in 1415 opened France to the foreign conqueror, allied with the Duke of Burgundy. A belated attempt to cooperate against the English foundered when the new leader of the Armagnacs, the dauphin Charles, sanctioned the assassination of John the Fearless in 1419. John's son, Philip the Good, swearing vengeance against the Dauphin, allied himself with Henry V and persuaded the pathetic Charles VI to sign the Treaty of Troyes in 1420 by which Henry V was made the heir to the French throne. Charles died at Paris on Oct. 21, 1422.

EDMUND H. DICKERMAN
University of Connecticut

CHARLES VII (1403–1461), king of France. He was born in Paris on Feb. 22, 1403, the son of Charles VI. His reign began inauspiciously, for his demented father had been persuaded by his Anglo-Burgundian tutors to disinherit him and to name Henry V of England heir to the throne in the Treaty of Troyes (1420). When Charles VI died in 1422, the dauphin Charles declared himself king from his domain south of the Loire. The Anglo-Burgundians referred to him contemptuously as the "King of Bourges," but he was recognized if not obeyed by most of his countrymen.

Charles showed no inclination to provide leadership to latent French patriotism. Instead, he and his incapable advisers stood paralyzed while the English regent, the Duke of Bedford, gradually conquered most of France north of the Loire. In 1428 the English began the siege of Orléans.

On March 6, 1429, Joan of Arc presented herself to Charles at Chinon. She described her visions of seeing him crowned and restored to his rightful place as King of France. Her sincerity moved Charles and his councillors, and the King briefly stirred himself from his lethargy. He raised an army, which Joan led to the relief of Orléans in May. Her success culminated in the King's march to Reims for his coronation, on July 17, 1429. When Joan was soon captured by the Burgundians and turned over to the English, Charles did not lift a finger to save her from being burned as a heretic. But her inspiring example served as a catalyst for a national resurrection that even royal sloth could not check.

England's grip on northern France gradually slipped, due to royal weakness and economic exhaustion. Patriotic insurrections accelerated the deterioration of the English position. When the able Bedford died in 1435, Philip of Burgundy, who had long contemplated a separate peace with Charles VII, deserted his English ally. The Peace of Arras, signed in 1435, was a turning point in French fortunes. Philip was recognized as a sovereign prince over his domains in France, free from any allegiance to the King; but his withdrawal from the English alliance allowed Charles to focus on his English foes. In 1436 the English were expelled from Paris. The Seine valley and large parts of Gascony were recovered by 1442. The *Praguerie*, an uprising of great nobles led by the dauphin Louis, was repressed in 1440.

The stiffening of the King's will late in life was probably due to the influence of new advisers and his mistress, Agnes Sorel. As a basis for France's revival, the King instituted financial reforms. After 1440 he collected salt taxes (*gabelles*), sales taxes (*aides*), and a direct property tax (*taille*), without the consent of the States-General. These new revenues allowed him to institute military reforms. The *ordonnances* of 1439, 1445, and 1446 established regularly paid royal companies of *gens d'armes* (heavy cavalry) and *francs archers* (bowmen). The best mercenary troops were enrolled in his service, and the rest of the plundering bands were scattered by force.

His new army enabled Charles to complete the expulsion of the English. He took the offensive in 1449, and by 1453 only Calais remained in English hands. By the time he died at Mehun-sur-Yèvre, on July 22, 1461, Charles "the Well Served" had served France well.

EDMUND H. DICKERMAN
University of Connecticut

CHARLES VIII (1470–1498), king of France. He was born at Amboise on June 30, 1470. Only 13 when his father Louis XI died, Charles was ill-equipped to rule. Of feeble body and weak intellect, he showed no ability for or interest in governing. Charles' able older sister, Anne of France (Anne de Beaujeu) was regent during his minority. She crushed a rebellion of nobles led by Duke Francis II of Brittany in 1485; and when Francis died, she assured Brittany's attachment to France by coercing his daughter and heir, Anne, to marry Charles.

The king assumed his majority in 1491. Freed from the threat of internal rebellion, he began planning an invasion of Italy. Charles had a vague claim to the throne of Naples, and when he was invited to intervene against King Ferdinand of Naples by Lodovico Sforza of Milan, he leaped at the opportunity. Charles secured the neutrality of England by a large subsidy and of Spain and the Holy Roman Empire by costly territorial concessions. Backed by the resources of a strong centralized state, Charles set out for Italy in October 1494 with an army of 30,000 men. The divided and militarily inferior Italian states acquiesced without opposition to his triumphant march down the peninsula. On Feb. 22, 1494, the young king entered Naples.

His triumph was short-lived, however, for Spain, Venice, the papacy, the empire, and Milan united against him and forced him to retreat. After fighting his way out of a trap at Fornovo in July 1495, Charles returned to France. Naples fell to Spain the next year. Charles spent the rest of his short life planning a return to Italy. A Franco-Spanish partition of Naples had been tentatively agreed upon when Charles died in an accident at Amboise on April 7, 1498.

Charles' reign saw the introduction of Italian Renaissance culture in France. But the king's foreign policy initiated 60 years of Franco-Habsburg warfare in Italy.

EDMUND H. DICKERMAN
University of Connecticut

CHARLES VII of France (portrait by Jean Fouquet).

GIRAUDON

CHARLES IX (1550–1574), king of France during the wars of religion. The son of Henry II and Catherine de Médicis, he was born in St.-Germain-en-Laye on June 27, 1550. He began his reign in 1560, when he was still a minor, with France on the brink of civil war. The mutual hatred of Catholics and Huguenots (French Calvinists) boded ill for France. Charles was frail in health and of mediocre intelligence. His one passion was hunting, about which he wrote a book. Even after being declared of age on Aug. 17, 1563, he left governing to his mother.

Catherine sought to avoid civil war by playing off the Huguenot and Catholic factions. But she was initially excluded from power by the ultra-Catholic Guise faction, which pushed Charles to war against the Huguenots. Catherine's efforts to reconcile theologians of both faiths failed. Religious war broke out in 1562. The assassination of the Duke de Guise on Feb. 24, 1563, restored Catherine's ascendancy over Charles, and she hastily granted the Peace of Amboise, which gave the Huguenots limited toleration.

For the next two years Catherine maintained peace and tried to secure the monarchy's grip on France. But full-scale war broke out again in 1568. Peace was restored only by granting the Huguenots further liberties and four fortified cities by the Peace of St.-Germain in 1570.

Charles IX had yet to rule. Only in 1572 did he attempt to throw off Catherine's domination. He and the Protestant leader Gaspard de Coligny hoped to reunite the nation in a war against Spain in the Low Countries, but the plan foundered on Charles' loss of nerve. He acquiesced to his mother's demand for the massacre of Huguenots, which occurred on St. Bartholomew's Day, Aug. 24, 1572. This bloodbath seems to have broken his spirit. He subsequently left governing to Catherine and devoted himself to hunting and to his mistress, Marie Touchet. He died of tuberculosis at Vincennes on May 30, 1574.

EDMUND H. DICKERMAN
University of Connecticut

CHARLES X (1757–1836) was the last Bourbon king of France. Charles Philippe, Count d'Artois, was born at Versailles on Nov. 9, 1757, the fourth son of the crown prince and the grandson of Louis XV. Artois' upbringing was neglected since he was only a distant heir to the throne. He was noted for his charm, his debts, and his dissipation. But beginning in 1785 he began to take an interest in affairs of state as a champion of absolutism.

The revolution of 1789 forced the unpopular Artois into exile. Until 1794 he lived at various Continental courts, organizing Royalist armies. After participating in a futile expedition to Brittany in 1795, he settled in Britain with his elder brother, Louis, who had become the Bourbon claimant to the throne.

Early in 1814, Napoleon's defeat offered Artois the chance to return to France "in the baggage train of the Allies." He roused enough popular support for the Bourbons to impress the victors and negotiated his brother's accession as Louis XVIII. Yet the two Bourbons differed on policy, and by 1815–1816 Artois was the leader of the ultra-Royalist faction. The ultras gained ground after the fall of the moderate royal favorite, Élie Decazes, in 1820. In 1822, Louis XVIII appointed Jean Baptiste, Count de Villèle, a politician acceptable to Artois, as prime minister.

When his brother died in 1824, Artois became king as Charles X. Though his first acts were conciliatory, his legislation favoring ex-émigrés and the church antagonized the liberals and moderates. After new elections in November, 1827, a dissident right combined with the left to force Villèle's dismissal. When the King's attempt to pursue his policy with less controversial ministers failed, he named a fighting ultra government under Jules de Polignac in August 1829.

Charles' foreign policy, though successful, failed to win over public opinion. When parliament refused to endorse the Polignac government, new elections again returned the opposition. In response the king issued the July Ordinances suspending freedom of the press, dissolving the new chamber, and rigging a new election. In the face of this threat of revived absolutism, Paris revolted on July 28–30, 1830. Charles fled from France, and Louis Philippe accepted the crown as a constitutional monarch. The remaining years of Charles' life were spent in exile. He died at Görz, Austria (now Gorizia, Italy), on Nov. 6, 1836.

PETER AMANN
State University of New York at Binghamton

CHARLES I, first of the line of emperors who became known as Holy Roman emperors. See CHARLEMAGNE.

CHARLES II (823–877), emperor of the Carolingian Empire, who is sometimes known as Charles the Bald. His reign was his dynasty's last great age, and during it the Carolingian Renaissance reached its zenith.

A grandson of Charlemagne, Charles was the son of Emperor Louis I (Louis the Pious) and his second wife, Judith of Bavaria. Charles' birth was a major cause of the splintering of the Carolingian Empire. In 817, Louis I had divided his empire among the sons of his first marriage, Lothair I, Louis the German, and Pepin of Aquitaine. After Pepin's death in 838, Judith persuaded Louis to provide for her son Charles. Civil wars plagued the empire and Louis I until his death in 840, and continued until Charles, Lothair (now emperor), and Louis the German divided the empire in 843 by the Treaty of Verdun.

Charles' portion of the empire corresponded generally with modern France. Breton revolts and Viking raids disturbed his reign, but the greatest danger came from his half brothers and their sons. Despite meetings that gave lip service to a "confraternal" form of government over the empire, war was a normal part of their family life. In 855, Lothair I died and was succeeded as emperor by his son Louis II, and as ruler of Lotharingia by his son Lothair II. On the death of Lothair II in 869, Charles and Louis the German fought over Lotharingia. Charles had himself crowned king of Lotharingia at Metz in 869. However, Louis the German forced him to share the realm by the Treaty of Mersen (870).

On Emperor Louis II's death in Italy in 875, Charles again outmaneuvered Louis the German, and he was crowned king of Italy and emperor. At Louis the German's death in 876, Charles attacked Germany but was defeated. In 877, Charles invaded Italy, but dangers of revolts in other parts of the empire brought an early retreat, during which he died.

K. F. MORRISON, *University of Chicago*

CHARLES III (839–888), emperor of the Carolingian Empire and last king of all the Franks. He is sometimes referred to as Charles the Fat. When his father, Louis the German, died in 876, Charles and his brothers, Carloman and Louis, inherited their father's East Frankish kingdom. Carloman was incurably ill and in 879 ceded his Italian claims to Charles. When both his brothers died (Carloman in 880 and Louis in 882), Charles inherited the entire East Frankish kingdom. The West Franks elected him their king in 884.

Charles marched to Rome in 881 and was crowned emperor by Pope John VIII. But Charles could give John little help in his war with the Saracens. Despite three more Italian expeditions, his authority was never generally acknowledged in Italy and his reign in France and Germany became increasingly ineffectual. The Diet of Trebur deposed Charles in 887. He died in prison.

K. F. MORRISON, *University of Chicago*

CHARLES IV (1316–1378), emperor of the Holy Roman Empire and king of Germany, was born in Prague on May 14, 1316, the eldest son of John of Luxemburg, king of Bohemia. Baptized Wenceslas, he received the name Charles in 1323 at the court of his uncle King Charles IV of France. The next year he married Blanche, the sister of the future French king Philip VI.

After serving his father in Luxemburg, Italy, and the Tyrol, Charles concentrated on developing political support from the German princes and the papacy to strengthen the position of the house of Luxemburg against that of Wittelsbach. These efforts secured his election as king of Germany on July 11, 1346. After his father was killed at the Battle of Crécy in August 1346, Charles became king of Bohemia.

In 1347, when the Wittelsbach emperor Louis IV died, Charles began pressing his claim to the imperial throne, and on Jan. 6, 1355, he was finally crowned emperor at Rome. The next year he attempted to bring speed and orderly procedures to future imperial elections, though ultimately without success, by issuing the Golden Bull of 1356. The chief gain for Bohemia was that it won recognition as an autonomous kingdom.

One of the last medieval emperors of the Holy Roman Empire with any power, Charles devoted most of his energies to expanding his kingdom of Bohemia. By the purchase of lands and by treaty he was able to enlarge the kingdom, even adding Silesia in 1368. However, he partially undid his work later by dividing his possessions among three sons and two nephews. Charles was also interested in ending the Babylonian Captivity, and he tried to persuade the popes to return to Rome from Avignon.

A cultivated man who knew Latin, French, German, Italian, and Czech, Charles patronized men of letters and invited the famous humanist Petrarch to his imperial capital at Prague. He constructed castles patterned after the French château style and hired German and French architects to complete the Cathedral of St. Vitus. In 1344 he had Prague created an archbishopric. One of Charles' most lasting achievements was his founding of the Charles University.

Charles died at Prague on Nov. 29, 1378. He had previously secured the election of his son Wenceslas as king of the Romans.

BRYCE LYON, *Brown University*

BRUCKMANN, FROM ART REFERENCE BUREAU

Charles V (detail from a painting by Titian, 1548).

CHARLES V (1500–1558) was emperor of the Holy Roman Empire from 1519 to 1556 and, as Charles I, king of Spain from 1516 to 1556. Charles inherited the largest empire ruled by a European monarch up to his own day, but the defense of his far-flung possessions brought him into perpetual conflict with the French house of Valois, with the Turks, and with the Protestants. To Charles, the wars of his reign were fought to defend the prerogatives of Catholicism and the Habsburg dynasty. To his enemies, however, they symbolized an unwanted medieval imperial spirit that blocked the new religious and nationalistic developments of the 16th century.

Charles' personality was shaped by his great historical role. He was preoccupied with warfare rather than with affairs of the court. An aloofness and lack of warmth, which may have resulted from his separation from his parents in early childhood, prevented him from maintaining rapport with the popes and sovereigns of his time.

Charles' Heritage. Born in Ghent on Feb. 24, 1500, Charles was the son of Philip, Duke of Burgundy (who later, as Philip I, was king consort of Castile) and the grandson of Emperor Maximilian I. His mother was Juana la Loca, daughter of Ferdinand of Aragon and Isabella of Castile. When Philip died in 1506, Charles fell heir to Philip's Burgundian possessions.

Though Ferdinand ruled Castile after Juana became mentally deranged in 1506, Ferdinand had no issue by his second wife. Thus Charles was assured the kingdoms of Aragon and Castile.

The confinement of Juana in Spain and the early death of Philip made Charles the charge of his aunt, Margaret of Austria, who was regent of the Habsburg Netherlands. Since her household was dominated by Burgundian culture, Charles was imbued with chivalric ideals, religious piety, and dynastic pride. He learned the art of government from the Burgundian nobleman Guillaume de Croy, Lord of Chièvres. His religious education was imparted by Adrian of Utrecht, who was later to become pope as Adrian VI. Both of these men fervently believed in the medieval concept of a universal and Catholic empire and both worked hard in the early years of Charles' rule to realize this dream.

Burgundy, Spain, and the Empire. In 1515, Charles reached his majority and became Duke of Burgundy. Less than a year later Ferdinand died, and a massive crowd in Brussels witnessed Charles' coronation as king of Spain on March 14, 1516. He delayed going to his new kingdom in order to conclude the Treaty of Noyon with France. By this treaty the French king, Francis I of the house of Valois, recognized Charles V as king of Spain in return for Charles' acknowledgment of the French seizure of the Duchy of Milan. This pact particularly antagonized Spain, which saw its vital interests in Italy sacrificed just as Charles' Burgundian advisers were appearing in Aragon and Castile. When the king arrived in Spain in September 1517, his reception was initially cold. In retaliation Charles summarily dismissed the regent, Cardinal Jiménez de Cisneros.

Charles was elected Holy Roman emperor on June 28, 1519. Since Francis I had also sought the imperial crown, Charles' election intensified the Habsburg-Valois struggle for hegemony in Europe. Furthermore, since Protestantism had made considerable headway in Germany, Charles was faced with religious dissension in the empire. Charles was invested at Aachen on Oct. 23, 1520. In the next year, by the Edict of Worms (May 26, 1521), he attempted to banish Protestants from the empire. At the same time, he was confronted in Spain with a revolt of the *communeros* in Castile (1520–1521), who sought Juana's restoration. Another uprising in Valencia aimed at strengthening local power over royal prerogatives. Charles returned to Spain in 1522, where he remained 7 years, determined to prevent further strife by centralizing Spanish administration. In 1526 he married Isabella of Portugal. Isabella gave birth to a son, Philip, and proved to be an able regent of Spain from 1529 until her death in 1539.

Meanwhile, the struggle with France for control of Milan had been renewed in 1523. Fighting lasted until 1525, when Francis I was captured at the Battle of Pavia on February 24. Had Milan remained the sole issue, the Peace of Madrid (Jan. 14, 1526) might have freed Charles to deal with German religious questions. But Charles also tried, though ultimately without success, to get Francis to renounce his claim to Burgundy. A new and strongly anti-Habsburg pope, Clement VII, joined the French king in the League of Cognac, and hostilities were renewed in Italy in 1527. The sack of Rome by imperial troops in May destroyed Charles' plans of ruling Europe jointly with the pope. Although he had strengthened himself militarily in Italy, Charles was the loser diplomatically, and his failure to extract a promise of internal church reform from Clement VII worsened the religious schism. On Aug. 3, 1529, Charles made peace with Francis by surrendering his claims to Burgundy, while Francis gave up Milan and Naples. Only then did time and improved relations with the papacy allow Charles to be crowned as Holy Roman emperor in Bologna on Feb. 24, 1530.

The Emperor was obliged to check the Ottoman Turks before attempting to pacify Germany. The Turks, who had already seized Belgrade in 1521 and Rhodes in 1522, now captured Algiers in 1529 and Tunis in 1534. After Charles had spent many months in creating a Mediterranean defense, Tunis was recaptured in 1535.

While the Emperor was thus occupied, the Protestant princes formed the Schmalkaldic League in 1531. The refractory Germans could no longer be attacked frontally, so the Emperor asked Pope Paul III to call a general church council in 1536 to consider reform. By this time France had regained its strength, and a new war over Milan disrupted the council. Only a resumption of Ottoman raids brought a truce among the European powers in May 1538. A new campaign against Algiers once again diverted Charles from his European concerns.

But in 1542, European affairs again were of critical importance. A succession dispute between Cleves and Gelderland erupted into war, pitting Francis I and Christian III of Denmark against Charles V, Margaret of Austria, and Henry VIII of England. The war was ended when a Franco-Turkish alliance turned opinion against Francis. He capitulated by the Treaty of Crépy-en-Laonnois in September 1544. France surrendered territory in Canada and agreed to a general church council. Charles was at long last free to seek a solution in Germany.

Charles and the Protestants. At the Emperor's instigation, the Council of Trent opened on Dec. 13, 1545. Charles declared war against the Schmalkaldic League the following July, and at the Battle of Mühlberg (1547) the Protestant elector of Saxony, John Frederick, was defeated. But Charles was soon criticized by Pope Paul III for tolerating the Protestants at the Diet of Augsburg in June 1548, and his religious zeal subsequently diminished.

Charles met with a further setback in 1551 when a number of German Catholic princes, hostile to the growth of imperial power and unwilling to agree to Charles' plan to have his son Philip succeed him, allied themselves with Henry II of France. French troops moved to the Rhine, and Charles was almost captured at Innsbruck in March 1552. That fall he was forced to grant further concessions to the Protestants.

After the death of Queen Isabella in 1539, Charles had been increasingly drawn toward religious mysticism. In 1554, tired and depressed, he gave his German territories to his brother Ferdinand. New campaigns by the French in Italy and the election of another hostile pope, Paul IV, convinced Charles he should retire completely. On Oct. 25, 1555, supremely discouraged, Charles abdicated the crown of the Netherlands in favor of his son Philip. He relinquished Spain, the Spanish Empire, and his possessions in Italy to Philip on Jan. 26, 1556. On September 4 Ferdinand became emperor. Charles entered the monastery at Yuste, in Estremadura, where he died on Sept. 21, 1558.

Evaluation. The imperial design of Charles V has been variously interpreted as an attempt to revive the medieval empire, as a plan to extend the empire of Ferdinand and Isabella, and as an effort to create a new world based upon a universal Christian spirit. Certainly at times Charles did seek to foster rule by a collaboration of emperor and pope, but his avoidance of any unification of the various states of his realm, except as they all acknowledged him their king, argues against any serious imperial scheme. Charles did have greater power than medieval emperors, but his resources were inadequate to do more than preserve what he had. Even though his was a world empire on a new scale, the Spanish treasure fleets from the Indies could not support both his dynastic and his religious goals. Charles had to call upon the financial centers of Antwerp, Augsburg, and Genoa for additional millions, supplied at interest rates up to 45% annually. By the time of his death, he owed 28 million ducats and left Spain all but bankrupt.

Economic problems hampered Charles at every turn and in the long run proved to be the greatest obstacle to his imperial concept. Moreover, the new nationalism represented by Francis I of France and by the German Protestant princes also prevented Charles from solidifying his control over the far-flung lands that he ruled. The rise of Ottoman power in the latter half of his reign was a third factor that utterly disrupted his calculations. Charles was never able adequately to meet the Ottoman challenge, yet he could not ignore it, since the Mediterranean Sea was a vital link in the chain of imperial communications.

Though Charles failed to achieve his imperial goals, his accomplishments are significant. The geography of his inheritance implied a Spanish-based Atlantic empire rather than a central European one, and his generally excellent administration of the Indies strengthened this new orientation. The institutions of *audiencias* (courts of appeal) and vice-royalties strengthened Spanish control in the New World, and his treatment of the American Indians was tolerant. So was, in retrospect, his attitude toward Protestantism, for he perceived weaknesses in the affairs of the Roman Catholic Church that made him press for general Catholic reform as a way of healing the breach.

Legacy in Spain. The fact that Charles was Holy Roman Emperor as well as king of Spain was in the long run to Spain's disadvantage. Charles frequently sacrificed the economic prosperity of Spain to meet the demands of his empire. It is true that the defense of Christendom against the Turk and the preservation of Christian unity in the face of the new Lutheran doctrine appealed to the religious zeal of Castile. But Charles increased taxes in Spain to finance these schemes, and in so doing he hurt Spain's economy and stifled the country's regional autonomy. Only in Spain did Charles pursue a strictly centralizing course, motivated by the memory of the revolts early in his reign.

One year after Charles' abdication Spain was bankrupt. And in the following decades reaction against Charles' centralizing policies was in full swing. Reasserting its ancient rights, the aristocracy gave its allegiance to the crown only as long as its privileges were respected. The central authority of the state, briefly enhanced by Charles, ultimately gave way before the particularist interests of the aristocracy.

Legacy in the Empire. Charles' division of his empire between Philip II and Ferdinand of Austria diminished Habsburg power almost at once. The rebellion of the Netherlands that began in 1565 gradually removed one of the richest areas from the Habsburg dominion, and the role of the emperor in German affairs declined. By the early 17th century the empire was to be strongly challenged by a revived France.

ROBERT W. KERN
University of Massachusetts

Further Reading: Brandi, Karl, *The Emperor Charles V* (New York 1954); Chudoba, Bodhan, *Spain and the Empire, 1519–1543* (Chicago 1952); Lynch, James, *Spain Under the Habsburgs* (London 1964).

CHARLES VI (1685–1740), was emperor of the Holy Roman Empire and (as Charles III) king of Hungary. Charles was born in Vienna on Oct. 1, 1685, the second son of Emperor Leopold I. When the Habsburg ruler of Spain, Charles II, died in 1700, Leopold put Charles forward as the heir to the Spanish throne. But the Bourbon Philip V had already been placed on the throne by his grandfather, Louis XIV of France. Fearing a union of France and Spain, England and the Netherlands went to war against France in 1701, siding with the Emperor. This War of the Spanish succession lasted until 1714. In 1703, in Vienna, Charles was proclaimed king of Spain as Charles III. With English aid he established his court at Barcelona. However, he never had much support outside of Catalonia. He was married in 1708 to Elizabeth-Christina of Brunswick-Wolfenbüttel; their daughter, born in 1717, was the future Empress Maria Theresa.

On April 17, 1711, Charles' elder brother Joseph I, who had been emperor since 1705, died without a direct heir, and Charles was summoned to assume the Austrian throne. Charles was reluctant to renounce his Spanish interests. It was not until September 27 that he could bring himself to depart, and even then he left his wife behind as regent in Spain to uphold his claim. He was elected emperor on Oct. 12, 1711, and crowned in Frankfurt am Main on December 22. England and the Netherlands now opposed his continued claim to the Spanish throne. They entered into negotiations with Louis XIV, leading to the Treaty of Utrecht (1713), which recognized Philip as King of Spain. Charles attempted to continue the war but had to conclude the Peace of Rastatt with France the following year. As compensation for relinquishing the Spanish throne, Charles received the Spanish Netherlands and the Italian territories of Naples, Sardinia, and Milan, formerly held by Spain.

In 1713, Charles informed his counselors of new regulations for the succession, which previously had devolved only on male members of the Habsburg family. Henceforth the Habsburg lands were to be "indivisible and inseparable," and in case Charles should have no male heir, his daughters and their issue should succeed him. This declaration, the Pragmatic Sanction, was approved by the various estates of his realm at different times. It had great constitutional significance, for by it each estate recognized the unity of the Habsburg territories and pledged the acceptance of a common sovereign. But it required many concessions to persuade the powers of Europe to recognize the Pragmatic Sanction.

As an ally of Venice, Charles VI became involved in a war with Turkey in 1716. By the Treaty of Passarowitz (July 21, 1718), he obtained Little Wallachia and Belgrade and a large portion of North Serbia. As a supporter of the Saxon kings in Poland, Charles was involved in the War of the Polish Succession (1733–1735). In the peace treaties of 1735 and 1738, Austria had to cede Naples and Sicily to Spain and a part of Milan to Savoy, receiving Parma-Piacenza in return. In alliance with Russia, Charles became involved in a new war with Turkey in 1736, and by the Treaty of Belgrade (Sept. 18, 1739) had to surrender nearly everything that had been gained at Passarowitz. By the time of Charles' death in Vienna, on Oct. 20, 1740, the dismemberment of the Habsburg patrimony had begun.

ERNST C. HELMREICH, *Bowdoin College*

CHARLES VII (1697–1745), emperor of the Holy Roman Empire and elector of Bavaria. He was born in Brussels on Aug. 6, 1697, the son of Elector Max Emanuel of Bavaria, a member of the Wittelsbach dynasty. In 1722, Charles married Maria Amalia, younger daughter of the late Emperor Joseph I and niece of the reigning Emperor Charles VI. Upon the death of his father in 1726 he took over the government of Bavaria as elector.

Charles inaugurated an active political reign designed to win for Bavaria a major role in European affairs, while at the same time he presided over a lavish court modeled on Versailles. His opportunity came in 1731 when Emperor Charles VI demanded sanction (the "Pragmatic Sanction") of his designation of his daughter Maria Theresa as heir to the Habsburg dominions. Though Bavarian assurance of this sanction had been given before Charles' marriage to Maria Amalia, Charles now claimed the Habsburg lands for himself on the strength of his advisers' interpretation of the will of Emperor Ferdinand I, from whom he, as well as Maria Theresa, was descended. Upon Charles VI's death in 1740 the complicated question of Maria Theresa's succession claim came into the open.

Charles joined Frederick the Great of Prussia in his assault on Austria in the War of the Austrian Succession, thinking himself in a good position to press his claim to the crown of the Holy Roman Empire. At first the war went well. Charles was able to occupy much of Austria and drive on to Prague. In January 1742, at Frankfurt, he was elected emperor. But this was the last of his luck. Austrian and Hungarian troops moved into Bavaria and occupied Munich, forcing Charles into exile, where he brooded on his ephemeral electoral and imperial titles. For a brief time the changing tides of war favored him again, and he was able to return to Munich, his capital, in 1744. But Austrian troops were back in Bavaria within a few months, and Charles died in Munich, a broken man, on Jan. 20, 1745.

GERALD STRAUSS, *Indiana University*

CHARLES I (1288–1342), king of Hungary. He was the grandson of King Charles II of Naples and the son of Charles Martel of Naples and his wife Clemencia. As Charles Robert he was Count of Anjou and of Provence. He claimed the Hungarian throne after the extinction of the Árpád dynasty in 1301. He had the support of Pope Boniface VIII, the Habsburgs, and a faction of the nobility for his claim. The majority of the great nobles of Hungary, however, favored Wenceslas III of Bohemia. In August 1301 they had Wenceslas crowned king of Hungary. But Wenceslas was unable to defend his position. In 1305 he returned to Bohemia, where he was murdered the following year. An attempt by the anti-Anjou faction to install Duke Otto III of Bavaria as king also failed. Finally, in October 1308 the Hungarian diet elected Charles as king.

Charles established a firm, though still feudal, basis for the Anjou dynasty. He reduced the power of the great nobles, confiscated their estates, and distributed the land to the lesser nobility. He introduced military and economic reforms. He increased the privileges of the towns and opened new trade routes for Hungarian merchants. Charles reorganized the mining industry, asserted the royal monopoly on coinage, and imposed direct taxes. His ambitious foreign policy was shaped by his desire to secure the succession to the thrones of Naples and Poland for his family. He had married Elizabeth of Poland in 1320. He married his younger son Andrew, aged seven, to Joanna, aged six, granddaughter of Robert of Naples, and in 1333 he gained an agreement that at Robert's death the crown should pass to Andrew. Similarly, because of his own marriage to Elizabeth and because of the aid he had given Poland in its wars with the Tatars and Lithuanians, Charles was able, in 1339, to reach an agreement with his brother-in-law King Casimir III of Poland (who was childless) that the Polish throne should pass to his son Louis.

Charles' reign—aside from his aid to Poland and some minor campaigns—was generally peaceful. He laid the foundations for the long and spectacular reign of his son Louis I, who became king of Hungary and Poland. Charles died at Visegrád, Hungary, on July 16, 1342.

GUNTHER E. ROTHENBERG
University of New Mexico

CHARLES II, king of Hungary. See CHARLES III, king of Naples.

CHARLES III, king of Hungary. See CHARLES VI, emperor of the Holy Roman Empire.

CHARLES IV, king of Hungary. See CHARLES I, emperor of Austria.

CHARLES III (1543–1608), duke of Lorraine. He was born in Nancy on Feb. 18, 1543, the son of Francis I of Lorraine and Christina of Denmark. Since Charles was only two years old when his father died, his mother and uncle acted as regents for him. In 1552, Henry II of France, distrustful of the regents' favoritism toward Emperor Charles V, carried the young duke off to the French court. Charles married Claude, the daughter of the French king, in 1559 and in 1560 returned to Nancy and assumed power.

Charles' long reign saw internal reforms based on the French model. His foreign policy was shaped by Lorraine's proximity to France. Charles remained on good terms with his French brothers-in-law until 1584, when he began to support the Catholic League in the wars of religion. Charles hoped to obtain the French crown for his son in place of the Protestant Henry of Navarre. But his pretensions went unheeded and brought war in 1592 with Henry of Navarre, who later became king of France as Henry IV in 1594. Lorraine's defeat ended Charles' dynastic ambitions. He died at Nancy on May 14, 1608.

EDMUND H. DICKERMAN
University of Connecticut

CHARLES I (1227–1285), the first Angevin king of Naples and Sicily, known as *Charles of Anjou*. He was the posthumous son of Louis VIII of France. By his father's will Charles was left the rich countships of Anjou and Maine, and in 1246 he became count of Provence through his wife Beatrice.

In 1265, Pope Clement IV, who was a Frenchman, chose Charles as candidate for the throne of the kingdom of Sicily, which included both the island of Sicily and southern peninsular Italy. Financed in part by the Guelph bankers of Florence and Siena, Charles gained the throne after disposing of the Hohenstaufen king of

Sicily, Manfred, in battle near Benevento (Feb. 26, 1266). His defeat of Manfred's 16-year-old nephew Conradin at the Battle of Tagliacozzo (Aug. 23, 1268) ended German influence in southern Italy.

Taking advantage of the imperial and papal vacancies, which after 1268 stripped the Italian factions of their natural leaders, Charles then extended his influence into northern Italy and into the Balkans, becoming by 1272 king of Albania and a threat to Byzantine Emperor Michael VIII. He was held momentarily in check by the new pope, Gregory X, who proclaimed the union of the Eastern and Western churches at Lyon in 1274. But Charles continued his plans to extend his power in the East, taking over the remnants of the kingdom of Jerusalem in 1277 and the principality of Achaea in 1278.

Charles next planned an expedition against Constantinople. But this was halted by the outbreak in Palermo, on March 30, 1282, of an uprising against French domination known as the Sicilian Vespers. The Sicilians proclaimed as king Peter III of Aragón, the husband of King Manfred's daughter Constance. As a result, the area of kingdom under Charles' control was limited to the mainland and was ruled from Naples. He died at Foggia on Jan. 7, 1285.

R. T. McDONALD, *Smith College*

CHARLES II (c. 1254–1309), king of Naples, known as *Charles the Lame*. He was the son and successor to Charles I. On the death of his father in 1285, he was a prisoner of the Aragonese. He was finally released in the fall of 1288 on condition that he reconcile the Franco-papal alliance with Alfonso III of Aragón.

Released from this vow by Pope Nicholas IV, Charles nevertheless continued to work for peace and finally persuaded Pope Boniface VIII to ratify the Treaty of Caltabellotta (1302), recognizing Frederick, brother of James II of Aragón, as king of Trinacria (insular Sicily), for Frederick's lifetime. Charles retained the title of king of Sicily and ruled southern peninsular Italy, with his capital at Naples. He died at Poggioreale on May 7, 1309.

R. T. McDONALD, *Smith College*

CHARLES III (1345–1386), king of Naples, known as *Charles of Durazzo*. He was the son of Louis, Duke of Durazzo, in the direct male line of Charles II of Naples. After his father's revolt against Queen Joanna I of Naples and subsequent death in prison (1362), Charles was placed under the care of his cousin King Louis of Hungary. In 1370, Charles married his first cousin Margaret, the niece of Queen Joanna and her potential heiress.

When Joanna acknowledged the Avignonese pope in 1378, Charles was offered her throne by the Roman pope Urban VI. Joanna thereupon adopted as her heir Louis, Count of Anjou and brother of Charles V of France. By August 1381, however, Charles of Durazzo was in possession of Naples. War followed in both Italy and Provence until the death of Louis of Anjou (Sept. 21, 1384). Charles was left in control of the kingdom of Naples but Provence had been lost. In 1385 he invaded Hungary, deposed Mary, King Louis' daughter, and was himself crowned king of Hungary as Charles II. He died in the castle of Visegrád, near Buda, on Feb. 24, 1386.

R. T. McDONALD, *Smith College*

CHARLES IV, king of Naples and Sicily. See CHARLES III, king of Spain.

CHARLES I, king of Navarre. See CHARLES IV, king of France.

CHARLES II (1332–1387), king of Navarre, who earned the sobriquet "the Bad." Ambitious and unscrupulous, he aspired to the throne of France, which he claimed as a relation of the last Capetians. During the early 1350's, Charles, conspiring with the English, forced the French king John II to reward him with extensive fiefs in Normandy. Later in the decade Charles supported Étienne Marcel's Parisian revolution and then helped to crush the French peasant uprising known as the Jacquerie, thereby extorting guarantees of his territories. These were recognized in the Peace of Brétigny of 1360.

When John II died in 1364, the new king, Charles V, forced him to cede most of his holdings. Charles never ceased to intrigue with England. But it was only in 1378, when he apparently planned to poison Charles V, that he lost his last possessions in France. He died on Jan. 1, 1387.

EDMUND H. DICKERMAN
University of Connecticut

CHARLES III (1361–1425), king of Navarre, known as *Charles the Noble*. He was born in Mantes, in northern France, the son of Charles II of Navarre and Jeanne of France. Charles' policies were the opposite of his father's. He was Francophile in outlook and peaceful by nature. When he disavowed his father's plot to poison Charles V of France in 1378, he was awarded his father's confiscated lands in Normandy and Champagne. Charles also sought unsuccessfully to mediate the dispute between the Armagnac and Burgundian factions at the French court.

In Navarre, Charles undertook economic improvements, including deepening rivers and digging canals. Peace was restored with Castile, and territory lost by his father was recovered.

Charles married Lenora of Castile in 1375. They had nine children, but only their daughter Blanche survived. She succeeded her father upon his death on Sept. 8, 1425.

EDMUND H. DICKERMAN
University of Connecticut

CHARLES I, king of Portugal. See CARLOS I, king of Portugal.

CHARLES I, king of Spain. See CHARLES V, emperor of the Holy Roman Empire.

CHARLES II (1661–1700), king of Spain, known as *Charles the Bewitched*. He was born in Madrid on Nov. 6, 1661, the son of Philip IV and Archduchess Mariana of Austria, and ascended the throne in 1665 at the age of four. Charles suffered from numerous ailments produced by generations of Habsburg inbreeding. No heir was expected of him, and as a result his reign was dominated by a French-Austrian struggle for the succession. In 1698, Charles named as his heir Joseph, Prince of Bavaria. But French pressure forced him in 1700 to name the Duke d'Anjou, Louis XIV's grandson, his successor. His death at Madrid on Nov. 1, 1700, ended the long period of Habsburg rule in Spain.

ROBERT W. KERN
University of Massachusetts

CHARLES III (1716–1788), king of Spain. He was born in Madrid on Jan. 20, 1716, the son of Philip V of Spain and his second wife, Elizabeth Farnese, daughter of the Duke of Parma. His ambitious mother, lacking a great inheritance of her own and seeing her children blocked from the Spanish succession by their two elder half brothers, zealously sought a crown for Charles in Italy. In 1733, Spain and France attacked Austrian Italy. Austria was forced to cede Naples and Sicily to Spain, and Charles became king of the Two Sicilies as Charles IV in 1735. When ill health brought about the premature deaths of his half brothers and made his mother's plotting unnecessary, he ascended the Spanish throne at the age of 43.

Foreign Policy. As a diplomat, Charles was frustrated by constant English rivalry over commercial rights in South America. Alliance with France was a vital necessity, and so a pact (the Bourbon Compact) was formed, renewed in 1761, and expanded in 1768 and 1779. War with Britain ensued each time, however, and in 1763, Spain was forced to cede Florida to Britain to secure the return of Havana and Manila, obtaining Louisiana from France in compensation. In 1769, Charles reluctantly acknowledged British occupation of the Falkland Islands. But during the American Revolution, Spain blockaded Gibraltar (1779), captured Mobile (1780), and permanently seized Minorca (1782). However, French weakness finally forced Charles to sign the Treaty of Paris with Britain in 1783, and the Bourbon Compact lapsed.

Domestic Policy. Domestically, Charles was much more successful. He was one of the most able rulers among the enlightened despots of the day. Faced with a rising population which necessitated a better use of land and industrial expansion, Charles developed new taxes and attempted to destroy obsolete institutions. When rioting broke out against one of the royal ministers, the Marquis of Squillace, in February 1766, the king appointed the Count of Aranda president of the Council of Castile. Aranda took drastic action against the church and the aristocracy in response to the common belief that they had led the riots. The Jesuits were expelled a year later and their property distributed to the landless. The powers of the Inquisition were limited in 1768 and 1784, and charities were reformed so that henceforth the government rather than the church monopolized welfare.

Aside from Aranda and the Count of Floridablanca, middle-class reformers like Pedro de Campomanes and Gaspar Melchor de Jovellanos formed an elite in the bureaucracy. They sponsored enlightened economic policies, improved colonial administration, and stimulated industrial growth through the famous *Sociedad Económica de Amigos del País*. This aspect of the reign more than made up for the misadventures abroad, and by the time of the king's death on Dec. 14, 1788, in Madrid, the long decline of Spain had been partly checked and the prototype of a modern state was in existence.

ROBERT W. KERN
University of Massachusetts

CHARLES IV (1748–1819), king of Spain during the French Revolution and the early years of the Napoleonic empire. He was born in Naples, Italy, on Nov. 11, 1748, the son of the enlightened Charles III, whom he succeeded as king of Spain in 1788. In 1792 he made several attempts to save his cousin Louis XVI from execution by the French Revolutionary government. Unsuccessful, he went to war against France in 1793. Spain was defeated and ceded half of Santo Domingo to France by the Peace of Basel in 1795.

Grievances against England soon drove Charles to revive the traditional Franco-Spanish alliance by the Treaty of San Ildefonso in 1796. The alliance was sealed by the later transfer of Louisiana to France. Henceforth Spain was a satellite of France in its revolutionary wars. The loss of Trinidad to England in 1797 and the destruction of the Spanish fleet at Trafalgar in 1805 greatly diminished the king's popularity.

Considerable responsibility for the failures of Charles IV must be attributed to Manuel de Godoy, allegedly a lover of Queen María Luisa and a court favorite, who was prime minister from 1792. Godoy was ambitious and vain, and his close identification with Napoleon brought him into rivalry with the heir to the throne, Prince Ferdinand. Charles was finally forced to abdicate in favor of Ferdinand on March 19, 1808. The French invasion of Spain and the Spanish War of Independence followed. Charles spent his last years as an exile in Rome, where he died on Jan. 20, 1819.

ROBERT W. KERN
University of Massachusetts

CHARLES IX (1550–1611), king of Sweden. He was born in Stockholm on Oct. 4, 1550, the third son of the great Swedish king Gustav Vasa (Gustavus I). At the age of 10, by his father's will, he was left a large duchy in central Sweden. Charles learned to use his independent position to institute agricultural and economic reforms and to build up his own power, and he played an important part in the rebellion that he and his brother John staged against their eldest brother, King Eric XIV, in 1568. When Eric was deposed in 1568, John became king as John III and for a time curtailed Charles' ducal rights.

When John's son Sigismund, a Catholic, became king of both Poland (1587) and Sweden (1592), Charles took up the task of defending Swedish nationalism and Protestantism. Although a Calvinist, he was the prime mover behind the Uppsala meeting of 1593 that solidified Lutheranism in Sweden. Then, in 1594, he had himself made regent of Sweden. When Sigismund arrived at last with an army from Poland, Charles defeated him at Stångebro in 1598. Charles then proceeded ruthlessly to consolidate his position, blending demagogic appeals with brutal suppression of the council and the higher nobility. In what came to be known as the Linköping Bloodbath, he executed the supporters of Sigismund in 1600. But he hesitated to take the royal title and was crowned only in 1607.

Charles repeatedly fought the Poles in the Baltic lands, and at his death on Oct. 30, 1611, at Nyköping, the Danes were almost ready to attack Sweden in the west. He was succeeded by his son, Gustav Adolphus (Gustavus II).

FRANKLIN D. SCOTT
Northwestern University

CHARLES X (1622–1660), king of Sweden, also known as Charles X Gustavus. He was born in Nyköping, Sweden, on Nov. 8, 1622. He was the son of Catherine, the eldest daughter of Charles IX, and of John Casimir of the Palatinate. For both romantic and political reasons Charles wanted to marry his cousin, Queen Christina. Although Christina decided not to marry anyone, she carefully manipulated matters so that Charles would succeed her on the throne, as he did on her abdication in 1654. He then married Hedvig Eleonora of Holstein-Gottorp.

Charles helped to start the process of recovering lands alienated to the great nobles. However, most of his 6-year reign was occupied with the twin problems of diplomacy and war.

Charles had fought on the continent in the latter part of the Thirty Years' War, and as king he carried through a number of brilliant campaigns. He dreamed of expanding the Swedish empire around the Baltic and perhaps as far as the Black Sea. His wars in Poland in 1655–1657, however, produced victories but no decisions, and when Denmark threatened from the west, he quickly shifted his forces. The most dramatic exploit of his career resulted. He and his army were in Jutland at the moment of a rare freezing of the waters of the Great Belt and Little Belt (Store Bælt and Lille Bælt); he led his forces over the ice in an island-hopping operation onto undefended Zealand (Sjælland) in 1658. The Danes bought peace by surrendering the rich provinces of Skåne, Halland, and Blekinge, which have remained in Swedish possession, and also Bornholm and large areas in the north, which were partially rewon by Denmark in a new war in 1660. Because of Dutch opposition, Charles lost the Delaware colony in America, and he lost to the Danes the Swedish holdings on the coast of West Africa. His conquest of the southern "breadbasket" was his lasting contribution to Sweden. Charles died in Göteborg on Feb. 13, 1660, while planning a campaign against Norway.

FRANKLIN D. SCOTT, *Northwestern University*

CHARLES XI (1655–1697), king of Sweden. He was born in Stockholm on Nov. 24, 1655. The son of Charles X, he inherited the crown in 1660 and assumed full powers in 1672 after a regency of 12 years. In 1680 he married Ulrika Eleonora, daughter of Frederick III of Denmark.

Sweden's subservient position to France and the near disaster of continental war shocked young Charles into concern about affairs of state. In a war with Denmark, he displayed bravery and power of leadership at the Battle of Lund in 1676. Thereafter his prestige and authority grew rapidly. By 1693 he was declared by the Estates of the Riksdag (Parliament) to be an autocrat who was "responsible to no one on earth for his actions, but has power and might according to his pleasure . . . to guide and govern his kingdom."

Through the "reduction" of the great estates given to the nobles by Gustavus Aldolphus (Gustavus II) and Christina, Charles reclaimed much land, at the same time forcing the deprived nobility into dependence on the crown for positions in the bureaucracy. To this revolution he added a reorganization of the military, freeing Sweden from dependence on foreign subsidies and establishing the obligation of military districts to supply a fixed quota of men for the army, to be locally trained and paid in kind (the *indelningsverk*). He also recreated the Swedish fleet. Charles died in Stockholm on April 5, 1697. He was a benevolent despot, who improved the position of the peasantry, promoted the iron and textile industries, and restored the state's finances.

FRANKLIN D. SCOTT, *Northwestern University*

CHARLES XII (1682–1718), king of Sweden, whose exploits made him a romantic hero. His dashing personality, his military genius, and his habit of enduring hardships with his soldiers won him the devotion of thousands through brief years of glory and a decade of decline.

Born at Stockholm on June 17, 1682, Charles was given a careful education, such as his father, Charles XI, had failed to receive. Tutors guided his innate curiosity and ability. He learned horsemanship and bear hunting from his father. He was thoroughly indoctrinated in the Lutheran faith, knew German, Latin, and French, became skillful in mathematics and military engineering, and was well versed in military history. But he never learned the art of compromise. Instead he was taught by his austere father to think of himself as the final arbiter of every question, the absolute ruler of his land.

War in Northern Europe. When his father died in 1697, Charles was not quite 15 years old, but within the same year he won full recognition as king. On Dec. 14, 1697, he put the crown on his own head. Other thrones, too, were changing hands, and the situation was ominous for Sweden. Peter the Great of Russia, who had become sole czar on the death of his half brother Ivan in 1696, began to look for new fields of action after ending a war with Turkey in 1699. In February 1700, less than three years after Charles ascended the Swedish throne, Peter and Augustus of Saxony, newly crowned king of Poland as Augustus II, started the Great Northern War, attacking Swedish positions in Livonia. Peter's army marched against Narva in Swedish Estonia.

Frederick of Holstein-Gottorp, who was married to Charles' sister Hedvig Sofia, was threatening Denmark at this time. When Frederick IV of Denmark countered the threat by attacking Holstein-Gottorp, Charles XII moved quickly, and with the support of an Anglo-Dutch squadron, landed an army on Danish Zealand. Denmark submitted at once, and Charles hurried his army across to the eastern front and routed the Russian forces that were besieging Narva. Although he was only 18 years old, he was already a genius in tactics and an outstanding leader of men. Having tasted glory, he launched on 18 years of campaigning. He shaped his strategic plans on the assumption that Poland was the base area he must control before moving into Russia, which he considered the overshadowing threat to Sweden and to Western civilization. He overthrew Augustus and won victory upon victory but could never achieve dependable support within Poland. Perhaps a more facile diplomacy could have won Prussian assistance.

Russia and Turkey. Charles thought he had a useful ally in the Cossack chieftain, Mazepa (Mazeppa), but the Russians crushed Mazepa before a junction of forces could be made. At Poltava, deep in the Ukraine, Charles led his troops against Peter and the Russians on June 28, 1709. However, Swedish reinforcements were waylaid, and the king himself was disabled. Peter and his army had learned much since Narva and now decisively defeated the young lion of the north. Charles retired into Turkey, and most of his army surrendered. Many of these were destined to suffer death or imprisonment.

The disaster of Poltava brought Sweden's enemies out of their various retreats, and they closed in from all sides. Three times Charles convinced the Turks to declare war on the Russians,

King Charles XII of Sweden

but his situation did not improve. After the strange *Kalabalik* (Turkish for "tumult") of Feb. 1, 1713, in which the Turks attacked and burned Charles' quarters at Bender and took him prisoner, he had little reason to stay in Turkey. In October 1714 he and two companions rode incognito across Europe, arriving in about 15 days at Stralsund in Pomerania. There he directed a last-ditch defense but had to withdraw to Sweden. He gathered a fresh army of 80,000 men, determined to win what he could as a means of bargaining for peace. While he was besieging the Norwegian border fortress of Fredriksten on Nov. 30, 1718, a bullet of unknown origin smashed through his head, killing him instantly. With his death, both the Swedish empire and the autocratic government collapsed.

Charles was genius with limitations. He lacked the good fortune of Gustavus Adolphus, who had Axel Oxenstierna as a partner. Toward the end of his reign the shrewd Baron Görtz of Holstein came to his aid, but it was too late to save Sweden by diplomatic means from a task that was militarily too great for her. Charles was shy with women and never married.

FRANKLIN D. SCOTT, *Northwestern University*

Further Reading: Bengtsson, Frans G., *The Life of Charles XII, King of Sweden, 1697–1718* (London and New York 1960); Haintz, Otto, *König Karl XII von Schweden*, 3 vols. (Berlin 1958).

CHARLES XIII (1748–1818), king of Sweden. He was born at Stockholm on Oct. 7, 1748, the second son of King Adolf Frederick and Queen Louisa Ulrika. Charles was kindly and sociable, but he was neglected by his mother in favor of his older brother, the more brilliant Gustavus III. Charles lacked self-confidence and was easily swayed by others; hence, he was frequently used as a tool by opposition elements.

After the assassination of Gustavus III, Charles was regent for the young king Gustav IV Adolf (Gustavus IV) between 1792 and 1796, but he turned over most of his authority to his friend Gustav Adolf Reuterholm. Charles was interested in the promotion of Freemasonry, and he became Grand Master in Sweden. Although he opposed the basic purposes of the revolutionists of 1809, he accepted the crown from them in that year when they forced the autocratic Gustav Adolf to abdicate. Charles was quickly won, in 1810, by the charm of the French marshal Bernadotte, whom he adopted as his son under the name of Charles John; and because of lack of interest and early senility, he surrendered political leadership to Charles John as crown prince. Charles XIII died in Stockholm on Feb. 5, 1818.

FRANKLIN D. SCOTT
Northwestern University

CHARLES XIV (1763–1844), king of Sweden and Norway, who attained fame as Marshal Bernadotte of France before being elected crown prince of Sweden as Charles John (Karl Johan) in 1810.

He was born Jean Baptiste Jules Bernadotte, in Pau, in the southwestern French province of Béarn, on Jan. 26, 1763. When he was 17, his father, a lawyer, died, and the boy had to give up plans for further schooling. He enlisted in the army and rose steadily through the noncommissioned ranks. Early in the French Revolution, he was made a lieutenant (1792), and by 1794 he was general of a division.

Marshal of France. In campaigns along the Rhine, Bernadotte distinguished himself as a disciplinarian and as an inspirer of troops in critical situations. In 1797 he led 20,000 men in support of Napoleon Bonaparte's Italian campaign. Bernadotte then served briefly as French ambassador to Vienna and for 10 weeks in 1799 applied his administrative skills as minister of war in Paris.

Bernadotte strongly disapproved of the Napoleonic coup of the 18th Brumaire (Nov. 9, 1799), but he waited in vain for the Directory to ask him to oppose the Corsican. Napoleon was tempted on this and other occasions to have Bernadotte shot, but Bernadotte had in 1798 married Désirée Clary, who had been Napoleon's fiancée and was the sister of Joseph Bonaparte's wife, Julie. Partly because of this relationship with the Bonaparte clan, but probably more because of his prestige and ability, Bernadotte was made a marshal by Napoleon in 1804, named Prince of Ponte Corvo in 1805, and appointed governor of Hannover and later of the Hanseatic cities. He participated in the major campaigns of the Emperor and continued to be trusted despite occasional differences with Napoleon.

Ruler of Sweden. The marshal's life was suddenly altered when in 1810 the crown prince of Sweden died, and Bernadotte was elected heir to the throne of the Vasas by the Swedish Riksdag. Sweden may have hoped thereby to gain Napoleon's favor. But though Napoleon gave Bernadotte permission to proceed to Sweden, neither had any illusions that Sweden and France would become firm allies, despite the two men's previous close association in France.

As Crown Prince Charles John, Bernadotte directed the affairs of Sweden, for Charles XIII was aged and infirm and left control in the hands of his capable adopted son. Within four years he had brought about a restructuring of Scandinavia: Finland was left in Russian hands; Norway was torn from Denmark and made a kingdom united with Sweden; Pomerania was sold to Prussia; and Sweden retired from the continent. This reorientation laid the basis for a prolonged era of peace in northern Europe. Charles John allied himself closely with Alexander I of Russia and helped plan the campaign of the last coalition, which led to the French defeat in the Battle of the Nations at Leipzig in October 1813. After Leipzig, he led his Swedish troops against Denmark and eventually against Norway to force Norway's acceptance of the union with Sweden.

When Charles XIII died in 1818, Charles John succeeded to the throne at Charles XIV. As ruler of the united kingdoms of Sweden and Norway, he showed a sincere paternalistic concern for the good of his subjects. He promoted agricultural reform and did what he could to curtail the excessive use of alcohol. However, the suspiciousness of his nature, aggravated and confirmed by his experiences in the French Revolutionary period, made him sometimes unreasonable. His liberal sympathies appeared in his acceptance of the Norwegian constitution of 1814, but this attitude often conflicted with the autocratic tendencies that grew with his power. In government, as in battle, he was extremely cautious, though in talk he sometimes indulged in violent boasting. Both skill and luck shaped the remarkable career of the lawyer's son from Pau who founded the only "Napoleonic" dynasty to outlive the Napoleonic era. He died at Stockholm on March 8, 1844.

FRANKLIN D. SCOTT, *Northwestern University*

Further Reading: Barton, Dunbar Plunkett, *The Amazing Career of Bernadotte 1763–1844* (London 1929); Höjer, Torvald, *Carl XIV Johan*, 3 vols. (Stockholm 1939–1960); Scott, Franklin D., *Bernadotte and the Fall of Napoleon* (Cambridge, Mass., 1935).

CHARLES XV (1826–1872), king of Sweden and Norway. He was born in Stockholm on May 3, 1826, the eldest son of Oscar I, whom he succeeded in 1859. Although good-hearted and popular, Charles came to the throne at a time when liberal forces were curtailing the powers of the monarchy. He long opposed parliamentary reform, but was persuaded to change his position by his minister, Louis de Geer, and in the end pushed vigorously for reform. Charles' Scandinavian sympathies and schemes led him to promise military support to Denmark in the Schleswig-Holstein affair, but he had to yield to the veto of his ministers. Charles was a writer of verse, an artist, and an art collector. He died in Malmö on Sept. 18, 1872.

FRANKLIN D. SCOTT, *Northwestern University*

CHARLES XVI, king of Sweden. See CARL XVI GUSTAF, the form of the name by which he is generally known.

CHARLES (1948–   ), Prince of Wales, the eldest son of Queen Elizabeth II of Britain and Prince Philip, Duke of Edinburgh, and heir to the throne of the United Kingdom of Great Britain and Northern Ireland. He was born at Buckingham Palace on Nov. 14, 1948, and was christened Charles Philip Arthur George. He became heir to the throne when Elizabeth became queen in February 1952, and he became Prince of Wales in 1958.

On his 18th birthday he was designated regent in the event that his mother was incapacitated. The Prince of Wales attended private schools in Scotland and Australia, was enrolled at Cambridge University in 1967, and in 1971 began a five-year career in the armed services.

CHARLES, shàrl, **Jacques Alexandre César** (1746–1823), French physicist, who is best known for the discovery of the law that relates the volume of a gas to its temperature. Charles was born at Beaugency on Nov. 12, 1746. After studying a variety of subjects he became an administrator in a government agency, but was discharged later during an economy drive. He then gave paid performances in which he repeated Benjamin Franklin's experiments, especially the one with lightning, and he continued giving such lectures with spectacular experiments for 30 years. From 1795 until his death in Paris on April 7, 1823, he was professor of physics at the Conservatoire des Arts et Métiers.

Although Charles investigated many topics, he did not pursue them in any depth. In 1783 he invented a spherical balloon made of taffeta and coated with a solution of rubber dissolved in turpentine, which he filled with hydrogen and used to make two ascensions. His great success earned him a pension from Louis XVI, a seat in the Academy, and a laboratory at the Sorbonne. His fame also saved his life during the French Revolution.

Charles wrote about the integral calculus (1784), electrical experiments (1787), and comparative thermometer scales (1787). He discovered the law of gases, sometimes known by his name, about 1787, when he measured the expansion of the gases oxygen, nitrogen, hydrogen, carbon dioxide, and air as the temperature increased from 0° to 100° C and found that the expansion was uniform. He was not the first to carry out experiments in this field, however, and he did not publish his results. Gay-Lussac, who learned about the experiments by chance, described them in his own meticulous publication on the expansion of gases, so Charles is usually named as codiscoverer of this gas law along with Gay-Lussac.

EDUARD FARBER, *Editor of "Great Chemists"*

CHARLES, Cape, the southern tip of Virginia's Eastern Shore, the peninsula between Chesapeake Bay and the Atlantic. The Chesapeake Bay Bridge-Tunnel links Cape Charles, at the north entrance to the bay, to a point about midway between Norfolk and Cape Henry.

CHARLES ALBERT (1798–1849), king of Sardinia. The Italian form of his name is *Carlo Alberto*. He was born in Turin, capital of the kingdom of Sardinia, on Oct. 2, 1798, the son of Carlo Emanuele of the Carignan branch of the house of Savoy and Maria Cristina, Princess of Saxony-Curland. Educated mainly in France, Charles Albert was commissioned in Napoleon's army early in 1814. After the collapse of the French Empire he returned to Turin as heir presumptive to the Sardinian crown.

Around 1820, Charles Albert met members of clandestine liberal organizations. In March 1821 he promised them that he would ask his uncle King Victor Emmanuel I to grant a constitution, but a military insurrection broke out before he could do so. The king abdicated in favor of his brother Charles Felix, who repudiated Charles Albert's offer of a constitution. Austrian intervention quickly crushed the insurrection. To regain prestige among supporters of absolutism, Charles Albert joined the French forces that defeated the Spanish liberal government in 1823 and pledged to respect Sardinia's traditional institutions.

Charles Albert became king on the death of Charles Felix in 1831 and was an efficient, hardworking administrator. A devout Catholic, he suppressed liberal agitation but later tolerated a measure of freedom of the press and of association. In the wake of the revolution in Paris in February 1848, demonstrators in Turin clamored for a constitution, which Charles Albert granted on March 4. On March 23, after an appeal from the Milanese, who were in revolt against the Austrians, Charles Albert declared war on Austria. Successes in April and May were followed by the defeat of Custoza in July 1848, which forced him to abandon Lombardy and Milan, and by the more severe defeat of Novara on March 23, 1849, which ended the war. On the evening of the defeat Charles Albert abdicated in favor of his son Victor Emmanuel II and went into exile. He reached Oporto, Portugal, on April 20 and died there on July 28, 1849.

Charles Albert was called the Italian Hamlet, less politely *Il Re Tentenna* (King Wobble). Like other rulers of the time he had been torn between the inimical aspirations of traditional absolutism and patriotic liberalism.

M. Salvadori, *Smith College*

CHARLES AUGUSTUS, ô-gus′təs (1757–1828), grand duke of Saxe-Weimar. He was born in Weimar on Sept. 3, 1757. His tutor, Christoph Weiland, a talented and cultivated poet, inculcated in him a liberal outlook and a respect for the world of the intellect. When Charles Augustus came to the throne in 1775, he called Goethe to Weimar as privy councillor, and under Goethe's influence he made Weimar one of the most progressive German states and the center of German intellectual life.

Charles Augustus instituted numerous legal and economic reforms. He modernized the collection of taxes and the administration of justice. He introduced scientific improvements in agriculture, forestry, and mining. Above all, he devoted himself to improving the educational system, a task he entrusted to the philosopher Herder. He lavished special attention on the university at Jena, where he appointed Schiller professor of history (1789) and the philosophers Schelling (1798) and Hegel (1801). Jena also attracted the early romantics, among them Ludwig Tieck, Novalis, and August and Friedrich Schlegel.

Interested in German unity, Charles Augustus became in 1785 an active member of the League of Princes (Fürstenbund), which aimed at limiting the ambitions of the Habsburg emperor Joseph II. After the Battle of Jena in 1806, at which Napoleon defeated the German princes, Charles Augustus was obliged to join Napoleon's Confederation of the Rhine. However, the wars of liberation against Napoleon (1813–1815) found him once again on the German side. For his military services the Congress of Vienna awarded him territory and the title of grand duke.

In 1816 he promulgated a liberal constitution in Weimar, the first in the German states, and came out in favor of the *Burschenschaften* (liberal and nationalistic student societies) and a free press. These policies made him suspect in conservative circles but earned him the gratitude and respect of his people. He died in Weimar on June 14, 1828.

C. M. Kimmich, *Columbia University*

Further Reading: Bruford, W., *Culture and Society in Classical Weimar* (Cambridge, Eng., 1962).

CHARLES BORROMEO, Saint. See Borromeo, Saint Charles.

CHARLES CITY, a city in northern Iowa, the seat of Floyd county, is situated on the Cedar River, 105 miles (168 km) northeast of Des Moines. The city is a trading center for an agricultural region. It has plant nurseries and produces tractors, pharmaceuticals, and wood products.

The first permanent settlement here was made in 1850, on a site originally known as The Ford. Upon incorporation, in 1869, the name of Charles City was adopted in honor of Charles Kelly, son of Joseph Kelly, the first settler. Government is by a mayor and a city council. Population: 9,268.

CHARLES D'ORLEANS. See Orléans, Charles d'.

CHARLES EDWARD. See Stuart, Charles Edward Louis Philip Casimir.

CHARLES LOUIS (1771–1847), archduke of Austria and duke of Teschen, who commanded Austrian armies against Napoleon Bonaparte. He was born in Florence, Italy, on Sept. 5,1771, the third son of Emperor Leopold II of the Holy Roman Empire. He served with distinction in the battles of Jemappes and Neerwinden and was made field marshal and commander of the Austrian forces on the Rhine in 1796. He won victories against the French in Germany in 1796–1797 and 1799–1801.

Charles Louis reorganized the Austrian army after its defeat at the Battle of Austerlitz in 1805 and created an efficient fighting force that won a notable victory at the Battle of Aspern in May 1809. After being defeated at the Battle of Wagram in July 1809, he retired and wrote on military history. He died in Vienna on April 30, 1847.

CHARLES MARTEL, mär-tel′, (689–741), grandfather of Charlemagne, was a powerful Frankish leader. Since his cognomen Martel means "hammer," he is sometimes known as Charles the Hammer.

He was the illegitimate son of Pepin of Heristal, who governed Neustria (northwestern France) and Austrasia (the eastern Frankish lands centering on Metz) in the name of the Merovingian dynasty. Charles' mother was named Chalpaïda.

From the mid-7th century on, the Frankish kings were political ciphers; the so-called "mayors of the palace" held real power. These mayors, including Pepin of Heristal, mostly belonged to the family of Arnulfinger (later called Carolingian), and they usually inherited the office of mayor.

On the death of Pepin of Heristal in 714, Pepin's nephews divided the Austrasian and Neustrian mayoralities, which he had united. Pepin's widow, Plectrude, imprisoned Charles Martel, to cool his ambitions. When rebellion began in Neustria, Charles escaped, raised an Austrasian army, and defeated the Neustrians in two campaigns (717 and 719), reuniting his father's offices.

Expansion to the East. Thereafter, Charles was involved in a series of campaigns to extend the Frankish kingdoms. A number of barbarian tribes lived along his eastern borders. Their brigandage endangered Charles' frontiers, and their political disunity at home invited Frankish expansion. Charles marched against the Frisians and Saxons (719–738), the Swabians (730), and the Bavarians (725–728). To reinforce his military gains, he encouraged Christian missionaries to go among the still-pagan tribes as Frankish representatives both in religion and in politics. The greatest of these missionaries was St. Boniface, "the Apostle of the Germans."

Threat of Islam. Dangers also threatened from the southwest. Charles overcame some of these by subduing the Duke of Aquitaine. However, more serious enemies appeared in Spain. In 710–711, Spain fell to the armies of Islam, and by 720 the danger of Islamic expansion into Gaul was imminent. In 725, Charles engaged an Arab force at Autun, and in 732 he repulsed another band of Arabs, probably reconnaissance troops, in the famous engagement at Moussais-la-Bataille (also known as the Battle of Tours) near Poitiers. All medieval history was affected when Islam's conquests were stopped at the Pyrenees.

Papal Alliance. Pope Gregory III, who was struggling to defend the papacy against the Lombards, saw Charles as a potential ally. In 739 he offered him the title of consul, at the same time requesting his military assistance. Though Charles declined Gregory's offer, since he himself sought an alliance with the Lombards, the proposal made it clear that Charles, rather than the Merovingians, was the ruler of the Franks. In fact, in 737, at the death of the Merovingian king Theodoric IV, Charles had simply neglected, as mayor of the palace, to name a new king.

Charles died at Quierzy-sur-Oise, France, on Oct. 22, 741. His policies had assured Frankish preeminence among the tribes of northern Europe; and Pope Gregory's proposal foreshadowed a series of alliances between popes and Franks that culminated in Charlemagne's coronation as emperor in 800.

K. F. MORRISON, *University of Chicago*

CHARLES OF ANJOU. See CHARLES I, king of Naples.

CHARLES OF DURAZZO. See CHARLES III, king of Naples.

CHARLES RIVER, in eastern Massachusetts. It rises in southwestern Norfolk county and follows a winding 60-mile (96-km) course to empty into Boston Harbor. The Massachusetts Institute of Technology and Harvard University, in Cambridge, are on its shores.

CHARLES UNIVERSITY, in Prague, Czechoslovakia, is the oldest and one of the best-known universities in central Europe. It was founded by King Charles IV, Holy Roman emperor, in 1348, and opened with colleges of divinity, law, medicine, and arts and a faculty divided equally among Czech, Saxon, Bavarian, and Polish scholars. In 1409 a decree promulgated during the rectorship of Jan Hus, gave the Czechs control. Between 1654 and 1791 the university was under Jesuit control. It was then taken over by the state and in 1882 divided into two sections: Charles and German universities. The Germans closed Charles in 1939. It was reopened in 1945 after the liberation as a state-maintained institution; the German unit was abolished.

The present university has faculties of law, philosophy, mathematics and physics, natural sciences, education, physical training and sport, culture and journalism, general medicine, medical hygiene, and pediatrics. The 5-year course of study may lead to a doctorate. Postgraduate degrees are Candidate of Science and Doctor of Science. Enrollment averages 20,000 full- and part-time students. Tuition is free.

MIROSLAV SOUKUP
Czech Classical Scholars Union

CHARLES WILLIAM FERDINAND (1735–1806), was Duke of Brunswick and a famous general. Charles William Ferdinand (German, Karl Wilhelm Ferdinand) was born at Wolfenbüttel, in Brunswick on Oct. 9, 1735. As a young officer he served with great distinction with Frederick the Great, King of Prussia, in the Seven Years' War (1756–1763). In 1780 he succeeded his father as ruler of Brunswick. His father's extravagance had left the duchy heavily indebted. Charles William Ferdinand reformed Brunswick's finances and improved the government to such a degree that he was regarded as a model of the 18th century "enlightened despot."

In 1787 he led the successful Prussian expedition against the Netherlands, and in 1792 he headed the Austro-Prussian campaign against the revolutionary government of France. In 1806, again in command of Prussian forces, he was mortally wounded in one of the actions that preceded Napoleon's crushing defeat of Prussia at Jena. He died at Ottensen, Germany, on Nov. 10, 1806.

A. G. STEER, JR.
University of Georgia

CHARLESBOURG, shärl-bŏŏr', is a city in Quebec county, Quebec, Canada, about 3 miles (5 km) north of Quebec City, of which it is a residential suburb. It is 6 miles (10 km) northeast of the Quebec airport at L'Ancienne-Lorette and has easy access to ski centers to the north in the Laurentian Mountains. The Quebec Zoo is in Charlesbourg.

The site of the city was originally part of a grant to the Jesuits in 1626. The first settlement was established in 1659. Charlesbourg was incorporated as a town in 1949 and as a city in 1960. Population: 33,443.

CHARLESTON, a city in eastern Illinois, the seat of Coles county, is 85 miles (136 km) southeast of Springfield. The city is situated in an agricultural and dairy-farming area. It has railroad shops and lumber mills, and its manufactured products include shoes, brooms, business forms, and ceramics for the steel industry. Charleston is the site of Eastern Illinois University, chartered in 1895.

The Lincoln Log Cabin State Park is nearby. One of the Lincoln-Douglas debates was held here in 1858. Charleston is governed by commission. Population: 16,421.

CHARLESTON, a city in southeastern Missouri, the seat of Mississippi county, is 125 miles (200 km) southeast of St. Louis. It is an important cotton center and also manufactures shoes. Big Oak State Park is nearby, and there are many Indian mounds in the vicinity. The city is governed by a council and manager. Population: 5,131.

CHARLESTON'S old section includes the Dock Street Theatre (*left*) and St. Philip's Episcopal Church (*at right*).

CHARLESTON, a major Atlantic seaport with a unique colonial heritage, is the center of South Carolina's second-largest metropolitan area (1970 population, 303,849) and the seat of Charleston county. Charleston signifies more than a geographic area. It is an attitude, uniqueness, color, independence, good taste, and culture. It is an area of contrasts. Much older than the nation, the city is proud of its historic homes, streets, alleys, forts, and churches. The city is equally proud of its role in the modern world, manifested in its defense installations, its harbor, its industrial establishments, and its commercial and financial institutions.

Most of the city lies between the Ashley and Cooper rivers which flow into the Atlantic Ocean (or according to Charlestonians, form the Atlantic). Although some area west of the Ashley River has been annexed, the old city is virtually hemmed in by sprawling North Charleston to the north, the town of Mount Pleasant and its suburbs east of the Cooper River, many suburban areas on the west, and the Atlantic Ocean on the south. Two thirds of the people in greater Charleston live outside the city.

OLD HOUSES lend charm to Charleston's Battery area.

Economy. The economy of Charleston is linked directly to national defense and to Charleston's advantageous location on the Atlantic. Charleston is the home of one of the Polaris submarine bases, a navy yard employing thousands, the headquarters for the Sixth Naval District, an Air Force Defense Command and airlift base, the regional office of the Corps of Engineers, and several other military installations.

The nonmilitary sections of the port of Charleston are maintained by the state. The port is a modern facility, and trade has grown rapidly since World War II, making it one of the major ports in the nation. The port adds substantially to the economy and interest of the area. Manufacturing facilities are varied and increasing. Major products include paper, fertilizer, chemicals, rubber products, textiles, foods, and aircraft parts. Truck farming and fishing contribute significantly to the metropolitan income. Drawn by the historic attractions and charm of the city, tourists, visitors, and conventions are a major factor in its economy and life. Charleston is the retail, wholesale, banking, and financial center for the coastal area of the state.

Urban Needs. As one of the major urban areas of the state, Charleston has its share of city problems. Great effort is exerted to meet urban needs, but finding solutions to problems is aggravated by the area's topographical nature, which complicates transportation and road patterns and encourages the flight of business from downtown to suburban shopping centers, the concentration of Negroes in certain sections, and the relatively brief stay of many of the military residents. There has been a movement, against strong opposition, to consolidate city and county governments so as to coordinate services. There is already a county-manager form of government, countywide subdivision regulations, a modern county police force, unified traffic, health, welfare, and library services, and area-wide water service by the city.

Transportation in the city has been aided significantly by major bridges across both rivers, the downtown extension of an interstate highway, and modern feeder roads into the interstate system. The U. S. Army Corps of Engineers continually works to improve the harbor channels.

Although the metropolitan area has many public housing programs, more are needed to relieve the depressed areas of the city and county. Much of the city's population is Negro. Negroes are active in politics and have been voting freely since World War II.

Institutions and Points of Interest. Among major institutions in Charleston are the Medical College of South Carolina and a Veterans Administration hospital; the College of Charleston, founded 1770, the oldest municipal college in the country; the Citadel, founded in 1842, a state-supported military college; Baptist College in Charleston Heights, founded in 1965; and a technical education center.

Charleston has survived major fires, earthquakes, hurricanes, and wars, and looks to the future but preserves the past. Charleston adopted the first historical-preservation ordinance in the country. The Historic Charleston Foundation exerts positive leadership in preserving and restoring buildings and areas, such as Ansonborough, a considerable section in the heart of the old city.

The residential area located generally between Broad Street and the Battery (now an esplanade) is one of the most unique in the country, featuring old homes and tasteful architecture and furnishings, ironwork, courtyards, piazzas, and delightful gardens. The old churches are beautiful, especially St. Philip's, St. Michael's, the French Huguenot, and St. Matthew's—rebuilt in the 1960's. The Dock Street Theatre, opened in 1736 and one of the earliest in the country, was restored in 1937 and is in use.

Also noteworthy are the Fireproof Building (1826), apparently the first in the United States; the Nathaniel Russell, the Miles Brewton, the Heyward-Washington, and other famous houses; the cobblestone streets; the slave market; City Hall and its art collection; and Fort Sumter, where the Civil War began. The Atlantic beaches on Isle of Palms, Sullivan's Island, and Folly Beach, the Cooper River bridges, the port, the Navy Yard, Hampton Park, the Citadel, and the shrimp fleet are of interest. Surrounding the city are a number of gardens, notably Cypress, Magnolia, and Middleton gardens.

History. Charleston began in 1670 with a settlement on the west bank of the Ashley by 150 English and Irish colonists. At first called Albemarle Point, it was renamed Charles Town for King Charles II. In 1680, for better defense, the settlement was moved to the tip of the peninsula between the Ashley and Cooper rivers. Charles Town was the state capital from 1776 until 1786, when Columbia was founded. The city was incorporated as Charleston in 1783; by 1775 it had become the major city and port south of Philadelphia. In Charleston were passed the Ordinance of Nullification on Nov. 24, 1832, and the first Ordinance Secession on Dec. 20, 1860. The first overt act of the Civil War was the firing of Charleston shore batteries on a ship trying to deliver supplies to Fort Sumter. The city was blockaded from May 1861 to February 1865 and then occupied by Union troops. In 1886 an earthquake damaged about 90% of the buildings. Industry and commerce have been expanding since 1920.

Charleston is governed by a mayor and 16 aldermen. Population: 66,945.

ROBERT H. STOUDEMIRE
University of South Carolina

HERBERT LANKS, FROM BLACK STAR

CHARLESTON, West Virginia, is the site of the state capitol, which was designed by Cass Gilbert.

CHARLESTON, in West Virginia, the capital and largest city of the state and seat of Kanawha county, is situated 255 miles (410 km) west of Washington, D. C. The Kanawha River, a navigable tributary of the Ohio, meets the Elk River near the heart of the city. The rivers have been beautified by the planting of thousands of flowering trees and shrubs along their banks since 1960.

The area is rich in bituminous coal, oil, natural gas, and salt, making Charleston the center of a large chemical-manufacturing industry, in which many major national companies participate. An important technical research center employs more than 2,000 persons. Other industries produce mine equipment, hand tools and farm implements, plate glass, brick and clay products, and military hardware.

Besides being the political capital and the industrial heart of West Virginia, Charleston is the state's commercial and distribution center, with service by several railroads, by a number of airlines at its mountaintop airport, by many interstate bus and truck lines, and by numerous river barges.

The chief educational institution is Morris Harvey College, which was founded in 1888 in Barboursville and moved to its large riverfront campus in Charleston in 1935. Cultural organizations include the Charleston Symphony, Light Opera Guild, Kanawha Players, and the Charleston Ballet. Sunrise, a cultural and educational center, overlooks the downtown section from South Hills. The state capitol is a limestone and marble building of Italian Renaissance design completed in 1932.

The plan to extend three interstate highways into the city in order to make Charleston the hub of east-west and north-south highway transportation in West Virginia sparked a major building boom in the late 1960's. Among the new structures were high-rise apartments, 500 public housing units, and two urban renewal projects near the downtown area. The Civic Center for athletic, cultural, industrial, and civic events was expanded, and the Municipal Auditorium was renovated.

History. In 1788, Col. George Clendenin erected a log fort on the present site of Charleston; he called it Fort Lee, after Gov. Henry Lee of Virginia. An important frontier post, it offered protection to incoming Scotch-Irish and German settlers. Marauding Indians for whom the valley was a hunting preserve fiercely resisted white settlement. Daniel Boone, who fished and trapped in the Kanawha Valley, was elected to the Virginia legislature from the newly formed Kanawha county in 1791. The settlement as originally chartered in 1794 by the Virginia legislature was called Charles Town, after Clendenin's father, but the name was shortened in 1818 to Charleston.

West Virginia became a separate state during the Civil War, and Charleston was its capital from 1870 to 1875, when Wheeling became the capital. In 1885, Charleston became the capital permanently. Charleston grew very slowly until industrialization of the Kanawha Valley began about 1900. The manufacture of chemicals on a massive scale began in the 1920's, and since then the city has grown rapidly and steadily. Government is by mayor and council. Population: 71,505.

CHARLES K. CONNOR
Charleston "Daily Mail"

CHARLESTOWN, a city in Indiana, is in Clark county, about 90 miles (144 km) south of Indianapolis. Farms in the area produce tobacco, livestock, and dairy products, and there are limestone quarries. Charlestown is the site of the Indiana Ordnance Works and the Hoosier Ordnance Plant. Population: 5,890.

CHARLESTOWN, a part of Boston, Mass., is situated between the Mystic and Charles rivers. It lies northeast of the city proper, to which it was annexed in 1874. Charlestown was settled about 1628. Less than a decade later it became a town, and in 1847 it was chartered as a city.

Charlestown was the scene of the Battle of Bunker Hill in the American Revolution. The battle actually was fought on Breed's Hill, near Bunker Hill, on June 17, 1775. The frigate *Constitution*, known as "Old Ironsides," lies in dock at the Boston Naval Shipyard, a U. S. naval yard established in Charlestown in 1800.

CHARLEVOIX, shär-lə-vwa´, **Pierre François Xavier de** (1682–1761), French Jesuit traveler and historian. He was born in St.-Quentin, France, on Oct. 24, 1682. He taught at the Jesuit college in Quebec from 1705 to 1709 and returned to Quebec from France in 1720, having been commissioned by the French government to report on the best route to the "Western Sea." Setting out for the West in May 1721, he worked his way slowly down the Mississippi Valley and visited all the posts that constituted the frontier of the French empire in North America. He reached New Orleans in January 1722 and returned to France in 1723.

Charlevoix spent the latter part of his life in literary work. His most notable book, *Histoire et description générale de la Nouvelle France, avec le Journal historique...* (3 vols., Paris 1744), was the first general narrative history of New France based on both source material and firsthand knowledge. The *Journal* was first published in English in 1761, a century before the *History* was translated and edited by John G. Shea (6 vols., New York 1866–1872; new ed., 1900). Charlevoix died at La Flèche, France, on Feb. 1, 1761.

MASON WADE, *University of Western Ontario*

CHARLEY HORSE is a popular term for some types of muscle tears in the leg, particularly in athletes. The origin of the term is not known, although some believe it originated in veterinary medicine, perhaps from the once common use of the name Charley for old, lame horses. In recent years, as a result of great interest in sports medicine, authorities have been trying to discourage the use of such vernacular terms in favor of specific terms that more accurately describe the pathologic condition.

The specific injury in a charley horse is a partial or complete rupture of the rectus femoris muscle, a hip flexor that runs along the front of the thigh from the knee to the pelvis. Treatment of this injury entails rest, hot applications, and enzyme drugs to dissipate accumulations of blood resulting from hemorrhaging and thereby reduce swelling.

JOHN J. GARTLAND, M. D.
Jefferson Medical College

CHARLEY'S AUNT, a farce by Brandon Thomas, first produced in 1892. It was the basis of the successful musical comedy *Where's Charley?* (1948) by George Abbott and Frank Loesser, with Ray Bolger as Charley. The musical was made into a film in 1952. Charley and a fellow Oxford student await Charley's aunt from Brazil, who is to chaperon a luncheon for their sweethearts in Charley's rooms. When she fails to appear, a friend of Charley's (in the play) or Charley himself (in the musical) impersonates her, with much hilarity.

CHARLOT, shàr-lō´, **Jean** (1898–), French-American painter and author. He was born in Paris on Feb. 8, 1898. After studying at the École des Beaux Arts in Paris, he served in the French Army. In 1920 he went to Mexico, where he painted several murals, including the *Fall of Tenochtitlán* (1922) at the National Preparatory School. These works are marked by their strong, massive figures and monumental, almost architectural design. From 1926 to 1929 he participated in an archaeological expedition to Chichén Itzá.

In 1929, Charlot went to the United States, where he taught at the University of Georgia, the Art Students League in New York, and elsewhere. In 1949 he was appointed professor of art at the University of Hawaii.

Charlot's work comprises easel paintings, lithographs, woodcuts, and illustrations for children's books. His books include *Art-Making from Mexico to China* (1950) and *Mexican Mural Renaissance* (1963).

CHARLOTTE (1896–), grand duchess of Luxembourg from 1919 to 1964. The daughter of Grand Duke William IV, she was born in Colmar-Berg, Luxembourg, on Jan. 23, 1896. A national plebiscite placed Charlotte on the grand ducal throne in 1919. In the same year she married Prince Felix of Bourbon-Parma. In 1964, after a long and popular reign, she abdicated in favor of her son, Prince Jean.

CHARLOTTE is a cultural center as well as an industrial nucleus for North Carolina. In the modern 2500-seat Ovens Auditorium, opera and theatrical performances are given regularly.

CHARLOTTE, shər-lot', a city in southern Michigan, the seat of Eaton county, is on Battle Creek River, 18 miles (29 km) southwest of Lansing. It is in a dairying and bean-growing area. Livestock is auctioned in the city. The city's industries include the manufacture of glass, lumber, road machinery, silos, aluminum appliances, iron products, wood products, and furniture, and the processing of foods.

Charlotte was settled in 1835; it was incorporated as a village in 1871 and as a city in 1891. Government is by mayor, city manager, and council. Population: 8,244.

CHARLOTTE, shär'lot, is the largest city in North Carolina. It is situated 125 miles (201 km) southwest of Raleigh and about 10 miles (16 km) north of the South Carolina border, and is the seat of Mecklenburg county. It is the nucleus of a prosperous industrial region, sometimes called the Carolinas Crescent, that extends in an arc from Raleigh to Greenville, S. C.

The city is a major distribution, retailing, and manufacturing center. It has more than 1,200 wholesale firms and nearly 100 trucking terminals and is served by several railroads and airlines. Textiles, including apparel and hosiery, lead among the city's manufactures, but there is a diversity of other products. Among these are canned foods, processed meat, bakery and dairy products, machinery, primary and fabricated metals, chemicals, aircraft parts, computers, paper products, and boxes. Charlotte also is an important banking center.

Charlotte is the seat of the University of North Carolina at Charlotte and of two colleges under Presbyterian auspices: Queens College, for women, founded in 1875, and Johnson C. Smith University (formerly Biddle University), founded in 1867 for Negroes. Central Piedmont Community College also is in Charlotte. The city has a symphony orchestra. Opera and other theatrical presentations are offered at the Ovens Auditorium. The city has art and nature museums.

The 13,000-seat Charlotte Coliseum has a full schedule of spectator sports, including basketball and ice hockey. Charlotte's baseball team, the Hornets, is a farm team of the Minnesota Twins. There are 22 parks. Public golf courses, country clubs, and a yacht club provide additional recreation and there are water sports and boating on nearby Catawba Lake and Lake Norman.

History. Charlotte was settled about 1750, largely by Scotch-Irish and German migrants from Pennsylvania, New Jersey, and Virginia. It was in-

corporated in 1768, and six years later it became the county seat and organized a regular town government. The city was named for Charlotte Sophia of Mecklenburg-Strelitz (1744–1818), queen of King George III of England. The county was named for her home duchy in Germany. Charlotte was chartered as a city in 1866 and again in 1907.

The Mecklenburg county safety committee took strong action for independence prior to the American Revolution in May 1775. The British general, Lord Cornwallis, occupied Charlotte for several days in 1780, and later in the year the American general, Horatio Gates, made it his headquarters. Presidents Andrew Jackson and James K. Polk were born in the vicinity.

The Confederate Naval Ordnance Yard operated in Charlotte during the Civil War from 1862 to 1865. The last full Confederate cabinet meeting, under President Jefferson Davis, was held in the city on April 10, 1865.

From about 1800 until 1848, gold mines in the Charlotte area were the main U. S. source for gold. A branch of the U. S. mint, opened at Charlotte in 1837, operated until 1913, except for the Civil War years. The building was razed in 1933 but was reconstructed and opened in 1936. Called the Mint Museum of Art, it has historical exhibits and an art collection. Since 1929, Charlotte has had a council-manager government with an elected mayor. Population: 241,178.

HUGH T. LEFLER, *University of North Carolina; Author of "History of North Carolina"*

CHARLOTTE AMALIE, shär'lət ə-mäl'yə, is the capital of the Virgin Islands of the United States. It is situated on the south central shore of St. Thomas, a former Danish island about 12 miles (19 km) long and 3 miles (5 km) wide, lying 40 miles (65 km) east of Puerto Rico. Charlotte Amalie, the only town on the island, retains much of the Danish flavor in its architecture and street names. Fort Christian, with its founding date of 1671 over the entrance, now houses the police department and allied activities.

Charlotte Amalie is a popular health and vacation resort and a port of call for many cruise ships. Temperatures range between 70° and 90° F (21° to 32° C) the year round, and the cooling trade winds are relatively constant.

Part of the town is built on hillsides overlooking the harbor. Many of the colorful old warehouses have been converted into stores. Tourism is the biggest industry, aided by the Virgin Islands' free port status and $200 duty-free al-

CHARLOTTE AMALIE, with its pleasant climate and fine harbor, is a major Virgin Islands tourist center.

lowance for Americans returning to the states. St. Thomas' numerous fine beaches are easily reached from Charlotte Amalie by car, and some of them by bus. Traffic drives on the left. The island's main airport is approximately a mile (1.6 km) from the center of town.

Charlotte Amalie was founded in 1691 and was named in honor of the queen of Christian V, the Danish king then reigning. The town was part of the Danish West Indies until 1917, when the islands were bought by the United States. The U. S. Navy has a submarine base near Charlotte Amalie. Population: 12,372.

ROLAND DICKISON
College of the Virgin Islands

CHARLOTTENBURG, shär-lôt'ən-bŏŏrkн, is a residential district of Berlin, Germany—now in West Berlin. Once a city in the state of Brandenburg, Prussia, it was incorporated into Greater Berlin in 1920. It was an important industrial center, noted especially for its porcelain factory, which was established in 1751. Porcelain is still manufactured in Charlottenburg as well as a number of other products, but the modern district is more significant as a cultural and residential area. The entire district suffered severe damage during World War II, after which it underwent extensive reconstruction.

Charlottenburg has a technical academy with a valuable architectural museum, schools of music and of plastic and graphic arts, a physical-technical institute, and several other museums. Its most famous art museum is housed in Charlottenburg Palace, begun in 1695, for which the district is named. First called Lietzenburg, the palace was renamed in honor of Sophia Charlotte, wife of Frederick III, elector of Brandenburg (later Frederick I of Prussia).

CHARLOTTESVILLE, shär'ləts-vil, an independent city in central Virginia, the seat of Albemarle county, is the site of the University of Virginia and is famous as the home of Thomas Jefferson. It is situated about 70 miles (102 km) west of Richmond. The city has a large law book publishing firm and many research and industrial administration offices. Albemarle county is a center for the raising of quality horses and beef cattle.

The university was planned by Jefferson and was founded by him in 1819. Jefferson's home, Monticello, is on the outskirts of the city. Among notable figures of American history who lived in Charlottesville were Presidents James Madison and James Monroe, the frontiersman George Rogers Clark and the explorers Meriwether Lewis and William Clark.

Charlottesville was settled about 1737. It was named for Queen Charlotte, consort of George III of Britain. It became a city in 1888 and has a council-manager government. Population: 38,880.

RAYMOND A. WILLIAMS, *McIntire Public Library*

CHARLOTTETOWN, shär'lət-toun, the capital of Prince Edward Island, Canada, is situated on Hillsborough Bay on the south side of the island province. It is an attractive city with many trees and well-kept homes. Besides being the seat of the provincial government, Charlottetown is a center of wholesale and retail trade and of tourism, with transportation facilities by land, sea, and air. There are several processing and packing plants. St. Dunstan's University and Prince of Wales College are in Charlottetown.

In 1720 the first French colonists sent by the Count de St. Pierre settled at Port La Joie near the present capital site. The British, taking over after the Treaty of Paris (1763), called the capital Charlottetown after the queen of King George III. The first formal discussion of Canadian confederation was held at Charlottetown in 1864. In 1964 the Fathers of Confederation Memorial Centre, comprising a theater, art gallery, museum, and library, was opened by Queen Elizabeth II. The theater holds a summer festival of music and drama. Charlottetown, incorporated in 1855, is governed by a mayor and council. Population: 19,133.

DOROTHY CULLEN
Prince Edward Island Libraries

CHARM, in anthropology, an amulet, talisman, or good-luck piece worn on the person primarily to ward off evil. It is also a magic spell or incantation, often used to give an amulet its protective power (see AMULET).

Charms as incantations are among the oldest written records left by the ancient civilizations of the Middle East and Far East and have been recorded from all parts of the world and all levels of society. They often take the form of verse and are handed down through generations. Charms may thus become unintelligible to the user, and this additional mystery is sometimes thought to increase their power. Such charms have at times been reduced to nursery rhymes, such as the familiar "Rain, rain, go away," or injunctions to a bride, for example, to wear "something old, something new, something borrowed, and something blue." Charms also play a great role in folk literature and fairy tales. The phrase "Open, Sesame!" in the tale of Ali Baba is a charm. Many literary works incorporate charms—for example, the witches' spell in Shakespeare's *Macbeth*.

ERIKA BOURGUINON, *The Ohio State University*

CHARNWOOD, chärn′wood, **1st Baron** (1864–1945), English public official and biographer. He was born Godfrey Rathbone Benson on Nov. 6, 1864, in Langtons in Alresford, Hampshire, England. He was educated at Winchester and at Balliol College, Oxford, and later lectured at Balliol. He served as a Liberal member of Parliament (1892–1895) with the sole purpose, as he claimed, of espousing Irish home rule. He was mayor of Lichfield from 1909 to 1911 and continued as councillor and alderman until 1938. In 1911 he was made a peer.

Lord Charnwood attained renown for his biography *Abraham Lincoln* (1916), which was for long the most popular and authoritative one-volume work on the American president. He also wrote a life of Theodore Roosevelt (1923). Other publications include *According to St. John* (1926) and *Tracks in the Snow* (1927), a detective story. Charnwood died in London on Feb. 3, 1945.

CHARNY, shàr-nē′, a town in southeastern Quebec, Canada, on the Chaudière River about 8 miles (13 km) southwest of Quebec city. It is an important railroad divisional point, where trains turn to cross the Quebec bridge to Quebec city. It was incorporated in 1924. Population: 5,175.

CHARON, kâr′ən, in Greek mythology, was the boatman who ferried the dead across the river Styx into Hades. He was the son of Erebus and Nyx (Night) and was traditionally represented as a coarse, bearded old man.

Charon would accept for passage only those whose bodies had received funeral rites and had the proper toll, which was a small coin (obol) placed under the tongue of the dead person. A living person was given passage only if he carried with him a golden bough obtained from the Cumaean sibyl.

In later Greek lore, Charon, known as Charos or Charontas, is represented as the black bird or winged horseman that carries people to the afterworld. Although Charon was not mentioned by Homer, he figures in such later works as Aristophanes' *The Frogs* and Virgil's *Aeneid*.

CHARPENTIER, shàr-päN-tyā′, **Gustave** (1860–1956), French composer, whose music is melodic, ingeniously orchestrated, and evocative of his beloved Paris. Charpentier was born at Dieuze, Lorraine, on June 25, 1860. He attended the Paris Conservatory from 1881 to 1887, studying chiefly with Massenet. In 1887 he won the Prix de Rome for *Didon*, a cantata. The most important of his early compositions was a cantata entitled *Fête du couronnement de la muse* (1898), which he later modified and introduced into Act 3 of his opera *Louise*.

Louise, first performed at the Opéra-Comique in Paris on Feb. 2, 1900, was his only real success. He wrote both text and music and contrived a story at once naturalistic and symbolic, describing the daily life of contemporary Parisian working people. A second opera, *Julien*, was first given at the Metropolitan Opera in New York in 1913, but even the presence in the cast of Enrico Caruso and Geraldine Farrar could not save it from failure. Charpentier spent his later years giving occasional lessons and working for a girls' home that he endowed with the royalties from *Louise*. He died in Paris on Feb. 18, 1956.

WILLIAM ASHBROOK, *Author of "Donizetti"*

CHARPENTIER, shàr-päN-tyā′, **Marc Antoine** (1634–1704), French composer, who helped to introduce the Latin oratorio into France. His music combines Italian ornamentation with French grace and elegance. Charpentier was born in Paris in 1634. While studying painting in Italy, he became acquainted with Giacomo Carissimi's oratorios and decided on a career in music. After a period of music study in Paris, he composed incidental music for several Molière plays, including *Le mariage forcé* (1672) and *Le malade imaginaire* (1673). He wrote 16 operas, the most important of which was *Médée* (1693).

Charpentier's most significant contribution was as a composer of church music. He completed more than 150 works of this type, including oratorios, masses, psalms, motets, *Te Deums*, and *Histoires sacrées* (dramatizations of Biblical episodes). From 1698 he served as chapel master of Ste.-Chapelle, in Paris, for whose religious services he created some of his most ambitious choral works. He died in Paris on Feb. 24, 1704.

DAVID EWEN
Author of "The World of Great Composers"

CHARPY TEST, shär′pē, a technique for determining the toughness of a material. It measures the energy absorbed by a small notched specimen, supported at its ends, when it is struck and broken by a heavy pendulum. Energy absorption is determined from the change in kinetic energy of the pendulum after it strikes the material.

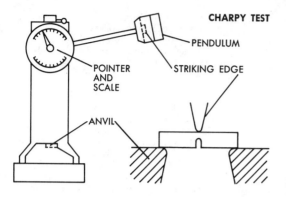

CHARPY TEST

PENDULUM

POINTER AND SCALE

STRIKING EDGE

ANVIL

Results on specimens of identical dimensions are useful in determining the effect of the processing history on the quality of materials. Results are also useful in establishing temperatures at which embrittlement is likely to occur. Notch-sensitivity, or sensitivity to abrupt change in cross section, is determined by testing specimens with a variety of notch designs.

CARL A. KEYSER, *University of Massachusetts*

CHARRAN. See HARAN.

CHARRIÈRE, shá-ryâr, **Isabelle Agnès Élisabeth de** (1740–1805), Swiss author. She was born on Oct. 20, 1740, at Zuylen, Utrecht, in the Netherlands, the daughter of Baron van Tuyll van Serooskerken van Zuylen. Intelligent and beautiful, she numbered James Boswell among her many suitors. In 1766 she married her brother's tutor and moved with him to Colombier, near Neuchâtel, Switzerland. Her married life there was dull and unhappy, though it was brightened somewhat by an intense intellectual friendship with Benjamin Constant.

Madame Charrière, who used the pen names "Zélide," "Abbé de la Tour," and "Belle de Zuylen," described her married life in several largely autobiographical novels, the best of which is *Caliste* (1787). She also wrote a lyric tragedy, comedies, and a number of advanced sociological works on such subjects as morality, poverty, and aristocratic privilege. She died at Colombier on Dec. 27, 1805.

CHARRON, shá-rôn', **Pierre** (1541–1603), French Roman Catholic philosopher. He was born in Paris. After studying and practicing law in Bourges, he entered the priesthood and became the personal preacher for Marguerite, consort of King Henry IV. In 1589 he met Michel de Montaigne (q.v.), the founder of the modern school of skeptical philosophy, and became his disciple. He died in Paris on Nov. 16, 1603.

Charron's major works are *Treatise on Three Truths* (*Trois vérités*, 1593), a polemic against Calvinism; *Christian Discourses* (*Discours chrétiens*, 1600), a discussion of prayer; and *Treatise on Wisdom* (*De la sagesse*, 1601), his major and most influential work. He used the "method of doubt" to prove that man could not rationally arrive at certain knowledge; therefore man must rely on natural impulse and free will to obtain "true wisdom," or moral ideals.

ROBERT M. SENKEWICZ, S. J.
Loyola Seminary, Shrub Oak, N. Y.

CHART. See NAVIGATION.

CHARTER, a document transferring rights, privileges, or immunities from the sovereign power of a state to its people, or to a group of them organized into a company, institution, or dependency. The term, from *charta* or *carta* (Latin for "written document"), originally had a broader meaning in England, encompassing all conveyances of land titles, including those between private individuals. Gradually the meaning was restricted to grants from the sovereign.

MEDIEVAL AND COLONIAL CHARTERS

Medieval charters, both in England and on the continent of Europe, were issued for various purposes. In 1215, king John of England regularized his feudal contract and accepted limitations on his authority in the Magna Carta (Great Charter). European monarchs also issued charters to merchant groups, guilds, and religious and educational institutions, which guaranteed certain privileges and immunities and sometimes provided specific arrangements for the internal conduct of the company's or institution's affairs.

In the 16th century, the British crown granted charters to merchants for overseas commercial activities. Because the crown controlled all new lands by right of discovery, these charters contained authorization for governing any outposts or colonies that the trading companies might establish. In the next century English charters of one kind or another formed the initial constitutional foundation for most of the English colonies in America. These charters bestowed land and governing rights on the grantees, reserved certain prerogatives to the crown, and often guaranteed "English liberties" to colonists who might settle within the grantees' jurisdiction.

Such colonial charters might take the form of a grant to a joint-stock trading company, such as the charters given to the Virginia Company (1606, 1609, and 1612) and to the Massachusetts Bay Company (1629). In these cases the land granted was described, and internal government of the company was arranged, with shareholders authorized to meet in "general courts" to pass ordinances and elect officers.

On petition, the crown might grant a charter to already existing settlements, where the colonists had organized themselves into self-governing communities by "covenants," but desired the legal status a corporate charter provided. Such was the case in Connecticut (1662) and Rhode Island (1663).

Another type of charter used in English colonization was the proprietary charter, or patent, which conveyed to the recipient (either one man or a group of men) hereditary rights to land and governing rights over those who settled on that land. The Council for New England (reorganized from part of the original Virginia Company) received such a charter in 1620, and Charles I extended a similar gift (Maryland) to Lord Baltimore in 1632. After the Restoration (1660), the proprietary charter became the principal instrument for creating new colonies. The Carolina patent (1663) to eight "lords proprietors," the gift of the future colonies of New York and New Jersey to James, Duke of York, and the grant of Pennsylvania to William Penn were examples. While the proprietary charter seemingly extended enormous powers to the grantee (over lands, church, taxation, courts, armies, and navies), qualifying restrictions on those powers stipulated that all laws must be in harmony with English laws, and all colonial citizens (freeholders) must be allowed a voice in legislation.

The charter for the colony of Georgia (1732) differed from all other American colonial charters. It was limited in duration to 21 years, and it granted only supervisory powers to the trustees, who would manage the colony's affairs but who did not "own" it.

These various charters, so useful to England in originating settlements, proved later to be problems when that country undertook to fashion its separate colonies into an integrated empire. In order to unify imperial control, English authorities attempted to reduce or cancel chartered rights. The Virginia Company charter was abolished by legal proceedings in 1624; the Carolina proprietorship was purchased by the crown; New Jersey's political powers were voluntarily returned; the Massachusetts charter was declared forfeit (1684), a new charter issued (1691), and alterations in it attempted in 1774.

By the time of the American Revolution, except for Massachusetts, only two corporate charters (those of Rhode Island and Connecticut) and two proprietary patents (Pennsylvania-Delaware and Maryland) remained. The other colonies were controlled directly by the crown. Even so, the Americans were to cite the original charter rights as justification for their stand during the American Revolution.

CARL UBBELOHDE
Case Western Reserve University

MUNICIPAL AND PRIVATE CHARTERS

In the United States, a municipal charter (as distinguished from a private, or corporate, charter) is a special law passed by the legislature of a state, or prescribed by the state constitution, authorizing a particular locality to govern itself and defining the powers and duties of the municipal corporation. In a sense, the municipal charter is to the city as the U. S. Constitution is to the federal government. Because the state is the political unit having residual powers, the municipal charter is, in theory, a delegation of a portion of the state's power for local self-government, and consequently the powers may be modified or, indeed, revoked by the state. The municipality has only those powers, express or implied, that are delegated, and these normally include the authority to tax and to pass local laws pertaining to health, property, education, and the like.

Some state constitutions give larger cities the privilege of framing and adopting their own charters by popular vote. These "home-rule" charters have been challenged, although mostly without success, as unconstitutional deprivations of the legislature's power to amend or repeal.

Municipal charters differ from private, or corporate, charters, which are also granted by the state, in two important respects. A charter issued to a private business corporation is a contract between the state and the corporation and thus cannot be revoked by the state; such was the lesson of the famous case, *Dartmouth College v. Woodward*, decided by the U. S. Supreme Court in 1819. In addition, the corporate charter is available to any person or any group meeting general statutory requirements, whereas the municipal charter requires a specific legislative authorization.

LINDA ALDEN RODGERS, *Columbia Law School*

CHARTER OAK, a white oak tree that formerly stood in Hartford, Conn., in the trunk of which the Connecticut colonial charter was said to have been hidden in 1687. The tree was blown down in a storm on Aug. 12, 1856. Its trunk was nearly 7 feet (about 2 meters) in diameter, and its age was estimated at possibly 1,000 years.

Late in 1686, Sir Edmund Andros, royal governor of New York, was empowered by James II of England to create a Dominion of New England, comprising all the New England colonies. According to tradition, the charter disappeared during a meeting in 1687 when Andros demanded its surrender by colonial officials, and it was concealed in the tree. Despite this incident, Connecticut submitted to the Dominion of New England, but the Dominion survived only two years.

CHARTERED COMPANIES were overseas trade associations that were granted charters that typically carried special privileges such as geographically defined monopolies for exploitation, trade, and colonization. Chartered companies, which were active from the 15th to the 18th century, often exercised legislative, military, and diplomatic authority in ways that made them virtual extensions of the homeland. The rise of European national states precipitated the growth of chartered companies, and these in turn enhanced the influence and wealth of the states.

Chartered companies introduced Europeans to commodities from distant lands, and they contributed significantly to European advancement by establishing overseas investment opportunities and markets for manufactures. Colonization carried out through these companies created empires and extended Western civilization to every continent.

The Hanseatic League and the 12th century Genoese associations for North African trade were predecessors of the chartered company. The sharing of risks and profits made such associations fundamental instruments of European commercial expansion. The merchants' joint ventures were accompanied by demands for special privileges. For example, the Merchants of the Staple held a monopoly on the export of English wool.

Noteworthy English chartered companies included the Eastland (formed in 1404), Muscovy (1505), Levant (1581), and East India (1600) companies. The Dutch East India Company (1602) and the French East India Company (1664) also were prominent.

Besides granting exclusive regional trading privileges, charters typically gave rights to export bullion for capital investment, to make laws, and to punish offenders. Military and treaty-making rights often were assumed.

Initially, subscriptions were obtained for each separate voyage, but this practice led to difficulties in accounting and in maintaining financial liquidity. Later, when the joint stock company came into existence, permanent general stock was issued. Some companies failed because of the vicissitudes of European politics, entanglement with local problems, piracy, poor management, and overexpansion. Domestic opposition—another cause of failures—arose from persons hostile to the export of gold and silver, from competitive industries disturbed by imports, and from rival merchants eager to break monopolies.

Many chartered companies operated in the Americas, most of them unsuccessfully. Sir

Humphrey Gilbert's colonizing hopes were crushed when he lost his fleet in the Atlantic, and Sir Walter Raleigh's Roanoke colony vanished mysteriously. But the London Adventurers' Jamestown settlement survived, and the Plymouth Adventurers' second colonizing effort succeeded. The Hudson's Bay Company endures today in Canada as a department store chain.

More than 70 French chartered companies, many mere extensions of the monarchy, operated in America in the 17th and 18th centuries, but most failed.

The Santo Domingo Company, successor to the Royal West India Company of France, developed Haiti. The Dutch West India Company developed the Antilles. Spain and Portugal, beset with backward economic organization, developed no strong companies.

RANDALL M. EVANSON
Wisconsin State University, Oshkosh

CHARTERHOUSE is a famous school and charitable foundation in Godalming, Surrey, England. The name is derived from a priory for Carthusian monks that originally occupied the site and was dissolved along with other monasteries in 1535. In 1611, Thomas Sutton endowed a hospital on the site and bequeathed money for the maintenance of a chapel and school. The new institution provided education for "poor scholars" and a home for "indigent gentlemen."

Charterhouse developed into one of the most noted preparatory ("public") schools in England. Among the well-known men educated at Charterhouse were Joseph Addison, Sir Richard Steele, John Wesley, Sir William Blackstone, and William Makepeace Thackeray.

CHARTERHOUSE OF PARMA, one of the most famous novels of Stendhal (q.v.). Its title in French is *La chartreuse de Parme*. It was written in Paris, where Stendhal was on leave from a diplomatic post in Italy, and published in 1839. Set in northern Italy, a region the author particularly loved, it centers on the character Fabrice del Dongo. The novel has an atmosphere of charming serenity, and the writing has moments of poetic rapture. The earlier part is noteworthy for a description of the Battle of Waterloo, shown in all its inglorious confusion through the eyes of the inexperienced Fabrice. The rest of the book deals mainly with the plots and counterplots in the petty princely court of Parma and their effect on Fabrice, who has the true aristocrat's disdain of ambitious calculations.

Fabrice's life takes on a trace of gravity and melancholy when he falls in love with Clélia Conti, who, though she returns his love, is forced to marry another. Fabrice rises to be archbishop of Parma, but after Clélia's death he renounces worldly honors and retires to a Carthusian charterhouse. Two other characters of importance are Gina, Duchess of Sanseverina, torn between conflicting emotions of amorous jealousy and maternal protectiveness toward her nephew Fabrice; and Count Mosca, Gina's middle-aged but passionate lover, the deft prime minister of Parma, whose characterization owes much to Stendhal's gift for self-observation.

F. W. J. HEMMINGS
University of Leicester, England

CHARTIER, shàr-tyā, **Alain** (c. 1390–c. 1440), French poet, prose writer, and diplomat. Chartier was born into a family connected with the court. After attending the University of Paris, he entered the service of Charles VI. Then in 1422, he became secretary of the royal household of Charles VII.

Chartier's earliest poem is the *Le livre des quatre dames* (1415). Other works, including *Quadriloque invectif* (1422) and *Traité de l'espérance* (1428), were written to rally the French in support of the royal house, following the English victory at Agincourt. In these didactic works he attacked the abuses of the nobility and clergy, exposed the sufferings of the peasantry, and called for a united effort against the English. Of more enduring value are his *Lai de plaisance* (1413–1414), *La belle dame sans merci* (1424), and *Breviare des nobles* (about 1424).

CHARTIER, shàr-tyā′, **Émile Auguste** (1868–1951), French philosopher and essayist. He was born in Mortagne, on March 3, 1868. Educated at the École Normale Supérieure, he became a professor of philosophy at the Lycée Henri IV in Paris. Through his teaching and extensive writings (under the pseudonym "Alain") he greatly influenced French thought between World Wars I and II. In his short aphoristic essays, the *propos*, Chartier embodied his views on ethics, stressing the importance of the individual conscience and the right of the citizen to resist power. Collections of his *propos* include *Cent un propos* (1908–1929), *Les propos d'Alain* (1920), *Propos de littérature* (1933), and *Propos de politique* (1934).

Among Chartier's other works are *Le citoyen contre les pouvoirs* (1925), *Éléments d'une doctrine radicale* (1925), *Les idées et les âges* (1927), *Les dieux* (1934), *Histoire des mes pensées* (1936), and *Les saisons de l'esprit* (1937). He died in Le Vésinet on June 3, 1951.

CHARTISM was a British working-class movement for social reform that formally came into existence after the publication of *The People's Charter* in May 1838. Drafted by William Lovett, a London working-class activist, and previously introduced as a bill in Parliament, the charter demanded six specific reforms: universal male suffrage, the secret ballot, annual Parliaments, abolition of property qualifications for members of Parliament, payment of members, and electoral districts of equal size.

The discontent that led to the charter arose from a radical tradition in England; working-class dissatisfaction with social and economic conditions in the new industrial society; and opposition to the Poor Law of 1834, which abolished outdoor relief and concentrated the poor in "workhouses."

In their campaigns, the Chartists relied on their own working-class leaders. An Irish demagogue, Feargus O'Connor, succeeded in uniting local movements of protest and offered national instead of local leadership. But his rise to power was associated with fierce factional fights and with bitter debates about the means—particularly the role of force—to secure Chartist objectives.

The first Chartist Convention, called in February 1839, was disbanded in September after a stormy history and complete failure to influence Parliament. Thereafter there was one limited attempt to use force—in Newport, Monmouthshire—and the imprisonment of many Chartist leaders. Attempts to influence Parliament by petitioning failed in 1842 and 1848, and during the mid-1840's much Chartist energy was diverted into a plan to resettle industrial workers on the land. The fiasco of the Chartists' attempt to capitalize on the Continental revolutions of 1848 proved decisive. Chartist activities continued after that date, but with radically diminished effect. However, within the next 70 years all the main Chartist objectives except annual Parliaments were secured in changed circumstances.

ASA BRIGGS, *University of Sussex, England*
Editor of "Chartist Studies"

CHARTRES, shàr'trə, is a commercial city in north central France, about 50 miles (80 km) southwest of Paris. It is the capital of the department of Eure-et-Loir and the most important town in the Beauce district. This district is a rich farming area, and is sometimes known as the "granary" of France. Cattle raising and some market gardening are also carried on. The city's manufactures include woolens, leather, hosiery, radio and television parts, and agricultural equipment.

The Cathedral. Chartres is primarily known for its magnificent Cathedral of Notre Dame, perhaps the finest example of French Gothic architecture, and said by some to be the most beautiful cathedral in France. This edifice was erected on the site of a basilica built by early Christians, which had burned down. Through the cooperation of nobles and peasants alike, it was built in the amazingly short time of 31 years (1194–1225), giving it an impressive and unusual degree of architectural unity. Only its main facade dates from another period, having been built in the middle part of the 12th century. This facade comprises the triple doorway and two splendid tall spires. The doorway, called the Royal Portal, is an unmatched example of late Romanesque religious art, consecrated to the glorification of Christ. Of the spires, the New Tower (actually the older, dating from 1134) was capped in the early 17th century with an elaborately ornamented second spire. The Old Tower, some 30 feet (9 meters) shorter, is simpler. It, too, is a marvel of Romanesque art.

The interior of the Chartres cathedral is also remarkable. The nave, wider than that of any other cathedral in France (52 feet, or 16 meters), is in the purest 13th century ogival style. In its center is a maze, the only one still intact in France, with 320 yards (290 meters) of winding passages, which the faithful used to follow on their knees. The warm glow of the light inside the cathedral results from the incomparably beautiful stained-glass windows, which date mostly from the 14th century. The clear blue that characterizes the three windows in the main transept and the well-known "Virgin of the Fine Window" is the famous "Chartres blue." Most of the glass came from the workshop of the glassmakers of St. Denis and of Notre Dame in Paris. The chancel screen, in sculptured stone, contains 40 groups representing scenes from the life of Christ and the Virgin. A huge crypt, the largest in France, underlies the nave and the chancel. It houses the statue of Our Lady Underground.

History. Chartres has had a colorful history. It has been of religious importance since ancient times. At first it was the site of Druid ceremonies, which were held around a well that was later discovered under the cathedral crypt. Later, a Gallo-Roman temple stood on the same spot. The early Christians erected a basilica there in

CHARLES ROTKIN-PHOTOGRAPHY FOR INDUSTRY

CHARTRES is best known for its famous cathedral, which towers over the oldest section of the city.

the 4th century, and St. Bernard preached the Second Crusade there in 1146. Chartres was the coronation site of Henry IV in 1594. Population: (1962) 31,085.

HOMER PRICE, *Hunter College, New York*

CHARTRES, Fort de, shàr'trə, a French fort on the Mississippi River and center of French government in the Illinois country from about 1720 to the close of the French and Indian War. In 1765 the fort was surrendered to the British, who destroyed it in 1772 because of erosion by the river. Parts of the fort, dating from 1753, have been reconstructed in Fort Chartres State Park near Prairie du Rocher, Ill..

CHARTREUSE, shär-trōōz, is a spicy, aromatic liqueur with a brandy base, made by monks at La Grande Chartreuse, headquarters of the Carthusian order, at Voiron, France, 14 miles (22 km) northwest of Grenoble. The secret formula for the liqueur was given to the Carthusians in 1607, and in 1757 it was perfected by a monk who was known as a "clever apothecary." Chartreuse is flavored with hyssop, angelica, orange peel, peppermint, and other ingredients. There are two types: yellow chartreuse, 86 proof, is colored with saffron; green chartreuse, 110 proof, with chlorophyll.

CHARTREUSE DE PARME. See CHARTERHOUSE OF PARMA.

CHARYBDIS. See SCYLLA AND CHARYBDIS.

CHASE, Edna Woolman (1877–1957), American editor. She was born in Asbury Park, N. J., on March 14, 1877, and was educated by tutors and at finishing schools. In 1895 she joined *Vogue* magazine, then an amateurish high-society weekly. When Condé Nast bought *Vogue* in 1909, Mrs. Chase was appointed its managing editor, and she became its editor in chief in 1914. In the same year she organized the first fashion show in America.

During her 60-year career Mrs. Chase became a major arbiter of women's fashions, and she transformed *Vogue* into one of the world's leading fashion magazines. With her daughter, the actress Ilka Chase, she wrote an autobiography, *Always in Vogue* (1954). She died in Sarasota, Fla., on March 20, 1957.

CHASE, Lucia (1907–   ), American ballet dancer and impresario. She was born in Waterbury, Conn., on March 24, 1907, and was educated at St. Margaret's School there and at the Theatre Guild School in New York City. In 1926 she married industrialist Thomas Ewing, Jr. She received her ballet training with Mikhail Mordkin, and as a member of the Mordkin Ballet from 1937 to 1939 she danced in such productions as *Giselle* and *La fille mal gardée*. In 1940 she helped found the Ballet Theatre (later the American Ballet Theatre), becoming a charter member and financial backer. She became the group's co-director in 1945, taking charge of administration and production policies. As a dancer, Lucia Chase was noted for her performances in such classic ballets as *Les Sylphides*, *Petrouchka*, and *Pas de quatre* and in such modern works as *Bluebeard*, *Judgment of Paris*, and *Tally-Ho*.

CHASE, Mary (1907–   ), American playwright. She was born Mary Coyle in Denver, Colo., on Feb. 25, 1907. After studying at the universities of Denver and Colorado, she became a reporter in 1924. She worked for the *Rocky Mountain News* from 1928 to 1931; then for four years she was a free-lance writer for International News Service and United Press. In 1928 she married Robert Lamont Chase.

Her first plays, *Now You've Done It* (1937) and *Too Much Business* (1938), were not very successful, but the New York production of *Harvey* in 1944 brought her wide acclaim. This play, about a drunkard with an invisible friend who happens to be a six-foot-tall rabbit, was awarded the Pulitzer Prize in 1945. Mary Chase's gift for combining comedy with fantasy was again shown in *Mrs. McThing* (1952), the story of a rich boy who wants to be a gangster and a girl whose mother is a witch. Later plays include *Bernardine* (1952), a comedy about teen-agers, and *Loretta Mason Potts* (1958).

CHASE, Mary Ellen (1887–1973), American author, noted for novels about New England. She was born in Blue Hill, Me., on Feb. 24, 1887. After taking her B. A. from the University of Maine in 1909 and her Ph. D. from the University of Minnesota in 1922, she taught English at Smith College from 1926 to 1955. She died in Northampton, Mass., on July 28, 1973.

Mary Ellen Chase's ability to derive themes of universal significance from regional subjects is best demonstrated in her novel *Dawn in Lyonesse* (1938), which is a modern parallel of the Tristan and Isolde story, with a New England setting.

Another celebrated novel is *Silas Crockett* (1935), which tells the story of a Yankee seafaring family through four generations. Her other fiction includes the novels *Mary Peters* (1934), *The Plum Tree* (1949), and *The Edge of Darkness* (1957), and the children's stories *Mary Christmas* (1926), *Gay Highway* (1933), and *Sailing the Seven Seas* (1958).

Among Miss Chase's other books are the critical study *Thomas Hardy from Serial to Novel* (1927), the biography *Abby Aldrich Rockefeller* (1950), the Biblical study *The Prophets for the Common Reader* (1963), and the autobiographical works *A Goodly Heritage* (1932), *A Goodly Fellowship* (1939), and *The White Gate* (1954).

DAVID GALLOWAY
Author of "The Absurd Hero"

CHASE, Philander (1775–1852), American bishop and college president. He was born in Cornish, N. H., on Dec. 14, 1775. After graduating from Dartmouth College, he was ordained a priest in the Episcopal Church in 1799. Chase organized several parishes in Ohio, and in 1819 he was consecrated bishop. Believing that the West must train its own clergy, he raised money for a theological seminary in Ohio. In 1824, Kenyon College, in what is now Gambier, Ohio, was established. Chase was president until 1831, when complaints from the clergy and faculty about his arbitrary management forced him to resign.

Chase lived in Michigan until, in 1835, he was named bishop of Illinois. In 1839 he established Jubilee College, a theological school, at Robin's Nest, Ill. Chase was elected presiding bishop of the Episcopal Church in 1843. He died at Robin's Nest on Sept. 20, 1852.

CHASE, Salmon Portland (1808–1873), American political leader, who was secretary of the treasury in Lincoln's Civil War cabinet and chief justice of the United States during Reconstruction. An outspoken opponent of slavery, he was a leader of the radical wing of the Republican party and a frequent aspirant to the presidency. He was an influential member of the cabinet, but differences with President Lincoln led to his resignation. As chief justice he expanded the power of the Supreme Court, and he conducted the impeachment trial of President Andrew Johnson with admirable restraint.

Early Career. Chase was born in Cornish, N. H., on Jan. 13, 1808. On the death of his father, when Salmon was nine years old, he was sent to Ohio under the guardianship of his uncle, Episcopal Bishop Philander Chase. In 1821 he entered Cincinnati College, of which Bishop Chase had become president. He transferred to Dartmouth College in 1824, graduating in 1826. For three years he ran a boys' school in Washington, D. C., and studied law.

Admitted to the bar in 1829, Chase began legal practice in Cincinnati in 1830. He established a solid reputation with the publication of the compiled *Statutes of Ohio* (3 vols., 1833–1835). At the same time he became active in the abolitionist movement, lecturing and writing. He also defended a number of escaping slaves, arguing before the courts that persons could not be claimed as property.

Chase was married and widowed three times: to Catherine Jane Garniss (1834–1835), Eliza Ann Smith (1839–1845), and Sarah Dunlop Ludlow (1846–1852). Of his six daughters, only two grew to maturity. The effervescent Catherine became her father's hostess and shared his political ambitions. She married Sen. William Sprague of Rhode Island in 1863, and for many years "Kate" was a reigning belle in Washington.

Politician. At first a Whig, Chase joined the Ohio Liberty party in 1840, and in 1848 he was prominent in the Free Soil movement. While vociferously antislavery, he felt himself at variance with the policies of the more radical abolitionists. In 1849 he was elected to the U. S. Senate by a coalition of Free Soilers and Democrats. As a senator, Chase attempted to turn the Democratic party toward opposition to slavery and campaigned against the Kansas-Nebraska bill of 1854. He then gravitated to the new Republican party, which nominated him for governor of Ohio in 1855. He was elected and then reelected in 1857.

At the first Republican convention in 1856, Chase attempted to obtain the presidential nomination, but stood little chance. He was elected to the Senate again in 1860 and was a presidential contender at the 1860 convention, representing the stronger antislavery elements of the Republican party. However, he was considered too controversial, and he lost to Abraham Lincoln.

Cabinet Member. President Lincoln appointed Chase secretary of the treasury, and he held that post from March 1861 to July 1864. While it is sometimes debated, Chase apparently was a capable secretary, and his policies enabled the Union to find the financial backing to fight the Civil War. Floating immense loans, handling trade in the war zone, suspending specie payments and issuing greenbacks, instituting a national banking system, increasing taxation, and dealing with the problems of confiscated property were major concerns in his conscientious administration of the Treasury.

Chase was an active cabinet member, participating in many discussions and decisions and often differing emphatically with the other secretaries and with the President. He was particularly firm in advocating the abolition of slavery, feeling that Lincoln did not go far enough in the Emancipation Proclamation. He also urged vigorous prosecution of the war, and he was free with advice on military matters.

Chase offered to resign on three occasions, but was turned down; he was probably surprised when Lincoln accepted his fourth resignation. The first two incidents, in December 1862 and May 1863, had to do with Chase's feeling that his policies and appointments were not being given proper weight. In February 1864 a paper known as the *Pomeroy Circular* was published, opposing Lincoln's renomination and calling for Chase for president. Chase may or may not have known of the circular, but he certainly knew of efforts to nominate him. He offered to resign a third time, but Lincoln refused, and nothing came of the boom for Chase's nomination. However, after a dispute over patronage in June, Chase tendered his resignation and Lincoln accepted it.

Chief Justice. On Dec. 6, 1864, after the death of Chief Justice Roger B. Taney, Lincoln nominated Chase to the post despite some doubts and their previous differences. Chase had indicated a desire for the position.

Coming as it did during the disruptive period of Reconstruction, Chase's term as chief justice required judicial capacity of the highest degree. One of his tasks was to preside at the impeachment trial of President Andrew Johnson in 1868. While not retreating from his strong stand politically,

Chase, as chief justice, handled this role with eminent fairness. He was against the quick reopening of federal courts in the South and in favor of some aspects of Radical Reconstruction, but he was reluctant to preside at the proposed trial of Confederate President Jefferson Davis, which never took place. The Radical Congress generally was opposed to Chase after the Johnson trial, and in some instances it appeared as though the Supreme Court was trying to avoid political entanglements.

A number of important cases came before the Supreme Court during Chase's tenure. In *Ex parte Milligan* (1866) the chief justice agreed with the majority that military commissions had no authority to try civilians in areas far from the theater of war, although he dissented over details. In 1870, Chase delivered the opinion that the Legal Tender Act of 1862 was unconstitutional, even though,

Salmon P. Chase

when in the Treasury, he had issued the greenbacks. He dissented in the Slaughterhouse cases (q. v.), which retained most civil rights under the protection of the states.

While chief justice, Chase again sought the presidency in 1868. He attracted no attention from the Republicans, who had Ulysses S. Grant as a candidate, so he tried for the Democratic nomination. His daughter Kate was active in Chase's behalf, but he lost out at the convention. In 1872, he appeared to be "available" for the Liberal Republican nomination, but his health was poor, and he failed again. He died of a stroke in New York City on May 7, 1873.

Handsome and impressive, Chase had a determined, powerful appearance. He was always strong in displaying religious and moral conviction. While not a profound scholar, he had some literary ability as is indicated by his diaries. Capable and honest in many ways, he was so swayed by flattery, so ambitious for the presidency, so aloof, so difficult to work with, so lacking in humor, and so self-righteous that his value to the country was diminished. Even so, he must be accounted one of the nation's leading cabinet members and justices.

E. B. LONG
*Director of Research, Bruce Catton's
Centennial History of the Civil War*

Further Reading: Belden, Thomas G., and Belden, Marva R., *So Fell the Angels* (Boston 1956); Donald, David, ed., *Inside Lincoln's Cabinet: The Civil War Diaries of Salmon P. Chase* (New York 1954); Hart, Albert B., *Salmon Portland Chase* (Boston 1899); Warden, Robert V., *Account of the Private Life and Public Services of Salmon Portland Chase* (Cincinnati 1874).

CHASE, Samuel (1741–1811), American patriot and judge. He signed the Declaration of Independence and served on the U. S. Supreme Court, being its only justice ever to be impeached. Although he early earned a reputation as a "foul-mouthed and inflammatory Son of Discord and Passion" and continued to be attacked for volatile conduct, his patriotism was as true as his talent for giving and receiving invective.

The son of an Anglican minister, Chase was born in Somerset county, Md., on April 17, 1741. He studied law in Annapolis and was admitted to the bar in 1761. In the early 1760's he joined Maryland's Country party, and in 1765 he led the colony's attack on the Stamp Act. He was a member of Maryland's colonial and state legislatures (1764–1784) and also served on its committee of correspondence and as a delegate to the Continental congresses (1774–1778 and 1784–1785). In 1776 he joined Benjamin Franklin and Charles Carroll in the futile mission to enlist Canadian support for the Revolution, but he returned in time to help secure Maryland's support for the Declaration of Independence.

Active on many congressional committees, he was forced to retire briefly in 1778, when Alexander Hamilton identified him as a speculator attempting to corner the market in flour. In 1783 he was sent to London to attempt (in vain) the recovery of Maryland stock in the Bank of England. He also drafted a commercial compact adopted by Virginia and Maryland in 1785. Uneasy with the U. S. Constitution, he voted against Maryland's ratification. In 1788 he was appointed chief judge of the Maryland Criminal Court, and in 1791 he also was named chief judge of the General Court, an instance of pluralism that aroused much criticism. In 1796, President George Washington appointed him to the Supreme Court.

Chase made useful contributions to American judicial history, particularly the doctrine of due process, but his political attacks on Jeffersonians tried under the Sedition Act (1798) led to the impeachment proceedings of 1804–1805. Narrowly acquitted by the Senate, he remained on the court for the rest of his life but was eclipsed by Chief Justice John Marshall after 1801. Chase died in Baltimore on June 19, 1811.

TREVOR COLBOURN, *University of New Hampshire*

CHASE, Stuart (1888–   ), American economist, semanticist, and author, whose work is primarily concerned with the problems of living in a wealthy, technologically oriented society. He was born at Somersworth, N. H., on March 8, 1888, and studied at the Massachusetts Institute of Technology and then at Harvard, where he graduated *cum laude* in 1910. He worked for several years in his father's accounting firm, then as an investigator for the Federal Trade Commission, and in the 1920's helped organize and direct the Labor Bureau, Inc., which gave technical economic advice to labor unions. A cofounder of Consumers' Research, he was later active in Consumers' Union.

Chase's books on the economic and social problems of 20th century life include *The Tragedy of Waste* (1925); *Your Money's Worth* (1927), written with Frederick J. Schlink; *A New Deal* (1932); and *Rich Land, Poor Land* (1936). *The Proper Study of Mankind* (1948) is a study of the science of human relations, and *American Credos* (1962) is a study of public opinion polls. In *Tyranny of Words* (1938) and *Power of Words* (1954), he dealt with the problems of communication and semantics.

ELMO ROPER, *Public Opinion Analyst*
Author of "You and Your Leaders"

CHASE, William Merritt (1849–1916), American painter, who was a distinguished member of the late 19th century realist school. He was also an outstanding teacher who had a great influence on the artists of the next generation.

Chase was born at Nineveh, Ind., on Nov. 1, 1849. After studying in New York City, he went to Munich and soon adopted the dark German style, but his style was brightened after a visit to Venice in 1877. Returning to the United States, he settled in New York City, where he taught for many years at the Art Students League and at his own studio, which became a center for artists who were trying to break the dominance of European styles in the United States. Chase died in New York City on Oct. 25, 1916.

Chase first made his reputation in Europe as a portrait painter. His later work includes interiors, still lifes, and landscapes. Examples of his paintings are *In the Studio* (1880–1883; Brooklyn Museum), *Alice* (1892; Art Institute of Chicago), and *A Friendly Call* (1895; National Gallery of Art, Washington, D. C.).

LORETTA GRELLNER
Chicago Public School Art Society

CHASE MANHATTAN BANK of New York City, is the second-largest privately owned bank in the world, with total assets that are exceeded only by those of the Bank of America in California. Chase Manhattan was formed in 1955 by a merger of the Chase National Bank with the Bank of the Manhattan Company. Chase National, named after Salmon P. Chase, secretary of the treasury during the Civil War, was chartered in 1879. The Bank of Manhattan was even older. The Manhattan Company was founded in 1799 to lay wooden water mains in New York City, an activity it subsequently abandoned in favor of banking.

After the merger, Chase Manhattan operated for 10 years under the Bank of Manhattan's New York state charter. In 1965, however, it was granted a national charter. The bank's full corporate title became *The Chase Manhattan Bank, National Association*. It has 95,000 stockholders.

Domestically, it operates about 140 offices in New York City and suburban Nassau and Westchester counties. Abroad, its own branches in about 20 countries and representatives' offices in more than 10 others, plus the facilities of affiliated and associated foreign banks available to it through its wholly owned subsidiary, Chase Manhattan Overseas Banking Corporation, give it access to over 1,400 banking locations in 50 countries.

CLIFTON H. KREPS, JR.
University of North Carolina

CHASSÉRIAU, shà-sā-ryō', **Théodore** (1819–1856), French painter. He was born in Samaná, Dominican Republic, on Sept. 20, 1819. He was influenced by Ingres, under whom he studied in Rome, but later became primarily a colorist under the influence of Delacroix and Delaroche. He painted murals in Paris in the churches of St. Merri (1843) and St. Roch (1854) and in the Cours des Comptes in the Palais d'Orsay. Fragments of his paintings that survived the burning of the Palais d'Orsay in 1871 are preserved in the Louvre. Chassériau's other works include *Caïn maudit* (1836), *Retour de l'enfant prodigue* (1836), *La chaste Suzanne* (1839), *Vénus Anadyomène* (1839), *Le Christ au jardin des oliviers* (1839), *Andromède attachée au rocher par les Néréides* (1841), *Esther se parant pour être présentée à Assuérus* (1842), *Captives troyennes* (1842), *Portrait équestre d'Ali-ben-Hamet, calife de Constantine*, and *Le Tepidarium* (1853). Chassériau died in Paris on Oct. 8, 1856.

CHASTELARD, shä-tlàr', **Pierre de Boscosel de** (1540–1563), minor French poet, grandson of the Seigneur de Bayard, the famous knight. He was born in Dauphiné, France. At the court of Francis II he fell violently in love with Mary, Queen of Scots, and was one of the party who escorted her back to Scotland in 1561 after the king's death. He was then obliged to return to France.

On a second visit to Scotland the next year, he hid under Mary's bed, where he was discovered by her maids of honor. Mary forgave Chastelard, but he rashly repeated his offense and was sentenced and hanged the following morning. He met his fate valiantly. His death inspired Algernon Charles Swinburne's tragic drama *Chastelard,* dedicated to Victor Hugo, written in 1862, and published in 1865.

CHASTELLAIN, shä-tlaN', **Georges** (1405?–1475), poet and court historiographer of the dukes of Burgundy. He was born in Alost (Aalst) in Flanders. After studies at the University of Louvain, he spent 10 years, from 1435 to 1445, at the French court. He entered the service of Philip the Good of Burgundy in 1446. After several diplomatic assignments, he was appointed court historiographer in 1455 and a councillor of state in 1457. In 1473, Chastellain was awarded membership in the Order of the Golden Fleece. He died at Valenciennes in February or March 1475.

Chastellain's major work was his *Chronique des Ducs de Bourgogne,* a history of the period 1419 to 1474. Knowing the men and events of his own day at first hand, he produced interesting sketches of leaders of the age. But his insights were limited by his idealization of chivalric society. Ignoring the rich Flemish burghers, he lauded the virtues of the Burgundian nobility even while describing their intrigues and treachery.

EDMUND H. DICKERMAN
University of Connecticut

CHAT, the name given to a variety of small Old World thrushes, such as the stonechats, robin chats and cliff chats. The designation is also given to a North American wood warbler, the yellow-breasted chat.

The yellow-breasted chat ranges from southern Canada through the United States and winters in Central America. It is more than 7 inches (18 cm) long and is plain olive-green above and bright yellow below. White eye-rings and white lines from the base of the bill to the eyes give it the appearance of wearing spectacles. The male and the female are alike in color.

A shy and secretive bird, the yellow-breasted chat favors dense thickets and tangled under-growths. It is a difficult bird to observe, but during the breeding season it is often heard giving a series of unmusical caws, chucks, grunts, and whistles. It nests in thick vegetation near the ground. The female lays from three to five brown-splotched white eggs in a bulky nest made of leaves, grasses, and wood stems. Incubation takes from 11 to 15 days, and both parents care for the young.

The yellow-breasted chat (*Icteria virens*) is a member of the family Parulidae in the order Passeriformes.

JOSEPH BELL
New York Zoological Society

CHÂTEAU. See CASTLES AND CHÂTEAUX.

CHÂTEAU D'IF, shä-tō' dĕf, is a famous castle in southern France. It stands atop a small limestone island opposite the harbor of Marseille, and its terrace affords a splendid view of the port.

Built by Francis I in 1524, the castle was used for several centuries as a state prison. Its inmates included the regicide Philippe Égalité and the mysterious Man in the Iron Mask imprisoned by Louis XIV. In Alexandre Dumas' novel *The Count of Monte Cristo,* the two heroes, Edmond Dantès and the Abbé Faria, are confined in the Château d'If.

CHÂTEAU-GAILLARD, shä-tō' gà-yàr', is a famous medieval castle in northern France. It stands on a massive rock above the Seine River at Les Andelys, 20 miles (32 km) southeast of Rouen. Once an important point of defense for the English in Normandy, the château is now an impressive ruin.

Château-Gaillard was built in 1196 by Richard the Lion-Hearted (Richard I), King of England and Duke of Normandy, in an attempt to defend Rouen from a French attack through the Seine Valley. The fortress served its purpose for several years, but after Richard's death, Philip II of France laid siege to it. The castle was demolished in a massive assault in March 1204, and three months later Rouen fell to the French.

CHÂTEAU-THIERRY, shä-tō' tye-rē', is a town in France, in the department of Aisne, on the right bank of the Marne River, 47 miles (75 km) east northeast of Paris. The town is built on the side of a hill, whose summit is crowned by the ruins of the old castle of Thierry, said to have been built by Charles Martel. The house in which the writer Jean de La Fontaine was born in 1621 is now a museum. The town has an active trade in champagne wines, and among the products manufactured there are musical instruments, agricultural tools, and woolen yarn. In addition, stone is quarried nearby.

Château-Thierry has been the scene of many important battles. It was captured by the English troops of Henry V in 1421 during the course of the Hundred Years' War, and by Emperor Charles V in 1544. Napoleon Bonaparte battled a Russo-Prussian army beneath its walls in 1814, and in 1870 it was seized by the Germans. In World War I the Germans occupied and pillaged it twice. The Marine Brigade of the American 2d Division won its first important victory near Château-Thierry, capturing the Bois de Belleau on June 25, 1918. This position served as a springboard for American participation in the July 18 offensive. Population: (1962) 9,356.

René de Chateaubriand

CHATEAUBRIAND, shà-tō-brē-äɴ', **François-René de** (1768–1848), French writer, whose novels, essays, books of travels, and celebrated autobiography deeply influenced the development of 19th century literature. His ardent individualism, his love of nature and the exotic, and his rediscovery of Christianity and of medieval art and history helped shape the romantic movement, as did his elaborate, magnificently rhythmic prose.

Early Years. Although it is difficult to disentangle fact and fiction in Chateaubriand's several accounts of his adventures and feelings, two determining influences on his temperament and career emerge: his Breton heritage and his membership in the impoverished nobility. He was born on Sept. 4, 1768, in the picturesque Breton harbor town of St.-Malo, long a den of corsairs, adventurers, and slave traders. Like most Celts he was independent and stubborn. He also was a dreamer, never at home in commonplace or sordid reality but prone to giving his imagination full play, and a melancholiac, easily bored.

These tendencies in Chateaubriand's personality were strengthened by a youth spent at the family château of Combourg, wandering through its empty forests and moors. His mother was loving but weak; his father was a strange, taciturn, authoritarian figure, who terrified his children. It was, therefore, with his gifted and nervous older sister Lucille, who encouraged his romantic yearnings and literary dreams, that Chateaubriand had his closest family relationship.

With no prospect of an inheritance, Chateaubriand became a lieutenant in the army, dreaming of travel and writing as a salvation from boredom. When the Revolution broke out in 1789, he refused to join either side and a year later he resigned his commission in order to go to the New World.

In July 1791 he landed in Baltimore and then went on to Philadelphia. (Although he did not actually meet Washington in Philadelphia, he later related an imaginary interview with the general.) He also traveled through what is today northern New York, where he met many Indians and probably visited Niagara Falls. (He did not go farther west, and his descriptions of the Mississippi and the Natchez country are based on books by earlier travelers.)

In December 1791, on receiving news of the arrest of Louis XVI, Chateaubriand returned penniless to France, where his family married him to a young heiress. He paid little attention to his wife, however, always preferring the company of other ladies, who were attracted to him by his talent and charm.

Chateaubriand joined the French émigré army in the Rhineland, was wounded during a siege, and with the help of his relations managed to escape to London. There he subsisted in penury by giving French lessons and doing translations. In 1797 he published the bulky, confused, anti-Christian *Essai sur les révolutions*. He also began to write *Les Natchez* (1826), a tale of the "noble savage" in the unsullied state of nature that Rousseau had praised.

Middle Years. In 1798, news of his mother's death led Chateaubriand to return to the Catholic faith that he had abandoned during his stay in the New World. Feeling that under the orderly, prochurch consulship of Napoleon the time was ripe for his reappearance in France, he went to Paris in 1800. There he completed a book begun in London, *Le génie du christianisme* (1802). This work, dedicated to Napoleon, who was just then concluding a concordat with the Pope and reopening the churches, was intended to rehabilitate Christianity from the low esteem to which it had fallen under the attacks of Voltaire and the Encyclopedists during the age of the Enlightenment. Replete with digressions and weak in theology, the *Génie* is not very logical or convincing as an apologetic. Nevertheless, it scored a great success in its appeal to the emotions at a time when people were tiring of the rationalism of the Enlightenment. By upholding Christianity rather than antiquity as the source of inspiration for European literature and art, the books led to the romantic rediscovery of Gothic cathedrals.

In 1801, Chateaubriand published *Atala,* the tale of a Christian girl vowed by her mother to perpetual virginity. The girl—Atala—falls in love with a Natchez Indian, but religion triumphs over passion, and she takes her own life in order to keep her vow. Chateaubriand's harmonious and caressing prose describing the lush Louisiana setting, the sentimental and highly civilized conversation of the Indians, and Atala's desert funeral was immediately praised as the magical gift of an enchanter.

René appeared in 1805. This novel portrays a melancholy romantic hero, who discovers that his beloved sister has entered a convent rather than surrender to her passion for him. He flees to America, where he wanders among moonlit forests, relating his grief to a sympathetic Indian and to a missionary. The hero, a thinly veiled transfiguration of the author, symbolized the emotional upheaval of the youth of the time.

Napoleon rewarded the author of *Le génie du christianisme* with a diplomatic post in Rome. There Chateaubriand wrote elaborate, melancholy letters on the ruins of the Eternal City and the Campagna. He broke with Napoleon in 1804, however, on learning that the Emperor had ordered the execution of the émigré duke of Enghien.

During the next few years Chateaubriand traveled in Greece and the Middle East. Then, although still considering himself an exile, he returned to France to write. In *Les martyrs* (1809), a poetical prose epic, he blended his humanistic love of classical antiquity, Virgil, and the Mediterranean landscape with his devotion to Christianity. But the story itself, of the early Christian martyrs persecuted by 3d century Roman emperors, pales before the historical evocation of the Romans and Franks. Equally vivid and warm was Chateaubriand s next work, *Itinéraire de Paris à Jérusalem* (1811), the fruit of his recent travels. He was elected to the French Academy in 1811.

Later Years. After the fall of Napoleon in 1814, Chateaubriand, who had written pamphlets attacking Napoleon's regime, was created a peer of the realm with the title Vicomte de Chateaubriand. He attempted to play an active political role in the restored monarchy, but Louis XVIII, distrusting his haughty pride and his literary prestige, sent him abroad as minister to Berlin and ambassador to London. From 1823 to 1824 he was minister of foreign affairs, but he antagonized the king's entourage and was forced to resign. Later, in 1828–1829, under Charles X, he was ambassador to Rome.

Although Chateaubriand was a constitutional monarchist, he disapproved of the monarchy of Louis Philippe that followed the Revolution of 1830. Retiring from politics, he spent much of his time in the company of his lady admirers, especially the aging but still beautiful Mme. Récamier. He also wrote, partly to recover from the financial ruin that resulted from his lavish style of living. *Les Natchez* appeared in 1826 and *Voyage en Amérique* in 1827. The latter, while factually unreliable, remains one of the most dazzlingly descriptive travel volumes on America ever written.

Chateaubriand's masterpiece, *Mémoires d'outre-tombe* (*Memories from Beyond the Grave*), appeared posthumously in 1849–1850. He had begun writing this work as early as 1803, while in Rome. His purpose was to relate the history of his feelings and ideas rather than that of his exterior life. The chapters on his youth in Brittany, on his lifelong idealization of women (who rewarded him generously for his cult of the eternal feminine), and on his love of nature and of the sea are, for their vividness and their depth of analysis, matched in French literature only by Rousseau's *Confessions* and Proust's memoir-novel *À la recherche du temps perdu*. The pages Chateaubriand devoted to Rome and to Venice, to the women he had loved, and to his haunting melancholy and contemplation of death are richly romantic. The last sections, on his political role after 1815, are more restrained and classical in their concise sharpness. Everywhere in the memoirs Chateaubriand displays his cherished ego; he is always, naïvely and proudly, at the center of his work.

Chateaubriand, who had romantically mourned the burden of living throughout his 80 years while enthusiastically pursuing the joys and honor of life, died in Paris on July 4, 1848. With France passing through yet another revolution, he was buried in the tomb he had built on the rocky island of Grand-Bé off the coast at St.-Malo.

HENRI PEYRE, *Yale University*

Bibliography
Evans, Joan, *Chateaubriand* (London and New York 1939).
Maurois, André, *Chateaubriand*, tr. by V. Fraser (London and New York 1938).
Moreau, Pierre, *Chateaubriand, l'homme et l'oeuvre* (Paris 1956).
Sieburg, Friedrich, *Chateaubriand*, tr. by V. M. Macdonald (New York 1962).
Tapié, Victor, *Chateaubriand par lui-même* (Paris 1965).

CHÂTEAUBRIANT, shä-tō-brē-äN′, is a town in northwestern France, in Loire-Atlantique department, 40 miles (64 km) north northeast of Nantes. It is an important market for livestock and has establishments that manufacture agricultural machinery, food products, and textiles. Châteaubriant's castle consists of the remains of the feudal Vieux-Château of the 11th to 15th centuries and of the Château-Neuf, constructed in the 16th century, which now houses a museum and law courts. Population: (1962) 9,985.

CHÂTEAUDUN, shä-tō-dûN′, is a town in north central France, situated on a plateau overlooking the Loir River, in Eure-et-Loir department, 28 miles (45 km) south southwest of Chartres. Rebuilt after a fire in 1723, it has straight streets terminating in a large square, the Place du 18 Octobre, to the north of which is a promenade providing a view of the Loir Valley. The castle of the counts of Dunois, built during the 12th to 16th centuries, is on a promontory to the west. Other notable buildings include the 12th century Church of the Madeleine, damaged in 1940 and since restored, and the Church of St. Valérien, erected during the 12th to 15th centuries. The town is a trading center for the surrounding agricultural region and has factories making telephone and optical equipment, machine tools, and dairy products.

Châteaudun has been in existence since the Gallo-Roman period. In the Franco-Prussian War it was captured by the Germans in 1870, after a heroic defense. Population: (1962) 11,107.

CHATEAUGAY RIVER, shat′ə-gē, in New York and Quebec, about 55 miles (88 km) long. In Canada it is called the *Châteauguay*. It rises in Lower Chateaugay Lake in the Adirondack Mountains of northeastern New York, flows northward across the international boundary and continues northeastward to empty into Lake St. Louis (an expansion of the St. Lawrence River) near the town of Châteauguay, opposite Montreal Island. It was the scene of important military operations during the war of 1812.

CHÂTEAUGUAY, Sieur de. See LE MOYNE—*Antoine le Moyne.*

CHÂTEAUGUAY, shä-tō-gā′, is a town in southern Quebec, Canada, on Lake St. Louis in the St. Lawrence River, near the mouth of the Châteauguay River, about 11 miles (17 km) southwest of Montreal. The town is a market for a mixed farming and dairying region. Population: 15,797.

CHÂTEAUGUAY-CENTRE, shä-tō-gā, is a residential town in Châteauguay county, Quebec, Canada, in a dairy- and truck-farming area. It is adjacent to the town of Châteauguay and about 15 miles (24 km) southwest of downtown Montreal, of which it is a suburb. The battle of Châteauguay, an engagement of the War of 1812 in which an invading American force was repulsed by Canadians, was fought nearby in 1813. The town was incorporated in 1960. Population: 17,942.

CHÂTEAURENAULT, shä-tō-rə-nō′, **Marquis de** (1637–1716), French admiral and marshal of France, who aided James II in his attempt to regain the throne of England in 1689. The name sometimes is spelled *Château-Renault*. He was born François Louis de Rousselet at Châteaurenault, France, on Sept. 22, 1637. He was made rear admiral in 1673. When James II moved against William III, who had succeeded him as king of England, Châteaurenault commanded the fleet that landed James' army in Ireland. Châteaurenault became vice admiral in 1701. The next year, escorting a fleet of Spanish treasure ships to Vigo Bay, Spain, he was defeated by an English fleet and lost part of the cargo. He was created a marshal of France in 1703. He died in Paris on Nov. 15, 1716.

CHÂTEAUROUX, shä-tō-rōō′, is a town in France, the capital of the department of Indre, on the Indre River 60 miles (96 km) southeast of Tours. It has factories manufacturing woolen goods, agricultural machinery, and paper, and processing food, tobacco, and leather. The home of Count Henri Gratien Bertrand, a general in the Empire, contains a museum of Napoleonic souvenirs, paintings, and other collections. Other points of interest are the Church of the Cordeliers (13th century), the Church of St. Martial (12th to 15th century), and the Château Raoul (15th century), which now houses the prefecture. The château is built on the site of a castle erected in the 10th century by Raoul le Large, lord of Déols, from which the town derives its name. From 1612 to 1736, Châteauroux was a duchy of the house of Condé, and from 1742 to 1744 of the Marquise de la Tournelle, who acquired the duchy and a princely income as mistress of Louis XV. Population: (1962) 44,227.

CHÂTELET, shä-tle′, **Marquise du** (1706–1749), French mathematician and translator, whose most important work was her translation of Newton's *Principia,* which appeared in 1756. She was born Gabrielle Émilie Le Tonnelier de Breteuil, in Paris, on Dec. 17, 1706, and married the Marquis du Châtelet-Lomont in 1725. In 1733 she met Voltaire, became his mistress, and provided him with the protection he needed when his *Lettres philosophiques,* published in 1734, incurred the wrath of the authorities.

The two retired to the Marquise's estate in Champagne, where Voltaire produced some of his most important works and Émilie wrote a memoir, *Dissertation sur la nature et propagation du feu,* which she submitted to a competition sponsored by the Academy of Sciences in Paris. Although it failed to win the prize, the academy published it in 1744. The Marquise died in childbirth on Sept. 10, 1749, in Lunéville, at the palace of King Stanislas of Poland, in the presence of her husband and Voltaire and the poet Jean François de Saint-Lambert, who was the father of her child.

L. Pearce Williams
Cornell University

CHATELPERRONIAN CULTURE, sha-tel-pə-rō′nē-ən, in archaeology, the first of the Upper Paleolithic series of cultures. It flourished in Châtelperron, in the Périgord region of central France, about 20,000 years ago. The Chatelperronians developed the earliest known blade culture. Their characteristic artifacts include knives made of flint blades, with one straight razorlike edge, and arrows, javelin points, and scrapers made of similar flints.

CHATHAM, Earl of. See Pitt, William (1708–1778).

CHATHAM, chat′əm, a municipal borough in Kent, southeast England, is 17 miles (27 km) east of the outskirts of London. It stands on the right bank of the winding estuary of the Medway River, 6 miles (10 km) southwest of its confluence with the River Thames.

Chatham is a shopping and business center bearing unmistakable marks of its long experience as a garrison town and naval base. The Royal Naval Dockyard, founded by Queen Elizabeth I, extends for 3 miles (5 km) and has built over 300 warships including such famous vessels as Horatio Nelson's *Victory,* HMS *Téméraire, Revenge,* and 6 ships named *Chatham.* A lofty naval war memorial stands among the obsolete defense works known as The Lines, built to defend the shipyard from landward attack.

The oldest building is the Norman St. Bartholomew's Chapel on High Street, used for many years as a dwelling but restored in 1896. The chapel was part of a hospital founded in 1078, whose present building stands on the hill above. Also on High Street is the almshouse founded in 1592 by Adm. Sir John Hawkins for "poor decayed mariners and shipwrights" and rebuilt in the 19th century. The demolition of excess military buildings has opened good views of the waterway, notably from the pleasant Riverside Gardens. Chatham figures in several books by Charles Dickens, who lived from 1817 to 1821 at 11 Ordnance Terrace. Population: (1961) 48,989.

Gordon Stokes
Author of "English Place-Names"

CHATHAM, chat′əm, is a port in eastern New Brunswick, Canada, on the south side of the Miramichi River, 12 miles (19 km) above its mouth, about 85 miles (137 km) northwest of Moncton. The river flows into the Gulf of St. Lawrence. Chatham carries on an export trade in lumber. The town was founded in 1800 and was named, according to tradition, in honor of William Pitt, 1st Earl of Chatham. Population: 7,883.

CHATHAM, chat′əm, a residential borough in northeastern New Jersey, is in Morris county, on the Passaic River, 11 miles (18 km) west of Newark. It is a residential suburb for commuters who work in Newark and New York City. The borough has some light industry, including the manufacture of chemicals and cement blocks. An inn that still stands in Chatham was visited by George Washington.

Chatham was settled in 1749. It was incorporated as a village in 1892 and as a borough in 1897. Government is by mayor and council. Population: 9,566.

CHATHAM, chat′əm, a city in southwestern Ontario, Canada, the seat of Kent county, is 65 miles (104 km) southwest of London, Ontario. It is situated on the Thames River, which empties into Lake St. Clair, permitting small craft to enter Lake Huron and Lake Erie. Chatham is the commercial center of an agricultural district that raises fruit, grain, tobacco, and livestock. There are natural gas deposits nearby. Its industries produce flour, woolen goods, and lumber. Chatham also has sugar refineries, canneries, dairies, and foundries and tobacco-processing and natural gas plants.

The site of Chatham was chosen by Lieutenant Governor John Graves Simcoe in 1795 and the town was founded in 1835. Population: 35,317.

CHATHAM ISLANDS, chat'əm, an island group in the South Pacific Ocean about 500 miles (800 km) east of New Zealand, of which it is a part. Chatham, Pitt, and Rangatira are the largest islands. The total land area of the group is 372 square miles (963 sq km). The islands rise from a submarine shelf that is geologically associated with New Zealand. Shallow lakes and swamps cover more than a fifth of the land, and there are extensive beds of thick peat. A dense forest, originally supported by the cool, moist climate, has been largely destroyed by fire and grazing.

Most of the inhabitants live in or near the villages of Waitangi and Owenga on Chatham Island. Many of the people are Maoris. Sheep farming and a limited fishing industry are the principal means of livelihood.

The islands were named by Lt. William R. Broughton, who discovered them while on the ship *Chatham* in 1791. The first known inhabitants were Morioris, the predecessors of New Zealand Maoris. Whaling and sealing bases were established in the islands in the early 19th century, and German missionaries settled in 1842. After 1865, New Zealand sheepmen moved in to produce wool.

Chatham Islands county is part of New Zealand, and residents vote in parliamentary elections.

Population: (1966) 520.

HOWARD J. CRITCHFIELD
Western Washington State College

CHÂTILLON-SUR-SEINE, shä-tē-yôn-sür-sân', is a town in France, 45 miles (72 km) northwest of Dijon. It is situated in the department of Côte-d'Or, on the Seine River, at the northern edge of the forest of Châtillon. The town's main industries are iron founding and the manufacture of machinery.

The ruined 13th-century castle of the dukes of Burgundy overlooks the forest of Châtillon. There is also a château built by Marshal Auguste F. L. Viesse de Marmont (1774–1852), who was born there. Other notable structures are the 10th century Church of St. Vorles and the 12th century Church of St. Nicholas.

In 1814 an abortive attempt at a peace settlement between Napoleon I and the coalition against him took place in Châtillon-sur-Seine. Population: (1962) 5,389.

CHATSWORTH, chats'wûrth, is an outlying section of the city of Los Angeles, in southern California in Los Angeles county. It is 25 miles (40 km) northwest of downtown Los Angeles at the western end of the San Fernando Valley. Formerly a semirural community in an area of small fruit farms, Chatsworth is now a suburban residential center with a variety of industrial concerns, primarily in the fields of space technology and missile systems. Manufactures include aircraft and missile components, printed circuits, precision instruments, and screw machine products.

Chatsworth owes its name to Spencer Compton Cavendish, 8th Duke of Devonshire, who, during a visit here in the 1870's, remarked that the region resembled Chatsworth Park, the site of his ancestral home in Derbyshire, England. The area is administered by the Los Angeles city government. Its population was estimated in 1970 at 42,100.

ROBERT MAYER
Chatsworth Branch Library

THE BRITISH TRAVEL ASSOCIATION

CHATSWORTH, in England, the home of the Duke of Devonshire, is one of the houses open to the public.

CHATSWORTH, chats'wûrth, an estate in Derbyshire, England, 20 miles (32 km) north of Derby, is the seat of the dukes of Devonshire. The original house was built in the mid-1500's by Sir William Cavendish and his wife, Bess of Hardwick, later Countess of Shrewsbury. Mary Stuart was imprisoned here for several years. The present Palladian mansion was begun in 1687 by William Cavendish, 1st Duke of Devonshire, after the design by William Talman. A north wing was added by Sir Jeffry Wyatville for the 6th Duke in 1820–1830. The mansion houses famous picture and sculpture galleries and a library. It is surrounded by formal gardens laid out by Sir Joseph Paxton. Chatsworth is open to the public.

CHATTAHOOCHEE, chat-ə-hōō'chē, is a town in northwestern Florida, in Gadsden county, on the Apalachicola River. It is 36 miles (58 km) northwest of Tallahassee and 2 miles (3 km) south of the Georgia border. Tobacco and truck crops are grown in the area and dairy cattle are raised. Fuller's earth is mined nearby. The town bottles soft drinks and makes cellulose products. Chattahoochee is the seat of the Florida State Hospital for the mentally ill, the largest hospital of its kind in the state, with a patient population of about 6,000. In 1681 the Spanish established the mission of Santa Cruz de Sabacola here. Chattahoochee was founded in 1828. Government is by mayor and council. Population: 7,944.

CHATTAHOOCHEE RIVER, chat-ə-hōō'chē, in the southeastern United States, about 435 miles (700 km) long. It rises in northeastern Georgia, flows southwestward and southward, forming about half the Georgia-Alabama boundary. Near Chattahoochee, Fla., it joins the Flint River to form the Apalachicola River. Several dams provide hydroelectric power and create man-made lakes.

335

CHATTANOOGA lies in a bend of the Tennessee River at the foot of Lookout Mountain, on which a historic Civil War battle was fought.

CHATTANOOGA, chat-ə-nōō′gə, an industrial city and port of entry in southeastern Tennessee, seat of Hamilton county, is situated on the Tennessee River, just north of the Tennessee-Georgia boundary. The immediate area is broken by numerous isolated hills and ridges and to the west is framed by escarpments of the Cumberland Plateau, through which the river penetrates in a deep canyon. Rail, air, river, and highway transportation give ready access to distant areas, while a new freeway system not only has changed the profile of the community but also provides quick access between the city and its suburbs.

As an urban center, Chattanooga has the problems of contemporary times made somewhat more complex by the city's proximity to two neighboring states (Georgia and Alabama), by the geographic contours of the area, and by its location within Appalachia (q.v.). The attack on the problems has taken several forms, including a 403-acre (163-hectare) urban renewal project known as the Golden Gateway, desegregation of city and county schools, an extensive railroad relocation project to remove rails from the central city, and air and water pollution studies.

Economy. Chattanooga is one of the most heavily industrialized centers in the southeastern United States. Its principal products include fabricated metals, textiles, synthetic fibers, processed foods, chemicals, power generated by steam and nuclear plants, and glass, wood, and leather products. Three insurance companies have home offices in the city. Commercial and industrial concerns make large use of electric power generated by the Tennessee Valley Authority. Tourists add about $50 million a year to the economy.

Education and Culture. In addition to its public schools, Chattanooga has parochial schools and three private schools—Girls' Preparatory School, and the McCallie School and the Baylor School, both for boys. The Chattanooga State Technical Institute and Chattanooga City College offer two-year programs. Tennessee Temple College is under Baptist auspices. The University of Chattanooga, founded in 1886, operates the Cadek Conservatory as one of its divisions. Cultural activities center around a symphony orchestra, an opera association, the Adult Education Council, the George Thomas Hunter Gallery of Art, and an outdoor art festival called "Plum Nelly."

Points of Interest. Chattanooga is known for its historic sites and natural beauty. Signal Mountain overlooks the rugged grandeur of the canyon of the Tennessee River. Lookout Mountain also affords mountain scenery and includes within its area such attractions as caves reached by elevator, a natural city of rocks known as Rock City, and a steep-incline railway. Point Park, on Lookout Mountain, is part of the Chickamauga and Chattanooga Military Park (with units in both Tennessee and Georgia), which was created in 1890 as the first national military park. Other units in Tennessee are on Signal Mountain, Orchard Knob, and Missionary Ridge.

History. Early settlers, in a town meeting in 1838, selected Chattanooga as the name for their community, since it was the Indian word meaning "rock that comes to a point" used for neighboring Lookout Mountain. The area had been within Cherokee territory for years before the American

CHICKAMAUGA DAM of the Tennessee Valley Authority controls the Tennessee River northeast of Chattanooga.

Revolution. In 1777 a band of antiwhite braves seceded from the tribe, moved from the Cherokee towns on the Little Tennessee River, and settled on Chickamauga Creek near present Chattanooga. Known as the Chickamauga, they fought under British guidance in the Revolution and continued constant warfare on frontier settlements until their power was broken in 1794. Thereafter the Cherokee concentrated in the Chattanooga area and made rapid progress toward civilization, especially as a consequence of the political leadership of Chief John Ross and the development of literacy in their own language (see SEQUOYA). About 1815 the site became a trading post called Ross' Landing. The Brainerd Mission, conducted by the American Board of Commissioners for Foreign Missions, served the Cherokee from 1817 until their forced removal to Oklahoma in 1838.

The site of Chattanooga was considered important because it was in an area where the corn country met the cotton country. Considerable river trade reached the town from the upper Tennessee, but the difficult waters in the canyon below Chattanooga were a major deterrent to trade. This fact made the opening in 1850 of the Georgia-owned Western and Atlantic Railroad from Atlanta to Chattanooga most important, as it gave Chattanooga an outlet to the Atlantic coast. In a decade the city became a major rail junction with lines to all points in the southeast.

On the eve of the Civil War, in 1861, Chattanooga had a population of about 2,500. In a state referendum on secession in that year, Chattanooga supported the Southern view, while Hamilton county voted to stay in the Union. This division was a prime concern of the area until 1863, when the military campaigns of Chickamauga and Chattanooga made Chattanooga a household word. At the close of the war a considerable number of soldiers from both sides returned to Chattanooga to make their permanent home. A spirit of harmony soon prevailed, reducing the problems of reconstruction at an early date.

In 1878, Adolph S. Ochs bought the Chattanooga *Times* and launched a publishing career that led to his purchase of the New York *Times*. Through his Chattanooga publishing activities, Ochs advocated a balanced economy and supported the iron and coal industries, which were the chief activities until about 1890, when the rich Birmingham, Ala., coal and iron fields were opened. About 1900, Chattanooga turned to textiles, insurance, metal fabrication, and the bottling of Coca-Cola, a process that originated in the city in 1899.

During the Spanish-American War the main sector of the Chattanooga and Chickamauga National Military Park was used as a training camp. Fort Oglethorpe (Ga.) about 5 miles (8 km) south of Chattanooga, established in 1904, was a major army post until 1946.

The creation of the Tennessee Valley Authority in 1933 not only effected control over floods, improved river navigation, and produced low-cost electrical energy but also brought some of the TVA's major offices to Chattanooga. The completion in 1940 of Chickamauga Dam 7 miles (11 km) above the city created Lake Chickamauga, about 60 miles (97 km) long, which has become an active recreation area and place for homesites.

Since 1911, Chattanooga has had the commission form of government. Population: 119,082.

JAMES W. LIVINGOOD
University of Chattanooga

CHATTANOOGA CAMPAIGN, chat-ə-noō′gə kam-pān′, in the American Civil War, fought in September–November 1863 in southeastern Tennessee. It was this decisive Civil War campaign that gained east Tennessee for the Union and opened the way for an advance into Georgia. The city of Chattanooga, Tenn., is almost entirely surrounded by high mountains that afford a magnificent view of the country, and by the Tennessee River, which makes a huge U-shaped bend just west of the city. Chattanooga was a key stronghold of the Confederacy and a major railway junction. The Civil War was the first large-scale war in which railroads played a vital part. Their importance was vividly illustrated in this campaign.

On Aug. 16, 1863, the Union Army of the Cumberland, led by Maj. Gen. William S. Rosecrans, advanced on Chattanooga. On September 9 the Confederates evacuated the city and Union troops occupied it, but Southern reinforcements, including a large part of Lt. Gen. James Longstreet's Corps from Virginia, had been rushed to the area. At the Battle of Chickamauga, fought 10 miles (16 km) south of the city on Sept. 19–20, 1863, Gen. Braxton Bragg's Confederate Army of Tennessee won an overwhelming victory. General Rosecrans army hastily retreated to Chattanooga; the Confederates followed and laid siege to the city.

Siege of the City. Several of the leading Confederate generals urged a crossing of the Tennessee River to strike at the Union line of communications to force the Northern army to retreat, but General Bragg chose to invest the city. This decision was to prove fatal to the Confederates' chances of winning the campaign. Although the siege was long and difficult for the beleaguered Union army—supplies ran short, the men were placed on half rations or less, and horses died by the score from starvation—General Bragg's inactivity gave Northern authorities the time they needed to rush reinforcements to the area.

Maj. Gen. Joseph Hooker was sent by rail from Virginia with two army corps. Maj. Gen. William T. Sherman was ordered from Mississippi with a large force. Maj. Gen. Ulysses S. Grant was given overall command in the West, and Rosecrans was replaced by Maj. Gen. George H. Thomas. Shortly after Grant's arrival in Chattanooga late in October, a new supply route was opened into the city from the west.

With all these forces assembling against him, General Bragg then made the incredible error of reducing the strength of his army by sending General Longstreet up the Tennessee Valley to attack Maj. Gen. Ambrose E. Burnside's Army of the Ohio at Knoxville, more than 100 miles (161 km) to the northeast.

Grant's Moves. The Confederates occupied Missionary Ridge east of the city, the commanding promontory of Lookout Mountain to the southwest, and the valley between. At first, General Grant planned to ignore Lookout Mountain and assault Missionary Ridge, but his plan was changed. The battles subsequently developed in three successive phases: Orchard Knob, November 23; Lookout Mountain, November 24; and Missionary Ridge, November 25.

General Grant's plan was to have Sherman move behind the city, cross the Tennessee River, and attack the north end of Missionary Ridge. While Sherman was getting ready, reports came that the Confederates were planning a retreat. Thomas' Army of the Cumberland was ordered to

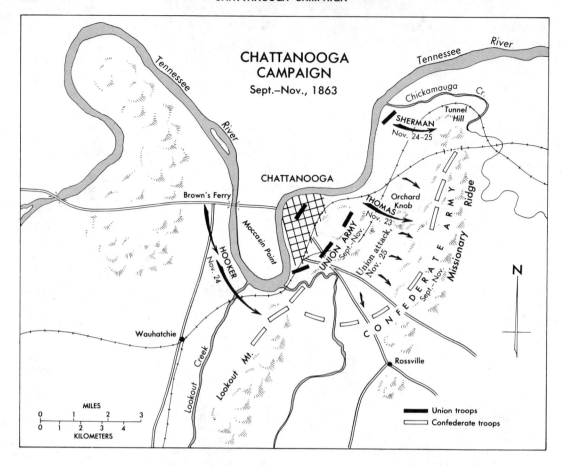

CHATTANOOGA CAMPAIGN
Sept.–Nov., 1863

Union troops
Confederate troops

attack Orchard Knob, a hill west of Missionary Ridge, on November 23. The army captured the position and the outpost line in front of Missionary Ridge.

On November 24, General Sherman attacked but made little progress. His assault was stopped at Tunnel Hill by Maj. Gen. Patrick R. Cleburne's Confederate division. Simultaneously, Hooker's troops, who outnumbered their opponents six to one, easily captured Lookout Mountain. This battle has been christened the Battle Above the Clouds.

Missionary Ridge. The climax came on November 25. Sherman and Hooker were both to attack; Thomas was to advance later, in the center. Sherman's assault came first, but was halted by Cleburne's command. Hooker was delayed. At this point Grant ordered Thomas to attack the trenches at the foot of Missionary Ridge. But to everyone's amazement, the men did not stop. Contrary to orders, they surged up the ridge. The Confederate left and center broke; only the right flank stood fast. The battle was suddenly over. The great strategic front of the Confederacy from Richmond, Va., to the Mississippi River was broken in the middle.

Losses. In these three battles the Union armies, totaling close to 60,000 men, lost about 5,800, mostly wounded. The Confederate army of some 37,000 men sustained approximately 6,700 casualties, the great majority captured or missing.

JOSEPH B. MITCHELL
Author of "Decisive Battles of the Civil War"

Bibliography

Esposito, Col. Vincent J., *The West Point Atlas of American Wars* (New York 1959).
Horn, Stanley F., *The Army of Tennessee* (Indianapolis 1941).
Johnson, Robert U., and Buel, Clarence G., eds., *Battles and Leaders of the Civil War*, vol. 3, rev. ed. (New York 1956).
Mitchell, Lt. Col. Joseph B., *Decisive Battles of the Civil War* (New York 1955).

CHATTEL, chat'əl, in law, is a term used broadly to denote property. It is defined generally as including all kinds of property except real estate. It is more comprehensive than "goods," since it includes animate as well as inanimate objects. In addition, a chattel may be tangible or intangible; an example of an intangible chattel is a bare right, such as evidence of a debt (for example, an I O U). The owner of a chattel may mortgage it (use it as security for the payment of a debt or the performance of some other act).

Tangible chattels often are subdivided into *personal chattels* and *real chattels.* Personal chattels, strictly speaking, are movable objects that the owner may carry about with him, such as household goods, jewels, or money. Generally, personal chattels include every type of property that is not annexed to the land and that lacks two essential characteristics of real estate—immobility and indeterminate duration. On the other hand, real chattels are property interests that arise out of, or are dependent on, real estate, such as leases. See also PROPERTY, LAWS OF.

PETER D. WEINSTEIN
Member of the New York Bar

CHATTEL MORTGAGE, chat'əl môr'gij, a written agreement that must be recorded, whereby the owner conveys personal property, other than real estate, to secure a debt. The *mortgagor* transfers his title to, but not possession of, the chattel (for example, an automobile or a television set) to another person, the *mortgagee.* If the mortgagor fails in his payments, the mortgagee may sell the property through proper legal proceedings to satisfy his claims. See also MORTGAGE.

In a *pledge,* unlike a chattel mortgage, title does not pass. A pledge transfers possession of personal property redeemable on certain terms, with an implied power of sale on default of payment. Also differing from a chattel mortgage is a *conditional sale,* in which the buyer makes a down payment and agrees to make other payments. If the seller is forced to retake the goods in case of nonpayment of the balance, he has the right to dispose of them at public auction or private sale.

SAMUEL G. KLING
Author, "The Complete Guide to Everyday Law"

CHATTERJI, chä'tər-jē, **Bankim Chandra** (1838–1894), Indian novelist, who laid the foundation of modern Bengali prose. He was born in Katalpara, Bengal, on June 27, 1838, of an orthodox Brahman family. After receiving his B. A. degree from Calcutta University in 1858, he embarked on a lifelong career as a civil servant.

Chatterji began to write poetry but soon abandoned it for prose. *Rajmohan's Wife* (1864), his first novel, was in English. His next work, *Durges-Nandini (Daughter of the Feudal Lord),* was in Bengali, marking a radical departure from the prevalent belief that literary works should be written only in Sanskrit or English. His early works were historical romances, but his later novels reflected his interest in social issues.

In 1872, Chatterji founded the *Bangadarshan,* a journal in which many of his novels were serialized. He was a firm advocate of Hindu orthodoxy and a champion of Bengali nationalism. *Bande Mataram (Hail to Thee, Mother),* the song that appeared in his novel *Ananda Math (Ananda Mission),* became the hymn of Hindu India in its struggle for independence. Many of his works have been translated into English, including *The Poison Tree* (Eng. tr., 1884) and *Krishnakanta's Will* (Eng. tr., 1895). He died on April 8, 1894.

CARLO COPPOLA, *Editor of "Mahfil, a Quarterly of South Asian Literature"*

CHATTERTON, Thomas (1752–1770), English poet, whose medieval interests, vivid imagination, and literary inventiveness place him among the precursors of the romantic movement. The drama of Chatterton's short life, involving poverty, literary forgery, and struggle for recognition, and ending in suicide at 17, made him the prototype of the misunderstood genius. His fame rests more on the pathos of unfulfilled promise than on his achievement.

Life. Chatterton was born in Bristol on Nov. 20, 1752, shortly after the death of his schoolteacher father. The boy entered Colston free school at 7, and at 14 was an attorney's apprentice drearily copying briefs. Meanwhile, however, Chatterton was creating his own world of solitary fantasy. Inspired by 15th century manuscripts and an old Bible, all of which he found in the Church of St. Mary Redcliffe, where members of his family were traditionally sextons, he taught himself to read Gothic lettering. He studied the early history of Bristol and constructed elaborate stories about the historical figure William Canynge, lord mayor of Bristol and original owner of the manuscripts, whom he pictured as the patron of an imaginary priest, Thomas Rowley. In pseudo-Middle English, Chatterton composed poems and historical accounts, which he attributed to Rowley.

When he was 12, Chatterton showed one of his teachers a Rowley poem, *Elinore and Juga,* and at 15, when a new bridge was opened in Bristol, he stirred excitement in a local journal with what he implied was a 12th century account of the opening of the old bridge. He also sold various forgeries to amateur Bristol antiquaries, some of whom may have connived at the deception. In 1769, Chatterton sent Horace Walpole a Rowley poem, which Walpole at first praised but then, growing suspicious, rejected coldly.

Chatterton next turned to writing contemporary political satire. Encouraged by several sales, he went to London in April 1770, where his youth and sharp wit won favorable attention from William Beckford, the popular lord mayor, and several journal editors. Success seemed assured, but Beckford died suddenly, the political tide turned, some journals suspended publication, and Chatterton was left with no prospects. On Aug. 24, 1770, he destroyed all the writings in his room, took arsenic, and died.

Writings. Chatterton's literary reputation rests on his medieval forgeries, published posthumously in 1777. The best known are *Bristowe Tragedie,* a ballad on the courage of a fictional knight facing unjust execution; *Ælla,* a short drama, with songs in various stanza forms, on a fictional Saxon chieftain's betrayal and death; and the *Excelente Balade of Charitie,* which contrasts the uncharitableness of a wealthy abbot with the generosity of a poor priest.

Many of Chatterton's contemporaries thought the Rowley poems authentic. For others the elaborately archaic vocabulary, pseudoarchaic spelling, and evidences in rhyme and meter of 18th century pronunciation marked the poems as imitations. The ensuing controversy, the genuine poetic feeling of the works, and the poet's youthful suicide made him a legend. Wordsworth, Coleridge, Shelley, and Keats admired him, and he was the subject of Leoncavallo's opera *Chatterton.*

GEORGIA DUNBAR, *Hofstra University*

Further Reading: Meyerstein, Edward H. W., *Life of Thomas Chatterton* (London 1930); Neville, John, *Thomas Chatterton* (London 1948); Wilson, Daniel, *Chatterton: A Biographical Study* (London 1869).

CHATTI, kat'ī, an ancient German tribe that lived north of the Main River. In 9 A. D. they joined the Cherusci and helped defeat Varus and destroy three Roman legions. In 69 they crossed the Rhine and besieged the Roman city of Moguntiacum (Mainz). In 83 they attacked the Romans on the Rhine near Moguntiacum. At this point Emperor Domitian assembled a large army and drove them from their lands into central Germany; the region north of the Main was annexed to the Roman Empire. In 162 and 170 the Chatti again made raids, and in 213 they fought against Emperor Caracalla. They were driven out of the Main basin by the Alamanni and disappeared from history.

ARTHER FERRILL, *University of Washington*

CHAUCER, chô′sər, **Geoffrey** (1343?–1400), English poet, who was the greatest literary figure of medieval England and one of the outstanding authors of world literature. He is most famous for the *Canterbury Tales,* a collection of stories told by a group of pilgrims traveling from London to the shrine of St. Thomas à Becket at Canterbury. Chaucer's pilgrims are typical members of late medieval English society, and their stories reflect his interest in contemporary attitudes toward religion, love, and marriage. But his concern with complex human situations gives Chaucer's art its main impetus. His works, marked by humor, warmth, insight, and understanding of human nature, comprise a rich tapestry of a lively and colorful period.

Chaucer grew up in 14th century London. As page to a daughter-in-law of King Edward III (reigned 1327–1377), he was exposed at an early age to life at a brilliant court devoted to the pageantry and ideals of chivalry. Through most of his adult life he occupied official positions that enabled him to acquaint himself with much of the contemporary social spectrum. He also pursued an independent literary career, but this is not mentioned in the extant records of his life.

During the period in which Chaucer wrote, English was reestablishing itself over French as the official language, and the dialect then spoken in London was the one from which modern English evolved. Chaucer's use of this dialect, with its close linguistic kinship to modern English, together with his brilliant narrative sense, his ability to create vivid characters, his insight into human problems, and the fluency of his mature style, has made him one of the most approachable and rewarding of the major poets.

LIFE

Early Years. Chaucer was born in London, probably in the early 1340's (in 1386 he referred to himself as "forty years old and more"). He was the son of a prosperous wine merchant, John Chaucer, who, like his own father and like his son after him, served a term as a customs official of the king. The elder Chaucer may have held other government posts, and it was probably through his influence that Geoffrey became a page in the household of Lionel, Earl of Ulster, the third son of King Edward III, in 1356. (This appointment is indicated in the earliest extant records of Chaucer's life.) In 1359–1360, Chaucer took part in a military campaign in France during the Hundred Years' War, was captured, and his ransom paid in part by King Edward.

From 1361 to 1366 there are no records of Chaucer's activities, but he may have been in the King's service for part of that time. It is also likely that by 1366 he had married Philippa de Roet, a lady in the service of the queen. (A document from Navarre, which has only recently been brought to light, indicates that Chaucer was in Spain early in 1366, possibly with the military, or as a pilgrim to the famous shrine of St. James in Santiago de Compostela.) Between 1367 and 1378, Chaucer made several trips abroad, notably to France and Italy. Some of these trips may have been diplomatic missions for the king; others dealt with financial matters and commercial treaties. On one of his journeys, to Italy in 1372, Chaucer went to Genoa to help negotiate a trade agreement, and then traveled to Florence, where he may have first read the works of Boccaccio and Petrarch that he subsequently made use of in his poetry.

Middle Years. In June 1374, Chaucer became a government official, serving as comptroller of customs for wool and leather at the port of London. He held this post for the next 12 years, during which time his income was supplemented by royal annuities and gifts, first from Edward III and later from Richard II. In addition, he received a rent-free dwelling, and he and his wife benefited from gifts and pensions bestowed upon them by John of Gaunt, Duke of Lancaster, whom both had served, and whose mistress (and later third wife), Catherine Swynford, was Philippa's sister. In 1382, Chaucer was granted the additional post of comptroller of petty customs.

In 1385, Chaucer lost his employment and his rent-free home, perhaps as a result of the political turmoil that plagued the reign of Richard II, who had become king in 1377. Chaucer, however, was not long without a post. Later, in 1385, he moved to Kent, where he was appointed justice of the peace. In the following year, he was elected to Parliament as a Knight of the Shire for Kent. Soon, however, he began to be plagued with personal ·and financial problems. His wife died in 1387, and records of 1388 indicate he was sued for debt and sold his annuity.

Final Years. In 1389, Chaucer reentered the service of the crown as clerk of the king's works. In his new position he was responsible for the upkeep and repair of government buildings and royal residences in and out of London, a post that required him to travel. Two years later he was appointed to the less taxing office of deputy forester of the royal forest of North Petherton, Somerset. He did not spend all his time in Somerset, however; records show that he was also active in Kent and London. In the 1390's he again received royal gifts and pensions.

When Henry IV seized the throne from Richard II in 1399, he confirmed and supplemented Chaucer's annual payments from Richard. (Chaucer's association with Henry's father, John of Gaunt, may have been a factor in Chaucer's continued good standing in the new reign.) In December 1399, Chaucer signed a lease on a house in London, on the grounds of Westminster Abbey. According to tradition, he died in London on Oct. 25, 1400. He was buried in Westminster Abbey, one of the first commoners and the first poet to be so honored.

Although the records of Chaucer's life reveal nothing about his art, he was known and praised as a poet by many of his contemporaries, among them the English poets Thomas Usk and John Gower and the French court poet Eustache Deschamps, who corresponded with Chaucer and whose works Chaucer on occasion imitated. Chaucer may also have known the French poets Guillaume de Machaut and Jean Froissart.

In his poetry, Chaucer rarely alludes to his personal life. Neither his wife nor his children are mentioned in any of his works, although he did compose a prose treatise on the astrolabe, an astronomical instrument, for one of his sons, Lewis, in 1391. Occasionally, however, Chaucer introduced himself into his poetry. His reading habits are described in Book Two of *The House of Fame,* and he included an unflattering self-portrait in the prologue to The Tale of Sir Thopas in the *Canterbury Tales.*

WORKS

In any examination and evaluation of Chaucer's work it essential to recognize his debt to the French and Italian literary traditions. First and foremost a narrative poet, Chaucer owed much to the courtly idealistic *romances* and the bourgeois-realistic *fabliaux* that were the dominant narrative genres in medieval French literature. (*Romances* were stories, either in verse or prose, about idealized love and chivalry; *fabliaux* were brief, frequently comic tales, written in verse and of a coarse and often ribald nature.)

Chaucer took his earliest narrative inspiration from the allegorical *Romance of the Rose*, begun about 1230 by Guillaume de Lorris and completed about 1280 by Jean de Meung. Guillaume detached the concerns of 12th century chivalric romance from the context of adventure. Using personified abstractions, he presented the lover's quest for his mistress' love (the rose) within the dream world of a walled, beautiful garden. Jean de Meun metamorphosed this golden world of love into a crowded setting, giving a sprawling, lively consideration of the central moral and philosophical problems of his day. Chaucer knew the *Romance of the Rose* intimately, translated it into English, and was deeply influenced by its unique and fascinating combination of idealized landscape, psychological allegory, philosophical concerns, and wide-ranging social commentary.

The Italian influence on Chaucer extends from ancient Rome to his own time. Ovid, the witty and worldly Roman love poet, provided him with numerous classical and mythological *exempla* of love's foibles. Chaucer read Boethius' *The Consolation of Philosophy*, an artful 6th century philosophical dialogue that examines the roles played by destiny and free will in the attainment of human happiness. He also borrowed the sources for some of his major works, notably *Troilus and Criseyde*, from the great 14th century Italian writer Giovanni Boccaccio.

However, indebted as Chaucer was to the works of others, he remained an entirely individual poet. Although he used literary sources and conventions, he gradually developed his own highly personal style and techniques. In his earlier works, he stressed theme rather than character delineation. In the course of the 1380's, however, he linked the significance of his poetry more closely to incisive character portrayal and the depiction of the individual psyche. Even in his most highly original works, however, it can be said that Chaucer perfected rather than abandoned medieval literary tradition.

Chaucer's concern with the narrator figure is perhaps the most unique characteristic of his poetry. His narrators, though, never represent Chaucer, the actual historical man, and in that respect he is one of the least intrusive of poets. His career can in a sense be summed up as that of a private man in search of a public voice. He handles his narrators with great inventiveness, imbuing them with life and strength, and achieves a variety of illuminating and often ironic effects.

"The Book of the Duchess." Chaucer's earliest poetry probably consisted of lyrics, secular and religious, in the French courtly manner. His first narrative poem, *The Book of the Duchess*, was inspired by the death of Blanche, first wife of John of Gaunt, in September 1369, and was probably written shortly after that date. At the beginning of the poem the narrator complains of his "sorwful ymagynacioun" that isolates him from the vitality of nature and fills him with despair and bleak fantasies. The cause and cen-

COURTESY OF THE CURATORS OF THE BODLEIAN LIBRARY, OXFORD

GEOFFREY CHAUCER, from a posthumous portrait by an unknown painter, in the Bodleian Library, Oxford.

tral image of his deviation from the normal rhythms of life is sleeplessness, a "sickness" that has affected the narrator for eight years. Finally, after reading an old retelling of the tragic love story of Ceys and Alcione (Ceyx and Halcyone from Ovid's *Metamorphosis*), he falls asleep.

In the radiant, fertile world of a dream, he meets a man in black, who is mourning for his beloved, "good, fair White" (French "Blanche"). A conversation then ensues in which the narrator's questions force (or permit) the grieving lover to recount, and therefore reexperience, the virtues of his lady and the story of his wooing. Finally the man in black declares that his beloved is dead. The narrator responds "Is that your loss? By God, it is routhe [a pity]," and the poem ends with the dreamer awakening, resolved to set down his dream in rhyme.

Throughout the work, Chaucer reveals his purposes allusively. The narrator is rescued from his "sickness" through his exposure to an old work of art (the legend), gains insight through his subsequent dream, and is finally moved to the creation of a new work of literary art. This poem moves less from grief to happiness than from personal isolation and artistic sterility to productive fulfillment. Unhappiness or grief is placed in its proper perspective in order that it may become a subject to liberate the artist's (narrator's) stifled creative faculties.

The Book of the Duchess is neither overly solemn nor philosophical. Its treatment of the ideal landscape of the courtly dream vision is lively, affectionate, and inventive. Chaucer's juxtaposition of vivid, contrasting images in the poem (for example, the green forest and the black-garbed man) is very effective. All in all, it is a successful and original first major work.

"The House of Fame." Chaucer's next important work was *The House of Fame* (written in three books between 1374 and 1385). The narrator, or poet, dreams that he is in a temple of Venus, the walls of which are decorated with the story of Virgil's *Aeneid*. He summarizes the *Aeneid*, stressing the tragic love of Queen Dido for Aeneas (an episode that Chaucer expanded by borrowings from Ovid's *Heroides*). When the dreamer leaves the temple, he finds himself in a desert from which he is rescued by a friendly but loquacious golden eagle.

In Book 2, the eagle carries the frightened narrator to the heavens. In the course of his conversation with the eagle, the poet reveals that he spends all of his spare time reading and is therefore unaware of what is actually going on in the world. He is especially ignorant of the affairs and intrigues of love. The eagle tells the narrator that he will now have the opportunity to hear "tidings" of "love's folk" as a compensation for having served Venus and Cupid long and unrewarded and that he is being transported to Fame's dwelling to learn about life at firsthand.

In Book 3, the narrator reaches the temple of the goddess Fame. There he finds that the goddess arbitrarily grants or refuses men's pleas for fame, either good or evil, or for obscurity. He then goes to the House of Tidings, which is full of reports, both true and false. As he looks for tidings of love, he sees a "man of great authority." Here the poem inexplicably breaks off. Perhaps the end of the work is lost; perhaps Chaucer was unable to find a statement worthy of utterance by the "man of great authority."

Throughout the poem the narrator's perplexity, skepticism, and detachment in the face of the rich insights, images, and doctrines offered to him in his dream seem to be a wryly comic comment on the confusion of the poet as he attempts to reduce to order the chaos of experience and imagination. As in *The Book of the Duchess*, Chaucer treats the relationship among books, dreams, and waking, but the component parts cohere far less in *The House of Fame* than in the earlier work. The chief irony of *The House of Fame* lies in its presentation of fame and love, which, instead of enlightening the dreamer, puzzle and even repel him. Since neither fame nor love fare well in Chaucer's delineation of them, the dreamer's skepticism in the face of his own vision is at once an unsatisfying and yet entirely justified reaction. *The House of Fame* delights by its exuberance and variety but puzzles by the obscurity of its larger design and meaning. It also provides evidence of Chaucer's wide reading, notably Dante's *Divine Comedy*, which probably furnished the prototype for Chaucer's eagle.

"The Parliament of Fowls" and Other Works. In *The Parliament of Fowls* (early 1380's?), Chaucer abandoned the traditional octosyllabic couplet of French courtly origin, which he had used earlier, for a 7-line stanza of his own invention. Again, as in *The Book of the Duchess* and *The House of Fame*, Chaucer links books and dreams, this time exploring the nature as well as the social ramifications of love. After reading a philosophical tract by Cicero, the narrator dreams that he is before a beautiful, walled garden over whose gate are two conflicting inscriptions. One beckons the reader to bliss and the other warns him of misery within. The dreamer enters and sees a temple full of famous, suffering lovers. Within the garden he also sees the goddess Nature surrounded by birds who, since it is Valentine's day, have come to choose their mates. Three aristocratic eagles vie for a beautiful female eagle. The other birds who are watching the proceedings offer a running commentary that ranges from sentimental praise to the sharp, realistic criticism of the lower classes of fowls, who must await the female eagle's decision before choosing their own mates. When the female eagle declares that she needs another year to make up her mind, Nature acquiesces in the delay, but meanwhile allows the lesser birds to make their matches. They then sing a hymn of praise to summer, the season of love, and the dreamer awakes.

In this poem the waking crisis or "sickness" that is purged by the dream-vision is the narrator's bewilderment and uneasiness at the power of love. The ambiguous quality of love is hinted at in the double inscription on the garden gate. However, the dreamer learns that the terrors of love are confined to a small corner of its garden (the temple). On the whole, love is a part of nature and society (the parliament of birds), in which, to be sure, it raises problems, but ones that can be handled.

As with the emotion of grief in *The Book of the Duchess*, Chaucer here is not so much explicating love as commenting on its ability to confer a liberating influence on the hitherto inhibited poetic imagination. The high good humor in which the parliament of the birds is described and the realistic voices of the lower fowl, which offer an amusing commentary on society, are special triumphs of Chaucer's sympathetic art.

In the 1380's Chaucer worked on several expanded narrative poems, returning to the conventional rhythms and meters of French courtly origin, and began the uncompleted epic *Anelida and Arcite*. At this time he also remade Boccaccio's Latin epic, the *Teseide*, into a shorter work that became the *Knight's Tale* of the *Canterbury Tales*. His prose writings in the early 1380's include his translation of Boethius' *The Consolation of Philosophy*, which is thought to have been done shortly before *Troilus and Criseyde* since its influence on that poem is quite clear.

"Troilus and Criseyde." This magnificent love story was Chaucer's greatest artistic achievement in the field of extended narrative. Chaucer's work was an adaptation of Boccaccio's *Filostrato*, which itself was an expansion of the original Troilus and Cressida episode in Benoît de Sainte-Maure's 12th century poem *Roman de Troie*. In reworking Boccaccio's version, Chaucer contributed memorable characterizations, especially the comic character Pandarus and the sensitive, finely drawn narrator, and constructed a brilliant and provocative complex of fate, fortune, and personal weakness that ultimately dooms the lovers' search for happiness.

Troilus and Criseyde is composed in five books in the 7-line stanza or "rhyme royal" used in *The Parliament of Fowls*. Criseyde is the daughter of Calchas, a Trojan soothsayer who flees to the Greeks when he realizes through his gift of foresight that Troy is doomed. Left behind by her father, she finds herself in an awkward and delicate position and is reluctant to accept the attentions of the valiant Trojan warrior-prince Troilus, who is deeply in love with her. Gradually, through the efforts of Pandarus, her uncle and Troilus' friend, she is persuaded to accept Troilus as her lover, and for three years they share a secret but profound felicity.

Calchas, however, convinces the Greeks to exchange an important Trojan captive for his daughter. Since neither Criseyde nor Troilus are prepared to expose their love by fleeing together, she goes to the Greeks but promises to return to Troilus in 10 days. However, finding it impossible to keep the promise, she convinces herself that a reunion with her beloved is not to be and gradually succumbs to the ardent suit of Diomede, a Greek. The faithful Troilus becomes deeply distraught when he learns of Criseyde's infidelity. Finally he dies in battle and his soul rises to the heavens, whence it can look down on earth and smile at the follies of man. The poem ends with the narrator's advice to young people to seek the eternal love of Christ, rather than to emulate Troilus and Criseyde.

In this work, Chaucer brilliantly and sympathetically explored the enormous complexity of a love relationship. Both as a sensitive human being and as an accomplished poet he was acutely aware of the problems encountered in presenting such a relationship credibly and fully. Ultimately, *Troilus and Criseyde* is less about love than about creating a love story—that is, about the relationship between art and experience. Both experience and art produce any great story, and the presence in *Troilus and Criseyde* of two artists—the intrusive Chaucerian narrator, and Pandarus, who creates the love affairs in a special sense—reveals Chaucer's great sensitivity to the counteraction of the two components.

The real protagonist of the work is Troilus—noble, earnest, self-doubting—quick to find in events the hand of irresistible powers, such as Love and Fortune, which rob him of his freedom of action. However, it has always been Criseyde who has most fascinated readers. She seems the quintessential woman—human, full of charm and ambiguous motives—at once appealing and pathetic, afraid of love at first, yet capable of great though impermanent devotion to Troilus.

The narrator does not condemn Criseyde outright for her infidelity to Troilus; she is, he says, "slydynge of corage" rather than opportunistic or wicked. Chaucer surely intended that she be seen as an example of the ambiguity of all experience. Her actions should not be sorted into a consistent, uniquely motivated pattern of behavior; rather, her portrait illustrates at once the triumph and the defeat of the artist in his attempt to comprehend and portray life and art.

"The Legend of Good Women." Shortly after completing *Troilus and Criseyde*, Chaucer began writing *The Legend of Good Women*. This work represented his first experiment with a collection of stories within a narrative framework. In a dream-vision prologue, the god of love accuses the poet of having slandered women in works such as *Troilus and Criseyde*. He commands the poet to undertake a series of "legends" (a word applied in Chaucer's day to pious tales) about "love's martyrs," faithful women who had suffered for their love. (The prologue offers yet another example of Chaucer's fascination with the relationship among books, dreams, and actual experiences; Chaucer later revised the prologue, leaving two versions that offer interesting comparisons in their artistic and thematic differences.) Chaucer planned to write 20 legends, but abandoned the work part way through the ninth tale.

"Canterbury Tales." About 1387, Chaucer began working on the *Canterbury Tales* (q.v.). Its composition involved the inclusion of tales which he had already written and the creation of new ones. He also worked out an ingenious narrative framework within which to present his stories—a pilgrimage originating in London, undertaken by some 30 people who are going to the shrine of St. Thomas à Becket at Canterbury. En route to and from Canterbury they amuse themselves by telling stories of all types.

The work, written for the most part in rhymed couplets, opens with an idealized description of the earth's joyful reawakening in spring. The narrator then discusses each of the pilgrims in a General Prologue, in which all of Chaucer's descriptive skills, as well as his powers of observation, his piercing irony, his sense of humor, and his ability to adapt and transform his source materials are brilliantly revealed. Some of the characters, such as the Prioress and the Wife of Bath, have their human weaknesses thoroughly but not viciously exposed. Through his portraits of other characters, including the Reeve, the Man of Law, the Physician, the Pardoner, the Summoner, and the Friar, Chaucer shows the relationship between the personal vices of the individual and the corruption that exists in the church and in other social institutions. Finally, there are a few ideal figures—the humble Parson, the worthy Knight, and the unworldly Clerk of Oxford. According to the rules laid down by Harry Bailly, the host of the tavern outside London where the travelers are staying, each pilgrim must tell two tales on the way to the shrine and two tales on the way back. The teller of the best tale (as judged by the host, who will accompany the assemblage to Canterbury) is to receive a free dinner.

Of the 120 tales provided for in this scheme, Chaucer wrote only all or part of 24. Among the outstanding tales are the ribald fabliaux of the Miller and the Reeve; the Knight's expansive philosophical romance; the Nun's Priest's Tale, a satiric beast fable; and the Parson's prose sermon on the Seven Deadly Sins. Several tales are concerned with marriage: The Wife of Bath uses marriage as the subject of her self-justifying theories of female sovereignty; the Merchant offers a bitterly ironic and corrosive story about matrimony; and the Franklin reveals an optimistic, genteel, middle-class vision of the sacrament.

As the pilgrimage unfolds, the participants engage in lively conversations and arguments between tales. There are also interruptions within tales during which the characters enter into relationships (usually of rivalry) with one another or develop and enrich by their actions the portraits presented in the General Prologue.

In many cases the interaction between the pilgrims, as well as the progressive revelation of character, color the tales themselves, heightening their import or their irony. For example, the prologue and tale of the Wife of Bath overtly serve to justify her wrenching of sovereignty from each of her five husbands in turn. Only thus, according to her, can there be bliss in wedlock. Yet both prologue and tale abound in points, unconsciously made by the Wife herself, that contradict her and expose her as a shrew for whom the pleasure in marriage is strife in and out of bed. Conversely, the Pardoner (a minor ecclesiastical official whose traffic in indulgences invited widespread corruption) revels in describing his villainy in the prologue and in underscoring it in his tale (a hypocritical sermon condemning his own special vice, greed for money). A superb actor, the Pardoner exaggerates his vices of character, while the Wife of Bath tries to reduce and to rationalize hers.

Chaucer reserves a special irony for his narrator, who is Chaucer himself in the role of a character accompanying the pilgrims. The naïveté of Chaucer the narrator and his apparently unsystematic descriptions of the pilgrims in the General Prologue enable Chaucer the poet to make telling points at his characters' expense. When it is the narrator's turn to relate a tale, he knows only one in verse, the inept popular romance of Sir Thopas, which the host interrupts in disgust, prompting the narrator to reply with a long, tedious moral tale in prose. Yet here, too, Chaucer's wit is double-edged, for Sir Thopas is actually a hilarious satire on popular romances, composed with malicious skill.

The *Canterbury Tales* ranks as one of the unquestioned masterpieces of world literature. It is outstanding for its immense variety, brilliant characterization, psychological insights, and gusto, and for the loving accuracy with which Chaucer delineates the human condition.

Shorter Poems. Chaucer's shorter poems, written at various times throughout his life, include translations and standard imitations of French ballades, and verses on love, politics, and religion. Two political poems, *Lack of Steadfastness* and *The Former Age*, written late in Chaucer's life, reflect his bitterness at England's decadence under Richard II. Of special interest among his shorter poems is *The Complaint of Mars*, a metaphorical treatment of the love of Mars for Venus in terms of the heavenly movements of the two planets bearing their names. Using this device, Chaucer puts the love affair in a double perspective—one human, personal, and pathetic; the other detached, scientific, and determined. Such an ambiguous attitude toward the failure of love inevitably recalls the larger aims of *Troilus and Criseyde*, which may have been composed during the same period.

Chaucer's Language. Although Chaucer's English and modern English are closely connected, there are several basic differences between them. (1) The vowels had values nearer those of modern Continental European languages than those of present-day English (after Chaucer's time, stressed vowels in English underwent diphthongization and shifts of position). (2) Consonants and consonant groups now silent or simplified were given full value. (3) Some Germanic grammatical forms—for example, the past participial prefix y- (compare German ge-)—have disappeared from modern English, and inflections of nouns and verbs have been simplified. (4) In many words ending in -e or -es, the unstressed "e" was pronounced, at least in Chaucer's poetic language. (5) English orthography has become much more regular than in the days before the introduction of printed books.

These divergencies from modern English can be illustrated in the following lines from the General Prologue of the *Canterbury Tales*:

A knyght ther was and that a worthy man,
That fro the tyme that he first bigan
To riden out, he loved chivalrie,
Trouthe and honour, fredom and courtesie.

In this example, (1) the stressed vowels of "tyme" and "riden" have the same sound as "team" in modern English; the stressed vowels of "loved" and "that" sound approximately like those of "foot" and "hot," respectively, in modern En-

glish. (2) The initial consonant of "knyght" is sounded, and the -gh- group has a value approximately that of the German -ch in "ach." (3) The infinitive ending -en in "riden" has been dropped in modern English ("ride"). (4) The final -e of "tyme" in line two must be pronounced to make the line scan, as must the final -ed in "loved" in line three (but the final -e of "trouthe" in line four is elided with the initial vowel of the following word. (5) The same vowel is orthographically represented by "y" in "tyme" and "i" in "riden."

There are also numerous differences in vocabulary between Chaucer's English and modern English. Many of the words he used are no longer current and others have acquired different meanings. Although some readers may welcome the challenge of enjoying Chaucer in the original Middle English, there are numerous renderings of his major works into modern English.

Influence. Chaucer's style and techniques have been imitated through the centuries, but rarely with much success. The 15th century "Chaucerians" were numerous and idolatrous, but most of them lacked poetic genius. The Elizabethan poet Edmund Spenser was influenced by Chaucer's versification. Shakespeare borrowed Chaucer's plot for his drama *Troilus and Cressida* but rejected the earlier master's tone and vision. In the 17th and 18th centuries, John Dryden and Alexander Pope modernized some of his tales.

Generally, however, from the 16th through the 18th centuries Chaucer was patronizingly revered as the "father of English poetry"—an untutored genius who accomplished miracles using a rude language in an uncultivated nation. It was not until the 19th century that his greatness was rediscovered, and even then Matthew Arnold denied him "high seriousness," a judgment accurate in one sense but revealing a certain insensitivity to the depths of Chaucer's comic genius. Chaucer's reputation has continued to grow in the 20th century, especially in the United States, where his work has been the subject of much scholarship.

ROBERT W. HANNING, *Columbia University*

Bibliography

Chaucer's Works are available in various editions, including **Donaldson, E. Talbot**, ed., *Chaucer: An Anthology for the Modern Reader* (New York 1958); **Robinson, Fred N.**, ed., *Complete Works* (Boston and London 1957); and **Tatlock, John Strong Perry**, ed., *The Modern Reader's Chaucer*, rev. ed. (New York 1938).
Baum, Paull F., *Chaucer: A Critical Appreciation* (Durham, N. C., 1958).
Bowden, Muriel, *A Reader's Guide to Geoffrey Chaucer* (New York 1964).
Brewer, Derek, *Chaucer*, 2d ed. (London 1958).
Bronson, Bertrand, *In Search of Chaucer* (Toronto 1960).
Clemen, Wolfgang, *Chaucer's Early Poetry* (London 1963).
Coghill, Nevill, *The Poet Chaucer* (New York 1949).
Crow, Martin M., and **Olson, Clair C.**, eds., *Chaucer Life Records* (Austin, Texas, 1966).
French, Robert D., *A Chaucer Handbook*, 2d ed. (New York 1947).
Kittredge, George L., *Chaucer and His Poetry* (Cambridge, Mass., 1915).
Lowes, John L., *The Art of Geoffrey Chaucer* (London 1931).
Muscatine, Charles, *Chaucer and the French Tradition* (Berkeley and Los Angeles 1959).
Payne, Robert O., *The Key of Remembrance: A Study of Chaucer's Poetics* (New Haven 1963).
Preston, Raymond, *Chaucer* (London and New York 1952).
Rickert, Edith, *Chaucer's World* (New York 1948).
Root, Robert K., *The Poetry of Chaucer*, rev. ed. (New York 1922).
Wagenknecht, Edward, ed., *Chaucer: Modern Essays in Criticism* (New York 1959).

CHAUDIÈRE RIVER, shō-dyâr', in southeastern Quebec, Canada. It rises in Lake Mégantic and flows northward about 120 miles (193 km) to the St. Lawrence River just west of Lévis. Its name, which means "cauldron" in French, refers to the rapids along its course, the largest of which is Chaudière Falls, 4 miles (6 km) above its mouth. In the American Revolution, the river was the route followed by Benedict Arnold's American forces on their way to attack the city of Quebec late in 1775.

CHAULIAC, shō-lyàk', **Guy de** (c. 1300–c. 1368), French surgeon and medical writer, who was the most famous surgeon of the Middle Ages in Europe and the author of an important text on surgery. Born at Chauliac in the Gévaudan region, he obtained a good medical education at the universities of Montpellier and Bologna. He specialized in surgery and became the personal physician to several popes.

Chauliac's book *Chirurgia magna* (*The Great Surgery*—the best modern edition, by E. Nicaise, was published in Paris in 1890) was the most important surgical text in its time, and it was often consulted in succeeding centuries. In it Chauliac recommends a thorough knowledge of human anatomy as a requirement for a surgeon. He also describes innovations in the surgical repair of hernias and cataracts, the removal of cancerous growths, and the diagnosis of bladder stones by means of a catheter. His remarks on dentistry and the history of surgery are also noteworthy. Although Chauliac made many contributions to the development of surgery, his advocacy of unnecessary surgical procedures also impeded its progress in some respects.

JERRY STANNARD, *University of Kansas*

CHAULMOOGRA OIL, chôl-mōō'grə, an oil once widely used in the treatment of leprosy. It is obtained from the seeds of a Far Eastern tree (*Taraktogenos kurtzii*). A closely related oil, hydnocarpus oil, is obtained from several trees of the genus *Hydnocarpus*. Both oils contain unsaturated fatty acids. Although these oils have been used for centuries in the treatment of leprosy, there is no conclusive evidence of their effectiveness, and they are being replaced by the sulfones.

ANDRES GOTH, M. D.
University of Texas Southwestern Medical School

CHAUMETTE, shō-met, **Pierre Gaspard** (1763–1794), French revolutionist, who was procurator general of the Commune of Paris. Born in Nevers on May 24, 1763, he outgrew the narrow provincialism that was characteristic of the rural French, and went to Paris in 1789 to study medicine. In the capital he joined the radical Cordeliers club and contributed to the *Révolutions de Paris*, Louis Prudhomme's newspaper. He signed the petition for the dethronement of Louis XVI at the Champs de Mars on July 17, 1791, and a year later was a member of the insurrectional commune that came into existence on Aug. 10, 1792.

As procurator general of the Paris Commune he worked extremely hard to improve the lot of the poor. Hospital reform was one of his chief projects. He sought to provide each patient with a bed, where previously up to six persons had shared one. He banned corporal punishment in the schools, regulated prostitution, provided the poor with decent burials, and opposed the circulation of obscene literature. These efforts and his own impeccable private life won him the respect of the ordinary Parisian.

On the national political level Chaumette favored a searching social revolution. He opposed the moderate Girondists, attacking them in the commune and before the Revolutionary Tribunal. A founder of the "cult of reason," he presented an actress dressed as the goddess of reason to the National Convention. He advocated the conversion of Notre Dame cathedral into the "foyer of reason," but Robespierre and the Convention reestablished freedom of worship.

When extremists in the Paris Commune menaced the authority of the Committee of Public Safety, the Committee suppressed them in 1794. Chaumette's attitudes had won him a host of powerful enemies, and he was arrested with the followers of the extremist Jacques René Hébert. He went to the guillotine in Paris on April 13, 1794.

RICHARD M. BRACE
Oakland University

CHAUMONOT, shō-mô-nō', **Pierre Joseph Marie** (1611–1693), Jesuit missionary. He was born on March 6, 1611, near Châtillon-sur-Seine, France. He ran away to study music and, after traveling through Italy, he settled in Umbria, where he tutored at the Jesuit secondary school and later taught at the university. In 1632 he entered the Jesuit novitiate of St. André in Rome to prepare for the ministry.

On Aug. 1, 1639, he arrived in Canada to work as a missionary among the Huron Indians. When the Iroquois warriors attacked the Huron tribe, Chaumonot led some 400 survivors to a new settlement on Isle d'Orléans opposite Quebec. In the interval between 1655 and 1658 he worked among the Onandoga, Oneida, and Cayuga Indians near Lake Cayuga, N. Y., where he founded the congregation of the Holy Family. Returning to Canada with 50 colonists, Chaumonot discovered that the Mohawk Indians had destroyed his mission at Isle d'Orléans. In 1688, accompanied by the last remnants of the Huron nation, he journeyed to Ancienne Lorette near Quebec, where he died on Feb. 1, 1693.

Before his death, Chaumonot wrote his *Autobiographie* (published in 1858) and also a valuable Huron grammar and a dictionary of dialects, which were translated into English in 1831.

DENNIS P. WOOD, S. J.
Loyola Seminary, Shrub Oak, N. Y.

CHAUMONT, shō-môn', is an industrial city and rail center in northern France. It lies on a steep headland between the Marne and Suize rivers, about 140 miles (225 km) southeast of Paris. Also known as *Chaumont-en-Bassigny*, it is the capital of the department of Haute-Marne.

Chaumont was built around the 10th century castle of the counts of Champagne. The castle now exists only as a ruin. Chaumont's church of St. Jean-Baptiste was built in the 13th century, and was greatly altered and expanded in the 16th century.

On March 1, 1814, Britain, Russia, Austria, and Prussia signed a treaty at Chaumont in which they pledged themselves to overthrow Napoleon and restore peace to Europe. During World War I, Chaumont was the headquarters of the American Expeditionary Forces under Gen. John J. Pershing. Population: (1962) 21,462.

CHAUNCEY, chôn'sē, **Isaac** (1772–1840), American naval captain, who served in the Tripolitan War (1801–1805) and the War of 1812. He was born in Black Rock, Conn., on Feb. 20, 1772. Chauncey joined the Navy as a lieutenant in 1799 and commanded several ships. He was commended for his conduct in the attack on Tripoli on Aug. 28–29, 1804.

At the outbreak of the War of 1812, Chauncey was chosen commander of the U. S. naval forces on Lake Ontario and Lake Erie. His headquarters were at Sackets Harbor, N. Y., where he established a naval base and built a fleet of small vessels. He supported the Army in several operations but did not succeed in maintaining naval supremacy over the British on the lakes. After the war he served on the board of navy commissioners in Washington, D. C., and was its president when he died there on Jan. 27, 1840.

CHAUNCY, chôn'sē, **Charles** (1592–1672), American clergyman and educator. Chauncy was born in Yardley Bury, Hertfordshire, England, in November 1592. He was educated at Westminster School and at Trinity College, Cambridge, where he was a fellow and professor of Greek. He was also a priest in the Church of England and was twice brought before ecclesiastical commissions for criticizing the church. In 1634 he was imprisoned for several months. In 1638, Chauncy fled to New England, where he preached at Plymouth and was pastor at Scituate, Massachusetts, still in conflict with the established church.

As Chauncy was preparing to return to England, a committee was sent from Harvard to ask him to be president, providing he would refrain from teaching his controversial doctrines. In 1654, Chauncy became the second president of Harvard, succeeding Henry Dunster. Chauncy was a successful president and remained in office until his death on Feb. 19, 1672.

CHAUSSON, shō-sôn', **Ernest** (1855–1899), French composer, who was a major figure in the postromantic movement in French music. He belonged to the group of French romantics who drew their inspiration from César Franck and in whose writing the Franckian traits of serenity, mysticism, and introspection predominate. However, there is also a strong Wagnerian influence in some of Chausson's orchestral pieces and works that he wrote for the stage.

Life. Chausson was born in Paris on Jan. 20, 1855, and was educated for the law. His first formal instruction in music did not take place until he was 25 years old, when, in 1880, he entered the Paris Conservatory and studied composition with Marie Duparc and Jules Massenet. The conservatory's strict academic procedures and curriculum soon forced him to leave, and he studied privately from 1880 to 1883 with César Franck, whose influence on Chausson as composer and as man was decisive and permanent.

Chausson was known as "a very talented amateur." He inherited a large personal fortune, which made it unnecessary for him to earn an income from his music. From 1889 he served as secretary of the Société Nationale de Musique, which he strongly supported and which introduced several of his works. Chausson died on June 10, 1899, from a fractured skull, the result of a cycling accident near his home in Limay.

Works. The impress of Franck on Chausson's music first became evident in *Viviane* (1882), an orchestral tone poem based on an Arthurian legend, and in *Poème de l'amour et de la mer* (1882–1892), a piece for voice and orchestra. Franck's influence is fully realized in two Chausson masterpieces completed in the 1890's: the Concerto for Piano, Violin, and String Quartet, which was introduced by Eugène Ysaÿe and his ensemble in Brussels on March 4, 1892; and *Poème*, a work for violin and orchestra, whose world premiere was given by Ysaÿe and the Colonne Orchestra in Paris on April 4, 1897. *Poème* became Chausson's most popular work and the one by which he is most often represented on concert programs. It also was used by Antony Tudor for his ballet *Jardin aux lilas* (1936; *Lilac Garden*).

Still another major Chausson work is his Symphony in B-Flat Major, which, though it was completed in 1890, did not have its first performance until April 18, 1898, in Paris. The symphony's chromatic harmonies and rich orchestration are evidence of Chausson's interest in Wagner, but in this work as in most of his other works, the gentle introspection and pervasive mysticism of Franck can be detected, particularly in the slow movement.

Chausson also wrote two unpublished operas, *Les caprices de Marianne* (about 1880) and *Hélène* (1884–1885); and a third opera, *Le roi Arthus*, which was first performed in 1903 in Brussels. He also composed many art songs, including some to texts by Verlaine, Villiers de L'Isle-Adam, and Maeterlinck, and a number of choral works, including several motets.

DAVID EWEN, *Author of* *"The Complete Book of Classical Music"*

Further Reading: Barricelli, Jean Pierre, and Weinstein, Leo, *Ernest Chausson: The Composer's Life and Works* (Norman, Okla., 1955); Cooper, Martin, *French Music* (London and New York 1951).

CHAUTAUQUA MOVEMENT, shə-tô'kwə, a broad system of popular adult education that took its name from a program established in 1874 on Lake Chautauqua, New York. The founders, Dr. John H. Vincent, secretary of the Methodist Sunday School and later bishop of the Methodist Episcopal Church, and Lewis Miller, a businessman active in church affairs, originally planned to train Sunday school teachers of all Protestant denominations in an attractive place during the summer. Within a few years, however, the chautauqua idea was extended to include lectures, discussions, and home readings reminiscent of the lyceum movement (see LYCEUM) founded by Josiah Holbrook in 1826. The wide scope of the chautauqua movement that developed through the years influenced the development of adult education in the United States and elsewhere for almost a century. Programs such as the adult summer school, university extension, correspondence courses, and "great books" discussion groups had their roots in chautauqua.

The Growth of the Movement. Known at first as the Chautauqua Sunday School Assembly, the new movement offered a combination of formal classes, informal conferences, recreation, and entertainment to over 1,000 participants during a 10-day period in August. Despite their affiliation with the Methodist Episcopal Church, the organizers did not identify the new program with their denomination.

The success of the initial year encouraged the expansion of the program. Hebrew and Greek were added in 1875, English literature in 1876, and French and German in 1878, along with in-service courses for public school teachers. Also in 1878, the Chautauqua Literary and Scientific Circle (C.L.S.C.) was organized as a 4-year plan of home reading in English, American, European, and classical history and literature. This plan is considered to be the first basic program of coordinated instruction on a national level for men and women in the United States. During any one year, all reading circles or classes studied the same works. Books were supplemented by a monthly magazine called the *Chautauquan*, published from 1880 to 1914, which included articles related to yearly themes, discussion questions, bibliographies, literary extracts, inspirational statements, and news. Those who successfully completed the 4-year course were awarded diplomas. Eminent literary figures, including William Cullen Bryant, Lyman Abbott, and Edward Everett Hale, supported the program, and within a short time, the enrollment of the C.L.S.C. increased from an initial 7,000 to 60,000 participants. By 1910, however, there were competing forms of adult education, and the C.L.S.C. enrollment decreased to about 10,000. The program ceased to operate on a national scale in 1914, but local reading circles based on it continued all over the United States.

The development of the Chautauqua summer school department, particularly between 1883 and 1897 under the direction of Dr. William Rainey Harper, paralleled the expansion of the C.L.S.C. The summer school ultimately offered courses in the schools of music, speech, physical education, domestic science, theater, theology, library training (set up by the great librarian Melvil Dewey), a normal school of languages, and a college of liberal arts. The instructors were often leading scholars and educators, and the program met with great success.

As professor of Hebrew at Yale College, Dr. Harper had inaugurated the first Chautauqua correspondence course in 1879 and later directed the entire Chautauqua correspondence study system. After becoming president of the University of Chicago in 1892, Dr. Harper organized correspondence study courses in the university's extension division. For some years Chautauqua conferred a limited number of degrees of bachelor of divinity and bachelor of arts on graduates of its correspondence study program, but as major universities instituted correspondence work, Chautauqua discontinued its own plan.

From 1902 onward, the movement was known as the Chautauqua Institution and was organized under a new charter. Its work was coordinated by departments of administration, instruction, grounds and buildings, and press. In 1909, Chautauqua had a summer resident population of 10,000 to 12,000 people who lived and worked in 30 buildings. Some 188 courses were offered to over 2,300 students. In addition to the formal program of instruction, Chautauqua offered popular lectures, literary readings, religious talks and sermons, concerts, and entertainment programs. In later years, conferences were organized on current literature and on contemporary social, political, economic, and religious issues. Social, athletic, and garden clubs were also organized, and concert and dramatic performances by noted artists increased.

Geographical Extent. By 1909 there were some 103 local centers based on the original Chau-

tauqua Institution throughout the United States. An authoritative estimate reported that close to two million people attended these centers. There was also a center in Canada and one in England. The popular programs offered at these local chautauquas varied in nature and effectiveness, but they frequently included classes in the Bible, elocution, cooking, and physical training. By 1924 it was reported that about one third of the population of the United States had had some contact with chautauqua programs, although only about 50,000 enrolled annually in the original institution on Lake Chautauqua. For some years summer courses for credit were conducted by the School of Education of New York University, and, more recently, by Syracuse University. In addition, courses in the arts have been offered on a noncredit basis.

Many people in the United States were put in touch with the chautauqua movement by the development of the "traveling chautauquas," groups that toured the country giving lectures and entertainment. These circuit groups were initiated in the early 1900's as a commercial venture and reached their height in the years just prior to World War I. Some traveling chautauqua meetings degenerated almost to a circus-type atmosphere and were highlighted by political and evangelical oratory and popular musical entertainment, with no intellectual or cultural pretensions. Nevertheless, the traveling chautauquas did bring some cultural stimulation to isolated communities.

Significance of the Movement. The significance of the chautauqua movement should be examined in light of the social and cultural situation of the 20th century United States. The growing influence of films and radio after 1910 tended to weaken the attraction of chautauqua programs. With the advent of television, the popularity of chautauqua lectures and entertainment declined still further.

Although the mass attraction of the movement has disappeared, the original Chautauqua center still continues its adult educational activity, and the movement as a whole has made a lasting imprint on the development of a peculiarly American culture.

WILLIAM W. BRICKMAN
The University of Pennsylvania

Further Reading: Case, Robert O., and Case, Victoria, *We Called It Culture* (New York 1948); DaBoll, Irene, and DaBoll, Raymond F., *Recollections of the Lyceum and Chautauqua Circuits* (Freeport, Me., 1966); Richmond, Rebecca, *Chautauqua, an American Place* (New York 1943).

CHAUTEMPS, shō-tän', **Camille** (1885–1963), French political leader. He was born in Paris on Feb. 1, 1885. A leader of the Radical Socialists, he held numerous ministerial posts in the 1920's and 1930's and was premier of France three times (1930, 1933–1934, and 1937–1938). Though he resigned the premiership in March 1938 upon Germany's annexation of Austria, he continued as vice premier until 1940.

Following the collapse of France in 1940, Chautemps served briefly in Marshal Pétain's cabinet and represented the Vichy government on a secret mission to the United States. Convicted of collaboration by the postwar French government, he remained in the United States until 1954, when the statute of limitations voided his 5-year prison sentence. He later returned to the United States from France, and died in Washington, D. C., on July 1, 1963.

CHAUVINISM, shō'və-niz-əm, a word derived from the name of Nicolas Chauvin, a soldier of the French Republic and the First Empire. His excessive admiration for Napoleon made him an object of ridicule among his comrades. In time the word "chauvinism" was coined from his name as a synonym for those who displayed extreme nationalism and national pride.

Chauvin was lampooned frequently on the French stage in the 1830's. The figure of Chauvin appeared in a play of Scribe's called *Le soldat laboureur* and in vaudeville sketches, including one by the popular playwrights Charles Théodore and Jean Hippolyte Cogniard called *La cocarde tricolore* (1831). The term "chauvinism" was soon picked up by French journalists and politicians.

CHÁVEZ, chä'väs, **Carlos** (1899–1978), Mexican composer, who drew on native Mexican and Mexican Indian sources to create a national musical art recognized throughout the world. Virtually single-handedly, he developed and modernized the musical culture of Mexico—as educator, conductor, and composer.

Life. Chávez was born in Mexico City on June 13, 1899. He acquired some training in piano and harmony from private teachers, but his basic musical education came from his study of textbooks and musical scores. In 1922–1923 he traveled in Europe, where he learned of the advances made by the modernists, notably Schönberg (Schoenberg) and Stravinsky.

Returning to Mexico in 1923, Chávez inaugurated concerts in which the works of European modernists were given their first Mexican performances. From then on the impact of his personality on Mexico's musical life and development was far-reaching. In 1928 he organized Mexico's first symphony orchestra to give regular series of concerts and was its conductor from 1928 to 1948. He also overhauled the system of music education in Mexico and was director of the National Conservatory from 1928 to 1934. From 1933 to 1939 he headed the department of fine arts of the ministry of education.

Chávez made many appearances as guest conductor throughout the United States. He wrote two books, *Toward a New Music* (Eng. tr., 1937) and *Musical Thought* (1960); the latter is a compilation of his lectures at Harvard University during 1958–1959. Chávez died in Mexico City on Aug. 2, 1978.

Works. Chávez began to compose when he was 18. He did not establish a personal musical viewpoint, however, until he freed himself of European influences and thought in terms of Mexican music. After making a firsthand study of his country's folk songs and dances and its native instruments, he assimilated into his own compositions the basic characteristics of Mexican and Mexican Indian folk music—the stark simplicity of the melodic line, the primitive force of percussive sounds and complex rhythmic patterns, and the abrupt contrasts of mood. These tendencies were apparent in his first work to gain recognition, the ballet *El fuego nuevo* (1921; *New Fire*).

Chávez' major works include symphonies, concertos, string quartets, sonatas, and various shorter works. His cultivation of native Mexican elements resulted in two highly successful symphonies, *Sinfonía Antígona* (1933) and *Sinfonía India* (1935). In the suite *Xochipilli-Macuilxochitl* (1940) and Toccata for Percussion (1942) he made extensive use of native Mexican percussion instruments.

Among Chávez' more sophisticated later works is his opera *Panfilo and Lauretta*, which had its world premiere in New York City in 1957. His other compositions include the Sixth Symphony, commissioned by the New York Philharmonic Orchestra and introduced under Leonard Bernstein's direction in 1964; *Invention;* for string trio, first performed in 1965 at the third Inter-American Music Festival in Washington, D. C.; and the Second Violin Concerto (1965).

DAVID EWEN, *Author of "Complete Book of 20th Century Music"*

CHAVEZ, shä'ves, **Cesar** (1927–   ), American labor leader, who organized the California grape pickers into the first important farm-workers union in the United States. Chavez was born in Yuma, Ariz., on March 31, 1927, and grew up in a series of migrant labor camps in Arizona and California. He served in the Navy in 1944–1945, and after World War II returned to migrant farm work. In 1952 he joined the Community Service Organization (CSO) in San Jose, Calif., and led voter registration drives, helped Chicanos with immigration problems, and organized CSO chapters in other cities. In 1958 he became general director of the CSO but resigned from the organization in 1962 when it refused to create a farm-workers union.

Chavez began to organize the National Farm Workers Association in 1962, and by 1965 he had enrolled 1,700 families in it. In September 1965 his union joined migrant Filipino grape pickers in a strike against the growers that was to last for several years. The wine growers capitulated early in the struggle, but the table grape growers held out into the 1970's. Under Chavez' leadership the union, now called the United Farm Workers (UFW) and affiliated with the AFL-CIO, organized boycotts of nonunion farm products. Jurisdictional conflicts with the Teamsters Union continued until agreement was reached in March 1977 on recruitment of members.

CHAVEZ, shä'ves, **Dennis** (1888–1962), American public official. Born on April 8, 1888, at Los Chavez, N. Mex., he left school at 13 and he worked in behalf of local Democratic candidates before he could vote. His services as a Spanish interpreter in Sen. Andrieus A. Jones' 1916 campaign won him a Senate clerkship. After earning his LL. B. at Georgetown University in 1920, Chavez entered law practice in Albuquerque. He served in the state legislature and later in the U. S. Congress (1931–1935).

In 1935, Chavez was appointed to the U. S. Senate to fill a vacancy. Elected to that seat in 1936 and reelected four successive times, he served continuously until he died in Washington on Nov. 18, 1962. In the Senate, Chavez regularly supported New Deal bills. He championed the American Indian and measures to benefit Puerto Rico, thereby winning the nickname "Puerto Rico's senator." He supported reciprocal trade agreements, notably with Latin America. His work in the 1940's produced the federal Fair Employment Practices Commission and a program of federal aid for maternal and child care.

DAVID LINDSEY
California State College at Los Angeles

CHAYEFSKY, chī-ef'skē, **Paddy** (1923–   ), American playwright, known chiefly for his original television plays. He was born Sidney Chayefsky in New York City on June 29, 1923, and was educated at City College. His first major success as a writer was in the new medium of television, when he wrote *Holiday Song* (1952), a play dealing with Jewish religious life. His best-known work is *Marty,* which he wrote first as a television play in 1953; the film version won four Academy Awards in 1955.

Chayefsky was praised for his naturalistic depiction of "the wonderful world of the ordinary" in *Marty* and such later television plays as *The Bachelor Party* (1954; filmed 1957) and *The Catered Affair* (1955; filmed 1956). The same realistic quality was apparent in his first Broadway play, *The Middle of the Night* (1958), and in his original screenplay for *The Goddess* (1958). His other Broadway plays include *The Tenth Man* (1959), a return to Jewish folk comedy; *Gideon* (1961), which has a Biblical theme; and *The Passion of Josef D.* (1964), a play about Stalin. *The Latent Heterosexual* (1968), first performed in Dallas, recounts how an invert marries for tax-dodging purposes. An anthology of Chayefsky's television plays was published in 1955.

HOWARD SUBER
University of California, Los Angeles

CHAYOTE, chä-yō'tē, a perennial, trailing vine bearing edible, fleshy fruits. The chayote (*Sechium edule*), a member of the gourd family (Cucurbitaceae), may grow to 100 feet (30 meters) in length and each vine may produce up to several hundred fruit. The chayote is native to tropical America and is an important food plant in parts of Mexico and Central America. It is also grown to a limited extent in the southeastern United States. In the tropics the tubers (enlarged tips of underground stems) as well as the fruits are used for food.

The pear-shaped, one-seeded fruits vary in color from ivory white to dark green and range in size from about 3 ounces (90 grams) to 2 pounds (900 grams) in weight. The surface of the fruit may be either smooth or corrugated; the flesh should be fiberless and delicately flavored. Chayote is propagated from seed or cuttings.

JOHN P. McCOLLUM, *University of Illinois*

CHAZYAN SERIES, shä-zē'ən, the second-oldest series of the Ordovician System of rocks in North America. Laid during the Chazyan Epoch, about 470 million years ago, it succeeds the Canadian Series and underlies the Bolarian, or lower Mohawkian. The typical rocks near Chazy, N. Y., have about 1,000 feet (300 meters) of fossiliferous limestone, which contains the first abundant record of bryozoans and clams. The faunas in the Chazy rocks are provincial; the St. Peter Sandstone of the Mississippi Valley seems of equivalent age, but was laid in conditions adverse for marine life. The Whiterockian Stage of Nevada may include all of the Chazyan, though some believe it is older. Correlations of the typical Chazyan with European rock series are evident in few places, but it seems to correlate with the uppermost Arenigian, the Llanvirnian, and the lower Llandeilan. See also ORDOVICIAN.

MARSHALL KAY, *Columbia University*

CHEAPSIDE, in London, England, is a historic section and street extending from St. Paul's Cathedral eastward to the Mansion House (residence of the lord mayor). About midway between these landmarks is the Church of St. Mary-le-Bow. During the Middle Ages the area was called the Chepe (from the Anglo-Saxon word *cēap,* meaning "sale" or "bargain") and was an open square where markets or fairs were held. Streets leading from it, such as Bread Street and the Poultry, still bear the names of products 'that were sold there. The Mermaid Tavern, meeting place of Elizabethan poets and playwrights, stood in this section.

CHEBOKSARY, chi-bo-ksä'ri, is the capital of the Chuvash Autonomous Soviet Socialist Republic of the USSR in central European Russia. Located on the south bank of the Volga, it lies between Gorky on the west and Kazan on the east.

First mentioned as a population center in 1371, it became a fortress city in 1555. However, its growth as a major city did not begin until 1939, when it was linked by rail with Moscow and Kazan. A manufacturing center, especially of electrical equipment, it also processes crops and lumber from the surrounding region. Population: (1972) 227,000.

CHEBOYGAN, shē-boi'gən, is a port city in northern Michigan, the seat of Cheboygan county, 150 miles (241 km) north of Bay City. It is on Lake Huron, on the South Channel of the Straits of Mackinac, at the mouth of the Cheboygan River. The city, in a dairying and mixed farming area, is a year-round resort especially popular with fishermen. Three large inland lakes, Mullet, Black, and Burt, provide excellent sturgeon fishing. Black Lake State Forest, Hardwood State Forest, and Wilderness State Park are nearby. Cheboygan's port ships fish and local farm produce. Leading industries are paper mills, tool and die works, and factories making wood furniture and record player cases. Cheboygan was an important lumbering center in the late 1800's.

Incorporated as a city in 1889, Cheboygan is governed by a city manager. Population: 5,553.

CHECHEN-INGUSH AUTONOMOUS SOVIET SOCIALIST REPUBLIC, chi-chen'in-goōsh', is an administrative subdivision of the Russian republic in the USSR. Located in the Caucasus, it is 7,450 square miles (19,400 sq km) in area. Its capital is Grozny, an oil-producing center. Its population comprises two closely related ethnic groups of the north slopes of the Caucasus, the Chechen and the Ingush. These people, under the leadership of Shamyl, long resisted Russian penetration of the Caucasus, not falling under Russian rule until Shamyl's defeat in 1859.

Under the Soviet regime, the Chechen and Ingush were established as autonomous oblasts, which were merged in 1934 and made an autonomous republic in 1936. In World War II, some Chechen collaborated with the German invaders. In retaliation, Joseph Stalin dissolved the Chechen-Ingush ASSR in 1944 and exiled the entire population to Central Asia. Under Nikita Khrushchev, the exiles were allowed to return, and their republic was restored in 1957. Population: (1967 est.) 1,033,000.

THEODORE SHABAD
Editor of "Soviet Geography"

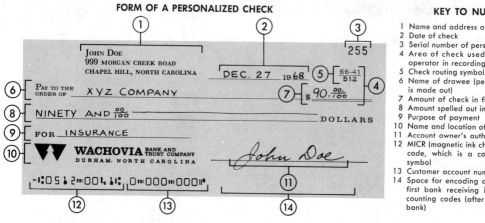

1 Name and address of account owner
2 Date of check
3 Serial number of personalized check
4 Area of check used by proof machine operator in recording and sorting checks
5 Check routing symbol
6 Name of drawee (person to whom check is made out)
7 Amount of check in figures
8 Amount spelled out in words
9 Purpose of payment
10 Name and location of bank
11 Account owner's authorized signature
12 MICR (magnetic ink character recognition) code, which is a coded transit routing symbol
13 Customer account number
14 Space for encoding amount of check (by first bank receiving it) and internal accounting codes (after receipt by drawee bank)

CHECK, a written order to the bank where the writer has his checking (demand deposit) account, telling the bank to pay a specific sum of money to a designated person or to "cash" (any holder of the check). By common estimate, over 90% of all money payments in the United States are made by check.

Writing a Check. Rules of proper check writing are few and simple: start writing at the extreme left end of each blank space, and use all the space provided; make sure the amount in numbers and the amount in words agree; sign your authorized signature; and write legibly and in ink. Penciled checks are legal, but they are easy for unscrupulous persons to erase and alter. Ink erasures are immediately detectable, however, on the tinted or patterned checks that most banks supply to customers.

Endorsement. A check made out to "cash" is already fully negotiable. A check drawn to a named person (the *drawee*) must be endorsed by that person, either in blank or restrictively, before its ownership can be transferred.

Endorsements are written on the back of a check, usually at its left-hand end. *Endorsement in blank* means that there is only the signature of the person to whom the check is drawn. *Restrictive endorsement* names the party to whom the check is being transferred; for instance, "Pay only to XYZ Company," followed by the drawee's signature, or "For deposit to my credit in Wachovia Bank and Trust Company," again followed by the drawee's signature. To avoid possible losses, careful check users prefer always to use restrictive rather than blank endorsements.

Collecting Checks. A check that is cashed at or deposited in a bank other than the one on which it is drawn must be presented to the "drawee bank" for payment (and deduction from its writer's account balance) by the bank that originally receives it. In the United States this process of presentation and payment takes place through the local clearinghouse if both banks are in the same town; otherwise, the nationwide check clearing and collecting facilities of the Federal Reserve System are used. To speed the payment of checks, especially nonlocal ones, each check has on it a check routing symbol and an MICR (magnetic ink character recognition) code.

Check Routing Symbol. Use of the check routing symbol by U. S. banks in sorting and routing checks for collection began in 1945. It appears as a fraction, in the upper right corner of each check, immediately above the "amount in figures" line. The numerator is the bank's American Bankers Association transit number; figures before the hyphen identify particular cities and states, those following it identify particular banks in those cities and states. In the illustrated check, for example, the transit number (66–41) specifies North Carolina (66) and, within North Carolina, Wachovia Bank and Trust Company (41).

The denominator is a Federal Reserve routing symbol, denoting the Federal Reserve bank or branch through which the check can be collected. It also shows whether the check will be received for immediate credit or deferred credit, according to Federal Reserve availability schedules. A sample schedule is shown below, with the symbols for the Fifth Federal Reserve District, including the 512 on the illustrated check.

Federal Reserve Bank of Richmond

Immediate Credit	510	Richmond
Deferred Credit	511	District of Columbia
	512	North Carolina
	513	South Carolina
	514	Virginia
	515	West Virginia

Baltimore Branch

Immediate Credit	520	Baltimore
Deferred Credit	521	Maryland
	522	West Virginia

Charlotte Branch

Immediate Credit	530	Charlotte
Deferred Credit	531	North Carolina
	532	South Carolina

Other Federal Reserve districts—there are 12 in all—follow similar patterns.

Electronic Check Processing. With a check's routing symbol printed just above its dollar amount in figures, a proof machine operator recording and sorting checks in a bank need only glance at the check's upper right-hand area to record and sort it for collection quickly. Still this process has proved too slow to handle the rapidly mounting volume of checks.

Fortunately, electronic equipment makes automated check handling feasible. Starting in 1956, checks began to carry (along their lower left-hand edge) an MICR code. The equipment "reads" the data fields of this code, and records and sorts checks automatically. The fields show the bank's routing symbol and condensed transit number (0512–0041 on the illustrated check). They also show the customer account number assigned by the bank. Space remains (under the signature) for the first bank receiving the check to encode its amount before processing it. Also, after receiving the check for payment, the bank it is drawn on may add internal accounting codes for its own use. See also BANKS AND BANKING— sections 1, 5, 7; FEDERAL RESERVE SYSTEM.

CLIFTON H. KREPS, JR.
University of North Carolina at Chapel Hill

CHECKERS is a game for two persons played on a board marked in 64 small squares of alternate colors (light and dark) in eight rows of eight squares each. Each contestant is provided with 12 disks, called *men* or *checkers;* the object is to move these pieces diagonally across the board in such a way as to capture all the opponent's men or block their progress. Because of the simplicity of its fundamentals, checkers is a popular children's game. At the expert's level, checkers ranks in profundity with the complicated game of chess.

Fundamentals of the Game. The players, designated as *black* and *white,* place the board between them so that each has a double corner of dark squares at his right. Each arranges his men on the first three rows of dark squares as shown in Fig. 1. The notation used in describing the game is based on numbering the squares as in Fig. 1. A move is denoted by the number of the square from which a piece starts, followed by the number of the square moved to, joined by a hyphen. In the notation, black and white moves alternate, and no distinction is made for color or captures.

Black makes the first move, and white counters. (There are 47 playable combinations of these first two moves.) Players alternate thereafter, moving on the dark squares only. The move is diagonally forward one square, if that square is vacant. For example, black might start by playing 11-15, or 9-13; and white might reply 22-18, or 24-20. A man may not move to an occupied square, but it may jump over and *capture* an adverse man on an adjacent square, if the square beyond is vacant. For example, if black opens 11-15 and white counters 22-18, then black must jump 15-22 and remove white's man on 18. White in turn must jump either 26-17 or 25-18,

BLACK

	1		2		3		4
5		6		7		8	
	9		10		11		12
13		14		15		16	
	17		18		19		20
21		22		23		24	
	25		26		27		28
29		30		31		32	

WHITE

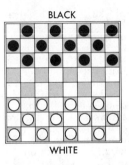

BLACK

WHITE

Fig. 1. Checkerboard shows men in place for start of the game. Checkers notation, as used with illustrations below, is based on numbering system given here.

and remove black's man on 22. If a jumping piece lands on a square from which another jump is possible it must continue to jump until it runs out of captures. A player must make a capturing move, if one is possible, but may choose if there is more than one. At the outset all checkers are *single men.*

The dark squares farthest from a player form the *king row.* A single man reaching one of these squares is crowned *king* by the opponent. The promotion is made by placing a second checker of the same color on top of the single one. A king may move both forward or backward one move at a time and jump one or more pieces in either or both directions. If a single man reaches the king row by capture, the turn to play ends with the crowning.

The winner is the first player to leave the adversary without a move, either by capturing or

PROBLEMS AND SOLUTIONS

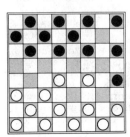

Fig. 2. White to play and win. Black has made only three moves here, but already has lost the game. *Solution:* 19-15, 10-19, 18-14, 9-18, 22-8, 4-11, 27-24, 20-27, 31-8 and white wins the game.

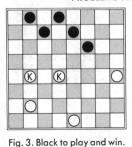

Fig. 3. Black to play and win. This shows the danger of "holes" where men are one square apart. Black sets up a stroke and captures three men in one play. *Solution:* 11-15, 18-11, 7-16, 20-11, 2-7, 11-2, 1-5, 2-9, 5-30. Black moves and wins the game.

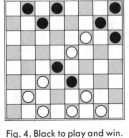

Fig. 4. Black to play and win. This is a situation where black forces the necessary holes in white's position, so that a winning stroke is possible. *Solution:* 6-10, 15-6, 1-10, 22-6, 2-9, 27-18, 8-29. Black gains a piece and wins the game.

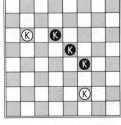

Fig. 5. Black to play and win. *Solution:* 15-18, 9-5, 10-6, 27-32, 19-23, 5-1, 6-9, 1-5, 9-14. Black forces an exchange and wins.

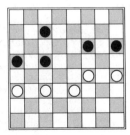

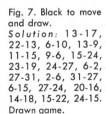

Fig. 6. Black to move and win. Black's plan is to force white's single man to square 13 and block him. *Solution:* 9-6, 5-1, 14-10, 1-5, 6-1, 5-9, 10-15, 9-5, 15-18, 5-9, 1-5, 9-6, 18-15, 21-17, 5-1, 6-9, 15-18, 17-13, 18-15, 9-14, 1-5, 14-17, 15-10, 17-22, 10-14, 22-25, 5-1, 25-22, 1-6, 22-25, 6-10, 25-22, 10-15, 22-25, 15-18, black wins.

Fig. 7. Black to move and draw. *Solution:* 13-17, 22-13, 6-10, 13-9, 11-15, 9-6, 15-24, 23-19, 24-27, 6-2, 27-31, 2-6, 31-27, 6-15, 27-24, 20-16, 14-18, 15-22, 24-15. Drawn game.

blocking all of his men. A game is drawn when both contestants agree that neither has a prospect of winning.

Strategy. A player seeks to maintain his *bridge*, in order to hamper adverse single men from becoming kings. The black bridge is formed by men on 1 and 3; white, by men on 30 and 32.

Because men have more mobility toward the center of the board, players try to control the *key squares:* 14, 15, 18, and 19. A man on either 14 or 19, for example, tends to cramp the opponent's move on that side of the board. On the other hand, black men on 21 or 28 or white men on 5 or 12 are isolated and thus weak.

The *move,* or opposition, is of tactical importance. Specifically, the move means having a chance to pin down the opponent. For example, with two men on the board—black on 11 and white on 23—if black moves he can trap white and win with 11-15; but if white moves, he wins with 23-19. When both players have the same number of men on the board, the move is calculated by totaling the men in either *system.* (Black's systems include all squares in files running from 1, 2, 3, and 4; white's systems include all squares in files running from 29, 30, 31, and 32.) If the total of black and white men in either system is odd, the player whose turn it is to play has the move. However, if a black man is blocked on square 28, or a white man is blocked on square 5, the move is against the player whose turn it is to play, when either system contains an odd number of men. If the blocked man is released, the regular determination applies. The move usually changes with each exchange of pieces, but it does not change if all jumps of the exchange are completed in the same system.

Many games are decided by maneuvers called *strokes* or *shots* that involve multiple captures, usually resulting in the gain of material. Strokes vary from simple plays to long and complicated series of moves, and skilled players can annihilate adversaries with them. Shots kill any player. Figs. 2, 3, and 4 show such plays.

Endings are a vital part of the game. For example, the inexperienced player will have trouble winning with three kings against two, if the weak side can reach the double corner where capture is not possible. The owner of the three kings can always force a position similar to that in Fig. 5, after which he should win easily.

Certain series of endings on which many others depend are called *positions.* Their technique decides the fate of many games between experienced players. First position (Fig. 6) is encountered frequently. It can come up in innumerable ways and shows how a slight advantage can be capitalized. Fifth position, shown in Fig. 7, also occurs frequently, and many games are lost because black fails to sacrifice by 13-17.

So many variations of play have been analyzed that, by choosing known lines of play, experts can play to a draw almost at will. For this reason, a two-move restriction may prevail for *openings* in championship games. This means that the first move on each side is determined by lot. To equalize, each match comprises two games, the contestants changing colors after the first.

Development of the Modern Game. The origin of checkers is not clear. Some historians believe that it was derived from chess during the Middle Ages, others say that it was played in Egypt at least as early as 1600 B.C. Scientific checkers, however, is comparatively modern, dating from

GAME No. 1. "Single Corner" (11–15, 22–18)

11–15	24–19	11–16	31–24	24–27
22–18	16–20	18–15	2–7	15–10
15–22	28–24	14–18	11–2	27–31
25–18(a)	8–12	23–14	16–20	22–18
8–11	32–28	9–18	2–9	31–27
29–25(b)	10–15	15–11(e)	5–30	18–14
4–8	19–10	18–23	24–19	27–23
25–22	7–14(c)	27–18	20–24	Black wins
12–16	30–25(d)	20–27	19–15	

(a) This constitutes the *single corner*, popular with all grades of players.
(b) 24–19, 9–13, 28–24 lead to an even game.
(c) An attempt to cramp the single corner with the idea of later playing against the double corner.
(d) The only good move. If 24–19, then black wins via 11–16.
(e) This natural looking move loses. White can draw 26–23, 3–7, 23–14, 6–10, 15–6, 1–26, 31–22, 7–10, 21–17, and so forth.

GAME No. 2. "Old Fourteenth" (11–15, 23–19)

11–15	26–23	15–22	25–21	15–24
23–19	9–14	23–18(e)	22–26	28–19
8–11	31–26	14–23	21–14	13–17
22–17	6–9(b)	27–18	26–30	8–4
4–8(a)	13–6	9–13	19–15	17–22
17–13	2–9	17–14	30–26	4–8
15–18	26–22	10–17	15–8	22–26
24–20	1–6(c)	21–14	26–22	19–15
11–15	22–17(d)	6–10	32–28	26–30
28–24	18–22	30–25	22–15	Drawn
8–11	25–18	10–17	24–19	

(a) This forms *old fourteenth,* one of the oldest and best-known openings. Several other openings start with the same first four moves.
(b) There are several possibilities here. 5–9 should draw; and 11–16 can draw also, though it is weak. Either 14–17 or 18–22 should lose for black.
(c) 3–8, 22–17 should draw, but if black plays 9–13 he is trapped in the famous big stroke.

9–13	23–14	22–26	24–15	15–11
20–16	10–17	15–10	31–24	7–2
11–20	25–2	26–31	15–11	20–24
22–17	17–22	29–25	24–19	22–18
13–22	19–15	12–16	11–7	11–16
21–17	21–25	25–22	19–15	21–17
14–21	30–21	16–19	2–6	White wins

The stroke itself ends with 25–2, but the ending is lost for black though pieces are even.
(d) 32–28, 3–8, 30–26, 9–13 lead to interesting lines where either side may get into trouble. But the game should be drawn.
(e) 17–13 looks strong but loses to 14–17, 21–14, 9–18, 23–14, 10–17, 32–28, 17–21, 19–16, 12–19, 24–8, 3–12, and so on.

the publication of *Introduction to the Game of Draughts* (1756), by William Payne, the English mathematician. (The British called the game *draughts,* a term referring to the pieces.) Payne's theories were largely incorporated in Joshua Sturges' *Guide to the Game of Draughts* (1800), which laid the foundation for innumerable later analyses.

Many national varieties of the game exist. In *Spanish draughts,* the 16th century forerunner of the Anglo-American game, a king may move any distance along an open diagonal. *Damenspiel,* the German game, permits the ordinary piece to move either forward or backward (as the modern kings move), while kings may move any number of squares, forward or backward. *Polish draughts,* in which the board has 100 squares, and each player has 20 men, is also popular in France, where another version, called *jeu des dames,* is common. English draughts, however, is the most widely popular game. The game's governing body in the United States is the American Checker Federation.

FRANK K. PERKINS, *Boston "Herald"*

Bibliography

Hopper, Millard, *How to Play Winning Checkers* (New York 1961).
Reisman, Arthur, *Checkers Made Easy* (New York 1964).
Wiswell, Thomas, *America's Best Checkers* (New York 1956).
Wiswell, Thomas, *Secrets of Checkerboard Strategy* (New York 1960).

CHECKOFF, an arrangement, usually based on a collective bargaining agreement, by which an employer deducts union dues and assessments from the wages of union members and sends them to the union treasury. The checkoff enables the union to receive the dues automatically, without the need for dues collectors. It guarantees the financial stability of the union.

The checkoff appears in collective bargaining agreements either by itself or with other union security provisions, such as the union shop, maintenance of membership, and agency shop provisions. The Labor-Management Relations Act of 1947 (Taft-Hartley Act) requires that dues checkoff arrangements be subject to the written authorization of the union member. The authorization may be revoked after one year or at the end of the collective bargaining agreement, whichever occurs first.

The checkoff evolved from collective bargaining between bituminous coal employers and the United Mine Workers in the Central Competitive Field Agreement of 1898. The employers in the agreement accepted the checkoff to enable the union to have the financial strength to enforce wage scales on companies not parties to the agreement. Although the checkoff became part of the collective bargaining agreement in many industries, it was resisted by some union members who favored the personal payment of dues weekly or monthly as a method for keeping in contact with the union business agent and guaranteeing his attendance to duty. In the United States, most industrial union contracts and a majority of craft union contracts have checkoff provisions. The checkoff is little used in other countries.

HARVEY L. FRIEDMAN
University of Massachusetts

CHECKS AND BALANCES are the constitutional controls whereby separate branches of government have limiting powers over each other so that no branch will become supreme. Perhaps the best known system of checks and balances operates in the U. S. government under provisions of the federal Constitution.

Most national, state, and local governments have at least the mechanics of a system of checks and balances. Even dictatorial governments, otherwise scorning restraints on powers, provide internal checks to insure proper performance by governmental agencies and to fix responsibility.

Theory of Checks and Balances. The concept of constitutional checks arose as an outgrowth of the classical theory of separation of powers, by which the legislative, executive, and judicial powers of government were held properly to be vested in three different units. The purpose of this, and of the later development of checks and balances, was to ensure that governmental power would not be used in an abusive manner. However, in its original form the concept involved social classes rather than government departments.

Classical political philosophers from Aristotle onward favored a "mixed" government combining the elements of monarchy, aristocracy, and democracy. The English theorist James Harrington in his *Oceana* (1656) derived a theory akin to separation of powers from the old idea of mixed government. Later, John Locke, in his second treatise *Of Civil Government* (1690), urged that the best way to avoid a perverted government was to provide constitutionally for separation of the legislative and executive powers. Montes-

quieu, in his *Spirit of the Laws* (1748), added the third power of the judiciary to this concept, and the modern expression of separation of powers came into being. The mechanics of checks and balances were refined by the founders of the American republic.

Provisions in the U. S. Government. The framers the U. S. Constitution were strongly influenced by the advantages of separation of powers and of checks and balances. These theories had been in practice in the governments of the American colonies, and they underlie the fundamental laws of the United States.

The Constitution distinctly separates the legislative, executive, and judicial branches of government. The federal system adds to the checking because power is divided constitutionally between the central government and the states. Further, the constitutional provisions for direct election of members of both houses of Congress and virtually direct election of the president puts two branches of the government under check of the electorate. However, procedural requirements in the Constitution ensure that even measures popular with the voters cannot be adopted without presumably adequate consideration.

The operation of checks and balances in the federal government is spelled out in the Constitution. The two houses of Congress legislate separately, and this legislation is subject to presidential veto; however, Congress, by a two thirds vote of each house, can override a presidential veto. The judicial branch, in determining cases, may declare legislation unconstitutional, but the judiciary itself is subject to executive and legislative checking through the appointment of judges and the passage of legislation governing organization, procedure, and jurisdiction of the courts. There also is a possibility of amendment of the Constitution to reverse judicial determinations. Other constitutional checks are the possible legislative removal of the president and of judges by impeachment and approval by the Senate of treaties and major presidential appointments. See also CONSTITUTION OF THE UNITED STATES.

PAUL C. BARTHOLOMEW
University of Notre Dame

Further Reading: Vanderbilt, Arthur T., *The Doctrine of Separation of Powers and Its Present-day Significance* (Lincoln, Nebr., 1953); Wahlke, John C., and others, *The Legislative System* (New York 1962).

CHEDDAR, ched'ər, is a village in southwestern England, in Somerset, 14 miles (18 km) southwest of Bristol, at the foot of the Mendip Hills. A fruit-growing and dairying center, it has been known since the 17th century for its cheese. Tourists visit the Cheddar Gorge, a picturesque pass between vertical limestone cliffs over 400 feet (120 meters) high and 2 miles (3 km) long. There are stalactite caves in which late Stone Age bones and tools have been found. Population: (1961) 2,845.

CHEDUBA ISLAND, shə-dōo'bə, is in the Bay of Bengal, about 20 miles (32 km) off the western coast of Burma. Historically, Cheduba, which is about 220 square miles (570 sq km) in area, served as a stepping-stone for the spread of Indian culture, especially Buddhism, into Burma. Trading craft from India and Pakistan still call at the small port, also named Cheduba, on the island's northeast coast. Cattle raising, fishing, and agriculture support the inhabitants. Population: (1960) 30,000.

CHEESE is a nutritious milk product that is usually made from curds that have been concentrated and ripened. It is high in protein and is also an important source of calcium and vitamin A. Cheese is generally richer than milk in butterfat, except for those cheeses made from skim milk or whey. Its high protein content makes it an excellent low-cost substitute for meat.

There are hundreds of different varieties of cheese, from very soft and perishable types to aged cheeses so hard they can be used only for grating. Most cheeses are made from cow's milk, although milk from sheep and goats is widely used in Europe and a few cheeses are made from the milk of water buffalo and reindeer.

The United States is the world's largest producer of cheese. Most of the cheese produced there is made in Wisconsin. Other leading cheese-producing states are Ohio, Michigan, Minnesota, Illinois, and New York. U. S. consumption averages about 10 pounds (4.5 kg) per person yearly.

Other major cheese-producing countries are Switzerland, France, Italy, the Netherlands, Denmark, Britain, and Ireland. France produces more different types of cheeses than any other country, especially soft and semisoft varieties.

MAKING CHEESE

All cheese starts as milk, but the milk may be sweet whole milk, a combination of sweet and sour milk, or a mixture of whole and skim milk. The first step in making cheese is to separate the whey (the liquid portion of the milk) from the curd (the solid particles). When milk is slightly sour, this may be done by placing the milk over very low heat for several hours. In modern manufacture, a culture of lactic acid-producing bacteria is added to sweet milk to cause the separation, and sometimes a combination of heat plus the culture and an extract of rennet may be used.

The next step in cheese making is pressing the curds to concentrate them and remove moisture. The amount of moisture extracted determines the texture of the cheese. The softer the cheese desired, the less moisture is extracted.

In making fresh, unripened cheese, such as cottage cheese, the curd need only be well drained, pressed or molded into shape, and then seasoned. Most cheese, however, is ripened, or cured. This means that the cheese undergoes a process of fermentation, after which it is stored in cellars, caves, or special rooms where the temperature and humidity can be controlled. The temperature at which the cheese is ripened and the length of time it is kept at that temperature are two of the many factors that determine the characteristics of the cheese. Other factors include the kind of milk used and the manner in which the curd is pressed. Many cheeses owe their distinctive character to various kinds of molds or other microorganisms that are either injected into the cheese or absorbed from the floor and walls of the caves. The blue-green veining of Roquefort, for example, is due to the mold *Penicillium roqueforti*, which is found in the humid mountain caves of southern France.

Cheese may remain in a ripening cellar for two weeks, two months, or nearly a year, depending on the variety. During this ripening period, the cheese is salted and turned frequently, and the exterior may be rubbed with oil or some other protective coating. Some cheeses are dry-salted, but others are immersed in brine. During the ripening period, various flavorings, such as caraway seeds, may also be added.

After ripening, some cheeses are further aged in special cellars for periods of six months to four years. With age, a cheese becomes sharper in flavor and firmer in texture and may also become darker in color.

Any ripened cheese, whether it is aged or not, is called a *natural cheese*. A *process*, or *pasteurized process, cheese* is a mixture of fresh and ripened cheese that has been shredded, mixed, heated to a liquid state, and then poured into sterile molds and sealed. *Pasteurized process cheese food* is a mixture of fresh and natural cheese to which nonfat dry milk, whey solids, and water have been added. It is softer than process cheese and spreads and melts more easily, but contains more moisture and less actual cheese. *Pasteurized process cheese spreads* are still higher in moisture content, sometimes containing only about 28% cheese, with vegetable gum added to give them a soft, chewy consistency.

HISTORY

The origin of cheese is unknown. It may have been discovered by shepherds—perhaps in the Indus Valley or Mesopotamia some 6,000 to 8,000 years ago. The shepherds carried milk in a pouch made from a sheep's or goat's stomach, and milk thus brought into contact with rennet from the stomach lining would coagulate into cheese. It is definitely known that cheese was a common food by 2000 B. C., for small cheese molds, with holes punched for draining the curds, have been found in ruins dating back to that period.

An extensive cheese industry existed in the Roman Empire. Pliny the Elder, in his *Historia naturalis* (77 A. D.), describes many of the cheeses prized by Roman gourmets, including a cheese believed to be the Swiss cheese called Sbrinz, a cheese that may have been the forerunner of Roquefort, and the firm sharp cheese of Cheshire favored by Roman legionnaires.

During the Middle Ages, cheese was made primarily by the monks in abbeys, and many monastery cheeses are still world renowned. Camembert cheese is mentioned in 12th century chronicles, but it was Napoleon who made it famous.

Beyond the walls of monasteries and great feudal estates, most cheese making was a family operation until the 15th and 16th centuries, when farmers in England began to "join their milk together" to make large wheels of cheese. Highway tolls in Europe contributed to the making of large cheeses, for tolls were levied according to the number of cheeses in a farmer's cart rather than by weight.

Factory cheese was produced in the United States in 1851 when a Rome, N. Y., farmer, Jesse Williams, urged other farmers to sell him their excess milk. Fifteen years later, 500 cheese factories were operating in New York state alone.

The first process cheese was developed in Switzerland in 1911, but a year later in Chicago a cheese peddler named James L. Kraft began experimenting with a method of pasteurizing cheeses. Approximately 75% of all cheese sold today in the United States is made by some adaptation of this basic method.

BETTY WASON
Author of "A Salute to Cheeses"

Further Reading: Marquis, Vivian, and Haskell, Patricia, *The Cheese Book* (New York 1965); Simon, André, *Cheeses of the World* (London 1956); Wason, Betty, *A Salute to Cheeses* (New York 1966).

THE KING OF CHEESES, as connoisseurs often call Roquefort, ripens in humid cellars in the southern French village that gave it its name. The blue-green veining in the cheese is produced by a mold of the penicillin family.

Principal Cheese Varieties

The number of different cheeses produced around the world is almost beyond count. The following list includes the varieties that are best known or most copied—for nearly all famous cheeses are imitated outside their countries of origin.

Allgauer is the name used for several cheeses produced in the Allgäu region of Germany. Most often it refers to a semifirm, large-holed cheese similar to Swiss Emmentaler.

American is a mild process cheese of the Cheddar type produced in the United States. It ranges in texture from semisoft to firm and is bright yellow in color. American cheese is often sliced before packaging.

Appenzeller is a semifirm, bright-yellow cheese produced in Switzerland in plate-shaped 15-pound (6.8-kg) wheels, which are marinated in cider or white wine during ripening. It is somewhat softer than Emmentaler and has small irregular holes.

Asiago is an Italian cheese originally made from ewe's milk but now made mostly from cow's milk. When young, it is semifirm, but when cured a year or longer, it becomes a hard grating cheese similar to Parmesan.

Bel Paese is a creamy Italian dessert cheese with a mild but distinctive flavor. An American version is produced in Wisconsin.

Bierkäse is a pungent semisoft German cheese sometimes marinated in beer during the ripening period.

Bleu is the French name for any blue-veined cheese.

Blue is a term applied to any blue-veined cheese.

Bondost is a firm yellow cheese of Swedish origin. An American version is now also made.

Brick is a semifirm natural cheese of American origin. It has a distinctive but not pungent flavor and is usually made in the form of a loaf.

Brie, one of the most renowned French cheeses, is often called the cheese of kings because so many monarchs have praised it. It is creamy-soft, almost runny in texture, with a soft white crust.

Caciocavallo is a firm Italian cheese similar to Provolone. In making Caciocavallo, the curd is pulled into a rope, sometimes braided, and is rubbed with oil as it ripens until the outside is light brown and waxy. It is also made throughout the Balkans, where the name is variously spelled *Kashkaval, Kachavelj,* or *Karschkavalj.*

Caerphilly is a semisoft, creamy-white Welsh cheese that is mild in flavor. It is a ripened cheese but very perishable.

Camembert is a delicious dessert cheese of French origin but now imitated in many other countries. Its characteristic flavor is due to the mold spread over the surface of the ripening curd.

Cantal is a firm yellow French cheese produced in France since Roman times.

Chantelle is a semisoft ripened cheese, pale in color and coated with red wax. It is produced in Illinois.

Cheddar cheese was first made in the English village of Cheddar but is no longer made there. Today the term is applied to about 80% of all the cheese produced in the United States, both natural and process varieties. It ranges in color from white to deep orange and in flavor from mild to very sharp. Some varieties are supple enough to slice easily, while others are crumbly or flaky.

Cheshire is a firm English cheese available in "red" (actually orange), "blue" (blue-veined), and white varieties.

Colby is a mild type of Cheddar made in Vermont.

Coon is a very sharp piquant Cheddar made in New York State. It has a crumbly texture and is almost white, with a black coating.

Cottage, the simplest kind of fresh cheese, is made by heating slightly sour or skim milk until the curd separates, then cutting and draining it. The curd is then usually blended with fresh cream and seasoned. Commercial cottage cheese is made from

CHEESES TAKE MANY FORMS

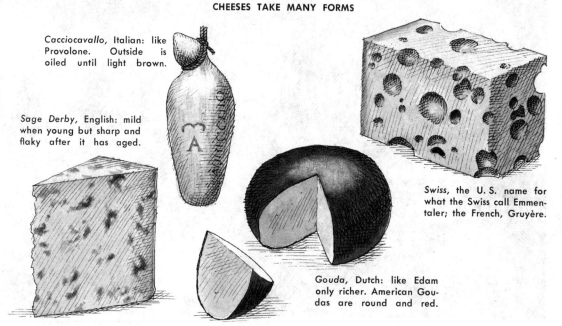

Cacciocavallo, Italian: like Provolone. Outside is oiled until light brown.

Sage Derby, English: mild when young but sharp and flaky after it has aged.

Swiss, the U. S. name for what the Swiss call Emmentaler; the French, Gruyère.

Gouda, Dutch: like Edam only richer. American Goudas are round and red.

reconstituted dried skim milk or nonfat dry milk solids, with lactic acid added to hasten the separation. Cottage cheese may also be known as *pot cheese, Dutch cheese,* or *schmierkäse.*

Coeur à la Crème is a delicate fresh French cheese made from naturally soured whole milk and cream and then pressed into heart-shaped baskets.

Cornhusker is a semifirm Cheddar cheese made in Nebraska. It is similar to Colby.

Coulommiers is a soft French cheese similar to Brie.

Cream cheese is a soft unripened cheese made of cream and sweet whole milk treated with a culture of lactic acid-producing bacteria.

Crema Danica is a soft ripened Danish desert cheese that has a very high butterfat content.

Creole, which is made in Louisiana, is an unripened cheese made of equal parts of cottage cheese and heavy cream.

Danablue, or **Danish Blue,** is a blue-veined cow's milk cheese from Denmark. It is the most popular imported blue cheese in the United States.

Derby is a firm English cheese, mild when young but flaky and sharp when aged. Sometimes it is flavored with sage and called Sage Derby.

Dunlop is a sharp firm Cheddar made in Scotland.

Edam, one of Holland's most famous cheeses, is semifirm in texture and is made in a round cannonball shape with a protective coating of red wax. Many Edam-type cheeses are now made in the United States, usually ranging in size from ¾ pound to 14 pounds (340 grams to 65 kg).

Emmentaler is the world-renowned, big-holed cheese commonly called "Switzerland Swiss" in the United States. Made in wheels weighing from 175 to 200 pounds (80 to 90 kg), it is cured for 6 to 10 months and then aged from 1 to 2 years. Although it was made originally in Switzerland, varieties of Emmentaler are now made also in Germany, Denmark, and France.

Farmer's cheese is a variety of cottage cheese in which the curd is cut into fine particles and pressed into a loaf. The name is also sometimes applied to any ripened cheese in the locality where it is produced.

Feta is a semisoft white flaky Greek cheese that is made from the milk of sheep or goats and marinated in brine.

Fontina, of Italian origin, is a semisoft to firm cheese made of ewe's milk, salted in brine, and usually cured about 2 months. If cured longer, it becomes a hard grating cheese. The name Fontina is also applied to a semifirm cow's milk cheese made in Wisconsin.

Fontinella is an Italian cheese similar to Fontina but firmer and sharper.

Gammelost is a semisoft, mold-ripened Norwegian cheese made of skim milk. The interior is brownish yellow with a blue-green tint, and the exterior is deep brown.

Gjetost, a Norwegian cheese, is made from the whey of goat's milk. It is brown in color and quite sweet.

Gorgonzola, the best of the Italian blue cheeses, is named for the village near Milan where the fungus that gives the cheese its particular flavor is found in the local caves. When young, Gorgonzola is creamy and semisoft, but with age it becomes firmer, sharper, and deeper in color. In the United States, domestic versions of this cheese are made in Michigan and Wisconsin.

Gouda, named for the Netherlands city where it originated, is similar to Edam but richer in butterfat and generally larger, ranging from 6 to 50 pounds (3 to 23 kg). Most Dutch Goudas have a golden outer coating and are loaf-shaped. Varieties made in the United States are usually round and have a red outer coating.

Gruyère, originally made in Switzerland, is similar to Emmentaler but has smaller holes, a more pronounced flavor, and a higher butterfat content. A kind of process Gruyère, which is made in both Switzerland and the United States, is usually packaged in wedges wrapped in foil.

Hand cheese, or **Handkäse,** is a pungent semisoft cheese made from skim milk curds that are molded by hand. Originally made in Germany, it is now also made in the United States by the Pennsylvania Dutch.

Harzkäse is a variety of hand cheese that is made in the Harz Mountains of Germany.

THEY PLEASE MANY PALATES

Provolone, Italian: firm and smoky. It is usually molded into a pear shape.

Roquefort, French: may be called a "blue" cheese for its blue-green veining.

Brie, French: creamy-soft, almost runny in texture, with a soft white crust.

Pineapple, a variety of Cheddar shaped by the net bag in which it is cured.

Havarti is a Danish cheese, firm in texture, with both large and small holes and a distinctive, moderately sharp flavor. It has been made for a century near the town of Havarti, Denmark.

Herkimer is a sharp natural Cheddar cheese made in Herkimer county, New York.

Kuminost, a spiced Scandinavian cheese, is firm and Cheddar-like, often flavored with cumin and caraway.

Lancashire is an English cheese similar to Cheshire but white in color, softer, and moister, with a more pungent flavor.

Leyden is a Netherlands spiced cheese similar in consistency to Gouda.

Liederkranz, one of the great American cheeses, was created by Emil Frey, a New York delicatessen man, in 1850 and named for his choral society. It is a mold-ripened, aromatic, soft dessert cheese, now produced in Ohio.

Limburger is a creamy soft pungent-smelling cheese of Belgian origin. Varieties of Limburger are now made in many countries, including Germany and the United States.

Manchego is a Spanish cheese with a flavor much like that of aged Swiss. Made from sheep's milk, it is semifirm and mild when young, growing firmer and sharper with age.

Manteca, a variation of Provolone, is a firm, flask-shaped cheese in which sweet butter (butter made from whey) is sealed in the center.

Maroilles is a soft to semisoft, robust-flavored cheese made in the Abbey of Maroilles in the Champagne district of France.

Monterey, or **Monterey Jack,** is a Cheddar type made originally in Monterey county, California. There are two varieties: a semifirm, creamy, pale cheese made of whole milk; and a firmer, zestier, aged cheese, bright in color and made only partially of whole milk.

Mozzarella, of Italian origin, is a mild, white, semisoft cheese that melts easily. In the United States a domestic variety is made of whole milk, but in Italy it is made of skim cow's milk and, to some extent, of buffalo milk. Originally it was made entirely of buffalo milk.

Munster, Münster, or **Muenster,** of Alsatian origin, is made in the Vosges Mountains of France. It is soft and pancake-shaped and has a pungent flavor. The American version is a mild semifirm cheese with small holes.

Mütschli is a semisoft cheese made in Switzerland. It is sometimes called *mountain cheese.* It melts easily and is used in preparing a kind of fondue known as *raclette.*

Mysost is a whey cheese of Scandinavian origin. Like Gjetost, it is brown in color and has a sweet flavor, but it is made of cow's milk, not goat's milk. An American version of this cheese is made in several Midwestern states.

Neufchâtel, as originally made in Normandy, France, is a soft, delicate, white cheese with a white crust, produced in both fresh and ripened versions. American Neufchâtel is a fresh cheese, similar to cream cheese but with a lower fat content. It is made by adding a lactic acid starter to fresh milk, with just enough rennet to coagulate the curd.

Nökkelost, a Norwegian spiced cheese, is similar to Kuminost and is made from skim milk or a mixture of skim and whole milk.

Parmesan, of Italian origin, is one of the most popular of all cheeses. A sharp, hard, grating cheese, it is cured for 14 months or longer and, when fully cured, keeps fresh almost indefinitely. After grating, however, it loses its flavor rapidly. In the United States the production of Parmesan-type cheese has increased greatly in recent years in Michigan and Wisconsin.

Pecorino Romano is similar to Parmesan cheese in flavor and texture but is always made from sheep's milk.

Petit Suisse is a very perishable, fresh cream cheese of France. It is made of whole milk to which cream has been added.

Pineapple is a variety of Cheddar that is cured in net bags that mold the cheese into the shape of a pineapple. During the ripening period the outer surface is frequently rubbed with oil to produce a hard, shiny surface.

Pont l'Évêque is a soft dessert cheese of Normandy whose unique flavor is due to a fungus found only in this region.

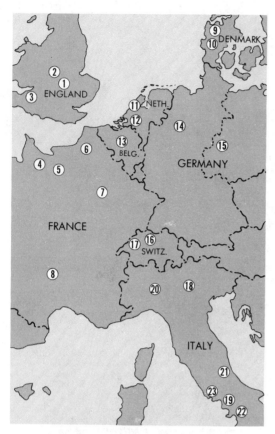

IMPORTANT CHEESES OF WESTERN EUROPE
(Number refers to area where cheese originated)

① STILTON	⑫ GOUDA
② DERBY	⑬ LIMBURGER
③ CHEDDAR	⑭ MUNSTER
④ PONT L'ÉVÊQUE	⑮ HARZKÄSE
⑤ CAMEMBERT	⑯ EMMENTALER
⑥ NEUFCHÂTEL	⑰ GRUYÈRE
⑦ BRIE	⑱ GORGONZOLA
⑧ ROQUEFORT	⑲ MOZZARELLA
⑨ DANABLUE	⑳ PARMESAN
⑩ CREMA DANICA	㉑ CACIOCAVALLO
⑪ EDAM	㉒ PROVOLONE

㉓ ROMANO

Port du Salut, or **Port Salut,** is a pungent soft cheese made first by Trappist monks in France in 1816. It is now produced in many countries, usually, but not always, under the supervision of Trappist monks.

Pot cheese is another name for cottage cheese.

Provolone is a firm Italian cheese with a smoky flavor. The curd is molded into pear-shaped forms that are hung in a room and smoked. After smoking, the cheese is either dipped in paraffin or oiled to a high gloss. Although Provolone can be used as a table cheese after 6 to 9 months of curing, it is usually cured for 14 months and used for grating. In the United States, a domestic variety of Provolone is made in a different manner and is softer.

Ricotta, as it is made in Italy, where it originated, is made from the whey left over from making sheep cheese. It may be a soft, firm, or very hard grating cheese. An American cheese of the same name is made from the whey of Cheddar cheese, blended with whole milk.

Romadur is a German cheese similar to Limburger but not as pungent.

Romano is a hard grating cheese that keeps almost indefinitely. The Italian cheese of this name is usually made of sheep's milk, but American Romano is always made of cow's milk.

Roquefort is one of the best known of all the blue-veined cheeses and is the only well-known one made solely of sheep's milk. By law, the name can be used only to designate cheese ripened in the Roquefort caves of France. Roquefort is so respected by connoisseurs that it is often called the "king of cheeses."

Saanen is probably the hardest cheese made anywhere. This cheese, which originated in Switzerland, is cured at least 3 years, sometimes as long as 7 years, and remains edible indefinitely.

Sapsago is a small, hard, pale-green cheese flavored with dried clover. It is also known as *Schabzieger.* It has been made in Switzerland since the 15th century. A version of this cheese is now made in Wisconsin.

Sbrinz is an extremely hard cheese made for centuries in Switzerland. It is similar to Parmesan but has a mellower flavor and higher butterfat content.

Smoked cheese is any cheese, usually American or Cheddar, that is flavored with liquid smoke, hung in smokehouses along with ham and bacon, or rubbed with smoke salt.

Stilton, named for the English town where it first acquired its reputation, is regarded as England's finest cheese. It is a firm, blue-veined cheese made from cow's milk. A cheese of the same name is now also made in Wisconsin.

Swiss, in the United States, refers to the big-holed cheese that the Swiss call Emmentaler and the English and French refer to as Gruyère. It is a firm, pale-yellow cheese with holes that may be as large as an inch (25 mm) in diameter. Made in wheels weighing between 160 and 200 pounds (72 to 91 kg), it is one of the most difficult cheeses to produce, requiring three species of bacteria to start the fermentation process, produce the large holes, and give the cheese its characteristic nutty flavor. The Swiss cheese industry in the United States was established by emigrants from Switzerland in 1850. Today it is the second most popular cheese in the United States.

Taleggio is a soft aromatic Italian dessert cheese. It is pale in color with a rosy crust.

Teleme, or **Telemi,** originated in the Balkans, where it is made with sheep's milk. The American cheese of the same name is made of cow's milk. Soft, white, and brine-marinated, it is somewhat similar to Feta.

Tillamook is a Cheddar cheese produced in Oregon. A special salt-free variety is semifirm in texture and has a pungent flavor.

Tilsiter is a semifirm cheese, piquant in flavor, with small irregular holes. It was made originally by Dutch emigrants who settled in Prussia. Varieties of this cheese are now produced in Germany, Switzerland, Denmark, Norway, and the United States.

Tomme is a family of skim milk cheeses made in the Savoie district of France. Sometimes it is flavored with fennel, raisins, or sweet wine.

Vacherin is a name used for several quite different cheeses produced in Switzerland and the bordering regions of France. They range in texture from soft to semisoft and in flavor from mild to pungent.

Weisslacker is a soft to semisoft German cheese similar to Limburger but much milder and with a lustrous white crust.

Wensleydale is a blue-veined Yorkshire cheese similar to Stilton but sharper in flavor.

CHEETAH, chē'tə, a medium-sized member of the cat family considered the fastest of all four-legged animals. Toward the end of the 19th century the cheetah still ranged from central India through the savannahs of Asia Minor, Arabia, and Africa. Today it is apparently extinct or nearly extinct in all these areas, except for east, central, and south Africa.

Characteristics. The cheetah has a very slender build, with long legs and a long tail. The muzzle and neck are short and the ears are round. The feet differ from those of all other cats in that the claws are not protected by skin sheaths and cannot be fully retracted. Cheetahs stand about 39 inches (1 meter) high at the shoulders and reach about 7¼ feet (2.25 meters) in length including the 2½-foot (75-cm) tail. Weights range from 110 to 140 pounds (50–65 kg).

The fur of the cheetah ranges from whitish-yellow to rich ochre, with underparts buff-white to white. The face is characteristically marked by two heavy black "tear streaks" running from the inner corner of the eyes to the corners of the mouth. The body is dotted with rather small spots that are dark brown or black. Male cheetahs may have a short mane along the nape of the neck. The tail is slightly bushy toward the end and has a number of black rings; the tip is usually bright white.

The gestation period of the cheetah is from 84 to 95 days. There are normally 2 or 3 cubs in a litter. The cubs are remarkable for having a rather long mane along the nape and back; the mane disappears toward the end of the first year.

Behavior. Cheetahs live in pairs, or in small family groups that are led by the strongest male. Cheetahs can attain a speed of 70 miles (110 km) per hour in short spurts. This swiftness evolved in connection with the cheetah's method of hunting. Like other cats, they first stalk their prey, crouching close to the ground. However, they begin the final onrush from a greater distance and outrun their prey. They beat it down with their forepaws and finally bite it through the nape of the neck or throttle and strangulate it.

Even when captured as adults, cheetahs can be tamed relatively easily with proper handling, at least to an extent. They have been trained as "hunting leopards"—mainly in India—to hunt and kill for their masters. (The favorite game is blackbuck.) The cheetah is hooded, chained on a wagon, and driven through the hunting grounds until a herd of antelope is sighted. The cap is then removed, and as soon as the cheetah spots its prey, the chain is released. On occasion, tame cheetahs have been used in the United States to hunt coyotes. Attempts to breed the cat in captivity have thus far had very limited success.

The single species, *Acinonyx jubatus,* is classified in the family Felidae, order Carnivora.

PAUL LEYHAUSEN
Max Planck Institute for Behavioral Psychology
Wuppertal, Germany

CHEEVER, chē'vər, **Ezekiel** (1615–1708), American educator, who was the most noted schoolmaster in colonial New England. He was born in London, England, on Jan. 25, 1615, and went to America in 1637. The head of various New England schools for 70 years, he achieved his greatest fame as master of the renowned Boston Latin School, in Boston, Massachusetts, where he served from 1670 until his death on Aug. 21, 1708. His renowned *Accidence, a Short Introduction to the Latin Tongue* was a standard text in New England schools for more than 100 years. Cheever's funeral sermon was delivered by one of New England's leading clergymen, Cotton Mather, and he was later celebrated in verse and story, most notably in Nathaniel Hawthorne's *Grandfather's Chair.*

RICHARD E. GROSS, *Stanford University*

CHEEVER, chē'vər, **John** (1912–   ), American writer, noted for his lively sense of comedy, acute moral perception, and versatility as a storyteller. He was born in Quincy, Mass., on May 27, 1912. His first short story was based on his expulsion from Thayer Academy in Massachusetts at the age of 17. A frequent contributor to leading American periodicals, particularly the *New Yorker,* Cheever published his first volume of short stories, *The Way Some People Live,* in 1943. However, he did not receive wide critical acclaim until the publication of his best-selling novel, *The Wapshot Chronicle* (1957), which received the National Book Award of 1958. This work and its popular sequel, *The Wapshot Scandal* (1964), trace an old New England family from the beginning of the 20th century to the 1960's.

Cheever is essentially a satirist, but an urbane and indulgent one, whose ultimate goal is to "celebrate a world that lies spread out around us like a bewildering and stupendous daydream." Realistic in manner but ironic in tone, his fiction, as in the *Wapshot* novels, is frequently concerned with the family as a social institution, with its intricate moral and emotional tensions. In his short fiction, Cheever appears as an increasingly stringent critic of American suburban life. Collections of his stories include *The Enormous Radio* (1953), *The Housebreaker of Shady Hill* (1958), and *The Brigadier and the Golf Widow* (1964).

DAVID GALLOWAY, *Author of "The Absurd Hero"*

CHEFOO. See YENTAI.

Cheetah

CHEHALIS, chē-hā′lis, a city in southwestern Washington, the seat of Lewis county, is about 80 miles (130 km) south of Seattle. It is situated in a timber and diversified farming region. It has lumber mills and processing plants for milk, fruit, and vegetables. Chehalis was incorporated in 1890. It has a commission form of government. Population: 5,727.

CHEJU ISLAND, chŭ′i-jōō′, is an island of South Korea in the East China Sea. It is about 90 miles (145 km) southwest of the Korean mainland, from which it is separated by Cheju Strait, and is Korea's largest island. Its area slightly exceeds 700 square miles (1,813 sq km). Its terrain is mountainous, and the highest point, Mt. Halla (6,398 feet or 2,773 meters), is an extinct volcano.

Once called *Quelpart Island,* and *Saishu-to* by the Japanese, Cheju was separated from South Cholla province after World War II and made into a separate province. Formerly used as a place of exile, the island received prisoners of war during the Korean War and many refugees afterward.

Cheju is noted for its tangerines and for its women divers, whose catches of seaweed, shellfish, and clamshells (for inlaid work) are exported. The chief industries are fishing, seafood processing, cattle raising, and farming. The city of Cheju on the north shore is a port and the provincial capital. Population: (1960) of the province, 281,720; (1965) of the city, 84,267.

CHEKA, chä′kä, is the shortened form of the Russian name for the Bolshevik secret police between 1917 and 1922—the "All-Russian Extraordinary Commission." The Cheka was established on Dec. 20, 1917, under the direction of F. E. Dzerzhinsky, to combat "counterrevolution, sabotage, and speculation." Designed as an instrument of revolutionary terror at a time of mounting violence and disorganization, it received its baptism in the crises that threatened Bolshevik rule in 1918. It soon became a byword of Bolshevik ruthlessness. Mounting criticism after the civil war led to its reorganization in 1922. This did not, however, diminish its arbitrary and autonomous powers. Under its new name GPU (OGPU from 1923), it grew into the Stalinist version of the Soviet secret police.

THEODORE H. VON LAUE
Washington University, St. Louis

CHEKE, chēk, **Sir John** (1514–1557), English classical scholar. He was born in Cambridge on June 17, 1514, and was educated at St. John's College, Cambridge. In 1540 he became first regius professor of Greek at Cambridge University, a post he held until 1551. Meanwhile, he was tutor to the Prince of Wales (later Edward VI) in 1544, was made provost of King's College, Cambridge, in 1548, and was knighted in 1551.

Because he was Lady Jane Grey's secretary of state during her 9-day reign, Queen Mary had him arrested in 1553. Released in 1554, Cheke went to Switzerland and Italy, then settled in Strasbourg, where he lived by teaching Greek. In 1556, after a visit to his wife in Brussels, he was seized and sent to England. There, through the threats of John de Feckenham, he recanted his Protestantism, and Cardinal Pole received him into the Roman Catholic Church. Cheke died soon after in London on Sept. 13, 1557.

Anton Chekhov

SOVFOTO

CHEKHOV, chek′ôf, **Anton Pavlovich** (1860–1904), Russian dramatist and short story writer, whose work exerted an immense influence on European and American literature. His realistic plays, noted for the new technique of indirect action, are an integral part of the world repertoire. Pitiless in his observation of the follies of man, Chekhov nevertheless shows a profound understanding of human nature that transcends mere compassion. This quality is chiefly responsible for the marvelous blend of the comic and the tragic that is so characteristic of his best work.

Life. Chekhov's grandfather was a serf who in 1841 bought the freedom of his family of eight for 3,500 rubles, the equivalent of about $40,000 at that time, which he had saved as manager of his master's estate. Chekhov's father, Pavel Yegorovich, settled in Taganrog on the Sea of Azov, marrying the daughter of a local cloth merchant and opening a small grocery shop. There Chekhov was born on Jan. 29, 1860.

At the age of seven, Chekhov was sent to a local school for Greek children, and two years later to the Taganrog secondary school. In 1876 his father went bankrupt and fled from his creditors to Moscow, leaving his son to fend for himself by tutoring. After passing his final school examinations in 1879, Chekhov obtained a scholarship from the Taganrog town council to study medicine at Moscow University. While he was a medical student, he supported himself and his family by writing short stories, which he published under the pseudonym Antosha Chekhonte.

Chekhov received his M. D. degree in 1884 and worked briefly in a hospital at Voskresensk, a small town near Moscow. He then continued his medical practice in Moscow, devoting most of his time, however, to writing. The summer of 1890 he spent on the island of Sakhalin, the site of a penal colony, and made a thorough study of convict life. His only "academic" book, *The Island Sakhalin* (1894), was based on this trip.

In 1892, Chekhov made his first journey abroad, visiting Venice, Florence, Rome, Paris, and Nice. On his return he bought a small farm near the village of Melikhovo in the Serpukhov district of Moscow province. There he spent the next six years with his parents and sister.

Chekhov had contracted pulmonary tuberculosis in the winter of 1883. After suffering a violent hemorrhage in March 1897, he spent the winter in Nice. He showed great interest in the trial of the French Jewish army officer, Alfred Dreyfus, and defended him against his Russian detractors.

In 1898, Chekhov sold his farm and settled in his own house in Yalta. In 1901 he married Olga Knipper, an actress of the Moscow Art Theatre, which produced some of his plays. His health deteriorated gravely during his three years in Yalta, and on June 15, 1904, he left with his wife for the German health resort of Badenweiler, where he died on July 14. He was buried in the cemetery of the Novodevichy Monastery in Moscow.

Short Stories. By the end of 1885, Chekhov had published over 300 short stories. His first volume, *Tales of Melpomene* (1884), contained six stories dealing with stage life. His first large volume of short stories, *Motley Stories* (1886), included such masterpieces as *Surgery* (1884), *A Living Calendar* (1885), *Grief* (1885), and *A Work of Art* (1886). This volume was followed by two more books of short stories, *At Twilight* (1887) and *Stories* (1888). *Stories* included, in addition to *Happiness* and *The Kiss*, his famous descriptive story *The Steppe*, and won for him the Pushkin Prize.

Between 1886 and 1889, Chekhov was a fervent follower of Leo Tolstoy, and he wrote a series of Tolstoyan propaganda tales, most of which he later refused to include in his collected works. In 1889, Chekhov wrote *A Boring Story*, a masterpiece that first revealed his great gifts as a creative artist and profound thinker.

It was the insight into the stark realities of human suffering he had gained during his brief stay on Sakhalin in 1890 that made Chekhov realize the inadequacy of Tolstoy's philosophy. His first challenge to Tolstoy's views appeared in *The Duel* (1891). In this long short story he attacked the idea, so strongly expressed in Tolstoy's *Kreutzer Sonata* (1889), that sexual love is incompatible with the ideal Christian life. In *Ward 6* (1892) Chekhov went on to condemn Tolstoy's firm belief in nonresistance to evil.

Chekhov's longest short story, *Three Years* (1892–1895), deals with the folly of a life devoted entirely to the pursuit of material success. This theme occurs frequently in his other stories of that period—*A Woman's Kingdom* (1893), *A Teacher of Literature* (1894), *My Life* (1897), *Ionych* (1898), *A Doctor's Visit* (1898), *Lady With Lapdog* (1899), and *In the Ravine* (1899). His faith in a new and better life is expressed most strongly in his last two stories, *The Bishop* (1902) and *The Betrothed* (1903).

Plays. The dream of "a new life" is one of the main themes not only of Chekhov's later short stories but also of his plays. His early dramas are mainly plays of direct action, in which the dramatic action takes place in view of the audience. They include his first major play, the extremely long *Platanov* (1881); a one-act naturalistic play, *On the Highway* (1885), which was banned by the censor as "sordid"; his more mature four-act drama *Ivanov* (1889); and his one-act farces *On the Harmfulness of Tobacco* (1886), *The Swan Song* (1888), *The Bear* (1888), *The Proposal* (1889), *The Wedding* (1890), and *The Night Before the Trial* (1891).

After the failure of Chekhov's attempt to write a Tolstoyan melodrama, *The Wood Demon* (1889), he evolved his brilliant plays of indirect action. In these, the main dramatic action takes place offstage, attention being concentrated entirely on the reactions of the characters to the dramatic events of their lives. These indirect-action plays are his great masterpieces: *The Seagull* (q. v., 1896), which was one of the first productions of the infant Moscow Art Theatre; *Uncle Vanya* (1897), which is a revised version of *The Wood Demon; The Three Sisters* (1901); and his most famous play, *The Cherry Orchard* (q. v., 1903). The essential feature of these plays is the gradual growth of dramatic tension in the first two acts, reaching a crescendo in the climax in the third act, and a gradual diminution of tension in the fourth act. The realistic touches help to give actuality and intimacy to the life of their characters, who, as a rule, belong to the educated section of Russian society.

In both *Platonov* and *The Cherry Orchard* the main theme is the passing of an old family estate into the hands of rich businessmen. In *The Cherry Orchard* above all, the comic element is fully developed and is perhaps best expressed in the intricate and contrasting love themes of the major and minor characters. In the finale of the play, the element of high comedy reaches its culmination in the way the old butler Fiers is abandoned in the locked-up empty house in which he had spent all his life as a devoted servant. The sound of the ax felling the cherry trees is merged with the dramatic realization of the born serf, who despised freedom, that the old order he so much admired was wrong and that the past he doted on is dead.

See also DRAMA—*The Modern Era* (Russia); RUSSIAN LANGUAGE AND CULTURAL LIFE—3. *Drama.*

DAVID MAGARSHACK
Author of "Chekhov: A Life"

Bibliography

Chekhov's Works were translated, in part, into English by Constance Garnet, 13 vols. (London and New York 1916–22).

Bruford, Walter Horace, *Anton Chekhov* (New Haven 1957).

Gerhardi, William Alexander, *Anton Chekhov: A Critical Study* (London 1949).

Magarshack, David, *Chekhov: A Life* (London 1952).

Magarshack, David, *Chekhov the Dramatist* (London and New York 1960).

Simmons, Ernest J., *Chekhov: A Biography* (Boston 1962).

Toumanova, Nina, *Anton Chekhov* (New York 1960).

CHEKIANG, ju′jē-äng′, one of China's eastern coastal provinces, is an area of picturesque hills, rich plains, and many coastal islands, including the Choushan (q.v.) archipelago. Under the Southern Sung dynasty (1127–1279), Chekiang's capital, Hangchow (then known as Linan), was the royal capital. In more recent times, Chekiang gained notice as the birthplace of Chiang Kai-shek, the Nationalist Chinese leader.

Chekiang has a total land area of 39,750 square miles (102,953 sq km). Its northern region, a thickly settled, richly productive agricultural area, is part of the Yangtze delta. The southern region, covering almost 70% of the province, is mountainous.

Chekiang's climate is humid and subtropical. Summer is hot, and winter is mild. The average temperature at Hangchow is 84° F (28° C) in July and 39° F (4° C) in January. The annual rainfall is more than 40 inches (1,000 mm).

Most of Chekiang's population is concentrated in the northern plain and in a few pockets of the coastal lowland. Agriculture is the predominant pursuit of the people of the northern plain, whereas fishing is the traditional occupation of the people of the coastal region and the Choushan archipelago. Chekiang's most populous cities are the capital, Hangchow, Chia-hsing, and Wuhsing (Huchow). All three are located in the northern plain, and all are centers of the silk industry, for which Chekiang is known. Ningpo (Yinhsien) in the north and Wenchow (Yungchia) in the south are important seaports.

The major crops of Chekiang, grown chiefly in the north, are rice, corn, wheat, tea, ramie, and mulberry trees (the last, by providing food for silkworms, are the basis of the silk industry). Plums and peaches are raised in the southern hills, and other products of the south are hardwood, bamboo, tung oil, and lacquer.

The province's mineral resources are modest, consisting of small coal, iron, and fluorite deposits. The chief traditional industries are silk and cotton textiles, tea curing, food processing, and wine and liquor brewing, all based on agricultural products. The yellow rice wine of Shaohsing and the cured ham of Chinhua are famous throughout the country. New industries, developed to a limited extent since 1950, produce iron and steel, chemicals, and machinery.

Chekiang's scenery is renowned, and the province boasts many resorts. Hangchow itself is located on the shore of West Lake, a famous and much-frequented beauty spot. At Putoshan in the Choushan archipelago are the many temples and monasteries of one of China's major Buddhist centers. Population of the province: (1957) 25,280,000.

CHENGTSU WU, *Hunter College, New York*

CHELAN, Lake, shə-lan', the largest natural lake in the state of Washington. It occupies a deep glacial gorge in the Cascade Range in the north central part of the state. Much of the lake, which is about 55 miles (88 km) long and about 2 miles (3 km) wide, lies in the Okanogan National Forest. Its southern outlet drains into the Columbia River near the town of Chelan. Lake Chelan State Park is situated near Chelan.

CHELATE, kē'lāt, a coordination compound in which the ligand contains two or more donor groups so that it forms with the central metal ion one or more heterocyclic rings. The name "chelate," first proposed by the British chemists Gilbert T. Morgan and Harry D. K. Drew in 1920, is derived from the Greek word meaning "claw." Morgan also suggested the terms "unidentate," "bidentate," "tridentate," and so on to denote ligands containing one or more donor groups. Unidentate ligands cannot, of course, form chelates.

Many dyes, such as alizarin, and pigments, such as phthalocyanines, are chelates. Chelates also play vital roles in plant and animal metabolism. Chlorophyll, hemoglobin, vitamin B_{12}, and cytochromes are chelates. Many new aminopolycarboxylic acids (acids containing NH_2 and COOH groups) that form water-soluble chelates have been used for removing metal ions, as in softening of water and clarifying of solutions. The most familiar of these sequestering agents is ethylenediaminetetraacetic acid (EDTA).

In general, chelates are more stable than related coordination compounds that do not contain rings. Thus, they are formed by ions of all the metallic elements even those such as sodium and calcium, which do not usually form stable complexes with unidentate ligands.

Chelating agents are quite numerous, but they are generally restricted to molecules or ions

ETHYLENEDIAMINE

$$H_2N — CH_2 — CH_2 — NH_2$$

OXALATE ION

GLYCINATE ION

$$H_2N — CH_2 — C$$

in which the donor atom is a nonmetal of periodic group V A or VI A, usually nitrogen, oxygen, or sulfur. The donor atom may be either neutral (coordinating group) or negative (acidic group). Hence, for bidentate chelates, the most common type, three combinations of donor atoms are possible: there may be two coordinating groups (ethylenediamine), two acidic groups (oxalate ion), on one coordinating group and one acidic group (glycinate ion).

A particularly important type of chelate, called an "inner complex salt," is formed when the coordination number and charge of the central metal ion are exactly balanced by the total number of donor groups and charges, respectively, of the chelating ligands. Since such chelates have no electrical charge, are frequently insoluble in water and soluble in nonpolar solvents, and exhibit intense colors that differ greatly from those of the unchelated metal ion, they are used extensively in chemical analysis. The brilliant scarlet precipitate of bis (dimethylglyoximato) nickel (II) formed by the interaction of dimethylglyoxime with as little as one part of nickel in two million parts of water is probably the best known compound of this type.

GEORGE B. KAUFFMAN
California State College at Fresno

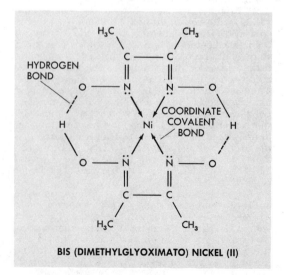

BIS (DIMETHYLGLYOXIMATO) NICKEL (II)

CHÉLIFF RIVER, shä-lĕf', is the principal river of Algeria. It rises in the Djebel Amour ranges of the Saharan Atlas Mountains and is about 450 miles (742 km) long. The river first flows north, crossing the Tell Atlas Mountains and then turns west and empties into the Mediterranean north of Mostaganem. The Chéliff was dammed for irrigation and hydroelectric power in 1942, and its lower valley has intensive agriculture. The name is also spelled *Sheliff*.

CHEŁM, кнelm, is a city in Poland, in Lublin province, about 40 miles (64 km) from the border of the USSR. Chełm (Russian, *Khelm*) is a rail junction and a processing and trade center for the farming region near the city. Machinery and furniture are manufactured in Chełm.

Chełm came under Austrian rule with the third partition of Poland in 1795. In 1815, Poland was revived as a kingdom under Russian rule, and Chełm has belonged to Poland since then. It was the site of a German victory over Russia in August 1915. In 1944 it was the first Polish city to be taken by the Soviet Army. The new Polish republic was proclaimed in Chełm on July 22, 1944. Population: (1964 est.) 33,500.

CHEŁMNO, кнelm'nô, is an industrial town in Bydgoszcz province, Poland. Chełmno (German, Kulm) is situated on the Vistula River, about 24 miles (39 km) northeast of the city of Bydgoszcz. Machinery and furniture are Chełmno's major manufactures. The town developed around a fort built by the Teutonic Knights in 1231. Chełmno was Polish from the 15th to the 18th centuries. It was held by Prussia and then Germany until 1919, when it was returned to Poland. Population: (1964) 17,100.

CHELMSFORD, chems'fərd. The titles of Viscount and Baron Chelmsford are borne by the head of the Thesiger family, which was founded in England by John Andrew Thesiger (1722–1783), a native of Saxony. His second son, Charles Thesiger (died 1831), was the father of Frederic (1794–1878), for whom the barony was created in 1858. Frederic was a British naval officer in the Napoleonic Wars; then, changing his profession, he was called to the bar in 1818. He became a king's counsel in 1834, and during 12 years in Parliament (1840–1852) was solicitor general (1844) and attorney general (1845–1852). He was lord chancellor in 1858–1859 and 1866–1868.

Frederic Augustus Thesiger (1827–1905), his son and successor as 2d Baron Chelmsford, had a distinguished military career. He served in the Crimean War, the Indian mutiny, and several colonial wars in Africa. In the Zulu War (1879) he narrowly retrieved victory from defeat after being superseded in his command.

His eldest son, Frederic John Napier Thesiger (1868–1933), 3d Baron Chelmsford, was a colonial governor in Queensland (1905–1909) and New South Wales (1909–1913) and viceroy of India (1916–1921). His name is commemorated in the Montagu-Chelmsford report (1918), which began self-government in India. He was created Viscount Chelmsford in 1921. His elder son died of wounds in World War I. His younger son, Andrew Charles Gerald Thesiger (1903–   ), succeeded him as 2d Viscount and Baron Chelmsford in 1933.

L. G. PINE, *Former Editor of "Burke's Peerage"*

CHELMSFORD, chems'fərd, a municipal borough in England, the county town of Essex, is at the confluence of the Chelmer and Cann rivers, 28 miles (45 km) northeast of London. Its cathedral, completed in 1424, collapsed and was rebuilt in 1800. The town developed in the 1st century as Caesaromagus. The grammar school dates from 1551. Chelmsford is an agricultural market town and manufactures radio and electrical equipment, ball bearings, and optical instruments. There is trade, especially in lumber and grain, and grain is milled. Population: (1961) 49,908.

CHELMSFORD, chemz'fərd, a town in northeastern Massachusetts, in Middlesex county, about 22 miles (35 km) northwest of Boston. It is in an agricultural region. Chelmsford has textile, wool-processing, and electronics plants, factories producing wooden boxes and reproductions of Colonial furniture, and a large gray-granite quarry. Places of interest include the Fiske House (1790), the Unitarian Church (1840), and the nearby Billerica State Forest. The town was settled about 1650 and incorporated in 1655. Government is by selectmen. Population: 31,432.

CHELSEA, chel'sē, in London, England, is an area on the north bank of the Thames River in a part of the city known as the West End. Chelsea was formerly a separate metropolitan borough of London, but it was merged in 1965 with the royal borough of Kensington to form the royal borough of Kensington and Chelsea.

Since the 1700's, Chelsea has been an artistic and literary quarter. Writers and artists associated with it have included Swift, Steele, Smollett, Turner, Whistler, Carlyle, George Eliot, and Oscar Wilde. The tradition continues in Chelsea's present Bohemian quarter.

Notable buildings include Chelsea Old Church and the Chelsea Royal Hospital. The church, parts of which dated to the 14th century, was ruined in World War II, although most of the Sir Thomas More Chapel survived. The Royal Hospital, for old and invalid soldiers, is a Christopher Wren structure begun in 1682 and completed 10 years later. The buildings are arranged in three courts set in gardens fronting the Thames.

CHELSEA, chel'sē, an industrial city in northeastern Massachusetts, in Suffolk county, is situated between the Mystic and Chelsea rivers, 2 miles (3 km) northeast of Boston, with which it is connected by the Maurice J. Tobin Memorial Bridge. The city's chief manufactures are rubber heels and soles, women's shoes, and slide projectors. Oceangoing tankers use the Chelsea River to reach oil storage yards in Chelsea.

The first permanent settlement was made in 1624 by English planters and was called Winnisimmet. It became the town of Chelsea in 1739. During the Revolutionary War siege of Boston by the Continental army, the left wing of Washington's forces was located in Chelsea. One of the first captures of a British vessel by the Patriots was made at the Battle of Chelsea Creek on May 27, 1775.

Chelsea was a summer resort for Boston residents until its industrial growth after the Civil War. On April 12, 1908, one third of the city was destroyed by fire. Chelsea is governed by a mayor and council. Population: 30,625.

MILDRED A. BROWN, *Chelsea Public Library*

COURTESY OF THE VICTORIA AND ALBERT MUSEUM, LONDON

CHELSEA red anchor mark tureen, from
about 1755, in the form of a hen and chicks.

CHELSEA FIGURINE, *The Girl in a Swing*,
made at Charles Gouyn's factory about 1752.

CHELSEA PORCELAIN, chel'sē pôr'sə-lən, is the
product of an English pottery factory founded
shortly before 1745 in Chelsea, which is now part
of London. The probable founders were Charles
Gouyn, a jeweler, and Nicholas Sprimont, a
noted rococo silversmith. They in turn may have
derived their original formula from Thomas Bri-
and, a chemist who demonstrated his porcelain
before the Royal Society in 1743.

Incised Triangle Mark. The earliest Chelsea
wares, often marked with an incised triangle,
were usually copies from contemporary rococo
silver, some perhaps from the design-books of
Juste Aurèle Meissonier, goldsmith to Louis XV
of France. Triangle-mark porcelain is extremely
glassy and, when held to the light, reveals many
points of brightness, called "pin holes." Specimens of this type are very rare, the most frequent
survival being a small cream jug called a "goat
and bee" jug from its molded decoration.

Gouyn dissolved his connection with the original factory about 1750 and started another nearby. Its products, very similar to those of the
parent organization, include the figure known as
"Girl in a Swing," which has given its name to
the entire production of Gouyn's short-lived
enterprise.

Raised Anchor Mark. Nicholas Sprimont, under
the patronage of the Duke of Cumberland, became proprietor of the Chelsea factory in 1750.
He began to produce a slightly less glassy porcelain, distinguished by circular patches, known as
"moons," that are visible when the piece is held
to the light. An anchor in raised relief on a small
oval pad marks this ware. From 1750 to 1754
the factory made a specialty of wares decorated
in enamel colors in the style of Japanese porcelains by Sakaida Kakiemon. Chelsea derived
some of its designs from products of the Meissen
factory in Germany, including harbor scenes by
the artist J. G. Heintze. It also used designs of
fables and animal subjects by the Irish miniature
painter Jeffryes Hamet O'Neale. Chelsea itself
produced a few figures of distinction, including
those based on drawings of birds from a book by
George Edwardes.

Red Anchor Mark. In 1752–1753 a new kind
of porcelain, usually marked with a small anchor
painted in red, was introduced at Chelsea. Less
glassy than either of the two earlier types, this

porcelain was commonly used for figures, many of
which were based on Meissen porcelains designed
by Johann Joachim Kändler and J. F. Eberlein.

The Chelsea factory eagerly adopted the late
rococo style, producing numerous tureens in the
form of animals, vegetables, and fruit. These
wares are the finest examples of Chelsea porcelain. The so-called "German flowers," based on
Meissen designs, occur sporadically during the
red anchor period, as well as close copies of natural flowers (known as "Hans Sloane flowers")
taken from the illustrations to the *Gardener's
Dictionary* by Philip Miller. Leaf-forms were employed for decorative dishes and tureen stands.
In 1755, under the inspiration of French porcelain made at Vincennes, Chelsea adopted an
underglaze blue ground color called Mazarine
blue and introduced gilding into its wares.

Gold Anchor Mark. The Chelsea factory was
closed from 1756 to 1758 because Sprimont was
ill. When the factory reopened, a gold anchor became the Chelsea mark, and the style of its wares
showed the strong influence of Sèvres porcelain.
Gold anchor ware, decorated with flowers and
exotic birds based on Sèvres designs, is notable
for a thick, rich glaze, sometimes crazed, which
was especially suitable for painting and ground-
laying. New ground colors were introduced, including claret (a version of Sèvres *rose Pompa-
dour*), turquoise, green, and yellow. Also, Chelsea products were made in much larger sizes than
formerly, and the production of decorative trifles,
known as Chelsea toys—scent bottles, *bonbon-
nières*, seals, and *étuis*—was greatly increased.

The effect of the full-blown rococo style of
gold anchor ware is seen in the scrolling curves
that form the handles of vases and ornament the
molded bases of figures. Vase paintings, superbly
executed, were sometimes based on the work of
rococo artists such as François Boucher.

Chelsea produced little work of importance
after 1763. Finally, in 1770, the factory was
bought by William Duesbury, who continued to
operate it until 1784 as an adjunct to his own
porcelain factory in Derby.

GEORGE SAVAGE
Author of "Porcelain Through the Ages"

Further Reading: King, William, *Chelsea Porcelain*
(London 1922); Savage, George, *Eighteenth Century
English Porcelain* (New York 1952).

CHELTENHAM, chelt'nəm, is a municipal borough in England, in Gloucestershire, on the River Chelt, 7 miles (11 km) northeast of Gloucester. Its mineral springs, discovered in 1716, became famous when George III visited them in 1788. An educational center, Cheltenham has three well-known privately endowed boarding ("public") schools: Cheltenham College (boys, 1841); Cheltenham Ladies' College (1853); and Dean Close School (boys, 1884); it also has teacher-training colleges and a grammar school founded before 1550. Manufactures are bricks, aircraft, anesthetics, and rubber goods. It is known for music and cricket festivals and horse racing. Population: (1961) 72,154.

CHELTENHAM, chel'tən-ham, a township in southeastern Pennsylvania, is in Montgomery county, about 9 miles (14 km) north of Philadelphia, of which it is a residential suburb. It includes the unincorporated communities of Elkins Park, Wyncote, Melrose Park, La Mott, Edge Hill, and Chelton Hills. The township is the site of Faith Theological Seminary, a 4-year coeducational institution, and the Tyler School of Art of Temple University. Cheltenham was first settled in 1690 and was incorporated as a township in 1900. It has the commission-manager form of government. Population: 40,238.

CHELYABINSK, chi-lyä'byinsk, in the USSR, is the second largest city of the Ural industrial region. The capital of Chelyabinsk oblast of the Russian republic, it is on the Miass River, 930 miles (1,500 km) east of Moscow.

Chelyabinsk is on the northern margins of a brown-coal basin and on the Soviet Union's major east-west railroad. A center of heavy industry, it has an iron and steel plant, a steel-pipe mill, a ferroalloys plant, and a zinc refinery. The city's factories manufacture tractors, press-forge equipment, machine tools and dies, road-building machines, hoisting equipment, and precision instruments. There are also chemical plants in Chelyabinsk.

Founded in 1736 as a Russian fortress, Chelyabinsk became a grain-trading and transportation center with the construction of the Trans-Siberian Railroad in the late 19th century. Industrial development of the city began in the 1930's and was intensified during World War II, when Chelyabinsk was one of the Soviet Union's arsenals for the war effort.

Chelyabinsk oblast, with an area of 29,300 square miles (87,900 sq km), occupies the southeastern part of the Ural Mountains and foothills. It is a mineral-rich area, with brown coal, iron ore, nickel, copper, zinc, and gold. One third of the territory is farmland. The industrial centers of the oblast, besides Chelyabinsk, the capital, are Magnitogorsk, Zlatoust, and Miass. Population (1966): of the city, 820,000; of the oblast, 3,263,000.

THEODORE SHABAD
Editor of "Soviet Geography"

CHELYUSKIN, Cape, chi-lyōōs'kin, the extreme northern point of Asia, on the Taimyr Peninsula in the USSR. It is also called Cape Severo or Cape Severo-Vostok (Northeast Cape). It was named Chelyuskin after a Russian officer who died there on an expedition that he led in 1742; it was not revisited until 1878, when Nils Adolf Nordenskjöld reached it in the *Vega.*

CHEMICAL ANALYSIS is the determination of the chemical components of a substance. Chemical analysis is the chemist's way of answering the question "What's in it?" The material to be studied may be anything from a carload of ore to the genetic material of a fruit fly; the information sought may range from the kinds and amounts of chemical elements present to the ways in which the atoms are arranged in their compounds.

Before the chemist can begin an analysis, he must obtain a representative sample of the material to be analyzed. He may, for example, be required to determine the composition of a carload of ore by analyzing a sample that weighs only a gram or two. If, as in this example, the material is not homogeneous, the selection of the sample may prove to be an extremely difficult procedure.

After a representative sample is obtained, two principal stages in its chemical analysis follow: (1) the separation of the sample into its constituent compounds, or even into its constituent elements, and (2) the measurement of the various constituents that have been separated. Of these two steps, separation takes the most time, and chemists try to avoid it by testing for single elements or compounds as part of the whole mixture. With complex materials this short-cut nearly always causes a loss of accuracy or sensitivity.

. **Separation.** The principal methods used in chemical separations are precipitation, distillation, solvent extraction, chromatography (including ion exchange), fractional freezing and zone melting, centrifugation, diffusion and electrodialysis, and electroplating and electrophoresis. Of all these methods, chromatography is the most commonly used for organic and inorganic compounds. In gas chromatography separation and measurement of substances are accomplished simultaneously by one instrument.

Precipitation is another important separation technique. In this method, a solvent is used to extract an element or compound whose presence is suspected, and the resulting solution is treated so that the element or compound is converted to an insoluble compound that settles out as a sediment, or precipitate. The precipitate is collected, washed, dried, and weighed. If it is a single pure compound, the determination is complete; if not, further separation of the mixture may be necessary. Precipitation is the basis of gravimetric analysis, which is accurate and selective, but it is a slow method and can be used to determine only one substance at a time.

Measurement. The chief methods of measurement are weighing, titration, spectroscopy by emission and absorption of radiation, measurement of radioactivity, and measurement of temperature and heat.

Titration involves the controlled addition of a substance that reacts selectively with the constituent to be measured until a signal indicates that all of the constituent present in the solution has reacted with the added substance. The signal may be the change of color of a trace substance, called an "indicator," or it may be a sharp change in electrical potential or current. Titration is usually done by adding a measured volume of a standard solution (volumetric analysis). However, the weight of the solution may be measured instead, or the reagent may be generated by a measured quantity of electricity. Titration methods are fairly precise; that is, they can be repeated on the same sample with very close agreement, but they lack sensitivity and cannot detect very small amounts of a substance.

Spectroscopic methods are the most frequently used for measurement of substances. They are fast and sensitive, but they are ordinarily not very precise. In *emission spectroscopy,* the test sample may be made to emit light or other radiation (ultraviolet, X-ray, or gamma ray) by various stimuli, including flames, an arc or a spark, the impact of electrons or neutrons, or high-energy radiation.

In *absorption spectroscopy,* which is widely used, the sample is made to absorb rather than emit radiation. Atomic absorption spectroscopy, in which a solution is sprayed into a flame through which a light beam passes, is excellent for measuring traces of metallic elements. Ultraviolet and infrared absorption provide identification of organic compounds and knowledge of their structure, as does the new and powerful technique of nuclear magnetic resonance.

Several newer electrical techniques, based on potential-current-time relationships (as is the older method of polarography), are used for oxidizable and reducible materials that contain traces of metal ions.

HAROLD F. WALTON, *University of Colorado*

CHEMICAL AND BIOLOGICAL WARFARE.

Toxic chemical and biological agents may be used in warfare to disable or destroy an enemy by direct effect or indirectly through the reduction of his food supply. Such warfare is waged by disseminating toxic chemicals or biological materials from the air or on the surface of the earth. The term "chemical and biological warfare" (CB warfare) also includes the defensive measures against such attacks.

In addition to toxic chemicals, chemical warfare includes the use of smokes for concealment and identification and of flame weapons, including thermite and magnesium incendiary munitions and the flamethrowers and napalm bombs in which thickened gasoline is the fuel.

The main method of attack with both chemical and biological weapons is to form a cloud of fine particles (an aerosol) of the material that remains airborne for a time during which people on the target inhale it. A secondary method of attack is to penetrate the skin with toxic chemical or biological agents.

Military Advantages of Toxic Weapons. Because of the nature of cloud attacks, chemical and biological agents can be effective over large areas. An aerosol penetrates buildings and fortifications and seeks out enemy personnel, even though the target has not been accurately located. If these people have not taken protective measures, a high percentage of casualties, perhaps up to 30%, may result. In addition, these weapons have the advantage of doing relatively little property damage, so that if a port or similar facility is captured it is usable immediately.

Another advantage of these agents is that it is not necessary to kill to accomplish the military purpose involved. Chemical compounds and biological materials may be developed which incapacitate temporarily with subsequent full recovery. No other weapons of war allow this predetermination of a minimum level of personnel damage and still permit the military task to be accomplished. These characteristics make such agents the most flexible of the weapons of war.

Chemical Agents. The *lethal chemical agents* of importance are the anticholinesterase compounds, the nerve gases. These agents kill rapidly by inhibiting the action of the enzyme cholinesterase, resulting in lack of muscular control and in respiratory paralysis. The dose required to kill a man is very small, about one milligram. The nerve gases are odorless and colorless and give no immediate, easily detectable physiological indication of their presence.

Tabun, US symbol GA (dimethylaminoethoxycyanophosphine oxide), and sarin, US symbol GB methylisopropoxy fluoro-phosphine oxide), the more volatile liquids of this class, kill mainly on inhalation. Both vapor and liquid are also lethal when absorbed through the skin or eyes. A relatively nonvolatile nerve gas is VX. Minute droplets on the skin can cause death, as most of the material is absorbed rather than evaporating. Aerosols of VX are effective on inhalation.

Botulin, a toxin formed by the bacterium *Clostridium botulinum,* is one of the most lethal poisons against humans. Possibly 0.03 milligram, inhaled or ingested, causes fatal botulism. The lethal agents of previous wars, chlorine and phosgene, are no longer considered effective war agents against protected troops.

Incapacitating chemical agents may be designed to attack any specific body system, reducing one's ability to function physically or mentally. BZ, an example of such an agent, causes apparent drunkenness, combining mental confusion with staggering and general loss of fine control of the body. One much-used group of the incapacitants is the riot-control agents. The tear gases CN (chloroacetophenone) and CS (o-chlorobenzylmalononitrile) and the vomiting agent Adamsite, DM (diphenylaminochloroarsine), have been used by most countries for controlling domestic riots, and in the war in South Vietnam. Agents can also be developed to cause effects such as those of heavy tranquilizers and morphine. The enterotoxin of *Staphylococcus aureus* causes acute gastroenteritis, which is rarely fatal.

Mustard, US symbol HD (2,2'-dichlorodiethyl sulfide), is primarily an incapacitating agent. It was called "king of gases" in World War I because of its effectiveness in causing casualties, although only about 2% died. Its military value lies in its toxicity on the skin as well as to the lungs and eyes. It is a liquid that volatilizes slowly, remaining in the target area up to several weeks, and the vapor is effective in low concentrations.

Biological Agents. Many diseases can be used for biological warfare. Investigation is necessary to determine whether the organism causing a given disease can be adapted to the purpose—whether it is hardy enough to be produced in quantity, withstand reasonable periods of storage, and live through the various stresses to which it would be subjected when disseminated from a munition (such as a bomb, artillery shell, or missile) and exposed to the elements. Organisms of any type—viruses, rickettsiae, bacteria, or fungi—may be suitable for biological warfare.

Chemical agents sometimes have a delay period before their effects appear, but biological agents always have an incubation period. This may range from a day to several weeks, depending on the organism. The period of disability may also vary, from a few days to several months, depending on the disease and the treatment. Rarely do disease organisms penetrate the unbroken skin, but this barrier can be breached by mechanical means—darts or shell fragments; or by insect vectors such as mosquitoes, ticks, or fleas.

Lethality is not as clear-cut a designation with biological agents as it is with chemical agents. Such factors as immunity, both innate and acquired, the portal of entry by which the disease organism enters the body, and treatment are all important in determining the result of exposure to biological agents; thus it is not simply a matter of supplying a sufficiently high dose to cause death.

One *lethal disease* with a relatively high fatality rate that could be considered for biological warfare is plague. Untreated, the disease could result in over 50% mortality among those who become infected. With treatment the rate could drop to less than 10%. Other diseases might include the encephalitides, such as Japanese B, which has a fatality rate of from 35 to 60% of persons infected, and Rocky Mountain spotted fever, which might result in a rate of over 50% deaths among those infected if untreated but less than 1% with treatment. These mortality figures are for those who contract the disease, in its naturally occurring form. Not all persons exposed become infected.

Among the *incapacitating diseases* that could be suitable for biological warfare are Venezuelan equine encephalomyelitis and dengue fever (breakbone fever), both with mortalities under 1%, and Q fever with a death rate of 1 to 4% untreated and less than 1% treated.

Diseases that are intermediate in severity and might be used in biological warfare are psittacosis (parrot fever) with a mortality of about 10% untreated and 2% treated, tularemia (rabbit fever) with fatalities of between 5 to 8% untreated but less than 1% treated, and brucellosis with a mortality of 2 to 5% untreated and less than 2% treated.

Military Uses. A chemical agent may be a solid, liquid or gas, although it would rarely be in a gaseous state in the munition as the amount contained would be small. The gas would be formed from a liquid upon detonation of the munition. If the agent is mainly intended to be inhaled, it would be disseminated from the munition either as an aerosol or a gas. If it is intended to be absorbed through the skin, it would be disseminated in larger droplets either to touch the skin directly or to contaminate vegetation or matériel so as to reach the skin indirectly. Attacking through the skin would circumvent the highly effective protection of the mask.

Biological agents may be in solid or slurry form, to be disseminated as an aerosol.

Chemical and biological agents may be disseminated upwind from the target so that the material drifts over the target achieving maximum surprise, or munitions may be placed directly on the target to establish a cloud of the agent rapidly before adequate defensive measures are taken. In the latter case, there would be an off-target effect as the agent drifts downwind.

A spray tank can be used to disseminate either an aerosol or heavier drops of chemical agent for ground contamination. The tank may be used on a plane, on a missile, or in a vehicle on land or sea. Agents can also be disseminated from shells, rockets, or land mines. Bomblets, scattered from airdropped clusters or missile warheads, are suitable for disseminating either chemical or biological agents for on-target attack.

Chemical agents of the more highly toxic materials such as the nerve gases can be used to attack areas of up to tens of square miles. Biological agents, because the organisms reproduce when established in a host, can be effective in much smaller doses and can be used to attack much larger areas, up to thousands of square miles. The size of the area affected by biological agents can be controlled by the amount of agent dispersed, through the diffusing effect of wind currents, and by the timing of the release, because most organisms live only a few minutes in sunlight.

The strategy controlling the use of toxic agents would generally dictate that lethal agents be used on targets manned entirely by soldiers. Targets peopled by soldiers and civilians would be attacked with incapacitating agents.

Both chemical and biological agents lend themselves to covert use.

Defense. The basic protection against either chemical or biological agents is the protective mask. The mask covers the entire face, and the air inhaled is purified by charcoal and fiber filters to ensure that both gases and particles are removed. If used in time and worn properly, it gives practically complete protection to the lungs and eyes. The difficulty lies in knowing when to put on the mask. There might be warning signs and devices to detect chemical agents, but at present there are no practical devices or physiological signs to warn of the presence of biological agents.

Other individual protective measures include both permeable and impermeable clothing. The permeable clothing normally would be the regular coveralls or uniforms the serviceman wears, treated to prevent penetration by chemical agents, liquid or vapor, or to accelerate the death of biological organisms. Gloves and hoods, either permeable or impermeable, can be worn, and boots can be treated to resist penetration by agents. Impermeable clothing is simply a plastic barrier between the man and the hostile materials. Collective protectors are available to purify the air drawn into buildings and fortifications.

If the various types of barriers fail in preventing the chemical agent from reaching the man, treatment measures are available. An ointment to protect against mustard can be used either prophylactically or immediately after contamination. Mustard burns are treated similarly to thermal burns. They heal very slowly, although they are relatively painless. A combination of artificial respiration and massive injections of an antidote, atropine tartrate, can reduce deaths from nerve gases. The most effective method of artificial respiration is mouth-to-mouth.

Against biological agents, the normal medical treatment for the disease would be used. However, many of the diseases have the same early symptoms as the common cold, and as a result treatment might be delayed until too late to be effective. Furthermore, adequate therapeutic measures are not presently available for all of the diseases of possible use in biological warfare. In addition, disease organisms can be developed that are resistant to antibiotics. Vaccines would be employed if available.

Decontamination measures and materials are available for use against both chemical and biological agents to clean contaminated persons, equipment, some food (particularly in containers), and limited areas of terrain. It is difficult to contaminate large bodies of water with chemical agents, but if exposed water has to be consumed, boiling it for 15 minutes and then chlorinating it normally makes it safe. Any food or water in a dustproof container is normally protected against biological agents. Again, boiling for 15 minutes makes it safe. Chlorination makes water safe against many biological agents, but not all of them.

Identification devices are available for chemical agents. Besides determining what agents may have been employed, they indicate when it is safe to unmask. Identification measures for biological agents are still too slow and not sufficiently specific to be generally valuable.

Antifood Warfare. Antifood warfare includes attacks on both crops and animals. It is potentially effective in any prolonged war. Anticrop agents may be either chemical or biological and include defoliating agents. The logical targets would be wheat, rice and other cereal grains, and potatoes, as these are the main foods of most of the peoples of the world.

The chemical agents, mainly of the herbicide variety, may also be used to defoliate trees and other vegetation in order to improve observation at ground level or from the air. The agents are 2,4-D (2,4-dichlorophenoxyacetic acid), 2,4,5-T (2,4,5-trichlorophenoxyacetic acid), and cacodylic acid, all of which are used in weed control. Their toxicity to humans is low.

The major biological antifood agents are the fungi. These include the cereal rusts, late blight of potatoes, and rice blast. These living organisms would be spread even beyond the large area of the initial attack by the natural formation of lesions that burst and shoot out spores to be carried by the wind.

Antianimal attacks would be with biological agents, and would not only reduce the food supply but would also reduce industrial and medical supplies, as well as a form of draft power and transport still important in much of the world.

National Capabilities. Any first-class military power is prepared to defend itself against chemical and biological warfare and, as a minimum, to wage chemical warfare. In addition, it can be expected that the major powers have the capability for offensive biological warfare.

Although it requires much research and testing to develop agents and weapons to wage sophisticated biological warfare, almost any nation could produce the required equipment to wage at least covert biological warfare effectively. The factories needed to produce the agents can be small, and if a country desires to violate any agreement banning production, they can be easily concealed. Modified commercial equipment could be used for the production and dissemination of agents.

Chemical warfare requires larger production plants and somewhat greater sophistication in weapons. Because of the large amounts of munitions required, production, testing, shipping, and storage of munitions would be far more difficult to conceal than with biological weapons.

History. Chemical warfare was first used on a large scale in World War I by the Germans at Ypres, Belgium, on April 22, 1915, although the French had fired gas grenades before that time. Gas was then used widely by both sides. Mustard, chlorine, and phosgene were used extensively, and many other agents were tried. The

gas mask was the main protective equipment developed. Casualties on both sides from gas were extensive, although the death rate was low. Col. Harry Gilchrist, M. D., of the U. S. Army Medical Corps, made an extensive study of comparative casualties from gas and other weapons in World War I and concluded that gas "is not only one of the most efficient agencies for effecting casualties but is the most humane method ever applied on the battlefield."

Gas was used by Italy against Ethiopia in the Abyssinian campaign in 1936 and by Japan against China from 1937 to 1943. Gas was not used in World War II after Japan used it. Since then riot-control agents have been used extensively around the world by various nations.

Biological agents have not been used in modern warfare on a large scale, but all through history diseased bodies have been thrown over city walls during sieges, and decomposing bodies have been used to contaminate sources of drinking water. The American Indians, particularly susceptible to smallpox, were intentionally infected with the disease by the Spanish, French, and British; large numbers of deaths resulted.

International Status. Until the 1970's the only major international agreements restricting chemical and biological weapons were the Hague Convention of 1899 and the Geneva Protocol (Chemical-Biological) of 1925. Both had been violated, and neither had been signed by the United States. On Nov. 25, 1969, President Nixon unilaterally renounced U. S. use of such weapons and ordered U. S. stocks destroyed. A treaty banning biological warfare, drawn up by the Geneva Disarmament Conference in 1971, was approved by the UN General Assembly on Dec. 16, 1971, and signed by the United States and some 70 other countries on April 10, 1972. This treaty and the 1925 Geneva Protocol were ratified by the U. S. Senate on Dec. 16, 1974.

JACQUARD H. ROTHSCHILD
Brigadier General, USA (Retired); Author of "Tomorrow's Weapons—Chemical and Biological"

Bibliography
American Chemical Society, *Nonmilitary Defense, Chemical and Biological Defenses in Perspective*, Advances in Chemistry Series, No. 26 (Washington 1960).
Rothschild, Jacquard H., *Tomorrow's Weapons—Chemical and Biological* (New York 1964).
U. S. Department of the Army, *Chemical, Biological, and Nuclear Defense*, FM 21–40 (Washington 1966).
U. S. Department of the Army, *Employment of Chemical and Biological Agents*, FM 3–10 (Washington 1966).
U. S. Department of the Army, *Military Biology and Biological Warfare Agents*, TM 3–216 (Washington 1956).
U. S. Department of the Army, *Military Chemistry and Chemical Agents*, TM 3–215 (Washington 1956).
U. S. Department of the Army, *Tactics and Techniques of Chemical, Biological, and Radiological (CBR) Warfare*, FM 3–5 (Washington 1958).
U. S. House of Representatives, Committee on Science and Astronautics, *Research in CBR (Chemical, Biological, and Radiological Warfare*, 86th Congress, 1st Session, H. R. No. 815 (Washington 1959).

CHEMICAL BOND. See BOND, in chemistry.

CHEMICAL COMPOUND. See COMPOUND.

CHEMICAL ELEMENT. See ELEMENT.

CHEMICAL ENGINEERING. See CHEMICAL INDUSTRIES—*Careers*.

CHEMICAL EQUATION. See EQUATION.

CHEMICAL EQUILIBRIUM. See EQUILIBRIUM.

A CHEMICAL PLANT producing ethylene lights the skyline at Texas City, Texas.

CHEMICAL INDUSTRIES. The chemical industries are based on the use of chemical reactions to convert relatively simple and inexpensive raw materials (such as coal, salt, petroleum, and air) into products that have much greater unit value. For example, from crude oil costing only about 1 cent per pound, the chemical industries make nylon yarn worth nearly $1 a pound.

One branch of the chemical industries produces thousands of "basic chemicals" that in turn are used to produce a host of "end products" for sale to other industries and to individual consumers. Thus from two principal raw materials, petroleum and natural gas, the organic chemical industry produces two primary ("building-block") chemicals, phenol and acetic anhydride. These are the two main "intermediate chemicals" used in the manufacture of a well-known end product, aspirin (acetyl salicylic acid).

SIGNIFICANCE OF CHEMICAL INDUSTRIES

Chemical industries help supply man's basic needs for food, clothing, and shelter; serve all other industries; and contribute to technical progress.

Supplying Man's Basic Needs. Products of the chemical industries are of fundamental importance to the industries that supply mankind with food, clothing, and shelter. The chemical industries produce fertilizers and pesticides that have greatly helped to increase production of food and fiber crops. They produce synthetic fibers, dyestuffs, and other chemicals for textile and clothing manufacturers. They produce paints and other products needed for the manufacture, use, and preservation of building materials such as wood, steel, glass, and concrete.

In addition, one branch of the chemical industries—the pharmaceutical industry—discovers and produces the antibiotics, vaccines, anesthetics, and other medicinal products that have helped conquer various diseases and have helped millions of persons to attain good health and long life.

Serving Other Industries. Most of the chemical industries' output is sold to other industries rather than directly to the public. For instance, the chemical industries sell oxygen and sulfuric acid for use in steelmaking, soda ash for use in glassmaking, and chlorine for use in papermaking. The chemical industries supply the auto industry

with paints, plastics, sealing compounds, hydraulic fluids, and other chemical products. Automobile tires usually are made with synthetic rubber and synthetic-fiber tire cords produced by the chemical industries.

For the food and beverage industries, the chemical industries furnish natural and synthetic flavors and colors, vitamins and minerals for proper nutrition, salt and other preservatives to prevent spoilage and rancidity, citric acid and baking soda to control the acid-alkaline balance, and synthetic sweeteners for special diet foods. For the textile and clothing makers, the chemical industries supply man-made and synthetic fibers, dyes, scouring and bleaching agents, and chemicals to impart nonshrink and wash and wear properties.

The chemical industries supply water-treatment agents that make water safe and pleasant to drink; they make uranium fuel rods for nuclear power stations; and they make special-grade adhesives and plastics for supersonic airplanes. They play a central role in the economy of every industrialized nation because they supply materials essential to all other industries.

Contributing to Technological Progress. Moreover, the chemical industries in every large nation contribute to overall technological progress. The contributions are made through the development of useful and profitable new products; through "technical service" work to help improve customers' products; and through "contract research" work to help solve scientific and engineering problems for industry and government.

Examples of achievements in these three lines of endeavor may be found in the work of chemists and engineers employed by the Du Pont chemical company. For their own company, they developed nylon polyamide synthetic fiber in 1935, climaxing a 10-year research effort that cost $27 million. For a customer company, in 1923, they helped launch the production of tetraethyl lead, the gasoline antiknock additive that contributed to the success of the gasoline-driven automobile. For the U. S. government during World War II, they helped make a success of the atomic bomb project by designing and operating chemical plants to produce plutonium.

The chemical industries serve as a reservoir of technical manpower that can be used to help solve public problems, such as mosquito control and sewage disposal, as well as problems of private industry, such the development of airplane seat upholstery that is lightweight and flame resistant.

INDUSTRY STRUCTURE

In the United States the chemical industries consist of some 11,000 corporations, more than 3,000 sole proprietorships, and some 700 partnerships, together employing about 1 million people. In the late 1960's these organizations operated some 13,000 manufacturing plants, in which about 600,000 of the industries' employees worked.

Manufacturers. The corporations account for some 90% of the industries' total shipments (worth about $40 billion per year). In the late 1960's they were investing some $3 billion each year for new plant and equipment in the United States and also about $3 billion a year in their foreign operations. They were spending about $1.5 billion each year for research and development work. Within the United States, average investment per employee was about $25,000, a sum considerably higher than in most other industries. It reflected a high degree of mechanization and automation with extensive use of electronic instruments and controls.

The largest manufacturers of chemicals and allied products in the United States in the late 1960's were Du Pont, Procter & Gamble, Union Carbide, Monsanto, Dow Chemical, Allied Chemical, Olin Mathieson, and the Celanese Corp. Each had annual sales of $1 billion or more.

The most profitable segment of the chemical industries in the second half of the 20th century has been pharmaceutical manufacturing. Among

FERTILIZER COMPONENTS are manufactured in immense facilities developed by the chemical industries.

the largest U. S. producers of ethical (prescription) drugs were Merck & Co., Eli Lilly & Co., Chas. Pfizer & Co., Abbott Laboratories, Upjohn Co., and Smith Kline & French Laboratories.

The industry also includes the chemical divisions of petroleum companies, of steel companies, and of companies in many other industries. Among companies with large and active chemical divisions are the Standard Oil Co. (New Jersey), the Eastman Kodak Co., and the United States Steel Co.

Many large U. S. chemical plants built since World War II are on the coastal plains of Texas and Louisiana, near oil and natural gas for petrochemical feedstocks (raw materials), near salt and other chemicals, and near both ocean and inland-waterway shipping. Other concentrations of U. S. chemical plants are along the Ohio River and some of its tributaries; at Niagara Falls and in the Tennessee River valley, where low-cost electric power is available; and in New Jersey, northern Ohio, and around Chicago, where there are large industrial markets and there is access to ocean or Great Lakes shipping.

Principal Products. Sulfuric acid continues to be produced in far greater volume than any other chemical; output in the United States is approximately 30 million tons per year. Chemicals ranking next in tonnage are anhydrous ammonia, caustic soda, chlorine, soda ash, nitric acid, and phosphoric acid. Among organic chemicals, those in largest production are benzene (about 4 million tons per year), ethyl alcohol, formaldehyde, styrene, and methanol. (Organic chemicals are carbon-containing compounds that are generally obtained from organic materials such as trees and other plants, animal tissues, coal, and oil.)

Production of industrial chemicals, including both organic and inorganic, is the largest segment of the chemical industries; sales of these basic chemicals average about $15 billion per year. Other main divisions of the chemical industries, in descending order of value of shipments, are synthetic materials (fibers, plastics, and rubber); cleaning and toilet goods, including soaps, detergents, polishes, and cosmetics; pharmaceuticals (ethical, proprietary, and veterinary drugs); paints and allied products; agricultural chemicals (mainly fertilizers and pesticides); and miscellaneous chemical products (such as glue and gelatin, printing inks, carbon black, and nonmilitary explosives).

Ranking of Nations. No precise comparison is possible, but on the basis of available data it appears that the nations with the largest chemical industries in the late 1960's ranked in this order: the United States, West Germany, Japan, Britain, the USSR, France, and Italy.

The U. S. chemical industries have attained great size because of their personnel, their rich markets, and their physical resources. Many enterprises failed; the success of those that survived and prospered can often be traced to the tenacity, technical skill, and business acumen of their leaders. The chemical industries have benefited from an abundance of natural riches in the nation. These include huge and readily worked deposits of coal, salt, sulfur, phosphate rock, potash, uranium, and other minerals; large reserves of petroleum and natural gas; vast acreages of croplands and timberlands; and great rivers that provide water for cooling and use in production processes, as well as for low-cost bulk transportation to major industrial and population centers.

ORIGIN AND DEVELOPMENT

In prehistoric times, men carried out simple operations that can be viewed as the beginning of the chemical industries. Limestone and some kind of alkali must have been refined by the craftsmen who made glass in the Middle East about 7000 B.C. The Egyptians must have extracted tannin from bark or leaves for leather tanning about 3000 B.C. The rulers of ancient Rome had their togas colored with a purple dye that the Phoenicians obtained from a kind of mollusk.

In late Roman times, the people of Greece, Italy, and Gaul made soap; a complete soapmaking factory was found in the ruins of Pompeii. By that time the Chinese had invented a kind of gunpowder. Chemical experimenting in the Islamic empire is evidenced by continued international use of chemical terms derived from Arabic words, such as alcohol and alkali.

In a sense the alchemists in medieval Europe carried out small-scale chemical manufacturing. This involved the three principal "mineral acids" (nitric, sulfuric, and hydrochloric acids), as well as salt, sulfur, lime, mercury, and two organic compounds (alcohol from wine, acetic acid from vinegar).

First Industrial Chemical Production. Some historians feel that the chemical industries—if these industries are defined as the conscious use of chemical technology in the hope of sustained economic gain—originated in France in 1790, when Nicolas Leblanc worked out a process for converting common salt into soda ash. This compound was of great use to the soap, glass, and textile industries. Previously soda ash had been obtained only in small quantities from the ashes of the Spanish saltwort plant or, also at great expense, from the natron lakes in Egypt.

Leblanc's process was little used in France. But it was introduced in England by James Muspratt, who built a plant near Liverpool in 1823, and it became the core of the British chemical industries for the next 70 years. Leblanc's required quantities of sulfuric acid, and the production of sulfuric acid in turn required saltpeter (potassium nitrate), so plants were built to produce both of those compounds. The muriatic (hydrochloric) acid that was produced as a by-product in the Leblanc process was a troublesome waste material until someone found that it could be reacted with manganese dioxide to produce chlorine and that the chlorine could then be reacted with lime to produce bleaching powder for the textile industry. Later, other plants were built to recover the sulfur and manganese for reuse.

The chemical industry quickly took root in America. In Boston, in 1635, only 15 years after the landing of the Pilgrims, saltpeter (needed for gunpowder) and alum (used in dyeing and tanning) were produced and sold by John Winthrop, Jr. The first U. S. patent was granted in 1790 to Samuel Hopkins, of Philadelphia, for an improved potash kettle.

Chlor-Alkali Processes. A characteristic of the chemical industries is that older processes are continually being replaced by new and still more efficient technology. The Leblanc process, which made obsolete the leaching of saltwort ashes, in turn was made obsolete by the ammonia-soda process developed in 1863 by Ernest Solvay of Belgium. In Solvay's process, two gases—ammonia and carbon dioxide—are dissolved

GOODYEAR TIRE & RUBBER COMPANY

SAMPLES OF A PAINT RESIN used to control the drying time and improve the quality of newly poured concrete are collected by a chemical plant employee.

in a water solution of common salt. Sodium bicarbonate forms as a white precipitate, which is then converted into soda ash by heating. Some of the soda ash is marketed as such; some is carbonated to produce baking soda; and some is reacted with slaked lime to produce caustic soda.

The Solvay process is giving way to more efficient technology. Caustic soda can now be produced more economically by the electrolytic process, in which an even more valuable chemical commodity—chlorine—is coproduced. This process —which requires large quantities of low-cost salt and electric power—was successfully demonstrated in 1890 in an experimental plant at Bellows Falls, Vt. It was based on the work of Ernest A. Le Sueur while he was a student at the Massachusetts Institute of Technology. Two men who were quick to employ the electrolytic method were Herbert H. Dow, founder of the Dow Chemical Co., of Midland, Mich., now the world's largest producer of chlorine and caustic soda; and Elon Hooker, who organized Hooker Chemical Corp., of New York, a pioneer in the use of low-cost hydroelectric power at Niagara Falls, N. Y., for large-scale production of chemicals.

Sulfuric Acid Processes. Sulfuric acid was produced "by the bell"—that is, in large, bell-shaped glass jars—in the 16th, 17th, and 18th centuries. In 1746, John Roebuck, a physician of Birmingham, England, showed that this useful but corrosive acid could be produced more economically in several large lead chambers than in many glass bell jars (which were expensive and easily broken). In 1749, in London, Joshua Ward patented the use of saltpeter to increase the "yield" in making sulfuric acid.

Although one contact-acid process had been

patented in England in 1831, it was not until the late 1890's that more practical methods were developed—notably in Germany, by Badische Anilin- und Sodafabrik A. G.; and in the United States by General Chemical Co., now part of Allied Chemical Corp. The essential reaction—converting sulfur dioxide into sulfur trioxide—is promoted by the use of either platinum or vanadium pentoxide as a catalyst.

In addition to being more efficient than the lead-chamber process, the contact-acid process was also able to produce highly concentrated acid, such as "fuming" sulfuric acid, which was then in short supply and in heavy demand for the production of valuable coal-tar dyes. The first contact-acid plant in the United States was built at Mineral Point, Wis., for the New Jersey Zinc Co., in 1899. This process now accounts for more than 90% of all the sulfuric acid produced in the United States.

Rise of the Organic Chemical Industry. Before 1850 there was little understanding of organic chemistry and there was only scant production of organic chemicals (carbon-containing compounds). Aside from soapmaking, the organic chemical industry then consisted of a few simple operations such as heating wood without air to obtain charcoal and acetic acid, distilling alcohol from fermented liquors, and treating alcohol with sulfuric acid to make ether for use as an anesthetic. The textile industry still used natural dyes, such as madder and indigo, which were difficult to use, usually expensive, and sometimes hard to get at any price.

Suddenly a new chemical industry was born. A few chemists had investigated the coal tar that was a by-product of the illuminating gas then made from coal in most large cities. Benzene was distilled from coal tar in an experiment in 1815. In 1843, August W. von Hofmann, a German chemist, showed that aniline made from benzene was the same as aniline made from natural indigo. This was an indication that molecules with dyeing properties might be found in coal tar.

Hofmann went to England in 1845 to teach at the Royal College of Chemistry, where he often conjectured that the chemical exploration of coal tar might lead to worthwhile discoveries—such as a way to make synthetic quinine. A student, William H. Perkin, set up a small laboratory in an attic and tried to do just that. The result was a murky precipitate that one might quickly throw away, but Perkin dipped a white cloth into the beaker, and the cloth turned lavender. He patented this first synthetic dye, which he called mauve, and in the following year (1857) began producing the compound.

Perkin's success prompted many other chemists, particularly in Germany, to seek coal-tar dyes. Several dozen useful new colors were developed by 1880. Even the two most widely used natural colors were swept into disuse: by 1890, alizarin from coal tar had almost completely replaced madder; and by 1910, synthetic indigo had fully replaced the natural product. Probably the first makers of synthetic dyes in the United States were Thomas and Charles Holliday, who began producing magenta and other coal-tar chemicals in Brooklyn, N. Y., in 1864. The largest U. S. producer of coal-tar dyes in the late 19th and early 20th centuries was Schoellkopf Aniline & Chemical Co., founded at Buffalo, N. Y., in 1879, a predecessor of Allied Chemical Corp.

Previously, coal tar had been used as a wood preservative, for waterproof roofing, and for road paving. But it became the raw material for a fast-growing industry in which researchers were seeking—and finding—coal-tar chemicals of value in dyeing and in other applications. Developments in 1879 included two synthetic perfumes, coumarin and heliotrope; a synthetic flavor, vanillin; and the first noncaloric sweetener, saccharin. The first synthetic plastic material, phenol-formaldehyde resin, was discovered in 1907 by Leo H. Baekeland, founder of the Bakelite Co., now part of the Union Carbide Corp., of New York.

In 1910 the German scientist Paul Ehrlich discovered that arsphenamine was effective in the treatment of syphilis. Prontosil, first of the sulfa drugs, was synthesized in 1932. And by 1900, military men were using two powerful coal-tar explosives: picric acid, adopted as a propellant for cannon projectiles by the British, French, and Japanese armies; and trinitrotoluene (TNT), chosen by the Germans.

Chemical Industry in World War I. Until World War I, the strength and aggressiveness of the German chemical companies gave them world supremacy in coal-tar chemicals. Then, when there was great need for explosives and other products, and when German chemicals were no longer available, the British and French governments turned to the United States for their supplies. The U. S. chemical companies experienced great growth in plant facilities and in manpower, acceleration of research and development work, and a rise in prestige. This momentum carried the U. S. chemical industries to a position of world eminence in volume and value of production and in number of product and process patents each year—a position they have held ever since.

Chemicals from Coke Ovens. Meanwhile, developments in other industries were changing the raw material base of the organic chemicals industry. Electric lighting was taking the place of gas lighting, so that there was a sharp drop in the production of illuminating gas and its by-product, coal tar. The loss was more than offset, however, by the steel industry's changeover from beehive ovens (which produced only coke for iron-making blast furnaces) to slot-type ovens that produced more coke per ton of coal consumed and also recovered the by-product chemicals—notably benzene, toluene, naphthalene, cresols, and ammonium sulfate. By 1930, slot-type ovens accounted for more than 90% of all coke produced in the United States and supplied more raw material than the organic chemical industry had ever had.

Petrochemical Industry. By 1930 an even more sweeping change in the organic chemical industry's raw material base was well under way. Prest-O-Lite Co., of Indianapolis, Ind., had been seeking a better way to make acetylene, the flammable gas in headlamps it was making for autos, bicycles, and miners. Some of the research work was assigned to the Mellon institute, Pittsburgh. From that research in 1912–1920 grew an idea for a whole new field of organic chemistry ("petrochemicals"), based on the hydrocarbons in natural gas and petroleum. After Prest-O-Lite and four other companies merged in 1917 to form the Union Carbide Corp., a new chemical subsidiary was organized to pursue that idea. The new company began producing ethylene glycol in South Charleston, W. Va., in 1925, and began building a larger plant on nearby Blaine Island, in the Kanawha River, in 1927. The Blaine Island plant—expanded many times since then—has been called the world's largest organic chemicals facility.

The production of chemicals from natural gas and petroleum now greatly exceeds the volume of chemicals produced from coal and coke. Petrochemical plants account for more than 80% of the benzene produced in the United States and for more than 90% of the toluene, xylenes, phenol, and styrene. In addition, petrochemical plants produce large quantities of noncyclic compounds —especially ethylene, propylene, and butadiene— that are not produced from coal.

Synthetic Rubber and Plastics. When World War II cut off the flow of natural rubber from Southeast Asia to the United States, the U. S. government called on industry to create a synthetic rubber industry. Within two years (by 1943), at a cost of $750 million, the nation had a new industry of 29 major plants and 22 smaller units, built and operated by 20,000 engineers and workmen, which produced about 860,000 metric tons of synthetic rubber per year—enough for U. S. requirements and for shipments to allied nations. This industry—entirely in private ownership since 1954—has continued to grow, mainly because synthetic rubber is preferred over natural rubber in many applications. Synthetic rubber production and consumption in the United States now amount to more than 2 million metric tons per year; consumption of natural rubber is less than one fourth of that volume.

Synthetic plastics, produced by another big branch of the organic chemicals industry, have become a part of everyday life. The resins or polymers manufactured in greatest volume are polyethylene, polyvinyl chloride, polystyrene, phenolic, urea and melamine, alkyd, and styrene copolymer resins.

Man-Made Fibers. The chemical industries have developed and produced a series of man-made fibers for use in clothing, carpets, draperies, and tire cord. First came the cellulosic fibers, such as rayon and acetate, that are made from wood pulp. Rayon was first produced in the United States in 1914 by the American Viscose Corp., of Philadelphia, now part of FMC Corp.

The first of the truly synthetic fibers—fibers synthesized from simpler molecules—was nylon-6,6, developed by Du Pont researchers headed by Wallace H. Carothers and placed on the market in 1940. The textile industry selects its fibers from a growing list that now includes acrylic, polyester, spandex, polypropylene, and several nylon types. Frequently two or more fibers are used together in blends. U. S. production of cellulosic fibers is more than 800 million pounds per year, or more than 25% of the world total. U. S. production of fully synthetic fibers is more than 2 billion pounds per year, or more than 35% of the world total.

For synthetic rubber, synthetic plastics, and synthetic fibers, the bulk of the raw material or intermediates comes from petrochemical plants. Examples of principal intermediates are butadiene and styrene for synthetic rubber; ethylene and vinyl chloride for synthetic resins; and cyclohexane and para-xylene for synthetic fibers.

The Quest for "Fixed" Nitrogen. Still another kind of synthetic material supplied largely by petrochemical companies is nitrogenous fertilizer. Nitrogen is one of the three elements essential for plant growth. The nitrogen in the air cannot

ALLIED CHEMICAL CORPORATION

PAPER DYES are matched to customer requirements.

be used by plants in that form, for nitrogen has to be "fixed"—that is, chemically combined with one or more other elements—before it can be taken up by plant roots.

Historically, farmers generally have not had nearly as much nitrogen fertilizer as they should have used for maximum yields. Also, nitrates and nitric acid have been needed in ever greater quantities for commercial and military explosives. During the Revolutionary and Civil Wars, American soldiers used gunpowder made with nitrates scraped from small deposits in caves.

The first American "fixation" enterprise that was both technically and financially successful was the American Cyanamid Co., organized in 1907 by Frank S. Washburn to use an electric-furnace process in a plant at Niagara Falls, Ontario, to make calcium cyanamide. Production began in 1909, and the plant was expanded eight-fold in the next five years.

The most widely used fixation process up to now is the one developed by Fritz Haber and Carl Bosch of Germany's Badische Anilin concern. Their process—using high temperature and high pressure to convert nitrogen and hydrogen into ammonia—was first used in a Badische plant built in 1913. Allied Chemical Corp. developed a somewhat similar process and built an ammonia plant at Hopewell, Va., in 1927. Since then, total U. S. ammonia capacity has risen rapidly.

In early ammonia plants, the hydrogen used came mainly from chlorine-caustic electrolytic plants, where it is by-product. But in 1929, Shell Oil Co. formed a subsidiary, Shell Chemical Co., to produce ammonia at Long Beach, Calif., using hydrogen obtained by "cracking" natural gas. This is now the standard hydrogen source for ammonia plants. Processing large quantities of natural gas, most of the large petroleum companies and several natural gas companies have entered the ammonia business.

The chemical and petroleum industries have become increasingly interconnected. Oil and gas companies have expanded and diversified their chemical operations; chemical companies have obtained "captive" supplies of hydrocarbon raw materials by acquiring smaller petroleum firms.

CAREERS IN THE CHEMICAL INDUSTRIES

To staff their offices, production facilities, and research laboratories, U. S. chemical companies in the late 1960's employed about 100,000 chemical engineers and chemists. In addition, they employed many other men and women holding college degrees in science and technology. Among these are electrical engineers, mining engineers, mechanical engineers, metallurgists, physicists, mathematicians, biologists, physicians, and veterinarians.

Many, though not all, officers and other executives of chemical companies joined the industry as chemical engineers and chemists. A company tries to assemble a team of executives with a broad range of managerial skills to make sure that the company's manpower, capital, plant, and equipment are used to best advantage.

A chemical engineering degree, which usually requires about five years of college study, was held in the late 1960's by some 60,000 people in the United States. Most of them are in the chemical industries, working in all of the companies' major branches: executive, marketing, production, and research. A chemical engineering student studies chemistry, mathematics, physics, and economics. In particular, he studies the "unit operations" used in chemical plants—such as heat transmission, distillation, and gas absorption—and the equipment used to carry out and control those operations. He learns how to design a new chemical plant, estimate the costs, and predict the profit that could be expected.

Hundreds of men and women with 4-year (bachelor's) degrees in chemistry are hired by U. S. chemical companies each year. Higher salaries are offered to those with 5-year (master's) degrees. Still higher salaries are paid to those who have earned doctoral degrees, such as a Ph. D. in organic chemistry. Such a degree usually requires at least three years of graduate study after the 4-year degree.

About half of all chemical companies' employees are production and maintenance workers, most of whom are paid at hourly wage rates under union contracts. Chemical industry wages are higher than those in most other manufacturing industries, except construction and mining.

HOWARD C. E. JOHNSON, *Editor-in-Chief*
HOMER STARR, *Assistant Managing Editor*
"Chemical Week"

Bibliography

Faith, William L., Keyes, Donald B., and Clark, Ronald L., *Industrial Chemicals*, 3d ed. (New York 1965).
Haynes, Williams, *American Chemical Industry*, 6 vols. (New York 1954).
Ihde, Aaron J., *The Development of Modern Chemistry* (New York 1964).
Leicester, Henry M., *The Historical Background of Chemistry* (New York 1965).
McGraw-Hill Publishing Co., *Chemical Engineering* (New York, biweekly).
McGraw-Hill Publishing Co., *Chemical Week* (New York, weekly).
Manufacturing Chemists' Association, *The Chemical Industry Facts Book* (Washington 1962).
Mark, Herman F., and Standen, Anthony, eds., *Kirk-Othmer Encyclopedia of Chemical Technology* (New York 1964).
Stanford Research Institute, *Chemical Economics Handbook* (Palo Alto, Calif., 1966).
Taylor, F. Sherwood, *A History of Industrial Chemistry* (New York 1957).

CHEMICAL SYMBOL. See ELEMENT.

CHEMICAL WARFARE. See CHEMICAL AND BIOLOGICAL WARFARE.

CHEMILUMINESCENCE, kem-ē-lōō-mə-nes′əns, is an emission of light from a chemical reaction in which very little heat is produced. It is commonly called "cold light." In chemiluminescence the compound producing the light is raised to an excited state by energy produced in a chemical reaction. The compound emits light when it reverts to its original energy state. The light that is emitted is of the same wave length or color as the light produced by fluorescence when the compound is irradiated with ultraviolet light. The luminescence produced by the slow oxidation of white phosphorus is an example of chemiluminescence. Other compounds may be oxidized, even in water solution, and produce an intense light with no noticeable heat. The two best-known compounds of this type are luminol (3-aminophthalhydrazide) and siloxene ($Si_6H_6O_3$), both of which luminesce if oxidized with a mixture of potassium ferricyanide and hydrogen peroxide in solutions of proper acidity. Luminol produces a white light and siloxene an orange color. The intensity of the light depends on the amount of each ingredient in the mixture. The luminol reaction is also sensitive to the presence of traces of copper or compounds which serve as catalysts. Oxalyl chloride and many hydrazides react in the same manner as luminol.

Chemiluminescent systems activated by oxygen from the air are receiving considerable attention for marking exits in case of electric failures and for assisting in air and sea rescues at night. In these cases, the chemical mixture may be covered with a plastic tape or stored in a plastic tube; the system is activated when the tape is removed or when air is admitted to the tube. Sufficient light is produced in these chemiluminescent systems to take a photograph in a dark room.

CHARLES WHITE, *University of Maryland*

CHEMIN DE FER, shə-man′də fâr, is a gambling card game. It is a variant of baccarat, which it has largely replaced. Any number of persons may play. The one offering the largest bank (fund against which bets are made) is the first banker, or he may be designated by lot. The banker may not withdraw any part of the bank or winnings but may retire after any coup (round of play). If the banker retires or goes broke, the right to be banker rotates to the right.

To start, the person to the banker's right bets any desired part of the bank's total. The next person bets any part of the remainder, and so on. However, any bettor may call "banco" and bet the entire amount of the bank, canceling other bets. The game is played with three to six standard decks shuffled together and placed in a dealing box. The banker deals two cards face down to the highest bettor (the "player"), who represents all bettors against the bank. The banker then deals himself two cards face down. The object is to get a hand whose total is as close to 9 as possible. Face cards count 0 and other cards their pip value, but only the last digit of the total count is significant (for example, 18 equals 8). If either hand counts 9 or 8, it is shown at once. Otherwise the player, and then the banker, may stand or draw one card face up, depending on his point count and the rules of the house. The banker wins all bets if his total is closer to 9 than the player's. Ties are a standoff.

FRANK K. PERKINS, *Boston "Herald"*

CHEMISTRY

The modern chemist must work with complex and delicate equipment, and must have a knowledge of other sciences.

CHEMISTRY, kem'is-trē, is the science of the nature of matter and its transformations. As a systematic discipline, chemistry is a comparatively young science, which had its beginnings at the end of the 18th century, when some of the basic concepts of modern chemistry were introduced. Actually, however, man had been transforming matter chemically ever since he began using fire several hundred thousand years ago.

CONTENTS

1. Origins of Chemistry

An empirical understanding of chemical materials was associated with the technological arts that arose in the river valley civilizations of the eastern Mediterranean basin about 5,000 years ago. By 1000 B. C. these arts included cookery and fermentation; the making of pottery, leather, glass, dyestuffs, and drugs; and the technique of smelting metals. Copper and tin, in the form of bronze, were in extensive use, and iron was being introduced. Silver and gold were used in coinage and ornaments, and mercury and lead were known.

The ancient Greeks were the first people to leave a record of their philosophical ideas regarding the nature of matter. Thales of Miletus, in the 6th century B. C., believed that water is the basis of all things. Others argued for air, fire, and numerical and geometrical relationships. Empedocles of Agrigentum developed a theory in which there were four elements—earth, air, fire, and water. Aristotle presented a system of the four elements, attributing to each a pair of qualities—fire was hot and dry; air was hot and moist; water was cold and moist; and earth was cold and dry. It was thought that through correct manipulation of qualities, one element might be transformed into another. This became one of the key beliefs of the alchemists.

Alchemy. Alchemy had its beginnings during the early part of the Christian era. While the alchemists were interested in many aspects of matter, the discipline became particularly concerned with the transmutation of base metals into silver and gold and the search for a drug to confer immortality. These goals were pursued in turn by the Greeks, the Arabs, and the scholars of the Latin West. None, of course, succeeded, but a sizable body of knowledge about matter and its manipulation was accumulated as a result of the work of the alchemists. Particularly important was the improvement of the distillation process about 1200 A. D., resulting in the production of both concentrated alcoholic beverages and mineral acids. By the 16th century, interest in alchemy began to wane, and attention turned to the preparation of medically useful materials through chemical processes.

Iatrochemistry. The years between 1500 and 1700 were dominated by the teachings of Paracelsus (the Swiss physician Theophrastus Bombastus von Hohenheim), who taught that the job of the alchemist was to prepare drugs rather than gold. His followers, known as iatrochemists (from Greek *iatros*, "healer") introduced many chemical preparations into medical practice. The iatrochemists came to think of the human body as a factory that operated by fermentation processes. Chemical medicines were strenuously opposed by traditional physicians, who pointed out that many of the substances used were highly poisonous. While some useful contributions were made by the iatrochemists, their approach to medicine was too simple, and by 1700 their activities were submerged in chemical developments of greater significance.

Metallurgy. Technological developments paralleling the iatrochemical period, particularly in metallurgy, were important because they made available a number of new chemical substances. Also, the introduction and development of assaying laid the foundations of analytical chemistry. The state of the mining and metallurgical technologies was carefully described about the middle of the 16th century by Vannoccio Biringuccio, an Italian mine superintendent, and Georg Agricola, a German physician. Their books included chapters dealing with the manufacture of mineral acids, saltpeter for gunpowder, alum for dyeing, glass, and alloys.

2. 17th and 18th Centuries

With the rise of the new attitude toward science that grew out of studies in astronomy and mechanics during the 17th century, there developed a new interest in the nature of matter. Although such studies were still dominated by alchemical ideas, the work of some scientists in this period revealed a tendency to depart from traditional viewpoints.

The chemical investigators of the 17th century began to show a more realistic attitude toward the identity of chemical substances than had their predecessors. Salts, acids, and alkalies from different sources or prepared in different ways were beginning to be recognized as identical. The Belgian chemist Jan Baptista van Helmont saw that samples of *gas sylvestre* (carbon dioxide) were identical, whether prepared from burning wood, fermenting grain, or the action of acid on sea shells or marble. His studies of gases were handicapped, however, by the lack of a suitable apparatus for the preparation and manipulation of gases produced by chemical reactions. It was not until a century later that the problem was solved by Stephen Hales, an English biologist, who created a "pneumatic trough" when he separated the generating vessel from the receiving vessel and collected gases by water displacement.

The great English chemist Robert Boyle further developed the idea of chemical identity when he laid the foundations of qualitative analysis through the use of vegetable colors as acid-base indicators. He also utilized precipitation reactions and color reactions for the identification of chemical substances. Boyle made studies of gases, particularly in connection with the vacuum pumps he built with Robert Hooke. The inverse proportion between the pressure and volume of gases at constant temperature was reported by Boyle in 1662. His studies of combustion revealed that substances do not burn in a vacuum and that air is somehow related to the process. His contemporaries Hooke and John Mayow also observed such a relationship.

Boyle is particularly noted for his book the *Sceptical Chymist* (1661), in which he questioned traditional concepts of the elements and suggested that elemental substances must be ". . . certain primitive and simple, or perfectly unmingled bodies, which not being made of any other bodies, or of one another, are the ingredients of which all those called perfectly mixt bodies are immediately compounded, and into which they are ultimately resolved." He failed, however, to give any examples, and the concept had no impact until the next century.

The Phlogiston Theory. The theory that air is involved in combustion was not pursued, however, partly because working with gases was difficult and partly because an alternate viewpoint of combustion, the phlogiston theory, became popular early in the 18th century. This theory, which was first suggested by the German chemist Johann Joachim Becher, was developed into a broad chemical system by Georg Ernst Stahl, a German chemist. Stahl suggested that combustible substances contained a subtle substance, phlogiston, which escaped when the substance burned. Other phenomena, such as the calcination of metals and the smelting of ores with charcoal, were explained by this theory. Although not universally accepted by scientists, the phlogiston theory served as a broad unifying chemical concept during a large part of the 18th century. As further knowledge was accumulated, the theory was altered accordingly, but not always in a convincing fashion.

Pneumatic Chemistry. Pneumatic chemistry—the chemistry of air and its components—moved ahead rapidly after the mid-1700's, particularly as a result of improvements made on Hales' pneumatic trough. Joseph Black, the Scottish chemist, showed that "fixed air" (carbon dioxide) could be prepared from chalk (calcium carbonate) or magnesia alba (magnesium carbonate) by heating or by the action of acids. He showed further that chalk could be obtained by the recombination of quicklime (calcium oxide) and "fixed air" and observed the conversion of strong alkalies into mild alkalies through absorption of the gas.

Henry Cavendish, an Englishman, made careful studies of the density and solubility of fixed air, and in 1766 he isolated and studied the light gaseous element hydrogen, which he called "inflammable air." Some chemists were of the opinion that this gas was phlogiston.

In 1774, Joseph Priestley, an English clergyman, prepared the gaseous element oxygen by heating the red calx of mercury (mercuric oxide). Since substances burned better in oxygen than they did in ordinary air, Priestley (who supported the phlogiston theory of combustion) believed that it was air without phlogiston and named it "dephlogisticated air." The same gas was independently discovered in Sweden by Carl Wilhelm Scheele, who named it "fire air." Scheele also discovered chlorine. Priestley discovered and studied ammonia, hydrogen chloride, three oxides of nitrogen, sulfur dioxide, and silicon tetrafluoride; he also worked with several other gases isolated by other chemists.

Refutation of the Phlogiston Theory. Cavendish, Priestley, and Scheele interpreted their experiments within the framework of the phlogiston theory. Their French contemporary Antoine Laurent Lavoisier was developing a skeptical attitude toward phlogiston, a position that was reinforced as new experimental evidence accumulated in the various laboratories. Lavoisier showed, when repeating experiments of Boyle, that lead and tin gain weight when heated and simultaneously the air is diminished in volume. Sulfur and phosphorus also gained weight on burning.

In 1775, after learning about Priestley's "dephlogisticated air," Lavoisier showed that heating mercury in air resulted in the formation of a red calx of mercury with a simultaneous decrease in the volume of the air by about one fifth. The residual air showed no capacity to support combustion. The red calx, on heating to a high temperature, decomposed into mercury and a gas identical with Priestley's "dephlogisticated air." Lavoisier reasoned that Priestley's gas was an important component of the ordinary air that combined with metals and combustible substances to form compounds. When he found that the compounds formed by the combination of nonmetals, such as sulfur, phosphorus, and carbon, with Priestley's gas were acidic, he introduced the name "oxygen" (from Greek words meaning "acid former") for the gas. He showed that carbonic acid (carbon dioxide) was formed during the respiration of animals as well as in the combustion of candles.

Contributing to the development of Lavoisier's theories was Cavendish's demonstration that water is produced when hydrogen and oxygen are exploded. Lavoisier decomposed water by passing it through a hot iron tube; the inside of the tube became coated with iron oxide, and hydrogen gas came out. Lavoisier proposed the name "hydrogen" (from Greek words meaning "water former") for this gas, which Cavendish had named "inflammable air." Cavendish also exploded air mixed with oxygen and showed that the resulting gas combined with alkali to form nitrate, the salt equivalent of nitric acid. The gas, nitrogen, had been shown to be present in air by the experiments of Daniel Rutherford, when he was a student of the Scottish chemist Joseph Black.

In 1783, Lavoisier began an open attack on the phlogiston theory, arguing that in chemical reactions like combustion and calcination it was not phlogiston but air that supported these reactions, and that the oxygen in air combined with the combustible material or the metal to form oxides.

In 1787, Lavoisier, together with the French chemists Claude Louis Berthollet, Louis Bernard Guyton de Morveau, and Antoine François de Fourcroy, published a book that was intended to reform chemical nomenclature. They discarded traditional names in favor of names that systematically indicated the chemical composition of a compound. This nomenclature forms the basis of inorganic chemical nomenclature today.

In 1789, Lavoisier published his *Traité élémentaire de chimie*, a book that organized the whole of chemical knowledge on the basis of Lavoisier's concepts and that had a profound effect during the next generation.

By 1785 several prominent French chemists had announced their support of Lavoisier's ideas, and during the next decade these ideas won additional support, notably from Joseph Black and Heinrich Klaproth, a German chemist. Others, including Priestley, refused to abandon the phlogiston theory. Their position was a futile one, however, since Lavoisier's views explained chemical phenomena more directly and simply than did the phlogiston theory. Younger chemists generally took up the newer view.

Analytic Techniques and the Discovery of New Elements. The concept of the chemical element had been given an operational meaning by Lavoisier, who suggested in his *Traité* that a substance should be accepted as elemental only if it could not be decomposed into simpler substances through analytical operations. Lavoisier listed 33 elements in his book, including heat and light; of these, 27 remain in the present list of elements.

Lavoisier also made use of the concept—now known as the "law of the conservation of matter" —that matter cannot be created or destroyed, and that the masses of reacting substances must be recoverable in the products. This concept, on which all chemical analysis is based, was first developed in a section of the *Traité*, but Lavoisier had made continuous use of the idea in his earlier work.

The last quarter of the 18th century was important, not only for the pneumatic studies but also for mineralogical studies that led to the improvement of analytical procedures and the discovery of additional elements. The Swedish chemist Torbern Bergman carried out exclusive analytical work on minerals, and other Swedish chemists were responsible for the discovery of the metallic elements nickel, manganese, and molybdenum. This work also stimulated mineralogical analysis elsewhere.

In Germany, Martin Heinrich Klaproth was particularly important in recognizing the basic criteria of quantitative analysis. By insisting on the use of pure reagents, accurate sampling, avoidance of contamination of the apparatus used, and complete reporting of results, he laid the foundation for successful gravimetric analysis. Through his analytical work he discovered uranium, zirconium, and cerium, and confirmed the discovery of titanium by William Gregor (English). Concurrently, other analysts were adding to the list of metallic elements: tellurium was discovered by Franz Joseph Müller von Reichstein (Austrian); tungsten, by Fausto and Juan José de Elhuyar (Spanish); yttrium, by Johan Gadolin (Finnish); beryllium and chromium, by Louis Nicolas Vauquelin (French); niobium, by Charles Hatchett (English); tantalum, by Anders Ekeberg (Swedish); palladium and rhodium, by William Wollaston (English); and osmium and iridium, by Smithson Tennant (English).

3. The 19th Century

During the first half of the 19th century, interest centered on atomic theory and the problems of determining atomic weights. During the second half of the century, most progress was made in the field of organic chemistry.

Development of the Atomic Theory. The first atomic theory that could be used as a basis for explaining chemical reactions was that of the great English chemist John Dalton. Atomic ideas were not new in science, having been introduced by the Greek Democritus about 400 B.C. Atomic theory became a part of Epicurean philosophy. The speculative nature of atoms, together with the general ill will toward the materialism of the Epicureans, resulted in a lack of interest in atoms until the 17th century. At that time, atomic theories interested a number of leading scientists (notably Pierre Gassendi, Boyle, and Isaac Newton) as possible explanations of the physical properties of matter, especially gases. However, these theories were of little significance in explaining chemical matters.

About 1789 the Irish chemist William Higgins, in a book supporting Lavoisier's ideas, developed a theory of chemical atoms. The book had little impact on the chemical world and appears not to have been responsible for Dalton's theory.

At the beginning of the 19th century, chemists were interested in theories of chemical affinity, that is, the forces that held elements together in compounds. They were also becoming aware of the fact that combination took place according to characteristic proportions. The early discussions of affinity were vague and frequently had recourse to mysterious forces. However, it was possible to establish experimentally that certain substances reacted more readily than others, and as early as 1718 the French apothecary Étienne François Geoffroy had prepared a table of relative affinities for various acids and bases.

In 1803, Claude Louis Berthollet published his *Essai de statique chimique*, in which he attempted to deal with problems of chemical affinity. He suggested that the composition of chemical compounds was variable, depending on the concentration of the reacting substances. A contrary position was taken by Joseph Louis Proust, a French chemist, who showed, as a result of careful analytical work, that properly purified compounds were constant in composition and that Berthollet was basing his conclusions on reactions between solutions, alloys, and other mixtures, rather than on reactions between pure substances. Proust's demonstration came to be known as the "law of definite proportions," and while it seems to have had no influence on Dalton's early thought, it contributed greatly to the acceptance of atomic theory.

John Dalton, a Quaker schoolmaster, was largely self-educated. He was well grounded in Newtonian philosophy and appears to have arrived at his atomic views through the study of weather phenomena and the solubility of gases in water. His friend William Henry, an Englishman, observed that the solubility of a gas in water is directly proportional to the pressure on the gas (Henry's law). Dalton formulated the "law of partial pressures" (Dalton's law), which states that the pressure exerted by each gas in a mixture is independent of the pressure exerted by the other gases, and that the total pressure of the mixture is equal to the sum of the pressures that each gas would have exerted if present by itself in the container.

Dalton began to suspect that solubility was a physical process, probably related to the complexity and weight of the gaseous particles. By 1803 his notebooks reveal an attempt to assign relative weights to "atoms" of various gases, both elemental and compound. By 1808, when the first part of his *New System of Chemical Philosophy* was published, Dalton recognized that the atomic viewpoint was significant, not only in explaining the solubility of gases but in understanding the weight proportions of the elements in compounds themselves. Dalton's theory assumed that elements are composed of small indivisible particles called atoms; all atoms of a particular element are alike in mass and other properties; atoms of different elements differ in mass and other properties; and atoms of different elements combine to form compounds.

At this point, an atomic theory was needed that would explain the weight relations in chemical combination in terms of the relative masses of component atoms. Besides considering the "law of definite proportions," attention could be directed to the "law of multiple proportions," which was discovered by Dalton. This law, first observed in oxides and hydrides of carbon, holds that when two elements form a series of compounds and the quantity of one element is set at a constant level in each compound, the weight of the other element varies in the ratio of small whole numbers.

Atomic Weights. Dalton recognized the significance of relative atomic weights, and his notebooks of 1803 contain tabulations in which the hydrogen atom is assigned a weight of one. Since it was not possible to weigh atoms, the determination of atomic weights had to be based on the combining weights of elements in pure compounds. Dalton assigned oxygen an atomic weight of 5.5, for according to the analytical values for water then available to him, 1 unit weight of hydrogen was combined with 5.5 unit weights of oxygen. Dalton assumed that the formula of water was 1 atom of hydrogen to 1 of oxygen. Since the atomic combining ratio (or formula) as well as combining weights are essential to the development of a reliable system of atomic weights, 19th century chemists were faced with a difficult problem because there was no basis for determining with certainty the formula of a compound. Dalton utilized the rule of greatest simplicity, assuming that the formula of the most common compound of two elements had an atomic ratio of 1:1, while a second compound of the same elements would have an atomic ratio of 2:1 or 1:2. While this rule was of some value, there were sufficient deviations from it to cause trouble. Water itself was ultimately shown to have two atoms of hydrogen to one of oxygen. Therefore, Dalton's atomic weight figures proved unsatisfactory, partly through misapplication of the rule of greatest simplicity, but mainly because of the unsatisfactory nature of the analytical figures used.

Gay-Lussac's Law of Combining Volumes. A new factor entered the picture in 1808, when the French chemist Joseph Louis Gay-Lussac reported that when gases react under identical conditions of temperature and pressure, the volumes involved are always in the ratio of small whole numbers; for example, two volumes of hydrogen react with exactly one volume of oxygen to form water. Gay-Lussac's law of combining volumes suggested that equal volumes of different gases must contain equal numbers of atoms. However, certain discrepancies caused some chemists, notably Dalton, to question the validity of the law.

Avogadro's Laws. The problem was resolved in 1811 by the Italian physicist Amedeo Avogadro, who proposed the hypothesis that bears his name. Avogadro assumed that equal volumes of different gases (at the same temperature and pressure) contain the same number of molecules and that molecules of gaseous elements may contain more than one atom. He went on to show that Gay-Lussac's law of combining volumes—when applied to molecules rather than atoms—was in accordance with the experimental evidence and met the criticisms directed against it if the molecules of the known elemental gases contained two atoms each (H_2, O_2, N_2). In spite of the logic of the hypothesis advanced by Avogadro, the theory was not favorably received at that time.

Berzelius. Jöns Jacob Berzelius, a Swedish chemist, perhaps more than anyone else, recognized the significance of the atomic theory to chemistry. He saw the need for reliable atomic weight figures and set out to make the accurate analyses that would lead to such figures. Comprehensive sets of values were published in 1814, 1818, and 1826. Berzelius' work reflected painstaking attention to analytical detail coupled with generally sound reasoning toward combining ratios. While some of his assumptions later proved unsound, his analytical work proved to be excellent. Berzelius made use of analogies in working out the most suitable formulas of compounds under consideration. For the metals, he set up certain arbitrary rules for the formulas of oxides. These rules worked satisfactorily for most metals but led to several erroneous atomic weights.

Petit-Dulong Law and the Law of Isomorphism. In 1819 two laws were announced that bore on the atomic weight problem. The law of Petit and Dulong (discovered by the French chemists Pierre Louis Dulong and Alexis Thérèse Petit) stated that the product of the specific heat and the atomic weight of an element was a constant. Although not a very precise law, it was useful for diagnostic purposes since it could be used to calculate the most probable formula for a compound containing an element whose atomic weight was being determined.

The law of isomorphism was reported by Eilhard Mitscherlich, a German chemist, who saw the similarity between crystals of arsenates and phosphates. When an element whose atomic weight was being determined formed compounds whose crystals were isomorphous (had the same shape) with the compounds of an element whose atomic weight was known, it could be assumed that the formulas of the compounds were similar.

Dumas' Vapor-Density Method. In 1826 a unique approach to atomic weights was introduced when the French chemist Jean Baptiste André Dumas developed a method for determining the vapor density of liquids and solids. If the density of an element's vapor is compared with the density of an equal volume of hydrogen gas at the same temperature and pressure, the difference in molecular weights should be proportional to the difference in the densities. Division of the molecular weight of the element's vapor by an appropriate small number should give the atomic weight. Dumas divided the molecular weight by two in every case, thereby falling into error since of the elements he studied, mercury is a monatomic vapor, sulfur is hexatomic, and phosphorus and arsenic are tetratomic. The existence of monatomic and other types of molecules was suggested by Marc Gaudin, a French scientist, in 1833, but it had no impact, and the vapor density approach to molecular and atomic weights was considered untrustworthy.

For the next several decades there was lack of agreement about atomic weights. Berzelius' values were accepted by some chemists. Others preferred to ignore the atomic concept or to use combining weight figures known as "equivalents."

Cannizzaro. The problem of atomic weights was not resolved until 1860 despite the attention given to the problem by some of the best chemists of the time. In 1860 more than a hundred leading chemists met in Karlsruhe, Germany, to discuss the problem of atoms, molecules, and formulas. A young Italian chemistry teacher, Stanislao Cannizzaro, described his course in which he utilized the assumptions of Avogadro's hypothesis in the development of chemical principles. Although Cannizzaro's message was not heeded at the conference, several of the leading younger chemists soon realized its importance. The application of Avogadro's hypothesis to data from vapor-density measurements made it possible to determine the molecular weight of compounds and elements, and through such information to arrive at accurate formulas.

Electrochemistry. Chemistry was profoundly influenced by studies of electricity at the end of the 18th century. About 1780 the Italian physiologist Luigi Galvani observed that a freshly dissected frog's leg in contact with a piece of metal twitched whenever a nearby static machine began operating. Further studies led him to develop a theory of animal electricity. These views were questioned by Alessandro Volta, an Italian physicist, who reported in 1800 that a flow of electricity can be produced by a pile of metal pairs separated by felt or blotting paper that had been soaked in salt solution. A current could also be produced by connecting a series of glasses containing salt or acid solution by pairs of metal strips soldered to one another.

A few months after Volta's reports, current electricity was used in England by William Nicholson and Anthony Carlisle to decompose water into hydrogen and oxygen. Berzelius in Sweden and Humphry Davy in England carried out extensive studies of the chemical effects of electricity. Both recognized the ability of electricity to decompose many chemical substances and observed that hydrogen and metals appeared at the negative pole of their cells, with oxygen and acidic substances at the positive pole. These observations led both to hypothesize that chemical affinities were electrical in character. Berzelius ultimately developed an elaborate, dualistic theory suggesting that atoms of elements have a characteristic polarity, and atoms of opposite polarities combine to form stable compounds. Berzelius even considered many compounds to be somewhat polar, leading to further combination to form more complex compounds. Although the dualistic theory ultimately proved to be misleading when applied broadly, it served as a stimulus to chemical thought for several decades.

Davy's electrochemical work led to the discovery, in 1807, of the chemically active metals potassium and sodium. During the next year Davy discovered barium, strontium, calcium, and magnesium by using a similar approach.

In 1833, Michael Faraday, Davy's former assistant, made a particularly important contribution to electrochemistry when he discovered the electrochemical laws. Faraday realized that the amount of an element liberated by a specific quantity of electricity is related to the equivalent weight of the element. For example, the quantity of electricity that liberates 1 gram of hydrogen will liberate 8 grams of oxygen, and 35.5 grams of chlorine—in each case one equivalent weight of the element. Faraday, aided by the historian of science William Whewell, developed the nomenclature of electrochemistry when he introduced the terms electrode, anode, cathode, ion, anion, and cation.

Chemical Symbolism. Modern chemical symbolism also had its beginning during this period. The alchemists had used various symbols for the substances they worked with, but their symbolism was not well systematized and served primarily as a kind of shorthand. Dalton introduced symbols for the elements, using various kinds of circles (hydrogen $\odot$, oxygen $\bigcirc$, carbon $\bullet$, nitrogen $\textcircled{1}$) to represent elements and combinations of these symbols to represent compounds. However, these symbols were not easy to write, and in 1814 Berzelius suggested that letters be used instead. Where two elements had the same initial letter, a second letter might form a part of the symbol of one of them. Thus, H came into use for hydrogen, O for oxygen, S for sulfur, C for carbon, Cu for copper (cuprum), and Fe for iron (ferrum). Berzelius also suggested that formulas of compounds might be represented symbolically; for example, carbon dioxide could be written as $C + 2O$. Ultimately the practice developed of representing the number of atoms in the molecule (if more than one) by subscripts following the symbol, as in H_2O, a practice that is still followed.

The Nature of Acids. Boyle had recognized acids as chemicals that changed the color of certain vegetable extracts such as syrup of violets, and it was well known in the 17th century that acids are sweetened by alkalies with the formation of salts. However, there was no serious attempt to formulate a theory of acidity until Lavoisier found that nonmetal oxides, such as those of phosphorus, sulfur, and carbon, possessed acidic properties. He suggested that oxygen was the acidifying principle. This viewpoint persisted for over two decades and caused chemists to look upon chlorine as an oxide since its water solution is acidic.

Davy challenged this view in 1810, when he found that it was not possible to remove oxygen from chlorine by the use of chemicals with a strong attraction for oxygen. His view that chlorine is an element was accepted slowly, but the French chemists Gay-Lussac and Louis Jacques Thenard soon found it necessary to admit that iodine and prussic acid (hydrocyanic acid) contained no oxygen. Gay-Lussac introduced the term "hydracid" for acids such as hydrochloric, hydriodic, hydrocyanic, and hydrosulfuric, to distinguish them from "oxyacids." Davy and Dulong believed that there was a single type of acidifying behavior rather than two types of acids. In 1815, Davy suggested that acidity depended not on a particular elementary substance but on peculiar combinations of various substances. Although Dulong admitted that an acid might be regarded as water plus acid anhydride (nonmetal oxide), he argued that it might as readily be looked upon as hydrogen plus an acid group. The former view, in agreement with the dualistic theory of Berzelius, was more widely held until the 1830's when Graham and Liebig carried out studies on poly basic acids.

Thomas Graham of Glasgow had already discovered in 1830 his "law of gaseous diffusion" (the relative rates of diffusion of gases are inversely proportional to the square roots of the densities) when he began his work on the phosphoric acids. He found that it was possible to distinguish three series of phosphate salts (meta, pyro, and ortho) derived from three phosphoric acids. The acids differed in the number of units of water that combined with a unit of oxide of phosphorus ($H_2O + P_2O_5$, $2H_2O + P_2O_5$, $3H_2O + P_2O_5$). Graham observed the same relationships in the arsenates and arsenic acids. Graham's representation of formulas followed

Berzelius' dualistic ideas. A few years later Justus Liebig, at Giessen, Germany, presented a clearer view. Applying Davy's ideas, he saw that acids vary in the number of atoms of replaceable hydrogen present in the molecule. (For example, the three phosphoric acids become HPO_3, $H_4P_2O_7$, and H_3PO_4.) An acidlike tartaric acid contains two replaceable hydrogen atoms and is capable of forming an acid and a neutral salt with the same metal.

The Periodic Table. Within three decades after Lavoisier introduced his operational definition of an element, there was an effort to find a basis for interrelating all the elements. This was also a fruitful period for the discovery of new elements. Between 1807 when Davy isolated the alkali metals and 1830 when Nils Gabriel Sefström, a Swedish physician and chemist, discovered vanadium, 16 new elements were discovered. In fact, new discoveries were announced so frequently that some chemists, including Davy, questioned whether all of the alleged elements were truly elemental. Davy felt that the number of truly elemental substances should be very limited, and at one time he even claimed to have found hydrogen to be a component of sulfur and phosphorus, presumably eliminating them from the list of elements.

In 1815, William Prout, an English physician, suggested that hydrogen might be the building block ("protyle") out of which all other elements were formed. He pointed to the fact that the densities of elemental gases appeared to be exact multiples of the density of hydrogen. He suggested that all atomic weights should be whole numbers. The Scottish chemist Thomas Thomson found the hypothesis very attractive and sought to fit atomic weights into the pattern. Berzelius, however, claimed that careful analytical work gave results that were inconsistent with the hypothesis, and it was abandoned except for sporadic revivals of interest.

In 1829, Johann Wolfgang Döbereiner, an Austrian chemist, introduced his concept of "triads," suggesting that elements should be classified in groups of three, with one of the elements having an atomic weight that is the arithmetic mean of the other two; for example, he formed triads of calcium, strontium, and barium and of chlorine, bromine, and iodine. The idea was useful in creating families of elements with similar properties, but there were numerous exceptions, and the theory had only limited usefulness.

Between 1830 and 1860 a number of other attempts were made to classify elements on the basis of atomic weights and similar chemical properties, but these attempts failed because of uncertainty regarding atomic weights. This shortcoming was resolved when Cannizzaro reintroduced Avogadro's hypothesis.

In 1862 the French geologist A. E. Béguyer de Chancourtois introduced the telluric helix, a system of plotting the elements according to atomic weights around the surface of a cylinder. Elements on the same vertical line on the cylinder were found to be chemically related. However, as there were some serious flaws in the execution of the idea and it was not clearly explained, it had no impact.

This was also true of the law of octaves conceived by John Newlands in 1865. Newlands arranged the elements in order of increasing atomic weight, using seven columns. He reported that the 8th and 15th elements were like the 1st, the 9th and 16th like the 2nd, and so forth, a relationship like that of the octave in music. Newlands' ideas were not well received by his English contemporaries.

A sound classification system finally grew out of the work of the Russian Dmitri Ivanovich Mendeleyev and the German Julius Lothar Meyer, beginning in 1869. The approach of Mendeleyev was tabular while that of Meyer was graphic.

Mendeleyev showed that if the elements are arranged in a series of rows, in order of increasing atomic weight, there is a periodic recurrence of properties. This is similar to what Newlands did, but Mendeleyev showed imaginative qualities, which Newlands lacked. Mendeleyev placed the lightest element, hydrogen, by itself and started the first full period with lithium. This avoided relating hydrogen to fluorine, chorine, and bromine as Newlands had done. He jumped a space in going from calcium to titanium, and jumped two spaces in going from zinc to arsenic. It was suggested that undiscovered elements would occupy the vacant spaces, and Mendeleyev predicted the properties that these elements would have. With the discovery of gallium by Paul Émile de Boisbaudran of France in 1875, scandium by Lars Nilson of Sweden in 1879, and germanium by Clemens Winkler of Germany in 1885, Mendeleyev's predictions were confirmed, and the periodic system gained new adherents.

Lothar Meyer arrived at a similar periodic relationship when he plotted curves showing the change of physical properties with increasing atomic weight. For example, when atomic volumes were plotted against atomic weights, the curve showed a succession of peaks and depressions. Each peak was occupied by an alkali metal. Elements with related properties occupied similar positions on successive undulations of the curve.

The periodic system proved to be an important unifying concept in chemistry. Although the Mendeleyev-Meyer tables underwent a sequence of modifications during the next century, the basic concept was sound. The classification scheme was capable of accepting newly discovered elements; in fact, a new family of elements—the rare gases—was discovered by John Strutt (Lord Rayleigh) and William Ramsay in the 1890's.

The periodic system was discovered on quite empirical grounds. There was no clue in 1869 as to why the elements might be arranged in this manner. A half century later, when atomic structure was being developed, the reason became evident.

Organic Chemistry. In the early days of chemistry only minor attention was given to the substances associated with living organisms. It was widely believed that vital forces outside the realm of physics and chemistry were involved. Even those chemists who refused to be awed by the theories of mysterious life forces found biological material difficult to study in a meaningful way.

Before 1800 only a few compounds had been isolated from plants and animals. The most notable were the organic acids isolated and studied by Scheele: oxalic, malic, citric, tartaric, lactic, uric, gallic, pyrogallic, mucic, and pyromucic acids. He also discovered glycerol as a saponification product of fatty oils. H. M. Rouelle discovered urea in human urine and hippuric acid in the urine of cows.

Carbohydrates. After 1800 there was a fairly steady isolation and identification of materials of biological origin as well as some conversion into materials not found in living organisms. Proust studied the saccharine juices of plants and identified three sugars: sucrose, glucose, and fructose. In Russia, Gottlieb Kirchhoff found that when starch is digested with sulfuric acid, glucose can be isolated from the resulting syrup. A few years later Henri Braconnot, a French chemist, found that glucose is also produced when linen rags are digested with sulfuric acid. Gay-Lussac and Louis Jacques Thenard showed by analysis that sugars, starch, and cellulose contain hydrogen and oxygen in the proportion of two atoms to one, the same as in water. The term "carbohydrate" was introduced for saccharine substances by Karl Schmidt in 1844.

Alkaloids. In 1805 the German pharmacist Friedrich Sertürner isolated a crystalline substance from opium, which he described in more detail in 1816. This substance, called morphine, contained nitrogen and was alkaline in character. During the next few years two professors at the Paris school of pharmacy, Pierre Pelletier and Joseph Caventou, isolated crystals of similar materials which were named "alkaloids." They obtained strychnine and brucine from St. Ignatius beans and quinine and cinchonine from cinchona bark. Hans Christian Oersted of Denmark obtained piperine from pepper, Friedlieb Ferdinand Runge isolated caffeine from coffee beans, Pelletier and François Magendie, a French physiologist, found emetine in ipecacuana root, and K. F. W. Meissner isolated veratrine from sabadilla seeds. The alkaloids all had physiological effects, and since they were readily obtainable in the form of pure crystals, they were of interest both medically and chemically.

Fatty Acids. Important studies of fatty oils were carried out by Michel Eugène Chevreul, a French chemist, between 1810 and 1823. He showed that saponification resulted in breakdown of fat by alkali with the production of soap and glycerol. Acidification of the soap resulted in the precipitation of fatty acids such as stearic, oleic, butyric, and capric. His work revealed that fats are mixtures of compounds of fatty acids and glycerol. In addition, he described a number of fatty acids and established general principles for examination of organic substances. Chevreul developed two research techniques of basic importance in the study of organic materials: he used inert solvents to separate chemical substances without altering their composition and he used successive crystallizations of the substance until the maximum melting temperature was reached.

Synthesis of Organic Compounds. The decline of the concept that organic chemistry was dominated by vital forces outside the realm of regular chemical laws is associated with an experiment conducted by the German chemist Friedrich Wöhler in 1828. Wöhler sought to prepare ammonium cyanate from an ammonium compound and a cyanate, both considered to be inorganic in character. Instead of the expected compound he obtained urea, hitherto known only as a compound isolated from the urine of mammals. While some chemists interpreted Wöhler's synthesis of urea as a disproof of vitalism, it could still be argued that an aspect of vitalism was present since ammonia and cyanates were frequently prepared from proteinaceous materials. Nevertheless, vitalism came to play less and less a role in organic chemistry, and it was largely eliminated by 1844 when Adolf Wilhelm Hermann Kolbe, a German chemist, synthesized acetic acid from compounds that could be prepared from the component elements.

In 1856 the Frenchman Marcellin Berthelot began studies demonstrating that it was possible to prepare from carbon disulfide and hydrogen sulfide (compounds that can be prepared from the elements) such compounds as methane, ethylene, and naphthalene. In 1862 he prepared acetylene by passing hydrogen through an electric arc produced with carbon electrodes. In 1866 he produced benzene by passing acetylene through heated tubes. In his book *Chimie organique fondée sur la synthèse* (1860), Berthelot argued that no distinction existed between organic and inorganic chemistry, that chemists could synthesize from inorganic materials the same compounds that are synthesized by plants and animals. After this, vitalistic doctrines no longer played a role in chemistry.

Analysis of Organic Compounds. The period between 1800 and 1850 was an extremely fruitful one for the isolation of new carbon compounds from plant, animal, and mineral (coal tar, coal gas) sources and for the manipulation of these compounds into derivatives not found in nature. As a consequence, many problems arose involving formulas, classification, and interrelationships. But many of these problems could not be resolved until accurate molecular formulas were developed along the lines of Cannizzaro's proposals. However, advances pertinent to these problems were made between 1820 and 1860.

Of particular importance was the improvement in the quantitative analysis of organic compounds. Measurements of the carbon, hydrogen, and nitrogen in organic compounds had been attempted from the time of Lavoisier, but these met with little success because everyone burned the samples and tried to measure the gases formed (carbon dioxide, water, and nitrogen) volumetrically. A successful method for measuring carbon and hydrogen was finally developed by Justus von Liebig of Germany in 1830. The sample was burned in a glass combustion tube containing copper oxide as an oxidizing agent. The water that formed was collected in a weighed drying tube and the carbon dioxide in a weighed bulb containing potassium hydroxide. The weights of hydrogen and carbon in the sample could then be calculated from the weights of water and carbon dioxide produced from the burned sample.

Liebig separated the nitrogen determination from the carbon-hydrogen determination and developed a method for nitrogen that utilized a separate sample. A better procedure for nitrogen was introduced by Dumas. He burned the sample in an atmosphere of carbon dioxide in a combustion tube containing copper oxide; nitrogen gas was then collected in a tube over a concentrated solution of potassium hydroxide, which absorbed the water and carbon dioxide formed during the combustion. The nitrogen was measured volumetrically, then calculated to a weight basis in order to arrive at the percentage of nitrogen in the sample.

The percentage of oxygen in a test sample was not determined directly; instead it was estimated by subtracting the percentages of the other elements from 100%. While this is not an ideal approach because it may reflect errors in the other determinations, it is still used because no convenient and reliable technique for oxygen determination has been developed.

Sulfur and halogens, which are occasionally present in organic compounds, also had to be determined. A number of procedures that were applicable to particular types of compounds were developed. The most universally useful, although hazardous, was the procedure introduced by the German chemist George Ludwig Carius in 1864. He oxidized the sample at furnace heat in a sealed tube containing fuming nitric acid. In the tube sulfur was converted to sulfate, which precipitated as barium sulfate; halogens were converted to silver halides and analyzed in that form.

Radical Theory. One of the earliest attempts to develop a unifying concept for organic chemistry was the radical theory. Dumas and Pierre Boullay, a French pharmacist, advanced the idea in the form of the etherin theory in 1828. They reported that compounds such as ethyl alcohol, ethyl ether, and the several ethyl esters could be regarded as an etherin (or ethylene, C_2H_4) radical combined with water, hydrogen chloride, nitric acid, and so forth. The idea was received with indifference until 1832, when Liebig and Wöhler reported their studies on oil of bitter almonds and introduced the benzoyl radical. They isolated a compound, benzoyl hydride (benzaldehyde, $C_6H_5 \cdot CHO$; formulated $C_{14}H_{10}O_2 \cdot H_2$ by Liebig and Wöhler), which could be converted into a variety of derivatives that appeared to differ only in the atoms attached to the benzoyl ($C_{14}H_{10}O_2$) radical, which remained intact throughout the various chemical conversions. During the next decade, additional radicals (methyl, cinnamyl, salicyl, cacodyl, and acetyl) were introduced.

"Nucleus" and Type Theories. Concurrently, the concept of a stable organic radical that could remain intact throughout a series of chemical changes was thrown into question by experiments in which chlorine was substituted for hydrogen in various compounds. Dumas postulated a "law of substitution" in 1834, indicating that when a compound containing hydrogen is exposed to chlorine, bromine, or iodine, for every atom of hydrogen lost an atom of halogen is found in the compound. The French chemist Auguste Laurent, working in Dumas' laboratory and also independently, confirmed these conclusions and in 1837 introduced his "nucleus" theory. This theory held that the properties of a compound are not necessarily due to the kind of atoms present, but to the physical structure, or "nucleus," of the compound. Therefore, atoms of one element may be substituted for another in the "nucleus" without significantly altering the properties of the compound. Although Dumas disclaimed belief in the "nucleus" theory when it was attacked by Berzelius and Liebig, he later introduced his type theory, which bore a striking resemblance to the "nucleus" theory. These theories had the general effect of throwing doubt on Berzelius' dualistic theory and turning organic chemists toward a unitary point of view, which suggested that an organic formula must be looked upon as a unit, not as a two-part compound.

The decade of the 1840's was one of confusion. Neither radicals nor types were satisfactory in developing an organizational scheme for chemistry. Many chemists were skeptical about atoms. Those who did accept atoms were inclined to accept the atomic weights of Berzelius, but there were enough uncertainties to raise doubts.

In 1842 the French chemist Charles Frédéric Gerhardt correctly concluded that Berzelius' atomic weights for silver, sodium, and potassium were incorrect, and he proceeded to halve them. Unfortunately, he also halved the correct values of a number of other metals. Analyses of carbon-rich compounds such as naphthalene ($C_{10}H_8$) led Dumas to realize that Berzelius' figure for the atomic weight of carbon was in error by more that 2%. Jean Stas of Belgium worked with Dumas in arriving at a more accurate value. Later in his career, Stas carried out very careful work on atomic weights that led to refinement of existing values.

Laurent and Gerhardt published extensively on organic theory during these years, and their ideas revealed considerable insight into the problems of atoms, molecules, equivalents, and formulas. However, they were not entirely consistent and unambiguous.

Work on organic nitrogen compounds, the amines, led to introduction of the ammonia type. August Wilhelm von Hofmann began working on amines while still an assistant in Liebig's laboratory, and he carried out extensive work on aniline. Charles Wurtz of France devised a procedure for the synthesis of simple amines in 1849, and Hofmann quickly proceeded to synthesize secondary and tertiary amines. Since amines are basic in character, Hofmann suggested that they might be classified as an ammonia type—that is, molecules in which one, two, or three of the hydrogen atoms of ammonia (NH_3) had been replaced by organic groups without destroying the basic properties of the compound.

In England, Alexander Williamson devised a procedure for preparing ethers and recognized that alcohols and ethers might be considered as water types in which one of the hydrogen atoms of water was replaced by an organic group in alcohols and both hydrogen atoms replaced by organic groups in ethers. Gerhardt developed the new type theory more extensively.

Valence. At this time Edward Frankland, an English chemist, was groping toward the concept of combining capacity, or valence. He found that zinc reacted with ethyl iodide to liberate what he considered to be ethyl (C_2H_5), a free radical (which was really butane, C_4H_{10}). A byproduct of the reaction was the highly reactive zinc ethyl, Zn $(C_2H_5)_2$, the first example of an organometallic compound. In interpreting the characteristics of chemical compounds, Frankland recognized that atoms and groups of atoms have a characteristic capacity for combination that may be expressed as a small whole number. For example, hydrogen, the ethyl group, and silver all have a valence of one. Since oxygen has a valence of two, an atom of oxygen must react with two atoms of hydrogen or silver, with two ethyl groups, or with an ethyl group and a hydrogen atom. Although the valence concept was accepted very slowly, it ultimately proved very useful in predicting and interpreting chemical formulas.

It was Friedrich August Kekulé, a German chemist, who caught the real significance of valence when, in 1858, he called attention to the tetravalence of the carbon atom and suggested that carbon atoms can combine with one another to form chains. Essentially the same ideas were conceived by the Scottish chemist Archibald Scott Couper, but Kekulé's paper was published earlier, and he made numerous additional contributions that enhanced his reputation.

Molecular Structure. The concept of valence coupled with the ideas of Kekulé and Couper and the proposals of Cannizzaro, formed a sound basis for progress. The results were particularly apparent in organic chemistry, in which the compounds always contain carbon and hydrogen, frequently oxygen, sometimes nitrogen, sulfur, phosphorus, or halogens, but seldom any other elements. Structural ideas developed very rapidly after 1860. In earlier decades such ideas were presented, but without conviction, and many chemists believed it would never be possible to learn the arrangement of the atoms in a molecule. Kekulé and the Russian chemist Alexander Butlerov were leaders in the development of structural concepts, although Couper, the Austrian Joseph Loschmidt, and the Scot Alexander Crum Brown had used structural formulas earlier.

With the use of structural formulas it became possible not only to account for some of the properties shown by particular types of compounds such as acids, alcohols, ethers, and amines, but to gain an understanding of isomerism, a phenomenon that had been encountered since the 1820's. At that time Wöhler assigned the same formula to cyanic acid as Liebig had assigned to fulminic acid. Berzelius suggested that this might be possible if atoms were arranged differently in their molecules. He recognized other cases where two compounds had different properties, yet appeared to have the same composition as revealed by analysis. Berzelius introduced the term "isomerism" for such cases. With the introduction of structural ideas it became possible to show that two compounds with the same molecular formula, for example, C_2H_6O, could differ structurally:

ethyl alcohol   dimethyl ether

Certain compounds such as ethylene (C_2H_4) and acetylene (C_2H_2) created problems because they did not contain sufficient hydrogen to satisfy the four valences of each of the carbon atoms. Some chemists sought to interpret the structure of ethylene by supposing that one of the carbon atoms had a valence of two. Crum Brown represented the situation by having each carbon joined to the other a second time (a double bond). Emil Erlenmeyer of Germany extended Brown's concept and introduced a triple bond for acetylene. Such compounds were termed "unsaturated" and had the capacity to add bromine, hydrogen bromide, and other reagents, a characteristic not observed in "saturated" compounds such as ethane (C_2H_6), where such reagents only acted by substitution, if at all.

ethane   ethylene   acetylene
(saturated)   (unsaturated)   (unsaturated)

A structural problem of major importance was associated with the aromatic class of compounds obtained from coal tar, a byproduct of the illuminating gas industry. The principal component, benzene, had been discovered by Faraday in 1825 in a condensate obtained from a gas produced from whale oil. Others soon found it in coal tar. After 1860 its molecular formula was established as C_6H_6, a formula that suggested a high degree of unsaturation. However, it did not react as an unsaturated compound; in reactions with halogens, there was a substitution of the halogen for hydrogen rather than an addition. Kekulé suggested, in 1865, that the structure might best be represented in the form of a "ring," or hexagon, with a CH group at each corner.

The Kekulé structure did not account for the fourth valence of the carbon atoms unless alternate double bonds were introduced. However, benzene shows none of the tendency of unsaturated compounds to add reagents. Albert Ladenburg, a German chemist, suggested a prism structure to eliminate the need for double bonds.

Kekulé structure   Ladenburg structure

Kekulé introduced an "oscillatory" concept, which had the effect of eliminating the existence of stationary double bonds, thereby "explaining away" the failure of additive reagents to react. Although the Ladenburg structure was able to account for the failure of common addition reactions, it was inconsistent with certain other properties of benzene, and the Kekulé structure proved most acceptable.

Stereochemistry. Another structural problem was associated with the property of optical activity shown by some compounds. The rotation of polarized light by quartz crystals was observed by Jean Baptiste Biot, a French physicist, in 1813. He later observed that liquids such as turpentine, lemon oil, and solutions of camphor rotated polarized light. An instrument, the polarimeter, was developed for measuring the extent of rotation. In the 1840's researchers began to use it to analyze optically active substances.

Isomerism. In 1848 the famous French chemist Louis Pasteur observed that the ammonium salt of tartaric acid crystallized into two forms of crystals that were mirror images. On sorting these crystals mechanically, he found that one type of crystal rotated polarized light to the right, the other to the left. Although he suspected that the cause must be due to molecular asymmetry he was unable to accomplish anything further in understanding the phenomenon.

In 1874 two young chemists, Jacobus Henricus van't Hoff of Holland and Joseph Achille Le Bel of France independently recognized that the isomerism was found in compounds where at least one carbon atom—called an asymmetric carbon atom—was attached to four different atoms or atomic groups. These four substituents can be arranged around an asymmetric carbon atom in two different patterns, giving structures that are mirror images. Van't Hoff introduced the tetrahedral model of the carbon atom, thus giving structural formulas a three-dimensional character.

a

b

Isomers of lactic acid are shown in the conventional manner, *a;* and in the tetrahedral form, *b*.

The tetrahedral model accounted for both optical and geometrical isomerism. Some unsaturated compounds were known to exist in two forms, which came to be known as *cis* and *trans;* an example of this type of isomerism is found in maleic and fumaric acids, $CH_2(COOH)_2$ Van't Hoff suggested that when two carbon atoms are joined by a single bond, rotation around the bond is possible, but when a double bond is present rotation is no longer possible, and two arrangements of substituent groups can be predicted.

HCCOOH   HCCOOH
‖   ‖
HCCOOH   HOOCCH

Maleic Acid (*cis*)   Fumaric Acid (*trans*)

The concepts of van't Hoff and Le Bel came to play an important role in structural studies, since many naturally occurring compounds are optically active or show *cis-trans* isomerism.

One of the most impressive uses of stereochemical principles is seen in the work of the German chemist Emil Fischer, who worked out the structure of glucose and related sugars about 1890. This proof of structure was particularly difficult since the glucose molecule contains 4 asymmetric carbon atoms, making it necessary to consider sixteen possible isomeric arrangements.

Tautomerism. Another structural problem was encountered with compounds that appear to possess two different sets of properties. The compound now known as acetoacetic ester was prepared independently by Johann Anton Geuther and by Frankland and B. F. Duppa in 1863. Geuther reported the salt-forming characteristics of the compound, while the English chemists found it to behave like a ketone. Other instances of compounds showing dual behavior were reported. It became evident that two compounds existed, with a small intramolecular shift bringing about a profound change in behavior. Conrad Laar introduced the term "tautomerism" for the phenomenon in 1885. The two forms of acetoacetic ester, termed *keto* and *enol*, were isolated independently in 1911 by the German chemists Ludwig Knorr and Kurt Meyer using

$$CH_3-\overset{\overset{\displaystyle O}{\|}}{C}-CH_2-COOC_2H_5 \rightleftarrows$$

keto form

$$CH_3-\overset{\overset{\displaystyle OH}{|}}{C}=CH-COOC_2H_5$$

enol form

temperatures of $-78°C$ ($-108°F$). As the temperature increased, migration of a hydrogen atom led to the formation of the other tautomer.

The last half of the 19th century was important for organic chemistry. Structural concepts were successfully introduced, and numerous synthetic techniques were developed. Many of the reactions used in organic synthesis are known for their discoverers, such as Perkin, Cannizzaro, Wurtz, Kolbe, Hofmann, Gatterman, Michael, Friedel-Crafts, Knoevenagel, Gabriel, Claisen, Curtius, and Grignard.

There was also a great deal of interest in compounds of natural origin. Besides research on fats and sugars, work of high quality was carried out on alkaloids, terpenes, purines, and the natural dyestuffs alizarin and indigo.

Dyes. The German organic chemists became particularly interested in dyestuffs, both natural and synthetic, after Hofmann's English student William Henry Perkin accidentally produced a synthetic purple dye, mauve, from impure aniline while trying to synthesize quinine in 1856. Perkin set up a successful manufacturing plant near London.

Within a short time, chemists produced other synthetic dyes from chemicals derived from coal tar. Germany became predominant in the production of synthetic dyes, and German organic chemists were active in mastering the fundamental nature of colored compounds. They learned what kinds of atomic groups introduced color, intensified color, and led to firm attachment of dye to cloth. Carl Graebe and Carl Liebermann synthesized the ancient dye alizarin (found in the madder root) in Adolf von Baeyer's laboratory in 1868, and it was in commercial production within a few years. Baeyer worked on the other principal natural dye, indigo, for more than a decade before he succeeded in establishing its structure and synthesizing the compound. The synthesis was not commercially practical. The German dye industry directed considerable research and development effort on the indigo problem before the Badische Anilin-und Soda Fabrik began commercial synthesis in 1898. By the end of the century most natural dyes were supplanted by synthetic aniline derivatives, except for alizarin and indigo, and even these were produced synthetically.

Biochemistry. Not only were chemists interested in the nature of the compounds occurring in biological systems, but they sought to gain an understanding of biological processes as well.

Photosynthesis. Although earlier investigators had associated plant growth with air and light, it was Joseph Priestley who first showed that plants have the capacity to improve air that had been "spoiled" by a burning substance or by animal respiration. Priestley assumed that plants abstracted phlogiston from the air, thereby improving it. The Dutch investigator Jan Ingenhousz showed in 1779 that green plants improve the air only when exposed to light. He also found that plants spoil the air in the dark and that the nongreen parts of plants cause the air to deteriorate. It was soon shown by the Swiss botanist Jean Senebier that plants give off oxygen during exposure to light.

The overall nature of the photosynthesis reaction was fully clarified by Nicolas Théodore de Saussure, a Swiss botanist, who in 1804 showed that the green parts of plants, in the presence of light, utilize carbon dioxide and water to form plant material and release oxygen as a product of the reaction. Pierre Joseph Pelletier and Joseph Bienaimé Caventou of France isolated the green pigment, chlorophyll, from plants in 1817, but its chemical nature and role in photosynthesis were too complex for them to study it effectively. Little more was learned of the nature of photosynthesis until the 20th century.

Plant Growth. Extensive studies were made during the 19th century to learn which elements are necessary for plant growth. The German chemist Carl S. Sprengel listed fifteen elements as essential. The Frenchman Jean Baptiste Boussingault established an experimental farm in Alsace and made extensive studies on the growth of plants and animals. He recognized the importance of nitrogen compounds in plant growth and demonstrated that leguminous plants left the soil enriched in nitrogen. It was not until 1890 that the role of nitrogen-fixing bacteria in root nodules of legumes was established by the Russian-born bacteriologist Sergei N. Winogradsky.

Justus von Liebig also took a deep interest in plant growth and emphasized the importance of phosphorus and certain other minerals. He supposed that plants obtained their nitrogen from atmospheric ammonia, failing to recognize the virtual absence of that compound in the atmosphere. From 1843 until 1900 John Lawes and Joseph Gilbert operated an agricultural experiment station at Rothamsted, England, where they extended the knowledge of soil fertility in relation to plant growth. They were very influential in the development of superphosphate fertilizers.

Foods. Extensive studies were made during the 19th century on the nature and energy value of foods and of the food requirements of various animals. William Prout suggested in 1834 that foods contain three essential classes of substances: saccharine, fatty, and albuminoid. The term "protein" was soon introduced for the latter by the Dutch chemist Gerardus Mulder. Through Liebig the idea was advanced that foods serve two physiological requirements: energy supply and tissue formation and replacement. Carbohydrates and fats supply energy needs, while proteins are necessary for tissue repair.

Important studies on animal calorimetry were made by Karl von Voit and Max von Pettenkofer in Munich and by Max Rubner of Marburg and Berlin. Rubner measured the energy value of foods when burned in a calorimeter and when consumed by animals. He showed that one unit weight of fat was equal to more than two units of protein or carbohydrate.

Fermentation. In the 1830's several biologists associated alcoholic fermentation with the presence of yeast cells in a saccharine medium. Chemists such as Liebig and Berzelius took issue with this; Liebig insisted that fermentation was merely a mechanical decomposition, and the presence of yeast was the result of fermentation rather than the cause. More than two decades later Liebig became embroiled in a bitter controversy with Pasteur, who was carrying out experiments that showed that without living yeast cells fermentation was impossible.

Moritz Traube of Germany suggested in 1858 that fermentation was caused by a soluble ferment such as the pepsin in the gastric juice or the diastase present in malt. No one found such a substance until 1897, when the German investigator Eduard Buchner ground up yeast cells, filtered them through a fine filter, and showed that the cell-free filtrate was able to ferment sugar. The name "zymase" was given to the active substance. Willy Kühne, a German protein chemist, had introduced the term "enzyme" in 1878 for a biological substance capable of catalyzing a biological reaction. His term originally was to designate such agents as pepsin and diastase, but it served equally well when applied to zymase.

Physical Chemistry. Among the early attempts to correlate physical properties with the chemical composition of a substance was the work of the German chemist and historian Hermann Kopp, between 1840 and 1860. Kopp recognized that related compounds showed characteristic changes in molecular volume, melting point, and boiling point. In 1845, Charles Frédéric Gerhardt had referred to homologous series of alcohols and organic acids—that is, compounds whose formulas formed a series differing by a CH_2 group, such as methyl, ethyl, propyl, and butyl alcohols, CH_3OH, C_2H_5OH, C_3H_7OH, C_4H_9OH. Kopp found that the physical properties of the members of such a series differed in a regular and systematic fashion.

Thermodynamics. Thermodynamics developed about the mid-19th century as a consequence of the activities of physicists such as J. Robert Mayer, Hermann Helmholtz, James Prescott Joule, William Thomson (Lord Kelvin), Ludwig Boltzmann, Rudolf Clausius, and James Clerk Maxwell. However, these men were interested primarily in the physical implications of heat changes and gave little thought to chemical relationships.

Chemists had long been interested in the heat changes associated with chemical reactions, and some had associated chemical affinity with the heat liberated during the formation of a compound. After 1852 extended studies on heats of reaction, in particular heat of combustion, were made by Julius Thomsen in Copenhagen and Berthelot in Paris. They soon realized that while evolution of heat during the formation of a compound was related to stability of the compound, affinity could not be correlated solely with heat energy.

The German investigator August Friedrich Horstmann undertook the application of thermodynamics to chemistry in 1868, when he applied the Clausius-Clapeyron equation to the change of vapor pressure of a liquid with change in temperature. He also applied the equation to heats of dissociation of carbonates and hydrates. Van't Hoff generalized the equation in 1889 to make it applicable to equilibrium conditions in gases and dilute solutions.

The American physicist Josiah Willard Gibbs also extended the application of thermodynamics in connection with the equilibria of heterogeneous substances. He introduced the "phase rule," which related the number of chemical components in a heterogeneous system to the number of phases and the conditions (such as temperature and pressure) necessary to describe the system. Gibbs' contributions were accepted very slowly since they were poorly understood when he presented them. Hendrik Roozeboom of Holland was one of the earliest chemists to make practical use of Gibbs' phase rule when he applied it to a gas-liquid equilibrium he was studying. He later made extensive use of the rule in the study of alloys.

Van't Hoff and the Frenchman Henri Le Châtelier applied the principles of thermodynamics to homogeneous equilibria; this was particularly helpful in predicting the nature of changes in a system when strains were introduced by changes in temperature, pressure, or concentration.

Using the principles of thermodynamics Fritz Haber, a German chemist, worked out the most practical conditions for the industrial production of ammonia from nitrogen and hydrogen. The Haber process had profound effects on warfare and agriculture because it permitted nitrates to be prepared from atmospheric nitrogen instead of from Chilean saltpeter.

The usefulness of thermodynamics was extended by Walther Nernst, a German chemist, who in 1906 suggested that the entropy (degree of randomness) of a substance is zero at a temperature of absolute zero. Although the Nernst theorem has never been proved conclusively, it has been widely used to calculate equilibria of chemical systems from a limited number of physical constants. Nernst, Haber, and the American Gilbert Newton Lewis were particularly active in this work.

Kinetic Molecular Theory. Concurrent with advances in thermodynamics was the development of kinetic molecular theory. This was first done in connection with gases, but was ultimately found applicable to liquids and solids as well. Although natural philosophers had speculated that gases were made up of particles in motion, it was not until after the mid-19th century that a convincing theoretical treatment of the subject was presented, primarily through the work of Clausius, Kelvin, and Maxwell.

It was possible to utilize the assumptions of kinetic theory (gases are composed of molecules in motion; the kinetic energy of the molecules is related to the temperature of the gas; and collisions between molecules are perfectly elastic) to derive such well-known relationships as Boyle's law, Charles' law, Graham's law of gaseous diffusion, and Avogadro's hypothesis. There was some concern, however, that at very high pressures or very low temperatures gases exhibit a noticeable deviation from the gas laws. Johannes Diderik van der Waals, a Dutch physicist, showed in 1873 that the deviation could be explained by taking into account the physical volume occupied by close-packed molecules and the attraction of the molecules for one another when in close proximity.

The kinetic theory was also of value in connection with the liquefaction of gases. Oxygen and nitrogen were liquefied in France in 1877. Large-scale operations were carried out six years later by James Dewar in London and by Sigmund Florenty von Wroblevsky and Karol Stanislav Olszevski in Cracow. Helium was finally liquefied in 1908 by Heike Kamerlingh Onnes in Leiden.

Ionization. Knowledge of the nature of solutions was advanced during the 1880's, particularly as a result of the theory of ionization. There had been little progress in the understanding of electrolysis since the time of Faraday except for the observation of the German physicist Johann Hittorf in 1857 that certain ions move through a solution faster in the presence of an electric current than others. In 1874, Friedrich Kohlrausch showed that every ion has a characteristic mobility.

In 1884, Svante Arrhenius of Sweden introduced his theory of ionization. He suggested that salts, acids, and bases dissociate into charged particles, or ions, when they dissolve in water, thus providing charged particles to carry a current of electricity through the solution. The ions lose their charge when they come into contact with an oppositely charged electrode, being deposited on the electrode (if it is a metallic ion) or escaping as a gas (if it is a nonmetallic ion). Arrhenius' theory also explained why salts have a greater influence on the osmotic pressure, vapor pressure, melting point, and boiling point of a solvent than do solutes like sugar and alcohol, which fail to conduct a current.

Discovery of Radioactivity. As the 19th century came to a close the discovery was made that the element uranium spontaneously emits radiation resembling X-rays. The French physicist Antoine Henri Becquerel made this observation somewhat accidentally in 1896 while studying the behavior of fluorescent substances. It soon became apparent that the radiation was associated with all forms of uranium. A Polish student living in Paris, Marie Sklodowska Curie, found that thorium compounds are also radioactive. She and her husband, Pierre, isolated two new radioactive elements—polonium and radium —before the end of the century.

4. The 20th Century

Radiochemistry and Atomic Structure. The study of radioactive elements quickly attracted the attention of leading chemists and physicists. Ernest Rutherford and his associates at McGill University, and later at Manchester and Cambridge, made a number of highly significant observations. By 1899 several investigators, including Rutherford, found that radiations were not homogeneous but were made up of an easily absorbed portion (alpha particles), a more penetrating portion that could be deflected by a magnetic field (beta particles), and a very penetrating portion resembling X-rays (gamma rays). The beta particles were shown to be identical with electrons, the negatively charged particles discovered by Joseph John Thomson, an English physicist, in 1897 during his studies on gas-discharge tubes.

Since helium gas is found in association with radioactive substances, it was suspected that helium might be related to the alpha particles. In 1903, William Ramsay, an English scientist, and his coworker Frederick Soddy observed that helium is liberated at a steady rate from radium chloride. In 1908, Rutherford and Thomas Royds proved that alpha particles are helium ions with a double positive charge (He^{+2}).

Concurrently, new radioactive elements were being discovered in the products of decay of uranium and radium. Rutherford and Soddy separated an active material named thorium X from thorium, leaving the latter inactive. The thorium X gradually lost activity, whereas thorium became active once more. Radioactive gases were isolated in several laboratories. Studies of decay rates showed a behavior that could be expressed in terms of half-life—the time during which one half the starting material disappears.

Discovery of Isotopes. Identification of elements isolated from decaying radioactive material suggested an identity with known elements. For example, radium D, a radioactive product in the decay series of radium, could not be separated from ordinary lead after being mixed with

that element. Rutherford and others began to suspect that radioactive elements were decomposing into other elements. Kasimir Fajans was responsible for making careful atomic weight determinations of lead from radioactive ores and ordinary ores. This revealed significant differences and suggested that, contrary to Dalton, not all atoms of a particular element are alike. In 1913, Soddy introduced the term "isotope" for atoms that differ in mass but otherwise have the properties of the same element. At that time Fajans, Soddy, and Alexander S. Russell independently introduced the radioactive-displacement law, which predicted the nature of the resulting atom when a radioactive atom decayed. The isotope concept was eventually found to hold for atoms of stable elements as well when J. J. Thomson and Francis Aston developed the mass spectrograph, an instrument for separating and recording the atoms of a particular element by their differing masses.

Subatomic Particles. The work on radioactivity was leading to the rejection of the Dalton atom as a small indivisible particle. Electrons were being found present in virtually all elements. In 1911, Hans Geiger and Ernest Marsden, working in Rutherford's laboratory, bombarded gold foil with alpha particles and observed a peculiar scattering of the particles. From this, Rutherford deduced that the atom must be made up of a positive nucleus surrounded by electrons moving in planetary orbits. He supposed that practically all of the weight of the atom was concentrated in the nucleus, which nevertheless made up only a tiny part of the volume of the atom. Rutherford's atom was primarily empty space.

The Rutherford model of the atom was inconsistent with classical electrodynamics since a revolving electron should quickly lose energy and collapse into the nucleus. The Danish physicist Niels Bohr treated the problem from the standpoint of quantum theory and developed a model for the hydrogen atom that restricted energy changes to electron displacements between certain energy levels. In this way he was able to correlate the paths of the electron in the hydrogen atom with the absorption and emission lines of the hydrogen spectrum.

The Bohr concept of the atom was extended to other elements with greater difficulty, requiring the introduction of various approximations. During the 1920's atomic models became more and more mathematical through the introduction of wave mechanical treatment by the French physicist Louis Victor de Broglie and the German physicist Erwin Schrödinger and of matrix mechanical treatment by Werner Heisenberg.

Rutherford treated the charge and mass of the nucleus in an empirical fashion at first. In 1913, Henry Moseley showed that the atomic number of an element, hitherto merely a place numeral associated with position in the periodic table, had physical significance. When he used various elements as the target of an X-ray tube, he found that the principal wavelengths of the X-rays decreased systematically as he substituted an element for the previous one in the periodic table.

In 1919, Rutherford bombarded nitrogen with alpha particles and brought about the transmutation of nitrogen into oxygen with the simultaneous emission of protons. The discovery of the proton, the nucleus of the ordinary hydrogen atom, made it possible to account for the positive charge of the nucleus. In 1932, James Chadwick discovered the neutron, a particle with approximately the same mass as the proton, but with no charge. The protons and neutrons together accounted for the mass of the nucleus.

Bonding Theory. Even before the discovery of the nuclear particles, chemists were developing concepts of chemical combination that involved the behavior of the outermost electrons in the atoms undergoing combination. The Americans Gilbert N. Lewis and Irving Langmuir and the German Walther Kossel independently developed their ideas on this subject beginning about 1916. They deduced that the outermost shell of electrons is most stable when it contains eight electrons, as is the case of the rare gases beyond helium. If metals, which contain 1, 2, or, at most, 3 electrons, give away their outer electrons, they expose a filled shell having 8 electrons while acquiring a positive charge. Nonmetallic elements have outer shells that can be filled by accepting 1, 2, or 3 electrons, while acquiring a negative charge. In the formation of salts, electrons are transferred from metallic atoms to nonmetallic atoms, producing positive and negative ions, which strongly attract one another. The resulting ionic compounds are said to be held together by ionic bonds.

In the case of nonmetallic compounds, the theory provided for the sharing of electron pairs between atoms, in such a way that each atom has 8 electrons in its outermost shell, thus creating a state of stability. The combinations that result are called covalent compounds, and the shared electron pair is called a covalent bond.

Biochemistry. Hormones and vitamins received particularly strong attention during the first 30 years of the century. Then, with the availability of isotopes as tracers, rapid progress was made in the understanding of fermentation, intermediary metabolism, photosynthesis, the role of enzymes, and biochemical genetics.

Nutrition. In 1912, F. Gowland Hopkins, working at Cambridge, England, introduced the concept of accessory food factors, and Casimir Funk, a chemist at the Lister Institute in London, introduced the word "vitamine." However, most discoveries in the field of nutrition resulted from research on animal diets at agricultural experiment stations. At a station in Connecticut, for example, the search for a basically adequate synthetic diet for white rats led Lafayette B. Mendel and Thomas B. Osborne to recognize the presence of trace organic nutrients in milk. E. V. McCollum at the Wisconsin station associated a growth factor (vitamin A) with the milk fat and a water-soluble factor (vitamin B) with the skim milk portion. Another water-soluble factor (vitamin C) was soon recognized in fresh fruits and vegetables as a preventative for scurvy.

Intensive nutritional research on laboratory animals ultimately unraveled a complex picture of organic compounds essential in trace quantities for adequate nutrition. The period between 1920 and 1940 was spent in isolating, identifying, and synthesizing the various fat-soluble and water-soluble factors occurring in foods. There was also much work done on the requirements for trace minerals and essential amino acids and their role in metabolism.

Hormones. The role of hormones as chemical regulators of bodily processes was first recognized in 1902, when the English physiologists

Ernest Starling and William Bayliss discovered secretin. This compound is secreted into the blood stream by the duodenum when food enters from the stomach. Upon reaching the pancreas, secretin initiates the secretion of pancreatic juice.

Insulin, which is produced by the islets of Langerhans in the pancreas, is a hormone associated with carbohydrate metabolism. In 1922 the Canadian physiologists Charles Banting and Charles Best prepared an insulin-rich pancreatic extract that alleviated the symptoms of diabetes when injected into diabetic animals. Improved purification of the hormone made it possible to use insulin obtained from beef pancreas in the treatment of human diabetes. The amino-acid sequence of insulin, which is a protein, was worked out by Frederick Sanger of Cambridge University in 1956. Beef insulin was synthesized by a Chinese team of chemists in 1964 and human insulin by an American team a year later.

Other hormones discovered during the first decades of the 20th century include adrenaline, thyroxin, pituitary hormones, hormones from the adrenal cortex, and sex hormones. Except for adrenaline and thyroxin, the hormones proved to be complex polypeptides or sterols.

Photosynthesis. The structure of chlorophyll was established in the 1930's by Hans Fischer at Munich. Fischer had already established the structure of the chemically related heme, the nonprotein portion of hemoglobin. Chlorophyll was synthesized independently in 1960 by research groups under the direction of Robert B. Woodward at Harvard and M. Strell at the Technische Hochschule in Munich. The nature of the photosynthetic process was unraveled very slowly. In the early 1900's it was shown that the reduction of carbon dioxide to sugar takes place in several steps and involves both light and dark reactions. Studies of reactions similar to photosynthesis in bacteria in the 1920's led to an understanding of the role of hydrogen acceptors in the transference of biological energy and work on the intermediary metabolism of carbohydrates shed further light on the photosynthetic process.

Isotopic Tracers. The introduction of isotopic tracers in the late 1930's made possible real progress in biochemistry. Although heavy isotopes could be prepared from stable elements, radioactive isotopes were much preferred because of the ease with which they could be detected and measured. They became available after the discovery of artificial radioactivity by Frédéric and Irène Curie Joliot in France in 1934. The introduction of the cyclotron made it possible to produce such isotopes as sulfur-35, phosphorus-32, iodine-131, and iron-55 in quantities sufficient for use as biological tracers. In 1941, Samuel Ruben and Martin Kamen at the California Radiation Laboratory discovered carbon-14, which has a half-life of 5,730 years and is well suited to biochemical tracer studies. Melvin Calvin's laboratory at the University of California used carbon-14 in establishing the sequence of compounds formed from labeled carbon dioxide in the process of photosynthesis.

Fermentation. In 1904, Arthur Harden and W. J. Young of the Lister Institute isolated a coenzyme from yeast juice, which is necessary for fermentation. About 10 years later, the German biochemist Otto F. Meyerhof showed that the coenzymes present during alcoholic fermentation are also present in muscle cells, where they are essential in carbohydrate metabolism. He and his associate, Gustav Embden, clarified the breakdown of phosphorylated 6-carbon sugars through phosphorylated 3-carbon fragments to pyruvic acid, acetaldehyde, and ethyl alcohol—a series of reactions known as the Meyerhof-Embden pathway.

Respiration. The role of oxygen in intermediary metabolism was studied by the German biochemist Otto Warburg. In 1923, Warburg improved the respiration manometer, making it possible to measure oxygen uptake in metabolizing systems. He believed that after oxygen is carried to the cells by the hemoglobin of the blood, it is picked up by a system of enzymes known as cytochromes. The cytochromes proved to be proteins combined with heme, which is the oxygen-carrying portion of the pigment hemoglobin.

Albert Szent-Györgyi of Hungary continued the respiration studies with minced pigeon muscle, which has a very high rate of oxygen uptake. He showed that the uptake rate can be maintained by the addition of salts of certain acids that might be intermediary products in carbohydrate metabolism. Hans A. Krebs added other acids (citric, α-ketoglutaric, pyruvic, glutamic, and aspartic acids) to the list of metabolic accelerators.

In 1937, Krebs, a German-British biochemist, postulated a metabolic cycle in which pyruvic acid is degraded to a 2-carbon fragment, which then undergoes a condensation with oxaloacetic acid to form citric acid. The citric acid is then involved in a cyclic series of reactions in which energy-carrying hydrogen atoms are liberated and carbon dioxide is given off. The cycle of reactions is completed with the formation of oxaloacetic acid, which then reenters the cycle. In 1951, Severo Ochoa of the New York University College of Medicine showed that the 2-carbon fragment originating from pyruvic acid is coenzyme A with an attached acetyl group. Although the Krebs citric-acid cycle, as this series of reactions is known, underwent minor modifications since its introduction, it presents a convincing mechanism for the conversion of pyruvic acid into carbon dioxide and water with the liberation of energy.

Enzymes. All steps in the citric-acid cycles, as well as in virtually all metabolic reactions, are carried out in the presence of enzymes. It was generally supposed that enzymes are proteins of a highly specific structure, but this was not conclusively demonstrated until 1926 when the American biochemist James B. Sumner succeeded in preparing crystalline urease, the enzyme that hydrolyzes the conversion of urea to ammonia and carbon dioxide. Shortly thereafter, the American John H. Northrup crystallized pepsin. By the mid-1960's more than 75 enzymes were crystallized; they have all been found to be proteins that are highly specific for a single type of reaction.

Biochemical Genetics. Although nucleic acids were first isolated in 1869 by Friedrich Miescher, a Swiss biochemist, their importance in biology was not conclusively proved until 1944, when three scientists at the Rockefeller University—O. T. Avery, C. M. MacLeod, and M. McCarty—showed that in bacteria, transmission of hereditary information is carried by deoxyribonucleic acid (DNA).

In 1953 the English biochemist Francis Crick and the American biochemist James Watson, working at Cambridge University, suggested that DNA consists of two strands of nucleotides joined in the form of a double helix. They theorized that the bases of the nucleotides in the opposite strands were joined by weak bonds, and that each strand could act as a template for the production of new DNA molecules. The Crick-Watson hypothesis was subsequently confirmed by many experimenters. DNA controls the synthesis of ribonucleic acids (RNA's), which are in turn involved in the synthesis of proteins, but the actual mechanisms of these reactions have not been determined.

Analytical Chemistry—Colorimetry. Absorption of light by colored solutions has been used as an analytical procedure for more than a century. For the most part, measurement was made by visual comparison of the color of a solution of unknown concentration with that of solutions of known concentration. Spectrophotometers came into practical use about 1940. These instruments utilize filters or other optical devices that make it possible to restrict illumination to a narrow range of wavelengths. Photocells are used to measure absorption. Concurrently, new colorimetric reagents, such as dithizone, came into use, greatly extending the scope of colorimetry.

Spectroscopy. The use of spectroscopy was expanded extensively in the mid-20th century. The spectroscope was developed in Germany in 1859 by Robert Bunsen and Gustav Kirchhoff. Its use in qualitative analysis was immediately recognized, both in the chemical laboratory and in astronomical observatories, where it is used for the identification of elements in stars.

The extension of spectroscopic techniques into the infrared region of the spectrum was particularly important in qualitative and quantitative analysis. The energies involved in many intramolecular vibrations associated with some atomic groups fall in the infrared range; therefore, infrared absorption spectroscopy has become useful in structural analysis and quantitative determination of complex compounds.

Ultracentrifuges. The ultracentrifuge, a device for measuring the sedimentation rates of substances in colloidal suspension, was developed in the 1920's. Through this method, it became possible to gain information about probable molecular weights and degree of heterogeneity of protein suspensions, starch, and polymeric materials. The early ultracentrifuges, developed by Theodor (The) Svedberg of Sweden, were heavy, expensive, oil-driven instruments of limited applicability. They have been supplanted by air-driven and electrically driven ultracentrifuges.

Electrophoresis. Electrophoresis is another valuable analytic technique. It involves the migration of electrically charged particles in an electric field and is used for the separation and identification of such material. Arne Tiselius of Sweden figured prominently in the application of this technique, which has been important in the study of proteins and high polymers.

Mass Spectrometry. The mass spectrometer developed from the work of Joseph J. Thomson and Francis Aston in Cambridge, England. They used a combination of magnetic and electrostatic fields for the separation of positive ions according to their masses. Until 1940 the mass spectroscope was used, for the most part, to study the distribution of isotopes among the various elements. When commercial instruments finally became available, the mass spectroscope came into widespread use as an analytical instrument.

Nuclear Magnetic Resonance. Nuclear magnetic resonance (NMR) has been developed since the 1940's. It is based on the response of nuclear spins to a magnetic field of regularly varying frequency. The behavior of hydrogen nuclei, for instance, in the magnetic field is influenced by the nature of the atoms to which the hydrogen atoms are bonded. NMR has significant value as a diagnostic tool in the study of molecular structure.

Chromatography. Chromatography was developed in 1903 by the Russian Mikhail Tswett, who sought to separate plant pigments by passing a solution through a column of solid adsorbent. It was popularized after 1931, when Richard Kuhn of Berlin used it for the separation of closely related biological pigments. Subsequently, other types of chromatography were developed, including paper chromatography, partition chromatography, and gas chromatography. These techniques have proved effective in the separation of complex organic compounds.

X-Ray Crystallography. X-ray crystallography was first used in 1912 by Max von Laue in Germany. At that time its use was limited to crystals of fairly simple compounds. However, with the availability of high-speed computers, it has become possible to analyze the structure of such complex crystals as vitamin B_{12}, DNA, and hemoglobin; inorganic compounds can also be analyzed by this technique.

5. Careers in Chemistry

In the mid-1960's more than 100,000 chemists and chemical engineers were employed in the United States alone. They were involved in many types of work, some of it peripheral to chemistry itself—for example, sales, management, journalism—but most were involved in teaching, research, development, or control work in one of six fields: analytical chemistry, physical chemistry, organic chemistry, inorganic chemistry, biochemistry, and chemical engineering.

Types of Chemists. *Analytical chemists* carry out work that leads to the identification of chemical substances (qualitative analysis) and estimates the quantities present (quantitative analysis).

Physical chemists are interested in the physical characteristics of chemical substances. They are continually searching for improved theoretical concepts to explain the structure of atoms and molecules and the mechanism of chemical reactions.

Organic chemists study the compounds of carbon in combination with hydrogen and other nonmetals. These compounds include not only those found in living organisms but also those found in minerals and compounds of purely synthetic origin.

Inorganic chemists are interested in all of the elements and their compounds, other than organic carbon compounds. This includes metals, radioactive elements, and the commercial acids, bases, and salts, which make up a very large part of the products of the chemical industry.

Biochemists are concerned with the compounds present in living organisms, how they are formed from simple materials, and how they are broken down by living cells. Their work includes phases of agricultural and medical chemistry.

Chemical engineers are involved in the production of chemical substances and the control of chemical processing operations. They also design and build chemical plants and carry out research and development work on processing operations. See also CHEMICAL INDUSTRIES—*Careers in the Chemical Industries.*

Employment. Most chemists are employed in industry. Many manufacturing plants support large research and development laboratories in which chemists develop new products, improve existing products, and develop and improve manufacturing processes.

The government also supports extensive research and development programs, particularly in the fields of medicine, warfare, space, and agriculture.

Many chemists are employed as teachers in both high schools and colleges. Those who teach in colleges frequently do research as part of their activities.

Educational Requirements. Anyone planning to become a chemist or chemical engineer should plan to obtain at least a bachelor's degree in college. This demands extensive study in the four basic fields of chemistry (inorganic, organic, analytical, and physical), in mathematics, and in physics. Students should enter college with as much mathematics and science as is practical. Many colleges also expect a chemistry major to gain a reading knowledge of one or two foreign languages (preferably German, Russian, or French). College graduates in chemistry or chemical engineering are sought by industry and government and are able, if they have taken required courses in education, to teach in high schools where science teachers are in very short supply.

Many students who have strong academic records go on to graduate school for a master's or doctor's degree. As graduate students they specialize in one of the branches of chemistry and spend a significant part of their time working on a research problem. Attainment of an advanced degree results in improved employment opportunities, with greater responsibility, higher salaries, and much greater opportunities for advancement.

Further information on career opportunities in chemistry may be obtained by writing to the following organizations: American Institute of Chemical Engineers, New York, N. Y.; American Chemical Society, Washington, D. C; Manufacturing Chemists' Association, Inc., Washington, D. C.; American Society of Biological Chemists, Bethesda, Md.

AARON J. IHDE, *University of Wisconsin*

Bibliography

Farber, Eduard, *The Evolution of Chemistry* (New York 1952).
Farber, Eduard, ed., *Great Chemists* (New York 1961).
Ihde, Aaron J., *The Development of Modern Chemistry* (New York 1964).
Leicester, Henry M., *The Historical Background of Chemistry* (New York 1956).
Leicester, Henry M., and Klickstein, Herbert S., *A Source Book in Chemistry* (New York 1952).
National Academy of Sciences–National Research Council, *Chemistry: Opportunities and Needs* (Washington 1965).
Nourse, Alan E., *So You Want to Be a Chemist* (New York 1964).
Partington, J. R., *A History of Chemistry*, 3 vols. (London 1961–1964).
Partington, J. R., *A Short History of Chemistry* (New York 1957).
Taylor, F. Sherwood, *A History of Industrial Chemistry* (London 1957).

CHEMNITZ. See KARL-MARX-STADT.

CHEMOSH, kē'mosh, was the national god of the Moabites, an ancient tribe akin to the Israelites. As indicated in the Old Testament and in Moabite, Assyrian, and Egyptian records, the position of Chemosh in Moab was similar to that of Yahweh in Israel. Sacrifices were offered to him on shrines or "high places" built in his honor. Military defeats were considered a manifestation of his displeasure; victories, a gift of his beneficence. A Biblical passage (Judges 11:24) indicates that Chemosh was also worshiped by the Ammonites, and a shrine built to Chemosh in Jerusalem by King Solomon seems to have been a place of worship for about 300 years, until it was destroyed by King Josiah. The Moabites, referred to in poetic utterance as "the people of Chemosh," often took the name Chemosh as part of their own, as in Chemosh-Nadav (Chemosh is bountiful).

RAPHAEL PATAI, *Theodor Herzl Institute*

CHEMOSURGERY, kem-ō-sûr'jə-rē, is the application of strong chemicals to localized areas of the body for the removal of diseased tissues. The widest application of this method of treatment is for the removal of small tumors, particularly of the skin. Chemosurgery is also used to remove badly infected or gangrenous tissues.

A wide variety of different chemicals may be used in chemosurgery, but special advantages are claimed for zinc chloride paste and phenol. Zinc chloride paste, in addition to killing the tissue, hardens and preserves it, facilitating its removal and subsequent microscopic examination. Studying the removed tissue through a microscope is particularly important in cases of cancer, helping the surgeon determine whether or not all the cancerous tissue has been excised. After the main mass of tissue has been removed, the surgeon excises bits of tissue from the surrounding organs and has them examined under a microscope. He continues to do this until the removed bits of tissue show no evidence of the disease.

ANDRES GOTH, M. D.
University of Texas Southwestern Medical School

CHEMOTHERAPY, kem-ō-ther'ə-pē, is the treatment of disease by administering drugs that injure or kill the disease-producing organisms without damaging the host. The term is also used more loosely to mean any use of drugs in the treatment of disease, and particularly of cancer. The more precise meaning given above derives from concepts introduced by the German bacteriologist Paul Ehrlich around 1900. While working with certain chemical dyes, Ehrlich found that they have a selective action against specific kinds of disease-producing organisms. Unlike vaccines, which destroy invading organisms indirectly (by increasing the body's natural defenses), these chemicals were found to destroy them directly. However, as Ehrlich noted, it is important that a chemotherapeutic agent have a high degree of selectivity against the invading organism if it is not to affect the body cells of the host. Thus, a selective action is the key to successful chemotherapy.

If enough information were available on the biochemical differences between disease-producing organisms and the host's body cells, chemotherapeutic agents could be produced at will. As it happens, however, the reverse is often the case.

A new drug having a curative effect is discovered more or less by accident, and by studying the drug's mode of action, scientists obtain new knowledge about the biochemical differences between the organism and the cells of the host. One of the best examples of this sequence of events is the history of the drugs known as sulfonamides. These drugs were generally useful in the treatment of infections long before anything was known about their selective action on bacteria. Later it was found that they destroy bacteria by taking the place of paraminobenzoic acid, a growth factor essential for bacteria but not for humans. When sulfonamide molecules are present, the bacteria absorb them instead of paraminobenzoic acid molecules; as a result, the bacteria cannot grow and multiply.

Mode of Action. Although all chemotherapeutic agents have some selective action against specific disease-producing organisms, their mode of action varies considerably. Penicillin and related antibiotics prevent bacteria from synthesizing their rigid cell walls. Since animal cells do not have cell walls, they are not harmed by these drugs. Other chemotherapeutic agents are injurious to the cell membranes of certain microorganisms; they also inhibit certain synthetic processes, such as the formation of proteins or nucleic acids.

In some instances, the selective effect of a drug is enhanced by its tendency to become localized in a particular region or tissue of the body. For example, the drug griseofulvin, which is used in treating some fungus infections of the skin, has a greater tendency to become localized in diseased skin than in normal skin, a fortunate circumstance that undoubtedly contributes to the drug's effectiveness.

While the ideal drug used in chemotherapy should kill the invading organisms, many valuable drugs simply inhibit their multiplication. Antibacterial substances of this type are commonly referred to as being *bacteriostatic*, rather than *bactericidal*, a term reserved for drugs that kill bacteria. Inhibition of multiplication is usually sufficient for treating a disease since the normal defense mechanisms of the body contribute to the eventual cure.

History and Research. The development of chemotherapy may be divided into two periods, with the year 1935 as the dividing point. In that year, the German biochemist Gerhard Domagk reported the curative effect of Prontosil (a sulfonamide derivative) against bacterial infections. Before this discovery, there were no known synthetic drugs that could cure a bacterial infection in man. Previously, chemotherapy had been limited largely to parasitic diseases. Quinine and quinacrine were used for malaria; emetine was helpful against amebiasis; arsenical drugs were effective against trypanosomiasis, syphilis, and amebiasis; and antimony compounds were used in treating schistosomiasis.

Since 1935, numerous sulfonamides, antibiotics, and newer synthetic drugs have revolutionized the treatment of many infectious diseases. Isoniazid and para-aminosalicylic acid are valuable in the treatment of tuberculosis, and other new drugs are effective in combating malaria and other parasitic diseases.

Present-day research in the field of chemotherapy is aimed largely at developing new drugs. One of the problems facing researchers is the ability of certain microorganisms to develop a natural resistance to the drugs used against them. Fortunately, however, not all species tend to develop rapid drug resistance and not all drugs are equally vulnerable to what may be termed a "bacterial counterattack." Nevertheless, drug resistance is a serious problem which may be minimized, though not completely overcome, by the rational use of existing drugs and the development of new chemotherapeutic agents.

Among the substances that have been studied as possible sources of new drugs are the various products of molds. One such product, cephalothin, appeared to be an effective antibiotic for people who are allergic to penicillin. Occasionally, researchers succeeded in modifying a natural product. Such an approach led to the development of a large number of semisynthetic penicillins, some of which were highly significant advances. Some of these penicillins are effective against microorganisms that have become resistant to the naturally occurring antibiotics. Many of them also have a broader antibacterial spectrum, making them effective against a wider variety of bacteria species.

In addition to developing new drugs, chemotherapy researchers are investigating the mode of action of many existing drugs. When it is learned how a chemotherapeutic agent works, the drug may become a valuable tool in the study of molecular biology. Studies using penicillin, for example, have provided insight into the way in which bacteria synthesize their cell walls. Puromycin and actinomycin are also widely used as experimental tools. These drugs block the synthesis of proteins or inactivate nucleic acids, thus preventing the formation of enzymes.

ANDRES GOTH, M. D.
University of Texas Southwestern Medical School

Further Reading: Barber, Mary, and Garrod, Lawrence, *Antibiotic and Chemotherapy* (Baltimore 1963); Cowan, Samuel T., and Rowatt, Elizabeth, eds., *Strategy of Chemotherapy* (New York and London 1958); Goldin, Abraham, and others, eds., *Advances in Chemotherapy*, 2 vols. (New York 1964–1965); Manson-Bahr, Philip H., and Walters, John, *Chemotherapy of Tropical Diseases* (Springfield, Ill., 1961).

CHEMOTROPISM. See TROPISM.

CHEMURGY, kem′ər-jē, is the applied science that develops new products, and new uses for old products, from agricultural materials. To be of economic importance, the products of chemurgy must be competitive in cost with items made from other raw materials. The most important uses for agricultural products are for human foods, animal feeds, and fibers for textiles and cordage. Products derived from agricultural materials also have long been used in industry and medicine, and since the 1930's there has been a rapid increase in the variety and importance of such products.

An organization for the promotion of chemurgy, the National Farm Chemurgic Council, was founded in Dearborn, Mich., in 1935. It has headquarters in New York City and serves as a clearinghouse for chemurgic information.

Food. One of the major results of advances in chemurgy is the development of thousands of new foods. Frozen concentrated orange juice and other citrus concentrates have revolutionized the entire citrus industry. The great improvements that have been made since World War II in processing dehydrated egg products have made many ready-mix and easy-to-prepare foods available on the grocery shelves today. The distribution of frozen bakery products has made it easy for housewives to serve freshly baked products.

Bulgur, a dried, crushed wheat product, is an ancient food of the Middle East which has been modernized and improved by the chemurgy. Rice now can be abraded, or scraped, to give a whiter kernel and a high-protein rice flour useful for enriching many food products.

Chemurgists have also developed many new foods for calorie-conscious consumers. Some of the newest are lower-calorie, protein-rich whole peanuts and low-fat cheese. A new process converts waste whey (the watery part of milk) to a nutritious dried dairy product.

A new foam-mat drying process produces dried powders from liquid and puréed foods that can be reconstituted in seconds to full-bodied products similar in flavor and appearance to the freshly prepared products. A new explosion puffing process makes dried fruit and vegetable pieces that cook completely in 3 to 5 minutes, with nearly all the flavor, nutrition, and taste of cooked fresh fruits and vegetables. Freeze-drying is gaining in popularity for specialty foods.

Livestock Feeds. The isolation and identification of growth factors (such as estrogenic, or female, hormones) in forages have contributed to greatly improved feeds. Fermentation processes now provide beta carotene (which is converted to vitamin A in the animal's body) and riboflavin (vitamin B_2) for widespread use in animal feeds. Other fermentative processes upgrade the nutritive value of wheat, barley, and other mill feeds.

Alfalfa, which once was dried solely by the sun, can now be dehydrated under controlled conditions in heated mechanical dryers. Antioxidant stabilizers, which reduce atmospheric-induced changes, are added to help retain much higher amounts of the original nutritive values than are retained in sun-dried alfalfa.

Scientists have also found ways to remove undesirable compounds from otherwise nutritious feed materials. For example, bitter saponins can be removed from forages, other bitter compounds can be removed from safflower seed, and poisonous gossypol can be removed from cottonseed.

Poultry feathers, once a costly disposal problem, are now used to increase the protein content of mixed feeds, and ways have been found to convert cannery wastes—also a disposal problem—into nutritive livestock feeds.

Fibers. The utility of cotton as a clothing textile has been greatly increased by the development of wash-and-wear fabrics. Cotton clothing also has been made much more versatile by treating for flame resistance, adding stretch characteristics, and imparting permanent creases.

Wool, also, can now be treated so that it can be laundered or dry-cleaned without distortion or the loss of its new appearance.

New ways of tanning make leather more suitable for garments, gloves, and shoe uppers since these specially treated leathers are resistant to wet-cleaning, dry-cleaning, and soiling.

Industrial Applications. The starch fractions of corn, wheat, and other cereal grains can now be converted to such useful items as urethane foams and dialdehyde starch. The foams, both flexible and rigid, are used as insulation materials and for many other purposes. The starch has application in adhesives, binders, drilling additives, gelatin conditioners, and textile processing.

Three corn sugar acids—gluconic, 2-ketogluconic, and saccharic acids—are now in commercial use in bottle-washing compounds, pharmaceuticals, veterinary medicines, and aluminum etchants. Corn sugar is now converted by fermentation to gumlike products utilized in cosmetics and paper and as thickening and stabilizing agents.

Scientists have found how to convert tallow to liquid detergents that can be broken down by microorganisms in soil and water. This may help solve the detergent waste-disposal problem. Animal fats have come to be applied extensively in the manufacture of plastics and plasticizing agents.

Linseed oil is now used to protect concrete highways, sidewalks, and bridge decks from the harmful effects of freezing and thawing and the action of de-icing chemicals. A successful new fire-retardant paint is based on chemically modified tung oil, which is derived from the seeds of tung trees. A new oil made from crambe—an oilseed obtained from a herb of the mustard family—is used as a mold lubricant for the continuous casting of steel. A new chemical derivative from turpentine, pinane hydroperoxide, helps in the manufacture of "cold" rubber, and derivatives of pine gum can be used as a filler for paper and paperboard.

Bagasse, or residue, of sugarcane, once burned as a fuel to avoid waste problems, is finding profitable outlets in the manufacture of insulating board, sound-absorbing board, and paper. Kenaf, a fast-growing fiber plant, originally from the East Indies, may prove useful for pulping and papermaking.

Medical Products. A little known outlet for agricultural materials is in the manufacture of medical products. For example, today's commercial processes for manufacture of penicillin owe much to agricultural materials and technology. A blood-plasma extender is made from dextran, a carbohydrate similar to starch made by fermenting sugar. A little-recognized use for cotton is the conforming cotton bandage that came into use during World War II. Rutin, a drug valuable in restoring weakened blood capillaries to overcome hemorrhagic conditions, has been made from tobacco and buckwheat.

CH'EN TU-HSIU, chun dōō shyōō (1879–1942),

was a scholar and a founder of the Chinese Communist party. He was born in Huaining on Oct. 8, 1879, and died in Kiangtsing, Szechwan, on May 27, 1942.

Ch'en studied in Japan and France, and he looked to the West for solution of China's problems. After 1915 he became famous for his essays on science and democracy and for his critiques of Chinese culture. He helped initiate China's literary renaissance and, while teaching literature at Peking University, was imprisoned briefly for his participation in the 1919 student demonstrations against the Versailles Treaty.

In 1921 he organized the Communist party in Shanghai with Li Ta-chao and served as its head until 1927, when he was blamed for the failure of the Kuomintang-Communist alliance. He organized a Trotskyite group, but was expelled from the Communist party in 1930. Imprisoned by the Nationalists from 1932 to 1937, he abandoned politics and devoted himself to classical studies.

JAMES R. SHIRLEY
Northern Illinois University

CHENAB RIVER, chĕ-näb', in West Pakistan, one of the "five rivers" of the Punjab. Its tributaries are the Jhelum and the Ravi. It rises in the Himalayan ranges of Kashmir and, entering Pakistan's Punjab region near Sialkot, flows in a southwesterly direction until it unites with the Sutlej River after a course of about 675 miles (1,085 km). The combined stream flows 50 miles (80 km) farther to the Indus. The Chenab is of great importance to the Punjab region of Pakistan because of its huge irrigation system: the Lower Chenab Canal and the Upper Chenab Canal irrigate some 2.5 million acres (1 million hectares) in the Rechna Doab area.

CHENEY, chĕ'nē, **Ednah Dow Littlehale** (1824–1904), American reformer and author. She was born in Boston, Mass., on June 27, 1824. An abolitionist and suffragette, she engaged in numerous social causes and was particularly active in welfare work during the Civil War. Besides several novels she wrote a biography of her husband, Seth Wells Cheney, one of Louisa May Alcott, and her own memoirs. She died in Jamaica Plain, Mass., on Nov. 19, 1904.

CHENEY, chĕ'nē, **Sheldon Warren** (1886–   ), American drama and art critic. He was born in Berkeley, Calif., on June 29, 1886. After graduating from the University of California in 1908, he became drama and art critic for several periodicals. In 1916 he founded the *Theatre Arts Magazine,* which he edited until 1921. He spent the next few years in New York City, principally with Equity Players (The Actors' Theatre). Thereafter he lectured and wrote on modern art, opposing all academicism.

Cheney's books include *A Primer of Modern Art* (1923) and *The Theatre: 3000 Years of Drama, Acting and Stagecraft* (1929; revised and enlarged edition, 1952), which is a standard history of the subject. Among his later books are *Expressionism in Art* (1934), *The Story of Modern Art* (1941; enlarged ed., 1958), *Men Who Have Walked with God* (1945), and *New World History of Art* (1956).

CHENG HO, jung hu (died c. 1435), was a eunuch official of the Ming dynasty (1368–1644) of China and a great explorer of the early 15th century. He was a Muslim from Yünnan province.

Cheng led seven extraordinary naval expeditions for the Ming emperor Yung Lo to Southeast Asia, India, Arabia, and Africa between 1405 and 1433. These voyages were lavish demonstrations of the power and navigational skills of the Chinese, surpassing any previous naval operations anywhere. The first voyage included 62 ships carrying about 27,800 men, and the others were of a similar scale. The purpose of the expeditions was probably the expansion of Chinese political influence overseas, and Cheng brought back exotic products to the Chinese court as evidence of his exploits.

Tribute missions from some of the countries visited came to China for about a generation, but Cheng's voyages were eventually stopped. Their cost was heavy and the eunuch's leadership in these expeditions was resented by regular officials. After Yung Lo's death the government readopted its isolationist policy. Temples commemorating Cheng Ho still exist in Southeast Asia.

JAMES R. SHIRLEY
Northern Illinois University

CHENGCHOW, jung'jō', is the capital city of Honan province, China. It is situated 10 miles (16 km) south of the Yellow River, and between two historical cities—Loyang, one of China's ancient capitals, 62 miles (100 km) to the west, and Kaifeng, 31 miles (50 km) to the east. Chengchow is an important junction of two major rail lines in North China—the north-south Peking-Canton Railway and the east-west Lunghai Railway, which extends from Lienyunchiang, a seaport on the Yellow Sea, westward to Singkiang. A small town before the construction of the railroads, Chengchow has become the political, economic, and cultural center of the province.

Located in the famous cotton region of China, Chengchow has become the largest cotton-textile center in Honan province. Other newly developed industries include textile machinery, food processing, and agricultural machinery. Population: (1958) 785,000.

CHENGTSU WU
Hunter College, New York

CHENGTEH, chung'du', is a city in Hopei province, China. It was the capital of former Jehol province, which was abolished by the Communist government in 1956. Railroads connecting with Peking and with Chinchow in western Manchuria make Chengteh an important trade center for furs and animal skins, silks, tea, fruits, and grains. Silk weaving is a traditional industry of the city, and oil extraction from oil shales is a new industry developed in the 1950's.

Located in the Jehol mountains, northeast of Peking, Chengteh enjoys a cool and pleasant summer climate. A beautiful summer palace of the former Manchu emperors was built in the northern part of the city. The famous Putala Temple inside the palace grounds was once a magnificent structure but is now tarnished for lack of proper maintenance. Population: (1958) 120,000.

CHENGTU, chung'dōō', the capital of Szechwan province, China, is located in central Szechwan, 170 miles (274 km) northwest of Chungking. The city is a river port lying astride the Ching Kiang, a tributary of the Min River, which is itself a tributary of the Yangtze.

Chengtu's chief importance is as an agricultural trade center. It lies in the fertile western Szechwan plain, one of China's most important farming regions, which has an irrigation system that dates from 250 B.C. The city is also the focus of trade routes linking the Szechwan basin with eastern Tibet, southern Kansu, and southern Shensi. Railroads connect Chengtu with Chungking and southern Kansu. Iron and steel, locomotives, and machinery are Chengtu's heavy modern industries. Chemicals, precision instruments, silk textiles, and processed foods are also produced.

Chengtu was the political, economic, and cultural center of Szechwan from 300 B.C. until the 20th century. It was twice the capital of the state of Shu during the Three Kingdoms period (220–265 A.D.). Wu-hou Tz'u, the shrine of Chu-ko Liang (q.v.), a famous statesman of Shu, is a popular tourist attraction. Chengtu remains a seat of scholarship, with more than 10 institutions of higher learning. The home of the poet Tu Fu is preserved as a provincial museum in Chengtu. Population: (1958) 1,135,000.

CHENGTSU WU, *Hunter College, New York*

CHÉNIER, shä-nyä', **André Marie de** (1762–1794), French poet, who wrote the finest French verse of the 18th century. His poetry has both classical and romantic elements, marking the end of the French neoclassical tradition and heralding the romantic revolution of the 19th century.

Life. Chénier was born in Constantinople on Oct. 30, 1762, the son of Louis de Chénier (1722–1795), the French consul general there. During his childhood he absorbed a love and knowledge of Greek culture from his mother, of Greek descent. In 1765 he went with his family to France, where from 1773 to 1781 he attended the Collège de Navarre. In 1783–1784, after six months in the army, Chénier toured Switzerland and Italy; he then settled in Paris, where he associated with writers and artists. In 1787 he became secretary to the French ambassador in London.

In 1790, Chénier's enthusiasm for the French Revolution caused him to return to Paris. There he grew embittered by the brutalities of the Reign of Terror and published a pamphlet, *Avis au peuple français sur ses véritables ennemis* (1790), attacking the Jacobins and calling for constitutional government. In 1793 he placed himself in jeopardy by assisting Malesherbes in the defense of Louis XVI, and the next year was arrested on Robespierre's order and guillotined, in Paris on July 25.

Works. Only two of Chénier's poems, both political, were published before his death. The first full edition of his works, which include bucolics, elegies, epistles, odes, hymns, and epic fragments, was published in 1819.

The classical influence is especially strong in Chénier's earlier poetry, notably the *Bucoliques,* which are reminiscent of the Greek Anthology. But all of his poems are marked by a classical purity of form and vigor of thought and expression. In fragments of two long poems, *Hermès* and *L'Amérique,* Chénier strove to unite these elements with 18th century rationalism.

Chénier's later poems, however, are his most famous—especially *La jeune captive* and the *Iambes,* both written during his imprisonment. These poems anticipate the romantic movement in their melancholy, personal sincerity, love of nature, and metrical innovations. Chénier's works influenced 19th century French poetry.

KENNETH DOUGLAS, *Author of*
"A Critical Bibliography of Existentialism"

Further Reading: Loggins, Vernon, *André Chénier* (Athens, Ohio, 1965); Scarfe, Francis, *André Chénier: His Life and Work, 1762–1794* (New York and London 1965).

CHÉNIER, shä-nyä', **Marie Joseph Blaise de** (1764–1811), French poet, dramatist, and revolutionary. The younger brother of the poet André Marie de Chénier, he was born in Constantinople (now Istanbul), Turkey, on Feb. 11, 1764. During the Revolution he became known for his tragedies, including *Charles IX* (produced in 1789 after having been forbidden by the censor for two years); *Henri VIII* (1791), his masterpiece; and *Caïus Gracchus* (1792).

He was a member of the National Convention, the Council of Five Hundred, and the tribunate. However, he was thought to be too moderate, and his *Caïus Gracchus* was banned in 1793. Chénier also wrote a work on the history of French literature and did translations of Greek, Latin, German, and English classics. He died in Paris on Jan. 10, 1811.

CHENILLE, shǝ-nēl′, is a kind of yarn made from cloth that has already been woven. The cloth is made with widely spaced groups of warp (lengthwise) yarns, usually made of cotton. The filling (crosswise) yarns are made of heavy wool. After the cloth is woven, it is cut into strips between the warp yarns, producing thick threads resembling tuft-covered caterpillars. The yarn thus produced may be used for tufting or fringes or may be woven into fabric.

ERNEST B. BERRY, *School of Textiles*
North Carolina State University

CHENILLE PLANT, shǝ-nēl′, a tall East Indian shrub, also known as the *red hot cattail* because of its long spikes of bright red flowers. Although the flowers are very small, the spikes may be 18

Chenille plant

J. J. SMITH

inches (45 cm) long and 1 inch (2.5 cm) wide. The chenille plant grows 15 feet (4.5 meters) tall. Its botanical name is *Acalypha hispida,* and it belongs to the spurge family.

DONALD WYMAN, *Harvard University*

CHENNAULT, shǝ-nôlt,, **Claire Lee** (1890–1958), U. S. Air Force general and pioneer air tactician, who led the Flying Tigers in China in World War II. He was born in Commerce, Texas, on Sept. 6, 1890. A high school principal, he joined the army in World War I, earned a commission in the Infantry Reserve in 1917, and won flier's wings in 1919. He commanded a fighter squadron in Hawaii for 3 years and by 1935 was chief of fighter training at Maxwell Field, Ala. He experimented with aerial tactics and hotly argued the value of fighters in *The Role of Defensive Pursuit* (1935), despite the War Department doctrine that bombers needed no protection.

He was retired for partial deafness in 1937 and became air adviser to the Chinese government. He built an air force, obtained U. S. aircraft, and proved his theories in combat against Japanese pilots. Lacking pilots, he rounded up in the United States men for the American Volunteer Group, which came to be called the Flying Tigers, and by original training methods made them a potent fighting force. In April 1942 he was recalled by the army and headed the U. S. air war in China until July 25, 1945.

Retired again, he returned to China in 1946 to establish the Civil Air Transport for Chiang Kai-shek, and he operated it until 1958. He died on July 27, 1958, at New Orleans.

ROBERT L. SCOTT, *Brig Gen., USAF (Retired)*
Author of "Flying Tiger: Chennault of China"

CHENONCEAUX, she-nôN-sō, is a village in west central France, in Indre-et-Loire department, on the Cher River, 18 miles (29 km) southeast of Tours. It is famed for its château, started in 1515 by Thomas Bohier, tax receiver under Francis I. It came into the hands of Henry II, who gave it to his mistress Diane de Poitiers. She was dispossessed by Catherine de Médicis after Henry's death (1559).

The château, outstanding for its beautiful setting, its gardens, and its Renaissance-style architecture, is on an islet in the Cher River. The château's famous wing that spans the river was built in 1560 by the celebrated French architect Philibert Delorme. Population: (1962) 285.

CHENOPODIUM, kē-nǝ-pō′dē-ǝm, is a genus of North American and Eurasian plants, many of which are serious weed pests. Chenopodiums belong to the goosefoot family (Chenopodiaceae). They have alternate, usually toothed leaves and small inconspicuous flowers. Each fruit is a single seed covered by a bladderlike membrane.

One of the most vicious pests is the lamb's-quarters, or pigweed (*Chenopodium album*). It reaches a height of 10 feet (3 meters) and its irregularly shaped leaves are whitish underneath and grow 4 inches (10 cm) long. Sometimes the young shoots are collected and used as salad greens. Another species, the American wormseed (*C. ambrosioides*), grows 3½ feet (about 1 meter) tall and bears aromatic lance-shaped leaves 5 inches (13 cm) long. It is widely distributed in the eastern and central United States. The Good-King-Henry (*C. bonus-henricus*) is a perennial plant often found in urban areas of the United States and sometimes grown as a potherb. The Jerusalem-oak goosefoot (*C. botrys*) grows 2 feet (60 cm) tall and is found chiefly in sandy soils.

DONALD WYMAN
The Arnold Arboretum, Harvard University

CHEOPS, kē′ops (reigned 2590–2568 B. C.), was an Egyptian king who built the Great Pyramid at Giza. Under the throne name *Khnum-Khufu* he ruled Egypt as the second king of the 4th dynasty. "Cheops" is the Greek form of his name.

From his father, King Snefru, Cheops inherited a strong and very wealthy kingdom over which he exercised absolute control. No important royal records have survived from his reign, but ample testimony to his wealth and power is borne by his known constructions at Giza. In addition to the Great Pyramid, which alone covers 13 acres and contains some 2,300,000 blocks of stone weighing from 2 to 15 tons each, these include royal mortuary temples and a causeway connecting the pyramid complex with the river bank; 3 queens' pyramids; beautifully carved and painted tombs for 8 of the royal children; and 64 large tombs for members of the court. It is estimated that building these structures occupied 100,000 men for 20 years.

Cheops is often characterized as impious and ruthless because he is so described in tales recorded more than 2,100 years after his death by the Greek traveler-historian Herodotus. No Egyptian evidence corroborates this judgment. See also PYRAMID.

CAROLINE PECK, *Brown University*

CHEPHREN is the Greek form of the name of the Egyptian ruler Khafre. See KHAFRE.

CHEQUERS, chek'ərz, in Buckinghamshire, England, 2 miles (3 km) southwest of Wendover, is the official country residence of British prime ministers. The 15th century house and 1,300 acres (526 hectares) of woods and farmland are set among the Chiltern Hills. Lord and Lady Lee of Fareham gave the estate to the nation in 1917, with a trust fund to maintain it. It was first occupied by Prime Minister David Lloyd George in 1921. It is not open to the public.

The house is a typical gabled Tudor building of mellowed red brick, which was extensively remodeled in the 1560's. A medieval long gallery was retained but an interior courtyard was roofed over to provide a lofty great hall. On the walls are some portraits of Oliver Cromwell's time. Chequers has been the scene of many historic international conferences. With the prime minister's London house at 10 Downing Street, it remains in constant use. The name Chequers is a reminder that as long ago as the beginning of the 13th century the estate belonged to Henry de Scaccario—the Latin for Henry of the Chequer (or Exchequer)—a government official.

GORDON STOKES
Author of "English Place-Names"

CHER, shâr, is a department in central France, 2,820 square miles (7,304 sq km) in area, comprising parts of the old provinces of Berry and Bourbonnais. Bourges, the capital, is 122 miles (196 km) south of Paris. The Cher River crosses it from southeast to northwest, and the Loire forms the greater part of its eastern border. In the northwest is a portion of the marshy region known as the Sologne, which has been drained for agricultural purposes. The Sancerrois Hills, in the northeast, are noted for their vineyards. The central plateau is flat and dry, but the south is rolling and verdant.

In addition to grapes, Cher raises grain, vegetables, cattle, and sheep. The major industrial centers are Bourges, an important producer of military ordnance, and Vierzon, which produces metals, chemicals, porcelain, and glassware. Population: (1962) 239,514.

CHERBOURG, a French port on the English Channel.

GEORGIA ENGELHARD, FROM MONKMEYER

CHER RIVER, shâr, is a river in central France, about 200 miles (320 km) long. It rises in the Massif Central east of Aubusson, in the department of Creuse, flows north to the industrial city of Montluçon, northwest through the department of Cher, past Vierzon, and then west until it empties into the Loire River south of Tours. It is navigable only from a point below Vierzon to its mouth but is paralleled by the Berry Canal along part of its upper course.

CHERAW, chĕ'rô, is a town in northeastern South Carolina, in Chesterfield county. It is situated on the Pee Dee River, 87 miles (140 km) northeast of Columbia. Cheraw is a shipping center for a farm area, and its factories produce cotton textiles, clothing, plywood, boxes, and brick. Points of interest include some historic residences and St. David's Church, built about 1770. Cheraw State Park is south of the town.

Cheraw was settled about 1750 by Welsh families from Pennsylvania and incorporated in 1768. Gen. Nathanael Greene assumed command of the southern division of the Continental Army here in 1780. During the Civil War the Confederates maintained a supply depot in the town. Cheraw is governed by a mayor and council. Population: 5,627.

CHERBOURG, sher-bōōr', is a French seaport and naval base on the English Channel, on the northern shore of the Cotentin Peninsula of Normandy. It is the largest city of the Manche department. Cherbourg's location on a wide embayment, greatly improved by a protecting jetty completed in 1853, affords a splendid harbor. It is the chief French Channel stop for transatlantic passenger liners, and many international maritime lines maintain offices in Cherbourg. Despite its fine natural and developed port facilities, its cargo trade and its general economic development suffer from the city's relatively isolated location. It is much farther than the other major Channel ports from the populous Paris Basin and from the Picardy-Nord industrial region. There is regular air service to Southampton, England, across the Channel. Cherbourg is also a popular seaside resort.

The city is dominated by Mount Roule, site of a fortress from whose terrace a magnificent panorama of the area may be seen. The naval base and arsenal (both open only to French citizens), the lush Emmanuel Liais park, with its impressive display of subtropical vegetation testifying to the effect of an extremely equable maritime climate, the Museum of Natural History and Ethnography, and the fishing quays are also of interest to tourists.

Cherbourg was founded as a Roman outpost and was under English rule until about 1200. It was periodically attacked or controlled by the English from the 13th through the 18th centuries. In World War II it was held by the Germans from June 1940 through June 1944. Its recapture was a decisive phase of the Battle of Normandy. Although the port was gravely damaged and its harbor mined in World War II, reconstruction began as soon as the Germans were driven out, and it was reopened quite swiftly for use as an Allied Military port. Population: (1962) 37,096.

HOMER PRICE
Hunter College, New York

CHERCHELL. See CAESAREA MAURETANIAE.

CHEREMKHOVO, chi-ryem-KHô′və, is a city in the USSR, in eastern Siberia. It is situated in Irkutsk oblast, on the Trans-Siberian Railroad, 75 miles (125 km) northwest of Irkutsk. Cheremkhovo is a major coal mining center, with underground mines and several large surface pits. The coal serves as a power-station fuel and as raw material for the chemical industry. A machinery plant produces mining equipment. The city has a branch of the Irkutsk polytechnic school and a mining school.

Cheremkhovo was founded in 1772 as a post-relay station on the Trans-Siberian trail. Its industrial development dates from the late 19th century, when the coal deposits began to be mined as a source of fuel for the Trans-Siberian Railroad. Population: (1966) 111,000.

THEODORE SHABAD
Editor of "Soviet Geography"

CHERENKOV, che-ren′kôf, **Pavel Alekseyevich** (1904–   ), Russian physicist, who was awarded the Nobel Prize in physics in 1958 for the discovery of Cherenkov radiation. Cherenkov was born in 1904 in the village of Novaya Chigla, Voronezh province, to a peasant family. He had to work for a living while going to school and did not enter college until he was 20. After graduating from Voronezh State University he became a postgraduate student in Moscow at the Physical Institute of the Academy of Sciences of the USSR under the direction of the well-known physicist Sergei Ivanovich Vavilov.

While studying the fluorescence of liquids induced by gamma rays, Cherenkov in 1934 discovered unexpectedly a new kind of radiation, and Vavilov designed a program for studying this phenomenon. As the radiation was very faint, the only means to observe it at that time was the highly sensitive human eye. To increase his sensitivity, Cherenkov spent from an hour to an hour and a half in complete darkness before every experiment. Cherenkov's experiments provided convincing quantitative proof for the theory of the new effect developed by Igor E. Tamm and Ilya M. Frank. In 1946 the Soviet state prize was awarded to Cherenkov, Vavilov, Tamm, and Frank for this work. The Nobel Prize was awarded in 1958 to Cherenkov, Tamm, and Frank (Vavilov had died in 1951).

In the following years Cherenkov made remarkable investigations in the physics of high energy. He is also known for his skill in the professional training of young research physicists.

J. G. DORFMAN, *Institute for the History of Science and Technology, Moscow*

CHERENKOV RADIATION, che-ren′kôf, is the emission of light by a transparent medium caused by the passage of charged particles through the medium at a speed greater than the speed of light in the medium. It was first observed by the Soviet physicist Pavel A. Cherenkov in 1934 while studying the emission of light by liquids under the action of gamma rays. This work was carried out under the direction of Sergei I. Vavilov, and the phenomenon is also sometimes called the Vavilov-Cherenkov effect.

Cherenkov radiation differs substantially from the usual fluorescence phenomena induced by ·X rays, ultraviolet light, or radioactive radiations. It is independent of temperature; it is produced not by gamma rays themselves but by electrons liberated by them; and it is not emitted symmetrically at random but only in directions inclined at a certain angle to the direction of motion of the electron.

In 1937 the Soviet scientists Igor E. Tamm and Ilya M. Frank developed a mathematical theory explaining the origin and all the features of the Cherenkov radiation. The speed of propagation of light in gases, as in nonmetallic liquids or solids, is less than that in a vacuum, being equal to the speed of light in a vacuum divided by the index of refraction of the substance. The theory states that Cherenkov radiation is emitted by any charged particle moving inside the substance with a velocity surpassing the speed of propagation of light in the same medium. J. V. Jelley in the United States showed experimentally in 1951 that other charged particles as well as electrons do in fact cause Cherenkov radiation. An analogous effect is found in acoustics. When a missile is moving in air with a velocity surpassing the speed of propagation of sound, a shock wave is emitted in directions inclined at a certain angle to the direction of movement of the missile.

J. G. DORFMAN, *Institute for the History of Science and Technology, Moscow*

CHEREPOVETS, chi-ryi-pə-vyets′, is a city in the USSR, in northern European Russia. It is situated in Vologda oblast, at the northern end of the Rybinsk Reservoir, 230 miles (380 km) north of Moscow. Since the opening of an iron and steel plant in 1955, Cherepovets has been one of the main metallurgical centers of the European part of the USSR, using iron ore from the Kola Peninsula and coking coal from Vorkuta. The city has shipyards on the Sheksna River, which forms part of the Volga-Baltic waterway.

Cherepovets was founded in 1777 on the site of a 14th century monastery. It became a trade center in the early 19th century with the completion of the Mariinsk waterway, replaced in the early 1960's by the modernized Volga-Baltic waterway. Population: (1966) 159,000.

THEODORE SHABAD
Editor of "Soviet Geography"

CHÉRET, shā-re′, **Jules** (1836–1932), French painter and lithographer, who pioneered modern poster techniques. He was born in Paris and studied lithography—a new method for reproducing colored designs cheaply—there and in London. Returning to Paris in 1866, he set up his own shop and, influenced by Japanese prints and impressionism, began printing striking theatrical posters. Realizing that posters are intended to sell what they advertise, he gave his particular impact by simplifying detail, creating clean, legible lettering, and presenting unframed scenes of figures caught in mid-action, which invited the viewer to participate. These principles of good poster design influenced Toulouse-Lautrec and are still followed. Chéret died in Nice in 1932.

CHERIMOYA, cher-ə-moi′ə, a tropical tree native to the mountains of Peru and Ecuador cultivated in warm regions for its round or conical edible fruits. The fruits are pale green on the outside and have an inner white pulp that tastes like pineapple. Each fruit is about 5 inches (13 cm) long and weighs about 1 pound (0.45 kg).

The cherimoya grows about 25 feet (7.5 meters) tall and bears deciduous alternate leaves about 10 inches (25 cm) long. The fragrant flowers are yellow and about 1 inch (2.5 cm) in

J. HORACE MCFARLAND

CHERIMOYA FRUIT has a rough, brownish skin and a delectable, aromatic, whitish pulp of soft texture.

length. In the United States, the cherimoya is grown only in Florida and southern California. It is propagated by budding and grafting and is cultivated in much the same way as citrus trees.

The cherimoya is known botanically as *Annona cherimola*. It belongs to the custard apple family (Annonaceae) and is closely related to the sweetsop (*A. squamosa*) and the soursop (*A. muricata*).

DONALD WYMAN
The Arnold Arboretum, Harvard University

CHERKASSY, cher-käs′sē, a city in the USSR, is the capital of Cherkassy oblast in the Ukrainian republic. It is situated on the right (south) bank of the Dnieper River, about 90 miles (155 km) southeast of Kiev. The city is the center of a sugar beet district, and has sugar-refining, canning and other food-processing industries. A factory producing artificial fiber was opened in the early 1960's. Cherkassy was founded in the 15th century, but its modern development dates from the late 19th century, when it became a major railroad crossing on the Dnieper River.

Cherkassy oblast lies on both banks of the Dnieper River's middle course. Its territory of 8,100 square miles (21,000 sq km) consists of the Dnieper lowland, rising in the west to the central Ukrainian uplands. Cherkassy oblast is primarily an agricultural region, producing sugar beets, winter wheat, barley, and corn. Cattle are raised both for dairy products and for beef. Industries are engaged mainly in the processing of farm produce. The only mineral resources of any importance are the brown-coal deposits of Vatutino (formerly called Yurkovka). The principal cities are Cherkassy, Smela, and Uman. The oblast was formed in 1954. Population: (1970) of the city, 159,000; of the oblast, 1,536,000.

THEODORE SHABAD
Editor of "Soviet Geography"

CHERKESS AUTONOMOUS OBLAST. See KARA-CHAI-CHERKESS AUTONOMOUS OBLAST.

CHERKESSIA. See CIRCASSIA.

CHERNIGOV, chir-nyē′gəf, a city in the USSR, is the capital of Chernigov oblast of the Ukrainian republic, 85 miles (137 km) northeast of Kiev. It is a port on the right bank of the Desna River, on the main railroad from Odessa to Belorussia. Its favorable location on transportation routes has promoted the city's industrial development. Chernigov produces woolen cloth and synthetic fiber, musical instruments, and other consumer goods.

One of the oldest cities in the USSR, it dates from the 8th or 9th century. Its Spasski Sobor (Cathedral of the Saviour), founded in 1024, is one of the oldest monuments in the Soviet Union. Chernigov became the seat of an independent principality in the 11th century, was destroyed by the Mongols in 1239, and passed to Lithuania in the 14th century. It came under Russian control early in the 16th century and, except for a period of Polish rule (1618–1667), remained under Russian sovereignty thereafter.

Chernigov oblast lies along the Desna River, a tributary of the Dnieper. The area is about 12,300 square miles (31,900 sq km). Chernigov oblast produces rye, oats, buckwheat, hemp, and flax; sugar beets and tobacco are grown in the southeast; its natural resources include lumber and peat. Industry is concentrated in Chernigov (the capital), Priluki, and Nezhin. Population: (1970) of the city, 159,000; of the oblast, 1,560,000.

THEODORE SHABAD
Editor of "Soviet Geography"

CHERNOVTSY, cher-nôf′tsē, a city in the USSR, is the capital of Chernovtsy oblast in the Ukrainian republic. Located on the Prut River, it is near the Rumanian border, 140 miles (225 km) southeast of Lvov. Chernovtsy (German, *Czernowitz;* Rumanian, *Cernăuţi*), is a regional commercial and industrial center, producing cotton and wool textiles and knitwear. A hosiery mill is the city's largest factory. There are also plants for machine building, wood processing, food preserving, and the making of footwear.

Chernovtsy is the cultural center of northern Bukovina, with a university (founded 1875) and a medical school. Although reputed to date from the time of Kievan Russia in the 12th century, it was first mentioned in the 15th century as an economic center of Moldavia under Polish control. In 1775 it passed to Austria. From 1918 to 1940 it was included in Rumania and in 1940 was annexed by the USSR, where it was first known as Chernovitsy. During World War II, when the city was occupied by the Germans and their Rumanian allies, most of the large Jewish population was exterminated.

Chernovtsy oblast is 3,100 square miles (8,000 sq km) in area. It was formed in 1940 from part of northern Bukovina, which was ceded by Rumania to the Soviet Union. The wooded slopes of the Carpathian Mountains in western Chernovtsy oblast drop to the rolling lowlands of the Prut and Dniester rivers in the east. Grains, potatoes, and sugar beets are the principal crops. Fruit growing is widespread, while sheep raising and lumbering are the main activities in the Carpathians. Woodworking and food processing are concentrated in the larger towns. Population: (1970) of the city, 187,000; of the oblast, 845,000.

THEODORE SHABAD
Editor of "Soviet Geography"

CHERNOZEM, cher-nə-zyôm', is the name of a zonal group of soils that have a dark brown or nearly black granular surface layer that is rich in organic matter or humus. The word *Chernozem,* which is Russian for "black earth," was established as a scientific term about 1880 by the Russian scientist Vasili V. Dokuchayev.

Chernozem soils develop under tall and mixed grasses in cool to temperate, subhumid climates. At a depth of 20 to 60 inches (0.5 to 1.5 meters) they have soft accumulations of calcium carbonate (lime) within reach of the grass root systems. They contain more major nutrients for crop plants than any other major kind of soil, and are highly productive in the growing of wheat and other cereals.

These soils dominate a belt of land extending eastward from near Kiev in the Ukraine for about 1,800 miles (2,900 km). In North America a similar belt runs north from eastern Kansas through eastern North and South Dakota, Manitoba, and Saskatchewan, and into northern Alberta. Such belts occur in other regions of comparable climate and similar vegetation. See also SOIL—*Soil Classification.*

CHARLES E. KELLOGG
U. S. Department of Agriculture

CHERNYSHEVSKY, cher-ni-shef'skē, **Nikolai Gavrilovich** (1828–1889), Russian political thinker and author, who was an important early member of the revolutionary movement in Russia.

Chernyshevsky was born in Saratov on July 24 (old style, July 12), 1828, the son of a priest. Trained at the University of St. Petersburg, he belonged to the intelligentsia who wanted to westernize Russia. As an editor of the radical journal *Contemporary* he wrote a series of vehement revolutionary essays. Influenced by the utilitarian John Stuart Mill, the materialist Feuerbach, and the socialists Fourier, Belinsky, and Herzen, he promoted socially relevant literature and art, denounced both czarist rule and Western capitalism, and urged the establishment of a democratic, socialist society of agrarian and industrial communes, based on a philosophy of materialism and enlightened egoism.

In 1862, in the wake of student riots and fires, the government arrested Chernyshevsky. While in prison he wrote his famous novel, *What Is to Be Done?* (1863), depicting the ways young socialist revolutionaries thought and acted. Partly directed against the portrait of a radical in Turgenev's *Fathers and Sons* (1862), the book was in turn attacked as naïve by Dostoyevsky in *Notes from the Underground* (1864). Without a trial, Chernyshevsky was exiled to Siberia and was allowed to return to Saratov only to die there, on Oct. 29, 1889. His works and martyrdom inspired Lenin and other revolutionaries.

FRANCIS B. RANDALL
Author of "N. G. Chernyshevskii"

CHEROKEE, cher'ə-kē, a city in northwestern Iowa, the seat of Cherokee county, is on the Little Sioux River, 59 miles (94 km) northeast of Sioux City, in a livestock and farming area. There are farm machinery works, railroad shops, and creameries. The city has its own symphony orchestra, a community theater, a museum, and the only planetarium in Iowa. It is the site of a state institution for the mentally ill. Cherokee was settled in 1856. Government is by mayor and council. Population: 7,272.

CHEROKEE INDIANS, cher'ə-kē, a large and powerful tribe who, at the time of European contact, lived in the region of the southern Allegheny and Great Smoky Mountains and adjacent areas of Virginia, North and South Carolina, Georgia, Tennessee, and Alabama. Their language is part of the Iroquoian family, although the Cherokee never joined the League of the Iroquois.

Village Life. The Cherokee were divided into seven clans with members in every village. A person had to marry outside his clan. Descent was matrilineal; after marriage a man usually resided with his wife's family. Before European contact the Cherokee lived in square or rectangular houses with upright poles forming a framework. The outer covering was bark, wood, or woven siding, coated with earth and clay. By the American Revolution, however, most Cherokee were living in log cabins similar to those used by whites. Each village was composed of one or more settlements, with a total population of 350 to 600.

The economy was based on the cultivation of corn, beans, and squash, though hunting and collecting wild food were also important. The Cherokee practiced slash-and-burn agriculture. They cleared the land by stripping the bark from trees and later burning the trees. Until the 1700's, when the whites introduced horses, the Cherokee's only domesticated animal was the dog.

Tribal Organization. Until the early 18th century, when the Cherokee began to unite into a tribal state, all political authority rested within the individual villages. Each had two complementary political bodies—the Red organization and the White, which governed during war and peace, respectively. The White organization was headed by the White Chief. His position was not hereditary, but certain clans seemed to furnish more chiefs than others. He could convene and preside over council meetings and supervise important community activities, particularly those concerning agriculture. Next in the hierarchy were a deputy chief and a "talking chief," or outstanding speaker. Then followed two councils: one was made up of representatives of the seven clans, and the other was a body of elders. The White organization also contained religious officials, minor government assistants, and some messengers. These officials avoided the use of direct coercion and acquired their authority largely through the love and respect of the council members.

In time of war the Red organization controlled the affairs of the town. The head of this body was the "Raven," or Red War Chief, who organized war parties. This official was elected from among the most illustrious warriors of the village. He was assisted by one deputy chief and a counselor of war from each of the seven clans. There were other war officials, including a speaker, a doctor, a standard-bearer, and priests. The scouts of the war party were divided into three classes, who patrolled to the right, left, and rear. Certain women who had distinguished themselves by heroic actions were permitted to speak in the war council and to determine the fate of prisoners.

Ceremonies and Customs. Ceremonies and ritual marked the changeover of rule between the Red and White organizations. Before departing for battle, warriors participated in a nightlong dance. They fasted and observed sex taboos. On their return from battle they underwent several days of ritual purification before resuming peaceful activities.

The Cherokee, like many North American tribes,

played a ball game with rackets, which was the forerunner of the modern game of lacrosse. As with warfare, ritual fasting and bleeding usually was associated with the game. The most important Cherokee ceremonies were those of the Autumn Green Corn, or harvest feast, and the New Fire, or New Year, observances. These lasted about three weeks and included ritual bathing, relighting of the perpetual fire in the village council house, and feasting. These rites were intended to eliminate all bad feeling among the villagers and revitalize their sense of unity. During these weeks, they held their village councils.

Later Cherokee Culture. Following the American Revolution the Cherokee increasingly sought to adopt white farming techniques along with other features of white economy. By the early 19th century there were many prosperous, privately owned Cherokee plantations. It is reported that in 1825 the Cherokee owned no less than 1,277 Negro slaves. Some of these plantation owners were of mixed blood; educated in American schools, many of them rose to positions of power in Cherokee political affairs. In 1821, Sequoya, a mixed-blood, introduced a Cherokee alphabet, and within a few years the Cherokee had started to develop a native literature. A body of elders headed by a traditional White Chief ruled until 1820, when a constitutional republic, modeled on the U. S. government, was instituted.

Dissolution of the Cherokee. As the white men's frontier advanced during the early 18th century, the Cherokee found it necessary to organize into a centralized tribal state. The important offices were held by priests, and the overall structure was patterned after the village Red, or war, organization. The warriors in charge were to enforce tribal agreements with South Carolina, and to restrain Cherokee individuals and villages from attacking white colonial settlements. South Carolina had threatened reprisals against all Cherokee for such acts, and the Cherokee realized that the whites were well-armed and could cause widespread ruin.

The tribal government was successful in these functions until the American Revolution. This event caused much bloodshed and vast destruction of Cherokee villages, followed by a rush of white settlers into the area. The Cherokee nation, with the exception of a faction of dissident warriors, sued for peace in 1782. These last moved to the region near present-day Chattanooga, where they were defeated by the whites in 1792. This factional split signaled the end of the centralized Gherokee tribal state.

In 1828 gold was discovered in the Cherokee country, and pressure by whites forced the removal of the Indians from their traditional lands. Pressure from the state of Georgia to enforce the removal of the Cherokee from their land resulted in the Indians petitioning the U. S. Supreme Court. In *Cherokee Nation* v. *Georgia* (1831), the court decreed that the Indians' title to their land was only that of occupancy. The court, therefore, upheld the extension of Georgia's laws over territory claimed as its own. Pressure for removal reached its peak in 1835 with the ratification by Congress of the Treaty of New Echota (signed by only a small minority of Cherokee), ceding their lands to the whites.

In 1838 a body of 7,000 troops arrived to enforce the fraudulent treaty and to remove the Cherokee to Indian Territory (now Oklahoma). Thus about 14,000 Cherokee set out on what has become known as the "trail of tears." About 4,000 of these died of exhaustion and cold on the way, and 1,000 managed to escape deportation and live as fugitives in the Great Smoky Mountains. In the following years these Indians reemerged and eventually reacquired about 56,000 of the 7,000,000 acres of land seized from them. Today this is a federal reservation.

In Oklahoma, the Cherokee became divided into two factions: the minority made up of "Old Settlers," who had voluntarily resettled before the Treaty of New Echota, and the majority Cherokee National Party, made up of later deportees. For many years the United States, represented by the Army, supported the minority faction. In spite of these pressures, the two factions eventually became reintegrated. Today, the Cherokee, particularly those on the Oklahoma reservation, display great tribal unity.

RICHARD A. GOULD
American Museum of Natural History

Further Reading: Fenton, William N., and Gulick, John, *Symposium on Cherokee and Iroquois Culture* (Washington 1961); Gearing, Fred, *Priests and Warriors* (Washington 1962); Gulick, John, *Cherokees at the Crossroads* (Chapel Hill, N. C., 1960).

CHERRY, any of some 50 species of trees and shrubs within the genus *Prunus,* of the rose family (Rosaceae), bearing small, smooth, long-stemmed fruits, each with a single, round pit, or stone. Cherries are native to Europe, Asia, and North America. The genus *Prunus* also contains plums, peaches, apricots, and almonds.

Cherry trees vary in growth characteristics from upright to weeping and range in size from small shrubs to forest trees reaching 100 feet (30 meters) in height.

Cherry blossoms are white or pinkish and, depending on the type of tree, are produced in either elongated (racemose) or small, flat-topped (corymbose) clusters. The cherry fruits, borne on stems up to 3 inches (7.5 cm) long, range from $\frac{1}{8}$ to $1\frac{1}{4}$ inches (3 to 32 mm) in diameter and are round to heart-shaped in form. Fruit flesh color varies from light cream to almost black.

Economically, the more important types of cherries are those having corymbose flower clusters. These forms, native to the Caspian-Black seas region of Eurasia and to the Orient, include the orchard varieties, the flowering cherries, and several types of wild cherries. The racemose cherries are mostly wild species, some of which are native to North America.

Orchard Varieties. The sweet cherry (*P. avium*), from western Asia, is a favorite home garden fruit. More than 85% of the United States commercial production of some 90,000 tons (81,700 metric tons), valued at $25 million, is grown in the states of California, Oregon, Washington, and Michigan. About 44% of the marketable production is canned; 35% is sold as fresh fruit; 20% is brined for maraschino, glacé, or candied products; and less than 1% is frozen.

Several hundred horticultural varieties are grown. Bing, Lambert, Napoleon (Royal Ann), and Black Tartarian are the leading varieties of sweet cherries in the western United States; Schmidt, Windsor, and Lambert are the most popular ones in the eastern United States. Napoleon, used extensively for brining, is the standard light-fleshed cherry. Lambert, Schmidt, and Windsor are dark-fleshed. Bing, with its large, firm, and dark-fleshed fruits, is the leading variety and the standard of quality.

ROCHE ROCHE

THE WILD CHERRY (*above left*) has clusters of tiny white flowers that are quite fragrant. The cultivated cherry (*above right*) has large pink double flowers that cloak the entire tree. At the far right is a close-up of the fruit of the cultivated cherry tree.

The sour cherry (*P. cerasus*), native to Europe and western Asia, is processed for pie filling, jams, and jellies. In the United States, Michigan grows more than 60% of the commercial crop; New York, Wisconsin, and Pennsylvania, about 30%. The remainder comes from other Great Lakes states. The commercial yield in the United States is about 160,000 tons (145,000 metric tons), valued at $23 million. The Montmorency, a clear-fleshed, red-skinned variety, accounts for nearly all of the commercial production.

The duke cherry, a sweet-sour hybrid, usually has an upright tree like the sweet cherry but a more acid fruit. It is prized for home gardens.

Flowering Cherries. A number of cherries are grown as ornamentals. Varieties of the Oriental species *P. serrulata* and others are well known for the beauty of their spring blossoms in Washington, D. C., and in Japan.

Wild Cherries. Several wild cherries have economic value. Most important of these is the wild black cherry (*P. serotina*), of eastern North America, which along with other similar species is used as a landscape tree and as a source of cherry fruitwood in furniture manufacture. Chokecherries (*P. virginiana*), sandcherries (*P. besseyi* and others), and the Korean cherry (*P. tomentosa*) are used for jams and jellies.

Cherry Growing. Commercial cherry varieties are grown upon the rootstock of either mazzard (wild sweet cherry) or mahaleb (*P. mahaleb*, the St. Lucie cherry). Mazzard usually is preferred by growers as understock because the budded trees generally grow larger and live longer. Mahaleb generally is preferred by nurseries because of the usually high percentage of germinating seed and the rapid growth of seedlings.

Cherry trees are either self-fertile or self-sterile. The flowers of self-fertile trees can be fertilized by their own pollen; self-sterile trees require pollen from another variety.

All of the commercial varieties of sweet cherry are self-sterile. In addition, Bing, Lambert, and Napoleon are intersterile; that is, they cannot be used to fertilize each other. Pollinizing varieties, such as Deacon, Republican, or mazzard, are planted in the ratio of about 1 per 9 orchard spaces (every third tree in every third row) to obtain the needed pollen. Sour cherries are self-fertile. Duke cherries usually require pollination by a sweet cherry.

HAROLD FOGLE, *U. S. Department of Agriculture*

CHERRY HILL is a township in western New Jersey, in Camden county, 4 miles (6 km) east of Camden. It is a residential suburb of Philadelphia, Pa. It manufactures telephone and telegraph apparatus, electrical and electronic equipment and computers; concrete blocks and bricks; athletic goods; and house furnishings. Its name was changed from Delaware to Cherry Hill in 1961. It has a council-manager form of government. Population: 64,395.

CHERRY LAUREL, any of several evergreen shrubs of the rose family. The most popular cherry laurels are varieties of *Prunus laurocerasus*. They grow to a height of 18 feet (5 meters) and bear, glossy leaves and clusters of small white flowers. They are native to southeastern Europe but are often grown in the United States as ornamentals and hedge shrubs.

DONALD WYMAN
The Arnold Arboretum, Harvard University

CHERRY ORCHARD, a play in four acts by the Russian dramatist Anton Chekhov, written and produced during 1903–1904, the last year of the author's life. Not an immediate success, the work is now recognized as one of the greatest modern plays.

In *The Cherry Orchard,* as in *The Three Sisters* (1901), Chekhov describes a comparatively minor incident that reflects the larger social fabric of Russian society. Beyond the disintegration of the Ranyevsky family, which is its central motif, the play affords a glimpse at the social reorganization of Russia in the last days of the 19th century.

The action of the play is deceptively simple. It reviews in desultory fashion the circumstances attending the forced sale of the Ranyevsky property, including the family's beloved cherry orchard. The family is on the verge of bankruptcy, and none of its members can do anything to prevent the collapse. Lopakhin, the wealthy grandson of a former serf, suggests to Madame Ranyevsky that she chop down the orchard and build houses on the land. The family refuses, in horror, and is eventually evicted from the land by Lopakhin, who proceeds, as the play ends, to destroy the orchard.

While *Cherry Orchard* may be interpreted as optimistic in part, demonstrating the movement of Russian society towards social equality, it is primarily concerned with the tragic destiny of a class that has outlived its usefulness but not its grace or nobility. This class, like the beautiful and unprofitable orchard that symbolizes it, is ripe for the ax. But its passing is hardly a cause for rejoicing, and the play derives its poignancy from Chekhov's identification with a gracious world, now old and ridiculously helpless, that must be demolished for the new.

MAURICE VALENCY, *Author of "The Breaking String: The Plays of Anton Chekhov"*

CHERRY VALLEY MASSACRE, in the American Revolution, carried out on Nov. 11, 1778, at the small frontier settlement of Cherry Valley, N. Y., 46 miles (74 km) west of Albany. In early 1778, Joseph Brant, the great Mohawk chief, who was a friend of the British, gathered many Indians at Unadilla and Oquaga villages on the Susquehanna River. On Sept. 17, 1778, he destroyed German Flats on the Mohawk River opposite Herkimer, N. Y. In response, a force led by Col. William Butler destroyed Unadilla and Oquaga on October 8 and 10.

Brant, reinforced by Loyalists under Capt. Walter N. Butler, determined to destroy Cherry Valley. The settlement had a fort garrisoned by 200 to 300 men, but Col. Ichabod Alden, its commander, was remiss in defensive preparations. On November 11, having obtained intelligence from a captured patriot scouting party, Brant and Walter Butler fell upon the unsuspecting village with 800 men. The attackers killed over 30 men, women, and children, burned houses and took 71 prisoners. They exchanged fire with the fort, killing 16 Continentals, but withdrew on the 12th after the belated arrival of 200 patriot militia. The settlement was abandoned.

PAUL C. BOWERS, JR., *Ohio State University*

CHERT, chûrt, is a dense, granular variety of quartz, the most common mineral. Chert is cryptocrystalline, that is, its crystals are too small to be seen even with a microscope. It may be any color but is usually light. Chert closely resembles the duller and usually darker flint, but has a more splintery fracture. In geology, however, chert is sometimes considered to include flint and all the granular, cryptocrystalline varieties of quartz.

Chert is found distributed through limestone and dolomite. It occurs in the form of nodules that range a few inches to a few feet in diameter, and also in the form of thick beds that extend for hundreds of miles.

CHERUB, one of the order of heavenly beings that in the angelic hierarchy are next to the seraphim. (See ANGEL.) Originally, in Mesopotamia, the word *cherub* referred to a winged sphinxlike figure with a human head and an animal body, placed at the entrances of sanctuaries and palaces as a divine intercessor and guardian. The use of cherub in Hebrew religion came from the Canaanites (II Samuel 22:11; I Kings 6:23; I Chronicles 28:18; Ezekiel 28: 14; Psalms 18:10; and Exodus 25:20, where they symbolize the power and majesty of Israel's God, Yahweh). The four "Living Creatures" in Revelation 4:6 are derived from later Jewish apocalyptic literature. Renaissance art misinterpreted them as winged children.

FREDERICK C. GRANT
Union Theological Seminary

CHERUBINI, kā-roō-bē′nē, **Luigi** (1760–1842), Italian composer, who contributed greatly to the development of 19th century French opera. As a forerunner of the romantic style in music, he also influenced numerous German composers, notably Beethoven. Cherubini was primarily a composer of opera and of church music. His style was marked by rich orchestral and harmonic color, intense rhythmic energy, and dramatic power. Cherubini was also one of the leading theorists and teachers of his age.

Life. Maria Luigi Carlo Zenobio Salvatore Cherubini was born in Florence, Italy, on Sept. 14, 1760. After being instructed by his father and several other teachers, he studied under Giuseppe Sarti, from whom he acquired his mastery of counterpoint. His first opera, *Quinto Fabio* (1780), like most of his succeeding dramatic works through 1788, was an *opera seria* in the old-fashioned florid Neapolitan style. In 1784–1786, Cherubini lived in London, where he produced four operas for the King's Theatre. For one year, in 1785–1786, he was composer to King George III.

In 1788, Cherubini settled permanently in Paris. His first French opera, *Démophon* (1788), reflects Gluck's important influence on him. *Lodoïska* (1791), his first success, was followed by *Médée* (1797), perhaps his masterpiece, and *Les deux journées* (1800), his most popular and influential opera.

In 1805–1806, Cherubini visited Vienna, where he produced his opera *Faniska*. There he met Beethoven, who considered him the greatest living composer. After his return to Paris, Cherubini, who was on bad terms with Napoleon, gradually withdrew from active musical life. From 1809 he composed mostly church music, including several masses and motets and two great Requiems, in C minor and D minor. He also wrote a symphony and chamber works.

In 1822, Cherubini was appointed director of the Paris Conservatory, with which he had been connected since its foundation in 1795. His *Treatise on Counterpoint and Fugue* (1835) became a classic. He died in Paris on March 15, 1842.

Music. Cherubini's best operas are the French works written in the last decade of the 18th century. Although they are classed as *opéras comiques* because they employ spoken dialogue in place of recitative, they are serious in tone, permeated with a lofty idealism inspired by the spirit of the French Revolution, and equally remote from both the serious and the comic operas of older tradition. Several of them belong to the class of "rescue" opera and served as models for Beethoven's *Fidelio*, which was based, like Cherubini's *Les deux journées*, on an incident during the Revolution.

Many features of Cherubini's music, including the employment of the *leitmotiv* and the use of local color—Polish in *Lodoïska* and that of the Savoy Alps in *Élisa* (1794)—anticipated the practice of romantic composers. In *Médée* he conveyed violent passion and emotional turbulence within a severely classical framework. However, a certain dryness and lack of lyrical warmth both in his operas and in his religious works prevent his music from attaining the highest rank. Despite moments of grandeur, something cool, almost academic, remains at its heart.

WINTON DEAN, *Author of "Handel's Dramatic Oratorios and Masques"*

CHERUSCI, kē-rus'ī, an ancient German tribe on the Weser River. In 9 A. D., under their leader Arminius and in alliance with other German tribes, they destroyed three Roman legions commanded by Varus in the Battle of the Teutoburger Forest. The Romans lost 20,000 men—more than in any battle since Cannae (216 B. C.). After this the Romans were forced to abandon hope of establishing their northern frontier on the Elbe River. Roman policy in Germany became defensive.

Because of their victory over the Romans, the Cherusci became very important in Germany. The Romans finally destroyed them by diplomacy rather than by military force. Other German tribes were encouraged to attack them, and jealousy within the royal house was promoted. By the end of the 1st century A. D. the Cherusci had disappeared from history.

ARTHER FERRILL
University of Washington

CHERVIL, chûr'vəl, is a name commonly applied to two plants of the parsley family, both of which are cultivated for food. The salad chervil (*Anthriscus cerefolium*) has leaves that are similar in taste and appearance to those of parsley. They are used as a salad green, a garnish, and as a seasoning in meat loaf, soup, and other dishes. They are also used to flavor vinegar. The salad chervil is native to the Caucasus region of Russia but has become naturalized from Quebec southward through the northeastern United States.

The turnip-rooted chervil (*Chaerophyllum bulbosum*) is a biennial European plant grown for its edible carrot-shaped roots, which are gray on the outside and yellowish white inside. They are eaten mostly in stews or as a boiled or fried vegetable.

LAWRENCE ERBE
University of Southwestern Louisiana

CHERWELL, chär'wel, **1st Viscount** (1886–1957), British physicist, who was scientific adviser to Sir Winston Churchill during World War II. He was born Frederick Alexander Lindemann on April 5, 1886, at Baden Baden, Germany. His father was an Alsatian engineer who became a British subject after the German annexation of Alsace in 1870; his mother was an American of Scottish extraction. Educated in Scotland and Germany, Lindemann did research in Berlin with Walther Nernst and was already known before World War I for the Nernst-Lindemann theory of specific heats and the Lindemann melting-point formula.

Returning to Britain in 1914, Lindemann joined the Royal Aircraft Establishment at Farnborough, where he showed theoretically how to stop an aircraft "spinning" fatally. He learned to fly and made the first tests himself.

In 1919 he became Dr. Lee's professor of experimental philosophy and head of the Clarendon Laboratory at Oxford. Aloof, a vegetarian, a nonsmoker, and a total abstainer from alcohol, he nevertheless became firm friends with Winston Churchill. Courage, humor, love of good language, prowess in sports (Lindemann competed in tennis at Wimbledon), and patriotism were qualities that each valued in the other. From 1932 the two fought to awaken Britain to the Nazi threat and to the need for effective air defense. In this, Lindemann quarreled over priorities with his former friend and supporter for the Oxford chair, Henry Tizard.

Lindemann was Churchill's scientific adviser throughout World War II and also gave advice on economic matters. He was created 1st Baron Cherwell in 1941 and made paymaster general in 1942. After the war he returned to Oxford, but he was again paymaster general under Churchill from 1951 to 1953 and was the chief sponsor of the Atomic Energy Authority during this period.

Cherwell retired from the Clarendon Laboratory in 1956 and was created viscount the same year. He continued to influence Churchill regarding technological education. Churchill College at Cambridge was one of the results. Cherwell died in Oxford on July 3, 1957.

R. V. JONES
University of Aberdeen, Scotland

Further Reading: Birkenhead, Lord, *The Prof in Two Worlds* (London 1961); Harrod, R. F., *The Prof* (London 1959).

CHESAPEAKE, ches'ə-pēk, a city in southeastern Virginia, is the fourth-largest city in area in the United States. It was formed on Jan. 1, 1963, by the merger of Norfolk county (population, 51,612) and South Norfolk (population, 22,035), the smallest of the three politically independent cities in the county. (The others were Norfolk and Portsmouth.) Norfolk county was abolished in the process. The consolidation was prompted by the county's desire to end a continuing loss of territory and population through annexations, and by South Norfolk's fear of encirclement by Norfolk.

The result was the creation of a rural-urban corporation with a total area of 372 square miles (963 sq km), containing about 40,000 homes, more than 800 farms, a large waterfront industrial zone (principally fertilizer plants and bulk oil depots), and a vast tract of the Great Dismal Swamp. Of the city's area, 28 square miles (72.5 sq km) covers portions of Hampton Roads and the Elizabeth River.

Government is by council-manager. At the time of its formation, the city's principal problems were a scarcity of taxable retail trade outlets and the difficulty of bringing city services to its rural residents, who still received the services of farm agents, game wardens, and foresters.

Norfolk county was settled about 1620, and records in the circuit court date to 1637. The Battle of Great Bridge (Dec. 9, 1775), in which American patriots defeated a British regiment, obliging Lord Dunmore, governor of Virginia, to flee the colony, was fought in what is now Chesapeake. Population: 89,580.

LLOYD H. LEWIS, JR.
Norfolk "Ledger-Star"

CHESAPEAKE AND DELAWARE CANAL, ches'ə-pēk, del'ə-wâr, in Maryland and Delaware, connecting the Elk River arm of Chesapeake Bay with the Delaware River. It is a link in the sheltered passage for shipping that is sometimes called the Atlantic Intracoastal Waterway, and will accommodate some oceangoing vessels. From its western end near Chesapeake City, Md., to its eastern end near Delaware City, Del., its length is about 19 miles (30 km). It was completed in 1829 by private builders and was bought by the U. S. government in 1919.

CHESAPEAKE AND LEOPARD INCIDENT, ches'ə-pēk, lep'ərd, an encounter between British and American vessels on June 22, 1807. It precipitated a crisis in Anglo-American relations that led ultimately to the War of 1812.

The incident began when the British man-of-war *Leopard* fired at the American frigate *Chesapeake* off Norfolk Roads, Va., killing 3 Americans and wounding 18 others. The British then boarded the *Chesapeake* and seized 4 sailors–allegedly deserters from the British navy–one of whom was subsequently hanged. War fever ran high in the United States following news of the attack. The *Chesapeake's* commander, Capt. James Barron, was court-martialed and found guilty of "neglecting . . . to clear his ship for action."

Friction between the United States and Britain was inevitable in 1807 as Britain and France waged an economic war of attrition that victimized neutral commerce. The most critical maritime issue between the United States and Britain was the British practice of impressment–inspecting vessels to recover deserters from the British Navy. To the United States the *Chesapeake* incident was an insult to national sovereignty. War was averted in 1807 because President Jefferson felt that his embargo of all foreign trade would be an effective economic weapon against Britain. The failure of the embargo set the stage for war in 1812, although by this time Britain had made reparations for the *Chesapeake* affair.

LAWRENCE S. KAPLAN, *Kent State University*

CHESAPEAKE AND OHIO CANAL, ches'ə-pēk, ō-hī'ō, a waterway along the Potomac River between Washington, D. C., and Cumberland, Md., in operation from 1828 to 1924. Work on the canal began as one of several attempts to establish an efficient, economical means of transportation between the Eastern seaports and the Middle West. The grand design of the project was to reestablish the Potomac route to the West, which the Ohio Company and Braddock's road had established in the 1750's and the Potomac Company and the National Road had restored in the 1800's. The success of the Erie Canal and the Pennsylvania Main Line of Public Works soon overshadowed the Potomac project, and the waterway was never completed beyond Cumberland.

The struggle between the canal and the Baltimore & Ohio Railroad was the first major test between waterway and railway. The railroad won, and the canal prospered only briefly as a vital coal carrier along the Potomac border during the Civil War. It declined rapidly after 1873, and the canal company became bankrupt and was taken over by the B & O Railroad in 1894. The government acquired the waterway in 1938 and established it as a National Monument in 1961.

WALTER S. SANDERLIN
Washington and Jefferson College

CHESAPEAKE & OHIO RAILWAY COMPANY, ches'ə-pē ō-hī'ō, a major east-west railroad system of the United States with 5,100 miles (about 8,200 km) of main line in 8 states, the District of Columbia, and also Canada. Many of C & O's earliest lines follow canal and wagon-road routes planned by George Washington to "smooth the road and make easy the way" between the Atlantic seaboard and the Midwest.

Current Era. The C & O has been one of America's most consistently prosperous railroads. In 1965 the C & O passed its 75th consecutive

year of profitable operation. In the 20th century a common stock dividend was paid every year except one (1915). Net assets in the late 1960's were about $1.3 billion.

An important carrier of bituminous coal and manufactured goods, the C & O in the late 1960's had gross annual revenues of about $400 million, of which 93% came from freight haulage. Coal was still king of the road, contributing 60% of total freight tonnage and 46% of freight income. An equally important factor in the C & O's prosperity was the high proportion of manufactured products in its freight mix. The manufactures-and-miscellaneous category accounted for 23.5% of gross freight tonnage and 38.8% of revenues. Passenger-service revenues, accounting for less than 5% of total income, were declining steadily. The C & O's equipment roster in the late 1960's reflected the dominance of freight in its operations: only 320 passenger cars remained on the lines, but there were 80,000 freight cars. Nearly all 1,000 locomotives were in freight service.

History. The present company was incorporated in 1868 following the consolidation of two small lines, the Virginia Central and the Covington & Ohio. In 1888, the C & O absorbed the Richmond & Alleghany and thus earned title to "all the rights and appurtenances" of George Washington's James River Company, of which Richmond & Alleghany was the owner. Already one of the great east-west lines, C & O in 1947 acquired, through merger, the Pere Marquette Railroad Company, thus extending its lines through lower Michigan, across Lake Michigan (by car ferry) to Wisconsin, and through Ontario, Canada, to Buffalo, N. Y.

The C & O substantially broadened its influence in transportation in 1963 by acquiring control of the Baltimore & Ohio Railroad, then in great financial difficulty. The Interstate Commerce Commission (ICC) rejected a rival bid of the New York Central System, and the C & O acquired most of the B & O's common and preferred stock. While stopping short of merger, the affiliated roads moved swiftly toward consolidated management and operation, to the point of sharing high-level corporate officers who shuttled between the C & O's system headquarters in Cleveland, Ohio, and the B & O's general offices in Baltimore, Md. A pending merger of the two eastern railroad giants, the New York Central System and the Pennsylvania Railroad, led the C & O in 1965 to enter into an agreement to merge with the Norfolk & Western Railway, subject to ICC approval.

LUTHER S. MILLER, *"Railway Age"*

CHESAPEAKE AND SHANNON, Battle of the, fought in 1813 between the frigates *Chesapeake* (U. S.) and *Shannon* (British) in the War of 1812. The *Shannon* was waiting off Boston, expecting the *Chesapeake* to come out and fight. Capt. James Lawrence took the *Chesapeake* to sea on the morning of June 1 and engaged the *Shannon* late in the afternoon. Early in the battle the *Chesapeake* was crippled by gunfire and drifted close to the *Shannon*. Lawrence was mortally wounded; his last order was "Don't give up the ship." Capt. Philip Vere Broke of the *Shannon* led a party that boarded the *Chesapeake*. A musket butt badly wounded his head, but the *Chesapeake's* crew was overcome. The *Chesapeake* was towed to Halifax as a prize and was converted into a British warship.

CHESAPEAKE BAY, ches'ə-pēk, is the most extensive indentation on the Atlantic coast of the United States. Wholly enclosed within the boundaries of Maryland and Virginia, it separates the main section of Virginia from its narrow coastal peninsula and nearly bisects Maryland. The bay reaches inland some 200 miles (320 km) from south to north. It varies in width from 4 to 30 miles (6 to 48 km) and is as much as 348 feet (106 meters) deep. Cape Charles and Cape Henry, which guard its entrance from the sea, are 12 miles (19 km) apart.

Several important rivers and many lesser streams empty into the bay. From Virginia flow the James, York, and Rappahannock; between Virginia and Maryland, the Potomac; and through Maryland, from Pennsylvania, the Susquehanna. The coastal outline is most irregular—a succession of points and bays with occasional islands—because Chesapeake Bay is the submerged valley of the Susquehanna. The other rivers were tributaries of the Susquehanna, and their present mouths are tidal estuaries, which combine with the configuration of the bay itself to make a shoreline of some 3,600 miles (5,800 km). The confused coastal outlines, together with the influx of the river, profoundly influence the tides, which vary in certain areas nearly 12 hours from normal, a difference as great as would normally occur halfway around the globe.

The many displays of charming coastline scenery and the numerous recreation centers on the bay are growing tourist attractions. Wildlife is abundant—ducks and other game fowl attract the hunter—while the waters are popular fishing grounds. Of commercial importance are alewives, squeteague, croakers, and shad. The bay is also a prolific source of oysters and crabs. The U. S. Department of Tidewater Fisheries maintains a fleet of powerboats to enforce fishing regulations.

Excellent harbors give Chesapeake Bay a great and growing commercial importance. Baltimore, Md., and Norfolk, Va., rank among the half dozen leading U. S. ports in volume of seagoing traffic. The Chesapeake and Delaware Canal, part of the Atlantic Intracoastal Waterway, provides an inland water route to Philadelphia.

The bay area has been the stage for much American history and military development. The first permanent English settlement in the New World was established at Jamestown, Va., in 1607. The wealthy planters of Tidewater Virginia played a leading role in the struggle for independence, and the surrender of Cornwallis at Yorktown in 1781 proved to be the decisive event in the Revolutionary War. The British attack on Baltimore in the War of 1812 provided the inspiration for the American national anthem, and the fight between the *Merrimack* and *Monitor* in Hampton Roads during the Civil War changed the concept of naval warfare. Hampton Roads, which includes the ports of Norfolk and Newport News, has long been a focal point of naval installations, and Annapolis, the capital of Maryland, is the site of the U. S. Naval Academy.

In the 1950's the first bridge across the bay was built at its narrowest point, near Annapolis (see CHESAPEAKE BAY BRIDGE). The Chesapeake Bay Bridge-Tunnel (q.v.) was opened at the mouth of the bay in the 1960's.

FERDINAND C. LANE
Author of "The Mysterious Sea"

CHESAPEAKE BAY BRIDGE, a bridge extending 4.4 miles (7.1 km) across Chesapeake Bay from Sandy Point, near Annapolis, Md., to Kent Island on the eastern shore of the bay. It provides a 28-foot (8.5-meter) wide, 2-lane vehicular crossing. The bridge has an overall length of 7.7 miles (12.4 km), including its approaches, and is a part of one important route for the heavy traffic between Washington D. C., and New York City. The bridge, which cost $44 million, was opened on July 30, 1952.

The bridge is composed of cantilever spans, a truss span, and a suspension span. The main part of the structure is a suspension bridge with a 1,600-foot (488-meter) main span. Its two towers are each 348 feet (106 meters) high, and its pile foundations go down 203 feet (62 meters) beneath the water. The main span is 186 feet (57 meters) above the channel for large ships going to and from Baltimore.

CHESAPEAKE BAY BRIDGE-TUNNEL, a combination of trestles, bridges, and tunnels that stretches 17.6 miles (28 km) across the entrance to Chesapeake Bay, providing a 2-lane vehicular crossing between Norfolk, Va., and the tip of Cape Charles. The crossing was built with tunnels rather than entirely above water to ensure that U. S. Navy and commercial ships would have clear channels into and out of Chesapeake Bay even if the crossings were bombed in time of war.

Two concrete-lined tunnels, each 24 feet (7 meters) in diameter and 1 mile (1.6 km) long, carry the roadway deep beneath the main chan-

THE THIMBLE SHOAL section of the Chesapeake Bay Bridge-Tunnel (see map), looking from south to north.

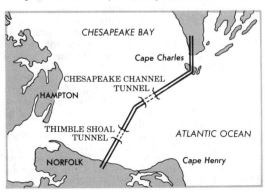

nels for ships. The ends of each tunnel are connected to man-made islands, 1,500 feet (450 meters) long; the four islands were built in water with an average depth of 40 feet (12 meters).

Other parts of the crossing are provided by two steel bridges. The high-level North Channel Bridge has a vertical clearance of 80 feet (24 meters) and a horizontal clearance of 300 feet (100 meters) for a clear channel. The medium-level Fishermans Inlet Bridge crosses a channel near Cape Charles.

The major length of the crossing is provided by 12.5 miles (20 km) of precast concrete pile trestles carrying the 31-foot-wide (9-meter) roadway 25 feet (8 meters) above mean low water; the trestles were designed to withstand 20-foot (6-meter) waves from Atlantic storms.

The Chesapeake Bay Bridge-Tunnel, which eliminated an 85-minute ferry trip, was opened for traffic in 1964.

ALBERT H. GRISWOLD, *New York University*

CHESAPEAKE BAY RETRIEVER, a medium-sized breed of sporting dog. Chesapeake Bay retrievers are strong swimmers and have remarkable endurance in rough, cold waters. The dog stands 21 to 26 inches (53–66 cm) at the shoulder and weighs 55 to 75 pounds (25–34 kg). The coat is short and thick, with a dense, woolly undercoat; the color ranges from brown to a faded, dead-grass shade.

The breed is one of the few developed in the United States. Two puppies rescued from a foundering English brig off the coast of Maryland in 1807 are generally considered to be the progenitors of the breed. The puppies—probably descended from Newfoundland stock—developed into excellent duck retrievers and were bred to each other and to other Maryland duck dogs.

WILLIAM F. BROWN
Editor of "American Field"

Chesapeake Bay retriever

EVELYN M. SHAFER

CHESHIRE, chesh'ər, a town in south central Connecticut, is in New Haven county, about 14 miles (22 km) north of New Haven. It is a residential community in a fruit-, truck-, and poultry-farming area. The town has manufactures of heavy machinery and brass and wood products. Cheshire is the home of Cheshire Academy, a private school for boys, established in 1794. The town is also the site of the Connecticut State Reformatory.

Settled about 1700, the community was named New Cheshire in 1724 after Cheshire, England. It was incorporated in 1780. In the first half of the 19th century, Cheshire was a copper- and barite-mining center; it has several old houses dating from this period. Government is by a board of selectmen. Population: 19,051.

CHESHIRE, chesh'ər, is a West Midland county of England, lying south of the Mersey River and east of the Irish Sea. Its county town is Chester, on the river Dee, about 15 miles (24 km) south of Liverpool. Running north and south through the center of Cheshire are the Peckforton Hills and the dense Delamere Forest. On the east are the outliers of the Pennines, a long range of hills. The central and southern parts of the county are rich undulating pastureland, where dairy farms abound. The county has many well-preserved medieval timber buildings, especially at Chester.

There are a number of important industries in Cheshire, particularly along the Wirral Peninsula, which runs out between the estuaries of the Dee and the Mersey for about 12 miles (20 km) to the Irish Sea. The great seaport and shipbuilding city of Birkenhead, at the tip of the peninsula, faces Liverpool across the Mersey. Merseyside docks and industrial installations line the banks for many miles. Near the base of the peninsula, Ellesmere Port and Stanlow have important oil installations.

Chemical works at Northwich are based on great subterranean deposits of brine. Macclesfield is famous for its silks; Stockport, for men's hats; and Crewe, for its railway works and men's clothing. At Jodrell Bank, near Congleton, are the world-famous radio telescopes of the Nuffield Radio Astronomy Laboratories of the University of Manchester. On the west and north shores of the Wirral Peninsula are long sandy beaches extending in front of Hoylake and New Brighton. Population: (1961) 1,368,979.

GORDON STOKES
Author of "English Place-Names"

CHESNUTT, ches'nut, **Charles Waddell** (1858–1932), American author and educator. Chesnutt was born in Cleveland, Ohio, on June 20, 1858. He was educated at the state normal school at Fayetteville, N. C., and became its principal in 1881. In 1884 he worked as a journalist in New York City while studying law. He was admitted to the Ohio bar in 1887.

Chesnutt is regarded as the first American Negro novelist. He is best known for his short stories based on folklore, as in *The Conjure Woman* (1899). His novels, among them *The House Beyond the Cedars* (1900) and *The Marrow of Tradition* (1901), expose the consequences of racial prejudice. He received the Spingarn Medal for his work. Chesnutt died in Cleveland on Nov. 15, 1932. A biography by Helen M. Chesnutt was published in 1952.

CHESS, ches, is a game of mental skill between two sides, using a set of figurines (chessmen) on a checkered board of 64 squares. It consists of alternate moves by each side, with the ultimate objective of trapping the enemy's king.

The Board and Chessmen. The chessboard has 32 light-colored and 32 dark-colored squares, all of which are used in the game. The 8 vertical rows are called *files;* the horizontal rows, *ranks.* Straight lines of the same-colored squares running in a slantwise direction are called *diagonals.* (See Fig. 1.)

Each side has a set of 16 chessmen. One set is light in color, for the White side; the other is dark in color, for the Black side. The 8 important men are called *pieces:* king, queen, 2 rooks (or castles), 2 bishops, and 2 knights. The other 8 men are called *pawns.*

The board is placed between the two players so that each has a white square at his right hand. At the start of the game, the two rooks occupy the extreme right and left squares of the first rank (the nearest row); the two knights stand next to the rooks; the two bishops are placed next to the knights; the queen is "on color" (white queen on a light square, black queen on a dark square); and the king stands on the one remaining square along the first rank. The pawns stand on the row directly in front of the pieces. Fig. 1. shows the chessboard set up for play.

Moves and Powers. Each type of chessman moves in a different manner. It may capture an opponent's man by moving onto the occupied square and removing the piece from the board.

A pawn may move straight forward only one square at a time, except on its first move, when it may move two squares (to the 4th rank). It also may move diagonally forward, but only to capture an opponent's man. If two opposing pawns meet on the same file, they stop each other; they can neither move nor capture the other. If a pawn manages to reach the other end of the board (the 8th rank), it is immediately promoted to any more powerful piece except the king (usually it is exchanged for a queen).

The knight's move is L-shaped; two squares in either a horizontal or vertical direction and then one square to its right or left. It can jump over pieces between its original square and the square to which it moves, but can only capture the opponent's piece on the square on which it finally lands. (See Fig. 2.)

The king may move in any direction, but only one square at a time. The remaining men may move any distance open along their lines of power but may not leap over any men: bishop, along the diagonal; rook, along a file and rank; queen, the most powerful piece of all, along the diagonal, file, and rank.

The powers of the chessmen are related directly to their mobility. The knight is usually most active on the board early in the game; the long-range pieces (bishop and rook) become more active as the board clears; and pawns are potentially more valuable as the chance of promoting them increases. In playing strength, the king and knight are equal to 3 pawns each; the bishop (roughly) to 3½ pawns; the rook, 5; and the queen, 9. A bishop, although it covers only half the squares of the board, still rates a fraction of a pawn better than a knight, and two bishops usually are better than two knights or even bishop and knight. But a bishop shut in by its own pawns may be almost valueless.

Special Powers. *En passant* (French for "in passing") is a special way of capturing with a pawn. It applies when the pawn moves forward two squares on the first move and passes by an opposing pawn that has reached its 5th rank on an adjoining file. On his next turn only, the opposing player may capture the advancing pawn as if it had moved only one square forward, and place his own pawn diagonally forward on his 6th rank.

There is one situation in which two pieces, a king and a rook, can be moved simultaneously. Once in a game a player may safeguard his king by *castling.* This maneuver permits a player to move his king two squares toward either rook (if the squares are clear) and then move the rook to the square jumped over by the king. Castling is legal only if neither king nor rook has moved previously; and only if the king is not under direct attack (check), does not move into such attack, and does not cross a square under attack by an opposing man.

Any move that threatens to capture a king is called a *check.* To guard his king from the threat, the player must either move his king to a safe square, capture the checking man, or interpose one of his chessmen between the king and the enemy piece. The opponent must not ignore the check. The game ends when the king is in check and there is no way for him to avoid capture. This is called *checkmate* or *mate,* and it means victory for the other contestant.

Notation. Moves in chess are described by a code. Every piece has a letter symbol: K-king, Q-queen; R-rook; N-knight (though sometimes Kt is used); B-bishop; and P-pawn. The pieces on the kingside of the board at the start of a game are called KR (king's rook), KN (king's knight), and KB (king's bishop). Those on the queenside are QR (queen's rook), QN (queen's knight), and QB (queen's bishop). A file takes the name of the piece that stands on that file at the start, for example, the QR file. Ranks are numbered 1 through 8. Each square is identified by its rank and file; for example, the first square on the queen's rook file, from White's side of the board, is called QR1 for White's moves but QR8 for Black's.

A move is recorded by identifying the piece moved, following it with a hyphen, and then naming the square on which it has been placed. Thus, a first White move of a pawn to the fourth rank before the queen is 1 P-Q4; Black's reply of knight to the third rank before his king bishop is 1 . . . N-KB3. Castling kingside is written O-O, and castling queenside, O-O-O. Captures require an "x" and the chessman taken; for example, RxKN (or RxN if only one knight can be taken). *En passant* is written PxP e.p. Check is an abbreviated "ch" after the move. An exclamation mark (!) signifies a brilliant move; one question mark (?), a poor move; and two question marks (??), a losing move.

ILLUSTRATIVE GAMES

This first game is the one that Paul Morphy, U.S. chess champion, played against the Duke of Brunswick and Count Isouard at the Paris Opera House in 1858, and it is the most celebrated game in all chess history. It is also highly instructive, displaying clearly the rapid development of all the pieces and with pressure on the center. In addition, it shows an attack on a badly developed position, a sacrifice as a means of

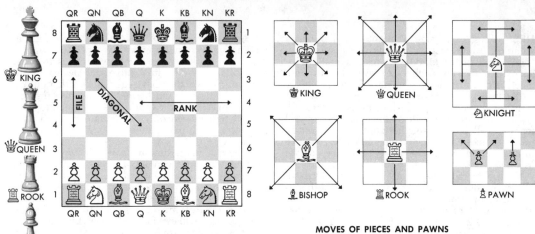

CHESSBOARD, MEN, AND NOTATION

Black (top) and White (bottom) pieces and pawns are in place for play. Directional arrows show lines of power: *file* (rows from player to player), *diagonal*, and *rank* (rows left to right). White's files are named as coded at bottom and ranks as numbered at the left. Black's ranks are numbered as at the right. A pawn is named by the file on which it stands; its designation changes when it shifts to a new file. Pieces retain their designations throughout the game.

MOVES OF PIECES AND PAWNS

Arrows indicate how chessmen move. The *king* can move only to a square next to the one it is on. The *queen* moves any number of squares on a file, rank, or diagonal. A *knight's* move is 2 squares on a file or rank, then 1 square to either side. A *bishop* moves any number of squares on a diagonal; it always remains on the color on which it starts. The *rook* moves any number of squares on a file or rank. A *pawn* moves either 1 or 2 squares straight forward on its first move; afterwards, only 1 square at a time and only forward. Pawns capture only by moving 1 square ahead on a diagonal. With the exception of the knight, no chessman may jump over another in its path. White always moves first.

---

tearing open the opponent's position, an intensification of pressure against pinned pieces, the power of rooks on open files, and the importance of safeguarding the king by castling early. 1 P-K4, P-K4 2 N-KB3, P-Q3 constitutes the *Philidor Defense*.

WHITE (Morphy)	BLACK (Allies)	WHITE	BLACK
1 P-K4	P-K4	10 NxP! (m)	PxN
2 N-KB3 (a)	P-Q3 (b)	11 BxNPch	QN-Q2 (n)
3 P-Q4	B-N5 (c)	12 O-O-O (o)	R-Q1 (p)
4 PxP	BxN (d)	13 RxN!	RxR
5 QxB	PxP (e)	14 R-Q1 (q)	Q-K3 (r)
6 B-QB4 (f)	N-KB3	15 BxRch	NxB
7 Q-QN3! (g)	Q-K2 (h)	16 Q-N8ch!	NxQ
8 N-B3 (i)	P-B3 (j)	17 R-Q8 mate	
9 B-KN5 (k)	P-N4 (l)		

(a) Piece deployment (strategic arrangement) with attack on the center.

(b) Philidor Defense: somewhat inferior as it shuts in the king bishop, whereas ... N-QB3 develops a piece while guarding the king pawn.

(c) Definitely inferior, as now Black must yield bishop for knight or else lose a pawn.

(d) Or 4 ... PxP?? 5 QxQch, KxQ 6 NxP.

(e) Black must recapture or be behind in material, but White's piece deployed is a gain of a tempo (time).

(f) White uses the tempo to threaten mate by 7 QxP. (White harasses his opponent with each move, so far as possible.)

(g) Moving a piece twice in the opening and attacking prematurely are violations of White's tenets but are justified here by Black's poor play. In fact, Q-QN3 sets up a winning double attack on king bishop pawn and queen knight pawn.

(h) Black defends his king bishop pawn: 7 ... Q-Q2 loses prosaically to 8 QxP and 9 QxR.

(i) White confidently keeps developing. 8 QxP wins a pawn but kills White's fine attack: 8 ... Q-N5ch 9 QxQ, BxQch. 8 BxPch, QxB 9 QxP wins outright but inartistically (see note o).

(j) Now Black defends his queen knight pawn.

(k) White mobilizes his last minor piece and pins Black's king knight to the queen.

(l) Under harassment, Black tries rashly to strike back. 9 ... Q-B2 relieves him of the pin and clears a diagonal for his bishop.

(m) A sacrifice to tear open the position.

(n) Now Black is paralyzed by pins.

(o) White has castled safely, intensified the pin on the queen knight and doubtless has precalculated the finish since before 10 NxP and quite possibly since before 8 N-B3.

(p) Black must guard against 12 BxNch.

(q) By forcing means, White has brought out all his pieces, still holds the paralyzing pins and threatens to win by 15 BxRch.

(r) Black unpins his knight. White can still win by 15 BxN, PxB 16 BxRch, but chooses to win elegantly instead.

This second game, played in the Interzonal Tournament at Stockholm in 1962, between Robert Fischer (White) of the United States and Gideon Barcza of Hungary, illustrates fine technique. Black picks the *Caro-Kann Defense* (1 ... P-QB3), a backward-seeming reply that aims to provoke a premature attack or a weakening overextension by White. But White's mobile pawn majority can promote to a queen in a pure king and pawn endgame; and so, as Black dare not trade off many pieces, White usurps control of the board until Black loses one pawn, then another.

WHITE (Fischer)	BLACK (Barcza)	WHITE	BLACK
1 P-K4	P-QB3	33 R-N5	P-N3
2 N-QB3	P-Q4	34 K-K3	K-B1
3 N-B3	PxP (a)	35 K-Q4	K-N1
4 NxP	N-B3 (b)	36 K-Q5	R-B3 (k)
5 NxNch	KPxN (c)	37 K-Q4	R-K3
6 P-Q4	B-Q3	38 P-QR4	K-B2
7 B-QB4	O-O	39 P-R5	Q-Q3ch
8 O-O	R-K1	40 B-Q5	K-B1
9 B-N3	N-Q2	41 PxP	P-B3
10 N-R4	N-B1 (d)	42 K-K3	NxP
11 Q-Q3	B-B2	43 B-N8 (l)	K-B2
12 B-K3	Q-K2 (e)	44 R-B5ch	K-N1
13 N-B5	Q-K5	45 BxP	N-Q4ch
14 QxQ	RxQ	46 K-B3	N-K2
15 N-N3	R-K1	47 P-R4	P-N3
16 P-Q5 (f)	PxP	48 R-N5	K-N2
17 BxQP	B-N3 (g)	49 P-R5	K-R3
18 BxB	PxB	50 P-B4	PxP
19 P-QR3	R-R4	51 BxP	R-Q5
20 QR-Q1	R-B4	52 P-QN3	N-B3
21 P-QB3	R-B2	53 K-K3	R-Q1
22 B-B3	R-Q2	54 B-K4	N-R4
23 RxR (h)	NxR	55 B-B2	P-R5 (m)
24 N-B5	N-B4	56 R-R5	K-R1ch
25 N-Q6	R-Q1	57 K-Q2	R-KN1 (n)
26 NxB	RxN	58 RxP	P-N4 (o)
27 R-Q1	K-B1	59 R-B4	PxP
28 R-Q4	R-B2	60 PxP	RxP
29 P-R3 (i)	P-B4	61 RxPch (p)	K-R2
30 R-QN4	N-Q2	62 K-B3	R-N5
31 K-B1 (j)	K-K2	63 P-B4	N-N2
32 K-K2	K-Q1	64 K-N4	Resigns (q)

(a) Initiating an exchange advances the opponent.

(b) 4 ... N-Q2, then ... KN-B3 avoids doubled pawns; but White develops and controls terrain.

(c) 5 ... NPxN weakens Black's kingside. The move actually made grants White a queenside majority and so permits White's program discussed above.

(d) 10 ... P-KN3 shuts out White's knight but again weakens Black's kingside.

(e) Black is heading for an endgame as will be seen, but White's strategy welcomes exchanges.

(f) White wisely does not try to control the whole board but clears lines for his pieces and maintains his compact pawn structure.

(g) Already Black must concede a new weakness in order to get his queen rook into play.

(h) The rook so laboriously developed (at cost of so many extra moves) is gone, and the endgame nears.

(i) 29 R-QN4, N-Q2, 30 B-N4, P-N3, 31 BxN, RxB, 32 RxP loses to 32 ... R-Q8 mate; but now 30 R-QN4 to win a pawn is a threat.

(j) As piece play is a standoff, the kings come into the game as fighting pieces.

(k) Black holds off White's king.

(l) Now White wins a pawn. Black may hope to trap the bishop, but White's rook pawn arrives (47 P-R4 and 49 P-R5) in time to release the bishop.

(m) Black's kingside pawns fall to 55 ... R-R1 56 R-KB4, R-R3 57 K-B3, 58 K-N3, and 59 K-R4.

(n) A counterattack: 58 ... RxP for 58 RxP.

(o) 58 ... RxP is met, however, by 59 R-B4, and then a second Black pawn falls.

(p) The end, long inevitable, is now imminent.

(q) It is clear that White cannot be restrained from the decisive queening of a pawn.

General Play. Because White moves first, he presses his initiative by trying to occupy or control the central squares from which pieces exert their maximum force. Each side tries to mobilize its pieces in the fewest possible moves; to control files, unobstructed by pawns, or outposts (squares in the center or near the opposing side from which a piece cannot be driven by pawns); to protect its men, especially its king.

A game is won occasionally by a surprise checkmate, but usually it comes by force, after one side has gained control of the greater part of the board through captures and by promoting its pawns. Once the other side is powerless to prevent checkmate or ruinous loss of men, it may concede the game by resigning (surrendering).

When neither side can gain a decisive advantage the game may be called a *draw,* by mutual agreement or because neither has men sufficient to force a checkmate. A draw also can be claimed (by the player who would otherwise be losing) if he can check the other's king perpetually, or if the other player cannot contrive to checkmate within 50 moves (if a man is captured or a pawn is moved, the count resumes), or if precisely the same position occurs for a third time. Another form of draw is the *stalemate,* in which the side whose turn it is to move cannot do so without exposing its king to check.

In official tournament and match play, the moves of the game are written down, and each side must make a required number of moves in a specified time (customarily, in the United States, 40 moves in two hours for each player and 20 in an hour thereafter). There are also "speed tourneys" at 10 seconds per move; and there are tournaments conducted by mail in which players have three days to respond to a move.

History of Chess. Most scholars believe that chess originated in northern India (West Pakistan) as an offspring of a Hindu game under the Sanskrit name *chaturanga* about A. D. 500, and then spread to Persia (Iran). The name chess is derived from the Persian word *shah,* which means "king," and checkmate from *shah mat,* which means "the king is dead." The Arabs learned the game when they conquered Persia in the 600's and they introduced it into Europe by way of Spain, Sicily, and Constantinople.

By the 16th century the moves of chess had assumed their modern form. François André Philidor of France (1747–1795) was the first (unofficial) champion of the modern game. Adolf Anderssen of Germany won the first modern international tournament in London in 1851. After he lost a match to Wilhelm Steinitz of Austria (1866), the latter claimed to be world chess champion. Emanuel Lasker of Germany became so by beating Steinitz (1894). In like fashion the following won the title: José R. Capablanca of Cuba (1921), Alexander A. Alekhine of France (1927), and Max Euwe of Holland (1935). Alekhine won again (1937) and died "intestate" (1946). From 1948 to 1952, the Russians Mikhail Botvinnik, Vassili Smyslov, Mikhail Tahl, Tigran Petrosian, and Boris Spassky held the world title. But in 1972, in a highly publicized match, U. S. champion Bobby Fischer took the title from Spassky. In 1975, Fischer was stripped of his title by the Fédération Internationale des Echecs (FIDE) after he refused to accept federation rules for a championship match. A Russian, Anatoli Karpov, gained the title by default.

FIDE, formed in 1946, formulates rules and governs tournaments. The U. S. Chess Federation regulates play in the United States.

JACK STRALEY BATTELL*
Coauthor of "The Best in Chess"

Bibliography

Chernev, Irving, and Harkness, Kenneth, *Invitation to Chess* (New York 1962).

Golombek, Harry, *Capablanca's 100 Best Games of Chess* (New York 1965).

Horowitz, Israel A., and Battell, Jack Straley, *Best in Chess* (New York 1965).

Réti, Richard, *Masters of the Chess Board* (New York 1958).

Wade, Robert G., *Soviet Chess* (New York 1968).

SELECTED GLOSSARY OF CHESS TERMS

Center. The four squares Q4, Q5, K4, and K5.

Closed Game. Type of position with pawns so blocked that most files cannot be opened.

Connected Pawns. Ones that can mutually support one another.

Development. Early phase of game requiring mobilization of pieces.

Discovered Attack (Check). Attack (on king) by the moving away of an intervening man.

Double Attack. One man threatening two points.

Double Check. A discovered check in which the man moved also checks.

Doubled Pawn. Two pawns of the same player on a file.

Fianchetto. To post a bishop at QN2 or KN2.

Fork. Attack by one man on two enemy points.

Hole. Any important square on which a piece can settle without being attacked by pawns.

Isolated Pawn. One deprived of protection by pawns of its own side. *Isolani* is the same, but denotes compensating value because of central location.

Major Piece. Rook or queen.

Majority. Larger group of pawns that opponent has on kingside, queenside, or center.

Minor Piece. Knight or bishop.

Minority Attack. Advance of pawns so supported by men as to disrupt the opponent's majority.

Open File. One with no pawns on it.

Outpost. A well-protected piece utilizing a hole that discomfits the opponent.

Overburdened Man. One that is perilously required to protect more than a single man.

Passed Pawn. One that is not opposed by an enemy pawn on its march to queening.

Pawn Storm. Attack spearheaded by pawn action.

Pin. To fix an adverse man by an attack so, if it moves, a more valuable piece behind it falls.

Tempo. Gain of time, particularly in developing.

Zugzwang. Situation of a player in which any legal move he may make must impair his position seriously.

Zwischenzug. A move interpolated, with a threat that the opponent cannot ignore, before a necessary or an expected move.

CHEST, in biology, the completely enclosed upper cavity of the body. The chest, also known as the *thorax,* is bounded by the ribs, sternum (breastbone), vertebrae, and the diaphragm. Contained within the chest are the trachea (windpipe), lungs, heart, esophagus (gullet), and several major blood vessels. In addition to protecting these organs from injury, the chest plays an important role in breathing. The membrane lining the chest is also the membrane covering the lungs, so that when the chest expands (in inspiration), the lungs are enlarged and air rushes into them. In expiration the chest contracts, forcing the air out of the lungs.

JEFFREY WENIG, *ENDO Laboratories*

CHESTER, George Randolph (1869–1924), American author, editor, and critic. He was born in Ohio. Chester worked at various jobs before becoming a reporter on the Detroit *News.* In 1901 he joined the Cincinnati *Enquirer,* and later was its Sunday editor. He began contributing stories to magazines, and in 1908 he quit journalism to write fiction. His fame rests on his invention of the character "Get-Rich-Quick Wallingford," a rascally but likable company promoter who was the hero of many of Chester's books, beginning with *Get-Rich-Quick Wallingford* (1908) and including *Young Wallingford* (1910) and *Wallingford in His Prime* (1913). With his second wife, Lillian De Rimo, Chester collaborated on several novels and plays. After World War I he entered the film industry as a writer and director but returned to magazine writing in 1921. He died in New York City on Feb. 26, 1924.

CHESTER, the county town of Cheshire, England, stands on a rocky hill above the river Dee some 7 miles (11 km) from its estuary and about 15 miles (24 km) south of Liverpool. Now one of the oldest and most attractive towns in England, Chester was the most important port in this part of Britain before the 15th century, when the Dee silted up. While it is no longer a major seaport, it remains a busy commercial and administrative center. The earldom of Chester has been conferred on the eldest son of the reigning British monarch since the 13th century.

The town was laid out by the Romans, and Chester is still entered by gates at the four points of the compass. Medieval walls nearly 2 miles (3 km) in length surround the city. The east wall and part of the north wall rest on Roman foundations. Near the east gate a Roman amphitheater has been excavated. Chester castle was rebuilt in the 1700's, but it retains the 13th century Agricola tower that now holds the museum of the Royal Cheshire Regiment. Other ancient remains are in the Grosvenor Museum. The red sandstone cathedral, built in the 13th to 15th centuries, incorporates remnants of a 10th and 11th century Benedictine abbey church. It became the cathedral of the new diocese of Chester in the 16th century, during the Reformation. Still standing are the monastic chapter house, refectory, and cloisters.

Chester's streets are noted for their fine half-timbered medieval buildings. Unique in the city's plan are the Rows—covered galleries running above the ground floors of shops and reached by stairways from the sidewalks. They provide traffic-free promenades and another level of shops. Population: (1961) 28,324.

GORDON STOKES, *Author, "English Place-Names"*

CHESTER, a city in southwestern Illinois, is on the Mississippi River, 55 miles (88 km) southeast of East Saint Louis. It is the seat of Randolph county. Chester is a trade center and manufactures hosiery, shoes, and flour. Fort Kaskaskia State Park, 10 miles (16 km) to the north, is on the site of an early trading post that became the first capital of Illinois. Government is by mayor and council. Population: 5,310.

CHESTER, a port city in southeastern Pennsylvania, is in Delaware county, 14 miles (22 km) southwest of Philadelphia, on the Delaware River. It is the trade and shipping center of a major industrial district and has large shipyards and dry docks. Chester's industries include steel mills, locomotive works, oil refineries, and factories manufacturing helicopters, electronic precision instruments, paper products, textiles, chemicals, and floor coverings.

The city is the seat of PMC Colleges, which include Pennsylvania Military College, a 4-year institution for men, and Penn-Morton College, a 4-year coeducational institution. Crozer Theological Seminary is also in Chester. Of interest are the Caleb Pusey House (1683), the oldest English-built house in Pennsylvania, and the Old Court House (1724), the state's oldest civic building.

Dutch settlers joined earlier Swedish settlers here in 1655 and founded the town of Upland. This was the second settlement in the state; the first, a temporary settlement on Tinicum Island in the Delaware River, disappeared shortly afterward. Deputy Governor William Markham, representing William Penn, established the seat of the colonial government of Pennsylvania here in 1681. Penn, who renamed the site, arrived the following year. Chester was county seat from 1789 to 1851. It was incorporated as a city in 1866. Government is by mayor and council. Population: 56,331.

EDITH S. MATTHEWS
J. Lewis Crozer Library

CHESTER, a city in northern South Carolina, the seat of Chester county, is 50 miles (80 km) north of Columbia. The city is a processing center, and has creameries and textile, lumber, and flour mills. It is also an important rail junction. Chester was settled and named by Pennsylvanians about 1756. It was incorporated as a town in 1849 and as a city in 1893. Government is by a city manager. Population: 7,045.

CHESTERFIELD, 4th Earl of (1694–1773), English diplomat and writer, who was the embodiment of English gentility in the Augustan age. His *Letters to His Son* are a classic of 18th century English literature.

Public Career. Chesterfield was born Philip Dormer Stanhope, in London, on Sept. 22, 1694. After a private education, he toured the Continent in his 20th year, spending a good deal of his time in Paris, where he imbibed much of the gallantry and aristocratic mannerliness that characterized the *beau monde* of the age. On his return to England in 1714, he embarked on a distinguished career in politics and diplomacy. He served in the House of Commons in the ruling Whig coalition from 1716 to 1726, when he succeeded his father as earl and entered the House of Lords. From 1728 to 1732 he was ambassador to The Hague, in the Netherlands, and during the rest of the 1730's he was increasingly active in forming an opposition to Sir Robert Walpole's seemingly unassailable ministry in the government.

In 1745, Chesterfield was appointed lord lieutenant of Ireland, an important post that he merited by having been generally recognized since 1739 as the leader of the opposition party in the House of Lords. Although he was in Ireland for less than a year, his tenure was auspicious, for during that year "Bonnie Prince Charlie," grandson of the deposed King James II, appeared in Scotland at the head of an army, determined to recapture the English throne. The attempt was crushed at the Battle of Culloden, but at any time before then sympathetic Ireland might have rallied to the pretender's cause had not Chesterfield's Irish policy of toleration encouraged compromise. He was so popular with the Irish, in fact, that they gave him on his departure, according to an 18th century historian, "the universal acclamations of the people who praised him, blessed him, and entreated him to return."

From 1746 to 1748, Chesterfield was one of the two secretaries of state of England. Failing in health, he surrendered his office but declined to accept either a dukedom or a pension from the government.

Literary Associations. Throughout his years of government service, Chesterfield maintained close connections with the literary world. He had been friendly with Alexander Pope since 1714 and through him with a great part of the Augustan literary establishment. He was a pallbearer in 1732 for the poet John Gay, and two years later he was at the deathbed of Dr. John Arbuthnot, physician, poet, and close friend of Pope.

Always a patron of the arts, Chesterfield is ironically most often remembered in this connection as the object of a notorious attack by Samuel Johnson. In 1748, Dr. Johnson had dedicated to Chesterfield his ambitious plan for an English dictionary. Through some oversight (most uncharacteristic of him), Chesterfield failed to acknowledge the dedication or encourage the project; later, on the eve of the dictionary's publication, Johnson wrote a letter to Chesterfield in which he exposed the emptiness of Chesterfield's patronage. Johnson's pique was certainly justified, but his accusations were hardly fair to the usually gracious and cooperative earl.

Composition of the Letters. When Chesterfield returned from his first diplomatic post, that in the Netherlands, in 1732, he brought his mistress with him. Their son, Philip, was born shortly after. For Philip, when he was less than six years old, Chesterfield began to write the famous *Letters* that even the truculent Dr. Johnson could admire ("Lord Chesterfield's Letters to his son, I think, might be made a very pretty book. Take out the immorality, and it should be put into the hands of every young gentleman.").

The letters extol the virtues of compromise, discretion, and the wisdom of always presenting a brave and mannerly appearance and of being, in short, the consummate civilized man in control of oneself and one's society. Chesterfield was describing the virtues that fitted him well for a diplomatic career. But the advice was lost on his son, who was graceless and clumsy; not even his knowledgeable and affectionate father could outfit him for an illustrious career. The letters continued to pour from Chesterfield's pen until Philip died in 1768, when Chesterfield undertook the education of his godson (also named Philip Stan-

Philip, 4th earl of Chesterfield, from Allan Ramsay's portrait.

BETTMANN ARCHIVE

hope), and composed the less well-known but similar *Letters to His Godson.*

Chesterfield lived in comfortable retirement at his country house in Blackheath and Chesterfield House in London, where he died on March 24, 1773.

His last moments on earth were characteristic of his courtesy and his aristocratic sense of decorum. His valet announced a visitor, a certain Mr. Dayrolles. Chesterfield's last words were, "Give Dayrolles a chair."

RICHARD E. HUGHES, *Boston College*

Further Reading: Chesterfield's *Letters to His Son,* first published posthumously in 1774, are available in a modern edition by Bonamy Dobree, 6 vols. (London 1932). The *Letters to His Godson* were first published in London in 1890 in an edition by Lord Carnarvon. Biographical studies include Willard Connely, *The True Chesterfield* (London 1939); and Samuel Shellabarger, *Lord Chesterfield and His World* (London 1935).

CHESTERFIELD ISLANDS, a group of 11 coral islets in the Coral Sea, 340 miles (547 km) northwest of New Caledonia. They are administered as part of the French overseas territory of New Caledonia. The area of the Chesterfield Islands totals about 4 square miles (10 sq km). Rich guano deposits are found on the islands.

CHESTERIAN SERIES, ches-tir'ē-ən, the youngest series of rocks deposited in the Upper Mississippian subsystem of the Carboniferous period, about 320 million years ago. It succeeds the Meramecian series and underlies the Morrowan series of the Lower Pennsylvanian subsystem. The series is named for Chester, Ill., the type region of the rocks.

The Chesterian rocks at Chester are distinctive in that they have alternating successions of sandy shale and limestone that thicken generally toward central Illinois and southward. They are overlain, with regional unconformity, by basal Pennsylvanian sandstones. The maximum thickness is more than 1,000 feet (300 meters). In West Virginia similar rocks in the lower part of the succession are overlain by about 5,000 feet (1,500 meters) of sandstone and conglomerate, which are thought to have been laid while erosion was proceeding in the interior of the continent.

Among the many kinds of organisms in the marine Chesterian rocks, the most distinctive and widespread are the small, spheroidal echinoderms called blastoids. See also CARBONIFEROUS PERIOD.

MARSHALL KAY, *Columbia University*

G. K. Chesterton (bronze bust by Maria Petrie)

CHESTERTON, Gilbert Keith (1874–1936), English author, who was one of the most genial, witty, controversial, and versatile men of letters of his time. He wrote poetry, plays, novels, and essays, as well as social and literary criticism. Perhaps his best-known works are his series of Father Brown detective stories.

Chesterton was born in London on May 29, 1874. After attending St. Paul's School in London, he studied art at the Slade School. He began his literary career by reviewing art books for *The Bookman* and went on to write for other journals, including the *Illustrated London News*. About 1899, Chesterton began his lifelong friendship with Hilaire Belloc, whose religious, social, and political beliefs were in such accordance with Chesterton's own that the two men were sometimes referred to as "The Chesterbelloc." In 1900, Chesterton published his first books, both collections of verse, called *The Wild Knight* and *Greybeards at Play.*

Many of Chesterton's works were in the field of social criticism. They included *The Defendant* (1901), in which he defended late Victorian conventionality in such an unconventional way that he came to be known as "the master of paradox." His fantasy novel *The Napoleon of Notting Hill* (1904) satirizes contemporary society. He also expressed his social and political views in such nonfiction works as *What's Wrong with the World* (1910) and *The Outline of Sanity* (1926), and in *G. K.'s Weekly,* a journal that he established in 1925.

By 1910, Chesterton had left London and established his household in Beaconsfield. There he started his series of detective stories about Father Brown, an engaging priest-detective. The series included *The Innocence of Father Brown* (1911), *The Secret of Father Brown* (1927), and *The Scandal of Father Brown* (1935).

Chesterton's humor and whimsy are also reflected in many of his poems, such as his famous lyric *The Donkey.* Much of his best verse was published in *New and Collected Poems* (1929).

He was also a prominent literary critic and wrote outstanding studies that included *Robert Browning* (1903), *George Bernard Shaw* (1909), and *Chaucer* (1932).

A major turning point in Chesterton's life occurred in 1922 when he was converted to Roman Catholicism. From this time on he vigorously championed his faith in many of his important works, including *St. Francis of Assisi* (1923), *The Everlasting Man* (1925), and *St. Thomas Aquinas* (1933). During his last years he conducted a weekly literary program for the British Broadcasting Corporation.

Chesterton died in Beaconsfield on June 14, 1936.

ANNE FREMANTLE
Author of "This Little Band of Prophets"

Further Reading: Chesterton, Mrs. Cecil, *The Chestertons* (London 1941); Chesterton, G. K., *Autobiography* (London 1936); Kenner, Hugh, *Paradox in Chesterton* (New York 1948); Ward, Masie, *G. K. Chesterton* (New York 1944).

CHESTERTON, a town in northwestern Indiana, is in Porter county, 14 miles (22.5 km) east of Gary, just south of Lake Michigan. The town manufactures metal products, die castings, and dresses. Indiana Dunes State Park on the Lake Michigan shore is 3 miles (5 km) north. Government is by a town board. Population: 6,177.

CHESTNUT, any of several shrubs and trees sometimes grown for their edible nuts. Chestnuts belong to the genus *Castanea* of the beech family (Fagaceae) and are widely distributed throughout the northern temperate zone.

Chestnuts generally range in height from 30 to 60 feet (9 to 18 meters) and have furrowed bark with toothed oval or lance-shaped leaves. The leaves are glossy green but turn bronze in the fall. The chestnut's staminate (male) flowers are borne in small spikes, called catkins, and the pistillate (female) flowers are hardly noticeable. The fruits are very spiny round burs usually containing 2 or 3 shiny dark brown nuts.

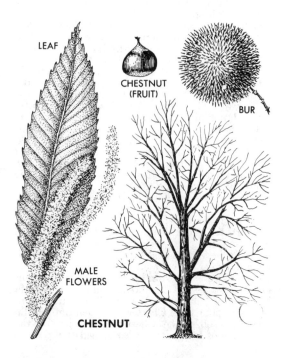

LEAF

CHESTNUT (FRUIT)

BUR

MALE FLOWERS

CHESTNUT

Species. The American chestnut (*C. dentata*) once ranged throughout the eastern half of the United States and was one of the commonest trees there. Its wood was widely used for making rail fences and its nuts were roasted and eaten by early settlers. In the 1930's, however, a destructive fungous disease called chestnut blight was introduced into the United States from Europe, and it soon killed all of the larger trees. Although some young trees of this species may be seen growing in woodlands, these too will inevitably be killed by the blight.

Today the species most widely cultivated are the Spanish chestnut (*C. sativa*), the Japanese chestnut (*C. crenata*), and especially the Chinese chestnut (*C. mollissima*), which, with its hybrids, is the most resistant to the chestnut blight and the most highly recommended species for cultivation. The Chinese chestnut grows about 60 feet (18 meters) tall, and its branchlets are often downy (pubescent). Its leaves grow from 3 to 7 inches (7.5 to 18 cm) long, and the nuts are about 1 inch (2.5 cm) across.

In the United States, most commercial chestnut nuts are imported from Europe, where they are obtained from the Spanish chestnut tree. However, sizable orchards of the Chinese chestnut are grown in the United States and are beginning to produce nuts for the American market. Although many people grow chestnut trees around their homes, the trees will not produce nuts unless several different varieties are planted together, so that they will be cross-pollinated.

Other "Chestnuts." The term chestnut is also commonly applied to several plants unrelated to the true chestnuts. The horse chestnut (*Aesculus hippocastanum*) belongs to the horse chestnut family (Hippocastanaceae), and the water chestnut (*Trapa natans*) is an aquatic plant of the evening primrose family (Onagraceae). The Cape chestnut is a tall southern African tree (*Calodendrum capense*) of the rue family (Rutaceae), while the Moreton Bay chestnut (*Castanospermum australe*) is a member of the legume family (Leguminosae).

DONALD WYMAN
The Arnold Arboretum, Harvard University

CHETNIK, chet′nĕk, was the name applied to members of a World War II Yugoslav resistance movement that was organized after the German invasion of Yugoslavia in March 1941. It was led by Gen. Draža Mihailović, who was also minister of war in the government-in-exile of King Peter. The group found its main support in Serbia. Soon after its formation it came into conflict with a rival resistance organization, the Partisans, composed of political groups to the left, particularly the Communists, under the direction of Josip Broz Tito. A three-way struggle developed between the Chetniks, the Partisans, and the German occupation forces. In this confused situation, the Allies, believing Tito be a more effective fighter, concentrated on supporting the Partisans. Mihailović was executed by the new Yugoslav regime in July 1946 on charges of treason.

BARBARA JELAVICH and CHARLES JELAVICH
Indiana University

CHETTLE, chet′əl, **Henry** (1560–1607), English dramatist and pamphleteer. Although thirteen plays have been attributed to Chettle's sole authorship, the only extant one is *The Tragedy of Hoffmann*, a melodrama of revenge, written in 1602 (printed in 1631). It is uncertain when he began writing plays. However, in Francis Meres' *Palladis Tamia* (1598) Chettle is mentioned as one of "the best for comedy amongst us," and from then until 1603 he wrote or collaborated on more than 40 plays.

Chettle's name first appears as the editor of Robert Greene's *Groats-worth of Wit* (1592), which refers to Shakespeare as an "upstart crow." Chettle later apologized for the insult in the preface to his *Kind-Hart's Dreame* (1593), a pamphlet satirizing the abuses of his age. Chettle's *Englande's Mourning Garment* (1603) is an elegy in prose and verse to Queen Elizabeth.

CHEVALIER, shə-vȧ-lyā′, **Maurice** (1888–1972), French actor and singer, celebrated for his engaging smile and buoyant delivery of impudent French songs. He was born at Ménilmontant, in Paris, on Sept. 12, 1888. He left school at the age of 10 and obtained his first singing job at the age of 11, touring the Parisian suburbs as "le petit Chevalier." He was the star of a group of young café entertainers in 1905, when he was discovered by the famous Mistinguett and taken into her act at the Folies-Bergère.

Chevalier first appeared in American films in 1929 in *Innocents of Paris* and achieved immediate success as a charming and debonair Parisian boulevardier. His jaunty straw hat became his trademark. A series of musical films followed, including *The Love Parade* (1929), *The Merry Widow* (1934), and *Folies-Bergère* (1935). At the peak of his success he returned to Paris.

During the German occupation of France in World War II, Chevalier worked only 12 weeks, preferring retirement to collaboration. In 1958 and 1963 he toured Europe and the United States in a one-man show called *An Evening with Maurice Chevalier*. His postwar American films included *Love in the Afternoon* (1957) and *Gigi* (1958), *Fanny* (1961), and *Jessica* (1962). He died in Paris on Jan. 1, 1972.

HOWARD SUBER
University of California at Los Angeles

Maurice Chevalier

BLACK STAR

CHEVALIER, shə-vå-lyā′, is a French title of nobility. The word has the same origin of the English "cavalier," derived from the Late Latin *caballarius*, "horseman." In the Middle Ages the title was bestowed upon nobles admitted to an order of chivalry; the medieval chevalier was roughly equivalent to an English knight. By the 18th century, however, the title had become largely honorary and was frequently bestowed upon younger sons of the French nobility, who were barred from deriving their titles from the family's estates.

In the French Legion of Honor, chevalier is the lowest rank.

CHEVERLY, she′vər-lē, is a town in central Maryland, in Prince George's county, near the Anacostia River. It is situated about 5 miles (8 km) east of Washington, D. C., of which it is a residential suburb. The St. George's General Hospital is in the town. Cheverly has a mayor-council form of government. Population: 6,696.

CHEVES, chiv′is, **Langdon** (1776–1857), American politician and banker, who rose from humble origins to become a political leader in his home state of South Carolina, speaker of the U. S. House of Representatives, and president of the Second Bank of the United States. Cheves was born on Sept. 17, 1776, in a fort in Abbeville district, S. C., where his mother had taken refuge from the Cherokee Indians. Self-educated, he was admitted to the state bar in 1797 and quickly established a reputation as an outstanding lawyer and an impressive orator.

Entering politics in the early 1800's, Cheves served as a state legislator (1802–1809) state attorney general (1809), U. S. congressman (1811–1815), and justice of the South Carolina court of appeals (1816–1818). In Congress he joined the nationalistic War Hawks, and he served as speaker of the House in 1814 and 1815.

In 1819, Cheves accepted the most challenging and important position of his career, the presidency of the Second Bank of the United States, in Philadelphia. Taking office when the bank was on the verge of financial ruin, he followed a severe contraction policy, curtailing all new bank loans and calling in loans already issued. As a result the bank was placed on a sound financial foundation, and it survived a period of depression. But the consequences suffered by debtors, particularly in the West and South, led one critic to charge that the "Bank was saved, and the people were ruined."

During the South Carolina nullification crisis in the early 1830's, Cheves took a moderate position favoring a Southern convention to discuss threats to states' rights. In 1850 he attended such a convention in Nashville, Tenn., at which he again urged Southern unity. He died in Columbia, S. C., on June 26, 1857.

JAMES ROGER SHARP, *Syracuse University*

Further Reading: Wright, D. M., "Langdon Cheves and Nicholas Biddle," *Journal of Economic History,* vol. 13, pp. 305–319.

CHEVIOT, shiv′ē-ət, is a suburban city in southwestern Ohio, in Hamilton county. On the western outskirts of Cincinnati, it is primarily a residential area, although packing boxes are manufactured. Cheviot was settled in 1878. It has a mayor and council form of government. Population: 11,135.

CHEVIOT HILLS, chev′ē-ət, a range of grass-covered ancient rocks, extending southwest to northeast for about 35 miles (56 km) along the border between England and Scotland, in Northumberland and Roxburgh counties. The highest peaks are the flat-topped Cheviot (2,676 feet; 816 meters), Peel Fell, and Carter Fell, where the Newcastle-Edinburgh road makes a dramatic crossing. The North Tyne, Tees, and Coquet rivers rise here. The hills provide pasture for hardy Blackface and Cheviot sheep. The hills were the scene of much Scots-English border warfare over the centuries.

GORDON STOKES
Author of "English Place-Names"

CHEVIOT SHEEP, shev′ē-ət, are one of the oldest breeds of sheep native to the British Isles. Bred both for meat and wool, Cheviots are active, hardy animals that are adapted to a harsh climate. They have blocky bodies and short legs. A ram weighs 150 to 220 pounds (70–90 kg), while a ewe weighs 90 to 165 pounds (40–75 kg). (The North Country Cheviot is considerably larger.) The gestation period is about 148 days.

The head and legs of Cheviot sheep are covered with short white hair, although small black spots may occur; the nostrils and hooves are black. Horns are usually absent and the ears are erect.

The wool of the Cheviot is medium in fineness and length. The weight of the fleece ranges from 7 to 12 pounds (3–5 kg) for rams, and from 5 to 8 pounds (2–4 kg) for ewes.

Cheviots originated in the Cheviot Hills of the border country between Scotland and England. They are now found in the British Isles and also in Sweden, Norway, Canada, and New Zealand. About 3% of the registered sheep in the United States are Cheviots. See also SHEEP.

CLAIR E. TERRILL
U. S. Department of Agriculture

CHEVREUL, shə-vrûl′, **Michel Eugène** (1786–1889), French chemist, who made notable contributions to the study of natural chemical products, and discovered the chemical nature of fats.

Chevreul, the son of a surgeon, was born on Aug. 31, 1786, at Angers. Educated there and at Paris, he became assistant to Vauquelin at the Muséum d'Histoire Naturelle and occupied the chair of chemistry there from 1830 until his death in Paris on April 9, 1889, at the age of 102.

In 1824 he became director of dyeing at the Manufacture Royale des Gobelins, France's national tapestry works. Here he studied the conditions necessary for effective color contrast and began the scientific standardization of color, obtaining precise definition of 1,442 different shades. It was out of this work that Seurat and Signac developed neoimpressionist painting.

From 1811 to 1823, Chevreul carried out his fundamental researches on fats. Having demonstrated the presence of two main constituents (oily and solid), occurring in different proportions in different fats, he showed that each was a combination of an organic acid with a sweet substance which he called glycerin. These investigations emphasized for the first time the importance of isolating and examining pure components of natural products and introduced the melting point as a criterion of purity for organic solids.

COLIN A. RUSSELL, *Harris College, England*

CHEVREUSE, shə-vrûz', **Duchesse de** (1600–1679), French political intriguer. Born Marie de Rohan in December 1600, she was the daughter of Hercule de Rohan, Duke de Montbazon. At the age of 17, after a turbulent and neglected childhood, she married Honoré Albret, Duke de Luynes. Though Marie captivated Anne of Austria, the Queen of France, she was expelled from the Court in 1622 by Louis XIII because of her ungovernable behavior. Her husband had recently died, and Marie, beautiful, charming, but entirely devoid of scruple, immediately married Claude de Lorraine, Duke de Chevreuse, and again took her place at court.

Becoming the mistress of Lord Holland, the English ambassador to France, she conceived a wild scheme to join Holland's friend Buckingham in an amorous union with the French Queen. Her success in this venture intensified the King's antipathy for Marie. Audacious to an extreme, Marie persuaded the Queen that, should Louis XIII die prematurely, Anne would marry the King's dashing brother, Gaston d'Orléans. A vast conspiracy soon formed, and Marie began an extraordinary career of intrigue and treason that drove her first to England in 1627 and then back to France in 1628, whence she was exiled again in 1634 for imparting to Spain state secrets acquired in the boudoir. Involved in several conspiracies against Cardinal Richelieu before his death in 1642, Marie was subsequently at the center of almost every plot against Cardinal Mazarin, Richelieu's successor, during the Fronde rebellion. After 1653, however, Marie lost all political importance. She died in Gagny, near Paris, on Aug. 12, 1679.

LIONEL ROTHKRUG, *University of Michigan*

CHEVROLET, shev-rō-lā', **Louis** (1879–1941), Swiss-American automobile racer and designer, who designed the first Chevrolet automobile. He was born in La Chaux-de-Fonds, Switzerland, was educated in France, and went to the United States in 1900 as a representative of a French manufacturing firm. He soon became a renowned racer and set records at tracks around the country.

As a member of the Buick racing team in 1909 he became associated with William C. Durant, the founder of General Motors Company. Durant sponsored his experiments in constructing a light car to compete with the Ford. In 1911 the first Chevrolet, a 6-cylinder car, was produced.

In a few years, however, the designer sold out to Durant and returned to his main interest—designing racing cars—as president of the Frontenac Company. Two models that he designed won the Indianapolis 500-mile race in 1920 and 1921. His later career included the designing of aircraft. He died in Detroit on June 6, 1941.

ELEANOR S. BRUCHEY
Michigan State University

CHEVROTAIN, shev'rə-tān, one of four species of small deerlike mammals found in forested regions of tropical Asia and neighboring islands, and in central Africa. Two Asian species are brown with white throat stripes; the third is tan with whitish spots and stripes running lengthwise along the body. These species stand 8 to 13 inches (20–33 cm) at the shoulder and are 17 to 22 inches (43–66 cm) long. The single African species, the water chevrotain, stands about 14 inches (35 cm) at the shoulder and is about 36 inches (90 cm) long. Its coat is rich reddish brown with white spots and streaks. When threatened, it plunges into a stream and runs along the bottom, to emerge beneath overhanging vegetation at the other side.

Chevrotains, often called "mouse deer," are only distantly related to the true deer. Neither sex bears antlers or horns, but the upper canine teeth of males are enlarged into long tusks. In captivity the larger Malayan chevrotain produces a fawn every 5 months, and the reproductive rate in the wild is probably similar. Predators take a heavy toll of these defenseless mammals.

The Asian chevrotains belong to the genus *Tragulus,* and the water chevrotain to *Hyemoschus;* together they constitute the family Tragulidae of the order Artiodactyla.

JOSEPH A. DAVIS, JR.
New York Zoological Society

CHEVY CHASE, che'vē chās, an unincorporated area in central Maryland, is in Montgomery county, east of the Potomac River. It is about 6 miles (10 km) northwest of downtown Washington, D. C., of which it is a fashionable residential suburb. Chevy Chase is situated on the lands of a former estate known as Cheivy Chace, owned by Joseph Belt (1690–1761), a member of the Maryland House of Burgesses and colonel of militia in the French and Indian War. The densely populated area includes two incorporated villages, Chevy Chase and Chevy Chase Section Four, as well as the unincorporated villages of Chevy Chase Lake and Chevy Chase Manor. Chevy Chase is under the jurisdiction of Montgomery county. Population: 16,424.

CHEVY CHASE, chev'ē chās, one of the most famous ballads in English. It celebrates in superbly simple style a bloody conflict in the Cheviot Hills between England and Scotland. "The lord Percy" (Sir Henry Percy, or Hotspur, son of the Earl of Northumberland) vows to hunt three days over the Scottish border. He is challenged by "the doughty Douglas" (James Douglas, 2d Earl of Douglas) to single combat, but Richard Witherington, an English squire, insists on fighting too. A tremendous battle ensues, in which both heroes are slain. The ballad may be based on the historic Battle of Otterburn (1388), in which Douglas was killed and Percy captured, or it may be a dramatic fusing of many border skirmishes. An oral tradition, probably from the 15th century, inspired a 16th century version called *The Hunting of the Cheviot;* there is also a 17th century version.

CHEWING GUM is a sweetened, flavored mixture of chicle and other natural gums used for chewing. From early times man has enjoyed chewing on various gummy substances. The early Greeks chewed gum from the mastic tree, and the Maya Indians chewed chicle more than a thousand years ago. Chewing gum made with chicle and other latex products was developed in the 1860's and soon attained wide popularity.

The manufacture of chewing gum begins with the preparation and blending of the gum base materials. Chicle, the natural gum obtained from the sapodilla tree (*Achras zapota*), is blended with similar latex products, such as sorva and jelutong, to provide a smooth, uniform chewing quality. In blending, these gums are first ground and then melted with pressurized steam. Next, the sterilized gum base is purified by means of

WYOMING TRAVEL COMMISSION

CHEYENNE'S FRONTIER PARK contains pioneer relics including Indian scout Jim Baker's rough-hewn log cabin.

centrifuge machines and fine mesh screens. In this state, the mixture looks very much like a thick syrup.

The next step in chewing gum manufacture is the addition of precisely measured amounts of finely powdered sugar, corn syrup, and flavorings to the gum base. The most popular flavorings are made with spearmint oil, peppermint oil, fruit extracts, and various spices. These ingredients, plus the gum base, are placed in huge mixing kettles, each holding 1,000 to 2,000 pounds (455–910 kg). When mixing is completed, the gum, which has the consistency of bread dough, is kneaded and passed through a series of rollers that gradually reduce it to a long flat continuous ribbon 19½ inches (50 cm) wide. The ribbon is then scored in a pattern of single sticks which are separated as the ribbon enters the wrapping machines. Sometimes the gum is made in small pillow-shaped pieces and coated with sugar or candy in rotating copper pans.

The final step in the manufacture of chewing gum is packaging. Sticks of gum are individually wrapped and gathered into packages that are then tightly sealed.

CHEWINK. See TOWHEE.

CHEYENNE, shī-an', is the capital of Wyoming and the seat of Laramie county. It is located in the southeast corner of the state, on rolling plains at the edge of the Laramie Mountains, 6,062 feet (1,848 meters) above sea level. Cheyenne retains much of the individuality and Western spirit of its colorful early history, but it has incorporated many changes into its life and economy since the mid-20th century. While mindful of its past in the annual pageantry of Cheyenne Frontier Days, and while preserving its historical importance as a railroad and livestock center, modern Cheyenne is a growing industrial city and a defense base of national importance.

Life and Economy. Cheyenne is Wyoming's largest city. Its metropolitan area is the home of nearly one out of five people in the state. It is the business center of an extensive cattle-raising, sheep-raising, and farming region. Three railroads, two interstate expressways, and two airlines converge here, the railroads providing a major source of employment. Unusually good transportation facilities have helped attract small industries, including oil refining, fertilizer processing, and the manufacture of electronic products, precision instruments, valves, and restaurant equipment. Despite this industrial development, the city is noted for its pure air and was cited for it by a U. S. Public Health Service survey in the 1960's. Federal and state government employment are important to the city's livelihood. Adjoining Cheyenne to the northwest is Francis E. Warren Air Force Base, a major installation of the Strategic Air Command.

Features of Interest. Cheyenne Frontier Days, celebrated the last full week in July each year, has been a prime tourist attraction since it was started in 1897. Locally managed and produced, it is one of the top shows in the rodeo circuit. Arena events include bronco busting, chuck wagon races, steer and calf roping, and bulldogging (throwing a steer by seizing its horns and twisting its neck). Indian dances, square dancing, carnival activities, and three mile-long parades entertain the visitors. The parades feature a large collection of antique horse-drawn vehicles.

Year-round points of interest in the city are the state capitol, with its unusual golden dome, and the Wyoming State Museum, which interprets the history of Wyoming and the American West through its collection of historical, ethnological, and archaeological materials. There are many scenic drives near the city.

History. Cheyenne was founded as a division point on the Union Pacific Railroad in 1867. It was named for an Indian tribe, the Shey-an-nah. Fort D. A. Russel was founded here at the same time, to protect settlers and railroad workers against marauding Indians. The post is now Warren Air Force Base.

In its early days Cheyenne was known as "Hell on Wheels" because of the rowdy gangs that followed the railroad construction crews. The town was the cattle headquarters of the West in the 1870's and 1880's. It has been the state capital since Wyoming entered the union in 1890. The city has a commission form of government, headed by a mayor. Population: 40,914.

KATHERINE HALVERSON
*Chief, Historical Division, Wyoming State
Archives and Historical Department*

CHEYENNE INDIANS, shī-an', an important Plains tribe, speaking a language belonging to the Algonkian family. Their name is derived from the Sioux Indian word that means "people of alien speech."

History. In 1804 the explorers Lewis and Clark met the Cheyenne tribe near the Black Hills of South Dakota, but there is evidence that before 1700 the Cheyenne had lived a more settled existence in Minnesota. By the mid-1800's the Cheyenne had become fully adapted to a nomadic way of life based on the hunting of big game, primarily bison and antelope. Fish, small game, and wild vegetable foods supplemented their diet. The Cheyenne lived in skin tepees and used skin clothing.

In the nomadic period, the Cheyenne engaged in almost continuous warfare with neighboring tribes and, after 1860, with the white men. Camps of friendly Cheyenne were attacked by U. S. Army troops at Ash Hollow and Sand Creek, and their women and children were slaughtered. In 1876 the Northern Cheyenne helped defeat Custer's force at Little Bighorn. Later, however, they met military reverses and ceased fighting after destruction of the camps of chiefs Dull Knife and Two Moons. After these defeats, the Northern Cheyenne were resettled in Indian Territory (now Oklahoma) along with the Southern Cheyenne, who had settled earlier in southern Colorado. Several attempts to leave Oklahoma failed; the last was in 1879, when 64 Indians were killed by troops and 78 recaptured. Later one reservation was established in Montana and another in Oklahoma.

Organization. The Cheyenne were organized into 10 main bands made up of family groups. These bands were led by a council of 45 peace chiefs, each a renowned warrior chosen for a 10-year term of office. Cutting across the bands were the military societies. Originally five in number, these increased to seven during the 19th century. They were not kin groups but tightly organized associations centered around common activities and war rituals. Each society had four war leaders, two serving as head chiefs and two as messengers to the Council of Forty-five and the other military societies.

Customs and Ceremonies. The importance of warfare was emphasized by the elaborate rituals and paraphernalia associated with it. Of special importance were decorated shields and feather bonnets, which, if treated by correct ritual, were believed to endow the owner with extra prowess in battle. Female chastity was honored by the Cheyenne, and daughters of the chiefs served as maids of honor in ceremonies and in council. However, in general, women had little real power or authority in tribal affairs.

The Cheyenne possessed a unique ceremony, the annual Renewal of the Sacred Arrows. The arrows symbolized the collective tribal existence, and their spiritual well-being brought prosperity to the tribe as a whole. Other important ceremonies include the Sun Dance, still performed each year, and the Animal Dance, which was unusual for the mimicry and clowning in it. Both of these were performed by other Plains tribes as well. The Peyote Cult has also become important among the Cheyenne today.

The cholera epidemic of 1849 reduced the Cheyenne by almost one third, but the population later began to grow. In the early 1960's over 3,000 Cheyenne lived on reservations.

RICHARD A. GOULD
American Museum of Natural History

Further Reading: Hoebel, E. Adamson, *The Cheyennes* (New York 1960); Lowie, R. H., *Indians of the Plains* (New York 1954).

CHEYNE-STOKES RESPIRATION, chān stōks, is an unusual abnormality in the rate and depth of breathing, caused by serious disorders of the heart, lungs, or central nervous system. In an episode of Cheyne-Stokes respiration, breathing is shallow at first but increases rhythmically until it becomes deep. It then decreases in depth until it stops completely for a brief period. Generally, one complete cycle lasts from 30 to 60 seconds.

RALPH TOMPSETT, M. D.
Baylor University Medical Center

CHIANG CHING-KUO, jē-äng' jing-gwô' (1910–), became the political leader of the Taiwan-based Republic of China in 1975. The eldest son of Chiang Kai-shek and his first wife, he was born in Chikow, Chekiang province, on March 18, 1910. In 1925, while the Kuomintang (Nationalist) party was allied with the Communists, he was sent to Moscow to study. Remaining in the USSR after his father broke with the Communists in 1927, he graduated from the military-political institute in Leningrad, worked in factories, and was married to a Russian. In 1937, he returned to China.

Beginning as an effective administrator in Kiangsi, Chiang gained political experience and became his father's trusted adviser. In the 1950's, after the move to Taiwan, he built up a strong internal security system. In 1965 he became defense minister, and in 1972 prime minister. When the elder Chiang died in 1975, Chiang Ching-kuo was elected to succeed him as leader of the Kuomintang.

While reasserting his father's goal of recovering the Chinese mainland, Prime Minister Chiang concentrated on bolstering the political ment of Taiwan. He also brought into positions of governmental authority more people who were born in Taiwan. In 1978, Chiang was elected president of the republic. He relinquished the premiership but remained Kuomintang chairman.

CHIANG, MAYLING SOONG, jē-äng' (1892–), the wife of Chiang Kai-shek, president of Nationalist China. She was born in Shanghai and was the third and youngest daughter of Sung Yao-ju (Charles Soong), an American-educated businessman. The Soong family became prominent and powerful in Chinese political affairs. Her brother, Soong Tse-wen (T. V. Soong), served as China's premier and her sister, Ai-ling, married Kung Hsiang-hsi (H. H. Kung), who was also premier for a time. Another sister, Ch'ing-ling, married Sun Yat-sen, the revolutionary leader, and was active in revolutionary politics herself. Ch'ing-ling split with the Nationalists in 1949 and became vice chairman of the Chinese Communist government.

Mayling Soong graduated from Wellesley College in the United States in 1917. She met Chiang Kai-shek when he was a young officer in Sun Yat-sen's military service. They were married on Dec. 1, 1927, and shortly after, Chiang became a convert to Christianity.

As the wife of Chiang, Mayling played a significant role in Chinese politics, although she held few official positions. She served chiefly as her husband's adviser and helped negotiate his release from Sian in 1936 when Chiang was kidnapped by troops under the command of Chang Hsüeh-liang. She was the director-general of the New Life Movement and was the first woman to be decorated by the Chinese government. On her many trips to the United States, Mme. Chiang acted as spokesman for the Nationalist government. She addressed the U. S. Congress in 1943, pleaded for aid in 1948, and visited the United States in the spring of 1966. Her published books include *Sian: A Coup d'État* (1937), *This is our China* (1940), and *China Shall Rise Again* (1941).

JAMES R. SHIRLEY
Northern Illinois University

Generalissimo and Madame Chiang Kai-shek

CHIANG KAI-SHEK, jē-äng'kï'shek' (1887–1975), was a Chinese military leader and the first constitutional president of the Republic of China. He was born to a merchant family in Chikou, Chekiang, on Oct. 31, 1887. He is also known by his other name, *Chiang Chung-cheng*.

Chiang received his training at the government military college at Paoting, where he formed attachments with other future military leaders, and in the Japanese army. While in Japan (1907–1911), he became a follower of the Shanghai revolutionary group under Ch'en Ch'i-mei, who introduced him to Sun Yat-sen (q.v.) and whose friends and relatives were later a chief bulwark of his power. He fought in Shanghai under Ch'en during the 1911 Revolution, the "second revolution" of 1913, and the antimonarchical movement of 1915–1916. After Ch'en's assassination in 1916, Chiang remained in Shanghai for two years, a period of his life about which little is known.

Rise to Power. Chiang joined the Kuomintang (KMT), Sun Yat-sen's revolutionary group, in Canton as a military officer in 1918. On the advice of Chiang and others, Sun decided to reorganize the party along Russian lines. In 1923, Chiang went to Russia to study Bolshevik military organization for three months. He received his first important appointment in 1924, when he became head of the Whampoa Military Academy, the training ground of many of China's future military leaders.

After Sun's death in 1925, a battle for party leadership ensued. Chiang consolidated his military position through alliances with the Communists and the Kuomintang left wing, and in 1926 he was appointed commander of the Northern Expedition forces. By a military coup of March 1926 he had broken the power of other party leaders and tried to suppress the Communists but did not make a final break until 1927. During the Northern Expedition, Chiang moved his army to Nanchang and gained the support of the Shanghai foreign communities and businessmen.

He broke the Communist stronghold in Shanghai by arresting the Communist leaders. When the Kuomintang left wing split with Russia over questions of policy, the Communists were expelled, and negotiations were begun with the right wing.

By this time, Chiang had suffered military reverses in the north and temporarily retired from government. However, political maneuvers and alliances with the remaining warlords enabled Chiang to become president of the revolutionary government in Nanking in 1928. He survived repeated crises until 1931, when he was forced to resign. By keeping control of his armies, however, he was able to retain a major share of his political power.

The Sian Incident. From 1931 on, China was beset by the Japanese, who took control of Manchuria. Chiang saw that China was not yet prepared for war with Japan and continued his attempts to suppress the Communists. By 1935 many Chinese favored an end to civil war and the establishment of an anti-Japanese front. When Chiang flew to Sian in 1936, he was arrested by the Manchurian military leader Chang Hsüehliang (q.v.) and held for two weeks. Communist negotiators obtained his release in return for a united front agreement.

During the Chinese-Japanese war (1937–1945), Chiang gained absolute control of the Kuomintang. When the war merged into World War II after Pearl Harbor, he became supreme commander of the allied air and land forces in the Chinese theater of war. In 1943 he again took the presidency of China.

The Civil War. The Japanese surrender in August 1945 was the signal for an immediate struggle between the Nationalists and the Communists for the former Japanese-held territory. When the American-inspired negotiations with the Communists failed in 1947, civil war resumed.

Chiang was elected the first constitutional president of China by the National Assembly in 1948, but his government was failing rapidly. He resigned on Jan. 21, 1949, leaving Vice President Li Tsung-jen to negotiate with the Communists, who had taken Manchuria and were moving south to the Yangtze River. Unable to secure additional aid from the United States, Chiang flew to Taiwan where he had organized a base and was joined by many of his troops and government officials. In 1950 he announced his resumption of the presidency, against Li's protests.

Retreat to Taiwan. Following the Communist victory in 1949, Chiang served as head of the government in Taiwan until his death in Taipei, April 5, 1975. As president, his authority was complete. Although Taiwan was replaced in the United Nations by Communist China in 1971, he never relinquished his claim to legitimate authority over all China. He was incapacitated during his final years.

Before his second marriage, to Mayling Soong, in 1927, he had two sons. The first, Gen. Chiang Ching-kuo, was named premier in the Taipei government in 1972. Chiang Wei-kuo, his other son, also followed a military career.

Among works published under his name are: *China's Destiny* (New York 1947); *The Collected Wartime Messages of Generalissimo Chiang Kai-shek, 1937–1945*, 2 vols. (New York 1946); and *Soviet Russia in China: A Summing-up at Seventy* (New York 1957).

JAMES R. SHIRLEY, *Northern Illinois University*

CHIANGMAI, chē-äng′mī, sometimes known as the northern capital of Thailand, is the country's only city except for Bangkok-Thonburi. Located 465 miles (750 km) north of Bangkok, in a valley amid forested hills, Chiangmai is accessible by road, rail, and plane. The city's architectural and natural beauty have brought it an increasing tourist trade, supplementing the income earned from such agricultural staples as teak, rice, tobacco, longan, peas, garlic, onions, and pepper and from such products of cottage industries as umbrellas, lacquerware, silverware, woodwork, and pottery. The fast-growing University of Chiangmai was founded in 1963.

Established in the 13th century as the capital of the Thai (Tai) prince Mangrai, Chiangmai ("new city") was long a bone of contention among Burmese and rival Thai rulers. Although the presence of Burmese craftsmen (victims of forays into Burma) greatly enriched the area, Burmese troops twice nearly destroyed the city—in the 16th century and again in the 18th century.

Modern Chiangmai has a land area 21 times that of Bangkok and a population of about 800,-000 in its metropolitan area. Population: (1960) of the city, 65,600.

PRACHOOM CHOMCHAI
Chulalongkorn University, Bangkok

CHIAPAS, chyä′päs, bordering the Pacific Ocean and Guatemala, is Mexico's most southerly state. Most of its area of 28,528 square mies (73,887 sq km) is part of the Chiapas-Guatemala highlands. The vegetation varies from tropical savanna, monsoon jungle, and rain forest to the pine and oak forests of the temperate highlands. The leading cities are Tapachula (1960 population 41,578) and Tuxtla Gutiérrez (41,244), the capital. Most of the state's inhabitants are mestizos, but about one third are Indians.

Chiapas is a leading agricultural and livestock state and is the chief Mexican producer of coffee and cacao. Construction of the Netzahualcóyotl dam and hydroelectric project on the Río Grande de Chiapa in the 1960's promised further economic development.

In Chiapas are the ruins of Palenque, Yaxchilán, Bonampak, and Toniná, among the most important archaeological sites of the Classic Mayan period.

Chiapas was conquered by the Spaniards in 1524–1527. In 1821 it broke away from Guatemala, and in 1824 it became one of the original 19 states of Mexico. Population: (1960) 1,210,870.

DONALD D. BRAND, *The University of Texas*

CHIARI, chē′ä-rē, **Roberto Francisco** (1905–   ), Panamanian president from 1960 to 1964. Born in Panama City on March 2, 1905, he was the son of Rodolfo Chiari, who was president of the nation from 1924 to 1928. In a varied political career, he served in the legislature and the cabinet, was vice president, and held the presidency for five days in November 1949.

Chiari was elected to a regular 4-year presidential term on May 8, 1960. At first he advocated close relations with the United States. However, he soon added his voice to the popular demand for revision of the treaty regulating U.S. control of the Panama Canal. Following a violent clash between Panamanians and U. S. forces in January 1964, he briefly broke off diplomatic relations with the United States.

LAURENCE R. BIRNS
The New School for Social Research, New York

CHIAROSCURO, kē-är-ə-skyōōr′ō, in painting, drawing, and graphics, is the relationship of light and shade in a work of art. The terms is derived from the Italian words *chiaro* (light) and *oscuro* (shade). Chiaroscuro involves the handling of values from white to black and determines the degree to which objects are modeled or give the illusion of three-dimensionality.

In Western art, Roman illusionist murals and mosaics are among the first works that show a concern with the effects of light and shade. Not until the 15th century, with Leonardo da Vinci's scientific examination of visual phenomena, did chiaroscuro become a prime consideration in art. It reached a climax in the late 16th and early 17th centuries in the canvases of Michelangelo da Caravaggio. His use of violently contrasting bright light and dark shadow serves to isolate and dramatize the figures and create a strong feeling of three-dimensional form.

Caravaggio's influence was felt throughout Europe. In Naples, chiaroscuro effects were adopted by Caravaggio's contemporaries Giovanni Battista Caracciolo and Massimo Stanzioni. Henrik Terbrugghen and Gerard van Honthorst carried Caravaggio's style to Holland, where it was transmitted to Rembrandt. Caravaggio's influence is seen in the work of the 17th century artists Francisco de Zurbarán and José Ribera of Spain and in that of Georges de La Tour of France.

The lightness and delicacy of the rococo style of the 18th century were a reaction against chiaroscuro effects. These effects, however, were revived by the neoclassic and the romantic painters. In Oriental art, which was never very much concerned with naturalistic representation, chiaroscuro effects are of little importance.

In the graphic arts chiaroscuro refers to a particular woodblock technique. Developed by Ugo da Carpi in the late 15th century, this form uses several woodblocks to achieve successive effects of dark to light.

WILLIAM GERDTS, *University of Maryland*

CHIAROSCURO is used strikingly in *St. Sebastian Nursed by St. Irene,* a painting by artist Georges de la Tour.

COURTESY OF THE DETROIT INSTITUTE OF ARTS

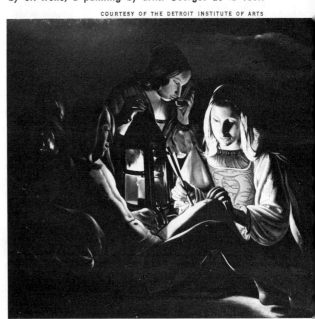

CHIBA, chē-bä, a city in Japan, is the capital of Chiba prefecture on Honshu island. It is located on Tokyo Bay, 25 miles (40 km) by rail east of Tokyo. Chiba has an 8th century Buddhist temple and a medical school. A large steel mill, built in 1952, is the major industrial plant in the city. Chiba also produces cotton goods and processes foods. Population: (1960) 241,615.

CHIBCHA, chib′chä, the native population of the high plateau of Bogotá in central Colombia at the time the region was discovered by Europeans. The Chibcha, also called *Muisca*, were a farming people, cultivating corn, potatoes, quinoa, and many other native Andean food crops. They lived in towns, some of them of considerable size; Chibcha Bogotá, for example, is reported to have contained 20,000 houses. The buildings in these towns were constructed of wood with walls of cane and mud, so that they have not produced the spectacular ruins found in areas like Mexico and Peru. The Chibcha wove cotton cloth for clothing, and they manufactured jewelry of gold and emeralds.

Politically, the Chibcha were organized into many small city-states, often at war with one another. In the early 16th century A. D., the Zipa dynasty of Bogotá under Nemequene and his nephew, Tisquesusa, built up a powerful feudal state in the southern third of Chibcha territory. The rival Zaque dynasty at Tunja provided the major opposition, but there were a number of lesser rulers involved as well. The Zipa dynasty enjoyed absolute power throughout the dominions it controlled.

Chibcha religion was rich in mythology, ceremonies, and organization. A number of the chief gods were nature deities, of whom the Sun was one of the most important; human sacrifices were made to him. Other deities received offerings of gold, emeralds, incense, corn, beer, and other prized materials. Fasting and ritual bathing were practiced, and public ceremonies included imposing processions. There was a professional celibate priesthood, and the Chibcha recognized a high priest of the entire nation, who was entitled Sugamuxi.

The Chibcha were conquered by Spanish armies between 1536 and 1541, and their religion and native political organization were soon suppressed. The Chibcha language became extinct in the 18th century, but the descendants of the Chibcha still form the basic rural population of their original homeland.

JOHN HOWLAND ROWE
University of California

Further Reading: Kroeber, A. L., "The Chibcha," *Handbook of South American Indians,* Bureau of American Ethnology, Bulletin 143, vol. 2, pp. 887–909 (Washington 1946); Pérez de Barradas, José, *Los Musicas antes de la conquista,* 2 vols. (Madrid 1950–1951); Steward, Julian H., and Faron, Louis C., *Native Peoples of South America* (New York 1959).

CHIBOUGAMAU, shi-boo′gə-moo, is a town in central Quebec province, Canada, in Abitibi county. It is 185 miles (298 km) northwest of Chicoutimi, on the northwest shore of Chibougamau Lake. It is a gold- and copper-mining center in a heavily wooded region. The town is the terminus of the 150-mile (240 km) highway from St.-Félicien, which cuts through the Chibougamau forest reserve. Mining was first carried on here in 1903. The town was laid out in 1950. Population: 9,701.

CHICAGO, shə-kä′gō, in northeastern Illinois, is the second most populous city in the United States and the center of the third-largest metropolitan area. As a focus of manufacturing, trade, and finance, its influence is felt throughout the nation.

Situated on Lake Michigan at the edge of relatively flat prairie country, the city's complex covers a large region. The Chicago standard metropolitan statistical area includes the counties of McHenry and Lake, on the border of Wisconsin, Kane and DuPage, west of the city, and Cook and Will counties, bordering on Indiana. The standard consolidated area also includes Lake and Porter counties in Indiana. In Lake county, Ind., is the Gary-Hammond-East Chicago industrial complex, dominated by steel mills.

1. Introduction

Viewed from Lake Michigan, the Chicago skyline presents a wall of skyscrapers springing up behind a lakefront area that has been kept virtually free of commercial activity to provide a well-kept "front yard" for Chicagoans. Upper- and middle-class homes hug the lakefront and spread outward toward the suburban fringes. The city's streets are laid out according to a conventional grid design, with only an occasional street deviating from the pattern by following an old Indian trail. The heart of the city is known as the Loop. Originally this signified the principal commercial area, which was circled by elevated trains. But with the coming of the subway, increased use of motor cars, and expansion of the commercial area, "the Loop" now refers generally to the central business district of the city.

Chicago has long been a vital transportation center. The world's largest rail terminal is in Chicago, oceangoing steamships dock at Chicago's wharves, and O'Hare Airport is the busiest in the world. Thriving businesses such as printing and publishing, electronics, iron and steel, and wholesaling and retailing form a large part of the economic activity in Chicago.

CHICAGO'S skyline has three of the world's tallest buildings: the Sears Tower (*far left*), Standard Oil (Ind.) Building (*center*), and John Hancock Center (*right center*).

Geography has greatly influenced Chicago's development. Its location as a natural portage between Lake Michigan and inland rivers brought settlers and trade, yet the same proximity to important waterways caused the land to be marshy and hard to develop. Chicago literally had to pull itself out of the mud to become the nation's second-largest city in a little over 100 years.

During this turbulent period of its growth, Chicago acquired certain characteristics that distinguished it from other American cities. It was a booming frontier town for a long time. Later it welcomed thousands of immigrants from overseas to spur the development of its industries and commerce. The city's roughness and raw force was glorified by the poet Carl Sandburg, who said Chicago was "Stormy, husky, brawling; City of the Big Shoulders." Some of the lawlessness of the earlier days was revived in the 1920's, during the prohibition era, when gangsters were powerful. But the progressive vitality of Chicago as manifest in its rich economy and the vigor of its people remains a treasured legacy of the frontier period.

The growth in Chicago's population from the Civil War until World War II was staggering. This growth has left its mark on the present character of Chicago, since much of it resulted from immigration, and many of the immigrants settled in racial or ethnic groups. The first large ethnic group to reach Chicago was the Germans. They were followed by the Irish, Italians, Mexicans, Puerto Ricans, Scandinavians, eastern Europeans, and, more recently, Southern blacks.

2. Urban Development

Chicago has shared with other metropolitan areas the dilemma of decay in the central city, as middle-class neighborhoods have surrendered to the encroaching slums and former inhabitants have fled to the newer suburban fringes. Since the late 1940's, when Chicago's growth rate diminished, the city has settled into a pattern that seems to characterize mature urban areas. Population declined 7% from 3,620,962 in 1950 to 3,369,359 in 1970, as white middle-class and working-class families migrated to the suburbs.

Unlike many large cities, however, Chicago has waged an effective war against internal dilapidation and seems to have turned the tide. Many new buildings and complexes are rising in Chicago, and older residential areas are being conserved.

Urban Renewal. Chicago is no stranger to the concept of urban renewal. As early as 1908, Daniel H. Burnham, a Chicagoan who was one of America's great architects, submitted a plan for urban growth that shaped Chicago's development for the next half century. In it Burnham proposed the city's now famous system of parks and forest preserves and a lakefront free of commercial activity. This was, however, primarily a visual plan. It was not concerned with the social and economic factors of metropolitan growth.

In the 1940's, urban decay caused widespread concern among government and civic leaders. This concern resulted in the clearance of about 23 acres (10 hectares) of slums but not in redevelopment of the area. More recent urban renewal efforts have been based on comprehensive urban planning. These developments were

---

INFORMATION HIGHLIGHTS

Location: Northeast Illinois, on southwest shore of Lake Michigan.

Population: City, 3,369,359 (2d in U.S.); *metropolitan area*, 6,978,947 (3d in U.S.).

Land Area: 224.2 square miles (575 sq km).

Elevation: 595 feet (180 meters) in business area.

Climate: *Mean temperatures,* 26.1°F (−3°C) in January; 75.7°F (25°C) in July. *Mean annual precipitation,* 33.18 inches (74 cm).

Government: Mayor and council.

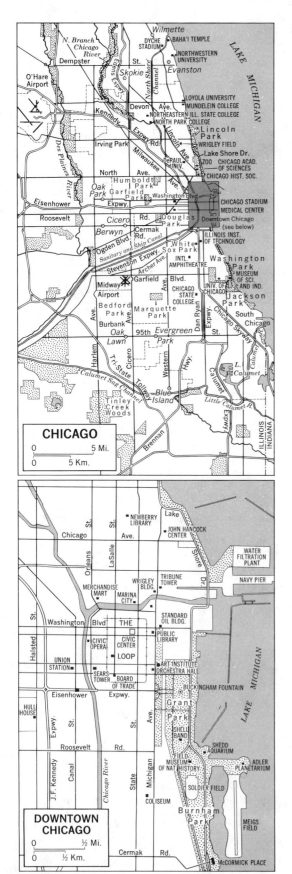

CHICAGO

0 ____ 5 Mi.

0 ____ 5 Km.

DOWNTOWN CHICAGO

0 ____ ½ Mi.

0 ____ ½ Km.

pioneered by the Illinois Institute of Technology and the University of Chicago. Both institutions have aided renewal in the areas surrounding their campuses.

Community development projects in Chicago have stressed selective demolition and the conservation and rehabilitation of property. Such projects have been prepared by the city of Chicago under the direction of its department of urban renewal. The department has developed the Comprehensive Plan of Chicago, which seeks to coordinate the rehabilitation of social, economic, and physical factors in the city. A series of plans for 16 areas of the city coordinates transportation, industrial development, recreational and educational opportunities, housing, medical facilities, and social rehabilitation.

The Comprehensive Plan has designated 21,-400 acres (8,660 hectares) in the north, south, and west parts of the city as major improvement areas. In other areas conservation and rehabilitation projects will renovate older neighborhoods. The object of this plan is to develop a city that will provide proper living conditions for all its citizens.

Despite gains made in redevelopment of housing in Chicago, low-income housing still remains a problem. Middle- and upper-income housing has been provided in such developments as Carl Sandburg Village, Prairie Shores (sponsored by the Illinois Institute of Technology), and Hyde Park-Kenwood (sponsored by the University of Chicago), and in rehabilitation areas like those on the West Side of Chicago. The Chicago Dwellings Association rehabilitates housing and sells it somewhat below market level to lower-middle-class buyers. But the poor of Chicago still live primarily in slums, and the new housing developments have not broken down the community pattern of racial segregation. The Rev. Martin Luther King chose Chicago to begin his first major northern civil rights campaign in 1966, saying that the slums of Chicago were "the prototype of those chiefly responsible for the Northern race problem." To combat these social and material problems, the city has acted to implement urban opportunity programs, education and job training, public housing, and social services.

Rapid Transit and Highways. Since 1974, mass transportation in the Chicago area has been coordinated by a Regional Transportation Authority (RTA) covering the six northeastern Illinois counties. Existing transportation systems—including the Chicago Transit Authority, which operated independently from 1945 to 1974—were consolidated into an independent public body that operates an efficient and coordinated mass-transit system throughout the metropolitan area. The RTA provides transportation close to almost every home and office in Chicago by bus, subway, commuter railroad, or rapid transit. This system is supplemented by a large fleet of taxicabs and by helicopter services.

In spite of the public transportation available, more than half of all personal trips in the Chicago metropolitan area are made by automobile, putting a great burden on Chicago streets and parking facilities. To meet these needs, several parking garages and a number of expressways have been built in and around the city. Chicago was the first city to install rapid-transit lines in the medians of expressways, thus utilizing valuable space.

STEEL MILLS, like this one in South Chicago, dominate the industrial complex that stretches eastward along the Lake Michigan shorefront to Gary, Indiana.

3. The Economy

The four main components of Chicago's economy are manufacturing, wholesale and retail trade, finance, and the provision of services. Trade, particularly in agricultural commodities such as grain and livestock, has historically been a fundamental of the Chicago economy. Manufacturing, now the dominant economic factor, was introduced by Cyrus McCormick when he built a plant in Chicago to manufacture his newly invented reapers in 1847. Now, with 3.8% of the nation's population, the Chicago area contributes 5.1% of the gross national product. Incomes in Chicago average approximately 142% of the national average income level.

Manufacturing. Manufacturing is the largest supplier of jobs in Chicago, employing about a third of those working in the city. Manufacturing enterprises are concentrated in the fields of metal and machinery—high output industries that provide good wages for the labor they employ. The four major iron and steel industries—electrical machinery, nonelectrical machinery, primary metals, and fabricated metals and instruments—become more important as continued regional dispersion brings a decline in Chicago's "export" industries, such as leather products and agricultural products.

Trade and Finance. Although the economy of early Chicago was based on wholesale and retail trade, today these enterprises make up a much smaller portion of Chicago's economic life. The Swift and Armour meat-packing companies have moved from Chicago, and the famous stockyards closed in July 1971. Most trading in agricultural commodities is now done on paper at the Chicago Board of Trade and the Mercantile Exchange. Wholesale and retail trade is still an important part of Chicago's economic life, however, employing nearly one fourth of those working in the city. Marshall Field, Carson Pirie Scott, and Sears Roebuck are still durable names in retailing. In the 1970's a number of new stores were located along what Chicago likes to call its "Magnificent Mile," the stretch of Michigan Avenue from the Chicago River north to Oak Street. Many of these stores are found in the Watertower Plaza.

Chicago is an important financial center in the Midwest. The Chicago Board of Trade acts as the price leader in grain and livestock futures for the entire country. The Chicago Mercantile Exchange, where contracts for perishable goods are bought and sold, is the largest in the world. The Midwest Stock Exchange, with 400 companies listed, is another of the city's important financial institutions. The banking industry is also a prosperous one in Chicago.

Transportation. Chicago is a hub of the federal interstate highway system in the Midwest, giving the city natural advantages as a trucking capital. It also forms a key point in the interstate railroad network, which, while it is not as vital to the nation as it was during World War II and earlier, still constitutes an important means of freight transportation. On a normal day, approximately 35,000 railroad freight cars, with an average capacity of 50 short tons (45 metric tons), are handled in the Chicago yards.

Chicago's natural advantages as a waterway transportation center have been improved by the construction of several strategically placed canals that increase the Great Lakes shipping traffic. The opening of the St. Lawrence Seaway in 1958 gave oceangoing vessels access to the port of Chicago via the Great Lakes. When ships arrive in Chicago they may dock at the port facilities of the Navy Pier, the Chicago regional port district, or the Chicago sanitary port district.

Chicago has risen rapidly as a center for air transportation. O'Hare International Airport is the busiest airport in the world, serving approximately 37 million passengers a year with daily operations averaging about 1,900 plane movements.

Midway Airport, which yielded to O'Hare its title of "busiest in the world," now receives few scheduled flights of major airlines. Its commuter traffic, however, is becoming more important. Of the three airports in Chicago, Meigs Field is the smallest. Known as a "businessman's airport," Meigs Field is situated only a few minutes from the Loop.

4. Education and Cultural Life

Chicago's system of public education from kindergarten through high school or trade school is governed by the Chicago board of education. The school system includes vocational high schools, technical high schools, and Washburne Trade School, which allows students to combine job training with part-time apprenticeship in a trade.

The Chicago Picasso, a five-story-high steel sculpture by the Spanish artist, stands in the Daley Plaza.

The Catholic archdiocese of Chicago maintains elementary and high schools. The Lutheran Church also educates a substantial number of Chicago youth, and a few other religious bodies maintain educational institutions below the college level or offer supplementary classes in religious education.

Higher Education. The University of Illinois in downstate Urbana has had a Chicago branch since 1893, when the medical center became part of the university. The medical center confers degrees at the associate, bachelor's, master's, certificate, first professional, and doctoral levels in 40 program areas. An undergraduate branch of the University of Illinois was opened in Chicago in 1946 and installed in the Navy Pier building. In 1965 the University of Illinois at Chicago Circle, a handsome new urban campus near the downtown Loop, replaced the Navy Pier accommodations. It offers graduate work in many fields, in addition to baccalaureate degrees.

The Chicago community college system comprises eight junior colleges. The board of governors of state colleges and universities administers three senior-level institutions in the city—Chicago State University, Governors State University, and Northeastern Illinois.

The University of Chicago—once a defunct Baptist college—has become a world-renowned center of learning. Contributing to its birth and growth were the monetary gifts of John D. Rockefeller and Marshall Field and the intellectual gifts of its first president, William Rainey Harper.

Northwestern University was founded in suburban Evanston, on the northern border of the city, in 1851. Many classes in the law, medical, and business schools are now held in downtown Chicago. The Illinois Institute of Technology, formerly Armour Institute, has played an important part not only in scientific and technical education but also in contributing a philosophy of urban renewal to the city.

The two major Catholic universities are De-Paul University and Loyola University. The Presbyterian Church operates Lake Forest College. One of the younger private institutions is Roosevelt University, which was formerly the Central YMCA University. It is housed in historic surroundings in the old Auditorium Hotel on Michigan Avenue.

Libraries. Chicago's public library system, which has about 70 branches, is supplemented by several distinguished private libraries. Chicago was without a public library until 1873, when British donors sent 7,000 volumes to establish one. The library was originally housed in a water tank behind the Rookery office building at Adams and LaSalle streets. The main public library building now stands on a beautiful site on Michigan Avenue, near the lakefront.

There are several libraries in Chicago famed for specialized collections. The Newberry Library, established in 1885, maintains an important collection in the humanities. It is complemented by the John Crerar Library, established in 1897, which has collections in the natural, physical, and social sciences. The Chicago Historical Society maintains a library of writings and documents of historical importance to the city, as does the Municipal Reference Library. The latter provides an archive of public documents and information concerning municipal government.

Museums. The Art Institute of Chicago, with a collection valued at more than $250 million, is one of the four largest art museums in America. It also maintains a library with important collections in art and architecture. In terms of numbers of visitors, the most popular of Chicago's museums is the Museum of Science and Industry, where scientific and industrial exhibits often permit actual participation or manipulation by the observer. The Field Museum, formerly the Chicago Natural History Museum, has occupied its location in Grant Park since 1921. Its exhibits embrace anthropology, geology, botany, and zoology, and like the Art Institute, it is heavily engaged in research, publication, and teaching. Near the Field Museum in Grant Park are the John G. Shedd Aquarium and the Adler Planetarium and Astronomical Museum. The Chicago Historical Society maintains a museum in Lincoln Park concerned with Chicago history and the era of Abraham Lincoln.

Cultural Organizations. Chicago's most famous musical organization is the Chicago Symphony Orchestra, which was established in 1891. Under a succession of fine directors, the symphony has achieved world renown. The Lyric Opera Company was established in 1954, but encountered financial difficulties.

During the summer months, concerts are given at Ravinia Park in Highland Park, a suburb of Chicago. Ravinia is an outdoor pavilion used for productions of various kinds. There are a number of theaters that present the productions of traveling companies. Also, the Goodman Memorial Theatre of the Art Institute gives several fine productions each year.

Architecture. Chicago was the birthplace of the famous Chicago school of architecture, which flourished in the late 19th and early 20th centuries. Daniel H. Burnham, William LeBaron Jenney, Louis Henri Sullivan, and Frank Lloyd Wright were some of the great architects connected with this school. They sought to free architecture from the shackles of classical tradition. The Monadnock Building, the Great Banqueting Hall of the Auditorium Hotel (now the library of Roosevelt University), the Rookery, Home Insurance Building, and the Carson Pirie Scott store are some of the most noted works of the Chicago school.

A spurt of building in the 1920's produced many of Chicago's present landmarks. The Gothic design of the Tribune Tower resulted from an international competition conducted by the Chicago *Tribune* in 1922. The twin towers of the white, ornately designed Wrigley Building remind many observers of a birthday cake. The Merchandise Mart, built in 1930, is the largest commercial building in the world, enclosing about 4 million square feet (370,000 square meters).

After the Depression, the first building of major importance to be built in the Loop was the Prudential Building, constructed in 1955. Since that time, the Chicago school of architecture has largely been replaced by the school of International architecture, exemplified by Ludwig Mies van der Rohe. Mies designed such buildings as Crown Hall on the campus of the Illinois Institute of Technology, Lake Shore Drive Apartments, and the Federal Center, all of which embody his functional and utilitarian type of design. The 31-story Civic Center, another example of modern architecture in Chicago, provides not only city offices and courtrooms but also a handsome plaza dominated by Pablo Picasso's great steel sculpture, 50 feet (15 meters) tall and weighing 163 tons.

The University of Illinois' Chicago Circle campus is another interesting architectural complex. Its concrete structures vary in height and design, and its 28-story University Hall is unusual in having a greater width at the top than at street level. It rises above the Exedra, or "Great Court," where classes may meet or students may gather in open-air surroundings. Standing on the campus, a renovated Hull House, the famous settlement house founded in 1889 by Jane Addams, reminds sightseers of a now-historic Chicago.

The Chicago Amphitheater is the home of the annual International Livestock Exposition and has been the site of several national political party conventions. McCormick Place, built on the lakefront in 1960 to assure Chicago's place as the primary convention and trade show center of the country, burned to the ground in January 1967. It has since been rebuilt.

Symbolic of the "new Chicago" are the twin round apartment buildings of Marina City. These tubular structures are part of a complex containing 900 apartments and complementary facilities.

Chicago now has three of the world's tallest buildings: the Sears Tower (1,454 feet, or 442 meters), the Standard Oil (Indiana) Building (1,136 feet, or 345 meters), and the John Hancock Center (1,127 feet, or 342 meters).

Newspapers. Chicago has two newspaper firms. The McCormick-Patterson interests own the Chicago *Tribune*. Field Enterprises publishes the *Sun-Times*. Its *Daily News*, which began operations in 1875, ceased publishing in 1978.

Chicago has become an important center for the black press. Publications such as the *Daily Defender, Ebony, Jet,* and the *Negro Digest* are directed at nationwide black audiences. The foreign language press, once very important in Chi-

CHICAGO TOURISM COUNCIL

ROUND TOWERS of Marina City, an apartment house complex, rise on the north bank of the Chicago River.

cago, has dwindled somewhat as more ethnic groups have become English-speaking.

Television and Radio. Chicago has nine television stations, including one educational station, and 28 radio stations. All of the major networks maintain both television and radio stations in Chicago.

5. Recreation

With its system of parks and forest preserves, for which Chicago long has been famous, and its spectator sports, the city has much to offer the seeker of outdoor recreation.

Parks and Forest Preserves. Lincoln Park, the largest of the city parks, contains several landmarks and museums as well as the Lincoln Park Zoo and the children's farm. At the Brookfield Zoo, west of Chicago, uncaged animals may be observed in seminatural habitats. In Jackson Park, which was developed on the lakefront for the Columbian Exposition of 1893, is the Museum of Science and Industry, housed in what was the Fine Arts Building of the exposition. North of Jackson Park are Grant Park and Burnham Park, the combination of parks that gives Chicago its famous "front yard" along the shore of Lake Michigan. In Grant Park are the Field Museum, the Shedd Aquarium, and Soldier Field, an outdoor arena. The Art Institute is in Burnham Park.

Sports. Chicago is one of the few remaining cities to sponsor two major league baseball teams, the Chicago Cubs of the National League and the Chicago White Sox of the American League. Chicago also has a professional football team, the Chicago Bears; a professional hockey club, the Chicago Black Hawks; and the Chicago Bulls of the National Basketball Association. Also prominent in sports in Chicago are five racetracks: Arlington, Washington, Hawthorne, Sportsmen's, and Maywood.

6. Government

The population of the Chicago metropolitan area represents about two thirds that of the entire state of Illinois. The city is the seat of Cook county, and some of the governmental functions of the city are shared with the county. At the same time the city, because of its unique size, often finds itself in political and legislative difficulties with the state government. There are no other large urban areas in Illinois, and Chicago is 30 times more populous than the next-largest city in the state, Rockford. The result is that for political purposes Illinois is considered to be divided between the Chicago area and "downstate," which means everything outside the metropolitan area.

City of Chicago. The city government is organized on a mayor-council plan. Chicago and other large Illinois cities have had their powers enhanced by "home rule," granted by the new state constitution that went into effect in 1970. Each of the 50 Chicago aldermen (councilmen) is elected from a ward on an officially nonpartisan basis, although usually both major political parties back slates of candidates.

The mayor, elected to a four-year term, is the chief executive officer of the city. He administers its 24 departments and prepares its budget. Since he also appoints (with the "advice and consent" of the city council) members of many governing boards, his sphere of influence in the city government is broad.

Chicago is the only remaining major urban area in the United States where a political machine has remained efficient enough to cope with urban problems while still surviving by the traditional means of patronage and political favors. The Democratic party machine is highly organized in Chicago, and greatly strengthens the power of any Democratic mayor.

Cook County. Nearly two thirds of the population of Cook county is within the Chicago city limits. Suburban Cook county contains much of the wealth and the middle-class population that has moved from the central city. These county residents, with few exceptions, are much opposed to becoming involved in the complex problems of the central city.

The principal governmental agency in the county is the Cook county board of commissioners. This is a 15-member board, with ten members elected at-large from Chicago and five at-large from the suburbs. The administrative head of the county is the board president. The board is empowered to lay and collect taxes and to issue bonds to support such services as highways, hospitals, and charitable institutions.

Board of Education. The 11 members of the board of education are appointed to five-year overlapping terms by the mayor with the "advice and consent" of the city council. After their appointment, members of the board are relatively free of any formal control by the city government.

Metropolitan Sanitary District of Greater Chicago. Because of the fragmentation of government in the Chicago area, some important governing bodies are at least semiautonomous and do not have boundaries coextensive with those of the city. The metropolitan sanitary district of Greater Chicago, whose officers are elected from the county on a partisan basis, is an example of such a government. The sanitary district was established in 1889, on the crest of public concern over the rise of waterborne diseases, to keep the city's Lake Michigan water supply pure.

Park and Forest Preserve Districts. The Chicago park district is a separate unit of government, legally independent of the city government except that the mayor appoints its five-member board of commissioners. The board controls 486 parks and playgrounds, including the 28 miles (45 km) of lakeshore. The lakeshore beaches, drives, and parks are situated on land that is about 60% man-made.

The forest preserve district, unlike the park district, serves all of Cook county. This agency is responsible for maintaining recreational facilities such as golf courses, hiking trails, and acres of forest preserve land.

7. History

Geography has played an important role in Chicago's growth throughout its history. Commonly used by the Indians as a portage, Chicago got its name from the Indian word *chicagou*, generally agreed by scholars to mean "strong" or "powerful." Chicago's position as a natural portage to the West and South drew traders and trappers from the East who became its first settlers. Louis Jolliet and Jacques Marquette, the French explorers, in 1673 became the first Europeans to visit the Chicago area. Jean Baptiste Point du Sable, a trader, lived on land that is now part of downtown Chicago. He left in 1796, leaving his trading business in the hands of John Kinzie, who became its first permanent white settler.

On Aug. 17, 1803, Capt. John Whistler of the U. S. Army arrived in the area with a company of soldiers, to build Fort Dearborn. At the beginning of the War of 1812 the fort was destroyed, and all its inhabitants except two women and a trader were massacred by Indians allied with the British. Largely because of its strategic location, the United States was determined to rebuild Fort Dearborn and sent Capt. Hezekiah Bradley with 112 men to reconstruct it in 1816. The presence of the rebuilt fort soon attracted new settlers to the area.

Chicago grew rather slowly until Aug. 4, 1830, when the community came legally into existence with the filing of a plat for 48 blocks and fractional blocks. Two years later, news of the Black Hawk War in Illinois drew attention to Chicago. The resulting boom was aided by an 1833 congressional appropriation of $25,000 to build a harbor there. Shortly thereafter, on Aug. 5, 1833, Chicago, with 43 houses and 200 inhabitants, was incorporated as a village. It was incorporated as a city in 1837.

Growth as a City. Chicago grew by seven-league steps in these early days, weathering a great boom and bust in land speculation from 1833 to 1839 to emerge as a city based firmly on trade. Afterward, Chicago kept growing at a rapid pace, without much regard for form or fashion. The streets were often seas of mud lined with hastily constructed buildings. In this condition Chicago launched its career as a convention city in 1847, when it was host to the Rivers and Harbors Convention. This was an auspicious beginning, for it brought to Chicago many businessmen, like Cyrus McCormick, who stayed to aid in the city's development.

Chicago became a convention city once again in 1860, when Abraham Lincoln was nominated for the U. S. presidency at the Republican National Convention. The campaign that followed found the sentiments of Chicagoans divided between the candidates. Lincoln was familiar to most people in the state because of his famous debates with Stephen A. Douglas in their campaign for the Senate two years earlier. Douglas, who won the Senate race, was Lincoln's unsuccessful opponent for the presidency.

The Civil War brought real prosperity and a place in the national economy to Chicago. Cyrus McCormick's reapers gained fame when Lincoln claimed they were worth an army of field hands. The Civil War also stimulated development of specialization in manufacturing and food processing.

The tumultuous growth of both the economy and the population during the Civil War days was aided by the growth of railroads. The Galena and Union Railway had been established in 1848. By 1853, Chicago was establishing itself as a primary terminal. Within two years there were nearly 3,000 miles (4,800 km) of track touching Chicago, owned by 11 branch lines and 10 trunk lines. The 96 trains a day brought immigrants into Chicago and took trade goods out. By the end of the Civil War, the population of Chicago had risen to 300,000.

Much of this transformation of Chicago was guided by Potter Palmer, a Quaker boy who had emerged from the land speculation era with a swampy piece of land he had bought for $25. On this land he created State Street, which he felt would become a prominent shopping area. He also built the Palmer House, one of the most sumptuous hotels of its day. In 1863 he formed a partnership with Marshall Field and Levi Z. Leiter, which later developed into the great merchandising firm of Marshall Field and Company.

The Great Fire. Most of the buildings erected in the previous half century were destroyed in 1871 by the Great Chicago Fire, which raged out of control from October 8 until October 10. One of the few surviving buildings was the Gothic water tower on the near North Side, which has become a sentimental landmark for Chicagoans. Many predicted the demise of Chicago, but with reserves of strength peculiar to young and vital cities, 6,000 temporary structures were put up by the end of the first week after the fire. The fire had given Chicago a chance to start over again with higher standards of construction and better planning. Businesses were quickly rebuilt, and Chicago returned to the economic life of the nation stronger than before.

Labor Difficulties. The rapid growth of Chicago's manufacturing industries was not accomplished without mounting difficulties between management and labor. In 1884 unemployment grew and greater frictions developed. In May 1886 violence broke out when a bomb was thrown into a meeting where 180 policemen had been dispatched to quiet a restless crowd. This so-called Haymarket Riot sparked a roundup of laborites and suspected anarchists, four of whom were hanged for the killing of seven policemen. Another famous labor incident, the Pullman strike, occurred in 1894, when workers of the Pullman railroad car company went on strike after George M. Pullman reduced wages but refused to lower prices in the town of Pullman (now part of Chicago), which was controlled by the company. The strike was eventually quelled by federal troops.

Columbian Exposition. A landmark in Chicago's development was the exposition that opened there on May 1, 1893, to commemorate the 400th anniversary of Columbus' discovery of the Western Hemisphere. The selection of Chicago as the site

THE 1893 WORLD'S FAIR was an important landmark in Chicago's development. Domed building at right is now the city's popular Museum of Science and Industry.

for the Columbian Exposition focused worldwide attention on the city.

The primary aim of the exposition was to illustrate scientific progress and its application to industry. The exhibits brought Chicago into contact with some of the most advanced ideas of the day. One direct result was the installation in Chicago of the first electric transit system in the United States. Besides the scientific and industrial displays, the exposition was composed of buildings designed by outstanding architects. The Midway, the amusement area of the exposition, introduced Chicago to such memorable novelties as Little Egypt, the "exotic dancer," and the Ferris wheel.

Cultural Renaissance. The period from 1890 until the 1920's is known as Chicago's cultural renaissance. In 1891 the Chicago Symphony was established under the direction of Theodore Thomas, who began building the fine reputation the symphony enjoys today. The first Chicago opera company was established in 1910. Its leading soprano, Mary Garden, with her unorthodox combination of dramatic style and musicianship, came to personify Chicago opera in these early days. Her efforts as a director led the company to financial ruin, however. In 1922 a second attempt to establish an opera company failed when its financial director, Samuel Insull, was discredited in the fall of his financial empire. Chicago was again without its own opera company until 1954, when the Lyric Opera was established with Maria Callas as its first star.

Chicago's literary community was probably most responsible for the city's cultural renaissance. Eugene Field, Peter Finley Dunne, Hamlin Garland, Henry Blake Fuller, Robert Herrick, Frank Norris, Theodore Dreiser, and Carl Sandburg are some of the writers whose names highlight the period. Several noteworthy literary magazines were established during this era. One of these was the *Little Review*, which was published in Chicago from 1914 to 1916, when it moved to New York, and another was *Poetry: A Magazine of Verse*.

World War I. World War I changed the course of Chicago's economic life from trade to manufacturing. Chicago rose to the escalating need for war materials by building up the iron and steel industries that remain foremost in Chicago's economy today. At the same time the agricultural industries began their steady decline. The once-dominant meat packers gradually moved away from Chicago, taking with them the dependent leather industries.

The rise in industrial activity drew many Southern blacks to Chicago in search of work and increased opportunities. As their numbers grew, racial tension mounted, and Chicago suffered five days of rioting in 1919 during which 38 were killed and 500 injured.

Prohibition. The 1920's brought prosperity, prohibition, and the gangland syndicate to Chicago. Johnny Torrio became the first big boss of the Chicago syndicate, but he soon began to fear for his life. Suffering from nerves, Torrio returned to Italy, leaving the organization in the hands of the notorious Al Capone. Capone systematically eliminated his enemies, culminating the purge by murdering seven henchmen of George "Bugs" Moran in the infamous St. Valentine's Day Massacre in 1929.

Depression Years. The economic Depression that began in 1929 struck Chicago as hard as it did other U. S. cities. However, Chicago celebrated its 100th anniversary with the 1933 World's Fair, called the Century of Progress Exposition. Though the effects of the Depression were being felt around the globe, the fair proved immensely popular. It was held over for another year in 1934 and attracted 100 million people.

In 1932 and 1940, when the Democratic party held its national convention in Chicago and nominated Franklin D. Roosevelt to his first and third terms, the city proved its popularity as a central site for conventions. When the United States entered World War II in 1941, Chicago contributed massive amounts of matériel and men to the Allied cause.

Political History. Chicago's political history has been as full of contrasts and incongruities as the city itself. Chicago's first mayor, William B. Ogden, who was president of the Union Pacific Railroad, used his personal fortune to pay Chicago's debts when the city was in severe financial straits during the panic of 1837.

In the early years of the city's history, mayors were elected chiefly on the basis of personality or fame, without benefit of political machines. After the Great Chicago Fire in 1871, Joseph Medill, publisher of the Chicago *Tribune*, ran for the mayoralty and won on a "fireproof" platform. Another mayor, Carter H. Harrison, caught the fancy of the citizenry at the turn of the century as he rode about town on a fine white horse, waving his hat to everyone. Called "our Carter" by all Chicagoans, he and his son, Carter H. Harrison II, each served five two-year terms as mayor.

As the city grew larger, the basis of political power became the political machine, which operates by giving patronage jobs to those who can assure a good turnout of the party vote on election day. John ("Bathhouse John") Coughlin and Michael ("Hinky Dink") Kenna controlled the first ward in this manner around the turn of the century. A citywide political organization was not developed until the 1930's, when Edward J. Kelly, a Democrat, built an organization that is still dominant in Chicago politics.

Democratic mayors of the 20th century included William Hale ("Big Bill") Thompson, a colorful but ineffective mayor. Thompson ended his third term in 1931 and was succeeded by Anton J. Cermak. During a visit to President Roosevelt in Miami, Fla., in 1933, Cermak was shot and killed by an assassin whose target was the president. Kelly, the organizer of the Democratic machine, was named to succeed Cermak and was later elected for four terms. Richard J. Daley, who, like Kelly, provided Chicago with a strong and reasonably progressive administration, began his long tenure as mayor in 1955. On Dec. 20, 1976, Mayor Daley died, ending one of the most important political careers in the city's history. A colorful person, Daley was elected to six terms, increasing his margin with each election. He was the last of the nation's big-city leaders who could deliver votes, and he played an important political role at both the Illinois and national levels. An astute politician, he reacted flexibly to changing conditions, but held his organization together.

At the time of Daley's death there was no heir apparent. A Chicago alderman, Michael Bilandic, was elected in June 1977 to fill out the mayor's unexpired term. But the county Democratic chairmanship, long held by Daley,

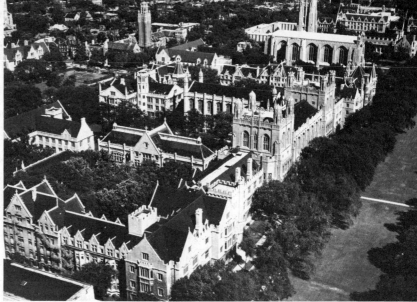

UNIVERSITY OF CHICAGO, showing the division of humanities quadrangle, Harper Memorial Library, and (upper right) Rockefeller Memorial Chapel.

went to George Dunne, chairman of the Cook county board.

SAMUEL K. GOVE, *University of Illinois*

Bibliography
Condit, Carl Wilbur, *The Chicago School of Architecture* (Univ. of Chicago Press 1964).
Havighurst, Robert James, *The Public Schools of Chicago* (Chicago Board of Education 1964).
League of Women Voters, *The Key to Our Local Government: Chicago-Cook County Metropolitan Area* (Citizens Information Service 1972).
Merriam, Charles Edward, *Chicago* (Macmillan 1929).
O'Conner, Len, *Clout: Mayor Daley and His City* (Regnery 1975).
Pierce, Bessie Louise, *A History of Chicago*, 3 vols. (McClelland 1940–1957).
Rakove, Milton, *Don't Make No Waves, Don't Back No Losers* (Indiana Univ. Press 1975).
Royko, Mike, *Boss: Richard J. Daley of Chicago* (Dutton 1971).
Siegel, Arthur S., ed., *Chicago's Famous Buildings* (Univ. of Chicago Press 1965).
Simpson, Dick, ed., *Chicago's Future* (Stipes 1976).
Solomon, Ezra, and Bilbija, Zarko G., *Metropolitan Chicago* (Free Press 1960).
Wagenknecht, Edward Charles, *Chicago* (Univ. of Okla. Press 1964).
Wolfert, Richard Jerome, *The Government of the City of Chicago* (Chicago Municipal Reference Library 1966).

CHICAGO, University of, shə-kä′gō, a private, nonsectarian, coeducational institution situated in the Hyde Park-Kenwood section of the South Side of Chicago, Ill. University buildings extend along both sides of the Midway Plaisance in Chicago's "cultural mile." Other units are in downtown Chicago.

Founding and Growth. The university was founded in 1891, financed by an initial gift of $600,000 from John D. Rockefeller and built on ground donated by Marshall Field. The University of Chicago succeeded a smaller, similarly named institution that flourished from 1857 to 1886 on a Chicago site donated by U. S. Senator Stephen A. Douglas. The American Baptist Education Society was instrumental in founding the new university, but the institution is now completely nondenominational.

Under its first president, William Rainey Harper, the present university began classes in 1892 with 594 students and 103 faculty members. By 1950 the student body numbered 9,266, and the faculty stood at 803. In the mid-1960's there were about 11,500 students, including 6,100 graduate and professional students, and there were 1,100 full-time faculty members.

Chicago is a relative newcomer to the ranks of great academic institutions, but its faculty has been distinguished from the start. The first faculty included eight former university and college presidents. Within a decade such scholars as John Dewey in philosophy, Thorstein Veblen in economics, and James Breasted in archaeology were added.

Many Nobel Prize winners also have been associated with the university: *in physics,* A. A. Michelson, Robert A. Millikan, Arthur H. Compton, James Franck, Enrico Fermi, Clinton J. Davisson, Ernest O. Lawrence, Werner Heisenberg, Tsung Dao Lee, Maria G. Mayer, Chen Ning Yang, Eugene P. Wigner, Julian S. Schwinger, and Owen Chamberlain; *in chemistry,* Harold C. Urey, Glenn T. Seaborg, Robert S. Mulliken, Karl Ziegler, and Willard F. Libby; *in physiology and medicine,* Alexis Carrel, Edward A. Doisy, Herman J. Muller, Charles B. Huggins, Edward L. Tatum, James D. Watson, Konrad E. Bloch, Sir John Eccles, and George Wells Beadle (Chicago's 7th president); and *in literature,* Lord Bertrand Russell.

An outstanding figure in university history was Robert Maynard Hutchins, who for 23 years was, successively, president and chancellor.

Divisions of the University. Components of the university are an undergraduate college, four graduate divisions (biological sciences, humanities, physical sciences, and social sciences), and seven graduate professional schools.

The undergraduate college is a coeducational residential school, noted for its general education. In 1966 it was reorganized into five collegiate divisions, each under the direction of a master. More than 75% of the college's graduates continue their studies toward an advanced degree.

The seven graduate professional schools serve a wide variety of interests. The Graduate School of Business is the first business school in the United States to offer a doctoral program. The school also sponsors a special nondegree executive program for business executives. The Divinity School represents 12 denominations. The Graduate School of Education utilizes the university's laboratory school complex of nursery, elementary,

429

and high schools in training and developing scholar-teachers, professional specialists, researchers, and administrators. The Law School traditionally concerns itself with the relationships between law and the social sciences. The Graduate Library School was the first library school in the country to offer the doctoral degree. The School of Medicine is an integral part of the Division of Biological Sciences and is noted for its teaching and research faculty. The School of Social Service Administration is a pioneer in social reform and social welfare studies and a leader in social work education.

Research Projects. The University of Chicago cooperates in basic research projects with many federal agencies, including the Agency for International Development and the Atomic Energy Commission. Faculty members serve as consultants to federal agencies. More than 50 major corporations use the services of the university's Industrial Relations Center.

Research facilities include the Oriental Institute, a center for archaeological study specializing in the Middle East; the Enrico Fermi Instiute for Nuclear Studies; the Computation Center; Yerkes Observatory (at Williams Bay, Wis.); McDonald Observatory (Fort Davis, Texas), operated jointly with the University of Texas; the Social Science Research Building; the Center for Policy Study; the Center for International Studies; the Center for Health Administration Studies; the Sonia Shankman Orthogenic School, for emotionally disturbed children; and La Rabida-University of Chicago Institute, for the study and treatment of major childhood diseases. Affiliated research-oriented institutions include the National Opinion Research Center and the Argonne National Laboratory, which is operated under a contract arrangement with the U. S. Atomic Energy Commission and Argonne Universities Association.

Several sites on the university campus have been designated by the U. S. Department of the Interior as national historical landmarks: Robie House (designed by Frank Lloyd Wright and now used by the Adlai Stevenson Institute); the site of the first controlled, self-sustaining nuclear chain reaction, Dec. 2, 1942 (marked by a commemorative statue designed by British sculptor Henry Moore); the Department of Art's Midway Studios (built by American sculptor Lorado Taft from sections of his 1906 campus studio); and the room in the George Herbert Jones Laboratory where plutonium was first weighed in 1942.

Library and Press. The university library has over 2.6 million volumes. Its manuscript and archival collection of over 3 million units includes photostats of the life records of Geoffrey Chaucer, the Bacon Manor rolls and manuscripts, New Testament manuscripts, and the personal papers of Stephen A. Douglas, André Gide, and Enrico Fermi. The new Joseph Regenstein Library, a graduate research facility in the social sciences and humanities, which can accommodate 3 million volumes, contains the offices and classrooms of the Graduate Library School.

The University of Chicago Press is the largest university press in the United States in terms of output. It publishes annually about 150 scholarly books and 30 learned journals.

CARL W. LARSEN, *The University of Chicago*

Further Reading: Goodspeed, Thomas Wakefield, *History of the University of Chicago* (Chicago 1916); Storr, Richard, *Harper's University* (Chicago 1966).

CHICAGO ART INSTITUTE. See ART INSTITUTE OF CHICAGO.

CHICAGO FIRE, shǝ-kä′gō, a disaster that destroyed 3½ square miles (9 sq km) in the heart of Chicago in 1871. It left some 120 persons dead and thousands homeless. The loss of 18,000 buildings and their contents was put at $200 million.

Chicago had suffered serious fires in 1839, 1849, and 1857, yet few precautions had been taken. In 1871 the month of October was unusually hot and dry, and the wooden structures and flammable contents of the many freight stations and warehouses were like a tinderbox.

The blaze began on October 8, about 8 P.M., in a barn behind the house of Timothy and Catherine O'Leary at 137 DeKoven Street. Legend has it that the fire was started when Mrs. O'Leary's cow kicked over a lantern. The fire spread northward, crossing the Chicago River twice, and not stopping until it reached Fullerton Avenue, on October 10. It followed a capricious course, aided by gale-force winds.

Few buildings survived the holocaust. Amazingly, one that did was the O'Leary home. Another, the now-famous Water Tower, stands today as a landmark revered by Chicagoans. As the fire spread, the Michigan Avenue Hotel was bought from its owner by John B. Drake when it appeared doomed; however, the demolition of adjacent buildings saved the hotel and made it a good bargain. On the North Side, only two homes were spared. Among the famous buildings that went up in flames were the sumptuous Palmer House (later rebuilt), the Field and Leiter store on State Street, the million-dollar courthouse, and Crosby's Opera House.

Many rang the death knell for Chicago after the disastrous fire. With astounding vigor, however, the city was quickly rebuilt, and it emerged stronger than before. At the end of the first week, 6,000 temporary structures already housed refugees and businesses. One of the immediate effects of the fire was to aid Joseph Medill's mayoral campaign on a "fireproof" ticket.

Of more long-lasting benefit was the new start that the fire gave to Chicago. Many of Chicago's early buildings were of poor quality, products of a rapidly expanding city erected with little planning. Some of the famous buildings in existence today are products of the post-fire building. They were designed by such noted architects as Louis H. Sullivan, Dankmar Adler, and Daniel H. Burnham, who helped to establish Chicago's reputation for architectural beauty.

SAMUEL K. GOVE, *University of Illinois*

CHICAGO HEIGHTS, shǝ-kä′gō hīts, an industrial city in northeastern Illinois, in Cook county, is 23 miles (37 km) south of Chicago, at the intersection of the Lincoln and Dixie highways. It is situated in an agricultural area that produces grain, soybeans, corn, and vegetables. The city has many manufactures including freight cars and railroad equipment, iron and steel products, glass, electrical equipment, textiles, chemicals, furniture, fertilizer, batteries, and automobile parts. Chicago Heights is the seat of Bloom Township Community College, a 2-year coeducational institution.

The site, originally located on the old Hubbard Trail, was settled in 1833. The community was first called Thorn Grove and was renamed Bloom in 1892. Its name was changed to Chi-

THE CHICAGO FIRE destroyed some 18,000 buildings. By the time the fire burned itself out, about 90,000 people were left homeless.

cago Heights in 1901 when it was incorporated as a city. Government is by commission. Population: 40,900.

VELIA LoBUE
Chicago Heights Free Public Library

CHICAGO OPERA. Chicago's first opera house opened in 1865 but was destroyed in the Great Fire five years later. A new house, the Auditorium, opened in 1889, and Emma Eames and Jean and Édouard de Reszke made their American debuts there in 1891—all in a single production of *Lohengrin*. In 1909 the soprano Emmy Destinn and the conductor Arturo Toscanini made their Chicago debuts jointly in *Aida*.

In 1910 the Chicago Grand Opera Company was founded under the musical direction of Cleofonte Campanini, with the financial backing of industrialist Harold McCormick. The same year Mary Garden, who was to dominate opera in Chicago for the next 20 years, returned to sing there. During her first season with the Chicago Grand Opera, she starred in *Pelléas et Mélisande*, *Louise*, and *Salome*—the last of which was closed after the second performance because of the alleged lewdness of Miss Garden's dancing (Chicago did not see *Salome* again for 11 years). The Chicago Grand Opera survived through the 1913–1914 season, then closed—a financial failure.

The third company established in Chicago was the Chicago Civic Opera (1922–1932). Mary Garden continued as the major artist, and Claudia Muzio, Louise Homer, and Feodor Chaliapin also were heard during this period. The company moved to a new home, the Civic Opera House, for the 1929–1930 season; there, in the following season, Lotte Lehmann made her first American appearance (in *Die Walküre*), and Mary Garden her last.

The Civic Opera was succeeded by another Chicago Grand Opera Company, the shortest-lived (1933–1935) of the city's opera ventures, though it survived long enough for Maria Jeritza and Lauritz Melchior to make their Chicago debuts on its stage. This company gave way to the Chicago City Opera Company (1935), which became the Chicago Opera Company and continued under that name until 1946, omitting the 1943 season. Singers introduced during this time included Ezio Pinza, Helen Traubel, Grace Moore, and Zinka Milanov; and two powerful conductors, Artur Rodzinski and Fritz Reiner, made their Chicago opera debuts.

Lyric Opera. After the demise of the Chicago Opera Company, the city was without a resident troupe until 1954, when the Chicago Lyric Theatre was founded. The principal mover in this undertaking was Carol Fox, a young Chicago socialite and voice student, who became general manager of the company. A production of *Don Giovanni* in early February 1954 gave evidence of the Lyric Theatre's artistry, and the company scored a coup the following November 1 with the American debut of Maria Callas (in *Norma*). In 1955 both Callas and Renata Tebaldi were signed: Callas for Bellini's *I Puritani*, a work not previously heard in the United States in more than 30 years; and Tebaldi for *Aida*. In 1956, Carol Fox changed the company's name to the Lyric Opera of Chicago.

In 1959 the Lyric Opera produced Leoš Janáček's *Jenufa* in English for the first time in the United States. Later, it revived Francesco Ciléa's *Adriana Lecouvreur* for Renata Tebaldi and Puccini's *Turandot* for Birgit Nilsson. The company's 1967 season was canceled because of a conflict with the American Federation of Musicians, but there was a complete 1968 season. Later seasons featured Wolf Siegfried Wagner's directing a new production (1969) of his great-grandfather's *Der fliegende Holländer* and the first staging in Chicago (1973) of Donizetti's *Maria Stuarda*.

SHIRLEY FLEMING
Editor of "Musical America"

CHICAGO RIDGE, a village in northeastern Illinois, in Cook county, is 15 miles (24 km) southwest of downtown Chicago. The village is primarily residential with some industry, including the manufacture of steel tanks and lumber. Argonne Forest, a Cook county forest preserve, is just west of Chicago Ridge. The village underwent an expansion in population of more than 500% between 1950 and 1960. It has the mayor-council form of government. Population: 9,187.

CHICAGO SANITARY AND SHIP CANAL, a channel for trade and for removal of sewage from Chicago. The 30-mile (48-km) canal, called the Chicago Drainage Canal when completed between Chicago and Lockport in 1900, follows a route up the Chicago River and across to the Des Plaines River. This route, first proposed by Louis Jolliet in 1673, was used for the Illinois and Michigan Canal, completed in 1848 solely to facilitate commerce.

In an effort to overcome a major pollution problem in 1871, the cut between the Chicago and Des Plaines rivers was deepened, so that water of Lake Michigan carried polluted Chicago River water southward instead of receiving it. Construction of the Drainage Canal was begun in 1892, primarily for the purpose of improving sewage disposal.

The volume of Lake Michigan water diverted to the canal led to concern by nearby states and Canada that the level of the Great Lakes would be lowered. The issue was settled in 1929 by a Supreme Court order limiting lake water diversion to 1,500 cubic feet (42 cubic meters) per second by 1939. The canal now is a section of the Illinois Deep Waterway, operated by the federal government since 1933 as part of the inland waterway between the Great Lakes and the Mississippi River.

WALTER S. SANDERLIN
Washington and Jefferson College

CHICAGO SYMPHONY ORCHESTRA,

the third-oldest symphony orchestra in the United States, founded in 1891 by the conductor Theodore Thomas. One of Thomas' aims was to house the Chicago Orchestra, as it was then called, in a hall of its own. His ambition was realized in December 1904 with the opening of Orchestra Hall, the first permanent auditorium for an American orchestra. Thomas lived to enjoy the hall only a few weeks, however; he caught cold rehearsing in the yet-uncompleted building, and died of pneumonia in January 1905. During his Chicago tenure, Thomas laid the foundations for an ensemble oriented basically to the German repertoire. He was a champion of the music of Richard Strauss, who appeared with the orchestra as guest conductor.

Frederick Stock, a violist who had become the Chicago orchestra's assistant conductor in 1901, was its permanent conductor from 1905 until his death in 1942. (From 1906 to 1912 the ensemble was called the Theodore Thomas Orchestra; it was then renamed the Chicago Symphony Orchestra.) Stock, while continuing Thomas' German traditions, also introduced the new French music of Debussy and Ravel and led premieres of works by American composers. He instituted childrens' concerts and a popular Saturday night series at low prices; in 1919 he established the Chicago Civic Orchestra, which still serves as a training ensemble for orchestral musicians. In 1941, to celebrate the orchestra's 50th anniversary, Stock commissioned works from Stravinsky (Symphony in C), Milhaud (Symphony No. 1), and Roy Harris (*American Creed*), among others.

Stock was succeeded as conductor by Désiré Defauw (1943–1947), Artur Rodzinski (1947–1948), Rafael Kubelik (1950–1953, following a series of guest conductors), Fritz Reiner (1953–1960, with limited appearances in 1960–1963), and Jean Martinon (1963–1968). In 1966 the orchestra's 75th anniversary was celebrated with two commissions: one from Gunther Schuller and one from Martinon himself (the symphony *Altitudes*). Martinon retired in 1968, and from 1969, Georg Solti was music director.

SHIRLEY FLEMING
Editor of "Musical America"

CHICAGO WORLD'S FAIR. See FAIRS AND EXPOSITIONS; WORLD'S COLUMBIAN EXPOSITION.

CHICANO, chi-kä′nō, a Mexican-American who is either a U. S. citizen of Mexican heritage or a Mexican citizen living in the United States. The term "Chicano" is of uncertain origin. It may have been derived from the Nahuatl pronunciation of Mexicano (Mexican-American). But whatever its origin, the term was applied by older Mexican residents of the U. S. Southwest to the refugees who flooded into the area after the revolution in Mexico in 1910. Other ("Anglo") residents of the Southwest began using the term in the 1930's, and "Chicano" took on a political connotation about 1965 in connection with the California grape workers' strike.

History. Since the 16th century, Spanish-speaking people have lived in what are now the states of the American Southwest (New Mexico, Arizona, and Texas) and California. The Anglo immigrants from the United States competed with the ruling Mexicans, cooperated with them for economic gain, or, in some cases, intermarried with them and became part of Mexican society. However, as American infiltration increased and Americans became the majority, antagonism between the two peoples rose, though the two groups tolerated each other as protection against the Indians.

By 1886 the Indians were under control, and by 1887 the railroads were bringing more than 120,000 Anglo settlers annually into California alone. Modest Mexican majorities were soon replaced by overwhelming Anglo majorities. By 1900, in all the border states except New Mexico, the Mexicans found themselves in the minority.

Reduced to landless laborers, politically and economically powerless, the Mexicans found work where they could. It was usually temporary or seasonal work, first on the cotton farms or in railroad construction, and then, with the coming of irrigated farming, on the great fruit and vegetable farms of the area.

Swelling the ranks of the Mexican workers already in the region, thousands more crossed the border from Mexico. Many entered legally, and those who arrived illegally (*wetbacks*) were tolerated by the authorities because their labor was needed. Those who entered legally (*braceros*) usually returned home after the agricultural season ended, and there was some supervision by the U. S. government of their living conditions. After World War II, however, the need for cheap imported labor decreased, organized labor's opposition to the *braceros* increased, and in 1964 the law permitting their importation was allowed to expire.

Urbanization. After World War II, as machinery replaced men on the large farms, Mexican-Americans began to seek work in urban areas, particularly in Los Angeles, Calif., and in El Paso, Bexar, and Hidalgo counties, Texas. In the 1970's, almost half of the more than 6 million Chicanos lived in central cities.

In part because of educational deficiencies—Chicanos tend to start school later in life and remain in school a shorter time than the general U. S. population—most urban Chicanos are semiskilled workers or laborers. Even within these categories, Chicanos work at the poorer jobs and for less money.

Most urban Chicanos, by choice or necessity, live in distinctive "Mexican" neighborhoods, the *barrios*. There, though most Chicanos are bilingual, Spanish is spoken in stores, gas stations, banks, and in religious services. The culture is

Mexican, with Spanish-language motion picture theaters and radio and television stations.

Political Activities. During most of their history the Chicanos had almost no political representation, received little aid from federal programs, produced few leaders, and protested little. Outbreaks of violence against them went largely unnoticed outside the Southwest.

In 1929 the League of United Latin-American Citizens (LULAC) was founded. For many years it remained a confederation of local social and civic clubs with programs restricted to providing citizenship education and encouraging the young to finish high school. After World War II, LULAC and other organizations—the Mexican-American Political Association (MAPA) and the Political Association of Spanish-speaking Organizations (PASO)—became concerned with equal-employment opportunities, voter registration, and the election of Chicanos to office.

In the 1960's two radically different Chicano leaders emerged—Reies Lopez Tijerina and Cesar Chavez. Tijerina's organization, the Alianza, claimed thousands of acres of land in the Southwest, asserting that this land, now owned by Anglos, rightfully belonged to the Spanish-speaking population. The claim was based on land grants by Spanish kings in the 17th and 18th centuries.

Chavez, better known nationally, organized the National Farm Workers Association, which in 1965 struck against the California grape growers. By 1969 the growers of wine grapes and by 1970 many of the growers of table grapes had recognized the union. See CHAVEZ, CESAR.

In the mid-1960's the first student forms of the Chicano movement appeared. Out of one of them, the Mexican-American Youth Organization (MAYO), José Angel Gutiérrez in 1970 established a new party, La Raza Unida ("uniting of the race"). La Raza took the position that Chicanos need their own political party so as to control the political, economic, and social life of some 20 counties in south Texas where Chicanos have large majorities. La Raza, however, saw its function as not merely political, but social as well—to promote *chicanismo*, a concept of pride in Mexican-American history and culture. La Raza was successful in electing Chicano candidates to Texas school boards and city councils.

Further Reading: Grebler, Leo, and others, *The Mexican-American People* (Free Press 1970); Moore, Joan Willard, and Cuéllar, Alfredo, *Mexican Americans* (Prentice-Hall 1970).

CHICHÉN ITZÁ, chē-chān' ēt-sä', is a famous Toltec Maya center, set on the plain of northern Yucatan, Mexico, about 72 miles (112.7 km) southeast of Merida. The name means "the mouth of the wells of the Itzá," a tribe probably descended from the original builders, and reflects their dependence on an underground water system.

History. The Spanish conquerors, under the early Spanish explorer Montejo, first came to the Yucatan in the 1530's, about a thousand years after the estimated founding of Chichén Itzá. At this time the city was already in ruins, though still an important pilgrimage and sacrificial center. Archaeological investigations indicate a period of occupation spanning the years from 600 to 1400 A.D. Specific dates for any building, however, can only be approximated within a range of 200 years.

Even before the major construction began, Chichén Itzá was probably a regional pilgrimage center. Whether it was also a city with a permanent concentrated population is unclear. A map surveyed in the 1920's covers a strip 1 mile (1.6 km) wide and extending 2 miles (3.2 km) south of the sacrificial well. Hundreds of structures appear in scattered clusters linked by raised causeways. These multi-chambered palaces, long colonnades, single-room shrines, and temples may be divided into two classes of architectural style, and the styles are thought to reflect two separate phases of occupation.

WILLIAM R. COE, FROM H. STANLEY LOTEN

CHICHÉN ITZÁ contains some well-preserved buildings, including the pyramid in the background known as the Temple of Kukulcan.

Architectural Periods. The first or early period covering the years from 700 to 900 A. D. (or 900 to 1050), is represented by buildings reflecting native Maya architecture. Typically, they are simple, rectangular stone structures with plain walls. Most of the buildings are widely dispersed.

The second architectural class, by far the more important, spans the years from approximately 900 to 1100 (or 1050 to 1150). Here are represented such monumental constructions as the Great Ball Court, the Temple Pyramid of Kukulcan or Castillo, and the Temple of the Warriors. The Mayans had no animals for transport, so the immense quantities of accurately hewn stones and the rubble fill were hauled by men. The walls were frequently decorated with painted and carved scenes of battles with Toltec warriors.

This and other architectural parallels with the Toltec site of Tula in Hidalgo, Mexico, seem to indicate a strong tie with the region of present-day Mexico City. Such interaction of forms is illustrated by the Caracol, a round tower 40 feet (12 meters) high and 22 feet (6.7 meters) in diameter which rests on two terraces. A spiral staircase winding up the inside leads to a series of radiating slots, indicating that the tower might well have functioned as a stellar observatory. The circular plan is more common in the central highland area, while the exterior moldings and the vaulted interior are representative of Maya architecture. The complete fusion of the two traditions is seen in the Temple of the Warriors. Here Maya masks of the rain god Chac are stacked on a pure Toltec dado, or base.

The Great Ball Court, a standard institution of the Toltecs and Aztecs, is found in superhuman proportions. Its immense stone walls are 270 feet (92 meters) long and 25 feet (7.6 meters) high. In the colossal alley ritualistic games were played with a hard natural rubber ball thrown through stone rings set in the masonry. The ceremonial ball games may have ended with the sacrifice of the losing team. The Well of Sacrifice, thought to be a central point in the city, is an enormous cavity in the rock, about 160 feet (48.8 meters) across its widest point. There is a sheer drop of 70 feet (21 meters) to the green water beneath.

The Maya were an agricultural people with many nature gods, such as the rain god Chac, who they thought would protect their crops from drought. Their chief god, often represented as a feathered serpent, was Kukulcan, keeper of the winds. The Maya regarded these beings as utterly indifferent to the fate of humanity, and their cooperation could only be purchased at extremely high prices. For example, beautiful maids, precious stones, and other prized objects were thrown into the sacrificial well to placate the rain god in time of drought.

Dating the Ruins. Archaeological investigations derived from a study of Mayan inscriptions, ceramics, and literature have been conducted by the Carnegie Institution of Washington, D. C., and the Mexican government since the beginning of the 20th century. The use of carbon-14, a method of dating whereby the amount of carbon present is measured, has helped to date the architecture. Not only a major tourist attraction, Chichén Itzá is of prime importance to an understanding of the complex events and concepts of pre-Columbian civilization.

H. STANLEY LOTEN
Royal Architectural Institute of Canada

CHICHERIN, chi-chä′ryin, **Georgi Vasilievich** (1872–1936), Russian aristocrat and revolutionary, who became the first Soviet commissar of foreign affairs. He was born in Tambov oblast. He was raised humbly in the provinces, and began his career in 1896 as an archivist in the czarist ministry of foreign affairs. Resigning in 1904, he left Russia for western Europe and entered the revolutionary movement, taking a position between the Mensheviks and the Bolsheviks. He soon held an important post in émigré politics.

Chicherin returned to Russia in early 1918 and joined the Bolshevik party. Recognizing his usefulness to the Soviet regime, Lenin put him in charge of Soviet diplomacy. In this capacity Chicherin established the continuity of Russian foreign policy from the czars to Stalin. By virtue of his linguistic ability, remarkable erudition, and diplomatic skill he stood out among his peers in other European governments. His position was made difficult by the Communist International, the revolutionary branch of Soviet foreign relations, which enjoyed greater prestige in party circles than the regular diplomatic corps. Yet, as the revolutionary tide receded after World War I, Soviet diplomacy gained. With the rise of Stalin, Chicherin's influence declined, and in 1930 he was replaced by Litvinov. He died in Moscow on July 7, 1936.

THEODORE H. VON LAUE
Washington University, St. Louis, Mo.

CHICHESTER, chich′əs-tər, **Arthur** (1563–1625), English administrator in Ireland, who founded the city of Belfast and was chiefly responsible for the "Plantation of Ulster." Chichester was born in Rawleigh, Devonshire, in May 1563 and was educated at Oxford.

As the youthful captain of an English warship, Chichester helped defeat the Spanish Armada in 1588 and aided in capturing the Spanish port of Cádiz in 1596. In 1598 he took a leading part in Queen Elizabeth's Irish wars, and from 1605 to 1614 he attempted to govern Ireland as the crown's lord deputy.

In that office, Chichester forcibly imposed English law and persecuted the Irish Catholics. He forced into exile the native Irish chiefs Hugh O'Neill, Earl of Tyrone, and Rory O'Donnell, Earl of Tyrconnell, and confiscated their estates with the intention of dividing them between Irishmen loyal to the English crown and colonists imported from Scotland and England. However, the crown awarded all the best lands to the colonists, and the native population was driven out. Thus was accomplished the "Plantation of Ulster," which brought Presbyterian Scots into six counties and gave them two million acres of Ireland.

In 1613, Chichester was raised to the Irish peerage as Baron Chichester of Belfast, and in 1615 he was recalled to England, where he died on Feb. 19, 1625.

GIOVANNI COSTIGAN
University of Washington

CHICHESTER, chich′əs-tər, **Sir Francis Charles** (1901–1972), British yachtsman and aviator, who at the age of 65 made a 28,500-mile (45,866 km) journey around the world alone in a 53-foot (16 meter) ketch. He left Plymouth, England, on Aug. 27, 1966, and reached Sydney, Australia, in 107 days. He returned by way of Cape Horn in 119 days. He had made a record solo crossing from Plymouth to New York in 1962 (33 days).

Sir Francis was born in North Devon, England, on Sept. 17, 1901, and was educated at Marlborough College. At an early age he piloted airplanes. He flew solo from England to Australia in 1929 and was the first to fly across the Tasman Sea from New Zealand to Australia (1931). He was a navigation officer in the Royal Air Force from 1941 to 1945. Among his publications are his autobiography, *The Lonely Sea and the Sky* (1964). Created a knight commander of the Order of the British Empire in 1967, he died in Plymouth, England, on Aug. 26, 1972.

BILL BRADDOCK, *New York "Times"*

CHICHESTER, chich'əs-tər, is a municipal borough and cathedral city in southern England, the county seat of West Sussex, about 55 miles (88 km) southwest of London. Chichester is a market center with medieval and Georgian buildings. Its old wall, built about 200 A. D., is still standing. The cathedral was built mainly in the early 12th century. Nearby are the remains of the 100-room palace of King Cogidubnus, who ruled the area in the 1st century A. D. on behalf of the Romans. A museum now stands on the palace site, which was discovered in 1960.

The site of Chichester was known during the Roman occupation as Regnum or Noviomagus. It was captured by the Saxons in the 5th century and renamed Cisseceaster for the Saxon king, Cissa. Chichester was important in the Middle Ages as a wool and grain market. Population: (1961) 20,124.

CHICK-PEA, chik'pē, a bushy annual plant widely grown for its round edible seeds. The seeds are about ⅜ of an inch (9.5 mm) in diameter and are white, red, or black. They can be boiled, roasted, or fried. Roasted seeds are used as a coffee additive or substitute.

The chick-pea has long been cultivated and is an important crop in India, the Middle East, and southern Europe. It is now extensively grown in parts of Africa as well. Central America, Mexico, and the southwestern United States also produce chick-peas. The chick-pea grows about 2 feet (60 cm) tall and has hairy stems and compound leaves composed of 9 to 15 pairs of leaflets. The white or pink flowers are borne singly on long stalks, and the rectangular pods, which are about 1 inch (2.5 cm) long, contain one or two seeds.

The chick-pea is known botanically as *Cicer arietinum*. Like its relative the garden pea, it belongs to the legume family (Leguminosae).

LAWRENCE ERBE
University of Southwestern Louisiana

CHICKADEE, chik'ə-dē, is the name applied to seven species of titmice found in North America. Chickadees are usually small, plump birds with stubby bills, short, rounded wings, longish tails, and small, strong feet. Both sexes are alike in coloring and usually have dark caps and bibs. The common chickadee of the northeastern and central United States is the black-capped chickadee, *Parus atricapillus*. It is a small bird, usually about 5 inches (13 cm) long, and has a gray body with a black cap and bib and white cheeks.

Although chickadees are usually nonmigratory, they may form small roving bands in the winter. Their call is a whistled *chickadee*. Chickadees are extremely active birds, often hanging upside down in their restless search for insects, seeds, and fruits. One chickadee may kill as many as

RUE, FROM MONKMEYER PRESS PHOTO SERVICE

Black-capped chickadee

500 caterpillars in a single day. Tame, unafraid birds, chickadees are easily trained to take food from one's hand.

In the spring chickadees form breeding pairs. Both parents or the female alone builds a nest in the cavity of soft or rotting tree stumps or posts. The female lays 5 to 9 white eggs, speckled with brown, and incubates the eggs for about 12 days.

Chickadees belong to the genus *Parus* of the family Paridae in the order Passeriformes. They are closely related to crows and jays.

CARL WELTY, *Beloit College*

CHICKAHOMINY RIVER, chik-ə-hom'ə-nē, in southeastern Virginia, about 90 miles (145 km) long from its source northwest of Richmond to its junction with the James River near Williamsburg. The Chickahominy is north of the James and flows generally parallel with it on a southeasterly course. In the Civil War the river was an important strategic feature in the Seven Days' Battles in June 1862.

CHICKAMAUGA, chik-ə-mô'gə, **Battle of,** in the American Civil War, fought Sept. 19–20, 1863, in the northwest corner of Georgia. It was the greatest Confederate victory of the war in the western theater. After the Battle of Gettysburg (July 1–3, 1863) and the surrender of Vicksburg (July 4), the attention of the entire country, both North and South, was focused on east Tennessee and on the city of Chattanooga, a railway center of great strategic importance.

Events Preceding the Battle. On Aug. 16, 1863, Maj. Gen. William S. Rosecrans, commanding the Union Army of the Cumberland, advanced upon Chattanooga from the northwest, leading a force of more than 60,000 men. The defending Confederate Army of Tennessee, commanded by Gen. Braxton Bragg, numbered about 44,000.

In four days Rosecrans' army reached the Tennessee River near Stevenson, Ala., 35 miles (56 km) southwest of Chattanooga. By September 4 it had crossed and was marching toward Chattanooga and north Georgia. The advance was in three columns: the 20th Corps (Maj. Gen. Alexander McD. McCook) on the right; the 14th Corps (Maj. Gen. George H. Thomas) in the center; and the 21st Corps (Maj. Gen. Thomas L. Crittenden) on the left. The right and center corps were directed over the mountains toward the rear of Chattanooga to cut the enemy supply line. The left corps (Crittenden's) was sent toward the city.

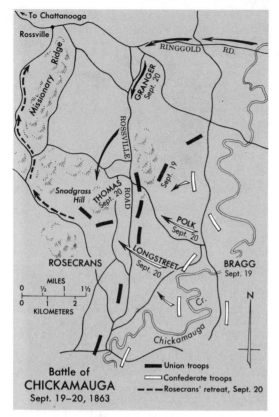

**Battle of
CHICKAMAUGA
Sept. 19–20, 1863**

Union troops
Confederate troops
Rosecrans' retreat, Sept. 20

On September 9 the Confederates evacuated Chattanooga. Upon receiving this news, Rosecrans urged his troops forward to cut off what he conceived to be a demoralized Confederate retreat, thus placing his widely separated columns in very grave danger. There were 40 miles (64 km) between the right and left columns and no good connecting roads. If attacked, they would be unable to assist each other.

Confederate Moves. Rosecrans' assumption that Bragg's army was in full retreat was very much in error. Bragg had evacuated Chattanooga and moved south toward La Fayette, Ga., to concentrate his forces and prepare for an attack. He had been joined by Maj. Gen. Simon B. Buckner's Corps from Knoxville, Tenn., and by additional reinforcements from Mississippi. Bragg was aware that Rosecrans had split the Union army into two widely separated parts, but had not been informed of the existence of the third, or right, column.

Bragg immediately saw the opportunity of overwhelming one of the Union columns before another could come to its assistance. On September 10 he ordered an attack against Thomas' 14th Corps in the center. Two days later he turned to strike at Crittenden's 21st Corps on the Union left. Neither effort succeeded. Bragg then decided to await the arrival of additional reinforcements. In the longest railroad troop movement undertaken by the Confederacy during the entire war, a large part of Lt. Gen. James Longstreet's Corps was being dispatched by rail via the Carolinas and Georgia.

Meanwhile Rosecrans had recognized his danger. Hastily he issued orders to bring his corps together, but it would be a matter of days rather than hours before this could be done. For both Rosecrans and Bragg this was a period of ex-

treme tension. Rosecrans needed time to concentrate his army; if attacked in force before his columns joined, disaster would be almost inevitable. Bragg also felt the pressure of time. Longstreet was coming by rail but Confederate rolling stock was in poor condition and his arrival time could not be predicted. The longer Bragg waited the more troops he would have, but each day gave his enemy more time to concentrate. Finally, on September 18, when three brigades of Longstreet's Corps arrived, Bragg issued orders for an attack.

In order to approach the main Union defense line the Confederates had to move through dense woods, over narrow mountain roads, and struggle across Chickamauga Creek, the Indian "River of Death." Many of the fords and bridges were strongly defended; only a few units were able to cross that evening. But during the night the Army of Tennessee pressed onward until, by daybreak, about three fourths had gained the west bank of the stream.

The Battle—September 19. The Confederate plan of attack was to envelop the Union flank on the northern side, to shove their opponents away from Chattanooga, and to destroy them against the wall of mountains to the south. However, on the morning of September 19 the Confederates were surprised to discover that their lines did not overlap the Union line to the north as expected. Thomas' corps had appeared on the field during the night and had extended the line in that direction. The fighting on September 19 was bitter and prolonged. It raged throughout the day as additional units came into action: McCook's 20th Corps arrived during the afternoon; the remainder of Bragg's army crossed the creek to take their part in that violent struggle. And late that night Longstreet appeared on the scene with two more of his brigades.

September 20. For the next day's battle, Bragg organized his army into two parts. Lt. Gen. Leonidas Polk commanded the right half, Longstreet the left. The plan of battle was the same, to envelop the Union left, and sweep the whole Army of the Cumberland back into the mountains toward the south. When the Confederates advanced on September 20, they found that their enemy had retreated slightly to a stronger position; nevertheless, Polk's men attacked vigorously, exhibiting the highest courage. But the Union left, commanded by Thomas, held firm.

Following the plan, of attacking progressively in order from right to left, Longstreet's men took up the assault to find, suddenly, a gap in the Union lines directly in front of them. Due to a misunderstanding, a Union division had left its place in line. The Confederates poured through the gap. Longstreet, immediately grasping the fact that the situation had changed drastically, discarded Bragg's plan. Contrary to orders, he swung his corps to the right and drove swiftly inward. Rosecrans and the entire Union right flank was swept from the field, leaving Thomas in command of the Union left, stubbornly resisting against greatly superior numbers.

By their swift turn to the right, Longstreet's men had almost finished the battle, but as they surged forward up the slopes of Snodgrass Hill other Union troops suddenly appeared. Maj. Gen. Gordon Granger, commanding Rosecrans' Reserve Corps on the Ringgold Road, had sent a division marching to the sound of the guns. With their help, Thomas' line stood firm.

Longstreet had grasped the changed character

of the battle, but Bragg had not. He refused Longstreet's requests for reinforcements. Polk and Longstreet were left to continue their attacks, uncoordinated and unsupported. Furthermore, they were facing a very stubborn, patient foe. Thomas was in command of all the Union troops remaining on the field, and inspired by his presence, the defenders were determined that the position would be held at all costs. From that day George H. Thomas became known as "the Rock of Chickamauga," in honor of his brilliant defense of the position, and for saving the Army of the Cumberland from complete disaster. It was not until almost dark that he was forced to withdraw.

Losses. Both sides suffered heavy losses. Union casualties were approximately 16,000 out of a total of almost 60,000 men engaged. The Confederate army of about 66,000 men sustained a loss of 18,000. After the defeats of Gettysburg and Vicksburg, the Battle of Chickamauga gave new hope to the Southern cause.

JOSEPH B. MITCHELL
Author of "Decisive Battles of the Civil War"

Bibliography

Esposito, Col. Vincent J., *The West Point Atlas of American Wars* (New York 1959).

Horn, Stanley F., *The Army of Tennessee* (Indianapolis 1941).

Johnson, Robert U., and Buel, Clarence G., eds., *Battles and Leaders of the Civil War*, vol. 3, rev. ed. (New York 1956).

Mitchell, Lt. Col. Joseph B., *Decisive Battles of the Civil War* (New York 1955).

Steele, Maj. Matthew F., *American Campaigns* (Harrisburg, Pa., 1942).

CHICKAMAUGA DAM, in southeastern Tennessee, on the Tennessee River 7 miles (11 km) northeast of Chattanooga. One of the major dams of the Tennessee Valley Authority, it was completed in 1940. One purpose of its construction was to aid navigation on the river, and the dam has a lock with a maximum lift of 53 feet (16 meters). The dam also aids flood control and supplies hydroelectric power. Its erection created Lake Chickamauga, 60 miles (97 kilometers) long, which is a popular recreation area.

CHICKASAW, chik′ə-sô, is a city in southwestern Alabama, in Mobile county. It is situated 6 miles (10 km) north of Mobile, on Chickasabogue Creek, an affluent of the Mobile River. A 25-foot-deep channel connects the city with Mobile Bay on the Gulf of Mexico. Chickasaw is located in a lumbering region, and its main economic activities are centered around the manufacture of paper. The city was incorporated in 1946. It has a mayor and council form of government. Population: 8,447.

CHICKASAW INDIANS, chik′ə-sô, a Muskhogean-speaking tribe, known in U. S. government records, along with the Choctaw, Cherokee, Creek, and Seminole, as one of the Five Civilized Tribes. In 1540 the Spanish explorer Hernando de Soto, who referred to them as the "Chicaza," met them in the region of what is today northeastern Mississippi. The Chickasaw language, along with the rest of their culture, was similar to that of the Choctaw, and was widely used along the lower Mississippi Valley for intertribal trade and communication.

Homes and Villages. The Chickasaw had a landing place on the Mississippi River, at the present site of Memphis, Tenn., which was connected to their settlements by a 160-mile trail.

The towns were up to 6 miles long, very narrow, and irregular in plan. Each family occupied a cluster of three buildings—a rectangular summer house, a granary for storing corn, and a circular house used during the winter. The summer houses were constructed by building a wooden frame of posts and saplings to which an outer covering of split boards and bark was attached. The winter house was a more substantial building of thick, upright posts covered by interwoven saplings and poles, and daubed over with a thick covering of clay and grass. By the American Revolution, however, the Chickasaw were living in log cabins like those of the whites along the frontier. Here they lived a sedentary life based on intensive maize agriculture.

Customs in Warfare. The Chickasaw were known as fierce warriors, and they fought constantly with neighboring tribes. In 1732 they routed an Iroquois war party that had penetrated their country. Their enmity with the French had begun when alliances were formed between the French and the Choctaw Indians. In 1736 the Chickasaw defeated the French at Amalahta, in Mississippi, and siding with the Natchez tribe, they continued to disrupt French efforts to conquer the region. The Chickasaw, however, did not attempt to subjugate Indian tribes but were interested mainly in protecting their own land and in staging daring attacks on enemy villages in order to give conspicuous displays of personal bravery. Women and children were frequently taken prisoner and eventually adopted into the tribe. Male prisoners, on the other hand, were elaborately tortured to death. The victim taunted his captors to demonstrate his bravery, while his torturers, mostly women, tried to crush his spirit before he died. Heads and scalps were taken as trophies in battle.

Resettlement of the Chickasaw. The boundaries of the Chickasaw territory were first recognized by the United States through the Hopewell Treaty of 1786. This set their northern boundary at the Ohio River. As early as 1822 some Chickasaw Indians began to settle west of the Mississippi, and treaties for the removal of those who remained were made in 1832 and 1834. Most of the Chickasaw were later resettled in Indian Territory (now Oklahoma), and in 1855 the government signed a treaty giving separate lands to the Chickasaw and Choctaw tribes in Indian Territory. There are estimated to be more than 3,000 Chickasaw Indians in Oklahoma.

RICHARD A. GOULD
American Museum of Natural History

CHICKASHA, chik′ə-shā, a city in central Oklahoma, the seat of Grady county, is 40 miles (64 km) southwest of Oklahoma City. It is situated on the Washita River, a tributary of the Red River. The surrounding country is predominantly agricultural. Cotton is the chief crop, but corn, wheat, alfalfa, and sorghum are also extensively grown. There are gas and oil wells in the area. The city's economy is centered mainly around cotton ginning and the production of cottonseed oil. Other products include flour and feeds, farm machinery, oilfield equipment, and dairy foods. In Chickasha are the Oklahoma College for Women and the Jane Brooks School for the deaf.

Chickasha was incorporated as a town in 1892 and as a city in 1898. The name is a Chickasaw Indian word meaning "rebel." Government is by council and manager. Population: 14,194.

CHICKEN, a species of fowl domesticated early in man's history. Its scientific name is *Gallus domesticus*, and it belongs to the family Phasianidae, which also includes Old World pheasants and partridges. Chickens are probably the most numerous birds in the world, largely because of their importance as a source of human food. In addition to their commercial importance, chickens are raised as a hobby by fanciers who breed them for their beauty and for other special characteristics. Fighting cocks, in countries where cockfighting is not prohibited by law, are highly prized, and these fierce, highly competitive gamecocks have been bred for many centuries.

In many countries a highly efficient industry engaged in the production, processing, and marketing of chicken meat and eggs has evolved, making the raising of chickens one of the most specialized and efficient industries producing food. World production amounts to approximately 8 billion annually, although precise estimates are impossible to obtain. The primary areas of production are North America and Europe, but chickens supply human food throughout the world. In a typical year in the mid-1960's over 2.7 billion chickens were produced in the United States. Most of these were broilers (2.3 billion), raised primarily for meat, while 375 million laying hens were raised as breeding stock or to produce table eggs. On the average, each person in the United States consumes about 33 pounds (15 kg) of chicken meat and over 300 eggs each year.

DOMESTICATION

As with many domestic animals, the origin of the present-day domestic fowl is somewhat obscure. Four species of wild jungle fowl—the red jungle fowl (*Gallus gallus*), the Ceylonese jungle fowl (*G. lafayettii*), the gray jungle fowl (*G. sonneratii*), and the black jungle fowl (*G. varius*)—probably contributed to the development of the domestic species we know today. These wild ancestors of the domestic chicken are found primarily in southeastern Asia, through north central and eastern India, Burma, Thailand, the Malay Peninsula, Ceylon, portions of China, the Philippines, and part of Indonesia.

The red jungle fowl has the widest distribution of the wild species and is considered by some to be the chief ancestor of modern chickens. However, certain breeds of domestic fowl, particularly those developed in Asia, differ considerably from the wild jungle fowl in having short wings, large body size, a wide drooping tail, and a very calm temperament. In addition, Darwin found differences in the skull between one domestic breed, the Cochin breed, and the red jungle fowl. These characteristics in certain breeds suggest that the chicken as we know it today may have had other ancestors now extinct.

Most available evidence, however, points to Asia as the place of origin of the domestic chicken. The chicken was known to the ancient civilization of the Indus Valley and was probably fully domesticated by 2000 B.C. The chicken spread rapidly over the ancient world and appeared in Egypt in the 15th century B.C. The tomb of the pharaoh Tutankhamen (about 1350 B.C.) contained the painting of a readily recognizable cock. Images of chickens on coins from northwestern India and on Assyrian seals suggest that domesticated chickens spread from India to Iran sometime during the 1st millennium B.C. Greece also quickly accepted the chicken. References to the cock or hen in Greek literature and images on coins and seals are common in the 4th and 5th centuries B.C.

Chickens were prized for many reasons in the ancient world. The cock was admired for his courage and pride, and his traditional early morning crow made him valued as a timepiece and symbol of the waking day. The ability of the hen to lay eggs prolifically made her a symbol of fertility. A rooster and a hen were traditionally carried in front of Jewish bridal couples.

Cockfighting apparently was a sport practiced well before the birth of Christ. In fact, chickens may have been domesticated as fighting birds even before they were prized for meat and eggs.

The most extensive records of the early domestic culture of chickens are in agricultural writings by the ancient Roman authors Cato the Elder (234–149 B.C.), Marcus Varro (116–27 B.C.), Columella (1st century A.D.), and Palladius (4th century A.D.). Both Varro and Columella suggested that a poultry farm should have about 200 chickens and gave detailed instructions for the construction of proper housing for chickens. Several breeds of chickens were known during the Roman era, including one breed that possessed five toes and was considered particularly good for producing eggs. Several 5-toed breeds still exist today.

Capons, that is, castrated males, were recognized in the ancient world for their desirable flesh. Aldrovandi, the 16th century Italian naturalist, refers to the recommendations of Aristotle (384–322 B.C.) concerning capon production. These recommendations were similar to those followed later by the Romans and described by both Varro and Columella. The capons were generally produced by burning the spurs with a red-hot iron and treating the resulting wound with potter's clay. This procedure for emasculating male fowl is certainly a baffling one, but apparently it was practiced for many years.

The breeding of chickens for special characteristics has been carried on for centuries. Bones found in excavations in the Indus Valley apparently came from chickens larger than wild fowls, suggesting that at a very early stage in the domestication of chickens, breeding for size had begun. As the chicken spread over the world, poultry keepers in different areas developed divergent ideas as to the desirable attributes of a domestic bird. Certain peculiarly striking characteristics appeared, probably by mutation, and were preserved by poultry breeders. This selective breeding led to the development of a large number of breeds of chickens.

BREEDS

Although there may be considerable variation in the appearance of individual chickens within a breed, a breed is usually defined as a group of fowl related by descent, and breeding true for certain characteristics recognized as distinguishing the breed. Within a breed, varieties may be recognized by differences in comb, plumage, color, beard, and other features.

The scope of poultry breeders' standards for chickens is attested to by the more than 200 breeds or varieties of chickens that are recognized today. These are generally classified on the basis of their geographical area of origin. Breeds within each of these classifications usually have

CHARACTERISTICS OF REPRESENTATIVE BREEDS OF CHICKENS

Breed	Standard Weight				Type of Comb	Earlobe	Body Skin	Shank[1]	Eggshell
	Cock		Hen						
	lb	kg	lb	kg					
American Breeds:									
Plymouth Rock	9½	4.3	7½	3.4	Single	Red	Yellow	Yellow	Brown
Wyandotte	8½	3.9	6½	3.0	Rose	Red	Yellow	Yellow	Brown
Rhode Island Red	8½	3.9	6½	3.0	Single and rose	Red	Yellow	Yellow	Brown
Jersey Black Giant	13	6.0	10	4.5	Single	Red	Yellow	Black	Brown
New Hampshire	8½	3.9	6½	3.0	Single	Red	Yellow	Yellow	Brown
Asiatic Breeds:									
Brahma (Light)	12	5.5	9½	4.3	Pea	Red	Yellow	Yellow[2]	Brown
Cochin	11	5.0	8½	3.9	Single	Red	Yellow	Yellow[2]	Brown
Langshan (Black)	9½	4.3	7½	3.4	Single	Red	White	Bluish black[2]	Brown
English Breeds:									
Australorp	8½	3.9	6½	3.0	Single	Red	White	Dark slate	Brown
Cornish (Dark)	10	4.5	7½	3.4	Pea	Red	Yellow	Yellow	Brown
Dorking (Silver-gray)	9	4.0	7	3.2	Single	Red	White	White	White
Orpington (Buff and white)	10	4.5	8	3.6	Single	Red	White	White	Brown
Sussex	9	4.0	7	3.2	Single	Red	White	White	Brown
Mediterranean Breeds:									
Leghorn	6	2.7	4½	2.0	Single and rose	White	Yellow	Yellow	White
Minorca (S. C. Black)	9	4.0	7½	3.4	Single	White	White	Dark slate	White
Ancona	6	2.7	4½	2.0	Single and rose	White	Yellow	Yellow	White
Andalusian (Blue)	7	3.2	5½	2.5	Single	White	White	Slaty blue	White
Hamburg (only breed in class)	5	2.3	4	1.8	Rose	White	White	Leaden blue	White
Continental Breeds:									
Campine	6	2.7	4	1.8	Single	White	White	Leaden blue	White
Lakenvelder	5	2.4	4	1.8	Single	White	White	Slate	White
Polish (only breed in class)	6	2.7	4½	2.0	V-shaped or absent	White	White	Blue or slate	White
French Breeds:									
Houdan	8	3.6	6½	3.0	V-shaped	White	White	Pinkish white	White
Crevecoeur	8	3.6	6½	3.0	V-shaped	Red	White	Leaden blue	White
La Fleche	8	3.6	6½	3.0	V-shaped	White	White	Dark slate	White
Faverolle	8	3.6	6½	3.0	Single	Red	White[2]	Pinkish white	Brown
Oriental Breeds:									
Sumatra	5	2.3	4	1.8	Pea	Gypsy	Yellow	Black	White
Malay	9	4.0	7	3.2	Strawberry	Red	Yellow	Yellow	Brown
Cubalaya	6	2.7	4	1.8	Pea	Red	White	Pinkish white	White

[1] Except for the breeds noted, the shanks are not feathered.
[2] Shanks feathered.

several common characteristics. The accompanying table lists some distinguishing features of representative breeds from various classes of chickens recognized by the American Poultry Association. Because of space limitations, not all breeds in each class can be listed, nor can the numerous varieties within each breed be described. Since there is much variation in color among the varieties, no characteristic color can be given for each breed.

In addition to the breeds listed on the table, bantams—that is, domestic fowl that are often miniatures of the standard breeds—are also bred. They are usually only about 25% as large as their full-sized counterparts. Also not listed are some particularly striking breeds, which are kept for their ornamental qualities, and several breeds and varieties bred as game, or fighting, fowl. The Chinese silky fowl, described by Marco Polo in the 13th century, resulted from a mutation of feature structure that gives it a peculiar "silky" or "woolly" appearance. Frizzled fowls are also the result of a particular mutation that affects feather structure. A Japanese breed, called the Yokohama, may have a tail up to 12 to 18 feet (4 to 6 meters) long; in average chickens the tail is 7 to 8 inches (18–20 cm) long. The Yokohama breed is the result of continued selection for this rather bizarre characteristic.

Egg-Producing Breeds. In modern poultry production, very few breeds of poultry are actually used extensively. Breeds used for egg production usually have quite different characteristics from those breeds that are most desired for meat production.

Egg-producing birds are usually bred for high rates of egg production and small body size. Ideally, the body size of a hen kept for egg production should be just large enough for her to produce large numbers of eggs of adequate size. Small hens are normally more efficient than larger ones because they require less feed to maintain their bodies. In the United States, the value of a hen for meat after she completes egg production is very small.

The White Leghorn is the breed used most extensively for egg production today. Its eggs have white shells. The hens used to produce eggs are the offspring of crosses of several strains of White Leghorns or of crosses of inbred lines. The hybrid offspring, like hybrid corn, are strikingly superior to the parent lines. Some strains or inbred lines, when mated, give offspring with particularly desirable characteristics, and breeders of commercial stocks of laying hens strive to produce commercial strains that may be mated with other strains having desirable attributes.

Most of the eggs sold in the United States have white shells. However, some markets, particularly in New England, prefer brown-shelled eggs. For these markets, New Hampshire or Rhode Island Reds or crosses of Rhode Island Reds and Barred Plymouth Rocks are used to a considerable extent for brown egg production.

Broiler Breeds. A chicken bred as a broiler must grow to market size very rapidly if it is to produce meat efficiently. This means that meat-producing birds have, at maturity, a large body size that is very inefficient for producing eggs. Pure breeds are seldom used for meat

Barred Plymouth Rock (male)

Rhode Island Red (male)

New Hampshire (male)

ALL PHOTOS, U. S. DEPARTMENT OF AGRICULTURE

Light Brahma (female)

production in the modern poultry industry; rather, most broiler chicks are crosses of two or more breeds. The most important meat-producing breed is the White Plymouth Rock. It is the predominant female parent of the modern broiler chick, while the male broiler parent is usually from the Cornish breed, which has had rapid feathering and a dominant white feather color introduced from crosses with other breeds.

PRODUCTION

Incubation. Chickens are well developed at hatching. They are covered with down and are able to feed themselves almost at once, but they must be protected from environmental extremes, especially cold, during the first weeks of life, given proper feed and water, and protected against disease.

Nearly all present-day chickens are hatched in incubators, which are constructed to maintain the proper temperature and humidity for the embryo to develop. Eggs are turned mechanically in these incubators to prevent embryonic death or malformation during incubation. The incubation period for chickens is 21 days.

Diet. More is known about the nutrition requirements of the young chicken than about that of any other species of animal. This has come about primarily because of the economic im-

portance of the chicken and also because of the usefulness of the chick as an experimental animal in basic studies in nutrition.

Chickens are known to require a dietary source of 13 vitamins, 14 inorganic elements, 13 amino acids, 1 essential fatty acid, a source of additional nitrogen, a source of energy, and water. These essentials are supplied to the chick in feeds containing natural feed ingredients as well as in concentrates or pure forms of some required nutrients.

The energy sources most used in poultry feeding are grains such as corn, milo, barley, wheat and wheat-milling by-products. Waste fats from the meat processing and the vegetable oil processing industries are also important sources of energy. The most important protein sources for chickens, in addition to those in the grains listed above, are soybean meal, meat meals, fish meal, cottonseed meal, and peanut meal. These protein sources must supply the required amounts of amino acids to the poultry. Growing chickens, from hatching to 6 weeks of age, require about 20 to 24% protein in their diets, whereas older chickens require somewhat less. Laying hens are fed diets containing about 16% protein, although the precise amount required depends on the amount of feed being consumed and the rate of egg production achieved.

Silver Cornish (male)

White Leghorn (male)

Yokohama (male)

ALL PHOTOS, U. S. DEPARTMENT OF AGRICULTURE

Silver Sobright Bantam (female)

Vitamin and mineral supplements are also used in poultry feeds to help provide these nutrients in proper amounts. Computers programmed with data on nutrient requirements, ingredient composition, and ingredient cost are used extensively to formulate commercial chicken feeds.

Broiler Production. The poultry industry is extremely specialized for the production of meat and eggs. The barnyard flock of the past no longer contributes significantly to the total production of chickens. Broiler, or meat, production in the United States is carried out largely by companies which have integrated many of the separate phases of production into one business complex. The hatching of chicks, the raising of broilers, the production of feed, and the processing and marketing of the final product may all be done by one company.

Broilers usually require 8 to 9 weeks to reach market size. The average weight of all broilers marketed in the United States in a typical year in the mid-1960's was 3.5 pounds (1.6 kg). This weight, under good conditions, can be reached on from 7 to 8 pounds (3.2 to 3.6 kg) of feed. In modern broiler housing, the environment can be closely regulated by proper use of heat and ventilation. Automatic mechanical systems for feeding and watering are also employed. Labor efficiency in raising broilers is very high.

Egg Production. Egg production is also highly specialized, although not all the necessary operations are as integrated as for broiler production. Hens begin to lay at about 22 weeks of age. They are kept for a full year of egg production, after which many are sold for meat and replaced by young hens. Modern housing for layers generally consists of windowless houses in which ventilation and light can be precisely regulated. A large percentage of new housing for laying hens makes use of laying cages in which hens are housed one to three per cage. Several tiers of cages may be used to make the best use of the space inside the laying house. Feed and water are supplied by automatic systems, and automatic egg-gathering equipment brings the eggs to a central location for processing and packaging. With such systems, one man may take care of up to 25,000 laying hens. Many very large egg-producing units with as many as several hundred thousand laying hens are now in existence.

The average annual production per layer in the United States is about 220 eggs. It is not unusual, however, to have large flocks producing 260 eggs per hen per year under good management. It usually requires an average of 4 to 4.5 pounds (1.8 to 2 kg) of feed to produce a dozen eggs.

ANATOMY AND PHYSIOLOGY

The chicken, in common with other birds, has numerous skeletal features that distinguish it from other animals. Many of these structures represent adaptation for flight that were useful to the chicken's wild ancestors. The skeleton is compact and light in weight, but very strong. Many bones contain air-filled cavities connected with the respiratory system. The wings are well developed and the breastbone, or sternum, has a keel-like structure to facilitate the attachment of powerful breast muscles useful for flight.

The body is covered with feathers, which make up from 4 to 9% of the weight of the chicken, depending on the age and sex of the individual. The feathers insulate the body of the chicken, making a regulated body temperature possible. They grow in definite areas of the skin called feather tracts. The typical parts of a body feather are the quill, which is continuous with the shaft throughout the length of the feather; the barbs, branching from the shaft; the barbules, branching from the barbs; and the barbicles, branching from the barbules. Feathers are replaced or molted in a regular sequence. At the end of the laying period, hens undergo an extensive molt.

Circulatory and Respiratory Systems. The circulatory and respiratory systems of the chicken are like those of other birds. The bird heart has four chambers, which serve to separate completely the arterial and venous blood streams. The respiratory system is distinguished by four pairs of air sacs on each side of the body. These air sacs are connected with spaces in the skeleton and also with the lungs, which are themselves closely attached to the spinal column and ribs. During inspiration and expiration air quickly passes through the lungs to the air sacs and then back through the lungs. The air sacs increase the buoyancy of the body, dissipate the heat resulting from the bird's muscular and metabolic activity, and increase the efficiency of the lungs.

Digestive System. Chickens take their food by means of a horny beak covering each jaw. The esophagus—the passage from the mouth to the stomach—is modified to form a crop, or pouch, in which food can be stored for some period of time following a large meal. The function of teeth in grinding and masticating food is taken over by the gizzard, a large muscular organ that forms part of the stomach. The gizzard has a rough, horny lining and retains small stones to aid in crushing large particles of food. Chickens are frequently given access to stones, called grit, to replenish the gizzard's supply.

Most of the digestion of food occurs in the small intestine, which is supplied with digestive enzymes from its own cells and from the pancreas. Bile from the liver and gall bladder also enters the small intestine through the bile ducts. At the junction of the large and small intestines there are two long blind pouches, called ceca, which play a minor role in digestion. The ceca may be 4 to 6 inches (10 to 15 cm) long in adults. The large intestine in chickens is extremely short and appears to have relatively little function other than as a passage from the small intestine to the cloaca. The undigested food wastes of the intestine and the products of the kidneys and reproductive organs all pass through a common chamber, the cloaca, which opens to the outside through the vent, or anus.

Reproductive System. As might be expected, the reproductive system of the hen is highly developed. The hen possesses two ovaries, although only the left ovary is functional. In a hen producing eggs regularly, the ovary appears as a cluster of follicles. These follicles contain the developing ovum, or yolk, in various stages of development, ranging from a nearly mature ovum to those hardly visible to the unaided eye.

When ovulation occurs, the follicular membrane ruptures, and the ovum, or yolk, is released from the ovary and enters the oviduct through a funnel-shaped structure known as the infundibulum. Below the infundibulum, the oviduct is divided into four main regions: the magnum, where the egg white is secreted; the isthmus, where the shell membranes are formed; the uterus, or shell gland; and the vagina, the passage to the cloaca.

The yolk requires 7 to 9 days to mature in the ovary. After ovulation, the white is secreted around the yolk in about 3 hours, the membranes are formed in about 1¼ hours, and the egg spends about 20 to 21 hours in the shell gland. If a hen is going to lay another egg the following day, ovulation occurs about ½ hour after an egg is laid.

Reproduction in chickens is affected markedly by changes in day lengths. Female chickens subjected to increasing periods of light will mature sexually much earlier than will hens given constant short periods of light or subjected to decreasing quantities of light. The hypothalamus, an area of the brain, is sensitive to light and in response to light causes the release of hormones which are responsible for ovarian development and ovulation.

The male chickens possess two testes, located high in the abdominal cavity along the back near the kidneys. Sperm passes from the testes through the ductus deferens to the cloaca. The male chicken has a rudimentary copulatory organ located on one of the transverse folds of the cloaca. The spermatozoa are introduced into the cloaca of the hen by the male and quickly find their way up the oviduct, where fertilization of the egg takes place, probably as the yolk passes the infundibulum.

DISEASES

In modern poultry production, thousands of chickens are raised in close proximity to each other. Under these circumstances, the spread of disease can be extremely rapid, and losses from disease can be serious. The monetary loss in the United States each year from chicken diseases has been estimated to be as high as $300 million. Disease control requires measures aimed at the prevention of outbreaks as well as the proper diagnosis and treatment of diseases. The most generally encountered diseases of poultry are the following:

Infectious bronchitis is a respiratory disease caused by a virus, which affects all ages of susceptible birds. It is characterized by coughing, gasping, nasal discharge, weakness, and depression. In young chickens, mortality may be very high, but in adults little mortality is observed. The disease is best controlled by vaccination with modified live-virus vaccines at regular intervals.

Newcastle disease is a highly infectious respiratory disease caused by a virus. It is also known as *avian pneumoencephalitis* and *fowl pest*. Both young and adult chickens are affected.

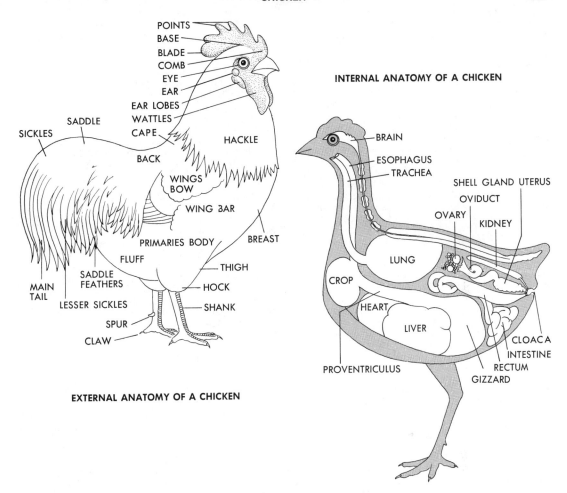

POINTS
BASE
BLADE
COMB
EYE
EAR
EAR LOBES
WATTLES
SADDLE
SICKLES
CAPE
HACKLE
BACK
WINGS BOW
WING BAR
PRIMARIES BODY
BREAST
FLUFF
MAIN TAIL
SADDLE FEATHERS
THIGH
LESSER SICKLES
HOCK
SPUR
SHANK
CLAW

EXTERNAL ANATOMY OF A CHICKEN

INTERNAL ANATOMY OF A CHICKEN

BRAIN
ESOPHAGUS
TRACHEA
SHELL GLAND UTERUS
OVIDUCT
OVARY
KIDNEY
LUNG
CROP
HEART
LIVER
CLOACA
INTESTINE
PROVENTRICULUS
RECTUM
GIZZARD

The most common symptoms are gasping, coughing, depression, loss of appetite, and nervous symptoms. Partial or complete paralysis of the limbs, muscular tremors, peculiar attitudes of the head and neck, and abnormal movements such as somersaulting, falling, and walking in circles may also be observed. Egg production in hens may completely cease. The disease is best controlled in countries where it is endemic by periodic vaccination with appropriate vaccines made from killed or modified live-virus preparations.

Mycoplasmosis is a respiratory disease caused by the bacteria *Mycoplasma gallisepticum*. It is also known as *air sac disease* or *chronic respiratory disease*. Those affected with the disease may show nasal discharge, watery eyes, and respiratory difficulty. This disease is often associated with other respiratory diseases. It is transmitted chiefly from infected hens to their chicks through the eggs. The disease can also be transmitted by contact with infected individuals, but it spreads very slowly in this manner. The disease can best be controlled by maintaining breeding flocks free of the disease by strict measures of isolation and sanitation. Chicks hatched from such flocks can begin life free of the disease.

Laryngotracheitis is a respiratory disease of chickens that is caused by a virus. The most characteristic symptom is gasping. When the affected chicken is inhaling, it often raises its head and neck and opens its mouth; and when exhaling, it draws its head back and lowers it.

Coughing and wheezing are also heard in affected flocks. In areas where the disease is prevalent, a vaccine is available to protect against the infection. However, since the vaccine is made from a live virus, it should not be given to animals whose exposure to the disease is unlikely, since it will introduce the live virus to the area.

Avian leukosis complex refers to at least two separate diseases, *Marek's disease* and *lymphoid leukosis*, both characterized by the growth of lymphoid tumors in many tissues of the body. These diseases cause the greatest economic loss to the poultry industry today.

Marek's disease is primarily a disease of young chickens from 2 to 5 months of age. It is also known as *fowl paralysis* and *neural lymphomatosis*. Nerve-tissue tumors that cause paralysis of both legs and wings are the most common form of this disease, but the tumors may also affect the viscera, eyes, and gonads. The disease is probably caused by a virus. To prevent the spread of the infection to young chicks, they should be isolated from older hens during the rearing period. No effective control method has been developed; breeding stock resistant to the disease may eventually be the most effective means of control.

Lymphoid leukosis is another disease characterized by the development of tumors in many organs of the body. It is also known as *visceral lymphomatosis*. The liver, spleen, heart, ovary, kidney, and intestine are often affected. In contrast to Marek's disease, lymphoid leukosis is most often observed in mature birds. This disease is also probably caused by a virus. The agent can be transferred from the hen to the chick through the egg. No effective control measures are known.

Coccidiosis is a very serious disease caused by protozoan parasites of the genus *Eimeria*. The parasite lives in various portions of the intestinal tract. It is transmitted to other chickens who ingest parasite oocysts passed in the droppings of infected birds. The oocysts are noninfective when they are originally passed in the droppings, but after 48 hours, when moisture and temperature conditions are suitable, the oocysts sporulate and become highly infective. When ingested, they develop in the intestinal tract and cause the active disease. The life cycle of the coccidia can be interrupted by keeping the house warm and dry and by removing infected litter daily to prevent reinfection. Chickens in wire cages or in pens with wire floors do not contract the disease since they do not have an opportunity to ingest sporulated oocysts in litter or droppings. After mild infections, chickens develop considerable resistance to coccidiosis. Many drugs, known as coccidiostats, can depress the development of coccidia with little harm to the chicken. These drugs, usually administered in the feed, are widely used to control coccidiosis.

Other diseases to which chickens are susceptible include pullorum disease, fowl pox, infectious coryza, fowl cholera, fowl plague, synovitis, avian encephalomyelitis, fowl typhoid, erysipelas, and blue comb. These are not so common as those described above, but they do cause serious losses. Chickens are also subject to internal and external parasites such as roundworms, tapeworms, cecal worms, gapeworms, several varieties of mites, lice, and fleas. These can be controlled by drugs effective against worms and by use of certain insecticides for the external parasites.

M. C. NESHEIM, *Cornell University*

Bibliography

American Poultry Association, *American Poultry Association Standard of Perfection* (Atlanta, Ga., 1953).
Biester, Harry E., and Schwarte, L. H., eds., *Diseases of Poultry*, 5th ed. (Ames, Iowa, 1965).
Bradley, Orlando C., *The Structure of the Fowl* (Edinburgh 1960).
Brown, Edward, *Races of Domestic Poultry* (London 1906).
Card, Leslie E., and Nesheim, Malden C., *Poultry Production*, 10th ed. (Philadelphia 1966).
Chamberlain, Frank W., *Atlas of Avian Anatomy*, Michigan Agricultural Experiment Station (East Lansing, Mich. 1943).
Cole, Harold H., ed., *Introduction to Livestock Production Including Dairy and Poultry* (San Francisco 1966).
Ewing, William, *Poultry Nutrition* (Pasadena, Calif., 1963).
Ghigi, Alessandro, *Poultry Farming as Described by the Writers of Ancient Rome* (Milan, Italy, 1949).
Hutt, Frederick B., *Genetics of the Fowl* (New York 1949).
Lind, Levi R., ed. and tr., *Aldrovandi on Chickens* (Norman, Okla., 1963).
Mountney, George J., *Poultry Products Technology* (Westport, Conn., 1966).
Oliver & Boyd Ltd., *British Poultry Science* (Edinburgh, 3 times yearly).
Poultry Science Association, *Poultry Science* (College Station, Tex., bimonthly).
Sturkie, Paul D., *Avian Physiology* (Ithaca, N. Y., 1965).
Titus, Harry W., *The Scientific Feeding of Chickens* (Danville, Ill., 1961).
Warren, Don C., *Practical Poultry Breeding* (New York 1953).
Winter, Alden R., and Funk, E. M., *Poultry: Science and Practice* (New York 1960).
Zeuner, Friedrich E., *A History of Domesticated Animals* (New York 1964).

CHICKEN POX is a highly contagious disease caused by a virus. It is characterized by a poxlike rash, and its name was probably derived from the word "chick-pea," because the skin lesions were thought to resemble the small round seeds of the chick-pea plant. In medical terminology, chicken pox is known as *varicella*.

Although chicken pox is generally considered to be a disease of children, it sometimes occurs in adults. It is most prevalent in children between the ages of 2 and 8, and it is estimated that about 50% of all children have had chicken pox by the time they enter kindergarten. Once a person has had chicken pox, he is usually immune to the disease for the rest of his life.

Cause. The virus that produces chicken pox is a tiny particle about 0.22 microns in diameter. (One micron equals about $\frac{1}{25,000}$ of an inch.) Because it appears to be identical with the virus that causes herpes zoster (an inflammatory disease of the nerves, also known as shingles, that produces small, blisterlike skin eruptions), it is frequently referred to as the varicella-zoster (V-Z) virus, and doctors believe that chicken pox and herpes zoster are actually two different forms of the same disease. This theory is supported by cases showing that children have developed chicken pox after being exposed to adults with herpes zoster. Chicken pox develops when a child is first infected with the V-Z virus. When the disease subsides the virus remains in the body in a latent, or inactive, form and may, for unknown reasons, become activated and produce herpes zoster many years later.

Symptoms. The incubation period for chicken pox ranges from 11 to 20 days, with an average of 14 days. The first symptom is usually the appearance of small, blisterlike lesions, called vesicles, on the skin. The vesicles vary in size from about $\frac{1}{16}$ to $\frac{1}{4}$ inch (1.5 to 6 mm) in diameter, and they first appear on the scalp, face, and trunk. Over the next few days, these lesions break open and become encrusted, while fresh lesions appear on the arms and legs. In most cases, the lesions disappear within 5 to 20 days.

Although patients with chicken pox usually complain of itching, they are otherwise fairly well and their temperature usually ranges from 100° F to 102° F (38° C to 39° C).

Complications arising from chicken pox are rare. Sometimes bacterial skin infections occur, and these may lead to impetigo, conjunctivitis, or other infections. Disorders of the nervous system are extremely rare complications of chicken pox.

Treatment. There is no specific treatment for chicken pox. Itching of the skin may be relieved by applying soothing liquids, such as calamine lotion or a dilute solution of sodium bicarbonate. In infants and small children, it is usually advisable to keep their fingernails short to prevent them from scratching.

The skin lesions can usually be protected against bacterial infection by careful washing with soap and water. If the vesicles become infected, antibiotics are administered. Because patients with chicken pox are considered to be contagious for five days after the rash has appeared, it is best to keep them isolated from other people during this period.

PHILIP BRUNELL, M. D.
New York University School of Medicine

CHICKEN SNAKE, a name used for some rat snakes. See RAT SNAKE.

R. A. SCHLEGEL

CHICKWEEDS include *Cerastium vulgatum* (left), also called mouse-ear chickweed; and *Stellaria media* (right).

CHICKWEED, chik'wēd, is a spreading annual European plant that has become naturalized throughout temperate regions and is a serious garden weed in North America. The chickweed, known botanically as *Stellaria media,* belongs to the pink family (Caryophyllaceae). Its stems grow about 12 inches (30 cm) long but are so weak that they often droop to the ground. The small white flowers are about ½ inch (12 mm) wide and are borne in loose, flat-topped terminal clusters. The leaves of the chickweed are opposite, oblong-oval, and about 2½ inches (6 cm) long.

In warm climates or during warm winters, the chickweed flowers and produces seed all year round. Although hand weeding and raking are recommended for controlling the pest, spraying the plants with 2-4-D, a common chemical weed killer, is also effective.

DONALD WYMAN
The Arnold Arboretum, Harvard University

CHICLAYO, chē-klä'yō, is a city on the arid coastal plain of northwestern Peru. It is the capital of Lambayeque department. The irrigated land around Chiclayo yields abundant crops of rice and sugarcane, and rice milling is one of the city's main industries. Other industries produce jute, leather, shoes, lumber, furniture, glassware, cement, canned fruit, beer, chocolate, and machine-shop goods. Chiclayo is connected by road and rail with the nearby port of Pimentel and by the Pan American Highway with Lima, the national capital, a 475-mile (760-km) drive down the coast. The city has a cathedral. Population: (1961) 95,667.

CHICLE, chik'əl, is the natural gum obtained from the sapodilla tree (*Achras zapota*). Chicle is an important ingredient in chewing gum. However, it is always blended with other gums, both natural and synthetic, to form the gum base. Sometimes these other gums are also called chicle.

Although the sapodilla tree is widely grown throughout Central America and other tropical regions, most commercial chicle comes from a relatively restricted area of the Yucatan peninsula, comprising portions of Mexico, Guatemala, and British Honduras. The gum is obtained from V-shaped cuts made in the trunk of the tree. The cuts are made about a foot (30 cm) apart up the side of the trunk until the lowest branches are reached. Very often the tapping cuts are

destructive to the tree. In addition to wounding the bark and the wood, they injure the cambium, (the layer of tissue that produces the wood and bark) so that the growth of new wood and bark is greatly retarded. A carelessly tapped tree yields very little chicle for several years afterward.

After the cuts are made, the gum that oozes from them is collected and heated in large kettles. When sufficiently thickened, it is poured into wooden molds. The resulting gum blocks are then wrapped for shipment.

LAWRENCE ERBE
University of Southwestern Louisiana

CHICO, chē'kō, a city in northern California, in Butte county, is situated in the Sacramento Valley, 90 miles (144 km) north of Sacramento. The surrounding area produces almonds, rice, fruits, field crops, and livestock. Chico's principal economic activities are the processing and packing of nuts and the production of lumber, matches, conveyor systems, and toothpaste tubes. The city is the seat of Chico State College, a coeducational institution, founded in 1889.

Chico was settled in 1847 and incorporated as a city in 1872. It has a council-manager type of government. Population: 19,580.

CHICOPEE, chik'ə-pē, is a manufacturing city in southwestern Massachusetts, in Hampden county, 8 miles (13 km) north of Springfield, on the Chicopee River. Situated in an industrial area, the city manufactures automobile tires and tubes, drop forgings, radio parts, sporting goods, cotton products, surgical bandages, knit goods, ladies' undergarments, plastic tile, paints, and box containers. It is the home of the College of Our Lady of the Elms, a 4-year institution for women, and was the birthplace of Edward Bellamy, author of *Looking Backward.* Westover Air Force Base is just northeast.

One of the oldest settlements in western Massachusetts, Chicopee was founded in 1641 as the

CHICLE is made from the sap of the sapodilla tree. This workman in Yucatan, Mexico, is cutting the bark.

EWING GALLOWAY

northern part of Springfield. With the establishment of textile mills and iron foundaries early in the 1800's, manufacturing became the predominant activity. A Chicopee factory was the first in the United States to cast bronze statues, and in 1835 the first friction matches in the country were made here. It became a township in 1848 and a city in 1890. Chicopee includes the communities of Chicopee Falls, Chicopee Center, Williamansett, Fairview, and Aldenville. Its name is an Indian word meaning "birch bark place." The city is governed by a mayor and a board of aldermen. Population: 66,676.

RITA BLANAN KUSEK
Chicopee Public Library

CHICORY, chik′ə-rē, a stout perennial plant, whose leaves are widely eaten as salad greens or as a cooked vegetable. The chicory, also known as witloof or witloof chicory, is probably a native of Europe and Asia. It ranges in height from 3 to 6 feet (90 to 180 cm) and bears bright blue flower heads about 1½ inches (38 mm) across. The fleshy roots of the chicory are sometimes dried, ground, and roasted to be used as a flavoring or adulterant in coffee.

When grown for its leaves, chicory seed is planted in the spring in rows 15 to 18 inches (38 to 45 cm) apart. Just before cold weather, the roots are harvested and the tops are cut off about 2 inches (5 cm) above the crown. The roots may be placed in cold storage until they are used. At that time they are all cut to the same length and placed upright in a trench or other forcing structure. They are planted about 2 inches (5 cm) apart and covered to the crowns with moist soil. About 6 or 8 inches (15 or 20 cm) of dry sand or sawdust is then placed over the crowns. This covering excludes light and ensures the formation of solid leafy heads. When kept at temperatures from 50° to 60°F (10° to 16°C), desirable heads from 4 to 5 inches (10 to 12 cm) long may be produced in about 3 weeks.

The chicory is known technically as *Cichorium intybus* and belongs to the composite family. It is closely related to the endive *(C. endivia)* and is sometimes also known as French endive.

JOHN P. MCCOLLUM, *University of Illinois*

Chicory (Cichorium intybus)

J. J. SMITH

CHICOUTIMI, shē-kōō-tē-mē′, is a city in southeastern Quebec, Canada, on the Saguenay River, about 120 miles (192 km) north of Quebec city. It is an important tourist center, the terminus of the Saguenay River steamship route. Hunting and fishing are attractions in the region. Chicoutimi's industries include machine shops and the manufacture of wood products, principally furniture, flooring, sashes, and doors. The city is near the site of a trade and mission post founded by the Jesuits in 1676. It was incorporated as a city in 1676. Population: 33,893.

CHICOUTIMI-NORD, shē-kōō-tē-mē′ nôr, is a city in south-central Quebec, in Chicoutimi county, on the north shore of the Saguenay River. It lies opposite the industrial and commercial city of Chicoutimi, to which it is connected by a highway bridge. It is principally a residential suburb of Chicoutimi and of Arvida, 5 miles (8 km) to the southwest.

The site was originally known as Ste.-Anne de Chicoutimi. The town was incorporated as Chicoutimi-Nord in 1955. It was incorporated as a city in 1961. Population: 14,086.

CHIDAMBARAM, chi-dum′bə-rəm, is a town in India, in southeast Madras state, 125 miles (200 km) southwest of Madras city. Rice and peanuts are processed here.

It was once a capital of the Chola dynasty (907–1279). Chidambaram is the site of many Hindu temples and pagodas, some of them gems of Dravidian art that attract many pilgrims each year. The most famous temple, the Kanak Sabha, or golden shrine, dedicated to the god Shiva (Siva), is said to have been erected in the 10th century by a Chola king who witnessed the god in his role of cosmic dancer. Population: (1961) 40,694.

CHIEF JUSTICE, in the United States, the presiding judge of the highest appellate court of a jurisdiction. Most often the title refers to the chief of the U. S. Supreme Court, but it is also accorded to the presiding officer of many of the highest state courts. A chief justice has the powers of a presiding officer and, in addition, often has administrative duties within his court system. However, he has no significant judicial power beyond that of any justice of his court.

The only specific mention of the office of chief justice of the United States in the federal Constitution is the provision that the chief justice shall preside in an action for impeachment of the president. The Constitution provides for presidential appointment and Senate confirmation of all judges of the Supreme Court. The Judiciary Act of 1789, which established the Supreme Court, simply states "That the supreme court of the United States shall consist of a chief justice and five associate justices." President George Washington, in a letter to John Jay upon the confirmation of the latter's appointment as the first U. S. chief justice, described the office as the "head of the department which must be considered as the keystone of our political fabric."

By tradition, the chief justice administers the oath of office to the president and vice president of the United States at their inauguration, although this function may be performed by any official authorized to administer oaths. At state occasions the chief justice is accorded the fourth rank of precedence, after the president, the vice president, and the speaker of the House of Representatives, in recognition of his role as the symbolic head of the federal judiciary.

Under present statutes the chief justice of the United States has the power to assign circuit and district judges to serve in other circuits and to assign retired judges to serve outside their former circuits. The chief justice also summons and presides over the Judicial Conference of the United States, an assembly of judges representing all the federal courts, which makes a comprehensive annual survey of the federal court system.

Within the Supreme Court itself, statutes give the chief justice power to supervise the operation of the offices of the clerk, the marshal, the reporter, and the librarian. The chief justice traditionally speaks first and votes last when the court is in conference. When he concurs with the decision of the court, he assigns the writing of the opinion to a justice or writes it himself.

The fame of the office of chief justice comes mainly from the vigor of the men who have held it. John Marshall, the fourth chief justice, generally is regarded as the greatest, having set his stamp on the office during his 34-year tenure.

Many of the court's most famous opinions were written by chief justices. These include

Chief Justices of the United States

John Jay, of New York, nominated by George Washington, Sept. 26, 1789; resigned 1795.
John Rutledge, of South Carolina, nominated by George Washington, 1795; presided summer term; nomination rejected by Senate, December 1795.
Oliver Ellsworth, of Connecticut, nominated by George Washington, 1796; confirmed March 4, 1796; resigned 1799.
John Marshall, of Virginia, nominated by John Adams, Jan. 20, 1801; confirmed Jan. 27, 1801; died July 6, 1835.
Roger Brooke Taney, of Maryland, nominated by Andrew Jackson, Dec. 28, 1835; confirmed March 15, 1836; died Oct. 12, 1864.
Salmon Portland Chase, of Ohio, nominated by Abraham Lincoln, Dec. 6, 1864; confirmed the same day; died May 7, 1873.
Morrison Remick Waite, of Ohio, nominated by Ulysses S. Grant, Jan. 19, 1874; confirmed Jan. 21, 1874; died March 23, 1888.
Melville Weston Fuller, of Illinois, nominated by Grover Cleveland, April 30, 1888; confirmed July 20, 1888; died July 4, 1910.
Edward Douglass White, of Louisiana, nominated by William Howard Taft, Dec. 10, 1910; confirmed Dec. 12, 1910; died May 19, 1921.
William Howard Taft, of Connecticut, nominated by Warren G. Harding, June 30, 1921; confirmed the same day; resigned Feb. 3, 1930.
Charles Evans Hughes, of New York, nominated by Herbert C. Hoover, Feb. 3, 1930; confirmed Feb. 14, 1930; resigned July 1, 1941.
Harlan Fiske Stone, of New York, nominated by Franklin D. Roosevelt, June 12, 1941; confirmed June 27, 1941; died April 22, 1946.
Frederick Moore Vinson, of Kentucky, nominated by Harry S Truman, June 6, 1946; confirmed June 20, 1946; died Sept. 8, 1953.
Earl Warren, of California, nominated by Dwight D. Eisenhower, Sept. 30, 1953; presided at session opening Oct. 5, 1953; confirmed March 1, 1954; resigned June 26, 1968, effective June 23, 1969.
Warren E. Burger, of Minnesota, nominated by Richard M. Nixon, May 21, 1969; confirmed June 9, 1969.

Marbury v. *Madison* (written by Marshall in 1803), affirming the power of the Supreme Court to declare laws of Congress unconstitutional; *Dred Scott* v. *Sandford* (Roger Brooke Taney, 1857), holding that an emancipated Negro was not a citizen of the United States and that an enslaved Negro did not become free by having been taken into a free state or territory; and *Brown* v. *Board of Education* (Earl Warren, 1954), declaring segregated public schools unconstitutional. See also SUPREME COURT OF THE UNITED STATES.

EDMUND W. KITCH, *University of Chicago*

CHIEM, Lake, kēm, the largest lake in Bavaria, Germany. Lake Chiem (German, Chiemsee) lies about 40 miles (64 km) southeast of Munich and about 30 miles (48 km) west of Salzburg, Austria. It covers an area of 31 square miles (80 sq km) and is 1,600 feet (488 meters) above sea level. The lake is drained by the Alz, a tributary of the Inn River. There are three islands in the lake: Herreninsel (with a castle built by King Louis II of Bavaria), Fraueninsel, and Krautinsel.

CH'IEN LUNG, chē-en' lŏong' (1711–1799), was the fourth emperor of the Ch'ing dynasty in China. His personal name was *Hung-li* and his dynastic title *Kao Tsung*. Born in Peking on Sept. 25, 1711, Hung-li ascended the throne in 1736 and reigned for 60 years. He formally abdicated in favor of his son, Chia Ch'ing, in order not to reign longer than his grandfather, the K'ang Hsi emperor, but he actually ruled until his death in 1799.

The Ch'ien Lung period marks the apex of the Ch'ing dynasty and the beginning of its decline. The empire reached its greatest extent, incorporating Tibet and Sinkiang, and there was general peace and prosperity. Much of the credit for the flourishing economy in these years, however, belongs to Ch'ien Lung's predecessors.

Ch'ien Lung's education was good and his interests wide, extending to European art and technology. Like his grandfather, he tolerated and employed the Jesuit missionaries, but he did not allow them to carry on religious activities. He was a poet and essayist of some quality. A mediocre painter but an avid and discerning art collector, he was largely responsible for the magnificent Palace Collection now in Taiwan. The great scholarly 36,000-volume Ssu-k'u chüan-shu (Imperial Manuscript Library) was compiled under his sponsorship.

In the last years of his reign China was still strong enough to refuse the trade concessions sought by the Macartney mission in 1793 and the Dutch mission in 1795, but weaknesses were developing. In his later years Ch'ien Lung fell under the influence of the corrupt and rapacious Hoshen. The increasing immorality of officials and declining prosperity brought social discontent that left China defenseless against foreign power in the 19th century.

JAMES R. SHIRLEY
Northern Illinois University

CHIFLEY, chif'lē, **Joseph Benedict** (1885–1951), Australian prime minister. He was born in Bathurst, New South Wales, on Sept. 22, 1885. He was elected to the federal House of Representatives as a Labour party member in 1928 and appointed minister of defense the following year. Chifley lost his parliamentary seat in the general election of 1931 but was reelected in 1940.

Chifley was appointed Commonwealth treasurer in October 1941. During World War II he introduced a comprehensive system of wartime financial controls, planning, and carrying through the greatest war loans in Australia's history. From 1942 to 1945 he also held the new post of minister for postwar reconstruction.

He became acting prime minister on April 30, 1945, and on July 4 he assumed the premiership, at the same time retaining his treasury post. Chifley's government was defeated in the 1949 elections. He died in Canberra on June 13, 1951.

CHIGA, chē'gə, a Bantu-speaking people living just east of Lake Edward in southwestern Uganda. They are part of a group referred to as the Interlacustrine Bantu. Numbering over 400,000 people, the Chiga inhabit an area in which population densities are as high as 720 per square mile (278 per sq km).

Most of the Chiga are Christians. They are primarily hoe cultivators of finger millet and sorghum. Until they came under British control in 1912, the Chiga lived in numerous autonomous communities, which relied on kinship groups for maintaining social control. They never united into a single political system.

ROBERT A. LYSTAD
Johns Hopkins University

CHIGASAKI, chi-gä-sä'kē, is a city in Japan, in Kanagawa prefecture, on Honshu island. It is on the northern shore of Sagami Bay, about 20 miles (32 km) southwest of Tokyo. Chigasaki was once a stage town on the Tokaido highway linking Tokyo with the Kyoto-Osaka district. In the 20th century it became a seaside resort and then a residential suburb of Tokyo and Yokohama. Light industry, especially electronics, is concentrated in the north along the main rail lines. Chigasaki became a city in 1947 and has had one of the highest urban growth rates in Japan. Population: (1965) 100,081.

DAVID H. KORNHAUSER, *University of Hawaii*

CHIGGER, chig'ər, a larval mite that is a parasite of land-dwelling vertebrates, including man. It has three pairs of legs and an ovoid, saclike body. Chiggers occur throughout the world. Some, called *redbugs* in the United States and *harvest mites* in England, bite humans, producing severe itching and inflammation. Others, in parts of Asia and on some Pacific Islands, transmit scrub typhus, a serious rickettsial disease.

After hatching, a chigger attaches itself to a host and feeds on the host's tissue fluids for several days. It then drops to the ground and burrows into the soil, where it molts into a nymph and then into an adult. The nymphs and adults are larger than the larvae and have four pairs of legs and a body shaped like a figure 8. They live in soil and litter, feeding on small arthropods and their eggs.

Chiggers belong to the family Trombiculidae in the order Acarina, class Arachnida. There are about 2,000 species. The term "chigger" is sometimes confused with "chigoe" (q.v.).

CONRAD E. YUNKER, *Rocky Mountain Laboratory, U. S. Public Health Service*

CHIGI, kē'jē, the name of an Italian noble family, known in history for its great bankers, ecclesiastics, and patrons of the arts. Beginning as bankers in Siena in the 13th century, the family attained European prominence with Agostino the Magnificent (1465?–1520), papal banker and merchant prince in Rome, who built a far-flung business empire, fraternized with princes, and spent lavishly as a patron of artists and writers. The elegant Roman residence called the Villa Farnesina, decorated with frescoes by Raphael, was built for Agostino.

In later generations the family rose to new heights through the church. Fabio Chigi became Pope Alexander VII (reigned 1655–1667). Seven Chigi became cardinals, and many members of the family acquired lands and titles in the Papal

States. As literary men and bibliophiles, Alexander VII and his descendants assembled the celebrated Biblioteca Chigiana, now part of the Vatican Library.

A Roman line of the family, the Chigi-Albani, survives, tracing its descent from Agostino II Chigi, a nephew of Alexander VII. One branch of the family remains in Siena, where the 14th century Chigi-Saracini Palace is the site of an academy of music.

RANDOLPH STARN
University of California at Berkeley

CHIGNECTO BAY, shig-nek'tō, in Canada, is an inlet, 50 miles (80 km) long and 8 miles (13 km) wide, at the northern end of the Bay of Fundy, between New Brunswick and Nova Scotia. The bay is noted for its tides, among the highest in the world, which can rise as much as 50 feet (15 meters). Chignecto Isthmus, 12 miles (19 km) wide, separates the bay from Northumberland Strait in the Gulf of St. Lawrence. In 1888 construction of a ship railway to carry vessels up to 5,000 tons across the isthmus was begun. The railway, which would have saved a run of several hundred miles around Nova Scotia, was never completed, for lack of funds. Fundy National Park is situated on the northern shore of the mouth of Chignecto bay.

CHIGOE, chig'ō, a tropical flea that infests many mammals, including man. The chigoe, also known as the *sandflea* or *jigger*, is less than $\frac{1}{25}$ inch (1 mm) long and is the smallest of all known fleas. Unlike most other fleas, it lacks comblike rows of bristles on its head or thorax, has a short, telescoped thorax, and has weak legs that are poorly modified for jumping.

An impregnated female chigoe burrows into the skin of a host—in man, usually under toenails or between the toes—producing itching, inflammation, and sometimes ulceration. In the burrow, her abdomen swells and about 100 eggs are deposited. These mature in a week and are expelled from the wound. After hatching, the larvae feed on organic debris in shaded sandy soil or earthen floors. They pupate in cocoons, and the adults emerge 17 days after the eggs are laid.

The chigoe, *Tunga penetrans*, belongs to the family Hectopsyllidae of the order Siphonaptera. The term "chigoe" is sometimes confused with "chigger" (q.v.).

CONRAD E. YUNKER, *Rocky Mountain Laboratory, U. S. Public Health Service*

CHIHFENG, chû'fung', is a city in North China, in the southeast part of the Inner Mongolian Autonomous Region. It is a trading center for the vast grazing region of the Liao River basin and is connected by railroad with the southern Manchurian region. Leather goods, wool, other animal products, grains, and herbs are exported. The people are mainly Mongols of the Ongniod Banner.

Inner Mongolia is divided administratively into eight leagues (*meng*), and Chihfeng is the seat of the Chaowuta (Jaoda) league. It is about 90 miles (150 km) from Chengte in Hopeh province and is connected with it by highway. The regional capital, Huhohot, is about 300 miles (500 km) to the west. Population: (1958) 49,000.

CHENGTSU WU, *Hunter College, New York*

CHIHUAHUA, chē-wä′wä, the largest state in Mexico, borders New Mexico to the north and is separated from Texas on the northeast by the Río Grande. The state's area is 95,400 square miles (247,087 sq km). The population is predominantly mestizo and white, but Chihuahua's 60,000 Tarahumaras compose the largest Indian tribe in northern Mexico. Casas Grandes, the best known prehistoric ruin in northern Mexico, is in Chihuahua.

The state is on the North Mexican plateau, the high western margins of which have been dissected by rivers flowing through deep gorges (*barrancas*). The pine and oak forests of these temperate highlands constitute the leading timber resources of Mexico. Eastward lie valleys and plains of steppe climate, and beyond them are desert plains and arid mountain ranges.

Irrigated agriculture and livestock raising, mining, manufacturing, forestry, and tourism characterize the economy. The major crops are maize, beans, cotton, oats, wheat, alfalfa, potatoes, and fruits. Chihuahua is Mexico's leading producer of metals (first in zinc, lead, and silver; second in copper, gold, and iron), besides being the chief lumbering state. Manufacturing is primarily the processing of products of field, pasture, forest, and mine. Most of it is carried on in the five leading cities—Ciudad Juárez, Chihuahua city, Hidalgo del Parral, Delicias, and Camargo—and in the cellulose manufacturing center of Ciudad Anáhuac.

Chihuahua city, capital of the state, was founded in the early 1700's after silver mines had been developed nearby. Located in the well-watered Chuviscar Valley, it is the commercial center for most of the state, the chief manufacturing center, and the site of the state university. Its cathedral is the finest example of colonial architecture in northern Mexico.

Probably the first Europeans to visit Chihuahua were Alvaro Núñez Cabeza de Vaca and his companions in 1536. Spanish settlement began in the 1560's with mining communities in the south. Ranching to supply the mines became important, and during the 19th century Chihuahua had the largest cattle ranch in Mexico.

Chihuahua became one of the original 19 Mexican states in 1824. For the next century economic development was held back by Apache and Comanche raids, U. S. and French invasions, and the disorders of the Mexican revolution. Since 1930, the construction of irrigation projects, cellulose plants, pipelines (bringing in natural gas and petroleum products), and the scenic Chihuahua-Pacific Railroad across the *barranca* country have stimulated the economy. Population: (1970) of the state, 1,612,525; of the city, 257,027.

DONALD D. BRAND, *University of Texas*

CHIHUAHUA, chə-wä′wä, is the world's smallest breed of dog and a popular member of the toy group. The graceful, vivacious Chihuahua weighs from 1 to 6 pounds (0.5 to 2.5 kg) and stands from 4 to 6 inches (10 to 15 cm) at the shoulder. It has a round skull and large popeyes that should be full but not protruding. The coat, which may be smooth or long, ranges from snow white to jet black; a smooth coat of solid color is preferred by dog fanciers. Terrier-like qualities may be observed in the behavior of the breed.

The Chihuahua originally descended from the small hairless Asiatic dog, and its ancestors include the long-coated Techichi of the Toltec and Aztec

EVELYN M. SHAFER

Smooth-coat chihuahua

Indians. The breed is named for the Mexican state where it again became popular, after having dropped from favor following the destruction of Montezuma's empire. The modern Chihuahua was developed about 1850. Its popularity in the United States began to soar in the 1950's, and the Chihuahua now ranks among the 10 most popular breeds of dog.

WILLIAM F. BROWN
Editor of "American Field"

CHILBLAIN, chil′blān, is a localized skin condition caused by repeated exposure to cold and dampness. Poor nutrition and impaired circulation are predisposing causes.

Chilblain, known medically as *pernio*, occurs mostly on the hands, feet, face, and ears. The affected parts become swollen and purplish, with sensations of itching, burning, and pain. They are usually also cold, sweaty, and tacky to the touch. Treatment of chilblain consists essentially of keeping the areas warm and improving the patient's diet. Sometimes, vasodilators (drugs that widen the blood vessels) are also administered.

SIDNEY HOFFMAN, M. D.
St. John's Episcopal Hospital, Brooklyn, N. Y.

CHILD, Julia (1912–   ), American food expert, author, and television personality. She was born Julia McWilliams in Pasadena, Calif., on Aug. 15, 1912. She graduated from Smith College in 1934 and worked with the OSS in Ceylon during World War II. At the time of her marriage to Paul Child in 1946 she knew little about cooking, but during the Childs' six-year stay in Paris, she attended the Cordon Bleu cooking school and acquired a wide knowledge of French cuisine. With two friends she began L'Ecole des Trois Gourmandes in Paris and, also with them, wrote *Mastering the Art of French Cooking* (1961). The book's success led in 1963 to her popular American TV series on French cooking.

CHILD, Lydia Maria Francis (1802–1880), American abolitionist and author. Lydia Maria Francis was born in Medford, Mass., on Feb. 11, 1802. In 1828 she married David Lee Child, a Boston lawyer. The Childs became ardent abolitionists, and Mrs. Child wrote one of the first antislavery books, *An Appeal in Favor of That Class of Americans Called Africans* (1833). From 1841 to 1849 she edited the *National Anti-Slavery Standard*, a New York weekly. She died in Wayland, Mass., on Oct. 20, 1880.

CHILD ABUSE is physical or emotional harm to children caused by their parents or guardians. In the United States alone, about 300 cases of physical child abuse per million people are reported each year. An approximately equal number of cases of serious neglect is reported. One third of all types of child abuse affects children under 1 year of age, one third from ages 1 to 3, and one third over age 3.

Every state of the United States has laws requiring physicians and other professionals to report suspected child abuse. Laymen are also strongly encouraged to report cases so that abused children can be found and helped.

Types of Abuse. Physical abuse of children includes intentionally inflicted bruises, fractures, burns, and other wounds. Such injuries collectively are sometimes referred to as the *battered-child syndrome.*

Some children are abused emotionally by being repeatedly terrorized, by being set up as scapegoats, or by rejection. In addition, children are sometimes subjected to sexual abuses ranging from molestation to incest. All types of emotional abuse may have serious and lasting effects on the child's personality.

A frequent symptom of child neglect is underfeeding, which is the most common cause of underweight in infancy. In extreme cases, children may be near death from starvation by the time they are brought to a hospital.

The Abusers. Parents who abuse children come from all ethnic, religious, geographic, socio-economic, and educational groups. Most child-abusing parents or guardians were themselves abused as children. They regard their child as someone who should satisfy his parents' psychological needs. When the child cannot do this, as he usually cannot, the parents may become violently angry. Most abusers are simply lonely, unloved, immature, depressed, and angry persons. Less than 10% of them are classified as psychotics or sociopaths.

Treatment. To break the cycle of violence, a nonpunitive approach to child-abusing parents is required. The abused child is usually hospitalized to guarantee his safety while a case investigator and other professionals decide the best long-range approach to caring for the child and treating his parents. The parents in child-abuse cases usually do not accept traditional psychotherapy. They respond better to therapists who actively reach out to them with guidance and emotional support, as well as to group therapy. Laymen trained as mothering aides or home-workers are often helpful. Day-care centers are important in giving the mother a part of her day free from the demands of her child.

In some cases the juvenile court awards temporary custody of the child to a child-protection agency. If the home is considered dangerous, the child is placed temporarily in a foster home. However, the ultimate goal is to reunite the family. In 90% of the cases in one large state, the children were returned to their own homes after their parents showed improvement. In only 10% of the cases were parental rights later terminated and the children released for adoption.

BARTON D. SCHMITT, M. D. and
C. HENRY KEMPE, M. D.
University of Colorado Medical Center

Further Reading: Kempe, C. Henry, and Helfer, Ray E., eds., *Helping the Battered Child and His Family* (Lippincott 1972).

CHILD DEVELOPMENT. The area of child development encompasses the physical, psychological, and social growth of the normal child from birth to adolescence. This area is studied by two branches of psychology. *Developmental psychology* tends to focus on developmental processes in lower animals as well as in children and on the genetic aspects of development. *Child psychology* typically pays more attention to the intellectual, personal, and social aspects of development. Interest in child development is certainly multidisciplinary—involving pediatricians, teachers, and all who work and live with children. Psychologists, however, have played a dominant role in doing research and spreading information about child development.

Regardless of one's viewpoint, a relatively regular, sequential process of physical growth and behavioral change can be observed in children. Given minimally adequate nourishment and reasonable protection from illness, injury, and other hostile aspects of the environment, physical development is in general predictable. The development of motor skills also follows a relatively orderly pattern.

DEVELOPMENT IN INFANCY

The newborn infant weighs approximately 7½ pounds and is approximately 20 inches long. Except for a slight loss of weight for a short period after birth, weight and height will increase with age until, or slightly beyond, the period called adolescence. The first year of life is marked by evidence of physical growth and maturation. All senses are operative at birth or shortly thereafter, but the motor capacities of the infant are extremely limited. Indeed, his behavior is dominated primarily by a number of primitive reflexes, most of which disappear by 3 to 4 months of age. One of these is the reflex sucking behavior that occurs in response to tactile stimulation around the mouth (rooting reflex). Another example is reflex postural adjustment involving the placement of the arms and legs according to the position of the head to the left or right (tonic neck reflex). Still another is the fanning of the toes when a finger is rubbed along the sole of the foot (Babinsky reflex). Such reflexes are evidence of the immaturity of the infant's nervous system.

As the infant develops over the first few weeks, it becomes easier to identify waking and sleeping periods that were hardly distinguishable during the first week except at the extremes of deep sleep or crying. Once the longer periods of wakefulness begin to occur, the infant is more visually alert. During this time one can observe the first social smiling and marked increases in vocalizations other than crying.

The period from 3 months to approximately one year is marked by a considerable elaboration of motor skills, perceptual ability, and vocalization, which culminates in walking and the beginning of talking. These achievements mark a new era for both infant and mother. At this time parents, psychologists, and others concerned with child development become increasingly concerned with the impact of the environment on the infant. This does not mean that the environment was necessarily unimportant before, but there is much greater opportunity for it to be influential after the first year, and its influence is more obvious. There are new problems of behavior control. The socialization process has already been

INFANCY

During the first few years of life children grow rapidly. They also develop such basic skills as walking and talking, and begin to learn how to live in the world with other people. Experiences at this stage are important influences on intellectual and social development, as well as on physical growth.

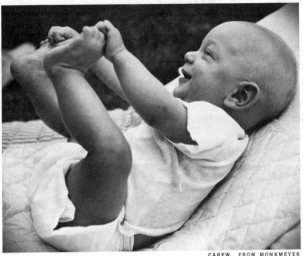

CAREW, FROM MONKMEYER

A baby's activities may seem to be limited to his immediate surroundings, but he soon learns to smile in response to attention.

FRITZ HENLE, FROM MONKMEYER

Once a child begins to walk, she begins to learn more about the world around her.

started with regard to feeding, but the do's and don't's pertaining to other behaviors increase geometrically once the child is walking and is more vocal. Likewise, perceptual and intellectual development take on new dimensions as the child's ability to interact with his environment increases overwhelmingly. Learning to talk and listen, a keystone in the process of intellectual and cognitive development, provides a particularly obvious example of behavior that is influenced by the environment. Language is acquired only in a social context, and the meanings of words are clearly related to what the child experiences.

By 3 years of age, the child is sufficiently adept in using words and muscles to be sent to a nursery school. His interactions with other children are characterized at best by play (with them or at least in company with them) and at worst by violent aggression, as when he decides the toy another child has is the one he wants most. An experienced mother or teacher knows that he can be distracted by suggesting an alternative activity or by presenting another toy. More adequate social behavior will soon develop with relatively minimal help from adults.

The decision to start nursery school at 3 years rather than earlier is probably determined more by the time of completion of toilet training than on the basis of what nursery schools might provide for a child at any particular time. In the USSR, school training for some children is started during the first year. Nurseries taking children at this age are concerned not only with caring for the infant but also with providing an enriched environment through a training program that concentrates on perceptual development.

Child development after 3 is not so easily divided into age periods. Developmental sequences can be discussed more readily in terms of major psychological processes and principles.

NATURE VS. NURTURE

A major issue among a generation of child psychologists was the nature vs. nurture controversy—the debate about the relative influence of heredity and environment on development. An American, G. Stanley Hall, sometimes called the father of child psychology, brought to child psychology the view that genetics is the determining factor. Among Hall's more influential students were Arnold Gesell, a pediatrician who was concerned with early behavioral development generally, and Lewis M. Terman, a psychologist who was concerned primarily with intellectual development.

The importance of inheritance in the determination of individual differences in physiognomy and physique has seldom been seriously questioned. But there has been much less certainty about the degree to which individual differences in social behavior and intelligence might also be genetically determined. Because of the difficulty of doing adequate research on genetic questions with human beings and the ease with which at least limited environmental effects could be demonstrated, the genetic viewpoint had been rather soundly rejected by the end of the first half of the 20th century. Since then, however, much more research has been done with lower animals, with which selective breeding is possible and on which more stringent environmental controls can be exercised. As a consequence, there is increasing support for the notion that genetic variables do contribute significantly to the development of intelligence and social behavior. Although there is considerable chance for error in generalizing about human beings from experiments on lower animals, enough is known about the process of genetic transmission to make psychologists feel somewhat more com-

451

fortable about such generalizations. Furthermore, the more reasonable "environmentalists" had always assumed some genetic contribution to behavior and were arguing only against the more extreme genetic position that asserted no environmental effects. It would be difficult to find anyone today who would take either of the extreme positions that were the source of so much research and debate until around 1940.

Recent research with dogs has shown genetic differences in temperament that are only minimally affected by environment. Differences in both the alertness and the irritability of infants are frequently noted, and these differences may not only remain dominant characteristics of behavior but may also determine the quality and character of many other experiences during infancy and childhood. For example, the child who cries easily may get a different amount and type of attention than one who cries very little. Just how the parent responds, however, is determined both by the baby's behavior and the parents' assumptions about the facts of development. A mother who assumes that the baby's crying is evidence of "his father's temper" is likely to let him cry, whereas a mother who is more "environmentally" oriented will seek to comfort the baby. Obviously the potential influence of such combinations of factors makes it difficult to do adequate research on the effects of parent-child interaction.

MATURATION VS. LEARNING

Anyone working with small children must realize that they cannot do certain things—sit up alone or walk, for example—until the nerves and muscles needed for these operations have reached the necessary stage of maturation. As the child gets older and its behavior more complex, however, there is less justification for assuming that behavior is a function of maturation alone. It is true, for example, that the infant may not walk at 3 or even 6 months of age because of soft bones and inadequate neural development. Nevertheless, he will have many experiences, as he first crawls and finally stands, that will facilitate the strengthening of muscles and the development of neuromuscular control needed to maintain balance. Thus, even in the first year when maturation tends to dominate, there is still a complex interaction between maturation and environment.

Toilet training is even more dependent on neurological maturation—a child cannot control his bladder and bowels until the nerves that regulate muscles in these areas have developed. Yet attitudes that are learned about toileting may facilitate appropriate behavior once the necessary maturation has occurred. Mothers who claim to have toilet trained their children at a very early age are apparently only adept at anticipating the child's toileting behavior.

Readiness for Learning Skills. The notion of readiness to learn has been freely applied to a number of other situations with somewhat less justification. By the time the child is 3 to 4 years of age, failure to perform is not so likely to be due to the lack of neurological maturation as it is to our inadequate knowledge of the techniques of training. Thus, even though we may say that the child is not ready to learn because he fails to learn by some traditional training technique, it may be a mistake to assume that he cannot be taught under different conditions and with different procedures. Frequently, what is required is not only better control of attention and motivation but also some information regarding the component skills involved in the task. That is, the child will not be able to learn skill B until he has learned skill A.

The Role of Practice and Motivation. It should be noted that there is no necessary virtue in many early achievements, and if a child is given a reasonably rich environment he will automatically profit from those experiences for which he is ready. For example, it would be difficult to indicate the precise sequence of experiences appropriate for learning to use a hammer to drive a nail. If one were to attempt to train a 3-year-old child directly, that is, with hammer, nail, and board, both the adult and the child would end up terribly frustrated if not injured. The child who has had no experience with a hammer will do a variety of things with the hammer, prior to using it properly, in spite of any and all instructions and demonstrations by the adult. Moreover, if he has not already had a certain number of manipulative experiences with small objects, it will take longer for him to use the hammer correctly than if he has had these experiences.

Not the least part of the problem is that of motivation. One reason that the child will not use the hammer properly is that he responds directly to the hammer rather than to the demonstration of its use. He must first investigate its properties; the noise it produces is likely to prove particularly enchanting. Some of the exploratory activities in which the child may indulge at this point are not of direct importance as component skills of hammering. Yet they are interests that have to be satisfied, responses that have to be made before he can go on to other responses, and therefore they are not unimportant. Once he has found out what he must find out, he will begin to engage in other activities that will lead more directly to the skill of using the hammer.

For example, hammering for the purpose of making noise, although annoying to the adult, provides the child with direct training in swinging the hammer. Inasmuch as the best noise comes as the result of an appropriate swing, such a swing will be rewarded more than other less appropriate moves, such as holding it by the wrong end, which he will also try.

It is only when the child is capable of using the hammer properly himself and is no longer entranced with its noise-making properties that he is likely to respond appropriately to any direct guidance regarding additional uses. Thus, although it may be fair to say that the child must be ready before he could learn to use the hammer, in this instance readiness is not the result of physiological maturation.

Much of the process of becoming ready involves a variety of experiences. Although some of these are not apparently relevant to the final goal, they may be important subskills or important in the development of appropriate motivation. That is, the child will not be interested in the more complex task until he has satisfied his own interests. It is also important to recognize that even the experiences that were not directly relevant to the task of hammering may have relevance to some other activity. For example, hammering different objects to make different noises may give a child his first meaningful ex-

Play is a child's work, particularly in the preschool years. That is, play is an important part of the child's education. Lifting and feeling things, piling them up, using them to hit with—these activities help the child learn the properties of the world he lives in.

CAMPBELL HAYS, FROM MONKMEYER

A 3-year-old may have his own ideas of what toys are for, but he can learn from following the advice and example of his parents.

ROY PINNEY FROM MONKMEYER

Driving pegs through a board may please a child because of the noise produced, and this play also teaches useful skills.

perience with differences in pitch.

It is highly probable that if we thought it important we could arrange to have children able to use hammers effectively at a much earlier age than they normally do. The wooden toy with large pegs that can be driven from one side to the other contributes markedly to the development of such a skill. The pegs provide a large target, and it is not necessary for children to master the task of holding the object to be driven as they attempt to drive it. Once they have learned to pound pegs through the board and are accomplished at swinging the hammer, they should find it much easier to pick up the skill of holding the nail.

This example of learning to use a hammer may seem relatively trivial, but it is a fact that children learn a great deal about the physical properties of the world through play. Therefore play is a serious part of their education.

INTELLIGENCE

Another concern of those who study child development is intelligence—what it is and what factors influence it. One group of psychologists maintained that intelligence is inherited and remains generally constant throughout a child's development. The notion of fixed intelligence was popularized by Lewis M. Terman, who also developed the widely used Stanford Revision of the Binet-Simon test of intelligence. This test yields the familiar IQ scores, with the "average" around 100. The availability of an objective measure, along with Terman's assertions regarding the nature of intelligence, made intelligence the most popular focus of the heredity-environment battle.

An adequate test of this issue requires that either heredity or environment be controlled while the other is varied. This was hardly possible with human beings, although there were some ingenious attempts. Correlations between the IQ scores of both identical and fraternal twins, raised apart, provided a relatively sound

test that tended to support the genetic point of view. Other investigators, however, found marked improvements in IQ scores following nursery school training or after placement in superior foster homes. The battle was long and strenuous but it never was won.

Those not involved in the debate accepted and promulgated the more reasonable position that intelligence reflects an interaction of heredity and environment. Furthermore, it is now generally assumed that it is not even possible to attribute a percentage to the contribution of either nature or nurture because of the complexity of this interaction.

Substantial effort has gone into defining intelligence and sorting it into its component parts, primarily in an effort to devise improved scales for measuring intelligence. These attempts, however, have not been notably successful. There is fairly good agreement as to the kind of behaviors one would identify as indicating intelligence. Yet there is still considerable discrepancy between what is measured by tests of intelligence and the accuracy with which school achievement can be predicted from a test score. Thus, although an IQ score provides a better estimate of school achievement than any other available measure, there is a fairly large potential for error in any prediction for the immediate future and even greater potential for error in predicting 4 or 5 years into the future. This is particularly true if the prediction is being made on the basis of a test given in early childhood.

Today many educators and psychologists are more likely to plan educational objectives for a child on the basis of an analysis of specific skills and "on the job" performance rather than on the basis of an IQ score. Greater concern for the child's demonstrated skill, rather than his estimated capacity to learn, allows increased flexibility in the schools. An educational plan can be tailored for both a child's strengths and weaknesses and will thus make irrelevant any estimate of general ability. Each child should be getting the best possible training regardless of any over-all conception of his ability; and the best possible training will be designed on the basis of what he can do now rather than in response to an abstract number.

COGNITIVE DEVELOPMENT

Research on such processes as perception, concept formation, and problem solving is frequently subsumed under the general term *cognitive development*. Typically, this research is concerned with the taking in and processing of information.

Two major theoretical viewpoints have influenced research on cognitive development. The first has its roots in the work of the Russian physiologist Ivan P. Pavlov and the American psychologist John B. Watson and is now usually called learning theory or sometimes neo-behaviorism. Pavlov and Watson provided the theoretical and methodological background for the strong environmentalistic position. It was reasonable to propose that all behavior is learned, and they provided the model (conditioning) for how that learning took place. See also BEHAVIORISM; CONDITIONING.

Learning Theory. According to this theory, learning is assumed to result from an associative bond or connection between a stimulus and response; the bond is strengthened by reward or reinforcement following the occurrence of a response in the presence of a stimulus. Thus, for a child to learn to discriminate a circle from a triangle, he must be reinforced for consistently choosing or responding in some way to one or the other stimulus. It has been demonstrated that such a procedure does indeed work and that discriminations that children do not already make can usually be learned under such conditions. Furthermore, the natural environment provides many situations that follow the principles used in the laboratory. We can account for the development of much discriminative behavior by these principles.

As the child grows older he begins to respond on the basis of abstract concepts, and his behavior can no longer be readily accounted for by the most simple principles of learning. This transition from simple to more complex behavior has been of particular interest to the child psychologist. The neo-behaviorists propose that language serves an important function in such behavior. If this is true, it is reasonable to expect that children too young to talk would respond in certain test situations as do lower animals (that is, not in terms of abstractions), whereas children who can talk would respond as adults do. Considerable research on this problem has shown that in general this is the case. For example, a chimpanzee may learn over a series of trials to choose the middle-sized box in a set of three regardless of its position. However, if he is presented with a new set of boxes, all of which are larger than the boxes in the original set, he will not necessarily choose the middle-sized box in this new set. A 4-year-old child might also have difficulty with the test set. A 6-year-old child, however, would have no trouble. If asked how he knew which one to choose, he would say that he knew it was the middle-sized one. The learning theorist assumes that the child can only respond to the relationship among the stimuli when he has the label for this concept. Without the label he, like the chimpanzee or any other lower animal,

would learn to respond only to the specific box to which responses were originally reinforced. He would therefore be unable to generalize, or transfer, what he has learned to a slightly different set of stimuli.

This notion of language as a mediator is a powerful one, and it provides a substantial basis for explaining more complex thought processes in relatively simple and manipulatable terms. Language is seen as intervening between the stimulus and the overt response, in that the overt response is made on the basis of a label or a set of labels rather than to the more concrete aspects of a stimulus. Thus, a label applied to an abstract property of a stimulus becomes the effective stimulus rather than a more obvious property of the stimulus. In the example cited, the words "middle-sized" represent a solution involving the recognition of a relationship among the stimuli. "It is not the large or the small so it must be the middle-sized one." But note that even the labels "large" and "small" represent concepts of a relative nature presumed to be beyond lower animals, who typically learn to respond to absolute rather than relative aspects of objects except under very special circumstances.

Cognitive Theory. The alternative to the learning theory approach is known as cognitive theory. This approach is typified by the work of the Swiss psychologist Jean Piaget, who has made extensive studies of the thought and language of children. It assumes that cognitive structures, which are the basis for intelligence, result from the child's interactions with the world. These structures are in a continuous process of organization and elaboration. The process by which structures become established Piaget calls *assimilation,* and the process that modifies existing structures to meet new situations he calls *accommodation.* Although he sees the process of assimilation and accommodation as continuous, he divides cognitive development into three major periods. These are the sensorimotor period, the period of concrete operations, and the period of formal operations. The period of concrete operations, being a long one, is divided into a preconceptual phase, an intuitive phase, and a concrete operations phase.

The Sensorimotor Period. The first of the three major periods is concerned with the elaboration of sensorimotor skills from the early reflex behavior of the first three months to the appearance of the first symbolic activity at not quite two years. During this period there occurs increased organization of response systems, which range from more adequate nursing behavior to walking and more adequate perceptual organization. The child learns to discriminate the nipple from a blanket or an adult finger and, when hungry, will reject both of the latter. His grasping response becomes more accurately shaped to an object before he touches the object. Piaget proposes that by eight months the concept of object permanence is demonstrated by the fact that the infant will for the first time actively search for objects when they are hidden from his view. The infant also begins to recognize means-ends relationships. That is, he seems to recognize that certain actions are necessary for certain effects to take place. With this progress it is also possible for him to begin to use objects as tools. For example, a stick that is first found to make a noise upon striking an object may be observed to move the object. The stick may now be used in new

PRIMARY SCHOOL YEARS

Children 6 to 8 years old are in the first stage of formal education. Although they still work best with concrete situations, they are beginning to develop an ability to think abstractly.

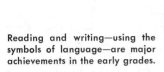

Reading and writing—using the symbols of language—are major achievements in the early grades.

and different situations as an instrument to move objects as well as to make noise. Subsequently the infant may explore the principles involved with other sticks, spoons, or even books.

Conflict between learning and cognitive theories arises because cognitive theory is more liberal than learning theory in what it attributes to the infant by way of intellectual development. The learning theorist insists that the cognitive theorist is gratuitously attributing to the child more intelligence than is necessary to account for the behavior he observes. In the instance of tool-using mentioned above, the learning theorist would use simple learning principles such as conditioning to account for this behavior. Piaget, on the other hand, spoke of a "stick schema." The learning theorist would say that the response of pushing with a stick is reinforced by the movement of the object. This response would generalize to other stimuli having sticklike characteristics.

In the latter part of Piaget's sensorimotor period, the child is observed to indulge in active exploration to discover new "means," and he begins to be curious about the process as well as the effect. The sensorimotor period ends as children begin to show inventiveness in their means-ends activities. They now begin to combine activities and objects, and their search behavior suggests a much more mature concept of object permanence. This in turn indicates the development of images or other representational processes. For example, the child can look for or talk about an object that is out of his sight. This capacity particularly marks the beginning of the preconceptual stage within the period of concrete operations. If Piaget has gratuitously assumed more complicated structures than are necessary to explain this type of behavior, the learning theorist has had little to say about the wide variety of activities and the degree of organization in behavior that is observed in children at this stage.

Concrete Operations. In the preconceptual phase of the period of concrete operations, the cognitive structures, although more abstract, lack generality and are yet too interrelated with the perceptions and actions for which they stand. This the learning theorist takes as evidence for the assertion noted earlier that behaviors at this age are the result of simple instrumental learning and stimulus generalization. Therefore, he maintains, they are no more complicated than the behavior of lower animals, which can be explained with these concepts.

Some tests that indicate movement to the concrete operations phase have been of particular interest to American psychologists. For example, a child of six, seven, or even eight years of age may not show an appreciation of the fact that certain properties of objects can remain unchanged in spite of the modification of other features of the object. A classic example involves placing in front of the child a row of egg cups with an egg in each. If he is asked if there are just as many eggs as egg cups, he will readily agree. But then the eggs are removed from the cups and placed in front of the egg cups, but spread out so that the row of eggs is now longer than the row of egg cups. When he is again asked whether there are the same number of eggs as egg cups, he will insist there are more eggs. Similarly, if one of two equal sized balls of clay is rolled out into a long sausage or flattened into a pancake, the child will no longer agree that the quantities are the same. This finding remains unchanged even when a variety of questions is used to avoid the child's possible failure to understand the notion of amount or quantity. For example, he may be asked whether the flattened clay would provide him just as much to eat if it were toffee or to select the piece of toffee that he would be willing to pay more for.

Numerous experiments by a variety of investigators have confirmed Piaget's findings in general. Piaget suggests that it is not until the child understands the reversibility of the process that he will be able to respond appropriately. It is interesting, however, that training directed toward demonstrating the reversibility of the process has not proved to have a lasting effect on the ability of children to respond to the abstract properties of objects. It is evident that in the intuitive phase the child finds it very difficult to ignore the more obvious form cues, such as length, width, and height, and is likely to respond to them regardless of the instruction he is given. Indeed, it is quite likely that he does not understand precisely what is requested. Even when he is asked a question like, "Which toffee would you pay the most money for?" it may be erroneous to assume that the child understands the price-quantity relationship so familiar and rational to the adult. Furthermore, he may recognize that there is no difference in quantity. But, having been asked to make a decision, he may decide he would prefer to pay more for the flattened toffee because it would be easier to bite, or more fun to eat, or because it is unusual.

Research that has concentrated on teaching the child to ignore the more prominent perceptual cues indicates that conservation behavior can be demonstrated considerably in advance of the age at which Piaget proposed it should occur. Furthermore, there is evidence that not only his estimates of the age of occurrence are wrong, which is a relatively trivial fact, but also that the more specific details of the theory as to the underlying structures for conservation may be questioned.

Piaget has a genius for selecting situations that may provide cognitive challenge to children. This has been due not only to his fertile imagination but also to some of the details of his theory. For example, Piaget ascribes the inability of the child to ignore the prominent perceptual cues to the child's inability to "decenter" his perception. That is, the child cannot respond to any but the most obvious cues. Although, on one hand, this says nothing more than what it describes, it does suggest a general problem. Another example of the lack of ability to decenter is indicated by the inability of children to place objects in a series according to some attribute such as length. To do this requires that the child take at least two relationships into account. That is, the object to be placed next must not only be longer than the shortest, but also shorter than the next longer, and so on.

Likewise, children who cannot decenter cannot understand part-whole class relationships. For example, suppose that a child has responded that a bead chain of 18 brown and 2 white beads is all wooden. Then, if he is asked whether a necklace made of the brown beads would be longer, shorter, or the same length as a necklace made of the wooden beads, the child in the early intuitive phase will say that there are more brown beads. This incorrect response appears to be the result of the child's inability to think simultaneously of the whole (wooden beads) and the parts (brown and white beads). To do so he would have to decenter from the part-part relationship. This situation, however, is duplicated to some extent when an adult, questioned whether the white of an egg is spelled y-o-k-e or y-o-l-k, responds "y-o-l-k." That answer, too, represents a failure to decenter; but it is not the result of the lack of potential for decentration but rather an indication that even adults frequently solve problems on the basis of the obvious features presented rather than with full comprehension of the question.

Formal Operations. With achievement of the ability to decenter thought, to understand reversibility, to conserve amount, number, and volume, to use rules in play, and to understand class relations a child moves from the concrete operations period to the final period of formal operations at about 10 to 12 years of age. This stage is typified more generally by a fuller capacity for abstract thought, the ability to use propositions—that is, "to operate with operations"—and to deal with the hypothetically possible, rather than to have thought occur only in response to concrete situations.

Piaget's theory of cognitive development has an interesting similarity to the more general genetic theories discussed earlier in that both assume that behavior is determined by the unfolding of structures. In the case of genetic theories, however, maturation is the critical variable and experience is incidental. For Piaget, although the order in which structures develop is a matter of logic and therefore fixed, experience is assumed to be essential to the development of each structure.

LANGUAGE

Although language is a particularly distinctive aspect of human behavior, it may not be language itself that distinguishes man from other animals but the potential for the development of language. Considerable effort has gone into the training of a variety of animals to speak, but with little success beyond the achievement of the pronunciation of a few simple words. Furthermore, in spite of a particular lower animal's ability to respond to verbal commands, there has been no evidence that it could use words to serve a communicative function. On the other hand, the human may develop language with little or no delay under relatively adverse circumstances. Given the opportunity to learn, he needs little by way of teaching. Even a child with below average intellectual ability can learn to talk.

The Beginnings of Speech. The infant's earliest vocalization is a cry, but over the first months of life other sounds are made in increasing variety. By six months the average American infant makes most of the vowel sounds and approximately half of the consonant sounds of the English language. He is not likely to have acquired all of the consonant sounds, however, even by 2½ years. Nevertheless, the change in frequency of occurrence of various speech sounds is in the direction of the frequency of occurrence of those sounds in adult speech. That this occurs even before the infant is using words to any significant extent indicates the influence of the infant's auditory environment on his speech development. In other words, the sounds the infant hears occur with increased frequency, and those sounds he does not hear occur with decreased frequency over the first two years. Other research has demonstrated that the amount of an infant's vocalization increased when an experimenter reinforced this behavior by smiling at the infant, making clucking sounds, and on occasions squeezing the infant's abdomen following such vocalization. When the reinforcements were discontinued, the amount of babbling decreased. Although it would seem likely that increasing the amount of babbling might facilitate the development of early speech, there is no evidence that this is necessarily true.

There is a considerable period of time between the identification of the first word and the appearance of useful language. Indeed, it is rather difficult to say precisely when the first word does appear. It is frequently heard only by the mother, and its meaning may be considerably less specific than the mother likes to think. The ease with which the sound combination "ma ma" is said has undoubtedly been influential in making this a relatively universal nickname for mother. Certainly mother would greet this utterance with considerable delight, although when it first occurs it is unlikely that it occurs as either a label or a call. Its effect, however, is dramatic in terms of the attention that ensues; thus the frequency of vocalization in general is likely to increase. But, inasmuch as reinforcement follows only "ma ma," these sounds will be strengthened more than other sounds and thus should occur with relatively higher frequency. The final establishment of the meaning of "ma ma" takes place when its production is reinforced only under

AGES 10 TO 12

Children of 10 to 12 have mastered some physical skills and have made great advances in abstract thinking and ability to follow directions. As at other stages, they learn both skills and social behavior by example.

A volunteer helps Boy Scouts in a suburb of Santiago, Chile, to enlarge their headquarters hut.

THE PEACE CORPS

specific circumstances—that is, in the presence of mother but not father. In that way the infant comes to learn that the approval occurs only under a select set of stimulus conditions. Such differential conditioning typifies the acquisition of meaning for words in general, particularly at this earliest level.

Sentences. The use of 2-word and 3-word sentences begins around 2½ years of age, with girls likely to be somewhat advanced over boys. There is some dispute about the basis for acquiring the ability to construct sentences and the notions of grammar. One group assumes that sentences, tenses, and so forth are learned in a manner relatively similar to that in which word meanings are learned—that is, through a process of reinforcement and shaping, as indicated above. Others insist that grammatical propositions are either acquired as such or may even be the result of inherent structures. Linguists are showing particularly strong interest in the early language of children. With better samples of children's speech and better linguistic analysis, it should be possible to design better experiments to test theories of the acquisition of speech.

The function of speech in thought remains unclear. The learning theorists, as noted earlier, have ascribed to speech a very central role with regard to thought processes. It is equally plausible to suggest that the capacity for abstract reasoning also makes language possible, rather than that language makes abstract reasoning possible.

SOCIAL AND PERSONALITY DEVELOPMENT

As with cognitive development, two main theories have been particularly important in determining the direction of thought and research in the area of social development.

Freudian Views. Of great influence historically is the theory of Sigmund Freud, which became particularly influential in the 1930's partly because it offered an antidote to the overly rigid views of John B. Watson. Not only was Watson the arch-environmentalist, but his concern for the influence of the environment on the child led him to propose the use of very rigid discipline from birth on. The infant was not to be "babied," "fondled," or "loved" for fear of creating a child that was too dependent upon his parents, a child with too much need for attention. These more

extreme aspects of Watson's viewpoint were not warmly received by the majority. Freudian theory supported the alternative view: the child should be loved; he should be given attention; he should not be frustrated. Adequate love was presumed to be essential for progress through the various stages of psychosexual development. Lack of love and inadequate gratification of needs was assumed to produce fixations at various stages of development. Such fixations were the source of neurotic behavior in later life. Even normal individual differences in personality were presumed to reflect differences in progress through the various stages of psychosexual development.

The Theory of Dollard and Miller. The social learning theory of two American psychologists, John Dollard and Neal Miller, an amalgam of psychoanalytic and learning theory, has been much more influential than Freudian views, particularly on research on social development. Although their theory, like psychoanalysis, also focuses on such events as weaning, toilet training, and the handling of aggression, the consequences of these events are explained in terms of the development of learned drives that influence later behavior rather than in terms of repressions and fixations. The fact that social learning is stated in terms that make it susceptible to confirmation or disproof by empirical research has made the Dollard-Miller concept a much more fertile framework for research on social development than psychoanalytic theories.

The earliest attempts at socializing the infant are concerned with toilet training, eating, the suppression of aggression, and the control of exploratory activities (for example, the infant must not touch the phonograph or pull on the curtains). Improper attempts at socialization are recognized by all theories as potent sources of later problems in social behavior. It is now well recognized that bowel and bladder control is possible only after maturation of the nerves to the appropriate sphincters. Thus punishment before there is any possibility for the child to exercise control over these functions can result only in anxiety. Moreover, anxiety may be associated through conditioning not only to the parent but also to all other stimuli present when punishment occurs.

The eating behavior of young children inevitably falls considerably short of adult standards. The child is quite likely to mix with the procedure of eating a self-instructional program on the physical properties of milk or cereal. This may be done by feeling, pouring, slapping, and so on. Such behavior is not socially acceptable, but it is difficult to know how to limit it without making the eating situation itself a source of conflict and anxiety. The fact that the most frequently voiced concern of mothers has to do with eating suggests that the situation is often mishandled. It is important to recognize that popular adult standards regarding just how one eats, and the order in which foods are eaten, are not only complicated but are also arbitrary. That the child's infractions of these rules can upset us is testimony to the residual anxiety we ourselves have from our own early training. It should always be remembered that the child has a long time in which to learn to eat according to adult customs. There are certain behaviors, such as throwing food, that cannot be countenanced. The suppression of such behaviors can be accomplished without making the whole situation uncomfortable if one concentrates on inhibiting only one such activity at a time and does not worry at the same time about less important matters such as drooling or eating with the hands.

The mother should realize that the child frequently may not understand why he is being scolded or punished. When that is the case, the effect of punishment may generalize to the total situation. If the eating situation does become anxiety producing, then the combination of anxiety, which can be controlled only by staying away from eating, and hunger, which can be satisfied only by eating, provides an approach-avoidance conflict. Such a conflict can be the source of a variety of other behaviors such as aggression or thumb-sucking. Whether these behaviors serve to reduce the conflict or are a natural consequence of it, they are clearly symptomatic of underlying conflict. The reduction of the original sources of conflict is not always readily accomplished, and attempts to suppress the symptoms may only lead to substitute symptoms.

It is also possible, however, that some symptomatic behaviors remain long after the reasons for their original occurrence have disappeared. Under such circumstances, various direct means of suppression may prove effective without untoward effects. The judgment of when this may or may not be possible, however, should in most instances be left to someone such as a pediatrician or child psychologist who is able to evaluate the situation more objectively than the parent.

With an infant's increased capacity to explore his environment, as well as increased pressures for socialization, there is also increased interference with his activities. The consequences are frequently frustration, anger, and possibly aggression. The older the child the more likely that interference will produce anger because the older child is less readily distracted. The adult is often very thoughtless with regard to how he interferes because the child's activities appear to be so unimportant. The child's reaction, however, emphatically indicates how important his activities are to him. Inasmuch as there are many situations where the parent must interfere without warning either to save the child from injury or an object from damage, he should attempt to anticipate other less urgent interruptions and either prepare the child for them by suggesting they are coming soon or distract him sufficiently from what he is doing that a new activity may be introduced without interfering with the old.

Use of Words in Training. There has been general agreement for some time that as much socialization training as possible should be left until the child is sufficiently verbal that the mother's displeasure with the behavior of the child can be associated with the appropriate stimuli through the use of word labels. This is another example of verbal mediation. For example, if in training a child not to pull books from shelves an association between "books" and punishment, or words that stand for punishment, is made, the sight of books should elicit the word "books," which in turn should elicit the anxiety associated with punishment. Thus, training will be optimized because punishment will be associated with the books rather than with mother or father. Furthermore, the punishment is verbally administered prior to the response rather than after the response is made. Recent research suggests that if punishment follows rather than precedes an unwanted response, the response is less likely to be inhibited, but the child has feelings of guilt.

Imitation or Modeling. Two American psychologists, Albert Bandura and H. H. Walters, have called attention to another important influence on the social development of children. This has to do with imitation or modeling, which is the result of identification with an adult or another child. It has long been apparent that children imitate the behavior of others. The important question is under what conditions will a child attempt this imitation. Although much work remains to be done on this issue, it is apparent that the child models his behavior after those persons who effectively exercise control, both over others and also over the environment more generally. For example, it is not uncommon for the child to want to toilet, to eat, to dress, and so on, as mother and father do. Less fortunately, he may also imitate the classroom bully. Parental punishment of the child's aggression only provides an additional aggressive model. As a consequence children punished for aggression are frequently found to be more aggressive, particularly away from home, than those who are not punished.

A matter of special concern to most parents is the development of conscience. Simple avoidance learning may serve as the basis for the control of some early behaviors, but the time comes when self-limitations are placed on behavior. The child now verbalizes the reasons for not doing certain things, he cautions himself before doing them, and he recognizes after a transgression that he should not have done what he did even in the absence of any untoward consequence. Such behaviors are thought to reflect the degree of identification with adult models. The standards the adult provides become the standards of the child insofar as he understands them and can implement them.

There has been some concern in the past as to how one can imitate behaviors in the absence of the model and also what constitutes the reinforcement for imitative behavior. One way to look at this question is to assume that a child has some image of the adult's behavior even in the absence of the adult. Insofar as his behavior approximates the image, that behavior is reinforced as the result of the fact that the child perceives himself as now behaving like his model. The importance of adequate models with which a child may identify should be obvious.

In spite of the influence of modeling on behavior one should not overlook the fact that much behavior is under control of relatively simple and straightforward reinforcement contingencies. That is, the child will tend to do those things that bring him attention or approval, and those behaviors that do not bring approval or gain attention will tend to decrease in frequency. Behaviors that gain attention but not approval, however, may be continued if the need for attention is great and approval is seldom achieved. This is not an uncommon circumstance in many homes.

Dependency. Two additional aspects of social and personality development that have received considerable attention are dependency and achievement. Dependency becomes a matter for concern when a child is found to be overly reluctant to leave his mother to play with other children or even to play by himself. Although some psychologists assume that such behavior indicates a high dependency drive that is the result of earlier maternal reactions to dependency, it may be more scientifically rigorous to assume that dependency responses reflect anxiety and a lack of security. The experiments of American psychologist Harry F. Harlow's work with monkeys is relevant. He was concerned with the variables that produced the bond between mother and infant. Earlier theories had proposed that this bond arose from the association of mother with the delivery of food, but Harlow demonstrated that the tactual sensations from being held by the mother were even more important. Infant monkeys that were deprived of their mothers but provided with adequate "contact comfort" ran to their "terry cloth mothers" (frames covered with towelling and warmed by light bulbs) in the face of threat rather than to the "wire-frame mothers" on which they were fed. Furthermore, once comforted by being able to cling to the "terry cloth mother" the infant monkey was capable of facing whatever threatened him with considerable belligerence. They derived no such strength, however, from the wire mothers on which they were fed.

Insofar as we may generalize from monkey to man, it would appear that the early comforting of a child by the mother, or mother substitute, is of considerable importance to the well-being of the child. It is of critical importance to understand that the infant monkey that receives sufficient contact comfort is neither overly dependent nor does he build up a strong need for attention. On the contrary, having had the early comfort experience, and with continued potential to return for comfort, he is somewhat better able to deal with the world and to assert some independence than the monkey who has never had such an experience. It does not seem unreasonable that the process with human infants would be similar. The child who is too fearful to interact with the environment will be overly dependent, whereas the child who is given all the warmth and protection he needs will be eager to leave mother and explore the world. In general, research with children has indicated that dependency is greatest in those children who are rejected by their mothers. Thus, dependency behavior is not a consequence of the availability of the mother, as might be expected from a simple learning point of view, but is rather a consequence of being insecure and anxious as the result of inadequate maternal attention.

Achievement. Achievement behavior, like dependency behavior, has also been assumed by some theorists to have its own drive state. But, as with dependency, it may not be necessary to propose a special drive to account for this behavior. The fact that some achievement strivings are oriented toward specific tasks suggests that at least some of these may be based on modeling and on the consistent reward of achievement by parental or peer encouragement and approval. When parents are overly concerned with achievement, and the child's failures are greeted with disapproval, this may make anxiety and the need for approval strong contributors to achievement behavior. When this anxiety is too strong, however, the child's preoccupation with, and anxiety over, potential failure may interfere with achievement and place him in a vicious circle from which the only apparent escape is to "drop out."

An advantage of most programmed learning situations is that the ratio of successes to failures is very high. Even though one child may be progressing more slowly than another, the level of success remains similar for both children. Thus the slower child is less likely to be discouraged. It is important to recognize that many achievements are independent of intelligence. It is unfortunate when failures resulting from improper educational experiences unduly influence an individual's conceptions of his capabilities.

Many of the problems and principles involved in development from birth to puberty are also important as the child grows older. See ADOLESCENCE.

W. E. JEFFREY
University of California, Los Angeles

Bibliography

Baldwin, Alfred L., *Theories of Child Development* (New York 1967).
Hoffman, Martin L., and Hoffman, Lois W., eds., *Review of Child Development and Research,* vol. 1 (New York 1964).
Hunt, Joseph McV., *Intelligence and Experience* (New York 1961).
Kessen, William, *The Child* (New York 1965).
Mussen, Paul H., Conger, J. J., and Kagan, J., *Child Development and Personality* (New York 1963).

For Specialized Study

Bandura, Albert, and Walters, R. H., *Social Learning and Personality Development* (New York 1963).
Bronfenbrener, U., "Soviet Methods of Character Education: Some Implications for Research," *American Psychologist,* vol. 17, pp. 550–564 (Washington 1962).
Bruner, Jerome S., and others, *Studies in Cognitive Growth* (New York 1966).
Dollard, John, and Miller, Neal E., *Personality and Psychotherapy* (New York 1950).
Flavell, John H., *The Developmental Psychology of Jean Piaget* (Princeton 1963).
Harlow, Harry F., "Love in Infant Monkeys," *Scientific American,* vol. 200, pp. 68–74 (New York 1959).
Hunt, Joseph McV., *Intelligence and Experience* (New York 1961).
Kagan, J., and Moss, H. A., *Birth to Maturity: A Study in Psychological Development* (New York 1962).
Kendler, H. H., and Kendler, T. S., "Vertical and Horizontal Processes in Problem-solving," *Psychological Review,* vol. 69, pp. 1–16 (Washington 1962).
Lenneberg, Eric H., *New Directions in the Study of Language* (Cambridge, Mass., 1964).
Scott, J. P., "The Process of Primary Socialization in Canine and Human Infants, *Monographs of the Society for Research in Child Development,* vol. 28 (Lafayette, Ind., 1963).
Sears, Robert R., Maccoby, E. E., and Levin, H., *Patterns of Child Rearing* (Evanston, Ill., 1957).
Yarrow, L., "Maternal Deprivation: Toward an Empirical and Conceptual Re-evaluation," *Psychological Bulletin,* vol. 58, pp. 459–490 (Washington 1961).

CHILD GUIDANCE CLINIC. See CHILD WELFARE.

A young girl labors in a cheerless South Carolina cotton mill in 1909.

CHILD LABOR is work performed by children that either endangers their health or safety, interferes with or prevents their education, or keeps them from play and other activity important to their development. Child labor of this character has long been considered a social evil to be abolished.

Child labor as a social problem is associated with the rise of industrial production and the appearance of capitalism. This is not to imply that children did not work in earlier ages. Children on the medieval manor helped in agriculture almost as soon as they could toddle; illustrated manuscripts show children working beside their parents in the field, and contracts between lord and serf specifically mentioned the obligation of children to work.

In the ancient world the vast majority of the population labored in field or city workplace, and children joined in as soon as they were able. The same is true of primitive societies today, although they make less of a distinction between "work" and "play" than highly developed societies do. Indeed, in cultures with low economic productivity, child labor of some sort was and is clearly inescapable. In such societies, however, the child was not physically separated from the care of the family or from the occupation of his parents. Children received some protection, and their labor was also a form of vocational training for the economic role they would assume as adults.

EARLY HISTORY OF CHILD LABOR

Industrial child labor first appeared with the development of the domestic system. In this type of production an entrepreneur bought raw material to be "put out" to the homes of workmen to be spun, woven, sewn, or handled in some other manner. This permitted a division of labor and a degree of specialization among various families. Pay was by the piece, and children were used extensively at whatever tasks they could perform. This system was important in England, on the Continent, and in North America from the 16th to the 18th century and lingers until the present in some industries and in some countries.

The domestic system was largely replaced by the factory system associated with the Industrial Revolution, which gained impetus in the 18th century. Machinery, driven by waterpower and later by steam, took over many functions formerly performed by hand labor and was centralized in factories situated at the source of the power. Children could and did tend the machines in ever increasing numbers from as early an age as five. Child labor also proliferated in coal mining. Half-naked children as young as six labored incredibly long hours in the damp and dark. Many of them carried coal in packs on their backs up long ladders to the surface.

Mistreatment of Children. In the 1830's the English Parliament set up a commission to look into the problems of working children. The testimony the commission took is revealing. One worker in a textile mill testified that he first went to work at the age of 8 and that he customarily had worked from 6 A. M. to 8 P. M., with an hour off at noon. When business was brisk, however, he worked a 16-hour span, from 5 A. M. to 9 P. M. When asked how he could be punctual and how he awoke, the boy said:

"I seldom did awake spontaneously; I was most generally awoke or lifted out of bed, sometimes asleep, by my parents."

A boy whose services had been sold by his parents to a mill owner (for 15 shillings for 6 years) testified that the child laborers in that mill were locked up night and day. He said that twice he ran away, was pursued and caught by his overseer, and was thrashed with a whip.

A girl who worked in the mines testified:

"I never went to day school; I go to Sunday school, but I cannot read or write; I go to the mine at 5 o'clock in the morning and come out at 5 in the evening; I get my breakfast of porridge and milk first; I take my dinner with me, a cake, and eat it as I go; I do not stop or rest any time for that purpose; I get nothing else until I get home, and then have potatoes and meat, not every day meat. I work in the clothes I have now got on, trousers and ragged jacket; the bald place upon my head is made by carrying the coal buckets. I carry the buckets a mile and more under ground and back; I carry 11 a day; I wear a belt and chain at the workings to get the buckets out; the miners that I work for are naked except for their caps; they pull off all their clothes; I see them at work when I go up; sometimes they beat me, if I am not quick enough, with their hands; they strike me upon my back; the boys take liberties with me; I would rather work in a mill than in a coal-pit."

Pauper Children. During the great social dislocations of the early Industrial Revolution, there were many children who had no parents or whose parents could not support them. Under the English Poor Law then in effect, local government officials were supposed to arrange for these children to become apprentices so that they would learn a trade and be cared for. In thousands of cases these so-called "pauper children" were simply turned over in large numbers to a distant mill owner by the local officials. After having been thus "apprenticed," they had virtually no one to care or intercede for them and were little better than slaves.

Other working children were indentured—their parents sold their labor to the mill owner for a period of years. Others lived with their families and worked for wages as adults did, for long hours and under hard conditions.

Effects of Economic Doctrines. The situation was made possible by the economic doctrines widely believed at the time. Employers, following Adam Smith, felt that the government should not meddle in business. They believed that economic affairs should be allowed to run according to their own "natural laws," much as the physical world was regulated by such laws as the law of gravity. One of the "natural laws" of economics that businessmen thought they perceived was the "iron law of wages"—it held that wages could not possibly rise above a subsistence level. So low wages and long hours seemed inevitable.

Furthermore, idle hands were looked upon as the devil's tools, while work was thought to be morally uplifting. Employers felt that they were doing the poor a favor by providing them with useful work. Such ideas were widely accepted. President Washington's secretary of the treasury, Alexander Hamilton, approved of child labor. In his *Report on Manufactures* (1791) to Congress he advocated a tariff and other policies to encourage manufacturing because, among other reasons, it would make possible wider employment of women and children.

In western Europe the factory system appeared later than in England. When it did become important—in the 1830's in France and a decade or two earlier in the Rhine provinces of Germany—conditions similar to the worst in England soon appeared.

REGULATION OF CHILD LABOR

The movement to limit child labor sprang from several sources. The crowded and unsanitary conditions existing when children lived in factory dormitories gave rise to epidemics that spread to the nearby population. Concerned medical men warned that the rigors of childhood employment resulted in a permanently weakened and damaged labor force. Some people were concerned because child laborers had no time for religious instruction. (Sunday schools, when they were first started, taught reading and writing as well as religious subjects. They were intended for working children who re-

ceived no other schooling.) There was concern about this lack of education and also about the immoral atmosphere of factory dormitories.

England and Europe. Some mill owners worked for the passage of regulatory laws because they disliked employing young children, but they could not stop unless their competitors also did—a situation that could be brought about only by legislation. England passed the first amelioratory legislation, the First Factory Act, in 1802, but it applied only to children who had been apprentices under the poor laws. At any rate, it was not enforced. But other factory acts followed in 1819, 1825, 1833, 1844, and 1878. These measures gradually widened and strengthened inspection, shortened the hours, and raised the age at which children might go to work.

In France children under 10 were barred from the mines as early as 1813. After an investigation by the French Academy of Sciences, a regulatory law curbed the worst features of child labor in that country in 1841.

In Prussia the government became concerned about child labor because the army complained that industrial employment made boys unfit for later military service. As a result, a regulatory law was passed in 1839.

Switzerland, the Low Countries, and the Scandinavian countries enacted legislation at about the same pace as France and Germany, but Spain, Italy, the Balkan countries, and Russia lagged far behind during the 19th century.

United States. Children worked in the American colonies, most of all on the family farm but also in various kinds of household industries, as apprentices, at sea, as indentured servants, and as slaves. In 1789 textile manufacturing on the English pattern was transplanted to the northern and middle states. As in England, children were the bulk of the labor force at first, but the United States did not have a great supply of pauper children as did England at the time, so that before long, women—many of them young—became the mainstay of the labor force in textiles.

State Legislation. Some states passed protective legislation, if it can be called that. In 1836 a Massachusetts law required that working children receive some schooling. In 1842, Connecticut and Massachusetts limited the work of children in textile factories to 10 hours a day. Pennsylvania in 1848 outlawed the hiring of children under 12 in the mills. The struggle for free compulsory public education that characterized the years before the Civil War was indirectly a campaign against excessive child labor.

Reliable statistics about child labor in the United States exist only from 1870. Beginning in that year the census reported child laborers as a separate category. About 750,000 workers 15 and under were reported in the 1870 census. Certainly it did not report many more who helped with family farms, stores, or other enterprises. Rapid industrialization came after 1870, and for the next 40 years child workers increased both in numbers and as a percentage of the child population. As a result the campaign for child labor laws became an important reform movement and remained so for more than fifty years.

By 1900 about half of the states placed some sort of restrictions on child labor, but only about 10 made a serious effort to enforce such laws as there were. The South was finally industrializ-

A child "hurrying coal" through a low passage in an English mine in the 19th century.

ing as textile manufacturing moved from New England to be close to its raw materials (and to take advantage of cheap labor). In the process, the South appeared destined to repeat all the horrors of the early Industrial Revolution. The number of child laborers in the South tripled between 1890 and 1900.

Elsewhere in the country, the glass industry employed young boys for 12-hour shifts in front of fiery furnaces. The domestic system lingered on in the garment industry where whole families labored for subcontractors in tenement sweatshops. In the coalfields, boys manned the "breakers." Here they sat hunched over chutes as coal poured beneath them, picked out the stone and slate, and breathed coal dust for 10 hours at a stretch. The tobacco industry employed thousands of children under 10 to make cigars and cigarettes. In silk spinning, artificial flower making, oyster shucking, berry picking, canning, and shrimp packing, the story was the same.

A number of organizations worked to eliminate child labor. The unions opposed it on both humanitarian and economic grounds. The National Consumers League, an organization of middle-class and well-to-do reformers founded in 1899, tried to use the economic and political pressure of consumers on behalf of many causes. The National Child Labor Committee, launched in 1904 by social workers in the settlement houses and joined by others, coordinated the battle. These progressive organizations plus the labor movement were responsible for such state laws as were passed.

National Legislation. The limited value of state laws soon became apparent. Labor and the progressives had little influence in a number of states, especially in the South, so that state laws there were out of the question. As a result businesses in such states had a competitive advantage, and this stiffened resistance to strengthening or even enforcing laws in more progressive states. A national law appeared to be the only answer, and a campaign for one began. Public support was mobilized by several of the "muckrakers," the journalists who exposed intolerable conditions. The cause was helped incalculably by an angry bit of verse penned by one of the reformers, Sarah N. Cleghorn:

> The golf links lie so near the mill
> That almost every day
> The laboring children can look out
> And see the men at play.

In 1912, Congress was persuaded to establish a Children's Bureau. The battle appeared won in 1916 when, during the high tide of the progressive crusade, President Wilson wrestled through Congress the Keating-Owen Act, which barred from interstate commerce articles produced by child labor. The victory was brief,

however, for a conservative Supreme Court in 1918 in *Hammer* v. *Dagenhart* declared the law unconstitutional because it infringed on states' rights and denied children the "freedom" to contract to work. Congress swiftly reenacted the measure as a part of the Revenue Act of 1919, this time outlawing products produced by children by putting a special tax on such products. In 1922 in the case of *Bailey* v. *Drexel Furniture* the Supreme Court again struck down the measure.

The only road still open was the tortuous one of a constitutional amendment. Congress proposed one in 1924 and sent it to the states for ratification. But the national mood in the 1920's was far different from what it had been 10 years before. Progressives were dispirited and divided; conservatism was in the ascendancy. Among those who opposed ratification of the proposed amendment were the American Farm Bureau Federation, the National Association of Manufacturers, and the southern textile industry. They were joined by most of the Roman Catholic hierarchy of the country, who argued that the amendment threatened parental discipline and invaded the privacy of the home. Faced with this weighty array of enemies, the amendment was defeated in most states. A White House Conference on Child Health and Protection in 1930 did help to keep attention focused on the problem. (Another such conference, the Mid-century White House Conference on Children and Youth, was held in 1950.)

During the New Deal years, the political pendulum had swung again, and new national efforts were made. Measures against child labor were included in the codes of the National Recovery Administration in 1933. The codes, too, were declared unconstitutional but not because of the child labor provisions. In 1938 the far-reaching Fair Labor Standards Act once again struck at child labor. This time the Supreme Court, its composition altered by time, upheld the law. This act, also known as the Wages and Hours Act, with its amendments, is now the basic child labor act for the United States. It bans employers engaged in interstate commerce from employing workers under 16 or under 18 in hazardous occupations. Under certain circumstances, children 14 to 16 may be employed after school hours. The states may further control child labor so long as their legislation does not conflict with federal law.

Canada. Child labor never became a serious problem in Canada because that nation remained predominately agricultural until well into the 20th century. The Canadian provinces have child labor laws that vary slightly among themselves but are generally comparable to U. S. legislation. In addition Canada has had since 1945 a family allowance system. This provides that all mothers are paid a sum each month to help in the maintenance of each child from birth through age 16. The allowance is paid only if the child remains in school. This program has virtually ended child labor in Canada.

CURRENT DEVELOPMENTS

In the United States child labor remains a problem in only one sector of the economy, agriculture. Federal law requires only that children under 16 may not be employed in agriculture during school hours. Therefore, small children may be worked long hours in farming during other times, especially because state laws covering child labor in agriculture are generally lax or nonexistent. Hardest hit are the children of migrant farm laborers. There were 400,000 migrant farm laborers in the United States in the late 1960's.

The attention of child labor reformers had switched in the late 1960's from combating child labor to the problem of helping older youngsters in the 16-to-21-year age group find employment. Automation of farm and factory had greatly reduced jobs available to young people who lacked good educations—the high school dropouts. The problem was particularly acute for young people in the Negro ghettos and for rural youth.

Child labor on the world scene first came under attack in 1900 when the International Association for Labor Legislation was founded. The cause has since been taken over by the International Labor Organization, established by the Treaty of Versailles and now a specialized agency of the United Nations. International conferences of the ILO recommend minimal legislation to member countries but do not have the power to obtain enactment. The UN General Assembly in 1959 adopted a Declaration of the Rights of the Child, but it, too, is only advisory. Virtually every nation now has excellent child welfare legislation on the books, but enforcement is often spotty or almost nonexistent. Perhaps the worst problems in the 1960's lay in countries (especially in much of Latin America) where there was a flood of immigration from the countryside to cities that could not grow fast enough to provide even minimal services. There was a shortage of schools, and many children entered various street trades to help piece out pitifully meager family incomes. Child labor also remained a problem under the commune system of agricultural organization in some parts of rural mainland China. In some areas there were insufficient schools or the labor of children could not be spared.

HUGH G. CLELAND
State University of New York at Stony Brook

Bibliography

Abbott, Grace, *The Child and the State* (Chicago 1938).
Bremner, Robert H., *From the Depths* (New York 1956).
Chambers, Clarke A., *Seedtime of Reform* (Minneapolis 1963).
Clopper, Edward N., *Child Labor in City Streets* (New York 1912).
Hammond, John L., and Hammond, Barbara, *The Town Laborer, 1760–1832* (London 1928).
Hunter, Robert, *Poverty* (New York 1904).
Markham, Edwin, *Children in Bondage* (New York 1914).
Spargo, John, *The Bitter Cry of the Children* (New York 1906).

CHILD PSYCHOLOGY. See CHILD DEVELOPMENT.

CHILD MARRIAGE. See MARRIAGE.

CHILD WELFARE is concerned with the well-being of children and with child-rearing problems, such as illegitimate birth, child neglect or abandonment, or with other aspects of parental incapacity or parent-child relationship around which specific *social services* have been developed.

Need for child welfare services cuts across lines of all kinds and is not confined to children who are poor or to children whose parents may be receiving help through one of the several kinds of social insurance or economic assistance programs. Very conservative estimates suggest that for about one in 20 children in the United States, there will be times when parents may be unable to give or secure the care their children require without special help. This may be true when circumstances or personal problems impair the adults' ability to perform their role as parents; when the child has special needs, handicaps, or problems with which no parent can be expected to cope; when the community lacks the resources required in modern society to supplement or to facilitate the child-rearing function of the family.

The importance of services and provisions to strengthen families and to shore up parental capacity as needed is basic to child welfare. The parents, the child, and the general society each have a role in developing child welfare.

In the United States, child welfare services are offered under a variety of governmental and voluntary auspices, whether or not there is a concurrent need for financial assistance. One of the most descriptive and comprehensive definitions found in the Social Security Act as amended in 1962 states that "*child welfare services* means public social services which supplement, or substitute for parental care and supervision for the purpose of (1) preventing or remedying, or assisting in the solution of problems which may result in the neglect, abuse, exploitation, or delinquency of children, (2) protecting and caring for homeless, dependent, or neglected children, (3) protecting and promoting the welfare of children of working mothers, and (4) otherwise protecting and promoting the welfare of children, including the strengthening of their own homes where possible or, where needed, the provision of adequate care of children away from their homes in foster family homes or day care or other child care facilities."

This definition is problem-focused, emphasizing prevention and remedy. It recognizes the value of strengthening a child's own home where possible. Where this is not possible, a variety of substitute living situations is provided.

TYPES OF SERVICES

Child welfare services are directed to the social problem of *deprivation of parental care*. As the accompanying chart illustrates, they are designed to help with society's child-rearing task in three important ways: (1) to substitute for parental care either partially or wholly according to a child's individual needs; (2) to supplement the care that a child receives, or to compensate for certain inadequacies or limitations in parental care; and (3) to support or reinforce the ability of parents to meet their children's needs.

Substitute Care. Service designed to substitute for natural parental care, either partially or completely, is still the predominant child welfare service. Of the total number of children receiving child welfare services in the United States, more than half are receiving service away from their own homes and their own families.

CHILDREN at a day care center in New York City eat a hearty lunch as part of a nursery school program.

Foster and Institutional Care. The term "foster care" is used to include care in any kind of facility, individual family, boarding home, adoptive home, group home, or children's institution. It is useful to think of adoption as separate from other kinds of foster family care, because adoption is a permanent substitute. Foster care, on the other hand, whether in the setting of an individual family home, in a group home, or in an institution, is never really permanent. The unsettling threat of change, or the promise of change, is always present. It must always be seen as a kind of interim care, awaiting the time when the problem that made placement necessary may be resolved and the child may return to his own home, or move on to a new "own" home on a permanent basis.

In the foster care program child welfare has developed and perfected a variety of methods or types of care and, within the range of available resources, it seeks to "fit" the type of care and method of service or "treatment" to the individual needs of a particular child or family. For example, family home care, of a particular quality, would usually be seen as the preferred care for an infant during the period of time needed to facilitate his placement for adoption. An agency-operated group home staffed with skilled "counselors" and other specialists, or a highly specialized institution, might be a better choice for a disturbed adolescent who had experienced serious rejection by a mentally ill mother.

Foster care in group settings rather than in family homes is more frequently experienced throughout Europe, in Israel, and in the Soviet Union. Many variations have been developed. One distinctive kind of institutional care, known as "children's villages," was first developed in Austria by Hermann Gmeiner. The typical village consists of ten to sixteen cottages each headed by a "mother" who cares—on what purports to be a permanent basis —for a group of eight or nine children ranging from babyhood to adolescent. The *Dorfleiter*, or village father, provides the only "fathering" that is available.

Many problems contribute to the gap between what child welfare seeks to give children through substitute care and what is actually happening to some children. Suffering most are children of minority status, the physically and mentally handicapped, older children, and the emotionally disturbed.

Adoption. About 10% of the total number of children receiving child welfare services are children living in homes where adoption is contemplated. A sound adoption is one that may be described as socially desirable and legally incontestable. For a child, adoption means opportunity for a permanent affiliation with a family other than the one in which he was born. For adoptive parents it means parenthood achieved by legal rather than biological means. Child welfare agencies have developed great skill and usefulness in arranging and facilitating sound adoptions. The number of children and parents so protected is very small in relation to the total need for the service. Nevertheless, the total number of child adoptions is gradually increasing, and child welfare agencies throughout the world are participating in a growing proportion of adoptions of children by nonrelated persons.

Supplementary Care—Day Care. The major types of supplementary care are day care and homemaker service. Day care is a method of supplementing parental functioning by providing care and training opportunities for children during some part of the 24-hour day. As with full-time foster care, a number of methods, kinds of settings, or types of program have been developed. One of the most widespread programs is *family* day care, individual care and "mothering" in the warmth and safety of a normal family home. In the United States family day care is viewed as most suitable for babies or very young children whose own mothers' must work and whose developmental needs require this kind of individual attention and continuity of relationship to one substitute mother person.

Many European countries maintain group day care for infants in day nurseries associated with a mother's place of empoyment, rather than family day care for an individual child. Particularly in eastern Europe, the factory crèche or infant nursery is very common. In Czechoslovakia, for example, over 50,000 children between three months and three years of age were being cared for in such facilities in the 1960's. In the United States, there are increasing group day care facilities, particularly under programs such as "Head-Start" and "Get Set," which have the objective of breaking the cycle of intergenerational poverty. These group day care centers may be called day nurseries, day care centers, child care centers, or nursery schools. Not all nursery schools are true day care centers, but any good day care program for children of nursery school age will have an educational component in its program indistinguishable from that of a good nursery school. Because sound early childhood education is an important feature of a good day nursery as well as of a good nursery school, the distinction between the two kinds of programs tends to blur.

Day care provisions are expanding all over the world, including the developing countries, and the United States lags behind many other highly industrialized countries. Israel has developed many outstanding services, and the Soviet Union, which reportedly had accommodations in nurseries and kindergartens for 3.4 million children in 1960, had nearly doubled that accommodation by 1963 and is expanding it further, according to the International Labor Office in Geneva. In Norway, in addition to day nurseries and infant "crèches," there is a large number of "park aunts" who look after children of preschool age in parks and playgrounds. The mother who needs to shop, visit a clinic, or "catch her breath" may safely leave her child with an "aunt" during part of the day.

There is in the United States deep concern over the dearth of day care services of good quality, at a time of ever-increasing need. One of the most serious situations is found in the urban ghettos where parents must often rely on facilities providing such substandard care as to constitute a "national scandal." The lack of good day care facilities in these areas derives from the fact that parents have too little money, too few choices, and often too little understanding of what is actually happening to children.

Homemaker Service. In the homemaker service program, a carefully selected and agency-trained parent substitute is sent into the child's own home instead of providing him with foster care or supplementary care outside his home. This method offers many advantages over foster care for some children and their families, and is often less costly. Homemaker service makes it possible for children to stay in their own homes and bridges the gap caused by the absence of the mother when she is incapacitated but in the home and, in some instances, when she has died.

Like day care, homemaker service has been much more highly developed in countries other than the United States. In the early 1960's, for example, Britain, with 25% of the population of the United States, had 55,000 homemakers available when a comparable figure in the United States was 4,000. Of these 4,000 homemakers, offering service to 10,000 families, not all were providing service to families with children. For although homemaker service development was pioneered as a child welfare service, it is also used in programs for the aged and the chronically ill. Several European countries have established formal training courses for homemakers.

In communities without homemaker service, the only alternative for the care of children when the mother is out of the home, and there are no close friends or relatives to step in and take over, is to place the children in foster care.

In the United States, the federal government supports a continuing trend toward greatly expanded homemaker service, particularly under the auspices of public welfare agencies and particularly in relation to problems of illness. About 75% of recently established homemaker programs were under the auspices of public welfare agencies.

There is an increasing trend to recruit homemakers from the social class and neighborhood of the families to be served. Representing the life style and values of the families to be helped, and in some instances having themselves successfully coped with the problems of poverty and ghetto living, these homemakers can be effective.

Other Supplementary Service Provisions. Although not included under the Social Security Act definition of child welfare services, the importance to child welfare of social insurance programs such as Old Age Survivors and Disability Insurance (OASDI), the Medicare and Medicaid provisions, and the financial assistance aspects of the Aid to Families With Dependent Children (AFDC), cannot be overemphasized. Yet it is in these programs, particularly in the social insurances, that the United States lags far behind other highly

developed industrial countries. In the Soviet Union, for example, as well as Australia, nearly all families are covered by some form of social insurance or family allowance provision.

The most frequent kind of social insurance program of direct interest to children, utilized in other industrialized countries, is a family allowance system. This system is not available in the United States. Originally adopted in France, this kind of provision has since spread to more than 60 countries. It was based on the idea that "the existence of dependent children should not give rise to undue inequities in family levels of living." The family allowance idea is predicated on the principle that family needs are based on the size of a family and that these needs may require more funds than the family income can provide. Thus, a family allowance system provides for a regular allowance to every family for the support of each child as a normal supplement to family income, in recognition of the fact that the family with children carries a heavier economic burden than the childless family. The net effect is to maintain or increase the families' standards of living through equalization of costs of maintaining dependents. The allowance provides benefits for adopted, foster, and natural children.

Services to Support or Reinforce Parental Capacity —Protective Services. The community's concern to protect children has resulted in the establishment of protective services. In carrying them out, the designated child welfare agency, which in most places in the United States is the public child welfare agency, acts on a complaint received from the police, or from schools, courts, neighbors, physicians, or other social agencies, by sending a child welfare worker to the family's home. He confronts the parents with the community's concern and tries to learn about the quality of child care they do or could provide. When the worker determines that the complaint is valid and the care is inadequate, the worker offers to help the family through counseling and other aids to improve their parental functioning in order to avoid juvenile court action and prevent the possible loss of their children's custody. The worker may continue to see the family for a short time or a longer time depending on the situation. He is not empowered to remove the children without their parents' consent, but if he thinks that the children cannot safely remain, his agency may petition the court, alleging neglect or abuse. If the court concurs, it may order the children's removal, and the agency would then be responsible for planning with the court and with the family for substitute care.

An analysis of child welfare cases handled by public child welfare agencies would indicate that the most important category of problems presented by the children served is that of neglect, abuse, and exploitation. It ranks third among the problems faced by children receiving service from voluntary agencies. Not all the instances of serious neglect, abuse, and exploitation are known to agencies equipped to give protective services, and there is growing reason to believe that the number of unprotected children in serious jeopardy far exceeds the number known to protective service agencies at this time. The most frequently encountered situation is that of a child who although not "abused" is receiving care of such substandard or "indifferent" quality as to put him in great danger. It is estimated that of all children needing protective services, from 5% to 7% are "abused" or "battered" children, and the remaining 90% plus are the seriously neglected. Because physical abuse of a child is so dramatic and shocking, and can have such grave consequences, it has received a disproportionate amount of public attention.

Recent studies of the characteristics of parents who "neglect," "abuse," or "batter" their children suggests a contrast between those parents who abuse and those who neglect. The physical abuse is more likely to involve parents with serious mental or emotional problems and is as likely to occur in families of higher socioeconomic levels as of lower. Two kinds of "stress" are characteristically found in many of the parents who seriously neglect their children: the stress of financial deprivation and the stress of living in a one-parent family. When these stresses are combined, the result is often overwhelming.

Services to Unmarried Parents. Illegitimacy is one of the major problems with which the child welfare field is concerned. It sees the out-of-wedlock child as a child "at-risk" and has built its service provisions around the goal of "assuring for him, in so far as possible, the care and protection that would have been his had he been born as a welcomed child into an already strong and stable family." Service ideally starts as long before the birth as possible, to assure for the mother the protection of good prenatal care; freedom from environmental and psychological stress during the pregnancy; acceptance and understanding counsel both before and after the child's birth to help the mother—and whenever possible the father also—to make early as well as sound decisions regarding care or relinquishment of the child; to work out plans for caring for the child; and to assist the parents in the solution of problems related to unmarried parenthood.

Unfortunately, a very small proportion of the out-of-wedlock children are receiving this kind of protection in the United States. A rough estimate is that probably less than one third of the unmarried mothers receive agency services near the time of the child's birth. Presumably the percentage is even less after the child is born. The girl least likely to receive needed service is nonwhite, and is poor, and usually keeps her baby.

Despite the serious problems in inequity and lack of coverage, the United States has developed highly specialized services of excellent quality to assure good prenatal and postnatal care, protection from disclosure, counseling, opportunities for continued schooling, and aids and comforts to someone facing the difficult experience of pregnancy without a husband. Where the United States has fallen down is in services to support, reinforce, and sustain parents who, though unmarried, maintain families that struggle against great odds to rear out-of-wedlock children.

Many countries, including Britain, the Scandinavian countries, and France are doing a far better job with this latter group. New Zealand has set universal service coverage as a goal and has statutory provisions that a child welfare worker must be notified in confidence in every case of out-of-wedlock birth. This gives the social agencies there the opportunity of making an offer of help in every case situation. Minnesota is one of the few states in the United States which for many years has had a similar provision.

UN CHILD WELFARE PROGRAM

The UN Declaration of the Rights of the Child states that what society owes to the child can be nothing less than the "best it can give." Yet in many of these countries poverty and great deprivation are the rule rather than the exception, and these are the conditions under which three fourths of the world's children live. As many as one third die before reaching their fifth birthday. Of those who survive, only half ever see the inside of a school. Far fewer than that receive the education and training needed to get along successfully in the rapidly changing world in which they live. Parental struggle under these circumstances, to meet even the most basic of children's needs—the need for survival—is almost too staggering to comprehend. Survival, however, is only the first of a child's needs and rightful expectations from his parents and from his society.

UNICEF (the United Nations Children's Fund) is the only branch of the United Nations devoted entirely to the welfare of children and to development of family and child welfare services. Its specific mission is to encourage and assist the governments of economically less developed countries in undertaking long-term measures to meet the outstanding needs of children. Funds currently allocated to UNICEF, like funds to support child welfare generally, are tragically inadequate, but are being used with great imagination and with very encouraging results.

The general condition of children in the developing countries may at times seem so grim that efforts to alleviate their plight on any significant scale may appear hopeless. In *Children in the Developing Countries*, UNICEF reports the findings of its survey done cooperatively with the countries concerned. It also reports on some very hopeful developments; on the specific work that is going on throughout the world; and on the sound achievements that are being made.

The UNICEF report, though concentrating on services in the less well developed countries, stresses one most important point that is equally applicable to child welfare in the more "advanced" countries: "Much more could be done . . . if children were accorded their due place in every country's planning for its future."

ROBERTA McLEAN HUNT*
Community Council of Greater New York

Bibliography

Billingsley, Andrew, and Giovannoni, Jeanne M., *Children of the Storm: Black Children and American Child Welfare* (Harcourt 1972).
Child Welfare Journal, Special Issue on Foster Care (1973).
Child Welfare Journal, Special Issue on Groups and Group Methods (1972).
Child Welfare League of America Staff, *CWLA Standards for Child Protective Service*, rev. ed. (Child Welfare 1973).
Day Care and Child Development Council of America, *Alternatives in Quality Child Care* (Acropolis 1972).
Edwin Gould Foundation for Children, *Our Troubled Children: Our Community's Challenge*, ed. by Russell B. Wright (Columbia Univ. Press 1967).
Kadushin, Alfred, *Child Welfare Services*, 2d ed. (Macmillan 1974).
National Program for Comprehensive Child Welfare Services: *A Statement Prepared by the Committee on Public-Voluntary Agency Relationships* (Child Welfare 1971).
Sherman, Edmund A., and others, *Children Adrift in Foster Care: A Study of Alternative Approaches* (Child Welfare 1973).
Steiner, Gilbert and Milius, *The Children's Cause* (Brookings 1976).
Stewart, Patricia R., *Children in Distress: American and English Perspectives* (Sage 1976).
Zietz, Dorothy, *Child Welfare Services and Perspectives*, 2d ed. (Wiley 1969).

CHILDBED FEVER. See PUERPERAL FEVER.

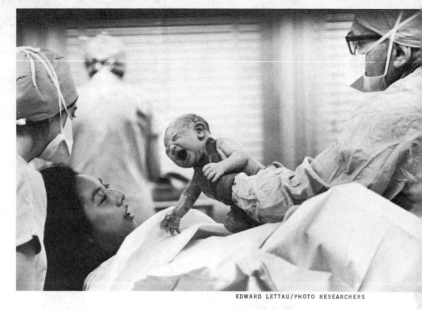

A newborn baby is shown to its mother minutes after it was delivered. If the baby is to be breast-fed, it can begin nursing right away. Close contact between mother and child during the first hours after birth establishes a bond that may last for years.

CHILDBIRTH is the biological culmination of the human reproductive process and the beginning of a baby's life as a member of society. In the United States and other Western societies in the 20th century the experience of childbirth has been shaped to a great extent by medical professionals. This shaping has been associated with increased safety for both mother and baby, decreased participation in the process of childbirth by the father and other family members, and the mother's diminished sense of being in charge of the childbirth process.

Since about 1950, hospital-and-doctor-dominated childbirth procedures have been slowly giving way to practices that seek to combine the medical advantages of hospital procedures with the psychological and social advantages of traditional family-oriented birth customs. These practices, often grouped together under the term natural childbirth, emphasize the participation of both parents in the events of labor and delivery. Typically they include prenatal classes for the mother and often for the father, exercises and relaxation techniques to make it easier for the mother to give birth, and minimal use of anesthetics or other drugs that may stupefy the mother and possibly injure her or her baby. See NATURAL CHILDBIRTH.

WAYS OF CHILDBIRTH

During the 1930's and 1940's, as births in the United States moved into the hospital and home birth attended by midwives or physicians became less available, a routine in birth management developed. Designed to spare women all pain and discomfort, the routine included liberal use of anesthetics and drugs to reduce discomfort and pain. Because the mother was usually given drugs to make her forget the experience, doctors and nurses felt the presence of family members to be an unnecessary hindrance to hospital procedures. Also, because the mother needed time to recover from the drugs, it was not safe to leave the infant with her for 12 to 24 hours after the birth. Therefore what is now recognized as a very desirable bonding between mother and infant often did not take place.

During the 1950's, in reaction to such well-intentioned but emotionally and socially unsatisfying hospital practices, there was a public ground swell in favor of "natural childbirth" methods. As a result, hospitals gradually began to offer parents the opportunity to be together throughout labor and delivery and to have their infant with them after birth (rooming-in). During these years, also, increasing criticism was directed at anesthesia, chemical induction of labor, and routine use of forceps, because of their effects on both mother and infant.

In the 1970's a movement for a return to home delivery began on the part of some couples who wished to play an active part in their own health care, and who saw a basic conflict between their goals and the goals of health-care providers. Such couples seek a family-centered, drug-free experience. Often the only helpers available to them are friends or self-taught "midwives." Such help can be dangerous, because special training is needed in order to detect some of the problems that may occur in pregnancy and delivery in time to obtain appropriate professional care for the mother.

Birth centers are units that provide a home-like setting for delivery, but with some of the safeguards of a hospital and an effective back-up arrangement for obtaining prompt medical care should complications occur. Many centers are staffed by teams made up of nurse-midwives and obstetricians. The first demonstration of such a center in the United States opened at the Maternity Center Association in New York City in September 1975. However, roughly similar centers have long existed in other countries, including France and the Netherlands.

For many families, out-of-hospital birth can provide emotional satisfactions difficult if not impossible to attain in most hospital settings. However, parents considering an out-of-hospital birth must weigh the alternatives carefully. Out of the hospital there is a greater risk of being unable to cope with one of the fairly rare obstetric emergencies that hospitals are designed to deal with. In the hospital there may be technology-oriented management of delivery, less opportunity to relate to the newborn, and a possibly increased likelihood of infection.

In the past, carefully designed home-birth programs such as that at the Frontier Nursing Service in Kentucky have had enviable records of safety. However, as of the late 1970's it was

Expectant mothers and their husband-coaches learn techniques of breathing and relaxation at a childbirth class.

not known whether out-of-hospital settings for delivery were more or less safe than in-hospital settings. Until more is known about the comparative advantages and disadvantages of the different ways of childbirth, expectant couples must exercise great care in exploring the choices available to them.

Choosing the Type of Care. The choice of a professional to assist with pregnancy and birth is based on the kind of experience desired and the state of the mother's health. Talking to couples or family members who have recently given birth can be helpful in reaching a decision. Couples should read several of the many books on pregnancy and birth and not rely on just one. It is wise to begin reading before the pregnancy is begun.

Once a decision is made, prenatal care can be started with the professional selected. The annual checkup can be used to evaluate the personality "fit" between the family and recommended professionals. Doctors skilled in obstetrics may be family physicians, board-certified specialists in obstetrics and gynecology, or physicians who are not certified specialists but limit their practice to obstetrics and gynecology. Some nurse-midwives provide general health care for women, and some become involved only in pregnancy, but a prepregnancy interview should be easy to arrange in either case. Names of nearby nurse-midwives can be obtained from the American College of Nurse-Midwives, 1000 Vermont Ave., N. W., Washington, D. C. 20005.

It is usually easy to find a doctor skilled in standard techniques of supervising pregnancy and delivery. However, if a family-centered childbirth is desired, local childbirth educators can be consulted for referrals to suitable hospitals, birth centers, or home delivery practitioners. Information also can be obtained from the following agencies:

International Childbirth Education Assn.
P. O. Box 5852
Milwaukee, Wis. 53220

Maternity Center Association
48 East 92d Street,
New York, N. Y. 10028

National Association of Parents &
Professionals for Safe Alternatives in Childbirth
Chapel Hill, N. C. 27514

Hospital care, private or clinic, is usually the most costly way to have one's child, with birth centers and home delivery considerably less expensive. There is great variation in childbirth services and facilities from institution to institution, and expectant parents should check out local hospitals or birth centers before selecting one of them.

Most babies, by far, are born in hospitals, where delivery and care of the newborn infant generally follow a course like that described in this section. However, many hospitals can accommodate natural childbirths—and in fact most natural childbirths do take place in hospitals. Also, hospitals that are more family-centered design their maternity care so that family members are together for long periods. In what is called "rooming-in," infants may remain with the mother for varying periods so that the mother can enjoy the baby and learn to care for it. To provide some of the advantages of home delivery, a few hospitals have opened birthing rooms where the father can stay with the mother throughout the whole process of delivery.

Preparation for Childbirth. During the period of pregnancy parents should investigate methods of infant care, with special attention to feeding methods. If a woman wishes to breast-feed her baby, she can obtain information and the names of people who can provide guidance from La Leche League, 9616 Minneapolis Ave., Franklin Park, Ill. 60131. Pediatric-nurse practitioners provide total infant- and child-health care, often in association with board-certified pediatricians or clinics.

For many couples, childbirth classes are an especially informative and anxiety-relieving introduction to the experience of childbirth. The classes provide information about the anatomy and physiology of pregnancy; labor and delivery; and techniques for self-help during the contractions of labor, including breathing and relaxation. Nutrition, activity and comfort in pregnancy, and adjustments of mother and father to pregnancy and parenthood are also usually included. Classes in infant care and feeding, though less widely available, are valuable, as are programs to help couples adapt to their new roles as parents. The agencies mentioned in the preceding section can provide referrals.

If a hospital birth is planned, the couple should tour the hospital's maternity unit. Attending childbirth classes at the hospital, if available, will help the couple become as familiar as possible with the hospital's personnel, policies, procedures, and setting. In some communities there are special classes for couples who are expecting their baby to be delivered by cesarian section.

Conventional Hospital Delivery. Typically, when labor appears to have begun, a couple notifies their physician or a hospital staff member, possibly a resident physician or nurse-midwife. The mother will probably be admitted to the hospital if contractions are five minutes apart in the case of a first baby or ten minutes apart for a mother who has given birth before, or if the membranes that enclose the baby rupture. The breaking of these membranes, known as the bag of waters, is signaled by a gush or trickle of watery fluid from the vagina. If labor is scheduled to be started artificially, the mother will enter the hospital at a preappointed time.

Procedures Following Admission. When the woman is admitted, urine and blood specimens usually are taken, a pelvic examination done, and in some hospitals a pubic shave and enema may be administered. The mother is assigned to a labor room of one or more beds and cared for by a maternity nurse, whose other duties may keep her from being in constant attendance. Eating and drinking are generally not permitted. Fluids may be given intravenously in order to prevent the mother from becoming dehydrated.

If the baby's heartbeat is to be monitored electronically, the membranes are ruptured so that electrodes can be passed through the vagina and fastened to the baby's scalp to record its heart rate. Fetal monitoring may be needed, for example, to check on the baby's condition if continuous anesthesia—described in a later section—is to be used. Although it is thought to be less sensitive, an external monitor may be used in place of an internal monitor. It is strapped around the mother's abdomen and requires her to remain on her back throughout labor. Some experts doubt the efficacy of monitors, and question whether they should be used routinely. Also, some studies have reported that the rate of cesarean sections increases when monitors are used—apparently because the tracings of the monitor are sometimes interpreted incorrectly.

Samples of blood from the baby's scalp may also be taken to provide more information about the baby's health, and a catheter may be introduced into the uterus in order to graph the mother's contractions.

Labor and Delivery Procedures. If permitted in the labor room, the father may remain throughout the first stage of labor, in which the cervix dilates. He is usually asked to leave the room during examinations. When the second (pushing) stage of labor begins, or shortly thereafter, the mother is wheeled to the delivery room and helped to move onto the delivery table, where she is positioned on her back with her legs placed in stirrups. The birth area is washed and covered with sterile drapes. The mother's hands are restrained so that she cannot touch the baby or drapes and contaminate the sterile area. Episiotomy, the surgical enlarging of the birth outlet by an incision in the tissue surrounding the vagina, is usually performed in order to expedite birth just before the baby's head appears. The father, if present, may be asked to leave at this point. If regional anesthesia effected through the spinal canal is under way at this time, it is continued throughout the rest of delivery. The mother is awake to see her baby born, but often forceps must be used to assist the baby's birth because the anesthesized mother is unable to sense the need to push and bring her natural forces to bear. An anesthetist is usually present to give supplementary gas anesthesia, should it be indicated, during the final stage of delivery.

After delivery, the baby is usually given to the mother for a short time before it is taken to a central nursery. Generally the nursing staff shows the baby to the father in the waiting area when it is taken to the nursery. Thereafter the mother sees the infant for feeding for periods of 20 to 30 minutes every four hours, five times a day from 6 A. M. to 10 P. M. At other times the infant is in the central nursery, where at specified times it may be viewed through an observation window by relatives and friends.

Delivery at a Birth Center. Out-of-hospital birth centers provide a homelike atmosphere where the whole family, including the infant, can remain together for their entire stay. No procedures are routinely performed nor drugs routinely used, and the mother labors and delivers in the same bed. If complications occur, transfer is made to a backup hospital. The wishes of the parents have high priority in planning the experience, and the attendants are expert assistants watchful for any abnormality. Brothers and sisters of the new baby may be present if the parents so choose. After the birth, the family returns home and is visited there by a public-health nurse during the baby's first week of life.

Delivery at Home. In home delivery, the doctor or midwife comes to the home for the delivery. In the United States, few professionals feel they can spend the time required for the entire labor and delivery, so families desiring a home birth must be independent and willing to assume major responsibility for their own health care. Good prenatal care is essential. Backup services in the event of complications must be arranged in advance. Candidates for both home-birth and birth-center delivery should be healthy and free from any sign of deviation from a normal delivery.

RUTH WATSON LUBIC
The Maternity Center Association, New York City

THE COURSE OF DELIVERY

Delivery is the act by which a baby is expelled from the uterus, or womb, through the vagina. Normally, a baby is born about 38 weeks (266 days) after it is conceived. In some cases, however, the baby may be born after only 26 weeks, and in others after as long as 41 weeks following conception. Generally, if a baby is born before 35 weeks after conception, it is considered to be premature.

It is not known exactly why a baby is born at a particular time. It is known, however, that just before the start of childbirth there is a withdrawal of the substances that have been exerting an inhibitory influence on the muscles of the uterus throughout the pregnancy. Once these substances are no longer produced, the uterine muscles become active and start the process of expelling the baby. These contractions of the uterine muscles are known as *labor pains*, and as childbirth progresses they become more frequent and stronger.

The onset of labor pains is usually an indication to an expectant mother that she is about to give birth. In many cases she is also forewarned of the approach of childbirth by a thick, pinkish mucous discharge (called a "show") or by the escape of a watery fluid from the vagina.

Stages of Normal Childbirth. The process of childbirth is usually divided into three separate stages. For a woman giving birth for the first time, the first stage lasts about 12 hours and the second stage about 50 minutes. For women who have had previous deliveries, the first stage lasts about eight hours and the second stage about 20 minutes. For nearly all women, the third stage lasts only a few minutes.

First Stage. The first stage of childbirth, known as the *stage of dilatation*, extends from the time regular contractions of the uterus occur until the time the cervix (the small opening between the uterus and the vagina) becomes wide enough to permit the passage of the baby through it. During this stage, the cervix increases in diameter from about half an inch (13 mm) to nearly 4 inches (100 mm).

At the onset of labor the contractions of the uterus are short and recur about every 10 to 15 minutes. They are accompanied by sensations of discomfort in the small of the back, and as the contractions become stronger and more frequent, these sensations become more severe and eventually spread over the entire abdominal area. Usually, at the end of the first stage, the fluid-filled sac surrounding the baby ruptures spontaneously and the fluid escapes. However, the sac often ruptures much earlier, sometimes even before labor pains begin. In some cases it does not break until the actual delivery of the baby.

Second Stage. The second stage, known as the *stage of expulsion*, extends from the time the cervix is sufficiently dilated until the time the baby is born. By the beginning of this stage, the contractions of the uterus are extremely intense, occurring every two or three minutes and lasting about one minute. At this time, the mother almost automatically begins contracting her abdominal muscles (known as "bearing down"), so that the baby is expelled by the involuntary action of the muscles of the uterus and the voluntary action of the muscles of the abdomen.

In about 95% of all pregnancies, the baby is born headfirst, a position known as a *vertex position*. About 4% are born with the feet or buttocks first, known as *breech positions*. The remaining few are born in abnormal positions, as with the arm or shoulder first. The vast majority of head presentations are born without any difficulty, although sometimes with the aid of an instrument known as obstetrical forceps.

Third Stage. The third stage of childbirth extends from the birth of the baby until the time that the afterbirth, consisting of the ruptured sac and placenta, has been expelled from the uterus. The placenta is a pancake-shaped structure through which the baby receives nourishment while it is in the uterus. This stage is known as the *afterbirth stage* or *placental stage*.

It is extremely important that all of the placental and sac tissues are expelled from the uterus. If parts of the tissue remain in the womb, serious complications, especially hemorrhaging, may result. Most often, the placenta and sac are delivered without any trouble, and they are then examined by the doctor to make sure that every bit of tissue has come out of the uterus. If parts of the placenta or sac are missing, the doctor removes them with his hand. As the final step in the process of childbirth, the doctor sutures the episiotomy cut and any tears that might have resulted from the delivery of the baby. Since a baby's head is the largest part of its body, when the head comes out first the rest of the body can follow quickly and easily. A breech baby is seldom delivered solely by the efforts of the mother and nearly always requires assistance from the doctor.

Anesthesia. During childbirth the contractions of the uterus often become so severe that many women are given drugs to relieve the pain. However, some women prefer to have their babies without anesthesia by one of the natural-childbirth methods. In cases of twins or premature babies, drugs are not used—or are used in very small amounts—because they may harm small babies.

Anesthetics are usually administered by hypodermic injection, but sometimes they are given orally or by a combination of both methods. For many women, only a local anesthetic such as Novocaine or Xylocaine is necessary. A *pudendal block*, which numbs the external genital area, is often used at the end of labor to eliminate birth pains. Sometimes the anesthetic is injected into the canal at the base of the spine so that it affects the pain fibers of the nerves to the uterus and cervix just after they leave the spinal cord. This kind of anesthesia, called a *saddle block*, numbs the whole birth area from belly to thighs. It cannot be used in every case, and it is given only at the very end of labor. Because of their occasional harmful effects on both mother and infant, saddle blocks are used by many physicians only for certain emergency deliveries. Two other types of local anesthesia, *caudal block* and *epidural block*, can be administered repeatedly throughout labor and delivery, and are known as continuous regional anesthetics. Great skill is needed for proper insertion of the needle through which the anesthetic will flow. Also, it is vital to monitor the condition of both mother and baby carefully—a service not all hospitals can provide. Epidural blocks are used more commonly than caudal blocks, largely because they are easier to administer. It is also true, however, that larger doses of anesthetic must be used for caudal blocks than for either saddle blocks or epidural blocks.

General anesthesia, in the form of a gas, is often given near the end of labor so that the woman will not be aware of obstetrical procedures such as episiotomy or use of forceps.

Artificial Induction of Labor. If labor is to be induced artificially the doctor usually breaks the membranous sac around the baby or injects into one of the mother's veins an artificial hormone that stimulates the uterine walls to contract. Often, both procedures are combined.

STAGES OF CHILDBIRTH

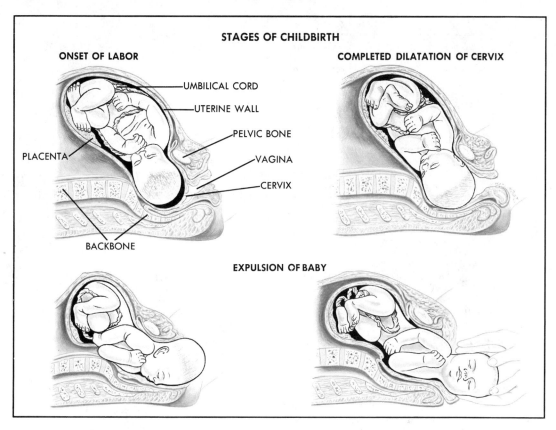

ONSET OF LABOR

UMBILICAL CORD
UTERINE WALL
PELVIC BONE
VAGINA
CERVIX
PLACENTA
BACKBONE

COMPLETED DILATATION OF CERVIX

EXPULSION OF BABY

Occasionally, childbirth is induced to preserve the health of the mother or to make certain that a live, healthy baby will be born—reasons known as medical indications. However, in most cases, childbirth is induced for the convenience of the mother or her doctor. Such an induction, known as elective induction, may have several advantages: the patient is well rested before labor begins; she is psychologically prepared; and her stomach is empty, thus limiting the danger of her vomiting while under anesthesia. Elective induction also avoids the risk of excessively rapid labor and the possible delivery of the baby while the mother is at home or on the way to the hospital. On the other hand, induction runs a risk of serious complications, including the delivery of a premature baby. It is generally agreed that because of inherent risks to the infant and mother this technique should be used only when medically indicated and not for reasons of convenience of the mother or her doctor.

Cesarean Section. In the vast majority of women, the space in the body pelvis is ample for a spontaneous, easy birth of the baby. In some cases, however, the space is too small, and the baby must be delivered through an operation called a cesarean section. Sometimes the need for a cesarean section is determined through physical examination, but usually it is determined by means of X-ray photographs that show the bones of the mother's pelvis and the bones of the baby's head. However, if there is still some doubt about the relative difference in the size of the pelvis and the baby's head, a "test of labor" is given. In a test of labor, the baby's head is permitted to progress to see if it will come into

the opening of the pelvis and descend into the vagina. If the head fails to come through, a cesarean must be performed at once. See also CESAREAN SECTION.

J. P. GREENHILL, M. D.*
Formerly, Michael Reese Hospital, Chicago

POSTNATAL CARE

After childbirth is completed, the doctor or a nurse remains with the mother for at least an hour. During this time, the mother is usually in a special ward or recovery room, where she is under close supervision. The purpose of this is to detect any excessive bleeding and to make sure that the mother recovers properly, especially if anesthetics or other drugs were administered during the delivery. While the mother is recovering, the baby is examined by a physician to make sure that its organs and limbs are functioning properly and to detect any obvious birth defects.

The baby can begin nursing almost immediately after birth. At this time the mother's breasts give the protein-rich milk known as colostrum. True lactation begins about two or three days after delivery, when the regular milk "comes in." The greatest stimulus to milk secretion is the baby's suckling. When the baby is taken off the breast, lactation will generally cease.

The uterus begins shrinking immediately after delivery and returns to its normal size after six weeks. The cervix gradually closes and the voluntary muscles of the pelvic floor gradually return to normal. The mother's average total weight loss from immediately before delivery to 12 days after delivery is about 17 pounds, mostly in fluids. During the first week after delivery exercise will help prevent circulatory problems and will improve respiration and bowel function.

During the first week after birth the baby will lose up to about 10% of its body weight by about the fourth day, but it will make up the loss by about the seventh day. Shortly after birth the baby's head and face may show wrinkling and other signs of the pressures of its journey down the birth canal. These signs usually disappear by the end of the first week. About half of all babies experience a slight jaundice about the third day, which disappears by the seventh day. As a result of the withdrawal of maternal sex hormones, a slight swelling of the breasts may occur in babies of both sexes, with leakage of milky fluid. The breasts should not be squeezed, or infection may occur. The cord stump becomes dry and shriveled by about the fifth day and usually falls off by the seventh. The baby's stools, dark green or tarry at first, become soft and greenish yellow by the fourth day. See also INFANCY AND INFANT CARE.

Most women get out of bed on the day of childbirth and leave the hospital when the baby is three to five days old. Usually it is recommended that the mother return to her physician for a checkup when the baby is about six weeks old.

DENIS CAVANAGH, M. D.
School of Medicine
University of South Florida

Bibliography

Bing, Elizabeth, *Six Practical Lessons for an Easier Childbirth* (Bantam 1969).
Boston Women's Health Collective, *Our Bodies, Ourselves*, rev. ed. (Simon & Schuster 1976).
Cavanagh, Denis, Woods, R. E. W., and O'Connor, T. C. F., *Obstetric Emergencies* (Harper 1978).
Greenhill, J. P., *Miracle of Life: The Story of a Baby from Conception to Birth and a Bit Beyond* (Year Book Medical Pub. 1971).
Guttmacher, Alan F., *Pregnancy, Birth, and Family Planning* (Viking 1973).
Hazell, Lester D., *Commonsense Childbirth* (Berkley Pub. 1976).
Kitzinger, Sheila, *The Experience of Childbirth* (Penguin 1972).
Klaus, H. Marshall, M. D., and Kennell, John H., M. D. *Maternal-Infant Bonding* (Mosby 1976).
La Leche League, *The Womanly Art of Breastfeeding* (1963).
Maternity Center Association, *A Baby Is Born*, 3d ed. (Grosset 1964).
Maternity Center Association, *Preparation for Childbearing*, 4th ed. (1973).
National Association of Parents and Professionals for Safe Alternatives in Childbirth, *Safe Alternatives in Childbirth* (1976).

CHILDE, child, Vere Gordon (1892–1957), Australian archaeologist and prehistorian, known for his comprehensive summation of European prehistory of the 3d and 2d millennia B. C. He was born, in Sydney, New South Wales, Australia, on April 14, 1892. He attended Sydney University and from 1919 to 1921 was private secretary to the premier of New South Wales. He studied archaeology at Queens College, Oxford, and at the University of Edinburgh, where in 1921 he joined the faculty as first Abercromby professor of prehistory. He left Edinburgh in 1946 to become director of the Institute of Archaeology of the University of London.

Childe's major interest was a study of the organization and character of the barbarian cultures of Europe and their relationship to the Middle East. He saw prehistory in terms of the social and technological advances whose stimulant effect upon each other resulted in the Urban Revolution. This marked the beginning of civilization, characterized by large urban centers, surplus wealth, the use of metals, and the development of writing and a numerical system. He believed that civilization developed first in Mesopotamia about 3000 B. C. and from there spread to the Indus Valley and Egypt and later to Europe. Childe thought that it may have occurred independently in China and, undoubtedly, in Meso-America.

Among Childe's numerous works are *Progress and Archaeology* (1944), *New Light on the Most Ancient East* (1952), and *The Dawn of European Civilization* (rev. ed., 1957). Childe did much to define and regularize archaeological terminology and to instill archaeologists with an international approach to prehistory. He died on Mt. Victoria, New South Wales, on Oct. 19, 1957.

PRISCILLA C. WARD
American Museum of Natural History

CHILDE HAROLD'S PILGRIMAGE is a poem by Lord Byron. Written in Spenserian stanzas, the work is divided into four cantos totaling about 4,500 lines. Cantos 1 and 2 were published in 1812; canto 3, in 1816; and canto 4, in 1818.

Childe Harold is weary of his life of dissipation and decides to seek distraction through travel. (Childe is an archaic word meaning "young lord.") In cantos 1 and 2 he journeys through Spain, Portugal, and Greece; canto 3 is devoted to Waterloo, the Rhine, and Switzerland; and canto 4 discusses Italy. With perception and insight, Byron describes and reflects on the landscapes, historical associations, great men and events, cities, buildings, and works of art of the places visited.

Childe Harold's Pilgrimage is autobiographical, with Byron's own travels furnishing its material. The poem's enduring quality is due not only to its evocative descriptions of the places visited but also to its eloquent pleas for liberty, justice, and social, political, and religious reform, which are interwoven among the descriptive passages.

CHILDE ROLAND TO THE DARK TOWER CAME, a poem in 34 six-line stanzas by Robert Browning, published in 1855. It is one of the most powerful and impressive of Browning's shorter poems.

The work is a dramatic monologue in which the hero, Childe (an archaic word meaning "young lord") Roland, a medieval knight, describes his search for the "dark tower." Many brave knights have attempted this adventure before him but none have returned from the quest. Childe Roland sets out on his dangerous and difficult search, traveling through a strange unidentified landscape, surrealistic in its configurations but sharply realistic in detail. After countless hardships, he finally reaches the tower and sees about him, like apparitions, the forms of those knights who have preceded him. As the poem ends, Childe Roland sounds a great blast on his trumpet to announce his arrival.

The symbolic significance of the dark tower is not explained in the poem. A possible interpretation is that it represents death, and that Childe Roland's quest is figuratively the journey through life, with its failures, successes, and perils, both real and imaginary, toward its inevitable goal.

CHILDREN'S AID SOCIETY, a nonsectarian organization serving all races and creeds, founded in 1853 by Charles Loring Brace to help orphaned, destitute, and homeless children in New York City. The society originally operated lodging houses and industrial schools, and pioneered in placing children in foster and adoptive homes rather than in institutions, the prevalent practice of the time. As its program developed it initiated visiting nurse services, free dental clinics, day nurseries for children of working mothers, and free hot lunches for schoolchildren.

Varied programs are offered to disadvantaged children and their families. Services include preschool; health and dental; psychiatric, psychological, and remedial education; adoption; family and vocational counseling; and homemaking and foster home care. In addition there are group work and recreational activities and employment programs. The society's summer camps include a special camp for handicapped children.

The affairs and business of the Children's Aid Society are managed by a voluntary board of trustees. Its work is financed by voluntary contributions, by reimbursement from public and private sources for service to children, and by the income from its endowment.

VICTOR REMER
The Children's Aid Society

CHILDREN'S BUREAU. See CHILD WELFARE.

CHILDREN'S COURTS. See CHILD WELFARE; JUVENILE DELINQUENCY—*Juvenile Courts.*

CHILDREN'S CRUSADE, the name given to a popular pietistic movement that flared up briefly in Europe in the late spring and summer of 1212. It apparently originated in the Rhineland. Although it was only one of many such movements during the Middle Ages, it attracted the attention of chroniclers, whose exaggerated accounts in turn fired the enthusiasm of later romantic historians. An unusually large number of children participated, many of them belonging to pastoral communities. The most important leader was a boy of Cologne named Nicholas.

Like other mass manifestations of popular piety, the Children's Crusade may be traced ultimately to a sharp increase in religious feeling among laymen during the 11th century. This growing lay piety affected public opinion in various ways, producing demands for higher moral standards of the clergy and an end to Muslim domination of the Holy Land. The Gregorian reforms, the austere monasticism of the Cistercians and Carthusians, and the early crusades were all influenced considerably by these attitudes.

In the 12th and 13th centuries popular religious feeling often took an emotional turn, drawing some persons to mysticism, giving rise to savage bursts of anti-Semitism, and stimulating the growth of anticlerical movements. There were periodic outbreaks of religious hysteria, often among rural people, such as the *pastoureaux* uprisings that troubled France in 1251 and 1320. The calling of the First Crusade in 1095 had given rise to the ill-organized popular expedition led by Peter the Hermit, which came to a disastrous end in Asia Minor shortly before the western feudal contingents took the field. The Children's Crusade forms part of this tradition of spontaneous popular movements.

In the early 13th century, people were becoming disillusioned with the leadership of the crusading movement. Jerusalem, lost in 1187, had not been regained by the Third Crusade. The Fourth Crusade in 1204 had scandalously plundered the Christian city of Constantinople. Since 1208 a bloody crusade had been waged against the Albigensian heretics of southern France.

It was amid efforts to recruit reinforcements for this campaign that the Children's Crusade was born. Bands of children in northern France assembled under the leadership of a shepherd boy named Stephen. These seem to have dispersed, but other groups began to come together around Liège, Trier, and Cologne in the spring of 1212. Persons of all ages were involved, but it was the large number of children that excited comment.

Proposing to rescue the Holy Sepulchre from the Muslims, these bands straggled up the Rhine Valley, through southern Germany, and across the Alps into Italy. At Genoa they failed to obtain passage across the Mediterranean. A few of them reached Marseille, where it is said that they fell into the hands of merchants who sold them into slavery in North Africa.

JOHN HENNEMAN
McMaster University, Hamilton, Ontario

CHILDREN'S LITERATURE. See LITERATURE FOR CHILDREN.

CHILDS, chīldz, **Marquis William** (1903–   ), American journalist, noted as a Washington correspondent. Born in Clinton, Iowa, on March 17, 1903, he earned degrees at the universities of Wisconsin and Iowa. After working for the United Press in Chicago, Detroit, New York, and St. Louis, Childs became a staff member of the St. Louis *Post-Dispatch* in 1926. There he remained, mostly as Washington correspondent, until 1944. For the next ten years, he was a columnist for the United Feature syndicate, writing from Washington and from Europe, where he did a three-month tour of battlefields during World War II. In 1954 he returned to the *Post-Dispatch* Washington Bureau, of which he became chief in 1962.

Childs' best-known book, *Sweden—The Middle Way* (1936), describes the Swedish economy as a middle way between uncontrolled capitalism and extreme socialism. He also wrote other books on public affairs, including *The Ragged Edge* (1955) and *Eisenhower, Captive Hero* (1958); *The Cabin* (1944), a semiautobiographical novel; and *The Peacemakers* (1961).

ROBERT W. DESMOND
University of California, Berkeley

CHILD'S GARDEN OF VERSES, a book of poems for children by Robert Louis Stevenson, published in 1885. Unusual in a day when children were just beginning to read anything but adult books or moral tales, *A Child's Garden* was planned to give children pleasure. The simple words and easy flights of imagination took off from situations every child knew: "At evening when the lamp is lit,/Around the fire my parents sit"; "I have a little shadow that goes in and out with me"; and "In winter I get up at night/And dress by yellow candle-light." Stevenson wrote many of these gay verses, enjoyed by generations of children, while he himself was an invalid.

CHILE

CHILE'S PRINCIPAL PORT, Valparaíso, is built on hills surrounding a spacious harbor. Private homes on the slopes overlook the city's business district.

J. ALLAN CASH, FROM RAPHO GUILLUMETTE

Coat of Arms of Chile

--- **CONTENTS** ---

CHILE, chil'ē, a republic in southern South America, is a country with a unique geography. Extending some 2,600 miles (4,200 km) along the Pacific coast, it has an average width of only 110 miles (180 km) between the ocean to the west and the towering peaks of the Andes to the east. Although 8th in size and 7th in population among the Latin American states, Chile is recognized as a leading nation of the region. It has one of Latin America's highest per capita incomes, and its more than 10 million people are intensely proud of their institutions and rich cultural life.

Chile's population is concentrated in a relatively tiny portion of the country—the fertile Central Valley, which extends between the Andes and a range of coastal mountains in Middle Chile. Near the valley's northern end lies Santiago, the capital. The forbidding Atacama Desert of the northern provinces isolates the country from Peru and Bolivia as the Andes cut Chile off from Argentina. Much of the southern

INFORMATION HIGHLIGHTS

Official Name: República de Chile.

Constitutional Head of State: President.

Constitutional Head of Government: President.

Legislature: Congreso Nacional—*upper chamber: Senado:* 45 members (elected for 8-year terms); *Cámara de Diputados:* 147 members (elected for 4-year terms).

Area: 292,256 square miles (756,945 sq km), excluding part of Antarctica claimed by Chile.

Boundaries: *West and south,* Pacific Ocean; *east,* Argentina; *northeast,* Bolivia; *north,* Peru.

Highest Elevation: Mount Ojos del Salado, 22,539 feet (6,870 meters).

Population: (1975 est.) 10,253,000.

Capital: Santiago (1975 est. population, 3,186,000; Greater Santiago, 3,262,990).

Major Language: Spanish (official).

Major Religion: Roman Catholicism.

Monetary Unit: Peso (worth 1,000 old escudos).

Weights and Measures: Metric system.

Flag: Lower half, red; upper half, a blue square on the left containing a white five-pointed star, and a white rectangular section on the right. See also *Flag.*

National Anthem: *Dulce patria, recibe los votos* ... (Sweet Fatherland, receive the vows ...).

region was not opened to settlement until the 1880's, when the fierce Araucanian Indians were pacified after a 350-year war.

Although plagued by frequent devastating earthquakes, Chile has been favored with an equable climate and rich soils in its central provinces and by abundant mineral wealth in regions unsuited to agriculture. The nation is largely dependent on its mineral exports, especially copper; but Chile is one of the continent's most industrialized regions and has vast timber resources as well as world-renowned vineyards and important cattle and sheep ranches.

Neglected by motherland Spain in the colonial period, Chileans acquired considerable experience in self-government before they won their independence in 1818. Most of the people are Roman Catholics, but the church has never dominated politics, and the church-state issue was less disruptive in the 19th century than in many other Latin American republics. Moreover, the military has seldom intervened in politics; it has been content to discharge its professional duties as the defender, rather than as the master, of constitutional administrations.

Chile's educational system and its celebrated national university are among the best in Latin America. The country has produced creative writers, historians, and musicians of the first rank, and many of them have won international reputations.

Despite the advantages of a superb natural endowment, political stability, broad individual liberties, and a productive intellectual life, Chile faces problems of great magnitude. Chronic inflation, low productivity in agriculture, and the conflict between the executive and legislative branches of government are among the most pressing problems. But increasingly in the last half of the 20th century, Chileans have been concerned by a fundamental paradox in national life: the coexistence of industrial, political, and cultural achievement with vast lower-class misery.

FREDRICK B. PIKE, *University of Notre Dame*

1. The People

The average Chilean is of Spanish descent (with some Indian forebears), speaks Spanish, and is at least nominally Roman Catholic. He enjoys a higher standard of living than the average Latin American. He lives in an urban community, where he is relatively well housed, reasonably well fed, and has had about six years of school.

Ethnic Groups. About two thirds of Chile's 9 million people are of mixed Spanish and Indian descent, and another one fourth are of Spanish descent alone. Despite the apparently large Indian element in the population, the overwhelming majority of Chileans are white. Because the Indians were never great in number, the Indian stock was quickly assimilated into the European mainstream of the population through intermarriage. In the mid-1960's only 3% to 5% of the total population was classified as Indian.

In addition, Chile has never experienced the mass migratory waves that flooded Argentina and Brazil. Some Germans settled in the southern Central Valley, and some Italians, British, and French primarily in the Santiago-Valparaíso region. Although immigration has contributed only a tiny percentage of the overall population, the minorities of non-Spanish European origin are more influential in national life than their numbers indicate.

Language and Religion. The Chileans speak Spanish. They pronounce it more carefully than Argentines, but their Spanish is considered less pure than that of urban Peru. Familiarity with Spanish extends to the Indian population as well. Close to 95% of the population is Roman Catholic, but the degree of adherence to the church varies. The most orthodox and traditional Chilean Catholics are those in the central area. An atmosphere of religious tolerance prevails, under a constitution that provides for freedom of worship.

Standard of Living. The overall standard of well-being, as reflected in per capita gross national product in the mid-1960's, put Chileans well above the average for Latin America. Per capita gross national product was $501, compared with $394 for Latin America as a whole. But distribution of income is unsatisfactory. The census of 1960 showed that 51.6% of the people received 16.5% of the income; 41.6% of the people received 45.1% of the income; and 6.8% received 38.4% of the income.

Increasingly, Chileans live in urban communities. In the mid-1960's, 68% of the population was estimated to be urban. About half of the urban population is concentrated in Greater Santiago, and the trend toward concentration continues. The proportion of agricultural workers in the economically active population is declining, but agriculture continues to be the chief economic support for about two thirds of the people.

Although a majority of Chileans enjoy adequate housing, a growing proportion of the population is ill-housed. In 1966, for example, it was estimated that 75,000 new dwellings were needed annually to keep pace with population growth and deterioration of existing units, but construction since 1960 had failed dismally to meet even the requirements for population growth alone.

Chileans are reasonably well-fed. The U.S. Department of Agriculture has estimated that

SANTIAGO, looking down past the stairs and terraces of Santa Lucía Hill toward Avenida Bernardo O'Higgins.

CARL FRANK

CHILE'S LAKE DISTRICT attracts fishermen and tourists. All Saints Lake, in the southern part of the district, is among the most beautiful of the lakes. Mount Tronador, rising in the distance, is on the border with Argentina.

daily per capita consumption was 2,610 calories in 1960 (compared with 3,140 for the United States) and would reach 2,680 in 1970. It found no nutritional deficits in the food supply. The availability of protein per capita (78.9 grams) exceeds minimum requirements.

Public-health facilities are comparatively good, especially as measured by the number of available physicians. The ratio of 7.3 doctors per 10,000 inhabitants in the early 1960's was exceeded in few countries of the Western Hemisphere. Urban Chileans are relatively fortunate in water supply. In the early 1960's, 78% of the urban population, but only 6% of the rural population, enjoyed satisfactory potable water services; and 40% of urban homes had sewer connections.

Population Growth. In the 1960's the population of Chile was increasing at the rate of 2.3% a year. Continued increase at that rate would double the population by the year 2000. Chileans are increasingly conscious of the challenge to economic development posed by the high birth rate, which in 1966 was 32.8 per 1,000 inhabitants (the death rate was 11.2). Thus they are increasingly alert to the potential of birth control, and in the late 1960's Chile had the most liberal birth control policy in Latin America.

About two fifths of the population is under 15 years of age, a slightly lower proportion than in Latin America generally. Life expectancy at birth—55 years for men and 60 years for women —is better than the regional average. Infant mortality is unusually high, but the ratio of 99.8 per 1,000 live births represented considerable improvement over the 164 per 1,000 in 1945.

SIMON G. HANSON
Editor, "Inter-American Economic Affairs"

2. The Land and Natural Resources

In climates and physical features, Chile resembles Pacific North America from Mexico to southern Alaska, the zone of equivalent latitudes. Extending along the western coast of South America, between the 18th and 56th parallels of south latitude, Chile actually lies due south of New England because of the curvature of the Pacific basin. The country is extremely well endowed in mineral resources other than fuels, and its Central Valley is one of the best pieces of farm real estate in the world.

Natural Regions. Chile's three main regions differ widely, both in climate and in natural wealth.

North Chile, from the Peruvian frontier to the city of La Serena, includes the Atacama Desert, one of the world's driest regions. In some sections no rainfall has ever been recorded, while in others the total for several decades hardly equals that of a summer thunderstorm. This is the region of Chile's unique deposits of raw nitrate. Here also are exploited the world's largest reserves of copper.

Middle Chile, from La Serena to Chiloé Island, is the heart of the nation. Particularly favorable to human settlement and economic advance, it contains 90% of the population, most of the manufacturing industries, and the best farm and pasture lands. The larger part, including the Central Valley extending from Santiago to Concepción, has a Mediterranean climate and vegetation. The fertile but semiarid valley, noted for its orchards and vineyards, resembles the Central Valley of California. Middle Chile south of Concepción is comparable to the Pacific Northwest of the United States. Rainy, with stormy winters and cool summers, it was originally covered by forests, which still occupy almost half the land. The country south of Temuco, with its many lakes and snow-capped volcanoes, is a prime resort area.

South Chile extends from Chiloé Island to Cape Horn, the southernmost point in South America. Mostly a region of fjords and mountains, high winds, and heavy rains, South Chile is much less favorable to economic progress than Middle Chile. In contrast to North Chile it is one of the world's rainiest areas; one becomes accustomed to rain on two out of every three days the year long. The area on both sides of the Strait of Magellan, including the Chilean part of the island of Tierra del Fuego, is referred to as Atlantic Chile. It is oriented to the Atlantic and even toward Argentine economic life. The climate is cold, dry, and windy. Sheep raising figures prominently in the economy, and there has been some exploitation of petroleum and natural gas deposits.

A number of South Pacific islands are part of Chile. The best known is Easter Island (q.v.). Chile also claims about 480,000 square miles (1,250,000 sq km) of Antarctic territory.

Natural Resources. Relative exploitation of resources does not reflect accurately the potential of Chile's endowment. Agriculture has lagged, despite a very favorable potential, because of long-standing deficiencies in public policy. The

CHILE

AGRICULTURE, INDUSTRY and RESOURCES

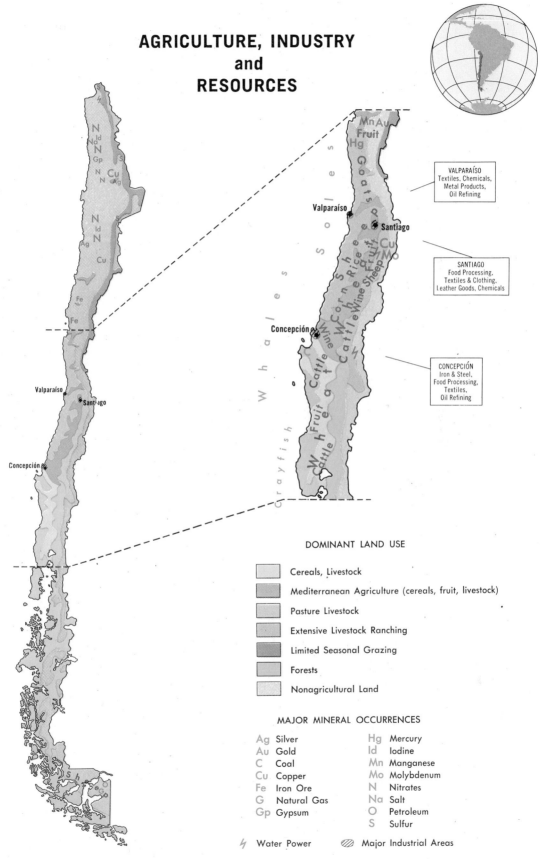

VALPARAÍSO
Textiles, Chemicals,
Metal Products,
Oil Refining

SANTIAGO
Food Processing,
Textiles & Clothing,
Leather Goods, Chemicals

CONCEPCIÓN
Iron & Steel,
Food Processing,
Textiles,
Oil Refining

Valparaíso

Santiago

Concepción

DOMINANT LAND USE

- Cereals, Livestock
- Mediterranean Agriculture (cereals, fruit, livestock)
- Pasture Livestock
- Extensive Livestock Ranching
- Limited Seasonal Grazing
- Forests
- Nonagricultural Land

MAJOR MINERAL OCCURRENCES

Ag	Silver	Hg	Mercury
Au	Gold	Id	Iodine
C	Coal	Mn	Manganese
Cu	Copper	Mo	Molybdenum
Fe	Iron Ore	N	Nitrates
G	Natural Gas	Na	Salt
Gp	Gypsum	O	Petroleum
		S	Sulfur

⚡ Water Power   ▨ Major Industrial Areas

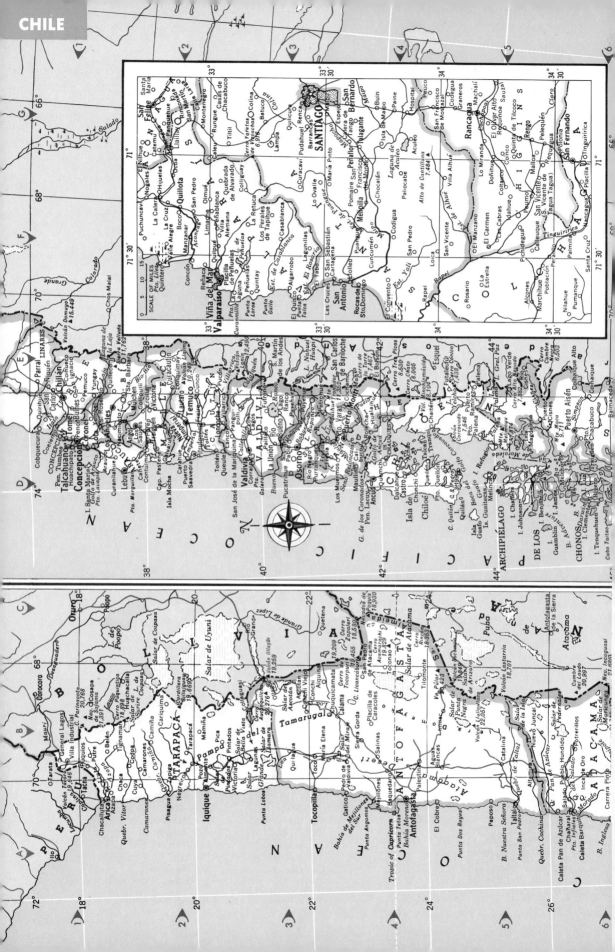

CHILE

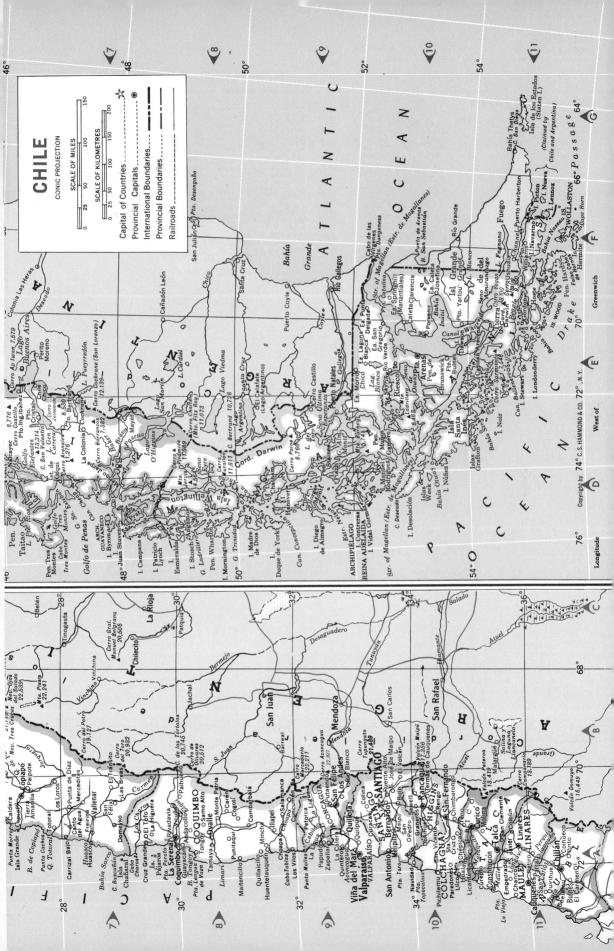

CHILE

TOPOGRAPHY

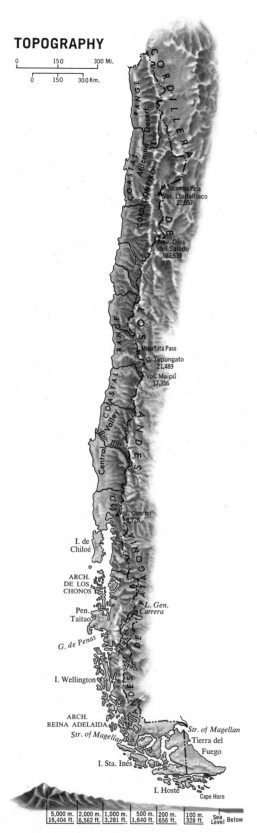

0   150   300 Mi.

0   150   300 Km.

CORDILLERA RANGE

COASTAL CORDILLERA

Atacama Desert

COND DOMEYKO

*Socompa Pass
Vol. Llullaillaco
22,057

Nev. Ojos
del Salado
22,539

Uspallata Pass
C. Tupungato
21,489

Vol. Maipú
17,356

Central Valley

Bío-Bío

COASTAL RANGE

A N D E S

Vol. Osorno
8,726

I. de
Chiloé

ARCH.
DE LOS
CHONOS

Pen.
Taitao

L. Gen.
Carrera

G. de Penas

I. Wellington

ANDES DE PATAGONIA

ARCH.
REINA ADELAIDA

Str. of Magellan

I. Sta. Inés

Str. of Magellan

Tierra del
Fuego

I. Hoste

Cape Horn

5,000 m.	2,000 m.	1,000 m.	500 m.	200 m.	100 m.	Sea	
16,404 ft.	6,562 ft.	3,281 ft.	1,640 ft.	656 ft.	328 ft.	Level	Below

© Copyright HAMMOND INCORPORATED, Maplewood, N.J.

Total Population, 9,566,000

PROVINCES

Aconcagua, 140,528 ....A 9
Aisén, 37,803 ....D 6
Antofagasta, 215,378 ....B 4
Arauco, 89,504 ....D 1
Atacama, 116,309 ....B 6
Bío-Bío, 168,837 ....D 1
Cautín, 394,785 ....E 2
Chiloé, 99,205 ....D 4
Colchagua, 158,543 ....A10
Concepción, 539,450 ....D 1
Coquimbo, 309,177 ....A 8
Curicó, 105,839 ....A10
Linares, 171,302 ....A11
Llanquihue, 167,491 ....D 3
Magallanes, 73,426 ....E10
Malleco, 174,205 ....E 2
Maule, 79,783 ....A11
Ñuble, 285,730 ....E 1
O'Higgins, 259,724 ....A10
Osorno, 144,088 ....D 3
Santiago, 2,436,398 ....A 9
Talca, 206,255 ....A11
Tarapacá, 123,064 ....B 2
Valdivia, 259,798 ....D 3
Valparaíso, 618,112 ....A 9

CITIES and TOWNS

Achao, 939 ....D 4
Alcones, 682 ....F 5
Algarrobo, 1,894 ....F 3
Ancud, 7,390 ....D 4
Andacollo, 5,381 ....A 8
Angol, 18,637 ....D 1
Antofagasta, 112,421 ....A 4
Arauco, 3,773 ....D 1
Arica, 43,344 ....A 1
Balmaceda, 735 ....E 6
Baquedano, 1,412 ....A 4
Barrancas, 13,787 ....G 3
Batuco, 1,125 ....G 3
Boco, 1,655 ....F 2
Buin, 5,269 ....G 4
Bulnes, 5,831 ....E 1
Cabildo, 3,479 ....A 9
Calama, 26,166 ....B 3
Calbuco, 2,532 ....D 4
Caldera, 2,715 ....A 6
Caleta Barquito, 932 ....A 6
Calle Larga, 1,872 ....G 2
Cañete, 5,487 ....D 2
Capitán Pastene, 1,669 ....D 2
Carahue, 5,891 ....D 2
Cartagena, 4,711 ....F 3
Casablanca, 3,937 ....F 3
Castro, 7,001 ....D 4
Catemu, 1,498 ....G 2
Cauquenes, 17,836 ....A11
Chaitén, 663 ....E 4
Chañaral, 5,210 ....A 6
Chanco, 1,966 ....A11
Chépica, 2,291 ....A10
Chile Chico, 1,926 ....E 6
Chillán, 59,054 ....A11
Chimbarongo, 3,982 ....A10
Chonchi, 1,453 ....D 4
Chuquicamata, 24,798 ....B 3
Cobquecura, 795 ....D 1
Codegua, 1,244 ....G 4
Coelemu, 4,546 ....D 1
Coihaique, 8,782 ....E 6
Coihueco, 1,844 ....A11
Coinco, 1,656 ....G 5
Colbún, 980 ....A11
Colina, 2,445 ....G 3
Collipulli, 5,572 ....E 2
Coltauco, 1,096 ....F 5
Combarbalá, 2,640 ....A 8
Concepción, 174,224 ....D 1
Concón, 5,381 ....F 2
Constitución, 9,536 ....A11
Contulmo, 978 ....D 2
Copiapó, 30,123 ....B 6
Coquimbo, 33,749 ....A 8
Coronel, 33,870 ....D 1
Corral, 3,740 ....D 3
Cunco, 3,342 ....E 2
Cuncumén, 1,052 ....A 9
Curacautín, 9,601 ....E 2
Curacaví, 4,116 ....G 3
Curanilahue, 12,117 ....D 1
Curepto, 1,699 ....A10
Curicó, 32,562 ....A10
Domeyko, 1,814 ....A 7
Doñihue, 1,622 ....G 5
El Carmen, Ñuble, 2,263 ....A11
El Carmen, O'Higgins, 625 ....F 5
El Convento, 733 ....F 4
El Manzano, 1,073 ....F 5
El Olivar Alto, 1,084 ....G 5
El Quisco, 1,019 ....E 3
El Tabo, 714 ....F 3
El Tofo, 1,175 ....A 7
Empedrado, 574 ....A11
Ercilla, 1,311 ....E 2

Espejo, 3,481 ....G 3
Estancia Springhill, 291 ....F10
Freire, 2,006 ....E 2
Freirina, 1,831 ....A 7
Fresia, 3,571 ....D 3
Frutillar, 686 ....D 3
Futaleufú, 616 ....E 4
Futrono, 981 ....E 3
Galvarino, 1,735 ....D 2
Graneros, 5,644 ....G 5
Guayacán, 1,514 ....A 8
Hijuelas, 897 ....F 2
Huachipato, †16,336 ....D 1
Hualañé, 1,712 ....A10
Huara, 885 ....B 2
Huasco, 1,902 ....A 7
Idahue, 1,832 ....F 5
Illapel, 10,395 ....A 8
Inca de Oro, 1,406 ....B 6
Iquique, 50,655 ....A 2
Isla de Maipo, 3,580 ....G 4
La Calera, 18,134 ....F 2
La Cruz, 3,000 ....F 2
La Higuera, 889 ....A 7
La Ligua, 5,095 ....A 9
La Serena, 40,854 ....A 8
La Unión, 11,558 ....D 3
Lago Ranco, 1,541 ....D 3
Lampa, 1,698 ....G 3
Lanco, 4,948 ....D 2
Las Cabras, 1,668 ....F 5
Las Cruces, 612 ....F 3
Lautaro, 10,448 ....E 2
Lebu, 6,248 ....D 1
Licantén, 1,368 ....A10
Limache, 14,488 ....F 2
Linares, 27,568 ....A11
Llaillay, 7,049 ....G 2
Llolleo, 9,846 ....F 4
Lo Miranda, 2,270 ....G 5
Loncoche, 6,619 ....D 2
Longaví, 2,625 ....A11
Lonquimay, 1,320 ....E 2
Los Andes, 20,448 ....B 9
Los Ángeles, 35,511 ....D 1
Los Lagos, 3,897 ....D 3
Los Muermos, 1,616 ....D 3
Los Sauces, 2,717 ....D 2
Los Vilos, 3,027 ....A 9
Lota, 27,739 ....D 1
Machalí, 3,008 ....G 5
Maipú, 16,740 ....G 3
Malloa, 926 ....G 5
Marchihue, 924 ....F 5
María Elena, 9,572 ....B 3
Maullín, 1,789 ....D 4
Mejillones, 3,363 ....A 4
Melipilla, 15,593 ....F 4
Molina, 7,621 ....A10
Monte Patria, 798 ....A 8
Mulchén, 10,729 ....E 1
Nacimiento, 3,823 ....D 1
Nancagua, 1,961 ....F 6
Navidad, 629 ....F10
Nogales, 2,797 ....F 2
Nueva Imperial, 6,442 ....D 2
Ocoa, 871 ....G 2
Olmué, 1,905 ....F 2
Osorno, 55,091 ....D 3
Ovalle, 25,282 ....A 8
Paihuano, 639 ....B 8
Paillaco, 3,539 ....D 3
Paine, 2,720 ....G 4
Paipote, 2,278 ....B 6
Palmilla, 1,136 ....F 5
Panguipulli, 4,708 ....E 2
Papudo, 1,292 ....A 9
Parral, 14,610 ....A11
Pedro de Valdivia, 11,028 ....B 4
Pelequen, 1,068 ....G 5
Pemuco, 1,667 ....E 1
Peñablanca, 5,586 ....F 2
Peñaflor, 10,699 ....G 4
Penco, 15,483 ....D 1
Petorca, 1,395 ....A 9
Peumo, 2,574 ....F 5
Pica, 1,646 ....B 2
Pichidegua, 841 ....F 5
Pichilemu, 2,227 ....A10
Pinto, 958 ....A11
Pitrufquén, 6,472 ....D 2
Placilla, 1,047 ....G 5
Placilla de Peñuelas, 1,495 ....F 2
Población, 1,026 ....F 5
Pomaire, 1,366 ....F 4
Porvenir, 1,956 ....E10
Potrerillos, 6,168 ....B 6
Pozo Almonte, 1,174 ....B 2
Pucón, 2,508 ....E 2
Pueblo Hundido, 2,123 ....B 6
Puente Alto, 43,557 ....B10
Puerto Aisén, 5,488 ....E 6
Puerto Cristal, 698 ....E 6
Puerto Ingeniero Ibáñez, 750 ....E 6
Puerto Montt, 41,681 ....E 3
Puerto Natales, 9,399 ....E 9
Puerto Quellón, 795 ....D 4
Puerto Saavedra, 805 ....D 2
Puerto Varas, 10,305 ....E 3
Puerto Williams, 302 ....F11

*City and suburbs. †Population of commune.

Total pop.—1969 off. est.; capital (with suburbs) & cities over 100,000—1965 off. est.; other pops—1960 final census.

mineral potential, on the other hand, has been more actively exploited to make Chile's mineral industry (exclusive of mineral fuels) the largest in South America.

Besides having the world's largest reserves of copper, Chile possesses huge reserves of medium-grade to high-grade (40% to 60% metal content) iron ore. Its nitrate deposits long provided the bulk of world requirements of nitrogen until the processes of making synthetic compounds were developed. Chile leads the world in production of iodine, which is obtained from the nitrate-bearing caliche beds. It accounts for less of the world's boron minerals production than it did early in the 20th century, when it produced half the world supply, but its known borax reserves in ulexite-type salina deposits and in the nitrate deposits are substantial. It has significant deposits of molybdenum and less important reserves of zinc, lead, gold, silver, and sulfur.

Chile is not so impressively rich in the mineral fuels. Coal showings, mostly bituminous, occur from Santiago to the far south, but the mines are difficult to work, are not located at optimum distances from consuming centers, and do not produce coal of completely satisfactory quality. Since oil was brought in on Tierra del Fuego, interest in petroleum has been active, but reserves are unimpressive for South America. Despite these deficiencies, Chile is estimated to have 4.9% of the overall energy potential of Latin America. Its hydroelectric potential is large and well distributed.

About one quarter of Chile's area is classified as forest land, half of which is readily accessible.

The forests consist of about 60 different species, mostly hardwood. The most significant development toward expansion of the promising pulp and paper industry has been the introduction of the Monterey pine (*Pinus radiata*) for reforestation.

SIMON G. HANSON
Editor, "Inter-American Economic Affairs"

THE ATACAMA DESERT in northern Chile is one of the driest regions in the world. In some parts no rain has been recorded. The region has rich mineral resources.

MIKE ANDREWS, FROM BLACK STAR

FAR TO THE SOUTH, in the cold, wet, windy territory of Chilean Patagonia, sheep are raised on ranches covering millions of acres.

CARL FRANK

3. The Economy

Chile's economy is popularly associated with mining because mineral products account for more than 80% of the country's exports by value (copper alone for two thirds). In terms of gross national product, however, mining contributes only 6%, whereas manufacturing accounts for 19% and agriculture for 10%. The accelerated pace of economic growth between 1950 and 1970 was impressive: gross national product rose at an average annual rate of about 4.5% during the 1960's, as compared with about 3.5% in the 1950's. However, the growth was uneven.

Growth and Planning. Manufacturing was the most dynamic area. It paced the economy with an average annual growth rate of about 9% through the 1960's. Agriculture, on the other hand, trended downward, suffering particularly during the late 1960's and into the 1970's as a result of droughts. Mining expansion was slowed by delayed decisions on the role of government. Toward the end of the 1960's, the administration was attempting to "Chileanize" mining by acquiring 51% ownership in what had been entirely foreign-owned and foreign-operated facilities. The election of a Socialist administration in 1970 led to nationalization of the copper interests and some other mining concerns in 1971.

The government has long accepted an active role in economic development. Since 1939 its development corporation has served as a catalyst for the substitution of domestic for imported manufactures. The government's role in communications, power, and transport has increased steadily. Chile is a leader in national planning. Its ten-year plan (1961–1970) called for a 5.5% annual growth of gross product and envisioned investments of some $10 billion.

Manufacturing. A scarcity of imported goods in World Wars I and II and a shortage of foreign exchange during the depression of the 1930's made the development of manufacturing a major concern of the Chilean government. Under policies geared to import substitution, Chile expanded from the production of simpler consumers goods to more sophisticated areas, topped by heavy industry in the form of an integrated steel mill.

Chilean industry tends to be high cost, which weakens the country's competitive position in the Latin American Free Trade Association (LAFTA), of which Chile is a member.

Agriculture. The agricultural sector of the economy is characterized by a concentration of landholdings, a scarcity of top-level entrepreneurial talent, low productivity of labor accompanying low levels of investment, inadequate mechanization, and inefficiencies in cultivation. On the other hand, agriculture is highly commercialized; transportation is not a limiting factor; and biological research on plants suitable for cultivation in Chile is far advanced, so that agriculture is not dependent on poor, obsolete varieties of grains, forage crops, and fruits.

Only 6.9% of the total number of farms comprise 78.5% of the total agricultural area, while 37% of the farms comprise only 0.3% of the area. Half of the 745,000 persons in agriculture in 1959 owned no land, and progress in land reform was slow until the late 1960's.

Mining. The mining industry is conspicuously efficient. About half of mining employment has been in the large copper, nitrate, and iron-mining operations.

Forestry and Fisheries. Chile has one of Latin America's most important forest products industries, but the industry is far from realizing its full potential. Maximum effectiveness will depend partly on development of an effective conservation program.

Strongly encouraged by the government, the fishing industry increased its catch sixfold between the mid-1950's and mid-1960's. Some $50 million was invested in the fish reduction industry from 1961 to 1963 alone, and an immense fish-meal trade has been developed.

Foreign Investment and Aid. Historically, foreign capital has played an important role in development in Chile. The book value of U. S. direct investments in the mid-1960's was over $800 million, chiefly in mining ($500 million). By the early 1970's, however, the tide of foreign investment had turned, largely as a result of new Chilean nationalization policies.

In the Alliance for Progress era, Chile was a major beneficiary. In the first five years of

478

GRANULATED NITRATE pours into railway cars at a mine in northern Chile. The value of this resource has declined since the introduction of artificial nitrates.

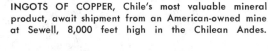

INGOTS OF COPPER, Chile's most valuable mineral product, await shipment from an American-owned mine at Sewell, 8,000 feet high in the Chilean Andes.

the Alliance, $690 million of aid was authorized for Chile, of which $605 million consisted of donations and soft-term loans. In addition, Chilean leadership has been conscious of the emphasis on planning, self-help, and other realities of the Alliance relationship.

Transport and Communications. Chile has a well-developed railway system, a good road network based on a hard-surface highway running the length of the country and good air service made especially important by the great length of the country. The government owns 80% or the railway system and the chief domestic airline, Línea Aérea Nacional (LAN). A state entity provides telegraph service. Telephone service has been provided largely by private companies, but the government has negotiated participation in ownership. A state entity is responsible for operating the basic telecommunications network.

Power. Consumption of electric power rose sharply in the 1960's. The trend is toward government ownership and operation, although in the mid-1960's only one third of the installed capacity was controlled by the government. Rural electrification was coming slowly, with less than 5% of the farms receiving electric service.

Public Finance. The public sector comprises several dozen decentralized agencies and social security funds as well as the ordinary official apparatus. The deficits of the state enterprises and autonomous agencies accounted for about 20% of fiscal outlays. The tax system is highly centralized. There are no provincial taxes, and revenues of municipalities are less than 10% as great as revenues of the central government. The proportion of government receipts derived from income tax revenues rose to 37% in the 1960's.

Foreign Trade. Chile's principal exports are copper, iron ore, nitrates, iodine, wool, rice, beans, lentils, fresh fruit, and fish meal. Major imports are machinery, transport equipment, metallurgical products, chemicals and related products, and farm products. Although the United States has been Chile's largest trading partner, there is a broadening relationship with Latin America (through LAFTA), an increasing outlet for exports in Japan, and continuing important relationships with Europe.

Labor and Social Security. Collective bargaining is general in unionized industries. Government control over the unions has been less extensive than in Argentina and Brazil, and there is an intimate relationship between the unions and political parties. Paternalism has been extensively practiced by employers but is becoming less pronounced. Because the extensive social security systems were legislated with political support rather than economic reality as the paramount consideration, their costs to the economy are generally conceded to be excessive. They cover two thirds of the economically active population, and the systems' receipts represent 8% of the gross national product.

SIMON G. HANSON
Editor, "Inter-American Economic Affairs"

4. Education

Education in Chile is compulsory for all children between the ages of 7 and 15. The structure of the educational system underwent considerable change following a study by a national planning commission. Under the new plan, which went into effect in 1966, the basic cycle of general education, which was formerly 6 years, was extended to 8 years with the intent to extend it to 9 years when circumstances should permit. The secondary cycle was divided into two types: (1) scientific-humanistic, to be completed in 3 years when the basic general cycle of 9 years is in full operation; and (2) technical-vocational to be completed in 2 or 3 years. Formerly the secondary cycle consisted of 6 years of academic studies or a technical-vocational program of 6 or 7 years. University courses range in length from 2 to 7 years, according to the profession studied.

Control of public education is highly centralized in a ministry of education, which also supervises private schools and exercises some control over public universities. Private schools, which account for about one third of the total elementary and secondary enrollment, receive a state subsidy for each person enrolled. In the late 1960's the administration was making great efforts to expand educational services so that every child of school age could be enrolled. For example, in 1966, President Eduardo Frei reported that in the previous 12 months 200,000 new pupils had been added; thousands of elementary teachers had been trained; 1,500 new schools had been constructed; and more than 90% of the pupils of elementary school age had been enrolled.

Higher education is offered at the University of Chile (in Santiago and Valparaíso), the State Technical University (Santiago), the Catholic University of Chile (Santiago), the Catholic University of Valparaíso, the University of Concepción, Southern University (Valdivia), Federico Santa María Technical University (Valparaíso), and the University of the North (Antofagasta). The first two are state universities; all the others are private.

The largest institution is the University of Chile, which accounts for more than half of the total university enrollment. One of the most promising developments toward extending higher education opportunities to new groups and regions is the university's network of university centers, which have been established in smaller communities. They prepare students for higher studies, offer preparation for technician-level professions, and serve the cultural interests of the community.

In keeping with the national goals of more rapid economic and industrial development, the universities are putting more stress on sciences, engineering, and business administration. In these areas and others they have received extensive aid from the U. S. government, UNESCO, and private foundations.

University students tend to be very active politically in Chile, as they are elsewhere in Latin America. At the University of Chile the same political parties prevailing throughout the country compete for control of the student federation. It is common for students to resort to direct action, such as demonstrations and strikes, to protest obsolete facilities and curricula, unpopular professors, and numerous other grievances.

Chile's educational system ranks among the best of all Latin America as reflected in the literacy rate of better than 80%. Yet it suffers from serious deficiencies, which the new educational structure hopes to reduce or eliminate. Some of these are a distressing dropout rate; lack of qualified teachers, school plants, and equipment; a rigid curriculum; inferior teaching methods and materials; insufficient attention to vocational education; and a lack of articulation among different levels of schools. Possibly the greatest need is to attune the educational system to the long-range goals of economic development already formulated.

CLARK C. GILL, *The University of Texas*

5. Cultural Life

Chile has one of the richest, most broadly shared cultural traditions of any Latin American country. Its long-standing dedication to political freedom has not only fostered creative expression among its own people but has attracted to Chile foreign intellectual leaders (often political exiles), who found Chile receptive to new ideas. Venezuelan-born Andrés Bello, who became the first rector of the University of Chile, and Argentine-born Domingo Sarmiento, the first director of the National Normal School, are examples of transplanted intellectuals whose educational and literary contributions have immensely enriched Chilean culture.

The Arts. Literature, particularly poetry, probably represents the area of Chile's greatest cultural contribution. Its beginnings can be traced to early colonial times with the publication of *La Araucana,* by Alonso de Ercilla y Zúñiga. This work, which gives the first artistic description of aboriginal life in Chile, is considered by some critics to be the most important epic poem in the Spanish language.

Chile's highest recognition in literature came in 1945, when the poet Gabriela Mistral won the Nobel Prize. The first Latin American Nobel laureate in literature, she was a teacher by profession. Following the award of the Nobel Prize, she was named a consul to the United States. Themes for her poetry include children, love, death, and nature. Her writing is variously characterized as being personal, subjective, mystical, lyrical, and sentimental. Two of her better known works are *Desolación* and *Los sonetos de la muerte* (*Sonnets of Death*).

Another 20th-century writer who has achieved worldwide distinction for his poetry is Pablo Neruda. Intensely committed to political causes, he joined the Communist party, under whose label he was elected to the Chilean senate in 1945. Some of his most famous collections are *Veinte poemas de amor y una canción desesperada* (*Twenty Love Poems and One Song of Despair*), written when he was only 20; and *Canto general,* a collection of his later works.

Chile has produced many distinguished novelists. Alberto Blest Gana, the most eminent of the 19th century, set the tradition of the realistic novel, which strongly influenced later writers. His best known work is *Martín Rivas.* In the 20th century, Joaquin Edwards Bello has portrayed the grim existence of the *roto* ("ragged"), the lowest of the urban social classes. The works of Manuel Rojas, poet, novelist, and short-story writer, also emphasize social problems. Two of his best known works are the novel *Hijo de ladrón* (*Son of a Thief*) and the short story *El vaso de leche* (*The Glass of Milk*). Eduardo Barrios, a master of the psychological novel, has portrayed characters suffering emotional torment as typified by the titles *El niño que enloqueció de amor* (*The Love-Smitten Boy*) and *Un perdido* (*A Lost Soul*).

Although Chileans are avid readers, their cultural interests extend far beyond literature to include the full range of artistic expression. Santiago is naturally the cultural capital with its Palace of Fine Arts and other museums, the National Library, the National Ballet, two symphony orchestras, the Experimental Theater of the University of Chile, and the Trial Theater of the Catholic University of Chile. Outstanding artists from Chile and abroad perform regularly in the Municipal Theater. Provincial capitals also have literary, theatrical, and musical groups. The extension program of the University of Chile and its university centers brings a rich cultural fare to the remote reaches of the country.

Folk music and folk dances are extremely popular. Best known of the dances is the *cueca,* a spirited dance of conquest and submission. Numerous religious festivals and other exhibitions that commemorate dramatic episodes from Chile's exciting past offer an attractive setting for folkloric expression. Rodeos with *huasos* (cowboys) in colorful costumes are especially popular as exhibitions of horsemanship and skill without resort to violence.

Among the contemporary contributors to culture of a nonliterary type, the following are especially noteworthy: Roberto Matta, the painter; Claudio Arrau, a distinguished pianist; Gustavo Becerra, a noted composer; Domingo Santa Cruz, formerly chairman of the UNESCO Commission on Music and promoter of the University of Chile's extension activities in music; and Isabel Barra, a moving force in the revival of folk music.

Sciences. Any nation committed to the goals of rapid industrialization must give high priority to scientific research and its dissemination. This Chile has tried to do mainly through its universities, using as the main vehicle for the task the Council of Rectors, composed of rectors of all the universities. By law a fixed percentage of customs duties is allocated to the council, which uses the funds for a variety of purposes: university construction; research designed to increase and improve the productivity of agriculture, industry, and mining; the promotion of an inventory and wise use of the country's resources; and the promotion of a better organization of the different economic activities. The council may propose research projects and designate the universities best able to execute them. The University of Chile, because of its prestigious science departments, bears the chief responsibility for scientific research. The Council of Rectors, through the Center of Information and Documentation, coordinates university research in scientific and technical subjects and collects and disseminates information on these subjects.

Press. More than 50 daily newspapers and more than a half-dozen weekly pictorial news magazines inform Chileans on local, national, and world affairs. Santiago alone has more than 10 dailies, each of a different political hue, ranging from the conservative, Catholic *El Diario Ilustrado* to the Communist party's organ, *El Siglo*. The most influential newspaper is *El Mercurio*, independent in its political views and highly respected for the fullness and fairness of its coverage. *La Nación* is government-owned and must change its policies with a change in government. The *South Pacific Mail*, a weekly, is the oldest English-language newspaper in Latin America. Many smaller communities maintain one or more thriving daily newspapers.

Numerous periodicals, of which several are devoted to literary, professional, and scientific subjects, are further evidence of Chile's high rate of literacy and the broad spectrum of tastes of its reading public. The Spanish edition of the *Reader's Digest* is the best seller of all the periodicals. Bookstores and newsstands are plentiful and well patronized.

Broadcasting. No commercial television stations are permitted in Chile. Authorized university outlets provide educational and cultural programs. Since television sets are extremely expensive, few people own them.

The impact of TV is minimal compared with that of radio. It is estimated that almost 90% of Chilean homes have a radio, making this medium a powerful disseminator of news, education, and entertainment. Radio has been a boon to rural education, where it has been used successfully by the Institute of Rural Education, a private organization subsidized by the government. The

ERNEST A. JAHN

A MODERN CATHEDRAL in Chillán, an important rail and industrial center, and capital of Ñuble province.

institute aims to improve the generally inferior conditions of rural living. Using the facilities of a network of broadcasting stations, it beams to rural schools a program complementary to that prescribed by the ministry of education. The impact far transcends the school because it reaches the rural community as a whole.

CLARK C. GILL, *The University of Texas*

6. Government

Until it was overthrown by a military coup d'etat and replaced by a junta in September 1973, a strong presidential government ruled Chile. Its patterns had been established by the 1925 constitution. The legislative branch had and used powers to block administration programs, and the proliferation of political parties made it difficult for a president to maintain the consistent support of a congressional majority. Before the coup d'etat of September 1973, the president, in addition to exercising administrative powers, could, in certain circumstances, decree laws. During times of internal disturbance, for example, the congress could grant to the executive extraordinary powers for a 6-month period. To meet internal disturbance or foreign attack, the executive, on his own if congress was not in session, could declare a state of siege, thereby suspending many constitutional guarantees. Elected by universal popular suffrage for a 6-year term, the president appointed and removed cabinet members without congressional approval. Indirect methods existed whereby congress could force the resignation of cabinet ministers.

The legislative branch consisted of a senate and a chamber of deputies (see *Information Highlights*). Congress enjoyed general legislative powers that included authority to approve or reject the budget. Except in a few prescribed instances, approval of bills was by absolute majority of both houses. Bills then had to be approved and published by the president, who was vested with broad veto powers. Congress had to give its consent before the president could leave the country. In 1967 it denied this consent for the first time in Chilean history, when the senate forced President Eduardo Frei to cancel a visit to the United States.

PRESIDENTS OF CHILE SINCE 1831

1831–1841	Joaquín Prieto
1841–1851	Manuel Bulnes
1851–1861	Manuel Montt
1861–1871	José Joaquín Pérez
1871–1876	Federico Errázuriz Zañartu
1876–1881	Aníbal Pinto
1881–1886	Domingo Santa María
1886–1891	José Manuel Balmaceda
1891–1896	Jorge Montt
1896–1901	Federico Errázuriz Echaurren
1901–1906	Germán Riesco
1906–1910	Pedro Montt
1910–1915	Ramón Barros Luco
1915–1920	Juan Luis Sanfuentes
1920–1925	Arturo Alessandri Palma
1925–1927	Emiliano Figueroa Larraín
1927–1931	Carlos Ibáñez del Campo
1931–1932	Juan Esteban Montero Rodríguez
1932–1938	Arturo Alessandri Palma
1938–1941	Pedro Aguirre Cerda
1941–1942	Jerónimo Méndez
1942–1946	Juan Antonio Ríos Morales
1946–1952	Gabriel González Videla
1952–1958	Carlos Ibáñez del Campo
1958–1964	Jorge Alessandri Rodríguez
1964–1970	Eduardo Frei Montalva
1970–1973	Salvador Allende Gossens
1973–	Augusto Pinochet Ugarte

Judiciary. A supreme court, consisting of judges appointed for life by the chief executive, was empowered to consider the constitutionality of legislative acts and could declare them inapplicable in specific instances. Appellate courts had original jurisdiction in certain cases and consisted of judges appointed by the president from a list of names submitted by the Supreme Court. Judges of lower courts were appointed by the president from a list of names presented by courts of appeals in particular districts.

Local Government. Under a highly centralistic system, each of the nation's provinces was under the direction of an intendant appointed by the president. Provinces were subdivided into departments headed by governors appointed by the president. Departmental subdivisions were called districts. Provincial assemblies provided for by the constitution had never functioned, but elections were held for municipal councils.

FREDRICK B. PIKE, *University of Notre Dame*

7. History

After the Spanish overthrew the Inca empire in 1533, Diego de Almagro led an unsuccessful expedition from Peru to conquer the Incas' southern domain in Chile. A second expedition, under Pedro de Valdivia, founded Santiago in 1541. To the north, the Indians were quickly subjugated; but to the south, the Araucanians were not completely pacified until 1883.

Although Chile failed to yield gold or silver, its central region proved suitable for farming and ranching. Settlers were often granted large estates, with claims on the labor of the resident Indians. But the danger of Araucanian attacks inhibited immigration from Spain, and the expense of maintaining a frontier army helped keep Chile a deficit area of the viceroyalty of Peru throughout most of the colonial period.

As in other parts of Spanish America, resentment against the motherland's restrictive economic and political policies, combined with intellectual ferment resulting from the spread of Enlightenment ideas and the examples of the French and American revolutions, stimulated desires first for reform and later for independence.

Napoleon's invasion of Spain in 1808 created the opportunity for revolt.

Independent Centralized Government. Initial Chilean attempts to achieve independence, undertaken in 1810, were suppressed in 1814 by Spanish troops from Peru. Afterward, many Chilean patriots went to Argentina and joined an army that was being trained in Mendoza by José de San Martín, an Argentine who intended to liberate Chile and Peru. In 1817, San Martín's army made a remarkable crossing of the Andes into Chile and routed the Spanish. The next year an independent Chile entrusted its political direction to Bernardo O'Higgins, a native-born hero of the revolutionary movement.

Hoping to effect a compromise between rival factions of conservatives and liberals, O'Higgins was unable to satisfy either group and was forced into exile in 1823. After seven years of chaos, conservative forces under a military officer, Joaquín Prieto, and a businessman, Diego Portales, crushed their opponents and ushered in the period of the "autocratic republic" (from 1830 to 1861). Although assassinated in 1837, Portales was the great architect and guiding genius of the autocratic republic. Conservative for pragmatic rather than doctrinaire reasons, he avoided fanaticism and established a tradition of firm-handed rule tempered by moderation.

Economic and Social Developments. During the period between 1830 and 1880, notable political stability and economic development were achieved. At the outset of the era a number of intrepid prospectors began to discover Chile's mineral resources. Impressive silver strikes were followed by the discovery of coal deposits. Then, in the 1870's, the nitrates of the northern desert region began to produce immense wealth for the republic. By 1881 approximately 80% of Chile's exports by value consisted of mine products, a figure that has remained fairly constant.

Mining helped trigger rapid economic expansion, which produced a social revolution. The landed aristocracy opened its ranks to the men of new wealth, and by the latter part of the 19th century the aristocracy was studded with new Chilean as well as English, Scottish, German, and French names. In 1883, *El Mercurio*, the leading daily of the major port city of Valparaíso, noted that of the 59 personal fortunes in Chile of over 1 million pesos, only 24 were of colonial origin. The remainder belonged to men who had begun their march toward fortune and social prestige in the postindependence period.

Liberalism. By the late 1840's a new generation of liberal intellectuals and statesmen had arisen. Led by José Victorino Lastarria, Francisco Bilbao, and Santiago Arcos, among others, they demanded decentralization of government, extension of suffrage, curtailment of presidential powers, and suppression of the Catholic church's temporal influence. As the Liberal party gained strength, it was staunchly opposed by the Conservative party. Avowedly confessional and somewhat ultramontanist, the Conservative party defended the church's right to intervene in politics and claimed to stand for continuation of the traditions established by Portales.

During the 1870's the Liberals found allies among members of the Radical party, which had elected its first deputies to congress in 1864. As a result of a Liberal-Radical alliance, the Conservative party entered a prolonged period of decline, and the republic's institutions were liberalized. Especially between 1865 and 1885 political practices and even the constitution, framed in 1833 under Portales' influence, were modifed to provide for a system in which ministers were largely responsible to congress. Suffrage was expanded, and the church was deprived of various privileges, including its power to control education.

Changes in Chile's political structure and church-state relationship were effected by peaceful and constitutional means. Political stability in turn contributed to an essentially uninterrupted process of economic development. These factors helped account for Chile's victory in the War of the Pacific (1879–1883) over the combined forces of Peru and Bolivia. Crushing its politically disorganized adversaries, Chile expanded its frontiers far to the north, acquiring vast new nitrate resources, and depriving Bolivia of its coast and Peru of its southernmost region.

Shortly after overcoming its military challenge from abroad, Chile succumbed to internal stress and for the first time since 1830 engaged in a civil war. Elected to the presidency in 1886, José Manuel Balmaceda feared that his overconfident country was in danger of slipping into inertia. Centralized economic planning was necessary, he felt, so that government revenue deriving from export taxes on nitrates would be invested in special development projects. Persuaded that only a strong president could institute changes of the nature he had in mind, Balmaceda became arbitrary and moved to curtail congressional powers. Led by naval officers and supported by British investors in Chilean nitrates, forces that believed in a parliamentary political system and the unregulated market economy precipitated a civil war and drove the president from power in 1891.

Parliamentary Government. The period of parliamentary government lasted from 1892 to 1920. During this time new social and economic problems appeared, labor unrest became commonplace, and strikes, some of them violently suppressed, increased in frequency. A basic cause of the problems was a rural-to-urban population shift, in the course of which the rural paternalism that had frequently characterized master-serf relations broke down, and rapidly swelling urban labor forces were subjected to intensive exploitation.

Alessandri and Ibáñez. For the 1920 presidential election, Arturo Alessandri Palma was the candidate of the Liberal Alliance, made up principally of Liberals and Radicals and enjoying significant support from burgeoning middle sectors. Waging a new type of campaign, Alessandri appealed to the lower classes, in effect promising to substitute a system of government-administered paternalism for a private paternalism of a bygone day. Elected by the narrowest of margins, Alessandri was unable to win congressional approval for a mild reform program. Following a brief period of military intervention, during which he was exiled, Alessandri was recalled in 1925 and presided over the adoption of a new constitution. The constitution reestablished presidential rule (although still assigning imposing powers to congress), provided for church-state separation, and embodied impressive-sounding social justice codes.

In 1927, Col. Carlos Ibáñez seized the presidency, ushering in a four-year period of mild dictatorship that witnessed many material accomplishments, largely under the stimulus of foreign (mostly U. S.) capital. When the world depression struck in 1929, Chile lost its markets and ready access to foreign investment and loan capital. The resulting economic crisis led to the overthrow of Ibáñez in 1931 and to a brief period of political instability.

Alessandri's reelection to the presidency in 1932 heralded Chile's return to constitutional order. Alessandri devoted himself to economic recovery rather than reform, supported by a newly formed alliance of the Liberal and Conservative parties, both committed to defense of the established social order. Although facing challenges from Fascists, Communists, and Marxian Socialists, Alessandri maintained order.

Popular Front and Centrist Regimes. For the 1938 presidential election a Popular Front was formed by the Radical, Socialist, and Communist parties. By a narrow margin, it elected Pedro Aguirre Cerda. Although the Socialists soon ceased to collaborate and Aguirre Cerda died in 1941, the front initiated three years of the most energetic administration that Chile had enjoyed since the Ibáñez rule. Extensive housing and school programs were undertaken, industry expanded under the stimulus of a government development corporation, and real wages advanced for the working classes.

Between 1942 and 1952, Chile was governed

CHRONOLOGY

1810 Chilean patriots under Bernardo O'Higgins and José Miguel de Carrera oust Spanish officials and declare provisional government.

1814 At the Battle of Rancagua, royalist forces crush the patriot armies, restoring Spanish authority.

1817 Patriot forces defeat the Spanish at Chacabuco.

1818 Chile declares its independence (February 12).

1830 Conservatives defeat liberals at the Battle of Lircai, inaugurating the "autocratic republic."

1837 Chile declares war on Peru-Bolivia confederation (formed in 1835) to restore balance of power.

1837 Diego Portales, architect of the autocratic republic, is assassinated by mutinous soldiers protesting the war.

1839 Chilean forces triumph at the Battle of Yungay (Peru), ending the Peru-Bolivia confederation.

1842 The University of Chile is established at Santiago.

1865 Non-Catholics are granted rights of private worship, as the liberal republic is launched.

1879 War of the Pacific begins (Chile against Bolivia and Peru) following dispute over Bolivia's taxation of Chilean nitrate concessionaires.

1880 Boundary settlement recognizes Argentina's ownership of most of Patagonia.

1883 Treaty of Ancón ends hostilities with Peru, recognizing Chile's ownership of Tarapacá and right to hold Tacna and Arica pending a plebiscite.

1884 Treaty of Valparaíso (confirmed in 1904) grants Chile control over Bolivia's coast.

1909 Valparaíso–Buenos Aires transcontinental railroad is completed.

1922 Socialist Labor party associates itself with the Third International, becoming Chile's first Communist party.

1929 Following failure of U.S.-inspired efforts to conduct a plebiscite, Tacna is restored to Peru but Chile retains Arica.

1945 Chile, neutral in World War I and hitherto neutral in World War II, declares war on Japan (April) and becomes charter member of United Nations (June).

1952 Women vote for first time in national elections.

1962 Chilean Catholic hierarchy issues joint pastoral letter setting forth the church's support of thorough socioeconomic reform.

1964 Election of Eduardo Frei Montalva as president ushers in era of social and economic reform.

1970 Socialist Salvador Allende becomes first elected Marxist head of state in Latin America.

1973 Allende government is overthrown.

UNICERSITY OF CHILE in Santiago overlooks the broad tree-lined Avenida Bernardo O'Higgins. The University, with centers in other cities, is Chile's largest institution of higher learning.

by two Radical party presidents, with the same party generally controlling congress. This period was notable primarily for mounting inflation (long one of Chile's main problems), for the lag of wages behind cost-of-living increases, and for proliferation of the bureaucracy. Disgruntled voters in 1952 supported the reform program offered by Carlos Ibáñez and elected the former dictator to the presidency by one of the largest majorities in the country's history.

Rise of the FRAP and Christian Democrats. As constitutional president, Ibáñez displayed little of the energy that had characterized his dictatorial rule. He filled his time mainly with political maneuvering and meeting a never-ending series of cabinet crises. When the 1958 presidential election took place, a large segment of the electorate expressed discontent with the preceding 16 years of inertia by voting for Salvador Allende, the candidate of the Popular Action Front (FRAP), a Communist-Socialist alliance. Allende failed by only 35,000 votes to defeat Jorge Alessandri Rodríguez, son of Arturo Alessandri and candidate of the Liberal and Conservative parties.

Although an efficient administrator of thorough integrity, Allessandri lacked personal magnetism. His extremely moderate reform programs were blocked by a Liberal-Conservative-Radical alliance, which controlled congress. Alessandri also failed to fulfill his major purpose, the curtailment of inflation. As the 1964 elections approached, Liberals, Conservatives, and some Radicals concluded that the charismatic Christian Democratic candidate, Eduardo Frei Montalva, offered the only hope for defeating Allende, again the standard-bearer of the FRAP. With 2.5 million going to the polls, Frei received 56% of the ballots and Allende 39%.

Particularly since 1957 the Christian Democrat party had urged basic social and economic changes, including land and tax reforms, leading to a "communitarian society" which would avoid the severely criticized extremes both of communism and liberal capitalism. This became the goal of the new administration, but its programs encountered much opposition. Although the Christian Democrats won an absolute majority of seats in the Chamber of Deputies in 1966, the party soon split into pro- and anti-Frei factions.

Nevertheless, the Frei government was able to introduce a program for Chileanizing the copper industry and set about buying controlling interests in the foreign-owned companies that had been providing nearly a quarter of the world's

supply of that commodity. The administration also expanded educational facilities dramatically and, in 1967, gained congressional approval of a sweeping land-distribution program. Frei's principal failure was his inability to cope with inflation.

The Move Toward Socialism. In 1970, opponents of Allende and the FRAP could not unite behind one presidential candidate. Constitutionally barred from renominating Frei, the Christian Democrats chose a less popular figure, Radomir Tomic, while the old-line Liberals and Conservatives, who had joined to form the National party, nominated the 71-year-old former president, Alessandri. The Marxist-Socialist Allende, running again with Communist support, received only 37% of the popular vote, but this was a plurality. In the absence of a majority winner, the election was thrown into Congress. Though controlled by Christian Democrats, the chamber was reluctant to break precedent by opposing the leader in the popular vote. Accepting Allende's pledge to respect Chile's democratic institutions and free press, the legislators named him president in November 1970—the first popularly-elected Marxist head of state in Latin American history.

Within a year, Allende's administration had expropriated the copper properties and was acquiring, through purchase, control of other mining operations, many foreign-owned manufacturing concerns, and all private banks. Land reform was greatly speeded.

However, in September 1973, after weeks of nationwide strikes and economic chaos, the socialist experiment came to a violent end. The military overthrew the Allende government and established a ruling junta. Allende was reported to have committed suicide.

FREDRICK B. PIKE, *University of Notre Dame*

Bibliography

Burr, Robert N., *By Reason or Force: Chile and the Balancing of Power in South America, 1830–1905* (Berkeley 1965).

Galdames, Luis, *A History of Chile* (Chapel Hill, N. C., 1941).

Gil, Federico, *Genesis and Modernization of Political Parties in Chile* (Gainesville, Fla., 1962).

Gil, Federico, *The Political System of Chile* (Boston 1966).

Gill, Clark C., *Education and Social Change in Chile* (Washington 1966).

Halperin, Ernst, *Nationalism and Communism in Chile* (Cambridge, Mass., 1965).

Pendle, George, *The Land and People of Chile* (New York 1960).

Pike, Fredrick B., *Chile and the United States, 1880–1962* (Notre Dame, Ind., 1963).

Silvert, K. H., *Chile Yesterday and Today* (New York 1965).

CHILE, University of, chil'ē, the national university of Chile, a public, coeducational institution of higher education in Santiago with a number of branch campuses throughout Chile. Founded in 1738 by King Philip V of Spain as the Universidad de San Felipe, it was reconstituted in 1842 by the Venezuelan scholar Andrés Bello and was reopened in 1843 with Bello as rector. A second reorganization in 1879 enlarged the university's functions, and in a 1931 reform of higher education it was made autonomous.

The university's original five faculties have been augmented extensively. Today there are faculties of agriculture, architecture, fine arts, music, economics, mathematics and physics, law and social science, veterinary medicine, philosophy and education, medicine, dentistry, chemistry, and pharmacy. Over 130 research institutes bring the university's special knowledge to bear on Chilean industry and government. Secondary education is under the guidance of the university's philosophy and humanities department, and degree candidates at other Chilean universities must be approved by the university. Over 50% of all Chilean university students attend the national university, which has a total of 22,700 students either at Santiago or branch units. The university library houses over 1 million volumes.

DIEGO BARROS ORTIZ, *The University of Chile*

CHILI. See CAPSICUM.

CHILKAT PASS, chil'kat, is in the Coast Mountains of northwestern British Columbia, Canada, about 50 miles (80 km) northwest of Haines, Alaska. It is crossed by Haines Highway, which runs from Haines across a narrow strip of British Columbia to Haines Junction, Yukon, where it joins the Alaska Highway. During the Yukon gold rush of the 1890's, Chilkat Pass and Chilkoot Pass, about 50 miles to the east, were routes followed by prospectors.

CHILKOOT INLET, chil'kōōt, is in southeastern Alaska, about 65 miles (105 km) northwest of Juneau. It extends inland for about 20 miles (32 km) from the head of Lynn Canal, a large inlet branching off Chatham Strait. A northern arm of Chilkoot Inlet is Taiya Inlet, on which the city of Skagway is situated. During the Yukon gold rush of the 1890's, prospectors sailed through Chilkoot and Taiya inlets to the beginning of the trail to Chilkoot Pass, which led to the goldfields.

CHILKOOT PASS, chil'kōōt, is in the Coast Mountains on the border between southeastern Alaska and northwestern British Columbia, Canada, about 20 miles (32 km) north of Skagway, Alaska. Its altitude is about 3,500 feet (1,065 meters).

The pass is famous as one of the principal routes used by prospectors after the discovery of gold in the Yukon in the 1890's. The route began at the head of Taiya Inlet, near the present site of Skagway. A good wagon road extended for 6 miles (10 km). Beyond the end of the road, a trail led for more than 4 miles (6 km) through a narrow, precipitous canyon, and then rose above timberline and continued for 4 miles over the summit. In places the trail was nearly perpendicular. After the Yukon Railroad was built through White Pass in 1900, traffic on the trail was greatly diminished.

CHILLAN, chē-yän', is a city in Chile, about 260 miles (420 km) by road southwest of Santiago. The rich farm and pasture lands around Chillán furnish raw materials for the city's industries—winemaking, flour milling, leatherworking, and distilling. There is skiing nearby in the foothills of the Andes. Termas de Chillán is a popular hot-springs resort in the hills.

The city, which was founded about 1580, is the capital of Ñuble province and Chillán department. It was the birthplace (1778) of one of the fathers of Chilean independence, Bernardo O'Higgins. Chillán was destroyed by an earthquake in 1833 and was rebuilt on a new site nearby. Another earthquake in 1939 caused much loss of life and damage to property. Population: (1960) 65,112.

CHILLICOTHE, chil-ə-koth'ē, a city in northern Missouri, the seat of Livingston county, is situated about 75 miles (120 km) northeast of Kansas City. It is a shipping point for an orchard, grain, and livestock area. The city's manufactures include air filters for road and farm machinery, structural steel, ornamental iron, ready-mix concrete, lumber, brick, tile, gloves, feeds, fertilizer, and dairy products. The State Training School for Girls is here.

Chillicothe was first settled about 1830 and laid out in 1837. It was incorporated as a city in 1855. It has the mayor-council form of government. Population: 9,519.

CHILLICOTHE, chil-ə-koth'ē, is a city in south central Ohio, the seat of Ross county, on the Scioto River near the mouth of Paint Creek. It is 45 miles (72 km) south of Columbus. The city is a trade and distribution center in a rich farming and grazing area. Hogs, cattle, corn, and dairy products are the chief sources of farm revenue. Principal industries include the manufacture of paper, shoes, aluminum household ware, floor tile, and steel railroad springs. Other industries make such products as building materials, flour, and potato chips.

Chillicothe is the seat of a branch of Ohio

UP THE STEEP CHILKOOT PASS, prospectors climbed in single file on their way to Yukon gold in the 1890's.

BROWN BROTHERS

University and the Ross County Historical Society, which maintains a museum. Adena, home of Thomas Worthington, sixth governor of Ohio (1814–1818), is about one mile (2 km) west of the city. It is believed to have been designed by Benjamin H. Latrobe and is a state memorial. Mound City Group National Monument, 3 miles (9 km) to the north, preserves prehistoric Indian mounds and artifacts. The Chillicothe *Gazette,* founded in 1800, is the oldest continuously published newspaper west of the Alleghenies.

Chillicothe was founded in 1796 and was incorporated as a city in 1802. It was the capital of Ohio from 1803 to 1810 and from 1812 to 1816. Chillicothe is a Shawnee Indian word meaning "town." The city has a mayor-council form of government. Population: 24,842.

Marie-Louise Sheehan
Chillicothe Public Library

CHILLIWACK, chil'ə-wak, is a city in southern British Columbia, Canada, on the Fraser River, 58 miles (93 km) east of Vancouver and 10 miles (16 km) north of the U. S. border. It is on the Trans-Canada Highway and the Canadian National Railways. Situated in the most productive farming area in the province, Chilliwack is the trading center for the eastern portion of the Fraser Valley, noted for dairying, poultry-raising, and horticultural specialties. Beef and dairy cattle are raised. Crops include hops, filberts, corn, peas, small fruits, hay, and oats.

When placer gold was discovered along the Fraser River in 1858, miners swarmed into the area. Settlement at Chilliwack began in 1862. The city grew rapidly after a system of dikes was completed in 1903 to guard against the annual flooding of the river. Chilliwack was incorporated in 1908. Population: 9,135.

CHILLON, shē-yôn', is a castle in Switzerland, at Territet (just south of Montreux) at the eastern end of Lake Geneva. It was once an important stronghold of the counts and dukes of Savoy. It stands on a rock that rises from the lake 22 yards (20 meters) from the shore, with which it is connected by a bridge. Chillon dates from the 13th century, when it was the favorite residence of Peter II of Savoy. It is famed as the prison of François de Bonnivard, prior of the Abbey of St. Victor, who was chained in one of its dungeons from 1530 to 1536, inspiring Lord Byron's poem *The Prisoner of Chillon.* Later it was used as a state prison and has since been restored as a historical museum.

Chimaera

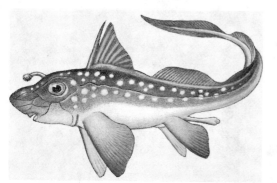

CHILON, kī'lon, was a Spartan ephor in about 556 B.C. He was considered one of the Seven Wise Men of early Greece and was credited with having raised the power of the five annually elected ephors to a level equal to that of the kings. Little else is known for certain about him, but he probably was responsible for making Spartan military training more rigorous and a change in foreign policy. During his lifetime the Spartans stopped acting as Dorian conquerors and claimed to be the legitimate successors of the Mycenaean kings of the Peloponnesus. They helped put down tyrannies in other cities and made alliances that led ultimately to the Peloponnesian League.

Donald W. Bradeen
University of Cincinnati

CHILOPODA. See Centipede.

CHILTERN HILLS, chil'tərn, a range of chalk hills in southern England noted for their splendid beech woods. They extend from the Thames River about 50 miles (80 km) northeastward through the counties of Oxford, Buckingham, Bedford, and Northampton. The highest point is Coombe Hill (850 feet, or 260 meters) near Wendover. The average height is about 500 feet (150 meters), and the average width 15 miles (25 km). The hills have a steep northwest escarpment and a more gradual fall to the southeast.

The Chiltern Hundreds is a political subdivision in the region. Its name has become well known because appointment as steward of the Chiltern Hundreds is a way of "resigning" from Parliament. Actually, a member may not resign from Parliament—but neither may he hold a salaried office. Therefore, if he is appointed to the stewardship, which carries a small salary, he automatically gives up his parliamentary seat.

Gordon Stokes
Author of "English Place-Names"

CHILUNG, jē'lŏong', the second-largest port of Taiwan, China, is located on the northern coast of the island. Important for its international commerce, Chilung is also the home port of a large fishing fleet. A large shipyard is located on the inner harbor, which is protected from the open sea by Hoping Island and two islets. Aside from shipbuilding, which is the leading industry, other main industries include the manufacture of chemicals and the processing of marine products.

Chilung has exceptionally heavy rainfall, averaging 122 inches (300 cm) on an average of 214 days a year. The city is about equally distant from Shanghai, Okinawa, Manila, and Hong Kong. Population: (1960) 226,373.

Chengtsu Wu
Hunter College, New York

CHIMAERA, kī-mir'ə, any of a unique group of primitive marine fishes, related to sharks and rays, that probably are divergent offshoots of a primitive sharklike ancestor. They are known as *ratfishes.* Chimaeras live in deep, cool ocean waters.

Like sharks and rays, chimaeras have cartilaginous skeletons. The male also has claspers that aid in copulation, and the female extrudes her eggs in cases. However, chimaeras also have other characteristics suggestive of higher bony fishes. For example, they have a single gill opening, separate anal and urogenital openings, and no spiracle.

Chimaeras have large heads that sometimes have pointed snouts; large eyes; exposed beaklike teeth in an undershot mouth; and conspicuous sensory canals. The fishes grow to a maximum length of 79 inches (2 meters) and a weight of 35 pounds (16 kg). Their bodies taper to pointed tails and have very large fan-shaped pectoral fins. The smooth, slippery skin ranges in color from silvery with stripes and spots to leaden or black, depending on the depth of their habitat. Chimaeras are slow-swimming, sluggish fishes, most active at night. They feed on small invertebrates and fish.

Some taxonomists place all 24 species of chimaeras in the family Chimaeridae, but others classify some of the species in the families Callorhinchidae and Rhinochimaeridae. All are in the order Chimaeriformes, class Chondrichthyes.

E. J. Crossman, *University of Toronto*

CHIMBORAZO, chĕm-bō-rä′sō, is a dome-shaped mountain mass in Ecuador, some 120 miles (190 km) from the Pacific. The name, from the Indian Chimpu-Raza, means "Mountain of Snow." The loftiest and most imposing of a group of volcanic peaks that includes Cotopaxi, it rises 20,561 feet (6,267 meters). It was once much higher, but the main crater has been worn away. Minor craters and even spirals of smoke have been reported, and hot springs gush from its sides, which are groined by 15 glaciers.

Alexander von Humboldt, whose efforts to climb it took him 1,668 feet (509 meters) short of the top in 1802, proclaimed it the loftiest mountain in the world, and it had this reputation for some 70 years. Edward Whymper finally climbed Chimborazo in 1880.

Ferdinand C. Lane
Author of "The Story of Mountains"

CHIMBOTE, chĕm-bō′tā, is an industrial city and seaport in Ancash department, Peru, 260 miles (420 km) northwest of Lima by the Pan American Highway. Economic development of the nearby Río Santa valley made Chimbote Peru's leading steel center, beginning in the late 1950's. The valley supplies coal, electricity, and limestone for the steel industry; iron ore is shipped in from the port of San Juan, south of Lima. Chimbote exports anthracite coal and agricultural products from the valley. It is also a major fishing port and producer and shipper of fish meal, which became the chief export of Peru in the 1960's. Population: (1970 est.) 90,000.

CHIMERA, kī-mir′ə, in Greek mythology, was a fire-breathing female monster that ravaged the countryside around Lycia. The forepart of her body was that of a lion; the middle, of a goat; and the hind part, of a dragon. Chimera (also spelled *Chimaera*) was finally killed by Bellerophon with the aid of the winged horse Pegasus.

According to one account, the monster had its origin in the volcano of Chimera, near Phaselis in Lycia, at the top of which lived lions; around the middle, goats; and at the foot, poisonous serpents. In another account, Chimera was the offspring of Typhon, a monster with 100 serpents' heads and fiery eyes, and Echidna, a monster that was half woman and half serpent. In time, Chimera came to denote any grotesque monster or any horrible creature of the imagination.

CHIMBORAZO is the highest Andes peak in Ecuador.

CHIMES AND CARILLONS, kar′ə-lonz, are fixed, cup-shaped bells for performing music. A carillon contains 23 or more bells, a chime less than 23. The most desirable range of carillons is four or more octaves (at least 48 bells); the lowest-tone bell is called the *bourdon*. For concordant harmonies to be played on many bells, the bells must be tuned to produce specific overtones. Carillon bells contain five main partials (see Harmonics): the strike, a minor third, a perfect fifth, the nominal (an octave above the strike), and the hum (an octave below the strike).

The carillon is played by means of a keyboard of wooden levers and pedals connected by wires and cranks to bell clappers. The levers are struck with the clenched hand, and a pedal board enables the bass bells to be played by the feet.

Chimes may be played from a similar keyboard, but usually the levers are much larger and there is no pedal board. Both chimes and carillons may be played electrically from piano keyboards, but this considerably reduces musical expression and increases maintenance expense.

Chimes. The word "chime" is derived from the Latin *cymbalum* (plural, *cymbala*) through the Old French *chimble*. A cymbala was a set of small bells hung from a rack and used for indicating pitches and accompanying chants (manuscripts of the 12th and 13th centuries show King David striking a cymbala with hammers). Eventually, the cymbala function was absorbed by the organ, which has resonant tone bars with such stop labels as "glockenspiel" and "celesta."

In medieval monasteries, bells were used to identify the devotional periods called canonical hours. By the 14th century it was common for bells to be attached to clock mechanisms in both church and secular towers. It became customary to ring a short tune, known as a clock chime tune, on several bells as a warning that the hour bell was about to strike. One of the best known of these is the Westminster tune, in which four bells sound each quarter hour and announce the hourly striking of Big Ben in London.

The bells in a chime are usually limited in number, intended for simple melodies only, and frequently not carefully tuned. Notable chimes

Manual playing of the carillon allows the carillonneur to take full advantage of the instrument's expressive qualities. James R. Lawson plays the clavier of Notre Dame University's carillon, the oldest in the United States (installed in 1856).

COURTESY NOTRE DAME UNIVERSITY

Carillon bells, arranged in chromatic series, at the Rockefeller Memorial Chapel, University of Chicago.

in North America include those at St. Thomas Church, New York City (21 bells); Cornell University, Ithaca, N. Y. (21 bells); and the University of California at Berkeley (12 bells).

Carillons. The word "carillon," according to one theory, derives from the Latin *quadrilionem* or *quaternis*, either of which would indicate that the set originally consisted of four bells. Some cymbala did contain four bells, but larger sets also were common. However, the derivation of the word "carillon" remains uncertain, and it is more likely that the carillon originated with the striking clock (the English word "clock" comes from the French *cloche*, meaning "bell"). The instrument is played by a *carillonneur*.

The carillon was developed in Flanders. By the 15th century it had eight or more bells, each playing a different note of the diatonic scale. The bells were suspended from a frame and struck by multiple hammers set in a large, weight-driven, rotating cylinder. When enough bells were arranged in chromatic series, whole tunes with harmonies could be played automatically.

Toward the end of the 16th century, keyboards (*claviers*) were added to many of the carillons in and around Antwerp. The carillon at Aalst is traditionally credited with acquiring the first keyboard (1481).

The 17th century was the golden age of the carillon in Europe, paralleling the development of change ringing in England. By the middle of the 17th century two Dutch bell founders, the brothers François (or Frans) and Pieter Hemony, succeeded in producing perfectly tuned carillon bells. Most of their carillons were of three octaves.

During the 19th century, the art of casting bells declined and few carillons were made. Early in the 20th century, the secrets of tuning were rediscovered, initially by English founders, and a renaissance of the carillon art began. In 1922, the first tuned modern carillons were made in England for the Portuguese Church in Gloucester, Mass., and the Metropolitan Church in Toronto, Canada. That same year, a training school for carillonneurs was established in Mechlin, Belgium, by Jef Denijn.

The world's oldest carillon is at the Rijksmuseum in Amsterdam, Netherlands (24 bells, dating from 1553). Perhaps the most famous is at St. Rombold's Cathedral in Mechlin (49 bells, of which 27 were cast by the Hemony brothers). The carillon at the Riverside Church, New York City, contains 74 bells, of which the 20-ton bourdon is the largest and heaviest tuned bell in the world. Other notable carillons in the United States are at the University of Chicago chapel (72 bells); the Shrine of the Immaculate Conception, Washington, D. C. (56 bells); and Mountain Lake Sanctuary, Lake Wales, Fla. (53 bells).

Imitation Carillons. After World War II, instruments called carillons, but actually something quite different, began to be manufactured, particularly in the United States. One such instrument consists of sets of large tubes similar to the chimes used in symphony orchestras; it is called a *tubular carillon*. It produces overtones, however, that are unsuited to the playing of true carillon music.

Another imitation carillon, called the *electronic carillon*, is similar in principle to the electronic organ; it imitates the sound of bells through the use of electronic equipment. Its source of tone is a set of rods that are struck by tiny hammers. The vibrations are amplified electrically and are subsequently broadcast through a system of loudspeakers. See also BELL; CHANGE RINGING.

JAMES R. LAWSON, *Carillonneur*
The Riverside Church, New York City

Further Reading: DeJong, Rinus, and others, *De zingende torens van Nederland* (Zutphen, Netherlands, 1966); Price, Frank Percival, *The Carillon* (London 1933); Rice, William Gorham, *Carillon Music and Singing Towers of the Old World and the New* (New York 1931); Rottiers, Jef, *Beiaarden in Belgie* (Mechlin, Belgium, 1952).

CHIMKENT, chim-kent', is a city in the USSR, in Central Asia. It is the capital of Chimkent oblast in the Kazakh republic. Chimkent is situated in the western foothills of the Tien Shan mountain system, 75 miles (120 km) north of Tashkent, in an oasis watered by a tributary of the Arys River.

A major industrial center, it has one of the Soviet Union's largest lead smelters, processing ore from all over Central Asia. Its chemical industry produces phosphorus compounds from a phosphate deposit in the nearby Karatau Mountains. Electric power for the city's industries was long furnished by stations burning brown coal from the nearby Lenger mines. But in the early 1960's, Chimkent was reached by a pipeline from the Bukhara natural gas fields and converted to the use of natural gas.

Founded in the 12th century on the Silk Road from China, Chimkent was ruled by the khans of Kokand until it passed to Russia in 1864.

Chimkent oblast, with an area of 46,600 square miles (120,600 sq km), is a desert territory, but grains, cotton, and fruits are produced on some of its irrigated lands. Sheep raising is also important. The principal mines serving the Chimkent smelter are at Kentau. Population: (1966) of the city, 209,000.

THEODORE SHABAD
Editor of "Soviet Geography"

<small>ERIC HOSKING, FROM PHOTO RESEARCHERS</small>

Chimney swift

CHIMNEY, a hollow vertical structure enclosing a flue for carrying smoke and gases upward for dispersion in the atmosphere. The hot, gaseous combustion by-products, because they are lighter than the cooler outside air, rise up the chimney, creating a vertical draft whose force is proportional to the height of the chimney.

Home Chimneys. In Europe before the 16th century, chimneys were outside attachments to the building structure. From the 16th century on, chimneys were placed within the building structure. In colonial New England, homes usually were built around a large central chimney that served several fireplaces used for cooking and heating. In the American frontier West, chimneys often were built of logs that were plastered inside to form a fire-resistant flue.

In modern dwellings, chimneys generally are used with fireplaces. From the ground up, the structure includes a foundation, a hearth and a fireplace, a throat to reduce the cross section and enhance the vertical flow, a damper to control the draft, a smoke shelf to block gusts of wind down the chimney, a smoke chamber, and a vertical flue. The most common construction is a brick fireplace with a terra-cotta flue surrounded by brick or stone.

Industrial Chimneys. Tall chimneys for industrial use were first built during the Industrial Revolution. Some modern chimneys are more than 300 feet (91 meters) tall. Building materials for industrial chimneys now include brick, concrete, reinforced concrete, steel, aluminum, and titanium.

Specifications for chimneys are becoming more strict in the effort to combat air pollution. Engineers can use wind tunnel tests to obtain design data for taller chimneys to meet the stricter surface-air-pollution standards. In this method, a scale model of the chimney and its surrounding terrain would be built and tested to evaluate aerodynamic and other design factors.

ROBERT L MOUNT, *Science Writer*

CHIMNEY SWIFT, a small, insect-eating bird found in eastern and midwestern North America. It breeds east of the Rocky Mountains from central Canada to Texas and central Florida. It is highly migratory and winters annually in Central and South America, as far south as Amazonian Peru.

Often referred to as a "cigar with wings," the chimney swift has a short neck, cylindrical body, and long tapering wings. It is about 5 inches (13 cm) long and is colored a uniform sooty brown except for slightly paler regions on its throat and chest. The sexes are alike in size and color.

The chimney swift nests in colonies and gets its name from its habit of building its nest in man-made chimneys. The bird constructs its half-saucer-shaped nest by attaching small twigs to the inside vertical wall of the chimney with a gluey saliva from its mouth. The saliva forms such a firm bond that even summer rains cannot dissolve the nest. Four to five pure white, glossy eggs are laid in the nest. Both the male and female incubate the eggs, and both care for the young. Since chimney swifts begin their southward migration to the American tropics early, the young birds are flying with the adults by July.

The food of the chimney swift consists entirely of insects, all of which are taken on the wing. The insects may range in size from beetles to winged ants and flies. A sudden cold spring rain that washes the air free of insects can be disastrous to chimney swifts, especially when there are young to be fed.

There is no truth to the popular belief that swifts are related to swallows; instead they are near relatives of hummingbirds. The chimney swift (*Chaetura pelagica*) is a member of the family Apodidae, which is in the order Apodiformes.

KENNETH E. STAGER
Los Angeles County Museum of Natural History

YLLA, FROM RAPHO GUILLUMETTE

CHIMPANZEES are sociable and responsive, and are among the most intelligent and versatile of all animals.

THE CHIMPANZEE can stand erect on its legs, and in some cases will walk short distances on its legs alone.

NATE SOCK, FROM BLACK STAR

CHIMPANZEE, chim-pan-zē', a great ape native to the dense forests and open woodlands of west and central equatorial Africa. The common chimpanzee is classified as a single species, *Pan troglodytes*, but there is as much variation among chimpanzees as among men. The pigmy chimpanzee is considered by many authorities to be a distinct species, *Pan paniscus*. Chimpanzees are highly intelligent social animals closely related to man, and for this reason they are valuable for use in medical and behavioral research.

Characteristics. Adult chimpanzees have few natural enemies other than disease, for they are large, powerfully built animals that stand about 4.5 feet (1.3 meters) high and weigh an average of 115 pounds (52 kg). There are wide individual differences, and the male tends to be somewhat larger and more robust than the female.

The gestation period of the chimpanzee is 7 months, and the newborn animal weighs about 4 pounds (1.8 kg). It is almost as helpless as a human infant. It clutches the hair on its mother's sides and back while it clings to her chest and stomach. Only the head has any appreciable amount of black hair at birth; there is a white tuft at the anal region, and another is often found at the chin. The hair tends to lighten with age, whereas the skin darkens. Some individuals develop black faces early in life, but others only develop a tan face color.

As the infant chimpanzee grows, it begins to explore the world; it starts to ride on the mother's back when she travels. A new infant is seldom born before the last one is two or three years old. Even at that age the juvenile chimpanzee remains closely associated with its mother, although it spends more and more time with its playmates and other members of its band. The chimpanzee reaches full stature at about age 12; few achieve the potential life-span of over 50.

Behavior. A band of chimpanzees, which usually contains 6 to 10 members, exists as part of a larger community of bands. These bands may exchange members, merge, or divide, depending on available food and other factors. Some bands consist only of adult males or of mothers and young, but individuals appear to come and go freely within the community.

Much of the life of the chimpanzees is spent in the trees, where they sleep and obtain the fruits that constitute the bulk of their diet. They also eat other vegetable matter and insects, and there are reliable reports of chimpanzees killing and eating small mammals. The apes seldom venture far from trees, and they avoid direct sunlight. A sleeping nest is built each night, and a resting platform may be built during the day.

The chimpanzee's long arms are suited to brachiation (swinging through trees), but most purposeful travel takes place on the ground. Chimpanzees walk on the soles of the feet and the middle phalanges of the flexed fingers. A chimpanzee can also stand erect on its short stocky legs. Some individuals may travel short distances on their legs only, especially when the hands are being used to carry an object. When excited, males often stand on their legs and also put on an impressive display. The display usually starts with swaying or stamping and with vocal sounds that reach a crescendo scream. This may be followed either with a final charge or the flinging of objects, or both. These displays, however, seldom express directed aggression.

Chimpanzees do not swim. Therefore the major rivers in the rain forests where they live may be effective barriers separating the different races of chimpanzees.

Intelligence. Chimpanzees are very responsive and easily excited animals, and they enter into many tasks with great exuberance. They display great versatility in the range of problems they can solve and in their ability to manipulate objects and fashion crude tools. Although their performances on particular tasks may be matched by some monkeys, no monkey tested has been able to equal the versatility of the chimpanzee.

Young chimpanzees often become strongly attached to their trainers, and even adult chimpanzees show partiality to certain people. The chimpanzee is, above all, an intelligent social animal requiring companionship and a sufficiently stimulating environment to keep it active and interested in life.

Chimpanzees are classified in the family Pongidae, suborder Anthropoidea, order Primates.

IRWIN S. BERNSTEIN, *Yerkes Regional Primate Center, Emory University*

Further Reading: Yerkes, Robert M., *Chimpanzee, a Laboratory Colony* (New Haven, Conn., 1943); DeVore, Irven, ed., *Primate Behavior* (New York 1965).

CHIMU, chē′mōō, was the name of two periods of pre-Incan civilization in Peru. The first, known as Mochica or early Chimu, flourished from about 500 to 1000 A.D., when it was absorbed by the Tiahuanaco. The late Chimu culture then emerged in the north, with its capital at Chan-Chan, and flourished until it was taken over by the Incas in the 15th century.

The Chimu periods were marked by great population increase and expansion. The first true cities developed, and numerous irrigation projects opened new terrain. Chimu ceramics, particularly of the early period, have been found in great abundance. These were noted particularly for their representational decorations. In the late Chimu period metalwork was outstanding. Bronze and copper were used for such utilitarian objects as digging sticks, needles, and knives; and silver and gold were hammered into goblets, plates, and ornaments. See also PERUVIAN ARCHAEOLOGY.

CH'IN DYNASTY, chin (221–207 B.C.). The Ch'in dynasty, which lasted only 15 years, welded China into a unified state. Its reign marks a revolutionary change in Chinese history. Feudalism was abolished, and the first Ch'in ruler took the title *Shih Huang-ti* (First Emperor) to emphasize his deliberate break with the past.

The Ch'in state, centered in modern Shensi, began wielding power in the 7th century B.C. Administrative and legal reforms instituted under the 4th century legalist minister Shang Yang undermined the feudal order and increased Ch'in power. The legalists further weakened the old system by encouraging private ownership of land, peasant armies, political centralization, and the development of trade and agriculture.

The Ch'in conquest of China was completed by Cheng (259–210 B.C.), who became king of Ch'in in 247 and who had vanquished all of his rivals by 222 B.C. Superstitious and impetuous, he was also a vigorous leader who closely supervised affairs and traveled widely within the empire. His chief aides were the legalist Li Ssu, a cold and calculating man who had studied with Hsün-tzu, and the brilliant general Meng T'ien.

Ch'in armies extended Chinese power as far south as Annam, and the nonfeudal social order, which was only partly developed in other states, was established throughout China. Disarmament was enforced by collecting weapons and melting them into huge bells and statues and by destroying walls. A harsh legal code was imposed, and thought control was attempted by a massive burning of books distasteful to the legalists.

The Ch'in ensured political centralization by a series of measures. They divided China into prefectures and counties with officials directly responsible to the emperor. They standardized weights, measures, and coins and reduced the various methods of writing Chinese characters to a single system. The capital at Hsienyang, near modern Sian, was made into a magnificent city, and several major construction works were carried out. Among the works were the completion of the Great Wall, which was carried out by Meng T'ien, and many roads, canals, and irrigation systems.

After the death of the Shih Huang-ti in 210 B.C., the throne was usurped by his second son, Hu Hai, with the aid of Li Ssu and Chao Kao, a powerful eunuch. Hu's reign was brief but disastrous. Incompetent and despotic, he killed Li Ssu, Meng T'ien, and many others. Although he inherited the resentment against his father's revolutionary changes, he added to it by increasing the stringent laws and heavy taxation. After his murder in 207 B.C., Ch'in rule collapsed into anarchy, and the Ch'in emperors became a symbol of evil to most Chinese, although they had established the basis of imperial China.

JAMES R. SHIRLEY
Northern Illinois University

Further Reading: Bodde, Derk, *China's First Unifier* (Leiden, Netherlands, 1938); Hsu, Cho-yun, *Ancient China in Transition* (Stanford, Calif., 1965); Watson, William, *China Before the Han Dynasty* (New York 1962).

CHIN, jin, the name of several Chinese ruling dynasties: the Western Chin (265–317 A.D.) and Eastern Chin (317–420), which together are referred to as the Chin dynasty, and the so-called Later Chin (936–947) of the Five Dynasties period. The name is also spelled *Tsin*.

Politically, the earlier Chin dynasty marked the final breakup of the Chinese imperial system, which had endured for some 450 years, and ushered in a period of disunion. In 265, Ssu-ma Yen, the founder of the dynasty, succeeded in giving the Chinese empire a semblance of reunification. But constant efforts throughout his reign to quell opposition in the south weakened the economic structure and military defenses of the North China plain. Chaos erupted upon his death and the northern territories were left open to successive waves of attack by nomadic tribes culminating in the destruction of the capital, Loyang, in 316. Fleeing south, members of the Chin house and aristocracy set up a new dynasty, the Eastern Chin, near present Nanking, and this lasted for a century more.

Culturally, the Chin period was a time of regeneration for Chinese civilization. During this period the alien religion of Buddhism first menaced and then was absorbed into the ideological basis of Chinese society. Literati such as Hsi K'ang and T'ao Ch'ien engaged in metaphysical speculation characteristic of both Taoism and Buddhism, and found in lyric poetry a satisfying mode of self-expression. It was also the period in which great artists such as Wang Hsi-chih and Ku K'ai-chih flourished.

CHARLES J. CHU, *Connecticut College*

CHIN, jin, the name of a Jurchen (Jürched) dynasty that ruled part of northern China from 1115 to 1234. The Chin (or Kin) dynasty rose to power by destroying the Liao dynasty (907–1125) in northern China and driving the followers of the Liao, the Khitan (Ch'i-tan), westward to Turkestan, where they founded the Kara-Khitai empire (1124–1211). Through their contacts with the Chinese Sung dynasty (960–1279), the Jurchens gradually adopted Chinese civilization. The Chin were finally overthrown by the Mongols.

CHIN HILLS, chin, a mountain range in western Burma. Situated between the Manipur Hills to the north and the Arakan Yoma to the south, the Chin Hills average 5,000 to 8,000 feet (1,545–2,440 meters) in elevation and reach their highest point in Mt. Victoria (10,016 feet, or 3,053 meters). The Manipur River cuts a north-south canyon through the hills before it joins the Myittha, a tributary of the Chindwin River. The hills are named after the Chin tribes who live there. See also KUKI-CHINS.

CHINA

CONTENTS

CHINA, occupying one of the pivotal geographical regions of the earth, is the most populous country in the world, containing almost one fourth of the human race. Since 1949 the country has been divided in fact into two separate entities, each of which claims legal jurisdiction over all of China: *Communist China* (the People's Republic of China), in control of the mainland, and *Nationalist China* (the Republic of China), in control of Taiwan.

1. Introduction

For some 3,000 years, China has been one of the main centers of the world. Rivaled for sheer power and sophisticated living only by the Roman imperial colossus, China's civilization exerted political and cultural influence throughout one of the few heavily populated regions of the world at the beginning of the Christian era. In subsequent centuries new empires rose and fell in many parts of the globe, while the nature of civilization underwent successive changes. Despite many vicissitudes, however, China continued to endure as a political entity, and in our own times it has once again surged to the forefront of international affairs.

The Oldest Contemporary Civilization. As the world's "oldest contemporary civilization," China has inherited a complex legacy of cultural pat-

terns from the past. In many instances the Chinese sought to preserve their cultural heritage intact and to transmit it to their descendants with a minimum of modification. But, as any inquiry into Chinese history soon reveals, the Chinese were not completely averse to innovation when circumstances seemed so to warrant it. Nor were the Chinese entirely reluctant to discard institutions and values which seemed no longer to fulfill social and cultural needs.

Furthermore, China's way of life did not serve the purposes of the inhabitants of China alone. The institutions, ideas, manners, and customs of the Chinese posed a perennial lure for peoples in neighboring lands—in Korea, Japan, the northern and western border regions, and the areas along the long southern frontier. Their cultures were given the lasting impress of things Chinese. It is noteworthy too that the "West" did not escape China's cultural influences. During the 18th century western Europe was swept by a fad for Chinese ways and fashions, the vestiges of which are still apparent.

The Apogee of Chinese Power. Traditional Chinese civilization reached its apogee of power and splendor for the fourth time—the Chou (about 1027–256 B.C.), Han (202 B.C.–220 A.D.), and T'ang (618–906) dynastic periods were the first three—during the 15th to mid–18th centuries. By almost all relevant criteria, China under the Ming (1368–1644) and the Ch'ing (1644–1912) was during these centuries indisputably one of the greatest states in the world. In effective command of their domains, the Ming and Ch'ing emperors justifiably took for granted foreign respect for their authority. But thereafter the Chinese empire entered into a steady decline. After much buffeting from foes at home and abroad, the last of China's imperial ruling houses and the imperial order itself collapsed in revolution.

Nationalist Revolution. Somewhat more meaningful than the actual downfall of imperial China in 1911–1912 were forces that had for many years generated revolution within the country. From the broader perspectives of history, the overthrow of the Ch'ing dynasty may be viewed as a by-product of a long, unfolding revolution. It slowly became apparent that the political elimination of the Manchus was no cure-all for the many social and cultural ailments of China and that even

WERNER BISCHOF, FROM MAGNUM

EMIL SCHULTHESS, FROM BLACK STAR

493

THE REPUBLIC OF CHINA

(Information Highlights)

Official Name: The Republic of China.

Head of State: President of the Republic.

Head of Government: President of the Executive Yüan (Premier).

Legislature: Legislative Yüan.

Capital: Taipei.

Area (de facto): 13,885 square miles (35,961 sq km).

Boundaries: Island group separated from mainland China by the Taiwan Strait.

Elevation: Sea level to 13,113 feet (3,997 meters).

Population: (1976) 16,352,987.

Official Language: Chinese.

Major Religions: Roman Catholicism has most adherents; others are Buddhism, Taoism, Islam, and Protestantism.

Monetary Unit: New Taiwan dollar (NT$ = 100 cents).

Weights and Measures: Metric system.

Flag: State emblem (a 12-pointed white sun in a blue sky) in the upper canton of a red flag.

National Anthem: *San Min Chu I (The Three People's Principles).*

People's Republic of China was an epochal event in the long history of the Chinese people. In preceding centuries the founders of new regimes, while occasionally shaking up the prevailing way of life drastically, had nevertheless striven to revitalize and preserve the empire's social and cultural heritage. The new Communist rulers of China, however, were unswervingly committed to building an entirely new way of life in keeping with their ideological convictions. Under their forced draft programs major upheavals were inspired throughout the length and breadth of the land. And with the passage of time an increasingly large percentage of the people of China were born and reared under conditions dissimilar to those known to the older generations. It is unlikely that these younger men and women can ever be inspired to return to a past which they have never known.

The creation of the Communist republic cast China in a fundamentally new historical role. Until very recent years China's leaders were content to restrict their concerns to the world of East Asia and to regions not far beyond. But by mid–20th century their international horizons had been vastly extended. Pride, ambition, and perhaps ideological dogma impelled them to pursue their goals in the world at large. Whether or not Communist China fulfills the aims of its foreign policies, its mere existence is one of the first facts of international life.

HYMAN KUBLIN
Brooklyn College
The City University of New York

greater struggles than had been anticipated would be required before a new nation and state could be constructed. Arousing the people of China to the need for an all-out campaign to unify a country ripped apart by self-seeking warlords and preyed upon by the imperialists was the final achievement of Dr. Sun Yat-sen.

The national revolutionary movement, spearheaded by Sun's Kuomintang (Nationalist party) scored many notable gains during the tempestuous years of the late 1920's. Much of central eastern China was unified by military action directed by Gen. Chiang Kai-shek, Sun's successor, and China's strongest government since the overthrow of the Manchus was established at Nanking. Yet the newly born Nationalist regime had many causes for concern. Warlords continued for many years to dominate huge parts of the country, while a weak but determined Chinese Communist party remained a thorn in the flesh of the Nationalists. Far more critical, however, was the persistent encroachment of Japan which, after overrunning Manchuria in 1931–1932, ceaselessly nibbled away at North China. The result was the outbreak of the Sino-Japanese War in 1937.

War with Japan. The modern political fate of China was shaped by the conflict with Japan. The devastating impact of the long, drawn-out hostilities upon economically and militarily weak China was a more serious consequence. Its toll in death and destruction after more than eight years of conflict was well-nigh incalculable. Perhaps even more ominous for the Nationalists was their confrontation by a Communist party whose ranks had been tremendously swelled during the Sino-Japanese struggle.

Communist China. The establishment of the

THE PEOPLE'S REPUBLIC OF CHINA

(Information Highlights)

Official Name: The People's Republic of China.

Head of State: None.

Head of Government: Premier of the State Council.

Legislature: National People's Congress.

Capital: Peking.

Area (de facto): 3,691,500 square miles (9,561,000 sq km).

Boundaries: (Clockwise from the north) Mongolia, USSR, North Korea, Pacific Ocean, Hong Kong, Macao, Vietnam, Laos, Burma, India, Bhutan, India, Nepal, India, Pakistan, Afghanistan, and USSR.

Elevation: Highest point—Mount Everest, 29,028 feet (8,825 meters); lowest point—Tufan Basin, Sinkiang, 928 feet (282 meters) below sea level.

Population: (1974) 800,000,000.

Official Language: Chinese.

Major Religions: Buddhism has most adherents; others are Taoism, Christianity, and Islam.

Monetary Unit: Yüan (Jen Min P'i).

Weights and Measures: Metric system.

Flag: Red, with 5 stars in canton area.

National Anthem: *I Yung Chun Chin Hsing Ch'ü (The March of the Volunteers).*

CHINA: People and Way of Life

2. The People

China has the largest population of any country in the world. In 1970 there were more than 697 million people, and of this number approximately 94% were Han-Chinese. The "men of Han"—referring to the Han dynasty (202 B.C.–220 A.D.) under whom China came of age culturally and politically—are usually called "the Chinese" by Westerners, and have a common history, culture, and written language. The remaining 6% of the people is composed of various minority groups, usually referred to as "minority nationalities" because of their diverse ethnic and linguistic backgrounds. They are generally found in China's border areas or in its marginal agricultural lands.

Population. The population of China is heavily concentrated in the most arable areas—on the Great Plain of North China, on the fertile central plateau of Szechwan, in the river valleys and deltas, and in the coastal areas. There are several large urban centers with populations of over two million people.

Perhaps more significant than the actual size of the population is the rate of growth and the ratio of people to arable land. The rate of growth is estimated at about 2.2% per annum. Although this rate is not among the world's highest, if such a relatively moderate rate is applied to the large base population, the annual growth exceeds 15 million people. Also, when the total land area of China is considered, the number of people per square mile is about 160 (60 per sq km), a rather low density. However, if specific areas of population concentration are studied, it is found that the population density of the North China plain, for example, ranges from 800 to 1,200 people per square mile (300 to 450 per sq km) and that the densities of the Yangtze River delta are as much as three times these figures. This means that there are too many people for the available cultivable land—about 1,500 persons per square mile (575 per sq km) of cultivated land or about 0.4 acres (1.6 hectares) per person.

(TOP TO BOTTOM) CAIO GARRUBBA, FROM RAPHO GUILLUMETTE; BOSSHARD, FROM BLACK STAR; HIL PABEL, FROM BLACK STAR; MARC RIBOUD, FROM MAGNUM; HARRY REDL, FROM BLACK STAR; EMIL SCHULTHESS, FROM BLACK STAR; GOKSIN SIPAHIOGLU, FROM PHOTO RESEARCHERS; AL LOWRY, FROM PHOTO RESEARCHERS.

Overcrowded conditions are found in large cities, such as Peking, Shanghai, Tientsin, and Shenyang (Mukden). In the 20th century, all have grown rapidly, as a result of industrialization and migration from overcrowded rural areas.

When it first achieved power, the Chinese Communist government refused to acknowledge that an overpopulation problem can exist, but in the 1960's, it adopted measures for population control that included raising the minimum ages for marriage and providing information about birth control. In addition, on numerous occasions, it attempted to alleviate the seriously overcrowded conditions of the cities by curbing migration from rural to urban areas. In recognition of the unequal distribution of population, the government attempted to move people into previously marginal agricultural lands inhabited by national minorities or into areas in which virgin agricultural lands were being developed and in which new industries were being built. With the spread of modernization, changes in the traditional attitudes toward family size occurred, but the population problem was far from resolved and, in fact, continued to grow.

China's huge population growth is not a new phenomenon. By the 1st century B. C., the population numbered around 50 million. China's population grew and declined cyclically. For example, the introduction of new crops from Champa (in modern South Vietnam) in the 11th century and new crops such as maize, sweet potatoes, and peanuts from the Americas in successive centuries after 1492 caused "population explosions" because these crops could be planted on formerly uncultivable or marginal lands. However, frequent periods of warfare and natural calamities decimated the Chinese population. Thus, it reached an estimated 100 million by 1200 A. D., but fell to 65 million by 1368 at the end of the Yüan (Mongol) dynasty. It mounted to 150 million by 1600, but natural disaster and famine reduced it to 100 million by 1680. The population soared to an estimated 430 million by 1800, but a 15-year period of famine, banditry, and rebellions left only 380 million. By the 1970's the decreased mortality rates resulting from modern preventive medicine caused the population to reach its new high of about 697 million people.

Early Development. China has the oldest continuous surviving civilization in the world although it is not the first to have developed. Peking man, a fossil man discovered in 1921 at the Choukoutien cave site southwest of Peking, lived about a half million years ago. He is the first ancient form of man found with cultural remains that give evidence of his use of fire, tools, weapons of stone and bone, and primitive hunting and gathering techniques. There are no signs, however, of a Chinese civilization or even of its earliest cultural forerunner, the Neolithic or agricultural stage, in the region until about 3400 B. C. The evolutionary development of early man and his culture in China appears to have been slow. Peking man lived over a wide area of Asia, but was not yet a Mongoloid racial type. For centuries, the population in northwestern Asia was primarily proto-Caucasoid, and it was not until the post-Pleistocene period (8000–6000 B. C.) or just prior to the development of agriculture in China, that part of the population first developed Mongoloid characteristics. The Mongoloids came to the northern part of

STERN, FROM BLACK STAR

PEKING pedestrians walking in the rain through a street where Communist slogans vie with advertisements.

China and apparently underwent adaptive changes as the glaciers retreated and the environment changed. These hunting and fishing people gradually came to resemble their present forms, with light yellow skin, medium stature, straight black hair, and eyes with the epicanthic fold. They spread to other areas and eventually migrated throughout East Asia and America.

It was in the area sometimes called the "cradle of Chinese civilization"—at the bend of the Yellow River (Hwang Ho) and in the Wei River valley—that the more rapidly developing Mongoloid peoples entered the food-producing stage, either through diffusion from the West or, more likely, through their own independent invention. Moreover, their modest agricultural beginning laid the foundation for China's later agrarian civilization and its spiraling development.

The Han-Chinese system of agriculture produced surplus food, which could sustain an increasing number of people and which would not have been possible with the meager returns of the earlier hunting and gathering forms of economic life. The spread of agriculture led to the development of agricultural technology, such as irrigation and flood control, which in turn led to a further elaboration of agriculture and, concomitantly, to the development of the sociopolitical systems necessary for operating and controlling an expanding and increasingly complex society.

The Chinese were surrounded in the arid north and northwest by the so-called "barbarians," peoples who were for the most part nomads speaking Altaic languages that were dissimilar to the various Chinese languages. Their agriculture was limited and their mobile life did not allow for the evolution of the stable and complex social institutions developed by the Chinese. The

SHANGHAI, China's biggest city, chief seaport, and industrial center, presents a typically modern skyline.

NANKING is on the Yangtze River, northwest of Shanghai. A canal passes through one of its poorer districts.

EMIL SCHULTHESS, FROM BLACK STAR

ANDREAS RAMER, FROM P. I. P.

presence of these frequently aggressive peoples, plus the unfavorable geography and climate to the north and west of the Yellow and Wei rivers, discouraged movement in those directions by the Chinese. Therefore, the rapidly expanding population migrated to the east, south, and northeast.

While the early Mongoloid inhabitants of the north were adapting and changing to an agricultural economy, another cultural tradition emerged in the south and southwest. It appears to have developed at a slower pace and to have been related to that of a proto-Negroid people who had moved into parts of Southeast Asia. At the time of the Chinese migrations, around 1100 B.C., the people to the south were still either hunters and gatherers, or people such as the Thai who had also developed agriculture. Thai agriculture, however, was less efficient and did not produce the large food surpluses necessary for early population growth and social complexity. As a result, they could not successfully compete with the more advanced Chinese and were forced to leave the area and settle in the various parts of mainland Southeast Asia, or were gradually absorbed by the Chinese. In this manner, the Chinese empire spread to its present borders and left the various unassimilated minorities in the marginal border areas.

Sinitic Language. All of the 700 million Han-Chinese speak Sinitic languages of the Sino-Tibetan language family. All of these languages are not mutually intelligible. Mandarin, spoken by well over 400 million, is China's official language and the one most extensively used. It originated in North China and spread with the migrations of the people to east-central and southwest China. Different local varieties of Mandarin are mutually understandable.

Sinitic dialects that are not mutually intelligible and those that do not resemble Mandarin

are found primarily in Taiwan and in southeastern China. This area is divided by mountains, valleys, and river systems, and is the last major one to have been incorporated into the Chinese empire. A major Chinese language, Wu or Soochow, is spoken by over 35 million people in several provinces south of the lower Yangtze River and is sometimes referred to as Shanghai speech. The Min dialects, spoken farther south by about 20 million people may be divided into the Southern Min group, represented by Amoy (spoken in southern Fukien), and Swatow (spoken in northeastern Kwangtung province and Hainan Island). Amoy is also the principal dialect spoken on Taiwan by the Chinese who migrated from Fukien between the mid-1600's and 1900.

The Hakka language is spoken by about 5 million people in the hilly areas that extend from Fukien province to Kwangsi Chuang Autonomous Region and northern Kwangtung. The Hakka (meaning guests) people were later migrants who were forced to farm in the hills. The Hakka are also numerous on Taiwan.

Yüeh or Cantonese is spoken in Kwangtung and Kwangsi by approximately 40 million people. It is also the Chinese language usually spoken by residents of emigrant communities in America and Southeast Asia.

Linguistic diversity has long been recognized as a problem in China. The single system of Chinese written characters has served as a means by which all literate Chinese can communicate. In the 20th century, an increasing number of the population has begun learning Mandarin. See also Section 13. *Language.*

Minority Groups and Languages. A language other than Chinese is a factor in identifying national minorities. Also taken into consideration are origin, continuous residence in specific areas, and distinctive economic and cultural traits. Marked physical differences are less important because physically different members who speak Chinese and who have been assimilated into the Chinese culture have often been accepted as Chinese.

Some of the languages spoken by minority groups belong to the Sino-Tibetan language family, although they are not Chinese languages. Included in this group is Thai. Thai is spoken in different forms by ethnic groups such as the Chuang of the Kwangsi region and the Paiyi of Yünnan province. There are over 9 million Thai speakers in China, mainly in Yünnan, and they are closely affiliated with the Thai of Burma, Thailand, and other countries of Southeast Asia. These groups have methods of farming and writing and social structures that frequently resemble those of the Thai in Yünnan who live near the Southeast Asian border. The Thai who live on the non-Chinese side of the border originally migrated from China. The approximately seven million Chuang of Kwangsi have no written language of their own and are polytheistic.

Other groups who speak non-Chinese Sino-Tibetan languages are the Miao of southeastern Kweichow and western Hunan provinces, and the Yao of Kwangsi, Hunan, Kwangtung, and Yünnan provinces. They live in the mountainous regions of these provinces, as well as in Vietnam, Laos, and Thailand. In China these groups number some 4 million people, who are in most ways culturally different from the Han-Chinese.

The other significant branch of the Sino-Tibetan language family spoken in China is Tibeto-Burman, which includes Tibetan, spoken in Tibet and western Szechwan by about 3 million people, and the language of the 3 million Lolo or Yi people of the mountain areas between Szechwan and Yünnan. The Tibetans fall into two basic groups. The larger group is composed of farmers who traditionally have worked as tenants on the agriculturally poor lands of the Lamaist monasteries or of Tibetan nobles. The other group includes the nomadic yak and sheep herders. Before the Chinese Communists moved into Tibet in 1959, 20 to 25% of the people were Lamaist priests who exercised great social and economic power.

The Lolo tribesmen, who speak a Tibeto-Burman language and live in the mountains, have strongly and successfully resisted the Chinese. They are polytheistic and animistic. The Lolo farm by dry agriculture, frequently abandoning soil exhausted by extensive double cropping, and herd sheep and goats. The Lolo of Yünnan, unlike those of Szechwan, have intermarried with the Chinese and have become highly Sinicized.

The languages of several large minority groups in China belong to the Altaic language family. Three main branches are represented—the Mongolian, Turkic, and Tungusic.

The largest Altaic group is formed by the Turkic-speaking Uigurs of Kansu province and of the Sinkiang Uigur Autonomous Region, formerly referred to as Chinese Turkestan. Sinkiang has a population of over 6 million people, and of this number 80% are Uigur. The remaining people are the nomadic Kazakhs, Kirghiz, Uzbeks, and Salar who mostly speak Turkic languages. Although the area is among the driest in the world, the oases of the Tarim Basin support nearly 4 million Uigurs who live by rainfall farming and who grow crops such as winter

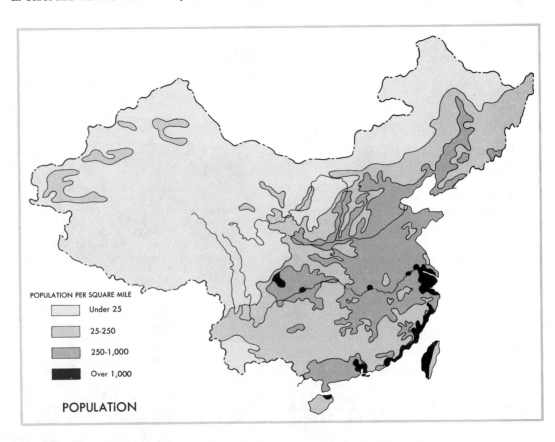

POPULATION PER SQUARE MILE

- Under 25
- 25-250
- 250-1,000
- Over 1,000

POPULATION

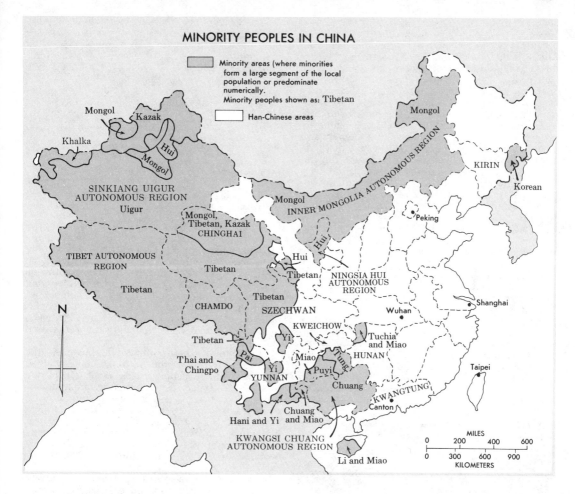

MINORITY PEOPLES IN CHINA

wheat and cotton. They have their own written language and are Muslim.

The aggressive and highly mobile Mongols invaded China many times and ruled it in the 13th and 14th centuries. In China approximately 1.5 million Mongolian-speaking people inhabit the Inner Mongolia Autonomous Region. The other Mongols, somewhat over one million people, live in the Mongolian People's Republic, an independent republic formerly known as Outer Mongolia. The Mongols in China have their own system of writing and engage in agriculture and nomadic and sedentary animal herding. The farmers have been agriculturally and culturally influenced by the Chinese who, over the years and especially after 1949, have infiltrated the area. Their expansion into the region has been so extensive that by the 1960's the Chinese outnumbered the Mongols 7 to 1. The Mongols are followers of Tibetan Lamaism, and until the establishment of Chinese Communist rule the lamas played a major role in Mongol life.

The more than 2.5 million Manchus who live in Manchuria and North China are considered a minority although they have almost completely lost their original identity. They ruled China from the 17th to the 20th century, during which time they absorbed much of Chinese culture. Thus, they follow much the same occupations and customs as the Han-Chinese and their Altaic Manchu language has been almost completely replaced by Chinese.

Some groups are more difficult to classify. Over one million Koreans live in the Yenpien Korean autonomous district in Kirin province. They have retained their own customs, which are similar to the Chinese, and although their language is not Sinitic, the written language contains many Chinese characters. The Hui of Ninghsia Hui Autonomous Region and of other parts of the northwest are Chinese Muslims. For the most part they are descendants of Turkic-Uigur soldiers and merchants who entered China over a thousand years ago. They mainly speak Chinese and number about 3.5 million.

There are many minorities that speak non-Chinese languages that belong neither to the Altaic nor the Sino-Tibetan group. These include the 14,000 Tajiks of southwestern Sinkiang, who speak an Iranic language of the Indo-European group, and the Wa and Puman people who speak an Austroasian language. The Wa and Puman are fierce tribesmen who live on both sides of the Yünnan-Burma border and number only about 100,000. The Austronesian or Malayo-Polynesian language is also spoken in China by various groups, predominantly in Taiwan. The several hundred thousand members are descendants of people who migrated to Taiwan from Southeast Asia long before the arrival of the Chinese. They speak various related languages and were animists and headhunters before their pacification by the Japanese in the early 1900's. Pushed by the Chinese to the interior mountain slopes, they hunt game and practice slash-and-burn agriculture.

Role of the Minorities. Over the centuries many of these minorities have threatened Chinese civilization. Relations between them have been strained, and the minorities have strongly resisted the spread of Chinese culture into their areas. Past governments and the 20th-century Nationalist and Communist governments have been concerned about controlling the large minority populations because the areas that they inhabit are often strategically important even though remote. It also has been recognized that the minorities serve as an important avenue of influence to surrounding countries that have similar peoples within their borders, and possibly they also serve as buffers.

The Chinese Communist government, rather than use force, has attempted to ease the traditional strain by creating autonomous regions, counties, and districts. The minority groups also have been encouraged to develop their own systems of communication, styles of life, and educational and writing systems. However, it is clear that the Chinese Nationalists on Taiwan and the Chinese Communists on the mainland still desire to integrate them into the Chinese civilization. The Chinese Communists have infiltrated so many people into areas such as Inner Mongolia and Tibet that they have overwhelmed the native cultures, controlled elections, and influenced the selection of minority leaders. In many areas communes have been organized to

COMMUNE of Hua Shan, north of Canton, raises turnips and other farm produce for sale in the market.

HARRY REDL, FROM BLACK STAR

influence ways of thinking and living. Also, these areas are usually sparsely settled and are possible relocation areas for China's expanding population.

BERNARD GALLIN, *Michigan State University*

Bibliography

Moseley, George, "China's Fresh Approach to the National Minority Group," *China Quarterly*, no. 24 (London 1965).
Schwartz, Henry G., "Chinese Migration to North-West China and Inner Mongolia 1949–1959," *China Quarterly* no. 16 (London 1963).
Shabad, Theodore, *China's Changing Map: A Political and Economic Geography of the Chinese People's Republic* (New York 1956).
Taeuber, Irene B., "China's Population—Riddle of the Past, Enigma of the Future," in *Modern China*, ed. by Albert Feuerwerker (Englewood Cliffs, N. J., 1964).
Wiens, Herold J., *China's March Toward the Tropics* (Hamden, Conn., 1954).

3. Social Life and Customs

In the 1930's, social scientists examining the societies of mainland China began concerning themselves not only with the nature of traditional (Confucian) Chinese society, but also with the degree to which China's rural and urban working classes participated in this society. The chief contribution of their research has been a recognition of the differences that existed between the styles of life of the ruling classes and the rural and urban workers.

In spite of these differences, however, the Confucian tradition and ideology have welded the Han-Chinese people into a single civilization for over 2,000 years. Therefore, if we are to understand the nature of the changes taking place in China today under communism, we must first understand what traditional Chinese society was like, what differences between the educated elite and the peasantry existed, and what changes were evolving in China even before the Communists came to power.

The Confucian Background. Confucian ideals, the enunciated values of Chinese society up until the Communist revolution, are grounded in the life and teachings of Confucius (q. v.), the great Chinese sage and philosopher, who was born in 551 B.C. The period when Confucius lived was one of social chaos, and he hoped to alleviate suffering among the people by restoring order and peace through moral and political reforms. The all-pervasive concern of his doctrine was social order and personal dignity, to be derived from right conduct and hence from social approval. In its acknowledgment that not all people are equal in their capabilities, Confucianism divided society hierarchically, the individual being subordinated within the family and within society by an established system of graded relationships. A scholar elite well-versed in Confucian values was to be created to take the reins of political and social leadership and by example spread the Confucian morality throughout every segment of society.

Through the centuries Confucian teachings set a pattern, or ideal, for the structure of the family and of Chinese society at large. However, although the Confucian elite was charged with the task of spreading Confucian ideals downward through society, the peasant classes had difficulty in learning and practicing the Confucian social pattern because of economic strictures on them. Still, these classes looked to the local elite who, being better off economically, could better practice the social and family duties preached by Confucius. This elite regularly played the role of buffer between the poor, uneducated peasantry, who were helpless in times of trouble, and the government, which did not function at the village level because of its small staff. Most rural families were dependent to a great degree upon the elite, who served as mediators when conflicts arose and generally provided service or leadership for their kinship organization, village, or area.

Village Life. Traditionally a great proportion of the Han-Chinese people lived as individual family units in village concentrations; agriculture was usually the primary basis of their economic life. Technology was based primarily on hand labor carried on by the family unit, which normally composed the work team. The implements necessary for farming were few and until the 20th century there was little technological innovation in this area of economic life.

In every village a large number of uneducated peasants worked relatively small portions of agricultural land, part of which they rented. Poverty stalked the Chinese countryside in times of war, natural disaster, or governmental instability and sheer survival was sometimes difficult in the face of disease and lack of food.

That small segment of the village population which was more secure was the educated, landholding elite, who often had enough land to rent large portions out to tenants. This landholding elite was usually composed of the wealthiest and most influential people in the area.

Although community consensus between the peasantry and the elite was a highly valued Confucian ideal, the peasantry were often passive participants in the running of the village. The peasants had little influence of their own, and so tended to accept the leadership of the elite. Therefore, throughout much of China's history, the rural political situation was probably in a precarious balance that depended on economic conditions and the degree of responsibility assumed by the elite and the government for the masses. Changes in this balance, in times of internal disorder, were sometimes a source of discontent or even of rebellion.

Cities and Towns. Members of the rural elite, through successful competition in the ancient system of civil service examinations, had the best opportunity and greatest likelihood of those in the rural area to move into the scholar-official class of the government, though according to the ideals of Confucius such advancement was open to rich and poor alike. The scholar-official class was based in the cities, which served as political and cultural centers, and also in the market towns, which served as points of distribution for goods to and from the rural hamlets and cities. They were a nationally recognized elite, a Confucian gentry of government officials, retired officials, and prospective officials. But the cities and towns in which this elite lived were also marked by the same extremes of wealth and education as were the rural areas. They often were centers of concentration of numerous other governmental staff people, soldiers, service workers such as artisans, shopkeepers, and merchants, laborers, and the wealthier landed people who preferred to live there rather than in the rural village areas where security and luxuries were scarce.

The Family. In traditional China the institution of prime importance was the family, and indeed the dominant principle of a righteous life was considered to be allegiance to one's parents (*hsiao*, translated "filial piety," was one of Confucius'

cardinal virtues). Confucian teachings regarding the sanctity of relationships between family members and setting forth mutually protective functions for them were at bottom the same as his ideals for government, which he conceived of as a kind of large family.

The family, as idealized in traditional China and, frequently, even today, was a joint family made up of several small patrilineally related units, covering perhaps five generations. This family lived under one roof and functioned as a single cooperating unit in all its activities—economic, religious, and social. Its members might work at a combination of occupations—agricultural, business, and governmental—and by such concerted effort the united family might be able to achieve wealth and prestige. The structure of this ideal family was hierarchical, according to generation, age, and sex. It was headed by the eldest male, who wielded complete power over all the family members. The headship usually passed to the eldest son, or sometimes to the son adjudged most worthy. Wives, brought into the husband's joint household through family rather than individual decision, were subservient to the husband's mother and to other family members.

Although for many this ideal pattern was within the realm of possibility, it was usually only the upper classes and well-to-do families that managed to cooperate and develop toward this end. Among the masses of the peasantry, economic insufficiency resulting from lack of land

DEMONSTRATIONS, like this one on the anniversary of Communist China, are very common on the mainland.

HENRI CARTIER-BRESSON, FROM MAGNUM

usually prevented the establishment of families large enough to conform to this pattern. Although many children were born, few survived. As a result, say modern demographers, the Chinese family averaged no more than five or six persons. Indeed, the peasant family sometimes had barely enough children to reproduce itself through successive generations—and to die without heirs was considered a sin.

The peasant family with sons enough to form a large joint family usually had insufficient land and resources to maintain this family. In the family with modest resources the father's position was often relatively weak because his grown sons might contribute more economically to the family than he did. The father thus had limited bases on which to assert his authority, prevent excessive competition between married sons for the family's limited resources, and make demands on his sons and their families that could hold a large family together. As a result, those peasant families with more than one married son under one roof usually did not remain in this condition for long.

Poverty threatened the unity of peasant families in still other ways. Because a thorough Confucian education required time, money, and leisure, it was rare indeed for peasant sons to be well indoctrinated with the Confucian values of filial piety or with the ideal degree of respect for parents and elders. Often the limited practice of the Confucian value of filial piety was often accompanied by a strengthened relationship between the family's sons and their wives, who usually were drawn together by the demands of economic necessity. The strengthening of the husband-wife relationship inevitably occurred only at the expense of the father-son relationship.

The result of this combination of conditions was that most peasant families went through a regular growth cycle. They might grow from very small and simple families to something approaching the ideal of a joint family consisting of several small family units. Such a joint family usually remained together a short time and then divided again into small component family units, each one hoping to begin its own growth cycle. However, family division often tended to weaken each family unit economically by fractionating the land.

The growth cycle for families with more economic resources, more education, and more influence in the community was different and more in conformity with Confucian ideals; division of such families was far less freuent. When these large and wealthy families eventually did divide, even the newly formed units were still quite large. These families were able to maintain their size, landholdings, and prominence over the years.

Cohesive Factors. Although family division generally did occur on all levels of society, it did not usually mean complete divorcement of the several newly independent family units. They still shared either the care of the old parents or sacrifices to common ancestors, or both. Custom and social pressure required that the separate units continue to come together on regular occasions — at least once or twice a year—for ancestor worship rituals.

In addition, factors of physical propinquity and economics provided a basis for certain amounts of cohesives. Because the system of inheritance dictated equal inheritance of the land by sons, brothers still normally retained and farmed adjacent fields even after land was divided by the family. They not only continued to farm land side by side, but they also shared an irrigation

system and all the other activities and problems associated with cultivation or farming. For example, they frequently had to share the use of large farm implements and animals. And a single room in the ancestral house containing the family altar and ancestral tablets continued to be the common property of all the separated families. The upkeep for this room and its accouterments was shared equally by all.

Kinship Groups. Elite families usually expanded steadily in numbers, ramifying into kin-related branches recognizing a common male ancestor. In numerous villages of southeastern China and, to a lesser degree in central China, all of the inhabitants are members of one kinship group and actually bear the same surname. However, most villages of China are composed of several kinship groups. The political and social competition within each village was based on competition among kinship organizations, and among the leading families within those organizations.

Another important kind of kinship group in traditional China was based on marriage ties among elite families of equivalent socioeconomic standing. Through marriages, local landed elite families built a large network of relationships with families of other descent lines who, like themselves, were often influential in business and politics in the area. These families' extensive relationship system clearly enhanced their value as leaders, mediators, and protectors to their local communities and to the local peasantry.

The peasantry, like the elite, normally married people outside their own villages and always with surnames different from their own. However, peasant families rarely had the opportunity to develop the extensive marriage networks necessary for the building of marriage-based kinship groups, nor were they usually able on their own to expand in numbers into kin-related organizations recognizing a common male ancestor.

The Lineage. In traditional China, it was quite common for a wealthy family group interested in solidifying and more effectively organizing its larger patrilineal kinship extension to donate some of its land to the group of male, kin-related relatives. The kinship group thus became a kind of landowning corporate organization, a lineage, commonly referred to as a "clan." In this way the group of patrilineal relatives with their single demonstrated common ancestor is given a strong basis for maintaining their relationship to this kinship-based organization.

Although the members of a lineage, which may sometimes number in the thousands, clearly base their relationship on common kinship, it is not at all certain that the organization is truly conceived to reinforce the relationship between kinsmen. Rather, kinship relationships are used as the basis for group cohesiveness so that the kinship organization, which cuts across class, can function as an economic and political manipulative force on behalf of its member families.

Religion. In addition to the family-oriented religious beliefs, which centered on ancestor worship, the activities of the folk religion were an almost daily concern of all the less educated people in the rural areas. It was also a concern of the common people in the cities who had continuing and close ties with the rural areas from which they or their ancestors had migrated. Usually, only the gentry members of the elite did not participate in the folk aspect of religion; frequently, they were agnostics and knew virtually nothing about the supernatural belief systems of Chinese folk religion, which were a complex mixture of Taoism, Buddhism, and animism.

Ritual activity always has existed in virtually all areas of Chinese life. Many temples, or at least altars, could be found in the villages and towns throughout the country. Each village and even urban neighborhood worshiped its own local deities who belong to a hierarchical pantheon of gods. Magical rites frequently were performed by shamans to cure the ill and exorcise demons, and divination and geomancy rites were employed as a guide to personal action or for determining building and burial sites. The organized village or neighborhood worship of the many deities and the magical rites helped provide an important source of village or neighborhood identification and cohesiveness.

In addition, rituals served as an occasion to bring relatives and friends together. Visits on such occasions took on a special significance for the elite because these exchanges reinforced and strengthened interfamily relations which then could be socially or economically helpful to their local kinship group and to their fellow villagers.

CHANGING CHINA

Pressures on the Chinese traditional way of life began with the arrival of the commercially aggressive Western powers in the mid-19th century. The impact of their technological culture challenged China's very existence. As early as the first two decades of the 20th century, many of the social reformers of the Chinese scholar class were reacting against the "evils" of traditionalism and asserting that China must reform or cease to exist. In their view, much of the Confucian ideal of the family-oriented society was incompatible with the requirements of the modern state and could only impede China's economic and political development.

These men advocated sweeping changes in the codes that affected marriage, divorce, and the status of women, all so important to the nature of the traditional family system, and thus presented the first serious challenge to the system. Nationalist Chinese government leaders were sympathetic to these new ideas because they realized that traditional family loyalty could be detrimental to the fostering of nationalism.

During these decades, however, other powerful influences of modernization were operating and tended to undermine the foundation of the traditional system. The growth of population, as a result of improved health facilities, better communications, and a burgeoning of industry and commerce all provided an opportunity for geographic and social mobility and a greater involvement in the market economy and with the government. Increased relationships beyond the family and new organizational groupings tended to usurp the traditional family functions.

Socioeconomic change has been in progress since the 1930's but it did not stem from a particular political ideology. It is a trend which was encouraged by the compelling desire of modern Chinese governments to develop a grass roots influence and to increase the social consciousness and relationship to the state of the general population. It is a trend which today is being accelerated by the Nationalist government on Taiwan and especially by the Communists on the mainland.

The Communist Regime. To further their ideological ends, the Chinese Communists embarked upon a program of universal education, including classes for adults and politically oriented mass associations in both rural villages and urban areas. Many of these activities have been directed against traditional religions, and as a result, religious practices of all forms have been greatly curtailed. In their highly directive manner, the Chinese Communists have striven to substitute a concern for the state for the people's traditional concern for family and local area. They also hoped to reshape such facets of the traditional Chinese mentality as the Confucian precept that those who performed mental labor, the elite, were meant to rule those who performed physical labor.

Immediately upon the take-over of the mainland, the Chinese Communists promulgated a countrywide land reform program in which they confiscated and distributed the lands of the old local elite. Much of the elite's wealth and prestige, which had been based on their large landholdings, were dissipated and the local landlord class and their power were destroyed. The land reform program also destroyed the strength and power of the lineages by confiscating the corporate landholdings upon which their authority had been built. The basis for the traditional political-organizational systems therefore were dissolved, and the result was a virtual power vacuum in rural China.

Cadres. This vacuum was quickly filled by the central government operating through the Communist cadres, groups of ideologically trained activists who carry out party policy. In the 1950's they were customarily brought in from outside the local area.

Cadres constitute the new elite class of both rural and urban China. As in traditional times they are still functionaries of the government, but now they also serve the Communist party. Thus, the concept of elitism still exists in China except that the dichotomy between people has been created entirely on the basis of expertise in ideological orthodoxy — Communism rather than Confucianism. (It will be interesting to see whether or not the idealized relationships between cadres and the masses will continue or will once again revert to the more traditional pattern of a dualistic society in which the elite was an entity separate and distinct from the peasants and urban workers.)

The influx of cadres to the rural areas facilitated the reorganization of the political structure and economy of these areas. This reorganization began with the formation of mutual-aid organizations, passed through stages of agricultural producers' cooperatives and collective farms, and culminated in the establishment of communes.

The Commune. As the basic administrative unit of the rural area, the commune combines a number of villages or urban neighborhoods both economically and politically. It has not been the economic success it was planned to be nor has the commune concept been completely accepted by the peasantry. In fact, in the mid-1960's, popular demand pressured the Communist government to allow commune member families to cultivate small, private plots of land. But the commune system has had profound effects on family organization and activities. One of its most important consequences has been the increasing dissolution of the family as the traditional economic unit. With the introduction of large farm labor teams, the individual farmer is no longer free to make his own decisions with regard to the use of his time.

The commune system also has seriously affected the family by assuming many of its traditional social functions. It assumes much of the care of the aged in old-age homes and of the young in child care centers. Thus, women are released from home duties for farm and factory duties. Through the influence of new laws and expanded government enforcement, women have also been given increased independence. Never before have the traditional family structure and traditional Chinese society been attacked so massively and directly as they have been since the advent of the Chinese Communists.

Taiwan. The aim of the Nationalist government, on the mainland before 1949 and now on Taiwan, has been to preserve traditional Chinese culture. Nevertheless, as a result of the influences of modernization and urbanization, the structure of Chinese society there is also changing.

An aggravating scarcity of land in Taiwan has caused migration to the cities and a gradual shift from a subsistence, village-based agriculture to greater participation in the market economy of the country. The increase in activities beyond the village has affected the continued operation of the traditional family system and has made the family as an economic unit look beyond the village and the kinship group for a livelihood. It has also fostered an increased independence of the individual from the family. Young people, including women, with new economic opportunities have achieved a new independence in marriage, for example, and ancestor worship shows a marked decline.

At the same time, the Chinese Nationalist government on Taiwan has, through its land reform program of 1949–1953, played a part in this process of change. No longer is the accumulation of land the most direct path to high economic status, prestige, and mobility in the social system. As a result, the emotional tie to the land has been greatly weakened.

This changed attitude toward the land and its value also has reduced the number of well-educated villagers who are active in village or local affairs, resulting in a decline of the traditional landlord leadership. Aspiring men from the middle peasantry are trying to fill this void. Land reform and increased educational opportunities have stimulated greater social and economic mobility, at least on the local level.

Summary. It is clear that Chinese traditional society is undergoing profound changes on the mainland and to a lesser degree on Taiwan. The central focus on large family orientation has been repudiated (on the mainland) and weakened (on Taiwan) as the traditional family structure has lost its customary economic and social functions. The economic role of the land as the significant road toward the achievement of social mobility and security has been reduced.

The prestige and power of both the traditional elite and the powerful corporate kinship organizations have been curtailed. Perhaps, finally, the historical and age-old concern of many Chinese governments over the potential danger to the state of overly powerful lineages and ambitious and powerful families in local areas is being resolved by both natural evolutionary developments in Taiwan and, more decisively, through revolutionary developments in Communist China.

The process of cultural change is not completely dependent on ideology. The Chinese Communist revolution has accelerated this process of change through strong government, the commune system, mass education and associations, and a smoothly functioning communications system just as the Nationalists, in a less drastic way, through their government programs, have acted as a catalyst to change. With or without these governments, China would be far from the traditional society it once was.

RITA SCHLESINGER GALLIN
BERNARD GALLIN
Michigan State University

Bibliography

Fried, Morton H., *Fabric of Chinese Society* (New York 1953).
Gallin, Bernard, *Hsin Hsing, Taiwan: A Chinese Village in Change* (Berkeley, Calif., 1966).
Lang, Olga, *Chinese Family and Society* (New Haven, Conn., 1946).
Myrdal, Jan, *Report from a Chinese Village*, tr. by M. Michael (New York 1965).
Schurmann, Franz, *Ideology and Organization in Communist China* (Berkeley, Calif., 1966).
Yang, C. K., *The Chinese Family in the Communist Revolution* (Cambridge, Mass., 1959).
Yang, C. K., *Chinese Village in Early Communist Transition* (Cambridge, Mass., 1959).
Yang, Martin, *A Chinese Village, Taitou, Shantung Province* (New York 1945).

4. Education

The Chinese people have traditionally set a high value on education and accorded respect and position to educated people. Since the earliest times, education has been considered a major function of government in China.

In the course of its long history, China suffered many invasions and was actually ruled by alien conquerors at times. Despite foreign conquests and separatist tendencies, the country has been held together, largely by cultural ties. The Chinese people are by no means homogeneous. Localism and provincialism have militated against national solidarity. Nevertheless, a common cultural heritage binds together the people of the vast land with common ideas and common attitudes in regard to human values, family traditions, human relations, and community life. Much of this commonality is the product of a common literature preserved in a common written language that transcends differences in dialect and the spoken tongue. Much has been said about the diversity of dialects as an obstacle to national unity in China. What has often been left unsaid is that the Chinese written language has remained stable for many centuries and that the common written language has been a powerful unifying force because it is understood by all regardless of dialectal differences and has ensured the preservation of common ideas and traditions despite political and social vicissitudes.

Ancient Period. The written language was already well developed and a body of literature in existence before the Chou dynasty (1027–256 B. C.). Confucius (551–479 B. C.), revered by the Chinese as their "Supreme Sage and Foremost Teacher," claimed only to be "a transmitter, not a creator" because in his day there was already a wealth of knowledge and wisdom to be passed on to the young generation. Different types of schools had been in existence to teach the young; some were designed to serve the needs of the princes and the sons of nobles and officials, while others existed for the education of the children of the common people.

The emphasis of education in the ancient period was on moral instruction. The "five human relationships," which subsequently occupied a prominent place in Confucian ethics, were

TAIWAN'S Roman Catholic Fujen University, in a suburb of Taipei, is strikingly modern.

considered essential for a harmonious society based on the patriarchal social system and the monarchical political system. A well-defined code of ethics governed the five human relationships: between ruler and minister, between father and son, between husband and wife, between brothers, and between friends. Religious instruction centered on the observance of rituals, in which music and dancing played a role.

In the education of princes and sons of nobles emphasis was placed on the philosophy and technique of government. The purpose of education was not limited to instructing the future rulers how to rule and how to conduct the affairs of government, but also to select, by examination, the best qualified candidates for government employment and, subsequently, to determine their eligibility for promotion or continuation in office. Inasmuch as political thinking stressed government by moral example, character education was as important to the future rulers as to the common people.

The concept of education was not unlike that of liberal education in the Western world. The content of the curriculum was broad. Its core was the "six arts," which may be comparable to the trivium and quadrivium of the liberal arts of Western education. They consisted of rituals, music, archery, charioteering, writing, and mathematics. Rituals meant the observance of customs and traditions as well as the laws of the land; they were the expression of good manners and propriety of conduct. Music included poetry and songs and dancing; it was supposed to have a salutary effect on the emotions and the inner spirit. The other arts indicated a concern for the development of both body and mind and the concept of the educated person as one having many-sided interests, including sports, physical skills, and artistic expression. The inclusion of mathematics is noteworthy; it reflects ancient China's interest in physical phenomena and accounts for such early achievements as a scien-

tifically arranged musical scale, the making of a calendar, alchemy, and technological inventions such as paper, gunpowder, the compass, the seismograph, and, in later centuries, printing with movable type.

The Golden Age. The subject matter of education was greatly increased with the rise of diverse schools of thought in what became known as the classical age of China. During the period from the 6th century to the 2d century B. C. several important major schools of thought appeared, each having its proponents who propagated their ideas by teaching. Each had offshoots and many variations; the Chinese spoke of "a hundred schools of thought" that carried on intellectual debates on problems of life, of government, and the nature of civilization.

The writings of the philosophers were incorporated into the literature to be passed on to the younger generation. The invention of papermaking in the 1st century A.D. made it easier to produce books and make knowledge available to more people.

Schools were established in the villages as well as in the prefectures and cities. A national university was established in 125 B. C. at the capital, Changan (now Sian); by the 2d century A. D., it had an annual enrollment of 30,000 students. In subsequent centuries, Chinese universities attracted students from neighboring countries and became the source of Chinese influences in Korea and Japan.

Advancement from lower schools to higher schools was determined by examinations. The most important examinations were administered by the state for the purpose of selecting competent scholars to fill government posts. Thus began the competitive examinations that laid the groundwork for the well-known civil service examination, and the selection of personnel by examination introduced a system of "government by scholars" that became a major characteristic of traditional China.

The competitive state examinations were given on different levels. The lower examinations were given in local and provincial centers, while the highest examinations were given in the national capital. Three major degrees—later given the names Hsiu-ts'ai, Chü-jen, and Chin-shih—were awarded; interestingly, they correspond to the bachelor's, master's, and the doctor's degrees in Western education. The most distinguished of those who were awarded the highest degree were invited to become members of the Han-lin Academy, the highest honor a scholar could attain. They achieved national fame and brought pride and prestige not only to their families but also to their native villages.

The examinations were administered according to strict rules and were, in general, fair and impartial. They provided an open road to suc-cess, available to all who would take the time to study and meet the requirements.

Evils of Formalization. Chinese classical education at the beginning was broad in scope and liberal in spirit. The system of competitive examinations engendered social mobility, enabling ambitious youth of humble origin to rise to the top by patient effort in acquiring an education. As time went on, however, the evils inherent in the examination system began to appear. The state tended to pay more attention to the administration of examinations than to the establishment of schools. For the students, the passing of the examinations became the sole objective of studying, and anything not directly related to the examinations was of little concern.

As a result, in subsequent dynasties, the content of education became narrower. The ascendancy of Confucianism as the state cult eventually crowded out other schools of thought.

In time, conservatism and formalism became dominant, and the creative spirit in education declined. The content of education became confined to Confucian classics and a narrow and rigid interpretation of these classics. The study of the classics degenerated into an uncritical memorization of texts. The situation was not unlike what was known as Ciceronianism in Western education, that is, the worship of a standardized style of writing to the neglect of thought. Young learners as well as mature scholars strove to follow prescribed styles of writing; form became more important than content.

Rise of Modern Education. This formalized system of education was obviously inadequate for the modern age. In the 19th century, China found itself in a modern world among nations with which it could not compete. Military defeats and political setbacks awakened the nation to the need of modernization. Thoughtful leaders, in the face of an exceedingly conservative and corrupt government, saw the need, for new knowledge and new ideas. Before the end of the century, new schools teaching modern subjects had appeared to challenge the old system. Selected students were sent abroad for study, and educational missions were sent to Western countries to acquire the know-how for educational reform. The first modern system of schools was adopted in 1903, and the old system of competitive examinations based on the classics and formalized styles of writing was abolished in 1905.

American education provided a strong stimulus. Chinese students studying in the United States brought back American ideas and American institutions. American missionary schools were among the most active and highly respected modern schools. With the establishment of the republic in 1912 and with a growing interest in modern democracy on the part of China's intellectuals, American influence increased rapidly. A reorganized system of schools, providing for six years of elementary education, six years of secondary education on two levels, and a 4-year college followed by graduate study, conformed with the American pattern.

Political instability in the early years of the republic forestalled a planned nationwide development of public education, but it did not prevent the influx of new ideas from abroad. As a matter of fact, World War I and subsequent years saw an intellectual awakening in China, which the Chinese call their "New Thought" movement, and which foreign observers have

PRIMARY SCHOOL in Shanghai. The poster on the wall shows a Communist soldier guarding Nanking Road.

PAN-ASIA, FROM BLACK STAR

named the "Chinese Renaissance." It was marked not only by an active interest in new ideas from abroad, but also a critical reevaluation and reinterpretation of China's past heritage in the light of modern needs and modern methods of scholarship. An offshoot of the "New Thought" movement was a student movement representing a demand on the part of youth for more freedom and for active participation in political affairs. This movement became an important factor in the subsequent development of education.

A "literary revolution" was launched. One of its specific tasks was to reform the written language and popularize a vernacular literature written in words corresponding to the spoken tongue. China's classics had been written in the "literary style." Though using the same words (characters), the literary style had a grammatical construction and form of expression very different from those of the spoken tongue, with the result that a learner could read the words without knowing their meaning. The proponents of the "literary revolution" proposed the wide adoption of vernacular writing, enabling readers to comprehend the meaning as soon as they learned the words. The publication of novels, popular writings, even scholarly books in the vernacular language made learning much easier and much more appealing. It paved the way for popular education, not only for school-age children but also for adults.

Education in Nationalist China. With the establishment of a unified government and the attainment of relative political stability, the Nationalist government inaugurated a period of long-range planning and national reconstruction. The state-supported schools, now more assured of funds and continuity, rose in national importance. Up to that time, private schools, especially those established under missionary auspices, had been the most stable schools and were generally superior to the public schools in educational standards. Now, the state schools and universities moved to the front and took their place among the best and most highly respected educational institutions of the country. A national system of public education was becoming a reality.

Notable progress was made in science studies and technical education. Engineering, medicine, agriculture, and other "practical" courses of study, as well as basic science courses in the universities, were given new emphasis. Effort was made to relate education to the pressing needs of a developing nation, particularly the need of trained personnel for the multitudinous tasks of national reconstruction.

Plans were made for adult education and the gradual liquidation of illiteracy. A program of "social education" included plans for libraries, museums, and community centers in rural and urban areas. Schools multiplied, and enrollments soared in schools of all levels.

A major achievement of the Nationalist government was the unification of the spoken language and the popularization of what was known as the *Kuo Yü* (literally, "national tongue"). It has been noted that China has always had a uniform written language. The same word, however, is pronounced differently in areas of different spoken dialects; so great are the differences in pronunciation that the spoken dialect of one area may sound like a foreign language to people in an area speaking another dialect. Dialectal diversity was not only an obstacle to national unity but also made language study more difficult.

The Nationalist government adopted effective measures to rectify this traditional shortcoming. Since more than 50% of the Chinese spoke dialects more or less similar to that of the Peiping (Peking) area (in North China), the Peiping dialect was officially declared to be the *Kuo Yü*, the standard pronunciation that the rest of the country was required to learn. In all schools, from the kindergarten up, this newly adopted national tongue (commonly known as Mandarin-Chinese) was a required subject of study and was soon made the official medium of instruction. School children in all parts of the country learned to read and speak in the national tongue.

PEKING UNIVERSITY zoology teacher (warmly dressed) uses both Roman alphabet and Chinese ideographs.

MARC RIBOUD, FROM MAGNUM

The learning of a standardized pronunciation was aided by the adoption of phonetic symbols equivalent to an alphabet. In Taiwan, these phonetic symbols continue to be used, with great success, to teach children to pronounce each written character according to the *Kuo Yü*. This unification of the spoken tongue was already making headway before World War II, but the migration of people into interior China during the war further hastened the trend. There was no doubt that the difficulties of dialectal diversity were being overcome.

In Taiwan, the government made educational progress part of the overall national plan for economic and social development. Greater emphasis was placed on investments in secondary school education and technical training programs to enable the country to achieve its economic development aims. Compulsory primary education was received by over 95% of school-age children, and the one-teacher school became a thing of the past, even in the most remote rural areas. In 1968 free compulsory education was extended to include three junior high school years. In the mid-1960's there were more than 75,000 students enrolled in 600 preschool establishments; more than 2,200,000 in 2,000 primary schools; 500,000 in 375 secondary schools; 100,000 in 120 technical schools; 4,000 in 8 teacher-training schools; and 65,000 in 35 higher educational institutions. During the same period approximately 85% of the primary school students were finishing the six-year program.

Education in Communist China. The establishment of the Communist regime was followed by an energetic effort to promote education. Adult education was given great emphasis because the new regime, by its very ideology of mass support, demanded that the entire population must be taught to understand and to support actively the policies of the state. Every available means was utilized to change the ideas and attitudes of the people in order to remake Chinese society and produce the "new type of man" needed to bring about the new society.

This required a comprehensive program that would merge formal and informal education and make no distinction between education and propaganda or indoctrination. The schools and the media of mass communication, such as the theater, the museum, the press, the radio, and demonstrations and campaigns of all kinds, would pursue the same objectives and work together under centralized direction.

New types of schools appeared: the "work-study" schools, in which students spend a part of their time in production and labor; the "spare-time" schools, attended by workers in their after-work hours and by peasants in their off-seasons; the "worker-peasant" schools, enabling adult workers and peasants to advance quickly from illiteracy to condensed forms of "secondary" and even "higher" education; schools for cadres; and many kinds of institutes and short-term, abbreviated courses designed to give training for specific tasks needed by the state and the party.

The Communists laid down three cardinal principles of education: it must serve "proletarian" politics; it must be combined with productive labor; and it must be under the direct supervision and control of the Communist party. Politics and production constitute the keynote. Political education aims to develop a strong "class consciousness," a determined effort to carry on the "class struggle," and wholehearted acceptance of Communist ideology and the party line. Education for production stresses the importance of labor and imparts the knowledge and skills needed to carry on the work of the farms, factories, mines, industries, and business enterprises. Science and technology are promoted; what is traditionally known as the humanities and the social sciences is relegated to a minor position, if not banished from the curriculum.

Taking into account the variety of schools and a nationwide network of propaganda agencies and media of mass communication, one observes a vast expansion of education in Communist China. The entire program is geared to the needs of the state and "the revolution." Since individualism is condemned by the Communist collectivist ideology, the purpose of education is not to promote individual welfare or fulfill personal ambitions; it is to serve the state, to which personal plans and desires must be subordinated. What a person does after the completion of a course of study depends on what the state and the party want him to do. Every student graduating from a school on any level is assigned a job, and he is expected to accept it without question, even if it is far removed from his home or personal interest. Further study is not approved unless it is considered necessary from the standpoint of the party-state.

It is the task of education to produce "Red experts." According to the Communist definition, an expert is one possessing the knowledge and skills needed in production and in the class struggle, and a person is "Red" when he is thoroughly committed to the Communist ideology. Education is more than knowledge; its efficacy is tested in action. The process of learning involves much more than books; participation in political activities, ranging from the collection of fertilizers to anti-imperialist campaigns, is an essential part of the experience of students. Consequently, the suspension of regular classes for political activities is not considered any interruption of schooling.

Building on the foundation laid in pre-1949 years, the Communists have pushed further the reform of the Chinese language. Continued progress has been made in the unification of the spoken tongue and the use of the vernacular language in newspapers, periodicals, posters, and propaganda materials. A new phase of the language reform is the simplification of the written characters. Characters with complicated component parts (strokes) have been replaced by abbreviated forms, which are easier to learn and to write. A phonetic alphabet, using the letters of the Roman alphabet, has been introduced to teach the pronunciation of the characters.

It is estimated that there are at least 200 million young people of elementary and secondary school age. The Peking government has not been consistent in announcing school enrollment figures. Primary school students are reported to be about 90 million, a figure representing nearly 90% of the children in the relevant age group. Only about 8 million of some 38 million in the 13–16 age bracket, however, are reportedly enrolled in the secondary schools. There are some 400 institutions of higher learning in Communist China, and each year the newly graduated number somewhere around 170,000.

THEODORE HSI-EN CHEN
University of Southern California

CHINA: The Land and Economy

5. Geography

China's location within the framework of the Eurasian landmass and the Pacific Ocean has influenced the country's history and is the basis of many of its present strategic, commercial, and climatic problems.

Traditionally, the Chinese have been preoccupied with their extensive interior boundaries and central Asian territories as well as with the nomadic Mongol and Turkic peoples along their frontiers. These peoples were threats at times, but at other times their lands were overrun by the Chinese. When the pressures of European, American, and Japanese seapower reached China's Pacific shores in recent centuries, China's attention became focused on its eastern seaboard. Today, mainland China must watch both its back door to central Asia and its front door to the Pacific, where it is confronted by the Soviet Union and the United States, respectively.

A change in China's routes of commerce paralleled the shift in focus of its strategic interests. During the Han dynasty, as early as the 2d century B. C., China used central Asia's caravan routes to trade with far-off Rome. Much later the blocking of these trade routes by the Saracens in the eastern Mediterranean and southwestern Asia brought the European traders by sea around Africa to China's shores.

It is in climate and its effects, however, that China's location has been of the greatest significance, for its vast north-south extent in the northern temperate zone gives it not only a great variety of climates, plants, and animals, but also some of the most productive agricultural regions of the earth. Northern Manchuria, a part of China lying on the latitude of southern Labrador, shares the intense cold of Siberia. But the southern extremity of China, Hainan Island, lies well within the tropics and grows coconut palms, coffee, and rubber trees. In between lie all the intermediate climates of the temperate zone. Each has its specialized effects upon vegetation and crops, providing a large array of products upon which the Chinese have used their ingenuity to create tasteful foods, artistic works, and functional objects.

Topography. In attempting to convey the complexity of China's topography, it is useful to draw imaginary lines dividing China into four quarters and to characterize each quarter in a general way. One might well characterize the northeast quarter as a region of great plains running down to shallow seas from bordering or surrounding mountains of moderate height. Through these plains run the great river systems of the Amur (Heilung), the Liao, the Hai, the Hwang (Yellow), and the Yangtze (Yangtzu). Their drainage areas support a large part of China's population, and the easy land communications in this region have led to a great measure of linguistic unity.

YANGTZE RIVER gorges, near the eastern border of Szechwan province, offer scenic beauty and a promise of hydroelectric power.

CAIO MARIO GARRUBBA, FROM RAPHO GUILLUMETTE

HWANG HO, or Yellow River, is second to the Yangtze as the country's largest river. Small sailboats dot its broad surface near Tsinan, in east-central China.

The southeast quarter, on the other hand, is a region of many steep hillsides, narrow river valleys, and small delta plains. The seacoast in this area is marked by numerous promontories and embayments. Although individual elevations do not exceed 5,000 to 6,000 feet (1,500–1,800 meters) and are generally much lower, this hilly terrain has tended to compartmentalize and isolate cultural minorities and to preserve ancient and various linguistic communities. Soils are thin and sterile on the slopes. Land communications are difficult and usually follow navigable rivers. Although pockets of fertile alluvia support dense concentrations of population, as on the Hsi River delta in and around Canton, these are separated by sparsely populated slopelands.

The southwest quarter is a region of high plateaus, the eastern half of which has been eroded by heavy rainfall and melting snows into great corrugations. These corrugations are oriented by mountain folds that run eastward and then bend southward. They present major obstacles to transport and communications between China on the one hand and Burma, India, and Tibet on the other. Elevations in the western half of these high plateaus average over 16,000 feet (4,875 meters). At these heights, most animals and plants cannot live, and there is such sparse rainfall that evaporation prevents depressions from filling up and overflowing to cut channels to the sea. It is a region rather of internal drainage, where salt lakes accumulate the minerals left by evaporation. Erosion has been minimal, and the areas between the mountain ranges have mild, rolling slopes with small elevation differences. In both the north and the south, the plateau edges have been compressed by tectonic forces into high ranges such as the Kunlun, Astin (Altyn) Tagh, Himalaya, and Karakorum. The plateau region's sparse population is localized in the eastern and southeastern section where lower heights and better-watered vegetation permit limited farming combined with the raising of horses, sheep, cattle, and yaks.

In the northwest quarter of China, an area marked by extensive desert basins draining peripheral mountain chains, a similar type of livelihood prevails, combined with intensive cultivation of intermittent oases in the basins. The Tsaidam Basin, 9,000 feet (2,750 meters) in elevation but still part of the Tibetan plateaus, is bounded by arms of the Kunlun system rising 10,000 feet (3,050 km) or more above the basin floor. In the Dzungarian and Tarim basins, at about a fourth the Tsaidam elevation, are areas that are suitable for agriculture. In these areas melting snow from the mountains has found its way to alluvial fans in the piedmont of the high Kunlun, Nan Shan, T'ien Shan, and Altai Shan systems. The fertile alluvial fans surround the vast dead hearts of the basins. To the east the basins narrow and then open out again onto the Mongolian plateaus, 3,000 to 5,000 feet (915-1,525 km) high. The Mongolian plateaus are poorly watered in the Great Gobi desert, which extends eastward toward the Great Wall of China, but grow increasingly moist toward the north and southeast. The moister areas are a nomad grazing realm, although around the Ordos Basin, along the western and northern regions of the Yellow River loop, are oases of intensively cultivated and irrigated land.

In this northwest quarter of China, climate rather than topography has been the limiting factor in communications, and the lines of piedmont oases have channeled trade routes of great antiquity, permitting the expansion of China along narrow corridors into the border mountains of Kashgar and Dzungaria and the Ili valley beyond. These great desert wastelands were not suitable for the sedentary agriculture of the Chinese, but would support the nomadic way of life of the Mongols and Turks. The great mobility of these peoples, however, made it difficult for them to be controlled, and the Chinese for their self-protection early built the Great Wall (see CHINA, GREAT WALL OF).

Climate. Although partly determined by latitude, China's climates are also affected by two opposite influences from east and west. On the one hand, the presence of the Pacific Ocean along China's eastern seaboard provides a moderating effect upon temperature extremes. On the other hand, the great central Asian spaces of western China and Mongolia, with little moisture and associated vegetation, radiate heat at a tre-

CHINA

AGRICULTURE, INDUSTRY and RESOURCES

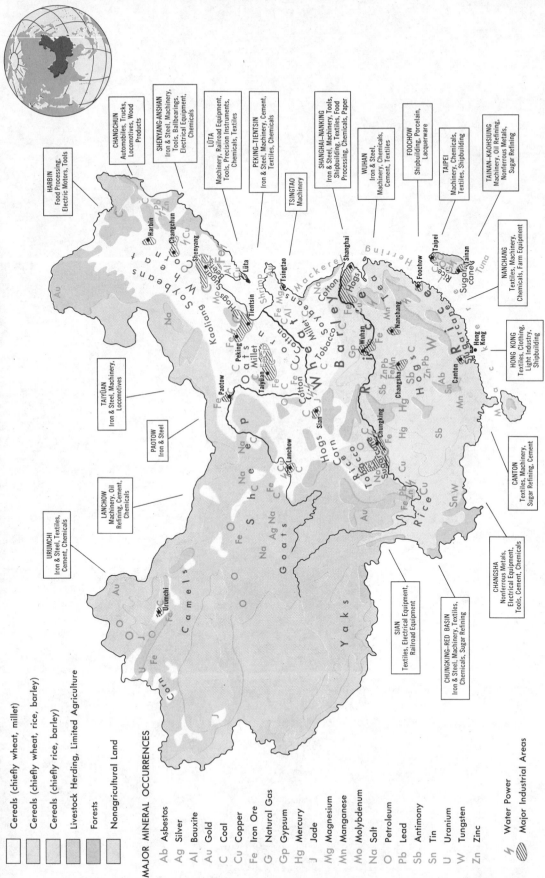

DOMINANT LAND USE

- Cereals (chiefly wheat, millet)
- Cereals (chiefly wheat, rice, barley)
- Cereals (chiefly rice, barley)
- Livestock Herding, Limited Agriculture
- Forests
- Nonagricultural Land

MAJOR MINERAL OCCURRENCES

Ab	Asbestos
Ag	Silver
Al	Bauxite
Au	Gold
C	Coal
Cu	Copper
Fe	Iron Ore
G	Natural Gas
Gp	Gypsum
Hg	Mercury
J	Jade
Mg	Magnesium
Mn	Manganese
Mo	Molybdenum
Na	Salt
O	Petroleum
Pb	Lead
Sb	Antimony
Sn	Tin
U	Uranium
W	Tungsten
Zn	Zinc

⚡ Water Power

▨ Major Industrial Areas

HARBIN
Food Processing,
Electric Motors, Tools

CHANGCHUN
Automobiles, Trucks,
Locomotives, Wood
Products

SHENYANG-ANSHAN
Iron & Steel, Machinery,
Tools, Ballbearings,
Electrical Equipment,
Chemicals

LÜTA
Machinery, Railroad Equipment,
Tools, Precision Instruments,
Chemicals, Textiles

PEKING-TIENTSIN
Iron & Steel, Machinery, Cement,
Textiles, Chemicals

TSINGTAO
Machinery

SHANGHAI-NANKING
Iron & Steel, Machinery, Tools,
Shipbuilding, Textiles, Food
Processing, Chemicals, Paper

WUHAN
Iron & Steel,
Machinery, Chemicals,
Cement, Textiles

FOOCHOW
Shipbuilding, Porcelain,
Lacquerware

TAIPEI
Machinery, Chemicals,
Textiles, Shipbuilding

TAINAN-KAOHSIUNG
Machinery, Oil Refining,
Nonferrous Metals,
Sugar Refining

NANCHANG
Textiles, Machinery,
Chemicals, Farm Equipment

HONG KONG
Textiles, Clothing,
Light Industry,
Shipbuilding

CANTON
Textiles, Machinery,
Sugar Refining, Cement

CHANGSHA
Nonferrous Metals,
Electrical Equipment,
Tools, Cement, Chemicals

CHUNGKING-RED BASIN
Iron & Steel, Machinery, Textiles,
Chemicals, Sugar Refining

SIAN
Textiles, Electrical Equipment,
Railroad Equipment

LANCHOW
Machinery, Oil
Refining, Cement,
Chemicals

PAOTOW
Iron & Steel

TAIYÜAN
Iron & Steel, Machinery,
Locomotives

URUMCHI
Iron & Steel, Textiles,
Cement, Chemicals

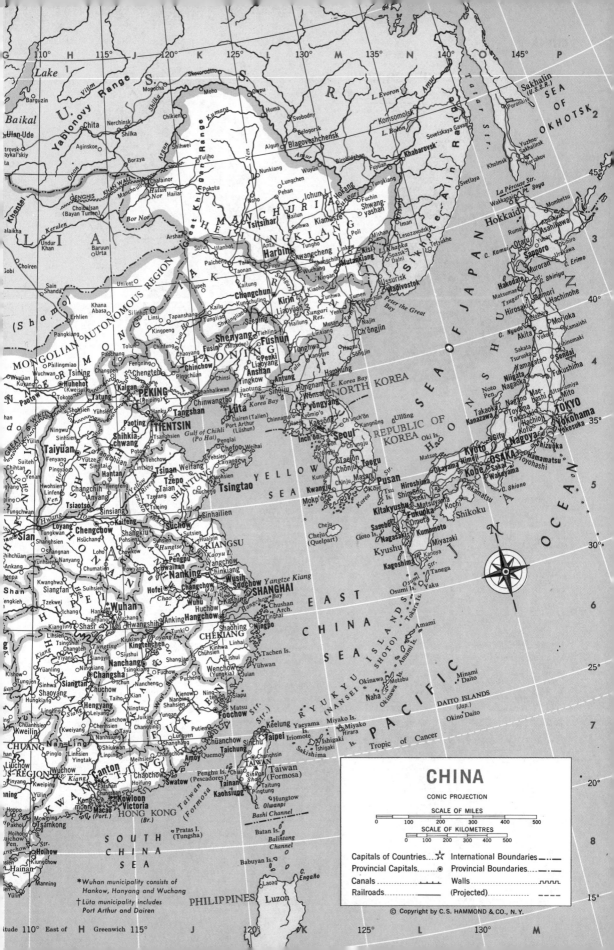

TOPOGRAPHY

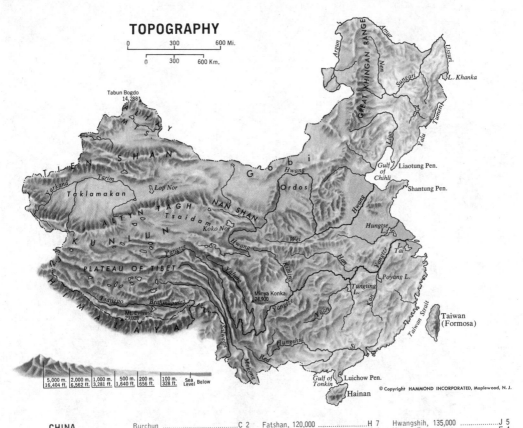

© Copyright HAMMOND INCORPORATED, Maplewood, N.J.

5,000 m. / 16,404 ft. | 2,000 m. / 6,562 ft. | 1,000 m. / 3,281 ft. | 500 m. / 1,640 ft. | 200 m. / 656 ft. | 100 m. / 328 ft. | Sea Level | Below

CHINA
Total Population, 800,292,000

INTERNAL DIVISIONS

Anhwei, 30,663,000 ....J 5
Chekiang, 22,865,747 ....J 6
Fukien, 13,142,721 ....J 6
Heilungkiang, 11,897,309 ....L 2
Honan, 44,214,594 ....H 5
Hopei, 43,348,000 ....J 4
Hunan, 33,226,954 ....H 6
Hupei, 27,789,693 ....H 5
Inner Mongolian Aut. Region,
  9,200,000 ....G 3
Kansu, 12,928,000 ....F 4
Kiangsi, 16,772,865 ....J 6
Kiangsu, 47,137,000 ....K 5
Kirin, 11,290,073 ....L 3
Kwangsi Chuang Aut. Region,
  17,591,000 ....G 7
Kwangtung, 36,740,000 ....H 7
Kweichow, 15,037,310 ....G 6
Liaoning, 20,566,000 ....K 3
Ningsia Hui Aut. Region,
  1,000,000 ....G 4
Shansi, 14,314,485 ....H 4
Shantung, 48,876,548 ....J 4
Shensi, 15,881,281 ....G 5
Sinkiang-Uigur Aut. Region,
  4,873,608 ....B 3
Szechwan, 65,685,063 ....F 5
Taiwan, 12,993,000 ....K 7
Tibet Aut. Region,
  1,270,000 ....C 5
Tsinghai, 1,676,534 ....E 4
Yünnan, 17,472,737 ....F 7

CITIES and TOWNS

Aigun ....L 1
Aihsien ....G 8
Amoy, 308,000 ....J 7
Ankang ....G 5
Anking, 129,000 ....J 5
Anshan, 833,000 ....K 3
Anshun, 40,000 ....G 6
Antung, 370,000 ....K 3
Anyang, 153,000 ....H 4
Aqsu ....B 3
Atushi, 5,000 ....A 4
Barkhatu ....B 4
Barkol ....D 3
Batang ....E 6
Bulak ....B 2

Burchun ....C 2
Canton, 1,867,000 ....H 7
Chalainor ....J 2
Chamdo ....E 5
Changchih, 180,000 ....H 4
Changchow, Kiangsu, 300,000 ....J 5
Changchow, Kwangtung, 81,200 ....J 7
Changchun, 988,000 ....K 3
Changpeh ....H 3
Changsha, 709,000 ....H 6
Changteh, 94,800 ....H 6
Changting ....J 6
Changyeh, 45,000 ....E 4
Chaochow, 101,000 ....J 7
Chaotung, 50,000 ....F 6
Chaoyang, 30,000 ....J 3
Charkhliq ....C 4
Chefoo, 140,000 ....K 4
Chendo ....E 5
Chengan ....G 6
Chengchow, 785,000 ....H 5
Chengkiang ....F 7
Chengteh, 120,000 ....J 3
Chengtu, 1,135,000 ....F 5
Chenhsien ....H 6
Chiai, 191,074 ....K 7
Chiehmo (Cherchen) ....C 4
Chihfeng, 49,000 ....J 3
Chihshui ....G 6
Chihtan ....G 4
Chikien ....K 1
Chimai ....F 5
Chinchow, 400,000 ....J 3
Chinkiang, 190,000 ....K 5
Chinsi, 45,000 ....K 3
Chinwangtao, 210,000 ....K 4
Chira ....B 4
Chomo Dzong ....D 6
Chowkow, 85,500 ....J 5
Chüanchow, 110,000 ....J 7
Chüanhsien ....G 6
Chuchow, 190,000 ....H 6
Chuguchak ....B 2
Chumatien, 45,000 ....H 5
Chunghsin ....K 7
Chungking, 2,165,000 ....G 6
Chungning ....G 4
Chungshan, 93,000 ....H 7
Chungtien ....E 6
Chushul ....D 6
Dairen (included in Lüta),
  766,400 ....K 4
Denchin ....E 5
Ed Dzong ....D 5
Erhlien ....H 3

Fatshan, 120,000 ....H 7
Fengfeng, 45,000 ....H 4
Fenghsien ....G 5
Fengkieh ....G 5
Fengning ....J 3
Fenyang, 25,000 ....H 4
Foochow, 623,000 ....J 6
Fowyang, 75,000 ....M 2
Fuchin ....J 6
Fuchow, 45,000 ....C 2
Fuhai ....K 2
Fularki ....K 2
Fushun, 1,019,000 ....K 3
Fusin, 290,000 ....K 3
Fuyü, 62,969 ....L 2
Fuyüan ....M 2
Gartok ....B 5
Golmo ....D 4
Gulo Gomba ....B 5
Gyangtse ....C 6
Gyatsa Dzong ....D 6
Hailar, 60,000 ....J 2
Hailun ....L 2
Hailung, 20,000 ....L 3
Hanchung, 70,000 ....G 5
Hangchow, 794,000 ....J 5
Hankow (incl. in Wuhan),
  750,000 ....H 5
Hanku, 75,000 ....J 4
Hantan, 380,000 ....H 4
Hanyang (incl. in Wuhan) ..H 5
Harbin, 1,595,000 ....L 2
Heiho ....D 5
Hengyang, 240,000 ....H 6
Hingi ....G 6
Hochih ....G 7
Hochwan, 75,000 ....G 5
Hofei, 360,000 ....J 5
Hofeng ....C 2
Hoifung ....J 7
Hoihow, 402,000 ....H 4
Hokang, 200,000 ....M 2
Hoppo, 80,000 ....G 7
Hotien (Khotan) ....A 4
Hsüchang, 58,000 ....H 5
Huaiyin, 77,000 ....J 5
Huchow, 120,000 ....J 5
Huhehot, 320,000 ....H 3
Huma ....L 1
Hunchun, 13,246 ....M 3
Hungkiang, 45,000 ....H 6
Hwainan, 280,000 ....J 5
Hwangchung ....F 4
Hwanghoyen ....E 4
Hwangling ....G 4

Hwangshih, 135,000 ....J 5
Hwangyüan ....F 4
Hweili ....F 6
Hwohsien ....H 4
Ichang, 81,000 ....H 5
Ichun, Heilungkiang, 200,000 ...L 2
Ichun, Kiangsi ....H 6
Ihsien ....K 3
Iliang ....F 7
Ining (Kuldja), 85,000 ....B 3
Ipin, 190,000 ....F 6
Jyekundo ....E 5
Kaifeng, 318,000 ....H 5
Kalgan, 480,000 ....J 3
Kanchow, 98,600 ....H 6
Kangting ....F 6
Kaohsiung, 623,869 ....J 7
Kaotai ....E 4
Karamai, 43,000 ....B 2
Kashgar, 100,000 ....A 4
Kashing, 132,000 ....K 5
Keelung, 285,716 ....K 6
Khabakhe ....C 2
Khana Abasa ....H 3
Khotan ....A 4
Kiamusze, 232,000 ....L 2
Kian, 52,800 ....J 6
Kiangling ....H 5
Kiaoho ....L 3
Kiaohsien ....K 4
Kienko ....G 5
Kienshui ....F 7
Kingku ....F 7
Kingpeng ....J 3
Kingtehchen, 266,000 ....J 6
Kingyang ....G 4
Kinhwa, 46,200 ....J 6
Kinta ....E 3
Kirin, 583,000 ....L 3
Kishow ....G 6
Kisi, 253,000 ....M 2
Kitai ....C 3
Kiuchüan, 50,000 ....E 4
Kiukiang, 64,600 ....J 6
Kiungchow ....H 8
Kokiu, 180,000 ....F 7
Kongmoon, 110,000 ....H 7
Kulang ....F 4
Kuldja, 85,000 ....B 3
Kumyan ....G 8
Kungchuling, 60,000 ....K 3
Kungyang ....F 6
Kunming, 900,000 ....F 7
Kurla ....C 3
Kütsing ....F 7
Kuyang ....G 3

*City and suburbs.

CHINA: Total pop. (mainland)—1967 off. est.; Taiwan total pop., cap. & cities (over 250,000)—1967 off. est.; other cities (Taiwan)—1956 final census; cities (mainland)—1958 off. est. & 1953 final census. **HONG KONG:** Total pop.—1969 off. est.; other pops—1966 census. **MACAO:** Total pop.—1965 off. est.; other pops—1960 final census.

mendous rate in winter, resulting in the development of high barometric pressures as heavy cold air settles over the land. In summer, the barren surfaces absorb heat easily during the hours of sunshine, bringing extraordinarily high temperatures, with expanded air rising buoyantly to create low barometric pressures. Such extremes of "continentality" contrast with the moderate and more gradual temperature changes occurring over the Pacific surface, and so air pressures in the interior are usually opposite to those prevailing in the coastal region. Thus, when winter high pressure develops in western China and Mongolia, the relative pressure over the Pacific is lower, and cold, dry air flows from the interior to the sea, bringing the onset of a country-wide dry season. When summer heat develops deep "troughs" of low pressure in the interior, the cooler ocean atmosphere takes on a relatively higher pressure. Air charged with ocean moisture thus moves onshore toward the centers of low pressures in the Gobi and Sinkiang deserts, bringing summer rains to the eastern parts of China over which it passes.

There is a general reversal of dominant winds between summer and winter, accompanied by the respective seasons of rainfall and drought. Summer winds are from the east and south; winter winds from the north and northwest. It is this seasonal reversal of prevailing winds that is referred to as the "monsoon wind system." The East Asia or China monsoons are most noteworthy for the long, cold, dry, and, in North China, often dusty winters. It is the moist, summer half of the year, however, that provides the rainfall that is essential to China's agriculture.

Although the summer brings onshore winds charged with moisture over eastern China, the condensation of this moisture into rainfall requires further "mechanisms." Mountain ranges may compel moist oncoming air to yield rains. Updrafts from overheated basins boxed in by mountains may bring on thunderstorms. Finally, cooler air masses hugging the land surface may force more buoyant oncoming moist air to rise and condense into rains. The clash of air masses with different temperature characteristics is the result of slow-moving cyclonic whirls of air many hundreds of miles in diameter, creating "fronts" of cloudiness and rainfall over wide areas. Although these "extra-tropical" storms affect most parts of China, their paths most frequently cross the central and northern portions. Their fluctuating paths are responsible for much of the variations in rainfall and temperature that occur in these regions. The success of much of China's yearly harvest depends upon the rainfall produced by these storms.

In China's southeast coastal regions, hurricanes known as typhoons may travel westward from the central Pacific tropics. Many of them follow the northward-curving route of the warm, moist air accompanying the Japan Current and passing over Taiwan and Okinawa to Japan. Others reach coastal mainland China, bringing deluges of rain that create floods and producing destructive winds that push "storm tides" over coastal embankments and low-lying fields, inundating them with salt water and temporarily destroying their fertility. The occurrence of

HIMALAYA MOUNTAINS of Tibet seen from the summit of Mt. Everest, highest peak in the world, on the Tibet-Nepal border. Rongbuk Glacier is in the center.

NATIONAL GEOGRAPHIC SOCIETY, FROM UPI

typhoons is usually limited to the region between Shanghai and Hainan Island. They account for an important part of the annual rainfall in this area, and the windward slopes of mountains in this part of China are especially wet.

Although the rainfall pattern over China exhibits a reduction in annual amount as one progresses from the coast inland and from south to north and northwest, local topographic features often affect local rainfall patterns. High mountains may not prevent buoyant air from rising over them, but they often prevent the passage of heavy cold air. They may, indeed, divert the flow of either warm or cold air. Certain major mountains of China are, in effect, climatic divides or boundaries, restricting much of the moisture to the windward slopes and shutting off severe cold waves from leeward regions.

The Himalaya mountains and other high east-west ranges of southwest China and Tibet restrict the entry of moisture from the Indian Ocean region into northwest China. The Great Hsingan and East Manchurian mountain chains and the Taihang range in eastern Shansi tend to limit the entry of moisture into China from the Pacific. Most important as a climatic divide between North and South China proper, however, is the Tsinling (Chinling) range, an eastward extension of the Kunlun system. Its 10,000 to 12,000-foot (3,050–3,650-meter) ridges in southern Shensi, together with lower extensions in the Tapieh Shan of Hupeh, make the annual rainfall north of the mountains about 25 inches (640 cm) lower than that south of the mountains. Farther south, the Nanling range is a lower and less significant climatic boundary separating the tropical provinces of Kwangtung and Kwangsi from the Yangtze valley.

The lengths of China's growing seasons, assuming that rainfall is plentiful, depend largely upon latitude and altitude. South of the Tsinling, in the Szechwan basin, the growing season is virtually year round. North of this range, crops grow only from one third to two thirds of the year. Where rainfall is abundant, a considerable variability in the annual amount of rainfall is not critical. But where the average annual amount for the region is already marginal, as in northern Shensi and Shansi, any decrease from the norm augments the risk of crop failure. Hence, northwest China and parts of north China are high-risk areas for agriculture, although soils may be relatively rich in mineral and organic nutrients for plants.

Plant Life. China has the greatest variety of flora of any region of comparable size and situation in the world. Over 15,000 species of seed plants have been identified for China. North American species north of Mexico number only 165 genera of broad-leaf trees compared with China's 260, and Europe has far fewer than North America. The introduction of Chinese flora into Europe, North America, and other regions has been extensive.

Millennia of exploitation and destruction through burning and clearing in shifting agriculture in the southern mountain lands have reduced China's commercial forests to 5% of its area, one of the poorest in the world for an area of its size. Prime forests remain only in China proper's frontier extremities in northern Manchuria and in western Szechwan and Yünnan. Other exceptions are the planted forests

of Chekiang and Fukien, the still extensive forests of Taiwan, and recently reforested areas, much of them in wind-shelter belts. In the rest of China, areas once in forests now have long been without seedstock and must be planted to restock. Other areas once in forests are now in permanent cultivation.

Uncultivated slopelands in South China are covered for the most part with coarse ferns and grasses unpalatable to domestic livestock and cut from time to time as household fuel. In much of North and Northwest China, however, rainfall is too low to support a forest cover where the land is uncultivated. There is some doubt that there ever was a natural forest covering the loess plateaus in Shansi, Shensi, and Kansu. Forest areas give way to grassland in the southwestern part of Manchuria and in the Mongolian fringelands, where grazing of domestic livestock takes the place of sedentary agriculture, though much of the best grasslands have been invaded by the farmer in recent times. Because of higher rainfall and snowfall in the east and lower evaporation in the north, large areas of the East Manchurian Mountains and the Great and Lesser Hsingan Mountains are covered by natural forests. Much was exploited during the Japanese occupation of Manchuria, and accelerated cutting has been going on since the Communist regime took over.

Animal Life. The fauna of China is widespread and varied, though a great proportion of the larger mammals are found in the north and west. There are several species of deer, among which the roe, musk, and sika have been hunted in the mountains of northern Shansi and Inner Mongolia. Wapiti and antelope, as well as

MARC RIBOUD, FROM MAGNUM

COLLECTIVE FARM near Chungking. Communes were set up on a grand scale in 1957–1958 but failed to improve farm output until divided into smaller units in 1962.

the wild sheep, wild ass, and wild boar, also are hunted. North China and Manchuria are the home of many fur-bearing animals of commercial importance. Among these are the badger, sable, marten, mink, weasel, wolverine, otter, fox, several kinds of squirrels, the marmot, and the raccoon dog. The raccoon dog resembles but is slightly smaller than the American raccoon and produces a fur called on the market Chinese coon. It is said that in normal times more fox skins are shipped from the port of Tientsin than from any other port in the world. Bears in China include the Tibetan black bear, the Manchurian black bear and grizzly, and the giant panda, found in Kansu, Tibet, and Szechwan. Other carnivora are the tiger, manul (a small wildcat), leopard, and wolf. There are several kinds of monkeys.

Fully one half of all the species of mammals in China are rodents. Many varieties of rats, mice, chipmunks, gophers, squirrels, and hares abound. Insectivora are few in North China because of its dry climate, but Central and West China are the habitat of many moles, hedgehogs, and shrews. Amphibia are represented by several species of toads and frogs, some like those of Europe. There are many species of snakes in China, most of them nonpoisonous. Among the venomous species is the cobra, which differs slightly from the Indian variety. Turtles and tortoises are well represented. The Chinese alligator, smaller than its congener in the Western Hemisphere, rarely reaches more than 6 feet (1.8 meters) in length.

An important item in the diet of many Chinese is fish. Shad, perch, bass, sturgeon, a variety called perch pike, and loach, found in mountain streams, are said to be the most edible, but many other kinds are used for food. Carp is raised in ponds in large numbers. Marine fishes are the major source of China's fish food.

China is particularly rich in birds. Of the birds of prey, several kinds of owls, hawks, falcons, and eagles abound. The vulture, buzzard, and carrion crow represent the scavengers. There are several varieties of pheasants, some of which are very beautiful. Other game birds are the partridge, quail, plover, and woodcock. Water birds are particularly numerous: one of them, the cormorant, has been domesticated and trained to catch fish. Other water birds are ducks, pelicans, geese, herons, bitterns, cranes, storks, gulls, terns, and ibis. Representative of the songbirds are the thrush, bulbul, and lark. There are several species of doves and pigeons, and woodpeckers, swifts, nightjars, ravens, starlings, finches, sparrows, swallows, martins, wrens, orioles, buntings, and bramblings are all represented.

Of the domesticated animals of China produced for food, those raised in large numbers include poultry, cattle, pigs, sheep, and goats. Cattle are raised chiefly in Inner Mongolia, Sinkiang, Chinghai, and Tibet. Draft animals in North China include camels, donkeys, mules, oxen, and, to a lesser extent, horses. In the far north, however, the Mongolian horse is bred in rather large numbers. In the mountains of the southwest, Chinese ponies, little larger than the Shetland, are raised for difficult transportation work. The water buffalo is used in South China for plowing. In Tibet the yak and its hybrid with the cow are economically important animals raised principally for food.

Mineral Wealth and Power Base. Influencing Chinese economic and cultural development are the fuels, water power, metallic ores, and nonmetallic minerals that provide the basis for political power and standards of living in the modern world. The distribution of these, in turn, is governed by geologic structures and occurrences of various rock types.

Vast areas of present-day China were swampland or were under sea water in ancient geologic times. Sedimentation buried former accumulated organic matter and peats, as well as organic reefs on the sea floor. Thicknesses of many miles of sediments carbonized organic material into lignite, bituminous coals, or anthracite, or squeezed out buried oil droplets into sandstones and shale to form oil shale and petroleum deposits. Coal-rich and oil-rich regions of China, thus, are the sedimentary basins and plains such as Szechwan, Dzungaria, Tsaidam, Tarim, and Manchuria, as well as other sedimentary regions warped into mountains and plateaus, such as Shansi and Shensi. It is in the more accessible of these regions that China today is building its large industrial complexes based upon coal power and petroleum.

Metal ores, however, were concentrated into deposits through different processes far in the depths of the earth under tremendous pressure, producing molten rocks and allowing metallic elements to sort themselves out. Such pressures frequently compressed horizontal strata into mountain folds. Long aeons of erosion removed the overlying mantle to expose the metal ores, particularly in mountain flanks. Metalliferous ores are found in many of China's mountainous regions such as the Great Hsingan, where gold is extracted, and the East Manchurian Mountains, where great masses of rich iron ores, copper, molybdenum, and other metals are mined. Large iron ore, uranium, and copper reserves are found along the northern slopes of the Tien Shan in Sinkiang. Gold is found in the Altai; iron in the hills of Hupeh, Szechwan, Fukien, and Anhwei; tungsten in the Nan Shan slopes of southern Kiangsi; antimony in the western hills of Hunan; nonferrous metals such as silver, lead, zinc, and copper in the southwestern borderlands of China; mercury in Kweichow's Talou Mountains; and tin throughout the southern provinces of China, but especially in southern Yünnan.

China has abundant coal fuels and is moderately to well supplied in petroleum and oil shale, providing a sound industrial base. Added to these is the potential and developed water power from numerous swift-dropping rivers, many with large reservoir spaces upstream. When looked at as a whole, however, a large part of this potential hydropower is situated badly—in the highlands of southwestern China and eastern Tibet, far away from the industrial cities most needing the power. Nevertheless, a large potential and some 4 to 5 million kw capacity of developed hydroelectric power are found in China's populous eastern half on such rivers as the Amur, Yalu, and Sungari in Manchuria, the central Yellow river gorgelands, the Yangtze river gorgelands (mostly in Szechwan), the Chientang, Ou, Min, and Hsi in southeastern China, and on Taiwan.

The basis for large-scale modern industrial development is present in China's known resources. Estimates of their extent are constantly being revised upward, and new geological surveys and exploration are continually adding to China's knowledge of its natural resource endowment and environment.

HEROLD J. WIENS, *University of Hawaii*

Bibliography

Cressey, George B., *Land of the 500 Million* (New York 1955).
Ginsburg, Norton, and others, *The Pattern of Asia* (Englewood Cliffs, N. J., 1958).
Pearcy, G. Etzel, *Geographic Regions of Asia: South and East* (Washington 1964).
Shabad, Theodore, *China's Changing Map* (New York 1956).
Shen, T. H., *Agricultural Resources of China* (Ithaca, N. Y., 1951).
Tregear, Thomas Refoy, *A Geography of China* (Chicago 1965).

6. Economy

To a man such as Marco Polo, the China of seven centuries ago appeared to be a land of great wealth. In comparison with Europe during the Middle Ages, China's cities were larger and

TAIWAN'S FARMS form an abstract pattern from the air. Nearly 90 percent of the farms are individually owned.

BIRNBACK

its upper classes were richer. But this apparent prosperity was only a superficial veneer, which was supported by the toil of tens of millions of peasant farmers. By modern standards China was a poor, underdeveloped country in Marco Polo's time, and it remains so today.

The industrial revolution that brought so much prosperity to Europe and America, and then to Japan, has only begun to raise China out of poverty. Since a century ago, when Chinese scholars and statesmen began to realize that the old ways could not meet the Western challenge, China's industrialization and economic growth have been constantly interrupted by international and civil war and other political upheavals.

COMMUNIST CHINA

Agriculture. Throughout recorded history, agriculture has been the key sector in China's economy. Farmers provided the surplus that supported Chinese art and scholarship in the past, and still provide the much larger surplus required by modern industrialization. Not only must the 20th century Chinese farmer feed himself, he must also produce enough to feed the growing working class in the cities. In addition, most of China's foreign exchange earnings come from the export of agricultural products, without which there could be no imports of machinery, and hence no industrialization.

From the early 15th century, China's population, freed from the repeated devastations—war, drought, and famine—of the previous two centuries, began to increase. There were fewer than 100 million people in China in 1400, but by 1800 there were 400 million, and by 1953 nearly 600 million. Whereas in 1400 there were great unsettled areas that could be brought under cultivation, by 1900 only Manchuria still had sizeable areas of empty land, and by the 1950's even Manchuria was well settled. To be sure, large regions of China were sparsely populated, but these were areas of high mountains, as in Tibet, or areas without water, as in the dry northwest in Sinkiang and in the Gobi Desert.

Even when the land was very densely populated, it was still possible within the context of the traditional farming system to increase output. Numerous irrigation schemes were promoted by both government officials and private individuals. In some areas more labor made it possible to grow two crops of rice a year, or one crop of rice followed by winter wheat. New and better seeds occasionally appeared or were brought to China from nearby foreign lands. By the 20th century these methods, too, had reached a point of sharply diminishing returns. Even at their best they were only able to raise farm output by one half of 1% a year.

Thus, when the Communists took over the Chinese mainland in 1949, the agricultural sector was nearly stagnant. This sector not only had to meet traditional consumption needs, but in addition had to support increased industrialization and a population that was growing by more than 2% a year. As in the rest of the world in the mid-20th century, public health conditions in China had caused a population explosion that was fast outstripping the agricultural sector's ability to provide food.

Before the winter of 1955 Chinese Communist agricultural policies were designed first, to consolidate the political power of the Communist party and second, to recover farm output from low Chinese-Japanese wartime (1937–1945) levels. The first objective was achieved by land reform carried out by the Communists as soon as they had secured a particular area. Before 1949 a little less than half of China's land had been owned by absentee landlords who rented out the land. All of this land was confiscated in the late 1940's and early 1950's and was redistributed to peasants, who previously had had little or no land of their own.

Recovery of farm output in this period was achieved mainly by the restoration of peace and order. In addition, special efforts were undertaken to increase the output of cash crops that had been particularly hard hit by war. The price of cotton was raised so that the textile mills of Shanghai and Tientsin could continue to meet China's clothing needs. Tea, silk, tobacco, and other crops were also stimulated by high prices and other incentives.

EMIL SCHULTHESS, FROM BLACK STAR

GAGGLE OF GEESE on a road in South China. Agriculture remains the key factor in China's economy.

Cooperatives and Communes: 1955–1960. In the winter of 1955–1956, Mao Tse-tung made a dramatic move to consolidate further his and the party's political power and to raise agricultural output by collectivizing Chinese agriculture. Virtually all of China's rural population was organized into cooperatives of 100 to 300 families each. Each family retained its house and a small plot of land, equivalent on the average to 5% of his previous holdings. All other land was owned and farmed by the cooperative collectively.

This new organization, it was believed, could raise farm output in several ways. New techniques, for example, could be quickly introduced because it was no longer necessary to persuade a conservative peasantry that they were desirable. Only the head of the cooperative had to be persuaded or directed. Even more important, the government felt, the existence of cooperatives would make it possible to mobilize large amounts of labor for constructing roads and irrigation works. It was recognized that there might be incentive problems caused by the fact that the individual farmer was no longer working for himself and his family alone. But these problems, it was hoped, could be overcome by an elaborate system of work incentives, such as paying a worker on the basis of the difficulty of the job he was doing, how hard he worked, and so on.

The anticipated rise in output, however, did not occur in 1956 or 1957. By 1957, in fact, the slow pace of agricultural development had become a drag on the rest of the economy. It was not that the cadres in charge of the new cooperatives failed to introduce new techniques. They did so, but in the process discovered that the traditional system was more sophisticated than they realized and the new techniques were minor improvements at best. Labor corvees were organized, but the results failed to live up to expectations. Furthermore, the incentive problem proved to be more intractable than was at first realized, and in late 1957 the government began to take steps to improve management.

In late 1957 there was a radical shift in the political climate within China that led to a quick reversal of the conservative policies of 1957. By the middle of 1958, it was believed that farm output could be successfully raised by means of an even more radical reorganization of rural society. The result was the formation of the "rural people's communes" in the latter half of 1958. The commune's principal feature was its size, 4,000–5,000 families as against 200 in the old cooperatives. Many Communists felt that the commune was a major step toward the establishment of a true Communist state, where people are paid according to their needs rather than according to how productively they work. Thus many of the incentive features built into the cooperatives were diluted or abandoned during the initial stages of the communes.

The great expectation about the communes was that they could mobilize vast amounts of labor that would transform the Chinese countryside almost overnight. Communal mess halls were set up so that even the women, freed from household chores, could join more fully in the effort. And there was, in fact, a vast outpouring of effort in 1958 and 1959, but there was little concern about whether the effort was productive or not. People were put to work digging irrigation ditches when workers were badly needed for the harvest.

ROLLING MILL in the steel center at Anshan, in Northeast China, the country's chief industrial region.

In the early stages of the commune movement the government and party had also taken steps to abolish the small, private plots that the farmers had been allowed to retain and to close the limited free market on which goods produced individually could be sold. These small plots, however, were the main source of the nation's vegetables and pork, as well as a number of lesser items. When the communes tried to produce the same items collectively, the result was a drop in output. The cadres in charge of the communes were too busy working on various construction projects and attempting to raise grain output to be bothered with lesser commodities such as vegetables. As early as 1959 it was becoming apparent that this situation would have to be rectified. In that year free markets began to be reopened, and a year or two later the small private plots were reestablished. In addition, farmers were allowed to keep the output from these plots for personal consumption and for sale on the free market.

By late 1959 it had become increasingly clear that something more basic was wrong with agriculture than the poor showing of a few products, such as vegetables and pork. Part of the crop failure was caused by poor weather. The 1959 fall harvest of grain was a poor one, but in spite of this the government continued to push its overall program and kept the communes intact. Throughout 1960 the situation failed to improve. Droughts continued, insect and animal diseases grew, and the weather remained poor until 1962. According to what the Chinese have told foreign visitors, grain output in 1960 was only 150 million tons, a decrease from the 185 million tons produced in 1957, which meant a drop of 20%. In 1961 it had increased to only 162 million tons.

Although the number who died as a direct result of inadequate grain supplies was small, the situation nevertheless was serious. In the latter part of 1960 and throughout 1961 the commune system was overhauled and reorganized almost out of existence, although the communes were never actually abandoned. Instead, more of their key functions were transferred to lower-level units. By early 1962, for example, most control over agricultural output had passed into the hands of a small "production team" of 60 to 80 families. Grain output and certain other activities were still handled collectively, but only within this small unit. There was no sharing of successes or failures with thousands of other families. Farm organization had in effect reverted to a level comparable in size to the first stages of collectivization in the winter of 1955.

The agricultural crisis of the years 1959–1961 also brought home to the government in Peking the realization that farm output could not be raised by organizational means alone. The first and second 5-year plans had given primary emphasis to heavy industry, with transportation and communications next, and agriculture, forestry, and water conservation third. Peking saw that, to some degree, resources for investment would have to be shifted away from heavy industries, such as machinery and steel, to industries that could help raise agricultural productivity. More rural electrification and the production of large numbers of irrigation pumps and insecticides were necessary, but the most important need was the development of a chemical fertilizer industry. The Chinese had begun building a chemical fertilizer industry, but the effort was not given a top priority until after the 1959–1961 crisis.

Beginning in 1961, Peking also started to import 5 to 6 million tons of grain a year from Australia, Canada, and France. These imports, although small relative to total Chinese grain output, allowed the government to reduce grain quotas and still feed the increased urban population. The reduced quotas in turn increased farmer incentives to raise output, since they knew that all the surplus they produced would not automatically be taken away from them.

The basic rural organizations and policies of 1962 continued in effect. Between 1962 and 1966, grain production rose to about 200 million tons a year, which in per capita terms was almost back to the levels of 1957. Until a much larger agricultural surplus was created, however, the pace of growth in farm output continued to limit the rate of growth in the rest of the economy.

Industrialization. If the level of farm output per capita has failed to change much during the past century, the same situation has not prevailed in modern industry in China. By 1967, China possessed a large industrial sector in absolute terms, one comparable in size to that of Japan a decade or so earlier. In per capita terms, Chinese industry was still very small and much like that of many other underdeveloped nations.

Chinese industrial development got off to a slow start in the last decades of the 19th century. A few Chinese officials encouraged the development of several arsenals, the China Merchants Steamship Company, and a few textile mills. Because of inadequate funds and constant government interference, these enterprises were mismanaged and barely solvent. By the beginning of the 20th century, however, private Chinese entrepreneurs had begun to build a number of textile and flour mills together with a variety of other light consumer-oriented industries. They were joined by an increasing number of Japanese firms, and throughout this period, and until the 1930's, the number and size of Chinese and foreign firms in China grew at about the same pace.

There was some heavy industry in China during this time, but most of China's steel and machinery development before 1949 took place in Manchuria under the aegis of the Japanese. When the Soviet Union briefly occupied Manchuria at the end of World War II, they dismantled much of this equipment and took it home with them. Thus, in 1949 the Communists inherited a fairly substantial light industrial base concentrated in such cities as Shanghai and Tientsin and a gutted heavy industrial establishment in Manchuria.

The task of rehabilitating Chinese industry was begun immediately and continued in spite of China's entry into the Korean War in late 1950. By 1952 the process of recovery had been completed, and the country was ready to launch new industrial development.

China's first 5-year plan, for the years 1953–1957, was patterned on the early 5-year plans of the Soviet Union. The core of industrial development was to be heavy industry, particularly steel and machine tools. The growth of these industries, it was hoped, would not only make for more rapid overall economic growth, but would also provide a base for increasing military power. Investment in industries and sectors that did not contribute directly to machinery and steel was kept to a minimum.

Because heavy industrial firms were more complex than those of light industry and because China's experience with such enterprises was limited, the government had to rely heavily on Soviet and East European technicians, thousands of whom came to China in this period. But the funds that paid for this industrial program came primarily from domestic resources. The Chinese Communist government used its great political power to introduce a sharp rise in taxes. As a result of these heavy taxes China's rate of gross investment was raised to over 20% of the country's national product, a rate matched or exceeded only by the much richer and more developed nations of Europe, America, and Japan.

By 1957, China's heavy industrial establishment had grown to 3½ times the level of 1952, or at a rate of nearly 30% per year, a remarkable performance if viewed in isolation. Even if the slower-growing consumer and handicraft industrial output figures are included, Chinese industry during the first 5-year plan nearly doubled in size. But it was also becoming increasingly apparent by 1957 that this rate of growth in industry could not be sustained using the methods previously followed. As already indicated, the slow pace of agriculture was beginning to hold back the entire economy.

In early 1958, even before the communes began to be set up in rural areas, there was a great surge in industrial activity. The second 5-year plan (1958–1962), originally drawn up for 1958 was abandoned and replaced by increasingly grandiose schemes. China was going to industrialize overnight.

The "Great Leap Forward" in industry, as the movement in 1958–1959 was called, had two major objectives. On the one hand, large-scale modern factories were to be built in even greater numbers while, on the other, small-scale handicraft firms were also to get a big push. This two pronged development was termed "walking on two legs." In a country such as China, with large supplies of labor and little capital, the constructive application of small-scale labor-using methods, where possible, is a way of saving capital. But in China in 1958, small-scale operations were pushed indiscriminately. Hundreds of thousands of backyard iron furnaces, for example, were set up across the country taking men and students away from more productive activities to make iron of such low quality that it was of little use. At the same time, large-scale enterprises were ordered to produce more and more goods without regard to whether the items produced were needed or not.

By 1960 output in most sectors had been raised enormously, but in such an uncoordinated way that further growth was becoming increasingly difficult. In the middle of 1960 the Soviet Union, in an attempt to bring China in line behind Soviet political leadership, withdrew all its technicians. Factories dependent on this technical support could no longer be built or their production easily sustained. Finally, in 1960, the effects of the agricultural crisis were being increasingly felt. Industries dependent on the raw materials of agriculture were operating well below capacity, and by early 1961, the "Great Leap Forward" in industry also had collapsed. The lack of statistics for this period makes it impossible to estimate precisely the magnitude of the decline in output, but it is likely that industrial enterprises on the average were operating at half their normal capacity, or even less.

The years 1961–1965 in industry were primarily ones of recovery. Emphasis had shifted to making existing factories produce efficiently rather than on building new enterprises. The only new plants established were related to the needs of agriculture or of the military. The break with the Soviet Union had increased China's military vulnerability and had shut off its major source of armaments. As a result the government in Peking began a crash program to fill the gap with a domestic armaments industry. Nuclear weapons and missiles were given a high priority, and by October 1964, China had exploded its first atomic bomb and by 1967, its first hydrogen bomb. There were comparable developments in the field of conventional armaments. For the first time, China was able to supply its petroleum needs, both military and civilian, from domestic sources.

By 1965 recovery had largely been achieved. Consumer goods industries were probably back up to the levels of 1957 and a little more, but heavy industries, including military enterprises, were producing about twice as much as in 1957. The government was ready to begin a new across-the-board development of industry, and the third 5-year plan was scheduled to start in 1966. The second 5-year plan had been replaced in early 1958 by the "Great Leap Forward" spirit, and hence China operated on annual plans only for the next eight years.

The year 1966 also marked the beginning of the "Great Proletarian Cultural Revolution." Chairman Mao Tse-tung called the revolution to revive the dwindling party élan and to purge the Communist leadership of increasing "revisionism." Since he was opposed by many military and high

MODERN PLANT produces chemical fertilizer to increase the yields of Taiwan's limited farming areas.

government leaders who wanted a less centralized economic policy with more material rewards for the individual, Mao called the youthful Red Guards out of schools to join in the intense power struggle that developed. Although a considerable and apparently successful effort was made to keep the Red Guards out of the factories until December of 1966, the political turmoil made it difficult to make decisions. Industrial growth continued throughout 1966, but in late 1966 and the early part of 1967, the Cultural Revolution entered the factories, and for a period of several weeks there was considerable disruption in industrial production. The government moved quickly, but restoring order proved more difficult than disrupting it had been.

Industrial Planning and Organization. Most of China's early industrial growth had been carried out by private entrepreneurs, both Chinese and foreign, operating in a free market. When the Communists came to power in 1949, however, the state immediately took control of all firms previously owned by the Japanese or by officials and others close to the Nationalist government, who had fled.

Private entrepreneurs who remained were encouraged to believe that they would continue to operate freely. Under the "Common Program" initiated in 1949 the government acknowledged the existence of an economic mixture: private enterprise as well as government, joint, public-private, and co-operative enterprises. By the early 1950's, however, the activities of private firms were being increasingly restricted by a system of controls, and the managers and owners came under political attack, with the beginning of the

"3-Anti" and "5-Anti" movements against the bourgeoisie. Key sectors, such as banking and large-scale commerce, were socialized first, and in 1955–1956, at the same time that collectivization was carried out in rural areas, most remaining industrial and commercial enterprises were brought under state control. The state determined the value of the assets of each capitalist and then paid him 5% of that value each year as compensation for his lost assets.

Thus, by 1956 the Chinese economy was fully socialized. To run this socialist economy, Peking drew on the experience of the Soviet Union. Before 1958 virtually the entire system of Chinese planning and control was copied from that of the Soviet Union.

The first element of this system was that each enterprise was to be independent of the others; that is, it was to be responsible for its own profits and losses, and could not share its profits or losses with other firms. At the head of each enterprise was the factory manager, appointed by the state and in China usually a Communist party member who had joined the party as a guerilla soldier in the 1940's or earlier. Each firm also had a party committee headed by a party secretary whose job it was to make sure that the enterprise and the individuals in it had the "proper" political attitudes.

Overall direction of these enterprises came not from the market as in a capitalist economy, but from a plan drawn up by officials in Peking. Plans for the long-run development of the country were formulated by the state planning commission, established in 1952. There were monthly plans, annual plans, and 5-year plans. In 1956 the State Economic Commission was created to draw up and to coordinate annual plans with longer-term plans. Plans for shorter periods were designed to provide specific day-to-day direction for the enterprise, while the 5-year plans were to give general guidance to the development program. In drawing up these plans the central planners in Peking used statistics that had been gathered by the State Statistical Bureau from each enterprise and covered the various aspects of its operations. These figures were then coordinated, and overall targets for the economy were determined.

Once the overall production targets were determined, they were then broken down so that each enterprise knew how large a share of the total it was expected to contribute. In addition, the enterprise was told the maximum number of workers it could hire, how fast its costs should be reduced, what its profits should be, and how much raw material and machinery it could have. The latter targets were designed to make sure that the firm did not attempt to meet targets by using men and materials wastefully.

During the years 1955 through 1957 this system worked reasonably well, although there was a tendency for controls either to be so tight they stifled initiative or so loose that there was considerable waste, as in 1956. This system of centralized controls was not well suited for encouraging or running numerous small-scale enterprises.

Changes in economic policy usually reflected shifts in political policy. By 1958 there were pressures to move away from the Soviet pattern of planning and control. When these pressures were combined with impatience at the top and a political shift to the left, the result was a major reorganization of industry that caused the already described anarchic industrial growth of the "Great Leap Forward."

The philosophy that governed the reorganization of industry in 1958 was taken in part from Mao's guerrilla warfare experiences of the 1930's and 1940's. In guerrilla war success was achieved by giving maximum authority to one's platoon commanders, not by centralizing decision-making in the hands of the generals. The equivalent of the platoon commander in industry was the factory's manager or party secretary. In 1958 and 1959 these individuals were directed to consult with their workers and to take whatever action they felt was desirable, provided that the action was in line with Maoist ideology. The central planners were pushed into the background and became little more than observers.

A market economy is also decentralized, but market forces, such as supply and demand, ensure that production is coordinated. If too much of one item is produced, its price falls, and enterprises cut back production so as not to lose money. China in 1958 abandoned coordination by the planners, but failed to provide a substitute, with the result that items were produced whether they were needed or not. To make matters worse, the system for collecting statistics was reorganized in such a way that widespread falsification of key data resulted. It is impossible for central planners to meet the objectives of their plan or even to run an economy unless they know what is happening. Before 1958, Chinese data had become increasingly standardized and reliable, but this effort was thrown away in the excesses of 1958 and 1959.

Employment methods at the lower levels were also badly supervised. When the government finally became aware of this disorganization and moved to restore order, the first step was to reestablish some form of centralized control over the individual enterprises. In 1961 there was a debate among economists as to just how this should be done, with some arguing that the government should move in the direction of increasing the role of market forces. But the actual steps taken were much more modest. For large-scale enterprises, such as the steel mills of Anshan, fully centralized planning and control were reestablished. For smaller firms and firms that produced directly for consumers, however, a degree of decentralization was retained. Because these smaller enterprises often obtained raw materials from nearby areas and sold their products in those same regions, all the necessary coordination could be handled at provincial and lower levels. There was no need to have Peking take over this role. In the years that followed, at least through 1966, the trend was toward putting more and more firms under the control of provincial, city, and county governments rather than Peking.

Wages and Incentives. In industry as well as in agriculture, the government has had to face the issue of how best to get workers and managers to work both creatively and hard. To a degree, Peking followed the experience of the Soviet Union and relied on large wage differentials to stimulate effort. Thus the highest paid engineers in a Chinese factory received about 10 times as much as the lowest category of unskilled worker. Even among the workers themselves, the wages of the highest paid were several times those of the lowest.

But the Chinese government has never been satisfied with the obvious conflict between large differences in wages and the Communist ideal of payment according to need. Partly for this reason, there have been various attempts to reduce the use of piece-rate wages (a worker, for example, is paid according to the number of screws he turns, rather than by the number of hours spent turning screws), which tended to increase differentials. As in the Soviet Union, various kinds of incentives were introduced, including frequent awarding of medals, trips to Peking, and even a brief meeting with Chairman Mao himself for particularly able workers. Unlike the Soviet Union, monetary bonuses for factory managers have not been used. Instead, it was assumed that a factory manager has been more deeply imbued with Communist ideology than the ordinary worker and hence, less in need of material rewards for his efforts. In spite of this, factory managers live much better than the laborer.

Generally, urban residents in China have a higher standard of living than those who live in rural areas. This fact together with collectivization has led to a steady stream of migrants away from farms into the cities, a flow far greater than could be absorbed by the needs of industrialization. To stop this migration, the government has lowered the wages of unskilled urban workers to make them comparable to incomes in rural areas and has set up elaborate controls to make it difficult for a peasant to leave the rural areas or to stay in the cities once he arrives. There have also been efforts to forcibly return many unemployed individuals to the countryside.

Transportation. Before the coming of the West to China in the middle of the 19th century, the country relied heavily on junks and sampans that plied China's major waterways for transportation. The alternative means of transport, and the only ones available where there were no water routes, were the backs of men and animals, animal driven carts, and wheelbarrows. But these methods were extremely expensive. A man or animal carrying grain, for example, soon ate up as much as he was carrying. Thus only goods of high value per pound could be carried long distances over land. Most large cities, as a result, were located on the Yangtze River or along the southeast coast where they could be supplied easily by boat. When the capital was established at Peking in the 15th century, various emperors found it convenient to obtain grain supplies via a man-made canal rather than by land or by ocean voyage around the Shantung peninsula.

Although the late 19th and 20th centuries saw the advent of the steamship, the automobile, railroads, and aircraft in China, it was the railroad that made the greatest change. The railroad meant cheap transport costs for areas not accessible by water, and hence opened large areas to commerce and industrialization, particularly in North China.

In 1949 the Communists inherited a railroad system that had been built largely by various foreign powers. On the whole, Peking's policy was to make fuller use of this existing system rather than to expand it. A few new tracks were laid, such as the lines between Paotow and Lanchow, and Yingtan and Amoy. Also the agricultural and industrial wealth of Szechwan was tapped by the extension of a line into the province. The Chengtu-Paoki line was completed in 1956 and tied in with the North China rail system. There was also the construction of the Lanchow-Sinkiang line, with an extension to

COTTON SPINNING plant at Sian, capital of Shensi province and one of the country's textile centers.

Aktogai in Soviet Asia in the early 1960's, but this line was designed as much to consolidate Chinese political power in the region as for economic purposes. By 1958 the railroads were being so heavily used that they had become a major bottleneck. The drop in output in 1961 temporarily alleviated this problem. Since 1961 there has also been an attempt to extend and improve China's neglected road system and to increase the number of trucks available for transport.

Foreign Trade and Aid. In the early 19th century China's trade involved the exchange of silver and opium for Chinese silk and tea for the markets of Europe and America. By the late 19th and early 20th centuries Chinese imports of cotton textiles from the mills of England, India, and Japan had largely replaced silver and opium. As for export, Chinese silk continued to be an important commodity, but tea gradually was replaced by supplies from India and Ceylon. In its place, China began to export a variety of other products, principally agricultural or animal products, such as soybeans and hog bristles. Most of this trade was with Western Europe, the United States, and Japan.

After the Communists came to power, both the direction and content of China's trade changed. The Soviet Union, which had had little trade with China previously, quickly became its largest trading partner by far, with the Eastern European nations also playing a significant role. The American embargo on all trade with China, which followed immediately after Peking's decision to enter the Korean War, only accelerated this shift in the direction of trade and did not really cause it.

The principal reason why China decided to alter the direction of its trade was to concentrate resources on building a heavy industrial base. To obtain the equipment for these industries, China stopped imports of all nonessential items. Ninety per cent of imports in the 1950's were for industrial and military programs. Exports, however, did not change significantly. China had to export those goods in which it had a comparative advantage, that is, mainly agricultural products.

This pattern of trade continued through 1959 and into 1960, but then the combined force of the agricultural crisis and the break with the Soviets caused major changes. Given the shortage of various foods at home, it was impossible to continue exporting such goods at previous levels. Peanut and other edible oil exports, for example, were virtually eliminated in the crisis years. Some foreign exchange earnings were maintained by expanding cotton textile exports. By 1961 and 1962 total trade had fallen to half the 1959 peak level and did not fully recover until 1966.

Imports not only fell off but their composition was also altered. The Soviet Union was no longer willing to ship complete plants and equipment; at the same time China could not have made good use of these items in the years 1961 and 1962 anyway. Instead, Peking began to import large quantities of grain to feed the urban population. In addition, the direction of trade began to shift away from the Soviet Union and eastern Europe to Japan and western Europe. By 1966, Japan had replaced the Soviet Union as China's principal trading partner. Trade between the United States and China, however, continued to be blocked by both the American embargo and China's unwillingness to deal with what it considered to be the world's major imperialist power.

The Chinese turn to Communism and, more importantly, Peking's decision to enter the Korean War ended any possibility that China could obtain economic aid, as contrasted to trade, from the United States or other Western powers. In the years 1950 to 1955, however, China did obtain the equivalent of about U.S.$2 billion from the Soviet Union. But over half of this sum was to help pay for Soviet military equipment used in the Korean War or to reimburse Moscow for Russian properties in Manchuria and in the northwest that had been turned over to the Chinese.

China received less than U.S.$1 billion in economic aid, mostly from the Soviet Union, during the 18 years after the Communists came to power. India, by contrast, receives approximately that much every year.

Although Soviet loans to China dwindled to negligible proportions after 1955, Soviet technicians and plans continued to play an important role until they too were cut off in the middle of 1960. With the Sino-Soviet break, China not only ceased to receive either loans or technical support from the Soviet Union, but actually began to pay back previous credits. Throughout the crisis years of the early 1960's China exported more to the Soviet Union than it imported from it, so that by the end of 1965 the entire Soviet loan had been repaid.

China, therefore, more than any other underdeveloped nation has had to rely on its own limited resources. This means that the rate of savings and taxation has continued to be high. The burden has been further increased by China's "go it alone" foreign policy, which has necessitated large military expenditures. Communist China also uses its foreign aid and trade to further its political interests, and has aided North Vietnam, Nepal, Cambodia, and Egypt, when it could little afford to do so.

NATIONALIST CHINA

For centuries before the beginning of Japanese rule in 1895, the island of Taiwan was an economic backwater that collected the surplus populations of the nearby provinces of Fukien and Kwangtung on the mainland of China. During the 50 years of Japanese colonial rule, progress was made in raising farm output, in the development of modern transport, and even to a limited degree in industrialization. Allied bombing and the general disruption of World War II and China's civil war caused sharp declines in the output of all sectors of the economy in the decade of the 1940's. Full recovery to prewar levels was not achieved until about 1953. Thus began a series of 4-year plans for developing the economy. The first (1953–1956) emphasized agricultural growth and the improvement of rural conditions, electric power, and transportation. The second (1957–1960) was designed to stimulate better trade, and the third (1961–1964) focused on the development of the mining and manufacturing industries and of power production. The fourth (1965–1968) aimed at a higher economic growth.

From 1953 to 1958, as a result of the infusion of large amounts of U.S. economic aid, the national income of Taiwan grew at the substantial rate of 5.6% per year. During the next seven years the importance of American economic aid dwindled as the economy relied increasingly on its own resources, growing throughout this period at the extremely rapid rate of 8.4% per year, a rate exceeded only by few of the world's other economies. In 1966 the gross national product was U.S.$3,121 million.

During most of the 1950's the pace of population increase cut into the effect of economic growth on living standards. Per capita income only rose from about U.S.$111 in 1953 to U.S.$123 in 1958. By 1966, however, this figure had risen to U.S.$190, a rate that, if continued, would remove Taiwan from the ranks of underdeveloped countries within a decade.

Agriculture. Taiwan's agriculture has had the double task of feeding the island's burgeoning population as well as providing a surplus for export. The key food crop was rice, which continued to be grown by the same intensive labor methods used on the Chinese mainland. A 40% increase in rice yields had been achieved under Japanese rule by the extension of irrigation, the introduction of improved rice seeds from Japan, and the increased use of fertilizer.

One of the first steps taken by the Nationalist government when it moved to Taiwan was to institute a major land reform. This reform included a law reducing farm rent to 37.5% of the annual main crop yield, the sale of government-owned land to the farmers who tilled it, and government purchase of land owned by landlords, which was then resold to the farmers. By the mid-1960's 87% of all Taiwan's farmers owned at least part of the land they cultivated as against 61% in 1949 when the Nationalist government moved to the island.

Other steps taken to improve yields have included the expansion of chemical fertilizer production, further seed improvement, and some mechanization. Tractors are of limited value when plots are as small as they are in Taiwan, but machines that save labor time during the planting and harvest, when everyone is fully occupied, make a significant contribution to productivity. By the mid-1960's these improvements and others had succeeded in raising rice yields another 40% above the levels of 1953. There was also an increase in the production of other grain crops, principally sweet potatoes.

Taiwan's major cash crop, most of which is exported abroad, is sugar. The island's sugar production and exports reached a peak, in the years before World War II, of 1.1 million tons, or one metric ton. During the war output fell sharply and, although production recovered after 1947, by the mid-1960's it had not quite been restored to prewar peak levels. Where before the war Taiwan was the 4th-largest sugar producer in the world, by the 1960's it had dropped out of the top 10.

Other farm products fared better. Tea and such tropical and subtropical fruits as bananas and pineapples greatly expanded production in the 1950's and 1960's. Overall, agricultural output in the mid-1960's was nearly double the level of the early 1950's, with large rises in the fisheries and animal husbandry industries.

Industry. Although the Japanese began building railroads almost as soon as they took control of the island, little else that could be associated with modern industrial development was begun until the 1930's. At that time, the Japanese began to develop sources of electric power, and industrial employment rose sharply.

After the war the loss of Japanese technicians and capital was quickly replaced by the influx from mainland China. Industry recovered rapidly from wartime destruction and total industrial employment by 1952 was well above prewar levels. The most dramatic change in the late 1940's and early 1950's was the rise of the cotton textile industry. Under Japanese rule this industry had been almost totally neglected, presumably because the Japanese government felt a need to insure its own textile industry. By the mid-1950's, Taiwan's textile industry had risen so rapidly that it accounted for 20% of all industrial production. By the mid-1960's this industry was a major foreign exchange earner.

The performance of textiles began to be copied by many other industries in the 1950's and 1960's. Food-processing firms also expanded, but a characteristic of the period was increasing industrial diversification. The chemical and metal industries began to play an important role, and the beginnings of domestic production of refrigerators and television sets were signs that Taiwan was leaving its rural peasant economy and social system behind. By 1965, in fact, about three fifths of the island's population lived not on the farm, but in cities and towns.

Government Policy. The economy of Taiwan is a mixed economy, with large shares owned by both the government and private individuals. Many of the key industrial enterprises are state-owned, but the share of the private sector in industry has been increasing steadily. During the 1950's state controls even over private enterprises were tight, but there was a gradual relaxation as prosperity grew.

The major influence of the government on the economy arises out of the large expenditures on the military. Over 10% of Taiwan's gross national product is consumed by the armed forces. If it were not for the more than U.S.$2 billion in U.S. military assistance, these expenditures would either have been sharply curtailed or they would have cut deeply into investment and growth. As it was, during the 1950's, government outlays on the armed forces were a constant source of inflationary pressure. Prices throughout the 1950's and into the 1960's often rose by 10% or more a year. By 1963, however, increasing prosperity caught up with prices, and from then on prices leveled off and even declined.

Communications. Taiwan has approximately 10,200 miles (16,311 km) of highways, reaching all parts of the island. In 1960 the completion of the 190-mile (306-km) cross-island highway enabled travelers to go directly from the east to west coast, rather than having to circle the Central Mountain range.

A large portion of Taiwan's 2,700 miles (4,500 km) of railroads is owned and operated by the Taiwan Sugar Corporation. All major cities and towns are connected by the government-owned railroad system, and there are two separate provincial systems, one for the east coast and one for the west coast.

Taiwan has several airlines, including the Civil Air Transport, China Airlines, and the Foshing Airlines, and is served by several international companies. The main airport is in Sungshan in suburban Taipei. The China Merchants Steam Navigation company is the oldest and largest shipping concern. The three international ports are Keelung in the north, Kaohsiung in the south, and Hualien on the east coast.

Foreign Trade and Aid. Taiwan's most dynamic performance has been in foreign trade. Exports and imports together grew from U.S.$320 million in 1953 to U.S.$838 million in 1964. More important, exports alone rose from U.S.$128 million to U.S.$439 million, an increase of 242%.

Without large scale imports of machinery and other key equipment, Taiwan's industrialization program would have been impossible. More than half of all such equipment could not be produced at home and had to be purchased abroad. During the 1950's, however, Taiwan's exports fluctuated between U.S.$93 and U.S.$157 million. To pay for imports that regularly ran over U.S.$200 million, the government had to rely heavily on American economic aid.

The rapid expansion of exports in the 1960's, when combined with a similar rise in domestic savings, however, greatly reduced the country's dependence on outside assistance. These developments led the United States government to the decision to end all economic (but not military) aid to Taiwan in 1965 since the money was no longer needed there.

The export expansion was not accomplished by finding new markets for old products. Sugar, for example, which provided 58% of all export earnings in 1954 accounted for only 20% in 1964–1965. Instead, various industrial products (textiles, lumber products, and so on) and processed farm products other than sugar, such as canned pineapples and mushrooms, increased in importance. Unlike so many small underdeveloped economies, Taiwan was no longer heavily dependent on the export of only one or two raw materials. This was just one more indication that the economy of Taiwan could no longer be considered in the ranks of the world's poor peasant economies.

DWIGHT H. PERKINS, *Harvard University*

Bibliography

Cheng, Chu-yuan, *Communist China's Economy, 1949–1962* (Seton Hall, N.J., 1963).
Eckstein, Alexander, *Communist China's Economic Growth and Foreign Trade* (New York 1966).
Fairbank, John K., *The United States and China* (Cambridge, Mass., 1958).
Jacoby, Neil H., *U.S. Aid to Taiwan* (New York 1966).
Li, Choh-ming, ed., *Industrial Development in Communist China* (New York 1964).
Mancall, Mark, ed., *Formosa Today* (New York 1964).
Wu, Yuan-li, *The Economy of Communist China* (New York 1965).

The Ming Tombs, the burial place of the last 13 emperors of the Chinese Ming dynasty (1368–1644), lie beyond this ornamental gateway in a valley north of Peking.

CHINA: History and Government

7. History

The archaeological record of man in East Asia begins some 500,000 years ago. At that time, a kind of ape-man inhabited northern China; with a brain capacity about two thirds that of modern man, this ape-man walked erect, could fashion simple tools, and lived by hunting and gathering. He may also have used fire. Until recently, the earliest representative of these proto-humans was the famous Peking man, discovered in a limestone cave southwest of Peking in 1927; in 1963–1964, however, an even earlier female cousin of Peking man was discovered considerably to the west, at Lan-t'ien, near Sian.

Prehistoric Period. The long evolution of these protohumans into modern man concerns more the history of mankind as a whole than the development of a specifically Chinese civilization. Let us merely note here the indefatigable efforts of Chinese archaeologists who are adding every year to our picture of China's prehistory. Many specimens of Neanderthal man (200,000–100,000 B.C.) and *Homo sapiens* (100,000–25,000 B.C.), the direct ancestor of modern man, have been unearthed in both North and South China; the area watered by the Yellow River, however, seems consistently to have been in the forefront of early cultural advance. In the late Neolithic period (from about 5000 B.C. onward), this area, with its fertile and easily worked soil and abundant water supply, proved especially hospitable to a people whose livelihood was coming to depend more and more on agriculture. Grouping into small communities, they lived in round or rectangular pits sunk into the earth, with thatch roofs supported by pillars. Besides hunting, fishing, and farming, they also raised pigs and dogs. Skillful in fashioning tools, they produced a wide variety of implements—from hoes, knives, arrows, and fishhooks to spindle whorls, pigment mortars, needles, and awls. Their pottery included a three-legged vessel called the *li* that became the ancestor of the beautiful bronze tripods of a later period.

Distinctive forms of this pottery help to identify two successive cultures that grew up in the late Neolithic period: (1) a Yang-shao culture (after a site in northwest Honan), characterized by reddish pots, often with geometric designs in black and (2) a Lung-shan culture (from the name of a site in Shantung), distinguished by the shiny black surface of its pottery. The technically superior Lung-shan pots show for the first time in China the use of the potter's wheel; many of them also bear potters' marks, though there is as yet no sign of literacy. Other indications of Lung-shan's cultural progress are the defensive walls of firmly packed earth that now began to surround the villages and the clearer social distinctions as shown, for instance, in the more ceremonial burials for members of the upper classes. Elaborate religious practices included a well-developed ancestor cult, agricultural rites, and scapulimancy, a means of divination in which the answers to previously asked questions are determined by interpreting the cracks induced by applying heat to animal bones.

The extent to which the rise of civilization in China was stimulated by contacts with earlier civilizations to the west is still unclear. Although seas, mountains, and deserts kept China relatively isolated throughout most of its history, this isolation was never complete. Furthermore, the North China plain, the so-called cradle of Chinese civilization, is precisely that part of the country which connects most easily by land with the rest of Asia. For the present, however, the evidence indicates that the civilization then was essentially a native growth. Borrowings of ideas and inventions from other civilizations notwithstanding, it never lost its distinctive, indigenous character.

Early Kingdom. The Shang dynasty (1523–1028 B.C.), according to one tradition, marks the beginning of China's Bronze Age as well as its history proper. Written sources, the earliest extant, now supplement archaeological remains. Certain inscriptions on daggers, sacrificial vessels, and pieces of jade probably preserve the most primitive form of Chinese writing. More important for historians, however, are more advanced forms of inscriptions on the bones and tortoise shells used in scapulimancy. Many of these were stored after use in a kind of state archive. Discovered at the end of the last century, these "oracle bones," with their questions and, sometimes, answers concerning favorable times for the planting of crops, chances of success in a coming military campaign, the meaning of the king's dreams, and the like, have greatly added to our picture of Shang society.

At its summit stood the Shang kings who dominated a loose confederation of chiefdoms; in their heyday, they may have exercised at least a precarious control over much of North China. Succession was at first from older brother to younger brother; only toward the end of the dynasty did a father-son succession become established as a heritage to all later dynasties. The talent for sophisticated political organization, a hallmark of Chinese civilization, had already revealed itself in the specialization of government functions. Religion, an important state activity, was monopolized by the priests—we know the names of more than one hundred of them—whose expertise in divination and responsibility for placating the spirits probably gave them great political power. Other officials were given such specific responsibilities as supervision of weapons, collection and allocation of tribute, construction of public buildings, and maintenance of irrigation works.

A great gulf separated the rulers, who alone controlled the new bronze technology, and the ruled. The king and his nobles lived in imposing palaces, while the commoners still huddled in subterranean pits. In the frequent warfare, nobles fought from chariots, commoners on foot; human sacrifice, especially of prisoners of war, was common. Kings continued to rule, in a manner of speaking, even after their deaths, surrounded by their harem, their bodyguards, and their slaves who were often buried alive with them.

The excavation of many widely scattered sites confirms that much of North China was unified culturally. A major achievement of this culture, after the invention of writing, was the casting of magnificent bronze sacrificial vessels whose beauty and metallurgical technique have never been surpassed in China or elsewhere. Another key invention was the calendar, with its division in the 10-day "weeks" and 60-day cycles used by the Chinese to measure time down into this century. Important in every agricultural society, regulation of the calendar became a major preoccupation of Chinese governments.

We do not know much about the political history of the Shang. Traditional accounts, reconstructed long afterwards, tell us that the dynasty was founded by a man called T'ang who rallied his fellow nobles and their followers to overthrow the evil and degenerate last ruler of the Hsia dynasty (supposedly established by the legendary flood-controller Yü but not yet confirmed by any archaeological discovery). For the rest of the dynasty, we must content ourselves with a list of king's reigns until, in 1027 B.C., the Chou, a former vassal of the Shang from the area of the Wei River in the western highlands, defeated their overlord and became the dominant power in North China.

Chou Dynasty (1027–256 B.C.). Chinese historians some centuries later justified the Chou conquest of Shang by the theory that the last Shang ruler was evil and had lost Heaven's mandate to rule. To reinforce this theory, the early Chou rulers were written up as paragons of virtue: Wen Wang (King Wen), who remained a loyal vassal despite wretched treatment by the last Shang tyrant; his son, Wu Wang (King Wu), who dutifully avenged his father by destroying the Shang; and the sagacious Chou Kung (Duke of Chou), who served as regent for King Wu's young son and established the institutions and customs of a golden age. These stories reveal the firm Chinese belief that rulers retained their right to govern only by conforming to the ways of Heaven (*T'ien*), the guiding force in the universe (a concept lying somewhere between but quite different from the Western notions of God and of fate). In expressing this belief, Chinese historians have always tended to see the dominant cause of dynastic change not so much in political, economic, or social conditions as in the personal moral defects of the ruler.

Western Chou. The first part of the Chou dynasty, known as the Western Chou because of its capital in the northwest near modern Sian, saw no significant rupture in the slow, steady development of Chinese civilization. The writing system continued to evolve; bronze vessels were

CHINESE DYNASTIES AND STATES

T'ang Kingdom (legendary)	...... 3d millennium B. C.	
Yü Kingdom (legendary)	.... 3d millennium B. C.	
Hsia Dynasty	.... c.1994 B. C.–c.1523	
Shang (Yin) Dynasty	.... c.1523 B. C.–c.1028	
Chou Dynasty	.... c.1027 B. C.– 256	
Western Chou	.... c.1027 B. C.– 770	
Eastern Chou	.... 770 B. C.– 256	
Spring and Autumn	.... 722 B. C.– 481	
Warring States	.... 403 B. C.– 222	
Ch'in Dynasty	.... 221 B. C.– 206	
Han Dynasty	.... 202 B. C.– 220 A. D.	
Western (Earlier) Han	.... 202 B. C.– 9 A. D.	
Hsin	.... 9 A. D.– 23 A. D.	
Eastern (Later) Han	...... 25 – 220	
Three Kingdoms	.... 220 – 265	
Shu	.... 221 – 264	
Wei	.... 220 – 265	
Wu	.... 222 – 280	
Chin (Tsin) Dynasty	.... 265 – 420	
Western Chin	.... 265 – 317	
Eastern Chin	.... 317 – 420	
Southern Dynasties	.... 420 – 589	
Liu Sung	.... 420 – 479	
Ch'i	.... 479 – 502	
Liang	.... 502 – 557	
Ch'en	.... 557 – 589	
Northern Dynasties	.... 386 – 581	
Later Wei	.... 386 – 535	
Eastern Wei	.... 534 – 550	
Western Wei	.... 535 – 556	
Northern Ch'i	.... 550 – 577	
Northern Chou	.... 557 – 581	
Sui Dynasty	.... 581 – 618	
T'ang Dynasty	.... 618 – 906	
Five Dynasties	.... 907 – 960	
Later Liang	.... 907 – 923	
Later T'ang	.... 923 – 936	
Later Chin	.... 936 – 947	
Later Han	.... 947 – 950	
Later Chou	.... 951 – 960	
Ten Kingdoms	.... 902 – 979	
Wu	.... 902 – 937	
Southern T'ang	.... 937 – 975	
Southern P'ing	.... 907 – 963	
Ch'u	.... 927 – 951	
Earlier Shu	.... 907 – 925	
Later Shu	.... 934 – 965	
Wu-yüeh	.... 907 – 978	
Min	.... 909 – 944	
Southern Han	.... 907 – 971	
Northern Han	.... 951 – 979	
Sung Dynasty	.... 960 – 1279	
Liao	.... 947 – 1125	
Northern Sung	.... 960 – 1126	
Hsi-hsia	.... 990 – 1227	
Chin (Kin)	.... 1115 – 1234	
Southern Sung	.... 1127 – 1279	
Yüan Dynasty (Mongol)	..... 1271 – 1368	
Ming Dynasty	.... 1368 – 1644	
Ch'ing Dynasty (Manchu)	.... 1644 – 1911	
Republic	.... 1912 –	

Typical utensils used in China around the first millennium B. C. (*Left*) Wine cup, or *chia*, from Shang dynasty (1523–1028 B. C.), the beginning of the Bronze Age. The cup could be placed over a fire to warm the wine, and picked up by its top handles (*Right*) Mao Kung Ting, a bronze food vessel from the Chou dynasty (1027–256 B. C.).

LUCY MAUD BUCKINGHAM COLLECTION OF THE ART INSTITUTE OF CHICAGO

BIRNBACK

still cast, if with declining artistic vitality; scapulimancy persisted, though it gradually gave way to other methods of divination. Politically, too, the Chou adopted Shang patterns; vassals enjoyed a free hand within their own domains but recognized the general military, political, and religious preeminence of the Chou. This preeminence was reinforced by a code of conduct for nobles that went far toward creating stability and balance in the political system. All legitimacy stemmed from the Chou kings, and vassals went regularly to the Chou court for the ceremony of investiture that confirmed them in their rule. The Chou kings also served as arbiters of disputes among the nobles. When warfare did break out, moral strictures comparable to chivalry, such as not killing a defeated enemy or not attacking an enemy before he had time to mobilize his forces, helped to mitigate its brutality. These rules of conduct, extended to public actions in general, created a feeling of solidarity among those who practiced them; all others were regarded as outsiders or "barbarians." So it has been throughout Chinese history: the Chinese have disdained barbarians not so much for racial reasons but mainly because of their failure to learn the superior Chinese order. A barbarian could always gain acceptance by showing the proper respect for the values of Chinese civilization.

Eastern Chou. The power of the early Chou rulers gradually waned until, by the 8th century, it had all but disappeared. In 771 B. C., defeated by a vassal who had allied with barbarians, the Chou court was forced to move its capital eastward to Loyang in Honan (hence the name "Eastern Chou" for the remainder of the dynasty). The Chou kings from then on retained some religious authority—disputes about sacrifices, successions and the like were still referred to the court—but no effective military and political power. With the tenuous unity of the earlier period gone and warfare among the states increasing, several leading vassals in the more highly civilized domains in the central part of North China contended for hegemony. Eventually, however, more dynamic states in the peripheral areas came to the fore. Larger, hardier, and less committed to the old cultural niceties, they introduced a new brutality into warfare, and profited from it. Annihilation of the enemy became the aim and seizure of territory the prize.

By the 5th century B. C., in the period of the Warring States, the struggle centered on the three most powerful remaining states: Ch'in, the northwestern state in the same area in which the Chou had risen; Ch'u, a southern state in the Yangtze River valley region that had developed a highly refined variation on the culture of the north; and Ch'i, grown strong by incorporating other states as well as barbarian tribes of the Shangtung peninsula. Ch'in snuffed out the hapless Chou in 256 B. C. and, in lightning campaigns from 230 to 221, destroyed the last six of its rivals, including Ch'u and Ch'i. For the first time in its history, China became a unified empire.

Military superiority gave Ch'in victory over its rivals. With greater effectiveness than they, it had, among other changes, replaced its chariots with cavalry and developed more effective methods of drafting troops. Nevertheless, numerous economic and political innovations bolstered the military strength. Agriculture made giant strides: the new ox-drawn, iron-tipped plow greatly extended the cultivable area per man; advances in irrigation and in fertilizers made possible permanent cultivation instead of the constant shifting from worn-out fields to new ones, thus providing a more dependable economic base. Instead of taxing a percentage of the harvest, which made the receipts of any given year difficult to predict, governments could now assess regular, fixed taxes on land holdings. Greater agricultural productivity also stimulated population rise, providing the manpower for further expansion and for the armies. Trade, too, expanded, funneling great wealth into those states that promoted it.

As the states that responded to these changes grew in size, power, and complexity, they required an increasing number of advisers, administrators, strategists, and diplomats. This emerging class of specialists included not only disinherited, exiled, or impoverished nobles but, more significantly, talented commoners who received an education directly or indirectly from these nobles. These specialists were the professional forerunners of the scholar-officials who would pilot the Chinese government throughout two millennia of imperial history. And the brilliant thinkers among them also made this period the golden age of Chinese philosophy (see CHINA–15. *Philosophy and Religions*).

Ch'in Dynasty (221–206 B. C.). Shih Huang Ti (The First August Sovereign), as the unifier of China now styled himself, sought to create a durable, centralized empire. The semi-independent feudal domains were replaced by commanderies and prefectures, each governed jointly by a civil, a military, and a supervisory official sent out by the central government and responsible to it. Former aristocrats were forced to migrate to the new capital near Sian (not far from the capital of the Western Chou), destroying in a single stroke their local-based power and enabling the central government to keep a watchful eye on them. Henceforth, nobility became a reward for military merit rather than a right by birth.

Recognizing that effective control demanded dependable communications, the emperor ordered the construction of highways linking the entire country to the capital; along the highways, inscribed stone tablets praised the regime's accomplishments. The writing system was standardized, as were weights and measures, coinage, and the calendar. To guard against revolts, only imperial soldiers were allowed to possess weapons.

Legalism became the state orthodoxy. In 213 B.C., the emperor decreed the burning of all undesirable books, especially various political writings such as Confucian works that lauded the ancient system. This act earned for the Ch'in founder excoriation by later Confucian scholars, but it was probably less destructive of earlier writings than the numerous wars of this period. Nor did it affect at all utilitarian works dealing with agriculture, medicine, pharmacy, and divination.

Externally, the Ch'in sought to defend its frontiers where necessary and to expand them where possible. Against the always dangerous nomads to the north and the west, the emperor linked up earlier walls built by the individual states into the Great Wall—as a solid barrier from the sea to the desert along the mountains that marked off China's northern limits. The Hsiung-nu, Turkish-speaking northern nomads, were driven beyond the Wall. To the south, China's relentless absorption of new territories continued; intensive cultivation of the area watered by the lower Yangtze River began, and Chinese armies for the first time brought some measure of imperial control to Fukien, Kwangtung, and Kwangsi.

The Ch'in new order, at first welcomed by a population wearied of war and devastation, soon collapsed. The peasants groaned under the conscription for the army and the corvées for the gigantic public works; all who served the state lived under the constant fear of severe punishment for the slightest offense; former noble elements seethed with revenge; and few were truly committed to the orthodox but crude Legalism. While he lived, the First August Sovereign was able to keep the lid on the widespread discontent; but immediately upon his death, palace intrigues brought instability and insurrections. The ruling house, meant to last for ten thousand years, was destroyed by its subjects in 206 B.C. Nevertheless, the Ch'in left an important legacy, the ideal of the unified empire, that motivated all Chinese governments, weak or strong, for the next two millennia.

Han Dynasty (202 B.C.–220 A.D.). Out of the widespread revolts that toppled the Ch'in, there eventually emerged two outstanding contestants for power: the brave and chivalrous Hsiang Yü, who championed the interests of the pre-Ch'in nobility; and Liu Pang, a commoner whose talent for leadership included the ability to control his generals effectively, a surer grasp of political actualities, and a realistic concern for the plight of the commoners. Having established his base in the historic Wei River valley, Liu finally triumphed in 202 B.C. and called his new dynasty the Han, deriving the name from the Han River (the Heavenly River).

Western (Earlier) Han. The governmental system of the new Han empire was a compromise. Over most of the country he restored the Ch'in political structure, in this way creating a strong, centralized government. The rest of the country he carved into semiautonomous fiefs for his sons and his leading generals. These fiefs were soon felt to be a potential threat to imperial authority, however. With rank ingratitude but superb political astuteness, Liu himself eventually cashiered most of the generals who had helped him achieve power and decreed that all further enfeoffments be limited to members of the imperial family. But, in 154 B.C., when seven imperial princes holding the largest fiefs rebelled, their defeat marked a major step in the consolidation of the government. By the end of the reign of Wu Ti (141–87 B.C.), the feudal lords had lost their last vestiges of autonomous power.

Han Wu Ti. Wu Ti (the "Martial Emperor") presided over an explosion of Chinese military power, much of it directed against the Hsiung-nu menace to the north. Earlier rulers had chosen to buy off the nomads with tribute. Liu Pang himself set the precedent by giving a Chinese princess in marriage to the Hsiung-nu chieftain. Wu Ti reversed this policy of appeasement and initiated a series of long and bitter campaigns that wore down the Hsiung-nu until, in 52 B.C., all the border tribes submitted to Chinese domination.

The wars of expansion also widened Chinese intellectual horizons. Hoping to outflank the Hsiung-nu, Wu Ti sent an officer, Chang Ch'ien, to negotiate an alliance with a central Asian people, the Yüeh-chih. A great explorer and adventurer, Chang brought back not a diplomatic success but a wealth of firsthand information on lands as far west as the fringes of the Hellenistic world.

Han expansion meant more than defeating the Hsiung-nu. The presence of Chinese military power in Fergana (now Russian Turkestan) enabled them to control much of the famed Silk Route over which passed goods destined for western Asia and the Roman world. To the northeast, the Chinese founded a colony in northern Korea (it eventually grew to 400,000 inhabitants). From there, Chinese influences then slowly seeped into still primitive Japan. Finally, in the south, a series of relatively easy campaigns spearheaded Chinese control into what are now parts of Yünnan and North Vietnam.

Military campaigns, however, put a severe strain on imperial finances. Consequently, the government resorted to a variety of economic measures, some dating back to the Chou and the Ch'in, designed to supplement the income from land taxes. Extortion of gifts from nobles; special taxes on merchants and artisans; government monopoly of iron, salt, and wine; commutation of legal punishments by the payment of fines; the sale of court ranks: few sources of added revenue were overlooked. The government even tried its hand at currency debasement. The Confucianists severely criticized such active interference in the economy as neither consonant with ancient practices nor befitting the paternal role of the government. But the noninterference policy they advocated could not obtain adequate revenues; eventually, their criticisms were muted and many of Wu Ti's measures gradually became standard procedures in the financial administration of later dynasties.

While the general tenor of Wu Ti's economic reforms may have been borrowed from the ideas of the Legalists of the Ch'in dynasty, concern for social order and acceptance by the intellectuals led him to sponsor as state ideology Confucianism or, rather, an amalgam of Confucian theory and generous borrowings from other philosophies that went under the name of Confucianism. From the early Han, men trained in Confucianism had assumed much responsibility in the government and had impressed the emperors with their learning, their expertise, and their undivided loyalty. What attracted Wu Ti even more were the cosmological interpretations and divinatory knowledge emphasized by a new breed of Confucian scholars. In good Legalist fashion, he chose not to honor Legalist scholars and established high court positions for the specialists in the Five Classics that were revered as the essence of Confucian wisdom. An Imperial University for training officials was established in 124 B.C.; three centuries later, it boasted of 30,000 students. Through official rewards for virtuous behavior, appointment of community leaders as officials, examinations in Confucian knowledge for the civil service, inscribing the Classics on stone (from which repeated rubbings could be made), sacrifices to Confucius on official occasions, and similar measures, the Han state assured the primacy of Confucian attitudes in the Chinese political order.

By the end of the first century B.C., Han prosperity had vanished. State revenues declined as powerful landlords accumulated not only more land but also servile peasants on their virtually tax-free estates. Peasants still on the tax rolls were left to bear the increasingly heavy assessments at a time when population increase was bringing land scarcity. At this point, Wang Mang, nephew of the late empress, whose family had dominated the court for decades, and one of the great political and social reformers in Chinese history, appeared on the scene. Usurping the throne in 9 A.D., he proclaimed his intention to make his Hsin dynasty a perfect Confucian state. Nevertheless, his efforts to restore effective government and to solve the financial crisis smacked more of Wu Ti's Legalist policies. In any case, his efforts failed. Revolts broke out, including that of the Red Eyebrows, the first of those semireligious, semi-bandit secret societies that would often play a leading role in the fall of later dynasties. Even before Wang was assassinated in 23 A.D., China had already fallen into anarchy.

Eastern (Later) Han. Two years later, an alliance of landlords and peasants had restored the throne to the house of Han. The successful contender, Kuang Wu Ti ("Illustrious Martial Emperor"), established his capital at Loyang, initiating the period known as the Eastern or Later Han (25–220 A.D.). Kuang Wu Ti successfully restored unity and peace but neither he nor his successors were able to establish full control over the powerful landlords. It is not surprising, then, that diminishing tax rolls again became a major problem for the dynasty. To this were added the machinations of the empresses, the intrigues of the eunuchs, and factional strife within the bureaucracy. The fall of the dynasty was in many ways a melancholy replay of the Western (Earlier) Han collapse, only worse: except for a short time in the late 3d century, China would not know unity again for 400 years.

Enhancing the splendor of the Han dynasty were its many cultural achievements. A vigorous prose style developed, perhaps best exemplified in the historical writings of Ssu-ma Ch'ien (d. 85 B.C.) and Pan Ku (32–92 A.D.). These histories were widely read for their literary excellence and undoubtedly helped reinforce the unusually keen sense of history among educated Chinese. Moreover, they also set the pattern for a series of official "dynastic histories" that make the written historical record of China unrivaled for continuity and richness. Many Han scholars worked on the restoration and emendation of ancient texts; the commentaries they added had a lasting influence, particularly in strengthening Confucianism. Lexicography also made a great step forward around 100 A.D. with the compilation of the *Shuo Wen* (Explanation of Writing), which for the first time classified Chinese characters according to the system still used in simplified form today. Technological advances included the invention of paper, protoporcelain, a crude seismograph, and the water-powered mill. Conscious of their enormous debt to this period, the Chinese to this day are proud to call themselves "men of Han."

Period of Disunion (220–589). The task of putting down the rebellions at the end of the Han fell to provincial military commanders, and almost all of them used the opportunity to keep powerful armies loyal to themselves. One of these warlords, Ts'ao Ts'ao, took over the tottering central government in 196. His son, Ts'ao P'ei, deposed the last Han emperor in 220 and established his Wei dynasty, which controlled most of North China. Bearing in mind the disorders that crippled the Han, the Wei rulers forbade empresses and eunuchs to interfere in the government.

The Three Kingdoms. Meanwhile, in 221, a member of a remote branch of the Han, aided by the astute Chu-ko Liang and the warrior Kuan Yü (who later became the god of war in Chinese popular religion), established the Shu dynasty in the Szechwan basin. In the following year, another general established the Wu dynasty in the southeast or lower Yangtze valley with its capital at Nanking. The appearance for the first time in that area of a capital with imperial pretensions marked the beginning of an intensive development that would eventually transform it into the new economic and cultural heartland of China.

The innumerable acts of bravery, cunning, and treachery recounted in a popular historical novel, *The Romance of the Three Kingdoms*, have made this period a delight and a fascination to generations of Chinese. None of the Three Kingdoms, however, could break the stalemate.

Chin Dynasty. It was another general, Ssu-ma Yen, who usurped the Wei throne, established the Chin dynasty, and brought a tenuous unity to China in 280. At his death in 290, however, civil war broke out. The greedy aristocrats and corrupt officials could not reestablish order, and in 316 a wave of invading nomads overran north China. The following year a Chin prince restored

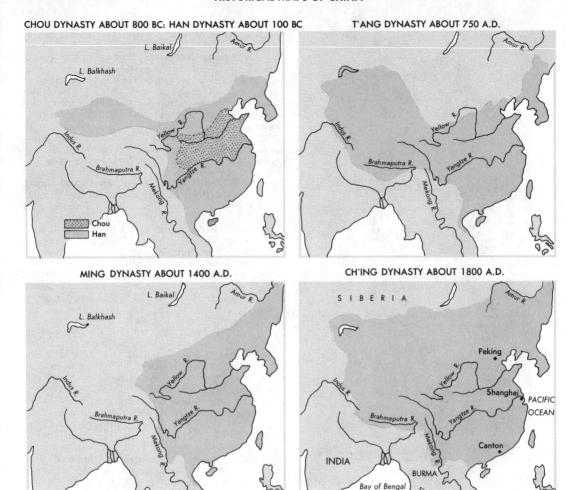

CHOU DYNASTY ABOUT 800 BC: HAN DYNASTY ABOUT 100 BC

T'ANG DYNASTY ABOUT 750 A.D.

MING DYNASTY ABOUT 1400 A.D.

CH'ING DYNASTY ABOUT 1800 A.D.

the dynasty at Nanking—a regime successful in defending the rest of China but too weak to recapture the north.

Southern Dynasties. The same was true for the four short-lived dynasties that followed it: the Liu Sung (420–479), the Ch'i (479–502), the Liang (502–557) and the Ch'en (557–589). Throughout this period, the court was seldom able to control more than the lower Yangtze region, the rest of the south being in the hands of powerful landlords. Seldom in China have so many rulers sat so insecurely on their throne; relatives, generals, and other nobles were ever ready to attempt a usurpation, and often did. The Han methods of choosing officials for their learning and proven ability gave way to an aristocratic monopoly (family patronage by rank) on the excuse that upbringing and access to experience should be the prerequisites for office. Many aristocrats, though privileged, were disillusioned and gave themselves over to alcohol, alchemy, poetry, and metaphysics. Nevertheless, these dynasties must be credited with achievements in literature and arts as, for example, the first collection of *belles lettres.* Meanwhile historical continuity was not lost: the Han remained the ideal that beckoned.

Northern Dynasties. The north from 316 on was at the mercy of repeated invasions by Hsiung-nu descendants, Mongols, and Tibetans. In the ka-

leidoscope of rising and falling regimes—at one time, nine ruling houses simultaneously contended for supremacy—terror and military despotism reigned. A notable exception, however, was the Tibetan Fu Chien, who was able to unify the north temporarily in the late 4th century by creating a Chinese-style administration and a well-trained Chinese infantry to supplement his cavalry. His chances of conquering the south appeared excellent, but, in 383, his army was repulsed at the historically crucial battle of the Fei River in Anhwei (Anhui). His defeat not only saved the south for the Chinese but also brought on renewed fragmentation in the north. Not until 439 did the Toba Tartars (proto-Mongols) restore peace throughout North China with their Northern (Later) Wei dynasty. Later in the century, Sinicization became their policy: they moved their capital to Loyang, ordered the nobles to adopt Chinese dress, customs, and surnames, and encouraged intermarriage with the Chinese. Slowly, the two halves of China were drawing together.

Buddhism gave a further stimulus to unity. From its homeland in India, it had barely reached China by way of central Asia during the Han dynasty. Not until the disorders and misery that overwhelmed China after the Han breakdown did it make rapid progress. One can overestimate the "rationality" or lack of deep religious concern of

COLLECTION OF THE NATIONAL PALACE MUSEUM, TAIPEI

T'AI TSUNG (627–650), first great emperor of the T'ang dynasty that lasted 300 years.

included the invention of gunpowder, the wheelbarrow, and the kite, as well as the first use of coal.

Sui Dynasty (581–618). Following the breakup of the Northern Wei, the north was again divided until a usurper successfully reunified it and, in 589, finally brought all of China under one government. The efforts of this vigorous Sui dynasty went beyond internal unification into external expansion, pursued by diplomacy and intrigue where possible and by military force when peaceful methods failed. The Great Wall was reconstructed, and, more importantly, various rivers and streams were widened and connected into an extended thoroughfare, the Grand Canal, that linked the traditional north and the Yangtze Valley into one integral area. The projects paid rich dividends in national unity and security, but there were other public works that did not, such as the building of palaces, parks, and other appurtenances of imperial grandeur. Moreover, all of them required oppressive tax and labor burdens. Reverses in the military campaign against Korea intensified popular resentment. An attack by the Eastern Turks in 615 sparked a number of internal rebellions that led inexorably to the dynasty's rapid disintegration.

It may be said that the Sui overreached itself, trying to accomplish too much too fast. What it did accomplish benefited not itself but the succeeding T'ang dynasty, which again unified China—a repetition of events eight centuries earlier when the Han rulers built their empire on the solid foundations begun by the Ch'in.

T'ang Dynasty (618–906). Reunification did not come easily. The Sui had kept China together for less than 30 years, an even shorter period than the fleeting Chin unification of the late 3d century. Its collapse might well have plunged the country once again into disunion. Fortunately, a more able leadership rose to the challenge; its astute policies repeated the success of its predecessors without repeating their mistakes. Much of the credit for this achievement must go to Li Shih-min, the ambitious son of a provincial governor in Shansi, who persuaded his vacillating father to revolt and then effectively took charge of the effort. After allying with the Turks, they captured Ch'ang-an (now Sian) in 617, founded the T'ang dynasty, and gathered at the court an increasing number of able generals and civilian officials. By 628, the empire had greatly expanded, and Li Shih-min, known to history as T'ang T'ai Tsung ("Grand Ancestor of T'ang"), had succeeded his father on the throne. This new empire that arose out of the shambles left by the Sui was destined to last, not for three decades but for three centuries.

T'ang T'ai Tsung. T'ai Tsung's reign (627–650) marks the first apogee of the T'ang. Chinese armies, well supported by their allies, the Uighur Turks, pushed deep into central Asia, Tibet, and even parts of northwestern India. The frontiers were guarded by military colonies (a system first tried during the Han) in which peasants served simultaneously as farmers and soldiers. Although the goal of self-sufficient frontier forces remained at best only partially achieved, the ideal of the system had such a strong attraction for Chinese rulers that military colonies reappeared often in later dynasties.

Peaceful foreign contacts, however, far exceeded in importance the T'ang military conquests. Peace and prosperity during the first half

the Chinese before this period—Taoist religious practices and a popular religion did after all enjoy wide adherence—but it is clear that a far more intense religious fervor gripped the Chinese at this time. In north and south, among nomadic conquerors and Chinese, nobles and commoners, Buddhism enjoyed a spectacular popularity.

Of great importance was the Buddhist impact on Chinese culture. Its colorful pantheon and ritual brought a host of new motifs to painting and sculpture. The cave temples cut into the cliffs at Yün-kang (near the earlier Northern Wei capital of Ta-t'ung) and at Lungmen (near the later capital, Loyang) still stand as great examples of Chinese sculpture. Buddhism also added new vocabulary to the Chinese language, new concepts to Chinese thought, and new methods in teaching. Its influence even penetrated deeply among the Confucianists. The desire to obtain authoritative texts of the various sutras impelled many Chinese monks to undertake the arduous pilgrimage to India; their return brought China new information on other parts of Asia. The progress of Chinese culture, however, was not entirely dependent on the Buddhist stimulus. Native arts, such as calligraphy, reached new heights. Scholars also compiled the first encyclopedias and local histories, genres that have added immeasurably to the richness of the Chinese historical records. Technological advances of the dynasty produced a truly remarkable cosmopolitanism, unprecedented and perhaps unsurpassed in Chinese history and rarely found elsewhere in the world. Buddhism continued to flourish within China as well as through Chinese pilgrims who journeyed to India for texts and instruction. Islam, Judaism, Manichaeanism, Zoroastrianism, and Nestorian Christianity entered China for the first time and developed unhindered. Many Buddhist monks and some laymen arrived from Japan to study the sutras as well as Chinese philosophy and literature, and to take back with them knowledge of T'ang political, economic, and social institutions. It was this cultural impact that moved the Japanese government to embark on a detailed imitation of T'ang patterns so that the T'ang plays in Japanese history a role analogous to Greece and Rome in Western civilization. Tibet and Korea likewise modeled their governments and a considerable part of their societies on the T'ang.

This cosmopolitanism was partially underpinned by commerce with the non-Chinese world, which expanded by leaps and bounds. Besides the overland trade with central Asia in which Uighur merchants played a prominent role, a considerable overseas trade, larger than ever before, grew up with Southeast, South, and West Asia. In this period of Islamic expansion, the intermediaries were chiefly the Arabs. Many of them came to live in China's coastal ports and the largest Arab colony, in Canton, had at one time as many as 100,000 inhabitants.

Cosmopolitanism rested squarely upon internal strength and a remarkable political stability. The government, incorporating with improvements some of the best features learned from the past, operated effectively. In the selection of officials growing reliance was placed on merit rather than on birth, although the hereditary privileges of the aristocracy continued to carry much weight, especially in local government. The revived Imperial University gave increasing numbers of officials a better training in the tenets of Confucianism than had been available since the Han.

Fiscally, the land taxes formed part of an extraordinarily detailed land system, the "equal field," that dated back to the Northern Wei. It sought to provide each peasant with sufficient land to support himself and his family, with regular redistribution of land to prevent excessive accumulation. Despite its extreme complexity and ambitious goals, surviving documents indicate, contrary to the skepticism of past historians, that the system was rigorously enforced at least in some parts of the empire for quite some time, an eloquent testimonial to the effectiveness of early T'ang administration.

Empress Wu. In the late 7th century, an event unique in Chinese history brought a short hiatus in the T'ang imperial line: a woman usurped the throne and declared herself founder of a new dynasty, the Chou (690–704). Castigated ever since by Chinese historians, Empress Wu must be considered a very capable if ruthless ruler, in some ways resembling Catherine the Great of Russia. On the one hand, for example, her effort to select officials obedient to herself rather than to the old aristocracy relied heavily on the examination system, thus strengthening the trend toward a bureaucracy of merit. On the other hand, excessive reliance on herself and a few favorites, as well as jealousies among the favorites, did not build up a solid loyalty to the new dynasty, which ended with her deposition in 704.

The Second Great Reign of T'ang. The stage was now set for the second great T'ang reign, that of Hsüan Tsung ("Profound Ancestor"), from 712 to 756—an era of splendid cultural advance. Under imperial patronage, Chinese lyric verse reached new heights in the poems of Li Po (705–762) and Tu Fu (712–770). Both figure and landscape painting flourished, as did the central Asian music that now replaced earlier Chinese forms. Delicate terra-cotta figurines, including noble ladies, musicians, dancers, and female polo players, vividly bring to life the sumptuous court life of this period.

All of this ended in catastrophe. Earlier military successes in central Asia gave way to reverses, including a disastrous defeat by the Arabs in 751 that shattered Chinese control over Turkestan. In 755, a revolt by An Lu-shan, a general of mixed blood who had enjoyed the patronage of the emperor and his consort, capped a growing internal crisis: the equal field system had disintegrated, causing government revenues to decline and the militia and corvée systems to become largely inoperative. With the help of "barbarian" troops, the dynasty resumed its rule, but its best days were over. No effort was made to revive the equal-field system; instead, a simpler biennial tax on land areas replaced the equal-field per capita levies, and the government gave up trying to control the ownership of land. The fiscal authorities also experimented with numerous new taxes in an effort to replace the loss of revenue from those areas over which military leaders had made themselves virtually independent satraps. Despite the relatively weak central government, however, much of the country enjoyed stability and peace. Commerce prospered and paper money made its first appearance. Blockprinting was invented, perhaps by Buddhists seeking a way to reproduce large numbers of prayers, charms, and sutras; once available, its use quickly spread to calendars, Confucian texts, lexicons, and books of all kinds. In literature, one of China's greatest prose masters, Han Yü (768–824), started Chinese prose away from the artificial and ornate style that had been in vogue for several centuries toward a more straightforward genre; in poetry, the simple style of Po Chü-i (772–846) won him an immense popularity not only in China but in Korea and Japan as well.

Chinese culture was not only flowering, it was also changing direction. Interest began to shift away from Buddhism and back to traditional Chinese concepts and values, especially those of Confucianism. Several reasons for this change may be suggested. The success of an imperial order based on Confucian values is an obvious one. On the other hand, Buddhism's decline was hastened by a great persecution in the years 841–845, in which other foreign religions also suffered. (Two earlier, smaller persecutions had occurred in 446 and 574 under the northern dynasties.) The major goal of the persecution was to break the economic power of the Buddhist temples; however, its effect was to send Buddhism on a downward slide from which it never recovered.

The Five Dynasties (907–960). The fall of the T'ang, made inevitable by the expanding power of the generals in various regions, ushered in what was to be China's last interval of prolonged political fragmentation. In the north, five dynasties followed each other in rapid succession; the longest one among them was the Later Liang (907–923), a mere 16 years. Despite prestige-borrowing devices such as calling themselves the Later T'ang (923–936) or the Later Han (947–950), power simply changed hands through a chain of usurpers, some defeated by their rivals and others overthrown by their subordinates. None was able to establish his authority over more than a part of North China. Meanwhile, in the south, several of the ten kingdoms that arose in the same period achieved not only longer life spans but also more powerful and prosperous reigns.

While the chaotic military and political events ran their course, the truly significant developments were taking place in the background. The power of the aristocrats, already weakened by the progress of the examination system, was irrevocably broken by the military upstarts who ruled in the north. Henceforth, China's elite would come from nonaristocratic origins. This development was further aided by the continuing Confucian revival, which was in turn facilitated by the spread of printing. The first woodblock edition (in 130 volumes) of the classics was printed under imperial patronage. A definite decline in the status of women can be observed in the strengthening of the taboo against the remarriage of widows, in the spread of concubinage (the taking of secondary wives), and in the beginnings of foot-binding.

Another important change was taking place along the northern frontiers. The great influence of the T'ang, spreading far and wide, had stimulated the progress of a number of nomadic tribes who learned to combine the possession of their own pastoral bases with the subjugation of nearby farming areas. Some of them soon acquired both the military power and the political expertise to establish and administer a Chinese-style empire. At this time, the Khitan, an eastern branch of the Mongols, won the cession of 16 prefectures below the Great Wall, regarded themselves as one of the legitimate successors to the T'ang empire, and made their Liao empire (947–1125) a lasting dynasty. Peking, its southern capital, was destined later to become the capital of other empires. The story of that renowned city is but one indication of a different pattern in Chinese history from this point on: the frequent presence of the alien dynasties of conquest, from the Liao down to the Manchus, who ruled as recently as 1911. For almost half of this period, a minority of conquerors of nomadic origin controlled the majority of the agricultural Chinese, who took comfort in assertion of cultural superiority, in the fact that even the "barbarian" conquerors had to respect the long, continuous culture native to their land.

Sung Dynasty (960–1279). When the general Chao K'uang-yin seized the throne in 960, his usurpation seemed no different from those that had preceded. However, his Sung dynasty, instead of being regional and ephemeral, succeeded in restoring both unity and stability to most of the country. With the coming of peace and prosperity, there appeared new social, political, and cultural patterns. Their significance can hardly be exaggerated; these patterns set the direction of Chinese life and thought for almost a thousand years.

Northern Sung. Chao himself initiated many of the policies that opened the road to unity. With a shrewd appreciation of the war-weariness of his people, he stressed in his reunification campaign humane treatment for the population and leniency toward surrendered rulers. As a result, most of China submitted quickly to Sung rule, and with a minimum of bitterness and ill-will. Perhaps because as a general and usurper he knew the perils of military power only too well, Chao decided that civilian scholar-officials must ultimately control the government, including supervision of military affairs. He did not, however, destroy the powerful generals under him as a number of previous founding emperors had done; instead, he cleverly persuaded them to do something unheard of: give up their military commands in exchange for retirement to luxurious sinecures. Moreover, he concentrated most of his best troops near the capital, leaving only small and weak garrisons in local areas. This general policy undoubtedly hampered the effectiveness of the army—even at the height of Sung power, parts of north and northwest China lay in the hands of the Khitan and Tanguts, respectively, to whom the Sung emperors sent yearly tribute. On the other hand, it accomplished the major goal: an end to over a century of militarism and regional separatism.

In these conditions, the economy boomed. Agriculture led the way, spurred on by the opening of new lands, better tools and irrigation methods, better rice strains, and more efficient organization of farming in the large estates that began to dominate much of the Chinese countryside. Commerce grew throughout the land, facilitated by improved transportation and increasingly available credit and banking facilities, including paper money. A remarkable diversification appeared in the Sung economy: the extractive industries produced ever larger amounts of salt, copper, gold, silver, lead, tin, and alum while textiles, metalware, printing, lacquers, and porcelains led the manufacturing trades.

A new social and political order arose, characterized by an openness through the breakdown of hereditary barriers, unprecedented in Chinese history. The stress on merit in the civil service, together with the greater educational opportunities made possible by more books and schools, opened government positions to a much wider segment of the population. While most of the officials continued to come from leisured families that could easily afford to put their sons through the long period of study necessary to pass the official examinations, it was no longer impossible or unreasonable for some talented but poor boys to aspire to an education and to eventual government service.

A tight lid on expenditures kept the Sung government in excellent fiscal health well into the 11th century. Gradually, however, higher military expenses, declining tax yields, and the higher costs of an expanding bureaucracy brought budget deficits. These and other problems led to various attempts at reform, the most thoroughgoing being Wang An-shih's in the years 1069–1085. Wang sought nothing less than a fundamental reorganization of the government's fiscal base, including budget reform, a more equitable land tax, state participation in commerce, and conversion of the corvée to cash payments. Wang's efforts to increase the state's economic and military strength were stunningly successful, but only temporarily. Ill-conceived military adventures and imperial extravagance soon ate up the budget surpluses. Even more important was

CULVER PICTURES

KUBLAI KHAN (1260–1294), Mongol ruler of the huge Asian empire founded by his grandfather Genghis Khan.

Wang's inability to rally most of officialdom behind his program. Many officials, including some of the most prestigious, saw these measures as excessive and un-Confucian. Ideological opposition was often reinforced by concern for their own privileged economic position, a factor that in part accounted for the extreme bitterness of these quarrels even after Wang had left the scene.

Southern Sung. Despite the resulting internal weakness, the Sung could not resist the temptation to try the age-old strategy of using barbarians against barbarians and entered into an alliance with the newly arisen Jurchen state of Chin (Kin) against the Liao. A dismal performance by the Sung army, together with bloated demands for a share in the spoils of the Chin victory, encouraged the Chin to turn on their erstwhile allies. In the ensuing campaign, they extended their control over the entire north, leaving the Sung to rule central and southern China. From this time onward (1127–1279), the dynasty is known as the Southern Sung, in contrast to the earlier Northern Sung.

The retreat of the Chinese government to the south recalls in many ways the beginning of the southern dynasties eight centuries earlier. The differences are more striking, however. Rather than a south on the threshold of development, the Sung found a well-developed area that had already established itself as the economic and cultural heartland of China. Not surprisingly, then, the Southern Sung enjoyed greater prosperity than the Northern Sung, despite the shrunken area under its control. Internal and overseas commerce continued to expand, bringing the government a higher percentage of its revenue from these sources than ever before or after. Culturally, the Confucian revival found its culmination in Chu Hsi whose genius as a synthesizer has often reminded Western scholars of St. Thomas Aquinas. The orthodoxy created by Chu Hsi dominated Chinese thought for the next several centuries. Just as in the Northern Sung, painting and literature flourished. In the latter, two new forms, popular drama and the novel, made

their appearance and enjoyed great popularity.

Yüan Dynasty (1271–1368). In the 12th century, while the Chin and Southern Sung dynasties divided China, the Mongols were still scattered and disorganized tribes to the northwest, without even a common name. The credit for unifying them and forging them into invincible conquerors belongs to Genghis (Chinggis) Khan. In about three decades before his death in 1227, he had put together an enormous empire stretching from Korea to the Volga and from Siberia to India. His successors added to his conquests, and, under his grandson Kublai (Khubilai, 1260–1294), the fattest plum of all, South China, fell to the Mongol armies.

Mongol Rule. The Mongol victory meant that all of China was, for the first time, in the hands of non-Chinese conquerors. Moreover, these barbarians brought with them attitudes and policies unlike anything ever experienced by the Chinese. The Chinese, in their isolation, might consider China as the center of the universe and Chinese civilization the standard for the world to emulate. The Mongols, however, had had wide experience with other countries and cultures. They made it painfully clear that they regarded China as only one part of their vast empire and Chinese civilization itself as only one among many.

The new regime was especially offensive to the scholar-officials. In place of their unchallenged mastery of the political order, they now found themselves supervised by all sorts of foreigners, Mongols, Turks, Iranians, Arabs, Georgians, and Armenians. At one point their social position sank so low that satirists ridiculed them as little better than beggars. Worst of all was the general barbarization that the Mongols brought to Chinese life. At court, throughout the administration, and ultimately in the society itself, civilized restraint gave way to cruelty, ruthlessness, and excesses of all kinds.

Foreign Visitors. China's incorporation into the vast Mongol empire led to many more contacts with the West than before. A steady stream of traders and diplomats from western Asia and Europe traveled to Peking, capital of the Great Khan. Many, including the Venetian, Marco Polo, returned home with fabulous tales about the glories of Cathay. Christian, Buddhist, and Islamic missionaries also came, taking advantage of the religious tolerance to proselytize in China; of these, the Muslims sunk the deepest roots, and sizable Muslim communities never completely Sinicized have persisted in China to this day. Chinese inventions and techniques, from movable type and the magnetic compass to playing cards and kites, made their way westward as did many Chinese themselves; Chinese quarters could be found in towns as far west as Novgorod, Moscow, and Tabriz. Chinese engineers taught the Mongols how to use gunpowder in weapons and built the ships for two unsuccessful attempts to invade Japan.

Despite the new worlds open to it, however, Chinese culture remained largely impervious to foreign influences. Painting (especially landscapes), poetry, and historiography continued along paths clearly marked out in earlier periods. Drama and the novel became even more popular than under the Sung, reflecting the growing influence of the lower classes on culture. Written in a style close to everyday speech rather than in the stilted and highly allusive classical style, novels and plays could be enjoyed by educated and uneducated alike. They also provided an outlet for many unemployed scholars who were willing to turn their talents to these not-quite-respectable literary forms.

The declining competence of Kublai's successors, Sinicization that drained the martial vigor of the Mongols, and, especially, internecine struggles within the leadership brought the Yüan dynasty to an early end. By the mid-15th century, droughts, floods, and famines had touched off widespread peasant revolts. Aimed first against the landlords, they soon metamorphosed into a national campaign to drive out the alien rulers. Nor did the Mongol court put up a determined fight to keep China; to them, it was more important in the long run to watch over developments in central Asia and to keep in touch with other Mongol branches farther west. Consequently, it chose to retire to the base in Mongolia that no Chinese army was capable of penetrating.

Ming Dynasty (1368–1644). Among the rebel leaders at the end of the Mongol era, there again emerged a sole victor: Chu Yüan-chang, an energetic, clever, and unscrupulous commoner from a peasant family, who eliminated his competitors and established the Ming dynasty at Nanking in 1368. He is known from his reign title as the Hung Wu ("Vast Military Power") emperor.

The founder of a Chinese empire or a vigorous emperor early in the line tended to set the tone of the entire dynasty. Ancestral respect required that later emperors conform as far as practicable to established precedents. In the Sung, the generous attitude toward the scholar-officials owed much to the policies of its founder. So, too, Hung Wu's dynamic 32-year reign, exercizing a powerful effect on later Ming history, was largely responsible for the autocracy of the Ming emperors.

Possibly a paranoiac, Hung Wu was hypersensitive to any real or supposed threats to his power. Although he adopted the general administrative structure of the Sung and Yüan, he added to it a secret police service whose investigations of suspected conspiracies led to the execution of hundreds of officials. To cow the bureaucrats still further, he continued the Mongol practice of public thrashings at court, even for high officials. When his prime minister was implicated in a plot in 1380, he simply abolished the post, took over its functions himself, and used mere secretaries as his aides, though decades later these secretaries became in fact the leading ministers.

Emperor Yung Lo. The Yung Lo ("Perpetual Happiness") emperor (1403–1424), who had usurped the throne from his nephew, was hardly the man to reverse the trend toward autocracy. An extremely capable ruler, he tried to erase the Mongol threat from the borders of China by personally commanding five massive military campaigns deep into central Asia: in the fourth, for example, his army consisted of 235,000 men with a supply train of 117,000 carts and 340,000 donkeys. Equally remarkable were a series of maritime expeditions that sent Chinese ships as far as the Persian Gulf and the east coast of Africa. Scholars still debate the motives behind these expeditions: whether, for example, Yung Lo was searching for the deposed nephew who might have escaped only to reappear some day to claim the throne. Or perhaps Yung Lo was after trade revenues and military intelligence about condi-

tions on the other side of central Asia. Whatever the reasons, these expeditions vividly illustrate the vitality of the early Ming. Particularly striking for an empire historically land-oriented was the enormous naval capacity that had developed since the Sung. As a result of these expeditions, Chinese prestige in Southeast and South Asia reached unprecedented heights; envoys and, in some cases, even the rulers of foreign countries were brought back to China to present tribute and to acknowledge the preeminence of the Chinese emperor. Chinese immigrants began to penetrate the cities in these lands. Only in recent years has the economic dominance established by these and later generations of "overseas Chinese" begun to break down under the assault of new, nationalistic governments.

The vigor of the Yung Lo reign knew few bounds. Public works projects included the reconstruction of the Great Wall, repair of numerous city walls, roads, and canals, and the extensive rebuilding of Peking. For strategic reasons, Peking became the primary Ming capital from 1421 on, reversing the centuries-long drift of the Chinese population toward the southeast. With many migrants pouring in, the north began to make new economic and cultural progress, though it never quite caught up with the south.

The Decline of Ming. After the Yung Lo reign, a long decline set in. Symptomatic was the tendency of later emperors, brought up in the seclusion of the palace and with little knowledge of the outside world, to rely on eunuchs, some of whom had been their companions since childhood. Eunuchs eventually came to play a major role throughout the Ming administration, a role that became particularly abusive when they also controlled the secret police. This inevitably brought on a bitter conflict with the scholar-officials who denounced this deviation and fought hard to restore their own preeminence in government service. Yet, the scholar-officials suffered from a major weakness of their own. When not struggling against the eunuchs, they dissipated their energies in bitter factional struggles among themselves instead of concentrating on improving general conditions. Fiscal difficulties added to the Ming plight. The costs of defense against the Mongols and against pirates along the southern coast, many of them Japanese, together with imperial profligacy and maladministration, drained the treasury despite a basically thriving economy. Agricultural productivity continued to grow, particularly with the introduction of New World crops such as peanuts, maize, and sweet potatoes. The population snowballed from something over 65,000,000 at the end of the 14th century to perhaps 150,000,000 around 1600. But creeping administrative paralysis eventually joined with natural disasters to produce the rebellions that signaled an impending transferral of the "heavenly mandate."

Cultural Achievements. Culturally, the Ming scored higher in technique than in creativity. The best efforts went into the variation, collection, classification, and assessment of the creations from earlier periods. Philosophy, however, made major progress: the school of Wang Yang-ming emerged to challenge the Chu Hsi orthodoxy. Influenced by Zen Buddhism, this Confucian school stressed meditation and intuitive knowledge rather than Chu Hsi's "investigation of things". Toward the end of the Ming, Jesuit missionaries appeared at the capital. Well-educated, they brought the learning of the Renaissance to China. Their explanations of European philosophy, science, and technology won them considerable admiration from some scholars. Western learning, however, did not take a firm hold in China; rather it was the Chinese civilization, through the reports of Jesuits, such as Matteo Ricci, that had a lasting influence on the West.

Ch'ing Dynasty (1644–1911). The Ming dynasty gave way to the second period of foreign rule over all China. But the Manchus, unlike the Mongols, achieved great success in adopting and ruling through traditional Chinese institutions. Despite Manchu emperors on the throne and both Manchu and their allied Mongol garrisons at key points throughout the country, the alien Ch'ing dynasty (1644–1911) represented in almost every way a prolongation and improvement over the Ming, rather than an abrupt break, thus strengthening the impression of China's cultural continuity.

The Manchus sprang from the same Jurchen stock that had produced the Chin dynasty five centuries earlier. In the late 16th and early 17th centuries, a forceful leader, Nurhachi (1559–1626), circumvented Ming efforts to keep the nomad tribes divided. After uniting the Manchus and dominating the Mongols, he and his successors were ready to embark on further conquest. Their golden opportunity came in 1644. China, torn by rebellion, had a rebel leader sitting briefly on the throne. Responding to the appeal of a Ming general to come through the Great Wall to help him put down the usurper, the Manchus acted with alacrity. Once in Peking, they refused to leave; instead, they overran the rest of the country. The military conquest was harsh, but political appeals were never neglected. The new ruler kept the government structure intact, promising to make it work better, for example, by eliminating eunuch interference. The only important change was the doubling of a number of key posts, one for a Manchu and the other for a Chinese. The obvious intentions were two: to fit the Manchus themselves into the traditional order and to rally many of the old bureaucrats to the new dynasty.

K'ang Hsi and Ch'ien Lung. The bulk of the period from 1644 to 1800 falls into the reigns of two great emperors: K'ang Hsi (1661–1722) and Ch'ien Lung (1736–1795). Ascending the throne at the age of seven, K'ang Hsi brusquely disposed of his regents at 13 and began his own energetic rule. Two of his major tasks were the consolidation of the Manchu rule and stabilization of the frontiers. In a bloody civil war from 1674 to 1681, he crushed a major revolt of leading Chinese generals in the south led by the same man who had invited the Manchus into China. Manchu forces also attacked Taiwan (christened "Formosa" or "The Beautiful" by the Portuguese) and, with the aid of a Dutch fleet, defeated in 1683 the grandson of the famous Cheng Ch'eng-kung (Koxinga) who had wrested the island from the Portugese earlier. For the first time, Taiwan was integrated into the empire. With the help of the Jesuit Gerbillon, the Chinese negotiated a satisfactory treaty at Nerchinsk with the Russians, demarcating their common border for the first time. In the early 18th century, Manchu armies entered Tibet. Expansion continued under Ch'ien Lung and led to Ch'ing control over a much wider area than Ming China or any previous dynasty, with the exception of the Yüan.

The Manchu emperors were well accepted by the Chinese. Their renowned patronage of Confucianism and scholarship won them the support of most scholars. K'ang Hsi commissioned, among other works, great encyclopedias and collections of literature. Ch'ien Lung was more subtle: on the one hand, literary inquisitions eliminated disloyal Chinese intellectuals and destroyed all works that spoke disparagingly of the Manchus and their "barbarian" predecessors; on the other hand, he excelled K'ang Hsi not merely as a patron of scholarship and art but also by being himself a prolific painter, calligrapher, and poet.

The Decline of Ch'ing. The tide of Manchu fortunes began to turn toward the end of the 18th century. Even before Ch'ien Lung abdicated in 1795 so as to refrain from achieving a longer reign than his grandfather, K'ang Hsi, the usual and quite unmistakable signs of dynastic decline had appeared. Enormous sums were sunk into military campaigns; corruption began to infest all levels of the government; and even the very success of their rule had begun to turn against the Manchus. The long period of peace and prosperity had led the population to soar to more than 300,000,000 by 1794. This population explosion began to outpace both the growth potential of the agrarian society and the capabilities of the traditional administration system. When rebellion broke out in the west in 1795, its temporary success revealed an alarming deterioration in the Manchu army. Apparently the Manchus had grown soft by sitting comfortably at the top of the society, enjoying the refinements of Chinese life and forgetting the discipline their founding leaders had extolled. In any case, the eventual loss of their identity by the Manchus has led to an exaggerated notion that the melting pot of Chinese civilization absorbs all conquerors.

Greater misfortunes lay ahead: dynastic decline came precisely when China would soon meet the greatest challenge in its history, the many-sided and overpowering impact of the modern West and the ultimate realization that tumultuous changes must take place to introduce an industrial way of life.

JAMES T. C. LIU, *Princeton University*
PETER J. GOLAS, *Harvard University*

MODERN HISTORY OF CHINA TO 1911

While early European evangelism, as typified by the Jesuit missionaries, finally had only a very small impact on the Chinese empire, European trade as it grew forced a fundamental change in the relationship between China and the West. Until 1842, however, this trade was nominally contained within the institutional framework of the system of tributary relations, whereby the Chinese government subsumed its relations with the European powers under the same system that it had for centuries applied to its smaller neighbors in Central and Southeast Asia.

The Opening of China. By the late 18th century, trade with the West had come to be concentrated in and limited to the port of Canton in South China. British trade had by far outstripped that of any other nation, and until 1834 the British East India Company held a legal monopoly of British commerce with China. The company purchased its silks and the especially important tea cargo for the home market through officially designated Chinese monopoly merchants, known collectively as the "Cohong." The Cohong became the sole means by which the foreign traders could communicate with

TZ'U HSI (1835–1908), dowager empress and de facto ruler of China, strove in vain to keep Manchus in power.

the Chinese government. The trade, though subject to numerous restrictions and unregulated exactions, was profitable to all concerned, and not the least to the Chinese imperial customs officers who supervised it. British efforts to obtain better trading arrangements and formal and equal diplomatic relations with China on the European model (Macartney embassy, 1793; Amherst embassy, 1816) were invariably rejected by the Chinese.

The growth of an illegal trade in opium, fostered by the East India Company, and the parallel growth of private British trade, which increasingly chafed at Chinese restrictions on commerce and official contact, led inexorably to open conflict. The ineptness of British diplomacy was matched only by the inadequate response of many of the Chinese officials. The smuggling of opium into China rapidly increased from 4,244 chests in 1820–1821 to 40,200 in 1838–1839 as the result of an expansionist production policy in India and the influx of private merchants to Canton after the abolition of the Company's monopoly. The Ch'ing court in Peking, after intense debate, dispatched Lin Tse-hsü (1785–1850) to Canton as Imperial Commissioner to extirpate the opium trade. Lin was an official of unquestioned probity and considerable ability but as ignorant as most of his colleagues of the motives and power of the European civilization whose representatives he was to challenge. He reached Canton in March 1839. Within a few days, by the threat of force, he compelled the foreign merchants to surrender the opium in their possession and, to the astonishment of Chinese and foreigners, sluiced into the river 20,000 chests valued at $6 million, mixed with salt, lime, and water. To the British, Lin's actions was not only piracy of trade but an insult to the crown, and his perfidy was compounded by an irreconcilable clash of legal sys-

tems arising out of the murder of a Chinese in a brawl with British and American sailors, and by the total stoppage of British trade.

The hostilities which followed, known to succeeding generations as the Opium War (1839–1842), were on a petty scale but ominous to the Ch'ing court, which feared the possibility of domestic rebellion in South China as much as it did the foreign encroachment. By mid-1842, a small British marine and naval force had seized the key point where the Grand Canal intersected the Yangtze River and threatened both Nanking and the grain supply of Peking. To preserve itself, the Manchu dynasty capitulated. On Aug. 29, 1842 the British forced Chinese acceptance of the Treaty of Nanking, which, together with the Supplementary Treaty of the Bogue in 1843 and the French and American treaties of 1844, established the principles that were to govern China's international status for a century.

By the Treaty of Nanking, the five ports of Canton, Amoy, Foochow, Ningpo, and Shanghai were opened to residence and trade; the island of Hong Kong was ceded to Britain; the Cohong monopoly of trade was abolished; the Chinese paid an indemnity for the opium destroyed and for the expenses of the war; diplomatic relations on the basis of equality were established between British consuls in the treaty ports and Chinese officials; and a uniform low tariff, the rates of which were to be fixed by mutual agreement, was established. The other treaties completed the new structure of relations by providing for extraterritorial jurisdiction in criminal cases enforced by foreign consuls, and for the principle of most-favored-nation treatment that in effect made the treaties of all the foreign powers into a single document of treaty law to which China was subjected.

T'ai-p'ing Rebellion. As a result of the Opium War the coastal periphery of China had been opened to Western influence. Before the second treaty settlement of 1858–1860, which greatly extended foreign privileges, there began a series of domestic rebellions that threatened the existence of the Ch'ing dynasty. The most important of these uprisings in size and consequences was the T'ai-p'ing Rebellion (1851–1864). Organized originally as a quasi-Christian sect by Hung Hsiu-ch'üan (1814–1864), who purported to be the younger brother of Jesus, the T'ai-p'ing movement rapidly attracted large numbers of disaffected peasants in South China. In 1851, Hung formally rebelled against the Manchus and declared his regime the "Heavenly Kingdom of Great Peace (T'ai-p'ing t'ien-kuo)" with himself as the "Heavenly King." Aided by poor harvests, communal dissension, and corruption of the Manchu government, the T'ai-p'ing movement easily overran the Yangtze provinces, accumulating hordes of followers en route. In March 1853 the T'ai-p'ing army captured Nanking and made it their capital.

The quasi-Christian beliefs of the T'ai-p'ing leaders, which in the early years of the uprising attracted sympathetic notice from some Western Christian missionaries, were combined with an even larger dosage of China's domestic sociopolitical tradition to furnish the rebellion with its ideology, program, and organization. In the initial phase of the rebellion, the T'ai-p'ing army formed a disciplined, egalitarian, military-religious society. Its puritanical zeal forbade slavery, opium, tobacco, and concubinage for the rank and file. Equality of the sexes was proclaimed, the abolition of footbinding was called for, and women were enrolled in separate labor and military units and appointed to some offices. The ideal T'ai-p'ing program called for a kind of communism in which the land would be divided equally among the tillers and the surplus product consigned to a common treasury. Little of this radical program was in fact put into practice; first, because the territory controlled was never securely held for any length of time, and second, because Hung and his chief subordinates took on traditional forms of status and hierarchy.

The early rebel victories baldly revealed the decay of the Manchu armies. The ultimate suppression of the T'ai-p'ing took 15 years of civil war, and can be attributed to (1) corruption and factionalism among the rebels; (2) the failure of the T'ai-p'ings to follow up the military advantage in 1853 by pressing northward; (3) the inability of the T'ai-p'ings to achieve an alliance with the other anti-Manchu forces, such as the Triad Society; and (4) the alienation of the scholar-gentry class by the rebels' wholesale attack on Confucianism and the entire social order based upon it. It was in fact Chinese officials, deeply imbued with Confucianism and loyal to the Ch'ing dynasty as the supporter of an orthodox Confucian society, who organized the new provincial Chinese armies that defeated the heterodox T'ai-p'ings.

With the grudging consent of the Manchu imperial court, Chinese officials such as Tseng Kuo-fan (1811–1872) and Li Hung-chang (1823–1901), organized new provincial militias. Equipped with foreign-style weapons and a Confucian indoctrination, these largely locally financed, gentry-led contingents gradually encircled and besieged Nanking, which fell in July 1864. Some T'ai-p'ing remnants fled northward to join the Nien rebels, who had been increasingly active in the North China plain since 1853. It was not until 1868 that Li Hung-chang was able to wipe out the last Nien bands, and not until some years later that revolts by Muslim minorities in Southwest China (1855–1873) and in the Northwest (1862–1873) were finally suppressed.

Second Treaty Settlement. The great mid-19th century domestic rebellions coincided with a second armed confrontation with the Western powers, the Anglo-French War (or Second Opium War) of 1856–1860. The underlying issue was whether China would concede an extension of the privileges won by the foreign powers in the first treaties. In practice, neither the commercial nor the diplomatic privileges exacted from China in the 1840's satisfied the Western powers. The Chinese, reacting to their immense domestic troubles and the seeming enormity of the concessions already made, refused negotiation until a strong Anglo-French naval force, dispatched to the north in 1858, forced the conclusion of the Treaties of Tientsin in June of that year. Only a further show of force, including the occupation and looting of Peking in 1860, produced final Chinese acceptance of the 1858 treaties.

By this second treaty settlement, and by new tariff and commercial negotiations at Shanghai in 1858, the entire Chinese empire was in effect opened to Western influence. Additional treaty ports were opened and foreign shipping was permitted on the Yangtze River. Permanent foreign legations were established in Peking; missionary residence and property holding were sanctioned in the interior; and a foreign-staffed maritime customs service was established. By the most-favored-nation principle, the United States and Russia, and subsequently other nations, secured identical privileges. Taking advantage of the Anglo-French threat to the Ch'ing dynasty, the Russians, moreover, were able to obtain Peking's acceptance of their annexation of Manchuria north of the Amur River and territory the Russians subsequently named the Maritime Province, situated between the Ussuri River and the Pacific (Sino-Russian Treaty of Peking, November 1860).

The T'ung Chih Restoration. The Hsien Feng Emperor, who had fled from Peking in 1860, died in August 1861. He was succeeded by his minor son, who took the reign title T'ung Chih (reigned 1862–1874). Hsien Feng's brother, Prince Kung (personal name, I-hsin; 1833–1898), had remained in the capital and had negotiated the 1860 treaties. By a coup d'etat that eliminated more antiforeign rivals, Prince Kung became the center of a revived Manchu-Chinese leadership which, for a time at least, appeared to cope more adequately with China's internal and external problems than its predecessors had. Prince Kung and the Chinese provincial leaders Tseng Kuo-fan, Li Hung-chang, and Tso Tsung-t'ang (1812–1885) were united in seeking a "restoration" of the traditional Confucian system.

More important to the restoration leaders than mere material means of suppression was the compelling need to reassert Confucian morality and civil government in the pacified areas. Tseng Kuo-fan reopened local academies and resumed the regular civil service examinations in territories recovered from the T'ai-p'ings. Efforts were made to make the examinations more practical in content and to restrict the sale of degrees, a revenue-producing practice greatly expanded in the 1850's by the fiscal needs of civil war. To regain the allegiance of the peasantry and local landholders, time-honored measures of moral exhortation, remission of tax payments in afflicted

SUN YAT-SEN (1866–1925) and Mme. Sun. He led the struggle to end the Manchu dynasty and form a republic.

WIDE WORLD

CHIANG KAI-SHEK (left), after winning North China in 1928, and Yen Hsi-shan (1883–1960), satrap of Shansi.

areas, and reduction of taxes were resorted to.

The immediate threat to the dynasty after 1860 was domestic rebellion. Tseng Kuo-fan, and especially Li Hung-chang (for his Huai Army), at first purchased foreign arms, then established arsenals of their own in several places, including the major Kiangnan Arsenal opened at Shanghai in 1865. In addition to weapons, ammunition, and machinery, numerous translations into Chinese of Western scientific and technical works were produced at Kiangnan. Tso Tsung-t'ang established another important arsenal and shipyard at Foochow in South China in 1866. The products of these and other smaller establishments were not adequate in quantity or quality to protect China from foreign aggression. But they did provide the material means for suppressing rebellion and maintaining a precarious domestic order.

In March 1861 a new "Office for the General Management of Affairs Concerning the Various Countries" (better known by its abbreviated name, Tsungli Yamen) was established to handle relations with the Western diplomats now resident in Peking. Despite opposition, an Interpreters College (T'ung-wen Kuan) was opened in Peking in 1862, its curriculum including mathematics and science as well as Western languages for China's future diplomats. Prince Kung, Tseng Kuo-fan, and the others had a more realistic appreciation than did their archconservative opponents of the strength of the Western powers who threatened their society even while now lending support to the weakened dynasty. By their hesitant adoption of Western techniques, however, they did not intend to "Westernize" China, but rather to strengthen it along traditional lines. Their apparent short-run success concealed acute contradictions.

While the Chinese provincial leaders were unquestionably loyal to the Ch'ing dynasty, it was nevertheless a fact that in the process of suppressing the rebels they had developed military forces and regional political and economic bases whose continued existence marked not only a shift of power in the provinces from Manchus to Chinese, but also an augmentation of the power and influence of the provincial governors at the expense of the imperial government in Peking. The dynastic central power, in a sense, owed its survival to the growth of regionalism. The best example of this phenomenon is Li Hung-chang, who with his Huai Army dominated Northeast China as governor-general of the key metropolitan province of Chihli for three decades from 1870 to 1895.

Localism in another context brought on numerous confrontations with the foreigner throughout the remainder of the dynasty. Restoration of Confucian morality and government in the post-T'ai-p'ing period meant in practice reinforcement of the authority of the local Chinese scholar-gentry class, whose ideology and social position made it least amenable to political innovation and social reform, and to the threatening presence of foreigners, especially foreign missionaries, which the treaties sanctioned. In hundreds of recorded anti-Christian incidents, the Manchu court was ground between the demands of the foreigner that the treaty rights of missionaries be observed and the increasing xenophobia of the scholar-gentry, whose passive support was essential for the survival of Manchu rule. Finally, the Confucian ideology, which sanctioned the T'ung Chih Restoration, allowed all too little room for a fundamental attack on the political inadequacies, social inequities, and technological backwardness which had been responsible both for military defeat at the hands of foreigners and for massive domestic disaffection.

"Self-Strengthening" and "Modernization" to 1895.
A slow process of adjustment to China's changed external circumstances continued to the end of the century under the rubric of "self-strengthening." Chinese diplomatic missions, a decade and a half after foreign ministers came to Peking, were established in London and Berlin (1877); Paris, Washington, and Tokyo (1878); Madrid and St. Petersburg (1879); and later elsewhere. Between 1872 and 1881, under the leadership of Yung Wing (1828–1912, an 1854 graduate of Yale), 120 Chinese students were sent to the United States to study. Smaller numbers were sent for technical training to England and France. Complementing the early arsenals, pioneer firms were established in several modern industries: shipping (China Merchants' Steam Navigation Co., 1872), mining (Kaiping Coal Mine, 1877), telegraph (Tientsin-Shanghai line, 1881), railroad (13 miles at Kaiping mines, 1882, later much extended), textiles (Shanghai Cotton Cloth Mill, 1890), iron and steel (Hanyang Ironworks, 1896). These firms and their imitators were often organized on the basis of "official supervision and merchant management," which meant in practice that private capital was sometimes augmented with official loans and concessions and the enterprises were managed by bureaucrats closely tied to such regional leaders as Li Hung-chang and Chang Chih-tung (1837–1909). Gradually, a modern national postal system emerged under the auspices of the Maritime Customs. Foreign newspapers in the treaty ports stimulated the development of a modern Chinese-language press. *Shun Pao,* the leading Chinese daily in Shanghai, was founded in 1872. If their evangelism was less successful than they hoped, Protestant missionaries through their schools, hospitals, and publications (presenting a wide selection of Western ideas) were an important "transmission belt" for Western culture. During the last half of the 19th century China's foreign trade rapidly expanded (total value in customs taels of silver, 1865: 54 million; 1899: 195 million) and with it grew the importance of the treaty ports and their foreign-controlled enclaves, especially Shanghai and its International Settlement, where foreign commercial, banking (such as the Hong Kong and Shanghai Banking Corporation, founded 1865), and cultural institutions proliferated. In the shadow of this China-based Western enterprise, there developed a semimodern Chinese mercantile com-

munity—compradors handling the Chinese side of a foreign firm's business, distributors of imports, processors of exports, and small bankers.

Almost imperceptibly change was taking place, but for the most part it was still confined to the periphery of Chinese society. Above all, the Ch'ing state, in Peking and in most of the provinces, remained governed by ideological inertia, vested political interests, and fiscal weakness which precluded radical innovation and reform. During most of the reign (1875–1908) of the Kuang Hsü Emperor, the court and government were dominated by his aunt, the Dowager Empress Tz'u Hsi (1835–1908). Clever, narrow-minded, and corrupt, the Dowager Empress' chief concern was to maintain the Manchu dynasty, not to modernize the Chinese nation.

Renewed Foreign Encroachment. The weakened ties between the Chinese empire and the states on its frontiers, which (through the "tribute system") for centuries had acknowledged a state of dependency on Peking, were shattered by renewed European encroachment after 1870 and by the appearance of a new Asian power—Japan. In 1871, Russia moved troops into Ili in central Asia to forestall the spread of British influence. After difficult negotiations China was able to recover part of Ili in 1881 (Treaty of St. Petersburg). The failure of the Tsungli Yamen to contest Japanese claims to suzerainty over the Liu-ch'iu (Ryukyu) Islands and the payment of an indemnity in 1874 for shipwrecked islanders murdered by Formosan natives meant the further loss of control. Although the tributary ties between Burma and China were tenuous, it was nevertheless a shock to be forced to recognize the *fait accompli* of the British protectorate in 1886. Much more important to the Chinese was the steady French absorption of Vietnam (Annam) in 1858–1885, which transformed that former tributary and cultural dependency of China into a French colony. Wavering Chinese resistance to the French culminated in the Sino-French War of 1884–1885 in Tongking (North Vietnam), and, despite several French reverses in the border fighting, China finally acknowledged the French protectorate in the Treaty of Tientsin (1885).

The ensuing loss of Korea was the *coup de grace,* which, in revealing the basic weakness and ineptitude of the Manchu dynasty, opened the floodgates of modern Chinese nationalism that swept the dynasty into history. A Sino-Japanese contest over Korea developed in intensity from 1876 when a Japanese treaty with Korea failed to acknowledge the traditional Chinese suzerainty. Under Li Hungchang, the Chinese attempted to revive their dormant influence in order to counter the Japanese. Endemic factionalism in the Korean court provided ample opportunity for the two adversaries to choose sides. The outbreak of civil war in Korea in 1894 and the dispatch of troops by both China and Japan led to the beginning of hostilities in July 1894. Contrary to widespread expectations, the Japanese won a succession of easy victories. By the Treaty of Shimonoseki (April 1895), China recognized the independence of Korea; ceded to Japan Taiwan, the Penghu (Pescadores) Islands, and the Liaotung Peninsula in southern Manchuria (which was later returned to China as a result of Russian, German, and French intervention); agreed to pay an indemnity of 230,000,000 taels; and granted to the Japanese (and hence to other foreigners) the right to engage in manufacturing in the treaty ports.

The revelation of China's helplessness had two consequences; it aroused a more radical reform

movement and an increase in the zeal and number of anti-Manchu revolutionaries; and it led to a "scramble for concessions" by the European powers and Japan. Germany seized Kiachow Bay (Chiaochouwan) and Tsingtao in Shantung province on the pretext of the murder of two missionaries (November 1897), and forced the Chinese to grant a 99-year lease on Kiaochow along with exclusive rights to develop railroads and mines in Shantung. In March 1898, Russia extorted a 25-year lease on the southern part of the Liaotung Peninsula, including Dairen and Port Arthur (now Lüta) and the right to construct a railroad in South Manchuria. France followed (April) with a 99-year lease on Kwangchow Bay (Kuangchouwan) in Kwangtung province and railroad rights in Yünnan. In the same month, China promised Japan not to alienate Fukien province (China's southeastern coast opposite of Taiwan) to any other power. Britain (June) secured a 99-year lease of the New Territories (on the mainland adjacent to Hong Kong), a nonalienation agreement for the whole Yangtze valley hinterland of Shanghai, and the lease of a naval base at Weihaiwei in Shantung. These "spheres of influence," much more menacing than the treaty port concessions of the past, appeared to foreshadow the outright imperialist partition of China, on the model of Africa, into a congeries of European colonies.

Reform and Revolution. Demands for more radical reform came from many scholar-gentry sources after 1895. The leader of the reform movement was a Cantonese scholar, K'ang Yu-wei (1858–1927), who had opposed the peace treaty with Japan in 1895. He had been exposed through translations to some aspects of Western history and political thought, and had developed a new interpretation of tradition in which he saw Confucius as a reformer who had himself written, rather than merely edited, the principal classics as a means of invoking an alleged golden age in antiquity to justify major institutional reform in his own time *(K'ung-tzu kai-chih k'ao [Confucius as a Reformer],* published 1897). K'ang, in effect, sought to establish a constitutional monarchy in the name of Confucius. In the unsettling atmosphere of the "scramble for concessions," K'ang caught the ear of the Kuang Hsü Emperor, and for a hundred days between June 11 and Sept. 21, 1898, a veritable stream of reform edicts inspired by K'ang or his principal follower, Liang Ch'i-ch'ao (1873–1929), poured from the imperial court. Vested conservative interests—Chinese and Manchu—felt seriously threatened; not the least among whom was the Dowager Empress. On September 22, Tz'u Hsi, with Manchu military support, seized and imprisoned the Emperor. K'ang, Liang, and other reformers fled to the safety of foreign concessions, and Kuang Hsü's reform edicts were revoked. Until her death in 1908, Tz'u Hsi was the effective ruler of China.

It was in part her pique with the foreign powers who prevented her from disposing of Kuang Hsü permanently, that led Tz'u Hsi and other high Manchus to support the Boxers (Yi Ho Ch'üan), armed bands of peasants in North China who from 1899 on attacked Christian missionaries and their converts. The interplay of foreign demands for suppression and equivocal responses from the court led in June 1900 to the outbreak of war. Through the efforts of the leading officials of Central and South China, fighting was restricted to North China and the fiction maintained that the court had not given its approval to the Boxer Rebellion. Tz'u Hsi fled Peking for Sian in the west, to return only in January 1902 after foreign troops had seized and looted the capital and China had been forced to accept the onerous Boxer Protocol of September 1901. It called for the punishment of pro-Boxer officials, payment over a 40-year period of an indemnity of gold amounting to $739 million, fortification of the legation quarter, and foreign garrisons along the railroad to the coast.

The return of the Dowager Empress to Peking by railroad symbolically marked the inauguration of a reform program—whose content was that of the 1898 edicts. A new school system was proposed and in 1905 the centuries-old examination system was abolished. Thousands of students went abroad to study, mostly to Japan. Yüan Shih-k'ai (1859–1916) and other modern military leaders began to rebuild China's shattered army along Western models. The administrative structure in Peking was partially reorganized, although no significant financial reform was accomplished. In 1908 the Dowager Empress even proclaimed a 9-year program which would lead to eventual constitutional government on the Japanese model. These reforms, especially the effort to reassert centralized government implicit in them, paradoxically prepared the way for revolution.

Three years before the abortive Hundred Days Reform of 1898, the leader of the republican revolutionary movement, Sun Yat-sen (1866–1925), organized his first uprising in Canton. Born in a village near Canton, Sun was educated partly in Hawaii and had a medical degree from a British hospital in Hong Kong. The 1895 plot of his Hsing Chung Hui (Revive China Society) failed, but Sun escaped to Japan and then to London, where his kidnapping by the Chinese legation became a *cause célèbre* and made him world famous as the leading anti-Manchu revolutionary. In the years that followed, Sun devoted his efforts to seeking financial support among the large overseas Chinese communities in Southeast Asia and America to finance revolts against the Manchu dynasty. While Sun was the most prominent adversary, he was not alone in seeking to overthrow the Manchus. After 1900, revolutionary groups and journals sprang up among students in the treaty ports and in Japan. In 1905, with the encouragement of Japanese supporters, Sun's followers and the revolutionary student groups in Japan combined to form the T'ung Meng Hui (United League) in Tokyo to fight for republicanism not only against the Manchus but also against the constitutional monarchist Liang Ch'i-ch'ao. The program of the T'ung Meng Hui was nominally Sun Yat-sen's Three Principles of the People (San Min Chu I): "nationalism," "people's rights" (parliamentary democracy), and "people's livelihood" (a vague socialism). What held the revolutionary society together, in practice, was an increasingly heavy dosage of anti-Manchu nationalism.

The repeated armed attacks of the next years, often under Huang Hsing (1873–1916), invariably were failures, but slowly republican anti-Manchu sentiment gained ground among the numerous Chinese students in Japan, in units of the New Army, in the provincial assemblies which were convened in 1909 as part of the Manchu constitutional program, and among provincial scholar-gentry who resented Manchu efforts at recentralization. Railroad centralization, in fact, was the immediate cause of the revolution which broke out at Wuchang, in Central China, on Oct. 10, 1911. Disaffected troops, loosely affiliated with the T'ung Meng Hui, who were scheduled to be sent to Szechwan to repress local riots directed against the nationalization of provincial railroads with funds raised from foreign bankers, rose in revolt when their plot was discovered. Declarations of independence from Peking followed rapidly in all the southern and central provinces as the T'ung Meng Hui, the New Army, and the provincial assemblies combined to oppose the Manchus. The court recalled to power

WIDE WORLD

JAPANESE INVASION of China began on July 7, 1937, at the Marco Polo Bridge near Peking, where this Chinese sentry is seen standing guard just before the attack.

Yüan Shih-k'ai, whom it had dismissed in 1909, since the best imperial troops were loyal to him. But Yüan came on his own terms, and covertly negotiated a settlement with the republicans. Sun Yat-sen, who had read about the Wuchang uprising in a Denver newspaper and had returned to China to be elected provisional president of the Chinese Republic, agreed to step down in favor of Yüan. On Feb. 12, 1912, the boy Emperor Hsüan T'ung (1906–1967, later known as Henry Pu-yi) announced his abdication, thus ending the Ch'ing dynasty and two millennia of monarchy and empire. Yüan Shih-k'ai was installed as president on March 10 in the city of Peking, which he controlled. This act inaugurated the Republic of China, which was to survive on the mainland for 37 years.

THE REPUBLIC OF CHINA

Warlordism. Until Yüan's death in 1916, the new republic retained a surface unity. With the aid of the 1913 "reorganization loan" of £25 million from Britain, Russia, France, and Japan, Yüan was able to suppress the parliamentary opposition. Following an abortive "Second Revolution" in July 1913 by supporters of Sun Yat-sen, parliament was dissolved and President Yüan began to take steps toward reestablishing the monarchy with himself as emperor. But the centrifugal tendencies of the late Ch'ing period had gone too far for the provinces to accept such a denouement. Rebellion by provincial military leaders, which began in Yünnan in December 1915, forced Yüan to withdraw his imperial plans. Yüan died on June 6, 1916 and was succeeded by the vice president, Li Yüan-hung (1864–1928), who reassembled the parliament of 1913, which Yüan had dispersed. In reality, control of the Peking government lay in the hands of the premier, General Tuan Ch'i-jui (1864–1936), whose troops and allies controlled North China. Warlord domination of the central government and military satrapies in the provinces characterized the period from 1916 to 1928.

Presidents and premiers—sometimes with captive parliaments to sanction their acts and always with the international trappings of sovereignty (recognition by the powers, access to the critical maritime customs revenue)—succeeded one another in Peking as rival groups of northern militarists contended for the symbols of power. Political power, in fact, at the national level and locally, was coterminous with the military force that the warlords, big and small, could direct against their rivals. Three principal warlord cliques emerged: Anfu (Anhui, Fukien) under Tuan Ch'i-jui; Chihli (Hopei) under Ts'ao K'un (1862–1938) and Wu P'ei-fu (1872–1939); and Fengtien (in Manchuria) under Chang Tso-lin (1873–1929). By 1922, civil government in China had hopelessly disintegrated and civil war was endemic.

In South China, "independent" of the North after 1917, the same scenario repeated itself, although on a more provincial scale and modified by recurrent attempts by Sun Yat-sen to find allies among the southern militarists.

Intellectual Revolution and Nationalism. Behind this political fiasco, however, profound changes in thought were occurring in China. Eventually they led to the reintegration of the Chinese nation and the birth of renewed political and intellectual forces that shaped the future. With the fall of the Manchus, the hold of Confucian orthodoxy was irrevocably broken. The disgust with warlord politics, exposure to new ideas in the West, the growth of native Chinese bourgeois and proletarian classes

SYD GREENBERG, FROM PHOTO RESEARCHERS

CHINESE RETURNING to Nanning in South China in 1945 after it had been held by the Japanese for a year.

during the temporary withdrawal of foreign interests during World War I, and the accumulated anger at imperialist exploitation and betrayal combined to foster an intellectual revolution and the growth of virulent modern nationalism.

The tenor of the new thought is exemplified by the monthly magazine *New Youth (Hsin Ch'ing Nien)*, founded in 1915 by Ch'en Tu-hsiu (1879–1942), which attacked the incubus of Confucianism and called on Chinese youth to follow "Mr. Science" and "Mr. Democracy" rather than the values and norms of tradition. Peking University —where Ch'en was dean of the liberal arts faculty and where Hu Shih (1891–1962), American-educated pragmatist and scholar, taught—became a center of a "literary renaissance" which advocated writing in the vernacular language (*pai-hua*) in order to reach and emancipate the masses. *New Youth* was joined by other journals and through them a bewildering variety of the philosophical, social, and literary theories then current in the West and Japan reached young Chinese intellectuals.

The intellectual revolution as a whole is often designated the "May Fourth Movement," from the student demonstrations in Peking on May 4, 1919, against the decisions of the Versailles Peace Conference confirming Japan's control of the German concessions in Shantung which Japan had seized in 1914. Japan's "Twenty-one Demands" of 1915, including control of Manchuria, important economic concessions, and a tutelary role in China's government, had already fostered a strong anti-Japanese nationalism among intellectuals and the middle class. The May Fourth demonstrations in Peking and the boycotts which followed in other cities were evidence that the most important product of the intellectual revolution would be nationalism.

Two political forces sought to harness this nationalism in their rivalry for hegemony in China. Sun Yat-sen began in October 1919 to reorganize his political party, the Kuomintang, and to recruit supporters from among the students. Almost simultaneously Communism made its appearance in China. Under the impact of the Versailles "betrayal" and the student demonstrations, Ch'en Tu-hsiu and Li Ta-chao (1888–1927), Peking University professor and librarian, moved to link nationalism and Communism. They organized the first unit of a Chinese Communist party in September 1920, and, in July 1921, 11 men, including Mao Tse-tung (1893–   ), met in Shanghai for what was later called the First Congress of the Chinese Communist party (CCP).

The Reunification of China. Russian representatives played a role in organizing and shaping the new Chinese Communist party. These same Comintern agents were soon in touch with Sun Yat-sen who, disillusioned with the Western powers who supported the northern warlords, was ready to accept aid wherever he could get it. In a joint statement issued in Shanghai on Jan. 26, 1923 by Sun and Adolph Joffe, representing the Soviet foreign ministry, the Russians promised support for China's reunification and acknowledged that China was not ripe for the Soviet system. This arrangement inaugurated an alliance between the Kuomintang (KMT) and the Soviet Union. The Third Congress of the CCP in June 1923 acquiesced to Russian pressure and agreed to join the much larger and more influential KMT as individual members, an arrangement formalized at the KMT First Congress in January 1924, which proceeded to reorganize that party along Leninist lines.

Sun Yat-sen and his followers had returned to Canton in February 1923. There, with the advice and assistance of Russian agent Michael Borodin (1884–1953), they began to construct the political and military forces with which they hoped to conquer the North. The KMT military and fiscal position in the South was gradually consolidated. Chiang Kai-shek (1887–   ), Sun's military aide, was sent to Moscow and on his return became head of the Whampoa Military Academy, where the officers for a KMT army were to be trained. Communists soon occupied high posts in the KMT, where they concentrated on propaganda and organizational activities among workers and peasants. While right-wing members of the KMT warned Sun of the dangers of CCP subversion, Sun was convinced that the practical importance of Russian support outweighed the risk. On their part, many Communists chafed at the subordination of their party and looked ultimately to capturing the KMT from within.

Sun Yat-sen died on March 12, 1925, in Peking. Civil leadership passed to Wang Ching-wei (1883–1944), leader of the nominal left wing of the KMT, but increasingly power concentrated in the hands of Chiang Kai-shek, the military commander. The beginning of the long-awaited Northern Expedition to smash the warlords and unite China in July 1926 greatly enhanced Chiang's position. The success of the KMT armies was phenomenal. One column swept rapidly toward the Yangtze and by October controlled the Wuhan cities, to which the Nationalist government, dominated by the KMT left wing, moved at the end of 1926. But, even while the Northern Expedition was advancing victoriously, an incipient split in the Nationalist leadership between Chiang Kai-shek, backed by the KMT right wing, and Wuhan was already apparent. In addition, militant Communist-led uprisings, preceding and following the advancing armies, increasingly disturbed the conservative military commanders associated with both Chiang and Wuhan. By now the whole matter of CCP strategy and tactics had

become inextricably intertwined with the struggle between Stalin and Trotsky in the Soviet Union so that the CCP, under constant pressure from the USSR, was unable to develop a consistent policy to salvage its ever more precarious position. On April 12, Chiang's troops bloodily destroyed the CCP organization and labor movement in Shanghai. On April 18, he established his own government in Nanking in defiance of Wuhan. Events moved swiftly to a climax. Having failed to win the support against Chiang of the warlord Feng Yü-hsiang (1882–1948), Wuhan in July broke with the CCP. Borodin and others left for the Soviet Union. Scattered military forces loyal to the CCP engaged in vain insurrections to the end of the year but were ruthlessly suppressed. Such of the CCP leadership as could escape fled to an underground life in the cities or into rural South China, where Mao and Chu Teh (1886–   ), began a new chapter in the history of the CCP on the Hunan-Kiangsi border in the spring of 1928.

By August 1927, Wuhan and Nanking had reached an accommodation. In April 1928, the Northern Expedition was under way again with Chiang in command. The fall of Peking (renamed Pieping after the capital was moved to Nanking) in June, and the adherence to the Nationalist government of the Manchurian warlord Chang Hsüeh-liang (1898–   ) in November signaled for the first time since 1916 the nominal unification of the Chinese republic.

The Nanking Government, 1928–1937. The new KMT-controlled government at Nanking had only one quasi-normal decade in which to prove itself before the all-out Japanese attack of 1937. Its accomplishments were noteworthy; its problems and failures were fatal.

Sun Yat-sen's political timetable had provided for a period of party "tutelage" after the military unification of the nation and before constitutional government could be instituted. The Nanking government was thus a one-party dictatorship—albeit superficial and often inefficient—dominated by the standing committee of the central executive committee of the KMT, and increasingly by one man, Chiang Kai-shek, who with consummate skill balanced the cliques, factions, and forces under him. However Nanking did not achieve real fiscal and administrative control outside of the Yangtze and southeastern provinces. Chiang's position was contested by Yen Hsi-shan (1883–1960) in Shansi, Li Tsung-jen (1890–   ) in Kwangsi, Chang Hsüeh-liang in Manchuria until 1931, local militarists in Yünnan, Szechwan, and Sinkiang, and CCP Soviets in Hunan-Kiangsi and then in Shensi. The presence of these domestic challenges to its authority, as well as the omnipresent menace of Japanese militarism, was a major factor in the growing militarist color of the KMT government. As much as half of the total annual national expenditures for 1928-1935 was devoted to military purposes.

Nanking's rule was based primarily on the southeastern coastal cities, not on the rural hinterland. The chief sources of government revenue were the maritime customs, commodity taxes, and the salt tax. The government hopefully experimented with an annual budget, and rather successfully refunded the huge foreign and domestic debt. However, time and the balance of domestic political power did not allow the Nanking government to cope with the fundamental problem of agricultural stagnation nor to promote significant industrial growth.

The Nanking decade was probably the most free and creative in scholarship, the arts, and sci-

CAIRO CONFERENCE of 1943, at which Chiang Kai-shek (*left*), President Roosevelt, and Prime Minister Churchill met. Madame Chiang is at the right.

ence in 20th century China. Such institutions as Peking and Tsing Hua universities were of the highest quality, and the researchers at the central government's Academia Sinica were active in a dozen scientific fields. Publishers and bookstores flourished. Literature, however, was increasingly dominated by left-wing writers such as Lu Hsün (1881–1936), Mao Tun (1896–   ), and Pa Chin (1904–   ). Nevertheless the overwhelming influence in cultural life was American and liberal. The eventual erosion of the support of the intellectuals during 12 years (1937–1949) of anti-Japanese war and civil war was a mortal wound from which the KMT never recovered.

The CCP and Japan were Nanking's two most formidable problems. Before 1937 the CCP had been relatively successfully contained, but with the outbreak of war with Japan in 1937 the context changed radically and the CCP was able to expand rapidly and challenge the KMT. After the debacle of 1927 and until sometime in 1931, there were in effect two centers of Communist power in China. The official leadership, including Li Li-san, Wang Ming, and the "Returned Student Clique," attempted from their underground headquarters to implement the Comintern line of organizing insurrections by the urban proletariat. In the mountainous regions on the Hunan-Kiangsi border, Mao Tse-tung, Chu Teh, and others were evolving a different strategy: establishment of a CCP-controlled territorial base in the countryside, by agitating for radical land reform among the peasantry, whose sons could be recruited into a disciplined and indoctrinated Red Army. Mao Tse-tung's domination of the CCP was achieved gradually in a process of intense political struggle with his rivals within the CCP and at a time when Chiang Kai-shek's "extermination campaigns" increasingly threatened the Communist power base. The fifth and last of these campaigns forced the CCP in October 1934 to evacuate Hunan-Kiangsi and to embark upon the harrowing 5,000-mile (8,000-km) "Long March," which brought the remnants of its forces to Shensi province on China's northwest frontier at the end of 1935. En route, at

Tsunyi in Kweichow province, Mao at last achieved unquestioned control of the CCP, which now began to rebuild its strength and to add the weapon of anti-Japanese nationalism to its political arsenal.

Sino-Japanese War and Civil War (1937–1949). Beginning with the Mukden Incident of Sept. 18, 1931, and the occupation of Manchuria, Japanese military influence was extended systematically to Mongolia and then to North China. The central government in Nanking under Chiang Kai-shek, believing itself unprepared to withstand the Japanese until it had eliminated its domestic enemies (in particular the CCP), was forced to make a series of humiliating concessions (Tangku Truce, 1933; Ho-Umetsu Agreement, 1935). This policy of "first pacification and then resistance" was ill-received by nationalist intellectuals and students ("December 9th Movement," student demonstrations in 1935–1936). Disaffection reached the Manchurian troops of Marshal Chang Hsüeh-liang who had been assigned to blockade the CCP-held areas in the northwest. When Chiang Kai-shek went personally to Sian to enforce his orders, in December 1936, he was kidnapped by Chang, and released largely as a consequence of the mediation of the CCP.

Japan's full-scale aggression began on July 7, 1937, near Peking, in a small town called Lukouchiao (Marco Polo Bridge). Shanghai was taken in November after valiant defense on the part of the Nationalist Army, and Nanking, with horrible Japanese atrocities, in December. By the end of 1938, Japanese armies controlled North and Central China, the main coastal cities, and modern lines of communication. The Nationalist government and armies, "trading space for time," withdrew to Szechwan in West China, where Chungking became the wartime capital. Except for a major Japanese offensive in 1944, the battle lines remained largely as they were in late 1938, and the war became one of grinding attrition which sapped the strength of unoccupied China, and of organizing anti-Japanese nationalism in occupied China into a potent political force, an assignment in which the CCP succeeded amply.

The "united front," apart from external formalities, did not last much beyond 1938. Both the KMT and the CCP concentrated much of their energies and resources in preparing for the confrontation that each expected would come once the Japanese were defeated. At the end of the Pacific War, in August 1945, the CCP was in control of an area in North China with a population of some 100 million, claiming an army of regulars and guerrillas of nearly 910,000, and leading a party of 1,200,000 members discipline and indoctrinated through "rectification" campaigns. It also possessed a persuasive party line expounded in Mao's 1940 pamphlet *On the New Democracy*, which promised a "bourgeois-democratic" revolution, albeit under proletarian hegemony, before proceeding toward a socialist society. The KMT, on the other hand, had had to bear the main burden of front-line fighting against the Japanese. Runaway inflation had damaged the morale of its civil servants, soldiers, and urban population. Cut off from the more modernized coastal areas of China from which it had once drawn its intellectual as well as economic strength, KMT ideology and program had ossified and increasingly lost touch with reality. While KMT's territory, military forces and equipment, and foreign support far exceeded those of the CCP, in reality the adversaries were much more evenly matched.

American efforts in 1946 (the mission of Gen. George C. Marshall) to mediate a political settlement of the incipient civil war were designed to deter Chiang Kai-shek from entering upon a military course from which, without sufficient time for political and economic reforms to strengthen the Nationalist government, he might not emerge victorious. In mid-1946, however, full-scale fighting began, and developed into one of the biggest wars in modern history. CCP tactics of maneuver and exploitation of the countryside against the urban areas, in which the large KMT armies were defensively entrenched, gradually turned the balance against the Nationalists. Having captured the cities of Manchuria and their enormous garrisons in the fall of 1948, the CCP began an all-out offensive which took Peking in January 1949. Mao's armies swept across the Yangtze, driving Nationalists who did not surrender toward South China, from where military remnants and political leaders fled to Taiwan in the latter part of 1949.

CHINA SINCE 1949

Chinese history since 1949 is the history of two Chinas: the Republic of China reestablished on Taiwan by Nationalist adherents who were able to escape from the mainland; and the People's Republic of China proclaimed by Mao Tse-tung on Oct. 1, 1949 in Peking, its capital.

Republic of China. The Kuomintang still dominates the government of the Republic of China on Taiwan, although under the constitution in effect since 1946 several minor parties now function. The Nationalist government retains its claim to be the government of all of China, of which it now controls only one province, Taiwan, while the other mainland provinces are seen as temporarily in the hands of an illegal Communist regime. A grossly overstaffed national bureaucracy, which provides a livelihood for many who fled from the mainland, and well-equipped armed forces numbering perhaps 600,000, which consume a very large share of annual expenditures, are evidence of a continued if probably unrealizable resolve to recover the mainland. In the national govern-

ment, in the officer corps of the army, and in the top levels of the educational system, the mainland Chinese are dominant. A genuine electoral process has gradually developed at the local level, and here the Taiwan Chinese hold most of the offices. Resentment on the part of the Taiwan-Chinese majority (about 14 million) against the dominant minority from the mainland (about 2 million) has not entirely disappeared, but the uglier forms of conflict are now little in evidence. As a result of a relatively uniform educational system, a process of homogenization may be said to be taking place among the youth.

The economic growth of Taiwan has been impressive. A successful land reform program was completed in 1964. Technical assistance and the expansion of credit to agriculture have been promoted. Output and both domestic consumption and agricultural exports have increased notably. Industrial production and exports—of increasingly sophisticated goods—have similarly expanded.

Although the Republic of China has strengthened the economy of Taiwan, its diplomatic position has declined. Most countries, and since 1971 the United Nations itself, have recognized the Peking government as the sole representative of China.

After the death of Chiang Kai-shek in 1975, his son, Premier Chiang Ching-kuo, succeeded him as leader of the Kuomintang. In 1978, Chiang Ching-kuo was elected president.

Communist China. Since 1949 the CCP has been "Maoist" in form and content to a degree matched perhaps only by that to which the Soviet Union was "Stalinist" at the peak of Stalin's hegemony. The "thought of Mao Tse-tung" was prescribed as the panacea for the difficult problems which the new regime faced: political integration and control, social transformation, economic development, and adjustment of its international status. Until the "Great Proletarian Cultural Revolution," which began in the summer of 1966, the overwhelming impression of informed observers was that Mao's regime was in effective control of the mainland and that, in spite of some setbacks, progress was being made along all these fronts.

The period 1949–1952 was one of consolidation of CCP control and economic rehabilitation. In February and March 1950, military, political, and economic agreements were concluded with the Soviet Union, providing external support for the new government. Land reform, already undertaken in areas long held by the CCP, was formalized in the Land Reform Law of June 1950 and extended in a harsh, often bloody, process to the rest of the country. Landlords, as a class, were wiped out as agricultural land, animals, and implements were divided among the peasantry. The "five-anti" campaign directed against the bourgeoisie, beginning in October 1951, although it was far less violent, was a major step in the collectivization of private enterprise. By the "three-anti" movement of 1951–1952, the party undertook to cleanse itself and to indoctrinate its new adherents as well as to attack bureaucratism, waste, and corruption in the state structure. Although China's involvement in the Korean War possibly delayed restoration of the economy, it also provided a patriotic context for the effective spread of CCP political control. By 1952 inflation had been halted, the transport system had been restored, and output was at about the prewar level.

The first five-year-plan period (1953–1957) which followed was characterized by a consolida-

WIDE WORLD

THE UNITED STATES sought to mediate between Chinese Nationalists and Communists in 1946. In front, from left, are Chou En-lai, Gen. George Marshall, Chu Teh, Chang Chih-chung (the only Nationalist), and Mao Tse-tung.

tion of the political structure, important advances in industrial production, agricultural collectivization, and a growth of China's international influence. The constitution adopted in 1954 centralized state authority in Peking. In the CCP, the abolition of the six regional bureaus into which the country had been divided since 1949 achieved a similar concentration. Chou En-lai continued as premier, and Mao, in addition to leading the party, became head of state, though he relinquished that office to Liu Shao-ch'i in 1959. The 1953–1957 plan emphasized heavy industry at the expense of consumer goods and agriculture. Social costs were large, but industry achieved a very high average annual rate of growth. While the Chinese process of collectivizing the agricultural land and capital (1953–1955) which had been distributed in the earlier land reform avoided the worst excesses of Soviet collectivization, changes in the organization of agricultural production did little to increase output.

The "Great Leap Forward" began in 1958, in effect an effort to solve China's economic problems —in particular the stagnation of agricultural output—by the application of increased labor (rural "people's communes") rather than capital. The result was a critical disorganization of the economy, characterized by food shortages and industrial decline. By 1962, however, the economy had begun to recover as the CCP retreated from its more radical policies. But the problem of fostering economic growth was not solved, and intense discussions between rival proponents of "political" and "economic" measures took place at the top levels of the party. The Great Leap coincided with the surfacing of long latent differences with the Soviet Union, in matters of domestic policy and the organization of the Communist bloc, but especially in their respective evaluations of the role that the USSR and China should play in supporting the revolutionary potential of the underdeveloped countries. By 1963, Soviet "revisionism" had become as loathsome an enemy of the CCP as American "imperialism." Sino-Soviet border skirmishes erupted at several places in 1969.

Economic strains, criticism of domestic and foreign policies, and progressive bureaucratization of the local party organizations were some of the factors that induced Mao to undertake his "Great Proletarian Cultural Revolution" in 1966. After three years of turmoil, Mao was able to remove many of his opponents, including Liu Shao-ch'i. Lin Piao was designated as Mao's potential successor, but he was reported killed in 1971 after leading an abortive coup against Mao. In 1974 an ideological campaign was launched against Lin and Confucius, who were linked as abettors of individualism and bureaucratism.

In 1967, China exploded its first hydrogen bomb, and in 1970 it orbited its first space satellite. Tension between Peking and Washington eased as U. S. forces were withdrawn from Vietnam. The United States backed the admission of the People's Republic to the United Nations in 1971, President Nixon visited China the next year, and diplomatic relations were established between the two nations in 1979. Japan had normalized its relations with China in 1973 and signed a treaty of peace and friendship in 1978.

In 1976, Chou En-lai died, followed by Chu Teh and then Chairman Mao himself. Hua Kuofeng, a moderate, succeeded Chou as premier. Mao's widow, Chiang Ch'ing, and three other leftist leaders were arrested, and Hua became party chairman as well as premier. Former deputy premier Teng Hsiao-p'ing, purged after Chou's death, was reinstated in 1977. In 1978 a new constitution incorporated features of an economic program designed to make China a modern country by 2000.

ALBERT FEUERWERKER[*]
University of Michigan

Bibliography

Chang, Hsin-pao, *Commissioner Lin and the Opium War* (Cambridge, Mass., 1964).
Ch'en, Jerome, *Mao and the Chinese Revolution* (London and New York 1965).
Chow, Tse-tsung, *The May Fourth Movement: Intellectual Revolution in Modern China* (Cambridge, Mass., 1960).
De Bary, W. T., Chan, Wing-tsit, and **Watson, Burton,** *Sources of Chinese Tradition* (New York 1960).
Feuerwerker, Albert, ed., *Modern China* (Englewood Cliffs, N. J., 1964).
Goodrich, L. Carrington, *A Short History of the Chinese People* (New York 1963).
Levenson, Joseph R., *Confucian China and its Modern Fate,* 3 vols. (Berkeley, Calif., 1958–1965).
McAleavy, Henry, *The Modern History of China* (New York 1967).
Reischauer, Edwin O., Fairbank, J. K., and **Craig, A. M.,** *A History of East Asian Civilization,* 2 vols. (Boston 1960, 1965).
Schram, Stuart, *Mao Tse-tung* (New York 1967).

REPRESENTATIVES at a meeting of the National People's Congress. Speeches are translated (note earphones) for minority groups, like the Mongols, Tibetans, and others.

8. Government

The People's Republic of China (Communist China) was formally proclaimed on Oct. 1, 1949. Its first constitution was adopted in 1954, its second in 1975, and its third in 1978. The Chinese Communist party (CCP), with its own constitution and administrative system, continued to exercise complete control over the government.

Organizational Theory. The Chinese Communists claim to be the true representatives of Marxism-Leninism, and the network of political organizations penetrating all sectors of society is based on Marx's "theory of contradictions." Simply stated, it is the belief that tensions and conflicts of interest are inherent in all situations. According to Mao Tse-tung, there are two types of contradictions, those that can be settled by violence ("antagonistic contradictions") and those that can be settled peacefully through appeal to reason ("nonantagonistic contradictions"). Since resolving these tensions moves history forward, animosity between groups and class struggle must be fostered rather than dampened. One of the major charges that the Chinese have leveled against the Russians is that the leaders of the Soviet Union have neglected class struggle with the result that Soviet society is no longer moving toward communism. The tasks of Chinese Communist rulers, under this theory, are to identify correctly the antagonistic and nonantagonistic contradictions in society, and to release the pent-up energies and emotions of groups and classes whose interests coincide with the building of socialism. Once this tension has been tapped, organizations should channel human activities in the directions deemed constructive by the top leadership. At the same time, coercive organizations must eliminate, reform, and weaken any group whose interests stand in opposition to the building of socialism.

Employing the theory of contradictions, the Chinese Communists have attempted to build the basic contradictions of their society into the state structure. The Communists hope that in this way their organizations will remain dynamic. One such tension is the conflict between central and local interests, which is reflected in the organizational principle of "democratic centralism." Another conflict, between vertical, hierarchical controls and geographic or territorial loyalties, is embraced in the principle of "dual control." Finally, the conflict between the values of the new Communist man and the values of the technically proficient expert is reflected in the organizational principle of "both red and expert."

Democratic Centralism. "Democratic centralism" attempts to reconcile the need for both central guidance and local initiative. One handbook on government describes it in this way: "Democracy seeks the direct participation of the masses in the affairs of state and has as its goal that all state activities must be in the interest of the masses." This definition envisions mass participation in administration. More importantly, although the theory calls for the rulers to act in the interests of the masses, the rulers and not the masses, decide what is in their interest. Once decisions are made, the handbook also states, centralism "demands that the part follows the whole, the lower level state organizations follow the upper levels, in order to guarantee the interests of the masses."

Mass Line. The CCP's vaunted "mass line," derived from its guerrilla heritage, embraces a number of specific leadership techniques intended to put "democratic centralism" into practice. These include (1) the participation by upper level officials in physical labor; (2) the frequent convening of national and provincial congresses of peasants and workers; (3) the development of an elaborate communications network which enables the leaders and the masses to know the demands of each; and (4) the attempt to convince, rather than to coerce. Through these practices, the CCP hopes to eliminate barriers between the party and masses, thereby enabling the leaders to remain sensitive to contradictions in their society.

Dual Control. According to the principle of "dual control," each agency is subject to two lines of control, one based on territory and another on function. A provincial level bank, for example, is controlled both by its provincial party committee, a territorial, horizontal chain of command, and by the national level bank, a functional, vertical chain of command. Every political unit in China is subject to these two types of control.

Red and Expert. Another conflict in Chinese society stems from the different skills and attitudes of the dedicated party official (the "red") and the technocrat (the "expert"). The Chinese Communists tend to distrust the "expert," claiming that he tends to be concerned with his own narrow interests and has a parochial view of the community's needs. On the other hand, the CCP fully trusts the "red." He is the party revolutionary, able to apply Mao Tse-tung's ideas to specific contexts and skillful in leading men. Since officials who are only "red," with no technical skills, cannot develop nuclear weapons, for example, the party hopes to create people who are both red and expert.

The organization of the army reflects one attempt to solve the "red-expert" dilemma. The army has two chains of command. One chain of command consists of political officers whose main job is to instill "redness" in the troops. Another chain of command, the regular field commanders or the "experts," is responsible for training the troops to be militarily proficient. This combination of political officers and field commanders aims at producing soldiers who are both politically correct and militarily able. But as a result of having two chains of command army politics appears to consist, in part, of conflict between the "red" hierarchy and the "expert" hierarchy.

Another source of creative tension, at least in theory, is the relationship between the government and the party. In accord with Leninist principles, the CCP stands at the apex of political power. The party claims to be the repository of the wisdom of the working class, and has seized the governmental apparatus in order to enforce the "dictatorship of the proletariat." This theory has led to the growth of two identifiable, large organizations: the party and the government. The tasks of the party are to retain its proletarian purity, to formulate policy, and to supervise the government. It leads in the resolution of "nonantagonistic" contradictions through extensive propaganda and educational activities, and it directs the struggle against the "antagonistic" enemies. The government apparatus is responsible for administration of the economy and the actual application of coercion against the enemies of the state. While the party protects its ideological purity by being rigorous and exclusive in its membership policy, the government remains responsive to all groups among whom exist "nonantagonistic contradictions."

Institutions—Party. The CCP, the government, and the army are the three main organizations in Communist China. In oversimplified terms, the party stands supreme. The CCP is hierarchically organized, led by its chairman.

Several small committees under the party chairman are the real centers of power, directing specific activities, but little is known about these committees. In the vaguest terms, the politburo is in charge of formulating broad policy guidelines; the secretariat is in charge of day-to-day administration of the policy guidelines; the military affairs committee directs the army; and temporary, ad hoc committees, such as the Proletarian Cultural Revolutionary Committee established in 1966, supervise special campaigns run by the party.

The chairman, politburo, and secretariat, in theory, are the products of a democratic electoral process, supposedly elected by the party's 196-member central committee. According to the party constitution, moreover, the central committee is elected by a national party congress, convened annually, which represents the will of the party's 19 million members. However, there was no national party congress for 10 years after the one held in 1958, and by 1968 well over half of the party's central committee selected at the 1958 party congress, had died or were purged. In fact, therefore, the exact process through which politburo, secretariat, and ad hoc committee members are selected remains unknown. A fair guess would be that the process of promotion is more personalized than institutionalized, and that the chairman and those close to him are in charge of appointments to positions of supreme power.

No less than nine tiers of organization separate an average party member from the central apparatus. Below the center are 6 party regional bureaus, 27 provincial level party committees, about 165 administrative district committees, nearly 2,000 county- and municipal-level committees, an unknown number of rural-district and urban-ward party committees, and over 100,000 township (commune) committees, urban-district committees, and factory committees. Below these are the party branches, subbranches, groups, and cells to which every party member belongs. The CCP also controls the nonparty mass organizations, which serve as "transmission belts" for policies. They include such groups as the All-China Federation of Trade Unions, All-China Democratic Youth, and All-China Federation of Democratic Women.

The party's political power is maintained through a number of techniques. Party cells,

DIVORCE COURT in Peking. Divorce is legal, but it is frowned on by most Chinese as inimical to the social order.

MAO TSE-TUNG (*standing, center*) greets enthusiastic crowds in Peking on International Labor Day, May 1, 1967. Mao led the People's Republic of China from its proclamation in 1949 until his death in 1976. Standing next to him is his then heir-apparent, Lin Piao, who was killed in 1971 after leading an attempted coup.

found in every government agency, army brigade, business, factory, school, and rural village, link these units to the party. The party cells lead and enforce central directives.

The party also has 10 functional departments, such as its finance and trade political department, propaganda department, and organizational department. These departments are organized under the central committee and extend to the county level, and supervise specific areas of government and army activity. For example, the party's finance and trade political department works closely with the government's ministry of finance when the latter draws up the annual budget. Party control is also ensured by the fact that party leaders hold several jobs. To cite two examples, a vice chairman of the party may also be minister of defense and leader of the military affairs committee. A member of the politburo and secretariat may at the same time serve as minister of finance.

Finally, party control is asserted through the use of ad hoc committees during "campaigns." These campaigns, in fact, are one of the distinctive features of the Chinese political system. The party leadership designates a certain goal as "central"—be it the elimination of illiteracy, the construction of backyard steel furnaces, or the study of Mao Tse-tung's writings. All activity of the bureaucracy is then directed toward the achievement of this goal. Campaigns disrupt normal chains of command, and lines of authority converge upon the party ad hoc committees established to direct the campaign.

Government. The activities of the central government are supervised by the state council. The head of the council is the premier, who is elected by the National People's Congress (NPC) on recommendation of the party chairman. The other council members are the several deputy premiers and the ministers of government departments and commissions. The council resembles a cabinet. As the executive organ of the NPC, it is the central people's government. Constitutionally it is responsible to the NPC and the NPC's standing committee.

The constitution leads one to believe that the state council is subordinate to the National People's Congress. The NPC is supposedly the highest governmental organ, elected every five years and convened annually. In fact, in many years it held no session. The standing committee of the NPC, according to law, exercises the power of the NPC when it is not in session, but there is no evidence to indicate that this is the case. Thus as is the case with the CCP, constitutional provision has been made for democratic participation in formulation of policy. In fact, however, this participation seems nominal.

Below the central government, more or less parallel to the party structure, are several levels of government: provinces, administrative districts, counties, districts, and townships (communes). There are also 3 independent municipalities directly under the central government and 5 autonomous regions: Tibet, Inner Mongolia, Sinkiang-Uigur, Ningsia-Hui, and Kwangsi-Chuang. Each of these units enjoys residual power in matters of tax collection and allocation of funds.

Rural Organization. The penetration of the governmental apparatus below the county level (a county in China has between 300,000 to 800,000 people) represents one of the real breaks with China's past. Prior to 1949, formal government stopped at the county level. The gentry class provided the link between the village and the government. Today, however, the government impinges directly upon the life of the average peasant. Propaganda, improved transportation, and increased educational opportunities have widened the peasant's horizons. At the same time, the government controls his life. For example, the peasant cannot travel without a permit, and his wages are determined by the labor he contributes to the production team and brigade.

The village is organized into brigades (subunits of the commune) and production teams (subunits of the brigade). With the exception of small plots retained by the peasant, land is owned by the team and brigade, and the peasant has little voice in deciding what is grown on this land. All activities of the brigade, whether military, political, medical, economic, or cultural, are directed by commune officials. While brigade ófficials are usually natives of the village they lead, the commune frequently has one or two nonnatives in its administration. These nonnatives, in theory, are more likely to remain loyal to the center, while natives will be tempted to defend the interests of their locality.

Judiciary. The Communist judiciary is not part of the "checks and balances" system, as are many Western judicial systems, but is under the supervision of the National People's Congress. Also, it often works closely with the ministry of public security. There are a supreme people's court and a supreme people's procuratorate, but members can be appointed and removed by the standing committee of the congress.

Military. The military apparatus in China is theoretically organized much like any military, with four exceptions. First, over the chiefs of staff looms the party's military affairs committee. Second, paralleling the regular chain of command, are the political officers. Third, below the platoon level is a structure of militia units, trained and commanded by the army, which exists in almost every commune. Fourth, while there are command positions, no ranks exist independent of the command post. Without a command post, a former commander is an ordinary soldier. These differences reflect the philosophy of the Chinese Communists—egalitarianism, with an emphasis upon political considerations.

Several important aspects of the Chinese army are not reflected in organizational charts. These relate to the functions of the military in Chinese society. The army plays an economic role, growing its own food and assisting the peasants in their activities. Moreover, military men head several key industrial ministries. The army has an important social role, serving as a source of upward mobility and providing technical education to rural youth. As a coercive instrument, it maintains order and unity in the country. Moreover, beginning in 1960, the army increasingly served as a source of ideological inspiration to the society. When the party began to lose its revolutionary élan, the army under Lin Piao apparently succeeded in re-creating the "spirit of Yenan" among its ranks. Finally, beginning in 1964, many leading army officials began to assume leadership posts in both the party and government. Also, the army played a major part in directing the course of the Cultural Revolution.

Theory and Practice. A comparison of the organizational principles with the actual governmental structure in Communist China reveals a discrepancy between principle and reality. The discrepancies point to some of the political problems faced by the Peking regime. The principle of "democratic centralism" has not been realized, and more "centralism" exists than "democracy." As a result, the leaders of Communist China have found it difficult to remain in touch with local developments. In addition, the principles of "dual control" and of the existence of two complex organizations—party and government— have produced a sluggish bureaucracy, replete with delay, buck-passing, and bureaucratic politics.

The close involvement of the party in administration, particularly noticeable after 1958, has caused the CCP to lose its "ideological purity." No longer the vanguard of a socialist movement, by the mid-1960's the CCP mirrored Chinese society, including within its ranks traditionalists and the new technocrats, as well as the "reds."

Finally, by the late 1960's, the utility of the theory of contradictions was open to question. The theory was applicable to China of the

WIDE WORLD

CHIANG KAI-SHEK and Mme. Chiang in the garden of the presidential residence at Shihlin, north of Taipei. Chiang served as president of the Republic of China from 1950 until his death in Taipei, April 5, 1975.

1930's and 1940's when there were long-standing economic and political grievances among the population, but by the 1960's, the real contradictions were between the people and their government over such questions as taxes, job opportunities, and freedom of expression. The leaders of China could not easily tap these conflicts without challenging their own structure of authority, that is, without calling their own legitimacy to rule into question. Whatever decisions they have made, the CCP leaders will continue for some time to be confronted with the difficult task of readjusting their organizational principles to a society that is less characterized by its contradictions than by its increasing unity.

MICHEL OKSENBERG, *Stanford University*

REPUBLIC OF CHINA

Late in 1949 the Nationalist government retreated to Taiwan and designated Taipei the "temporary capital" of the Republic of China. Since then, this relocated government has exercised effective control over the island-province of Taiwan, including 14 islands in the Taiwan group and 64 islands in the Penghu (Pescadores) group, with a combined area of 13,885 square miles (35,962 sq km), and some lesser islands (Quemoy and Matsu islands and their surrounding islets) off the Chinese mainland. The Nationalists continued to claim their government to be the sole legitimate ruling authority for the whole of China, to maintain diplomatic relations with nations that did not recognize the Peking government, and, until 1971, to represent China in the United Nations. In anticipation of a victorious return to the mainland, the Nationalist government also continued to retain essentially the same makeup it assumed in Nanking under the Constitution of 1946.

Structure and Form of the National Government. As head of state the president of the republic is vested with extensive constitutional powers. These include the emergency powers granted the office under the *Temporary Provisions* adopted in 1948. The vice president, in contrast, is not invested with any actual constitutional powers but is authorized to act for the president or succeed to the presidency should that office become vacant.

Both the president and vice president are elected to 6-year terms by the National Assembly. This representative body is composed of delegates previously elected on the mainland and alternates appointed in Taiwan. The over 1,500 existing members have had their terms of office extended indefinitely. In addition to its regular function as an electoral college, the National Assembly, in 1960, revised the *Temporary Provisions* so as to overcome the constitutional 2-term limitation imposed on presidential incumbents. Subsequently, this body reelected Chiang Kai-shek president for his third, fourth, and fifth terms. Chiang died in Taipei on April 5, 1975, and was succeeded by Vice President C. K. Yen. Chiang's elder son, Chiang Ching-kuo, retained the post of premier until his election as president in 1978.

The national government is organized on the basis of five governing powers, in accordance with Sun Yat-sen's political theory. These powers are exercised through five independent branches called "yüan" (councils). Besides the executive, legislative, and judicial yüan, an examination yüan is in charge of civil service matters, and a control yüan exercises powers of consent, impeachment, censure, and auditing.

The executive yüan contains eight ministries and two commissions and operates under a modified cabinet system. Its president functions as the premier presiding over the ministers of state appointed to his council.

The legislative yüan fulfills a parliamentary role but does not enjoy the full status of a national parliament. Its members were elected by popular vote in their respective mainland constituencies. However, in Taiwan the 500 or so available members have had their terms of office extended without elections, as in the case of the assembly delegates.

The judicial yüan serves as the highest state tribunal and is empowered to interpret the constitution, as well as laws and ordinances. Its council of grand justices, after having been reactivated in 1952, has rendered a number of important decisions concerning adjustment problems the government wishes resolved in accordance with the provisions of the constitution.

Local Government. Although government on the national level adheres in principle to the 1946 constitution, provincial government in Taiwan has not been granted the full powers of self-government enumerated in that document. The governor is still appointed by the president of the republic, upon the recommendation of the premier, while members of the provincial council are appointed by the executive yüan. However, popular elections are held for provincial assemblymen, and since 1959 the powers of the provincial assembly have been enlarged. Self-government is more in evidence in the 16 counties (hsien) and 5 municipalities of the province.

Furthermore, since Taiwan is in reality the only province in which the Nationalist central government exercises its normal functions, the province is faced with a situation of dual administrations—a national government superimposed on a single provincial government. In recent years provincial authorities have gradually assumed control over more administrative functions. Even though under the constitution there is no strict limitation to the powers of the central government in relation to those of the local governments, the central government may, as in Taiwan, delegate the power of administration over a wide range of matters to lower levels.

The Role of the Kuomintang. Government on the national level also is closely restrained under the Nationalist regime. Power rests with those who are affiliated with the Kuomintang. The Kuomintang exercises control over the government. Chiang Kai-shek, until his death, and Chiang Ching-kuo, from 1978, stood at the apex of the Nationalist power structure by serving concurrently as director general (*tsung-ts'ai*) of the Kuomintang and president of the republic.

HARRY J. LAMLEY, *University of Hawaii*

Bibliography

Barnett, A. Doak, *Cadres, Bureaucracy, and Political Power in Communist China* (New York 1967).
Gittings, John, *The Role of the Chinese Army* (London and New York 1967).
Lewis, John W., *Leadership in Communist China* (Ithaca, N.Y., 1963).
MacFarquhar, Roderick, *China Under Mao* (Cambridge, Mass., 1966).
Schurmann, H. Franz, *Ideology and Organization in Communist China* (Berkeley, Calif., 1966).
Townsend, James, *Political Participation in Communist China* (Berkeley, Calif., 1967).
Tung, William L., *The Political Institutions of Modern China* (The Hague 1964).

The Great Wall, begun 2,000 years ago to protect China from invasion, extends for over 1,500 miles.

CHINA

The imperial summer palace in a suburb of Peking became a public park after the revolution of 1911-1912.

In the center of Peking's ancient Forbidden City stands the Hall of Supreme Harmony, now a public museum.

Traffic on the Whangpoo River at Shanghai, China's largest city and port on the East China Sea.

PLATES 2 AND 3

A woman skillfully plucks young and tender tea leaves at Meichiawu plantation, near Hangchow.

Curiously shaped mountains characterize the landscape near Kweilin in southern China's Kwangsi province.

An army of workers, with banners flying, gather to celebrate the completion of the great Ming Tombs Dam.

Fertile, loamy slopes along the Yellow River are terraced to facilitate and increase the harvest of wheat.

RIBOUD, FROM MAGNUM

The world's largest statue of Buddha is said to be this figure in Changhua.

PLATE 4

TAIWAN

The modern architecture of the provincial government buildings in Taichung, Taiwan's fifth-largest city, shelters the interiors from the rays of the sun.

Hakka women transplant rice in southern Taiwan. They are descendants of early settlers from mainland China.

Famous Buddhist sculptures of Lungmen, of the 8th and 9th centuries, have been a favorite gathering place in modern times for students interested in China's cultural history.

CHINA: Philosophy, Religion, and Science

9. Philosophy and Religion

Religion has not played an all-important part in the life of the Chinese people. Philosophy, especially Confucian ethics, has provided the spiritual and moral basis of Chinese civilization. Philosophy in Chinese civilization corresponds to religion in other civilizations.

The history of Chinese philosophy may be divided into five periods: early ancient period (to about 200 B. C.); late ancient period (about 200 B. C. to 400 A. D.); medieval period (about 400 to 1000 A. D.); early modern period (about 1000 to 1800); and contemporary period (since about 1800).

EARLY ANCIENT PERIOD

Chinese mythology points to an indefinitely long period of time. It claims that the earliest rulers consisted of three sovereign groups, namely, the celestial sovereigns, the terrestrial sovereigns, and the human sovereigns, each reigning for hundreds or thousands of years. In this openly extravagant claim is to be found, however, its prototypal insistence on the importance of man. Man is so important that he is matched from the beginning of time with heaven and earth to form a cosmic triad. The Chinese term for the triad of heaven-earth-man is *san-ts'ai*, meaning three powers, three forces, three origins, or any number of comparable interpretations. A notable characteristic of Chinese philosophy is humanism.

Reliable history begins with the Shang dynasty (1523–1028 B. C.), when religion rather than philosophy was still the controlling force over the minds of men. Departed ancestors acted as intercessors between men and spirits, and the various spirits were ruled over by *Shang-ti*, the Supreme Lord. Elaborate systems were devised for consulting the will of spirits and ancestors, and courses of action were determined in line with the oracles obtained. Replacing the Shang as the ruling house, the Chou dynasty (1027–256 B. C.) brought with it the belief in *T'ien*, or Heaven. The assimilation of *Shang-ti* in *T'ien*, signified an amalgamation of the concept of an anthropomorphic God with the concept of an ultimate cosmic force or principle.

The ancient Chinese classics, consisting of the *Classic of Poetry*, the *Classic of History*, the *Classic of Changes*, and the *Classic of Ceremonials*, are the literary remains of the Chou period. Spanning the several centuries from the beginning of the Chou dynasty to about 500 B. C., the anthological material in these volumes contains a number of philosophical ideas and ideals in embryonic form: the notion of the five elements in the *Classic of History*, the notion of *Yin-yang* in the *Classic of Changes* in terms of *Ch'ien-k'un*, and the notions of benevolence, righteousness, and such matters scattered through many passages. With the coming of the Chou dynasty, there was a perceptible shift from dependence on divine direction in human affairs to human endeavor. Talent and virtue, in theory at least, were upheld as the basis of the well-defined feudalistic hierarchy. As time passed, the feudalistic structure began to decay and crumble, at-

LAO TZU, founder of Taoism, as portrayed by Chao Meng-fu (1254–1322), an artist of the Yüan dynasty.

tended by a notable rise in the value of the common people with a corresponding increase of disenfranchised nobility. The result was the appearance of a new class, the middle class, consisting of scribes, counselors, and teachers, many of them with an aristocratic background. To this middle class belonged practically all the philosophers of the ancient period, and the best known among them was Confucius.

The period of classical philosophy was so vigorous and creative that it is more generally known among the Chinese as the period of "the hundred philosophers." Oddly, Mao Tse-tung used the popular adage "Let the hundred philosophers contend together and let the hundred flowers bloom together" when in 1956 he urged the population to speak their mind about the Communist government. In the classical age of China the hundred philosophers did indeed contend together, each advocating his independent ideas free from fear. It was not until the 2d century B. C. that the historian Ssu-ma T'an classified the various philosophers into six schools —Confucianists, Taoists, Moists, Logicians, Diviners (Yin-yang), and the Legalists. This classification has been a convenient device for presenting classical Chinese philosophy.

Confucianism. The most influential philosophical system not only in China but also in Korea, Japan, and Vietnam, Confucianism goes back to the personality as well as the teachings of Confucius (551–479 B. C.). The chaos and confusion of the later Chou dynasty was the burning issue confronting all thinkers of the classical age. To reestablish order out of chaos, Confucius undertook, by teaching and personal example, to revive the life of benevolence and righteousness as the ideal for the individual and society. Though proclaiming himself "a transmitter and not an innovator," Confucius was a revolutionary without fanfare. He was a born teacher. With an unswerving conviction in the native integrity and capacity of the individual, he observed: "By nature all men are alike; it was by custom and habit that they are set apart." He went on to say: "In education there is no distinction of classes." Confucius was the first professional teacher in China who conducted the first school that kept an open door to the lowborn as much as to the highborn. The Chinese have honored Confucius as their "Supreme Sage and Foremost Teacher," and when a Teachers' Day was instituted in modern China, Confucius' birthday was chosen.

Even as Confucius carried over certain ideas and ideals from antiquity, he put the stamp of his own genius on the system by introducing the unitary principle of jen, for which benevolence, love, manhood, human-heartedness have been used as English equivalents. A number of Confucius' sayings on jen are preserved in his Analects; the simplest of these reads: "Jen is to love all men." An ancient commentary says in amplification: "Jen is to love men joyously and from the innermost of one's heart." The Chinese character for jen indicates ideographically "that which is common in two men," therefore the essence of humanity. It is jen in man that makes a man human, according to Confucius. Jen is inborn in all men and its fulfillment constitutes their destiny; thus jen may be said to be the alpha and omega of man. Jen is the measure of the true worth of an individual as well as the demarcation between man and animal. The preservation of jen is more important than the preservation of life itself, and a superior man is one who would hold fast to jen under all circumstances without ever acting contrary to it. So central is the concept of jen in the system of Confucius that it may be said to be the philosophy of jen, or the way of human-heartedness.

When a man's life is rooted in jen, it is natural that he will be practicing the virtue of filial piety at home and reciprocity and loyalty abroad. "What one does not wish to be done unto, do not do to others" is a well-known saying of Confucius. Less well known is the saying "wishing to be established oneself he assists others to be established; wishing to be successful oneself he assists others to be successful." Fundamental as it is, the virtue of *jen* should be accompanied by the grace of decorum, just as a building should have a beautiful façade together with a solid foundation. When these qualities are properly cultivated and combined in the individual, there is the superior man. Like the Western term "gentleman," the Chinese term *chün-tzu* (literally "son of a ruler") has also shifted from describing a man of noble birth to denoting a man of noble character. This important transformation is another achievement of Confucius, the revolutionary without fanfare. Government, according to Confucius, should be based on moral force rather than contractual relationship or legal authority. Since the most effective form of moral persuasion is personal example, the position of the sovereign may be likened to that of the schoolmaster and the state to the schoolhouse. In the system of Confucius, ethics, politics, and education work hand in hand, and the super virtue of *jen* is the unifying principle.

In the *Analects* of Confucius are collected and preserved notes and records of the sayings and doings of the master kept by his disciples. Supplementing the *Analects* are two small but basic Confucian texts, namely, the *Great Learning*, attributed to an immediate disciple, Tseng Shen, and the *Doctrine of the Mean*, attributed to Tzu Ssu, who was Confucius' grandson. Emphasizing the concept of *ch'eng*, or sincerity, as the basic truth and reality for man and the universe, the *Doctrine of the Mean* stands as the most metaphysical of all Confucian texts, and suggests a notable element of mysticism in its tone. In the *Great Learning* is found the well-known program of development from the inner life of the individual to world peace, with the eight steps indicated as follows: investigation of things, extension of knowledge, sincerity of thoughts, rectification of the heart, cultivation of the self, regulation of the family, government of the state, and peace in the world.

The doctrine of *jen*, coupled with the concept of *yi*, or righteousness, was extended by Mencius (about 372–289 B.C.), the greatest follower of Confucius. In support of his theory of the natural goodness of man, Mencius argued vigorously for the inborn "seeds" of the four cardinal virtues of *jen*, *yi*, decorum (*li*), and wisdom (*chih*). Human nature was good, urged Mencius, and all men had the capacity to become like Yao and Shun, the great ancient sage-kings. He said further: "All things are within me" and "He who knows his own nature knows Heaven." With such a firm conviction in the integrity and capacity of the individual, Mencius stood out as the most outspoken champion of the rights of the common man. He said, in feudalistic China of the 3d century B.C.: "The people rank the highest, the spirits of land and grain come next, and the ruler counts the least."

Balancing the idealistic Confucian wing of Mencius was the realistic wing of Hsün Tzu, (about 306–212 B.C.). To Hsün Tzu, human nature was evil; the goodness in man was acquired as a result of accepting the admonition of wise teachers and the commandments of the sage-kings. Heaven was but nature proceeding with predictable regularity, completely unconcerned with human affairs; this was all the more reason why man should help himself. Hsün Tzu agreed with Mencius, however, in advocating perfection or sagehood as the goal of life. Even-

NATIONAL MUSEUM OF HISTORY, TAIPEI

CONFUCIUS (551–479 B. C.) as portrayed by Wu Tao-tsu (c. 700–760 A. D.), an artist of the T'ang dynasty.

tually Mencius was elevated to the position of Second Sage of China, while Hsün Tzu remained as one of the hundred philosophers, and the Confucius-Mencius orthodoxy dominated the Chinese mind as the established school of Confucianism throughout the ages.

Taoism. Whereas Confucianism attracts the reformers and progressives, Taoism holds its appeal for hermits and recluses. In patterns of alternation and supplementation these two systems, so different and distinct from each other, have combined to mold Chinese thought and culture. The founders of Taoism were Lao Tzu (about 575–485 B. C.) and Chuang Tzu (about 369–286 B. C.), with the *Tao Te Ching* and the

Chuang Tzu regarded as their respective texts and their teachings deal with the central notion of the *Tao*. *Tao*, meaning literally "path" or "road," has come to signify, in the philosophical context, the basic principle that pervades man and the universe. Hence the English word "way" furnishes an apt translation for "*tao*." The *Tao* is eternal and absolute, infinite and immutable. It is nonbeing, that is, above all being, and therefore beyond description—"illusive and evasive, evasive and illusive." The female and the child and water are the favorite metaphors employed in the *Tao Te Ching*, emphasizing thereby the axiom of strength in weakness and honor in humility.

The exhortation of humility and quietude is coupled with the denunciation of force, pride, and self-assertion. Just as *wu*, or nonbeing, is the final reality in the realm of existence, so *wu-wei*, or nondoing, is the highest ideal in the realm of conduct. "The Tao does nothing and yet there is nothing left undone," says the *Tao Te Ching*. Nondoing means nonassertion, nonimposition, noninterference. To let things alone is to let things happen, and Taoism is a philosophy of "live and let live." Governments and conventions do no good, and wars do worse than no good. True social harmony can only be derived from cosmic harmony of the *Tao*.

The *Tao* is the original uncarved block, and the *Te,* or the essence, is the expression of *Tao* in individual men and things. All men are exhorted to preserve the original simplicity of nature and their human nature. The blessed ones might achieve an identification of the individual with the *Tao* in an experience of naturalistic mysticism. To Chuang Tzu, the world of daily life is a realm of relativity where differences and distinctions abound, but in the realm of the absolute, or the *Tao*, prevail unconditional freedom, complete equality among all men and things, and even indifference to life and death.

In the subsequent development of Taoism into a popular religion, the conquest of death through philosophical unconcern was turned into a cult which preached the literal conquest of death—the achievement of physical longevity through deeds and rites and the acceptance of a whole array of gods. The spirit of classical Taoism, however, has pervaded many aspects of Chinese culture, such as art and literature, particularly landscape painting and nature poetry, endowing them with a tone of peace and serenity.

Moism. For several centuries in ancient China, Moism was spoken of together with Confucianism as the two eminent schools of philosophy. Founded by Mo Tzu (about 470–391 B.C.), an exact contemporary of Socrates in ancient Greece, Moism distinguished itself by its doctrine of universal love. Partisanship lay at the root of the chaos in the empire, according to Mo Tzu, and the Confucian doctrine of *jen* was at best an ineffective cure. Mo Tzu condemned offensive war and engaged himself in defensive constructions and tactics. Holding to a firm belief in the will of heaven, Mo Tzu proclaimed what heaven desired to see was universal love prevailing among all men.

In regard to government, Mo Tzu also favored virtue and talent as the basis for public leadership and appointment, but he considered "identification with the superior" necessary for group action. His zeal for "promoting what is beneficial and removing what is harmful" led to his advocacy of thrift and his condemnation of music and ceremonials. Moism has been regarded by some as a system of utilitarianism.

An organized community of Moists with duly appointed leadership and its own code of conduct persisted for a considerable period of time, but Moism had been all but forgotten for some 2,000 years until its revival in the mid-20th century.

The School of Logicians. Running counter to the general indifference toward logic as a systematic discipline among Chinese thinkers are the logicians. Though constituting a minor school, they distinguish themselves for their purely intellectual interests. The Chinese reference to the school is *Ming Chia*, or "name philosophers," because they stress so much the importance of names. Of the Name Philosophers, Hui Shih (about 380–300 B.C.) and Kung-sun Lung (about 320–250 B.C.) are regarded as representatives, with a small text, the *Kung-sun Lung Tzu*, extant from the writings of the latter and only limited fragments from the former. The discourses of the logicians deal with such problems as the one and the many, substance and attributes, the nature of knowledge, and the function of names. But the designation "school of logicians" should be understood in a very broad sense, since the discussions concern dialectics, sophisms, and paradoxes as well as logic.

The School of Diviners. Represented by Tsou Yen (about 340–260 B.C.), the diviners include the philosophers who teach the doctrine of the *Yin-yang* and those who teach the five elements. Appearing first in the *Classic of Changes* and the *Classic of History*, respectively, the *Yin-yang* and the five elements doctrines betoken early attempts among the Chinese at developing a metaphysics, or theory of final reality, and a cosmology, or a theory of the origin of the universe. *Yin-yang* as a concept consists of two polar elements referring originally to the shady and sunny sides of a valley or a hill, and eventually to such contrasting pairs as female-male, negative-positive, cold-hot, wet-dry, and weak-strong. The five elements consist of metal, wood, water, fire, and earth. In both doctrines the elements are to be thought of not as inert material entities but as dynamic forces, powers, or agencies, subsisting in a constant flux, alternating between phases of harmony and contradiction, production and overcoming. The doctrines of *Yin-yang* and the five elements, loaded with a component of occultism, have been closely associated with astrology, alchemy, and fortune-telling. Rather than maintaining a distinctive system of thought by themselves, the teachings of the diviners have exercised their influence as a permeating ingredient in Chinese life and thought.

Legalism. Grounded on the view that human nature is evil and that government consists of power manipulation, Legalism advocated a system of political thought in ancient China not dissimilar to that propounded by Niccolò Machiavelli in Renaissance Europe. Wei Yang, or Prince Yang of Shang (about 400–338 B.C.), and Han Fei (about 280–233 B.C.) were the leading spokesmen of this system of political realism, each leaving behind a work bearing the name of the author. Han Fei learned from his teacher Hsün Tzu the lesson that human nature is evil. Whereas Hsün Tzu, the Confucianist, prescribed the "straightening and bending" of the individual to help him achieve sagehood, Han Fei, the Legalist, prescribed the same drastic procedure to produce a mass submission of docile subjects to the state and the ruler. He could see neither goodness nor intelligence in the ordinary man. Since to consult the will of the people is to court disaster, the ruler must resolutely make all decisions by himself and exact from the people unquestioning obedience. Among all Chinese philosophies, Legalism stands alone in its advocacy of the precedence of the state over the individual and national prestige over the welfare of the people. For the realization of these objectives the Legalists placed their emphasis on statecraft, power, and law, supported by a penal code of the severest kind. With neither respect to traditional values nor to human feelings, the Legalists seized every opportunity to strengthen the position of the state and increase the enjoyment of the ruler. They had little use for benevolence and righteousness (*jen* and *yi*), so much emphasized by the idealists, such as the Confucianists. The fact that both Wei Yang and Han Fei died violent deaths has confirmed in the Chinese minds the feeling that he who lives by the sword dies by the sword. Perhaps practical politics can never be completely divested from some of the manipulations suggested by the Legalists, but no politician or political thinker in China since the time of Han Fei has dared to identify himself openly with the school of Legalism as a system of political theory.

LATE ANCIENT PERIOD

The period of the six schools was characterized by a notable abundance of vigor and vitality and a great variety of original thinking. All "hundred philosophers" stood on equal footing; their status was determined solely by the merit of their teachings. There was neither patronage nor persecution, neither orthodoxy nor heterodoxy. This healthy state of affairs came to an end when the Ch'in dynasty reunified the empire in 221 B. C., giving way to a period characterized by the syncretism of the schools and ascendancy of Confucianism.

Ascendancy of Confucianism (200 B. C.–200 A. D.). Tung Chung-shu (about 179–104 B. C.), popularly regarded as the greatest Confucian scholar of his day, was an outstanding representative of both these trends. Continuing the Confucian tradition, Tung codified the set of five cardinal virtues, namely, benevolence (*jen*), righteousness (*yi*), decorum (*li*), wisdom (*chih*), and trustworthiness (*hsin*). He underlined the first three of the five social relations–those between sovereign and subject, father and son, husband and wife, brother and brother, friend and friend–designating them as the "three major cords." The five cardinal virtues and the three major cords have been controlling ideals in the Chinese ethic ever since. Tung Chung-shu believed in the all-pervasive operation of the *Yin-yang* forces and an item-by-item correspondence of man and the universe, that is, the theory of macrocosm and microcosm. This synthesis of Confucianism with the *Yin-yang* school may be regarded as an example of the prevailing eclectic trend among ·the philosophical schools of the time.

It was a combination of enthusiastic promotion by scholars like Tung Chung-shu and self-seeking patronage by the imperial court that launched Confucianism on its snowballing course of ascendancy. Once the choice was made, political, social, and educational institutions were developed according to Confucian principles, and such institutions and usages in turn strengthened the position of Confucianism. The establishment of the civil service examination system (136 B. C.) and the Imperial University (124 B. C.), with Confucian classics as the official syllabus, were notable factors in the elevation of Confucianism to its position of supremacy. In the end, a Confucian temple stood side by side with a school in every county in China, honoring and perpetuating the memory of "Confucius, the Supreme Sage and Foremost Teacher." The state cult of Confucianism is sometimes referred to as a religion. The success of Confucianism has been attained at the expense of the other schools of philosophy. Only Taoism has survived and persisted as a complementary system to Confucianism.

Renaissance of Taoism (200–400 A. D.). The alternating prevalence between Confucianism and Taoism corresponds closely to the cyclic alternation between order and chaos in Chinese history. In times of peace and prosperity Confucianism flourishes and occupies the foreground of the intellectual stage, with Taoism kept in the background. When order is overtaken by chaos, Confucianism and Taoism exchange places. The Han dynasty collapsed at the beginning of the 3d century A. D., and the Chinese empire fell into a state of disorder and dismemberment for a period of several centuries. While Confucianism came to a halt in its course of ascendancy and Buddhism was getting acclimatized to the Chinese soil, Taoism enjoyed a Renaissance in three phases—romantic Taoism, religious Taoism, and philosophical Taoism.

In line with the spirit of Lao Tzu and Chuang Tzu, the Taoist romantics attempted to lead a life of complete freedom from care and responsibility. Disdaining appointment to public office, they would do only as their spirit led. Spontaneity became the cardinal virtue, and imitation and conformity irredeemable vices. Supreme joy was found in "pure conversation" about "super-wisdom" in the company of like-minded friends, enlivened by the wine bottle. Remarkably, several of the romantic Taoists ranked among the greatest geniuses in literature, art, and music.

The religion of Taoism started as a semisecret religious and political organization, thrived on the increasing suffering of the people, and developed into a folk belief of occultism and animism. Flaunting the teachings of transcendence over life and death of classical Taoism, it cultivated ardently the search for longevity and the elixir of life and evolved a rich cult of fairies and immortals.

The philosophical Taoists in the Taoist renaissance movement displayed a twofold emphasis, namely, syncretism of Taoist teachings with those of other schools and a radical reinterpretation of classical Taoist texts. The *Huai-nan Tzu*, a Taoist work of the 2d century B. C., regarded *Yin-yang* as the expression of the *Tao* and incorporated in its system also the ceremonials and ethical ideals of Confucianism. Among the ancient Chinese classics, the Taoists paid special attention to the *Classic of Changes*, establishing thereby a kind of dual claim with Confucianism over this great book. Their reinterpretation of the Taoist texts was so radical that they are sometimes called Neo-Taoists. According to the celebrated commentary on the *Tao Te Ching* by Wang Pi (226-249), for instance, the concept of *wu*, customarily understood to mean nonbeing, or that which lies at the basis of being, meant simply nothing. With *Tao* having become nothing, the all-pervading principle back of all things was said to be *tzu-jan* or "self-so," that is, spontaneity. The sage was the man who had achieved his union with the *Tao*, and was best suited to be king. In the end, the true sage for these Neo-Taoists turned out to be not Lao Tzu or Chuang Tzu, but Confucius. This was because Taoist leaders like Lao Tzu were still wrestling with the union with the *Tao*, but Confucius had completely forgotten to bother about it. In abundant evidence was the syncretic trend of the day among the schools of thought.

MEDIEVAL PERIOD

Spread of Buddhism. The introduction of Buddhism into China constitutes a major event in the history of cultural relations between China and India, an event comparable in importance to the spread of Christianity in the Western world. By the 3d century, Buddhist thought began to play an increasingly important role in Chinese philosophy, the development of which had been, up to this point, completely indigenous. During the ensuing centuries and until the flourishing of Neo-Confucianism in the 10th century, the best Chinese minds were attracted to Buddhism. Several schools of Buddhism were imported from India, and several more developed in China. The majority of the 13 schools of Buddhism in China belong to the Mahayana branch, but the Theravada · (Hinayana) branch is also represented. While the Wei-shih and the San-lun schools propound the Indian emphasis on analysis and abstraction, the indigenously developed T'ien-t'ai and Hua-yen (Ten-dai and Kegon in Japan) schools espouse preference for synthesis and harmonization. The philosophies evolved by T'ien-t'ai and Hua-yen, in their attempts at dealing with such contrasting concepts as particular and universal, subjective and objective, external and internal, generally minimize differences in favor of identities, and exemplify the doctrine of "one-in-all and all-in-one." A well-known dictum of Chinese Buddhist philosophy says, "Form (*rupa* in Sanskrit and *se* in Chinese) is not different from void (*sunyata* in Sanskrit and *k'ung* in Chinese), nor void from form." Freed from the Hindu insistence on the endless course of transmigration and iron-clad caste stratification, Buddhism in China significantly champions the idea of universal salvation and makes ample room for sudden enlightenment. As Buddhism infiltrates Chinese culture, it is itself infiltrated by Chinese cultural elements like Confucianism and Taoism. In the series of translations over the centuries of the all-important Buddhist term *nirvana*—starting with "release through extinction" and ending with "perfection complete"— it is easy to see the influence of Confucianism at work. "Extinction" is inherent in the etymology of the Sanskrit term, but "perfection" is much more palatable to the Chinese mind. The most outstanding product of this intellectual intercourse is the Ch'an school (Ch'an, pronounced "Zen" in Japanese, is the Chinese transliteration of Dhyana in Sanskrit), which might be said to be Indian Buddhism with a Chinese Taoist look.

Emergence of Ch'an Buddhism. Traditionally the beginning of Ch'an is traced back to the responsive smile between the Buddha and disciple Mahâkasyapa, and its importation into China is attributed to Bodhidharma. Ch'an Buddhism as a school flourished in China from the 5th to the 10th century and was then exported to Japan; it is, for the most part, a philosophic-religious creation of the Chinese mind. Commencing with emphasis on meditation, the school evolved such radical creeds as "teaching without words," "pointing directly to the mind," "becoming Buddha by realizing one's true nature," and "becoming Buddha here and now." The essence of Ch'an Buddhism consists in the insistence that the mind should be freed from distractions and distortions and kept pure and clear so that it can apprehend the basic truth of this fleeting universe, achieving thereby Buddhist nature, nirvana, or salvation. Historically, a southern and a northern school arose within Ch'an Buddhism, emphasizing respectively sudden and gradual enlightenment. Ch'an Buddhism, with its distinctly Chinese Taoist accent, has exercised a profound influence on Chinese art and literature as well as on Chinese attitudes towards life and the universe. The emergence of Neo-Confucianism, though a repudiation of Buddhism on the surface, is to no small measure due to the stimulation and challenge of Ch'an Buddhism.

Buddhist philosophy has always reflected much of its Indian background and origin, but in adapting to the Chinese soil it has undergone various transformations in the direction of simplicity, practicality, and catholicity.

MODERN PERIOD

In spite of its obvious acclimatization in China, there is always something foreign about Buddhism to the Chinese mind—its outlook on the universe and all existence as void, its lack of concern about society, and its emphasis on the mystical experience in personal cultivation. Not until the 10th century in the Sung dynasty, however, did Confucian scholars suceed in launching a movement in protest now known as Neo-Confucianism.

Rise of Neo-Confucianism. Neo-Confucianism is Confucianism revived and revised in response to the metaphysical and epistemological problems and propositions presented by Buddhism and, to a lesser extent, Taoism. The two basic tenets of Neo-Confucianism are nature (*hsing*), especially human nature, and principle (*li*). In fact, among the Chinese the movement is generally referred to as the Hsing-li learning of the Sung and Ming dynasties.

Chou Tun-yi (1017–1073) heralded the new learning by displaying a diagram in which the universe was shown to proceed from the Non-Ultimate to the Supreme Ultimate, which engenders Yin-yang and the five elements and through them the myriad transformations and good and evil. A more theoretical contribution was made by Chang Tsai (1020–1077) with his doctrine of the *ch'i*, the Ether, or material force. The Ether as substance is the Supreme Ultimate with its two phases of condensation and dispersion, which may be spoken of as the *Yang* and the *Yin*, and it is through these two phases of the Ether that all things are formed and dissolved. The Ether in its state of dispersion constitutes the Great Vacuity, but the Great Vacuity is not the same as the void of Buddhism or the nonbeing of Taoism. For the Ether in its phase of dispersion, that is, the Great Vacuity, is at the same time in its readiness for the next phase of condensation and creation. The world of existence is definitely not just the creation of the mind, as taught by

TEMPLE of Confucius in Taipei, one of many throughout Japan, Korea, and Vietnam, as well as China.

Buddhism, but a real world, as has been assumed by all Chinese philosophers, especially the Confucianists. The Ether or material force as function, in its alternating phases of activity and quietude, constitutes the Great Harmony. The Great Harmony and the Great Vacuity are themselves two aspects of the Ether. Here we see an example of a reassertion of the Confucianist position against the challenges of Buddhism and Taoism.

Brief mention should be made of the two Ch'eng brothers. They were the first ones to teach the concept of *li* as a principle that is self-evident, everywhere present, governing all things, and a universal process of creation and production. The *li* is endowed in all things, in a blade of grass as well as in man. It is this endowment that constitutes the natures of things and man, and therefore both nature and human nature are originally good. The elder brother, Ch'eng Hao (1032–1085), particularly saw the *li* as the vital principle in the ongoing process of production and creation of all things. He identified the creative quality of *li* with the *jen* of Confucius and thus extended the concept of *jen* to a cosmic scope. Both brothers asserted that the man of *jen* "forms a union with heaven and earth." The younger brother, Ch'eng Yi (1033–1107), developed a more minute program for the cultivation of one's character and one's mind. It was the tradition started by Ch'eng Yi that Chu Hsi continued and expanded.

Chu Hsi (1130–1200). Generally regarded as the representative spokesman for Neo-Confucianism, Chu Hsi was a great synthesizer of the several contributions made by his predecessors. He proposed a pair of concepts regarding the world of existence, namely *ch'i* (Ether or material force) for the physical world and *li* (Reason or rational principle) for the metaphysical world.

Ch'i is tangible but not intelligible, whereas *li* is intelligible but not tangible. *Li* in its totality constitutes the intrinsic nature of all things and is the Supreme Ultimate, while individuated *li*, united with *ch'i*, accords each thing its actual existence. The metaphysical interest shown here suggests Buddhist inspiration. In ethics, Chu Hsi distinguishes between the human mind and the cosmic mind. The latter, consisting of *li* only, is always good and pure, whereas the former, consisting of *ch'i* as well as *li*, can be good and pure but also evil and turbid, varying with the quality of the *ch'i* that is endowed in the individual. It is the duty of man so to cultivate his nature, with all its desires and passions, as to harmonize with the cosmic mind. Thus Chu Hsi attempted to uphold the orthodox Confucianist assumption of the goodness of human nature and at the same time account for the possibility of evilness in man. Chu Hsi was a great scholar as well as a great thinker. His commentaries on the Chinese classics were regarded as authoritative for centuries.

Mind School of Neo-Confucianism. Rivaling the Cheng Yi and Chu Hsi wing of Neo-Confucianism is the wing represented by Lu Chiu-yuan (1139–1193) and Wang Shou-jen (1472–1529). In contrast to Chu Hsi's dualism of *li* and *ch'i*, Lu Chiu-yuan, a contemporary and critic of Chu Hsi, insists on the monism of *hsin*, or the mind. To Chu, knowledge begins with investigation of external things; to Lu, all knowledge consists of the investigation of one's own moral nature. "Even the Six Classics are but commentaries of my mind," says Lu Chiu-yuan.

Wang Shou-jen, or Wang Yang-ming, continued Lu's line of thought, namely the "mind" school of Neo-Confucianism. Claiming that the mind is *li* and that *li* is good, Wang Shou-jen teaches that man by nature is good; that is, man has innate knowledge of the good and innate ability to do good. Knowledge is achieved not by investigation of external things but by removing impediments which clutter up the mind, and it is completed only by practice. Knowledge is the beginning of action, and action is the completion of knowledge. This promising line of thought which keeps knowledge and action in a wholesome relation was influential in China for a while, but it later lost its vitality.

Reaction Against Neo-Confucianism. The Manchus overran China and set up the Ch'ing dynasty in 1644. Many Chinese blamed Neo-Confucianism, the system that had dominated the Chinese mind for the preceding centuries, for the national disaster. Yen Yuan (1635–1704), a spokesman of the movement of revolt against Neo-Confucianism, denounced the system for being too much cut off from actual experience. When it is not too bookish, he charged, it is too introspective. In contrast, classical Confucianism is not only a system of teaching but also of conduct. Neo-Confucianism is so much preoccupied with meeting the challenge of Buddhism that it has taken up the Buddhist habit of contemplation and speculation. While Neo-Confucianists tried to make people understand principles by teaching principles, Confucius did it by helping people to perform their tasks and live their lives. The revolt against Neo-Confucianism might be regarded as a revival of classical Confucianism. The philosophy of Tai Chen (1723–1777), one of the revival's leading thinkers, is best preserved in an elaborate commentary on the *Mencius*. To Tai Chen the basic characteristic of the universe is production and reproduction. "Life reproducing life is *jen*," says Tai Chen. Since the reproductive processes of life involve desire, desire in human nature should be regarded as continuous with and not contrary to the cosmic mind, with nothing evil about it. Insisting on academic thoroughness, Tai stands also as a representative of an age distinguished for its superb scholarship in Chinese textual criticism. It was about this time that Western science and philosophy were first introduced into China.

CONTEMPORARY PERIOD

Impact of Western Philosophy and Science. The marine route between Europe and east Asia brought about a Western impact on China and turned a new chapter in the development of Chinese philosophy. In the late 19th century, there started a very vigorous effort at translating the works of such writers as Aristotle, Euclid, Adam Smith, John Stuart Mill, Darwin, and Herbert Spencer, and introducing such systems of philosophy as those of Schopenhauer, Haeckel, Kropotkin, Nietzsche, Rudolf Eucken, and Bergson. At the same time, Western teachers taught Western ideas in missionary schools, and Chinese students were sent to study in Europe and America.

The May Fourth Movement of 1919 is evidence of the seething vitality resulting from the Western impact on the Chinese mind. It is notable that John Dewey, Bertrand Russell, and Hans Driesch were on extended lecture tours in China during this period. In the 1920's, furthermore, a raging debate between science and metaphysics involved a number of participants, pitching the realists and materialists on the one side against the idealists and spiritualists on the other. Almost all the major schools of Western philosophy had their Chinese proponents, notably pragmatism by Hu Shih, neorealism by Chin Yueh-lin, and Neo-Kantian idealism by Chang Tung-sun. There was also a devoted and partisan group advocating the dialectical materialism of Karl Marx.

Reconstruction of Indigenous Systems. Under the impact of these contemporary movements of thought, adherents of both Buddhism and Confucianism attempted to bring about revivals of their philosophies. The 1920's and early 1930's witnessed Ou-yang Ching-yü's effort to revitalize Buddhist idealism. Much more significant was the publication in 1947 of the *Hsin Wei-shih Lun* (*A New Treatise on Radical Idealism*) in 4 volumes by Hsiung Shih-li. The roots of this lifetime study by Hsiung go back to *Vijñaptimātrasiddhiśāstra*, an idealistic version of Mahayana Buddhism propounded by Asaṅga and Vasubandhu in India and amplified by Hsuan Tsang and K'uei Chi in 7th century China. Hsiung's reflections broadened his horizon in the direction of Confucianism and Taoism. His central thesis is that reality is a vital spiritual process, continuous and unified, dynamic and plastic. Hsiung's treatise was a remarkable attempt at achieving a metaphysical conception of reality from Buddhist, Taoist, and Confucian sources, which, he hoped, would transcend the dualisms of Western philosophy and even of Buddhism.

Another notable indigenous philosopher is Liang Su-min, who also had an early love for Buddhism but shifted almost completely to Confucianism. Liang's discourses on Chinese civilization and his analysis of the Confucian forces in Chinese society and culture won many admirers for their brilliance and penetration. He is regarded as the spokesman of Neo-Confucian intuitionism, and his thought is noted for its integrity and independence. Mention should also be made of Fung Yu-lan, who is fundamentally a historian of Chinese philosophy. Fung's system is a combination of Neo-Confucianism and Western realism and logic that might be called Neo-Confucian rationalism.

Sway of Communism. The first half of the 20th century was a vigorous and stirring period in the development of Chinese philosophy. With the establishment of the Communist government in China in 1949, however, all the schools of philosophy, whether developments from classical Chinese systems or adaptations from Western system, were branded as "idealisms" and banished in favor of the one and only true philosophy, namely the system of dialectical materialism of Marx and Lenin. Thus, for example, Fung Yu-lan renounced his former philosophical position and attempted to make a system of dialectics of the *Tao Te Ching* and to represent Confucius as an exponent of materialism. The Yang Hsien-chen affair is a good illustration of the confused situation. An elderly philosophy professor at the Higher Party Institute of the Chinese Communist party's central committee, Yang stressed the doctrine of "combining two into one," which, under normal conditions, could very well be considered as one of the orthodox interpretations of the Marxist dialectic as well as of the indigenous Chinese concept of *Yin-yang*. But in the early 1960's, when Yang propounded this view, the Sino-Soviet split was growing in intensity and gathering momentum. The official doctrinal emphasis was on "dividing one into two," and

Yang's emphasis on "combining two into one" was roundly denounced as expressing the view of revisionism, and the elderly theoretician of the party was purged. It is evident that no thought, not even Communist thought, except "the thought of Mao Tse-tung" can be expressed in Communist China without risks, and "the thought of Mao Tse-tung" is cited and interpreted to suit the Communist party's strategy of the moment.

Renewal of Chinese Thought Overseas. Owing to the political situation, a considerable number of Chinese philosophers have left their homes and positions on the Chinese mainland to live and work more freely elsewhere—in Taiwan, Hong Kong, and abroad. Perhaps the most active group of Chinese teachers and writers congregated in Hong Kong. T'ang Chun-i, supported by Mu Tsung-san and others, founded the movement of humanistic idealism. The doctrine is formulated on the basis of Confucianism and affirms anew the rationality and dignity of man as an individual and as a member of the organized human community. It is a frontal denial of the deterministic materialism that turns man into a unit of production or a pawn of the state. It is anti-Communist on the ground that communism in the last analysis dehumanizes man, replacing humanity by inhumanity.

Chinese philosophy in the second half of the 20th century is thus in an odd situation. Its pursuit flourishes not at home but away from it. Mainland China has come under the sway of an ideology that is in every respect foreign to the Chinese mind and soul. Chinese philosophy abroad displays much vigor and variety. It has also shown a marked trend toward a revival of Confucianism.

Y. P. MEI, *State University of Iowa*

Bibliography

Chan, Wing-Tsit, *Chinese Philosophy, 1949–1963: An Annotated Bibliography of Mainland China Publications* (Honolulu 1967).
Chan, Wing-Tsit, *An Outline and an Annotated Bibliography of Chinese Philosophy* (New Haven 1959).
Chan, Wing-Tsit, *A Source Book in Chinese Philosophy* (Princeton 1963).
Creel, Herrlee G., *Chinese Thought From Confucius to Mao Tse-tung* (Chicago 1953).
De Bary, William T., *Sources of Chinese Tradition* (New York 1960).
Fung, Yu-lan, *A History of Chinese Philosophy*, tr. by D. Bodde, 2 vols. (Princeton 1952–1953).
Fung, Yu-lan, *A Short History of Chinese Philosophy*, tr. by D. Bodde (New York 1948).

10. Science and Technology

During most of its history, China has maintained a high level of cultural and technological development. Its early science was unmatched in the world. The time lag between the recorded appearance of many important technological developments in China and later in Europe is measured in centuries; for example, 12 centuries for porcelain, 10 for papermaking and iron casting, 6 for block printing, and 4 for gunpowder and magnetic instruments.

The Chinese conducted systematic observations and investigations in astronomy, mathematics, medicine, optics, acoustics, and various natural sciences. As early as the 4th century B. C., Chinese astronomers had charted the positions of some 800 stars, formulated rules for prediction of eclipses, and recorded the complex phenomenon of the precession of equinoxes. Magnetic declination was recorded and studied in China long before Europe became aware even

of magnetic polarity. The first practical seismograph was constructed in China about 130 A. D.

China did not experience prolonged periods of lost learning, corresponding to the Dark Ages in Europe. On the contrary, until the 17th century, China exhibited a pattern of cumulative learning and scholarship unsurpassed in the world prior to the Renaissance in Europe and the ensuing upsurge of science there. Unfortunately for China, this technological development soon leveled off into a period of stability and then deteriorated into an era of indifference. The resulting contrast between the East and the West was heightened by the dynamic upsweep of science and technology in Europe that took place during and after the age of discovery.

Equally unfortunate for China was the fact that social conditions have not been favorable to the emergence, or even acceptance, of modern science in China, as illustrated by its response to the four waves of Western scientific influence that successively washed the shores of China beginning about 1600, 1800, 1900, and 1950. A negative factor has been the fact that Western intellectual and ideological influences arrived at the same time as Western military pressures, and thus the Chinese have shown greater interest in the technology of military science than in pure science and other fundamental ideas.

First Major Experience with Western Science. China's first sustained encounter with modern, though pre-Newtonian, science began four centuries ago, with the arrival in Canton in 1582 of an Italian Jesuit missionary, Matteo Ricci, who was well versed in mathematics, mechanics, astronomy, and map making, as well as in jurisprudence and theology. Increasingly, Jesuit missionaries came to be employed as technical advisers and assistants.

During the Ming dynasty and its successor, the Ch'ing, or Manchu, dynasty, beginning in 1644, some 70 Western books on mathematics, astronomy, engineering, geography, and other subjects were introduced into scholarly circles in Peking, but they fell into disuse as Western influence declined sharply with the death of Emperor K'ang Hsi in 1722. The fervor of the European Renaissance, with its new outlook on the natural world and the universe, had been carried to China by the learned European missionaries but failed to take root there.

As an educational undertaking, the effort to introduce elements of Western culture, including science, was at best tolerated. What was accepted and utilized was Western knowledge of weaponry. Why was China so resistant to Western learning and the scientific outlook? One explanation is that China's feeling of its own cultural preeminence engendered indifference to and disdain for foreign ways. The traditional Chinese view was that science is technology, that is, utilitarian, but not an essential part of culture. This outlook gradually changed. However, the fact that science was associated with the foreigner and his misdeeds prolonged the rejection of science as a foreign influence.

Second Major Encounter with Western Science. The second wave of Western scientific influence may be dated roughly from the introduction of smallpox vaccination in Canton in 1805 by a British physician. The first Protestant missionary to China, Robert Morrison, arrived in Canton in 1807, and during the following decades various schools, clinics, and hospitals were founded in connection with missionary work. As a result, medical education and modern medical practice became the leading scientific profession in China. This wave, however, was limited severely by Chinese conservatism and by the great political turmoil in China during the 19th century.

The Chinese government establishment remained fearful and resistant to Westernization, but pressures upon it for action continued to mount. What hastened the adoption of modern technological institutions was an unmistakable demonstration that nothing would suffice short of adopting the technology of modern military and industrial power. This demonstration was the fall of Peking to an Anglo-French expeditionary force in 1860. As a result, military academies, arsenals, and shipbuilding and other facilities were founded. Training schools attached to these institutions began to translate and publish Western works on technology and science. At the same time, other schools were founded using foreign teachers to give instruction in geography, biology, mathematics, chemistry, physics, anatomy, and mechanics.

Defeat by Japan in the war of 1894–1895 came as a shock to the Chinese, who increasingly were faced with the realization that more would be required than the acquisition of Western military hardware. In 1898 the government launched the "Hundred Days of Reform," a frantic effort, marked by a flurry of imperial edicts issued at a bewildering rate, directing the founding of agricultural schools, use of scientific methods in agriculture, opening of mines, building of railroads, and a crash program to translate books of Western learning. The movement was halted by the Empress Dowager Tz'u Hsi, who placed Emperor Kuang Hsü in virtual house arrest and executed or banished the young emperor's advisers, the modern reformers. Two years later the violent Boxer Rebellion lashed out against all foreign persons, property, and influence.

When Japan defeated Russia in 1905, it became a model for China despite the fact that Japan had been regarded as a long-standing enemy. As a model of successful resistance to a European power, Japan attracted China's attention as a source of modern education, and Chinese students streamed to Japan at the rate of more than 500 a month. By 1910 more than 30,000 Chinese were studying in Japan.

Third Wave of Western Influence. The third wave of Western—American and European—scientific influence began after the suppression of the Boxer Rebellion and spanned the first half of the 20th century. It accelerated during the early years of the Chinese republic, founded in 1911, an era marked by a new spirit. Modernization proceeded in education and in industry and radiated into other spheres. An important step was the establishment of the American-patterned Tsinghua College in 1908. By 1914 there were nearly 1,000 Chinese students in the United States, and by 1925 an estimated 2,500.

After the Nationalist government subdued the provincial warlords and established the central government at Nanking in 1927, scientific institutions sprang up rapidly. The Academia Sinica, founded in 1928, came to include 11 institutes in major fields. The highest governmental scientific authority in China, it conducted research and also advised government on scientific matters. In rapid succession dozens of scientific organizations and research and training institutions were founded, and several made noteworthy contributions to science despite limited resources and personnel.

Science was a subject of intense interest on the part of intellectuals in China in the 1920's and 1930's, and there was an upsurge of scientific education, research, and publishing during the 1930's and early 1940's. In many ways the early 1930's can be regarded as the start of a modern renaissance, which had long been delayed by China's conservatism and its ingrained negative reaction to Western influence. But this renaissance was cut short by the diversion of national energies to confront Japan's military invasion.

World War II had a mixed effect on China's scientific and technological growth. Although

AUTOMATED controls in a seamless tube factory in Peking are handled by a woman industrial worker.

TECHNOLOGY STUDENTS in the Hsin Hua (New China) school in Peking learn to operate the controls of an electronic panelboard.

technology was advanced, science and the economy suffered. One effect of Japan's war on China was to drive a large number of China's educators, scientists, technical specialists, and students into the hinterlands, where they set up new institutions, some of which later became permanent, either independently or as branches of central organizations that moved back to Peking or Shanghai from wartime bases.

Communist Take-over. The Communists took over the reins of government in 1949, inheriting most of the existing scientific facilities. The greatest loss, by far, to the Chinese Communists was caused by the exodus of 500 or more scientists with advanced degrees. Efforts to attract them back to China were largely unsuccessful. A few of those who did return, however, helped China attain strength in the fields of nuclear physics and modern rocketry.

Brilliant records were established by many Chinese entering scientific fields in the United States; for example, the two Nobel Prize winners in physics, Tsung-dao Lee and Chen-ning Yang, who received their undergraduate education in China. These achievements reaffirm the belief that China's cultural heritage may well prove to be a deciding factor in the development of the country's scientific capabilities. Communist China has inherited the assets, as well as the limitations, provided by the traditions of Chinese scholarship and practical ingenuity. A significant resource, used by the Communists in building their expanded scientific establishment, has, in fact, been the scientific research institutions founded in China prior to 1949.

Russian Scientific and Technological Assistance. The fourth and by far the largest wave of Western scientific and technological influence to penetrate into China came between 1954 and 1960, when the Soviet Union initiated in China an ambitious program of scientific modernization that has no parallel in history. Under the Chinese-Russian scientific and technical agreement announced in 1954, scientists of both countries drew up detailed plans for scientific development in China. The first planning effort involved 200 Chinese and 20 Soviet scientists. In 1957 a task force of over 600 Russian scientists in some 25 different fields reviewed the plan, which is reported to have contained nearly 600 research and development projects, 100 of which the Chinese chose as priority items for Russian assistance.

Soviet scientific influence was paramount. Hundreds of Soviet scientists and engineers were in China before the end of 1957. Russian language texts were widely introduced into the educational system. According to a Chinese report, nearly 40,000 Chinese were sent to the Soviet Union for various kinds of training, some 2,000 at the graduate level.

The Chinese made great strides during their first five-year plan (1953–1957) and during the following years into 1960. Research installations were doubled and came to number in the hundreds. Many technological projects were undertaken, including major works such as dams, factory complexes, and communications facilities. Of particular interest to the Chinese was

MARC RIBOUD, FROM MAGNUM

the development of atomic energy, to which they assigned top priority. Evidence points to a Russian-Chinese disagreement on this point. While the Soviets emphasized economic objectives, the Chinese opted for atomic energy and weapons development.

Chinese Technological Advancement. In 1960, in the wake of the ideological dispute between the Soviet and Chinese Communist parties, the Soviet Union abruptly terminated its economic and military aid and withdrew its scientific and technological advisory teams from China. Despite the serious setback caused by the Soviet withdrawal, the Chinese Communists maintained a top priority for nuclear development, and in October 1964, China detonated its first atomic test device. During the months between its first and second atomic explosions (October 1964–May 1965), China came to be acknowledged as a nuclear power, the fifth and only non-Western nation to achieve this status. What did this signify in terms of China's overall development in science and technology? Had there been comparable achievement in other fields, or was this just a single *tour de force?*

Without question there has been a great change in the scale of scientific endeavor in China under the Communist regime. Scientific modernization has become a prime slogan of the regime, and the nation has constantly been exhorted to be scientific, that is, to employ scientific experimental methods. Spectacular growth in the total number research institutions—from roughly 100 to between 1,500 and 2,000—is also an indicator. The number of persons trained in Chinese educational institutions for scientific and technological professions sharply increased under the government's massive drive in education. While difficult to verify and to evaluate, Peking's claims give an indication of the scale of the education effort. According to a New China News Agency statement in August 1963, college graduates in China since 1949 totaled over one million, including 370,000 engineers, over 110,000 physicians and pharmacologists, over 100,000 agronomists and foresters, 325,000 teachers, and more than 70,000 natural scientists. By Western standards, a large proportion of these graduates would be considered low-level technicians rather than scientists and qualified professional people, but China is unmistakably in a new era in terms of the number of persons trained in modern scientific and technical subjects.

There were about 85,000 scientists in China at the beginning of 1965, excluding specialists in agriculture and medicine. As of the same date, the estimate for engineers was 450,000. Despite these numbers, marking an astonishing increase over a relatively short period, the Communist government has been confronted with a major weakness in its scientific capabilities. This arises from the fact that relatively few persons have been trained to replace China's senior scientists, the majority of whom were trained in Europe and the United States.

Politics and Science. The shortage of senior scientific and technological personnel to direct research and development projects in China has been compounded seriously by politics. Communist ideological activity has dominated every facet of life in China, and the foreign-trained intellectuals, including scientists, have been very hard hit. The "mass approach" glorifies the peasant and worker and advocates a "people's science." Antiforeign and anti-intellectual campaigns have humiliated and interfered with the functioning of the already undermanned corps of senior scientists. These moves were intensified in the "Proletarian Cultural Revolution" beginning in the mid-1960's. Practically every major scientific publication in China was suspended as of the latter half of 1966.

It is difficult to achieve a full perspective on China's erratic movement toward modernization. On one hand, China has exploded nuclear devices and is on its way to having a rocket delivery system for nuclear warheads. On the other hand, the nation's agriculture has failed to show a great response, and agricultural output in the late 1960's was only slightly above levels attained in peak years in the 1950's. There has been a great increase in the number and kinds of factories, and China is exporting industrial products, including machine tools, but these products for the most part are conventional trade items, reflecting the arrival of the industrial revolution rather than the scientific revolution in China.

China's advancement technologically is overshadowed by progress elsewhere in the world, but this should not obscure the considerable rate at which changes have occurred within the Chinese context. A country that only recently began its industrialization, China is building aircraft and merchant and naval vessels, including submarines, and constructing sophisticated research equipment, such as electron microscopes. The nuclear bombs, particularly the hydrogen bomb, constitute China's most complex technological feat, but this has been achieved at tremendous cost in terms of funds and personnel diverted from tasks of economic development in a still poor and basically agrarian society.

China's greatest modern scientific achievement was the synthesis of bovine insulin, the first major scientific feat since the Communist regime assumed control. In a statement early in 1967, Peking indicated that Chinese scientists had been working for six years and nine months to achieve their breakthrough, which was announced in November 1965. There is no doubt in world scientific circles that the Chinese have made a most significant contribution, producing the complex giant molecule of 777 precisely arranged atoms to constitute the bovine form of insulin. As a result the synthesis of human insulin is in the offing, whether in China or elsewhere.

Prospects. The prospects for scientific advancement in China, and therefore for science-based technologies, will continue to be affected deeply by the political leadership, which, despite its lip-service to science, constitutes a major obstacle to the emergence of a strong Chinese scientific community. The present group of Communist party veterans knows far better how to tear down social institutions than how to build them up. Its lack of scientific background and appreciation of the needs of scientists may continue to hold China back. Ultimately there will be a fifth scientific wave for China, and in a sense it has already begun. This time it is coming from within and from below, because the new generations of Chinese are learning their science at home, from fellow Chinese. As their numbers grow, and as time goes by, the old political leadership will be replaced by people who have had greater exposure to modern education than Mao Tse-tung and his colleagues, who were born under the Manchu dynasty. As science education continues to expand and as China modernizes, China will increasingly embrace science and the scientific outlook, and in turn China will itself be embraced by science.

ROBERT BRUCE SHEEKS
National Academy of Sciences

Bibliography

Cheng, Chu-yüan, *Scientific and Engineering Manpower in Communist China (1949–1963)*, National Science Foundation, NSF-65-14 (Washington 1965).

Fairbank, John K., Reischauer, Edwin O., and Craig, Albert M., *East Asia: The Modern Transformation* (Boston 1965).

Gould, Sydney H., ed., *Sciences in Communist China*, American Association for the Advancement of Science, Publication No. 68 (Washington 1961).

Haskins, Caryl P., *The Scientific Revolution and World Politics* (New York and Evanston, Ill., 1964).

Hudson, Geoffrey F., *Europe and China: A Survey of Their Relations from the Earliest Times to 1800* (Boston 1961).

Klochko, Mikhail A., *Soviet Scientist in Red China*, tr. by Andrew MacAndrew (New York 1964).

Lach, Donald F., *Asia in the Making of Europe* (Chicago 1965).

Reischauer, Edwin O., and Fairbank, John K., *East Asia, The Great Tradition* (Boston 1962).

Teng, Ssu-yu, and Fairbank, John K., *China's Response to the West: A Documentary Survey (1839–1923)*, (Cambridge, Mass., 1965).

Winter, Henry T. T., *Eastern Science* (London 1952).

CHINA: Arts, Language, and Mass Media

11. Art and Architecture

This section deals with architecture, painting, and sculpture. For an account of the Chinese art of porcelain, pottery, and bronze, see *Porcelain; Pottery; Bronze and Brass in Art*.

ARCHITECTURE

Although the ancient Chinese never considered architecture a fine art, in China as in the West it has been the mother of the fine arts. It was through the medium of architectural decoration that painting and sculpture matured and gained recognition as independent arts.

Technique and Forms. The architecture of China is an indigenous system of construction which was conceived in the dawn of Chinese civilization and has been developing ever since. Its characteristic form is a timber skeleton or framework standing on a masonry platform and covered by a pitched roof with overhanging eaves. The spaces between the posts and lintels of the framework may be filled in with curtain walls whose sole function is to separate one portion of the building from another, or the interior from the exterior. The walls of the Chinese building, unlike those of the conventional European building, are free from the weight of the upper floors and the roof, and may be installed or omitted as required. By adjusting the proportion of the open and walled-in spaces, the architect may admit or exclude just the amount of light and air appropriate to any purpose and to any climate. This high degree of adaptability has enabled Chinese architecture to follow Chinese civilization wherever it has spread—to Korea and Japan in the east, to Sinkiang in the west, to Indochina in the south, and to the Siberian border in the north.

As the Chinese system of construction evolved and matured, rules like the orders of classical European architecture were developed to govern the proportion of the different members of the building. In buildings of a monumental character the order is enriched by *tou-kung*, sets of brackets on top of the columns supporting the beams within and roof eaves without. Each set consists of tiers of outstretching arms called *kung*, cushioned with trapezoidal blocks called *tou*. The *tou-kung* are functional members of the structure, carrying the beams and permitting the deep overhang of the eaves. As they evolved, they assumed different shapes and proportions. In earlier periods they were simple and large in proportion to the size of the building; later they became smaller and more complicated. Hence they serve as a convenient index to the date of construction.

SIMPLE ELEGANCE distinguishes the art and architecture of China—for example, this graceful pagoda in the Li Gardens, near Wuhsi.

The planning problem of the Chinese architect is not that of partitioning a single building, since the framing system makes the interior partitions mere screens, but of placing the various buildings of which a Chinese house is composed. These are usually grouped around courtyards, and a house may consist of an indefinite number of such courtyards. The principal buildings are usually oriented toward the south, so that a maximum amount of sunlight can be admitted in winter, while the summer sun is cut off by the overhanging eaves. Apart from the variations required by special topographical conditions, the same general principles apply to all domestic, official, and religious architecture.

Historical Development. The oldest architectural remains in China are some tombs of the Han dynasty. Both the burial chamber and the *ch'üeh*, or gate piers, include translations into stone of timber construction, showing a highly accomplished carpenter's art rendered by an equally masterful touch of the sculptor's chisel. The important role played by the *tou-kung* is seen even in that early period.

No timber structure built during the long interval up to the middle of the 8th century A. D. has as yet been found standing in China. Yet glimpses of the outward appearance of such structures may be gathered from the details of construction in some of the cave temples and from the paintings on their walls. In the caves of Yunkang, near Tatung, Shansi, constructed about 452–494 A. D., and in those of Hsiangtang Shan, on the border of Honan and Hopeh provinces, and Tienlung Shan, near Yanku (Taiyüan), Shansi, which were built about 550–618 A. D., the façades and interiors are treated architecturally, carved from the rock cliffs to emulate the contemporary timber structures. On the tympanum of the west portal of the Tz'u-ên Ssŭ pagoda (701–704 A. D.), in Sian (Changan), Shensi, is an engraving showing in accurate detail a Buddhist temple hall. The frescoes on the walls of the 6th to 11th century caves at Tunhwang, Kansu, are paradise scenes with elaborate architectural backgrounds. These relics are graphic records of the architecture of a period that has left us no standing specimens. Here, too, we notice the importance of the *tou-kung*, whose evolution may be clearly traced.

Such indirect evidence of the character of early Chinese architecture is well supported by groups of buildings still standing in Japan. They were erected in the Suiko (Asuka), Hakuhō, Tempyō, and Kōnin (Jogan) periods, corresponding to the Sui and T'ang dynasties in China. In fact, until the middle of the 19th century the architecture of Japan reflected as in a mirror the changing styles of continental builders. The early Japanese structures may justifiably be called colonial Chinese, and some are actually known to have been erected by continental architects. Earliest of these is the Hōryūji group, near Nara, which was constructed by Korean builders and completed in 607. Another is the Kondō of the Tōdaiji, Nara, built by the Chinese monk Ganjin (Chien-chên, died 763) in 759.

The oldest extant wooden structure in China itself is the main hall of the Buddhist temple Fo-kuang Ssŭ, Wutai, Shansi. It is a one-story building of seven bays, with *tou-kung* of gigantic size, showing an unparalleled vigor and dignity in proportion and design. The temple was built in 857, shortly after the nationwide Buddhist persecution of 845. It is the only wooden structure known to date from the T'ang dynasty, the golden age of Chinese art. The hall houses specimens of sculpture and calligraphy and a fresco frieze, all of the same period. The congregation in one spot of all the major arts of T'ang date makes this temple and its contents a unique treasure in China.

Wooden structures of later periods are found in increasing numbers. A few of the more outstanding monuments may be chosen to represent the Sung dynasty, together with the contemporaneous Liao and Chin dynasties.

The Hall of Kuan-yin (Goddess of Mercy) of the Tu-lo Ssŭ, Chihsien, Hopeh, was built in 984. It is a two-story structure containing an eleven-headed Kuan-yin, standing upright. A mezzanine story is inserted between the two main stories, so that the structure is actually built of three superposed "orders." Here the function of the *tou-kung* is shown to best advantage.

The group of buildings at Tsintzu, near Yanku, was built about 1025. The two principal buildings are each one story in height, but the main hall has double-decked eaves. The main hall of the Hua-yen Ssŭ, Tatung, is a huge single-story structure with single-decked eaves. Built about 1090, it is one of the largest Buddhist structures in China. Of considerably later date (1260) is the main hall of the Pei-yüeh Miao, Chuyang, Hopeh. The inner structural members supporting the upper part of the roof have been extensively rebuilt, but the lower part and the outward appearance of the building as a whole are essentially unaltered.

A comparative study of these few examples reveals that the *tou-kung* tends to become smaller and smaller in proportion to the building. Another common characteristic is an increase in the height of the columns toward the corners of the building. This latter refinement brings about a gentle curvature of the eave line (with the exception of the Hua-yen Ssŭ hall), and of the roof ridge, giving an appearance of elegance.

With the coming of the Ming dynasty, the subtle refinements disappeared. This trend is

PEKING'S "Temple of Heaven," a 700-acre enclosure, includes this interesting building of the Ming dynasty.

FORBIDDEN CITY in Peking encloses imperial palaces, audience halls, temples, and apartments and illustrates the typically Chinese skill of planning on a grand scale.

especially noticeable in the monuments built under imperial patronage, and is best exemplified in the sacrificial hall at the tomb of Emperor Yung Lo, built in 1425 at Changping, Hopeh, 25 miles (40 km) north of Peking. Here the *tou-kung* has shrunk to insignificance; its presence can be detected only at close view.

Despite the retrogressive features of individual buildings of the Ming and Ch'ing dynasties, we have in the imperial palaces of Peking a superb example of planning on the grandest scale, showing the aptitude of the Chinese for conceiving and executing a design of colossal proportions. The hundreds of audience halls and apartments within the Forbidden City, a walled enclosure measuring about 3,350 feet (1,020 meters) by 2,490 feet (760 meters), are mainly structures of the late Ming and the Ch'ing dynasties. The entire area was conceived as a single architectural unit, with one main axis dominating the Forbidden City and the entire Imperial City surrounding it. The halls, pavilions, verandas, and gates are grouped in innumerable courtyards connected by colonnades. The buildings themselves are raised on white marble terraces. Columns and walls are generally painted red, while the *tou-kung* are decorated with intricate designs in blue, green, and gold, forming a cool belt which accentuates the deep shady overhang of the eaves. The whole structure is crowned by a roof of glazed yellow or green tiles. The ingenuity of the Chinese in applying color to architecture on an all-inclusive scale has never been equaled.

Multistoried Timber Structures. Because of the limitations of the material, high structures in timber are rare. The best known is the Ch'i-nien Tien of the Temple of Heaven, Peking. It is a building of circular plan, standing on three tiers of white marble terraces and crowned by three tiers of blue glazed tile roofs, the uppermost of which converges into a cone whose apex is about 108 feet (33 meters) above the ground.

The finest example of multistoried timber construction in China is the little-known wooden pagoda of Yinghsien, Shansi. Erected in 1056, it is a five-story structure with four additional mezzanine stories, built on an octagonal plan.

Each of its main and mezzanine stories is a complete "order" in itself. The pagoda as a whole therefore comprises nine superposed "orders." Scarcely any of its members is idle: every timber has its part in supporting the building. The top roof, which is an octagonal cone, is surmounted by a wrought iron spire whose tip is 215 feet (65 meters) above the ground. Although most of the early pagodas were of wood, this is the only one of its kind still standing in China.

Masonry Pagodas. The early wooden pagodas have disappeared, but many of their counterparts in brick—or, in rare cases, stone—have survived the destructive forces of man and nature. Contrary to the general assumption, the design of the Chinese pagoda was not imported from India; rather, it is a cross between the architectural ideas of the two civilizations. The body is entirely Chinese, the Indian element finding expression only in the spire, which is derived, often in much modified form, from the stupa. Many of the pagodas are brick and stone translations of wooden prototypes embodying the traditional Chinese architectural conceptions.

Chinese masonry pagodas may be divided into five principal types:

One-Story Pagodas. A stupa is a monument marking the site where some Buddhist relic is buried; the tomb stupa of a deceased monk may properly be called a pagoda. Most of the tomb stupas of the 6th to the 12th centuries are small, square pavilionlike structures, one story high, with one or two strings of cornices. The earliest examples of the one-story form is the Ssŭ-mên T'a (which is not a tomb), built in 544 near Tsinan, Shantung. More typical is the tomb of Hui-ch'ung at Ling-yen Ssŭ ('mid-7th century), Changching, Shantung.

Multistoried Pagodas. The multistoried pagoda retains most of the characteristics of the indigenous multistoried building. Counterparts in wood are still extant in Japan, but only brick structures of this type remain in China. One of the earliest and best examples is the Hsiang-chi Ssŭ pagoda, built in 681, near Sian. It is a square pagoda of 13 stories, 11 of which are intact. The stories are marked by strings of corbeled cornices; and the exterior walls of each story, in addition to their doorways and windows, have delicate reliefs of simple pilasters and architraves supporting *tou*.

In the Sung dynasty the octagonal plan became general. Representation of columns or pilasters on the walls is often omitted, but the cornices are in most cases supported by numerous *tou-kung*. In some instances, such as the twin pagodas of Tsohsien, Hopeh (about 1090), the outward appearance of the wooden pagoda has been faithfully reproduced in brick.

Multieaved Pagodas. The multieaved type seems to be a mutation of the single-story pagoda, produced through increasing the number of cornices. In appearance, it presents a high main story crowned by a great number of closely decked eaves. The earliest example is the 12-sided, 15-story pagoda of Sung-yüeh Ssŭ, built about 520, on Sung Shan, a sacred mountain in Honan. During the T'ang dynasty the square plan was the only one chosen for this type of pagoda. The pagoda of Fa-wang Ssŭ (about 750), also on Sung Shan, is an excellent example.

The octagonal plan was introduced about the middle of the 9th century and after the 11th century became accepted as the standard shape for a pagoda. A great number of pagodas of this type, enriched by *tou-kung* under the eaves, were built in north China from the 10th to the 12th centuries. The best-known example is the pagoda of the T'ien-ning Ssŭ, Peking, a structure of the 11th century which has been much repaired.

Stupas. The stupa in its original Indian form, though known in China through the early Buddhist missionaries, was never transplanted there. When the stupa finally did become established in China, in much modified form, it arrived through Tibet in conjunction with the spread of Lamaism. The Tibetan stupa is generally bottle shaped and raised on a high base. The best example is the stupa of Miao-ying Ssŭ, Peking, which was built in 1260 by Kublai Khan. Later the bottle became more slender, particularly the neck. This part, which originally resembled a truncated cone, came to resemble a smokestack. Typical of the later stupas of the Tibetan type is the one in North Sea Park, Peking, built in 1651.

Diamond-Based Pagodas. The *chin-kang pao-tso t'a*, or diamond-based pagoda, consists of a group of pagodas on a common base. Its development was foreshadowed as early as the 8th century in the pagoda group of Yün-chü Ssŭ, Fangshan, Hopeh, which is composed of a large pagoda and four small ones on a single, very low platform. The form did not reach full architectural maturity until the Ming dynasty. An excellent example is the Wu-t'a Ssŭ (Five Pagoda Temple), built in 1473 outside one of the west gates of Peking. This structure reminds the observer in various ways of the 8th century Borobudur in Java.

P'ai-lou. In most of the towns and on many of the country roads of China are found monumental archways called *p'ai-lou*. Although the *p'ai-lou* is considered a purely Chinese architectural concept, one cannot fail to notice an analogy between this form and the gateways of the railings surrounding certain Indian stupas, such as those of Sanchi. In south China stone *p'ai-lou* are common; in northern cities the street scene is often enlivened by gaily painted timber ones.

Bridges. The building of bridges is an ancient art in China. Early examples were either simple timber structures or pontoon bridges, and it was not until the middle of the 4th century A. D. that the arch was used to span a water barrier. The most notable example of Chinese bridge building is the Great Stone Bridge, Chaohsien, Hopeh. This is an open-spandrel bridge (one with small arches piercing the triangular space between the roadway and the ends of the main arch) whose principal arch has a span of 123 feet (37 meters). Built in the Sui dynasty, it is a feat of engineering to amaze even a modern engineer. The more common type of bridge, exemplified by the celebrated Marco Polo Bridge near Peking, uses intermediate piers. Suspension bridges are often employed in the mountainous regions of southwestern China, and bridges with huge stone lintels, sometimes measuring 70 feet (20 meters) or more, are not uncommon in Fukien.

PAINTING

Painting as an art first appeared in China in the form of decorations on banners, dresses, gates, walls, and other surfaces. The aesthetic appeal and suggestive power of this medium were utilized by kings and emperors of the earliest days as a convenient means of teaching and governing the people.

Pre-T'ang Painting. In the Han dynasty the art of painting reached technical maturity, and murals were used to decorate the interiors of halls and palaces. In 51 B. C., Emperor Hsüan Ti (reigned 73–49 B. C.) ordered portraits of 11 of his ablest generals and ministers, who had brought about the surrender of the *shan-yü* (king) of the barbarian Hsiung-nu, painted on the walls of Ch'i-lin Ke—an indication that portrait painting had already become a recognized art. Paintings were executed on walls and on silk. A considerable number of paintings on silk are reported to have been included in the imperial collections of the T'ang dynasty, but these have disappeared.

A painted brick discovered in a tomb at Naknang (Lolang), Korea, which was the capital of a Chinese province from 108 B. C. to 313 A. D., is in the Museum of Fine Arts, Boston. It affords a glimpse of painting in a frontier province of the great Han empire. Numerous stone slabs with designs engraved or in relief also provide indirect but valuable evidence of the character of Han mural painting.

The oldest existing Chinese scroll painting, attributed to Ku K'ai-chih (344?–?406 A. D.), is treasured in the British Museum in London. Ku K'ai-chih was a celebrated painter of the Chin (Tsin) dynasty. The scroll, probably a T'ang copy, is labeled *Admonitions of the Instructress to the Court Ladies* and depicts scenes illustrating a series of proverbs or morals. The figures are painted with a brush on silk, in lines of great accuracy and dexterity, but no attempt was made to set them against a background. The painting shows conceptions of the human form and of space which still adhere to some extent to the archaic methods of presentation on the Han relief stone slabs. Yet it also contains the essential characteristics of the 5th and 6th century Buddhist sculpture.

Painting of the T'ang Dynasty. Painting, like other branches of art, blossomed into its full glory during the T'ang dynasty. Yen Li-teh and his brother Yen Li-pên (about 600–673) are the first of a long list of great T'ang painters.

Horses and Groom by T'ang painter Han Kan is dated about 750, with inscription by Sung Emperor Hui Tsung (reigned 1101–1125).

Li-teh was also an architect, while Li-pên was the greater painter. Attributed to the latter is the scroll *Portraits of Emperors and Kings,* in the Museum of Fine Arts, Boston, in which many of the characteristics of the Ku K'ai-chih scroll are traceable.

Wu Tao-tzǔ (about 700–760) became the most celebrated Chinese painter. The first to make full use of the flexibility of the brush, he employed undulating lines varying in thickness, with third-dimensional effects. This was a radical departure from the wirelike lines of the earlier painters and gave him greater freedom of expression. "Wu's wind-blown draperies" became a phrase familiar to every student of Chinese painting, and succeeding painters depicted movement ever more vividly. Wu, with his free and masterly brush, excelled in painting subjects of all kinds, sacred and secular—figures, animals and plants, landscape, and architecture. The number of his murals recorded in the *Li-tai Ming-hua Chi (Famous Paintings of All Ages)* by Chang Yen-yüan (late T'ang) totals more than 300. Most have been destroyed.

By the T'ang dynasty, decorating temple walls with paintings had become almost a universal practice. Several hundred items are recorded in the *Li-tai Ming-hua Chi:* scenes of paradise and hell, images of Buddha, Bodhisattvas, lokapalas, demons, and other legendary beings. And these were from collections in the two capitals only—from Sian and Loyang (Honan). There were also many paintings by lesser artists in other cities and on the sacred mountains. Almost no works of this kind have been preserved in the central provinces, but the caves of Tun-hwang on the Silk Road are a rich source of information on Buddhist mural painting in a frontier province.

By the beginning of the 8th century landscape, which was to become the noblest form of Chinese painting, had freed itself from its role as a mere background to figure painting. Li Ssǔ-hsün, who was born about 651 and died in 716 or 720, and his son, Li Chao-tao, are generally recognized as the liberators of landscape paint-

ing. Known as the Two Li Generals, they founded the Li or northern school of painting. The work of this school is characterized by careful, wirelike drawings colored with bright blue and green and accented with specks of gold and vermilion. It is highly decorative but somewhat stiff, with every detail minutely and laboriously depicted. While the Two Li Generals were perfecting this style, Wu Tao-tzǔ painted on the walls of the Tatung palace, in one day, in ink and only faintly tinted with colors, the panoramic *Three Hundred Li on the Chialing River*—a work widely different in technique and style from the products of the Li school.

About a half century later, the poet-painter Wang Wei (699–759) was to be hailed as the master of ink landscape. His work, in contrast to the rigid draftsmanship of the Li school, is characterized by boldness and freedom. Wang Wei excelled in depicting mist and water and was the first to succeed in capturing atmosphere in nature. It is said of him that there are pictures in his poetry and poetry in his pictures. He, too, had his followers, and was hailed by Ming critics as the founder of the southern school of landscape painting, just as the Li Generals were called the founders of the northern school.

Among other great T'ang painters were Ts'ao Pa and Han Kan (about 750), both celebrated for their pictures of horses, and Chou Fang and Chang Hsüan (late 8th century), who depicted domestic and feminine scenes. A copy of one of Chang's scrolls, made by Emperor Hui Tsung (reigned 1101–1125) of the Sung dynasty, is in the Museum of Fine Arts, Boston.

Five Dynasties and Sung. During the chaotic Five Dynasties period there flourished a number of artists who heralded the great Sung painters. Ching Hao, who lived at the end of T'ang and the beginning of this period, was the master of the great landscapist Kuan T'ung who exerted a tremendous influence on the landscape painting of the Sung dynasty. The monk Kuan-hsiu, who was active about 920, was famous for his figures, particularly lohans. Hsü Hsi and Huang Ch'üan were painters of birds and flowers.

567

Mural painting, though less popular than it had been in the T'ang period, was still common during the Northern Sung dynasty, and a few Sung murals have escaped destruction and survived for posterity. In the Tunhwang caves are examples of the work done in a frontier province.

Working at the court academy under imperial patronage were such great painters as Kuo Hsi (about 1020–1090) the landscapist, and Huang Chü-ts'ai, son of Huang Ch'üan, who like his father painted birds and flowers but was a finer artist.

Among the scholar painters of the early Sung period, Li Ch'êng and Tung Yüan (late 10th century) are generally recognized as the greatest landscapists. Another painter, Fan K'uan, often covered his hilltops with heavy vegetation, and placed high, rugged cliffs along riverbanks. Mi Fei (1051–1107) filled his scenes with heavy mists and clouds, and rendered his protruding hilltops with the horizontal, broad, short "eggplant" strokes so much imitated by later painters. Li Lung-mien (Li Kung-lin, 1040–1106) is well known to the Western world. His line drawings of figures and horses, executed with extreme facility and dexterity, are examples of the highest achievement in draftsmanship.

Toward the end of the Northern Sung dynasty, Emperor Hui Tsung, himself an accomplished artist who aimed at extreme naturalism, became a great patron of art. Nevertheless, though he devoted far more attention to the academy than had earlier emperors, it did not produce any outstanding artist.

While painting in general flourished in the Southern Sung dynasty, Buddhist painting receded into almost complete obscurity. By this time Buddhism had died out in the land of its origin. Confucian scholars launched merciless attacks on it, and the Buddhists themselves, now dominated by the Ch'an (Zen) sect, while not entirely iconoclastic, substituted meditation for image worship. Buddhist painters of this period preferred such themes as "Kuan-yin in White Dress by the Moonlit Pool," "Meditating Sages," or "Sixteen Lohans"—themes which were not bound by rigid rules calling for dignity and symmetry, as were the religious paintings of earlier periods.

In a world dominated by neo-Confucianism and Ch'an Buddhism, painters turned to landscape as their preferred medium of expression. In the late 12th and early 13th centuries the academy numbered a host of great landscape painters, including Liu Sung-nien, Liang K'ai (about 1203), Hsia Kuei (about 1195–1224), and Ma Yüan (about 1190–about 1225). Liu Sung-nien excelled in landscape of the blue-and-green (Li) style, and Liang K'ai was a master of the technique of line drawing of human figures against a landscape background, also in line. But the two great figures in ink landscape of the Southern Sung dynasty were Hsia Kuei and Ma Yüan. Hsia Kuei's strength and boldness are best seen in his famous Ten Thousand Li of the Yangtze River. Ma Yüan, who placed his horizons rather low, is more readily appreciated by Westerners. His landscapes, in contrast to those of Hsia Kuei, are marked by tranquility and delicate atmosphere, best illustrated by a pine tree silhouetted against a misty background, a motif familiar to every student of Chinese painting. Up to his time, Chinese landscape painters had tried to include all they saw. Ma Yüan's compositions show merely a few rocks and one or two trees. This pattern—simple in construction and sparse in detail—is perhaps closer to the Western conception of landscape painting than the all-inclusive pattern. It profoundly influenced the painting of the Yüan dynasty.

Yüan Painting. The comparatively short Yüan period had a number of great painters. Chao Mêng-fu (1254–1322), best known as a painter of human figures and horses, was equally at home with landscape. He was also a calligrapher of the first rank. His best-known work is the Horse with Groom. Among the scholars who avoided Mongol officialdom was Ch'ien Hsüan (1235–about 1290), renowned as a painter of flowers, birds, and insects.

Wu Chên (1280–1354), Huang Kung-wang (1264–1354), Ni Tsan (1301–1374), and Wang Mêng (died 1385) are honored as the Four Great Masters of Yüan. They were all landscape painters. Wu Chên treats his material somewhat heavily, but he has a keen sense of space. He is also well known for his bamboos. In striking contrast are the airy scenes of Huang Kung-wang and Ni Tsan, who used washes very sparingly, obtaining their effects with lines consisting mainly of dry brush strokes. This is particularly true of Ni Tsan, who emphasized this style through his choice of extremely simple subjects. Wang Mêng painted his scenes heavily, building them up laboriously with individual strokes.

Ming and Ch'ing Dynasties. The Ming dynasty, relatively recent, has left us many paintings. Mural painting became rare, but some examples which have come down to us, such as those in the Fa-hai Ssŭ, near Peking, show superlative craftsmanship. Yet connoisseurs and critics do not classify these murals as art, looking to the scrolls alone for the work of the great masters. Early Ming academicians strove to emulate T'ang and Sung paintings, but the spirit of their work is entirely different. Wu Wei, the landscape painter, who modeled himself on Ma Yüan, became the founder of the so-called Che (Chekiang) school. Pien Wên-chin (Pien Ching-chap, about 1430) and Lü Chi (about 1500) were well known for their flowers and birds in the manner of Huang Ch'üan and Huang Chü-ts'ai; Lin Liang founded a school in which the same subjects were treated in an extremely facile and sketchy manner. The leading exponent of the Che school is Tai Chin (Tai Wên-chin, about 1430–1450), originally an academician, but expelled from the academy through the intrigues of jealous colleagues. Like all painters of the period, he modeled himself upon Sung masters—specifically, on Ma Yüan—but created a style of his own, simple and articulate in stroke, light in rendering.

Both the academic and the Che schools gradually died out, the latter being reincarnated in the "literary man's style," best represented by the Four Masters of Ming: Shên Chou (1427–1509), T'ang Yin (1470–1523), Wên Chêng-ming, and Tung Ch'i-ch'ang (1554–1636). Ch'iu Ying (about 1522–1560), who learned his craft as a lacquer pianter, was a master of detail. In his paintings we see the pleasures of everyday life exquisitely and faithfully recorded. A salient characteristic of Ming painters is their masterly manipulation of the brush. It does not merely make a line or a wash; it conveys tone, strength, and spirit. In this dynasty the technique of the brush attained perfection.

Pines and Mountains in Spring by Sung artist Mi Fei (1051–1107) is typical of his landscapes with hilltops rising above white clouds.

Ch'ing dynasty art is a continuation of the Ming tradition. Early in this period the southern school of landscape painting, best represented by the four Wangs—Wang Shih-min (1592–1680), Wang Chien (1598–1677), Wang Hui (1632–1717), and Wang Yüan-ch'i (1642–1715) —came into prominence. Wang Shih-min and Wang Chien, who took Tung Yüan and Huang Kung-wang as their masters, formed the vanguard of Ch'ing painting. The former is known for his bold brush strokes. Wang Hui was a disciple of Wang Shih-min, and excelled him in control of the medium. He is said to have combined the northern and southern schools, and was proclaimed by his master as the Sage of Painting. Wang Yüan-ch'i, grandson of Wang Shih-min and the most learned of the four, best caught the spirit of Huang Kung-wang. He is known for his landscapes with light tinges of color.

Ch'ên Hung-shou (1599–1652) originated a style in which, despite an appearance of carelessness, each stroke is skillfully conceived and precisely executed. He had many imitators. Shih T'ao was another "careless" painter of landscapes and bamboos. Both men reached maturity in the Ming dynasty, but they lived into the early years of Ch'ing, and their influence on later painters places them as artists of the later rather than of the earlier dynasty.

SCULPTURE

Sculpture, like architecture, was not accorded due recognition by the Chinese. While we know the great painters, the sculptors are anonymous.

Early Sculpture. The oldest specimens of Chinese sculpture were found in the Shang dynasty tombs at Anyang. The owl, tiger, and turtle are favorite motifs, and the human figure also appears occasionally. These marble pieces are in the round, some of them being architectural elements. Their surfaces are decorated with patterns like those found on the contemporary bronzes. In decorative pattern, in basic concepts of form and mass, and in spirit, the sculpture and the bronzes are one. Bronze masks have also been found, some of the *t'ao-t'ieh*, some of human beings. They are often well modeled.

Human figures and animals in the round began to be used as decorative motifs on the bronzes around 500 B. C. The human figures were first carved in the kneeling position, molded in strict conformity with the *law of frontality*, but the art soon freed itself to portray action. In general, the human figures are short and stubby, rendered with little feeling for modeling, but the animal forms show keen and subtle touches of the chisel, based on careful observation of nature.

Han, Three Kingdoms, Six Dynasties. In the Han dynasty sculpture gained importance in conjunction with architecture. Reliefs decorate interior wall surfaces, such as those found in a number of tomb shrines, notably the tombs of the Wu family at Chiahsiang, Shantung. Human figures and animals (lions, lambs, and chimeras) in the round stand in pairs flanking the avenues leading to tombs, temples, and palaces. At Ch'üfu, Shantung, the human figures are typically rigid, lumpy, and ill-modeled, bearing only a vague resemblance to the human form. Yet the animals are in general well modeled, robust, vigorous, and animated. The lions and chimeras are usually winged. (Since figure sculpture, animal or human, had never been employed by the Chinese of earlier times as guardian monuments to an architectural approach, it is possible that the idea was imported from the Occident through contact with the barbarian tribes of the west and north.) On some of the contemporary *ch'üeh* in Szechwan are found reliefs of birds, dragons, and tigers that rank with the best decorative sculpture.

With the spread of Buddhism during the period of the Northern and Southern dynasties, anthropomorphic sculpture assumed an important role. A few small images of the early 5th century have come down to us. The first important monuments are in the caves of Yunkang, near Tatung, first capital of the Northern Wei dynasty (386–535 A. D.). These are undoubtedly Chinese versions of Buddhist caves in India. Yet, aside from decorative motifs (the acanthus leaf, the frets, the beads, and even the Ionic and Corinthian capitals) and the basic conception of the caves themselves, there seems to be no traceable Indian influence to give the sculpture an Indian or otherwise un-Chinese character. There are a few characteristically Indian figures, but the group remains essentially Chinese.

The work on the caves near Tatung was begun by imperial order in 452 and stopped abruptly in 494, when the capital was moved south to Loyang. The plan of some of the caves is fairly similar to the chaitya caves of India, with the chaitya, or stupa, in the center. The architecture and sculpture, however, are basically Chinese. The earliest, and larger, figures, some measuring over 70 feet (21 meters) in height, are heavy and sturdy. The pleated draperies cling to the body. Later the figures grew more slender, and the head and neck became almost tubular. The eyebrows are arched and join with the bridge of the nose. The wide forehead is almost flat, turning sharply back at the temples. The eyes are mere slits; the lips, thin, forever smiling. The chin is often sharply pointed—a feature especially noticeable in some bronze statuettes of the period. The draperies no longer cling to the body, but hang from it, often flaring out at ankle level, and are arranged symmetrically on the right and left, with the pointed, almost knifelike, ends of the folds spread out like a bird's wings. (It is not by accident that pointed ends are also characteristic of the strokes of the calligraphy of the period.) The Bodhisattvas of these statuary groups, whose Indian counterparts wear princely attire, are stripped of most of their ornaments. They wear a simple tiara and a heart-shaped necklace, and from the shoulders of each figure hangs a long sash, the ends crossing through a ring hung in front of the thighs.

A project similar to that at Tatung was begun by the Wei emperors about 495 at Lungmen, near Loyang, on the cliffs of the I (Yi) River. Here the heads are less tubular and more rounded, and the draperies less pointed and more fluent, though still symmetrically arranged, achieving a superb decorative effect. The walls of some of the caves are decorated with reliefs representing the emperor on one wall and the empress on the opposite one, each attended by an entourage, forming compositions of the highest order. The activity of the cliff sculptors at Lungmen continued until the latter part of the 9th century.

The Northern Ch'i (550–557) rulers were devout but extravagant Buddhists. Yet it was not until nearly the end of their brief dynasty that they began the caves at Tienlung Shan. Most of the figures of these caves assume a standing posture. Their heads are almost round. The forehead is markedly lower; the eyes, though still very narrow, are wider. The nose and lips are fuller, with the enchanting smile of earlier periods almost completely suppressed. The draperies are simpler, hanging vertically.

Sculpture of the Sui and T'ang Dynasties. In the Sui dynasty the standing figures begin to show a peculiar protrusion of the abdomen. The head has become smaller in proportion to the body, and the jaws and nose are fuller. The eyes, though still narrow, show some convexity in the upper lids, emphasizing the presence of the eyeballs. The slightly convex surface intersects the curved plane under the brow in a gentle "valley." The line of intersection appears as a wide arc, repeating the rhythm of the brow and the eye. The subdued smile is produced by more fully modeled lips, and the mouth is smaller. The neck has assumed the peculiar shape of a truncated cone, protruding sharply from the chest and joining the head with similar abruptness. The cone is circumscribed about halfway up by a groovelike fold. The drapery is shown in more

natural folds, and the hem rarely flares. In contrast to the costume of Buddha, which is austerely draped in all periods, that of the Bodhisattvas has become more gaudy. The tiara and the necklace are now bedecked with jewel-like ornaments. Strings of beads, hanging from the shoulders and interrupted at intervals with pendants, reach far below the knees.

Sculpture, especially Buddhist sculpture, reached its zenith in China in the T'ang dynasty. The work begun at Lungmen by the Wei Tatars attained new heights, and the creation of Buddhist images was advanced with similar zeal throughout the empire. About the end of the 9th century, however, cave sculpture seemed to lose the interest of the worshipers of central China. It was continued at Tunhwang, but the center for China proper shifted to Szechwan, which contains many late T'ang caves. The activity in that province continued through the Sung and Yüan periods into the Ming dynasty.

It is difficult to differentiate sharply between the Sui and early T'ang styles, but toward the middle of the 7th century T'ang characteristics definitely emerged. The figures have become more naturalistic. The S-curve appears in most of the standing figures, which are balanced on one leg, with the hip of the relaxed leg and the shoulder on same side slightly lowered. To maintain equilibrium, the head is tilted slightly toward the side of the supporting leg. The body is more fleshy, although the waist remains slim. The face, especially that of the Bodhisattva, is pleasingly plump. The gracefully arched eyebrow is not carried quite so far as in the previous periods, but curves naturally, clearly defining the temple. The ridge of the eyebrow is now seldom incised with a groove. The area of the upper eyelid extends farther up, and the curved plane below the brow is narrower. The nose is shorter and less sharply ridged. The lips are definitely sensuous, and the distance of the upper lip from the nose is markedly shortened. The hair is now carried very low, reducing the height of the forehead. The Bodhisattvas of this period are less garishly ornamented. The tiara is often simplified, but the hair is drawn into an enormous knot on top of the head. The garments are modeled to conform closely to the body, and the beads, though still often worn, are bare of most of their former pendants.

About the beginning of the 8th century a very earthly type of Buddha was introduced. He is represented as a complacent, fat creature of this world, with a flabby chin, scarcely any neck, and a full, protruding abdomen—a most unusual conception of the ascetic who wandered the woods of Buddh Gaya. Not many figures of this type have been found, but all are evidence of superlative achievement in the plastic representation of the human form.

Toward the end of the T'ang dynasty, in the caves of the secluded Szechwan area, there appeared a type of sculpture characterized by the iconographic tributes and fantastic physiology of the newly popular *mi-tsung* or *mi-chiao* (secret sect or religion). In its treatment of the human form and of the draperies, however, it shows no perceptible break with T'ang tradition. An entire wall area is often used for a single subject. The paradise scene, which is pictured over and over again in the contemporary mural painting at Tunhwang, is here executed in relief, forming a single composition—a plastic conception never

Landscape, by Ch'i Pai-shih, illustrates the revival of scholarly painting that took place in China during the 20th century.

MICHAEL SULLIVAN

found in cave sculpture of earlier periods.

T'ang sculptors were extremely skillful in portraying animal forms, many examples of which have been preserved in the grounds of the T'ang imperial tombs. Some smaller pieces are on view in museums of the United States and European countries.

Sung Sculpture. With the fall of the T'ang dynasty the creation of Buddhist images in stone almost ceased. Statues in Sung temples were carved in wood, modeled in clay, or, rarely, cast in bronze. The only exceptions are found in the caves of Szechwan. Few of the bronze images escaped melting down in later periods. One notable exception is the 70-foot statue of Kuan-yin in Chengting, Hopeh, cast by order of the first Sung emperor, T'ai Tsu (reigned 960–976). Clay figures are numerous. A superb example of this work is the altar group in the Hua-yen Ssŭ, Tatung. The eleven-headed Kuan-yin of the Tu-lo Ssŭ, Chihsien, closely follows the T'ang tradition; it measures about 60 feet (18 meters) in height and is the largest clay figure in China. Many wooden statues of the Sung period have found their way to the museums of the West.

The most noticeable characteristic of Sung statues is the rounding of the face. The forehead is broader than in previous periods. The nose is short and almost bulbous. The eyebrows are less arched, and the convex surface above the upper lid is even wider, reducing to a narrow strip the concave plane under the eyebrow. The lips are thicker, and the mouth is very small. The smile has almost vanished. The neck is rendered naturally, emerging above the chest and supporting the head without any demarcation.

The S-curve of the T'ang Bodhisattvas seems to have been forgotten. Even when the figure is not completely rigid, the ease with which T'ang figures carry their weight, and the consequent lowering the the relaxed side of the body, seem beyond the grasp of the Sung sculptors. The Ch'an Buddhists introduced a new pose for the Kuan-yin, showing the goddess seated on a rock with one leg hanging down and the other foot resting on the rock. This complicated pose presented the sculptor with new problems of arrangement of the body and the draperies.

Szechwan cave sculpture of the Southern Sung period shows evidence of a decline in the sculptor's art. This is especially noticeable in some of the Bodhisattvas. By this time they have taken on an unmistakably feminine appearance. They are gaudily dressed and overburdened with jewelry and ornaments. The pose is rigid, almost frigid; the expression is blank. The best example of this work is the group of young, matronlike Bodhisattvas in Tatsu.

Yüan, Ming, and Ch'ing Sculpture. During the Yüan dynasty, Lamaist Buddhism was introduced from Tibet. With it came sculptors whose influence was to last through the Ming and Ch'ing periods. Most of their figures are shown sitting cross-legged. The waist is almost wasp-like, the chest is broad, and the shoulders are square. The head has become more squat, but the rhythm of the torso is repeated in the broadening of the forehead. The top of the head is flattened and surmounted by a grossly elongated *ushnisha,* the hump characteristic of the sculptured heads of Buddha.

The Ming and Ch'ing dynasties were a sad period for sculpture in China. The statuary of these periods shows neither the robust vigor of Han, nor the archaic charm of the Six Dynasties, nor the mature self-assurance of T'ang, nor even the rococo elegance of Sung. The sculptor's art had degenerated into uninspired manual labor.

LIANG SSU-CH'ENG
Academia Sinica, Peking

MODERN DEVELOPMENT

Architecture, painting, and sculpture all in various ways reflect the revolution that took place in Chinese civilization in the first half of the 20th century.

Architecture. In the hundred years following the "opening up" of China to Western influence in the 1840's, many buildings put up in cities penetrated by Western influence were uneasy mixtures of Chinese and Occidental styles. The Chinese timber frame does not adapt to traditional Western brick and stone, and architects often achieved a pseudo-Chinese flavor simply by capping a Western-style building with a Chinese roof. Government buildings erected in Nanking and Shanghai in the 1930's, and some universities, show a better understanding of traditional architecture, although this "Chinese Renaissance" style was still a compromise.

Since the Chinese Communists came to power in 1949, a vast amount of building has been carried out, most of which is simple and functional with no particular architectural character. During the 1950's Peking became burdened with a number of public buildings in the Soviet "wedding-cake" manner—neither modern nor Chinese in style. Later, however, Chinese architects rejected this disastrous influence and at the same time made great advances on the technological level. Their most spectacular achievement was the Great Hall of the People in Peking, seating 10,000 people; it was built in less than a year in 1959. But it seems that a productive marriage of Chinese traditional architecture and modern techniques will be achieved only when it is realized, as it has been in Japan, that the basis of Oriental architecture is not the roof, but the frame, which is ideally suited to modern methods.

Painting. The tradition of scholarly painting which flourished in the 17th and 18th centuries lost its impulse as the Ch'ing dynasty declined. But in the 20th century it has undergone a revival, partly perhaps as a response to the Western challenge. Leading figures in this revival were Wu Ch'ang-shih (1844–1927), Ch'i Pai-shih (1863–1957), and Huang Pin-hung (1864–1955). With the founding of the art schools after the republican revolution of 1911–1912, traditional techniques were taught along with the Western, and now painting in the Chinese medium has ceased to be a pastime only for the gentleman and has begun to be a truly popular art.

The teaching of Western painting began shortly before the revolution of 1911–1912. After the end of World War I many young men went to Europe to study art, notably Liu Hai-su, who founded the school which later became the Shanghai Academy of Art, and Hsü Pei-hung (1895–1953), who taught in National Central University in Nanking and later became head of the Academy of Art in Peking, in which he was succeeded on his death by his pupil Wu Tso-jen. These painters and their students worked very skillfully in both oils and in Chinese ink; Hsü Pei-hung, particularly, became noted for his realistic brush studies of horses.

Meantime another school was founded in Canton in 1917 by Kao Chien-fu (1881–1951), dedicated to depicting modern industrial society, and even warfare, in the traditional medium. Both this Cantonese school and the woodcut movement, inaugurated by Lu Hsün in 1929, were given official approval in 1949 as reflecting the "socialist realism" demanded in arts by the People's Republic.

During the 1950's artists such as P'ang Hsün-ch'in and Lin Feng-mien, having returned from France, were beginning to create a new style that was both Chinese in feeling and in tune with the modern international movement. The outbreak of the war with Japan in 1937, however, cut short this promising development. As artists became refugees in the remote western provinces and nationalism replaced Montparnasse as their inspiration, their work became much more Chinese in theme, and often in style as well.

The years between the end of World War II and the establishment of the new regime in 1949 were too brief and chaotic for any significant developments to take place. Since then, apart from Fu Pao-shih (1904–1966), the most interesting painters have been those living outside China, such as Chao Wu-chi in Paris, Tseng Yu-ho in Honolulu, and the Fifth Moon group in Taiwan, who, partly under Western influence, have rediscovered the abstract, calligraphic elements in Chinese painting.

Meanwhile, in Communist China abstract "bourgeois formalism" and expressionism have been firmly discouraged for ideological reasons. On the other hand, painters have generally been guaranteed prestige and security provided that they painted in a manner that all could understand. Building on the earlier experiments of the Cantonese realists, they have successfully depicted the new society and changing landscape of China in traditional techniques. Most painters today are understandably cautious, but Li K'o-jan and Ch'eng Shih-fa have shown in their work how much vigor and individuality were possible within these limits. Future developments will depend on the amount of control over artists.

Sculpture. With the decay of Buddhism in China, the art of sculpture sank to a low level. Since 1900 there has been a growing demand for monuments and portrait busts, though very little concern with sculpture as an art form in its own right. In the 1930's, Hua T'ien-yu, Liao Hsin-hsüeh, and Liu K'ai-ch'u returned from Paris to set up studios in Shanghai, but because there was no living sculptural tradition in China their work remained essentially Western in style. Since 1949 traditional handicrafts such as wood, jade, and ivory carving have been much encouraged. Craftsmen, organized in cooperatives, have a secure livelihood and standards of workmanship are very high. But there is little originality. The village craft of clay sculpture also underwent a sudden revival, of which the most striking example is a rendition in Szechwan, where the rent collectors and suffering peasants are modeled life-size in clay with dramatic realism.

MICHAEL SULLIVAN, *Stanford University*

Bibliography

Bachhofer, Ludwig, *A Short History of Chinese Art* (London 1947).
Hájek, Lubor, Hoffmeister, Adolf, and Rychterová, Eva, *Contemporary Chinese Painting* (London 1961).
Priest, Alan, *Aspects of Chinese Painting* (New York 1954).
Sickman, Laurence, and Soper, Alexander, *The Art and Architecture of China* (Baltimore 1956).
Siren, Osvald, *Chinese Painting: Leading Masters and Principles* (New York 1956).
Sullivan, Michael, *Chinese Art in the Twentieth Century* (London 1959).
Waley, Arthur, *An Introduction to the Study of Chinese Painting* (New York 1958).
Willetts, William, *Chinese Art* (Harmondsworth, Middlesex, England, 1958).

SIX STYLES OF calligraphy (described in the text), written by Chao Meng-fu, a great painter of the Yüan dynasty (1271–1368). Each column, reading from top to bottom, contains four words: "autumn harvest, winter store."

12. Calligraphy

Chinese calligraphy is the art of brush writing. It is closely allied to painting and has been practiced by both the literati and artists in China for centuries.

The origins of calligraphy can be traced back to the ideographs and symbols carved on oracle bones during the Shang dynasty (about 1523–1028 B.C.). Of the approximately 2,000 ideographs that appear on the nearly 100,000 extant bones, more than 1,300 have been clearly identified as the earliest forms of characters used in modern written Chinese.

Subsequent inscriptions on metal and stone indicate that a process of simplification took place during the first millennium B.C. The first major change, the *ta chuan* (great seal style), descended directly from the Shang logographs—symbols representing entire words—and appeared during the Chou dynasty (about 1027–256 B.C.). As shown in the accompanying illustration, it is characterized by balanced, rounded strokes in complicated but regular forms. Further modification came during the Ch'in dynasty (221–206 B.C.), when Li Ssu introduced the style known as *hsiao chuan* (small seal style), which is still used on seals today. Small-seal characters are written in uniform size, and its strokes are of even width. Its cumbersome rigidity and formalism were softened by the next innovation, *li shu* (clerical style), which facilitated the execution of characters. Since this early formative period, there has been no basic change in the structure of words; later emphasis was placed on the style of strokes. Also, improvements in the manufacture of writing brushes and in materials, such as paper, silk, and ink, helped turn the technique of writing into an art.

During and immediately following the Han dynasty (202 B.C.–220 A.D.) various distinctive scripts, such as *k'ai shu* (model style), *hsing shu* (running style), and *ts'ao shu* (cursive or grass style) appeared. The *k'ai shu* became, and still is, the official style in which books, magazines, or similar materials, are printed. The running and cursive scripts have been reserved for personal notes and calligraphic purposes.

Calligraphers of repute have appeared in every dynasty. Some were known for the beauty of their lines, some for their vigorous and bold strokes, and others for their relaxed mannerisms. Chang Chih and Ts'ai Yung of the Han dynasty,

So Ching of the Chin dynasty, and Mi Fei and Su Shih of the Sung dynasty were only a few of the great calligraphers. The grand master of Chinese calligraphy, however, was Wang Hsi-chih (321–379), whose handwriting in the *Lan T'ing Hsü* (*The Orchard Pavilion*) is an example of calligraphy executed with great rhythmic skill and vitality.

Handwriting is judged by the quality of the brushwork, by the abstract·beauty of the dots and lines that are formed. Wang Hsi-chih listed and defined what he thought were the four requirements for good calligraphy:

Brush power (*li*) is the basis for the calligraphic structure: turning and twisting (*chuan*) of the brush balances the shape. Deftness (*ch'iao*) is the key to composition, and the characters must be artistically spaced (*ch'eng*).

What this means is that the artistry of a character is judged by the length and thickness of the strokes, the manner in which the strokes are joined, their rhythm and vitality, and the amount of pressure that is used. Every Chinese schoolchild learns to hold the brush properly, with fingers in a fixed position, wrist steady, and hand flexible. It is usual to learn a model script before tackling the running or cursive styles, and characters have been copied for centuries from standards books such as the *Thousand Character Classic* (see accompanying illustration).

Calligraphy is not merely elegant penmanship. It is the total artistic product of the individual. For this reason calligraphy is practiced by both masters and intellectuals and is treasured by all. Examples and reproductions are hung in the home, sometimes in pairs, and are customary forms of gifts. Also, poems are often written in various calligraphic styles on paintings as artistic, philosophical, and literary complements to the picture. The invention of the ballpoint pen and of the typewriter may have reduced the popularity of calligraphy, but it remains a viable art form to this day. See also CHINA—13. *Language*.

CHARLES J. CHU, *Connecticut College*

Further Reading: Ch'en Chih-mai, *Chinese Calligraphers and Their Art* (Melbourne 1966); Chiang Yee, *The Chinese Eye; an Interpretation of Chinese Painting* (New York 1960); Waley, Arthur, *An Introduction to the Study of Chinese Painting* (New York 1958); Yang Lien-sheng, *Chinese Calligraphy*, catalog of the exhibition of Chinese calligraphy and painting in the collection of John M. Crawford, Jr. (New York 1962).

13. Language

Chinese is one of the major languages of the world, spoken by approximately 700,000,000 people. It is the chief member of the Sino-Tibetan family of languages.

Word Formation. Chinese is often described as a monosyllabic language, but the validity of this statement depends upon what we regard as a word in Chinese. The language has two types of units, each of which has some, but not all, of the features of a word in other languages. The first type is the monosyllable, called in Chinese *tzŭ*, which almost always operates as a meaningful unit and thus corresponds closely to what is known in linguistics as a morpheme. Partly because the *tzŭ* is written with a single character, it is frequently mentioned in everyday speech. People talk about learning *tzŭ*, using the right or wrong *tzŭ*, paying so much for 10 *tzŭ* in a telegram, or receiving so much money per 1,000 *tzŭ* for contributing to a periodical. The second type is the syntactical unit. It can be spoken independently and combined with a high degree of freedom, and therefore acts more nearly as a word in the linguistic sense. It may consist of a single *tzŭ* or of a close-knit combination of two or more *tzŭ*. In short, we can say that the Chinese language is monosyllabic or polysyllabic, depending upon whether we base our definition on the morpheme or on the syntactical unit. In this article we shall speak of words in both senses, but we shall distinguish when necessary between root words and syntactical words.

The Chinese syllable has a rather simple phonetic structure. Except for a few words that begin with vowels, each syllable begins with a consonant or a consonant cluster. The cluster is usually simple, consisting at most of a stop, a fricative, an aspiration, and a semivowel: for example, *ts'u-* (*ts'w-*) in *ts'uan*. There are no words of the *str-* or *spl-* type. After the consonant or consonant cluster there is a main vowel, with or without a final consonant or semivowel. In most parts of China there are only two semivowel endings, *-i* and *-u* (forming diphthongs like *ai* and *ou*), and three consonant endings, *-n*, *-ng*, and *-r*. In ancient times there were other endings—for example, *-m*, *-p*, *-t*, *-k*, *-b*, *-d*, and *-g*—but these have largely disappeared, except a few in the southeast dialects.

In addition to consonants and vowels, there is a third constituent element of the Chinese word. This is the height and movement of the fundamental pitch of the voice, known as tone. Tones have often been described as a device to distinguish words. This is true only in the sense that differentiation between vowel sounds is a device to distinguish the English word "met" from "mat," and differentiation between consonants is a device to distinguish "mat" from "mad." Actually, of course, the tones in Chinese have evolved from unpremeditated natural causes. The sounds of the four tones in Mandarin, or Standard Chinese, are (1) high level, (2) high rising, (3) low rising (or low dipping), and (4) high falling to low. Occasionally words differing only in tone are etymologically related—for example, *hao*[3] (good) and *hao*[4] (fond of), which are related in somewhat the same way as "man" is related to "men." But the majority of words that differ only in tone are quite unrelated— *fei*[1] (fly); *fei*[2] (fat); *fei*[3] (bandit); *fei*[4] (waste, spend)—as in the case of "mat" and "met." In most parts of China there are four tones. The same words are usually grouped in the same class, but the pitch pattern of each class varies sharply from one locality to another.

Grammar. Most Chinese sentences have a subject and a predicate, although minor sentences, corresponding to such expressions as "What a nuisance!" and "Never heard of such a thing," are less unusual in Chinese than in English. The subject in Chinese is literally the subject matter and need not represent the agent performing the action. For example, *cher yao k'ai p'u-tzŭ*, which is translated "They will open a store here," means literally "This place will open store." or more analytically, "As for this place, there will be opened a store." Within either the subject or the predicate the words are arranged in four main types of construction: (1) coordinate construction, often without conjunctions or even pauses, as in the expression *tung nan hsi pei* (east, south, west, and north); (2) qualifier-qualified construction, with the parts always in that order, as in *huai jên* (bad men), *hên k'uai tê p'ao* (very quick-ly run—run very quickly), or *kang tsou tê jên tê mao-tzŭ* (just left kind of man's hat—the hat of the man who has just left); (3) verb-object construction: *hsieh hsin* (write letters) or *wên t'a chao shei* (ask him look-for who—ask him whom he is looking for); and (4) verb-complement construction—*sao-kan-ching t'a* (sweep-clean it—sweep it clean) or *ta-p'o* (strike-broken —smashed).

The parts of speech in Chinese are similar in many respects to those in English, but there are two important differences. First, words denoting qualities do not have special grammatical features of their own but behave like other intransitive verbs: *t'iar hao* (weather fine—the weather is fine). Secondly, there is a class of particles or enclitics which are attached to words or to sentences to express moods or aspects. In addition, there is considerable overlapping of function among Chinese words, just as in English the word "cut" can be used as a noun, a verb, or an adjective. The common belief that Chinese has no parts of speech is a gross exaggeration. Most words have only limited functions: *chih* (paper) is always a noun; *t'i* (kick), always a transitive verb; *tsao* (early), always an adverb or quality verb.

While the above sketch gives the main structural features of the Chinese language, it will be of interest to the general reader as well as the practical student to see how the formal features of an Occidental language like English would be translated into Chinese. In the first place, an English word corresponds in translation much more closely to the syntactical word in Chinese than to the monosyllabic morpheme: *ti-pan* (ground-board—floor), *huo-ch'ê* (fire-vehicle—train), *hsien-tsai* (appear-exist—now), *t'u-shu-kuan* (charts-books-institution—library). Chinese nouns are not distinguished by number, the notion of number being expressed, when necessary, by numerals or by words like "many" or "several." There are no articles, but most nouns designating individual persons or things have specific numeratives or classifiers which must be attached to a preceding numeral or demonstrative: for example, *i-t'ou niu* (one head of cattle); *chei-ko jên* (this piece man). Definiteness and indefiniteness are expressed by specific words, and there is a strong tendency to place words of definite references in the subject position and words of indefinite reference in the object position. *Shu hai mei k'an* means "The book has not yet been read," but *hai mei k'an shu* means "(One) has not yet read (any) book." Personal pronouns have no case or gender, *t'a* meaning "he," "him," "she," "her," or "it." There are a few prepositions, such as the semiliterary *yü* (at), but most spatial and temporal relations are expressed by substantive forming locatives *u-li yu ren* (room-inside has people—there are people in the room); *shan-shang tê shui* (hilltop's water —water on the hill).

Chinese verbs have neither tense nor voice, and notions of time or received action are expressed, when necessary, by adverbs or other explicit means. Completed action or change of state, whether in the past, present, or future, is expressed by the particle *lê*. Progressive action is expressed by the particle *chih* or *chê* (-ing), the adverb *chêng tsai* (right at), or the final particle *nê*. The verb *shih* (to be), is normally used before predicate nouns, as in the expression *wo shih jên* (I am a man), but it is not required before adjectives, since these are themselves verbs. Because the qualifier always precedes the qualified word, an adverbial clause always precedes the main clause, as in *yao-shih ni lai, wo chiu lai* (If you come, I then come—I shall come if you do).

Historical Development. The preceding description covers the principal features of the Chinese language. In a country as large as China, however, there are many dialectal variations, and there have also been changes through the centuries. This is especially true of sound, less so of vocabulary (the choice of words out of a common root stock), least of all of grammatical structure.

In the period represented by Confucius (c.551–479 B. C.), the Chinese language possessed a rather rich system of consonants and vowels, and probably only three tones. There were four grades of initial consonants (for example, *p, p', b, b',* like the Sanskrit *p, ph, d, dh*) and a variety of consonant endings (*-m, -n, -ng, -p, -t, -k, -b, -d, -g, -r*), but no final semivowel. There were also occasional consonant clusters like *kl-* and *pl-*. Later, as we learn from a dictionary published in 601 A. D. and from other sources, the four grades of consonants were reduced to three: *p, p',* and *b'*. The final consonants *-b, -d, -g,* and *-r* were dropped, and final semivowels appeared, to form diphthongs with the main vowel. The number of tones increased to four. In the majority of the modern Chinese dialects there are usually only two grades of consonants (*p* and *p'*) and, as we have noted, three consonant endings (*-n, -ng,* and a modern *-r*). The four tones of modern Chinese differ from those of ancient Chinese in that the old first tone has been subdivided into the modern first and second tones and the old fourth-tone words have been distributed among the other modern tones.

The monosyllables functioned more as independent words in ancient Chinese than in the language at later stages. Moreover there are in the old texts traces of inflection, as in the use of *ngo* for "I" and *ngâ* for "me." The cognate modern words, *wu* and *wo*, have no such distinction. In general, however, there has been remarkably little structural change in the Chinese language.

The chief dialects into which ancient Chinese has developed may be classified into nine groups: Cantonese, Kan-Hakka, Amoy-Swatow, Foochow,

STERN, FROM BLACK STAR

THE ROMAN ALPHABET, as posted here, has been introduced in China to simplify the written language.

Wu (Kiangsu-Chekiang region), Hsiang (Hunan province), and Northern, Southern, and Southwestern Mandarin. The first six groups, which are concentrated in the five or six provinces on or near the southeast coast, have preserved more features of the ancient pronunciation than the others. The last three groups, which are spoken in three fourths of the area of China proper and by two thirds of the entire population, are characterized by relative uniformity of pronunciation and vocabulary. For this reason it is possible for a resident of Pinkiang (Harbin), Manchuria, to understand a resident of Kunming, Yunnan Province, without too much difficulty. Standard Chinese, variously called Mandarin, *kuo-yü* (national language), or *p'u-t'ung-hua* (ordinary language), belongs to the Northern Mandarin group, and its standard of pronunciation is that of Peking.

A development of great cultural significance in the history of Chinese has been the growth of a literary language along with the spoken language. We have evidence that at least as early as the 9th century A. D. there were two divergent idioms, one quite similar to present-day Mandarin, and the other like the writing of previous centuries. Through the centuries the spoken language, which was rarely written, changed more and more in pronunciation and vocabulary, whereas the written language, because all literate Chinese read a common body of literature, remained almost uniform. Such changes as have occurred in the written language have taken place throughout the country, that is, uniformly with respect to diction and composition, though not with respect to pronunciation. Hence every educated Chinese has one system of pronunciation, that of his present local dialect, whether Mandarin or one of the other groups, but two idioms, his local spoken idiom and the literary idiom common to the whole country. The literary idiom does not merely exist on paper but is learned through reading aloud, and the Chinese read and compose aloud or sotto voce to a greater extent than other peoples. Although literary Chinese is never spoken, it is an actual language or idiom (quite apart from the fact that there is a uniform system of writing for all the variant pronunciations).

In 1917, Hu Shih (1891–1962) and other scholars initiated a movement to have Chinese written in the spoken idiom rather than in the literary idiom. There already existed a small body of Mandarin literature, mostly in the form of novels. The movement was encouraged by the educational authorities, who ordered that the school curriculum through the sixth grade be taught in the spoken style of Mandarin, called *pai-hua* (plain talk). This step had two purposes. In the first place, it would be possible for two thirds of the country's children, those from the Mandarin-speaking provinces, to read and write in a close approximation to their mother tongue rather than in an additional literary idiom. Secondly, the remaining one third would learn the standard dialect, thereby helping to unify the spoken language. While the *pai-hua* movement made relatively slow progress from a quantitative point of view, by the 1930's it had succeeded in establishing the prestige of the spoken idiom. It had been most successful in literature and science, though somewhat less so in the fields of business and government.

Writing. The Chinese system of writing consists of characters representing the *tzŭ*, or monosyllabic root words. Speech elements smaller than a syllable do not normally correspond to elements in the characters. According to the traditional system of classification, there are six categories of characters: pictographs, simple ideographs, compound ideographs, phonetic loans, phonetic compounds, and derivative characters. Examples of the first five categories are: (1) 山 (*shan*, mountain); (2) 二 (*êrh*, two); (3) 明 (*ming*, bright), consisting of the characters for "sun" and "moon"; (4) 無 (*wu*, have not), a pictograph for a word with the same sound meaning "dance," it being impossible to picture the idea of "have not"; and (5) 柿 (*shih*, persimmon), consisting of a significant part, 木 (tree), and a phonetic part, 市 (*shih*, market). The sixth class contains few members and is not important.

There is only a rough correspondence between the spoken word and the written character. A character often represents words which have the same sound but different meanings. For example, the character 未 represents two words: *wei* (not yet) and *wei* (the first double hour after noon). A much more important divergence between word and character has taken place because the number of characters has been increased to indicate extensions of meaning of what is linguistically the same word. Thus the word *yüan*, meaning "primary," "original," or "source," for which the same character, 元, was used in the ancient texts, has come to be written with three different characters— 元, 原, and 源 —for its three meanings. In this way the number of characters used for most words in Chinese has multiplied to several times the number of the words. In a large dictionary there are about 40,000 or 50,000 characters, and the telegraph code book contains nearly 10,000. One kind of Chinese typewriter has 5,400; a list of characters for use in the first four grades of school has 2,741; and the basic list of Yen Yang-

chu (James Y. C. Yen, 1894–   ) has 1,200. The number of root words in the speech of an illiterate adult is estimated at 2,500 to 3,000 *tzŭ*.

Characters are arranged in dictionaries according to sound or form. The oldest dictionaries grouped characters according to tones, rhymes (vowel and ending), and initial consonants, so that all characters with the same sound appeared under the same heading. Modern dictionaries that arrange characters by sound reverse the order: initials, finals, tone. A more frequently used system is the arrangement of the characters according to the 214 radicals, or recurrent parts. These correspond roughly to the significant parts of phonetic compounds. The radicals are arranged in ascending order of number of strokes, and the characters under each of the radicals are arranged in ascending order of the number of the remaining strokes. In addition a system of arrangement based on the four corners of the characters is often used in library catalogues.

Language Reform. What is commonly known as language reform in China refers to reform both of the language itself and of the writing system. Under reform of the language fall such movements as the 1917 movement for vernacular literature and the movement for unification of the national language through the standardizing and teaching of Mandarin. There has been steady progress in both directions in spite of, and at times because of, the political and social changes in the middle of the 20th century. In most parts of China even public documents and newspapers are now written in *pai-hua*. As to the spread of Mandarin pronunciation, there is general agreement that Mandarin, with the pronunciation of Peking as the norm, is Standard Chinese, and it is not only to the national interest to spread Mandarin, but also to the individual's advantage to acquire it.

In the matter of writing reform, there has been, on the one hand, a slow, continuous movement toward the simplification of the characters and, on the other hand, a radical movement for the adoption of an alphabetic form of writing. To the former category belongs the early change from the "great seal" to the "small seal" characters under the Ch'in dynasty (221–207 B.C.), and the later spread of the so-called simplified characters, as recorded in a study in 1930 on *Vulgar Characters Since the Sungs and the Yüans* (that is, since 960 A.D.). The latest movement for simplification consists mainly of the legalizing of those vulgar characters and, to a lesser extent (10–15% of the cases), the creating of new simplified forms.

Because of the radical nature of the proposed changes, the official position on alphabetization has been cautious. The national phonetic letters (introduced in 1919) with their 37 initials and finals, the National Romanization (1928), and the Pinyin system (revised in 1958) have all been officially adopted under various authorities, but they have been used as a form of writing only on a limited scale, and no action has been taken to abolish the characters in favor of an alphabetic form of writing.

Since the concise literary idiom based on the language of past ages, in which there was a rich variety of sounds, is no longer completely intelligible to the ear when read with a modern pronunciation, it will not be completely intelligible to the eye if written phonetically with the modern Mandarin pronunciation, with its relatively few sounds. The use of an alphabetic system must therefore be limited to writing the spoken idiom. The adoption of such a system, its opponents argue, would mean a break with the past, as represented in the literary idiom. They also fear that if people wrote their dialects alphabetically, the unity of the written language would be destroyed, and written Chinese in Shanghai, Taipei, and Canton would look as different as Italian, French, and Spanish. Those who favor alphabetization, on the other hand, contend that its adoption would hasten the vernacular literature movement and thus spread the knowledge of Standard Chinese.

Romanization and Pronunciation. Modern methods of language teaching have reduced the time needed for learning to speak Chinese from 5–10 years to 2 or 3. For the general reader who does not intend to learn the language, an acquaintance with the so-called Wade-Giles system is useful. This form of romanization is used in some European publications, and even official documents and publications in China, both from Taipei and from Peking, where the National Romanization and the Pinyin systems are the legal forms, follow the Wade-Giles system whenever the main text is in English. The approximate equivalents of the Chinese sounds of the letters in this system are as follows:

a	father		police
ai	aisle	ih	vocalized
ao	out		r
ch(i), ch(ü)	jeep	k	goat
ch(ih), ch(other)		k'	coat
vowels	dry	p	beak
ch'(i), ch'(ü)	cheese	p'	peak
ch'(ih), ch'		t	deem
(other vowels)	try	t'	team
ê	up, leng-	ts, tz	Windsor
	thened	ts', tz'	it's hot
eh	oh yeah	u	rule
ei	eight	ü	French
êrh	err, Middle		usine
	Western	û	buzz
hs	she; German	Other letters as in
	ich	English

Y. R. CHAO, *Agassiz Professor of Oriental Languages and Literature, Emeritus University of California at Berkeley*

Bibliography

Chao, Y. R., *A Grammar of Spoken Chinese* (Berkeley, Calif., 1967).
Chao, Y. R., *Mandarin Primer*, with Folkways Records (Cambridge, Mass., 1948).
Chao, Y. R., and Yang, L. S., *Concise Dictionary of Spoken Chinese* (Cambridge, Mass., 1947).
De Francis, John, *Beginning Chinese*, rev. ed. (New Haven 1963).
Forrest, Robert A. D., *The Chinese Language* (London 1948).
Karlgren, Bernhard, *Grammata Serica Recensa* (Stockholm, Sweden, 1964).
Karlgren, Bernhard, *The Chinese Language* (New York 1949).
Mathews, Robert H., *Chinese-English Dictionary* (Cambridge, Mass., 1943).
Simon, Walter, *A Beginner's Chinese-English Dictionary of the National Language* (London 1947).
Simon, Walter, and Lu, C. H., *Chinese Sentence Series*, with Linguaphone Records (London 1942).
Tewksbury, Malcolm G., *Speak Chinese*, rev. ed. (New Haven 1955).

14. Literature

Chinese literature dates approximately from the 15th century B. C. Although belles-lettres is the chief concern of this account, works of history, philosophy, allegory, and aphorism, especially of the early periods, are so closely woven into the fabric of all later literature that they too must be discussed.

Although Chinese literature traditionally has been divided into four departments—canons, history, philosophy, and miscellany—it is more profitable to consider the whole body of this literature with respect to the following five characteristics:

(1) Although in most dynasties the court was the center of literary fashion, folk creation was the important life-giving force of literary innovations. Foreign influence on poetry and fiction often took roots first in folksongs or folklore.

(2) The ancient Chinese had a rich mythology, but left no full-fledged epic poetry to portray its heroes and gods. Rather, they became idealized men of worldly moral deeds, celebrated in didactic prose.

(3) Pacifist spirit predominates. The Chinese word for literature, *wên*, is the exact opposite of the word for militarism, *wu*.

(4) Romantic otherworldliness, passionate pursuit of love, and tragic conflicts of will and fate are seldom carried far. Spirituality develops in the physical world and pervades it. Hence, faithful representation of simple mundane experiences and spontaneous expression of intuitively grasped natural beauty gain breadth and depth of meaning.

(5) The peculiar qualities of the Chinese language—the logographic writing and the determination of word meaning by exact tonal modulations—ally the literature closely with the fine arts and music. In poetry the monosyllabic written characters make it easy to achieve extremely neat patterns of meter and rhyme; and prose, in the classical style at least, often rises to the level of poetry.

THE CLASSICAL AGE (15TH TO 3D CENTURIES B. C.)

The earliest authenticated writings of the classical period of Chinese literature are inscriptions on bronze vessels and oracle bones, the oldest of which date from about the 15th century B. C., during the Shang dynasty. They are remarkable for their calligraphy, simplicity, symbolism of intense religious devotion, accurate recording of dates and events, and occasional sonorous rhymes. The first real flowering of Chinese poetry is found in the *Book of Odes* (*Shih Ching*), produced between the 10th and 7th centuries B. C. Extant in the book are 305 poems—lyrical, ritual, satirical, and narrative—refined from remote folk origin and closely associated with music. The poems are spontaneous, vivid, and realistic expressions of social life and customs. Metrical schemes vary, but tend to follow the 4-word line, with frequent rhymes. These poems enchant the reader with word music from the hearts and souls of a people singing of their love, courtship, reverence, worship, despair, lamentations about bad times, and protests against tyranny and war. They remain living embodiments of natural objects lighted by vivified senses of man at poetry's dawn.

Four other works, chiefly products of the classical age, are grouped with it in a collection known as the Five Canons or Classics. The *Book of Change* (*I Ching*) consists of a set of symbols and texts for divination, perhaps first formulated about the 11th century B. C., with later commentaries. It presents in abstract form the original Chinese conception of the dual forces that had set the universe in motion. The *Book of Historical Documents* (*Shang Shu*), sometimes called the *Book of History* (*Shu Ching*), consists of decrees, counsels, and admonitions of ancient kings, princes, and ministers, and other semilegendary records, attributed to a period from the dawn of history to about the 7th century B. C. In solemn, didactic prose, it portrays the thought and action of great ancient Chinese, who, it was said, having struggled with nature and learned its secrets, set moral standards by personal example, formed benevolent governments, vindicated the people against tyrants, and so became prototypes of the ideal sage to inspire the philosophical and literary mind of later ages. The *Spring and Autumn Annals* (*Ch'un Ch'iu*), brief records of current events from 722 to 481 B. C., because of the meticulous choice of "correct terms" in their definitions, have influenced historiography, literary history, and literary criticism. Finally, some ancient ritual codes and principles of government compiled about the 2d century B. C., together with a number of Confucian dissertations, constitute the *Book of Rites* (*Li Chi*). The Five Canons, despite misinterpretations, interpolations, and forgeries, represent the primary forms of ancient Chinese literature and mark the beginnings of the Chinese literary tradition.

Between the 6th and 5th centuries B. C., Chinese literature entered a new stage of development, marked by increasingly elaborate description, interesting anecdotes, suggestive observation, and illuminating critiques. Of the numerous schools of philosophy that emerged during this period, two, the Confucian and the Taoist, became leading sources of spiritual guidance for later generations. The Confucianist, while acquiescing in man's fate as directed by some invisible power, seeks not to know the nature of that power beyond this world. Man's highest standard is set in humanity itself, symbolized by the ideal human sage, the perfection of the best of human nature. Much of Confucian-influenced Chinese literature is enlivened by a humanistic this-worldliness, and subsequent creative Chinese writers claim kinship with the classical tradition.

Confucius (c. 551–479 B. C.) himself is believed to have written little. Even the traditional claim that he edited some of the Canons has been questioned. It is certain only that his aphorisms and short discourses were recorded by his disciples in the *Analects* (*Lun Yü*). Two dissertations by his followers—*The Great Learning* (*Ta Hsüeh*) and the *Doctrine of the Mean* (*Chung Yung*)—expound his philosophy in a better organized form.

The Taoist school, supposedly founded by the philosopher Lao Tzu (c. 604–531 B. C.), represents a reaction against Confucianism. The canon of this school, *The Canon of the Way and of Virtue* (*Tao Te Ching*), shows that it emerged no earlier than the late 5th century B. C. According to Taoist thought, there exists above the physical universe a higher power, called the way or *tao*. It is not a personified god, but a transcendental force above all existence and nonexistence—the absolute—which is manifest in the perfect, natural state of things, the highest that man may hope to attain—the supreme good. To the Taoist all discriminations are artificial; all commonly accepted virtues presuppose prevalent evils ("Not until the Sage is forever dead can the Bandit be completely put out. . . ."). Strong and pervasive Taoist influence on Chinese literature has nurtured the spirit of freedom from all conventions, enabling poets and other writers to develop the faculty for self-abandonment and keen insight into nature.

Among the philosophers of the two leading schools, Mencius (372?–?289 B. C.), the Confucian protagonist, left behind eloquent passages of oratory, and Chuang Tzu (4th to 3d centuries B. C.) wrote unsurpassed Taoist allegorical essays that form an inexhaustible source of subtle metaphor and simile.

As the classical age drew to a close amid incessant wars, sensitive men felt a keen *Weltschmerz*. Late in the 4th century B. C. appeared richly imaginative and colorful works of pure sentiment by poets of great individuality, who cultivated their art consciously through the best use of words, independent of music. Most of this new poetry was written in the Yangtze River area, the picturesque southern region of abundant flora and fantastic landscape. The earliest works of this type are attributed to Ch'ü Yüan (c.343–?289 B. C.), once a minister and then an exile of the Ch'u state. His chief follower and imitator was Sung Yü (296–?240 B. C.), also of Ch'u; hence the name Ch'u rhapsody or elegy (*Ch'u Tz'ŭ*) is applied to this style. A lengthy prose-verse mixture, with interwoven dramatic dialogue, fanciful narratives and descriptions, and soaring lyrics, it has maintained lasting influence on later imaginative literature. Sung Yü and the northern philosopher Hsün Tzŭ (c.300–235 B. C.) also called their writings after this style *fu* (exhibitory essay), which was to develop into a very important genre in the Han age.

THE MIDDLE EPOCH
(2D CENTURY B. C.–7TH CENTURY A. D.)

At the beginning of this literary period, which coincides with the major part of the Chinese medieval period, the country entered an era of national consolidation, expansion, and prosperity. The short-lived Ch'in dynasty had unified China and laid the foundations for the enormous development of the Han empire. The flourishing literature of the Han dynasty combined court refinement with robust folk elements. Its growth was nourished and stimulated through foreign contacts—with the Hsiung-nu in the north, the Tungus in the northeast, the Pacific coastal and island tribes, and the countries of central Asia. Foreign melodies and musical instruments were introduced, and exotic customs and landscapes were portrayed and discussed with growing inspiration. Now the *fu*, as court literature reflecting the new vision and material splendor of the age, unfolded at its best a panorama of rich colors and gorgeous imagery. Its greatest master was Ssŭ-ma Hsiangju (179–117 B. C.). Other distinguished writers of the *fu* were Mei Shêng (died 140 B. C.), Yang Hsiung (53 B. C.–18 A. D.), Pan Ku (32–92 A. D.), and Chang Heng (78–139 A. D.).

As the *fu* developed, creativeness gradually gave way to stereotyped floridity. Not until the 11th century, the age of great prose, did this form, liberated from slavish imitation and artificial metrical restrictions, become a lucid but impassioned prose poem. Yet beginning with the Western (Earlier) Han dynasty, lyric and narrative poetry, derived directly from folk literature, developed with fresh vigor. Many works of this type, often anonymous, are great poetry, comparable in directness, spontaneity, and profundity to the *Book of Odes*. Collected, edited, and sung in the Imperial Conservatory, they became recognized as an influential poetic genre, known as the Imperial Conservatory or *yüeh-fu* style. Their metrical schemes at first were as varied as the

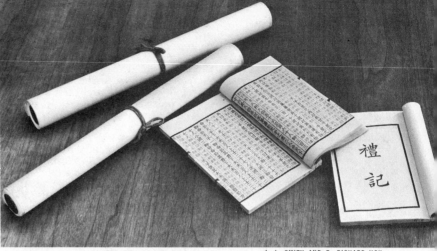

LITERATURE in two forms: Long paper scrolls, carefully hand-lettered, and often inscribed to an individual; and paperback books, such as this Confucian text, *The Book of Rites*, published in the Sung dynasty (960–1274).

musical forms of the age, but a tendency toward regularity gradually emerged. Out of a sound pattern with five characters to a line came the *ku shih* (old-style poetry).

Although both folk and more sophisticated works in the Imperial Conservatory tradition had flourished in earlier Han times, most of those still extant date from the Eastern (Later) Han dynasty. Most remarkable of the anonymous works are the *Nineteen Old Poems* and *The Wife of a Prefect Clerk*, a narrative poem in 360 lines. The latter tells the story of the devoted love of a husband and wife, frustrated by a domineering mother, and ending in tragedy. Among the many authors were the poetess Pan Chao and the poet Fu Yi (both of the 1st century A. D.), Chang Heng (78–139 A. D.), and Ts'ai Yung (133–192 A. D.). Much of Han poetry was tinged with Confucian moralism or Taoist mysticism, but it excelled in the objective description of social life and customs and in a deep understanding of the sorrows and joys of humble people.

Although literary forms like the *fu*, the *yüeh-fu*, and the *ku shih* grew so luxuriantly that belles-lettres began to form a major category of its own and individual genius shone more brilliantly in this field than ever before, the writings of the great Han historian Ssŭ-ma Ch'ien (145–?87 B. C.) are also important. In the classical age, history had consisted of the fragmentary record of events or of a mixture of anecdote, oratorical harangue, and short didactic discourse. With Ssŭ-ma Ch'ien's *Historical Memoirs* (*Shih Chi*), history developed into lucid, systematic narrative. The traditional anecdotes were objectively examined, and historic figures became living personalities. In his masterly prose, Ssŭ-ma Ch'ien depicts persons of the lower classes as well as kings and emperors. The *Historical Memoirs* are considered the first comprehensive Chinese history and the prototype of subsequent biography. Ssŭ-ma Ch'ien's follower and imitator Pan Ku, in his *History of the Former Han Dynasty*, set an example for later dynastic historians with his erudition and thorough treatment of all cultural subjects.

Three other aspects of Han intellectual life have had a lasting influence on Chinese literature:

(1) The rediscovery in fragmentary form of ancient canons, lost in wars and destruction, engaged many scholars in philological research and textual reconstruction. Excellent results were obtained in such works as the *Etymological Dictionary* (*Shuo-wên*) of Hsü Shên (died c.120

A. D.), and the *Survey of Dialects* (*Fang-yen*), attributed to Yang Hsiung. But fabrications and distortions of the ancient texts, largely by Liu Hsin (50 B. C.?–23 A. D.) and his contemporaries, perpetuated many misconceptions and superstitions about ancient China.

(2) The elevation of Confucianism to the rank of a state philosophy marked the beginning of its manipulation by the rulers of successive dynasties. These rulers evolved dogmatic orthodoxies from it to suit their purposes, obscuring its humanistic philosophy with religious mysticism.

(3) Indian Buddhism began to compete with Taoism in popularity, giving rise to many superstitious cults and enriching Chinese folklore. Such Indian ideas as cycles in future worlds and Nirvana, introduced in Eastern Han, were not as yet thoroughly digested. Mythical thinking and fanatic faith prevailed in influential circles. The crisis in philosophic thinking provoked Wang Ch'ung (27–97 A. D.) to write his *Animadversions* (*Lun Hêng*), in which he analyzed and evaluated the spirit of the age. Championing literary creativeness and vigorously attacking bigotry and pedantry, he produced one of the most important contributions to Chinese philosophical and literary criticism.

With the decline of the Han dynasty the second literary cycle began to wane. Nevertheless, the strife-torn times were brightened by a flash of literary creation. The leading figures were Ts'ao Chih (192–232 A. D.) and the Seven Greats of the Chien-an period (196–220), and Emperor Wên Ti (Ts'ao P'ei, reigned 220–226), first of the Wei dynasty, the first successful experimenter with a new poetic pattern of seven characters to a line. In this brief but memorable period all the literary forms popular since the Western Han dynasty reached new heights. Its writings were individual and tender, rich in true feeling and vigorous expression. Some of them, voicing the spirit of the age, show emotional depth and spiritual exaltation. The Wei dynasty (220–265 A. D.), one of the Three Kingdoms, was supplanted by the Chin, or Tsin (265–420 A. D.), which in the year 317 was pushed southward by barbarian tribes. In its new southern center at Chienkang (near modern Nanking), the capital of the defunct Wu dynasty (222–280 A. D.), the Chin and four succeeding dynasties maintained a precarious existence under constant threats from the north. Here in the Yangtze Valley, through the Six Dynasties period, ending in 589 A. D., a picturesque, fanciful, sentimental, and highly artificial literature developed, stamping with its characteristic decadence the decline of a literary cycle.

At the same time, northern China, occupied by barbarian tribes, produced little creative literature. Yet there were some charming folk verses, and the warlike spirit of the nomadic peoples occasionally burst into heroic song. The northern landscape, seen afresh under foreign rule, was sometimes depicted with barbaric beauty, sometimes with deep melancholy. These sporadic writings enriched Chinese literature.

In the south, the efforts of the literati to achieve painstakingly cultivated workmanship and mature literary criticism prepared the way for the Chinese literary renaissance. In both prose and poetry there was an extreme development of line-for-line and word-for-word parallelism. The parallel prose (p'ien wên) is unique, with virtues and vices of which only the Chinese language is capable. The standardization of the four tones of the language, which contributed much to later formalism, must also be credited to the early part of this period. Great literary craftsmen wrote treatises on the art of writing, such as the *Essay on Literature* (*Wên Fu*) by Lu Chi (261–303). Hsiao T'ung (501–531) made the first comprehensive anthology of Chinese creative literature, *Literary Selections* (*Wên-hsüan*), in which he meticulously classified 38 separate forms and further subdivisions. And against the background of an artificial age, the critic Liu Hsieh (late 5th–early 6th centuries) produced his *Literary Mind* (*Wên-hsin tiao-lung*, c.480), a penetrating reevaluation of the past and a sober criticism of the contemporary scene.

A few creative writers, too, made superb contributions. In a painful period of disunion and chaos, the famous Seven Worthies of the Bamboo Grove produced memorable poetry of escape. Their prodigious wine drinking, fantasies about the cosmos, and spiritual escapades were celebrated in inspired verse. But the uniquely great poet of the period was T'ao Ch'ien, or T'ao Yüan-ming (372–427), known as the "Renowned Recluse," who pictured a profound harmony between nature and life, fate and human will, in a flow of effortless and placid verse which was later often emulated but never equaled.

THE RENAISSANCE AND NEOCLASSICISM (7TH TO 10TH CENTURIES A. D.)

When the brief Sui dynasty, which reunited China, was succeeded by the T'ang, literature entered a new cycle in a splendid age of Chinese history, an age worthily called the renaissance.

T'ang Poetry. The poetry of this age developed in four stages: early (c.620–710); heyday (c.710–780); middle (c.780–830); and late (c. 830–906).

The Early Period. This period was marked by a demand for a return to classical simplicity and clarity. Although the vogue of artificiality inherited from the preceding age persisted, it was infused with new life by a rising generation of poets. Two favorite courtiers of Emperor Chung Tsung (reigned 684; 705–710)—Shên Ch'üan-ch'i (died c.713) and Sung Chih-wên (died c.710)—extracted from the essence of technical poetic theories a form called *lü shih* (regular poetry), which was to develop into one of the finest T'ang types. Although the 4-line stanza could be infinitely multiplied to make a *p'ai lü* (extended form), 8 lines were the norm, and all had to be of equal length, with 5 or 7 characters. The middle 4 lines were always strictly parallel couplets with contrasting tones; the other lines were comparatively free. This form was equally suited to the artificer and to the serious poet who preferred a formal structure. The outstanding poet of the early period was Ch'en Tzŭ-ang (656–698), who was recognized by the master poets of the heyday as their only pioneer.

The Heyday of T'ang. In this period T'ang poetry rose to its zenith. Its ascent was prepared by increasing social development and prosperity in China, and accelerated by conflict and suffering. Emperor Hsüan Tsung, or Ming Huang (reigned 713–756 A.D.), with whom this period began, was a great patron of poetry and the arts during the internally peaceful early years of his reign.

The poets of this period identified themselves with its tragedies and its felicities. The most distinguished were Li Po (701/705–762) and Tu Fu (712–770), who are commonly recognized as the master spirits of Chinese poetry. Both reacted against the immediate past and claimed kinship with the classics, but they were entirely different in temperament. Tu Fu stood for Confucian this-worldliness. He was a great secular poet whose works are realistic etchings of a tormented humanity. In them, exquisite scenery and lovely human forms appear in relief against a background of mundane life. Li Po had an affinity for Taoist transcendental naturalism. In his poems magnificent landscape, female beauty, and earthly love are mirrored in the eternal spirit of the cosmos. The finest works of Tu Fu were written in *lü shih* style, which best suited his exactness and precision of expression. Li Po was most successful in his freely improvised *ku shih* and in the *chüeh chü* (curtailed poem), a short song form popular in the T'ang age which was restricted to four even lines but was capable of suggesting infinite overtones.

Among the many other celebrated poets of the T'ang heyday were Wang Wei (699–759), the painter, famous for evoking "poetry in his painting and painting in his poetry"; Mêng Hao-jan (689–740), who wrote some of the period's tenderest lyrical verses; Wang Ch'ang-ling (c.700–765), master of the *chüeh chü;* and Ts'ên Shên (715–770) and Kao Shih (c.700–765), who left memorable verses about battles and expeditions on the rugged frontiers.

The Middle Period. During the middle period pacification of internal turmoil and resistance to invasion were alternately successful and frustrated. In this Indian summer of the T'ang dynasty, poetry developed in a new way with the emergence of two great figures—Han Yü (768–824) and Po Chü-i (772–846)—representing two new schools. Han Yü, celebrated chiefly as a leading advocate of neoclassical prose and a champion of Confucianism, was also an innovator in poetry. His works, which are sometimes marred by argumentative tirades and moral preaching, contain lines of strange beauty, with grotesque images, dissonant tones, and freakish rhymes. Occasionally the ugly and the horrible hold a fascination for him. The most extraordinary talent among Han Yü's friends and followers was that of Li Ho (790–816), whose imaginative power in weaving together the most diverse subjects, and superb sensibility for word music and vivid imagery, earned him the name of "ghost genius."

Po Chü-i, who led the other school of this period, had a style so simple and clear that it came close to the language of the people. His famous long poems are touching romances in melodious speech. Despite the apparent easy grace and intimate charm of his verses on almost every detail and triviality of daily life, Po was a poet of very serious purpose. With his vernacular diction and commonplace rhymes, he spoke for ordinary people in a way they could understand. Closely associated with him were Yüan Chên (779–831) and Liu Yü-hsi (772–842).

The Late Period. Toward the end of the T'ang dynasty the imperial court was crumbling, and signs of disintegration appeared everywhere. Yet this sunset of a glorious age of poetry was not without splendor. The three leading poets of the period were Tu Mu (803–852), known for his heroic style, Li Shang-yin (813–858), and Wên T'ing-yün (mid-9th century), whose works were distinguished by their elegance and colorful imagery. The artificiality of their poems, however, was a sign of approaching decadence.

T'ang Prose. Essays and fiction showed great distinction in the T'ang age. Han Yü and Liu Tsung-yüan, the great middle T'ang poets, were recognized leaders in neoclassical prose writing. Both opposed the florid parallelism which had been in vogue for 500 years. While Han, an ardent Confucianist, wrote vigorous polemic and expository works, Liu, who was more detached, drew sharply outlined portraits of persons and crystal-clear landscape sketches. The two men perfected many forms of the modern Chinese essay.

The first real fiction was also developed in the T'ang dynasty. Earlier works had been mere fables or naïve tales; in the T'ang short stories intriguing plots and vivid characterizations were developed. Among these stories, which were modestly called *ch'uan ch'i* (curious traditions), are gems comparable to the best Western medieval romances. The two most important writers were Yüan Chên, the poet, and Li Kung-tso (770–c.850). Love, chivalry, social satire, fanciful ideas about Buddhist visions, and Taoist mystical experiences were among their favorite subjects. These stories retained their influence on later fiction and drama, continuing to add spice and color to popular beliefs. But their form and content attest the creativeness of the T'ang age, which lifted superstition to the level of imaginative literature.

Contemporary literary criticism is found mainly in the casual but illuminating remarks of the poets and prose writers in their conversations, letters, and private journals. During the declining years of the age, which were marked by a belief in art for art's sake, there developed a vogue for gleaning famous lines of great masters in handbooks called *shih chü t'u* (samples of poetic patterns). Some of the editors of these books showed sound critical sense, but the great critic of the age was Ssŭ-k'ung T'u (837–908). In the twilight of T'ang, as if for its swan song, he wrote in superb, impressionistic verse, with the choicest metaphors and similes, a book of criticism called *Poetic Characteristics* (*Shih P'in*), in which he presented the 24 qualities to be desired in poetry. Because of its trenchant aphorisms and melodious style, his work became a kind of formula for Chinese poets.

THE AGE OF REASON AND THE RISE OF THE DRAMA AND THE NOVEL (10TH CENTURY TO 1900)

The end of adventurous expansion and the achievement of internal unity ushered in an age of inner reconstruction and philosophical contemplation. The Sung dynasty was an age of masterly prose. In this period the ideas of Confucianism, Taoism, and Buddhism, which had stirred men's hearts in the lyrical T'ang age, were mulled over and subjected to scientific scrutiny. Poetic forms perfected in T'ang now became conventional, but the rarefied music of a form of pure poetry, the *tz'ŭ*, developed since the decadence of the previous age, came into full flower.

Sung Prose. Foremost of the Sung prose writers was Ou-yang Hsiu (1007–1072), a classicist who reacted against artificial parallelism and floridity and favored a return to simplicity and directness. His major accomplishment lay in making prose serve the uses of his time. The flowing style of his political treatises, philosophical dissertations, and essays had a flexibility of rhythm and a clarity of structure unattainable in poetry. His followers included Wang An-shih (1021–1086), the great political reformer, distinguished for his wit and penetrating observation, and the poet Su Shih, or Su Tung-p'o (1036–1101), whose prose writings were brilliantly variegated. Like his master, Su Shih left unsurpassed prose poems. His father, Su Hsün (1009–1066), his brother, Su Chê (1039–1112), and their contemporary, Tsêng Kung (1019–1083), all achieved great distinction. These six, with Han Yü and Liu Tsung-yüan of the T'ang dynasty, are known to Chinese schoolboys as the Eight Masters of T'ang and Sung. Prose writers of the Yüan, Ming, and Ch'ing dynasties imitated or criticized their classical style but never surpassed it.

Rationalist philosophers of the Sung dynasty expressed in placid and deliberative prose their ideas of the order of the universe and their theories of knowledge. The commentaries and discourses of Chu Hsi (1130–1200), Lu Chiu-yüan (1139–1193), and others, written in the plainest vernacular, are memorable contributions to the lucidity and naturalness of informal style.

Sung Tz'ŭ Poetry. The development of the *tz'ŭ* is another instance of the close relationship between folk and polite literature. It first emerged during the T'ang dynasty as a group of folksongs and instrumental tunes, was gradually taken over by the courtiers and literati, the verses imitated or polished, and the tunes converted into poetic sound patterns. The first important works in *tz'ŭ* forms were written in the age of chaos and despair of the last decades of the T'ang dynasty and the Five Dynasties period. An offspring of the most extravagant years in the T'ang court and society, it first thrived in a period of spiritual ruin, when fainthearted kings and officials, particularly in the south, drugged themselves with exquisitely voluptuous poetry and dolorous music. Men of great talent, such as Li Yü (937–978), last king of the Southern T'ang dynasty (937–975), produced fine *tz'ŭ* poems. In the Sung dynasty the *tz'ŭ* became the most distinguished genre. Its softly vibrating tonal structure and gentle melodies made it the most suitable type for the portrayal of picturesque scenery and feminine beauty and for the expression of delicate feelings and tender thoughts. Many of the masters of the lofty and vigorous Sung prose, revealing a hidden side of their natures in an age of reason, were adepts in this type of effeminate verse.

The first distinguished *tz'ŭ* writer of lasting influence was Yen Shu (991–1055). A favorite of the Sung court in its heyday, he wrote *tz'ŭ* verses imbued with the riches and splendor of his time, yet with an implicit sense of the transitoriness of rapture and beauty. Fan Chung-yen (989–1052) wrote touching pieces on the familiar themes of parting and desolation. Ou-yang Hsiu, statesman, historian, and revered master of prose, shows most clearly the dual personality characteristic of many famous Sung writers. His *tz'ŭ* verses, with their implied longing for romantic love, excelled in the reproduction of virgin beauty in varied natural settings. Then came Liu Yung (c.1035) and Su Shih, who in their different ways enriched and liberated the *tz'ŭ* genre. Liu, repudiated by the court as a vulgarian, but beloved as a popular bard of singsong girls, townsfolk, and villagers, wrote in the vernacular on the universal theme of love. Su Shih, unrestrained by elaborate rules, burst into bold songs, some heroic and others of an ethereal beauty. The vernacular *tz'ŭ* verses of Huang T'ing-chien (1045–1105), disparaged by his contemporaries as overly rustic, were relished in later times. The last great *tz'ŭ* writer of the Northern Sung dynasty (960–1126) was Chou Mei-ch'êng (1057–1121), who developed many novel techniques.

After the Jurchen invasion the Southern Sung dynasty (1127–1279) was established in the Yangtze Valley. Overlapping the Northern and Southern Sung periods were two writers of great talent. Emperor Hui Tsung (reigned 1101–1125) wrote *tz'ŭ* verses about the vanishing splendors of an imperial court seen through the eyes of a ruler and a great artist.. His later verses, written in captivity under the Jurchens, were plaintive melodies. The poetess Li Ch'ing-chao (1081–c.1140/1145) transformed the commonplace into the spiritual with her incomparable natural eloquence.

At the beginning of the Southern Sung period, in the midst of the struggle for national existence, two patriotic poets, Lu Yu (1125–1210) and Hsin Ch'i-chi (1140–1207), wrote verses in a heroic strain. With peace, poetry returned to virtuosity and craftsmanship, and only intermittently came outbursts of heartfelt anger and sorrow, protests against an iron age. Chiang K'uei (c.1155–1235) was the most accomplished craftsman of this period. Finally, during the last years of the dynasty, came quaintly elegant *tz'ŭ* verses reflecting the futility and apathy of a lost generation of literati. Yet throughout this period the people, who continued to assimilate foreign elements, were preparing a great new trend in vernacular literature—the rise of the popular drama and novel.

The Rise of the Drama. From the ancient combination of singing, dancing, and impersonation portraying historical or legendary characters, spectacular vaudevilles for court entertainment had become highly developed since the Han dynasty, foreshadowing the modern Chinese theater. It was not until the Sung dynasty, however, that actors in town and country began to form organized troupes and to adopt specialized roles (clowns, ladies and gentlemen, and other characters), and it was only in the late 11th century that complete stories were enacted on the stage. The earliest dramatic work with a definite plot is traceable to Chao Tê-lin of the late Northern Sung dynasty. The first rich flowering of dramatic literature was in the *tsa chü* or *tsa hsi* (miscellaneous play) of the Southern Sung. When the *tz'ŭ* reached its limit as a poetic genre, talented writers turned to playwriting. Adopting some of the elaborate *tz'ŭ* technique, they brought to the drama pure poetry revitalized and enriched by folk vernacular and motifs. The traditional Chinese drama has since remained colloquial and poetic, constituting a fusion of song and dialogue enlivened with gestures and acrobatic dances.

Under Mongol role during the Yüan dynasty, large numbers of intellectuals were deprived of their positions with the civil service and began to assimilate folk art. As a result, the theater flourished. The most distinguished Yüan playwrights were Kuan Han-ch'ing, Ma Chih-yüan, Pai P'u, Chêng Kuang-tsu, and Wang Shih-fu, all of the 13th century. Perhaps the most celebrated work of this period was Wang Shih-fu's *Romance of the Western Chamber* (*Hsi Hsing Chi*), a love story with dramatic plot in exquisite verse.

In the Ming dynasty attempts at innovation in other literary forms ended in imitation of the past, but the drama and the novel, sustained by the living vernacular, continued to develop. Ming drama was enriched by the tunes and dialects in the revitalized Southern Sung tradition. In the earlier plays singing was usually monopolized by the leading character in each scene; in the new form solo singing could be alternated with singing by two or more characters to form lively musical dialogues. Among the most distinguished works of the southern school of drama are *The Story of the Lute* (*P'i P'a Chi*) by Kao Ming (mid-14th century), and *Peony Pavilion* (*Mu Tan T'ing*) by T'ang Hsian-tsu (1550–1617). Southern drama, refined and invigorated by the rise of the *k'un-ch'ü* school in the 16th century, reached its heyday in the early Ch'ing (Manchu) dynasty. Among the best playwrights were the Ch'ing period were Li Yü (1611–?1680), versatile writer and great dramatic critic; K'ung Shang-jên (1648–1718), author of *The Peach Blossom Fan* (*T'ao Hua Shan*); and Hung Shêng (1646?–1704), whose *Immortal Palace* (*Ch'ang Shêng Tien*), the romantic love story of Emperor Hsüan Tsung, excelled all other plays on this popular theme.

Chinese dramatic literature and stagecraft were. often at secret odds. External effects of dazzling costumes, gorgeous makeup, shrill declamations, and acrobatic stunts tended to obscure the poetry. After the middle of the 18th century the Chinese drama in more recent forms became so ostentatious that, despite musical and dialectal changes, dramatic literature dwindled to almost nothing. Acting, though remarkable for subtle symbols and gestures, almost eclipsed playwriting. The drama as literature took flight, to return only in the 20th century, with the rise of realistic spoken drama (*hua chü*).

The Development of the Novel. The Chinese novel, in its traditional form of innumerable episodes leading to a denouement, developed about the 11th century, during the Sung dynasty. Professional storytellers, already known in T'ang times, flourished in many towns and villages. Through summer evenings and winter days they poured out their endless tales. Historical events were found to be the most suitable themes, but chivalry, domestic scenes, love affairs, and the supernatural were all favorite topics. In their interminable harangues the storytellers relied mainly on a good memory and a ready wit. Out of the crudely written versions of their tales, prepared for reference when memory failed, grew the rudimentary form of the Chinese novel.

Between the Yüan and Ming dynasties the art of novel writing began to mature. Most of the great works of this period were based on old stories, already popular in Sung times, which were now polished or rewritten. The first successful work of this kind, *The Water Margin* (*Shui Hu Chuan*), translated into English as *All Men Are Brothers*, is a picaresque novel about the adventures of 108 chivalrous robbers who rebelled against corrupt government in the late Northern Sung dynasty. Its author preferred anonymity. Later research revealed that he was Shih Nai-an, who lived in the middle of the 14th century, when the overthrow of the Yüan dynasty was under way. The vivid characterization and forceful style of this novel gave it so strong a popular appeal that, according to some critics, it contributed much to the revolutionary spirit of the Chinese common people. Next to appear was a historical novel, *The Three Kingdoms* (*San Kuo*), by Lo Kuanchung of the late 14th century. Some of its heroes, originally historical personages, were so vividly drawn that they became in later folk tradition either deities or prototypes of villains.

In the 16th century appeared *Pilgrimage to the West* (*Hsi Yu Chi*), translated into English as *Monkey*, a mythological novel of rich and brilliant imagination. Crude versions of the story, passing through several hands, were perfected by Wu Ch'êng-ên (c. 1510–c. 1580). *The Gold Vase Plums* (*Chin P'ing Mei*), translated into English as *The Golden Lotus*, an acridly realistic novel about domestic life, was published in 1610. In its descriptions of avarice, lechery, and corruption, and in the subtle psychology of its characterizations of officials, fops, rogues, and licentious women, it surpassed all other works of the kind.

About 1765 there appeared in Peking bookstores the *Story of a Stone* (*Shih T'ou Chi*), an unfinished work in 80 chapters. The genius evident in this anonymous book at once attracted the attention of the best writers of the age. Soon 40 additional chapters were "found and edited" by a certain Kao Ê. The 120 chapters were published in 1792 as *The Dream of the Red Chamber* (*Hung-lou mêng*). Its author was identified as Ts'ao Chan, or Ts'ao Hsüeh-ch'in, (1719?–1763). The story of the rise and decline of a great Chinese family, its superb characterizations, thrilling episodes, and panoramic representations of intricate human relationships and everyday experiences place it among the world's greatest novels.

Three series of short stories are also important: *Spectacular Stories, Ancient and Modern* (*Chin Ku Ch'i Kuan*), compiled about 1640; *Strange Stories from a Chinese Studio* (*Liao Chai Chih I*), by P'u Sung-ling, or P'u Liu-hsien (c.1640–1715), consisting mainly of tales about fox spirits and ghosts, written in the style of the T'ang romances; and *Unofficial History of the Literati* (*Ju Lin Wai Shih*), a series of brilliant satires by Wu Ching-tzǔ (1701–1754), which exerted great influence on all later Chinese satire.

20TH CENTURY LITERATURE

With the overthrow of the Ch'ing dynasty and the establishment of the Chinese republic, efforts were made to adapt the time-honored Chinese civilization to the modern world and to reassert the rights of the people. On May 4, 1917, a cultural movement began. It was led by Hu Shih (1891–1962) and Ch'ên Tu-hsiu (1879–1942) with many followers mainly from the National University of Peking. Owing largely to their efforts the modern vernacular (*pai-hua*) was ac-

corded public recognition as the sole medium for creative literature and as the official language for school textbooks. A reevaluation of China's heritage was attempted, and interest was aroused in other literatures. Translations, chiefly of Western romanticists, Russian novelists, and writers of oppressed eastern European nations flooded the Chinese book market.

In the years following the revolution of 1911 the most important of the few creative writers who gained national recognition was Chou Shu-jên (pen name Lu Hsün, 1881–1936). His poignant satirical novelettes, short stories, and essays brought him prominence as the most influential critic of modern Chinese society. Hsü Chih-mo (1895–1931) and Wen I-to (1899–1946) were among the first of the modern Chinese poets who successfully employed the contemporary vernacular to create new poetic forms. Kuo Mo-jo (1891–   ), novelist, playwright, poet, and activist since the 1920's, moved from Goethean romanticism to historical materialism. But the keynote of the so-called May Fourth spirit was liberal humanism, which was championed by Chou Tso-jên (1888–   ) in his *Humane Literature* (1918).

In the 1930's and 1940's, before and during the Sino-Japanese War, plays and novels characterized by social consciousness and faithful realism were written in increasing numbers. The plays of Wan Chia-pao (pen name Ts'ao Yü, 1909–   ), which have been translated into several foreign languages, won him acclaim as China's most important contemporary dramatist through his mastery of rich and fluent expression in the vernacular, and his penetrating observations of Chinese society in transition.

The works of four novelists of this period before the next political cataclysm are especially memorable. Shu Ch'ing-ch'un (pen name Lao Shê, or Lau Shaw, 1898–   ) wrote, in the purest Peking colloquial idiom, lively satires and sympathetic portrayals of intellectuals and plebeians. Shen Yeu-ping (pen name Mao Tun, 1896–   ), with sedulous craftsmanship patterned on Western naturalism and realism, and with great sensitivity, depicted social agony and convulsion. Li Fei-kan (pen name Pa Chin, or Ba Kin, adapted from *Bakunin* and *Kropotkin*, 1904–   ), the prolific anarchistic idealists, appealed most to restive youth. Shen Ts'ung-wen (1902–   ), a confirmed individualist of superior talent and fine discrimination, attained incomparable lyricism and pathos in his works in the new humanist tradition.

In 1949, China came under Communist rule. With it the slogan "Politics takes command!" began to exercise its effect. Literature and all the arts were required to serve such political purposes as the party dictated. Chairman Mao Tse-tung's *Talks at the Yenan Forum on Literature and Art* (1942) became the master plan for literary policy, whose enforcement was hailed by the party as the "second, even more sweeping and profound literary revolution" than the one of 1917.

The remarkable fact about Chinese literature in the 3d quarter of the 20th century is that Mao's literary theory produced so many results. Politics indeed took supreme command, at the immeasurable cost of literary value. Sporadic but strong protests were quickly silenced. The leading maverick in the ranks of Communist writers was Hu Feng, who cried, "There is the garish fact that literature is not wanted. . . . Don't compel writers to lie, don't do dirt to life!" He was liquidated in 1955, with hundreds of others in continuous waves of purges. But Mao's formula did produce an immense quantity of literature by forced growth. Within his definition of "national form" the *yang ko* or "sprout song," an old Chinese folksong form, spawned numberless folk operas and musicals. The new mass literature —composed by workers, peasants, and soldiers, illiterate or semiliterate, collaborating with "awakened" professional writers and zealous students—appeared in thousands of tabloids all over the country.

It is a commentary on the "Second Literary Revolution" under total Communist control that the severest purges were of those writers and critics who had made the most of the Marxian appeal to humanitarianism and revolutionary fervor, and had thus contributed most to the Communist winning of totalitarian rule. The courageous, dissident woman writer Ting Ling was placed in abject "labor reform," and Hu Feng was liquidated, as were Ai Ching, the talented poet, and scores of their like. Writers whose literary life somehow survived during the third quarter of the 20th century produced, at the party's behest, stereotypes of positive heroes and class enemies and hymns in adulation of Mao and his regime. They had to be constantly on the alert to adapt themselves to the frequent changes of propaganda targets under the banner of "Politics takes command!" In hundreds of publications new names of authors appeared, but since individuality was anathema under collectivism, their personal style and character were as indistinguishable as if the writing was anonymous. The "particle of art" (Pasternak's phrase) in rare cases maintained a surreptitious existence beneath some works, where the writer's fidelity to art and life, despite himself and the party, underlay the propaganda. Notable examples were Chou Li-po's *Changes in a Mountain Village* (1958), Wu Ch'iang's *Red Sun* (1959), and Yang Mo's *Song of Youth* (1960).

Inhibition of individual creative expression since the early 1950's diverted a part of Chinese intellectual energy to the safer sanctum of literary-historical research. Though such work was not free from ideological control either, China's old cultural heritage is too rich not to yield valuable finds. Occasionally, ancient classical texts were discovered and notably edited by competent hands. Even some of the reinterpretations of classical works for popular consumption, when stripped of ideological veneer, were not without value. However, setbacks in these fields, too, were suffered during the Red Guard movements of 1966–1967, which recklessly attacked all traditional values and achievements. That the renowned historian Wu Han and the senior playwright T'ien Han, long known as subscribers to Communist causes, should have become initial victims of these movements because they drew political-moral lessons from history was proof that even the past was no longer a sanctuary for the Chinese writer of the 1960's.

The third quarter of the 20th century saw the most totalitarian control of literature known in Chinese history. Hardly any creative work of quality by individuals can be recorded. But the immense quantity of work ground out by the party-controlled literary machine, catering to a vast population to serve the regime's immediate political purposes, is impressive. And when the immediate purposes were served, the accelerated rate of growing literacy would continue to have its effect on coming generations, whether under the same or a different regime.

SHIH-HSIANG CHEN
University of California at Berkeley

Bibliography
Birch, Cyril, and Keene, Donald, eds., *Anthology of Chinese Literature* (New York 1965).
Bishop, John L., ed., *Studies in Chinese Literature* (Cambridge, Mass., 1965).
Ch'en, Shou-yi, *Chinese Literature: A Historical Introduction* (New York 1961).
Hsia, C. T., *History of Modern Chinese Fiction* (New Haven 1961).
Liu, Wu-chi, and Li, Tien-yi, eds., *Readings in Contemporary Chinese Literature* (New Haven 1964).
Watson, Barton, *Early Chinese Literature* (New York 1962).

15. Theater

In the traditional Chinese theater singing is at least as important as acting. The Chinese refer in ordinary conversation to the drama as either *chü* (song) or *chi* (play), their conception of the art standing in significant contrast to the Western conception of drama as action.

Dramatic writing, an art long despised and neglected, had a late growth in China. The literati, who took to writing for the theater as a last resort, did not deign to learn the craftsmanship required by the form, but merely exploited it as a vehicle for the exhibition of their literary achievements and imaginative ingenuity. At its best this kind of dramatic writing contains scenes of true sentiment, rich in poetic beauty and dramatic at fleeting moments. Yet, with few exceptions, Chinese plays of the old school are not well constructed. Victims of overattention to poetic justice, neglect of the logic of character, and indulgence in long-winded narrative, they lack the balance demanded by Western dramatic standards. Nevertheless, a study of the techniques used in producing these plays shows that, while generally lacking in realism, they can soar into flights of unhampered imagination and impart a feeling of pure theater.

The old Chinese theater is an art based on music. It combines singing, dancing, acrobatics, pantomime, and highly stylized acting. To appreciate its grace and beauty and its sense of theatrical truth, one must bear in mind the fundamental conception of the Chinese playgoer that the theater is at best an illusion of life, to be evoked by the suggestiveness of acting and music and by the imagination of the spectator. The Chinese stage is almost as bare as the Elizabethan stage. It has a protruding square platform with no scenery and no curtain, and is faced on three sides by the audience. In the center hangs a decorative backdrop with openings at right and left for entrance and exit. The orchestra, which sits on the right side, is conducted by the player of the small drum, the sounds of which accentuate, with meticulous precision, every movement of the actors. Usually the orchestra comprises a "civil" part, with a Chinese violin, a flute, a Chinese moon guitar, and a Chinese cornet; and a "military" part, consisting of a big drum, a big gong, a small gong, and cymbals. The property man, who sets up the chairs, tables, kneeling cushions, and other simple properties, is never obtrusive and, so far as the audience is concerned, scarcely exists.

The acting is entirely conventional. But its patterns seem beautiful and convincing when they are enlivened by the well-disciplined art of accomplished actors. The character parts, also con-

PEKING OPERA actors, wearing typically colorful costumes and enacting traditional roles, perform a scene from a historical play about the Three Kingdoms.

ventional, are divided roughly into four major types of roles; the *shêng,* or male characters; the *tan,* or female characters; the *ching,* or characters with painted faces; and the *ch'ou,* or comedian. Until the revolution of 1911, all these characters were played by men. With an oar standing for a boat, a whip for a horse, a table for a hill, a flag with the picture of wheels for a cart, and a painted cloth for a city wall, the genius of the Chinese theater succeeded in presenting, in its every aspect, the many-sided life of old China.

Ancient Origins. Chinese drama can be traced back to the enchantments practiced by the ancient seers. In the Shang dynasty (about 1523–1028 B. C.), the *hsi* (sorcerer) and *wu* (sorceress), impersonating deified ancestors and gods, performed ceremonial songs and dances to propitiate the gods and spirits, invoking them to drive out pestilence, send abundant crops, and effect other miracles. The spectators at these performances were moved to join in the dancing. Out of these religious rites and folk dances arose a group of performers and musicians—brothers, historically, to the Chinese acting profession of modern times—employed by the court for the amusement of the emperors and the nobility.

The activity of the court entertainers reached its height in the Han dynasty (202 B. C.–220 A. D.), when clowns, wrestlers, acrobats, singing girls, and musicians, disguised as gods, fairies, warriors, tigers, leopards, bears, dragons, white elephants, divine turtles, and gigantic birds, enacted mythological stories before Emperor Wu Ti (reigned 140–87 B. C.) and foreign tribute bearers from the western regions.

Formative Period. Because of the invasion of China by western tribes the music and dance of central Asia had a distinct influence on performances during the period of the Southern (420–589 A. D.) and Northern (386–581 A. D.) dynasties, as seen in the warrior dance *Mask of the Duke of Lan Lin,* the revenge dance *Tiger,* and the comic dance *Drunkard's Wife.*

In the T'ang dynasty Emperor Hsüan Tsung (reigned 713–756 A. D.) showed his interest in the theater by founding at Changan (now Sian)

the Pear Orchard, a place for training actors, musicians, and dancers. During the same dynasty there arose a new type of short comic sketch in dialogue form, called *ts'an chün hsi,* using two actors, the *ts'an chün* (leading player) and the *ts'ang hu* (supporting player). These comic pieces, like the other singing and dancing media of the period, had little story interest. They were satires in disguise, sustained by the wit and humor of talented actors and sometimes interlarded with timely political thrusts.

Under the Sung dynasty, with the rising influence of professional storytellers, the *ts'an chün hsi,* by that time known as *tsa chü* or *tsa hsi* (miscellaneous play), gradually shed its satirical and bantering quality and adopted story form. The various stories in a *tsa chü* performance were episodic and unrelated to one another, but the form became more complicated, with four principal characters and two subordinate characters. The dancing and singing that accompanied the performance became essential features of the Chinese legitimate theater. This simple type of *tsa chü* was the forerunner of the theater of the southern school, which flourished in Hangchow.

Yüan Drama. After a period of incubation in northern China under the alien Chin dynasty, there arose during the Yüan dynasty the theater of the northern school, which represented a great advance over the *tsa chü.* Prosperity and peace created an unprecedented demand for the theater. Although the arts in general were ignored by the Mongol rulers, the theater, being responsive to a less cultivated but wider public than other art media, became the most vital literary expression of the time. When the Mongols abolished the civil service examinations, many Chinese scholars, for want of a better means of self-expression, turned to writing for the theater. By this time the drama of the northern school had evolved into its mature form, with four acts, a prologue, an epilogue, and an interlude for the exposition of a full-length story. In the hands of the dramatic talent of the day, action held the stage in place of narration, dialogue became dramatic, and metrical forms were much more varied.

The age of Yüan was unrivaled in its abun-

dance of excellent plays. Among the best known are *The Sorrows of Han* by Ma Chih-yüan; *The Sufferings of Tou-E* by Kuan Han-ch'ing; *The Slave of the Treasure,* Chinese counterpart of Molière's *L'Avare; The Orphan of the Chao Family,* a tragedy distinguished by sublimity of conception and character; and *The Romance of the Western Chamber (Hsi-hsiang chi),* a romantic play of youthful love, written with rare beauty and inimitable literary flourish by Wang Shih-fu. These plays have been published in various languages, the earliest translation being Voltaire's adaptation of *The Orphan of the Chao Family,* which he called *L'Orphelin de la Chine.* The Yüan play which has been performed most frequently in Europe and the United States is *The Chalk Circle* by Li Sing-tao.

At the end of the Yüan dynasty, as the theater of the northern school began to decline, Kao Ming (courtesy name Kao Tsê-ch'êng; mid-14th century), the earliest scholar of the theater of the new southern school, wrote his immortal play *The Story of the Lute (P'i-p'a chi),* a complicated 42-act (in some versions, 24-act) development of the theme of filial piety, depicting the life of Chao Wu-liang, the idealized daughter-in-law of a scholar's family. In 1945 this play was presented in a form considerably shortened in the New York musical success *Lute Song.*

Drama in the Ming and Ch'ing Dynasties. In the Ming dynasty, Wei Liang-fu (mid-16th century), a musical genius of the south, introduced the epoch-making *k'un-ch'ü* school of singing. It became at once admired and influential and gradually forced the northern school theater of the Yüan period out of existence. During the ascendancy of the *k'un-ch'ü* school, T'ang Hsientsu, or Tang Shien-chu (1550–1617), one of its great masters, wrote his five romantic plays. Of these, *Peony Pavilion (Mu-tan t'ing),* in 55 acts, is the best example of his exuberant imagination and of his aptitude for portraiture and literary embellishment. Among the writers who tried to emulate his writing, and to excel him in metrical harmony, was Yüan Ta-ch'êng (died 1645), a high official of the declining Ming dynasty. His best work was the play *The Swallow as Gobetween,* the love story of a singsong girl. In the Ming period the theater of the southern school reached its zenith.

The *k'un-ch'ü* school of singing continued to hold an indisputable position among numerous Chinese theater troupes during the first 150 years of the Ch'ing dynasty. Authors who professed allegiance to the Ming dynasty rather than to the foreign Ch'ing dynasty gave vent to their repressed sentiments in dramatic form. The most notable works of this period are *The Palace of Eternal Life (The Immortal Palace, Ch'angshêng tien)* by Hung Shêng (1646?–1704), a play based on the tragic love of Emperor Hsüan Tsung and his mistress Yang Kuei-fei, and *The Peach Blossom Fan (T'ao-hua shan)* by K'ung Shang-jên (1648–1718), on the theme of love and patriotism—a dirge among the ruins of the fallen dynasty.

After a short period of imperial patronage at the court of Emperor Ch'ien Lung (reigned

ILLUSION is basic to the traditional Chinese theater, and is enhanced by the extravagant makeup of actors, like these men in their dressing room at the Peking Opera.

CAIO MARIO GARRUBBA, FROM RAPHO GUILLUMETTE

1736–1794), the theater of the *k'un-chü* school began to fall out of public favor because of its overelaborate poetic language and excessive refinement. Out of the melting pot of many theater troupes the *p'i-huang* school of the theater emerged to take the fancy of the common people. Its plays, still cherished as the most popular form of entertainment in China, are rarely of literary value; yet they have attracted accomplished actors including Mei Lan-fang (1894–1961).

Modern Chinese Drama. In the modern era Chinese dramatic presentation has broken away from the traditions of the classic Chinese theater. Differing from the old in both form and spirit, it represents a revolution in dramatic technique. About 1900, politically conscious intellectuals, in an effort to depose the Manchu regime and to modernize their country, turned to the Western theater for inspiration and support. A great number of Western plays, including those of Henrik Ibsen, George Bernard Shaw, Anton Chekhov, and Eugene O'Neill, as well as the classics of every age, were translated, and some of them performed. Borrowing Western techniques of playwriting and production, talented dramatists and directors initiated a new theater, called *hua chü* (spoken drama), as distinguished from the old school of music drama. A drama of social significance, its topical themes and varied production techniques have won the approval of the modern Chinese public. The new theater, alert to the impress of reality, reflects the life and thought of the people of China in their own everyday speech, in striking contrast to the classical verse of the old theater, with its stories of scholars, warriors, and kings. The new theater endeavors to be modern in form, yet distinctly Chinese in content. *Hua chü* occupies an unprecedented position in modern Chinese literature, exerting a far-reaching influence over the common people in their adjustment to the contemporary world. See also DRAMA; ORIENTAL THEATER.

CHIA-PAO WAN
Dramatist and Teacher

16. Music

The spirit of Chinese music is deeply rooted in Confucian philosophy. To this philosophy, music is the harmony of heaven and earth and the flowering of spiritual understanding in man. Its belief is that tones are the substance of music, whereas melody and rhythm are merely the appearance of tones. Thus, unlike the music of other cultures, emphasis in Chinese music is on the single tone: its articulation, timbre, and inflection.

This concept is manifest in *ya yüeh* (ritual music) and the music for *ch'in* (zither). *Ya yüeh* is closely related to the idea of order in the universe and to the elements in nature. Pitches and instruments, when carefully ordered, are believed capable of regulating the affairs of state and the minds and passions of people. *Ch'in* music is especially associated with man's spiritual life. Each excitation of the strings and subsequent inflections in pitch and timbre are controlled to express poetic and philosophical contemplations. Besides the dominating influence of Confucianism, the solo music for *ch'in* and other instruments also bears the imprint of Taoist and Buddhist thought.

Prehistory. According to prehistoric legends, music began with the mythical emperor Fu Hsi.

PAINTED FACE (*Hua-lien*) is a name for this familiar character—usually a military man—in Peking Opera.

The 12 pitches of the octave were first established by Ling Lun at the command of Huang Ti, the Yellow Emperor of the 27th century B.C. Actually, history and archaeology prove that the foundations of Chinese music were laid during the Shang dynasty (about 1523 to about 1028 B.C.). Several significant instruments were already in existence—the pitched sonorous stone (*ch'ing*), the pitched bronze bell (*chung*), the globular flute (*hsüan*), the panpipes (*p'ai hsiao*), and the reed mouth organ (*sheng*).

Ya Yüeh. Ritual music, regarded as a regulator of the universe and of the state, was the most significant and the best-documented music of Chinese antiquity. While archaeological excavations have unearthed a remarkable number of Shang dynasty instruments, the earliest sources on *ya yüeh* are the classics of the Chou dynasty (about 1027–256 B.C.). They provide a general idea of the principles of this music and the methods of performance by instrumental ensembles, singers, and dancers.

After the fall of the Han dynasty (202 B.C.–220 A.D.), due to almost four centuries of continuous invasion and internal upheaval, the tradition of this music was gradually lost. Each succeeding dynasty, however, endeavored to restore it. The greatest revival occurred during the Sung dynasty (960–1279), and subsequent dynasties followed the theories and practices established during this time. Many important treatises were published during the Ming dynasty (1368–1644), but ritual music continued to lose its force until, by the end of the Ch'ing dynasty (1644–1911), it was totally neglected. In modern times, it may still be heard in some Confucian temples and in Korea, where it is known as *a ak*. Among the instruments used are those of the Shang dynasty already mentioned and two kinds of zither, *ch'in* and *se*.

Su Yüeh. This term refers to the music of the people and is similar to the term "secular music" in the West. The earliest known form of *su yüeh* again dates from the Chou dynasty. Wu Ti, an emperor of the Han dynasty, created the Imperial Office of Music to collect, edit, and classify the ancient music still preserved among the people. Most significant in the collection was the form that had become known as *ch'ing shang yüeh*, for voice and instrumental ensemble, and sometimes with dance.

From the Han dynasty until the end of the T'ang dynasty (618–906 A.D.), China's contacts with India and central Asia increased. Music brought back from and written in the style of these other cultures became popular and helped establish the T'ang dynasty as the "golden age of *su yüeh*." The T'ang form called *ta ch'ü* represented the highest achievement in ensemble music and remained popular through the Sung period, after which it was eclipsed by theater music. Traces of its influence, however, can still be detected in some ensemble music today. In Japan, for example, *gagaku* is recognized as having preserved much of this type of music.

The instruments used in *su yüeh* ensembles often include the cross flute (*ti*), the vertical flute (*hsiao*), the short lute (*p'i p'a*), and zithers. In modern times the long lute (*yüan hsien*), the flat lute (*yüeh ch'in*), the unfretted long lute (*san hsien*), the dulcimer (*yang ch'in*), and the two-stringed fiddle (*erh hu*) are also used.

Dramatic Music. The *k'uei lei* (puppet show) and the *ying hsi* (shadow play) were early dramatic forms that flourished from the Han through the Sung dynasties. They were accompanied by the *ch'ing shang yüeh*. An important form of musical drama, the *chu kung t'iao*, appeared in the 11th century. It was sung without action. It was popular until the emergence of the first true musical theater, the *tsa chü* of the Yüan dynasty (1271–1368).

Tsa chü, usually referred to as *pei ch'ü* (northern drama), had four acts and was strict in form. The southern drama, first known as *hsi wen* and later as *ch'uan chi*, flourished throughout Ming and Ch'ing times. Effusive in style, it had scores of scenes, with different modes used even within each scene. In the 16th century a new singing style was adopted in the performance of *ch'uan chi*, which became known as *k'un chü*. By the early 19th century it was replaced in popularity by *ching hsi* which was a merger of various provincial schools of drama. Although *ching hsi*, the Peking opera, has much folk influence in its music and remains popular today, *k'un ch'ü* persists as a revered classical form and can still be heard. The principal instrument for *k'un ch'ü* is the *ti;* for *ching hsi*, the *hu ch'in*.

Modern Developments. Jesuit musicians began performing European music in China by the end of the 16th century and were soon patronized by the court. However, this music never reached the people and declined by the end of the 18th century. A more broadly based interest did not develop until about a hundred years later. By the turn of the 20th century, Chinese students began studying music in Europe and the United States, and soon afterward Western orchestras and music schools were established in China. Meanwhile, there was a strong effort to revive and reform Chinese traditional music. Under the Communist regime there has also been an attempt to integrate Western techniques with Chinese musical concepts and forms. Thus the cultivation of Western music, the reform of traditional music, and the revival of lost musical practices apparently have all been undertaken in an effort to create a new national music.

Instruments. Because of the great variety of timbre used in Chinese music and of the philosophical interest in relating these timbres to the elements in nature, the instruments were classified early in Chinese history according to the eight kinds of material—stone, metal, silk, bamboo, wood, skin, gourd, and clay—prominently featured in the instruments.

The most commonly used solo instruments are the *ch'in, p'i p'a, cheng,* and *hsiao.* The *ch'in,* the long zither, is capable of innumerable inflections in pitch and timbre. The favorite instrument of scholars and artists since the time of Confucius, it is the most characteristic Chinese musical instrument. Over 100 symbols are used to indicate the subtle inflections that give the music its elusive quality. These symbols, called *chien tzu,* indicate how the strings are to be plucked, tapped, or pulled and how the left-hand fingers should glide over the strings to produce microtonal changes in pitch and the many types of vibratos and tremolos. They also suggest poetic images for tone quality or the execution of details. For example, a certain portamento should suggest "a flying seagull touching down," and a tap by the left finger "the echo in an empty valley."

The *p'i p'a*, a short lute, was introduced from Central Asia during the Southern and Northern dynasties of the 4th to 6th centuries A.D. It became popular during the T'ang dynasty and developed into a virtuosic solo instrument. Among the other solo instruments are the *cheng,* a long zither with movable bridges, and the *hsiao,* a vertical flute made of bamboo, introduced by the Tibetans during the Han dynasty.

Theory of Music. The Chinese tonal system is founded on the 12 pitches of the octave, called *lü lü,* calculated from the cycle of fifths. This cycle of fifths, similar to the Pythagorean, was first described by Kuan Tzu (died 645 B.C.). Either a pentatonic (5-tone) or a heptatonic (7-tone) scale is built on each of the 12 pitches. Each of the scales then serves as the gamut for five pentatonic or seven heptatonic modes called *t'iao.* All together, 60 pentatonic and 84 heptatonic modes are possible. All are used in *ya yüeh* and considerably less in *su yüeh,* depending on the dynasty.

Temperament. The philosophical significance attached to the tones in Chinese music led to the belief that the determination of a fundamental absolute pitch (the *huang chung,* or yellow bell) and the generation of the other pitches from this fundamental one was a matter of first importance to each dynasty.

In the application of the cycle of fifths, 12 fifths are equal to 7 octaves in theory, but in actuality are not. The discrepancy, which is about a quarter of a semitone and which is known as the Pythagorean comma, caused the West to adopt the equal temperament system to facilitate modulation to all keys. In China, however, several systems were proposed. An approximate equal temperament system was recommended by Ho Cheng-t'ien as early as the 5th century A.D., but Chu Tsai-yü was the first to arrive at the correct mathematical solution in a treatise of 1584, almost half a century before Marin Mersenne's exposition in 1636. Among the notable other systems was the 53-tone system with an imperceptible comma. It was proposed by Ching Fang in the 1st century B.C. and by Nicolaus Mercator in the West in the 17th century A.D.

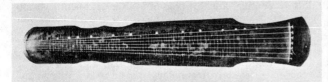

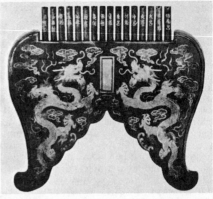

CHINESE MUSICAL INSTRUMENTS

The *ch'in*, or long zither (*above*), is the most characteristic Chinese instrument. A favorite since Confucius' time, it is capable of subtle inflections in pitch and timbre. Others are: the *p'ai hsiao*, or pan pipes (*above right*); *p'i p'a*, or short lute (*below left*); *yüeh ch'in*, or flat lute (*center*); *erh hu*, or fiddle.

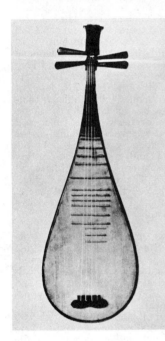

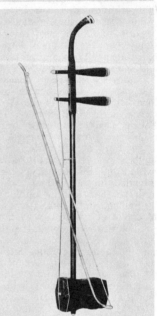

ALL PHOTOGRAPHS FROM CHOU WEN-CHUNG

Notation. A pitch notation employing the names of the 12 pitches has evolved since the Chou dynasty and was used for *ya yüeh*. During T'ang and Sung times a notation with simplified Chinese ideograms, called *tzu p'u*, was used in *su yüeh*. It was similar in principle to the letter notation of the West, but since the Ming dynasty another related notation called the *kung ch'ih p'u* has been in use.

CHOU WEN-CHUNG, *Columbia University*

Further Reading: Levis, John H., *Foundations of Chinese Musical Art* (New York 1964); Van Aalst, J. A., *Chinese Music* (New York 1964).

17. Communications Media

Written communications played an enormous role in the development of Chinese culture. Inscriptions from the Shang dynasty (1523–1028 B.C.) reveal the existence of an advanced system of writing. Records of important events, as well as an extensive literature and philosophy, were recorded in the Chou dynasty (1027–256 B.C.). With the development of the Chinese state from the Ch'in-Han period (221 B.C. to 220 A.D.) communications were increasingly tied to political affairs since most literate people were in or aspired to government service.

The first newsletters originated in the Han dynasty when information was sent to provincial authorities in the form of a "metropolitan gazette," or *ti pao*—known as *tsa-pao* in the T'ang dynasty (618–906 A.D.), as *ch'ao-pao*, *pien-pao*, and *hsiao-pao* in the Sung (960–1279), and as *ching-pao* and *kuan-pao* in the Ch'ing (1644–1912). An elaborate system of military roads and post relays, using both horses and foot couriers, with stations 10 *li* (about 3 miles) apart existed from the Ch'in–Han period on. The average speed of transmission was 300 *li* (100 miles) a day, although faster time could be made, using relays. This communications system developed further in the T'ang dynasty with the establishment of a bureau of official reports (*chin tsou yüan*, later *t'ung cheng ssu*) and by the Sung and later dynasties there were several kinds of gazettes and tabloids containing news from all corners of the empire. Special events were also described in bulletins, on wall posters, and by itinerant storytellers.

An important development in the spread of communications in China resulted from the invention of paper in the Han period (202 B.C.–220 A.D.) and of printing in the T'ang. By the 7th century, full-page wood-block texts or pictures were being run off, and an entire Buddhist sutra was printed as early as 868 A. D. In the 10th century, authorities undertook to print all the Chinese classics and the Buddhist religious texts, and soon thereafter the Taoist canon. Movable type was developed in the 11th century, although block printing remained the dominant form in China. Books of all types were printed in large numbers during the Sung dynasty and thereafter by both public and private printing houses. In fact, it has been estimated that in the 18th century more written records were extant in Chinese than in all other languages put together. One of the largest works ever compiled in a single edition, the *Complete Library of Four Treasures* (*Ssu K'u Ch'uan Shu*), comprising 3,450 complete works in 36,000 volumes, was completed in the late 18th century. Censorship, which was practiced frequently in China, also reached a peak at this time when the Manchu emperors sought to remove all seditious interpretations of the classics, and some 2,300 works were ordered suppressed.

Emergence of Modern Communications. The development of modern mass media in China followed the intrusion of the Western countries into China in the 19th century. The traditional-style Peking gazette, a court transcript (*kung-men ch'ao*), a provincial official paper (*yüan-men ch'ao*), and even private newsletters specializing in the news of the court, edicts, and memorials, existed in 19th century China, but they were intended for officialdom and not for the public at large. The reading public was at most 10 to 20 million, and perhaps several tens of thousands of copies of gazettes were circulated.

The first Western-style publications in China, started by Protestant missionaries, were intended for the general public. Such were a Chinese monthly (*Ch'a Shih Shu Mei Yueh T'ung Chi Ch'uan*), published in Malacca in 1815–1821, and the first periodical published on the mainland (*Tung Hsi Yang K'ao Mei Yueh T'ung Chi Ch'uan*), issued at Canton in 1833–1837. The earliest Chinese daily was the *Chung Wai Hsin Pao*, the Chinese edition of the *China Mail*, published in Hong Kong from 1858. The oldest Chinese-run daily was the *Hua Tzu Jih Pao*, published there from 1862. The largest pre-World War II paper, the *Shen Pao*, was founded in Shanghai in 1872, while Wang T'ao, called the father of Chinese journalism, began the *Hsun Huan Jih Pao* in Hong Kong in 1874.

By the end of what is considered the first period of the development of a modern Chinese press, on the eve of the Sino-Japanese War (1894–1895), there were an estimated dozen modern-style newspapers in the principal port cities of China. The *Shen Pao* and *Hsin Wen Pao* at Shanghai survived as important papers into the 20th century, while a new group of revolutionary papers, influenced by the famous writer Liang Ch'i-ch'ao, emerged in Shanghai, Hong Kong, and Japan in the late 1890's and early 1900's. Among those papers that survived the fall of the Manchus, the Tientsin *Ta Kung Pao* was the most famous. The leading publishing house of pre-Communist China, the Commercial Press (*Shang Wu Yin Shu Kuan*) was founded in Shanghai in 1896 and began to publish the periodical *Eastern Miscellany* (*Tung Fang Tsa Chih*), in 1901.

Spreading literacy—which increased from perhaps 5% to 20% by the first third of the 20th century and to over 50% after mid-century—and urbanization greatly increased the audience for mass communications in China. China, however, has remained overwhelmingly rural, and modernization has been delayed, first by a conservative tradition and then by revolution and war.

Western technology played a key role in the development of mass communications in China. The British-owned Great Northern Telegraph Company linked Hong Kong and Shanghai by cable in 1871 and shortly thereafter opened lines to Japan. The Chinese government founded the Chinese Telegraph Company in 1881, and cables were laid to Tientsin (1879–1881), Peking (1884), and Hankow (1882–1884). The government took over all telegraph lines in 1902 and in 1906 established a ministry of posts and communications (Yu Ch'uan Pu, later Chiao T'ung Pu). By 1937 there were over 59,230 miles (95,320 km) of cable, and the figure had doubled by the mid-1950's. Local telephone service was begun in Shanghai in 1881, and long distance service came into use after 1900. By 1937 there were 33,415 miles (53,775 km) of telephone line, while some 90,000 miles (145,000 km) were in use by the late 1950's. Wireless communications developed after 1905, and radio transmitters and receivers were introduced in some of the port cities by the 1920's. In the 1930's many private and public broadcasting stations came into operation, and they blanketed the country by 1950. The Chinese post office, founded in 1896, replaced the old postal system and by 1944 maintained 25,795 post offices covering 242,422 miles (390,130 km) of delivery.

The radical press, most notably the *New Youth* (*Hsin Ch'ing Nien*), founded in Shanghai in 1915, played a key role in the development of the Chinese Communist revolution. Periodicals of all types appeared at an increasing rate, and by 1921 there were 550 dailies, 46 10-day periodicals, 54 fortnightlies, 300 monthlies, and 4 quarterlies. Ten years later an estimated 900 periodicals, including 300 important dailies, were being read by over 30 million people. In the early 1930's, the Shanghai *Shen Pao* and *Hsin Wen Pao* had the largest circulation, with about 150,000 subscribers each, and the *Tung Fang Tsa Chih* led among periodicals, with 45,000 readers in 1931.

Censorship in pre-Communist China varied according to local conditions. There was rigorous censorship during the last years of Manchu rule and under Yüan Shih-k'ai (1914–1916). During the 1930's and 1940's the Nationalist government suppressed leftist and Communist writers and critics of the government generally. The Kuomintang maintained a central publicity department and a censorship department, but its power varied from province to province. Nationalist press controls continued to a lesser extent on Taiwan after 1949. The government there publishes the *Central Daily* (*Chung Yang Jih Pao*) and runs a central broadcasting station. Mass communications have developed greatly on the island where there were 19 dailies, 145 radio stations, and 2 television stations in the mid-1960's.

Communications in Communist China. Under the Communists since 1949, the press has been controlled to an unprecedented degree. All expression is considered political, and all citizens are expected to "speak out." Many pre-1949 books are proscribed, and mass organizations practice "positive censorship," proclaiming the virtues of socialism. In 1951 the Communist party alluded to 1.5 million active propagandists, a number that later increased greatly. Their job is to publicize the themes of a succession of mass campaigns involving every citizen of the People's Republic. The more important of these campaigns were the 1951 "Resist America, aid Korea campaign" and its counterpart for the communications media, the attack on the movie praising a 19th century reformer, Wu Hsun; the 1954–1955 campaigns against several prominent intellectuals and against standard interpretations of the famous novel *Dream of the Red Chamber;* the 1956–1958 antirightist campaigns; and the "Great Proletarian Cultural Revolution" beginning in the mid-1960's. The latter grew out of a series of "learn from the army" campaigns, all of which involved an unprecedented use of the mass media. These devoted almost all their space and time to the campaigns, while reading and discussion groups ensured the attention of the populace. Wall posters became an important source of information for the populace and for foreign newsmen, and they also were the instruments through which political trial balloons were launched and official pronouncements were issued. They served as the public arena in which the relative strength of the opposing factions in the political struggle were tested.

As early as the 1930's, the Chinese Communists published 34 journals in South China, and during World War II they circulated over 100 periodicals in the north. The New China News Agency (Hsin Hua She) was founded in 1937, replacing the Red China News Agency whose history went back to 1929. The party newspaper, *Jen Min Jih Pao* (*People's Daily*), with a circulation ranging from about 500,000 to 750,000, began publication in 1948. The authoritative party journal *Hung Ch'i* (*Red Flag*) was founded in 1958 to supersede *Hsüeh Hsi* (*Study*). Since 1957, other important visual communications have been carried in the big character posters (*ta tzu pao*). Popular literature, opera, and theater also convey government propaganda to the masses. The propaganda department of the central committee of the Chinese Communist party is the highest decision-making information body in China, while the government maintains a ministry of culture and a ministry of communications as well as the New China News Agency.

Some 83 radio stations and 1 million receiving sets existed on the mainland in 1950. By 1956 there were 1.5 million receivers, and the number had increased to an estimated 8 million by 1963, with signals being transmitted from 450 broadcasting stations. In addition, radio loudspeakers constantly relay programs in most gathering places in China.

An average of a dozen films a year were shot in the early 1950's. Production increased to 82 films in 1959, and these were shown at an estimated 1,200 movie houses and by 14,500 mobile projector teams. The estimated movie attendance rose from about 1.4 billion in 1956 to 4 billion in 1960, the largest in the world. Television has developed slowly in China since the 1950's, and by 1964 there were an estimated 30 television stations.

Periodical production has varied from about 400 titles in 1921 to perhaps 900 titles in 1934,

HARRY REDL, FROM BLACK STAR

POSTERS have been used by the Communist government to inform people about the "cultural revolution."

275 titles in 1950, and an estimated 310 titles in 1961. The 98 publishing houses that existed in 1950 were reduced to 82 by the mid-1960's, but book production rose from 12,000 titles in 1950 to over 30,000 in about 1.8 billion copies in 1956 and 46,000 titles in 2.4 billion copies in 1959. It fell again to 5,180 titles in 1964. In addition, 20,000 serial picture books in 600 million copies were published annually in the 1950's. There were about 90 regular newspapers in 1950, over 800 in 1957, and about 1,900 in 1959, with a circulation of almost 5 billion. However, the number of newspapers declined in the 1960's.

Publications concentrate on technical or ideological subjects. Of the former many are translations, of which some 27 million copies were distributed in 1957. Ideologically, the mass media are devoted to the inculcation of major Marxist tenets such as the theory of the class struggle, the dictatorship of the proletariat, and the building of socialism.

JAMES P. HARRISON
The City University of New York

Bibliography

Britton, Roswell S., *The Chinese Periodical Press, 1800–1912* (Shanghai 1933).
Carter, Thomas F., *The Invention of Printing in China and Its Spread Westward*, rev. by L. C. Goodrich (New York 1955).
Chu, Chia-hua, *China's Postal and Other Communication Services* (London 1937).
Houn, Franklin W., *To Change a Nation* (Glencoe, Ill., 1961).
Hsieh, Jan-chih, *The Press of Free China* (Taipei 1959).
Nunn, G. Raymond, *Publishing in Mainland China* (Cambridge, Mass., 1966).
Pye, Lucien W., ed., *Communication and Political Development* (Princeton, N. J., 1963).
Yu, Frederick T. C., *Mass Perusasion in Communist China* (New York 1964).

CHINA, Great Wall of, the largest defensive barrier ever built by men. About 1,500 miles (2,414 km) long, it stretches from Shanhaikuan on the Gulf of Chihli (Po Hai), along the northern frontier of China, to Chiayukuan in Kansu province in the west.

In the 3d century B. C., the first Ch'in emperor connected the walls that had been built by feudal lords during the Chou dynasty. Repairs and extensions were made in various periods, notably during the Ming dynasty, from which time most of the present wall dates. Many sections no longer exist.

The wall is built mostly of rubble, although the western sections are of tamped earth and important passes are of brick or masonry. The width varies from 15 feet (4.6 meters) to 40 feet (12.2 meters) at the base, and from 12 feet (3.7 meters) to 35 feet (10.7 meters) at the summit. Its height ranges from 20 feet (6.1 meters) to 50 feet (15.2 meters). Watch towers were set at regular intervals, and troops summoned by beacon fire could be transported quickly along the top of the wall.

JAMES R. SHIRLEY
Northern Illinois University

CHINA GRASS. See RAMIE.

CHINA LAKE is an unincorporated community in south central California, in Kern county, 112 miles (180 km) northeast of Los Angeles. It is the post office and town for the U. S. Naval Weapons Center (formerly U. S. Naval Ordnance Test Station), an important center of rocket and guided missile experimentation, and is entirely within the base area. China Lake is administered by the Navy. Population: 11,105.

CHINA SEAS, arms of the Pacific Ocean off the east and south coasts of China.

East China Sea. The sea skirts the eastern coast of China from the Yellow Sea to the northwest south to Taiwan. It is bounded on the north by Korea, and on the east by Kyushu Island and the Ryukyu archipelago. The Korea and Tsushima straits connect the East China Sea with the Sea of Japan on the northeast. Approximately 485,-000 square miles (1,256,000 sq km) in area, the sea ranges from 100 to 600 feet (30 to 180 meters) in depth, except near the Ryukyus where it reaches about 9,000 feet (2,700 meters). The chief ports are Shanghai, Ningpo, and Foochow on the Chinese mainland coast, Keelung (Chilung) in Taiwan, and Nagasaki in Japan.

South China Sea. About 895,400 square miles (2,320,000 sq km) in area, the South China Sea is separated from the East China Sea by the Taiwan Strait. The sea extends southwest from Taiwan to Vietnam, Cambodia, Thailand, and the Malay Peninsula, and is bounded in the south by the secondary islands of Indonesia and Borneo. The Philippine Islands form the eastern boundary. The two major extensions of the sea are the Gulf of Siam and the Gulf of Tongking. On the east the Mindoro and Balabac straits connect it with the Sulu Sea; on the southwest the Strait of Malacca connects it with the Andamon Sea, and the Karimata Strait connects it with the Java Sea. Overlying a continental shelf (the Sunda platform) in the south, the sea is about 600 feet (180 meters) deep, but reaches 15,000 feet (4,600 meters) in the north. Known for its violent typhoons, the South China Sea is studded with islands and reefs, and is a major shipping lane from Europe to East Asia. Major ports are Swatow, Canton and Chankiang (Tsamkong) in China; Kaohsiung in Taiwan; Hong Kong; Macao; Haiphong in North Vietnam; Chalon in South Vietnam; Singapore; and Manila in the Philippines.

DAVID H. KORNHAUSER
University of Hawaii

CHINABERRY, chī'nə-ber-ē, a Chinese tree widely planted in the southern United States as an ornamental and shade tree. The chinaberry, known botanically as *Melia azedarach*, belongs to the mahogany family. It reaches a height of 45 feet (13.5 meters) and bears long clusters of fragrant lilac-colored flowers. Its fruits are yellow berries, ½ inch (13 mm) across, that remain on the tree during the early fall and winter. Birds are greatly attracted by these berries. The chinaberry's leaves, which may be 3 feet (1 meter) long, are composed of many leaflets from 1 to 2 inches (2 to 5 cm) long.

DONALD WYMAN
The Arnold Arboretum, Harvard University

CHINAN. See TSINAN.

CHINAWARE. See CERAMICS; PORCELAIN; POTTERY.

CHINCH BUG, chinch, a small destructive insect found throughout the United States, Canada, Mexico, Central America, and the West Indies. It is mainly a pest of corn and sorghums, although it may attack small grains and other plants belonging to the grass family.

The chinch bug has a slender black body about ³⁄₁₆ inch (0.6 cm) long. The base of the antennae and the legs are reddish or yellowish brown. The wing covers are whitish and are marked at the middle of their outer margins with a triangular patch of black.

Adult chinch bugs hibernate in almost any kind of ground cover, including clumps of native prairie grass, hedgerows, grassy fence rows, and along roadsides. They remain in hibernation until the temperature rises above 70° F (21° C) for several hours while the sun is shining. They then fly or walk to fields of small grain or to early-planted corn or sorghums. There, within a 3- or 4-week period, each female lays from 200 to 300 eggs in the ground or on the leaf sheaths or roots of crop plants. The bug requires from 30 to 40 days to complete its development. There are two or more generations annually.

Chinch bugs are controlled by plowing a furrow around the margin of the grain field and applying creosote to the furrow each day for about 2 weeks. Burning their hibernating quarters is of value in some areas where the insects overwinter in bunch grasses and debris.

Chinch bugs belong to the order Hemiptera, family Lygaeidae. The technical name of the species is *Blissus leucopterus*.

HOWARD L. MCKENZIE
University of California, Davis

CHINCHILLA, chin-chil'ə, a genus of South American rodents found from southern Peru and Bolivia to southern Chile. Chinchillas live at altitudes of from 3,000 to 15,000 feet (1,000 to 4,000 meters). They grow a remarkably soft dense fur of long, silky hair. The fur, which is said to have more hairs per square inch than that of any other animal, is colored bluish, pearl, or brownish gray, with light blackish-tinged marks. The underparts are yellowish white. Chinchillas have bushy tails marked with brown or black and long white or black vibrissae ("mustaches"). The head is broad, with large eyes and ears. Chinchillas range from 9 to 15 inches (23 to 38 cm) long, plus a tail of 3 to 10 inches (7.5 to 25 cm), and weigh from 1 to 2 pounds (450 to 900 grams). The females are larger than the males.

Chinchillas are gregarious; colonies of up to 100 individuals used to be frequent, but years of uncontrolled hunting—by natives for meat and by traders for skins—left the animals on the verge of extinction. They are nocturnal animals and strictly vegetarian, eating the plants that grow on the barren rocks of the Andean highlands, especially the iro, or spiny grass (*Festucca*). Water is obtained from dew that collects on plants.

Life Cycle. Chinchillas take a single mate for life. The female is the active partner during courtship. Litters of 1 to 6 are born after a gestation period of 112 days; from 1 to 3 litters are born in a year. In captivity the estrous cycle lasts 24 days, with two days of estrus, or heat. The young nurse for 45 days, leave the parents at 10 weeks of age, and become sexually mature at 5 to 8 months. The life-span in the wild is about 10 years; in captivity, up to 20 years.

Fur Commerce. Chinchilla pelts are among the highest-priced in the international fur market. During the period of heaviest demand, some 200,000 skins were exported from South America in a single year. Fur coats of wild chinchilla have been sold for as high as $100,000. Practically extinct in Peru and nearly exterminated in Argentina, Chile, and Bolivia, chinchillas are now protected by law in those countries. The establishment of fur farms has also helped save them from complete extinction. The first farm was established in 1923 near San Antonio de los Cobres, Argentina, with a colony of 36 animals. This pioneer enterprise was not successful. In 1924 a few animals were taken from Chile to Inglewood, Calif. This new farm soon became the largest chinchilla ranch in the world and was the source of the animals used to establish sev-

HEDGECOCK, FROM MONKMEYER

Chinchilla

eral other farms in North America and Europe. The raising of chinchillas in captivity has lowered the price of the skin, but it still remains the most expensive pelt in the fur trade, considering its size and weight.

Classification. There are two species of chinchilla and a few local races. *Chinchilla brevicaudata* is the largest in total length. It once ranged from the high Andes of Peru to northwestern Argentina, but it is now extinct in the northernmost part of its range. *Chinchilla lanigera* is smaller in total length, but in contrast to *C. brevicaudata*, its tail is longer than the combined length of the head and body. It is found in northern Chile to about 30° south latitude. The chinchillas and the viscachas (*Lagidium* and *Lagostomus*) constitute the family Chinchillidae.

FERNANDO DIAS DE AVILA-PIRES
Universidade do Brasil

Further Reading: Hodgson, Robert G., *Modern Chinchilla Pens and Equipment* (New Hartford, N.Y., 1956); Houston, John W. and Prestwich, *Chinchilla Care* (Gardena, Calif., 1951).

CHINCHÓN, chēn-chôn', **Conde de** (1590?–1647), Spanish colonial governor. Luis Gerónimo Fernández de Cabrera Bobadilla Cerda y Mendoza, was born in Madrid. He was viceroy of Peru from 1629 to 1639. During this period the useful properties of cinchona bark—which was named *Cinchona* in his wife's honor—were discovered, and important explorations of the Amazon were made. Spanish cruelties caused a revolt among the Urn Indians near Lake Titicaca, which Cabrera had difficulty in suppressing. He died near Madrid in 1647.

CHINCHOW, jin'jō', is a city in the western part of Liaoning province, China, on the western Manchurian plain. The Shenyang-Chengte and Peking-Shenyang railroads pass through Chinchow, giving it considerable strategic importance. In the past, Chinchow was a trade center linking the southern part of the Manchurian plain with the mountainous Jehol region. In addition to its present importance as a hub of transportation, Chinchow is a center of oil refining and the production of chemicals, machinery, and textiles. Population: (1957) 400,000.

CHENGTSU WU, *Hunter College*

CHINDWIN RIVER, in northwestern Burma, the chief tributary of the Irrawaddy River. Approximately 550 miles (885 km) long, it rises in the Patkai and Kumon mountains of the north and flows through the Hukwang valley and the Naga Hills. The river follows a southwesterly course until it reaches Kalewa, where it turns east and then continues southeast to join the Irrawaddy north of Pakokku. The main stream is navigable to Kindat (240 miles, or 385 km) in the dry season and as far as Homalin (380 miles, or 610 km) during the rainy season.

CHINESE CABBAGE. See CABBAGE.

CHINESE CHECKERS is a game played by 2 to 6 players with colored marbles on a hexagonal checkered board. It is a modern version of the 19th century English *Halma* (a Greek word meaning "leap"), and became popular in the United States in the 1930's. Generally the board is manufactured in two sizes. The smaller size accommodates 10 marbles (men) in the starting base, or *pen* (a triangular enclosure). The larger board has places for 15 men in each pen. Each player receives 10 (or 15) marbles of a distinctive color and places them in the depression in the pen. Contestants may compete individually or as partners. If the latter, the players sit directly opposite each other and assist each other in play. The object of the game is for a contestant to move all of his men to the pen directly opposite his starting point. The first player or side to complete this transfer wins the game.

The players move one piece at a time, in turn; the move of any man may be a *step* or a *hop*. The step is a move to an unoccupied adjacent square in any of six directions. The hop is a jump over a man on an adjacent point to an unoccupied point beyond, adjacent and on the same line. The pieces hopped may be either friendly or adverse, but the men jumped are not removed from the boards. A player starting a hopping move may continue to jump as long as he can, but he may not combine a step and a hop on the same turn. In addition he is not compelled to make a hopping move or continue hopping farther than he wishes.

The quickest way to advance is to string out some of the men to form a *ladder* from the original base toward the goal and to advance rearmost pieces by hops up the ladder.

FRANK K. PERKINS, *Boston "Herald"*

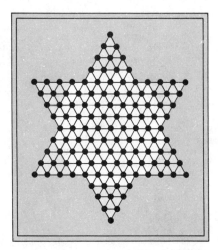

Chinese checkers can be played on a board shaped like a hexagram. The one shown here has starting enclosures for 10 marbles for each person playing.

CHINESE COOKING. Within the realm of culinary art, Chinese cooking is one of the most popular and highly praised. Its influence embraces all Far Eastern nations and reaches as far west as the Hawaiian Islands. In everyday food preparation it can be timesaving and inexpensive; for formal occasions it can be sophisticated, infinite in variety, and extravagant. The essence of Chinese cooking lies in the insistence that food must satisfy taste and provide flavor, however humble and simple the ingredients.

Characteristics. The use of many different parts and forms of food, such as bamboo shoots, water chestnuts, lotus roots, shark's fin, bird's nest, turtle meat, duck's tongue, bear's paw, fish lips and gills, and lily blossoms, has given Chinese dishes an exotic reputation. Most of the dishes consist of a mixture of foodstuffs. Meat and vegetables are often prepared together, with seasonings and flavorings added during the cooking. Meticulous cutting of the food into small pieces is stressed, because small pieces not only can be handled better with chopsticks (q.v.), the implements used in eating, but also have more surface areas exposed to heat and seasonings. In addition, with small pieces cooking time can be shortened and fuel saved. The different shapes and sizes add to the appearance of dishes, providing harmony or rendering variety as the occasion requires.

In very ancient times the Chinese, like all other primitive peoples, relied on fishing and hunting for food. As time progressed, both animal meat and farm products became part of the Chinese diet. Still later there was a tendency toward a diet heavy in plant food; and with the introduction of Buddhism, which frowns on killing any living thing, and with China's great population increase during the T'ang and Sung dynasties, this tendency toward a predominantly vegetarian, and, therefore cheaper, diet became pronounced.

The modern Chinese diet, based on an agricultural economy that is squeezed by a huge, ever-increasing population, continues to consist mostly of foods of plant origin, supplemented by small amounts of meat. Instead of butter and other animal fats, Chinese cooking employs vegetable oils, such as cottonseed, corn, soybean, and peanut. A number of bean products are present at almost every Chinese meal, in the form of bean sprouts, bean curd, soybean milk, and soy sauce. Among the grains, rice is of primary importance, especially south of the Yangtze River. Other mainstays for Chinese meals are wheat and millet. Corn, barley, and *kaoliang* (a variety of grain sorghum) are used extensively in the north. Fresh seafood is used widely along the coastal areas, but not inland because of difficulties in transporting this food. Dehydrated and salted sea products are used in inland cooking, and they are often considered as delicacies or as therapeutic food.

Chinese food varies considerably throughout the nation, but methods of food preparation have long been standardized. Methods common to all regions include stewing, braising, simmering, deep-fat frying, roasting, and barbecuing, double-boiler cooking, and steaming. Baking rarely occurs in the home; boiling in a large amount of water is practically nonexistent. Blanching, however, is employed as a step in preparation of ingredients prior to cooking.

The proper cutting and preparation of food, quick intense heat, and accurate timing are essential elements in Chinese cookery. Upon these three items rests the success of the unique cooking method called *ch'ao,* which implies fast cooking in little fat over a quick fire accompanied by constant stirring. The oil, heated to a high temperature, quickly sears the meat to preserve the flavor, juiciness, and tenderness; it also preserves the crisp texture and attractive color of the vegetables. Fat also acts as a flavor extender, giving meat the fragrance of the accompanying vegetables and, in turn, giving the vegetables the flavor of the meat.

To develop or enhance the flavor of a Chinese dish, soy sauce is often used along with salt. Other common seasonings are monosodium glutamate in small amounts, sugar, honey, wine, mustard, hot pepper, curry, sesame paste, and oil. Common spices include Chinese peppercorn, star aniseed, cinnamon, and clove. Fresh ginger root, scallion, garlic, and leek are indispensable flavoring agents.

Types. There are five major schools of Chinese cooking: Shantung, Honan, Szechwan, Fukien, and Kwangtung (Cantonese). The Shantung and Honan schools represent northern regional cooking, where wheat flour is the staple. Shantung is noted for dishes prepared with wine stock; Honan is famous for sweet-and-sour sauce. Szechwan food is characterized by hot and peppery seasonings; this school of cooking produces the best dishes using ham and mushrooms. Fukien dishes utilize considerable amounts of seafood; the specialties are delicate in taste and light in body. This school is partial to sugar and *hung tsao* (red wine dregs) as seasonings.

The Cantonese school, offering the most variety and grandeur in its dishes, uses more expensive ingredients and herbs. Concentrated, rich stock is the base of many of its dishes. Cantonese cooking was the first to reflect foreign influence, and it played a major role in popularizing Chinese food in foreign lands. *Chop suey,* a dish which does not exist in China, was first improvised by early Cantonese restaurants abroad to cater to foreign tastes. While sweet-and-sour pork, *chow mein, wonton,* fried rice, and egg roll originated with other Chinese schools of cooking, they became popular Chinese food in the United States through Cantonese cuisine.

Non-Cantonese restaurants frequently carry a regional designation; they may specialize in Shanghai, Mandarin, or Szechwan cooking. Shanghai represents the cooking and foods along the Yangtze River; Mandarin, north of the Yangtze; and Szechwan, inland.

In restaurants featuring these types of cooking, various forms of steamed bread (*man t'ou, pao tzu*), noodles (*mein*), and other pastas (*ping, chiao tzu, wonton*) are available in addition to rice. In Cantonese restaurants these foods are served more often as appetizers or refreshments.

DOROTHY C. LEE
General Foods Kitchens

Bibliography
Chen, Joyce, *Joyce Chen Cook Book,* rev. ed. (New York 1967).
Chu, Grace Z., *The Pleasures of Chinese Cooking* (New York 1962).
Lee, Beverly, *The Easy Way to Chinese Cooking* (New York 1963).
Ma, Nancy Chih, *Mrs. Ma's Chinese Cookbook* (Rutland, Vt., 1961).
Miller, Gloria B., *The Thousand Recipe Chinese Cookbook* (New York 1966).
Wong, Ella-Mei, *Chinese Cookery* (New York 1967).

CHINESE EASTERN RAILWAY is a railroad line in northeastern China connecting Chita on the Trans-Siberian Railway with Vladivostok on the Sea of Japan. It crosses the Chinese provinces of Heilungkiang and Kirin and is about 918 miles (1,418 km) long. By secret Russo-Chinese treaties in 1896 and 1898, Russia secured concessions to build the railroad and a branch line from Harbin to Dairen and Port Arthur (the last two form present Lüta). The lines were completed in 1903 and were called the Chinese Eastern Railway. After the Russo-Japanese War of 1904–1905, Japan acquired the southern section of the railroad as far as Changchun and renamed the lower section the South Manchurian Railway.

The Chinese Eastern Railway was at first operated solely by the Russians, but, in 1924, China and Soviet Russia agreed to manage the line jointly, with a Russian as president. In 1935, four years after the Japanese invaded Manchuria, the USSR sold its interest to the Japanese. At the end of World War II, by a treaty in 1945, the Russians regained their interest in both railroads and operated them jointly as before. In 1950 a treaty with the Chinese Communists provided for the end of Russian control, and by the end of 1952 the entire Soviet interest had been turned over to Communist China.

CHARLES J. CHU, *Connecticut College*

CHINESE EVERGREEN, a popular houseplant closely related to the jack-in-the-pulpit. The Chinese evergreen (*Aglaonema modestum*) belongs to the arum family. It is native to the Philippines, where it grows 12 to 20 feet (3.5–6 meters) tall. The leaves are alternate and are 6 to 10 inches (15–25 cm) long, with long petioles that encircle the stem. The flower is a small greenish spike about 2 inches (5 cm) long and is hooded by a green to whitish leaflike structure similar to that of the jack-in-the-pulpit.

The Chinese evergreen makes a very good houseplant because it grows well in water or soil and does not require much direct sunlight. It is propagated by cutting off a piece of leafy stem and placing the base of it in water. After roots have sprouted, however, the plant grows better in soil than in water.

DONALD WYMAN
The Arnold Arboretum, Harvard University

ROCHE

Chinese evergreen

CHINESE-JAPANESE WARS, a series of armed conflicts between China and Japan from 1894 to 1945. The disputes generally centered on the control of northeastern Asia and were part of Japan's thrust for empire.

The War of 1894–1895. Traditional Japanese interest in Korea was strengthened as Japan modernized in the late 19th century. Korea had been under Chinese suzerainty for centuries, but the relationship had not been defined by treaty and was vague according to international law, as Japan realized. Japan forced a treaty of independence on Korea in 1876, and China, having no intention of relinquishing its traditional, dominant role, countered Japan's moves with a series of political maneuvers. The revolt of a Korean secret society in 1894 threatened the government and forced the pro-Chinese king to call for Chinese troops. The Japanese also sent troops, and war broke out on Aug. 1, 1894.

The modern military forces of Japan easily crushed the Chinese. The treaty of Shimonoseki (April 17, 1895) ended Chinese influence in Korea and gave Taiwan (Formosa), the Pescadores, the Liaotung Peninsula, and a large indemnity to Japan. Japan's quick success alarmed some of the Western powers, and the triple intervention of France, Germany, and Russia forced Japan to return the Liaotung Peninsula.

The war demonstrated China's weakness and set off a scramble for foreign concessions that threatened to dismember China. The shock of defeat stimulated reform and revolutionary movements among the Chinese. Russian attempts to intervene in Korea were defeated when Russia lost the Russo-Japanese War of 1904–1905. Japan acquired special rights in southern Manchuria and finally annexed Korea in 1910.

Japan's desire to protect and extend its position in North China caused more conflict. An attempt to establish a protectorate over China by the Twenty-one Demands of 1915 failed, but Japan obtained the former German rights in Shantung Province by the Versailles Treaty of 1919. Outraged sentiments in China strengthened Chinese revolutionary movements. The growth of Chinese nationalism and communism threatened Japan's interests in China at a time when growing Japanese patriotism demanded the extension of Japanese power.

The Mukden Incident. The Japanese patriotic movement was centered among officers of the Kwantung Army stationed in Manchuria. In 1929 the Manchurian warlord Chang Hsüeh-liang (q.v.) declared allegiance to the Chinese central government in Nanking and began working against Japanese interests. The Kwantung Army leaders, against government orders, staged a bombing incident near Mukden on Sept. 18, 1931, and used it as a pretext for the conquest of Manchuria. Since the Chinese government was unwilling to risk war with Japan, resistance was slight. On Feb. 18, 1932, the Japanese installed P'u-yi, the former Ch'ing (Manchu) emperor, as the puppet emperor of Manchukuo in March 1934. The League of Nations failed to take action despite the Lytton Commission's criticism of Japan.

The Shanghai Incident. Strong anti-Japanese sentiment against the Mukden Incident was expressed by a Chinese boycott of Japanese goods. Partly to force an end to the boycott, Japanese troops were landed at Shanghai on Jan. 28, 1932. Chinese forces resisted for more than a month, but finally had to withdraw. An agreement on May 5, 1932, established a demilitarized zone around Shanghai and ended the boycott.

From 1932 to 1937, Japan gradually encroached on Chinese sovereignty in northern China by a series of minor incidents. The failure of the Chinese government to resist these incursions led to increased attacks on the government by both Chinese Nationalists and Communists. On Dec. 12, 1936, Chang Hsüeh-liang and others kidnapped Chiang Kai-shek in Sian and held him for two weeks. With Communist support they forced him to accept a policy of united Chinese resistance against Japan.

The War of 1937–1945. The united front agreement marked the end of Chinese nonresistance. On July 7, 1937, a minor incident at the Marco Polo Bridge (Lukouchiao) near Peiping brought full-scale but undeclared war. During the next 18 months, Japanese forces captured most major cities, sealed off the Chinese from the sea, and forced the government to retreat to Chungking in western China. Only Russia provided assistance to China. Japan wanted a quick end to the war and made moves for a negotiated settlement. The Nationalists refused.

The low point of the Chinese resistance came in late 1938. By then, Japanese bombing of civilians, the rape of Nanking (December 1937), and the heroic actions of ill-equipped Chinese troops had moved world sentiment against Japan. When Britain and the United States announced the beginning of aid to China in December, morale improved.

The war was stalemated after 1938 and Japan turned to Southeast Asia and the realization of its Greater East Asia Co-Prosperity scheme. After the sneak attack on Pearl Harbor (Dec. 7, 1941) and Chiang Kai-shek's formal declaration of war on Japan the next day, the Chinese-Japanese War merged into World War II. Except for a limited offensive in 1944, the Japanese tried only to hold their positions. They controlled the major cities and lines of communication, although Chinese guerrilla bases behind Japanese lines harassed them constantly. The Nationalists held the southwest and west, while the Communists controlled the northwest. Tension between the Chinese forces sometimes erupted into open battle and was a hindrance to the Chinese war effort.

Results of the War. Japan surrendered unconditionally on Aug. 14, 1945. The American defeat of Japan stripped it of empire and left it subject to foreign occupation until 1952.

The war in China caused perhaps 50 million deaths and widespread destruction. Government morale was undermined by the war and the Nationalists proved incapable of solving the problems left in its wake. The dislocation of normal patterns of authority provided scope for Communist organization of peasant discontent and by 1945 about one fourth of the population lived under Communist-led regimes. An American mediation attempt under Gen. George C. Marshall failed in 1946, and by 1949 the Communists controlled all of China, except for Nationalist-held Taiwan (Formosa) and a few other, much smaller islands.

JAMES R. SHIRLEY
Northern Illinois University

Further Reading: Clyde, Paul H., *The Far East: A History of the Impact of the West on Eastern Asia,* 3d ed. (Englewood Cliffs, N. J., 1958); Lu, David J., *From the Marco Polo Bridge to Pearl Harbor* (Washington, D. C., 1961). Smith, Sara R., *The Manchurian Crisis, 1931–1932* (New York 1948).

CHINESE LANTERN, a popular perennial garden plant grown for its large red bladderlike fruit pods. Each pod is 2 inches (5 cm) long and contains a cherrylike ball in which the seeds are embedded. Sometimes the pods are dried and used as ornaments. The Chinese lantern, known botanically as *Physalis alkekengi,* ranges in height from 1 to 2 feet (30 to 60 cm) and spreads quickly by means of underground stems. Its oval leaves may be 3 inches (7 cm) long and the whitish flowers are nearly 1 inch (2.5 cm) across. The Chinese lantern is native from southeastern Europe to Japan.

DONALD WYMAN
The Arnold Arboretum
Harvard University

Chinese lantern (*Physalis alkekengi*)

CHINESE NEW YEAR is the most important and popular of Chinese festivals. Its date is fixed traditionally according to the Chinese lunar calendar as the second new moon after the winter solstice. Thus it falls somewhere between January 21 and February 19 on the Gregorian calendar. The Chinese New Year festival is still celebrated by the Chinese all over the world, although the Gregorian calendar has been China's official calendar for over 50 years.

No one knows how far back New Year celebrations go in Chinese history. Their religious background involves clearing away the bad luck of the old year and obtaining a new slate for the next. It was also believed that the various godlike spirits had to report on the past year to the ruler of heaven, the Jade Emperor. Many Chinese still open the celebrations by burning a paper image of Tsao Wang, the hearth god, thus sending him on his way one week before the new year. The fireworks that continue through the new year period begin at this time.

In keeping with the idea of clearing out the old, the New Year was thought to be an appropriate time for a thorough housecleaning and for the payment of debts. It is also a time for giving alms to the poor and for eating special lucky foods.

Usually on the day before New Year's Eve, men pay ceremonial visits to friends and associates, wishing them luck with the traditional greeting *kung-hsi fa-ts'ai,* meaning "happy greetings and may you gather wealth." On the last day of the year, final preparations are made for the family's New Year's Eve feast, the highlight of the celebration. Before the meal, all doors are sealed with paper strips to prevent the entrance of evil, and no one may enter or leave until these are removed shortly before dawn. After the meal, gifts are exchanged, and at midnight solemn greetings and family ceremonies occur.

For days after the New Year begins, businesses are shut down, and the time is devoted to rest or recreation. It is an especially exciting time for children because they receive presents of money in red envelopes. Birthdays are not celebrated in the same way as in the West, and since ages are figured from the New Year, this replaces the birthday. A child is one year old at birth and two years after the New Year, so that an infant may become two years old in a matter of hours.

Traditionally, the festivities last 15 days until the Lantern Festival, a time for parades of elaborate paper lanterns and street dances by dragons or "lions." For many of the poor, however, the celebrations only last a few days.

Each Chinese year is popularly known by one of the 12 animals of the Chinese Zodiac in the following order: rat (Aries), ox (Taurus), tiger (Gemini), hare (Cancer), dragon (Leo), serpent (Virgo), horse (Libra), sheep (Scorpio), monkey (Sagittarius), cock (Capricorn), dog (Aquarius), and boar (Pisces). These names provide a ready reference to the recent past, especially for the illiterate, because each name is used only once in 12 years.

JAMES R. SHIRLEY
Northern Illinois University

Further Reading: Eberhard, Wolfram, *Chinese Festivals* (New York 1952).

CHINESE NEW YEAR is ushered in with joyous festivities to celebrate the start of the lunar year. A paper dragon is carried through the streets to mark the start of the year of the dragon.

CH'ING DYNASTY, ching, the Manchu dynasty that ruled China from 1644 to 1912. Ch'ing means "pure" and is a short form of Ta Ch'ing.

The dynasty's origins reach back to Nurhachi (1559–1625), a chieftain of the Aisin Goro clan of the Ju-chen people in Manchuria. Nurhachi created the powerful military-economic Eight Banner System and began the conquest of Manchuria. The task was completed by his son, Abahai, who in 1635 forbade use of the term Ju-chen and replaced it with Mánchou (Manchu). He declared himself first emperor of the Ta Ch'ing, but it was his son, Fu-lin, who was enthroned in Peking in 1644 as the first Ch'ing emperor, the Shun Chih Emperor.

The Manchu conquest of China was facilitated by rebellions and by defectors who helped the Manchus take Peking. Final victory, however, proved difficult and was not achieved until 1683, when the Formosan regime founded by Cheng Ch'eng-kung (Koxinga) was destroyed.

The Ch'ing controlled China by stationing Manchu garrisions throughout the provinces. Official support of Confucianism legitimized their rule in Chinese eyes, while retention of the social order and sharing of power with Chinese leaders neutralized opposition. The dynasty was further stabilized by two intelligent and able emperors, K'ang Hsi (q. v.) and Ch'ien Lung (q. v.), who each ruled for 60 years. They expanded the empire so that, except during the Yüan dynasty, it reached its greatest extent.

EMPERORS OF THE CH'ING DYNASTY

Personal name		Temple name	Reign title	Reign years
Fu-lin	1638-1661	Shih Tsu	Shun Chih	1644-1661
Hsüan-yeh	1654-1722	Sheng Tsu	K'ang Hsi	1661-1722
Yin-chen	1678-1735	Shih Tsung	Yung Cheng	1723-1735
Hung-li	1711-1799	Kao Tsung	Ch'ien Lung	1736-1796
Yung-yen	1760-1820	Jen Tsung	Chia Ch'ing	1796-1820
Min-ning	1782-1850	Hsüan Tsung	Tao Kuang	1821-1850
I-chu	1831-1861	Wen Tsung	Hsien Feng	1851-1861
Tsai-ch'un	1856-1875	Mu Tsung	T'ung Chih	1862-1875
Tsai-t'ien	1871-1908	Te Tsung	Kuang Hsü	1875-1908
P'u-yi	1906-1967		Hsüan T'ung	1909-1912

Although the culminating period of Chinese traditional culture, the Ch'ing compares favorably with other periods in only a few aspects. Important developments were made in the ceramic arts and in philosophy, and one of China's greatest novels, the *Hung Lou Meng* (translated as the *Dream of the Red Chamber*), was written at this time. Officially sponsored works include the *K'ang hsi* dictionary and the 36,000-volume *Ssu-k'u ch'üan-shu (Imperial Manuscript Library)*.

By the early 19th century, China fell subject to internal decay. Increasing penetration by the West brought changes unprecedented in Chinese history, and the failure of the Ch'ing rulers to recognize the significance of occurrences helped bring an end to Imperial China. A series of defeats by foreign powers began with the Opium War, and the T'ai-p'ing Rebellion, although quelled, revealed the failure of Manchu power. In spite of natural disasters, internal disorders, and increasing foreign pressure, the Ch'ing dragged on until overthrown by revolutionaries in 1911.

JAMES R. SHIRLEY
Northern Illinois University

Further Reading: Giles, Herbert A., *China and the Manchus* (Cambridge, Mass., 1912); Hummel, Arthur W., *Eminent Chinese of the Ch'ing Period, 1644–1912*, 2 vols. (Washington 1943–1944); Latourette, Kenneth S., *The Chinese: Their History and Culture*, 4th rev. ed. (New York 1964).

CHINGHAI, ching'hī, is a large province of western China. The province's 278,378 square miles (721,000 sq km) are bordered on the southwest and south by Tibet. The name Chinghai, which is often spelled *Tsinghai*, means Blue Sea, and is derived from China's largest salt lake, Chinghai or Koko Nor (q. v.), located in the northeastern part of the province.

In the northeastern corner of Chinghai is the valley of the Hwang Ho (Yellow River) and Hwang Hsui. In the northwest are the brackish marshes of the Tsaidam Basin. In addition to alkaline marshes, the basin is marked by extensive grasslands and by belts of gravel and coarse sand. The Chinghai Plateau, in southeastern Chinghai province, is part of the Tibetan Plateau. This very extensive area has an average elevation of about 13,000 feet (4,000 meters).

More than half of Chinghai's population is Chinese; the balance is made up of Mongols, Tibetans, Kazakhs, Hui, Turkomans, and Salars. Sining, the provincial capital, is the main center of Chinese population. Since 1950 many new cities have been developed in the Tsaidam Basin, with Guermo the main industrial center.

Because of Chinghai's cold, dry climate, agricultural development is limited. Sheep grazing has been the traditional occupation of the people of the grassland. Modern industries include petroleum drilling and the making of machinery and chemicals. Woolen textiles and dairy products are industries of older date. Population: (1964) 2,500,000.

CHENGTSU WU, *Hunter College, New York*

CHINGHIZ KHAN. See GENGHIS KHAN.

CHINKIANG, jin'jē-äng', a city of Kiangsu province, China, is an important river port on the lower Yangtze. Located approximately 42 miles (68 km) east of Nanking, the city lies astride the Nanking-Shanghai railroad and is also traversed by the Grand Canal. Chinkiang functions as a trade link between northern and southern Kiangsu. Since it is located in the Yangtze delta, which is a densely populated and agriculturally very productive region, Chinkiang is one of the historical urban centers in this area.

Chinkiang's climate is hot and humid in summer, but spring and autumn are pleasant. The scenery of the area is beautiful. In Chinese literature "spring in Kaingnan" (the lower Yangtze plain) connotes the lovely springtime landscape of this region. Chao Shan, Peiku Shan, and King Shan are the famous scenic areas in the vicinity of the city. Chao Shan, a small island in the middle of the Yangtze, is especially well known for its scenery.

Traditional industries in Chinkiang include food processing, handicrafts, and silk. A special kind of silk fabric (called "Chinkiang silk"), rice vinegar, and preserved vegetables are the famous specialties of the city.

The history of Chinkiang goes back about 2,000 years. Marco Polo tells of the town and of the establishment of Nestorian Christian churches there, a fact confirmed by a Chinese record of about 1333. It was held from 1853 to 1857 by the T'ai-p'ing rebels, who left it a ruin, but the city was rebuilt after being opened to foreign trade under the Treaty of Tientsin (1858). From 1928 to 1949, Chinkiang was the capital of Kiangsu. Population: (1958 est.) 190,000.

CHENGTSU WU, *Hunter College, New York*

CHINOISERIE decoration was used (above) inside the lid of a French harpsichord (1754) and (right) on the panels of a late 18th century French secretary.

CHINLING, chin'ling', a mountain range in northern China, an eastern branch of the Kunlun Mountains. The name is also spelled *Tsinling.*

The Chinling runs in a east-west direction between the Wei and Han rivers across southern Kansu, southern Shensi, and western Honan provinces but is mainly in Shensi. It is part of the barrier that separates the northern loess land from the southern forest soils and historically often has checked invading tribes from the north. The southern slopes are gradual, while the northern peaks are rugged and almost impassable. The highest peak is Taipai Shan (about 12,000 feet, or 3,650 meters), about 75 miles (120 km) southwest of Sian.

CHINO, chē'nō, a city in California, in San Bernardino county, is 37 miles (60 km) east of Los Angeles. It is the center of an agricultural area, engaged in dairy farming, the raising of livestock and Thoroughbred horses, and the production of fruit, vegetables, hay, grain, and roses. The California Institution for Men, a state prison, is located nearby. The city is becoming increasingly suburban as the population pressures of Los Angeles move eastward.

Chino was founded in 1887 and incorporated as a city in 1910. It is governed by a mayor and council. Population: 20,411.

CHINOISERIE, shēn-wäz-ə-rē', the Oriental influence that affected European art and decoration, especially during the 17th and 18th centuries. The term also applies to the objects showing this influence. The arts of China were the chief source of inspiration for chinoiserie, but other Eastern countries also contributed their influence.

Early Chinoiserie. Since the time of Marco Polo's visit to China in the 13th century, the Western world has been fascinated by the exotic products of the East, and by stories of the splendors of the Orient. The artists of Italy were the first in the West to reflect this interest by incorporating Chinese motifs into their interior decoration and furniture design. By the 17th century this taste was well established in Italy; indeed, nearly all of the few surviving pieces of Venetian lacquer furniture from this period are decorated with raised gilt chinoiserie figures.

In England the taste for chinoiserie was well developed by the mid-17th century. The East India Company, quick to recognize the growing taste for Oriental objects, imported large quantities of lacquers and porcelains into England. It

became fashionable to install lacquer or porcelain plaques into room paneling and furniture forms. Oriental porcelains often were mounted in rich settings of gold or silver by European craftsmen. The diarist John Evelyn and other 17th century English writers describe houses furnished with Indian screens or paneled in the finest "japan," a term employed loosely to include lacquer imported from the Orient as well as the European imitation of it. In 1688, two Englishmen, John Stalker and George Parker, published *A Treatise on Japaning and Varnishing.* This extremely influential work included patterns for Oriental designs as well as a complete description of the manufacture of lacquer.

The English economist John Pollexfen, in his *A Discourse of Trade, Coyn and Paper Credit* (1697), refers to a group of artisans sent to China about 1670 to introduce patterns that would help Chinese artisans make their products more acceptable to the prevalent European taste. About 1700 another group of craftsmen went to India with a large quantity of English patterns to teach the Indians how to manufacture goods designed especially for the European market. Because it was popularly, but erroneously, believed that lacquer came from India (rather than from China) lacquerwork was often referred to as India work or Coromandel work, from the Coromandel coast of southeast India.

Later Chinoiserie. France, like England, embraced the taste for chinoiserie during the 17th century, and lacquer was used to decorate the furniture of the great *ébénistes* (makers of ebony furniture) of the period. The fashion for chinoiseries reached its height during the Louis XIV period, and remained popular during the 18th century, when it became an integral part of the Louis XV, or rococo, style. Fanciful Chinese figures, often combined with landscapes, were applied as ornamentation to furniture and other decorative art forms. *Ébénistes,* such as Bernard van Risenburgh, Mathieu Criaerd (Criart), and Jacques Dubois, made a specialty of lacquered furniture.

599

The rococo style was developed in England by Thomas Chippendale and other 18th century cabinetmakers and designers. The publication of Chippendale's book of designs, *The Gentleman and Cabinet-Maker's Director* (1754) provided patterns for furniture in the Chinese taste and for many kinds of ornamentation inspired by the Orient. The rococo style, which had spread throughout Europe by the mid-18th century, completely embraced chinoiserie details.

A taste for Oriental objects continued throughout the 18th century in both Europe and the American colonies. Chinese porcelains were especially prized and there was an active trade in porcelains made exclusively for the Western market.

In England, from about 1800 to 1830, there was a revival of chinoiserie, in the Regency style. The remodeling of the Royal Pavilion at Brighton (begun in 1817) stimulated a craze for Oriental art and furniture as well as English-made decorations in the Chinese manner. The taste for chinoiserie, though on a much diminished scale, continued through the entire 19th and into the 20th century.

JOSEPH T. BUTLER
Sleepy Hollow Restorations, Tarrytown, N.Y.

Further Reading: Fastnedge, Ralph, *English Furniture Styles from 1500 to 1830* (Harmondsworth, England, 1955); Honour, Hugh, *Chinoiserie: The Vision of Cathay* (London 1961); Symonds, Robert W., *Furniture Making in 17th and 18th Century England* (London 1955).

CHINON, shē-nôn', is a historic town in west central France. It is situated on the Vienne River, in the department of Indre-et-Loire, 25 miles (41 km) southwest of Tours.

Above the river, crowning a lofty rock that had been fortified by the Romans, are the ruins of the Château de Chinon. This ancient castle once belonged to the Plantagenet kings of England, and Henry II of England died here in 1189. The old town, beneath the castle, has changed little since the Middle Ages; medieval buildings are crowded on narrow, winding streets.

Chinon was the residence of several French sovereigns, and remained the seat of the court until 1450. Here, in 1429, Joan of Arc presented herself to Charles VII and revealed her mission of expelling the English from France. Across the river, at La Devinière, is the farmhouse in which the author François Rabelais was born. Population: (1962) 5,122.

CHINOOK, shi-noŏk', in meteorology, a warm, dry wind in the Great Plains of North America, blowing eastward from the Rocky Mountains in winter. "Chinook" is the local name of the *foehn*, which may occur on the leeward side of mountains anywhere in the world.

The chinook's characteristic warmth and dryness are the result of changes that an air mass undergoes as it crosses the Rocky Mountains. On the windward side of the mountains, wind carries the air up the slope. Decreasing atmospheric pressure at increasing altitudes cools the air and condenses much of its moisture, which precipitates as rain or snow. The latent heat of the condensing water vapor is added to the air; and as the air descends on the leeward side of the mountain, it is compressed and warmed. Thus, in the chinook, the air has lost moisture and has gained heat.

The temperature at a given location may rise as much as 50° F (about 28° C) in less than an hour after the onset of the chinook. Snow on the ground is melted or sublimed (evaporated before melting). The clearing away of the snow cover permits cattle to graze after the chinook. This result is a boon to ranchers because they need not store as much food for the cattle in the fall. See also WINDS.

JAMES E. MILLER
New York University

CHINOOK INDIANS, shi-noŏk', a tribe of North American Indians that lived mainly along the north side of the Columbia River in Washington. They spoke a language of the Chinookan family, which served as the basis for the Chinook jargon, the principal trade language used by Indians and whites along the Pacific coast from California to Alaska.

The Chinook were famous as middlemen in the early trade along the Columbia River between the whites on the coast and the Indians living in the interior. They levied tolls on other tribes using the river and transshipped goods, mainly furs, to European and American ships. It was through Chinook hands that most of the firearms, beads, flour, blankets, knives, and other European trade articles passed to the tribes of the interior.

Although their existence was known earlier, the Chinook were first described by the explorers Lewis and Clark in 1805. At that time the Chinook lived in large houses made of wooden planks and accommodating several families. Their economy was based largely on hunting, fishing (mainly of salmon), and collecting of wild vegetable foods. For hunting and fighting they used a bow with a layer of dried sinew attached to the back to increase its power. They were noted for their large dugout canoes, which served as a principal means of transportation.

Another outstanding feature of Chinook culture was the practice of head deformation. Infants' heads were flattened by pressing and binding a padded board against the forehead. The Chinook considered it a disgrace not to have a head flattened in this way.

The tribe was always small. Lewis and Clark estimated that there were 400 Chinook living on the Columbia River. By the mid-1800's the number had been reduced to about 100 as a result of a disastrous epidemic as well as mixing with the Chehalis Indians to the north, with whom they have since completely fused.

RICHARD A. GOULD
American Museum of Natural History

CHINQUAPIN, ching'kə-pin, any of several native American shrubs and trees closely related to the chestnut. Chinquapins belong to the beech family (Fagaceae). In the eastern United States the name is most often applied to *Castanea pumila,* a shrub or small tree that ranges from Pennsylvania to Florida and Texas. Its elliptical leaves grow from 2½ to 6 inches (6 to 15 cm) long and have toothed edges, with each tooth ending in a bristle. The fruits are round, very spiny or bristly burrs about 1½ inches (4 cm) across. Each burr usually contains only one small nut.

In the western United States, the term evergreen chinquapin is applied to *Castanopsis chrysophylla,* a giant tree native to Oregon and California. It reaches a height of 100 feet (30 meters) and bears broad, lustrous, dark green leaves from 2 to 5 inches (5 to 12 cm) long. The underside of each leaf is covered with short

CHINQUAPIN

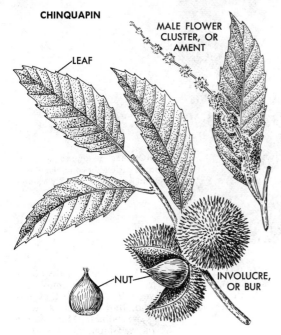

MALE FLOWER CLUSTER, OR AMENT

LEAF

NUT

INVOLUCRE, OR BUR

yellowish hairs. The fruits of this species are small prickly burrs about 1 inch (2.5 cm) in diameter. Enclosed in each burr is usually a solitary edible nut about ½ inch (13 mm) wide. Unlike the nuts of the chestnut, which ripen in one year, the nuts of the evergreen chinquapin take two years to mature. This species is valued because it grows well in poor, dry soils.

DONALD WYMAN
The Arnold Arboretum, Harvard University

CHINTZ, chints, is a fabric that receives its name from the glazed finish it is given. Chintz is used for summer draperies, kitchen and bathroom curtains, slipcovers, and summer dresses.

Chintz is usually made from a plain woven cotton cloth, generally printcloth or lightweight sheeting. The fabric may be printed with a small geometric design or a large floral pattern. It is then given a glaze or highly lustrous finish that is characteristic of this fabric.

Chintz glaze is sometimes made of wax or starch. Although chintz finished in this way is cheaper, the glaze is not permanent and will be removed when the fabric is washed or dry-cleaned. A permanent type of glaze is made with resin. Chintz made with a resin glaze is more expensive.

ERNEST B. BERRY, *School of Textiles*
North Carolina State University

CHINWANGTAO, chin'hwäng'dou', is a city in Hopeh province, China, located on the Gulf of Chihli (Po Hai), about 120 miles (195 km) northeast of Tientsin. Because it has a deep, ice-free natural harbor and good rail connections with southern Manchuria and Tientsin, Chinwangtao has in the 20th century become a major commercial port and naval base. An expansion of mining activities at the Kailan coal mines, some 60 miles (95 km) to the west, in the 1950's has enhanced the industrial importance of the entire region, increasing exports from Chinwangtao and bringing new industries — notably glass, light metals, and chemicals — to the city.

The popular beach resort of Peitaiho is located just southwest of Chinwangtao, and the historic city of Shanhaikwan, where the Great Wall of China (q.v.) starts, is a short distance to the northwest.

Opened to foreign trade in 1907, Chinwangtao was much frequented by European and American shipping and was used by the U. S. Navy during World War II. Since 1949, Chinwangtao has been a major naval station of the Chinese Communists. Population: (1957) 210,000.

CHENGTSU WU
Hunter College, New York

CHIOGGIA, kyôd'jä, the second-largest city of the lagoon of Venice, is one of Italy's leading fishing ports and a colorful seaside settlement. Its economy has for centuries been based on fishing. The fishing barges of Chioggia, flat-bottomed, with lateen sails made of orange-colored cloth, are well known in the Adriatic area. The suburb of Sottomarina, on the coastal sandspit *(lido)* that separates the lagoon from the open sea is a small but popular seaside resort.

Chioggia consists of a single island about 3,900 feet (1,200 meters) long and about 1,100 feet (350 meters) wide. It is divided into two parts by a canal. Narrow streets, called *calli,* run at right angles to the canal and create an outline resembling the spinal structure of a fish.

The chief attraction of Chioggia lies in its narrow streets, old houses, and colorful waterfront. The cathedral was originally built in the 11th century but was completely reconstructed by Longhena in 1674. Chioggia's oldest church, San Martino, was finished in 1392. Its outstanding feature is a 14th century polyptych by Paolo of Venice. The most interesting civic building is the Granaio (originally a grain warehouse), of the 14th century, now the fish market.

Chioggia, probably of Roman origin, was already a town second in importance only to Venice in the 8th century. The highlight of its long history was its siege, in 1379, by the fleet of Genoa. Although the city had to surrender and was sacked, the Venetians blockaded the Genoese there soon after and forced their surrender, thus winning a final victory over their great rivals. Population: (1966) 47,451.

GEORGE KISH, *University of Michigan*

CHIOS, kī'os, is an island in Greece, in the eastern Aegean Sea, close to the western shore of Turkey. The modern Greek form of the name is *Khíos.* The island has an area of 321 square miles (831 sq km) and forms, with neighboring islands, the department of Chios. Chios is also the name of the island's chief city.

Modern Chios is known for its cereals, olive oil, tobacco, citrus fruits, and especially for mastic, a resin used in the production of gum, varnish, and a Chiote liquor. The island has suffered from many earthquakes; particularly destructive ones occurred in 1389, 1546, and 1881.

History. Chios is said to have been the birthplace of Homer. In Classical and Byzantine times it was famous for its wine. A much fought-over commercial center, Chios was held by the Persians, the Romans, the Byzantines, the Arabs, the Venetians, the Genoese, and the Ottoman Turks. During the Genoese occupation, which lasted from 1304 to 1329 and from 1346 to 1566, Chios became an important link in the Genoese commercial routes that stretched to the Black Sea. Following the

CHIOS has a rugged shoreline that is visible beyond the Greek Orthodox church of this village.

Turkish capture of the island in 1566, native Chiote merchants traded as far afield as Holland, England, and Russia, and Chiote business firms became far-flung enterprises. Chios built up a great commercial fleet. The Turks granted the island an autonomous system, which allowed for the local collection of taxes. The mastic tree plantations were assigned to the mother of each sultan of Turkey (the Validé Sultan), who annually received a fixed sum from the revenues they brought in.

In 1822, after the outbreak of the Greek war for independence, a rebellion (which did not have the backing of a majority of the islanders) began in Chios. In retribution for this and for Greek uprisings in the Peloponnesus, the Turks landed a military force, which mercilessly slaughtered the islanders. Of the estimated population of 100,000, about 20,000 were killed, and more than 45,000 were sold into slavery; other thousands fled. Reports of the slaughter helped stir up anti-Turkish, pro-Greek sentiments in western Europe. In 1824 the French artist Eugène Delacroix added to the general indignation in Europe by depicting the massacre in a painting. But Chios remained Turkish.

With the outbreak of the first Balkan War in 1912, Greece took the island. During World War II it was occupied by German and Italian troops. It was liberated by British and Greek forces in 1944. Population: (1961) of the department, 62,223; of the island, 60,061.

GEORGE J. MARCOPOULOS
Tufts University

buds, seeds, berries, and nuts, and occasionally of small animals. Active by day, chipmunks depend mainly on their eyesight. Although they forage mainly on the ground, they also climb well. Litters of 1 to 8 young are born in May after a gestation period of 31 days. Chipmunks hibernate during the winter, but arouse themselves at regular intervals to eat some of their cached larder and to perform their toilet in a special corner.

Chipmunks are classified in the family Sciuridae, order Rodentia. A closely related species (*Eutamias sibiricus*) is found in regions of the Far East.

A. W. F. BANFIELD
National Museum of Canada

Chipmunk

CHIPMUNK, chip'mungk, any of 17 species of small, ground-dwelling North American squirrels. The slender body of a chipmunk is 8 to 12 inches (22–30 cm) long, including the 4-inch (10-cm) tail. The coat is short and fine, and the tail has a short, flattened brush. The flanks and tail are tawny, and the belly is white. Five black stripes run down the back, separated by gray or creamy stripes; the cheeks are streaked with brown. The single species of eastern North America (*Tamias striatus*) is distinguished from the western chipmunks (genus *Eutamias*) by its heavier build, creamy flank stripes, and lack of a third premolar.

Chipmunks are primarily solitary animals, except during the spring breeding season. Their burrows have one or two entrances and are up to 12 feet (4 meters) long. Their diet consists of

CHIPPAWA, chip'ə-wä, a village in southern Ontario, Canada, is on the Niagara River, about 2½ miles (4 km) above Niagara Falls. The water intake for the large Queenston plant of the hydroelectric power commission of Ontario, 6 miles (9.6 km) below the falls, is at Chippawa. The principal industry of the village is the manufacture of artificial abrasives.

Chippawa was founded by United Empire Loyalists in 1784. The name is a popular adaptation of Ojibway, a numerous and widely distributed tribe of Algonkin Indians. The site of the village was the upper landing place of the great portage around Niagara Falls. In the War of 1812, American forces defeated the British in the Battle of Chippawa near here on July 5, 1814. Population: 3,749.

CHIPPENDALE, Thomas (c.1718–1779), English furniture designer and cabinetmaker, whose name became identified with the style of furniture popularized by his book *The Gentleman and Cabinet-Maker's Director*. . . . Chippendale's name is generally associated with furniture in the rococo taste—carved and asymmetrical with cabriole legs. This is the style he termed "French," drawn in part from Louis XV designs. But Chippendale also drew heavily from many design sources, including Gothic, Chinese, and neoclassic. The influence of his book gave rise to further variations of his style, such as Irish Chippendale and American Chippendale.

Life. Chippendale was born about 1718 at Otley, Yorkshire, the descendant of a family of joiners and cabinetmakers. He served his apprenticeship under his father, who about 1727 moved the family business to London. Shortly after his marriage to Catherine Renshaw in 1748, Thomas Chippendale opened his own cabinet-making shop in Conduit Lane. In 1753 he moved to 60 St. Martin's Lane, a center of furniture making in London, where he remained thereafter.

In his shop, which probably was not so large as the shops of several competitors, Chippendale employed craftsmen for every branch of the business. He formed a partnership with James Ranni that lasted until Ranni's death in 1766. In 1779 he took another partner, Thomas Haig, who, after Chippendale's death in 1779, continued the business with Chippendale's son.

"The Director." Chippendale's greatest contribution to furniture design, *The Gentleman and Cabinet-Maker's Director* . . . , was first published in London in 1754. A second edition appeared in 1759, a third, revised and enlarged edition, was published in 1762.

The publication of *The Director* did more than stimulate a vogue for furniture in the rococo manner. The book eventually was used by cabinetmakers throughout England, and started a competition to further elaborate Chippendale's fanciful designs. Its influence spread far beyond the British Isles. A particularly successful and florid version of the style flourished in Portugal, and Irish and American cabinetmakers evolved distinctive variations of the Chippendale style.

Chippendale's Work. Bills and correspondence from Chippendale's shop are almost the only means of authenticating pieces from Chippendale's own firm. He had many important clients, including the Duke of Atholl, the Duke of Portland, the Earl of Pembroke, and the Earl of Dumfries. It is curious that some of the best furniture that can be definitely ascribed to Chippendale is not in the rococo taste of *The Director* but rather in the neoclassical taste of the Adam style. This includes the furniture made between 1766 and 1770 for Harewood House, Yorkshire, for Sir Edwin Lascelles. See also CHIPPENDALE FURNITURE.

JOSEPH T. BUTLER
Sleepy Hollow Restorations, Tarrytown, N. Y.

Bibliography
Editions of Thomas Chippendale's *The Gentleman and Cabinet-Maker's Director* include a facsimile of the 3d edition (1762), published in New York in 1939; and *Thomas Chippendale: A New Edition of Thomas Chippendale's The Gentleman and Cabinet-Maker's Director*, with an introduction by Ralph Edwards (New York 1958).
Brackett, Oliver, *Thomas Chippendale* (London 1924).
Edwards, Ralph, and Jourdain, Margaret, *Georgian Cabinet-Makers* (London 1955).
Layton, Edwin J., *Thomas Chippendale: a Review of His Life and Origin* (London 1928).

CHIPPENDALE FURNITURE is furniture in the style of Thomas Chippendale (q.v.), the most famous English cabinetmaker of the second half of the 18th century. This period, the golden age of English furniture design and craftsmanship, was dominated by Chippendale, who designed and manufactured fine furniture at his shop in St. Martin's Lane, London. Chippendale's book of designs, *The Gentleman and Cabinet-Maker's Director* . . . , first published in London in 1754, had enormous influence on furniture design throughout Europe and in the United States, and its influence is still felt in the 20th century.

"The Director." *The Gentleman and Cabinet-Maker's Director* . . . went through a second edition with only minor changes in 1759, and a revised, expanded edition in 1762. The copperplate engraved illustrations in *The Director* were all in the nature of fashion plates and were not intended to be actual working drawings. Most of the pieces were shown with at least two different decorative treatments; a side chair, for instance, might have one front leg cabriole shaped and carved, the other square and fretted, and the seat rail half plain and half fretted. Many of the chairs are shown with an arm at the right and none at the left, thus serving to depict the design as either an armchair or a side chair. Some of the French commode tables show two variations for the same piece, one with full-width drawers and the other with a pair of hinged doors concealing the drawers contained within. With one of the designs for a chest-on-chest, four decorative treatments are shown and most of the plates for pedestal desks show at least two design variations.

The three editions of *The Director* present designs for 162 pieces of furniture, 41 decorative accessories, such as girandoles, hanging shelves, and brackets, and 42 details, such as cornices, fretwork, and shields for pediments. To one piece, a breakfast table with narrow drop leaves that Chippendale made for the Earl of Pembroke, he gave the name of his client. As a result "Pembroke" became the standard designation for this type of table during the furniture periods that followed, and still continues to be used.

Relatively few pieces of furniture can be assigned with certainty to Chippendale or his shop. Bills of sale and correspondence from Chippendale are frequently the only means of distinguishing his own work from that of other cabinetmakers who followed the designs of *The Director* in London and other leading European cities.

Characteristics of the Style. The chief characteristics of the Chippendale school of furniture are structural soundness and solidity, made graceful by the use of flowing lines and well-executed carved details. In scale the pieces are ample enough for comfort and, structurally, they are well adapted to the purposes for which they were made.

Details include bold cabriole legs terminating in claw-and-ball feet, straight molded legs, plain, fluted, or reeded on the outer sides, sometimes ending in the square Marlborough foot; pierced and carved back splats for chairs; serpentine or bowed fronts for chests of drawers and other case, pieces; and broken pediment tops surmounting such tall pieces as secretaries and, in America, highboys and chests-on-chests. Carved ornamentation is done in such motifs as shell, scroll, foliage, and gadroon or Chinese frets. Mahogany was used almost to the exclusion of other woods,

CHIPPENDALE furniture in the Chinese manner is exemplified by a black lacquered sideboard at the left and by the mahogany chair below.

except in the American colonies, where some pieces were made of walnut by Philadelphia craftsmen, and of cherry by cabinetmakers of New England.

In general line and proportion the Chippendale style was developed from Early Georgian furniture design which, in turn, was derived from the furniture of the Low Countries with its inherent stiff heaviness. This was replaced by more graceful curves and flowing lines in the early Chippendale. As this style developed, almost simultaneously its breadth and scope were enhanced by elaborate adaptations from furniture of the Louis XV period, known as French manner Chippendale; the Chinese Chippendale in which details were adapted from ornamentation and architecture of the Celestial Empire, and the Gothic Chippendale wherein lines and details reflected Gothic architecture.

The four basic styles of Chippendale furniture are French rococo, Chinese, Gothic, and neoclassic or Adam. Outstanding designs include neoclassic French commode tables, china cabinets and elaborate canopy beds in the Chinese manner, and Gothic breakfront bookcases and sideboard tables.

Influence. In *The Director*, Chippendale presented ideas for furniture design that had not previously reached beyond fashionable London. A considerable number of provincial cabinetmakers subscribed to the book, and thus his genius as a designer was followed by many working outside the London area.

Eventually, Chippendale's influence spread beyond England. His followers and imitators became so numerous in Ireland and the American colonies that they developed variations of the style that came to be known as Irish Chippendale and American Chippendale. In the American colonies especially, the cabinetmakers of Philadelphia and some of the master craftsmen of New England produced skillful adaptations of Chippendale styles for local tastes. They evolved some of the finest American furniture designs. Distinctive were the highboys and lowboys and cabriole-leg chairs with pierced back splats that came from shops of such Philadelphia craftsmen as William Savery and Benjamin Randolph. See also FURNITURE—*English*; FURNITURE, AMERICAN.

THOMAS H. ORMSBEE, *Author of* "*Field Guide to Early American Furniture*"

Bibliography

Baker, John Percy, *Chippendale and His School* (London and New York, 1925).

Bond, Harold Lewis, *An Encyclopedia of Antiques* (Boston 1937).

Cescinsky, Herbert, and Hunter, George Leland, *English and American Furniture* (New York 1930).

Eberlein, Harold D., and McClure, Abbot, *The Practical Book of Period Furniture* (Philadelphia 1914).

Hayward, Helena, ed., *World Furniture: An Illustrated History* (New York 1965).

Heal, Ambrose, *The London Furniture Makers from the Restoration to the Victorian Era, 1660–1840* (London 1953).

Honey, W. B., and Turner, W. J., *British Craftsmanship* (London 1948).

Jourdain, Margaret, *English Interior Decoration, 1500 to 1830* (London 1950).

Kimball, Sidney Fiske, and Donnell, Edna, "Creators of the Chippendale Style," *Metropolitan Museum Studies*, vol. 1, pp. 115–154 (New York 1928–1929).

Macquoid, Percy, and Edwards, Ralph, *The Dictionary of English Furniture from the Middle Ages to the Late Georgian Period*, 2d rev. ed., 3 vols. (London and New York 1954).

Ward-Jackson, Peter, *English Furniture Designs of the Eighteenth Century* (London 1958).

CHIPPENHAM, chip′ən-əm, is a municipal borough in Wiltshire, England, on the Avon River, 12 miles (19 km) northeast of Bath on the Great Western Railroad. Its name, derived from the Saxon *cyppan,* to buy, indicates its early existence as a market town. Listed in Domesday Book (1085) as a crown manor, its records go still further back to the 9th century and the Danish invasion. An ancient stone bridge of 22 arches, a 15th century parish church, and an old town hall are among its points of interest. It is in a dairying region; cheese is processed and bacon is cured in the area. The borough manufactures agricultural machinery and makes leather and furniture. Population: (1961) 17,543.

CHIPPEWA FALLS, chip′ə-wä, a city in west central Wisconsin, the seat of Chippewa county, is situated on the Chippewa River, 10 miles (13 km) northeast of Eau Claire. It is a lake resort near Lake Wissota, the state's largest artificial lake. The city is also a trade and industrial center in an agricultural and dairying area. Its creameries make high-grade butter and other dairy products. Its factories produce computer parts, electrical components, hydraulic pumps, fishing lures, plastics, shoes, doors and sashes, beer, bottled spring water, and packed meats.

In 1836, French Canadians built a sawmill and dam here. The following year the Indians gave up their right to the Chippewa Valley, and the town became a busy lumbering center. Chippewa Falls was incorporated in 1869 and is governed by a mayor and council. Population: 12,351.

CHIPPEWA INDIANS, chip′ə-wô, a large North American tribe, speaking a language of the Algonkian family. At the time of European contact they lived near Sault Ste. Marie in present-day Michigan. Later they settled around and to the north of Lake Superior. The Chippewa are also known as the *Ojibwa* and *Saulteaux.*

The Chippewa pursued a nomadic life. They lived in dome-shaped oval shelters of about 15 by 20 feet (4½ by 6 meters) made of a framework of saplings covered with strips of birch bark. These were known as wigwams and were constructed by the women, who carried the birch bark in rolls from one campsite to another. The Chippewa's main subsistence was hunting, fishing, and collecting wild plant food, although some of the southern groups had a limited maize agriculture. Maple sugar and wild rice were harvested regularly. Each season the headman divided the maple groves and rice beds into allotments to be harvested by individual families.

The Chippewa's dependence on hunting and trapping resulted in their having a loose social organization and enabled small groups to function alone for long periods of time. Their prowess as hunters, using bow and arrow, snares, and traps, was exceptional. It was reported that one winter a band killed 2,400 moose using only snares. During the summer, fishing, particularly for whitefish and sturgeon, was more important, and bands of Chippewa often congregated near good fishing spots.

The finest Chippewa craftsmanship was demonstrated by their birch bark canoes. These were easily carried from one waterway to another, and their construction has been widely imitated by whites. Birch bark was also used in making bags and containers.

The Chippewa were greatly influenced by the early British and French fur trade. They secured large numbers of beaver pelts and other furs, which they exchanged for a variety of European goods, and they came to depend on European goods more and more. As the headmen became more powerful and acquired greater prestige and influence through their dealings with white traders, the post of headman became patrilineally inherited.

Ceremonies and Culture. Interest in the supernatural greatly influenced the ceremonial life of the Chippewa. Their anxieties over sorcery and their fear of starvation were projected into a supernatural, cannibal monster, the Windigo, which they feared would capture them. Ceremonial life centered around the Midewewin, or Grand Medicine Society. Novices who had experienced supernatural visions were initiated into the society at an annual ceremony, the aim of which was to bring novices and members into direct contact with the spiritual world. Sick people were sometimes initiated into the society, and, if cured, they would become life members since the society had supplied them with supernatural knowledge.

Many of the traditional Chippewa stories were collected and transcribed by the early anthropologist and Indian expert Henry Rowe Schoolcraft. These later formed the basis for Longfellow's *The Song of Hiawatha.*

In the late 1960's there were estimated to be more than 15,000 Chippewa living on reservations carved out of their original territory.

RICHARD A. GOULD
American Museum of Natural History
Further Reading: Kinietz, Vernon W., *The Indians of the Western Great Lakes, 1615–1760* (Ann Arbor, Mich., 1940); Quimby, George I., *Indian Life in the Upper Great Lakes* (Chicago 1960).

CHIPPING SPARROW. See SPARROW.

CHIQUINQUIRÁ, chē-kēn-kē-rä′, is the market town of a small highland basin in Boyacá department, north central Colombia. It is situated about 90 miles (150 km) north of Bogotá, with which it is connected by railroad. Coffee, grain, and cattle are the mainstays of its economy. There are emerald deposits near Muzo, to the southwest. Emerald mining, though unimportant now, dates back to before the arrival of the Spanish, who founded Chiquinquirá in 1586. The city is also noted for the toys handcrafted by its artisans. The Shrine of Our Lady of Chiquinquirá is in a church built of marble quarried in the vicinity. Population: (1964) 16,926.

CHIQUITO INDIANS, chē-kē′tō, a group of tribes occupying the plains of the same name in eastern Bolivia. These Indians lived in fortified villages, which were politically autonomous. An undetermined number of them spoke languages of the Chiquitoan stock. They were discovered in 1543 by an expedition led by Álvar Núñez Cabeza de Vaca that ascended the Paraguay River in search of the mythical El Dorado and were conquered by another such expedition in 1557–1560. Released from Spanish rule in 1595, when the city of Santa Cruz was moved westward, they reverted to their aboriginal mode of life. They suffered heavily from slave raids until the coming of Jesuit missionaries in 1691. The Jesuits grouped the Chiquito into eight large and prosperous missions, but these were abandoned when the Jesuits were expelled in 1767, and the Indians slipped back into a half barbarous condition, in which they have remained. First studied in 1908, they were discovered to be good agriculturalists and basket makers. Although they had adopted many modern customs, they still played a native ball game, and during Christian feasts they danced with their faces hidden by cloth masks and their bodies covered with ostrich feathers. In 1766 the Jesuits calculated the population of Chiquito at about 24,000; in 1831 it was 15,000. The present number of Chiquitos is not known.

IRVING ROUSE
Yale University

CHIRICO, kē′rē-kō, **Giorgio de** (1888–1978), Italian painter, who founded *pittura metafisica*, or metaphysical painting, a movement that captured in paint the mysterious quality of dreams. During his metaphysical period Chirico painted deserted city squares that conveyed a unique mood of melancholy and foreboding, and disturbing still lifes of oddly juxtaposed objects in distorted perspective. These early works deeply influenced the surrealist movement, with its emphasis on the psychological and irrational, and are Chirico's great contribution to the development of painting. He later repudiated the metaphysical style and returned to academic art.

Early Years and Metaphysical Painting. Chirico was born in Volos, Greece, on July 10, 1888. His father, an Italian engineer working in Greece, taught his son to draw. Chirico studied art at the Polytechnic Institute in Athens and then in Munich, where he was influenced by Nietzsche's antirealist aesthetics and by German romantic painters, especially Arnold Böcklin.

In 1909–1910, Chirico lived in Turin and Florence, cities whose warm light and striking architecture inspired his early metaphysical style. He continued this style in Paris, where he moved in 1911. In his smooth-surfaced "Italian piazza" paintings, such as *Enigma of an Afternoon, Nostalgia of the Infinite,* and *Enigma of an Autumn*

CHIRICO'S *The Mystery and Melancholy of a Street.*
COURTESY OF THE MUSEUM OF MODERN ART, NEW YORK

Evening, severe buildings in exaggerated perspective cast strange long shadows on empty squares punctuated by statues. Such works, exhibited at the Salon d'Automne (1912–1913) and the Salon des Indépendants (1913–1914), were championed by the poet and art critic Guillaume Apollinaire and profoundly affected the emerging surrealist movement.

Conscripted into the Italian Army in 1915, Chirico was stationed in Ferrara. There he met the painter Carlo Carrà, and the two further developed the style Chirico now began to call *pittura metafisica.* According to his brother Andrea, a surrealist novelist and poet who became the theoretician of *pittura metafisica,* the style tried to represent a new reality that, by posing objects in startling new relationships, appealed directly to the unconscious and thereby provoked a reexamination of man's concept of the real world. In his metaphysical paintings of this period, such as *Jewish Angel, Sweet Afternoon,* and *Toys of a Prince,* Chirico presents faceless mannequins or statues, fish, rubber gloves, and engineer's tools, incongruously combined and strangely distorted.

Later Years and Repudiation of Modern Art. After 1919, Chirico's work took several directions. In Rome, in an effort to understand such earlier masters as Michelangelo and Titian, he copied their paintings or adopted their styles. By the time he returned to Paris in 1924, Chirico's paintings were beginning to be dominated by classical motifs—gladiators and horses, villas and ruins. Nevertheless, he was hailed by the emergent surrealists and exhibted with them, and he wrote the "dream novel" *Hebdomeros* (1929), one of the major works of surrealist literature. He also designed sets and costumes for the Suédois and Monte Carlo ballets.

After 1930, Chirico finally repudiated surrealism and all modern art. He returned to Italy to study the techniques and painting mediums of the great Renaissance and baroque masters. He died in Rome on Nov. 21, 1978.

WILLIAM GERDTS
University of Maryland

Further Reading: Soby, James Thrall, *Giorgio de Chirico* (Mus. of Modern Art 1955).

CHIRON, kī′ron, in Greek mythology, was the son of Cronos (Saturn) and the nymph Philyra, one of the Oceanides. He was regarded as the wisest of the Centaurs. Chiron was born a Centaur (half man, half horse) because his father had changed himself into a horse and Philyra into a mare to deceive his wife, Rhea.

Chiron was raised and educated by Apollo and Artemis (Diana), who taught him the arts of medicine, music, prophecy, and hunting. In turn, Chiron was the teacher of such eminent Greek heroes as Jason, Hercules (Herakles), Aesculapius, and Achilles.

In a battle between Hercules and the Centaurs, Chiron was accidentally wounded in the knee by a poisoned arrow. Hercules, who had learned medicine from Chiron, tried to cure the wound, but it would not heal. Although Chiron was immortal, he suffered great pain from the wound and retired to a cave in Malea, wishing to die. Chiron was released from his misery by giving his immortality to Prometheus, after which Zeus (Jupiter) placed him among the stars as the constellation Sagittarius.

CHIROPODY. See PODIATRY.

CHIROPRACTIC, kī-rə-prak'tik. The term "chiropractic" is derived from two Greek words—*cheir*, meaning "hand," and *praktikos,* meaning "effective." Practitioners of this form of drugless therapy hold that the nervous system integrates all of the body's functions, including its defenses against disease, and that when the nervous system is impaired in any way—as by pressure on a nerve—it cannot perform properly. As a result there is a lowered resistance to disease, aches, pains, and other disorders.

The core of the nervous system is the spinal cord, which runs inside the 24 movable vertebrae of the backbone. Between these vertebrae are small openings through which nerves branch out to every part of the body. Chiropractors contend that even a slight displacement of the vertebrae (called a subluxation) can cause mechanical interference with the spinal cord and nerves. Their aim, therefore, is to eliminate the interference by manipulating or adjusting the misplaced vertebrae. With the nervous system thus repaired, they believe that the body is then able to remedy the ailment. Although most adjustments are made on or in the region of the spine, where misalignments and dislocations are more likely to occur, treatment may extend to the pelvis or any area where manipulation of bones, muscles, and other tissues will remove the "nerve interference."

Chiropractors claim notable success in treating many disorders, including lumbago, slipped discs, arthritis, hay fever, and high blood pressure. Leading practitioners contend that, contrary to popular belief, reliable chiropractors do not claim to cure such diseases as cancer, heart disease, or blood disorders. Nor do they perform surgery or intrude into areas outside their province of training. For example, chiropractors do not prescribe drugs. However, chiropractors themselves disagree on the scope of their methods of treatment. Those belonging to the International Chiropractors Association want chiropractors to treat patients only by spinal manipulation, while members of the American Chiropractors Association think that treatment should be broadened to keep pace with advances in physiotherapy and related fields. They use diathermy, psychological counseling, and dietary measures along with spinal manipulation.

History. Chiropractors say that they can trace their treatment methods to Hippocrates and other noted physicians of ancient Greece and Rome. Indeed, early manuscripts of the Egyptians, Hindus, and Chinese do reveal incidents of this form of treatment. However, modern chiropractic is said to have been founded by a Canadian-born Iowa merchant, Daniel David Palmer, who is credited with having performed the first chiropractic adjustment in 1895. Three years later, Palmer established the Palmer College of Chiropractic in Davenport, Iowa, and in 1910 his textbook, *The Science, Art and Philosophy of Chiropractic*, was published. In this book Palmer explained that chiropractic is "the science of adjusting by hand any and all luxations of the articular joints of the human body; more especially, the articulations of the spinal column, for the purpose of freeing any and all impinged nerves which cause deranged functions."

Before his death in 1913, Palmer's son, Bartlett Joshua, had joined him in developing the methods of modern chiropractic. Bartlett's son, David Daniel, took over after his father's death in 1961, emphasizing manual manipulation of the spine as the principal chiropractic procedure.

Since its founding, the field of chiropractic has grown considerably. According to the Bureau of the Census, there were 14,360 chiropractors in the United States in 1960. By the mid-1960's, chiropractic associations stated that there were many more, perhaps as many as 30,000.

Training and Licensing. There are 16 colleges in the United States that offer the Doctor of Chiropractic degree (D. C.), and their enrollment is estimated at about 10,000. Admission to most chiropractic colleges requires a high school diploma or its equivalent. In some states, students are also required to take 2 years of training at a liberal arts college.

To obtain a D. C. degree, a student must enroll in a 4-year course and take more than 4,000 hours of instruction in basic medical sciences and chiropractic subjects. A typical curriculum of basic science courses include histology, anatomy, embryology, chemistry, diagnosis, pathology, physiology, bacteriology, symptomatology, pediatrics, gynecology, and public health. Chiropractic subjects include spinal analysis, palpation, X-ray interpretation, and chiropractic principles and techniques. Some colleges offer more than 400 hours of X-ray studies.

Mississippi and Louisiana are the only states that do not license chiropractors. In most other states a chiropractor is required to pass the same basic science examination as a medical doctor before receiving his D. C. degree.

Opposition. Chiropractic has long been the target of heavy attack from the medical profession. The American Medical Association has charged that "chiropractic constitutes a hazard to rational health care in the United States because of the substandard and unscientific education of its practitioners and their rigid adherence to an irrational, unscientific approach to disease causation." The AMA has further charged that no chiropractic school is accredited by recognized accrediting bodies; most chiropractic instructors lack college degrees and are not qualified to teach the basic sciences; and chiropractors are barred from practicing in any hospital accredited by the Joint Commission on Accreditation of Hospitals.

A study of admission practices at seven leading chiropractic colleges was made by the AMA's department of investigation in 1964. Results of this study declared: "The actual admitting practices followed by 5 of the 7 schools contacted do not meet the professed standards set up by the two chiropractice organizations, as well as those standards that the schools have set for themselves according to their own catalogues."

Chiropractors claim that such charges are motivated by fear of economic competition. They insist that their theories and methods are misunderstood and that their educational requirements have been vastly improved in recent decades. In addition, reputable chiropractors often refer patients to medical doctors when the patient's illness lies outside the realm of chiropractic.

Although chiropractors are not employed by the U. S. Public Health Service and state health departments, their widespread acceptance is attested to by the fact that many insurance companies and workmen's compensation laws honor claims for treatment by chiropractors. It is estimated that four million people obtain the services of a chiropractor each year.

MIRIAM G. HILL, *University of Alabama*

CHIRU, chir′ōō, a rare, little-known antelope of the Tibetan and Ladakh plateaus in Asia. It is also called the *Tibetan antelope.* The male stands 32 inches (81 cm) at the shoulder and weighs 100 pounds (45 kg). The slender, almost straight horns—found only in the male—are up to 27 inches (68 cm) long. The snout of the male has a swollen appearance. Both sexes have a short, thick, woolly coat of a pinkish tan color. Like most mountain-dwelling species, the chiru descends to lower altitudes in winter.

The single species, *Pantholops hodgsoni,* is in the family Bovidae, order Artiodactyla.

JOSEPH A. DAVIS, JR.
New York Zoological Society

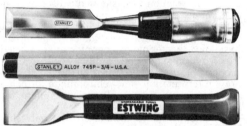

(TOP AND CENTER) STANLEY TOOLS;
(BOTTOM) ESTWING MANUFACTURING COMPANY

CHISELS: *(Top to bottom)* Wood chisel, cold chisel for cutting metal, and rock chisel used by geologists.

CHISEL, chiz′əl, a steel tool, based on the principle of the wedge, that is used for cutting wood, metal, or stone. A chisel consists of a metal bar with one end beveled to one or more sharp edges. The other end is fitted with a handle or is made blunt so that it can be struck with a hammer.

Chisels vary in shape and size. Many are designed for specific applications. Wood chisels include the *firmer chisels,* with sturdy blades for making gouges; *paring chisels,* with thinner blades for lighter work; and *butt chisels,* with short wide blades for making depressions for butt door-hinges. *Cold chisels,* or *chipping chisels,* are used with a hammer to cut cold metal. They include *flat chisels,* with broad edges for cutting flat surfaces, and *cross-cut chisels,* with sturdy narrow blades for cutting grooves.

CHISELMOUTH, chiz′əl-mouth, a freshwater fish found from southwestern Canada to Nevada. It is abundant in the Columbia River drainages of Oregon and Washington and in the Fraser River system of British Columbia. The chiselmouth is also called the hardmouth or squaremouth because of the cartilaginous, or horny, materials in its upper and especially its lower jaws.

An elongated, carplike fish, the chiselmouth reaches a length of 1 foot (30 cm). It has numerous small, fine scales, a relatively long and narrow posterior portion of the body, and a deeply forked caudal fin. It is generally dark brown spreckled with darker pigments, but the belly is lighter, and there is orangy pigment under the bases of the pectoral and pelvic fins.

The chiselmouth, *Acrocheilus alutaceus,* belongs to the family Cyprinidae (carps and minnows) in the order Cypriniformes.

JAMES C. TYLER
Academy of Natural Sciences of Philadelphia

CHISHOLM, chiz′əm, **Shirley Anita St. Hill** (1924–   ), American congresswoman. She was born in Brooklyn, N. Y., on Nov. 30, 1924, and graduated from Brooklyn College (B. A.) and Columbia University (M. A.). After working as a teacher and director in New York City nursery schools and day care centers, she entered politics as a member of the New York State Assembly (1964–1968). Her first election to Congress as Democratic representative from New York made her the first black woman member of the House of Representatives. In the 1972 presidential race she won 10% of the Democratic convention votes. She wrote an autobiography, *Unbought and Unbossed* (1970), and *The Good Fight* (1973).

CHISHOLM TRAIL, chiz′əm, the principal route over which Texans drove longhorn cattle to markets at Midwestern rail points, mainly in Kansas, following the Civil War. From the middle of the Indian Territory (Oklahoma) to Wichita, Kans., it followed the earlier wagon tracks of Jesse Chisholm (c. 1806–1868), a Scotch-Cherokee trader, and the trail eventually took its name from him.

Before the war, small Texas herds had been trailed to New Orleans, a few to California, and some north over the Shawnee Trail through Dallas and the eastern edge of the Indian Territory to Sedalia, Mo., and elsewhere in the Midwest. In 1866 further use of the Shawnee Trail was opposed by Midwestern farmers, who objected to the tick fever spread by longhorns, which were themselves immune to it. Joseph G. McCoy (q.v.), a young stock dealer in Springfield, Ill., saw the need for a new trail west of most of the farm settlements. In 1867 he established a cattle depot in the village of Abilene, Kans., and invited Texas drovers to bring their cattle there to be shipped by rail to market. Within a short period the Chisholm Trail became the chief route to Abilene from the south.

The main course of the Chisholm Trail ran through San Antonio, Austin, Fort Worth, the Indian Territory, and Wichita to Abilene. Feeder

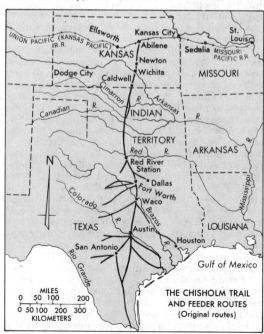

THE CHISHOLM TRAIL
AND FEEDER ROUTES
(Original routes)

trails led into it. Cattle on the trail lived on grass alone. After 1871 — the peak trailing year, in which 600,000 Texas cattle were taken north afoot — Ellsworth and Wichita became the chief Kansas cattle markets for several years; then Caldwell and Dodge City replaced them. In 1876 a rival Western Trail branched off at Belton, Texas, and led past Fort Griffin direct to Dodge City.

The westward push of farmers, with their barbed-wire fences, caused trailing to diminish rapidly in the 1880's and to give way to costlier rail transport. Over all of the trails from Texas, however, had gone an estimated 9 to 10 million cattle in probably the largest migration of domestic animals in history. Use of the cattle trails enabled Texas ranchmen to recover from the economic blows of the Civil War, to stock new ranches to the north, to help satisfy the nation's growing demand for meat, and to make beef, rather than pork, the country's chief meat item. The trails also led to the rise of Chicago and Kansas City as packing centers, and they spurred Western rail extension and the development of refrigerator cars. In 1967 elaborate celebrations were held to commemorate the centennial anniversary of the Chisholm Trail.

WAYNE GARD
Author of "Rawhide Texas"
Further Reading: Gard, Wayne, *The Chisholm Trail* (Norman, Okla., 1954).

CHISUM, chiz'əm, **John Simpson** (1824–1884), American cattleman. He was born in Hardeman county, Tenn., on Aug. 15, 1824. He moved with his family to Texas in 1837, worked as a contractor and builder, and was clerk of Lamar county. In 1854, with a partner, he entered the cattle business, later shifting his operations to New Mexico. He drove herds, sold beef to government contractors for Navaho and Apache reservations, and prospered despite Indian raids, rustlers, and periodic depressions.

The owner of between 60,000 and 100,000 head of cattle by the 1870's, he was the largest individual owner of cattle in the United States — probably in the world — and was known as the "cattle king of America." In 1880 he was instrumental in having Pat Garrett elected sheriff to bring an end to lawlessness and range wars. He died in Eureka Springs, Ark., on Dec. 23, 1884, leaving an estate of half a million dollars.

CHITA, chi-ta', is a city in the USSR, in eastern Siberia. It is the capital of Chita oblast in the Russian republic and is situated on the Trans-Siberian Railroad, 400 miles (650 km) east of Irkutsk. Chita's principal industries are coal mining and metalworking. The mines are situated in the western outskirts of the city and supply both power stations and the railroad. The city's principal factory is a locomotive and car shop. Other factories produce compressors, refrigerating equipment, and machine tools. As the center of a sheep-raising area, Chita also has a meat-packing plant and a sheepskin factory.

Chita is a cultural center of the Transbaikalian region of Siberia, with a branch of the Academy of Sciences, a teachers college, and a medical school. It has a drama theater and a puppet theater, and its regional museum is well known.

Founded originally as a Russian strongpoint in the conquest of Siberia in 1653, Chita first assumed significance in 1826 as a center of exile of the Decembrists. Its modern development dates

from 1897 when it was reached by the Trans-Siberian railroad and when its coal mines began to be developed as a source of fuel.

Chita Oblast. The oblast is situated on the borders of Mongolia and Manchuria and has an area of 143,800 square miles (431,500 sq km). Largely mountainous, the oblast is rich in minerals, notably tin, tungsten, molybdenum and fluorspar. Balei is a gold-lode mining center, and Petrovsk-Zabaikalski has a small steel plant. Although some spring wheat is grown in the short Siberian growing season, sheep raising is the principal nonindustrial activity. In the extreme south, adjoining Mongolia, camels are also raised. The stockherders are mainly Buryat Mongols, who account for 4% of the population and are settled in the Aga Buryat National Okrug, named for the Aga River which passes through it. The vast majority of the population is Russian. The oblast was formed in 1937. Population: (1966) of the city, 201,000; of the oblast, 1,095,000.

THEODORE SHABAD
Editor of "Soviet Geography"

CHITAL or **CHITRA.** See AXIS DEER.

CHITIN, kī'tin, is a nonliving, noncellular organic compound found primarily in insects and other animals of the phylum Arthropoda. It is found also in certain sponges, coelenterates, and annelids. Chemically, chitin is mainly a sugar derivative known as a glucosamine polysaccharide; it also may include waxy compounds. Chitin is secreted by the epidermis of the animal and is used in the structural development of the exoskeleton (outer skeleton), biting jaws, stomach, grinders, sensory organs, copulatory organs, lenses of the eye, organs of defense, and walking appendages. In some arthropods, the chitin remains soft, while in others it forms a suit of armor.

DAVID A. OTTO
Stephens College

CHITON, kī'tən, a marine mollusk that lives mostly in intertidal rocky areas. It is one of the most simply constructed of all mollusks.

The chiton has eight dorsal plates of shell

CHITON'S overlapping plates are encircled by a fleshy girdle sometimes covered with bristles or tiny spines.
ANNAN PHOTO FEATURES

that protect its soft body parts. The plates are overlapping and are held together by an encircling girdle, which may be adorned with beads, hairs, spicules, or warts. The animal's flat, powerful foot is used to clamp down on rocks. The foot is surrounded by the mantle, which covers the soft parts and also secretes the shell plates. The chiton's small head lacks tentacles and eyes, but in some chitons eyelike organs in the shell plates respond to changes in light. Chitons range in size from less than 1 inch to over 1 foot (2.5–30 cm). The largest chitons, including the 14-inch (35 cm) Steller's chiton of California, are found along the Pacific coast of the United States.

Chitons are usually slow-moving. They feed during the night, mainly on marine algae. Some species, such as the veiled Pacific chiton (*Placiphorella*), are able to lift the front part of the mantle and snap it down on live shrimp. Most chitons have a homing ability and after a night of foraging return to their original resting place.

Chitons belong to the class Amphineura in the phylum Mollusca; there are about 400 species. They are used as bait and food in some West Indian Islands but otherwise have no economic value.

R. TUCKER ABBOTT
The Academy of Natural Sciences of Philadelphia

CHITRAL, chi-träl, a former princely state, is a territory in the Malakand agency of Northwest Frontier province, West Pakistan. It is also the name of the headquarters of the area. Strategically located, the 5,727-square mile (14,833-sq km) territory is bounded on the northwest by Afghanistan and on the northeast by Kashmir, and is close to the Soviet Union and China.

Chitral is mountainous, with deep, narrow valleys made fertile by the streams of the Indus River system. Transportation facilities are sparse and there is little communication with the outside world. Fruit orchards are abundant, and wheat and barley are grown on irrigated land. Other economic activities include animal herding and the manufacture of embroidered cloth, daggers, and sword belts.

The predominantly Muslim population is composed of the indigenous Kafir and the Khos tribesmen, whose Knowar language is the lingua franca of the region and who belong to the Khoja sect ruled by the Aga Khan. The principal family of Chitral since the 16th century bears the title of Mehtar, or prince, and claims descent from Baba Ayub, a grandson of the Mughul emperor Babur. Population: (1951) 105,724.

BRIJEN K. GUPTA, *Brooklyn College*

CHITTAGONG, chit'ə-gông, is a major port and the second-largest city of Bangladesh. Situated on the Karnafuli River, 12 miles (19 km) from the Bay of Bengal, it is an important rail terminus and the headquarters of Chittagong division.

Since the creation of Pakistan in 1947, the city's commerce and industry have grown enormously, and port installations have been expanded. Because Chittagong has a natural harbor and good transportation facilities, much of East Bengal's ocean trade, which previously went through Calcutta, has been funneled through Chittagong. The city is connected by rail, air, and water with the rest of Bangladesh. New industrial plants include jute and cotton textile mills, petroleum refineries, and iron and steel plants. Other industries are fruit canning, leather

processing, and shipbuilding. The Chandraghona paper mill is 30 miles (48 km) east on the Karnafuli River, and just above it is the Karnafuli hydroelectric project.

Chittagong began as a fishing village. After the 8th century A. D. it was controlled by various Buddhist, Muslim, and Hindu princes. The port was also used by the Arakans, Arabs, Persians, Portuguese (who called it Pôrto Grande), and Mughuls (who called it Islamabad). The Mughuls occupied Chittagong in 1666, and in 1760, Nawab Mir Kasim Ali ceded it to the East India Company. It became part of East Pakistan (now Bangladesh) in 1947. Pop.: (1974) 416,733.

ROBERT C. KINGSBURY, *Indiana University*

CHITTENDEN, chit'ən-dən, **Thomas** (1730–1797), American political leader, who was the first governor of Vermont. He was born in East Guilford, Conn., on Jan. 6, 1730. After a brief career at sea, he settled in Salisbury, Conn., in 1749. He remained there for 25 years, holding various public offices and representing the town in the provincial assembly. In 1774 he moved to a grant of land bordering the Winooski River in Vermont. Thereafter he was active in establishing the state of Vermont.

Early in 1777 he tried, unsuccessfully, to have the Continental Congress recognize Vermont as a state. Later that year, as president of the council of safety, he helped draw up Vermont's constitution, and in 1778 he was elected governor. Except for the year 1789–1790, Chittenden held this office until his resignation shortly before his death in Williston, Vt., on Aug. 25, 1797. In 1791 his efforts to secure Vermont's admission to the Union were successful.

CHIUSI, kyōo'sē, is a town and commune in central Italy, situated 38 miles (60 km) southeast of Siena and just southwest of Lake Trasimeno at an elevation of 1,300 feet (400 meters). Chiusi grew out of the Etruscan city of *Clusium*, earlier known to the Umbrians as *Chamars*. Located in the mountainous district of northeastern Etruria, Clusium was built almost entirely on volcanic ash. It was well fortified and was one of the most powerful of the 12 cities in the Etruscan religious federation. The city never completely lost its pre-Etruscan character; evidence exists of cremation here long after burying of the dead became customary in the rest of Etruria. Like other Etruscan cities, Clusium was ringed by tombs, forming a veritable necropolis.

Clusium entered into the history of Rome on two important occasions. Lars Porsena, the king of the city at the time of the establishment of the Roman Republic (509 B. C.), attacked Rome in an attempt to restore the exiled Tarquinius Superbus to power. Supposedly, Rome held out against Porsena. There is good evidence, however, that the city was actually taken, and perhaps Porsena himself was instrumental in the defeat and exile of Tarquinius. On the second occasion, about 390 B. C., Rome assisted Clusium against the invading Gauls led by Brennus. The Romans' intervention brought down the wrath of the Gauls on their own city, which fell to the invaders.

Modern Chiusi is a rather prosperous market town. Tourism is gradually becoming its most important industry. Population: (1961) of the town, 2,510; (1966 est.) of the commune, 8,848.

RICHARD E. MITCHELL, *University of Illinois*

KNIGHTS in single combat submitted settlement of their dispute to God's will (note angel hovering above) as in this 15th century miniature.

CULVER PICTURES

CHIVALRY

CHIVALRY, shiv′əl-rē, was the system of values and ideals of conduct held by knights in medieval Europe. In its institutional form, chivalry was an informal, international order to which many, but not all, of the ruling class (nobility) belonged. The word is derived from the Latin *caballus* (horse) through the French *chevalier* ("horseman" or knight).

Origins. The origins of chivalry are difficult to ascertain. Probably the custom of investing youths with armor as practiced by the Germanic tribal chieftains provided the foundations of the system. But a more certain origin was feudalism, the social-political system that governed early medieval Europe. At first the feudal noble spent most of his time fighting for land, plunder, and ransom. But as political stability replaced anarchy, there gradually appeared certain ideals more exalted than love of carnage. The vassal's loyalty to his lord and his prowess in defending his lord's cause became the principal feudal virtues. By the 12th century these military qualities had been elaborated into an ethical code that defined the characteristics of the ideal knight. The virtues were prowess in arms, courage in battle, courtesy toward one's enemies, and generosity toward one's social inferiors. Glory, the knight's highest aspiration, was earned in combat. Honor was gained by living according to the chivalric code. All nobles invested with knighthood considered themselves a part of the international order of chivalry.

Chivalry's code was rough-hewn, for courage, prowess, and generosity were not far removed from arrogance, brutality, and prodigality. But a majority of knights undoubtedly honored the ideal, for it was admirably suited to the demands of feudal warfare. Two institutions, the Christian church and the noble courts, attempted to mitigate feudal chivalry's military harshness by offering reformulations of the chivalric code.

The Church. The church constantly sought to temper the anarchy of feudal warfare and to transform the feudal warrior into a Christian knight who would fight only the infidel or the heathen. The Truce of God (forbidding warfare on certain days) and the Peace of God (forbidding war on the helpless of society) were frequently invoked by the 11th century. By the 12th century, ecclesiastics like John of Salisbury lauded battle in service of the faith, urged charity toward the weak (the poor, women, and orphans), and, most importantly, preached that the knight who violated these rules was no knight at all. The Crusades, championed by the church, aimed at freeing the Holy Land from Muslim control and provided a Christian outlet for the knight's martial energies. The church's ideal of knighthood was summed up in the famous epic poem, *The Song of Roland.* Roland, the hero, served church, emperor, and God simultaneously.

The Crusades inspired the formation of chivalric orders that combined knightly and monastic ideals. Composed solely of knights who had taken monastic vows, these orders produced many of the best warriors of the day. The Knights Templar and the Knights Hospitaller arose in the 12th century and played an important part in the conquest and defense of the Holy Land. The Teutonic Knights fought first in the Middle East, then in the Baltic region to free Prussia from heathen control. In Spain and Portugal, the orders of Santiago and Calatrava fought until the late 15th century to expel the Moors from Iberia.

The attempts of the church to influence chivalry were only partially successful. True, many knights were also good Christians, but the class as a whole was not transformed. Rape, slaughter, and brutality were never eliminated.

The Court. The second institution tending to modify the military-political ethic of chivalry was the feudal court and its noble ladies. As peace and relative stability increased in the 12th century, life became less barbaric and leisure increased. A new ideal, that of courtly love, was elaborated by the ladies and their minstrels. They called on the knight to treat women with refined courtesy and said that it was to win his lady's love that the knight strove for fame on the battlefield and in tournaments. Social skills—gentle conversation, dancing, and competence on a musical instrument—were added to the qualities

CULVER PICTURES

THE ACCOLADE of knighthood, a sword touched to the shoulders, might reward bravery in battle. The kneeling warrior is about to be knighted by his commander.

and skills expected of the knight. Contemporary literature focused on the ideal of courtly love and in turn helped shape it. The *chansons de geste,* poems celebrating a knight's devotion to glory, God, and his lady love, were recited at courtly entertainments. Troubadors and minstrels in southern France and minnesingers in Germany eulogized and popularized this new facet of chivalry. The tales of writers like the Frenchman Chrétien de Troyes and poems of courtly love like the *Roman de la rose* gained enormous popularity. The ideal of courtly love helped civilize the crude knights and enhanced the position of women in society. But it was also fraught with moral problems, for the ideal of romantic love was outside the bounds of Christian marriage.

Mature chivalry, a loose coalescence of feudal, religious, and courtly love ideals, demanded many compromises from the knights. Those qualities which brought glory on the battlefield were not always compatible with excellence in the company of ladies. And Christian morality did not easily accept the martial virtues and courtly love. To many churchmen, the knights' quest for glory and courtly love seemed dangerously close to the sins of vainglory and lust. The reconciliation of these often contradictory aspects of chivalry depended upon the character and conscience of the individual knight.

Training. Preparation for knighthood began early. At about the age of seven the noble youth was sent to serve as a page in the castle of another noble. At 14 he became a squire and began his training in knighthood. He learned the use of arms and horsemanship. He also engaged in endless physical exercises such as swimming and wrestling. The squire was attached to a knight, whom he served and accompanied in battle. Usually at 21, the squire was knighted by his lord, by a churchman, or, in cases of exceptional bravery, by his commander on the battlefield.

Decline. Chivalry, in both its ideals and practices, declined in the late Middle Ages. The reason was clear: the forms of warfare had changed. Traditionally the knight had fought for honor and glory, not ransom or wages. Combat

had been on a small scale, between members of an international brotherhood, who treated each other with courtesy and generosity. But when the institutions of war changed, the ideals of chivalry became outmoded. Wars became longer, larger, and more impersonal, and new arms and tactics appeared. Infantry (pikemen and archers) and artillery, when used wisely, proved capable of defeating the best feudal knights. The battles of Crécy (1346), Poitiers (1356), and Agincourt (1415) testified to the end of the armored knight's military monopoly. These large-scale battles of the Hundred Years' War rendered obsolete the knight's quest for individual glory. Victory, not fame, became the object of war. Monarchs like England's Edward II and France's Charles V found that victory was best gained with mercenary troops led by professional captains. They were more reliable and would serve indefinitely if promptly paid. Furthermore, long-term inflationary trends brought reduced income from noble estates just as expenses for arms, armor, horses, and attendants increased. Many nobles could not afford the trappings of knighthood and preferred to remain squires, serving as mercenaries. Newly aroused patriotism in France and England also helped to dissolve the bonds of international chivalry. By the 15th century, only a minority of French and English nobles were knights.

Like most declining institutions, chivalry grew more rigid and formalized as it lost its usefulness. A sign of its decadence was the creation of the late medieval orders of chivalry. These were not spontaneous groupings of knights, but were formed by rulers to inspire loyalty in their nobles. Edward III of England established the Order of the Garter in 1349, and John II of France created the Order of the Star three years later. The most famous order, that of the Golden Fleece, was formed by Philip of Burgundy in 1429. These artificial constructs formalized the etiquette of chivalry, even as it was being outmoded. Luxury of dress, heraldry, and endless tournaments and banquets were designed to keep the fading institution intact. Tournaments had been common since the 12th century, but they reached their peak as chivalry was declining. The early melees had been dangerous to both man and beast, but later tournaments were designed to avoid bloodshed. Blunted lances and padded armor assured safety from everything but unforeseen accidents. Equipment became elaborate and costly, so winners were rewarded with money ransoms as well as their lady's smile. Jousting (single combat between knights) became popular, and champions took on all challengers in mock battles with sword and lance. The tournaments symbolized the decadence of chivalry, for combat, which had once been spontaneous and grim, had become stylized and harmless.

The legacy of medieval chivalry was significant, for the knight was the ancestor of the modern gentleman. To chivalry's religious, courtly, and military ethic, the Renaissance added a classical education and courtly polish. When, in the 18th and 19th centuries, the nobility was eclipsed by the bourgeoisie, it was from the Renaissance ideal of the courtier that the bourgeoisie derived their concept of the gentleman.

EDMUND H. DICKERMAN
University of Connecticut

Further Reading: Kilgour, R. L., *The Decline of Chivalry* (Cambridge, Mass., 1937); Painter, Sidney, *French Chivalry* (Baltimore 1940).

CHIVASSO, kē-väs′sō, is a town and commune in Italy, situated in the Piedmont region, in Torino province, 13 miles (21 km) northeast of Turin. It lies at the junction of the Cavour Canal and the Po River. It is the market town for cereals and hemp produced in the vicinity, and has steelworks, textile mills, and tanneries. There are sulfur baths at nearby San Gesio. The cathedral, begun in 1415, has a richly ornamented facade. An octagonal tower is all that remains of the palace of the marquises of Montferrat, who ruled the town until 1431, when it passed to the house of Savoy. Population: (1961) of the town, 11,806; (1966 est.) of the commune, 22,795.

CHIVE, chīv, a perennial onionlike plant, whose pungent grasslike leaves are commonly used for flavoring salads, soups, cheese, and omelettes. The chive, known technically as *Allium schoenoprasm*, belongs to the amaryllis family (Amaryllidaceae). It grows in thick tufts and produces small oval bulbs. Its small purplish flowers are borne in clusters, but they produce few seeds. Consequently, the plant is generally propagated by division of the tufts.

The chive is native to Europe and is commonly found in European gardens. In the United States it is cultivated to only a limited extent. In commercial plantings, the chive is harvested and divided into clumps, which are placed in small clay pots, and the old leaves are cut off. When new leaves form, the pots are crated and marketed. The consumer then grows the plants at home, cutting off leaves as they are needed.

JOHN P. McCOLLUM, *University of Illinois*

CHIVERS, chiv′ərz, **Thomas Holley** (1809–1858), American poet. He was born near Washington, Ga., on Oct. 18, 1809, the son of a wealthy planter. He was a medical doctor, but practiced only briefly, and was married and divorced before he was 20. A mystic who claimed to have angelic visions, Chivers brought out his first book of verse, *The Path of Sorrow*, in 1832. Two years later he went north, where he spent much of his remaining life. He died in Decatur, Ga., on Dec. 18, 1858.

In 1840, Chivers began to correspond with Edgar Allen Poe, whose aesthetic theories were very like his own. Chivers developed a musical verse technique very much like Poe's, and in *Enochs of Ruby* (1850), one poem, *Isadore*, echoed Poe's *Raven*. In *Virginalia* (1853), Chivers developed musical metrics even further than Poe had, repeating refrains and carefully suiting sound to sense. Chivers was accused of plagiarizing Poe, but who stole from whom is still a matter of debate.

CHKALOV, chə-kä′lôf, **Valeri Pavlovich** (1904–1938), Soviet aviator. He was born in Orenburg, Russia, on Feb. 2, 1904. He became a military test pilot and in 1935 received the Order of Lenin for his work. In the next year he commanded a nonstop flight from Moscow to Nikolayevsk, Siberia, along a difficult Arctic route, proving the feasibility of such flights.

Chkalov was the chief pilot of a Soviet plane that made a pioneer nonstop flight from Moscow to Vancouver, Wash., over the North Pole in June 1937. The distance of approximately 5,400 miles (8,700 km) was covered in about 63 hours. Chkalov was killed while testing a new plane near Moscow on Dec. 15, 1938.

BURPEE SEEDS

Chives

CHKALOV. See ORENBURG.

CHKHEIDZE, chкнā-ē′dze, **Nikolai Semyonovich** (1864–1926), Russian political leader, who was prominent in the Georgian Social Democratic party. He was born in the Caucasian city of Kutaisi. In the 1890's he became an active Marxist and from 1907 to 1917 served with distinction in the third and fourth Russian dumas as leader of the Menshevik faction. When the February Revolution erupted in 1917, he became the chairman of the Petrograd soviet of workers' and peasants' deputies.

After the Bolsheviks seized power in the October Revolution, Chkheidze returned to his native Caucasus to help form a Menshevik government in Tiflis. Elected president of the Georgian constituent assembly, he took part in drafting a constitution for the new republic. In 1921, however, the Bolsheviks occupied Georgia, and Chkheidze emigrated to France, disheartened. He committed suicide near Paris on June 13, 1926.

PAUL H. AVRICH, *Queens College*

CHLADNI, kläd′nē, **Ernst Florens Friedrich** (1756–1827), German physicist, who made fundamental contributions to the study of sound. Chladni was born in Wittenberg, Saxony, on Nov. 30, 1756. He first studied law, graduating from the University of Leipzig in 1782. After his father's death, he turned to science and became a pioneer in the investigation of sound and meteorites. He died in Breslau on April 3, 1827.

Chladni was the first to analyze sound waves mathematically and is therefore often called the "father of acoustics." He set thin plates covered with a layer of sand to vibrating. Sand remained in curved lines where the plate did not vibrate. The symmetrical patterns ("Chladni's figures") that fascinated audiences, and in 1809 a demonstration was given for Napoleon.

Chladni measured the velocity of sound in various gases by filling organ pipes with the gases. The pitch of the notes sounded by the pipes was used to determine the period of vibration of the column of gas, and from that the velocity of sound in each gas was determined.

Chladni also studied meteorites and was one

of the first to maintain that meteorites really fell from the sky, as many observers claimed (but as scientists denied). He even suggested they were remnants of an exploded planet.

He invented a musical instrument, the euphonium, made of glass rods and steel bars that were sounded by being rubbed with a moistened finger.

ISAAC ASIMOV, *Author of*
"The Intelligent Man's Guide to Science"

CHLOASMA, klō-az′mə, a discoloration of the skin, occurring mostly in women and appearing usually on the face. Chloasma is most often associated with pregnancy, at which time there is also a darkening of the nipples, areola, and vulva. The facial discolorations generally have an irregular outline and are not elevated above the surrounding skin surface. They range in color from yellowish to dark brown and occur mostly on the cheeks, forehead, and the bridge of the nose. It is believed that chloasma in pregnant women is caused by the combined action of sunlight and circulating hormones (estrogen, progesterone, and the melanocyte-stimulating hormone produced by the pituitary gland). After the woman gives birth, chloasma may fade or disappear entirely. However, it is often permanent.

Chloasma may also occur in women who are not pregnant and sometimes even in men. It may be due to chronic illnesses, malnutrition, or hypothyroidism. The use of contraceptive pills, which contain female sex hormones, may also produce chloasma in nonpregnant women.

STEPHEN E. SILVER, M. D.
University of Oregon Medical School

CHŁOPICKI, KHŁȯ-pēts′kē, **Józef** (1771–1854), Polish general. He was born Grzegorz Józef Chłopicki on March 14, 1771. At the age of 14 he joined the Polish Army and in 1794 served with Tadeusz Kościusko in the rebellion that followed the second partition of Poland. Entering the service of Napoleon I, Chłopicki fought in Italy, Spain, Prussia, and Russia. Returning to Poland after the defeat of Napoleon, he was made a general in the Russian army, in which he served until 1818. He resigned after a quarrel with the Russian grand duke Constantine. At the outbreak of the Polish revolution of 1830, Chłopicki was chosen dictator. However, he soon resigned because of his opposition to the policies of the revolutionary leaders and joined the army fighting the Russians. Wounded in February 1831, he retired from the army. Chłopicki died at Cracow on Sept. 30, 1854.

CHLORAL, klôr′əl, or *trichloroacetaldehyde,* is a colorless oily liquid with a strong penetrating odor. Its formula is CCl_3CHO. The most important industrial use of this substance is in the manufacture of the insecticide DDT. Chloral is also used in the synthesis of other organic compounds and as a liniment.

Chloral is made by the chlorination of ethyl alcohol followed by the addition of sulfuric acid and distillation. It may also be produced by the chlorination of acetaldehyde.

Chloral is soluble in alcohol, ether, and chloroform, and it combines with water to form chloral hydrate, a soporific compound commonly known as "knockout drops." The melting point of chloral is −57.5° C (−71° F), and its boiling point is 97.7° C (207° F). Both the liquid and its vapor are extremely hazardous to handle, as inhalation of the substance may cause severe injury to the lungs.

Additives and Derivatives. Chloral additives are chloral alcoholate, chloral ammonia, and chloral caffeine. The most important chloral derivative is chloral hydrate (see CHLORAL HYDRATE). Chloralformamide and chloralimide are chloral derivatives that are sometimes substituted for chloral hydrate.

Chloralformamide, $Cl_3CCHOHNHCHO$, is a soporific slower and safer in its action than chloral hydrate. Chloralimide, $(Cl_3CCH{=}NH)_3$, prepared by the reaction between chloral and ammonium chloride, is a tasteless, odorless crystalline material that is employed as an antipyretic and analgesic. Butyl chloral, $CH_3CHClCCl_2CHO$, is a substance similar to chloral that is used in medicine as a sedative.

CHLORAL HYDRATE, klôr′əl hī′drāt, is a sleep-inducing drug. In therapeutic doses, it produces natural-like sleep, lasting up to 8 hours. However, the drug is irritating to the skin and mucous membranes and should be taken only under medical supervision.

Toxic doses of chloral hydrate cause respiratory depression, a fall in blood pressure, and damage to the heart. Combinations of liquid chloral and alcohol, known as "knockout drops" or as "Mickey Finns," can produce an acute poisoning. Taken habitually, chloral hydrate produces addiction, or physical dependence, and the chronic user usually has gastritis.

Chloral hydrate is a crystalline powder produced by the addition of water to chloral (q.v.).

CHLORAMPHENICOL, klôr-am-fen′ə-kôl, is an antibiotic that is effective against a wide variety of disease-causing microorganisms but can also cause serious illness. It is widely known by its trade name Chloromycetin.

The drug acts by blocking protein synthesis in bacteria. It is the preferred drug for the treatment of typhoid fever, and it can also be used to treat rickettsial, urinary tract, and other infections, but safer antibiotics are preferred for most infections. Caution in the use of chloramphenicol is necessary because the drug can cause serious and even fatal reactions, including a severe depression of the bone marrow and a resulting disappearance of blood cells. Very young babies are especially vulnerable to severe reactions.

Chloramphenicol has been prepared synthetically, but its isolation from cultures of the fungus *Streptomyces venezuelae* is more economical.

ANDRES GOTH, M. D.
University of Texas Southwestern Medical School

CHLORDANE, klôr′dān, is a powerful insecticide of the chlorinated hydrocarbon class. A viscous liquid with the formula $C_{10}H_6Cl_8$, it is soluble in many organic solvents but insoluble in water. Its primary uses have been for veterinary purposes in controlling lice, ticks, fleas, and mange; in sprays to kill household insects; and in agriculture to control various insects, especially on corn.

Chlordane is a toxic chemical and should be handled with care. It is poisonous if inhaled, swallowed, or absorbed through the skin. Its manufacture and sale by manufacturers for most uses were banned in July 1975 because of its cancer-causing properties.

CHLORINE, klōr′ēn, a nonmetallic element, symbol Cl, is a member of the halogen family. The discovery of chlorine is generally attributed to Carl Wilhelm Scheele, a Swedish chemist, who called the gas "dephlogisticated marine acid air." In 1810, Sir Humphry Davy proved that the gas was an element and named it chlorine, from the Greek word for greenish yellow, *chloros.* However, because it was difficult to make and impossible to handle or transport, chlorine remained a laboratory curiosity for many years. In 1823, Michael Faraday produced liquid chlorine for the first time. Only after a method for manufacturing liquid chlorine on a commercial scale was found were its many uses realized.

Properties. Liquid chlorine is a clear, amber fluid, which in contact with the eyes, skin, or clothing may cause severe burns. The liquid vaporizes readily to a greenish yellow gas that is about 2½ times as heavy as air. The gas has a characteristic, sharply penetrating odor. In concentrations of about 3 to 5 parts per million in air, it can be readily detected by most people. In such low concentrations the gas irritates the mucous membranes, the respiratory system, and the skin. Fifteen to 30 parts per million causes more severe irritation of eyes, coughing, and labored breathing. In high concentrations, difficulty in breathing may increase to the point that death occurs from suffocation. Although it is extremely hazardous, chlorine produces no known cumulative effects.

The atomic number of chlorine is 17, and its atomic weight is 35.45. The diatomic element, Cl_2, has a molecular weight of 70.9; it solidifies at $-101°C$ ($-149.8°F$), and it boils at $-34°C$ ($-29.2°F$). Liquid chlorine is 1½ times as heavy as water. Chlorine occurs naturally in two isotopic forms—Cl^{35}, which makes up 75% of the chlorine found in nature, and Cl^{37}, which makes up about 25% of naturally occurring chlorine. In addition, at least five other isotopes of chlorine have been produced synthetically. These are Cl^{33}, Cl^{34}, Cl^{36}, Cl^{38}, and Cl^{39}. Cl^{36} is used as a tracer in studies of the chemical effects of chlorides and in studies of the reaction mechanisms of chlorine-containing compounds.

Like other members of the halogen family, including fluorine, bromine, and iodine, chlorine has a high electronegativity and forms negative ions. Under specific conditions, chlorine unites with most of the other elements. In the presence of heat or moisture the reaction may be extremely rapid. Chlorine reacts with many inorganic compounds—in some cases with explosive violence, and frequently with the evolution of heat. Small amounts of chlorine will dissolve in water, forming hypochlorous acid, HOCl, and hydrochloric acid, HCl; the chlorine is readily released by these compounds. In attacking metals, for example, corrosion is caused primarily by the powerful oxidizing action of the hypochlorous acid and the dissolving action of the hydrochloric acid formed through hydrolysis. For this reason chlorine is usually handled and stored under cool, dry conditions. It is generally kept in iron, steel, or copper containers.

Uses. The most important use of chlorine is in the synthesis of chemical intermediates of products that contain no chlorine. The largest single use is in the manufacture of ethylene oxide, H_2COCH_2 and ethylene glycol, $HOCH_2CH_2OH$. These two organic chemicals are key compounds in the manufacture of syn-

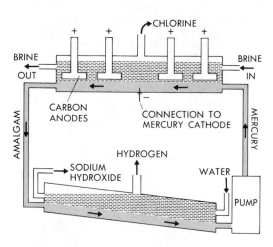

In mercury-cathode cells, salt water is electrolyzed and chlorine gas is given off at the anode. Alkali metal forms an amalgam with the mercury cathode, and the amalgam is then decomposed to yield caustic soda.

thetic fibers and antifreeze fluids, and as intermediates in organic synthesis.

Chlorine is also employed in the synthesis of intermediates for the preparation of propylene glycol, which is used in the manufacture of polyester resins and cellophane. Similarly, chlorine is used in the synthesis of intermediates of glycerol, which is used in making resins and explosives.

Inorganic Chlorine Compounds. The most common inorganic compounds of chlorine are sodium chlorine, NaCl, which is common table salt, and hydrogen chloride, a colorless gas that readily dissolves in water to form hydrochloric and hypochlorous acids. The reaction of chlorine with water to form the acids is the basis for the use of chlorine to kill bacteria in drinking water and swimming pools and in sewage-treatment systems.

Chlorine generally forms negative, univalent ions, but it also exhibits positive oxidation states in compounds such as sodium hypochlorite, $NaClO$, sodium chlorite, $NaClO_2$, sodium chlorate, $NaClO_3$, and sodium perchlorate, $NaClO_4$. The hypochlorites NaClO and CaClO are important products in making bleaching powder for the paper and pulp industry.

Organic Chlorine Compounds. Among the most important organic compounds of chlorine are the chlorinated alkanes and alkenes. These include carbon tetrachloride, CCl_4, chloroform, $CHCl_3$, methylene chloride, CH_2Cl_2, trichloroethylene, $CHCl=CCl_2$, and tetra-chloroethylene, $CCl_2=CCl_2$. Such compounds are used in the manufacture of cleaning solvents, paint removers, degreasing and metal-cleaning solutions, and in the dry cleaning industry. Carbon tetrachloride and chloroform are also important starting materials in the manufacture of fluorocarbons, such as the Freons, for refrigerants and aerosol propellants.

Chlorine is used extensively in the preparation of 1,2=dichloroethane, which is commonly known as ethylene dichloride. This substance is added to gasoline that contains tetraethyl lead to improve the antiknock properties of the fuel. Ethylene dichloride is also used in the preparation of vinyl chloride, $CH_2=CHCl$, an important commercial monomer used in making plastic and resin products.

Chlorine is also an important ingredient in many pesticides, including such compounds as dichlorodiphenyltrichloroethane (DDT), benzene hexachloride (BHC), 2,4-dichlorophenoxyactic acid (2,4-D), lindane, and chlordane. Monochloroacetic acid ($CH_2ClCOOH$) is used in herbicides and also in detergents, pharmaceuticals, and in the preparation of thioglycolic acid ($HSCH_2COOH$), which is used in permanent wave lotions.

Occurrence. Because of its extreme reactivity, chlorine is not found in nature in the free state. It is found only in the combined state, chiefly with sodium as common salt, NaCl. It is also found as the minerals carnallite, $KCl \cdot MgCl_2 \cdot 6H_2O$, and sylvite, KCl.

Production. During the last half of the 19th century, chlorine was produced commercially by oxidation of hydrogen chloride either with manganese dioxide (the Weldon process) or with air (the Deacon process). Today, however, most chlorine is produced by the electrolysis of brines. This method was initially utilized for the preparation of caustic soda, or sodium hydroxide, and the chlorine that was produced was considered to be a useless by-product. During the early 1850's several British patents indicated that there was some understanding of the potential value of commercial electrochemical production of chlorine. However, because electricity was exceedingly expensive at that time, this method was not adopted until the early 20th century.

Two general types of electrochemical cells are now in common use — the diaphragm cell and the mercury-cathode cell. The diaphragm cell is used in the production of about 75% of the chlorine made in the United States. In a diaphragm cell a sheet of material, usually asbestos, is used to separate the anode and its surrounding fluid from the cathode and its fluid. This prevents the products of the electrolysis — chlorine and sodium hydroxide — from interacting. In an operational diaphragm cell, sodium chloride brine is continuously fed into the solution surrounding the anode, where chlorine gas is being liberated from the solution and then collected for industrial use. Some of the brine flows through the diaphragm into the solution surrounding the cathode. At the cathode, hydrogen is liberated. Evaporation of the aqueous solution yields sodium hydroxide, which is also known as caustic soda.

The mercury-cathode cell, which is used in most countries other than the United States, is composed of two essential parts — an electrolyzer and a decomposer. In the electrolyzer an aqueous solution of the salt undergoes electrolysis. Chlorine gas is evolved at the insoluble graphite anode, and an alkali metal is deposited at the surface of the mercury cathode, in which it dissolves to form a liquid mercury amalgam. The amalgam flows into the decomposer, where it is broken down with water to form caustic and hydrogen gas.

DONALD J. BURTON
University of Iowa

CHLORIS, klō′ris, in Greek legend:

(1) The daughter of Amphion, king of Thebes, and Niobe. When Niobe boasted of her fertility (having had, by most accounts, seven sons and seven daughters) she enraged Leto, wife of Zeus, who had only two children, Apollo and Artemis. As punishment for Niobe's arrogance, Apollo and Artemis shot arrows at her children, all of whom were killed except Chloris and her brother Amyclas, who managed to escape.

(2) The wife of Neleus, king of Pylos, by whom she had 12 sons, all of whom except Nestor were slain by Hercules.

(3) The goddess of bowers and the wife of Zephyrus, god of the west wind. She was known to the Romans as Flora.

CHLORITE GROUP, klōr′īt, a mineral group of hydrous magnesium silicates such as prochlorite, clinochlore, and penninite. Aluminum and iron substitute for magnesium and silicon to varying degrees in different minerals of the group, all of which have similar chemical and physical properties.

The crystals of chlorite minerals are transparent to opaque and have a glassy or pearly luster. They are usually various shades of green, but sometimes are reddish, yellow, or white, because of the presence of elements such as manganese or chromium. The minerals of the chlorite group are common and widespread. Their presence in many slates and schists accounts for the green color often observed in those rocks.

Composition, $Mg_3(Si_4O_{10})(OH)_2 \cdot Mg_3(OH)_6$ (general formula); hardness, 2–2.5; specific gravity, 2.6–2.9; crystal system, monoclinic.

CHLOROFORM, klôr′ə-fôrm, is an anesthetic agent. It was one of the first anesthetics to be used, but in the United States it has now been almost completely supplanted by other, safer anesthetics. Chloroform is, however, still used in some parts of the world, particularly in tropical areas where the heat would cause ether dispensed by the opendrop method to evaporate too quickly.

About eight times as potent as ether in producing anesthesia, chloroform is used only in low concentrations. The margin of safety between anesthetic and lethal doses is small. Chloroform may cause serious circulatory depression (low blood pressure), fatal disturbances in heart rhythm, and liver damage. It is rapidly absorbed from the skin and mucous membranes, and it is highly toxic. Prolonged use of chloroform may result in vomiting, jaundice, coma, and possibly death.

In addition to its former use as an anesthetic, especially in obstetrical procedures, chloroform was also used as a component of liniments and cough mixtures. However, this use was not based on any scientific evidence, and most physicians today do not include chloroform in their prescriptions. However, there are still several over-the-counter cough mixtures and liniments that contain chloroform.

The chemical formula of chloroform, or trichloromethane, is $CHCl_3$. A heavy, colorless liquid at ordinary temperatures, chloroform boils at 141°F (61°C). At 77°F (25°C), it dissolves in 210 volumes of water and has a specific gravity of 1.476. It vaporizes readily. Soluble in fats and oils, chloroform is an excellent organic solvent that can be used in several chemical procedures. Chloroform itself does not burn, but in the presence of a flame it converts to phosgene, a toxic war gas.

Chloroform was discovered in 1831–1832 independently by three men: Samuel Guthrie of the United States, Eugène Soubeiron of France, and Justus von Liebig of Germany. Its value as an anesthetic agent was discovered by the obstetrician Sir James Y. Simpson of Scotland in 1847, and its use was subsequently popularized in England by John Snow.

SOLOMON GARB, M.D.
University of Missouri Medical School

CHLOROMYCETIN, a trade name for chloramphenicol. See CHLORAMPHENICOL.

CHLOROPHYCEAE and **CHLOROPHYTA.** See ALGAE—*Green Algae.*

CHLOROPHYLL, klôr'ə-fil, is the green pigment that plants use to carry out the process of photosynthesis. Its function is to absorb the light energy used in photosynthesis for the reduction of carbon dioxide to sugars and other plant materials. The chlorophyll of the plant cells is contained within the organelles called the chloroplasts (see CHLOROPLAST).

Chemistry of Chlorophyll. Chlorophyll is actually a group of substances that are closely related to one another but are distinguishable by the colors of light that they absorb. For example, chlorophylls *a* and *b,* which occur in higher plants, absorb light that has maximum wavelengths of 675 and 650 millimicrons (1 millimicron = $\frac{1}{25}$ millionth inch) respectively, while the two kinds of chlorobium chlorophyll in green photosynthetic bacteria absorb light maximally at wavelengths of 725 and 747 millimicrons respectively.

Structure of a molecule of chlorophyll *a*

All chlorophylls are porphyrins; that is, their chemical structure consists of four simple pyrrole rings, each of which contains four carbon atoms and one nitrogen atom. The pyrrole rings are joined by carbon bridges, forming a larger ring. Chlorophyll is distinguished from other porphyrins occurring in nature by two characteristics—the magnesium atom found in the center of the chlorophyll porphyrin rings and the long-chain phytol group bound to it. The magnesium atom appears to play a determining role in the photosynthetic function of chlorophyll. Chlorophyll also is characterized by the number and nature of the simpler chains arranged around the periphery of the porphyrin nucleus.

Chlorophyll and Photosynthesis. The fact that chlorophyll is essential to photosynthesis can be demonstrated in a number of simple ways. First, it is possible to show that the nongreen portions of variegated leaves and the nongreen leaves of variegated plants do not carry on photosynthesis.

Next, it can also be shown that photosynthesis takes place within the cells of the leaf only when the light falls directly on the chlorophyll-containing bodies, the chloroplasts. Finally, the comparison of the absorption spectra of the colors of light absorbed by chlorophyll with the effectiveness of these same colors of light in inducing photosynthesis by the leaf confirms that chlorophyll is essential to the photosynthetic process.

To be active in photosynthesis, chlorophyll must be bound to proteins, which in turn are constituents of the organized membranes (lamellae) of the chloroplast. The same chlorophyll, for example chlorophyll *a,* may be bound to more than one type of protein in the chloroplast, giving rise to chlorophyll *a*'s of different absorption spectra and different photosynthetic activity. One such form of chlorophyll *a,* known as chlorophyll-*a*-P700, although present in the chloroplast only in small amounts, is believed to be responsible for one of the basic photosynthetic acts in which light energy is converted to chemical form.

Although chlorophyll is required for photosynthesis, other pigments also play a role in the process. These accessory pigments are able to absorb light energy and transfer it to chlorophyll *a.* The accessory pigments increase the range of wavelengths of light that can be used fruitfully by the plant for the conduct of photosynthesis. See also PHOTOSYNTHESIS.

JAMES BONNER
California Institute of Technology

CHLOROPICRIN, klôr-ə-pik'rən, is a colorless, slightly oily liquid of the formula CCl_3NO_2. It is highly poisonous if inhaled, and it is used for military purposes as a poison gas; it is also used in organic synthesis, in fumigants, in fungicides and insecticides, and for the extermination of rats.

Chloropicrin is a relatively stable liquid that is not decomposed by mineral acids. It is soluble in alcohol, benzene, and carbon disulfide but is insoluble in water. Chloropicrin is prepared either by the reaction of picric acid with calcium hypochlorite or by the addition of nitrogen to chlorinated hydrocarbons.

CHLOROPLAST, klôr'ə-plast, a chlorophyll-containing body found in the cytoplasm of plant cells. Chloroplasts are responsible for conducting the entire process of photosynthesis in plants. Cells in the green portions of the higher plants contain 20 to 50 chloroplasts each, while cells of algae contain fewer chloroplasts, and often only one chloroplast per cell.

Structure and Function. Algal chloroplasts commonly have unusual shapes; for example, the single chloroplast of *Spirogyra* is helical. The chloroplasts of the higher plants are saucer-shaped, and each is 5 to 20 microns (0.005–0.02 mm) in diameter and 1 to 2 microns (0.001–0.002 mm) thick. Each chloroplast is bounded by a semipermeable membrane and contains a highly ordered system of membranes arranged in pancakelike stacks called grana. The membranes bear large numbers of particles—the quantasomes—composed of protein and lipids. These particles contain all of the chlorophyll of the chloroplast.

The photosynthetic reactions by which light is captured and its energy converted into forms suitable for reducing carbon dioxide all take place in the quantasome. The spaces between the grana in the chloroplast contain the enzymes

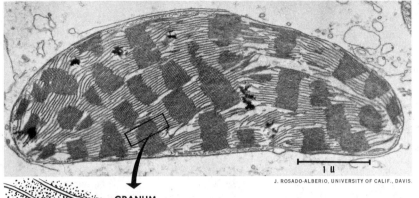

(Left) Electron micrograph of chloroplast showing many grana. (Below) Diagram of granum with its stacked lamellae, and a cross section of a single lamella showing one suggested molecular structure.

J. ROSADO-ALBERIO, UNIVERSITY OF CALIF., DAVIS.

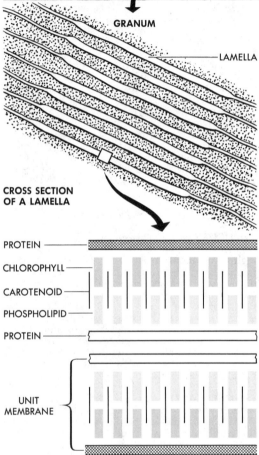

GRANUM

LAMELLA

CROSS SECTION
OF A LAMELLA

PROTEIN

CHLOROPHYLL

CAROTENOID

PHOSPHOLIPID

PROTEIN

UNIT
MEMBRANE

in many strains of plants they are known to be passed from one generation to the next only through the maternal line. In general, proplastids do not appear to be passed on through the male, or pollen, line.

Chloroplasts as Symbionts. In many respects chloroplasts are semiautonomous, self-replicating entities that live symbiotically within their host plant cell. They resemble single-celled organisms in that they contain their own genetic material (DNA) and produce their own ribosomes (small particles that are the site of protein synthesis). The chloroplast ribosomes differ in size and chemical composition from those of the host cell; they synthesize many, and perhaps all, of the enzymes used in photosynthesis. It is also possible to demonstrate that when two chloroplasts bearing different genetic markers (characters that identify a particular mutant) reside in the same cell, they may undergo fusion, sexual union, and recombination of their genetic markers, just as do other single-celled organisms.

Since the properties of chloroplasts of all plants, from algae to the higher plants, are remarkably similar, it would appear that the cells of plants were infected by some now extinct creature—the ancestor of the chloroplasts—long ago in evolution. The symbiotic relationship between chloroplasts and plant cell proved so profitable that it has been maintained largely unchanged to the present day.

JAMES BONNER
California Institute of Technology

CHLOROQUINE, klôr′ō-kwīn, an important synthetic drug, is used primarily for the treatment of malaria, but it also has other valuable medical uses. It was developed in the United States during World War II in an effort to find a synthetic antimalarial drug superior to the ones then available. The drug also turned out to be valuable in the treatment of amebic infections, and it may have value in some other diseases, including some forms of arthritis.

The antimalarial effectiveness of chloroquine depends on the strain of protozoa causing the malarial infection. In infections caused by *Plasmodium falciparum*, chloroquine cures the infection, except for a few resistant cases, while in infections caused by *P. vivax*, chloroquine suppresses the attacks but fails to eradicate the infection. In ameba infections, the drug is valuable when the liver and other organs outside the intestine are affected. Chloroquine may cause some adverse effects, including visual disturbances, gastrointestinal difficulties, itchiness, and headache.

ANDRES GOTH, M. D.
University of Texas Southwestern Medical School

that are responsible for the use of this energy in manufacturing carbohydrates.

Reproduction. Chloroplasts arise only from chloroplasts, and thus they are self-replicating, or self-reproducing. In algae the chloroplast divides at the time of cell division, and each daughter cell receives one of the daughter chloroplasts. In the higher plants, chloroplasts develop from smaller, colorless, immature forms called proplastids. During cell division in the higher plants the proplastids divide but mature chloroplasts do not. The development of the proplastids into chloroplasts is controlled genetically by each plant, or host, cell containing them.

Although all cells of the plant body presumably contain proplastids, the development of the proplastids into mature chloroplasts takes place only in certain of the plant cells, such as those of the leaf, and only in the presence of light. Proplastids occur in the cytoplasm of eggs, and

CHLOROSIS, klə-rō'sis, is a term once commonly applied to a form of iron-deficiency anemia. This type of anemia occurred mostly in young girls and was characterized by weakness, fatigue, nervousness, pounding of the heart, and digestive upsets. In addition, the patient's skin appeared pale, and because some people thought the skin had a greenish tint, the disorder was also commonly known as *green sickness.*

For many years, physicians failed to understand the true nature of the disease and attributed it to causes ranging from neurosis to tight corsets. Around 1900 the disorder became recognized as a form of iron-deficiency anemia, and the term "chlorosis" slowly disappeared from use.

ERNEST BEUTLER, M. D.
City of Hope Medical Center, Duarte, Calif.

CHLORPROMAZINE, a tranquilizing drug. See TRANQUILIZING DRUGS.

CHLORTETRACYCLINE, an antibiotic commonly known by its trade name Aureomycin. See ANTIBIOTICS.

CHMIELNICKI, KHmyel-nēts'kē, **Bohdan** (1595?–1657), Ukrainian national hero, who was a Cossack leader. The Ukrainian form of his name is Bohdan Khmelnytzkyi, and the Russian form is Bogdan Khmelnitsky. He was born into the petty gentry of the Ukraine. Captured by the Turks in the Polish-Turkish war of 1620–1621, he returned to his estate after two years in Constantinople and apparently took up the ways of a landowner, loyal to the Polish crown.

For most Ukrainians, who were Eastern Orthodox, Polish rule meant oppression by Polish Catholic landlords. For the Cossacks, it meant they would have to struggle to retain privileges granted them for military service. Discontent caused sporadic rebellion among them, which was harshly repressed. Chmielnicki often argued the Ukrainian case, quite loyally, to the Polish authorities. However, after a punitive detachment of Poles sacked his estate, abducted his wife, and murdered his son, he turned against the government and became a rebel leader. Although his diplomacy and the prowess of the Cossacks enabled him to defeat the Poles many times, indecision, the heterogeneity of the movement, and the unreliability of his allies deprived him of success. He was granted Russian aid in 1654 in return for his recognition of the czar's sovereignty. He died at Subotov on Aug. 6, 1657.

EDWARD KEENAN, *Harvard University*

CHOATE, chōt, **Joseph Hodges** (1832–1917), American lawyer and diplomat. He was born on Jan. 24, 1832, in Salem, Mass., into an old and distinguished New England family. He graduated from Harvard College in 1852 and Harvard Law School two years later. In 1855 he was admitted to the bar, and he moved to New York City, where he became a leading lawyer. His cases ran the gamut from courts-martial to antitrust suits, from disputes over wills to claims under the *Alabama* award. In his most famous case, he argued successfully against the constitutionality of the income tax law of 1894 before the U. S. Supreme Court in 1895.

A well-known "club man" and popular after-dinner speaker, Choate was active in New York cultural and humanitarian undertakings. A Republican, he helped organize the Committee of Seventy that was responsible for the overthrow of the Tweed Ring. He was president of the New York constitutional convention of 1894. Appointed ambassador to Britain in 1899, he served in that post for six years and helped settle the Alaska boundary dispute. In 1907, Choate was named head of the American delegation to the Second Hague Conference. When World War I broke out, he ardently supported the Allies and was active in urging American intervention. He died on May 14, 1917, in New York City.

JOHN BRAEMAN, *University of Nebraska*

CHOATE, chōt, **Rufus** (1799–1859), American lawyer and political leader, who was deeply devoted to the law and phenomenally successful at its practice. George F. Hoar compared his power over jurymen with the fascination of a snake for a bird, and Wendell Phillips called Choate "a man who made it safe to murder." Tall, with wild hair, unearthly eyes, and a voice that ranged from a whisper to a roar, Choate suited an age that liked picturesque heroes and purple oratory.

Born in Essex, Mass., on Oct. 1, 1799, Choate graduated from Dartmouth College in 1819, first in his class. Worship of Daniel Webster, the hero of the Dartmouth College case (1818), won Choate over to the practice of law. Admitted to the Massachusetts bar in 1823, he started his practice at Danvers, Mass., later moving to Salem and then to Boston.

Unlike many attorneys, Choate preferred the life of a lawyer to that of an officeholder. He served in both houses of the Massachusetts legislature (1825–1831), in the U. S. House of Representatives (1831–1833), and in the U. S. Senate (1841–1845), but he retired gratefully and declined appointments to the Massachusetts supreme court and the U. S. Supreme Court. His political views reflected the economic needs of his state, and his nationalism was another form of New England sectionalism. His law practice included famous cases argued before the U. S. Supreme Court, such as the License and Passenger cases (1847 and 1849), but criminal law was his forte.

A lifelong scholar, Choate accumulated an 8,000-volume library and wrote and lectured on a multitude of subjects. He died en route to Europe, at Halifax, Nova Scotia, on July 13, 1859.

JOSEPH C. BURKE, *Duquesne University*

CHOCANO, chō-kä'nō, **José Santos** (1875–1934), Peruvian poet and revolutionary nationalist. He was born in Peru on May 14, 1875. His early years are obscure. He was an active journalist, diplomat, and politician and spent some years in Colombia, Spain, Mexico, and Guatemala. He was an adviser to the Mexican guerrilla Francisco Villa and to President Manuel Estreba Cabrera of Guatemala. Not long after returning to Peru in 1921, he killed one of his political enemies. Thereafter he lived in exile in Santiago de Chile, where he himself was murdered on Dec. 13, 1934.

Chocano's poetry, generally rich, vigorous, and musical, is derived from both the Indian and Spanish traditions and defends Latin America against "Yankee imperialism." The best known of his volumes, *Alma América* (1906), influenced the Nicaraguan poet Rubén Darío in the development of native American themes. Chocano's poem ¿ *Quién sabe?* (1913) stimulated the *indianista* tendency in Latin American literature.

CHOCOLATES are formed on sheets by the depositor.

CHOCOLATE, chok′lət, is a solid or semisolid food prepared by the fine grinding of roasted, shelled beans of the cacao, or cocoa, tree. As the beans are ground, a free-flowing liquid is produced. This liquid, called *chocolate liquor,* is the basis for all chocolate products.

Chocolate liquor consists largely of fat called *cocoa butter,* which makes up slightly more than half its weight. It also contains carbohydrates, protein, a small amount of mineral matter, and about 1% residual moisture. Its rich brown color is derived from the natural bean pigments and its unique aroma is due to the bean's various essential oils.

Although chocolate and cocoa are commonly regarded as very different foods, they differ only in the amount of cocoa butter they contain. When chocolate liquor is subjected to hydraulic pressure until its cocoa butter content is reduced from about 54% to 24% or less, the residue forms a solid mass called *press cake.* This cake is broken, pulverized, cooled, and sifted, producing commercial *cocoa powder.* Chocolate is made with chocolate liquor whose fat content has not been reduced.

Kinds of Chocolate. In the chocolate factory the three products—chocolate liquor, cocoa powder, and cocoa butter—are converted into an almost endless variety of consumer products. Most chocolate manufacturers closely guard their formulas and procedures for blending the beans and their methods of processing added ingredients. However, according to the Definitions and Standards of the Federal Food, Drug, and Cosmetic Law of 1944, all forms of chocolate sold in the United States must be manufactured within the limits of the regulations set forth.

Milk chocolate is by far the most popular kind of chocolate. As defined by law, several types of dairy products may be used in making milk chocolate, but fluid and powdered whole milk are the traditional and most widely used products. Similarly, a variety of sweeteners may be used, since unsweetened chocolate is too concentrated in flavor to be eaten as such and would have little appeal if made into a sugarless product. By law,

milk chocolate must contain not less than 12% milk solids and not less than 10% chocolate liquor. Certain optional ingredients are permissible, but they must all conform to the prescribed standards.

Sweet chocolate differs from milk chocolate in that it contains no milk solids, but it must contain not less than 15% chocolate liquor. *Bittersweet chocolate* is sweet chocolate that contains not less than 35% chocolate liquor. *Baking chocolate,* or *bitter chocolate,* contains no milk solids or sweeteners.

Chocolate Manufacture. The manufacture of chocolate begins with the delivery of dried, fermented cocoa beans to the factory. The beans arrive in large burlap bags weighing an average of about 140 pounds (64 kg). The first step in the manufacturing process is cleaning the beans, by using screens and air currents to remove extraneous material. The different kinds of cocoa beans may then be blended, although this step sometimes occurs after roasting. During roasting, the beans are placed in rotating cylinders through which air, heated by gas or oil, is forced. The temperature of the air exceeds 500° F (260° C), and the entire process, in which the moisture of the beans is reduced from 7% or 8% to about 1%, is completed in about one half to three quarters of an hour.

After cooling, the beans are cracked or shattered and the shell, which is lighter than the inner material, is removed from the cracked bean by air currents. The remaining particles, called *nibs,* are then ground by one of several processes to obtain the chocolate liquor.

Once the chocolate liquor is collected, a portion of it is sent to the hydraulic presses, not only to produce cocoa powder but to obtain cocoa butter, which is later used in making milk chocolate and sweet chocolate. The remaining portion of the chocolate liquor is added to various mixtures to make different kinds of chocolate. For milk chocolate, the chocolate liquor is combined with either powdered milk mixed with pulverized sugar, or with a mixture of fluid milk and dissolved sugar that has been reduced to a powder by boiling under high vacuum at low temperatures to prevent caramelization. For sweet chocolate, the chocolate liquor is mixed with pulverized sugar.

After the various mixtures are blended, they are usually subjected to their first fine grinding by steel roll refiners. After this initial grinding, the cocoa butter obtained in the hydraulic presses is added to convert the fine powders into pastes of desired consistency. Spices and flavorings are usually added at this stage, and further grinding and flavoring procedures are carried out with or without the application of heat. The only processes that remain are those of viscosity standardization, tempering, molding into bars, blocks, or cakes, and the wrapping, packaging, and shipping of the chocolate. All these procedures are conducted under strict controls because of the perishable nature of most chocolate products when subjected to exposure and particularly to heat.

History of Chocolate. The words "cacao" and "chocolate" stem directly from the languages of the Maya and Aztec Indians of Central America. It is not known exactly when cacao trees were first cultivated, but it is known that cacao beans played an important role in these Indians' lives— as a form of currency and as the chief ingredient of a cold sugarless beverage that they called *cacahuatl,* enjoyed by members of the upper class.

In the early 1500's Spanish explorers in Central America noted the popularity of the drink but were not attracted to it because of its bitterness. Being familiar with sugar, they sweetened the drink to produce a new kind of beverage, served hot. Named *chocolatl* by the Indians to distinguish it from *cacahuatl,* it was brought back to Spain by Hernán Cortés.

During the next two centuries, as the popularity of the drink spread from the Spanish court to the courts of other European countries, it became the fashion to serve chocolate to royal guests. In 1720 the Swedish botanist and taxonomist Carolus Linnaeus gave the cacao tree the scientific name *Theobroma cacao,* derived from Greek words meaning "cacao, the food of the gods." The food value of the drink, however, had been recognized two centuries earlier by Cortés who, in a letter to his emperor, Charles V, wrote that *chocolatl* is "the divine drink that builds up resistance and fights fatigue."

In the late 18th century, French and Dutch processors began experimenting with methods of defatting chocolate liquor, leading to the manufacture of chocolate powder. The idea of adding finely ground sugar to the residual cocoa butter followed, and it is believed that the first solid eating chocolate was sold in England in the mid-1800's. The food value of the solid chocolate was soon recognized. Chocolate bars were included as standard rations items for troops in the South African War and World Wars I and II. Today, the U. S. Army Field Ration "D"—an emergency starvation preventive—is a 4-ounce (125 gm) bar of special chocolate fortified with vitamin B_1 (thiamine) and containing 600 calories.

Production and Consumption. The production of chocolate and cocoa is usually measured in terms of cocoa bean grindings. The total world production of cocoa bean grindings is about 1.5 million tons a year. The largest chocolate- and cocoa-producing country is the United States, which produces about 21% of this total. Other leading producers include West Germany, which produces about 11% of the world total; the Netherlands, about 9%; and Britain, about 8%. The most outstanding increase in chocolate production has occurred in the Soviet Union, where the amount produced rose from 5,600 tons in 1939 to 95,200 tons in 1967.

During the 20th century, western Europe and the United States have been by far the world's largest consumers of chocolate and cocoa. The tropical countries, where the entire supply of cocoa beans is grown, consume very little of the finished products, owing to the difficulty of preserving chocolate in a hot climate.

In the United States the consumption of chocolate and cocoa is about 330,400 tons a year. This is equivalent to about 3½ pounds (1.6 kg) per person. About 94% of this total is produced in the United States; the rest is imported almost entirely from Europe. In the United States the leading state in the production of chocolate is Pennsylvania.

SAMUEL F. HINKLE, *Former President*
The Hershey Chocolate Corporation

Further Reading: Chatt, Eileen M., *Cocoa: Cultivation, Processing, Analysis* (New York 1954); Clarke, Tresper, *Sidelights in the History of Cacao and Chocolate* (Toronto 1961); Cook, L. Russell, *Chocolate Production and Use* (New York 1963); Hinkle, Samuel F., *Interesting Aspects of Chocolate* (Philadelphia 1947).

CHOCTAW INDIANS, chok'tô, an important North American tribe, speaking a language of the Muskhogean family. At the time of European contact they lived in the central and southern areas of what is now Mississippi.

The Choctaw were less warlike than their neighbors and traditional enemies, the Chickasaw. Instead, they devoted their energies to agriculture. The staple crop was maize, which they produced in a number of varieties. Beans, pumpkins, sweet potatoes, and sunflowers (grown for the seeds which were ground into flour) were also raised, along with tobacco. They cleared the land by girdling the large trees and burning the underbrush. They used digging-sticks to make holes for planting the seeds, and for hoeing they used an implement made from the shoulder blade of a bison or, sometimes, by attaching a shell or stone blade to a wooden handle. Children camped in small shelters near the fields to chase crows away. Special huts were built to store the corn.

The Choctaw depended mainly on hunting for fresh meat. For this they used bow and arrows or long blowguns made of hollow cane. After European contact, horses became important, especially for transporting game killed on the hunt.

Ceremonies and Traditions. The Choctaw society was split into two divisions, which ruled, respectively, during war and peace. Little is known about these, but it is thought that they corresponded to the Red and White divisions of neighboring tribes, such as the Cherokee. Each division had the role of handling funeral duties for members of the opposite division. Choctaw funeral practices were elaborate. Bodies were wrapped in skins and left outdoors, sometimes on a scaffold, until most of the flesh was gone. Then the bones were cleaned by special priests who allowed their fingernails to grow long for this purpose. The clean bones were deposited together in a bone-house, above which were scaffolds from which were hung hoops, wreaths, and carved images to assist the spirits of the dead. When the bone-houses were filled, there was a general "feast of the dead" in which the relatives assembled to wail and bury the remains, forming a small conical mound of earth over them. The burial was followed by general feasting.

The Choctaw played a ball game using rackets and a small ball of stuffed deerskin. The game of "chunkey" was also popular. In one of its variations, competitors hurled sticks after a rolling disk, each trying to make his stick land closest to the stone when it stopped. These games were played with great competitive spirit and were accompanied by elaborate ritual dances.

History. During the 18th century the Choctaw allied themselves with the French, thus incurring the enmity of the Chickasaw tribes. Some of the Choctaw Indians began moving west of the Mississippi as early as 1780, where they clashed with the Caddo Indians. They ceded their lands to the United States government in 1830, and from 1831 to 1833 the majority of the tribe moved to Indian Territory (now Oklahoma). In the late 1960's there were about 11,000 Choctaw on reservations in Oklahoma and Mississippi.

RICHARD A. GOULD
American Museum of Natural History

Further Reading: Cotterill, R. S., *The Southern Indians* (Norman, Okla., 1954); Swanton, John R., *Source Material for the Social and Ceremonial Life of the Choctaw Indians* (Washington 1931).

CHODOWIECKI, кнō-dō-vyets′kē, **Daniel Nickolaus** (1726–1801), German painter and engraver, who was one of the most popular illustrators of his time. His work is distinguished for its sensitive designs and for its striking realism, which has been compared to Hogarth's. His engravings comment perceptively and sympathetically on contemporary manners and morals.

Chodowiecki was born in Danzig, Poland, on Oct. 16, 1726. He worked in business, first in Danzig and after 1743 in Berlin. In 1754 he turned to painting, beginning by painting snuffboxes and then progressing to enamels and miniatures. His set of miniatures *The History of the Life of Jesus Christ,* commissioned by the German Academy of Sciences in Berlin, established his reputation.

After 1757, Chodowiecki worked chiefly as an engraver, executing more than 2,000 engravings before his death. These included illustrations for Rousseau's *Nouvelle Héloïse,* Goethe's *Leiden des jungen Werthers,* Schiller's *Räuber,* Cervantes' *Don Quixote,* Sterne's *Sentimental Journey,* and Goldsmith's *Vicar of Wakefield,* as well as works by Lessing, Klopstock, Voltaire, and Shakespeare. In 1797 he became director of the Berlin Academy of Arts. Chodowiecki's engravings were in great demand throughout his life. He died in Berlin on Feb. 7, 1801.

CHOERILUS, kir-′i-ləs, the name of several Greek poets. Choerilus of Athens (6th–5th century B. C.) was a tragic poet who began writing plays in 523 B. C. According to Suidas, the 10th century lexicographer, Choerilus wrote 150 tragedies—13 of them prize-winners—and competed with Aeschylus, Pratinas, and Sophocles. He is said to have effected changes in the tragic mask and costume. Of his tragedies nothing but the name of one— *Alope*—survives.

Choerilus of Samos (late 5th century B. C.) composed an epic poem, *Perseis,* celebrating the victory of the Greeks over Xerxes I. He was a friend of Herodotus and, according to Suidas, fled Samos after him. Later he celebrated the feats of Lysander. He died at the court of Archelaus of Macedonia. *Perseis* (sometimes called *Persika*) is notable for its celebration of a historical rather than a mythological subject. Only fragments of *Perseis* are extant.

CHOFU, chō-fōō, in Japan, is a residential and industrial suburb of Tokyo on the island of Honshu. Located west of Tokyo along the banks of the Tama River, Chofu was originally a stage town on the Koshu Highway, a major artery linking Edo, the feudal capital, with the western Kanto Plain and beyond. Population expansion began with the spread of interurban transit in the 1920's and spurted after World War II. Chofu became a city in 1955. Population: (1965) 118,004.

DAVID H. KORNHAUSER
University of Hawaii

CHOIR, kwīr, in architecture, that part of a church intended primarily for the presiding clergy and the organized group of singers, or choir. Ordinarily the choir separates the sanctuary, or area surrounding the main altar, from the nave, where the congregation worships. Because most medieval churches were oriented with the main altar at the east end, the term "choir" came to be used to refer also to the whole eastern part of the building.

In pre-Reformation times the persons who sang the various church services were usually monks or canons and, as part of the clergy, were provided with an area in the church apart from that of the laity. In early Christian basilicas they probably occupied the bema, or transepts. (The apse, around the altar, was reserved for the higher clergy, and the nave for the laity.) As singers became more numerous, the choir was enlarged. In San Clemente, Rome (12th century), where there are no transepts, the choir occupies a considerable part of the nave and is divided from the rest of the nave by a low parapet wall.

In Romanesque and Gothic churches the choir is an additional unit that begins at the eastern side of the transepts and ends at the sanctuary. It is raised above the level of the nave by a step, or, where there is a crypt underneath the choir (as in San Miniato, Florence, or in Canterbury Cathedral), by a full flight of stairs. The choir is further isolated from the transepts and from its own side aisles by carved screens, considered especially important where the choir was composed of monks.

Although the laity had neither chairs nor pews, the members of the choir, who spent many hours daily at church services, were provided with choir stalls. Generally there are two or three rows of stalls on either side of a central aisle facing each other, each row raised a step or more above the one in front of it. The seats are often hinged, and have on their undersides a small bracket called a *misericord*. When the seat is folded up, the occupant standing in front of it can support some of his weight on the misericord. Most frequently misericords were simply carved moldings, but occasionally they were animal or human figures. A particularly interesting set is preserved in Beverly Minster, Yorkshire, England. Often the stalls of the back row, where the more important clergy sat, bore canopies with decorative wood tracery to suggest shelter.

EVERARD M. UPJOHN, *Columbia University*

CHOIR, in music. See CHORAL MUSIC.

CHOISEUL, shwȧ-zùl′, **Étienne François de** (1719–1785), French diplomat and statesman. He was born on June 28, 1719, the son of the Marquis de Stainville. As a young man, then known as the Count de Stainville, he entered the army and served with distinction in the War of the Austrian Succession, achieving in 1748 the rank of lieutenant general. In 1750, Stainville married one of the most delightful women of the 18th century, Louise Honorine Crozat.

Stainville's personal wealth and influence at court helped him to win the ambassadorship to Rome in 1753. For his services he was awarded the decoration of the Holy Spirit—and was appointed ambassador to Vienna in March 1757. He concluded the second Treaty of Versailles in May 1757, joining France and Austria in an offensive alliance to recover Silesia for Austria. At this time he was made Duke de Choiseul and a peer of France. On Dec. 3, 1758, during a critical juncture in the Seven Years' War, he succeeded Cardinal Bernis as minister for foreign affairs. He later served as minister of the navy, of colonies, and of war and *surintendant des postes* as well.

Choiseul's diplomatic skill saved France from the worst consequences of the disastrous Seven Years' War with Britain. On the one hand, he limited France's commitments in order to prepare for a separate peace with Britain; on the other hand, he prolonged the war by enticing Spain into the conflict in 1761 on France's side. Finally, at the Peace of Paris (1763), Choiseul gained valuable concessions for France from Britain at Spain's expense. He greatly expanded the navy and initiated army reforms that persisted until the Revolution.

Choiseul did not actively seek the expulsion of the Jesuits from France, as is often alleged. But, indifferent to the order and wearied by the diplomatic complications of its presence in France, he took no measures to save it. Increasing opposition from friends of the Jesuits and from critics of his naval and military programs brought about Choiseul's fall on Dec. 24, 1770. He was exiled to his estates in Touraine. He was allowed to return to Paris in 1774 but never recovered political power. He died in Paris on May 8, 1785.

LIONEL ROTHKRUG
University of Michigan

CHOISEUL, shwȧ-zûl', an island in the western Pacific Ocean, is part of the Solomon Islands. It is located about midway between Bougainville and Santa Isabel islands. Choiseul covers an area of about 1,500 square miles (3,885 sq km). It is volcanic and densely forested. The inhabitants are Melanesians, whose economy is based on copra.

Choiseul was under German control from 1886 to 1899, when it was taken over by Britain. It was occupied by the Japanese during World War II.

CHOKE, an electric circuit element that has many turns of insulated copper wire wound on a form. A choke has the property of inductance which is the ability to oppose a change in the electric current. A *smoothing choke,* which has a heavy steel core, is used to reduce fluctuations in the direct-current output of a power supply. An *audio-frequency choke,* which has a steel core, reduces current variations in circuits used at audio frequencies (20–20,000 hertz). A *radio-frequency choke,* which has an air core or a powdered iron core, is used to block radio-frequency currents.

E. NORMAN LURCH
State University of New York, Farmingdale

CHOKEBERRY, any of several eastern North American shrubs sometimes planted for ornament. Chokeberries belong to the genus *Aronia* of the rose family (Rosaceae). The most popular species is the red chokeberry (*A. arbutifolia*), named for its small, bright red, applelike fruits and its leaves, which turn red in the fall. The red chokeberry grows about 9 feet (2.7 meters) tall and bears small, white, 5-petaled flowers similar to those of the strawberry. It is often found in woodlands and grows well in almost any soil.

DONALD WYMAN
The Arnold Arboretum, Harvard University

CHOKECHERRY, a shrub or small tree, whose small round edible fruits have been used in making wines, sauces, and jellies. The chokecherry is known botanically as *Prunus virginiana,* and it belongs to the rose family (Rosaceae). It ranges from Newfoundland to Saskatchewan and south to North Carolina and Missouri.

JOHN J. SMITH

Chokecherry

The chokecherry grows up to 30 feet (9 meters) in height. Its alternate leaves vary from ¾ to 4½ inches (20–115 mm) long and contain a substance that is poisonous to cattle and other animals. The small white flowers of the chokecherry are borne in spikes from 2½ to 5 inches (6–12 cm) long, and the fruits vary in color according to the variety. Most chokecherries have dark purple fruits, but those of the variety *melanocarpa* are black while those of the variety *xanthocarpa* are yellow.

DONALD WYMAN
The Arnold Arboretum, Harvard University

CHOKING is a sensation that occurs in the throat when the flow of air into the lungs is partially or completely obstructed. The obstruction may be present in the back of the throat (pharynx), the voice box (larynx), or the windpipe (trachea), and it may be caused by objects within these structures or as a result of outside pressure on them. Choking may also occur if a person inhales an extremely irritating gas, causing a sudden reflex action that prevents breathing. In any of these circumstances, the reaction is acute anxiety or panic, with violent attempts to expel the occluding objects, to remove anything constricting the throat or chest, and to overcome suffocation by breathing hard.

Choking most often occurs during eating or drinking, when solid food lodges in the pharynx or larynx or when liquid is inhaled into the larynx and trachea. As a rule, the expulsive force of coughing is sufficient to remove the obstructions. Obstructions that cannot be coughed up may be removed manually or with a special instrument. If a completely obstructing object cannot be removed immediately, breathing may be restored by making a surgical opening in the trachea below the obstruction.

In the "Heimlich maneuver" for relieving choking, the rescuer wraps his arms around the victim's waist from behind, makes a fist with one hand and holds the fist with the other hand between the navel and rib cage, and presses the fist forcefully into the victim's diaphragm to expel the food. See also FIRST AID.

RALPH TOMPSETT, M. D.°
Baylor University Medical Center

CHOLA, chō′lə, a south Indian Tamil dynasty that ruled almost all of peninsular India in the 11th century A. D. The Cholas arose in the Cauvery River valley in the areas around Tanjore and Tiruchirapalli. In the 2d century B. C., Prince Elara conquered Ceylon, but the Cholas were soon checked by the surrounding peoples. The Cholas' rise to empire did not begin until centuries later, when King Aditya (reigned c. 871–907) defeated the Pallavas and when King Parantaka I (reigned 907–953) vanquished the Pandyas. Rajaraja the Great (reigned 985–1014) extended the empire from the Deccan to Ceylon, and his successor Rajendra I (reigned 1014–1044) completed the conquest of Ceylon. He also sent his armies as far north as the Ganges River, and launched a spectacular raid across the Bay of Bengal against the Srivijaya empire of Sumutra in 1025. The Cholas' empire then included nearly all of southern India, the eastern Deccan, and the Laccadive, Maldive, and Nicobar islands, and dominated parts of the Malay Peninsula and Indonesian islands. The Chalukyas, Pandyas, and the Sinhalese rose against the Cholas, and by the 13th century their power was reduced. The dynasty ended in 1279.

The Cholas were patrons of Hinduism and were great temple and monument builders. They beautified Tanjore, Gangagikondapuram, and Kanchi with splendid monuments in the Dravidian style. The most famous is the Saiva temple in Tanjore. They also developed ornate gateways called *gopuras,* and built extensive irrigation works. A remarkable feature of their administration was the role played by village assemblies in local affairs.

B. G. GOKHALE, *Wake Forest University*

CHOLECYSTITIS, kō-lə-sis-tī′tis, is an inflammation of the gall bladder, most often associated with the presence of gallstones. Although cholecystitis may occur in either sex and at almost any age, it is most frequently found in women, especially obese women over 40.

Symptoms. Cholecystitis often lasts over a period of years. Many persons have no symptoms or suffer only such mild symptoms as indigestion and heartburn, which occur mostly after eating fried or fatty foods. Some patients occasionally suffer severe attacks of discomfort or episodes of nausea and vomiting. These, too, are generally provoked by eating fried, greasy, or fatty foods. Sometimes when a patient has gallstones, a stone may pass out of the gall bladder and lodge in the common bile duct, obstructing the outflow of bile and causing jaundice.

When cholecystitis occurs as an acute disease the patient suddenly develops a severe pain in the upper right part of the abdomen. Often there is also a pain in the back or left shoulder blade. During the attack the patient often becomes nauseated and vomits. If the gall bladder becomes infected, the patient may develop fever and chills and sweat profusely. Usually an attack of acute cholecystitis is precipitated when a gallstone lodges in the small duct (cystic duct) leading from the gall bladder to the common bile duct.

Treatment. Most often cholecystitis is treated by the surgical removal of the gall bladder. In some chronic cases, however, if the risk of surgery is high or if the symptoms are not severe, the doctor may simply recommend a diet that is low in fat.

LOUIS J. VORHAUS, M.D.
Cornell University Medical College

CHOLERA, kol′ə-rə, is an acute diarrheal disease of the gastrointestinal tract caused by the ingestion of *Vibrio cholerae* bacteria. The incubation period ranges from a few hours to 5 days after the bacteria are ingested. If the disease is untreated, the victim's chances of survival are only 40%, but in cases where patients receive proper treatment, the chance of survival is greatly increased. In several large epidemics a survival rate of 100% has been shown.

History. One of the earliest known descriptions of cholera is found in a Tibetan Sanskrit manuscript believed to have been written in the 9th century. In Pakistan and India the common delta of the Ganges and Brahmaputra rivers has been a known focus of cholera since it was described there by a Portuguese traveler in the early 16th century. Until the 19th century, cholera was confined to Asia, almost exclusively to India, but between 1817 and 1899 successive epidemics spread throughout Asia, Europe, Africa, and the Americas. The fear of cholera during this period drove nations to work together for their common protection, and in 1851 at the First International Sanitary Conference in Paris an agreement for quarantine measures was drawn up.

The first major advance in controlling cholera occurred in 1854, when the British physician John Snow showed that an outbreak of cholera in a London neighborhood was related to the drinking of contaminated water from a single water pump. It was not until 1883 that the disease was traced to a specific organism. In that year, the German bacteriologist Robert Koch, who was then working in Egypt, identified the bacterium *V. cholerae* as a cholera-producing organism.

In 1905, in the El Tor quarantine camp on the Red Sea, several unusual *Vibrio* strains were isolated from the bodies of pilgrims returning from Mecca. The pilgrims showed no symptoms of cholera but in the laboratory these organisms, termed *V. El Tor,* were found to be nearly identical with *V. cholerae.* Because the pilgrims had not developed cholera it was thought that this biotype of *V. cholerae* was not capable of producing the disease. In later years this belief was disproved, and in 1961 cholera caused by *V. El Tor* began spreading through many countries in the western Pacific and in southeastern Asia.

Symptoms and Diagnosis. Although some cholera victims have no apparent symptoms at all, others may suffer severe dehydration from massive diarrhea. The sudden onset of profuse, effortless, and painless diarrhea is typical of symptomatic cholera. The diarrhea is described as "rice-water stool," a continuous, light-gray, watery stool with flecks of mucous material in it, but containing no blood or pus.

Shortly after the onset of diarrhea most victims have sudden bouts of vomiting, and about 75% of all cholera patients also suffer severe muscular cramps, usually confined to the extremities. Marked dehydration is indicated by sunken eyes and cheeks, dryness of the tongue and mucous membranes, hoarseness, and drawn, withered skin on the hands, face, and feet. The lips are bluish in color and the skin becomes cold and clammy.

The diagnosis of cholera largely depends on the isolation and identification of the disease-producing bacteria from the patients stools. Stool samples are placed in special culture media, and within 18 hours the *Vibrio* colonies become apparent. Under a microscope, each bacterium appears as a short, comma-shaped rod with a single flagellum, or whiplike hair, at one end of the cell. Final identification requires the use of special biochemical tests.

Pathogenesis and Treatment. After the cholera-producing bacteria are ingested they multiply in the jejunum and ileum (the middle and last portions of the small intestine) where they produce a toxic substance that probably interferes with the functioning of the intestinal membrane. Normally, this membrane allows the exchange of water and salts between the intestine and body tissues, but when this function is disturbed the water and salts are not absorbed and are eliminated from the body in a watery diarrhea. Thus, even if the patient drinks large quantities of water, the water will not be absorbed through the intestinal wall and consequently the diarrhea will not subside.

The treatment of cholera consists of intravenous replacement of the lost fluids and salts. Once the initial losses are restored, maintenance therapy is continued by replacing the amount of stool produced with an equal amount of water and salt solutions. Prompt replacement results in a rapid improvement of all symptoms except for the continuing diarrhea. Oral antibiotics, such as tetracycline, chloramphenicol, and streptomycin, will reduce the duration and amount of diarrhea by about 50%. Tetracycline, in adequate dosage, will completely eradicate the bacteria.

Prevention. Cholera is generally confined to people of lower socioeconomic groups living in tropical and subtropical regions where there is poor sanitation. Careful hygiene provides the most certain protection against the disease since it is transmitted through foods and beverages that are contaminated with the disease-producing bacteria, usually from the stools of cholera victims. Apparently, ingestion of a large number of bacteria is essential to produce the disease, and the infection of medical workers caring for cholera patients is rare in places where even elementary sanitary precautions are adopted.

Although there is a cholera vaccine, it is only about 50% effective and then its protection lasts only from 6 to 18 months. When the disease does develop in a vaccinated person, the illness is just as severe as in a person who has not been vaccinated. Thus, the best method of controlling cholera depends largely on sanitary measures with adequate water supplies and proper methods of sewage disposal.

CRAIG K. WALLACE, M. D.
The Johns Hopkins University School of Medicine

Further Reading: Carpenter, C. C. J., "Cholera" in *A Manual of Tropical Medicine,* by George W. Hunter and others (Philadelphia 1966); De, S. N., *Cholera: Its Pathology and Pathogenesis* (Springfield, Ill., 1961); Pollitzer, R., *Cholera* (World Health Organization, Geneva, 1959); Rosenberg, C. E., *The Cholera Years* (Chicago 1963).

CHOLESTEROL, kə-les′tə-rôl, is a sterol with the empirical formula $C_{27}H_{46}O$. (See STEROIDS.) It is widely distributed in animal tissues, but is found in highest concentrations in nerve and brain tissue. Medical interest in cholesterol is based both on its role in normal body physiology and on its relationship to disease.

Although the exact role of cholesterol in the normal body is unclear, there are several indications that it must have considerable importance. Its high concentration in all nerve tissues suggests that it plays a vital role in nerve conduction.

Cholesterol is similar in chemical structure to the sex and adrenal cortical hormones, which are derived from cholesterol by the body. Cholesterol is also a precursor of bile salts. The liver normally synthesizes large quantities of cholesterol.

Cholesterol in Disease. Cholesterol is of considerable importance in a number of diseases. Gallbladder stones are composed mainly of cholesterol; in fact, gallstones may be more than 90% cholesterol. However, the actual cause and process of formation of gallstones is not known. In the condition known as xanthomatosis, there are abnormal cholesterol deposits in various tissues, including the skin.

Deposits of cholesterol are found in the lining of arteries in a group of diseases of the blood vessels and heart. These deposits, which may be quite thick, roughen the interior of the arteries and make clot formation more likely . Sometimes the deposits are so thick that the blood flow past them is decreased to such an extent that the tissues supplied by the vessel do not receive an adequate amount of blood. With greater blockage of the vessel, parts of the organs deprived of blood may die (infarct). Sometimes the deposition of cholesterol so greatly reduces the elasticity of the arterial wall that the wall splits and bleeding occurs.

Diseases related to cholesterol deposition in the arteries include arteriosclerosis, angina pectoris, myocardial infarction (coronary thrombosis, heart attack), cerebral vascular disease, stroke, and dissecting aortic aneurysm.

Cholesterol in the Diet. It is thought that a reduction in the dietary intake of cholesterol might be helpful in preventing and controlling diseases of the blood vessels. Although the liver produces far more cholesterol (endogenous cholesterol) than is usually eaten in food (exogenous cholesterol), it appears that the dietary cholesterol is more likely to be deposited in the arteries than the endogenous cholesterol. Accordingly, some doctors now advise limitation in the intake of high-cholesterol foods such as brains, egg yolk, liver, kidney, sweetbreads, butter, cream, and some cheeses.

Importance of Unsaturated Fats in the Diet. It has been found that the kind and amount of fat in the diet influence the rate at which the body produces cholesterol, the rate at which the cholesterol is deposited, and the incidence of heart attacks. In general, those fats that are considered saturated because there are few double bonds between their carbon atoms tend to increase the deposition of cholesterol. Such fats include coconut oil and those that are hard at ice-box temperatures. The unsaturated fats, with several double bonds between carbon atoms, include most vegetable oils that have not been hydrogenated; fish oils also belong to this group. These fats remain liquid at icebox temperatures. Chicken fat is intermediate between these two groups in degree of saturation.

The evidence that substituting unsaturated for saturated fats in the diet will lower the incidence of heart attacks and other cardiovascular diseases is not yet conclusive, but it is impressive. Experimental evidence on several species of animals and preliminary results on studies in man support this theory. Therefore, many doctors now recommend the substitution of unsaturated fats for saturated fats in the diet.

SOLOMON GARB, M. D.
University of Missouri Medical School

CHOLLA, choi'ə, is a name commonly applied to any of several very spiny cacti native to the southwestern United States and Mexico. The species most often referred to is *Opuntia cholla*, a treelike cactus growing about 10 feet (3 meters) tall with a trunk diameter of 6 inches (15 cm). Unlike many related species that have flat joints, or segments, this species has rounded segments that bear many spines when the plant is young. At maturity, however, most of the spines are shed. The flowers of the cholla are deep purple and about 1 inch (2.5 cm) wide. Chollas can be propagated either by seed or by placing one of the segments in the ground as a cutting.

DONALD WYMAN
The Arnold Arboretum, Harvard University

CHOLON, chu'lun', is a city in South Vietnam, in the prefecture of Saigon, on the southwest outskirts of the capital and in close proximity to the thriving port of Saigon. Located at the center of a network of canals, it dominates the river traffic of southern Vietnam. It has a predominantly Chinese population.

Cholon thrived during the French colonial period (1883–1954), when the Chinese controlled most of the local commerce and monopolized the rice trade. After South Vietnam gained its independence in 1954, the Ngo Dinh Diem government conferred citizenship on most of the Chinese business community. When the United States entered the war against the Vietcong, the Chinese, who have the most effective distribution and marketing system in southern Vietnam, began to specialize in imported goods from the United States.

Cholon, whose name means "Great Market" in Vietnamese, was founded by Chinese merchants and immigrants in the 18th century. It has been jointly administered with Saigon since the post-World War II period when the rapid growth of both cities eliminated the distance between them.

ELLEN J. HAMMER
*Author of "The Struggle for Indochina" and
"Vietnam: Yesterday and Today"*

CHOLULA, chō-lōo'lä, is an ancient city on the central plateau of Mexico, 6 miles (10 km) west of Puebla. It was a center of the Toltec civilization before the coming of the Aztecs and is said to have had 100,000 inhabitants at the time of the Spanish conquest. Cortés massacred many of its citizens in 1519 and destroyed its 400 temples.

Officially *Cholula de Rivadabia*, it is now a small agricultural trading and processing center, but a place of unusual architectural interest. The central attraction is the ruin of a large truncated pyramid of unknown antiquity. It was sacred to the Toltec and Aztec god Quetzalcoatl, whose temple stood at the top. A Christian church has replaced the temple. Cholula has about 70 other churches, whose spires and domes dominate the skyline. Population: (1960) 12,833.

CHOMEDEY, Paul de. See MAISONNEUVE.

CHOMO LHARI, chô'mô hlä'rē, is a mountain peak of the Himalayas on the Tibet-Bhutan border. It has an altitude of 23,997 feet (7,314 meters) and is directly east of the Tangla Pass, the gateway to Lhasa, Tibet, from India. Chomo Lhari means "the Mountain of the Goddess" in Tibetan and the peak is sacred to the people of Tibet. It was first climbed in 1937 by Lt. Col. F. Spencer Chapman and the Sherpa Pasang Dawa Lama, both of whom survived a hazardous descent. Since World War II no further ascents of the mountain have been made.

CHONDRIOSOME. See CELL.

CHONDRODITE, kon'drō-dīt, is a magnesium fluosilicate, the most common of a number of similar minerals known as the chondrodite group. It is found embedded in iron deposits or crystalline limestones in the form of grains or, sometimes, as crystals. The crystals are yellow to red-brown, have a glassy luster, and are transparent to translucent. The fluorine may be replaced to some extent by the hydroxyl (OH) group.

Chondrodite occurs most abundantly in the United States, near Brewster, N. Y. Other deposits are found in Sweden, Italy, and Finland.

Composition, $Mg_5(SiO_4)_2(F,OH)_2$; hardness, 6–6.5; specific gravity, 3.1–3.2; crystal system, monoclinic.

CHONGJIN, chŭng'jin', is an ice-free port in northeastern North Korea, on the Sea of Japan. It is an industrial and rail center. In the 1930's Chongjin was a fishing village; but because of its closeness to the Musan iron mines, the Japanese, who then controlled Korea, developed Chongjin into an iron and steel center. Its industrial installations were dismantled after World War II but were restored before the Korean War (1950–1953). Badly damaged by the UN forces, Chongjin was rapidly rebuilt after 1953. No population figures for Chongjin have been available from the North Korean government since the division of the country following World War II. Population: (1940) 184,301.

CHONGJU, chung-joo, a city in central South Korea, is the capital of North Chungchong province. It is located approximately 70 miles (113 km) southeast of Seoul and is a marketing and processing center for rice, soybeans, cereals, and tobacco grown in the surrounding area. Chongju's industries include the brewing of sake (rice wine), textile milling, meat packing, and canning. Population: (1960) 92,342.

CHONJU, jŭn-joo, is the capital of North Cholla province in South Korea. The city is surrounded by the country's richest rice land, and the area around Chonju is the most densely populated in South Korea. It is an old city whose people have maintained their ancient traditions; the founder of the Yi dynasty, the last imperial line, is buried there. Handicraft industries include the production of fans and fine paper and the processing of specialties such as ginger and dried persimmons. Population: (1960) 188,726.

CHONOS ARCHIPELAGO, chō'nōs, a group of about 1,000 semibarren islands in the Pacific Ocean, off the southern coast of Chile. They extend about 130 miles (210 km) from north to south and are separated from the mainland by Moraleda Channel. The islands are part of the Chilean provinces of Chiloé and Aisén. They are inhabited mainly by a small number of Chonos Indians. There is a small settlement at Puerto Lagunas, on Melchor Island.

CHOP SUEY. See CHINESE COOKING.

CHOPIN, shō-paN', **Frédéric** (1810–1849), Polish-French composer and pianist, who wrote almost exclusively—and with consummate mastery—for his own instrument. In this apparently limited field his poetic genius displayed astonishing variety, vastly enriching the technique and idiom of the piano and exerting an influence on every composer for that instrument until well into the 20th century.

After Beethoven's sonatas, which are so different in intent and scope that no comparison is possible, Chopin's output is the most important contribution to the literature of the piano. That of Schumann is not comparable in variety, nor did he extend the technical vocabulary and idioms of the piano in anything like the same way. As for later piano composers from Liszt to Scriabin and Szymanowski—with the single exception of Brahms—their styles would have been very different if Chopin had not preceded them.

Life. Frédéric François Chopin was born at Żelazowa Wola, near Warsaw, probably on Feb. 22, 1810. His father was a Frenchman from Lorraine, who had settled in Poland in 1787. His mother was of an upper-class but impoverished Polish family. In October 1810 the Chopins moved to Warsaw, where, when he was 7, Frédéric began to take piano lessons from Wojciech Żywny, a local piano and violin teacher. In the same year he composed a little Polonaise in G minor. (Most of his juvenilia were polonaises and, after he heard genuine folk music, mazurkas.) Chopin first appeared publicly as a pianist when he was 8 and from that time onward was feted as a prodigy. Fortunately, however, his general education was not neglected, and he attended the Warsaw Lyceum. He also studied composition with Józef Elsner, director of the Warsaw Conservatory, and completed a normal 3-year course there in 1829. In August of that year, three weeks after leaving the conservatory, he made a brilliant debut in Vienna. In 1830 he played his two piano concertos in Warsaw.

On Nov. 2, 1830, Chopin left Warsaw to give concerts in western Europe, never to return to Poland. At the end of the month the Polish insurrection broke out, and his traveling companion, Titus Woyciechowski, went home at once to take part in the struggle. Chopin, however, stayed in Vienna, inactive and tortured by anxiety for his loved ones. He made one public appearance the following April and then decided to move, reaching Paris in mid-September 1831.

Paris was then the most exciting cultural center in Europe, and Chopin was quickly welcomed not only by eminent musicians and the leading Polish exiles but also by such men as Heinrich Heine, Alfred de Vigny, and Eugène Delacroix. He made his first public appearance in Paris on Feb. 26, 1832, and soon established himself as a teacher of numerous rich and aristocratic pupils. His compositions, which were published in France (by Schlesinger) and usually at the same time in England and Germany, were enthusiastically received by the critics—Schumann above all —and also contributed to his material prosperity.

After his first visit to London in July 1837, Chopin embarked on an affair with the novelist George Sand (q.v.). Liszt had introduced them in the autumn of 1836, and although Chopin was not at first attracted to her, they became intimately involved by the early summer of 1838. In November they and her children went to Majorca, where they spent three months in wretched con-

GIRAUDON

FRÉDÉRIC CHOPIN, in a portrait by his friend, the great French romantic painter Eugène Delacroix.

ditions. In Majorca, Chopin began to show symptoms of what is generally supposed to have been tuberculosis. Although the trip was in every way a failure, Chopin spent the summers of 1839 and 1841–1846 at Mme. Sand's country house at Nohant, near Châteauroux, in Berry, France, where he did most of his composing. He spent the rest of the year in Paris.

Chopin made no public appearance between February 1842 and Feb. 16, 1848, when he gave his last concert in Paris. However, he was able to live in quiet luxury on his fees as a teacher. By this time the passion between him and Mme. Sand had cooled, but she continued to guard him in a quasi-maternal way. The strains in their relationship that led to a final break in July 1847 were caused by the jealousies and intrigues of her children and perhaps by Chopin's own difficult, hypersensitive character.

Chopin's health deteriorated rapidly after the break. He composed only two more works— the Mazurka in G Minor (Opus 67, No. 2) and the Mazurka in F Minor (Opus 68, No. 4), which were published posthumously. (The latter was put together by Auguste Franchomme from Chopin's sketches.) The Revolution of 1848 ended the Orléanist monarchy and with it a substantial part of Chopin's patronage. He went to London in April 1848, and although very ill, he played before Queen Victoria and performed twice in public. After spending the summer in Scotland and northern England, he played for the last time in public on November 16, in London, returning to Paris on November 23. Unable to teach or compose, he died there on Oct. 17, 1849.

Musical Style. Chopin's piano compositions created something approaching a revolution in writing for that instrument, although like most revolutions it was heralded by signs and portents. Early composers for the pianoforte, notably Johann Christian Bach and Mozart, had written *cantabile* passages and movements for the instrument, but they concealed its inability to sustain tone by the old harpsichord and clavichord device of ornamenting a note instead of sustaining it. The composers of the generation after Mozart —above all J. N. Hummel and John Field—were more ingenious in exploiting the pianoforte's sonority, but it remained for Chopin to invent "melodies that would be actually ineffective if sung or played on an instrument capable of sustaining tone but which, picked out in percussive points of sound each beginning to die as soon as born, are enchanting and give an illusion of singing that is often lovelier than singing itself" (G. Abraham, *A Hundred Years of Music*).

Chopin's pseudosinging melodies were strongly influenced by the Italian opera arias of his day, but instead of imitating opera melody he stylized it. His delicate ornamentation—more plastic than that in most earlier piano music—is a stylization of vocal coloratura, not a copy of it. Vocal portamento, for instance, is transmuted into chromatic scale. In the mature Chopin, ornamentation is not something added to the melodic line but an indispensable part of it; one cannot distinguish between melodic substance and decoration.

The supporting background of Chopin's melody is similarly plastic and even more specifically pianistic. Its most obvious feature is the wide spread of the left hand, whose range is so greatly extended beyond the ordinary octave or tenth of classical figuration that the resulting sonority is qualitatively new. Moreover, Chopin's widespread arpeggios are seldom merely broken chords. Their chordal basis is veiled and diversified by nonessential, often chromatic, notes. They sometimes embody melodic lines and thus produce what has been called "singing figuration." Above all, Chopin frequently disguises and diversifies the clear tonal chords and modulation schemes of classical arpeggios with shifting harmonics and subtle chromatic progressions. Indeed such harmonic conceptions frequently seem to have been the starting point of Chopin's thoughts, and they constitute perhaps the most individual and important feature of his style.

Works. It is often said that Chopin was not a master of large-scale musical architecture. Nevertheless the two piano concertos—Concerto in F Minor, called No. 2 (Opus 21, 1829) and Concerto in E Minor, called No. 1 (Opus 11, 1830)—are by no means as conventional or as feebly orchestrated as it is sometimes asserted. Furthermore, the three mature sonatas—B-Flat Minor (Opus 35, 1839) and B Minor (Opus 58, 1844) for piano, and G Minor for piano and cello (Opus 65, 1845–1846)—not only contain a great deal of fine music but are marked by such ingenuities in construction as the reentry of the second subject as the climax of the development section of the B-Flat Minor Sonata. Of the larger single-movement works, the scherzos and impromptus are little more than skillfully expanded ternary structures, but the ballades and such later works as the F-Minor Fantaisie (Opus 49, 1840–1841) and the Polonaise-Fantaisie (Opus 61, 1845–1846) show Chopin feeling his way toward a new conception of free but organic musical form. The first two ballades, in G Minor (Opus 23, 1831–1835) and F Major (Opus 38, 1836; revised 1839), show him experimenting with a new form evolved from sonata form, perhaps under the influence of unacknowledged literary programs. (We have it on Schumann's authority that Chopin's ballades were inspired by the narrative poems of Adam Mickiewicz, and a musicologist of the standing of Zdisław Jachimecki has identified

the F Major precisely with the poem *Switezianka*.) The Ballade in A-Flat Major (Opus 47, 1840–1841) and F Minor (Opus 52, 1842) are the consummation of this form.

Chopin's other works, in which he reveals the full variety of his genius, may be divided roughly into two classes: the idealized dances (mazurkas, polonaises, and waltzes) and the free lyrical poems (nocturnes, the Berceuse, the Barcarolle, and the études). The preludes include examples of all these miniature forms. Classification, however, quickly breaks down. Many of the dances are lyrical poems. Nor can one describe these groups as miniatures, though they include some of the most exquisite miniatures in all music. The C-Sharp Minor Mazurka (Opus 50, No. 3, 1841), the F-Sharp Minor Polonaise (Opus 44, with its interpolated mazurka, 1840–1841), and the C-Minor Nocturne (Opus 48, No. 4, 1841), for instance, are certainly not miniatures; in each case the content explodes the confines of its genre.

The mazurkas are the most Polish of all Chopin's compositions, the closest to folk music (in such details as the use of the major scale with the fourth degree sharpened, triplets interpolated in the melodic line, the snap of grace notes). However, Chopin seldom used actual folk melodies in his mature works; the Christmas lullaby in the middle section of the B-Minor Scherzo (Opus 20, 1831–1832) is one of the rare instances.

The polonaise is an aristocratic processional dance, with no element of folklore. In Chopin's hands it becomes a patriotic call to arms, almost as surprising as the transmutation of the mazurka into something that Bach almost might have written (the opening of Opus 50, No. 3). As for the waltzes, they are, as Schumann said of the Waltz in A-Flat Major (Opus 42, 1840), "for countesses to dance to."

The nocturnes and such nocturnelike pieces as the *Berceuse* (Opus 57, 1843), the E-Major Étude (Opus 10, No. 3, 1829–1832) and Preludes Nos. 13, 15, and 21 (Opus 28, 1836–1839) have exercised a slightly ambiguous influence on the world's estimate of Chopin. Their melancholy, Italianate sweetness—often heavily exaggerated by bad pianists—has given a false impression of effeminacy. But even the sweetest of nocturnes may end with a stroke of tragic drama, as in Nocturne in B Major (Opus 32, No. 1, 1836–1837), or the sweetness may be reserved for the very end of a bitter and passionate piece, as in Nocturne in C-Sharp Minor (Opus 27, No. 1, 1834–1835).

GERALD ABRAHAM
Author of "Chopin's Musical Style"

Bibliography

Abraham, Gerald, *Chopin's Musical Style*, rev. ed. (London 1960).
Brown, Maurice J. E., *Chopin: An Index of His Works in Chronological Order* (London 1960).
Hedley, Arthur, *Chopin* (London 1947).
Hedley, Arthur, tr. and ed., *Selected Correspondence of Fryderyk Chopin* (London 1962).
Hipkins, E. J., *How Chopin Played* (London 1937).
Huneker, James, *Chopin: The Man and His Music* (New York 1900).
Jonson, E. Ashton, *Handbook to Chopin's Works* (London 1908).
Kelley, E. Stillman, *Chopin the Composer* (New York 1913).
Kobylańska, Krystyna, ed., *Chopin in His Own Land: Documents and Souvenirs* (New York 1956).
Niecks, Frederick, *Frederick Chopin as a Man and Musician*, 2 vols. (London 1888).
Walker, Alan, ed., *Frédéric Chopin: Profiles of the Man and the Musician* (London 1966).
Weinstock, Herbert, *Chopin: The Man and His Music* (New York 1949).

CHOPIN, shō'pan, **Kate O'Flaherty** (1851–1904), American author. She was born on Feb. 8, 1851, in St. Louis, Mo., of Irish and French parents, and graduated from a convent school. At 19 she married Oscar Chopin, with whom she moved first to New Orleans and then to a Red River plantation. After her husband's death, she returned to St. Louis and began to write. She died there on Aug. 22, 1904.

Mrs. Chopin's stories, such as *Désirée's Baby* (collected in *Bayou Folk*, 1894) and *A Night in Acadie* (1897), translate her plantation memories into vivid prose and rank among the best of the regional works then fashionable. She wrote unsentimentally in a Gallic manner, drawing clear, sharp, subtle pictures of Creole and Cajun characters. Her work is judiciously flavored with dialect. She stopped writing after the publication in 1899 of her sensuous, polished novel *The Awakening* because it aroused much controversy for its handling of adultery and mixed marriage.

CHOPPER, a device used to convert a slowly varying signal into a rapidly varying alternating one that can be amplified easily and accurately.

An electromechanical chopper consists basically of a coil connected to an alternating current supply and a reed that is vibrated by the coil. As the reed vibrates, it switches back and forth between two contacts, periodically interrupting the direct-current signal. The resulting intermittent signal is easily converted into a proportional alternating-current signal which can then be amplified.

In *optical choppers* a beam of light is interrupted at regular intervals by placing rotating fan blades between the light source and a light detector. Variations in the amount of light on the detector are converted to an alternating-current signal which can then be amplified.

E. NORMAN LURCH
State University of New York, Farmingdale

CHOPSTICKS is the English name for eating utensils (Chinese, *k'uai-tzu*) that have been used in China since at least the 4th century B. C. and later in the other countries of East Asia. The word "chop" is a corruption of *k'uai*, which means means "quick" or "speedy." Chopsticks are

Chopsticks

COULTER, FROM BLACK STAR

pairs of narrow sticks approximately 8 inches (20 cm) long, although the size varies. The upper half of the stick is squared, making it easier for it to be grasped securely. The lower half is rounded. Often, in Japan, the sticks are shorter and the lower ends come to a blunt point. Japanese restaurants sometimes use prepackaged pairs whose upper ends have to be separated before use.

Chopsticks are usually made of bamboo, although modern ones may be of plastic. More elaborate pairs are made of enameled wood, ivory, or bone, and in Korea, of brass or silver. They also may be inscribed with poetry or may be decorated.

Chopsticks are held in one hand. The first, or lower, stick is held stationary between the base of the thumb and the fourth finger. The second, or upper, one is held by the thumb and the second and third fingers, and it is this stick that is manipulated, pinching the food against the stationary chopstick. Because the food is cut into small pieces before being served, knives are not needed and therefore are not set on the table as in the West.

CHARLES J. CHU, *Connecticut College*

CHOQUETTE, shô-ket, **Robert** (1905–   ), French Canadian writer noted for his poetry describing the Canadian scene. He was born in Manchester, N. H., but lived most of his life in Canada. He was first a magazine editor and an art librarian and then became a writer and producer for radio and later for television. His novels, including *Le curé de village* (1936), *Les Velder* (1941), and *Élise Velder* (1958), present popular pictures of French Canadian rural life.

Far more important than his prose is Choquette's poetry. At 20 he published *À travers les vents* (1925), lyrical poems about northern Canada that won the Prix David. There followed *Metropolitan Museum* (1931), *Les poésies nouvelles* (1933) and, after 18 years' labor, the epic *Suite marine* (1953). Critics said that Choquette's early works had vigor but lacked polish; ironically, his later *Suite marine*, although praised for its sweep and ambition, was thought to be too polished. Choquette was elected to the French Canadian Academy.

CHORAGUS, kə-rā'gus, among the ancient Greeks, a wealthy Athenian who was selected by rotation to pay for equipping and instructing one of the choruses in the competitive dramatic and religious festivals of the ten Attic tribes. The term is also spelled *choregus*. Each poet or playwright was assigned a choragus, whose generosity was often a significant factor in the outcome of the competition, in which the chorus played a significant role. Thus there was rivalry among the choragi, and the one judged to have supported the best chorus received an ornamental tripod inscribed with his name and the names of the poet and the master who had trained the chorus. These tripods were placed on public monuments. (In Athens, the choragic monument to Lysicrates survives.) The office of choragus was eliminated around 300 B. C.

In music, the term choragus has been used to refer to a conductor or leader of a music or drama festival.

CHORAL LYRIC. See GREECE—*10. Greek Literature* (The Classical Period): Lyric or Subjective Poetry.

CHORAL MUSIC, kôr′əl, is music for a group of singers who are divided into several sections according to voice range, each section singing one line of the vocal score. The conventional voice ranges are soprano and alto (high and low female voices) and tenor and bass (high and low male voices). Some choral works call for instrumental accompaniment; others are written to be sung *a cappella*. Although some choral music is scored for female voices only or for male voices only, most choral works call for a mixed choir or chorus (from Greek *choros*, a group of chanters), combining all four parts. The singing of each vocal line by many unified voices distinguishes choral music from vocal ensemble music, in which only one person sings each vocal line.

Choral music has been written in every period since the 15th century, in almost every country of the Western world, and by nearly every major composer. It was almost always closely connected with the church until the 19th century, when the growth of singing societies created a new demand for secular choral works. Today, in addition to church choirs, there are amateur choral societies and smaller professional choirs. These groups inherit from past centuries a tremendous library of choral music, much of it still unexplored; and this stock is constantly being added to by contemporary composers. It is essential for performers and listeners to understand the various styles and purposes of this music as it has developed in Western culture.

As early as the 4th century, when plainsong (later called Gregorian chant) was the only music of the Christian church, groups of singers (*scholae*) began to be trained as choruses to sing the chants that were too difficult for the congregation. Choir schools (*scholae cantorum*) were established at large churches and monasteries.

Composers of the 9th century developed a form of polyphonic music called organum (q.v.), which added a vocal line following the plainsong in parallel fifths or fourths. Organum gradually became more complex, incorporating solo voices that added florid countermelodies to the unison chant sung by the choir. This tendency culminated with two composers of the school of Notre Dame in Paris—Léonin (late 12th century) and Pérotin (late 12th and early 13th centuries)— leading ultimately to the motets of Philippe de Vitry (1291–1361) and Guillaume de Machaut (c. 1300–c. 1377). Machaut's *Notre Dame Mass* (?1364) is the first known setting of the Ordinary of the Mass by a single composer. Most of this polyphonic music, like the medieval secular music (French *chanson* and Italian *caccia*), was intended for one voice on each part, usually supplemented by instruments.

RENAISSANCE

The 15th Century. In the early 15th century musical styles circulated between France and England, with cathedrals, churches, colleges, and royal chapels vying with each other in the excellence of their music. The result was the development of true choral music, with two or more singers to each part. The most famous composers were Gilles Binchois (c. 1400–1460) and Guillaume Dufay (c. 1400–1474) of the Burgundian school, and Lionel Power (died 1445) and John Dunstable (died 1453) of the English school. Dunstable and Power composed the first musically unified masses, with the various movements built on a plainsong tune (*cantus firmus*). Also at this time the English carol became a polyphonic form, with verses for soloists and refrain (*burden*) for chorus.

In the late 15th century appeared a group of English composers including John Browne, Walter Lambe, Richard Davy, and Robert Wilkinson, whose choral works—mostly antiphons and *Magnificats*—are found in the Eton College choirbook. Their compositions, large, polyphonic, and technically demanding, employ a florid style and a wealth of detail in the vocal parts. These works mark an early peak in choral music.

The leading composers of the 15th century Flemish school were Jean d'Okeghem (c. 1430–1495), Jacob Obrecht (1450–1505), and Josquin Desprès (c. 1450–1521). Josquin's 24 masses and roughly 100 motets display four-voice writing of wonderful clarity, balance, and expressiveness.

The 16th Century. Because the Catholic Church was the chief patron of the arts, the most common choral forms of the 16th century were the mass (a set form of five movements for the invariable texts of the Ordinary: the Kyrie, Gloria, Credo, Sanctus, and Agnus Dei) and the motet, a shorter work with words from Scripture or the liturgy. The choirs consisted usually of fewer than 20 male voices. (Women were not allowed in church choirs until the 18th century.) The choral sound was not massive; instead it emphasized clarity and balance. Choirs furnished music daily for the celebration of the Mass and for the eight canonical hours.

English composers of the early 16th century included John Taverner (c. 1495–1545), John Redford (died 1547), Robert Fayrfax (1464–1521), William Cornyshe (c. 1465–1523), and Christopher Tye (c. 1500–c. 1573). All of these men wrote great numbers of masses and motets.

Musical leadership in the second half of the 16th century belonged to Italy, where a Roman, Giovanni Palestrina (c. 1525–1594), was the most important composer. His works are the supreme models of the ideal liturgical style: restrained, balanced music, masterfully blending beautiful melody, harmony, and rhythm. Palestrina composed 105 masses and some 500 motets; the *Missa Papae Marcelli* (about 1560) for six voices is his most famous work.

Venice was next in importance after Rome as a music center. The school of Venetian music began with Adrian Willaert (c. 1490–1562), who developed a form of antiphonal scoring that was especially effective at St. Mark's Basilica and became a Venetian specialty. This form was further evolved by Andrea Gabrieli (c. 1520–1586) and brought to its culmination by Giovanni Gabrieli (c. 1554–1612), whose magnificent motets include the *In ecclesiis*. The younger Gabrieli supplemented his polychoral arrangements with independent instrumental parts, providing a great variety of musical color.

English composers of the late 16th century were confronted with the special task of writing music with English texts for the new Anglican Church liturgy. Thomas Tallis (c. 1505–1585) wrote motets in a simple, chordal style. In 1550, John Marbeck (c. 1510–c. 1585) supplied music for the Book of Common Prayer in one-note-to-a-syllable fashion. The motet was gradually replaced in Anglican services by the anthem, which was developed by Thomas Morley (1557–1602) and Orlando Gibbons (1583–1625). Although Gibbons was active well into the 17th century, his music generally follows the 16th century style.

The same is true of the versatile William Byrd (c. 1543–1623), perhaps the greatest of all English composers, who wrote services and anthems for the Church of England, Catholic Church music, and many secular and instrumental works. Byrd's *Great Service* and his three masses (for three, four, and five voices respectively) are among the classics of the age. His Latin motets, including the *Ave verum corpus,* show his genius for bold, emotional writing.

The most popular forms of Renaissance secular music were the *chanson* and the madrigal, ensemble music scored for one singer to a part. The most important composer of the French *chanson* was Claude Le Jeune (1528–c. 1600). The Elizabethans, especially Morley, Gibbons, and Byrd, wrote many madrigals for chamber performance by small vocal ensembles. In Italy the madrigal, which usually used romantic poetry for its texts, was refined in the early 16th century by Philippe Verdelot (died about 1550), Costanzo Festa (1490–1545), and Jakob Arcadelt (c. 1505–c. 1567). The greatest masters of the Italian madrigal were Cipriano de Rore (1516–1565), who also wrote many motets; Philippe de Monte (1521–1603), who wrote 1,200 madrigals; Luca Marenzio (c. 1553–1599), whose 17 books of madrigals show masterful use of word-painting; and Carlo Gesualdo (c. 1560–1613), who wrote madrigals for virtuoso singers.

Renaissance choral music reached its highest point in the work of the Flemish composer Roland de Lassus (c. 1532–1594). Lassus, master of the Italian madrigal and the French *chanson,* also composed 53 extant masses and some 500 motets. In his works he fused northern and southern European elements as well as the religious and secular influences of his time, integrating the entire Renaissance musical world. Among his incomparable motets are the *Penitential Psalms,* published posthumously in 1604.

The 16th century marks a great climax in the development of choral music, with each voice line independent and important to the total effect. Instruments were generally used with the voices, supplementing the vocal sound as well as playing independent parts.

BAROQUE ERA

The 17th Century. Choral music as the dominant form of composition was replaced at the beginning of this period by opera and instrumental music. The writing of motets and masses in the old manner continued, but the new style of opera permeated and transformed sacred music as it did theatrical music. Even so, musicians of the baroque period regarded the old polyphonic style as specifically "sacred" and consciously distinguished it from the new homophonic theatrical style.

Claudio Monteverdi (1567–1643), whose career spanned the end of the Renaissance and the beginning of the baroque, combined the austere polyphonic style with all the new techniques of the 17th century. His modern, imaginative, and expressive music includes polyphonic masses, magnificent psalm settings, many books of soloistic madrigals, and the *Vespers* (1610), perhaps his greatest work.

Giacomo Carissimi (1605–1674) first used the chorus as an important element in the oratorio, a form developed at the beginning of the 17th century. Carissimi employed the chorus dramatically,

especially in his oratorios *Jephtha* and *Jonah.* His masterful choral writing served as a model for Handel and other composers.

Heinrich Schütz (1585–1672), the 17th century's greatest German Protestant church composer, combined the Italian and German styles in his early book of madrigals and his opera *Daphne* (1627), as well as in the voluminous sacred music to which he devoted the rest of his life. Great originality distinguishes his *Psalms of David* (1619), written in the Venetian style for voices and instruments; the *Resurrection Story* (1623); and the *Seven Last Words* (about 1645). In 1666, at the end of his career, Schütz composed three Passion settings, from the Gospels of St. Luke, St. Matthew, and St. John, in the unaccompanied style of the earliest Lutheran composers, mostly solo recitatives with vivid and dramatic choruses. For most other German composers of this period the chorale was the focal point of Protestant church music.

The greatest of the north Germans was the Danish-born Dietrich Buxtehude (1637–1707), organist of St. Mary's Church in Lübeck from 1668 until his death. Buxtehude's large-scale compositions, showing his mastery of secular and sacred idioms, were performed at his *Abendmusiken,* a series of Advent concerts that attracted to Lübeck such composers as Handel and J. S. Bach. Characteristic works by Buxtehude include his *Missa Brevis* in polyphonic style, the *Benedicam Dominum* in the Venetian manner, and *In dulci jubilo,* one of his 124 surviving cantatas.

In France, Jean Baptiste Lully (1632–1687) and André Campra (1660–1744), primarily writers of opera, composed motets that are really cantatas for soloists, chorus, and orchestra. Marc Antoine Charpentier (1634–1704), a pupil of Carissimi's, introduced the oratorio form to France in such works as his *Judicium Salomonis,* with its dramatic use of chorus. François Couperin (1668–1733) wrote accompanied motets that are gems of delicacy, sweetness, and elegance. Michel Richard de Lalande (1657–1726), the most distinguished French church musician of his day, continued the Lully tradition with his 42 motets, including the *Dixit Dominus.* Lalande's exciting, brilliant style anticipates Handel.

English music after the Restoration (1660) was dominated by Pelham Humphrey (1647–1674), John Blow (1648–1708), and Henry Purcell (1659–1695). These composers, writing for cathedral choirs of men and boys, developed the "full" anthem (entirely for choir without independent accompaniment) and the "verse" anthem (with sections assigned to solo voices with independent accompaniment). Purcell, organist of Westminster Abbey from 1679 to his death, was a versatile composer of operas, ceremonial music, Latin motets, and anthems ranging from the profound eight-part *Hear My Prayer* (about 1681) to the cheerful *Rejoice in the Lord Alway* (about 1683).

Bach and Handel. The 18th century was dominated by Bach and Handel, who were masters of nearly every known form of music. Johann Sebastian Bach (1685–1750) excelled in church music, in which he incorporated all the techniques and styles of the baroque era. His extant sacred cantatas number about 200 (some 100 others have been lost), written for performances at the Lutheran Sunday services at St. Thomas' Church, Leipzig, where Bach was cantor from 1723 to 1750. Incorporating arias, chorales, recitatives, orchestral sinfonias, and choruses, the cantatas cover a tremendous range of technique and expression. Bach also wrote a *Magnificat* (1723), a *St. John Passion* (1723), a *St. Matthew Passion* (1729), the great B Minor Mass, written over a number of years, and several motets, usually arranged for double choir. The two passions, with their combination of lyricism and drama, transcend the ecclesiastical purposes for which they were written. Mendelssohn's revival of the *St. Matthew Passion* in 1829 began the Bach cult that has permeated the musical world.

George Frideric Handel (1685–1759), mainly an opera composer, was trained in Germany and Italy before settling in England (1712), where he wrote a series of occasional works. These were festal anthems for solo voices, chorus, and orchestra: the *Utrecht Te Deum* (1713), *Chandos Anthems* (1716–1718), *Wedding Anthem* (1736), *Funeral Anthem for Queen Caroline* (1737), and *Dettingen Te Deum* (1743).

From 1738 to 1752, Handel turned his great operatic talent to the writing of oratorios, with texts based on the Bible, that were intended for performance in the theater during Lent. These were primarily works of entertainment, not religious or liturgical music as such. Their form was adopted from opera, incorporating recitatives, arias, concerted numbers, instrumental interludes, and choruses; the distinctive element was the predominant choral participation. The *Messiah* (1742), *Judas Maccabaeus* (1747), *Susanna* (1749), and *Theodora* (1750) are based on texts drawn from the Old Testament, the New Testament, and the Apocrypha; the other oratorios take their texts exclusively from the Old Testament and include *Saul* (1739), *Samson* (1742), *Joseph* (1744), *Belshazzar* (1745), and *Jephtha* (1752). These are exciting and dramatic works that have been revived in modern times.

The *Messiah*, Handel's universally popular oratorio, differs from his other oratorios in that it is pictorial and devotional rather than dramatic. It was first presented in Dublin in 1742, with about 40 singers in the chorus and an orchestra of similiar size. When the *Messiah* was given later in London it was coolly received, the subject being considered too religious for entertainment. Yet the *Messiah* remains one of the greatest compositions of all time, despite misguided efforts by later musicians, including Mozart, to "improve" it with enriched orchestration.

CLASSICAL AND ROMANTIC PERIODS

Haydn and Mozart. The two greatest composers of the second half of the 18th century, Haydn and Mozart, were predominantly interested in instrumental music; but they also wrote much choral music, mostly for the Catholic Church. This music is now considered too theatrical and operatic for church services and is performed only in concerts.

Franz Joseph Haydn (1732–1809) wrote 12 masses, of which six are early works and the other six mature masterpieces. The early masses are lyrical and charming but not particularly personal. In the later, less conventional masses Haydn wrote in a dramatic, frequently polyphonic style. The *Paukenmesse* (*Drum Mass*; 1796), also called the *Mass in Time of War*, was so named because of the extraordinary use of trumpets and tympani in the "Agnus Dei." The *Nelson Mass* (1798), named in honor of Lord Nelson's victory in the Battle of the Nile, uses a curious orchestration without woodwinds; it contains much strong choral music. The *Theresienmesse* (1799), the *Creation Mass* (1801), and the *Harmony Mass* (1802) are impressive works with a mixture of solo and chorus writing.

In 1791–1792 and again in 1794–1795, Haydn visited London. There he was inspired by Handel's oratorios, and after returning to Vienna he composed *The Creation* (1798), a dramatic oratorio with brilliant orchestration, expressive arias, and splendid choruses. Its beautiful imitations of nature have made it Haydn's most popular work. *The Seasons* (1801), Haydn's other large-scale choral work and his last major work, has a secular text divided into four sections: Spring, Summer, Autumn, Winter. Its naïve scene painting points to the romantic writing of later composers.

Most of the church pieces of Wolfgang Amadeus Mozart (1756–1791) are early works written on a small scale (usually for four solo voices, chamber orchestra, and chorus). Mozart's sacred works include 17 masses written at Salzburg, among them the great *Coronation Mass* (1779). He also wrote four litanies, two sets of Vesper psalms, and many motets, including the splendid *Ave verum corpus* (1791).

Mozart never completed his two greatest masses, the C Minor Mass (1782) and the *Requiem* (1791). The C Minor Mass was probably filled out with movements from Mozart's other masses before its first performance in Salzburg. However, the sections completed by Mozart are sufficient for a nonliturgical performance. Only the first two movements of the *Requiem* were completed by Mozart, although he wrote about half of the remainder in vocal score. This material was orchestrated by his friend Franz Xaver Süssmayr, who also composed three movements. The total effect of the *Requiem*, with Mozart's first two movements repeated at the conclusion, is moving and beautiful, poignantly expressing the composer's contemplation of death.

Beethoven and Schubert. The finest composers of choral music in the early 19th century were Beethoven and Schubert. Ludwig van Beethoven (1770–1827), primarily a composer of orchestral and chamber music, also wrote considerable choral music. The Mass in C (1807), commissioned for liturgical use, combines classical forms with new and dramatic effects. Beethoven developed his deep personal convictions in his several cantatas, the oratorio *Christ on the Mount of Olives* (1801), and the *Choral Fantasia* (1808) for chorus, piano, and orchestra. Beethoven's masterpiece, the *Missa Solemnis* (1823), achieves a complete blending of voices and instruments: it is not a choral work with instrumental accompaniment, but a work in which choir and orchestra are coequal. This technique, which Beethoven also used for the *Ode to Joy* finale of his Ninth Symphony (1824), results in a work of great power and expression. It inspired many later composers, who tried, with varying degrees of success, to reproduce it.

Like Beethoven, Franz Schubert (1797–1828) unites the classical tradition of the 18th century with the novel characteristics of 19th century romanticism. Schubert wrote much choral music, both secular and sacred. His mass in G (1815), composed when he was only 18, is ingenuous and charming. In his maturity Schubert wrote two large-scale masses, of which the Mass in A Flat (1819–1822) is the more successful. This work, rich in melody and beautiful harmony, is his most personal treatment of the sacred text.

Later Romantic Composers. Choral music, which had long been the province of church and cathedral choirs, widened its scope in the 19th century with the growth of choral societies in England, continental Europe, and the United States. Much of the credit for this development belongs to Felix Mendelssohn (1809–1847), the most popular of 19th century composers. Although Mendelssohn pioneered in the writing of cantatas with secular texts, his two greatest choral works are sacred oratorios. *St. Paul* (1836) is a fine work, but it lacks the dramatic movement of *Elijah* (1846), in which Mendelssohn beautifully combined music and drama.

Hector Berlioz (1803–1869) specialized in colossal and spectacular musical effects that called for large choirs and a huge orchestra. His *Mass for the Dead* (1837), better known as the *Requiem,* and his *Te Deum* (1849) contain excellent and original choral music. Berlioz also wrote an oratorio, *L'enfance du Christ* (1854), which is full of gentle, poetic, pastoral charm.

The outstanding choral composer of the late 19th century was Johannes Brahms (1833–1897). In his *German Requiem* (1868) Brahms fused the lyrical style with the symphonic. He also composed shorter works for chorus and orchestra and several *a cappella* motets in conscious imitation of Bach's style.

The *Te Deum* (1884) and the F Minor Mass (1890) of Anton Bruckner (1824–1896) reflect the colorful devotion of his native Austrian Catholicism. The *Requiem* (1874) of Giuseppe Verdi (1813–1901) is a work of genius, a personal rather than ecclesiastical expression. Although Antonín Dvořák (1841–1904) was not primarily a choral composer, his *Stabat Mater* (1877), *Requiem* (1890), and *Te Deum* (1892) are full of lyric beauty and sincere expression. Gustav Mahler (1860–1911), in his *Resurrection Symphony* (1894) and Symphonies No. 3 (1896) and No. 8 (1907), was the most successful of the many composers who have followed Beethoven's example by introducing choral music into their symphonic works.

THE TWENTIETH CENTURY

Europe. A number of European composers, including Arnold Schönberg (1874–1951), Igor Stravinsky, Paul Hindemith (1895–1963), and Béla Bartók (1881–1945), introduced iconoclastic methods and revolutionary ideas to choral music, making significant additions to the repertory. Because many of their works were experimental, the public was often slow to accept them.

However, some Europeans wrote in a conservative style. These included the Swiss composers Ernest Bloch (1880–1959), whose *Sacred Service* (1930–1933) has a Jewish liturgical text, and Frank Martin, who wrote several sacred oratorios.

Many of the foremost 20th century composers in the choral field have been English. The outstanding choral works of Ralph Vaughan Williams (1872–1958) include his *Sea Symphony* (c. 1905–1910), the unaccompanied Mass in G Minor (1922), and the mystical oratorio *Sancta Civitas* (1926). Gustav Holst (1874–1934) composed the *Hymn of Jesus* (1917), the *First Choral Symphony* (1923–1924), and a *Choral Fantasia* (1930), as well as several hymns for chorus. The most notable choral work by William Walton

is the oratorio *Belshazzar's Feast* (1929–1931). Diversity is especially evident in the works of Benjamin Britten, which include the *Ceremony of Carols* (1942), the cantata *Saint Nicholas* (1948), and the *War Requiem* (1962). Other contemporary British choral composers are Edmund Rubbra, Michael Tippett, Peter Racine Fricker, Anthony Milner, and John Joubert.

Arthur Honegger (1892–1955) of France achieved worldwide acclaim with his dramatic oratorio *King David* (1921), his opera *Judith* (1926), and the oratorio *Joan of Arc at the Stake* (1934–1935). Other French composers made enormous contributions to modern choral literature—Darius Milhaud, with his more than 30 choral works, Gabriel Fauré (1845–1924), with his serenely spiritual *Requiem Mass* (1887), and Francis Poulenc (1899–1963), with his excellent motets, unaccompanied Mass (1937), *Stabat Mater* (1937), and *Gloria* (1959).

The choral works by continental composers frequently express national characteristics through the use of folk song. The *Glagolitic Mass* (1926) by Leoš Janáček (1854–1928) expresses his Slavonic heritage, and the *Psalmus Hungaricus* (1923) by Zoltán Kodály (1882–1967) is distinctly national in feeling. Soviet choral music includes cantatas with patriotic themes, such as *Alexander Nevsky* (1938) by Sergei Prokofiev (1891–1953).

Anton Webern (1883–1945), the Austrian serial composer, wrote three important cantatas. A German, Carl Orff, composed the *Carmina Burana* (1936), a cantata with optional staging and dance, written in a highly individual manner with special emphasis on rhythmic percussion effects. From Italy came notable choral compositions by Luigi Dallapiccola and Goffredo Petrassi.

United States. In the United States a great interest in choral music developed after World War II. American choral music covers a tremendous range in type and quality, and the permanent value of much of it cannot yet be judged. Charles Ives (1874–1954) was one of the most daring composers at the beginning of the 20th century. His choral music foreshadowed many techniques developed later, and its polytonality continues to shock audiences. Important contemporary choral composers include Virgil Thomson, Randall Thompson, Aaron Copland, William Schuman, Alan Hovhaness, Norman Dello Joio, and Daniel Pinkham, who employ varied styles with differing stresses of folk song, jazz, 12-tone technique, and polyphony. The vast range of technique and expression covered by their music makes it representative of the spirit of their country.

CHARLES N. HENDERSON
St. George's Church, New York

Bibliography

Bukofzer, Manfred F., *Music in the Baroque Era* (New York 1947).
Bukofzer, Manfred F., *Music in the Middle Ages* (New York 1940).
Dean, Winton, *Handel's Dramatic Oratorios and Masques* (London 1959).
Einstein, Alfred, *Mozart, His Character, His Work,* tr. by Arthur Mendel and Nathan Broder (New York and London 1946).
Geiringer, Karl, *Johann Sebastian Bach, the Culmination of an Era* (New York and London 1966).
Jacobs, Arthur, ed., *Choral Music* (Baltimore 1963).
Láng, Paul H., *Music in Western Civilization* (New York 1941).
Wienandt, Elwyn A., *Choral Music of the Church* (New York 1965).
Young, Percy M., *The Choral Tradition* (London 1962).

CHORAL SPEAKING, kôr'əl, is the dramatic recitation of poetry or prose by a trained group of people speaking in unison or in careful alternation of voices. Choral speaking, or "choric speech," groups, like singing groups, are divided into sections by voice quality. Usually the leader "orchestrates" each selection, assigning parts to a section or to a voice.

Choral speaking by the chorus was an important part of ancient Greek drama. It was not used again until Marjorie Gullan of London reintroduced it at the Glasgow Music Festival in 1922. Choral speaking then gained in popularity as a teaching aid in schools and for public performances.

CHORALE, kə-ral', a choral song, especially a hymn of a type introduced during the Protestant Reformation in Germany. The term derives from the Gregorian *cantus choralis,* which denotes that part of the chant sung by the congregation, as opposed to the *cantus accentus,* or solo part.

When Martin Luther launched the Reformation, he perceived that Protestantism would be strengthened by greater congregational participation in the service. Gregorian plainsong was unsuitable for such a purpose, and the chorale was developed to replace it. The chorale, which substituted German for the Latin of the plainsong, replaced the flowing, unharmonized Gregorian melodies with brisk and regular tunes in duple and triple meters. Chorale texts were usually translations or paraphrases of liturgical texts and Latin psalms and hymns; some of the melodies were original, but most were drawn from folk songs and pre-Reformation hymns.

Luther himself wrote the words and melodies for many chorales, including *Vom Himmel hoch da komm' ich her* and probably the famous *Ein' feste Burg ist unser Gott.* Some of these appeared in the first two published collections of chorales, both issued in 1524 by Luther's friend Johann Walther: the *Achtliederbuch* and the 2-volume *Enchiridion.* The Protestant custom at first was to sing the chorales in unison, but harmonizations were soon developed, conventionally giving the melody to the tenor part.

The popularity of chorales increased during the 17th century for several reasons. The prevailing "Italian" style in music depreciated the polyphonic techniques of earlier vocal music; the chorale melodies came to be allotted to the soprano part, which was more easily recognizable; and the development of the organ supplied an instrument sufficient in both volume and variety to support the melodic line and supply the harmony. At the same time it became fashionable to replace the original meters of the old chorales with the now-familiar steady succession of equal notes, a practice that was often detrimental to the music.

The chorale attained its last important development, as well as its most elaborate, in the work of J. S. Bach. Bach probably composed no original chorales, but he wrote more than 400 arrangements of traditional hymns. He also used the chorale as the foundation of much of his religious music. Both the *St. John Passion* and the *St. Matthew Passion* include familiar chorales, which are introduced at appropriate points in the text. But Bach's most important use of the chorale was as the inspiration for his church cantatas, which often employ these hymns as the bases for choruses, arias, and recitatives. Probably the best known of these is the "Wachet auf" Cantata No. 140, based on a chorale written by Philipp Nicolai (1556–1608).

Many other musical forms were derived from the chorale, most of them intended for the organ; these include the chorale prelude, chorale fantasia, chorale partita, and chorale fugue. Excellent examples of all these forms appear in the works of Bach. Later composers who used chorales in their compositions include Mendelssohn, Théodore Dubois, and Benjamin Britten. Many chorales, usually in their 17th century forms, may be found in contemporary hymnals.

HELEN N. MORGAN
North Shore Branch, New England Conservatory

CHORD, in music. See HARMONY.

CHORDATA, kôr-dā'tə, a phylum that includes all animals with backbones (the vertebrates) together with a few more primitive animals. At some stage of their existence, all chordates possess a rodlike structure called the notochord, from which the group gets its name.

Chordate Characteristics. The chordates primarily are animals that swim, although the most primitive kinds, known as the ascidians, or sea squirts, do so only when they first develop from the egg into the tadpolelike larvae. Many other chordates long ago abandoned life in the water as fish, to become creatures of the land and air. However, as animals that swim and feed in water, the chordates all have certain distinctive features. These are: a band of muscle extending along each side of the body or tail, which supplies the power of swimming; a stiffening rod (the notochord or its replacement), which prevents the muscles from contracting the body or tail like a concertina; gill slits on each side, which allow water that has entered the mouth to escape without passing all the way through the intestine; and a central nervous system, which is essentially a hollow tube lying above the notochord and extending the length of the body. These features are found in some form at some stage in the development of all chordate animals from sea squirts to man.

Chordate Divisions. The phylum Chordata is divided into three subphyla: Tunicata, or Urochordata, which includes the sea squirts and their close relatives; Cephalochordata, which has only lancelets such as amphioxus, and Vertebrata, which includes the whole vast community, present and past, of vertebrates, ranging from the primitive jawless lamprey eels to the highly developed birds and mammals.

Tunicates. In the adult state the sea squirts are generally inconspicuous marine animals that occur from the intertidal zone to the greatest depths of the ocean. They always attach themselves to the surface of rocks, weeds, pilings, or the sea floor itself by means of an external supporting layer of celluloselike substance. Internally, sea squirts consist largely of a complex water-sifting feeding apparatus with two siphons opening to the exterior, one for water intake and the other for water ejection.

At one time, sea squirts were classed with bivalve mollusks, such as clams and oysters, since anything less like a swimming vertebrate was hard to imagine. However, sea squirts do possess numerous gill slits, which allow the water taken in through the mouth siphon to be eliminated without passage through the gut. Also, the tad-

CHORDATE CHARACTERISTICS

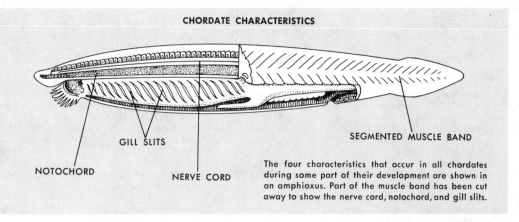

NOTOCHORD

GILL SLITS

NERVE CORD

SEGMENTED MUSCLE BAND

The four characteristics that occur in all chordates during some part of their development are shown in an amphioxus. Part of the muscle band has been cut away to show the nerve cord, notochord, and gill slits.

pole-shaped larva that develops from the egg possesses a swimming tail consisting of a central notochord rod, a muscle band on each side, and a fine nerve tube above the rod. Thus the sea squirts have all the qualifications for membership in the chordate phylum. However, the truly chordate tadpolelike larvae exist as such for only a few hours and serve merely to select a suitable spot on which to settle and grow as a sedentary sea squirt.

Cephalochordates. The other kind of nonvertebrate chordate, the lancelets, inhabit the shallow seas and live, much as do the sea squirts, on the sea floor. They sift food particles from a steady stream of water taken in through the mouth and passed outward again through numerous gill slits along each side of the throat. Unlike the sea squirts, lancelets are not actually attached to some solid surface but remain imbedded in loose sand with only the forward end of the body projecting into the water. Also, they retain their structure and capacity for swimming throughout life, in contrast to the sea squirt larvae, which resorb their tails when they become attached. The lancelet retains its notochord, lateral bands of locomotory muscle, and nerve tube, and at any time can either swim out of the sand and imbed itself in a more suitable area or wriggle through the loose, wet sand without actually emerging.

Both the lancelets and the attached sea squirts, however, feed in essentially the same way. The food-laden water taken in through the mouth is sifted as it passes through the gills. A film of mucus, secreted from a midventral gland (the endostyle) in the large throat, passes over the inner walls of the gill region and entraps small food particles; the mucus and particles then pass along to the intestine. The same elaborate food-collecting mechanism is used by the young lamprey eels, which are true vertebrates and are far more advanced than the nonvertebrate chordates. The presence of the endostylar feeding mechanism in juvenile lampreys indicates almost certainly that this was the general feeding method and mechanism employed by all early chordates and ancestral vertebrates at a time before the true fishes had evolved.

Primitive Vertebrates. Juvenile lampreys, which grow to lengths of about 6 inches (15 cm) are not parasitic predators on fish, as they are when mature; instead, they live much like the lancelets. They inhabit fresh water rather than the sea, and live imbedded in the soft mud and in shallow water along the banks of rivers and lakes. Here they

draw in water through the mouth, filtering out the contained food particles and eliminating the filtered water through the gill slits at the side of the throat. By means of their muscular bodies and tails they can move freely through the soft mud and occasionally in the water alone. But although they live in this primitive way, their body structure has all the complex and essential organs and systems common to all backboned animals. They lack jaws, which are not needed by filter feeders, and they lack paired fins, but they possess virtually all other vertebrate features. The notorchord persists as a large and substantial structure stiffening the body, and it is reinforced by rings of cartilage, which constitute a vertebral column around the notochord. Even in human embryos, at a very early stage of development, a notochord is formed first and then the vertebral column develops around it.

Evolution. The chordates, as a whole, appear to have evolved in two main phases. The first phase was the evolution of marine filter feeders, which consisted entirely of soft body structures and had only a temporary or intermittent need to swim. The second phase was the evolution of the swimming stage into the true vertebrate state; this probably occurred in fresh waters and led to the subsequent evolution of fishes and their terrestrial descendants, the land vertebrates. Throughout chordate evolution the notochord has played a dominant role—as the essential stiffener of the first swimming tail, as the basis for the construction of a vertebral column, or backbone, and finally as a vitally important tissue in the early development of all higher vertebrates.

See also AMPHIOXUS; TUNICATA; VERTEBRATA.

N. J. BERRILL
McGill University

CHOREA, kə-rē′ə, is a human disorder characterized by an almost continuous involuntary jerking of various parts of the body. The term is derived from the Greek word *choreia,* meaning "dance," and the jerking movements associated with the disorder have a surprisingly close resemblance to some of the frenetic social dances of the 1960's.

The most common varieties of chorea are Sydenham's chorea and Huntington's chorea. The former, also known as St. Vitus's dance, was first well described by the English physician Thomas Sydenham in 1685. The latter was first clearly described in 1872 by the American physician George Huntington.

Sydenham's Chorea. Sydenham's chorea usually occurs in children between the ages of 5 and 15, and is more common in girls than in boys. When it occurs in a young pregnant woman, it is called chorea gravidum, although it is indistinguishable in other respects from Sydenham's chorea.

The first signs of Sydenham's chorea are muscular movements that may seem simply to be those of ordinary restlessness. However, they gradually increase in number and severity, becoming abrupt, brief, aimless jerks of various parts of the face, neck, trunk, and extremities. They occur irregularly, as often as every few seconds, but vary widely in tempo and intensity. They cease completely during sleep. In some cases the movements are almost entirely restricted to the limbs on one side of the body. Emotional instability is a common accompaniment of this disorder, but it rarely becomes severe. Fever is unusual.

Generally, Sydenham's chorea runs its course within a few weeks or months and finally subsides completely. Treatment is nonspecific, aimed directly only at reducing the symptoms through bed rest and administering sedatives.

Since many patients have symptoms of acute rheumatic fever either before or after an attack of Sydenham's chorea, it is believed that this disorder is often a part of the rheumatic process, possibly a delayed reaction to the streptococcal infection. However, final proof of this relationship is still lacking. It is known, though, that Sydenham's chorea is associated with various types of injury to the nerve cells and small arteries in many parts of the brain.

Sydenham's chorea is sometimes incorrectly suspected in children who have spasmotic twitchings called tics. These involuntary movements are restricted to single muscle groups and occur repeatedly in a stereotyped form.

Huntington's Chorea. Unlike Sydenham's chorea, Huntington's chorea leads to progressive disability and death. It is a rare hereditary disease that has been traced in the United States to a single family that migrated from England in the 17th century.

Huntington's chorea starts in middle life, usually with a few scattered jerking movements or minor defects in coordination. The disease progresses gradually, and within a few years the jerks become grotesque and violent, and finally disabling. In almost every case, mental deterioration soon develops, producing memory loss, emotional outbursts, slovenly behavior, and severe dementia. In a few individuals the mental changes appear only late in the disease, and sometimes they never occur at all.

During the course of the disease, extensive degenerative changes develop in many portions of the cerebral cortex and areas deep within the brain, but the precise nature of the underlying biochemical disorder is unknown. No therapy will halt the progress of Huntington's chorea, but the jerky movements can be partly eased for a time by the administration of certain sedatives.

Other Varieties. Much rarer than Sydenham's chorea or Huntington's chorea are varieties that may appear during acute viral encephalitis or result from brain injury, either before or after birth or as a result of senility. In these forms of chorea, the symptoms are more complex, often including other kinds of abnormal movements.

E. CHARLES KUNKLE, M. D.
Maine Medical Center

CHOREGUS. See CHORAGUS.

CHOREOGRAPHY, kôr-ē-og'rə-fē, is the art of creating a dance: selecting steps, gestures, and other movements and arranging these movements in sequences to make a series of formal patterns. The term also refers to the sequences and patterns themselves.

Characteristics. Choreography may be a community or an individual creation. For example, it can be the result of a tradition developed by the people of a geographic area or cultural community, as in ethnic, folk, or modern social dancing. The age-old patterns of the Pueblo Indian Corn Dance are still repeated in dusty village plazas in the American Southwest. Choreography of this kind is generally an expression of community feeling, whether religious, military, or festive.

An obvious example of individual choreography is the personal victory dance of a primitive hunter. Also, a single choreographer is the creator of a formal ballet, modern dance composition, or other theatrical dance work. The theatrical choreographer is always a trained dancer who knows what the body can do and understands how to combine such elements of dance as rhythm, dynamics, and direction into the ordered, purposeful movement that makes a work of art.

Choreography draws inspiration from a variety of sources. Very often the inspiration is a form of sound, which the choreographer transforms into movement. He may start simply by responding kinetically to the beating of a drum or the turning of an egg beater at different speeds, or he may walk to the rhythm of the canon *Three Blind Mice*. Rhythm also is the basis for precision dancing in unison, such as that of the Rockettes at Radio City Music Hall in New York City. On another level, a choreographer may express his personal reactions to music, as George Balanchine did in his abstract ballet *Palais de cristal* (1947), set to Bizet's Symphony in C.

Closely related to sound as a source of inspiration are other dance forms. A choreographer may develop one of the early European court dances, such as the pavane, galliard, or saraband, to create an elaborate ballet. Many choreographers observe ethnic and folk dances, edit them, and dramatize them for theater, as Pearl Primus has done with African dances, the Moiseyev Dance Company with Russian dances, and the Ballet Folklórico de México with Mexican dances.

Rich sources of inspiration for choreographers are stories, ideas, or emotions, which may come from fairy tales, books, or poems. The choreography of a dramatic ballet, such as Marius Petipa's *Sleeping Beauty* (1890), or of a musical comedy, such as Jerome Robbins' *West Side Story* (1957), is designed to advance the plot line, define character, and convey mood. Choreography may also make social commentary, as in Eugene Loring's *These Three* (1966), based on the martyrdom of three murdered civil rights workers, and in L. A. Larchiune and Vasily Tikhomiroff's *Red Poppy* (1926), about the political situation in China. Occasionally a choreographer may work without music or story, in complete silence. Jerome Robbins' *Moves* (1959) is an example.

History. Choreography predates man; some birds and animals have mating dances that are rhythmic rituals. The primitive man who made up a dance to explain, through mimetic gesture, the events of a battle or a hunt, or to display his physical prowess to attract a woman, was choreographing. When David danced before the Lord "with all his might," he determined how to dis-

CHOREOGRAPHER George Balanchine rehearses some dancers of the New York City Ballet.

FRED FEHL

play that might and was thus a choreographer. The movements of the chorus in ancient Greek drama required choreography, as did the folk dances that developed in medieval Europe.

At the 16th century French court, the Italian-born Balthasar de Beaujoyeulx choreographed the first ballet, which he defined as "a geometric arrangement of numerous people dancing together under a diverse harmony of many instruments." The term "choreography", or "choregraphy" (literally "dance writing"), however, originated in the late 17th century and meant the recording of previously composed dance steps by notation. Some modern choreographers still refer to their work as "writing a ballet."

Until recent times choreography was instinctive. Those with an inborn talent for making patterns of movement developed their art through trial and error. In the United States in the late 1920's, however, dancers began to explore choreography as a science. Classes in dance composition were launched in the field of modern dance (but not in ballet), and students experimented with various sources of inspiration.

Most of the work of early choreographers was preserved only through direct imitation by their pupils, since early systems of dance notation were difficult and little known. But in the 20th century the Hungarian Rudolf von Laban invented a workable system of dance notation, which, with the later Benesh system, made it possible to record the choreography of any dance for the use of future dancers and choreographers.

WALTER TERRY
Author of "The Ballet Companion"

Further Reading: Humphrey, Doris, *The Art of Making Dances* (New York 1958); Martin, John, *Introduction to the Dance* (New York 1939); Terry, Walter, *The Ballet Companion* (New York 1968); Van Praagh, Peggy, and Brinson, Peter,, *The Choreographic Art: An Outline of Its Principles and Craft* (New York 1963).

CHORION. See EMBRYOLOGY—*Extraembryonic Membranes.*

CHOROID. See EYE.

CHORUS, in Greek drama, a group that participates in a play or comments on the action. The Greek word *choros* originally meant "a dancing-place," and since dancing in ancient Greece was almost always associated with singing, it came to mean a group of singers and dancers and the composition performed. Such compositions reached the height of literary perfection about 600 to 400 B.C.,

JEROME ROBBINS, noted choreographer of ballets for both stage and screen, demonstrates a dance movement.

FRED FEHL

when paeans were sung in honor of the god Apollo, dithyrambs were sung in the processions honoring Dionysus, trained groups of maidens sang hymns to goddesses, and choruses sang specially commissioned odes to greet victors in athletic games. The best-known composer of the victory odes, and indeed of choric odes in general, was Pindar.

Choric odes (as distinct from lyric or monodic odes performed by one person) were usually of unparalleled metrical complexity. The first stanza, called the *strophe*, was followed by a second, metrically equivalent stanza, the *antistrophe*. The antistrophe, in turn, was sometimes followed by a metrically different *epode*. This pattern, strophe-antistrophe-(epode), might be repeated indefinitely.

Choric performances led to the development of the Greek drama. In Athens, in the 530's B.C., the legendary Thespis is supposed to have been the first performer to step forward and deliver the speeches appropriate to the characters in whatever myth the chorus was narrating. In fully developed Greek tragedy and comedy the chorus remained the backbone of the dramatic structure, and every play consisted of some half-dozen formal choric odes interspersed with dramatic scenes, or *episodes.* Occasionally the chorus might perform antiphonally with an actor.

The relevance of the chorus to the action varied. Sometimes it had the chief role, such as Danaus' 50 daughters in Aeschylus' *Suppliants;* sometimes its role was vital but subsidiary, such as Dionysus' followers in Euripides' *Bacchae;* sometimes its relevance was tenuous, as in Euripides' *Phoenissae,* where the chorus consists of visitors. Occasionally the leading chorister (*coryphaeus*) had a brief speaking role.

In general, the chorus in tragedy commented rather indirectly on the deeper meanings of the play. In Aristophanic comedy it was common to dress the chorus in symbolic costumes (*The Wasps, The Clouds*), or divide it (men versus women in *Lysistrata*), or have it address the audience at one point as the poet's mouthpiece (*parabasis*). After 400 B.C. the chorus gradually disappeared from comedy.

RICHMOND Y. HATHORN
Author of "Handbook of Classical Drama"
Further Reading: Bieber, Margarete, *The History of the Greek and Roman Theater,* 2d ed. (Princeton, N. J., 1961); Webster, Thomas B. L., *Greek Theatre Production* (London 1956).

CHORUS, in music. See CHORAL MUSIC.

CHORZÓW, KHÔ′zhoōf, is a Polish city in the province of Katowice, lying 165 miles (226 km) southwest of Warsaw. Located in the heart of the Upper Silesian industrial region, it is a working-class city, dominated by the Kościuszko iron and steel works, which lie in the center of the city. Chorzów also has an important chemical industry.

In the late 18th century the Prussian government (which then ruled Upper Silesia) established an iron-works near Chorzów to use the local iron ore and the abundant reserves of coal. A settlement called Königshütte (Polish, Królewska Huta) grew up near the works. Upper Silesia was transferred to Polish rule after World War I, and in 1934 the present city of Chorzów was formed by merging Królewksa Huta, Chorzów, and certain other villages. Population: (1965 estimate) 154,000.

NORMAN J. G. POUNDS, *Indiana University*

CHOSEN. See KOREA.

CHOSHU, chō-shoō, was formerly a feudal clan of Japan, in southern Honshu. Its domain was reorganized into the Yamaguchi prefecture. Choshu, or the house of Mori, became one of the most powerful of the outer *han* (baronies) during the Tokugawa shogunate (1600–1868) and was instrumental in bringing about the downfall of the Tokugawas.

The *han* administration introduced fiscal and economic policies which made Choshu solvent when most of Japan suffered from economic adversity. A system of forced savings and investment enabled Choshu to import weapons and acquire Western technology. Monopolies in such products as paper, wax, cotton, and indigo, and the expansion of agricultural output also contributed to its economic strength.

The defeat of the Choshu at Shimonoseki in 1864 by a combined European fleet and one American ship, in retaliation against Choshu's firing on the American vessel *Pembroke,* resulted in the opening of the Straits of Shimonoseki to foreign ships. The Choshu militia included men of all classes, rather than being limited to samurai, and at the end of the Tokugawa era they effectively fought the shogun's forces. A year after the Meiji Restoration (1868), the daimzo of Choshu, Satsuma, Hizen, and Tosa voluntarily relinquished their fiefs and put their forces at the disposal of the emperor. For years, Choshu and Satsuma alternated at the helm of government. Choshu leaders, such as Ito Hirobumi and Inoue Kaoru, helped establish constitutional government in Japan, and Yamagata Aritomo was influential in creating the modern Japanese army, controlled by Choshu until after World War I.

JOYCE LEBRA, *University of Colorado*

CHOU DYNASTY, jō, was the Chinese dynasty that ruled from about 1027 B.C. to 256 B.C. This period was a time of great intellectual ferment and during its last 200 years was one of constant warfare.

The account of the origins of the Chou people and their early rule are legendary. They probably lived to the west of the territory controlled by the preceding ruling dynasty, the Shang, and may have been recently settled nomads. According to tradition the evil Shang ruler Chou Hsin made war on Wen Wang (King Wen) of Chou but was overthrown by Wen's virtuous sons, Wu Wang (King Wu) and Chou Kung (the Duke of Chou). Wu Wang established his capital near present-day Sian in 1027 B.C., although some scholars date its founding a century earlier. This marked the beginning of the Chou dynasty. The period until 770 B.C., when the capital was moved east to Loyang, was called the Western Chou and the period after this, the Eastern Chou.

The Chou dynasty was the earliest source of the *T'ien Ming,* the mandate of heaven theory, according to which Chinese sovereigns ruled only as agents of heaven. The Chou order, however, was based on feudal principles. Those who had assisted in the conquest of the Shang were granted fiefs and became hereditary aristocrats, monopolizing power, and owing loyalty in return. The states that were formed had unstable boundaries, and war developed as they vied for power. There were two major periods of warfare. The first was the "Spring and Autumn" period (722–481 B.C.) named after the *Spring and Autumn Annals* that covered these years, and the next was the "Warring States" period (403–222 B.C.). Chou power steadily declined during these times until 249 B.C., when the King of Ch'in annexed the last Chou territory.

Striking social changes accompanied this turmoil, and produced revolutionary thought in response, especially during the Warring States period. This was the golden age of Chinese philosophy, when the "hundred schools" debated the nature of man, the world, and society, attempting to find means of restoring peace. In addition to being the classical age of prose and poetry, the Chou dynasty was a time of scientific advance. Astronomical data were collected and by 444 B.C., the year was calculated to have 365¼ days. Iron displaced bronze, money was first coined, and the ox-drawn plow appeared. Other refinements of life that were introduced included lacquerware and chopsticks. Out of this welter of thought and change came the basic philosophical and political principles and the social patterns that were to dominate Chinese life up to the 20th century.

JAMES R. SHIRLEY, *Northern Illinois University*

Chou En-lai

EASTFOTO

CHOU EN-LAI, jō'en'lī' (1898–1976), premier of Communist China. A man of great charm and exceptional diplomatic skill, Chou became a major figure in the early 1920's and eventually attained third rank in the Communist party hierarchy. He is usually classed as a moderate.

Chou was born into a family of the provincial gentry in Shaoshing, Chekiang, but moved to Huaian, Kiangsu, while still very young. After receiving a traditional education, he went to Waseda University in Japan in 1917 and returned to study at Nank'ai University in 1919. During the May Fourth Movement, Chou joined the protest-and-study activities in Peking and was imprisoned for six months. There he met his future wife, Teng Ying-ch'ao. Although introduced to Marxist ideas in Japan, Chou did not become a Communist until after leaving for France in 1920. There he studied and worked, and helped recruit members for the Chinese Communist party that was taking shape at home.

On his return in 1924, Chou became a political commissar in the Whampoa Military Academy and in Chiang Kai-shek's First Army. It was Chou who organized the workers' uprisings that delivered Shanghai to Chiang Kai-shek in 1927. He narrowly escaped from Chiang's suppression of the Communists in Shanghai in April 1927 and fled south, where he became active in organizing the Communists in Nanchang, Swatow, and Canton.

Chou was first elected to the political bureau of the Communist party in 1927. He spent 1928 in Russia and at the end of the year returned to Shanghai, where he worked with Li Li-san until 1931, when the party leadership passed from Li. Chou then went to Mao Tse-tung's rural base in southern Kiangsi and has remained closely associated with Mao ever since. He became a political commissar under army commander Chu Teh, a vice chairman of the Revolutionary Military Council, and a political officer on the 6,000-mile "long march" to Yenan in northwestern China in 1934–1935.

Chou's negotiating skill was demonstrated in 1936, when he initiated the events leading up to Chiang Kai-shek's kidnapping at Sian by disaffected warlords. Chou persuaded them not to kill Chiang and helped set the conditions that resulted in his release. Chou flew to Nanking to negotiate the united front against Japanese aggression, and when the Chinese-Japanese War broke out in 1937 he headed the Communist delegation at the Nationalist capital. He also represented the Communists in the abortive American-inspired negotiations under Gen. George C. Marshall at the end of World War II.

From 1949 to 1958, Chou was foreign minister as well as premier of the state council. Although he relinquished his post as foreign minister in 1958 to Ch'en Yi, he remained premier and the major spokesman on foreign policy. He headed the Chinese delegations to the Geneva conference on Indochina in 1954 and to the Asian-African conference of 1955 in Bandung. In 1956 the Communist party elected him one of its four vice presidents. During the Cultural Revolution of the 1960's he supported the Maoists while attempting to curb the excesses of the Red Guards. Afterward, although Lin Piao remained the party's only vice president, Chou continued as third-ranking member of the Politburo's Standing Committee.

Chou traveled widely through much of the world, including Africa. In 1969, in order to cope with what he saw as a growing Soviet threat across the border, he launched a vigorous program of normalizing his government's relations with countries of the Western world and Africa. Two years later, in 1971, he succeeded in arranging for a visit to Peking by U. S. Secretary of State Kissinger, during which preparations were made for the historic visit by President Nixon in February 1972. Shortly afterward he became ill and appeared less frequently at official functions. He died of cancer in Peking on Jan. 8, 1976.

JAMES R. SHIRLEY*
Northern Illinois University

CHOU KUNG, jō'gŏong', the Duke of Chou and the son of King Wen of the Chou dynasty (1027–256 B. C.), was China's original philosopher-king.

According to tradition, Chou Kung lived in the late 12th century B. C.; some scholars place his lifetime a century later. He is reputed to have aided his brother, King Wu, in completing the defeat of the Shang dynasty in 1027 B. C. and is thought to have been chiefly responsible for establishing Chou authority, suppressing a rebellion, and organizing the new state system. After Wu's death Chou Kung acted as a regent for his nephew, King Ch'eng, and has been greatly acclaimed not only for training the young king wisely, but for relinquishing his power when Ch'eng came of age. Falsely attributed to him are the editorship of the *Rites of Chou* and part authorship of the *Book of Changes.*

JAMES R. SHIRLEY
Northern Illinois University

CHOUAN, shōō-än', is the name for the insurgents from Brittany who waged a guerrilla war against the French Revolutionary government, beginning in 1792. Their name is probably derived from *chat-huant* (screech owl), whose call they imitated in order to gather their forces at night. Led by the Cottereau brothers, the insurrection spread to Poitou and Maine, but was suppressed by Napoleon Bonaparte in 1800.

CHOUART, Médart. See GROSEILLIERS.

CHOUSHAN ARCHIPELAGO, jō'shän', a group of 180 Chinese islands in the East China Sea at the mouth of Hangchou Bay. They are part of Chekiang province. The name is also spelled *Chusan.* The main island is Choushan.

CHOUTEAU, shōō-tō, a family of New Orleans origin closely connected with the founding of St. Louis, Mo., and the history of the trans-Mississippi West.

(RENÉ) AUGUSTE CHOUTEAU (1749–1829) was a fur trader and cofounder of St. Louis. He was born in New Orleans, La., in September 1749. In August 1763 he left New Orleans for the Illinois country as clerk to Pierre de Laclède, who, with others, had obtained a grant of the fur trade on the Upper Mississippi and Missouri rivers. On Feb. 15, 1764, under orders from Laclède, the boy, directing 30 workmen, began clearing the site of St. Louis. After 1768 he operated as Laclède's partner. Following Laclède's death in 1778, Chouteau emerged as the citizen of first importance. Though he held no office, he was much consulted by Spanish officials, particularly with respect to the important Osage tribe, whose trade he controlled for many years with his half brother Pierre. After the transfer of Louisiana to the United States, Chouteau served as judge of the court of common pleas, justice of the peace, president of the first board of trustees of St. Louis, lieutenant colonel of the militia, member of the legislative council of the Missouri territory, and also served as U. S. commissioner for various Indian treaties. He died on Feb. 24, 1829, in St. Louis.

(JEAN) PIERRE CHOUTEAU (1758–1849), half brother of Auguste and son of Pierre de Laclède, was a fur trader and Indian agent. He was born in New Orleans on Oct. 10, 1758. He arrived at St. Louis in September 1764 and later became active in the fur trade. In 1794 the half brothers obtained an exclusive grant of the Osage trade for 6 years. To control this trade, Pierre built Fort Carondelet in southwest Missouri. In 1804 he was named U. S. agent for all tribes west of the Mississippi; later he was agent for the Osage. One of the organizers of the St. Louis Missouri Fur Company, he remained active in the fur trade for many years. He was captain and major of militia, justice of the peace, and one of the first trustees of St. Louis. He died on July 10, 1849, in St. Louis.

AUGUSTE PIERRE CHOUTEAU (1786–1838), eldest son of Pierre, was a fur trader and Indian treaty commissioner. He was born in St. Louis on May 9, 1786. Graduated from the United States Military Academy in 1806, he soon resigned from the army to take his place in the family business, becoming a partner in various family-owned companies. During the last 20 years of his life he concentrated on trade in the Oklahoma area. He served frequently as commissioner for Indian treaties in the Southwest. He died at Fort Gibson, Okla., on Dec. 25, 1838.

PIERRE CHOUTEAU, JR. (1789–1865), brother of the preceding, was a fur trader and financier. He was born in St. Louis on Jan. 19, 1789. He was in the fur trade with his father as early as 1805, eventually becoming head of the American Fur Company, and engaged in many other enterprises. He died on Sept. 6, 1865, in St. Louis.

JOHN FRANCIS MCDERMOTT
Southern Illinois University
Editor of "The Early Histories of St. Louis"

Further Reading: McDermott, John Francis, ed., *The Early Histories of St. Louis* (St. Louis 1952); id., *Private Libraries in Creole Saint Louis* (Baltimore 1938); Oglesby, Richard E., *Manuel Lisa and the Opening of the Missouri Fur Trade* (Norman, Okla., 1963); Sunder, John E., *The Fur Trade on the Upper Missouri, 1840–1865* (Norman, Okla., 1965).

EVELYN M. SHAFER

Chow Chow

CHOW CHOW, a medium-sized breed of nonsporting dog. The chow chow is striking in appearance, with a distinctive rough coat of deep solid color, lionlike mane and paws, plumed tail curled over the back, erect ears, and stilted gait. It stands 18 to 20 inches (46–51 cm) at the shoulder and weighs 40 to 65 pounds (18–29 kg). The most unusual feature of the breed is the blue-black color of the tongue and mouth lining. The coat is usually black or red, but other colors are acceptable.

The chow chow, descended from the wild dogs of far northern regions, is probably one of the most ancient breeds of dog. The first record of the breed appears in a bas-relief from the Han dynasty of China, about 150 B. C., depicting its use as a hunting dog. The chow chow has also been used as a guard dog and for other work, but in the United States—to which it was introduced in 1890—it is principally a pet and show dog. Most chow chows are aloof rather than affectionate, but some are playful.

WILLIAM F. BROWN
Editor of "American Field"

CHOW MEIN. See CHINESE COOKING.

CHOWN, choun, **Samuel Dwight** (1853–1933), Canadian clergyman. He was born in Kingston, Ontario, on April 11, 1853, and educated at Victoria University (then in Cobourg, now in Toronto). He was ordained a Methodist minister in 1879, and during the succeeding 25 years he had charge of important congregations in Montreal, Toronto, and other major cities.

Chown was a leading advocate of church union, and as early as 1906 he served on a joint committee to study this question. As general superintendent of the Methodist Church, he used his influence to bring about the union of the Presbyterian, Methodist, and Congregational churches on which the United Church of Canada is based. The union was finally completed in 1925, and today it is the largest of Canadian Protestant groups. Chown was the author of *Story of Church Union in Canada* (1930). He died in Toronto on Jan. 30, 1933.

CHRÉTIEN DE TROYES, krã-tyaɴ′ də trwä′, French poet of the late 12th century, the earliest French author of extant Arthurian romances. Very little is known of his life. Chrétien (or Chrestien) was probably born at Troyes about 1130. Two of his *roman courtois* are dedicated to Marie de Champagne, daughter of Louis VII, and to Philippe d'Alsace, Count of Flanders; he probably enjoyed their patronage and may also have spent many years at Marie's court at Troyes. He died about 1185.

Chrétien's five Arthurian poems are *Erec et Énide* and *Cligès,* composed between 1160 and 1164; *Lancelot ou le chevalier de la charrette* and *Yvain ou le chevalier au lion,* composed between 1164 and 1172; and *Perceval* or *Le conte del graal* (about 1180). He also wrote translations of Ovid (some now lost); a romance, *Roi Marc et Iseut la blonde* (lost); a few lyric poems; and possibly *Guillaume d'Angleterre,* a saint's legend. His works, which are usually written in rhymed couplets containing eight syllables, are distinguished by their remarkably expert narrative technique.

Chrétien's Arthurian poems are drawn mostly from Geoffrey of Monmouth's *Historia regum Britanniae* (c. 1147) and Wace's *Roman de Brut* (1155). But Chrétien transformed the Arthurian legends by introducing three major elements: the character Lancelot; courtly love (q.v.), which is centrally important in *Lancelot;* and the mysterious special significance of the Holy Grail. His works, and especially these innovations, have enormously influenced later versions of the Arthurian legends. See also ARTHURIAN ROMANCES; GRAIL.

ELIE R. VIDAL
California State College at Hayward

CHRISM, kriz′əm, is usually a mixture of olive oil and balsam that is used in the Roman Catholic and Eastern Orthodox churches. "Chrism" literally means "anointing," and is derived from the same verb, *chiro,* as is the term Christ, "the Anointed One." Chrism is consecrated by the bishop on Holy Thursday in accordance with a custom that was followed as early as the Council of Carthage (390). In the East, the patriarch consecrates chrism, which, in addition to oil and balsam, may include as many as 50 other ingredients.

The use of oil in the consecration of priests and kings, as well as things, was a common practice in the Old Testament. Its symbolism is related to sports and hygiene. In the Christian tradition it is used in the three sacraments that confer a "character" and that can be received only once. At baptism it is placed on the crown of the head to indicate that the new Christian has been spiritually healed. At confirmation it makes the Christian an "athlete of Christ." Although both these sacraments confer participation in the "royal priesthood" (I Peter 2:9), at holy orders the anointing imparts a fuller share in the ministry of Christ. Chrism is also used in the consecration of churches, altars, chalices, patens, and in the solemn blessing of church bells and baptismal water.

CLEMENT J. MCNASPY, S. J.
"America" Magazine

CHRIST, Jesus. See CHRISTIANITY; JESUS CHRIST.

CHRIST, Disciples of. See DISCIPLES OF CHRIST.

CHRIST OF THE ANDES stands at the summit of Uspallata Pass on the Argentina-Chile border.

CHRIST OF THE ANDES, a bronze statue of Christ on the Argentina-Chile border in the Andes, dedicated in 1904, as a symbol of perpetual peace between the two countries. It was erected jointly by Argentina and Chile at the summit of Bermejo (La Cumbre; Uspallata) Pass, 12,572 feet (3,832 meters) above sea level, 85 miles (135 km) northeast of Santiago, Chile. It commemorates the final settlement of a long and bitter boundary dispute which more than once had threatened war.

Molded from old Argentine cannon, the statue is the work of the Argentine sculptor Mateo Alonzo. The figure of Christ, more than twice life-size, stands on a hemisphere and faces north; the left hand supports a great cross; the right arm is raised in benediction. A plaque on the base quotes a passage in Spanish from the dedicatory address: "These mountains will fall before Argentines and Chileans break the peace sworn at the feet of Christ the Redeemer."

CHRISTABEL, kris′tə-bel, an unfinished poem by Samuel Taylor Coleridge (q.v.), is one of his three most famous poetical works (with *The Rime of the Ancient Mariner* and *Kubla Khan*). The poem, published in 1816, consists of two cantos written in 1797 and 1800, respectively, totaling 677 lines. Coleridge's plan for two additional cantos was revealed in James Gillman's *Life of Coleridge* (1838).

The supernatural action of the poem, set in medieval times, involves an unspecified threat to the heroine, the virtuous maiden Christabel, posed by the beautiful but sinister Lady Geraldine. According to Coleridge's plan, Christabel's absent lover was ultimately to return to save her from Geraldine's evil influence. The poem, which involves elements of popular romance and legend, is founded on the theme that the power of good can surmount and redeem evil. *Christabel*'s unusual metrical system relies on the number of accents (four) per line rather than on the number of syllables.

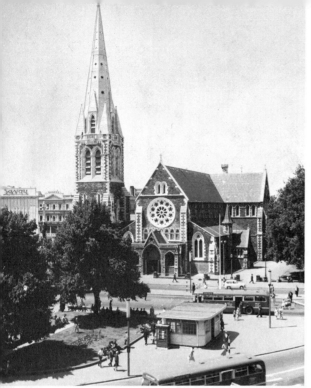

IN CHRISTCHURCH, NEW ZEALAND, the Anglican cathedral dominates Cathedral Square, in the business district.

CHRISTADELPHIANS, kris-tə-del'-fē-ənz, a small body of Christians founded in America in 1848. They were originally called *Thomasites,* for the English-born physician John Thomas. The name "Christadelphian" (Greek for "Christian brethren") was adopted in 1864. Thomas opposed the existing churches, regarding them as apostate. He wished to restore primitive Christianity and the beliefs of the earliest disciples, using the Bible as the only rule of faith and practice.

Christadelphians do not accept the conventional view of the Trinity, believing that the Holy Spirit is not a person, but an effluence of divine power. They believe that Jesus Christ will return and rule the world. They also believe that because of sin the total man is mortal, and that at the second coming only those who believed in the Gospel will become immortal. The unfaithful shall then be destroyed, while those who never heard the Gospel shall never see the light of resurrection. There is no ordained ministry. Local congregations are autonomous and their "serving brethren" work gratuitously.

CHRISTCHURCH, a municipal borough, in southern England, is in Hampshire, just east of Bournemouth on the English Channel. The oldest part of the borough is at the confluence of the Avon and Stour rivers, where the large and admirable Augustinian Priory Church (11th–16th centuries) and the remains of a castle and Norman house, both of the 12th century, are situated.

Modern Christchurch includes the villages of Mudeford and Highcliffe. Its lagoon-like harbor, a favorite for pleasure boats, is sheltered by the curving arm of Hengistbury Head, which is popular with local archaeologists and birdwatchers. Population: (1961) 26,336.

GORDON STOKES
Author of "English Place-Names"

CHRISTCHURCH, in New Zealand, is the largest city of South Island. It is located on the coastal margins of the Canterbury Plains at the northern base of Banks Peninsula. It is the chief manufacturing center of South Island and the principal administrative and commercial center of the Canterbury provincial district.

The winding Avon River flows through Christchurch, which has been called the "Garden City of the Plains." Spacious parks, gardens, treelined avenues, and picturesque bridges on the river give the city a very English appearance. The central business district surrounds Cathedral Square, the site of the Anglican Cathedral and focus of bus transport. Immediately to the west are the Canterbury Museum, McDougall Art Gallery, the Botanic Gardens, and 479-acre (184-hectare) Hagley Park. The University of Canterbury was established in 1873.

Industries in the city and its suburbs include meat-freezing works, woolen mills, sawmills, and engineering and railroad workshops. Factories produce machinery, fertilizer, rubber products, clothing, shoes, electrical goods, and furniture. Christchurch is connected with its port at Lyttelton by a railroad tunnel and a road tunnel through the Port Hills. The main South Island railroad extends north and south of Christchurch and a branch connects it with the west coast. Christchurch International Airport is at Harewood, 7 miles (11 km) northwest of the city.

Christchurch was founded as a Church of England settlement by John Robert Godley, who named it for Christ Church College of Oxford. The first settlers arrived at Lyttelton in 1850 and walked over the Port Hills to the site of the present city. From 1852 until the Abolition of the Provinces Act of 1875, Christchurch was the capital of Canterbury province. Population: (1961) 151,671.

HOWARD J. CRITCHFIELD
Western Washington State College

CHRISTIAN I (1426–1481), king of Denmark, Norway, and Sweden. As a youth, he spent some time at the court of Emperor Frederick III of the Holy Roman Empire. When Christopher of Bavaria (Christopher III) died in 1448, Christian was elected king. The house of Oldenburg, to which he belonged, was to rule Denmark until 1863. On his election, Sweden withdrew from the union with Denmark, and Karl Knutsson (Charles VIII) was elected king of Sweden. Norway acknowledged Christian's kingship in 1450. Christian was later elected to the Swedish throne, in 1457, but his efforts actually to rule ended with his defeat by the Swedes at the Battle of Brunkeberg in 1471. The treaty of Kalmar of 1472 allowed him to retain the throne in title, and his last years were peaceful.

When Christian was elected ruler of Schleswig-Holstein in 1460, the Danish empire reached its greatest extent since the time of King Canute (about 994–1035), encompassing in title, if not in fact, Norway, Sweden, Finland, Schleswig-Holstein, Iceland, and the Shetland, Faeroe, and Orkney islands, together with other possessions.

In domestic affairs the era is noted for the entry of Renaissance culture into Scandinavia, the increasing consolidation of the church's power, and the founding of the University of Copenhagen. Christian died in Copenhagen on May 21, 1481.

RAYMOND E. LINDGREN
California State College at Long Beach

CHRISTIAN II, kris'chən (1481–1559), king of Denmark, Norway, and Sweden. He was born at Nyborg, Denmark, on July 1, 1481. Through the efforts of his father, the Danish king John (Hans), and through his own studies, Christian was well educated and steeped in the humanist tradition. He spent some time in Norway as viceroy before he succeeded to the Danish throne in 1513, when he also became king of Norway and ruler of Schleswig-Holstein.

The first years of his reign were peaceful, but a conflict relating to the death of his Dutch mistress, Dyveke Villemssoon, and his strong support of the peasants and burghers against the nobility led to open controversy with the latter. In 1518 he attacked Sweden to assert his claim to the Swedish throne. Christian besieged Stockholm and, after its capitulation, carried out a "blood-bath" in which 82 persons were put to death. He was crowned king of Sweden in 1520, but a successful revolt in Sweden separated the two countries in 1523, and Gustav Eriksson Vasa (Gustavus I) took the Swedish throne.

War with the Hanseatic League and revolts in Schleswig-Holstein caused Christian to leave Denmark in search of aid, and his uncle Frederick I seized the Danish throne in 1523. After some years of exile and poverty, Christian landed in Norway in 1531, with the aid of the Hanseatic League, hoping to win support and regain the Danish crown. The effort failed miserably, and Christian was turned over to the Danes for imprisonment. After many years in prison at Sønderborg and Kalundborg castles, he died at Kalundborg on Jan. 25, 1559. During his reign, Denmark had imported a rich culture from the Netherlands, new laws had been promulgated, administration improved, and the Renaissance flowered.

RAYMOND E. LINDGREN
California State College at Long Beach

CHRISTIAN III, kris'chən (1503–1559), king of Denmark and Norway. He was born at Gottorp Castle, in Schleswig, on Aug. 12, 1503, the son of King Frederick I. In his early years he was influenced greatly by Johan Rantzau, a noble of Holstein. Christian attended the Diet of Worms in 1521, where he heard Martin Luther. He served as viceroy first in Schleswig-Holstein and later in Norway.

Frederick I died suddenly in 1533, and Christian was elected king the following year. He gathered burghers and Lutheran nobles in an alliance to wrest control from the Catholics at court and to seize Copenhagen, which resisted Christian's rule. It fell in 1536 after a year's siege. In addition, he fought the Hanseatic towns. The civil war and the invasion of Denmark by forces from Lübeck cost the kingdom heavily, and only the strong support of Johan and Melchior Rantzau permitted Christian to fight off his enemies.

From 1536, Denmark became Lutheran by the King's decrees, and the crown expropriated church properties. In addition, state administration was thoroughly reformed under the guidance of Johan Rantzau and Johan Friis; both burghers and nobles were now offered opportunities for advancement in the civil administration. An exemplary monarch, Christian supported schools, churches, hospitals, and other institutions. He died at the Castle of Koldinghus on Jan. 1, 1559.

RAYMOND E. LINDGREN
California State College at Long Beach

CHRISTIAN IV, kris'chən (1577–1648), king of Denmark and Norway. His reign was a period of greatness for his kingdom, and intellectual and cultural life blossomed. Christian was born at Frederiksborg Castle, in Denmark, on April 12, 1577. His father, King Frederick II, died in 1588, and during Christian's minority his mother controlled the regency. In 1596 he assumed crown.

Foreign Policy. Christian struck out for empire with a bold foreign policy and the expansion of commercial enterprises. But in doing so he plunged Denmark heavily into debt. The Kalmar War with Sweden in 1611–1613 cost the Danish crown both money and influence, even though it ended without loss of territory. In 1625, Christian intervened in the Thirty Years' War, hoping to become the leader of the Protestant forces and to establish Danish supremacy. However, he failed disastrously against the imperial armies, and he relinquished his hopes for Protestant leadership by the Treaty of Lübeck in 1629.

Christian was forced to stand by while Gustavus Adolphus (Gustavus II) of Sweden assumed a position of leadership in European affairs and thus threatened Danish security. In 1643–1645, Christian fought stubbornly and bravely against the Swedes (Torstensson's War). Denmark lost heavily in this conflict, for the provinces of Herjedalen, Jämtland, Gotland, and Halland went to Sweden. For a fixed period Sweden was also granted freedom from the tariffs imposed by Denmark on ships using the Øresund.

Domestic Policy. Christian sought to encourage commercial growth and financial stability, while at the same time he spent large sums on war and buildings. Administrative reforms improved the Danish government for a time, and the codification of laws aided the farmers and burghers in their conflict with the nobility. The Danish East and West Indies companies were founded, and many new public buildings were constructed, including Rosenborg Palace and the Round Tower in Copenhagen and a new Frederiksborg Castle.

In the first years of Christian's reign, much was accomplished. After 1629, however, the King repeatedly found himself at odds with the council and nobility as Denmark's ability to sustain the heavy debt and public expenditures diminished. Yet he has remained popular with Danes, and his life is the subject of legends and anecdotes. He died at Copenhagen on Feb. 28, 1648.

RAYMOND E. LINDGREN
California State College at Long Beach

CHRISTIAN V, kris'chən (1646–1699), king of Denmark and Norway. He was born at Flensburg, in Schleswig, on April 15, 1646, the son of King Frederick III. After private tutoring, Christian traveled abroad. He became king in 1670. Of limited intelligence, Christian was guided by his ministers in most matters. He enjoyed sports and the company of his mistress, Sophia Amalie Moth.

Denmark fought against Sweden and France in 1675–1679 and won mastery of the seas but gained little else except debts and financial problems. During Christian's reign, government leaders developed a sound administration, reformed the law, encouraged cultural development, and tried to maintain fiscal stability. Christian died at Copenhagen on Aug. 25, 1699.

RAYMOND E. LINDGREN
California State College at Long Beach

CHRISTIAN VI, kris'chən (1699–1746), king of Denmark and Norway. He was born at Copenhagen on Nov. 30, 1699, the son of Frederick IV. Influenced by the Pietistic teachers J. G. Holstein and J. W. Schroeder, he developed a sense of responsibility and dedication.

Crowned in 1730, Christian depended heavily on his wife and advisers for aid in ruling. His reign was peaceful, but Denmark suffered economically while the king built such costly royal symbols as Christiansborg Palace and the hunting lodge of Eremitagen. The major institutional change of his reign was the adoption in 1733 of a type of serfdom, *Stavnbåndet*. This system protected the large property owners by preventing the small farmers and agricultural workers from leaving their places. Christian died at Horsholm on Aug. 6, 1746.

RAYMOND E. LINDGREN
California State College at Long Beach

CHRISTIAN VII, kris'chən (1749–1808), king of Denmark and Norway. He was born at Copenhagen on Jan. 29, 1749, the son of Frederick V, whom he succeeded on the throne in 1766. Christian had a mental collapse in 1770, and his physician, Johann Friedrich von Struensee, gained control of the government. Struensee ruled until 1772, when a conspiracy by the Queen Mother and jealous ministers, and Struensee's scandalous liaison with Caroline Matilda, the Queen, led to his fall. After that date the Queen Mother, the Crown Prince, and the ministers controlled Danish affairs. Christian spent his last years in isolation and died at Rendsburg, in Holstein, on March 13, 1808.

RAYMOND E. LINDGREN
California State College at Long Beach

CHRISTIAN VIII, kris'chən (1786–1848), king of Denmark, is associated with Denmark's loss of Norway and with the final years of absolutism in Denmark. He was born at Copenhagen on Sept. 18, 1786, the son of Prince Frederick, stepbrother of Christian VII. He received an excellent education and possessed considerable intelligence but proved to be an incapable administrator.

As viceroy in Norway in 1813–1814 Christian faced a Swedish attack, and he defended Norwegian independence as Norway's elected king in 1814. When he relinquished the Norwegian throne in the same year, a treaty was negotiated that started the union of Norway and Sweden. After his return from Norway, he spent years in despondent isolation as governor of the island of Fyn, since his cousin, King Frederick VI, distrusted his liberalism, which he had evidenced in his rule of Norway.

After succeeding Frederick VI as king of Denmark in 1839, Christian espoused conservative rather than liberal ideas and refused to yield to demands for a constitution. The liberal ferment of the times found some outlet in local government reform, improvement of education, the Grundtvigian theological movement, and Scandinavianism. But Christian insisted on leaving the crown as he inherited it. After his death at Copenhagen on Jan. 20, 1848, the surge of liberal revolt ended absolutism in Denmark.

RAYMOND E. LINDGREN
California State College at Long Beach

CHRISTIAN IX, kris'chən (1818–1906), king of Denmark. He was born at Gottorp on April 8, 1818, the son of Duke William of Schleswig-Holstein-Sønderborg-Glücksburg. When Christian succeeded Frederick VII in 1863, he was confronted by the German-Danish conflict of interest in the duchies of Schleswig-Holstein. The duchies revolted against a constitution, sanctioned by Christian, that integrated them with Denmark. Austria and Prussia intervened, and a short war followed in 1863–1864. The war ended with Denmark relinquishing its rights to the duchies.

Bitterness generated by this inauspicious start of Christian's reign was at first directed toward the King. However, by the end of his reign he had become quite popular as a constitutional monarch. He approved the revised constitution of 1866, which provided for limited parliamentary rule, later expanded under pressures from new political parties. During his reign Denmark experienced an agricultural revolution, industrialization and urbanization, the rise of socialism and labor unions, and the development of strong political parties. Amid this turmoil Christian lived a quiet life, while his sons and daughters occupied thrones in Russia, Greece, England, Norway, and Sweden. He died at Copenhagen on Jan. 29, 1906.

RAYMOND E. LINDGREN
California State College at Long Beach

CHRISTIAN X, kris'chən (1870–1947), king of Denmark and Iceland. He was born at Charlottenlund Castle, near Copenhagen, on Sept. 26, 1870, the son of the Crown Prince, later King Frederick VIII.

Christian succeeded to the throne in 1912 and faced difficult problems during World War I in trying to preserve Denmark's neutrality. In 1918 he became king of Iceland, when it was established as an independent kingdom united with Denmark. In 1920 his intervention in the "Easter crisis" caused popular demonstration against the crown. The monarchy regained popular support when a new cabinet was formed. In the 1920's and 1930's the King did not play a strong role in government, although he shared in many cabinet decisions.

With the German invasion of Denmark in 1940, Christian X became a symbol of Danish resistance, especially after he was virtually made a German prisoner in 1943. With the liberation of Denmark in 1945, he emerged a hero. Although his reign encompassed two great wars, a depression, the advent of socialist government, and the end of the Danish-Icelandic union in 1944, the bond between the monarchy and the country remained strong. He died at Copenhagen on April 20, 1947.

RAYMOND E. LINDGREN
California State College at Long Beach

CHRISTIAN AND MISSIONARY ALLIANCE, a Protestant group whose major objective is foreign missionary work. The alliance was formally organized in 1887 in New York City by a Presbyterian minister, A. B. Simpson, to increase the pace of Christian evangelization. In the late 1960's it had about 125,000 members and adherents in the United States and Canada and about 900 missionaries and 3,000 national ministers in 24 other countries.

GERALD SMITH
Christian and Missionary Alliance

CHRISTIAN CHURCHES (DISCIPLES OF CHRIST). See DISCIPLES OF CHRIST.

CHRISTIAN ENDEAVOR, International Society of, an international movement with societies for all age groups in Protestant churches. It serves as a training school for the church, and it aims to promote an earnest Christian life among its members and to make them more useful in the service of God.

The first Christian Endeavor Society was organized on Feb. 2, 1881, by the Rev. Francis Edward Clark (q.v.) to serve the needs of his Congregational church in Portland, Me. In 1885 the United Society of Christian Endeavor was founded under Clark's leadership. The name was officially changed in 1927. By the 1960's there were thousands of local societies, representing 80 denominations in 50 countries. These societies provide courses in religious leadership and work in many areas of human welfare. The headquarters of the International Society and the World's Christian Endeavor Union, with which it is affiliated, are in Columbus, Ohio. In the early 1960's there were about 1 million U.S. members and a world total of 4 million.

CHRISTIAN KNOWLEDGE, Society for Promoting, one of the oldest religious associations connected with the Church of England. It was founded in England in 1698 by four laymen under the direction of the Reverend Thomas Bray. Its objectives were to promote the establishment of charity schools in all parts of Britain; to disperse Bibles and religious tracts both at home and abroad, and to advance the honor of God and the good of mankind by promoting Christian knowledge. Under the society's auspices many church schools and teachers' training colleges have been built. SPCK maintains an important publishing house which provides translations of the Bible and the Book of Common Prayer as well as grammars, dictionaries, and general literature for the missionary field.

CHRISTIAN REFORMED CHURCH, a church established in western Michigan by immigrants from the Netherlands. A wave of immigration beginning in 1846 was composed largely of families that had participated in a secession from the state church of the Netherlands in 1834. The immigrants joined the Reformed Church in America in 1850. Because of dissatisfaction with what were considered doctrinal errors and loose practices in the Reformed Church, some of the immigrants formed the new denomination in 1857.

The principal source of growth, other than family growth, has been immigration. This growth was especially large during the last two decades of the 19th century. After World War II some immigration resumed, particularly to Canada, where about one fourth of the membership now resides. The Dutch language was used exclusively at first in the worship services. The change to English was gradual, with the turning point coming shortly after World War I. Total membership in the late 1960's was about 275,000.

The Christian Reformed Church maintains Calvin College and Seminary in Grand Rapids, Mich. Foreign mission work is maintained in Nigeria, Japan, Mexico, Argentina, and elsewhere. Beginnings have been made in inner-city work in various locations.

J. H. KROMMINGA
The Christian Reformed Church

Further Reading: Kromminga, J. H., *In the Mirror* (Hamilton, Ontario, 1957).

CHRISTIAN SCIENCE headquarters, in Boston, Mass., are in the Mother Church. The original church structure at the right was dedicated in 1895. The larger, domed extension was added later and was dedicated in 1906.

CHRISTIAN SCIENTISTS are members of the Church of Christ, Scientist, a Protestant denomination that first received a state charter in Massachusetts in 1879. Unlike many of its 19th century religious neighbors, the Church of Christ, Scientist, did not evolve gradually from a complex English and European lineage. It took its basic organizational form in a period of less than 30 years and was shaped largely through the efforts of a single religious pioneer, a New England woman named Mary Baker Eddy. The church is an heir of the broad Christian tradition, but broke with the orthodox creeds of its time. Unique elements of theology still set Christian Science apart from traditional Protestantism.

Mary Baker Eddy, the Founder. Mary Baker Eddy was raised in the severe Calvinist tradition only slightly modified in the New England Congregationalism of the early 1800's. She became a religious rebel at an early age, specifically protesting the doctrine of foreordination, which inexorably destined some to be saved by the Deity and others to be hopelessly lost in endless torment.

After harsh early years of sickness, the death of her first husband after only six months of marriage, separation from her only child, and the untimely death of an especially well-loved elder brother, her early independence of thought and character emerged decisively.

She had searched stubbornly but without success for practical means to relieve her own growing invalidism. She had looked into homeopathy, the so-called water cure, and had investigated the methods of a man named Phineas P. Quimby who cured by a mixture of mental suggestion and rudimentary psychology.

In 1866, when she was in her 45th year, she had an experience which she considered similar in importance to the "falling apple" episode that reputedly led Sir Isaac Newton to a major discovery. She received a remarkable physical healing through the spiritual inspiration that came to her in reading the account in the Gospel of Matthew of Jesus' healing of the paralyzed man (Matthew 9:1–8). Mary Baker Eddy later wrote of the occasion that she had gained an illumined sense of "Life in and of Spirit; this Life being the sole reality of existence" (*Miscellaneous Writings*, p. 24). With a greatly expanded consciousness of the reality and supreme goodness of God had come physical healing.

For three years afterward she studied the Bible more intensely and tested her growing sense of spiritual discovery against the hardest facts of everyday living. She found that she could heal others and teach them to heal in turn. As early as 1870 she explained her views in small classes of instruction. In 1875, nine years after her initial experience of spiritual healing, she shared her views in a book on the subject, later to become the denominational textbook of Christian Science, called *Science and Health with Key to the Scriptures*. Throughout her long life (she lived until 1910) she continued to revise the book, pouring into it her experience and elaborating the theology of Christian Science. See also EDDY, MARY BAKER.

Establishment and Growth of the Church. Those who became interested in Christian Science were at first mostly members of evangelical churches. Frequently they attended services at their own churches as well as meetings and classes of the Christian Science movement. In 1879, however, a distinct church organization was formed with the vote to "organize a church designed to commemorate the word and works of our Master, which should reinstate primitive Christianity and its lost element of healing" (*Church Manual*, p. 17).

By 1892 the church had assumed its present-day structure. Expanding swiftly outward from its Boston birthplace, the denomination quickly gained local or branch churches in Great Britain, Europe, and Canada. Approximately one third of the 3,300 Christian Science churches are located outside the United States.

Theology and Practice. The healing practice of Christian Science is better known than the theology from which it springs, but the theology must be considered as giving unique force and direction to the denomination and the lives of its members. Through the emphasis upon study and spiritual instruction basic to the movement from its beginnings, Christian Scientists are usually well informed about the theology and metaphysics of their religion. Although Christian Scientists do not usually employ medical services, except in connection with childbirth, they do not consider their religion simply a substitute method of healing or faith cure. A total spiritual discipline, rather than an isolated will to believe, is emphasized. Daily prayer, continuing communion with God, study, and spiritual regeneration are notable aspects of this way of life.

Church services are very simple in form, without ritual or symbolism. Hymns, the Lord's Prayer, Scriptural selections, and congregational responsive reading are included. The place of a traditional pastor's sermon is taken by the Lesson-Sermon, a reading of correlated selections from the Bible and *Science and Health*. This service is the same in Christian Science churches throughout the world. Midweek evening meetings similar in form provide for spontaneous sharing of personal witness and testimonies of healing by the congregation in the latter half of the service.

No visible sacraments are performed in the church, though the spiritual significance of baptism and communion remain vital in the theology of Christian Science.

Christian Scientists believe that in the life of Jesus Christ men find the way of fulfillment. Much more than a good man, Jesus is the incarnation of the Christ. Through his pure obedience, or perfect oneness with God, he gave to men a transforming and healing view into the deepest reality of being.

Christian Scientists do not accept the world at face value. Evil, pain, disease, and matter itself are considered less substance and fact than the solid, habitual impressions of the sinful, carnal mind of which St. Paul spoke. To break free of these limited views through prayer and profound Christian regeneration—and Christian Scientists acknowledge the depth and severity of this challenge—is to begin to experience the spiritual reality that is also ultimate scientific fact.

This process of spiritual awakening brings healing in the whole range of human experience and is an integral part of Christian life. Thus men learn of their potential, their actual nature, source, and destiny. "God is the Principle of man, and man is the idea of God," states the denominational textbook of Christian Science. "Hence man is not mortal or material.... When speaking of God's children, not the children of men, Jesus said, 'The kingdom of God is within you'" (*Science and Health*, p. 476).

Organization and Operations. The Church of Christ, Scientist, is organized along simple lines, without ecclesiastical hierarchy. There are no ordained clergy, and all members of the church have equal status. The denomination as a whole is governed by principles stated in the *Church Manual* and administered by a five-member Board of Directors. All local church offices are filled by election from the local congregation. Executive boards handle branch church affairs, and services are conducted by two Readers, usually a man and woman, who have been elected to the position.

The denomination provides Protestant chaplains for the armed services of the United States, and branch churches send field workers to prisons and mental institutions. Christian Science nurses receive a three-year training course in nonmedical nursing, and the church maintains two large sanatoriums and a home for those of advanced years.

The church does not have social agencies nor does it advance policy and position statements for its membership. But rather than taking a traditional pietist position, it stresses living "in the world" as committed and concerned lay Christians in business, in politics, the arts, or sciences. Some 7,000 Christian Scientists listed in the church directory as practitioners are engaged in a public ministry of spiritual healing.

The *Christian Science Monitor* is an international daily newspaper read regularly by Christian Scientists and by many nonmembers who respect its high journalistic standards. It is not an "official" church voice.

DAVID E. SLEEPER
The First Church of Christ, Scientist

Further Reading: DeWitt, John, and Canham, Erwin D., *The Christian Science Way of Life* bound with *A Christian Scientist's Life* (Englewood, N. J., 1962); Peel, Robert, *Christian Science: Its Encounter with American Culture* (New York 1958).

CHRISTIANITY

CONTENTS

CHRISTIANITY, kris-chē-an'ə-tē, is the religion instituted in Palestine in the person and work of Jesus Christ and the fellowships of his immediate followers. Subsequently this faith was widely adopted in many nations, and it is now professed by about two sevenths of the world's population. Present-day Christianity exhibits three main divisions, Roman Catholic, Protestant, and Eastern Orthodox. These are convenient names rather than full official titles, and some Christian groups do not fall within any of the three. Despite long separation and much variety, all three main divisions share certain identifying characteristics of typical Christianity. These include adoration of Jesus Christ as the second person in the Trinity of God the Father, the Son, and the Holy Spirit; the use of sacred rites, of which the most important are designated sacraments; reverence for the Old and New Testaments as authoritative Holy Scripture; the requirement of a morally disciplined life; and the maintenance of a structure of church government and a body of trained clergy.

The expansion of Christianity as a professed religion has been a marked though somewhat discontinuous feature of Western history. As a result of modern, especially 19th century, missionary effort, it became the adopted religion of an increasing minority in Asia and Africa and in other areas where it had been virtually unknown. It has been repressed but not extinguished in the Communist nations; elsewhere it continues to have a somewhat reduced rate of growth. Statistics of membership are far from exact, but of the three main divisions Roman Catholics easily outnumber the other two combined, and Protestants exceed Eastern Orthodox in a ratio of rather more than three to two. An injurious divisiveness has weakened the force of Christianity, but this is now yielding to a unitive trend of extraordinary force and promise.

1. Doctrine and Practices

This summary of Christian doctrine and practice describes things that are common to most Christians but also notes differences between the major divisions. More detailed statements on doctrine and activities can be found in articles on specific churches.

BELIEFS

The apostolic preaching in which early Christianity was nurtured gave origin to an orderly

FRANK HURLEY, FROM RAPHO GUILLUMETTE

BASILICA OF THE NATIVITY in Bethlehem, overlooking the hills of Judea, marks Christ's birthplace.

and comprehensive body of teaching and belief, which, with varying degrees of emphasis, has been familiar to instructed Christians in all centuries. An index to this is best seen in the Apostles' Creed, which from beginnings in slightly divergent 2d century forms of baptismal confession (the Rule of Faith) reached its final wording in southern Gaul about 500 A.D. Most later statements of doctrine, having general authority or more limited acceptance, may be thought of as expansions of this formula, and until recent times the theological work of countless Christian scholars has been shaped by its clauses. The theologians have utilized the works of interpreters of doctrine before them, and ultimately have turned for authority to the Christian Bible. In addition to the Jewish canon of sacred books, the Bible contains the 27 books of Christian origin that constitute the New Testament. The special emphases in belief that have marked certain eras of reform and revision have been, as a rule, consciously based on a fresh reading of the Bible. The Bible was habitually read, however, in the light of the "analogy of faith," a general sense of its teaching that accorded with the Apostles' Creed. See also APOSTLES' CREED; BIBLE.

The Christian body of belief has been characteristically stable without becoming stagnant. This distinction is not always perceived in the crises of change, but it becomes apparent on reflection over protracted periods of development. The principle derived from Leviticus 6 by Origen in the 3d century, that teachers of the Word of God are "not to set forth stale doctrines according to the letter, but by God's grace ever to bring forth new truth," has controlled the main course of doctrinal history, often when it was not consciously espoused. The enduring elements of belief take fresh color in every age from current philosophical thought and human conditions. In certain instances this involves painful adjustment to new knowledge. The simple apostolic message had to undergo a confrontation with Hellenic thought patterns. Medieval theology met the shock of the impact of Aristotelianism. The new cosmology of Copernicus and his even more alarming successors in astronomical science was but slowly assimilated to Christian thinking, and the dismay that arose in some circles because of 19th century evolutionary biology and Biblical criticism still finds echoes. In each instance some have been alienated from Christian belief. As decades pass, however, the majority have accepted the new light of attested scientific scholarship with a grateful sense of the emancipation and enlargement of cherished doctrines rather than of their invalidation.

Beliefs About God. Cradled as it was in Judaism, Christianity from the first showed a deep consciousness of the reality of God. Christian teaching about God took from Judaism its notions of divine creation and providence, but it was also marked by increased emphasis on the fatherhood of God, a theme vividly presented in the recorded teachings and prayers of Jesus. At the foundation of the Christian structure of belief is the affirmation of God in terms of creation and of fatherly concern for man. Man is clearly conceived as in all nations one, and (apart from imprecise ideas about the angels) man is the crowning work of God's creation. The doctrine of God, now a special area of debate, has in past centuries often been the occasion of disputes. With changed concepts of the universe and of man's participation in the natural order, the point of contact between God and his handiwork becomes more difficult to establish, or even to conceive. The futility of learned search in this sector of theology is expressed in the phrase "God is dead"; but even those who find truth in this language continue their search for a living God. See AGNOSTICISM; ATHEISM.

Christians have always, not without awe and wonder, believed, on the testimony of Scripture and the evidence of man's perversity, that the winning power of God's love does not extend equally to all individual men. Yet they have been moved to carry to all the invitation to come within the circle of its benefits and to join the fellowship of those who know God's fatherhood. Christian belief in "God the Father Almighty, maker of heaven and earth" so rests upon experience beyond the range of syllogisms that for most Christians it is likely to be little affected by contrary rational arguments.

Belief in Christ. Belief in Christ has always been the essential point of difference between Christianity and the other great religions. Typically a high concept of Christ pervaded the Christian mind, signalized by such terms as "Son of God" and "Our Lord and Saviour." The New Testament accounts of his birth of a virgin (Matthew and Luke) and identification of him with the Logos, or creative and light-giving Word of God (John), together with the reports of his teaching, death, resurrection, ascension, and destined return to earth, entered into the early teaching and are crisply affirmed in the received creeds. The language of the Nicene-Constantinopolitan Creed of 381, "Who for us men and for our salvation came down ... and was made man" represents a cherished element of faith. The supernatural factors in the accepted teaching about Christ were not without difficulty from the beginning. But there was no less difficulty in excluding them. The church's authoritative doctrine of Christ as divine and human came to rest in the Chalcedonian formula of 451. For many Christians Christ's "two natures in one person" has been an undisputed commonplace, to others an unresolved mystery and object of meditation. There are always a great many Christians who neglect theological definitions in their approach to the person of Christ and are content with the way of piety and devotion. A profound reverential love of Jesus, expressed in a variety of devotional writings, has been and remains a notable aspect of the Christian religion. See also CHRISTOLOGY.

Belief in the Holy Spirit. Belief in the Holy Spirit has always been affirmed and has been most intense in times of group emotion. The place of the Spirit in the Trinity has been defined in somewhat different terms. The council

648

of 381, to counter the *Pneumatomachi* (antagonists of the Spirit) led by Macedonius, deposed bishop of Constantinople, who regarded the Holy Spirit as a creature like the angels, declared that the Spirit "proceeds from the Father." In the West, following St. Augustine's view, the word *"filioque"* (and the Son) was inserted after "from the Father" in liturgical texts. The change was deeply offensive to the Eastern church. It was, however, retained in the Reformation, so that Protestantism agrees with Roman Catholicism rather than with Orthodoxy at this point. In the 20th century the question of how the Holy Spirit proceeds from the Father and the Son has come under review by Roman Catholic and Orthodox theologians.

Beliefs About the Church. Some form of belief about the church is common to all varieties of Christianity, although there has been in general a weakness of theological definition in this area. Jesus had much to say of the Kingdom of God, which in his teaching was both a society of the faithful into which men were being recruited and an expected life to come. Little that is specific is discernible in his teaching about the church, a name that largely replaced "Kingdom" in the Christian vocabulary. His word to Peter "Thou art Peter, and upon this rock I will build my church" (a passage variously explained by the Church Fathers), has been interpreted, along with the early tradition of Peter's ministry in Rome, as authorizing the papal rule of the church. Controversy over this and other matters of clerical ranks and authority has diverted attention from efforts to describe the church in its essential nature. The Protestant Reformers taught that in the Apostles' Creed "holy Catholic Church" and "Communion of Saints" refer to the same entity. The evidence seems conclusive that, whatever of church authority was felt among early Christians, the church arose out of their spontaneous brotherly communion in Jerusalem. The visitation of the Holy Spirit on Pentecost served as confirmation and enhancement of the apostolic message most effectively spoken at the time by Peter.

A new interest attaches to the doctrine of the church as a result of ecumenical discussion, and Vatican Council II advanced far toward defining it for Roman Catholics in language that does not exclude other Christians. Many issues concerning the orders of ministers in the church have hitherto been treated too much in connection with denominational claims. For example, some churches hold to the authority of bishops as successors of the Apostles, while others reject this succession. These issues are coming under more unbiased and historically informed discussion, and this offers promise of a clarification of the nature and functions of the ministry, which should promote its future development in response to need.

Ethics. A Jewish inheritance, including a reverential acceptance of the Ten Commandments, has strongly influenced Christian ethics; but what distinguishes it from any other body of ethical teaching is its appropriation of the teachings of Jesus and its continuity with the early fellowship of believers as interpreted by St. Paul. The motivation of ethical behavior lies not in meeting detailed prescriptions of conduct but in realizing a manner of life morally worthy of holy fellowship in Christ.

In actuality the behavior of Christians has

CHAP. IX.

1 Saul going towards Damascus, 4 is striken downe to the earth, 10 is called to the Apostleship, 18 and is baptized by Ananias. 20 He preacheth Christ boldly. 23 The Iewes lay wait to kil him: 29 So doe the Grecians, but hee escapeth both. 31 The Church hauing rest, Peter healeth Æneas of the palsie, 36 and restoreth Tabitha to life.

AND Saul yet breathing out threatnings & slaughter against the disciples of the Lord, went vnto the high Priest,

2 And desired of him letters to Damascus, to the Synagogues, that if hee found any of this way, whether they were men or women, hee might bring them bound vnto Hierusalem.

3 And as he iourneyed he came neere Damascus, and suddenly there shined round about him a light from heauen.

4 And he fel to the earth, and heard a voice saying vnto him, Saul, Saul, why persecutest thou me?

5 And he said, who art thou Lord? And the Lord said, I am Iesus whom thou persecutest: It is hard for thee to kicke against the prickes.

KING JAMES BIBLE account of St. Paul's conversion, in Acts, Chapter 9, verses 1–5, in the 1611 edition.

unquestionably been affected by other considerations. These include the Scriptural teaching on the fall of man and human sinfulness, concern about future punishment and reward, treatises and sermons on the sins and the virtues, systems of discipline and penance, the teaching of moral philosophers and casuists, and contemporary social standards. But more characteristic are the elements clearly derived from Jesus and St. Paul. Jesus differentiated his teaching from that of his predecessors by affirming that the religious man's love extends even to enemies and that one is to forgive an offending brother not seven times but unceasingly (Matthew 5:43–44; 18:21). In the letters of St. Paul life is transformed for Christians by the fact that they are "members one of another." Since they "walk in love," immorality and covetousness are not even to be mentioned among them. They are to be "subject to one another out of reverence for Christ." In various epistles Christians are enjoined to be active in good deeds, to be gentle toward all, to follow peace, and to "walk honestly towards outsiders." Paul's lofty paean on. *agapē* (I Corinthians 13), the divinely inspired love that unites the Christian community, is unique in literature. The Christian's basic understanding of social ethics arises as an extension of this bond of unity and obligation within the communion of believers.

WORSHIP AND SACRAMENTS

The disciples of Jesus, meeting with his mother and brothers after his departure, "with one accord devoted themselves to prayer" (Acts 1:12–14). The first Christians on occasion met "for the breaking of bread," that is, to celebrate the Eucharist. Admission to membership in the fellowship was by baptism. Common worship, and the specially significant rites historically known as sacraments, are thus attested from the earliest period. Although a hostile environment forced the choice of unfrequented places and inconvenient hours for Christian worship, routines of worship were established. Long before the liberation of the church under Constantine, we find habitual use of certain liturgical elements that have persisted. In the Middle Ages, especially at the greater ecclesiastical centers, the services were marked by multiple variations for seasons and occasions, and by colorful and dramatic pageantry. Anxious criticism of the trend toward elaboration was voiced by some at the time. The Reformation, appealing to Scripture and the early church, brought about in many areas of the West a great simplification of worship. See also WORSHIP.

Routines of Worship. Sunday morning, associated in Christian memory with the Resurrection of Christ, has always been the favored time of worship. This has been made convenient by the recognition under most governments of Sunday as the weekly day of rest. Although the conditions of modern life tend to annul this provision, Sunday still remains the great day of Christian assembly the world over. There is, of course, no attempt to confine common worship to Sundays. Frequent occasions for it are provided on other days. Monasticism developed a detailed system of conventual worship, with seven times ("hours") of prayer and psalmody daily. The Breviary ("abbreviation"), containing these services, was first called by that name when it was revised about 1080 under Pope Gregory VII. Through later revisions it has retained its characteristic use of the Scriptural Psalms, and the singing or reading of Psalms,

which has been a leading feature of Reformed and Anglican worship.

The routines of worship are not only weekly, but also involve the annual round of solemn occasions collectively known as the Christian Year. The great feast of Easter has been celebrated in remembrance of Christ's Resurrection from the earliest times. Lent, the period of 40 days (not counting Sundays) before Easter, came to be kept as a season of special penitential abstinence, ending with Holy Week, when the passion of Christ is vividly recalled in special acts of worship. Easter Day has traditionally brought a great release of gladness, with pealing bells and chanting choirs. The Christian Year begins, however, with the Advent season, which includes the four Sundays preceding Christmas Day. The date, December 25, was that formerly celebrated as the birthday of Mithra, the sungod, and the feature of friendly gifts reflects other pagan festivities of the winter solstice. A body of later medieval Christmas carols, now familiar in modern form, testifies to the devout happiness that has attended the celebration of Jesus' birth. See also CALENDAR—7. *Church Calendar.*

Popular elements in worship have taken many directions, including the veneration of innumerable martyrs and saints on the traditional days of their deaths. These days being more numerous than the days of the year, All Saints' Day was introduced and since the 8th century has been celebrated on November 1 in the West. Relics of saints have been treasured, often for miraculous powers. The cult of the Virgin Mary has been largely promoted by popular devotion. The worship practices of many sects and revival movements feature popular spiritual stimulation, which at its best has flowered in Negro spirituals.

Forms of Worship. Christian worship, despite its modern variety, generally retains certain of its earliest features. It reflects the influence of the synagogue in the public reading of Holy Scripture, normally with comment or exposition. In 2d century worship the Gospels and Epistles were treated as authoritative Scripture. The Eu-

All Saints day.

even the Spirit of truth, which proceedeth from the Father, he shall testifie of me. And yee also shall bear witnesse, because ye have been with me from the beginning.

All Saints day.

The Collect.

Almighty God, which hast knit together thy elect in one Communion and fellowship in the mysticall body of thy Sonne Jesus Christ our Lord : grant us grace so to follow thy holy Saints in all vertuous and godly living, that wee may come to those unspeakeable joyes, which thou hast prepared for them that unfainedly love thee, through Jesus Christ our Lord. Amen.

THE COLLECT for All Saints' Day from a 1637 edition of the Book of Common Prayer. Collects are prayers appointed for use through the church year.

charist was preceded by the Kiss of Peace and the collection for the poor. The prayer of consecration began with thanksgiving (*eucharistia*) for redemption, brought to remembrance Christ's passion, and invoked a blessing on the bread and wine. Very early such enduring liturgical elements as the *Sursum corda* (Lift up your hearts) the *Sanctus,* and the Lord's Prayer found a stated place in the service. Elaborate and nobly phrased liturgies followed by the 4th century, notably at Rome, Alexandria, and Antioch, the clergy using a written text. But stability and uniformity were not attained. In the West the Gallican Rite, a prolix liturgy with local variations, gave place about 600 A. D. to the Roman, by comparison simple and concise. In time, however, increasing variety of forms and ceremonies for different occasions, and the use of Latin when it was not understood by most worshipers, tended to make public worship an impressive spectacle enacted by the clergy rather than, as earlier, a reliving in faith of the New Testament events. In the 11th century the wine of the sacrament was, probably to avoid profanation, withdrawn from the laity, and from 1215 laymen were required to communicate only at the Easter communion. The sacraments recognized in the Middle Ages and in modern Roman Catholicism and Orthodoxy are: baptism, confirmation, the Eucharist, penance, extreme unction (anointing of the sick), ordination, and marriage. See also CATHOLIC CHURCH, ROMAN —1. *Doctrine* and 3. *Liturgy.*

Protestantism, seeking to base worship on Scripture and early church practice, has from its beginnings used in its liturgies the language of the people. It tends to view negatively all ceremonial accretions, and reduces the sacraments to baptism and the Lord's Supper. (See also COMMUNION SACRAMENTS.) Luther's *Formula missae* (1523) laid a foundation for Lutheran worship, stressing the Words of Institution (Matthew 26:26–28) and authorizing lay Communion in both kinds. Zwingli in 1525 and Luther in his German Mass (1526) introduced vernacular worship. The Strasbourg liturgy of Martin Bucer, based on a Protestant adaptation of the Roman rite, was revised by Calvin in his Form of Prayers . . . according to the Use of the Ancient Church (1540), from which stem many liturgies of Reformed churches. The Anglican Book of Common Prayer—despite learned criticism, one of the best-loved books of worship and not fundamentally changed since it left Cranmer's hands in 1552—makes selective use of medieval materials and authorizes traditional vestments, which the Puritans rejected. Disputes about public worship have dealt with vestments, postures, gestures, and other externals more than with the words used. In the 20th century, particularly in the 1960's, both Protestants and Catholics have shown a willingness to reconsider long-sanctioned practices.

PROPAGATION OF THE CHRISTIAN FAITH

Prompted by explicit New Testament injunctions, Christianity has taken as its field of mission the whole human race. A desire to bear testimony to his faith and way of life is an expected characteristic of each Christian. The expansion of Christianity has been accomplished not less by incidental private contacts, talk, and example than by organized and directed missions. Believers put to flight by persecution have often

been agents of conversion among those who gave them refuge, and the testimony of martyrs has been a potent persuasive. Political decisions favorable to Christianity have brought about innumerable nominal conversions and have often afforded opportunity for a genuine work of evangelism. On the other hand, adverse political policies have in extreme instances prevented the permanent growth of a Christian community.

Where church and state have been closely associated, the Christian witness to universality has sometimes failed to such a degree that the state's enemies were regarded as candidates not for conversion but for death by the sword. The church, having without any violence won its way to recognition in the ancient world, was more concerned eight centuries later to kill the Muslims than to win them. It was at the close of the Crusades that the learned Franciscan missionary Raymond Lully (died 1315) pleaded for educational missions employing the languages of the Muslim peoples. "Victory," he declared, "can be won only as Christ sought it, by love and prayer and self-sacrifice." The use of coercion in the promotion of Christianity is wholly rejected by modern Christians, though in some countries discrimination is still practiced in favor of a state-supported church. Under Communist governments Christian means of propagation are narrowly restricted. International Christian missions have become an important phase of modern Christianity.

Preaching. In early times preaching, or proclamation, was the characteristic means of spreading Christianity. This method was in the tradition of Jewish prophecy and had long been used by traveling Greek sophists. Preaching became an essential part of worship, and has indeed been largely confined to church pulpits and formal services. Outdoor informal preaching, however, has been a feature of medieval and modern revival movements. The radio and television preaching of today is also usually detached from liturgical worship, and is frequently addressed to non-Christians. A number of the Church Fathers excelled as eloquent preachers able to convince pagan hearers. The 17th century saw an impressive development of pulpit oratory, and this has remained a tradition, especially in France and Scotland. But preaching in its traditional form has now lost some of its importance for the propagation of Christianity. It is in part replaced by dialogue in various forms.

Education. Under the aegis of Christianity, learning has flourished, except when impaired by untoward social conditions. While inviting the uneducated into its membership, the Christian church has normally expected of them a preparation by study of the elements of Christian belief. For this purpose the early church devised "catechetical schools," which in some instances reached a remarkable academic maturity. It has habitually taken the initiative in the establishment of schools, not only of theology but also of elementary and advanced learning in other fields. Its doctrinal positions have often been challenged by its own trained scholars, and in former times ecclesiastical authorities adopted strong measures to discourage theological deviation. But there was never a serious inclination to repudiate learning itself. Christian schools have everywhere accompanied Christian missions, and in some countries have greatly expanded the range of education among all classes of the population, making it available to youth of social ranks formerly excluded from educational privileges. Christians have differed, however, in their attitude to literary and scientific studies. Some Christian educators, such as John Amos Comenius, had no hesitation in maintaining that all ascertained knowledge can be harmoniously related to Christian doctrines. Others in past centuries have fought the entrance of unfamiliar knowledge as a challenge to Christianity itself. This polarization has existed since the days of the early Church Fathers. Some of them, in "apologetic" writings addressed to pagans, sought their readers' approval of Christianity on the grounds that it was anticipated by Plato and made the most of pagan parallels to Christian teachings, while others denounced all pagan thought. The divergence here is apt to be particularly embarrassing where the Christian message to non-Christians is involved.

After the invention of printing, religious texts were for many decades the major output of the press. In the early period many small medieval treatises and devotional guidebooks, which had already been circulated in manuscript, found a widened circulation in print. The Reformation movement was greatly aided by the enterprise of countless printer-publishers; nor did the Counter-Reformation lack the same service. It was only with the rise of the sciences and of secular fiction that Christianity lost its preeminence in the book trade.

The output of books concerned with Christianity is larger than ever today, though not proportionately so. Bible societies and missionary agencies distribute the Scriptures and theological and devotional literature in quantity throughout the world (see BIBLE SOCIETY). Denominational and nondenominational journalism, learned and popular religious periodicals, and publicity through releases to newspapers have been channels for the spread of Christian propaganda. The modern film and record industries, and broadcasting by radio and television, have already been utilized extensively to promote Christian belief. However, in contrast to early printing, these new inventions have been chiefly employed for other than religious ends. Christian leaders see a crucial task ahead in using the changing means of communication to make a Christian impact upon the world.

Charity. Such scriptural admonitions as "Love thy neighbour" and "Do good unto all men" have borne fruit in a concern for the well-being of "all sorts and conditions of men." Christian benevolence toward the needy was early noted with surprise and disapproval by pagan writers and has been fostered at all periods in the church. Over against this, however, the focus of some Christians on preparing for an expected end of the world led them to feel that social action was irrelevant. There has also not infrequently been a fantastic mingling of apocalyptic and utopian elements in Christian attitudes toward social issues. The medieval church, despite its theory of a just war and its practical attempt to limit the ravages of feudal warfare by the Truce of God, in blessing the crusades cancelled any progress toward the abolition of war. Modern Christianity has likewise failed to check the forces that make for war. A few smaller Christian denominations, notably the Quakers, have affirmed the principle of pacifism; and Christians generally are among the most active supporters of the agencies for international peace. The churches systematically encouraged the emancipation of slaves, which was often ceremonially enacted in a service at the altar. From the 4th century Christian hospitals were provided in cities; their number became large during the high Middle Ages. The duties of the clergy included care of the local poor; but the abolition of poverty is a more modern concept. Christians have never been content with the society about them. They have rebuked its evils and worked for its betterment, but sometimes in well-meaning ignorance they may have worsened conditions.

ORGANIZATION

Early Christianity, with members recruited from diversified classes of people, faced problems of discipline and order. As an inevitable alternative to confusion, the early church took on a structure of government. There is no indisputable evidence of a universally accepted procedure either of admission to clerical rank or of the settlement of disputes. In Acts 6, helpers in ministration to widows were chosen by "the whole multitude" and ordained by the Apostles. In Acts 15 a council of the Apostles and elders at Jerusalem decided against certain requirements of Jewish ceremonial. In Acts 20 and in I Clement 44, it seems implied that bishops and presbyters were not differentiated, but Ignatius (about 112) clearly distinguishes them. At Rome bishops were chosen by popular election at a time when at Alexandria they were selected by the presbyters from among themselves. Cyprian taught (251) that the episcopate is a universal corps, in succession to the Apostles, of divinely authorized interpreters of doctrine. But widely variant views of episcopal authority continued to find expression.

Roman Catholic and Orthodox Churches. Within Roman Catholicism the unique authority accorded to the pope placed the episcopate in a somewhat ambiguous doctrinal position. However, Vatican Council II in 1964 declared bishops the successors of the Apostles, exercising as one body, though never without the Roman pontiff, a collegiate power, and called to be solicitous for the whole church. The hierarchical structure of the church grew in response to practical needs. In the imperial age provincial, or metropolitan, sees were elevated above others "since all who have business gather to the metropolis," as stated in a council of 341. The still higher dignity of patriarch was accorded to the bishops of Jerusalem, Constantinople, Antioch, Alexandria, and Rome, each with a prescribed authority over several metropolitans. An important practical measure was the creation in 1059 of the college of cardinals as a body of available Roman clergy empowered to elect a pope and so to counter injurious feudal and imperial pressures. See also BISHOP; CARDINAL; CLERGY.

In the West, church power pyramided up to the papacy; but in the East there was no such centralization, and the patriarchates were disturbed by mutual rivalry and weakened by the Muslim expansion. In the 19th century they were freed from both these causes of deterioration, and they have in some degree recovered status and leadership. The Russian church, an important branch of Eastern Orthodoxy, and the smaller Orthodox units in states now Communist, are tolerated under severe restrictions.

Protestant Church Organization. Protestant churches offer considerable variety in organization and ministry. Lutheran and Reformed communions have generally been indifferent or antagonistic to hierarchical episcopacy. But Luther and the other Reformers had no objection to bishops as such. It was the opposition of most bishops to reform that called forth the Reformers' harsh, condemnatory utterances against the episcopal order. In German Lutheranism the principal governing units have been territorial consistories, related in origin to the medieval episcopal courts but under the authority of the civil government; the members are jurists, theologians, and area superintendents. But an episcopal succession was maintained in the Swedish Reformation, and episcopal organization was adopted in Denmark and Norway. Lutheranism in America has everywhere adopted synodical government. It was under the influence of the Pietist Henry Melchior Mühlenberg that the first American Lutheran synod was held (1748), a majority of those present being laymen. A constitution of 1778 for the Evangelical Lutheran Church of North America secured synodical rule with lay representation. The Scandinavian branches of Lutheran churches in America are also governed synodically and without bishops.

Calvin fully approved of the episcopate as it was developed in the early centuries and did not object to contemporary bishops if they adopted evangelical principles; but the bishop of Geneva had been expelled before Calvin came, and there was no desire to have the office renewed. At the close of the Reformation era the introduction of bishops in Scotland by royal appointment called forth a strong antiepiscopal movement. The Reformed church of Hungary, on the other hand, calls its chief officers bishops. Generally the Reformed and Presbyterian churches have been guided and governed by elective assemblies. In French Protestantism there emerged, in ascending order of authority, the local consistory, the colloquy for a number of congregations, the provincial synod, and the national synod.

In Scottish Presbyterianism the local session of lay elders with the minister presiding, the presbytery of neighboring ministers and representative elders, the provincial synod, and the general assembly constitute a similar series. Each of these ruling bodies has its own defined range of authority, and each consists of ministers and laymen. The governing decisions are thus made by regularly constituted representative bodies, in no case by an individual person. The system may be described as "conciliar," and can be related historically to medieval conciliarism and many other pre-Reformation experiments in representative government in church and state. One of the most consistent medieval examples is seen in the Dominican order with its similarly stratified governing chapters. A recent trend in Protestantism is to make increasing use of specially appointed departmental secretaries and experts, who attend to administrative matters for which synodical action would be inconvenient.

Anglicanism in all its branches has been consistently episcopal, though with considerable adaptation to national and local conditions.

Criticism of the Organized Church. From the time when Christianity became the religion of the Roman Empire until modern times most churches have been "established" in the sense of being state-connected and -maintained. This has often involved a large measure of state control, which in turn has been met by protests and exaggerated ecclesiastical claims. The Christian conscience can never equate its standards with those of public opinion or of political expediency.

Side by side with the historic established churches there have been countless separated communions, whose leaders were moved to reject practices approved or tolerated in the state church. In some instances these have testified through centuries against what they regard as an inferior type of Christianity. In this way Quakers and Methodists and various Nonconformist and secessionist bodies have made a cumulative impression even upon the churches they have left. The early Christian ascetics, by their adoption of a life of hardship, similarly offered a criticism of successful and relaxed Christianity; and later religious orders showed, in the formative stage at least, an earnestness not prevalent in the routine life of the church. A number of these dedicated groups, especially Franciscans, Dominicans, and Jesuits, made it their task to impart new reality to the life of the hierarchical church itself. A vast number of voluntary group movements have also stimulated the Protestant churches from within, producing their own organizations in more or less harmonious relation with the ecclesiastical structure. See also CATHOLIC CHURCH, ROMAN—4. *Organization;* PROTESTANTISM.

COMPARISON WITH OTHER MAJOR RELIGIONS

Christianity has never ceased to be in contact with Judaism and is now in direct confrontation with Hinduism, Buddhism, and Islam. Statistics, merely approximate, make Christians almost as numerous as the combined membership of the other four faiths. Together with them, Christianity is today challenged by materialism and militant atheism, a situation that tends to create a bond of sympathy between religions even where differences are fully recognized.

The centrality of Christ as the divine-human agent of salvation has no parallel in the other world religions, though his ethical teaching appeals to individuals in them all. Hinduism retains primitive elements uncongenial to Christianity, though its principle of *ahimsa,* or nonviolence based on reverence for all life, has appealed to some Christians, and some modern Hindu sects incorporate elements of Christian teaching. The Buddhist way of salvation—that of emancipation, without the aid of any deity, from the cravings that cause man's suffering and from the unhappy cycle of rebirth—is remote from Christian concepts. But Buddhism has greatly changed with its historical expansion. The Zen Buddhism of Japan, with its intense meditation in quest of the decisive enlightenment within this life, has fascinated some Christian minds. Today, however, Buddhism seems entering on an activist and political trend. Islam, worshiping "no god but Allah" and peculiarly resistant to Christian persuasion, has been during recent decades actively engaged in missions, chiefly in Africa. While tolerance and mutual appreciation grow, contrasts also stand out the more with deepening acquaintance, and no future coalescence among the great religions now indicated. See RELIGION and articles on major religions.

2. History

This survey of the history of Christianity begins with the spread of the church in the ancient world. The very beginnings of Christianity are described in other articles. See BIBLE—*14. New Testament History;* GOSPELS; JESUS CHRIST.

EARLY CHRISTIANITY

When Christianity arose, imperial Rome had provided a system of roads and sea-lanes by which cultural and religious influences could readily move through every province. The people of the empire were hungry for a satisfying religion. A score of mystery religions were attracting some from all ranks of society. No doubt a knowledge of their sacred rites and savior gods led the pagan mind nearer to Christian concepts. The shrines of new and old deities were perplexing in number. Many texts reveal that pagans felt an unanswered need to escape an addiction to sin. Some cults engaged in frenzied penances, and on another level, philosophers became the guides of troubled souls. A vaguely monotheistic belief arose among philosophical writers, who habitually spoke of God in the singular number. Everywhere some men were turning to Judaism and attending synagogues. Many of these Gentile "God-fearers" were early won over to the Christian community. The artificial cult of the emperor failed as a unifying element amid religious confusion. Christianity came with a more profound answer. Appropriating to itself the sacred books of Israel and the values of Jewish monotheism, it soon added to its treasury of authoritative texts the books of the New Testament, which convey a trinitarian view of deity, a concept less startling than Judaism offered to prospective converts from polytheism.

Judaism had secured the right to exist through the empire, and so long as Christians were mainly recruited from Gentiles who frequented the synagogues, they were mistaken for a Jewish sect. But it was soon recognized that, quite without state authorization, a vigorous new religion had arisen, addressing itself to every race and class. Its growth was alarming to old-fashioned people, who deplored the Christian desertion of the temples, rejection of animal sacrifices, avoidance of pagan festivals, and strict and distinctive morals. Slanderous rumors were circulated ascribing to the Christians loathsome rites and treasonable intentions. Christian apologists wrote effective refutations of these falsehoods and made a brilliant plea for the legal recognition of Christianity. From their treatises, together with a few extant lively literary attacks on Christianity, we glimpse a protracted contest in persuasion. The treasures of Hellenic philosophy as well as Judaic faith were being drawn into the stream of Christian thought. Clement of Alexandria and especially his pupil Origen made a masterly use for the Christian cause of the learning of earlier ages.

Expansion and Development. The early documents tell us little of other apostolic missions than those of Paul. The tradition of Peter's sojourn and leadership in Rome is strong, but specific facts are meager. There seems some possibility that the see of Alexandria was founded from Rome by Mark, acting for Peter. It is typical that, about 112, Pliny as governor of Bithynia (now part of Turkey) found that province teeming with Christians, though we have no evidence of previous missionary effort there. A similar lack of information baffles us in other areas, some of them beyond the bounds of the empire. About 200 A. D., Tertullian wrote airily of "places of the Britons not reached by the Romans but subjugated to Christ," while far across the Roman world, in northwestern Mesopotamia, King Abgar IX held Christian teachers in special favor. The planned or unplanned beginnings of Christianity in such localities must remain unknown. Traditions that assign mission fields to Andrew, Thomas, Bartholomew, and other apostles or their associates are at most unverified possibilities.

Organization varied with place and circumstances. Prevailingly in churches of synagogue origin the leaders were called *presbyteroi* whatever their functions, and among these the presbyter who conducted the worship was called *episcopos*, bishop. Another important task of the bishop was the supervision of the deacons in the administration of funds. In an early stage of the Christian ministry we find a class of itinerant evangelists, who brought through their visits a spiritual stimulation, and others, known as prophets, whose charismatic utterances sometimes became ecstatic. Soon, however, these ministers lost their usefulness, and what was of value in the functions they exercised devolved chiefly upon the bishops. When not prevented by persecution, synods of bishops were held to settle troublesome issues. But it was later, under the patronage of Christian emperors, that the church's network of organization became general.

The Church, the Empire, and the Councils. The pagan emperors gave no consistent answer to the problem posed for them by Christianity. Many of them adopted repressive measures but avoided general persecution. The serious effort of Decius and Valerian (249–260) to destroy the church was followed by the "long peace" instituted by Gallienus. But in 303 Diocletian and the fanatical Galerius resumed with enhanced cruelty the policy of suppression. From 305, when Diocletian abdicated, Galerius added thousands to the army of martyrs. But in 311 the dying persecutor acknowledged defeat and asked the Christians for their prayers. It remained for Constantine, coming victoriously from Britain and Gaul, to introduce, in 313, the new era of recognition and preferential treatment of the church. The rise of an entirely peaceable religion, within three centuries, to this point of triumph over the supreme secular power remains one of the most impressive phenomena of history.

Intimate relations between church and empire were at once established. But differences and rivalries within the church now came to the surface, and Constantine found himself mediating between Christians who had lately risked their lives together. The Donatist schism over the readmission of those who had lapsed in persecution, and the Arian controversy over the place of Christ in the Trinity, each led to a council of bishops convoked by the Emperor. The second of these, held at Nicaea in Bithynia in 325, is the first of those councils regarded as "ecumenical." Most of the 300 bishops present were from Eastern parts, but the able Hosius of Córdoba was in the Emperor's confidence, and the pope was represented by legates. Constantine himself joined intimately in the discussions and actually proposed the acceptance of the disputed word *homoousios* (consubstantial), by which the council affirmed against the Arians the equality of Christ with the Father. See also CONSTANTINE I; NICAEA, COUNCILS OF.

Theodosius I summoned the second ecumenical council, held at Constantinople in 381. A very significant ecumenical council was the fourth, convened at Chalcedon in 451. The presence of Emperor Marcian and Empress Pulcheria at decisive moments was a factor in its success. This council, to close a long controversy, declared the dogma of the unconfused and unseparated divine and human natures in Christ (see CHALCEDON, COUNCIL OF). However, the Monophysite (one nature) schism ensued, severing from orthodox unity Egypt, Syria, Palestine, and, a little later, Abyssinia and Armenia.

During the period before Chalcedon most of the eminent Christian scholars known as the Church Fathers lived and wrote, leaving a lasting treasury of theology and ethics. Their use of nonscriptural terms from Greek thought both clarified and complicated Christian theology. See also FATHERS OF THE CHURCH.

Early Monasticism. Christian life and literature in this period felt the rising influence of an ascetic movement that, though not wholly Christian in origin, reached its fullest expression in Christian monasticism. Reacting against worldliness in the church, ascetics went to desert solitudes in Egypt for meditation and prayer. As their numbers multiplied, they drew together in companies and accepted guidance from experienced leaders such as Anthony (died 356) and Pachomius (died 346). The Rule of Pachomius was followed by many settlements in and beyond Egypt. But it was the Rule of Basil of Caesarea (died 379) that became normative for Eastern monasticism; while Benedict of Nursia (died about 555) in his *Regula monachorum* furnished the enduring pattern for that of the West. See BASIL, ST.; BENEDICT, ST.; MONASTICISM.

Architecture and Church Art. During the persecutions most buildings for Christian worship were destroyed. In the 4th century numerous large churches were built in an adaptation of the basilica, or palace, style. They were oblong and had the table, or altar, at the eastern end with a semicircular apse behind it, and some, including St. John Lateran at Rome, had a spacious *atrium* between the narthex, or porch, and the nave. Very different is the great domed cathedral of Hagia Sophia (Holy Wisdom) in Constantinople, the finest of many structures of its kind, planned for Emperor Justinian by Anthemius of Tralles and completed in 547. A simple though varied Christian art had flourished, especially in catacomb tombs at Rome and elsewhere, since the 2d century, and pictorial art, chiefly in mosaics on walls and floors of churches, was employed with increasing freedom. In Hagia Sophia mosaics on gold background and a variety of metal ornaments provided splendor and instruction. Christian sculpture had its beginnings chiefly in figures chiseled on marble sarcophagi. They treat with vigor Biblical themes, often in series, using Old Testament incidents with allegorical allusion to Christian beliefs. Rounded figures were avoided as suggestive of pagan idols. See ARCHITECTURE; CATACOMBS; CATHEDRALS AND CHURCHES.

MEDIEVAL CHRISTIANITY

The Emergence of Christendom and the Conversion of New Nations. The word "Christendom" is here used of the aggregate of territories in which the church and the secular authority constituted two organs of one society. Not long after Emperor Julian's futile promotion of a pagan revival (361–363), the suppression of paganism became, under Theodosius, a fixed imperial policy (392). Ulphilas brought Christianity in its Arian form to the Goths, and it reached the other early Germanic invaders before they entered the empire. The Briton Patrick, in a great missionary career, planted orthodox Christianity firmly in Ireland in the 5th century. The powerful Franks and Anglo-Saxons came into Gaul and Britain, respectively, as pagans, to be afterward converted to Nicene orthodoxy. Missionary monks sent to Canterbury by Gregory I in 597 had a limited success in southern England, but the conversion of the English owed more to Irish monks, who came either from their famous Scottish center in Iona (founded in 563) or directly from Ireland. A long-continued Irish monastic migration to the Continent (about 500–1000) contributed immensely to the actual Christianization of Europe and shed a light of learning in the "dark age." See also IRISH CHURCH HISTORY.

Although a good many English missionaries had been trained by Irish teachers—including Willibrod (died 734), church founder in Frisia —Boniface of Crediton (died 754), "Apostle of the Germans," was not one of them. Strongly bound to the papacy, and a great organizer, he was unfavorable to the individualistic Irishmen.

Some Eastern monks too were distinguished missionaries. Moravia received Christian instruction from Cyril and Methodius, Greeks from Salonika, who for their translations created a Slavonic alphabet. It was mainly on the initiative of kings and rulers that Christianity came to be adopted in Bohemia, Bulgaria, Poland, Hungary, Russia, and Prussia. The undeniably sincere piety of Vladimir I of Russia (baptized 988) and of Stephen I of Hungary (997–1038) earned for them recognition as saints. The Celtic, Germanic, and Slavic peoples that the Roman Empire had encountered on its frontiers were thus by about 1000 A. D. within the borders of Christendom.

The Church and Secular Powers in Alliance and Conflict. The alliance of ecclesiastical and secular power was far from harmonious. Emphatic claims of their superiority to princes were stated from time to time by vigorous popes, most explicitly by Gelasius I in 494; and the ecclesiastical statesmen Leo I (reigned 440–461), Gregory I (reigned 590–604), and Nicholas I (reigned 858–867) gave high importance to the papal office. But such distinction was not maintained. Most of the popes had to adjust their policies to those of princes who treated them as subjects or at most colleagues. Charlemagne wrote to Leo III, who had crowned him emperor, comparing himself to Moses and Leo to Aaron. The Western empire so created proved weak and unstable both as ally and as adversary of the papacy. In the East, Justinian (reigned 527–565) regarded himself as head of the Christian society, which embraced both church and state. The pattern thus presented remained characteristic of the lands of Eastern Orthodoxy. A few courageous

Greek and Russian prelates affirmed some measure of church autonomy, but without cumulative effect.

In the 11th century the papacy was rescued by the empire from subservience to local factions. Taking on new vigor, it broke from imperial control and, in the vivid personality of Hildebrand (Pope Gregory VII, reigned 1073–1085), asserted authority over emperors and kings. The habitual investiture of bishops with their symbols of office by secular rulers, with its implication of subjection to the lay power even in things spiritual, was intolerable to Hildebrand and his successors. Hildebrand joined battle with Emperor Henry IV, who to secure his throne underwent a humiliating act of penance. Improving on Gelasius, Hildebrand regarded himself as the head of Christendom and indeed of the world, with a universal right to depose princes and absolve their subjects from allegiance. He met with reverses, but his claims were insistently reasserted by later popes. Agreements for England (1107) and for Germany (1122), by which both powers were to share the ceremony of investiture, did not close the controversy, since it left the underlying question of the right to appoint bishops unresolved. Also involved were disputes over the exemption of clerical offenders from trial in secular courts, a major factor in the struggle between Archbishop Thomas à Becket (died 1170) and King Henry II. The proud emperor Frederick Barbarossa, defeated in a long war, knelt in surrender to Alexander III (1177). The policy of Innocent III (reigned 1198–1215) included a free use against recalcitrant rulers of both excommunication of the person and interdict, which deprived the people from the sacraments until submission should follow. The lapse of the imperial office from 1254 to 1273 and its reduced importance thereafter transferred the struggle to national ground. Rejection by the French king Philip IV of the high demands of Boniface VIII occasioned Boniface's downfall (1303), ending an era of papal ascendancy. See also CATHOLIC CHURCH, ROMAN —2. History; biographies of GREGORY VII and other popes.

Christendom Against Islam: Great Wars of the Middle Ages. After the first great era of Muslim military expansion, relations between Christendom and Islamic states remained hostile. In the 8th century the horns of a great Muslim crescent were pointed toward Constantinople in the east and Frankish Gaul in the west. Slowly the Christian kingdoms that arose in Spain gained strength to roll back the invaders. Having united politically under Ferdinand and Isabella (1469), the Spaniards captured the stronghold of Granada, extinguishing Muslim power (1492).

In the East the Turks had centuries earlier replaced the Arabs as assailants of the Christian frontiers, had snatched most of the Byzantine territory in Asia Minor, and then approached Constantinople. Western pilgrims to the Christian holy places in Palestine were molested, and tales of their sufferings aroused deep resentment. In 1095, Eastern Emperor Alexius appealed to Pope Urban II for Western help. Urban's rhetoric at the Council of Clermont launched the first of the series of Crusades that for two centuries were to drain off into foreign wars the predatory feudal militarism of the West. Jerusalem was twice won and twice lost by the Crusaders. Constantinople was taken by the

Venetians in 1204 but recovered in 1261 by the Eastern Christians, who thereafter defended their diminishing empire till 1453. The historic capital then fell to the Ottoman Turks, and the Balkan Peninsula later came wholly under their sway. See CRUSADES.

During the same era Mongols from central China, who before 1250 became Muslims, exchanged atrocities with the Turks in Asia Minor and overran most of Russia, which they ruled and ravaged (1224–1480). The heroic leadership of St. Sergius of Radonezh (died 1392) turned the tide in favor of Christian Russia. Centered now in Moscow, Russian Christianity entered a new era of development. After 1453 Russia regarded itself as heir to the Byzantine state and church, and Moscow as the Third Rome.

Medieval Faith and Morals. The flowering of medieval culture was delayed until the disorders of the age of invasion had given place to more stable conditions. The names of Photius (died 891), worldly patriarch and historical scholar, and Michael Psellus the Younger (died about 1078), a Platonist of prodigious learning, are sufficient to suggest the intermittent flame of intellectual glory in the Greek church. In the West the great scholastics had their forerunners. The Irishman Johannes Scotus Erigena (died about 877), the first Western scholar since the 5th century to make effective use of Greek sources, outclassed and alienated his contemporaries; but the Platonic cast of his thought was not without influence. Plato, also, through Augustine, enlivened the mind of Anselm of Canterbury (died 1109) and made possible his ontological argument that God exists since God is "the highest thinkable."

After Anselm, intellectual advance was cumulative. Prefaced by the rise of monastic and cathedral schools with instruction in the seven liberal arts, the early universities of Salerno, Bologna, Paris, and Oxford afforded protracted studies in medicine, law, and theology. Their teachers were stimulated by the challenge of a body of learned texts that reached them through Arabic and Jewish scholars in Spain and Sicily. At the center of this new learning were Aristotle's scientific writings with the commentaries of Averroës of Córdoba (died 1198). It was the achievement of the Dominicans Albertus Magnus and Thomas Aquinas to capture Aristotle for theology while straining out the Averroistic "eternity of matter" and denial of immortality. But the scholastics differed among themselves hardly less than modern thinkers. The Franciscan Bonaventure (died 1274) represents a mystical Platonic-Augustinian strain, asserting the reality of universal ideas. But Platonic realism also had its perils for theology, inducing a trend to pantheism. Some later scholastics, notably William of Occam, were content to sever theological from philosophical truth. Christian doctrines were for faith, not for rational proof. A strong emphasis on divine predestination was voiced by the Oxford scholar Thomas Bradwardine (died 1349).

The condemned heresies of scholars were numerous and varied, as were also the popular movements stamped as heretical. The Waldenses and Lollards, with their devotion to the Bible, in some respects anticipated the Reformation. The Albigenses rather looked backward to the dualistic Bogomils of early centuries (see ALBIGENSES). The Inquisition, which took its origin as a legal substitute for lynching, was from 1232 engaged in a vast effort to detect and punish heretics, using the harsh court procedures of the age and, with the cooperation of "the secular arm," dooming countless thousands to death by fire.

In other ways church authority reached the laity more helpfully. In the preaching of the friars and in many writings addressed to pastors and preachers, not only expositions of the Creed and Commandments but also directions for the moral guidance of laymen on such topics as the deadly sins, the cardinal virtues, and the works of mercy were made familiar.

Schism of East and West. Craving unity, the church was plagued with schism. The Monophysites resisted Byzantine approaches (432, 638, 648) and, with numerous sectarian variations, continued to spread. The Patriarch John the Faster drew the shocked condemnation of Pope Gregory I by assuming the title "Ecumenical Bishop." The papal coronation of Charlemagne, a challenge to the Eastern empire, increased the alienation of East and West. The Western insertion of the term *filioque* in the Nicene Creed was ably attacked by Photius (about 885) and thereafter by numerous Greek and Russian theologians. The final schism between East and West took place in 1054 and was enacted in Constantinople between emissaries of Leo IX and Patriarch Michael Cerularius, who had earlier assailed the Westerns for the use of unleavened bread in the Eucharist. Attempts to end the schism at the first Council of Lyons (1274) and the Council of Florence (1439) were futile. The Greeks at Florence, hoping for aid against the Turks, surrendered most of their earlier contentions, but their concessions were angrily repudiated in the East.

The papacy itself was frequently disturbed by the elevation of antipopes subservient to emperors. From 1080 to 1180 this was a prominent feature of imperial policy. The causes of the Great Western Schism were also political. The popes had resided in Avignon from 1309, where they were under French influence. Pope Gregory XI, urged by Catherine of Siena and others, courageously removed to Rome in 1377. His successor alienated the French cardinals, who pronounced his deposition and elected their own pope (1378). Residing at Avignon, the schismatic popes for 40 years contested with Rome for the allegiance of Europe.

Conciliarism. From the time of Boniface VIII various proposals had been made to settle papal affairs by means of a general council. Thus was developed the doctrine of conciliarism, the supremacy of representative councils. When other attempts to end the papal schism failed, the conciliar arguments of John Gerson and Peter d'Ailly, doctors of Paris, induced a group of cardinals from either side to cooperate in preparing the way for the Council of Pisa (1409). Dismissing two popes, it elected a third, unexpectedly making the schism triple. But the great Council of Constance (1414–1418) induced the Roman Pope to abdicate and successfully deposed the other claimants. In 1417 the cardinals present elected Martin V, who in 1420 brought the united papacy back permanently to Rome. See also CONSTANCE, COUNCIL OF.

Medieval Art, Architecture, and Music. Byzantine architecture exhibits continuity with little prog-

ress, the most marked change being the frequent use of a ground plan in the shape of a Greek cross, the arms being of equal measurements. Russian churches imitated the various Byzantine models, featuring interior splendor. In the West, church architecture made repeated and surprising advances. About 1000 A. D., after an era in which more churches had been destroyed than built, a new "array of white sanctuaries" appeared. These were in the sturdy Romanesque style, and were often large, though, using as they did the rounded arch, they could not be high. They were improved with a clerestory, whose windows admitted sufficient light, and with a wide transept, which with the long nave gave them the form of a Latin cross. There was much variety and experimentation. See ROMANESQUE ARCHITECTURE.

In Normandy an approach to Gothic is seen in the introduction of ribbed vaulting and an elementary flying buttress. The successful use of the pointed arch, the determinative feature of Gothic, was developed in the 12th century by men of great talent in the Île de France. The height of the structure could now be greatly increased and the walls lightened to become mere framework for stained glass windows glowing with countless pictured lessons for the faithful. The lofty cathedrals with their towers and flying buttresses produced an external view unmatched by any other type of edifice, leading eye and thought toward high heaven. The arts of the sculptor and metalworker were employed with increasing freedom, which permitted a mingling of humor with symbolism. See GOTHIC ARCHITECTURE; GOTHIC SCULPTURE.

In the same era, church music was intensely cultivated and attained new variety and sophistication. From the earlier single-line melody of the Gregorian chant, composers moved to polyphonic forms of increasing complexity. In the 15th century these forms tended to be more delightful than devotional. See GREGORIAN CHANT.

The Later Middle Ages: Decline and Attempted Reform. With all its fruits of religious genius, the medieval period ended with a sense of frustration. The word "reform" rings through the literature concerned with the welfare of the church and of Christendom. The failure of the Crusades in their original purpose, the prevalence of abuses in the life of the clergy, the decline of the religious orders from their early zeal, and the entanglements of the papacy in worldly affairs all tended to create a mood of disillusionment and distrust. Laymen were becoming more literate and more vocal in criticism of ecclesiastics. The literature of satirical exposure and proposed reformation became abundant everywhere. Earnest preachers continued to testify to the essentials of Christianity, and in many homes there was Christian instruction and prayer. The greatly expanded pilgrimage life of the 15th century marks the rising religious anxiety of the time. The powerful hymn *Dies irae*, sung at funerals, gave utterance to the foreboding that had replaced the early note of joyous faith. When printers, long before Luther, began to publish vernacular Bibles, the demand was far greater than the supply.

The Biblical pre-Reformers, Wyclif in England and Hus in Bohemia, lacking the help of printers, had little success (see HUSSITES). The conciliarists were concerned for a fundamental reform of the church, yet it was the conciliarists at Constance who were responsible for the death of Hus (1415). That council's elaborately prepared reforming decrees were designed to reduce the pope's control and to correct detailed abuses; but the revived papacy was to condemn conciliarism and neglect most of these reform measures. In the century after Constance no pope made the spiritual and moral condition of the church his chief concern. The most zealous of reforming spirits before Luther was Savonarola, who in his denunciation of clerical misconduct had the passion of a Hebrew prophet. His agitation for a new reformed council set the train of events leading to his death in 1498.

CHRISTIANITY IN MODERN TIMES

Many forces, both religious and secular, combined to produce the Protestant revolt and the Reformation. The history of the Reformation era is covered in PROTESTANTISM; REFORMATION; CATHOLIC CHURCH, ROMAN—2. *History;* and related articles such as LUTHER, MARTIN; and CALVIN, JOHN.

Change and Reform Since the Reformation. During the past four centuries Christianity has undergone great changes. The Reformation movement, in its reliance on the Bible and its emphasis on the principles of justification by faith, the communion of saints, and the priesthood of believers, gave answers to religious problems that were satisfying to many. It was not, however, a single movement in organization, but arose spontaneously in various nations, taking over the old parishes and uniting them nationally or territorially where governments were favorable, and elsewhere organizing local congregations and drawing them together in a national or territorial connection. From the churches so formed numerous new movements emerged in separate units, to issue in our time in hundreds of denominations. Some of these are so naïve in their self-approval as to be largely indifferent to the Holy Catholic Church visible outside their ranks ("Catholic" here meaning universal and implying the fellowship of all Christians). However, this attitude is rapidly breaking down as all sects are exposed to similar problems and the flow of common ideas. Indeed it has been among the characteristic teachings of Protestantism that the church reformed is still to be reformed, and accordingly that advance in the appropriation of truth is a normal element in Christian life. In the historic tendency of Protestantism to split into new units it is not easy to evaluate motives. In many instances, however, there was a sincere effort to reach a new level in the realization of essential Christianity, even if this was somewhat mixed with willful disregard of the values of fellowship.

Another feature of the religious scene is the growth of strong cult movements, such as Christian Science, Mormonism, and Jehovah's Witnesses. These have their own sacred scriptures and did not originate in the Reformation, but recruit their membership largely from among nominal Protestants. Protestantism has been widely affected by certain movements that were not by intention separative, though in some instances resulting eventually in autonomous churches, notably English and American Puritanism, Dutch and German Pietism, and the Evangelical Revival with Methodism as its product.

Roman Catholicism recovered religious energy in the Counter-Reformation but lost its political status as a result of the Thirty Years' War (1618–1648) and subsequent national movements. It suffered inner conflicts over Jansenism, Gallicanism, Febronianism, Liberalism, and Modernism, but was able to avoid serious losses from schisms and to move into the 20th century with impressive strength.

Eastern Orthodoxy was drawn into discussion with Lutherans in the 16th and Reformed and Anglican theologians in the 17th centuries, but until the 19th century it remained largely unaffected by, and without influence in, Western Christian thought. The Russian church was stirred by controversy over liturgical reforms, in course of which the brilliant and impulsive Patriarch Nikon (died 1681) was deposed for his revision of liturgical texts. The Westernizing and secularizing policy of Peter the Great was countered by the piety of the Elders (*Startsy*), who for two centuries practiced a ministry of soul-guidance to countless pilgrim inquirers.

Churches and Secular Rulers. In modern times there have been numerous church-state conflicts; these have been attended by fresh thinking and have brought some solutions that may be expected to have permanence. When the modern era began, the concept of a church detached from the state was unfamiliar and unattractive. The state-connected Lutheran churches of Germany were subject to a large measure of control by the princes, who in Luther's thought had been charged with responsibility in church matters in time of difficulty. The tie with government remained firm despite political changes. The Reformed churches contended for autonomy against state control. Where governments were favorable, as in Geneva, this meant cooperation, with defined separate functions, rather than detachment.

In Scotland there was a protracted conflict in which the church repeatedly rejected the royal policy. In the 18th and 19th centuries a crucial struggle took place over patronage in the appointment of ministers as against the free call of the congregation and action by presbyteries. A number of secessions from the Church of Scotland took place, while the dominant "Moderate" party preferred patronage to controversy. But in 1843 occurred the "Disruption," in which more than one third of the ministers left the General Assembly, surrendering their livings, to organize the Free Church.

The Church of England, having lost its exclusive status by the Toleration Act of 1689, suffered unwholesome influences from government intervention. In 1717 a Whig administration abruptly suppressed its chief organ, the Convocation of Canterbury; it was revived only in 1852. Meanwhile ecclesiastical abuses mounted, most of them connected with the state's influence. The spell was broken by the Tractarian Movement, which began with Keble's denunciation of "the national apostasy" in 1833.

French Protestantism after long harassment was suppressed in 1683. Most known Protestants fled abroad, but a remnant persisted in France until freed in the French Revolution. In their *Declaration of Gallican Liberties* (1682) the French Roman Catholic clergy in collaboration with Louis XIV denied the secular claims of the papacy and asserted the superiority of a general council over the pope.

In German areas Febronianism corresponded to Gallicanism. Bishop Nicholas von Hontheim ("Febronius") in *The State of the Church* (1763) argued that the pope is not "universal bishop" but is subject to councils. The book shaped the policy of Joseph II of Austria, whose edict of toleration (1781) freed his Lutheran, Calvinist, and Orthodox subjects to worship as they wished.

Many Roman Catholics favored the freer atmosphere of the age, since it accorded to the church independence in its own sphere. The famous slogan of Cavour, "a free church in a free state," was borrowed from Montalembert, lay leader of the Liberal Catholic party in France. But the papacy under Pius IX reasserted papal supremacy, and the first Vatican Council affirmed the infallibility of the pope in 1870. After new setbacks in republican France, Leo XIII's policy alleviated the church-state tension, but a widespread anticlericalism prevailed to bring disestablishment of the French church in 1905. In Germany, Leo succeeded in allaying the strife that his predecessor had waged with Bismark (the Kulturkampf); but he remained at odds with the new Italy, which had seized the papal states in 1870. See also ANTICLERICALISM; CHURCH AND STATE.

In Russia, Peter the Great in 1721 set up the Holy Synod as an instrument for the control of the church. But the imperial policy was unstable. The mystical Alexander I founded (1815) the Holy Alliance, which till 1830 functioned feebly in an absolutist spirit. Moscow's one great metropolitan, Philaret Drozdov (died 1867), felt compelled to live in solitary retirement. He is credited, however, with the draft of the 1861 proclamation freeing the Russian serfs. After 1917 the Soviet regime attempted to destroy the national church and the numerous sects of Russia. But Christianity proved tenacious. During the war crisis (1943) the Orthodox Church was permitted to elect a patriarch; but its potential leaders were in exile.

During the century prior to 1914 the political liberation of the Balkan nations from Turkish rule made possible the establishment of national Orthodox churches in Greece, Bulgaria, Rumania, and what is now Yugoslavia. These were dissociated from Constantinople, which remained in Turkish hands, and with the exception of Greece have since formed special relations with Moscow.

Christian Missions and Migrations. From Christian communities and churches missions have gone forth to all parts of the globe. If the first three centuries of our era witnessed the Christian infiltration of the Roman Empire, the last four centuries (the 17th to 20th) have achieved a like result throughout the world. Christians do not look for any international government to arise that will give their faith preferred treatment or attempt the suppression of others. But nothing in the modern history of Christianity is more important than its mission in new fields, where it has been instrumental in changing conditions in a degree far greater than would be indicated by a count of adherents.

It was not the Crusades but the age of discovery and colonial settlement that set the stage for the rise of modern missions. The Spaniard Bartholomé de las Casas (died 1566), who in course of his labors became a Dominican, set a pattern of missionary devotion in South and Central America, befriending the Indians against their Spanish masters. The early Jesuits with extraordinary zeal carried on missions in China, Japan, the Philippines, and the Spanish and Portuguese colonies of Africa and South America. Important for Roman Catholicism was the establishment of the Congregation of the Propaganda (*Congregatio de propaganda fide*) in 1622, coordinating the church's missions throughout the world. (See CATHOLIC CHURCH, ROMAN—5. *Activities.*) The early 18th century saw the spread of Russian Orthodoxy, with Russian government, from the Urals to the Bering Strait.

The Reformation leaders were not indifferent to missions—Calvin's Geneva actually sent a dedicated band of missionaries to Brazil in 1556. Yet it was later that Protestant nations made colonial settlements that could be footholds for mission work. The beginnings of a continuous foreign missionary movement may be seen in the German Pietist mission in India (1709) and the widespread work of groups of Moravians led by Count Zinzendorf, starting in 1732. But it was British and American evangelicals of various denominations who took the leadership in the expansion of mission effort and organization through the 19th century. The story of their work shows a long roll of brilliant and devoted missionaries, a series of missionary societies, church missionary boards, and other supporting agencies in the sending countries, and a vast amount of printed material including translations of the Bible and other books into some 1,300 languages, many of which had never before been reduced to writing. Modern missions for the most part exhibit rare, unselfish dedication. Though some missionaries have been glad of the protection of colonial powers, colonial commercial interests have sometimes resented their presence as possible defenders of the people against exploitation. Schools, universities, and medical centers have accompanied most Christian missions. Church-supported schools have contributed to a general rise in literacy; moreover, a large proportion of the national leadership of many African and Asian states has come from those educated in Christian schools. See also MISSIONARY MOVEMENTS.

Revival Movements. All parts of the modern church have been stimulated by revivals of various kinds. Some of these have begun in ways that surprised all concerned, as when Jonathan Edwards was astonished in 1734 by responses from concerned hearers of an argumentative sermon. Unexpected manifestations of religious emotion attended the intinerant preaching of Howel Harris in Wales in 1735 and George Whitefield's outdoor sermons at Bristol in 1739. During the same decade, preaching stirred the parishes of western Scotland. Somewhat earlier Theodore Jacob Frelinghuysen had begun among his Dutch Reformed people in Raritan, New Jersey, a sober revival that spread through the work of Gilbert Tennent to Pennsylvania Presbyterians. Whitefield, a dramatic orator, paid seven visits to America, where his preaching is a distinct feature of colonial religious history from 1739 to 1770. He and his friend John Wesley differed on the doctrine of predestination. Both were Anglicans at the outset. Wesley's dedicated labors, riding, preaching, writing, and organizing, created the Methodist Church, which in England was recruited largely from those whom the Church of England had neglected. See also METHODISM.

Robert Haldane, a Scottish seagoing merchant, having devoted his wealth to religious causes, went in 1815 to Geneva, where he led groups of students, imparting to them an evangelical zeal which later bore fruit in revival campaigns led by César Malan and others in France, Germany, Belgium, and the Netherlands. Opposition forced the revivalist evangelicals to form free churches in Geneva, Bern, Zürich, Basel, Lyon, Paris, and a number of places in Germany.

With some exceptions, later revivals tended to be managed campaigns, with less of spontaneity, but they long remained an effective means of converting the negligent to a positive Christian stand. Preaching a simple gospel, in which hellfire was an ingredient, revivalists stirred up the frontiersmen in Kentucky and the Carolinas. A cumulative effect was obtained by means of camp meetings, with relays of preachers from different denominations. See also CAMP MEETING.

Revivals have always been criticized by both dogmatists and liberals, and their defects are easily discerned. They have aimed at bringing about conversions by a directed process involving fear and guilt followed by assurance of salvation, and their leaders have usually presented Bible texts with uninformed literalism. But it is undeniable that they promoted good relations among denominations and greatly enlarged active church membership at a period when irreligion was rife. One of the most effective of revivalist figures was Dwight L. Moody. Unselfish, tolerant, and wisely constructive, he left a lasting influence in America and Britain.

In Roman Catholicism revival methods are very different. The attempt has been to revive the local parish through the services of members of religious orders under hierarchical direction. The missioners have been sent for short periods, but at fairly frequent intervals, to preach in the parishes and counsel inquirers. The missions have been designed to quicken the spiritual life of laymen, and have been concerned more with instruction than with conversion. Voluntary movements in the same direction have generally been brought under clerical guidance. After 1848 the German bishops employed Jesuit and Capuchin missioners to preach plainly on sin and repentance, with impressive results. The Missionary Society of St. Paul (Paulist Fathers), founded in 1858, was a result of Isaac Hecker's mystical call to a similar work in America. Missions of this sort have become more general and frequent. The term "Catholic Action" has been applied, especially since 1928, to the apostolate of laymen in their communities, notably in efforts to affirm Christian standards in labor, the arts, the press, and literature. Vatican Council II approved the many organizations that have arisen in this connection, describing their purpose as "the evangelization and sanctification of men, and the formation in them of a Christian conscience."

Christianity Confronts Science and Marxism. In the 19th century, science offered an embarrassing challenge to Biblical theology. One of the most trying adjustments was demanded by Charles Darwin's presentation, with abundant data, of the theory of biological evolution. Most theologians were at first alarmed and hostile. But some Biblical scholars began to apply the principle of evolution in their interpretation of revelation itself. As Christian thinkers progressively made terms with the new science, opposition to it was aroused and became active, especially in America. Twelve volumes entitled *The Fundamentals* (1910–1915) were distributed in millions of copies and occasioned the Fundamentalist Controversy in the Protestant churches at the same time that a Liberal theology on good terms with science was developing in the seminaries.

In Roman Catholicism the problems raised by new knowledge were hardly less acute. Gregory XVI in 1832 and Pius IX in 1864 sternly rejected the Liberalism of their era, and in 1907, Pius X condemned the Modernists for errors that included an evolutionary view of history and Scripture. Some of the Modernists attributed their central ideas to John Henry Newman's *Development of Doctrine* (1845), the thesis of which they extended to combat the Thomist structure of theology prescribed by Leo XIII (1879).

Protestant Neoorthodoxy stood in the same loose relation to Søren Kierkegaard that Modernism did to Newman. Its chief prophet, Karl Barth, electrified the theological world by his *Romans* (1919), introducing a "theology of crisis," which, in rejection of Liberalism, reaffirmed Pauline, Augustinian, and Reformation doctrines of the divine initiative and the Bible as God's Word. In America, Reinhold Niebuhr similarly returned from Liberalism to Biblical and early Protestant points of emphasis.

The antireligious dialectical materialism of Karl Marx (set forth in *Das Kapital*, 1867), which sees history as primarily economic struggle, came at a time when Christians showed little interest in those economically oppressed, and Marxism may have helped to arouse Christian social concern. Institutionalized in Communist states, engaged in constant revolutionary propaganda, and representing itself as man's ultimate system of belief, materialism both menaces and stimulates Christianity.

Educational and Social Work. The record of the church as teacher and founder of schools has been maintained from medieval into modern times, though educational standards have not always been high. In the United States an attempt to provide education for the spreading frontier settlements resulted in the founding of some 500 denominational colleges before the Civil War. A majority of them also failed before the war. In the surviving schools, and those later founded, denominationalism has largely vanished, and standards have been raised. Theological seminaries have multiplied, and a few of them have attained high scholarly standards, not without the contribution of many teachers trained in Europe. Public school education has increasingly excluded religion, leaving, for most Protestants, the religious instruction of children to the home and the Sunday school. Parochial schools, promoted especially by Roman Catholics in the 19th century, have given prominence to religious subjects.

In Germany, Christian instruction has been given in state schools, and this plan was maintained under new regulations in West Germany after World War II. German schools of theology were very active in the 19th century, and in the later 20th century have recovered much of the intellectual strength they lost in the war period.

England has provided Christian teaching for the young since the government assumed the control of education in 1870, maintaining continuity with the work done previously in parish schools. In 1944 an agreement was reached by which non-Anglican churches have a voice in the syllabus for religion used in each county. Scotland's system of parish schools was maintained under church control until 1918, and religious instruction has been continued in the national schools under the guidance of the Joint Committee for Religious Education. The Religious Education Association has worked in America since 1903 "to inspire religious forces with the educational ideal and educational forces with the religious ideal," and a similar purpose prevails widely elsewhere. See also RELIGIOUS EDUCATION; THEOLOGICAL EDUCATION.

Innumerable medieval hospitals, and relief foundations by Reformation, Puritan, and Pietist Christians, testified to the Christian sense of social duty. The group of Anglican Evangelicals derisively called "the Clapham Sect" initiated many philanthropies and began the movement for the emancipation of slaves, a reform achieved for the British dominions in 1834. Nationally influential leaders of the antislavery cause in America included William Lloyd Garrison and Theodore Dwight Weld. Christian educational and relief agencies distribute funds on an increasing scale, and with planned intent to ensure permanent benefits to the receiver. Numerous British writers from about 1850 sought to apply the notion of the Kingdom of God in Jesus' teaching to social and economic issues.

In America the term "Social Gospel" came into use in the 1890's to designate a type of Christian social teaching that arose amid the industrial struggles of that era. It challenged the assumption of laissez-faire business that the poor were to blame for their poverty and proposed reforms in favor of the working class. Begun by Congregational and Baptist ministers, the Social Gospel penetrated most communions. These came to adopt "social creeds" and to set up departments of social service. The theological weakness of the movement was in part amended by Walter Rauschenbusch in *A Theology for the Social Gospel* (1917). But an age of world struggle called for a more critical theological analysis of social problems, and this was introduced by Reinhold Niebuhr, notably in *The Nature and Destiny of Man* (1941). Roman Catholicism also manifested a greatly intensified activity in social reform.

Art, Literature, and Music. Renaissance art, inspired by classic models, turned from symbolism to naturalism, portraying the human form in the colorful garb of the age, or in the nude, with a realism that was controlled only by the sheer love of visual beauty. Artists were self-conscious and ambitious: leaving behind medieval anonymity they wrote spiritedly about their work. Religious themes were treated not without reverence but in a new humanist spirit. Leonardo da Vinci studied the Apostles as historical persons and depicted them as men of character sharing a dramatic moment. See RENAISSANCE ART.

In the baroque era, Rembrandt and Rubens treated biblical themes under Calvinist and Roman Catholic influence respectively. The 18th century rococo style turned not only to excessive ornamentation but to scenes of dramatic emotion.

In music, a noble hymnody arose under Luther's inspiration, and sacred chorales were popular, the words being in some instances devout parodies

on popular songs. The French Psalter was the contribution of Calvin's Geneva, Louis Bourgeois and Claude Goudimel providing the music for Clement Marot's and Theodore Beza's verse translations. Enthusiastic outdoor psalm singing came to be a feature of the spread of Calvinism in France and the Netherlands. The most learned musician of the age was Giovanni Palestrina, who as choir director of St. Peter's, Rome, wrote masses in great numbers, many of them, in accordance with decisions of the Council of Trent, based on themes from Gregorian chant. The early 18th century was the era of a vastly enriched and assuredly immortal church music in the works of Bach and Handel.

The growth of humanist literature, as in the works of Boccaccio, Chaucer, and Shakespeare, led away from exclusive concentration on religion. The 18th century saw the popularity of authors indifferent or cynically hostile to traditional Christianity in fields of historical scholarship (notably Diderot, Voltaire, and Gibbon), anecdotal biography, and fiction. Friedrich Schleiermacher was addressing a potentially vast reading public in his *Discourses on Religion to its Cultured Despisers* (1799). One phase of the romantic movement in literature was a nostalgia for medieval scenes (exemplified by Chateaubriand, Scott, and Coleridge), and romanticism played a part in the formation of Schleiermacher's theology of feeling. But the new science of subsequent decades, and the interpretation placed upon it by some philosophers (for example, Herbert Spencer), enhanced the general trend toward materialism and secularism in 19th century thought. Nevertheless the materialist epitaph on Christianity, pronounced most vociferously by Friedrich Nietzsche, was illusory.

RECENT PHASES

Updating. The revolutionary changes of our era have made Christians more than ever conscious of the need to bring their message and methods abreast of the times. This has been strikingly evident in Roman Catholicism, especially since 1958 when John XXIII became pope. Viewing the gravity of the world's problems as well as those of the church, Pope John summoned the Second Vatican Council (1962–1965) specifically with the intent of bringing about a modernization, or updating, of the church in all its parts as an instrument of grace in the world. Its agencies of service and social action, relations with other churches and with non-Christians, methods and emphases in teaching, liturgical worship, the functions of persons in religious orders and of lay members—indeed all the church's essential components—were scrutinized and regulated. Numerous Orthodox and Protestant observers were in constant attendance and were cordially welcomed.

The texts of the council's debates and decisions are impressive both for their matter and for the evidence they offer of the openness of mind and charitable concern for all that have replaced the armed dogmatism of most earlier councils. There is no retreat from earlier positions, but there is a new emphasis and a new, chastened, and teachable spirit. Atheistic communism is "sorrowfully but firmly repudiated"; but there are no anathemas or loftily uttered denunciations. The episcopal order has "a collegiate character" as shown by the historic role of bishops in ecumenical councils. As successors of the apostles,

PROPER OF THE SEASON

SEASON OF ADVENT

FIRST SUNDAY OF ADVENT   *I classis*

Statio ad S. Mariam maiorem.

Entrance Antiphon
Ps. 24, 1-3

To you I lift up my soul; in you, O my God, I trust; let me not be put to shame; let not my enemies exult over me. No one who waits for you shall be put to shame. *Ps. ibid. 4* Your ways, O Lord, make known to me; teach me your paths. ℣. Glory be to the Father and to the Son, and to the Holy Spirit. As it was in the beginning, is now, and ever shall be, world without end. Amen. To you I lift up my soul: in you, O my God, I trust; let me not be put to shame; let not my enemies exult over me. No one who waits for you shall be put to shame.

This way of repeating the Entrance Antiphon is followed throughout the year.
The Gloria is not said in Masses of the Time from this Sunday until the vigil of Christmas, inclusively.

Ad te levávi ánimam meam: Deus meus, in te confído, non erubéscam: neque irrídeant me inimíci mei: étenim univérsi qui te exspéctant, non confundéntur. *Ps. ibid., 4* Vias tuas, Dómine, demónstra mihi: et sémitas tuas édoce me. ℣. Glória Patri, et Fílio, et Spirítui Sancto. Sicut erat in princípio, et nunc, et semper, et in sǽcula sæculórum. Amen.

Quo finito, repetitur Ad te levávi *usque ad psalmum.*
Hic modus repetendi antiphonam ad Introitum servatur per totum annum.
Non dicitur Glória in excélsis *in Missis de Tempore ab hac dominica usque ad vigiliam Nativitatis Domini inclusive.*

ROMAN MISSAL for the United States, in English, with accompanying Latin text. This shows a transitional phase from Latin to the vernacular, which is now used in public Masses.

BENZIGER BROTHERS, INC.

bishops are associated with the pope in his infallible deliverances. The measure of autonomy they exercise in their pastoral office is enlarged; specifically they are not "vicars of the Roman pontiffs." The position and functions of the laity are specially examined "in view of the circumstances of our time." Laymen are admonished to make Christ known "especially by a life resplendent in faith." Irrespective of race or sex, all lay members of the church, which in its entirety is "a priestly community," are to be joined in one lay apostolate, by which in family life, daily work, and eucharistic worship they "consecrate the world itself to God." Laymen participate in the evangelization of the world, and by the quality of their work and the equitable distribution of its products, they help to make moral values prevail in society. Many new regulations for religious communities are approved; their manner of life is to be "adapted to modern circumstances"—physical, psychological, social, and economic. To effect suitable changes, bishops are enjoined to hold territorial conferences under rules of their own approved by the pope. No doubt some cautious decentralization is intended in such decisions. The radical alteration, effective January 1, 1968, of the constitution of the Roman Curia distributes its membership geographically and provides for a renewal of key personnel at each papal election. Certainly a comprehensive spiritual and administrative renewal was begun; and Vatican II affirmed principles that would seem to make impossible any future stage of immobility in Roman Catholicism. See also VATICAN COUNCIL, SECOND.

The active features of recent Protestantism include many that continue 19th century impulses. The 1880's saw anticipations of a later wide development of organizations for youth, and also the settlement movement, providing friendly aid to immigrants and disadvantaged persons. Later social action has taken many forms in slum areas, including storefront churches with modest institutional equipment and coffeehouses under church auspices. Many prayer groups have been springing up, some with a social concern. Christians have supported, sometimes through church action, the causes of civil rights and world peace, and virtually all units of the church give substantially to funds for international relief.

Mention of the well-known names of Karl Barth, Paul Tillich, Dietrich Bonhoeffer, and Reinhold Niebuhr calls attention to the variety, liveliness, and challenge of 20th century Protestant theology. Nikolai Berdyaev in Orthodoxy, and Pierre Teilhard de Chardin in Roman Catholicism have been no less impressive. All of these have found an ecclesiastically unrestricted public and have helped to set the trend of contemporary thought.

Liturgical Renewal. Since 1900 a revival of liturgical worship has been a feature of church life. While the liturgical renewal is historically informed, it is far from reactionary, but rather daringly progressive. From 1954 Pope Pius XII introduced a number of liturgical reforms, including evening Masses, lay responses, and congregational singing. Vatican II set forth clearly the principles of public worship, authorizing several departures from earlier use. Liturgical studies are to receive major attention in seminaries; priests are to instruct their people in worship; and the people are to participate with "acclamations, responses, psalmody, antiphons and hymns." Adaptations to national cultures may be made, and the use of the mother tongue in the Mass is to be extended at the discretion of the bishops' conferences. A large use of the vernacular is also encouraged in baptism, the anointing of the sick, and matrimony. There are provisions for the improvement of sacred music and of the art objects and furnishings in churches. The reforms authorized are comprehensive, and not less impressive is the expectation conveyed that such reforms are to continue. See also CATHOLIC CHURCH, ROMAN—3. *Liturgy.*

In the Anglican Church the worship ideals of the Tractarian movement were largely lost in a tendency to magnify ritual details of gesture and incense; but the deeper message of the Tractarians slowly bore fruit in a revived concern for reality in worship affecting many Protestant communions. The Scottish church was awakened by the innovations, at the time startling rather than persuasive, of Robert Lee, who founded the Church Worship Society in 1865. The changes that followed in Scottish and worldwide Presbyterianism were gradual. The Reformed and Presbyterian churches were by 1900 at an early stage of liturgical reform. Most of them have since published revised books of worship and hymnals, and experimental variations have been much in vogue. Lutheran reform in worship has been cumulative since about 1850 and shows a trend to the judicious use of "the liturgies of the ecumenical church" under the guidance of modern scholarship, as agreed by most Lutheran churches in America (1954).

In several instances the union of two or more churches has occasioned the production of a new manual of worship. This has occurred in the United Church of Canada in 1932, the Church of South India in 1947, and the United Evangelical Lutheran Church of Germany in 1948. New standards have been reached in instrumental church music, and the quality of hymn texts shows some needed improvement. These improvements rest upon service rendered by eminent musicologists and editors as well as composers.

The Ecumenical Movement. The principle of Christian unity has been incorporated in all typical theologies and has always had its eager exponents. In former centuries the advocates of action for unity were hindered by political and geographical barriers, and still more by the theological disputes that have continued to rend the church. But the 20th century has witnessed a reversal of the divisive trend. Since the World Missionary Conference held at Edinburgh in 1910, most churches have been drawn into a movement that seeks the worldwide spiritual and corporate unity of the Christian church and people. Since 1937 it has been called the Ecumenical Movement. Nathan Söderblom, its prophetic leader of the 1920's, spoke of it as the Ecumenical Revival, a term that is well applied, since it has brought to life anew the church consciousness and spirit of communion of apostolic times. It has been stimulated by study of the early church and no doubt also by the dangers that confront the severed parts of the church in a world of secular power. Its organizational aspect should not be mistaken for the movement itself, which is basically spiritual and is born of a greatly deepened sense of the reality of unity in Christ.

The movement has made itself visible in many local forms of intercourse across denominational lines, comity and cooperation in missions and social work, national and regional councils of churches, and a successive series of worldwide conferences. These led up to the formation of the World Council of Churches, after delays caused by war. Starting in 1948 with 144 member churches, the council grew to more than 200 by the mid-1960's. Representatives of the chief Protestant and Orthodox churches and of the ancient regional churches of the Middle East mingle in committees and conferences with those from churches of modern mission origin. The council's offices in Geneva embrace many commissions and departments and are in touch with church problems and projects everywhere.

The council, however, does not directly initiate or promote the union of denominations. Scores of such acts of union have taken place spontaneously, and many are under negotiation. The papacy, at first unfavorable, has become friendly to the movement, and many Roman Catholics have been in helpful contact with ecumenically minded Protestant and Orthodox churchmen, participating with them in study and worship and in causes of civil betterment.

Christianity addresses itself with alertness to the modern world, renews its life of worship, and moves toward unity of spirit and purpose. But it is confronted by new perils and by the constant requirement of interior reform and renewal.

JOHN T. MCNEILL
Union Theological Seminary

Bibliography

Adeney, Walter F., *The Greek and Eastern Churches* (Edinburgh 1908).
Baillie, John, McNeill, John T., and Van Dusen, Henry P., general eds., *Library of Christian Classics*, 26 vols. (London and Philadelphia 1953–).
Barry, Coleman J., *Readings in Church History*, 2 vols. (Westminster, Md., 1960–1964).
Baum, Gregory, ed., *The Teachings of the Second Vatican Council* (Westminster, Md., 1966).
Beach, Waldo, and Niebuhr, Richard, *Christian Ethics* (New York 1955).
Beaver, R. Pierce, *Ecumenical Beginnings in Protestant Missions* (New York 1962).
Bennet, John C., *Christian Social Ethics* (New York and London 1966).
Bethune-Baker, James F., *Introduction to the Early History of Christian Doctrine*, 5th ed. (London 1933).
Bouquet, Alan C., *The Christian Faith and the Non-Christian Religions* (New York 1958).
Brauer, Jerald C., *Protestantism in America*, rev. ed. (Philadelphia and London 1966).
Catholic University of America, *New Catholic Encyclopedia*, 15 vols. (New York 1967).
Cullmann, Oscar, *Early Christian Worship*, tr. by A. S. Todd and J. B. Torrance (London 1953).
Dawley, Powel Mills, *Chapters in Church History*, rev. ed. (New York 1963).
Dillenberger, John, and Welch, Claude, *Protestant Christianity* (New York 1954).
Fedotov, George P., *The Russian Religious Mind* (Cambridge, Mass., 1946).
Ferm, Robert L., *Readings in the History of Christian Thought* (New York and London 1964).
Grant, Robert McQueen, *The Bible in the Church* (New York 1960).
Hughes, Philip, *A History of the Church*, 3 vols., rev. ed. (New York 1947–1949).
Latourette, Kenneth Scott, *A History of Christianity* (New York 1953).
Lehmann, Paul H., *Ethics in a Christian Context* (New York 1963).
Lietzmann, Hans, *A History of the Early Church*, tr. by Bertram E. Wolf (New York 1961).
Neill, Stephen Charles, *Colonization and Christian Missions* (London 1966).
Nichols, James Hastings, *History of Christianity 1650–1950* (New York 1956).
Nygren, Anders, *Agape and Eros*, tr. by Philip S. Watson (London and Philadelphia 1953).
Petry, Ray C., and Manschreck, Clyde L., *A History of Christianity; Readings*, 2 vols. (Englewood Cliffs, N. J., 1962–1964).
Rouse, Ruth, and Neill, Stephen C., *History of the Ecumenical Movement, 1517–1948* (Philadelphia 1967).
Schmemann, Alexander, *The Historical Road of Eastern Orthodoxy*, tr. by Lydia W. Kesich (New York 1963).
Sherrard, Philip, *The Greek East and the Latin West* (London 1959).
Spinka, Matthew, *Christian Thought from Erasmus to Berdiaev* (Englewood Cliffs, N. J., 1962).
Thompson, Bard, *Liturgies of the Western Church* (New York 1951).
Walker, Williston, *History of the Christian Church*, rev. by C. C. Richardson, W. Pauck, and R. T. Handy (New York 1959).

FRITZ HENLE, FROM PHOTO RESEARCHERS

CHRISTIANSTED, capital, port, and shopping center of the island of St. Croix, U. S. Virgin Islands.

CHRISTIANSTED, kris′chən-sted, is the principal city of St. Croix, one of the Virgin Islands of the United States, 40 miles (65 km) south of St. Thomas. The city is on the north central coast at the head of a large basin; its original name was Bassin. It came into existence in 1733, when the French sold St. Croix to Denmark, and served briefly as capital of the Danish West Indies.

The town prospered as a provisioning station for ships and as a center of the cane sugar and rum industries, but its economy suffered with the advent of technological advances in shipping and the emancipation of slaves in 1848. Cane cutters were imported from Puerto Rico; today almost half the population is Puerto Rican, although tourism has replaced sugar as the major industry. Other industries, such as aluminum and oil, and the island's agriculture, help to stabilize the economy. Population: 2,966.

ROLAND DICKISON
Dean of the College of the Virgin Islands

CHRISTIE, kris′tē, **Dame Agatha** (1890–1976), English novelist and playwright, famous for her detective stories, many of which feature the egotistical Belgian detective Hercule Poirot or the English village spinster-sleuth Jane Marple. Her published works include approximately 100 titles, some 60 of which were full-length detective stories, 19 were collections of short mystery stories, and 14 were detective-story plays. Others included nonfiction, a book of poetry, and several romantic novels written under the name Mary Westmacott. Many of her books were translated and were made into plays or motion pictures. The most successful include *The Mousetrap* (1952), one of the longest-running plays in London theater history, *Witness for the Prosecution* (1953), and *Murder on the Orient Express* (released as a motion picture in 1974).

Agatha Mary Clarissa Miller was born in Torquay, Devon, England, on Sept. 15, 1890. She studied voice in Paris but abandoned a singing career and turned instead to writing. In 1914 she was married to Col. Archibald Christie, whom she divorced in 1928. Two years later she was married to archaeologist Max (later Sir Max) Mallowan, with whom she made several trips to the Middle East. She was made Dame Commander, Order of the British Empire, in 1971.

Dame Agatha's first novel, *The Mysterious Affair at Styles,* appeared in 1920 and introduced Hercule Poirot, but she did not achieve fame until 1926, when her sixth book, *The Murder of Roger Ackroyd,* was published. Jane Marple was introduced in *Murder at the Vicarage* (1930). The novel *Ten Little Niggers* (1939) appeared in the United States as *And Then There Were None* (1940) and as a play (*Ten Little Indians,* 1943) and three motion pictures. Detective Poirot's death occurred in *Curtain,* published in 1975. In the following year, on Jan. 12, 1976, Dame Agatha died in Wallingford, England.

CHRISTIE, kris′tē, **Loring Cheney** (1885–1941), Canadian lawyer, diplomat, and confidential adviser to several prime ministers. Born in Amherst, Nova Scotia, on Jan. 21, 1885, he was educated at Acadia University (B. A., 1905) and Harvard University (LL. B., 1909). Christie worked in the office of the attorney general of the United States for several years before 1913, when he returned to Canada to become legal adviser to the department of external affairs, a post he held until 1923. During the later stages of World War I and the following peace conferences, he was Prime Minister Robert L. Borden's closest confidential adviser. Distrusted by Liberal Prime Minister W. L. Mackenzie King, who won office in 1921, Christie resigned in 1923, accepting employment with a London financial house.

By 1935, when he returned to external affairs in a senior capacity, his views had come to coincide closely with those of Mackenzie King, and Christie helped reinforce Mackenzie King's determination to avoid any transatlantic entanglements, including commitments to Britain. In September 1939, during the critical first days of World War II, he was appointed the minister to Washington, where his experience and strong American sympathies proved invaluable. Incapacitated by illness in November 1940, Christie died in New York City on April 8, 1941.

D. G. G. KERR, *University of Western Ontario*

CHRISTIE'S, kris′tēz, is the popular name of Christie, Manson & Woods, Ltd., the world's oldest firm of fine art auctioneers. The firm's headquarters are in London, with branch offices in New York and Geneva. Christie's was established in 1776 by James Christie (1730–1803). The grandsons of James Christie took new partners in 1859, and the firm acquired its present name.

In 1778, Christie negotiated the sale of pictures from the Sir Robert Walpole collection to Catherine the Great of Russia; these became the nucleus of the Hermitage collection. Since then the firm has disposed of many of the major European estates and collections, including the Spanish Gallery of King Louis Philippe of France; the Hamilton Palace collection of the Duke of Hamilton; the jewels of Madame Du Barry; and J. P. Morgan's collection of miniatures. Christie's has also sold out the studios of most major British artists, including Gainsborough, Reynolds (both personal friends of James Christie), Romney, Raeburn, Landseer, and Augustus John.

JANE SABERSKY, *Christie, Manson & Woods*

CHRISTINA, kris-tē'nə (1626–1689), queen of Sweden, was born in Stockholm on Dec. 17, 1626, the daughter of King Gustavus Adolphus and Maria Eleanora of Brandenburg. The death of her father when she was six and the incapacity of her mother resulted in her being educated in a manner that befitted a male heir to the throne. During Christina's minority the sober and wise chancellor, Count Axel Oxenstierna, acted as regent. Christina spent her early teens at the rural estate of Stegeborg with the family of her aunt Catherine, the wife of Johann Casimir, prince of the Palatinate. There she played and studied languages and statecraft with her cousins, Charles Gustav, four years her senior, and Maria Eufrosyne. Christina developed such an affection for Charles Gustav that she agreed to marry him. But soon after he went off to war, Christina resolved she would never marry.

In 1639 her aunt Catherine died, and Christina moved into Stockholm. Increasingly she showed an independent spirit and an unusual keenness of mind. The guardianship of Oxenstierna irked her, and the preaching of Lutheran ministers bored her. In 1644, Christina reached her 18th birthday and was proclaimed queen. She bestowed high offices and extensive estates upon favorites. Christina was interested in philosophical speculation and invited foreign men of letters to her court, among whom the most notable was René Descartes. Though intelligent and sincere in her pursuit of philosophy, and though she wrote sage aphorisms, she could not be classed as a profound thinker. Christina tried conscientiously to do her duty as queen and enjoyed the authority that went with her position; but she was bored by the sessions of the council and the everyday business of governing.

In the aftermath of the Thirty Years War, which ended in 1648, many of the Swedish nobles had become very wealthy and had built great palaces. The lesser nobility and the farmers, however, objected to their increased taxes and resented the tax-free status of the magnates. In the *Riksdag* (parliament) of 1650 the three estates of clergy, burghers, and farmers attacked the nobility and demanded reforms and the reversion to the crown of lands given to the nobles. Although the queen had herself donated many of these lands to the magnates, she appeared sympathetic to the cries for reform. Christina shrewdly played one party against the other until she had manipulated the nobles into accepting Charles Gustav, her cousin, as her heir. Thereafter she refused to take any action to reduce the nobles' estates.

Having secured the succession of her cousin to the throne, Christina renounced the crown on June 6, 1654. Her desire to abdicate has never been satisfactorily explained. The feeling that a man should rule may have played some part in her decision. Furthermore, pressure on her to marry and produce an heir had been annoying. But her decision was certainly strongly influenced by her increasing interest in the Roman Catholic Church, which was encouraged by Descartes, the Jesuits, and emissaries of the Catholic powers. In Lutheran Sweden she could not be both queen and Catholic. Carefully keeping secret her leanings to the Roman church, she at last persuaded the Council to accept her abdication. Her cousin succeeded her as King Charles X Gustavus. After her abdication Christina proceeded slowly to Rome, and at Innsbruck, just before entering

PORTRAIT BY DAVID BECK—BETTMANN ARCHIVE
Queen Christina of Sweden

Italy, she publicly renounced the Lutheran faith and became a Roman Catholic. This was a coup for the Pope and a shock to the Swedes and to Protestants everywhere.

Twice later Christina returned to Sweden to check on the properties that had been granted her for her maintenance. But both times she was received coolly and with suspicion. Though she had no country, she was still a queen, and not only the Pope but the kings of France and Spain tried to use her for their own ends. At one point it seemed she might become queen of Naples, but the project foundered, perhaps because of the treason of her secretary, Giovanni Monaldeschi, or perhaps because she had the traitor killed. After 1659, Christina maintained a court in Rome, where she cultivated the arts and sciences, collected a notable library and gallery of art, and served the papacy. She died in Rome on April 19, 1689, and was buried in St. Peter's Basilica.

FRANKLIN D. SCOTT, *Northwestern University*

Further Reading: Weibull, Curt, *Christina of Sweden,* tr. by Alan Tapsell (Göteborg, Sweden, 1966).

CHRISTINE DE PISAN, krēs-tēn' də pē-zäN' (1364–?1431), French author. She was born in Venice but was sent to France to live with her father, Thomas de Pisan, who had become physician and astrologer to Charles V. Married at the age of 15 to Étienne du Castel, she was widowed at 25 and supported herself and her three children by writing.

Equally adept in prose and poetry, Christine wrote ballads, love poems, and more than 15 books on history, war, philosophy, customs, and morals. She carried on a vigorous polemic against Jean de Meung's *Roman de la rose,* which she asserted was contemptuous of women. In *Épître au dieu de l'amour* (1399) and in *Le Trésor de la cité des dames* (1402), an allegorical poem, she extolled the virtues and heroism of women. Christine died in France in 1431 or soon thereafter.

CHRISTMAS LIGHTS adorn Oxford Street in London.

CHRISTMAS, kris′məs, is a Christian festival commemorating the birth of Jesus Christ. The name derives from the Old English *Christes Mæsse,* or Christ's Mass, and the present spelling probably came into use about the 16th century.

All Christian churches except the Armenian Church observe the birth of Christ on December 25. This date was not set in the West until about the middle of the 4th century and in the East until about a century later. The Armenians follow the old Eastern custom of honoring Christ's birth on January 6, the day of the Epiphany, commemorating in the West chiefly the visit of the Magi to the infant Jesus, and in the East, Christ's baptism. (See EPIPHANY.) Some churches hold their most elaborate festivals on January 6, and in parts of the United States this date has been celebrated as "Old Christmas" or "Little Christmas."

Origins of Christmas. The reason for establishing December 25 as Christmas is somewhat obscure, but it is usually held that the day was chosen to correspond to pagan festivals that took place around the time of the winter solstice, when the days begin to lengthen, to celebrate the "rebirth of the sun." Northern European tribes celebrated their chief festival of Yule at the winter solstice to commemorate the rebirth of the sun as the giver of light and warmth. The Roman Saturnalia (a festival dedicated to Saturn, the god of agriculture, and to the renewed power of the sun), also took place at this time, and some Christmas customs are thought to be rooted in this ancient pagan celebration. It is held by some scholars that the birth of Christ as "Light of the World" was made analogous to the rebirth of the sun in order to make Christianity more meaningful to pagan converts.

Many early Christians decried the gaiety and festive spirit introduced into the Christmas celebration as a pagan survival, particularly of the Roman Saturnalia. They considered the birth of Christ a solemn occasion. But almost from the first, Christians have generally regarded Christmas as both a holy day and a holiday. For Christ's birth brought a new spirit of joy into the world, and from the first recounting of the story of the Nativity, man has fashioned endless variations—not only in words, but in art, song, dance, and drama—and has even created special symbolic holiday foods. Customs of all lands have been added through the centuries, making Christmas today the greatest folk festival in the world.

Development of Customs. The English adapted many older folk festivals to their Christmas. In the Middle Ages, English Christmases were times of great hilarity and good cheer, and vast banquets and pageantry celebrated the occasion. It was in this period that the idea of the Lord of Misrule reached its greatest expression. A common person or a servant of a great lord was chosen to rule with absolute authority during the Christmas season, and often his "rule" resulted in uncontrolled frivolity. This tradition may have originated during the Saturnalia, when slaves became the equals of their masters.

Burning the Yule log was adapted to English custom from the ancient Scandinavian practice of kindling huge bonfires in honor of the winter solstice. The idea of using evergreens at Christmastime also came to England from pre-Christian northern European beliefs. Celtic and Teutonic tribes honored these plants at their winter solstice festivals as symbolic of eternal life, and the Druids ascribed magical properties to the mistletoe in particular. The evergreen holly was worshiped as a promise of the sun's return, and some say that Christ's crown of thorns was made of holly. Legend tells that the berries were once white, but when the crown was pressed upon Jesus' brow, the drops of blood turned the berries bright red. The Christmas wreath is thought by some to have originated from this legend.

Other well-known Christmas customs originated in various lands. While there are many ideas about the origin of the Christmas tree, it is widely believed that Martin Luther began the custom in Germany. The sight of an evergreen tree on Christmas eve, with stars blazing above, is said to have made a great impression on him, and he put a similar tree, decorated with lighted candles, in his home. Some scholars hold that the evergreen tree, a symbol of life to the pagans, became a symbol of the Saviour and thus an integral part of the celebration of his birth.

A well-loved Christmas custom is the singing of Christmas carols. The word "carol" is thought to have originally denoted a dance accompanied by singing. Thirteenth century Italy is considered the birthplace of the real Christmas carol, and St. Francis of Assisi, who led songs of praise to the Christ Child, is thought to be the father of this custom. St. Francis is also credited with first introducing the crèche, or Nativity scene of the Baby Jesus in the manger. Elaborate wood-carved crèches, often requiring years of work, are now traditional Christmas symbols. Among the Pennsylvania Dutch, descendants of Bohemian and Moravian settlers in the United States, such a scene is called a *Putz*.

The beloved image of Santa Claus as a fat, jolly, bearded old man derives from St. Nicholas, an austere-looking 4th century Christian bishop of Asia Minor, who was noted for his good works. The idea of gift giving associated with this saint spread from Asia Minor to Europe and was brought to the United States by early Dutch settlers. The American writer Washington Irving contributed to the concept of St. Nicholas as a laughing holiday figure, and in 1822, Clement Moore composed his *Visit from St. Nicholas* (" 'Twas the night before Christmas") with its noted description. But the image of Santa in fur-trimmed dress that ultimately captured the imagination was drawn in the United States by the cartoonist Thomas Nast in 1863.

FRITZ HENLE, FROM PHOTO RESEARCHERS

CHRISTMAS PAGEANT in St. Croix, Virgin Islands.

Christmas has not always been remembered with gaiety and good cheer. Excessive frivolity had always been frowned upon by some, and Christmas was not celebrated by the Puritans or Calvinists. When the Puritans came to power in England under Oliver Cromwell in 1642, Christmas celebrations were banned as evidences of antireligious, Royalist sentiment. Penalties were exacted for celebrating Christmas, and for staying home from work on Christmas day. The Puritan tradition was brought to New England, where Christmas did not become a legal holiday until 1856. Nevertheless, in other areas of the United States, the festive season was celebrated with joyousness by immigrants, who brought their holiday traditions from their homelands. It is this tradition of "joy to the world" that today marks the spirit of Christmas nearly everywhere in the world.

MARGUERITE ICKIS, *Author of "The Book of Religious Holidays and Celebrations"*

PUBLIFOTO, FROM BLACK STAR

CHRISTMAS DECORATIONS at Rockefeller Center in New York feature a huge Christmas tree.

CHRISTMAS CACTUS is an epiphytic type of cactus (*Zygocactus truncatus*) that has drooping branches with flattened, shiny joints. It bears red blossoms and fruit, often during the Christmas season. See also HOUSEPLANTS.

CHRISTMAS CAROL, kris'məs kar'əl, a story by Charles Dickens, published in 1843. It concerns Ebenezer Scrooge, a miserly London businessman, and the family of his exploited clerk, Bob Cratchit. Dickens wrote *A Christmas Carol* in the fall of 1843, in an attempt to relieve his increasing financial difficulties. Although the book shows signs of hasty writing, it was an immediate success. In relation to Dickens' major novels, the story must be regarded as slight. However, it has always been popular, partly because of its warmth, gaiety, and appeal to the spirit of Yuletide charity, and, ironically, partly because of its defects—sentimentality and crude characterization.

On Christmas eve, Scrooge is visited by the ghost of his late partner, Marley, who warns him that his meanness will bring retribution. That night a vision of Christmas Past recalls his youth; a vision of Christmas Present shows him the poor but cheerful Cratchit family, including the appealing cripple Tiny Tim; and a vision of Christmas Yet To Come depicts Scrooge's possible unmourned death. Scrooge awakens on Christmas morning filled with love and gives the Cratchits the happiest Christmas they have ever had.

JAMES REEVES
Author of "English Fables and Fairy Stories"

Further Reading: Chesterton, G. K., *Criticisms and Appreciations of the Works of Charles Dickens* (London 1933); Osborne, Eric A., *The Facts About "A Christmas Carol"* (London 1937).

CHRISTMAS ISLAND, kris'məs, in the Indian Ocean, is 223 miles (359 km) south of Java Head. It is about 11 miles (18 km) long, 4½ miles (7 km) wide at its narrowest point, and 60 square miles (155 sq km) in area. The Chinese and Malayan population is mainly employed in the island's only industry, extracting and exporting phosphate.

Christmas Island was annexed by the British in 1888, placed under control of the Straits Settlement in 1889, and incorporated in the settlement of Singapore in 1900. On Oct. 1, 1958, Britain transferred sovereignty over the island to Australia. Population: (1966) 3,381.

CHRISTMAS ISLAND, kris'məs, one of the Line Islands, is the largest atoll in the Pacific Ocean. It is approximately 160 miles (255 km) southeast of Fanning Island and is 222 square miles (575 sq km) in area. The island was discovered by Capt. James Cook in 1777, annexed by Britain in 1888, and in 1919 was included in the Gilbert and Ellice Islands colony (since 1976 the Gilbert Islands). The United States also claims the island, which is on long-term lease to a copra plantation worked by the British government. Nuclear tests were conducted there by the British in 1957–1958 and by the United States in 1962.

CHRISTMASBERRY (*Heteromeles arbutifolia*), is an evergreen shrub of California that has glossy leaves, clusters of small white flowers in early summer, and bright red, hollylike berries that often persist through December. See also TOYON.

DONALD WYMAN, *The Arnold Arboretum*

CHRISTOFFEL, kri-stöf'əl, **Elwin Bruno** (1829–1900), German mathematician, who introduced covariant differentiation in the study of higher dimensional geometry. He was born in Montjoie (now Monschau), near the Belgian border, on Nov. 10, 1829. Christoffel studied at the University of Berlin and was strongly influenced by Dirichlet and the works of Riemann. He graduated from Berlin in 1856. In 1862, Christoffel succeeded Dedekind as professor at the Polytechnicum in Zürich and then helped to establish a department of mathematics at the University of Strasbourg when it reopened in 1872 as a German university following the Franco-Prussian War of 1870–1871.

Christoffel published memoirs on the theory of functions, where the important Schwartz-Christoffel formula bears his name, and he completed a long paper on the theta function only a few weeks before his death at Strasbourg on March 15, 1900. In a paper of 1869 on quadratic differential forms he introduced the expression, later called covariant differentiation by Ricci, that became basic to the study of the differential calculus of higher dimensional surfaces. The ideas of this paper have important applications in tensor analysis, where they lead to the "Riemann-Christoffel curvature tensor," which is well known in general relativity theory.

CARL B. BOYER
Brooklyn College

CHRISTOLOGY, kris-tol'ə-je, is the doctrine of the person and work of Christ. Christology is concerned with Christ's nature, both human and divine, His incarnation, His revelation of God, His miracles, or "mighty works," His death (which effected the atonement, or redemption of mankind from sin), His resurrection and ascension, His glorification, His heavenly intercession, and finally His coming again in glory to hold the Last Judgment.

This is the teaching of the Apostles' Creed, the oldest of the Christian creeds. Its beginning, as the simple affirmation of belief made at Baptism in Rome about the middle of the 2nd century, implied that it set forth the apostolic teaching as contained in the New Testament (see APOSTLES' CREED and CREEDS AND CONFESSIONS). Its final form dates from the 7th or 8th century. It has many translations. The one found in the *Book of Common Prayer* is almost a century older than the King James Version of the Bible—hence its archaic (and beautiful) style and its slight divergences from the Latin original. This creed was designed originally to repudiate such false teachings as Gnosticism or Docetism, which would have denied the true humanity of Jesus.

The Nicene Creed, also found in the Prayer Book in an equally archaic translation, was the work of the Council of Nicaea (325) supplemented by Constantinople (381) and Chalcedon (451). It reaffirmed and amplified the Apostles' Creed and was designed to refute Arianism, which made Christ a creature, "the firstborn of all creation." It became the standard creed of both East and West but led to dissension, as the Eastern formula read: the Holy Spirit "proceeds from the Father *through* the Son," while the Western Church insisted on "*and* the Son." This change was one of the causes leading to the separation between East and West in 1054.

The so-called Athanasian Creed, a 6th century formula, is chiefly concerned with the exact definition of the relations between the Father, the Son, and the Holy Spirit—the three "persons" in the Blessed Trinity. It takes for granted the earlier statements on Christ's deity, as at Nicaea, Constantinople, and Chalcedon. Christ has two natures, human and divine, which are united "inseparably" in the Incarnation, and yet "unconfusedly"; he is both "truly" God and "perfectly" man. These four terms set the boundaries of speculation and definition for all later orthodox theology. Later creeds and confessions, Orthodox, Roman Catholic, Protestant, Anglican, and other, have not altered the doctrines relating to Christology.

But it is not only in the creeds, or in the systematic theology which expounds them, that the doctrine of Christ is set forth. Hymns, prayers, homilies and sermons, the liturgy, devotional books, and works of art likewise state it; two important examples are *The Imitation of Christ* by Thomas à Kempis and Johann Sebastian Bach's *Jesu, Joy of Man's Desiring*. Like all basic or fundamental religious doctrines, the doctrine of Christ too is no mere result of theological speculation or of rational inference from sacred texts; it expresses the deep personal conviction and faith which lie at the heart of the Christian religion.

Conceptions and Titles of Christ. The origin of this conviction can be traced in the New Testament. The disciples of Jesus, who at first looked upon him as a teacher and prophet, "mighty in deed and word before God and all the people" (Luke 24:19; Acts 10:36–38), came to believe that he was the Messiah (or Anointed), the glorious future king of Israel who was to inaugurate the reign of God over the whole world (Mark 11:9–10; John 12:12–16; 1:41; Acts 1:6). As reflected in the Gospels, this growing faith was essentially a religious conviction, derived from the impression of Jesus' teaching, character, and "mighty works" of healing and exorcism, and the authority (Matthew 7:29) with which he spoke and acted as God's agent and representative. His works of healing and exorcism were proofs, not of personal prerogatives so much as of the approach of the divine reign or "the kingdom of God" (Matthew 12:28), although the implication that Jesus is "more than a prophet" is also clear (as in Matthew 11:2–6, where Jesus does not define his own title explicitly—he is simply "the coming one").

In lieu of signs and wonders, which men desired to see as evidences of supernatural authority, Jesus himself was the "sign" to his generation (Mark 8:11–12; Luke 11:29–32). The heart of Jesus' message was the proclamation of the near arrival of the kingdom of God; his mission consisted in preparing men to enter it, in "binding the strong man," and in rolling back the powers of darkness. It was all but inevitable that his disciples should look upon Jesus as the destined Messiah (Mark 8:27–30).

At the same time the Gospels bear witness to the early use of another term, "The Son of Man," which had even more exalted supernatural connotations (Mark 13:26). In the Jewish Bible, the term "son of man" meant simply "human being" (Ezekiel 3:10; Psalms 8:4); but the title "The Son of Man" (derived from Daniel 7:13) had come to mean, in some areas, as in the apocalyptic First Book of Enoch (46:3–6), the heavenly being who was with God when He created the world and who will come on the clouds of heaven to judge the world on the Last Day (Matthew 25:31–33)—a figure reminiscent of Zoroastrian speculation. In the Gospels (for example, Mark 8:38; 14:62) this title is implicitly claimed by Jesus, although the references to his impending rejection, sufferings, death, and resurrection (as in Mark 8:31; 9:31; 10:32 ff.) only hint at the identification, and may be later insertions into the tradition. They stress the tremendous paradox of the cross: the divine, heavenly Son of Man must die. Whether or not the disciples already looked upon Jesus as the Son of Man, in addition to viewing him as the Messiah, is uncertain, as is also the precise sense in which Jesus used the term. But after the Resurrection there was no hesitation in ascribing to him the more transcendent title, with its connotations of exaltation, divine rank, and future coming (*parousia*) to hold the final judgment.

In the earliest stage of Christian doctrinal development, in the early Christian-Jewish communities in Palestine, this concept was normative. The ancient Aramaic invocation that survives in I Corinthians 16:22 attests this early Christology: *Marana tha,* meaning "Our Lord, come!" (cf. Revelation 22:20; Didache 10:6.) The title is not so much theological as religious, and reflects the faith of the early Christians in Jesus as a divine, supernatural being, upon whom all their hopes of salvation, both here and hereafter, depend. This faith requires expression, and the only adequate term available to the early Palestinian Christian-Jews, who were monotheists, and whose Bible was the Old Testament, was this transcendental one found in contemporary apocalyptic writings.

It was when the church spread beyond the borders of Jewish territory, to the east and west outside Palestine and also outside the settlements in the Jewish Diaspora, especially in the west, that other terms or titles became necessary. "Son of Man" was not understood by Greek-speaking Gentiles. To them it seemed to mean "the son of the man" or "son of a man," since they were unfamiliar both with Semitic idiom and with the Jewish apocalypses. Even the term "Messiah" was meaningless; it meant, literally, "anointed with oil" (*chrism*), and was either merely transliterated into Greek or, if translated, was understood either as a proper name or as a bizarre Oriental title, *Christos,* often confused with the Greek word *chrēstos* (gentle).

In the letters of Paul and also in Hebrews, "Christ" is used almost exclusively as a proper noun, part of the name "Jesus Christ," and no longer as a title, although its divine connotations are retained. Paul never uses the title "Son of Man," "Messias" (the Greek transliteration of Messiah), or "King of Israel," nor does he use the title "Rabbi" for Jesus. The great Christological passage in Philippians 2:5–11 might suggest the title "Son of Man," but instead the title used is "Lord." (I Corinthians 15:47 is sometimes cited as an example; but here no title appears, and the passage is an exposition of Genesis 2:7.)

It was inevitable that the Greek-speaking Gentile churches should use Greek religious terms and titles, and they chose those that were richest in meaning. "Son of God," which was not a common Messianic title among the Jews in spite of Psalms 2:7, was perhaps the earliest to be adopted. "Saviour" (*Sōtēr*), another such title, had the advantage of being equally applicable to a divine or to a human being, and therefore to one who was both. Commonest of all, in the early Gentile churches, was "Lord" (*Kyrios*), which meant, in religious circles, the head of a cult, a divine being who was worshiped by a group, such as a city, a nation, or, later, a church. It was also known to Greek-speaking Jews and Christians as the translation of the Hebrew name for God (*YHWH*) in the Septuagint. The earliest Gentile creed was probably simply "Jesus is Lord" (I Corinthians 12:3) or possibly *Kyrios Christos* ("Christ is Lord"). The consequence of the adoption of this title, which could not have been adopted in Palestine, was that many passages in the Old Testament referring to God were interpreted as referring to Christ. Finally, in circles where Gnostic or theosophical speculation was growing, the term "Logos" (Word, Thought, Reason, Purpose, or Utterance of God) was adopted (John 1:1–14; in Colossians 1:15–20 the idea is present, but not the term).

The term "Logos" was originally derived from philosophical speculation, and was widely popularized by Stoic teaching; however, its use in the 1st century was not limited to the philosophers. The idea of a divine Logos was found in many different cults and sects, as an expression of the principle of mediation between God and the world, not only in creation but also in the maintenance of the universe (Colossians 1:17).

Other titles were used in the Gentile churches, some of them derived from the Old Testament, as Mediator, Sacrifice, Lamb of God, Passover, High Priest, Prince, Captain, Child of God, Servant of God. Others came from the noblest religious teaching and aspiration in the Gentile world, as Invincible Sun, Splendor of God, Life, Light, Water of Life, Living Bread, Master, King, and King of Kings.

The variety in the titles applied to Christ by the early church is surprising. They match, and even exceed, those ascribed to the other deities in the ancient world. The church was entering upon its whole inheritance, not only from Judaism and the Old Testament, but also from the age-old religious devotion and aspiration of the entire civilized world. It used to be maintained that the church abandoned the purity of its pristine faith, as it spread through the Greco-Roman world; that it accommodated itself to Greek, Roman, Egyptian, and Syrian mythology, and let its message be silenced or neutralized by philosophical speculation, until centuries of controversy completely stifled the original gospel of Jesus.

But modern scholarship recognizes that these controversies were inevitable. The variety in the conceptions of Christ set forth even in the New Testament, the philosophical or scientific problems which they set (chiefly the profoundest problem of all: How can one person be both God and man?), the necessary reinterpretation of the Old Testament from the standpoint of the Christian view of Christ (especially as "Lord"), the requirement of a whole new set of terms for expressing the Christian dogma (or of old terms, such as "nature," "person," "substance," "will," with new meanings) — all these were problems which no Greek or Hellenist of the 2d to 5th century could leave unsolved.

Moreover, modern research in social psychology and the history of religions has shown that the symbols used by the early church (especially those of Messianic King, Divine Teacher, Perfect Man, Saviour, Redeemer, Revealer, Lord, Final Judge, Son of Man, Logos, and High Priest) have deep and permanent significance for the total life of mankind. They belong to the primeval structure of human thinking; what the church did was to provide for these basic needs a supernatural satisfaction.

Christological Controversies. The Christology of the 2d century was partly adoptionist; that is, Christ became God by virtue of His noble character, pure teaching, and martyr death. This view simply applies the popular euhemerist explanation of the pagan gods as deified men, who had been founders of cities, inventors of arts, benefactors of mankind, or heroes. It was also partly monarchian, viewing God as a single Person, a unitary mind or will, who nevertheless manifested himself in different modes (hence modalism), such as the Father, Son, Spirit, Saviour, or Lord. This view reflects the influence of another type of pagan thought, syncretism, in which Zeus, Jupiter, Jove, Amon, and Baal were merely different names for the one true God, who was known to different nations under these different names. But as against both adoptionism and modalism (modalistic monarchianism), the church insisted on the true deity of Christ and his distinction in person from the Father. Neither monarchianism nor Gnosticism (also rife in the 2d century) contributed, except negatively, to the development of Christology.

The long period of Christological controversy opening in the 4th century was inaugurated by the attempt of Arius to define Christ as the "first of creatures," meaning a created and not an eternal being. Arius took his start from Paul's phrase "the first-born of all creation" (Colossians 1:15), from which his inference followed that "there was a time when the Son was not." This view provoked widespread controversy, the orthodox doctrine being defended almost singlehandedly by Athanasius of Alexandria (*Athanasius contra mundum*). The Arian doctrine was branded as heretical and rejected at the Council of Nicaea in 325. See also ARIANISM.

Once the relation of the Son (Christ) to the Father was defined—the Son being viewed as eternal, begotten before all creation, and distinct in person from God the Father though one with Him in substance, nature, and will—it became necessary to define the relation between the divine nature and the human in the Incarnation of the Son. Although the controversies were complicated by political motives and by the rivalries of different schools and patriarchs, the main alternative answers were theological. Some held it impossible to think of the divine and human natures of Christ as distinct: God could not be a child, or have a mother, or grow in grace. Therefore, Christ's divine nature must have swallowed up the human, as a drop of water is merged in the ocean. Alternatively, the divine nature must either embrace or supplement the human, with a resulting unity and homogeneity, or form a single new nature combining both.

But the church as a whole, clinging firmly to Scripture and tradition, refused to accept any of these alternatives and thus to sacrifice the historical reality of Jesus' true human nature and the distinction of his human personality from God, and from all human beings.

The resulting definition of the nature of Christ (strongly influenced by the dogmatic letter which Pope Leo I sent to Flavian of Constantinople in 449, just before the Council of Chalcedon in 451) was highly metaphysical and difficult to conceive—like many of the formulas in mathematics and physics. However, the definition safeguarded (1) the cardinal and essential monotheism of the Christian faith; (2) the truth of divine revelation; (3) the historical reality of Jesus' human nature, character, life, and teaching; and (4) the distinction between the divine Persons in the Blessed Trinity. The solution was not a compromise but a safeguard of the essential truths of the Christian faith. Although strictly unimaginable and indescribable, the distinction between the divine Persons and the union of the two natures in Christ were principles which (granted the meaning of the language used in that long era of controversy) simply could not be abandoned if Christianity was to continue to be what it had been from the beginning: faith in God as revealed in Christ.

There were later developments in Christology. Monothelitism found the unity of Father and Son in the unity (identity) of two wills. Unitarianism has held that Christ is entirely human, though possessing divine qualities of character, leadership, and heroism. In such modern theories as Ritschlianism, Christ has the "value" of God. In the view of William Sanday, Christ's relation to the Father existed in his "subconscious." Other views range from the concept of Christ as one *avatar* in a long series of divine manifestations to the projection of a "Christ Idea," the "Christ myth" theory of the early 1900's. None of these later views, however, is characteristic of the main stream of historical Christian theology. Nor are the various philosophical interpretations set forth in modern times, beginning with Hegel, any more satisfactory. The presuppositions of present-day thought are too remote from those of the Bible and of the early church fathers and theologians to provide a satisfactory equivalent to the ancient doctrines. Ancient Christology presupposed ancient philosophy, not modern.

See also BIBLE—15. *Religion and Theology of the New Testament;* CHRISTIANITY; INCARNATION; JESUS CHRIST.

FREDERICK C. GRANT
Union Theological Seminary, New York

Bibliography

Bultmann, Rudolf K., *The Theology of the New Testament,* 2 vols. (New York 1954).
Dibelius, Martin, *Gospel Criticism and Christology* (London 1935).
Fuller, Reginald H., *The Foundations of New Testament Christology* (New York 1965).
Harnack, Adolf von, *History of Dogma,* 7 vols. (New York 1958).
Knox, John, *The Humanity and Divinity of Christ* (New York 1967).
Mackintosh, Hugh R., *Doctrine of the Person of Jesus Christ* (New York 1912).
Neve, Juergen L., *History of Christian Thought,* 2 vols. (Philadelphia 1946).

CHRISTOPHE, krēs-tôf', **Henri** (1767–1820), Haitian king, who was a leader in the struggle for independence against France. A liberated slave, born in Grenada, in the British West Indies, on Oct. 6, 1767, he joined the antislavery rebellion in Haiti at its outset in 1791 and became an intrepid fighter for independence. His valor attracted the attention of the leader of the struggle, Toussaint L'Ouverture, who made him one of his commanders.

After the French captured Toussaint in 1802, Christophe served as a general under Jean Jacques Dessalines. In 1806 he participated in the conspiracy against his leader and gained control over the northern portion of the country. Thereafter he engaged in an inconclusive conflict with Alexandre Pétion, who controlled the southern region. Although in possession of only part of the country, Christophe proclaimed himself Henri I, King of Haiti, in 1811. He ruled until Oct. 8, 1820, when, during a period of revolt and while suffering from partial paralysis, he committed suicide, allegedly using a silver bullet.

An archdisciplinarian, Christophe required all able-bodied men to work in the fields, thereby reviving the coffee and sugar economy and adding considerable wealth to his treasury. An admirer of the court of Louis XIV, he instituted elaborate protocol and noble titles. To satisfy his love of the grandiose he had constructed the citadel at La Ferrière and his palace of Sans Souci at Cap-Haïtien, the capital. Although uneducated, he surrounded himself with scholars from abroad. He built schools, encouraged the theater, established newspapers, and proclaimed a body of laws, the *Code Henri.*

LAURENCE R. BIRNS
The New School for Social Research. NewYork

Further Reading: Adams, Russell L., *Great Negroes, Past and Present,* 3d ed. (Afro Amer. Pub. Co. 1969); Cole, Hubert, *Christophe, King of Haiti* (Viking 1967).

CHRISTOPHER, kris'tə-fər, **Saint,** Christian martyr and patron of travelers. Extraordinary legends have developed about him to an extent scarcely equaled in hagiographic literature, but nothing is known with any certainty about him. He was reputedly martyred somewhere in the East. By the 5th century, he was venerated.

In the East he was pictured as a converted pagan warrior, originally called Reprobus, who preferred death by cruel torture to apostasy. Western medieval legend, playing probably upon the name Christopher, meaning "Christ-bearer," described him as a giant who, after conversion, stationed himself at a riverbank to perform charitable works by carrying travelers across the stream on his shoulders. One of his passengers, a child whose weight became heavier with each step until it seemed equal to that of the whole world, proved to be Christ Himself.

July 25 became his feast day in the West; the Eastern churches celebrate it on other days. Because of doubts about his existence, his feast was dropped from the universal liturgical calendar of the Roman Catholic Church in 1969.

CHRISTOPHER, kris'tə-fər, antipope in 903–904. A Roman cardinal priest of St. Damasus, he led a revolt against Pope Leo V, whom he imprisoned. Christopher had himself installed as pope but was in turn deposed and imprisoned by Sergius, who had returned to Rome after being excommunicated and exiled by Pope John IX. One source states that Sergius put Christopher to death. He is buried in St. Peter's.

JOSEPH S. BRUSHER, S. J.
University of Santa Clara, Calif.

CHRISTUS, kris'təs, **Petrus** (1410?–1472 or 1473), Flemish painter, who was a leading artist of the early Netherlandish school. Influenced by Jan van Eyck and Rogier van der Weyden, he treated religious subjects in a smoother, more realistic manner than did painters of the earlier Gothic school. By intuition and experiment he completed the development toward realistic perspective that was one of the great achievements of 15th century art.

Christus was born in Baerle, Flanders, about 1410. In 1444 he settled in Bruges, where he may have worked in the studio of Van Eyck. Only a few works known to be by Christus survive. They suggest Van Eyck, although they are not so highly polished. Among them are the moving *Lamentations* (Musée Royaux des Beaux-Arts, Brussels) and fine portraits, such as that of a Carthusian monk (Metropolitan Museum of Art, New York City). Others include the *Madonna with Saints Francis and Jerome* (Städelsches Kunstinstitut, Frankfurt) and the *Exeter Madonna* (Staatliche Museen, Berlin). Christus died in Bruges in 1472 or 1473.

WAYNE DYNES, *Vassar College*

CHRISTY, kris'tē, **Howard Chandler** (1873–1952), American painter and illustrator. He was born in Morgan county, Ohio, on Jan. 10, 1873. After attending school at Duncan Falls, Ohio, he went to New York in 1893 to study art under William

FREDERIC LEWIS

Drawing of a "Christy Girl" by Howard Chandler Christy.

M. Chase. He soon decided to be an illustrator. He went to Cuba during the Spanish-American War (1898) and drew pictures of Theodore Roosevelt's "Rough Riders" in action. His illustrations appeared in *Harper's* and *Scribner's* magazines and in *Collier's Weekly*. His reputation grew with his *Men of the Army and Navy* series and his illustrations of the books of James Whitcomb Riley and Richard Harding Davis.

Christy is best known for his creation of a feminine type, the "Christy Girl," used in his magazine illustrations. After 1920 he concentrated on painting portraits of prominent contemporaries. He also painted *Signing the Constitution*, in the Capitol at Washington. He died in New York City on March 3, 1952.

CHRISTY MINSTRELS, kris'tē, one of the most successful troupes in the history of the minstrel show; for it, Stephen Foster wrote some of his greatest ballads, including *Swanee River*. The company was organized in 1842 in Buffalo, N. Y., by Edwin P. Christy (1815–1862) and was first called the Virginia Minstrels. It made its New York City debut on April 27, 1846, and was an immediate success.

Christy established the minstrel show format: the circle of "blackface" performers surrounding the white interlocutor (Christy himself), with "end men" serving as butts for the jokes. The three sections of the show were the "olio," or variety show; the free fantasia, in which individual performers did routines; and the burlesque, in which earlier routines were satirized. Later minstrel shows adhered to this pattern.

DAVID EWEN, *Author of "The Story of America's Musical Theater"*

CHROMATE. See CHROMIUM.

CHROMATIC ABERRATION. See ABERRATION, OPTICAL.

CHROMATICISM, krō-mat'ə-siz-əm, in musical composition, is the use of pitches extraneous to the diatonic scale. In 20th century usage, chromaticism also means the system of harmony in which all 12 semitones of the scale have equal importance.

In the West, chromaticism (from Greek *chrōma*, "color") first occurred in Greek music, probably as a result of the influence of Oriental music. In the Middle Ages the use of accidentals (chromatic notes) in Gregorian plainsong was formalized as *musica ficta* or "false music." *Musica ficta* was viewed at first as a corruption of musical purity, but it came into common use in the 14th century, marking the end of strictly modal plainsong.

The rise of the madrigal, a polyphonic vocal setting of romantic poetry, increased the use of chromatic figures, which lent themselves to certain dramatic effects. The first composer to use chromaticism extensively was Adrian Willaert; its harmonic uses were extended by Gesualdo and Monteverdi in their madrigals.

In the 18th century equal-temperament tuning replaced mean-temperament tuning, introducing a scale consisting of 12 equal semitones within the octave. Thus E-flat and D-sharp, for example, were sounded as the same pitch, but they continued to be notes capable of performing two different harmonic functions. See HARMONY—TONALITY.

Chromaticism became increasingly popular in the 18th century. It was used in fugues and in dramatic music (oratorios, cantatas, and operas), in which chromatic figures were often employed to express grief or lamentation. Also, the harmonic ambiguity of chromatically altered tones made them useful as pivot notes for modulations between keys, as in the *Marche Funèbre* in Beethoven's Piano Sonata No. 26. During the 19th century the diatonic framework progressively weakened. César Franck experimented freely with chromatic techniques, and harmonies in Wagner's operas are often quite free of tonal centers. By 1900, Debussy's ambiguous chords had fathered the French impressionistic school, with its marked chromaticism.

The serial techniques of Arnold Schoenberg introduced pure chromaticism, in which no tone serves as a tonic center. However, the music of some later composers, including Bartók and Hindemith, alternated chromaticism with diatonic or modal harmonies, and that of others, among them Stravinsky and Poulenc, exemplified a reaction against excessive 12-tone chromaticism.

HELEN N. MORGAN
North Shore Branch, New England Conservatory

CHROMATIN. See CELL; CHROMOSOME.

CHROMATOGRAPHY, krō-mə-tog′rə-fē, is a method of separating chemical substances that depends on their partition between two media. One medium, or *phase,* is stationary, and the other is moving; the first may be a solid or liquid, and the second may be a liquid or gas. The substances to be separated move with the moving phase, and the greater the proportion in the moving phase, the faster they move. Different substances move at different rates and eventually become separated from one another.

The word "chromatography" comes from the Greek and means "color writing." The technique was first described by the Russian botanist Mikhail Tswett in 1903. He dissolved the pigments of green leaves in a mixture of petroleum ether and alcohol, poured some of the resulting deep green solution onto powdered chalk (the stationary phase) packed in a vertical glass tube, let it soak in, and then added more solvent (the moving phase). The colored constituents of the leaves were washed down the tube. The carotins, which are weakly adsorbed by the chalk, moved ahead, while the chlorophylls, which are strongly adsorbed, moved more slowly. Soon the tube showed bands of color—orange, green, and yellow —separated by white areas of clean chalk.

The same principle serves to separate colorless substances. It is not necessary to see bands on the column; more often fractions of the solution flowing from the tube are collected and the concentration pulses examined as each constituent emerges. Moreover, the adsorbent need not be packed into a tube; it can be spread on a sheet of glass or held between the fibers of a piece of paper. Several different chromatographic techniques have been developed, and the method used depends on the type and quantity of the substances to be separated.

LIQUID COLUMN CHROMATOGRAPHY

Adsorption. In adsorption chromatography, which was developed by Tswett, the solid packed into the tube, or column, has a large surface area. The substances to be separated are adsorbed on this surface and desorbed again as fresh solvent passes. Separations depend on the balance of affinity between the solvent and solid adsorbent. Some common adsorbents include aluminum oxide, silica gel, carbon, and powdered sugar. The solvents range from polar liquids, such as alcohols, to nonpolar liquids, such as hexane. Chromatography on aluminum oxide will separate aromatic from aliphatic hydrocarbons.

Partition. In partition chromatography the stationary phase is a film of liquid that coats the particles of a solid support. The liquid is usually water. The moving phase is a liquid that is insoluble in water. However, it is possible to use a support such as a Teflon polymer that is preferentially wetted by the organic liquid. Partition chromatography in columns has only limited use; partition chromatography on paper (paper chromatography), which is very widely used, is described later in this article.

Ion Exchange. In ion-exchange chromatography the stationary phase is a material of high molecular weight with a molecular structure resembling honeycomb or fish net. The net includes negative or positive electrically charged atomic groupings called ions. A hydrogen ion may be replaced by a sodium ion, or two hydrogen ions by one doubly charged ion such as zinc. This process is called ion exchange.

The materials used in ion exchange show preferences for one kind of ion over another. The ion-exchange resins in common use hold potassium ions more firmly than sodium. If a small amount of solution containing sodium and potassium salts is poured on a column of resin and then dilute hydrochloric acid is passed, the hydrogen ions of the acid displace the sodium and potassium ions, which then travel down the column. The sodium ions travel faster and emerge as sodium chloride before the potassium chloride.

Complexing Agents. The selectivity of ion-exchange resins toward metals can be enhanced by the addition of a complexing agent to the solution that flows down the column. The complexing agent combines with positively charged metal ions to form complex negative ions. Negative ions are repelled by cation-exchange resins (which have fixed negative charges) and attracted by anion-exchange resins (with positive charges).

One of the best ways to separate metallic elements is to dissolve them in hydrochloric acid, which acts as a complexing agent, and pour

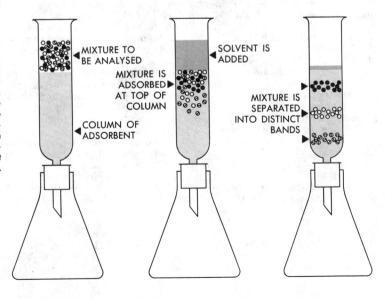

ADSORPTION CHROMATOGRAPHY

A solution containing several compounds is poured into a column of adsorbent material, and a solvent is then added to it. The solvent carries the compounds from the solution down the column at varying rates. The compounds become separated from each other as a result of their different degrees of adherence to the adsorbent and varying solubility in the solvent.

◄ MIXTURE TO BE ANALYSED

◄ SOLVENT IS ADDED

MIXTURE IS ADSORBED ► AT TOP OF COLUMN

► COLUMN OF ADSORBENT

MIXTURE IS ► SEPARATED INTO DISTINCT ► BANDS

the solution into an anion-exchange resin column. Many metals form negatively charged chloro-complexes and are retained by the resin, but the complexes differ enormously in stability and in their attraction to the resin. By first passing concentrated hydrochloric acid (which stabilizes the complexes) and then successively weaker solutions, the metal salts are washed out of the column one by one, and a great number of separations can be made.

Inorganic Ion-Exchange Materials. The newer inorganic exchangers, such as zirconium phosphate, offer better selectivity than resins for certain ions; they can be used to separate cesium from rubidium, which is an important process in atomic energy. Other specialized exchangers have been developed, such as the modified cellulose used to separate large ions. Though most applications of ion-exchange chromatography are in inorganic chemistry, cation-exchange resin columns are used routinely in medical laboratories to analyze mixtures of amino acids from proteins.

GAS-LIQUID CHROMATOGRAPHY

Gas-liquid chromatography is currently the most commonly used and most important type of chromatography. It is used to separate volatile compounds of all kinds, and it is especially valuable in the petroleum industry. Gas chromatography has revolutionized the organic-chemical industry by making it possible to check ongoing reactions by rapid analysis of the constituents. Also, it has provided an entirely new view of the complexity of natural products; for example, the essence of fresh coffee can be resolved into more than 300 chemical constituents.

The columns for gas chromatography are generally metal tubes about 0.2 inch (0.5. cm) long. The tubes are folded to save space and are mounted in a chamber that can be heated. They are packed with ground firebrick or diatomaceous earth that has been thinly coated with a layer of a liquid of high boiling point, such as squalene or a silicone. This liquid film is the stationary phase. The moving phase is a gas, usually helium but occasionally hydrogen or nitrogen. This is called the *carrier gas*. Samples are added to the gas just before it enters the column. Liquid samples are injected by a hypodermic syringe through a rubber septum; they strike a heating element and vaporize immediately. On entering the column the molecules of the sample travel back and forth between the gas and liquid phases. The more soluble they are in the liquid, the more slowly they travel. Different substances travel at different rates and leave the column at different times, each producing a concentration pulse which is detected and recorded on moving graph paper. The number of peaks appearing on the graph shows the number of constituents present; the position of the peaks (compared with known compounds) shows what they are; and the height of the peaks shows the quantity of each substance. Sometimes the fractions are passed into a mass spectrometer for further examination.

The detection device that reveals the presence of something other than pure carrier gas in the gas leaving the column is usually an electrically heated wire mounted in a small cylinder. The better the gas conducts heat, the cooler the wire. Hydrogen is the best heat-conducting gas and helium (which is preferred as a carrier because it is nonflammable) is nearly as good. If any other gas is added, the conductivity drops and the temperature of the wire rises. This changes its electrical resistance and sends a signal to the recorder.

Another very sensitive device used to detect the presence of a gas other than the carrier gas is the *hydrogen flame ionization detector*. This will easily measure 0.01 microgram (one one-hundred millionth of a gram or 3.5 ten billionths of an ounce) of an organic compound. It is used with the recently developed open capillary columns, some of which are 1,000 feet (300 meters) long and have very high resolving power.

Commercial gas chromatographs come equipped with interchangeable columns made with different kinds of liquid coatings. If the test substances cannot be separated on one type of column, they may be tried on another. Temperature is another factor which can be controlled to achieve the desired separations.

Gas chromatography has two great advantages over liquid chromatography—speed and resolution. Molecules diffuse much faster in gases than in liquids, giving sharper bands and permitting faster flow rates. On the other hand, gas chromatography is not well adapted for the analysis of aqueous solutions. Nonvolatile samples cannot be run directly but must first be converted to volatile derivatives. For example, amino acids may be converted to their N-trifluoroacetyl methyl esters.

PAPER CHROMATOGRAPHY

The technique of paper chromatography was developed in the 1940's by the British chemists Archer John Porter Martin and Richard Laurence Millington Synge, who shared the 1952 Nobel prize in chemistry for their discovery. In paper chromatography, the stationary phase is a piece of absorbent paper. The sample is placed as a spot near one end of a paper strip, and this end is dipped into the liquid that will be the moving phase. The liquid rises by capillary action and takes the constituents of the sample along with it. The substances move at different rates, depending on their partition between the fixed and moving phases. When the liquid is close to the top, the paper is removed and dried. The different constituents are made visible by spraying the paper with a reagent that forms colored compounds with them; amino acids are sprayed with ninhydrin, giving red, purple, or yellow spots. The position of the spot indicates the kind of amino acid present and the size gives an approximate measure of the amount.

If the paper is very dry the process will not work. It is the invisible film of water absorbed from moist air that is the actual stationary phase; the cellulose fibers of the paper act as support. Paper chromatography is actually a kind of partition chromatography.

If one solvent does not separate a pair of substances, another will. In two-dimensional paper chromatography a square piece of paper is used and the sample placed near one corner. First the paper is dipped in one solvent, making the constituents run along one edge of the square. Then it is dried, turned at right angles, and dipped in the second solvent. The constituents end up as spots all across the paper and may be identified by comparison with known substances. The technique of autoradiography is used to locate spots tagged with radioactive isotopes.

With paper chromatography only minute quantities of the test substances are needed, which makes it a useful technique for biochemical analysis. Another application is in geochemical prospecting, where traces of metals are sought in soils and streams.

THIN-LAYER CHROMATOGRAPHY

In this relatively new technique, a solid adsorbent is mixed with plaster of paris or starch (which acts as a binder), ground very fine, spread on a glass or plastic plate, and dried. The sample is spotted on the plate, and thereafter the technique is very similar to paper chromatography. However, it is faster and gives sharper spots and is therefore replacing paper chromatography in many laboratories.

DISPLACEMENT CHROMATOGRAPHY

In the analytical procedures described above a small sample sufficient to load a small fraction of the column is applied. It is moved by passing a solvent that is more weakly adsorbed than the sample down the column. This procedure is called *elution chromatography*. For separating large quantities of the material, displacement chromatography is better. A sample large enough to saturate over half the column is used, and then a displacing solution is passed that is more strongly adsorbed than the sample. This drives the most weakly held constituents ahead, followed by the others in order of their adsorption strength. They leave the column one after the other in pure form, except for narrow zones of mixing. Displacement chromatography on cation-exchange resin columns is used to separate the rare earth elements, some of them in tonnage quantities.

HAROLD F. WALTON, *University of Colorado*

CHROMATOPHORE, krō-mat'ə-fôr, a star-shaped, pigment-containing cell present in all vertebrate animals. Chromatophores are found chiefly in the deep layers of the skin, the mucous membranes, and the choroid layer of the eye. In contrast to melanocytes, which are found in epithelial tissue and produce their own pigment, chromatophores are located in connective tissue and appear to obtain their pigment granules from surrounding tissues.

Although chromatophores are present in mammals, including man, they are most abundant in reptiles, fishes, and amphibians, which they help protect by enabling them to lighten or darken the color of their skin. Although the size of the chromatophores does not change, the distribution of the pigment granules in them can be altered. The granules may be dispersed evenly throughout the cells, giving the animal a darker appearance, or they may be concentrated in the center of the cells, making the animal appear lighter. Among the factors controlling granule distribution are two hormones, adrenaline and intermedin, the latter secreted by the pars intermedia (middle portion) of the pituitary gland. Experiments with mammalian intermedia have shown it to have an effect on fish and amphibian chromatophores. However, its effects on mammalian chromatophores are not known.

JEFFREY WENIG, *ENDO Laboratories*

CHROME PIGMENTS, krōm, a group of pigments containing chromium. They include chrome greens, chrome oxide green, chrome red, chrome yellows, molybdate orange, and zinc yellow.

Chrome greens are widely used in paints and enamels. The pigments are produced by mixing chrome yellow and iron blue; a wide variety of green hues is produced by varying the proportions of the component colors. Chrome greens are sensitive to alkali, but they are not sensitive to light and have good opacity.

Chrome oxide green is an almost indestructible pigment made of chromic oxide. It is produced by burning sodium dichromate with a reducing agent. Chrome oxide green is very resistant to the action of both acids and alkalis.

Chrome red (chromate red, Chinese red, chrome orange, American vermilion) is a paint pigment composed of basic lead chromate ($PbCrO_4 \cdot PbO$). The color of chrome red varies from red to orange. The pigment is resistant to light, but it is darkened by exposure to sulfur or hydrogen sulfide. Chrome red is used wherever an orange pigment is needed. It is also used in the manufacture of rust-inhibitive paints.

Chrome yellows (permanent yellow) are used in paints and enamels. They are made of lead chromate ($PbCrO_4$). Chrome yellows range in color from a bright medium yellow to a light greenish yellow, but they darken on exposure to light and turn black in the presence of sulfides. Because they are sensitive to alkali, they cannot be used on alkaline surfaces, such as cement.

Molybdate orange (molybdenum orange, molybdate chrome orange) is a chrome-containing pigment used in paints, plastics, and printing inks. It is a fine powder of dark orange or light red and is a solid solution of lead chromate, lead molybdate, and lead sulfate.

Zinc yellow (zinc chrome, zinc potassium chromate, citron yellow, buttercup yellow) is a greenish yellow chrome-containing pigment used in the manufacture of rust-inhibitive paints.

CHROMIC ACID, krō'mik, is the common name for the oxide of chromium in the $+6$ oxidation state. It is also known as *chromium trioxide* or *chromic acid anhydride*. True chromic acid, H_2CrO_4, exists only in aqueous solutions of chromium trioxide. However, it is an unstable compound and reacts spontaneously to form dichromic acid, $H_2Cr_2O_7$.

Chromic acid (CrO_3) is a reddish purple crystalline solid with a specific gravity of 2.67 to 2.82. It melts at 197° C (386.6° F) and then slowly decomposes while molten. It is very deliquescent and highly soluble in water and organic solvents such as acetic acid, pyridine, and ether. Crude chromic acid precipitates out from a mixture of concentrated sulfuric acid and concentrated sodium dichromate, $Na_2Cr_2O_7$. The product is purified by recrystallization and then melting. Chromic acid is a strong acid and a powerful oxidizing agent. It is highly destructive to animal and plant tissues. If brought into contact with reducing agents or organic substances, a serious explosion may result.

Chromic acid is used in the chemical industry in the manufacture of chromates, which are salts of chromic acid, or as an oxidizing agent or catalyst. Most of the chromic acid produced is used in chromium plating. It is also used in medicine as a caustic agent, in process engraving, in ceramic glazes and colored glass, in metal cleaning, in the manufacture of inks and paints, and as a pigment in rubber.

HERBERT LIEBESKIND
The Cooper Union, New York

CHROMITE, krō′mīt, is the only important ore of chromium, although this element appears in many other minerals. Chromite is essentially an oxide of iron, magnesium, chromium, and aluminum, and is a member of the *spinel* group of minerals. It is observed in compact masses or as grains disseminated in rock, but rarely as distinct crystals. The mineral is black and has a metallic to submetallic luster.

Occurrence. Chromite occurs in peridotite, a rock composed primarily of the silicate minerals pyroxine and olivine, or in serpentine formed by alteration of peridotite. It may also occur in the peridotite parts of layered intrusive rocks. The chromite deposits in peridotite and serpentine are usually irregular or lenticular masses that range in size from a few pounds to one in the Philippine Islands that originally contained 10 million tons. Chromite bodies in the peridotitic parts of layered igneous rock complexes are usually larger and more continuous, hence easier to locate and mine. The most important ore sites are in the USSR, the Republic of South Africa, Southern Rhodesia, Turkey, the Philippine Islands, and Cuba. There are no major deposits of chromite ore in the United States.

Uses. Chromite has three main fields of use: it is used in metallurgy, in the manufacture of refractories, and in the production of chromium chemicals.

The major metallurgical application is the conversion of chromite to alloys of iron and chromium. These alloys then serve as additives in making stainless, high-speed, and other special-use steels, and high-temperature and other special alloys. (A relatively small amount of chromite ore is used to add directly to stainless steel melts.) The addition of chromium to iron alloys enhances their resistance to corrosion, oxidation, wear, and impact. Another important, although small, metallurgical use of chromite is in the production of chromium alloys with nickel. These "nichrome" alloys have high electrical resistance and high resistance to corrosion. Alloys with cobalt are used in the manufacture of cutting tools, as a hard facing to prevent abrasive wear and corrosion, and in high-temperature applications. Other special-purpose chromium alloys are made in combination with elements such as aluminum, copper, and titanium.

An important use of chromite is in the manufacture of refractories, largely in the form of chromite brick. Raw chromite ore is used directly for this purpose. The ore is ground, mixed with a binder, and pressed into bricks under a pressure of 10,000 to 15,000 psi (about 700–1,000 kg per sq cm). Chromite refractories, being chemically neutral, are used in lining parts of furnaces for steelmaking, nonferrous-metals refining, glassmaking, and cement manufacture. A major use is along the slag line of basic open-hearth steel furnaces.

The production of chromium chemicals—principally sodium bichromate—is still another important use of chromite, although the quantity of ore consumed for this purpose is relatively small. The major industrial applications of chromium chemicals are in the manufacture of pigments, leather tanning, textiles, and electroplating. See also CHROMIUM.

Composition, (Fe,Mg) (Cr,Al,Fe)$_2$O$_4$; hardness, 5.5; specific gravity, 4.6; crystal system, isometric.

GEORGE SWITZER
Smithsonian Institution

CHROMIUM, krō′mē-əm, symbol Cr, is a metallic element. The French chemist Louis Nicolas Vauquelin isolated it from lead chromate in 1797. The name of the element is derived from the Greek word *chrōma,* meaning "color," because many of the compounds of chromium are very highly colored.

Properties. Chromium is a hard, blue-white metal with a brilliant luster. Its melting point is 1550°C (2822°F), and its boiling point is 2482°C (4500°F). Chromium is a transitional element located in column VIB of the periodic table. Its atomic number is 24, and its atomic weight is 51.996. There are four naturally occurring isotopes of the element—^{50}Cr, ^{52}Cr, ^{53}Cr, and ^{54}Cr. The most abundant isotope is ^{52}Cr.

In the ground state the electronic configuration of the chromium atom is 1s^2, 2s^{2}2p^6, 3s^{2}3p^6, ^{3}d^{5}4s^1. Because all the electrons from the 3d and 4s levels can take part in chemical reactions, the oxidation state of chromium varies from 0 to +6. However, the most common oxidation numbers are +2, +3, and +6.

Ordinarily chromium dissolves in dilute hydrochloric and sulfuric acids. However, if it is first treated with concentrated nitric acid, hydrogen peroxide, or a strong oxidizing agent, it becomes insoluble in dilute acids. This state, in which the metal is said to be passive, is the result of a firmly held oxide coating on its surface that renders it chemically inactive. The passive condition is only temporary and disappears when the metal is heated, subjected to mechanical strain, or brought in contact with active metals. Chromium exhibits greater passivity than any other metal. Because of this tenacious oxide coating, it oxidizes and corrodes more slowly than iron.

Occurrence. Approximately 0.037% of the igneous rock in the earth's crust is chromium. Because chromium is such an active element, it is not found in the free state in nature. The most important commercial source of chromium is the mineral chromite, or ferrous chromite, which contains iron in the divalent state and chromium in the trivalent state. The chemical formula of the ore can be represented either as FeO·Cr$_2$O$_3$, FeCr$_2$O$_4$, or Fe(CrO$_2$)$_2$, but in each case there is about 68% Cr$_2$O$_3$ and 32% FeO. Virtually all high-grade chromite ore is from the Transvaal, in South Africa; low-grade ores are mined in Montana, California, and Oregon.

Production. Chromium metal is produced from chromite in several ways. First chromite is roasted with soda ash to form sodium dichromate (Na$_2$Cr$_2$O$_7$) which is then reduced by heating with coke to form green chromic oxide (Cr$_2$O$_3$). In the Goldschmidt, or thermite, process the chromic oxide is intimately mixed with aluminum, and the mixture is heated. During the reduction of chromic oxide a large quantity of heat is developed. The heat melts the chromium, and metal that is 97 to 99% pure is recovered.

In an alternate method pure chromium may be obtained by reduction of the chromic oxide by either carbon or silicon in an electric arc furnace. By electrolysis of either chrome alum or chromic acid solutions, a deposit of approximately 99.8% metallic chromium can be obtained at the cathode. As its purity increases, chromium becomes more ductile, and the pure metal can be worked by rolling, forging, or extrusion at high temperature.

Low-grade chromium, which is used mainly in the manufacture of chrome steel, is obtained by the treatment of chromite with coke in an electric furnace. The chromite is reduced to a mixture of chromium and iron, and this alloy is known as *ferrochrome*.

Chromium Compounds. Although the most stable oxidation state of chromium is +3, the +6 compounds are the most important industrially. Chromous compounds such as chromous chloride ($CrCl_2$) are representative of the +2 state. These compounds are powerful reducing agents. The +3 state is characterized by octahedral coordination of negative ions or neutral molecules around the central chromium ion. Therefore, the ion $Cr(H_2O)_6^{+3}$ is typical of the thousands of coordination complexes of +3 chromium. The oxide of +3 chromium is Cr_2O_3. It is called chromic oxide green and is one of the most permanent and indestructible pigments known.

The principal industrial compounds of chromium are sodium chromate, Na_2CrO_4, sodium dichromate, $Na_2Cr_2O_7$, ammonium dichromate, $(NH_4)_2Cr_2O_7$, and chromic acid. All of these compounds are acidic and are strong oxidizing agents. They are used in the bleaching of fats, oils, and waxes; in leather tanning; in the textile industry; in the manufacture of catalysts; in photomechanical processes; in fungicides; as corrosion inhibitors in dry cells; and in the manufacture of refractories.

Uses of Chromium Metal. Chromium is used in the metallurgical, refractory, and chemical industries. The predominant industrial application of chromium is in the manufacture of alloy steels. For this purpose chromium, in the form of ferrochrome, is added to steel. The chrome steels thus produced are used in the manufacture of ball bearings, armor plate, and projectiles and in many other processes involving high temperature and pressure.

Up to 3% ferrochrome may be added to steels to improve mechanical properties and increase hardenability of the steels. Steels made from 5 to 6% ferrochrome have greatly enhanced corrosion and oxidation resistance, and consequently they are used in the oil industry.

When more than 10% chromium has been added, the steels are called stainless steels because of their high resistance to corrosion, oxidation, and the effects of many chemicals. A typical stainless steel contains 74% iron, 18% chromium, and 8% nickel. Stainless steels with a low carbon content are used to manufacture cutlery, while those with a high carbon content are used to make special tools and dies.

Because of its brilliant luster and resistance to corrosion, chromium is used to plate metals. Decorative coats of chromium between 0.00001 and 0.00002 inch thick can be electroplated over a layer of electrodeposited nickel. Hard coatings of layers between 0.001 and 0.010 inch can be electroplated to increase the wear resistance of metals or to produce a low coefficient of friction between plates.

Nichrome is an alloy of nickel, chromium, and iron used to make electrical resistors for heaters. *Chromel* is an alloy of nickel and chromium used for the same purposes, while *stellite* is a hard alloy of chromium, tungsten, and cobalt used in the manufacture of cutting tools.

HERBERT LIEBESKIND
The Cooper Union

CHROMOLITHOGRAPHY. See LITHOGRAPHY– *Chromolithography.*

CHROMOSOME, krō'mə-sōm. Chromosomes are microscopic bodies found in the nuclei of cells of most plants and animals. They carry hereditary materials, units of which have been called genes and which determine the growth, development, and characteristics of an organism. The name "chromosome" was derived from the Greek words *chrōma* (color) and *sōma* (body), since chromosomes are deeply colored by certain stains.

Chromosome Number. The number and size of the chromosomes in a cell vary with the species, but the chromosome number for a given species is generally constant. There is no relation between the chromosome number and the complexity of an organism. Thus, while Mendel's garden pea has 14 chromosomes per cell and human cells have 46 chromosomes each, some single-celled animals have several hundred chromosomes.

Usually the gametes (the sperms and eggs) have half as many chromosomes as do normal body cells, and they are therefore said to have the *haploid number* (n) of chromosomes. In the body cells of sexually reproducing organisms, which arise directly or indirectly from the union of two sex cells, the chromosomes occur as homologous pairs, and the cells are said to have the *diploid number* (2n) of chromosomes. In man the diploid number is 46, and the haploid number 23.

Biochemical Composition. Chromosomes typically contain a complex chemical compound called deoxyribonucleic acid (DNA) together with several types of protein. It is the DNA that carries the cell's genetic information and thus controls the activities of cells, including metabolism, tissue differentiation, and cell division. The relatively simple nuclear material of some bacteria and viruses have been shown by autoradiography and other techniques to consist entirely of DNA.

The amount of DNA in the cell can be estimated by applying stains that are highly specific for DNA and then measuring the amount of stain present. From these measurements it can be shown that the amount of DNA doubles during interphase of cell activity, with a subsequent halving at the following cell division. The halving can also be shown beautifully by experiments in which the DNA is labeled with radioactive elements. Cells which have either half of the normal chromosome number, such as gametes, or which have an excess of chromosomes can be shown to have proportional amounts of DNA.

Structure. In the colon bacillus, *Escherichia coli*, which contains two to four nuclei, the genetic material is simply a double-stranded helix of DNA whose ends are joined to form a circle. In higher organisms the chromosome's structure is considerably more complex and changes from one stage of cell division to another. During interphase, a metabolic stage between cell divisions, chromosomes of higher organisms are present in the nucleus in the form of a dispersed network of very fine filaments, which is generally not visible under the light microscope. During cell division the chromosomes become tightly coiled like a spring and thickly coated with a deeply staining nucleoprotein material known as the *matrix*. In this form, after proper staining, they are easily visible under the light microscope.

Each chromosome consists of strands or threads called *chromonemata* (singular *chromonema*). The chromonemata are made up of material called *chromatin*. On the basis of staining behavior chromatin is divided into the more uniformly staining euchromatin, which comprises the bulk

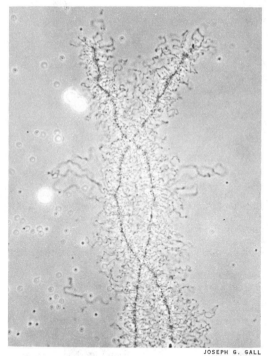

JOSEPH G. GALL

PART OF A GIANT LAMPBRUSH CHROMOSOME from a developing newt oocyte. The many loops extending from the backbone of the chromosome are strands of DNA.

of the chromosome and contains most of the hereditary material, and the heterochromatin, staining lighter or darker, which is found near the centromere and is relatively inert genetically.

Some regions of the chromosome do not coil during cell division. These uncoiled segments appear as constrictions and give each chromosome its characteristic shape. One such region is the *centromere* (or kinetochore), which is associated with chromosome motility. It is at this point that the spindle fibers attach to the chromosome during cell division. Along the chromosome there are areas known as *chromomeres*, which appear as darkly staining thickenings on the chromosome axis. These are thought to be related to the activity of genetic units.

In some special types of chromosomes, where the DNA is actively synthesizing gene products, as in salamander eggs (oocytes), strands of DNA loop out at regular intervals from the backbone of the chromosome. It is not known whether the DNA in ordinary chromosomes occurs in similar loops, or is part of a continuous thread that extends the length of each chromonema, or is attached to the chromosome in some other way. The number of double strands of DNA in chromosomes of higher organisms is a matter of controversy, but the diameter of the chromosome can certainly accommodate many DNA molecules.

Function of the Chromosomes. The primary function of the chromosomes is to carry the genetic material – DNA – which controls much cellular activity. During interphase, when the cell is not dividing and the chromosomes are not readily visible, DNA transmits information for the process of protein synthesis by which all of the enzymes of the cell are produced. It is through the enzymes that DNA controls the cell's activities.

The key components of the double-stranded DNA molecule are pairs of purine and pyrimidine bases that are linked together. It is now thought that several of these pairs of bases at a specific location on the DNA molecule transmit the relevant information for development and functioning of particular structures. In the salivary gland cells of the larva of the fruit fly *Drosophila* the chromonemata replicate many times without separating to produce multistranded, or polytene, chromosomes, which are enormous compared to those in other types of tissue. These chromosomes are so large that they can be seen with the naked eye. Along the length of these polytene chromosomes knobs or puffs appear and disappear at definite times during larval growth. These swellings probably represent regions of "gene" activity; if this is so, it suggests that the "genes" are not all active at the same time. It is possible that the activity of different segments at different times during development may lead to an explanation of how the cells of an embryo can differentiate into nerve, muscle, and other cell types, in spite of the fact that each has the same genetic material.

The determination of the sex of an individual illustrates the role that whole chromosomes play in the development of organisms. In the fruit fly *Drosophila melanogaster,* which has eight chromosomes in each of its cells, the female differs from the male in that the female body cells possess two rod-shaped chromosomes, known as X chromosomes, while the male body cells have one X chromosome and one J-shaped chromosome, known as a Y chromosome. Thus, of the haploid sperm cells, half contain three chromosomes plus an X chromosome and half contain three chromosomes plus the Y chromosome. All of the eggs of the female contain one X chromosome. Consequently, if an egg is fertilized by a Y-bearing sperm, the result will be a male; if the sperm has an X chromosome, the offspring will be female. Half the progeny are therefore male and half are female. A similar mechanism is responsible for the 50% male – 50% female theoretic sex ratio in humans. (Actually the human sex ratio at conception is about 108 males to 100 females.)

Chromosome Replication. Cell division is a continuous process that enables the organism to grow and expand and also to maintain itself by replacing old or worn-out cells with new ones. One type of replication, division, and assortment of the chromosomes into new cells is known as *mitosis.*

Near the beginning of mitosis each of the chromosomes replicates, forming a double structure loosely attached at the centromere region; at this stage each half chromosome is called a *chromatid.* The original pair of chromosomes and their replicated units thus make up a four-chromatid unit, the *tetrad.* The chromatids of each pair then separate and move apart to opposite ends of the cell, and the cell splits in half producing two daughter cells, each with approximately the same complement of chromosomes as the original cell.

In *meiosis,* which occurs during the formation of the eggs and sperms, the chromosomes double once but the cell divides twice, and the four cells that are produced are haploid. Each cell has one set of chromosomes, that is, half the full chromosome number (including one member of each of the chromosome pairs). When two gametes unite, the diploid chromosome number is restored.

Each generation may be regarded as a cycle in which diploid individuals produce haploid gametes which combine to form a new diploid

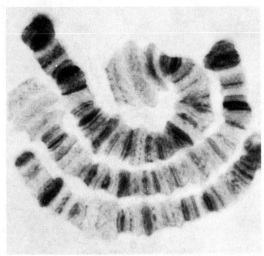

OAK RIDGE LABORATORY—UNION CARBIDE—AEC

(Above) Portions of giant chromosomes from the salivary glands of the larvae of a fruit fly. The chromosomes are marked with characteristic bands and puffs, which may indicate localized genetic activity. *(Right)* Chromosomes of a human male during mitosis. Each chromosome consists of a pair of chromatids. In the photograph the sex chromosomes are labeled X and Y.

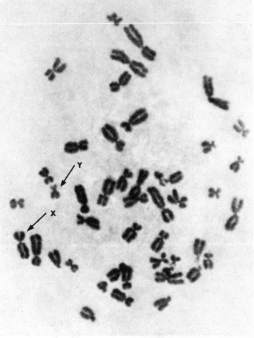

MEMORIAL HOSPITAL, NEW YORK

generation. For a more detailed description of cell division, see Mitosis.

Chromosome Aberrations — *Abnormal Chromosome Number.* Ordinarily each cell has two segments of genetic material controlling a particular physical trait or function, one on each of the two homologous chromosomes. The machinery of the cell is attuned to this balance, and any disturbance will usually disrupt normal functioning. If the cell is upset by the loss of a chromosome during division because of a failure to move to one of the poles, perhaps 400 to 1,000 structural features or functional activities are affected; the cell is thrown out of balance and usually dies.

In man, when chromosomes are present in abnormal numbers, the individual is grossly defective and usually is stillborn or dies shortly after birth. An exception is mongolism, a severe type of mental and physical deformity caused by the presence of a specific extra chromosome. Mongoloids may live 40 or 50 years, but most die young.

Other exceptions occur in the case of the sex chromosomes. Normally, females have two X chromosomes, and males one X and one Y. Individuals with varying combinations of X and Y chromosomes usually survive and may even produce offspring. Females with Turner's syndrome have only one X chromosome and no second sex chromosome; such females are underdeveloped sexually and are always sterile. Males with Klinefelter's syndrome have two X chromosomes and one Y, and are underdeveloped males. Also, in certain leukemias the normal chromosomes complement is changed to include a new small chromosome, different from those usually found in man.

In some species, particularly in plants, chromosomes may appear in multiples of the haploid number greater than two; this is called polyploidy. Tobacco and wheat are two well-known polyploids. Polyploids may also be produced experimentally, and when produced from two separate species they may have characteristics of both original

types. Thus, the polyploid hybrid between cabbage and radish has the leaf structure of the radish and the roots of the cabbage. Tetraploids of the water shrimp *Artemia* and of the roundworm *Ascaris* are examples of polyploidy in animals.

Structural Abnormalities. The normal structure of chromosomes may be changed in several ways. Errors may occur in the synthesis of the DNA during replication of the chromosomes, or the chromosome may fragment spontaneously with a subsequent rearrangement of the broken segments. Cells exposed to high-energy radiation such as X rays or gamma rays generally show widespread chromosomal damage. Although in some rare instances broken chromosomes may rejoin correctly, usually new and deleterious combinations result. In most cases chromosomal fragments without centromeres will be lost at the next cell division because they will be unable to attach to the spindle fibers. If in the case of two fragments that have rejoined, both carry centromeres, the chromosome will be pulled apart during division if the centromeres go to opposite poles. Damage of this type results in an unbalanced chromosome complement and death to the daughter cells.

History. Chromosomes were probably first identified as distinct cell structures by the Czech biologist Walther Flemming in 1873. The name "chromosome" was given to these structures by the German biologist Wilhelm von Waldeyer in 1888.

During the latter half of the 19th century the behavior of chromosomes during cell division was carefully studied and described by the Belgian biologist Edouard van Beneden and by the German biologists Oskar Hertwig and Theodor Boveri. During the same period, the relationship of the chromosomes to inheritance was explored by the German biologists August Weismann and Eduard Strasburger and others. In 1900, Mendel's classic study of the genetics of garden peas, which had been ignored since its publication 35 years earlier, was rediscovered by Tschermak, Correns, and De Vries. In this work Mendel had postulated the existence in gametes of hereditary "factors," which were later correlated with the "genes" carried by the chromosomes.

In the years following 1900, many important discoveries in genetics were made by American biologists. In 1903, Walter S. Sutton presented the first clear explanation of the relationship between the theory of hereditary factors and the microscopically visible chromosomes. A year earlier Clarence Erwin McClung had studied the behavior of the X chromosome in the grasshopper. Nettie Stevens, Edmund Beecher Wilson, and others soon established the relationship of specific chromosomes to sex determination in many other organisms.

Many of the most significant early discoveries concerning chromosomes were made through genetic experiments with the fruit fly *Drosophila*. In 1910, Thomas Hunt Morgan described the inheritance of white eyes in *Drosophila*, which proved to parallel the heretofore puzzling inheritance of such characteristics as color blindness and hemophilia in man; these are now known to be sex-linked characteristics. In 1913, Alfred H. Sturtevant used a breeding experiment to show that the hereditary factors, the genes, could be "mapped" in a linear sequence on the chromosomes. And, in 1916, Calvin Bridges discovered that abnormal chromosome numbers could occur by the failure of chromatids to separate during meiosis; he gave the name "nondisjunction" to this phenomenon.

In 1941, Edward L. Tatum and George W. Beadle made a breakthrough in biochemical genetic analysis, enunciating the now famous "one gene—one enzyme" hypothesis, and using as an experimental organism the bread mold *Neurospora* (then relatively new to genetic investigations). See also BEADLE, GEORGE WELLS; GENETICS.

ALFRED NOVAK
Stephens College, Columbia, Mo.

Further Reading: Bourne, Geoffrey H., *Cytology and Cell Physiology* (New York 1964); De Robertis, E. D. P., Nowinski, W. W., and Saez, F. A., *General Cytology* (Philadelphia 1965); Herskowitz, Irwin H., *Genetics* (Boston 1962); Swanson, Carl P., *Cytology and Cytogenetics* (Englewood Cliffs, N. J., 1957).

CHROMOSPHERE, krō′mə-sfir, the bright reddish layer of gas in the atmosphere of the sun. It lies between the photosphere and the corona and is the site of many important solar phenomena. See SUN—*Chromosphere.*

CHRONICLE, kron′i-kəl, a record of historical events in the order of their occurrence, in which there is no personal interpretation of facts or conscious literary art in the manner of presentation. The term usually refers to works produced in unsophisticated eras or works directed toward a popular audience that may be unable to appreciate more complex treatises. Chronicles can be charming in their lack of artifice and fascinating in their revelation of the outlook of the age in which they were written.

The writer of a chronicle seldom cites his sources of information and often uses tradition and legend without regard to authenticity. When writing about his own time, he is unselective, reporting major events and minor oddities in equal detail. Nevertheless, in the absence of original documentation, chronicles can be extremely valuable as the only sources of important historical information, and they often prove acceptable when tested against other types of evidence. The greatest number of important chronicles originated in all parts of Europe in the Middle Ages, though some examples date from as late as the 17th century.

History. The earliest chronicle in the Christian era was an abstract of universal history written by Eusebius of Caesarea about 325 A. D. Translated into Latin by St. Jerome, it became a model for later chronicles. The *Chronica* of Sulpicius Severus (360?–410) was a summary of sacred history from the creation to 403 A. D., and this type was continued for six centuries by Byzantine scholars, the most important being the 7th century *Paschal Chronicle*. These chronicles based their early sections on the Old Testament, starting with the story of Adam, and were intended to promote Christian teaching.

The first chronicles in western Europe began a century after the fall of Rome. Flavius Magnus Aurelius Cassiodorus, an aide of the Gothic king Theodoric, compiled a *Chronica* in 519. The earliest Welsh historian, Gildas, wrote his *De Excidio Britanniae* before 547. The *Anglo-Saxon Chronicle* was begun under Alfred the Great shortly before 892 A. D. and continued until 1154.

Most surviving chronicles, however, do not date back beyond the 11th century. The *Chronicon* of Marianus Scotus, covering universal history up to 1082, was widely used and imitated. The major record of Charlemagne's exploits, formerly attributed to Turpin, bishop of Reims (about 753–800), was really composed about 1150. The fullest Welsh chronicle is the *Historia Regum Britanniae* (about 1136) of Geoffrey of Monmouth (1100?–1154). Scholars in Ireland maintained chronicles for six centuries, culminating about 1636 with *The Annals of the Four Masters*.

Late in the 12th century, chronicles began to pass from Latin into the vernacular and from monkish authors to lay scribes. Some of the newer chronicles were composed in verse, for example, the *Roman de Brut* by the Anglo-Norman Wace of Jersey and the summary of French history by the Belgian Philippe Mousket. Later, detailed prose records of national history were written by chroniclers, including the Frenchman Jean Froissart and the Elizabethan Raphael Holinshed, from whose work Shakespeare derived material for a number of plays.

LIONEL STEVENSON, *Duke University*

CHRONICLE PLAY, kron′ə-kəl, in English literature, a play based, more or less accurately, on history. Chronicle plays generally draw their source material from medieval and Renaissance chronicles, such as that of Holinshed (1578) and, like them, present a series of loosely related events from one king's reign. Such Elizabethan and Stuart dramatists as Shakespeare, Marlowe, Jonson, Dekker, Heywood, and Ford wrote chronicle plays, at a time when an awakening sense of national self-esteem after the defeat of the Spanish Armada (1588) inspired a new interest in national origins.

Chronicle plays brought England's history to life, unrolling the splendid pageant of kings and warriors from before the Norman conquest to the time of Elizabeth I. They borrowed their history whole, mistakes and all, but they transformed it, making their real hero England itself.

CHRONICLES, I and II, kron'i-kəlz. The First and Second books of Chronicles are canonical books of the Old Testament. The name "Chronicles" was first used about the late 4th century A. D., in its Latin equivalent, by St. Jerome (q.v.). The Septuagint, the Greek version of the Old Testament compiled in the 2d century B. C., uses the name *Paralipomena,* or "things omitted" (from other biblical books). The Hebrew name for Chronicles is *Dibre Hayamim,* meaning annals, or history. In the Greek, Latin, and most Bibles in modern languages, the books of Chronicles are placed between Kings and Esdras or Ezra-Nehemiah; in the Hebrew Bible, it comes at the very end.

I and II Chronicles originally were one book. The division, which dates back to the Septuagint, was adopted in the Hebrew Bible in the late Middle Ages. There is also evidence, in the Bible itself, that Chronicles and Ezra-Nehemiah originally formed one book.

Structure and Composition. Four sections can easily be recognized in Chronicles by their content: (1) genealogical lists from Adam to David (with appendices; I Chronicles 1 to 9); (2) the death of Saul (I Chronicles 10) and the history of David's reign (I Chronicles 11 to 29); (3) the history of Solomon (II Chronicles 1 to 9); and (4) the history of the Kingdom of Judah (II Chronicles 10 to 36). The last two verses duplicate the opening of the Book of Ezra, which as previously noted is thought to have formed the continuation of Chronicles. These verses contain the beginning of the proclamation of King Cyrus of Persia permitting the Jews to return to their land from the Babylonian captivity.

The material that Chronicles comprises is quite varied. Excerpts from earlier historical Old Testament books (notably Genesis) for the genealogy, and from Samuel and Kings for the history from David to the end of the Judean monarchy, form the basic component. Chronicles often follows these sources closely, even literally, yet there are many characteristic deviations (which are discussed below in the section on the philosophy of Chronicles). For the history from David on, and particularly that of the Judean kingdom, the narrative parallels that of Samuel and Kings. Much more limited is the material from extra-Biblical sources. Chronicles refers explicitly to a number of them, for example, "The Book of the Kings of Judah and Israel" (II Chronicles 16:11), or "The Words of Samuel, the Seer . . ." (I Chronicles 29:29). It is a moot question how many, if any, of these citations refer to genuine sources, and how many to inventions of the Chronicler, the author, who wished to embellish his work by imitating similar but authentic references in Kings. Other sources, not referred to as such, may have been employed.

Another component of Chronicles is the personal contributions of the Chronicler, including notes intended to correct his sources or to change their meaning; narratives; prayers; sermons; and lists. These, and the author's biased selection from earlier Biblical books, reveal his philosophy and his purpose.

Later additions to the book of the Chronicler are, for the most part, found in the genealogies and the history of David. Their extent and intent are a matter of debate, linked with the question of the date of the book. If passages claimed to originate in the 2d century B. C. (for example, I Chronicles 24) are additions, the orig-

inal book can be dated to an earlier period. Most scholars do acknowledge later additions, and the prevailing opinion gives a 4th century B. C. date of authorship.

Philosophy. The philosophy of Chronicles is best discerned in the focus of four themes: legitimacy, short-range retribution, cult, and Davidism.

Legitimacy in Chronicles has been epitomized by Professor Robert North as follows: "In order that the will of God be done, it is important that the right people be in charge." This is the raison d'être of the first 405 verses (virtually only names).

The philosophy concerning retribution is that man is rewarded for his good deeds and punished for his bad deeds, and the sooner requital comes, the more clearly the doctrine is proved. By extension, this doctrine impels the Chronicler to read the cause and effect sequence backwards, seeing in the historical events effects for which he constructs religiomoral causes. This quest for causes leads him to a radical rewriting of Biblical history. For example, II Kings 21, the source of II Chronicles 33, has only bad things to say about King Manasseh. To Chronicles, this is incompatible with Manasseh's long and peaceful reign. Chronicles therefore tells that Manasseh was exiled for his sins, whereupon he repented, returned to the throne of his country, and thenceforth led a good life (II Chronicles 33:11–13).

The ideas of cult and Davidism are interrelated. The Jerusalem Temple, with its Levitical clergy, and the Davidic dynasty are to Chronicles the institutional foundations of the people and the religion of Israel. The book, totally unsupported by ancient sources, tells that David prepared the construction of the Temple in every detail–blueprints, funds, materials, and personnel–and that Solomon was concerned only with the mechanical implementation of the plans. Furthermore, according to Chronicles, David instituted the Temple music and organized the priestly guilds for the sacred service. David and his dynasty are the outstanding symbol and pledge of the grace God shows to Israel, besides which little else deserves notice.

What results from this philosophy is a totally new view of Israelite history and religion. Only the history of the Judean, the Davidic, monarchy is told; the sister Israelite, or Ephraimite, monarchy is thought to have no history worthy of record. Messianism, as developed by the prophets, has left no trace in Chronicles. The dynasty of David has in its history come so close to the perfect order of things as to render the longing for the ideal future unnecessary. Most important, the pivotal events and personalities of Old Testament history are virtually ignored outside of quotations or genealogies. The Exodus from Egypt, Sinai, the conquest of Palestine, go almost unmentioned, as do the patriarchs or Moses. Zion (David's stronghold in Jerusalem) and David have usurped their roles. According to Chronicles, it appears that God made no covenant with Abraham on Canaan or with Israel on Sinai, only with David on Zion. With this theology, Chronicles has moved itself to the fringes of the Bible, and no interpretation has succeeded in bringing it closer to the core. See also BIBLE: *Table of the Books of the Bible; 5. Growth of the Old Testament Literature.*

MATITIAHU TSEVAT
Hebrew Union College, Cincinnati

WRIST CHRONO-GRAPH designed for use by skin divers. The movable bezel around the rim gives a convenient reading of elapsed time spent underwater.

LONGINES-WITTNAUER WATCH CO. INC.

CHRONOGRAPH, kron′ə-graf, a device used to measure, and to produce visual or permanent records of, the duration of events lasting from fractions of a second up to 12 hours. Chronographs that are used to measure and give a visual indication of short time intervals are often called *chronoscopes.*

Chronographs fall into two general classifications: watch chronographs, which are entirely mechanical in action; and electromagnetic, electronic, cathode ray, and flashing chronographs, each of which uses a highly accurate crystal-controlled clock or a marine chronometer as a time base. The first type is widely used by engineers, time-and-motion-study experts, doctors, and judges of many sporting events. The second group is more applicable in the scientific and military fields, where extremely precise time determinations are required, and is also used for precise timing of some sporting events.

Watch-type chronographs have hour, minute, and second hands that show conventional time. Chronographs that do not indicate the time of day are referred to as *timers.* In addition to the usual clock hands, chronographs have an independent second hand, called the chronograph hand. It revolves about the dial center and extends almost to its edge. Push buttons are used to start, stop, or return the chronograph hand to zero. Sixty divisions of one second each, subdivided into fifths or tenths, are engraved around the edge of the dial. Chronographs have a small dial usually located on the main dial near the position of the 3 on an ordinary clock dial. This small dial has 30 divisions, and a hand on it advances one division for each revolution of the chronograph hand, thus recording elapsed time up to 30 minutes. Many chronographs also have dials near the 6 position that permit recording elapsed time up to 12 hours. Split-second chronographs have two chronograph hands that can be operated independently to allow for the timing of overlapping events.

Prior to use, all chronograph hands are set at zero by pressing a button. When the event being timed begins, the button that starts the chronograph hand is pushed. When the event terminates, the button is pushed again to stop the hand, and the time is shown. If the action is interrupted—rather than terminated—the hand can be restarted when the action resumes, so that only the actual time of the event is monitored.

The more accurate chronographs incorporate means of reducing errors in observation and in the rate of the time base and make possible readings to much smaller fractions of a second.

JAMES J. O'SHAUGHNESSY
Longines-Wittnauer Watch Company

CHRONOLOGY, krə-nol′ə-jē, is the science of dating that arranges time into periods or divisions, and places events in the proper places within the arrangement. Chronologists employ two main types of dating:

Relative dating places a period, event, or object in relation to an established sequence, showing that it is earlier than certain periods and later than others, although its actual date in years is unknown. Events or periods that occurred at the same time are said to be *synchronic.* Those occurring at different times are called *disynchronic.*

Chronometric dating places an event either on a time-line (10,750 B.C., for instance) or in a time-bracket (12,000 to 10,000 B.C.). Some authors use the term *absolute dating,* but that term is increasingly rejected because it makes no distinction between placing an event on the line or in the bracket.

The attainment of chronometric correctness is the goal of those who would make history an exact science, but for most periods the goal is nowhere in sight. Nevertheless, several modern techniques make it possible to fix the approximate dates of ancient materials. The methodology includes *radiocarbon dating,* which measures the amount of carbon-14 (which decreases in an organism at a fixed rate after its death) in materials that were once alive; *obsidian dating,* in which the hydration layer left on the obsidian by the absorption of water from its surroundings is measured; *thermo-remanent magnetism,* in which the remanent magnetism caused by heat (usually in an ancient hearth or kiln) is compared with the ever-changing direction and intensity of the earth's magnetic field; *thermoluminescence,* in which light, emitted from heated ground pottery through the release of energy stored as electron displacements, is studied and related to pottery samples of known dates; *fluorine testing,* in which the contemporaneity of bones in the same deposit can be assessed by their fluorine content; *pollen analysis,* in which the identification and enumeration of the types of pollen present in a sample can be used to tie that sample to a time scale; and *varve counting,* in which layers of sediment released by glaciers are counted and correlated with similar data from elsewhere.

Although all of these techniques are being improved and refined constantly, none yields precise dates. Only *dendrochronology,* which allows the scientist to date wooden materials by comparing their growth rings with the known pattern of growth rings in trees dating back to about 3,000 years, is exact, and then only within its narrow limits.

Man's first awareness of recurrent phenomena marking divisions of time came from simple observations of nature. Divisions of the year were probably not just made according to four seasons but to two—heat and cold. The year began with the awakening of spring and closed with the onset of winter. Division of the year into four seasons was based on observations of the stars or constellations. One of the oldest of existing farmers' calendars, Hesiod's *Works and Days,* prescribes plowing and sowing operations according to the rising and setting of constellations. Because religion also required close observation of recurring celestial phenomena, formal reckoning of time and the development of calendars came into the hands of the priest class. Calendars all

Reproduction of the Aztec Calendar Stone in the National Museum of Anthropology in Mexico City.

over the world began as cycles of religious feasts, and feast and fast days observed in religious calendars today are a surviving feature from the earliest calendars.

Chronologists usually deal with historical times, but in the early period, even in countries such as Egypt and Babylonia where abundant records have survived and where careful observations of celestial phenomena were made, they often encounter great difficulty.

Egyptian Chronology. In the early period Egyptians dated by outstanding events associated with the reign of a pharaoh, such as "the year of smiting the northerners." Later they used the more precise system of reckoning according to regnal years, such as "the twelfth year of Sesostris III." In the absence of complete king lists, it is impossible to establish an exact chronology. Partial lists have been found: the *Turin Papyrus* (about 1200 B. C.); the *Palermo Stone* (about 2600 B. C.); the royal lists of Abydos, Karnak, and Sakkara; and the *Aegyptiaca* of Manetho, an Egyptian high priest who about 280 B. C. wrote a history of Egypt in Greek from earliest times to 323 B. C. He had access to complete king lists and detailed records, but unfortunately his work is fragmentary. He set up a system of arranging all Egyptian rulers—from the first historical king, Menes, to Alexander the Great—into 31 dynasties, with larger divisions of Old, Middle, and New Kingdoms. The system is still in use.

Other bases for Egyptian chronolgy are records of synchronous events and astronomical observations. The Amarna letters and the Boğazköy records have provided numerous synchronisms between Egyptian, Babylonian, Assyrian, and Hittite chronologies.

From very early times, Egyptians celebrated the heliacal rising of Sirius with a feast, because this was the harbinger of the annual flooding of the Nile. On this event they established their calendar of 365 days, divided into 12 months of 30 days each, with 5 feast days at the end of the year. Every 4 years the calendar was 1 day short and every 1,460 years it righted itself. Such a period was called a Sothic-period, from the Egyptian name for Sirius. This discrepancy was known to the Egyptians, and in 238 B. C. a reform was proposed in the Decree of Canopus by which a day was to be inserted every fourth year. This proposal was the basis of the reformed Julian calendar of Julius Caesar.

Dates of the earlier periods are approximate. Beginning with dynasty 12, records of Sothis and lunar observations enable scholars to date with nearly absolute correctness.

The conspectus of Egyptian dynasties given here follows the table that appears in EGYPT—*Chronology.*

Period	Dates	Dynasties
Prehistoric	c. 4500–3100 B. C.	
Early Dynastic	3100–2665	1–2
Old Kingdom	2664–2155	3–6
First Intermediate	2154–2052	7–10
Middle Kingdom	2134–1786	11–12
Second Intermediate	1785–1554	13–17
New Kingdom	1554–1075	18–20
Late	1075–657	21–25
Saite	664–525	26
First Persian	525–404	27
Last Egyptian Kingdom	404–341	28–30
Second Persian	341–332	31
Greek	332–30 B. C.	
Roman	30 B. C.–A. D. 364	

Early Babylonian. Chronology of Sumerian and Akkadian dynasties is usually based on estimated dates of Hammurabi's reign. Around that time greater reliance can be placed upon synchronisms and records of astronomical observations. By working backward through existing king lists it is possible to set up a system of earlier Babylonian dynasties whose dating is at best roughly approximate.

The early Kish and Uruk (Erech) dynasties of the king lists are now referred to the first half of the 3d millennium B. c., a period called Early Dynastic. The king lists become more reliable with the 1st dynasty of Ur, beginning with the reign of Mes-anne-pada (about 2525 B. C.). This is the dynasty of the Royal Tombs of Ur and is said to have lasted 177 years. It ruled over most of Babylonia. The next ruler to enjoy wide hegemony was Lugal-zaggisi (about 2289–2264). He was defeated by Sargon I, an Akkadian, about 2264. Sargon ruled at Agade (about 2277–2221). His grandson, Naram-sin (about 2197–2160), attained still greater glory and acquired a larger domain. An invasion by a barbarian horde of Guti followed a brief period of anarchy, and after about 90 years, the Guti were driven from Babylonia by the king of Uruk (about 2060). Next came the 3d dynasty of Ur (about 2053–1944), under which Sumerian culture reached its highest development. After a period of rival dynasties of mixed rulers at Isin and Larsa, the 1st dynasty of Babylon was established; Hammurabi (about 1728–1686), the sixth king of that dynasty, brought the early Babylonian empire to its greatest glory. It soon crumbled before a Kassite subjugation (about 1677) that was to last intermittently for more than 500 years.

Minoan Chronology. Sir Arthur Evans set up a system that was long standard for Aegean chronology; he based his scheme on synchronisms with Egypt according to the Egyptian dating in Eduard Meyer's *Aegyptische Chronologie.* Evidence has tended to confirm Evans' dating of the Early Minoan Periods, but little chronological weight can be attached to subdivisions that he made in the last two periods of his system, which often overlap considerably. The Minoan chronology given here follows that of J. L. Caskey and F. Matz in the revised edition of the *Cambridge Ancient History.*

Early Minoan I	3200–2800 B. C.
Early Minoan II	2800–2200
Early Minoan III	2200–2000
Early Palace Period	2000–1700
Late Palace Period	1700–1400

Assyrian Chronology. This is founded on abundant sources of information that are for the most part corroborative. As a result the period from 911 to 626 B. C. is established with possible discrepancies amounting to one year in some reigns. From 911 to 1068 B. C. the margin of error may be as much as 10 years, and beyond the latter date the possibility of error increases. Among the important sources are the so-called limmu lists for the years 890–648 B. C., which are tables of archons whose years of office were designated by their names. Lists of Assyrian kings covering the period from the 24th century to 746 B. C. were found in the palace of Sargon II at Khorsabad. Of these, the *Synchronous History* records relations between Assyria and Babylonia for eight centuries preceding 800 B. C., and the *Gadd Chronicle* gives a good account of the closing years of the Assyrian Empire and the rise of the Late Babylonian Empire. The *Canon of Ptolemy* is a list of Babylonian and Persian kings, with the length of their reigns, from Nabonassar (747 B. C.) to Alexander the Great. The era of Nabonassar begins in 747 because in February of that year the Babylonians instituted an astronomical calendar, consisting of a 19-year cycle with 7 intercalated months within the cycle, which closely approximates a true astronomical calendar. The Greek astronomer Ptolemy used this calendar as the basis for his canon. Dates of some important Assyrian kings, according to Albert T. Olmstead's *History of Assyria* are:

Tiglath-pileser I	1115–1102 B. C.
Ashurnasirpal II	885–860
Tiglath-pileser III	746–728
Sennacherib	705–681
Ashurbanipal	669–633

Hebrew Chronology. Probably the chronology of no people has received greater scholarly attention than that of the Hebrews. Furthermore, not only was it customary practice to base Biblical chronology on the fairly well established chronology of the Assyrians, but in the accounts of the reigns of the kings of Israel and Judah, the duration of each reign was recorded with cross references telling in what year of the reign of a king of Judah a king of Israel came to the throne, and vice versa. Nevertheless, Biblical chronology has remained a perplexing tangle of seemingly insoluble problems.

To begin with, the recorded years of the reigns of the kings of Judah to the fall of Samaria amount to 31 more than the years of the kings of Israel over the same period, and no cross references after the first two reigns are correct. The years from the First Temple to the Second number exactly 480. The years of the kings of Israel number 240. The period from Abraham's departure from Ur to the Exodus was 480 years and from the Exodus to the First Temple was 480 years. The Hebrew chroniclers were evidently seeking symmetry, not accuracy.

It is now believed that the reigns of the monarchy period were stretched to make them conform to the 480-year span, that the period of the exile of the Hebrews in Egypt was extended to make it coincide with the Hyksos invasions, and that the Greek translators of the Septuagint, when they learned from Manetho's recently published (about 280 B. C.) *Aegyptiaca* of the early date of the first Egyptian king Menes, lengthened the lives of the patriarchs to make Hebrew history antedate the Egyptians. Using a synchronism to fix 853 as the last year of Ahab's reign, Edwin R. Thiele has worked out a very precise chronology for the kings of Judah and Israel in *The Mysterious Numbers of the Hebrew Kings* (1951).

Late Babylonian and Early Persian (Achaemenid) Chronology. In contrast to other early chronologies, this can be presented with assurance of a high degree of correctness.

Tables for translating dates from the Babylonian-Persian calendar to the Julian calendar for the period 626 B. C. to A. D. 75 are contained in *Babylonian Chronology 626 B. C.–A. D. 75*, by Richard A. Parker and Waldo H. Dubberstein. According to the authors, the tables are in almost all cases astronomically correct to the day.

Hindu Chronology. The Hindu civil year is based on a sidereal solar year that does not take into account the precession of the equinoxes. Hence there is a slight discrepancy between their year and a true astronomical tropical year. Moreover, the Hindus are divided in their allegiance to 3 different figures for a solar year: 365 days, 6 hours, and 12½ minutes, according to the astronomer Aryabhata; 365 days, 6 hours, 12 minutes, and 30.915 seconds, according to the *Rājamrigāka;* 365 days, 6 hours, 12 minutes, and 36.56 seconds, according to the *Sūrya-Siddhānta.* Aryabhata's year exceeds the Julian year by 5 days in 576 years. His civil year begins as the sun enters Mesha (Aries). In 603 A. D. that was on March 20; now, because of precession, it is occurring in April.

Of the many chronological eras recognized in different parts of India, six are most important. (1) The Kaliyuga era, an astronomical system that is still referred to but that is not now used for civil purposes. It appears to have been adopted in the 4th century after Christ, but its epoch is reckoned from Feb. 18, 3102 B. C. A. D. 1970 marks the 5,072d year of the era. (2) The Vikrama Samvat era of northern India began on Feb. 23, 57 B. C.; 1970 marks the 2,027th year of the Vikrama era. (3) The Saka era of southern India, with its epoch of March 3, A. D. 78, is in general use in many parts of India; 1970 is the 1,892d year of the Saka era. (4) The Saptarshi era, used in Kashmir and the northeast, dates from the moment when the Saptarshi were taken into heaven and became stars of the Great Bear in 3076 B.C. (5) The Buddhists reckoned from the reputed date of the death of Buddha in 543 B. C., although he actually died in 483 B. C. This era is still used in Ceylon, Burma, and Thailand. (6) The epoch of the Jains was the death of Vardhamāna Mahāvīra, the founder of their faith, in 527 B. C.

Chinese Chronology. Sometime before 2000 B. C. the Chinese adopted a lunar calendar for their civil year and, by intercalating months, adjusted the lunar calendar to an astronomical year, which they recognized as being 365¼ days in duration and in which they intercalated a day every 4 years. From 206 B.C. the civil year began with the first day of that lunation during which the sun entered the Chinese sign for Pisces. At the same time the Chinese adopted a 19-year cycle, with 12 common years of 12 lunations each, and 7 intercalary years with 13 lunations. The months were of 29 or 30 days' duration, but it is not known how these were distributed. Each lunar month was designated by the name of the sign that the sun entered during that lunation. As often as the sun did not enter a new sign during a lunation, an intercalary month was inserted, which kept the name of the preceding month. The Chinese were able to devise a system of reckoning by cycles of 60. Each of the days in the cycle had a particular name and a date could be noted by the name of the day, month, and year. This practice is helpful to students in verifying Chinese chronology. The Chinese reckon the first year of the first cycle as the 81st year of Emperor Yao's life (2277 B. C.).

Beginning in 163 B.C. records were kept according to Nien-hao. These were periods of regnal years, each emperor decreeing that the years were to be known as the first, second, third, and so on, of his reign or of some other name. To convert a Chinese date into one in a Western era, it is only necessary to refer to a conversion table of Nien-hao.

When the Chinese Republic was established in 1911, the Gregorian calendar was adopted. Until 1930 the old and new systems were used side by side, but since then publication and use of the old lunar calendar have been prohibited.

Even so, it is still in use to some extent. An official calendar corresponding to the Western calendar is published each year by the Academia Sinica at Peking.

Japanese Chronology. There are various ways of reckoning eras among the Japanese:

(1) By a continuous era beginning with the first year of the reign of Jimmu (660 B. C.).

(2) By reigns of emperors, beginning with the first civil year of the new emperor. At the death or abdication of an emperor the current year was usually counted in his reign, and the reign of his successor began the following year. On rare occasions when the official enthronement of an emperor was delayed for some years after his actual accession, his reign was reckoned from the official enthronement.

(3) By periods, called Nengo. The Japanese adopted this system in 645 A. D. from the Chinese, that is, counting by periods of no fixed length, each with a distinctive name. The first period was called Taikwa, and the system has been in use with a few intermissions ever since. In 1872 it was decided that each emperor's reign should henceforth have only one Nengo.

(4) According to sexagenary cycles, also borrowed from the Chinese. The 60-year cycles of five 12-year periods began A. D. 424.

The Japanese calendar is Gregorian, in all respects like the Western calendar.

Accurate tables of the various Japanese reckonings are easily accessible.

Greek Chronology. Contemporary records are necessary for establishing precise chronologies. Such records do not exist for early Greece, and consequently estimates of early dates often vary by a century or more.

During most of the ancient period the Greeks did not observe an era but designated each year by a local magistrate in office at the time: at Athens the first archon, at Sparta the first ephor, at Argos by the priestess of Hera, a lifetime office. The names of ephors are recorded from 757/756 B. C. and of archons from 683/682 B. C. The ancient Greek historians recognized the handicap of dating by local officials; and during the 4th century B.C. a system of dating from the traditional date of the first Olympiad (776 B. C.) began to be adopted. An Olympiad began with the quadrennial celebration of the Olympic games, held on the first new moon after the summer solstice.

To convert Olympiads into modern dating, one multiplies the number of Olympiads by 4; if the result can be subtracted from 780, the remainder gives the year B. C. when the *1st* year of the given Olympiad begins; for the 2d, 3d, or 4th years of the Olympiad, 1, 2, or 3 must be added before the subtraction is made. Thus the 3d year of Olympiad 75 is 477 B. C. (780 minus 303). For a date in the Christian era, 779 should be subtracted from 4 times the number of the Olympiad. Thus Olympiad 293 begins in the middle of A. D. 393 (1172 minus 779). Because the Olympiads began about July 1, double years are used to express entire Olympic years in modern dates. If an event in Greek history is known to have occurred in the first or last half of our calendar year, the customary double year used by historians is unnecessary.

Although each city-state in Greece had its own calendar, with its own names for the months and its own time for beginning the calendar year, the structure of all their calendars was the same.

They were lunisolar, with the year divided into 12 months, alternating in length between 29 and 30 days, the lunar year being 11¼ days shorter than the solar year. In order to reconcile lunar and solar years, the Greeks adopted at some unknown date (in central Greece perhaps as early as the Mycenaean age) an 8-year cycle, with 3 intercalated months during each cycle (octaeterid). During the 4th century B. C. a more precise scheme, taken from the Babylonians by Meton, was introduced into Athens. This was the 19-year (Metonic) cycle of years of 12 lunar months, with an intercalated month in the 3d, 5th, 8th, 11th, 13th, 16th, and 19th years. In the cycle, 110 months were "hollow" (29 days) and 125 were "full" (30 days). This makes the average duration of a year 365⁵⁄₁₉ days.

Roman Chronology. All European countries have borrowed their civil calendars from the Romans. Tradition reports that the second Roman king, Numa Pompilius, added 2 months, January and February, to the earliest Roman calendar, bringing the number of months to 12 and the days of the year to 355; and, to overcome the discrepancy of 10¼ days between the lunar and solar year, he ordered that an intercalary month of 22 or 23 days (alternately) be inserted every 2d year between the 23d and 24th of February. A 4-year period thus contained 1,465 days, and the mean length of the year was 366¼ days. Another correction was introduced at an unknown date, according to which every 3d period of 8 years, instead of containing 4 intercalary months totaling 90 days, should contain only 3 months, consisting of 22 days each. This Roman lunisolar calendar had a mean year of 365¼ days.

Nevertheless, the Roman calendar was permitted to stray far from the astronomical year. The priests, who had the power to intercalate months, abused this power for political reasons. Cicero, suffering the anguish of a political exile while serving as governor of Cilicia in 51 B. C., wrote his friend Atticus to use his influence to prevent an intercalary month—which would extend his tenure—from being inserted at that time.

Caesar put an end to the confusion when, as dictator, he decreed in 46 B. C. that the civil year be regulated entirely by the sun. Assisted by Sosigenes, he fixed the mean length of the year at 365¼ days, and arranged that every 4th year should have 366 days. The year 46 B. C., instead of having 355 days, had 445 days to reconcile it with the astronomical year. Caesar arranged that the months should have 30 and 31 days alternately, with 29 (or 30) for February, but his successor, Augustus, to gratify his vanity, named the 8th month after himself, took a day from February and added it to his own month, and revised the number of days in September, October, and November to complete the calendar in use today. The first Julian year began on Jan. 1, 46 B. C. The astronomical year is not exactly 365¼ days, and in 1582 Pope Gregory XIII took steps to make the calendar year coincide with the astronomical year. The Gregorian calendar was not adopted by Great Britain and the English North American colonies until 1752, and the Julian calendar is still used by adherents of the Greek Orthodox Church.

The Romans in Republican times designated the years by the names of the consuls of the year. This awkward system was an annoyance to historians who sought to establish a chronological epoch. Different dates for the foundation of Rome were set by Quintus Fabius Pictor, Polybius, Marcus Porcius Cato, Marcus Verrius Flaccus, and Marcus Terentius Varro. A knowledge of these dates is necessary in order to reconcile Roman historians with each other and with modern dating. Livy, for instance, at times uses the epoch of Cato and at other times that of Fabius Pictor. Modern chronologers adopt Varro's date for the founding of Rome (April 21, 753 B. C.). Because the year 753 A.U.C. (*anno urbis conditae,* "from the founding of the city") is the year 1 B. C. and 754 A.U.C. is the first year of the Christian era, in order to convert a date A.U.C. into modern reckoning, one must, if it is smaller than 753, subtract its number from 754, for a B.C. date, or, if larger than 753, subtract from it the number 753 for a year since the birth of Christ.

Islamic Chronology. The Islamic era is reckoned from July 16, A. D. 622, the first day of the lunar year (according to the pre-Islamic Arabians) in which the Hegira (Ar. *hijrah*), or emigration of Mohammed from Mecca to Medina, occurred. Hegira years are used for religious matters throughout the Muslim world, but their use for other matters is largely restricted to the Arabian Peninsula. This system was adopted by the Caliph Omar I (ʻUmar ibn-al-Khaṭṭāb, reigned 634–644) in about the 17th year of the new era.

The Muslim calendar is lunar: the years consist of 12 months, each containing 29 or 30 days arranged alternately. An intercalated day comes at the end of the 12th month in appointed years in each cycle of 30 years. The purpose of this intercalated day is to reconcile the first day of the month with the day of the new moon. In each cycle of 30 years, 19 are common and contain 354 days and 11 are *kabīsah* and contain 355 days.

To ascertain whether a Hegira year is common or *kabīsah,* divide it by 30. The quotient gives the number of completed cycles, and the remainder indicates the place of the year in the cycle in question. If the remainder is 2, 5, 7, 10, 13, 16, 18, 21, 24, 26, or 29, the year is *kabīsah* and consists of 355 days.

The 12 months that comprise the Hegira year are Muḥarram (30 days), Ṣafar (29), Rabīʻ I (30), Rabīʻ II (29), Jumāda I (30), Jumāda II (29), Rajab (30), Shaʻbān (29), Ramaḍān (30), Shawwāl (29), Dhu al-Qaʻdah (30), and Dhu al-Ḥijjah (29 or 30). Reliable conversion tables of Islamic dates are easily obtained.

Medieval Chronology. A man who traveled in the Middle Ages must have been confused by the numerous systems of reckoning time that varied from town to town and country to country.

Under the Roman Empire years were indicated by the names of the consuls; in the West no consuls were appointed after A. D. 534, and in the East, after 541. Thereafter, years were designated *post consulatum Paulini* in the West and *post consulatum Basilii* in the East. In 566 the Byzantine Emperor Justin II assumed the consulship himself, and thereafter Imperial years were reckoned from the January 1 following the emperor's accession. Monarchical countries in Europe reckoned by regnal years, but the practice differed. The Franks counted regnal years from the king's accession, but Charlemagne dated from his coronation, and this practice was usually observed by the French kings. In Germany reckoning for kings was usually from the date of accession, and, if they became emperors, from their coronation, or sometimes from both. In England reckoning was originally from the coronation date, but after Henry III regnal years were counted from the accession. The pontifical years of the popes began not with election but with ordination.

Various indiction cycles were employed. The most important were the Greek, or Constantinopolitan, Indiction, beginning on September 1; the Imperial Indiction, or Indiction of Constantine (also known as the Indiction of Bede), beginning on September 24; and the Roman, or Pontifical, Indiction, beginning on December 25, sometimes on January 1. See also INDICTION.

The most important eras were the Spanish era, beginning Jan. 1, 38 B.C., the era of Diocletian, beginning Aug. 29, A.D. 284, the era of the Armenians, beginning July 9, 552, and the Christian era, which, during the Middle Ages, was a confusing system because the beginning of the year was set at different days in different countries. Some countries reckoned the beginning of the era during the year before, others during the year after, the birth of Christ. Dionysius Exiguus, the originator of the era in the 6th century, set its commencement on Annunciation Day, March 25, nine months before the traditional date for the birth of Christ. Other days for the beginning of the Christian Era were January 1, March 1, Christmas Day, and Easter. Modern scholars have not reached agreement on the actual date of the birth of Christ. Many favor 4 B.C., others 6, 7, and 8 B.C.

Mayan Chronology. The ancient Mayas of the Yucatán Peninsula in Mexico seem to have been the first people in the world to realize the indispensability of setting a fixed starting point from which to reckon their chronological era. By making observations from their lofty pyramid temples with a clear sweep of the horizon in all directions, and by carefully marking risings and settings of celestial bodies along the horizon, the Mayas were able to arrive at a figure for the duration of an astronomical year that is actually more accurate than the figure of our Gregorian calendar:

Astronomical year	365.2422 days
Mayan calendar year	365.2420 days
Gregorian calendar year	365.2425 days
Julian calendar year	365.2500 days

The Mayas were so exact in their time reckonings that it is possible to date their monuments with respect to each other to the precise day. Difficulties arise when it comes to translating Mayan chronologies into modern chronologies. A number of systems have been developed, each based on reasonable arguments. The zero date of the Mayan chronological era, "4 Ahau 8 Cumhu," was set at Feb. 10, 3641 B.C., by Charles P. Bowditch and Thomas A. Joyce, at Oct. 14, 3373, by Herbert J. Spinden, and at Aug. 13, 3113, by John Eric Thompson (see *Bibliography*).

Sylvanus G. Morley, in *The Ancient Maya* (1946), divides the history of the Mayas into three major epochs: Pre-Maya (2500 B.C.?–A.D. 317); Old Empire (317–987); and New Empire (987–1697). He also offers correlation tables of Mayan and Gregorian chronologies.

See also BIBLE—6. *Old Testament History Including Archaeology and Chronology;* CALENDAR; ERA.

WILLIAM H. STAHL, *Brooklyn College*
Revised by EDWARD L. OCHSENSCHLAGER
Brooklyn College

Bibliography

Bury, John B., Cook, S. A., and Adcock, F. E., eds., *Cambridge Ancient History* (London 1925); rev. ed. issued in fascicles (1967–   ).
Ehrich, Robert W., ed., *Chronologies in Old World Archaeology* (Chicago 1965).
Kubitschek, Wilhelm, *Grundriss der antiken Zeitrechnung* (Munich 1928).

Egyptian

Hayes, William C., *The Scepter of Egypt*, 2 vols. (New York 1953–1959).
Parker, Richard A., *The Calendars of Ancient Egypt* (Chicago 1950).

Minoan

Hutchinson, R. W., "Notes on Minoan Chronology," *Antiquity*, pp. 61–74 (Newbury, Berkshire, England, June 1948).

Assyrian

Brinkman, J. A., "Mesopotamian Chronology of the Historical Period," appendix in Leo A. Oppenheim, *Ancient Mesopotamia* (Chicago 1964).
Dubberstein, Waldo H., "Assyrian-Babylonian Chronology 669–612 B.C.," *Journal of Near Eastern Studies*, pp. 38–42 (Chicago, January 1944).
Olmstead, Albert T., *History of Assyria* (New York 1923).
Poebel, A., "The Assyrian King List from Khorsabad," *Journal of Near Eastern Studies*, pp. 247–306 and 460–492 (Chicago, July and October 1942).

Hebrew

Olmstead, Albert T., *History of Palestine and Syria* (New York 1931).

Late Babylonian-Early Persian

Brinkman, J. A., "Mesopotamian Chronology of the Historical Period," appendix in Leo A. Oppenheim, *Ancient Mesopotamia* (Chicago 1964).
Olmstead, Albert T., *History of the Persian Empire* (Chicago 1948).
Parker, Richard A., and Dubberstein, Waldo H., *Babylonian Chronology 626 B.C.–A.D. 75* (Providence, R. I., 1957).

Hindu

Eggermont, P. H. L., *The Chronology of the Reign of Asoka Moriya* (Leiden, Netherlands, 1956).

Chinese

Hoang, Pierre, *Concordance des chronologies mnémoniques chinoise et européenne* (Shanghai 1910).
Moule, Arthur C., *The Rulers of China 221 B.C.–A.D. 1949*, with an introductory section on the earlier rulers c. 2100–249 B.C. by W. P. Yetts (London 1957).
Tchang, M., *Synchronismes chinois . . .*, 2357 B.C.– 1904 A.D. (Shanghai 1905).

Japanese

Bramsen, William, *Japanese Chronological Tables . . . 645 A.D.–1873 A.D.*, with an Introductory Essay on Japanese Chronology and Calendars (Tokyo 1910).
Reischauer, Edwin O., *Chronological Chart of Far Eastern History*, on China, Japan, and Korea (Cambridge, Mass., 1947).
Tsuchihashi, Yachita, *Japanese Chronological Tables from 601 to 1872 A.D.* (Tokyo 1952).

Greek

Forsdyke, Sir Edgar John, *Greece Before Homer:* vol. 1, *Ancient Chronology and Mythology* (London 1956).
Pritchett, William K., and Neugebauer, O., *The Calendars of Athens* (Cambridge, Mass., 1947).
Thomson, G., "The Greek Calendar," *Journal of Hellenic Studies*, vol. 63, pp. 52–63 (London 1943).

Islamic

For day-to-day conversion tables, consult Romeo Campani, *Calendario Arabo* (Modena, Italy, 1914); for ordinary conversion tables, consult Wolseley Haig, *Comparative Tables of Muhammadan and Christian Dates* (London 1932).

Medieval

Poole, Reginald L., *Medieval Reckonings in Time* (London 1918).

Mayan

Bowditch, Charles P., *The Numeration, Calendar Systems, and Astronomical Knowledge of the Mayas* (Cambridge, Mass., 1924).
Spinden, Herbert J., *The Reduction of Mayan Dates* (Cambridge, Mass., 1924).
Thompson, John Eric, *A Correlation of the Mayan and European Calendars* (Chicago 1927).

HAMILTON WATCH COMPANY

THE MARINE CHRONOMETER is mounted in gimbals to minimize the effect of a ship's pitch and roll at sea.

CHRONOMETER, krə-nom′ə-tər, a clock that measures time with great accuracy and is used in navigation to provide the time of observations of celestial bodies for determining position at sea. Chronometers are set to Greenwich mean time, the basic time used in celestial navigation.

A chronometer differs from an ordinary clock or watch principally in that it is considerably more accurate because it contains a variable lever device and a temperature-compensating balance. The variable lever regulates the power transmitted by the mainspring so that it remains uniform as it unwinds. The balance, formed by a combination of metals of different coefficients of expansion, compensates for changes in temperature and makes the rate of losing or gaining approximately uniform at all temperatures. To reduce the effect of the ships motion on the chronometer, it is hung in gimbals to keep it in a horizontal position. It is fitted in a special wood box with a glass top that is usually airtight. This box is placed in a second cloth-padded box to protect the instrument from vibrations and temperature changes.

The chronometer's face is the same as that of an ordinary clock or watch. It has an hour and a minute hand. However, it has two additional superimposed dials—one with a second hand that moves every half second, and the other with a hand that indicates numbers of hours since the last winding. Chronometers are wound daily at the same time and are checked for accuracy every day by means of radio time signals. A careful record is kept of the chronometer's error and the daily change in the error, which is called daily rate. The United States Navy will not issue a chronometer which loses or gains more than 1.55 seconds a day, or which has a daily rate of more than 0.50 second.

The chronometer was invented in 1735 by John Harrison, a self-educated English horologist, who subsequently spent 30 years refining and perfecting his instrument.

WILLIAM SEMBLER
State of New York Maritime College

CHRYSALIS, kris′ə-ləs, the resting, or pupal, stage in the life cycle of a butterfly. During the chrysalis stage, the insect changes from a caterpillar, or larva, into an adult. Although the chrysalis appears to be a mummylike structure that remains in one place and seems to be inactive, it is undergoing many complex physical and chemical changes. During this stage each larval structure is broken down, and adult structures are formed. The exact chemical processes involved in this transformation are not entirely understood.

Characteristics. Each chrysalis is tightly enclosed in a thin shell-like covering, and although some movement is possible, it is restricted to slight movements in the abdominal region. The color of the chrysalis varies greatly according to the species, ranging from dull brown to brilliant shades of green and yellow, sometimes with metallic gold or silver markings. A few days before the adult emerges, the butterfly's color pattern may sometimes be seen through the thin pupal shell.

At the end of the chrysalis' abdomen is a specialized spiny process, called a cremaster. The tip of the cremaster is attached to a tiny pad of silk that was spun by the caterpillar on a leaf, branch, or other support. Thus, the chrysalis is suspended with its head pointing downward. In some species, however, the chrysalis is supported in a more or less upright position by a thin silken band, called a girdle, that passes around the thorax and is attached to the support.

The duration of the chrysalis stage varies among different species and sometimes even fluctuates among members of the same species. In some butterflies it may last only 7 to 10 days, while in others it may last more than a year. Several northern species spend the entire winter in the chrysalis stage.

Moth Pupae. Structurally there is little difference between a moth pupa and a butterfly pupa, although the term "chrysalis" is never applied to the resting stage of a moth. All moth pupae are typically smooth and rounded, while butterfly pupae often have angular body projections. In addition, the butterfly chrysalis is rarely enclosed in a cocoon or buried underground, as is the moth pupa.

DON R. DAVIS, *Smithsonian Institution*

CHRYSANDER, кнrü-zän′dər, **Friedrich** (1826–1901), German music scholar and editor. He was born in Lübtheen, Mecklenburg-Schwerin, on July 8, 1826. He studied philosophy at the University of Rostock but later devoted himself exclusively to music. From 1868 to 1871 and again from 1875 to 1882 he edited the *Allgemeine musikalische Zeitung.* He also edited *Die Jahrbücher für musikalische Wissenschaft* (2 vols., 1863–1867) and, with others, the *Denkmäler der Tonkunst* (5 vols., 1869–1871) and the *Vierteljahrsschrift für Musikwissenschaft* (1884–1894).

The work for which Chrysander is best known is his and Georg Gervinus' monumental 100-volume edition of the works of George Frideric Handel, published from 1859 to 1894 under the auspices of Germany's Handel Society, which he founded in 1856. Chrysander completed only two volumes and the first part of a third (1858–1867) of an extensive projected biography of Handel. He died in Bergedorf (now part of Hamburg) on Sept. 3, 1901.

CHRYSANTHEMUM, kri-san'thə-məm, a large genus of annual and perennial plants native to temperate regions, mostly in Europe and Asia. Generally, chrysanthemums have alternate, strongly-scented leaves and flower heads consisting of fertile disk flowers in the center and petal-like ray flowers around the outside. Some species have been cultivated for so many centuries that their central flowers have become modified in size and shape so that they resemble the ray flowers. It is these species, with their huge ball-like flower heads that are widely cultivated in gardens and sold by florists.

Although many species, including the feverfew (*Chrysanthemum parthenium*), the common field daisy (*C. leucanthemum*), and the Shasta daisy (*C. maximum*) all belong to the genus *Chrysanthemum,* the term "chrysanthemum" in popular usage refers only to the large-flowered types, especially those with similar ray and disk flowers. One of the best known of these species is the florist's chrysanthemum (*C. morifolium*), which originated in China, and whose flower heads range in color from white and yellow to pink and red. Sometimes the flower heads are solid colors, but often they are combinations of colors or varying shades of the same color.

The many different varieties of the florist's chrysanthemum and other popular species are divided into several classes. The most important of these classes are: the *exhibition* types, whose ball-like flower heads are 6 inches (15 cm) in diameter; the so-called *decoratives*, with reflexed (backward-bending) petals and flower heads from 1½ to 4 inches (3.8 to 10 cm) wide; the *singles*, with flower heads resembling those of daisies; the *semidoubles* and *anemones*; the *pompons*, with spherical flower heads not more than 4 inches (10 cm) in diameter; the *spoons*, which have spoon-shaped ray flowers; the *azaleamums*, or *cushion* types, which are dense, dwarfed plants bearing many flower heads; and the *cascades*, which have weak stems and can be trained to grow downward if they are cultivated properly.

Cultivation. Garden chrysanthemums are hardy in the northern United States, but often they bloom so late in the fall that the flower buds are frozen before they blossom. In the central states they are also hardy, but sometimes they need to be covered with a cloth at night to protect them from the frost.

Chrysanthemums are propagated by cuttings or by merely dividing the plants after they have finished blooming. The pinching back of young shoots is essential for making bushy plants, the end buds being removed several times until July. Although chrysanthemums are all fall-blooming plants, they may be forced to bloom early by completely covering them in late summer with black cloth. Commercial chrysanthemum growers have perfected this technique so that they can produce blooming plants at almost any time of the year.

The chief insect pest of chrysanthemums is the aphid, which usually attacks greenhouse plants, not those grown outdoors. The chief plant diseases are wilt disease, leafspot, mildew, and a virus disease that stunts the plants' growth. However, chrysanthemums are actually very easy to grow and can be kept in good condition by lifting and thinning the clumps every few years.

DONALD WYMAN
The Arnold Arboretum, Harvard University

CHRYSAROBIN, kris-ə-rō'bin, is an orange-yellow powder used in dilute form as an ointment for certain skin diseases such as psoriasis. It is obtained from a substance found in the wood of a tree (*Andira araroba*) native to India and Brazil. It may irritate the skin if it is not diluted before application. Chrysarobin leaves a stain on skin and clothing.

CHRYSEIS, krī-sē'əs, in Greek legend, was the daughter of Chryses, a priest of Apollo. During the Trojan War, before the siege of Troy, the Greeks took many prisoners, of whom Chryseis was given to Agamemnon and Briseis to Achilles. When Agamemnon refused Chryses' plea for his daughter's return, Apollo sent a plague against the Greeks. At a Greek council, the soothsayer Calchas advised that the maiden be returned. Agamemnon agreed but at the same time insisted that Briseis be awarded to him for giving up Chryseis. Achilles submitted but withdrew in rage from the war, his wrath being the theme of Homer's *Iliad.*

CHRYSANTHEMUM TYPES (*l. to r.*): Pompon (Fortune); spider (Peggy Ann Hoover); and irregular incurve (Mrs. Kidder).

ROCHE

CHRYSIPPUS, krī-sip′əs (c. 280–c. 205 B.C.), Greek philosopher, who was called the second founder of the Stoic school, after Zeno, because of his systematization of Stoic doctrines. Chrysippus was also famed for his dialectical skill and for his defense of Stoicism against the Epicureans and the members of the Greek philosophical Academy. Though he is reputed to have written over 700 works, only fragments remain.

Chrysippus was born in Soli in Cilicia. About 260 B.C. he went to Athens, where he attended the lectures of Arcesilaus and subsequently became the disciple of Cleanthes, whom he succeeded in 232 as leader of the Stoics.

CHRYSLER, krīs′lər, **Walter Percy** (1875–1940), American industrialist, who established the Chrysler Corporation, one of the "Big Three" automobile manufacturers in the United States. He was born in Wamego, Kans., on April 2, 1875, and began his career as a railroad machinist, rising eventually to become the head of a locomotive factory. In 1912 he became plant manager for the Buick Motor Company, the principal unit of General Motors. In 1916 he was named president of Buick and a vice president of General Motors at an annual salary of $500,000. He resigned in 1920 over a policy difference with William Durant, president of General Motors.

During a recession in 1920 and 1921, Chrysler was retained by a banking syndicate to reorganize Willys-Overland, a motor company in financial difficulty. After a spectacular success he was called upon to restore to solvency the Maxwell Motor Corporation, which produced Maxwell and Chalmers cars. While doing so, he supervised the design of the first Chrysler automobile, which was first shown in 1924. The success of this model encouraged Chrysler's financial backers, and in 1925, with their support, he reestablished Maxwell Motor Corporation as the Chrysler Corporation. In 1928, Chrysler acquired the Dodge Brothers Company, and later added Plymouth and DeSoto to his line. Chrysler remained president of the corporation until 1935, when he became chairman of the board. He died at Great Neck, Long Island, N. Y., on Aug. 18, 1940.

WILLIAM GREENLEAF
University of New Hampshire

CHRYSLER CORPORATION, krīs′lər, a U. S. automobile manufacturer with other diversified manufacturing interests in 19 countries on 6 continents. Formed in 1925, the Detroit-based corporation is named for Walter P. Chrysler (q.v.), who had risen to a position of leadership in the automobile industry. With associates he created the Chrysler Corporation to take over the property and business of the Maxwell Motor Corporation, which he had reorganized.

In its first full year of operation, Chrysler Corporation offered four models—a "50," "60," "70," and Imperial "80." Speed, acceleration, beauty, and performance won these cars wide acceptance, and in 1927, Chrysler held 5th place in the American automobile industry. In 1928, Chrysler acquired the extensive properties of the Dodge brothers. The new Dodge Division, manufacturing automobiles and trucks, increased the Chrysler Corporation more than fivefold and brought it into close competition with the industry's leaders, General Motors and Ford.

Despite the Depression of the 1930's, Chrysler management succeeded in eliminating the indebtedness incurred by its expansion. Although expenditures were cut sharply, there were no reductions in the research budget. Among Chrysler's innovations were rubber-insulated engine mountings, oil filter and air cleaners, and 4-wheel hydraulic brakes.

Like its competitors, Chrysler became active in the overseas automobile market. Many of these activities were placed under Chrysler International, S. A., organized in 1958 with headquarters in Geneva, Switzerland. In the same year Chrysler acquired a 25% interest in the French company manufacturing the Simca compact car. By 1963 this interest had been increased to 64%. Chrysler also acquired Farco A. G., a Greek company manufacturing lightweight trucks, and subsequently gained a controlling interest in Roote Motors, Ltd., of Britain.

For the domestic market, the Chrysler Corporation offers a complete line of cars (Valiant, Plymouth, Dart, Dodge, Chrysler, and Imperial) and trucks. Most manufacturing activities are situated in Michigan and Ohio, with assembly plants and complementary facilities spread throughout the country near population centers. Sales through over 6,500 dealers are aided by the Chrysler Credit Corporation. Over 2 million units were sold annually in the mid-1960's.

Diversification characterizes the corporation's activities. The Chrysler Outboard and Chrysler Boat corporations cater to the boating market, and Chrysler has long provided inboard marine engines for pleasure and commercial craft. Through its Airtemp Division, Chrysler supplies heating, cooling, and air conditioning equipment. A Chemical Division concentrates on needs of the transportation industry, and through its Amplex Division, Chrysler manufactures Oilite, a powdered metal. The Defense-Space Group continues Chrysler's record of participation in government work.

With net sales exceeding $5 billion annually in the late 1960's, Chrysler ranked 6th among the world's industrial companies in terms of sales.

ARTHUR M. JOHNSON, *Harvard University*

CHRYSOBERYL, kris′ə-ber-əl, is a rare beryllium-aluminum oxide mineral, finer varieties of which are important as gemstones. The mineral always occurs as tabular crystals that are very hard, transparent, and have a glassy luster. They are yellowish to emerald-green, grayish, or brown. True *cat's-eye*, or *cymophane*, is a variety that has an opalescent luster and shows a narrow beam of light across its surface. *Alexandrite* is a valuable emerald-green variety that appears red by transmitted light. The primary sources of chrysoberyl are Ceylon and Brazil; the alexandrite variety is found in the Ural Mountains.

Composition, $BeAl_2O_4$; hardness, 8.5; specific gravity, 3.6–3.8; crystal system, orthorhombic.

CHRYSOCOLLA, kris′ə-kōl-ə, is a hydrous copper silicate mineral, and a minor ore of copper. It usually occurs in massive form, with microscopically small crystals. Pure chrysocolla is green to greenish-blue or blue, and the crystals have a glassy luster. However, the mineral varies greatly in water content and is often impure, with a brown or black color. Chrysocolla is found in copper deposits in all parts of the world.

Composition, $CuSiO_3$, with varying amounts of H_2O; hardness, 2–4; specific gravity, 2–2.4; crystal system, possibly orthorhombic.

CHRYSOLITE, kris'ə-līt, is a magnesium-iron silicate in the series of minerals known as olivine. It is a rather common rock-forming mineral that is found in granular masses. Crystals of chrysolite are transparent to translucent, have a glassy luster, and are olive green to yellow. Fine transparent varieties used as gemstones are called *peridot;* the chief source of the latter is the island of Geziret Zabargad in the Red Sea. In the United States, chrysolite occurs in New Mexico and Arizona. See also OLIVINE.

Composition, $(Mg,Fe)_2SiO_4$; hardness, 6.5–7; specific gravity, 3.3–3.4; crystal system, orthorhombic.

CHRYSOLORAS, kris-ō-lō'rəs, **Manuel** (1355?–1415), Greek scholar and pioneer in the teaching of Greek in the West. He was born in Constantinople. In 1393 the Byzantine Emperor sent him to Italy to seek Western aid for the defense of Constantinople against the Ottoman Turks. He traveled in Europe, becoming known for his learning, and in 1397 he was invited to teach Greek in Florence. The response to his teaching was enormous; among the many scholars he attracted were such humanists as Leonardo Bruni, Poggio Bracciolini, and Francesco Filelfo.

Among Chrysolaras' contributions to the field of literature and Greek scholarship was his *Erōtēmata sive quaestiones,* the first Greek grammar used in western Europe; it was based on the new theory of teaching language by questions and answers. He translated Homer and Plato's *Republic* into Latin. It was through Chrysoloras that scholars were able to rediscover the Greek classics, and the basis of western humanism was laid.

Chrysoloras was also engaged in public affairs. He was active in trying to arrange a general council to discuss the union of Greek and Latin churches. At the time of his death, on April 15, 1415, he was on his way to the Council of Constance as representative of the Greek church. His nephew and companion in Italy, Johannes Chrysoloras, was also a Greek scholar.

CHRYSOPHYTA. See ALGAE—*Golden Algae.*

CHRYSOPRASE, kris'ə-prāz, is an apple-green variety of chalcedony that receives its color from nickel oxide. It occurs in Silesia and, in the United States, in Oregon and California. Brilliant chrysoprase is semiprecious. See CHALCEDONY.

CHRYSOPSIS, krə-sop'səs, any of a group of short North American plants with hairy leaves and large yellow daisylike flower heads. They are also known as *golden asters* and are sometimes cultivated as garden plants.

CHRYSOSTOM, kris'əs-təm, **Saint John** (3. 354–407), patriarch of Constantinople and Doctor of the Church, whose writings mark him as the most distinguished representative of the Antiochene school of theology. His pulpit eloquence was equalled by no one in Christian antiquity and, perhaps, by few since then.

He was born in Antioch into a Christian family of nobility and wealth. Antioch was a center of Greek culture, and as a boy John received an excellent education, studying Greek philosophy under Andragathius and rhetoric under the famous pagan sophist Libanius.

Following a practice common at the time, John deferred baptism until about the age of 18 and about the same time entered the monastic school near Antioch directed by Diodore of Tarsus. Some three years later he became a monk, dwelling first with an elderly hermit on the heights above the city and then in solitude in a cave on Mt. Sylpios. So rigorous were his penances there that they permanently impaired his health, and he had to return to Antioch, where he was ordained a priest in 386. From his 12 years as a priest at Antioch his unequaled reputation as preacher and the name Chrysostom ("golden mouth"), used since the 6th century, derive. The sermons he gave are a remarkable source of information on the times.

Patriarch of Constantinople. In 398, at the urging of the imperial minister Eutropius, Emperor Arcadius consecrated the unwilling priest bishop and patriarch of Constantinople. As patriarch, John was revered for his saintliness, incomparable eloquence, and passion for social justice. In his pastoral zeal he engaged in charitable works that drained much of the see's income, and his refusal to curry official favor or to engage in the notorious intrigues of the Byzantine court roused highly placed opponents to conspire for his downfall. His lack of realism and diplomacy in executing clerical and monastic reforms and his sometimes tactless excoriations of the wealthy served the cause of his opposition.

With the backing of Empress Eudoxia, Theophilus, patriarch of Alexandria, who sought primacy for his own see, convened the illegal Synod of the Oak, which declared John deposed in 403. John was banished from Constantinople but almost immediately recalled. Soon, however, Eudoxia became infuriated at John's supposed unflattering references to her in a sermon, and she engineered his deposition and permanent exile in 404.

After being detained for three years at Cucusus in Little Armenia, John was consigned to the more remote Pityus. While on a forced march to this place, he died near Comana in Pontus on Sept. 14, 407. In 438 his body was brought back to Constantinople. After the Venetians plundered the city in 1204, they sent his remains to St. Peter's in Rome. His feast day is January 27 in the West and November 13 in the Greek Church.

Works. Chrysostom's writings comprise several treatises (notably *On the Priesthood*) composed before 386; some 236 letters written during his exile; and his sermons from Antioch. The homilies contain permanently valuable commentaries on Biblical books interpreted according to the principles of the Antiochene school.

JOHN F. BRODERICK, S. J., *Weston College*

Further Reading: Baur, Chrysostomus, *John Chrysostom and His Times,* tr. by M. Gonzaga, 2 vols. (Westminster, Md., 1960–1961).

CHRYSOTILE. See ASBESTOS.

CHU HSI, jōō'shē' (1130–1200) was one of China's later Confucian philosophers and scholars. He wrote more than 100 works, including commentaries on almost all the Confucian classics. Chu Hsi grouped the *Confucian Analects,* the *Great Learning,* the *Doctrine of the Mean,* and the *Book of Mencius* into the Four Books. These books and his commentaries became the standard texts and official interpretations on which the civil service examinations were based for some 600 years. His philosophy also spread to Japan and Korea where, as in China, it dominated social and political thought for centuries.

Chu Hsi synthesized the philosophies of the Neo-Confucianists of the early Sung dynasty (960–1279) and was particularly influenced by Ch'eng Yi. His school, therefore, was called the Ch'eng-Chu School or the School of Li ("law" or "principle"). According to Chu Hsi's philosophy, abstract law or principle permeates the universe and makes things one. Each thing shares this universal "Great Ultimate," but it also has a particular principle of being, or nature, of its own. Bodily form is given by material force (ch'i). His belief that man is basically good and able to extend his knowledge through objective study reinforced the Confucian emphasis on scholarship.

WING-TSIT CHAN, *Chatham College*

Further Reading: Chan, Wing-tsit, ed. and tr., *A Source Book in Chinese Philosophy* (Princeton 1963); Fung Yu-lan, *A History of Chinese Philosophy*, tr. by Derk Bodde, vol. 2, (Princeton 1953).

CHU KIANG. See PEARL, river, China.

CHU-KO LIANG, jŏŏ'gŏŏ' lyäng' (181–234), one of China's greatest heroes, was a military strategist and statesman of the Three Kingdoms period (220–265 A. D.). He became famous as a scholar-recluse at a young age but spent much of his later life trying unsuccessfully to restore to power Liu Pei, king of the state of Shu and one of the pretenders to the Han dynasty throne usurped by Ts'ao Ts'ao. Chu-ko Liang led seven military campaigns against the usurpers and, as prime minister of Shu, was the mainstay of the state. Shu, in fact, lasted only a short while after his death.

The popular historical novel *San Kuo Chih Yen I (The Romance of the Three Kingdoms)*, written by Lo Kuan-chung during the Ming dynasty (1368–1644), deals with the deeds and valor of Chu-ko Liang.

CHU TEH, jŏŏ'du' (1886–1976), Chinese Communist leader, who played a major role in the formation of the Chinese Red Army. He was born in Ilung, Szechwan province, on Dec. 18, 1886. Chu led the life of a warlord from 1916 to 1921 and went to study at Göttingen University in Germany in 1922. While in Europe, he met Chou En-lai, who persuaded him to become a Communist.

Chu was deported to China via the Soviet Union in 1925. In 1927 he participated in the Nanchang uprising, the event from which the Chinese Red Army's beginning dates. Defeated by Chiang Kai-shek, he led a few soldiers into Mao Tse-tung's guerrilla base in Kiangsi and spent the following years organizing the Communist forces.

From 1931 to the mid-1950's, Chu was a close associate of Mao and commander in chief of the Communist armies. He led them through the Long March of 1934–1935 and to victory in 1949. After 1949 he held many high-ranking posts, including chairman of the National People's Congress. He died in Peking on July 6, 1976.

JAMES R. SHIRLEY, *Northern Illinois University*

CHÜANCHOW, chü-än'jŏ', is a city in Fukien province, China, on the left bank of the lower Chin River. Chüanchow was once one of China's major seaports, but oceangoing ships no longer can reach the port. The city is still the economic center of the Chin River basin, however.

Chüanchow's traditional industries make lacquer ware and embroidery and do bamboo weaving. Modern industries include sugar refining and machine building. Population: (1958) 110,000.

CHUANG TZU, jŏŏ-äng'dzu' (c. 369 B. C.–c. 286 B. C.), or *Chuang Chou,* was the greatest Taoist philosopher after Lao Tzu. He was born in the state of Meng, which was on the border between the present provinces of Shangtung and Honan. Little is known about him, except that he was a minor official in Meng and lived most of his life as a recluse.

His philosophy is embodied in the *Chuang Tzu,* although many chapters of the book were not written by him, but by his disciples and their followers. Chuang Tzu's beliefs may be summed up by the titles of the book's first two chapters, "Wandering at Leisure" and "The Equality of Things." According to him, the universe is in perpetual flux, with every end followed by a new beginning. Since there is no proof that the Supreme Being that appears to be directing this ceaseless transformation actually exists, men must follow nature and not impose their artificiality on it.

For complete happiness and spiritual freedom, such as the true sage enjoys, man must discard knowledge and "travel beyond the mundane world" to abide with enduring values and permanent reality. This permanent reality is the *tao,* the Absolute that unites all things. Distinctions, discriminations, and opposites such as life and death, right and wrong, beauty and ugliness, and success and failure are all merely manifestations of subjective points of view.

He did not expect people, except in rare cases, to become hermits, but he felt that relative happiness could be attained by adhering to transcendental values in earthly affairs. The degree of happiness depends on the extent to which the individual accepts the transitoriness of life and freely develops his natural ability (te).

Lao Tzu believed that nongovernment is the best form of government because nonaction is the best form of action. Chuang Tzu agreed because he thought laws suppress freedom and distort nature and therefore lead to human misery. But Chuang Tzu concentrated more on the individual than Lao Tzu and made more of a distinction between what is of nature and what is of man. He wanted not so much to reform things as to rise above them. Chuang Tzu's imagery, metaphors, philosophical anecdotes, wit, and biting criticism of Confucianism and society remain unsurpassed in Chinese literature. His stress on individual freedom, on imagination and a broad perspective, and on unity with nature exerted an immense influence on later Chinese landscape painting and poetry. See also TAOISM.

WING-TSIT CHAN, *Chatham College*

Further Reading: Chan, Wing-tsit, ed. and tr., *A Source Book in Chinese Philosophy* (Princeton 1963); Fung Yu-lan, *A History of Chinese Philosophy*, tr. by Derk Bodde, vol. 1 (Princeton 1952); Watson, Burton, tr., *Chuang Tzu, Basic Writings* (New York 1964).

CHUB, a common minnow of southern England, Europe, and the USSR. It is found from the Gulf of Finland, south to the Euphrates River and from England east to European Russia. The chub is a coarse and bony fish that is not valued highly as food, although it is taken commercially to some extent in Russia. It is, however, a highly regarded sport fish.

A small, cylindrical fish with small fins, the chub's average weight is 2 to 3 pounds (0.9–1.2 kg), but some chubs may reach a weight of 12 pounds (5.5 kg) and a length of 30 inches (75 cm). The chub is gray-green to gray-brown on the back, yellow to metallic bronze on the sides, and buff to white on the underside. The fins are dusky with pink streaks.

Chubs normally inhabit the surface waters of rivers or rapid streams but occasionally may live in ponds. The smaller chubs live in schools and feed on small animals and plants, whereas the larger ones are solitary and predatory on other fishes. The chub spawns from April to June, and in this period the female may lay as many as 200,000 eggs.

The chub, *Leuciscus cephalus*, is a member of the family Cyprinidae, which is in the order Cypriniformes.

The name "chub" is also applied to some whitefishes (genus *Coregonus*), sea chubs (genera *Kyphosus* and *Girella*), and other minnows (genera *Gila, Hemitremia,* and *Hybopsis*).

E. J. CROSSMAN
University of Toronto

CHUBB, Thomas Caldecot (1899–1972), American writer of poems, biographies, and juvenile books. He was born in East Orange, N.J. on Nov. 1, 1899. Graduating from Yale in 1922, he had already published two books of poetry: *The White God* (1920) and *Kyrdoon* (1921). Chubb was deeply interested in ships and the sea. He was ship news reporter in New York and Paris for the New York *Times* (1925–1929) and worked as chief of the port section of the OSS during World War II. His later activities included the racing of the yawl *Victoria*. He died in Thomasville, Ga., on March 20, 1972.

Chubb wrote many volumes of flowing musical poetry, including *Ships and Lovers* (1933) and *Cornucopia* (1953). He also published *The Months of the Year* (1960), his translation of sonnets on the seasons by the 14th century Italian poet Folgore da San Geminiano. In his biographies of Boccaccio (1930), Aretino (1940), and Dante (1967), he brought the Italian Renaissance to life.

Chubb's books for young readers include *The Byzantines* (1959), *Slavic Peoples* (1962), and *Northmen* (1964).

CHUBB CRATER. See NEW QUEBEC CRATER.

CHUCK-WILL'S-WIDOW, a nocturnal bird that inhabits the eastern United States from Kansas and New Jersey southward through Texas and Florida. It is from 11 to 13 inches (28–33 cm) long and has reddish brown feathers that are lined and mottled with black. The sexes are alike in color except that the male has large patches of white on his outer tail feathers.

The chuck-will's-widow, which is heard but seldom seen, is best known for its nocturnal call, which sounds like its name. The bird feeds chiefly on night-flying insects such as moths, beetles, and winged ants; occasionally it has been known to eat small birds.

The chuck-will's-widow does not build a nest; instead it lays two eggs on a carpet of dead leaves on the ground. The pinkish cream eggs are glossy and heavily blotched and spotted with shades of brown and lavender. They are incubated by the female.

The chuck-will's-widow (*Caprimulgus carolinensis*) belongs to the family Caprimulgidae, which includes the nighthawks, whippoorwills, and nightjars, in the order Caprimulgiformes.

KENNETH E. STAGER
Los Angeles County Museum of Natural History

Chuckwalla

CHUCKWALLA, chuk'wol-ə, a herbivorous lizard found in rocky desert areas of southeastern California, western Arizona, and adjacent areas. Various species also inhabit limited ranges in Baja California and on islands in the Gulf of California.

A very bulky lizard, the chuckwalla reaches an overall length of about 16 inches (40 cm); its thick tail is as long as its head and body. The chuckwalla has folds of loose skin on the sides of its neck and body. In adult males, the foreparts and limbs are usually black and the rest of the body red or light gray. The young are cross-barred, a condition also existing to some extent in females.

When pursued, the chuckwalla takes refuge in narrow rock crevices. It inflates its lungs to increase the size of its body, thus making its removal from a hiding place difficult. Certain anatomical structures apparently help these desert lizards to cope with the dryness and the excess of salt in their plant food. The female lays about eight eggs, but little else is known of the behavior of chuckwallas.

Chuckwallas make up the genus *Sauromalus* in the family Iguanidae. The common chuckwalla found in the United States is *C. obesus*.

CLIFFORD H. POPE
Author of "The Reptile World"

Chuck-will's-widow

CHUGACH MOUNTAINS, chōō′gach, in southern Alaska, extending parallel to the coast for about 300 miles (480 km) eastward from near Cook Inlet to the western end of the St. Elias Mountains. They are part of the Coast Ranges. The highest point is Mt. Marcus Baker (13,250 feet; 3,962 meters). Chugach National Forest is on the southern slope of the range.

CHUKAR. See PARTRIDGE.

CHUKCHI, chōōk′chē, a Siberian Arctic people of the USSR, who live in northeastern Siberia across the Bering Strait from Alaska. Together with the Koryak people to the south and the Kamchadal people of the Kamchatka Peninsula, the Chukchi form the Paleo-Asiatic language group. These languages have some common traits with Eskimo and North American Indian languages. Of the Soviet Union's almost 12,000 Chukchi, nearly 10,000 live in Chukchi national okrug, a subdivision of Magadan oblast. Most others live in Koryak national okrug to the south, a subdivision of Kamchatka oblast.

In terms of mode of living and economic pursuits, the Chukchi fall into two categories: nomadic, reindeer-raising Chukchi, who live inland in the tundra; and coastal dwellers, who fish, hunt seals, and raise sled dogs. The reindeer-raising Chukchi also hunt birds and trap fur-bearing animals. The coastal Chukchi, who account for about one fourth of the total number, live in permanent villages along the coasts of the Chukchi Sea, an arm of the Arctic Ocean, and along the Bering Strait and the Bering Sea. The reindeer Chukchi wander with their herds in the interior. The traditional religion of the Chukchi is animism.

In the 1920's Soviet scholars developed a literary language for the Chukchi, whose spoken language is called Luoravetlan. A Latin alphabet was devised, and the first book in Chukchi was published in 1932. In the late 1930's, the Latin alphabet was supplanted by a new alphabet based on the Russian Cyrillic alphabet, in keeping with a general alphabet reform among non-Russian minorities. Since then a small body of literature, mainly primers and political writing, has been published in Chukchi.

THEODORE SHABAD
Editor of "Soviet Geography"

CHUKCHI NATIONAL OKRUG, chōōk′chē, ôk′-rōōg, a political subdivision of the USSR, in northeastern Siberia, facing Alaska across the Bering Strait. The Chukchi (Russian, *Chukotski*) national okrug, which is part of Magadan oblast of the Russian republic, is named for the Chukchi people, who are the principal Siberian native minority in the okrug. Most of its area of 284,-800 square miles (737,700 sq km) consists of wooded tundra (in the south) and treeless tundra (in the north). Long, cold winters limit the growing season to two short summer months. The capital Anadyr (1966 population, 5,000) is situated at the mouth of the Anadyr River, which drains the central part of the okrug.

The native peoples, consisting of 10,000 Chukchi and 1,000 Eskimo, raise reindeer (numbering more than 500,000 head) and hunt fox, squirrel, and other fur-bearing animals. The Russian inhabitants engage in the mining of gold, tin, and coal, and they staff the Arctic research stations and supply ports along the coast, especially Pevek in the north and Providenia in the east. The national okrug was formed in 1930. Population: (1966) 84,000.

THEODORE SHABAD
Editor of "Soviet Geography"

CHUKCHI SEA, chōōk′chē, part of the Arctic Ocean between Alaska and Siberia, north of Bering Strait, which connects it with the Bering Sea. The Chukchi Sea merges with the Arctic Ocean at the edge of the continental shelf to the north.

CHULA VISTA, chōō′lə vis′tə, is a city near the southwestern tip of California, in San Diego county. It is an industrial and residential community, 8 miles (13 km) southeast of San Diego, of which it is a suburb. The city's chief industry is the manufacture of missile and aircraft parts. Other products include structural steel, hardware, and fertilizer. Tomatoes, celery, and flowers are grown nearby, and the packing and shipping of vegetables is an important activity. Southwestern College, a 2-year coeducational institution, is in Chula Vista. The city was laid out in 1888 and incorporated in 1911. Government is by manager and council. Population: 67,901.

CHULALONGKORN, chōō′lä′lông′kôn′ (1853–1910), was the Siamese monarch responsible for modernizing Siam (now Thailand). His dynastic name was *Rama V*.

Chulalongkorn was born in Bangkok on Sept. 20, 1853. He succeeded his father as king in 1868, but the country was governed under a regency until 1873. Despite his traditional upbringing (including Buddhist monkhood), he quickly grasped the significance of Western culture. Threatened by foreign imperialism, Chulalongkorn maintained Siam's independence by making sagacious concessions to foreign powers and simultaneously introducing sweeping social and governmental changes.

His social revolution emphasized modern education and the abolition of slavery. He laid the foundation for a modern economy by launching public works, railways, and postal and telegraph services. His modernized government administration and judiciary paved the way for revision of the unequal treaties forced on Siam by foreign powers through the years.

PRACHOOM CHOMCHAI
Author of "Chulalongkorn the Great"

CHUMACERO, chōō-mä-ser′ō, Alí (1918–   ), Mexican poet, whose special concern was poetic form. At 22, Chumacero was one of four editors of the review *Tierra Nueva* (1940–1942), which promoted the view that poetry is an art rather than a vehicle of social protest.

Chumacero edited two collections of poems, *Poesia romantica* (1941) and *Cuentos y crónicas* (1944), and published three remarkable volumes of his own poems—the relatively spontaneous *Páramo de sueños* (1944), the more guarded *Imágenes desterradas* (1948), and the highly disciplined and concentrated *Palabras en reposo* (1956). Chumacero's meditations on love, time, death, and the struggle of the soul are intelligently constructed and enclosed in strict yet lovely measures that are lyrical without being too sensual, and modern without being jangled. As one critic put it, Chumacero "takes possession of himself in the poetic form and is calm."

CHUNGKING, chŏŏng'king', the leading industrial center of Southwest China, is on a promontory at the confluence of the Yangtze and Chialing rivers in eastern Szechwan province. It occupies a commanding position in water transportation in the Szechwan Basin and serves as a gateway to the lowland regions of central China. In Chinese, Chungking is also known as *Pahsien.*

The iron and steel works at Tsuchikou and the coal industry at Paimiaotzu, both on the Chialing River, near Chungking, laid the foundation upon which Chungking became the center of heavy industry in Szechwan. The city also manufactures cotton, paper, matches, and chemicals. Two major highways link Chungking with Northwest China and Soviet Turkestan, and with the southwestern provinces and Burma.

The first major railroad across the basin was completed in 1952, linking Chungking with Chengtu. This line was later connected with the Lunghai Railway in Shensi province by the completion of the Paochi-Chengtu Railway in 1956. A bridge across the Yangtze at Paishato, west of Chungking, was built in 1962.

Chungking was the center of the ancient Pa kingdom, which was absorbed by the state of Chin toward the end of the 4th century B.C. Thereafter Chungking tended to be overshadowed by Chengtu, except when rebellious leaders at the end of the Yüan (Mongol) and Ming dynasties used it as a base of operation. In 1890, by the Treaty of Peking, Chungking was made an open port, and attained municipal status in 1923.

In November 1937, when Nanking fell to the Japanese, Chungking was chosen as the wartime capital. The city was under prolonged and heavy aerial bombardment during 1939–1941, resulting in severe destruction of life and property. As the war intensified in eastern and central China, many industries were moved west to Chungking and reestablished there to support the war effort. Under the Communist regime the iron and steel industry has expanded so greatly that Chungking is Southwest China's leading steel producer. Population: (1958) 2,165,000.

KUEI-SHENG CHANG
University of Washington

CHUQUICAMATA, chōō-kē-kä-mä'tä, a mining town in northern Chile, is famous for its open-pit copper mine, one of the largest in the world. More than 10,000 feet (3,050 meters) above sea level on the western slope of the Andes, the town exists primarily to house and serve the 7,000 men who dig and refine the copper ore.

Although it was long known that there was copper in the region, and several small mines were in operation in 1900, it was not until 1911 that large-scale facilities were planned. In that year the Guggenheim family, mining promoters in the United States, paid $25 million for the property. They sold their holdings to their competitor, The Anaconda Company, another U.S. firm, for $70 million. Anaconda paid higher than prevailing wages to its Chilean workers and built schools, hospitals, and housing. In 1967 a new arrangement, called "Chileanization of copper" was agreed to. Anaconda promised greater investment and production, also stock for the Chilean government, in return for tax relief and guarantees against early nationalization. Population: (1960) 24,798.

LAURENCE R. BIRNS
The New School for Social Research, New York

CHUNGKING'S Assembly Hall, built in 1954, has seating accommodations for more than 4,000 people.

CHUR, kōōr, is a city in Switzerland, the capital of Graubünden (Grisons) canton. Chur (French, *Coire;* Italian, *Coira;* Romansch, *Cuera*) is located 74 miles (119 km) southeast of Zürich, on the Plessur River, just above its junction with the Rhine, at an altitude of 1,952 feet (595 meters). The city is a tourist resort and commercial center but has industries that include woodworking, printing, and the manufacture of flour, beer, chocolate, metal goods, and textiles. The inhabitants are mostly German-speaking and Protestant.

Originally a Roman settlement, Chur became a bishopric as early as 452, and in 1170 its prelates became princes of the Holy Roman Empire. Their rule was ended in 1464, and the city accepted the Reformation in 1524–1526, although the Roman Catholic bishopric remains. Points of historical interest are the bishop's court, built on the site of a Roman fort; the 8th century St. Margaret's Church; the 12th to 13th century Cathedral of St. Lucius, built on the site of an earlier church, and containing the tomb of the Swiss soldier and political leader Georg Jenatsch (1596–1639); the 15th century town hall; and the Rhaetian Museum. The sacristy of the cathedral also houses many items of artistic and historical interest. Population: (1960) 24,825.

CHURCH, Benjamin (1734–?1778), American physician and traitor. He was esteemed in Massachusetts professional, social, and political circles until his double-dealings were uncovered in 1775.

Church was born in Newport, R.I., on Aug. 24, 1734. After attending Harvard, he studied medicine in England and then returned to practice in Boston. Church wrote and spoke in defense of colonial rights and served in the Massachusetts provincial congress and on the colony's committee of safety. He became director general of hospitals for Washington's army in July 1775.

Patriot authorities discovered his traitorous

activities two months later, when they decoded his letter to the commander of a British vessel, containing information on the strength of the American forces. For several years, Boston patriots had suspected him of British sympathies. Much later, a historian discovered documents confirming that he had been passing on intelligence to British Gen. Thomas Gage as early as May 1775.

Church's denial of the charges was not convincing. He was convicted by court-martial on Oct. 4, 1775. After confinement he was allowed to leave the country on a ship that presumably was lost at sea in 1778. As a result of his arrest and conviction, Congress made death the maximum penalty for communicating with the enemy.

Don Higginbotham, *University of North Carolina*

CHURCH, Benjamin (1639–1718), American soldier, who fought in several colonial wars. Born in Plymouth, Mass., he became a carpenter. In 1674 he purchased land at Sogkonate (Little Compton), R. I., where he befriended neighboring Indians. During King Philip's War (1675–1676), commanding small detachments of Plymouth troops and friendly Indians, he defeated Philip at Great Swamp (near Kingston, R. I.) in December 1675. He continued pursuit until Philip was ambushed and shot on Aug. 12, 1676.

Later, in Plymouth colony, Church served as a local magistrate. During King William's War (1689–1697) and the early years of Queen Anne's War (1702–1704), he took part in five expeditions against the French and Indians in Nova Scotia and Maine. He retired in 1704 and died on Jan. 17, 1718, near Little Compton.

CHURCH, Frederick Edwin (1826–1900), American painter of romantic, exotic landscapes. He was born in Hartford, Conn., on May 4, 1826. He was a pupil of Thomas Cole in Catskill, N. Y., and belonged to the Hudson River school of landscape painting. Discontented with local subjects, however, Church traveled about the Western Hemisphere and Europe seeking spectacular landscapes, to which he brought an impressive technique. His masterpiece, *Niagara Falls* (1857), impressed critics as well as the public; Ruskin remarked that it contained effects of light on water never before known to art. Church's panoramas, such as *Heart of the Andes* (1855), *Jerusalem* (1870), and *Morning in the Tropics* (1877), made him rich as well as world famous.

When rheumatism struck his painting arm in 1877, Church learned to paint with the other arm, but it too was soon crippled. He died on April 7, 1900, at Olana, his home on the Hudson.

CHURCH, Sir Richard (1784–1873), British army officer, who commanded the Greek Army in the Greek War of Independence. He was born in Cork, Ireland, and enlisted in the British Army at the age of 16. Later he was commissioned and served in various posts in the Mediterranean area. He was knighted by George IV of England in 1822.

His interest in Greek freedom from Turkish rule brought him command of the Greek Army in 1827. He drove the Turks from the western provinces of Greece. After the war, he resided in Greece and was active in the revolution of 1843. He was appointed a senator in 1843 and a general in the Greek Army in 1854. He died in Athens on March 30, 1873.

CHURCH. The word "church," in its most limited meaning, denotes a building in which Christians meet for religious worship. In a wider sense it denotes a variety of relationships, ranging from that of a group of Christians professing a particular creed to the whole body of the faithful, either in the practice of their faith or in their dealings with the state. Derived from the Greek adjective *kyriakon*, meaning "belonging to the Lord," the term "church" originally designated the place where the apostles and evangelists gathered believers together for worship and mutual support.

As converts became more numerous, they were grouped in a series of parishes, or churches, under the guidance of a bishop, or overseer. Since he was the integrating authority, his pronouncements on church matters were made *ex cathedra*, that is, from his official seat (Greek *kathedra*, chair). Therefore, the church where he resided became known as a cathedral. When, at times, the bishop met with other bishops in council to determine a common rule of Christian life or practice, their decisions were issued as coming from the church, in this case, the clergy.

In time the church as a whole developed a duality of ritual and practice in its Eastern and Western segments. This led, eventually, to a separation of the two parts. In the East several autocephalous, or self-governing, patriarchates emerged, in Constantinople, Alexandria, Antioch, Jerusalem, and later in Moscow. In the West the bishop of Rome claimed primacy over other bishops as the successor of Peter and, thus, sole vicar of Christ, with final authority in matters of doctrine and discipline. From this separation came the two divisions known as the Eastern Church and the Roman Church, with "church" in this instance meaning the entire body of the faithful and bishops within each area.

These remained the major divisions of the church until the Reformation of the 16th century. After this time many Christians of the Church of Rome separated into dissenting denominations or sects, each of which came to be known as a particular church (Anglican Church; Presbyterian Church; Methodist Church). Each remained within the Christian tradition but proclaimed a distinctive creed and ritual. Similar divisions within the Eastern Church emerged as the Armenian Church, the Coptic Church, and the Orthodox Church. One thing all shared in common, however, was a varying relationship to the state, ranging in turn from coordination (Holy Roman Empire—Roman Church; Established Church of England) to widely disparate attitudes often resulting in persecution (Quakers; Pilgrims; Jehovah's Witnesses). From such conditions a complex pattern of relations emerged that has come to be defined under the general title of Church and State. See also Christianity; Church and State; articles on denominations; and Index entries under *Church*.

Church Architecture. Church buildings tend to follow the prevailing architecture of the region in which they are located. Thus, Eastern churches favor Byzantine architecture; Western, Gothic or Romanesque. Modern trends in church architecture are moving toward a synthesis of styles and a general simplicity of detail that can only be defined under the generic term of church architecture. See also Cathedrals and Churches.

James H. Smylie
Union Theological Seminary, Richmond, Va.

CHURCH AND STATE is a phrase that refers to the continually varying relations between organized religion and organized government, which for centuries has troubled rulers, churchmen, philosophers, and common men. The underlying questions are simple. Do earthly rulers and their people believe in some god or group of divinities whose power exceeds that of secular governors? And does a select class of men—priests or other experts in divinity—uniquely understand the divine laws and wishes? If so, should not secular rulers—kings or parliamentarians—conform their rule to the divine will as understood and expounded by the priestly adepts? Or should secular rule hold itself strictly aloof from all religious questions?

These questions, however simple as stated, are infinitely complex when related to the public and private organization of men's lives. The terms *church* and *state* have elusive significance. Men primarily familiar with Anglo-American and European cultures inevitably think of "church" as an entity having some structure like the Roman Catholic Church, or the Church of England, or some less closely organized sect such as the Methodist or Baptist churches in the United States. They think of "state" as a separate entity. Church-state relations, as these concepts have come to carry meaning in Western civilization, require political and churchly institutions somewhat resembling those that developed in medieval and modern Europe and in America. Before a church-state problem in these terms can arise, there must be a church sufficiently organized and active to influence temporal government, and a secular rule—a lay state—competing with churchly magnates for ecclesiastical influence.

Even without a structured church, there may still be an establishment of religion and thus the possibility of a church-state problem. There might be a secular government that favored some amorphous belief or disbelief, giving that creed a preference over others. There might be a citizenry jealous of religious favoritism in government and wishing to exclude government from any religious concerns. Although Hinduism, Buddhism, and Confucianism were immensely influential religious philosophies, they never developed a centralized and disciplined ecclesiastical organization like that of the medieval papacy. Nevertheless, suspicious resentment between sects in India caused the drafters of the 1949 Indian constitution to decree governmental neutrality toward all religions.

Establishment and Separation. Two contrasting types of church-state arrangements have appeared in Western societies. In one situation, government assumed that it should join forces with some organized church, but contention arose as to which church among two or more it should choose. Thus Henry VIII of England broke with Rome in 1531, created a Church of England separate from the Roman Catholic Church, and became a "Protestant" ruler, though he probably never so considered himself. His son and heir, Edward VI, continued that course, but Edward's half sister Mary, who succeeded him in 1553, married Philip of Spain the next year and re-established Roman Catholicism. Elizabeth succeeded Mary in 1558 and made England's government Protestant again. In 27 years, England changed its state religion three times.

Although governmental favor for one religion may involve intolerance of other creeds, it does not necessarily do so. Where a church is "established"—is favored by a ruler—his government may still tolerate dissenters, as Louis XIV of France did until 1685. On the other hand, it may insist on adherence to the established church, as Louis XIV did after that year. State favor for one creed inevitably makes the outsiders apprehensive; they sniff the approach of tyranny in every breeze.

The second type of arrangement between church and state is a complete divorce of the two. Separation appears to have been the direction of constitutional development in modern states since the "enlightenment" of the 18th century. The principle of separation, consistently adhered to in the United States, appears in the constitutions of a number of nations that have adopted written fundamental laws since 1945. Japan, India, and Italy are examples.

Pre-Reformation Conflict. Church-state relations in Europe during most of the past 1,500 years followed the first of these two patterns—that of union or close relation between the established church and the state. In the 6th century, religious and secular rule were so closely united in the authority of the Roman emperor Justinian that he undertook to decide on the competing orthodoxy of Monophysite and Nestorian Christians; taking Pope Vigilius captive in 548 A. D., he obliged the pontiff to concur in the emperor's churchly authority.

The European conflict between *imperium* (dominion of the secular rule) and *sacerdotium* (priestly authority) continued with varying fortunes through the Middle Ages. In the latter part of the 11th century and first quarter of the 12th, the contest appeared as the "investiture controversy" over the power to select and put in office church magnates.

A bishop often held great estates as feudal tenant of a secular overlord. When an episcopate fell vacant, the emperor, king, duke, or other lay magnate asserted his right to select his new vassal for himself and to establish or "invest" him in his churchly dignities. Popes, on the other hand, contended that high church dignitaries were primarily religious, and papal authority should select and vest them in office.

In 1075, Pope Gregory VII forbade lay investiture. The next year the Holy Roman emperor Henry VI and a group of bishops loyal to him declared void Gregory's own election as pope. Gregory excommunicated Henry and purported to depose him from the imperial throne—a pretext for actual deposition that Henry's secular rivals seized. Henry, fearing the loss of his throne, submitted to Gregory at Canossa in Italy in 1077. The penitent waited for three days outside the papal gate, barefoot and in sackcloth, until the pope absolved him. Following a second purported deposition in 1080, Henry returned to Italy with an army, captured Rome, and in 1084 installed an antipope who reinstated Henry's imperial credentials. Gregory died, out of power, a year later.

Repudiation of Papal Authority. Contests over secular control of Catholic clergy continued for the next four centuries. But in the early 1500's an even more serious movement began in northern Europe. In 1517, Martin Luther, an Augustinian monk in Wittenberg, Germany, attacked the institution of papal "indulgences," which purported to remit some of the consequences of man's sin. Luther's attack offended church discipline, and in 1521 he was excommunicated.

Emperor Charles V, a Habsburg king of Spain who sympathized with the papacy, sentenced him to outlawry. But Luther refused to recant, and, with the support of powerful German princes, he continually gained adherents. The Reformation had begun.

The liberty of every man to think out his own relation to God, which Luther both preached and exemplified, worked powerfully to separate much of northern and western Europe from Roman Catholicism and subsequently to shatter the unity of Protestantism. Individual freedom to choose a religious belief inevitably led to independent judgment on political theory as well—a long step on the road away from kingship.

Hence in 1604 when James I of England heard a group of his leading clergy discuss toleration of antiepiscopal Puritans within the Church of England, he protested, "No Bishop, no King," and added that the Puritans would either conform to the establishment or he would "harry them out of the land or else do worse." James' words were prophetic. During his reign many Puritans were harried out of England to America, where during the next century and a half they got on without a bishop, and at the end of that time got rid of their English king.

Disestablishment in America. The 17th and 18th centuries saw a concurrent growth of scientific knowledge and of religious rationalism in England, on the European continent, and ultimately in British America. Men who perceive that the universe operates according to an undeviating system of scientific principles may find difficulty in believing in an anthropomorphic divinity whose earthly favors can be attracted and whose earthly penalties can be deflected by appropriate rituals. Scientism and skepticism set the tone of 18th century "enlightenment," and neither was likely to strengthen governmentally established religions.

In America each of the thirteen colonies, except perhaps Rhode Island, originally had a government that fostered one or more religions. But establishment never got a good hold because of the diversities of religions among the predominantly Protestant settlers and the freedom with which they moved among the different settlements. In the 17th and 18th centuries, Baptists went to Anglican Virginia, Catholics to Maryland, Jewish immigrants to New York and Rhode Island. With such a mixture of religions, governmental favoritism became difficult.

During the 18th century much of the fierceness of religious rivalries in British America disappeared. After they became independent in 1776, the new states repealed most of their legislation supporting one or another religion. The first clause of the 1st Amendment, proposed by James Madison to Congress in 1789 and adopted in 1791, set the tone for the American attitude toward separation of church and state thereafter—"Congress shall make no law respecting an establishment of religion, or prohibiting the free exercise thereof . . ."

Madison submitted another proposed amendment that read in part: "No State shall violate the equal rights of conscience, or the freedom of the press, or the trial by jury in criminal cases." He prophetically told the House of Representatives, "I think there is more danger of those powers being abused by the State governments than by the Government of the United States." Congress, however, did not adopt, then or later, Madison's proposal.

Until 1868, when the 14th Amendment was ratified, the several states remained free to do as they chose about religion. The 14th Amendment forbade any state to "deprive any person of life, liberty, or property without due process of law" and to "deny to any person within its jurisdiction the equal protection of the laws"—vague guarantees whose content was not clearly apparent. But during the next century the Supreme Court construed them to include disestablishment.

The most conspicuous 20th century controversies concerning government's relation to religion in the United States have involved religion in relation to public education and legislation limiting Sunday labor. Without an explicit federal constitutional prohibition against state religious legislation, the Supreme Court nevertheless held in *Cantwell* v. *Connecticut* (1940) that the concept of freedom embodied in the 14th Amendment included the liberties guaranteed by the 1st Amendment. In *Everson* v. *Board of Education* (1947) the court, although upholding a New Jersey law that provided for the use of public bus transportation both for Catholic parochial school and public school pupils, nevertheless uttered the extremely influential dictum: "The 'establishment of religion' clause of the First Amendment means at least this: Neither a state nor the Federal Government can set up a church. Neither can pass laws which aid one religion, aid all religions, or prefer one religion over another. Neither can force nor influence a person to go to or to remain away from church against his will or force him to profess a belief or disbelief in any religion. No person can be punished for entertaining or professing religious beliefs or disbeliefs, for church attendance or non-attendance. No tax in any amount, large or small, can be levied to support any religious activities or institutions, whatever they may be called, or whatever form they may adopt to teach or practice religion. Neither a state nor the Federal Government can, openly or secretly, participate in the affairs of any religious organizations or groups and vice versa. In the words of Jefferson, the clause against establishment of religion by law was intended to erect 'a wall of separation between Church and State.'"

The principle of this sweeping pronouncement has not prevented government from giving incidental aid to religion when the aid supports a purpose that is essentially secular—school buses, which keep children safe from traffic, and Sunday legislation, which affords a common day of leisure. It bars religious exercises in public school, such as prayer or Bible reading for worship. Though application of the court's pronouncement may pose problems, its general principle remains clear: government must not undertake religious activity, and churches must not attempt any part of secular government.

ARTHUR E. SUTHERLAND
Harvard University Law School
Author of "Constitutionalism in America"

Further Reading: Brinton, Crane, Christopher, John B., and Wolff, Robert L., *A History of Civilization,* 2d ed., 2 vols. (Englewood Cliffs, N. J., 1960); Gwatkin, H. M., and Whitney, J. P., eds., *The Cambridge Medieval History,* 8 vols. (New York and London 1911); Peasley, Amos J., *Constitutions of Nations,* 2d ed., 3 vols. (The Hague 1956); Stokes, Anson Phelps, and Pfeffer, Leo, *Church and State in the United States,* rev. ed. (New York 1964).

CHURCH ARCHITECTURE. See CATHEDRALS AND CHURCHES.

CHURCH ARMY, a primarily British organization affiliated with the Church of England and founded in 1882 by the Reverend Wilson Carlile. Like the Salvation Army, which it resembles, it does evangelistic and social work. Missions and "Labour Homes" have been established in the slums of London and other large cities to house and care for vagrants and the unemployed. The Church Army also does considerable work in the rehabilitation of prisoners about to be discharged. The army gives only remuneration—in money, food, or shelter—in return for work, and never free gifts. Branches of the Church Army exist in other parts of the Commonwealth and in the United States.

CHURCH CALENDAR. See CALENDAR—7. *Church Calendar.*

CHURCH FATHERS. See FATHERS OF THE CHURCH.

CHURCH MUSIC. See ANTHEM; CHANT; CHORAL MUSIC; HYMNS; and Index entry *Church Music.*

CHURCH OF CHRIST, SCIENTIST. See CHRISTIAN SCIENTISTS.

CHURCH OF ENGLAND. See ANGLICAN COMMUNION; ENGLAND, CHURCH OF; GREAT BRITAIN AND NORTHERN IRELAND—*Religion;* and the Index entry *England, Church of.*

CHURCH OF GOD, the name given to at least 200 independent religious bodies formed at the end of the 19th century in the United States. They are Holiness, or Pentecostal, churches, the offspring of Methodism, and teach the doctrine of holiness or sanctification to be obtained by a "second blessing" of justification or forgiveness. They believe in God as the only founder of the church, yet as fundamentalists they emphasize personal religious experience. Most are governed by the congregational system.

The largest of the churches is the Church of God in Christ, organized in Arkansas in 1895, which had an estimated membership of 425,500 in the late 1960's. The Church of God (Cleveland, Tenn.) was founded in 1902 and had a membership of more than 200,000 in the late 1960's. The Church of God (Anderson, Ind.) had more than 140,000 members in the late 1960's.

CHURCH OF IRELAND. See GREAT BRITAIN AND NORTHERN IRELAND—*Religion;* IRELAND, CHURCH OF.

CHURCH OF SCOTLAND. See GREAT BRITAIN AND NORTHERN IRELAND—*Religion;* SCOTLAND—*Religion and Education.*

CHURCH OF THE NAZARENE. The Church of the Nazarene was organized in its present form on Oct. 13, 1908, at Pilot Point, Texas, by the union of several small religious bodies. The principal groups were the Church of the Nazarene, founded in Los Angeles, Calif., by P. F. Bresee in 1895; the Association of Pentecostal Churches of America, Brooklyn, N. Y. (1896); and the Holiness Church of Christ, Pilot Point, Texas (1905).

The government of the church is representative. Each local church may call its own pastor and manage its local affairs. Local churches, however, are subject to the counsel of superintendents, who are elected by district assemblies. The General Assembly, composed of equal numbers of ministerial and lay delegates from the various assembly districts, is the supreme legislative body of the church. General superintendents, elected by this assembly and a general board, have supervision of the entire denomination.

Nazarenes subscribe to 15 articles of faith, which are similar to those held by other evangelical religious bodies and especially those aligned with the Wesleyan-Arminian theological tradition. Special emphasis is placed on the doctrine of entire sanctification.

Nine liberal arts colleges and one Bible college are maintained in the United States and Canada. Missionary work is conducted in 45 world areas. The publishing house, the graduate theological seminary, and the denominational headquarters are located in Kansas City, Mo.

B. EDGAR JOHNSON, *Church of the Nazarene*

CHURCH SCHOOL. See CATHOLIC CHURCH, ROMAN—5. *Activities;* RELIGIOUS EDUCATION; SUNDAY SCHOOL.

CHURCH STATES, the land, chiefly in Italy, ruled by the popes. Scholars disagree in assigning territorial boundaries to church or papal states since different popes pursued radically diverse temporal policies in Italy, Asia Minor, and Europe.

Papal temporal rule, known as theocracy, developed as a result of the disintegration of the Roman Empire. In the face of invasions and the need to secure fiscal independence, the popes assumed temporal as well as spiritual authority. Eventually, constant pressure from the Lombards forced the papacy to seek aid and land from the Franks. King Pepin granted lands to the papacy in 754, and title to these was confirmed by Charlemagne in 774. This territory, in addition to the Patrimony of St. Peter (land belonging since early times to the Church of Rome) and the land that had accrued to the church after the Peace of Constantine in the 4th century, formed the nucleus of the papal domain which grew to include Ravenna, Pentapolis, and Romagna. The territorial endowments and income from this land enabled the Holy See to assume economic and social functions which the secular leaders had relinquished during the turbulent Middle Ages. Gradually, the popes effectively executed the duties once discharged by the imperial government.

By the 16th century, church states ribbed mid-Italy from sea to sea and included the March of Ancona, the duchies of Parma, Piacenza, Modena, Romagna, Urbino, Spoleto, Castro, and the provinces of Bologna, Perugia, and Orvieto. It has been estimated that the area embraced 17,000 square miles (44,030 sq km) and 3 million people. These states experienced economic and political decline long before the revolutions of Europe curtailed the monarchies. A chief sign of demise was the increasing secularization of the old patrimonies. In 1860, Italy annexed Romagna, Ancona, and Umbria, leaving the pope only the city of Rome and the province of Latio. Ten years later King Victor Emmanuel took Rome and eliminated church states forever. Henceforth the pope's personal sovereignty and his right to diplomatic representation replaced temporal rule.

In 1929 the Lateran Treaty was concluded by which Italy recognized the pope as both the temporal and spiritual ruler of Vatican City. This area, less than one square mile (2.6 sq km) in size, contains the Vatican palace, annexes, and gardens and the basilica of St. Peter. This spate of land has not been regarded as a restoration of the church states. The pope, often styled "the Prisoner of the Vatican," concurs in this view. "It will, we hope," remarked Pius XI, "be clear that the Sovereign Pontiff has no more material territory than is indispensable for him . . . to exercise the spiritual power entrusted to him for the good of mankind . . . we are pleased that the material domain is reduced to so small an extent." In the 20th century the papal income is partially supplied by Peter's Pence, the annual offering made by Catholics the world over. The sum, administered by a commission of cardinals, helps the Holy See meet local and universal church needs.

HARRY J. SIEVERS, S. J.
Loyola Seminary, Shrub Oak, N. Y.

CHURCHES OF CHRIST, churches that were originally part of the Disciples of Christ but became a separate body in 1906. They are strictly congregational and have no central organization. In the late 1960's there were approximately 18,000 churches with a membership of 2,500,000. See also DISCIPLES OF CHRIST.

CHURCHILL, chûr'chil, **Charles** (1731–1764), English poet and satirist. He was born at Westminster, London, in February 1731. Churchill forfeited a fellowship at Cambridge University for an early marriage and was ordained an Anglican priest in 1756, succeeding to his father's parish in 1758.

Soon, however, Churchill left the church (he had by this time achieved a reputation as a rake), and in 1761, the year he separated from his wife, he achieved a huge success with his poetical satire *The Rosciad*, a witty and severe attack on most of the prominent theatrical personalities of the day. Churchill turned also to political satire, writing *The Prophecy of Famine* (1763) and contributing to the *North Briton*, a periodical published by the political agitator John Wilkes. In 1763, after the *North Briton* published an attack on George III, Wilkes fled to France; Churchill, however, remained in England, where he continued to pillory such prominent figures as the artist William Hogarth (*An Epistle to William Hogarth*, 1763, against which Hogarth retaliated with a famous cartoon of Churchill as a debauched clergyman) and Samuel Johnson (*The Ghost*, 1763).

In 1764, en route to meet Wilkes in France, Churchill contracted typhoid fever. He died in Boulogne on Nov. 4, 1764.

RICHARD E. HUGHES
Author of "Literature: Form and Function"

Further Reading: Brown, Wallace C., *Charles Churchill: Poet, Rake, and Rebel* (Lawrence, Kan., 1953).

CHURCHILL, JOHN. See MARLBOROUGH, 1ST DUKE OF.

CHURCHILL, chûr'chil, **Lord Randolph Henry Spencer** (1849–1895), British political leader. Third son of the 7th Duke of Marlborough, he was born at Blenheim Palace, Oxfordshire, on Feb. 13, 1849, and was educated at Eton and Oxford University. In 1874 he became Conservative member of Parliament for Woodstock. In the

same year, despite strenuous parental opposition, he married Miss Jennie Jerome, a famous beauty, of New York City.

During the next four years his attendance in Parliament was intermittent, for he often served as secretary to his father, who had been appointed by the prime minister, Lord Beaconsfield, as viceroy of Ireland. These visits gave young Churchill a close understanding of Irish politics and society at a critical time. When the Beaconsfield government fell in 1880, he returned to London to hurl himself with feverish intensity into domestic politics.

He quickly became the acknowledged leader of a group of four independent Conservatives known as "the Fourth Party," who were as disenchanted with their nominal leader, Sir Stafford Northcote, as with Gladstone's Liberal government. The Fourth Party and its daring young leader quickly attracted notice. In 1883–1884, Churchill captured the National Union of Conservative Associations and then came to terms with Lord Salisbury, whom he had always championed. In June 1885, when Salisbury replaced Gladstone as prime minister, Churchill became secretary of state for India, in which office he completed the British annexation of Burma. He had by now developed a sometimes insolent but strikingly original political style and was the most articulate advocate of "Tory Democracy."

In the winter of 1885–1886 he saw, and utilized, the potentialities of Ulster feeling when Gladstone turned to Irish Home Rule; his phrase "Ulster will fight, Ulster will be right" became the rallying cry of the North. He played a vital part in the creation of the Unionist coalition that defeated Home Rule. August 1886 found him chancellor of the exchequer and leader of the House of Commons, unquestionably second only to Salisbury. But he had many enemies. In December 1886 he threatened to resign over a cabinet disagreement on military expenditure. To his surprise, his challenge was accepted, and his influence declined forthwith. He died in London on Jan. 24, 1895, leaving a dazzling promise unfulfilled, and a son, Winston Churchill, to vindicate his memory.

ROBERT R. JAMES
All Souls College, Oxford University

CHURCHILL, chûr'chil, **Winston** (1871–1947), American novelist. He was born on Nov. 10, 1871, in St. Louis, Mo. He graduated from Annapolis and in 1895 moved to Cornish, N. H.

Churchill is best known today for his early works, thoroughly researched historical romances including *Richard Carvel* (1899), set in the days of the American Revolution; *The Crisis* (1901), laid in St. Louis during the Civil War; and *The Crossing* (1904), about Kentucky pioneers. In his own day, however, he was admired for his later novels, which attacked bossism and corruption and urged the need for religion in the modern world. These books were based on Churchill's own experience as a member of the New Hampshire legislature (1903–1905) and as an unsuccessful candidate for governor in the allegedly crooked election of 1912. *Coniston* (1906) shrewdly draws the character of the fictional corrupt boss Jethro Bass, and *The Dwelling Place of Light* (1917) uses the backdrop of a factory strike in a New England town in developing philosophical ideas. Churchill died on March 12, 1947, in Winter Park, Fla.

CHURCHILL, Sir Winston (1874-1965), British leader. English on his father's side, American on his mother's, Sir Winston Leonard Spencer Churchill embodied and expressed the double vitality and the national qualities of both peoples. His names testify to the richness of his historic inheritance: Winston, after the Royalist family with whom the Churchills married before the English Civil War; Leonard, after his remarkable grandfather, Leonard Jerome of New York; Spencer, the married name of a daughter of the 1st duke of Marlborough, from whom the family descended; Churchill, the family name of the 1st duke, which his descendants resumed after the Battle of Waterloo. All these strands come together in a career that had no parallel in British history for richness, range, length, and achievement.

Churchill took a leading part in laying the foundations of the welfare state in Britain, in preparing the Royal Navy for World War I, and in settling the political boundaries in the Middle East after the war. In World War II, he emerged as the leader of the united British nation and Commonwealth to resist the German domination of Europe, as an inspirer of the resistance among free peoples, and as a prime architect of victory In this, and in the struggle against communism afterward, he made himself an indispensable link between the British and American peoples, for he foresaw that the best defense for the free world was the coming together of the English-speaking peoples. Profoundly historically minded, he also had prophetic foresight: British-American unity was the message of his last great book, *A History of the English-Speaking Peoples*.

His dominant qualities were courage—he did not know what fear was—and imagination. Less obvious to the public, but no less important, was his powerful, original, and fertile intellect. He had intense loyalty, marked magnanimity and generosity, and an affectionate nature with a puckish humor. Oratory, in which he ultimately became a master, he learned the hard way, but he was a natural wit. The artistic side of his temperament was displayed in his writings and oratorical style, as well as in his paintings. He was a combination of soldier, writer, artist, and statesman. He was not so good as a mere party politician. Like Julius Caesar, he stands out not only as a great man of action, but as a writer of it too. He had genius; as a man he was charming, gay, ebullient, endearing.

As for personal defects, such a man was bound to be a great egoist—if that is a defect. So strong a personality was apt to be overbearing. He was something of a gambler, always too willing to take risks. In his earlier career, people thought him of unbalanced judgment partly from the very excess of his energies and gifts. That is the worst that can be said of him. With no other great man is the familiar legend more true to the facts. We know all there is to know about him; there was no disguise.

Young Churchill: 1874–1900. He was born on Nov. 30, 1874, at Blenheim Palace, the famous palace near Oxford built by the nation for John Churchill, 1st duke of Marlborough, the great soldier. Blenheim, named after Marlborough's grandest victory (1704), meant much to Winston Churchill. In the grounds there he became engaged to his future wife, Clementine Ogilvy Hozier (b. 1885). He later wrote his historical masterpiece, *The Life and Times of John*

WINSTON CHURCHILL flashes his famous "V for victory" signal during his World War II prime ministry.

Churchill, Duke of Marlborough, with the archives of Blenheim behind him.

His father, Lord Randolph Churchill, was a younger son of the 7th duke of Marlborough. His mother was Jennie Jerome; and as her mother, Clara Hall, was one-quarter Iroquois, Sir Winston had an Indian strain in him. Lord Randolph, a brilliant Conservative leader who had been chancellor of the exchequer in his 30's, died when only 46, after ruining his career. His son wrote that one could not grow up in that household without realizing that there had been a disaster in the background. It was an early spur to him to try to make up for his gifted father's failure, not only in politics and in writing, but on the turf. Young Winston, though the grandson of a duke, had to make his own way in the world, earning his living by his tongue and his pen. In this he had the comradeship of his mother, who was always courageous and undaunted.

In 1888 he entered Harrow, but he never got into the upper school because, always self-willed, he would not study classics. He concentrated on his own language, willingly writing English essays, and he afterward claimed that this was much more profitable to him.

In 1894 he graduated from the Royal Military College at Sandhurst. He then was commissioned in the 4th Hussars. On leave in 1895, he went for his first experience of action to serve as a military observer and correspondent with the Spanish forces fighting the guerrillas in Cuba.

Rejoining his regiment, he was sent to serve in India. Here, besides his addiction to polo, he went on seriously with his education, which in his case was very much self-education. His

WITH HIS MOTHER, the former Jennie Jerome of New York City, Churchill is pictured at the age of six.

mother sent out to him boxes of books, and Churchill absorbed the whole of Gibbon and Macaulay, and much of Darwin. The influence of the historians is to be observed all through his writings and in his way of looking at things. The influence of Darwin is not less observable in his philosophy of life: that all life is a struggle, the chances of survival favor the fittest, chance is a great element in the game, the game is to be played with courage, and every moment is to be enjoyed to the full. This philosophy served him well throughout his long life.

In 1897 he served in the Indian army in the Malakand expedition against the restless tribesmen of the North-West Frontier, and the next year appeared his first book, *The Story of the Malakand Field Force.* In the same year, 1898, he served with the Tirah expeditionary force, and came home to seek service in General Kitchener's campaign for the reconquest of the Sudan. Once again young Churchill managed to play the dual role of active officer and war correspondent. As such he took part at Omdurman in one of the last classic battles of earlier warfare—cavalry charges, a thin red line of fire against clouds of fanatical dervishes. The Battle of Omdurman was the end of a world. Once more Churchill wrote it up, and the whole campaign, in *The River War* (2 vols., 1899), a fine example of military history by an eyewitness. He made enemies among the professional soldiers by his frank criticisms of army defects. He entertained himself by writing a novel, *Savrola* (1900), which curiously anticipates later developments in history, war, and in his own mind.

On the outbreak of the South African War in 1899, he went out as war correspondent for the London *Morning Post.* Within a month of his arrival, he was captured when acting more as a soldier than as a journalist, by the Boer officer Louis Botha (who subsequently became the first prime minister of the Union of South Africa and a trusted friend). Taken to prison camp in Pretoria, Churchill made a dramatic escape and traveled, with a price of £25 on his head, via Portuguese East Africa back to the fighting front

in Natal. His escape made him world-famous overnight. He described his experiences in a couple of journalistic books and made a first lecture tour in the United States. The proceeds from the tour enabled him to enter Parliament (M. P.'s were not paid in those days).

Rising Politician: 1901–1915. On Jan. 23, 1901, Churchill became member of Parliament for Oldham (Lancashire) as a Conservative. But he had returned from South Africa sympathetic to the Boer cause, and his army experiences had made him extremely critical of its command and administration, which he proceeded to attack all along the line. The tariff proposals of Joseph Chamberlain completed his alienation from the Conservative party, and in 1904 Churchill left the party to join the Liberals. In consequence he was for years execrated by the Conservatives, and was unpopular with army authorities.

As Liberal M. P. for Northwest Manchester (1906–1908) and for Dundee (1908–1918), he was in a position to share in the long Liberal run of power and to take his place in one of the ablest British governments in modern times. As undersecretary of state for the colonies he played a considerable part in making a generous peace with the Boers. In 1906 he published his authoritative biography, *Lord Randolph Churchill* (2 vols.), and in 1908, *My African Journey,* a first-class example of his lifelong flair for journalism. In this year, 1908, he married and, in his own words, "lived happily ever afterwards." By his marriage to Clementine Hozier there were one son (Randolph) and four daughters (Diana, Sarah, Mary, and one who died in infancy).

As president of the board of trade (1908–1910) and home secretary (1910–1911), he contributed largely to the early legislation of the welfare state. He helped to create labor exchanges, to introduce health and unemployment insurance, to prescribe minimum wages in certain industries, and to limit working hours. As first lord of the admiralty (1911–1915), he was in a key position, as German naval power rose to its peak and modernization of the British fleet became an urgent necessity. Churchill's collaboration with Admiral Lord Fisher to this end was historic: it produced the changeover to oil-fueled ships from coalburning vessels, the creation of a naval air service, and the first development of the tank. With war approaching, Churchill, on his own responsibility, kept the fleet fully mobilized.

With the German onrush through neutral Belgium in 1914, he led a naval detachment to Antwerp, but failed to stem the tide. In 1915 he made himself responsible for the campaign to force the Dardanelles, with the aim of pushing Turkey out of the war, of linking up with Russia, and of taking the Central Powers in the rear. The campaign foundered, partly through bad luck, partly through lack of experience in combined operations. Churchill was made to take the responsibility, and when a coalition government was formed in May 1915, the Conservatives made it a condition that he should be dropped as first lord of the admiralty.

Changing Political Fortunes: 1916–1939. The Dardanelles failure seemed the end of his political career. He took up painting as a hobby and a consolation, and he remained devoted to it for the rest of his life. His accomplishment in the art should not be underestimated. In 1916 he went back to the army, gallantly volunteering for active service on the western front, where he commanded the 6th Royal Scots Fusiliers. But his energy and ability could not be dispensed with, and Prime Minister Lloyd George called him back to become minister of munitions.

At the end of the war, Churchill became secretary of state for war and also for air (1919–1921). In this post he pushed through army reforms and the development of air power, and became a pilot himself. He involved himself in much controversy by backing the efforts of the counterrevolutionaries against the Bolsheviks in Russia. As secretary of state for air and colonies (1921–1922), he took a leading part in establishing the new Arab states in the Middle East, while supporting a Jewish national home in Palestine as an act of historic and humanitarian justice. He was also closely concerned in the negotiations to establish the Irish Free State, and thus earned further Conservative distrust.

Having lost his seat in Parliament in the 1922 elections, Churchill lived in the political wilderness for the next two years. He was able to go forward with his memoirs, *The World Crisis* (5 vols., 1923–29), a large canvas. After various attempts to form a central, antisocialist grouping, he went back to the Conservative party in time to become chancellor of the exchequer in Prime Minister Stanley Baldwin's government (1924–1929). He was least happy in this office and ill at ease with economic affairs. Churchill was responsible for returning Britain to the gold standard, with the pound sterling set at $4.88 parity. This step was in conformity with the best expert advice, though Churchill's instinct was against it, and the policy was disastrous. It led to the coal strike, which precipitated the general strike in 1926. The general strike left a legacy of ill will and justified resentment throughout the labor movement, in particular a distrust of Churchill. It helped to bring about widespread unemployment, and was a factor in creating the world economic crisis that undid the recovery from World War I, promoted Hitler's rise to power in Germany, and brought about World War II.

UPI

INSPECTING BOMB DAMAGE after Nazi air attacks, Churchill inspired spirit of resistance among British.

During the whole of this disastrous period of 1929–1939, Churchill was out of office. During these years of political frustration he wrote his major works: *Marlborough* (4 vols., 1933–38); the first draft of *A History of the English-Speaking Peoples* (4 vols., 1956–58); a vivid and characteristic autobiography, *My Early Life* (1930); a revealing and suggestive book, *Thoughts and Adventures* (1932); and a volume of brilliant, if generous, portrait sketches, *Great Contemporaries* (1937). He also began to collect his speeches and newspaper articles warning the country of the wrath to come.

No one would take heed of his reiterated warnings of the folly of attempting to appease Hitler and of the necessity to bring together a "Grand Alliance" against the aggressor powers

UPI

AT YALTA with President Roosevelt of the United States *(center)* and Premier Stalin of USSR *(right)* in February 1945, Churchill discusses war strategy and postwar plans.

before it was too late. Baldwin and Chamberlain were too solidly entrenched in power to shift. Churchill tried to rally the right-wing Conservatives against Baldwin's liberal Indian policy, and he backed Edward VIII against Baldwin at the time of the king's abdication in 1936. These weapons broke in his hands, and only lost him support. Appeasement went on to the bitter end.

When war came in 1939, Churchill was inevitably recalled, as first lord of the admiralty. The signal went round the fleet, "Winston is back," a quarter of a century after his first going to the post. But the first wave of German military power overwhelmed Poland in September, and in the spring of 1940 the tidal wave overwhelmed northwestern Europe, followed shortly afterward by the fall of France.

War Leader: 1940–1945. On May 10, 1940, in the midst of this cataract of disasters, Churchill was called to supreme power and responsibility by a spontaneous revolt of the best elements in all parties. He, almost alone of the nation's political leaders, had had no part in the disaster of the 1930's, and he really was chosen by the will of the nation. For the next five years, 1940–1945—perhaps the most heroic period in Britain's history—he held supreme command, as prime minister and minister of defense, in the nation's war effort. At this point his life and career became one with Britain's story and its survival.

At first, until 1941, Britain fought on alone. Churchill's task was to inspire resistance at all costs, to organize the defense of the island, and to make it the bastion for an eventual return to the continent of Europe, whose liberation from Nazi tyranny he never doubted. He breathed a new spirit into the government and a new resolve into the nation. Upon becoming prime minister he told the Commons: "I have nothing to offer but blood, toil, tears, and sweat.... You ask, what is our policy? I will say: It is to wage war, by sea, land, and air, with all our might. ... You ask, what is our aim? I can answer in one word: Victory."

ELECTION VICTORY that returned Churchill to power in 1951 pleases him and his wife, Clementine.

UPI

Meanwhile he made himself the spokesman for these purposes among all free peoples, as he made Britain a home for all the faithful remnants of the continental governments. These included the Free French, for Churchill had himself picked out Charles de Gaulle as "the man of destiny." But Churchill's personal relationship with President Franklin D. Roosevelt was Britain's lifeline. Britain had lost most of her army equipment in the fall of France and during the evacuation of the British Expeditionary Force from Dunkirk in June. Roosevelt rushed across the Atlantic a supply of weapons that made a beginning.

By the autumn of 1940, Churchill was convinced that Germany could not bring off the invasion of Britain. Secure in this conviction, he took the momentous decision to send one of the only two armored divisions left in Britain to Egypt, to hold the land bridge to the East. Submarine warfare had placed a severe strain on the British navy, and Roosevelt again came to Britain's aid with the lease of 50 destroyers. Churchill took the grievous decision to cripple the French fleet at Oran, Algeria. He could not take the risk of the French navy's being taken over by the Germans, for this probably would have been the end for Britain.

The turning point of the war came in 1941, when Churchill took advantage of his opponents' mistakes. Hitler's invasion of Russia brought Russia into the war, and Churchill seized the opportunity of welcoming a powerful ally with both hands. Japan's attack on Pearl Harbor brought the United States into the war, and Hitler made the mistake of declaring war on the United States. Churchill's unforgettable speech to Congress after Pearl Harbor expressed something of the inspiration and high resolve in the face of mortal danger that he had given his countrymen while they had fought on alone for over a year.

The "Grand Alliance" to combat aggression that he had had in mind from the 1930's was now a fact. Churchill made himself the linchpin, journeying uncomplaining between Roosevelt and Stalin, though an older man than either. It was possible now to plan the liberation of the world from the aggressors. He and Roosevelt set forth their war aims in the Atlantic Charter, signed aboard the U.S.S. *Augusta* off Newfoundland in August 1941.

The first results of Allied cooperation were the landings in North Africa, the rounding up of the Nazi forces there, and the invasion of Sicily and Italy, "the soft under-belly of the Axis." It proved harder going than was expected, supporting Churchill's opposition to the opening of a second front in the west. Not until the summer of 1944 were the preparations complete for the invasion of Normandy, to break open Hitler's Europe. Churchill had always had an acute personal interest in combined operations, and he regarded the mobile "Mulberry" harbors as in large part his own idea. Only the personal order of King George VI prevented the prime minister from landing with the landing forces on D-day.

The last year of the war saw the famous partnership between Churchill and Roosevelt dissolving. Churchill looked to the shape of things that would emerge after the war, with the immense accession of strength to Russia and to communism in Europe. At the summit conferences in Teheran and Yalta, Churchill was grieved to find the president not supporting him in his struggle with Stalin to contain Russian expansion after the war. On the surrender of Germany in May 1945, Churchill rode around London in the victory celebrations, but, as he wrote, there was foreboding in his heart.

Peacetime Leader: 1945–1955. Before the surrender of Japan, Churchill's wartime government broke up, and the Labour party won a large majority in the general election of July 1945. Churchill was deeply affected ·by this blow, though it was in no sense a vote of censure upon him but upon 20 years of Conservative rule. He continued to enjoy esteem as leader of the opposition Conservative party.

He turned to writing a personal history, *The Second World War* (6 vols., 1948–1953), and to painting, exhibiting regularly at the Royal Academy. Though he was out of office, his prestige was a major asset to his country. In his famous "iron curtain" speech at Westminster College in Fulton, Mo., he warned the West against Russia's aims and the aggrandizement of communism, making a plea for cooperation between the English-speaking peoples as the only hope of checking it. This aroused a storm of controversy in the United States, but events soon confirmed Churchill's view of the world picture.

On Oct. 26, 1951, at the age of 77, he again became prime minister, as well as minister of defense. As the Conservatives held a very small majority and Britain faced very difficult economic circumstances, only the old man's willpower enabled his government to survive. He held on to see the young Queen Elizabeth II crowned at Westminster in June 1953, himself attending as a Knight of the Garter, an honor he had received a few weeks earlier. In 1953, also, he received the Nobel Prize in literature. On April 5, 1955, in his 80th year, he resigned as prime minister, but he continued to sit in Commons until July 1964.

Last Years. Churchill's later years were relatively tranquil. In 1958 the Royal Academy devoted its galleries to a retrospective one-man show of his work. On April 9, 1963, he received, by special act of the U. S. Congress, the unprecedented honor of being made an honorary American citizen. When he died in London on Jan. 24, 1965, at the age of 90, he was acclaimed as a citizen of the world, and on January 30 he was given the funeral of a hero. He was buried at Bladon, in the little churchyard near Blenheim Palace, his birthplace.

A. L. ROWSE
All Souls College, Oxford University

Bibliography

Avon, Earl of, *Memoirs of the Right Honorable Sir Anthony Eden*, 3 vols. (London 1960–1965).
Bonham-Carter, Lady Violet, *Winston Churchill* (New York 1965).
Broad, Lewis, *Winston Churchill: A Biography*, 2 vols. (Englewood Cliffs, N. J., 1958–1963).
Bryant, Sir Arthur, *The Turn of the Tide* (New York 1957).
Churchill, Randolph S., *Winston S. Churchill: Youth (1874–1900)* (Boston 1966).
Cooper, Alfred Duff, *Old Men Forget* (London 1953).
Eade, Charles, ed., *Churchill by His Contemporaries* (New York 1954).
Guedalla, Philip, *Mr. Churchill* (Mystic, Conn., 1950).
Ismay, Lord, *Memoirs of General Lord Ismay* (New York 1960).
Moran, Lord, *Churchill: Taken From the Diaries of Lord Moran* (Boston 1966).
Rowse, A. L., *The Early Churchills: An English Family* (New York 1956).
Rowse, A. L., *The Churchills: From the Death of Marlborough to the Present* (New York 1958).

CHURCHYARD, church'ərd, **Thomas** (1520?–1604), English poet. He was born at Shrewsbury and spent most of his life·as a soldier, fighting in campaigns in France, Flanders, Ireland, and Scotland, and as a courtier. Between 1560 and 1603 he wrote considerable prose and poetry, including court pageants for Queen Elizabeth in 1574 and 1578. However, a passage printed in his collected verse, *Churchyard's Choice* (1579), so offended Elizabeth that he was forced to take refuge in Scotland for three years. Churchyard was buried in London on April 4, 1604.

Churchyard's poetry is highly mannered, with a great deal of alliteration and exaggerated figures of speech. His best work is the long narrative poem *The Legend of Shore's Wife* (published in the 1563 edition of *A Mirror for Magistrates*). His other writings include the antiquary study *The Worthiness of Wales* (1587).

CHURL, chûrl, in Saxon England, a member of the lowest rank of freemen. In caste standing, churls were beneath the classes of nobles and above the class of slaves. Many churls were reduced to slavery after the Norman Conquest (1066). See ANGLO-SAXONS—*Social Structure*.

CHURN, chûrn, a vessel in which butter is made by agitating milk or cream so as to separate the liquid from the oily globules of fat. Buttermaking was one of many food processes discovered in the Neolithic period. Churning may have begun with the swinging of milk in a skin container, a method still practiced by nomadic peoples. The oldest surviving churns are pottery imitations of these skin containers, but stirring in bowls of wood or earthenware was the method of churning adopted by European agriculturists. The churn became household equipment in Europe, especially in the form of the dash churn, a covered wooden tub in which the milk was dashed by hand with a paddle.

The dash churn was brought to America by the first settlers, and was still widely used on 19th

OLD STURBRIDGE VILLAGE

CHURNS, such as this 18th century American dash churn for the making of butter, were in general use until the 1900's.

CHURRIGUERA'S retable for San Esteban in Salamanca. The twisted columns are characteristic of his style.

century farms. It was often made of tinplate. U. S. patents from 1790 to 1893 include 2,440 for churns. Among them are box-shaped churns with a handle to turn the paddles; swing churns, like those of the nomads; pneumatic churns; and revolving drums.

Dairies now use power-driven rotatory churns, or centrifuges, to make butter and drain the buttermilk. The butter produced by these machines has uniformity of texture, moisture-content, and taste. See also BUTTER—*Commercial Buttermaking* (Churning).

THOMAS KINGSTON DERRY
Coauthor of "A Short History of Technology"

CHURRIGUERA, cho͞or-rē-gä′rä, **José Benito de** (1665–1725), Spanish architect, who is the best-known member of a family that developed a distinctive variant of Iberian baroque architecture. The term "Churrigueresque" is sometimes improperly extended to the extravagant late baroque style in Spain and its American colonies. However, the work of the chief members of the Churriguera family is relatively restrained, even conservative by the standards of the period. The most distinctive feature is the chunky twisted column—a motif modeled on a set of celebrated, late-antique columns preserved in St. Peter's, Rome.

José Benito Churriguera was born in Madrid, on March 21, 1665. From his father, a Catalan

altarpiece maker, he acquired a style that blended forms from Catalan wood sculpture with more grandiose classical elements derived from Roman baroque architecture. In 1689 his award-winning design for Queen Maria Luisa's funeral monument (later altered) in the Church of the Encarnación, Madrid, brought him to the attention of the royal family. In 1690 he became architect of the Cathedral of Salamanca, for which he created one of his most influential works—the carved retable, or altarscreen, of San Esteban.

After 1696, when he was appointed palace architect, Churriguera was active mainly in Madrid. His important commissions there included the Church of Santo Tomás and the Goyeneche Palace (now the Academia de San Fernando). Both of these buildings were remodeled in the neoclassic style during the 18th century; some of Churriguera's other work was destroyed.

Still surviving, however, is the greatest masterpiece of Churriguera's maturity, the town of Nuevo Baztán, built under the patronage of the banker Juan de Goyeneche. Its central administrative block, overlooking spacious plazas on three sides, includes a palace and a church. Churriguera died in Madrid, on March 2, 1725.

His younger brothers, Joaquín (1674–1724) and Alberto (1676–?1750), assisted José Benito in a number of his works. Alberto also designed the Plaza Mayor of Salamanca (1728) and the chapel of Santa Tecla in Burgos Cathedral (1736).

WAYNE DYNES, *Vassar College*

Further Reading: Kubler, George, and Soria, Martin S., *Art and Architecture in Spain and Portugal and Their American Dominions, 1500 to 1800* (Baltimore 1959).

CHUSHAN. See CHOUSHAN.

CHUTE, cho͞ot, **Marchette** (1909–), American author, noted for her biographies of English authors and for her historical romances for children. She was born in Wayzata, Minn., on Aug. 16, 1909, and studied at the Minneapolis School of Art and the University of Minnesota.

Miss Chute's biographies include *Shakespeare of London* (1950) and *Ben Jonson of Westminster* (1953), both of which won the New York Shakespeare Club award in 1954; *Geoffrey Chaucer of England* (1946); and *Two Gentle Men: The Lives of George Herbert and Robert Herrick* (1959).

Her books for children include *Rhymes About the Country* (1941), a volume of verse; *Around and About* (1957) and *Innocent Wayfaring* (1955), both illustrated by herself; and *Jesus of Israel* (1961).

Miss Chute was appointed a member of the executive board of the National Book Committee in 1954 and was elected vice president of the National Institute of Arts and Letters in 1961.

CHUTNEY, chut′nē, is a sweet, somewhat acidic condiment with a jamlike consistency, that is served with many foods, particularly curry dishes. It originated in India but is now made throughout the world.

Although the basic ingredient of chutney may vary slightly, they usually include apples, seeded Malaga raisins, preserved mangoes, lemon peel, onion, and chilies. Among the spices and other flavorings often added are ginger, mustard, and cayenne pepper. The ingredients are first pounded together in a mortar and then boiled in white vinegar for about 10 minutes.

CHUVASH AUTONOMOUS SOVIET SOCIALIST REPUBLIC, chŏō-väsh', a political subdivision of the USSR, in central European Russia, on the right bank of the Volga River, west of Kazan. Its area of 7,100 square miles (18,300 sq km) is a rolling lowland, heavily dissected by gullies and karst (limestone) formations.

The climate is moderately continental with a cold winter and hot summer and an annual precipitation of 20 inches (50 cm). The growing season of six months allows the cultivation of spring wheat, rye, buckwheat, and peas. Hemp is widely cultivated, and hops are a distinctive crop. Cattle are raised for beef and dairy products; other livestock include hogs, sheep, and poultry. Beekeeping is a common farm occupation. Mineral resources are limited to limestone, clays and sands, peat, oil shale, and phosphate rock.

One third of the republic's area is in forests, which support a furniture industry and the manufacture of prefabricated housing. Industry is concentrated in the capital, Cheboksary (1966 population: 170,000). Its manufactures include electrical goods and chemicals. Kanash, a railroad hub in the center of the republic, has car repair shops, and Alatyr, another railroad town in the southern part of the republic, has locomotive shops.

The republic is named for the Chuvash people, who account for 70% of the total population. This ethnic group was formed from the 10th to the 15th century through the merger of the Turkic-speaking Volga Bulgars and a local Ugro-Finnic population. The Chuvash language belongs to the Turkic group of the Altaic language family and is related to two dead languages, Khazar and Volga Bulgar. Although most Chuvash still speak their native language, they have largely been assimilated with the Russians; many have adopted the Russian Orthodox religion. Russians make up 25% of the total population of the republic. When ethnic political subdivisions were established in the Soviet Union, the Chuvash were first assigned the status of an autonomous oblast in 1920. The present autonomous republic dates from 1925. Population: (1966) 1,177,000.

THEODORE SHABAD
Editor of "Soviet Geography"

CIANO, chä'nō, **Galeazzo** (1903–1944), foreign minister of Italy during the Facist regime. He was born in Livorno (Leghorn) on March 18, 1903, the son of Costanzo Ciano (whose title of Count of Cortellazzo he also bore), an Italian admiral and hero of World War I who was instrumental in bringing fascism to power in 1922. Young Ciano received an LL.D. from the University of Rome in 1925, and entered the diplomatic corps soon afterward. After assignments that took him from Latin America to China, he met and married, in 1930, Edda Mussolini, the daughter of the dictator, Benito Mussolini. From that moment on, Ciano's career advanced spectacularly. In 1932 he became minister to China; in 1933, head of Mussolini's press office; in 1935 undersecretary for press and propaganda; and after serving in the air force in the Ethiopian War (1935–1936), minister of foreign affairs in 1936. He also became a member of the Supreme Council of Fascism.

Ciano was less of an extremist than many of the other Fascist leaders. Though he personally disliked and distrusted the Germans, he imple-

mented Mussolini's policy of friendship with Hitler's regime, culminating in the "Pact of Steel," which he signed in 1939. It was generally believed that he was the heir presumptive to Mussolini's position as the dictator of Italy. Nevertheless, Ciano was so overshadowed by the personality of his father-in-law that he could do very little to modify the course steadily and stubbornly followed by Mussolini. He contributed, however, to Mussolini's decision not to enter World War II as Germany's ally when war broke out in September 1939. But by June 1940, with France on the verge of defeat, Mussolini could no longer be restrained.

With the demonstration of Italy's military weakness in the first months of the war, Ciano's fears of the Germans were soon justified by Hitler's treatment of his ally. Ciano wrote in his diary: "We have always been treated as servants, not as allies . . . ." He was instrumental in the coup of July 25, 1943, which overthrew Mussolini and provoked the collapse of Italian fascism. Ultimately he had to flee to Germany with his family. Eventually, on direct orders from Hitler, he was sent back to Verona, to serve in Mussolini's ephemeral new Fascist puppet state. He was arrested, tried, and shot for high treason on Jan. 11, 1944.

Ciano left behind a few letters, written in jail while he was awaiting execution, and a diary covering the years from 1939 to February 1943. The diary is historically extremely important, as it presents an inside view into events and developments concerning the alliance of Mussolini with Hitler. His widow, Edda, passionately defended his memory after his death.

SERGIO BARZANTI
Fairleigh Dickinson University

CIARDI, chär'dē, **John** (1916–   ), American poet and critic, an important champion of modern, idiomatic language in poetry. He was born to an Italian immigrant family in Boston, Mass., on June 24, 1916, and studied at Bates College, Tufts College, and the University of Michigan. He later taught English literature at the University of Kansas City, Harvard, and Rutgers. In 1956 he was appointed poetry editor of the *Saturday Review,* where he became a leading, often controversial, spokesman for contemporary verse.

Writings. Though Ciardi uses traditional lyric forms, his vision is often satirical, and he is intensely conscious of the mutability of things. His poetry is witty and facile, and at its best converts the occasional subject into one of universal moment, combining clever, vernacular diction with a deep and dedicated humanism.

Ciardi's *Other Skies* (1947), a volume of poetry about his experiences as an aerial gunner during World War II, is among the best American poetry to come out of the war. His other books of verse include *Homeward to America* (1940), *From Time to Time* (1951), *As If* (1955), *I Marry You* (1958), *39 Poems* (1959), *In the Stoneworks* (1961), and *You Know Who* (1964). He also wrote the collections of critical essays *How Does a Poem Mean?* (1959) and *Dialogue with an Audience* (1963); the children's books *I Met a Man* (1961) and *The Wish-Tree* (1962); and distinguished translations of Dante's *Inferno* (1954) and *Purgatorio* (1961).

DAVID GALLOWAY, *Author of "The Absurd Hero"*

Further Reading: White, William, *John Ciardi* (Detroit 1959).

CIBBER, sib'ər, **Colley** (1671–1757), English actor and playwright. As an actor, he excelled in the delineation of fops; as a playwright, he is best remembered for two or three high comedies that set a new fashion with their sentimental, seemingly moral endings. He also was joint manager of the Drury Lane Theatre in London for much of his life. In addition, Cibber is perhaps entitled to be called a drama critic. In his famous autobiography, *An Apology for the Life of Colley Cibber, Comedian* (1740), his descriptions of the best players of his own and the previous generation (particularly of Betterton and Mrs. Bracegirdle) are invaluable vivid records in the best tradition of drama criticism.

Career. Colley Cibber was born in London on Nov. 16, 1671. He went on the stage early in life, and by 1696 he was playing in his own comedy *Love's Last Shift*, creating the part of Sir Novelty Fashion. (Vanbrugh developed Sir Novelty into Lord Foppington in his play *The Relapse* [1696], and Cibber played that part, too.) Cibber also excelled in the portrayal of such senile characters as Fondlewife in Congreve's *The Old Bachelor* (1693) and Justice Swallow in Shakespeare's *King Henry the Fourth, Part II*.

Cibber wrote nearly every kind of play, libretto, and burlesque. The best of his plays—for example, *She Would and She Would Not* (1702) and *The Careless Husband* (1704)—have been revived successfully in the 20th century. Cibber altered Shakespeare's *King Richard the Third* for David Garrick, and this version was performed until 1871, when Henry Irving removed the Cibber alterations as impertinences. Yet some of Cibber's lines in *Richard the Third* are dramatically effective; for example, "Off with his head— so much for Buckingham!" and "Conscience, avaunt, Richard's himself again!" Laurence Olivier reintroduced several of them in his 1956 film version of the play, on the perfectly safe assumption that no film critic would recognize the lines as anything other than Shakespeare's.

In 1730, Cibber, a Whig, was rewarded for his political activities by being appointed poet laureate, although his flat occasional effusions in verse earned him Pope's derision in *The Dunciad* (1743 version). Charles Reade, in his romantic novel *Peg Woffington* (1852), depicts Cibber in his old age as an unvenerable fop, but Cibber's self-portrait in his autobiography is clearer and fairer. He was an avid devotee of the theater until his death, in London, on Dec. 12, 1757.

Family. Colley's father, Caius Gabriel Cibber (1630–1700), was a Danish sculptor of some note, who did his best work in England under the direction of Sir Christopher Wren. Colley's son, Theophilus Cibber (1703–1758), an actor-manager, was a wild and extravagant individual, who drowned while on a trip to Ireland. Theophilus's wife, Susanna Cibber (1714–1766), a sister of the composer Augustine Arne, was an excellent singer of Handel's music and a tragic actress good enough to play leading parts with Garrick. Her stage name was simply Mrs. Cibber. Colley's youngest daughter, Charlotte Charke (died 1760), the wife of a professional musician, was a notorious tomboy who specialized in male roles on the stage. She described her own racy autobiography, first published in 1755, as "some account of my unaccountable life."

ALAN DENT
Author of "Mrs. Patrick Cambell"

CÍBOLA, Seven Cities of, sē'bō-lä, Zuñi Indian towns of northern Mexico and the southwestern United States that were reputed to possess great riches. Inspired by reports of their magnificence and wealth, the Spanish explorer Coronado undertook to find them in 1540. He actually discovered a Pueblo Indian town that was described by a fellow Spaniard as "a little, crowded village, looking as if it had been crumpled all up together." There was no sign of the treasure mines or the golden halls they had expected.

Excavations of the principal town, Hawiku, in what is now New Mexico, were first attempted in 1917. Several stages of occupancy were discovered, ranging from the earliest nomadic hunters to increasingly sophisticated Indian tribes. The study of Cíbola has thus added to the knowledge of North American Indians and of the anthropology of this region.

CIBOTIUM, si-bō'tē-əm, any of a small genus of tropical treelike ferns sometimes grown in greenhouses in the northern United States. Probably the most cultivated species is *Cibotium schiedei*, which is native to Mexico and Guatemala. It grows about 15 feet (4½ meters) tall and has fronds about 5 feet (1½ meters) long made up of deeply cut segments 8 inches (20 cm) long. The fronds are borne on dark-brown, hairy stalks, and the segments are deep green above and bluish green below.

VERA JOHNSTON, FROM NATIONAL AUDUBON SOCIETY

CIBOTIUM grows profusely in the shade of a dense rain forest in Hawaii Volcanoes National Park, Hawaii.

Another cultivated species, known as the Scythian lamb (*C. barometz*), is a trunkless tree fern with fragrant, graceful fronds composed of segments 6 inches (15 cm) long.

Cibotiums belong to the tree fern family (Cyatheaceae) of the order Filicales in the division Filicophyta (ferns).

DONALD WYMAN
*The Arnold Arboretum
Harvard University*

CICADA, si-kā'də, any of a group of medium-sized to large insects that are common in tropical and subtropical countries. In North America they are abundant throughout the eastern United States. Although cicadas are sometimes called "harvest flies" or "locusts," they are not related to the flies or the locusts.

DEVELOPMENT OF THE 17-YEAR CICADA—MATURE NYMPH TO ADULT

After 17 years underground, the fully grown cicada nymph emerges (*upper left*). The nymph then attaches itself to a plant and molting begins. The adult insect works its way out of the nymphal case (*upper right*) and waits while its wings harden and its body becomes dry (*lower left*). After a day the cicada is ready to fly (*lower right*). The adult insect lives for 30 to 40 days, but the empty nymphal case may cling to its support for months.

The cicada is about 1 to 1½ inches (2.5–3.8 cm) long. It typically has a stout body with a proboscis arising from the head, bristlelike antennae, and two pairs of membranous, many-veined wings. The male cicadas are well known, especially during the hot summer months, for the shrill, buzzing sound they produce with the drumlike membranes on the sides of their abdomen.

Types of Cicadas. There are two races of the periodical cicada that inflict damage on fruit trees. One of these has a 13-year life cycle, and it occurs only in the southeastern United States. The other race, the 17-year cicada, or 17-year "locust," occurs in abundance in the northeastern part of the United States; as its name implies, it has a 17-year life cycle. The common "harvest fly," or dog-day cicada, is believed to have a 2-year life cycle.

In the Western states, cicadas are generally smaller. While common, they are never present in great numbers. These species are reported to remain in the ground for one, two, or more years, depending on the species.

Life History. The 17-year locust has the longest developmental cycle of any known insect. In late May, June, and early July the female uses the sawlike ovipositor at the end of her abdomen to make roughened punctures in twigs and small branches; she deposits her eggs into these holes. As many as 400 to 600 eggs are laid by each female, 12 to 20 in each insertion beneath the bark.

The eggs hatch within 6 to 7 weeks into young, wingless cicadas called nymphs. Some nymphs drop to the ground and crawl several inches into soil cracks. Others move to the base of trees, where they dig small cells near a tree rootlet and suck the plant sap. The growth of the nymphs is slow, and although great numbers feed on tree roots, they seem to have little effect on tree vigor. The nymphs remain underground until they reach maturity, which may take from 13 to 17 years.

The full-grown nymphs burrow up to the soil surface and gradually work their way through small holes. They finally crawl up a tree trunk or stem of weed, on which they firmly affix themselves. Molting soon takes place, and the adult insect gradually works its way out of the nymphal case. The following day, after the wings have hardened and the bodies have become dry, the insects are ready to take flight. The empty nymphal skins continue to cling to the tree trunks and other supports for several months.

Tremendous populations of cicadas, from 20,000 to 40,000, may emerge from the ground beneath a single large tree. They fly during the day, mate, and pump sap from the twigs of trees with their sucking mouthparts. Within a few days after emergence, the male starts its shrill buzzing. The adults live for 30 or 40 days and usually disappear by mid-July in the Midwest.

Cicadas belong to the order Homoptera, family Cicadidae. The 17-year "locust," or periodical cicada, is *Magicicada septendecim.*

HOWARD L. McKENZIE
University of California, Davis

CICELY, sis′ə-lē, or *sweet cicely,* any of several anise-scented perennial herbs of the genus *Myrrhis* (native to Europe) or the closely related genus *Osmorhiza* (native to America and eastern Asia) of the parsley family. Cicelies grow up to 3 feet (1 meter) tall and bear clusters of small white flowers. The aromatic leaves of *M. odorata* are used in salads and soups. Some species have fleshy flavorful roots that are eaten raw or boiled.

LAWRENCE ERBE
University of Southwestern Louisiana

BUST IN THE MUSEO CAPITOLINO, ROME—ALINARI, FROM
ART REFERENCE SERVICE

Marcus Tullius Cicero

CICERO, sis′ə-rō, **Marcus Tullius** (106–43 B. C.),
Roman statesman, orator, and author, who was
one of the most active politicians and scholars of
his time. He was born in the town of Arpinum
in the Italian countryside on June 3, 106 B. C.
His family was of equestrian rank. This denoted
wealth and standing in Arpinum, but the equestrian rank was at a social level below that of the
Roman senatorial class. Arpinum was also the
birthplace of the general Marius, who was consul
in Rome seven times. Marius, who was at the
height of his prestige during Cicero's formative
years, may have been an inspiration to Cicero's
family, who were related to the Marii. Sometimes
in the early 90's B. C., Cicero's father moved his
family to Rome, which offered education, opportunity, and the possibility of a political career.

Education. Young Cicero, an avid and tireless
student, received the best education that money
or influence could obtain. The gentle Greek poet
Archias inspired him with a love of literature and
learning. Cicero also observed and emulated
Rome's finest orators, Lucius Licinius Crassus
and Marcus Antonius. Even in those early years
he practiced and polished his oratorical delivery. He received training in civil law from the
jurist Quintus Mucius Scaevola (the Pontifex
Maximus). His philosophic training was eclectic
and thorough: he was exposed to Diodotus the
Stoic, Phaedrus the Epicurean, and Philo of the
Platonic Academy. Those school years also
brought him into contact with Titus Pomponius
Atticus, a fellow student who became a lifelong,
intimate friend.

The decade of the 80's was a difficult one in
which to mature. The violent struggle for supremacy between the factions of Marius and
Sulla dominated the political scene. Cicero's family connections were with Marius, but several of
Cicero's friends and contacts in Rome were associated with Sulla. Victims on both sides aroused
his sympathy: the Marians slew his teacher Scaevola; the Sullans executed his relative Marius
Gratidianus. Cicero sought to be neutral, but

when that proved impossible he worked on the
side of Sulla, although he did not take up arms.

Sulla's victory in 82 brought dictatorship, but
it also brought stability and order. The courts
were restored and reorganized after a decade of
chaos. For Cicero that meant the resumption of
a budding oratorical career. In 80 he appeared
for the first time in a criminal case, the murder
trial of Sextus Roscius. Cicero's speech for Roscius was primarily an attack on Chrysogonus, an
ex-slave of Sulla who was abusing his influence,
bypassing due process, and enriching himself at
the expense of his enemies. The speech was a
masterpiece. Chrysogonus was crushed, Sulla
washed his hands of his ex-servant, and the freedom of the courts seemed assured.

In 79, Cicero went abroad for reasons of
health and also in order to further his education.
He studied in Athens with the renowned philosopher Antiochus of Ascalon and in Rhodes with
Molo, the foremost professor of rhetoric. By 76
B. C., at the age of 30, his formal education was
complete.

Political Ascent. Cicero was prepared to embark on a political career. His oratorical talents
and his connections helped, as did his marriage to
Terentia, a woman of some means who brought
with her a substantial dowry. In 75, Cicero was
elected to the quaestorship, the lowest office in
the hierarchy of magistrates. This position gave
him automatic access to the Roman Senate. The
tenure of his office was served in Sicily, where
he impressed the inhabitants with his generosity,
integrity, and learning. Those qualities stood out
all the more sharply by contrast with those of
Gaius Verres, a later governor of Sicily who
ruthlessly exploited the populace and the island.
When the Sicilians instituted legal proceedings
against Verres in Rome, they naturally applied to
Cicero to represent them in court. Cicero's brilliant prosecution of Verres in 70 unquestionably
established his reputation as Rome's finest orator.
Verres fled into exile. Cicero had outmaneuvered
the defense counsel, Hortensius, previously regarded as the leader of the Roman bar. This
victory was a great stimulus to Cicero's career.
He advanced up the magisterial ladder, reaching
the aedileship in 69 and the praetorship in 66.

Cicero was now nearing the summit of political ambition, the consulship. But that office was
jealously guarded by the old nobility. It was rare
indeed for a man of equestrian origin to reach
it. Cicero needed powerful assistance. To obtain this, he developed closer ties with Pompey
the Great, with whom he had served in the military in 89. During Cicero's term as praetor in
66, a political contest emerged over the appointment of Pompey to a major command in the war
against Mithridates VI, king of Pontus. Cicero
delivered a compelling speech in Pompey's behalf
and overcame the opposition of men like Hortensius and Catulus. At the same time Cicero
was serving his own interests and those of his
class, the equites, whose financial investments in
the East were seriously threatened by Mithridates.
Therefore, as a candidate for the consulship in
63, Cicero could count on a wide following. Men
from the Italian aristocracy outside Rome considered him one of their own. The business classes,
headed by Cicero's wealthy friend Atticus, showed
their gratitude. As an advocate of Pompey,
Cicero took advantage of the general's reflected
glory. And he campaigned tirelessly. Finally, he
spread reports that his opponents, Catiline and

Gaius Antonius, were planning violence. Cicero was swept in at the head of the polls.

Consulship. As so often happens to the "new man" who reaches positions normally closed to his class, Cicero, once in office, grew more conservative and became a staunch defender of the status quo. His goal was a *concordia ordinum,* an alliance of the senatorial class and the wealthy equites as the state's most responsible and experienced leaders. Beyond this he advocated a *consensus omnium bonorum,* a coalition of the upper classes in Rome and throughout Italy to maintain stability and sound government. When an agrarian bill to purchase land and distribute it to the needy was presented early in his consulship, Cicero delivered a series of denunciatory speeches that crushed the effort. Its defeat must have driven many men who were in debt or without property to seek desperate measures. Catiline, beaten once more in the elections for the consulship of 62, took advantage of this growing discontent and organized a conspiracy, which included sabotage in Rome and armed insurrection in Etruria. Cicero's network of agents kept him informed of the plot and enabled him to thwart an attempt on his life. He denounced Catiline to the people and to the Senate and received full powers to deal with him summarily. Nevertheless, Cicero hesitated. According to rumors, Catiline was secretly backed by Julius Caesar and Marcus Crassus, two of Rome's most powerful men. Cicero himself had many jealous rivals in the aristocracy, who refused for a long time to believe his stories about Catiline. It was only after Catiline had openly joined his armed compatriots in Etruria, and after conclusive evidence had emerged about his plans, that Cicero could arrest the leaders of the conspiracy in Rome. The Senate debated their fate in December 63, Caesar arguing for imprisonment, Cato for execution. When Cato's speech won the day, Cicero as consul swiftly carried out the execution. The conspiracy collapsed: Catiline and his remaining followers were defeated and slain on the battlefield early in 62. Cicero regarded his actions here as the greatest of his triumphs: he had saved the state and had molded the coalition of senators and equites that he had long contemplated—with himself at its head.

Exile and Return to Rome. But Cicero's expectations turned out to be an illusion. He was soon to come under sharp attack by politicians who sought popularity by accusing him of executing Roman citizens without trial. Pompey returned from the Eastern wars late in 62 and was cool to Cicero, refusing to praise him for his actions against Catiline. The alliance between Senate and equites broke down when Cato attacked the business classes for defaulting on a tax contract. Instead of winning Pompey over to his coalition, Cicero saw the general, who wished to secure land allotments for his veterans and to thwart the conservatives in the Senate, draw closer to Caesar and Crassus in 60 and 59. Worse yet, criticism of Cicero for his execution of the conspirators was growing. In 58 the demagogic tribune Publius Clodius presented a broad popular program, turned opinion decidedly against Cicero, and with the aid of armed bands drove the orator into exile. Cicero spent the next 15 months abroad, much of the time in Thessalonica. This was the grimmest period of his life. His letters are filled with spite, lamentations, and despair. In Rome, however, the situation was changing. Clodius had abused his power and turned his fire on Pompey. The general gathered armed bands of his own, checked Clodius, and effected the recall of Cicero in August 57.

Cicero was escorted home with wild enthusiasm. It was a great personal triumph. He delivered some of his most vitriolic speeches against Clodius and other enemies in the months after his return. Cicero had high hopes of a revival of his influence, but political realities dictated otherwise. His efforts to detach Pompey from Caesar and Crassus (the alliance of the three is known as the First Triumvirate) and win him for the establishment backfired. The triumvirs renewed their alliance in 56 and cowed their opposition into helplessness. Cicero lost all independence of action. He had to deliver a speech supporting Caesar's command in Gaul in 56 and other speeches defending his own former enemies. Cicero largely withdrew from politics and spent most of his time in study and writing. Some of his most important philosophical and rhetorical works were produced between 55 and 51.

In 51, Cicero was called out of his semiretirement to serve as governor of Cilicia in Asia Minor. He accepted most reluctantly, for he hated to leave Rome, the center of political and intellectual life. Nonetheless, he carried out his duties scrupulously, preserving the province from outside attack, reconciling the interests of provincials and tax collectors, and producing a surplus for the treasury.

Civil War. Shortly after Cicero's return to Rome late in 50, civil war erupted between Caesar and Pompey. Cicero was thrust into a tortuous dilemma. He had nothing but contempt for Caesar's cause, which represented revolution and chaos, but several of his friends, as well as his son-in-law, were in Caesar's camp. Many of the old nobility were with Pompey. Although Cicero's sympathies were with the Pompeian cause, he feared that Pompey himself would bring devastation and autocracy. For months the orator wavered; finally he joined Pompey in Greece in June 49. But his activities there were limited, and most of Pompey's generals profoundly distrusted him. After Pompey's defeat at Pharsalus in 48, Cicero sadly returned home, assured of Caesar's clemency.

Last Years. The years 47 to 44 were bitter ones for Cicero. Little political life remained under Caesar's dictatorship. Cicero delivered only three speeches, all in praise of Caesar. But his private correspondence shows his distaste for the regime and reveals his inner isolation. These were also the most painful years of his personal life. He divorced his wife of 30 years; he became estranged from his brother; and he lost his daughter, to whom he had always been devoted. As usual, his only solace was in intellectual pursuits. He immersed himself in the writing of philosophical and oratorical treatises.

Cicero had no hand in the assassination of Caesar in 44, but he rejoiced in the deed. He collaborated afterward with Caesar's slayers Brutus and Cassius in order to restore the Republic. While the tyrannicides were in the East, Cicero worked assiduously in their behalf. This involved him in conflict with Mark Antony, who headed the Caesarian faction. In late 44 and early 43, Cicero recovered his old fervor and exercised more influence than ever. He delivered 14 blistering speeches, the *Philippics,* against Antony. These were among his most powerful orations, and with them he won the backing of much of the Senate. But when Antony allied himself with Octavian, Caesar's adopted son whom Cicero had hoped to play off against Antony, the orator's efforts proved in vain. A proscription list was drawn up; Cicero's name was on it. Antony's henchmen hunted him down and murdered him at Formiae on Dec. 7, 43. The vindictive Antony then ordered Cicero's head and hands cut off and had them exposed on the rostra in the Forum.

Works. Although Cicero experienced frustrations and defeats in his political career, his literary production was prodigious, completely dwarfing in volume that of any other Latin writer. The range and variety of his writings are extraordinary. Oratory, of course, was his principal occupation. Of his speeches 58 survive. They include orations in both civil and criminal cases, speeches to the Senate, and harangues to the people. They range from the most bitter invective, as in the speeches against Catiline, Lucius Calpurnius Piso Caesoninus, and Antony, to the warmest eulogies, as in the speeches for Pompey and Archias. There are important political speeches as well as intricate legal discussions. The mastery of all forms, the ease in handling the most difficult cases, and the subtlety and humor combined with compelling power make Cicero without question the foremost Roman orator.

Cicero's rhetorical works vary in quality. Two, however, stand out. *Brutus* is an invaluable history of Roman oratory, and *De Oratore* is a worthy effort to lift oratory from academic pedantry to the level of genuine humanism. Works of political theory also occupied Cicero's attention. The *De Republica* and *De Legibus*, an intellectualizing of Roman political and constitutional ideals, essentially are adaptations of Platonic theory to the Roman experience. They were the vehicles for his firm belief in the rule of law and the guidance of an enlightened governing class. Cicero's philosophical tracts are largely paraphrases of Greek models, primarily Stoic and Academic. Though lacking originality, they possess great significance, for it was Cicero alone who was responsible for creating a philosophical literature in Latin. His works have survived to exercise a profound influence on succeeding centuries, whereas the works of his Greek predecessors have perished for the most part. His talent in expression and style brought Latin prose to a height not achieved before or since.

Cicero's poetry has not endured. Ancient critics found it wanting. He seems to have been more a versifier than an inspired artist. Yet Plutarch reports that Cicero in his younger days was regarded as Rome's finest poet.

In the midst of an incredibly full political and scholarly life, Cicero found time also to engage in a prolific correspondence. Of his letters to Atticus 16 books are preserved, as are 16 books of letters to other friends, 3 books to his brother Quintus, and 2 books to Brutus, a total of about 925 letters from Cicero and another 125 written to him. The scope and variety of subjects touched on are limitless. The letters are without parallel in classical literature. Since they were not meant for publication, they often reveal Cicero in intimate and unguarded moments. As a consequence there is no one else in antiquity of whom we know so much: his fears, his hopes, his innermost thoughts and feelings. His other works show Cicero the politician, the author, the thinker. His letters show Cicero the man.

Evaluation. Cicero has always been among the most controversial figures in history. Criticism of him has concentrated on his vacillation, his indecision, his insincerity, and his excessive self-laudation. Much of the criticism is misguided. Cicero's egotistic expressions were tempered by an ability also to laugh at himself on occasion. His shifts of political stance usually reflected changes in the political scene of the late republic. He was flexible in his allegiances and attitudes, but he did not lack ideals. A belief in constitutional government and the rule of law, together with an abhorrence of violence and civil war, remained constant convictions throughout his life.

ERICH S. GRUEN
University of California at Berkeley

Bibliography

Cowell, Frank R., *Cicero and the Roman Republic* (New York 1948).
Dorey, Thomas A., ed., *Cicero* (New York 1965).
Haskell, Henry J., *This Was Cicero* (New York 1942).
Hunt, Harold A. K., *The Humanism of Cicero* (Melbourne, Australia, 1954).
Petersson, T., *Cicero, a Biography* (Berkeley, Calif., 1920).
Sihler, E. G., *Cicero of Arpinum* (New York 1914).
Smith, Richard E., *Cicero the Statesman* (New York and London 1966).

CICERO, sis′ər-ō, a town in northeastern Illinois, is in Cook county, just west of Chicago, of which it is a suburb. Cicero is primarily residential, but about one fourth of its area contains one of the greatest industrial concentrations in the world, with more than 150 factories in an area of 1.75 square miles (4.5 sq km). The largest of these factories produces communications and electronic equipment. Other industries include the manufacture of printing presses, malleable and steel castings, tool and die makers' supplies, forgings, and rubber goods.

Cicero was founded in 1867. Its charter from the state of Illinois grants it rights, powers, and privileges of self-government enjoyed by no other Illinois town except East St. Louis. Government is by town president and town trustees. Population: 67,058.

LEROY J. LAWNICZAK, *Cicero Public Library*

CICHLID, sik′ləd, any of a family of about 600 primarily freshwater species of fishes native to South and Central America and Africa. One genus is also found in India and Ceylon, and one of the Central American species ranges northward into Texas. Although native only to these areas, certain species have been introduced into many other parts of the world and have established permanent populations. Since cichlids are often brightly colored and have a variety of shapes, they are popular aquarium specimens.

Although they resemble perches in their general appearance, cichlids have only a single nostril on each side of the head. They are considered freshwater fish, but many can live in brackish water. Most cichlids prey on smaller fish and invertebrates, but others are specialized for plant feeding. Often quarrelsome fish, many cichlids stop fighting at breeding time when mated pairs undertake elaborate courtship ceremonies. Most cichlids show some parental care for their offspring.

Cichlids are found in numerous genera in the family Cichlidae in the order Perciformes.

JAMES C. TYLER
Academy of Natural Sciences of Philadelphia

CID, The, sid, in history, the popular title of the medieval knight Rodrigo Díaz de Vivar (about 1043–1099), the great military leader of the Spanish *Reconquista.* It is derived from the Arabic word *sidi* (lord). He is also called Rodrigo el Campeador (the Champion) or El Cid Campeador.

The Cid was born about 1043 in Vivar, near Burgos, the son of a minor landowner. He grew up at the court of Ferdinand I of Castile, as a ward of the King's eldest son, Sancho. His own lifetime saw the beginnings of the Christian *Reconquista* against the Muslim domination of Spain, which had lasted since 711. In about 1060 the young Rodrigo participated in a military campaign against the Aragonese for domination of the Muslim state of Saragossa. He had already shown considerable ability in combat, and medieval romances are eloquent about these early exploits. By the time of Ferdinand's death in 1065, the Cid had become the foremost knight in Castile, and enjoyed an influence out of proportion to his relatively humble rank.

According to the royal will, Ferdinand's territories were divided among his three sons: Castile went to Sancho, León to Ferdinand's favorite, Alfonso, and Galicia to García. In the next several years the Cid's military talents were indispensable to Sancho as the King first satisfied his territorial ambitions in the east, and then turned upon his younger brothers to regain what he regarded as his rightful inheritance; by 1071 García had been defeated, and Alfonso was deposed and exiled to Muslim Toledo. However, at the siege of Zamora in 1072, Sancho was assassinated, and Alfonso returned to claim the thrones of both León and Castile.

The loss of his protector put the Cid in a difficult position. Alfonso attempted to win his loyalty, however, by arranging his marriage to a royal niece, the Asturian princes Doña Jimena. The Cid remained at court for nine years, but was now surrounded by his old rivals and was forced to give up the position of preeminence that he had enjoyed under Sancho. In 1081 he captured García Ordóñez, the king's favorite, in battle. The Cid's capture of so notable a personage reawakened Alfonso's suspicions. Shortly thereafter, when the Cid took an unauthorized initiative against Toledo, the King used this as a pretext to banish him from Castile.

The *Poema de mio Cid,* an anonymous epic written in the 12th century, begins at this point. It relates how, with money raised by a clever trick, and with only 300 men, the Cid waged a victorious campaign in Aragón. Turning south, he then attacked the rich Muslim Levant region. These campaigns facilitated new Castilian victories against the Muslim Caliphate of Córdoba, and the Cid and Alfonso were reconciled in 1090. Two years later the Cid captured the fortress-city of Valencia by routing Yusuf Ibn Tashfin. The poem closes with the Cid's revenge over the Infantes of Carrión, relatives of his old rival Ordóñez. His champions defeated them in single combat to avenge their affronts to his two daughters, to whom they had been married with Alfonso's consent. According to the *Historia Roderici,* a Latin narrative believed to have been compiled about 1110, the Cid governed Valencia until his death on July 10, 1099. See also CID, THE, in literature.

ROBERT W. KERN, *University of Massachusetts*

CID, The, sid, in literature, the hero of a number of Spanish poems, chronicles, romances, and dramas. The character is based on Rodrigo Díaz de Vivar, El Cid Campeador, an 11th century Spanish nobleman.

Poema de mio Cid. The first known literary treatment of the Cid is the anonymous *Poema de mio Cid* (about 1140), the earliest extant Spanish epic. The language of the *Poema* is rough-hewn and primitive, and a considerable amount of vivid dialogue contributes to the work's dramatic quality. The verse is characterized by assonance and has lines of varying length, 14-syllable lines predominating. The poem is not only movingly human but highly original, despite some stylistic borrowings from the *Chanson de Roland.*

The *Poema,* also called *Cantar de mio Cid,* is distinguished for its realistic touches, adherence to fact, and sobriety. The Cid, whom critics commonly regard as a symbol of the Spanish national character, is portrayed as loyal, generous, humane, sober, democratic, brave, religious, and devoted to his family. His unswerving loyalty to the king of Castile, the nucleus and unifying force of the Spanish nation, is related to Spanish nationalism. The work's antiquity and realism give it great archaeological interest; but the *Poema* is a living literary document.

After a period of fame, the poem was gradually forgotten, a result of the public's growing preference for the fictions of the *Cantar de Rodrigo,* a work about the Cid, written in the 14th or 15th century. The *Poema* was rescued from oblivion in 1779, when Tomás Antonio Sánchez published a 1307 copy of it. The romantic age restored the work to its former esteem; Southey praised it, and Hallam considered it the best epic poem written between the end of classical antiquity and the appearance of the *Divine Comedy.* The so-called "Spanish Generation of 1898," keenly interested in Castile as the soul of Spain, added their praises. Although it was unknown too long to have directly influenced the majority of later works about the Cid, the *Poema de mio Cid* is the greatest Spanish treatment of the theme.

Other Versions. The *Cantar de Rodrigo* (also known as *Las mocedades del Cid*) is mainly responsible for the accretion that the Cid slew the father of Ximena, the heroine, and for converting the restrained and mature Spanish hero of the *Poema* into the young, passionate braggart found in subsequent versions. It also accounts for the love interest and for the increased importance of Ximena in these subsequent accounts. The many *romances* (ballads) about the Cid reflect these innovations, as does the Golden Age play *Las mocedades del Cid* by Guillén de Castro y Bellvis (q.v.). One of the better-known 20th century works about the Cid is Eduardo Marquina's play *Las hijas del Cid* (1908).

The most famous non-Spanish work about this great epic hero is Corneille's play *Le Cid* (1637), which is based, not on the *Poema de mio Cid,* but on Guillén de Castro's play. Corneille borrowed from Castro much of the characterization of Ximena, as well as the idea of centering his plot on the conflict between love and duty. Massenet's opera *Le Cid* (1885) is based mostly on Corneille. Other non-Spanish authors who have used the Cid include Johann Gottfried von Herder, Southey, and Hugo.

LEONARD MADES
Hunter College, City University of New York

CIDER is a beverage made from the juice of apples. In Europe the term generally means a beverage made from fermented apple juice, but in the United States, unless specifically labeled as "hard" cider, it is made of unfermented apple juice. In France, in Normandy and Brittany, a fermented and aged cider is the native "wine" of those districts. In England, cider rivals beer in popularity in the southern and western sections of the country; cider is also a popular beverage in such countries as Germany, Spain and Switzerland.

In the United States and Canada, homemade cider is usually not processed, and has a sweet flavor somewhat heartier than that of apple juice. However, if it is kept in a warm place or neglected for too long a time, it begins to ferment and becomes sharp and vinegary.

Commercially made cider has a uniform flavor, though the characteristic taste of different brands may vary according to the types of apples used. In producing commercial cider, whole apples are grated in a mill and the juice is extracted by means of a press. Preservatives are then added and the cider is pasteurized before being bottled.

Frozen concentrated cider was introduced in the 1960's. The method used to obtain cider for freezing is similar to that used to obtain cider for bottling. Before freezing, however, the cider is subjected to low temperatures in a high vacuum to remove most of the water. The concentrated cider is then canned and frozen. Before serving, it is mixed with water.

The degree of fermentation of apple juice in commercial processing is highly controlled and can be initiated or halted at desired times. Through these controls and distillation processes other cider products are obtained. A strongly fermented cider produced by distillation is called cider brandy or applejack.

CIEGO DE ÁVILA, syä′gō thä ä′vē-lä, is a city in Cuba. It is situated in Camagüey province, on the Central Highway and main-line railroad, about 65 miles (105 km) northwest of Camagüey. Ciego de Ávila is a transport, trading, and processing center for a fertile region producing sugarcane, tropical fruit, and cattle. Its nearest port is Júcaro, about 15 miles (25 km) south, on the Caribbean. Population: (1953) 35,178.

CIÉNAGA, syä′nä-gä, is a seaport on the Caribbean coast of Colombia, in Magdalena department, 17 miles (27 km) south of Santa Marta. It serves an agricultural region whose main crops are cacao, bananas, cotton, and tobacco. It is also a fishing port. Ciénaga is linked with Colombia's interior cities by the Atlantic railroad, completed in 1961. Population: (1964) 47,719.

CIENFUEGOS, syän-fwä′gōs, a town and municipality in Cuba, in the province of Las Villas, is situated on the south central coast of the island, about 140 miles (225 km) southeast of Havana. Cienfuegos is a sugar port, built on a peninsula in Cienfuegos (or Jagua) Bay of the Caribbean Sea. The surrounding agricultural area produces sugar cane, coffee, tobacco, and cattle. Industries of Cienfuegos include sugar factories, coffee-processing plants, sawmills, and a rum distillery. The climate from May to November is hot and humid, but the winter months are agreeable, with warm daytime temperatures and cooler nights.

Cienfuegos is known as a handsome city, with wide, well-shaded streets and one of the finest plazas in Cuba. Important buildings include the municipal palace, the cathedral, and the Terry Theater. To the east there are views of the Trinidad Mountains. Across the bay to the southwest, guarding the narrow entrance to the bay, is the fortress Castillo de Jagua, built by Spain in the 1740's as–a defense against pirate attacks. Cienfuegos is connected by road and railway with Santa Clara, capital of the province, about 40 miles (64 km) to the northeast.

The harbor of present Cienfuegos was visited by Columbus in 1494, but there was little settlement of the bay area until the 1700's. Although the date of Cienfuegos' founding is uncertain, its development as a port began in the early 1800's. Population: (1953) 57,991.

CIERVA, thyer′vä, **Juan de la** (1895–1936), Spanish aviator, who invented the autogiro. Cierva was born in Murcia, Spain, on Sept. 21, 1895. He was educated in Madrid at the Escuela Especial de Caminos, Canales y Puertos and made a study of theoretical aerodynamics on his own.

After an unsuccessful experience with conventional airplane design in 1919, he began work on rotating-wing machines. On Jan. 19, 1923, he flew the first successful gyroplane (to which he gave the name Autogyro) for a distance of 200 yards (about 180 meters) at Getafe, Spain; he later repeated his flight at Madrid. By 1925 the autogiro was ready for commercial production, and Cierva became the technical director of the Cierva Autogyro Company, Ltd., in England. He continued to demonstrate the autogiro and received many awards for his accomplishments. He died in an airplane crash at Croydon, England, on Dec. 9, 1936.

CIGAR. The cigar originated in the Caribbean islands as tobacco leaves in a corn husk and, after Christopher Columbus observed it in 1492, spread to the Iberian Peninsula and into various Spanish possessions. In about 1670 it was taken to India by the Portuguese. Its entry into northern Europe resulted from the mingling of British and French troops in Spain in the Peninsular War.

Kinds of Cigars. Cigars are classified basically by shape. The kinds include *Coronas* (round, straight, roundly blunt head), *Panatelas* (long, slender with straight sides, ends pointed or blunt), *Perfectos* (thick in the middle, slightly tapering at ends), *Londres* (cylindrical, blunt on one end), *Bouquets* (medium-sized with large belly, tapered at both ends), and *Clubs* (full-bodied, large). *Cheroots* and *stogies*, made of tobacco not used in standard cigars, are open at both ends and have no heads. Countless modifications exist, largely as a result of the use of machinery.

Cigars once were assorted into six colors, but by 1930 they could be mechanically assorted into 32 shades. Better cigars once were made of filler fragments as long as the cigar; low-priced cigars used short filler. This changed, however, when the industry began using reconstituted leaf (good-quality elastic leaf made of scraps and stems).

For cheap cigars, Pennsylvania, Ohio, and Manila filler is used with Connecticut and Wisconsin binders, along with Sumatra leaf or shade-grown wrappers from the United States. The finest cigar has a Cuban filler, binder, and wrap-

CIGAR MAKING includes sorting wrapper leaves for size (*left*) and rolling them on a suction die (*right*).

per (but Sumatra wrappers constitute the highest standard of grade uniformity in wrappers). Besuki binder, grown in eastern Java, is the best quality binder. Havana (or Cuban) leaf, once deemed indispensable in the cigar industry, has been replaced by flavorings, blended grades of leaf, or substitute leaf.

How Cigars Are Made. The cigar remained largely handmade until soon after Rufus L. Patterson, of North Carolina, developed bunching and rolling machines in 1917. Before that, production equipment consisted of a board, a gauge, and a knife.

Manufacture has remained basically unchanged except for the application of machinery. Roughly the steps include rendering the leaf pliable with moisture, assorting it, spraying with flavorings, removing the midrib, fabricating the bunch, or inner central part of the cigar, applying the binder leaf to give shape, encasing the bunch in the wrapper leaf, pasting the head, and cutting the cigar to the proper length. The end that goes in the mouth is the head; the other end is the tuck. Wrapping begins at the tuck and continues to the head, where the wrapper is fastened with a paste, usually of gum tragacanth.

History. By 1850 the English had developed a wooden mold that doubled cigar production, and the mold had gained general acceptance by 1880. In the 1890's machines were introduced for partial removal of midribs of leaf and for stacking the leaf flat (in books). The suction table, also introduced in the 1890's, aided in cutting the wrapper but, even more significantly, it moved the industry from homes to factories. At this stage the cigar, originally spread by soldiers, sailors, and immigrants from Europe, became the object of advertising.

Patterson introduced his complete cigar-making machine in 1917, and within five years it was used by virtually all large cigar manufacturers. The Universal Tobacco Machine Company developed a bunch machine, and soon it also in-

troduced a superior rolling machine that put wrappers on the bunches. Its other new devices banded cigars and wrapped each in cellophane at the rate of more than 4,200 per hour. Cellophane wrapping preserves the flavor and maintains a uniform moisture content.

During the 1950's and 1960's reconstituted filler, binder, and wrapper leaf were developed. They reduced waste, eliminated some minor hand operations, and produced a more uniform blend and more even burning. By the 1960's the manufacture of cigars was almost completely automated, and the industry was concentrated in relatively few factories.

Manufacturing Centers. The first center of the cigar industry was Seville, Spain, headquarters of the Casa de Contratación, which controlled the tobacco industry in the 1700's. About 1800 the center of the industry gravitated to Havana but remained under rigid Spanish control. After 1820, London developed a considerable industry. Tiring of Spanish restrictions, Cuban cigar workers began moving to Key West, Fla., about 1830. In 1868, Vincente Ibor and Eduardo Gato led a group of Cuban cigar makers to Florida and founded Tampa, now a center of the industry.

Other cigar-making centers are New York City, eastern Pennsylvania, the Connecticut Valley, Philadelphia, Baltimore, Cincinnati, St. Louis, and Albany, all in the United States, and Manila in the Philippines. Cheap cigars have long been manufactured from Palatine or Dutch leaf in Belgium and Germany. Using tobacco cultivated in what is now Indonesia, various cities of the Netherlands, including Amsterdam, Rotterdam, and Utrecht, became important centers.

Marketing. Major changes have occurred in cigar consumption in the United States. Until about 1800, cigars were smoked primarily by men of wealth, but then cheap cigars were introduced from Belgium and Germany. Demand for better quality became greater by 1865, and by 1904, Americans spent more for cigars than for any

CIGARETTE TOBACCO is dispensed from machines in shredded condition suitable for pressing and cutting.

PHILIP MORRIS

other tobacco product. In the 1960's, however, cigars held only a small share of the market, and they accounted for less than 3% of the nation's annual tobacco tax revenue.

NANNIE M. TILLEY, *Author of*
"The Bright-Tobacco Industry, 1860–1929"

CIGARETTE. The cigarette originated in the New World, where Spanish explorers found it among the Aztecs in 1518. It spread rapidly to the Iberian Peninsula and other Mediterranean areas but did not reach northern Europe until the 1850's, when the British brought it back from the Crimean War. By 1865 the cigarette had reached the United States, where it eventually became important commercially through two innovations: application of machinery to its manufacture (1880) and development of domestic blends (1913).

On a world scale, the cigarette industry rose phenomenally throughout the 20th century. In the late 1960's the largest cigarette-producing countries, in descending order, were the United States, USSR, Japan, Bulgaria, and Britain.

Kinds of Cigarettes. Cigarettes may be classified by tobacco, by flavor, or by length. Prior to 1913 the leading types were *first-class Turkish*, *straight Turkish*, *pseudo-Turkish* (packaged and adorned to resemble Turkish cigarettes), *straight Virginias* (made of flue-cured leaf of Virginia and the Carolinas), and *miscellaneous* (consisting of mouthpiece and uncased straight Burley). The *American* type (domestic blend and a small amount of Turkish tobacco) was introduced in 1913 and has become dominant. See also TOBACCO.

Smokers in Hispanic-American countries prefer cigarettes made of dark, strong leaf, while those of eastern Europe smoke a lighter Turkish type. English cigarettes are generally manufactured with a high moisture content; immediately after production they are placed in a drying room so that they emerge in a hardened condition. In the USSR the favorite is the *papirosa*, which is only about one third tobacco, the rest being a hollow tube. Generally cigarette manufacturers use the tobacco produced in their own countries, but many who must import leaf prefer the milder Burley and flue-cured with a small proportion of Turkish tobacco.

In the flavor classification, the *menthol* type predominates. In length, the 70-millimeter (about 2.8 inches), or regular size, prevailed almost exclusively until about 1939, when the first 85-millimeter (3.4-inch), or king-size, length came into vogue. The 100-millimeter length (4 inches) entered the market in 1966.

How Cigarettes Are Made. An important part of the manufacture of cigarettes lies in preparation of the leaf. Preparation includes making the leaf pliable, grading it, removing the midrib, flavoring it, and storing it for aging. Different types of tobacco for a blend are assembled and shredded by powerful cutters slicing through the leaf, which is thoroughly mixed before entering the cigarette machine. There the shredded leaf falls on a continuous roll of paper, and the cigarette rod is formed, fastened, and cut into proper lengths.

A device for packaging and wrapping in cellophane is attached. In the 1960's the most modern cigarette machine generally produced 1,400 per minute. Electrically counted and routed, cigarettes number 20 to the package, 10 packages in each carton, and 60 cartons in each case.

Smokers in many areas roll their own cigarettes. In some jungle areas of Hispanic America, smokers often roll their tobacco in corn husks as their ancestors did 500 years ago.

History. The cigarette found in Mexico in 1518 resembled the 20th century product, although the crushed tobacco was stuffed into a hollow reed or wrapped in a vegetable product, probably corn husk. According to tradition, paper-wrapped cigarettes were developed in the 16th century by beggars of Seville, Spain, who rolled discarded cigar butts in scraps of paper. The cigarette, this time in paper, returned to Mexico well before 1765 when Visitor General José de Gálvez confiscated large quantities of cigarette paper in Jalapa and established a government tobacco monopoly. Meanwhile the cigarette, along with the production of tobacco, had spread into the Middle East. When cigarettes entered France early in the 19th century, they were wrapped in paper manufactured in Barcelona, Spain. As early as 1845, French smokers preferred America's Maryland or Virginia tobacco because that grown in France was too acrid. In southern Russia as early as 1840 native-grown leaf was mixed with Maryland, Ohio, and Kentucky leaf.

The date when factory production of cigarettes began is not known for certain. It is known that Baron Josef Huppmann established the Ferme cigarette factory in St. Petersburg, Russia (now Leningrad), in 1850; opened a branch house in Dresden, Germany, in 1872; and established the Monopal cigarette works in New York City in 1882. In London, Robert Peacock Gloag, impressed with the cigarette he had seen used by the Russians in the Crimean War, manufactured some in the 1850's from Latakia (Turkish) tobacco and yellow tissue paper, which he called Don Alphonso Spanish Whiffs. Gloag used the awkward method of constructing a paper tube and then inserting the crushed tobacco through a thin metal pipe.

Eventually Americans emulated the English and began the manufacture of cigarettes in 1864. Almost 20 million were made that year, but production immediately declined. After 1869, Greeks, Turks, and Egyptians began the manufacture of cigarettes in Britain and the United States. Cigarette smoking at this time interested only the more sophisticated, who often rolled their own. In 1869 the F. S. Kinney Company of New York imported Polish and Russian cigarette rollers, some of them from London, to instruct American girls in the art of making cigarettes by hand. The Panic of 1873 discouraged the smoking of expensive cigars but greatly increased demand in the United States for cigarettes because they were cheaper. Factory production increased as New York manufacturers moved into the Southern tobacco-producing areas and as Southern manufacturers took up cigarette production.

An expert roller, with helpers, made 40 cigarettes per minute by handwork techniques. Each roller sat before a table containing a small trench —a small cut in the surface—the length of the cigarette. When fitted in the trench, the paper projected its lengthwise edges slightly above the smooth tabletop. A pinch of shredded tobacco was placed on the paper. Then the worker, wearing a strip of felt over the palm of the hand, rubbed the felt over the trench, catching a protruding edge of the paper so that the cigarette was whirled into shape by one deft rolling motion. Paste was used for fastening the edges.

The invention in 1860 of the Pease cutter, which shredded tobacco leaf instead of pulverizing it, proved the first step in applying machinery to cigarette production. The most successful among the many attempting to develop a cigarette-making machine was James Albert Bonsack of Virginia who, by 1880, developed a machine containing three fundamental parts: the feeder that apportioned the tobacco uniformly; the forming tube where the cigarette was shaped into a continuous roll; and the knife for cutting the cigarette rod into equal lengths. The Bonsack machine was improved slightly by William T. O'Brien and James B. Duke in Duke's factory at Durham, N. C. By 1886, Duke's daily output reached 4 million at a reduction in cost of 50 cents per 1,000. By the end of 1889, Duke dominated the

cigarette industry, and his company continued to do so until its patents expired.

Until 1913, Turkish leaf—cultivated in various countries around the eastern Mediterranean—was used so extensively in cigarettes that the mistaken belief arose that tobacco originated in Turkey and that only Turkish or Egyptian cigarettes were superior. (In the United States and Britain, however, a blend of flue-cured leaf and a small amount of Turkish became popular.) In 1913, Richard J. Reynolds changed the cigarette industry significantly when he developed what is generally called the first American cigarette. He began manufacturing cigarettes in Winston-Salem, N. C., using a domestic blend of Burley and flue-cured leaf (soon adding Maryland tobacco) that he mixed with a small amount of Turkish tobacco. This cigarette was successful immediately, and other manufacturers were forced to copy it. The popularity of this cigarette was spread greatly during the two world wars.

Three major developments arose in the cigarette industry from 1913 to World War II: (1) The Arenco packer, a Swedish machine used to pack matches, was adapted in the late 1920's to create a small machine that combined making the package, packing the cigarettes, and affixing revenue stamps. This move reduced the cost of packaging to less than 1 cent per 1,000. (2) Moisture-proof cellophane was adopted in 1931 as wrapping for packages to preserve the freshness of cigarettes between manufacture and use. (3) Three large American manufacturers cooperated in the 1930's in developing a new source for cigarette paper, which had long been made of linen rags and was produced chiefly in France. By using seed flax and experimenting for six years, the firms produced excellent cigarette paper in the United States. The new paper plant in Brevard, N. C., began production in 1939, and it made possible the tremendous expansion of the cigarette industry that occurred immediately after World War II ended.

FINISHED CIGARETTES are inspected as they roll off the end of a high-speed cigarette-making machine.

During the 1950's large-scale manufacturers developed reconstituted leaf (excellent leaf made of scrap tobacco and stems and processing elasticity), adopted a satisfactory mechanical method for removing the midrib from the leaf, and began manufacture of filter-tipped cigarettes to remove gases and minute particles. Reconstituted leaf and removal of the midrib by the thrashing process, both developed in the United States, made for great economy. Filter-tipped cigarettes were developed in western Europe and quickly adopted in the United States by means of machinery evolved in England and Germany. The popularity of filter-tipped cigarettes stemmed from the health controversy over cigarette smoking. In the United States the controversy began in 1952 and reached a climax with the surgeon general's adverse report issued in 1964. See also SMOKING AND HEALTH.

Marketing. The major U. S. cigarette-manufacturing center is the North Carolina-Virginia area—Winston-Salem, Durham, and Reidsville, N. C., and Richmond, Va. Many cigarettes are made in New York City, London, various European Common Market countries, and in Russia.

Before the adoption of machinery, sales approaches were mild. But after the advent of Bonsack's invention and its evolution into an intricate and effective cigarette-making machine, the industry steadily increased its expenditures for advertising.

Taxes. No tobacco product is taxed more heavily than cigarettes. The U. S. federal government in the late 1960's was collecting more than $2 billion annually from its taxes that amounted to 8 cents a pack. State cigarette taxes varied from nothing in North Carolina (where the bulk of the industry is situated) to 11 cents per pack in New Jersey, Texas, and Washington. In addition, many city governments also tax the sale of cigarettes. Elsewhere over most of the world, cigarettes are heavily taxed.

NANNIE M. TILLEY, *Author of*
"The Bright-Tobacco Industry, 1860–1929"

A longitudinal section of several cilia shows the basal bodies beneath the cell membrane, the stalks extending from the bodies, and the filaments that are in the stalk.

D. W. FAWCETT

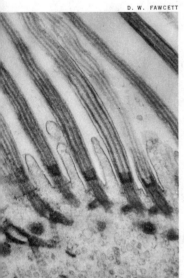

CILIA

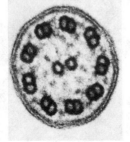

Cross section of a cilium shows the two central filaments surrounded by nine pairs of filaments. Cilia of both plants and animals exhibit this structure.

D. W. FAWCETT

Bibliography

Boyd, William K., *The Story of Durham: City of the New South* (Durham, N. C., 1927).
Brooks, Jerome E., *Tobacco, Its History Illustrated by the Books, Manuscripts and Engravings in the Library of George Arents, Jr.*, vol. 1 (New York 1937).
Jenkins, John W., *James B. Duke: Master Builder* (New York 1927).
Tilley, Nannie M., *The Bright-Tobacco Industry, 1860–1929* (Chapel Hill, N. C., 1948).
Young, W. W., *The Story of the Cigarette* (London and New York 1916).

CIGOLI, chē'gō-lē, **Lodovico Cardi da** (1559–1613), Italian painter and architect. He was born in Castelvecchio, Italy, on Sept. 21, 1559. He lived in Florence and studied painting with Alessandro Allori and Santo di Tito and architecture with Bernardo Buontalenti.

Influenced by Michelangelo, Pontormo, Andrea del Sarto, and particularly by Correggio, Cigoli developed a personal style that led to the assertion that he originated baroque painting in Florence. His *Martyrdom of St. Stephen* (Uffizi, Florence) is considered his masterpiece. Other notable works are *St. Peter Healing the Lame Man* (St. Peter's, Rome), *St. Francis Receiving the Stigmata* (Florence), *Nativity* (Pistoia), and *Story of Cupid and Psyche,* a fresco in the Villa Borghese, Rome.

Cigoli's work in architecture is not of the same importance as his painting. He died in Rome on June 7, 1613, grief-stricken over his failure on a fresco painting for a Roman church.

CILÈA, chē-lā-ä, **Francesco** (1866–1950), Italian opera composer. He was born in Palmi, Calabria, on July 26, 1866. He wrote his first opera, *Gina* (1889), while studying at the Naples Conservatory. He then taught at Florence, at Palermo, and at Naples, where he was director of the conservatory from 1916 to 1935.

Cilèa's first well-known work was *L'Arlesiana,* a tragic opera about Provençal peasants, which was adapted from a drama by Alphonse Daudet and produced in Milan in 1896. Cilèa's best-known work, *Adriana Lecouvreur,* was presented in Milan in 1902 with Caruso. The opera, which recounts the tragic love of a French actress for the Count of Saxony, has been called by one critic "a work of incontrovertible mediocrity"; nevertheless it remains popular. Cilèa died at Varazze, near Genoa, on Nov. 20, 1950.

CILIA, sil'ē-ə, are microscopic hairlike projections found on the surface of some living cells. They are among the specialized cell structures known as organelles, and occur in a wide variety of cell types, ranging from protozoa to cells lining the human trachea. Cilia generally function either in cell locomotion or in assisting the passage of material over the surface of the cell. In protozoa the cilia cover the entire surface of the organism; they move back and forth like oars, with a synchronous beat, thereby propelling the organism through its liquid surrounding. In the stationary cells of the trachea the beating of the cilia helps in removing foreign material from the windpipe.

Structure. Cilia from all types of cells have very similar structures. The stalk, which extends from the body of the cell like a hair, is about 0.0002 mm in diameter and about 0.005 to 0.015 mm in length. The cytoplasm of the stalk is continuous with that of the cell, and the stalk is surrounded by an extension of the cell membrane. Within the cell, at the base of the stalk, there is a dense basal body. In some cell types a rootlet fiber coming from the basal body extends into the cell's interior. Eleven filaments originate from the basal body and extend upwards through the stalk. The filaments are usually arranged with a pair in the center and the nine others in a circle around them.

Some organisms possess cilia that have been modified to the extent that they conduct impulses but do not move. For example, it is thought that the sensory rods and cones of the vertebrate eye have evolved from cilia. Rods and cones possess the basic ciliary structure in the form of a highly modified stalk with a basal body and rootlet fiber. Similarly modified cilia are found in the eyes of some mollusks and the brains of fishes. The ultrastructure of cilia is similar to that of two other cell organelles—the centriole and the flagellum.

DAVID A. OTTO, *Stephens College*

CILIATES, sil'ē-ətz, a large class of microscopic one-celled, or acellular, animals which, except during encystment, have short whiplike lashes, called *cilia*, arranged in rows along the length of their bodies. The cilia beat back and forth and are used for locomotion. They also produce water currents that bring food particles to the mouth.

Although some ciliates are parasites, living in or on other organisms, most are free-living, inhabiting moist soil as well as fresh and salt water. Many are omnivorous, feeding on a wide array of bacteria and algae as well as other protozoa.

Characteristics. Ciliates range in length from about 0.004 to 0.12 inch (0.01 to 3.0 mm) and vary greatly in shape. In all species, however, the body is covered by a thin, semirigid, membranous sheet, called the pellicle, through which the cilia protrude. On one side of the body there is usually a mouth opening leading to a tubular gullet. When masses of food particles reach the end of the gullet they are enclosed in small bubble-like structures, called food vacuoles, which move about through the body. As the vacuoles circulate, digestive enzymes break down the food particles into substances that can be used by the ciliate. Any remaining undigested matter is voided through the cytophage, another opening in the body surface. Excess water is removed by the contractile vacuoles.

All ciliates have two kinds of nuclei. One is a large nucleus, called a macronucleus, which directs metabolism and development. The other, the micronucleus, is smaller and controls heredity.

Through extensive studies with light and electron microscopes, scientists have discovered the complex structure of the ciliate's ciliary system. Each cilium was found to have a sheath surrounding 11 longitudinal fibers, with 9 of the fibers arranged in a circle around a central pair. The 11 fibers are attached to a granule, called a kinetosome, at the base of the cilium. Extending from each kinetosome is a long fibril, called a kinetodesmose, which overlaps with those from adjacent kinetosomes, forming compound fibrils that run beneath each row of cilia. In some ciliates, a ciliary coordinating center, called a neuromotorium, has been found.

In many ciliates there is a layer of tiny carrot-shaped bodies, called trichocysts, underneath the pellicle. When discharged, each trichocyst forms a long sticky thread. Usually, trichocysts are discharged as a means of defense, but sometimes they are used as an anchor.

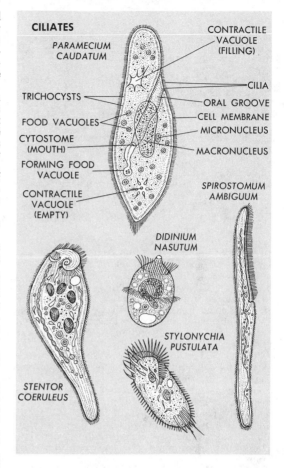

CILIATES

PARAMECIUM CAUDATUM

TRICHOCYSTS

FOOD VACUOLES

CYTOSTOME (MOUTH)

FORMING FOOD VACUOLE

CONTRACTILE VACUOLE (EMPTY)

CONTRACTILE VACUOLE (FILLING)

CILIA

ORAL GROOVE

CELL MEMBRANE

MICRONUCLEUS

MACRONUCLEUS

SPIROSTOMUM AMBIGUUM

DIDINIUM NASUTUM

STYLONYCHIA PUSTULATA

STENTOR COERULEUS

In studies of *Paramecium aurelia*, scientists have discovered that certain individuals contain unusual cell particles. These particles, known as kappa particles, produce a substance called paramecin, which is lethal to those members of the species that lack the particles. The paramecia with the kappa particles are known as killer paramecia while those without them are called sensitive paramecia. Although the presence or absence of kappa particles is under genetic control, they can be passed to the next generation only through the cytoplasm.

Reproduction. Ciliates reproduce by two methods. In binary fission, one cell divides into two equal halves, producing two identical daughter cells. In conjugation, two individuals come together and exchange nuclear and, in rare cases, cytoplasmic material. They then separate and each one then undergoes many divisions before conjugation occurs again. Each of the new cells formed contains hereditary material from both the original parent cells.

It has been found that many species of ciliates have distinct mating types, which can be classified into groups called syngens. Within any syngen there are generally two mating types that will mate (conjugate) only with each other, not with members of any other syngen. In *Paramecium aurelia*, 16 syngens have been found.

Classification. The class Ciliata belongs to the subphylum Ciliophora of the phylum Protozoa. There are at least 6,000 species.

W. D. BURBANCK, *Emory University*

CILICIA, si-lish′ə, is the classical name for the eastern Mediterranean coastal region of Asia Minor, corresponding to the provinces of İçel and Adana (Seyhan) in present-day Turkey. The area is separated from the central Anatolian plateau by the high ranges of the Taurus Mountains. In its eastern part it gradually widens into a broad, fertile plain watered by several rivers. The Amanus Mountains of northern Syria form the region's eastern boundary. Despite this geographic confinement, Cilicia has never been culturally isolated: the famous defile of the Cilician Gates affords communication with the northern hinterlands, while the shoreline of the Gulf of Issus and the Amanian Gates connect it with northern Syria. The ancient cities of Adana, Mersin, and Tarsus still retain their importance.

History. The earliest historical mention of Cilicia dates from about the 14th century B.C., when the region was referred to under the name of Kizzuwatna as a Hittite vassal state. Widely distributed finds of Mycenaean pottery attest to contemporary Greek influences arriving by sea. In 715 B.C. it was conquered by the Assyrians, who referred to it as Que; and with the invasions of the Achaemenid Persians in the middle of the 6th century B.C. it became a semi-independent satrapy of the Persian empire.

After the defeat of Darius by Alexander the Great in 333 B.C., Cilicia was shared between Alexander's political heirs, the Seleucids and the Egyptian Ptolemies. As their power declined, the various cities of the region assumed independence. The Romans sent an expedition there under the command of Pompey in 67 B.C. to stop piratical activity by the peoples of the mountainous western regions. Cilicia was absorbed into the Roman Empire and was governed from Syria until it became a separate province in 74 A.D.

The region was early converted to Christianity—Tarsus was the birthplace of St. Paul—and it remained a Byzantine province until it was conquered by the Arabs in the 9th century. In the 11th century the Armenians, driven from the east by the Turks, founded the state of Little Armenia here. This fell to the Egyptian Mamluks at the end of the 14th century, and they, in turn, lost it to the Ottomans in 1516.

JOHN R. WALSH
University of Edinburgh

CIMA, chē′mä, **Giovanni Battista** (1459?–?1517), Italian painter of the Venetian school. He is often called *Cima de Conegliano*, after his birthplace at Conegliano in the Alps. Cima is believed to have studied with Bartolomeo Montagna in Vicenza and with Giovanni Bellini in Venice. As is shown by his first work, *La Madonna della Pergola* (Vicenza), he early perfected the austerely beautiful style that characterizes all his large altarpieces of madonnas and saints. He excelled in an airy, luminous handling of color and in landscapes closely observed from nature and painted as backgrounds for his rather stiff figures. A later painting is *La Madonna sotto l'Arancio* (Venice). Cima died in Venice about 1517.

CIMABUE, chē′mä-boo′ä, **Giovanni** (c. 1240–1302), Italian painter, who was the first great master of the Florentine school. He has been regarded traditionally as the teacher of Giotto, but beyond this his career was very shadowy until modern scholars succeeded in isolating a

ANDERSON–ART REFERENCE BUREAU

CIMABUE'S altarpiece depicting the Madonna and Child.

small nucleus of authentic works from a varied collection of more or less plausible attributions.

The enormous superiority of Cimabue over his Florentine predecessors, such as Coppo di Marcovaldo and the Master of Vico l'Abbate, seems to be due largely to his determination to come to grips with the various painting trends that were dominant in his time. During a stay in Rome in 1272, he studied the powerful classical style that had developed under the leadership of Pietro Cavallini. Cimabue's work also shows that he was familiar with the aristocratic Byzantine style of Constantinople and with the more expressive and emotional manner cultivated by provincial Byzantine masters. Cimabue could have seen both of these Byzantine styles in Italy in imported art objects and in the works of itinerant craftsmen. Despite these influences, however, Cimabue remained mindful of his own Tuscan tradition, with its strong compositional clarity and its emphasis on human dignity.

Works. Cimabue's most famous work is the great altarpiece of the *Madonna and Child Enthroned with Angels and Prophets* (Uffizi Gallery, Florence), probably painted in the early 1280's, for the Church of Santa Trinità, Florence. The figures are disposed in and around a quasi-architectural setting of a stepped throne. Although it is a fully mature work, the altarpiece pays homage to Byzantine tradition in the abstract pattern of the gold striation on the garments of the two chief figures. Belonging to about the same period is the extensive cycle of frescoes in the Church of San Francesco at Assisi. Despite the poor condition of these frescoes, the artist's remarkable skill in the building up of dramatic effects is clearly evident in the narrative scenes of the *Crucifixion* and the *Life of the Virgin*.

Among Cimabue's other major works are two large painted crosses, notable for their powerful expressive stylization. The first of these is in the Church of San Domenico, Arezzo. The second is the magnificent cross in the Church of Santa Croce. (The cross was badly damaged by floods in 1966.) The last known work of Cimabue, executed about 1302, is the mosaic in the apse of the Cathedral of Pisa, of which only the upper half of the figure of St. John has survived unrestored.

Reputation. In his own time Cimabue's fame was very great, as we know from the contemporary reference to him in Dante's *Divine Comedy*. However, his reputation was obscured in succeeding centuries by the conventional comparison of his work with that of Giotto, whose achievement in eliminating the lingering traces of the Byzantine manner was so much lauded by Giorgio Vasari. But as the earlier development of medieval painting came to be better understood, Cimabue's achievement was reassessed, and he is now considered not merely a precursor but a fountainhead of the great age of Italian painting.

WAYNE DYNES, *Vassar College*

Further Reading: Nicholson, Alfred, *Cimabue* (Princeton 1932); White, John, *Art and Architecture in Italy, 1250 to 1400* (Baltimore 1966).

CIMAROSA, chē-mä-rô′zä, **Domenico** (1749–1801), Italian composer, who excelled in *opera buffa*, or comic opera. His comic operas are remarkable for their wit, charm, and melodic richness. Cimarosa is especially noted for his superb handling of vocal parts, particularly ensembles. His most popular and best-known work is his comic opera *Il matrimonio segreto*.

Life. Cimarosa was born in Aversa, near Naples, on Dec. 17, 1749. He displayed his musical gifts at an early age, and in 1761 won a scholarship to the Conservatory of Santa Maria di Loreto in Naples. There he studied violin, piano, clavichord, and voice for the next 11 years under Antonio Sacchini and other distinguished teachers. After graduation in 1772, Cimarosa produced, in Naples, his first operatic work, *Le stravaganze del conte*. Although this comic opera met with only moderate success, his next opera, *La finta parigina*, produced in 1773, also in Naples, was well received and established him as a popular favorite in Italy. Six years later, with the production in Rome of his opera *L'Italiana in Londra*, he achieved international renown.

Until 1781, Cimarosa divided his time between Naples and Rome, composing operas specifically for each city, as was the custom of the day. As a masterstroke he presented, in 1781, two operas in Naples, one in Rome, and two in Turin. Soon he became one of the most sought-after composers of his time, and his works, translated into many languages, were performed in London, Dresden, Vienna, Paris, Warsaw, and other leading cities.

In 1787, Cimarosa was invited to St. Petersburg by Catherine the Great to succeed the Italian composer Giovanni Paisiello as her court composer. During his four years there he is said to have composed some 500 musical pieces, including three operas. However, Catherine was displeased with Cimarosa's choral works, and he left Russia in 1791.

On his way back to Italy, Cimarosa stopped in Vienna, where Emperor Leopold II appointed him imperial chapelmaster. It was in Vienna in 1792 that he produced his masterpiece, *Il matrimonio segreto*. The opera's charming libretto was written by Giovanni Bertati, who took his inspiration from the play *The Clandestine Marriage* (1766) by the English dramatists George Colman and David Garrick. *Il matrimonio segreto* was an instant success, overshadowing the works of all Cimarosa's contemporaries, including Mozart.

After the Emperor's death in 1793, Cimarosa returned to Italy, where he continued to compose and to enjoy great success. His fortunes turned, however, in 1799 when he was imprisoned and condemned for openly supporting a short-lived liberal revolution in Naples. A pardon was secured at public insistence, and he went to live in Venice, where he died on Jan. 11, 1801. A rumor that Cimarosa had been poisoned because of his revolutionary views aroused general concern, but the Pope's physician, sent to examine the body, swore that Cimarosa had died of natural causes.

Works. Cimarosa was an incredibly prolific composer, producing almost 80 operas, both comic and serious. Among his most important operas, in addition to *Il matrimonio segreto*, are *La ballerina amante*, *L'impresario in angustie*, *Le vergine del sole*, and *Gli Orazi e Curiazi*. Cimarosa also composed masses, oratorios, cantatas, and symphonies. A cantata, the lively *Maestro di Cappella*, an amusing parody of 18th century style, had a revival as late as the 1950's.

JOSEPH C. FUCILLA, *Northwestern University*

CIMARRON, sim′ə-rōn, **Proposed Territory of,** an area 34 miles wide and 168 miles long, now known as the Oklahoma Panhandle, but in frontier days called the *Neutral Strip* or *No-Man's Land*. After Texas ceded its claim to this area to the United States in 1850, the strip was at first ignored when the boundaries of surrounding territories were formed. Cattlemen brought in herds to graze its land, and the absence of law attracted criminals. Farmers came and built sod houses but were harassed by outlaws and were unable to record their land claims.

In 1886 some squatters began to try to establish law and land registry. They drew plans for a Territory of Cimarron, adopted the laws of Colorado, and in 1877 held elections and sent Dr. Owen G. Chase as a delegate to Congress to seek recognition. But bills to establish Cimarron Territory died in committee, and in 1888–1889 drought, dust storms, and the opening of homestead land to the east reduced the population of the strip from about 12,000 or 14,000 to less than 4,000.

In 1889, Congress included the area in the jurisdiction of a federal court at Muskogee, thus identifying it as part of the embryo Indian Territory and thereby including it in the subsequent Oklahoma Territory.

WAYNE GARD, *Author of "Frontier Justice"*

Further Reading: Rister, Carl Coke, *No Man's Land* (Norman, Okla., 1948).

CIMBRI, sim′brī, a Germanic tribe that threatened Rome in the late 2d century B. C. The Cimbri and the Teutones left their homes in Jutland and migrated southward in search of lands to settle. By 113 B. C. the Cimbri had reached Illyricum, where they defeated a Roman consular army. Turning westward, they invaded Gaul and, when refused a homestead by the Roman Senate, defeated another consular army in 109. They fought intermittently with the Romans in the next few years. In 105 they defeated the Romans at Arausio (Orange). About 80,000 Romans reportedly fell; it was their worst defeat since the Battle of Cannae (216).

The Cimbri migrated to Spain, were defeated by the Celtiberi, and returned to Gaul, where they joined the Teutones in a combined assault on Italy. In 101 B. C. at Vercellae, in Cisalpine Gaul, the Romans, commanded by Marius and Catulus, defeated first the Teutones and then the Cimbri, who had taken a longer route through the Brenner Pass.

RICHARD E. MITCHELL
University of Illinois

CIMMERIANS, sə-mir'ē-ənz, an ancient half-mythical, half-historical people. They were first mentioned in the *Odyssey,* by Homer, who said they lived in Oceanus in a region shrouded by mist and clouds, where the sun never shone. From this comes the term "Cimmerian gloom."

The historian Herodotus regarded the Cimmerians as early inhabitants of Russia. Supposedly, they were driven by the Scythians through the Caucasus mountains into Asia. The Cimmerian Bosporus, ancient name for the Kerch Strait, was named after them. History gives little additional certain knowledge. Most scholars agree that the Cimmerians were several groups of people who lived north of the Caucasus and the Sea of Azov in the 8th century B. C. They spread over Asia Minor and destroyed the Phrygian dynasty, becoming a great power for about 30 years. They were finally defeated by the Lydians in the 7th century B. C. They are said to have inhabited a large city in what is now the Crimea.

CIMON, sī'mən (c. 510–450 B. C.), Athenian general. A member of the aristocratic Philaid family, he was the son of Miltiades, the victor of Marathon, and Hegesipyle, daughter of the Thracian king Olorus. In 489 B. C., Cimon paid the 50-talent fine imposed by the Athenians upon his father, who had failed in a punitive expedition against Paros. During this expedition Miltiades had received a wound that led to his death.

Cimon is said to have fought well at the Battle of Salamis (480). He was elected one of the 10 Athenian generals in 478 and probably held this position during most of the next 17 years. He became the leading commander of the combined fleets of Athens and the Delian League, which had been formed to fight the Persians. He encouraged the league members to contribute money rather than men and ships, thus increasing the power and efficiency of Athens' fleet while weakening the allies. This process ultimately led, after Cimon's death, to Athens' turning the league into an empire.

Cimon expelled the Persians from Eion about 476, winning for Athens part of the rich Thracian coast. Shortly thereafter he captured the island of Skyros from pirates and returned with what were purported to be the bones of the legendary Athenian king Theseus. The bones were then buried in a shrine near the Agora. About 469, Cimon led a large fleet to the east and won, in a single day, a spectacular double victory over the Persians on land and sea at the river Eurymedon in Pamphylia, Asia Minor. He used the spoils, and perhaps part of his own fortune, to beautify Athens.

When Thasos tried to withdraw from the Delian League in 465, Cimon besieged the island and took it in 463. On his return the lead-ers of the growing democratic element in Athens, Ephialtes and Pericles, accused him of accepting bribes. They were suspicious of Cimon's conservatism and his friendship with Sparta. But Cimon was acquitted and in the next year convinced the Athenians to send aid to Sparta against the Messenian helots, who had revolted. When Cimon and the Athenian troops arrived, however, they were told by the Spartans to return home The Spartans suspected that most of the Athenians secretly sympathized with the enemy. This insult to Athenian pride doomed Cimon politically. Ephialtes and Pericles stripped the conservative Council of the Areopagus of its political powers, which were transferred to the democratic juries and Council of Five Hundred. Cimon was ostracized in 461.

Although there is a story that he was soon recalled, it is far more likely that he served the whole 10-year period of banishment; at least there is no sign of his presence during this period when the Athenians were trying to fight Sparta and Persia simultaneously. But in 451, Cimon made a 5-year truce with Sparta. He was again elected general and in 450 led a major expedition to Cyprus. He defeated the Persian fleet and besieged Citium, but died there of unknown causes. The expedition withdrew, and in the next year Athens made peace with Persia.

DONALD W. BRADEEN
University of Cincinnati

CINCHONA, sin-ko'nə, a genus of evergreen trees that are the source of quinine and other important alkaloids used in medicine. The dried bark of the stem or the roots of the cinchona tree is known as "cinchona bark," "Peruvian bark," and "Jesuits' bark."

Native to the Andes region of Ecuador and Peru at elevations of 3,000 to 9,000 feet (1,000 to 3,000 meters), cinchona trees are tall, and some may have trunks of more than 2 feet (60 cm) in diameter. The trees have been cultivated extensively in the East Indies and India; the chief source of cinchona today is Java.

It is not known whether the Peruvian natives knew the medicinal effects of cinchona or the early Spanish explorers discovered its value as an antipyretic. There are many conflicting stories concerning the initial use of the bark, but its use spread rapidly, and a controversy regarding its effectiveness existed in Europe for many years. Soon the bark was in great demand, and many trees were abused to obtain the bark and the root. In recent years, cultivation of cinchona trees and the scientific stripping of the bark have ensured a lasting supply.

The powder made from cinchona bark is light brown to moderate yellowish brown. It has a faint aromatic odor and an astringent bitter taste. Cinchona contains a mixture of about 25 alkaloids, of which quinine, quinidine, cinchonine, and cinchonidine are the most important. Quinine is, however, responsible for most of the effects of cinchona.

Cinchona has been used as a tonic, as an antiperiodic against recurring episodes of malarial fever, and as an antipyretic. It can produce derangement of the hearing and also of vision. The principal use of cinchona is as a source of its two important alkaloids: quinine, which is used to treat malaria, and quinidine, which is used to treat atril fibrillation.

JOHN C. KRANTZ, JR., *"U. S. Pharmacopeia"*

Cincinnati, second-largest city in Ohio and its chief port on the Ohio River (*foreground*), as seen from Covington, Ky.

EWING GALLOWAY

CINCINNATI, sin-sə-nat'ē, a city in Ohio, the seat of Hamilton county, is in an amphitheater of hills above the Ohio River. Sir Winston Churchill once described it as "the most beautiful of the inland cities of the Union." In the 19th century the poet Henry Wadsworth Longfellow hailed it as "Queen City of the West," and it has proudly kept that title.

Cincinnati is the largest city on the Ohio River and, next to Cleveland, the largest in Ohio. The river, which brought coal and iron from the Appalachian fields and aided the early development of the city, continues to play an important role in Cincinnati's economy.

The city derives its name from the Society of the Cincinnati, an association of former Continental Army officers of the American Revolution named in honor of the great Roman general Lucius Quinctius Cincinnatus. Gen. Arthur St. Clair, a member of the society and the first governor of the Northwest Territory, in 1790 gave the name to the settlement adjoining the headquarters of the Army of the Northwest Territory. He also named Hamilton county after Alexander Hamilton, successor to George Washington as president general of the Cincinnati society.

The Economy. Cincinnati is a major manufacturing center employing about 150,000 people, with an annual payroll amounting to approximately $1 billion. It leads the world in the manufacture of three very different products—machine tools, soap products, and playing cards. It is also an important supplier of cans, chemicals, clothing, building materials, furniture, mattresses, radios, cosmetics, malt and distilled liquors, paper products and printing, jet engines, and packaged meats.

The city's retail sales amount to nearly $1.5 billion annually, and the wholesale trade accounts for more than triple that sum. Foreign trade has become important in the area's economy. Unlike most other American cities, where sales to foreign buyers are not financially noteworthy, Cincinnati has more than 250 firms doing business in foreign countries. Commercial banks in Cincinnati and Hamilton county conduct business in more than 100 offices and branches, and their resources amount to nearly $1.5 billion.

Because of its geographic location, Cincinnati has become the hub of transportation in the Ohio Valley, and the city is a terminus for many bus lines, railroads, and airlines. It is the only city in the United States that owns (and leases) its own

---

INFORMATION HIGHLIGHTS

Location: Southwestern Ohio, on Ohio River, 16 miles (25 km) east of Indiana border.

Population: *City,* 452,524; *metropolitan area,* 1,-104,668 (section in Ohio only).

Land Area: 72.4 square miles (187.5 sq km).

Elevation: 550 feet (168 meters) in downtown business area.

Climate: *Mean temperatures,* 36°F (2°C) in January; 79°F (26°C) in July. *Mean annual precipitation,* 39.51 inches (100.3 cm).

Government: Mayor, council, and city manager.

723

railroad—the Cincinnati Southern Railroad. The Greater Cincinnati Airport is across the Ohio River in Kentucky. The river has been navigable throughout the year, since the completion of a system of locks and dams in 1929. It carries more commerce than any other inland waterway in the world, 16 million tons (15 million metric tons) more annually than the Panama Canal. The largest and most modern barges are accommodated at the port of Cincinnati.

Urban Development and Renewal. The original settlement of Cincinnati was along the waterfront, in the area now known as the Basin. During the 19th century the population pushed its way up to the tops of the surrounding hills. Today the city stretches 25 miles (40 km) along the river and a maximum of 15 miles (25 km) up from the river.

Cincinnati's urban renewal needs were visualized in its Master Plan, prepared in 1948, but work was not actually begun until the 1960's. Naturally a beginning had to be made in the Basin area. The earliest population of the city had built row houses along the Basin's narrow streets, and by the 1960's it had become drab and grimy. The first district to be rehabilitated was the West End. Formerly a monotonous square mile of slum, this area was completely transformed. Century-old tenements were torn down and replaced by modern aluminum, brick, and stainless steel buildings. Directly west of Cincinnati's central business district, the area has ready access to parking lots, railroad sidings, and loading docks.

In 1962, Cincinnati voted $150 million toward a complete revitalization of its downtown core area as the second phase in its urban renewal. Portions or all of eight major downtown blocks were to be demolished and replaced. The first new buildings to be completed were the Convention Hall; Provident Towers, an office building; an underground garage beneath Fountain Square,

TYLER DAVIDSON FOUNTAIN, at Cincinnati's center, has figures cast in Munich, Germany, in 1871.

focal point of the central business district; and a multistory parking garage. These were to be followed by a Federal Reserve Bank Building, major office structures, and, adjoining the core renewal area on the riverfront, a $40 million sports stadium for the Cincinnati Reds baseball team and an American Football League team.

Cincinnati is careful, however, to preserve its cultural past even as the new buildings are erected. Such rarities as a block of Dayton Street, in the West End, have been retained and are being renewed. Formerly an avenue of graceful Victorian homes of first-generation German burghers, Dayton Street preserves the aura of mid-19th century gentility.

Cincinnatians in the 19th century built their structures of solid brick and painted them red when the soot and smudge of their industries discolored them. Their descendants still favor brick houses and still prefer the single-family type— 58% of the city's housing units are single-family structures. Besides one-family homes, however, Cincinnatians have accepted high-rise apartment houses. Taking advantage of the beautiful views from its hills, Cincinnati has constructed 15- and 20-story apartment buildings, with balconies and picture windows facing the river and the hills.

The peculiar configuration of the hills on which Cincinnati has been built has separated the community into many different neighborhoods, each with a distinct character, which has, however, altered with the years. Mt. Adams takes its name from a visit by former president John Quincy Adams in 1843, when he dedicated an astronomical observatory on the hill. Impressed by his speech of dedication, the residents renamed the site in his honor. Originally German and Irish families built their homes there, but as they moved on the district was taken over by a lower-income group. Today Mt. Adams is enjoying a renaissance influenced in part by the nearby art museum and academy. The quaint 19th century houses on narrow, precipitous streets have been transformed into smart apartments and shops that still preserve the charm of the past.

Visiting Cincinnati in 1842, Charles Dickens wrote, "I was quite charmed with the appearance of the town, and its adjoining suburb of Mt. Auburn; from which the city, lying in an amphitheatre of hills, forms a picture of remarkable beauty, and is seen to great advantage." It was on Mt. Auburn in 1857 that President William Howard Taft was born. Today his home has been restored as it was the day of his birth. Because of its central location, Mt. Auburn has become a center for medical services, with a number of hospitals and doctors' offices.

Education and Cultural Life. Cincinnati is the home of two major universities offering graduate and undergraduate degrees—the University of Cincinnati, the oldest municipal university in the United States, and Xavier University. The University of Cincinnati was founded in 1819 as Cincinnati College. There are now more than a dozen colleges in the university with a combined enrollment of more than 25,000. The cooperative system of education (the work-study program) was initiated by the university in 1906.

Xavier University, a Roman Catholic institution of higher learning for men (coeducational for graduate students) was founded in 1831 as the Athenaeum, a "literary institute." It is the oldest Catholic university in Ohio. Catholic colleges for women in Cincinnati are the College of

TAFT MUSEUM, an art gallery, was built in 1820 and was the home of President William H. Taft's brother.

Mt. St. Joseph-on-the-Ohio, begun in 1906 and operated by the Sisters of Charity, and Our Lady of Cincinnati College, founded in 1931 and administered by the Sisters of Mercy.

Other Cincinnati colleges are the Ohio College of Applied Science, a two-year technical institute founded in 1928 as the Ohio Mechanics Institute, and Hebrew Union College, founded in 1875 by Rabbi Isaac M. Wise, one of the leaders of Reform Judaism. It is a rabbinical school of American Reform Judaism and is the oldest Jewish theological school in the United States.

Elementary schools in Cincinnati date from one year after the city's founding, in 1789. At that time the settlement of Columbia, now a part of the city, started a subscription school. Not until 1828, however, were elementary public schools established. In 1847 the first high school accepted students, and nine years later the first evening classes for adults were begun. Today Cincinnati has a citywide network of more than 100 public schools and an extensive Roman Catholic school system. Schools are also maintained by Lutherans, Jews, and Baptists.

Libraries. The Public Library of Cincinnati and Hamilton County contains 2.5 million volumes in its central building and about 40 branches. It houses outstanding collections of books in art, music, religion, and genealogy, and is a depository of United States and Ohio documents. The library's Inland Rivers Collection was established in 1956 by the Sons and Daughters of Pioneer River Men to preserve the record of river life in the flatboat and steamboat eras.

Cincinnati's unique Lloyd Library and Museum has special collections dealing with botany, mycology, pharmacy, chemistry, the natural sciences, eclectic medicine, agriculture, entomology, and pharmacopoeia. The Cincinnati Historical Society Library contains the special James A. Green collection on U. S. President William Henry Harrison as well as one on Ohio. The University of Cincinnati Library has the largest collection of volumes in modern Greek of any outside of Athens. Its other collections include materials on American Indians, classical archaeology, and geography.

Museums. The Taft Museum on Pike Street, previously the home of President Taft's brother Charles Phelps Taft, is a fine example of Federal American architecture, in which paintings and art objects are displayed. The Cincinnati Art Museum in the Eden Park district houses a wide range of collections of famous works of art. Since 1869 it has operated an art academy. Nearby, the Cincinnati Museum of Natural History offers a planetarium, a wilderness trail, and a reproduction of a cavern.

Music and Drama. Music has been an integral part of Cincinnati's cultural life since its settlement. Martial music was played for a Fourth of July celebration in 1799 by a band of French and German musicians, and the settlement's first newspaper, *Liberty Hall,* reported meetings of a "harmonical society" in 1815. The huge German immigration to Cincinnati in the mid-19th century provided a new musical form, and between 1838 and 1882 the city knew only German choral singing. In 1848 a Swiss singing group was organized, the Schweizer Verein. Cincinnati's most durable singing organization, the May Festival Association, has continued to the present day. In 1873 its first biennial May Music Festival included 1,083 voices of German, English, Welsh, Swiss, and other choral societies and an orchestra of 108 instruments.

In 1895 the Orchestra Association presented the Cincinnati Symphony Orchestra in its first season of 20 concerts with Frank van der Stucken conducting. Among other conductors in the first 75 years of the orchestra have been Leopold Stokowski, Fritz Reiner, Eugene Goossens, Thor Johnson, and Max Rudolf.

In 1960 the founding of two dramatic groups encouraged appreciation of the legitimate theater in Cincinnati. They were Edgecliff Academy of Fine Arts of Our Lady of Cincinnati College and Playhouse in the Park, a company of talented actors. The Association of Community Theatres (ACT) in Cincinnati is composed of 13 civic theater groups, presenting well-known plays.

Communications Media. Cincinnati has two daily newspapers. The Cincinnati *Enquirer* (morning) was founded in 1841, succeeding the old *Advertiser*. The Cincinnati *Post* (evening) was an early link in the chain of newspapers established by E. W. Scripps. In 1958 the newspaper bought the Taft family's Cincinnati *Times-Star* and merged it with the *Post*.

The Greater Cincinnati area is served by commercial television stations affiliated with the major broadcasting companies, and by Ohio's first educational television station, the seventh in the United States. There are also more than a dozen radio stations. Both the University of Cincinnati and Xavier University operate their own stations.

Parks and Places of Interest. Cincinnati enjoys an extensive park system of 3,869 acres (1,550 hectares). The largest park, Mt. Airy Forest, contains 1,476 acres (590 hectares) and features an arboretum. Eden Park, only a 5-minute ride east of downtown Cincinnati, affords spectacular views of the Ohio River and the nearby Kentucky hills.

The city's zoo, maintained by the Zoological Society of Cincinnati, was opened in 1875. Its verdant parklike setting has attracted such cultural activities as the annual Zoo Arts Festival, an exhibit of original art in various media inaugurated in the 1960's, and a summer opera season featuring artists from the Metropolitan Opera and great European companies.

The Tyler Davidson Fountain is one of the most notable Cincinnati landmarks. It was erected in 1871, the gift of Henry Probasco to the city in honor of his brother-in-law, Tyler Davidson. Its bronze sculptures were cast in Munich, Germany. Replacing a dilapidated old market, the fountain has served ever since as the hub from which distances are measured in Cincinnati. Even as urban renewal swirls around it, citizens have demanded that the fountain be retained as a graceful reminder of a gentler past. The Fort Washington Monument now stands on the original site of that frontier outpost.

History. Cincinnati originated as a settlement in the Territory Northwest of the Ohio River, as the Continental Congress called the land east of the Mississippi River, south of the Great Lakes, and west of Pennsylvania that was ceded to the United States by the British after the Revolutionary War. In 1788 a town was planned in the area that is now Cincinnati and was called Losantiville, a name made up by its surveyors. Trouble with Indians in the Northwest Territory prompted the federal government to build Fort Washington just outside the settlement's boundaries in 1789. The next year General St. Clair gave the settlement the name Cincinnati. Indian attacks in 1790 and 1791 nearly caused abandonment of the settlement.

Cincinnati was incorporated as a town in 1802 and received its city charter in 1819. The city began to develop in 1827, when the Miami Canal, paralleling the Great Miami River and connecting Cincinnati with Ohio communities north of it, was completed. While the city grew during the canal era in the early 19th century, it was not until the coming of the railroads that it developed rapidly. By 1850, Cincinnati was a major rail terminal and shipping center.

As the slavery issue began to divide the United States, Cincinnati found itself in a difficult position. Only the Ohio River separated it from the Southern states on which it depended for trade, yet the city was an important station on the Underground Railroad for escaping slaves. Harriet Beecher Stowe, author of *Uncle Tom's Cabin* (published in 1851), began to write that antislavery best seller while she lived in Cincinnati, from 1832 to 1850. When war came, Cincinnati remained firmly on the side of the Union.

After the Civil War, Cincinnati found its position as the most important city in the "West" threatened by Chicago and St. Louis. The Suspension Bridge across the Ohio, connecting the city with Kentucky, was opened in 1867. As river shipping yielded in importance to the railroads, Cincinnati decided on a drastic step. In 1880 the city built its own railroad into the South—to Chattanooga, Tenn. This is the railroad that the city still owns and leases to a private company.

In the early years of the 20th century, Cincinnati's municipal government was riddled with graft and corruption. However, in 1922 a nonpartisan reform movement was begun and was able to win the election of 1924. At that time the city's present charter was adopted. Cincinnati was less severely affected by the Depression of the early 1930's than some other American cities, but it suffered a disastrous flood in 1937. The rapid expansion in the city's development during and after World War II necessitated the Cincinnati Master Plan for urban renewal that was later put into operation.

Among famous residents of Cincinnati and Hamilton county were the following. The ninth president of the United States, William Henry Harrison, was an early resident of Hamilton county. He was elected by a great electoral majority in 1840, but succumbed to pneumonia only one month after taking the oath of office. William Howard Taft, the 27th president, was the only American to serve as both president and chief justice of the United States. He also founded a political dynasty. His son, Robert A. Taft, served three terms in the U. S. Senate and his grandson, Robert Taft, Jr., was elected U. S. representative from Ohio. Both were born in Cincinnati.

Nicholas Longworth, another Cincinnatian, was speaker of the U. S. House of Representatives from 1925 to 1931. In 1906 he married Alice Roosevelt, daughter of President Theodore Roosevelt. In the field of education, William Holmes McGuffey is remembered not so much as an educator but as a compiler of the famous McGuffey *Eclectic Readers*, which were published in Cincinnati in 1836 and 1837. All told, about 122 million copies of the reader were sold. The Reverend Mr. McGuffey became president of Cincinnati College in 1836.

Government. Cincinnati is governed by a 9-member city council elected every two years. The council elects one of its own members as mayor, another as vice mayor, and a third as president pro tempore to preside over the council in the absence of the mayor and vice mayor. It also appoints a city manager. The council enacts the laws for the city, but the city manager administers them. He has a seat in the council but cannot vote on matters coming before it. There are six major departments in the city administration—the departments of public works, public utilities, finance, urban development, safety, and law.

ERNEST I. MILLER
The Public Library of Cincinnati

Further Reading: Cincinnati Planning Commission, *The Plan for Downtown Cincinnati* (Cincinnati 1964); Harlow, Alvin F., *The Serene Cincinnatians* (New York 1950); Hessler, Iola O., *Cincinnati Then and Now* (Cincinnati 1949); Tucker, Louis L., *Cincinnati's Citizen Crusaders* (Cincinnati 1967).

CINCINNATI, The Society of the, sin-sə-nat′ē, the oldest hereditary military society in North America. It was founded on May 10, 1783, by officers of the American Revolutionary army stationed in the Newburgh-Fishkill area of New York state, before the disbanding of the army.

The society's objectives were to perpetuate the ideals of the Revolution, to maintain the friendships formed among the officers on the battlefield, and to extend help "towards those officers and their families who, unfortunately may be under the necessity of receiving it." The name "Cincinnati" was adopted in honor of a famous Roman general, Lucius Quinctius Cincinnatus, the first individual in recorded history to advocate the concept of the citizen-soldier, trained for military service, who returns to civilian status at the close of a military emergency. The city of Cincinnati, Ohio, was named after the society.

George Washington was the first president general of the society. Membership was restricted to those commissioned officers of the continental line forces of the United States and France who had served as commissioned officers at least 36 months during the Revolution. The order was made hereditary and originally was passed on from father to oldest son; at present, if the original line has died out, a qualified Revolutionary War officer may be represented by the oldest male descendant of a collateral line.

The general society is made up of 14 constituent societies, one in each of the 13 original states and one in France. An individual is a member of the constituent society to which his ancestor either belonged or could have belonged.

With about 2,350 members in the late 1960's the society was stronger numerically than at any other time in its history. Primarily concerned with historical research and endowing scholarships, it maintains an outstanding Revolutionary War museum at its national headquarters, Anderson House, in Washington, D. C.

CHARLES WARREN LIPPITT
The Society of the Cincinnati

CINCINNATI, University of, sin-sə-nat′ē, a municipally sponsored, state-affiliated institution of higher education in Cincinnati, Ohio. Chartered in 1819 as Cincinnati College, the school was established as a municipal university by act of the Ohio General Assembly in 1870 and was voted municipal tax support in 1893.

Units of the university are: McMicken College of Arts and Sciences (founded 1870); colleges of medicine (1819), engineering (1900), education and home economics (1905), nursing and health (affiliated 1916), law (founded 1819), design, architecture, and art (1922), business administration (1906), and pharmacy (affiliated 1954); the Graduate School (1906); the Evening College (1920); University Research Foundation (1943); College-Conservatory of Music (affiliated 1955); and University College (a 2-year institution founded in 1960). The main library houses over 1 million volumes. Between 1945 and the mid-1960's enrollment increased from 6,000 to 27,000.

The university sponsors research programs in astronomy and space, laser surgery, chemistry, and medicine (the Sabin polio vaccine was developed at the medical center by Dr. Albert Sabin), and in the study of human environment.

RICHARD B. BAKER
University of Cincinnati

CINCINNATI SYMPHONY ORCHESTRA, sin-sə-nat′ē, an orchestra in Cincinnati, Ohio, founded in 1895 under the auspices of the Cincinnati Orchestra Association. In 1929 it was incorporated within the Cincinnati Institute of Fine Arts. The orchestra's first permanent conductor was Frank van der Stucken, who directed it from 1896 to 1907. In that year it was disbanded because of a dispute with the American Federation of Musicians. Two years later, however, the orchestra again began to perform under the baton of Leopold Stokowski, who conducted it until 1912. He was followed by such distinguished conductors as Ernst Kunwald (1912–1917), Eugène Ysaÿe (1918–1922), Fritz Reiner (1922–1931), Eugene Goossens (1931–1948), and Thor Johnson (1948–1958). Max Rudolf was appointed permanent director of the orchestra in 1958. Guest conductors have included Richard Strauss and Igor Stravinsky.

CINCINNATIAN SERIES, sin-sə-nat′ē-ən, the uppermost series of the Ordovician System of rocks in North America. The series was formed about 450 million years ago, during an epoch that lasted about 20 million years. The Cincinnatian, typically exposed in southwestern Ohio and adjacent states, has hundreds of feet of richly fossiliferous marine shales. These have been separated into the Edenian, Maysvillian, and Richmondian stages of rocks.

The principal Cincinnatian deposits in eastern North America are sediments that reach a thickness of nearly 3,000 feet (900 meters) in

CINCINNATIAN SERIES of rocks contains shells of brachiopoda of the *Sowerbyella* and other genera.

CINDERELLA tries on the slipper, from a wood engraving (1861) after the original by Gustave Doré.

central Pennsylvania. The upper, stream-laid red sandstone and conglomerate of these deposits were derived by erosion from rising lands in a late stage of the Taconian mountain-building period. Silurian sandstone overlies these rocks. The Cincinnatian series over most of the western and Arctic regions is represented by limestones that are a few hundred feet thick.

Late Ordovician rocks have not been identified or adequately studied in the tectonic belts on the coastal borders of the Atlantic and Pacific oceans. However, intrusions that have been determined to be of Cincinnatian age by radiodating methods are known in Newfoundland. Similar rocks underlie Silurian deposits in New England and New Brunswick and form boulders in Silurian conglomerates in central Newfoundland.

MARSHALL KAY, *Columbia University*

CINCINNATUS, sin-si-nā′təs, **Lucius Quinctius,** Roman general and statesman of the 5th century B. C. According to tradition, he was *consul suffectus* in 460 and was twice dictator, in 458 and in 439.

Cincinnatus was appointed dictator in 458 to relieve the troops of the consul Minucius, besieged by the Aequi at Mt. Algidus. Found plowing in the field and told of his command, Cincinnatus assumed the required dress, came to Rome, took command of the troops, and went to the rescue. Within 15 days he had won a victory, celebrated a triumph, and was back on his farm.

Rome took great pride in its simple country folk who conquered the world, and Cincinnatus, farmer, soldier, and politician, was the model Roman. Later historians embellished the stories concerning Cincinnatus, and probably little they related is historically valid.

RICHARD E. MITCHELL, *University of Illinois*

CINDERELLA is a traditional European fairy tale. An early version appeared in Charles Perrault's *Histoires et contes du temps passé,* subtitled *Contes de ma mère l'oye (Mother Goose's Tales),* published in 1697. It became popular in the English-speaking world in the translation by Robert Samber in 1792.

The story according to Perrault concerns a poor, neglected girl, Cinderella ("little cinder girl"), who is forced by her cruel stepmother and stepsisters to be their servant. She is rescued from her plight by her Fairy Godmother, who sends her to a ball in a pumpkin magically transformed into a coach. At the ball the prince of the kingdom falls in love with her. Obliged to return home at midnight, Cinderella loses a tiny glass slipper in her flight. Searching his kingdom for the owner of the slipper, the prince finds Cinderella and marries her. The tradition of the "glass" slipper is probably the result of misreading the French *vair,* a kind of fur, for *verre,* meaning "glass." In other versions of the tale, Cinderella is helped by her dead mother, who appears in the form of a cow or goat.

This lucky folk heroine, embodying the concept of duty and humility rewarded, figures in the folklore of countries from India to South America. Variants of the Cinderella legend include the tales *Catskin* and *Cap o' Rushes.* The tale has been adapted for several operas and ballets, notably Gioacchino Rossini's opera *La Cenerentola* (1817), which omitted the supernatural elements, and the Sadler's Wells Ballet's *Cinderella* (1948), with music by Sergei Prokofiev. The Cinderella story is the subject of the most popular of all Christmas pantomimes.

JAMES REEVES
Author of "English Fables and Fairy Stories"
Further Reading: Cox, Marian Roalfe, *Cinderella: Three Hundred and Forty-five Variants* (London 1893); Perrault, Charles, *Fairy Tales,* tr. by Norman Denny (London 1951).

CINEMA. See CARTOON, ANIMATED; MOVING PICTURES; PHOTOGRAPHY—10. *Motion Picture Photography.*

CINEMASCOPE is the trade name for a motion picture process in which an image is projected on a wide, curved screen to create a slight illusion of depth. The general range of vision provided by the screen approximates the range of vision of the human eye. A stereophonic sound system is used with the process to enhance the 3-dimensional effect.

The CinemaScope process involves a method of distortion photography known as *anamorphic distortion,* in which the filmed image is magnified or compressed along different directions that are perpendicular to one another. Such distortion can be achieved by a variety of techniques. In the case of CinemaScope a cylindrical lens is mounted on the motion picture camera. The lens takes in a scene that is twice as wide as the viewing area that can be photographed by an ordinary lens. However, the cylindrical lens compresses this wide image horizontally (but not vertically) by 50%, so that the film does not have to be of unusual size. In fact the process uses film of standard 35-mm width, although the sprocket holes are narrower than usual in order to provide space for four soundtracks.

A single projector is required by the CinemaScope process. The distorted image on the film is corrected before it reaches the screen by a compensating anamorphic lens in the projector; the lens expands the compressed image to its normal horizontal dimensions. The film is provided with both photographic and magnetic soundtracks to permit it to be played in theaters equipped with either kind of sound-reproducing system.

An anamorphic filming process was demonstrated and theatrically presented in New York City as early as 1930 by an American scientist, Henry Newcomer. However, the invention of the process that was later revised and used in CinemaScope is generally credited to Henri Chrétien, a French optical scientist. Chrétien exhibited his anamorphic system at the Paris Exposition in 1937, but his work generated little interest at that time. However, the chief of technology for 20th Century Fox, Earl I. Sponable, observed Chrétien's work. His organization bought the process in 1952, developed it to make it suitable for commercial use, and renamed it CinemaScope.

The CinemaScope process made its first public appearance on Sept. 16, 1953, with the premiere of the motion picture *The Robe* in New York City. The wide-screen filming technique was a critical success with the viewers, and CinemaScope was adopted thereafter by 20th Century Fox for all its productions. The success of the process also led to the development of a number of other anamorphic filming techniques, such as Panavision and Superscope, which are compatible with CinemaScope equipment.

CINEMATOGRAPHY. See MOVING PICTURES; PHOTOGRAPHY—*4. Motion Picture Photography.*

CINERAMA, sin-ə-ram′ə, is a motion picture projection technique that creates the illusion of a 3-dimensional image. The cinerama screen covers an arc of approximately 146°, thus including the area of peripheral vision of the human eye, and it is curved to conform to normal perception of depth. A picture projected on the screen thereby gains the illusion of depth and loses the appearance of being framed.

Cinerama was first developed by a U. S. motion picture producer and inventor, Frederic Waller, who demonstrated his process at the 1939 New York World's Fair. During World War II the U. S. government supported him in the development of a gunnery trainer for airmen that used a 360° screen on which a continuous picture was projected by 11 machines. After the war the stereophonic sound system that is used in Cinerama was developed; and the first commercial picture, *This Is Cinerama,* was brought out very successfully in 1952.

The first cinerama pictures were photographed on 35-mm film through three separate 27-mm lenses set at 48° to one another, so that each lens covered about one third of the entire image. The images were kept clear by means of special focal depth lenses. Three projectors were used to throw the separate images on their respective thirds of the screen, where they merged into a single huge, panoramic picture. The screen was made up of hundreds of perforated strips angled like the slats of a Venetian blind, set on end. A multichanneled speaker system was set up behind the screen and along the sides and rear of the auditorium. At first there were some difficulties in merging the three images on the screen, but these have since been overcome by projecting the film from a single negative. Cinerama film is now exposed in 65-mm cameras.

Cineraria (Senecio cruentus)

CINERARIA, sin-ər-ar′ē-ə, any of several plants derived from the florist's cineraria (*Senecio cruentus*). The florist's cineraria, a native of the Canary Islands, has been considerably modified through cultivation, and many modern varieties are grown as greenhouse ornamentals. The plants have many daisylike flower heads that may be as wide as 3 inches (7.5 cm). Their coloring ranges from white to pink, blue, or purple, usually with a bit of white in the center. Sometimes the flower heads are double.

Cinerarias are raised as annuals, and for winter and spring blooming the seed should be sown in midsummer. The plants are usually grown in a cool greenhouse and need a lot of moisture.

DONALD WYMAN
The Arnold Arboretum, Harvard University

CINGOLI, chēng′gô-lē, is a town and commune in Italy, in Macerata province, in the Marches region of central Italy. It is near the Musone River, about 15 miles (25 km) northwest of Macerata. There are textile mills and a macaroni factory.

Julius Caesar, in his *De bello civili,* attributes the founding of the town, called Cingulum, to one of his lieutenants, Titus Labienus, in 63 B. C. The town was nearly destroyed during the invasions of the Goths and Lombards (5th and 6th centuries). Some remains of the ancient walls still stand. There is a Gothic church, which was rebuilt in 1278. Population: (1961) of the town, 2,268; (1966 est.) of the commune, 12,031.

CINNA, sin′ə, **Gaius Helvius,** Roman poet of the 1st century B. C., most of whose poetry, fashioned on Alexandrian models and extremely obscure, has been lost. The *Zmyrna,* or *Smyrna,* an epic poem which survives in fragments, deals with the incestuous love of a girl for her father Cinyras. A *Propempticon Pollionis* is attributed to him.

It has been generally accepted, though there is some doubt, that this was the Cinna killed by the mob at Julius Caesar's funeral in 44 B. C. Shakespeare in *Julius Caesar* follows Plutarch in his account of the lynching of Cinna. Despite his protestations that he is "Cinna the poet" he is taken to be Lucius Cornelius Cinna, the younger, who had conspired in plotting Caesar's murder.

CINNA, sin′ə, **Lucius Cornelius** (c. 130–84 B. C.), Roman statesman. After an uneventful career, he burst upon the pages of Roman history in 88 and 87 B. C., in the period of civil conflict between Marius and Sulla. Sulla had expelled Marius and his followers from Rome in 88 and proceeded to the East. Cinna, meanwhile, reached the consulship in 87 and took advantage of Sulla's absence to advocate full equality for Rome's new citizens. Expelled in turn by his fellow consul Gnaeus Octavius, Cinna made common cause with Marius, and by the end of the year 87 the two men controlled Rome. A massacre of their enemies followed, for which Cinna must be held at least partially responsible.

After Marius died in early 86, Cinna directed affairs, holding the consulship from 86 to 84. Dissent and political activity were stifled. Not surprisingly, Cinna's name is blackened in the ancient tradition. But Rome did enjoy three years of peace and stability under his leadership. His reforms included measures designed to appeal to debtor and creditor alike, and he effected the full enfranchisement of the Italians. Overtures to Sulla, however, proved abortive. In 84, with Sulla's return from the East imminent, Cinna mobilized for war. But his rigorous military discipline offended the troops, who rose in mutiny and killed him. His daughter Cornelia was the first wife of Julius Caesar.

ERICH S. GRUEN
University of California at Berkeley

CINNA, sin′ə, is a tragedy by the French dramatist Pierre Corneille. In Corneille's time, *Cinna, or the Clemency of Augustus* (1640 or 1641) was considered his masterpiece. Although the play is set in ancient Rome, it centers, like Corneille's other tragedies, on the universal theme of conflicting emotions, and it is intended to apply particularly to the political situation in 17th century France.

Cinna is torn between his respect for Emperor Augustus, who trusts him, and his love for Amélie, who urges him to overthrow Augustus for killing her father. Augustus is torn between justice and mercy for the traitors. The play debates the respective merits of monarchy and republicanism, justice and mercy, loyalty toward and revolt against a tyrant. Parisian audiences saw Amélie as a contemporary lady who combined love with intrigue against the tyrannies of Cardinal Richelieu.

CINNABAR, sin′ə-bär, is a mercury sulfide mineral and the only important ore of mercury. It is found near recent volcanic rocks and hot springs as vein fillings and rock impregnations, apparently desposited there by solutions that rose from far below. Pure crystals of cinnabar are transparent to translucent, vermilion red, and have a diamondlike luster. Crystals that are mixed with impurities such as clay and bitumen are brownish and dull. Commercially produced cinnabar is known also as *vermilion.*

Although cinnabar is the leading ore of mercury, large deposits occur at relatively few localities. These include Almadén, Spain; Idrija, Yugoslavia (formerly Idria, Italy); Huancavelica, Peru; and Kweichow and Hunan provinces in China. In the United States the leading deposits are at New Idria and New Almaden in California.

Composition, HgS; hardness, 2.5; specific gravity, 8.1; crystal system, hexagonal.

CINNAMIC ACID, sə-nam′ik, is a white crystalline compound that occurs naturally in Peru and Tolu balsams and in styrax. It is a benzene derivative with the formula $C_6H_5CH = CHCOOH$; it is soluble in benzene, ether, acetone, glacial acetic acid, and carbon disulfide, and it is insoluble in water. The melting point of cinnamic acid is 133° C (271° F) and the boiling point is 300° C (572° F).

Cinnamic acid may be prepared by heating benzaldehyde with sodium acetate in the presence of acetic anhydride (the Perkin reaction). It is most commonly used in perfume production. It is also used in medicines and as a chemical intermediate.

CINNAMIC ALCOHOL, sə-nam′ik al′kə-hôl, is a solid compound that crystallizes in the form of white needles. It has the formula $C_6H_5CH = CHCH_2OH$. Cinnamic alcohol may be derived either from oil of cinnamon or oil of cassia or by the reduction of cinnamic aldehyde. The melting point of the compound is 33° C (91° F), and its boiling point is 257° C (495° F). It is soluble both in alcohol and in ether.

Cinnamic alcohol has an odor similar to that of hyacinths. It is most commonly used in the manufacture of perfumes, particularly for the production of lilac and other floral scents. It is also used as a flavoring agent.

CINNAMIC ALDEHYDE, sə-nam′ik al′də-hīd, is a volatile yellowish liquid that is the major component of oil of cinnamon. It has the characteristic spicy odor of cinnamon. Cinnamic aldehyde is obtained from Ceylonese or Chinese cinnamon oils, or it may be synthesized commercially by the condensation of benzaldehyde and acetaldehyde. Cinnamic aldehyde is soluble in alcohol; however, the compound is only slightly soluble in water.

Because of its pleasant odor, cinnamic aldehyde is used to mask the taste and odor of various drugs. It is also used as a fragrance for perfumes and soaps, as a food flavoring, and in the manufacture of beverages.

CINNAMON, sin′ə-mən, is the dried, highly aromatic, reddish or yellowish brown bark of tropical trees of the genus *Cinnamonum*, especially that of the Ceylon cinnamon tree (*C. zeylanicum*). Cinnamon has long been valued as a spice. The ancient Greeks and Romans obtained it from Arabian traders. The Portuguese, in their attempt to find the sources of cinnamon and other costly spices, discovered the route around Cape Horn to India and Ceylon in 1505. Cinnamon from wild trees was the first important export of Ceylon, but the trees were apparently not cultivated there until more than 100 years after the Dutch gained control of the island in the year 1656.

Wild cinnamon trees may attain a height of 30 feet (9 meters) or more, but under cultivation they are severely pruned to produce shrubby plants with many slender stems. When the shoots are about 6 to 8 feet (1.8–2.4 meters) high, they are cut off near the ground. Harvesting is done during the rainy season, because the bark is more easily stripped from shoots that are undergoing rapid growth. To facilitate stripping, the bark is slit along the length of the stem on each side. The bark is then pried loose at one end of the shoot and peeled off. The strips

CINNAMON TREES, pruned to bush size, are harvested at the base of the shoots.

(Left) CINNAMON BARK is peeled from a branch. (Above) Cinnamon chips are collected in bags, while the quills (visible behind the bag) are baled for shipment.

are heaped together and covered with sacks to promote fermentation, which loosens the corky outer layer of bark so that it may be readily scraped off. It is the inner bark (secondary phloem tissue) that contains the aromatic properties. Scraping is done with a curved knife, and the bark is held rigid by being placed against a smooth stick. The scraped inner bark dries into "quills," which are baled for export by placing the smaller quills inside the larger ones. Broken quills are used for making ground cinnamon.

Cinnamon trees, in addition to yielding the spice cinnamon, also yield cinnamon oil. The oil is obtained by the distillation of shoots and low grade bark. Cinnamon oil is used mostly as a flavoring in medicines. It may also be used as an astringent or to relieve excess gas in the stomach and intestines.

LAWRENCE ERBE
University of Southwestern Louisiana

CINNAMON FERN, sin'ə-mən, a coarse, stiff fern native to Asia and the Americas. The cinnamon fern, known botanically as *Osmunda cinnamomea*, has two types of fronds (leaves): sterile fronds, which may be 5 feet (1.5 meters), and fertile fronds, which bear spore sacs and are 2 feet (60 cm) long and cinnamon brown in color. The fern's roots are often dug up in blocks, dried, and sold as "osmunda fiber" for growing orchids.

DONALD WYMAN
The Arnold Arboretum, Harvard University

CINO DA PISTOIA, chē'nō dä pēs-tō'yä (1270?–1336) Italian jurist and poet. He was born in Pistoia, Italy. His full name was Guittoncino dei Sinibaldi or Sighibuldi. He received his doctorate from the University of Bologna and taught law at the universities of Siena, Florence, Perugia, and Naples. His most important legal work was *Lectura in codicem* (1312–1314), a commentary on the Justinian Code which blended pure Roman law with contemporary statutes and customary and canon law, thereby initiating Italian common law. He wrote some 200 lyric poems notable for purity of language and harmony of rhythms, most of them dedicated to a woman named Selvaggia. Dante, in *De vulgari eloquentia*, praised his poetry. Cino died in Pistoia in 1336.

CINQ-MARS saN-mar', **Marquis de** (1620–1642), French courtier, who was executed by Louis XIII. Born Henri Coiffier Ruzé d'Éffiat, he was the second son of the Marquis d'Éffiat. Cardinal Richelieu, Louis XIII's chief minister, prepared Cinq-Mars from adolescence to become the king's favorite. He was appointed grand master of the wardrobe on his 18th birthday. A year later he was officially the royal favorite. Cinq-Mars enraged Richelieu, on the one hand, by refusing to recount to him the king's secrets, and, on the other hand, exasperated the King by balking at his role as a foil for Louis' complicated emotions. Pulled in contrary directions, Cinq-Mars in 1641–1642 entered a conspiracy to overthrow Richelieu. The plot was discovered and the cardinal laid proofs of Cinq-Mars' treason before Louis XIII. Cinq-Mars, who confessed, was condemned to death and executed at Lyon on Sept. 12, 1642.

LIONEL ROTHKRUG
University of Michigan

CINQUE PORTS, singk'pôrts, a confederation of towns on the southeast coast of England that originated in an 11th century grant of royal privileges to towns that would provide ships and men for the protection of England, before the existence of the Royal Navy. At first there were but three ports in the confederation—Sandwich, Dover, and New Romney. With the addition of Hythe and Hastings there were five, and they were given the Norman French name meaning "five ports." Later, Rye and Winchelsea were added as "head ports," but the name remained unchanged—even when the group included over 30 ports.

The most valued privilege granted the Cinque Ports by the crown was the right to hold court and to retain the revenue therefrom. The court of Shepway, common to the ports, was the equivalent of a shire, or county, court. It was in existence in the 12th century and is still convened, although its duties are nominal. Only Dover, of the original group, remains a recognizable seaport. The honorary office of Lord Warden of the Cinque Ports has been held by many eminent men, including the Duke of Wellington and Sir Winston Churchill.

GORDON STOKES
Author of "English Place-Names"

CINQUEFOIL

Three cinquefoils, of the genus *Potentilla*: (top left) common cinquefoil (*P. canadensis*); (top right) Norway cinquefoil (*P. norvegica*); (left) rough-fruited cinquefoil (*P. recta*).

J. J. SMITH

CINQUEFOIL, singk'foil, any of a large group of annual and perennial plants and shrubs with small white, yellow, or red flowers. Cinquefoils are mostly native to temperate and arctic regions of the world. Their leaves are usually composed of 3 leaflets; their flowers, which consist of 5 petals, ripen into dry capsules. In general, cinquefoils are easily propagated by seed or by division.

Cinquefoils comprise the genus *Potentilla* of the rose family. The common cinquefoil (*P. canadensis*) is a drooping plant native to North America. It has small yellow flowers and leaves made up of 5 leaflets. The shrubby cinquefoil (*P. fruticosa*) is a 4-foot (1.2-meter) shrub native to North America, Europe, and Asia. Its flowers vary from white to deep yellow and its leaves are composed of 3 to 7 leaflets.

DONALD WYMAN
The Arnold Arboretum, Harvard University

CINTRA. See SINTRA.

CIPHER AND CODE WRITING. See CRYPTOGRAPHY.

CIRCASSIA, sər-kash'e-ə, is a historical area in the northwest foothills of the Greater Caucasus Mountains in the Russian republic of the Soviet Union. Circassia (also Cherkessia) is administratively divided into the Adyge Autonomous Oblast and the Karachai-Cherkess Autonomous Oblast. The latter was formed in 1957 by the merger of the Cherkess Autonomous Oblast and the area inhabited by the Karachai people. The Adyge Oblast lies mainly in the valley of the Belaya River, a tributary of the Kuban. Its capital is Maikop, the center of a huge oil field and a city with food-processing and wood-working industries.

To the east is the Karachai-Cherkess Oblast. Its capital is Cherkessk, which has food-processing industries, but is better known as the northern terminus of the highway across the Greater Caucasus Mountains to Sukhumi on the Black Sea coast. Both regions have a mild, moist climate, and consist geographically of northern lowlands and southern mountains. Grain and sunflowers are the main crops on the lowlands, where there is considerable dairy farming. Livestock raising on mountain pastures is the chief upland occupation, but timber cutting is an important industry. The lowland population is predominantly Russian, with Circassians largely confined to the mountains.

The Circassians (more properly Adyges or Cherkess) follow the Muslim religion and are related to Georgians and Armenians. They are a sturdy, handsome people, and Circassian men are among the finest equestrians in the world. Before World War I many Circassian women were found in Turkish harems, where they were highly prized for their beauty.

The origins of the Circassians are lost in antiquity. During the Middle Ages they occupied much of the northwest of the Greater Caucasus Mountains, with their capital at Sukhumi. From the 10th to the 13th centuries Circassia was under the rule of Georgia. Thereafter the Circassians maintained a precarious independence for several centuries, fighting and occasionally paying tribute to the Crimean Tatars. In the 16th century czarist Russia began to aid Circassia in this struggle. By 1705, the Tatars were finally defeated, after which the Russians themselves began slowly encroaching on Circassian territory. Russia seized all Circassia in 1829, on the legal pretext that it was territory ceded by Turkey as a result of a Russo-Turkish war. Actually Turkey never had ruled Circassia, but had merely maintained a trading station on the coast.

The Circassians rebelled against Russian occupation and fought a valiant, but hopeless, battle for independence until 1864, largely under the leadership of the great Caucasian hero Shamyl. Local patriotism was so intense that, when the Russian armies finally won, most Circassians refused to remain in the Caucasus and emigrated to Turkey. Possibly as many as 500,-000 thus resettled in Asia Minor, Bulgaria, and Serbia. Much of Circassia was depopulated, later to be settled by other Caucasian races and Russians.

ELLSWORTH RAYMOND, *New York University*

CIRCE, sûr'sē, in classical mythology, was a sorceress who lived on the island of Aeaea. She was the daughter of Helios (the Sun) and Perse, the daughter of Oceanus. Odysseus (Ulysses) and his crew came to her island after 11 of his ships were destroyed by the Laestrygones during his homeward voyage after the Trojan War.

On landing on the island, Odysseus sent out a scouting party led by Eurylochus. They came to the palace of Circe, who gave them food and wine but turned them into swine with a touch of her magic wand. Only Eurylochus escaped.

On his way to the palace to rescue his men, Odysseus was given a magic herb by Hermes (Mercury) that made him immune to Circe's magical powers. He forced her to restore his men to human form, but he remained with her for a year, after which she bore him a son, Telegonus. Circe then advised Odysseus to summon the shade of the blind seer Tiresias, from whom he received instructions for his homeward journey.

CIRCLE, the set of all points that lie in a given plane, and whose distance from a fixed point O in the plane is a given positive number r. The point O is called the *center* of the circle, and r is called the *radius*. A circle determines two regions in the plane. The set of all points in the plane whose distance from O is less than r is the interior of the circle, and the set of all points whose distance from O is greater than r is the exterior of the circle. The term *circumference* is often used to designate the curve itself.

The following terms are also often used in connection with the circle: *secant*—a line cutting the circle in two points; *chord*—a segment of a secant whose endpoints are points of the circle; *diameter*—a chord through the center of the circle; *tangent*—a line that lies in the plane of the circle and intersects the circle in one and only one point, called the point of tangency; *arc*—a part of the circle bounded by two given points of the circle; *segment*—the region bounded by a chord and the arc cut off by the chord; *central angle*—an angle formed by two radii at the center of the circle; *sector*—a region bounded by two radii and the arc cut off by them.

The length of the circumference of a circle is equal to $2\pi r$, or πd, where d is the diameter. The area enclosed by a circle is equal to πr^2. The number π is an irrational number, that is, it cannot be expressed as the ratio of two whole numbers. One complete revolution around the center of a circle is equal to 360 degrees. A central angle subtended by an arc equal in length to the radius is 1 radian. Thus, 360° equal 2π radians.

A circle may be determined by conditions other than specifying the center and radius. Thus, three points not on the same line determine a circle—one and only one circle can be drawn through these three points. Also, only one circle can be drawn with a given point as center and tangent to a given line. If a plane cuts a sphere in more than one point, the plane figure determined by the points of intersection is a circle. If the plane contains the center of the sphere, the circle formed is called a great circle; otherwise it is called a small circle.

Representation in Analytic Geometry. In rectangular Cartesian coordinates, the equation of a circle with center at the point (h,k) is given by $(x - h)^2 + (y - k)^2 = r^2$, where r is the length of the radius. This is the *standard form* of the equation. If the center of the circle is at the origin, $h = k = 0$, and the equation reduces to $x^2 + y^2 = r^2$. The *general equation* of a circle is given by $x^2 + y^2 + ax + by + c = 0$, where a, b, and c are constants. It can readily be reduced to standard form to give

$$\left(x + \frac{a}{2}\right)^2 + \left(y + \frac{b}{2}\right)^2 = \frac{a^2 + b^2 - 4c}{4}$$

showing the center to be at $(-a/2, -b/2)$. In polar coordinates, the general form of the equation of a circle with center at point (r_1, θ_1) and radius a is given by $a^2 = r^2 + r_1^2 - 2rr_1 \cos(\theta - \theta_1)$, which reduces to $r = a$ if the center is at $0,0°$).

Circle of Inversion. Given a circle with center O and radius r and any point P other than the center of the circle, the inverse of P with respect to the circle is the point P_1 lying on the line OP (or OP extended) such that the length OP times the length OP_1 is equal to r^2. The circle is called the *circle of inversion.*

History. The circle is one of the figures studied extensively by the ancient Greek geometricians. Hipparchus (d. 126 B.C.) is believed to have been the first to divide the circle into 360°, probably based on the Chaldean division of the Zodiac.

Hippocrates of Chios is credited with discovering that the area enclosed by a circle divided by the square of its radius is a constant. This constant is designated by the Greek letter π (pi). Hippocrates did not try to determine the value of π, but Archimedes (d. 212 B.C.) was able to arrive at the approximation that π is between $3\frac{10}{71}$ and $3\frac{1}{7}$. In his attempt to determine the value of π, Archimedes considered the circle as the limit of a regular polygon with an infinite number of sides. For a given length of perimeter, the circle includes the largest possible area of all closed plane curves. As the number of sides of an inscribed regular polygon increases, the area of the polygon increases to that of the circle, and, similarly, the area of a circumscribed regular polygon decreases to that of the circle. Since he knew how to work with regular polygons, Archimedes was able to approximate the area of the circle by using polygons of many sides and thus obtain an approximation for the value of π. Later mathematicians developed formulas capable of giving the value of π to any desired degree of accuracy. One simple formula is the infinite series given by Leibniz:

$$\frac{\pi}{4} = 1 - \frac{1}{3} + \frac{1}{5} - \frac{1}{7} + \cdots$$

One of the great problems of antiquity was concerned with the circle, namely, by use of compass and unmarked ruler to construct a square whose area is equal to that of a given circle. Many discoveries in geometry were occasioned by attempts to solve this problem. However, in 1882, Ferdinand Lindemann, using concepts unavailable to the ancient geometers, showed that π is a transcendental number, thus proving such a construction to be impossible.

FRANCIS A. GREENE, S. J.
Xavier University, Cincinnati

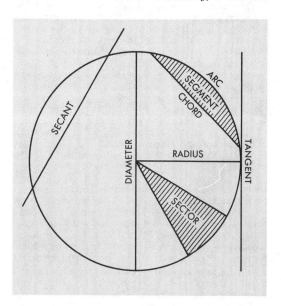

CIRCLEVILLE, a city in south central Ohio, the seat of Pickaway county, is situated on the Scioto River, 25 miles (40 km) south of Columbus. Just south of the city are the high, fertile Pickaway Plains, where corn, poultry, and hogs are raised. The city produces paper, fluorescent lamps, livestock feeds, and molded plastics. The Public Library Memorial Hall has a miniature of the octagonal Indian fortifications that stood on the site of Circleville.

Nearby are Logan Elm State Park, marking the traditional spot where Logan, the Mingo Indian chief, called for war on white settlers in 1774; and the sites of Cornstalk town and Camp Charlotte, notable in the Indian wars.

Circleville was laid out on a circular plan in 1810 and was replatted in 1841, after a fire. It became a city in 1853. Government is by mayor and council. Population: 11,687.

CIRCUIT, Electric. See ELECTRICITY.

CIRCUIT, Electronic. See ELECTRONICS.

CIRCUIT, Judicial, in the United States, a federal court area comprising a number of federal district courts and a court of appeal. There are 11 such federal judicial circuits in the United States. The term "circuit court" is sometimes used also for state trial courts. (See COURT, JUDICIAL.) Both usages reflect the early practice of "riding circuit," in which judges traveled from town to town in an established district, holding court in each community.

The practice of riding circuit was well adapted to the American colonial and frontier situation, where transportation was difficult and disputes usually involved parties from a single community. It was easier for the judge – and often for the lawyers as well – to travel to the community than for the parties and their witnesses to travel to the judge. Circuit riding had earlier roots in England, where it dated at least to the reign (1154–1189) of Henry II.

The most ambitious system of judicial circuit riding was set up in the United States by the Federal Judiciary Act of 1789. The act established three circuits, which together ran the length of the eastern seaboard. Each justice of the U. S. Supreme Court was required to sit on circuit twice each year in addition to fulfilling his duties on the Supreme Court. In 1792 the justices protested to President George Washington against the burdens imposed by circuit riding. These duties subsequently were reduced, then died by attrition, and finally were officially abolished in 1911. Although the obligation no longer exists, each Supreme Court justice is empowered to sit as a circuit judge and is so designated for a particular circuit.

Lawyers often traveled with the circuit-riding judge, taking cases in each community where court was held. Although this mode of professional life was rugged, it had its attractions. An Illinois practitioner and justice of the Illinois supreme court, John D. Caton, writing in 1893, described circuit riding as follows: "[The lawyers], with the judge, traveled on horseback in a cavalcade across the prairies from one county seat to another, over stretches of from 50 to 100 miles, swimming the streams when necessary. . . . The lawyer would, perhaps, scarcely alight from his horse when he would be surrounded by two or three clients requiring his services . . . . One would require a bill in chancery to be drawn. Another an answer to

be prepared. A third a string of special pleas, and a fourth a demurrer to be interposed, and so on, and all of this must be done before the opening of the court the next morning."

The writer, however, called it a "jolly life on the border," mentioning the nighttime storytelling at log cabin camps, "in which Mr. Lincoln became so proficient."

EDMUND W. KITCH
University of Chicago

CIRCUIT BREAKER, a switch that protects electrical equipment from damage by opening a circuit whenever there is an excessive current. It has contacts that open automatically, usually when an overload or short circuit causes an excessive current. Circuit breakers, which perform the same function as fuses, are commonly installed in boxes in residential, commercial, and industrial buildings. Small circuit breakers provide protection for household wiring and appliances; large ones provide protection for machines, transformers, transmission lines, and other electrical equipment.

The most common circuit breaker operates electromagnetically. If the current exceeds the value at which the circuit breaker is designed to open, a coil causes separation of the contacts. Resetting of the contacts is done automatically or manually. One advantage of a circuit breaker is that it can be reset, whereas a fuse must be replaced. Television sets, for example, now have small circuit breakers instead of fuses.

MARVIN BIERMAN
RCA Institutes Inc.

CIRCUIT COURT OF APPEALS. See UNITED STATES–*Judicial System.*

CIRCUIT RIDER, a traveling preacher, usually of the Methodist Church, who visited rural communities that were without churches. The circuit rider was an important agent in helping to mature a civilization on the American frontier.

In 1785 the Baltimore Conference of the Wesleyan Society in America created seven circuits to be organized along the spreading frontiers of the West and the South. The idea was suggested by John Wesley. These lonely missionaries would go forth to organize churches and congregations. From time to time other circuits were organized as population spread westward. In remarkably short time the circuit rider became as much a fixed character on the frontier as the hunter and the land speculator. Although he is usually pictured as gaunt, poorly clad, and riding a bony mount, the circuit rider had a nose for the location of religion-starved settlers.

The first major circuit rider was Francis Asbury (1745–1816), a plain, conscientious man who in time rode over western Virginia and North Carolina into Tennessee, Kentucky, and Ohio. On his heels came hundreds of fledgling·ministers who served their apprentice years riding the hard circuits. They rode into the backwoods virtually without scrip or purse, living off the rugged fare of the new country. Most were single men who had to live on annual salaries that ranged from $64 to $100. This was scarcely enough to keep them mounted and in clothes. For bed and board they depended on hospitable settlers.

Two of the most famous circuit riders were James B. Finley and Peter Cartwright. Finley rode circuit in Kentucky, Ohio, and Indiana and served as missionary to the Wyandot Indians. Cartwright served in Kentucky, Ohio, Indiana, and Illinois. Often, these pioneer ministers confronted ruffians and bullies who disrupted meetings and sought to prevent the organization of churches. Cartwright is known to have dealt with them directly with his fists.

The success of the Methodist Church in America in the first half of the 19th century was due largely to the work of the circuit rider. Other denominations copied this form of missionary work, and they too sent missionaries west. By mid-century, however, churches had been established, and the circuit rider now settled in a specific "charge."

THOMAS D. CLARK, *University of Kentucky*
Author of "Pioneer America"

CIRCULAR LETTERS, in American history, were issued frequently by colonial assemblies during the pre-Revolutionary struggle as a means of mobilizing opposition to British laws. Such letters had been used earlier by British administrators to instruct colonial officials and to obtain information. During the French and Indian War (1754–1763), Britain often circularized the American governors on military problems, and William Pitt, as secretary of state, sent formal messages to them in circular letters.

Massachusetts was a leader in using the circular letter as a revolutionary device. Its letter of June 8, 1765, calling for a Stamp Act congress was distributed by its legislature to those of the other colonies, thus initiating a practice that was to be imitated widely.

The Massachusetts Circular Letter of Feb. 11, 1768, the most famous of the letters, denounced the Townshend Acts (q. v.) as a violation of the principle of "no taxation without representation." It was written by Samuel Adams at the request of the Massachusetts House of Representatives. Although more or less affirming the supremacy of Parliament, the letter flatly denied the legality of British taxation in America. It declared British rule of the colonies to be limited by the immutable laws of nature, and it rejected, as interference in local affairs, the British practice of paying officials.

The letter aroused British officials, particularly the secretary of state, the Earl of Hillsborough, who demanded withdrawal of the letter under penalty of dissolution of the legislature. By a vote of 92 to 17, the Massachusetts House of Representatives refused to repudiate its action, and the assembly was thus dissolved. Other colonial legislatures accepted the letter and suffered the same fate. In April, Hillsborough dispatched to the colonies a circular letter full of threats and warnings. This letter served to further intensify bitterness toward Britain, and that summer British troops were sent to Boston.

Their assembly dissolved, about 90 Massachusetts towns responded to a circular letter of the selectmen of Boston, dated Sept. 14, 1768, by electing delegates to an extralegal convention, which met briefly in place of the assembly and in defiance of the governor.

JOHN A. SCHUTZ
University of Southern California

CIRCULATORY SYSTEM, the body system that consists of the heart and the blood vessels—including the network of arteries, veins, and capillaries. See also ANATOMY, HUMAN—THE CIRCULATORY SYSTEM.

CIRCUMCISION, sûr-kəm-sizh'ən, is an operation involving, in males, the removal of the penis foreskin. In females, parts of the external genitals are removed.

Male circumcision, is first attested to in ancient Egypt. According to Herodotus, not only the Egyptians but the Syrians and other Asian peoples practiced it, and according to Jeremiah 9:24-25, so did the Edomites, Moabites, and Ammonites. The Philistines, Canaanites, Elamites, and Sidonians were uncircumcised, according to statements in the Bible.

Among the Biblical Hebrews, circumcision was a very ancient rite, as shown by reports of its performance with flint knives (Joshua 5:2, compare Exodus 4:25). At an early date the tradition developed that circumcision was commanded by God to Abraham, to be performed on every male of his progeny on the 8th day after birth, as the token of an "everlasting covenant" between God and the seed of Abraham (Genesis 17:9-14). At the same time, circumcision came to be considered the sign of belonging to the community of Israel, from which uncircumcised foreigners were excluded to the extent of making intermarriage between them and the Children of Israel impossible (Genesis 34:14). Another meaning attributed to circumcision among the Hebrews was that it was a protection against the wrath of God (Exodus 4:24-25), as in the Canaanite myth told by Philo of Byblos (Philo Byblius) according to which the god Chronos had himself and his warriors circumcised in order to put an end to a pestilence. The Hebrew prophets utilized the concept of circumcision to express the idea that man must humble himself before God, and they speak of the "circumcision of the heart" to represent this humility (Jeremiah 4:4, 9:25; Ezekiel 44:9). In the New Testament the circumcision of the flesh was pronounced superfluous (Galatians 5:6, 6:15; Acts 15:1-20), and only circumcision of the heart, of the spirit, was insisted upon (Romans 2:29).

In the 2d century A. D., Roman authorities in Egypt prohibited circumcision except for priests. The Arabs practiced it in pre-Islamic times, and with the spread of Islam the custom was adopted in all Muslim lands. In modern times, circumcision has been practiced by almost all Jews and Muslims and by many tribes in Africa, America, and Australia. In most of these tribes it is performed at or prior to puberty.

Although ritual circumcision had originally nothing to do with hygienic considerations, the removal of the foreskin has long been known to help prevent infection of the penis. This led to a widespread adoption of clinical circumcision among non-Jews in western Europe and America. In recent years it has also been found that circumcision helps prevent cancer of the penis.

Female circumcision is a relatively rare folk custom, practiced in ancient and modern Egypt, Sudan, Ethiopia, and Libya and by some African, Indonesian, Australian, and Peruvian Indian tribes. It consists of the excision of the labia minora and the clitoris (clitoridectomy). The reasons given for female circumcision often involve the wish to diminish sexual desire, to remove what is considered a blemish in the female body, and to facilitate intercourse or conception, or both. The operation may be performed at varying times from the 7th day of life to puberty, or immediately preceding marriage.

RAPHAEL PATAI
Theodor Herzl Institute

CIRCUMFERENCE, a term used in geometry in connection with the circle. It appears in Euclid's *Elements* in definitions 17 and 18 of Book I. No geometrical definition is given for the term by Euclid. He uses it in the general sense of contour or outline, in phrases such as "circumference of a circle," to emphasize that he is talking about the circle itself and not, for example, the diameter or the interior. The modern use of the term is also for emphasis—that is, the circumference of a circle is the circle itself; but in some instances the word refers to the total length of a circle.

The length of the circumference of a circle is equal to the product of π times the length of the diameter, or π times twice the radius; in symbols, $C = \pi d = 2\pi r$. The value of π is approximately 3.14159. The symbol π was first introduced by William Jones in 1706 and is the first letter of the Greek word for circumference (*periphéreia*).

FRANCIS A. GREENE, S. J.
Xavier University, Cincinnati

CIRCUMSTANTIAL EVIDENCE is indirect evidence that seeks to prove certain facts by proving other circumstances and events. *Direct* evidence, such as the testimony of any eyewitness to a particular happening, goes to the precise question in issue. *Circumstantial* evidence is evidence that, according to the common experience of mankind, usually and reasonably tends to establish the truth of the principal fact in issue, by offering proof of collateral or supporting facts. Thus, evidence that a piece of rock embedded in a wrapped loaf of bread is the same type of rock as that found in the immediate vicinity of a bakery is circumstantial evidence that reasonably tends to establish the principal fact that the stone found its way into the bread during manufacture, leading to the conclusion that the bakery was negligent.

The distinctions between the two types of evidence have developed over many years in the history of Anglo-American law. These distinctions have been defined in case law, that is, in the course of court rulings on the acceptability of evidence in particular trials, and also sometimes by statute.

Despite a popular tendency to look down on the quality of circumstantial evidence, the law gives it weight equal to that of direct evidence. Properly presented, circumstantial evidence may be as conclusive in its power to convince as the direct testimony of an eyewitness. However, the collateral facts in circumstantial evidence must be consistent with the main fact sought to be proved and must be inconsistent with any other reasonable theory. For example, in a prosecution for murder by poison, the facts are often established by such circumstantial evidence as proof of earlier, similar unexplained deaths in the same household; the presence of abnormally large quantities of poison in the victim's body (testified to by toxicological experts); and recent purchase by the accused of quantities of poison. However, proof that poison had long been used to kill rodents in the accused person's home would be inconsistent with the inference of guilt from the accused's purchase of poison. Thus, such proof required that his purchases of poison be rejected as evidence of homicide.

M. MARVIN BERGER
Associate Publisher, "New York Law Journal"

CIRCUS, a form of entertainment featuring animals and skilled performers, presented within a circular enclosure that is surrounded by an audience. The enclosure, commonly called the "ring," is usually about 40 feet (about 13 meters) in diameter. It was originally devised as a running course for horses ridden bareback. A circus performance generally consists of bareback riding and other equestrian acts, as well as routines by trained animals, tumblers, wire walkers, jugglers, aerial gymnasts, and clowns. Often circuses feature spectacular "thrill" acts, such as a man shot from a cannon. The courageous and daring feats seen in most circus shows generate an aura of excitement that has made the circus one of the most popular forms of entertainment in the world.

Origins of the Circus. Performing skills, such as juggling, acrobatics, and wire walking are of ancient origin. The Romans, especially, were avid enthusiasts of entertainment that involved great physical skill and endurance. (The word "circus," Latin for "ring," was used to refer to the chariot races of ancient Rome.) After the fall of Rome in 476, acts that had formerly been seen in the arenas were perpetuated for centuries by itinerant animal trainers and entertainers. The modern concept of the circus as a ring show was not developed until the late 18th century.

Development of the Modern Circus. Philip Astley (1742–1814), an Englishman, is generally regarded as the "father of the circus." He was the first to demonstrate a variety of equestrian and acrobatic skills within a ring. In 1768 Astley founded a riding school in London. To advertise his establishment he exhibited his own riding skills in an open ring enclosure. These shows were very successful, and Astley gradually supplemented the equestrian acts with tumblers, acrobats, tightrope and slack wire artists, and a troupe of dancing dogs.

Encouraged by Astley's success, Charles Hughes, who had been a member of Astley's company, also opened a riding school. In 1782, together with Charles Dibdin, a dramatist, he organized a show like Astley's and called it "The Royal Circus," borrowing the Latin word. Thus Hughes gave the "circus" the name by which it is known today.

Astley, meanwhile, continued to develop and enlarge his circus. In 1782 he went to Paris, where he had first performed in 1774, and established an amphitheater. The circus began to be a popular form of entertainment throughout Europe. It is believed that the first public circus in Russia was introduced there by Christoph de Bach about 1810.

Early American Circuses. Although animals had been exhibited in colonial America, the Revolutionary War delayed the importation of the exciting new ring show that had taken Europe by storm. It was not until 1792 that the famous English horseman John Bill Ricketts produced the first real circus in the United States, building amphitheater, modeled on one designed by Astley, in Philadelphia. The show Ricketts presented was a great success, attracting many distinguished visitors, including George Washington. As the new nation developed, the circus moved westward with the population.

Traveling Circuses. American showmen quickly departed from traditional European methods of presenting circuses. European circuses of the 18th century were nontraveling shows, usually

THE SINGLE-RING CIRCUS has been traditional in Europe for centuries. A lithograph of the 1850's shows an equestrian performance in the lavish Cirque Olympique in Paris.

produced in large permanent buildings. American circus owners realized, however, that few cities in the United States were capable of supporting such shows. To meet the demands of the predominantly rural American population, circus entrepreneurs developed traveling shows that wandered in search of an audience. The early traveling shows were crude affairs, but with their menageries, thrills, and magic allure, they provided a break from the monotony of dull and uneventful lives, and people flocked to them. For many years, the circus was the principal form of amusement known to most Americans, especially in rural areas.

The Circus Tent. In 1826, Nathan Howe and Aaron Turner were the first to present their shows beneath a canvas tent. The mobility provided by the great portable tents helped give the American circus its peculiar character and rendered it altogether unlike the circus shows in the Old World.

The Circus Parade and Other Innovations. The circus parade was another institution that orig-

inated with the 19th century American circus. The first circus parade is believed to have taken place in Albany, N. Y., in 1837. Circus showmen were quick to realize the commercial benefits of spectacular street processions as advertisements, and parades remained popular until the 1920's. Colorful and elaborate parade wagons were constructed and soon circus press agents compared the lavish cavalcades to the triumphal pageants of the Roman emperors. The steam calliope, a boisterous musical instrument, was invented in 1855 and rapidly became a familiar sight in circus parades.

Another American innovation came into being in 1853, when a racecourse, or "Hippodrome track," was placed around the ring enclosure. This enabled showmen to enhance their programs with elaborate processions, or "spectacles," and chariot races. The menagerie, or exhibition of animals, had developed along with the circus. However, it remained independent until the late 1860's when it was combined with the circus.

The final break with European circus tradi-

THREE RINGS filled with activity are featured by the Ringling Brothers-Barnum and Bailey Circus.

TRAINED ELEPHANTS and their girl riders perform for spectators at the Ringling Brothers-Barnum and Bailey Circus during an appearance in New York City.

WILD ANIMAL ACTS bring circus audiences a sense of danger and a taste of the exotic. Here a tiger leaps through a flaming hoop at the command of its trainer.

tion came when a second ring was added to circus shows; a third ring was added to some shows later. To this day the European circus uses only one ring, always stressing the artistic value of the individual performance. In the United States, on the other hand, the circus developed a kind of rough-and-tumble character, in which the quantity of performers and animals in a given show was highly stressed.

Barnum and After. One of the best-known names in American circus history is that of P. T. Barnum (q.v.). Before actually entering the circus business, he had become renowned for his exhibitions of freaks, such as the famous midget "Tom Thumb." In 1871, Barnum was induced by William Coup and Dan Castello to join them in organizing a circus. (It was Coup who in 1873 introduced the second ring.) Thanks to Barnum's prestige and Coup's managerial brilliance, the resulting company was a great success. In 1881, Barnum combined with James A. Bailey (q.v.), a clever and imposing competitor, to create the Barnum and Bailey Circus—a name that became a household word.

In 1907, Barnum and Bailey's Greatest Show on Earth was purchased by the Ringling Brothers, who had their own highly successful circus. The two great shows operated separately until the spring of 1919, when the combined Ringling Brothers-Barnum and Bailey Circus opened in New York City.

In the meantime, numerous American circuses had come into being. By 1909 there were 98 touring companies, including such famous outfits as Forepaugh, Hagenbeck-Wallace, Sells-Floto, Al G. Barnes, Sparks, and John Robinson. Wild West shows, too, notably the Western hero "Buffalo Bill" Cody's, enjoyed great popularity.

Today only about a half dozen shows still exhibit under canvas, traveling by truck and tractor trailer. In 1956, Ringling Brothers-Barnum and Bailey abandoned tents and began to play in buildings, thus limiting its tour to population centers with large arenas. Numerous other indoor circuses are staged throughout the United States, but these generally consist of a program of acts contracted for one or more exhibition dates, with the performers furnishing their own wardrobe, rigging or properties, and transportation from town to town.

The American circus continues as a three-ring presentation and, whether performed indoors or beneath canvas, is well attended. Many of the acts seen in today's circuses are imported from abroad, thus maintaining the international flavor of American circuses. Also, television has made millions of Americans familiar with the one-ring European shows. As a consequence, some American showmen have predicted that this growing familiarity with the one-ring show may result in a trend in the United States toward the classical circus tradition in which one act is performed at a time.

MEL MILLER
Ringling Museum of the Circus, Sarasota, Fla.

Further Reading: Ballantine, Bill, ed., *Wild Tigers and Tame Fleas* (New York 1958); Chindahl, George L., *History of the Circus in America* (Caldwell, Idaho, 1958); Fox, Charles P., *Circus Parades* (Watkins Glen, N. Y., 1953); May, Earl C., *The Circus from Rome to Ringling* (New York 1932).

CIRENCESTER, sī'rən-ses-tər, is a town and urban district in England, in Gloucestershire, 15 miles (25 km) southeast of Gloucester. It is situated in the Cotswold Hills, once a noted sheep-raising district, and the town's handsome stone buildings date from the time when it was the center of the Cotswold wool trade. Cirencester's 16th century church has a splendid 3-story porch so large it was once the town hall.

During the Roman occupation of Britain, Cirencester (then called Corinium) was the second-largest town in Britain, after London. The town has a museum devoted to Corinium. An abbey was built in the town in the 12th century, but only a stone arch remains. In the great park on the west side of the town is a famous 5-mile (8-km) avenue of chestnut trees, and just beyond is the Royal Agricultural College, founded in 1846. Population: (1961) 11,834.

GORDON STOKES, Author, "English Place-Names"

CIRQUE, sûrk, a steep, amphitheater-shaped basin in mountain slopes and at the heads of valleys. A cirque is formed when a glacier develops in a mountain valley and starts to flow. Frost action in the deep crevasse at the head of the glacier breaks rock from the headwall of the valley. The cirque is broadened and deepened as the debris is carried away by the ice; the debris eventually is deposited in moraines along and down the valley. If there are parallel valleys in the mountain slope, the intervening ridges are cut away by the ice and form sharp rugged crests, or *aretes*. When the glacier melts, a lake, or *tarn*, may remain in the floor of the cirque.

Cirques are abundant at the heads of present glaciers in the Canadian Rocky Mountains and Alaska, and on Mt. Rainier in Washington. Formerly glaciated valleys of the higher western ranges, such as the Colorado Rocky Mountains, also have cirques; and a few cirques are seen in the highest eastern ranges, such as the White Mountains of New Hampshire. See also GLACIER.

MARSHALL KAY, Columbia University

CIRRHOSIS, sə-rō'səs, is a disease of the liver in which bands of fibrous tissue form throughout the liver, causing the organ to become hardened and to have an irregular surface. The growth of these fibrous bands is associated with the death of many liver cells, whereas other areas of the liver undergo regeneration.

Causes. Cirrhosis is a leading cause of death in people between the ages of 25 and 65. In the United States, cirrhosis is commonly associated with alcoholism. Although alcoholic cirrhosis has been attributed to the malnutrition frequently associated with alcoholism, it has been shown that alcohol itself can lead to an excess deposition of fat in the liver (fatty liver), and this condition is often followed by cirrhosis.

Recent research has also shown that the toxins produced by some fungi that contaminate food in tropical areas may cause cirrhosis. Occasionally, viral hepatitis may also lead to cirrhosis, and a prolonged obstruction of the bile ducts may cause secondary biliary cirrhosis. A similar condition, known as primary biliary cirrhosis, is thought to be due to an autoimmune reaction in the liver, although the exact cause is unknown. Rare causes of cirrhosis include severe heart failure, hemochromatosis (a disorder of iron metabolism), and Wilson's disease (a disorder of copper metabolism).

Symptoms and Treatment. Cirrhosis begins with a loss of appetite and general weakness. The disease, especially the alcoholic form, can be arrested at an early stage if the patient's consumption of alcohol ceases.

If the disease is not arrested, signs of impaired liver function later develop. The most conspicuous of these is a yellowing of the skin (jaundice) due to the liver's inability to rid the body of bilirubin, a bile pigment normally removed from the blood by the liver. Spider-shaped marks appear on the skin. The patient may also have a tendency to bleed, due to the lack of clotting factors normally produced by the liver. In men, there may be a development

CIRQUES in the Uinta Mountains, Utah, are the result of glacial erosion in the last Ice Age.

FROM "GEOLOGY ILLUSTRATED" BY JOHN S. SHELTON (W. H. FREEMAN AND COMPANY, © 1966)

of the mammary glands accompanied by a wasting away of the testicles and impotence with a loss of pubic and axillary hair.

Because the flow of blood through the liver is obstructed, it may bypass the liver through veins that become enlarged in the wall of the abdomen or along the esophagus. These veins may rupture, often causing death. In some cases, surgery may be used to shunt the flow of blood from the portal vein (which carries blood from the intestine to the liver) to the vena cava (which empties into the heart). If ascites (the accumulation of fluid in the abdomen) develops due to high blood pressure in the portal veins, it is treated by restricting the patient's intake of salt and administering diuretics (drugs that increase the production of urine). Mental abnormalities (including coma) may result from the liver's inability to detoxify harmful substances originating in the intestine. Antibiotics are administered in such cases.

CHARLES S. LIEBER, M. D.
Cornell Medical Division, Bellevue Hospital

CIRROSTRATUS. See CLOUDS.

CIRRUS. See CLOUDS.

CIRTA, sûr′tə, an ancient city in North Africa, is the site of modern Constantine (q.v.), Algeria. It was founded by Carthage and became a prosperous commercial city.

Noted as a fortress, the city was the capital of the Numidian kings at the height of their power in the 2d century B. C. Later it became a flourishing Roman colony. Cirta was destroyed during the civil war between Maxentius and Constantine I in 311 A. D. It was rebuilt by Constantine, who renamed the city for himself.

CISALPINE REPUBLIC, sis-al′pîn, a nominally independent state created by Napoleon Bonaparte in northern Italy in 1797 after victories there by the French armies. The original republic consisted of part of the former duchy of Milan in Lombardy, which had been under French occupation since 1796. Napoleon dictated a constitution and installed a progressive group of Lombards to administer the area in the French interest.

By the Treaty of Campo Formio (Oct. 17, 1797) France secured Austrian recognition of an enlargement of the original republic to include the remainder of Lombardy and the duchy of Modena. The state was further enlarged that year by the addition of the Cispadane Republic (a similar French satellite state), Mantua, Romagna, and part of Venetia. The frontiers of the enlarged republic extended to the river Adige in the north and the Valtellino in the northwest. Lost to the Austrians in 1799, it was recaptured and restored by the French in 1800.

The satellite state underwent numerous structural and administrative changes as French demands for its manpower and natural resources increased. In 1802 the Cisalpine Republic was superseded by the Italian Republic, proclaimed at Lyon by a carefully selected *consulta* of staunch Bonapartists, who named Napoleon its president. In continued to exist in this form until 1805, when Napoleon was proclaimed king of Italy.

RICHARD M. BRACE
Oakland University, Rochester, Mich.

CISCO, sis′kō, any of several freshwater fishes that occur throughout the colder waters of the Northern Hemisphere. They are closely related to the whitefishes (q.v.).

All ciscos have a small fatty fin behind the dorsal fin and a distinctive axillary scale at the base of each pelvic fin. They are silvery in color, and they lack the strong teeth on the tongue and jaws that characterize many other fishes (such as salmons, trouts, and chars) of their family. Since ciscos vary greatly in body form and hybridize freely, it is very difficult to differentiate the various species.

Although ciscos vary in their habits and habitats, most live in open waters of deep lakes and feed on plankton and small organisms. They spawn in the autumn months, either on reefs or in streams.

Many ciscos are commercially important. They may be marketed fresh, but they are especially esteemed when smoked. For many years, several ciscos supported an important commercial fishery in the Great Lakes, but recently the cisco population in the Great Lakes has been greatly reduced by overfishing, habitat changes, and the invasion of the sea lamprey and enormous populations of the alewife.

Ciscos are classified in various genera in the family Salmonidae, which also includes salmons, trouts, and chars.

R. WELDON LARRIMORE
Illinois Natural History Survey

CISSOID, sis′oid, a curve invented by the Greek mathematician Diocles (about 150 B. C.) in his solution of the problem of doubling the cube. The cissoid of Diocles may be constructed as follows. Let C be a circle in a plane with center O, t a line tangent to C at the point A, and B the point on C diametrically opposite A. Draw a line through B intersecting the circle at point P_1 and the tangent at point P_2. Let P be the point on this line such that the distance from B to P is equal to the distance P_1 to P_2. The locus of all such points P is the cissoid of Diocles. If B is the origin and BA the x-axis, the Cartesian equation of the cissoid is $y^2(2a - x) = x^3$, where a is the radius of the circle.

The *general cissoid* is obtained by replacing the circle and the tangent in the definition above by any two given plane curves and taking B as any fixed point in their plane. The name "cissoid" comes from the Greek word for "ivy," since the portion of the curve inside the circle bears a close similarity to the shape of an ivy leaf.

FRANCIS A. GREENE, S. J.
Xavier University, Cincinnati

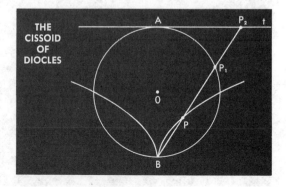

THE CISSOID OF DIOCLES

CISTERCIANS, sis-tûr′shənz, a monastic order in the Roman Catholic Church. Because of their robes they are also called Gray or White Monks. The order was founded by St. Robert de Molesme, who in 1098 established a community at Cîteaux, in France, dedicated to the literal observance of the rule of St. Benedict (see BENEDICTINES). It was above all the prudence and zeal of the third abbot of Cîteaux, English-born St. Stephen Harding (died 1134), that made possible the expansion of the struggling community into a vigorous new order. Under his rule the first four daughter houses of Cîteaux (La Ferté, Pontigny, Clairvaux, and Morimond) were established between 1113 and 1115, and in 1119 he drew up the *Carta caritatis*, a code of statutes for the government of the whole order.

The subsequent rapid expansion of the Cistercians was inspired largely by the genius of St. Bernard, who joined the order in 1112. At his death in 1154 there were some 280 abbeys, and by the end of that century some 530, over 60 of them in England and Wales (see BERNARD, SAINT).

Rule. The Cistercian life was one of poverty, prayer, and arduous labor. There were long fasts and little sleep. Golden ornaments and rich cloths were banished from the altars and the churches themselves were unadorned with sculpture and painting. In aiming at simplicity, the Cistercians achieved a pure and beautiful style of architecture; the best surviving example is at Pontigny.

Apart from the austerity of the monks' lives, the Cistercian Order differed from the older forms of Benedictine monasticism in both its constitutional structure and its economic organization. Each house elected its own head but was subject to visitation by the abbot of the founding house, while all the abbots of the order met together once a year in general chapter. (Cîteaux itself was visited by the abbots of the first four daughter houses.) The monasteries were supported by the labor of the monks themselves who often undertook the cultivation of great tracts of wasteland. To help with this work, and to provide a form of religious vocation for the illiterate peasant, numerous lay brothers were recruited. Through their agricultural activities the Cistercians came to play an important part in the economic life of medieval Europe, especially in the growth of the English wool trade and the opening up of arable land in eastern Europe.

Decline and Revival. By the middle of the 13th century, however, there were signs of decline from the fervent zeal of the early days, and the circumstances of the 14th century, with its wars, plagues, and schism, hastened the process of decay. In the later Middle Ages there was a general relaxation in standards of austerity, but also repeated attempts at reform, one of the most notable being that of the Abbot de Rancé of La Trappe in the 17th century. The Protestant Reformation and the later upheavals of the French Revolution produced a suppression of nearly all Cistercian houses in Europe, but during the 19th century there was a substantial revival.

In 1892 the order was divided into two observances, the Cistercians of the Common Observance—called the Sacred Order of Cistercians (SOCist)—and the Order of Cistercians of the Strict Observance (OCSO), often called Trappists. The latter order was formed by a union of several Trappist congregations. By the mid-1960's there were about 1,600 Cistercian monks of the Common Observance. See also TRAPPISTS.

BRIAN TIERNEY
Catholic University of America
Further Reading: Bouyer, Louis, *The Cistercian Heritage*, tr. by E. A. Livingstone (Westminster, Md., 1958); Lekai, Louis J., *The White Monks* (Okauchee, Wis., 1953).

CITADEL, The, sit′ə-del, a state-supported liberal arts military college on the Ashley River, in Charleston, S. C. The official name of the institution is The Citadel, The Military College of South Carolina. Undergraduate degrees are offered in liberal arts, business administration, engineering, and physical science. The cadets wear uniforms, live in barracks on campus, and are subject to military regulations. Coeducational summer school and evening programs are also offered. Each cadet is given a choice of training in either the Army or the Air Force Reserve Officers Training Corps and qualifies for military commission upon graduation.

The Citadel was founded in 1842. The college was known as the South Carolina Military Academy until 1910, when the present name was adopted. In the mid-1960's, about 2,000 cadets were enrolled.

MARK W. CLARK
President-Emeritus, The Citadel

CITATION, in law, a writ issued by a court, commanding a person to appear before the court at a particular time. It may order him to perform a specified act or show cause why he should not do so. As a type of summons or notice to a party to appear and answer at a proceeding, a citation is most frequently used in cases arising in probate and matrimonial courts.

The term is also used in reference to legal writing, where it means a legal authority such as a reported case, a statute, a constitution, or a treatise. Such citations appear in briefs, memoranda of law, and other documents, to establish the proposition set forth.

PETER D. WEINSTEIN
Member of the New York Bar

CITHARA, sith′ə-rə, a stringed musical instrument that was widely used in ancient Greece. Similar in shape to the lyre, it had from five to eleven strings that were plucked with a plectrum or with the fingers. The guitar and the zither derive their names from the cithara.

A CITHARA, held by Apollo, as depicted on a 5th century B. C. Greek vase in the red-figured style.

, THE METROPOLITAN MUSEUM OF ART (GIFT OF MR. AND MRS. LEON POMERANCE)

CITIES OF REFUGE, places of asylum in ancient Israel for persons who had committed unintentional murder. The Bible contains several references to places that were to serve as asylums. In Exodus 21:12–13, God tells Moses that He would "appoint a place" where such a criminal might flee. In Deuteronomy 4:41–43, Moses names three cities, Bezer, Ramoth, and Golan, to the east of the Jordan River, as cities of refuge. In Deuteronomy 19:1–13, Moses instructs the Israelites to "separate three cities" of refuge, without naming them. Numbers 35:14–15 and 24–28 indicate that there were to be six cities of refuge, three to the east and three to the west of the Jordan. If the "congregation" decided that a murder was unintentional, the killer could be sheltered in one of the cities. If the murder was judged premeditated, the dead man's kin could kill him. On the death of the high priest, the unintentional murderer could return home. Finally, in Joshua 20, six cities are named: Kadesh, Schechem, and Kiriath-Arba (Hebron) to the west of the Jordan, and the three cities named in Deuteronomy to the east. The procedure of admission to such a city is specified.

It has not been established whether the cities of refuge were actually functioning institutions in ancient Israel or merely representative of a legal provision never put into effect.

RAPHAEL PATAI, *Theodor Herzl Institute*

CITIUM, sish´ē-əm, was an ancient city on the southeastern coast of Cyprus. The site lies near the modern town of Larnaca, which is the administrative center of the *eparchy* (district) of Larnaca. Larnaca was founded by Frankish Crusaders and was called both Larnacas and Alykes (after the salt marsh that was worked for salt both in antiquity and in modern times). The town was the main port of the island during the period of Turkish domination. A small village about 6 miles (10 km) west of Larnaca preserves the name of the ancient site.

The founding of Citium is traditionally ascribed to Phoenician settlers. Graves from Mycenaean times (about 1560–1100 B.C.), however, have been found nearby. Citium remained one of the chief cities of Cyprus throughout antiquity, and parts of the ancient fortification wall and moat are preserved. The Athenian statesman and general Cimon died while besieging the city in 449 B.C. The city was the birthplace of the philosophers Zeno, Persaeus, and Philolaus. The fortunes of the city diminished in late Roman times, but Citium gradually returned to prominence under the Byzantine Empire.

JAMES R. WISEMAN, *University of Texas*

CITIZEN KANE was the first motion picture directed by Orson Welles. The film, released in 1941, tells the life story of a newspaper tycoon. (It has been suggested that William Randolph Hearst served as the inspiration.) Welles, who was then 25, cast himself as the tycoon, Charles Foster Kane. *Citizen Kane* explores its protagonist's motivation as a psychological mystery, with a clue buried deep in his early childhood and uncovered to the audience only after his death. The film's reputation rests primarily upon its brilliant technique, the use of a highly mobile camera, deep-focus photography, and exceptionally fluid montage.

CITIZENS BAND RADIO. See CB RADIO.

CITIZENSHIP is a relationship between an individual and a state involving the individual's full political membership in the state and his permanent allegiance to it. Other persons may be subject to the authority of the state and may even owe it allegiance, but the citizen has duties, rights, responsibilities, and privileges that the noncitizen shares to a lesser degree or not at all. The status of citizen is official recognition of the individual's integration into the political system.

More or less permanent allegiance to the state is an important element of citizenship. Even though he may leave the territory of his state, the citizen is bound by this tie unless he loses the status of citizen. At the same time, the state possesses certain responsibilities toward its citizens, which also are permanent and on which the citizen may normally rely.

Citizens, Nationals, and Subjects. For purposes of international relations, the term *national* is preferred to citizen, although in most states the two concepts are virtually the same. The nationals of a given state are all persons who owe it allegiance, including those who are not allowed to become citizens. The only significant group of U. S. nationals not admitted to citizenship consists of the native inhabitants of American Samoa. Many other states make this distinction with regard to their colonial populations, and some countries have denied citizenship to certain ethnic groups.

The state may treat citizens and noncitizen nationals differently in its domestic jurisdiction, just as it may discriminate between both of these groups and *aliens*—persons present on its territory and subject to its authority but owing it no allegiance and remaining nationals of a foreign state. In dealing with other governments, however, the state is obligated to afford protection to all of its nationals, citizens and noncitizens alike, and foreign governments customarily recognize its authority to do so.

In Britain and most other monarchies, the term "citizen" is used less often than *subject*. The latter word emphasizes the subordinate position of the individual relative to the monarch; however, as monarchs retain few personal political powers under constitutional monarchy, there is little practical distinction between citizen and subject. The category of British subject includes the citizens of the independent states of the Commonwealth, but a British subject is not entitled to citizenship in any particular Commonwealth country unless he qualifies under its citizenship laws. A Canadian citizen, for instance, automatically is a British subject, but a British subject from Britain, Australia, India, or from another of the Commonwealth nations may become a Canadian citizen only by meeting Canadian naturalization requirements.

Rights and Duties. In a modern democratic state, the rights and duties of citizenship are inseparable, as each stems from the other. Democratic theory holds that the state deserves, gains, and retains the loyalty of its citizens by affording them the opportunity—through their influence on the political system—to gain the maximum achievement of their own goals.

The citizen, by his own participation in the political sphere, makes it more likely that his needs and wishes will be taken into account in the making of policy. The primary right of citizenship in a democracy is the right to meaningful political participation. It is the freedom, in company with his fellow citizens, to hold the government—its officers, its policies, and its actions—responsible to him.

But the citizen in a democracy has some special responsibilities too. In addition to such requirements as obedience to law and payment of taxes, which characterize all societies, democracy necessitates political participation and obligates the citizen to accept responsibility for the results of governmental action. Citizenship in a democracy must be active. It is made meaningless by the citizen who avoids participation and declines to accept responsibility for what government does, thinking of politics in terms of "we" who are governed and "they" who govern. There necessarily must be politicians and civil servants who accept professional responsibility for the conduct of government, but they respond to the public influence in a democracy, and the public is to blame if results are unsatisfactory.

In a nondemocratic society, citizenship, if the term is used, means something else. The emphasis shifts toward duties, rather than rights, though there may be no total extinction of the latter. The loyalty of the population to the state may be just as great as in a democracy, but it is based on factors other than active political participation.

The allegiance of a citizen to his country is his most fundamental political loyalty. In a pluralistic society this can coexist with a variety of other loyalties, including those to family, church, private groups and organizations, political and social ideals, and even to subordinate political institutions or international organizations. Each of these may lead to conflict with one's national allegiance, but does not necessarily do so. In a totalitarian society, in which the state demands the total commitment of its citizens, such conflict is inevitable for anyone who has alternative loyalties.

HISTORICAL DEVELOPMENT

Throughout history, wherever the term "citizenship" was used, it implied a combination of obligations and privileges in the relationship between an individual and his state. The major differences involved the size and importance of the citizenry relative to the population and the extent of the rights and privileges conferred on citizens. These varied greatly.

Ancient Concepts. The concept of citizenship first became important in some of the cities of ancient Greece. There it was restricted to a small minority of the population. The extent of actual political participation varied from city to city and from time to time, but in each case citizens possessed rights and privileges denied both to foreigners and to a large majority of the city's population.

Roman citizenship at first was a device for distinguishing between the Romans themselves and the inhabitants of the territories incorporated within the Roman Empire. Later, in order to promote loyalty to Rome, inhabitants of a conquered territory might be admitted to Roman citizenship; this came to be done so frequently that the idea of citizenship as a distinction of natives of Rome disappeared. Citizenship conferred special legal privileges of great significance—a notable example being the successful claim of St. Paul that, as a Roman citizen, he could be tried only in Rome and not by the authorities in Palestine.

In medieval times the concept of allegiance was important in the feudal system. However, the term citizenship was not applied to the reciprocal rights and duties involved; its use at the time was confined largely to city-states. In certain cities, especially in Germany, citizenship was a bulwark for some economically privileged persons against the claims and demands of feudal overlords. Merchants relied on their status as citizens not merely as an avenue to influence within their own cities but as a promise of protection in their dealings with other cities and with the feudal aristocracy. The later extension of the idea of citizenship to the national level can be explained largely in terms of the economic importance of the urban middle class at the time of the transition from feudalism to the national state.

Modern Concepts. The American and French revolutions were the events through which national citizenship gained its modern significance. As citizenship in the medieval city-state had signified freedom from feudal domination, so national citizenship in the United States and France symbolized the end of monarchy. The distinction between citizen and subject no longer may be vital but it was to revolutionaries of the 1700's.

Citizenship held by all, in contrast with earlier rankings, conformed to the egalitarian ideal. In France distinguishing titles of address were abolished for a time, and everyone was addressed simply as "Citizen _____." As the revolutionary ideology spread, citizenship began to be viewed as an instrument for the promotion of popular government, individual liberties, and political equality. From this base grew the modern concept of citizenship.

QUALIFICATIONS FOR CITIZENSHIP

Citizenship normally is acquired at birth, but it may be acquired subsequently—usually by a process known as "naturalization" in which the state confers its citizenship on immigrants who meet specific requirements. For the most part, native and naturalized citizens have identical rights and duties.

Citizenship by Birth. The laws of virtually every country follow one or the other of two broad rules—or a combination of the two—in determining citizenship by birth. One rule is *jus soli*, according to which all persons born within the territory of a given state, except the children of foreign diplomats, are citizens of that state. The alternative rule is *jus sanguinis*, under which the place of birth is irrelevant and every child acquires the nationality of his parents—usually of the father if the parents are of different nationalities.

The United States, Britain, most other common law countries, and most Latin American states base their nationality laws primarily on the *jus soli*. The rest of the world, including the major states of continental Europe, tends to rely on the *jus sanguinis*.

Either of these in its pure form is rare, however. Britain, for instance, exempts from the *jus soli* children born in Britain to enemy aliens in wartime. But it also accords British nationality (with some exceptions) to anyone born abroad whose father was a British citizen at the time of the birth. Canada has similar rules. Virtually anyone born in Canada, except the child of a foreign diplomat, is a Canadian from birth. A child born outside Canada has Canadian citizenship from birth *jure sanguinis* if either parent was a Canadian citizen at the time of the birth and if the birth was registered with the appropriate Canadian authorities within two years. Such citizenship is lost at the age of 24 unless the person is then domiciled in Canada or has, after reaching the age of 21, formally registered his intention to remain Canadian.

Acquisition and Loss of Citizenship. In rare instances, citizenship may be acquired through adoption by a citizen of another state or through legitimation or recognition of paternity. By the laws of some countries, marriage automatically makes a woman a citizen of the country of her husband. This was formerly the rule in both Britain and the United States, but their laws were changed to end the loss of citizenship for a woman on marriage to an alien. Citizenship also may be gained by the acquisition of territory through annexation, conquest, or purchase. The entire population of the newly incorporated area may be made citizens of the acquiring state, although inhabitants of the territory sometimes are given an option of retaining their former citizenship.

By far the most common method of acquiring citizenship other than through birth is naturalization—conferring citizenship on an individual who has emigrated to the state and who voluntarily accepts its nationality. Almost all countries have some provision for naturalization, but requirements vary widely. Furthermore, some countries —often those which determine citizenship *jure sanguinis*—insist on the "indelibility" of their citizenship and deny the validity of naturalization proceedings for their citizens in any other country. This was the British rule until 1870, and the impressment into the British fleet of native Englishmen naturalized in the United States but still claimed as British subjects was one cause of the War of 1812.

The loss of nationality also is governed by widely varying laws. In some states nationality may be renounced. Certain other steps may be held to imply the renunciation of nationality, including naturalization in a foreign state, service in its armed forces, entry into its public service, or marriage to an alien. Deprivation of citizenship may be a penalty for crime or for other actions, often including prolonged residence abroad. At times states have deprived all members of a given ethnic group of their citizenship.

DUAL CITIZENSHIP AND STATELESSNESS

Conflicting nationality and citizenship laws of different states sometimes result in dual or multiple citizenship or in statelessness. Considerable international effort has been directed toward avoiding these situations and their concurrent problems.

Conflicting Citizenship. A person born in a state applying the *jus soli* to parents who are citizens of a state with the *jus sanguinis* is a national of each state by its own laws. In the reverse case he is a citizen of neither and hence is stateless. Marriage between citizens of two states produces either dual citizenship or statelessness if one state provides that a wife take the nationality of her husband while the other does not. Naturalization leads to dual nationality if the country of former nationality refuses to permit its citizenship to be lost or renounced. Deprivation or loss of citizenship means statelessness to an individual who has not become a national of any other country.

Problems. Tax payment, obligations to military service, the citizenship of children, and protection in dealings with foreign governments are some of the problems that may be affected by the lack of citizenship or by dual or multiple citizenship. Compulsory military service, for instance, ought to be required of an individual in no more than one country, and every individual ought to have one state where he is entitled to live and which will afford him protection in international relations.

The Hague Conference of 1930 dealt with some aspects of these situations and declared "that every person should have a nationality and should have one nationality only." Article 15 of the Universal Declaration of Human Rights states: "Everyone has the right to a nationality. No one shall be arbitrarily deprived of his nationality or denied the right to change his nationality."

Citizenship in a Federation. In a federation, such as the United States, dual citizenship in the nation and a constituent state is inevitable; but this seldom leads to serious problems, as control of citizenship is the responsibility of the national government. The Soviet Union, at least nominally, is an exception to this rule: both the USSR and the constituent "union republics" may confer citizenship.

CITIZENSHIP IN THE UNITED STATES

Matters relating to citizenship have always been of concern in the United States, primarily because it is a nation of immigrants. In the early days of the republic there also was a problem of conflicting federal and state responsibilities in this area.

Native and Naturalized Citizens. American citizenship at birth is gained primarily *jure soli,* but children born abroad to American parents generally are entitled to American citizenship also. Naturalization requirements have changed frequently. Until the 1920's they generally were designed to encourage large-scale immigration. Thereafter immigration was restricted stringently, both in total numbers and according to national origins. Immigration restrictions and naturalization requirements are closely related, so that permanent entry to the United States generally is limited to those eligible to become citizens.

Naturalized citizens legally are equal in almost all respects to persons who have been Americans from birth. The only constitutional disqualification of naturalized citizens is for the offices of president and vice president of the United States. However, naturalized citizens have been subject to loss of citizenship on grounds not applicable to the native-born.

Naturalized citizens who subsequently are believed to have been members of allegedly subversive organizations sometimes have been charged with falsifying their original applications for citizenship; in these cases they have been subjected to possible revocation of citizenship and deportation. American law also has provided for denaturalization of naturalized citizens who take up permanent residence abroad within five years after naturalization. In addition, the Immigration and Nationality Act of 1952 (the McCarran-Walter Act) provides for the loss of American citizenship of any naturalized citizen who later resides abroad for five years or for three years in the country of his birth or previous nationality. The purpose of these provisions is to deny U.S. citizenship to the alien who does not transfer his permanent allegiance to the United States in good faith. In practice, however, they impose restrictions on the naturalized citizen that do not apply to the native-born.

Loss of Citizenship. Several actions have been legal cause for loss of U. S. citizenship for any American, native or naturalized. These include voluntary naturalization in a foreign state, taking an oath of allegiance to a foreign state, unauthorized service in foreign armed forces, employment by a foreign government under certain circumstances, voting in a foreign election, formal renunciation of American nationality (with some limitations), desertion, treason, and draft avoidance.

The U. S. Supreme Court has held unconstitutional the desertion provision (*Trop* v. *Dulles* 356 U. S. 86 [1958]) and the foreign elections restriction (*Afroyim* v. *Rusk* 387 U. S. 253 [1967]) and has cast doubt on the validity of all other provisions withdrawing citizenship except when it is voluntarily relinquished. However, naturalization in a foreign state still may be held to constitute such relinquishment. In the Afroyim case, the Supreme Court referred to the basic nature of democratic citizenship: The individual rights bound up in the concept of citizenship were held to be a fundamental element of democracy, which could not be abrogated unilaterally by the state; only with his own consent can a person cease to possess the character of citizen.

National Versus State Citizenship. The U. S. Constitution made naturalization the responsibility of the national government, but otherwise left the determination of citizenship to the individual states. This proved awkward. All state citizens were also citizens of the United States, but it was possible that a naturalized U. S. citizen might not be accepted as a citizen by any of the constituent states. Furthermore, although the states could not naturalize, they had the right to admit anyone to virtually all the privileges of state citizenship whether or not he was a U. S. citizen.

The most serious problem involved the Negro. In the Dred Scott case (1857), the U. S. Supreme Court held that no Negroes, free or slave, were citizens and that neither the states nor the national government had the power to make them citizens. This decision, intimately related to the conflicts leading to the Civil War, was reversed after the war by the 14th Amendment to the Constitution. The amendment deprived the states of authority over the determination of their citizens, as follows: "All persons born or naturalized in the United States, and subject to the jurisdiction thereof, are citizens of the United States and of the State wherein they reside."

See also ALIEN; CITIZENSHIP EDUCATION; NATURALIZATION.

MURRAY CLARK HAVENS
University of Texas

Bibliography
Bar-Yaacov, Nissim, *Dual Nationality* (London 1961).
Brogan, Denis, *Citizenship Today* (Chapel Hill, N. C., 1960).
Jones, J. Mervyn, *British Nationality Law* (London 1956).
Parry, Clive, *Nationality and Citizenship Laws of the Commonwealth and of the Republic of Ireland* (London 1957).
Roche, John P., *The Early Development of United States Citizenship* (Ithaca, N. Y., 1949).
Weis, Paul, *Nationality and Statelessness in International Law* (London 1956).

CITIZENSHIP EDUCATION consists of the formal and informal methods by which citizens are enabled to understand and contribute to the effective working of their society. All nations are their schools to promote effective citizenship. The schools attempt to develop young persons who have the necessary knowledge and understanding and who hold the values and ideals that will lead them to satisfying and competent roles as citizens of the state. Central to such education is the furthering of the nationalistic and patriotic goals of the society. This is true in closed societies as well as in democracies.

Citizenship education has come to mean much more than the teaching of the facts of governmental structure and function, and in a broad sense the promotion of good citizenship can be considered the major and all-pervading purpose of education. In a free society, schools have a particularly heavy responsibility. They must teach the student to understand and believe in democracy as a living, changing process rather than as a set of rigid beliefs to be memorized without question.

Education in citizenship also takes place outside schools. The church and home, of course, are important in helping to form basic opinions, and informal influences such as television and newspapers have an important effect on a person's basic attitudes toward civic affairs. Political activities such as election campaigns are also a source of information, particularly the widely publicized contests for national offices.

CURRENT THEORIES

In the United States and elsewhere in the world there has been great controversy since the early 1900's concerning the kind of basic civic education most fitting for the development of socially competent individuals. Many educators agree that the schools must teach more than the traditional curriculum subjects and political civics. There is, however, a considerable disagreement about the new content and particularly about the methods by which the revised objectives are to be reached. There seems to be emerging, though, a consensus as to certain appropriate essentials of such training in the United States.

Most U. S. educators feel that citizenship education programs should be comprehensive, spreading across all the years of schooling, based upon a thorough knowledge of U. S. history and government, including an emphasis on the Constitution and the nation's political institutions. The heart of the program, it is felt, should be centered in the social studies, but civic experiences in all subjects and work of student councils, clubs, and other such school-wide organizations are also important.

Such programs should, of course, have dedicated teachers, who would reiterate the fact that every civic right has a corresponding social duty. The attempt to make civic education functional by relating learning experiences to everyday life in the school and the local community is also thought to be important, as well as a realization that the modern world demands citizens who understand peoples and cultures in every part of the earth. Young people require a better understanding of the role their nation plays in the international scene. To gain such an international outlook, the student must study other governments and varying economic systems, other societies, past and present, as well as the relationship between man and his environment. There is also a growing concern to have citizenship education point up the importance of improvement in group relations and minority rights.

Other significant factors of new programs are concentration on controversial current affairs and the fostering of healthy emotional adjustment among students through studies such as personal development, home and family life, social psychology, and mental hygiene.

HISTORY OF EUROPEAN CIVIC EDUCATION

General political education and concern with the development of civic responsibility was evident in the city-states of ancient Greece. The education systems in Sparta, and particularly in Athens, fostered the development of responsible citizens and laid the foundations for modern educational practices. Service to the state was a prominent aspect of life under the emperors of ancient Rome, and this aspect of Roman education was adopted in many areas as the Roman Empire expanded.

In medieval Europe, citizenship education was tied closely to the church and to religious education, a characteristic that has persisted. In some Protestant areas of Germany, for example, Lutheran influence is reflected in provisions for religious instruction. In Spain and in Italy the state and the Catholic church have been partners in education for centuries. Such religious influence in public education has declined, however, in a number of countries.

In the Renaissance, with the rise of nationalism and the growth of an economically influential middle class, the need became ever more apparent for the state to become actively involved in the educational process. Naturally, the content of education has varied greatly throughout history, depending on a nation's philosophy, its stage of development, and its form of government. The education of Spartan youth was, for example, quite different from the upbringing of the youth of Athens. Modern totalitarian nations that believe, as did the Spartans, that the individual exists for the state, have instituted educational programs based on the leadership-follower principle. Their schools entail practices that are radically opposed to those followed in nations that derive their political systems from Athenian democracy and are dedicated to majority rule, liberty of the individual, and faith in the reason of the common man.

U. S. CITIZENSHIP EDUCATION

Political education in U. S. schools was started near the end of the 18th century. By the 1820's, when public elementary and high schools were established, political history was a standard subject. A great stimulus to the teaching of national political and democratic ideals at that time was the need to initiate great numbers of immigrants into the American political and social system.

Through most of the 1800's the responsibilities of citizenship were taught as a part of American history, but toward the end of the century a series of studies by the National Educational Association led to the introduction of courses in civics and its broader implications. A pattern for the social studies program that is still widely followed was introduced in 1916.

This program included a full-year civics course in the 9th grade and a course in problems in American democracy in the 12th grade.

According to a government survey, about 112,500 students were enrolled in civics and government courses in grades 9 through 12 of U. S. schools in 1900. By 1922 the figure had reached more than 416,000. The category of community civics was added to the curriculum by 1928, bringing the total enrollment in civics courses to more than 610,500. In 1934 about 891,000 students were enrolled in such courses, and by the early 1960's the figure had reached almost 2 million.

About 18% of U. S. students in grades 9 through 12 were taking government or civics courses in the early 1960's, and 14 states required the taking of such courses. Many other states required similar studies as part of American history classes. Approximately two-thirds of the students enrolled in the 12th grade were taking courses in advanced civics and problems of democracy.

Experimental Programs. Experiments in citizenship education marked the decade following World War II. These studies attempted to explore new approaches and helped chart the means toward increasingly effective civic education.

Many examples of such experimental programs were reported in a survey published in 1967 by the National Council for the Social Studies. The survey concluded that three major needs must be met by the schools in the field of civic education: (1) They must create an informed citizenry; (2) develop an analytical citizenry; and (3) promote a committed and involved citizenry.

An example of a program to create an informed citizenry is a project carried out by a 9th-grade class at Hopkinton High School in New Hampshire. The class, in attempting to make a town survey, sent a questionnaire to the community government and also consulted government officials and studied statutes and records. The results of the study were published by the students and circulated throughout the community. The experiment thus furnished civic information not only for the students, but for members of the whole community.

In an attempt to develop an analytical citizenry, high school students in Woodside, Calif., were enrolled in a brief program designed to promote tolerance to nonconformity by comparing their responses to a questionnaire with the responses obtained from a cross section of the adult population. In analyzing and comparing these responses, the students became aware of their own and other people's prejudices.

To further the development of a committed and involved citizenry, many U. S. schools sponsor programs in which students work outside the classroom to help others in the community. At West Leyden High School in Illinois, for example, students of the Mental Health Organization Club visit the Chicago State Hospital regularly to talk with and entertain mentally ill patients. School and hospital officials are enthusiastic about the program, which helps develop a sense of social commitment in the students as well as offering consolation to the patients.

Studies Since 1950. A mounting number of reports and articles have appeared in professional journals and popular magazines since 1950. Important among these have been the yearbooks of influential societies, such as the National Council for the Social Studies' *Education for Democratic Citizenship* in 1951 and the American Association of School Administrators' *Education for American Citizenship* in 1954. Pamphlets, teaching aids, and units were sponsored by such diverse groups as the National Association of Manufacturers, the American Legion, the Tufts Citizenship Center, and the National Education Association. In 1954 the Citizenship Education Project, sponsored by Columbia University Teachers College and the Carnegie Fund, involved about 1,500 secondary schools throughout the United States in a program of citizenship education practices in schools and communities. Its publications provided a great deal of tested information on civic laboratory practices.

Results of the various studies substantiated what educational reformers had been claiming for years: traditional subject matter presented by traditional methods alone held little promise for improving students' chances of attaining the aims of citizenship education. A citizenship study made in Detroit, Mich., pointed out that the attitudes and understandings of democratic citizenship are acquired as a result of a many-sided process. The report of the study cautioned that until more certain insight was gained, the schools should maintain a balanced relationship among the techniques of teaching democracy. The Detroit study found that the attributes of democratic citizenship were developed in five ways: by the intellectual process, through participation in democratic activities, via emotional appeals, as a result of cultural assimilation in intimate home and community groups, and as the products of emotionally balanced individuals.

In the late 1950's, after the launching of Sputnik I, public attention in the United States shifted to the natural sciences, mathematics, and to the promotion of competence in foreign languages. The National Defense Education Act contributed millions of dollars to the development of curricular areas that had minimal responsibilities in civic education. A decade later, however, with a new generation reacting violently against numerous conditions at home and abroad, national concern began to focus once again on the social studies and civic education.

There was much evidence of this renewed interest. The Robert Taft Institute of Government was created and carried out a national study of citizenship requirements in the schools. Indiana University established a high school curriculum center in government, and professors at several major institutions carried on research to identify relevant factors in the political socialization of children. National testing agencies attempted to establish specific objectives for the better assessment of the attainment of civic aims, and cities such as Louisville, Ky., established summer institutes in government for teachers as well as students.

The amended Federal Elementary and Secondary Education Act began to provide funds for social studies and for teacher education in civics. And finally, the National Council for the Social Studies, sensing public alarm and even professional disillusionment as to the efficacy of school programs, conducted a national survey, the results of which were published in 1967 in *Promising Practices in Civic Education.*

RICHARD E. GROSS, *Stanford University*

CITRANGE, sit'rənj, a hybrid of the trifoliate orange (*Poncirus trifoliata*) and the sweet orange (*Citrus sinensis*). The trifoliate orange is a hardy ornamental, with sour, inedible fruit, used as rootstock on which to bud the more tender citrus varieties; the sweet orange is the popular orange of commerce.

Citranges were first produced in Florida in 1897 by W. T. Swingle, U. S. Department of Agriculture botanist, to extend the northern range of citrus fruits. There are many varieties, with no two alike. In character, citranges are midway between the cold-hardy, deciduous, compound-leafed *Poncirus* and the subtropical, evergreen, single-leafed *Citrus*. The greenish flesh of the citrange has a high juice content and the vitamins and minerals of *Citrus*, but it retains a slight acridity from *Poncirus*.

The fruit produces a "citrange-ade," and several varieties have usefulness as quality-increasing rootstock for other citrus.

Crossing of the citrange with the kumquat (*Fortunella*) produces the citrangequat, with the combined heritage of the three groups.

LOUIS W. ZIEGLER
University of Florida

CITRIC ACID, sit'rik as'əd, is a common, naturally occurring organic compound found in the tissues of both plants and animals. Its formula is $HOOCCH_2C(OH)(COOH)CH_2COOH \cdot H_2O$. Citric acid plays a vital role in the energy-producing processes of all cells (see also CITRIC ACID CYCLE). The greatest concentrations of citric acid are found in the citrus fruits, particularly in lemons and limes.

Citric acid solidifies in the form of colorless, translucent crystals or as a white powder. The compound is odorless but has a strong acid taste. It is soluble in water, alcohol, and ether; it melts at 153° C (307° F), but decomposes before reaching the boiling point.

In the past most citric acid was extracted from lemon or lime juice. Today it is most commonly made by the fermentation of a carbohydrate, usually molasses made from sugar beets, by the action of a species of the mold *Aspergillus*. The acid that is produced during fermentation is precipitated in the form of its calcium or barium salt, then liberated from the salt and refined.

In addition to its role in cell metabolism, citric acid functions as a food additive and industrial processing agent. It is used in soft drinks, flavoring extracts, confections, effervescent powders, cheese processing, electroplating, medicines, and alkyd resins. It is also used as an acidifier, as a sequestering agent to remove trace metals, as a mordant in dyeing to brighten colors, as an antioxidant in foods, and as a cleaning and polishing agent for metals such as stainless steel.

CITRIC ACID CYCLE, the last stage in the oxidation of all foodstuffs in living cells. A continuation of the Embden-Meyerhof pathway (in which glucose is broken down into pyruvic acid), its major function is the liberation of energy from foodstuffs to provide the cell with most of the energy required for its metabolic processes, especially biosyntheses. Also known as the *Krebs cycle* and the *tricarboxylic acid cycle*, the citric acid cycle is one of the metabolic processes that occur in all forms of life.

The citric acid cycle was formulated in 1937 by the British biochemists Hans A. Krebs and

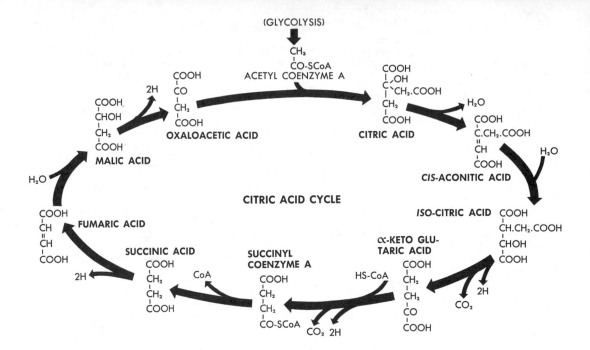

(GLYCOLYSIS)

CITRIC ACID CYCLE

CH₃
CO-SCoA
ACETYL COENZYME A

OXALOACETIC ACID

MALIC ACID

CITRIC ACID

CIS-ACONITIC ACID

FUMARIC ACID

SUCCINIC ACID

SUCCINYL COENZYME A

α-KETO GLUTARIC ACID

ISO-CITRIC ACID

William A. Johnson. They showed that its reactions are in a continuous cycle in which the end products provide materials for the repetition of the process.

Preparation of Foodstuffs for the Cycle. Food is prepared in the gastrointestinal tract for the enzymic reactions of the cycle. The main components of foodstuffs—proteins, carbohydrates, and fats—are hydrolyzed into a soluble form; the proteins yield amino acids, carbohydrates yield simple sugars, and fats yield glycerol and fatty acids. Then the amino acids, sugars, glycerol, and fatty acids are transported to the tissues of the body where they enter the cells. In the cells, these substances are partially oxidized; the main product of this reaction is a reactive form of acetic acid known as acetyl coenzyme A. Other products of the partial oxidation are carbon dioxide and some of the intermediate substances of the citric acid cycle.

The Main Steps of the Cycle. The citric acid cycle consists of a series of enzymic reactions in which acetic acid is oxidized to carbon dioxide and water; about two thirds of the energy contained in the foodstuffs is released here. Intermediate products of the cycle also provide a supply of simple precursors from which complex cell materials can be synthesized.

The first step of the Krebs cycle (see diagram) is the condensation of acetic acid (which is reacting as acetyl coenzyme A) with oxaloacetic acid to form citric acid. The citric acid molecule is rearranged in the next step to form isocitric acid, which then is changed to ketoglutaric acid. In the fourth step, which is the formation of succinyl coenzyme A, a molecule of coenzyme A is needed in the reaction, and a molecule of carbon dioxide is lost. Succinic acid is formed in step five when an enzyme splits off the coenzyme A from the succinyl coenzyme A. In the next step, succinic acid loses two hydrogen atoms to form fumaric acid. It is then hydrated to form malic acid. Oxaloacetic acid is formed in the next step when two hydrogen atoms are removed from the malic acid. With this reaction the cycle is completed. The oxaloacetic acid formed may begin another cycle by condensing with another molecule of acetyl coenzyme A.

Thus the citric acid cycle results in the regeneration of oxaloacetic acid, and the net result of one cycle is the complete combustion of one molecule of acetic acid, which is summarized in the following equation:

$$CH_3COOH + 2H_2O \rightarrow 2CO_2 + 8H$$

Production of Energy by the Cycle. The hydrogen produced during the citric acid cycle is transferred to special acceptor compounds (pyridine nucleotides and flavoproteins), which are involved in some of the enzyme reactions in the cycle. Reoxidation of these compounds by molecular oxygen liberates energy, and the energy produced is stored in a high-energy phosphate compound known as adenosine triphosphate (ATP). ATP is the basic unit of biologic energy, and its energy can be released when the organism needs energy for biosynthetic reactions.

During the oxidation of a molecule of glucose a total of 38 molecules of ATP can be produced. Of these 38 molecules, 2 are produced by glycolysis in the Embden-Meyerhof pathway, 2 are produced during the citric acid cycle proper, and a maximum of 34 can be produced by oxidative phosphorylation when the hydrogen-acceptor compounds produced in the preceding stages give up their electrons.

The enzymes required for the citric acid cycle and the reactions involved in the production of ATP are found in a cell organelle called the mitochondrion. This highly organized structure is known as the power plant of the cell. The number of mitochondria in the cell depends on the type of cell, but there may be several hundred per cell.

PATRICIA LUND
Oxford University

CITRINE, si'trēn, is a light yellow quartz. Because this transparent semiprecious stone resembles topaz, it is also known as *false topaz* and sometimes is sold as topaz; it is, however, less hard than true topaz. Citrine occurs naturally as crystals and can be produced artificially by heating some other varieties of quartz.

CITROEN, sē-trô-en', **André Gustave** (1878–1935), French industrialist and engineer, who popularized the mass-produced automobile in France. His production and marketing techniques made him known as the "French Henry Ford."

Citroen was born in Paris on Feb. 5, 1878, and graduated as an engineer from the École Polytechnique in 1898. He achieved fame during World War I as director of the arsenal at Roanne, where he dramatically increased French munitions production. After the armistice of November 1918, the Roanne plant was rapidly converted to automobile production, and the first Citroen was built in May 1919. By 1929 the Citroen company had 10 large plants producing 120,000 cars a year. Citroen lost control of the company when it went bankrupt in 1934. The company was later reorganized and is again a major automobile producer. Citroen died in Paris on July 3, 1935.

WILLIAM GREENLEAF
University of New Hampshire

CITRON, sit'rən, a small bushy tree, whose large lemonlike fruits have a thick fragrant rind that is used in making candies and in fruitcakes. The citron is native to Asia and was cultivated in the Mediterranean region as early as 300 B. C., where it was introduced from Persia. The citron, which is easily injured by cold and must be cultivated only in frost-free areas, is grown as a commercial crop in Corsica, Sicily, Greece, and the West Indies. The annual production is about 6,000 tons (5,500 metric tons).

The citron's toothed leaves range in length from 4 to 7 inches (10–18 cm), and the small white and purple flowers are borne in clusters. The yellow fruits are 6 to 10 inches (15–25 cm) long. Inside each fruit is a greenish pulp containing many seeds.

The citron is known botanically as *Citrus medica,* and it belongs to the rue family (Rutaceae). It is closely related to the grapefruit, the sweet orange, and the tangerine.

LOUIS ZIEGLER, *University of Florida*

CITRONELLA OIL, sit-rə-nel'ə, is a pale yellow, light oil that is obtained from the steam distillation of citronella grass, *Cymbopogon nardus,* which is grown in Java and Ceylon. The oil, which is soluble in alcohol, has a pungent, citruslike odor.

Citronella oil serves as a source for the manufacture of geraniol, citronellol, and citronellal, all of which are employed as flavoring agents and in perfumes. Citronella oil is also used in medicine, in perfumed disinfectants and soaps, and in insect repellents.

CITRUS FRUITS, sit'rəs, commercially, are the fruits of plants in the genera *Citrus, Poncirus,* and *Fortunella,* of the rue family (Rutaceae). These plants, native to Southeast Asia, are characterized by winglike appendages on the leaf stalks; oil glands in the leaves, in the rinds of the fruits, and in the bark of green twigs; an abundance of white or purplish, usually fragrant, flowers; often spiny trees; and a distinctive fruit —botanically, a type of berry called a hesperidium (leathery rind and parchmentlike partitions).

World production of commercial sweet oranges, tangerines, grapefruit, lemons, and limes approximates 585 million boxes annually (a box varies from about 47½ to 90 pounds— 21.5 to 41 kg—depending on the kind of fruit and where it is grown). The value of the world citrus crop is conservatively estimated at from 1 to 2 billion dollars (U. S.), with about half of this amount going to the farmers.

Citrus fruits are cultivated throughout the world, primarily in subtropical areas. The United States is the main producer of citrus fruits. Florida, with about 800,000 acres (324,000 hectares) of groves, leads in world production. The Mediterranean region, particularly the nations of Spain, Italy, and Israel, is the second-largest center. Mexico, Brazil, Argentina, Japan, and India have major citrus industries.

Citrus fruits are eaten fresh, preserved as sweets, squeezed for their juices for drinks and flavorings, and processed for vitamins and other substances. Citrus by-products include the dried pulp used as cattle feed and citric acid used for flavoring.

The genus *Citrus* comprises many species and includes the sweet orange (*C. sinensis*); the sour orange (*C. aurantium*); the mandarin, tangerine, and Satsuma oranges (*C. reticulata*); the King orange, which is believed to be a sweet-mandarin hybrid; the bergamot (*C. bergamia*); the lime (*C. aurantifolia*); the lemon (*C. limon*); the grapefruit (*C. paradisi*); the shattuck, or pomelo (*C. grandis*); the citron (*C. medica*); and the calamondin (*C. madurensis*).

Poncirus contains one species, the trifoliate orange (*P. trifoliata*), used primarily as rootstock for other citrus.

Fortunella, the kumquats, includes several species, three of which are in cultivation.

The citrus hybrids include the tangelo (tangerine × grapefruit), limequat (lime × kumquat), orangequat (sweet orange × kumquat), citrange (trifoliate orange × sweet orange), tangor (tangerine × sweet orange), and others. See also CITRANGE; LEMON; LIME; ORANGE.

LOUIS W. ZIEGLER, *University of Florida*

CITTERN, sit'ərn, a stringed instrument of the guitar family, with a pear-shaped body, flat back, and fretted neck. It was invented in the Middle Ages and reached the height of its popularity in Elizabethan England. The cittern was played by plucking, either with the fingers or with a plectrum. It had wire strings whose number varied but usually was eight or nine. The term has many variant spellings, including *cithern* and *cithren.*

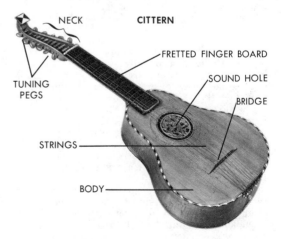

NECK   CITTERN

FRETTED FINGER BOARD

SOUND HOLE

BRIDGE

TUNING PEGS

STRINGS

BODY

CITY. The term "city" has various meanings, depending on whether it is defined by demographers, politicians, economists, sociologists, or historians. To the student of Greek and Roman history it means not only the walled town such as Athens or Rome but the territory surrounding it, the inhabitants of which enjoyed the privileges of citizenship — in other words, a city-state. In England, the term sometimes is used to designate a borough that is also a bishop's see, a carry-over from an archaic ecclesiastical terminology. In the United States, a city is, in legal terminology, a particular type or class of municipal corporation. As commonly used most everywhere, however, city merely means a relatively dense aggregation of population of considerable size, in which the conditions of life can be described as urban in contrast with the rural life of the open country.

In this sense cities are a universal phenomenon of civilized society. They have been found in every country beyond the stage of pastoral economy, whether or not it was industrially or technologically advanced.

It is impossible to draw an accurate line as to where country leaves off and city begins. No specific population or degree of density can be set down as necessary to constitute a city. For statistical purposes the United States census bureau classes all municipalities with populations over 2,500 as urban. Many places of 2,500, however, are obviously rural. The reader may assume that when this article speaks of cities it means built-up communities of at least 5,000 people.

DEVELOPMENT OF CITIES

Cities had their beginnings in the need of naturally gregarious mankind to seek safety and mutual protection in some easily defensible location. The inaccessible rock of the Acropolis determined the site of Athens. Rome owed its start to its seven hills surrounded by the marshes of the Tiber. The defense motive alone, however, would never have produced sizable cities. It was the development of trades and crafts behind the protection of the city walls, and the exchange of their products for food and raw materials, on which city growth was fed. The earliest large cities dating from about 3500 B.C. were found in the Tigris-Euphrates and Nile valleys, where easily navigable streams enabled this exchange of goods to take place over a wide and fertile area. Thus, thousands of years ago, the main forces that produced cities in later times — industry, commerce, transportation, and markets — already were manifest in Babylon, Nineveh, Memphis, and Thebes.

Location. In primitive times, accessibility to water transportation was of primary importance to city growth. It was not accidental that the famous cities of classical antiquity dotted the shores of the Mediterranean. In later times, railways, highways, and airways usurped, to considerable degree, the place of water transportation in determining the sites and size of cities. Several of the world's greatest cities — Moscow, Berlin, and Paris, for example — are situated far from the sea, with only minor streams and canals to serve them. There can be no doubt, however, that the great ports of Tokyo, New York, and London, have played a major part in making them the world's largest cities.

The sites where land and water or ocean and river transportation meet are places where merchants thrive. Commerce, the exchange of goods, is an important supplement to industry, the pro-

duction of goods, in building up the wealth and population of cities. Of the twelve largest cities in the United States, five — New York, Los Angeles, Philadelphia, Baltimore, and San Francisco — are ocean ports, and another, Houston, is connected by ship canal with the Gulf of Mexico. Four more — Chicago, Detroit, Cleveland, and Milwaukee — are Great Lakes ports, while St. Louis and Washington are situated on navigable rivers. This circumstance had little to do with the growth of Washington, but it had much to do with the early prosperity of St. Louis, and it remains a factor in its commercial life.

Other Factors. A variety of factors have contributed to the growth of cities. Some have gained importance as centers of religious devotion — Rome and Jerusalem being striking examples. Others have profited from their reputations as centers of learning or art. Paris for centuries has drawn students from all parts of the world to its ateliers and universities, and tourists to its galleries and museums. Climate has been a powerful lure in drawing population to such cities as Nice, Miami, and Los Angeles.

By far the most important of these noneconomic factors is government. Imperial Rome produced almost nothing but government, which it exchanged for tribute from its far-flung provinces. In modern times, the growing tendency to centralize the rapidly increasing activities of government in national capitals has had much to do with the swollen

ATHENS under Roman rule in the 2d century A.D. The Acropolis, surmounted by the Parthenon is at the upper right; the Olympieum is at the center left.

proportions of London, Berlin, Paris, Washington, and Moscow. Into these vortices of power and administration are drawn not merely the agents of government but those who seek its services and favors. Particularly striking has been the growth of Washington, which in 1900 had only 278,718 inhabitants and which rose to 763,956 in 1960 — 2,323,000 inhabitants in the metropolitan area including adjacent districts in Maryland and Virginia.

CITIES IN HISTORY

Though the life and achievements of cities stand out preeminently in the earliest pages of recorded history, it has only been in the 20th century that they have assumed the character and proportions with which we are familiar.

Ancient World. The cities of ancient times were mostly small, densely populated areas surrounded by defensive walls. Politically such a center was completely intergrated with the surrounding countryside as a city-state. Judged by modern standards, the truly urban area within the walls was very limited in extent and population. These ancient cities looked large to contemporary writers, and they brought down to our day an exaggerated impression of city size. Exact figures as to the population of ancient cities are not available, but estimates of scholars put the population of Athens at the height of its glory at from 40,000 to 140,000; Jerusalem at 30,000; and Carthage at not more than 300,000. Rome in the Augustan era, gener-

ally agreed to have been the largest city of that time, is estimated at not more than 800,000. Indeed, providing for 800,000 people in a city without any mechanical means of passenger transportation except the chariots and litters of the rich was not the least of the marvels of the capital of the ancient world.

Dark Ages. Following the barbarian invasions beginning in the 4th century after Christ, cities virtually disappeared from western Europe for a period of several hundred years known as the Dark Ages. They did not all go at once. Some were destroyed by the invading hordes, who had no use for cities except to pillage them. They would probably have sprung to life as have cities battered in modern wars had it not been that trade routes were broken and that the simple agricultural economy and rigidly formal social organization of feudalism discouraged urban concentration. A few Mediterranean ports continued some shadow of urban life on the basis of trade with the East. Rome was a long time reaching its low point of 17,000 inhabitants about the end of the "Babylonian Captivity" in 1377, but most cities died more promptly. Constantinople, at the extreme eastern limit of Europe, was the only European city to survive the Dark Ages with a population of 100,000.

Urban Revival. The rebirth of cities began with the revival of trade in the 10th century. Slowly at first, and then with increasing rapidity, the famous cities of medieval Europe rose. The city

ROME DURING THE REIGN OF THE EMPEROR AURELIAN (270–275 A. D.)—BETTMANN ARCHIVE

ROME was the largest city of the ancient world. The Capitoline Hill is in the center with the Forum and the Colosseum behind it. The Pantheon is at the left.

republics of Italy, the Hanseatic cities of Germany, and the flourishing cities of the Low Countries in the course of a few centuries played a major role in history. They threw off the shackles of feudalism and introduced modern systems of law and justice. They contended in the field with armies of kings and princes. They developed a life so rich and pleasant as to cause some writers to look back to the 12th and 13th as the best of centuries. They were, however, of no great size compared with the modern metropolis. At the beginning of the 16th century there were but six European cities — Constantinople, Paris, Naples, Venice, Milan, and Lisbon — with more than 100,000 population. Ghent at that time boasted 50,000 people; London and Bruges 40,000 each; and Brussels, Louvain, and Liège 20,000 to 30,000 each.

Modern Cities—Effect of Trade and Transport. The period of exploration and discovery, beginning in the 15th century, heralded a new era in urban development. World trade replaced local trade. Cities that could exchange manufactured goods for the food and raw materials of distant continents had almost unlimited growth potential. The die was cast for an urban revolution when the ships of the early navigators first entered the bays and rivers of the New World, and the impetus given city growth by Columbus' voyage never relaxed its force until the New World became an old world with a mature economy of its own.

Other influences combined with worldwide trade to cause the extraordinary growth of modern cities, some of which remain powerfully operative. The development of mechanized means of land transportation beginning in the 19th century—and later of air transit — made huge urban complexes

like New York and London logistic possibilities. The city worker could live far from work, amusements, and shopping, and goods could be moved to and from cities.

Effect of Industrialization and Mechanized Agriculture. Another force contributing to urban growth was the vastly increased productivity of labor in industry. Beginning with the Industrial Revolution, machines driven at first by water, then by steam, and then by electricity, replaced old-time hand labor. Machine production meant, in fact, city production, as large-scale industry, even if not originally situated in a city, quickly builds up a city around it.

Still another factor was the revolution in agricultural technology. The significance of this will be realized when it is remembered that the modern plow did not come into general use until well into the 19th century. Until that time such cultivation as a growing crop received was by the application of muscle to a hoe handle; grain was cut with a scythe, raked by hand, and threshed on the barn floor with a flail as in Biblical days. Modern agricultural machinery and improved breeding of animals and plants enabled a much smaller proportion of the world's population to supply the food for city people.

All of these forces are still operating. The rate of city growth is accelerating in underdeveloped countries, and, although it has slackened somewhat in highly industrialized nations, cities there are still growing, and the proportion of city dwellers to country folk is increasing.

The Age of the City. Cities of 100,000 population are scattered over the world, and at least 40 cities, representing all the continents, had populations exceeding 2,000,000 in the 1960's. Especially in the United States and western Europe, city life has become the characteristic form of existence for a majority of the people. In the United States almost 70% of the population was classified as urban in the 1960 census — and this figure was exceeded in the more densely populated western European countries. About 63% of the U. S. population lived in 212 metropolitan areas in the 1960's, and half the U. S. population lived in just 13 megalopoli.

Comparative figures are not available for other countries, but from the number of great cities that are found everywhere outside the equatorial jungles and polar icecaps it is clear that the dominant position of the city is a worldwide phenomenon. Whether this period is called the age of steel, the age of electricity, the age of the automobile, or the atomic age, it certainly may be called the age of the city.

URBAN LIFE

The history of the city is the history of civilization itself. In the beginning cities furnished the first opportunity for extensive division of labor and opened the door to inventions and industrial progress. They suffered an eclipse in the Dark Ages, but the few that contrived to exist kept alive the traditions of ancient skills, and in the 10th century civilization once more started its upward spiral

from the little cities that sprang up at the foot of a castle, just outside the precincts of an abbey, or at the head of navigation of some stream. Thereafter, leadership in industry, commerce, art, and literature has been found in the cities. Many individual leaders, it is true, have been country born and bred, but almost without exception it has been the city that has supplied the inspiration and opportunity for their genius.

City Government. It is well to remember this when pessimists decry the city's influence on its people and deny its capacity for self-government. This negative attitude of mind was reflected in the United States in a widespread gerrymandering of legislative districts to permit farms and small towns to dominate the cities — not remedied to any extent until the push for legislative reapportionment in the 1960's. There is no denying that cities from the earliest times often have been turbulent, revolutionary, and corruptly governed. American city government was labeled in 1888 by James Bryce in his *American Commonwealth* as "the one conspicuous failure of the United States." At this time American city government was at a low ebb and the label stuck, although the condition improved considerably.

Cities early developed democratic means of meeting the problems that faced them, but they sometimes succumbed to tyrants and bosses from

PIAZZA DELLA SIGNORIA, civic center of Florence, Italy, in the Renaissance, showing the Duomo (far left), the Palazzo Vecchio (middle right), and the Loggia dei Lanzi (far right).

THE EXECUTION OF SAVONAROLA, BY AN UNKNOWN 15TH-CENTURY FLORENTINE ARTIST—BETTMANN ARCHIVE

within, or to the centralizing tendencies of kings and dictators from without. The career of the cities has been a checkered one; yet there are no more glorious pages in the story of the struggle for popular self-government than those written by the Italian city republics of the early Middle Ages, the Flemish cities of the 12th century, the Boston town meeting in its controversy with the British crown, or the people of Cincinnati when they threw out a boss and wrote themselves a new and admirable form of government in 1924.

Urban Problems. Cities have repeatedly demonstrated their capacity, when released from the leading strings of centralized government, to handle their own affairs. There is no reliable evidence to show that man cannot successfully adjust himself to the conditions of city life without either physical or moral deterioration. Even the bad effects of city slums can be overcome by health, recreational, and educational programs.

Cities, historically speaking, have had a compactness and unity that has enabled them to grapple vigorously with crises. Means of communication by press, radio, and mouth-to-ear contacts have always been more effective in the city than in the country. The greatest internal handicap under which American cities have suffered has been the diversity in race and language in their populations. Integrated public opinion is difficult to secure among ethnic groups whose backgrounds differ widely and to whom demagogic appeals of a racial character are most effective.

This problem has been corrected to a large extent under the leveling influence of mass media, but another difficulty confronts the great urban communities in dealing with their complex problems. This arises from the tendency of urban population to overrun legal city boundaries. Where the political city and the economic and social city no longer coincide, it is difficult to secure coherent and effective action.

This condition exists in all great population centers, and it never has been more than partially solved by annexation or consolidation. In fact, the outlying units of government over which the population of a modern metropolis sprawls generally are adamant in their resistance to absorption by the central city. How serious this problem has become is apparent from the fact that New York's metropolitan area extends into three states, Chicago's into two states, and Detroit's into two counties. In many of the largest metropolitan areas in the United States the nucleus cities actually have been declining in population while the adjoining suburban communities are increasing.

The cause of this outward movement of population is the obsolescence of homes in the close-in sections of the nucleus cities and the gradual deterioration of old residential neighborhoods, plus the facility afforded by the automobile and public commuter transportation of living miles away from one's work. The results are the spread of blight and slums in the nucleus cities, and a serious threat to the financial soundness. Worst of all, however, is the inability of a metropolitan region, made up of dozens or even hundreds of independent local governments, to devise means of meeting its common problems.

A solution of these related problems of urban sprawl and urban deterioration is being sought, on the one hand, in regional government authorities and, on the other hand, in accelerated programs of urban renewal. The U. S. government in 1965 created the Department of Housing and Urban Development in order to participate more effectively in urban affairs.

See also MUNICIPAL GOVERNMENT; URBAN PLANNING; URBAN RENEWAL.

THOMAS HARRISON REED
Municipal Consultant

Further Reading: Gutkind, Erwin A., *An International History of City Development*, 10 vols. (New York) (1964–   ); Mumford, Lewis, *The City in History* (New York 1961); Schneider, Wolf, *Babylon is Everywhere: The City as Man's Fate* (New York 1963); Tunnard, Christopher, and Reed, Henry Hope, *The American Skyline* (Boston 1955).

LONDON before the great fire of 1666 showing St. Paul's *(background left)*, Tower of London *(background right)*, and London Bridge, spanning the Thames.

CITY COLLEGE, a publicly controlled coeducational institution in New York City. It is officially known as The City College of The City University of New York and is the oldest and largest of the senior colleges in the City University.

The City College is made up of three schools: liberal arts and science; education; and engineering and architecture. All the schools offer undergraduate degrees and the master's degree. The college also participates in doctoral programs offered by the City University in a number of academic fields. The City College does not charge tuition fees to matriculated undergraduates who live in New York City.

The institution was founded in 1847 and began to grant degrees in 1853. It became known as The College of the City of New York in 1866 and as The City College in 1929. It was the oldest of the seven municipal colleges that were united to form the City University of New York in 1961.

Enrollment at The City College exceeds 20,000.

CITY MANAGER, an executive appointed by the legislative body (council) of a local government—city, town, village, or county—to serve as its chief administrative officer. Unlike a mayor, the city manager is not popularly elected, but he is responsible to the elective council, which can remove him from office.

A city manager generally has professional training and experience in local government. His duties include appointing and supervising administrative personnel, submitting the annual budget to the council, making recommendations to the council on policy matters and keeping it advised of the financial condition and future needs of the city, and seeing that all laws and ordinances are enforced.

The city council of Staunton, Va., created the post of "general manager" in 1908, but the council-manager plan, as it is known today, was first adopted by Sumter, S. C., in 1912. By 1925 nearly 250 cities and towns in the United States had adopted this plan, and by the late 1960's it was the leading form of local government among U. S. cities with populations over 25,000—surpassing the mayor-council plan and the commission plan. More than 2,100 municipalities were using the council-manager plan by that time. It was in effect in 46% of cities with populations over 100,000, 53% of those in the 50,000–100,000 range, and 51% of the 25,000–50,000 group. In addition, 1,850 local governments in Finland, Germany, Ireland, Norway, and Sweden had adopted the council-manager plan. See also MUNICIPAL GOVERNMENT.

ORIN F. NOLTING
International City Managers' Association

CITY OF GOD, a great religious, philosophic, and literary classic of the 5th century, written by Augustine of Hippo. Begun in 412 and finished in 426, *De Civitate Dei* (*The City of God*) was occasioned by the fall of Rome in 410, which the pagans interpreted as sign of the gods' anger at Constantine's recognition of Christianity. In 412 the philosopher Volusanius declared to Marcellinus, a Christian Roman official in North Africa, that good Christians could not be good citizens; Marcellinus asked Augustine to respond to the charge.

Of the 22 books of *The City of God*, the first 10 answer the pagan accusation by showing that neither demons nor gods bring happiness here or hereafter, and that vices within the empire rather than Christianity brought Rome's collapse. The last 12 books show Augustine as the father of "philosophies of history," as he gives a religious interpretation of human history in the light of Biblical revelation. In these books he traces the origin, development, and destiny of the City of God and of "Babylon," city of conflict and confusion, from the fall of Adam to the end of time. Book 19 contains a theology of peace; books 20–22 provide a Christian eschatology.

Augustine's city of God is an invisible society, a communion of saints both living and dead. Its order is founded on the love of all its citizens for God; those who prefer themselves to God form "the other city" of Babylon. After the Last Judgment these two cities became Heaven and Hell. Augustine identified neither with the temporal state. See also AUGUSTINE, SAINT.

MARY T. CLARK, *Manhattanville College*

CITY PLANNING. See URBAN PLANNING.

CITY-STATE, a sovereign political unit in which all major activities are concentrated at one focal point, usually an urban community. In view of the concentration of political life, city-states have tended to be small, comprising the urban center and surrounding rural districts. Because this form of political organization normally appeared in early stages of civilized societies, citizens were also grouped in a tight social, religious, and economic bond.

History. City-states flourished in three major periods of Western civilization: the ancient Near East, the classical period of Greece, and medieval and Renaissance Europe. The first organized states known to history were the city-states of Sumer (lower Mesopotamia), such as Ur, Lagash, and Erech. Some 14 Sumerian city-states existed by about 3000 B. C., each with a walled, urban center. In Egypt, on the other hand, the rise of civilization brought a unified kingdom, and from the time of the conqueror Sargon of Akkad (about 2250 B. C.) the Mesopotamian city-states, too, were generally combined under the control of an overlord. In the first millennium B. C., the Phoenician coast was divided into the city-states of Tyre, Sidon, Byblos, and others.

The Greek city-state, or *polis,* which emerged out of the early Homeric tribal societies, became by about 700 B. C. the dominant vehicle of political life. Athens, the largest Greek city-state, covered 1,000 square miles (2,600 sq km); at the other extreme, the island of Ceos, 10 by 6 miles (16 by 10 km), was divided into four city-states. Classic Hellenic civilization flourished in these small political units, and Aristotle argued that a man was a "political" animal in the sense that truly cultured life was possible only in the *polis.* However, rivalries eventually exhausted the Greek city-states, and under the Macedonian kingdom, beginning about 350 B. C., and subsequent Hellenistic kingdoms only a few *poleis* were truly independent.

The Greek colonies in the Mediterranean and Black seas, established between 700 and 500 B. C., were also organized as city-states, especially in Italy, where a number of Etruscan and native city-states appeared in imitation of the Greek *poleis.* The most famous of these colonies, Rome, eventually conquered the Mediterranean world and ended the period of the ancient city-states.

During the Middle Ages and Renaissance there came the third era of city-states, often called "communes." In Italy the autonomous cities of Milan, Venice, Genoa, and Florence flourished and became centers of art and letters very much like the Greek *poleis*. Other communes appeared in Flanders from the late 11th century, but soon fell under the rule of territorial princes. The great German trading centers of Bremen, Hamburg, Lübeck, and others became independent in the 12th century, and late in the next century they grouped themselves in the Hanseatic League (q.v.), which eventually had more than 70 members. Geneva, another famous city-state, was the center of Calvinism during the Reformation. The rise of the nation-states of modern Europe ended this period. Venice and Geneva, however, retained their sovereignty until the French Revolution, and the free cities of Germany survived, in part, until the unification of Germany in 1871.

Characteristics. City-states were absolutely independent, regardless of size, and pursued their own policies in war and peace. However, several might group themselves into leagues for mutual advantage. The Greeks formed such groupings after 499 B.C. to resist the Persians and other enemies, and the German Hanseatic League protected the trade of its members. The use of coinage appeared in the Greek city-states a little before 600 B.C.; there and in medieval Europe each state coined its own issues and sought economic independence. City-states could be imperialistic in favorable circumstances, although in view of their small size the resulting empires were usually sea-based. Both Athens and Venice failed when they sought to expand into

Cerro Bolívar, a mountain of iron ore near Ciudad Bolívar, is one of Venezuela's principal iron deposits.

VENEZUELA-UP-TO-DATE

neighboring areas by land. City-states often existed in a larger cultural matrix, which they expressed with local variations.

The citizens of a city-state usually numbered fewer than 10,000. They felt themselves tightly bound together, often under the divine protection of a particular god or saint. In Mesopotamia the god was believed to own the city-state and to appoint earthly representatives to administer it. Government there was theocratic as it was later in Calvin's Geneva. In early Greece kings ruled, but most often political control of a city-state was in the hands of an oligarchy based on landed possessions or, less often, on commercial wealth (as in Venice). Yet, from Greek times, the free members of a city-state were considered to have certain inalienable rights under the rule of law, the root of Western political ideals. In Athens the assembly of the citizens had full powers after 508 B.C., but such democratic government was unusual.

In a city-state a fairly extensive rural area always lay about the political center. In ancient Sparta this center was no more than a group of villages, but normally the city proper was a tight nucleus, with a fairly extensive population. Industrial and commercial classes plied their professions at and near the market. A meeting place for the council and other officials was usually provided, and every city also boasted a temple or cathedral as magnificent as the wealth and piety of its citizens permitted. Some farmers lived in the city; others lived in villages, which might have some local self-government, in minor matters. Generally the peasants, even if they possessed the right to vote, played a lesser role in political life, although their crops were vital to city dwellers.

The small size of city-states and their limited resources in men and wealth tended to lead to their disappearance whenever an area became capable of larger organization. Yet this form of political organization was of great significance in the birth of civilization in the Near East, encouraging the rise of monumental architecture and the use of writing. In Greece and in Renaissance Italy the small city-states greatly stimulated intellectual activity. The concept of the modern city as a self-governing–though not sovereign–entity also owes much to the ancient and medieval city-states, which retained local powers even after losing their sovereignty to larger political units.

CHESTER G. STARR, *University of Illinois*

Further Reading: Fowler, William Warde, *The City State of the Greeks and Romans* (Macmillan, N. Y., 1960); Fustel de Coulanges, Nuna Denis, *Ancient City* (Doubleday 1956); Hammond, Mason, *City-State and World State* (Harvard Univ. Press 1951); Ullmann, Walter, *Principles of Government and Politics in the Middle Ages* (Barnes & Noble 1961).

CITY UNIVERSITY OF NEW YORK. See NEW YORK, CITY UNIVERSITY OF.

CIUDAD BOLÍVAR, syōō-thäth′ vō-lē′vär, is a seaport in Venezuela, on the narrows of the Orinoco River, 250 miles (400 km) from its mouth. The port, a focal point of trade for a vast region of grassplain and forest, ships cattle, meat, hides, and a variety of tropical forest products. Handcrafted gold objects are a specialty of the city. Though one of the world's richest sources of iron ore is nearby, industrial development has centered on Ciudad Guyana, to the east.

Ciudad Bolívar is the capital of Bolívar state. Founded in 1764, the city was at first named Angostura ("narrows"). In 1819 the Congress of Angostura formed a union of what are now Venezuela, Colombia, and Ecuador, with Simón Bolívar as its president. Angostura bitters, a popular flavoring made from tree bark, originated in the city in 1824 but is no longer made there. Population: (1971) 103,728.

CIUDAD GUAYANA, syōō-thäth' gwä-yä'nä, a city in eastern Venezuela, is an industrial center and port at the confluence of the Caroní and Orinoco rivers, 325 miles (525 km) southeast of Caracas. The city was founded in 1961 by the Corporación Venezolana de Guayana (CVG), a government agency formed as part of a policy to invest oil royalties in projects that would diversify the economy against the day when oil reserves would be depleted. The CVG designed a community with beauty and efficiency in mind.

The major impetus for creating the city came from the discovery in 1947 of vast reserves of easily mined high-concentrate iron ore in the Cerro Bolívar, a ridge 75 miles (120 km) distant. Besides iron ore, geologists have found within 200 miles (320 km) of Ciudad Guayana extensive reserves of coal, oil, natural gas, manganese, nickel, chromium, gold, industrial diamonds, bauxite, and kaolin.

Another incentive for making Ciudad Guayana a major industrial center was the enormous hydroelectric potential of the Caroní River. Much of the power for the industrial complex comes from two dams on the river, the Macagua (generating capacity 360,000 kilowatts) and the Guri (525,000 kilowatts). The capacity of the Guri Dam will eventually be increased to 6 million kilowatts.

Government investment assistance, mineral wealth, and cheap power have stimulated a rapid expansion of industry since 1960. Ciudad Guayana has a large steel mill, an iron-ore reduction plant, an aluminum works, and numerous light industries. Pulp and paper mills have been established to make use of the area's extensive forest resources.

Ciudad Guayana, which is also known as Santo Tomé de Guayana, includes several older communities, such as Puerto Ordaz and San Félix. Population: (1970) 143,240.

CIUDAD JUÁREZ, syōō-thäth' hwä'räs, is a city in Mexico, on the Rio Grande (Río Bravo del Norte) opposite El Paso, Texas. Juárez, as the Mexican city is usually called, is the commercial center of a cotton-growing district in Chihuahua state. It derives a considerable income from the tourist industry, which is served by many small shops, restaurants, bars, and cabarets. Sports attractions are bullfighting, greyhound racing, and jai-alai. Points of interest include the Mission of Our Lady of Guadalupe (founded 1659) and the Museum of Art and History.

The city was founded in the 17th century as El Paso del Norte and was renamed in 1888 for Mexican President Benito Juárez. In 1967 the disputed international boundary here was relocated under the terms of an agreement reached in 1963. Mexico gained a net total of 437 acres (177 hectares) north of the Rio Grande. In 1968 the river was diverted to a channel that had been constructed along the new border. Population: (1970) 407,370.

CIUDAD REAL, thyōō-thäth' rä-äl', a city in south central Spain, is the capital of Ciudad Real province, in the historic region of New Castile. It was designated "Villa Real" by its founder, King Alfonso X of Castile, in the 13th century and raised to the status of city (Spanish, *ciudad*) by King John II of Castile in 1420. Once famed for its leathercraft, Ciudad Real is now mainly an agricultural center.

The province of Ciudad Real is typical meseta (high plateau country), rising in the south toward the Sierra Morena range. A particularly desolate region known as La Mancha—made famous in Cervantes' novel *Don Quixote*—stretches through much of the province.

Despite its climate—characterized by little rain, hot summers, and cold winters—Ciudad Real is one of the leading provinces in Spain in the production of grapes and of wheat and other grains. Olives are grown in several places. Much livestock, especially sheep, is raised, but it is necessary to move the flocks between winter and summer pastures. Almadén, in the west, supplies much of the world's mercury. Puertollano, in the south, is a growing city with coal deposits, a smelting works, and an iron foundry. In the heathlike regions of the province, birds are trapped to be sold as pets, and lavender, thyme, rosemary, and other plants are cultivated; their flowers also support beekeeping. Population: (1970) of the city, 41,708; of the province, 507,650.

M. M. LASLEY, *University of Florida*

CIUDAD TRUJILLO. See SANTO DOMINGO.

CIVET, siv'ət, any of about 30 species of small to medium-sized carnivores in the family Viverridae, which also includes the mongooses. The name civet, or civet cat, is applied in particular to those species that are hunted or raised for the musk—also known as civet—secreted by the civet's anal glands.

Civets vary greatly in appearance, from the weasel-shaped linsangs to the shaggy binturong, but most are about the size of a domestic cat and have a long foxlike snout. The head-and-body length ranges from 16 inches (400 mm) in the fanaloka or Malagasy civet (*Fossa*) to 38 inches (965 mm) in the binturong of Southeast Asia. In most species the tails are about as long as the head and body.

African palm civet (*Nandinia binotata*)

The civets are basically predatory and carnivorous, but most also eat carrion as well as fruit and other vegetable matter. Most are good climbers, and some even have retractile claws like the cats. Two species, the water civet (*Osbornictis*) of the Congo and the otter civet (*Cynogale*) of Southeast Asia, are partially aquatic.

At or near the anus in all civets are large scent glands that secrete the musk civet into a pouch. Civet is prized as an ingredient in perfume, and in the Orient it is believed to have medicinal properties. Civets have been widely hunted for their musk, and in some parts of Africa they have even been caged and "milked" periodically. The chief source of commercial civet is the African civet (*Viverra civetta* or *Civettictis civetta*).

The civets—including the binturong, the genets, and the linsangs—make up the subfamilies Viverrinae, Paradoxurinae, and Hemigalinae. These subfamilies, together with the mongooses (subfamily Herpestinae), make up the family Viverridae, order Carnivora.

CIVICS AND CIVICS TEACHING. See CITIZENSHIP EDUCATION.

CIVIL AERONAUTICS ADMINISTRATION (CAA),
a former government bureau concerned with the regulation and development of civil aviation in the United States. Originally part of the Civil Aeronautics Authority (established 1938), the Civil Aeronautics Administration became a bureau in the Department of Commerce under a reorganization of 1940, which also created the Civil Aeronautics Board as a separate agency. By the Federal Aviation Act of 1958, the CAA was absorbed into the new Federal Aviation Agency.

During its existence, the CAA enforced safety regulations, operated air traffic control services and navigational aids, encouraged the development of a national system of airports, and allocated navigable airspace over the United States and its territories. It also fostered air commerce abroad through technical assistance to foreign governments.

CIVIL AERONAUTICS BOARD, an independent
federal agency charged with the economic regulation and promotion of commercial air transportation within, as well as to and from, the United States. The CAB's activities include the regulation of tariffs, public rates and fares, and mail rates; of agreements and interlocking relationships among air carriers and between carriers and other aeronautical enterprises; and of air carrier accounting and periodic reporting of finances and operation. Its jurisdiction also extends to awards of operating authority, government subsidy of carriers, and enforcement of applicable laws and regulations. The promotional aspects of the CAB are of considerable importance, as is its work in encouraging competition to the extent necessary to assure the sound development of air transportation.

In the late 1960's the CAB's authority extended to 55 air carriers operating under certificates of public convenience and necessity. Of these, 11 were domestic trunkline carriers, including several with international routes; 2 U. S. flag carriers operating only international and territorial routes; 13 local service carriers providing air service to the medium-sized and smaller cities and connecting to the major communities of interest; 13 supplemental air carriers, or charter specialists; 2 all-cargo carriers; 2 Hawaiian carriers; 7 intra-Alaskan carriers; 2 carriers in the Caribbean; and 3 helicopter operators.

The CAB is an outgrowth of the Civil Aeronautics Authority, established in 1938 to develop and promote air transportation in the United States. Under a reorganization two years later the authority was renamed the Civil Aeronautics Board; the Civil Aeronautics Administration was transferred to the Department of Commerce; and the Air Safety Board's functions were assumed by the CAB. The Federal Aviation Act of 1958 transferred the board's safety regulatory powers to the new Federal Aviation Agency, but the CAB was continued as the investigator of civil aircraft accidents. However, on April 1, 1967, the Bureau of Safety, which was the accident investigation arm of the CAB, became part of the new Department of Transportation that was activated on that date.

The board is made up of five members (no more than three from the same political party) appointed by the president of the United States for 6-year terms. The president designates a chairman and a vice chairman from among the board membership each year. Except for presidential approval required for board decisions involving foreign air operations, the CAB functions independently of any other arm of the executive branch.

CHARLES S. MURPHY
Chairman, Civil Aeronautics Board

CIVIL AIR PATROL (CAP), a federal chartered,
nonprofit corporation, whose mission is to further the aeronautics and space position of the United States through an aerospace education and training program. Formed in 1941 to enlist volunteer civilian airmen for wartime tasks, the organization was transferred to the War Department in 1943 and established as a civilian auxiliary of the U. S. Air Force (USAF) in 1948. It is governed by a national board of senior officers, including the national commander, an Air Force general officer who supervises USAF-CAP liaison activities. A national headquarters at Maxwell Air Force Base (Montgomery, Ala.), 8 regional offices, 52 wings (one in each state, the District of Columbia, and Puerto Rico), and small community-level units constitute the 2,300 organizations of the CAP. In the late 1960's more than half the 80,000 male and female members were cadets (minimum membership age is 13).

CAP's aerospace education program provides academic instruction and textbooks for cadets, sponsors more than 200 college workshops annually for teachers, and holds training sessions for adults. Among the cadet activities are an international exchange program with about 25 countries; orientation courses in jet aircraft, space missiles, and air traffic management; and flying encampments in gliders and powered aircraft. The emergency services program includes the operation of 4,700 light aircraft, 4,000 vehicles, and a 16,600-station radio network in air search and rescue operations. It also carries out civil defense missions. The Office of Information publishes the monthly CAP *Times* and various public service materials. The CAP works closely with the Federal Aviation Administration and the Red Cross.

BRIG. GEN. WILLIAM W. WILCOX, USAF
National Commander, Civil Air Patrol

CIVIL DEFENSE is the system that provides passive defense for the civilian population and for private and public property against strategic or tactical military operations carried out by an enemy. The purpose of civil defense (CD), in the strict sense, is the protection of noncombatant civilian populations and noncombatant property. It is clear that in total war the civilian population and civilian resources are as likely to become military targets as any military installation or unit.

The emphasis in civil defense is on passive defense measures. Civil defense personnel in Western nations maintain law and order among the affected population, provide shelter and food, conduct and assist in rescue operations, offer first aid, and generally take part in welfare-oriented aspects of civil government during the periods of crisis and recovery. It is primarily oriented toward protecting the population against the effects of nuclear weapons delivered by long-range missiles and aircraft.

Civil defense organizations in totalitarian nations, however, often take on a paramilitary aspect. In these areas, civil defense measures provide protection against conventional explosives, delivered by aircraft and by naval gunfire.

Development of Civil Defense. The idea of providing the population with passive defensive measures can be traced to the Bronze Age and the beginning of fortified towns. The massive medieval castles owed their size in part to the requirement that the fighting nobility shelter civilians against external threats.

Historically the militia, craft and trade guilds, and religious institutions performed civil defense functions. Now volunteer fire companies, citizens' welfare committees, civil air patrol, scout organizations, rescue squads, ham radio networks, and neighborhood civic associations all perform functions related to those of civil defense organizations.

Civil defense as a standing organization on the national level, however, did not arise until World War I and the advent of relatively long-range aerial bombing and long-range artillery. German attacks on Britain with bomber aircraft and dirigibles underlined the need for efforts to protect noncombatants and handle the nonmilitary aspects of defense. But it was not until World War II that civil defense came into its own as aerial bombardment assumed a major role.

U. S. civil defense in World War II was patterned after the British model but was neither as well organized nor as well trained, although many able people devoted much time and effort to the program. Civil defense personnel in U. S. coastal regions enforced blackout restrictions. The lights of coastal towns and cities, if not extinguished, would have provided an excellent background against which U-boat skippers could see U. S. and Allied ships in silhouette.

The development of atomic and nuclear weapons and the means to deliver them (intercontinental-range aircraft and, subsequently, intercontinental missiles) after World War II totally changed the nature of warfare and the entire world geopolitical situation. No nation could regard itself as immune from attack, nor could any civilian population expect to be spared the devastating effects of nuclear weapons. With the onset of the cold war, it became clear to most of the world powers that the protection of the civilian population and nonmilitary property and resources had become a major responsibility of national defense establishments.

The program of the early 1960's to encourage homeowners to build fallout shelters or develop shelter areas in their homes received little response. Further, a credible civil defense effort needs more than shelters, but many towns have no CD organization, and most have only a minimal one. Evaluation of radiation hazards is a key part of CD work, yet there are very few radiation-rate meters and dosimeters available, and even fewer people who know how to read and interpret them. However, civil defense is supervised by the Department of Defense, and hence most civil defense functions in time of war would probably be carried out by the military.

Steps in Event of Attack. The civil defense picture is by no means static: advances in weaponry and political developments change the situation continually. In view of the changing nature of the threat, it is impossible to set forth rules for action during an attack. However, a few steps may be noted. One must keep in mind that these rules may have to be revised in light of new developments and that the rules apply only in the case of nuclear attack.

One should first determine the location of shelter facilities in his neighborhood, place of business, and other areas where significant time is spent. The status of shelter supplies and equipments in these areas should then be determined. Plans for reaching the shelter areas should also be established.

Warning of a nuclear attack may come through the mass media or by CD sirens. In any event, time between warning and attack may be brief, so it is best to proceed to any specially constructed shelter that is available or to any heavily built structure, preferably below ground level, or in areas without windows. Even extensive, highly complex warning systems, such as those employed by the United States, are not totally effective against a surprise attack. The first warning of this will be the blinding flash of the weapon detonation, followed by a shock wave of highly compressed air and debris moving out from the point of detonation at about the speed of sound. Upon sensing the flash, one should take cover on the spot and remain there until the shock wave passes. Taking cover will protect one against flying debris hurled by the impact of the shock front. After the shock front has passed, one should get to a shelter.

Following the detonation there will be a period of about 10 minutes or more before radioactive fallout begins to return to earth. During this period one should seal up openings to the outside (through which nuclear radiation may enter the shelter space) and gather in water supplies and food. All available clean receptacles should be filled with water, and bottled beverages and canned juices should be collected. As soon as fallout begins (in the form of coarse sandlike grains, visible on clean, light-colored surfaces in daytime or in a flashlight beam at night) all persons should take shelter, taking care to brush off all fallout particles.

During the shelter stay, occupants should organize and share the necessary tasks. The decision to leave the shelter is a difficult one. If radiation measurement devices are available and qualified personnel present, the risk involved in leaving the shelter can be gauged. If not, one should remain as long as supplies permit.

CIVIL DISOBEDIENCE is a strategy of non-violent resistance to governments or laws deemed to be unjust or discriminatory. Narrowly construed, the term denotes mere refusal to obey the commands of government and thus is almost synonymous with passive resistance. In a broader sense it includes gratuitous acts undertaken in defiance of laws for the purpose of rendering them ineffective.

Scattered instances of passive resistance were recorded in pre-Christian eras. For example, slaves in the ancient world on occasion lay down on the ground and accepted beatings rather than perform such work as building pyramids or palaces. Individual action or nonaction of this sort was usually without direction and ineffective.

The idea of civil disobedience, on the other hand, is a creation of religious and philosophical thought and derives, at least remotely, from the teachings of Jesus. It implies an organized effort to achieve a well-defined goal. Although individual acts of disobedience may have a dramatic impact, massive civil disobedience is more likely to have practical consequences.

THEORETICAL BACKGROUND

Civil disobedience has been used in preference to other forms of resistance both on moral and on practical grounds. Its advocates have generally argued that it is both right and effective.

Religious Teachings. In some ways the teachings of Jesus, and the church he founded, were grounded in passive resistance and constituted a campaign of civil disobedience. In the Sermon on the Mount, Jesus radically revised the militant doctrine of traditional Judaism. "Ye have heard that it hath been said, 'An eye for an eye, and a tooth for a tooth': but I say unto you, Resist not evil: but whosoever shall smite thee on thy right cheek, turn to him the other also" (Matthew 5:38-39). Following this precept, the early Christians passively resisted the power both of the unconverted Jews and of Rome itself. The tradition of individual martyrdom, initiated by Jesus, was advanced by some of the most articulate of the Church Fathers, while wholesale martyrdom occurred when Christians were thrown into the arena to be torn to pieces by wild animals. The belief that there are two realms of experience, a here and a hereafter, a natural and a supernatural, was so dramatically fostered by the teachings and life of Jesus himself and by the conduct of his disciples that passive resistance to punishment, quiet refusal to obey imperious commands, and meek acceptance of discriminatory regulations became the conventions of early Christianity.

The pacific tradition has never died out in the Christian community. On the contrary, it has become the basis of the Quaker refusal to bear arms and of the reform tendencies of other groups. In the 20th century, pacifism, as well as passive resistance in peacetime, has been characteristic of Quaker action in public affairs. While the American Friends Service Committee, the voluntary relief organization of American Quakers, does not as an organization preach disobedience, it does encourage emphasis on the sacredness of the individual and the superiority of the ways of peace to such an extent that it often clashes with the forces of government, both in the United States and abroad.

Nevertheless, the Christian churches have not normally rested their moral plea on the pacifism derived from the Sermon on the Mount. Jesus himself was not at all times a pacifist. He threw the moneychangers out of the temple, and thereby sanctified a militant tradition that has not only paralleled but more often superseded the pacific. It is an essential paradox of Christianity that both the Crusades, among the most savage wars in history, and the "battles" of Martin Luther King's nonviolent Southern Christian Leadership Conference were fought in the same God's name.

The great religions of the East parallel the Christian experience. While Hinduism and Buddhism have tended to inculcate the tradition of nonviolence that prepared the way for the political campaigns of Gandhi, Islam has tended toward militancy in asserting what it holds to be true. At bottom the degree of pacifism found in a given religion depends on the priority assigned to the individual soul, without qualification, as against the assertion of the divine dispensation of a particular body of doctrine. If the principal tenet to be defended is that each human being is in some sense divine, it will follow that to take life is an evil and that neither individual violence nor war may be condoned. Civil action against presumed injustice must, therefore, be pacific. Alternatively, if the tenet to be defended is that believers in a particular body of doctrine, followers of a particular prophet, are charged with a divine mission to propagate that doctrine anywhere and everywhere, lest the forces of evil triumph over good, it may follow that militant and violent means are appropriate and that individual human life is less sacred than the destiny of a people and its revelation. Thus the Moslem cry of "Jehad" (holy war) is at the opposite religious extreme from the Buddhist retreat into the monastery or Christian nonviolent resistance.

Nonreligious Theories. Passive resistance and civil disobedience have been justified also in nonreligious, philosophical terms by many individual thinkers and by certain groups and movements. At the height of the dispute over slavery that preceded the American Civil War, Ralph Waldo Emerson and Henry David Thoreau advocated, on philosophical grounds, disobeying the laws and governing bodies that condoned or supported slavery. Agitating in 1850 against the newly enacted Fugitive Slave Act, which among other things enjoined citizens to assist in capturing escaped slaves, Emerson told his audiences, "The law is suicidal, and cannot be obeyed . . . he who writes a crime into the statute-book digs under the foundations of the Capitol to plant there a powder-magazine, and lays a train." The key word is "suicidal." Emerson believed that all men, regardless of race or color, are fundamentally equal by nature, and that a society that attempts to legislate inequality and discrimination commits suicide by self-contradiction. Daniel Webster, the immediate object of Emerson's attack, had invoked the Constitution to justify a compromise calculated to preserve the Union, but Emerson and other abolitionists agreed with William H. Seward that "there is a higher law than the Constitution"—the natural law of human dignity and equality.

At a different level of political action, civil disobedience was a favored tactic of anarchists. The Russian anarchist Prince Pyotr Kropotkin, following the lead of Jean Jacques Rousseau, argued that human beings are naturally good but corrupted by governments. He believed that refusal to obey government would eventually force it to disintegrate, leaving men free to live in the peace and benevolence that he presumed to be their natural state. A similar doctrine was taught by Count Leo Tolstoy, who proposed a form of Christian anarchism whose principle tenet was refusal to cooperate in the organized violence of governments. But the world anarchist movement that flourished from the later 19th century until after World War I was seldom pacific. Experience proved that anarchism inevitably conflicted with established authority, and in that event the anarchists generally fought back.

In general, the proponents of civil disobedience maintain that refusal to obey unjust laws or autocratic officials poses an insoluble problem for government just to the extent that a civil disobedience campaign enlists great numbers of people. On a small scale such a campaign may be crushed by the arrest of the disobedient, but when very great numbers are involved, arrest becomes impractical. Ultimately, they believe, the only solution will be for the government to revise or repeal the offending laws or for the offending officials to resign. In addition, they maintain, nonviolence is preferable to violence because it places the moral burden on the upholders of the law.

CIVIL DISOBEDIENCE IN PRACTICE

Civil disobedience has its best chance to succeed when the authorities being resisted respect established law and individual rights under it.

Failures. In modern totalitarian societies, as in ancient authoritarian societies, the tactics of civil disobedience have never been truly successful. The army or the police of a dictatorial regime enforces the decrees of the regime without hesitation, because the status of the enforcing officials depends on the regime, not on the established law. Thus in Rome not only Christians but other disobedient or nonconfessing sectarians were put to death so systematically that mass campaigns could not be organized.

Peasant resistance to Stalin's agricultural program in the Soviet Union during the early 1930's was more effective but failed in the end, and the cost in human lives has been variously estimated at from 5 to 10 million. Organization of the disaffected farmers under the prevailing Soviet dictatorship was impossible; and because their forces were never concentrated and they never succeeded in penetrating the bureaucracy or the army, they became ineffective victims of the tyranny.

Gandhi and Indian Independence. On the other hand, during the same period Indian leaders, inspired by Gandhi's dedication, were able to organize immense demonstrations against British rule. Thousands of demonstrators, gathered in one place, would lie in the street or across a railroad track, daring the police to arrest them. British respect for law and due process made countermeasures exceedingly difficult. Commonly the British response was to arrest the leaders while the masses gradually dispersed. But once jailed, such men as Gandhi and Jawaharlal Nehru, the charismatic leader of the revolutionary Congress party, quickly assumed an even more effective image in the public eye. On several occasions Gandhi, himself inspired by the writings of Thoreau, undertook fasts until the British yielded at least to some degree on issues posed by the tension between their rule and Indian claims to independence. Gandhi's death, in fact, seemed more dangerous to authorities than the living man.

Civil disobedience may not have been the decisive factor in the success of the Indian revolution, but its force, as a means both of educating the Indian masses to understand the issue and of directing action against the British, was certainly a major contributing element.

Disobedience and Negro Equality in the United States. In the United States, civil disobedience was only a sporadic and sometimes quixotic gesture in the struggle against slavery. But without doubt the refusal of some Northerners to obey the fugitive slave laws contributed to the ultimately intolerable irritation of Southerners and dramatized throughout the country the degradation occasioned by slavery and the courage of fugitive slaves, who were protected by the disobedience campaigns. The Underground Railroad, the institution built by Northern peaceful resisters against slavery, became a persuasive symbol of the abolitionists' cause.

A century later perhaps the most clearly successful campaigns of civil disobedience were mounted in the cities of the southern United States. The "sit-ins" at segregated restaurants, libraries, transportation terminals, and other public facilities, and the "freedom rides" of integrated groups on interstate buses were well organized and well publicized. Their purpose—to make certain discriminatory regulations impossible to enforce—was accomplished by posing the threat of an endless stream of court cases and by appealing to the sympathies of fair-minded men throughout the country. The campaigns followed in the wake of the Supreme Court's decision in *Brown* v. *Board of Education* (1954), in which public school segregation was finally ruled to be in conflict with the nation's constitutional doctrine of equal rights. Thereafter, one by one, the discriminatory practices in Southern states were tested in the courts and found to be in violation of the Constitution. By court orders and by a series of civil rights acts (passed by Congress in 1957, 1960, 1964, and 1965), the goals of the disobedience revolution were consolidated.

It was a bitter and sometimes violent struggle. State and local authorities often sought to end acts of disobedience by mass arrests, and beatings by police were common. Private citizens, working singly and in organized groups, sought to terrorize the demonstrators by bomb scares, actual bombings, murders, and lynchings, as well as by threats of economic or other reprisal. But as the arrested demonstrators provided the necessary cases on which the courts could act, not only the judicial process but the political process came to the support of the civil rights movement. By the late 1960's, equal rights for Negro Americans had been mostly secured in the courts, and the movement increasingly turned toward converting those rights into equal opportunities.

STUART GERRY BROWN, *University of Hawaii*

Bibliography

Henry David Thoreau's essay *Civil Disobedience* (published as *Resistance to Civil Government* in 1849) is the classic statement of the doctrine. Also of great importance for their relation to massive organized civil disobedience in the 20th century are Mohandas K. Gandhi's *Non-Violent Resistance* (*Satyagraha*, 1935) and Jawaharlal Nehru's *Toward Freedom* (1940).

King, Martin Luther, Jr., *Stride Toward Freedom: The Montgomery Story* (New York 1958).

Lynd, Staughton, ed., *Nonviolence in America: A Documentary History* (Indianapolis 1965).

Miller, William R., *Nonviolence: A Christian Interpretation* (New York 1964).

CIVIL ENGINEERING is one of the most diverse branches of engineering. The civil engineer plans, designs, constructs, and maintains a large variety of structures and facilities for public, commercial, and industrial use. These structures include residential, office, and factory buildings; highways, railroads, airports, tunnels, bridges, harbors, channels, and pipelines. They also include many other facilities that are a part of the transportation systems of most countries, as well as sewage and waste disposal systems that add to our convenience and safeguard our health.

The term "civil engineer" did not come into use until about 1750, when John Smeaton, the builder of the famous Eddystone lighthouse near Plymouth, England, is said to have begun calling himself a "civil engineer," to distinguish himself from the military engineers of his time. However, the profession of civil engineering is actually as old as civilization.

HISTORY

Engineering in ancient civilizations included the construction of bridges, highways, canals, tunnels, irrigation and drainage systems, water supplies, docks, and harbors. Some of the best-known works of early engineers and architects are the Great Pyramid in Egypt (3000 B. C.); King Solomon's Temple in Jerusalem (about 1000 B. C.); the Parthenon in Greece (432 B. C.); the Colosseum in Rome (80 A. D.); and Roman bridges, aqueducts and roads.

Babylonia and Assyria. There is evidence that the Babylonians and Assyrians struggled with problems of hydraulic engineering involving dams, levees, and canals. They solved problems concerning the sides of right triangles, and they also solved simple algebraic equations. They computed areas of land, volumes of masonry, and cubic contents of excavation necessary for canals. The first organized road building was done in the Assyrian Empire, and the first bridge of technical importance was constructed over the Euphrates River in the 6th century B. C.

Egypt. In ancient Egypt the simplest mechanical principles and devices were used to construct many temples and pyramids that are still standing, including the Great Pyramid at Giza and the temple of Amon-Ra at Karnak. The Great Pyramid, 481 feet (146.6 meters) high, is made of 2.25 million stone blocks having an average weight of more than 1.5 tons (1.4 metric tons). Great numbers of men were used in the construction of such monuments. The Egyptians also made obelisks by cutting huge blocks of stone, some weighing as much as 1,000 tons (900 metric tons). Cutting tools of hard bronze were used.

The Egyptians built causeways and roads for transporting stone from the quarries to the Nile. The large blocks of stone that were erected by the Egyptians were moved by using levers, inclined planes, rollers, and sledges.

Greece. The Egyptians were primarily interested in the know-how of construction; they had very little interest in the theory of the why-for of use. In contrast, the Greeks made great strides in introducing theory into engineering problems during the 6th to the 3d centuries B. C. They developed an abstract knowledge of lines, angles, surfaces, and solids rather than referring to specific objects. The geometric base for Greek building construction included figures such as the square, rectangle, and triangle.

The Greek *architekton* was usually the designer, as well as the builder, of architectural and engineering masterpieces. He was an architect and engineer. Craftsmen, masons, and sculptors worked under his supervision. In the classical period of Greece all important buildings were built of limestone or marble; the Parthenon, for example, was built of marble.

Rome. In its heyday in the 2d century A. D., Rome ruled the world from Scotland to Persia. As the Romans conquered other nations, they borrowed their captives' ideas and practices, and the engineers of Rome are therefore considered developers rather than originators. The Greek influence is especially noticeable. However, the Roman arch construction employing a central keystone at the top indicates that Roman engineers were familiar with masonry under compression, although they had no written or formal knowledge about equilibrium of forces.

The work of the Roman *architectus*, or technical expert, included the design and construction of bridges, aqueducts, highways, and buildings for public use. Under the Romans the art of road building reached its highest level until modern times. Besides the Via Appia, major roads built in Italy include the Via Flaminia, the Via Aurelia, and the Via Aemilia. The Romans also built tunnels for roadways, aqueducts, and stone arch bridges that are still standing, and harbors, docks, and lighthouses. See also AQUEDUCT —*History* (Roman Aqueducts); BRIDGES—*History* (Roman Bridges).

Medieval and Renaissance Europe. Bridges, cathedrals, and castles were outstanding among the engineering works built during medieval times. For the most part, bridge building continued in the Roman tradition, using stone arches. Bénezet built the famous Pont St.-Bénezet at Avignon on the Rhône River during the period 1178–1188, and the Old London Bridge was built across the Thames in 1209. During the Renaissance, which began in the 15th century, there was little civil engineering because of the lack of demand for public works.

France. The demands for public works, such as bridges, canals, roads, and water supplies, gradually became very great in Europe, particularly in France and England, as strong nations with centralized governments developed during the 17th and 18th centuries. The transition of the military engineer to civilian pursuits to satisfy these demands brought the engineer, and particularly the civil engineer, great opportunities. During this period, France was the leader in the development of engineering.

Early civil engineers, as a general rule, had very little formal education. The earliest formal training program for civil engineers was that offered by the École des Ponts et Chaussées to prepare men to serve in the Corps des Ponts et Chaussées, formed in 1716 for the scientific advancement of bridge building and road building.

Britain. After the Napoleonic Wars, engineering leadership developed in Britain. The first engineering technical society, the Institution of Civil Engineers, was established in Britain in 1818, but it was not incorporated by royal charter until 1828.

Civil engineering and architecture became identified as separate professions in about the middle of the 19th century. The architect was recognized for the emphasis he placed on aesthetic aspects of design, while the civil engineer was developing more rationalized, scientific designs. Tradition, intuition, and appearance, which controlled the work of the architect, were of secondary consideration to the engineer.

United States. The age of engineering in the United States is considered to have begun with the founding of the American Society of Civil Engineers in 1852. It was the time of the opening of the West, and there was tremendous activity in surveying new regions, developing water power, and building railroads and canals. Also, the discovery of rich mineral deposits caused mining to become an important activity.

Many of the early engineering opportunities in the United States were for civil engineers. The success of the Erie Canal (completed in 1825) inspired the construction of many other canals in the eastern part of the country. After a brief heyday, canals were largely displaced by railroads, starting with the completion of the Baltimore and Ohio Railroad in 1830.

The building of railroads employed the major portion of the trained civil engineers in the 19th century. However, it was not long until the demands of urban communities in need of water supplies, sanitation, and improved roads and streets required much of the attention of civil engineers. Consulting firms of civil engineers were organized to design municipal facilities throughout the fast-developing country.

Schools. The first American engineering school was at the United States Military Academy at West Point, established in 1802 as the headquarters of the engineering corps of the Army. It remained a school entirely for the training of Army engineers until 1866.

A tremendous growth in the number of schools offering engineering courses came after the Civil War with the opening of the West and the expansion of U. S. industry and business. The Morrill Act of 1862 established the land-grant principle, and many land-grant colleges and universities developed programs in agriculture and mechanics arts. The mechanics arts of that day have become the engineering of today. Civil engineering was usually the first branch of engineering to be set up because it was still the only recognized engineering program in the United States.

American Society of Civil Engineers. The counterpart of Britain's Institution of Civil Engineers in the United States is the American Society of Civil Engineers (ASCE), the country's first engineering technical society. It was founded on Nov. 5, 1852, with James Laurie as its first president. It was organized by civil engineers who felt the need for an exchange of "the benefits of their experience and studies."

MODERN CIVIL ENGINEERING

Like other branches of engineering, civil engineering is ". . . a profession in which a knowledge of the mathematical and natural sciences gained by study, experience and practice is applied with judgment to develop ways to utilize economically, the materials and forces of nature for the benefit of mankind" (from the 1962 definition adopted by the Engineers' Council for Professional Development).

The present-day civil engineer is involved in the exploration of space, the use of thermonuclear energy, the building of ballistic missile facilities, and the control of air and water pollution—the development of materials and systems for ac-

complishing things that seemed quite remote even a decade ago. He will always be needed for the earlier occupations of building bridges, roads, canals, aqueducts, dams, airports, and water distribution systems. Better ways will be developed for accomplishing the old tasks, while new problems of greater complexity will continue to arise to challenge him.

Branches. The technical activities of the civil engineer are varied and overlap the ASCE's technical divisions, which are used to classify areas of civil engineering in the United States. The divisions are air transport, construction, engineering mechanics, highway, hydraulics, irrigation and drainage, pipeline, power, structural, surveying and mapping, urban planning and development, and waterways and harbors.

The enrollments in these technical divisions show that the principal interest of the members of the ASCE is in some phase of building. The activities of all of the technical divisions involve construction, even if that is not their major role. Building remains the basic job of civil engineers.

Education. The bachelor of science degree in civil engineering in the United States normally requires four years of study beyond high school graduation, although there are a few schools that have gone to a 5-year curriculum. Recognition has been given to the need for more advanced technical and scientific training, along with a broader education that contains a reasonable amount of social-humanistic content. A 4-year B. S. degree in civil engineering, with four years of appropriate engineering experience, will qualify a young person to apply for registration as a professional engineer.

Licensing. Civil engineers have played a prominent part in protecting the public from the practice of incompetently trained engineers. In the United States, civil engineers also played a leading role in the passage of the first state licensing provision for registering professional engineers in Wyoming in 1907. All states now have such laws; Puerto Rico, the Panama Canal Zone, and the District of Columbia also have licensing provisions. In 1920, the state boards of registration for professional engineers formed an organization called the National Council of State Boards of Engineering Examiners. In 1967, that name was shortened to the National Council of Engineering Examiners.

GEORGE F. BRANIGAN
University of Arkansas

Bibliography

Abbott, R. W., *American Civil Engineering Practice* (Wiley 1956–1957).
Beakley, George C., and Leach, H. W., *Engineering—An Introduction to a Creative Profession* (Macmillan, N. Y., 1967).
Bucksch, H., *Dictionary of Civil Engineering and Construction Machinery Equipment* (Adler 1968).
Finch, James K., *The Story of Engineering* (Doubleday 1960).
Hammond, Rolt, *A Career in Civil Engineering* (Sportshelf and Soccer Assoc. 1966).
Johnson, Lee H., *Engineering: Principles and Problems* (McGraw-Hill 1960).
Kemper, John D., *The Engineer and His Profession* (Holt Rinehart & Winston 1967).
Kirby, Richard, and others, *Engineering in History* (McGraw-Hill 1956).
Merritt, Frederick S., *Standard Handbook for Civil Engineers* (McGraw-Hill 1968).
Sandstrom, G. E., *Man the Builder* (McGraw-Hill 1970).
Smith, Ralph J., *Engineering as a Career* (McGraw-Hill 1956).
Urquhart, Leonard C., *Civil Engineering Handbook* (McGraw-Hill 1959).
Williams, Clement C., and Farber, E. A., *Building an Engineering Career* (McGraw-Hill 1957).

CIVIL LAW. The legal systems of the contemporary Western world are usually divided into two groups—the *common law* and the *civil law*. The common law, developed originally in England, forms the general basis for the legal order of the United States. The civil law emerged on the European continent and is in effect today in such countries as France, Germany, and Italy.

The two great legal systems have spread far beyond their original homes, carried both by colonizing efforts and by the West's economic and political power. Today the legal systems of Latin America, of parts of Africa, and of much of Asia are considered to be within—or strongly influenced by—the civil law tradition. In North America, the law of Louisiana is still significantly affected by French law, and the legal system of Quebec continues in large areas of private law the system that it received from France.

As a description of the law in force in the modern world, the civil law-common law classification is incomplete. Some legal systems, such as the Scandinavian, do not fit readily into either category. Furthermore, with the emergence of Communist states in eastern Europe the civil law systems of those countries underwent profound changes. Nonetheless, if the need for appropriate qualification is kept in mind, an understanding of the general characteristics of the civil law system can serve as an introduction to the legal orders of many contemporary societies.

In comparisons of the civil law and the common law, two points of difference are usually emphasized. First, in the civil law systems large areas of private law are codified. Codification —the systematic and comprehensive statement of the rules and principles that form the starting point for legal reasoning and for the administration of justice—is not typical of the common law. Second, the civil law was strongly influenced by Roman law in many ways. In the common law, the Roman influence was less striking and in no way pervasive. However, such points of difference must not obscure the extent to which the civil law and the common law share a common tradition. Both systems were developments within western European culture; they hold many values in common. Both are products of Western civilization.

Roman Law. To understand why continental European countries share a common legal heritage in the civil law, and to grasp the meaning of that heritage, one must consider the history of the civil law, with its roots in Roman law.

Over its long history, Roman law was brought to a high level of juristic development. The Romans, with their genius for institution and their practical sense, achieved excellent solutions for practical problems and combined these solutions into a remarkable body of law. This law, reflecting the relatively high development of Roman political, economic, and social life, met the requirements of a culturally and economically advanced society. However, the Roman juristic tradition and the corpus of Roman law did not pass immediately and full blown to the societies of western Europe.

When the German tribes shattered the Western Roman Empire and the last of the line of imperial rulers in the West was deposed in 476, western Europe disintegrated. Those highly effective organs of social control, the Roman courts and administrators, were replaced by relatively weak and imperfect institutions. In large areas of human activity, there had ceased to be government under rules of law maintained by centralized authority. In addition, the rise of Islam in the 7th century destroyed western Europe's commercial structure by closing the Mediterranean to trade. With the consequent collapse of urban life, western Europe slipped back into a localized, agrarian society.

The legal and political order that had been appropriate for Rome's highly developed commercial civilization could not survive Rome's political and economic collapse. The relatively sophisticated Roman law was hardly needed in the rural society, based on an estate economy without markets, that emerged. However, Roman law was not entirely lost nor forgotten during this period. In memory, or as familiar custom, elements of Roman law persisted. The church preserved in its law and culture much of Roman civilization. The system of personal law prevailing in the German kingdoms subjected the Roman element of the population to Roman law, though this law became obscure and vulgarized. See also ROMAN LAW.

Corpus Juris Civilis. The most important single event for the subsequent history of Roman law in western Europe—the event that made it possible for the Roman law to have a strong and pervasive effect upon the development of the modern civil law—occurred, oddly, after the fall of the Western Roman Empire. The empire continued in the East with its seat in Constantinople, and it was there, in 528, that Emperor Justinian decreed the great compilation, systematization, and consolidation of Roman law later known as the *Corpus Juris Civilis*.

The *Corpus Juris* comprises the Institutes, the Digest, the Code (a collection of imperial enactments), and the Novels (a collection of later imperial enactments). The Institutes, the Digest, and the Code were promulgated in 533 and 534. The Novels, containing imperial legislation enacted after the Code was issued, were never officially collected.

The Digest, also known as the Pandects—a poorly arranged compilation of extracts from the writings of the great Roman jurists, especially those of the classical period—came to be the most important part of the *Corpus Juris* for the subsequent history of the civil law. The extracts from the classical jurists consist of comments on the solution of actual or hypothetical cases, with reasons stated tersely. As the Digest was to state the law of Justinian's time, the original texts were appropriately revised by a committee of 16, under the Roman jurist Tribonian (died about 545). Another part of the *Corpus Juris* that later acquired considerable influence was a short systematic treatise, the Institutes, intended for the use of law students.

Introduction in Western Europe. The *Corpus Juris* was first brought to western Europe in 544, when the Eastern Empire reconquered Italy, but for more than 500 years the *Corpus Juris* was hardly known in the West. Its pervasive influence on Western law began with the 12th century "revival" of the study of Roman law at Italian universities. With this revival the specific history of the civil law system begins.

It was probably the Italian lawyer Irnerius who gave, at Bologna in the 12th century, the first lectures on the Digest. These lectures mark the discovery of the great compilation of Roman law and begin the development of legal science on the basis of that body of material. Irnerius' lectures came at a time when profound political and economic changes were already under way in western Europe. The Mediterranean trade routes had been reopened, and commerce was expanding along both the Mediterranean coast and the northern coasts of western Europe. Towns were becoming commercial centers and a money economy was emerging.

A new law was needed for the new conditions of economic and social life. The creation on the Continent of this new law—and of its corollary, a new legal science—was a long, complex process that forms a part of the general history of the economic, political, and intellectual development of western Europe. The new law was woven from many strands—the customs of merchants, canon law, the revived Roman law, and, at a later stage, natural law philosophies. Various professions contributed to its elaboration—practitioners, judges, administrators, scholars, men of affairs, churchmen, and philosophers.

Evolution of Contract Law. The revived Roman law was not completely foreign to 12th and 13th century Europe, but rather a part of a shared and not entirely forgotten past. Nevertheless, the civil law as it developed came to have many ingredients not found in the *Corpus Juris Civilis*. For example, the modern law of obligations—tort and contract law—bears very little resemblance to the comparable areas of law found in the Institutes and the Digest. But the development of the law of contractual obligations in the civil law illustrates one form of the influence of Roman law on the various national laws that gradually emerged in continental Europe.

In its beginnings, the law of contracts on the continent of Europe was unsuited to the commercial and industrial societies that emerged. The formless, entirely unperformed agreement, so necessary for developed trade and commerce, was not enforced. The slowly reviving economic life of the Continent had to flow, as a trading economy began to develop, within the legal framework of the formal contract and of the half-executed transaction, that is, an agreement fully performed on one side.

The new law of contracts began its growth not on the basis of Roman law but through the practices of merchants. These practices early developed into a *jus mercatorum* (mercantile law) administered by courts of merchants. At first, politically organized society did not endorse these practices and courts, and their effectiveness derived mainly from group pressures and understandings. Later, particularly as the towns obtained judicial autonomy, becoming islands of independent jurisdiction outside the territorial custom, the law merchant was officially sanctioned.

Mercantile practice, which prevailed over divergent customary law, developed informal and flexible transactions appropriate for active commercial life. And the merchant courts provided expeditious procedures and prompt justice administered by men who were themselves merchants and thus aware of mercantile problems.

By the 12th and 13th centuries, speculative and systematic thought—and with it Roman law materials—played a role of growing importance in developing the new law of contracts. From these beginnings may be traced the general characteristics of the theory of formation of contract and of the approach to formal requirements found today in such civil codes as those of France, Germany, and Italy.

The most sustained and important theoretical and systematic influence upon the development of contract law in Europe from the 12th century on was the study of Justinian's *Corpus Juris Civilis*. Thus, when the church supported as a moral precept the proposition that a simple, formless promise should be binding (*pacta sunt servanda*), the canonists wrote that even the "nude pact," a Roman law concept covering certain unenforceable agreements, should be enforced, at least by penitential discipline. In the development of the canonists' thinking the notion of *causa*, which had played such a limited role in Roman law, came to be used as a new *vestimentum* (garment). A continuity was thus maintained with Romanist teaching by fitting the canonist doctrine of *pacta sunt servanda* into the framework of the *pacta vestita* (clothed pact); also, a substitute was provided for formal requirements by ensuring, through the requirement of a cause, that a serious intent to assume a legal obligation had existed.

A good part of the history of contract in the civil law is the history of how the Roman law's limitation on the number of recognized types of enforceable, purely consensual transactions was overcome. This was the result in part of misunderstanding and in part of a conscious effort to shape a system more responsive to commercial needs and practices. In large measure, the pressure came from the practical requirements of commerce. The speculative thought of churchmen and, later, of natural law philosophers also was important. Roman law influenced these developments not only by providing the starting point but also through the legal thinking and legal science that had gradually grown up around the study of the *Corpus Juris*. To explain the form this latter influence took, one must consider the Roman influence upon the general patterns of thought of the civil law system.

Legal Science in Transition. Between 1100 and 1500 the Roman law became the basis for legal science in continental Europe. By the end of the 12th century, students from the Italian universities were carrying the new learning throughout western Europe. The study of the revived Roman law was carried on by three schools. The first in point of time—the Glossators—expounded the individual texts of the *Corpus Juris*. They were succeeded in the second half of the 13th century by the Commentators, who went beyond glosses on individual texts to systematic comments on legal problems. They did not ignore the law that was currently in effect but achieved a synthesis with it, thereby contributing to the introduction into practice of various specific rules and solutions contained in the *Corpus Juris*. The third school was called the Humanists, whose beginnings were in Italy in the 15th century. The Humanists brought a historical sense to the study of Roman law, undertaking to reconstruct the classical Roman law from the amended passages contained in the Digest. Theory and practice became increasingly separated because of the direction taken by legal scholarship and the high degree of learning required. In consequence, the universities became further removed from the practice of law than they had been when the Glossators and the Commentators were the dominant schools.

This separation of theory from practice probably operated to encourage systematic and speculative thinking about law. In addition, the *Corpus Juris* provided a body of material for study and explanation that was, particularly in the earlier centuries, in advance of contemporary social and economic requirements in many respects. At all events, by the 16th century speculative and systematic thinking developed out of the limited contractual types of Roman law a general theory of contract grounded upon agreement. By the end of the 18th century the specifically Roman elements had, by and large, disappeared from the general law of contracts. The enforceability of formless contracts was generally recognized, and most legal writers supported the proposition that arrangements entirely unperformed on both sides were actionable regardless of whether they fell within a contractual type known to the *Corpus Juris*.

In the field of contracts—as in other branches of the law—the crucial Roman influence on the modern civil law thus derived from the habits of thought, analysis, and presentation that were developed by university study of Roman law rather than from the specifics of that law. Men could transact more freely in terms of their needs and desires. In this way the intellectual ground was prepared in the field of contracts—and in the law generally—for the great codifications of the 19th century.

It is harder to generalize about the contributions of Roman law to modern civil law at the level of specific rules and solutions. The degree of Roman influence differed in the various fields of law and in the various parts of the Continent. In France, Roman influence was greater in the southern part of the country (the *pays de droit écrit*, land of the written law) than in the north (the *pays de coûtumes*, land of customary law). In Germany, a decree of Maximilian I in 1495 formally "received" the *Corpus Juris*, glossed by Italian scholars, as part of the law to be applied in the newly organized imperial court of justice, the Reichskammergericht. Roman law, thereby, did not become a general law. Particularism was recognized in the maxim that "Town's law breaks land's law, land's law breaks common law." The example of the Reichskammergericht was soon followed by the high courts of the various German principalities, states, and towns, but the law administered in the German courts was never fully romanized.

A fact of crucial importance to the modern civil law—one that reinforced the systematic and speculative tendencies that arose in legal thinking in the universities—was the failure of continental European countries until modern times to develop a law common to the emerging political and economic units. Germany and Italy did not achieve internal political unity until late in the 19th century. Even France, which had achieved political unity relatively early, was unable to develop a unified body of private law applied nationwide. Jean Portalis, writing of the French scene on the eve of the promulgation of the Civil Code in 1804, described the consequences of this failure to achieve legal unity: "What a spectacle opened before our eyes! Facing us was only a confused and shapeless mass of foreign and French laws, of general and particular customs, of abrogated and non-abrogated ordinances, of contradictory regulations and conflicting decisions; one encountered nothing but a mysterious labyrinth and, at every moment, the guiding thread escaped us. We were always on the point of getting lost in an immense chaos."

Codification. Continental European countries thus faced in relatively recent times the problem of establishing legal unity. With a desire to achieve results quickly and with a legal tradition that emphasized systematic analysis and statement of legal rule and principle, these countries naturally had recourse to codification. The resulting codes contain relatively complete and systematic statements—often at a fairly high level of generality—for the chief areas of law.

Five French codes were prepared at the beginning of the 19th century: the Civil Code (*Code Napoléon*, effective 1804), the Commercial Code (1808), the Code of Civil Procedure (1807), the Criminal Code (1811), and the Code of Criminal Procedure (1811). See also FRANCE—8. *Law.*

The French pattern was followed by other countries. Germany, for example, has the same five basic codes, the most important and influential being the Civil Code (Bürgerliches Gesetzbuch), effective in 1900. Italy follows the same pattern, except that it does not have a separate commercial code.

Although the continental European countries share a common legal tradition, there are many differences in their contemporary legal systems. For example, the German Civil Code is organized quite differently from the French Civil Code, being much more "scientific" in style and arrangement and aspiring to a comprehensive thoroughness to which the French Civil Code lays no claim. Switzerland, in its codifications—principally the Civil Code (1907) and the Code of Obligations (effective 1912)—has sought to take advantage of both French and German experience in respect to codification technique.

Although efforts have been made, especially in France, to draft new civil codes, neither France nor Germany has replaced its original code as Italy did in 1942. And considering the age of the French and German civil codes and the degree and depth of social and economic change since their original enactment, remarkably few changes have been made by legislation.

Decisional Law. In many areas, however, very significant change has been brought about through judicial decision. This form of change is interesting. First, it contradicts the premise on which the civil law systems, especially the German, originally sought to operate—that the courts were simply to apply the law, lawmaking being strictly reserved for the legislature. Secondly, the increasing importance of decisional law has rendered the law less systematic and ordered than it was originally conceived to be. Finally, the emergence of decisional law in the civil law systems demonstrates the importance in all systems of this technique—of developing and adapting the law—so familiar to the world of common law.

An interesting and extreme example of decisional law is offered by the interpretation given to a few words contained in Article 1384 of the French Civil Code: "A person is liable ... for the damage ... caused by the act ... of things that he has under his guard." Until the end of the 19th century this language had no independent significance; rather, it was regarded as introductory to certain rules imposing liability contained in articles 1384 and 1385. The general principle that regulated actions to recover damages for personal injuries was the one that is familiar in the common law—that is, the plaintiff must establish that the defendant willfully or negligently caused the damage. However, in a series of decisions beginning in 1896 by the highest French court for civil matters, what amounts to a rule of strict liability was applied, first to industrial accident cases (later covered by special legislation) and then to litigation arising out of automobile accidents. By 1927 the principle was clearly established that a plaintiff could recover for personal injuries by showing that these had been caused by an object—for example, an automobile—under the defendant's ultimate direction and control. By a law passed in 1909, Germany had introduced substantially the same rule for automobile accidents, except that recovery was limited by a statutory schedule.

Private Law Areas. In private law fields the continental European countries generally reach results that are close to those found in the common law, although the rules and principles that produce and explain the result are often very different from those of the common law. Civil law systems do not have arrangements comparable to the trust, though some of the purposes served by that institution can be achieved in other ways. Traditionally, these systems have restricted a person's freedom of testation (the right to bequeath property) more sharply than does the common law, by providing forced shares for the members of the deceased's immediate family. Some form of joint or community property typically obtains between husband and wife unless another arrangement is provided in the marriage contract. Finally, it can be noted that some civil law countries, such as Italy, do not permit divorce.

Procedure. Both the substantive law and procedural rules are on a national basis in the major civil law countries of continental Europe. West Germany has some federal elements in the structure of its judiciary, as all except the highest courts are state courts. However, Germany has a single judicial hierarchy as distinguished from the separate and often parallel system of state and federal courts that exists in the United States.

Civil law systems do not use a jury except for certain criminal matters. Civil litigation is handled either by a single judge or, in more important litigation, by a panel (usually three judges). The direction and control of the proceeding tends to be in the hands of the judge, who typically does most of the questioning of witnesses. In part because of the absence of a jury, relatively few exclusionary rules of evidence have been developed; the court takes evidence offered, so long as it is neither irrelevant nor simply cumulative, and gives it the weight that it deserves in reason. This avoids the problems that arise in the common law from exclusion of hearsay testimony.

Expert witnesses tend to be appointees of the court and so may present their views in a more impartial fashion than do the experts who, in usual American practice, are selected and paid by one of the parties. Fees for litigation are typically fixed by law or schedule and are regularly assessed against the losing party. Many civil law countries have well-developed systems of legal aid for those unable to afford counsel.

Two levels of review are usually provided. At the first level, the entire case can be redone, including the rehearing of testimony and the taking of new testimony. The second level of review is limited to questions of law, rather strictly defined.

The Two Systems Compared. In many respects the civil and common law systems are closer today in their general methods and approaches than they were in earlier periods. On the one hand, the common law has become far more systematic and speculative in its approach, due in large measure to the influence and efforts of academic legal scholarship. On the other, the systematic quality of a code inevitably decreases with the passage of time as decisional law comes to play a significant role.

Each system has thus come in recent decades to an appreciation of the other's traditional strength. The common law has grown to understand the economy of effort and the values of intellectual order that flow from an effort to state legal rules in a systematic, fairly generalized form. The civil law has increasingly perceived the virtue of testing, refining, and developing rules and principles in the light of precise fact situations.

Important differences in intellectual style still remain. These are reflected in legal writing and in legal education. Writers on the civil law tend to produce treatises; in the common law, effort is generally concentrated on less ambitious monographs. Continental legal education proceeds essentially by a lecture system designed to give a comprehensive description of existing rules and institutions. Common law legal education—at least in its American form—uses a discussion, or "case," method designed to explore the importance of policy and factual considerations in the decision-taking process. The Continental approach thus emphasizes structure and system while the American stresses the difficulties and unresolved problems in the law, sometimes at the expense of system and intellectual order.

Finally, to a greater degree than in other legal systems, civil and common law alike, the American lawyer seeks to anticipate possible legal difficulties and to devise arrangements that avoid potential legal, economic, and human hazards from which future disputes could grow.

ARTHUR VON MEHREN
Harvard University Law School

Bibliography

Association of American Law Schools, *A General Survey of Events, Sources, Persons and Movements in Continental Legal History*, Vol. 1, Continental Legal History Series (Boston 1912).
Buckland, William W., and McNair, Arnold D., *Roman Law and Common Law*, 2d ed., rev. by Frederick H. Lawson (New York 1952).
Cappelletti, Mauro, and others, *The Italian Legal System* (Stanford, Calif., 1967).
David, René, and de Vries, H. P., *The French Legal System* (Dobbs Ferry, N. Y., 1958).
Dawson, John P., *Unjust Enrichment: A Comparative Analysis* (Boston 1951).
Lawson, Frederick H., *A Common Lawyer Looks at the Civil Law* (Ann Arbor, Mich., 1955).
Lawson, Frederick H., *Negligence in the Civil Law* (London and New York 1950).
Schwartz, Bernard, ed., *The Code Napoleon and the Common-Law World* (New York 1956).
von Mehren, Arthur, *The Civil Law System: Cases and Materials for the Comparative Study of Law* (Boston 1957).
von Mehren, Arthur, ed., *Law in Japan: The Legal Order in a Changing Society* (Cambridge, Mass., 1963).
Yiannopoulos, Athanassios, ed., *Civil Law in the Modern World* (Baton Rouge, La., 1965).

A. DEVANEY

CIVIL RIGHTS AND LIBERTIES

CIVIL RIGHTS AND LIBERTIES. The terms "civil liberties" and "civil rights" have no fixed and uniform definition. Often they are used broadly and interchangeably. One way of distinguishing the two phrases is to say that a person enjoys a civil "liberty" when he is protected against some government action, but enjoys a civil "right" when the law confers upon him a positive power to do something. Thus the right to speak freely would be a civil liberty; the right to use public facilities on an equal basis would be a civil right.

In common usage "civil rights" often refers specifically to the rights of minority groups to equal treatment, and sometimes the phrase is used to mean nonpolitical rights granted by law, such as the right to own property. However the line is drawn between them, civil liberties and civil rights taken together encompass freedom of speech and religion, the rights afforded to criminal suspects, the rights of citizens to participate in the political process, and the right to equal treatment under law. Civil rights, in certain contexts, may also be meant to include basic economic and social rights.

Civil liberties and civil rights are considered a cornerstone of a free society. They indicate the ways in which a society protects individual freedom. But "freedom" also has many meanings. The word may be used to mean the absence of external restraint. In that sense, poor persons in the United States as well as rich ones are free to travel to Europe. A second meaning of freedom requires that a person have the opportunity to do something before he can be considered free to do it. In that sense, only those who can pay are free to go to Europe. A third sense of freedom is the freedom to do what is right. Some thinkers have reasoned that a man is genuinely free only when he believes what is true and does what is morally correct. They argue that the freedom to believe error and to do wrong is not true freedom. A fourth use of freedom refers to the absence of psychological problems that inhibit individual action.

The first two of these senses of freedom are associated with the relationship of individuals to government in a liberal democratic society, and they are the only senses in which the term will be discussed here. In a libertarian society preventing the dissemination of error and reducing immoral acts to a minimum are not considered central functions of government. Nor is eliminating, or reducing, psychological tensions—an end that might be accomplished best by a sharp limitation on freedom in the ordinary senses.

Although freedom—and the liberties and rights that protect it—is an important good, it may conflict with other goods. The speaker's freedom is maximized if he is allowed to incite a riot, but the peace of society may require restraint. In many circumstances different kinds of freedom conflict, as in the clash between a store owner's claim to serve whom he pleases and the claim of a member of a racial minority to equal treatment. Another example is the taxation of the rich for the benefit of the poor; the freedom of the rich to spend their money in the way they choose is restrained, but the freedom of the poor, in the sense of broader opportunity, is enhanced.

The civil liberties and rights granted by the law of any particular society reflect how that society has accommodated the inevitable clashes of values. While most discussion, and this article, focuses on how that adjustment is made by law, private institutions also play an important role in determining the practical bounds of individual freedom. If, for example, major private companies discharged employees who expressed unpopular opinions, many persons would hesitate to exercise their legal privilege to speak freely. More subtle influences, such as possible rejection by friends and acquaintances, also constrain uninhibited discussion.

THEORY AND HISTORY

The kinds of civil liberties and rights enjoyed in the United States and other democracies are the product of an essentially modern view of the nature of man and society. It is by no means the only modern view. Dictatorships, for example, whether Fascist or Communist, rest on other conceptions.

Liberal Democratic View. The liberal democrat believes that every man has inherent worth. Fulfillment of the individual may include participation not only in political and social life but also in religious, artistic, intellectual, and other activities that should not be subject to control by government. Individuals should have the chance to work out their own destiny, insofar as that is possible and consistent with the interests of others.

Because truth and justice in political and social affairs are difficult to ascertain, they are generally best arrived at by free and open discussion. Unrestrained discussion is not only a legitimate outlet for dissent, but it reduces the likelihood of more violent forms of social protest. Because government officers are sometimes arbitrary, and because the majority of the people may disregard claims of individual liberty in times of crisis or supposed crisis, the claims of individual

768

liberty should be protected either by legal rules that bind the legislature and executive, as in the United States, or by historical traditions that restrain those in power, as in Britain.

Each man's interests are entitled to equal consideration. Some libertarians believe that the government should only avoid promoting inequality; others contend that the government should reduce inequalities, at least to the extent of positively trying to provide opportunities for those who are disadvantaged.

In the United States and to a lesser extent in western Europe there is considerable agreement on the tenets of freedom, but there is sharp dispute over their philosophic underpinnings, their meaning and application to particular problems, and the weight they should be given as compared with other social interests, such as the preservation of society from outside attack.

Historical Antecedents—Athenian Democracy. Although the civil liberties and rights of liberal democracies reflect a distinctly modern conception of man, important elements of that conception have been drawn from earlier periods, and members of older societies had rights and liberties that resembled in varying degrees those of the present. In Athens and other Greek city-states ordinary citizens participated in the processes of government. In fact, given ancient Athens' small size and population (probably somewhat more than 300,000 people), direct participation could be, and was, much more extensive than in the modern nation-state. In Athens all male citizens were entitled to attend the Assembly, which held the ultimate power to govern. Magistrates and officials who ruled as representatives of the people were selected by democratic means, had short terms, and could not be reelected. These election procedures and the large popular juries of the courts assured wide citizen involvement in governing. Although most of the important political powers rested with the Council of Five Hundred, the council was subject to control by the Assembly.

The democratic ideal of the city-state—that the government's good is inseparable from the citizens' and that both goods can be assured best by citizen participation—seems to liberal democrats a great advance from the autocratic forms of government existing outside Athens. But from the perspective of today the democracy of Athens appears flawed in important respects. About one third of the population were slaves with virtually no rights at all. Furthermore, because Athens had no procedure for conferring citizenship on foreigners who had moved there or on their offspring, another considerable group of residents had no political voice.

Finally, the city-state was founded on the idea that fulfillment as a human being and fulfillment as a citizen are identical. In his *Funeral Oration*, which nobly summed up the ideals of Athenian democracy, Pericles said, "We . . . regard a man who takes no interest in public affairs, not as a harmless, but as a useless character. . . ." The notion that individuals might realize their potential in essentially private concerns, commercial, artistic, or religious, outside the concern of government, was alien to the city-state philosophy. Both Plato and Aristotle adhered to the Athenian conception of the social nature of man and the organic nature of society, in which all human concerns are closely interrelated.

Roman Law. At periods in its history, Rome had democratic institutions, and Roman law reflected the idea of private right to a greater extent than the city-states' did, but perhaps its most important contribution to the modern conception of individual rights was its recognition of the unity of the human race. The bases of Roman citizenship were broadened and by the Edict of Caracalla (212 A. D.) became worldwide.

The development of Roman institutions, particularly its law, was influenced by the theory of natural law, which originated with the Greek Stoics and was expounded by Cicero. According to this theory, the world is governed by a universal law of nature. In the light of this law, all men are equal. Human beings are obligated to obey this law, and legislation that contravenes it is morally wrong. By emphasizing the moral responsibility of rulers and the subjection of their acts to the judgment of a higher law, natural law doctrine provided at least a theoretical limitation on the powers of governors.

Christian Idealism. Christianity, in its early stages, had little effect on political principles. Although its basic doctrine asserts a radical equality of all men, because God loves the poor and weak as much as the rich and powerful, neither Jesus nor the early church leaders tried to apply this principle to political goals.

Christians did, however, claim for their religion a paramountcy over earthly concerns that was quite different from the civic-oriented or mystical religions of the Greeks and Romans. The Christians' claim did not lead immediately to tolerance of religious diversity by the church, but it did conflict with the Greek idea that civic activity is the highest form of human fulfillment.

During the medieval period a synthesis of Christian doctrine and natural law was achieved. On a theoretical level rulers were subject to the moral limits imposed by natural law and the responsibility of the church for man's spiritual side. Practically, both the power of the church and the essentially contractual obligations of the feudal system prevented a monopoly of the exercise of secular power.

The Magna Carta of 1215, a landmark in the development of English liberties, was primarily the result of efforts of nobles to stop encroachments by the crown. Nonetheless, it contained the guarantee that free men could be condemned only by the lawful judgment of their peers or by the law of the land. The idea it reflects of orderly procedures and judgments that are not arbitrary is fundamental to any system of rights and liberties, because rights that are unsure are little better than no rights at all.

Humanism and Natural Rights. The Renaissance and the Protestant Reformation both emphasized human individuality. Although the original reformers were no more tolerant of what they thought was heresy than the Roman Catholic Church was, the rapid development of religious pluralism in the 16th and 17th centuries demanded greater toleration in the interest of preserving the social order. In 1598, for example, after fratricidal wars between Protestants and Catholics, Henry IV of France issued the Edict of Nantes, which guaranteed unrestricted liberty of conscience, though not of worship, to the Protestant Huguenots.

One of the first Protestant sects to approve religious toleration as a desirable principle of government was the Independent, or Congregationalist, element of the English Puritans of the mid-17th century. Roger Williams, the Puritan founder of Rhode Island, took one of the most libertarian positions and established the first government based on general toleration.

English rights in the 17th century were expanded by both the Petition of Right (1628) and the Bill of Rights (1689). Writing in defense of the Glorious Revolution (1688), John Locke elaborated a theory of government that greatly influenced the development of civic rights in England and the United States.

Locke argued that natural law bestowed on men in the state of nature certain basic and indefeasible rights. The formation of society, he said, could be viewed as a social contract in which some rights are given up so that fundamental rights may be protected. The existence of natural rights and the limited grant of power to government given by the social contract restricted, in Locke's view, the extent to which individual rights may be infringed. If a government oversteps these bounds, resistance is justified.

Somewhat similar principles were developed by thinkers of the 18th century French Enlightenment, and the Declaration of Independence of the United States drew from both these sources. Written by Thomas Jefferson, it declared ". . . that all men are created equal, that they are endowed by their Creator with certain unalienable Rights; that among these are Life, Liberty, and the pursuit of Happiness. . . ." The same philosophy is expressed in the Declaration of the Rights of Man and of the Citizen (1789), issued by the National Assembly of France at the outset of the French Revolution.

The theory of natural rights is still widely accepted in the United States as the basis for civil liberties and rights, but probably not by most American social philosophers. They tend to rely on the more utilitarian argument that individual fulfillment is best promoted by restricting the powers of government. John Stuart Mill made the best-known defense of freedom of speech on these grounds in his book *On Liberty*, published in 1859.

CIVIL LIBERTIES AND RIGHTS IN THE UNITED STATES

The basic charter of civil liberties and rights in the United States is the Constitution of the United States. As adopted in 1789, it contained important safeguards of liberty, such as prohibitions against ex post facto laws and bills of attainder and a guarantee of the right of habeas corpus (see HABEAS CORPUS). But the most significant protections were added in 1791 by the Bill of Rights, the first 10 Amendments to the Constitution. The Bill of Rights originally bound only the federal government, but most of the states adopted similar guarantees.

Originally the Constitution of the United States recognized slavery. The Emancipation Proclamation of 1863 declared all slaves within areas of rebellion free, but only ratification of the 13th Amendment in 1865 made slavery unconstitutional. The 14th Amendment, ratified three years later, was designed primarily to guarantee the rights of freed slaves. It provides that no state shall "deprive any person of life, liberty, or property, without due process of law; nor deny to any person within its jurisdiction the equal protection of the laws." The 15th Amendment, ratified in 1870, was passed to protect the right of Negroes to vote. In 1920 the 19th Amendment, prohibiting voting discrimination against women, was ratified.

Constitutional provisions concerning individual rights and liberties are supplemented by federal and state statutes, but except in the area of racial discrimination these laws do not significantly add to the basic constitutional scheme. This scheme has been developed from the words of the Constitution itself by judicial decision. In the United States, but not in some other liberal democratic countries, the written Constitution is legally binding on the legislature, and a court will invalidate an improper legislative act if that act comes before it in a case. Because the words of the Constitution are short and simple, the courts, and particularly the Supreme Court of the United States, must decide how they apply to a variety of circumstances, and the body of constitutional law that has grown up is to be found by examining Supreme Court cases.

Freedom of Speech and of the Press. Probably the most fundamental liberty in libertarian democracies is freedom of speech. The framers of the Bill of Rights, concerned by the periodic suppression of dissent in 17th century England, prohibited Congress in the 1st Amendment from "abridging the freedom of speech, or of the press; or the right of the people peaceably to assemble, and to petition the Government for a redress of grievances."

The language of the amendment clearly does not protect every verbal expression. Words that are the essence of ordinary crimes for example, such as the words used in offering a bribe or inciting a riot, can be punished. Furthermore, even protected expression may be regulated without "abridging" the freedom provided for in the amendment. Speeches in the middle of Main Street during rush hour may be prevented in the interest of effective traffic control.

First Amendment Guarantees. The Supreme Court decisions on freedom of expression deal with two basic inquiries: What kinds of expression can be prohibited altogether because of their content? And, what interferences are permissible with expression whose content is protected? In *Gitlow* v. *New York* (1925), the court assumed that freedom of speech and of the press "are among the fundamental personal rights and liberties protected by the Fourteenth Amendment from impairment by the States." Since that time, jurists have taken for granted that whatever restrictions the 1st Amendment placed on the federal government are also applicable to the states of the Union.

A central problem for the court in dealing with freedom of speech is the extent to which society can prohibit expressions that threaten social harm because they advocate illegal acts. In *Schenck* v. *United States* (1919), Justice Oliver Wendell Holmes formulated the "clear and present danger" test to deal with a conspiracy to obstruct the draft. Under this test, speech can be punished only if it creates a clear and present danger that it will bring about a substantive evil that the government has a responsibility to prevent. If the evil is not imminent or its likelihood is slight, the state may not act.

In some subsequent cases the court declined to follow Holmes' standard, but most justices have accepted it. The test does not, however, give simple answers to difficult cases, because judges will disagree about the likelihood and imminence of particular dangers and will also disagree over how likely and imminent they must be before they are "clear and present."

In *Dennis* v. *United States* (1951), a case involving leaders of the Communist party convicted under the Smith Act (1940), the test was revised to allow suppression of advocacy of illegal action when the danger is very serious, in that case a revolution, even if it is not imminent. Four justices concurred in a plurality opinion that the courts "must ask whether the gravity of the 'evil,' discounted by its improbability, justifies such invasion of free speech as is necessary to avoid the danger." This revision, severely criticized for giving insufficient protection to speech, probably will be considered applicable, if at all, in the future only in cases involving major subversive movements.

The clear and present danger test has also been employed in cases in which the press publishes appeals that are designed to influence judges or juries or may have that effect. This is an area in which important liberties come into conflict. The right of the press to publish facts and opinion, which is from another perspective the right of the public to be informed, must be weighed against the right of litigants, particularly criminal defendants, to an impartial hearing. In the opinion of many jurists Lee Harvey Oswald could not have received a fair trial had he lived to stand trial for the assassination of President John F. Kennedy. Nevertheless, the question arises whether the preservation of that possibility was more important than giving the public the fullest available information about the assassination of the President, an event of grave concern to the entire country.

Although the Supreme Court has overturned convictions in which extensive and lurid pretrial publicity made a fair trial doubtful, it has not determined clearly to what extent such publicity can be curbed by statutes or judicial rules that do not conflict with the 1st Amendment.

Obscenity Rulings. For many years, it was assumed that suppression of obscenity did not violate the 1st Amendment. It is still true that obscenity itself is not protected, but in *Roth* v. *Alberts* (1957), the Supreme Court decided that whether material is obscene is itself a constitutional question. The justices have differed over the proper standard, but the prevailing view is that to be obscene a work must appeal predominantly to a prurient interest, be patently offensive, and utterly without redeeming social importance. Almost everything that is not "hard-core pornography" is protected under one of these three standards, and works of authors like Henry Miller and Edmund Wilson that were once banned in many states now enjoy constitutional protection.

Although states may take special precautions to prevent objectionable material from reaching young people, they may not ban material altogether for that reason. If the 1st Amendment is considered primarily as a means of assuring free and open discussion of important public issues, one can argue that artistic and literary works are outside the core of its concern, but the court's decisions in the obscenity area indicate that the amendment protects free expression concerning all subjects of human interest.

Libel Rulings. Another area to which the Supreme Court has extended the amendment is the common law of libel. In *New York Times Co.* v. *Sullivan* (1964), it rejected the traditional position that false and defamatory matter enjoys no protection. The court recognized that heavy judgments for libel might be imposed by unsympathetic jurors on newspapers that publish controversial matter. In the Alabama case before it a judgment of $500,000 in damages had been rendered against the New York *Times* for its publication and distribution of an advertisement by civil rights leaders that contained inaccuracies. The court held that when material is published relating to the official conduct of a public officer damages cannot be recovered unless the publication is made with "'actual malice'—that is, with knowledge that it was false or with reckless disregard of whether it was false or not. . . ." This rule was extended in *Associated Press* v. *Walker* (1967) to cover discussion of public figures as well as officials.

One of the more troublesome problems in the free speech area is posed by group libel laws, which deal with defamatory statements made about whole classes of persons, usually racial or religious groups, rather than individuals. Sweeping denunciations of whites, Negroes, Catholics, Protestants, or Jews do little to further intelligent social discourse and they may create or intensify social hostilities. They may, when directed against disadvantaged groups, interfere with the achievement of equal rights granted by the Constitution or by statute. Yet to permit punishment of the purveyors of racial and religious hatred is to inhibit free expression, and socially beneficial speech may be interfered with in the process. Moreover, the terms used in such laws are necessarily vague, and may be abused by those who wish to silence unpopular positions. In *Beauharnais* v. *Illinois* (1952), the Supreme Court, by a 5 to 4 margin, sustained a conviction under a "group libel" law.

Limitation of Prior Restraint. Of the various methods for curtailing unprotected speech, prior restraints are among the most severely condemned. Authorities have argued that the 1st Amendment was primarily intended to prohibit prior restraints, the traditional form of censorship. The absence of previous restraint is what William Blackstone meant by liberty of the press.

The usual prior restraint is a system in which all works are submitted to an executive official who decides whether they may be published. By placing the burden on the citizen to come forward with his work and by preventing the censored material from reaching the public, such a system is much more likely to discourage protected expression than penalties that operate after publication. States have not attempted to impose this sort of censorship on the press, and the cases with which the Supreme Court has dealt have generally involved more limited prior restraints.

The exception to the general rule is the regulation of moving pictures. Because the impact of even one movie showing is great, and because the considerable time between production and premiere makes submission to a "censor" feasible, the court has refused to hold that all prior review of the content of movies is forbidden. It has clearly stated, however, that movies are a form of communication to which the 1st Amendment applies, and it has laid down rigorous guidelines that must be met before a scheme of review will be upheld.

Speech whose content is protected may not be protected in all forms and at all times. In exceptional circumstances the police may silence a speaker whose words incense his audience to the point of violence, although ordinarily they must shield the speaker and prevent the outbreak of violence by means other than stopping the speech. If policemen were allowed to halt any speaker who angered his listeners, the result would be a sharp limitation on the expression of unpopular views.

More commonly, difficulties arise over government attempts to regulate the time and manner of speech. Carefully drawn regulations to prevent interference with traffic or with the peace and quiet of residents are constitutional. Thus a city may regulate the times and places at which massive demonstrations will be permitted or forbid the use of sound trucks making loud and raucous noises. But it may not adopt limitations on speech or press that are too comprehensive. Ordinances prohibiting the distribution of all handbills and circulars have been held to be unconstitutional, for their interference with expression is regarded as much too high a price to pay for the limited social gain of reducing littering.

Similarly, any system for regulating the times and places of demonstrations or parades must set out clear criteria for officials and not leave unfettered discretion to municipal authorities. If officials could refuse applications on any grounds they choose, they could use their power to promote speech they agree with and prevent speech they disagree with.

Picketing as a form of communication poses a special problem. Though it is expression in the ordinary sense, it is often something more. It may be a signal to other union members to act in a particular way simply because a picket line has been formed. The Supreme Court has held that picketing is an activity covered by the 1st Amendment and has invalidated a complete ban on picketing, but it has allowed Congress and the state legislatures flexibility in deciding what kinds of picketing conflict with public interests.

Curtailment of Indirect Interference. Sometimes the threat to freedom of speech takes the form not of outright prohibition or regulation but of indirect interference. One form of interference is the legislative investigation. The legitimate scope of such investigation is very broad, and in the course of an inquiry a witness may be asked about his political activities and organizational membership. The 5th Amendment privilege against self-incrimination protects a witness from having to make incriminating statements, but often the danger to him is public ridicule and possible loss of employment, rather than criminal prosecution.

The court has stated that exposure for its own sake is not a legitimate legislative purpose, but establishing in court the existence of such a purpose is difficult. In a series of decisions the court has held that the authority of the committee must be clear, that questions must be pertinent, and that the witness must be clearly informed of the purpose of the investigation. In *Gibson* v. *Florida Legislative Investigation Committee* (1963), a case involving the refusal of the president of the Miami branch of the National Association for the Advancement of Colored People to turn over the local organization's membership list to committees of the Florida legislature investigating subversive activities, the court reversed his conviction. It declared, "it is an essential prerequisite to the validity of an investigation which intrudes into the area of constitutionally

protected rights ... that the State convincingly show a substantial relation between the information sought and a subject of overriding and compelling state interest."

Another form of indirect interference is denial of public employment to persons of particular political persuasions or those who refuse to sign loyalty oaths. The court has been compelled to work out an accommodation between the government's need to assure that its employees are devoted to public service and the chilling effect on expression and association of tests of loyalty. In recent years it has greatly circumscribed the permissible use of loyalty oaths.

Right to Remain Silent. As this discussion has suggested, the right of free speech includes the right to remain silent about one's beliefs if one chooses. In *West Virginia Board of Education* v. *Barnette* (1943), the court held that a child could not be compelled to salute the flag if doing so was against his conscience and that of his parents. Another aspect of the 1st Amendment, also implied above, is the right to associate freely for legitimate purposes.

Freedom of Religion and Separation of Church and State. The beginning of the 1st Amendment reads: "Congress shall make no law respecting an establishment of religion, or prohibiting the free exercise thereof...." The amendment was supported both by those who believed in freedom of religion and church-state separation in principle and by those who simply wished to leave these matters to the states. A number of states still had established churches at the time of the Constitution's adoption.

Not until 1940 did the Supreme Court hold the free exercise guarantee applicable against the states. In part, this was because relevant cases rarely arose. Most states have their own guarantees, and the idea that people should be free to worship or not in any way they choose is so generally accepted in this country that it is unlikely to be disregarded.

However, certain problems occur when the claim to free exercise takes the form of activity thought to be antisocial or self-destructive, such as polygamy, snake-handling, the use of illicit drugs, or the refusal to be vaccinated or accept a blood transfusion. Passing on antipolygamy laws, the Supreme Court held, in *Reynolds* v. *United States* (1878), that such laws were supported by a valid secular interest and were constitutional. The same theory has been used in cases involving vaccination.

A different approach was used by the California supreme court when it considered the use of peyote by Navaho Indians in religious ceremonies. It weighed the secular interest in stopping the use of peyote against the importance of the use for religious purposes and held in favor of the users.

Sunday closing laws do not prohibit the free exercise of religion by those who observe the sabbath on Saturday, but they do interfere with worship indirectly. The court has upheld these laws on the ground that a uniform day of rest is desirable. It has also held, however, that unemployment benefits may not be denied to someone who refuses to take employment that requires him to work on Saturday when his reasons for refusal are religious.

In regard to draft exemptions Congress has gone farther than the Constitution requires and exempted from combatant military service those who conscientiously oppose participation in war because of their religious training and beliefs. Religious belief, for this purpose, is defined as a belief in a relation to a Supreme Being. No exemption is given to those who are opposed to particular wars, even when their reasons are religious, or to those who are opposed to all wars for nonreligious reasons. The Supreme Court has interpreted "Supreme Being" so broadly, however, that it is hard to conceive of anyone who is opposed to all war who is not "religious" for this purpose.

The guarantees of free exercise of organized religious worship and of freedom of speech assure that the public assertion of diverse religious beliefs will enjoy the same protection as private worship. The requirement that there be no establishment of religion complements the free exercise guarantee. If the government favors one denomination or sect, the free exercise of members of the others may be impaired.

At some points, however, the two guarantees may seem to conflict. For example, if religious conscientious objectors are exempted from military service, is that a discrimination against nonreligious objectors and therefore an establishment of religion? If army chaplains of major denominations are provided by the government, is that an establishment of those denominations?

Although the 1st Amendment originally left states free to establish churches if they chose, the Supreme Court unanimously held in 1947, in *Everson* v. *Board of Education,* that the "no establishment" clause was made applicable to the states by the 14th Amendment. Relying heavily on the authority of Thomas Jefferson and James Madison, it declared that the clause was intended to do more than forbid an established church and that it means at least:

"Neither a state nor the Federal Government can set up a church. Neither can pass laws which aid one religion, aid all religions, or prefer one religion over another. . . . No tax in any amount, large or small, can be levied to support any religious activities or institutions.

". . . [T]he clause against establishment of religion by law was intended to erect 'a wall of separation between church and State.'"

Despite this broad language, the court sustained the payment of public funds for the bus transportation of children to parochial schools, on the theory that busing was part of a general program to help parents get their children to school. Since the Everson case, debate has been sharp, in Congress and the state legislatures as well as in public discussion, over the breadth of the holding and the extent to which parochial institutions may benefit from the use of public funds for educational or other purposes. The Federal Elementary and Secondary Education Act of 1965 provided various types of aids to parochial and other private schools. (A threshold difficulty that must be met by parties in establishment clause cases is the requirement that a litigant must show some direct injury to himself resulting from the challenged practice.)

In accord with the principles of Everson, the court has since invalidated religious instruction, Bible reading, and prayers in the public schools. Each of these decisions has met with considerable popular protest by persons who believe that limited forms of state encouragement of religion are desirable. Although Everson forecloses direct financial aid for religious purposes, churches are in virtually every state exempt from property taxes, and private religious contributions are generally tax deductible. These and other practices, such as the provision of chaplains in the armed forces and in jails, have been justified as a permissible accommodation to religious exercise.

Rights of Criminal Suspects. The Bill of Rights contains a number of guarantees for persons suspected of, or tried for, crimes. The necessity for fair and orderly procedures for ascertaining criminal guilt was recognized long before freedom of speech and religion in the modern sense were even conceived, much less put into practice. Most of the protections in the Bill of Rights were drawn out of the English common law, although in some instances they go beyond it.

Every society must balance the need for efficient apprehension and conviction of criminals against the need to protect citizens from arbitrary intrusions by the government. The protections in the Bill of Rights are designed to prevent undue interference with individual privacy and to minimize the possibility of unfair treatment of criminal suspects. For some time the court held that its specific guarantees applied only to federal government procedures, the states being bound only to meet standards "implicit in a concept of ordered liberty." During the 1960's, however, the court held most of the important provisions of the Bill of Rights applicable to state procedures.

Fourth Amendment Guarantees. The 4th Amendment forbids unreasonable searches and seizures. It is interpreted to mean that the police may ordinarily search a person or his property only if they have a search warrant or if the search is pursuant to a valid arrest. A warrant may be issued only if there is probable cause to believe that specific relevant evidence will be found, and arrest must be based on probable cause that the arrested person has committed a crime. If something is seized in violation of this requirement, it may not be used in evidence against the person searched, even if it shows conclusively that he is guilty of a crime. This limitation on the use of evidence is not found in the amendment. It has been read into the amendment by judicial interpretation as the only effective way to enforce the amendment.

Fifth Amendment Guarantees. The framers of the 5th Amendment, which contains the privilege against self-incrimination, were particularly wary of institutions like the English Star Chamber that compelled witnesses to testify against themselves. The 5th Amendment privilege may be invoked before legislative committees and administrative bodies as well as in criminal trials. In *Miranda* v. *Arizona* (1966), the court went beyond the practice of any state or the federal government and held in a highly controversial decision that no police questioning may take place unless a suspect has been warned of his right to remain silent and either has a lawyer present or has waived the right to counsel.

Among other protections in the 5th Amendment are a safeguard against double jeopardy—trying a person twice for the same crime—and the guarantee that no one shall be deprived of life, liberty, or property without due process of law. The latter is meant to assure fair proceedings in both criminal and civil cases.

Sixth and Eighth Amendment Guarantees. The 6th Amendment provides for a public trial and for trial by jury in criminal cases. Trial by a jury of one's peers has been considered a basic element of Anglo-American justice since Magna Carta, although the functions of the jury have changed considerably. The 6th Amendment also grants a right to counsel in criminal cases, and it has been held that the states must provide counsel for criminal defendants who cannot afford their own. The 8th Amendment forbids excessive bail, excessive fines, and cruel and unusual punishment.

Right to Privacy. Privacy is generally regarded as a basic civil liberty, and the courts, especially in recent years, have assumed an important role in its defense. But, strictly speaking, there is no such right as a right to privacy in the sense of the rights just discussed. The 1st Amendment, the prohibition on unreasonable searches, and the privilege against self-incrimination, and the due process clause all protect aspects of privacy.

In an important case, *Griswold* v. *Connecticut* (1965), the Supreme Court responded to the interest in privacy and invalidated a state law forbidding doctors and others to give advice about birth control. It did so even though the state law was not obviously in conflict with any particular constitutional provision. Many states allow persons whose privacy has been invaded in ways defined by statute or decisions to recover damages in court.

Private Property and Economic Rights. The 5th Amendment contains one specific guarantee in favor of private property—that it cannot be taken for public use without just compensation. Just compensation has been held to mean compensation amounting to the full value of what is taken. The provision has been applied to state eminent domain cases, and nearly every state has a parallel requirement. Together with due process and equal protection clauses of the 14th Amendment, the 5th Amendment clause prevents arbitrary deprivations of private property by any government agency in the United States.

In the early 20th century these clauses were used by the Supreme Court to strike down state and federal schemes of economic regulation, but now the court defers almost completely to legislative judgments.

Political Rights. The right to speak on public questions and the right to participate in the political process by voting are fundamental in a democracy. The first of these has been discussed. The second, the right to vote, is not guaranteed in the federal Constitution, although discrimination based on color or sex is forbidden.

The states set voters' qualifications and commonly exclude minors, felons, and illiterates. Some states formerly had property qualifications. Arbitrary discrimination, however, is forbidden by the equal protection clause of the 14th Amendment, and in 1966 the court relied on that clause to invalidate the poll tax. The court, in the Reapportionment cases (1964), has also read that clause to provide substantial equality of representation for those who do vote. That holding has resulted in reapportionment of at least one house of the legislature in almost every state.

Equal Treatment of the Races. Often when people refer to "civil rights," they mean the guarantees of equal treatment for Negroes and other minority groups. Inequality of treatment has been perhaps the most deep-seated problem in American democracy, and although legal guarantees have greatly expanded since 1950, the experience of the 1960's suggests that the problem is still a long way from solution. (It should be noted that laws forbidding discrimination in employment, for instance, or in the sale of housing, necessarily limit the freedom of some in order to promote the long-term freedom, in terms of opportunity, of the persons who would otherwise be discriminated against.)

Although the disparity between slavery and the principles of the Declaration of Independence was obvious to some at the time, slavery was recognized in the Constitution. In the Dred Scott case (1857), a contributing cause of the Civil War, the Supreme Court held that Congress had no power under the Constitution to forbid slavery in the territories, as it had attempted to do in the Missouri Compromise.

The 13th Amendment (1865) abolished slavery. Some justices have read the amendment as prohibiting as well a variety of kinds of unequal treatment, on the theory that these are incidents of slavery. But most jurists have not accepted that position, and the great majority of civil rights cases have been decided under the 14th and 15th Amendments.

The 14th Amendment guaranteed citizenship for ex-slaves and provided that states shall not deprive persons of due process of law or deny them the equal protection of the laws. The 15th Amendment prohibits denial of the vote on racial grounds.

The ineffectiveness of these amendments to promote genuine equality for nearly a century after their ratification was the result both of some narrowing judicial decisions and lack of acceptance of the decisions that did protect Negroes' rights. Even when the court made it clear in the aftermath of ratification that racial discrimination in voter registration and the selection of jurors was unconstitutional, systematic exclusion of prospective Negro juries and of Negro voters continued in many Southern states.

Among the narrowing pronouncements was the Supreme Court's decision in the Civil Rights Cases (1883). These invalidated a federal law prohibiting racial discrimination by inns, hotels, and railways. It declared that the 14th Amendment applied only to "state action" and that in enforcing the amendment Congress could not forbid private acts of discrimination. Finally, in 1896, in *Plessy* v. *Ferguson*, the court upheld state-imposed segregation because laws requiring separation "do not necessarily imply the inferiority of either race to the other...."

The pattern of racial segregation in the South was not significantly disturbed until *Brown* v. *Board of Education* (1954), in which the court declared separate educational facilities to be inherently unequal because they give Negro children a sense of inferiority and retard their educational and mental development. It has since struck down every kind of state differentiation of treatment on racial grounds that has come before it, including laws against interracial marriages. At the same time it has expanded the concept of state action to encompass individual acts of discrimination that are supported by the state in some way. For example, it has held that a court may not enforce a private contract to discriminate on racial grounds.

Constitutionally guaranteed civil rights have been strengthened and supplemented by congressional and state legislative action, as well as by executive orders forbidding discrimination within the government itself. Overcoming vigorous Southern opposition, including extended fili-busters, Congress passed the Civil Rights Act of 1964 and the Voting Rights Act of 1965. The former contains a public accommodations section proscribing discrimination by hotels and restaurants and a fair employment section forbidding businesses connected with interstate commerce to discriminate in choosing their employees. The latter contains a complex scheme to circumvent devices for voting discrimination and to use the Department of Justice more fully in enforcing voting rights.

Both of these acts represent a greater involvement of the federal government in promoting equal rights than any since Reconstruction. The public accommodations section was approved unanimously by the Supreme Court as valid under Congress' power over commerce. Thus it overruled in effect, though not in theory, the Civil Rights cases of 1883.

In sustaining the Voting Act, the court has expanded the powers of Congress under the 14th Amendment, and in a separate case a majority indicated that Congress can prohibit private acts of discrimination that interfere with the assertion of constitutionally guaranteed rights.

Many of the Northern states have actively promoted civil rights. State public accommodations and fair employment laws preceded the federal act. A number of states and cities also have fair housing laws, prohibiting racial discrimination in the sale and rental of housing. In regard to public education, such devices as busing of pupils and merging of school zones have been used in New York and other states to overcome the effects of de facto racial segregation based on residential patterns.

Although attempts to redress inequality by law increased tremendously in the 1950's and 1960's, some of the laws are not effectively enforced, and there remains a demand for more positive programs to produce genuine equality of opportunity.

CIVIL LIBERTIES AND RIGHTS OUTSIDE THE UNITED STATES

All of the Western democracies recognize freedom of speech, but in most the limits are not as broad as in the United States. In Britain, for example, certain kinds of criticism of the monarch and members of Parliament are forbidden, and censorship of the theater has been more extensive than in the United States. Although Communist countries recognize a right to free expression within limits, it must be exercised, in the words of the Czechoslovak constitution, only in a way "consistent with the interest of the working people." Freedom of speech, as most Westerners understand it, is absent in Communist countries.

The developing countries generally accept in principle the liberal approach to freedom of speech, but in many of them critics of the regime in power are suppressed. It may well be that the limited consensus on political values that exists in some of the countries of Africa, for example, precludes full freedom of speech.

The right to worship freely is now generally recognized, although it has evolved only slowly in Spain and some other countries. Few countries outside the Communist world, however, separate church and state as strictly as the United States does. Government aid to the institutions of the predominant religion, and sometimes minority religions as well, is common.

All countries have safeguards for criminal suspects, but the nature and flexibility of the safeguards vary. France, for instance, has no privilege against self-incrimination, and its system of criminal justice relies heavily on questioning the suspect. In some of the developing countries there are "preventive detention" acts that allow the government to circumvent the ordinary safeguards in placing persons in jail. Enemies of the state have not always been afforded the usual protections in Communist countries.

The constitutions of the Communist and developing countries commonly place more emphasis on economic and social rights of a positive kind, such as the right to work and the right to be educated, than does the U. S. Constitution, which was formulated at a time when the function of government was considered to be largely negative.

With the exception of the Union of South Africa, the major countries of the world consider racial discrimination wrong and in varying degrees forbid it by law.

A variety of attempts have been made to protect human rights internationally, but these have had much less practical significance than the efforts of particular states. The Universal Declaration of Human Rights, drafted by the United Nations Human Rights Commission and adopted by the General Assembly in 1948, covers both traditional civil and political rights and the newer economic, social, and cultural rights, but it is not legally binding. The Assembly has adopted more limited conventions that do bind signatories on such subjects as genocide, statelessness, refugees, slavery, nationality, marriage, and forced labor.

In December 1966 two United Nations covenants that would be binding on signatories were adopted and opened for signature by the General Assembly. One is the Covenant on Civil and Political Rights, the other the Covenant on Economic, Social, and Cultural Rights. Even if the necessary number of states sign them, however, no enforcement mechanisms will work effectively for some time. Nonetheless they will help, as the Declaration and other efforts of the United Nations have helped, to create an international atmosphere in which observance of basic human rights is more consistent throughout the world.

On a regional level, the European Convention for the Protection of Human Rights and Fundamental Freedoms has been adhered to by 15 states. Its machinery includes a court that hears claims by individuals against member states. Similar institutions have been proposed for other multinational regions. In the foreseeable future, however, the primary guarantor of civil liberties and rights will continue to be the nation state.

See also CENSORSHIP; CHURCH AND STATE; CIVIL RIGHTS MOVEMENT; PRIVACY.

R. KENT GREENAWALT
School of Law, Columbia University

Bibliography
Becker, Carl, *The Declaration of Independence* (New York 1942).
Chafee, Zechariah, *Free Speech in the United States* (Cambridge, Mass., 1941).
Gellhorn, Walter, *American Rights* (New York 1960).
Greenberg, Jack, *Race Relations and American Law* (New York 1959).
Kauper, Paul G., *Civil Liberties and the Constitution* (Ann Arbor, Mich., 1962).
Mill, John Stuart, *On Liberty* (London 1859).
Stokes, Anson Phelps, and Pfeffer, Leo, *Church and State in the United States* (New York 1964).

CIVIL RIGHTS for Negroes received a symbolic expression of popular support in the August 1963 march on Washington, D. C., where Martin Luther King and others addressed more than 250,000 marchers.

PICTORIAL PARADE

CIVIL RIGHTS MOVEMENT, a campaign by a number of organizations, supported by many individual citizens, to achieve equality for American Negroes. Informally, "the movement" was a term used to refer to the activities of organizations in the forefront of the struggle during the 1950's and 1960's, when efforts to attain voting rights, access to public accommodations, and better educational and economic opportunities for Negroes were intensified.

As a result of the adoption of the 13th, 14th, and 15th amendments to the Constitution (1865–1870), the Negro was, in theory, a free and equal citizen. Congress in 1866 and 1875 passed civil rights acts aimed at guaranteeing Negro rights in courts and equal access to public accommodations. But in 1883 the Supreme Court declared unconstitutional the 1875 act, contending that the 14th Amendment did not prohibit the invasion of civil rights by individuals. The ruling doomed hopes of Southern Negroes for equality. In fact, the status of three fourths of the American Negroes—those in the former slave states—tended to worsen as the Southern white conservative leadership adopted laws and supported policies that effectively circumvented constitutional guarantees. See NEGRO IN AMERICA.

Negroes migrated to the North to escape oppression and to seek greater economic opportunity, and the civil rights leadership was assumed by the National Association for the Advancement of Colored People (NAACP) and the National Urban League (NUL). The NAACP, formally organized in 1910 and strongly committed to the ideals of democracy, sought through legal means to gain equality for all persons within the American political system. The *Crisis*, edited for many years by W. E. B. DuBois, forcefully publicized the organization's position, while the Legal Redress Committee provided counsel and served as the chief instigator of suits for those who were denied their legal rights. The committee became the Legal Defense and Educational Fund in 1939, and as a separate corporate entity it was more flexible and able to provide help for other agencies that were less financially stable. Many whites viewed the NAACP as radical and as a troublemaker because of the numerous litigations it brought; some Negroes looked on it with suspicion, feeling it was manipulated by whites. Although the organization was not popularly based, it was for a half century the most important and most effective civil rights agency. By its activities —and judicial acceptance of its position–a climate of opinion favorable to the growth of more activist organizations was created.

The National Urban League, one year younger than the NAACP, directed its efforts chiefly in behalf of working-class Negroes, for it was designed to help them adjust to urban areas. It instructed the migrants in how to live in cities, found lodgings and jobs, developed training programs, led boycotts against businesses in an effort to have Negroes employed, and provided leadership in relations with labor unions. The NUL and the NAACP were—and remained through the 1960's—the best financed of the agencies; they were nonrevolutionary and "orderly" and did not arouse the opposition of a large portion of the white power structure.

The Congress of Racial Equality (CORE), founded in Chicago in 1942, was the seedbed for the growth of ideas and tactics widely employed after 1956. This group believed that legalism alone would not bring uncompromising equality. It sought to end discrimination through interracial, nonviolent, direct action. CORE staged sit-ins in Chicago in 1943, bus rides and stand-ins at the Palisades Park pool in 1947 and 1948, and the "Journey of Reconciliation" (the first Freedom Ride testing desegregation of interstate transportation) in the South in 1947. In that year it considered undertaking a major effort against lunch counters and other public accommodations but the organization decided that the time was not ripe.

By mid-century, gains had been made by a threatened "march" on Washington in 1941; by various state laws; through Supreme Court decisions on political primaries, graduate and professional education, transportation, and real estate covenants; by presidential appointment of a Civil Rights Commission; and executive ordering of integration of the armed forces. But Congress— like the public—seemed more interested in lip service to democracy than in the achievement of actual equality. Inequity of opportunity and treatment in the political, economic, educational, housing, and public accommodations areas amply demonstrated that Negroes were still second-class citizens. Groups seeking to remove those inequalities were small, Northern-based, elitist, and inadequately financed (by whites primarily).

World War II and its aftermath effected great changes. Large numbers of Negroes moved west and north to share in the wartime prosperity and gave the minority problem a national rather than a sectional character; urbanization was rapidly accelerated; large numbers of Negroes who fought in the armed services against tyranny and injustice abroad more keenly felt injustice at home; independence for colonial peoples made realization of the ideals of democracy a domestic as well as an international issue; and the successful use of nonviolence by Gandhi in India underscored the efficacy of "creative disorder" as a means of achieving certain goals. By the mid-1950's a new generation was coming to maturity that had known only the changing conditions of the war and postwar years. Even so, it is doubtful that a major breakthrough in the struggle to attain equal rights for Negroes could have been achieved had not the U. S. Supreme Court handed down a watershed school desegregation decision in 1954.

School Desegregation and Its Aftermath. Although Negroes were denied formal education while in slavery, they participated enthusiastically in public education for a brief period during Reconstruction. Then, as a result of a Supreme Court ruling (*Plessy* v. *Ferguson*) Negroes after 1896 were confined to "separate but equal" schools in the South and in many other localities across the country. Manifestly unequal by every yardstick, these de jure and de facto segregated schools provided an education far inferior to that offered whites. Disadvantaged in education, Negroes were inevitably disadvantaged in almost every other area.

Beginning in the late 1930's, the Supreme Court chipped away at the 1896 doctrine as it applied to higher and professional education, and in May 1954 it tore the wall down. In *Brown* v. *Board of Education*, the court cited psychological and sociological data of Kenneth Clark and others and declared separate schools inherently unequal. Clark, a Negro educator and psychologist, had contended that segregation was harmful to both Negro and white students. In 1955 the justices remanded all cases on tax-supported schools to the district courts, ordering that Negroes be admitted to the public schools "on a racially nondiscriminatory basis with all deliberate speed." By then, some upper South and border states had moved toward desegregation, but in the deep South sentiment polarized around the "desegregation now" and "desegregation never" extremes. Many state and local authorities, mostly in the South, adopted many kinds of delaying schemes. Most Southern congressmen denounced the *Brown* decision, and White Citizens' Councils and other groups pledged to preserve white supremacy, sprang up in many states. Slowly, painfully, with much litigation, considerable violence, frequent use of federal marshals and occasional use of federal troops (notably at Little Rock, Ark., in 1957), and with "any perceptible movement" often construed as "all deliberate speed," desegregation had been accomplished by 1965 in 1,160 of the 3,028 Southern school districts containing white and Negro pupils. Nearly 316,000 Negroes—about 10%—were attending schools with whites.

The record in the publicly supported colleges and universities was better than in the secondary and elementary schools, but federal troops had to quell serious disorders at the University of Mississippi in the fall of 1962 and force the enrollment of James Meredith. The Civil Rights Act of 1964 required school districts to comply with its provisions against discrimination or lose federal funds provided for education.

Frontal Assault on Southern Discrimination. The Supreme Court decisions of 1954 and 1955 had a profound effect. Segregation, legal for more than 50 years, was suddenly illegal, and the machinery of the existing power structure would now be used to carry out the new legality. What, then, of the many things that had long been legal but long denied by existing local governments to so many citizens? If the central government had "changed the rules" in one area, would it permit change in other areas by new methods? Congress in 1957 signaled its willingness to help effect change by passing its first civil rights law in more than 80 years. The act dealt rather ineffectively with voting rights.

By 1957 a significant new organization and the most influential civil rights leader of the decade had emerged. Continued discrimination on the Montgomery, Ala., buses was met by ministerial leadership in the formation of the Montgomery Improvement Association, and a successful boycott of the bus lines followed. The Rev. Martin Luther King, Jr., was catapulted to the front, and under his leadership the Southern Christian Leadership Conference (SCLC) was organized in Atlanta in 1957. The charismatic King was totally committed to nonviolent direct action that would "create such a crisis and foster such a tension" that a community which had constantly refused to negotiate would be forced to "confront the issue." King, a moderate, stood between the forces of complacency and the forces of hatred and bitterness that were close to advocating violence. His methods were Gandhian but with more emphasis on love of those guilty of injustice. In contrast to Gandhi, King and his followers were members of a minority group; the success of assertive nonviolence thus depended in great measure on the inherent goodwill of the white majority.

The SCLC tactics were adapted from CORE, which under the leadership of James Farmer began to expand rapidly in the late 1950's. But it took a new organization, the Student Nonviolent Coordinating Committee (SNCC)—which King helped organize—to inject a more zealous tone into the movement. Beginning with four students sitting-in at a lunch counter in Greensboro, N. C., on Feb. 1, 1960, SNCC was formally organized at Shaw University in Raleigh the following April. The sit-ins, which SNCC was designed to coordinate, had already spread throughout the South, and those engaged in this activity were carefully selected and trained to endure all kinds of verbal and physical abuse without resorting to counterattack. The composure of the blue-denimed youth won much sympathy and admiration, and their actions were upheld by the Supreme Court in December 1961.

By that time a stronger civil rights bill had been passed in 1960. John F. Kennedy—not yet fully committed to civil rights but providing more moral leadership than his predecessor—had become president, and the Freedom Rides had begun in early 1961. Started by CORE, which expected to finish the rides with about 13 people, this action to test segregation in bus terminals serving interstate passengers mushroomed when SNCC joined, and it reached jail-overflowing proportions when hundreds of volunteers—white and black—reacted to the burning of one bus and the abuse and beating of the occupants of another. More than 600 federal marshals were sent into the area for protection of the riders, and the Legal Defense and Education Fund saved CORE from financial disaster by providing bail bonds and counsel. The next summer, CORE successfully conducted its Freedom Highways campaign aimed primarily at desegregating accommodations in restaurant chains.

The summer of 1962 also saw several organizations—on the initiative of SNCC—form the Council of Federated Organizations, which under the leadership of Robert P. Moses sought to teach Negroes in Mississippi what they needed to know to register to vote, to persuade them to try to register, and through orderly procedures to get officials to register them. But rebuffs, reprisals, and dilatory tactics prevented significant numbers of Negroes from joining the registration rolls.

Sit-ins, wade-ins, freedom rides, limited boycotts, demonstrations, marches, and other types of creative disorder were gaining public acceptance and convincing many white persons of the legitimacy and morality of the Negroes' demands, but events in highly segregated Birmingham, Ala., in April and May 1963 probably did more than any other single thing to gain widespread public support for the civil rights movement. Picketings and sit-ins at some stores resulted in the jailing of 2,400 persons. Dogs and fire hoses—by order of Police Commissioner Eugene "Bull" Connor—were directed at a large crowd of street demonstrators that included many high school and younger students. The photograph of a police dog leaping at the throat of a schoolboy outraged public sentiment, brought nationwide financial and political support, and fostered pressure for action by the federal government.

In June 1963, President Kennedy called for new legislation. More than 200,000 people, led by the mayor, marched in Detroit to demand immediate steps for equality. The degree of public support for civil rights was best exhibited by the march on Washington, D. C., on Aug. 28, 1963. More than 250,000 persons from all over the nation gathered in almost religious attitude at the Lincoln Memorial and demonstrated by their presence the intensity of the nation's "moral crisis."

Even as such nonviolent tactics received wide public support, white extremists in the South stepped up their reprisals. Medgar Evers, field secretary for the NAACP, was shot to death at his home in Jackson, Miss., on June 12, 1963. On September 15, four Negro girls were killed in a church bombing in Birmingham. The violence continued in 1964. For their "Mississippi Summer," COFO sent 1,000 students, teachers, social workers, lawyers, ministers, and other persons into the Magnolia State to encourage, train, and sustain Negroes in registering and voting. Harassed in every conceivable fashion—even to bombings and beatings—the freedom workers endured much. On June 20 three of them were murdered near Philadelphia, Miss.

Congress Responds. The civil rights bill had made no material progress in 1963. But then, after President Kennedy's assassination on November 22, President Lyndon Johnson called on Congress to pass his predecessor's legislative program. Administration pressure combined with public indignation finally proved effective, a Senate filibuster was broken, and the "Magna Carta" for the Negro, the Civil Rights Act of 1964, was passed and signed into law on July 2. The law forbade discrimination in the use of most public facilities. As the tactics of the rights groups had changed, so had the approach of Congress: The equal accommodations section of the law was based on the commerce clause of the Constitution rather than on the 14th Amendment, and the government at long last had declared for equality.

A "white backlash" against the civil rights movement developed during the presidential campaign in 1964. Negro leaders closed ranks against Barry Goldwater, the Republican candidate, who was the beneficiary of the backlash sentiment. The backlash proved not so strong as many had anticipated, and President Johnson was reelected. But the civil rights movement seemed to be making little progress. Negroes were having great difficulty registering in many places, and the situation in Alabama was especially bad. In March 1965 a march to dramatize the demand for voting rights was halted with bloodshed just outside Selma, Ala. President Johnson then went before Congress to make an impassioned plea for a voting rights law, and Congress responded with the act of August 6, which permitted federal examiners to register Negroes under certain circumstances. The salutary effect of the measure was undeniable; by the summer of 1967 more than half of the eligible Negroes had been registered in Alabama, Mississippi, Louisiana, Georgia, and South Carolina.

To the casual observer, the Negro seemed closer to achieving equal rights than ever before. Then, violence erupted again, in a new quarter.

Negro Violence and the Fragmentation of the Movement. In the Watts (Negro) section of Los Angeles, an outburst of rioting between Aug. 11 and 15, 1965, resulted in 34 deaths, more than 1,000 injuries, about 4,000 arrests, and $40 million in property damage. The riot was born of frustration that seemed rooted in the urban ghetto conditions: high unemployment, stalling of poverty programs, miserable housing, exploitation by business establishments, ill health, lack of hope, and insufficient efforts to channel frustration into nonviolent, creative disorder.

To unskilled and poverty stricken Negroes, the various provisions of the 1964 act were a mockery. Such Negroes had no training that would enable them to share in the booming economy and rapidly automating society. Many were disheartened and frustrated by the slow results of nonviolence and social disorder; a large number were alienated from the values of middle-class America; communication between them and constituted authorities as well as with civil rights leaders was poor.

A foretaste of the Watts disaster had come a year before. In the summer of 1964, riots erupted in New York City's Harlem; later, Rochester, N. Y., some New Jersey cities, and Philadelphia, Pa., suffered similar disturbances. Almost invariably an instance of alleged police brutality triggered the riots, and civil rights leaders insisted that police brutality and the hopeless poverty of the ghettos had to be abolished.

A serious division among civil rights organizations began to appear in 1966. In May a shakeup in SNCC resulted in the replacement of

John Lewis as chairman by the more radical Stokely Carmichael. Carmichael sanctioned retaliatory violence as a legitimate weapon. One month later, James Meredith was shot and wounded while leading a "March Against Fear" in Mississippi; Carmichael, one of the leaders who then took up the march, began to talk of Black Power (q.v.); he repudiated integration and directed more and more of his appeal to the masses in the ghettos. Many members of both races withdrew from the organization. SNCC gained some ideological identification with the Black Muslims (q.v.), and Black Power seemed to move toward Black Nationalism. Burning, destruction, rioting, and guerrilla tactics were freely spoken of by Carmichael and H. Rap Brown, who succeeded him in 1967. SNCC seemed to be evolving into a propaganda agency, with less emphasis on positive programs.

CORE, under the national chairmanship of Floyd B. McKissick, had become less conservative and in 1967 made the first significant move toward becoming the unifying group for activist Negro organizations when it eliminated "multiracial" from its membership description. McKissick considered the civil rights movement dead and the "black revolution" under way.

Efforts by King to end discrimination in housing and employment in Chicago through mass demonstrations and marches were unsuccessful in 1966. The SCLC leader found himself caught between the new legalism of NAACP and the growing radicalism of CORE and SNCC. His nonviolent philosophy and intellectualism impaired his chances of becoming a leader of the most alienated elements within the ghettos. Moreover, he did not improve his position—or help the civil rights cause—by denouncing his government's military intervention in Vietnam. His position on Vietnam apparently violated a tacit agreement with leaders of the older organizations, though Carmichael had earlier and more vigorously condemned U. S. involvement in Vietnam.

The more militant elements within the Negro community seemed close to a philosophy of nihilism in the summer of 1967. Registering voters, desegregating lunch counters, and finding a few jobs for Negroes had not made significant headway toward curing the ills of the cities. A summer of rioting in Newark, Detroit, and 30 other cities left nearly 100 persons dead and more than 2,000 others injured.

President Johnson appointed a National Advisory Commission on Civil Disorders, with Illinois Gov. Otto Kerner as chairman, to investigate the riots. On March 2, 1968, the commission reported that unemployment and underemployment constituted the most serious grievances, and that unfulfilled hopes and defiance of law helped create a climate that encouraged violence, but that white racism must bear the chief blame for the conditions that sparked riots. The commission denied the conspiracy theory of the riots and cited the strong desire of blacks for a cultural identity within a white society. It warned, however, of a trend toward the creation of two societies. The commission recommended sweeping programs for housing, job creation and training, education, and welfare. The proposals reflected the shifting of focus from guaranteeing constitutional rights to an assault on economic barriers.

Dr. King's Death and Its Impact. The assassination of Martin Luther King, Jr., on April 4, 1968, touched off new rioting in at least 46 cities. On April 11, the President signed a measure providing penalties for those who attempt to interfere with an individual's exercise of his civil rights and for those who use interstate and foreign commerce to incite, organize, participate in, or further a riot. The act forbade discrimination in most housing, but this provision was made obsolete in June. The Supreme Court, citing the 1866 Civil Rights Act, prohibited discrimination in the rental and sale of all housing.

Another act, signed on Aug. 1, 1968, authorized the construction or rehabilitation of more than 1.7 million housing units within three years. Federal subsidies would greatly reduce both rental and purchase costs.

The National Urban League took steps to help ghetto residents organize, choose leaders, identify grievances, and work out means of compelling merchants, city officials, and others to take corrective action. The emphasis on self-determination, pride, and self-respect indicated disillusionment with tactics that had led to violence. CORE was shaken in 1968 by dissension between advocates of reform and revolution.

The Rev. Ralph D. Abernathy succeeded King as president of SCLC and led the Poor People's Campaign that King had conceived. The two-month encampment in Washington and the marches on government offices failed to achieve the ill-defined goals. Issues had changed, and the old strategies seemed less effective; SCLC had probably played its major role under King. However, a strike by sanitation workers in Memphis, Tenn.—an action which King had supported—succeeded in achieving employee demands. For the first time, in such a confrontation, city officials faced an effective coalition of labor, civil rights, and religious groups.

Nixon Administration. Dubious of Richard Nixon's commitment to civil rights, blacks overwhelmingly supported Hubert Humphrey for president in 1968. Charges of a "Southern strategy" appealing to whites gained credence when in 1969 the Nixon administration sought to delay scheduled integration of certain Southern school districts. Open rebellion by lawyers in the Civil Rights Division of the Department of Justice proved as embarrassing as the Supreme Court's unanimous declaration in 1969 that segregation end "at once." Nearly 35% of Southern black students attended desegregated schools by 1970, but tempers flared North and South over the busing of students out of their school districts to achieve integration.

The Congress in 1970 rejected administration attempts to "water down" an extension of the Voting Rights Act of 1965, a law largely responsible for doubling black voters since 1960 and for electing 528 Southern black officials in 1969. But racial tension grew as black unemployment rose during a business recession in 1970 and as violence increased between blacks and police. Chicago police killed two leaders of the Black Panther party in 1969, and many persons supported Panther charges of a national conspiracy to eliminate their leaders. When police killed six Negroes in Augusta, Ga., and two at Mississippi's Jackson State College in 1970, blacks accused the Nixon administration of creating an atmosphere of violent repression.

CHASE C. MOONEY
Indiana University
BARRY GROSSBACH
Philadelphia Community College

CIVIL SERVICE, the organized body of paid, civilian government employees appointed to office rather than elected. It is often synonymous with the "merit system," under which employees are hired on the basis of their qualifications, as determined by their achievements in competitive examinations, and not because of their political affiliation.

The civil service is most typically viewed as an organ of a central government, but there are also state, provincial, local, regional, and international civil services. The precise categories of personnel officially included in a civil service vary somewhat from nation to nation. Also, popular and legal usages of the term may differ. However, custom and law everywhere exclude elected officials and members of the armed forces from civil service.

The civil service performs a complex and continuing service in most modern nations. Although enduring governments have always had officials who assisted the ruler, the modern civil service is generally distinguished by the precision and permanence of its general organization. The trained personnel of a civil service are essential to the carrying out of governmental functions, and as the needs of modern governments have grown more complex there has been a trend toward professionalization of civil servants.

U. S. CIVIL SERVICE

Since World War II, the merit system has covered more than 95% of federal full-time civil servants. In addition, more than two thirds of the states and many cities have full or partial merit systems. Employees in the civil service provide a vast range of services and include police officers, fire fighters, clerks, sanitation workers, administrators, technicians, and social workers. Virtually every occupation can be found in the civil service.

Reform Act of 1978. Until 1978 the U. S. Civil Service Commission was responsible for the management of the federal civil service. It provided examinations for job applicants, established job classifications, and was responsible for personnel management. The 1978 reform act replaced the commission with two new agencies—the Office of Personnel Management and the Merit Systems Protection Board. The new law also made it possible to reward good performance with merit pay raises and permitted supervisors to fire incompetent workers if they could show substantial evidence to support their claims. Pay increases also were tied to performance for some managers.

Job Classifications. The most distinctive features of U. S. civil services lie in their complex systems of job classification and availability to persons seeking employment. Generally there is a very detailed classification of jobs based on relative difficulties of duties and responsibilities, to which commensurate pay is usually quite closely tied.

Federal civil service employees are grouped according to jobs and pay scales into 18 General Schedule grades—GS-1 to GS-18. Salaries are comparable to those in private industry. The civil service is a career system, and employees may be promoted or transferred without any loss of their civil service rights. There has been a tradition of "lateral entry," with persons entering the civil service at all ages and levels, and frequently moving back and forth between the government and private enterprise.

Merit System. Most applicants for federal jobs must take civil service examinations, which vary according to the position being tested for. Examinations are required to be as practical as possible, and applicants may enter the civil service at any level for which they qualify. The exams may be oral or written, and some include a test of specific skills. For some occupations, applicants are evaluated on the basis of their education, training, and experience. All federal agencies have some positions not subject to civil service laws, including department and agency heads who are politically appointed and thus likely to support administration policies.

Applicants who pass the examinations are placed on a list in the order of their grades. Armed forces veterans are given extra credits. When a federal agency has a vacancy, it may hire one of the first three persons on the eligible list. The government investigates the background of applicants to determine their suitability, and there are loyalty and security requirements for positions involving national security. All but top policy makers are prohibited from taking an active part in partisan politics.

OTHER COUNTRIES

Britain. The national civil service in Britain is largely a "closed career system," with little lateral entry. The Civil Service Commission recruits and examines personnel and conducts examinations, but general personnel management is regulated by the treasury. Outside the central civil service are the employees of nationalized industries and of local governments.

The civil service is divided into a number of separate hierarchies, among which there is not much movement. There are four principal classes —administrative, executive, specialist, and clerical and typist. There is some promotion upward between the classes, but little lateral entry into any group. Entrance is at the bottom at a relatively early age.

Applicants are given academic essay-type examinations and general orals, both keyed to general rather than technical educational levels. While there is a limited admission of professional and technical personnel into posts near the top, the highest career positions and most of those leading to them are allocated to the administrative-class generalists.

France. France, too, has long had an essentially closed career system for its central government. Its system is proportionately larger than in Britain or in the United States because its highly centralized government has many responsibilities —such as education, police, and civil engineering —that in other countries are regulated by local units.

The French civil service is divided into classes that generally resemble the British system. Personnel management, including most recruitment, is departmental. Most members of the highest civil service class are chosen through the École Nationale d'Administration. Other specialized schools that prepare graduates for the technical services include the École Polytechnique for science and the École Nationale des Impôts for finance.

Canada. The Canadian Civil Service Commission was established in 1918 in an attempt to end patronage appointments by politicians. Most jobs in the government are under the merit system. Like the British system, the Canadian civil service is regulated by the treasury, but its classification system follows the U. S. pattern. There is a national civil service as well as one for each province.

INTERNATIONAL CIVIL SERVICE

The United Nations Secretariat and its specialized agencies are staffed by a worldwide civil service. Personnel management in the Secretariat is conducted by an office of personnel headed by an undersecretary reporting directly to the secretary general of the United Nations. Wage and salary administration and position classification are fiscal functions.

A main problem in the staffing of the civil service is the need to balance UN charter requirements that personnel be selected on a basis of both competence and geographical representation. Therefore there are area quotas. Written examinations are required only for lower-level positions. Basically, the system is an open one and represents mixed U. S., British, and French experience. Careers are encouraged, but there is also much fixed-term and temporary employment at all levels.

There is necessarily a complex system of pay and perquisites, generally based on the principle that such a body should receive pay in accordance with that of the highest-paid national services. There is a coordinating body to see that remuneration in the Secretariat and the specialized agencies is similar.

HISTORICAL BACKGROUND

The creation of national states in western Europe during the 15th and 16th centuries provided the preconditions and the impetus for the development of a civil service. But many modern practices can be traced to ancient and medieval times. Egypt, Greece, Rome, and China all contributed some of the elements of modern administration.

The evolution of the modern civil service in western Europe and in the United States took place in several stages. The first, or royal, stage saw the growth of the embryonic concepts of modern government, including a civil administrative system and a corps of personnel to manage it. This stage was largely complete by 1750 in Britain, France, and Prussia, and their experience was to have the greatest impact elsewhere.

The royal establishments were gradually converted into constitutional institutions responsive to the new authority of parliaments and politicians. The new institutions also served to meet the demands of a growing electorate for an impartial, economical service not limited to members of the aristocracy. They also provided the necessary professional skills to cope with new complexities.

Prussia and France. The development of civil services was most rapid in France and Prussia. By the mid-17th century, Frederick William, elector of Brandenburg, had established an efficient military bureaucracy. Its members were chosen on a competitive basis and were responsible for financial and economic matters, refugee settlement, and trade. The 18th century Prussian civil service is often considered the first modern civil service system.

In France, the French Revolution and the Napoleonic administrative reforms replaced the royal service with a public service by the early 19th century. The Napoleonic features of hierarchy, centralization, and competence became models for the reform of other government administrations.

Britain. By the mid-18th century in Britain, much of the power of the throne had been transferred into the hands of factions and parties. In the process the civil offices and their salaries and perquisites became open to the corrupting type of patronage manipulation that was soon to be known in the United States as the "spoils system."

However, by the middle of the 19th century there was so heightened a concern about corruption, economy, and efficiency, as well as popular rights to office, that modern civil service soon came full scale to Britain. The Civil Service Commission was established in 1855 to examine applicants nominated by the various departments. The merit system became a reality in Britain in 1870 with the requirement that there be open competition for most initial appointments to the civil service.

United States. The civil service in the United States has been deeply influenced by the democratic aspirations and social mobility of its people, and especially by the idea of equality of opportunity. At first, U. S. presidents made appointments on the basis of an individual's qualifications, regardless of party. But by the early 19th century it had become common practice for an incoming president to replace large numbers of government workers with members of his own party, regardless of qualifications.

The "spoils system," as this policy was known, was strongly supported by President Andrew Jackson. He fostered the growth of that system by his firm belief in personal and party loyalty as conditions for holding office. The system reached its peak in the years immediately after the Civil War, when corruption became a serious problem at all levels of government.

A movement for reform of the system led Congress to pass legislation in 1871 giving the president the authority to establish tests for persons applying for federal jobs. But the reform attempt was aborted in 1873, when Congress failed to provide additional funding. Public demands for reform intensified after the assassination of President James Garfield in 1881 by a disappointed office seeker.

Garfield's death led to passage of the Pendleton Federal Civil Service Act of 1883. The act created a Civil Service Commission and firmly established the merit system in the national government on a partial basis. A series of statutes and executive orders extended the system, eventually placing most jobs under civil service regulations. Many states and local jurisdictions followed the federal example, so that merit system practices became similar nationwide.

Bibliography

Barker, Ernest, *The Development of Public Services in Western Europe, 1660–1930* (Shoe String 1966).
Gartner, Alan, and others, eds., *Public Service Employment: An Analysis of its History, Problems, and Prospects* (Praeger 1973).
Gladden, Edgar N., *History of Public Administration*, 2 vols. (Cass 1972).
Golembiewski, Robert T., and Cohen, Michael, eds., *People in Public Service: A Reader in Public Personnel Administration* (Peacock 1970).
Hoogenboom, Ari, *Outlawing the Spoils: A History of the Civil Service Reform Movement, 1865–1883* (Peter Smith 1968).
Rosenberg, Hans, *Bureaucracy, Aristocracy, and Autocracy: The Prussian Experience, 1660–1815* (Harvard Univ. Press 1958).

CIVIL WAR

CONTENTS

CIVIL WAR, in American history, the conflict between the Northern states (the Union) and the 11 Southern states that seceded from the Union and were organized as the Confederate States of America. It was not a civil war in the usual sense of opposing sides contending for control of one government, but rather a conflict precipitated by one side's creation of a separate nation. In the South the Civil War is frequently called the *War Between the States.* It is also known as the *War of the Rebellion* and the *War of Secession.*

The hostilities that began with the firing on Fort Sumter on April 12, 1861, climaxed a sectional rift that had been widening for decades. And although the war ended with Robert E. Lee's surrender to Ulysses S. Grant at Appomattox Court House on April 9, 1865, its legacy of animosity lasted long beyond the period of Reconstruction and the readmission of the rebellious states to the Union.

The Civil War was immensely costly in both lives and dollars. It left the South devastated. It also represented the victory of a strongly centralized federal government over the advocates of states' rights, brought about the abolition of slavery, and spurred American industrial development.

1. A Heritage of Sectional Differences

The Southern attack on Fort Sumter at Charleston, S. C., on April 12, 1861, began the Civil War, but a sectional rift had existed for generations. During the colonial period southern colonies were more agrarian, had more plantations, depended more on staple crops, and possessed more slaves than did the colonies to the north. Although these differences were frequently troublesome during the Revolutionary period, independence was possible only through cooperation. The advantages of cooperation were so apparent that the founding fathers sought a "more perfect union" through the federal Constitution.

Union, however, did not eliminate sectionalism; as the republic grew older and stronger, differences between the North and the South grew more pronounced. Sectional differences, however, coexisted and competed with nationalism. The "mystic chords of memory"—to use Abraham Lincoln's phrase—of a common cause in the past and a common destiny for the future were as real as the present material blessings of a common market, currency, army, navy, and foreign policy. The Civil War came only when American obsession with sectional problems obscured the advantages of union.

DIVISIVE FORCES AND ISSUES

Westward Expansion. Westward expansion accentuated sectional differences. Territories were sources of future power, and both Northern and Southern states were eager to secure allies. The existence or nonexistence of Negro slavery determined whether a territory would be oriented toward the South or the North, and Congress determined the status of slavery in a territory. The slavery symbol was convenient but dangerous; of all the differences separating the North and the South, slavery was most open to attack.

When, in 1819, Missouri sought admission to the Union as a slave state, the issue provoked a passionate debate that Thomas Jefferson found

The Civil War began when the Confederates fired on Fort Sumter in April 1861. The Federal fort on an island off Charleston, S. C., surrendered, and the Rebel flag flew over it most of the war. South Carolina declared the Union dissolved in ordinance of Dec. 20, 1860.

as alarming as a "fire-bell in the night." Northern and Southern congressmen reached agreement in the Missouri Compromise (1820), which admitted Missouri as a slave state and Maine as a free state and stipulated that all remaining Louisiana Purchase territory north of the southern border of Missouri would be free. Although the South won Missouri, only two potential slave states remained in the Louisiana territory, while the North could carve numerous free states from the vast expanse north and west of Missouri. In time the South realized that to maintain its power, slave states would have to be acquired from Mexican territory.

The Tariff and Other Issues. Sectionalism manifested itself in other issues. Anxious for easy credit, the South and the West united in opposition to the Second Bank of the United States (a powerful, privately controlled institution dominating the nation's banking industry), while the Northeast tended to support it. Because it consumed rather than produced manufactured goods, the South opposed the protective tariff, while the industrial Northeast supported it, as did many Westerners who concluded that the tariff would promote home markets for agricultural produce and would finance internal improvements.

Although the West wholeheartedly supported the use of Federal funds to build needed roads

CHARLESTON

MERCURY

EXTRA:

Passed unanimously at 1.15 o'clock, P. M., December 20th, 1860.

AN ORDINANCE

To dissolve the Union between the State of South Carolina and other States united with her under the compact entitled " The Constitution of the United States of America."

We, the People of the State of South Carolina, in Convention assembled, do declare and ordain, and it is hereby declared and ordained,

That the Ordinance adopted by us in Convention, on the twenty-third day of May, in the year of our Lord one thousand seven hundred and eighty-eight, whereby the Constitution of the United States of America was ratified, and also, all Acts and parts of Acts of the General Assembly of this State, ratifying amendments of the said Constitution, are hereby repealed; and that the union now subsisting between South Carolina and other States, under the name of "The United States of America," is hereby dissolved.

THE

UNION

IS

DISSOLVED!

The economy of the South between 1820 and 1860 was based largely on cotton, grown on large plantations with a labor force consisting chiefly of slaves.

and canals, and favored the liberal distribution of public lands and the granting of preemption rights to settlers illegally "squatting" on land, attitudes toward these issues in the Northeast and the South ranged from outright hostility to lukewarm support.

The South and the Cotton Economy. The impact of cotton culture on the South and industrialism on the North widened the gulf between the two sections. Cotton was a hardy plant that grew widely in a variety of soils throughout most of the lower south; its production did not require elaborate tools or techniques. Cotton could be raised successfully by both free labor on small farms and by slaves on large plantations. Men could begin raising cotton with little capital and could expand production as they accumulated funds for land and slaves. The multiplying cotton production (doubling each decade from 1820 to 1860) demanded more land and more slaves and differentiated Southern society from the rest of American society.

The South's greatest and most vulnerable difference was its "peculiar institution"—Negro slavery. Slavery did not root well in arid climates, barren soil, or mountainous regions. Indeed, the overwhelming majority of Southern agriculturalists had modest farms, and three fourths of the white Southerners had no direct connection with slavery. Centers of slavery, however, were usually centers of economic, social, and political leadership; a small planter class (only 8,000 landowners held 50 or more slaves in 1850) dominated the South.

Economically, slavery failed to benefit the Negro, the nonslaveholding white, and the South as a whole, but high returns on cotton-belt plantations, enabling that section to import slaves from the worn-out upper South and seaboard areas, made slavery profitable for most planters. The sale of surplus slaves not only aligned the upper South with the cotton kingdom but also produced one of slavery's least defensible features—the thriving domestic slave trade. Whether profitable or not, slavery was a way of life that virtually all white South-

erners accepted and defended. It regulated a biracial society to their satisfaction, for they could not conceive of millions of free Negroes living in their midst.

As the spread of cotton culture made slavery more profitable and intense opposition to protective tariffs and resentment over Northern attacks on slavery grew, embattled Southerners argued that their society was perfect and became increasingly sectional, until in the 1850's they proudly called themselves "Southrons." "The South," declared Alexander H. Stephens, who was to become vice president of the Confederacy, "is my home—my fatherland . . . there are my hopes and prospects; with her my fortunes are cast; her fate is my fate, and her destiny my destiny."

The Industrial North. More diversified economically, the North was not so conscious of sectional differences as the South. Despite the expansion and prosperity of agriculture and commerce in the North, political power was shifting from agrarians and merchants to factory owners. Adept at overcoming labor and capital shortages and technological difficulties, Northerners by 1860 produced everything from pins to locomotives. The factory owners grew wealthy and powerful, but within their factories, "wage slaves" toiled long hours for low pay.

Humanitarian reformers, already critical of defects in Northern society, found Southern Negro slavery intolerable. Although led by an eloquent agitator, William Lloyd Garrison, and by an efficient organizer, Theodore Dwight Weld, extreme abolitionists attracted few sympathizers. There were, however, degrees of antislavery sentiment. Extremists demanded immediate, uncompensated emancipation. More moderate leaders called for gradual, compensated emancipation. Others proposed simply the prevention of the expansion of slavery. Despite their small numbers, abolitionists did arouse antislavery sentiment and helped to make slavery a political issue and to organize an antislavery bloc in Congress.

TOWARD THE DISRUPTION OF THE UNION

Compromise and Contention. Making slavery a political issue meant taking steps toward both its extinction and the disruption of the Union. Neither Whigs nor Democrats wished to take a stand on slavery; but after the acquisition of the Southwest from Mexico, Congress had to decide whether to introduce or to prohibit slavery in that territory. Although disruptive passions threatened to destroy hope for accommodation, Henry Clay, who helped frame the Missouri Compromise and sponsored the Compromise Tariff of 1833, brilliantly patched together the Compromise of 1850.

The calm ensuing the Compromise of 1850 vanished in 1854, when Congress, led by Stephen A. Douglas, passed the Kansas-Nebraska Act. Repealing the Missouri Compromise and leaving the question of slavery in those territories to the inhabitants (the doctrine of popular sovereignty), the Kansas-Nebraska Act aroused passions, killed the Whig party, and inspired a conglomeration of Whigs, antislavery Democrats, and Free Soilers to form the Republican party.

A guerrilla war followed in Kansas with outrages perpetrated by proslave, Missouri-based "border ruffians" and antislave Northern-supported fanatics like John Brown. "Bleeding Kansas" won converts to the Republican party, which although only two years old nearly elected the explorer and soldier John C. Frémont president in 1856 on a platform excluding slavery from the territories.

The "Wedges of Separation." The "wedges of separation" were driven deeper during the administration of President James Buchanan (1857–1861). The Supreme Court's Dred Scott decision (1857), which maintained that Congress could not prohibit slavery in the territories, inflamed the North. Buchanan further enraged the North by urging Congress to admit Kansas as a slave state under the Lecompton constitution. Outraged by the denial of popular sovereignty in a territory where free-state men outnumbered slave-state men nearly two to one, Douglas vigorously opposed the Lecompton constitution, broke with the administration, and split the Democratic party.

The rift among the Democrats deepened in 1858, when Douglas debated Abraham Lincoln, the Republican contender for Douglas' Senate seat. The Republicans found a new leader in Lincoln, who balanced his moral indignation and reform zeal with fundamental conservatism, while Southern Democrats were further alienated by Douglas' "Freeport Doctrine." Douglas declared that it mattered not what the Supreme Court said about slave property in the territories because "slavery cannot exist a day ... unless it is supported by local police regulations."

By the 1850's the issues dividing North and South had become emotionalized. Fugitive slave rescues, Kansas atrocities and debates, the widespread Northern acceptance of Harriet Beecher Stowe's portrait of slavery in *Uncle Tom's Cabin*, Southern attempts to reopen the African slave trade, and inflammatory speeches by lead-

The economy of the North was industrial and more readily adapted to the waging of war. In this painting, ironworkers forge a shaft in a New York foundry.

THE METROPOLITAN MUSEUM OF ART, GIFT OF LYMAN G. BLOOMINGDALE, 1901

The Lincoln-Douglas debates, between rival candidates for the Senate from Illinois in 1858, clarified the issues in the long dispute over slavery. Lincoln condemned slavery as evil, but Douglas said that the people of each territory should decide the slavery issue for themselves.

ing politicians were capped by John Brown's raid (Oct. 16–18, 1859), on the Harpers Ferry arsenal in Virginia (now West Virginia).

Supported by a handful of abolitionists, Brown failed in his attempt to foment a slave rebellion and was hanged. Southerners magnified the threat of Brown's scheme and blamed the entire Republican party rather than the extreme, radical abolitionist fringe. By the spring of 1860 the lower South was resolved to secede from the Union if a "black Republican" were elected president, and some states began military preparations.

Lincoln's Election. The election of a Republican in 1860 was virtually assured when Northern and Southern Democrats failed to reunite and nominated separate candidates—Douglas and John C. Breckinridge, respectively. The Republicans nominated Lincoln on a platform excluding slavery from the territories and calling for a protective tariff, a homestead law, internal improvements, and a Pacific railroad. Republican strategy broke the Northwest's traditional Southern ties; Lincoln swept all the North except New Jersey, and was elected.

Secession and Fort Sumter. Remaining consistent to its threat, the lower South (South Carolina, Alabama, Mississippi, Florida, Georgia, Louisiana, and Texas) seceded, established the Confederate States of America, named Jefferson Davis president, and seized nearly all federal forts and arsenals within its borders. Although he felt powerless to prevent it, Buchanan did not condone secession and refused to withdraw troops from Fort Sumter in Charleston Harbor.

For a month after Lincoln became president (March 4, 1861), his administration wrestled with the problem of whether to reinforce Fort Sumter and precipitate war or to withdraw and postpone, perhaps indefinitely, a confrontation. Lincoln ultimately elected to provision (not reinforce) the hungry garrison and to let Jefferson Davis make the next move. Davis and his cabinet decided to take the fort, and war came. Lincoln neither hoped for war nor confidently expected peace. He ran the risk of war but made certain that if war came the Confed-

erates would start it in the worst possible way by firing on "bread."

When Lincoln called for 75,000 volunteers to put down the "insurrection," the upper South (Virginia, North Carolina, Tennessee, and Arkansas) joined the Confederacy. To retain control of the strategic Border States, Lincoln insisted that the war was to preserve the Union and not to annihilate slavery, made arbitrary arrests in Maryland, respected Kentucky's neutrality until the Confederacy violated it, and when fighting broke out in Missouri supported

Uncle Tom's Cabin, a novel by Harriet Beecher Stowe, intensified antislavery feelings in the North.

pro-Union forces. Delaware and the western counties of Virginia (forming West Virginia in 1863) were emphatically loyal to the Union. By saving the critical Border States for the Union, Lincoln made the ultimate conquest of the South possible.

ARI HOOGENBOOM, *Brooklyn College*

Bibliography

Craven, Avery O., *The Coming of the Civil War*, 2d ed. (Cambridge 1957).

Current, Richard N., *Lincoln and the First Shot* (Lippincott 1963).

Donald, David, *Charles Sumner and the Coming of the Civil War* (Knopf 1960).

Dumond, Dwight L., *Antislavery Origins of the Civil War in the United States* (Univ. of Mich. Press 1939).

Elkins, Stanley M., *Slavery* (Univ. of Chicago Press 1959).

Filler, Louis, *The Crusade Against Slavery, 1830–1860* (Harper 1960).

Foner, Eric, *Free Soil, Free Labor, Free Men* (Oxford 1970)

Gray, Lewis C., and Thompson, Esther K., *History of Agriculture in the Southern United States to 1860*, 2 vols. (Carnegie Institute 1933).

Milton, George F., *The Eve of Conflict: Stephen A. Douglas and the Needless War* (Houghton 1934).

Nevins, Allan, *The Emergence of Lincoln*, 2 vols. (Scribner 1950).

Nevins, Allan, *Ordeal of the Union*, 2 vols. (Scribner 1947).

Nichols, Roy F., *The Disruption of American Democracy* (Macmillan 1948).

Phillips, Ulrich B., *Life and Labor in the Old South* (Little 1929).

Potter, David M., *Lincoln and His Party in the Secession Crisis* (Yale Univ. Press 1942).

Pressly, Thomas J., *Americans Interpret Their Civil War* (Princeton Univ. Press 1954).

Stampp, Kenneth M., *And the War Came* (Louisiana State Univ. Press 1950).

Stampp, Kenneth M., *The Peculiar Institution* (Knopf 1956).

Sydnor, Charles S., *The Development of Southern Sectionalism, 1819–1848* (Louisiana State Univ. Press 1948).

2. Manpower and Resources

Neither North nor South was prepared for war, especially so ruthless and total a conflict as a civil war. In 1860 the U. S. Army numbered only 16,367 officers and men, most of whom were stationed at remote outposts on the western frontier. Sectional loyalties within those thin ranks precluded any semblance of cohesiveness. With the exception of two aged generals, Winfield Scott and John E. Wool, not an officer then on active duty had ever commanded a unit larger than a 1,000-man brigade.

The U. S. Navy was equally unprepared for hostilities. Largely inactive since the War of 1812, the American fleet consisted of 90 ships. Only 42 were in active service at the outbreak of civil war; of this number, 11 fell into Confederate hands in the April 1861 capture of the naval base at Norfolk, Va. The remaining Federal vessels were scattered throughout the world. Not even the high command remained intact; 230 of 1,400 naval officers resigned their commissions to join the Confederacy.

Advantages of the North. In a comparison of the Northern and Southern nations, the Union seemed to possess every advantage. Twenty-three Northern states and seven territories, containing 22 million people, were arrayed against 11 Southern states with 9,105,000 people. An important correction must immediately be noted, for 3,654,000 of those Southerners were Negro slaves—of doubtful value to the Southern cause. Besides this great difference in population, a steady flow of European immigrants into the Northern states gave the Union a tremendous advantage in manpower.

THE UNITED STATES IN 1861

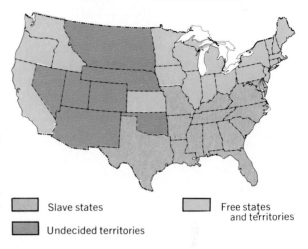

▨ Slave states	▤ Free states and territories
▨ Undecided territories	

The North's economic superiority was almost incalculable. Natural resources abounded, from Midwestern dairy products to New England timber. At Federal disposal were 110,000 manufacturing plants and 1,300,000 industrial workers. The Confederacy could rely only on 18,000 manufacturing establishments and 110,000 skilled workers. The commodities manufactured annually by the state of New York alone were four times greater in value than those produced by the entire Confederacy.

The North produced 97% of all firearms in America and 96% of the nation's railroad equipment. Over 70% of America's 31,300 miles of railroads were located in the North. The North not only possessed 81% of the country's bank deposits; the prewar South's banking and foreign exchanges were in New York City and were therefore promptly closed at the outbreak of the war.

Finally, the North possessed an established government with inherited foundations, proven machinery, and functioning diplomacy. The South had only hope and enthusiasm to substantiate its experiment in confederation.

Balancing Factors. Since the Civil War lasted four years, the inequality between the two sections obviously was not so pronounced as simple comparisons indicate. Indeed, the South enjoyed a number of favorable conditions. It was waging a defensive war, so it did not require as many men as the North, which needed troops for both battle and occupation. As Federal forces continued to attack and to enlarge the area of military operations, the Northern superiority in manpower became proportionally less because of the double drain on its strength.

The Confederacy had the psychological advantage of fighting for independence and "defense of hearth and home." Moral righteousness rested at first with the Southerners; for until Negro emancipation became an issue late in 1862, Federal forces were likened to oppressors attempting to force a free people into accepting an unwanted government.

The South also possessed a greater martial spirit. Its youths were better outdoorsmen, marksmen, and horsemen. Deeply imbued with a love of the military, Southerners traditionally had been outstanding graduates of military academies and leaders of America's fighting forces.

Northern and Southern troops marched off to war amid scenes of general rejoicing. Hardship and grief came later. Thomas Nast painted New York's 7th Regiment.

In purely military terms, the Confederacy had two out of three chances of winning. It could defeat the Federal armies in battle or fight them to a stalemate. Either way, the Southern nation would remain independent. Federal forces, on the other hand, had but one choice: they could restore the Union only through a physical conquest of the South. This would entail destroying the resources and will to fight of 5,400,000 people (excluding slaves) who occupied an area of 846,000 square miles (2,190,000 sq km). The Southerners unquestionably faced formidable odds in 1861; yet their prospects of victory were certainly superior to those of their forefathers in the American Revolution.

The Armies. The average Civil War soldier was a farm boy between 18 and 30 years of age. He possessed little formal education, and by modern-day standards his military training was superficial. He was more fighter than soldier, and he tended to scoff at military discipline and other formalities of army life.

Several factors prompted his voluntary entrance into the army. Intense patriotism, the determination to fight for one's particular cause, the enticement of enlistment bounties, or the simple love of adventure were all strong inducements. Yet when the war did not end as quickly as many expected, and enlistments dwindled as popular enthusiasm began to wane, both governments resorted to conscription.

The first Confederate draft law, enacted in April 1862, called for the induction of able-bodied men between the ages of 18 and 35 for an army term of three years. These age limits later were expanded to 17 and 50. Northern conscription began in March 1863, and called for the drafting of men between 20 and 45 for 3-year terms of duty.

Conscription was highly unpopular and only partially successful. In the North numerous draft riots erupted, notably an outburst of mob terrorism in New York City in July 1863. The drafted men were often of doubtful quality; the majority of men executed by sentence of courts-martial were draftees convicted of desertion. Glaring inequities existed in the conscription laws. The Confederacy granted exemption to large planters and slaveholders. On both sides a man could avoid the draft by paying a substitute to go in his place. Soon, from America's lower classes, the cry arose that the conflict was "a rich man's war but a poor man's fight."

A total of 1,556,000 men served in the Federal army, as compared to no more than 900,000 who fought for the Confederacy. The Southern armies reached a peak strength in 1863, then declined sharply thereafter. In contrast, the Federal forces continued to grow in size. By the end of the war, 800,000 Federal troops were matched against 200,000 Confederates.

To become a soldier, a man normally joined a military company being raised in his own locality. This company then went to a state training camp and joined similar units preparing for war. At the completion of basic training, 10 companies were banded together as a regiment and mustered into national service. Orders followed, assigning the regiment to duty in the field.

Pay and Equipment. The Federal private received $13 a month and a clothing allowance of $42 a year. Customarily, his uniform was dark blue. "Billy Yank's" equipment included rifle, ammunition, knapsack, blanket, haversack, canteen, bayonet, and cartridge box. He usually lived in a tent, cooked meals with his messmates, and was personally responsible for the good condition of his equipment.

His Confederate counterpart, "Johnny Reb," never enjoyed such abundance. In addition to his musket—often acquired from a dead soldier on the battlefield—the Confederate carried a blanket slung over one shoulder, canteen, knife, and cartridge box. For him, a tent was a luxury. Shoes were highly coveted because they were so few in supply. Although gray was the color of the official Confederate uniform, not many soldiers had such clothing. Many instead wore uniforms taken from dead or captured Federals and dyed a light brown ("butternut") in a solution of acorns or walnut hulls. The Southern private received $11 monthly until 1864, when his pay was raised to $18 because of widespread inflation.

Negroes in the Armies. Approximately 186,000 Negroes became Federal soldiers. They served under white officers and often suffered discrimination in such matters as pay and bounties. But they proved courageous fighters in several of the battles in which they participated.

Confederate officials were shortsighted in failing to use slaves as soldiers. Many Confederate leaders feared an uprising once the Negroes were given arms; others opposed the use of slaves on grounds that the Negroes were ill-prepared for such high responsibility. Not until March 1865 did the Confederate government authorize the recruitment of 200,000 Negroes as soldiers. A few all-black units were mustered into Southern service, but none was sent into combat.

Military Leaders. Both presidents, Abraham Lincoln of the Union and Jefferson Davis of the Confederacy, overplayed their roles as commanders in chief. In a sense, however, both were forced to do so until each had obtained generals of proven ability. Thereafter, Lincoln was fairly content to let his field commanders handle the armies.

Such was not the case with Davis. A West Point graduate and former secretary of war, Davis stubbornly concentrated on military affairs at the expense of civil matters. His intrusions were a source of embarrassment to field generals such as Lee and the two Johnstons. Davis never realized that the Confederacy, blessed with good generals, needed the effective political guidance that the president could have given but did not.

Generals of the North and South made many mistakes in the first months of the war. The officers were simply too inexperienced, the fighting forces too large, the tactics too revolutionary, and the objectives too sweeping. Moreover, while the generals who commanded field armies were professional soldiers, their West Point training had not prepared them for the unorthodox, intricate problems posed by an intranational struggle. Civil War generals had to learn their jobs, and this learning process proved painful to them and often disastrous to the troops they commanded.

That the U. S. Army permitted its officers to resign with honorable discharges and volunteer their services to the South explains in great part the initial military effectiveness of the Confederacy. A total of 182 former U. S. Army officers attained the rank of brigadier general or higher in the Confederate forces. Included in this number were Robert E. Lee, Joseph E. Johnston, Albert Sidney Johnston, Samuel Cooper, James Longstreet, John B. Hood, and Joseph Wheeler. Of 425 Confederate officers who attained a general's rank, 77 were killed in action.

Blacks served in both armies under white officers. They fought effectively for the North, but Southern leaders armed their slaves only in desperation in 1865.

THE BETTMANN ARCHIVE

COOK COLLECTION, VALENTINE MUSEUM

Confederate camp life, as depicted in the lithograph above, seems like a pleasant outing, but behind the lines, disease took a tremendous toll of lives. Nor were the Confederates always as well dressed as those shown at left. Shoes, uniforms, and weapons often were taken from the dead.

while Lee perfected the 500-year-old concepts of war with limited objectives. Lincoln paid Grant perhaps the highest compliment with the remark: "I can't spare this man. He fights." Three quarters of a century later, Winston Churchill voiced universal opinion when he termed Lee "one of the noblest Americans who ever lived, and one of the greatest captains known to the annals of war."

In addition to these two foremost commanders, the Civil War produced other generals whose fame transcends the ages. On the Union side, for example, were the excitable William T. Sherman, first practitioner of blitzkrieg and psychological tactics; the slashing, bantam-sized Philip H. Sheridan; and the eccentric but reliable George H. Thomas. Among the heroes of the Confederacy were Thomas J. (Stonewall) Jackson, a master of mobility and the war's most brilliant infantry commander; the defensive strategists Joseph E. Johnston and James Longstreet; Nathan Bedford Forrest, the greatest cavalry leader in the war; and J. E. B. (Jeb) Stuart, the spectacular cavalryman.

The great commanders of the Civil War emerged after a costly trial-and-error process. Early in the war, civilian leaders on both sides chose commanders on the bases of recommendation, hearsay evidence, or political considerations. Too often the results were catastrophic.

Minor Officers. Capable leaders in the lower echelons of command were developed also only after trial and error. Especially in the early stages of the war, regimental officers were chosen through political channels, and company commanders were elected by the companies on the basis of popularity. Hard experience of war weeded out most of the incompetents.

The Federal armies had 583 general officers, of whom 47 died in battle. The youngest general in the Civil War was a Pennsylvanian, Galusha Pennypacker. Born in 1844, Brevet Maj. Gen. Pennypacker did not reach voting age until after the war. The oldest general on active duty was John E. Wool of New York, who was 77 when the war began.

Commanding Generals. Any contrast of Northern and Southern officers inevitably devolves into a comparison of U. S. Grant and Robert E. Lee. The short, slovenly, cigar-smoking Grant was a product of the Midwest. Lee, 15 years older than Grant, was a stately representative of one of Virginia's oldest families.

Military analysts often assert that Grant was "the first of the modern generals" and Lee "the last of the old-fashioned commanders." It was Grant who introduced all-out, total warfare,

Winslow Homer was one of a number of notable artists and photographers who recorded the Northern side of the Civil War. *A Rainy Day in Camp* suggests some of the boredom that filled the time between battles. Union soldiers, like those at the right, were better armed than their opponents.

Weapons—*Small Arms*. The weapon most used by Civil War infantrymen on both sides was known officially as the United States Rifle Musket, Model 1861. Soldiers called it the "Springfield," as most of these guns were made at the arsenal in Springfield, Mass. The Springfield was a percussion-cap, muzzleloading smoothbore, caliber .58, weighing 9¾ pounds (4.4 kg). Its effective range was 250 yards (229 meters). It fired a soft lead Minié bullet—called a "minnie ball." More than 670,000 Springfields were issued to Union forces during the war. The Confederates took many in captured arsenals and from captured or dead Union Soldiers.

The Civil War also brought marked developments in breechloaders, which fired ready-made bullets more rapidly and more accurately than the muzzleloaders. Among such weapons were the 7-shot Spencer repeating carbine, the Sharps carbine, and the 15-shot Henry repeater. The Henry repeater was the forerunner of the famous Winchester carbine. Unfortunately for the North, red tape and the political conservatism of its leaders, who were reluctant to accept novel weapons, prohibited the wide and prompt adoption of the repeating rifle.

Bayonets, sabers, swords, knives, pikes, and lances existed in profusion, especially early in the war. But they proved to be more decorative than destructive. Of approximately 250,000 Federal soldiers treated for wounds, only 922 were victims of edged weapons. Moreover, as one authority has stated, most of these wounds "originated in private quarrels, or were inflicted by camp guards in the discharge of their duty."

Artillery. More than 48 different types of artillery field pieces were used by both sides in the war. The two most popular cannon were the

12-pounder (5.4 kg) Napoleon smoothbore howitzer and the 10-pounder (4.5 kg) Parrott rifled gun. The former fired a 12-pound (5.4 kg) shell and had an effective range of 1,500 yards (1,372 meters); the latter used a smaller shell but was accurate to 3,000 yards (2,743 meters).

Artillerymen used various types of shells, depending on the action in which they were engaged. Solid shot was employed for battering a fortification or for striking an enemy column in flank. Explosive shells and "spherical case" blanketed an area with what is known today as shrapnel. Canister, a thin-shelled projectile filled with lead balls the size of plums, was deadly for close action up to 300 yards (274 meters).

The basic Civil War artillery unit was known as a battery. It normally consisted of four to six guns commanded by a captain.

During the war the North experimented with

LIBRARY OF CONGRESS

CULVER PICTURES

New weapons, such as the machine gun, were tested during the war, but cannon still played a central role. The Federal equipment at the left is held in readiness at Yorktown, Va., in 1862.

a number of new weapons, including the machine gun, improved mortars, and cannon such as Rodmans, Columbiads, and Dahlgrens. Yet to gunners on both sides, the Napoleons and Parrotts remained the "old reliables."

Further Reading: Futch, Ovid L., *History of Andersonville Prison* (Univ. of Florida Press 1968); Gates, Paul W., *Agriculture and the Civil War* (Knopf 1965); Shannon, Fred A., *The Organization and Administration of the Union Army 1861–1865*, 2 vols. (Smith, P. 1965); Turner, George Edgar, *Victory Rode the Rails* (Bobbs 1953).

3. The Military Campaigns

The American Civil War was the largest and most costly struggle ever waged in the Western Hemisphere. Americans of North and South clashed in more than 3,000 engagements; the number of dead is unmatched in the nation's military history. Because each side fought for what it considered the true American way of life —each seeking to preserve a common heritage of freedom and opportunity—the war had to be fought to the bitter end. The Civil War thus became the first total war of modern times—a conflict of complete conquest and uncompromising objectives.

Weapons and tactics changed so markedly during the four years of combat that the Civil War is often termed "the most transitional conflict in history." This war brought such military innovations as the telegraph, aerial reconnaissance, hand grenades, land mines, the machine gun, rifled muskets and cannon, trench warfare, and wire entanglements. It was the first war in which railroads were widely used to move troops and supplies. The highly developed rail system in the North proved a great advantage to the Union armies.

Basic Strategy. Yet basic strategy, at least for the first three years, seldom varied. Each side amassed large armies, then moved against a vital point (usually a city) of the opponent. The de-

fending army would take a position between the invading force and its objective. Open battle would follow.

Few such engagements were decisive in a military sense. Owing to troop exhaustion and other factors, commanders seldom followed up their victories. After a battle one or both armies would retire, reorganize, reposition itself, and invite battle anew. This monotonous indecisiveness gave the campaigning an unending, purposeless quality.

Sieges and heavily fortified battlefronts were uncommon in the Civil War. Pitched battles one or two days long, with changes of base thereafter, were the general practice. Inadequate coordination existed between army segments; the high commands too often were more hesitant than heroic; political meddling into military affairs prevailed on both sides; civilian dissatisfaction was constant. At times the war seemed to possess an aura of mass confusion and fatal uncertainty.

Geographical Theaters. In addition, simple geography heightened the complexities of the war by dividing campaigns into three distinct and separate theaters.

The two major areas of operation were between the Mississippi River and the Atlantic Ocean. But the Appalachian Mountains, extending in an almost unbroken line from Pennsylvania to Alabama, prevented armies from moving freely from the eastern states of Virginia and the Carolinas into such western or trans-Appalachian states as Kentucky and Tennessee. As a result, separate armies in the East (east of the mountains) and in the West (west of the mountains) campaigned independently of one another until 1864, when the Union at last began to coordinate movements in the two theaters.

The third and least significant theater lay west of the Mississippi River. Isolated by the river from the others, it included Louisiana,

Texas, Arkansas, and Missouri (with its strong centers of Southern sentiment). Whoever controlled the Mississippi virtually held the key to this region, known as the Trans-Mississippi Department.

Military strategy in the 1860's, as in wars of former centuries, centered on the seizure of the enemy's key cities. For the Federal armies, which conducted most of the offensives, five Confederate cities became primary objectives. In the East were Richmond, the Confederate capital, and the vital railroad center of Atlanta; in the West were New Orleans and Vicksburg, both strongholds on the all-important Mississippi, and the railroad junction of Chattanooga.

Events of 1861. The war began on a tiny artificial island in the harbor of Charleston, S.C. The island contained a partially completed, pentagonal installation known as Fort Sumter. There, on Dec. 26, 1860, a Federal detachment of 128 men under Maj. Robert Anderson took refuge after South Carolina's secession from the Union.

Equipment to fight a war. A battery on tracks used by a Northern railroad to protect workmen repairing burned bridges; a balloon to scout Confederates along the James River; Northern telegraph wire strung during the battle of Fredericksburg.

In the weeks thereafter, Anderson refused repeated demands that he surrender the fort to Confederate authorities. The plight of the Federal garrison grew desperate, and Southern patience grew thin. The Sumter crisis loomed ominously when Abraham Lincoln, the North's new president, took office. Unwilling to stand by and do nothing, Lincoln shortly announced his intention to supply the Federals at Fort Sumter with food.

Confederates manning the Charleston batteries interpreted this decision as an act of aggression. Accordingly, on April 12, 1861, Southern guns opened fire on the fort and its defenders. Some 4,000 shells pounded Fort Sumter in the course of a 34-hour bombardment that reduced the fort to flaming rubble. Anderson was helpless and had no alternative but to surrender his command.

The firing on Fort Sumter prompted Lincoln to issue a call for 75,000 troops to suppress those forces that had fired on the American flag.

The Confederacy then committed a grave mistake by transferring the Southern capital late in April from Montgomery, Ala., deep in the South, to Richmond, Va. The new capital, only about 100 miles (160 km) south of Washington, became the foremost Federal target. Virginia became the major battleground of the Civil War.

The fight for control of Virginia in general and Richmond in particular began only a few weeks after war exploded. Federal forces made three thrusts into the Old Dominion. The first probe, by inexperienced troops, moved from Ohio into the pro-Northern counties of western Virginia. There they collided with Confederate units equally untrained in the ways of war. In a series of small battles, notably Philippi (June 3), Rich Mountain (July 11), and Corrick's Ford (July 13), the Federals gained victories. Fighting in this region continued intermittently until 1863, when the whole area entered the Union as the loyal state of West Virginia.

The other Federal invasions of Virginia met with disaster. The main Confederate defenses of the state stretched from Norfolk northward to the Potomac River, thence westward to Harpers Ferry. Early in June 1861, Federal Gen. Benjamin F. Butler, a lawyer-turned-soldier, left Fort Monroe with a small force and struck at Richmond by way of the peninsula of land between the James and York rivers. At Big Bethel Church, just west of Yorktown, Butler encountered the entrenched 1st North Carolina Infantry, and on June 10 ordered an attack. The Federals, many in gaudy Zouave uniforms, became demoralized before the battle and nervously began firing at one another. Exasperated officers finally got the men stumbling forward toward the Confederate lines, where their feeble thrusts were hurled back in confusion in less than 20 minutes.

First Battle of Bull Run. The third and major Federal drive resulted in the largest battle of the war's first year. In mid-July, bowing to public and political pressure, Gen. Irvin McDowell marched southward from Washington with 35,000 Federal recruits. His objective was Richmond; but to protect his rear, he had first to capture the railroad junction of Manassas, 30 miles (48 km) southwest of the Northern capital. Through espionage agents in Washington the Confederates quickly learned of McDowell's intentions. The Confederate generals P. G. T. Beauregard and Joseph E. Johnston quickly concentrated 30,000 Southern troops north of Manassas.

On July 21, an extremely hot Sunday, McDowell assailed the Confederate lines near a stream called Bull Run. By early afternoon the Federals seemed at the point of victory. Yet a determined stand by a brigade of Virginians under Gen. Thomas J. Jackson and timely reinforcements from the Shenandoah Valley enabled the Confederates to launch a counterattack that turned impending defeat into a stunning triumph. The Southern hero of the day became known as "Stonewall" Jackson.

This First Battle of Bull Run (or First Manassas) was little more than a collision between two large, armed mobs. Organization and tactics dissolved in the heat of battle. At times total confusion prevailed. Yet the battle had several important effects. Victorious Southerners became convinced that Yankees were poor fighters and that the war would be brief. On the other hand, Northerners were awakened to the reality that destroying the Confederacy would take longer than anticipated. Thus, while Southerners tended to become lethargic over a great success, Northerners mobilized in earnest for full-scale war.

Other Actions. The Union suffered another setback in the East before the year 1861 ended. On October 21, a Federal scouting party on the upper Potomac River was ambushed at Ball's Bluff near Leesburg, Va., and almost annihilated. Among the dead was Col. Edwin D. Baker, former Oregon senator and close friend of Lincoln. This disaster led to the creation of the Congressional Committee on the Conduct of the War. Seven U. S. congressmen comprised this investigative body. No member had any military training, yet the committee continually pried into army affairs and never hesitated to embarrass field commanders.

On November 7, the North scored its first significant success. An amphibious operation captured Port Royal, S. C., gaining a beachhead on the South Atlantic coast.

While Confederates in 1861 won most of the battles, Lincoln and the Northern people were by no means ready to concede defeat. Shortly after the July setback at Bull Run, Lincoln called to Washington the victor of western Virginia, Gen. George B. McClellan. In autumn McClellan succeeded the aging Winfield Scott as general-in-chief of the U. S. Army and began organizing a fighting force of 150,000 volunteers. It was the largest army that had ever been assembled in America.

Events of 1862 in the West. At the beginning of 1862, some 48,000 Confederate soldiers guarded a 600-mile (960-km) line stretching westward from Cumberland Gap, Va., through Bowling Green, Ky., to New Madrid, Mo., on the Mississippi River. Soft Federal probes convinced the Union high command that the Southern defenses were thinly manned. Early in February, therefore, Gen. U. S. Grant departed from Cairo, Ill., with 15,000 troops to attack the center of the Confederate line and to gain control of two important rivers, the Tennessee and the Cumberland.

To protect these rivers the Confederates had constructed twin forts in Tennessee just south of the Kentucky border. Fort Henry guarded the Tennessee; Fort Donelson, 12 miles (19 km) to the east, protected the Cumberland. On Febru-

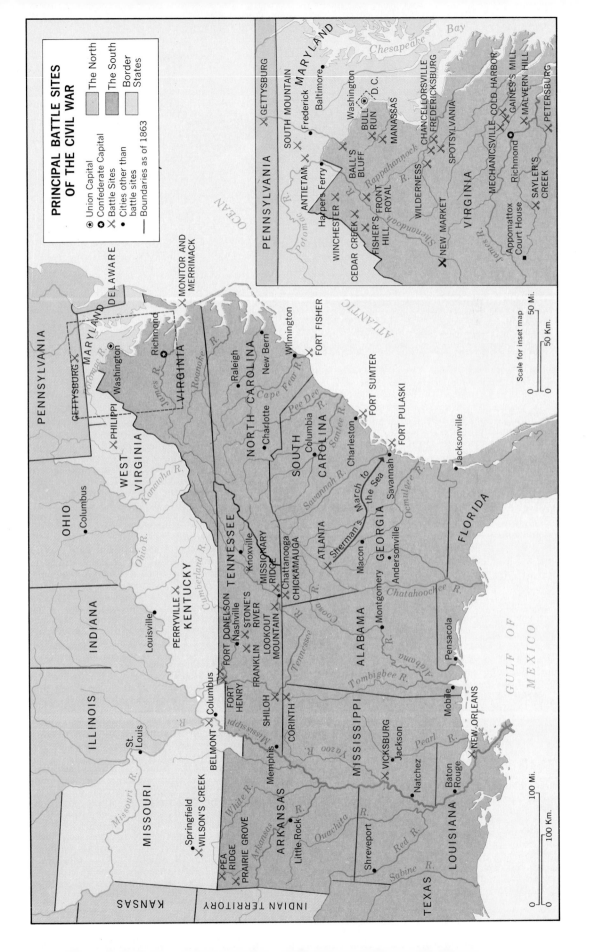

PRINCIPAL BATTLE SITES OF THE CIVIL WAR

⊙ Union Capital
✪ Confederate Capital
✕ Battle Sites
• Cities other than battle sites
— Boundaries as of 1863

The North
The South
Border States

Gilbert Gaul's *The Skirmish Line* is a realistic portrait of a small Yankee force in action. Most battles of the Civil War were fought by small units like this.

ary 6, a Federal river fleet battered 12-gun Fort Henry into submission. A week later, Grant surrounded the stronger Fort Donelson. Severe fighting (February 13–15) trapped most of the Southern garrison. To its besieged commander's query of surrender terms, Grant replied with his now-famous "no terms but unconditional surrender." The Confederates capitulated on February 16.

Grant's triumphs at Henry and Donelson brought great rejoicing in the North. The Union had achieved its first resounding victories; Kentucky was secure; all of Tennessee, Mississippi, and Alabama were open to Federal invasion; Southern morale suffered a severe blow; and the North had a new hero, who himself had a new nickname—"Unconditional Surrender" Grant.

After the capture of Fort Donelson, Grant's 43,000 Federals advanced southward through Tennessee toward Corinth, Miss., Albert Sidney Johnston's new base of operations. Even though most of his 40,000 Confederates were ill-trained and ill-equipped, Johnston resolved to drive Grant from Tennessee by a surprise attack.

Battle of Shiloh. The Battle of Shiloh (April 6–7), one of the war's most costly engagements, ensued. The initial Confederate onslaught caught Grant by surprise. It bent but never quite broke the Federal lines. By nightfall after the first day's fighting, Johnston had bled to death from a leg wound, the Confederate command system had broken down, and Federal reinforcements were filing into position. Grant delivered a strong counterattack the following morning. The Southern troops retreated to Corinth, but were forced a month later to abandon the city.

For the next four months the opposing armies of Grant and Braxton Bragg (who succeeded Johnston) warily eyed each other. Yet while these two great armies played a maneuvering game, four significant events transpired elsewhere in the Western theater.

New Orleans Captured. One was the Federal capture of New Orleans. Two weeks after Shiloh a fleet under Flag Officer David G. Farragut blasted its way into the mouth of the Mississippi and seized not only New Orleans but Baton Rouge and Natchez as well. The fall of New Orleans, soon after the defeat at Shiloh, was a crippling blow to the South. The one consolation to the Confederates in this campaign was the failure of a Federal river attack against the bastion of Vicksburg.

The Andrews Raid. A second event in the West materialized into one of the boldest raids in American history. In April a Federal espionage agent, James J. Andrews, and 21 Northern soldiers sneaked through northwestern Georgia to Big Shanty Station, only 30 miles (48 km) from Atlanta. There they stole the locomotive "General" and two cars of a Western & Atlantic passenger train. The Federals' plan was to race up the tracks to Chattanooga, tearing up the road behind them as they went.

The coup almost succeeded. However, a handful of soldiers and civilians gave chase and captured the Northern raiders halfway to their objective.

Andrews and seven of his men were subsequently hanged in Atlanta. Six of the surviving raiders later became the first recipients of the Congressional Medal of Honor.

The Morgan Raids. Southern cavalrymen soon gained a measure of revenge for the Andrews' foray. In July 1862, Confederate Col. John Hunt Morgan led his "Kentucky Cavaliers" on a 2-week slash through the Bluegrass country. Morgan won four small battles, captured 1,200 Federals, and returned safely to Tennessee with less than 100 casualties. In December, Morgan struck again into Kentucky. This "Christmas Raid" netted 1,900 prisoners, several hundred needed horses, and large quantities of military stores.

Bragg's Invasion of Kentucky. Shortly after Morgan's first Kentucky raid, General Bragg launched an invasion into the same state with his Confederate Army of Tennessee. Bragg hoped to occupy Kentucky's principal cities and, by "military persuasion," unite this border state with the Confederacy. Bragg's inherent caution soon overcame his daring strategy. He gained a tactical victory at Perryville (October 8) over Federal forces under Gen. Don Carlos Buell, then withdrew to Tennessee. Bragg's offensive was the last major Confederate effort to wrest Kentucky from the Union.

Other Moves. The Southerners made a desperate attempt that same autumn to recapture Corinth, Miss. Gen. Earl Van Dorn led his Confederate troops in a 2-day assault (October 3–4) on the city. Gen. William S. Rosecrans and his Federal defenders successfully repulsed the attacks. For his stand at Corinth, Rosecrans was given command of the Federal army opposing Bragg.

Meanwhile, Grant had started southward from Tennessee through Mississippi to Vicksburg, the chief Confederate stronghold on the Mississippi River. Grant planned to deliver a two-pronged attack: Gen. William T. Sherman was to strike Vicksburg from the north, while Grant assailed the city from the east.

The plan backfired. Confederate horsemen under Gen. Earl Van Dorn destroyed Grant's main supply base at Holly Springs, Miss. Grant had no alternative but to fall back to Memphis. Sherman, thus left alone, delivered a series of futile and costly assaults (December 28–29) at Chickasaw Bayou, north of Vicksburg. Grant then began preparations for moving his entire army down the Mississippi and seizing Vicksburg by renewed attack or long siege.

The final Western engagement of 1862 began on the last day of the year. The armies of Rosecrans and Bragg met at Stone's River, on the northern outskirts of Murfreesboro, Tenn. For the better part of four days the two mighty hosts waged a desperate but indecisive fight. Bragg finally broke off the battle and retired southward. The Federal forces at Stone's River suffered 31% losses, as compared to 25% casualties for the Confederates. Rarely has a drawn battle been so expensive in human life.

Events of 1862 in the East. McClellan's creation, the huge Army of the Potomac, spent seven months of inactivity around Washington, D. C. Finally, Lincoln, his patience exhausted, issued direct orders for McClellan to advance into Virginia. The 35-year-old commander vetoed the dangerous overland route to Richmond that McDowell had attempted the preceding year. Instead, he proposed to transport his army by water to Fort Monroe, and from there to Richmond by way of the same peninsula where Butler's earlier probe had met defeat. McClellan was confident that he could land his army on the peninsula and traverse the 70 miles (112 km) inland to Richmond before Gen. Joseph E. Johnston could disengage his Confederate forces stationed along the Manassas-Fredericksburg line.

Lincoln reluctantly agreed to the plan. But the President ordered McDowell's corps of 37,-000 men to remain on guard in the vicinity of Fredericksburg to protect Washington. Thus was the stage set for the Peninsular Campaign.

Start of the Peninsular Campaign. By early April all of McClellan's 105,000 soldiers were massed on the toe of the Virginia peninsula. Yet a thin Confederate screening force at Yorktown became so magnified in McClellan's cautious eyes that he initiated a one-month siege of the historic

Albert Bierstadt, renowned for his sweeping and romanticized landscape paintings, adapted his style to this scene of Yankee sharpshooters ambushing some Southern irregular soldiers.

Gen. Philip Sheridan leads a successful Union charge (1864) at Winchester, Va., a town that changed hands 84 times.

IMPORTANT BATTLES OF THE CIVIL WAR

Antietam, Sept. 17, 1862, fought in western Maryland about 55 miles (180 km) northwest of Washington, D. C. This was the climax of Gen. Robert E. Lee's first invasion of the North. Gen. McClellan's Army of the Potomac intercepted the invading Confederates at Sharpsburg. The ensuing struggle was the bloodiest one-day battle of the war. The armies fought to a stalemate, but Lee retired to Virginia. Federal losses were 2,108 killed, 9,549 wounded, and 753 missing. Confederate casualties totaled 2,700 killed, 9,024 wounded, and about 2,000 missing.

Atlanta Campaign, in Georgia, May 7–Sept. 2, 1864. Starting from Chattanooga, Tenn., Gen. William T. Sherman's Union army fought its way through the battles of Dalton, Resaca, Kingston, New Hope Church, and Kennesaw Mountain to the outskirts of Atlanta. The Federals repulsed Confederate counterattacks northwest and east of Atlanta, then forced the defenders from the city after a victory at Jonesboro. The key city of the Deep South was taken. In the campaign, the Federals lost 4,428 killed, 22,882 wounded, and 4,442 missing. Confederate losses were 3,044 killed, 21,996 wounded, and 12,983 missing.

Bull Run, First, July 21, 1861, fought in Virginia about 30 miles (48 km) west of Washington, D. C. It was the first major land engagement of the war. Approximately 35,000 raw Federal recruits under Gen. Irvin McDowell attacked an equally inexperienced Confederate force of 30,000 men under Gen. P. G. T. Beauregard and Gen. Joseph E. Johnston. A determined stand early in the afternoon by the Virginia brigade of Gen. Thomas J. ("Stonewall") Jackson and the timely arrival of Confederate reinforcements brought victory to the South. Federal losses were 418 killed, 1,011 wounded, and 1,216 missing; Confederate casualties numbered 387 killed, 1,582 wounded, and 12 missing.

Bull Run, Second, Aug. 29–30, 1862, fought on virtually the same ground as First Bull Run. Gen. John Pope, leading a Federal army of 45,000 men into Virginia, was flanked by "Stonewall" Jackson's corps and then assailed by the combined forces of Jackson and Lee. The Federals were decisively defeated and suffered casualties of 1,724 killed, 8,372 wounded, and 5,958 missing. Confederate losses were 1,481 killed, 7,627 wounded, and 89 missing. This victory gave Lee the momentum to embark on his Maryland (Antietam) Campaign.

Cedar Creek, Oct. 19, 1864, fought in Virginia about 60 miles (96 km) west of Washington, D. C. Gen. Philip H. Sheridan's Federal forces were resting at Middletown when Gen. Jubal Early's Confederate army, outnumbered more than two to one, attacked the Federal flank at dawn. The Southerners were successful at first but lost their impetus. In the lull that followed, Sheridan dramatically arrived on the field from Winchester and led a victorious counterattack. The victory ended Confederate control of the Shenandoah Valley. Early lost 2,910 men, most of his artillery, and all of his wagons. Sheridan's losses totaled 5,665 men.

Chancellorsville, May 1–4, 1863, fought in the Wilderness of north-central Virginia, about 50 miles (80 km) southwest of Washington, D. C. It is considered by many to be Lee's greatest victory. Gen. Joseph Hooker with a huge Federal army launched a drive on Richmond by trying to encircle both flanks of Lee's army encamped at Fredericksburg. Lee countered by dispatching "Stonewall" Jackson to flank one wing of Hooker's army while he held the other in check. Jackson's brilliant flank assault opened fighting that lasted three days and extended over a 10-mile (16-km) area. Hooker's stunned army ultimately abandoned the field. Union casualties totaled 17,275 men. Lee's victory cost him 12,821 men, including the irreplaceable Jackson.

Chattanooga, Battles Around, Nov. 23–27, 1863, waged on the heights north and east of the strategic city of Chattanooga, Tenn. After winning the Battle of Chickamauga, Confederate Gen. Braxton Bragg besieged the Union army in Chattanooga. But with the arrival first of Gen. U. S. Grant and then reinforcements, the Federals assaulted the Southern positions at Orchard Knob, Lookout Mountain, and Missionary Ridge. After the last battle the Confederates fled in disorder to Dalton, Ga. Union losses were 753 killed, 4,722 wounded, and 349 missing. Confederate casualties were 361 killed, 2,160 wounded, and 4,146 prisoners.

Chickamauga, Sept. 19–20, 1863, fought in the northwest corner of Georgia. After occupying Chattanooga, Gen. William S. Rosecrans' Union army started eastward in pursuit of Bragg's Confederates. The two forces collided along the banks of Chickamauga Creek. On the second day's fighting, the Southerners smashed the Federal right flank and forced half of Rosecrans' army to flee the field. A determined stand on the left flank by Gen. George H. Thomas averted a complete disaster. Bragg's failure to follow up his advantage allowed the Federals to withdraw to Chattanooga. Each side suffered 28% losses in the battle.

Cold Harbor, June 3, 1864, fought 10 miles (16 km) northeast of Richmond, Va. It was Grant's worst defeat of the war. After 4 weeks of trying in vain to turn the right flank of Lee's army in the battles of the Wilderness and of Spotsylvania (see below), Grant rashly ordered 3 Federal corps to drive straight at the center of Lee's entrenched lines. The Federal repulse was almost a massacre: more than 6,000 men fell in less than an hour of fighting. Lee's losses did not exceed 1,500 men. This battle was the last major victory of the Army of Northern Virginia.

Fort Henry and Fort Donelson, Feb. 6–16, 1862. The forts were earthen Confederate redoubts guarding the Tennessee and Cumberland rivers, respectively, in northern Tennessee. Neutralizing these forts to gain control of the two rivers was the first step in the Federal offensive in Tennessee. On February 6, a Federal river fleet battered Fort Henry into submission. Gen. U. S. Grant secured the works, then moved overland with his army and assaulted Fort Donelson. After 3 days of fighting, the Confederate garrison surrendered. The Federals inflicted 2,000 casualties and took 14,623 prisoners at a cost of 500 killed; 2,108 wounded, and 224 missing. These were the first major victories for the Union.

Franklin, Nov. 30, 1864, fought about 18 miles (28 km) south of Nashville, Tenn. Gen. John B. Hood with 22,000 Confederates attacked 23,000 men led by Gen. John M. Schofield, who was moving northward to join Gen. George H. Thomas' army at Nashville. The Federals hurled back a series of Confederate assaults and then withdrew to Nashville. Federal casualties were 189 killed, 1,033 wounded, and 1,104 missing; the Confederates lost 534 killed (including 5 generals), 1,744 wounded, and 417 missing. Hood's continued pursuit ended in disaster 2 weeks later at Nashville.

Fredericksburg, Dec. 13, 1862, fought in eastern Virginia, midway between Washington, D. C., and Richmond. Gen. Ambrose E. Burnside, new commander of the Army of the Potomac, attempted to rush past Lee's right flank by crossing the Rappahannock River at Fredericksburg. Since Burnside's pontoon bridges did not arrive on time, Lee had a chance to entrench on commanding heights southwest of the city. Burnside launched an all-day series of costly frontal assaults, which the Confederates repulsed easily. Burnside's losses exceeded 12,600 men; Lee's killed and wounded numbered 5,300.

Gettysburg. July 1–3, 1863, fought in southern Pennsylvania about 110 miles (176 km) west of Philadelphia. The battle is regarded by many as "the high-water mark of the Confederacy." Late in June, Lee's army swept northward on a desperate invasion. The Army of the Potomac, under its new commander, George G. Meade, gave pursuit and intercepted the Confederates at Gettysburg. For 3 days Lee unleashed one assault after another on the Federal lines. The climactic charge, by the division of Confederate Gen. George E. Pickett, failed and terminated the battle. Casualties were extremely heavy: Federal—3,070 killed, 14,497 wounded, 5,434 missing; Confederate—2,592 killed, 12,706 wounded, 5,150 missing.

Manassas, First and Second. See *Bull Run, First and Second.*

Monitor and Merrimack, March 9, 1862, fought in Hampton Roads, Va. It was the first engagement in naval history between ironclad ships. The *Merrimack,* originally a Federal steamer, was captured by the Confederates, rechristened the *Virginia,* and converted into a floating citadel 263 feet (80 meters) long and carrying 10 guns. In appearance the ship resembled "a floating barn roof." The U. S. S. *Monitor,* 172 feet (52 meters) long, bore 2 guns in a 140-ton revolving turret. It looked like "a tin can on a shingle." For 3 hours the ironclads fought an indecisive duel. This battle rendered obsolete every wooden navy in the world.

Nashville, Dec. 15–16, 1864, fought just south of Nashville, Tenn. Following defeat at Franklin, Hood's weakened Confederate army moved on to Nashville, where the Federal army was based. Gen. George H. Thomas, with an army twice the size of Hood's force, moved out of the city and assailed the Confederates on three fronts. Hood barely managed on the second day to extricate his broken army. Federal losses were 387 killed, 2,562 wounded, and 112 missing. Total Confederate losses are unknown, though Thomas reported the capture of 4,462 men.

Pea Ridge, March 7–8, 1862, fought in the northwestern corner of Arkansas. Federal forces under Gen. Samuel R. Curtis that had driven from Missouri a heterogeneous Confederate army that included some Indians, withstood a 2-day series of assaults by troops under Gen. Earl Van Dorn. This was one of the few fights in which Indians were used as soldiers. The Federals lost 203 killed, 980 wounded, and 201 missing. Confederate losses were 1,000 killed and wounded and 300 captured. This Federal victory preserved Missouri for the Union.

Peninsular Campaign, March 17–July 3, 1862, waged in southeastern Virginia on the peninsula between the James and York rivers. Union Gen. George B. McClellan disembarked his Army of the Potomac on the peninsula's tip and advanced slowly westward toward Richmond. Outnumbered Confederates under Gen. Joseph E. Johnston stung the Federals at Williamsburg, then stopped McClellan's advance at the twin battles of Seven Pines and Fair Oaks. Johnston was wounded at Fair Oaks and was succeeded by Gen. Robert E. Lee, who promptly launched a series of counterattacks known as the Seven Days' Campaign (see below). The Confederates drove the Federal army to the banks of the James, ending this Federal thrust at Richmond.

Petersburg Campaign, June 14, 1864–April 2, 1865, outside Petersburg, Va., 25 miles (40 km) south of Richmond. This was the longest siege operation of the war. Thwarted in repeated attempts to capture Richmond, Gen. U. S. Grant shifted his Union army in mid-June to the south bank of the James River and attacked Petersburg, which was a vital rail junction. The Confederate lines held. Grant then laid siege to Petersburg and Lee's army. Many battles were fought in the 9-month siege. The most notable were the Crater, Ream's Station, Hatcher's Run, Fort Stedman, and Five Forks. Grant's losses in the siege were 42,000; Lee's were 28,000.

Seven Days' Campaign, June 26–July 1, 1862, fought in southeastern Virginia. This was the climax of McClellan's Peninsular Campaign. Lee resolved to end the Federal threat to Richmond by attacking in force the isolated right wing of McClellan's army, then rolling up the other Federal elements. The Union army checked Lee's thrust at Mechanicsville on June 26, but broke under heavy attacks the next day at Gaines's Mill. In the battles that followed—Savage Station, Frayser's Farm, White Oak Swamp, and Malvern Hill—McClellan managed to avoid disaster and reach the safety of his base on the James River. Total Union casualties were 15,849 men, as compared to the Confederates' 20,141.

Shiloh, April 6–7, 1862, fought in southwestern Tennessee near the Mississippi border. It was named for the old Shiloh Church, near Pittsburg Landing. Grant, advancing toward Corinth, Miss., was suddenly attacked by Confederates under Gen. Albert Sidney Johnston. The Confederates were victorious the first day, but Johnston's death and the arrival of Federal reinforcements turned the tide and enabled Grant to deliver a successful counterattack on the following day. The Confederates withdrew to Corinth. Union losses were 1,754 killed, 8,408 wounded, and 2,885 missing; Confederate losses were 1,723 killed, 8,012 wounded, and 959 missing. This was the first battle in the Western Hemisphere in which 100,000 men were engaged.

Spotsylvania, May 10–12, 1864, the second major engagement in Grant's drive into Virginia, fought about 60 miles (96 km) southwest of Washington, D. C. In spite of the Federal defeat in the Wilderness, Grant continued pushing southward toward Richmond, trying to encircle Lee's right flank. At Spotsylvania the Federals struck Lee's lines, first in a series of probes and then in a full-scale assault in the rain on May 12. Lee's lines were bent but never broken. Fighting was severest in a sector known as "The Salient," or "Bloody Angle." Federal losses were 10,920 men; Confederate losses were about 6,000 soldiers, including 8 generals killed, wounded, or captured. In this battle the famous "Stonewall Brigade" was all but destroyed.

Stone's River (or Murfreesboro), Dec. 31, 1862–Jan. 2, 1863, fought about 30 miles (48 km) southeast of Nashville, Tenn. Gen. William S. Rosecrans moved southward from Nashville in search of Gen. Braxton Bragg's Army of Tennessee. At Stone's River the Confederates unleashed a series of furious assaults that turned and buckled—but never broke—the Federal lines. Rosecrans lost 1,677 killed, 7,543 wounded, and 3,786 missing; Bragg's casualties numbered 1,294 killed, 7,945 wounded, and 2,300 missing. The 3-day engagement accomplished nothing to compensate the cost in human life. Bragg retired from Murfreesboro, and Rosecrans did not renew operations until the following June.

Vicksburg Campaign, March 29–July 4, 1863, conducted for control of Vicksburg, Miss., the last major Confederate port on the Mississippi River. Skillfully maneuvering his 5 corps to the east side of the river, Grant fought his way to the outskirts of Vicksburg. Several attacks failed to shatter the city's defenses; Grant then began a 47-day siege that ended on July 4 in Vicksburg's surrender. Confederate losses were 8,000 killed and wounded, plus 29,936 men captured in Vicksburg; Union losses were 1,514 killed, 7,395 wounded, and 453 missing.

Wilderness, May 5–6, 1864, fought in north-central Virginia about 50 miles (80 km) southwest of Washington, D. C. Grant led the massive Army of the Potomac across the Rapidan River on May 4 and started toward Richmond. In the thick trees and underbrush of the Wilderness Lee attacked with his outnumbered army. Fighting raged for 2 days before Grant broke off the engagement. The Federals lost 17,666 men; Confederate casualties totaled about 7,750 men. Hundreds of soldiers, too badly wounded to crawl to safety, died in fires blazing in the dry woods. On May 7, Grant began moving southeastward toward Spotsylvania.

Winchester, 1861–1865, a strategically situated city at the lower (northern) end of the Shenandoah Valley in western Virginia. During the war, the city changed hands 84 times. Major battles were fought in and around Winchester on May 25, 1862; June 13–15, 1863; July 23–24, 1864; and Sept. 19, 1864. Winchester served as chief headquarters for Confederate Gen. "Stonewall" Jackson during the 1862 Valley Campaign.

The Battle of Antietam, depicted in the lithograph above, claimed more casualties than any other one-day battle of the war. Much of the action centered on the Burnside Bridge. Just before Antietam, nearby Harpers Ferry (below) fell to Confederate Gen. Stonewall Jackson after a damaging battle.

city. Johnston used this period of Federal immobility to get his 60,000-man army into position on McClellan's front. The Confederates abandoned Yorktown just as the Federals prepared to unleash a heavy bombardment. McClellan inched forward in pursuit. On May 5, in the rain at Williamsburg, Johnston began a delaying action that developed into an all-day major battle. The Confederates then continued retiring slowly toward Richmond.

Throughout April, driving rains had turned the countryside into a vast sea of mud. Both armies struggled against the elements to maintain their positions. By the end of May, McClellan's Army of the Potomac had reached Seven Pines. The church spires of Richmond were visible 9 miles (14 km) away.

Seven Pines was as close as McClellan ever got to the Confederate capital. Johnston, a superb defensive general, noticed that the flooded Chickahominy River had divided the Federal army into two parts. On May 31–June 1, the Confederates delivered at Seven Pines and Fair Oaks a series of attacks on McClellan's left (southern) flank. Wounded soldiers drowned in the mud as McClellan desperately clung to his positions. But Federal initiative was destroyed; McClellan's doubts overcame his determination. Johnston was seriously wounded in the fighting at Fair Oaks. Jefferson Davis, over the opposition of some of his advisers, named Robert E. Lee the new commander of what was to become shortly thereafter the Army of Northern Virginia.

Jackson in the Shenandoah Valley. In western Virginia at this time, Gen. "Stonewall" Jackson was performing brilliantly. Jackson had been entrusted with the security of the Shenandoah Valley, control of which was vital to both sides. This narrow slit of land between two ranges of the Blue Ridge Mountains was a direct avenue into both North and South. Neither side could move safely between the mountains and the coast unless the valley's northern door—the region around Winchester and Harpers Ferry—was shut.

Thus, when McClellan started up the peninsula, Gen. Nathaniel P. Banks with another Federal army advanced southward into the valley. Jackson had only 8,500 men at his command. His assignment was to hold Banks at Winchester and McDowell at Fredericksburg so as to prevent either from reinforcing McClellan in front of Richmond. On March 23, Jackson attacked part of Banks' army at Kernstown, just south of Winchester. The Federals hurled back the assaults; but Jackson's aggressiveness so alarmed officials in Washington that neither Banks nor McDowell was permitted to aid McClellan.

Soon three Federal armies entered the valley for the sole purpose of destroying Jackson's little band. Quickly reinforced by Gen. Richard S. Ewell's division, Jackson and his "foot cavalry," as his fast-marching infantry were called, began a campaign that is still studied at military academies throughout the world as a model of mobility and flexible striking power. The full impact of Jackson's successes in the valley campaign can best be seen from statistics. In 11 weeks between March 22 and June 9, 1862, Jackson's Confederates marched 630 miles (1,013 km) over rough terrain; fought 4 major battles and numerous skirmishes; defeated 3 Federal armies totaling more than 62,000 troops; inflicted 7,000 casualties; and captured 10,000 muskets, 9 cannon, and valuable railroad stock. Jackson's own army, never exceeding 17,000 men, lost 3,100 men and 3 cannon. And all the while, Jackson kept Washington under threat of attack—and prevented reinforcements from joining McClellan.

The Seven Days' Campaign. In mid-June, with the valley safely in Confederate control, Jackson moved rapidly to Richmond to assist Lee in a counteroffensive against McClellan. Lee had ascertained that the Federal army was still dangerously astride the swollen Chickahominy River. Lee's information came from his colorful cavalry chief, Gen. J. E. B. Stuart, who had just returned with his 1,200 horsemen from a spectacular 3-day raid all the way around McClellan's huge army. This was the first of several dramatic escapades by the fun-loving "Jeb" Stuart.

On the basis of Stuart's report, Lee resolved to assail McClellan's exposed right flank north of the Chickahominy, then drive the outflanked Federal army southward to the James River. The battles that followed comprise the Seven Days' Campaign.

The Confederates launched their offensive on June 26 at Mechanicsville, 9 miles (14 km) northeast of of Richmond. They suffered defeat from Federal troops under Gen. Fitz-John Porter. Lee struck again on June 27 and finally broke the Federal lines at Gaines's Mill after a severe all-day fight. McClellan quickly issued orders for his army to retire to Harrison's Landing, the Federal supply base on the James River. Lee tried desperately to destroy the Army of the Potomac before it could reach the protection of Union riverboats. Yet the Federals managed to hold back Lee at Savage Station (June 29), Frayser's Farm (June 30), White Oak Swamp (June 30), and Malvern Hill (July 1). McClellan made good his escape, but this second major attempt to seize Richmond had failed.

Second Bull Run Campaign. A few weeks later, another Federal threat confronted Lee, which led to the Second Bull Run (or Second Manassas) Campaign. Gen. John Pope began moving overland from Washington with 45,000 men of the newly formed Army of Virginia. Pope's target was Richmond; his approach was over the same route employed by McDowell a year earlier. Lee dispatched "Stonewall" Jackson's division northward to block this new Federal advance. On the afternoon of August 9, Jackson struck the van of Pope's army at Cedar Mountain, south of Culpeper. Each side delivered vicious assaults. At sundown the Federals limped from the field. Lee's main army joined Jackson's forces shortly after. Then, while Lee held Pope's attention, Jackson—followed a day later by the division of Gen. James Longstreet—swung around Pope's right flank and captured the Federals' all-important supply base at Manassas. An outraged Pope swung his army around and started in pursuit of Jackson.

Pope soon found Jackson entrenched, but at almost the same time the other half of Lee's army pounced on Pope. The August 29–30 Second Battle of Bull Run (or Second Manassas) ensued. The Federals suffered a severe defeat. Pope managed to check a final thrust by Lee at Chantilly (September 1) before retiring to the safety of Washington.

Lee's Invasion of Maryland. For the first time since the Civil War began, Virginia was temporarily clear of Federal invaders. The time was opportune, Lee reasoned, to strike into the North. Success might secure Maryland for the Confederacy and bring official and badly needed recognition to the Southern nation from England and France. Such recognition would come in the form of supplies and possibly troops.

Lee's gray-clad brigades waded across the Potomac early in September. At Frederick, Md., Lee divided his army. Jackson marched south to neutralize a Federal garrison at Harpers Ferry and to open up the Shenandoah Valley in the event that Lee had to withdraw from Maryland. Lee and the remainder of his army proceeded north toward Hagerstown.

Meanwhile, an alarmed Lincoln assigned what was left of Pope's army to McClellan and dispatched "Little Mac" in pursuit of the Confederate invaders. On September 14, McClellan fought his way through the passes at South Mountain, Md. The next day, as McClellan's troops converged on Lee, Jackson seized Harpers Ferry. Jackson then hastened northward and rejoined Lee late on September 16.

The following day produced the bloodiest one-day battle ever fought on American soil—the Battle of Antietam. From sunrise until dusk that Wednesday, Sept. 17, 1862, Federal brigades along Antietam Creek made repeated vicious assaults on Lee's lines. Had McClellan thrown his entire army against Lee's defenses, sheer weight of numbers might have carried the day for the Federals. Instead, the Union commander shifted his attacks from one sector to another. Casualties on both sides mounted frightfully in such areas as the East Wood, Sunken Road, and Burnside's Bridge. By nightfall Lee's army still held its position. The Federal army had suffered 12,400 casualties; the Confederates' casualties had been 13,000.

Further Fighting in Virginia. The check at Antietam Creek forced Lee back into Virginia.

The historic colonial town of Fredericksburg, Va., came under Union attack on Dec. 13, 1862, but Northern troops were thrown back with heavy losses by defenders led by Lee. (*Below*) During a lull to bury the dead, Rebels (at the end of the bridge) pose for a Brady photograph.

When McClellan seemingly made little effort to resume the campaign against Lee, Lincoln early in November removed him from command. McClellan's successor at the head of the Army of the Potomac was Gen. Ambrose E. Burnside, who did not feel himself competent to command so large an army.

Burnside's doubts proved well founded in a mismanaged campaign a month later. With Lee's army occupying the Winchester-Culpeper line, Burnside resolved to drive at Richmond by crossing the Rappahannock River at Fredericksburg. If the Federals could cross the river quickly, they would be squarely between Lee's army and the Confederate capital. Burnside's entire strategy depended on speed. He lost that advantage when

pontoon boats for crossing the Rappahannock failed to arrive promptly.

By the time Burnside got his 114,000 men across the river, Lee had nullified the Union's numerical superiority by selecting an almost ideal defensive position on heights southwest of Fredericksburg. Burnside, undaunted, delivered six large-scale but futile assaults against Lee's entrenched army on December 13. Federal casualties soared to more than 12,600 men; Lee's losses were less than half. At the height of the Federal massacre, Lee commented gravely: "It is well this [war] is so terrible. Otherwise, we should grow too fond of it."

Events of 1863 in the West. Cavalry raids by both sides occupied the early months of the third year of conflict. One of the longest was that of Col. Benjamin H. Grierson and 1,700 Federal horsemen. Leaving La Grange, Tenn., in April, Grierson's troopers wrecked railroads and supply depots all the way to Baton Rouge, La. The raid lasted two weeks and helped clear the way for Grant's campaign against Vicksburg.

On the other hand, Gen. Nathan Bedford Forrest and his Confederate cavalry made a series of lightning attacks in Tennessee throughout March and April. Gen. John Hunt Morgan followed these with a summer foray through Kentucky, southern Indiana, and across Ohio.

Vicksburg Campaign. During the first six months of 1863, Grant slowly descended on the Confederate stronghold of Vicksburg. Five Federal corps, with 75,000 men, moved down the west bank of the Mississippi and crossed the river below Vicksburg. Grant then skillfully maneuvered his army northward and interposed his Federals between the Confederate forces of Gen. John C. Pemberton near Vicksburg and of Gen. Joseph E. Johnston at Jackson. While Sherman's corps held Johnston at bay, Grant drove Pemberton's Confederates into Vicksburg itself.

A series of assaults (May 16–22) failed to crack the Southern defenses of the city. Grant thereupon resorted to siege operations. For six weeks the Federals isolated the city. Confederate soldiers inside Vicksburg were reduced to eating rats, mules, and grass in an effort to stay alive.

With escape hopeless, Pemberton surrendered the city and its 30,000 defenders on July 4. A joyful Lincoln proclaimed that "the Father of Waters again goes unvexed to the sea." The mighty Mississippi, from Minnesota to the Gulf, was at last in Union control. The Trans-Mississippi had been sheared from the Confederacy.

Chattanooga Campaign. As Grant accepted the surrender of Vicksburg, General Rosecrans and his Army of the Cumberland advanced south from Murfreesboro. To capture Chattanooga and defeat Bragg's Army of Tennessee, which was based in the city, Rosecrans' strategy was to swing in a wide arc through northern Alabama, then approach Chattanooga from the south. Such a move by 60,000 Federals would block the escape route of Bragg's 47,000 Confederates. But Bragg learned of the strategy and retreated 15 miles (24 km) out of Chattanooga to Chickamauga Creek in Georgia. Rosecrans seized Chattanooga, veered eastward after Bragg, and stumbled into one of the major battles of the war.

The desperate conflict at Chickamauga (September 19–20) took place in dense woods and thick undergrowth. On the first day, Confederates assaulted but failed to break Rosecrans' lines. That night, Gen. James Longstreet arrived from Lee's army with fresh reinforcements. Bragg renewed the attack the following morning. After several hours of intense fighting, the Confederates pierced the Federal position. Rosecrans' right flank fell back in disorder to Chattanooga and Rosecrans went with it. However, the Federal left flank, under Virginia-born Gen. George H. Thomas, held fast until darkness ended the battle.

Bragg's victory proved hollow when the Confederate general failed to pursue the shattered Federal army. Rosecrans was given time to reorganize his ranks and fortify Chattanooga. Grant arrived shortly after and assumed command of all Federal operations in the West. Thomas replaced Rosecrans as 20,000 reinforcements under Gen. Joseph Hooker rushed westward from the Army of the Potomac. Meanwhile, Bragg's army had taken positions on the major hills overlooking Chattanooga.

From November 23 to November 25, the Federals delivered a series of heavy assaults on Lookout Mountain, Orchard Knob, and Missionary Ridge. In the end, and for the first time during the war, Confederate soldiers by the hundreds fled in panic from the field. The Southerners continued their flight all the way to Dalton, Ga. There they encamped for the winter while President Davis sought a new commander to replace Bragg.

Grant's Chattanooga campaign not only cleared Tennessee of all major Confederate forces, but it also enabled the Federals to convert Chattanooga into a strategic base of operations. Figuratively speaking, the city became a dagger pointed at the heart of the Confederacy.

Events of 1863 in the East. Midway through January, Burnside tried to compensate for the disaster at Fredericksburg by a secret march around Lee's left (western) flank. Heavy rains and bottomless mud reduced the advance to a crawl. This "Mud March" finished Burnside as commander of the army. Lincoln replaced him with Gen. Joseph Hooker, who promptly rejuvenated the army's physical and moral condition in preparation for a spring campaign.

The two mighty armies of Hooker and Lee spent the remainder of the winter warily eying each other from opposite banks of the Rappahannock River. Elsewhere in Virginia, cavalry on both sides remained active. On March 8, John S. Mosby, a cold-eyed wisp of a man, led his Confederate troopers in a midnight raid on Fairfax Court House, only a few miles south of Washington. The most important capture by the Southerners at Fairfax was the garrison commander, Gen. Edwin Stoughton, who was taken prisoner while asleep in bed. In subsequent months, Mosby's Partisan Rangers so dominated the northern Virginia area that the region became known as "Mosby's Confederacy."

In April, Federal horsemen led by Gen. George Stoneman cut a swath of destruction from Fredericksburg to the outskirts of Richmond. Using this cavalry in an attempt to weaken Richmond's defenses deprived the Army of the Potomac of its scouts, and enabled Lee to win what many historians consider his greatest victory.

Chancellorsville Campaign. Hooker started south toward the end of April with an army of 133,000 soldiers. His strategy, on paper, seemed almost perfect. Outnumbering Lee by better than two to one, the Federal general planned a double envelopment of the Confederate army's flanks. Each of the two Federal flanking forces would be larger than Lee's army; and, like giant pincers, the two forces would isolate and destroy the Army of Northern Virginia.

The line of march of Hooker's right wing was through a thickly wooded, forbidding region known as the Wilderness. Lacking cavalry reconnaissance, Hooker left himself vulnerable to surprise attack. Lee soon discerned Hooker's strategy. He daringly left a screening force to protect his right flank at the old battlefield of Fredericksburg and marched west with two thirds of his small army to confront Hooker's right wing of five corps. On the afternoon of May 2, Jackson's corps rushed from the pine thickets and underbrush and delivered a savage surprise attack on Hooker's lines at a crossroads junction known as Chancellorsville.

Intense and confused fighting lasted three days and extended from Chancellorsville east to the outskirts of Fredericksburg. Hooker lost the campaign and 17,000 men. The Army of the Potomac, again defeated, limped up familiar roads toward Washington.

Chancellorsville, however, was a pyrrhic victory for Lee. His Army of Northern Virginia suffered 12,800 casualties, including the incomparable Jackson, who died of complications from bullet wounds inflicted accidentally by his own men.

Battle of Gettysburg. Nevertheless, Lee felt compelled to launch a second invasion of the North. The capture of an important city such as Harrisburg or Baltimore might relieve the pressure on Vicksburg and possibly effect a triumphant peace. A great victory on Northern soil

The Battle of Gettysburg, July 1863. Gettysburg, Pa., was as far north as the Confederate troops advanced in the Civil War. Lee (*right*) was defeated but escaped with his army. Winston Churchill wrote, "He had lost only two guns, and the war."

might also lead to European mediation in the struggle. Coupled with these possibilities were Lee's desires to transfer the war front from ravaged Virginia and to secure badly needed supplies for his destitute soldiers.

With his army at a peak strength of 76,000 men, Lee in mid-June crossed the Potomac River. Hooker's caution in giving pursuit led Lincoln to replace him with Gen. George G. Meade. By the end of June, the 90,000-man Federal army was marching rapidly through Maryland toward Pennsylvania. As the Federals pushed north in search of Lee, the Confederates turned back south in quest of supplies. Advancing from opposite directions, these two great armies collided at Gettysburg, Pa.

For three days (July 1–3) Lee delivered one determined assault after another against the Federal lines. The Union army held firm. The climax of the battle came on July 3, when 15,000 Southerners under Gen. George E. Pickett charged across an open field against the mile-long center of the Federal defenses. Pickett's suicidal assault failed and brought an end to a battle in which casualties on both sides exceeded 43,000. But after three years of bloody fighting, the Army of the Potomac had won its first clear-cut victory.

The Southern defeat at Gettysburg, coupled with the loss of Vicksburg on July 4, marked a turning point in the Civil War. Never again did the Confederacy possess the power sufficient either to invade the North in force or to impose peace through victory on the battlefield. The

South was reduced to defensive war. Such a war it would wage for two more years.

Lee made good his retreat to Virginia, as Meade seemed content merely to force the Confederates from Northern soil. Both armies then took strong positions on opposite sides of the Rapidan River. Cavalry clashes and infantry skirmishes occupied the remaining part of the year.

Events of 1864 in the West. In this third full year of the war the Federal military machine began to move efficiently. The two men most responsible for this acceleration were Abraham Lincoln, who on March 9 named U. S. Grant the supreme army commander, and Grant himself, who immediately laid plans for an all-out offensive on all fronts. The ever-weakening Confed-

Ulysses S. Grant (*below*) was determined to capture Richmond, Va., the Confederate capital. Unlike previous Union generals, he refused to be deterred by bloody fighting such as that at Spotsylvania (*above*). During the battle he wrote, "I propose to fight it out on this line, if it takes all summer."

eracy, Grant felt, would not be able to withstand constant pressure at every point.

Grant went east to campaign with the Army of the Potomac. He entrusted command of the Western forces to his eccentric but competent lieutenant, William T. ("Cump") Sherman. Yet while the two generals perfected plans for their two-pronged offensive against the South, Confederate cavalrymen under General Forrest were creating havoc in the West. On April 12, Forrest's troopers stormed Fort Pillow, Tenn., and killed most of the Negro soldiers garrisoned there. Sherman dispatched all available Federal cavalry to rid Tennessee of the elusive Forrest. The climax of this counteroffensive was the Battle of Brice's Cross Roads, Miss., on June 10, in which Forrest won his most decisive victory.

In spite of the harassing activities of such Confederate cavalrymen as Forrest, Morgan, Mosby, and Stuart, Generals Grant and Sherman moved ahead with their concerted drives. By the spring of 1864 the main Confederate defenses extended from northwestern Georgia along the eastern edge of the Appalachians to Winchester, Va., and south from there across Virginia through Fredericksburg and Richmond. Early in May both Grant and Sherman struck southward with their respective armies.

Sherman's Drive on Atlanta. Sherman, leading 3 armies and 4 cavalry divisions—more than 100,-000 veterans from the Midwest—struck for the key city of Atlanta. Opposing this force were the 2 corps and 1 cavalry division of Gen. Joseph E. Johnston's reorganized Army of Tennessee. Johnston realized that his 53,000 ill-equipped soldiers would be no match for Sherman's forces in a pitched battle. The Confederate commander therefore resorted to delaying actions and defensive battles, while Sherman attempted flanking movements and sharp thrusts in futile efforts to trap Johnston.

Although it took Sherman 74 days to traverse 100 miles (160 km), by mid-July he had forced Johnston into the trench fortifications of Atlanta. On July 18 a dissatisfied Jefferson Davis replaced Johnston with Gen. John B. Hood who, in spite of the loss of a leg and a crippling wound in an arm, maintained a reputation as a tough fighter. Two days after assuming command, Hood counterattacked—first at Peachtree Creek

(July 20) and then east of Atlanta (July 22). Sherman's men repulsed both assaults, then began tightening the noose of besiegement around Atlanta. Federal victories at Ezra Church (July 28) and Jonesboro (August 31–September 1) compelled Hood to abandon the city. The fall of Atlanta, occurring when it did, proved a determining factor in Lincoln's reelection that autumn.

The March to the Sea. Sherman was not content with the capture of Atlanta. He felt keenly that the war had to be carried to the Southern people themselves before the Confederacy would collapse. He therefore made plans to slash through the heart of the South. His subsequent campaign is known as the March to the Sea.

The Federal commander first transferred part of his army under Gen. Thomas to Tennessee in order to watch Hood, whose Confederates had moved northward in the hope of forcing Sherman to leave Georgia and follow them. With Thomas blocking Hood, Sherman on November 16 left Atlanta in flames and started east toward the coast with 62,000 veteran fighters. His 4 corps were spread over an area 60 miles (96 km) wide. They ravaged the countryside, and only token opposition slowed his advance. On December 22, Sherman reached the sea. He telegraphed Lincoln: "I beg to present you, as a Christmas gift, the city of Savannah, with 150 heavy guns and plenty of ammunition. . . ." Sherman had bisected the Deep South. The campaign had the strongest psychological impact of any in the war.

The Confederacy Diminished. Meanwhile, Hood's strategy in swinging into Tennessee backfired tragically. At Franklin, Tenn., on November 30,

The Union high command, seated on pews from a nearby church, plans the Battle of Cold Harbor, Va. Grant (far left) leans over the back of a pew to consult a map.

TIMOTHY O'SULLIVAN, LIBRARY OF CONGRESS, GAF CORPORATION

his assaults against part of Thomas' army were hurled back and cost the Confederacy 6,000 men, including 5 generals. Undeterred, Hood moved his army to the outskirts of Nashville, where Thomas was based. But before the ragged Confederates could mass for an assault, Thomas moved out to launch an attack (December 15–16) in heavy force and all but destroyed the Army of Tennessee.

Sherman's offensives of 1864 were immeasurably successful. The Confederacy had been cut in two, the Army of Tennessee shattered. At the end of the year all that remained of the Confederacy were Virginia, the Carolinas, and isolated areas in the Deep South.

Events of 1864 in the East. Simultaneously with Sherman's advance into Georgia in May, Grant and the 118,000-man Army of the Potomac retraced Hooker's steps through the Wilderness in a new "On to Richmond" drive. This offensive was not merely a simple invasion by a single army. Grant's plans actually called for a three-pronged attack. The Army of the Potomac would move directly against Lee and drive him southward; Gen. Benjamin F. Butler with the newly created, 25,000-man Army of the James would advance along the south bank of the James River, cut Lee's supply lines, and threaten Richmond; a third Federal force, under Gen. Franz Sigel, would carry out a series of destructive raids in the Shenandoah Valley, applying more pressure on Lee's forces.

From the Wilderness to Petersburg. Grant encountered no opposition until the Army of the Potomac had crept deep into the dense undergrowth of the Wilderness. There, in a near repetition of Chancellorsville, Lee's forces struck suddenly and furiously. Two days (May 5–6) of savage fighting momentarily blunted Grant's advance and cost him 17,000 men.

Yet, unlike every past commander of the Federal army in the East, Grant had no thought of retreating after this defeat. Rather, he introduced the radical policy of continuing to hammer at Lee as he edged closer to Richmond. For Grant this 1864 campaign was to be a fight to the finish.

To neutralize harassments on his flanks by Confederate cavalry, Grant dispatched a large contingent of horsemen under Gen. Philip H. Sheridan on a foray toward Richmond. "Jeb" Stuart's troopers had no alternative but to give pursuit. Cavalrymen fought a number of running engagements, climaxed on May 11 by a severe battle at Yellow Tavern, just north of Richmond. Stuart was killed in this engagement, and Lee's cavalry arm thereafter was never so free-swinging.

The Army of the Potomac pushed toward Richmond by attempting persistently to encircle Lee's right flank. The Confederates won victories but could not stem the Federal advance. Lee's soldiers momentarily checked Grant's movements in the desperate conflicts of Spotsylvania (May 12), North Anna (May 23), and Cold Harbor (June 3). At Cold Harbor, 6,000 Union soldiers fell in less than an hour of fighting.

Cold Harbor convinced Grant that he could not take Richmond by direct approach. The frustrated general bypassed the capital. His army crossed the James and moved on Petersburg, a strategic rail junction 25 miles (40 km) south of Richmond. At Petersburg, meanwhile, a makeshift Confederate force under Gen. P. G. T. Beauregard had repelled Butler's stab from the

Gen. William Tecumseh Sherman (*above*) commanded the Union forces at the Battle of Atlanta. He virtually leveled the city, and on Sept. 2, 1864, he sent a wire to Lincoln stating "Atlanta is ours, and fairly won."

east (May 15–19). Then Beauregard successfully held back the lead elements of Grant's army until Lee's infantrymen could file into position.

Grant was forced to turn again to siege tactics. For the next 9 months the two opposing armies peered at each other from behind intricate entrenchments. Each side stabbed several times at the other's defenses. The most spectacular of these attempts occurred on July 30. It is known as the Battle of the Crater.

Coal miners in the 48th Pennsylvania Regiment dug a long tunnel to the Confederate lines and detonated 8,000 pounds (3,629 kg.) of black powder beneath the Southern positions. But the Federal assault in force that was to have followed the explosion broke down from lack of coordination. The attack failed and cost Grant another 4,000 casualties. Thereafter, Grant concentrated on strengthening his siege lines.

In the fighting from the Wilderness to Petersburg, the Federal army suffered 60,000 casualties—more men than were in Lee's army. But Grant knew that Lee at last was pinned down. Moreover, there was small chance that Lee could find replacements for his 32,000 losses in the campaign. The well-equipped and confident Federal army could now afford to wait.

Action in the Shenandoah Valley. While Grant was pushing through the Wilderness, Sigel and his 8,000 Federal troopers advanced up the Shenandoah Valley as far as New Market. There they encountered a hastily assembled force less than half the size of Sigel's division. The highlight of the battle was the successful charge against the bluecoats by 225 young cadets from the Virginia Military Institute. Sigel's force suffered an embarrassing defeat and fled northward down the valley.

Both Lee and Grant recognized the importance of the valley, but neither could afford to dislodge his army from Petersburg in order to secure the region. Grant attempted to resolve the issue by dispatching into the valley a separate army under Gen. David G. Hunter. Grant directed Hunter to "eat up Virginia clear and clean as far as [you] can go, so that crows flying over it for the balance of this season will have to carry their provender with them."

To counter this threat, Lee rushed a detachment westward under Gen. Jubal A. Early. Hunter burned and looted his way as far as Lynchburg before Early's embittered Southerners sent them scurrying over the mountains into West Virginia. Early then decided to wage an offensive of his own. Sweeping down the valley, he crossed the Potomac and advanced to the outskirts of Washington. Early's raid (July 4–20) failed when he balked at attacking the capital.

Early's near-success with this counteroffensive embarrassed and infuriated Grant, who promptly sent a second and larger army into the valley. At the head of these 45,000 seasoned troops was General Sheridan, with orders to destroy all Confederate resistance in the Shenandoah. Early's 20,000 impoverished Confederates contested Sheridan's steady advance in this Second Valley Campaign. Yet Federal victories at Winchester (September 19), Fisher's Hill (September 22), and Cedar Creek (October 19) gave the Union undisputed control of the valley. At the end of the year, Confederate power in Virginia rested solely in the thin ranks of Lee's army.

Events of 1865. The end of the war came with more relief than fanfare. After a month's rest at Savannah, Sherman struck northward through the Carolinas on February 1 to unite with Grant in

LEE'S SURRENDER at Appomattox Court House, Va., on April 9, 1865, ended major Confederate resistance. The scene of the surrender was the home of Wilmer McLean (*right*). Lee (*seated left, above*) talks terms with Grant (*seated right*). The members of Grant's staff are grouped near him. Maj. Gen. Philip H. Sheridan, Union cavalry leader, stands at extreme right. After the surrender formalities, Confederate troops stacked their arms. The area around the surrender setting is preserved in the Appomattox Court House National Historical Park.

Virginia. The remnant of the Army of Tennessee, again under Gen. Joseph E. Johnston, was the only opposition in Sherman's path.

Johnston could offer only feeble resistance to Sherman's forces. Federal troops occupied Charleston without a fight. They were in control of Columbia, South Carolina's capital, when the city was wrecked by fire. On March 10, Sherman seized Fayetteville in central North Carolina, brushed back part of Johnston's weakened command six days later at Averysboro, and successfully withstood a Confederate attack at Bentonville (March 19–21). Federal troops then occupied the state capital at Raleigh.

The End in Virginia. Grant had spent the winter months of 1864–1865 in mustering his forces for a final, climactic drive against Lee's sagging defenses. At the same time, Grant had methodically extended his own lines around Petersburg farther to the south and west. Lee had no choice but to stretch his own lines accordingly. The Confederate defenses soon were drawn out to the breaking point. This was the precise situation Grant had sought to achieve.

On April 1, Federal troops stormed Lee's position at Five Forks, 16 miles (25 km) southwest of Petersburg. The Confederate line held valiantly but broke when Grant renewed the assault on the following day. That night, the Army of Northern Virginia abandoned the Richmond-Petersburg trenches and slowly retreated westward. President Davis transferred the Confed-

erate capital to Danville, near the North Carolina border. Lee's major hope was to rendezvous at Danville with Johnston's army, still falling back through North Carolina in the face of Sherman's advance. Together, Lee speculated, he and Johnston might be able to defeat first Sherman and then Grant.

This plan never materialized because of Grant's persistence. Federal brigades harried the rear elements of Lee's army and inflicted telling blows at Amelia Court House (April 4–5), Sayler's Creek (April 6), High Bridge (April 7), and Farmville (April 7). Sheridan's Federal cavalry then swept around Lee's flank and severed the Confederate escape route near Appomattox Court House. The Army of Northern Virginia, reduced to 28,000 ragged soldiers, was hopelessly surrounded. On Palm Sunday, April 9, Lee surrendered his command to Grant.

A Maine officer wrote of the scene as the defeated Southerners stacked arms in front of Federal ranks: "On our part, not a sound of trumpet more, nor roll of drum; nor a cheer, nor word nor whisper of vain-glorying . . . but an awed stillness rather, and breath-holding, as if it were the passing of the dead."

Lee's capitulation left Johnston's army with no place to go. On April 26, near Durham, N. C., Sherman accepted the surrender of this last major Confederate force.

The Trans-Mississippi Theater, 1861–1865. The campaigns of the Trans-Mississippi Theater followed no set pattern. This western region was so vast, and the contending forces so scattered and small, that battles and raids were desultory.

The first major engagement in this area took place on Aug. 10, 1861, when a Federal army under Gen. Nathaniel Lyon attacked Gen. Sterling Price's Confederates at Wilson Creek, Mo. In this battle, often called the "Bull Run of the West," Lyon was killed and his inexperienced Federals were repulsed. The Confederates secured Springfield and a month later seized Lexington, Mo.

Early in November of that year, Gen. U. S. Grant led a Federal army into northeast Missouri on a counteroffensive. A heterogeneous Confederate force beat back Grant's attacks at Belmont (November 7) and forced the Federals to retire to the Mississippi.

The contest for control of Missouri continued until March 7–8, 1862, when a makeshift Confederate army that included a brigade of Indians assailed the Federal forces of Gen. Samuel R. Curtis at Elkhorn Tavern and Pea Ridge, Ark., on the Missouri border. The fighting degenerated into mass confusion. Curtis ultimately succeeded in driving the Southerners from the field. This Federal triumph decisively cemented Missouri to the Union.

The Confederate forces in Arkansas were reorganized, but on Dec. 7, 1862, at Prairie Grove, near Fayetteville, Ark., they suffered a staggering defeat. Gen. Frederick Steele followed up his Federal victory by slashing across Arkansas in July 1863, and seizing Little Rock, the state capital. A counterraid 3 months later by Confederate Gen. Joseph O. Shelby covered considerable distance but accomplished little.

In 1864 an expedition initiated in conjunction with advances by Grant and Sherman became one of the fiascos of the war. Gen. Nathaniel Banks, 30,000 Federal soldiers, and 50 ships started up the Red River in Louisiana early in March. The objectives were to gain firm control of Louisiana and east Texas, to counteract threats from Emperor Maximilian in Mexico, and to seize large stores of cotton. The Federal thrust failed so completely that Banks was promptly removed from command.

That autumn, the indomitable Sterling Price made one final and desperate effort to secure Missouri for the Confederacy. Starting on October 20, Price and 12,000 men drove through Missouri until they were stopped by the outer fortifications of St. Louis. Price then swerved westward, failed in a thrust at Jefferson City, but successfully fought his way to the outskirts of Kansas City. At the battle of Westport (October 23), Federal elements forced the Southerners to retreat. Price waged a series of running fights all the way to Kansas. With the termination of Price's raid, heavy hostilities in the Arkansas-Missouri theater ended.

At Shreveport, La., on May 26, 1865—seven weeks after Lee's surrender at Appomattox—Gen. E. Kirby Smith surrendered himself and 43,000 scattered Confederates of the Department of the Trans-Mississippi to Gen. E. R. S. Canby.

THE NAVAL WAR

Naval affairs were among the most critical problems facing each side at the outbreak of the war. The Federal Navy was small and widely scattered. Moreover, the Confederate seacoast extended 3,500 miles (5,600 km) from the Chesapeake Bay to the Mexican border, and it contained hundreds of bays, inlets, and river openings. Not even a greatly enlarged fleet could adequately patrol such a vast shoreline.

The Union Blockade and Coastal Operations. Lincoln and his secretary of the navy, Gideon

In the Battle of Mobile Bay, Admiral Farragut directs the fire from the rigging of his flagship *Hartford*.

The first battle between ironclads pitted the *Monitor* against the *Merrimack* at Hampton Roads, Va., on March 9, 1862.

Welles, resolved early to weaken the South by blockading its chief ports. Many months passed before Union squadrons were large enough to enforce this blockade. Yet the cordon of Federal ships strengthened as the war progressed. This allowed Federal forces to peck away at Southern coastal defenses.

In 1861, Federal amphibious operations led to the capture of Fort Hatteras, N. C., and Port Royal, S. C. During the next year, Roanoke Island, New Bern and Fort Macon, N. C., Fort Pulaski, Ga., Pensacola, Fla., and New Orleans fell into Federal hands. The Confederates rallied briefly in 1863 and managed to hold their remaining coastal works, notably Charleston, S. C.

Northern fleets, however, continued to apply pressure all along the Southern shore. Two engagements marked the effectiveness of coastal attacks. On Aug. 5, 1864, Adm. David Farragut led a Federal squadron into mine-infested Mobile Bay with the battle cry: "Damn the torpedoes! Full speed ahead!" Five months later, on Jan. 15, 1865, Federal forces stormed and captured Fort Fisher, N. C., the last great Southern defense on the Atlantic coast.

On the Rivers. Federal navies also performed much service on the Mississippi River. A wide assortment of vessels campaigned against such Confederate strongholds as Memphis, Tenn., and Vicksburg, Miss. Some were little more than steamboats converted into warships by means of steel plating and deck guns. Others were sailing craft, with high decks and tall masts. A new Federal gunboat, the steam ram, had its baptism in the Mississippi campaigns. This little ship was fast and maneuverable, and its principal weapon was a heavy prow used to sink a vessel by ramming it broadside.

The Confederate Navy. The Confederacy was born without a navy, and the Southern nation was never able to develop a fleet that could challenge the growing Federal navy. Funds and shipbuilding facilities were lacking. The construction of Confederate warships in Great Britain was blocked at last by effective Union diplomacy. Confederate naval efforts were restricted for the most part to operations by privateers and blockade runners and undertakings by individual ships.

Most of the 20 Confederate raiders that were commissioned achieved considerable fame before they were destroyed. For example, the C. S. S. *Florida*, under Capt. John Newland Maffitt, captured 34 ships before she herself was seized in Brazil in 1864. The English-built *Alabama*, commanded by Raphael Semmes, took 62 prizes in two years on the high seas. On June 19, 1864, the *Alabama* was sunk off the coast of France in a historic duel with the U. S. S. *Kearsarge*.

Capt. James I. Waddell's steam raider the *Shenandoah* roamed the Pacific and bagged 40 ships—including 8 seized after the war on land had ended. On Nov. 6, 1865, the *Shenandoah* furled its colors in Liverpool, England.

The First Ironclads. The most famous Civil War naval battle was fought on March 9, 1862, in Hampton Roads, Va., between the U. S. S. *Monitor* and the C. S. S. *Virginia* (formerly the U. S. S. *Merrimack*, captured at the Norfolk navy yard and rebuilt). It was the first battle between ironclad ships. For 3 hours each tried vainly to sink the other. The engagement was indecisive, but it foreshadowed the day when wooden ships would be obsolete. See also MONITOR AND MERRIMACK.

Confederate Innovations. The Confederates made several notable innovations in naval warfare. One was an ironclad ram, the *Arkansas*, built hastily in the summer of 1862 to combat Federal ships on the Mississippi. Constructed of wood, railroad rails, wire, and pieces of iron collected from all over the South, the monster-like vessel created momentary havoc among Federal gunboats. However, its captain was forced to scuttle the ship near Baton Rouge, La., after its engines failed.

The Confederacy also boasted the first submarine of modern design. The 35-foot (10.6-meter) *H. L. Hunley* sank four times with its crews during trial runs. Nevertheless, on the night of Feb. 17, 1864, the little vessel torpedoed and sank the U. S. S. *Housatonic* in Charleston harbor. The *Hunley* and its fifth crew of seven men perished in the explosion.

In addition to the submarine, Confederates also developed the water mine and the torpedo boat. The latter was a small vessel propelled by a steam engine. It drifted along the surface with a torpedo suspended from a long spar. The first of these torpedo boats, the *David*, appeared in Charleston harbor in October 1863 and seriously damaged the blockading warship *New Ironsides*.

Such innovations were ineffectual in overcoming the constant and painful pressure of large Federal fleets all along the Southern coast. The ultimate victory of the Union in the Civil War is attributable in great measure to the contributions of the U. S. Navy.

CASUALTIES OF THE WAR

More Americans died in the Civil War than in all of America's other wars combined. Approximately 618,000 men perished in four years of fighting—an average of 423 deaths for each day of the war.

The North lost 360,022 soldiers. Of that number, 67,058 were killed in action and 43,012 died later of battle wounds. A total of 275,175 Federals received wounds while fighting.

Accurate figures do not exist for the Confederate side. The total number of Southern soldiers dead was close to 258,000. About 94,000 were killed or fatally wounded in battle.

In the famous British cavalry charge at the Battle of Balaclava in the Crimean War, the Light Brigade suffered 37% losses. Yet at Gettysburg, on July 2, 1863, the 1st Minnesota Infantry lost 82% of its strength. At Antietam the 1st Texas suffered 82% casualties in a few hours of fighting. The 27th Tennessee had 54% losses at Shiloh and, 6 months later, 53% casualties at Perryville. In the course of the Civil War, no less than 63 Federal and 52 Confederate units suffered 50% losses or higher in a single engagement.

Other statistics of fatalities add to the tragedy. Over 400,000 Civil War soldiers died of sickness and disease. Almost as many Federal soldiers (57,265) succumbed to dysentery and diarrhea as were killed outright on the battlefield (67,058). Since conditions in the Confederate armies were worse, the number of Southern deaths from sickness was probably higher.

Sanitation and Health. Army life in the 1860's had many and severe hardships. Improper diet and unsanitary conditions often prostrated half a regiment's membership. In both armies, a soldier who did not have his share of lice and fleas was a rare exception.

The fact that most of the soldiers came from rural communities made them highly susceptible to such "city sicknesses" as smallpox and chicken pox. The death rate from these diseases was unbelievably high. In the Federal armies, sickness and disease accounted for 7 of every 10 deaths. One authority has estimated that among the Confederates three men perished from disease for every man killed in battle.

Soldiers suffered, also, because of the limited medical knowledge of that era. Blood transfusions, X-rays, antibiotics, sterilization, vitamins, vaccines, and wonder drugs all came after the Civil War. No assured treatment existed for

Trains carried the sick and wounded from the battlefields to this Union field hospital at City Point, Va.

CULVER PICTURES

ALEXANDER MCCOOK CRAIGHEAD COLLECTION, THE WEST POINT MUSEUM COLLECTION

The Civil War ends. Lee's soldiers furl the Stars and Bars
for the last time, in R. N. Brooke's painting *Furling the Flags.*

typhoid fever, yellow fever, measles, or pneumonia, and no one was sure of the proper way to stop a hemorrhage. Most bone fractures, and all wounds of the joint, usually meant amputation.

In the Korean conflict of the 1950's the chances of surviving a wound were 50 to 1; in the Civil War, only 7 to 1.

Prisoners. Neither North nor South had the knowledge and facilities for handling large numbers of prisoners. The Civil War marked the first time that the nation had to contend with prisoners in any sizable number. Therefore, policies and treatment varied greatly—and often fatally.

In the course of the war the Confederates captured about 211,000 Federal soldiers. Of this number, 16,000 accepted battlefield paroles, that is, they signed promises not to bear arms again. Federal forces took as prisoners some 215,000 Confederates.

At various times throughout the war, both sides made efforts to establish a workable program of prisoner exchange. But owing to misunderstandings, violations of terms, and Grant's determination late in the war to bring the South to its knees at all costs, prisoner exchange was slight and sporadic.

The most notorious Southern prisons were Libby and Castle Thunder, converted warehouses in Richmond; Belle Isle in the James River, Virginia; "Camp Sorghum" at Columbia, S. C.; and Camp Sumter at Andersonville, Ga. Among the worst of the Northern compounds were Elmira Prison Camp in southwestern New York state; Point Lookout on Chesapeake Bay; Johnson's Island, in Lake Erie, a few miles offshore from Sandusky, Ohio; Camp Douglas, near Chicago; and Rock Island Prison Camp, on the Mississippi River between Illinois and Iowa.

Every major Civil War prison, judged by present-day standards, would have been con-

demned as uninhabitable. The suffering among the prisoners was universal and severe.

In the 9-month history of the huge stockade at Andersonville, Ga., 45,613 Federals in all were jammed into 16½ barren acres (6.7 hectares) containing one polluted stream, few shelters, less food, and no sanitation. More than 12,900 prisoners died of disease, exposure, and starvation. Similarly, the North's prison camp at Elmira, N. Y., existed for a little less than a year. During that period, 2,963 of 12,123 Confederates died of sickness and neglect.

The chief of the U. S. Record and Pension Office reported in 1903 that 25,976 Southerners and 30,218 Northerners perished in Civil War prisons.

JAMES I. ROBERTSON, JR.
*Virginia Polytechnic Institute
Former Executive Director
U. S. Civil War Centennial Commission*

Bibliography

Boatner, Mark M., *Civil War Dictionary* (McKay 1959).
Catton, Bruce, *Glory Road* (Doubleday 1952).
Catton, Bruce, *Mr. Lincoln's Army* (Doubleday 1951).
Catton, Bruce, *A Stillness at Appomattox* (Doubleday 1953).
Freeman, Douglas S., *Lee's Lieutenants*, 3 vols. (Scribner 1942–1944).
Henry, Robert S., *The Story of the Confederacy*, rev. ed. (Bobbs 1957).
Horn, Stanley F., *The Army of Tennessee* (Univ. of Okla. Press 1953).
Jones, Virgil C., *The Civil War at Sea*, 3 vols. (Holt 1960–1962).
Ketchum, Richard M., ed., *The American Heritage Picture History of the Civil War* (American Heritage 1960).
Naisawald, L. Van Loan, *Grape and Canister* (Oxford 1960).
Nevins, Allan, *The War for the Union*, 4 vols. (Scribner 1959–1971).
Wiley, Bell I., and Milhollen, Hirst D., *They Who Fought Here* (Macmillan 1960).
Williams, Kenneth P., *Lincoln Finds a General*, 5 vols. (Macmillan 1949–1959).
Williams, T. Harry, *Lincoln and His Generals* (Knopf 1952).

4. Political, Social, and Economic Developments

Boasting the same heritage and schooled in similar political, social, and economic institutions, the North and the South reacted similarly to the crisis of civil war. With nearly identical governments, the Union and the Confederacy each had to decide how much to respect civil liberties for dissenters and rights for states. All levels of Northern and Southern society sacrificed a frightful number of lives; and many persons, particularly in the South, suffered material privations as well. Facing a manpower crisis, both the North and the South utilized the Negro and in return moved toward the extirpation of slavery.

Despite the striking economic contrast between the North and the South, both sections issued paper money to meet obligations, both initially purchased supplies in Europe, and both converted existing industrial facilities and developed new ones to meet emergency demands. Although similar problems suggested similar solutions, the South was less adept at executing these solutions than the North. The South's commitment to a traditional society—states' rights, slavery, and agrarianism—inhibited its capacity to revolutionize its political, social, and economic structure to meet the demands of war.

POLITICAL DEVELOPMENTS IN THE SOUTH

More than two months before the Confederates fired on Fort Sumter, delegates from the lower South convened on Feb. 4, 1861, at Montgomery, Ala. (on May 21, 1861, the capital was moved to Richmond, Va.), wrote a constitution, chose a provisional president (Jefferson Davis) and vice president (Alexander H. Stephens), and acted as a provisional legislature for the Confederate States of America. The Confederate Constitution closely resembled the U. S. Constitution, although safeguards for states' rights and slavery and the prohibition of a protective tariff were included. The provisional government adopted all U. S. laws as of November 1860 that were not contrary to the Confederate Constitution, employed former U. S. postal and customs officers, and modeled its executive branch on that at Washington.

Although able, Davis' cabinet was weakened by frequent change and lacked outstanding Southern leaders, many of whom preferred military to administrative service. Davis relied most on Judah P. Benjamin, initially attorney general, later secretary of war, and finally secretary of state. Only Navy Secretary Stephen R. Mallory and Postmaster General John H. Reagan served in their departments throughout the entire struggle. Six men headed the crucial War Department, four served as attorney general, and two South Carolinians—Christopher G. Memminger and George A. Trenholm—headed the important Treasury Department.

Congress, under the permanent Confederate government (inaugurated on George Washington's birthday in 1862), proved to be an ineffective body overshadowed by the executive. Mediocre but excessively proud members were immersed in details when not absent, drunk, or brawling among themselves. Congress held secret sessions, alienating itself from the people; it was too timid to levy taxes or to shape fiscal policy and was divided bitterly between the supporters and the opponents of Davis.

In November 1861, Davis and Stephens were unanimously elected to fill 6-year terms of office, but by early 1862 many blamed Davis for recent Confederate military disasters. The influential Charleston *Mercury* and the Richmond *Examiner* went into opposition against Davis, while the tirades of Representative Henry S. Foote, an old political enemy, ultimately "provoked violence in Congress in which bowie knives flashed and pistols and fists were used," according to the historian Clement Eaton.

The Conscription Act of March 28, 1862, brought the contrary notions of Southern nationalism and states' rights into conflict, and added to and confirmed the opposition of such doctrinaires as Gov. Joseph E. Brown of Georgia and Vice President Stephens. Thinking "in terms of states' rights and civil liberties," Stephens, Eaton observes, did the Confederacy "incalculable harm" by opposing "conscription, the suspension of the writ of habeas corpus, the funding act, and the impressment of supplies"—all vital to war effort. After 1863, Stephens attacked Davis publicly for "seeking to establish a military despotism."

Davis' Leadership. Davis, in fact, deeply respected the rights of individuals. He suspended the writ reluctantly, with congressional approval, and only in certain local areas. Despite the powerful opposition, Davis retained a congressional majority until disasters at Gettysburg and Vicksburg produced an administration setback in the fall elections. The Confederate Congress that assembled in May 1864 was bitterly

Jefferson Davis is inaugurated as president of the Confederacy in Montgomery, Ala., on Feb. 18, 1861.

THE BETTMANN ARCHIVE

hostile to Davis, but lacking concrete proposals of its own generally acceded to his requests. Congressional sniping ultimately forced Davis in 1865 to drop Secretary of War James A. Seddon and to appoint Lee overall commander.

Although the states' rights position in the midst of a desperate war for independence was absurd and the fear of military dictatorship wholly unfounded, Davis had faults. He was unable to work with other Confederate leaders, could not communicate with the people, was a poor administrator, and failed as commander in chief. Davis was a man of intelligence and will, courage and honor, duty and energy, self-sacrifice, and religion. However, he was also stiff, inflexible, proud, sensitive to criticism, humorless, ill, irritable, and tense. "The most difficult man to get along with" that Seddon "had ever seen," Davis could not utilize the services of men who were able but tactless. Robert Kean of the Confederate war department observed that Davis wasted an inordinate amount of time on "little trash which ought to be dispatched by clerks," and Davis exasperated Mallory with "his uncontrollable tendency to digression" that prevented him from concentrating on essentials.

Convinced of his military genius, Davis (who had been U. S. secretary of war under President Franklin Pierce) was in effect his own secretary of war, and as commander in chief he centered overall military command in himself until Congress forced him to appoint Lee head of all Confederate armies. Davis bears responsibility for the reasonably sound strategy of the "offensive-defensive" stressing counterattacks, for the faulty organization of military departments along geographical lines, and for dispersing his forces to defend territory rather than concentrating armies to destroy the enemy. He occupied a very difficult position and with all his faults Davis was more qualified for the presidency than any other Confederate political leader.

More damaging than the inept political leadership of Davis, Stephens, the cabinet, and the Congress was the absence of a viable two-party system. Southerners mistakenly thought party strife a disadvantage; but without a loyal, constructive opposition to formulate and to develop alternative policies and leaders Southern criticism remained rash, vindictive, myopic, narrow, negative, and destructive.

POLITICAL DEVELOPMENTS IN THE NORTH

Lincoln made a better war leader than Davis. He possessed many of Davis' virtues and few of his faults. He was pragmatic, flexible, humble, magnanimous, able to take criticism, willing to admit mistakes, humorous, relaxed, and tactful. He constructed a cabinet with outstanding, strong-minded political leaders—many of whom were rivals for the presidential nomination and for control of the Republican party. William H. Seward was secretary of state; Salmon P. Chase, secretary of the treasury; Simon Cameron, and later Edwin M. Stanton, secretary of war; Gideon Welles, secretary of the navy; Caleb B. Smith, secretary of the interior; Montgomery Blair, postmaster general; and Edward Bates, attorney general.

Although Seward assumed he would dominate Lincoln, he soon realized that "Executive force and vigor are rare qualities" and that "the President is the best of us." Lincoln's personal characteristics enabled him to get along with and to utilize this difficult but able set of men. Though Lincoln rarely consulted his cabinet members on major policy decisions, he allowed them to shape crucial policies within their departments. "You understand these things," he once told Chase; "I do not." Loose bureaucratic

Fugitive Negroes ford the Rappahannock River in Virginia on their way north in August 1862, just months before the Emancipation Proclamation set them free.

TIMOTHY O'SULLIVAN, GAF CORPORATION

notions may not have promoted a unified administration in Washington, but these procedures did free Lincoln to concentrate on conducting the war.

As commander in chief, Lincoln actively intervened in military affairs, but his strategy frequently was sounder than that of his generals. ". . . Lee's army," he admonished Gen. Joseph Hooker, "and not *Richmond,* is your true objective. . . ." Searching for victory, Lincoln appointed and removed many generals and once even ordered an offensive to begin. Nevertheless, Lincoln recognized his own limitations and appointed successively Winfield Scott, George McClellan, Henry Halleck, and U. S. Grant to positions of overall command. And when he finally found the right commander he wrote Grant, "The particulars of your plans, I neither know nor seek to know."

A brilliant political realist, Lincoln attempted to occupy positions that would alienate neither Republican Radicals who would destroy slavery nor conservatives who would simply restore the Union. Championing Chase and Seward respectively, these factions fought within the Republican party, while the Democrats split into War Democrats, who supported the administration to save the Union but not to abolish slavery, and regular, antiadministration Democrats, who thought success impossible under Republican leadership. Military failure complicated Lincoln's task of holding together squabbling Republicans and keeping War Democrats in the coalition Union party.

To save the Border States in 1861, Lincoln overruled Gen. John C. Frémont's antislavery proclamation and later removed him from command. Discouraged that Lincoln would not use the war to extirpate slavery, antislavery men in particular and Northerners in general were further disenchanted throughout most of 1862 by military failures, administrative inefficiency, and high casualties. Reversing his direction, Lincoln issued the preliminary Emancipation Proclamation on Sept. 22, 1862, and on September 24, with no congressional authorization, suspended the writ of habeas corpus throughout the North and provided that those accused of disloyalty be tried in military courts.

Unlike Davis, Lincoln unhesitatingly assumed war powers, suppressed the constitutional rights of the accused, and arbitrarily arrested and imprisoned thousands. The Emancipation Proclamation and arbitrary arrests deeply offended moderate and conservative elements. The Union party, retaining only a small majority in Congress and losing majorities in Pennsylvania, New York, Ohio, Indiana, and Illinois, suffered a severe setback in the 1862 elections.

Defeat at the polls followed by disaster at Fredericksburg disturbed the radically oriented Republican senatorial caucus. Influenced by Chase, it blamed these reverses on differences within the administration and on Lincoln's lack of policy and demanded, in December 1862, a reconstituted, unified, vigorous cabinet, presumably without Seward. Although Seward resigned, Lincoln maneuvered Chase into stating that the cabinet was harmonious and also into resigning. Lincoln then maintained his balanced cabinet by accepting neither resignation.

The new year brought little comfort. Defeat at Chancellorsville added to Radical discontent and fanned conservative hostility to conscription,

arbitrary arrests, and martial law. Victories at Gettysburg and Vicksburg were offset by draft riots in New York City and by Gen. George Meade's inactivity. Disaffected Radicals boomed Chase for the 1864 nomination but failed because of mismanagement and because Chase's cabinet position prevented him from actively campaigning against his chief.

The 1864 Election. Lincoln was a superb politician who used his power and control of the patronage to dominate the Republican party. Although a group of extreme Radicals meeting in Cleveland nominated Frémont, the Republican convention meeting in Baltimore on June 7 unanimously nominated Lincoln. Andrew Johnson, a War Democrat from Tennessee, balanced the ticket as the vice-presidential nominee.

Meeting at the end of August, Democrats nominated McClellan on a peace platform that declared the war a failure. Virtually repudiating this platform, McClellan, like Lincoln, insisted on fighting for union. By late August, Republicans appeared to have lost the election, but in September the outlook changed. William T. Sherman captured Atlanta, giving Northern morale a lift and making the "peace" or "Copperhead" plank a liability to the Democrats. Frémont withdrew from the race, and Radicals and conservatives fell in line behind Lincoln. On election day Lincoln carried all the Union states except Kentucky, Delaware, and New Jersey. Although most of his supporters were moderates, Lincoln would move in the future as he had in the past toward the Radical program of transforming Southern society as well as restoring the Union.

THE NEGRO AND THE CIVIL WAR

Radical arguments for emancipation and for full Negro participation in society were underscored by military necessity. Lincoln, his generals, and Congress came to realize that to deprive the Confederacy of Negro manpower and to utilize it for the Union demanded social change. Even before the Emancipation Proclamation, slavery had received heavy blows. Although Lincoln and Congress initially did not plan to disturb slavery in the states, war in a slave-holding region decreed otherwise. Runaway slaves headed for Union lines, and on May 24, 1861, Gen. Benjamin F. Butler set a policy by refusing to return to their owners three fugitive slaves because slaves were erecting Confederate fortifications and were therefore "contraband."

The Emancipation Proclamation. On July 17, 1862, Congress anticipated the Emancipation Proclamation in the Second Confiscation Act, which declared all slaves of rebels free. On April 16, 1862, Congress abolished slavery in the District of Columbia with compensation and on June 19 in the territories without compensation. The preliminary Emancipation Proclamation, which Lincoln issued on September 22, declared all slaves in Confederate-controlled territory would be free on Jan. 1, 1863 (the date of the definitive Emancipation Proclamation).

Although Lincoln justified the proclamation "upon military necessity" and although it freed no one immediately, it had great impact. It increased the flow of runaway and abandoned slaves to Union lines, stimulated the abolition of slavery in loyal states, infuriated the South, which thought it an invitation to servile revolt,

The ruins of Richmond, Va., the capital of the Confederate States of America.

alienated Northern conservatives, and improved the North's image abroad. Its enthusiastic reception in Britain and France made recognition of the Confederacy, which had seemed imminent, only a remote possibility and ultimately moved a desperate South itself to propose Negro emancipation to improve chances for European recognition.

Although renowned for the Emancipation Proclamation, Lincoln preferred gradual, compensated emancipation coupled with voluntary colonization, but his plan proved impossible. Loyal slaveowners rejected the former, and the freedman rejected the latter. By the end of the war, state action had destroyed slavery in West Virginia, Tennessee, Maryland, and Missouri, leaving it untouched only in Delaware and Kentucky. Adoption of the 13th Amendment to the federal Constitution on Dec. 18, 1865, completed the task of abolishing slavery and settled the legality of military emancipation.

Negro Soldiers. Both the Confederacy and the Union utilized Negro labor, but neither was eager to use Negro soldiers. Mounting casualties and waning enlistments convinced the Union and ultimately, when it was too late, the Confederacy to arm Negroes. Certain Union officers had used Negro soldiers from the start of the war, and the War Department officially approved the enlistment of 5,000 Negroes on Aug. 25, 1862. After the Emancipation Proclamation, Negroes were freely enlisted, and the 178,895 who served were in Lincoln's words "very important, if not indispensable." Negro soldiers, however, received lower pay and bounties than white soldiers, and Confederates occasionally slaughtered captured Negro troops.

After the fall of Chattanooga in late 1863, some Confederate officers proposed that the South use Negro soldiers, but Davis, fearing its effect on morale, attempted to keep the idea secret. A year later, after the fall of Atlanta, Lee and Davis advocated arming slaves and promising them emancipation in return for faithful service. After a bitter struggle, the Confederate Congress approved the enlisting of Negroes but refused to promise them emancipation. A few Negroes were enlisted but not in time to be used in combat.

SOUTHERN SOCIAL AND ECONOMIC DISINTEGRATION

The war strained the South's economy. Blockaded and unable to import freely from abroad, the Confederacy had to supply itself with war materials. It set up arsenals, foundries, and powder mills; let contracts to private firms, including the famous Tredegar Iron Works of Richmond; and by 1863 could supply itself with arms and munitions. Although it established several uniform and shoe factories, the Confederacy was less successful in providing clothing for its soldiers. Despite the abundance of food in the South, where farmers had shifted from cotton and tobacco culture to cereal production, Confederate armies were frequently hungry because of poor transportation facilities.

Southern railroads, comprising a number of small lines, were neither integrated into a system nor into the war effort. Without "a single bar of railroad iron" being rolled in the Confederacy, its railroads also disintegrated for want of repair. Davis exhorted but did not coerce the railroads to pool their equipment, control their rates, and coordinate their schedules. Only in 1865, when it was too late to matter, did the Confederacy move to supervise its railroads effectively.

Disintegration in the crucial area of finance severely damaged the war effort. The Confederacy could tax, borrow, or print treasury notes to finance the war. Fearful that taxation would create disloyalty, the Confederacy raised only about 1% of its income in this way, while it realized 39% from loans, and 60% ($1½ billion) from the printing press. As the Confederacy issued more and more paper money and suffered reverses on the battlefield, treasury notes declined in value. Inflation accompanied by skyrocketing prices devastated creditors, people with fixed incomes, and wage earners, and destroyed the people's faith in Confederate finance. Soldiers received only $11 a month in depreciated currency until June 1864, when their pay was raised to $18. In July 1862 a cabbage cost $1.25 in Richmond. By the spring of 1864, boots were $200 a pair and flour $275 a barrel, and by the end of the war flour had increased to $1,000 a barrel.

Life Behind the Confederate Lines. Although the South embraced the war joyously, the holiday atmosphere had disappeared by 1862. Men were dying, manufactured goods were scarce, and crops were not being sold. Rural areas fared better than towns unless they were in the path of a defending or invading army. Foraging armies left not only empty smokehouses, barns, and corncribs but also a wake of lawlessness and degeneracy. With courts disrupted and law enforcement a mockery, vice and crime multiplied. Remote Southern landholders fed themselves adequately on sweet potatoes, peas, cornbread, and pork. But the solitude, the absence of able-bodied men, and the fear of slave rebellions compounded their anxieties.

The coming of Union armies also freed the slaves. Although no large-scale slave revolt occurred during the war, the quality of slaves' work deteriorated, and when liberated they frequently looted their former masters' houses. Slaves earnestly desired freedom and quickly seized it when the opportunity came.

Destitution damaged Confederate morale. The central government made no provision for soldiers' dependents. Slight aid from some states and charitable individuals did not solve the problem. During the last year and a half women began to break under the strain. Unable to extract a living from the family farm and facing starvation, many women implored their husbands to desert the Confederate Army. "Before God, Edward, unless you come home we must die!" wrote one. "Last night I was aroused by little Eddie's crying. . . . He said 'Oh, Mamma, I'm so hungry!'" And yet most of those at home sustained the war to the end. Besides managing farms, women sewed, clerked, spied on the enemy, and nursed the wounded.

NORTHERN SOCIAL AND ECONOMIC DEVELOPMENT

The Northern economy expanded with the demands of war. Although the war began during a business depression, high tariffs cutting off imports from abroad and huge government expenditures created a boom by 1862 that continued for the duration of the war. The Morrill tariffs of March 2, 1861, Aug. 5, 1861, July 14, 1862, and June 30, 1864, raised rates until they averaged 47% or more than double what they had been in 1857, and also raised the cost of the war because the government was the country's largest consumer.

Contractors made fabulous fortunes filling war orders, and from 1861 to 1865 the twofold increase in farm prices handsomely rewarded agriculturalists. Prices in general increased almost as rapidly as farm prices (80% from 1861 to 1865), but Northern inflation, although real, was mild compared with Southern inflation. Considering the absence of rationing, price controls, and central banking, Chase managed the Union economy remarkably well.

The Union's financial problems were similar to but not so acute as the Confederacy's. Fearful of alienating support, the Union raised only 20% of its revenue through taxation. It acquired the remainder by issuing $432 million in greenback paper money and also through a bewildering variety of loans (many marketed by private banker Jay Cooke for a commission) paying different rates of interest for different lengths of time. Greenbacks depreciated and fluctuated in value, gave rise to speculation, and were essentially a forced loan without interest from the people.

To rectify financial chaos (7,000 different kinds of banknotes, many spurious, circulated and fluctuated in value), congressional legislation on Feb. 25, 1863, and June 3, 1864, established a national banking system that required member banks to have at least one third of their capital in government bonds and provided for a stable but inelastic currency based on those bonds.

Not all Northerners shared in the war profits. Despite the labor shortage (which the low wartime rate of immigration failed to alleviate), real wages in January 1865 were only 67% of what they had been in January 1860. Although there was little organized labor at the beginning of the war, unions grew until 69 trades were organized with 300 locals. Organized labor, however, was bitterly opposed by employers who broke strikes by using Negroes (thereby laying the groundwork for race riots in New York, Brooklyn, and Cincinnati) and federal troops. Furthermore, the Contract Labor Law (July 4, 1864), permitting employers to import laborers under contract to work a maximum of one year to pay for their passage, distressed labor leaders. Wartime prosperity and unions yielded the laborer meager returns; his condition by the end of the war was worse than in 1860.

Wartime Life in the North. The prosperity, anguish, and dislocations of war stimulated extravagant living, frantic amusements, vice, and crime. Particularly ostentatious and offensive were the *nouveaux riches* and the "shoddy" rich who had waxed fat from war contracts. "Shoddy"—a reclaimed inferior wool substituted by dishonest manufacturers who attained great profits—came to denote any contractor who made exorbitant profits by supplying the government with inferior goods. Most businessmen were honest and conscientious, but even legitimate profits were very high.

Entertainment flourished. Theaters featuring comedy were jammed; and parties, balls, and receptions cheered both the indifferent and the afflicted of war. Vice flourished in cities and near army camps, and Lincoln observed that in the wake of war "Every foul bird comes abroad, and every dirty reptile rises up. These add crime to confusion. . . . Murders for old grudges, and murders for pelf, proceed under any cloak that will best cover for the occasion."

On the other hand, humanitarianism flourished and intellectual life was not neglected. The United States Sanitary Commission and the Christian Commission of the Young Men's Christian Association not only helped care for the wounded but also improved the morale of able-bodied soldiers. On the home front, colleges, lyceum lecture series, magazines, and newspapers continued to disseminate culture and information to all levels of Northern society.

In short, Northern society suffered heavy losses, but it was large, strong, and flexible enough to absorb the shock of civil war and continue to expand. Congress encouraged internal improvements by granting land, loans, and military protection to the transcontinental Union Pacific and Central Pacific Railroads (July 1, 1862, and July 2, 1864), Western settlement by the Homestead Act (May 20, 1862), and higher education by the Morrill Land Grant Act (July 2, 1862). Farmers brought new lands under cultivation while cities expanded and built not only new houses but new churches and public buildings as well. That the North had sufficient energy to complete the unfinished dome of the Capitol illustrates Northern capacity and will to grow despite civil war.

THE LEGACY OF THE CIVIL WAR

The Civil War subordinated the rights of states to the rights of the nation, abolished slavery, broke the South's economic and political power, organized Northern industry, left a heritage of hate and intolerance, and saddled the nation with the unfortunate psychological baggage of what Robert Penn Warren calls the "Treasury of Virtue" and the "Great Alibi." Sacrifice and victory in a "righteous" cause redeemed the North from past and future shortcomings and left it pharisaically alive to Southern failure to integrate but unconcerned with the ghettos of Chicago's South Side or of New York's Harlem. "Inevitable" defeat gave the South an explanation for failure, an excuse for inaction, and a unity it had never possessed before. It was conquered but not convinced or contrite, defeated but still defiant, and determined to salvage as much of its caste society as possible. Its "lost cause" reinforced the South's resolution to maintain its ideas, its institutions, its way of life.

ARI HOOGENBOOM, *Brooklyn College*

Bibliography

Chestnut, Mary B., *A Diary from Dixie*, ed. by Ben Ames Williams (Houghton 1949).
Cornish, Dudley T., *The Sable Arm: Negro Troops in the Union Army, 1861–1865* (Longmans 1956).
Coulter, Ellis M., *The Confederate States of America, 1861–1865* (Louisiana State Univ. Press 1950).
Donald, David, *Lincoln Reconsidered* (Knopf 1956).
Donald, David, ed., *Why the North Won the Civil War* (Louisiana State Univ. Press 1960).
Eaton, Clement, *A History of the Southern Confederacy* (Macmillan 1954).
Fite, Emerson D., *Social and Industrial Conditions in the North During the Civil War* (1910; reprint, Smith, P. 1930).
Lincoln, Abraham, *Collected Works*, ed. by Roy P. Basler and others, 9 vols. (Rutgers Univ. Press 1953–1956).
Nevins, Allan, *The War for the Union*, 4 vols. (Scribner 1959–1971).
Quarles, Benjamin, *The Negro in the Civil War* (Little 1953).
Ramsdell, Charles W., *Behind the Lines in the Southern Confederacy*, ed. by Wendell H. Stephenson (Louisiana State Univ. Press 1944).
Randall, James G., and Donald, David, *The Civil War and Reconstruction*, 3d ed. (Heath 1969).
Randall, James G., *Lincoln the President*, 4 vols. (Dodd 1945–55; vol. 4 with R. N. Current).
Roland, Charles P., *The Confederacy* (Univ. of Chicago Press 1960).
Thomas, Benjamin Platt, *Abraham Lincoln* (Knopf 1952).
Warren, Robert Penn, *The Legacy of the Civil War* (Random House 1961).
Wiley, Bell I., *The Plain People of the Confederacy* (Louisiana State Univ. Press 1943).
Williams, Thomas H., *Lincoln and the Radicals* (Univ. of Wis. Press 1941).

5. Diplomatic Developments

For the U. S., or Union, government the major diplomatic problem of the Civil War was to prevent foreign recognition, particularly by Britain and France, of the Confederate States as an independent nation. President Lincoln's government wanted to isolate the war, deny the Confederates foreign help, gain international acceptance of a naval blockade of the South's coastline (proclaimed on May 19, 1861), and forestall foreign intervention. The Confederacy's goal was to win foreign recognition, mainly through European intervention in the war itself.

Beginning with Britain on May 13, 1861, the European nations recognized the belligerency of the Confederate States. This was a limited recognition—the Europeans believed the Confederacy deserved the status of a nation for the purpose of fighting a war.

Questions of Maritime Rights. The fact that the Europeans treated the civil conflict as a true war also quickly raised old questions of maritime rights between belligerent and neutral nations. During the Civil War the traditional maritime roles of the United States and Britain were reversed. Britain had been the big naval belligerent who insisted on belligerent rights at the expense of the small naval belligerent, or neutral, and the United States had been the major maritime neutral. Now the Union was the major naval belligerent and Britain the foremost neutral.

In August 1861, in an effort to strengthen the Confederacy's diplomatic offensive, President Jefferson Davis sent James M. Mason and John Slidell to England and France as special commissioners. After running the Union blockade they took passage on the *Trent*, a British mail steamer, for a neutral port. On November 8, Capt. Charles Wilkes, commanding the Union warship *San Jacinto*, stopped the *Trent*, removed Mason and Slidell, and took them to Boston.

The English believed that Wilkes had violated international law and had insulted their flag. Before the crisis came to a head Secretary of State William H. Seward ordered the release of Mason and Slidell. His move averted possible war with England and overcame the Lincoln government's first major diplomatic crisis of the war. See also TRENT AFFAIR.

"King Cotton." The Confederate government relied far more on the economic power of raw cotton than on agents in dealing with Britain and France. English and French textile industries, and the incomes of millions of people, were dependent on cotton from the American South. Southerners were convinced that for cotton the English and French would recognize Southern independence and perhaps intervene in the war on the Confederate side. This was the theory of "King Cotton."

The theory failed in practice. It failed because English and French warehouses at the beginning of the war had a large 2-year supply of raw cotton; because manufacturers found substitutes, such as Indian cotton, for the Southern product; because the British needed Northern wheat as much as Southern cotton; because England profited from its neutrality by selling goods to the North; and because the English people in particular were too divided in opinion for the government to risk war. England's upper classes, like those of France, favored the Confederate side, but the masses and liberal humanitarians sided with the Union.

Forcible Mediation. In the fall of 1862 the attitude of the British ruling class contributed to another diplomatic crisis. It grew out of the idea of forcible mediation whereby Britain, or France, would demand an end to the fighting in the United States on the basis of a permanently divided nation.

After a crushing Union defeat in the Second Battle of Bull Run on Aug. 29–30, 1862, British leaders became convinced that the Northern cause was hopeless. They then wanted to propose a joint British and French mediation of the war that would have given the Confederate states recognition as an independent nation. But several weeks later a Union victory at Antietam caused the British to hold up their offer of mediation. Since British and French intervention depended on Southern military successes, and Antietam revealed Confederate weakness, that engagement was a diplomatic turning point and one of the decisive battles of the war.

The Slavery Issue. With England the issue of slavery had a deep effect on wartime diplomacy. Many Englishmen detested the South because it appeared to be fighting for the perpetuation of slavery.

At first, Europe's liberals and humanitarians were disappointed because Lincoln had not announced the Civil War as a crusade against slavery. So in part to strengthen the Union's moral and diplomatic position in Europe, Lincoln on Sept. 23, 1862, issued his preliminary Emancipation Proclamation. The effect of this and the final proclamation on Jan. 1, 1863, on the peoples of Europe was good.

Naval Blockade. A weapon more effective against the Confederacy than European sympathy for the Union was the Union's naval blockade. When the Civil War began, the blockade, stretching over 3,500 miles (5,630 km) of coastline, was hardly effective. Later, as the Union threw more ships into the cordon, it hurt, though the Confederates argued that the blockade was never effective enough to be binding under international law.

Since Britain was the world's foremost naval power, other nations followed its lead. Thus, the main problem for the Union in maintaining the blockade was whether Britain would respect it. Even though most of the ships the Union navy seized for intended breach of blockade were British, the British government accepted the blockade as legally binding. It did so because English statesmen believed their country would gain long-term benefits from having the United States committed to upholding the principle of a loose but legal blockade.

Ships for the Confederacy. Far less favorable to the Union cause was the role of Englishmen in assisting the Confederate States to construct a navy. Since the South had no navy and no truly adequate means within its territory of building one, it planned to buy one in neutral countries, mainly Britain. The Confederacy made arrangements with British firms for the building of commerce destroyers, such as the *Alabama*. Along with the *Florida, Shenandoah,* and other cruisers, the *Alabama* burned and sank over 250 Union ships.

The Confederates also contracted for construction of two armored steamers with an iron "ram" at the bow. These ironclads, capable of crushing wooden blockade ships and smashing the naval cordon, would have been a greater menace to the Union than the commerce raiders.

As the rams became ready for delivery in the autumn of 1863 they touched off the last major diplomatic crisis of the Civil War. Charles Francis Adams, the American minister in London, demanded that the British government seize the rams. The crisis subsided when the British took possession of the rams and adopted a tighter policy of neutrality.

Actions of Spain and France. Spain and France tried to take advantage of America's civil distress and regain lost influence in North America. Spain temporarily reannexed the Dominican Re-

public. Seward protested the annexation as a violation of the Monroe Doctrine. Spain ignored the protest, but a revolt of the Dominicans forced Spain, by July 1865, to give up its control and withdraw all its troops.

France tried to maintain a puppet empire in Mexico. The effort began in January 1862 when French troops, along with Spanish and English detachments, landed in Mexico to collect debts. The British and Spaniards ultimately pulled out, but the French soldiers remained and conquered much of Mexico. The Emperor of the French, Napoleon III, persuaded Archduke Maximilian of Austria to become emperor of Mexico.

Lincoln's government refused to recognize Maximilian's government, but while the war lasted Lincoln did nothing more that might anger the French. When the war ended, however, Seward applied pressure. Finally, in March 1867, Napoleon withdrew his soldiers from Mexico. The French withdrawal and the end of the monarchy marked an impressive victory for the Monroe Doctrine.

Postwar Claims. Just as Unionists were hostile to the French in Mexico, they resented Canada's alleged sympathy for the South. All through the war Confederate agents used Canada as a base for anti-Union activities and even for raids against Northern border towns. Some Americans consequently demanded the conquest and annexation of Canada. Some urged annexation as compensation for damage against the Union by Confederate cruisers.

Americans argued that Britain had to pay for the depredations of the *Alabama* and other raiders because by allowing these ships to be delivered to the Confederates it had been lax in enforcing its neutral obligations. Protracted negotiations between the United States and Britain in Washington resulted in a treaty (1871) calling for arbitration of the *Alabama* claims and of other differences between the two countries. In 1872 the tribunal awarded the United States an indemnity of $15.5 million, which blunted American demands for Canada and settled the last major diplomatic problem stemming from the Civil War. See also ALABAMA CLAIMS.

ALEXANDER DeCONDE
University of California, Santa Barbara

Bibliography

Adams, Ephraim D., *Great Britain and the American Civil War,* 2 vols. (Longmans 1925).
Bernath, Stuart L., *Squall Across the Atlantic: American Civil War Prize Cases and Diplomacy* (Univ. of Calif. Press 1970).
Case, Lynn M., and Spencer, Warren F., *The United States and France: Civil War Diplomacy* (Univ. of Pa. Press 1974).
Corti, Egon C., *Maximilian and Charlotte of Mexico,* tr. by Catherine A. Phillips, 2 vols. (Knopf 1929).
Duberman, Martin B., *Charles Francis Adams, 1807–1886* (Houghton 1961).
Jones, Wilbur D., *The Confederate Rams at Birkenhead: A Chapter in Anglo-American Relations* (Confederate Pub. 1961).
Jordan, Donaldson, and Pratt, Edwin J., *Europe and the American Civil War* (Houghton 1931).
Monaghan, James, *Diplomat in Carpet Slippers: Abraham Lincoln Deals with Foreign Affairs* (Bobbs 1945).
Nevins, Allan, *Hamilton Fish: The Inner History of the Grant Administration,* 2 vols., rev. ed. (Ungar 1957).
Owsley, Frank L., *King Cotton Diplomacy: Foreign Relations of the Confederate States of America,* 2d ed., rev. by H. C. Owsley (Univ. of Chicago Press 1959).
Stern, Philip Van Doren, *When the Guns Roared: World Aspects of the American Civil War* (Doubleday 1965).
Winks, Robin W., *Canada and the United States: The Civil War Years* (Johns Hopkins Press 1960).

CIVIL WAR, English, the fighting period of the English Revolution of 1640–1660. The First Civil War extended from 1642 to 1646; the Second Civil War was fought in 1648, and further campaigns to subdue Ireland took place from 1649 to 1652.

The causes and issues of the Civil War were neither clear nor simple. In the background lay nearly 40 years of growing disharmony between the Stuart kings and their subjects. The reasons for strife were many. By Charles I's reign (1625–1649) they included a wide range of arbitrary taxes, a religious policy that was soft toward Roman Catholics and harsh toward Puritans, a foreign policy that after 1630 favored England's old enemy Spain, various injuries to the interests of merchants, and a royal court that was expensive, parasitic, and fatally indifferent to the ideals and prejudices of most Englishmen.

Contemporaries noted a growing division in the ruling class between "the Court" and "the Country," the former including all who served the crown for profit or preferment, the latter all the gentry who felt their religious and political aspirations—and their own chances of public service—frustrated by a coterie of "evil counsellors" and nest-feathering courtiers. The Country's opposition reached such a pitch that Charles ruled without a Parliament from 1629 to 1640. Yet his government depended on the cooperation of the gentry who ruled the counties through such offices as justice of the peace, and by the later 1630's the relations between the central government and the county communities were steadily breaking down.

BEGINNING OF REVOLUTION

The crisis came in 1638 when the Scots rebelled against the imposition of a new prayer book on their basically Presbyterian church. Charles rapidly lost control over both church and government in Scotland, and he tried unsuccessfully to regain it by war (see BISHOPS' WARS). The financial strain caused him to summon the Short Parliament in April 1640. So uncompromising were its demands that he dissolved it after three weeks and staked his dwindling credit on one more campaign against the Scots. This ended disastrously, with the Scottish army in occupation of northern England. He was forced to call another Parliament, and with both Scottish and English armies to pay and his coffers empty, he was powerless to resist its demands.

The Long Parliament. Yet the Long Parliament, when it met on Nov. 3, 1640, had no thought of a civil war in England. It broke up the king's former ministry, bringing capital charges against his chief minister, the Earl of Strafford, and against the principal agent of his Scottish church reforms, Archbishop Laud, and driving others into exile. It passed momentous acts to secure regular triennial Parliaments, abolish the courts of star chamber and high commission, and outlaw all forms of nonparliamentary taxation. By the late summer of 1641 it had made personal rule by the king impossible, and with the country largely rid of Scottish and English troops, men looked forward hopefully to a fresh start on firm constitutional foundations.

Parliament's Demands. In October a violent rebellion in Catholic Ireland changed the whole scene. The massacres of Protestant settlers were exaggerated a hundredfold in the telling. With the English overlordship dwindling daily, an army had to be raised once more. The question

was, could the king be trusted with it? The prevailing alarm and anger enabled John Pym, the masterly leader of parliamentary opposition to the Court, to carry two demands more radical than any advanced before: that the king's councillors and ministers of state must be approved by Parliament and that Parliament (not the king) should dispose of the nation's militia. Here lay the seeds of civil war, and they were forced by the heat of popular excitement. Charles hastened the process on Jan. 4, 1642, by going in person to the House of Commons with an armed retinue to arrest five leading members. They were forewarned and escaped arrest.

Yet even then there was nothing inevitable about the drift toward war, except possibly Charles' practice of covertly encouraging appeals to force while publicly speaking peace, or Pym's ruthless exploitation of the grounds for distrust that the king too plainly offered. By March, however, the situation was almost irretrievable. In the Militia Ordinance, Parliament finally staked its claim to control the armed forces and to legislate without royal assent. Charles withdrew from London to York, and as more and more Royalist members departed to join him there, Parliament's demands became more extreme, both in church and state matters. Both sides began raising forces, and on August 22, Charles made his formal appeal to arms by raising his standard at Nottingham.

Split Between Crown and Parliament. Some historians have tried to depict the Civil War as primarily a social conflict between opposed classes or economic interests. But economic issues were not primary, and the social lineup varied from county to county. Although more peers were Royalist and more merchants and citizens were Parliamentarian, there were large exceptions in both categories. The "middling sort" below the gentry tended to be Puritan and Parliamentarian. But the landed gentry, who counted most in both politics and the conduct of the war, were not unevenly divided. Many stayed as neutral as they dared. The split ran right through the broad ruling class, and there was not much difference between moderate Royalists and moderate Parliamentarians, either materially or ideologically. Parliament, however, was strongest in the east and south, the king in the poorer north and southwest and in Wales.

THE FIRST CIVIL WAR

Both sides expected a short war, but the early rounds dashed their hopes. The confused and indecisive Battle of Edgehill in October 1642 left the way to London open to the king, and he was stopped only by a massive turnout of the city militia at Turnham Green. The shaken Parliament men began desultory peace negotiations during the opening months of 1643. Pym knew they would be futile. Patiently, painstakingly, he carried through Parliament the financial and administrative measures that would be needed to sustain a long struggle.

Early Royalist Victories. Parliament commanded the greater material resources and a much more efficient organization for exploiting them, but in 1643 the Royalists came near to winning the war. The Earl of Newcastle beat the Yorkshire Parliamentarians at Adwalton Moor in June and contained Lord Fairfax in Hull. In the west, Royalist victories at Stratton, Lansdown Hill, and Roundway Down prepared the way for

Prince Rupert's storming of Bristol on July 26. Parliament's main army under the Earl of Essex lay at Reading, decimated by sickness. Many lukewarm men at Westminster were ready to talk Parliament into a craven peace.

But the west was not all lost yet, and the king decided to besiege Gloucester before advancing further. Newcastle, too, settled down to a feeble siege of Hull. Essex, reinforced by six London militia regiments, managed to relieve Gloucester and (on the return march) to survive a battle with Rupert at Newbury. Even more promisingly, Parliament at the same time engaged the Scots as allies. The Solemn League and Covenant between the two nations (1643) pledged England, as part of the price of military aid, to establish a Presbyterian national church.

In the same month of September, Charles signed a truce with the Irish that compromised him more deeply and brought him no comparable military advantage. Ireland was ruled by a Roman Catholic confederacy, and the king seriously damaged his cause in the eyes of his violently anti-Catholic English subjects.

Parliament's last and gravest loss in 1643 was Pym himself, who died of cancer in December. He had built the machinery that sustained the war effort, rallied the flagging spirits of his troubled colleagues, and held together a broad middle group of members that prevented Parliament from splitting into a conservative peace party and a radical war party. The moderate center continued to hold, but within a year the rifts in Parliament's ranks deepened dangerously.

Parliamentary Successes. Meanwhile, in January 1644, the promised Scottish army of 21,000 crossed the border under Alexander Leslie, Earl of Leven, and Sir William Waller relieved the pressure from the king's forces in the south, with a victory at Cheriton. Thereafter, the center of warfare steadily shifted northward. Although Rupert drubbed the Parliamentary forces besieging Newark, Lord Fairfax, his son Sir Thomas, and young John Lambert led a great recovery in Yorkshire. By April the Scots had Newcastle's men retreating to York. Three armies converged on the city: Leven's Scots, Fairfax's northerners, and the Eastern Association army under the Earl of Manchester, with Oliver Cromwell, the fiery member of Parliament for Cambridge, in command of the cavalry. Charles could not afford to let York fall, and he sent Rupert to relieve it with every regiment he could gather on the way. The result was the biggest battle of the war, at Marston Moor, where Cromwell's and the Scots' cavalry clinched a crushing victory. On that day, July 2, 1644, the king lost the north.

Divisions in Parliament. Parliament's aristocratic generals squandered the chance of total victory that year. Rather than join Waller in forcing the king's main army to a decisive battle, Essex marched off to conquer the southwest and lost all his infantry, through death or surrender, in the depths of Cornwall. Manchester evaded every opportunity to engage the enemy until forced to fight at Newbury in October, when he let Charles' much outnumbered troops get away.

In fact, Essex and Manchester and their conservative supporters at Westminster did not want to bring the king to total defeat. They distrusted the radical spirit at work among Cromwell's cavalry, the famous Ironsides, and among the more extreme Puritan sects. They wanted a negotiated peace and a return to traditional monarchical rule, tempered by suitable constitutional guarantees.

The New Model Army. Cromwell brought the issue to a head in November 1644 by charging Manchester, his own general, before the House of Commons with "backwardness to all action." A full investigation substantiated the charge—and then Cromwell himself urged the House to drop it. He and the war party were intent not on a personal vendetta but on two constructive measures that would change the whole conduct of the war. The first, the Self-Denying Ordinance, required members of both houses to resign their military commands and civil offices. The second, the New Model Ordinance, proposed to fuse what was worth keeping of the Parliament's existing, semi-local armies into a single fighting force that would march wherever it was ordered and fight for total victory. After prolonged debates both measures were carried, and the result by the spring of 1645 was the New Model Army, with Sir Thomas Fairfax as general and (eventually) Cromwell as lieutenant general in command of the cavalry. It would not only win the war but change the course of the English Revolution.

Surrender of Charles. After a fumbling start in the campaigns of 1645, Rupert's terrible sack of Leicester in May jolted the Parliament into giving Fairfax his head and staking the New Model Army on a decisive battle. And the Battle of Naseby on June 14 was decisive, thanks again to Cromwell's cavalry. When Lord Goring's western Royalists were beaten next month at Langport, the king had no field army left. By April 1646 he was under siege in Oxford. He slipped through the lines, preferring to surrender to the Scots. By June, the First Civil War was over.

DIVISIONS AMONG THE VICTORS

Parliament and the Parliamentarian gentry emerged from the war deeply divided. The split was partly political, between conservatives, who wanted only a return to the status quo with appropriate safeguards, and the militant party, which aimed at a more decisive transfer of sovereignty from king to Parliament. It was also religious. The majority favored a single, exclusive national church, Presbyterian in character but subject to Parliament. Their opponents, the Independents, stood for a looser ecclesiastical framework and greater liberty of conscience. Farther to the left, and drawn from further down the ranks of society, stood a growing number of radical Puritan sects that disliked any national church and demanded full religious toleration.

The political and religious groupings did not split along identical lines, but on both sets of issues the opposing parties were labeled Presbyterian and Independent. In the country at large the conservative, Presbyterian wing included more of the ruling county families, while the Independents drew more upon the lesser gentry and thrusting townsmen. The New Model Army was strongly Independent and tolerationist, and that is why the Presbyterian Scots hated it so.

Conflicting Peace Aims. The Scots were prepared to help Charles back to his throne if he would swear to the Covenant of 1643 and accept a Presbyterian Church of England, but that he would not do. For this and other reasons he also held out against the severe peace terms that the Long Parliament put before him. He had high hopes of playing on the divisions among his enemies, but in January 1647 the Scots handed him over to the custody of the English Parliament.

The divisions he hoped for appeared very soon. In the spring, the Presbyterian-dominated Parliament tried to disband most of the army and to send the rest to Ireland. It proceeded so tactlessly and with so little regard for the soldiers' rights to their back pay and indemnity that the regiments spontaneously elected "Agitators" from the rank and file.

Factional Fighting. Early in June the regiments defied Parliament's orders to disband, marched to a single rendezvous at Newmarket, and carried the king off with them. Cromwell, who had tried to avert this breach, fled from Westminster to Newmarket, where the army published striking manifestos, refused to disband until its grievances were satisfied, and claimed a voice in the settlement of the kingdom. It demanded that Parliament expel its leading Presbyterians, declare a date for its own dissolution, and provide for future assemblies more truly representative of the people. A few weeks later it stifled resistance from Parliament and city by marching into London.

Its generals did not yet aim to depose Charles. Instead they tried to negotiate with him for his restoration on their own terms, which were more liberal than the Parliament's. He foolishly temporized with them, still hoping for armed support from outside England.

Increasing Radicalism. The generals could not deal with Charles indefinitely, for their own subordinates were growing restive. A powerful new popular movement known as the Levellers had arisen among the smaller traders and craftsmen of London and was busy indoctrinating the soldiery in favor of radically reformed biennial Parliaments elected by every "free-born" Englishman. There was no place for king or lords in their proposed Agreement of the People.

Just when the rift in the army was becoming serious, however, Charles temporarily healed it by making his escape to the Isle of Wight. There in the last days of 1647 he concluded a secret pact with commissioners from Scotland, where the government had changed in his favor. Unless Parliament promptly restored him, a Scottish army would march to his assistance and he would call his Cavaliers once more to arms.

THE SECOND CIVIL WAR AND THE FINAL CAMPAIGNS

Early in 1648, as the plan leaked out, Parliament broke off negotiations with Charles, and the army closed its ranks against "Charles Stuart, that man of blood." The Royalist risings began in South Wales and ranged from Kent to Cumberland, but unhappily for Charles they spent their force before the Scots were ready. When the Scottish army did invade, Cromwell fell on it at Preston and destroyed it (Aug. 17–19, 1648).

Capture and Execution of the King. The Royalist effort collapsed, but the Parliament, more distrustful than ever of its own army, promptly began to deal with the king again. The army, however, was intent on bringing him to trial. It captured Charles once more, marched into London, expelled the Presbyterians from Parliament, and left the Independent Rump to erect a high court of justice. This tribunal sentenced Charles to death, and a shocked crowd witnessed his execution before Whitehall Palace on Jan. 30, 1649. England became a republic.

Ascendancy of Cromwell and Resolution of the War. The fighting had not ended, however. In the spring the Levellers, cheated of their democratic commonwealth, raised mutinies in the army, and Fairfax and Cromwell had to lead the loyal regiments in suppressing them. A more serious threat already loomed from Ireland, for whose aid young Charles II's agents concluded a treaty. Cromwell landed an expeditionary force at Dublin in August. His bitter campaign included terrible massacres of the defenders of Drogheda and Wexford, but by the time he left in May 1650 the conquest of Ireland was well under way, and within two more years it was complete.

Cromwell was called home because Charles II had landed in Scotland, swallowed the Covenant, and put his cause into the hands of his father's old enemies, the Scottish Presbyterians. To forestall an invasion by them, Cromwell led an army northward. He was at last the commander in chief, for Fairfax resigned rather than attack his former allies under the Covenant. Their general, David Leslie, almost brought the invading army to defeat, but at Dunbar on September 3, Cromwell snatched an overwhelming victory against all the odds. Yet Charles II was still at large, and Scotland was not yet conquered. As a climax to the 1651 campaign the young king gambled everything on a march into England, hoping to rally both Cavaliers and Presbyterians in united resurgence. But few joined him, and Cromwell was on his track. His road ended in final defeat at Worcester—final, that is, until his bloodless restoration nearly nine years later. Only the devotion of many lowly but loyal subjects enabled him to escape to France.

Worcester ended the Civil Wars, but it did not inaugurate a settled peace. The Rump that ruled the Commonwealth—the purged remnant of a Parliament first elected in 1640—was not the kind of government for which Cromwell's Ironsides had fought. Their New Jerusalem needed other builders. Yet the Rumpers would not relinquish power until Cromwell turned them out in 1653. There followed an experiment with a nominated Parliament, and when that failed, Cromwell felt obliged to assume the headship of the state as Lord Protector. Even the Protectorate, however, failed to survive Cromwell's death in 1658 for long, and perhaps its most lasting legacy was the Englishman's profound suspicion of standing armies. The Great Rebellion had progressed far beyond the intentions of its first authors, and the face of politics never was the same again after their victory. Not even the spirit of reaction at the Restoration could put Britain back on the road to absolutism that so many European states were treading in the later 17th century.

AUSTIN WOOLRYCH
The University of Lancaster, England
Author of "Battles of the English Civil War"

Bibliography

Ashley, Maurice, *Oliver Cromwell and the Puritan Revolution* (New York 1958).

Davies, Godfrey, *The Early Stuarts, 1603–1660*, 2d ed. (New York 1959).

Gardiner, Samuel Rawson, *History of the Great Civil War, 1642–1649*, 4 vols. (London 1893).

Roots, Ivan, *Commonwealth and Protectorate: The English Civil War and Its Aftermath* (New York 1966).

Wedgwood, Cicely Veronica, *A Coffin for King Charles* (New York 1964).

Wedgwood, Cicely Veronica, *The Great Rebellion*: vol. 1, *The King's Peace, 1637–1641* (New York 1955); vol. 2, *The King's War, 1641–1647* (New York 1958).

Woolrych, Austin, *Battles of the English Civil War* (London 1961).